The Tree of Jesse, from the Book of Hours of Charles V, fifteenth century.
(© Archivo Iconografico, S.A./CORBIS)

NEW
CATHOLIC
ENCYCLOPEDIA

NEW CATHOLIC ENCYCLOPEDIA

SECOND EDITION

14
Thi–Zwi

GALE®

THOMSON
™
GALE

Detroit • New York • San Diego • San Francisco • Cleveland • New Haven, Conn. • Waterville, Maine • London • Munich

in association with
THE CATHOLIC UNIVERSITY OF AMERICA • WASHINGTON, D.C.

The New Catholic Encyclopedia, Second Edition

Project Editors
Thomas Carson, Joann Cerrito

Editorial
Erin Bealmear, Jim Craddock, Stephen Cusack, Miranda Ferrara, Kristin Hart, Melissa Hill, Margaret Mazurkiewicz, Carol Schwartz, Christine Tomassini, Michael J. Tyrkus

Permissions
Edna Hedblad, Shalice Shah-Caldwell

Imaging and Multimedia
Randy Bassett, Dean Dauphinais, Robert Duncan, Leitha Etheridge-Sims, Mary K. Grimes, Lezlie Light, Dan Newell, David G. Oblender, Christine O'Bryan, Luke Rademacher, Pamela Reed

Product Design
Michelle DiMercurio

Data Capture
Civie Green

Manufacturing
Rhonda Williams

Indexing
Victoria Agee, Victoria Baker, Sylvia Coates, Francine Cronshaw, Lynne Maday, Do Mi Stauber, Amy Suchowski

While every effort has been made to ensure the reliability of the information presented in this publication, The Gale Group, Inc. does not guarantee the accuracy of the data contained herein. The Gale Group, Inc. accepts no payment for listing; and inclusion in the publication of any organization, agency, institution, publication, service, or individual does not imply endorsement of the editors or publisher. Errors brought to the attention of the publisher and verified to the satisfaction of the publisher will be corrected in future editions.

LIBRARY OF CONGRESS CATALOGING-IN-PUBLICATION DATA

New Catholic encyclopedia.—2nd ed.
    p. cm.
        Includes bibliographical references and indexes.
        ISBN 0-7876-4004-2
        1. Catholic Church—Encyclopedias. I. Catholic University of America.
    BX841 .N44 2002
    282′ .03—dc21
    2002000924

ISBN: 0-7876-4004-2 (set)
0-7876-4005-0 (v. 1)
0-7876-4006-9 (v. 2)
0-7876-4007-7 (v. 3)
0-7876-4008-5 (v. 4)
0-7876-4009-3 (v. 5)
0-7876-4010-7 (v. 6)
0-7876-4011-5 (v. 7)
0-7876-4012-3 (v. 8)
0-7876-4013-1 (v. 9)
0-7876-4014-x (v. 10)
0-7876-4015-8 (v. 11)
0-7876-4016-6 (v. 12)
0-7876-4017-4 (v. 13)
0-7876-4018-2 (v. 14)
0-7876-4019-0 (v. 15)

For The Catholic University of America Press

EDITORIAL STAFF

Executive Editor
Berard L. Marthaler, O.F.M.Conv., S.T.D., Ph.D.

Associate Editor
Gregory F. LaNave, Ph.D.

Assistant Editors
Jonathan Y. Tan, Ph.D.
Richard E. McCarron, Ph.D.

Editorial Assistant
Denis J. Obermeyer

Director of The Catholic University of America Press
David J. McGonagle, Ph.D.

CONTRIBUTING EDITORS

John Borelli, Ph.D., Associate Director of Secretariat for Ecumenical and Interreligious Affairs, United States Conference of Catholic Bishops, Washington, D.C.

Drew Christiansen, S.J., Ph.D., Senior Fellow, Woodstock Theological Center, Washington, D.C.

Anne M. Clifford, C.S.J., Ph.D., Associate Professor of Theology, Duquesne University, Pittsburgh, Pennsylvania

Raymond F. Collins, M.A., S.T.D., Professor of New Testament, The Catholic University of America, Washington, D.C.

Cyprian Davis, O.S.B., S.T.L., Ph.D., Professor of Church History, Saint Meinrad School of Theology, Saint Meinrad, Indiana

Dennis M. Doyle, Ph.D., Associate Professor of Religious Studies, University of Dayton, Dayton, Ohio

Angelyn Dries, O.S.F., Ph.D., Associate Professor of Religious Studies, Cardinal Stritch University, Milwaukee, Wisconsin

Arthur Espelage, O.F.M., J.C.D., Executive Coordinator, Canon Law Society of America, Washington, D.C.

Eugene J. Fisher, Ph.D., Associate Director of Secretariat for Ecumenical and Interreligious Affairs, United States Conference of Catholic Bishops, Washington, D.C.

Foreword

This revised edition of the *New Catholic Encyclopedia* represents a third generation in the evolution of the text that traces its lineage back to the *Catholic Encyclopedia* published from 1907 to 1912. In 1967, sixty years after the first volume of the original set appeared, The Catholic University of America and the McGraw-Hill Book Company joined together in organizing a small army of editors and scholars to produce the *New Catholic Encyclopedia*. Although planning for the *NCE* had begun before the Second Vatican Council and most of the 17,000 entries were written before Council ended, Vatican II enhanced the encyclopedia's value and importance. The research and the scholarship that went into the articles witnessed to the continuity and richness of the Catholic Tradition given fresh expression by Council. In order to keep the *NCE* current, supplementary volumes were published in 1972, 1978, 1988, and 1995. Now, at the beginning of the third millennium, The Catholic University of America is proud to join with The Gale Group in presenting a new edition of the *New Catholic Encyclopedia*. It updates and incorporates the many articles from the 1967 edition and its supplements that have stood the test of time and adds hundreds of new entries.

As the president of The Catholic University of America, I cannot but be pleased at the reception the *NCE* has received. It has come to be recognized as an authoritative reference work in the field of religious studies and is praised for its comprehensive coverage of the Church's history and institutions. Although Canon Law no longer requires encyclopedias and reference works of this kind to receive an *imprimatur* before publication, I am confident that this new edition, like the original, reports accurate information about Catholic beliefs and practices. The editorial staff and their consultants were careful to present official Church teachings in a straightforward manner, and in areas where there are legitimate disputes over fact and differences in interpretation of events, they made every effort to insure a fair and balanced presentation of the issues.

The way for this revised edition was prepared by the publication, in 2000, of a Jubilee volume of the *NCE,* heralding the beginning of the new millennium. In my foreword to that volume I quoted Pope John Paul II's encyclical on Faith and Human Reason in which he wrote that history is "the arena where we see what God does for humanity." The *New Catholic Encyclopedia* describes that arena. It reports events, people, and ideas—"the things we know best and can verify most easily, the things of our everyday life, apart from which we cannot understand ourselves" (*Fides et ratio,* 12).

Finally, I want to express appreciation on my own behalf and on the behalf of the readers of these volumes to everyone who helped make this revision a reality. We are all indebted to The Gale Group and the staff of The Catholic University of America Press for their dedication and the alacrity with which they produced it.

Very Reverend David M. O'Connell, C.M., J.C.D.
President
The Catholic University of America

Preface to the Revised Edition

When first published in 1967 the *New Catholic Encyclopedia* was greeted with enthusiasm by librarians, researchers, and general readers interested in Catholicism. In the United States the *NCE* has been recognized as the standard reference work on matters of special interest to Catholics. In an effort to keep the encyclopedia current, supplementary volumes were published in 1972, 1978, 1988, and 1995. However, it became increasingly apparent that further supplements would not be adequate to this task. The publishers subsequently decided to undertake a thorough revision of the *NCE,* beginning with the publication of a Jubilee volume at the start of the new millennium.

Like the biblical scribe who brings from his storeroom of knowledge both the new and the old, this revised edition of the *New Catholic Encyclopedia* incorporates material from the 15-volume original edition and the supplement volumes. Entries that have withstood the test of time have been edited, and some have been amended to include the latest information and research. Hundreds of new entries have been added. For all practical purposes, it is an entirely new edition intended to serve as a comprehensive and authoritative work of reference reporting on the movements and interests that have shaped Christianity in general and Catholicism in particular over two millennia.

SCOPE

The title reflects its outlook and breadth. It is the *New Catholic Encyclopedia,* not merely a new encyclopedia of Catholicism. In addition to providing information on the doctrine, organization, and history of Christianity over the centuries, it includes information about persons, institutions, cultural phenomena, religions, philosophies, and social movements that have affected the Catholic Church from within and without. Accordingly, the *NCE* attends to the history and particular traditions of the Eastern Churches and the Churches of the Protestant Reformation, and other ecclesial communities. Christianity cannot be understood without exploring its roots in ancient Israel and Judaism, nor can the history of the medieval and modern Church be understood apart from its relationship with Islam. Interfaith dialogue requires an appreciation of Buddhism and other world religions, as well as some knowledge of the history of religion in general.

On the assumption that most readers and researchers who use the *NCE* are individuals interested in Catholicism in general and the Church in North America in particular, its editorial content gives priority to the Western Church, while not neglecting the churches in the East; to Roman Catholicism, acknowledging much common history with Protestantism; and to Catholicism in the United States, recognizing that it represents only a small part of the universal Church.

Scripture, Theology, Patrology, Liturgy. The many and varied articles dealing with Sacred Scripture and specific books of the Bible reflect contemporary biblical scholarship and its concerns. The *NCE* highlights official church teachings as expressed by the Church's magisterium. It reports developments in theology, explains issues and introduces ecclesiastical writers from the early Church Fathers to present-day theologians whose works exercise major influence on the development of Christian thought. The *NCE* traces the evolution of the Church's worship with special emphasis on rites and rituals consequent to the liturgical reforms and renewal initiated by the Second Vatican Council.

Church History. From its inception Christianity has been shaped by historical circumstances and itself has become a historical force. The *NCE* presents the Church's history from a number of points of view against the background of general political and cultural history. The revised edition reports in some detail the Church's missionary activity as it grew from a small community in Jerusalem to the worldwide phenomenon it is today. Some entries, such as those dealing with the Middle Ages, the Reformation, and the Enlightenment, focus on major time-periods and movements that cut across geographical boundaries. Other articles describe the history and structure of the Church in specific areas, countries, and regions. There are separate entries for many dioceses and monasteries which by reason of antiquity, size, or influence are of special importance in ecclesiastical history, as there are for religious orders and congregations. The *NCE* rounds out its comprehensive history of the Church with articles on religious movements and biographies of individuals.

Canon and Civil Law. The Church inherited and has safeguarded the precious legacy of ancient Rome, described by Virgil, "to rule people under law, [and] to establish the way of peace." The *NCE* deals with issues of ecclesiastical jurisprudence and outlines the development of legislation governing communal practices and individual obligations, taking care to incorporate and reference the 1983 *Code of Canon Law* throughout and, where appropriate, the *Code of Canons for the Eastern Churches.* It deals with issues of Church-State relations and with civil law as it impacts on the Church and Church's teaching regarding human rights and freedoms.

Philosophy. The Catholic tradition from its earliest years has investigated the relationship between faith and reason. The *NCE* considers at some length the many and varied schools of ancient, medieval, and modern philosophy with emphasis, when appropriate, on their relationship to theological positions. It pays particular attention to the scholastic tradition, particularly Thomism, which is prominent in Catholic intellectual history. Articles on many major and lesser philosophers contribute to a comprehensive survey of philosophy from pre-Christian times to the present.

Biography and Hagiography. The *NCE,* making an exception for the reigning pope, leaves to other reference works biographical information about living persons. This revised edition presents biographical sketches of hundreds of men and women, Christian and non-Christian, saints and sinners, because of their significance for the Church. They include: Old and New Testament figures; the Fathers of the Church and ecclesiastical writers; pagan and Christian emperors; medieval and modern kings; heads of state and other political figures; heretics and champions of orthodoxy; major and minor figures in the Reformation and Counter Reformation; popes, bishops, and priests; founders and members of religious orders and congregations; lay men and lay women; scholars, authors, composers, and artists. The *NCE* includes biographies of most saints whose feasts were once celebrated or are currently celebrated by the universal church. The revised edition relies on Butler's *Lives of the Saints* and similar reference works to give accounts of many saints, but the *NCE* also

provides biographical information about recently canonized and beatified individuals who are, for one reason or another, of special interest to the English-speaking world.

Social Sciences. Social sciences came into their own in the twentieth century. Many articles in the *NCE* rely on data drawn from anthropology, economics, psychology and sociology for a better understanding of religious structures and behaviors. Papal encyclicals and pastoral letters of episcopal conferences are the source of principles and norms for Christian attitudes and practice in the field of social action and legislation. The *NCE* draws attention to the Church's organized activities in pursuit of peace and justice, social welfare and human rights. The growth of the role of the laity in the work of the Church also receives thorough coverage.

ARRANGEMENT OF ENTRIES

The articles in the *NCE* are arranged alphabetically by the first substantive word using the word-by-word method of alphabetization; thus "New Zealand" precedes "Newman, John Henry," and "Old Testament Literature" precedes "Oldcastle, Sir John." Monarchs, patriarchs, popes, and others who share a Christian name and are differentiated by a title and numerical designation are alphabetized by their title and then arranged numerically. Thus, entries for Byzantine emperors Leo I through IV precede those for popes of the same name, while "Henry VIII, King of England" precedes "Henry IV, King of France."

Maps, Charts, and Illustrations. The *New Catholic Encyclopedia* contains nearly 3,000 illustrations, including photographs, maps, and tables. Entries focusing on the Church in specific countries contain a map of the country as well as easy-to-read tables giving statistical data and, where helpful, lists of archdioceses and dioceses. Entries on the Church in U.S. states also contain tables listing archdioceses and dioceses where appropriate. The numerous photographs appearing in the *New Catholic Encyclopedia* help to illustrate the history of the Church, its role in modern societies, and the many magnificent works of art it has inspired.

SPECIAL FEATURES

Subject Overview Articles. For the convenience and guidance of the reader, the *New Catholic Encyclopedia* contains several brief articles outlining the scope of major fields: "Theology, Articles on," "Liturgy, Articles on," "Jesus Christ, Articles on," etc.

Cross-References. The cross-reference system in the *NCE* serves to direct the reader to related material in other articles. The appearance of a name or term in small capital letters in text indicates that there is an article of that title elsewhere in the encyclopedia. In some cases, the name of the related article has been inserted at the appropriate point as a *see* reference: (*see* THOMAS AQUINAS, ST.). When a further aspect of the subject is treated under another title, a *see also* reference is placed at the end of the article. In addition to this extensive cross-reference system, the comprehensive index in volume 15 will greatly increase the reader's ability to access the wealth of information contained in the encyclopedia.

Abbreviations List. Following common practice, books and versions of the Bible as well as other standard works by selected authors have been abbreviated throughout the text. A guide to these abbreviations follows this preface.

The Editors

Abbreviations

The system of abbreviations used for the works of Plato, Aristotle, St. Augustine, and St. Thomas Aquinas is as follows: Plato is cited by book and Stephanus number only, e.g., Phaedo 79B; Rep. 480A. Aristotle is cited by book and Bekker number only, e.g., Anal. post. 72b 8–12; Anim. 430a 18. St. Augustine is cited as in the Thesaurus Linguae Latinae, e.g., C. acad. 3.20.45; Conf. 13.38.53, with capitalization of the first word of the title. St. Thomas is cited as in scholarly journals, but using Arabic numerals. In addition, the following abbreviations have been used throughout the encyclopedia for biblical books and versions of the Bible.

Books

Acts	Acts of the Apostles
Am	Amos
Bar	Baruch
1–2 Chr	1 and 2 Chronicles (1 and 2 Paralipomenon in Septuagint and Vulgate)
Col	Colossians
1–2 Cor	1 and 2 Corinthians
Dn	Daniel
Dt	Deuteronomy
Eccl	Ecclesiastes
Eph	Ephesians
Est	Esther
Ex	Exodus
Ez	Ezekiel
Ezr	Ezra (Esdras B in Septuagint; 1 Esdras in Vulgate)
Gal	Galatians
Gn	Genesis
Hb	Habakkuk
Heb	Hebrews
Hg	Haggai
Hos	Hosea
Is	Isaiah
Jas	James
Jb	Job
Jdt	Judith
Jer	Jeremiah
Jgs	Judges
Jl	Joel
Jn	John
1–3 Jn	1, 2, and 3 John
Jon	Jonah
Jos	Joshua
Jude	Jude
1–2 Kgs	1 and 2 Kings (3 and 4 Kings in Septuagint and Vulgate)
Lam	Lamentations
Lk	Luke
Lv	Leviticus
Mal	Malachi (Malachias in Vulgate)
1–2 Mc	1 and 2 Maccabees
Mi	Micah
Mk	Mark
Mt	Matthew
Na	Nahum
Neh	Nehemiah (2 Esdras in Septuagint and Vulgate)
Nm	Numbers
Ob	Obadiah
Phil	Philippians
Phlm	Philemon
Prv	Proverbs
Ps	Psalms
1–2 Pt	1 and 2 Peter
Rom	Romans
Ru	Ruth
Rv	Revelation (Apocalypse in Vulgate)
Sg	Song of Songs
Sir	Sirach (Wisdom of Ben Sira; Ecclesiasticus in Septuagint and Vulgate)
1–2 Sm	1 and 2 Samuel (1 and 2 Kings in Septuagint and Vulgate)
Tb	Tobit
1–2 Thes	1 and 2 Thessalonians
Ti	Titus
1–2 Tm	1 and 2 Timothy
Wis	Wisdom
Zec	Zechariah
Zep	Zephaniah

Versions

Apoc	Apocrypha
ARV	American Standard Revised Version
ARVm	American Standard Revised Version, margin
AT	American Translation
AV	Authorized Version (King James)
CCD	Confraternity of Christian Doctrine
DV	Douay-Challoner Version

ERV	English Revised Version		NJB	New Jerusalem Bible
ERVm	English Revised Version, margin		NRSV	New Revised Standard Version
EV	English Version(s) of the Bible		NT	New Testament
JB	Jerusalem Bible		OT	Old Testament
LXX	Septuagint		RSV	Revised Standard Version
MT	Masoretic Text		RV	Revised Version
NAB	New American Bible		RVm	Revised Version, margin
NEB	New English Bible		Syr	Syriac
NIV	New International Version		Vulg	Vulgate

T

THIEL, BERNARDO AUGUSTO

Second bishop of San José, Costa Rica; b. Elberfeld, Germany, April 1, 1850; d. San José, Costa Rica, Sept. 9, 1901. He completed his first studies in the Royal Gymnasium of Elberfeld and continued them in the Lycée of Neuss. In Cologne he entered the Vincentians, but that did not prevent his being drafted during the Franco-Prussian war, in which he served as a male nurse in the field hospital. The religious persecution of the Kulturkampf forced him to Paris where he completed his studies for the priesthood. In 1874 he was sent by his superiors to Ecuador where he directed the professors of theology in the Conciliar Seminary. The political upheaval after the death of García Moreno (1876) caused him to leave for Costa Rica, where he also devoted himself to teaching. He was appointed bishop on Feb. 27, 1880, and was consecrated on September 5. The first bishop of Costa Rica, Anselmo Llorente Lafuente, had died on Sept. 22, 1871, and political uncertainty of the time had given rise to the prolonged vacancy of the see. In 1884 political opposition to the Church intensified. Bishop Thiel was expelled along with the Jesuits. Authors like Ricardo Fernández Guardia attributed the situation to the machinations of Freemasonry, although others maintained that the lodge was very weak in Costa Rica.

In a report to the Holy See, Sept. 26, 1884, Thiel explained his expulsion, saying that Pres. Próspero Fernández was his friend, but that certain people had abused his kindness in order to secure the decree. In a letter written to Thiel from Seville on March 23, 1885, the historian León Fernández stated that the president of Guatemala, Justo Rufino Barrios (a staunch Mason), had arranged a revolution in Costa Rica for his own purposes, and that the bishop had been the victim of that revolution.

During his exile Thiel lived in Rome and in Germany, and he later went to Panama where he received an amnesty from the government of Costa Rica (May 9, 1886), and returned to his see of San José. He restored the seminary, placing it in charge of the Vincentian Fathers. On July 31, 1897, he founded the review *El Mensajero del Clero*. He built the archiepiscopal palace, and once again dedicated himself to historical research and to research on Costa Rican native folklore. As a reparation for the injustices committed against him by previous governments, the Congress of the Republic of Costa Rica gave him the title of ''Benemérito de la Patria.'' A culmination of his studies was the publication in 1882 of his notes on Costa Rican native lexicography: languages and dialects of the Talamancas, Viceitas, Terrabas, Borucas, and Guatusos. In 1896 he began to prepare his *Datos cronológicos para la historia eclesiástica de Costa Rica durante el siglo XIX*. His other works include *Términos de origen costarricense que se encuentran en documentos de los siglos XVII y XVIII; Explicación del catecismo de la doctrina cristiana,* based on the work by José Deharbe (Freiburg im Breisgau 1891); and a sacred history, as well as circulars, pastoral letters, and other short treatises.

Bibliography: V. SANABRIA MARTÍNEZ, *Bernardo Augusto Thiel: segundo obispo de Costa Rica* (San José, Costa Rica 1941). R. FERNÁNDEZ GUARDIA, *Cartilla histórica de Costa Rica* (3d ed. San José 1926).

[L. LAMADRID]

THIEMO, BL.

Benedictine abbot of the monastery of SANKT PETER, Salzburg, and later archbishop of Salzburg; b. Megling (birth date unknown); d. Ascalon, Sept. 28, 1102. Although of a family of Bavarian counts from Megling, Thiemo (Theodmarus) became a monk at NIEDER-ALTAICH, where he achieved considerable success in sculpturing, painting, and brass work. As abbot of Sankt Peter, he gained renown for his zeal in promoting material and spiritual improvements, according to Cluniac norms at ADMONT. Elected archbishop of Salzburg by members of the cathedral chapter loyal to Urban II, he took part in the synod of Piacenza (1095), the resolutions of which he carried out rigidly. Hard pressed by the rival imperial bishop Berthold of Moosburg, and defeated in battle at Saaldorf *c.* 1096, he fled to Carinthia, but was captured; when liberated after five years' imprisonment he entered a Swabian monastery. In 1101 he joined the Bavarian Duke Welf in a crusade to the Holy Land. After the defeat at Heraklea he fell into the hands of the Seljuk Turks and suffered an excruciating death at Ascalon. Thiemo was never canonized, though he is venerated as blessed since the 12th century. In 1884 his cult was approved for Admont and other Benedictine monasteries.

Feast: Sept. 28.

Bibliography: C. GREINZ, *Lexikon für Theologie und Kirche,* ed. M. BUCHBERGER, 10 v. (Freiburg 1930–38) 10:105. A. M. ZIMMERMANN, *Kalendarium Benedictinum: Die Heiligen und Seligen des Benediktinerorderns und seiner Zweige* 3:84. P. KARNER, *Die Heiligen und Seligen Salzburgs* (Austria Sancta 12; Vienna 1913) 2:1135.

[M. J. STALLINGS]

THIERRY OF CHARTRES

Teacher, philosopher, scientist, theologian, master and chancellor of Chartres, and defender of the liberal arts. B. Brittany; d. *c.* 1155.

Life. Little is known of the early years or even his year of birth. Thierry of Chartres signed documents as schoolmaster in the records of Chartres Cathedral in 1119 and 1121. He may have been the brother of Bernard of Chartres and may be the Thierry mentioned by Abelard, in his *History of My Calamities,* as having attended the Council of Soissons in 1121 and assisting the papal legate, Bishop Geoffrey of Chartres. It is the belief of most scholars that Thierry taught at Chartres until he became chancellor himself in 1142. He may have continued teaching after taking on the chancellorship. He replaced Gilbert who then became bishop of Poitiers. There is indication that Thierry also taught at Paris during the 1130s. He moved away from teaching what he calls the "ignorant mob" that students in the schools had become after the rise of the Cornifician movement of reform. He is mentioned in the writings of several students, including John of Salisbury, Adalbert, and Clarembald of Arras. Thierry obtained renown in his own time as a master of the liberal arts. Herman of Carinthia dedicated his translation of Ptolemy's *Planisphere* to Thierry, and Bernard Silvester dedicated his *Cosmographia* to him. Herman describes him, in 1143, as "Thierry the Platonist," and Bernard, in 1147, calls him "the most famous teacher." John of Salisbury, in his *Metalogicon,* calls him the "most studious investigator of the arts."

Thierry also served as archdeacon at Dreux, where his name appears on surviving official documents from 1136–42. Thierry attended the Consistory of Reims in 1148, where Gilbert's Trinitarian theories were on trial. Otto of Freising (*Chronica, Patrologia Latina,* ed. J. P. Migne [Paris 1878–90] 188, 1250) speaks of Thierry in the past tense in 1156, and a new archdeacon was named at Dreux in 1155. Little was known of Thierry's final days until, in 1946, an epitaph of him was discovered and edited by André Vernet ("Une épitaphe de Thierry de Chartres," in *Recueil de travaux offerts á M. Clovis Brunell* [Paris 1955] 660–670). This revealed that Thierry retired to an unnamed monastery, although not before bequeathing all his books—some seventy volumes—to the library at Chartres.

Works. Thierry wrote glosses on the theological works of Boethius, Cicero's *De inventione,* and the pseudo-Cicero *Ad Herennium.* Since the gloss was primarily a teaching tool, it lent itself to natural development and additions. This helps to explain the variety of separate glosses on the same work. Nikolaus Haring has identified three separate texts of Thierry's which gloss Boethius's *De Trinitate.* Each has both overlapping and distinct content. These are respectively referred to as *Commentum super Boethii librum De Trintate, Lectiones super Boethii librum De Trintate,* and *Glosa super Boethii librum De Trinitate.* In the same volume Haring includes critical editions of Thierry's commentary on Boethius's *Hebdomadibus* and his *Contra Eutychen.* Thierry uses these glosses as a platform for expounding on his own ideas. Haring also has several texts and textual fragments that are attributed to unnamed students of Thierry who are collectively known as the School of Thierry of Chartres. Thierry also wrote a short treatise titled *Tractus de sex dierum operibus.* Although the content is offered as an historical and literal exegesis on the opening of the book of Genesis, Thierry presents the story of creation through the interpretative lens of the natural sciences of his day. This work, like William of Conches' *Philosophia mundi* and *Dragmaticon,* offer the reader insight into not only the content of Chartrian science, but its integration into philosophy and theology. Finally, Thierry put together the still unedited massive volume entitled the *Heptateuchon,* the book of the seven arts. This contained almost fifty individual works that ought to be studied or consulted as part of the pursuit of study in the liberal arts. This seems to have been Thierry's first response to those seeking to shorten the course of study in the schools. It was never completed.

Thought. Thierry was a great defender of the liberal arts and believed in the integration of secular and sacred knowledge. He taught that the trivium gave expression to the quadrivium, through which we could obtain knowledge of the Creator. The sciences were tools or instruments for unlocking theological truths, and their study led to a better understanding of God. Although he was schooled in the Aristotle that was available during his lifetime, Thierry was a Platonist. Hermann of Carinthia refers to him as "the soul of Plato granted once again by heaven to mortals" (*De essentiis,* ed. C. Burnett [Leiden 1982] 347).

Thierry's originality was expressed in a vocabulary of his own making. He speaks of the creation as an unfolding (*explicatio*) of God and the universe as enfolded (*complicatio*) in God who is perfect simplicity. God is the form of forms and the unity out of which all plurality and all otherness comes. Thierry's concept of *intelligibilitas* is also original. By it Thierry claims a power for the soul that Boethius did not articulate. He argues that human beings have an innate power—that most people do not use—that enables them to contemplate the universal simplicity of God directly. This concept goes beyond contemplation of the forms or ideas—Thierry uses these terms interchangeably—and can only be described as a kind of intellectual mysticism where the distinction between the subject and the object ceases to exist.

The importance of Thierry's thought on his generation and those that came after him can be measured by the large number of students he taught, by those he inspired in their own writing, and by the number of patrons who had his writings copied.

Bibliography: Sources: *Tractus de sex dierum operibus* ed. N. HARING, in *Commentaries on Boethius by Thierry of Chartres and His School* (Toronto 1971). This critical edition also includes *Commentum super Boethii librum De Trintate, Lectiones super Boethii librum De Trintate, Glosa super Boethii librum De Trinitate,* and Thierry's commentary on Boethius' *Hebdomadibus* and *Contra Eutychen. Commentarius in librum Ciceronis de Inventione* ed. K. M. FREDBORG, in *The Latin Rhetorical Commentaries by Thierry of Chartres* (Toronto 1988). "Le Prologus in Eptatheucon de Thierry de Chartres," ed. E. JEANUEAU, in *Lectio philosophorum,* ed. E. JEANUEAU (Amsterdam 1973) 37–39. Literature: N. M. HARING "Chartres and Paris Revisited," in *Essays in Honor of Anton Charles Pegis,* ed. J. R. O'DONNELL, (Toronto 1974); 268–329; "The Creation and Creator of the World according to Thierry of Chartres and Clarembaldus of Arra," *AHDLMA* 22 (1955): 137–216; "Thierry of Chartres and Dominicus," *Mediaeval Studies* 26 (1964): 271–86. ANDRÉ VERNET, "Une épitaphe de Thierry de Chartres," in *Recueil de travaux offerts á M. Clovis Brunell* (Paris 1955) 660–670. A. ZIMMERMANN, "Die Kosmogonie des Thierry von Chartres," in *Architectura Poetica,* ed. U. ERNST, (Köln 1990) 107–118. P. DRONKE, "Thierry of Chartes," in *A History of Twelfth-Century Philosophy,* ed. P. DRONKE, (Cambridge 1988) 358–388.

[P. ELLARD]

THIERRY OF FLEURY

Thierry of Fleury or Thierry of Amorbach, hagiographer; b. *c.* 950; d. *c.* 1018. A contemporary of ABBO OF FLEURY, this 10th–century writer was at first a diocesan priest but eventually became a Benedictine at Fleury, now SAINT BENOÎT–SUR–LOIRE. There he compiled his *Libelli duo de consuetudinibus et statutis monasterii Floriacensis,* describing the customs of that abbey *c.* 995. In 1002 he went as a pilgrim to Rome, and there composed a *Life* of Pope MARTIN I (*Bibliotheca hagiographica latina antiquae et mediae aetatis* 5596) as well as accounts of SS. Tryphon and Ruspicius (*Bibliotheca hagiographica latina antiquae et mediae aetatis* 8340), the FORTY MARTYRS of Sebaste, and St. Anthimus of Nicomedia. He lived for a time at MONTE CASSINO, where he wrote a biography of Firmanus, Abbot of Fermo (*Bibliotheca hagiographica latina antiquae et mediae aetatis* 3001). From 1010 to 1018 he resided at the Abbey of Amorbach, and here he produced his best known work, the *Illatio sancti Benedicti* (ed. Dümmler, *Abhandlungen der Deutschen (Preussischen, to 1944) Akademie der Wissenschaften zu Berlin* 1894). Other writings included a hymn in honor of St. MAURUS and an explanation of the Catholic Epistles, now partly lost.

Bibliography: M. MANITIUS, *Geschichte der lateinischen Literatur des Mittelalters,* 3 vol. (Munich 1911–31) 2:449–455. A. MANSER, *Lexikon für Theologie und Kirche,* ed. J. HOFER and K. RAHNER, 10 v. (2nd ed. Freiburg 1957–65) 10: 51–52. P. SCHMITZ, *Histoire de l'Ordre de Saint–Benoît,* 7 v. (Maredsous, Bel. 1942–56) v.2.

[A. G. BIGGS]

THIETMAR (DIETMAR) OF MERSEBURG

Bishop and chronicler: b. July 25, 975; d. Merseburg, Germany, Dec. 1, 1018. Descended from the noble Saxon house of Walbeck and related to the imperial family, Thietmar was educated at Quedlinburg and Magdeburg. After ordination in 1004, he was appointed second bishop of Merseburg (1009), a see reestablished by the Emperor Henry II to facilitate the conversion of the West Slavs. Eager to revive the ancient boundaries of his diocese, he began (1012) a chronicle of Merseburg; its eight books were later enlarged into a history of the Empire covering the days of Henry I, the Ottos, and part of the reign of Henry II. This work is an important source for the period in which Thietmar was a contemporary witness, especially for the Church in central Germany and its relation with the West Slavs, with whose language Thietmar was familiar. The writings of WIDUKIND OF CORVEY and the QUEDLINBURG Annals were his sources for the period of the early Ottos. The chronicle is useful also for its insights into the folk practices and beliefs of his day; it was later revised at the abbey of Corvey.

Bibliography: THIETMAR OF MERSEBURG, *Chronicon,* ed. L. SCHMIDT (Dresden 1905), autograph reproduction; ed. F. KURZE, *Monumenta Germaniae Historica: Scriptores rerum Germanicarum* 54 (1889); ed. R. HOLTZMANN, *Monumenta Germaniae Historica: Scriptores rerum Germanicarum* new series 9 (1935). M. MANITIUS, *Geschichte der lateinischen Literatur des Mittelalters* (Munich 1911–31) 2:265–268. W. WATTENBACH, *Deutschlands Geschichtsquellen im Mittelalter,* ed. R HOLTZMANN (Tübingen 1948) 1.1:52–58. N. FICKERMANN, ''Thietmar von Merseburg in der lateinischen Sprachtradition,'' *Jahrbuch für die Geschichte Mittel- u. Ostdeutschlands* 6 (1957) 21–76.

[O. J. BLUM]

THING

A very general term variously used by philosophers. In its broadest sense, it designates all that can be thought, or supposed, or to which existence of any type can be attributed, whether this be real or apparent, stable or transient, known or unknown. More strictly, it designates either a particular kind of reality or a transcendental attribute of being. Although most common among realists, the term is employed also by proponents of other epistemological positions in their attempts to account for its general usage. This article treats the etymology and meaning of the term and its use for a special kind of reality; it discusses also the status of thing as a transcendental and concludes with a survey of various epistemological positions relating to its concept.

Etymology and Meaning. The English word thing is a translation of the Latin *res,* which is derived from the verb *reor,* to calculate or to judge. The parallel derivation in English would link the substantive ''thing'' with the verb ''to think,'' just as in German it would link *Ding* with *denken.* In its primary etymological sense, therefore, thing becomes equivalent to thought and indicates anything that can be the object of thought or of judgment. From its Latin usage in such expressions as *quam ob rem* (for which reason) and *qua re* (why), however, *res* seemingly acquired a derived meaning roughly equivalent to cause (Latin *causa*); it is this that has led to the neo-Latin and Italian *cosa* and to the French *chose,* both equivalents of the English ''thing'' and both having somewhat the same realist connotations.

Because the primary derivation leaves open the question of extramental existence, medieval thinkers noted the distinction between *res realis* and *res rationis* (see Saint Thomas Aquinas, *In 2 sent.* 37.1.1, *De pot.* 9.7; Saint Bonaventure, *In 2 sent.* 37.1). *Res realis* designates anything that exists outside the mind, whereas *res rationis* designates anything that has existence in the mind alone. It has been more usual, however, to restrict *res* to the meaning of *res realis* and to make it roughly equivalent with *ens* (being) in the ontological sense. In this usage, the word is said primarily of substance and only secondarily of any ACCIDENT that inheres in substance; it is said also of a PRIVATION, although less properly, as when blindness and sin are referred to as things.

Particular Kind of Reality. As a particular kind of reality that is opposed to other kinds, thing designates a concrete existing individual (Greek τόδε τι), the first SUBSTANCE of Aristotle, which as concrete and existing is opposed to the essence of substance abstractly considered and as individual and substance is opposed to an accident or a group of accidents. More precisely, it applies to an entity that is complete in itself and is capable of subsisting, and as such is opposed to an intrinsic PRINCIPLE of being that is either incomplete or incapable of subsisting. Thus the tree and the cat are things, whereas the primary matter and substantial form of which both are composed are not (*see* MATTER AND FORM). Similarly, both potency and act and essence and existence are principles of things but are not themselves things. The scholastics made this distinction more explicit by speaking of *ens quod* (the being that), which is equivalent to the thing, and the *ens quo* (the being by which), which is a principle entering in some way or other into the composition of the thing (see Saint Thomas, *De virt. in comm.* 11; *In 7 meta.* 7.1414, 1423; *In 8 meta.* 3.1716, 1721).

John DUNS SCOTUS makes a distinction between thing (*res* or *ens*) and entity (*entitas*), regarding matter and form as entities and not as things, although his conception of matter and form differs from Aquinas's. For Scotus, entities are pure formalities or aspects of things by which they come under a SPECIES or GENUS (*natura communis*). For him, as for Aquinas, a real distinction is not convertible with a distinction between things; Scotus, however, speaks of a special type of real distinction *a parte rei* (on the part of the thing) that exists between formalities and between the divine attributes, which is not admitted to be a real distinction by Thomists (see DISTINCTION, KINDS OF).

A more common philosophical usage is the employment of thing to designate a concrete existent individual that lacks rationality and as such is opposed to PERSON. The scholastics refer to this as the *suppositum,* which as such is differentiated from the *persona;* they regard both as individual substances that are capable of subsisting (*see* SUBSISTENCE). In contemporary thought this distinction has been revived, although along different lines, and it figures importantly in philosophies such as PERSONALISM and EXISTENTIALISM. L. W. Stern, for example, makes use of it in elaborating his personalist philosophy (*Person und Sache,* 3 v., Leipzig 1906–24). J. P. SARTRE touches on it when drawing a distinction between being-in-itself (*l'en sol*) and being-for-oneself (*le pour-soi*), the former corresponding to the thing and the latter to the human being or person. Somewhat analogous is the distinction made by M. Heidegger between the subject that has being or is in being (*das Seiende*) and the subject who is peculiarly human (*Dasein*).

Status as a Transcendental. Thing (*res*) is sometimes said to be one of the TRANSCENDENTALS, i.e., one of the notions or properties that are themselves convertible with BEING. This identification is not made in the classical Aristotelian tradition, but appears in the West as early as 1232 in the *Summa theologica* of ROLAND OF CREMONA, who enumerates *aliquid* and *res* as transcendentals along with *unum* (H. Pouillon). Saint THOMAS AQUINAS draws on the teaching of Avicenna, who had previously used the terms, and explains the latter's basis for distinguishing between *ens, res,* and *aliquid.* As Aquinas explains Avicenna, the term *ens* is taken from the act of existing, whereas the term *res* expresses the QUIDDITY or ESSENCE of what exists; *aliquid,* on the other hand, is regarded as being equivalent to *aliud quid* (the etymology is erroneous) and is related to *unum*—just as *ens* is said to be *unum* insofar as it is undivided in itself, so *ens* is said to be *aliquid* insofar as it is divided from others and thus is viewed as another *quid* (*De ver.* 1.1).

The questions arise (1) whether Saint Thomas actually taught that *res* is a transcendental and, if he did or not, (2) whether *res* is to be enumerated among the transcendental properties of being. Both questions are commonly answered by introducing a distinction between a transcendental notion and a transcendental property. A transcendental notion is any notion that is coextensive with the common notion of being, whether it itself designates a formality that is equivalent to the notion of being or a formality that is consequent on that notion. A transcendental property, on the other hand, is a notion that expresses a formality in some way different from the notion of being, but immediately and necessarily connected with that notion; it adds a modality that is not indicated in the notion of being, and yet that is found wherever being is found. From these definitions it follows that every transcendental property is a transcendental notion, but not every transcendental notion is a transcendental property.

The common Thomistic reply to the foregoing questions is (1) that Saint Thomas taught that *res* and *aliquid* are merely transcendental notions and (2) that, as such, they are not to be enumerated among the transcendental properties of being. *Res* is not a property of being because it signifies nothing more than *ens* itself, viz, that which has *esse*; its formality is thus equivalent to that of *ens* and is coextensive with it (see *In 1 sent.* 25.1.4; *In 2 sent.* 37.1.1). Similarly *aliquid* may be understood as ''some-thing,'' in the sense of ''not nothing'' (*non-nihil*), and in this sense is equivalent to *ens;* or alternatively, *aliquid* may be taken to mean *aliud quid* and thus indicates only a general modality of being. In either case it indicates nothing distinctive that is immediately connected with the notion of *ens* and thus cannot be enumerated as a transcendental property.

Epistemological Positions. From the point of view of EPISTEMOLOGY, three basic positions may be noted with respect to thing, viz, the realist, the phenomenalist, and the idealist.

The realist position maintains that things exist extramentally and can be known by the human mind as they exist (*see* KNOWLEDGE; TRUTH). This position necessarily entails a definition of truth as an adequation or conformity between intellect and reality, itself recognized or known by REFLECTION, and ultimately dependent on the INTENTIONALITY involved in the knowing process. It need not imply, however, that the human mind can know the extramental thing in all its essential notes or specific details. (*See* REALISM.)

The phenomenalist position dissociates the PHENOMENA or the appearances from the thing, maintaining that the mind knows only the phenomena and is incapable of attaining the thing directly. Pushed to its extreme, PHENOMENALISM degenerates into SKEPTICISM; in various forms it is refined and defended by the proponents of EMPIRICISM and POSITIVISM. It plays an important role in the thought of I. Kant, for whom the distinction between phenomena and NOUMENA, or the thing-in-itself (*das Ding an sich*), is pivotal. As Kant sees it, man can know phenomena, but he is incapable of grasping noumena; he may know the existence of the thing-in-itself, but its essence always remains hidden from him. (*See* KANTIANISM.)

The idealist position rejects the possibility of any reality transcending thought and thus regards the thing-in-itself as a contradiction. In its extreme form, it holds that the thing is nothing more than the activity of the ego, or of mind, or of Absolute Spirit. (*See* IDEALISM.)

See Also: KNOWLEDGE, THEORIES OF

Bibliography: V. MIANO, *Enciclopedia filosofica*, 4 v. (Venice-Rome 1957) 1:1249–55. P. FOULQUIÉ and R. SAINT-JEAN, *Dictionnaire de la langue philosophique* (Paris 1962) 92–93. R. EISLER, *Wörterbuch der philosophischen Begriffe*, 3 v. (4th ed. Berlin 1927–30) 1:275–85. M. GARCIA-FERNÁNDEZ, *Lexicon scholasticum philosophico-theologicum . . .* (Quaracchi-Florence 1910). J. MARITAIN, *Existence and the Existent*, tr. L. GALANTIÈRE and G. B. PHELAN (New York 1948). L. M. RÉGIS, *L'Odyssée de la métaphysique* (Montreal 1949). S. DUCHARME, ''Note sur le transcendental *res* selon saint Thomas,'' *Revue de l'Université d'Ottawa* 10 (1940) 85*–99*. H. POUILLON, ''Le premier traité des propriétés transcendentales . . . ,'' *Revue néo-scolastique de philosophie* 42 (1939)

40–77. M. DEANDREA, *Praelectiones metaphysicae* (Rome 1951). E. ADICKES, *Kant und das Ding an sich* (Berlin 1924).

[W. A. WALLACE]

THINKING WITH THE CHURCH, RULES FOR

Written by St. IGNATIUS OF LOYOLA, the Rules for Thinking with the Church are proposed to the individual as one of various practical means to attain the overall purpose of the SPIRITUAL EXERCISES. Since the rules were written for Catholics of the 16th century, their intrinsic nature and interpretation reflect somewhat the religious atmosphere of the time.

The Rules for Thinking with the Church are not a theological treatise. No effort is made to establish absolute principles. Certain biblical truths are presupposed, but the rules in themselves are nothing other than practical means for Catholics to remain faithful to the Church and defend themselves against the innovations of the reformers. Rules 1 to 9 are for all Catholics. Rules 10 to 18 are primarily for those who have charge of instructing the faithful.

In the light of their historical origin, a summary of the rules can be forthright and clear. Rule 1 reminds Catholics that the understanding of the divine law is given to them by the Church rather than through private and subjective interpretation of Scripture. Rules 2 and 3 encourage the faithful to receive the Sacraments of Penance and Holy Eucharist, to partake in liturgical and other services, including the Divine Office and other prayer at fixed times. Rules 4 and 5 reaffirm the excellence of the religious life with its vows of obedience, poverty, and chastity. Rules 6 to 8 encourage the faithful to the continued practice of traditional Catholic piety outwardly expressed by the veneration of saints, pilgrimages, indulgenced works, and external penance. Rule 9 concludes this first group with the exhortation to praise and understand the laws of the Church, to defend them, not criticize them.

In the second group rule 10 counsels teachers and preachers against dwelling on the shortcomings of those in authority. Public criticism in sermons fosters murmuring and scandal among the faithful. Rule 11 recommends positive theology, as well as the scholastic method in theology and the scholastic theologians. They are excellent means for understanding and defending the divine truths. That vanity among preachers and teachers may be avoided, rule 12 forbids all comparisons between the living and the saintly geniuses of the past. Rule 13 contains the famous hyperbole with which St. Ignatius stresses uncondi-

tional submission to the teaching of the Church. In case of conflict between the latter and one's own intellect, the defined teaching of the Church must prevail: "What seems to me white, I will believe to be black if the hierarchical Church so defines." Rule 14 recommends moderation in dealing with the nature of predestination, faith, and grace. Immoderate emphasis of these elements of salvation may lead the faithful to fatalism, neglect of good works, and underestimation of the power of man's free will (rules 15, 16, 17). Finally, granted that the supreme motive for a Christian life is the pure love of God, when this fails to be a motive Catholics should be moved to the observance of the law by the filial and even servile fear of God (rule 18). Although written in the 16th century, these rules have never lost their practical value for Catholics even to the present time.

See Also: IGNATIAN SPIRITUALITY.

Bibliography: J. DE GUIBERT, *The Jesuits: Their Spiritual Doctrine and Practice,* ed. G. E. GANSS, tr. W. J. YOUNG (Chicago 1964). P. DUDON, *St. Ignatius of Loyola,* tr. W. J. YOUNG (Milwaukee 1949). W. SIERP, "Recte sentire in ecclesia," *Zeitschrift für Aszese und Mystik* 16 (1941) 31–36.

[P. RIVERA]

THIOFRID OF ECHTERNACH

Benedictine abbot and hagiographer; d. Echternach, April 3, 1110. Invested in Rome (Nov. 19, 1083) as abbot of ECHTERNACH, he was a reformer who restored regular observance and improved the physical well-being of his monastery. His hagiographical writing, frankly inspirational and interlarded with miraculous events in the careers of his pre-Carolingian heroes, is nevertheless noteworthy for the simplicity of its style, embellished by the use of CURSUS and rhymed prose. He was surprisingly uninfluenced by the authors and biographical techniques of antiquity. His works include the following: *Vita Liutwini,* written *c.* 1078 [ed. W. Lampen ('s Hertogenbosch 1936)]; *Vita s. Irminae* (*Monumenta Germaniae Scriptores* 23:48–50); *Flores epitaphii sanctorum* (*Patrologia Latina,* ed. J. P. Migne, 217 v. 157:297–404); *Vita Basini* (*Acta Sanctorum* March 1:315–320); and *Vita Willibrordi* (*Acta Sanctorum* November 3:459–500). The evidence for Thiofrid's authorship of the *Vita Liutwini* is well established. For the life of Basinus, however, it is argued that its author was so dependent on the prior vita of LIUTWIN, which he cites and even enlarges, that only Thiofrid could have produced it. Writing some 300 years after the death of his subjects, Thiofrid nevertheless provided the oldest extant evidence for the lives of Archbishops Liutwin and Liutwin's nephew Basinus, and for their contribution to the church of TRIER.

Bibliography: W. LAMPEN, *Thiofrid von Echternach* (Breslau 1920). E. WINHELLER, *Die Lebensbeschreibungen der vorkarolingischen Bischöfe von Trier* (Bonn 1935). M. MANITIUS, *Geschichte der lateinischen Literatur des Mittelalters,* 3 v. (Munich 1911–31) 2:478–482.

[O. J. BLUM]

THIONVILLE (DIEDENHOFEN), COUNCILS OF

In 806 CHARLEMAGNE announced his intention of dividing his empire between his three sons, Pepin, Charles, and Louis. After his death in 814, three ecclesiastical-political synods were held at Thionville (Theodonis Villa, Germ. Diedenhofen) near Metz, the last two of which, in fact, concerned quarrels between descendants of Charlemagne.

(1) In October 821, on the occasion of the marriage of Lothair, the eldest son of Louis the Pious, a synod of 32 bishops issued four decrees respecting the maltreatment of subdeacons, deacons, priests, and bishops; the decrees were then confirmed by Louis and Lothair.

(2) In February 835, 15 months after Louis had abdicated at Soissons under extreme pressure from Lothair and had done penance for alleged crimes, he was rehabilitated at a synod of 43 bishops at Thionville, each bishop presenting, at the request of Louis, a written opinion on the advisability of his restoration. On receiving a unanimous vote, Louis was escorted to Metz and crowned there (Feb. 22, 835), after which he and the synod returned to Thionville to pronounce sentence upon Abp. EBBO OF REIMS and other bishops who, siding with Lothair, had harassed Louis.

(3) Four years after the death of Louis his three surviving sons, Lothair, Louis the German, and the young Charles, their disputes settled, solemnly approved at Thionville in October 844 six decrees that appealed to the princes to keep the peace among themselves (can. 1), to fill vacant sees with worthy men and to recall all exiled bishops (can. 2), to see that monasteries were taken out of lay hands (can. 3, 5), to ensure that Church property be restored (can. 4), and to reaffirm the ancient dignity of the clerical state (can. 6).

Bibliography: J. D. MANSI, *Sacrorum Conciliorum nova et amplissima collectio* (Graz 1960) 14:389–394, 657–670, 807–808. *Monumenta Germaniae Historica: Leges* 1:228–229. *Monumenta Germaniae Historica: Concilia* 2.2:696–703. *Monumenta Germaniae Historica: Capitularia* 2.1:112–116. C. J. VON HEFELE *Histoire des conciles d'après les documents originaux,* tr. and continued by H. LECLERQ (Paris 1907–38) 4.1:31–34, 89–92, 116–117. *Histoire de l'église depuis les origines jusqu'à nos jours,* ed. A. FLICHE and V. MARTIN (Paris 1935) 6:213–214, 224–225, 272.

[L. E. BOYLE]

THIRKELD, RICHARD, BL.

Priest, martyr; b. Cunsley (Coniscliffe?), Durham, England; d. hanged, drawn, and quartered at York, May 29, 1583. After studying for a time at Queen's College, Oxford (1564–65), Thirkeld studied at Rheims, where he was ordained priest, April 18, 1579. Almost immediately he left for the English mission, where he labored in Yorkshire (1579–83). Among his penitents was St. Margaret CLITHEROW. He was arrested Aug. 14, 1583, while visiting a Catholic prisoner in the Ousebridge Kidcote, York. He freely admitted to his captors and the mayor that he was a Catholic priest. The next day he wore his cassock and biretta at his indictment during which he was charged with reconciling to popery the queen's subjects. He was found guilty on May 27, and condemned the following day. He spent his last night on earth teaching and encouraging his fellow inmates. Bede Camm summarized six of Thirkeld's extant letters. He was beatified by Pope Leo XIII on Dec. 9, 1886.

Feast of the English Martyrs: May 4 (England).

See Also: ENGLAND, SCOTLAND, AND WALES, MARTYRS OF.

Bibliography: B. CAMM, ed., *Lives of the English Martyrs,* 2 v. (New York 1904–05). R. CHALLONER, *Memoirs of Missionary Priests,* ed. J. H. POLLEN (rev. ed. London 1924; repr. Farnborough 1969). J. H. POLLEN, *Acts of English Martyrs* (London 1891).

[K. I. RABENSTEIN]

THIRTY-NINE ARTICLES

The Thirty-Nine Articles of the Church of England are a series of statements of Anglican beliefs concerning certain religious teachings, some of which were subjects of great controversy in Europe in the sixteenth century. These articles are not a complete summary of the Christian faith for Anglicans (*see* ANGLICANISM).

In 1536 Henry VIII directed the Convocations of Canterbury and York to approve the Ten Articles, which were then issued under royal authority with a preface by the King. In 1539 the promulgation of the Six Articles Act defined six beliefs. Any opposition to this act by either Catholics or Protestants was to be punished by burning the offender alive. In the reign of Edward VI, Archbishop Cranmer published in 1553 with royal sanction the Forty-two Articles. These articles, which were influenced by Lutheran teaching, attacked the doctrines of both Catholics and extreme Protestants, like the Anabaptists. They were revised by Convocation in 1563 and reduced to 39. A further revision, attributed to ELIZABETH I, caused some small changes, together with the striking out of article 29 as being too hostile to Catholicism. Nevertheless, when these articles were again officially promulgated later in Elizabeth's reign, in 1571, No. 29 was restored. Since that time the Thirty-Nine Articles have been an official statement of the beliefs of the Church of England with regard to the doctrines touched on in them. A wholehearted acceptance of them was demanded of every ordinand in that church and until 1871 of every OXFORD and CAMBRIDGE graduate. Notable among the articles was one that declared that Holy Scripture contained all necessary teaching for salvation. The traditional creeds were to be received as they were proved by Scripture. General councils were declared to be not necessarily infallible. Much fundamental Christian teaching on the Holy Trinity, and the Incarnation and the Redemption achieved by Jesus Christ was included. Only two sacraments, Baptism and the Lord's Supper, were recognized. The Tridentine doctrine of transubstantiation was categorically denied. Catholic teachings on purgatory, indulgences, and the invocation of saints were said to be false and repugnant to God's word. What Catholics believed about the Mass was stigmatized as "a forged fable and dangerous deceit."

Cranmer's Forty-two Articles of 1553 had declared the King to be supreme head on earth, next under Christ, of the Church of England and Ireland. In the 1571 edition of the Thirty-nine Articles this declaration of the royal supremacy was restated as follows: "The Queen's Majesty hath the chief power in the Realm of England and other her dominions, unto whom the chief government of all estates of this Realm, whether they be Ecclesiastical or Civil, in all causes doth appertain, and is not, nor ought to be, subject to any foreign jurisdiction." The articles also stated that the Bishop of Rome had no jurisdiction in the realm of England.

In 1841 John Henry NEWMAN, then vicar of St. Mary's, Oxford, a leader of the Tractarian Movement, wrote in his famous *Tract 90* concerning the Thirty-Nine Articles that "it is often urged . . . that there are in the Articles propositions or terms inconsistent with the Catholic faith . . . the following Tract is drawn up with the view of showing how groundless the object[ion] is." Despite the great influence of Newman his tract was condemned by the heads of the various Oxford colleges and more importantly, by Newman's ecclesiastical superior, Richard Bagot the Bishop of Oxford, who pressured Newman into promising to write no more tracts. This incident had a great effect on TRACTARIANISM and contributed to Newman's decision to enter the Catholic Church in 1845.

Anglican ordinands are no longer required to give a wholehearted assent to the articles. It is now sufficient if they subscribe to them in the sense of regarding them as not contrary to the word of God and on the assumption that they will not publicly attack them.

Bibliography: A. P. FORBES, *An Explanation of the Thirty-Nine Articles with an Epistle Dedicatory to the Late Rev. E. P. Pusey,* 2 v. (5th ed. London 1887). C. A. HARDWICK, *A History of the Articles of Religion* (Philadelphia 1852), E. J. BICKNELL, *A Theological Introduction to the Thirty-Nine Articles* (New York 1919).

[E. MCDERMOTT]

THIRTY YEARS' WAR

The series of protracted religious-dynastic wars that afflicted the Holy Roman Empire and most western European states from 1618 to 1648. The Thirty Years' War had complex and diverse origins but religion was perhaps the most important, and religious motivation was an integral part of the political, economic, and dynastic policies that formed and reshaped the course of Europe in the 17th century. Frederick V, Ferdinand II, and Gustavus II Adolphus were political leaders with dynastic ambitions, but religious principles also played a decisive part in the role that these men filled during the wars. This confluence and concurrence of many motivations persisted throughout the conflict, and if the conclusion of the struggle primarily reflected political and dynastic interests, religion and its consequences were everpresent and influential at the Peace of WESTPHALIA in 1648.

The years following the Peace of AUGSBURG (1555), which had established the principle of "cujus regio, ejus religio," guaranteeing the Lutheran and Catholic confessions throughout the Empire, also witnessed the rise of Calvinist influence and strength, especially in the Palatinate and Brandenburg. Seeking privileges and rights enjoyed by Catholics and Lutherans, the Calvinists clashed with a rising tide of Catholic reaction. The Austrian Hapsburgs, encouraged by Jesuits, Capuchins, and Spanish zeal, fostered a militant policy of religious conquest and conversion. In this Catholic reformation, the Catholic League of Princes organized by Maximilian I of Bavaria in 1609 played a formidable part. Alarmed by growing Calvinist strength, Maximilian tried to rally the Catholic princes and to inspire the weak, ineffectual Emperor Rudolph II (1576–1612) to oppose the designs of the Protestant Union organized by Christian of Anhalt and Frederick IV of the Palatinate in 1608. The decade from 1608 to 1618 provided a crystallization of attitudes that ended in war.

The Bohemian War (1618–23). The death of Rudolph and the inability of his brother and successor, Matthias, raised the question of succession in the imperial lands. The childless Emperors had chosen their zealous and militant cousin Ferdinand of Styria as their heir. An ardent Catholic, Ferdinand was unacceptable to many Protestants, especially those of Bohemia. Despite their lukewarm pledge in 1617 recognizing Ferdinand's right of succession, the Bohemians searched for a new candidate, and discovered him in the ruler of the Palatinate, Frederick V (1610–32), son-in-law of James I of England, and a leader of the Protestant Union. In 1618, when the Bohemian estates accused the imperial government of violating their sovereign rights and privileges, they forcibly ejected the imperial emissaries by the defenestration of Prague, thereby proclaiming their rebellion against Hapsburg rule. Frederick was offered the crown of Bohemia by the provisional government. Ambition and religious commitment led Frederick to accept election and along with Count Matthew of Thurn and Ernst von Mansfeld, the new King took command of the Bohemian armies. The dying Matthias (1612–19) permitted Maximilian of Bavaria and the Catholic League to defend the cause of monarchical legitimacy and Catholic orthodoxy.

In 1619, Ferdinand II (1619–37) ascended the imperial throne and joined the League in an all-out war against the Bohemians. The Protestant Union, annoyed at Frederick's illegal acceptance of the Bohemian crown and divided between Lutheran and Calvinist factions, did not aid the Bohemian rebels. Frederick, left only with poorly paid, disorderly troops, saw his army and ambitions crushed by an army led by Count Johann Tilly and Duke Maximilian at White Mountain, Nov. 8, 1620. The brief reign of ''the winter king'' came to an end. While Frederick vainly sought aid at European courts, Bohemia underwent sweeping changes and reforms. Death sentences, imprisonment, and confiscation of land eradicated rebel opposition and weakened Protestant strength. The Jesuits were given charge of the education of the Bohemian nobility and of the task of converting Bohemia to Rome. The Palatinate fared little better. The electoral dignity and the Upper Palatinate were granted to Maximilian of Bavaria (1623). Personal aggrandizement became a fixed part of the religious and constitutional struggle which had spread to adjoining territories with the renewal of the war between the United Provinces and Spain.

The Danish War (1625–29). The Twelve Years' Truce (1609), which had brought a halt to Dutch-Spanish hostilities, expired in 1621. Colonial rivalry in the East Indies, added to religious and national differences, contributed to the war's renewal and continuance until 1648. Since the similar religious and dynastic interests of the Austrian and Spanish Hapsburgs encouraged cooperation and coordination between the two powers, the Dutch naturally turned to Protestant Germany for support in an effort to resist the Hapsburg offensive. The Bohemian

Army camp during Thirty Years War. (©Bettmann/CORBIS)

defeat, however, forced the anti-Hapsburg German diplomats to look more to Scandinavia than to Holland for aid. Christian IV (1588–1648), the Danish King, and Gustavus Adolphus of Sweden (1611–32) were the likeliest sources of assistance. Gustavus, engaged in a Polish war, could do little, but Christian, a prince of the Empire by virtue of his ducal title to Holstein, did intervene. Politically inspired but backed by the religious sentiments of his people, Christian accused the Emperor of unconstitutional acts against the Elector-Palatine. Using this as a pretext, Danish armies entered the Empire. Opposing them were Albrecht von Wallenstein, Duke of Friedland, an imperial general who led a personal army of 24,000 men, and Count Tilly, the League general. The Danish armies were defeated by Wallenstein at Dessau and by Tilly at Lutter in 1626. Wallenstein proceeded to occupy most of Denmark thereby forcing Christian to sue for peace. After the prolonged siege of Stralsund and several months of negotiations, Christian signed the peace of Lübeck (May 22, 1629) by which he renounced all claims to German territory and surrendered his legal membership in the lower Saxon district of the Empire, yet managed to avoid an indemnity and to retain Jutland, Schleswig, and Holstein. The terms, arranged by Wallenstein and approved by Ferdinand II, were mild and considerate largely because there was a new threat to Hapsburg hegemony. Gustavus Adolphus, ''the lion from the north,'' was looking toward the Empire, and his appearance was to change the course of the war.

Swedish Intervention (1630–35). The victory of Hapsburg arms inspired Ferdinand II to issue his Edict of RESTITUTION (1629). This comprehensive religious settlement not only represented the height of Catholic reaction but it also inspired further Protestant resistance to Vienna. Many Protestant princes joined the struggle and appealed to Sweden for help. Fearing imperial designs on the Baltic and its trade, Gustavus Adolphus, a remarkable monarch and brilliant soldier, concluded a treaty with Poland at Altmark in 1629 and the following year led his army into Germany. Aided by the able statesmanship of his chancellor, Axel Oxenstierna, Gustavus rallied the Protestant princes and inspired a counteroffensive against the imperialists. In this he was aided by the Emperor's dismissal of Wallenstein from the imperial service. Fearful of his general's growing power and personal ambitions, Ferdinand relieved the duke of his command. With Wallenstein's removal, Ferdinand was left with an army inferior to that of the Swedes in leadership and morale. Within a year, the Swedish forces conquered Pomerania, won cooperation from George William, the previously aloof Elector of Brandenburg, and overcame the suspicions of some of the Protestant leaders who saw little difference between a Swedish absolutist and an Austrian one. Gustavus's motives are not completely clear. His personal ambitions were strong; his religious convictions, sincere; and his political aspiration, genuine.

Gustavus, aided by a large French subsidy obtained from Cardinal RICHELIEU by the treaty of Bärwalde (1631), marched to relieve the city of Magdeburg, then besieged by Tilly, but not before the place was destroyed (May 1631) in one of the worst holocausts of a war full of horrors. King Gustavus, supported by the Saxons, engaged Tilly's army at Breitenfeld (Sept. 7, 1631), routing the Catholic forces. The King's tactical deployment of cavalry, light artillery, and superior infantry gave him a spectacular victory. Instead of marching on Vienna, the Swedes conquered Bamberg, the Upper Palatinate, Mainz, and Würzburg in rapid succession. At the same time, Gustavus advanced his political plan for a general union of the Protestant states with Sweden. The proposal was not well received. The princes feared the political consequences of such a union for their autonomy. Moreover, Richelieu looked with disfavor on a strong Protestant confederation across the Rhine. Gustavus also

announced his peace terms asking for Swedish Pomerania, an imperial title, revocation of the Edict of Restitution, and a general redistribution of Hapsburg territory. Wallenstein, who had been restored by Ferdinand in an effort to halt the Swedish advance, rejected the terms, and instead, invaded Saxony in the hope of weakening the Protestant alliance. Gustavus pursued him and both armies joined battle at Lützen near Leipzig, on Nov. 6, 1632. The imperialists were routed again but Gustavus lay dead on the battlefield.

His chancellor, Axel Oxenstierna, continued the war but with little success. Even the murder of the scheming Wallenstein, apparently with imperial approval (1634), failed to turn the war to the Swedish advantage. The overwhelming defeat of the Swedes and German Protestants at Nordlingen in September 1634 permitted the Hapsburgs to press their campaigns with greater zeal and advantage. Southern Germany was reconquered, forcing the Protestant princes to conclude a separate peace at Prague in 1635. This agreement reached by Saxon and Austrian diplomats revised the Edict of Restitution enforcing changes in ecclesiastical reservations as of Nov. 12, 1627. It also provided for an army for the entire Empire as well as for the removal of foreign forces. The peace was an effort to obtain the support of all the German princes for the ancient constitution and to unite them against foreign influences. Many German states subscribed to the treaty; a few, fearful of Swedish or French retaliation, declined to do so.

The Swedish-French War (1635–48). Cardinal Richelieu, alarmed at the peace of Prague, finally declared war on the Austrian Hapsburgs and Spain. Despite Richelieu's subsidies, the Swedes never regained the initiative even after the succession of Emperor Ferdinand III (1637–57). The war continued for 13 years, during which time an internal revolt was transformed into an international conflict. French armies under Marshal Henri, Vicomte de Turenne and Louis II de Bourbon, Duke d'Enghien, invaded Spanish territory and crossed into Germany. Despite the French success at Rocroy (1643) and preliminary overtures toward peace, the war dragged on. These years marked probably the most destructive period of the struggle. Plundering armies and ravaging mercenaries leveled German cities and destroyed the countryside. Atrocities and epidemics compounded the miserable lot of the homeless and starving peasantry. Five years of negotiations finally brought the Peace of Westphalia in 1648, although France and Spain continued their war until the Peace of the Pyrenees in 1659.

The Thirty Years' War left behind it a trail of destruction and death. Bohemia, Saxony, Thuringia, and Württemberg were devastated. Cities, towns, and villages were burned and plundered; some of them disappeared. The Empire was depopulated; the German states were fragmented and divided. Religious life was demoralized and political institutions badly weakened. Germany ceased for some time to play an important role in the affairs of Europe. Religious ideals had been overwhelmed by reasons of state. The conclusion of the Thirty Years' War marked the last of the great religious conflicts of the sixteenth and seventeenth centuries. From this point onward plans to re-establish the universal world of medieval Christiandom—a world ruled spiritually by the Pope and temporarily by a Christian Emperor and princes—were to seem unrealizable and archaic. Instead a modern Europe, divided into and governed by sovereign, territorial states emerged in the years following 1648.

Bibliography: F. C. DAHLMANN and G. WAITZ, *Quellenkunde der deutschen Geschichte,* ed. H. HAERING, 2 v. (9th ed. Leipzig 1931–32). G. FRANZ, *Bücherkunde zur deutschen Geschichte* (Munich 1951). M. RITTER, *Deutsche Geschichte im Zeitalter der Gegenreformation und des Dreissigjährigen Krieges,* 3 v. (Stuttgart 1889–1908). A. T. ANDERSON, *Sweden in the Baltic, 1612–1630: A Study in the Politics of Expansion under King Gustav Adolphus and Chancellor Axel Oxenstierna* (Doctoral diss. unpub. Univ. of Calif. 1947). M. ROBERTS, *Gustavus Adolphus: A History of Sweden, 1611–1632,* 2 v. (New York 1953–58). H. HOLBORN, *The Reformation,* v.1. of *A History of Modern Germany* (New York 1959–). G. FRANZ, *Der Dreissigjährige Krieg und das deutsche Volk* (2d ed. Jena 1943). G. PAGÈS, *La Guerre de Trente Ans* (Paris 1939). P. Geyl, *The Netherlands Divided,* tr. S. T. BINDOFF (London 1936). D. OGG, *Europe in the Seventeenth Century* (6th ed. London 1954). D. ALBRECHT, *Lexikon für Theologie und Kirche,* ed. J. HOFER and K. RAHNER, 10 v. (2d, new ed. Freiburg 1957–65); suppl., *Das ZweiteVatikanische Konzil: Dokumente und kommentare,* ed. H. S. BRECHTER et al., pt. 1 (1966) 3:570–572. H. HAUSER, *La Prépondérance espagnole, 1559–1660* (Paris 1933). B. CHUDOBA, *Spain and the Empire, 1519–1643* (Chicago 1952). C. V. WEDGWOOD, *The Thirty Years War* (New Haven 1939). R. G. ASCH, *The Thirty Years' War* (New York 1997). G. FRANZ, *Der Dreissigjährige Krieg und das deutsche Volk* (Stuttgart 1979). J. V. POLISENSKY, *The Thirty Years' War,* R. EVANS, Trans. (Berkeley 1971). H. U. RUDOLPH, *Der Dreissigjährige Krieg* (Darmstadt 1977). G. SCHORMANN, *Der Dreissigjährige Krieg* (Göttingen 1985).

[P. S. MCGARRY]

THMUIS

A titular see in Augustamnica Prima, lower Egypt, and a suffragan of Pelusium, founded before the beginning of the fourth century in the Delta on the canal east of the Nile River. Herodotus and Ptolemy noted the city as the capital of a nome. In the fourth century it still had its own civil administration, separate from Alexandria. It survived through the Arabian conquest as Al-Mourad, but disappeared in the Turkish conquests. Nine early bishops of Thmuis have been identified: St. PHILEAS, first known bishop, martyred at Alexandria in 307; St. Dona-

tus, his successor, martyr; Liberius, who attended the Council of Nicaea I (325); St. Serapion, most noted of the bishops (*c.* 338–359); Ptolomaeus, perhaps an Arian usurper, who attended the Council of Seleucia (359); Aristobulus, who attended the Council of Ephesus (431); and three Monophysites in the Middle Ages.

Bibliography: M. LE QUIEN, *Oriens Christianus* (Graz 1958) 2:537. E. AMÉLINEAU, *La géographie de l'Égypte à l'époque copte* (Paris 1893) 286, 500. J. QUASTEN, *Patrology* (Westminster MD 1950) 2:117; 3:57–59, 80–85. F. VAN DER MEER and C. MOHRMANN, *Atlas of the Early Christian World,* ed. and tr. M. F. HEDLUND and H. H. ROWLEY (New York 1958).

[M. C. MCCARTHY]

THOMAR (TOMAR), MONASTERY OF

Twenty miles from Fatima, founded in 1160 for defense and administration of the district's repopulation. Tomar was the seat of the TEMPLARS in Portugal and of the ORDER OF CHRIST. For many years after 1455 its prior, usually the king, had ecclesiastical authority for territories overseas. Under Henry the Navigator the monastery and town flourished. In 1530 Anthony of Lisbon introduced reforms. Thomar was an abbey *nullius diocesis* until 1882, even after being abandoned in 1834. Today it is a national monument of unusual mixed architecture.

Bibliography: *Definições e estatutos da ordem de Christo* (Lisbon 1628, 1671, 1717, 1746). W. C. WATSON, *Portuguese Architecture* (London 1908). F. M. DE SOUSA VITERBO, *A ordem de Christo e a musica sagrada* (Coimbra 1911). F. DE ALMEIDA, *História da igreja em Portugal,* 4 v. (Coimbra 1910–22); *História de Portugal,* 4 v. (Coimbra 1922–26). J. VIEIRA GUIMARÃES, *A ordem de Christo* (Lisbon 1936). *Grande enciclopédia portuguesa brasileira* (Coimbra 1935–60) 31:894–925.

[E. P. COLBERT]

THOMAS, APOSTLE, ST.

One of the TWELVE (Mk 3:16–19; Mt 10:2–4; Lk 14–16; Jn 20:24; Acts 1:13). The lists of the Twelve in the Synoptic Gospels always locate Thomas in the second group of four, usually paired with Matthew. But Acts 1:13 pairs him with Philip. The synoptic tradition only mentions the name of Thomas but gives us no further details. Almost all our information about Thomas, his personality, and his character, comes to us from the Fourth Gospel. In the Fourth Gospel Thomas appears in four passages (Jn 11:16; 14:5; 20:24–28; 21:2) and plays an important role in the theological development of the gospel.

The Greek τωμᾶς is a transliteration of the Aramaic word *te'ômâ,* meaning "twin." The latter word finds no

"Saint Thomas the Apostle," painting by Diego Velasquez.
(©Archivo Iconografico, S.A./CORBIS)

attestation as a surname in the Semitic world while its Greek translation, δίδυμος, is widely used as a surname in the ancient world. Quite naturally one would inquire about Thomas' twin. Given the fact the biblical literature is silent on the matter several later texts, including the third century apocryphal *Acts of Thomas* alleged that Thomas was Jesus' own twin.

In two passages that have no parallel in the synoptic tradition, the Gospel according to John introduces Thomas as a disciple of Jesus. In the first, Jn 11:16 portrays Thomas as the fearless disciple, prepared to follow Jesus to his death and encouraging the other disciples to do the same. In the second passage, however, Thomas appears confused when confronted with Jesus' prediction about his own death. In the second, Thomas' misunderstanding of Jesus' mission then becomes the occasion for Jesus' proclamation that he is "the way, the truth and the life" (Jn 14:6). It is in the final two passages that we find the most popular portrayal of the Apostle Thomas as 'doubting Thomas'. In these passages the Fourth Gospel omits the scene in the synoptic accounts where the disciples collectively express doubt when presented with the testimony of the first witnesses to Jesus' Resurrection (Mt 28:17; Mk 16:13; Lk 24:10–11).

The importance of Thomas as a character in the Fourth Gospel gave rise to many popular traditions about the career of the Apostle. According to the *Coptic Gospel of Thomas* Thomas was the recipient of secret revelations from Jesus after the Resurrection. These revelations have a distinctly Gnostic character. The *Acts of Thomas* offers a legendary description of the apostle's missionary activity in India. The tradition embodied in these legends have been maintained by Christians in India for centuries, and the existence of primitive and distinctive Christian communities in India prior to the arrival of Western colonial missionaries provide some oblique support for these traditions.

Feast: Dec. 21 (Latin Church).

Bibliography: R. E. BROWN, *The Gospel According to John,* 2 v., Anchor Bible Commentary. (Garden City, NJ 1966–1970). R. F. COLLINS, "The Representative Figures of the Fourth Gospel," *Downside Review* 94 (1976): 26–46, 118–132. J. P. MEIER, "The Circle of the Twelve: Did it Exist During Jesus' Public Ministry?" *JBL* 116 (1997): 635–72.

[C. MCMAHON]

THOMAS À KEMPIS

Spiritual writer; b. Kempen, near Düsseldorf, the Rhineland, 1379 or 1380; d. Zwolle, the Netherlands, Aug. 8, 1471. À Kempis was the younger of two sons of a peasant family, Hammerken; his name, À Kempis, was derived from his native village. His first schooling he received in Kempen, possibly in the school for local children conducted by his mother. From 1393 to 1398 he was a student in Deventer, under the patronage of FLORENTIUS RADEWIJNS, successor of Gerard GROOTE, founder of the Brothers of the Common Life. In 1399, instead of joining the Brothers of the Common Life as he had planned, he entered Mt. St. Agnes, a newly founded monastery of the CANONS REGULAR OF ST. AUGUSTINE, where his brother, John, 15 years his senior, was prior.

À Kempis was not clothed as a novice until 1406, a fact sometimes alleged as evidence that he was a dullard, but the delay was due to the unfinished state of the buildings. In 1413 he was ordained, and the remainder of his long life he spent at Mt. St. Agnes, except for a period of three years when the community moved because of an interdict. Little is known of his activity, aside from his transcription of manuscripts and composition of numerous works. He was subprior in 1425 and again in 1448, and for a time acted as master of novices.

Besides the copying of numerous manuscripts, including one of the Bible, Thomas is most commonly credited with the authorship of the *IMITATION OF CHRIST.*

He also wrote many works of devotion, collections of sermons, and contemporary chronicles. He is considered the most complete and outstanding representative of DEVOTIO MODERNA. This is evident especially from his treatises on the life of the soul and his spiritual conferences. Outstanding among these are: *Soliloquium animae*, considered one of the most characteristic works of the WINDESHEIM school, which contains practical counsels on fidelity to the movements of grace; *De tribus tabernaculis*, considerations on poverty, humility, and chastity; *De fideli dispensatore*, counsels to a contemplative in charge of the material goods of the monastery; *Sermones ad novicios*, 30 conferences for the novices at Mt. St. Agnes, concerned with the common life, keeping guard over the senses, the spiritual combat of the religious, and devotion to Our Lady.

À Kempis wrote a number of chronicles and lives of the saints. Among these are: *Vita Gerardi Magni*, an account of the life of Gerard Groote; *Vita Florentii*, a life of Gerard's successor; *Chronica Montis Sanctae Agnetis*, a history of Mt. St. Agnes, one of the principle sources for À Kempis's life. His works have been published in a critical edition: *Opera Omnia* ed. M. J. Pohle (7 v. Freiburg 1910–22).

Bibliography: J. MERCIER, *Dictionnaire de théologie catholique* 15.1:761–765. A. HYMA, *The Brothers of the Common Life* (Grand Rapids, Mich. 1950).

[P. MULHERN]

THOMAS AGNI

Dominican author, religious superior, bishop, patriarch of Jerusalem; b. Lentini, Sicily; d. Acco, Palestine, Sept. 22, 1277. He became a Dominican *c.* 1220, and founded the priory of San Domenico in Naples in 1231 and became its first prior. As prior he conferred the religious habit on (St.) THOMAS AQUINAS. In 1255 (not 1247) he was provincial of the Roman province. Thomas governed the following dioceses: Bethlehem, from Sept. 4, 1255; Messina, from 1262; and Cosenza, from April 4, 1267. From March 19, 1272, until his death he was patriarch of Jerusalem. As patriarch he settled the conflict over the kingship of Jerusalem in favor of Hugo II of Cyprus and appealed to King Henry III of England for help in the Holy Land. He wrote a life of St. PETER MARTYR of Verona.

Bibliography: J. QUÉTIF and J. ÉCHARD, *Scriptores ordinis praedicatorum* (New York 1959) 1.1:358–360. M. CONIGLIONE, *Archivum fratrum praedicatorum* 2 (1932) 443. H. C. SCHEEBEN, *ibid.* 4 (1934) 129. A. PAPILLON, *ibid.* 6 (1936) 26.

[C. LOZIER]

Thomas À Kempis. (©Bettmann/CORBIS)

THOMAS AQUINAS, ST.

Italian Dominican theologian, Doctor of the Church, patron of Catholic schools; b. Roccasecca, near Monte Cassino, *c.* 1225; d. Fossanuova, near Maenza, March 7, 1274; honored under the scholastic titles of Doctor Communis (13th century), Doctor Angelicus (15th century), and many others. [*See* DOCTOR (SCHOLASTIC TITLE).] He is the most important and influential scholastic theologian and philosopher, one whom the Church has made "her very own" [Pius XI, *Studiorum ducem, Acta Apostolicae Sedis* 15 (1923) 314]. This article treats of Thomas's life and doctrine, the ecclesiastical approval that has been accorded him, and his works and their English translations. (For a synthetic statement of Thomas's doctrinal positions and of his influence, *see* THOMISM.)

Life and Doctrine

The youngest son of Landolfo of Aquino (*c.* 1163–Dec. 24, 1245[?]), master of Roccasecca and Montesangiovanni, justiciary of FREDERICK II, and his second wife, Teodora of Chieti (d. 1255), of Lombard origin, Thomas had five sisters (Marotta, a Benedictine abbess of Santa Maria di Capua in 1254; Teodora, wife of Count Roger of San Severino and Marsico; Maria, wife of Guglielmo of San Severino; Adelasia, wife of Count Roger of

Manuscript page showing "littera inintelligibilis," written and autographed by St. Thomas Aquinas.

and grammar, although he never mastered calligraphy, which in part accounts for Thomas's notorious *littera inintelligibilis*. The struggle between Pope and Emperor reached a climax in 1239, when Frederick, infuriated by a second excommunication, exiled foreign monks and sent troops to occupy Monte Cassino as a fortress. By the spring of 1239 the new abbot sent the oblates, including Thomas, to one of the two Benedictine houses in Naples, San Demetrio or San Severino, to complete their studies at the imperial university of Naples, founded by Frederick II in 1224 as a rival to Bologna and other papal institutions.

At the University of Naples, where Thomas remained until 1244, he had Master Martin for grammar and logic and Peter of Ireland for natural philosophy [William of Tocco, *Ystoria,* 6; in *Ystoria sancti Thome de Aquino,* ed. Claire Le Brun-Gouanvic. (Toronto 1996)]. It was at Naples that Thomas was first introduced to ARISTOTELIANISM and the recently translated commentaries of Averroës. By 1243, at the latest, Thomas had become attracted to the DOMINICANS with their ideal of evangelical poverty, study, and service to the Church without ecclesiastical preferments. Deciding firmly to abandon family plans for him, he offered himself at the priory of San Domenico in Naples and received the mendicant habit toward the end of April 1244, at the age of 19. Normally Thomas would have completed his novitiate year at the priory in Naples, but Neapolitan Dominicans, having had previous experience (1235) with sons of noble and determined families, rushed Thomas immediately to Rome. Early in May 1244, Thomas set out on foot from Rome to Bologna in the company of John of Wildeshausen, Master General, and other friars en route to the general chapter, held annually at Pentecost.

Learning of her son's entry into a mendicant order, Donna Teodora hastened to Naples, then to Rome, only to learn that Thomas was traveling north to Bologna on the Via Cassia. She sent word to her older son, Rinaldo, camping at Frederick's temporary headquarters at Terni, near Acquapendente, to intercept Thomas and return him home, forcibly if necessary. Rinaldo encountered the traveling Dominicans a few miles north of papal territory near Acquapendente and forced Thomas to return by horseback to the family castle of Montesangiovanni, then to Roccasecca. The adamant arguments and appeals of Donna Teodora were of no avail even after many months. Thomas was determined not to be an abbot or any other ecclesiastical dignitary, but simply a Dominican friar, no matter what family plans had been made for him when he was a child.

Although Thomas spent most of his novitiate at home, it is incorrect to call this an imprisonment or cap-

Aquila; and one killed by lightning *c.* 1230), three older brothers (Aimone, soldier of Frederick II until 1233, when he began supporting the papal cause; Rinaldo, troubadour and soldier of Frederick until 1244, when he joined papal troops; and Landolfo), and at least three half brothers (Giacomo, Filippo, and Adenolfo). The family castle where Thomas was born, midway between Rome and Naples in Terra di Lavoro, was situated in the northern portion of the Kingdom of Sicily, ruled by the Hohenstaufen Emperor Frederick II from 1220 to 1250. Landolfo and his older sons were soldiers and civil officials in the service of Frederick, who was in almost continuous warfare with armies loyal to Popes HONORIUS III (1216–27) and GREGORY IX (1227–41). Political and religious loyalties rendered the position of the Aquino family very precarious. Amid political unrest, Thomas spent his first five years at the family castle of Roccasecca under the care of his mother and nurse.

Monte Cassino and Naples (1231–45). At the age of five or 6 (1231) Thomas was given (*oblatus*) to the Benedictine abbey of Monte Cassino by his parents in the hope that he would eventually choose this way of life and become abbot of the ancient monastery. A distant relative, Landolfo Sinnibaldo, was then abbot (1227–36). At Monte Cassino the oblate learned the elements of piety

Sacred Doctrine. What it is and to what it extends. All things are treated in it under the idea of God, either because they are God Himself or because they have some relation to God.							Item	Question
							1. Sacred doctrine	1
Part 1	**1. GOD** *(Threefold consideration)*	1st Concerning things that pertain to the divine essence					2. The one God	2–26
		2d Concerning things that pertain to the distinction of Persons					3. The Most Holy Trinity	27–43
		3d Concerning those things that pertain to the PRODUCTION of CREATURES by GOD	1st The PRODUCTION OF CREATURES				4. The creation	44–46
			2d The DISTINCTION of CREATURES	1st The distinction of things *in general*			5. The distinction of things in general	47
				2d The distinction of things in particular	(a) The distinction of *good and evil*		6. The distinction of good and evil	48–49
					(b) The distinction of corporeal and spiritual creatures	1st The *creature purely spiritual*	7. The angels	50–64
						2d The *creature purely corporeal*	8. The creature purely corporeal	65–74
						3d The *creature composed of body and spirit, i.e., man*	9. On man	75–102
		3d The PRESERVATION and GOVERNMENT OF CREATURES					10. The conservation and government of creatures	103–119
Part 2	**2. The ADVANCE of the RATIONAL CREATURE to GOD** *(Twofold consideration)* Those things should be considered by means of which man attains to or deviates from his end, i.e., HUMAN ACTS. But because singular things are the objects of operations and acts, therefore every operative science is perfected by the consideration of things in particular. Therefore a moral consideration of human acts must be given:	**1a 2ae IN GENERAL** — THE END OF MAN	1st The ACTS THEMSELVES	Some acts are peculiar to man; some are common to man and other living creatures; and since beatitude is the peculiar good of man inasmuch as he is rational, the acts that are peculiar to him have a more intimate connection with that good than those that are common to man and living creatures.	(a) Acts that are PECULIAR TO MAN		11. The end of man and beatitude	1–5
				(b) Acts that are COMMON TO MAN and other ANIMALS			12. Human acts	6–21
							13. The passions	22–48
			2d The PRINCIPLES of ACTS	(a) INTRINSIC PRINCIPLES — The intrinsic principles are POWERS of the soul and HABITS; but powers have already been treated in the 1st part. Therefore, now the consideration of HABITS:	1st HABITS IN GENERAL		14. Habits in general	49–54
					2d HABITS IN PARTICULAR	*Good* habits, *i.e., virtues*	15. The virtues	55–70
						Evil habits, *i.e., vices*	16. On vices and sins	71–89
				(b) EXTRINSIC PRINCIPLES — The extrinsic principle of GOOD is GOD, who instructs man by His *law* and helps and moves man by *grace*. The external principle of *evil* is the DEVIL. But he was treated in the 1st part; therefore it remains to treat of:	1st Laws		17. On laws	90–108
					2d Grace		18. On grace	109–114
		2a 2ae IN PARTICULAR	1st ACTS that pertain to ALL CONDITIONS of life (the virtues and vices affecting all men)	(a) THEOLOGICAL VIRTUES	(a) In the *intellect* — Faith		19. Faith	1–16
					(b) In the *will* — Hope, Charity		20. Hope	17–22
							21. Charity	23–46
				(b) CARDINAL VIRTUES	*Prudence*		22. Prudence	47–56
					Justice		23. Justice	57–122
					Fortitude		24. Fortitude	123–140
					Temperance		25. Temperance	141–170
			2d ACTS that pertain in a SPECIAL MANNER to SOME men.	(a) Graces gratuitously given (*gratiae gratis datae*)			26. Graces gratuitously given	171–178
				(b) *Active* and contemplative *life*			27. The active and contemplative life	179–182
				(c) The various *offices* and *conditions of men*			28. The various offices and conditions of men	183–189
Part 3	**3. CHRIST** Since Our Lord and Savior Jesus Christ, redeeming His people from their sins, has shown in Himself the way to truth, by which man, arising from the dead, is able to arrive at the happiness of immortal life, it is necessary to attain the scope of all theology, after considering the final end of men and the virtues and vices, to consider the Savior of all and the benefits He has conferred on man. Therefore, a consideration of:	1st The SAVIOR HIMSELF, i.e., the mystery of the Incarnation, what He did and suffered					29. The Incarnation	1–59
		2d The SACRAMENTS, which have their efficacy from the Incarnate Word.	(a) In GENERAL				30. The Sacraments in general	60–65
			(b) In PARTICULAR	Baptism			31. Baptism	66–71
				Confirmation			32. Confirmation	72
				Eucharist			33. Eucharist	73–83
				Penance			34. Penance, Qu. 84–90. Supplement	1–28
				Extreme Unction			35. Extreme Unction	29–33
				Orders			36. Orders	34–40
				Matrimony			37. Matrimony	41–68
		3d IMMORTAL LIFE, the end man attains through Christ, both God and man, suffering, dying, and rising from the dead						38. The Resurrection and Four Last Things	69–99

Chart of "Summa Theologiae," by St. Thomas Aquinas. (The Catholic University of America)

tivity, although his abduction was irregular and improper. There seems to be no historical truth to the legends of an attempt to seduce Thomas with prostitutes or of his miraculous girding with an angelic cord of chastity, edifying as they may have seemed to THOMAS OF CANTIMPRÉ, William of Tocco, and other hagiographers. Teodora and Landolfo (if he was still alive), aware of the change of political affairs and their inability to alter Thomas's decision, finally allowed him to rejoin the friars in Naples by the summer of 1245. Frederick II was deposed as Holy Roman Emperor at the Council of Lyons on July 17, 1245. The family of Aquino, accused of plotting his downfall, fled northward to Montesangiovanni in papal territory; Rinaldo was executed by Frederick and was considered a martyr by the Aquino family.

Early Studies in the Order (1245–52). In 1245 or 1246 Thomas resumed his northward journey to Paris, then to Cologne. Some scholars (e.g., A. Walz, I. T. Eschmann) maintain that Thomas was sent directly from Paris to Cologne for his early studies in the order. Others (e.g., P. Mandonnet, M. Grabmann, V. J. Bourke) maintain that Thomas studied under St. ALBERT THE GREAT at Saint-Jacques in Paris between 1245 and 1248. And others still (e.g., R.-A. Gauthier, J.-P. Torrell) are convinced that Thomas did study in Paris, but studied philosophy at the Faculty of Arts, as well as some tutelage under Albert.

It is certain that when Albert returned to Cologne in the summer of 1248 to organize and direct the *studium generale* ordered by the 1248 general chapter of Paris, he really "discovered," befriended, and sponsored Thomas, undoubtedly choosing him as his bachelor, i.e., assistant, in the newly organized *studium.*

Between 1248 and 1252 Thomas was Albert's pupil at Cologne, reporting Albert's extraordinary *Quaestiones super librum ethicorum* (at least 4 MSS extant) and *Quaestiones in librum de divinis nominibus Dionysii* (autograph, Naples, Bibl. Naz. B. 1, 54). It is probable also that as bachelor under Albert he read "cursorily" his *Expositio in Jeremiam, Expositio in threnos Jeremiae,* and part of *Expositio in Isaiam* (ch. 12–50). At Cologne Thomas was ordained to the priesthood at an early age, *etate adhuc juvenis* (bull of canonization; *Codificazione orientale, Fontii* 5:520).

In 1252 John of Wildeshausen asked Albert to recommend a suitable candidate for the doctorate at Paris, the Dominicans having two chairs at the university, one for Dominicans of the province of France (since 1229), the other for foreign Dominicans (since 1230). Albert recommended Thomas. Despite Thomas's youth and the growing antipathy toward mendicants at Paris, the master general was persuaded by Albert and Cardinal HUGH OF SAINT-CHER to assign Thomas to Saint-Jacques in Paris

Thomas Aquinas.

to read the *Sentences,* "ad legendum Sententias" (Tocco, *Ystoria,* 15; *Codificazione orientale, Fontii* 2:80).

Paris and University Conflicts (1252–56). Arriving in the fall of 1252, Thomas began lecturing on the *Sentences* under his new master, Elias Brunet de Bergerac, who had succeeded Albert in the Dominican chair for foreigners (1248–56). Tension between secular and mendicant masters at the university started at the university before the arrival of Thomas, but he and Dominicans in general were the center of the increasing storm (Y. M. J. Congar, 35–151). Jealous of the growing popularity of mendicant masters, the secular clerics, conspicuously unproductive in the middle of the 13th century, resented mendicant independence, concern for their own needs, and appeals for Roman dispensations, privileges, and special considerations. The mendicants, concerned with the education of their own men for the wide apostolate of revitalizing Christendom in a new age, were indifferent to local concerns of Parisian clerics. When secular masters voted to stop lecturing (March 1253), Dominican and Franciscan masters refused to comply; when secular masters urged an oath of retaliation against townsmen for killing a cleric in a brawl, mendicants refused and were expelled from the "consortium magistrorum" (September 1253). The second Dominican chair, for which Thomas was preparing, was particularly resented. More

important, secular clerics, having no clear concept of the new mendicant way of life in a changing world, confused friars with monks and objected to their desire to teach, preach, and care for souls.

Early Writings. During the growing conflict, Thomas prepared his lectures on the *Sentences* and wrote two youthful though significant works that expressed his clear, perceptive originality, *De ente et essentia ad fratres et socios* and *De principiis naturae ad fratrem Sylvestrum.* The former, purporting to clarify intricate logical concepts, is a highly original and unequivocal expression of (1) a real distinction between created essence and existence, (2) the pure potentiality of primary matter, (3) denial of materiality in separated substances, (4) participation of all created reality, material and immaterial, in the divine being, and (5) the Aristotelian dependence of logical PREDICABLES and abstracted forms (*forma totius* and *forma partis*) on existing individual realities. *De principiis naturae* is a brief, simple explanation of Aristotle's MATTER, FORM, and PRIVATION as principles of change, with an emphasis on the pure potentiality of primary matter.

Papal Intervention. In 1254 the Franciscan Gerard de Borgo San Donnino published an *Introductorius in Evangelium Aeternum,* applying the prophesies of Abbot JOACHIM OF FIORE to the mendicant orders, particularly to Franciscans. St. FRANCIS OF ASSISI was seen as the new Christ who inaugurated the new and last age of humanity, the age of the Spirit and the eternal gospel. The critical stage of evolution wherein the material institutions of Christ would give way to the spiritual Church of the Holy Spirit was declared to be at hand in the 1250s. This work provoked WILLIAM OF SAINT-AMOUR and other secular masters to open warfare against the mendicants. William's *Liber de antichristo et eius ministris* listed 31 heresies in the *Introductorius* and declared mendicants to be the precursors of ANTICHRIST foretold by Abbot Joachim. A university delegation under William was sent to persuade Pope INNOCENT IV to revoke all mendicant privileges, which he did in the bull *Etsi animarum* (Nov. 21, 1254). Innocent died on December 7. His successor, ALEXANDER IV, immediately annulled his predecessor's action by the bull *Nec insolitum* (Dec. 22, 1254). Infuriated, William continued to debate the issues at Paris, particularly with St. BONAVENTURE. In March 1256 William published the first version of his devastating attack, *De periculis novissimorum temporum.*

In this tense atmosphere Alexander IV ordered the chancellor of the university to grant Thomas Aquinas the license to teach (*licentia docendi*), even though he was under age, and to arrange for his inaugural lecture as soon as possible (*Chartularium universitatis Parisiensis*

1:307, dated March 3, 1256). On June 17, 1256, Alexander again ordered that Thomas be allowed to hold his inaugural lecture as master (ibid. 1:321). When Thomas finally gave his lecture (*principium*) on the text of Ps 103.13, he and his audience had to be protected by soldiers of St. LOUIS IX.

Although both Thomas and Bonaventure lectured for some months in their respective colleges as regent masters, the university refused to recognize their status. On Oct. 23, 1256, Pope Alexander sent a lengthy letter to the university, sternly commanding the recalcitrant administration, among other things, "to receive, insofar as it is within their power, into the academic community and into the University of Paris, the Friars Preachers and Minors now stationed in Paris, and also their students; and in particular and by name, the Friars, Thomas of Aquino, of the Order of Preachers, and Bonaventure, of the Order of Minors, as Doctors of Theology" (*Chartularium universitatis Parisiensis* 1:339). Actually it was not until Aug. 12, 1257, that the two friars were grudgingly admitted by Canon Christian of Verdun, the delegate of Bishop Reginald, to full magistral privileges in the university. The formal ceremony took place in the hall of the Franciscan house, the bishop and most secular masters being conspicuously absent.

Although excluded from the society of Parisian masters, both Thomas and Bonaventure replied pointedly to William of Saint-Amour's *De periculis,* which appeared in five versions between March and August 1256. Thomas attacked the doctrine in two disputations (*Quodl.* 7.7.1–2) and in a lengthy hurried reply, *Contra impugnantes Dei cultum et religionem* (between September and November 1256). William's book was condemned by the Holy See on October 5; the author was exiled permanently to his native town of Saint-Amour. Temporarily subdued, the conflict was revived ten years later by Gerard of Abbeville, an ardent disciple of William, between whom there was continuous correspondence during the interval.

First Paris Professorship (1256–59). Outstanding as Thomas was as a bachelor, lecturing between the Hours of Tierce and Sext (9 A.M. to 12 M.), he matured enormously as a master. Although young, he took his responsibilities seriously. "In his lectures he presented new problems, discovered a new and clear way of solving them, and he used new arguments in making these solutions" (Tocco, *Ystoria,* 15; *Codificazione orientale, Fontii* 2:81). As master his task was to lecture doctrinally on the Bible between the Hours of Prime and Tierce, resolve disputed questions in the afternoon, and preach to university clerics on special occasions. During his first three years at Paris as master, according to Mandonnet and oth-

ers, Thomas lectured on Isaiah and Matthew, but this is not historically certain (Eschmann, 395–397); in fact, the lectures on Matthew are almost certainly later (Torrell, 55–57).

The most masterful and important product of Thomas's first Parisian professorship was the disputed questions *De veritate* (1256–59) and the supervision of young bachelors assigned to him. Although present published versions cannot be considered actual classroom disputations, but polished, formalized versions of them, it is probable that *De ver.* 1–7, dealing with divine truth, were disputed and determined in the academic year 1256–57; *De ver.* 8–20, dealing with created truth, both angelic and human, originated in 1257–58; and *De ver.* 21–29, dealing with appetitive powers and grace, originated in 1258–59. Exceptionally conversant with current translations of source materials, Thomas adjusted many fundamentally Platonic and Augustinian views to his personal Aristotelian approach to Christian mysteries. As other great masters of the day, Thomas held quodlibetal disputations (*Quodl.* 7–11) during Advent and Lent. (*See* SCHOLASTIC METHOD; EDUCATION, SCHOLASTIC.)

During his first Parisian professorship Thomas seems to have had a fellow Dominican, Raymond Severi, as *socius,* i.e., secretary, confessor, Mass server, and general companion. By 1259 Thomas had a well-organized staff of other secretaries to copy needed texts and to take dictation. He also had at least two bachelors to train in theology, William of Alton, an English Dominican of Southampton, who succeeded Thomas as regent master in 1259–60, and a particularly close friend, HANNIBALDUS DE HANNIBALDIS, regent master (1260–62), who was created cardinal by Pope Urban IV in December 1262. Hannibaldus's commentary on the *Sentences* so closely followed the teaching of Thomas that it was once considered a work written by Thomas "ad Hannibaldum" and was published among his works (ed. Parma 22:1–436).

Completing his regency in Paris, Thomas was summoned to the general chapter at Valenciennes, midway between Paris and Cologne, in June 1259 under HUMBERT OF ROMANS. Appointed to a special commission on studies together with four other masters of Paris (Albert the Great, Bonhomme, Florent of Hesdin, and Peter of Tarantaise, later Pope INNOCENT V), Thomas helped to devise the first Dominican *ratio studiorum.* This emphasized the necessity of philosophical formation, the establishment of *studia artium* in Dominican provinces, the necessity of bachelors to assist lectors, and the importance of readily granting dispensations from other obligations for the sake of study (*Chartularium universitatis Parisiensis* 1:385–386). By 1259 many young men had entered the order who lacked a university training in arts.

The requirements of theology and the demands of Parisian masters were met by the new *ratio*.

Maturity in Italy (1259–68). After the chapter at Valenciennes, Thomas returned to the Roman province, where he was given REGINALD OF PIPERNO as his constant *socius*. The reasons for his return to Italy are much discussed by scholars. Thomas's personal motives aside, it seems that the needs of his order were best served there, particularly since his chair of theology at Paris was to be turned over to a new Dominican theologian and he was a member of the Roman province.

Chronology. The chronology of Thomas's stay in Italy is not at all clear. Most recent writers follow that suggested by Mandonnet, according to which Thomas first taught at Anagni from 1259 to 1261, this being where the papal Curia resided during the last years of Alexander IV's pontificate; then from 1261 to 1265 he passed the school years in Orvieto, the residence of Urban IV, with whom Thomas was on particularly friendly terms; then from 1265 to 1267 he taught in Rome at the Dominican priory of Santa Sabina; and finally, from 1267 to the fall of 1268, when he returned to Paris to begin his second regency, he served with the Curia of Clement IV in residence at Viterbo [*Revue des sciences philosophiques et théologiques* 9 (1920) 144].

Several observations are to be made with regard to this common account. Although there is no doubt that Thomas was highly regarded by both Urban IV and Clement IV, it seems improbable that he was ever master of the sacred palace in the modern sense or even lector in the papal curial school that was founded by Innocent IV in 1245. Likely as not, Thomas taught in Anagni, Orvieto, and later in Viterbo, but in each case at the Dominican priory that happened to be near the Roman Curia. This interpretation is strengthened by an ordination of the general chapter of Bologna in 1267 to the effect that the superior of the Roman province should take care always to have a competent prior and a competent lector in the priory near the papal residence.

Again, some documentary evidence suggests that in 1260 Thomas was made a preacher general in his province. This title was not only a sign of distinction; it also authorized him to take part in the provincial chapters that were held each year. Since the places of these chapters are known, one is able to reconstruct where Thomas probably was each year, in the early summer, for a limited period.

A second fact, probably one of the best documented in Aquinas's life, is that Thomas was in charge of a *studium* at Rome in 1265. An ordination of the provincial chapter of 1265 in Anagni, in fact, enjoined Thomas, "in remission of his sins," to inaugurate and direct such a *studium* in the priory of Santa Sabina. BARTHOLOMEW OF LUCCA mentions this in his biography of Thomas, and leads one to understand that two of Aquinas's major enterprises, the *Summa theologiae* and the commentaries on Aristotle, were intimately connected with this regency in Rome. It could well be that the erection and organization of the *studium* at Santa Sabina was Thomas's main, if not his only, scholastic activity in Italy.

A third document bearing on this period is more mysterious. It is a letter of June 9, 1267, from Clement IV enjoining Thomas to assign two brethren to serve with the Dominican bishop of Jibleh in Syria, Walter of Calabria (A. Potthast, *Regesta pontificum romanorum inde ab a. 1198 ad a. 1304* 20037). Since Thomas, as far as is known, never had any jurisdictional authority over other friars, the letter can only give evidence of the special relationship that obtained between Thomas and Clement IV, probably not unlike that between him and Urban IV.

Writings. Additional information on Thomas's life may be gleaned from the works composed during this period. He continued work on the *Summa contra gentiles,* begun in Paris (1.53 completed there), which many scholars attribute to a request made of Thomas by RAYMOND OF PEÑAFORT, to assist Spanish missionaries in their debates with cultivated Muslims and Jews. Expressing the intent of this highly original *summa,* Thomas said, "My intended purpose is to show, within the limits of my capacity, the truth that the Catholic faith professes, by means of the refutation of the errors opposed to it" (*C. gent.* 1.2.). The result was a theological synthesis that departed radically from the *Sentences* of Peter Lombard. Thomas wrote this work by hand, the last he would so compose, a possible indication that he had more time at his disposal in Italy than he had had at Paris.

Another significant work dating from this period is the *Catena aurea* (golden chain), as it was called from the 14th century on; Aquinas himself referred to its as the *Expositio continua in Matthaeum, Marcum, Lucam, et Johannem.* This work was commissioned by Urban IV, to whom the part on Matthew is dedicated. Urban died in 1264, and a manuscript of this portion fixes the date of its composition in 1263. The remaining portions were dedicated to a former student, the Dominican Cardinal Hannibaldus de Hannibaldis, and thus were not completed until after the death of Urban. The *Catena* is a gloss in the technical medieval sense, i.e., a string of passages selected from the works of various writers and arranged for the elucidation of some portion of Scripture, in this case, the four Gospels. It was an immediate success, and is among the most widely diffused works of Aquinas in both the manuscript and the early printed editions. Although a mere compilation, containing not one word of Thomas himself, the *Catena* seems to mark a turning point in Aquinas's thought. For beginning with the gloss on Mark, Aquinas's research into Greek patristic sources became more and more intense; he seems even to have procured new translations of certain Greek Fathers. Indeed, some of his treatises in the *Summa theologiae* are differently constructed from the corresponding ones in the commentary on the *Sentences* precisely because of the influence of Greek theology.

A related work of Aquinas, *Contra errores Graecorum,* grew out of a request of Urban IV, who asked Thomas for an expert opinion of a work by Bp. Nikolas of Cotrone that attempted to show a harmony between the Greek Fathers and the main points of Latin orthodoxy. The Latin version of Nikolas misrepresented the Greek; and Thomas, although not questioning the authenticity of the text, was evidently ill at ease with expressions contained in it. Thomas's evaluation was written probably in the summer of 1263.

According to Bartholomew of Lucca, the plan of the *Summa theologiae* was conceived in Rome in 1265, and the *prima pars* was almost certainly finished before Thomas left Italy to teach again in Paris. The fact that the *Summa,* as Aquinas himself notes in the prologue, was written for students of theology, and that it departed radically from the conventional theological syntheses of the time seems to confirm that it was written for use in the *studium.* Here Thomas could present an innovation in theological learning that might have been unacceptable at Paris but that could now be ventured in his order and within the confines of his home province.

Bartholomew holds also that Aquinas composed his commentaries on the Aristotelian corpus while at Rome. But this is questionable, since recent scholarship shows that the greater part of these commentaries were composed at a later date. Yet it appears that the plan of the enterprise was conceived, and its foundation laid, while Aquinas was in Italy. When he returned to his province in 1259, his knowledge of Aristotle, impressive as this was, was largely second-hand and based on translations from the Arabic rather than from the Greek. While in the company of Urban IV, who had been in the East before becoming pope, Thomas became more aware of the need for direct translations. Already in the *Contra gentiles* (e.g., 2.21) Aquinas showed a preoccupation with the *littera* and the *intentio* of Aristotle. Tradition credits him also with the initiative in regard to new, more accurate translations both of Aristotle and of his Greek commentators. His chief translator was WILLIAM OF MOERBEKE, a Flemish Dominican who had been in Greece and was later to become archbishop of Corinth, with whom Aqui-

nas worked personally, possibly during the pontificate of Urban IV, but certainly during the reign of Clement IV. The written exposition of the commentaries, although perhaps based on lectures given in Rome, was not finished until later.

Bartholomew of Lucca is the basis also for the attestation that Aquinas, at the mandate of Urban IV, composed the Office of the feast of Corpus Christi. This must have been prior to 1264, when the feast was inaugurated. Modern liturgical scholars question Bartholomew's accuracy, since the feast was celebrated earlier in Belgium and several of the hymns antedate Aquinas. Yet as William of Tocco records, "[Thomas] wrote the Office of Corpus Christi at the command of Pope Urban, in which he expounded all the ancient forms of this sacrament and compiled the truths that pertain to the new grace" (Tocco, *Ystoria,* 18). Tocco speaks of the work as a compilation, and thus it is quite clear that it was not an original composition. It seems that Thomas functioned there as an editor, working under the direction of the Pope, and that he should be credited with this work. The liturgical text used in the 20th century, it may be noted, is not identical with what Thomas compiled, being based on interpolations introduced in later centuries.

Second Paris Professorship (1269–72). Exactly when, and under what circumstances, Thomas began his second term of teaching at the University of Paris is not clear. It is certain, however, that he was already in Paris in May of 1269 (the school year ran until June), for he was present at the general chapter in Paris at that time. Moreover, he was there not as a delegate of his province but rather as a master present in Paris. Thus at this time he must have been teaching in Paris. Mandonnet argues that it is probable that Thomas had completed one quodlibetal disputation, viz, Easter 1269, when he appeared at the general chapter. He may even have left Italy earlier, as some have argued, and arrived in Paris in the fall of 1268.

Either date for the beginning of Thomas's second professorship at Paris raises the question as to why he would have left Italy in the midst of a school year to go to Paris. The answer that some have proposed—that the Dominican holding the chair for foreigners was sick or died, and thus a substitute had to be found—will not stand close scrutiny. More plausible, perhaps, is the explanation of H. C. Scheeben that the master general, JOHN OF VERCELLI, in view of the disputed status of Aristotelianism at the university, had invited Albert the Great to return to Paris [*Albert der Grosse* (Vechta 1931) 91]. His invitation reached Albert rather late, i.e., some weeks before Sept. 1, 1268, and Albert, who was then about 75 years old, declined. Thus the plan concerning the chair at Paris had to be recast, and there was some delay; according to this interpretation, Thomas was a second, if a more fortunate, choice.

Augustinian Orthodoxy. Whatever the details, the motivation behind this assignation of an eminent Dominican to a second term at Paris is fairly clear. The crisis provoked by the rise of Latin Averroism at the university was already sufficient reason, but there was the additional concern of defending the philosophy and theology that had been developed among the Dominicans generally, mainly through the efforts of Albert and Thomas, against the older type of doctrine that may be characterized as Augustinian. Gilson, considering the latter situation, puts his finger on St. Bonaventure, who was the superior of the Franciscan Order with his headquarters at Paris, as the source of the difficulty [*The Philosophy of St. Bonaventure,* tr. I. Trethowan and F. J. Sheed (New York 1938) 23]. Yet Bonaventure never came out directly against Thomas. That there was a personal friendship between them, as tradition affirms, seems doubtful; whether there was or not, Gilson correctly detects ''fairly good grounds for maintaining that any esteem that may have existed between them did not extend to each other's ideas.''

Although Bonaventure did not criticize Thomas openly and directly, the Franciscan JOHN PECKHAM, who was then at Paris, did. The doctrinal controversies between Thomas and SIGER OF BRABANT were in fact preceded by a violent discussion between Peckham and Aquinas. And behind Peckham there was of necessity the figure of Bonaventure, who was directly opposed to the type of theological Aristotelianism that Albert and Thomas were standing for. Thomas in particular was maintaining against Augustinianism that one of his own doctrines, a doctrine that seemed to concede most to the principles of Latin Averroism, viz, that of creation in time, cannot be philosophically demonstrated, since philosophically there is no contradiction in the notion of a world created from eternity. In any event, this is the type of controversy that could well have caused the master general to take such an unprecedented step as this second assignment of a master to the University of Paris.

Mendicant Controversy. Apart from the question of Augustinian theology, the issue raised earlier against the mendicants by William of Saint-Amour continued to be disputed. In 1266–67 a voluminous encyclopedia, *Collationes catholicae et canonicae scripturae,* had appeared; this was nothing but a considerably enlarged revision of *De periculis novissimorum temporum.* Thus, when Thomas returned to Paris, he found the atmosphere quite uncongenial. In the summer of 1269 a pamphlet of anonymous authorship was directed against the Franciscan THOMAS OF YORK; its writer was later revealed to be GE-

RARD OF ABBEVILLE, a secular master at Paris, who turned out to be the main figure in this second phase of the controversy. Against Gerard, Bonaventure wrote his *Apologia pauperum contra calumniatorem.* At the same time, Thomas entered the arena with his opusculum *De perfectione vitae spiritualis.* The major part of the work is a systematic theological treatise on the perfection of the Christian life, but the concluding chapters (21–26) are clearly a rejoinder to Gerard. This opusculum, dating from the beginning of 1270, soon enjoyed great popularity at the university.

Another secular master who involved himself in the controversy was Nicholas of Lisieux, who wrote the pamphlet *De perfectionibus status clericorum.* Apparently on the occasion of this, Thomas composed his *Contra pestiferam doctrinam retrahentium pueros a religionis ingressu,* a work that reflects concern also with other pamphlets, sermons, and academic discussions. His concluding words are worthy of note, for they reflect the gravity of the situation. Thomas cautioned that these problems are not solved simply by discussing them with young students and so misleading them; rather they should be worked out in writing, according to strict reasoning, and with the most careful consideration.

Other of Thomas's writings contain elements that belong to the Geraldinist (so named after Gerard or Gerald of Abbeville) controversy. Among these may be enumerated some of the questions of the 2a2ae of the *Summa theologiae, Quodlibets* 1, 3, 4, 5, and 12, and a series of sermons edited by T. Käppeli [*Archivum Fratrum Praedicatorum* 13 (1943) 59–94]. Despite such efforts on the part of the mendicants, Nicholas of Lisieux would not give in, but wrote a special pamphlet entitled *Contra Thomam et Pecham.* Thus the battle went on, although it did relax somewhat after the death of the main protagonist, Gerard of Abbeville, on Nov. 8, 1272.

Latin Averroism. Another controversy in which Thomas became involved during his second professorship at Paris concerned his interpretation of Aristotelian philosophy; this was challenged by a group of professors in the arts faculty, led by Siger of Brabant, who came to be known as Latin Averroists (*see* AVERROISM, LATIN). These thinkers saw in Aristotle conclusions that contradict Christian doctrine; they were good students of Aristotle, but in fairness to Thomas it must be noted that, in drawing their conclusions, they were also influenced by non-Christian thinkers such as Averroës, Avicenna, and PROCLUS, and by Neoplatonic treatises such as the *LIBER DE CAUSIS.* Their interpretation was influential in the arts faculty and soon drew the opposition of the theologians. The situation came to a head on Dec. 10, 1270, when the bishop of Paris, Étienne TEMPIER, drew up a list of 18 errors and condemnable propositions that contained the essence of Averroistic teaching (*Chartularium universitatis Parisiensis* 1:486).

In the condemnation of 1270 Thomas's Aristotelianism was in no way mentioned. Propositions 10–12 are directed against the negation of divine providence in the order of contingent things; prop. 5–6, against the eternity of the world; prop. 1, 2, 7, 8, and 13, against the thesis that there is numerically only one human intellect; and prop. 3, 4, and 9, against negations of free will. This syllabus was clearly addressed to an exaggerated Aristotelianism, viz, that of the Averroists and not that of Albert and Thomas. Yet there are intimations that the traditionalist theologians, e.g., the Augustinians led by Bonaventure, were convinced of the futility of using Aristotle in any way in theology, and thus were implicitly attacking Thomas's doctrine. In fact, the project of the condemnation of 1270 had already included two more propositions that corresponded to Thomas's teaching, viz, prop. 14, concerning the doctrine of one substantial form in man, and prop. 15, concerning the simplicity of spiritual substances. These propositions were withheld in the actual condemnation, and Thomas was never excommunicated during his lifetime. But in a later condemnation, that of 1277, not only the two omitted in 1270 but at least thirteen more propositions relating to Thomas's teaching were included. It is a sad commentary on Tempier that his syllabus of 1277 is a disordered jumble of theses with no distinction between heretical error and controversial school opinion. True, it contains sound warnings against a pagan philosophy that could not be tolerated in Christendom, but it is even more emphatically the manifesto of a party, the self-defense of one particular school, viz, that of Augustinian traditionalism.

Thomas intervened in the Averroistic controversy with his famous *De unitate intellectus,* written probably before the condemnation, but not long before it, in 1270. In two manuscripts this polemical writing bears the phrase *contra Sigerum;* from the conclusion of this work, it seems probable that Thomas was answering an Averroistic treatise that thus far has not been discovered.

Another treatise that grew out of the controversy but that is directed against the Augustinians is the polemical *De aeternitate mundi contra murmurantes.* The *murmurantes,* or murmurers, were the overorthodox, overzealous, integralist theologians who were muttering complaints about their colleagues who, on the basis of Aristotelian doctrine, held that an eternally created world is not inconceivable or, in other words, that creation in time (and not CREATION as such) is an article of faith. Aquinas, in his usual fashion, discusses the arguments of these integralists serenely and objectively, but cannot refrain from uttering what is perhaps the most biting criticism in all his works: "they speak as though they alone were rational beings and wisdom had originated in their own brains." This opusculum, according to a good but probable conjecture, was composed in the beginning of 1271.

It should be noted, however, that Aquinas's proper contribution to such questions is not to be found in his special works, least of all in his polemical writings, but is to be found in all that he wrote, in these years especially, when constructing his philosophical and theological synthesis. The Aristotelian commentaries may here be mentioned first, for the greater part of them was finished or elaborated at this stage. Thus he produced his detailed expositions of the *Physics,* the *Nicomachean Ethics,* the *Politics* (to 1280a 7), *On Interpretation,* the *Posterior Analytics,* and possibly part of *On the Heavens and Earth.* Thomas's literary activity in these years assumed almost incredible proportions. Among his scriptural writings is the commentary on St. John (the first five chapters written by Thomas himself, the rest a *reportatio*); possibly the commentary on Matthew; and part of the commentary on the Epistles of St. Paul (Rom 1.1 to 1 Cor 7.9). Of the works of theological elaboration, the *Quaestio disputata de virtutibus* is almost certainly from this period, as are six, if not seven, of the quodlibets. Work on the *Summa theologiae* progressed steadily in these years; although the 1a2ae was probably begun in Italy, the remainder of the *secunda pars* and some 30 questions of the *tertia pars* were probably done at Paris. The 2a2ae, Thomas's most original contribution to theology, is surely a work of the second Parisian period.

Naples and Death (1272–74). Thomas left Paris in 1272 shortly after Easter, which fell on April 24. On the feast of Pentecost, June 12, 1272, he was already at Florence, where a general chapter of the order was being held in conjunction with a provincial chapter. The latter entrusted to Aquinas the erection of a *studium generale* in Naples. Thus he moved on to that city, where he resided until Feb. 12, 1274.

In Naples Thomas held class, lectured, and directed disputations in the halls of the still existing priory of San Domenico Maggiore, which was then next door to the University of Naples. At the time, Charles I of Anjou, reigning over the Kingdom of Sicily, was attempting to inject new life into the university. Thomas may have been recalled from Paris at his insistence, but it seems unwarranted to say that Aquinas became a professor at the university. He taught at the Dominican *studium,* which, together with similar institutions of the Franciscans and the Augustinians, were independent faculties. Their lecturers were appointed not by the king but by their own ecclesiastical superiors. Thomas was not the King's professor, and yet Charles I paid his prior 12 ounces of gold per year, the same stipend as was given the professors in the constitutional faculties.

In the Neapolitan period, Thomas's literary activity diminished considerably. His lectures on the Psalms belong in this period; he also commented on Aristotle's *On Generation and Corruption,* probably finished the commentary on *On the Heavens and Earth,* and possibly commented also on the *Meteorology.* He also preached a Lenten cycle of sermons in Naples during 1273 that formed the basis for the *De duobus praeceptis caritatis et decem legis praeceptis;* his exposition of the Our Father and the Hail Mary also seem to date from this period.

Thomas likewise continued his work on the *tertia pars* of the *Summa theologiae,* though the rhythm of its composition seems to have slowed down. The treatise on the Incarnation was completed and that on the Sacraments begun. The work progressed through the Sacraments in general, Baptism, and Holy Eucharist, and then stopped in the midst of the treatment of Penance. The date was Dec. 6, 1273, the feast of St. Nicholas, in whose chapel Thomas usually said Mass. In the words of Bartholomew of Capua something extraordinary happened: "After the Mass, he never wrote nor dictated anything, in fact he hung up his writing instruments"—an allusion to the Scriptures, for the Jews in their captivity hung up their musical instruments. This occurrence in the life of a man whose habit it was, after Mass and thanksgiving, to spend the whole day writing, dictating, or teaching, was indeed a surprising change. His *socius* Reginald inquired as to why he had given up his work. Thomas replied, "I cannot go on. . . . All that I have written seems to me like so much straw compared to what I have seen and what has been revealed to me" (Tocco, *Ystoria,* 47; *Codificazione orientale, Fontii* 4:376–377). He may have had a breakdown of some type; medieval hagiography would not disclose such particulars, but the fact remains that his productive life had come to an end.

The rest of Thomas's life may be related briefly. He had been summoned to the second Council of Lyons, which was to treat of the union of Latins and Greeks; his health was obviously not good, so he left Naples in due time to allow for the long journey to France. The only fixed points of this trip are, according to Tocco, Maenza and Fossanuova, both a few miles north of Terracina, near the Via Appia. In the castle of Maenza Thomas fell sick with a mortal illness. When he felt his end nearing, he had himself transported to the nearby Cistercian Abbey of Fossanuova. There are, as may be expected, many details recorded about Thomas's last days and hours, some of which are only legendary. It is frequently said, for example, that he dictated a commentary on the

Song of Songs to the Cistercian monks, this notwithstanding the experience of Dec. 6, 1273. The absence of a manuscript tradition for this commentary would argue that the work possibly never existed. Other details convey the general impression of a holy death. Two are especially noteworthy, viz, Thomas's emphatic insistence on his faith in the Real Presence and his submission of all his theological doctrines to the judgment of the Church. He died before he was 50 years old. Few men in history have been able to look back on so productive, fruitful, and holy a life.

Ecclesiastical Approval

The holiness of Thomas's death at Fossanuova, and the miracles that accompanied it, soon led to his being venerated as a saint in the monastery and its vicinity. He was buried in the abbey, and peasants began to bring the sick and infirm to his tomb, where many cures were reported. His memory was also alive and revered in his own order, particularly at Naples, where the priory of San Domenico became a center of devotion to him. Reginald of Piperno returned to Naples after preaching at the funeral at Fossanuova, and there seems to have stimulated William of Tocco and Bartholomew of Capua to document Thomas's life and preserve his cult. The Neapolitan tradition was likewise furthered by Bartholomew of Lucca, who had studied under Thomas at Naples and who was at San Domenico when news came of the master's death.

Canonization. Meanwhile, as early as May 1274, the arts faculty at Paris had requested the master general to send Thomas's body to the university. Yet his teaching continued to meet stiff opposition in the faculties of theology at both Paris and Oxford. At Paris, as has been seen, Tempier's condemnation of 1277 was at least implicitly directed against Thomas; at Oxford two successive archbishops of Canterbury, ROBERT KILWARDBY, himself a Dominican, and John Peckham, Thomas's former antagonist who had since been elevated to the episcopacy, continued the attack against him. The Dominicans generally, however, were closing their ranks around their greatest teacher. By 1316, when the prospect of Thomas's canonization was already being entertained, the Dominican JOHN OF NAPLES was publicly upholding his doctrine at Paris "with respect to all its conclusions." And in 1325, two years after the canonization, Stephen Bourret, Bishop of Paris, formally revoked Tempier's condemnation, so far as it "touched or seemed to touch the teaching of Blessed Thomas" (K. Foster, 4).

The initiative for the canonization possibly came from the Pope, JOHN XXII, but more probably from the Italian Dominicans. William of Tocco was commissioned in 1317 to collect materials for the Holy See. Several subsequent inquiries were instituted by John XXII, the last of which was conducted in November 1321 to examine Thomas's postmortem miracles. The canonization itself took place at Avignon with exceptional solemnity on July 18, 1323. It was a great public occasion, attended by King Robert of Sicily, and John XXII did not hesitate to create the impression that he was glorifying Aquinas as much for his doctrine as for the holiness of his life.

The canonization was the first step of a movement that developed and grew stronger in the course of history. Some two centuries later, Thomas was elevated to the dignity of a Doctor of the Church by Pope PIUS V (*Mirabilis Deus,* April 11, 1567; see J. J. Berthier, 97–99). Finally, in 1918, St. Thomas became an institution in the Church with his being mentioned in the Code of Canon Law—this is the only name in the Code—with the injunction that the priests of the Catholic Church should receive their philosophical and theological instruction "according to the method, doctrine and principles of the Angelic Doctor" (1917 *Codex iuris canonicis c.* 1366.2; cf. *c.* 589.1).

Other Approbation. This culmination of the Church's approval, of course, would not have been possible without a long history of endorsement by popes and Church councils. Shortly after the canonization, in 1344, CLEMENT VI praised the Order of Preachers for producing St. Thomas, and bore witness to the fact that his teaching was spreading throughout the entire Church; the same Pope proclaimed to a Dominican general chapter (Brives 1346) that no friar was to dare depart from the common doctrine of Aquinas (Berthier, 55–56). URBAN V praised St. Thomas's excellence as a Scripture scholar, and in 1368 enjoined the masters and doctors of the University of Toulouse to follow his doctrine (ibid. 53–65). Both NICHOLAS V in 1451 and ALEXANDER VI in 1496 testified that Thomas's teaching was enlightening the universal Church (ibid. 76, 84); in this they were merely echoing the sentiments of their predecessors. PIUS IV, in 1564, also acclaimed Aquinas, and St. Pius V declared him "the most brilliant light of the Church" (ibid. 96, 98). In 1603 CLEMENT VIII praised him as the angelic interpreter of the divine will and claimed that no error was to be found in his work (ibid. 109, 112); 11 years later, PAUL V cited him as the "defender of the Catholic Church and conqueror of heretics" (ibid. 117). In 1724 BENEDICT XIII pointed out that his was the "surest rule of Christian doctrine" (ibid. 147); and BENEDICT XIV, who himself had written many learned works, confessed in 1756 that any good to be found in them must be ascribed wholly to the Angelic Doctor (ibid. 158). In 1777 PIUS VI commended his doctrine as most consistent with Sacred Scripture and the Fathers (ibid. 170).

In a letter to the Dominican Raymond Bianchi, dated June 9, 1870, PIUS IX observed "that the Church, in the ecumenical councils held after his death, so used his writings that many of the decrees propounded found their source in his works; sometimes even his very words were used to clarify Catholic dogmas or to destroy rising errors" (ibid. 177). This statement may be substantiated by a study of the councils and their enactments (ibid. 281–319; G. M. Manser, 75–79). The Council of Vienne (1311–12), for example, condemned the teaching of PETER JOHN OLIVI for holding that the intellect of soul is not *per se et essentialiter* the form of the human body, which was one of Aquinas's teachings. Martin Luther himself remarked that at the Council of CONSTANCE (1414) it was Thomas Aquinas who had prevailed over John Hus (Berthier, 287). The Council of FLORENCE (1439–45) has been observed to be little more than a compendium of the *Summa theologiae* of Aquinas (ibid. 289). When the Fifth LATERAN COUNCIL reopened the question of the teaching on the human soul that had been treated by the Council of Vienne, it again reaffirmed Aquinas's doctrine (ibid. 294–295). And LEO XIII, describing Thomas's influence on the Council of TRENT (1545–63), was substantially correct when he said that "the Fathers of Trent, in order to proceed in an orderly fashion during the conclave, desired to have opened upon the altar, together with the Scriptures and the decrees of the supreme pontiffs, the *Summa* of St. Thomas Aquinas whence they could draw council, reasons, and answers" (*Aeterni Patris*). The *Summa* was not actually on the altar, as the sequel proved, but for all practical purposes it might as well have been. That Aquinas had a similar influence on VATICAN COUNCIL I (1870) is universally agreed.

Apart from the approbation of the Roman Church, many of Aquinas's works have been translated into Greek and have thus exerted an influence on Eastern theology (see Manser, 72–74). And ecclesiastical approval aside, even non-Catholic philosophers and theologians have praised his doctrine. According to ERASMUS, there was no theologian equal in industry, or more balanced in genius, or more solid in learning. G. W. LEIBNIZ admired the solidity of his doctrine, and C. WOLFF praised the keenness of his intelligence. A. von HARNACK attested to his brilliance, as did R. Eucken in giving at least indirect testimony to the strength of the Thomistic revival that was taking place in his lifetime (ibid. 85–89; S. Ramírez, 20).

But it remained for the more recent popes, from Leo XIII to Pius XII, to accord the fullest possible approbation to the teaching of St. Thomas Aquinas. The encyclicals *AETERNI PATRIS* of Leo XIII, *Studiorum Ducem* of Pius XI, and, less explicitly, the HUMANI GENERIS of Pius

XII all affirm and endorse Thomism as the Church's answer to the most pressing problems of the day (*see* SCHOLASTICISM, 3).

Authority of St. Thomas. So unique and unanimous an endorsement, along with the prescription of the Code of Canon Law, has conferred a special authority on the teachings of Aquinas. And yet, as the discussions surrounding the renewal of VATICAN COUNCIL II have witnessed, such authoritative ordinations have not been without their undesirable side effects. Through the centuries, there have always been those who have sought to acquire authority for themselves by invoking the patronage of the officially recognized Thomas. And there have also been the less ambitious, the mentally lazy and the mediocre, who have been content to read their own limited thoughts into the mind of the Angelic Doctor. Against such abuses it need perhaps be insisted that the emphatic recommendation of St. Thomas by ecclesiastical authority is neither a form of political conservatism nor a disciplinary means of assuring uniform mediocrity. Thomism is not, and never was, a canonically prescribed doctrine in the sense of being a system of propositions that can be well circumscribed, polemically established, and faithfully transmitted from generation to generation. Were it so, it would be difficult to see how SCOTISM and SUAREZIANISM could ever have survived in the Church or how a Catholic thinker could learn anything from other philosophies and theologies.

The official adoption of Aquinas's teaching by the Church can be understood only in terms of the inner harmony, the essential compatibility, that exists between his thought and her doctrine. And the Church approves him before all others because in his writings, as in no others, the totality of truth has found a unique expression, an expression of exemplary value. Thomas himself professed no doctrinal particularity; he belonged to no school; he was content with no existing synthesis. He undertook, rather, the grandiose project of choosing everything, of seeking the deeper intentions of an Aristotle and of an Augustine, of probing the ultimate meaning of both human reason and divine faith. He knew the limitations of human minds, his own included. And yet he searched for a wisdom that would incorporate and transcend all earthly knowledge, confident that such wisdom was to be found in the bosom of his Church. With reason, perhaps, that same Church finds in him the outstanding exemplar of the Catholic saint and scholar, and has never hesitated to recommend his study to her children.

Works And English Translations

The following catalogue of the writings of Aquinas classifies his works within the categories of theological syntheses, academic disputations, expositions of Sacred Scripture, expositions of Aristotle, other expositions, polemical writings, treatises on special subjects, expert opinions, letters, liturgical pieces and sermons, and works of uncertain authenticity. In each case a generic characterization of the writing is given, then its place in the various editions, and finally, if available, its English translation. The standard editions of the works of Aquinas are referenced as follows: Leonine, i.e., *S. Thomae Aquinatis opera omnia, iussu Leonis XIII edita* (Rome 1882–); Parma, i.e., *S. Thomae opera omnia,* 25 v. (Parma 1852–73; photographic reproduction, New York 1948–49); Vivès, i.e., *D. Thomae Aquinatis opera omnia,* ed. S. E. Fretté and P. Maré, 32 v. (Paris 1871–80); Turin, i.e., *Editio Taurinensis,* the various editions published by Marietti in Turin and Rome; Turin phil, i.e., *D. Thomae Aquinatis opuscula philosophica,* ed. R. M. Spiazzi (Turin and Rome 1954); Turin theol., i.e., *D. Thomae Aquinatis opuscula theologica,* ed. R. A. Verardo, R. M. Spiazzi, et al., 2 v. (Turin and Rome 1954); Mandonnet, i.e., *S. Thomae Aquinatis opuscula omnia,* ed. P. Mandonnet, 5 v. (Paris 1927); and Perrier, i.e., *S. Thomae Aquinatis opuscula omnia necnon opera minora,* v.1, ed. J. Perrier (Paris 1949); Busa, *S. Thomae Aquinatis opera omnia: ut sunt in Indice Thomistico, additis 61 scriptis ex aliis medii aevi auctoribus,* 7 v., ed. Roberto Busa, SJ (Stuttgart 1980).

Theological Syntheses. These writings include Aquinas's systematic exposition of the *Sentences* of Peter Lombard and the two *summae* for which he is most known, the *Summa contra gentiles* and the *Summa theologiae.*

Scripta super libros Sententiarum. A theological synthesis elaborated while Aquinas was lecturing at Paris on the *Sentences, c.* 1256. Editions: Parma, v.6–8; Vivès, v.7–11; Mandonnet (bks. 1–2), 2 v. (Paris 1929); M. F. Moos (bks. 3–4 to dist. 22), 2 v. (Paris 1933–47); Busa, v. 1.

Summa contra gentiles. A synthesis covering the entire range of Catholic truth specifically for defending the faith, apparently intended for the use of Dominican missionaries in Spain; begun possibly in 1258, completed certainly by 1264 (Grabmann, 270–272). Edition: Leonine, v.13–15 (Turin manual, Rome 1934); Busa, v. 2. English: *On the Truth of the Catholic Faith,* tr. A. C. Pegis et al., 5 v. (New York 1955–56).

Summa theologiae. Aquinas's main work, written for students of theology to replace conventional theological syntheses of the time; unique in its plan, whereby theology first attained the status of a science; begun in 1265 or 1266 and left incomplete in 1273; the supplement that purposes to bring the work to its completion is extracted mainly from bk. 4 of Aquinas's writings on the *Sentences*. Editions: Leonine, v.4–12 (Turin manual, 4 v. Rome 1948); Vivès, v.1–6; Ottawa Institute of Medieval Studies, 5 v. (Ottawa 1941–45); Busa, v. 2. English: English Dominicans, 22 v. (2d ed. New York 1912–36); Blackfriars edition, with facing page translation, ed. T. Gilby et al., 60 vols., (New York 1964–).

Academic Disputations. These are divided into two classes, the regular disputations, or *Quaestiones disputatae,* which were held in the school of the master, and the solemn disputations, or *Quaestiones de quolibet,* which were open to the public and were held twice a year, viz, during Advent (the Christmas quodlibet) and during Lent (the Easter quodlibet). The writings are not recordings of the actual disputations but rather stylized compositions written by the master, in this case Aquinas, on the basis of the scholastic performance.

Quaestiones disputatae. These include the regular disputations *De potentia Dei, De malo, De spiritualibus creaturis, De anima, De unione Verbi incarnati, De virtutibus,* and *De veritate;* their chronology is difficult to determine; with the exception of *De veritate* (Paris 1256–59), *De potentia* (Italy 1259–68), and *De virtutibus* (Paris 1269–72), there is no substantial agreement on the dates of their composition. Editions: Parma, v.8–9; Vivès, v.13–14; Mandonnet, 3 v. (Paris 1925); Turin, 2 v. 1953; Busa, v. 3. *De veritate,* Leonine, v. 22. *De malo,* Leonine, v. 23. *De anima,* Leonine, v. 24/1. *De spiritualibus creaturis,* Leonine, v. 24/2. English: *On the Power of God,* tr. English Dominicans (London 1932–34; Westminster, Md. 1952); *On Evil,* tr. Jean T. Oesterle (Notre Dame 1995); *The De malo of Thomas Aquinas,* tr. Richard Regan (Oxford, 2001); *On Spiritual Creatures,* tr. M. C. Fitzpatrick and J. J. Wellmuth (Milwaukee 1949); *The Soul,* tr. J. P. Rowan (St Louis 1949); *On the Virtues in General,* tr. J. P. Reid (Providence 1951); *On Charity,* tr. L. H. Kendzierski (Milwaukee 1960); *Truth,* tr. R. W. Mulligan et al., 3 v. (Chicago 1952–54); *Disputed Questions on Virtue,* tr. Ralph M. McInerny, (South Bend 1999).

Quaestiones de quolibet. Twelve such questions are traditionally ascribed to Aquinas; all seem to have been disputed at Paris, *Quodl.* 1–6, and possibly 12, from 1269 to 1272, and *Quodl.* 7–11 from 1256 to 1259. Editions: *Quaestiones de quolibet,* Leonine, v. 25; Parma, v.9; Vivès, v.15; Mandonnet (Paris 1926); Turin 1949; Busa, v. 3.

Expositions of Sacred Scripture. These are here listed according to the canonical order of the books commented on and not according to their chronology, which has been worked out in some detail by Mandonnet (*Revue thomiste* 1928–29). Busa, v. 5, contains texts of all the scripture commentaries, but the editions reprinted are of doubtful use.

Expositio in Job ad litteram. A typically Thomistic exposition, making a use of all the philosophical and scientific resources available at the time; its central theme is God's providence; completed probably during the pontificate of Urban IV (1261–64). Editions: Leonine, v.16; Parma, 14:1–147; Vivès, 18:1–227.

In psalmos Davidis expositio. The literary style of this commentary indicates that it is a lecture transcript; it exposes 54 Psalms of the first four nocturns (i.e., the nocturns of Sunday to Wednesday) of the Office then in use, and is incomplete; the lectures were probably given in Naples, 1272–73. Editions: common text with 51 Psalms in Parma 14:148–353 and Vivès 18:228–556; three more Psalms (52–54), ed. A. Uccelli (Rome 1880).

Expositio in canticum canticorum. If Aquinas wrote an exposition of Solomon's Song of Songs, the text has been lost. The two works printed in Parma 14:354, 387, and in Vivès 18:557, 608, are not authentic; the first was composed by HAIMO OF AUXERRE and the second by GILES OF ROME.

Expositio in Isaiam prophetam. A commentary with some theological developments (ch. 1–11), but whose latter parts are little more than a literal gloss of the text (ch. 12 to end); an autograph fragment (ch. 34–50) exists; composed probably 1245–52, although some assign 1269–72. Editions: *Expositio super Isaiam ad litteram,* Leonine, v. 28; Parma, 14:427–576; Vivès, 18:688–821, 19:1–65; A. Uccelli (Rome 1880).

Expositio in Jeremiam prophetam. A "literal exposition" of Jeremias that is finished only to ch. 42; Mandonnet gives its date as 1267–68. Editions: Parma, 14:577–667; Vivès, 19:66–198.

Expositio in threnos Jeremiae prophetae. A literal explanation of the lamentations of Jeremias, with no doctrinal investigations; one MS ascribes the work to AUGUSTINE (TRIUMPHUS) of Ancona; Mandonnet dates it in 1267. Editions: Parma, 14:668–685; Vivès, 19: 199–225.

Catena aurea. A stringing together of selected passages from the Fathers and ecclesiastical writers; from Mark on, it shows a remarkably good knowledge of Greek authors; composed between 1262 and 1268. Editions: Parma, v.11–12; Vivès, v.16–17; 2 v. Turin 1953. English: *Catena Aurea* (Oxford 1841–45).

Expositio in evangelium s. Matthaei. A lecture transcript regarded by most authors as originating at Paris,1256–59; it may, however, date from 1269–72. Editions: Parma, 10:1–278; Vivès, 19:226–668; Turin 1951.

Expositio in evangelium Joannis. One of Thomas's best scriptural expositions, originating at Paris 1269–72.

Editions: Parma, 10:279–645; Vivès, 19:669–842, 20:1–376; Turin 1952.

Expositio in s. Pauli epistolas. The common text is composed of several heterogeneous pieces that reveal the editorial policies of Thomas's early disciples; it is based on lectures in Italy but some parts were written by Aquinas himself; variously dated 1259–65 and 1272–73. Editions: Parma, v.13; Vivès, v.20–21; 2 v. Turin 1953.

Expositions of Aristotle. These comprise a series of commentaries on the more important works of Aristotle composed toward the end of Thomas's life. Busa, v. 4 contains all the commentaries on Aristotle (an others) from older editions.

In libros peri hermeneias expositio. An unfinished exposition that makes use of the commentary of Ammonius, whose Greek-Latin version was completed by William of Moerbeke on Sept. 12, 1268; dates probably from Paris, 1269–72. Edition: Leonine, v.1 (2nd edition, 1989) (Turin manual, 1955). English: *Aristotle on Interpretation. Commentary by St. Thomas and Cajetan,* tr, J. T. Oesterle (Milwaukee 1962).

In libros posteriorum analyticorum expositio. A commentary based on the translation of James of Venice but made probably with the help of a corrected version by William of Moerbeke; date unknown. Edition: Leonine, v.1 (2nd edition, 1989) (Turin manual, 1955). English: *Exposition of the Posterior Analytics of Aristotle,* tr. P. Conway (Quebec 1956).

In octo libros physicorum expositio. A commentary based on the older Latin versions in its earlier portions and later on the text of William of Moerbeke; written probably between 1268 and 1271. Edition: Leonine, v.2 (Turin manual, 1954). English: *Commentary on Aristotle's Physics,* tr. R. J. Blackwell et al. (New Haven 1963 [reprint: South Bend 1999]).

In libros de caelo et mundo expositio. One of Aquinas's best works as a commentator, composed probably in Naples, 1272–73. Edition: Leonine, v.3 (Turin manual, 1952).

In libros de generatione et corruptione expositio. An unfinished commentary, believed to be Thomas's last work in philosophy; dates from Naples, 1272–73. Edition: Leonine, v.3 (Turin manual, 1952).

In libros meteorologicorum expositio. Another unfinished commentary, composed sometime between 1269 and 1272. Edition: Leonine, v.3 (Turin manual, 1952). English: Excerpt (1.8–10) in L. Thorndike, *Latin Treatises on Comets* (Chicago 1950) 77–86.

In libros de anima expositio. A commentary based on the text of William of Moerbeke; the first book seems to be a *reportatio* of 1268, the last two a direct composition by Aquinas (1270–71). Editions: Edition: Leonine, v.45/1; Parma, 20:1–144; Vivès, 24:1–195; Turin 1949. English: *Aristotle's De Anima with the Commentary of St. Thomas Aquinas,* tr. K. Foster and S. Humphries (New Haven 1951).

In librum de sensu et sensato expositio. In librum de memoria et reminiscentia expositio. Two commentaries based on the text of Moerbeke and composed probably at the same period as the foregoing commentary. Editions: Leonine, v.45/2; Parma, 20:145–214; Vivès, 24:197–292; Turin 1949.

In duodecim libros metaphysicorum expositio. A commentary composed of various parts (lectures given at different times?), completed probably at Naples in 1272. Editions: Leonine, v.46 (in press as of 2001); Parma, 20:245–654; Vivès, 24:333–649, 25:1–229; Turin 1950. English: *Commentary on the Metaphysics of Aristotle,* tr. J. P. Rowan, 2 v. (Chicago 1961).

In decem libros ethicorum expositio. A commentary based on the version of Robert Grosseteste as revised by Moerbeke, seemingly done at the same time as *Summa theologiae* 2a2ae (1271–72). Editions: Leonine, v.47; Parma, 21:1–363; Vivès, 25:231–614, 26:1–88; Turin 1949. English: *Commentary on the Nicomachean Ethics,* tr. C. I. Litzinger, 2 v. (Chicago 1964).

In libros politicorum expositio. The authentic composition of Aquinas terminates at 3.6; composed probably during the same period as the foregoing. Editions: Leonine, v.48; Parma, 21:364–716; Vivès, 26:89–513; Turin 1949. English: selections tr. E. L. Fortin and P. D. O'Neill, *Medieval Political Philosophy: A Sourcebook,* ed. R. Lerner and M. Mahdi (New York 1963) 297–334.

Other Expositions. St. Thomas's other expositions deal with two theological tractates of BOETHIUS, a Neoplatonic work on the divine names, and the *Liber de causis.*

Expositio super librum Boethii de Trinitate. Not a commentary in the usual sense but a scholastic discussion of questions arising out of the text; important for its discussion of the nature and division of the sciences and their methodology; composed before 1260–61. Edition: Leonine, v.50; B. Decker (Leiden 1955). English: q. 1, *On Searching into God,* tr. V. White (Oxford 1947); qq. 5–6, *Division and Method of the Sciences,* tr. A. Maurer (Toronto 1953).

Expositio in librum Boethii de hebdomadibus. An exposition important for understanding Aquinas's notion of participation; composed about the same time as the previous work. Editions: Leonine, v.50; Parma, 17:359; Vivès, 28:468; Mandonnet, 1:165; Turin theol., 2:391.

Expositio in Dionysium de divinis nominibus. Aquinas's first attempt at a direct exposition of a Platonic work with a critical assessment of its value; composed after 1268. Editions: Parma, 15:258; Vivès, 29:373; Mandonnet, 2: 320; Turin 1950.

Super librum de causis expositio. Another of Thomas's encounters with Platonism, possibly his last; written after 1270. Edition: H. D. Saffrey (Fribourg 1954).

Polemical Writings. These comprise the works written specifically against the secular masters, the Latin Averroists, and the traditionalist theologians at Paris.

Contra impugnantes Dei cultum et retigionem. A refutation of the attack of William of Saint-Amour on the mendicants; written in 1256. Editions: Leonine, v.41; Parma, 15:1–75; Vivès, 29:1–116; Mandonnet, v.4; Turin theol., v.2. English: *An Apology for the Religious Orders,* tr. J. Procter (London 1902; Westminster, Md.1950).

De perfectione vitae spiritualis. A response to the attack of Gerard of Abbeville on the mendicants; written in 1269–70. Editions: Leonine, v.41; Parma, 15:76–102; Vivès, 29: 117–156; Mandonnet, v.4; Turin theol., v.2. English: tr. in three unpublished M.A. dissertations, by G. J. Guenther, C. G. Kloster, and J. X. Schmitt (St. Louis University 1942–44).

Contra pestiferam doctrinam retrahentium pueros a religionis ingressu. A work directed against Gerard of Abbeville and his followers; written in 1270. Editions: Leonine, v.41; Parma, 15:103–125; Vivès 29:157–190; Mandonnet, v.4; Turin theol., 2:159. English: tr. J. Procter, *op. cit.*

De unitate intellectus contra Averroistas. A treatise directed against the Parisian Averroists and particularly against Siger of Brabant; written in 1270. Edition: Leonine, v.43; L. W. Keeler (Rome 1936), in Turin phil., 63. English: *The Trinity and the Unicity of the Intellect,* tr. R. E. Brennan (St. Louis 1946).

De aeternitate mundi contra murmurantes. Thomas's treatment of the possibility of an eternally created world; written between 1270 and 1272. Editions: Leonine, v.43; Parma, 16:318; Vivès, 27:450; Mandonnet, 1:22; Perrier, 53; Turin phil., 105.

Treatises on Special Subjects. These comprise a variety of writings on particular problems in philosophy and theology.

De fallaciis ad quosdam nobiles artistas. If authentic, it would be one of Thomas's earliest compositions, written *c.* 1245. Editions: Leonine, v.43; Parma, 16:377; Vivès, 27:533; Mandonnet,4:508; Perrier, 428; Turin phil., 225.

De propositionibus modalibus. If authentic, an early work of Thomas, composed before 1252. Edition: Leonine, v.43; I. M. Bocheński (Rome 1940).

De ente et essentia. A significant work on an important theme; composed before 1256. Editions: Leonine, v.43; M. D. Roland-Gosselin (Le Saulchoir 1926, Paris 1948); L. Baur (Münster 1926, 1933), in Turin phil.; Perrier. English: *On Being and Essence,* tr. A. Maurer (Toronto 1949).

De principiis naturae ad fratrem Sylvestrum. A treatise on matter and form and the four causes; same chronology as the preceding. Edition: Leonine, v.43; J. J. Pauson (Fribourg 1950). English: *The Pocket Aquinas,* tr. V. J. Bourke (New York 1960) 61–77; R. Kocourek (St. Paul 1948).

Compendium theologiae ad fratrem Reginaldum socium suum carissimum. A brief compilation of the whole of theology; incomplete; date of composition disputed. Editions: Leonine, v.42; Parma, v.16; Vivès, v.27; Mandonnet, v.2; Turin theol., v.1. English: *Compendium of Theology,* tr. C. Vollert (St. Louis 1947).

De substantiis separatis, seu de angelorum natura. One of the most important of Aquinas's metaphysical writings; date uncertain. Edition: Leonine, v.40; F. J. Lescoe (West Hartford, Conn. 1962). English: *Treatise on Separate Substances,* tr. F. J. Lescoe (West Hartford, Conn. 1960).

De regno (De regimine principum) ad regem Cypri. A political work addressed to the King of Cyprus; composed *c.* 1267. Editions: Leonine, v.42; Perrier; Parma, 16:225; Vivès, 27:336; Mandonnet, 1:312; Turin phil., 257. English: *On Kingship,* tr. G. B. Phelan, ed. I. T. Eschmann (Toronto 1949).

Expert Opinions. These are a series of replies of Thomas to queries from the pope, the master general, and the general chapter held at Paris in 1269. They include: *Contra errores Graecorum,* addressed to Urban IV (Leonine, v.40; Parma, 15:239; Vivès, 29:344; Mandonnet, 3:279; Turin theol., 1:315); the *Responsio . . . de articulis CVIII ex opere Petri de Tarentasia,* addressed to the Master General, John of Vercelli (Leonine, v.42; Parma, 16:152; Vivès, 27:213; Mandonnet, 3:211; Turin theol., 1:223); the *Responsio . . . de articulis XLII,* addressed to the same, which is of particular importance for the difference of opinion it reveals between Aquinas, Albert the Great, and Robert Kilwardby, all of whom were sent the same questions (Leonine, v.42; Parma, 16:163; Vivès 27:248; Mandonnet, 2:196; Turin theol., 1:211); *De forma absolutionis,* likewise addressed to the master general (Leonine, v.40; Turin theol., 1:173); and *De secreto,* a reply to a question that arose in the general chapter (Leonine, v.42; Mandonnet, 4:497, repr. in Turin theol., 1:447).

Letters. These include the texts of 15 letters written by Thomas on various occasions; for a complete listing, see I. T. Eschmann, "Catalogue . . . ," 417–423. *De articulis fidei et ecclesiae sacramentis* was written to the archbishop of Palermo, *c.* 1262 [Editions: Leonine, v.42; Parma, 16:115; Vivès, 27:171; Mandonnet, 3:1; Turin theol., 1:141; tr., in part, J. B. Collins, *The Catechetical Instructions of St. Thomas Aquinas* (New York 1953)]. Of interest for its scientific content is *De motu cordis,* written to a Master Philippus, who was a physician and professor at Bologna and Naples, *c.* 1270 (Leonine, v.43; Perrier, 63; Parma, 16:358; Vivès, 27:507; Mandonnet, 1:28; Turin phil., 165). Similarly important for its views on usury and credit is *De emptione et venditione ad tempus,* written to the Dominican John of Viterbo, probably in 1262 [Edition: Leonine, v.42; Turin theol., 1:185; English: A. O'Rahilly, "Notes on St. Thomas on Credit," *Irish Theological Quarterly* 31 (1928) 164–165]. Also of significance for its views on financial policy is a letter to the Duchess of Brabant (actually, Margaret of Flanders), *De regimine Judaeorum* [Editions: Leonine, v.42; Perrier, 213; Parma, 16:292; Vivès, 27:414; Mandonnet, 1:488; Turin phil., 249; English: tr. J. Dawson, *Aquinas' Selected Political Writings,* ed. A. P. d'Entrèves (Oxford 1954) 85–95]. Finally, for its discussion of magnetism and similar "occult" phenomena, one should read *De occultis operationibus naturae* [Editions: Leonine, v.43; Perrier, 204; Parma, 16:355; Vivès, 27:504; Turin phil., 159; English: J. B. McAllister, *The Letter of St. Thomas Aquinas De Occultis Operibus Naturae* (Washington 1939)].

Liturgical Pieces and Sermons. Apart from the Office for the feast of Corpus Christi, the *Adoro te,* etc., the most significant is the Lenten cycle of sermons given at Naples in 1273, *De duobus praeceptis caritatis et decem legis praeceptis* (Edition: J.-P. Torrell, "Les *Collationes in decem preceptis* de saint Thomas d'Aquin. Édition critique avec introduction et notes," *Revue des sciences philosophiques et théologiques* 69 (1985): 5–40; 227–263; Turin theol., v.2; English: J. B. Collins, *op. cit.*). Eschmann lists some 20 more sermons delivered on various occasions ("Catalogue . . . ," 424–428).

Works of Uncertain Authenticity. These are philosophical treatises, *De instantibus, De natura verbi intellectus, De principio individuationis, De natura generis, De natura accidentium, De natura materiae,* and *De quatuor oppositis* (Edition: Turin phil.). For a critical discussion, see Eschmann, "Catalogue . . . ," 428–430. Two other philosophical works, *De fallacies* and *De propositionibus modalibus,* long thought to be early

products of Thomas's, are almost certainly not his. (See Torrell, 11.)

The original authors (W.A. Wallace and J.A. Weisheipl) acknowledged their special debt to I.T. Eschmann, OP, of the Pontifical Institute of Mediaeval Studies, Toronto, whose unpublished lecture notes on Aquinas were used in preparing the original article. Since the publication of the original article, Weisheipl published his own biography on St. Thomas (listed below), which was the definitive account of St. Thomas's life and works until the appearance in 1993 of J.-P. Torrell's biography (also below).

Bibliography: Life and Doctrine. J.-P. TORRELL, OP, *Saint Thomas Aquinas: The Person and His Work,* trans. R. ROYAL (Washington, DC 1996), being an English translation of Torrell's *Initiation à saint Thomas d'Aquin, vol. 1: Sa personne et son oeuvre,* (Fribourg 1993), which Torrell followed with his *Initiation à saint Thomas d'Aquin, vol. 2 Maître Spirituel,* (Fribourg 1996); S. TUGWELL, OP, "Thomas Aquinas: Introduction," in *Albert and Thomas: Selected Writings,* (New York 1988) 201–267; J. A. WEISHEIPL, OP, *Friar Thomas d'Aquino: His Life, Thought, and Work,* (Garden City 1974), second edition with *corrigenda et addenda,* (Washington, DC 1983); V. J. BOURKE, *Aquinas's Search for Wisdom* (Milwaukee 1965). K. FOSTER, ed. and tr., *The Life of Saint Thomas Aquinas: Biographical Documents* (Baltimore 1959), includes tr. of selections from *Codificazione orientale, Fontii* 1–6, William of Tocco's *Vita,* etc. F. STEGMÜLLER, *Repertorium biblicum medii aevi,* 7 v. (Madrid 1959–61) 5:322–353. F. STEGMÜLLER, *Repertorium commentariorum in Sententias Petri Lombardi,* 2 v. (Würzburg 1949) 1:393–410. J. QUÉTIF and ÉCHARD, *Scriptores Ordinis Praedicatorum,* 5 v. (Paris 1719–23); continued by R. COULON (Paris 1909–); repr. 2 v. in 4 (New York 1959) 1.2:271–347. Y. M. J. CONGAR, "Aspects ecclésiologiques de la querelle entre mendiants et séculiers dans la seconde moitié du XIIIe siècle et le début du XIVe," *Archives d'histoire doctrinale et littéraire du moyen-âge* 36 (1961) 35–151. A. WALZ et al., *Dictionnaire de théologie catholique,* ed. A. VACANT et al., 15 v. (Paris 1903–50; Tables générales 1951–) 15.1:618–761. G. K. CHESTERTON, *St. Thomas Aquinas* (New York 1933). R. M. COFFEY, *The Man from Rocca Sicca* (Milwaukee 1944). F. C. COPLESTON, *Aquinas* (Pelican Bks. Baltimore 1955). G. M. MANSER, *Das Wesen des Thomismus* (Thomistische Studien 5; 3d ed. Fribourg 1949). J. MARITAIN, *St. Thomas Aquinas,* tr. and rev. J. W. EVANS and P. O'KELLY (New York 1958). H. MEYER, *Thomas von Aquin* (2d enl. ed. Paderborn 1961). J. PIEPER, *Guide to Thomas Aquinas,* tr. R. and C. WINSTON (New York 1962). A. G. SERTILLANGES, *St. Thomas Aquinas and His Work,* tr. G. ANSTRUTHER (London 1933; repr. 1957). G. VANN, *Saint Thomas Aquinas* (New York 1947). A. M. WALZ, *Saint Thomas Aquinas: A Biographical Study,* tr. S. BULLOUGH (Westminster, Md. 1951). **Ecclesiastical Approval.** J. J. BERTHIER, *Sanctus Thomas Aquinas "Doctor Communis" Ecclesiae* (Rome 1914). S. RAMÍREZ, "The Authority of St. Thomas Aquinas," *Thomist* 15 (1952) 1–109. K. RAHNER, introd. to J. B. METZ, *Christliche Anthropozentrik* (Munich 1962). **Works.** G. EMERY, OP, "Brief Catalogue of the Word of Saint Thoams Aquinas," in J.-P. Torrell's *Saint Thomas Aquinas* (English trans., cited above) 330–361, whose content and format mirrors that of Weisheipl, and is ultimately dependent upon I. T. ESCHMANN, "A Catalogue of St. Thomas's Works: Biographical Notes," in É. H. GILSON, *The Christian Philosophy of St. Thomas Aquinas* (New York 1956) 381–439. V. J. BOURKE, *Introduction to the Works of St. Thomas Aquinas*

(New York 1948), repr. from Parma ed. of *Opera omnia*, v.1. M. D. CHENU, *Toward Understanding St. Thomas*, tr. A. M. LANDRY and D. HUGHES (Chicago 1964). M. GRABMANN, *Die Werke des heiligen Thomas von Aquin* (3d ed. *Beiträge zur Geschichte der Philosophie und Theologie des Mittelalters* 22.1–2; 1949). **Selected Writings.** THOMAS AQUINAS, *Basic Writings*, ed. A. C. PEGIS, 2 v. (New York 1945); *Introduction to Saint Thomas Aquinas*, ed. A. C. PEGIS (New York 1948); *The Pocket Aquinas: Selections from the Writings of St. Thomas*, tr. and ed. V. J. BOURKE (New York 1960); *Philosophical Texts*, tr. and ed. T. GILBY (New York 1951; pa. 1960); *Theological Texts*, tr. and ed. T. GILBY (New York 1955); *Selected Writings*, ed. M. D'ARCY (New York 1940).

[W. A. WALLACE/J. A. WEISHEIPL/M. F. JOHNSON]

THOMAS BELLACI, BL.

Franciscan lay brother; b. Florence, Italy, *c.* 1370; d. Rieti, Oct. 31, 1447. He is known also as Thomas of Florence, of Linari, of Rieti, and of Scarlino. After a youth spent in profligacy, Thomas repented and entered the FRANCISCANS of the Observance at Fiesole, *c.* 1392. Though only a lay brother, he soon became master of novices. In 1414 the Commissary General of the Observant Reform took him to the kingdom of Naples, where he worked for six years. At the request of Pope Martin V, he joined Anthony of Stroncone in opposing the heretical FRATICELLI (1422–30). From 1430 to 1439 his headquarters were at Scarlino. In 1439 he accompanied Albert of Sarteano to the East, whence he was ransomed by Pope Eugene IV in 1444; he returned to Rome the next year. His cult was confirmed by the Holy See in 1771.

Feast: Oct. 31.

Bibliography: *Acta Sanctorum* Oct. 13:860–892. A. MERCATI and A. PELZER, *Dizionario ecclesiastico*, 3 v. (Turin 1954–58) 3:1148. D. STÖCKERL, *Lexikon für Theologie und Kirche*, ed. M. BUCHBERGER, 10 v. (Freiburg 1930–38) 10:123. L. WADDING, *Scriptores Ordinis Minorum*, 86 v. (Lyons 1625–54); 11:336–346.

[F. D. LAZENBY]

THOMAS BRADWARDINE

English theologian, mathematician, and precursor of modern science, honored under the scholastic title of *Doctor profundus;* b. Bradwardine?, near Hertford, *c.* 1300; d. Lambeth, Aug. 26, 1349. He received his training in the arts and theology at Oxford, earning the B.A. before Aug. 2, 1321, and the M.A. *c.* 1323. First a fellow of Balliol College, he transferred to Merton College where he remained fellow from 1323 to 1335, when he joined the learned circle of RICHARD OF BURY. He was proctor of the university from 1325 to 1327. In 1337 he was made chancellor of St. Paul's, London, and from 1339 served as chaplain and confessor to Edward III. In 1348 he was elected archbishop of CANTERBURY, but Edward refused to ratify the election. When the new incumbent died shortly after taking office, Bradwardine was consecrated archbishop at Avignon, July 19, 1349.

During his regency in arts, Bradwardine's interests were chiefly mathematical and scientific. From this period come his *Arithmetica speculativa* (Valencia 1503), *Geometria speculativa* (Paris *c.* 1530), and the *Tractatus de proportionibus* (Paris 1481; new text and tr. by H. L. Crosby, Madison, Wisconsin 1955).

But Bradwardine's chief claim to fame rests upon his theological works, which include *De futuris contingentibus* [partial ed. B. M. Xiberta in *Festschrift für M. Grabman* (Münster 1935) 1169–80], *Sermo Epinicius,* and the famous *De causa Dei contra Pelagium et de virtute causae causarum ad suos Mertonenses* (ed. H. Savile, London 1618). The *De causa Dei,* Bradwardine's chief work covering nearly 900 folio pages, is a kind of summa, but it lacks the comprehensiveness of its antecedents, being concerned mostly with the burning issues of the day: grace, merit, predestination, God's knowledge of future contingents, and man's freedom. It is a sustained attack directed principally against the views of some influential 14th-century theologians whom Bradwardine calls the "modern Pelagians" (tentatively identifiable as DURANDUS OF SAINT-POURÇAIN, WILLIAM OF OCKHAM, ROBERT HOLCOT, THOMAS OF BUCKINGHAM, and ADAM WODHAM).

In his fight against these theologians, Bradwardine takes up the cause of God's sovereignty. He opposes the exaggerated independence granted to man, stating that "God is the necessary coproducer (*coeffector*) of every act of the created will" (*De causa Dei* 540). In all created activity, the action or movement of God is "naturally prior"; "in a sense, God necessitates every created will to elicit its own free act" (*ibid.* 646), yet the will remains free. "God wills," he says, "that man's will should not be forced or impeded by any necessity in its willing and not willing" (637). Throughout the work Bradwardine stresses the necessity of created grace: for him, the habit of grace and the will are the efficient cause of every good and meritorious work (364). He stresses too the need of good works (318). In the quarrel over future contingents, he defends the certainty and immutability of God's knowledge and human freedom (685). He regards Holcot's suggestion that Christ could have been deceived about the future as blasphemous (785–787).

Bradwardine is generally regarded as a theological determinist; this view has yet to be proved. Even more precarious is the thesis that he was a prereformer.

Bibliography: A. B. EMDEN, *A Biographical Register of the University of Oxford to A.D. 1500* (Oxford 1957–59) 1:244–246.

G. LEFF, *Bradwardine and the Pelagians* (Cambridge, Eng. 1957). H. A. OBERMAN, *Archbishop Thomas Bradwardine, a 14th-Century Augustinian* (Utrecht 1957). M. CLAGETT, *The Science of Mechanics in the Middle Ages* (Madison, Wis. 1959).

[J. J. PRZEZDZIECKI]

THOMAS CORSINI, BL.

Servite lay brother; b. Orvieto, Italy, *c.* 1260; d. June 21, 1343. There is very little to record of Thomas's life, since it was outwardly uneventful. Our Lady appeared to him in a vision and urged him to take up her cause. At first he was doubtful and attributed the vision to hallucinations, but when it was repeated, he decided to join the SERVITE Brothers. Despite his noble origin, he preferred to remain a simple lay brother, and he afforded miraculous proofs of virtue, self-abasement, and desire for the contemplative life. He heroically took upon himself the rigorous hardships of begging alms for his community. His cult was confirmed in 1768.

Feast: June 23.

Bibliography: A. MERCATI and A. PELZER, *Dizionario ecclesiastico*, 3 v. (Turin 1954–58) 3:1148. L. FISCHER, *Lexikon für Theologie und Kirche*, ed. M. BUCHBERGER, 10 v. (Freiburg 1930–38) 3:93. *Annales Ordinis Servorum Mariae* (Florence 1618). C. LAZZARINI, *Compendio della vita del bº Tommaso di Orvieto* (Orvieto 1858). B. M. SPOERR, *Lebens-Bilder aus dem Serviten-Orden*, 4 v. (Innsbruck 1892–95) v.1. *Monumenta Ord. Servorum S. Mariae*, ed. A. MORINI et al., 20 v. (Brussels-Rome 1897–1930) v.11. A. GIANI and A. M. GARBI, *Annales Sacri Ordinis Fratrum Servorum B. Mariae Virginis*, 3 v. (2d ed. Licca 1719–25) v.1. A. BUTLER, *The Lives of the Saints*, rev. ed. H. THURSTON and D. ATTWATER (New York, 1956) 2:626–627.

[F. D. LAZENBY]

THOMAS GALLUS OF VERCELLI

Known also as Thomas of Saint-Victor, Augustinian Canon of Saint-Victor, first abbot of S. Andrea di Vercelli, mystical theologian; b. probably in France, before 1200; d. Ivrea or Vercelli in Piedmont, Dec. 5, 1246. Thomas's early life is unknown. He became a member of the distinguished parisian Abbey of Saint-Victor, and was chosen in 1218 by Cardinal Guala Bicchieri to assist in founding of the richly endowed Victorine abbey and hospital of S. Andrea in Vercelli. He took an active part in directing the construction of the abbey, where he was first prior and then abbot. There he continued to expound and correlate Dionysian texts and Scripture with mystical themes, in the form of commentaries, synopses, and tracts, which were broadly acclaimed. He also brought Dionysian themes into his commentaries on the Song of Songs. His reputation was such that he drew the Franciscan *studium generale* from Padua to Vercelli in 1228. Loyalty to his benefactor's family in Guelf-Ghibelline politics forced him in 1243 or 1244 into exile and excommunication in the neighboring Ghibelline town of Ivrea, where he went on writing until his death. His tomb is in S. Andrea di Vercelli. A 16th-century edition of his *Extractio* of Dionysian works was reprinted in vv. 15 (29–275; 369–395) and 16 (39–349; 454–469; 578–583) of the Carthusian *Opera Dionysii* (Tournai 1902). His commentaries on Isaiah and the Song of Songs have now been presented in modern editions, although much of his writing still remains in manuscript.

Bibliography: THOMAS GALLUS. *Commentaries du Cantique des Cantiques*, ed. J. BARBET (Paris 1967); "Commentaire sur Isaïe de Thomas de Saint-Victor," ed. G. THÉRY, *La Vie spirituelle* 47 (1936) 146–162. J. WALS, "The *Expositions* of Thomas Gallus on the pseudo-Dionysian Letters," *Archives d'histoire doctrinale et littéraire du moyen-âge* 30 (Paris 1963) 199–220, text and bibliog. G. THÉRY, "Thomas Gallus: Aperçu biographique," *ibid.* 14 (1939) 141–208, biog. and bibliog. J. BARBET, *DS* 15 (1991) 800–81, bibliog. P. GLORIEUX, *Dictionnaire de théologie catholique*, ed. A. VACANT et al., (Paris 1903–50; Tables générales 1951–) 15.1:773–777, bibliog. of Théry's authoritative pioneer studies. R. JAVELET, "Thomas Gallus et Richard de St. Victor, mystiques," *Recherches de théologie ancienne et médiévale* 29 (Louvain 1962) 206–233; 30 (1963) 88–121; "Thomas Gallus ou les écritures dans une dialectique mystique," in *L'Homme devant Dieu; melangess offerts au Henri de Lubac* (Paris 1963–64) 99–110. J. BARBET, *Abbas vercellensis, Thomas Gallus: Le commentaire du Cantique des Cantiques 'Deiformis animae gemitus.' Étude d'authenticité et edition critique* (Paris and Louvain 1972); "Un Apocryphe de Thomas Gallus. Le Commentaire *Deiformis animae gemitus* du Cantique des cantiques," *Divinitas* 11 (1967) 471–490; "Un Apocryphe de Thomas Gallus Le Commentaire *Deiformis animae gemitus* du Cantique des cantiques," in *Miscellanea Andre Combes*, 2 vols. (Rome 1967). F. RUELLO, "Depassement mystique du discours theologique selon saint Bonaventure," *Recherches de sciences Religieuses* 64 (1976) 217–270; "La mystique de l'Exode (Exode 3:14 selon Thomas Gallus, commentateur dionysien, d 1246)," in *Dieu et l'etre*, ed. A. CAQUOT (Paris 1978) 213–243. F. STEGMÜLLER, *Repertorium biblicum medii aevi*, 5 (Madrid 1955) 387–81.

[P. EDWARDS/G. A. ZINN]

THOMAS HÉLYE, BL.

Preacher and teacher; b. Biville, Normandy, France, 1187; d. Vauville, France, Oct. 19, 1257. Thomas dedicated himself first to teaching school and catechism in his native town. He was invited to teach in the nearby town of Cherbourg, but illness later forced him to return home. Here he observed the strictest regularity in his life and was early ordained a deacon by the bishop of Coutances. After pilgrimages to Compostela and Rome, he went to the University of Paris, where he studied theology and four years later was ordained a priest. More austere than ever, Thomas continued his mission of catechizing, preaching, and pastoral care in regions surrounding his native district. There is no reliable evidence, however, that he was a chaplain to (St.) LOUIS IX. His cult was confirmed in 1859, and his relics are in the church at Biville.

Feast: Oct. 19.

Bibliography: *Acta Sanctorum* Oct. 8:592–622. A. MERCATI and A. PELZER, *Dizionario ecclesiastico*, 3 v. (Turin 1954–58) 3:1148. ''Thomas Hélye,'' *Lexikon für Theologie und Kirche*, ed. J. HOFER and K. RAHNER, 10 v. (2d, new ed. Freiburg 1957–65); suppl., *Das Zweite Vatikanische Konzil: Dokumente und Kommentare*, ed. H. S. BRECHTER et al., pt. 1 (1966) v.10. A. BUTLER, *The Lives of the Saints*, rev. ed. H. THURSTON and D. ATTWATER (New York, 1956) 4:151–152. *Analecta Bollandiana* 22:505.

[F. D. LAZENBY]

THOMAS JORZ

Dominican cardinal and theologian; d. Grenoble, France, Dec. 13, 1310. Probably an Englishman (he is called *Anglus* or *Anglicus*), he became a Dominican in England; he was made regent master of theology at Oxford *c.* 1292, prior there from 1294 to 1297, and provincial of England (1297–1304). He successfully settled disputes between the Exeter priory and the cathedral chapter and between the Cambridge priory and the university, arranged for episcopal licensing of friars as confessors, and at the chapter of Marseilles in 1300 petitioned for the arrest of vagabond friars. In 1304 Jorz was granted royal safe conduct for two years to go to Rome on the order's business. He was made adviser and confessor to King Edward I and acted on behalf of both Edward I and Edward II at the Roman Curia. While on a royal diplomatic mission to Lyons, Dec. 15, 1305, he was created cardinal priest of S. Sabina by Clement V. En route to Henry VII of Germany as Clement's legate, Jorz died; he was buried at Blackfriars, Oxford. Extracts from his Commentary on the *Sentences* embody concise and complete refutation of DUNS SCOTUS's attacks on the teachings of THOMAS AQUINAS. Many works once ascribed to Jorz are now known to be those of THOMAS WALEYS, also called *Anglus* or *Anglicus*.

Bibliography: A, B. EMDEN, *A Biographical Register of the University of Oxford to A.D. 1500* (Oxford 1957–59) 2:1023. A. G. LITTLE and F. PELSTER, *Oxford Theology and Theologians, c.* A. D. *1282–1302* (Oxford 1934) 187–188. J. QUÉTIF and J. ÉCHARD, *Scriptores ordinis praedicatorum* (New York 1959) 1.2:508–510. H. HURTER, *Nomenclator literarius theologiae catholicae* (Innsbruck 1903–13) 3 2:462.

[A. DABASH]

THOMAS OF BAYEUX

Archbishop of York; b. Bayeux, Normandy; d. Nov. 18, 1100. Thomas was the son of Osbert (a priest of noble family) and a clerk in the household of Bp. ODO of Bayeux. Educated at Odo's expense, he attended schools in France, Germany, and Spain before being appointed treasurer of Bayeux cathedral. In 1066 he accompanied Odo to England, where he became a royal chaplain under William the Conqueror and, in 1070, archbishop-elect of YORK. His consecration was delayed by the dispute over the primacy of CANTERBURY and Archbishop LANFRANC's demand for a profession of obedience. The legatine council of Winchester, Easter 1072, declared in favor of Canterbury, but in 1093 Thomas refused to consecrate Lanfranc's successor, ANSELM, until the latter agreed to the title of metropolitan rather than primate of all England. Thomas claimed that his profession to Lanfranc had been personal and was not made ex officio.

Bibliography: HUGH THE CHANTOR, *The History of the Church of York,* tr. C. JOHNSON (New York 1961) 1–33.

[R. S. HOYT]

THOMAS OF BUCKINGHAM

English theologian, chancellor of Exeter cathedral; fl. mid-14th century. Originally from the Diocese of Lincoln, he was a fellow of Merton College, Oxford, in 1324, being a doctor of theology by 1346. He became chancellor of Exeter cathedral in 1346, canon and prebendary there in 1347. He is remembered chiefly for his *Commentary* on the *Sentences* (Paris 1505) and his *Quaestiones* (still in manuscript). Basically, he opposed the predestinarian tendencies that were in evidence in Oxford in the 1350s. His *Quaestiones* contain a mild reproof of a ''reverend doctor'' (RICHARD FITZRALPH?) who ''publicly says many things that are not in harmony with the sayings of saints and have not been commonly heard in schools'' (Oxford, New College, Manuscript 134, folio 395ᵛ). The tenor of his doctrine may be extracted from the *Quaestiones,* where he attempts to show that a middle, Catholic way can be found between the errors of Pelagius (*see* PELAGIUS AND PELAGIANISM), CICERO, and DUNS SCOTUS, ''and that the eternal predestination, preordination, prevolition and concourse of God is consistent with the freewill and merit of the creature'' (*Quaestiones,* folio 324ʳ).

Bibliography: W. A. PANTIN, *The English Church in the 14th Century* (Cambridge, England 1955). M. D. CHENU, ''Les *Quaestiones* de T. de Buckingham,'' *Studia mediaevalia in honorem . . . R. J. Martin, O. P.* (Bruges 1948) 229–241. A. B. EMDEN, *A Biographical Register of the Scholars of the University of Oxford to A.D. 1500,* 3 v. (Oxford 1957–59) 1:298–299. J. A. ROBSON, *Wyclif and the Oxford Schools* (Cambridge, England 1961) 32–69.

[V. MUDROCH]

THOMAS OF BUNGEY

Also known as Thomas of Bungay; Franciscan theologian; fl. 1270s; d. Northampton, England. Thomas is said to have entered the FRANCISCANS at Norwich, but the date of his entry is not known. He became tenth Franciscan master at Oxford (*c.* 1270–72), eighth minister provincial of the province of England (1272–75), and 15th Franciscan master at Cambridge (*c.* 1275–79). The time of his death is unknown, but he is said to have been buried at Northampton. He is the first provincial described in the lists as *magister,* but no details of his provincialate have survived.

In the famous MS Assisi 158, 33 *quaestiones* are either expressly attributed to Bungey (14) or attributed to him on other grounds (19). All were probably disputed at Cambridge. Most of them concern speculative theology, for example, the Trinity, creation, the Annunciation, the Incarnation, the Real Presence, Satan, sin, virginity, and the Last Judgment. One MS of a commentary on the *De celo et mundo* also survives. A copy of his *Commentary on the Sentences,* now lost, once existed in the library of SAINT AUGUSTINE ABBEY at Canterbury. Extracts from what appears to be a commentary on the Epistle to the Romans have recently been edited (Walmsley). His connection with Roger Bacon seems to have been entirely legendary.

Bibliography: A. G. LITTLE and F. PELSTER, *Oxford Theology and Theologians, c. A. D. 1282–1302* (Oxford 1934). J. R. H. MOORMAN, *The Grey Friars in Cambridge 1225–1538* (Cambridge, Eng. 1952). C. WALMSLEY, "Extracts from an Unknown Work of Thomas de Bungeye, O.F.M.," *Annali dell'Istituto Superiore di scienze e lettere 'S. Chiara'* 5 (1954) 217–238. A. B. EMDEN, *Biographical Register of the Scholars of the University of Cambridge before 1500* (Cambridge, Eng. 1963) 106.

[T. C. CROWLEY]

THOMAS OF CANTELUPE, ST.

Bishop of Hereford (1275); b. Hambledon, England, *c.* 1218; d. Orvieto, Italy, Aug. 25, 1282. A nephew and protégé of WALTER OF CANTELUPE, bishop of Worcester, Thomas was educated at Oxford, Paris, and Orléans. From 1261 to 1263 he was chancellor of the University of OXFORD, where he taught canon law. Two years later (Feb. 22, 1265) he became chancellor of England under the influence of Simon de Montfort. In August 1265, upon the defeat of the baronial party, he resigned from court and went back to Paris, where he lectured on theology until 1272. He then returned to Oxford where he was chancellor of the university for a second time, 1273–74. As bishop he gained a reputation for reform (though himself a pluralist by papal dispensation) and as a champion

of episcopal jurisdiction against that of the archbishop of Canterbury. His quarrel with Abp. JOHN PECKHAM over testamentary jurisdiction culminated in his excommunication (1282), a sentence against which Thomas appealed to the pope. He died before obtaining judgment in his case. Popularly regarded as a saint soon after death, he was canonized on April 17, 1320, the last Englishman to be canonized in the Middle Ages. His remains were returned to England and, after temporary interment in the Church of the Bonshommes at Ashridge, were translated to the Lady chapel in the cathedral of Hereford.

Feast: Oct. 3.

Bibliography: *Acta Sanctorum* Oct. 1:599–705. *Register of Thomas of Cantelupe,* transcribed R. G. GRIFFITHS, introd. W. W. CAPES (Canterbury and York Society; 1907). A. B. EMDEN, *A Biographical Register of the University of Oxford to A.D. 1500,* 3 v. (Oxford 1957–59) 1:347–349.

[R. S. HOYT]

THOMAS OF CANTIMPRÉ

Hagiographer and encyclopedist; b. S. Pieters-Leeuw (Brabant), *c.* 1201; d. Louvain, *c.* 1270–72. Born of the family of De Monte or Van Bellinghen in Brabant, Thomas was often called "Brabantinus" and was thus confused by early historians with his Flemish contemporary, the famous translator, WILLIAM OF MOERBEKE, also a "Brabantinus." After schooling at Liège, Thomas in 1217 joined the Canons Regular of St. Augustine at Cantimpré (Cambrai), hence his more familiar name. About 1230 he transferred to the Dominicans at Louvain and then studied in the School of COLOGNE, perhaps under ALBERT THE GREAT, and at Paris. By 1246 he was subprior at Louvain, and presumably died in this community.

His writings include a life of John, first abbot of Cantimpré, a supplement to the life of Bl. MARY OF OIGNIES by JACQUES DE VITRY [*Acta Sanctorum* 5 June (1867) 573–581], a life of St. Christine, the miracle worker of Saint-Truiden [ActSS 5 July (1868) 650–660], a life of St. Lutgart [ActSS 4 June (1867) 189–210], and a life of Bl. Margaret of Ypres.

Thomas's fame, however, rests especially on his *De natura rerum* (On the Nature of Things), and on his *Liber de apibus* (Book of the Bees). In the *De natura,* an encyclopedia of the natural sciences, the result of 15 years of work (*c.* 1228–44), Thomas undertook to compile all that was known about the nature and properties of creatures, with suitable moral applications for the use of preachers. He listed his sources as Aristotle, Pliny, Ambrose, Basil, Isidore, Jacques de Vitry, Palladius, Galen, Matthaeus Platearius, and Aldhelm; also the Physiologus, the Experimentator, and a Modernus. The complete work contains 20 books: books 1 to 3, man; books 4 to 9, animals; books 10 to 12, plants; book 13, water; books 14 to 15, stones and metals; books 16 to 18, astronomy, astrology, and meteorology; book 19, elements. There are at least two redactions, a longer and a shorter, in the MSS. The work was widely copied in the Middle Ages and made use of by Albert the Great (to whom it was occasionally attributed) and by Vincent of Beauvais. It was translated at least partially, into Dutch, French, and German.

The *Liber de apibus,* which, along with the *Vitae fratrum* of Gerard de Frachet, was commissioned by Master General HUMBERT OF ROMANS (resigned 1263) to record the earliest activities of the Order of Preachers, contains many anecdotes of first-generation Dominicans, including Thomas Aquinas. The work was widely circulated in MS and, from 1472 to the 17th century, in printed editions. G. Colvener prepared the best Latin edition in 1597. Many extant MSS contain excerpts of this work.

Bibliography: A. KAUFMAN, *Thomas von Chantimpré* (Köln 1899). L. THORNDIKE, *A History of Magic and Experimental Science* (New York 1923–58) 2:372–400. G. SARTON, *Introduction to the History of Science* (Baltimore 1927–48) 2.2:592–594. A. HILKA, ed., *Eine altfranz. moralisier. Bearbeitung des Liber de monstruosis hominibus orientis aus Thomas v. Cantimpré "De naturis rerum"* (Berlin 1933). P. AIKEN, "The Animal History of Albertus Magnus and Thomas of Cantimpré," *Speculum* 22 (1947) 205–225. A. C. CROMBIE, *Medieval and Early Modern Science,* 2 v. (2d rev. ed. Garden City, N.Y. 1959).

[J. C. VANSTEENKISTE]

THOMAS OF CELANO

Franciscan hagiographer; b. Celano, Italy *c.* 1190; d. Tagliacozzo, *c.* 1260. Thomas was born into the noble family of the Conti dei Marsi. His solid training in the rhetorical, hagiographical, and theological tradition supports the opinion that he studied at Monte Casino, Rome, or Bologna. He entered the Franciscan Order in 1215. In addition to his literary career he served as vicar of all the brothers of Germany. In 1221 he was among the first brothers to arrive in Germany where he spent time in Worms, Speyer, and Cologne. It is not known when he returned to Italy, but his dramatic and vivid narration of the canonization of St. Francis suggests he was back in Assisi for that occasion on July 16, 1228.

Brother Thomas was the first to write a life of St. Francis and the first to offer information about Francis's early followers and the development of the early fraternity. He composed four works that laid the foundation for the rich Franciscan literary tradition of the 13th century: *The Life of Saint Francis,* commonly referred to as *The First Life [Vita Prima]* in 1229; *The Legend for Use in Choir* in 1230; *The Remembrance of the Desire of a Soul,* commonly referred to as *The Second Life [Vita Secunda]* in 1247; and *The Treatise on the Miracles.*

Thomas wrote *The Life of Saint Francis* at the request of Pope Gregory IX on the occasion of Francis's canonization. He enthusiastically announces Francis as a new saint who is no longer a "dear hearer" of the Gospel but, a bold announcer of the Word of God who makes his hearers "children of peace." Thomas draws from the classic rhetorical and hagiographical tradition to frame this new saint in the tradition of Christian holiness, but he also relies on "trustworthy witnesses" and situates Francis in real places connected to concrete historical contemporaries. The first of the three books or divisions in the text develops Francis's conversion and his formation of the early brothers. The second book describes his mystical experience of the stigmata on Mt. La Verna in 1224 and provides a description of his death in 1226. The "humility of the Incarnation" characterizes the spirit of the first book and the "charity of the Passion" captures the dynamic of the second book. The third book is filled with the spirit and the new life in the Church that fills the account of Francis's canonization in 1228.

The Remembrance of the Desire of a Soul, written nearly 20 years later, is radically different from the earlier text. *The Remembrance* is a collection of memories gathered by the brothers and edited by Thomas, which he develops thematically in book two. In book one he also uses *The Legend of the Three Companions* as a source to develop a thematic illustrating Francis's conversion. In both books, Thomas keeps in mind the burning issues of the fraternity struggling to interpret their life, especially various provisions of *The Rule* that Francis left them.

Toward the end of his life, Brother Thomas was pressured to write *The Treatise of the Miracles.* This is a comprehensive collection of reported miracles attributed to the intercession of St. Francis. Remarkable about this text are the fresh and direct accounts of the life and experiences of ordinary people in their fields, town squares, and homes. His authorship of the celebrated *Dies Irae* is doubtful.

Bibliography: R. ARMSTRONG, J. HELLMANN, AND W. SHORT, eds., *Francis of Assisi: Early Documents,* 3 v. (New York 1999–2001), 1:171–179, 311–318; 2:233–238, 397–398. E. GRAU, "Thomas of Celano: Life and Work," tr. X. J. SEUBERT, *Greyfriars Review* 8 (1994): 177–200.

[J. A. HELLMANN]

THOMAS OF CLAXTON

Dominican theologian at Oxford in the early 15th century. On Feb. 26, 1404, at Oxford, he was a witness in a court action. He served on the university committee of 12 that in March of 1411 addressed a letter to the convocation of Canterbury in condemnation of 267 errors in the works of John WYCLIF. He was also a theologian at the Council of Constance, at least in 1414. Two works survive: a commentary on the *Sentences* (more exactly, a collection of questions according to the order of Peter Lombard) and a *Quodlibet*. Both works are in manuscript at the Florence National Library (manuscript Conv. B 6 340; *see* Quétif-Échard, *Scriptores Ordinis Praedicatorum* 1:730), while his own copy of the commentary on the *Sentences* is at Cambridge (Emden). Two important quodlibetal questions have been edited by Grabmann.

Thomas had a good grasp of Thomistic metaphysics. As is clear from the edited texts, he appreciates the importance of St. Thomas's positions on BEING. He views existence (*esse*) as "the actuality of essence" and defends the real distinction between essence and existence in creatures in order to safeguard the doctrine of creation. He holds that essence and existence are not to be regarded as distinct things (see Grabmann, "Thomae de Claxton. . ." 123), and defends the Thomistic doctrine of ANALOGY.

Bibliography: M. GRABMANN, "Thomae de Claxton, O.P., (*ca.* 1400) Quaestiones de distinctione inter esse et essentiam reali atque de analogia entis," *Acta Pontificae Academiae Romanae S. Thomae Aquinatis* 8 (1941–42) 92–153; *Mittelalterliches Geistesleben,* 3 v. (Munich 1925–56) 3:372–373. A. B. EMDEN, *A Biographical Register of the Scholars of the University of Oxford to A.D. 1500,* 3 v. (Oxford 1957–59) 1:426. É. H. GILSON, *History of Christian Philosophy in the Middle Ages* (New York 1955) 746.

[J. J. PRZEZDZIECKI]

THOMAS OF COBHAM

English scholar, bishop of Worcester; b. Kent, England, *c.* 1255; d. 27 August 1327. The sixth son of a Kentish knight, he was regent of three universities, being an M.A. of Paris, doctor of Canon Law of Oxford (where he was regent in 1291), and doctor of theology at Cambridge by 1314. He had a distinguished career as a scholar and diplomat and was regarded by his contemporaries as so outstanding in learning and virtue that the monks of CANTERBURY elected him archbishop (1313) on the death of Abp. ROBERT OF WINCHELSEA. King Edward II, however, gained the archbishopric for his chancellor, WALTER REYNOLDS, Bishop of Worcester. Pope JOHN XXII persuaded Cobham to renounce his claims to Canterbury; Cobham in turn was rewarded by provision to the See of Worcester in March 1317. Although consecrated at Avignon, he was not enthroned at Worcester until October 1319. He is buried in Worcester cathedral. During his lifetime he provided money for a congregation house

with a library upstairs, to be built against the university church of Oxford, but his intention of endowing the library and leaving his own books to it was frustrated, and they went to Oriel College. They came into the University's possession in 1410, however, and together with the collection of Humphrey, Duke of Gloucester, form the nucleus of the Bodleian Library.

Bibliography: W. STUBBS, ed., *Chronicles of the Reigns of Edward I and Edward II,* 2 v. (*Rerum Britannicarum medii aevi scriptores*; 1882–83). E. H. PEARCE, *Thomas de Cobham* (Society for Promoting Christian Knowledge; 1923); ed., *The Register of Thomas de Cobham* (London 1930). A. B. EMDEN, *A Biographical Register of the University of Oxford to A.D. 1500* (Oxford 1957–59) 1:450–451.

[J. L. GRASSI]

THOMAS OF CORBRIDGE

Archbishop of York; b. Corbridge, Northumberland, England; d. Laneham, Nottinghamshire, Sept. 22, 1304. Probably a member of the family that had long served the archdiocese of York, he was a doctor of theology, probably of Oxford, when he became a canon of York (by 1277) and then chancellor of York *c.* 1280 under Abp. WILLIAM WICKWANE. In 1290 he became sacrist of the chapel of St. Mary and Holy Angels in York Minster by papal PROVISION. Elevated to the archbishopric of YORK on the death of HENRY OF NEWARK, he was consecrated at Rome in 1300. He promptly became involved in a quarrel with King Edward I over the appointment of his successors as sacrist and as prebendary of Stillington (York), a quarrel that was still unsettled at the time of his death. In the few years that he was archbishop he left his see only to attend Parliament and achieved the remarkable feat of almost completing two very thorough visitations of York. He was described as a profound, deeply learned, exemplary, and prudent diplomat, and an admirable doctor of theology and incomparable professor of all the arts. He was buried in Southwell Minster.

Bibliography: W. H. DIXON, *Fasti eboracenses: Lives of the Archbishops of York,* ed. J. RAINE (London 1863). *The Historians of the Church of York and its Archbishops,* ed. J. RAINE, 3 v. (*Rerum Brittanicarum medii aevi scriptores* 71; 1879–94) 2:411–412. *Willelmi Rishanger . . .Chronica et annales. . .1259–1307,* ed. H. T. RILEY (*ibid.* 28.2; 1865) 476–477. *The Register of Thomas of Corbridge,* ed. W. BROWN and A. H. THOMPSON, 2 v. (Surtees Society 138, 141; London 1925–28). T. F. TOUT, *The Dictionary of National Biography from the Earliest Times to 1900,* 63 v. (London 1885–1900) 4:1137–38. R. BRENTANO, *York Metropolitan Jurisdiction and Papal Judges Delegate,1279–1296* (Berkeley 1959). A. B. EMDEN, *A Biographical Register of the Scholars of the University of Oxford to A.D. 1500,* 3 v. (Oxford 1957–59) 1:485.

[J. L. GRASSI]

THOMAS OF ECCLESTON

English chronicler, who joined the Friars Minor shortly after their arrival in England; dates of b. and d. unknown. About 1232 he began collecting materials for his *Tractatus de adventu Fratrum Minorum in Angliam,* which he finished about 1258. Nothing is known about him except the little that can be gathered from his chronicle; even his name "of Eccleston" is not recorded before the 16th century. He studied at Oxford, but does not seem to have traveled outside England. The chronicle consists of a series of notes and stories; apart from one section on the ministers general, it details the life, teaching, progress, and organization of the Order in England. Within its limits it is very valuable; Thomas was honest, accurate, and well-informed in describing the friars in their ordinary life.

Bibliography: P. BEGUIN, *Chronica Fratris Iordani, Tractatus de Adventu Fratrum Minorum in Angliam, Espistola de Transitu Sanctae Clarae* (Louvain 1990); bibliography. P. HERMANN, "Thomas of Eccleston: The Coming of the Friars Minor to England," *XIIIth Century Chronicles* (Chicago 1961).

[R. B. BROOKE]

THOMAS OF FARFA, ST.

Restorer of Farfa Abbey; b. Maurienne (Savoy), France, *ca.* 648; d. Dec. 10, *ca.* 720. The *Chronicon* of Farfa claims that Thomas was already a monk and a priest when he left his homeland for a pilgrimage to Rome and the Holy Land. The Blessed Virgin reportedly appeared to him in a vision in Jerusalem and bade him go to FARFA in the Duchy of Spoleto.

Farfa, founded by St. Lawrence Siro in the fourth century, was then in ruins. Thomas returned to Italy and began the difficult task of rebuilding the abbey, in which he was aided by the Lombard Faroaldo II, duke of Spoleto, who introduced him to Pope John VII. Thomas's sanctity brought the restored abbey many vocations, including the three noble Benevantans, Paldo, Taso, and Tato, who later founded the Abbey of SAN VINCENZO AL VOLTURNO. Thomas cared for his own sanctification and for the spiritual growth of his disciples, while faithfully administering the abbey's temporalities. In its liturgy Farfa invoked him among the saints of the monastery. SANT' EUTIZIO DI NORCIA and San Vincenzo al Volturno followed suit. The Congregation of Rites approved his feast for Farfa (2d class) in 1921.

Feast: Dec. 10.

Bibliography: GREGORIO DI CATINO, *Il Chronicon Farfense,* ed. U. BALZANI, 2 v. (Rome 1903). J. MABILLON, *Acta sanctorum ordinis S. Benedicti,* 9 v. (Paris 1668–1701; 2d ed. Venice 1733–40) 3:276–282. I. SCHUSTER, "Spigolature Farfensi," *Rivista storica benedettina* 5 (1910) 42–88; *Martyrologium Pharphense* (Maredsous 1910); *L'imperiale abbazia di Farfa* (Rome 1921). A. M. ZIMMERMANN, *Kalendarium Benedictinum: Die Heiligen und Seligen des Benediktinerorderns und seiner Zweige,* 4 v. (Metten 1933–38) 3:414–416. P. PIRRI, *L'abbazia di Sant'Eutizio* (Rome 1960).

[S. BAIOCCHI]

THOMAS OF JESUS (DE ANDRADA)

Preacher and writer; b. Lisbon, 1529; d. Morocco, 1582. A protégé of Luis de Montoya, OSA, Thomas entered the Augustinian Monastery of Our Lady of Grace, Lisbon, in 1534 and later pursued his studies at Coimbra. He won fame as a preacher, was at one time master of novices, and unsuccessfully attempted a reform of his order in Portugal, modeled after the Observantine practice obtaining in other provinces. He accompanied King Sebastian on his unfortunate expedition to Africa in 1578. Captured by the Moors, he was sold to an earnest Moslem who endeavored, first by kindness and then by torture, to draw him from Christianity.

During this period of his captivity he wrote *Os trabalhos de Jesus* by the faint light that penetrated his cell and without, apparently, the assistance of any books. Freed from this master through the intervention of the Portuguese ambassador, he went to Morocco and thence to Sagena where he ministered to the Christian slaves. His apostolic labors bore much fruit in encouraging the faithful and recovering apostates, some of whom suffered martyrdom. Thomas resisted the efforts of his family and members of the court to effect his release, preferring to remain where he felt needed. Finally, worn out by illness and work, he died, still a captive.

The *Os trabalhos de Jesus,* known in English as *The Sufferings of Our Lord Jesus Christ,* is made up of meditations on the Passion and is marked by both unction and solid piety. Thomas suggests a method of meditation, and each reflection is followed by a fervent colloquy. It was first published in Lisbon (pt. 1, 1602; pt. 2, 1609). The first American edition of the English translation was published at Philadelphia in 1841, the latest at Westminster, Maryland in 1961.

Bibliography: P. ELSIUS, *Encomasticon Augustinianum* (Brussels 1654). A. F. C. BELL, *Hispanic Review* 1 (1933) 50–54. A. ZUMKELLER, "Thomas von Jesus," *Biogrs- bibliogr. Kirchenlexikon* 11:1390–1392.

[R. J. WELSH]

THOMAS OF JESUS (DÍAZ SANCHEZ DE AVILA)

Discalced Carmelite, founder of the Carmelite deserts, mystical and missiology author; b. Baeza, Jaen, Spain, 1564; d. Rome, May 24, 1627. Thomas received his doctorates in law and theology from the University of Salamanca. In 1585, after reading the autobiography of St. Teresa of Avila, he entered the Discalced Carmelite novitiate at Granada. There he made a copy of the *Spiritual Canticle* of St. John of the Cross, who was prior at Granada at that time. Thomas made his profession, April 3, 1587, at Valladolid.

He served as professor and vice rector at the famous College of Alcalá. Later he directed his dynamic activity toward fostering the eremitical spirit within the order by establishing "deserts," at Bolarque in 1593 and at Las Batuecas in 1599. At the close of his tenure as provincial of Castile (1597–1600) he served as the first vicar, and later prior, (1606) of Las Batuecas. While prior of Zaragoza (1607), he was called to Rome by Paul V, thus becoming a member of the Italian congregation.

As a member of the Italian congregation, he devoted himself to fostering the missionary spirit of the order. He founded the Missionary Congregation of St. Paul that received papal approval on July 22, 1608. This congregation was suppressed by the same Pope in 1613. By this time Thomas was engaged in establishing the Discalced Carmelite Order in Belgium with new foundations at Brussels (1610), Louvain (1611), Douai (1612), Lille (1616), and Cologne (1613) and a desert at Marleine (1619). Within his lifetime he saw the erection of the Belgian and German provinces. He was appointed first provincial of the Belgian province in 1617. In 1623 he returned to Rome, where he was elected general definitor. He was reelected to this office in 1626, but died the following year.

His intellectual prowess was as extensive as his religious activity. His writings on history, mystical theology, and missiology were first compiled and published in two volumes at Cologne (1640). *De procuranda salute omnium gentium* was his classic treatise. Others of his works have been translated into various languages and reprinted many times. So great was his esteem within the order that one of the celebrated *SALMANTICENSES* referred to him as the "omniscient Thomas of Jesus."

Bibliography: B. ZIMMERMANN, *Les Saints déserts des Carmes Déchaussés* (Paris 1927). FELIPE A VIRGINE CARMELI, *La soledad fecunda* (Madrid 1960). JOSÉ DE JESÚS CRUCIFICADO, "El P. Tomás de Jesús, escritor místico," *Ephemerides Carmeliticae* 3 (1949) 305–349. J. ORCIBAL, *La Rencontre du Carmel Thérèsienne avec les mystiques du Nord* (Paris 1959). E. A. PEERS, *Studies of the Spanish Mystics,* 3 v. (v.1, 2d ed. Naperville, Ill. 1951; v.2–3, repr. 1st ed. 1960). TOMMASO DI GESÙ PAMMOLI, *Il P. Tommaso de Gesù e la sua attività missionaria all'inizio del s. XVII* (Rome 1936). A. SALAVILLE, "Un Précurseur de la Propaganda Fide et apôtre des missions, le P. T. de J., carme déchaussé," *Études Carmelities* 5 (1920) 301–323; in *Pensiero missionario* 5 (1933) 225–247. *Spiritualité Carmelitaine* 4 (Brussels 1939), special issue.

[O. RODRIGUEZ]

THOMAS OF PAVIA

Franciscan chronicler; b. Pavia, northern Italy, *c.* 1212; d. between 1280 and 1284. Thomas spent his childhood and youth in Pavia. Already a FRANCISCAN in 1229, he attended (St.) ANTHONY's funeral services at Padua in June 1231. In 1245 he attended the Council of Lyons as the companion of Bonaventure of Iseo, a vicar of the Minister General Crescentius. From 1249 to 1256 he was a lecturer in theology in the province of Bologna, then Parma, Bologna again, and finally Ferrara. This did not prevent him in 1253 from traveling through Romania, Dalmatia, Bohemia, and Germany. His *Dictionnarium bovis* was written in Bologna *c.* 1254. In 1266 he assisted at the general chapter at Paris as provincial of Tuscany, an office he held from 1258 to 1270. While in Tuscany, he was on friendly terms with King Charles I of Anjou. In 1278 he wrote his chronicle of emperors and popes.

His works are: (1) *Assidua,* legend about St. Anthony of Padua; (2) *Dialogus de gestis ss. Fratrum Minorum (c.* 1245), a little-noted collection of miracles; (3) *Dictionnarium bovis,* extensive source for preachers (The author does not believe in the Immaculate Conception; he exercises a prudence regarding the prophecies of JOACHIM OF FIORE that is not found in John of Parma. He also quotes the rhythmic Office of JULIAN OF SPEYER composed for St. Francis.); (4) *Tractatus sermonum,* probably the *Ars concionandi* that is referred to by SALIMBENE (*Bonaventure, Opera omnia* 9:8–21); (5) *Gesta Imperatorum et Pontificum,* a verbose chronicle [ed. Boehmer in *Fontes rerum Germanicarum* 4:609–672 and Ehrenfeuchter in *Monumenta Germaniae Historica: Scriptores* (Berlin 1826–) 22:483–528]. Salimbene speaks of him as a holy man, wise and of sound judgment, humble and meek, but verbose in his writings.

Bibliography: THOMAS OF PAVIA, *Dialogus de gestis sanctorum fratrum minorum,* ed. F. M. DELORME (Quaracchi–Florence 1923), v.5 of *Bibliotheca Franciscana ascetica medii aevi.* SALIMBENE, *Cronica, Monumenta Germaniae Historica: Scriptores* (Berlin 1826–) 32.2:429–430. G. GOLUBOVICH, *Biblioteca bio-bibliografica della Terra Santa e dell'Oriente Francescano,* 5 v. (Quaracchi–Florence 1906–23) 1: 309–312. R. DAVIDSOHN, *Forschungen zur älteren Geschichte von Florenz,* 4 v. (Berlin 1896–1908) v.4. E. LONGPRÉ, "Les *Distinctiones* de Fr. Thomas Pavie, O.F.M.," *Archivum Franciscanum historicum* 16 (1923) 3–33. S. DA CAMPAGNOLA, "Santi Francescani e Culti Poplari," in

Francescanesimo nell'Umvria Meridionale nei Secoli XIII–XIV (Narni, Italy 1985), 67–89.

[J. CAMBELL]

THOMAS OF STRASSBURG

Known also as Thomas de Argentina, Augustinian theologian; b. Hagenau (Alsace), *c.* 1275; d. Vienna, *c.* 1357. He entered the order at Hagenau and taught at Strassburg for several years prior to 1335, when he went to the Augustinian convent in Paris. He obtained the doctorate in theology two years later. His commentary on the *Sentences* dates from about 1337; it is possibly the first Augustinian commentary on all four books. In 1345 Thomas was elected prior general, the first non-Italian to hold the office, and was still general at the time of his death. As prior general, he vigorously promoted religious discipline and was mainly responsible for the revision of the constitutions of his order. Unfortunately, his program, which included careful provisions for the intellectual training of clerical candidates, was compromised by practical measures imposed by the ravages of the Black Death.

Doctrinally, Thomas belongs to the Augustinian tradition that stems from GILES OF ROME, whose teachings, as well as their defense, had been made mandatory for members of the order by the General Chapter at Florence in 1287. But Thomas differs from Giles on such matters as predestination, the Immaculate Conception, meritorious acts, and the theory of sovereignty. With Giles, he adopts and defends fundamental Thomistic theses, such as the real distinction between essence and existence and between the soul and its faculties, the unicity of substantial form, and the validity of a posteriori demonstrations alone for proving the existence of God. Something of the eclectic spirit of the age can be discerned in certain of his doctrines, notably, in his theory of knowledge. During his generalate, the teachings of WILLIAM OF OCKHAM were condemned by general chapters of the Augustinians in 1345 and 1348.

See Also: AUGUSTINIANISM.

Bibliography: THOMAS OF STRASSBURG, *Commentaria super quatuor libros Sententiarum* (Venice 1588). É. H. GILSON, *History of Christian Philosophy in the Middle Ages* (New York 1955). J. L. SHANNON, *Good Works and Predestination According to Thomas of Strassburg* (Westminster, Md. 1940). D. TRAPP, "Augustinian Theology of the Fourteenth Century," *Augustiniana* 6 (1956) 146–274. K. WITTE, "Thomas von Strassburg," *Die deutsche Literatur des Mittelalters: Verfasserlexicon* 9 (1995) 889–892.

[R. P. RUSSELL]

THOMAS OF SUTTON

English Dominican and foremost among the early defenders of St. THOMAS AQUINAS at Oxford; b. near Lincoln, *c.* 1250; d. *c.* 1315. Before his entrance into the order he was a fellow of Merton College. He was ordained deacon by Walter Giffard, Archbishop of York, on Sept. 20, 1274. His inception as master was probably *c.* 1285.

Sutton's academic and literary career extended over some 30 years. Among his early works are the *Contra pluralitatem formarum, de productione formae substantialis,* and the question *Utrum forma fiat ex aliquo.* A short polemical work, *Determinatio contra emulos et detractores fratrum predicatorum,* must also be assigned to him, as well as three sermons preached in 1292 and 1293. Sutton also completed St. Thomas's commentaries on the *Perihermenias* and *De generatione et corruptione* and wrote the *Quaestiones super librum sextum metaphysicorum.* The catalogue of Stams (early 14th century) attributes other works to him, but these are either unknown or not definitively identified.

But of the certainly authentic works, the four *Quodlibeta* and the 36 *Quaestiones ordinariae* or *disputatae* are by far the most important. The first two quodlibets and many of the *Quaestiones ordinariae* were written after 1287, as is clear from references to Henry of Ghent; the last two quodlibets and at least *Quaestiones ordinariae* 27–35 belong to the period between 1300 and 1310, as is clear from the references to certain views of DUNS SCOTUS [see J. Przezdziecki, "Thomas of Sutton's Critique on the Doctrine of Univocity," *An Etienne Gilson Tribute* (Milwaukee 1959) 190–192].

From the standpoint of doctrine, Thomas of Sutton is one of the most penetrating of the early Thomists. He defends St. Thomas on a wide variety of questions against many contemporary opponents, but chiefly against Henry of Ghent and Duns Scotus. And his defense of Thomistic positions, especially in the lengthy *Quaestiones ordinariae,* is masterful. He does not often quote St. Thomas, for he prefers to develop doctrines in his own way, but the supreme source of his inspiration is the writings of the great Aquinas. In his hands, Thomism is a living thing, a heritage to be preserved, developed, and passed on to posterity.

Bibliography: É. H. GILSON, *History of Christian Philosophy in the Middle Ages* (New York 1955). F. J. ROENSCH, *Early Thomistic School* (Dubuque 1964). W. A. HINNEBUSCH, *Early English Friars Preachers* (Rome 1951) 396–410. J. J. PRZEZDZIECKI, "Selected Questions from the Writings of Thomas of Sutton, O.P.," *Nine Mediaeval Thinkers,* ed. J. R. O'DONNELL (Toronto 1955) 309–378.

[J. J. PRZEZDZIECKI]

THOMAS OF TOLENTINO, BL.

Martyr; d. April 9, 1321, near Bombay, India. He entered the FRANCISCANS in early youth and became renowned for his apostolic vigor. In 1290 he was sent to ARMENIA where he converted many infidels and reconciled many schismatics. Thomas was entrusted with various diplomatic assignments to Europe and was finally summoned by Pope CLEMENT V to plan missions into Tartary and China. While making for Ceylon and Cathay, his ship was driven ashore on Salsette Island near Bombay, and here he was captured by Saracens, tortured, and beheaded. Bl. ODORIC OF PORDENONE discovered his body and took it to Zayton in China. Thomas's head was sent to Tolentino, Italy; in 1894 his cult was confirmed by LEO XIII.

Feast: April 9 (in Franciscan Order, September 5).

Bibliography: *Acta Sanctorum* (Paris 1863–) April 1:51–56. L. WADDING, *Scriptores Ordinis Minorum,* 86 v. (Lyons 1625–54); continuation by J. M. FONSECA et al., 25 v. (2d ed. Rome 1731–1886); continuation by A. CHIAPPINI (3d ed. Quaracchi-Florence 1931–) 6:676–677. G. PELLOSO, A. MERCATI and A. PELZER, *Dizionario ecclesiastico,* 3 v. (Turin 1954–58) 3:1148. L. OLIGER. *Lexikon für Theologie und Kirche,* ed. J. HOFER and K. RAHNER (Freiburg 1957–65) 10:133. *Bibliotheca hagiographica latina antiquae et mediae aetatis,* 2 v. (Brussels 1898–1901; suppl. 1911) 2:8257–68. *Analecta Franciscana* 3 (Quaracchi-Florence 1897) 474–479, 597–613; 4 (1906) 332–334. M. BIHL, ''De duabus epistolis fratrum minorum,'' *Archivum Franciscanum historicum* 16 (Quaracchi-Florence 1923) 89–103. A. C. MOULE, ''Textus duarum epistolarum fratrum minorum,'' *ibid.* 104–112.

[F. D. LAZENBY]

THOMAS OF VILLANOVA, ST.

Augustinian scholar, archbishop of Valencia; b. 1486, Fuenllana, Spain; d. Sept. 8, 1555, Valencia, Spain. Tomás García Martínez was born of Alonso Tomás García and Lucía Martínez Castellanos in Fuenllana in the province of Toledo, Spain. His family came from the city of Villanova (now Villanueva) de los Infantes, from which, according to the custom of his time, he derived his surname. At age 16 he enrolled at the University of Alcalá (1502–1512), obtained his degree in theology in an exceptionally short period of time, and was immediately invited to become part of the teaching faculty of his alma mater (1512–1516). The University of Salamanca, offered Thomas a professorship in 1516. Thomas declined the offer, announcing instead his intention to become an Augustinian friar. He professed religious vows in the Order of Saint Augustine on Nov. 25, 1517 and was ordained a priest on Dec. 18, 1518. His fellow Augustinians, recognizing both his gifts and his holiness of life, soon chose him to be local superior or prior. He was prior

of the monasteries of Salamanca, Burgos, and Valladolid, and visitor general and reformer of the Province of Castile (1525–1527) at the request of Emperor Charles V. When the Province of Spain was divided he became the first prior provincial of the Province of Andalusia (1527–1529); he was prior provincial of the Province of Castile (1534–1537). Concerned about the spiritual state of the people in the far reaches of the Spanish empire, he promoted the organization of a missionary group of Augustinian friars to minister to the people in the new world.

In 1542 the King of Spain and Holy Roman Emperor, Charles V, asked Thomas to become the bishop of Granada. He declined the offer. In 1544, while Thomas was prior of Valladolid, the king again offered Thomas an episcopal see—this time that of the wealthy archdiocese of Valencia. Again Thomas refused. But the king pressured Thomas' religious superior to force him to accept the position. Fray Francisco de Nieva, prior provincial of Castile and a former student of Thomas at Salamanca, ordered him to accept the position in virtue of his vow of obedience, and Thomas accepted. On Jan. 1, 1545, at the age of 59, he became archbishop of Valencia. He established boarding schools and high schools. For young girls he provided dowries, enabling them to be married in dignity. For the hungry, he turned his bishop's palace into a kind of soup kitchen. For the homeless he provided a place to sleep, offering them the shelter of his own home. It is thus for good reason that the common folk called him the ''Beggar Bishop'' and ''Father of the Poor.''

In 1545, the year that Thomas was appointed archbishop, he was summoned to attend the Council of Trent in Italy, but was not able to be present because the needs of his newly acquired diocese, which had not had a resident bishop since 1427, were urgent. Six years later, he was again asked to be present at the council; again he was unable to attend, for now he was too ill. On Aug. 28, 1555, the feast of Saint Augustine, Thomas celebrated Mass for the last time. Over the next 12 days he grew gradually weaker. As he was nearing death, he distributed to the needy what few personal belongings he still possessed; he even gave away the straw mattress on which he slept, asking only that he be allowed to borrow it until his death. Thomas died on Sept. 8, 1555. He was beatified in 1618 and canonized in 1658. Centuries later, a score of churches, schools, and universities bear his name. A congregation of sisters, devoted to charity, founded in France, was also named after him. In 1959 he was declared patron of studies in the Augustinian Order.

Feast: Sept. 18; Oct. 10 (Augustinians).

Bibliography: *Acta Sanctorum* (Paris 1863–) Sept. 5:799–992. THOMAS OF VILLANOVA, *Obras: Sermones de la Virgen* *y obras castellanas* (Madrid 1952). *The Works of Saint Thomas of Villanova,* The Augustinian Series, Volume 20, Part 1: Sermons, Advent, with an introduction by A. TURRADO, O.S.A.; Part 2: Sermons, Christmas; Part 3: Sermons, Lent; Part 4: Sermons, Easter; Part 5: Sermons, Sunday; Part 6A: Saints; Part 6B: Saints; Part 7: Marian Sermons; Part 8: Other Works; Part 9: **Literature.** *Saint Thomas of Villanova. A Biography* (Villanova 1994–2001). K. HOFMANN, *Lexikon für Theologie und Kirche,* ed. M. BUCHBERGER, 10 v. (Freiburg 1930–38) 10:134–135. P. JOBIT, *L'eveque des pauves* (Paris 1961). S. BACK, *The Pelican. A Life of Saint Thomas of Villanova* (Villanova 1987). A. CHAFER, ''La llamada universal a la santidad en Santo Tomas de Villanueva'' *Revista Augstiniana* 35 (Madrid 1994), 171–204; A. CHAFER, *Santo Tomas de Villanueva. Fidelidad evangelica y renovacion eclesial* (Historia viva, 11) Madrid, Ed. Revista Agustiniana 1966 (422). J. STOHR, and A. ZUMKELLER, T. VON VILLANOVA, *Marienlexikon* 6 (St. Ottilien 1994), 413 – 415. A. TURRADO, *Santo Tomas de Villanueva, Maestro de teologia y espiritualidad agustinianas* (Perfiles 3) Madrid, Ed. Revista Agustiniana, 1995 (91).

[J. ROTELLE]

THOMAS OF WILTON

English theologian (known also as de Wylton); fl. 1288 to 1327. This scholastic was known on the Continent as Thomas Anglicus or, after 1317, as Cancellarius London. A master in arts at Oxford, he was fellow of Merton College from 1288 to 1301, or later. In April 1304 he was granted license to study at a university in England or abroad, and this license was continuously renewed until November 1322. It is not known when he went to Paris, but by 1311 he was teaching there as a bachelor. From *c.* 1312 to 1322 he was a master in theology at Paris, where his disciples included WALTER BURLEY. In many ways an independent and tortuous thinker, more devoted to scholastic disputations than to Biblical exposition, he was, nevertheless, deeply influenced by his countryman, DUNS SCOTUS. His *Quaestiones disputatae* indicate the extent of Scotus's influence on secular masters at Paris within a decade of the death of the Subtle Doctor. In August 1320 Thomas officially became chancellor of St. Paul's, London, and functioned from 1322 until 1327.

Bibliography: A. MAIER, ''Das Quodlibet des Thomas de Wylton,'' *Recherches de théologie ancienne et médiévale* 14 (1947) 106–110. M. SCHMAUS, ''Thomas Wylton als Verfasser eines Kommentars zur aristotelischen Physik,'' *Sitzungsberichte der Bayerischen Akademie der Wissenschaften zu München* (1956) heft 9. J.M.M.H. THIJSSEN, ''The Response to Thomas Aquinas in the 14th Century'' *Eternity of the World* (Leiden 1990).

[J. A. WEISHEIPL]

THOMAS OF YORK

Franciscan philosopher and theologian; d. *c.* 1260. First mentioned in a letter written by ADAM MARSH, dated 1245, Thomas was at that time already a member of the English province. In 1253 he became a master of theology at Oxford, although he apparently had not obtained the customary degree in arts prior to his inception. He seems to have held his post at Oxford until 1256. He was then transferred to Cambridge where he became the sixth master of the Franciscan studium, succeeding WILLIAM OF MELITONA.

Thomas of York's only major work is the *Sapientiale,* an encyclopedic philosophical treatise in seven books. A shorter work, *Comparatio sensibilium,* may represent a first draft of the *Sapientiale.* Of the other writings attributed to Thomas, *Manus quae contra omnipotentem* is of particular interest. This is a defense of the mendicant orders in their controversy with the seculars and, in particular, with WILLIAM OF SAINT-AMOUR.

A characteristic feature of Thomas's method in the *Sapientiale* is his extensive and accurate citation of sources, whether they be Greek, Latin, Arabian, Jewish, or Christian. He attempts to reconcile various traditions and teachings and to present unified solutions to problems. The *Sapientiale* itself aims to be a concordance between the exponents of natural wisdom, the *sapientes mundi,* and the exponents of Christian wisdom, the *sapientes Dei.* Thomas utilizes the contributions of the former, particularly ARISTOTLE, but only when they conform with Christian wisdom. Thus he accepts the Aristotelian doctrine of nature, but rejects Aristotle in favor of St. AUGUSTINE when treating of the origins of human knowledge. Like St. BONAVENTURE, but unlike St. THOMAS AQUINAS (for whom an autonomous philosophy is possible), Thomas of York was convinced that philosophy requires completion, in its own order, from the truths of revelation; without this special aid, in his view, it inevitably falls into error.

Bibliography: M. WILKS, ''Thomas Arundel of York: the Appellant Archbishop,'' in *Life and Thought in the Northern Church 1100–1700.* D. WOOD, ed. (Woodbridge, England 1999) 57–86. J. A. MERINO, ''Tomas de York,'' in *Historia de la Filosofia Franciscana* (Madrid 1993) 373–75. B. TIERNEY, ''From Thomas of York to William of Ockham: The Franciscans and the Papal Sollicitudo Ominium Ecclesiarum,'' in *Comunione Interecclesiale Collegialita-Primato Ecumenismo* (Rome 1972) 607–58. E. SCULLY, ''The Power of Physical Bodies According to Thomas of York: Potency and Act,'' *Sciences Ecclesiastiques* 14, no. 1 (1962), 109–134.

[J. P. REILLY]

THOMAS II OF YORK

Archbishop; d. Beverley, England, Feb. 24, 1114. The son of Samson, afterward bishop of Worcester (d. 1112), he was also the brother of Bp. Richard of Bayeaux and the nephew of Abp. Thomas I of York (d. 1100), who brought him up and looked to his education. Through the favor of his uncle he became provost at Beverley in 1092, and one of the royal chaplains. King HENRY I was about to appoint him to the vacant See of London (Pentecost 1108) when, at the death of Archbishop Gerard, YORK also became vacant; Henry then nominated Thomas to York instead of London. He was elected by the chapter of York, but for more than a year was not consecrated because he refused to swear obedience to Abp. ANSELM OF CANTERBURY. With the backing of his cathedral chapter and the apparent support of the king, Thomas delayed his recognition of Canterbury's primacy, hoping in the meantime to receive the PALLIUM from Rome. From his deathbed Anselm suspended Thomas from his priestly office and refused consecration until he submitted. After Anselm's death (April 21, 1109), Thomas at length yielded to episcopal and royal pressure, made his profession, and was consecrated June 11, 1109. Although still a young man, Thomas was limited in his activity by a disease that caused him to become enormously fat. He was reputedly religious, liberal, of good disposition, learned, and eloquent. He is buried in York Minster near the grave of his uncle.

Bibliography: EADMER, *Historia novorum*, ed. M. RULE (*Rerum Brittanicarum medii aevi scriptores* 81; 1884). W. HUNT, *The Dictionary of National Biography from the Earliest Times to 1900*, 63 v. (London 1885–1900) 19:643–645. R. W. SOUTHERN, *Saint Anselm and His Biographer* (New York 1963).

[O. J. BLUM]

THOMAS WALEYS

English theologian; b. *c.* 1287; d. England, after February 1349. As a Dominican at Oxford he lectured on the *Sentences* of Peter Lombard (*c.* 1314–15), became regent master in theology (*c.* 1318–20), and composed his well-known *Moralitates* on the Old Testament. By 1326–27 he was lector in Bologna, where he lectured on Psalms 1–38.2, preached against the Franciscan doctrine of poverty, and wrote an impressive commentary on St. AUGUSTINE's *De civitate Dei*. As chaplain to Cardinal Mattèo Orsini at Avignon he preached a sermon in the Dominican priory (Jan. 3, 1333) opposing the view of JOHN XXII on the BEATIFIC VISION. The Franciscan Walter of Chatton charged him with six erroneous statements, and he was cited by the papal inquisitor (January 11) and confined to a cell in the priory. On September 7 another case was brought against him, and he appealed to the Holy See (October 12), whereupon he was transferred to the papal prison. Despite the intervention of Philip VI of France and John XXII's retraction of his own thesis, Thomas was held prisoner for 11 years without trial. Released

soon after 1342, he returned to England where he wrote *De modo componendi sermones*. In February 1349 he described himself as "broken down by old age." His works were highly regarded for their theological content and humanistic style.

Bibliography: J. QUÉTIF and J. ÉCHARD, *Scriptores ordinis praedicatorum* (New York 1959) 1.2:509, 597–602. T. KÄPPELI, *Le procès contre Thomas Waleys, O.P.* (Rome 1936). B. SMALLEY, "Thomas Waleys O.P.," *Archivum fratrum praedicatorum* 24 (1954) 50–107. F. STEGMÜLLER, *Repertorium biblicum medii aevi* (Madrid 1949–61) 5:8234–60. A. B. EMDEN, *A Biographical Register of the University of Oxford to A.D. 1500* (Oxford 1957–59) 3:1961–62. T. M. CHARLAND, *Artes praedicandi* (Ottawa 1936).

[J. A. WEISHEIPL]

THOMASSIN (LOUIS D'EYNAC)

Theologian, historian, and canonist; b. Aix-en-Provence, Aug. 28, 1619; d. Paris, Dec. 24, 1695. He entered the Oratory at Aix in 1632, was ordained there in 1643, and became professor of theology at Saumur in 1648. In 1668, at the Seminary of Saint-Magloire in Paris, he distinguished himself by his public lectures in positive theology. After the publication of the *Dissertationes in concilia generalia et particularia* (Paris 1667) and *Mémoires sur la grâce* (3 v. Louvain 1668), he gave up his teaching position. Thus freed, he devoted himself to his great works: the *Ancienne et nouvelle discipline de l'Église touchant les bénéfices et les bénéficiers* (3 v. Paris 1678–79; Latin tr., 1682); *Dogmata theologica* (3 v. Paris 1680–89); *Traités historiques et dogmatiques sur divers points de la discipline de l'Église et de la morale chrétienne* (7 v. Paris 1680–97). Along with D. Petau, Thomassin was one of the masters of positive theology.

Bibliography: A. INGOLD, *Essai de bibliographie oratorienne* (Paris 1880–82). L. BATTEREL, *Mémoires domestiques pour servir à l'histoire de l'Oratoire*, ed. A. INGOLD and E. BONNARDET, 5 v. (Paris 1903–11) v.3. A. MOLIEN, *Dictionnaire de théologie catholique*, ed. A. VACANT, 15 v. (Paris 1903–50; Tables générales 1951–) 15.1:787–823. P. NORDHUES, *Der Kirchenbegriff des Louis de Thomassin* (Leipzig 1958).

[P. AUVRAY]

THOMISM

As a theological and philosophical movement from the 13th century to the 20th, Thomism may be defined as a systematic attempt to understand and develop the basic principles and conclusions of St. THOMAS AQUINAS in order to relate them to the problems and needs of each generation. As a doctrinal synthesis of characteristic tenets of philosophy and theology, it is more difficult to define because of the variety of interpretations, applications, and concerns of different generations and individual Thomists. The Aristotelian-Christian synthesis of St. Thomas originated in opposition to 13th-century Augustinianism and Latin AVERROISM. Thomism likewise developed, floundered, and revived in the midst of opposing currents of thought. Thus Thomists, in developing and defending the basic insights of their master, could not help but be affected by problems and polemics of their day. Consequently the term ''Thomism'' applies to a wide variety of interpretations of St. Thomas by those who have professed loyalty to his thought and spirit.

Notion. Since the 13th century Thomism has come to represent one of the most significant movements in Western thought, particularly in the Catholic Church. Revived in the 16th century, it was espoused by leading theologians and philosophers of various religious orders in defense of Catholic teaching. Its revival in the 19th century as Neothomism, sometimes identified with neoscholasticism, was enthusiastically encouraged by Pope LEO XIII and his successors as offering the soundest means of combating modern errors and solving modern problems, particularly in the social order. Far from advocating a safe, closed system, the pontiffs have encouraged rigorous philosophical analysis and the confronting of contemporary problems with the wisdom of St. Thomas.

In a wide sense Thomism is the philosophy or theology professed by anyone who claims to follow the spirit, basic insights, and often the letter of St. Thomas. In this sense, medieval Augustinianism, SCOTISM, PROTESTANTISM, NOMINALISM, IDEALISM, and MATERIALISM are not Thomistic, whereas SUAREZIANISM is. In the strict sense Thomism is a philosophy and theology that, eschewing eclecticism, embraces all the sound principles and conclusions of St. Thomas and is consistent with the main tradition of Thomistic thinkers. In this sense Suarezianism, MOLINISM, CASUISTRY, and other forms of eclecticism are not Thomistic. Because of professed eclecticism, Francisco Suárez, Luis Molina, Gabriel Vázquez, and others are not considered Thomists in the strict sense. On the other hand, Tommaso de Vio Cajetan, Domingo Báñez, Jacques Maritain, and others are considered Thomists despite divergent interpretations of particular points and occasional defense of views rejected by the Thomistic tradition. Clearly Thomism is an analogical term embracing various interpretations and developments more or less faithful to the mind and spirit of St. Thomas.

Basic Doctrines. The basic doctrines of Thomism can best be appreciated in the historical context of concrete concerns of an age or polemic. Both in philosophy and in theology, however, certain principles are common-

Thomassin (Louis D'Eynac).

ly recognized as characteristic. These characteristics are discussed briefly before the historical development of Thomism is examined.

St. Thomas clearly distinguished between the realm of nature and the realm of supernature: the first is the domain of reason and PHILOSOPHY, the second is that of faith and THEOLOGY. Although Thomas Aquinas wrote strictly philosophical works, such as commentaries on Aristotle and short treatises, his most original contributions were made in the course of theological speculation wherein a personalized Aristotelian philosophy served as the handmaid to his theology. Thomists, recognizing the importance of philosophy, consider certain principles of Thomistic philosophy as indispensable for Thomistic theology.

Thomistic Philosophy. In the Thomistic order of teaching the first SCIENCE to be studied after the LIBERAL ARTS is natural philosophy, then moral philosophy, and finally metaphysics. No attempt is made here to indicate all the basic principles of these sciences, but the more important are noted briefly.

1. All physical bodies are composed of a purely passive principle called primary matter and an active principle of nature called substantial form in such a way that the first actualization of pure potentiality

is the unique substantial form and nature of a body (*see* FORMS, UNICITY AND PLURALITY OF; MATTER AND FORM).

2. Each physical body is rendered numerically unique solely by determined MATTER (*materia signata*), and not by form, *haecceitas,* or any collection of accidents (*see* INDIVIDUATION).

3. Since primary matter is the principle of individuation, of quantity, and of corruptibility, there can be no ''spiritual matter'' in separated substances and no multiplication of individuals within their species. In Thomistic doctrine each separated substance, or angel, is unique in its species, necessarily existent by nature, but contingent by creation and preservation.

4. In all created substances there is a real distinction between activities, powers or faculties, and essential nature; this is also true of FACULTIES OF THE SOUL, both sentient and intellective (*see* ACCIDENT; DISTINCTION, KINDS OF; SUBSTANCE).

5. The unique substantial form of man is his rational soul, which has three spiritual powers, a thinking INTELLECT, an agent intellect, and a WILL that freely determines itself. The activities of these faculties and powers of the soul demonstrate the spirituality and immortality of the soul (*see* SOUL, HUMAN; IMMORTALITY).

6. By nature man has the right to cooperate with other men in society in the pursuit of personal happiness in the common good; this pursuit of happiness is guided by conscience, laws both natural and positive, and virtues both private and public (*see* ETHICS).

7. Rejecting both idealism and POSITIVISM, a realist metaphysics recognizes universal ideas as existing only in the mind of creatures and God; individuals possessing similar characteristics in nature, however, proffer a legitimate foundation for universal knowledge (*see* UNIVERSALS). This epistemological position presupposes the psychological principle that nothing exists in the intellect that was not first in sense knowledge (*see* EPISTEMOLOGY; KNOWLEDGE).

8. From the visible things of the universe the human mind can know the existence of God as the first efficient, supreme exemplar, and ultimate final cause of all creation (*see* GOD IN PHILOSOPHY, 2; GOD, PROOFS FOR THE EXISTENCE OF).

9. God has no nature other than the subsistent fullness of pure actual being (*esse*), having no potentiality or limitation of any kind. Every creature, on the other hand, is characterized by a disturbing distinction between his inner nature and his actuality of borrowed existence (*esse*). (*See* ESSENCE AND EXISTENCE; POTENCY AND ACT.)

10. The metaphysical concept of BEING (*ens*) is analogically, and not univocally, said of God, substances, and accidents, such that each is recognized to be radically (*simpliciter*) different, and only relatively similar in some respect (*see* ANALOGY).

Thomistic Theology. While recognizing the unique position of the Bible in Christian theology, Thomistic theology, like other scholastic theologies, is an attempt to systematize revealed truths in a human manner so as to make revelation better appreciated by the orderly, logical, scientific mind. In matters of divine faith there is no difference between Thomistic theology and any other Catholic theology, but in the matter of undefined dogmatics there are certain conspicuous characteristics of Thomism that may be briefly listed.

1. Beyond the order of nature there is a higher, supernatural order of reality, including truths of revelation, grace, merit, predestination, and glory, that man could never know unless God revealed its existence (*see* REVELATION, THEOLOGY OF; SUPERNATURAL).

2. This supernatural order of divine reality is not simply modally (i.e., *quoad modum*) beyond the powers of nature, but substantially (i.e., *quoad substantiam*) in such a way that pure nature can neither strive toward nor attain it (*see* GRACE AND NATURE).

3. Notwithstanding the essential transcendence of faith and grace, there is a harmony between faith and reason and between grace and nature, for there is only one author of both. Thus there can be no contradiction between faith and reason, and grace perfects nature (*see* FAITH AND REASON).

4. Although reason can, objectively speaking, demonstrate the existence of God, providence, the immortality of the human soul, and other *praeambula fidei,* it can in no way demonstrate the saving truths of revelation, such as the INCARNATION, PREDESTINATION, life everlasting, and the Trinity. On the other hand, reason can in no way disprove them (*see* APOLOGETICS).

5. Man is not only a true secondary cause, but he is a free agent. Nevertheless whatever good man accomplishes is due to the grace of God, while whatever sin man commits is due to himself. God's universal causality in no way deprives man of his freedom, for God moves all things according to their natures, and man's nature is to act freely (*see* PREMOTION, PHYSICAL).

6. Predestination of certain persons to grace and glory is a free gift of God's mercy. Divine foreknowledge of the predestined is not through *SCIENTIA MEDIA* or through a foreknowledge of how man will react to

grace, but simply through God's free choice (*see* PREDETERMINATION).

7. The primary motive of the Incarnation of the Word is the Redemption of fallen mankind so that if Adam had not sinned, God would not have become man. (*See* REDEMPTION [THEOLOGY OF].)

8. The SACRAMENTS as an encounter with the Passion and death of Christ are not only symbols of faith, but also instrumental causes of grace in the soul and in the Church. Since Christ is the true minister of all Sacraments, they effect what they signify *ex opere operato* (*see* INSTRUMENTAL CAUSALITY).

9. The Church as the Mystical Body of Christ is the sole custodian of faith and the Sacraments. Sent to preach the Word to the world, the true Church of Christ must preserve unblemished the purity of divine revelation and the integrity of the Sacraments. This guardianship is in no way contrary to the development of doctrine under the Holy Spirit (*see* DOCTRINE, DEVELOPMENT OF).

10. Eternal life consists essentially in seeing God face to face, from which vision flows the fullness of happiness. Thus the essence of beatitude consists in the intellectual vision. In order to receive this beatific vision, however, the created intellect must be elevated by the light of glory (*lumen gloriae*).

One characteristic of Dominican Thomism, long since abandoned, was its opposition to the doctrine of the IMMACULATE CONCEPTION. Bound by an oath of loyalty to the basic teachings of St. Thomas, the majority of Dominican theologians and preachers believed that St. Thomas had denied the doctrine defended by John DUNS SCOTUS and popularized by the laity. Whatever may have been the true mind of St. Thomas, faced as he was with the special circumstances of the 13th century, it is historically certain that Dominican opposition in later centuries was unfortunate and unfaithful to his spirit. The doctrine that developed in later centuries was more orthodox than that opposed by St. BERNARD OF CLAIRVAUX, St. ALBERT THE GREAT, St. BONAVENTURE, and St. Thomas himself.

Since the many variations of philosophy and theology that may be labeled Thomistic can be understood only in their historical context, most of the remainder of this article is devoted to a general historical survey of Thomism from the death of St. Thomas to the end of the 18th century. The renewal of Thomism in the 19th and 20th centuries is treated mainly elsewhere (*see* NEOSCHOLASTICISM AND NEOTHOMISM).

General Survey

Apart from the Thomistic revival in the 19th century, the two major phases of Thomism may be designated as "early Thomism," which extends from the death of St. Thomas to the beginning of the Protestant Reformation, and "second Thomism," which extends from the Reformation to the 19th-century renewal.

Early Thomism. The death of St. Thomas on March 7, 1274, was deeply mourned by the city of Naples, the vicinity of Fossanova, the Roman province of the Dominican order, and the schools of Paris. Miracles connected with his death and burial initiated a cult centered largely in Naples. Lamentations, panegyrics, and letters extolling his learning and sanctity expressed profound grief at his passing (Birkenmajer, 1–35). Shocked by news of his death, the faculty of arts at Paris (including SIGER OF BRABANT and PETER OF AUVERGNE) addressed a moving letter on May 3 to the general chapter of the order meeting in Lyons. They requested that the body of so great a master be given permanent resting place in the city that "nourished, fostered, and educated" him; they further requested that certain philosophical writings begun but not completed at Paris and other works promised by Thomas be sent without delay (*ibid.* 4).

St. Thomas, however, left no immediate disciples worthy of his genius. His first successor at Paris, HANNIBALDUS DE HANNIBALDIS, followed Thomas faithfully in his commentary on the *Sentences* (1258–60), but he was created cardinal in 1262 and died in 1272. Thomas's second successor was ROMANO OF ROME (d. 1273), who was more Augustinian than Aristotelian or Thomistic (Grabmann, *Geschichte,* 61). REGINALD OF PIPERNO, Thomas's constant companion and confessor, for whom he wrote a number of less profound treatises, gave posterity no indication of his grasp of Thomas's teaching. Peter of Auvergne and other masters in the faculty of arts who eagerly read Thomas's philosophical commentaries could not have attended lectures in the theological faculty, where he was teaching. Even the earliest Thomists who may have known him personally, such as WILLIAM OF MACCLESFIELD, GILES OF LESSINES, BERNARD OF TRILLE, and Rambert dei Primadizzi, were never enrolled under Thomas as their master. Consequently there was little, if any, academic continuity between Thomas and those who later defended his teaching.

The "innovations" of Thomas Aquinas were strongly opposed during his lifetime, particularly by Franciscans, secular masters in theology, and Dominicans trained in the older Augustinian tradition. This tradition, influenced by the *Fons vitae* of Avicebron, claimed: (1) the identification of matter with potentiality and form with actuality, thus positing a *forma universalis* and a *materia universalis* in all creatures; (2) a certain actuality, however slight, in primary matter; and (3) that substantial form confers only one determinate perfection. From this followed the *famosissimum binarium Augustinianum,* namely, the hylomorphic composition of all created being, both spiritual and corporeal, and the plurality of substantial forms in one and the same individual. Thomas, on the other hand, maintained: (1) that matter and form are principles only of corporeal substances; (2) that primary matter is a purely passive, potential principle, having no actuality whatever; and (3) that in a single composite there can be only one substantial form conferring all perfections proper to it. Since these "innovations" were inspired by the "new Aristotelian learning" and supported by the growing menace of Latin Averroism, it was natural for the old school to associate Thomas with Averroists in the faculty of arts, even though he had explicitly attacked the fundamental errors of Latin Averroism.

More than any other Thomistic innovation, denial of universal HYLOMORPHISM and of plurality of forms aroused strongest opposition from the old school. For JOHN PECKHAM, Franciscan regent master from 1269 to 1271, both denials led to heresy. Denial of universal hylomorphism apparently eliminated the distinction between God and creatures; denial of plurality led to denial of the numerical identity of Christ's body on the cross and in the tomb. In a famous disputation with Thomas in 1270 over plurality of forms, Peckham was apparently unable to convince the masters of Paris, and possibly Bp. Étienne TEMPIER, of the heretical implications of Thomas's view. Nevertheless Peckham persisted in his conviction.

Condemnation of Thomistic Teachings. At the height of the first Averroist controversy in 1270, Thomas's systematic use of Aristotle could not be ignored; it was not ignored by the Franciscans, particularly not by Bonaventure. After Thomas's death Averroists disregarded the condemnation of 1270 and even the prohibition of 1272 against discussing theological matters in the faculty of arts. By 1276 Albert the Great was apprised of the growing tendency to associate Averroism with all who used Aristotle in theology. To avert rash condemnation of his own efforts and those of Thomas, Albert journeyed from Cologne to Paris in the winter of 1276–77. This arduous journey was of no avail. Word had reached Rome of dissensions in Paris, and JOHN XXI ordered Bishop Tempier to conduct an investigation. On March 7, 1277, acting on his own authority, Tempier proscribed 219 propositions, excommunicating all who dared to teach any of them (*Chartularium universitatis Parisiensis,* ed. H. Denifle and E. Chatelain, 4 v. [Paris 1889–97] 1:543–555). Although no person was mentioned in the decree, it was clear to all that the condemnation was directed principally against Siger of Brabant, BOETHIUS OF SWEDEN, and Thomas Aquinas. Of the 16 propositions generally considered to be Thomistic, the only serious

issue, mentioned four times, is the denial of universal hylomorphism and its ramifications. The Paris condemnation made no mention of the unicity of substantial form. Because of this deliberate omission, ROBERT KILWARDBY, Dominican archbishop of Canterbury, issued a condemnation of 30 theses on March 18, 1277, in a special convocation of masters in Oxford (*ibid.* 1:558–559). Of the 16 propositions in natural philosophy, five bear directly on the unicity of substantial form and six logically presuppose or follow from it. Whoever deliberately defended the propositions condemned was to lose his position in the university.

Reaction to the Condemnation. On April 28 John XXI endorsed the decree of Tempier and implemented its measures. Kilwardby's action, however, was quickly resented by the Dominican order. On receiving news of this action Peter of Conflans, Dominican archbishop of Corinth, disapproved strongly, protesting the inclusion of theses that were not heretical. In reply Kilwardby insisted that he wanted only to prevent the theses from being taught in the schools "because some are manifestly false, others deviate philosophically from the truth, others are close to intolerable errors, and others are patently iniquitous, being repugnant to the Catholic faith" (*ibid.* 1:560). The last phrase clearly referred to the doctrine of unicity of substantial form. Kilwardby's arguments against the doctrine were answered in 1278 by Giles of Lessines in his *De unitate formae.* On April 4, 1278, NICHOLAS III created Kilwardby cardinal bishop of Porto with residence in Rome.

The Dominican general chapter meeting in Milan on June 5, 1278, appointed two visitators, Raymond of Meuillon and John Vigoroux, to investigate and to take action against the English Dominicans "who have brought scandal to the Order by disparaging the writings of the venerated Friar Thomas Aquinas" (*Monumenta Ordinis Fratrum Praedicatorum historica,* ed. B. M. Reichert [Rome-Stuttgart-Paris 1896–] 3:199). With the appointment of John Peckham to the See of Canterbury on Jan. 28, 1279, the doctrinal estrangement of the two orders became inevitable. On May 21 of that year the Dominican general chapter meeting in Paris strictly forbade all irreverent or unbecoming talk against Thomas or his writings, no matter what the personal opinion of individuals might be. Thus reverence for the person and writings of Thomas Aquinas was imposed on the whole Dominican order.

Franciscan Opposition. As early as 1272 Franciscans, emphasizing the Augustinian orthodoxy of Bonaventure, compiled lists of doctrines "in which Bonaventure and Thomas disagree." Toward the end of 1279, WILLIAM DE LA MARE, successor to Peckham in the

Franciscan chair at Paris, completed a *Correctorium fratris Thomae* in which 117 passages of Thomas Aquinas were "corrected" according to Scripture, Augustine, and Bonaventure. This work was officially adopted by the general chapter of the Franciscans held at Strassburg on May 17, 1282, when it forbade diffusion of the *Summa theologiae* of Thomas except among notably intelligent lectors, and then only with the corrections of William in a separate volume reserved for private circulation (*Archivum Franciscanum historicum* 26:139).

Two years after the Franciscan capitular decision at Strassburg, Archbishop Peckham renewed Kilwardby's prohibition at Oxford on Oct. 29, 1284. In a letter to the masters of Oxford, November 10, he insisted that it was not Thomas who had originated the dangerous doctrine of unicity but the Averroists. In private letters to the chancellor of Oxford, Dec. 7, 1284, and to the bishop of Lincoln, June 1, 1285, Peckham reiterated his personal objections to the unicity of form in man.

In the schools of Paris and Oxford Thomist doctrines, particularly of unicity and individuation, were attacked as heretical and "condemned" by the Franciscans ROGER MARSTON, RICHARD OF MIDDLETON, PETER JOHN OLIVI, MATTHEW OF AQUASPARTA, and WALTER OF BRUGES. It was against this background that the early Thomist school developed.

Dominican Legislation. From 1286 until the canonization of St. Thomas (1323), the Dominican order did everything possible to promote the study and defense of Thomistic teaching among its members. The Paris chapter of June 11, 1286, strictly commanded every friar to study, promote, and defend the doctrine of Thomas Aquinas; those who acted contrary were to be deprived of whatever office they held and penalized. The chapter of Saragossa, May 18, 1309, determined that all lectors were to teach from the works of Thomas and resolve questions according to his doctrine. Disregard of this legislation by DURANDUS OF SAINT-POURÇAIN and JAMES OF METZ prompted the chapter of Metz, June 3, 1313, to forbid any friar openly to lecture, resolve questions, or answer objections contrary to what was commonly held as the opinion of the venerable doctor. The chapters of London (1314) and Bologna (1315) reiterated the regulation of Metz, adding that superiors should be particularly vigilant that nothing be taught or written contrary to the teaching of Aquinas. By such legislation the order established Thomism as its official teaching.

Early English School. One of the earliest defenders of Thomas in England, though more in an administrative than academic capacity, was WILLIAM DE HOTHUM, who incepted at Paris in 1280 and was elected provincial of the English Dominicans in 1282. He is said to have written a treatise *De unitate formarum,* but he is best known for his defense of RICHARD KNAPWELL, who incepted at Oxford in 1284. By his own admission Knapwell became convinced of Thomistic doctrine only gradually. At the time of his inception, over which Hothum presided, Knapwell had become a convinced Thomist. He vigorously defended the doctrine of unicity of form in the schools of Oxford in opposition to Roger Marston, notwithstanding the prohibition of Peckham. Denounced to the archbishop for publicly determining a *quaestio* in favor of unicity, Knapwell was summoned to present himself in London on April 18, 1286. On the advice of Hothum he did not answer the summons, presumably on grounds of exemption from jurisdiction. Having written *Correctorium corruptorii "Quare"* (1282–83), he was convinced that there was nothing heretical in the teaching of Thomas Aquinas. On April 30, 1286, Peckham convoked a solemn assembly, condemned eight theses of Knapwell as heretical, and excommunicated him and all who aided or counseled him. Hothum, who was present, protested on grounds of privilege of exemption and lodged an appeal to the pope. Knapwell went to Rome personally to plead his case, but the Holy See happened to be vacant until the election of NICHOLAS IV, a Franciscan. When the appeal was finally entertained in 1288, the Franciscan pope imposed perpetual silence on Knapwell, who is reported to have died in Bologna a broken man (*see* CORRECTORIA).

At Oxford the defense was continued by ROBERT OF ORFORD, who wrote his *Correctorium "Sciendum"* before becoming a master about 1287. In his *Quodlibeta* (1289–93) he refuted the attacks of GILES OF ROME and HENRY OF GHENT against the teaching of Thomas Aquinas.

THOMAS OF SUTTON wrote *Contra pluralitatem formarum* before becoming a Dominican in 1282. Being trained in philosophy outside the order, he maintained a predilection for the pure Aristotle and an independence of interpretation. Nevertheless a number of his writings were thought to be so Thomistic as to circulate as authentic works of Thomas Aquinas (Roensch, 46–51). He even completed Thomas's unfinished commentary on the *Perihermeneias* and *De generatione.* As a Dominican master in theology (after 1293) he confronted the new attacks of Duns Scotus, ROBERT COWTON, and Henry of Ghent and took part in the controversy between Franciscans and Dominicans on whether evangelical poverty belongs to the essence of Christian perfection or is only a means to it. Many historians consider Sutton to have been the most eminent of early English Thomists, even though his later writings were restricted by the exigencies of controversy.

Sutton's contemporary was the eminent controversialist William of Macclesfield, who incepted under Sutton at Oxford *c.* 1299. Before 1284 he composed *Correctorium corruptorii "Quaestione"* against William de la Mare and a defense of the unicity of form. During his academic career he defended the teaching of Thomas Aquinas against Henry of Ghent and GODFREY OF FONTAINES.

Thomistic teachings were also defended by NICHOLAS TREVET in his *Quodlibeta* and *Quaestiones disputatae* as well as by THOMAS WALEYS. After 1320 the influence of WILLIAM OF OCKHAM was strongly felt in England even among Dominicans, notably by ROBERT HOLCOT. A conspicuous exception was THOMAS OF CLAXTON, who in his commentary on the *Sentences* (*c.* 1400) strongly defended the real distinction of essence and existence (*esse*) in creatures and the analogy of being.

Early French School. After Peter of Auvergne, Bernard of Trille, and Giles of Lessines, the most prominent and versatile French Thomist was JOHN (QUIDORT) OF PARIS. He not only defended the teaching of Thomas in his *Correctorium "Circa"* (before 1284), two treatises on the unicity of form, and vigorous replies to Henry of Ghent, but he developed the Thomistic doctrine of separation of Church and State in his celebrated *De potestate regia et papali* (*c.* 1302). He fully appreciated the Thomistic doctrine of essence and existence, but he was less Thomistic in his views concerning the Eucharist; these were twice censured and twice defended without satisfactory results. A popular preacher called *Predicator monoculus,* he was well aware of contemporary trends and abuses of justice and warned of the proximity of anti-Christ.

Among the more vigorous opponents of Henry of Ghent and Godfrey of Fontaines was the Dominican BERNARD OF AUVERGNE, who acutely understood and ardently defended Thomas, his "master."

The most prolific French Dominican was HARVEY NEDELLEC, a polemicist who later became master general. Having studied Aristotle outside the order, he never appreciated the Thomistic distinction between essence and *esse* in creatures. As a theologian he wrote a valuable *Defensio doctrinae fr. Thomae* (1303–12) and remained a polemicist throughout his life, attacking the doctrines of Henry of Ghent, PETER AUREOLI, and his own confreres James of Metz and Durandus of Saint-Pourçain for departing from the teaching of Thomas Aquinas. Apart from his Aristotelian rejection of the real distinction of essence and *esse,* he had a profound and subtle understanding of Thomas. He lived to see the canonization of St. Thomas, which he helped to bring about. He was known by the scholastic title of *Doctor rarus.*

One of the best representatives of the French Thomistic school was WILLIAM OF PETER OF GODIN, whose *Lectura Thomasina* (1292–98), a commentary on the *Sentences,* manifested a calm and profound understanding of all traditional Thomistic doctrines (Grabmann, *Mittelalt. Geist.* 2:572–575). The principal controversy in his career involved the Franciscan view of the absolute poverty of Christ. A younger contemporary, Armand de Belvézer, wrote an influential commentary on Thomas's *De ente et essentia* (1326–28) and firmly opposed the view of JOHN XXII concerning the beatific vision, as had all Thomists. PETER OF LA PALU was an enthusiastic promoter of Thomas whose knowledge of Thomism left something to be desired. A nobleman by birth, Peter was deeply involved in legal and moral questions of the day, notably papal and regal power, privileges of mendicants, Franciscan poverty, and the trial of Peter John Olivi.

Carmelites. Early Carmelite theologians, though favorably disposed to defend Thomas, were more eclectic than Dominicans and some seculars. The *Quodlibeta* and *Summa* of Gerard of Bologna (d. 1317) manifest the influence of Thomas, Henry of Ghent, and Godfrey of Fontaines. The most outstanding early Carmelite master at Paris was Guy Terrena of Perpignan (d. 1342), who was more influenced by Godfrey than by Thomas. More Thomistic, but still eclectic, was JOHN BACONTHORP, lecturer at Oxford and Cambridge.

Early German School. German Dominicans of the 13th century were strongly influenced by St. Albert the Great. Albert's disciples preferred to develop the mystical and Neoplatonic elements of his thought. According to Grabmann the earliest representatives of Thomism in Germany were JOHN OF STERNGASSEN, Gerard of Sterngasse, and NICHOLAS OF STRASSBURG, all of whom depend heavily on Thomas for their commentaries on the *Sentences* and for their *Quaestiones disputatae* (Grabmann, *ibid.* 1:393–404). JOHN OF LICHTENBERG, master in theology at Paris, 1311–12, borrowed many passages from the *Summa theologiae* for his commentary on the *Sentences.* Henry of Lübeck (d. 1336), writing after the canonization of St. Thomas, was less hesitant to cite "venerabilis doctor beatus Thomas de Aquino, qui omnibus allis cautius et melius scripsit." Even at Paris Henry openly taught the doctrine of Thomas Aquinas on the principle of individuation, the real distinction, and the interpretation of Augustine "secundum doctorem Thomam" (Grabmann, *ibid.* 1:421–424).

Early Italian School. After Hannibaldus de Hannibaldis, the most faithful defender of Thomas was Rambert dei Primadizzi of Bologna (*c.* 1250–1308), possibly a disciple, who replied to the *Correctorium* in his *Apologeticum veritatis* of 1286–87. The foremost promoter of the cause in Italy was the octogenarian BARTHOLOMEW OF LUCCA, who studied under Thomas in Rome, accompanied him to Naples in 1272, and there received word of his death. Initiative for the canonization of Thomas came with the establishment of a separate province for Naples and Sicily in 1294. Bartholomew supplied much biographical information to William of Tocco (c. 1250–1323), promoter of the cause, and to BERNARD GUI, procurator general, when the cause was first introduced at Avignon in 1318. Bartholomew was a historian and a political theorist rather than a speculative theologian; he played no small role, however, in vindicating Thomas. In 1316 the Dominican JOHN OF NAPLES defended the thesis in Paris that the doctrine of Friar Thomas ''could be taught at Paris with respect to all its conclusions'' (*Xenia Thomistica* 3:23–104). REMIGIO DE' GIROLAMI is considered by Grabmann to have been a disciple of Thomas and the teacher of DANTE ALIGHIERI, at least by way of public lectures in Florence. The theology of the *Divina Commedia* is mainly Thomistic, although the cosmology is more Albertinian and Neoplatonic.

The practical theology of Thomas Aquinas was disseminated in Italy through the *De officio sacerdotis* of Albert of Brescia (d. 1314), the *Compendium philosophiae moralis* of BARTHOLOMEW OF SAN CONCORDIO, and the alphabetical handbook *Pantheologia* of Raynerius of Pisa (d. 1351). Italians, having no sympathy for the condemnations of 1277, did everything possible to popularize St. Thomas and his teaching.

Canonization and Vindication. Thomas Aquinas was canonized with exceptional solemnity by John XXII at Avignon on July 18, 1323. In a general congregation of all Parisian masters specially convoked on Feb. 14, 1325, Stephen Bourret, bishop of Paris, formally revoked his predecessor's condemnation so far as it ''touched or seemed to touch the teaching of blessed Thomas'' (*Chartularium universitatis Parisiensis,* 2:280). With this vindication of St. Thomas, his followers turned to the diffusion of his doctrine in opposition to other schools, particularly Scotism and nominalism. About 1330 a certain Durandellus, probably a disciple of John of Naples, composed an *Evidentia Durandelli contra Durandum.* Later DURANDUS OF AURILLAC forcefully promulgated the teachings of Thomas Aquinas. This diffusion, however, was temporarily halted by the black plague, the Western Schism (1378–1417), and the general decline of learning and religious life in the second half of the 14th century.

Diffusion of Thomism. The establishment of new universities in Italy, Spain, Portugal, Germany, Bohemia, Vienna, Cracow, and Louvain, the religious reform of the Dominican order under Bl. RAYMOND OF CAPUA (c.

1330–99), and the multiplication of manuscripts of St. Thomas contributed to the diffusion of Thomism. In the 14th century the *Summa theologiae* was translated into Armenian, Greek, and Middle High German. By the 15th century Thomism occupied a respected place in theological thought. St. ANTONINUS of Florence, self-taught in Thomistic theology, faced new moral problems in his *Summa theologiae moralis.* The Dominican general chapter of 1405 renewed norms for teaching in the order. At the Council of Constance (1414–18) the Dominican general, Leonardo Dati (d. 1425), developed and defended the supremacy of pope over council. Opposition to John WYCLIF and John HUS, occasioning the Council of BASEL (1431–38), stimulated John Nider (c. 1380–1438), John Stojkovic of Ragusa (c. 1390–1442), and John Torquemada (1388–1468) to develop a notable ecclesiology that helped to overcome the conciliarist movement. At the University of Cologne secular masters, such as HENRY OF GORKUM and the Belgian John Tinctor (fl. 1434–69), began lecturing on the *Summa* of St. Thomas. Henry of Gorkum wrote an introduction to the *Summa* (*Quaestiones in partes S. Thomae*) and a number of original Thomistic treatises, *De praedestinatione, De iusto bello,* etc.

The most remarkable of early 15th-century Thomists was John Capreolus, who incorporated a profound knowledge of St. Thomas into his *Defensiones theologiae Divi Thomae,* a commentary on the *Sentences,* in which he ably refuted the doctrines of Duns Scotus, Durandus of Saint-Pourçain, GREGORY OF RIMINI, and Peter Aureoli. The brilliance of this work merited for him the title of *Princeps Thomistarum.*

During the second half of the 15th century many Dominican and secular professors in German universities lectured on the *Summa* of St. Thomas, e.g., Kaspar Grunwald in Freiburg, Cornelius Sneek and John Stoppe in Rostock, and Leonard of Brixental (d. 1478) in Vienna. At Cologne the most outstanding defenders of Thomism against Albertists were Gerard of Heerenberg (de Monte, d. 1480), Lambert of Heerenberg (de Monte, d. 1499), and John Versor (fl.1475–85). One of the most noteworthy Dominican lecturers on the *Summa* at Cologne in this period was Gerhard of Elten (fl. 1475–84). Toward the end of the 15th century the Hungarian Dominican Nicholas de Mirabilibus wrote the treatise *De praedestinatione,* which presented the traditional teaching of the Thomistic school.

In this period a remarkable commentary on the *Summa* was written by a prolific Belgian of Roermond, DENIS THE CARTHUSIAN, known as *Doctor exstaticus;* he manifested a profound grasp of Thomistic, patristic, and biblical teaching.

The invention of printing helped to spread not only the text of St. Thomas's major works, but also numerous Thomistic commentaries, expositions, manuals, and defenses. In Italy significant contributions were made by PETER OF BERGAMO, regent at Bologna, whose *Tabula aurea* (1473) is the only complete index to the works of St. Thomas; he also wrote one of the last concordances of Thomistic doctrine (*Concordantia conclusionum*). Among his disciples were DOMINIC OF FLANDERS, whose *Summa divinae philosophiae* was the best-known commentary prior to that of Conrad Köllin; Tommaso de Vio Cajetan; and Girolamo SAVONAROLA, whose *Triumphus crucis* was an adaptation of the *Summa contra gentiles* and an early Thomist manual of apologetics.

PETER NIGRI (SCHWARZ), rector of the University of Budapest in 1481, wrote a large *Clypeus Thomistarum,* which is a strong defense rather than an exposition of Thomistic teaching, and numerous polemical works against the Jews.

Among notable editors of St. Thomas's works were Paul Soncinas (d. 1494), who also published a compendium of Capreolus, and the Venetian Antonio Pizzamano.

Despite the strength of the Thomistic school, it had to compete with Scotism and the growing popularity of nominalism. The Protestant REFORMATION brought Thomism to an end in countries lost to Rome, but it gave impetus to ''second Thomism'' in countries that remained Catholic.

Second Thomism. With the Reformation Thomism received new vitality in Spain and Italy. Doctrinal problems raised by reformers forced theologians to reexamine basic questions in terms of Sacred Scripture, apostolic tradition, and systematic theology. The outstanding characteristic of this phase was the gradual replacement of the *Sentences* by the *Summa theologiae* of St. Thomas. Begun in Germany in the 15th century, it spread to Paris, then to Spain and Italy. The Council of TRENT (1545–63) not only introduced needed reforms, but it also reenforced the teaching of theology and philosophy in Catholic universities and seminaries. New religious orders founded during the COUNTER REFORMATION frequently claimed St. Thomas as their official teacher; and even older orders, reformed in the spirit of Trent, made serious efforts to teach Thomistic doctrine. Diocesan seminaries as well, fulfilling the spirit of Trent and of Roman pontiffs such as PIUS V, introduced manuals of philosophy and theology that were in some way ''ad mentem S. Thomae Aquinatis.'' The outstanding characteristic of Thomism after the Council of Trent was the multiplication of manuals that claimed to be more or less Thomistic.

The initial harmony of reform and revival met serious obstacles both from within and from without (*see*

SCHOLASTICISM, 2). The first internal obstacle was the controversy between Dominicans and Jesuits concerning grace in the *Congregatio de auxiliis* (1598–1607). The deadlock that ensued produced centuries of mutual mistrust in philosophy and theology. The second internal obstacle was the rise of a new moral theology in the 17th century known as casuistry. This divided theologians into probabilists, probabiliorists, and Jansenists; it also diverted attention from fundamental principles to particular cases, quantitative distinctions, and legalism that led to an academic moral theology in following centuries. At the center of this development stood St. ALPHONSUS LIGUORI, whose *Theologia moralis* (1753–55) influenced all later moralists and disputants. The third internal obstacle for Thomism was the writing of textbooks in philosophy that would be relevant to modern philosophers and scientists. After Trent textbooks of Thomistic philosophy were written for seminaries; these were largely summaries of Aristotle or adaptations of the *Summa theologiae.* With the birth of modern science and philosophy in the 17th century one of two courses was generally followed: ignoring modern science or abandoning ancient philosophy. After I. Newton and C. WOLFF modern science and philosophy won the day in Catholic seminaries and universities. By the middle of the 18th century the Thomistic school was dead; the name of Thomas was rarely seen in seminary textbooks of philosophy, and even the name ''Thomists'' had to be defined as ''those who follow blessed Thomas'' (*Phil. Lugdunensis: Metaph.* [Lyons 1788] 308).

Before Trent. Prior to the reorganization of the University of Paris under Louis XI, an innovation was made by the Belgian Dominican Peter CROCKAERT. Originally a secular professing OCKHAMISM, Crockaert became a Dominican at Paris in 1503 and finally became a Thomist who was sympathetic to humanism. In 1509 he began lecturing on the *Summa* of St. Thomas instead of the *Sentences* of Peter Lombard. Among his illustrious disciples was Francisco de VITORIA, with whom he edited the *Summa theologiae* 1a2ae. At Cologne Conrad KÖLLIN, the most prominent Thomist of his day and first opponent of Martin Luther's doctrine on marriage, followed the German practice of lecturing on the *Summa* and in 1512 published a substantial commentary on the 1a2ae in Cologne, the influence of which extended far beyond Germany.

In Italy Tommaso de Vio CAJETAN lectured on the *Summa* at the University of Pavia (1497–99) at the invitation of Duke Sforza. His published commentary, however, was written between 1507 and 1520, when he was general of the Dominican order and cardinal priest of St. Sixtus. This commentary not only revived Thomistic studies in Italy but influenced the interpretation of many

Thomistic doctrines. In other writings Cajetan denied that reason could demonstrate the immortality of the human soul. Consequently many of his contemporaries and successors disagreed with his views, notably the Dominicans Ambrogio Catarino (1487–1553), Bartolomé Spina (*c.* 1480–1546), Giovanni Crisostomo JAVELLI, Bartolomé de MEDINA, Melchior CANO, Domingo BÁÑEZ, and "many theologians" of the Sorbonne in 1533 and 1544. Cajetan's influence on Thomism increased when Pius V ordered the publication of his commentary with the complete works of Thomas Aquinas in 1570 and Leo XIII ordered it to be published in the critical edition of St. Thomas (v. 3–12; Rome 1888–1906). The Italian revival of Thomism was augmented by FERRARIENSIS (Francesco Silvestri of Ferrara), also general of the Dominican order, who is best known for his commentary on the *Summa contra gentiles,* which is also included in the Leonine edition of St. Thomas (v. 13–15; Rome 1918–30). A penetrating commentary on the *Summa theologiae* 1a was written by Javelli; into this he inserted a *Quaestio de Dei praedestinatione et reprobatione,* in which he departed from traditional Thomistic teaching in his efforts to pacify Luther. Moreover, Javelli wrote one of the first manuals of philosophy "ad mentem S. Thomae" in three volumes, later entitled *Totius rationalis, divinae ac moralis philosophiae compendium;* this was printed many times in Venice and Lyons between 1536 and 1580.

Spain was the principal center of second Thomism. Having taught at Paris, Francisco de Vitoria returned to Spain, bringing with him Peter Crockaert's method of lecturing on the *Summa theologiae.* As professor in the principal chair of theology at Salamanca, succeeding the Thomist Diego de Deza (*c.* 1443–1523), he exerted considerable influence directly on the University of Salamanca and indirectly on the Universities of Valladolid, Seville, Evora, Alcalá, and Coimbra. The precision, lucidity, and humanist flavor of his lectures can be seen in his published commentary on the *Summa theologiae* 2a2ae (7 v.; Salamanca 1932–52). From 1526 to 1541 Vitoria conducted a series of conferences (*Relectiones theologicae* 12) on problems of current interest dealing with ecclesiastical and civil power, relation of pope to council, conditions in the New World, causes of just war, and the divorce of HENRY VIII (3 v.; Madrid 1933–35). Spanish universities henceforth had three distinct chairs of theology: Thomist, Scotist, and nominalist. Among outstanding disciples who continued Vitoria's work were Domingo de SOTO, Cano, Pedro de Sotomayor (d. 1564), and Martin de Ledesma (d.1574). Domingo de Soto, constantly concerned with current problems, wrote exhaustively on law in *De jure et justitia* and Pelagianism in *De natura et gratia,* and defended Bartolomé de LAS CASAS in the controversy with Juan Ginés de Sepulveda con-

cerning American Indians. Cano, an aggressive opponent of the Jesuits, was the first to give serious consideration to the sources of theological speculation in his *De locis theologicis.* Medina, disciple of Cano and father of probabilism, wrote a lengthy commentary on the whole *Summa,* only part of which has been published.

The Thomistic revival extended beyond the Dominican order to seculars, Augustinians, reformed Carmelites, and JESUITS, whose society was approved in 1540.

Early Jesuit Legislation. In the early constitutions composed between 1547 and 1550 St. IGNATIUS OF LOYOLA wrote, "In theology the Old and New Testaments and the scholastic doctrine of St. Thomas are to be read, and in philosophy Aristotle" (*Const.* 4.14.1). His own training at Alcalá, Salamanca, and Paris brought him into close contact with St. Thomas and Dominicans. The section *De sacrae theologiae studiis* specified that the *Summa* of St. Thomas was to be covered by two professors in a period of eight years, two years being devoted to the 2a2ae. Early professors, such as Claude LE JAY and Francisco de TOLEDO, a disciple of Domingo de Soto, were Thomists in philosophy and theology. Ignatius, however, expressed hope for a new work "more accommodated to our times"; Gerónimo NADAL, a companion, claiming to find prolixity in St. Thomas, hoped that some day a new theology would be written that would conciliate Thomist, Scotist, and nominalist factions. These desires inspired later Jesuits to seek greater freedom to depart from the teaching of St. Thomas (Beltrán de Heredia, 392–393). The Ratio Studiorum of 1586 under the fifth superior general, Claudius ACQUAVIVA, granted more liberty to depart from St. Thomas, particularly where he differed from current views, such as those respecting the Immaculate Conception and clandestine marriages. New legislation and problems of the Counter Reformation produced a radical departure in *Concordia liberii arbitrii cum gratiae donis* (Lisbon 1588) by Luis de MOLINA. This departure was continued by Gabriel VÁZQUEZ and by Francisco SUÁREZ, the most influential of all Jesuit writers. By a decree of 1593 Jesuits were ordered to return to the doctrine of St. Thomas; henceforth no one who was not truly zealous for the doctrine of St. Thomas was to teach theology (*nullus ad docendum theologiam assumatur, qui non sit vere S. Thomae doctrinae studiosus*). A thoroughly Thomistic *Summa philosophiae* (5 v.; Ticino 1618–23) was compiled by the Italian Jesuit Cosmo ALAMANNI. Belgian Jesuits, notably Robert BELLARMINE, applied Thomistic principles to problems of the day.

Trent and Thomism. The Council of Trent, convoked to define Catholic doctrine and to reform the Church, was guided inevitably by the mind and spirit of

St. Thomas (Walz, 440). Contrary to legend, the *Summa* of St. Thomas was not enshrined on the altar with the Scriptures. Nevertheless, Tridentine decrees followed closely the wording and teaching of Thomas Aquinas, especially concerning justification, Sacraments in general, and the Eucharist in particular. Outstanding Thomist theologians at the council were Domingo de Soto, Cano, Bartolomé Spina, Ambrogio Catarino, Franscesco Romeo (d. 1552), Bartholomew of the Martyrs (1514–90), Pedro de SOTO, Francisco FOREIRO, Bartolomé de CARRANZA, Giacomo NACCHIANTI, Ambrose Perlargus, Jerome Oleaster, Thomas Stella, and Peter Bertano.

One far-reaching effect of the disciplinary decrees of Trent was the establishment of seminaries for better education of the clergy. After the first Catholic university was established in Dillingen (1549), others were established rapidly in Germany, Austria, France, Belgium, and the New World (Manila 1611). This created a demand for good teachers of philosophy and theology as well as for orthodox textbooks. In 1562 petition was made for a catechism that would give a clear explanation of Catholic doctrine. This work was entrusted to Cardinal Seripandus; three Dominicans, Leonardo Marini (1509–73), Egidio Foscarari (1512–64), and Foreiro; and Mutio Calini, bishop of Zara. After the death of Seripandus in 1563, direction was given to Cardinal Charles BORROMEO. This *Catechismus Romanus* was published by order of Pius V in 1566 and was the basis for all Catholic catechisms up to the 20th century.

In 1567 Pius V declared Thomas Aquinas a Doctor of the universal Church and ordered that his complete works be collected and published in Rome with the *Tabula aurea* of Peter of Bergamo (Rome 1570–71). This Piana, or first Roman edition of the *Opera omnia,* added greatly to the diffusion of Thomistic teaching.

Congregatio de Auxiliis. Molina's *Concordia* of 1588 was condemned by the Spanish Inquisition, banned in Spain, and vehemently attacked at Salamanca by Báñez and Pedro de LEDESMA. In 1594 the opposing positions concerning grace and free will were publicly debated in Valladolid by the Jesuit Antonio de Padilla and the Dominican Diego Nuño. Soon heated debates were held throughout Spain.

Two issues were prominent: efficacy of grace in the free will of man and God's foreknowledge of man's free actions. Molina, rejecting the teaching of St. Thomas, posited a middle knowledge (*scientia media*) whereby God sees all possible reactions of individual men in various circumstances. Knowing how man will react, God gives grace accordingly. Insisting on man's free choice of grace, contrary to John CALVIN, Molina taught that God offers grace to all men. If man accepts grace, God concurs simultaneously (*concursus simultaneous*) with man in meritorious actions. Báñez, and Dominicans generally, insisted on the primacy of God's universal causality and taught that free will cannot choose grace unless it is physically premoved by God to do so (*praemotio physica*). God foreknows those who will be saved because He gives intrinsically efficacious grace to those whom He wills. To Dominicans the Jesuit position appeared to be Pelagian. To Jesuits the Dominican position appeared to be Calvinist.

Between 1594 and 1597, 12 reports were forwarded to Rome, where CLEMENT VIII established a commission under the presidency of Cardinals Madrucci and Arrigone. On March 19, 1598, and again in November, the commission submitted its report condemning Molina's book. Fearing to make a hasty decision, Clement VIII requested the Dominican and Jesuit generals to appear with their theologians. On Feb. 22, 1599, began the long series of conferences called *CONGREGATIO DE AUXILIIS.* From March 19, 1602, onward, the debates took place in the presence of the pope. Defenders of the Dominican position were Diego ÁLVAREZ and Tomás de LEMOS. The debates continued under PAUL V, who presided over the last session, in which ten cardinals voted for the condemnation of Molina and two voted against, namely, Bellarmine and Duperron. After 20 years of debate and 85 conferences before two popes no official verdict was given; but in a decree of Aug. 28, 1607, Paul V forbade each side from charging the other with heresy and from using inflammatory language. In 1611 the Holy Office required that all books concerning grace be examined in Rome before publication. In 1612 Aloysio Aliaga, confessor to the king of Spain, requested a decision on the controversy; but Paul V replied that "more circumspect deliberations are still needed." Numerous ponderous tomes were in fact published. The Belgian Dominican Jacques Hyacinthe Serry (1658–1738), disciple of Alexander Natalis, wrote a detailed account of the proceedings in his large *Historia congregationum de auxiliis* (Louvain 1700; definitive ed. Antwerp 1708) under the pseudonym A. Le Blanc. Serry continued the controversy in numerous writings, notably *Schola Thomistica vindicata* (Cologne 1706) against the Jesuit historian Gabriel Daniel.

17th-Century Commentaries and Textbooks. The tragic case of Galileo GALILEI and the new philosophy of René DESCARTES isolated rather than challenged Thomist thinkers. Theologians, divorced from scientific movements of the day, produced extensive commentaries and summaries of St. Thomas, often repeating their predecessors. Philosophers, clinging to the orderly universe of Aristotle, used Thomistic theology to explain Aristotelian philosophy in isolation from contemporary issues. The

Jesuits of Coimbra, known as Coimbricenses, composed a college text of Aristotelian philosophy (1592–1606). The reformed Carmelites of Alcalá, known as COMPLU-TENSES, cooperated in a *Cursus artium* (7 v.; 1624–28) that was used at Salamanca since 1627 and in many seminaries. The Carmelites of Salamanca, known as SALMAN-TICENSES, began to write a cooperative commentary on the *Summa* in 1631 that was not completed until 1704, *Cursus theologiae* (20 v.; Paris 1870–83), and a *Cursus theologiae moralis* in seven volumes between 1665 and 1709.

The most outstanding Thomist of the early 17th century was JOHN OF ST. THOMAS, who wrote a *Cursus philosophicus thomisticus* that expounded Aristotelian logic and natural philosophy; ethics and metaphysics were studied in theology. He also compiled an extensive commentary on the *Summa* called the *Cursus theologicus.* A contemporary of Cornelius Otto JANSEN, he was the last of the great line of Iberian commentators in second Thomism. Among his better-known contemporaries were Jerome de Medices (d. 1622), John Paul Nazarius (d. 1646), Francisco de Araujo (d. 1664), Mark Serra (1581–1645), John Ildephonse Baptista (d. *c.* 1648), Antonio de Sotomayor (*c.* 1558–1648), and a Belgian secular, Francis SYLVIUS. In this period mystical theology was developed by Tomás de VALLGORNERA in his *Mystica theologia Divi Thomae* (1662).

Probabilist Controversy. PROBABILISM is the theory of moralists who admit as a legitimate rule of conduct an opinion that is only probable even when there is current an opinion that is recognized as more probable. It entered the Thomistic school in 1577 with the publication of Medina's commentary on the *Summa theologiae* 1a2ae. While admitting the strength of the traditional Thomist view that the safer opinion ought always to be followed, he declared that it is morally licit to follow any probable opinion even though the opposite is more probable (in *Summa theologiae* 1a2ae, 19.5–6). All Spanish and Portuguese Dominicans after Medina taught probabilism until 1656, when it was explicitly forbidden by the general chapter of Rome. The last Dominican probabilist was Pedro de Tapia (1582–1657).

Probabilism entered Jesuit theology with Gabriel Vázquez, who explicitly quoted Medina. Thereafter Jesuit theologians defended probabilism in the battle against Jansenist rigorism. The laxist view of probabilism quickly degenerated into casuistry, notably in the writings of the Jesuits Tomas SÁNCHEZ, Antonio de Escobar y Mendoza, Juan CARAMUEL LOBKOWITZ, and the Sicilian Theatine Antonino DIANA. Jansenist opposition to probabilism and casuistry, which lasted for more than two centuries, was renewed by Pasquier Quesnel. Probabi-

lism, first condemned by INNOCENT XI in 1665, was frequently condemned by the Holy See and by later Thomists. St. Alphonsus Liguori, who considered himself a disciple of St. Thomas, reached a compromise in his *Theologia moralis* (1753–55) that allowed licit choice of contradictory moral opinions only when they are equally probable (equiprobabilism). A detailed history of probabilism and rigorism was written by the Italian Dominican Daniel CONCINA.

Decline of Second Thomism. Even before the French Revolution and the Napoleonic occupation brought "second Thomism" to an end, there was little vitality among philosophers and theologians. In Spain the Thomist school was represented mainly by Discalced Carmelites and the Dominican cardinal Pedro de GODOY. In France the tradition was carried on by Guillaume Vincent de CONTENSON, Antonin Reginald, Jean Baptiste GONET, Antoine GOUDIN, and Antonin MASSOULIÉ. In Belgium the outstanding representative was Charles René BILLUART, whose principal work was a commentary on the *Summa* in 18 volumes. In Italy Thomism was best represented by the Jesuit philosopher Sylvester MAURUS and by the Dominican Vincenzo GOTTI (1644–1742), whose principal work was *Theologia scholastico-dogmatica iuxta mentem D. Thomae* (16 v.; Bologna 1727–35). In Germany the Benedictines of Salzburg fostered Thomistic studies, notably Ludwig Babenstuber (1660–1715), who wrote *Philosophia thomistica* (Salzburg 1706) and *Cursus theologiae moralis* (Augsburg 1718); Paul Mezger, who wrote *Theologia thomistico-scholastica Salisburgensis* (Augsburg 1695); Alfons Wenzel (1660–1743); Placidus Renz senior (d. 1730); and Placidus Renz junior (d. 1748). In Switzerland the Cistercians Raphael Königand Benedict Hüber published a *Harmonia* of theological philosophy and philosophical theology "consonant with the doctrine of St. Thomas and Thomists" (2 v.; Salem 1718).

By the second half of the 18th century the complete works of St. Thomas had been printed eight times, the last being the second Venice edition (1745–88), begun by Bernard M. de Rossi (1687–1775). By then there was little interest in reading the text of St. Thomas outside the Dominican Order.

(For the Thomistic revival in the 19th and 20th centuries, *see* SCHOLASTICISM, 3.)

Bibliography: R. VERARDO, *Enciclopedia filosofica,* 4 v. (Venice-Rome 1957) 1:1709–13. *Bulletin Thomiste* (1924–). R. GARRIGOU-LAGRANGE, *Dictionnaire de théologie catholique,* ed. A. VACANT et al., 15 v. (Paris 1903–50) 15.1:823–1023. H. HURTER, *Nomenclator literarius theologiae catholicae,* 5 v. in 6 (3d ed. Innsbruck 1903–13) v. 2–4. J. QUÉTIF and J. ÉCHARD, *Scriptores Ordinis Praedicatorum,* 5 v. (Paris 1719–23); continued by R. COULON (Paris 1909–); repr. 2 v. in 4 (New York 1959). P. WYSER, *Der*

Thomismus (Bibliog. Einführungen in das Studium der Philosophie 15–16; Bern 1951). M. GRABMANN, *Die Geschichte der katholischen Theologie seit dem Ausgang der Väterzeit* (Freiburg 1933); *Mittelalterliches Geistesleben*, 3 v. (Munich 1925–56). A. M. WALZ, *Compendium historiae ordinis praedicatorum* (2d ed. Rome 1948). K. WERNER, *Geschichte des Thomismus*, v. 3 of *Der hl. Thomas von Aquino* (Regensburg 1859); *Die Scholastik des spáter Mittelalters*, 5 v. (Vienna 1881). F. J. ROENSCH, *Early Thomistic School* (Dubuque 1964). M. BURBACH, ''Early Dominican and Franciscan Legislation Regarding St. Thomas'' *Mediaeval Studies* 4 (1942) 139–158. V. BELTRÁN DE HEREDIA, ''La enseñanza de Santo Tomás en la Compañía de Jesús durante el primer siglo de su existencia,'' *Ciencia tomista* 11 (1915) 387–408. C. GIACON, *La seconda scolastica*, 3 v. (Milan 1944–50); *Le grandi tesi del tomismo* (2d ed. Milan 1948). A. BIRKENMAJER, *Vermischte Untersuchungen zur Geschichte der Mittelalterlichen Philosophie, Beiträge zur Geschichte der Philosophie und Theologie des Mittelalters* (Münster 1891–) 20.5 (1922). D. A. CALLUS, *The Condemnation of St. Thomas at Oxford* (2d ed. Oxford 1955). S. SZABÓ, ed., *Xenia thomistica*, 3 v. (Rome 1925). G. M. MANSER, *Das Wesen des Thomismus* (Thomistische Studien 5; 3d ed. Fribourg 1949). N. DEL PRADO, *De veritate fundamentali philosophiae christianae* (Fribourg 1911). A. G. SERTILLANGES, *Les Grandes thèses de la philosophie thomiste* (Paris 1928), Eng. *Foundations of Thomistic Philosophy*, tr. G. ANSTRUTHER (St. Louis 1931), É. H. GILSON, *The Christian Philosophy of St. Thomas Aquinas*, tr. L. K. SHOOK (New York 1956); *The Spirit of Thomism* (New York 1964). B. DAVIES, *The Thought of Thomas Aquinas* (Oxford 1992). R. INGARDIA, *Thomas Aquinas: International Bibliography, 1977–1990* (Bowling Green, Ohio 1993). T. F. O'MEARA, *Thomas Aquinas Theologian* (South Bend, Ind. 1997). J.-P. TORRELL, *Initiation a saint Thomas d'Aquin*, v. 1, *Sa personne et son oeuvre* (Fribourg 1993), v. 2, *Saint Thomas d'Aquin, maître spirituel* (Fribourg 1996). R. CESSARIO, *Les thomisme et les thomistes* (Paris 1999). J. F. WIPPEL, *The Metaphysical Thought of Thomas Aquinas: From Finite Being to Uncreated Being* (Washington, D.C. 2000).

[J. A. WEISHEIPL]

THOMISM, TRANSCENDENTAL

Speculative thought on the verge of the 20th century confronted the traditional rational foundations of Christian faith with a formidable array of adversaries, primary among which was KANTIANISM and POSITIVISM. Two Catholic thinkers pioneered the radical rethinking called for: Cardinal MERCIER and Maurice BLONDEL. Désiré Mercier inaugurated the movement known as NEOSCHOLASTICISM. He assumed in 1882 the chair of Thomistic philosophy, established at the insistence of Leo XIII, and later in 1889 founded the Institut Supérieur de Philosophie—both at the University of Louvain. From the beginning, the movement was preoccupied with the epistemological problem that Mercier preferred to call ''criteriology.'' Seeking a *rapproachment* with modern thought and science, he began with a sharp critique of earlier dogmatism; this found sympathetic echoes in the Institut Catholique at Paris and in the Italian neo-Thomist school represented by Agostino Gemelli and Giulio Canella.

Mercier, opposing on one hand the universal methodical doubt of Descartes and on the other the naive realism of the tradition, sought a new criterion of truth to ground the objectivity and the certitude of knowledge, one moreover intrinsic to the activity of the intellect itself. He concluded that the certitude of indemonstrable truths rested on a reflex act of the intellect grasping the relationality of its own act to reality. This amounted to an inference—i.e., the intellect could, after recognizing sensations in a psychologically irresistible experience as passive impressions, and through invoking the principle of causality, infer the existence of extra-mental reality. Some influence of the German Joseph Kleutgen can be detected here; its weak point is perhaps the failure to do justice to experience (as over against reason) and the empirical judgment. As a reaction against KANTIANISM it represents a limited success largely because Mercier, like all his Catholic contemporaries, interpreted Kant psychologically, viewing his thought as subjectivism rather than as the transcendentalism intended by Kant himself. In the end, the contribution was the traditional answer but presented in a newly critical way that opened up the problem to more radical rethinking, soon to come in a younger colleague of Mercier's at Louvain—Joseph MARÉCHAL.

Maurice Blondel confronted this same skepticism in an independent and decidedly distinct way, working from assumptions not explicitly Thomistic. In his *L'Action* (first published in 1893) he sought an answer to the problem of truth from the quite distinct province of human action—not in the pragmatist sense of altering the world but, emphasizing immanent action, more in the Aristotelian sense of consummating thought in achieving self-fulfillment. The wellspring of such action was the will, which Blondel saw as energized by an instinctual drive to the Absolute (*la volonté voulue*) which underlay in an unconscious way every instance of actually willing a concrete good (*la volonté voulante*). Openness to this a priori in free decision constituted a dynamism toward truth, ultimately to faith in Christian truth. Blondel's approach, accused of an implicit ''theologism,'' did recapture the domain of experience and, in spite of the intellectualist alternative to it proposed by the French Dominican Ambroise Gardeil and by Joseph de Tonquédec, was decisive in opening the way to transcendental Thomism.

Confrontation with Kant. More than any other, it was the shadow of KANT that lay upon the early 20th century, heralding the movement of Western philosophy into the unexplored realms of subjectivity, temporality, and relativity. His critical philosophy called into question the realist foundations of thought and the receptive character of knowledge. In their place, Kant introduced what he called ''transcendental philosophy'': a search for the unknown presuppositions underlying all knowledge, for its a priori conditions. Kant himself was content to conclude to the rejection of metaphysics, but the question refused to go away, and his endeavors only pushed deeper the problem as to the origin of human understanding and the kind of being affirmed thereby. FICHTE opened the era of German idealism with recourse to a self-positing Ego; SCHELLING retreated further to an Absolute, prior to both Ego and non-Ego, and explaining both; and HEGEL carried the project to its conclusion by viewing the activity of Ego or Mind as mere moments of Absolute Spirit, i.e., of an all-embracing subject-intentionality.

Joseph Maréchal (1878–1944), a Belgian Jesuit at the scholasticate of his society in the environs of the University of Louvain, and working to a degree in collaboration with Pierre Scheuer, took the challenge of critical philosophy seriously; and his original and profound endeavors gave rise to the movement that has come to be loosely known as transcendental Thomism. Earlier, a fellow Jesuit at the Institut Catholique in Paris, Pierre Rousselot, had published in 1908 *L'Intellectualisme de saint Thomas,* a clear effort to root the ideas of Blondel in Thomas Aquinas. This mediated Blondelianism offered Maréchal the fresh starting point he was searching for, and later the same year he published the first installment of ''Le sentiment de présence chez les profanes et les mystiques'' [*Revue de Questions scientifiques* 64 (1908) and 65 (1909)], in which he attempted a repudiation of phenomenalism by first distinguishing the representational from the existential character of knowledge, and then locating the latter in the judgment as the intellect's activity not of receiving its object but of ''structuring'' it from sense data. Knowledge was here a dynamism of projecting conceptual contents onto the domain of the real through the judgmental act; the grounds for this was an innate tending of the intellect toward intuition of the Absolute.

But it was Maréchal's masterwork, *Le point de départ de la métaphysique* (the first of five *cahiers* appeared in 1922), that seriously initiated his efforts to rehabilitate metaphysics. Opposition to his sympathetic treatment of Kant in the early *cahiers* led him to put off *Cahier* 4 (later published posthumously) and to attempt a direct confrontation of Thomism with Kantianism in *Cahier* 5, entitled *Le thomisme devant la philosophie critique* (Louvain and Paris, 1926; 2d ed. 1949). Here, Maréchal accepts Kant's own starting point—the immanent object—but insists that this constitutes the juncture between the subject and the real world. Kant was content to remain with a static and purely formal critique of knowledge, whereas his own starting point in fact leads one into realism (2d ed. p. 4). At the outset, Maréchal denies intellectual intuition: the mind neither has innate ideas nor simply contemplates the extra-mental thing (p. 351). He equally disal-

lows a realism based on experience, denying that the intellect is aware of a passivity induced within itself by the thing known; rather intellection is immanent activity attaining an intelligible object not to be confused with the external, material object of sensation (pp. 440–441). At the same time, Maréchal thought it necessary to temper the voluntarism that lay at the root of the kind of dynamism toward the real proposed by Blondel. He found a substitute in the act of judgment as an affirmation of absolute reality, at least implicit and necessary in all intellection, which formed the logical presupposition of there being any finite objects at all (p. 346 ff.). Underlying this was the distinction between the intellect's form (concept) and its act of judgmental affirmation (p. 519). Affirmation is a dynamism that objectifies the form and so grasps it as being, i.e., beyond the finite determinations of the representation, the intellect is made aware of a further intelligibility precisely by its own tending, in a dynamism unleashed by the concept itself, toward something infinite and absolute. The intelligence is enabled to grasp its forms as the forms of an act (existence), but only in virtue of its own finality to such an act—but not the concrete act of existing of the thing, rather the infinite act of existing which is in fact God (pp. 307–315). In this way, the intellect ''constitutes'' its object as belonging, in a finite and participatory way, to the realm of the real.

INTENTIONALITY as such then, i.e., formally as cognitive and representative, bespeaks the real order. By real here is meant not actually existing (this calls for a further and different kind of judgment) but necessarily able to exist. Maréchal is talking about essences, not about existence, but *real essences,* i.e., possible realities which he understands as grounded in prior actually existing reality—not finitely existing, however, but infinitely existing. In this there comes to light Maréchal's conviction that the possibility of God is in fact the argument for His existence: ''affirmer de Dieu qu'il est possible, c'est affirmer purement et simplement qu'il existe, puisque son existence est la condition de toute possibilitié'' (p. 450).

Critically, Maréchal grounds all of this in evidence. The evidence, however, lies not in the thing known, nor in the intellect's reflex grasp of its own relationship to reality (Mercier), but in the very judgment itself; i.e., an analysis of judgment shows that to refuse the affirmation of reality is to fall into a contradiction, namely, that of affirming that there is no affirmation (p. 496 ff.).

An initial charge of cryptic idealism was rather convincingly repudiated by Maréchal in a 1931 article: ''Le problème de dieu d'après M. Edouard Le Roy'' [*Nouvelle revue théologique* 58 (1931)]. It cannot be denied, however, that he did throw a pronounced emphasis upon the subjective, a priori conditions to knowledge; moreover, he reduced these conditions to a noncognitive factor, sc., the innate *élan* of the intellect to its end. Of even greater influence was the direction of his thought from an ontology of being as naively objective to an ontology of being as realized within consciousness. Among Maréchal's immediate disciples are Auguste Grégoire, André Marc, Joseph de Finance, and Andre Hayen. In reaction to his work was the newly critical development of a more traditional Thomistic epistemology by such thinkers as the Dominicans M.D. Roland-Gosselin and R. GARRIGOU LAGRANGE as well as Jacques MARITAIN and Etienne GILSON.

Dialogue with Heidegger. Post-Kantian and post-Hegelian thought attempted to rethink being not, however, as traditional metaphysics but rather as a philosophy of man in his historicity. This reintroduced the tension between idealism and realism, much of the latter being of Thomist inspiration. The effort to surmount this resulted in a new transcendentalism originating with Edmund HÜSSERL (1859–1938) called PHENOMENOLOGY. Hüsserl, however, bracketed (*epoché*) the question of real existence and concerned himself with a reductive analysis of what "came to appearance" on the horizon of consciousness, which he saw not as mere phenomena but as reality itself—thus developing an eidetic science of pure essences. Martin HEIDEGGER (1899–1976) rescued this method from Sartrean existentialism and transposed it into a philosophy in which Being (*Sein*) confers its beingness upon the beings (*Seiendes*) by a "lighting up" process which comes to pass within human consciousness (*Dasein*); an ontology of existence in which Being is clearly finite and historical.

A new generation of Catholic thinkers brought Maréchal's innovative understanding of Thomism to bear upon this new Heideggerian outlook—shared differently by W. DILTHEY, K. JASPERS, M. MERLEAU PONTY, etc. Heidegger's appeal to contemporary theology (expecially Protestant) lay in what he saw as his "overcoming" of metaphysics; the project of the new Maréchalians was the structuring from within a modified phenomenology of a neoclassical metaphysics in which Being would reappear as absolute and infinite, explaining finite and historical being. The achievement came principally from two sources: one German, the other Anglo-Saxon. In Germany the preeminent name was that of Karl RAHNER (1904–1984), who, however, received considerable support from the more purely philosophical endeavors of two fellow Jesuits: Johannes B. Lotz ("Die Unterscheidung von Wesenheit und Sein," *Der beständige Aufbruch,* Przywara Festschrift, 1959) and Emerich Coreth [*Metaphysik* (Innsbruk, Vienna, Munich 1961); available in a shorter English version by Joseph Donceel, *Metaphysics* (New York 1968)].

Rahner's prodigious output began with a basic philosophical work, *Geist in Welt* [(Innsbruck 1939); 2d ed. by J. B. Metz (1957); English translation *Spirit in the World,* by W. Dych (New York 1968)], which he saw not as a study but as a linear development of St. Thomas's metaphysics of knowledge, and culminated in his ongoing *Schriften zur Theologie* [(Einsiedeln, Zurich, Cologne); Eng. tr. *Theological Investigations* (London and Baltimore, 23 v.)] extending to all areas of theology. A significant alternative to this approach is to be found in the Canadian Jesuit Bernard J. F. LONERGAN (1904–1984) in whose work the direct influence of Heidegger gives way to that of studies in modern science (e.g., Herbert Butterfield) and in the philosophy of history (e.g. R. G. Collingwood). Noteworthy too is the work and spirit of Newman, whose role in Lonergan's thought parallels that of Blondel in the Continental thinkers. Beginning with genetic studies of St. Thomas on operating grace and later on the problem of knowledge (both published in *Theological Studies* in 1941–42 and 1946–49, respectively; each now available in book form) and progressing to *Insight: A Study of Human Understanding* (London 1957; New York 1965) and *Method in Theology* (New York 1972), Lonergan's consuming interest has been the detailed construction of a critical cognitional theory.

From Rahner and Lonergan has come a new metaphysics in which the being investigated is that which occurs within consciousness. They tend to view being as more phenomenal in kind and closely assimilated to meaning and knowledge. Coreth writes of "an immediate unity of being and knowing in the very act of knowing" (*Metaphysics* p. 70). From this being there is extrapolated the being of the cosmos. Lonergan, e.g., looks upon being as "whatever is to be known by intelligent grasp and reasonable affirmation" (*Insight* p. 391) and progresses from the structures of consciousness as sensation, concept, and judgment to the structures of extra-mental being as matter, form, and existence [cf. "Isomorphism of Thomist and Scientific Thought," *Collection* (New York 1967)]. Phenomenology had effected the decisive turn to subjectivity (better expressed in Heidegger's term "subject-ness," *Subjektitat,* precluding individualism), making man a "co-constitutor of his world of meaning" (Merleau-Ponty). This occasioned a subtle transformation of metaphysics into philosophical anthropology, which when the Christian implications of Maréchal's thought are brought to bear upon it can be made to function as a fundamental theology. Thus the work of Rahner and Lonergan brings the work of Maréchal to full flower as theological syntheses.

The decisive factor in this—common to all the transcendental Thomists—is the finality of consciousness. Analysis of the performance of the human spirit discloses at its very core an innate drive to being as absolute and really existing; this is the very nature of man as "spirit in the world" or finite transcendence. On this basis, the judgment (as an affirmation, however, and not merely as the *enuntiabile*) asserts the real beingness of the finite object, represented in the concept, and is a situating of it on the spectrum of real analogical being. In affirmation the spirit "performs" being—in contrast to more traditional realists theories in which intelligence "discovers" being; a performance Rahner locates in the activity of the "*intellectus agens*" (*Spirit in the World* pp. 187–226). The underlying finality is non-cognitive and appears in the early writings as rooted in the will (following Maréchal), though Lonergan of late prefers to speak only of distinct moments of knowing and loving unified in human spirit, eschewing the Aristotelian faculty theory of the soul. Nonetheless all transcendental Thomists afford a certain primacy to the conative and the volitional; for Rahner, "human spirit as such is desire (*Beigie rde*), striving (*Streben*) . . ." (*Spirit in the World* p. 281); for Lonergan, "Being is the objective of the unrestricted desire to know" (*Insight* p. 348).

Rahner explains the implications of this by recourse to his notion of the *Vorgriff*, i.e., a prehension or anticipation by the soul of being which, while conscious, is preconceptual, nonobjective, and unthematic in kind; all a posteriori knowledge is an objectification an thematization of this (*Spirit in the World* p. 142). Somewhat differently, Lonergan allows that man can think about being before knowing it; the former bespeaking "notions" of being and its transcendental properties but not the concepts realized in objective and explicit knowledge: "prior to every content, it [being] is the notion of the to-be-known through that content" (*Insight* p. 356). The being in question throughout all of this is unlimited, unconditioned, ultimate-absolute being as the unrestricted horizon of the pure desire to know, not, however, *the* Absolute Being which the believer can come to recognize (in faith) as its ground. This is not ontologism because the being objectified in the affirmation is not God but finite being as it points to the divine.

At the heart of this kind of thinking lies the "transcendental method": first, attention is directed not to objects to be known but to the intentional acts of subjects in their very knowing; secondly, what is sought thereby in a reductive (rather than inductive or deductive) analysis are the a priori conditions for the very possibility of knowing finite objects in any objective way. This represents an epistemological move beyond moderate realism into critical realism. Its starting point is the "question": man is ceaselessly driven to question everything except the very fact of his questioning. But this heuristic character of consciousness is inexplicable unless one admits

some sort of a priori "awareness" of what it is that the question seeks. One cannot ask "what is it" without betraying some sort of nonobjective prehension of the range of being; being (not "for us" but "in itself") is the horizon of the question (Coreth, *Metaphysics* p. 64). From within a more detailed gnoseology Lonergan offers a distinct explanation of this phenomenon: reacting against an older conceptualism in which understanding was reduced to the formation of the concept, he views it rather as the occurrence of "insight" allowing for a "higher viewpoint" on which basis concepts, as subsequent objectifications of insights, undergo constant revision. This brings into play his original theory of judgment in which the at least partial truth value of concepts is verified by assuring that the judgments involving such representations are "virtually unconditioned"—i.e., the intellect judges reflectively that the conditions for the verification of the affirmation have been reasonably met (*Insight* pp. 549 ff., 672). The resultant intelligibility is not one of rational necessity but, in an abandonment of the Aristotelian model of science, that of "emergen probability" (*ibid* p. 121 ff.). Differing from Coreth, however, Lonergan delimits metaphysics to the objective pole of the horizon of being, denying its extension to the subjective pole, sc., the method of performing, which has to be sought in a transcendental doctrine of methods [cf. Lonergan, "Metaphysics as Horizon," *Collection,* and Coreth's reply in *Language, Truth and Meaning,* ed. Philip McShane (Notre Dame, Indiana 1972)].

Doctrine of God. Transcendental Thomism reaches the traditional God of Catholic theism, and by an act of intelligence, but one rooted in love. The intellect in fact is "the faculty of the real only because it is the faculty of the divine" (Pierre Rousselot, *L'Intellectualisme* p. v). Due to its orientation to the Beatific Vision, it is enabled in this life to "perform" being, which is to say that every performance of being is at least an implicit and anonymous attaining to God. In this perspective, Rahner maintains that every human consciousness grasps the reality of God in an unthematic, preconceptual way as Absolute Mystery. The authentication of this in reflection is not probative but ostensive; the believer does not strictly demonstrate God's existence but interprets ordinary experience, common to himself and nonbelievers, as grace and thematizes them accordingly. But only in love, as man's response to God's prior loving of him, does man come to this nonobjective awareness of the Absolute Mystery; which love of God "as the deepest factor of knowledge is both its *condition* and its *cause*" [*Hearers of the Word,* tr. by M. Richards (New York 1969) 101]. More painstakingly, Lonergan reasons that man's capacity to know reality demands as its condition the infinite identity of being and knowing, who is God. If consciousness has an unrestricted horizon which is absolute being, this demands reasonably acknowledging *the* Absolute Being as an unrestricted act of understanding. This rests upon the virtually unconditioned judgment that unless God exists, reality is not fully intelligible (*Insight* p. 672). Again, the insight whence the argument proceeds is rooted in love, in Lonergan's term "conversion," i.e., it results from an intellectual conversion to a higher viewpoint explained by "horizon shifts" arising from prior religious and moral conversions [cf. *Method in Theology* (New York 1972) pp. 237–45; *Doctrinal Pluralism* (Milwaukee 1971) p. 34 ff.].

Theological Themes. Rahner's theory of man's openness to the divine means that man "stands before the possibility of the free action of God upon him, thus before the God of a possible material revelation" (*Hearers of the Word* p. 91). Should God choose not to speak, then that very silence would be His revelation; but through faith the believer finds this revelation publicly and historically in the Christ event. This undergirds several theological themes: The "anonymous Christian," sc., man as the recipient of a transcendental but not yet categorical revelation; the "supernatural existential," in which prior to the state of justification man is not in a state of pure nature but in an already graced state *existentially,* i.e., due to the ontological, not ontic, structures of consciousness; the historically conditioned character to the formulas of public revelation and its transmission—beneath which however the preconceptual remains as a transcultural element. More specifically theological are Rahner's important doctrines on Christ as the "real symbol" of the Father, on Uncreated Grace, and on the identity of the "economic" and the "immanent" Trinity.

Lonergan, apart from earlier Latin treatises on Christ and the Trinity, preoccupied himself with the nature and method of theological science, gradually working out in detail a new ideal of science, empirical rather than logical in Aristotle's sense, in which fixity gives way to the ongoing process, certitude to probability, necessity to verifiable possibility, knowledge to hypothesis. Here theology becomes itself method rather than, as for St. Thomas, theory. Among the fruits of this, Lonergan hoped for some overcoming of theological pluralism, a position Rahner viewed with reserve, condsidering pluralism as irreducibly given.

As a school, transcendental Thomism has clearly entrenched itself. Disciples are legion: foremost in Rahner's case is perhaps Johannes B. Metz [e.g., *Christliche Anthropozentrik* (Munich 1962)]; among Lonergan's many followers are his fellow Canadian Jesuit, also his editor, Frederick Crowe, and the American David Tracy [*The Achievement of Bernard Lonergan* (New York 1970)]. In

the United States, the editings and writings of Joseph Donceel have contributed notably to advancing the movement.

Critique. Probably no significant Catholic thinker in the West fails to feel the influence of transcendental Thomism; nonetheless reaction to it has been constant since its birth. Hans Urs von BALTHASAR (especially in *Cordula oder der Ernstfall* (2d ed. Einsiedeln 1966) has insisted at length that the movement gives an ultimacy to autonomous human freedom alien to Catholic theology in general. While some express doubts on its TRANSCENDENTALISM, seeing it as precritical (e.g., S. Ogden, H. Holz, R. Heinz), the more insistent question has been the genuineness of its Thomism. Leslie Dewart insists that "when Thomism takes a 'transcendental turn' it abrogates its title to Thomism" [*Foundations of Belief* (New York 1969) app. 2, p. 501]. Certainly, both Rahner's and Lonergan's notion of consciousness marks a radical departure from the *Weltanschauung* of Aquinas; with the latter viewing being in itself and not in the condition of luminosity it gains within human spirit. J. B. Metz, though probably overstating his thesis that this *Denkenform* is potentially in the thought of St. Thomas, does point the way to a resolution. Transcendental Thomism is not historical Thomism if one means by that unreconstructed Thomism. For one thing it never intended a linear development of Aquinas but a critical confrontation of his thought with modern questions. Still that thought in its depth and originality is creative in a way that challenges to a continual rethinking of being; this is something that lies less with the explicit content of his thought than with the contact of intelligence with the real that it allows. Thomas's doctrine on being, e.g., while itself ahistorical, does in its emphasis on act (*esse*) point the way toward appropriating its historicity.

Granting that Thomism is at least the matrix of this new world view, more to the point is the charge that the latter amounts to an idealistic interpretation of Aquinas. This stems largely from the neo-Thomist school of Garrigou-Lagrange, Gilson, and Maritain, all of whom advocate an abstractive intuition of the intelligible—as an alternative to spirit's "performance" of being. Agreeing with the transcendentalists in resting the objectivity of knowledge upon the judgment, they understand the latter not as a virtually unconditioned affirmation of reality after the conditions demanded for such intelligibility have been met (Lonergan), but as the act ("knowing") of intelligence living in its own order of intentionality, the act ("being") of the extra-mental thing (Jacques Maritain, *Degrees of Knowledge*). James Reichman ["The Transcendental Method and the Psychogenesis of Being," *Thomist* (October 1968)] has underscored this same criticism, stressing that the human intellect has as its proper object the quiddities of material things. Metaphysics needs a rational not a transcendental method, since "as chthonic, as a fromand-in-this-world science," it appropriates being from singular sensible things and not through an inner vision of its own potentiality as the faculty of being (p. 506, ff.). For the new Maréchalians, being seems to inhere in the mind of the knowing subject rather than in things known, and this raises the question of metaphysics as a science of the real. Also, it is not clear how such being, achieved in a grasp of the intellect's illuminative power, is anything other than potential being. Again, since being so viewed is not abstracted from existing essences on distinct levels of reality, why is not its commonness univocal in kind rather than analogical? Interpreting metaphysical finality in terms of an innate presence of being to the mind from the very dawn of consciousness (even granting that this is nonobjective in kind) also reduces considerably the sense in which abstracting the intelligible species from the plantasm can be said to be *strictly* necessary. The question can at least be asked if full justice is being done here to the bodily dimension of human spirituality. While not discrediting the direction set out upon by transcendental Thomism, these are at least serious reservations to which it will have to address itself.

One viable alternative to the premises of transcendental Thomism on one hand, and neo-Thomism on the other, has been worked out philosophically by Dominic De Petter ["Impliciet intuitie," *Tijdschrift v. Phil.* 1 (1939) pp. 84–105] and appropriated theologically by Edward Schillebeeckx ["The Non-Conceptual Intellectual Dimension in our Knowledge of God According to Aquinas," *Revelation and Theology* v. 2, tr. by N. D. Smith (New York 1968) pp. 157–206]—both Flemish Dominicans. This theory of "implicit intuition" conceives knowledge as a dynamism, but one entirely objective in kind rather than subjective as in the case of that inspired by Maréchal. It derives not from any unrestricted *desire* to know but from strictly cognitive elements. Here concepts as such are denied any value of the real, and knowledge is basically a nonconceptual awareness of reality—but one inseparable from concepts which, while not grasping the real by themselves, do refer to reality and so possess truth value, by supplying the objective determination within which alone the intuition can occur as something implicit. In this theory, a dynamism of the knowing subject gives way to a dynamism of the contents of knowledge.

Bibliography: G. VAN RIET, *L'Epistémologie Thomiste* (Louvain 1946), English tr. *Thomistic Epistemology*, 2 v., by G. FRANKS, D. MCCARTHY, and G. HERTRICH (St. Louis, London 1963–65). *Mélanges Joseph Maréchal: Oeuvres et Hommages*, 2 v. (Brussels 1950). J. DONCEEL, ed. and tr., *A Maréchal Reader* (New York 1970). E. DIRVEN, *De la forme à l'acte* (Paris 1969). M. CASULA,

Maréchal e Kant (Rome 1955). On Karl Rahner: a detailed bibliography of his writings from 1924 to 1964 arranged chronologically and systematically by G. MUSCHALEK and F. MAYR can be found in *Gott in Welt, Festgabe für Karl Rahner. Hrsg. von Johannes Baptist Metz [et al. Schriftleitung: Herbert Vorgrimler]* 2 v. (Freiburg 1964) 29.00–941. Two prestigious editorial achievements of Rahner are *Lexikon für Theologie und Kirche,* 11 v. including index with J. HÖFER (Freiburg 1957–67), three additional volumes since 1967 with others; and *Sacramentum Mundi,* a theological encyclopedia, 6 v., with 13 other ed. (New York 1968), published simultaneously in six languages. D. GELPI, *Light and Life: A Guide to the Theology of Karl Rahner* (New York 1966). L. ROBERTS, *The Achievement of Karl Rahner* (New York 1967). On Bernard Lonergan: a complete bibliography of his writings up to 1964 prepared by F. E. CROWE can be found in *Spirit as Inquiry: Studies in Honor of Bernard Lonergan, Continuum* 2 (1964); the later writings up to 1969 have been added to this list by D. TRACY, *The Achievement of Bernard Lonergan* (New York 1969) 271–78. P. MCSHANE, ed., *International Lonergan Congress,* v. 1 *Foundations of Theology,* v. 2 *Language, Truth, and Meaning* (Notre Dame 1972). O. MUCK, *The Transcendental Method* (New York 1968). K. BAKER, *A Synopsis of the Transcendental Philosophy of Emerich Coreth and Karl Rahner* (Spokane, Washington 1965). W. J. HILL, *Knowing the Unknown God* (New York 1971). C. BENT, *Interpreting the Doctrine of God* (Glen Rock, New Jersey 1969). G. MCCOOL, "The Philosophical Theology of Rahner and Lonergan," in *God Knowable and Unknowable* (New York 1973).

[W. J. HILL]

THOMPSON, FRANCIS

English poet and critic; b. Preston, Lancashire, Dec. 18 (or 16), 1859; d. London, Nov. 13, 1907. His family was deeply concerned with religious matters. His father, a surgeon, and his mother had been converted to Catholicism before their marriage. His father's two brothers were Anglican clergymen; one of them became a Catholic; and two of their sisters became Catholic nuns. Of the poet's two younger sisters, one became a nun. The family moved to Manchester in 1864.

Thompson entered the seminary at Ushaw College in 1870 but was not found suited to the priesthood. In 1877 he turned to Owens College, later part of Manchester University, to study medicine. He found it repugnant, his health declined, he twice failed his examinations, and he abandoned the study in 1883. He failed as a salesman and was rejected by the army. His mother had died in 1880, and in 1885 he quarreled with his father and left for London. He had been addicted to opium since about 1880, and in London he lived the life of a derelict in the streets and alleys. A pious Evangelical churchman, John McMaster, supported him for more than a year, but then Thompson reverted to the streets.

He submitted some poems to Wilfrid MEYNELL, editor of *Merry England*, and one was published in 1888. Meynell sought out the poet, now near death and in despair, and sent him to a private sanitarium where after a year he was cured of his drug addiction. He spent nearly another year with the monks of the Priory at Storrington before returning in 1890 to lodgings in London near the Meynells.

The period of purgation was a fruitful one. Thompson published "Ode to the Setting Sun" (1889) and his famous "The Hound of Heaven" (1890). Near the end of 1892 he visited the Franciscan monastery at Pantasaph in Wales. There he prepared his first volume of poetry for publication (1893), and there Coventry Patmore visited him (1894) and began their long friendship. *Sister Songs* were published in 1895 and *New Poems* in 1897.

Thompson is generally thought of as a Catholic poet whose verse seems florid and ornate by modern standards, but his "mysticism" and his vision of nature are supported by a hard core of objectivity and accurate theology. Love and poetry itself are his other subjects. He wrote nearly 500 reviews and critical essays during his last ten years. In his taste for the metaphysical poets and his grasp of the possibilities of myth and symbol he was in advance of his time. He also completed a life of St. Ignatius Loyola (1909) and of St. John Baptist de la Salle (1911) before he succumbed to tuberculosis at 47.

Bibliography: *Poems,* ed. T. L. CONNOLLY (rev. ed. New York 1941); *Literary Criticisms,* ed. T. L. CONNOLLY (New York 1948). P. VAN K. THOMSON, *Francis Thompson* (New York 1961). J. C. REID, *Francis Thompson: Man and Poet* (Westminster, Md. 1960). V. MEYNELL, *Francis Thompson and Wilfrid Meynell* (New York 1953).

[C. T. DOUGHERTY]

THOMPSON, JAMES, BL.

Priest, martyr; *alias* Hudson; b. Yorkshire; hanged at Knavesmire in York, Nov. 28, 1582. He entered the seminary at Rheims, Sept. 19, 1580. By special dispensation he received all the minor orders and was ordained priest in 12 days at Soissons in May 1581. His entry into the English mission, however, was delayed until August due to an illness. He was arrested just a year later (Aug. 11, 1582). Thompson's frank admission of his priesthood before the Council of the North amazed everyone, because he had been away from England for less than one year. Thereafter he was imprisoned, loaded with double irons. When he could no longer pay for his private cell, he was confined to the castle. On November 25 he was condemned for high treason. During his hanging three days later, he raised his hands to heaven, then beat his breast with his right hand, and finally made a great sign of cross. In spite of his sentence, he was neither disemboweled nor quartered. His remains were buried under the gallows. Thompson was beatified by Pope Leo XIII on May 13, 1895.

Feast of the English Martyrs: May 4 (England).

See Also: ENGLAND, SCOTLAND, AND WALES, MARTYRS OF.

Bibliography: R. CHALLONER, *Memoirs of Missionary Priests,* ed. J. H. POLLEN (rev. ed. London 1924; repr. Farnborough 1969). J. H. POLLEN, *Acts of English Martyrs* (London 1891).

[K. I. RABENSTEIN]

THOMSON, WILLIAM, BL.

Priest, martyr; *alias* Blackburn; b. *c.* 1560 at Blackburn, Lancashire, England; hanged, drawn, and quartered April 20, 1586, at Tyburn. He was ordained at Rheims in 1584. Returning to England, he worked in and around London until his arrest in the home of Roger Line, the husband of St. Anne LINE, while saying Mass. He was indicted on April 17, 1586, at the Old Bailey with Bl. Richard Sergeant and condemned for his priesthood. Thomson was beatified by Pope John Paul II on Nov. 22, 1987, with George Haydock and Companions.

Feast of the English Martyrs: May 4 (England).

See Also: ENGLAND, SCOTLAND, AND WALES, MARTYRS OF.

Bibliography: R. CHALLONER, *Memoirs of Missionary Priests,* ed. J. H. POLLEN (rev. ed. London 1924). J. H. POLLEN, *Acts of English Martyrs* (London 1891).

[K. I. RABENSTEIN]

THOREAU, HENRY DAVID

Transcendentalist, essayist, and social critic; b. Concord, Mass., July 12, 1817; d. there, May 6, 1862. To his contemporaries, Thoreau was either the "literary echo" of Ralph Waldo EMERSON or an advocate of primitivism, intent on nullifying civilization. Yet posterity finds him a creative artist both bold and original, and the just castigator of a society that had neglected its needs to serve its desires.

Thoreau, the son of parents of narrow means was educated at considerable family sacrifice at Concord Academy and Harvard (graduating 1837). For four years after graduation he taught in Concord and, at the same time, became the disciple of Emerson, his fellow townsman. In 1841, he moved into Emerson's house, earning his keep as a man of all work, and eventually helping Emerson to edit the *Dial,* the organ of the Transcendentalists (*see*

TRANSCENDENTALISM, LITERARY). In 1843, he lived briefly in the home of Emerson's brother William, on Staten Island, N.Y., tutoring his children, while he tried unsuccessfully to win his way in New York City as a professional journalist. On his return to Concord he adopted the mode of life he followed thereafter. Man, he believed, could find true contentment only by obeying higher laws, knowledge of which, while innate, was discerned best by cultivating a nearness to nature. Taking occasional jobs as surveyor, gardener, and carpenter to meet his few needs, he began extended philosophical inquiries into nature. The journal that preserves his account of these inquiries finally grew to 39 volumes, totaling two million words.

In July 1845, Thoreau built a hut at Walden Pond, in Concord; he lived in it for two years. He went to Walden not to escape society but "to drive life into a corner and find out whether it was a mean or a noble thing." *Walden; or, Life in the Woods* (1854), the book in which he tells what his sojourn taught him, addresses itself to all mankind. Even as its flawless organization and gracious style attest its merits as literature, its perceptions attest its worth as a spiritual document. Yet his contemporaries gave it scant notice, and *A Week on the Concord and Merrimack Rivers* (1849), the only other book he published during his lifetime, actually stirred their disdain. The essay "On the Duty of Civil Disobedience" (1849), which the 20th century, following M. K. GANDHI'S lead, hails as "a key document in the history of individualism," and his noble "Life Without Principle" (1863) did not fare better. During his last years, Thoreau, ravaged by tuberculosis, consoled himself that lack of recognition let his confrontation of self continue unhampered. Publication of his MSS, begun after his death, soon filled 20 volumes.

To a society oppressed by wasteful, aimless, material commitments, Thoreau's works offer both rebuke and challenge. In a famous phrase, he says in *Walden:* "The mass of men lead lives of quiet desperation." Convinced that this desperation finds its genesis in man's subservience to possessions, he sought to turn man away from "the inert finite to the resurgent infinite." His negations prefaced affirmatives.

Bibliography: H. D. THOREAU, *Writings,* ed. B. TORREY and F. B. SANBORN, 20 v. (Boston 1906); *Correspondence,* ed. W. HARDING and C. BODE (New York 1955); *Consciousness in Concord,* ed. P. MILLER (Boston 1958). H. S. CANBY, *Thoreau* (Boston 1939). F. O. MATTHIESSEN, *American Renaissance* (New York 1941). J. L. SHANLEY, *The Making of Walden* (Chicago 1957). W. HARDING, *Days of H. T.* (New York 1965).

[J. J. MCALEER]

Henry David Thoreau.

THORLÁK THÓRHALLSSON, ST.

Bishop; b. Fljótshlíeth, Iceland, 1133; d. Skálholt, Iceland, Dec. 23, 1193. He was a CANON REGULAR OF ST. AUGUSTINE, educated in Iceland, France, and England. He was superior of the Augustinian house in Thornykkvibær from its foundation in 1168 until he became bishop elect in 1174. He was consecrated bishop of Skálholt, July 1, 1178. As bishop, he, like Archbishop Eysteinn, pursued a firm, but not always successful, policy of asserting the claims of the Church against the State. His sanctity was recognized very soon after his death, and in 1198 he was formally canonized by the local bishops (no papal confirmation was sought). His cult never spread far beyond ICELAND. Besides SS. Thorlák and JON ÖGMUNDSSON, medieval Iceland venerated Guðmund the Good (1161–1237, feast: March 16) as a saint. Though he was the most popular of all Icelandic saints, he was never formally canonized though he was possibly beatified ca. 1376. The process for Guðmund's canonization was reopened in 1522 but was suspended at the Reformation.

Feast: December 23; July 20 (translation).

Bibliography: H. BEKKER-NIELSEN, "A Note on Two Icelandic Saints," *The Germanic Review* 36 (New York 1961) 108–109. O. WIDDING et al., "The Lives of the Saints in Old Norse Prose: A Handlist," *Mediaeval Studies* 25 (Toronto-London 1963) 294–337.

S. SIGURDARSON, *Thorlákur helgi og samtíd hans* (Reykjavík 1993), with biblio.

[H. BEKKER-NIELSEN]

THORMAN, DONALD JOSEPH

American journalist, author, and publisher of the *National Catholic Reporter*; b. Cicero, Illinois, Dec. 23, 1924; married, Barbara Lisowski, 1952, seven children; d. Kansas City, Missouri, Nov. 30, 1977. Thorman was the third and last child of Harry and Adophine Leverman Thorman; his father died when Thorman was two. The young Thorman, growing up during the Depression, began working at an early age to help support himself. He attended public elementary schools in Oak Park, Illinois, attended Oak Park High School. He spent his senior high school year at St. Philip's High School, Chicago, run by the Servite Fathers, and, upon graduation, entered the Servites' Mount St. Philip Monastery, Granville, Wisconsin for a year, before joining the U.S. Marine Corps (1942). He left the Marines in 1946, joined the Viatorian Fathers for a year, then entered De Paul University. He began teaching at Loyola University, spent a portion of the year 1950 at the University of Fribourg in Switzerland, and received an M.A. in sociology from Loyola that same year. He enrolled in Fordham University to begin work on a doctorate, but returned to Chicago after one year to help his family when his brother-in-law was stricken with terminal cancer.

In 1952, Thorman became managing editor of *The Voice of St. Jude* (now the *U.S. Catholic*), marrying Barbara Lisowski the same year. In 1956, Thorman became managing editor of *Ave Maria* magazine; in 1962, he was publisher and director of development for the Spiritual Life Institute of America; and in 1963, he formed his own company, Catholic Communications Consultants. In Dec. 1965, he became publisher of the *National Catholic Reporter*, which was then just over a year old.

Author of *The Emerging Layman* (Garden City, N.Y. 1962), Thorman was a major figure in the post-Vatican II U.S. Church, especially as publisher of the *Reporter,* a newspaper founded by a group of lay people in 1964, with Robert G. Hoyt as editor, in the belief that an independent press is a vital and healthy asset to the Church. Thorman and the newspaper's role were also important in ecumenical and interreligious affairs. He was active in the National Conference of Christians and Jews. To a generation of Catholics, especially those familiar with the Chicago Catholic tradition arising from the social encyclicals, the Catholic labor movement, and the Christian Family Movement (whose journal he and his wife edited for ten years), Thorman epitomized that era and helped establish a positive, active role for the laity in the Church. His other books include *Christian Union* (Garden City, N.Y. 1967), *American Catholics Face the Future* (Wilkes Barre, Pa. 1968), and *Power to the People of God* (Paramus, N.J. 1970).

[A. JONES]

THORNEY, ABBEY OF

Former BENEDICTINE monastery, earlier known as Ancarig, in the county of Cambridge, and the ancient Diocese of LINCOLN, England. It was founded *c.* 972 by ETHELWOLD OF WINCHESTER with the patronage of King EDGAR THE PEACEFUL, on the site of a hermitage destroyed by the Danes. It was dedicated to the Blessed Virgin and to St. BOTULPH, whose shrine was there. Under the first abbot, Godeman, the abbey became a center of intense literary activity. Fulcard of Saint-Bertin wrote lives of the Old English saints, and developed a school of calligraphy. Abbot Gunther (1085–1112) began rebuilding the church and his work was continued in the 13th century by Abbot David. When the abbey was suppressed in 1539 under King HENRY VIII, the abbot and 20 monks were pensioned. The nave of the abbey church became the parish church.

Bibliography: W. DUGDALE, *Monasticon Anglicanum* (London 1655–73) 2:593–613. *The Victoria History of the County of Cambridgeshire and the Isle of Ely,* ed. L. F. SALZMAN (London 1938) 2:210–217. D. KNOWLES, *The Monastic Order in England, 943–1216* (2d ed. Cambridge, England 1962).

[F. R. JOHNSTON]

THORP(E), ROBERT, BL.

Priest, martyr; b. in Yorkshire; hanged, drawn, and quartered May 15, 1591 at York. He studied at the English College in Rheims, where he was ordained in April 1585 by Cardinal Louis de Guise. He worked for about ten years in Yorkshire, renowned for his devotion and constancy. He was in bed very early on Palm Sunday 1595 when authorities came to arrest him in the Menthorpe home of Bl. Thomas WATKINSON. Someone supposedly observed him gathering palms the night before and reported his actions to the local justice of the peace. Thorpe was condemned as a traitor for being a priest. He was beatified by Pope John Paul II on Nov. 22, 1987, with George Haydock and Companions.

Feast of the English Martyrs: May 4 (England).

See Also: ENGLAND, SCOTLAND, AND WALES, MARTYRS OF.

Bibliography: R. CHALLONER, *Memoirs of Missionary Priests,* ed. J. H. POLLEN (rev. ed. London 1924) I, 86. J. H. POLLEN, *Acts of English Martyrs* (London 1891) 200–202.

[K. I. RABENSTEIN]

THOU, NICOLAS AND JACQUES AUGUSTE DE

Nicolas, Bishop of Chartres; b. Paris, 1528; d. Villebon, Nov. 5, 1598. Nicolas was the brother of Christophe de Thou, first president of the Parlement of Paris. He became canon of the Cathedral of Paris in 1547 and was designated bishop of Chartres in 1573. He shared the anti-League, pro-Gallican, *politique* sentiment of his family that caused trouble when the people of Chartres gave their support to the Duke of Mayenne in 1589. After 1591 Nicolas openly supported the candidacy of Henry IV for the French throne. He was appointed the representative of the archbishop of Reims at the coronation of Henry IV in 1594.

Jacques Auguste (Thuanus), French historian and government official; b. Paris, Oct. 8, 1553; d. Paris, May 7, 1617. Jacques was the son of Christophe de Thou. He studied law at Orleans, Bourges, and Valence and succeeded his uncle Nicolas as canon of Notre Dame, although he never received clerical orders. From 1572 to 1576 he accompanied Paul de Foix, Archbishop of Toulouse, to Rome. In 1578 he entered Parlement, and in 1581 he began a series of travels in southern France where he met Montaigne and the future Henry IV. Upon his return he was appointed *président à mortier* of the Parlement of Paris in 1586 and a councilor of state in 1588. Beginning in 1589 he actively supported Henry IV and in 1598 played an important role in drawing up the Edict of Nantes. During the regency of Marie de' Médicis, he was still active in the government, but was less effective because of the influence of the ultra-Montanists who opposed his historical writings and his stand against the acceptance of the decrees of the Council of Trent.

Thou had been horrified by the massacre of ST. BARTHOLOMEW'S DAY, and this played a part in forming his desire to understand how the Europe of his time had come to be. He began to build a collection of books in the 1570s, and in 1587 he opened a private library. From the resources of this library and through correspondence with foreign scholars, he acquired the material for his *Historia sui temporis.* He began this work in 1593, and the first part, covering the years 1545 to 1560, was published in 1604. It was immediately scrutinized by the ultra-Montanists and former Leaguers for the slightest hint of heterodoxy. A few objectionable phrases were found, and when the second part, covering the years 1560 to 1572,

appeared without praise for St. Bartholomew's Day, his enemies appealed to Rome. Despite the efforts of Cardinals DUPERRON and Ossat, Thou's history was placed on the Index in 1609. By this time two more volumes, covering the period to 1584, had appeared. The fifth and final volume, which brought the narrative to 1607, appeared posthumously in 1620.

Though Thou made errors, his work is the result of careful study. His history and his memoirs reflect the Gallican sentiment of his family and the ideas of the *politiques* who sought peace and toleration in France.

Bibliography: H. HARRISSE, *Le Président de Thou et ses descendants* (Paris 1905). H. DÜNTZER, *J. A. Thou's Leben, Schriften und historische Kunst* (Darmstadt 1837). K. HOFFMAN, *Lexikon für Theologie und Kirche,* ed. M. BUCHBERGER (Freiburg 1930–38) 10:146–47.

[J. M. HAYDEN]

THOUGHTS, MORALITY OF

The act of thinking is, in itself, amoral, although it is a spiritual activity proper only to a person. All moral activity involves thinking, but it also involves volition. In speaking of the morality of thoughts, therefore, thinking must be understood to include, or to be associated with, some activity on the part of the will.

Affective Element. WILL is involved, first of all, by the possible dependence of thought upon volition for its existence. Involuntary thoughts, where attention is focused upon certain objects, not because one wants to consider them, but because they violently obtrude themselves into consciousness and cannot be ejected, have no moral character. Similarly, if thoughts are in some degree, but not completely, involuntary, their moral character is proportionately lessened. Second, will is involved by reason of the affective response to the value, positive or negative, perceived in the object of one's thought. Both these modes of involvement of the will are expressed by saying that when a thought is freely conceived or dwelt upon, and when the heart is freely committed to the moral values or disvalues represented in it, the act of thinking can be good or evil.

In spite of the volitional element in thought to which morality is attributed, thoughts are nevertheless to be distinguished from desires. In thoughts, the affective response is directed simply to the object as it is mentally represented. Desire, on the other hand, is a wish or decision to make the contemplated object actual.

Christianity and the Morality of Thoughts. The morality of thoughts is intelligible only in the context of morality as a whole. There are those who hold that nothing is moral or immoral except that which helps or hurts another. Genuine morality, however, is primarily a matter of the heart, or of the interior of a person. It is true that the intensity and duration of internal self-affirmation and a repetition of the subject's consent may be effected by the external act, but these are secondary considerations. The essence of morality is interiority; the kingdom of God is within. This is not to say that commitment to external goals is of little worth. Love must flow outward to others. Rather it asserts that the essential worth of external commitment is the immanent love with which one gives himself to service. Thoughts, then, pertain to the very heart of morality along with desires and other internal acts.

This conception of the morality of thought is in accord with the Judeo-Christian tradition as found in the Bible. "You shall love the Lord, your God, with all your heart . . ." (Dt 6.5); Jesus reiterated this theme, added love of neighbor as of oneself, and said these two great teachings express the whole of God's law (Mt 22.37–40). Our most moral thoughts then are those of love of God and man. Nor does this interpretation do violence to the text, for "heart" (καρδία) in the Bible is the source of knowledge as well as the affections. And "to know God" is to experience His presence in an encounter leading to love (Jn 14.17; 10.14; 2 Jn 1.2). Our thoughts should also be those of gratitude, obedience, etc., in a word all that is meant by authentic religion (Hos 2.19–20; Jer 9.24). "Whatever things are true, whatever honorable, whatever just, whatever holy, whatever lovable, whatever of good repute, if there be any virtue, if anything worthy of praise, think upon these things" (Phil 4.8–9). And according to a familiar theme, these interior sentiments are more pleasing to God than exterior sacrifice and prayer of the lips. The mind also is the source of evil. "For out of the heart (καρδία) come evil thoughts, murders, adulteries, immorality, thefts. . ." (Mt 15.19). The importance of thoughts that are right before God is clear

What is inculcated in the Scripture is not just good thoughts but, more importantly, good attitudes and a basic commitment to the good. The primacy of attitude and orientation over acts is found in the teaching on change of heart (μετάνοια) and in the Pauline theme of the new man and the putting on of Christ: "Be renewed in the spirit of your mind, and put on the new man" (Eph 4.23–24).

Moral Theology. In their explicit consideration of the morality of thoughts, the attention of Catholic moralists has centered chiefly upon evil rather than upon good thoughts because the moral excellence of good thoughts is obvious, and no speculative difficulty is involved in their recognition and evaluation. With regard to evil thoughts, however, the case is not so clear. Mere knowledge of, or thought about, an evil thing is not sinful. It becomes important, therefore, to determine as precisely as possible the conditions under which thought about something bad is sinful. Thus St. Thomas Aquinas's most explicit treatment of the morality of thoughts is to be found in the context of his treatment of the subject of sin (*Summa theologiae* 1a2ae, 74). Other moralists also have been preoccupied with this aspect of the morality of thought, which is understandable if it is remembered that their teaching was intended largely to prepare the clergy for the ministry of sacramental confession.

What makes thought of an evil thing sinful is the attitude of the will toward what is contemplated. There are two types of morally objectionable responses by the will, and there are in consequence two general kinds of "bad thoughts." One involves complacence of will with regard to the object of thought (*delectatio morosa*), and the other involves joy (*gaudium*). Both complacence and joy are concerned with objects that have internal reality only, and are not conceived as having external existence, for example, revenge, lewdness, or theft imagined with approval. The difference between them is that complacence has an object that has no incarnation in time, whereas joy has as its object a historical act, i.e., something actually experienced in the past. Accordingly, joy is considered to include within the ambit of its approval the attendant circumstances of the act as it occurred. This is not true of complacence, for in imagining an act that has had no historical reality, the mind can prescind from circumstances.

The pertinent moral judgments of the theologians can be briefly stated. Both complacence and joy, when their object is evil, are sinful. The quality of the sin is the same as that of the corresponding exterior act, e.g., an actual murder. The gravity of the sinful approval depends objectively on the importance of the value sinned against; hatred is worse than unchastity because charity is a higher value than continence. Subjectively, the gravity depends on the clearness or obscurity of the subject's perception of the evil and the greater or lesser degree in which the liberty of the subject is engaged. Sinful circumstances present to the subject's consciousness add their malice to the act of entertaining the thoughts.

Bibliography: B. HÄRING, *The Law of Christ: Moral Theology for Priests and Laity,* tr. E. G. KAISER (Westminster, Md. 1961–) v.1. J. BEHM and E. WÜRTHWEIN, G. KITTEL, *Theologisches Wörterbuch zum Neuen Testament* (Stuttgart 1935–) 4:961–965. F. BAUMGÄRTEL and J. BEHM, *ibid.* 3:609–616. A. SNOECK, "De delectatione morosa uti est peccatum internum," *Periodica de re morali canonica liturgica* 40 (1951) 167–209. G. GILLEMAN, *The Primacy of Charity in Moral Theology,* tr. W. F. RYAN and A. VACHON (Westminster, Md. 1959).

[R. H. SPRINGER]

THOURET, JOAN ANTIDA, ST.

Foundress of the Sisters of Charity of St. Joan Antida; b. Sancey-le-Long, France, Nov. 27, 1765; d. Naples, Italy, Aug. 24, 1826. Her parents, François Thouret and Joan Claudia Labbe, were pious proprietors of a small farm. When Joan was 16 her mother died, and she assumed the management of her father's household. In 1787 after opposing all her father's attempts to make her marry, she obtained his permission to join the Daughters of Charity in Paris. The dispersal of religious communities caused by the FRENCH REVOLUTION compelled Joan to return home, where she devoted herself to nursing the sick, educating the young, and securing aid for persecuted priests. After the fall of Robespierre, she entered a new Congregation of Charity, which had established itself in Switzerland because of conditions in France. For two years she shared this group's precarious existence and hardships, journeying with it from Switzerland to Germany and Austria, and returning with it to Switzerland. Heeding the advice of two *emigrés* French priests, she went to Besançon where she opened a school for poor girls and a hospital (April 11, 1799). Soon, joined by other young women, Joan Antida wrote the rules and constitutions of her institute, which the archbishop of Besançon approved. In 1810 Madame Letizia, mother of Napoleon I, offered to the congregation the house of Regina Coeli in Naples; and Joan went with eight sisters and established schools and hospitals in Italy. Joan's close adherence to the Holy See, and Pius VII's approval of the rule in 1819 resulted in bitter opposition toward her and her institute from the clergy of Besançon, who were tinged with Gallicanism. The foundress had to endure attacks on her reputation and was even denied admission to her first French foundations. After her death in the Regina Coeli convent in Naples, she was buried in the chapel there. She was beatified on May 23, 1926, and canonized on Jan. 24, 1934.

Feast: May 23.

See Also: CHARITY, SISTERS OF

Bibliography: J.–A. THOURET, *Sainte Jeanne-Antide Thouret, fondatrice des Soeurs de la charité, 1765-1826: lettres et documents* (2d ed. Besanccedil;on 1983). F. TROCHU, *La Bienheureuse Jeanne Antide Thouret* (Paris 1933; s.l. 1970). *Santa Giovanna Antida Thouret* (Rome 1934); *Saint Jeanne Antide Thouret*, tr. J. JOYCE (London 1966).

[J. A. GIGANTE]

THREAT

The expression of an intention to inflict evil or punishment on another, usually made for the purpose of dissuading him from doing, or of influencing him to do, something. A threat can be just or unjust, good or bad, depending upon whether the threatened retaliatory measure is morally justifiable. God threatened His chosen people with calamities if they rejected His Commandments (Lv 26.14–43). The SANCTION normally attached to positive law is, in effect, a threat of punishment to be inflicted upon its transgressors. To threaten punishment may therefore be reasonable and virtuous, and a parent, a teacher, or a custodian of the law, would fail in his duty if he neglected in some circumstances to threaten punishment. PRUDENCE, of course, must dictate the norms to be observed in making justifiable threats. To threaten a child with exaggeratedly dire and frightening consequences of misbehavior is imprudent, because the threat can be more damaging than helpful to the child. On the other hand it is bad for the young to be threatened with punishment that is not actually intended.

If one really means to carry out a threat of inflicting unjust harm or injury on another, he is guilty interiorly of the injustice he is determined to commit. Even apart from any real intention to carry out the threat, it is always sinful to threaten harm one may not lawfully inflict, or to threaten to evil purpose, e.g., as in extortion. In these cases a threat is akin to violence or duress and is an unjust attack upon another's freedom, tranquillity, and personal dignity.

Bibliography: THOMAS AQUINAS, *Summa theologiae*, 1a2ae, 64–66; 2a2ae, 101,102, 116. W. R. FARRELL, *Companion to the Summa*, 4 v. (New York 1938–42) 3:331–353.

[P. MULHERN]

THREE CHAPTERS

Sixth–century theological controversy dealing with three Antiochene churchmen, THEODORE OF MOPSUESTIA, THEODORET OF CYR, and Ibas of Edessa. The term is taken from the Edict of Justinian (544) anathematizing certain chapters (*kephalia*) of their writings, and came to be applied also to the authors.

Theodore of Mopsuestia. The problem began with the condemnation of NESTORIANISM at the Council of EPHESUS by ST. CYRIL OF ALEXANDRIA in 431, when Rabbula of Edessa (d. 436), who suspected Theodore of Mopsuestia as the originator of the heresy, opposed the spread of his books in Armenia. He elicited the *Tome* of Proclus of Constantinople that condemned the Antiochene distinction between the Son of God and son of man, insisting on a unity of person in Christ.

In 438 Proclus requested the condemnation of Theodore, whom he named as author of the passages refuted in his *Tome,* but John of Antioch refused to anathematize one ''who had died in the peace of the Church''—an argument that would reappear frequently in the controversy. Cyril advised Proclus not to press the matter, and Theodore was not mentioned in the Council of Chalcedon.

Theodoret and Ibas. At the request of John of Antioch, Theodoret of Cyr had refuted the 12 Anathemas of Cyril and ascribed Apollinaristic leanings to Cyril in a letter to the Oriental Monk (*Epistolae,* 151). Theodoret had refused to accept the condemnation of Nestorius at the Council of Ephesus, accepted the union of 433 with reluctance, and wrote his *Eranistes* (447) against Eutyches and his supporters. Censured by imperial edicts in 448, he was deposed at the robber synod of Ephesus in 449 but rehabilitated at the Council of Chalcedon in 451 (11th session, Oct. 26).

In response to the attacks of Rabbula, Ibas, master of the School of Edessa and bishop from 448, wrote a *Letter to Maris* the Persian, defending Theodore of Mopsuestia and criticizing Cyril's Christology. Although he was deposed at the robber council, he likewise was restored at Chalcedon when his orthodoxy was recognized by the papal legates.

Monophysite Agitation. This agitation against Nestorianism and the Council of Chalcedon occasioned the compromising HENOTICON of Zeno (482); it was continued under Anastasius I (491–518). In his Monophysitic polemic, Severus of Antioch named Diodore of Tarsus and Theodore of Mopsuestia as the true fathers of Nestorianism. Severus was abetted by Philoxenus of Mabbugh, who called for the condemnation of Theodoret and Ibas along with Nestorius. By way of reaction, in 520 a ceremony honoring the memory of Diodore, Theodoret, and Nestorius was held at Cyr, and the bishop, Sergius of Cyr, was reprimanded by the government. In 532 at the Colloquy of Constantinople between the orthodox and Severian Monophysite bishops, the latter asserted that the Council of Chalcedon had erred in exonerating Theodoret and Ibas. In 542 Theodore Ascidas, seeking to counteract the repression of ORIGENISM, persuaded Justinian that by condemning the three deceased bishops, he would destroy Nestorianism at its roots.

Justinian. While attempting to safeguard the authority of Chalcedon, which had exonerated two of the three, Justinian published a theological tract in the form of an edict against the Three Chapters (544). He brought Pope VIGILIUS to Constantinople in 547 to persuade him to acquiesce in the condemnation; after considerable discussion the pope issued his *Judicatum* (April 11, 448) condemning the person and writings of Theodore, the *Letter to Maris,* supposedly written by Ibas, and the writings of Theodoret against the faith and St. Cyril. Forced by Western opposition led by the deacons Rusticus, Facundus of Hermiane, the future Pope Pelagius I, and many African and Dalmatian bishops, the pope withdrew the *Judicatum* after promising Justinian secretly that he would work for the condemnation.

Council of Constantinople. In July 551 Justinian published a profession of faith with 13 anathemas against the Three Chapters. When Vigilius objected, he was twice maltreated and had to take refuge in a church to escape outright persecution. Having decided to convoke a Council, Justinian requested judgment from the pope on a florilegium of texts culled from the works of the three incriminated bishops. Aided by Pelagius, Vigilius set to work, but on May 5, 553, the Council of CONSTANTINOPLE II opened without the pope and without the Western bishops residing in Constantinople who had refused repeated invitations to attend. On May 14 Vigilius published his *Constitutum* anathematizing propositions, *prout sonant*—as they read—attributed to Theodore, but he refused to condemn him as a heretic. The *Constitutum* repudiated certain propositions said to represent the thought of Theodoret and Ibas, but upheld the orthodoxy of the two men as vindicated at Chalcedon.

In its eighth session (June 2, 553) the Council condemned the person and writings of Theodore (c. 12), the writings of Theodoret against Cyril (c. 13), and Ibas's *Letter to Maris* (c. 14). Eight months later the emperor forced Vigilius to accept the condemnations (Dec. 8, 553), and in his *Constitutum* II (Feb. 23, 554) the pope confirmed this judgment.

Aftermath. Pelagius the deacon immediately attacked the pope in a Refutatorium (not preserved) and in his *In defensione trium capitulorum* based on a similarly named work by Facundus of Hermiane. However, upon the death of Vigilius (June 7, 555), Justinian chose Pelagius as pope, and he had great difficulty in taking possession as bishop of Rome until he took an oath of allegiance to the four ecumenical councils and named Theodoret and Ibas as ''venerable bishops,'' without mentioning the recent Council of Constantinople.

In Africa the majority of bishops rejected ''Justinian's Council'' and were exiled by the imperial government. They included Victor of Tunnuna, Facundus of Hermiane, Reparatus of Carthage, the deacon Liberatus (*Breviarum*), and Felix of Gillitanum (*Synodicum*), all of whom had written in defense of the Three Chapters.

In Italy the provinces of Milan and Aquileia, joined by Illyricum, separated from communion with Rome, having been aided in their opposition by the Lombard invasion. Milan soon returned to communion (*c.* 572), but despite the efforts of succeeding popes, including GREGO-RY I, the break with Aquileia was healed only under SERGI-US I (687–701).

Bibliography: É. AMANN, *Dictionnaire de théologie catholique*, ed. A. VACANT et al. (Paris 1903—50) 15.2:1868–1924. L. DUCHESNE, *L'Église au VIᵉ siècle* (Paris 1925). PELAGIUS I, *Pelagii diaconi ecclesiae romanae In defensione trium capitulorum*, ed. R. DEVREESSE (*Studi e Testi* 57; 1932). R. DEVREESSE, *Essai sur Théodore de Mopsueste* (*Studi e Testi* 141; 1948). E. SCHWARTZ, *Drei dog. Schriften Justinians* (Munich 1939). H. M. DIEPEN, *Douze dialogues de christologie ancienne* (Rome 1960). P. T. CAMELOT, A. GRILLMEIER, and H. BACHT, *Das Konzil von Chalkedon: Geschichte und Gegenwart* (Würzburg 1951–54) 1:213–242. C. MOELLER, *ibid.* 1:637–720. JUSTINIAN I, *On the Person of Christ: The Christology of Emperor Justinian*, tr. K. P. WESCHE (Crestwood, N.Y. 1991).

[F. X. MURPHY]

THREE WAYS, THE

The three ways comprise the classical purgative, illuminative, and unitive ways in Christian SPIRITUALITY. This article defines the meaning of this phrase in its historical development and present-day usage.

According to St. BONAVENTURE and the Franciscan school the three ways are "hierarchical actions," i.e., different orientations given spiritual exercises in order to achieve the elements that make up Christian perfection. Each way fulfills a particular role; and the three ways, followed more or less simultaneously, lead to interior order and loving union with God. Thus the three ways are not successive stages of spiritual development, but parallel methods of action at every stage. In *The Triple Way,* for example, St. Bonaventure shows how meditation can be organized to achieve purification, illumination, and union; he then shows how the same ends can be achieved by the exercise of prayer and by contemplation.

The earliest occurrence in Christian writing of the terms purgation, illumination, and union is found in PSEUDO-DIONYSIUS (fl. *c.* 550), who applied them to the mystical experience. According to Dionysius the three acts are thearchic (i.e., divine) and hierarchic (i.e., ordered) ways to mystical union. They describe, moreover, not only complementary functions, but also successive activities; being successive they correspond to the three stages of mystical growth set down by EVAGRIUS PONTICUS (d. 399). More will be said below of Evagrius's categories. HUGH OF BALMA, a Carthusian of the 13th century, correlated the Dionysian ways and the three ages—beginners, proficients, and the perfect—designating the degrees by the corresponding Dionysian terms. Each degree was denominated by its predominant emphasis. Thus beginners are those who endeavor to pu-

rify themselves of sin and its effects; proficients seek illumination, i.e., growth in virtue; and the perfect exercise union with God. Spiritual writers have come to accept this identification of ways and degrees, a usage followed in the present article.

The fact of growth is evident in Scripture (Prv 9.6; Eph 4.12–16; Phil 3.14). Christians are to grow to maturity in Christ. But although the Scriptures assert the necessity of growth, they do not mark out the traditional three stages. St. Paul speaks of two stages, infancy and adulthood, leaving aside the middle phase of adolescence (1 Cor 3.1–3; Heb 5.12–14). At the same time he indicates the practical usefulness of such divisions when he defines children as those who can assimilate only the milk of basic teachings but not the strong meat suitable for adults. Divisions of growth are thus a framework for spiritual direction according to the needs and possibilities of different people.

The Fathers. The divisions found in the works of the earliest Fathers are likewise twofold rather than threefold. St. Clement of Alexandria (d. 220) and Origen after him (d. 255) took over the Platonic categories of active and contemplative life from Philo (d. *c.* 40) and applied them to Christian life. The active life (βίος πρακτικός) consisted in the exercise of the moral virtues for the purification and ordering of the soul. The contemplative life (βίος θεωρητικός) was the highest human activity, the contemplation of God, and hence the exercise of the theological virtues. The contemplative life presupposed and crowned the active life. This original concept of the two lives in Christian literature continued in the works of SS. Augustine (d. 430) and Gregory the Great (d. 604).

But a second meaning of the two lives found its way into the thought of Augustine: the lives were identified with external modes or styles of living. This new sense became confused with the original signification by Gregory; ever since, ambiguity has plagued this terminology (E. Mason, *Active and Contemplative Life* [Milwaukee 1961]). But in Augustine the active life corresponded to what later became the purgative and illuminative ways, and the contemplative life was the unitive way. Augustine also used the triple division for spiritual progress of beginning, developing, and perfect charity. Other authors, such as GREGORY OF NYSSA (d. 394) and Cassian (d. 435), singled out the predominant virtues of fear, hope, and love as the distinguishing characteristics of the degrees.

The teaching of Evagrius, however, is the key to understanding the history of the three ways. While he used the twofold division of active and contemplative life, attributing to the first stage the active way of the *praktikē* aimed at moral perfection, or *apatheia,* he subdivided the contemplative way of *gnōsis* into a lower form of contemplation called *physikē theoria* and a higher form called *theologia.* These two degrees of contemplation came to specify and distinguish the illuminative and unitive ways in tradition.

Later Spiritual Writers. Classic authors such as Bl. Jan van RUYSBROECK (d. 1381) and St. JOHN OF THE CROSS (d. 1591) and many modern writers such as R. GARRIGOU-LAGRANGE, OP (d. 1964), and Louis Bouyer lay down the same basic characteristics of the three ways as Evagrius. For them as for Evagrius, both the illuminative and unitive ways represent states of mystical contemplation. Other modern writers, however, adapt this mystically oriented pattern to a more ascetical emphasis. They expand the Evagrian purgative way, which now becomes the purgative and illuminative stages, and they telescope the Evagrian illuminative and unitive degrees into a single stage, the unitive way, which alone has contemplation as its prayer form. Generally speaking, ascetical writers of this group consider the higher form of Evagrius's contemplation, called "mystical theology" or the mystical experience as an extraordinary gift and not necessary for high sanctity. A. TANQUEREY, SS, and J. de GUIBERT, SJ, are examples of writers of this school. Their works reflect descriptions of the three degrees of charity such as that found in the *Summa theologiae* of St. Thomas Aquinas (1a2ae, 24.9), even though they utilize the terminology of the ways. Present-day usage follows either one of these two general interpretations and can be exemplified in Garrigou-Lagrange and De Guibert.

Garrigou-Lagrange. For Garrigou-Lagrange the purgative way is ascetical; i.e., it is characterized by the action of the virtues, which always manifest the "human mode" of reason and deliberation. The beginner strives to know God and know himself; his prayer life is that of meditation. If he is generous to the inspirations of grace, he quickly brings order into his moral life and his prayer becomes more affective and more simple. Through faithfulness to active purification he enters the dark night of the senses and passive purification. This dark night is the door to the illuminative way and the beginning of manifest mystical life. The gifts of the Holy Spirit, which always act in a "superhuman way" according to the divine manner and measure, now predominate in the prayer and life of the proficient. Contemplation, especially the exercise of the gift of UNDERSTANDING, which penetrates divine mysteries, specifies the prayer life. But the proficient is not yet perfect. A still more radical purification must occur, the dark night of the spirit. This is the transition into the way of the perfect, which in turn is characterized by the highest infused contemplation, that of the gift of WISDOM, which gives a quasi-experimental knowledge of God. The classifications are those of John of the Cross,

the theological explanations those of Thomas Aquinas as interpreted by JOHN OF ST. THOMAS.

De Guibert. The more ascetical conception of the three ways, illustrated by De Guibert, identifies the beginner as the converted Christian who by meditation and mortification is endeavoring to eradicate the effects of sin and consolidate himself in God's grace. He enters the illuminative way when he has overcome habitual deliberate venial sin, and ordinarily his prayer life in the second stage will be affective prayer. Whereas the beginner is concerned primarily with fulfilling the demands of the law, the proficient emphasizes interiority and inner renovation. Hence recollection, humility, purity of heart, and self-abnegation are the virtues to be stressed. The crucial point in this second degree is the call to total abnegation. It is the fork in the road that separates the pedestrian Christian from the incipient saint. Those who hear this call are in the category of pious souls but become "mediocre" Christians if they make no further progress. Such persons, however, are not to be equated with the tepid or the retarded, both of which groups belong to the purgative way. But neither are they the fervent souls, who have the will to surrender completely to God. Only those in this last group negotiate the crisis of total abnegation and thus enter the unitive way. This last stage is the way of perfect charity, either heroic or ordinary; the fulfillment of charity rather than any special contemplative prayer is the specific mark of the perfect.

Each of these formulations of the three ways has its own advantages for spiritual direction in different settings and vocations to Christian life.

Bibliography: BONAVENTURE, "The Triple Way, or Love Enkindled," in v.1 of his *Works,* tr. J. DE VINCK (Paterson, N.J. 1960) 59–94. L. BOUYER, *Introduction to Spirituality,* tr. M. P. RYAN (New York 1961) 243–285. R. GARRIGOU-LAGRANGE, *The Three Ages of the Interior Life,* tr. M. T. DOYLE, 2 v. (St. Louis 1947–48). F. JURGENSMEIER, *The Mystical Body of Christ,* tr. H. G. STRAUSS (New York 1954). J. DE GUIBERT, *The Theology of the Spiritual Life,* tr. P. BARRETT (New York 1953) 255–301.

[E. E. LARKIN]

THULES, JOHN, BL.

Priest, martyr; b. ca. 1568 at Whalley, Upholland, Lancashire, England; hanged, drawn, and quartered March 18, 1616, at Lancaster under James I. He began his studies at Rheims and then completed them at Rome, where he was ordained (April 1592). Immediately thereafter he returned to his homeland to begin a 20-year apostolate. He was a prisoner at Wisbeach Castle, Cambridgeshire, for some years but later escaped. He labored in Lancashire until he was arrested by Earl William of Derby and was committed to Lancaster Castle, where fellow-martyr Bl. Roger WRENNO was confined. A curious metrical account of the martyrdom of Thules and Wrenno, as well as portions of a poem composed by Thules, are included in Pollen's *Acts of the English Martyrs,* 194–207. He was beatified by Pope John Paul II on Nov. 22, 1987, with George Haydock and Companions.

Feast of the English Martyrs: May 4 (England).

See Also: ENGLAND, SCOTLAND, AND WALES, MARTYRS OF.

Bibliography: R. CHALLONER, *Memoirs of Missionary Priests,* ed. J. H. POLLEN (rev. ed. London 1924). J. H. POLLEN, *Acts of English Martyrs* (London 1891).

[K. I. RABENSTEIN]

THURSTAN OF YORK

Archbishop; b. Condé sur-Seulles, near Bayeux, France, *c.* 1070; d. Priory of Pontefract, Yorkshire, England, Feb. 6, 1140. Thurstan was the son of a married priest. Soon after his father was made a canon of St. Paul's, London, Thurstan became one of the English king's chaplains. King HENRY I appointed Thurstan's brother to the bishopric of Evreux in 1113 and Thurstan himself to the See of YORK in 1114. Because he refused to give an oath of obedience to the archbishop of Canterbury, who was supported by the king, Thurstan spent several years in exile and did not enter into full possession of his see until 1121. Himself deeply ascetic, Thurstan became spiritual adviser to many, including the famous CHRISTINA OF MARKYATE; under his guidance the CANONS REGULAR OF ST. AUGUSTINE flourished in the province of York, as did the CISTERCIANS. It was his intervention on Oct. 17, 1132, at St. Mary's, York, that led to the exodus from that Benedictine house of certain monks who founded the Cistercian Abbey of FOUNTAINS with his help. In his efforts to exert metropolitan jurisdiction over the Scottish bishops he was not successful; but the See of CARLISLE (founded 1133) can be regarded as a by-product of those efforts. In 1138 Thurstan inspired the northern English to throw back the marauding Scots at the Battle of the Standard near Northallerton.

Bibliography: D. KNOWLES, *The Monastic Order in England, 943–1216* (2d ed. Cambridge, England 1962) 230–239, *passim.* D. NICHOLL, *Thurstan, Archbishop of York* (York 1964).

[D. NICHOLL]

THURSTON, HERBERT

English writer; b. London, Nov. 15, 1856; d. there, Nov. 3, 1939. The only child of Dr. George Thurston, he was educated at St. Malo, France; Mount St. Mary's (near Sheffield); Stonyhurst College; and London University. On Sept. 28, 1874, he entered the Society of Jesus at Roehampton, near London. He taught at Beaumont College from 1880 to 1887. After theological studies at St. Bueno's, North Wales, and ordination there (1890), he held briefly a number of temporary appointments until in 1894 he joined the staff of the journal, the *Month,* in London, and held that post until his death. His contributions to that magazine and to others total more than 760 items; in addition, he contributed more than 180 articles to the *Catholic Encyclopedia* (1907–12 and supplements). His revision of Butler's *Lives of the Saints* in four volumes (v.1, 1926; v.2, with Norah Leeson, 1930; v.3, with Donald Attwater, 1932; v.4, with Attwater, 1938) is probably the greatest monument to his learning and industry (*see* BUTLER, ALBAN).

Thurston's interests were mainly historical, liturgical, and hagiographical. Through his writings (many of them unsigned), he had great influence in checking the growth of spiritualism after World War I, and through his exact scientific method, skeptical turn of mind, wide learning, and manifest desire for the truth, he attained a position of eminence and authority among scholars of his day both in England and on the Continent. His three most notable books, collected from contributions to the *Month* and published posthumously, concern the interrelationship of psychic phenomena and sanctity: *The Physical Phenomena of Mysticism* (1952), *Ghosts and Poltergeists* (1953), and *Surprising Mystics* (1955).

Bibliography: J. CREHAN, *Father Thurston: A Memoir with a Bibliography of His Writings* (New York 1952).

[P. CARAMAN]

THWING, EDWARD, BL.

Priest, martyr; b. *c.* 1565 at Heworth (or Hurs, near York), England; hanged, drawn, and quartered July 26, 1600 at Lancaster. He was the son of Thomas Thwing and his wife Jane Kellet of York, and may have been related to Bl. Thomas THWING (d. 1680) also of Yorkshire. He studied at Rheims and spent an interval with the Jesuits at Pont-à-Mousson. At Rheims he was a reader in Greek and Hebrew and a professor of rhetoric and logic. He was ordained priest at Laon, Dec. 20, 1590. In 1597, he was sent on the English Mission and immediately was arrested and imprisoned at Wisbeach, whence he escaped with Bl. Robert NUTTER to Lancashire. They were arrested in May 1600, tried at the next assizes, and condemned for being priests. Both were beatified by Pope John Paul II on Nov. 22, 1987, with George Haydock and Companions.

Feast of the English Martyrs: May 4 (England).

See Also: ENGLAND, SCOTLAND AND WALES, MARTYRS OF.

Bibliography: R. CHALLONER, *Memoirs of Missionary Priests,* ed. J. H. POLLEN (rev. ed. London 1924). J. H. POLLEN, *Acts of English Martyrs* (London 1891).

[K. I. RABENSTEIN]

THWING, THOMAS, BL.

Priest and martyr; b. 1635, Heworth Hall (near York), North Riding, Yorkshire, England; d. hanged, drawn, and quartered at York, Oct. 23, 1680. Thomas, the grand-nephew of Bl. Edward THWING, was the son of Sir George Thwing of Kilton Castle and Heworth and Anne Gasciogne of Barnbrow Hall. Following his education at St-Omer, Douai, and ordination, Thomas returned to England (1664).

There he was chaplain at Carlton Hall, the seat of his Stapleton cousins (1664–68), and opened a school in their dower-house at Quosque (April 1668). In 1677, he became chaplain at Dolebank to the Institute of Mary to which three of Thwing's sisters belonged. The community was founded in the house donated by Sir Thomas Gasciogne, where Fr. Thwing was arrested in 1679.

About the time of the Titus Oates Plot, disgruntled former Gasciogne servants sought vengeance and reward by alleging that their former master and his associates, not including Thwing, plotted to assassinate the king. Nevertheless, Thwing was apprehended with Gasciogne and others. All were taken to Newgate for trial and all were acquitted, except Thwing.

On July 29, 1680, Thwing was tried at York before a partisan jury, and found guilty on the same evidence upon which his relatives had been acquitted. Although he declared his innocence and the king initially reprieved him, a death warrant was issued the day after Parliament met. On the gallows he prayed for the king and asked for prayers, before uttering his dying words, "Sweet Jesus, receive my soul!" He was buried in the churchyard of St. Mary, Castlegate; however, some relics are preserved at the Bar Convent in York and at Oscott College. He was beatified by Pius XI on Dec. 15, 1929.

Feast of the English Martyrs: May 4 (England).

See Also: ENGLAND, SCOTLAND, AND WALES, MARTYRS OF.

Bibliography: R. CHALLONER, *Memoirs of Missionary Priests,* ed. J. H. POLLEN (rev. ed. London 1924; repr. Farnborough 1969). H. FOLEY, *Records of the English Province of the Society of Jesus,* 7 v. (London 1877–82). J. H. POLLEN, *Acts of English Martyrs* (London 1891).

[K. I. RABENSTEIN]

THYRÄUS, HERMANN

Jesuit theologian and preacher; b. Neuss in the Rhineland, 1532; d. Mainz, Oct. 26, 1591. He studied at Cologne and in 1552 at the Collegium Germanicum, newly founded by Pope Julius III on August 31 of that year. On May 26, 1556, he was accepted as a novice in the Society of Jesus by (St.) Ignatius Loyola and in the same year began a four–year term as lecturer in theology at Ingolstadt. In 1560 he taught at Trier, becoming rector of the college in 1565, provincial of the Rhineland province in 1571, and finally rector of the college at Mainz in 1578. Besides theological writings that include the valuable *Confessio Augustana* (Dillingen 1567), he left several volumes of sermons that attest to his renown as a preacher.

Bibliography: C. SOMMERVOGEL et al., *Bibliothèque de la Compagnie de Jésus,* 11 vol. (Brussels-Paris 1890–1932) 8:10–11. B. DUHR, *Geschichte der Jesuiten in den Ländern deutscher Zunge,* 4 v. in 5 (St. Louis 1907–28).

[E. D. MCSHANE]

TIARA, PAPAL

A bee-hive shaped headdress, high and round, made of cloth of silver, with three diadems, usually enriched with precious stones, with two lappets (*infulae*) hanging down the back, historically worn by the pope as an extraliturgical insigne. The tiara is, or was, frequently called *triregnum* or *corona.*

Use. Although never considered a liturgical vestment, the tiara was historically used to crown the newly elected pope. The tiara was also worn by the pope for solemn entries, especially at St. Peter's or the Lateran Basilicas, when he wore the long papal cope. A very ancient usage required that the pope be crowned with the tiara, not by the dean of the Sacred College, as would seem suitable, but by the first assistant cardinal deacon, who was usually also the first of the cardinal deacons. The reason was that the pope is not crowned by the College of Cardinals, but crowned himself, the assistant deacon acting as a simple minister, helping the pope to put on the tiara. A formula of coronation, recited by the deacon, was added at a later date. The precious stones are not preceptive, and for his coronation Paul VI, the last pope to be crowned with a tiara, received a tiara made according to the old Lombard crowns, with fleurons but no stones on the diadems.

It is difficult to write the history of the papal tiara, since its shape has changed greatly. Its origin is closely related not only to the Latin MITER but also to the stiff Oriental one. In his *Antiquities of the Jews* Josephus says that the high priest's miter had a "golden crown polished, of three rows, one above another" [3.7.6; tr. W. Whiston, (London 1822) 1:140]. An ancient tiara, said to have been given to Silvester I (d. 335) by the Emperor Constantine, has a long history attached to it and is said to have been worn for the last time by Nicholas V (d. 1455) at his coronation (Müntz, 248). In about the 10th century the tiara became a stiff headdress, definitely distinct from the miter, but having only one circle or coronet. Boniface VIII (d. 1303) added a second diadem. However, very soon a third one and the lappets were added, giving it its present form. The Avignon popes followed the custom probably introduced by Benedict XI (d. 1304), and retained the triple diadem. With the Renaissance popes the tiara was transformed into a very precious papal ornament. Julius II (d. 1513) ordered the papal jeweller, Caradosso, to make him a precious tiara that cost approximately ten million francs. It was also at this period that the custom was introduced of having two other precious tiaras and one or two precious miters carried in front of the papal procession before the pope's pontifical Mass.

At the closing of the Second Vatican Council, Pope Paul VI descended the steps of the papal throne in St. Peter's Basilica and laid the tiara on the altar in a gesture of humility and renunciation of pomp, human glory and power. On Feb. 6, 1968, this tiara was presented to the National Shrine of the Basilica of the Immaculate in Washington, D.C. by the Apostolic Delegate to the U.S., where it is on permanent display in the Memorial Hall below the Great Church along with the stole of Pope John XXIII which he wore at the opening of Vatican II. Pope Paul VI was the last pope to be crowned with a papal tiara. Subsequent popes have affirmed this renunciation of pomp and glory, emphasizing instead their calling to be the Servant of the Servants of God.

Bibliography: E. MÜNTZ, *La Tiare pontificale du VIII au XVI siècle* (Paris 1897) best study and bibliog. B. SIRCH, *Der Ursprung der bischöflichen Mitra und der päpstlichen Tiara* (St. Ottilien 1975). A. MALOOF, "Eastern origin of the papal tiara," *Eastern Churches Review* 1 (1966) 146–149. C. E. POCKNEE, "Mitre and the papal tiara," *Church Quarterly Review* 167 (1966) 491–495.

[J. NABUCO/EDS.]

TIBERIUS, ROMAN EMPEROR

Reigned A.D. 14 to 37; b. Nov. 16, 42 B.C.; d. Misenum, March 16, A.D. 37. He was the son of Tiberius Claudius Nero and Livia Drusilla, who divorced her husband in 38 to marry Octavian (Augustus). After a brilliant military career (20–6 B.C.), Tiberius retired to Rhodes until A.D. 2, probably piqued over Augustus's failure to recog-

Pope Innocent III wearing a papal tiara.

nize him as his successor. On June 26, A.D. 4, after the death of Augustus's grandsons, Gaius and Lucius Caesar, Tiberius was adopted by his stepfather. Augustus died Aug. 19, A.D. 14, and after an interim rule in virtue of the *imperium* he already possessed, Tiberius was proclaimed emperor on September 17. In general, he followed the social, political, and foreign policies of Augustus. He refused, however, divine honors and enriched the treasury by a stricter economy. Under the influence of Sejanus, he became cruel and tyrannous. In A.D. 26 he took up residence in Capri.

Tiberius is explicitly mentioned in the Gospel of Luke (3.1), and it was during his reign that the public preaching of St. JOHN THE BAPTIST, the CRUCIFIXION, and the Resurrection of Jesus Christ took place, as did the martyrdom of St. STEPHEN and the conversion of St. PAUL. It is quite possible that the coin of tribute shown to Christ (Mt 22.19) was a silver piece decorated with the image of the emperor and the inscription: *Ti(berius) Caesar Divi Aug(usti) F(ilius) Augustus.* The legend reported by OROSIUS (*Hist. adv. paganos* 7.4; *Patrologia latina* 31:1066–1069) that on being informed of Christ's death and Resurrection by PILATE, Tiberius wanted to proclaim Him a god is apocryphal, however, (see Tertullian, *Apol.* 5; *Patrologia latina* 1:290–292).

Pope Boniface VIII, wearing papal tiara. (Archive Photos, Inc.)

Bibliography: M. P. CHARLESWORTH, *The Cambridge Ancient History* 10:607–652. F. B. MARSH, *The Reign of Tiberius* (New York 1931; repr. 1959). E. CIACERI, *Tiberio successore di Augusto* (2d ed. Rome 1944).

[M. J. COSTELLOE]

TIBESAR, ANTONINE

Scholar; b. Quincy, Illinois, 1909; solemn profession in the Franciscan order, 1927; ordained 1934; d. 1992. One of the most influential scholars in Latin American Church history in the mid-twentieth century. His early career involved teaching Latin and European history at the major seminary of the St. Louis province of the Franciscans. At the onset of World War II, he was assigned to pursue graduate studies at the CATHOLIC UNIVERSITY OF AMERICA where he had first received an M.A. in medieval history, and subsequently a Ph.D. in Latin American history in 1950.

This assignment to Catholic University was at the request of the wartime delegate general of the North American Franciscans, Father Matias Faust, who wanted to establish a Franciscan center for the study of Franciscan experiences in the Western Hemisphere. Father Faust's initiative established the Academy of American Francis-

can History, with which Father Antonine's career was intertwined for the bulk of the remainder of his life. He resided at the Academy from 1947 until 1988, and was its director on two occasions, 1954–63 and 1970–82. Beginning in 1948 he also taught in the history department at Catholic University, retiring as professor emeritus in 1974. He then went on to a second career at the University as a professorial lecturer in the department of church history until 1988.

His contributions to the field include numerous articles and monographs on the Franciscan experience in Peru, a four volume edition of the collected writings of Fray Junípero Serra, the California missionary, and a critical edition of the narrative of the seventeenth-century Peruvian missionary, Fray Miguel Biedma. He was also the associate editor responsible for Latin American topics in the 1967 edition of the *New Catholic Encyclopedia*. In the absence of any contemporary survey of the history of the Church in Latin America, this collection of entries, with key ones written by Tibesar himself, became the starting point on Latin American Church history for scholars and students of the late 1960s and 1970s.

As director of the Academy of American Franciscan history, he made the institution a major force in the field through its publication series, its sponsorship of scholarly meetings, and its patronage of scholarship and research. In addition to personally guiding the yearly publication of monographs, collections of letters of Franciscan missionaries in California, and the republication of important narrative accounts by missionaries in that series, Tibesar began an effort which continues to index the North American papers of the archives of the Congregation for the PROPAGATION OF THE FAITH in Rome. Between 1970 and 1988, he also edited *The Americas: A Quarterly Review of Inter-American Cultural History* and was responsible for making it the second leading journal of Latin American history in the United States. He retired to a Franciscan parish in Louisiana in 1988 where he died in March 1992.

Bibliography: J. D. RILEY and V. PELOSO, "The Intellectual Odyssey of a Franciscan: The Early Career of Father Antonine Tibesar," *The Americas*, 44:3 (January 1988) 343–62. *Franciscan Beginnings in Colonial Peru* (Washington, D.C. 1953). *The Writings of Junípero Serra* In 4 (Washington, D.C. 1955–56). M. BIEDMA, *La conquista franciscana del Alto Ucayali* (Lima 1981) "The "Alternativa": A Study in Spanish–Creole Relations in Seventeenth–century Peru" *The Americas* (1955) 229–83. "The Franciscan Doctrinero versus the Franciscan Misionero in Seventeenth–century Peru" *The Americas* (1957) 115–24. "The Franciscan Province of the Holy Cross of Española, 1505–1559" *The Americas* (1957) 377–89. "The Shortage of Priests in Latin America: A Historical Evaluation of Werner Promper's Priesternot in Latein Amerika" *The Americas* (1966) 413–20. "The Peruvian Church at the Time of Independence in the Light of Vatican II." *The Americas* (1970) 349–75. "The Lima Pastors, 1750–1820:

Their Origins and Studies as Taken from Their Autobiographies'' *The Americas* (1971) 39–51. ''Raphael María Taurel, Papal Consul General in Lima, Peru, in 1853: Report on Conditions in Peru'' *Revista Interamericana de Bibliografía* (1981) 36–69. ''The Suppression of the Religious Order in Peru, 1826–1830 or the King Versus the Peruvian Friars: The King Won'' *The Americas* (1982) 205–39. ''The King and the Pope and the Clergy in the Colonial Spanish–American Empire'' *The Catholic Historical Review* (1989) 91–109.

[J. RILEY]

TIBET, THE CATHOLIC CHURCH IN

Located in Central Asia, Tibet is situated on a difficult-to-access plateau averaging 16,000 ft. in height that is known as the ''Roof of the World.'' An autonomous region of CHINA since 1959, Tibet (Chinese Xizang) is bound on the north by Sinkiang Uighur and Tsinghai, on the east by Szechwan, on the southeast by Yunnan and Burma, on the south by Nepal, Bhutan and Sikkim, and on the south and west by India. Northern Tibet borders the Kunlun Mountains, while in the south the Tsangpo plain is separated from its neighbors by the Himalayas. Several rivers flow through the region, and numerous lakes are located within Tibet's central plateau. Agricultural produce includes barley, millet, peas and rice, while natural resources include hydropower, chromate, lithium, copper and gypsum.

From the 13th century until 1959 Tibet was a theocracy, with the highest political authority in the hands of the Dalai Lama. Intermittently controlled by China for 12 centuries, Tibet became increasingly independent after the mid-19th century. After becoming communist, China renewed its efforts to occupy the region in 1950 and took full control of the officially renamed Tibet Region and Chamdo (Changtu) Area in 1959. In 1965 the region became an autonomous region within the People's Republic of China. About 85 percent of Tibet is uninhabitable. Its population is concentrated in the south and depends largely on a pastoral economy. Another 2¾ million Tibetans dwell in neighboring provinces of China.

Overwhelmingly Buddhist, by the early 20th century almost 20 percent of Tibetans were celibate lamas (monks) belonging to the dominant Gelug, or ''Yellow Hat'' sect dating from the 15th century. The Dalai Lama, revered as the reincarnation of Buddha, was forced to flee to India in 1959, whereupon the Chinese government appointed the Panch'en Lama in his stead.

History. Christianity never won more than a tiny following in Tibet. Syrian missionaries reached its northern territory in the 7th century, and influenced the lamaist ritual. They were followed by Jesuits from India who at-

Bust of the Emperor Tiberius. (Anderson–Art Reference/Art Resource, NY)

tempted to establish a mission in Tsaparang in western Tibet *c.* 1624–35. In 1661 two Jesuits traversed the country journeying from China to India, and Ippolito Desideri, SJ, worked in Lhasa from 1716–21. Between 1707 and 1745 Capuchins made three different attempts to organize a mission in Lhasa, but persecution drove them out and Tibet was closed to foreigners. Tibet was officially annexed to China as a province in 1720.

Although Tibet came under the authority of the vicariate apostolic of Hindustan in 1792, no more missionaries arrived until a brief 1844 visit to Lhasa by Lazarists Evariste HUC and Joseph Gabet. Two years later the PARIS FOREIGN MISSION SOCIETY (MEP) was given charge of the Tibetan mission and the newly created Vicariate Apostolic of Lhasa. Its heroic attempts to penetrate this area resulted in the 1854 murder of two MEP priests, Nicholas Krick and Auguste Bourry, and succeeded only in opening a few precarious stations near the borders. Protestant missioners from the United States and the China Inland Mission labored from the end of the 19th century, but gained few converts. Renewed outbreak of hatred for foreigners at the turn of the 20th century sparked further persecution and resulted in the death of four missioners and many lay Catholics, as well as the almost complete destruction of the mission. By 1910 there were 21 European

Capital: Lhasa.
Size: 471,660 sq. miles.
Population: 2,682,400 (est.) in 2000.
Languages: Tibetan, Chinese; U-Tsang, Kham, and Amdo dialects are spoken in various regions. Religions: 780 Catholics (.03%), 2,679,120 Tibetan Buddhists (Lamaists) (99.9%), 2,500 Muslims (.09%).
Diocese: Kangting, China, created in 1946 out of the Vicariate Apostolic of Tatsienlu, erected in 1924. Suffragan to the Archdiocese of Chungking (Chongquing).

priests and 2,407 Catholic Tibetans. Although the Canons Regular of the Grand St. Bernard sent a dozen priests between 1933 and their expulsion in 1952, Catholics in Tibet numbered less than 1,200 at the time the communist government came to power. Another 3,000 Tibetan Catholics lived in China.

Tibet under Communism. The Dalai Lama fled into exile in 1959, following one of several popular uprisings against Chinese rule. His authority was viewed as a threat to the communist government of Mao Zedong, and during the Cultural Revolution of 1966–76 China began patient yet methodical efforts to eradicate religion from Tibet. Freedom of worship was abolished and over 6,000 churches, temples and other places of worship were destroyed. The Chinese Catholic Patriotic Society, which had been established in 1957 in defiance of the Holy See, continued to ordain bishops in an effort to build a pseudo-faith attractive to members of the Church. While Christian worship was once again permitted after 1980, social unrest continued; a 1987 revolt by Tibetans lasted for two years before it was suppressed through martial law. In May of 1995 the government attempted to undercut the power of the Dalai Lama by denying access to ten-year-old Gendhun Chokyi Nyima, who, as the reincarnation of the Panchen Lama was the second most important figure in Tibetan Buddhism. On Dec. 6, 1995, the government installed Gyaltsen Norbu, son of a government official, as the Panchen Lama and demanded his recognition by Buddhist monks. Nyima and his family were never seen again, and rumors that the boy had perished in prison were circulating in late 1999.

Into the 21st Century. Throughout the 1990s the Chinese government continued to discourage both Tibetan nationalism and religion, and its efforts extended to minority populations, such as Catholics who refused to join the Catholic Patriotic Association. In 1997 a concerted effort to teach socialist rather than spiritual values was underway in Tibet, while monks were forced to undergo a "reeducation" program to make them of use to society. In 1995 two Tibetan monks were imprisoned for demonstrating in Llasa, prompting the government to prohibit other monks from entering the city and closing the Jokhang, a religious site. In addition to detentions, the use of torture against such political prisoners persisted, sometimes resulting in death. In May of 1996 the Dalai Lama met with Pope John Paul II and discussed the situation facing both faiths in communist China. Repeated efforts by the Dalai Lama to win Tibet a limited degree of autonomy were ignored by the Chinese government, as were efforts by the Vatican to ensure the safety of all Catholics still living in the country. According to official sources, communist-mandated family planning—one child per family— while imposed on Tibet, did not apply to peasants or herdsman, who accounted for 88 percent of the population. However, reports from China in 2000 claimed that among the human rights abuses ongoing in Tibet was the compulsive sterilization of rural women.

Bibliography: C. H. DESGODINS, *Le Thibet d'après la correspondance des missionaires* (2d ed. Paris 1885). A. LAUNAY, *Histoire de la mission du Thibet*, 2 v. (Lille 1903). C. WESSELS, *Early Jesuit Travellers in Central Asia, 1603–1721* (The Hague 1924). E. D. MACLAGAN, *The Jesuits and the Great Mogul* (London 1932). C. DA TERZORIO, *Le missioni dei Minori Cappuccini,* 10 v. (Rome 1913–38) v.8. F. CALLAEY, "Missionnaires capucins et civilisation thibétaine," *Études franciscaines,* 46 (1934) 129–139. P. CROIDYS, *Du Grand-Saint-Bernard au Thibet* (Paris 1949). G. M. TOSCANO, *La prima missione cattolica nel Tibet* (Parma 1951). *I missionarii italiani nel Tibet e nel Nepal,* ed. L. PETECH, 4 v. (Rome 1952–53). K. S. LATOURETTE, *A History of the Expansion of Christianity,* 7 v. (New York 1937–45) v.3, 6, 7. T. SCHMID and H. MOTEL, *Die Religion in Geschichte und Gegenwart*[3], 7 v. (3d ed. Tübingen 1957–65) 6: 883–884. C. A. BELL, *Tibet, Past and Present* (Oxford 1924); *The Religion of Tibet* (Oxford 1931). A. M. CABLE et al., *The Challenge of Central Asia* (London 1929).

[E. R. HAMBYE/EDS.]

TIEFFENTALLER, JOSEPH

Jesuit missionary and noted geographer in Hindustan; b. Salurn (Bolzano, Italy), April 27, 1710; d. Lucknow, July 5, 1785. He entered the Society Oct. 9, 1729, and in 1743 went to the East Indian mission, where he held various positions, particularly within the Empire of the Great Mogul. After the suppression of the Society of Jesus (1773), he remained in India and was the main support of the mission. He was a fine scholar with an unusual talent for languages. He was the first European to write an exact description of Hindustan, and is the author of numerous studies on Hinduism, astronomy, natural sciences, and history. Tieffentaller sent his works in manuscript partly to the Danish scholar Dr. Kratzenstein at Copenhagen, and partly to the celebrated geographer A. H. Anquetil-Duperron. The latter gave due credit to the value and importance of the works and made them in part accessible to the learned world in his *Recherches hist. et géogr. sur l'Inde* (1786) and also in his *Carte*

A group of young Christian Tibetan women photographed in the late 19th century. (©Hulton-Deutsch Collection/CORBIS)

générale du cours du Gange et du Gogra dressée par les cartes particulières du P. T. (Paris 1884). A part of the manuscripts at Copenhagen were obtained by Johann Bernoulli of Berlin who used them in connection with the *Recherches* of Anquetil in the great work: *Des P. J. Tieffentallers der Gesellschaft Jesu und Apostol. Missionarius* in *Indien historisch-geographische Beschreibung von Hindustan* (3 v. Berlin 1785–87), French edition *Description hist. et géorgr. de l'Inde* (Berlin 1786–91).

Bibliography: R. STREIT and J. DINDINGER, *Bibliotheca missionum* 6:140–142. C. SOMMERVOGEL, *Bibliotèque de la Compagnie de Jésus,* 11 v. (Brussels-Paris 1890–1932) 8:21–24.

[J. WICKI]

TIERNEY, RICHARD HENRY

Editor, publicist; b. New York, NY, Sept. 2, 1870; d. New York, Feb. 10, 1928. He was the sixth of eight children of Richard and Bridget (Shea) Tierney, whose home in Spuyten Duyvil often served as a mission station for Catholics of that section of New York City. After graduating in 1892 from St. Francis Xavier College, New York City, he entered the Jesuit novitiate at Frederick, Maryland, continued his studies at Woodstock College, Woodstock, Maryland, and was ordained June 27, 1907. He taught philosophy and pedagogy at Woodstock from 1909 to 1914, when he was named editor-in-chief of *America,* the weekly Jesuit publication. He quickly brought the review to increased public attention by his forceful stand on controversial issues. He was critical of Pres. Woodrow Wilson's policy on Mexico and published damaging facts about the religious persecution of the Carranza regime there. This service was recognized by Benedict XV in a letter of March 17, 1915, to Cardinal James Gibbons. Under Tierney's direction, *America* was neutral in reporting World War I issues until the U.S. entered the war. He was deeply interested in the cause of

Irish independence. An editor of strong views who shrank from no controversy, he maintained the review at a high level until failing health forced his retirement in 1925.

Bibliography: R. J. PURCELL, *Dictionary of American Biography,* ed., A. JOHNSON and D. MALONE, 20 v. (New York 1928–36) 18:532–533. F. X. TALBOT, *Richard Henry Tierney* (New York 1930).

[T. N. DAVIS]

TIKHON, PATRIARCH OF MOSCOW

Nov. 10, 1917 to April 7, 1925; b. Toropets, in Pskov, Russia, Jan. 19, 1865; d. Moscow. The son of a Russian Orthodox priest, Vasily Ivanovich Bellavin studied in the Pskov Ecclesiastical Seminary and the St. Petersburg Theological Academy, was ordained, taught theology in the Pskov Seminary (1888–91), and in 1891 became a monk, exchanging his baptismal name Vasily for that of Tikhon (Tychon). He served in various administrative posts, first as inspector, then rector of the seminaries in Kazan and Kholm. In 1897 he became bishop of Lublin. From 1898 to 1907 he was in the United States organizing the Russian Church of North America. Made an archbishop in 1905, he was appointed to the Russian Sees of Jarosław (1907) and Vilna (1913). In Vilna he was noted for his tact in harmonizing relationships between the Polish Roman Catholics and the Russian Orthodox. Invading Germans forced him to flee his see during World War I. In 1917 he was elected archbishop of Moscow, and soon after given the title of metropolitan. He organized the Pan-Russian synod that met in Moscow on Aug. 15, 1917, and reestablished the patriarchal dignity suppressed by Peter the Great. After Tikhon was elected patriarch, his clash with the Bolshevik regime over its secularization of marriage, nationalization of schools, confiscation of Church property, and desecration of churches and monasteries caused his imprisonment (May 1922–June 1923). He was released after formally recognizing the legitimacy of the Soviet regime in the hope of mitigating the persecution of his Church. After this he directed his efforts against the conformist "Living Church" rather than against the government, and sought to consolidate ecclesiastical administration amid internal conflicts and severe external oppression.

Bibliography: F. MCCULLAGH, *The Bolshevik Persecution of Christianity* (London 1924). G. MACEÓIN, *The Communist War on Religion* (New York 1951). M. SPINKA, *The Church in Soviet Russia* (New York 1956).

[G. A. MALONEY]

TILLARD, JEAN-MARIE ROGER

Dominican theologian, ecumenist; b. Sept. 2, 1927, St. Pierre - Miquelon; d. Nov. 13, 2000, Ottawa, Canada. Born Roger Tillard, the son of Fernand Tillard and Madeleine Ferron. He was on his mother's side related to Monsignor Auguste Diès, editor of Plato in the Guillaume-Budé Collection, and specialist in ancient philosophy. He began his studies at St. Pierre-Miquelon, at the Collège Saint-Christophe of the Holy Ghost Fathers. However, the Second World War interrupted the activities of the College, and he was sent to Canada to the Collège Saint-Alexandre, maintained as well by the Holy Ghost Fathers, at Limbour, near Ottawa. He obtained his B.A. in 1948. He asked to be received in the Dominican order of Canada, Sept. 14, 1949.

Following his novitiate in St. Hyacinthe, Quebec, he made his profession in simple vows Sept. 15, 1950, with the religious name "Jean-Marie." He received a doctorate in philosophy at the Angelicum, in Rome, in 1953, with a thesis entitled: "Le bonheur selon la conception de S. Thomas d'Aquin" ("St. Thomas Aquinas's Conception of Happiness"). He then studied theology at the Saulchoir, where he was ordained a priest, July 3, 1955. The Saulchoir had for some time been applying the historical method to the study of Thomistic texts, attempting to restore to prominence in the reading of St. Thomas his use of Scripture, patristic texts, and conciliar decisions, as well as the events or situations which had led Thomas to his positions. Tillard received the license and lectorate in theology from the Saulchoir in 1957.

Returning to Ottawa in 1957, he was assigned to teach Trinitarian theology, Christology, and Sacramental theology. In 1968 he established the Dominican College's "Theological Saturdays," for which he remained in subsequent years the principal collaborator. His research was directed principally towards two domains of dogmatic theology: from 1961 to 1975, the theology of the religious life; and from 1975 to the end of his life, ecclesiology, in particular ecumenical problems. His publications include 20 volumes and some 250 journal articles. In 1967 the Dominican General Chapter named him Master of Sacred Theology.

Tillard was frequently called upon to participate in theological research groups or to act as a theological advisor. From 1962 to 1967 he was an expert and theological advisor for the Canadian Episcopate at Vatican Council II. From 1965 to 1968 he was president of the Société canadienne de théologie. From 1974 to 1980, he was a member of the International Theological Commission. However, it was on the ecumenical plane that his contribution was most important, through his active participation in diverse commissions: on the national level, from 1969 he was a member of the National Commission for the Union of the Roman Catholic and Anglican Churches, Ottawa, Canada; on the international level, he served in various commissions: from 1969, he was a member of the International Joint Commission for the Organic Unity of the Roman Catholic Church and the Anglican Communion (Rome-London); he was a consultant for the Secretariat for the Unity of Christians (Rome); in 1977, he became a member of the International Commission for Dialogue with the Disciples of Christ (Rome- Indianapolis); in 1978, he was elected vice-president of ''Faith and Order,'' World Council of Churches (Geneva); and in 1979 he was chosen to be a member of the International Commission for the Union of the Orthodox and Roman Catholic Churches (Rome-Constantinople). From 1981 to 1985, he was a member of the directive council of the Ecumenical Institute, Tantur (Jerusalem).

Bibliography: J.-M. R. TILLARD, *L'Eucharistie, Pâque de l'Église* (Unam Sanctam 44; Paris 1964); *Devant Dieu et pour le monde. Le projet religieux*, (Cogitatio Fidei 75; Paris 1974); *L'Évêque de Rome* (Paris 1982), Eng. tr. *The Bishop of Rome* (London 1982); *Église d'Églises: L'ecclésiologie de communion* (Cogitatio Fidei 143; Paris 1987), Eng. tr. *Church of Churches* (Collegeville, Minn. 1992); *Chair de l'Église, chair du Christ: Aux sources de l'ecclésiologie de communion* (Cogitatio Fidei 168; Paris 1992); *L'Église locale: Ecclésiologie de communion et catholicité* (Cogitatio Fidei 191; Paris 1995); *Credo nonostante: Colloqui d'iverno con Francesco Strazzari* (Bologna 2000). G. R. EVANS and M. GOURGUES, *Communion et réunion: Mélanges Jean-Marie Roger Tillard* (Bibliotheca Ephemeridum Theologicarum Lovaniensium, CXXI; Leuven 1995), bibliography for 1961–1994.

[G.-D. MAILHIOT/L. DEWAN]

TILLEMONT, LOUIS SÉBASTIEN LE NAIN DE

Historian; b. Paris, Nov. 30, 1637; d. Tillemont, near Paris, Jan. 10, 1698. He was educated at PORT-ROYAL under P. NICOLE and read classical authors, especially Livy, and the *Annals* of BARONIUS. At 18, he began a scrupulous collection of literary and historical data concerning early Christianity to A.D. 513. Although a member of the Jansenist sect (*see* JANSENISM), Tillemont took no part in its controversies. Directed by M. de Sacy, he entered the seminary at Beauvais in 1661, and was ordained in 1676. After 1665 he helped G. Hermant in the composition of the lives of SS. Athanasius, Basil, Gregory of Nazianzus, and Ambrose; and after 1669 he collaborated in Paris with others in the edition of patristic texts (Origen, Tertullian, Augustine). In 1667 he took up residence at Port-Royal, but the persecution of 1679 forced him to leave for Tillemont, where, except for a trip to Holland, he followed a regime of seclusion, studying Church history. A pious, usually retiring and humble

Louis Sébastien le Nain de Tillemont.

man, he never accepted ecclesiastical office and willingly allowed his own work to be published under others' names. At Tillemont, he spent leisure moments catechizing children and aiding the poor. His work is characterized by great thoroughness and exactness. The first volume of his *Histoire des empereurs* (6 v., 1690–1738), which was intended as an integral part of his great Church history, had to be published separately because a censor asked for changes in his ''Histoire ecclésiastique.'' Other censors, however, approved the work as *Mémoires pour servir à l'histoire ecclésiastique des six premiers siècles* (16 v., 1693–1712); volume five was in press at Tillemont's death and the remaining volumes appeared at subsequent intervals. He also compiled a compendious life of St. Louis, published in a pirated edition by Filleau de la Chaise (1688), and edited in its original form by J. de Gaulle (6 v., Paris 1847–51). Though limited by the contemporary state of historical studies and inadequate editions of the sources, as well as by his total neglect of archeological evidence, Tillemont's ecclesiastical history is still unsurpassed for its comprehensiveness and exactitude of detail. The *Mémoires,* delated to the Holy Office, were vindicated by Pope CLEMENT XI, and acknowledged by Edward Gibbon as the guide whose ''inimitable exactitude'' led him through the rocky paths of later Roman history with the sure-footed sagacity ''of an Alpine mule.''

Paul Tillich.

Bibliography: H. LECLERCQ, *Dictionnaire d'archéologie chrétienne et de liturgie,* ed. F. CABROL, H. LECLERCQ, and H. I. MARROU, 15 v. (Paris 1907–53) 6.2:2624–38. G. BARDY, *Dictionnaire de théologie catholique,* ed. A. VACANT et al., 15 v. (Paris 1903–50; Tables Générales 1951–) 15.1:1029–33.

[F. X. MURPHY]

TILLICH, PAUL

German-American Lutheran theologian; b. Starzeddel, Brandenburg, Germany, Aug. 20, 1886; d. Chicago, Oct. 22, 1965. The son of an Evangelical Lutheran pastor, Tillich studied theology at the universities of Berlin, Tübingen, and Halle, obtaining his Ph.D. from the University of Breslau (1910) and his Licentiate of Theology from Halle (1912). He was ordained an Evangelical Lutheran pastor and served as chaplain in the German army during World War I. After the war, he taught at the universities of Marburg, Dresden, Leipzig, and Frankfurt (1919–33) before becoming the first non-Semitic German professor to lose his chair because of his condemnation of National Socialism. He was invited to Union Theological Seminary in New York by Reinhold NIEBUHR and taught there from 1933 to 1955. After retiring, he was appointed to the distinguished position of University Professor at Harvard (1955–1962), spending his final years at the Divinity School at the University of Chicago (1962–65).

Tillich published over 500 works, including the three-volume *Systematic Theology* (Chicago 1951–1963). He was committed to the synthesis of faith and culture, a Christian apologist, the "Apostle to the Intellectuals." Influenced by 19th century German IDEALISM (HEGEL, SCHELLING, BOEHME) and EXISTENTIALISM (KIERKEGAARD, HEIDEGGER), with a solid foundation in the history of philosophy and theology, he forged a theological system that, by 1935, had moved away from the dominant dialectical, kerygmatic theology of Karl BARTH. His method of correlation "explains the contents of the Christian faith through existential questions and theological answers in interdependence" (*ST* I, 68), seeking "common ground" with the secular world (*ST* I, 7). This method is presented and actualized in *Systematic Theology.* Each of its five parts begins with specific existential questions that are then answered by the symbols of Christian faith: (i) the question of human rationality is answered by Logos, revelation; (ii) finite existence, being (asked theoretically by philosophy, existentially by theology), is answered by God the Creator; (iii) human sin, estrangement, is overcome by Jesus as the Christ, the "New Being" (iv) ambiguity of life is answered by the Spirit; (v) and human destiny, the meaning of history, is answered by the Kingdom of God. The "point of contact" between religion and science was of special concern to Tillich, since the division between these disciplines had led to a "schizophrenic split in our collective consciousness" (*Theology of Culture* [New York 1959], 3). He found the common ground in "the philosophical element of both" (*ST* I, 18) and sought nothing less than a rational theistic synthesis for the scientific age, indeed, a full theology of culture.

Tillich's Platonic-Augustinian ontological approach opposed the cosmological method of Aristotelian-Thomism. The latter used a method of correlation to harmonize natural and revealed theology, but this is quite distinct from Tillich's question-and-answer approach (cf. *Theology of Culture,* ch. 2). Many of Tillich's critics have expressed a resistance to any philosophical theology that forces the kerygma into a mold determined by the categories of philosophy. By his own account, Tillich deliberately did not write a *Summa,* a final theology, since this would have violated what he calls "the Protestant principle" (see *The Protestant Era* [Chicago 1948]) that Christianity is not to be identified with any of its historical manifestations. Other criticisms focus on problems regarding his interpretation of God (as "beyond the God of theism," the "ground of being," "Being-Itself," "our Ultimate Concern," etc.) and his understanding of religious language as symbolic, "deliteralized" rather than taken literally, or "demythogized." Barth objected to his universalism of revelation, and Niebuhr rejected his interpretation of the fall and sin in terms of alienation and estrangement. Others have rejected his Christology, his epistemology, his ontology, his philosophy of history, and his method of correlation, among other ideas. Nonetheless, his pervasive influence continues in the mediation of faith and culture, seen most prominently in disciples like David Tracy and Langdon Gilkey.

Bibliography: P. TILLICH, *On the Boundary: An Autobiographical Sketch* (New York 1966). W. and M. PAUCK, *Paul Tillich: His Life and Thought* (New York 1975). J. B. COBB, JR., *Living Options in Protestant Theology* (Philadelphia 1962). A. DULLES, *Apologetics and the Biblical Christ* (Westminster, Md. 1963). D. KEEFE, *Thomism and the Ontological Theology of Paul Tillich* (Leiden 1971). C. KEGLEY and R. BRETALL, eds., *The Theology of Paul Tillich* (New York 1964). A. J. MCKELWAY, *The Systematic Theology of Paul Tillich* (New York 1964). G. TAVARD, *Paul Tillich and the Christian Message* (London 1962).

[B. WHITNEY]

TIME

The term nominally means duration, an interval of motion, or the measure of either. Some philologists, tracing the word to an Old Teutonic root denoting "to extend," give time the etymological sense of extent of motion. Greek and Roman expressions are derived from Sanskrit roots meaning light and burning.

This treatment of time is divided into two parts. The first sketches the history of the concept of time, dealing with representative ancient, medieval, modern, and contemporary opinions. The second, or analytical, part then discusses natural time and its definition, measure, perception, existence, unity, and irreversibility—all from the viewpoint of Aristotelian-Thomistic philosophy.

History of the Concept of Time

Some vague knowledge of time is as old as man, but the rule of cultural development, *primum vivere deinde philosophari* (live first, then philosophize), kept the earliest cultures and civilizations for tens of thousands of years from probing the theoretical character of time. Unreflective awareness then, like the idea of time provided by common sense, remained preanalytic and practical in bent; time served to date lives and to inflect verbs.

Ancient period. The Babylonians refined methods of time-reckoning and the pre-Socratics groped toward the foundations of natural change, but it was not until PLATO that Western thought achieved a detailed and coherent theory of time. Plato's predecessors, like HERACLITUS and PARMENIDES, did not detach time from change; or, like ZENO OF ELEA, treated it only dialectically; or, like the Pythagoreans and DEMOCRITUS, sketched only fragmentary or superficial definitions. Aristotle, Plotinus, and St. Augustine were the only thinkers in the ancient world after Plato to propound theories at least equal, perhaps superior, to his. The views adopted by Epicurus, Chrysippus, and Zeno the Stoic seem to be imprecise residues of Aristotle's analysis. The Stoic doctrine of recurrent conflagrations, like every myth of eternal return, is strictly not a theory of time but a cyclic conception of cosmic destiny.

According to Plato (*Tim.* 37C–39E, 46C–47B), time is "the moving image of eternity" or "the everlasting image revolving according to number." In particular, time is the movement of the sphere of the fixed stars, whose unvarying circular course imitates the unchangeable life of the Living Creature. Its revolutions mark out or number the intervals called days. In their wandering but regularly repeated motions, the seven planets serve as instruments of time, determining and preserving the numbers or fixed intervals of time.

Particular defects in this view, like the implicit equivalence of part and whole, did not escape Aristotle (*Phys.* 217b 29–224a 16). But its radical fallacy lies in its metaphysicism; it obtrudes a metaphysical explanation on what wants natural induction, i.e., it tells what time is in virtue of what it is not. For Aristotle time is "the number of motion according to before and after." (This celebrated and controverted definition is examined below in the analytical section.)

A Platonic rebuttal had to await PLOTINUS (*Enn.* 3.7.7–13). Making time number, he argues, answers only how much but not what time is. Because nature is within time but time outside nature, time properly resides in the discrete operations of the Soul insofar as the Soul successively makes and sustains nature. The stars in their courses manifest and measure the quantity of time that remains essentially one with the generative life of the Soul. Though this grand metaphysical stroke liquidates some problems, Plotinus's metaphysicism, like Plato's, has its defects: the gulf between the Soul and nature is unbridged; and proper time is spiritual and discrete, while its natural counterpart is unaccountably continuous and material.

An acknowledged debt to Plotinus did not prejudice St. AUGUSTINE against a natural psychological solution (*Conf.* 11.14.17–11.28.38). If time is the measure of CHANGE, it demands a present beyond the fleeting instant and above bodily motion. Time, he shows inductively, is a distension of the soul, with future and past segments stretching bilaterally from the distended present of attention. Many have misread this quasi-physical time line as an offshoot of Plotinus or a forebear of Kant or Bergson. But in contrast to Plotinus and Kant, Augustine scrupulously transcribes the empirical data, and his interior spatializing of time differs essentially from Bergson's treatment. Augustine's closest kin is Aristotle. Though the two part company on the physical primacy of the now, they join hands on the totality of time, where both assign the soul's activity to hold all at once fluent parts unable to exist all at once.

Medieval period. With "the master of those who know" bestriding their world like a colossus, medieval thinkers devoted themselves to elucidating the Aristotelian text. The exegeses of Avicenna, Averroës, St. Albert the Great, St. THOMAS AQUINAS, and William of Ockham differ on the meaning of number, the perceived unicity, and the objective reality of time.

AVICENNA (*An-Najat.* 186–192) ascribes the number of parts to motion itself and considers time the measure of passage from one part to another, while the observer, imaginatively making cuts in the flux, gives being to instants. As the measure of all possible change, time is indirectly applicable to everything affected by mutability.

AVERROËS (*In 4 phys.* 98–132), anxious to reconcile the letter of Aristotle with time's universality, takes number to mean a mathematical entity. Next, the unicity of time seems to clash with concrete awareness: if time is subjectified in the primary motion, how can anyone not knowing this know time? Perceiving change, each notes himself changing, he answers, and through self-consciousness indirectly gains hold of primary motion. As regards the existence of time, Averroës introduces the seminal idea that time, potential in motion, becomes actual number through the soul's numbering of motion.

St. ALBERT THE GREAT (*In 4 phys.* 3.3–17) departs from Averroës on two counts but agrees with him on unicity. Averroës's formal number mathematicizes time, he maintains, whereas time is number *sui generis,* both formal and material. Next, awareness of inward change contains a virtual awareness of the primary motion, because this latter is "habitually" operative in all other motions. However, flatly opposing Averroës, Albert declares time to be materially as well as formally independent of the soul. In the view, to be elaborated below, of his fellow Dominican, St. Thomas Aquinas (*In 4 phys.* 15–23), the nows rather than continuous parts are numbered before and after; the primary motion exists secondarily in other motions; and time is primarily a being of nature, needing the soul to fix its totality.

WILLIAM OF OCKHAM (*Phil. nat.* 4.1–16) generally reproduces Averroës in a logically elegant dress. Though signifying principally what motion signifies, time consignifies both the soul and its judgment of the before and after. Time is predicated per se of its subject, the primary motion, as risible is predicated of man. Measurement of the primary motion renders all things formally temporal; time is virtually everywhere. Although time enjoys the same objective reality as a branch on a tree, the soul must intervene if primary motion and the branch are to serve as measures, i.e., the soul completes the being of time only when actually using the primary motion to measure passage.

The Renaissance scholastic F. SUÁREZ (*Disp. meta.* 50) shifts to the metaphysical plane in defining time as the successive duration of a material being. Time is formally continuous, i.e., in accord with Averroës, time as number is constructed by the soul's actual numbering of the parts of motion. Since every entity possesses an intrinsic duration, time is not one but intrinsically many and diverse. Oddly, early in the 20th century, D. Nys refurbished the opinion of JOHN OF ST. THOMAS (*Curs. phil.* 2.369–376), who substantially champions Suárez on this point, and presented it as that of Aquinas, so that many textbooks in natural philosophy still force physical time into the frame of metaphysical duration.

Modern period. Duration comes to the fore again, now in mathematical garb, in the monumental natural philosophy of Sir Isaac Newton. "Absolute, true, and mathematical time, of itself and from its own nature, flows equably without regard to anything external, and by another name is called duration." "Absolute" differentiates duration from the relative public time of particular observers; "true" means that it is the cosmic standard; "mathematical" means that it is quantity subsisting apart from particular subjects; "of itself" denotes that it is nature's intrinsic metric; and "equably" refers to perfectly uniform and unalterable passage.

G. W. LEIBNIZ, Newton's stoutest antagonist, holds that absolute time violates the metaphysical principles of sufficient reason and the identity of indiscernibles. For in a time divorced from events, the interchangeability of before and after instants renders temporal sequence irrational, and the plurality of instants vanishes. Time is, like number, independent of particulars and hence distinct from duration, which characterizes particular intervals. Elliptically put, time is the order of inconsistent and successive possibles; Socrates's walking today, for example, cannot simultaneously occur with his walking tomorrow. His polemic against Newton does not rescue Leibniz from an absurdity that his own mathematicized time-order inflicts on him—a temporal aspect at once a part of events and apart from events.

I. KANT transplants absolute time into human sensibility. Newtonian time, of itself prior to anything external, becomes an a priori sensuous form empirically real but transcendentally ideal. Unlike space, time is a one-dimensional successive continuum and an inner form directly arranging internal perceptions. If before, after, and simultaneous are added to content, Kant argues, the mind must antecedently supply them. Again, if one can think of time apart from objects and not vice versa, time is an a priori intuition. However, the assumed absolute time is self-refuting, for no abstract quantity can flow. Again, the alleged antecedence suggests only that time is objectively necessary to events. Finally, a time cut off from events is a preposterous void, for the fact is that awareness of motion precedes awareness of time.

Contemporary period. H. BERGSON starts with a critique that deposes rather than presupposes the reigning mechanism. A closed system of mechanical causation, he thinks, suppresses change and totally spatializes time. Man recovers real time, in contrast to clock time, in the primacy of change. Each state of unceasingly changing psychic life melts into its neighbor in an unbreakable flow. The intuition of change as pure duration is at one stroke the intuition of the time itself: real time is convertible with pure duration. However, dialectical brilliance cannot nullify the facts that successiveness always stamps process and that the flow involves a spatial environment. Pure change, moreover, is change turned into homogeneous duration.

A. N. WHITEHEAD celebrates process more sweepingly but less lucidly than Bergson. He discovers in total experience organically interrelated actual occasions, space concretely fused with time, and epochal durations as fundamental temporal quanta. Nature displays a becoming of continuity but no continuity of becoming: a becoming of continuity, for extended regions, not instants, coincide with the creative advance ultimate in things; but no continuity of becoming, for time, like the actual occasions it measures, comes in atomic droplets or pulsations. Whitehead's crude union of time with motion engenders a brood of paradoxes: multiple yet simultaneous time-regions; an irreversible time in reversible processes; one time made many in different events; and durations distinct without distinguishing instants.

In contrast to the Western tradition, M. HEIDEGGER derives his conception from practical or human time. Because Dasein or human being is a being-toward-death, the future is primary in primordial time. Man becomes fully man by projecting himself into the future to illumine the banal present and transfigure the inertial past; he becomes truly free by integrating the ecstasies of present-future and present-past firmly oriented toward death. However, it is pure sophistry to declare human time naturally prior to a world-time that clearly preexists and postdates individual human life. It is boldly fallacious also to link values essentially with time; a Jack the Ripper may confront death in the authentic Heideggerian manner while forging an inhuman or morally inauthentic destiny.

Aristotelian-Thomistic Analysis

Time means many things to many minds. First, time is deemed a practical condition or instrument for realizing human goods. A religious outlook meditates on the sacramental value of each moment for eternity, the historian dates the glories and tragedies of social man, and in a businessman's civilization believing "time is money," social time is like raw material to be harnessed by capital. Second, primitive "lived time" or I-time is the felt sense of duration in the person shaped by his past and advancing toward his future. Third, biological time regulates the build-up and breakdown of tissues, the length of cicatrization, the life-span of mayfly and tortoise. Fourth, mathematical-physical time, sometimes called public time, constitutes a metric intersubjectively applicable to every change. Each of these branches out from natural time. The religious, historical, and social significations take for granted a prior temporal structure measuring the human condition. The succession of inner states in psychic time is rooted in matter and motion. Biological time presupposes a deeper-lying periodicity within life-processes. The metric of mathematical-physical time abstractly imitates a primordial regularity built into nature.

Natural time. The definition of natural time develops from three inductive determinations: time as something of motion, time as continuous, and time as number.

Time and Motion. Disparity of attributes rules out the fusion of time and MOTION avowed by process and causal theories. Motions are either specifically or particularly diverse, but time is physically universal, i.e., not wholly circumscribed by one species or particular subject. Again, unlike motion, time is uniform. To predicate fast or slow of time amounts to the fruitless measuring of time elapsed by the identical time elapsed. Rather, time inevitably accompanies motion. Tales in world literature concerning the monk rapt in contemplation and Rip Van Winkle illustrate that awareness of time is indissolubly wedded to awareness of motion. Concomitance in awareness mirrors concomitance in nature.

Time as Continuous. Time is a CONTINUUM because it resides in motion that traverses continuous magnitude. A continuum is formally one and materially partitive; the parts joined to one another make up an order of local before and after. Not motion as such, but motion concretized in the spatial continuum, is properly called motion according to before and after. Data from nature and art attest that man estimates time by noting motion according to before and after. Time's passage is punctuated by the sun's rising and setting, the moon's phases, the here and there of star and planet, the ebb and flow of tides, and for urban man by bells, whistles, and hands on a dial.

Where nominally defined (Aristotle, *Cat.* 4b 24), time is classified, along with magnitude, as a proper measure, but a strictly physical inquiry discovers that time, like motion, shares secondarily and derivatively in the continuity proper to magnitude. Thus one may speak of a time line or time dimension in the broad acceptation. The fourth dimension of relativity mechanics means nothing more than that a particular measurement of time is necessary to describe exactly events in a particular coordinate system. It is irresponsible to rhapsodize with H. Minkowski that space and time, being themselves "shadows," henceforth fuse into a hyphenated third entity.

One indirectly demonstrates the observed continuity of time by showing the absurdities its denial entails; e.g., if indivisibles make up the time line, no body can be measured as faster or slower than another. The famous paradoxes of Zeno of Elea impugning observed continuity rest upon the erroneous assumption that what is infinitely divisible into smaller parts is already actually divided into an infinity of partless units. Turned about, the paradoxes ironically establish the realistic view: if time is a string of discontinuous nows, then all motion and time are illusions. B. RUSSELL and A. Grünbaum have recently tried to answer Zeno, but in basing their solutions on G. Cantor's transfinite number, both implicitly concede Zeno's fatal assumption that a continuum is actually composed of discontinuous elements.

Time as Number. The insight that time is number completes the definition. Number is a MULTITUDE measured by unity; its plurality arises from the division of the continuum. Time springs from the division of the motion-continuum by the nows bounding its passage. The pluralized motion is raised to the estate of number when one visualizes before and after under the common aspect of the now and counts them as two nows. The full-fledged definition emerges when the mind says, in effect, now . . . now. The nows, the correlates of the before and after in motion, are the numbered terminals of a continuum that may be diagrammed.

Three corollary remarks may help dispel certain misinterpretations. First, the words "before" and "after" do not render the definition circular. Despite the fact that current usage may accord them a fundamental temporal reference, before and after primarily denote the order of parts to magnitude. The here-before and the thereafter-ward of space underlie the positional character of the time line terminated by the before-now and the after-now. Second, the illusion persists that before and after are convertible with past and future. Man does perceive time, but both past and future, being nonactual, are strictly unper-

ceivable. Too, past and future denote part-times in the scheme of time, whereas before and after signify not parts but the partless nows numbered in motion. Third, number does not mean absolute or mathematical number divorced from passage. Time is numbered number, part and parcel of the process as the number of and in motion. It is indeed the numbered terminals indissociable from the flux, the very nows numbered before and after.

Scope of the definition. One attains the definition of time at the level of the general science of nature, i.e., the PHILOSOPHY OF NATURE, which aims to systemize concepts concerned with the most general features of nature. At this level, the mind achieves a quasi-abstraction from more concrete modes of natural philosophy. Thus a definition of time as an all-pervasive feature of common experience does not depend upon contemporary physical research, but it is analyzed out of the universal fact of motion that modern physics presupposes rather than supersedes. It is foolish, then, to comb the fundamental definition for hints about time in relativistic or quantum mechanics, but it is no less illusory, conversely, to imagine that the basic definition is toppled by revolutions that overturn the status quo in the more concrete provinces of natural science.

Measure of motion. Since time is number and measure is the property of number, time's principal property is to be the measure of motion; it is the standard that manifests the proper quantity of motion. Time and motion measure each other along different causal lines. Time in itself is the primary existential measure, while *quoad nos* man may determine unit-intervals of time by motions like the sun's apparent orbit or the movements of a quartz crystal clock.

Time measures motion alone in the per se sense. Everything else in nature is in time inasmuch as it is connected with motion. Hence, not the very substance of mobile being but only its duration or concrete length of existence is temporally determined. To make mobile being subject to time entails, of course, the suppression of substance. As natural substance, however, a mobile being enjoys an existential duration from generation to corruption properly measured by time. Generation-corruption itself, marking the outer bounds of duration, is measured by the limiting now.

The relation of the human soul to time is less clear-cut. Because the human soul qua spiritual is per se supra-temporal, its intransmutable substance is measured by the aevum. The operations that the soul coauthors with the body are subjectively under time; physical time necessarily governs sensory cognitions and desires that involve motion. Spiritual or discrete time properly measures purely intellectual operations. Yet these immaterial operations are extrinsically related to natural time; objectively, in the dependence of the INTELLECT on the PHANTASM; associatively, in the termination of the enunciation in the *ipsum esse rei,* the existential mode that includes a determined time.

In addition, one may truly call time a per se cause of corruption in the sense that it is number imbedded in a motion that betokens the essential indeterminateness of matter. Now, matter possesses its own, an absolute, necessity determining all things to breakdown and destruction. But time's causality remains no more than extrinsic and formal, for though one may list old age as a cause of death and imagine time bearing a scythe, time is merely incidental to the agent precipitating the destruction.

Perception of time. The perception of time matches its peculiar mode of existence. Since time coexists with motion in magnitude, man coperceives it with motion across extensive magnitude. In sensing time, he senses not just motion but the successiveness within motion, which bespeaks units before and after. The sense of time, then, comes down to the sense of concrete number in local motion. Furthermore, man formally perceives time in virtue of the *sensus communis* or CENTRAL SENSE, which refers the time line cognized to ongoing process. Time is first impressed on the central sense, then reimpressed on the IMAGINATION. The imaginative impress, because worked by the central sense, is said to be the proper effect of the central sense. The imagination is, in this case, materially causative; it retains its image in the service of the outward-directed central sense. Imagination plays, nonetheless, a significant role. Only imagination, among the internal senses, represents singularized quantities, such as lines and circles. Subsequently, the imagination detaches the numbered local motion from its qualitative surroundings, so that it appears as *this* time, as a quasi-mathematical entity of one dimension. Yet its later refinement in the imagination does not isolate the species of time from reference to sensible matter, for what is represented as a line answers to a flowing continuum in nature. Moreover, where contact with the outer flux is occasionally broken off, time-awareness arises from internal sensory activity. The COGITATIVE POWER embraces every sensory power, internal as well as external, within its cognitive reflection; awareness of inner time is simply a special case of this self-awareness.

Existence of time. The totality of time, the primitive schema present to perception and conception, depends on the soul to combine in one whole never coexistent parts as if they were coexistent. Time in its quantitative totality is a relation of reason; one, however, different from a sheerly logical relation constructed to order concepts. It faces outward and bears on the natural universe. Despite its dependence on the soul, time is first and foremost a being of nature and only secondarily, from the viewpoint of definitional totality, a being of reason. It is permissible, though ambiguous, to state that time does not exist without the soul, but it is more exact to hold that time exists without the soul. Time is rooted and has imperfect being in the now. The incomplete being of time copies the imperfect existence of motion; the fleetingness of the now imitates that of the indivisible moment. Time is, then, as physically real as motion: it shares motion's imperfect mode of being that needs the supplementary work of the mind to eke out its totality. This realistic answer diverges sharply from the Averroistic account, still strongly favored by scholastics, that time exists formally in the mind but fundamentally in motion. This self-contradictory formulation is tantamount to saying that time is formally a relation of reason but fundamentally a relation of reason; motion in its totality cannot serve as time's physical foundation, because it is no less a relation of reason than time.

Unity of time. It is self-refuting to regard time as specifically one but diversified according to its varied embodiments in motion. If two concurrent motions demand different times, equal times (hours or days) must simultaneously coexist. However, two divisions of time the same in every way are not two, but one time. Thus the notion of pluralized times entails the numerical unity of time supposedly done away with. Time, then, is not an abstractly universal continuum; it must properly reside in a numerically one subject.

This one time must be situated in the most basic of motions, a local motion. This primary subject also must be maximally regular among motions, primary among local motions. Fundamental natural analysis reveals one more trait: the primary motion belongs to the universal physical cause (*see* MOTION, FIRST CAUSE OF). The inherent causal inadequacies of univocal agents necessitate a universal physical cause. Such agents are of themselves powerless to produce substantial changes; a horse's parents that were its per se adequate cause would be at once causative of the equine species itself and of their own existence. It is the overriding influence of the universal physical cause also that maintains species outlasting their individual instances. Plainly, the ubiquity and uniformity of time are mediated by the primary motion of the universal physical cause. Insofar as its number resident in the primary motion is secondarily exhibited in every other motion, time stretches to the farthest reaches of the cosmos; it is coterminous with an efficacy equivocally exercised by the universal cause. Yet it remains uniform because the primary motion possesses a quasi-perpetual invariance. Here warranted knowledge stops; man cannot put his finger on which motion is the primary subject of time. It must be stressed that the foregoing propositions have been scientifically analyzed out of a general experience of nature unaffected by the vicissitudes of specialized observations; they are no more open to discard than are the general hylomorphic make-up of natural entities and man's soul-body composition because of the extinction of the ancient theory of the four elements.

A crude commingling of the general and specialized sectors of natural science underlies certain attempts to equate Einstein's special theory of relativity with a fundamental relativization of time itself. Relativity theory applies only to the measurement of natural time. Time as measured is always pluralized according to coordinate systems; time as measured is always relative to the measurer; time as measured never discloses simultaneous events. So-called time-dilatation is an elliptical way of expressing the retardation of a clock in motion relative to an observer; not time itself but clocks and their observed readings vary from system to system. Second, as a sophisticated hypothesis of time-measurement, relativity theory must assume an antecedent analysis. Its second postulate, the constancy of the velocity of light, depends on prior awareness of time, for velocity is roughly the ratio between distance and time. Again, relativistic simultaneity presupposes the natural unity and simultaneity of time. Were there no uniformly one time implied in the comparison, it would be meaningless to compare varied interpretations of the earlier-later relations of two light signals flashed to observers in various coordinate systems. Moreover, the statement that one cannot measure the simultaneity of two events involves some knowledge, at least vague, of what coinstantaneous occurrence means.

Irreversibility of time. It is a misunderstanding to base irreversibility on entropy and cause-effect sequences. A thermodynamic reversal would not involve the reversal of before and after, for man measures the normal or reversal course of entropy according to before and after. So also with one-way causal sequences: even if an extranatural agency reversed the cause-effect order, the reverse would be measured by an irreversible relation of before and after.

That time cannot recur follows from its unity. No power in heaven or on earth can undo the fact that Socrates sits down after he has run. Reversing time in this sense amounts to claiming that what is unique and determinate is really nonunique and indeterminate; in a word, a reversible time-order means the destruction of time. Irreversibility is, at bottom, necessary because it bespeaks the before and after that are properties of time. Time is necessarily unidirectional because each phase of the primary motion is numerically distinct from its neighbors before and after. One whole revolution may be constantly repeated, but the identity of the successive revolutions is specific rather than numerical. A time sheerly number would include an interchangeable past and future, and a time identical with motion would be reversible as process. But time is numbered number, imbedded primarily in one particular motion, so that the date of each event, its position on the time line, is always irrevocably different. Indeed, the very now terminating an event uniquely determines the event; that is to say, time is irreversible because the now, its principle and measure, is always formally other.

See Also: ETERNITY.

Bibliography: General. M. F. CLEUGH, *Time and Its Importance in Modern Thought* (London 1937). J. A. GUNN, *The Problem of Time* (London 1929). J. SIVADJIAN, *Le Temps* (Paris 1938). M. J. ADLER, ed., *The Great Ideas: A Syntopicon of Great Books of the Western World* (Chicago, Ill. 1952) 2:896–914. A. ALIOTTA, *Enciclopedia filosofica* (Venice-Rome 1957) 4:1124–31. R. EISLER, *Wörterbuch der philosophischen Begriffe* (Berlin 1927–30) 3:646–664. Particular. H. L. BERGSON, *Time and Free Will*, tr. F. POGSON (New York 1910; repr. 1950). J. F. CALLAHAN, *Four Views of Time in Ancient Philosophy* (Cambridge, Mass. 1958). A. GRÜNBAUM, *Philosophical Problems of Space and Time* (New York 1963). M. HEIDEGGER, *Being and Time*, tr. J. MACQUARRIE and E. ROBINSON (London 1962). A. MANSION, "La Théorie aristotélicienne du temps chez les péripatéticiens médiévaux," *Revue néoscolastique* 36 (1934) 275–307. B. R. RUSSEL, *Human Knowledge* (New York 1948). A. N. WHITEHEAD, *Process and Reality* (New York 1929).

[J. M. QUINN]

TIME (IN CANON LAW)

Time plays a prominent part in the legislation of the Church, not only in liturgical matters, such as the determination of Easter, but also in the disciplinary laws. Time is nowhere the efficient cause of rights, but it is often the medium through which rights are acquired or lost. In certain cases time affects the validity of an act. If, for instance, the age prescribed for admission to the novitiate (CIC c. 643 §1, 1°; CCEO cc. 450, 4° and 517 §1), for religious profession (CIC c. 656, 1°; cf. CCEO cc. 464, 1° and 527, 1°) or for matrimony (CIC c. 1083 §1; CCEO c. 800 §1), has not been reached, these acts are *ipso facto* null and void.

Before the promulgation of the 1917 Code of Canon Law there were no general norms for the reckoning of time; the matter was never treated under one heading by the authors. Commentators were not agreed upon the course to follow even when a single question was considered. One principle, however, seems to have guided the authors in the reckoning of time; to restrict odious things and amplify favorable things. This followed the rule of law, *"Odia restringi, et favores convenit ampliari."*

Available time (*tempus utile*) could be considered exceptional. Time is of its nature continuous, but available time does not run if one was ignorant of his rights or was unable to act within the determined time period (CIC c. 201 §2; CCEO c. 1544 §2).

The law defines the length of the various time units in common use. In the course of time these units have varied in length. Thus, day was once opposed to night and lasted about 12 hours. Now the day is made up of 24 hours reckoned continuously from midnight to midnight. The week is made up of seven days. The month and the year are made up respectively of 30 and 365 days unless these units are taken as they are in a specific calendar (CIC c. 202 §1; CCEO c. 1545 §1).

Bibliography: C. CALÀ, *Tractatus absolutissimus de feriis, solennibus, repentinis, et indictis* (Naples 1675). A. J. DUBÉ, *The General Principles for the Reckoning of Time in Canon Law* (Washington 1941). J. LACAU, *De tempore, dissertatio philosophico-scientificio-iuridica* (Turin 1921). G. MICHIELS, *Normae generales juris canonici. Commentarius libri I. Codex iuris canonici,* 2 v. (2d ed. Paris-Tournai-Rome 1955) 2:221–278. A. VAN HOVE, *Commentarium Lovaniense in Codicem iuris canonici 1,* v.1–5 (Mechlin 1928–); v.1, Prolegomena (2d ed. 1945) 1.3. P. W. WILSON, *The Romance of the Calendar* (New York 1937).

[A. J. DUBE]

TIME (IN THE OLD TESTAMENT)

The Biblical notion of time is related to the Israelite conception of history. Because of the concreteness of Hebrew thought nothing approximating a philosophic definition of time is found in Sacred Scripture. The fact that the Septuagint (LXX) translated the Hebrew '*ēt* (time) only on rare occasions by χρόνος supports this statement. The inspired authors, however, did have a concept of time that was not necessarily inferior because it was more concrete.

There is ample evidence that one of the meanings that the Israelites had of time was the familiar one of a period or duration (Ex 12.40; 1 Kgs 6.1; Lk 2.46; Acts 9.9). Time, however, was given another and far more significant meaning in the Bible, although there is strong disagreement on the methodology used to establish this richer meaning. James Barr attempts to point out the fallacies in the approach and the conclusions of John Marsh and Oscar Cullmann. In the case of Marsh, Barr attacks the distinction made between χρόνος and καιρός, i.e., between time as duration and time as fulfillment. In the case of Cullmann, Barr attacks the distinction made between καιρός and αἰών, i.e., between time as having content and time as an extended indefinite period. Irrespective of the divergent deductions, the three authors agree that the in-

spired writers employed the concept of time in a pregnant sense that emphasized the content, i.e., what transpired in time. In a word, time is event-full.

This quidditative (*see* QUIDDITY) concept of time is at once the fundamental and most meaningful one in Sacred Scripture. For example, in a calendar discovered at Gazer (Gezer) the months are associated with what takes place in them, e.g., one month with seeding, another month with harvesting. In the same vein Noemi and Ruth "arrived in Bethlehem at the beginning of the barley harvest" (Ru 1.22). Again, the cultic rites of the Feast of the PASSOVER (the same emphasis on content is present in other feasts also) bring about the reliving of the hour of deliverance from Egypt (Ex 12.26–27). What happened before happens again.

Through the theological perspective of sacred history the sense of time as the action it holds (i.e., God's activity) fully emerges. The beginning of heaven and earth is God's creative activity. The Exodus is the day that Yahweh "brought up Israel out of Egypt" (1 Sm 10.18). The Exodus as a saving act of God is a type and forerunner of the saving act of God spoken of by Isaiah (Is 25.9). It commences its fulfillment with the ultimate self-manifestation and involvement of God with man in the Incarnation.

From the beginning to the end of sacred history, time is the medium for God's saving acts. Each act is in some way the day of the Lord, and each day of the Lord is a type and anticipation of the eschatological DAY OF THE LORD, i.e., the PAROUSIA (1 Tm 6.15). This indwelling concept of time as linear, i.e., as pointing to the foreshadowing of Christ in the Old Testament and to His final coming in the New Testament, is supported by 1 Cor 10.1–11. Preeminently, therefore, time in the Bible connotes God's control of all history and His salvific acts; and reciprocally, time for man is his opportunity to respond to God that His saving acts may for him be efficacious: "there is a time for every affair and on every work a judgment" (Eccl 3.17).

Bibliography: J. BARR, *Biblical Words for Time* (London 1962). L. CĔRNÝ. *The Day of Yahweh and Some Relevant Problems* (Prague 1948). O. CULLMANN, *Christ and Time,* tr. F. V. FILSON (rev. ed. Philadelphia 1964). W. EICHRODT, *Theology of the Old Testament,* tr. J. A. BAKER (Philadelphia 1961–). E. JENNI, "Das Wort 'ô lām im A.T.," *Zeitschrift für die alttestamentliche Wissenschaft* 64 (Giessen-Berlin 1952) 197–248; 65 (1953) 1–35. J. MARSH, *The Fullness of Time* (New York 1952). C. TRESMONTANT, *A Study of Hebrew Thought,* tr. M. F. GIBSON (New York 1960).

[P. C. BERG]

TIME (IN THE NEW TESTAMENT)

The authors of the New Testament texts use two Greek terms for time: *chronos* and *kairos*. Although they do not engage in philosophical speculation about time, it is quite evident that their perspective is solidly rooted in the Jewish understanding of time as linear. That is to say, for the New Testament authors, time moves forward, and events can be certainly located in their own historical context. That linear notion of time, however, is not without a theological perspective: that God's activity has been discernible within the history of the Jewish people—from the creation to the rebuilding of the Temple—is now discerned within the life, death and resurrection of Jesus the Christ. Moreover, there is a view of time forward to the ultimate fulfillment of the age, which will not so much bring an end to time *per se*, but at which time God will reestablish the idyllic state of creation.

This linear, chronological sense of time is most evident in the Greek word χρόνος (*chronos*), which means "time" or "span of time." Χρόνος is used 54 times in the New Testament. It seems fair to say that the author of the Gospel of Luke and Acts of the Apostles finds this term most fitting for his grand two-part narrative, since he uses χρόνος seven and seventeen times, respectfully—much more frequently than any other New Testament author. For some examples, see the use of χρόνος in Mt 2.7, 16; Mk 2.19; 9.21; Lk 1.57; 4.5; 8.27; 18.4; 20.9; 23.8; Jn 5.6; 7.33; 12.35; 14.9; Ac 1.6, 21; 3.21; 7.17, 23; 8.11; 13.18; 14.3, 28; 15.33; 17.30; 18.20, 23; 19.22; 20.18; 27.9; Rm 7.1; 16.25; 1 Co 7.39; 16.7; Ga 4.1; Hb 4.7; 5.12; 11.32; 1 Pt 1.17; 4.2, 3; Rv 2.21; 6.11; 20.3.

There is, however, another Greek term which can be used as a synonym for χρόνος in the sense of "time" or "span of time," namely, καιρός (*kairos*; used 85 times in the New Testament; cf. Ac 1.7 and 1 Th 5.1 where both terms are used in the plural: "[the] times and [the] seasons"). Despite that usage, καιρός often carries much more theological freight than is normal for χρόνος. καιρός can mean "the proper time," or "a decisive moment," "a moment of grace," "a time requiring a decision and commitment." St. Paul uses both terms (as well as αἰών [*aiwn* = eon]), but while χρόνος normally designates a chronological, linear sense of time, καιρός "frequently refers to 'eschatologically filled time, time for decision'" (Baumgarten, 232; cf. Rm 3.26; 5.6; 8.18; 9.9; 11.5; 13.11; 1 Co 4.5; 7.5, 29; 2 Co 6.2 *bis*; 8.14; Gl 4.10; 6.9, 10; 1 Th 2.17; 5.1). For the New Testament authors, the "time" of Jesus is more than just a chronological moment in history, it is a time that demands a decision, a time that fulfills the meaning of the time that has gone before and the foretaste of the consummation of all time.

Although the biblical authors believe that God is present and active in χρόνος, that very belief calls one to recognize God's presence and to decide for God, in other words, to grasp the καιρός.

Bibliography: "καιρός" and "χρόνος" in W. BAUER, W. F. ARNDT, and F. W. GINGRICH, *A Greek-English Lexicon of the New Testament and Other Early Christian Literature*, rev. and ed. by F. W. DANKER, (Chicago 3rd ed., 2000). Gerhard Delling, "καιρός" and "χρόνος", in G. KITTEL, ed., *Theological Dictionary of the New Testament* trans. and ed., G. W. BROMILEY, 10 vols. (Grand Rapids, MI 1964–1976) v. III, 455–464 and v. IX, 581–594, respectively. J. BAUMGARTEN, "καιρός", in Horst Balz and Gerhard Schneider, eds., *Exegetical Dictionary of the New Testament*, 3 vols., (Grand Rapids, MI 1990) v. 2, 232–235. H. Hübner, "χρόνος", *idem.*, 488–489.

[T.A. FRIEDRICHSEN]

TIMON, JOHN

First bishop of Buffalo, New York; b. Conewago Township, Pennsylvania., Feb. 12, 1797; d. Buffalo, April 16, 1867. John was three years old when his family left a log-cabin home to settle in Baltimore, Maryland. At 15 he enrolled at Mt. St. Mary's College, Emmitsburg, Maryland. In 1818 the family migrated to Louisville, Kentucky, and the next year he went on to St. Louis, Missouri, where Timon came under the influence of the Vincentian Felix De Andreis. Timon went to study for the diocesan priesthood with Bp. Louis Dubourg of St. Louis, but in July 1822 he transferred to the Vincentian seminary, St. Mary-of-the-Barrens in Perry County. He pronounced his vows on June 10, 1825, and on Sept. 23, 1826, he was ordained by Bp. Joseph Rosati. During the next ten years Timon was occupied with administrative duties at the Vincentian seminary, and also served as parish priest and traveling missionary. In 1835 he was designated first superior or visitor of the American Vincentians, just constituted an autonomous province. For 12 years (1835–47) he was the Vincentian superior and also vicar-general of the St. Louis diocese. Moreover, as prefect apostolic of Texas (1839–41) he was largely responsible for reestablishing the Church in the Lone Star Republic and earned the title "Apostle of Texas."

On April 23, 1847, Pius IX appointed him to Buffalo, a see recommended for erection by the Fifth Provincial Council of Baltimore in 1846. This was the seventh attempt to make Timon a bishop, and he accepted only because he feared that another refusal might brand him an intractable priest. He also feared that he might otherwise be commanded to become coadjutor of Louisville, a post he wished to avoid since slavery, which he detested, existed in Kentucky. He was consecrated by Bp. John Hughes on Oct. 17, 1847, in old St. Patrick's Cathedral, New York City, and arrived in Buffalo five days later. Since there was no episcopal residence, Timon lived at

St. Louis Church, the oldest in Buffalo. When the trustees evicted him a month later, he moved to St. Patrick's and made it his procathedral. The trustees' action, taken because of Timon's interest in the title deed of the church property, precipitated a long, bitter feud. In 1855 the state legislature passed the Church Property (Putnam) Bill forbidding property to be left to any ecclesiastical officer. Timon succeeded in having this law repealed, and in 1863 the Church Trustee Law, a model for other states, was enacted.

With funds from Pius IX, European monarchs, and other sources, Timon erected St. Joseph's Cathedral (1851–55), where he was buried.

Bibliography: Archives of the Diocese of Buffalo, N.Y. R. BAYARD, *Lone-Star Vanguard: The Catholic Reoccupation of Texas, 1838–1848* (St. Louis 1945). C. G. DEUTHER, *Life and Times of the Rt. Rev. John Timon, D.D.* (Buffalo 1870). I. F. MOGAVERO, *That All May Know Thee: Centennial History of Niagara University, 1856–1956* (Philadelphia 1956).

[I. F. MOGAVERO]

TIMOTHEUS I, NESTORIAN PATRIARCH

Reigned 780 to 823; b. Ḥazza, Ḥedaiyab (in modern Iran), about the middle of the 8th century; d. Baghdad, 823. After studying under Abraham bar Dashandad at Bāshūsh, Timotheus was first a monk, then bishop of Bēth-Bāghāsh, and finally patriarch of the Nestorian Church, following a much-discussed synodal election. He was highly regarded by the Muslim Caliphs al-Mahdī (775–785) and Harūn ar-Rashīd (785–809), both of whom allowed him to carry on remarkably successful missionary enterprises in India, Turkestan, China, Yemen, and the region around the Caspian Sea. He organized the hierarchy of the Nestorian Church on the basis of six provinces; he exercised decisive influence in the separation of the hierarchy in Persia from the see of Rome; and in the synods of 790–791 and 804 he insisted on the purity of Nestorian doctrine.

He was one of the most prolific writers of his age. His works, all written in Syriac, include a treatise on astronomy, and a volume on Church matters, besides juridical canons, synodal canons, homilies for every Sunday of the year, a commentary on the writings of St. GREGORY OF NAZIANZUS, and two volumes of almost 200 letters. One of these letters contains a long apologia of Christianity spoken by Timothesus before the 'Abbāsid Caliph al-Mahdī. In all his writings Timotheus manifested a keen interest in Aristotelian philosophy, Biblical studies, juridical Church questions, and the works of St. Gregory of Nazianzus.

See Also: NESTORIANISM.

John Timon.

Bibliography: TIMOTHEUS I, *Epistolae,* ed. and tr. O. BRAUN, 2 v. (*Corpus scriptorum Christianorum orientalium* 74, 75; 1914–15). A. BAUMSTARK, *Geschichte der syrischen Literatur* (Bonn 1922). A. MINGANA, ed. and tr., *The Apology of Timothy the Patriarch before the Caliph Mahdi* (Cambridge, England 1928).

[J. M. SOLA-SOLE]

TIMOTHEUS I, PATRIARCH OF CONSTANTINOPLE

Reigned 511 to 518; b. ?; d. April 5, 518. He was a presbyter and Keeper of the Sacred Treasures of the Great Church, whom Emperor ANASTASIUS I selected (October 511) to replace the deposed, pro-Chalcedonian patriarch Macedonius II. Timotheus attempted to pursue religious policies acceptable to the Monophysites of the Byzantine Empire, but this proved difficult. His attempt to restore relations with John III Nikeotes, Monophysite patriarch of Alexandria, failed when John insisted that Timotheus explicitly condemn Chalcedon and the Tome of Leo.

Many of the clergy and laity at Constantinople and in the provinces refused to accept the deposition of Macedonius as legitimate. On November 4 and 6, 512, the attempt of Anastasius to introduce the Monophysite formula *crucifixus pro nobis* into the TRISAGION caused serious rioting. Timotheus ultimately adopted a more definite MONOPHYSITE policy. In 515 he apparently accepted the acts of the Synod of Tyre (514–15), which abrogated Chalcedon, and he expressly condemned that council in letters to Elias of Jerusalem and later to John of Jerusalem. He ordered the recitation of the NICENE CREED in the liturgy (previously it had been said only on Good Friday). His own personality does not emerge clearly. He never succeeded in becoming more than a malleable tool of the Emperor Anastasius.

Bibliography: V. GRUMEL, *Les Regestes des actes du patriarcat de Constantinople* (Kadikoi-Bucharest 1932–47) 1.1:193–205. L. DUCHESNE, *L'Église au VIe siècle* (Paris 1925) 25–42. J. LEBON, *Le Monophysisme sévérien* (Louvain 1909) 50–57, 63, 65. P. CHARANIS, *Church and State in the Later Roman Empire* (Madison, WI 1939) 36–77.

[W. E. KAEGI, JR.]

TIMOTHY, ST.

Disciple of St. Paul. He was born in Lystra, Lycaonia, of a pagan father and a pious Jewish mother Eunice, who taught him the Scriptures (Acts 16.1; 2 Tm 3.15). St. Paul, in A.D. 50, on his second trip to Lystra, found his young convert so esteemed by the local Christians that he took him as a coworker. Since Timothy had a Jewish mother, Paul circumcised him as an accommodation to Jewish scruples (Acts 16.2–4). Timothy was officially consecrated to the ministry (1 Tm 4.14) and became Paul's constant companion and his envoy for special missions (1 Thes 3.2–6; 1 Cor 4.17; Acts 19.22). Timothy is cowriter of Thessalonians, 2 Corinthians, Philippians, Colossians, and Philemon. His release from some imprisonment is noted in Heb 13.23. Paul assigned him to a special teaching office at Ephesus (1 Tm 1.3), but later urged him to come quickly to Rome, where Paul was suffering a lonely imprisonment.

St. John Damascene states that Timothy, first Bishop of Ephesus, witnessed Mary's departure from this world (*Hom. 2 de Dormitione; Patrologia Graeca* 106:749). Tradition tells of his martyrdom in A.D. 97 under Nerva. In 356 Constantius moved his remains to Constantinople.

Timothy was somewhat timid (1 Cor 16.11; 2 Tm 1.7–8) but affectionate (2 Tm 1.4). He was of frail health (1 Tm 5.23) and young at the time of Paul's final captivity (c. A.D. 63: 2 Tm 2.22). Paul shows fatherly concern for him in the two PASTORAL EPISTLES addressed to him and praises him as his beloved son (1 Cor 4.17), loyal imitator (Phil 2.19–20), coworker (Rom 16.21), and a dearly loved friend (2 Tm 1.4).

Feast: Jan. 24.

Bibliography: C. SPICQ, *Saint Paul: Les Épîtres pastorales* (*Études bibliques*; 1947).

[R. G. BOUCHER]

TIMOTHY AELURUS, MONOPHYSITE PATRIARCH

Of Alexandria, 457 to 460, 476 to 477; d. Alexandria, July 31, 477. A priest and supporter of the Patriarch DIOSCORUS, Timothy was called Aelurus (the Cat) because of his stealthy movements. With Peter Mongos he had attended the Robber Council of EPHESUS in 449, but he remained faithful to Dioscorus after the patriarch's condemnation. As a strong partisan of the terminology of St. CYRIL OF ALEXANDRIA, he organized the rebellion against PROTERIUS, the patriarch of Alexandria, and considered Pope LEO I a Nestorian. On the death of the Emperor MARCIAN (457) Timothy was consecrated patriarch of Alexandria by Eusebius of Pelusium and Peter the Iberian of Maiuma (March 16, 457). Dionysius the governor expelled him from the city but had to recall him after the sedition that followed the assassination of Proterius (March 28). Timothy held a synod at Alexandria that excommunicated Pope Leo I and the Patriarchs ANATOLIUS OF CONSTANTINOPLE and Basil of Antioch, and attempted to install his followers as bishops in all the dioceses of Egypt.

In October 457 the Emperor Leo I sent a questionnaire to the bishops of the Oriental provinces asking whether the Council of CHALCEDON should be upheld and Timothy recognized as patriarch, and he was unanimously rejected as an intruder. Despite Emperor Leo's conciliatory tactics Timothy would not retract his anti-Chalcedonian convictions and repulsed the representations of the imperial Count Rusticus. Amid a popular uprising in his favor, he was sent into exile to Gangra in Paphlagonia, whence he continued to write to his partisans, and was finally sent to Cherson on the Crimea where he wrote his "Against Those Who Speak of Two Natures."

On the accession of the intruding Emperor BASILISCUS (Jan. 9, 475) Timothy was amnestied and received in honor by the court at Constantinople. He attended a synod at Ephesus that declared that diocese a metropolitan see with the right to consecrate bishops in the province of Asia, thus contradicting the canonical decisions of Chalcedon, and accepted the compromising encyclical of the Emperor Basiliscus. On his triumphal return to Alexandria his Catholic successor Timothy Solafaciol (of the white turban) retired to a monastery in Canopus and received a small pension. Timothy Aelurus returned the remains of Dioscorus for honorable burial in the patriarchs' crypt in Alexandria and died shortly after the restoration of the Emperor ZENO. His many writings have been preserved only in fragments but indicate that he was not a thorough Monophysite. His opposition to Chalcedon was based on his intransigent devotion to the terminology of St. Cyril of Alexandria; and he opposed both the Eutychians and the followers of Julian of Halicarnassus.

Bibliography: A. FLICHE and V. MARTIN, eds. *Histoire de l'église depuis les origines jusq'à nos jours* (Paris 1935) 4:279–287. EVAGRIUS, *Historia ecclesiasticae* bk.2, ch.5–9. J. LEBON, *Le Monophysisme Sévérien* (Louvain 1909); ''La Christologie de T. A. d'après les sources syriaques inédites,'' *Revue d'histoire ecclésiatique* 9 (1908) 677–702. A GRILLMEIER and H. BACHT, *Das Konzil von Chalkedon: Geschichte und Gegenwart* (Würzburg 1951–54) 1:425–508, 637–676. T. SCHNITZLER, *Im Kampfe um Chalcedon* (Analecta Gregoriana 16; 1938).

[F. CHIOVARO]

TIMUR (TAMERLANE)

Also Timur Lang, or Timur the Lame; the Muslim conqueror and devastator of Muslim Asia; b. Kesh, Transoxania, 1336; d. Utar (Otrar), Central Asia, January, 1405. Descended from Turkish (not Mongol) stock no longer migratory, Timur began his career with an attempt to free his native Transoxania from the barbarian Mongol nomads who had overrun it during the invasion of Genghis Khan in 1220. Since Mongol authority in Transoxania was already weakened, Timur, by his ability and ruthlessness, made himself one of the leading Mongol vassals and, swearing allegiance to a puppet Khan of his own choosing, joined with the native prince of Balkh to expel the Mongol Khan and his army in 1363 (*see* MONGOLS). In these efforts he had the energetic support of the Muslim '*Ulamā*' (clergy) of Samarqand and of the Islamic population. Timur then seized the throne of Balkh, had his ally assassinated, made himself the champion of the Muslim settled people against the still half-pagan nomads, and freed Khwarizm (Khiva) and the Oxus Valley of Mongol domination in successive campaigns from 1370 to 1380.

While much of his life was spent in wars against the Mongols, Timur did not break with Mongol political theory. In fact, he issued decrees in the name of a Khan who was really his prisoner, married Mongol princesses of the line of Genghis Khan, and even claimed himself to be of Genghisid descent.

In 1381 his mounting ambition led him to attack cities of Persia, slowly recovering from Mongol devastation and misrule. The rest of his career was a series of great campaigns in all directions, in which he sacked and destroyed the chief cities of Islam in Asia, although he posed as a model of Muslim piety. He looted the Muslim Sultanate of Delhi in 1398 to ''punish'' it for living at peace among Hindus and crushed the forces of the Ottoman Empire for not attacking Christian Europe with sufficient vigor. He avenged hostility toward his troops with savage reprisals against the local populations; deliberately massacred the Christian populations of cities in Syria, Mesopotamia, Anatolia, and Georgia; nearly obliterated Nestorian Christianity, once flourishing under the Mongols; and burned and plundered capitulated Damascus in 1401 for having supported Mu'āwiya against ALĪ 740 years earlier.

Pyramids of human heads and ruined cities were not his only monuments; the scholars and artisans of conquered cities were carried off forcibly to Transoxania to make Samarqand Asia's most splendid capital. In the 15th century his descendants, the Timuri Dynasty, while dissipating their power in fratricidal struggles, sponsored a brilliant revival of Persian Islamic culture in Eastern Iran. In 1526, a prince of their house, Baber, conquered Delhi to found the Great Mughal Dynasty of India. Timur died while on a campaign to loot the Ming Empire of China.

Bibliography: E. G. BROWNE, *A Literary History of Persia*, 4 v. (2d ed. Cambridge, Eng. 1929) v.3. A. J. TOYNBEE, *A Study of History* (London 1934) 4:491–501. R. GONZALEZ DE CLAVIJO, *Embassy to Tamerlane 1403–06*, tr. G. LE STRANGE (London 1928).

[J. A. WILLIAMS]

TINCTORIS, JOHANNES

Renaissance theorist; b. Nivelles or Poperinghe, Flanders, *c.* 1435; d. Nivelles, Flanders, 1511. Tinctoris studied at the University of Louvain and at his death was a canon in the church of Nivelles; he was learned in mathematics, theology, and law as well as in music. He tutored Beatrice of Aragon, daughter of Don Ferrante (King Ferdinand I) of Naples and dedicated to her his celebrated dictionary, *Terminorum musicae diffinitorium* (*c.* 1474). This was followed by 11 more treatises written during his next 12 years (1474–86) at the Neapolitan court. His works on notation, modes, counterpoint, proportions, and instruments constitute a *summa* of early Renaissance music. In the *Liber de natura et proprietate tonorum* (1474) he proposes that modes in polyphony are best determined from the tenor voice. The *Liber de arte contrapuncti* (1477) treats of consonance and dissonance in polyphony, and formulates eight general rules for good counterpoint. His progressive attitude is clear from the preface, in which he states that no polyphony older than

40 years is worthy of attention and credits the English, chiefly John DUNSTABLE, for this new art. The few Masses, motets, and chansons he left are less significant than his theoretical writings.

Bibliography: *Opera omnia,* ed. F. FELDMANN (*Corpus mensurabilis musicae,* ed. American Institute of Musicology, 18; 1960–); *Tractatus de musica,* H. COUSSEMAKER, *Scriptorum de musica medii aevi nova series,* 4 v. (Paris 1864–76) 4:1–200; *Dictionary of Musical Terms,* tr. C. PARRISH (New York 1964); *Proportionale musices,* O. STRUNK, ed., *Source Readings in Music History* (New York 1950) 193–196; *Liber de arte contrapuncti, ibid.* 197–199. G. REESE, *Music in the Renaissance* (rev. ed. New York 1959) 137–150. H. HÜSCHEN, *Die Musik in Geschichte und Gegenwart,* ed. F. BLUME (Kassel-Basel 1949–). A. CŒURDEVEY, ''Contrepoint et structure contrapuntique de Tinctoris à Zarlino,'' *Analyse Musicale* 31 (1993), 40–52. H. HÜSCHEN, ''Johanne Tinctoris'' in *The New Grove Dictionary of Music and Musicians, vol. 18,* ed. S. SADIE (New York 1980) 837–840. D. M. RANDEL, ed., *The Harvard Biographical Dictionary of Music* (Cambridge 1996) 918. A. SEAY, ed., *Johannis Tinctoris Opera theoretica* (Rome: ''Corpus scriptorum de musica, vol. 22'' American Institute of Musicology, 1975–1978). R. WOODLEY, ''The Proportionate Musices of Johannes Tinctoris: A Critical Edition, Translation and Study'' (Ph.D. diss. Keble College, Oxford University, 1983); ''The Printing and Scope of Tinctoris's Fragmentary Treatise *De inventione et vsv mvsice,*'' *Early Music History* 5 (1985), 259–68.

[E. R. LERNER]

TINTERN, ABBEY OF

Former CISTERCIAN abbey on the River Wye, four miles north of Chepstow, Monmouthshire, west England, Diocese of HEREFORD (Latin, *Tinterna Major*). It was founded in 1131 by Walter Fitz Richard, Lord of Chepstow, with monks from L'Aumône, Diocese of Chartres, France. As early as 1139 Tintern sent a colony to Kingswood, Gloucestershire, and in 1200 another to Tintern Minor, County Wexford, Ireland. During the 13th century the abbey was completely rebuilt: the refectory and other claustral offices were begun in 1220; work on the church started in 1270 and ended about the beginning of the 14th century. This church, 245 feet long with transepts of 110 feet, and today almost perfectly preserved except for the roof, ranks with FOUNTAINS ABBEY as the most beautiful ruin in England. Tintern was damaged in 1223 during the war between Richard Marshall and King Henry III, and as compensation was allowed to pasture 40 mares with their foals for three years in the forest of Dene. Between 1265 and 1282 the abbot performed important royal commissions and acted as collector of tenths in the Diocese of Llandaff, Wales. This eventually involved the abbey in financial losses, and in the 14th century exemption from this office was granted. Tintern actually played little part in Welsh affairs, though local disputes arose about its weirs, which hindered navigation

along the River Wye to Monmouth. Even beyond the income from its wool trade, Tintern prospered through its possessions in Wales, Norfolk, and Kent, the most lucrative being the churches of Magor and Lydd, originally belonging to Santa Maria di Gloria, Diocese of Anagni, Italy, and granted to Tintern by Pope Gregory IX. At the dissolution under King HENRY VIII there were 13 monks at Tintern, the last abbot being Richard Wych.

Bibliography: W. DUGDALE, *Monasticon Anglicanum* (London 1655–73); best ed. by J. CALEY, et al., 6 v. (1817–30) 5:265–274. *Calendar of the Close Rolls Preserved in the Public Record Office, London (1227–1468). Calendar of the Patent Rolls Preserved in the Public Record Office, London (1232–1467).* F. A. GASQUET, *The Greater Abbeys of England* (New York 1903) 190–197. E. A. FOORD, *Hereford and Tintern* (London 1925). O. E. CRASTER, *Tintern Abbey* (London 1963).

[C. H. TALBOT]

TIRIDATES III, ARMENIAN KING

Reigned 282 to *c.* 330, scion of Parthian Nero–imposed Arsacid dynasty of Armenia. He regained the throne from the Sassanids of PERSIA with help of the Roman Emperor DIOCLETIAN, who imbued Tiridates with hatred of Christianity. Tiridates engaged in drastic persecution of the Christians in Armenia until his conversion (*c.* 302), when he was baptized by (St.) GREGORY ILLUMINATOR, who had miraculously cured him of a serious illness. Tiridates then made Christianity the official religion of the kingdom, gave Gregory large donations for building churches, and arranged Gregory's consecration as bishop of Armenia. Tiridates was hated by the Armenian nobles friendly to Persia and was killed by his majordomo. Often designated as ''Constantine of Armenia,'' Tiridates is listed among the saints of the Armenian Church; his feast is celebrated on the Monday after the fifth Sunday after Pentecost.

Bibliography: H. F. TOURNEBIZE, *Histoire politique et religieuse de l'Arménie* (Paris 1910). L. ARPEE, *A History of Armenian Christianity* (New York 1946).

[N. M. SETIAN]

TIRON, ABBEY OF

Former monastery, head of the BENEDICTINE congregation of Tironian monks, properly called La Sainte-Trinité de Tiron (Thiron, Tyron; Latin, *Tyronium*) in the Diocese of Chartres, department of Eure-et-Loir, commune of Thiron-Gardais, France. It was founded by (St.) BERNARD OF TIRON in February 1114 in the parish of Gardais, near the Thironne stream. A monk at Saint-Cyprien of Poitiers, which had been reformed by the Abbey of

Tintern Abbey in Wales. (Archive Photos)

CHAISE-DIEU, Bernard had become abbot and then left to become a hermit. Eventually he settled his 500 disciples in the forest of Le Perche, where he founded Tiron. His monks, who followed the strict BENEDICTINE RULE, avoided material wealth, living in great poverty, supporting themselves by some agriculture and placing much emphasis on craft work. Chanting was subordinated to meditation. After Bernard's death in 1117 his successors gradually abandoned his ideals and inclined increasingly toward Cluniac usages (*see* CLUNIAC REFORM). Between 1114 and 1191 Tiron founded nine abbeys in France, and five in Scotland, and nearly 100 priories, thus forming the Congregation of Tiron, which held annual chapter meetings. Tiron was burned by the English in 1428 and by the Protestants in 1562. In 1629 Tiron, experiencing a period of decline, was united to the MAURISTS. It maintained a college of 150 students. The abbey was suppressed in the French Revolution (1790). Today the abbey church and a few buildings remain.

Bibliography: L. MERLET, ed., *Cartulaire de l'abbaye de la Sainte-Trinité de Tiron,* 2 v. (Chartres 1882–83). *Acta Sanctorum* April 2:220–254. *Gallia Christiana,* v.1–13 (Paris 1715–85), v.14–16 (Paris 1856–65) 8:1257–77. L. H. COTTINEAU, *Répertoire topobibliographique des abbayes et prieurés,* 2 v. (Mâcon 1935–39) 2:3162–63. D. KNOWLES and R. N. HADCOCK, *Medieval Religious Houses: England and Wales* (New York 1953) 102.

[J. LAPORTE]

TIRRY, WILLIAM

Irish martyr; b. Cork, 1609; d. Clonmel, May 12, 1654. He became an Augustinian about 1627, and studied at Valladolid and Paris, where he qualified for admission to the faculty of theology in 1635. He returned to Ireland before 1640, and was probably prior of Fethard when in 1646 he was appointed provincial secretary. He became prior of Skryne in 1649, but because of the Cromwellian persecution he remained at Fethard. He was a man of great holiness; he was arrested while saying mass on April 4, 1654. He was condemned to death and executed at Clonmel under the anti-Catholic law of Jan. 6, 1653. Miracles were attributed to him by contemporaries.

Bibliography: F. X. MARTIN, "The Tirry Documents in the Archives de France, Paris," *Archivium Hibernicum* 20 (1957) 69–97. M. B. HACKETT, "The Tirry Documents in the Augustinian General Archives," *ibid.* 98–122.

[M. B. HACKETT]

TISCHENDORF, KONSTANTIN VON

Lutheran theologian and Biblical textual critic; b. Legenfeld, Saxony, January 18, 1815; d. Leipzig, December 7, 1874. He studied theology at Leipzig (1834–38), where he was especially influenced by J. G. B. Winer in joining a careful study of New Testament philology with a great veneration for the Bible. Though nominally belonging to the theological faculty of Leipzig (associate professor, 1845; professor of theology and Biblical paleography, 1859), he was chiefly concerned after 1837 with textual criticism, and he spent a large part of his life in the libraries of Europe and the Near East in search of unpublished manuscripts. He is famous for his dramatic recovery of the *Codex Sinaiticus* at the Monastery of St. Catherine at Sinai, which he visited three times between 1841 and 1869. The first folios were published in 1846 as the *Codex Frederico-Augustinus.* After the discovery in 1859 of almost the complete manuscript, it was published as *Bibliorum Codex Sinaiticus Petropolitanus* (Leipzig 1862). Other important manuscripts edited by Tischendorf were the *Codex Ephraemi rescriptus,* which he was the first to decipher (1843–45); the *Codex Amiatinus* (1850); and the *Codex Claromontanus* (1852). Between 1841 and 1869 he published eight editions of the Greek New Testament, the last of which still remains a basic standard book of reference for the Greek New Testament.

Bibliography: C. BERTHEAU, S. M. JACKSON, ed., *The New Schaff-Herzog Encyclopedia of Religious Knowledge,* 13 v. (Grand Rapids, MI) 11:451–453. W. SCHRAGE, *Die Religion in Geschichte und Gegenwart,* 7 v. (3rd ed. Tübingen 1957–65) 6:904–905.

[D. W. MARTIN]

TISCHNER, JÓZEF CASIMIR

Priest, philosopher; b. March 12, 1931, Stary Sącz, in the southern mountain region of Poland; d. June 28, 2000 in Kraków. Ordained a priest in 1978. Studied philosophy at the Jagiellonian University in Krakow, where Karol Wojtyła (the future JOHN PAUL II) and the phenomenologist Roman Ingarden were among his teachers. Beginning in the 1950s, Tischner contributed to the Catholic weekly *Tygodnik Powszechny,* which was at one time during the Communist era the only opposition newspaper in POLAND, providing a forum for many of Poland's intellectuals. Using his position as head of the Papal Theological Academy in Kraków, Tischner brought academics and other intellectuals together for discussions that Archbishop Wojtyła hosted in the archbishop's palace. In 1983, Tischner was instrumental, with the financial support of Cardinal Franz KÖNIG of Vienna, in organizing the first of the biennial seminars at Castel Gandolfo that provided Pope John Paul an opportunity for conversation with intellectual leaders and academics in various disciplines.

An early supporter of the Solidarity movement, Tischner served as chaplain to its first congress in Gdańsk, September 1981. The sermon he delivered at the Mass anticipated by two weeks John Paul's social encyclical "On Human Work" (*Laborem exercens*) and touched on many of the same themes. Later that year, when the Communist regime imposed martial law, he wrote *The Spirit of Solidarity,* which endeavored to expound philosophically the motive spirit behind this extraordinary social and political movement. This work set out to subtly demonstrate the errors underlying the ideology and practice of the Communist regime as concerns democracy, work, progress, and human dignity. The regime, he argued, had seriously undermined the meaning of these important concepts in the public discourse, and so Solidarity must, building on the common bonds between people, and their common concerns (which Communism sought to obscure), restore them to their proper sense, that is, to show their full ethical dimension. In 1993, in another one of his works, *The Unfortunate Gift of Freedom,* Tischner chided people who, dissatisfied with the rapid changes underway, blamed the nation's newly won freedom for the threat of consumerism, abortion, pornography, and other social evils.

Like his teacher and friend, Karol Wojtyła, Tischner is notable as a philosopher and academic who never lost the ability to speak to ordinary people. Many of his nine books were widely read and well received by a broader public.

Bibliography: J. TICHNER, *The Spirit of Solidarity* (Cambridge, Mass 1982). J. TICHNER and J. ŻAKOWSKI, *Tischner czyta Katechizm* (Kraków 1997).

[P. RADZILOWSKI]

TITHES

In Christian usage, the tenth or other part of a person's income that was required by law (ecclesiastical, civil, or both) to be paid to the Church for the maintenance of its institutions, the support of its ministers, the promotion of its works, and the relief of the poor.

Truck carrying notice protesting paying of tithes to British Anglican Church, London, 1936. (©Hulton-Deutsch Collection/CORBIS)

In the Bible. The custom of giving a certain percentage of the harvest annually to the deity or the king was quite widespread in antiquity. Among some peoples, tithes were also levied on the spoils of war (Gn 14.16–20), commercial profits, and other revenues.

Israelite laws on the giving of a tithe (Heb. *ma'śēr,* tenth part) are usually found in the context of various types of offerings to be made to Yahweh. Thus the tithe was basically a religious offering rather than a tax as such, although in 1 Sm 8.15, 17 a warning is given that the king will levy a tithe on grain, vineyards, and cattle—a practice of neighboring kingdoms that is attested by UGARIT texts.

The Biblical origins of the tithe are obscure, and the lack of uniformity in the laws makes it virtually impossible to trace its evolution with accuracy. Two of the oldest laws are silent (Ex 23.19; 34.26), but the custom must have been in use even before the Deuteronomic Code of

the eighth century B.C., for this was primarily a reform of existing laws and customs. In the Deuteronomic Code the tithe is limited to grain, wine, and oil (Dt 12.6, 11, 17; 14.22). These texts more or less equate the tithe with other ritual offerings and sacrifices. At the designated sanctuary a joyful sacred banquet was prepared from these gifts and shared with the Levite of the suppressed local sanctuaries (12.18–19). However, if the distance was too great, tithes could be sold locally and the money used to purchase banquet supplies at the central sanctuary (14.24–27). Every three years the tithes were given directly to the local LEVITES as additional compensation (14.28–29). Even then the tithes retained their sacred character, for the worshiper was to appear at the sanctuary and make the declaration prescribed in Dt 26.12–15.

The Priestly Code of postexilic times extends the tithe to the fruit of trees, herds, and flocks, but permits it to be redeemed (Lv 27.30–32; (see also 2 Chr 31.5–6). However, only a tithe of grain, wine, and oil is mentioned in Neh 10.39; 13.12. In Nm 18.21–32 the tithe becomes a sort of tax for the benefit of the Levites, but they, in turn, must give to the priests a tithe of the tithes (v. 26; see also Neh 10.38; 12.44), that is to be regarded as an offering of first fruits to Yahweh (Nm 18.27–29). Nehemiah 10.38–39 permits the Levites themselves, under the supervision of a priest, to collect the tithes. Despite the Chronicler's idealistic picture (2 Chr 31.5–6, 12), the people did not always bring in full tithes (Mal 3.7–10; Neh 13.10–14; Sir 35.8). The tithe continued to be paid (Jdt 11.3; 1 Mc 3.49), but later interpretation of the laws led to a triple tithe (Tb 1.6–8). The scrupulosity of the Pharisees in paying tithes (Mt 23.23; Lk 11.42) often led to vain boasting (Lk 18.12). No law of tithing is found in the New Testament, although the principle of Church support is laid down in Mt 10.10 (see also Lk 10.7) and echoed in 1 Cor 9.13–14.

In the Early Church. The early Church had no tithing system. The tithes of the Old Testament were regarded as abrogated by the law of Christ. It was not that the need to support the Church did not exist or was not recognized, but rather that other means appeared to suffice. Irenaeus and Origen spoke rather disparagingly of the institution of tithes as though there was something mean in it and unworthy of the generosity of Christians. As the Church expanded, however, and its material needs grew more numerous and complex, it became necessary to adopt a definite rule to which people could he held either by a sense of moral obligation or by a precept of positive law. The tithing of the Old Law provided an obvious model, and it began to be taught—more commonly in the West, however, than in the East—that the faithful should give tithes of their income.

When this view began to get sufficient support, it found legislative expression. The Council of Mâcon in 585 ordered payment of tithes and threatened excommunication to those who refused to comply. Other local councils made similar enactments, but their repetition and the warnings of penalties to be imposed upon delinquents suggest that the tithes were paid with some irregularity and reluctance. One of the capitularies of Charlemagne toward the end of the eighth century made the payment of tithes obligatory under civil law. In earlier practice, tithes were paid simply of the fruits of the earth (praedial tithes), but toward the 13th century they were extended to certain other kinds of profits and wages, and precise rules were elaborated for the determination of what was tithable and what was not, the conditions of exemption, etc. The Council of Trent declared that the payment of tithes was due to God, and that those who refused to pay them were to be excommunicated and were not to be absolved until full restitution had been made (Sess. 25.12). Nevertheless, as a general practice of the Church

in Europe, the institution was not destined to continue long. In the secularization of the state that followed the Reformation and the attendant circumstances of social and economic change, the system as it was known in earlier times became unworkable. The French Revolution brought tithing as a general method of Church support to an end. In the present law of the Church there remains no commonly applicable provision for tithes, although canon 1502 of the Code declares that particular laws or customs existing in some areas with regard to the payment of tithes were to be observed.

In the United States. In the U. S. no tithing system was ever generally employed except in the North Central and Mississippi Valley area where it was introduced by the Frehch and continued to be observed under English rule according to the provision of the Quebec Act. It was brought to an end when these lands were acquired by the U. S.

The Church in the U. S. has been supported in the main by voluntary contributions. In the early 19th century there was a disposition on the part of some to urge and enforce the obligation in conscience of the faithful to contribute to the Church by the imposition of certain ecclesiastical penalties. The First Synod of Baltimore considered those who failed to contribute to be unworthy of the Sacraments. The intervention of the Congregation for the Propagation of the Faith mitigated this severity. Instead of a compulsory method of Church support, the spirit of free-will offerings was advocated [May 13, 1816, pub. in Collect. of Congregation for the Propagation of the Faith (Rome 1907) n. 713 ad 2]. A decree of the Third Plenary Council of Baltimore reflected this attitude (Acta, 292).

Bibliography: G. LEPOINTE, *Dictionnaire de droit canonique*, ed. R. NAZ (Paris 1935–65) 4:1231–44. M. N. KREMER, *Church Support in the United States* (Catholic University of America Canon Law Studies 61; Washington 1930). C. PIONTEK, "Pennies Collections and Other Free-Will Offerings in the Code of Canon Law," *American Ecclesiastical Review* 109 (1943) 190–199, 272–279, 358–365. J. SELINGER, "Church Revenue by Assessment," *ibid.* 60 (1919) 439–441. F. J. CONNELL, "The Obligation of Paying Tithes," *ibid.* 146 (1962) 346–350. J. A. MACCULLOCH, *Encyclopedia of Religion and Ethics*, ed. J. HASTINGS (Edinburgh 1908–27) 12:347–350.

[P. K. MEAGHER/D. DIETLEIN]

TITULAR BISHOP

Formerly called *episcopus in partibus infidelium,* is a prelate invested with the episcopal character who has been given title to a see that no longer exists. After the 12th century when entire regions fell under the rule of the Turks, the Holy See continued to nominate bishops to

Latin sees in which the bishops were unable to govern or to reside. Many of these bishops undertook to assist other prelates in the government of large dioceses or in the exercise of pontifical functions and also to substitute for the bishops when these were absent from their dioceses. The assisting bishops were known as *vicarii in pontificalibus.* They also came to be known as bishops *in partibus infidelium.*

Since the 16th century bishops have been assigned also to sees that had long been suppressed. The reason given for this is that the abuse of appointing bishops without any determined title or see had to be corrected.

An encyclical letter of the Congregation of Propaganda, March 3, 1882, abolished the expression *in partibus infidelium* and substituted "titular see" and "titular bishop."

Many of the prelates of the Roman Curia—e.g., nuncios and apostolic delegates—are titular archbishops and bishops.

Titular bishops may be appointed by the pope as auxiliaries and coadjutors to diocesan archbishops and bishops or as an honor for distinguished service.

Since a titular bishop has received episcopal consecration, he validly exercises all the functions that by divine or ecclesiastical law belong to the episcopal order. He cannot exercise any jurisdiction in the diocese of his title.

Bibliography: F. J. MCELROY, *The Privileges of Bishops* (Washington 1951). J. ABBO and J. HANNAN, *The Sacred Canons,* 2 v. 2d ed. (St. Louis 1960) 1:348–349.

[F. J. WINSLOW]

TITULAR SEE

Is conferred on a prelate by way of title only, no concomitant jurisdiction being given in the respective diocese. In the early centuries of the Church, and in some cases well into the Middle Ages, these dioceses were flourishing residential sees; but later, ravaged by schism, persecution, and invasion, they had to be abandoned and became known as dioceses *in partibus infidelium.* In order to conserve the memory of these ancient sees the practice was begun, at the time of the Fifth Lateran Council (1512–17), in the pontificate of Leo X, of conferring them titularly on cardinals of the Roman Curia who would request the privilege. Later the custom evolved, as it exists today, of conferring these titles on certain bishops who are not diocesan bishops (e.g., auxiliary bishops and bishops attached to the Roman Curia). In the latter part of the 19th century, being informed that the designa-

tion *in partibus infidelium* had become offensive to the governments of some of the lands in which these sees were located, the Holy See, by a decree of 1882, changed it to "titular sees." The *Annuario Pontificio* of 2000 lists more than 1,500 such sees, located principally in ancient Asia Minor, Palestine, Syria, and Africa.

Bibliography: F. CLAEYS-BOUUAERT, *Dictionnaire de droit canonique,* ed. R. NAZ, 7 v. (Paris 1935–65) 5:574–575. *Annuario Pontificio* (Rome 1912–) (1964) 501–707, 1553–54.

[I. FOLEY]

TITUS, ST.

Gentile Christian of the apostolic Church, companion and helper of St. Paul, and recipient of one of St. Paul's epistles. Although Titus is not mentioned in Acts, Paul's epistles supply much information concerning him. When he went with Paul to Jerusalem *c.* A.D. 50, Paul did not feel compelled to circumcise him (Gal 2.1, 3), as he did TIMOTHY (Acts 16.1–3), since Titus was born of Gentile parents. Replacing Timothy at Corinth, Titus restored obedience, reconciled the Corinthians to Paul (2 Cor 7.15), and began the collection for Jerusalem (2 Cor 8.6). He went with Paul to Crete and was left there to organize the Church (Ti 1.5). Later Paul called him to Nicopolis (Ti 3.12) and sent him to Dalmatia (2 Tm 4.10). Tradition says Titus later lived in Crete and died there at the age of 93. His remains were transferred from Gortyna to St. Mark's, Venice. Titus was a decisive, efficient, zealous, yet kindly man whom Paul sent to trouble spots. The warmth shown by Paul in his letters to Timothy is lacking in that to Titus, but a greater trust in Titus's competence is clear.

Feast: Feb. 6.

Bibliography: C. SPICQ, *Saint Paul: Les Épîtres pastorales* (*Études bibliques*; 1947), xxxvi–xxxviii.

[R. G. BOUCHER]

TITUS OF BOSTRA

Fourth-century bishop of Bostra, Arabia; fl. *c.* 362 to 378. Titus is known mainly from a letter of JULIAN THE APOSTATE (362; *Ep.* 52) urging the people to expel their bishop from Bostra; he signed the HOMOOUSIAN formula in the Synod of Antioch under Meletius in 363. Jerome says he died during the reign of Valens (363–378; *De vir. ill.* 102) and praises his four books *Against the Manichees* (Jerome, *Ep.* 70), a work that is mentioned by Theodoret of Cyr (*Patrologia Graeca,* 83:381) and has been preserved in Syriac with portions in Greek (ed. Lagarde, 2d ed. Hanover 1926; *Patrologia Graeca,* 18:1059–1256).

Ruins of the Byzantine church of St. (Ayios) Titus, Gortyna, Crete. (©Michael Nicholson/CORBIS)

Titus argues against the Manichean dualistic teaching (bk. 1) and refutes the notion of an eternal existence for matter and the devil by a consideration of divine providence (bk. 2); defends the Old Testament (bk. 3); and explains the meaning of the New Law (bk. 4). Utilizing the Scripture, and implicitly Plato and the Stoics, Titus attempts an interesting synthesis of Hellenism and Christianity, which he opposes to Oriental dualism. The texts he quotes from Mani, however, are more likely from Mani's disciple Adda, according to Heraclian of Chalcedon (Photius, *Bibl.* cod. 85). Titus's ideas on the Trinity and Incarnation are worthy of consideration. Of his exegesis, only fragments are known through the *catenae,* and remains of a *Homily on Luke* indicate an early Antiochene leaning toward literal interpretation. Syriac fragments of an *On the Epiphany* seem to be his; but the *Homily on Palm Sunday* (*Patrologia Graeca,* 18:1263–78) and the *Parable of the Unjust Judge* (ed. Fronto du Duc, 1624) are not authentic.

Bibliography: J. SICKENBERGER, *Titus von Bostra: Studien zu dessert Lukashomilien* (TU new ser. 6.1; 1901); *Biblische Zeitschrift* 1 (1903) 182–193. R. P. CASEY, *Paulys Realenzyklopädie der klassischen Altertumswissenschaft,* ed. G. WISSOWA et al. (Stuttgart 1893) 6A.2 (1937) 1586–91. J. QUASTEN, *Patrology* (Westminster MD 1950) 3:359–362. B. ALTANER, *Patrology* (New York 1960) 360–361.

[P. CANIVET]

TIXERONT, JOSEPH

Sulpician theologian, educator, patrologist; b. Ennezat, France, March 19, 1856; d. Lyons, Sept. 3, 1925. Having studied theology at the seminary of Lyons, he was ordained there in 1879. Tixeront was trained in historical and theological method under L. DUCHESNE; then taught theology at the seminary from 1884 to 1898, and patrology at the University of Lyons from 1898 till his death. His most important work is his *History of Dogmas in Christian Antiquity* (3 v. 1905–12; English tr. of 5th ed. 192630), in which he traces the development of early Christian religious beliefs and doctrine with historical objectivity. His dissertation, *Les Origines de l'Èglise d'Èdesse et la légende d'Abgar* (1888; English tr. 1934), was followed by: *Vie mondaine et vie chrétienne à la fin du IIe siècle* (1906), *La Vie monastique en Palestine au Ve et VIe siècle* (1911), *Le Sacrement de Pénitence dans l'antiquité chrétienne* (1914), *La Démonstration de la prédication apostolique de St. Irénée* (1916), *Précis de patrologie* (1918), *Mélanges de patrologie et d'histoire des dogmes* (1921), and *L'Ordre et les ordinations* (1924). A conscientious scholar, he contributed immeasurably to the formation of an objective viewpoint in tracing the history of Christian doctrines back to their origins.

Bibliography: C. E. PODECHARD, *Joseph Tixeront* (Lyons 1925).

[F. X. MURPHY]

TLAXCALA, MARTYRS OF, BB.

Also known as Blessed Cristobal (Christopher), Antonio (Anthony), and Juan (John), protomartyrs of the New World; d. *c.* 1527–29 in Tlaxcala (now the Archdiocese of Puebla), MEXICO; beatified May 6, 1990, by John Paul II in the basilica of Our Lady of Guadalupe, Mexico City.

Tlaxcala, which is about sixty-five miles from Mexico City and twenty miles from Puebla, was the fifth diocese established in New Spain, the second in Mexico. The Franciscans evangelized the warrior Tlaxcalans, who were the first to enter a treaty with Hernán Cortés and assist the Spanish *conquistadores*. Although Cortés stood as godfather for four of the leading men of Tlaxcala in 1520, Christianity was not readily accepted by all. The three youths Cristobal, Antonio, and Juan were the first to die in America *in odium fidei*.

Cristobal (b. *c.* 1514, Atlihuetzia near Tlaxcala; d. 1527) He was the principal heir of Acxotécatl, a high-ranking nobleman. Following his baptism, Cristobalito served the Franciscans catechists as interpreter and repeatedly harassed his father to convert. His father reacted by beating his son and burning him over a fire. Cristobal died of his injuries the following morning.

Antonio (b. Tizatlán, *c.* 1516; d. Cuauhtinchán, 1529) Another Tlaxcalan noble and interpreter for the Franciscans, he was the grandson of Xicohténcati and heir to his title and estates. He was clubbed to death for destroying idols in the town of Tepea*c*.

Juan (b. Tizatlán, *c.* 1516; d. Cuauhtinchán, 1529) He was servant to Antonio and died with his master.

In his beatification homily, Pope John Paul II said these martyrs were drawn at a tender age ''to the words and witness of the missionaries and they became helpers, as catechists for other indigenous people. They are sublime and instructive examples of how evangelization is a task of all God's People, excluding no one, not even children.''

Feast: Sept. 23.

Bibliography: Congregatio pro Causis Sanctorum, *Cristobalito, Antonio y Juan: niños mártires de Tlaxcala* (Mexico City 1990). G. DE MENDIETA, *Historia eclesiástica indiana*, ed. J. GARCÍA ICAZBALCETA (Mexico City 1980). T. DE BENAVENTE MOTOLINIA *Historia de los indios de la Nueva España*, ed. E. O'GORMAN (Mexico City 1979), 176–81. *L'Osservatore Romano,* English edition (14 May 1990): 5–6.

[K. I. RABENSTEIN]

TOBIT (TOBIAS), BOOK OF

A deuteroncanonical book of the OT, written originally in Hebrew or ARAMAIC, but wholly extant only in Greek and other versions. This article treats of its title; canonicity; language, texts, and recensions; structure; literary genre and purpose; sources; and time of composition.

Title. In the more ancient Greek manuscripts this work is entitled Τωβίτ or Τωβείτ (Tobit), while later editions give as its title βίβλος λόγων Τωβίτ (Book of the Words of Tobit). The Latin Vulgate title is *Liber Tobiae* (Book of Tobias). This discrepancy is due no doubt to a confusion of the names of father and son in the story itself. The Greek text clearly distinguishes between Tobit (the father) and Tobias (the son), while the Vulgate (incorrectly) calls both Tobias.

Canonicity. St. Jerome did not consider this book inspired (see, e.g., *Patrologia Latina,* 29:23–24). Similar views were expressed by Athanasius, Cyril of Jerusalem, Epiphanius, Gregory of Nazianzus, and Hilary. Other Fathers, however, such as Polycarp, the *Pastor Hermae,* Clement of Alexandria, Origen, Cyprian, Ambrose, and Augustine, cite Tobit without reservation or qualification. The book is also found in the great Greek manuscripts of the 4th century. The first official declaration of canonicity came from the provincial council of Hippo (393). The same view was restated by the councils of Carthage (397 and 419) and has been reaffirmed by the ecumenical councils of Florence (1411), Trent (1546), and Vatican I (1870).

Language, Texts, and Recensions. Until recent years only the Greek text (and translations of it) were available. Scholars had already concluded from their

"The Angel Departing from the Family of Tobias," by Rembrandt Harmensz van Rijn. (©Historical Picture Archive/CORBIS)

study of this text, however, that the original language must have been Semitic. Their conclusion has been confirmed by the discovery at Qumran of both Hebrew and Aramaic fragments of Tobit. It is not yet possible to determine which of these languages is the original, though some scholars give a slight preference to the Aramaic. (See, e.g., J. C. Greenfield, *Journal of the American Oriental Society* 82 [1962], 293.)

The Vulgate version of Tobit is a hasty translation of an Aramaic text (now lost), though Jerome was strongly influenced by the Old Latin version that, like all other known translations, derives from the Greek text. The Greek version itself exists in two rather divergent forms. The more elegant (but less reliable) Received Text is best represented by Codex B and Codex A. The more primitive and presumably better text is found in Codex S. These two types of text can be found, e.g., in Alfred Rahlfs's *Septuaginta*. Verse references in this article are made according to the Greek text.

Structure. The story begins with an account of the trials and virtues of an exiled Jew, Tobit. His exemplary conduct, particularly in his unselfish concern for less-fortunate compatriots, is rewarded by a fortuitous and ri-

diculous twist of fate that leaves him blind and exposes him to the abuse and mockery of his wife and friends.

The scene then changes abruptly to a distant land, where a Jewish maiden named Sara is sorely afflicted by a demon who had successively killed her seven bridegrooms on the first night of their married life. She too is subjected to cruel mockery and ridicule but takes refuge in fervent prayer.

At this point God sends an angel, Raphael, posing as a guide and companion of Tobit's son, Tobias, who has been directed to retrieve some money for his father from a distant land. There Tobias meets Sara, and, under the angel's expert guidance, they are married and the demon is routed. They return to Tobit, whose blindness is cured by a remedy prepared by Raphael. The story ends with a prayer by Tobit, who praises God's strange but wonderful ways and proclaims the divine sovereignty in human history, which assures the eventual glory of Jerusalem.

With exceptional skill and sensitivity the author portrays the drama of two souls who wrestle with the apparent disarray of salvation history, like two "loose ends" seeking the meaning of life. As the plot develops, these two loose threads are deftly woven into the fabric of

God's loving design for His people. This happy conclusion reveals the author's purpose: his story is an illustration of the wisdom of faith.

Literary Genre and Purpose. The Book of Tobit is a good example of sapiential literature. The heroes and heroines are models of piety; the action pauses at times to permit the insertion of sage instructions for the unwary and inexperienced; and the happy outcome is a convincing demonstration of the wisdom of faith. It may best be described therefore as an edifying or didactic story.

The many references to precise locations (Thisbe, Nineveh, Jerusalem, Ecbatana) and to historical personages (Salmanasar V, Sennacherib, Asarhaddon) may appear to indicate an intention to write serious history. It is well to bear in mind, however, that this was the usual ancient manner of providing "realism." Moreover, such references often cause insurmountable difficulties when one attempts to relate them to a consistent outline of history. Thus, for example, the tribe of Nephtali was not deported during the reign of Salmanasar V (1.2), but rather during that of Tiglath-Pileser III; the schism in Israel occurred long before the time of Tobit (in spite of 1.4), and the "two-days journey" from Rages to Ecbatana (5.6) is in fact a trek of some 185 miles.

These considerations, joined with a better knowledge of ancient literary forms and a more tolerant attitude toward a sane and temperate criticism, have caused most scholars to abandon the attempt to defend the historicity of Tobit. They see in it rather a story that, while quite probably reflecting and alluding to plausible historical situations, is in fact created primarily to illustrate a profound and eminently true religious doctrine.

This religious truth is in essence a statement of the ultimate and inevitable vindication of the life of faith as contrasted with a life "prudently" adapted to the demands of a seemingly erratic course of history. Tobit and Sara have committed themselves to a philosophy of faith and, in the beginning, this decision brings them nothing but mockery and reproach. But all the while God is guiding the forces of history behind the façade of Raphael and through the exemplary obedience of Tobias. At the end, it is seen that what had appeared to be a crazy quilt of meaningless episodes was in reality the perfectly consistent pattern of an all-wise God, who rules history with sovereign ease and who grants to His persevering servants a share in the final vision of the triumph of His wisdom.

Such an interpretation of history was particularly appropriate during the postexilic period of the Old Testament, when the Jewish nation was successively bullied and harried by a series of oppressors. Tobit and Sara represent Israel herself, apparently helpless on the senseless wheel of history, whereas God works quietly to bring her to her promised glory. It is in a somber context of discouragement and bewilderment, therefore, that the author sets before his people a story that illustrates the trustworthiness of Israel's ancient faith.

Sources The author of Tobit manifests a rather intimate familiarity with various OT books. His knowledge of the Patriarch stories of Genesis is particularly notable. Many of the religious values that are highlighted there are emphasized in Tobit also: marriage within the tribe (cf. Gn 24.3–4 with Tb 10.12), hospitality (cf. Gn 18.3–8 with Tb 8.19), filial piety (cf. Gn 43.27 with Tb 2.4), chastity (cf. Gn 39.9 with Tob 8.4), and fatherly blessings (cf. Gn 27.27 with Tb 14.11). One may legitimately surmise that this clearly intentional parallel was meant to remind the contemporary Israelites that they, like the Patriarchs, were living on hope, and therefore could scarcely do better than to adopt the Patriarchal virtues and attitudes toward life and history.

Many scholars have also noted points of similarity between Tobit and various non-biblical legends. The biblical author was undoubtedly aware of the Story of Ahikar, who is presented as Tobit's nephew in this book (1.21–22; 2.10; 11.17–18; 14.10, 15), and was influenced by some of the maxims attributed to that famous sage. It is very hazardous, however, to conclude that even such superficial dependence exists in the case of such legends as the Ungrateful Dead or the Poisonous Maiden stories (see R. H. Pfeiffer, *A History of New Testament Times* [New York 1949] 269–271). Such themes are only partially relevant, and they would appear to be too much the patrimony of all mankind to be traceable to any specific source.

Time of Composition. Most authors agree that the Book of Tobit was composed about 200 B.C. The general atmosphere of the narrative (e.g., the prominence of angels and the emphasis on legal prescriptions) suggests a date toward the end of the postexilic period. On the other hand, the absence of any hint of the Maccabean successes would appear to demand a date prior to that period (early 2d century B.C.). It should be remarked, however, that a few scholars, noting the fine "Imperial Aramaic" of the Qumran fragments, have raised the possibility of an earlier (perhaps 4th century) date (see J. Bright, *A History of Israel* [Philadelphia 1959] 417–18).

Bibliography: C. MOORE, *Tobit,* Anchor Bible v. 40A (New York 1996). I. NOWELL, "Tobit," *New Jerome Biblical Commentary* (Englewood Cliffs, N.J. 1990) 568–579. J. FITZMYER, "The Aramaic and Hebrew Fragments of Tobit in Cave 4" *Catholic Biblical Quarterly* 57, 655–675. P. DESELAERS, "Das Buch Tobit," *Orbis Biblicus et Orientalis,* 43 (Freiburg 1982).

[D. DUMM]

Capital: Lomé.
Size: 22,000 sq. miles.
Population: 5,018,500 in 2000.
Languages: French; Ewe and Mina are spoken in the south, Kabye and Dagomba in the north.
Religions: 1,104,070 Catholics (22%), 602,220 Sunni Muslims (12%), 351,295 Protestants (7%), 2,960,915 follow indigenous beliefs or are without religious affiliation.
Archdiocese: Lomé, with suffragans Sokodé, Atakpamé, Aného, Dapaong, Kara, and Kpalimé.

TOGO, THE CATHOLIC CHURCH IN

The Togolese Republic is located in West AFRICA, and borders the Gulf of Guinea at the Bight of Benin on the south, GHANA on the west, BURKINA FASO on the north and BENIN on the east. A tropical, humid, predominantly agricultural country, Togo is characterized by a rolling savanna in the north that rises to hills in the central region before falling to a low, marshy coastal plain at the Bight of Benin. Natural resources include phosphates, limestone and marble, while agricultural products consist of coffee, cocoa, cotton, yams, cassava, corn, beans, rice and millet.

A German protectorate from 1884 until 1919, Togo then fell under French supervision as French Togoland, a mandate of the League of Nations and United Nations trust territory. In April of 1960 it gained its independence. In 1967 a bloodless military coup gained power, positioning General Gnassingbe Eyadema as president. The government continued to control the country through 2000 despite the legalization of political parties in a new constitution drafted in September of 1992 and rioting during the 1998 election. Charges of military harassment of opposition leaders surfaced, clouding Eyadema' supposed ''democratic victory.'' Most of the country's labor force was employed in agriculture, and efforts to reform the economy that began in 1990 had slowed by mid-decade due to political unrest and the drain on government coffers due to its need to fund a strong military in order to stay in power. By 2000 the region was again experiencing modest economic growth, although the government was operating in the red, with payments months in arrears.

History. The region was originally inhabited by Voltaic and Kwa peoples, and these were joined by Ewé immigrants in the 14th century and the Mina two centuries later. Danish slave traders controlled the southern coast during the 1700s. Togo received its first Catholic missionaries in 1863, when priests of the AFRICAN MISSIONS SOCIETY (SMA) came from Dahomey (modern Benin) to visit coastal villages. Two priests settled 104 miles inland at Atakpamé in 1886, but their mission was abandoned within a year, after both were twice poisoned, one of them fatally. In 1892 the region—now under German control as Togoland—was separated from the vicariate apostolic of Dahomey and became a prefecture apostolic, entrusted to the Society of the DIVINE WORD (SVD), which by 1914 had sent there 76 priests and 33 brothers, almost all German born. Togo had 19,740 Catholics when it became a vicariate in 1914. When Germany lost its protectorate after losing World War I, the SVD missionaries were gradually deported, along with the HOLY SPIRIT MISSIONARY SISTERS, who had sent 51 members to Togo since 1897. SMA missionaries again took charge. In 1922 the first native priest received ordination. After World War II, when the region fell under French authority, Franciscans, Benedictines and several religious congregations of men and women entered the mission. The hierarchy was established in 1955, with Lomé as metropolitan. Togo established diplomatic relations with the Holy See in 1981.

By 2000 there were 121 parishes in Togo tended by 234 diocesan and 109 religions priests. Other religious included approximately 175 brothers and 590 sisters, who helped run the nation's 454 primary and 38 secondary schools and engaged in an active and vibrant mission. In an effort to establish credibility with the Togolese people, the military government appointed Lomé archbishop Philippe Kpodzro as president of the legislative assembly that drafted Togo's new constitution, which guaranteed religious freedom while establishing no state religion. Kossi Kpodzro was eventually removed from his position after complaints that he used his position to advance the stature of the government; Church leaders more recently refrained from injecting sermons with political statements, and also declined the president's invitation to attend the ecumenical Day of National Liberation festival celebrating the installation of the government in 1967. Togolese bishops were members of the Regional Episcopal Conference of French-speaking West Africa, and Church representatives also served as part of the Togolese Human Rights Commission, which reviewed charges of religious discrimination brought against the government. Islamic-Catholic programs existed, as did the Biblical Alliance, which brought together Catholics and Protestants in discussion of their respective faiths. Many Togolese Catholics attended Mass in addition to maintaining their traditional tribal faith, a situation that the Church viewed with some concern. During his ad limina visit with Togo bishops in 1999, Pope John Paul II commented on the rising divorce rate in Togo, and noted that such ''irregular marital situations . . . do not allow 'people' to receive the sacraments.''

Bibliography: K. MUELLER, Geschichte der katholischen Kirche in Togo (Kaldenkirchen 1958). Bilan du Monde 2:852–855. An-

nuaire des Diocèses d'Expression Française pour l'Afrique . . . et Madagascar (Paris 1955—). *Annuario Pontificio* (1964) 244, 422–423, 775.

[R. M. WILTGEN/EDS.]

TOLEDO, COUNCILS OF

Eighteen national councils were celebrated in Spain between 400 and 702 that are collectively called the Councils of Toledo. Although local and peculiar to Spain, they were designated as general or universal councils; and as Perez de Urbel has indicated, several were purely provincial synods. Toledo III (589) specified that provincial synods be held every year, but there is no record that this rule was carried out with regularity. The *acta* of the last council in 702 have not been preserved.

Unique in their composition, these Visigothic councils were fundamentally an assembly of the bishops for ecclesiastical legislative purposes, but they dealt also with political and civil matters of the kingdom, and the later ones were attended by the princes and functioned as supreme tribunal for civil and juridical as well as ecclesiastical and liturgical affairs.

Councils I to III. At Toledo I (*c.* 400), 18 bishops under the presidency of Patronus (Patruinus), Archbishop of Toledo, considered the scandalous diversity of opinion among the bishops on the subject of ordinations in the light of the regulations of the Council of NICAEA. Several canons (1, 3, 4, 6, 9, 16, 19) concerned the evolution of the concept of celibacy and chastity in the Church. The order of penitence is an obstacle to entering the clergy (c.2). Those who have fought in war are excluded from major orders (c.8). Marriage with a woman of inferior condition (concubinage) is only forbidden to the Christian already married (c.17). The council condemned PRISCILLIANISM and concluded its deliberations with 18 anathemas. It made decisions relative to the reconciliation of bishops, priests, or clerics guilty of Priscillianism.

Toledo II (*c.* 527 or 531), under the Metropolitan Montanus, brought together an unknown number of bishops, probably five from the province and one from outside it. The question of the number of bishops present is complicated by the fact that the absent ones later signed the acts of the council. The first three canons concern the education of clerics, their fidelity to their bishops, and the obligation of celibacy. Canon 4 assures clerics of the lifetime tenure of the land and crops that they cultivated. The last forbids consanguinous marriage. Two letters of Bishop Montanus relative to the consecration of Holy Oil as reserved to the bishop are annexed to the acts of the council.

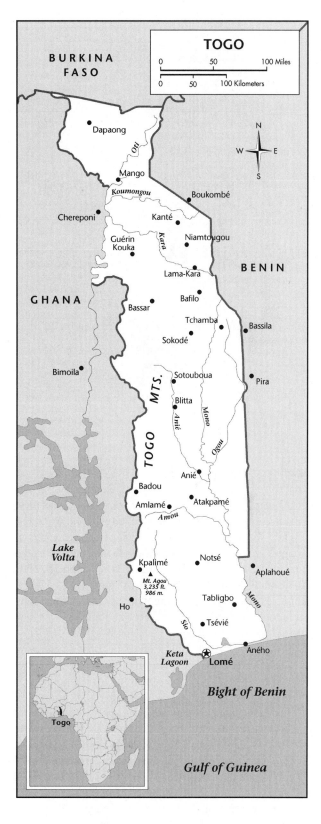

Toledo III (589) was preceded by two other synodal assemblies. In 582 the Arian King Leovigild had convoked a council of Arian bishops, which decreed that

Manuscript illumination of the Council of Toledo during Visigothic Rule. (©Archivo Iconografico, S.A./CORBIS)

Catholics becoming Arians need not be rebaptized and made use of the formula "Glory to the Father by the Son, in the Holy Spirit." Evidence of this Arian synod was given by various members reconciled with the Church at Toledo III. In 587, likewise, the Arian King Reccared arranged a conference between Catholic and Arian bishops at Toledo, evidently in preparation for Toledo III. Here the Catholics stressed the nature of saintliness, of which miracles are the proof, but this evidence proved unacceptable to the Arians. However, Reccared himself was converted and received into the Church by his uncle St. LEANDER OF SEVILLE. This made Toledo III of great importance in the religious and political life of Spain, for the King's conversion occasioned the reconciliation of a number of Arian bishops. A detailed verbal account of the council indicates that the King read a profession of faith including the procession of the Holy Spirit *a patre FILIOQUE*. He exhorted the people to convert with him and reminded the bishops of their duty to instruct the people. He anathematized Arius; recognized the Councils of Nicaea, Constantinople, Ephesus, and Chalcedon; and recognized the professions of faith of Nicaea, Constantinople I, and Chalcedon. The bishops drew up 23 anathemas and 22 disciplinary canons. A 23d anathema was added by the Arian bishops as a collective subscript. The King proposed the usage of recitation of the symbol or

creed to affirm orthodox faith (c.2). The remainder of the canons concerned mainly temporal administration, the lives and celibacy of clerics, the profession of chastity of widows or virgins, and dispositions relative to Jews. The council invited the clergy and civil magistrates to unite in abolishing certain abuses and accused some bishops of cruel treatment of clerics. It eliminated certain funeral practices and forbade improper dances and songs on feast days. Canon 18 prescribed an annual provincial council.

Councils IV to VI. Toledo IV (633), preceded by a synod in 597 and a provincial council in 610, was convoked by Sisenand, successor of Suintila, under (St.) ISIDORE OF SEVILLE with 62 bishops of Spain and the area of Gaul Narbonensis. Seventy-five canons were promulgated, along with 75 disciplinary chapters that are of importance for liturgy and the ecclesiastical discipline of monks. All had bad political significance. The Acts bears the signatures of six metropolitans, among them Isidore of Seville and Julian of Braga. Fifty-six bishops and seven representatives of bishops signed after them. A number of the canons concerned the admission of clerics to orders. The council equally insisted on penitential fasting and proposed principles of monastic discipline. Several canons concerned the temporal administration of churches, and a number of liturgical points were covered, including the ceremonial for the opening of councils, contained in canon 4.

At Toledo V (636), 22 bishops and two proxies met under the presidency of Eugene I, the new archbishop of Toledo. Except for canon 1, which dealt with the date of the Rogation procession (Dec. 14), the other seven canons were political in bearing. The decrees of the council were approved and published by King Chintila in his ordinance of June 30, 636.

Toledo VI (638) was convoked by King Chintila, brother of Sisenand; 52 bishops with four metropolitans-Julian of Braga, Eugenius of Toledo, Honorius of Seville, and Selva of Narbonne, who presided—promulgated 18 canons, of which the first is a new profession of faith, an amplification of that of Toledo IV. The other canons are ecclesiastical or politico-religious. Royal authority was strengthened, and Jews were excluded from the civil life of the country. Several canons concerned with public penitence completed and made precise the dispositions of Toledo IV.

Councils VII to IX. Toledo VII (646) consisted of 24 bishops with the metropolitans of Mérida, Seville, Toledo, and Tarragona, who met to remedy the troubles of the Church and State. The preface of the conciliar collections should be attached to canon 1, whose object, it explains, is to punish perturbators of national peace and protect against similar troubles. Canons 2 to 5 concern points of discipline or liturgy. The last canon is a homage of the clergy rendered to the King of Spain.

Toledo VIII (653) was convoked by King Recceswintn, who succeeded his father Chindaswintn in 652. The metropolitans of Merida, Seville, Toledo, and Braga were present, along with 48 bishops, a large number of abbots, representatives of bishops, and 16 counts and dukes. The *Tomus regius,* or book of royal edicts, around which discussion centered, demanded a revision of canon 75 of Toledo IV. Canons 4 to 7 concerned the continence of clerics, their instruction (c.8), and their fasting (c.9).

At Toledo IX (655), Eugene II of Toledo presided over 15 bishops and six abbots, and added to the conciliar collection 17 canons concerning the administration of ecclesiastical goods and serfs. Canon 10 listed penalties for incontinent clerics.

Councils X to XII. Toledo X (656) was a gathering of 20 bishops and five representatives of bishops, in the presence of the three metropolitans—Eugene II of Toledo, Fugitivus of Seville, and Fructuosus of Braga. They promulgated seven canons. Canon 1 fixed the celebration of the feast of the ANNUNCIATION eight days before Christmas. The other six canons concerned discipline; canons 2 and 7 were concerned with the civil organization of Spain.

Toledo XI (675) was convoked by King Wamba, successor of Recceswintn. The metropolitan Quiricius presided, and 17 bishops, two representatives for absent bishops, and six abbots made a famous profession of faith. Of the 16 disciplinary canons that repeated previous ones, canons 11 and 12 are notable: canon 11 concerned communion of the sick; canon 12, public penitence.

Toledo XII (681) declared legitimate the succession of Erwig to the Spanish throne and enacted 13 *capitula.* The archbishop of Toledo was given the power to install candidates he deemed worthy in vacant bishoprics in any province, but after royal designation. Legislation against Jews was reinforced.

Councils XIII to XV. Toledo XIII (683) was a *concilium mixtum,* or political assembly, as well as a council, including 48 bishops and archbishops, 27 representatives of absent bishops, abbots, and 26 nobles. The primacy of Toledo was confirmed (c.9). Most of the canons were political in object.

At Toledo XIV (684), JULIAN OF TOLEDO presided over 17 bishops, vicars of the metropolitans of five provinces, six abbots, and two representatives of suffragan (auxiliary) bishops of Toledo. They met to sign the decrees of the Council of CONSTANTINOPLE III against MONOTHELITISM.

Toledo XV (688) was convoked by Egica, successor of Erwig. The assembly of 61 bishops, several abbots, representatives of absent bishops, and 17 nobles considered the *Tomus regius* and was concerned with problems of personal conscience. A ruling was passed on Spanish orthodoxy in a dogmatic difficulty raised by Pope BENEDICT II and answered by Julian of Toledo, whose responses had been confirmed by Pope SERGIUS I in 687.

Councils XVI to XVIII. Toledo XVI (693) resulted when Julian of Toledo died in 690 and was succeeded by the Abbot Sisebert, who conspired against the throne and was seized and brought before a gathering comprised of 59 bishops, five abbots, three representatives of absent bishops, and 16 counts. The King presented a *Tomus* concerned with spreading the orthodox faith, points of discipline, care of country churches, the destruction of pagan superstitions and Judaism, and a letter for the punishment of Sisebert. The ignorance of the clergy and the chaotic state of Spain at the time is evident. Sisebert was deposed, excommunicated, and exiled. Felix, Archbishop of Seville, was transferred to Toledo.

Toledo XVII (694) was occasioned by a conjuration of Spanish Jews who had received Baptism hypocritically. The council comprised many bishops and nobles of the kingdom, the names of whom are lost. Canon 1 is a timid reaction against the invasion of the councils by the laity; previously the first three days of a council had been reserved for questions of faith and ecclesiastical discipline. Canons 2 to 6 ruled on points of liturgy. Canon 7 renewed ancient laws concerning the surety of the royal family. Canon 8 considered the repression of a Jewish plot.

Toledo XVIII (702) was held under King Witiza and Gonderic, Archbishop of Toledo. The Acts of the council are lost.

Bibliography: C. J. VON HEFELE, *Histoire des conciles d'après les documents originaux,* tr. and continued by H. LECLERQ (Paris 1907–38) v.3.2. R. D'ABADAL I VINYALS, "Els concils de Toledo," *Homenaje a Johannes Vinke* (Madrid 1962–63). M. TORRES, in *Historia de Espanña,* ed. R. MENÉNDEZ PIDAL, v.3 (Madrid 1940) 265–325. Z. GARCÍA VILLADA, *Historia eclesiástica de España,* 3 v. in 5 (Madrid 1929–36). T. ANDRÉS MARCOS, *Constitución, transición y ejercicio de la monarquía hispano-visigoda en los Concilios Toledanos* (Salamanca 1928). A. K. ZIEGLER, *Church and State in Visigothic Spain* (Washington 1930). A. MICHEL, *Dictionnaire de théologie catholique,* ed. A. VACANT et al (Paris 1903–50) 15.1:1176–90. P. D. KING, *Law and Society in the Visigothic Kingdom* (Cambridge 1972).

[I. E. ALBERCA]

TOLEDO, FRANCISCO DE

First Jesuit cardinal; b. Córdoba, Spain, Oct. 4, 1532; d. Rome, Sept. 14, 1596. After his philosophical studies

Francisco de Toledo.

at Valentia, he studied theology at Salamanca. He was ordained in 1558 and entered the Society of Jesus the same year. Called to Rome by Jesuit General Francis Borgia in 1559, he taught philosophy at the Roman College until 1563, and then theology. In 1569, Pius V appointed him preacher at the papal court, an office he held for 24 years. During his years at the Roman College, De Toledo wrote many works on philosophy, Scripture, and theology, most significant among which was his *In summam theologiae S. Thomae Aquinatis enarratio* (4 v. Rome 1869–70). An independent thinker, he opposed many of Cajetan's interpretations of Thomas Aquinas and was the first at the Roman College to teach predestination in view of foreseen merits. Highly esteemed by successive popes for his learning and diplomatic resourcefulness, De Toledo was sent on many papal missions, most important of which was to Louvain (1580) to promulgate the bull of Gregory XIII, *Provisionis nostrae,* concerning the errors of Baius (*see* BAIUS AND BAIANISM). Through De Toledo, Henry IV made his reconciliation with the Church, and at Henry's request Clement VIII made him a cardinal (Sept. 17, 1593). In his last years he played an important role in the revision of the Vulgate.

Bibliography: A. ASTRAIN, *Historia de la Compañia de Jesús,* 7 v. (Madrid 1902–25) 2:64–65; 3:595–604; 4:56–59. L. KOCH, *Jesuiten-Lexikon: Die Gesellschaft Jesu einst und jetzt* (Paderborn 1934); photoduplicated with rev. and suppl., 2 v. (Louvain-Heverlee 1962) 1761–62. C. SOMMERVOGEL, *Bibliotèque de la Compagnie de Jésus,* 11 v. (Brussels-Paris 1890–1932) 8:64–82.

[G. VAN ACKEREN]

TOLERANCE

Generally, tolerance means allowing, without intending either to approve or encourage, what one holds to be an evil or a questionable good. It implies at least interior reprobation of the evil and a refusal to use force to repress it. Tolerance therefore should be distinguished from indifference, which permits something merely because it is thought unimportant. Tolerance, however, is often used in a more positive, maximal sense to refer to respect, sympathy, and charity for persons holding views different from one's own.

We commonly speak of two types of tolerance, doctrinal (dogmatic) and personal (practical). Doctrinal tolerance is the permitting of error to be spread unopposed. Practiced systematically, this would be reprehensible because it becomes equivalent to INDIFFERENTISM or RELATIVISM. Truth is a primary human value, to be cherished and protected. We cannot, then, accept error on a par with truth or allow it to be propagated unchallenged. Instead, we must combat it while maintaining an unflagging love for its proponents. Personal tolerance is the permitting of others to hold and put into practice views that diverge from one's own. A crucial case concerns the toleration of different religions by the state: how and to what extent can it be justified?

Some ways of vindicating it are unsound. Indifferentists defend it on the grounds that one religion is as good as any other; but while every man may save his soul by following his conscience, obviously the Church founded by God for this purpose can help us attain our end more surely and easily than any other. Relativists hold that every religion uncovers a different aspect of the truth, and that they are all necessary, therefore, for the possessing of truth in its fulness. Although every religion mirrors the truth to some degree, we cannot say that each one has a different parcel of it; moreover, the most full and adequate possession of it is necessarily to be found in the Church established by God as a vehicle for His revelation.

Catholics are divided in regard to personal tolerance. Some maintain the more conservative "thesis-hypothesis" theory. The "thesis" refers to the ideal: a state in which all or a large majority of the citizens are Catholic and Catholicism is the official, privileged religion; in harmonious cooperation Church and State help each other attain their respective ends; hence, to maintain the one true faith, the disruption of which would be a serious spiritual evil and detrimental also to civil life, the state must not ordinarily tolerate heretical teachings. Under the "hypothesis" that there is not a Catholic majority, a state may licitly tolerate a variety of beliefs to preserve peace.

The more liberal position is that it is not tolerance, but religious liberty for everyone that should be accepted as a matter of principle by every state, for religious liberty is a natural right that is violated by mere tolerance. It is required by the very nature of the act of faith as a personal and free commitment, which would be contravened by any direct or indirect pressure brought against it. The ends and the functions of the state are limited to the temporal order and cannot validly be extended into the spiritual. We also know from past experience that ecclesiastical reliance on the secular arm inevitably tends to bring about regrettable excesses and situations.

Vatican Council II gave the theory and practice of tolerance a meaning quite different from that of the formerly common Catholic position. In its *Declaration on Religious Freedom,* the Council explicitly acknowledged it to be a natural right that as rational and free agents all men should be able to respond, freely and responsibly, to the truth as each perceives it (*Dignitatis humanae* 2–4).

The implication is that tolerance is not the issue so much as fellowship: in fraternal dialogue, all should seek to understand and learn from each other. In a polarized society tolerance may be the minimal safeguard against injustice, but such is not the ideal or the norm. Instead of merely tolerating each other, religious groups should have remorse over their divisions and accept one another with respect and affection. The function of the State is not to *tolerate* any Church but to guarantee the full freedom of all within the requirements of the common good (cf. ibid. 6).

See Also: CHURCH AND STATE; FREEDOM OF RELIGION; FREEDOM, SPIRITUAL.

Bibliography: A. VERMEERSCH, *Tolerance,* tr. W. H. PAGE (New York 1913). LEO XIII, "Immortale Dei" (Encyclical, Nov. 1, 1885) *Acta Sanctorum* 18 (1885) 161–180, Eng. *Catholic Mind* 34 (Nov. 8, 1936) 425–429. J. A. RYAN and F. J. BOLAND, *Catholic Principles of Politics* (New York 1940). PIUS XII, "Ci riesce" (Address, Dec. 6, 1953) *Acta Apostolicae Sedis* 45 (1953) 794–802, Eng. *Catholic Mind* 52 (April 1954) 244–251. *Tolerance and the Catholic: A Symposium,* tr. G. LAMB (New York 1955). J. MARITAIN, *Truth and Human Fellowship* (Princeton, N.J. 1957). A. F. CARRILLO DE ALBORNOZ, *Roman Catholicism and Religious Liberty* (Geneva 1959). R. J. REGAN, *American Pluralism and the Catholic Conscience* (New York 1963). P. RIGA, *Catholic Thought in Crisis* (Milwaukee 1963).

[G. J. DALCOURT]

TOLERATION ACTS OF 1639 AND 1649, MARYLAND

These legal enactments played a major role in the story of religious liberty in America. The 1639 act passed beyond even the contributions of George and Cecil CALVERT, the Catholic founders of MARYLAND, in the breadth of its provision for religious toleration.

Acts of 1639. The Maryland ordinance of 1639, which included the Toleration Act of that year, grew out of a controversy between Cecil Calvert, the second Lord Baltimore and proprietor of Maryland, and the Maryland assembly. The Maryland Charter, fashioned by his father, George, had been a preamble that looked to a more precise set of laws to govern affairs in the colony. The ordinance of 1639, with its toleration and other acts, marked the first complete step in this direction, the assembly prevailing over Lord Baltimore in taking it.

Very early in the planning and settling of Maryland the proprietor and his assemblymen interpreted the charter to mean that they were free from the laws that governed Englishmen through Parliament. Among these were statute laws, many of which were hostile to Catholics and others dissenting from the Established Church of England because they required profession of belief and Anglican ritual. By what were known as the Privileges of Durham, awarded directly by the king to the colonizing proprietor himself, Maryland was freed from such statute laws and was bound only by those that the colonial assembly specifically accepted. Yet as Englishmen they must be under certain other laws that the colonists together with the proprietor judged suitable.

There was disagreement over what these laws should be and who should initiate them. Lord Baltimore sent a code of laws to the colony when he learned that the assembly had independently initiated legislation for basic laws. Efforts at compromise in the Baltimore code failed. The assembly finally formulated its own ordinance of 1639, in which were found acts of toleration.

Holy Church, said one such act, "shall have all her rights and liberties." Although sectarianism divided the Church at this time, the term in current language included all of its divisions as being of the "Christian religion" to which the charter referred. Toleration would thus be assured to the protected Church or Christian religion and its adherents.

Another ordinance passage carried toleration further. An Act for the Rights of the People guaranteed that "the inhabitants of this province shall have all the rights and liberties according to the Great Charter." In the contemporary discussion by Catholics and other dissenters of the early 17th century the Englishman's liberties included freedom of religion regardless of any lack of connection with a church. Non-Christians could thus hope for equality before the law. Reference to being a Christian had been proposed by Baltimore, but was eliminated from the act.

One further guarantee was given to religious freedom by the assembly. It refused to legislate against blasphemy, sorcery, sacrilege, etc., though such laws were common practice at this time, particularly in New England. Baltimore's code had proposed similar laws, but they were rejected by the assembly's committee. The state was thus confined in the exercise of its authority in a spirit of separation of civil and religious authorities.

All these meanings of the Toleration Acts of 1639 are clear from sources other than the enactment itself. Comparison with the rejected code of Baltimore substantiates the intent of the assemblymen. They were dominantly Catholic, and many were of the educated gentry. Their thinking on Church-State relationship is to be understood against the distinctive theoretical development among English Catholics rather than among Spaniards. The oath controversy with James I and a remonstrance of grievances sent by the laity to Rome reveal that English Catholics were rejecting the prevailing theory of a confessional state. A pamphlet, *Objections Answered,* applied these emerging concepts of religious freedom and separation of Church and State specifically to the Maryland colonial enterprise in justification of its liberal practices.

It appears that the assemblymen had greater liberty than Cecil Calvert in pursuing this ideal. Lord Baltimore was somewhat confined to the legal formulations of England in his code. In the 1640s and 1650s, he was in conflict with the Puritans both in Maryland and in England. It was out of this situation that he tried to salvage at least a minimum of the freedom established before this time. The Toleration Act of 1649 was the chief outcome of his efforts in this situation.

Act of 1649. Contrary to what is generally written, this legislation was not the high point in religious liberty in Maryland but a decline from the acts of 1639. It was likewise less representative of the tradition behind the founding of the colony and its first legislative enactments. It clearly asserted for the first time in Maryland the practice of profession of belief as a condition for enjoying the rights of Englishmen and freedom of conscience. "Whatsoever person," it stated in Puritan fashion, "shall from henceforth . . . deny Our Saviour Jesus Christ to be the Son of God . . . shall be punished . . ." This would seem to bind those who publicly attacked Christian orthodoxy. The vast majority, who were Trinitarian believers, were thus assured that none of them would "from henceforth be in any ways troubled . . . for or in respect of his or her religion. . . ."

The act of 1649 achieved toleration among Christian sects in a way generally unknown in Western civilization except in Rhode Island at this time and Pennsylvania somewhat later. It attained its immediate defensive purpose since it protected Catholics and Protestants who had dissented from the Puritan creed behind Cromwell's Commonwealth. Certain measures passed by the Puritan majority of the Maryland assembly after 1650 were nullified by appeal to the Toleration Act of 1649.

When the Puritan regime fell, however, there was a return to the broader liberty found in the 1639 toleration act. A Jew, Jacob Lumbrozo, was accorded legal protection of law and served in public office. A Catholic priest successfully defended his right to public preaching by appeal to the 1639 ordinance providing for the freedom of the Church. Even more than 100 years after its passage, Marylanders disfranchised for their religious beliefs appealed to the Toleration Act of 1639. By 1700, however, the era of its influence had passed. The Church of England had been established in Maryland, and the colony was put under the statute laws of Parliament.

See Also: CHURCH AND STATE IN THE U.S. LEGAL HISTORY, 1.

Bibliography: M. P. ANDREWS, "Separation of Church and State in Maryland," *American Catholic Historical Review* 21 (Washington 1935–36) 164-176. T. O. HANLEY, *Their Rights and Liberties: The Beginnings of Religious and Political Freedom in Maryland* (Westminster, MD 1959); "Church-State Concepts in the Maryland Ordinance of 1639," *Church History* 26 (Philadelphia 1957) 325–341. *Archives of Maryland,* ed. W. H. BROWNE et al. (Baltimore 1883–). *Calvert Papers,* 3 v. (Maryland Historical Society, Fund Publication 28, 34–35; Baltimore 1889–99).

[T. O. HANLEY]

TOLKIEN, J. R. R.

Novelist; b. England, Jan. 3, 1892; d. Bournemouth, England, Sept. 2, 1972. Tolkien's father died when the boy was very young but his mother, a former missionary to Africa, raised him to love both adventure and words. These two interests form the basis of his extremely popular works of fiction. When John Ronald Reuel Tolkien was 12 his mother died, and since the parents had converted to Catholicism, Tolkien became a ward of a priest in Birmingham.

He graduated from Oxford in 1915 and served in World War I, where he was wounded. Having married, he returned to Oxford for an M.A. and worked on the *Oxford Dictionary.* In 1921 he began teaching at the University of Leeds. His reputation as a teacher developed and he published several scholarly pieces. In 1925 he joined the faculty at Oxford. He continued to write learned articles, among them ''Beowulf, the Monster and the Critics,'' and ''Chaucer as a Philologist.''

He is known best as the author of *The Hobbit* and a half-million word trilogy, *The Lord of the Rings* (*The Fellowship of the Ring, The Two Towers, The Return of the King*). These books sold enormously well in the United Kingdom and the U.S. (250,000 copies of the trilogy were sold in less than a year in the U.S.). Filled with men, dwarfs, hobbits, elves, wizards, and goblins (Orcs), the trilogy is essentially the story of a war pitting ultimate good against ultimate evil. Tolkien vigorously denied that his books were allegories and also insisted that his were not children's books—even after *The Hobbit* won a Herald Tribune prize in the U.S. as the best children's book of the year.

Other Tolkien works include *Tree and Leaf* (which incorporates an essay on the fairy-story genre); *Farmer Giles of Ham,* the fortunes of an unheroic farmer who attempts to capture a dragon; and the verse of *The Adventures of Tom Bombadil.*

Bibliography: R. J. REILLY, ''J.R.R. Tolkien and *The Lord of the Rings,''* in *Romantic Religion* (Athens, Ga. 1971). R. C. WEST, *Tolkien Criticism: An Annotated Checklist* (Kent, Ohio 1970).

[H. J. CARGAS]

J. R. R. Tolkien. (AP/Wide World Photos)

TOLSTOI, LEO NIKOLAEVICH

Russian novelist and moralist; b. Yasnaya Polyana, his estate in the Tula province, Sept. 9, 1828; d. Astapovo, Nov. 20, 1910.

Tolstoi, who was of aristocratic landowning stock, received his early education from French tutors, matriculated at the University of Kazan in 1844, but left in 1847. After some dissipated years in Moscow, he joined the army (1851–57), then traveled abroad, and finally settled (1861) on his estate, where he experimented briefly in education for peasant children along lines similar to those of Rousseau. From then on, he was completely occupied in writing. His earlier works include *Istoriĩa veherashnego dnĩa* (1851, *The Story of Yesterday*), *Detstvo* (1852, *Childhood*), *Dva Gusara* (1856, *Two Hussars*), *Lucerne* (1857), *Tri Smerti* (1858, *Three Deaths*), and *Kholstomer* (1861), all adumbrating the philosophy that was to come to flower in his masterpieces.

Tolstoi recollects in *Ispoved* (1879–82, *My Confession*) that he had from conviction abandoned the Russian Orthodox faith when he was 16. Nevertheless pure reason held him to belief in God, and he even made several unsuccessful efforts to regain his lost faith. He denied Christ's divinity, the claims of Orthodoxy or of any organized religion to be true Christianity, and the immortality of the individual. He rewrote the Gospels according to his own rationalistic standards and founded his own religion, described as Christian naturalism. The Holy Synod finally excommunicated him in 1901.

The chief influences on Tolstoi's intellectual development were ROUSSEAU's belief in the natural goodness of man and the corruptive effects of society, SCHOPENHAUER's pessimism with regard to man's inability to understand the irrational forces in life, and Joseph Marie de MAISTRE's distrust of secular and liberal reform programs. His two cardinal principles, to him the essence of the only true Christianity, were love of one's neighbor and nonresistance to evil. He idealized the simple life of the Russian peasant as an expression of the first, but rejected the authority of the state, which is based on force, as a violation of the second. Thus he was an anarchist and a religious populist. He inveighed against property, oaths, military service, war, and capital punishment. He also condemned contemporary art and literature for lacking popular moral and religious motivation.

Tolstoi is consistently didactic even in his novels. His greatest *Voina i mir* (1867–69, *War and Peace*), re-

Leo Nikolaevich Tolstoi, 1897.

cords the fate of the Russian gentry during the Napoleonic era, but it is also a philosophical argument by example, maintaining that great events, e.g., the battle of Borodino, are caused not by the conscious acts of history's heroes, but by the union of irrational forces and the unconscious acts of ordinary men. His other great novel, *Anna Karenina* (1875–77), contrasts the joys of simple country life with the evils of sophisticated Western society as these are embodied in Anna's illicit love. This novel enunciates Tolstoi's conviction of the unbreakable bond between human happiness and the observance of God's laws.

Bibliography: *Works,* tr. A. and L. MAUDE, 21 v. (Oxford 1928–37). E. J. SIMMONS, *Leo Tolstoy* (Boston 1946). I. BERLIN, *The Hedgehog and the Fox: An Essay on Tolstoy's View of History* (New York 1953). G. STEINER, *Tolstoy or Dostoevsky* (New York 1959).

[W. J. MCBREARTY]

TOMÁS DE SANTA MARÍA

Dominican composer and theorist of the Renaissance, whose treatise on keyboard technique is still of prime value; b. Madrid, *c.* 1510–20; d. Valladolid?, 1570. Fray Tomás obtained a royal printing license in 1557 for his bulky treatise, *Arte de Tañer Fantasía, assi para Tecla como para Vihuela* (Valladolid 1565), but publication was delayed eight years because of a paper shortage. The work, which is divided into two independent parts of 90 and 124 folios, contains more musical examples than any other treatise issued in 16th-century Spain, and reveals that he consulted with numerous "learned and skilled practitioners of the art, especially with the eminent royal musician, Antonio de Cabezón." Although Tomás considered his instructions for playing the *monacordio* (clavichord) merely preliminary to part 1, it is these instructions that have been translated (by E. Harich-Schneider and R. Boadella as *Anmut und Kunst am Klavichord;* Leipzig 1937) and cited in manuals for performing on old keyboard instruments. His method for fingering, graces, and rhythmic variants finds no parallel in his century and is so explicit that many so-called innovations of English virginal technique can now be traced to Spanish practice. Part 2 (ch. 16) included a group of *favordones* (*fabordones*) transcribed by F. Pedrell to show how Vesper Psalms were chanted in accompanied four-part harmony in the 16th century. Although on the title page he promises to teach "the art of playing with imagination, on keyboard instruments as well as *vihuela*" (six-course guitar), Tomás is in his best element when dealing with the keyboard.

Bibliography: F. PEDRELL, ed., *Hispaniae schola musica sacra,* 8 v. (Barcelona 1894–98) v.6. O. KINKELDEY, *Orgel und Klavier in der Musik des 16. Jahrhunderts* (Leipzig 1910). E. HARICH-SCHNEIDER, *The Harpsichord* (St. Louis 1954). E. HARICHSCHNEIDER and R. BOADELLA, "Zum Klavichordspiel bei Tomás de Santa María," *Archiv für Musikforschung* 2 (1937) 243–245. J. DE MARIETA, *Historia Eclesiástica de todos los Santos de España* (Cuenca 1596) pt. 2, fol. 211, no. 102. S. KASTNER, *Die Musik in Geschichte und Gegenwart* 11:1378–79. G. REESE, *Music in the Renaissance* (rev. ed. New York 1959).

[R. STEVENSON]

TOMÁŠEK, FRANTIŠEK

Cardinal, archbishop of Prague; b. June 30, 1899, Studénka, Moravia; d. Aug. 4, 1992, Prague, Czechoslovakia. Tomášek's father was a teacher and director of the local school; he died in 1906 at the age of 40. In order to provide a good education for her six children, his mother moved the family to Olomouc. There Tomášek did his elementary and secondary studies and served a stint in the army during the First World War. He entered the seminary of Olomouc in 1918 and was ordained to the priesthood on July 5, 1922. For the next 27 years he exercised his pastoral ministry in the archdiocese of Olomouc, joining the Cyril-Methodius theological faculty in 1934; he obtained a doctorate from the faculty in 1938.

The Nazi occupation of the country and the closing of all the universities in Moravia and Bohemia interrupted his priestly and teaching activities. At the end of the war in 1945, he was able to resume teaching, and continued to do so until 1950 when the Communist authorities closed the faculty. During these years he published his most important work, the best-selling *Katolicky katechismus*.

On Oct. 12, 1949, Tomášek was elected titular bishop of Buto and appointed auxiliary of Olomouc. His election and consecration were kept secret because of the religious persecution of the Church by the Communist regime. Bishop Tomášek was imprisoned in the concentration camp of Zeliv from 1951 to 1954. After his release, he resumed his pastoral work as a parish priest in Moravaska Huzova. He was the only Czech bishop allowed to go to Rome to participate in the Second Vatican Council. When the Communist authorities sent Archbishop Josef Beran to exile in Rome in 1965, Bishop Tomášek was named apostolic administrator of Prague. He embraced the reforms of the ''Prague Spring'' of 1968, establishing a Movement for Conciliar Renewal; this was repressed when the state suppression of the Church was reasserted following the Soviet invasion later that year.

Pope Paul VI created Tomášek a cardinal in the consistory of 1976, but reserved his name in pectore until June 27, 1977 when his name was published and he received the titular church of SS. Vitale, Gervasio e Protasio. Later that year he was promoted to the metropolitan see of Prague. His cautious approach to the ''Charter 77'' movement that was trying to gain concessions from the government produced dismay among Catholic intellectuals. He later took a firmer stand towards the regime and the dissatisfaction faded.

Cardinal Tomášek participated in the two conclaves of 1978, as well as in four assemblies of the Synod of Bishops. In 1985, he led the Church in Czechoslovakia in the celebration of the 1,100th anniversary of the death of St. Methodius, even as Pope John Paul II issued the encyclical *SLAVORUM APOSTOLI* to celebrate the evangelization of the Slavic nations by Sts. CYRIL AND METHODIUS. He supported the ''Velvet Revolution'' of 1988, insisting on the use of non-violent methods to peacefully oust the Communist government. He hosted Pope John Paul II's visit to Czechoslovakia in 1990; the following year, the pope accepted his resignation of the pastoral government of the archdiocese. He died on Aug. 4, 1992 in Prague and was buried in the crypt of the metropolitan cathedral of St. Vitus.

A letter of Tomasi to a niece, the Princess of Lampedusa.

See Also: CZECH REPUBLIC, THE CATHOLIC CHURCH IN.

[S. MIRANDA]

TOMASI, GIUSEPPE MARIA CAROL, ST.

Cardinal, liturgical scholar, priest of the Clerks Regular of the Theatine; b. Sept. 12, 1649, Alicata, Sicily, Italy; d. Jan. 1, 1713, Rome.

Eldest son of the duke of Palermo; four of his sisters including Ven. Maria Crucifixa (1645–99), became Benedictines. Rather than attaching himself to the Spanish Court as his father desired, he renounced his inheritance, joined the Theatines in Palermo in 1665 and was ordained in 1673.

Delicate health prevented his engaging in the sacred ministry, so he dedicated himself to study at Messina, Ferrara, and Rome. He was fluent in the classical as well as many Oriental languages.

Energetic in research, he drew from the Vallicellian and Vatican Libraries' treasures of unedited works, among them: *Codices Sacramentorum nongentis annis antiquiores* (Rome 1680), containing the Sacramentarium Gelasianum (7th c.), Missale Gothicum, Missale Francorum, Gallicanum Vetus; *Psalterium* (Rome 1683), a comparison of the Gallican and Roman psalters; *Responsalia et Antiphonaria Romanae Ecclesiae* (Rome 1686), manuscripts of the 9th to 12th centuries; *Sacrorum Bibliorum tituli* (Rome 1688); and *Antiqui libri Missarum Romanae Ecclesiae* (Rome 1691), containing the Antiphonary and Lectionary of St. Gregory; *Officium Dominicae Passionis* (Rome 1695), used by Greeks on Good Friday and translated into Latin; *Speculum* (Rome 1679); *Exercitium Fidei, Spei et Caritatis* (Rome 1683); *Breviarium Psalterii* (Rome, 1683); *Vera Norma di Glorificar Dio* (Rome, 1687); *Fermentum* (Rome, 1688); *Psalterium cum canticis* (Rome, 1697); *Indiculus Institutionum Theologicarum Veterurn Patrum* (3 vols., Rome, 1709, 1710; 1712), an exposition of theological theory and practice, derived from original patristic sources.

Tomasi di Lampedusa's profound erudition and critical power are apparent in the introductions and the dissertations he wrote for his editions of manuscripts. His scholarship would lay the groundwork for the science of liturgical studies that enabled the revision of the missal and breviary following Vatican II.

Tomasi was a consultor on many of the Roman Congregations, and on May 19, 1712, was created a cardinal by Clement XI, his friend whom he had encouraged to accept the Chair of Peter.

Beyond his erudition and nobility, Tomasi was a humble man of great charity toward the poor. Many of his works were published under the pseudonym *Carus*. He introduced Gregorian chant and taught in his titular church, S. Martino ai Monti, Rome.

He fell ill on Christmas Eve 1712. Upon his death one week later, he was buried in his titular church. He was beatified by Pius VII, June 5, 1803, and canonized by John Paul II, Oct. 12, 1986.

Pope John Paul II commented that his canonization was timely because of Tomas's "importance in the field of liturgical worship, which he greatly promoted in his life and with his learned writings. . . . The saint whom we proclaim today helps us to understand and bring about this renewal [Second Vatican Council] in its proper sense." Patron of liturgy and liturgists.

Feast: Jan. 3.

Bibliography: P. A. RULLÁN, *Ephemerdies Liturgicae* 72 (1958) 181–98. I. SCICOLONE, *Il cardinale Giuseppe Tomasi di Lampedusa e gli inizi della scienza liturgica* (Rome 1981). *L'Osservatore Romano,* Eng. ed. 42 (1986) 8–9.

[A. BUGNINI/EDS.]

TOMMASO DA CORI, ST.

Baptized Francesco Antonio Placidi; Franciscan priest; b. Cori, Latina, Italy, June 4, 1655; d. Civitella (today Bellegra), Italy, Jan. 11, 1729. After the death of his parents when he was fourteen, Tommaso cared for his sisters and his flock of sheep in the Roman Compagna, while holding silently in his heart a desire to live totally for God through the Franciscan life. Once his sisters were married, he entered the Observant Franciscan novitiate in Holy Trinity Friary at Orvieto (1677), completed his theological studies, and was ordained priest (1683). He spent most of his life (1684–1729) in the friary of Civitella (today Bellegra) hidden among the mountains around Subiaco. Immediately after his ordination, he was assistant novice master at Orvieto, and for a six-year period, he was guardian at Palombara. He established hermitages at Civitella and Palombara. These were individual communities in which the Rule was observed strictly and austerely. He was renowned as a preacher, confessor, and miracle-worker throughout the Subiaco region. His entire life centered around the Eucharist. Although Tommaso was beatified in 1785, the decree for his canonization was not issued until July 2, 1999. He was canonized by John Paul II on Nov. 21, 1999.

Feast: Jan. 19.

Bibliography: *Lettere inedite del B. Tommaso da Cori dei frati minori,* prepared by U. V. BUTTARELLI (Assisi 1993). Vatican Information Service (July 2, 1999). *L'Osservatore Romano,* English edition, no. 47 (November 24, 1999): 2.

[K. I. RABENSTEIN]

TONGERLOO, ABBEY OF

Premonstratensian abbey near Westerloo in the Diocese of Antwerp, Belgium; founded *c.* 1130 by Giselbert of Kasterlee as a daughterhouse of St. Michael's in Antwerp. One of the most famous abbeys of the Netherlands, known for pastoral care and agricultural improvements, it came to minister 59 churches. Its abbot was the first in the Netherlands to receive the miter (late 14th century). It escaped the commendatory system with difficulty in the 15th century but was incorporated into the new Diocese of's Hertogenbosch (1569–90). In 1626 it founded a Premonstratensian college in Rome that lasted until 1812. The BOLLANDISTS published volume seven of the *Acta Sanctorum* (1793) at Tongerloo. When suppressed in 1796 the abbey had 125 canons. The Gothic church and most of the cloister, but not the abbot's residence and the gatehouse, were then demolished. Tongerloo was revived (1835–40) and became an abbey (1868), regaining its former prominence. In 1872 it founded stations in

Manchester, Crowle, and Spalding (England) and in 1896 a mission in Buta, Congo. It founded the priory of Kilnacrott, Ireland (1924), restored the Abbey of Leffe (1931), and took over the priory of Storrington, England (1940). Tongerloo was rebuilt after a fire in 1928.

Bibliography: H. LAMY, *L'Abbaye de Tongerloo depuis sa fondation jusqu'en 1263* (Louvain 1914); "L'Oeuvre des bollandistes à l'abbaye de Tongerloo," *Analecta Praemonstratensia* 2 (1926) 294–306, 379–389; 3 (1927) 61–79, 156–178, 284–312. C. L. HUGO, *S. Ordinis Praemonstratensis annales,* 2 v. (Nancy 1734–36) v.2. N. BACKMUND, *Monasticon Praemonstratense,* 3 v. (Straubing 1949–56).

[N. BACKMUND]

TONGIORGI, SALVATORE

Jesuit philosopher whose works constitute a major contribution to the textbook, or manual, tradition of modern scholasticism; b. Rome, December 25, 1820; d. there, Nov. 12, 1865. He entered the society at 17 and, after completing his own early studies, spent the next five years teaching rhetoric at Reggio and humanities at Forli. Upon completion of his theological studies in 1853, he was assigned a chair in philosophy at the Gregorian University. During this period he wrote his famous textbook, *Institutiones philosophicae* (3 v. Rome 1861–62; 9th ed. Paris 1879), devoted to logic, ontology, cosmology, psychology, and theology. Written explicitly in the spirit of Christian philosophy, this follows the old scholastic traditions in matters not connected with the physics of the day, where the moderns are sympathetically heeded. Tongiorgi rejected the Aristotelian teaching on matter and form as outdated and ordered his treatise in a sequence that departed radically from that of the older scholastics. Following C. WOLFF, for example, he divided ONTOLOGY into general and special parts.

See Also: SCHOLASTICISM.

Bibliography: J. L. PERRIER, *The Revival of Scholastic Philosophy in the Nineteenth Century* (New York 1909). *L'Università Gregoriana del Collegio Romano nel primo secolo dalla restaurazione* (Rome 1930) 188–189. C. SOMMERVOGEL, *Bibliotèque de la Compagnie de Jésus,* 11 v. (Brussels-Paris 1890–1932) 8:96.

[N. J. WELLS]

TONIOLO, GIUSEPPE

Professor of economics and a founder of Christian Democracy in Italy; b. Treviso, March 7, 1845; d. Pisa, Oct. 7, 1918. From 1863 to 1867 he studied at the University of Padua and was deeply influenced by the political economist Angelo Messedaglia. In 1878, the year of his marriage to Maria Schiratti, who bore him seven children, he began to teach at the University of Pisa, where he continued until his death. During his early years in this position he did extensive research on the economic theory and practice of medieval Tuscany. This undoubtedly influenced the evolution of his socioeconomic thought. Among his students was Werner Sombart, the German economic historian.

To promote Christian social ideas, Toniolo established the Unione Cattolica per gli studi sociali (1889), the Società Cattolica per gli studi scientifici (1899), and the journal *Rivista internazionale di scienze sociali e ausiliarie* (1893). Between 1906 and 1909 he headed, at Pius X's request, the Unione Popolare. His reputation as a social thinker rests mainly on *La democrazia cristiana; concetti e indirizzi. . .*(Rome 1900).

The basic premise of Toniolo's theory is the primacy of ethics in the socioeconomic sphere. According to his teachings, the Christian social order rests upon three sets of social institutions: private, civil, and juridical. The private institutions are man, the family, and private property. The civil institutions are the hierarchical class organizations and the territorial associations. For those in industry and commerce, the class organizations take the form of corporations of arts and crafts; for those in agriculture, there are associations of landed proprietors and of farmers and rural workers. The settlement of the classes in specified territorial zones is the task of the territorial associations, from whence are derived communes and other autonomous entities. The juridical institutions are the State and the Church, two societies that are distinct yet harmonious. The separation of Church and State is an aberration that would do great harm to the public welfare. Christian democracy he defined as "that civil order in which all the social, juridical, and economic forces, in the plenitude of their hierarchical development, cooperate proportionally for the common good and in the last analysis to the advantage of the lower classes" ["Il concetto cristiana della democrazia," *Rivista internatzionale di scienze sociali* 14 (July 1897) 330].

Although he never admitted his collaboration, Toniolo probably contributed to Leo XIII's RERUM NOVARUM (1891). His school of thought had achieved considerable importance in the period immediately preceding the encyclical's appearance. Some of the ideas in the encyclical are very similar to those expressed by Toniolo in works published between 1886 and 1889.

Toniolo lived an exemplary life; the cause for his beatification was introduced in 1951.

Bibliography: *Opera omnia,* 19 v. (Vatican City 1947–53). F. VISTALLI, *Giuseppe Toniolo* (Rome 1954).

[E. A. CARRILLO]

16th-century painting by Juan Correa de Vivar depicting Saint Benedict Blessing Saint Maurus; both wear the tonsure of St. Peter.

TONSURE

From the Latin *tondere* (to shear), tonsure referred the rite of cutting the hair by which a layman was admitted to the clerical state. Tonsure was not an order but rather a ceremony of initiation required for the reception of orders. Originally it was not a distinct rite, but was part of the first of the minor orders to be received. In 1972, as part of the reorganization of the minor orders, Pope Paul VI abolished the requirement of tonsure.

History. There is no evidence of a ceremony of tonsure before the 8th century, and then only in Gallican documents. Essentially, the rite of tonsure consisted in the cutting of the hair of the candidate by the officiating prelate and the recitation by the candidate himself of the prescribed form. The ceremony of investing with the surplice, which appeared for the first time in the Pontifical of Durand at the end of the 13th century, is of only secondary importance, but it may never be omitted.

The wearing of the tonsure was an outgrowth of the Eastern custom of cutting the hair of slaves. It was adopted first by the monastic orders and later by the secular clergy for its symbolic value in manifesting the dedication of the cleric to the service of the Church. Until the 9th century there were three types of tonsure. The "crown" tonsure consisted in shaving the entire head except for a small ring of hair encircling the head and was commonly called the tonsure of St. Peter. The second type was prevalent among monks of both East and West

and seems to have been more ancient. It consisted of cutting the hair close, and was called the tonsure of St. Paul. Among the Celts the so-called tonsure of St. John was in vogue, whereby only the front of the head, from ear to ear, was shaven; the hair on the remainder of the head was allowed to grow long. This third type occasioned harsh discussions and was called in Rome the "tonsure of Simon Magus." None of these forms, however, can actually lay claim to apostolic origin. Among Gallican clerics there developed rather early in the Middle Ages the custom of shaving only a small circle on the top of the head, and this practice came to be universally accepted in the high middle ages.

Bibliography: "De tonsura clericorum," *Appendix ad omnia venerabilis Bedae opera, Patrologia Latina,* ed. J. P. MIGNE, 217 v. (Paris 1878–90) 95:227–332. P. GOBILLOT, "Sur la tonsure chrétienne et ses prétendues origines païennes," *Revue d'histoire ecclésiastique* 21 (1925) 399–454.

[T. J. RILEY/EDS.]

TOOLEN, THOMAS JOSEPH

Archbishop; b. Baltimore, Md., Feb. 28, 1886; d. Mobile, Ala., Dec. 4, 1976. Ordained to the priesthood by Cardinal James Gibbons in Baltimore, Sept. 27, 1910, after studies at St. Mary's Seminary there, he spent a year studying canon law at the Catholic University of America and then served St. Bernard's Parish, Baltimore, for 15 years. Toolen was appointed archdiocesan director of the Society for the Propagation of the Faith in 1925, and on May 4, 1927, consecrated by Archbishop Michael Curley as the sixth bishop of MOBILE.

The diocese of Mobile in 1927 contained 66 counties in Alabama and ten in northwest Florida with a Catholic population of 48,000 served by 48 diocesan and 94 religious priests. Diocesan schools had a census of 7,800 and from 11 communities 339 sisters staffed schools, hospitals, and orphanages. The 43 years of Toolen's leadership saw the diocese grow threefold. Catholics numbered 135,600, and clergy, 200 diocesan, 210 religious. The bishop gave priority to Catholic education so that diocesan schools enrolled 23,000 and Confraternity of Christian Doctrine programs were organized for both children and adults. Religious communities of women active in the diocese grew to 37, and 885 sisters worked not only in traditional ministries but also in such new fields as centers for social service at Mobile, Birmingham, Pensacola, Montgomery, and Huntsville. As the South emerged from the Great Depression, Toolen set about a program of rebuilding and expansion. More than 700 units of new construction marked his administration, including 189 churches, 112 elementary and high schools, and 23 health care facilities. Missions were opened and parishes established in rural areas to bring Catholic life for the first time to 28 counties.

A strong spokesman for Catholics in the face of KU KLUX KLAN attacks in the late 1920s, the bishop also championed racial justice in a segregated society. Parochial facilities and educational opportunities for African Americans were improved and pioneer efforts in social service and hospital care made racial history in Alabama. Both Pius XII and John XXIII cited Toolen for this work, the former pontiff conferring upon him the title of "Archbishop *ad personam*" in 1954. He took forceful action by ordering the integration of all Catholic schools in the diocese in 1964, stating in a pastoral letter, "I know this will not meet with the approval of many of our people, but in justice and charity, this must be done." The archbishop's refusal to endorse black activism often connected with violence in the 1960s diminished his effectiveness in the eyes of many.

Upon Toolen's resignation in 1969, his see, designated in 1954 as "Mobile-Birmingham," was divided to form a diocese for north Alabama. The archbishop remained active in religious, civic, and social affairs until his death. Flags flew at half-mast throughout the state to mark his funeral in Mobile.

[O. H. LIPSCOMB]

TOOTELL, HUGH (CHARLES DODD)

Historian of the Church in England, critic of the Jesuits; b. Lancashire, 1671; d. Harvington Hall, Worcestershire, 1743. He studied at Douai and in Paris, and was ordained in 1697. He worked in Lancashire and for a time served as an army chaplain overseas. From 1722 he was in England in the household of Sir Robert Throckmorton. He was a prolific writer and more than 60 of his MSS are listed in Joseph Gillow's *Bibliographical Dictionary of English Catholics*. His *History of the English College at Doway* (1713) and *The Secret Policy of the English Society of Jesus* (1715) involved him in fierce controversy with the Jesuits and have been characterized as "partisan and poisonous." His monumental three-volume *Church History of England from 1500 to 1688,* however, was a valuable, well-documented pioneer study. Mark Aloysius Tierney (1795–1862), who undertook to edit it, took to heart the words of Tootell's preface that his history was meant to be "an inducement to better performers . . .to be improved and built upon by posterity."

Bibliography: J. GILLOW, *A Literary and Biographical History or Bibliographical Dictionary of the English Catholics from 1534 to the Present time*, 5 v. (London-New York 1885–1902; repr.

New York 1961) 5:549. T. COOPER, *The Dictionary of National Biography from the Earliest Times to 1900*, 63 v. (London 1885–1900; repr. with corrections, 21 v., 1908–09, 1921–22, 1938; suppl. 1901–) 5: 1052–55. P. GUILDAY, *The English Catholic Refugees on the Continent, 1558–1795* (New York 1914). J. B. CODE, *Queen Elizabeth and the English Catholic Historians* (Louvain 1935).

[P. MCGRATH]

TORELLO, BL.

Hermit; d. March 16, 1282. He lived at Avellaneto near Poppi in Tuscany and was buried in what was at one time the Vallombrosian monastery of S. Fedele. Both the VALLOMBROSANS and Franciscans claim him as one of their members, but their claims are without historical foundation. He is invoked as a protector of children and of women in childbirth. His cult was approved by Pope Benedict XIV. He is usually represented in art as a hermit with a wolf and a small child.

Feast: March 16.

Bibliography: *Acta Sanctorum* March 2:493–499. A. M. ZIMMERMANN, *Kalendarium Bendictinum: Die Heiligen und Seligen des Benediktinerorderns und seiner Zweige*, 4 v. (Metten 1933–38) 1:337–338. A. ZIMMERMANN, *Lexikon für Theologie und Kirche*, ed. M. BUCHBERBER, 10 v. (Freiburg 1930–38) 10:209. L. BERRA, A. MERCATI, and A. PELZER, *Dizionario ecclesiastico*, 3 v. (Turin 1954–58) 3:1155. *Enciclopedia de la Religión Católica*, ed. R. D. FERRERES et al., 7 v. (Barcelona 1950–56) 7:257. G. GORETTIMINIATI, *Vita di S. Torello da Poppi* (Rome 1926).

[K. NOLAN]

TORNAY, MAURICE, BL.

Religious priest, martyr; b. La Rosière, near Orsières, Valais Canton, Switzerland, Aug. 31, 1910; d. To Thong, Tibet, Aug. 11, 1949. After completing school at St. Maurice Abbey, Maurice Tornay entered the novitiate of the Canons Regular of Great St. Bernard (Congregatio Ss. Nicolai et Bernardi Monti Iovis) (1931), made his solemn profession (1935), then volunteered for the Chinese missions (1936). He completed his theological studies while learning the local dialects at Weixi, Yunnan, China. Following his ordination at Hanoi (1938), he was given charge of the students at the minor seminary at Houa-Lo-Pa, China.

In 1945, Tornay was assigned to Yerkalo, the only parish in the autonomous Himalayan theocratic kingdom of Tibet. Here, he met with opposition from Buddhist monks, who forced him to abandon his parish. Undaunted, Tornay maintained contact with his persecuted parishioners from a hiding place in Pamé. Finally, he decided to seek an edict of toleration from the Dalai Lama in order to protect the Christians. He was murdered (with his servant) by armed men—agents of the Lamistic monks—who had offered to escort him to Lhasa.

During the beatification homily, May 16, 1993, Pope John Paul II remembered Tornay as a man "who wanted to teach children and lead them to holiness."

Feast: Aug.11.

Bibliography: R. LOUP, *Martyr au Thibet: Maurice Tornay, chanoine régulier du Grand-St-Bernard* (Fribourg 1950); *Martyr in Tibet: The Heroic Life and Death of Father Maurice Tornay, St. Bernard Missionary to Tibet,* tr. C. DAVENPORT (New York 1956). C. MARQUIS-OGGIER and P. DARBELLAY, *Maurice Tornay: Ein Schweizer Märtyrer im Tibet,* 2d ed. (Martigny 1999).

[K. I. RABENSTEIN]

TORNIELLI, BONAVENTURE, BL.

Servite; b. Forlì, Romagna, 1412; d. Udine, March 31, 1491. He was the son of Jacques Tornielli of a noble family in Forlì. Bonaventure entered the SERVITE order and completed his studies at Venice. He practiced severe austerities, making rapid progress in the spiritual life. He devoted himself with great success to preaching in the principal cities of Italy. In his order he held the positions of prior, provincial, and vicar-general. In 1483 when he was prior of the Convent of St. Marcel in Rome, Bonaventure decided to retire with six other religious to a hermitage. However, Pope Sixtus IV named him apostolic preacher shortly afterward, thus obliging him to continue in the apostolate. While preaching a series of Lenten sermons in the cathedral at Udine he died, on Holy Thursday. He was buried at Udine, but his body was later transferred to the Servite Church at Venice. Pope Pius X beatified him in 1911.

Feast: March 31.

Bibliography: *Monumenta Servorum Sanctae Mariae,* ed. P. SOULIER et al., 20 v. (Brussels 1897–1930) v.3. F. CORNARO, *Ecclesiae Venetae antiqua monumenta . . . illustrata . . . ,* 13 v. (Venice 1749) v.2. F. APOLLONIO, *Il beato Bonaventura Tornielli* (Rome 1912). G. ZINKL, *Lexikon für Theologie und Kirche,* ed. M. BUCHBERGER, 10 v. (Freiburg 1930–38) 10:209–210. L. BERRA, A. MERCATI and A. PELZER, *Dizionario ecclesiastico,* 3 v. (Turin 1954–58) 1:405.

[M. B. MORRIS]

TORQUEMADA, JUAN DE

Dominican cardinal, illustrious theologian, defender of papal authority against the conciliarists at Basel; b. Valladolid, Spain, 1388; d. Rome, Sept. 26, 1468. With Louis of Valladolid, UP, he attended the Council of CONSTANCE (1417–18). After studies at Paris he taught in Spain and was successively prior of Valladolid and of Toledo. From 1432 to 1437 he attended the Council of BASEL as orator for King John II of Castile, as procurator of the Dominican Order, and as theologian for Pope EUGENE IV. There he vindicated papal rights in a series of treatises. As a consultor, he reported favorably on the revelations of St. BRIDGET (1433) and censured some propositions of Augustine of Rome (1435). Against the HUSSITES, he wrote a treatise on the Eucharist. He made a collection of passages from the works of Thomas Aquinas in favor of papal authority. He was opposed to the doctrine of the IMMACULATE CONCEPTION, a fact reflected in his *De veritate conceptionis B.V.M.* (1437), first printed at Rome in 1547, and reissued in London (1869) by the Anglican E. B. Pusey 15 years after the definition of the doctrine. For his services to the papacy Torquemada was appointed master of the Sacred Palace in 1434.

When Eugene IV transferred the Council from Basel to Ferrara (Sept. 18, 1437) he sent Torquemada to King John of Castile to enlist the King's support for this move. At Ferrara Torquemada was active in discussions with the Greeks, especially on the question of purgatory. From there he was sent to Germany on a papal mission, for which he composed two treatises intended for delivery at the Diet of Nuremberg (October–November 1438) and the Congress of Mainz (March–April 1439). These works contain the first complete and systematic statement of the papal primacy of jurisdiction over the whole Church, even when the Church is assembled in a general council. [*See* CONCILIARISM (HISTORY OF).] In January 1439, the Council was transferred from Ferrara to FLORENCE, and Torquemada took part in the final redaction of the decree of union with the Greeks, which was signed on July 4, 1439. Some three months later, at the request of Pope Eugene IV, he undertook a public disputation in defense of the PRIMACY OF THE POPE against Cardinal G. CESARINI, a former adherent of the conciliarists, of whom a remnant still held out in opposition at Basel. The resounding success of Torquemada's *Oratio synodalis de primatu* won him the title of Defender of the Faith.

He was created cardinal Dec. 18, 1439, and led a papal mission to Bourges to assist in the negotiations for peace between France and England. In 1441 he composed his magisterial *Apparatus super decretum Florentinum unionis Graecorum,* a historical and doctrinal commentary defending the decree of union with the Greeks. In 1448–49 he wrote his chief work, *Summa de ecclesia* (no modern edition), defending the Church against both heretics and conciliarists. He was appointed bishop of Palestrina by Callistus III in 1455, and of Sabina by Pius II in 1463. He was universally venerated for his learning and probity of life. He was buried in the Church of the Minerva, Rome.

Bibliography: Critical editions and bibliog. J. DE TORQUEMADA, *Apparatus super decretum Florentinum unionis Graecorum,* ed. E. CANDAL, v.2.1 of *Concilium florentinum: Documenta et scriptores* (Rome 1940–); *Oratio synodalis de primatu,* ed. E. CANDAL, v.4.2 *ibid.* J. QUÉTIF and J. ÉCHARD, *Scriptores Ordinis Praedicatorum.* (Paris 1719–23) 1.2:837–843. J. F. STOCKMANN, *Joannis de Turrecremata, O.P., vitam ejusque doctrinam de Corpore Christi mystico . . .* (Bologna 1952). J. GILL, *The Council of Florence* (Cambridge, Eng. 1959).

[F. COURTNEY]

TORQUEMADA, JUAN DE

Franciscan historian; b. Spain, 1563?; d. Mexico City, 1624. Eleven years after Gerónimo de MENDIETA's death, Torquemada published his own monumental history of the Franciscan missionary work in Mexico, the *Monarquía indiana.* Torquemada, who held the office of provincial superior (1614–17), was both a disciple and an admirer of Mendieta. Torquemada was ordered by his superiors to make full use of all the available historical works, especially the unpublished MS of Mendieta. Hence modern charges that Torquemada plagiarized Mendieta's text are misleading if not unhistorical. Skillfully reorganizing the *Historia eclesiástica indiana,* he made a radical revision of the spirit and the meaning of Mendieta's material. Torquemada looked back nostalgically to the great age of the early friars, but unlike Mendieta he was resigned that the golden age could not be restored. He implied that conditions were neither so idyllic before 1564, nor as bleak and somber after 1564, as Mendieta described. He recognized that there was a decline after 1564, but Mendieta's sharp contrast between the ''golden age'' of Charles V and the ''Babylonian Captivity'' of Philip II was completely eliminated. Despite his sincere admiration for Mendieta, Torquemada belonged not to the extremist wing whose most articulate spokesman was Mendieta himself, but to the moderate wing among the mendicants who strove to reach a *modus operandi* between the indigenous people, the colonists, and the Crown.

As a consequence of Joaquin García Icazbalceta's discovery that Torquemada had borrowed the greater part of it from Mendieta, the *Monarquía indiana* fell from a position of preeminence to one of neglect among scholars. Torquemada borrowed not only from Mendieta, but also from other contemporary chronicles. In addition to including new material of his own, he often reinterpreted what he took from others. As such, the *Monarquía indiana* is a vast mosaic of Franciscan missionary historiography of early Mexico.

[J. L. PHELAN]

Manuscript page with illustration from ''Meditationes seu contemplationes devotissimae,'' 1479 edition, by Juan de Torquemada, printed at Mainz by Johann Neumeister.

TORQUEMADA, TOMÁS DE

Grand inquisitor of the Spanish INQUISITION; b. Valladolid, 1420; d. Avila, Spain, Sept. 16, 1498. The son of Pedro Fernández de Torquemada and nephew of Cardinal Juan de TORQUEMADA, Tomás De Torquemada entered San Pablo Dominican convent at Valladolid, from which he graduated in theology. He became prior of Santa Cruz convent, Segovia (1452), confessor to the royal treasurer Hernán Núñz, and confessor (1474) to Queen ISABELLA I and King Ferdinand V.

Although of Jewish descent, Torquemada probably encouraged the monarchs to attack both the orthodox Jews and those crypto-Jews who had been insincerely or forcibly converted to Christianity but continued to practice Judaism in secret. He helped draft the first royal request for an inquisition into the crypto-Jews (1478) and was one of eight Dominicans appointed (Feb. 11, 1482) to moderate the unjust inquisitors first appointed. On the advise of Cardinal Pedro González de MENDOZA, Isabella persuaded Pope SIXTUS IV to unify the whole Inquisition for Castile (Aug. 2, 1483) and Aragon (Oct. 17, 1483) under Torquemada's control, giving him power to appoint, dismiss, and hear appeals from other inquisitors. Thus empowered, Torquemada organized the Inquisition under five territorial tribunals, with one supreme appellate council under himself; he issued (Seville, Nov. 29, 1484) the *Ordinances,* which, as supplemented in 1484, 1485, 1488, and 1498, regulated inquisitorial procedure in SPAIN for the three succeeding centuries.

From 1483 on, Torquemada used this efficient police instrument to investigate and punish crypto-Jews, apostates, witches, and other spiritual offenders on an unprecedented scale; approximately 2,000 people were executed and vast numbers otherwise punished. Complaints to the Pope were ineffective since Isabella and Ferdinand supported Torquemada. Pope ALEXANDER VI actually appointed four extra inquisitors general to try to restrain him (June 23, 1494), but Torquemada remained in control even during his retirement (1494–98) in the convent of Santo Tomás that he had built at Avila. Exceptionally intolerant even for his times, Torquemada publicized an alleged ritual murder at La Guardia to encourage the expulsion of the Jews (1492) and tried far more suspects than any of his successors. But even though his successors reduced actual arrests, the spiritual police system Torquemada had organized effectively guarded Spanish thought throughout succeeding generations.

Bibliography: F. FITA, "La inquisición de Torquemada," *Boletín de la Real Academia de la historia, Madrid* 23 (1893) 369–434. H. C. LEA, *A History of the Inquisition of Spain,* 4 v. (New York 1906–07). E. LUCKA, *Torquemada und die spanische Inquisition* (Leipzig 1926). T. HOPE, *Torquemada, Scourge of the Jews* (London 1939). W. T. WALSH, *Characters of the Inquisition* (New York 1940). H. DEL PULGAR, *Crónica de los reyes católicos,* ed. J. DE M. CARRIAZO, 2 v. (Madrid 1943). N. LÓPEZ MARTÍNEZ, *Los judaizantes castellanos y la Inquisición en tiempo de Isabel la católica* (Burgos 1954). M. DE LA PINTA LLORENTE, *La Inquisición española y los problemas de la cultura y de la intolerancia,* 2 v. (Madrid 1953–58).

[D. W. LOMAX]

TORRES, CAMILLO

Colombian priest, sociologist, and revolutionary guerrilla; b. Bogotá, Colombia, Feb. 3, 1927; d. Feb. 16, 1966. Camillo Torres Restrepo was born into a branch of one of Colombia's few ruling families. After a rather free social life he decided to enter the diocesan seminary in Bogotá. Ordained a priest in 1953, he then went to the Catholic University of Louvain, where his work was exemplary if unoriginal. After a brief period as rector of the

Latin American College in Louvain he returned to Colombia in 1958 to study the socioeconomic conditions of Colombia, a study which was to form the basis of his doctoral dissertation.

Appointed chaplain of Bogotá's National University, Torres gradually became more actively involved in criticizing, and then attempting to rectify, the inequities that he personally perceived and that had become the object of his disciplined investigation. His initial assumption that needed reforms could be effected within the existing social and political structures developed into a belief that the structures themselves demanded change through radical action.

In 1964 Torres formed a United Front into which he attempted to bring people of widely divergent political views. The radical measures he proposed attracted national attention and, within both the government and the Catholic hierarchy, strong opposition. His calls for a revolution made a formal rupture almost inevitable, and he was granted laicization in June 1965. He campaigned with great energy for the United Front until Oct., when he joined a guerrilla movement of the left. In February of the following year, as he participated in an ambush on a military patrol, he was killed. His place of burial remains unknown.

Bibliography: C. TORRES, *Biografia, plataforma, mensajes* (Medellin 1966). G. GUZMÁN, *Camilo, el cura guerillero* (Bogotà 1967); *Revolutionary Priest,* ed. and with an introduction by J. GERASSI (New York 1971). W. J. BRODERICK, *Camilo Torres: A Biography of the Priest-Guerrillero* (New York 1975).

[J. FINN]

TORRES, FRANCISCO

Controversial theologian and patrologist (known also as Turrianus); b. Palencia, Spain, *c.* 1509; d. Rome, Nov. 21, 1584. After having studied philosophy and theology at the University of Alcalá, he entered the service of Cardinal Salviati in Rome in 1540 and worked on manuscript collections in Roman libraries. He edited a number of Greek Fathers, including the orations of Anastasius Sinaita, John Damascene, and Leontius of Byzantium, and took part in the theological disputes of the day. Pope Pius IV appointed him a papal theologian for the third step of the Council of Trent, and he took part in the debates on the Eucharist, the Sacrifice of the Mass, the Sacraments of Orders and Matrimony, celibacy, and episcopal residence. On Jan. 6, 1567, he entered the Society of Jesus. He wrote tracts on episcopal residence, papal authority, and scripture.

Bibliography: H. HURTER, *Nomenclator literarius theologiae catholicae,* 5 vol. in 6 (3rd ed. Innsbruck 1903–13) 3:281–284. C.

SOMMERVOGEL, et al., *Bibliothèque de la Compagnie de Jésus,* 11 v. (Brussels–Paris 1890–1932) 8:113–126. C. GUTIÉRREZ, ed. and tr., *Españoles en Trento* (Valladolid 1951).

[I. ONATIBIA]

TORRES, LUIS DE

Jesuit theologian; b. Alcalá de Henares, Spain, 1562; d. Madrid, 1655. Although prolific in his publications, Torres was not a theologian of conspicuous merit. His principal work was *Disputationes in 2am2ae D. Thomae: De fide, spe, charitate et prudentia* (Lyons 1623). He was quick to condemn opinions contrary to his own as dangerous, without taking the trouble to acquaint himself sufficiently with their foundations, a fault that caused the Jesuit general, Mutius Vitteleschi, to have his *Disputationes selectae* (Lyons 1634) withdrawn from circulation. He is remembered chiefly for the embarrassment in which he found himself when he had one of his students, D. de Oñate, defend the thesis that it was not of Catholic faith that a particular person, for example, Clement VIII (the then-reigning pontiff), was the legitimate pope. This happened in 1601, at the height of the stormy debates centering around the *CONGREGATIO DE AUXILIIS*, the sessions of which were soon to begin. It was falsely charged that the thesis cast doubts upon the legitimacy of Clement's title to the papacy. Torres and the unfortunate Oñate were jailed by the Inquisition, but were released in 1603 with a stern reprimand.

Bibliography: C. SOMMERVOGEL, *Bibliotèque de la Compagnie de Jésus,* 11 v. (Brussels-Paris 1890–1932) 8:129–131. H. HURTER, *Nomenclator literarius theologiae catholicae,* 5 v. in 6 (3d ed. Innsbruck 1903–1913) 3:883–884. A. ASTRAIN, *Historia de la Compañia de Jesús en la Asistencia de España,* 7 v. (Madrid 1902–25) 4:316–331. J. P. GRAUSEM, *Dictionnaire de théologie catholique,* ed. A. VACANT, 15 v. (Paris 1903–50; Tables générales 1951–) 15:1241.

[P. K. MEAGHER]

TORRES ACOSTA, MARÍA SOLEDAD, ST.

Baptized Bibiana Antonia Manuela, foundress of the Sisters SERVANTS OF MARY; b. Madrid, Spain, Dec. 2, 1826; d. there, Oct. 11, 1887. Bibiana was educated by the Daughters of Charity. Prevented from entering a Dominican community because of delicate health, she was attracted to a project of Don Miguel Martínez Sanz, pastor in Chamberi (Madrid), to provide home care for the sick poor. With six companions she founded the Sisters Servants of Mary on Aug. 15, 1851, and assumed in religion the name María Soledad. The dedication of this small group was quickly proved during a cholera epidemic in Madrid. The early years of the institute were most difficult because of a significant number of defections from the congregation, the government's refusal to recognize the foundress's rule, and the loss of Don Martínez as spiritual director. María Soledad was subjected to grave slanders and deposed as superior general. The community was near extinction when the new spiritual director, Don Gabino Sanchez, had the foundress reinstated. Stability finally came to the new institute, which received the Holy See's definitive approval in 1876. By 1881 there were sisters in Cuba; and by 1887, when the foundress died, there were 47 houses in Europe and Latin America. María Soledad was beatified on Feb. 5, 1950, and canonized Jan. 25, 1970.

Feast: Oct. 11.

Bibliography: J. A. ZUGASTI, *La madre María Soledad Torres Acosta y el Instituto de las Siervas de María,* 2 v. (Madrid 1916). P. ALVAREZ, *Santa María Soledad Torres Acosta* (Rome 1969). E. FEDERICI, *Santa María Soledad Torres Acosta* (2d ed. Rome 1969). J. M. JAVIERRE, *Soledad de los Enfermos: Soledad Torres Acosta* (Madrid 1970). P. PANEDAS GALINDO, *Con María junto a la cruz: Santa María Soledad y las Siervas de María, su espiritu* (Madrid 1984). G. PRADO, *Madre Soledad* (Madrid 1953).

[I. BASTARRIKA]

TORRES BOLLO, DIEGO DE

Founder of the REDUCTIONS OF PARAGUAY; b. Villalpando, Spain, 1551; d. Chuquisaca (now Sucre), Bolivia, Aug. 8, 1638. He became a Jesuit on Dec. 16, 1571, and in 1580, when he was already ordained, went to Peru. He was superior of Juli, rector in Cuzco, Quito, and Potosí, and secretary to the provincial and to the visitor. In 1600 he was sent to Rome and Madrid to discuss important matters of his province, to which he returned in 1604. A year later he founded the vice-province of New Granada (Colombia) and in 1607 the province of Paraguay. At the request of the bishop and the governor he started the Guaraní Reductions of Paraguay, on December 8, 1609, with the dispatch of the first two missionaries from Asunción. In 1611–12 he collaborated with *oidor* Alfaro in making peace with the indigenous peoples. At the end of his term as provincial, in 1615, he was named rector of the school at Córdoba (Argentina), and in 1628 he departed for Chuquisaca.

Bibliography: P. LOZANO, *Historia de la Compañia de Jesús en la Provincia del Paraguay,* 2 v. (Madrid 1754–55). R. VARGAS UGARTE, ''El P. Diego de Torres Bollo y el cardenal Federico Borromeo: Correspondencia inédita,'' *Boletín del Instituto de investigaciones históricas, Universidad nacional, Buenos Aires* 17 (1933–34) 59–82.

[H. STORNI]

TORRES LLORET, PASCUAL, BL.

Lay martyr, builder; b. Jan. 23, 1885, Carcaixent (or Carcagente), Valencia, Spain; d. there, Sept. 6, 1936.

Following the February 1936 elections in Spain, the climate in Carcagente became increasingly hostile to the Church. In mid-May, the convents of the Dominicans, Franciscans, and Immaculatas were sacked and burned; parish churches were attacked and religious objects were destroyed. On May 14, when the Dominican convent was attacked, its cemetery was profaned, bodies taken and publicly exposed until nightfall without retribution by the civil authorities. Two days later, municipal authorities sent teams of masons to block the entrances to churches; priests were prohibited from wearing their clerical garb; and the Franciscan and Dominican religious were expelled from their houses. In the escalating violence following the July revolution, 115 Catholics were assassinated in Carcagente, including BB. María del Olvido Noguera Albelda, Juan Gonga Martínez, and Pascual Torres Lloret—all members of Catholic Action.

Torres Lloret, born into poverty, was baptized in Assumption Parish, Carcagente, two days after his birth. On Oct. 5, 1911, he married Leonor Pérez Canet with whom he raised four children: Pascual, Teresa, Leonor, and José María. He was known as a kind man, who fulfilled his familial duties. Although he had a family to support, his sense of social justice would not permit him to accept the tithe from the salaries of his construction workers to which he was entitled by custom. Torres was highly esteemed by his clients for his honesty and fairness.

Torres was a man of profound faith, who daily attended Mass, received Communion, and recited the rosary with his family. As a close collaborator with his pastor at Assumption Church, he participated frequently in Nocturnal Adoration of the Blessed Sacrament. He served his parish as a catechist and social apostle, and belonged to various lay religious associations, including the Society of St. Vincent de Paul and Catholic Fathers of Families. In 1932 he helped establish the first branch of Catholic Action for youth.

At the time of the proclamation of the Second Republic in 1931, Torres was conscious of the likely persecution in store for the Church and her adherents. In July 1936, he redoubled his family prayers for peace, rather than seeking refuge in a safe haven. He remained at home and continued his religious activities even after it became dangerous to be identified as a Catholic.

After the expulsion of the religious from their convents, Torres took two sisters of the Immaculata into his home. When the churches were closed, he was privileged also to house the Blessed Sacrament. Throughout each night until his arrest, he and his wife took turns kneeling before the Eucharist in vigil. He himself also took the Eucharist to the sick. To prevent the profanation of sacred objects he used his skills as a builder to hide many of the church's treasures in a trench near the parish and in the walls of the rectory.

Both before and during the Revolution, he expressed his hope for martyrdom. This hope was fulfilled after the onset of the Spanish Civil War. Seven times he was questioned by the Committee, sometimes after being detained overnight. Yet he remained serene. He was first arrested with Juan Gonga while assisting at the Mass of Fr. Enrique Pelufo, vicar of Carcagente on July 25, and incarcerated for four days at the Colegio de María Inmaculada, whose chapel had been converted into a prison. On September 5 he was arrested in his home a second time. During the following night he was taken to the cemetery and shot to death. His body was thrown into a common grave. After the war it was translated to the cemetery in Valencia.

Pascual was beatified by Pope John Paul II with José Aparicio Sanz and 232 companions on March 11, 2001.

Feast: Sept. 22.

See Also: SPAIN, THE CATHOLIC CHURCH IN.

Bibliography: V. CÁRCEL ORTÍ, *Martires españoles del siglo XX* (Madrid 1995). W. H. CARROLL, *The Last Crusade* (Front Royal, Va. 1996). J. PÉREZ DE URBEL, *Catholic Martyrs of the Spanish Civil War,* tr. M. F. INGRAMS (Kansas City, Mo. 1993). R. ROYAL, *The Catholic Martyrs of the Twentieth Century* (New York 2000). *L'Osservatore Romano,* Eng. 11 (March 14, 2001) 1–4, 12.

[K. I. RABENSTEIN]

TORRES MORALES, GENOVEVA, BL.

Religious, foundress of the Sisters of the Sacred Heart of Jesus and the Holy Angels (Angelicas); b. Almenara, Castile, Spain, Jan. 3, 1870; d. Saragossa, Spain, Jan. 5, 1956. Young Genoveva endured many tragedies during her lifetime: by the time she was eight, four of her siblings and both her parents had died, and her left leg was amputated to the thigh (1883). Spiritual reading and prayer strengthened her fortitude. Because of her disability, she was barred from joining the Carmelites of Charity, in whose Mercy Home she had lived from 1885 to 1894. Canon Barbarrós encouraged Genoveva and the two women with whom she lived to form a religious community to assist needy women. Thus, Genoveva founded the Angelicas in Valencia (1911). Despite the numerous obstacles of a new enterprise, the community soon spread to other parts of Spain: Barcelona, Bilbao, Madrid, Pamplona, Santander, and Saragossa. Several years before

Mother Genoveva's death, the institute of the Angelicas received papal approval (1953). Mother Genoveva was beatified in Rome by Pope John Paul II, Jan. 29, 1995.

Bibliography: *Escritos personales de la Rdma. Madre Genoveva Torres Morales*, ed. B. LLORCA (Barcelona 1973). B. LLORCA, *Angel de la soledad: la madre Genoveva Torres Morales fundadora de las Hermanas del Sagrado Corazón de Jesús y de los Santos Angeles* (Zaragoza 1970). M. A. MARRODÁN, *Loores a la madre Genoveva* (Tarragona 1996).

[K. I. RABENSTEIN]

TORRÓ GARCÍA, MANUEL, BL.

Lay martyr; b. July 2, 1902, Onteniente (Ontinyent), Valencia, Spain; d. Sept. 21, 1936, Benisoda, Valencia. After finishing his elementary studies in the local public school, Manuel was apprenticed to a surveyor and continued other studies at home under the direction of his uncle, Prudencio Alberto Estan. Always studious, he finished his schooling with the Franciscans before his marriage to the nurse, Rosario Romero Almenar. They had one son who died hours after birth.

His spiritual life was fed through daily reception of the Eucharist and prayer, especially the family rosary. He belonged to the Youth of Catholic Action of which he was president of his parish chapter, the Third Order of St. Francis, and other confraternities. He founded and was president of the Nocturnal Adoration Society. Manuel taught the faith by word as a catechist and by action as a hospital volunteer through the Association of St. Philip Neri. He is described as a serious, hard-working, reliable man, who was especially gifted by the Holy Spirit with serenity, charity, and prudence.

Although not himself a laborer, Torró collaborated with the Catholic Labor Union. Just before the revolution, he was asked to serve as mediator and successfully negotiated terms to avoid a strike.

Prior to 1931 his hometown of Onteniente was considered profoundly Catholic, dedicated to the Immaculate Conception and Christ in Agony. Thereafter hostility grew toward the Church. On May 12, 1931, the religious of several monasteries were evicted. The hostility intensified following the elections of Feb. 16, 1936, when the Popular Front attained power. Catholics were arrested and churches and convents destroyed, as were the parish records of San Carlos. The parochial center of Catholic Action was converted into a theater. Twelve priests and 90 lay people who were born or worked in Onteniente were assassinated for their religious beliefs, eight of whom were included in the beatification process in the archdiocese of Valencia.

This was the atmosphere in which Manuel Torró García consciously chose to risk martyrdom, rather than hide his faith. Just days before the revolution the mayor asked Torró, president of the Nocturnal Adoration Society, for a list of members. Recognizing that appearance on the list meant probable martyrdom, he asked the permission of each to include his name. All but two wanted to be identified as members; all were assassinated before 1939.

On Sept. 20, 1936, he spent the day at his parents' home in La Clariana as was usual on Sundays. At midnight the militiamen arrived at the door to take him in for questioning. At that time Torró told his wife that he would be martyred, but that he was prepared. Prior to his execution that same night, Torró offered cigarettes to his assassins, then asked permission to sing the *Salve*. He was shot together with Vicente GALBIS GIRONÉS, two brothers named Velázquez, and a female employee of the brothers. A priest who covertly witnessed the execution related that it occurred about 2 AM near the highway between Albaida and Benisoda. As he lay dying of wounds to his stomach, before the shot in the head, Torró wrote the word ''salve'' in the dirt with his finger.

Torró's mortal remains were buried in Benisoda's cemetery until after the Spanish Civil War when they were transferred, July 18, 1939, to an individual niche in the new cemetery at Onteniente. He was beatified by Pope John Paul II with José Aparicio Sanz and 232 companions on March 11, 2001.

Feast: Sept. 22.

See Also: SPAIN, THE CATHOLIC CHURCH IN.

Bibliography: V. CÁRCEL ORTÍ, *Martires españoles del siglo XX* (Madrid 1995). W. H. CARROLL, *The Last Crusade* (Front Royal, Va. 1996). J. PÉREZ DE URBEL, *Catholic Martyrs of the Spanish Civil War*, tr. M. F. INGRAMS (Kansas City, Mo. 1993). R. ROYAL, *The Catholic Martyrs of the Twentieth Century* (New York 2000). *L'Osservatore Romano*, Eng. 11 (March 14, 2001) 1–4, 12.

[K. I. RABENSTEIN]

TORRUBIA, JOSÉ

Franciscan missionary, historian, and natural scientist; b. Granada, Spain, 1698; d. Rome, 1761. Torrubia entered the Franciscan Order in 1714 and left for the missions in the Philippines in 1719. There his gifts as a careful observer and writer soon brought him posts of distinction both within and outside the order, as well as the jealousy of some friars. In 1733 he was sent to Spain to recruit friar missionaries, and he gathered 72. While these went to the islands, Torrubia stayed in Mexico because of charges made against him in Manila. By 1750 these charges had been heard and dismissed by the order, the Holy See, and the king. In 1752 he was named archivist and chronicler of the order, an appointment that superseded an earlier one (1738) as chronicler of the order for Asia. As archivist and chronicler, Torrubia continued the Chrónica begun by Damián Carnejo in 1682 and carried forward by Eusebio González de Torres. In 1756 Torrubia published the ninth part of this chronicle. It is generally considered by far the best part because of the abundant documentation and the critical spirit of the author. Unfortunately, the tenth part, which he said he was preparing in 1759, was never printed. In that year he did publish his very important *I Moscoviti nella California o sia dimostrazione della veritá del passo all'America Settentrionale nuovamente scoperto dei Russi* (Rome 1759). Besides some important studies on the internal history of the order in Spain, Torrubia published his *Aparato para la historia natural española* (Madrid 1754). A second volume of this valuable study was never published. He was commissary general of the order at the Holy See at the time of his death.

Bibliography: L. PÉREZ, "Fray José Torrubia, procurador de la provincia de San Gregorio de Filipinas," *Archivo Ibero-Americano* 36 (1933) 321–364.

[L. G. CANEDO]

TORTURE

This article is concerned only with the use of torture as a means of obtaining a confession or other testimony in a judicial inquiry. Torture in the punishment of crime is dealt with elsewhere (*see* PUNISHMENT).

History. Torture, although in use among many peoples from antiquity, was not employed by the Jews, and there is no mention of it in the Old Testament. The Greeks subjected slaves to torture, but exempted freemen, except in cases of conspiracy and murder. Roman law sanctioned its use, although there were attempts—ineffective for the most part—to restrict its application. With the barbaric invasions, resort to torture in the investigation of crime declined. It is questionable whether the barbarians made any use of it before their contact with the Roman world, but in any case they favored the ORDEAL in their judicial processes. Then, under the influence of Germanic customs and concepts, torture was little used from the nineth to the 12th centuries, but with the revival of Roman law, the practice was reestablished in the 12th century. The English common law did not recognize the legality of torture except for the *peine forte et dure,* which was a torture by pressure of weights that could be inflicted upon a prisoner who, out of malice, refused to plead. There were few instances in which torture was inflicted by order of a common-law judge, but its use by order of crown or council or extraordinary tribunal

was common in the 16th century. The use of torture was abandoned in England by the middle of the 17th century.

Torture and the Church. In the early Church voices were raised against the practice (*see* Tertullian, *De corona* 11; *De idololatria* 17; St. Augustine, *Civ.* 19.6). It was proscribed for the Bulgarians in 866 by Nicholas I (d. 648). With the revival of its practice in Europe under the influence of Roman law, canonists and moralists appeared to regard it as too integral a part of the juridical system to be abolished without endangering the whole structure. In 1252 Innocent IV sanctioned the infliction of torture by the civil authorities upon heretics, and torture later came to have a recognized place in the procedure of the inquisitorial courts. According to the Church's existing legislation, force is not used to secure a confession from an accused person, and it is expressly stated that a person is not required to reveal the truth when interrogated judicially about a crime committed by himself. (1917 *Codex iuris canonics* c.1743.1).

Theory. After the revival of the use of torture in the 12th century, no attack of note upon the theoretical basis of the practice was made until the 16th century, when various influences—notably, among others, the harshening of penal law under the absolutist governments of the time and the extravagances of the witch hunts and trials—caused thoughtful men to seek a fresh view of the barbarous practice; it was not until the 18th century, however, that the budding protests bore fruit.

The use of torture as a means of uncovering the truth appears so futile, so unjust, and so revolting, that it is difficult for the modern mind to understand how it could have been tolerated by a civilized people. The barbarity cannot be objectively justified, and it is only when it is seen against the background of the times that it is possible to understand why people did in fact accept it. Nothing contributed more to its toleration than the fact that it was a part of the heritage of Roman law, which was held in great veneration. Again, it must be remembered that a different concept prevailed with regard to the position of the accused. He was not, as now in Anglo-American law, presumed innocent until convicted. Under Roman law, on the contrary, a credible accusation established a presumption of guilt, and this made it possible to view the suffering of an accused person under torture as being in some sense a punishment for his crime. Moreover, the accused was not exempt from an obligation to make self-incriminating statements. When questioned by a magistrate, even about his own guilt, he was bound to respond truthfully (*see* St. Thomas Aquinas, *Summa theologiae* 2a2ae, 69.1). Finally, it must also be remembered that during the centuries when the use of torture was an accepted judicial procedure, there was little squeamishness about resorting to cruelty in the interests of justice, as is evident in the savage penalties inflicted upon convicted criminals.

While not denying the right of an individual to immunity from violence, those who wrote in defense of the use of torture saw the right of immunity as yielding before the greater right of the state to discover guilty secrets that menaced its welfare or existence. If the state were not empowered to use torture to get at the truth, greater harm would result than would come by violating the liberty and persons of individuals (*see* Juan de Lugo, *De iustitia et iure* 37.13). Although the practice was thus defended by some, they laid stress upon the safeguards and limits that had to be observed if the use of torture was to be accounted licit (*see* St. Alphonsus Liguori, *Theologia moralis* 4.3.3). However, to the modern mind the defense is insufficient, because it weighs the damage done to the common good by an individual's obdurate silence only against the injury done to that individual when he is subjected to torture, whereas much damage is done to other individuals and to the common good itself when there is resort to torture. The use of torture has always been attended by grave abuses, against which protest and other forms of legal and moral counteraction have invariably proved ineffective. It lessens the majesty of law and weakens the security of all men who must see themselves as potential victims of similar mistreatment.

Bibliography: R. NAZ, *Dictionnaire de droit canonique*, ed. R. NAZ (Paris 1935–65) 5:1418–26. E. VACANDARD, *Dictionnaire de théologie catholique*, ed. A. VACANT et al., (Paris 1903—50) 7.2:2016–68, G. NEILSON, *Encyclopedia of Religion and Ethics*, ed. J. HASTINGS (Edinburgh 1908–27) 12:391–393. F. HELBING, *Die Tortur* (Berlin 1926). A. MELLOR, *La Torture* (Paris 1949).

[P. K. MEAGHER]

TOSCANINI, ARTURO

Distinguished opera and symphony conductor; b. Parma, Italy, March 25, 1867; d. New York City, Jan. 16, 1957. Son of Claudio (a tailor) and Paola Toscanini, Arturo studied cello and graduated with honors from the Parma conservatory in 1885. In 1897 he married Carla dei Martini, and was the father of Walter and two daughters, Wally and Wanda (later the wife of the piano virtuoso Vladimir Horowitz). While a cellist in a Rio de Janeiro opera orchestra, he was unexpectedly called upon to conduct Verdi's *Aïda*. Subsequently he was musical director or chief conductor of the Metropolitan Opera, La Scala (Milan), the New York Philharmonic, the Salzburg and Bayreuth festivals, and the NBC Orchestra (which he had organized). Toscanini had a phenomenal memory, was a stern and temperamental disciplinarian, and achieved

Arturo Toscanini.

performances of high perfection. He introduced works by PUCCINI, RESPIGHI, Moussorgsky, Kodály, the American Samuel Barber, and others. He refused an honorary doctorate from Oxford but accepted the One World award for music (1947). His funeral Mass took place in St. Patrick's Cathedral, New York City, in the presence of Cardinal Francis Spellman.

Bibliography: D. EWEN, *The Story of Arturo Toscanini* (rev. ed. New York 1960). T. W. GERVAIS, *Grove's Dictionary of Music and Musicians*, ed. E. BLOM 9 v. (5th ed. London 1954) 8:517–519. H. TAUBMAN, *The New York Times* 106 (Jan. 20, 1957) 2:7.1. N. BRODER, *Die Musik in Geschichte und Gegenwart*, ed. F. BLUME (Kassel-Basel 1949–) v.13 (in press). D. CAIRNS, "Arturo Toscanini" in *The New Grove Dictionary of Music and Musicians, vol. 19*, ed. S. SADIE (New York 1980) 85–88. D. M. RANDEL, ed., *The Harvard Biographical Dictionary of Music* (Cambridge 1996) 922–923. N. SLONIMSKY, ed., *Baker's Biographical Dictionary of Musicians, Eighth Edition* (New York 1992) 1898. R. WERBA, "Toscanini in Österreich: Versuch einer politisch-humanitären Demonstration," *Österreichische Musik Zeitschrift* 53 (1998) 26–35. F. ZIMMERMAN, "Arturo Toscanini," in *International Dictionary of Opera* 2 v., ed. C. S. LARUE (Detroit 1993) 1347–1351.

[H. E. MEYERS]

TOSTADO, ALONZO

Exegete and theologian; b. Madrigal, near Ávila, Spain, 1400?; d. Bonilla de la Sierra, near Ávila, September 3, 1455. His studies completed *c.* 1425, he began in 1433 to teach philosophy, theology, and law in Salamanca. In 1443 Pope Eugene IV summoned him to Siena, where he was condemned for heresy, notably for a strict teaching on the forgiveness of sins. He retracted immediately and later replied to an attack on him by Cardinal Juan de TORQUEMADA, a member of the tribunal at Siena. It is doubtful that Tostado was at the Council of Basel. For three months he was a Carthusian novice at Scala Dei until John II of Castile made him royal chancellor in 1444. In 1449 Nicholas V approved him as bishop of Ávila, where he served with zeal and holiness until his death. Diligent and endowed with a prodigious memory, he wrote some 70 works in 60,000 pages—mostly exegesis of Scripture and theological treatises in Latin, but also works in Spanish on the Mass and confession. There is still confusion about a complete list of his works, many of which are in manuscripts in Salamanca and Madrid. The few instances in which he indulges in philosophy show Platonic influence. His alabaster tomb in the cathedral of Ávila is one of the most beautiful in Spain.

Bibliography: *Opera* omnia, ed. R. BOVOSIUS, 13 v. (Venice 1569; reprint 1728). H. HURTER, *Nomenclator literarius theologiae catholicae,* 5 v. in 6 (3d ed. Innsbruck 1903–1913) 2:918–921. *Enciclopedia universal illustrada Europeo–Americana,* 70 v. (Barcelona 1908–30; suppl. 1934–) 62:1581–83. E. MANGENOT, *Dictionnaire de théologie catholique,* ed. A. VACANT, 15 v. (Paris 1903–50; Tables générales 1951–) 1.1:921–923. S. BOSI, *Alfonso Tostado: Vita ed opere* (Rome 1952).

[J. PÉREZ DE URBEL]

TOSTI, LUIGI

Benedictine, historian; b. Naples, Feb. 13, 1811; d. Monte Cassino, Sept. 21, 1897. After completing his studies at Monte Cassino, he joined the BENEDICTINES there and took his vows as a monk (Feb. 17, 1832). While lecturing on theology at MONTE CASSINO ABBEY, he published his *Storia di Monte Cassino* (1842). Together with GIOBERTI, Balbo, Carlo Troya, and other leaders of NEO-GUELFISM, Tosti planned to publish *L'Ateneo Italiano,* a historical and literary review; but the censors of the Kingdom of the Two Sicilies prohibited its publication. Within the next few years appeared his *Storia di Bonifacio VIII* (1846); *Storia della Lega Lombarda* (1848); *Salterio del soldato* (1848); and *Il Veggente del secolo XIX* (1848), supporting Gioberti's Neo-Guelf program and a federation of Italian states under the presidency of the pope. Tosti became a favorite of PIUS IX. In 1849, during the Pope's exile in Gaeta, Tosti urged him to return to Rome and to abandon his temporal power. To prevent French armed intervention against the Roman Republic, Tosti negotiated with the French minister in Rome. He also acted as mediator between Mazzini and Pius IX. After a brief asylum in Tuscany, he returned to Monte Cassino and concentrated on his studies. He later published *Storia di Abelardo* (1851), *Storia del Concilio di Costanza* (1853), *La Contessa Matilda e i Romani Pontefici* (1859), and *I Prolegomeni alla storia universale della Chiesa* (1861). When the Kingdom of the Two Sicilies was annexed to the Kingdom of Italy (1860), Tosti sought to effect a conciliation between Church and State in the peninsula. His famous pamphlet *La Conciliazione* (1887) envisaged a peaceful settlement of the ROMAN QUESTION. In 1890 he urged Bishop STROSSMAYER to suggest to the Vatican a treaty with Italy under the sponsorship of the Central Powers.

Bibliography: A. CAPECELATRO, *Commemorazione di don Luigi Tosti* (Monte Cassino 1898). A. QUACQUARELLI, *Il P. Tosti nella politica del Risorgimento* (Genoa 1945). A. C. JEMOLO, *Church and State in Italy, 1850–1950,* tr. D. MOORE (Philadelphia 1960).

[H. R. MARRARO]

TOTEMISM

A social institution through which divisions of a tribe (totem groups) are systematically and permanently associated with species, usually of animals, but sometimes of plants or inanimate objects, that are their totems. The word totem is of North American origin; but according to Émile DURKHEIM, seconded in this by A. R. Radcliffe-Brown, Australia is its "classic land." In its current more general sense the word has no equivalent in any Australian aboriginal language, although there are local terms for particular manifestations.

Applied to aboriginal Australia it signifies a view of the word that is human-centered but not human-dominated. It is a view that assumes a mystic and spiritual relationship between man and his nonhuman environment, not separating man sharply from natural species and natural elements, but stressing his part in the total scheme of things, his sharing of the same essential quality of being. The beginnings of this relationship are traced, both for precedent and for validation, to the mythical or creative era, the Eternal Dreamtime, as it is sometimes called, with emphasis upon the aspect of continuity.

Social Function. The mystical bond is translated for everyday practical purposes into personal and social relationships that take many forms and can be classified in various ways. Probably the most important hinges on whether affiliation with a natural object such as a totem derives from (1) membership in a specific social group that defines a person's relationship in totemic terms to everyone within his social perspective, whether with ritual ramifications (cult totemism) or not (social totemism), or (2) a personal experience or revelation that confers special attributes, as on a native doctor or songman (individual totemism). The rule of totemic exogamy is not universal in Australia and relates only to social totemism. Taboos on eating the flesh of one's totem, when the totem is represented by an edible species, are significant in some areas, but rarer than suggested by early reports. A person's relationship with his totem symbolizes a range of associations. It links him with the great ancestral and spirit beings and gods, with the sacred world of myth, with the immortal and eternal, in a complex of belief and action, that, traditionally, gives purpose and meaning to human existence. In this sense totemism is, symbolically, an expression of the basic value inherent in the aboriginal way of life.

See Also: RELIGION (IN PRIMITIVE CULTURE).

Bibliography: R. M. and C. H. BERNDT, *The World of the First Australians* (Sydney 1964). E. DURKHEIM, *The Elementary Forms of the Religious Life,* tr. J. W. SWAIN (London 1915; repr. Glencoe, Ill. 1954). A. P. ELKIN, *Studies in Australian Totemism* (Sydney 1938; Garden City 1964); *The Australian Aborigines* (Sydney 1938; 2d ed. Garden City 1964). J. G. FRAZER, *Totemism and Exogamy,* 4 v. (London 1910). S. FREUD, *Totem and Taboo* (1918), in *The Standard Edition of the Complete Psychological Works,* ed. J. STRACHEY, 24 v. (London 1953–) v.13. W. A. LESSA and E. Z. VOGT, eds., *Reader in Comparative Religion* (Evanston, Ill. 1958). C. LÉVI-STRAUSS, *Le Totémisme aujourd'hui* (Paris 1962). A. R. RADCLIFFE-BROWN, *Structure and Function in Primitive Society* (London 1952). R. L. SHARP, ''Notes on Northeast Australian Totemism,'' in *Studies in the Anthropology of Oceania and Asia,* ed. C. S. COON and J. M. ANDREWS (Cambridge, Mass. 1943). W. E. H. STANNER, ''Religion, Totemism and Symbolism,'' in *Aboriginal Man in Australia,* ed. R. M. and C. H. BERNDT (Sydney 1965).

[R. M. BERNDT]

TOTH, ALEXIS

Priest, Russian Orthodox leader in the U.S.; b. Prešov, Carpathian Ruthenia, 1854; d. Wilkes-Barrie, Pa., May 9, 1909. After ordination Toth (or Tovt) worked in the Prešov diocese as an Eastern Catholic priest until 1889, when he came to the United States after his wife's death, to minister to immigrant Catholics of the Ukrainian (Ruthenian) rite. Ukrainians in the U.S. then had nine Catholic parishes, chiefly in the coal-mining region of Pennsylvania. Until 1913 they were subject to the jurisdiction of the local Latin-rite bishops who were averse to having married priests work among the immigrants. Archbishop John IRELAND of St. Paul refused to accept Toth as pastor of the Ruthenian Catholic parish in Minneapolis because he had previously been married. The parishioners decided to follow Toth into Orthodoxy, and the Russian Orthodox Bishop Vladimir of San Francisco per-

sonally received 360 of them into his jurisdiction (March 25, 1891). In 1893 Toth was transferred to Wilkes-Barre, Pennsylvania, site of the largest Ruthenian colony in the country. With financial and moral support from Russia he established 17 Orthodox parishes for those whom he enticed from the Catholic faith. In a popular book, *Hde iskati i hyadati Pravdu?* (Where to Look to Find the Truth?), he argued that the lack of understanding and sympathy shown by Latin bishops for distinctive rites and customs, especially those permitting married clergy, was sufficient reason for leaving the Roman communion. The Orthodox promised Toth's followers their own hierarchy. Toth's activity has been thought ultimately responsible for the apostasy of nearly a quarter-million Slavic Catholics. He has been termed the Father of Orthodoxy in America because more than half of the 400,000 Russian Orthodox followers in the United States are descendants of his converts.

See Also: UKRAINIAN CATHOLIC CHURCH.

Bibliography: B. BOYSAK, *The Fate of the Holy Union in Carpatho-Ukraine* (privately pr.; Toronto, New York 1963).

[G. A. MALONEY]

TOUL, COUNCILS OF

A series of local councils held in Toul, France. (1) About 550 the bishops of Austrasia were convoked by King Theodebald to a council at Toul, whose bishop had complained to him against certain nobles. The archbishop of Reims claimed that the bishop should have appealed to him, not the King, and refused to attend; the council is known only from his correspondence. (2) In 859 Savonnières, a royal villa near Toul, was the site of a council of the Frankish Church, attended by bishops from 12 provinces. REMIGIUS OF LYON attempted to have his position on PREDESTINATION, as expressed at VALENCE (855) and just revised at LANGRES (859), approved by the council; but the matter was deferred and settled at Tuzey (860). (3) CALLISTUS II sent a cardinal legate to investigate reports that Gottfrid, Archbishop of Trier (1124–27), was guilty of simony. At mid-Lent, March 13, 1127, the legate and three bishops met in council at Toul for a preliminary hearing. Many accusers appeared, but since none were Gottfrid's peers (i.e., fellow bishops), the legate decided that the archbishop need only purge himself of infamy at a council at Worms three months later (May 15). There he did not attempt compurgation, but swore he was innocent and the next day resigned. Various diocesan synods were held also, e.g., 838, 1123, 1359, 1515.

Bibliography: C. J. VON HEFELE, *Histoire des conciles d'après les documents originaux,* tr. and continued by H. LECLERCQ,

10 v. in 19 (Paris 1907–38) 3.1:164–165 (for *c.* 550); 4.1:217–220; 4.2:1338–42, 1384–86 (for 859); 5.1:667 (for 1127).

[R. KAY]

TOURAINE REFORM

The Carmelite province of Touraine was established in 1384, during the WESTERN SCHISM. It was situated in west-central France, and embraced Orléanais, Maine, Anjou, Brittany, and Aunis. Especially as a result of the so-called religious wars, which in the second half of the 16th century brought France to the brink of ruin, the province in about 1600 presented a picture of a weak and far from spotless monastic life. General impoverishment and housing problems occasioned by the ravages of war had an unfavorable effect on community life and observance of the rule. With the establishment of peace under King Henry IV (1594–1610), a material and spiritual restoration got underway. The baroque movement and the COUNTER REFORMATION made their entrance into France. Theology and spirituality flourished, and there was a marked development of activity in the social field and in charity. New religious orders arose, and in practically all the older orders reform movements were in evidence. The Carmelites of the province of Touraine, who at this time were engaged in the restoration of their 16 monasteries, participated in this reform activity.

The Reform. The pioneer in this reform was Pierre Behourt (1564–1633), an energetic man who was hard on himself and on others. He struggled tirelessly and sternly to realize his ideals: the restoration of the old observance of the rule and of community life. At the age of 24, in 1588, he was made prior at Orléans and with the energy of youth, he there began his reform program. His effort at Orléans failed, and his following efforts at reform elsewhere were likewise destined to fail again and again. After ten years of futile struggle, he saw that he must put his hope in young religious. He sent a number of them to Paris, and two others he took with him to Ploërmel, where he was made prior in 1599. In the following year they renounced all personal possessions and thereby laid the foundations for the reform.

Behourt still had his mind set on the old Observant ideal of the 15th century. The situation was entirely different in the case of the young religious whom he had sent to Paris. In that center of religious renewal, they became acquainted with new, contemporary ideals and with new forms of religious life, and were deeply impressed and filled with a desire to embrace what they found. Philip Thibault (1572–1638) was the most distinguished member of the group. He was prudent and moderate, even somewhat timid by nature, but he possessed a strong sense of reality. Thanks to his diplomatic qualities, his gifts of leadership, and his financial ability, he was to succeed in introducing the new ideals and the current forms of spirituality into the reform. For the time being, however, the two groups went their own ways. Through the intervention of Henricus Sylvius, general of the order, Behourt's group, at the provincial capital of Nantes in 1604, received control over a monastery of their own, namely, that of Rennes.

Nevertheless, Behourt was never able to formulate concretely and carry out his own plan of reform. All his experiments with the rules of the Discalced Carmelites and of others failed. The Paris group, who were still in a state of uncertainty, went to Rome in the jubilee year (1600) in order to seek a solution for their difficulties. They did not get their solution, but received some encouragement. Back in France they tried, but without success, to get control over a monastery of their own. Behourt heard of this, and at his invitation a large part of the Paris group joined the group at Rennes in 1606. At the beginning of 1608, Thibault came also. His influence produced a split between the reformers, since his modern ideas seemed to be in conflict with Observant ideals of the older man. In November 1608 Thibault's program triumphed. Under his leadership the reform now really began to take on its characteristic features. Accordingly, the Tourainers defined their attitude in respect to the order. They did not wish to break away from membership in the order or from the province, nor did they wish to abandon the existing rule and constitutions, with their historically grounded adjustments or adaptations. However, they objected to the presence of reformed and non-reformed members in the one monastery, and they desired to give to every reformed monastery the right to direct its own organization.

The main point of the new program was really in the field of spirituality. Basing their plan on the existing legislation, the reformers adapted the old Carmelite ideal to the demands of their age, but without violating it in any essential way. They deliberately selected certain elements from the new ideas and modern forms of piety. In the years from 1608 to 1615, the revision was given form that found expression in the "Rules and Statutes" of 1612, and ultimately in the *Exercitia Conventualia* of 1615; these were officially approved at Rome. Down to the last detail, this codification mirrored the concepts and the customs of the reformers. Consequently it was very closely connected with their own age. Meanwhile, the membership increased rapidly. The movement spread out to the monasteries of Angers and Loudun, and at Chalain a new foundation was begun. The year 1615 marks the completion of the first and most important phase in the development of the reform. It spread very quickly. By

1636 all the 16 original monasteries of the province were reformed, and seven new foundations had been made. From 1618 the reform passed into the other five Carmelite provinces of France and Belgium, and around 1650, into Germany and Poland.

Influence and Characteristics. The reform exercised a great influence on the whole order, for at the general chapter of 1645 the constitutions of Touraine (developed out of the *Exercitia Conventualia* from 1615 to 1635) were prescribed for all reformed monasteries of the order. In Belgium the reform bore rich fruit (Michael a S. Augustino, Daniel a Virgine Maria, Maria Petyt). The province of Touraine itself sent out many missionaries to Central America. However, in the 18th century, the Touraine Reform declined rapidly, and after the French Revolution it had a rather feeble continuance in the monastery of Boxmeer (Netherlands). Nevertheless, the Touraine constitutions and customs exercised a great influence, which is reflected even in the present constitutions of the order.

The character of the Touraine Reform reflects the 17th century to a marked degree. Its most typical features may be summarized as follows: (1) An ideal of individual piety. Great emphasis was placed on interior prayer and on the human aspects of conscious communication with God, on improvement of one's spiritual life, and on pious practices. (2) Method in the spiritual life. This included methodical meditation and examination of conscience as a community exercise and means of sanctification, practice of the omnipresence of God, and aspirational prayer. (3) Preference for the unusual or striking: penitential practices, the cult of humility, great concern for outward impression. (4) New spiritual and monastic practices and devotions: meditations, examination of conscience, ten-day retreats, renewal of vows, Forty Hours Devotion, monthly patron, monthly virtue, devotion to the Child Jesus, etc. (5) Excessive regulation of life within and outside the monastery. (6) Strong devotion to Mary: Marial life (*Directoires des Novices*), Marial mysticism (Jean de Saint-Samson, Michael a S. Augustino, Maria Petyt), and the spread of the scapular devotion.

Outstanding writers of the movement were Jean de Saint-Samson, Dominique de Saint-Albert, Léon de Saint-Jean, Marc de la Nativité, Pierre de la Résurrection, Mathieu de Saint-Jean, Maur de l'Enfant Jésus, Michael a S. Augustino, Daniel a Virgine Maria, and Maria Petyt.

Bibliography: S. M. BOUCHEREAUX, *La Réforme des Carmes en France et Jean de St-Samson* (Paris 1950). P. W. JANSSEN, *Les Origines de la réforme des Carmes en France au XVIIᵉ siècle* (The Hague 1963). J. MACÉ, *Delineatio Observantiae Carmelitarum Rhedonensis* (Paris 1645). G. MESTERS, *Die rheinisehe Karmeliter-provinz während der Gegenreformation, 1600–1660* (Speyer 1958).

[P. W. JANSSEN]

TOURNÉLY, ÉLÉONOR FRANÇOIS DE

Founder of the Society of the SACRED HEART OF JESUS; b. Laval, Brittany, Jan. 21, 1767; d. Hagenbrunn, near Vienna, July 9, 1797. After priestly studies at Saint-Sulpice Seminary, Paris, where his piety, zeal, and attractive personality were remarked, the young aristocrat heeded the advice of Jacques ÉMERY, head of the seminary, and fled the French Revolution in 1791 to Luxembourg and Belgium. Dedicating his life to labor for the restoration of the JESUITS, suppressed by Clement XIV in 1773, he established a religious institute with this as its main purpose (May 8, 1794), and acted as its superior until his death. Together with his followers he eluded the armies of the French Revolution by moving to Cologne, Augsburg, and Vienna (August 1796), where he died of smallpox. Death overtook him before he could organize a religious congregation of women devoted to the education of girls and modeled on the Jesuits; but Father VARIN passed on his ideas to (St.) Madeleine Sophie BARAT, who then founded the Society of the SACRED HEART. This institute honors Tournély as the forerunner and ultimate inspiration of its foundress, and transferred his remains to its chapel in Vienna (Sept. 23, 1868).

Bibliography: F. SPEIL, *P. Léonor Franz von Tournély und die Gesellschaft des heiligen Herzens Jesu* (Breslau 1874). A. GUIDÉE, *Vie du R. P. Joseph Varin* (2d ed. Paris 1860). L. KOCH, *Jesuiten-Lexikon: Die Gesellschaft Jesu einst und jetzt* (Paderborn 1934); photoduplicated with rev. and suppl., 2 v. (Louvain-Heverlee 1962) 1763–64.

[J. F. BRODERICK]

TOURNELY, HONORÉ DE

Theologian; b. Antibes, near Nice, Aug. 28, 1658; d. Paris, Dec. 26, 1729. Tournely received a Doctorate of Theology at Paris in 1688, and after four years of teaching at the University of Douai, where he showed himself a strong anti-Jansenist, he was appointed Professor of Theology at the Sorbonne where he taught for 24 years (1692–1716). His principal work was *Praelectiones theologicae* (16 v. Paris 1725–30). There were numerous editions of it, as well as abridgements for use in seminaries. A notable abridgement of the whole work was published under the title *Honorati T. cursus theologicus scholastico-dogmaticus et moralis* (10 v. Venice 1731–46). His writings show Tournely to be an able and most influential theologian.

Charles Thomas Maillard de Tournon.

Forced by law to teach the Four Articles of 1682, he has been considered a moderate exponent of Gallicanism. He was, however, careful to imply that these principles were only opinions and exposed the opposing views. His personal activity in the Faculty of Theology of Paris, where he supported the condemnation of Maria d'Agreda (1697) and opposed the Chinese rituals (1700), associate him with the Ultramontane anti-Jansenist party. This is confirmed by his strenuous defense of the bull *Unigenitus*, both in 1714 on occasion of its registration at the Sorbonne and in 1729–1730 on the renewal of this registration.

Bibliography: J. HILD, *Tournely und seine Stellung zum Jansenismus* (Freiburg 1911). J. CARREYRE, *Dictionnaire de théologie catholique*, ed. A. VACANT et al. (Paris 1903–50) 15.1:1242–44. H. HURTER, *Nomenclator literarius theologiae catholicae* (Innsbruck 1903–13; 1926) 4:1111–13. P. FÉRET, *La Faculté de théologie de Paris. Époque moderne* (Paris 1910). M. SCHMAUS, "Die Kirchengliedschaft nach Honoré de Tournely," in E. ISERLOH and P. MANS, *Reformation Schicksal und Auftrag* (Baden Baden 1958). J. MAYR, *Die Ekklesiologie Honoré Tournelys* (Essen 1964). J. M. GRESGAYER, *Théologie et pouvoir en Sorbonne* (Paris 1991).

[P. K. MEAGHER/J. M. GRES-GAYER]

TOURNON, CHARLES THOMAS MAILLARD DE

Patriarch of Antioch, cardinal, apostolic visitor to the Far East, whose ill-fated China legation was followed by long government hostility to the Church; b. Turin, Dec. 21, 1668; d. Macau, June 8, 1710. Only 33 years old, but already distinguished at the Roman Curia, Tournon was chosen by Clement XI as papal plenipotentiary, with the title of patriarch and the comprehensive powers of legate *a latere* (Dec. 5, 1701) for an extremely difficult mission to the East Indies and the Sino-Manchu Empire. One key objective of the mission was solution of the CHINESE RITES CONTROVERSY. The legate, favored by the Catholic princes, sailed eastward from Cadiz on Feb. 9, 1703, and after extended sojourns at Pondichery (coast of India) and Manila, entered Beijing with honors on Dec. 4, 1705. Rome was electrified by his initial success when Tournon's report reached there a year afterward, and on Aug. 1, 1707, Clement elevated his envoy to the purple.

Three events of far-reaching consequence make Tournon's China career a decisive turning point in modern history. First, though the great Hsüan-Yeh emperor welcomed the pope's representative with unprecedented cordiality (first audience, Dec. 31, 1705), six months later he peremptorily warned him against any interference with the age-old national customs (second audience, June 29, 1706, with a curt dismissal reception the following day). This intransigence, further emphasized by several truculent decrees, doomed hopes of a Rome-Beijing entente on peaceful acceptance of a policy negative to the rites. Second, after the patriarch's departure south (August 28), the crisis at court came to a head. By edict of December 17, the Manchu sovereign ordered all missionaries to subscribe to the Matteo RICCI tradition of tolerance or suffer expulsion from the country (the *piao*, or residence permit test). Invoking Rome's secret decision of Nov. 20, 1704, Tournon countered the imperial despotism with an opposite mandate (Nanjing, Jan. 25, 1707), binding the same missionaries *sub poena excommunicationis* to repudiate the ceremonies in question as gravely illicit. Against this decree, and to stave off threatened ruin, the majority of the mission personnel appealed to the Holy See over the head of the legate; but all appeals were dismissed, and Tournon's ruling was upheld (1709). Third, for his Nanjing action Tournon was relegated to the Portuguese outpost of Macau, where he arrived on June 30, 1707. The three years to 1710, which he spent in detention there, were marked by a humiliating duel with the Catholic colonial officials, secular and ecclesiastical, who rejected his legatine authority as a violation of the Crown *padroado*. Long plagued by a painful abdominal malady, the indomitable prince of the Church quickly succumbed to apoplexy on Pentecost Sunday, six months after investiture with the red hat. His remains were taken back to Rome by the second Apostolic Visitor, Carlo Ambrogio MEZZABARBA, and interred in 1723 in the chapel of the Propaganda College.

Bibliography: [D. PASSIONEI,] *Memorie storiche dell' Eminentiss. Monsignor cardinale di Tournon,* 8 v. (Venice 1761–62), highly critical of the China Jesuits. R. C. JENKINS, *The Jesuits in China and the Legation of Cardinal de Tournon* (London 1894), follows the *Memorie,* but more objective in interpretation. L. PASTOR, *The History of the Popes From the Close of the Middle Ages,* 40 v. (London-St. Louis 1938–61): v.1, 6th ed.; v.2, 7th ed.; v.3–6, 5th ed.; v.7–8, 11–12, 3d ed.; v.9–10, 4th ed.; v.13–40, from 1st German ed. *Geschichte der Päpste seit dem Ausgang des Mittelalters,* 16 v. in 21. (Freiburg 1885–1933; repr. 1955–) 33:428–453, for Beijing negotiations uses contemporary Jesuit diary. A. S. ROSSO, *Apostolic Legations to China of the Eighteenth Century* (South Pasadena, Calif. 1948) 149–186, with tr. of relevant Chinese documents, 231–294. F. A. ROULEAU, "Maillard de Tournon, Papal Legate at the Court of Peking," *Archivum historicum Societatis Jesu* 31 (1962) 264–323.

[F. A. ROULEAU]

TOURNUS, ABBEY OF

Former Benedictine monastery, France (Departement Saône-et-Loire), founded in 875, perhaps in a castle attached to a church dedicated to the martyr St. Valerian (d. 177). The church was presented by Charles the Bald to the monks from the Abbey of Noirmoutier who fled the Normans in 836 and brought with them the relics of St. PHILIBERT, who became, after Our Lady, the secondary patron; hence the name Saint-Philibert de Tournus. Pope John VIII approved the foundation in 877; in 937 the monastery was burned by the Hungarians. Tournus was a center of intellectual life from the 10th to 13th centuries; in the 15th century it became a commendatory abbey. It was plundered in 1562 by the HUGUENOTS, and in 1627 it was converted into a secular collegial foundation of the Diocese of Chalon-sur-Saône until its suppression in 1785. The three-nave basilica was constructed between 1000 and *c.* 1120.

Bibliography: G. ALLEMANG, *Lexikon für Theologie und Kirche,* ed. M. BUCHBERGER, 10 v. (Freiburg 1930–38) 10:238. L. H. COTTINEAU, *Répertoire topobibliographique des abbayes et prieurés,* 2 v. (Mâcon 1935–39) 2: 3189–90.

[P. VOLK]

TOURON, ANTOINE

Historian; b. Graulhet, near Castres, France, Sept. 5, 1686; d. Paris, Sept. 2, 1775. He became a Dominican in Toulouse in 1706, master of novices at St. Dominic's in Paris (*c.* 1731), and theologian at the Casanate in Rome (1750–51). It seems he spent the rest of his life in Paris. At 50 years of age, he began his studies of the Dominican Order: the lives of St. Thomas and St. Dominic (Paris 1737, 1739) and especially his *Histoire des hommes illustres de l'ordre de Saint-Dominique* (6 v. Paris

Saint-Philibert in Tournus: Nave. (©Vanni Archive/CORBIS)

1743–49), still in part a valuable work. Touron then turned to apologetics and attacked the skepticism of Enlightened philosophy in a treatise *De la providence* (1752), *La main de Dieu sur les incrédules, ou histoire abrégée des Israélites* (3 v. 1756), and *Parallèle de l'incrédule et du vrai fidèle* (1756). After *La vie et l'esprit de S. Charles Borromée* (1761), he undertook his *Histoire générale de l'Amérique depuis sa découverte* (14 v. 1768–70), based on Spanish works and concerned especially with religious aspects.

Bibliography: A. PAPILLON, "Antoine Touron historiographe dominicain," *Archivum fratrum praedicatorum* 7 (1937) 320–329.

[A. DUVAL]

TOURS, ARCHDIOCESE OF

Metropolitan see in central France since *c.* 400. Thanks to GREGORY (540–594), Archbishop of Tours after 573, Tours' religious beginnings are well known.

St. Gatien Cathedral, Tours, France, c. late 1900s. (©Michael Maslan Historic Photographs/CORBIS)

He gives St. Gatian (*Catianus*) as the first bishop, sent by the pope *c.* 250; but the date is too early, for Gregory himself says the fourth bishop died in 385.

The glory of Tours began with the episcopacy of St. Martin (372 to Nov. 8, 397), known for two facts of fundamental importance: he evangelized the Tours countryside, establishing in villages (*vici*) the first six rural parishes in France; and he gave monks an important role in this apostolate. On the right bank of the Loire across from Tours he founded the monastery of MARMOUTIER, and Sulpicius Severus says that 2,000 monks were at his burial (Nov. 11).

For centuries afterward Tours was especially known for the shrine of St. Martin, the most popular and famous pilgrimage center in Christendom. Gregory recounts the miracles worked there. Clovis, after his victory over the Visigoths, came as a pilgrim to Tours in 507 and received there the message of the Emperor of the East, who gave him the title of (honorary) consul. Some historians have claimed that Clovis was baptized in Tours and not in REIMS. A sumptuous basilica that had been built on the tomb of Martin was dedicated in 472. Clovis's queen, CLOTILDE (d. 545), came to Tours to end her days. An important monastery continued that was founded by Martin and cared for pilgrims. Its most famous abbot, ALCUIN, who came from England on Charlemagne's request, founded a school and a calligraphic SCRIPTORIUM there that produced excellent MSS in the script called Caroline minuscule, the model for modern type. The kings of France preserved Martin's cape (*cappa, chape*), whence the word CHAPEL, the shrine where it was kept. In 853 the Norman threat caused St. Martin's relics to be moved to AUXERRE; they were returned Dec. 13, 885, but had to be kept protected within Tours' walls until 919.

After Alcuin's death (804), the Abbey of St-Martin became a chapter of canons, the most famous in France. The kings kept the title Abbot of St. Martin, and the canons were powerful lay lords, richly endowed. Popes came on pilgrimage: Urban II (1096), Pascal II (1107), Callistus II (1119), and Alexander III (1163). All the kings of France came there and were received as collegiate canons. The 11th-century basilica dedicated in 1108 was rebuilt after 1175. The pilgrimage of St. Martin lost importance *c.* 1200, as ROME, the Holy Land, SANTIAGO DE COMPOSTELA, and MONT SAINT-MICHEL became more popular. During the French Revolution the chapter was abolished and most of the basilica was destroyed. In 1860, thanks to M. Dupont (1797–1876) and Abp. Joseph Guibert (1857–71), the body of St. Martin was rediscovered (Dec. 14); a new basilica was built, and the pilgrimage continues.

Many Merovingian and Carolingian Church councils were held in Tours; Urban II presided in 1096, and Alexander III in 1162 when Frederick I Barbarossa was excommunicated (attended by St. Thomas Becket). The numerous saints from Tours include Maurus and Brigitte (fourth century), Flovier (fifth century), Ursus (508), and Avertinus (*c.* 1189). More recent are Bl. JEANNE DE MAILLÉ (d. 1414), and St. FRANCIS OF PAOLA (d. 1507). François PALLU (d. 1684) was a founder of the PARIS FOREIGN MISSION SOCIETY. Tours' prelates include: PERPETUUS (*c.* 461–491), advocate of vigils, fasts, and the veneration of saints; VOLUSIANUS (491–498); the poet HILDEBERT OF LAVARDIN (1125–33); Elias of Bourdeille (1468–84), who assisted at the Estates General in Tours in 1468; Georges d' Armagnac (1548–51); Alexander FARNESE (1553–54); and BOISGELIN DE CUCÉ (1802–04). The council of 1054 condemned the heretic BERENGARIUS, enemy of the school of BEC, who taught grammar, rhetoric, and perhaps medicine in Tours. In and around Tours there are many religious monuments and châteaux. There is no religious history of the diocese.

Bibliography: *Gallia Christiana* (Paris 1856–65) v.14. E. R. VAUCELLE, *La Collégiale de Saint-Martin de Tours* (Paris 1907). *Revue d'histoire de l'Église de France* 47 (1961) i–xiv, 1–221, articles by various authors in connection with the Année martinienne. P. BATAILLE and E. R. VAUCELLE, *Saint-Martin de Tours* (Paris 1925). R. FIOT, *Jean Bourdichon et Saint François de Paule* (Tours 1961). D. BEAUNIER, *Abbayes et prieurés de l'ancienne France*, ed. J. M. L. BESSE., v.8 (Paris 1920). *Annuario Pontificio* (Rome 1964) 455, 1410.

[E. JARRY]

TOUSSAINT, PIERRE

Former slave, hairdresser, entrepreneur, philanthropist; b. 1766, the French colony of Saint Domingue (in modern day Haiti); d. June 30, 1853, New York City.

Toussaint's mother and maternal grandmother were house slaves on a plantation in the Artibonite River Valley, near Saint Marc. The owner, Pierre Bérard, a devout Catholic treated his slaves in a humane manner. As a young child, Toussaint was baptized and not put into the fields, but worked as a house slave and was taught how to read and write. Allowed access to Bérard's library, Toussaint perfected his knowledge of French by reading the classical sermons of 17th century preachers, and in the process acquired a deep attachment to his Catholic faith.

After Pierre Bérard returned to France, his son Jean-Jacques took over the Artibonite plantation. In 1787, as the political situation in Saint Domingue worsened, Jean-Jacques brought his wife and five slaves, among them Toussaint, his younger sister Rosalie, his aunt Marie Bouquement and two other house slaves to New York City to ride out the crisis. In 1788, Jean-Jacques passed away suddenly of pleurisy on a visit to Saint Domingue to regain his properties. Toussaint came to the rescue of the now penniless Marie Elisabeth Bérard. Having been apprenticed to a local hairdresser by Jean-Jacques before he returned to Saint Domingue, Toussaint opened his own hairdressing business. A skillful hairdresser who was in great demand by the New York socialites, Toussaint was quickly able to earn enough as a hairdresser to support Marie Elisabeth, himself and the other slaves in the household. He was finally freed shortly before her death in 1807.

Toussaint achieved economic success as a renowned hairdresser in New York in the first half of the 19th century, rendering services to prominent socialites. He was able to purchase the freedom of his sister, Rosalie, and a fellow slave from Saint Domingue, Marie Rose Juliette, whom he married in 1811. When the married and subsequently abandoned Rosalie died, he and Juliette, who was childless, adopted their niece, Euphémie.

In addition to investing his wealth in stock and property, he also donated generously to various charities in the City. A devout Catholic, he attended Mass every morning and visited the Blessed Sacrament at the end of each day. Toussaint jumped over the barricades to nurse the sick and abandoned in times of pestilence. He and his wife nursed back to health a priest suffering from typhus. He provided shelter for homeless black youths, teaching them how to play the violin. He was generous with his funds both to whites and blacks alike. He was deeply in love with his wife, and among the few letters from his own hand are those sent to his wife when they were briefly separated. Among the most interesting of the letters found among his papers are several letters from George Paddington, a black man from Dublin, who was ordained a priest by Bishop England to serve as a priest in Haiti. The letters sent to Pierre Toussaint and preserved among his papers provide the best testimony of the honor and respect in which he was held.

Like all blacks in antebellum New York, Toussaint experienced racial discrimination despite his position as a man of substance. He and his wife were refused access to St. Patrick's Old Cathedral by an usher. Nevertheless, after his death almost immediately many persons of the time began to speak of his reputation for sanctity. Toussaint died in New York City on June 30, 1853. Cardinal John O'Connor introduced his cause for beatification in 1990. Pope John Paul II declared him Venerable in 1997.

Bibliography: The Pierre Toussaint papers, comprising about 1,200 items are kept in the New York Public Library. H.F.S. LEE, *Memoir of Pierre Toussaint: Born a Slave in St. Domingo* (Boston 1854, reprinted 1992). H. BINSSE, ''Pierre Toussaint: A Catholic Uncle Tom,'' *Historical Records and Studies* 12 (1918) 90–101. L. R. RYAN, ''Pierre Toussaint: God's Image Carved in Ebony,'' *Historical Records and Studies* 25 (1935) 39–58. A. SHEEHAN and E.O. SHEEHAN, *Pierre Toussaint, A Citizen of Old New York* (New York 1955). N. M. DORSEY, *Pierre Toussaint of New York: Slave and Freedman: A Study of Lay Spirituality in Times of Social and Religious Change* (Rome 1986). T. J. SHELLEY, ''Black and Catholic in Nineteenth-Century New York: The Case of Pierre Toussaint,'' *Records of the American Catholic Historical Society of Philadelphia* 102 (Winter 1991) 1–18. C. DAVIS, *The History of Black Catholics in the United States* (New York 1993). M. N. L. COUVE DE MURVILLE, *Slave from Haiti, A Saint for New York? : The Life of Pierre Toussaint* (London 1995). E. TARRY, *Pierre Toussaint: Apostle of Old New York* (Boston 1998).

[C. DAVIS]

TOVINI, GIUSEPPE ANTONIO, BL.

Married lawyer, journalist, politician, lay Franciscan tertiary; b. March 14, 1841, Cividate Camuno (near Brescia), Italy; d. Jan. 16, 1897, Brescia.

Giuseppe, the eldest of the seven children of Mosè Tovini and Rosa Malaguzzi, attended schools at Breno and Lovere (1852–58). His priest-uncle, Giambattista Malaguzzi, obtained a scholarship for him at a school in Verona, and then at the diocesan seminary. Following the death of his father (June 1859), Giuseppe enrolled in the law faculty at the University of Padua (1860–64). He continued his legal studies at the University of Pavia (1864–65) while working as an assistant director and teacher in a secondary school. Returning to Brescia in 1867, he worked in the law firm of Giordano Corbolani, whose daughter Emilia he married in January 1875. They had ten children, one of whom became a Jesuit and two who because religious sisters.

As mayor of Cividate (1871–74) he initiated several important public works, including the Bank of Vallecamonica (Breno) and a railroad connection to Brescia. From 1877, Giuseppe was especially involved in the Catholic Movement of Brescia. He collaborated in the creation of a Catholic daily paper, *Il Cittadino di Brescia*, where he later became manager. The paper's editor was Giorgio Montini, father of future Pope Paul VI. As president of the diocesan committee of *Opera dei Congressi*, a program designed to counter repression of the Church and anticlerical sentiment, he travelled throughout the region forming parochial committees. He later had regional (Lombardy) and national leadership roles in the organization. Beginning in 1879, he encouraged Catholic involvement in Brescian politics, invoking the ire of the liberal intelligentsia. He was elected provincial councilman for the district of Pisogne (1879) and city councilman in Brescia (1882). It was from these political positions that he able to defended the weak and poor people of his district.

In 1881, Tovini became a member of the Third Order of Saint Francis, which he found a providential way of living and serving in the world—living a life of voluntary poverty. Tovini became prior of the congregation in 1884, a post he held until his death. Of seemingly boundless energy and wanting to imbue every aspect of labor and industry with Catholic values, Tovini organized local and national Catholic congresses, founded charitable institutions, initiated the *Banco Ambrosiano* (1896), *Banco S. Paulo* (Brescia, 1888), and an agricultural union. In 1881 he disseminated constitutions for the establishment of societies of Catholic workers, small farm loan banks, and mutual aid societies.

Tovini's other important contributions were in the educational arena. He defended religious education in the schools and advocated free education in order to form youth to fulfill their civic and social responsibilities. For this purpose he founded (1882) a kindergarten (*l'Asilo San Giuseppe*), an association of fathers of families, the *Società Cesare Arici*, and an academy (*l'Istituto venerabile Alessandro Luzzago*); invited the Canossian Sisters

to open a girls school in Cividate Camuno (1894); and promoted and raised funds for the establishment of the Saint Antony of Padua University (1884), Artigianelli Institute (1891), and an international Catholic university in Rome (1891). He collaborated in the formation of the *Unione Leone XIII*, which was the foundation of the Federation of Italian Catholic Students (FUCI). Tovini used the media to spread Catholic faith by establishing pedagogical and religious periodicals, such as *Fede e Scuola* (from 1891), *Scuola Italiana Moderna* (from 1893), and *La Voce del Popolo* (from 1893).

Tovini, who had suffered from poor health throughout his life, died at age 56. His mortal remains were solemnly translated to the church of San Luca at Brescia, Sept. 10, 1922. He was declared venerable April 6, 1995. Pope John Paul II beatified Tovini at Brescia, Sept. 20, 1998, at the end of the centenary celebration of the birth of Pope Paul VI, who spoke often of Tovini.

Feast: Jan. 16 (Franciscans).

Bibliography: *Acta Apostolicae Sedis* 20 (1998): 956–958. *L'Osservatore Romano,* Eng. ed. 28 (1998): 1–2.

[K. I. RABENSTEIN]

TOWER OF BABEL

In this traditional expression the Hebrew word, *bābel,* for the city of BABYLON, is retained. The story of the Tower of Babel is told in Gn 11.1–9. This article will consider the literary structure of this story, its Mesopotamian coloring, and its significance in the book of GENESIS.

Literary Structure. The story begins abruptly with only a vague reference to what has gone before. It does not fit smoothly after the Table of the Nations (ch. 10), which supposes a distribution of mankind over the earth and even mentions historical Babel or Babylon (10.10). The tower incident could not have come immediately after the story of the FLOOD (ch. 6–9) and before the Table of the Nations because a greater number of men are involved than were in the ark with NOAH. And if a period of time were supposed to have elapsed, with a consequent increase in population, the ranging of all nations under Noah's three sons would have lost its meaning. In itself the account is a well-knit unit, but it betrays evidence of two formerly separate strands. There are two distinct invitations to begin the work (v.3, v.4). There are two building operations: one of a city that men build in order not to be scattered; the other of a tower that they erect in order to make a name for themselves. In opposition to the former purpose Yahweh scatters them over the earth; to frustrate the latter purpose Yahweh confuses their speech.

Ziggurat at Ur, viewed from the northwest.

The story is an ETIOLOGY, offering a reason for mankind's dispersion over the earth and the great differences in human languages. It also provides a popular, though erroneous, etymology of the name of Babylon. In Akkadian the name of this city, *bāb-ili*, means "the Gate of God." But the corresponding Hebrew word, *bābel*, is taken to mean "mixture, confusion," as if from the root *bll* (v.9). While the present story retains these various strands, it subordinates them to the comprehensive theme of the PRIMEVAL AGE IN THE BIBLE (see discussion below).

Local Color. The Mesopotamian origin of the story can be seen in its local coloring. The event is said to have taken place in "a valley [Hebrew *biq'â,* low-lying plain] in the land of Sennaar [Hebrew *Šin'ār*]" (v. 2). This is ancient Sumeria, extending from slightly north of modern Baghdad to slightly south of Nasiriyeh (cf. Gn 10.10; 14.1, 9). The use of baked clay bricks for large buildings, while strange in Palestine, was normal in the alluvial plain of Mesopotamia, where stone was scarce. The author emphasized the material chosen, since his audience would have considered it particularly ill-suited for a large and permanent structure.

The tower can refer only to one of the huge stepped towers or ziggurats (to use the ancient term) associated with the various sanctuaries of ancient Mesopotamia. The towers may have been stylized "mountains of god" or stairways to heaven (cf. Gn 28.12). The ziggurat of Marduk, in Babylon, the *é-temen-an-ki,* "House of the Foundation of Heaven and Earth," more than 297 feet high, was one of the most famous of these towers (*see* MESOPOTAMIA, ANCIENT). The Biblical narrative probably is connected with this or some other ziggurat that was temporarily in ruins. But the story as such is not one a native Mesopotamian would be likely to tell about the most imposing monuments of his land. In the eyes of the Israelites these gigantic structures and the cities whose culture produced them were signs of a human resourcefulness and pride that ill prepared men to acknowledge the supreme sovereignty of God in all their affairs.

Significance of the Story in Genesis. Driven by ambition and by the need for security and permanence on the earth, men began to use their ingenuity and pooled their resources to do together what they could never accomplish singly. While the city and its lofty tower were to be admirable accomplishments, there is no indication that they were planned as an assault on heaven. The story may once have contained a motif of divine jealousy in the face of human accomplishments, but there is no sure trace of that now. In fact, the reason for Yahweh's action in dispersing the men and confusing their tongues is obscure and unsatisfying. The suggestion of prevention (v. 6–7) does not imply that Yahweh was afraid of what man might later do to Him. The present dispersion of men and their inability to communicate easily with one another because of language barriers are indeed attributed to divine action rather than to natural causes, but the precise reason for the action is not given.

Within the wider context of the primeval history of Genesis, however, the divine preventive action makes more sense. According to Genesis, ch. 1 to 11, every advance in civilization has been accompanied by a corresponding increase of human sin. The divine intervention on the plain of Sennaar, then, is a preventive measure designed to obviate a further increase in sin once the city and tower were finished.

Taken together with the Table of Nations, which the author has deliberately juxtaposed, the Tower of Babel incident contributes to a rounded understanding of man's life in the world of cities and nations. The separation of mankind into different nations and peoples is something natural and good, the result of normal human life (ch. 10). At the same time, the disharmony and lack of understanding among peoples is not so natural. It has been willed by God, but because of man's sinful nature. It is both a punishment on man for the sins of his forebears and a striking reminder of his human limitations and of his need for divine guidance and aid.

Finally, the narrative in Gn 11.1–9 draws the primeval history of the YAHWIST to a close on a note of divine punishment and human need. The peoples of the earth are scattered, cut off from one another and from God. The answer to their need is found in SALVATION HISTORY, the account of God's special acts of grace in human time. The first of these is His choice of ABRAHAM, one man out of the scattered peoples, in whom all the families of the earth would eventually be blessed (12.1–3). From this time on, the divine activity would be manifest in various ways, reaching its perfect expression in the life, death, and Resurrection of Jesus Christ.

Bibliography: B. VAWTER, *A Path Through Genesis* (New York 1956). G. VON RAD, *Genesis: A Commentary,* tr. J. H. MARKS (Philadelphia 1961). A. PARROT, *The Tower of Babel,* tr. E. HUDSON (New York 1955).

[K. G. O'CONNELL]

TOZZO, ST.

Bishop of Augsburg; d. *c.* 777, probably at Augsburg. As a Benedictine monk of Murbach, Tozzo (Tosso)

according to legend was instrumental in gaining recognition for MAGNUS (first abbot of Füssen) from WIKTERP, bishop of Augsburg, who ordered Tozzo to conduct Magnus to Füssen. After helping him to establish a church and monastery there, Tozzo labored nearby at Waltenhofen as a parish priest. Tozzo succeeded Wikterp as bishop of Augsburg *c.* 772. Nothing is known of his administration. He was buried in the church of St. AFRA in Augsburg. Tozzo is usually represented with a torch in hand.

Feast: Jan. 16.

Bibliography: A. ZIMMERMANN, *Lexikon für Theologie und Kirche,* ed. M. BUCHBERGER, 10 v. (Freiburg 1930–38) 10:242. M. COENS, ''La Vie de S. Magne de Füssen, par Otloh de Saint-Emmeran,'' B. DE GAIFFIER, *Analecta Bollandiana* 81 (1963) 159–227; ''Une Vie-panégyrique de saint Magne de Füssen,'' *ibid.* 321–332. F. ZOEPFL, *Das Bistum Augsburg und seine Bischöfe im Mittelalter* (Munich 1956).

[M. J. STALLINGS]

TRACT

A section of Gregorian chant, ornate in style, that was historically sung during a penitential period in place of the Alleluia before the liturgical reforms of Vatican II. This included: (1) the Sundays and certain privileged ferial days of Lent (the use of the Tract *Domine non secundum,* repeated on the Mondays, Wednesdays, and Fridays of each week in Lent, originated in the 11th century), as well as the Easter Triduum until Holy Saturday (on this day, however, as an exception, it was sung with the Alleluia and immediately after it); (2) on the feasts of saints that fell in Lent; (3) on On Ember Saturdays, and (4) at requiem masses. Traditionally, the Tract was sung alternately by the two sides of the choir although it was sometimes sung by a soloist with the full choir, or by a group of singers with the full choir.

Origin of the Term. According to Amalarius (see text below), the difference between the Tract and the Gradual lay in its execution: the Tract was chanted without a response from the choir, whereas the Gradual was sung as a responsory. Performed by a soloist, the Tract was sung in one stretch—in Latin *tractim*—somewhat like a recitation [MS Paris, Bibl. Nat. nouv. acq. 1541, fol. 110, that uses *tractim* for the recitation of the Passion; this same word is studied by L. Kunz in *Kirchenmusikalisches Jahrbuch* 334 (1950) 8]. It should be noted, however, that certain Tracts of the second mode (see below) in the oldest MSS are designated by the expression *Responsorium graduale*—or more simply, according to Amalarius (*Liber officialis,* 1.2, ed. Hanssens, *Studi e Testi* 139) by the word *responsorius* (see Hesbert). For Holy Saturday Tracts the MS uses the term *canticum* (see

Hesbert LX); indeed, the Tracts for this day were taken not from the Psalms, but from the Canticles of the Old Testament (Ex 15; Is 5; Dt 32). The medieval Tract melody replaced an older one executed in responsorial form of which there remains only one example: the canticle *Vinea* [*Revue Grégorienne* 31 (1952) 131; *Sacris erudiri* 6 (1954) 100].

Medieval Texts Referring to the Tract. Amalarius in his *Liber officialis* (3.12; *loc. cit.* p. 299) pointed out the basic difference between Gradual and Tract: *Hoc differt inter responsorium cui chorus respondet et tractum cui nemo* ("This is the difference between the response [the Gradual] to which the choir answers and the Tract to which there is no reply"). In general, the *Ordines Romani* (ed. M. Andrieu, *Ordo I* and ff.) and the *Expositiones Missae* by known authors (RABANUS MAURUS, FLORUS OF LYONS, REMIGIUS OF AUXERRE) or by anonymous authors (Wilmart's list in "Expositio Missae," *Dictionnaire d'archéologie chrétienne et de liturgie*. ed. F. Cabrol, H. Leclercq and H. I. Marrou [Paris 1907–53] 5.1:1015) all mentioned the Tract, especially in the description of Good Friday and Holy Saturday. In this respect it should be noted that the Good Friday Tract, *Eripe me,* was mentioned as *nuperrime compilatum* ("very recently compiled") by the pseudo-Alcuin (*De Divin. officiis* 18; *Patrologia Latina*. ed. J. P. Migne [Paris 1878–90] 101:1209), who wrote at the beginning of the 10th century. In fact, this Tract does not appear in any of the oldest Graduals. William DURANTI (The Elder) in his *Rationale* (4:21) attributes a shade of sadness to the Tract.

Musical Analysis. The Tract, whether it be a question of the second or eighth mode, had its own formula of intonation, at times very beautiful (for example, the *Commovisti*), that was not used in the rest of the composition and terminated with another very full concluding formula (*cauda*). The verses used formulas that began with an intonation, continued with a recitative part (at times syllabic or slightly ornate, such as by means of an "embroidered *pes*"), and ended with a melismatic cadence.

There were only two melodic types of Tracts, one of the second mode and one of the eighth. The choice of mode was not contingent upon expression (the eighth mode might express joy; the second, sorrow), but instead depended upon the length of the text (Ferretti, 142–43). In fact, the melody of the Tract in the second mode offered a much wider choice of formulas and was consequently better suited to long Tracts and allowed leeway for greater variety. The eighth mode, poorer in formulas, was used for shorter Tracts. Of the 21 Tracts of the "primitive repertory" (Hesbert, 244), 15 belonged to the eighth mode and only six to the second. The Tracts that were composed later (*Nunc dimittis,* 9th–10th Century; *Tu es Petrus, Audi Filia,* and *Gaude Maria,* 11th century) likewise follow one of the two modal types mentioned.

Bibliography: P. M. FERRETTI, *Estetica gregoriana* (Rome 1934–) 1:142–165. J. FROGER, "Les Chants de la messe aux VIIIᵉ et IXᵉ siècles," *Revue Grégorienne* 26 (1947) 221–228. R. J. HESBERT, ed., *Antiphonale missarum sextuplex* (Brussels 1935). E. JAMMERS, *Musik in Byzanz, im päpstlichen Rom und im Frankenreich* (Heidelberg 1962). J. A. JUNGMANN, *The Mass of the Roman Rite,* tr. F. A. BRUNNER, 2 v. (New York 1951–55). W. APEL, *Gregorian Chant* (Bloomington, Ind. 1958). D. HILEY, *Western Plainchant: A Handbook* (Oxford 1993) 76–82. J. MCKINNON, "The Gregorian Canticle-Tracts of the Old Roman Easter Vigil,"*Festschrift Walter Wiora zum 90. Geburtstag,* ed. C.-H. MAHLING and R. SEIBERTS (Tutzing 1997) 254–69. T. KARP, *Aspects of Orality and Formularity in Gregorian Chant* (Evanston, IL 1998).

[M. HUGLO/EDS.]

TRACTARIANISM

A doctrinal system held by a group of Anglican clergymen who led the OXFORD MOVEMENT, intended to revive the Anglo-Catholic tradition of the Church of England. The name was derived from the widely circulated, extremely influential tracts or pamphlets propagating their ideas that were published from 1833 to 1841. The leaders, NEWMAN, KEBLE, R. H. FROUDE, and PUSEY, opposed the theological LIBERALISM and ERASTIANISM of their age, and reaffirmed the divine authority of the Church of England as a branch of the historically continuous Catholic Church. They stressed the importance of the sacraments as indispensable means of grace, and insisted on the authority of the bishops as successors of the Apostles. Tractarianism met opposition from political and religious leaders, principally for its alleged tendencies toward Rome. A major crisis occurred with the publication of Newman's *Tract 90,* which maintained that the THIRTY-NINE Articles were not directed principally against Roman dogmas, but against abuses in the Roman system. When the bishops repudiated this tract, Newman, W. G. WARD, and others submitted to Rome, but the movement under Pusey and Keble survived to have a profound influence on the Church of England (*see* ANGLICANISM; HIGH CHURCH).

Bibliography: J. WALSH and C. HAYDON, *The Church of England, c. 1689-c. 1833: From Toleration to Tractarianism* (Cambridge, England 1993). national

[T. S. BOKENKOTTER/EDS.]

TRADITION (IN THE BIBLE)

There are two concepts designated by the term tradition: the body of beliefs accepted by a society that gives it continuity with past generations and unity within itself and the process by which these beliefs are transmitted.

In the Old Testament. Israel's history, beginning with the Patriarchs, covered more than a millennium and a half. It was by the transmission and development of Israel's tradition that unity of spirit and growth in understanding were made possible.

Formulation. Tradition needs to be formulated in some manner that will make transmission possible. The formulation will take different forms depending on time and place and the circle within which it takes place. Thus, the acts and requirements of Israel's God may be incorporated into historical narrative, poetry, prophetic oracles, or legislation. In addition to the spoken or written word, tradition may be incorporated into liturgical acts that recall the events of the past in cultic celebration. Since the main purpose of tradition is to actualize the events of the past and put the believer in contact with the saving work of God, this method is extremely important. Note the use of the term "memorial" for some of these rites (Ex 12.14) and the similar intent of the Last Supper in the New Testament (1 Cor 11.24–26).

Content. The essence of Old Testament tradition lies in the history it recounts and the inspired interpretation given it; this is the content of the summaries of faith ("cultic credos") in Dt 6.20–24; 26.5–9; Jos 24.2–13. The cultic act was accompanied by an explanation that is explicitly commanded to be repeated to each new generation (Ex 12.26–27).

Tradition was capable of growth and reformulation. As new insights into God's plan were acquired, they were incorporated into the very recital of the events of the past. Such reformulation was not a falsification of ancient truths, but was rather a means of approaching more truly to God's eternal plan. The account of the call of Abraham in Genesis, for example, while resting on an early tradition, reveals insights acquired in the light of later events. Thus, there is a close connection between tradition and revelation.

The transition from oral tradition to written documents was gradual and is largely hidden in obscurity. National calamities in which the very structure of society was threatened, such as the fall of Judah in 587 B.C., would have given great impetus to committing traditions to writing. Scholars of the Uppsala school tend to hold that little of the Old Testament was written before exilic times, but their views have not been universally accepted.

In the New Testament. Tradition in the New Testament builds on the Old Testament, but is unique in many ways. Its essential content is the saving work of God in Jesus Christ. The period from its beginning to the completion of the New Testament was brief, well under a century.

Beginning and Formulation. Studies of H. Riesenfeld, B. Gerhardsson, and others have related New Testament tradition to rabbinic practice. The great rabbis gathered disciples who memorized their teachings and passed them on to others. Christ, too, was known as a RABBI (Mk 9.4; 11.21 etc.), a term that the New Testament usually renders as διδάσκαλος (teacher), gave special care to the formation of His close followers, who were called DISCIPLES (μαθηταί), and formulated His sayings in a manner apt for memorization by the use of parallelism, rhythm, and other techniques (see Mt 7.24–27). The institution of the Lord's Supper suggests that Jesus expected a lengthy period before His return, and if He wanted His teachings proclaimed to others and His work actualized for them, the formation of such a group was essential. Thus the kernel of New Testament tradition stems from the words of Jesus on the one hand and from the accounts of eyewitnesses to His ministry on the other.

In the Early Church. The first act of the Apostles after the Ascension was to choose a replacement for Judas; the function of the TWELVE was to bear witness to the work of God in Christ, especially to the ministry and Resurrection (Acts 1.15–26). The Twelve acted as a *collegium* with the duty of instructing and forming new converts; this was accomplished by the spoken word, but also by liturgical rites and prayers (Acts 2.42). Form-critical studies have shown that many of the Gospel narratives were formulated in this earliest community. The selection and formation of Gospel materials was not done mechanically, however, but with an eye to the needs of the community. (*See* FORM CRITICISM, BIBLICAL.)

The early existence of Christian tradition is attested also in the New Testament Epistles; this is important, for those of St. Paul, on the whole, are the earliest writings of the New Testament. Paul did not know Jesus in the flesh, but was called to the apostolic ministry after the Ascension. For this reason he often had to defend his authority as an Apostle. Yet, even in his earliest writings, it is clear that he submits his teaching to those who were Apostles before him (Gal 2.1–10) and bases it not only on the revelation made to him, but also on what had already been established as tradition. For example, A. M. Hunter has found in Paul's Epistles creedal formulas (1 Cor 15.3–7; Rom 1.3–5; 10.8–9), hymns (Eph 5.14; Phil 2.6–11), stereotyped catechetical instruction, called τύπο ν διδαχῆς (pattern of teaching; Rom 6.17), and allusion to or citation of sayings of Christ (1 Cor 7.10; 9.14; 11.24–25), all of which he must have received from those who were Christians before him. C. H. Dodd has shown that even Paul's utilization of the Old Testament exhibits a pattern common to other New Testament writers. (*See* TESTIMONIA.)

St. Paul, himself the product of strict rabbinical training, uses the technical terms of the rabbinic tradition-process in their Greek equivalents: παραδιδόναι (for Heb. *māsar*), to pass on, correlative to παραλαμβάνειν (for Heb. *qibbēl*), to receive, in 1 Cor 11.23 and 15.3; κρατεῖν and κατέχειν, to hold fast, and many others. Although Jesus had rejected purely human tradition (Mk 7.1–13), He is the new Moses (as shown in His Sermon on the Mount), and His word is to be held and kept as the new Torah (Law). Christ Himself is, in fact, the content of Christian tradition (Col 2.6).

Role of the Holy Spirit. In 1 Cor 11.23 St. Paul asserts that he received "from the Lord" what, clearly, he had received from the community. The preposition (ἀπό) has generally been taken to refer to the ultimate, rather than to the immediate, source. O. Cullmann, however, sees here a reference to the glorified Christ acting immediately in and through the apostolic tradition as its immediate author, an action that is virtually identified with that of the Spirit (2 Cor 3.17); any other tradition, he holds, would have to be regarded as a tradition of men. Even if all this could be granted, it would be wrong to look to Paul for the final answer to the problem of the role of Christ and the Spirit in tradition, because it hardly arose for Paul. J. L. Leuba has pointed out that as long as the expectation of an immediate Parousia prevailed, there was no need felt to distinguish between Christological tradition and the action of the Spirit; later New Testament authors, however, found it necessary to make the distinction. St. Luke elaborated a theology of the "middle time," the career of Christ seen as the period between that of Israel and that of the Church; knowledge of the historical Christ, necessary for saving faith, is made present for men by the eyewitness testimony of the Apostles, closely related to the action of the Spirit, but distinguished from it. St. John goes a step further in establishing a decisive difference between the time when Jesus lived and the time when He is no longer on earth. The work of the risen Christ is also clearly distinguished from that of the Spirit, who is "another" PARACLETE (Jn 14.16). Here, too, there is an interim period in which the Lord acts both through the witness of men and the action of the Spirit (15.26–27), who will reveal to them the deepest significance of what they have witnessed (16.13).

Tradition can be considered a deposit (παραθήκη; 1 Ti 6.20; 2 Ti 1.14). This means something that remains the goods of another, committed in trust, and which cannot be appropriated. Yet it need not be static. The servant who buried his lord's talent was blamed (Mt 25.24–30);

the scribe of the kingdom of heaven brings forth new things and old (Mt 13.52). The presence of the Spirit in the Church guarantees new insights and faithful continuity.

Bibliography: *Encyclopedic Dictionary of the Bible*, tr. and adap. by L. HARTMAN (New York 1963) 2843–87. Y. M. J. CONGAR, *La Tradition et les traditions*, 2 v. (Paris 1960–63). O. CULLMANN, *La Tradition* (Neuchâtel 1953). B. GERHARDSSON, *Memory and Manuscript*, tr. E. J. SHARPE (Uppsala 1961). A. M. HUNTER, *Paul and His Predecessors* (rev. ed. Philadelphia 1961). E. NIELSEN, *Oral Tradition* (Chicago 1954). H. RIESENFELD, *The Gospel Tradition and Its Beginnings* (London 1957). P. BENOIT, "La Tradition selon O. Cullmann," *Exégèse et théologie*, 2 v. (Paris 1961) 2:309–317. L. CERFAUX, "La Tradition selon saint Paul," *Recueil L. Cerfaux*, 2 v. (Gembloux 1954) 2:253–263. J. L. LEUBA, "La Rapport entre l'Esprit et la tradition selon le N. T.," *Verbum Caro* 13 (1959) 133–150. D. M. STANLEY, "Pauline Allusions to the Sayings of Jesus," *The Catholic Biblical Quarterly*, 23 (1961) 26–39. D. A. KNIGHT, "Tradition History," *Anchor Bible Dictionary* 6:633–638.

[J. JENSEN]

TRADITION (IN THEOLOGY)

Tradition is the communication by the living Church of the Christian reality and the expression, either oral or written, of that reality. The Christian community in the post-Apostolic era, because it is the continuation of Israel and of the risen Christ through space and time, presents the reality of the Biblical message and of the institutions of Christ, which that message fixed once and for all.

In the name of tradition and in a spirit of fidelity to their heritage, some Christians have been inclined toward conservatism, and by the same token others have made attempts at innovation and leaned toward novelty. This dual spirit raises several questions. (1) What is the meaning of tradition? Whatever it is, it requires, if it is to transmit the Christian message and reality faithfully, an authentic organ or agent. (2) Single or multiple, what is the organ of tradition? Tradition that is living and dynamic must, by the law of life itself, undergo change. The danger arises, however, that the Christian tradition of today may no longer be that of yesterday, that it has meanwhile lost its homogeneity. (3) If living tradition must maintain its continuity and identity with the past, does it still allow for some sort of progress? Not all Christians have attached the same value and authority to it. Some have claimed that its very fluidity, the handing down of the Christian message by word of mouth, endangers its truth and subordinates it to Scripture. (4) How, then, do tradition and Scripture compare? The comparison of the two leads ultimately to the question of the interrelation of Scripture, tradition, and the Church. Here lies the crux of the Protestant-Catholic debate over tradition.

Meaning of Tradition. Tradition begins with the gift of God the Father at that moment of SALVATION HISTORY when He intervenes and reveals Himself by event and word to His people, and it is accomplished by the incarnate and personal intervention of Jesus Christ, Son of God. The Apostles first experience REVELATION in the Person and work of Jesus, and then under the guidance of the Holy Spirit they bear witness to their experience. "The Apostles," wrote St. Clement of Rome, "preached to us the gospel received from Jesus Christ, and Jesus Christ was God's ambassador. Christ, in other words, comes with a message from God, and the Apostles with a message from Christ. Both these orderly arrangements, therefore, originate from the will of God" (1 Cor 42.1–2). Both the realities and the testimonies of faith compose the deposit of revelation.

Real and Verbal. There is a real and a verbal tradition. The deposit of Christian revelation is more than a message; it is the total Christian reality. Verbal tradition as a mode of transmission other than Scripture expresses the Christian revelation but does not contain the totality of it. Real tradition is that life and activity of the Church by which she presents the whole redemptive mystery. The Church, for example, accepts the gospel message of the Eucharist and celebrates it unceasingly upon her altars. She teaches the sign of the cross and imparts it. Verbal and real tradition are so complementary in her that the real is declared verbally and the verbal is clarified by the real.

Oral and Written. Just as in Israel the great Exodus and other saving events were told in memory of Yahweh's gracious intervention for His people, then later committed to writing, so in the early Church an oral tradition preceded the written tradition collected together into Sacred Scripture. The Bible is a document of tradition, the NT an embodiment of the KERYGMA, or preaching, of Jesus and His followers, of His life, and that of the early Christian community. Oscar Cullmann, a Protestant scholar, agrees that the oral tradition prior to the first writings was certainly quantitatively richer than the written tradition. Whether the written tradition had for its purpose the delimiting of the oral tradition, so as to establish the written Apostolic witness as a definitive norm for the Church, as he maintains, is a moot question. His opinion is that the oral tradition had normative value till only about the year 150, because it was confined to the period of the Apostles, who were eyewitnesses to the Christevent. Beyond that period Scripture was supposedly the only rule of faith (*see* RULE OF FAITH).

Yet St. IRENAEUS, writing about the year 180, taught that the law of tradition was most essential to the Church and would suffice for her if it alone existed. "And what if not even the Apostles themselves had left us any Scriptures? Ought we not to follow the course of that tradition which they delivered to those whom they entrusted with the Churches?" (*Adversus haereses* 3.4.1.) "And to this rule consent many nations of the gentiles, those I mean who believe in Christ, having salvation written by the Spirit in their hearts, without paper and ink, and diligently keeping the old tradition" (*ibid.* 3.4.2). In a sense, a gospel was prior to the Gospels. "For by no others have we known the method of our salvation than those by whom the gospel came to us: which was both in the first place preached by them, and afterwards by the will of God handed down to us in the Scriptures, to be the ground and pillar of our faith"(*ibid.* 3.1.1).

Three Types. Theology has recognized three types of tradition according to varying origins, namely, divine, Apostolic, and ecclesiastical. The moments of origin undoubtedly differed: God or Christ initiated divine tradition, the Apostles who were enlightened by the Holy Spirit began Apostolic tradition, and the post-Apostolic Church originated the ecclesiastical. The period of the origin of the deposit was different from the communication of the deposit in a spatio-temporal continuity. This fact causes difficulty in clearly distinguishing specific traditions from the unwritten Apostolic traditions.

The Council of TRENT (1545–63) affirmed the existence of unwritten Apostolic traditions but refrained from drawing up a list of them (*Enchiridion symbolorum* 1501). Historically speaking, such traditions represent the sacramental rites, the liturgy, ecclesiastical discipline, and practical conduct of Christians through the centuries. The historic form of one or another may have been of Apostolic or even divine origin. For example, the Sunday obligation to worship and the annual Easter Communion are ecclesiastical precisions of a divine or Apostolic law.

Organ of Tradition. Tradition demands a living bearer of the Christian message and reality, one who assumes the responsibility for its authenticity. This, in the first place, is the transcendent and invisible role of the Holy Spirit. The promise of Christ was to send the Holy Spirit to guarantee infallibly the retention of the deposit and its development.

Holy Spirit and Church. The Holy Spirit is, for the Church and her preaching and evangelical witness, a principle of identity, being one and the same and always active in the Church so that she can be the means of realizing the history of salvation. St. Irenaeus had this insight when he wrote: "The preaching of the Church is on all sides consistent and continues like itself, and has its testimony from the Prophets and Apostles and from all Disciples: as we have traced out our proof . . . through the whole economy of God and His ordinary way or working for the salvation of man, which is by faith. Which faith, received in the Church, we guard, and which, coming of the Spirit of God, is like some noble treasure in a precious vessel, continually reviving its youth and causing the very vessel which holds it to revive in like manner . . . for where the Church is, there also is the Spirit of God; and where the Spirit of God is, there is the Church and all grace: but the Spirit is truth'' (*Adversus haereses* 3.24.1).

In the visible and historical order, then, the Church is the beneficiary of the revelatory and redemptive work of Christ, the inheritor of the total Christian reality. Apart from this deposit she has no autonomy; she exists only in virtue of it. Her deposit includes the realities that are present to her historic life: the Apostolic ministry, the sacramental liturgy, the indwelling of the Holy Spirit, the fellowship of the saints, etc. The Church, then, is the instrument or means by which Christianity is mediated to the world.

Fathers of the Church. Among the early members of the Church who contributed much to her life and consciousness, who helped her to convey the Christian message and reality, were the Greek and Latin FATHERS OF THE CHURCH. The faith of the early Church came down to us elaborated and enriched by their writings. They were the men of tradition who kept the pulse-beat of the Church's life in their day. First and essentially commentators on Sacred Scripture, they wrote, especially in the 4th and 5th centuries, the history of salvation as it took place. Then it was that the Church defined her faith in the face of Trinitarian and Christological controversies, when she established her great liturgies, drew up the first religious rules and conciliar canons. Through the Fathers' articulation of the faith, the Church reflected upon and witnessed to the Bible. As the eyes and ears and voice of the Church, they were privileged witnesses to tradition, though they were not tradition itself (*see* CHRISTOLOGY; CONTROVERSIES ON; TRINITY, HOLY, CONTROVERSIES ON).

Faithful. The faithful, too, express the mind of the Church, perhaps more today that ever before in her history. By their understanding of the faith, their response to the preaching and teaching of the clergy, under the Holy Spirit's enlightenment, they give living witness to tradition (*see* WITNESS, CHRISTIAN). Theirs is a tradition of fidelity to the faith of previous Christian generations, for they conserve tradition in Christian practice. They transmit the faith from baptized to baptized, from parent to child, building up a consensus of the faith. The Sacraments of Baptism and Confirmation, in particular, enable them to share in Christ's priesthood, to participate in the Eucharistic liturgy, and so to enjoy the Christian reality.

The fidelity of the faithful is dependent upon and interacts with the tradition of the official TEACHING AUTHORITY OF THE CHURCH (MAGISTERIUM). Christ appointed the Apostles to shepherd His flock, and they were succeeded in their task by the local bishops. Between the two, shepherd and flock, there is a communal activity, the one member influencing the other.

For example, the better understanding of the Marian mysteries is due in large part to the growth in Marian piety among the faithful. As their consciousness of a Christian truth and reality develops, they accompany it with a living practice. In this way they contribute something original to tradition.

Liturgy. Nowhere is tradition more vital among the clergy and laity alike than in the liturgy. Christ speaks and acts in the liturgy, for it embodies the Scriptures and reenacts the saving events of His life and death, His Resurrection and Ascension. Because He is personally the new covenant between God and man, combining as He does in Himself the divine and the human, He is now able, through the extension of Himself in His MYSTICAL BODY, to re-present and reactualize that covenant. The liturgy mirrors the whole Christ especially in that it interprets the Scriptures in their original setting, the liturgical assembly, and brings to life the doctrine therein expressed. That is why it has been called ''the principal instrument of the Church's tradition.''

Magisterium. The Church, the Fathers, the faithful, the liturgy—all are the media of communication by which Christianity is delivered to the present generation. But what assurance do the PEOPLE OF GOD have that their Christianity is authentic? Christ endowed His Church with an official teaching body, the magisterium composed of the episcopal college united with the pope, who is the head of this college as Peter was of the Apostolic college. The magisterium's duty, as enunciated by VATICAN COUNCIL I (1869–70), is to guard faithfully, judge authentically, and declare infallibly the content of the revealed deposit (*Enchiridion symbolorum* 3020, 3069). The hierarchy and faithful form, corporatively and organically, the one as the voice and the other as the echo, the authentic organ of tradition. Their first duty is to guard faithfully, that is, witness to the revealed deposit.

The Spirit-assisted magisterium does not set itself up against the Apostolic rule of faith as an independent rule; its service is only secondary and subordinate—to provide believers with a security against error in the transmission of the deposit. Far from claiming to be an indispensable screen between God and His faithful, or between the Bible and the believer, the magisterium assumes a real value for the sure and uniform understanding of divine revelation.

If, in the past, mainly after the religious cataclysm in the 16th century, some theologians tended to identify tradition with the magisterium, there are reasons to explain their narrow outlook. For one thing, they reacted to the Reformers who attempted to overthrow the hierarchical priesthood. Their reactions led them to conceive the Church too much in terms of the hierarchy, and that is the reason for their overemphasizing the hierarchical structure in their ecclesiologies. On the other hand, writing in favor of an oral tradition, they involved themselves in a polemic against the Protestant teaching of the sole-sufficiency of Scripture. History has proved how reactions often end in extreme positions.

Continuity and Progress. The Christian message and reality, once lying remotely and somewhat blurredly in the deposit of revelation, can, if it is kept alive, continue to emerge homogeneously from the past, grow, and mature. Tradition is verified in the progress from the embryonic to the finally mature; across space and time it forms a continuum with the kerygma of the early Church.

The principle of continuity and progress was observable to the first Christians, though they did not have the historical perspective of a later Church and hence could not gauge the rate or amount of progress. The principle was laid down in unmistakable terms by the early 5th-century writer St. VINCENT OF LERINS in his *Commonitorium* (23.1). Vatican Council I quoted him to affirm the principle in its constitution on the Catholic faith: "Let there be growth . . . and all possible progress in understanding, knowledge, and wisdom whether in single individuals or in the whole body, in each man as well as in the entire Church, according to the stage of their development; but only within proper limits, that is, in the same doctrine, in the same meaning, and in the same purport" (Denz 3020).

The three great dogmatic definitions of 1854, 1870, and 1950 (the Immaculate Conception in *Ineffabilis Deus,* papal infallibility at Vatican Council I, and Mary's Assumption in *MUNIFICENTISSIMUS DEUS*) were prime instances of dogmatic development and its justifiability by the Church's appeal to a sense of faith or a consciousness steeped in tradition and Scripture. So far, however, theology has only started to theorize about doctrinal development; the constitution *Munificentissimus Deus,* in particular, pointed up the need of theory for a better understanding of the developmental process.

Contemporaneously with the development of the Marian dogmas and the crisis of MODERNISM, Catholic theology investigated the nature of doctrinal development. J. A. MÖHLER and his disciples at the University of Tübingen made the most significant breakthrough by their studies of tradition in terms of the Church's con-

sciousness. Möhler compared it to the genius of a people or national spirit, a *"Volksgeist"* (see his *Die Einheit in der Kirche,* 1832). It is the living bond between the past and present, is incarnated in the ecclesial community, and is expressed in its monuments of faith. While J. H. NEWMAN viewed doctrinal development historically and psychologically (*An Essay on the Development of Christian Doctrine,* 1845), J. B. FRANZELIN, SJ, took a positive theological approach to the problem (*Tractatus de divina traditione et Scriptura,* 1870). The former saw doctrine developing by stages and staying clear of corruptions; the latter felt that the only touchstone for homogeneous growth is the magisterium. L. BILLOT, SJ, faced the Modernist crisis with *De immutabilitate traditionis contra modernam haeresim evolutionismi* (1907), in which he opposed an extreme theory of doctrinal evolutionism and held that the Apostolic deposit must be kept essentially immutable.

Tradition and Scripture. The relationship between tradition and Scripture has been a chronic problem in the history of the Church. The problem originated with the value assigned to the Scriptural canon. If Christ intended His teaching to be consigned only to writing, then, without question, oral tradition cannot be normative in the life of His Church. But if tradition was meant to coexist with Scripture in the Church, then one is forced to ask what its authority is.

To assert that Sacred Scripture always has sovereign rule and is not subject to any other is not to claim that it is the only rule of faith. Tradition and Scripture are both wholly divine and wholly human. With the aid of the Holy Spirit, tradition remains a rule of belief as it was in the time of the early Church. The Church controls, verifies, proves, and even criticizes her tradition by Scripture. She holds no truth on the basis of Scripture alone, independently of tradition, nor on the basis of tradition alone, independently of Scripture.

The Council of Trent was the historical occasion when the problem of correlating tradition and Scripture came to a head. The original draft of the Tridentine decree (April 8, 1546) stated that revelation is contained "partly in written books, partly in unwritten traditions" (*partim . . . partim*). To appease a theological minority who objected to the phrasing, the decree was changed to read: "The council is aware that this truth and teaching are contained in written books *and* in the unwritten traditions" (*Enchiridion symbolorum* 1501, italics added). The final decree had what seemed to be an inoffensive "and" replacing the "partly . . . partly."

Meaning of Prior Draft. The first formulation affirmed the view that the saving gospel is contained partly in the Scriptures and partly in oral Apostolic traditions—

two quasi-independent sources of revelation. A generation after the council some of the leading theologians who retained this teaching were Melchior CANO, OP (*De locis theologicis,* 1563), St. Peter CANISIUS, SJ (*Catechism,* 1555), and St. Robert BELLARMINE, SJ (*De controversiis,* 1586). In a series of articles (Greg, 1959–61) H. Lennerz, SJ, vigorously defended the *partim . . . partim* theory and opposed it to the Protestant "scripturistic principle." Neither tradition nor Scripture contains the whole Apostolic tradition. Scripture is materially (i.e., in content) insufficient, requiring oral tradition as a complement to be true to the whole divine revelation.

Second View. Theologians équally numerous and erudite have proposed, both before and after the Council of Trent, that divine revelation is contained entirely in tradition and entirely in the Scriptures. Their position was given historical support in the study of Prof. J. R. Geiselmann of Tübingen, *Die Heilige Schrift und die Tradition* (Freiburg-Basel-Wien, 1962). He and a host of German theologians contended that the whole revealed deposit is found in Sacred Scripture. Their argument for the material sufficiency of Scripture is unlike that of the Protestant Reformers—that all revealed truths are only Biblically demonstrable. They simply mean that such truths are at least implicit in or based upon Scripture. Many disciplinary matters and customs in vogue in the Church cannot be traced to Scripture.

Intermediate Theory. A third theological theory, intermediate between the above two, has developed that regards it essential that Scripture and tradition be harmonized and unified without mutual detriment. J. Beumer, SJ (see his articles in *Scholastik,* 1941–61), drew upon the works of Möhler and M. J. SCHEEBEN to evolve the theory that Scripture is relatively sufficient as a mode of transmission other than tradition. It transmits in a written form not a part but the substance of revealed truth, so that all revealed truths are somehow traceable to its content. According to this theory, Scripture and tradition link, as it were, into concentric circles, tradition encompassing all that Scripture holds substantially. Tradition interprets Scripture and is likewise a more complete expression of the life and teaching of the Church.

The reason for their correlation is that whenever the Church confronts the Biblical text, she finds true and unequivocal understanding of it only in the light of her tradition and the internal witness of the Holy Spirit. Without a living tradition, the Bible lends itself to a variety of interpretations, not a few of which appear contradictory. Tradition is a helpmate to Scripture; in its interpretive role it helps to determine the contents of the Apostolic deposit. Irenaeus, CYPRIAN, ORIGEN, TERTULLIAN, and other ecclesiastical writers are emphatic in their teaching that the Scriptures should be read in the Church and that ecclesial tradition is "the exposition of the Scriptures."

Protestant-Catholic Convergence. Protestant scholars are increasingly more willing to admit that the slogan "Scripture alone" (*sola Scriptura*) couches only a half-truth—Scripture has only the primacy of truth. Protestants and Catholics are growing in the agreement that the early Church got along without Scripture *alone.* Granted that tradition anteceded Scripture, the scriptural documents are invaluable historical records through which the Holy Spirit introduces the believing reader and the whole Christian community to Christ. Aside from these areas of agreement, Protestants remain hesitant to accept the ecclesiastical traditions that arose before and after the Biblical period.

The problematic relationship of tradition and Scripture, complex as it is, narrows down to a question of ECCLESIOLOGY: do the two belong to the Church that Christ founded or do they not? The Catholic response is that the ecclesial community is in possession and command of both. God in Christ has chosen a people and given it oral and written guidance under the Holy Spirit. Each of the two represents a value and is normative. As rules of faith they are mutually inclusive and coinhere in the Church. Rather than oppose the one to the other or isolate them, the Church, by means of the two, transmits in a living authentic way, till the end-time, the Christian message and reality.

Although to some extent the Scripture-tradition problem still divides Catholicism and Protestantism, the mutual concerns over their correlation are beginning to converge. Scripture is read and interpreted within the tradition of the Church. It is highly significant that VATICAN COUNCIL II, by a two-thirds majority vote on Nov. 20, 1962, refused to adopt the expression "two sources of revelation." The revised schema spoke of the one source, divine revelation itself, which is presented orally and in written form by the Church.

See Also: DEPOSIT OF FAITH; DOCTRINE, DEVELOPMENT OF; PRESCRIPTION, THEOLOGICAL USE OF; REVELATION, FONTS OF.

Bibliography: A. MICHEL, *Dictionnaire de théologie catholique,* ed. A. VACANT et al (Paris 1903–50) 15.1:1252–1350. H. G. GADAMER et al., *Die Religion in Geschichte und Gegenwart,* 6 v. (3d ed. Tübingen 1957–63) 6:966–984. "Tradition," *Lexicon für Theologie und Kirche,* (Freiburg, 1957–66) v.10. Y. CONGAR, *La Tradition et la vie de l'église* (Paris 1963), Eng. *The Meaning of Tradition* (New York 1964). *La Tradition et les traditions,* 2 v. (Paris 1960–63) v. 1 *Essai historique,* v. 2 *Essai théologique.* G. MORAN, *Scripture and Tradition* (New York 1963) bibliog. 89–98. J. P. MACKEY, *The Modern Theology of Tradition* (New York 1963) bibliog. 209–216. G. TAVARD, *Holy Writ or Holy Church* (New York 1960). C. BALIČ, *De scriptura et traditione* (Rome 1963). P.

LENGSFELD, *Überlieferung: Tradition und Schrift in der evangelischen und katholischen Theologie der Gegenwart* (Paderborn 1960). O. CULLMANN, *The Early Church,* tr. A. J. B. HIGGINS and S. GODMAN (London 1956). W. BURGHARDT, "The Catholic Concept of Tradition in the Light of Modern Theological Thought," *Catholic Theological Society of America. Proceedings,* 6 (1951) 42–75.

[J. A. FICHTNER]

TRADITIONALISM

A philosophical and theological doctrine, disseminated through parts of Europe of the 19th century, according to which the principal truths of a metaphysical and moral nature can be attained by man through God's revelation alone. According to traditionalism, human reason by itself is not capable of coming to these truths; it needs external instruction—in the last resort, divine revelation. God must teach man not only supernatural truths but also the natural truths of His existence, the immortality of the soul, the moral law, the nature of authority, and the concept of being. God's revelation is diffused among men by tradition, that is, by oral and social instruction.

Origin. Traditionalism had its origin in the search after a stable and infallible principle of order in a world shaken by the French Revolution and by the widely diverging philosophies of the 18th century. Some thinkers blamed the existing instability on man's reliance on human reason, which on the one hand claimed to solve all mysteries, even those of faith, and on the other hand undermined all certitude, since the rationalistic Cartesian doubt contained in itself the seed of agnosticism (*see* RATIONALISM; CARTESIANISM). There was felt a great need of simply indicating a principle of stability rather than of discovering it. On this ground some Catholic thinkers came to the conclusion that the errors of the ENLIGHTENMENT and of the Revolution had their source in the conviction that the principles of political and intellectual order are of human origin. They thought, on the contrary, that these principles transcend human reason, defy its analysis, and therefore must be revealed by God and handed down to men.

Schools. Traditionalism developed into two main forms or schools: one rigid, the other moderate. The former was represented mainly by L. de BONALD (1754–1840), F. de LAMENNAIS (1782–1854), and J. de MAISTRE (1753?–1821); the latter, by A. BONNETTY (1798–1879), G. VENTURA (1792–1861), N. Laforêt (1823–72), and G. Ubaghs (1800–75). Moderate traditionalism was advanced chiefly by the professors of the University of Louvain; it is, therefore, also known as the Louvain school of traditionalism. However, in the midst of their discussions the traditionalists sometimes modi-

fied their views; besides, some of them, such as the moderate L. BAUTAIN (1796–1867), were affected by ONTOLOGISM. All this makes it more difficult to classify them accurately. With this qualification one can also number among moderate traditionalists J. HIRSCHER in Germany, J. DONOSO CORTÉS in Spain, V. GIOBERTI in Italy.

Doctrine. De Bonald, systematizer of the doctrine, presented his ideas in numerous works, particularly in his fundamental work *La Législation primitive* (Paris 1802) and in *Recherches philosophiques sur les premiers objects de nos connaissances morales* (Paris 1818). He maintained that man's ideas are somehow imprinted on his mind by its Author, and yet without voice, speech, or language there would still be no knowledge, at least of suprasensible truth. This language could not be invented by an individual or even by a society. It was given to man along with the notions of the first truths by the Author of man's reason. Consequently certain knowledge is founded on authority and ultimately on God's speaking to man. The first man who accepted these truths had to transmit them to others by instruction; and this transmission has been taking place down to modern times.

Similar doctrine was advanced by de Lamennais in his *Essai sur l'indifférence en matière de religion* (4 v. Paris 1817–23), particularly volume 2. He argued that human reason can err; thus, man is never certain that his reason does not err in each particular case. Therefore, one must look for an infallible principle if he wants to be certain. This principle must be accepted without argument, that is, by faith. Such faith is common to all men, not just proper to an individual. But the authority of universal reason, which expresses itself in common sense, is infallible, although it cannot be demonstrated and must be accepted by faith. If it were not infallible, one would fall into skepticism. The most universal truths that men commonly profess are God's existence and the fact of His revelation to mankind. These truths are the basis of all philosophy. For man in himself has no reason of his existence; he has it in God. The essence of reason, however, consists in possessing truth. Therefore, God, when creating intelligent beings, bestowed upon them a knowledge of basic truth, together with the language that man by himself could not invent; this truth was then handed down to others by speech, and its transmission continues because of the divine assistance. As a result, the belief in the testimony of the human race gives to the individual the greatest certitude; and belief in the testimony of God assures the only certitude for all mankind.

This doctrine was closely connected with the social and political philosophy of the traditionalists. De Maistre was interested mainly in this aspect of traditionalism, which he elaborated chiefly in the following works: *Du pape* (2 v. Lyons 1819); *Essai sur le principe générateur des constitutions politiques* (Petrograd 1809); *Les Soirées de Saint Pétersbourg* (2 v. Paris 1821). His fundamental idea was that man by himself is incapable of finding the true principle of political and social order, just as he is incapable of discovering ultimate truth. Corrupted by original sin, and yet associated with others, man must be governed. The kind of government, however, is not the result of his will; it is imposed by the divine sovereignty, which is reflected in the sovereignty of the popes and monarchs. The principle of order established by God is manifested to men through history, which shows that true order lies with hereditary monarchy and not with a government elected by the people. The supreme monarch is infallible in the temporal order as the pope is infallible in the supernatural order. The monarch should use even radical means to compel man to observe the law. Lamennais was less stable in his social and political philosophy. He changed his views from the absolute authority of the pope [*Religion considérée dans ses rapports avec l'ordre politique et civil* (2 v. Paris 1825–26); *Progrès de la révolution et de la guerre contre l'église* (Paris 1829)] to a liberal Catholicism and democratic order [the journal *L'Avenir,* founded in 1830; *Les Paroles d'un croyant* (Paris 1834)].

The moderate traditionalists modified the position of rigid traditionalism by asserting that some kind of instruction is necessary for the development of human reason that it may obtain the knowledge of God and of moral principles. However, this instruction is not an efficient cause but only an indispensable condition of such knowledge. As air, warmth, and moisture are necessary for the development of life in the seed, so instruction is necessary for man's certitude about fundamental truth. The necessary instruction can be provided by voice, writing, gesture, or any other means in the possession of human society. After such an instruction and, ultimately, after God's revelation, man can prove His existence and other fundamental truths [see *Collectio Lacensis: Acta et decreta sacorum conciliorum recentiorum,* ed. Jesuits of Maria Laach, 7.1:129; H. Lennerz, *De Deo uno* (Rome 1955) 16–17].

Ecclesiastical Decrees. Traditionalism was widely held and brought about the convocation of many provincial councils to warn against its teachings. Most of these councils took place in France between 1845 and 1869; two of them convened at Tours and Avignon in 1849 and in 1850 at Aix and Toulouse (*Collectio Lacensis: Acta et decreta sacorum conciliorum recentiorum* 4:842). Lamennais's doctrine was condemned as leading to anarchy by the encyclicals *Mirari vos* (1832) and *Singulari nos* (1834). The traditionalist doctrine about blind faith was

rejected by the encyclical *Qui pluribus* (1846). Bonnetty had to renounce his teaching by signing in 1855 four theses proposed by the Congregation of the Index. They contradict some passages of his works (H. Denzinger, *Enchiridion symbolorum,* ed. A. Schönmetzer, 2811–14). Bautain previously signed similar theses for his bishop, Nov. 18, 1835 (*Enchiridion symbolorum* 2751–56); he renewed his rejection of these errors on several occasions. The Holy Office, March 6, 1866, condemned traditionalist opinions of G. Ubaghs' *Theodicea* and *Logica* (see *Enchiridion symbolorum* 2841, introduction). Exaggerated traditionalism was condemned also in its doctrine concerning man's knowledge of God's existence by Vatican I (*Enchiridion symbolorum* 3004, 3026). An implicit condemnation of traditionalism can be found in the encyclical *Pascendi* (Sept. 8, 1907) and HUMANI GENERIS (Aug. 12, 1950).

Objections and Significance. The main objections against the traditionalist doctrine are reducible to the following. Traditionalism disagrees with the teaching of the Bible, particularly with Wisdom 13.1–9 and Romans 1.19–21. It makes man's faith irrational; irrational faith leads in its ultimate analysis to complete religious relativism. Traditionalism teaches blind faith as the answer to the philosophical problems that require a rational solution. Furthermore, men do not accept something as true because the human race agrees upon it, but because it is intelligible in itself. The traditionalists proved one-sidedly from history that human reason alone is incapable of forming successful institutions in the intellectual and social order. Yet, if one were to grant that human reason does not in fact reach truth, still it would not necessarily follow that reason is incapable of attaining it. Finally, language and voice cannot produce concepts, since words are but arbitrary signs that manifest concepts. The traditionalists exaggerated in general the dependence of man's reason on language, education, society, and revelation.

The traditionalists, however, were right in bringing out the role of faith at the time of exaggerated belief in reason, an exaggeration that led to the abolishing of all the mysteries of faith and of respect for legitimate authority. They were also correct in their conviction that faith is morally necessary for reaching the ultimate truths.

See Also: FIDEISM; ONTOLOGISM

Bibliography: T. GRANDERATH, *Constitutiones dogmaticae Concilii Vaticani* (Freiburg 1892). G. SANTINELLO, *Enciclopedia filosofica,* 4 v. (Venice-Rome 1957) 4:1277–78. H. LENNERZ, *Natürliche Gotieserkenntnis* (Freiburg 1926). L. LERCHER, *Institutiones theologiae dogmaticae* (5th ed. Barcelona 1951). É. BRÉHIER, *Histoire de la philosophie,* 2 v. (Paris 1926–32). H. HOCEDEZ, *Histoire de la theologie au XIXe siècle,* 3 v. (Brussels-Paris): v.1, 1800–31 (1948); v.2, 1831–78 (1952); v.3, 1878–1903 (1947). G. BOAS, *French Philosophies of the Romantic Period* (New York 1964). M.

FERRAZ et al., *Histoire de la philosophie en France au 19e siècle* (3d ed. Paris 1882). J. HENRY, "Le Cardinal Sterckx et la condamnation du traditionalisme," *Collectanea Mechliniensia* 16 (1927) 181–202; *Le Traditionatisme et l'ontologisme à l'Université de Louvain (1835–65)* (Louvain 1922). J. LUPUS, *Le Traditionalisme et le rationalisme,* 3 v. (Liège 1858). H. MÉDINE, *Esquisse d'un traditionalisme catholique* (Paris 1956). B. MENCZER, ed., *Catholic Political Thought (1789–1848)* (Westminster, Md. 1952). B. F. WRIGHT, "Traditionalism in American Political Thought," *The International Journal of Ethics* 48 (1937) 86–97.

[S. A. MATCZAK]

TRADUCIANISM

From the Latin *tradux,* a shoot or sprout, sometimes called generationism. There is no consistency or unanimity in the terminology, divisions, and definitions of traducianism and generationism. Generally traducianism and generationism (sometimes synonyms) denote a group of theories concerning the origin of the human soul from the parents and its simultaneous transmission with the body. In this sense it is opposed to creationism, preexistentism, EMANATIONISM. Traducianism is either a generic term including generationism, or a term connoting a materialistic view that the human soul is germinally contained in the bodily sperm and is transmitted by organic generation, or that the parents generate from an inanimate matter both body and soul of a child. Generationism connotes a spiritualistic view that the soul originates from the substance of the soul of the parents, or signifies the creative power of the soul received from the Creator to produce another soul and to transmit it to the child.

History. The Bible is not explicit on the origin of the human soul, because it knows no strict anthropologic dichotomy [C. Tresmontant, *A Study of Hebrew Thought,* tr. M. Gibson (New York 1960)]. Patristic teaching is mostly obscure, difficult to interpret, and not unanimous (*see* CREATIONISM). Tertullian taught materialistic traducianism (*De anima* 9–41). Those who seem to have favored traducianism or generationism were: Arnobius the Elder (*Adv. nat.* 2.36), Apollinaris, Gregory of Nyssa (*De hom. opif.* 29), Faustus of Riez (*Epist.* 3); some hesitated, e.g., Bachiarius (*Lib. de fide* 4), Rufinus (*Apol. ad Anast.* 4). Augustine rejected the traducianism of Tertullian (*Epist.* 190.4.14), hesitated (because of Pelagianism) in respect to creationism (*Epist.* 166.8.26), and favored spiritual generationism (*Epist.* 190.4.15). His authority led many Latin Fathers into indecision. In the Middle Ages only Averroists and Luciferians (Catharist sect) defended generationism and traducianism. Inspired by Augustine, Luther and many other reformers renewed generationism and traducianism and are followed by the majority of the contemporary Protestant theologians. Only in recent times have several Catholic theologians revived generationism in modified forms, e.g., G. Ubaghs, G. Hermes, H. Klee, F. X. Dieringer, J. Oischinger, P. Mayrhofer, Kolschmid, etc. J. Frohschammer taught a "secondary creationism" (parents do not generate, but create the soul), and A. de Rosmini-Serbati defended "generatocreationism" (development of a spiritual soul from a sensitive one; H. Denzinger, *Enchiridion symbolorum* 3220–24). There is no solemn teaching of the Church concerning the origin of the human soul. The ordinary magisterium teaches creationism (*ibid.* 190, 360, 685, 3896) and condemns traducianism and generationism (*ibid.* 360–361, 1007,3220–24).

Theology. Traducianism and generationism oppose the spirituality and simplicity of an individual soul and the transcendent dynamism of the Creator. However, they point out the necessity of reinterpreting an oversimplified creationism, which sins against the mystery of the origin of the whole man as a person in both spiritual and biological aspects and who receives his existence wholly from God (primary cause) and wholly from his parents (secondary cause), but in a different manner.

See Also: EVOLUTION; SOUL, HUMAN; SOUL, HUMAN, ORIGIN OF.

Bibliography: A. MICHEL, *Dictionnaire de théologie catholique,* ed. A. VACANT et al. (Paris 1903–50) 15.1:1350–65. A. MITTERER, *Lexikon für Theologie und Kirche,* ed. J. HOFER and K. RAHNER (Freiburg 1957–65) 4:668–669. P. OVERHAGE and K. RAHNER, *Das Problem der Hominisation* (Freiburg 1961). M. J. SCHEEBEN, *Handbuch der katholischen Dogmatik* (Freiburg 1961) 3:151. R. C. ZAEHNER, *Matter and Spirit: Their Convergence in Eastern Religions* (New York 1963).

[P. B. T. BILANIUK]

TRAJAN, ROMAN EMPEROR

Reigned from A.D. 98 to A.D. 117; b. Italica, southern Spain, Sept. 18, 53; d. Selinus, Cilicia, *c.* Aug. 8, 117. After a successful military career and a term as consul in 91, Trajan (Marcus Ulpius Traianus) was adopted by the Emperor Nerva (96–98), who wished to strengthen his own position. On the death of Nerva, Trajan, consul for the second time, took over the rule. He was popular with the army and careful not to offend the sensibilities of the senate. From the year 100 unofficially, and from the year 114 officially, he enjoyed the title of *optimus princeps.* His reign was marked by an extensive building program in Rome and in the provinces, and a strict control over provincial governors. His conquests in Europe, Africa, and Asia brought the Roman Empire to its maximum extent. A rescript that he sent to Pliny (Pliny *Epist.* 10.97) on the proper manner of dealing with Christians established a policy, even if not so intended, that was largely followed during the succeeding century: unsigned accusations against Christians should not be accepted; Christians should not be sought out, but if denounced and found guilty they were to be punished; those who denied they were Christians and adored the gods should be pardoned even if they had been suspect in the past. These provisions were in keeping with his general policy of a serious but not fanatical concern for traditions.

Bibliography: R. PARIBENI, *Optimus Princeps: Saggio sulla storia e sui tempi dell'imperatore Traiano,* 2 v. (Messina 1926–27); *Enciclopedia Italiana di scienzi, littere ed arti,* 36 v. (Rome 1929–39; suppl. 1938–) 34:154–157. R. P. LONGDEN, *The Cambridge Ancient History,* 12 v. (London and New York 1923–39) 11:199–252. R. HANSLIK and M. BONARIA, ''M. Ulpius Traianus,'' *Paulys Realenzyklopädie der klassischen Altertumswissenschaft,* ed. G. WISSOWA et al. suppl. 10 (1965) 1035–1113.

[M. J. COSTELLOE]

Trajan, Roman Emperor, illustration of a coin. (Archive Photos)

TRANCHEPAIN, MARIE ST. AUGUSTIN, MOTHER

Missionary, first superior of the Ursuline nuns of New Orleans, La.; b. Rouen, France; d. New Orleans, Nov. 11, 1733. Her parents were Protestant members of the French aristocracy. After her conversion to Catholicism, she left home to seek instruction from the Ursulines of her native city; she entered the convent there in 1677. Her aspirations to missionary work were encouraged by the Jesuit Nicolas I. de Beaubois, who arrived in France in 1726. Early the following year Mother St. Augustin and ten companions set out for New France, arriving in New Orleans Aug. 7, 1727, to begin their charitable work for the betterment of all classes, rich and poor, whites, African Americans, and Native Americans. During her administration the first boarding school for girls within the present limits of the United States was opened, and the first free school was established, the first orphanage, and the first sodality of the Blessed Virgin. The nuns also assumed charge of a military hospital and sponsored the first retreat for the ladies of the colony.

Bibliography: Archives, Ursuline Convent, New Orleans, La.

[M. C. RIVET]

TRANSCENDENCE

From the Latin *transcendere,* meaning to climb over, to surpass, or to go beyond, a term describing the relation existing between two things when one is superior and extrinsic to the other, e.g., God and the world, animal and plant, and knower and thing known. It implies an aspect of discontinuity, hiatus, or break between both the realities involved and the means of passing from the one to the other, and this either in reality or in knowledge. Transcendence is opposed to IMMANENCE, which stresses remaining within or under, although the two can be regarded as complementary. Thus God is transcendent, since He is above the world as the highest being and the ultimate cause; He is also immanent, since He is present in the world through PARTICIPATION and through causality. The notion of transcendence is basic in theology and religion in their treatment of God and to philosophy in its treatment of knowledge and of being.

Kinds. An understanding of the notion of transcendence requires that one distinguish its various meanings, namely, cosmological, ontological, epistemological, phenomenological, and mathematical.

Cosmological Transcendence. The first meaning of transcendence is one of relative comparison. It indicates a certain hierarchy, whether in place or time, or of being or activity. The transcendence is determined by the way one thing is related to another and can lead from the existence of the one to the existence of the other. Thus ''going beyond'' in this sense suggests the hierarchical steps passed over in a dialectical consideration of realities from the lower type to the highest—e.g., the ideas of Plato transcending the world of appearances. Another instance is that based on the relationship between effect and cause; thus St. Thomas Aquinas's ''five ways'' conclude to the existence of an ultimate being who, as ultimate efficient cause, transcends all beings (*see* GOD, PROOFS FOR

THE EXISTENCE OF). Similarly, the existence of a transcendent being without causal implications may be established (*via eminentiae*). In each case there is a factual transcendence in the relationship of a multiplicity of beings to a higher being beyond them. This is opposed to the notion of cosmological immanence, which stresses, for example, that God is in fact within the universe even though He is qualitatively a higher type of being.

Ontological Transcendence. Transcendence is used also to indicate the value or quality that makes one being superior to another and to explain why this is so. It is primarily concerned with degrees of perfection (*see* PERFECTION, ONTOLOGICAL). Ontological transcendence thus has reference to the above average or the above normal, and is determined by what the transcendent thing is in itself or in its ontological value. God is transcendent as the being who is greatest in perfection, considering that perfection absolutely; all limitation in perfection is denied of Him (*via negationis, via remotionis*).

Epistemological Transcendence. Transcendence also signifies what is beyond thought as its object, i.e., something known or knowable by man. Epistemological transcendence signifies ''going beyond'' mind either (1) to some being known as an object existing in reality, (2) to some reality beyond sense data such as an underlying SUBSTANCE or the exercise of CAUSALITY, or (3) to some being above the world, such as God. It is opposed to the immanence of knowledge, i.e., the enclosing of self within the mind, and frequently implies a rejection of PHENOMENALISM, MATERIALISM, and naturalism.

Phenomenological Transcendence. Transcendence also signifies something beyond CONSCIOUSNESS as its object. Phenomenological transcendence stresses the value of INTENTIONALITY in the knowing subject and assures both the OBJECTIVITY of the activity of knowing and the objective REALITY of the thing known. It analyzes human subjectivity to discover the contents of man's awareness and their extramental foundations. Phenomenological transcendence thus aims at overcoming the difficulties of the critique of reason that lead to epistemological immanence.

Mathematical Transcendence. Finally, transcendence is used in mathematics to designate functions and numbers that are transfinite or indefinite according to particular operational norms. Thus a transcendental number is defined as a number that is not the root of an algebraic equation with rational coefficients.

Problem of Transcendence. The problem of transcendence consists in finding out whether there is an absolute transcendent being, and, if so, in determining what this being is and why it is higher and better, yet knowable, or enigmatic yet attainable. The ABSOLUTE that is conceived as transcendent may be considered in many ways, namely, (1) simply as a more perfect nature that stands apart from this world (PLATO); (2) as a justification of the value of human knowledge in its truth, necessity, and certainty (St. AUGUSTINE); (3) as the cause of this world in its beginning and in its continuance, as regards both its existence and its essence (St. THOMAS AQUINAS); (4) as the object implied in human consciousness that demands the presence of the other, namely, as cause of and horizon for the meaningfulness in one's consciousness (PHENOMENOLOGY); or (5) as the explicit infinite reality that is implicit in any knowledge or expression concerning the finite universe (St. BONAVENTURE).

The dialectical movements and the reasoning processes that lead to the absolute as an existent whose reality cannot be denied vary according to the framework in which thought about the transcendent is developed. Such inquiry is prominent in contemporary thought, with its concern over the ontological question of extramental existence and the related epistemological question of the possibility of knowing anything beyond consciousness. Both in contemporary thought and throughout history, however, philosophers vary greatly in the solutions they offer.

Historical Solutions. A survey of various theories of transcendence may best be given in terms of the answers of philosophers to questions concerning the possibility of mind's transcending itself (1) to know anything other than itself, (2) to know substance or soul, and (3) to know God.

Objects beyond Thought. Is there any thing or object beyond thought? *''Un au-delà de la pensée est impensable''* expresses the negative answer of E. LE ROY and of L. BRUNSCHVICG. Greek thinkers such as Plato and Aristotle and medieval thinkers such as Bonaventure, St. Thomas, and J. DUNS SCOTUS accepted as a matter of fact that knowledge can grasp things existing in the world. Modern philosophy, beginning with R. Descartes's reflective *Cogito, ergo sum,* introduced a chasm between mind as spirit and matter as extension. The objectivity of knowledge thenceforth had to be certified or guaranteed by a higher power that did not depend on the very activity of knowing. The agnostic attitude of British EMPIRICISM had its influence on the phenomenalism of I. Kant, who limited valid knowledge to the PHENOMENA of verifiable sense perception.

The theory of intentionality developed by St. Thomas served as a metaphysical explanation of the nature of KNOWLEDGE. His theory of REFLECTION on the activity of knowing and its subject also provided the psychological means of verifying knowledge by a process within the range of human activity. Contemporary phenomenology, readapting the theory of intentionality, seeks to recover the objectivity of knowledge by a reflection on subjectivity; this opens, through intentionality, to objectivity itself. Such intentionality assures the presence of the object known as something in reality and avoids the Kantian formalities of sensation and thought that serve as substitutes for the existent in the elaboration of knowledge. The subject-object dichotomy, with its hiatus requiring a jump from the self to the other, is there replaced by a subjectivity-objectivity couplet that is linked, from within, by intentionality.

Substance and Soul. Ancient and medieval thinkers for the most part accepted the possibility of the human mind's grasping intrinsic principles or transphenomenal factors in the universe. Yet the late Middle Ages, as seen in WILLIAM OF OCKHAM and NICHOLAS OF AUTRECOURT, proposed theories that questioned the power of the human mind to grasp UNIVERSALS, underlying substance, and intrinsic principles such as the SOUL. The history of the concept of substance from R. DESCARTES to D. HUME again shows a slow disintegration of the notion and a questioning of its validity. With Kant, theoretical knowledge of any object not verifiable by sense perception becomes impossible. The critical problem of the possibility of knowing the thing-in-itself or its underlying principles has been accentuated by the skeptical stands taken by proponents of LOGICAL POSITIVISM and of linguistic analysis.

God. Can the mind transcend itself to know something beyond both the world of material reality and itself, namely, God? Again theories of intentionality and self-reflection seek to assure the objectivity of knowledge and to extend its validity further into the realm of the immaterial. Yet the God suggested in Plato and Aristotle and affirmed as discoverable by medieval Christian thinkers has slowly come to be regarded as beyond attainment. Reasons alleged by later thinkers include that such a being would be meaningless as an object of thought or irrelevant as an explanation of the universe or simply would involve a contradiction. Again, the need of appealing to God to explain or justify the world seems no longer to be felt. The basic choice has become that between God and the self: the existence of God seems to imply, for some, an alienation and a belittling of self. Thus AGNOSTICISM and ATHEISM have developed as modern rejections of transcendence.

On the other hand, the existence of a transcendent God is affirmed in the many forms of religious and philosophical transcendentalism, albeit with great variations as to God's knowability. Some, considering God to be knowable only by way of negation, hold that nothing positive can be known about God; others, considering God to be knowable by analogy and by causality, hold that God is knowable as an ideal toward which man must tend; still others, considering human knowledge to be a simple participation of God's knowledge, feel that an adequate understanding of God is attainable through the development of human insights; and finally some, despairing of attaining God through reason, seek the pathway to a transcendent God through the heart and through human emotions.

The "five ways" of St. Thomas serve as a basis for developing a knowledge of God by way of causality, of remotion, and of superexcellence and through the use of analogy of attribution, of participation, and of proportionality. Contemporary personalist and existentialist philosophers, avoiding the problems posed by causality and starting their philosophizing with things and objects, attempt to develop proofs for the existence of God through reflection on the person and consciousness. Whereas for modern philosophers the notion of a transcendent God was unacceptable, for many contemporary thinkers the affirmation of a transcendent God is again considered meaningful and legitimate. The ontological God of the earlier philosophers, however, tends to give way to a living God in the tradition of biblical thought. Again, with the phenomenological investigations of M. Heidegger and K. Jaspers, a new approach to the transcendent is visible, even though this is not properly theistic (*see* EXISTENTIALISM, 2, 5). Somewhat similar is the effort made within PERSONALISM to rediscover, by use of new methods and with different emphases, a personal God who is truly transcendent.

See Also: MOTION, FIRST CAUSE OF;
TRANSCENDENTAL (KANTIAN);
TRANSCENDENTALISM; TRANSCENDENTALS.

Bibliography: P. FOULQUIÉ and R. SAINT-JEAN, *Dictionnaire de la langue philosophique* (Paris 1962) 731–734. D. MACKENZIE, *Encyclopedia of Religion and Ethics,* ed. J. HASTINGS, 13 v. (Edinburgh 1908–27) 12:419–425. A. CARLINI, *Enciclopedia filosofica,* 4 v. (Venice-Rome 1957) 4:1289–94. G. GIANNINI, *ibid.* 1297–1306. H. BLUMENBERG, *Die Religion in Geschichte und Gegenwart,* 7 v. (3d ed. Tübingen 1957–65) 6:989–997. A. DONDEYNE, *Contemporary European Thought and Christian Faith,* tr. E. MCMULLIN and J. BYRNHEIM (Pittsburgh 1958; repr. 1963). H. SPIEGELBERG, *The Phenomenological Movement,* 2 v. (The Hague 1960). A. BANFI, *Immanenza et trascendenza come antinomia filosofica* (Alessandria 1924). G. BONTADINI, "Critica dell antinomia di trascendenza e di immanenza," *Giornale critico filosofia italiana* 10 (1929) 226–236. P. THÉVANEZ, "La notion de transcendance vers l'intérieur," in his *L'Homme et sa raison,* 2 v. (Neuchâtel 1956) 1:29–55.

[B. A. GENDREAU]

TRANSCENDENTAL (KANTIAN)

Transcendental (Kantian) is a methodological term employed by I. KANT, founder of transcendental IDEAL-ISM. Kant's ideas were further developed in a systematic way by the German idealists, but in doing so the latter departed on important subjects from Kant's original intentions. The earmark of Kantian idealism is the transcendental method. As Kant himself describes it: "I apply the term transcendental to all knowledge which is not so much occupied with objects as with the mode of our cognition of these objects, so far as this mode of cognition is possible a priori" (*Critique of Pure Reason,* A 11). Behind this is the so–called Copernican revolution that implies a "new method of thought" (*ibid.* B xviii): a priori knowledge of objects is not possible on the basis of the traditional assumption that all man's knowledge should conform to objects: one must start rather from the supposition that objects should conform to man's knowledge (*ibid.* B xvi). Kant looks for the conditions that make a priori knowledge possible, a knowledge distinguished by its necessity and universality. These conditions are not found in the object, but only in the forms that already inhere in the subject before it receives impressions from without. It is only through these forms that PHENOMENA and objects are constituted or produced. Hence man is only able to know a priori as much of things as he himself projects into them (*ibid.* B xviii). To these forms belong in particular the two pure perceptions of the sensitive faculties, the twelve concepts or categories of the intellect, and the three ideas of reason. The central element of the transcendental method is the transcendental deduction of purely rational concepts; this method shows that the "conditions of the possibility of experience" are also the conditions "of all objects of experience" (*ibid.* B 161), that is to say, of objects–for–us but not of things–in–themselves. Therefore, "no a priori cognition is possible for us, except of objects of possible experience" (*ibid.* B 166), i.e., of human experience.

Contemporary philosophers, unlike modern thinkers, recognize that the transcendental method realizes its full implications only in surmounting the limits set by Kant himself. There really are elements in the subject that condition the possibility of human knowledge, for the formal objects of the soul's faculties correspond to the a priori forms of Kant, as J. MARÉCHAL has shown. But the investigation must be pushed further, through the conditioning factors of the sense faculties and of the discursive power to the highest conditioning factor, that of the intellect, viz, BEING itself. It is this latter that is missed by Kant. From the vantage point of being, both the thing–in–itself and the realm of metaphysical reality open up to the human mind.

See Also: KANTIANISM; NEO–KANTIANISM.

Bibliography: J. MARÉCHAL, *Le Thomisme devant la philosophie critique* (Louvain 1949), v. 5 of his *Le Point de départ de la métaphysique.* J. B. LOTZ, "Die tranzendentale Methode . . . ," in *Kant und die Scholastik heute* (Pullach 1955) 35–108; *Metaphysica operationis humanae . . . methodo tr. explicata* in *Analecta Gregoriana* 94 (Rome 1961); *Ontología* (Barcelona 1962). E. CORETH, *Metaphysik* (Innsbruck 1961).

[J. B. LOTZ]

TRANSCENDENTAL MEDITATION

Transcendental Meditation or TM is an artful combination of an initial simplicity of technique with a final complexity of theory and practice. It was introduced in the United States in the early 1960s by Maharishi Mahesh Yogi, a Hindu monk with a degree in physics from Allahabad University. Maharishi studied Vedic teachings and the philosophy of Shankara in the Himalayas under Swami Brahmanand Saraswati ("Guru Dev"). The TM technique involves the silent repetition of a mantra or sound derived from the Vedic tradition, practiced 15 to 20 minutes twice daily, and is taught for a fee. In 1976 Maharishi introduced the TM-Siddhi program, which is based on the Yoga Sutras of Patanjali. It stabilizes the experience of transcendental consciousness gained through TM and develops mind-body coordination. TM officials estimate that currently there are about 3.5 million TM practitioners worldwide, one million of whom are in the U.S.—more than there are in India. There are about 50,000 practitioners of the TM-Siddhi program.

Unlike meditation techniques which emphasize the importance of effort and the enduring of painful sitting postures for extended periods of time, TM sees meditation as a relaxing and effortless technique which "mechanically" reduces stress and nervous excitation.

Maharishi contends that he is promoting science and not religion, but this is somewhat misleading. The VEDAS are Hindu religious documents, and Maharishi himself in 1963 characterized TM as an "approach to God realization." The theology being promoted is a scientifically informed and nonmonastic version of Shankara's Advaita Vedanta. As for the TM technique itself, it is quite similar to the practices advocated by John Cassian, the Hesychasts, the author of THE CLOUD OF UNKNOWING, and, more recently, Dom John Main, OSB.

According to Maharishi's Vedic psychology, the TM technique exploits the natural tendency of the mind to seek greater happiness and intelligence. During the practice of TM the mind spontaneously attends to increasingly subtle levels of consciousness because they are increasingly attractive. The mind eventually begins to "transcend," i.e., leave behind mental activity and attain a fourth level of consciousness which is different from waking, dreaming, and sleeping. In 1963 Maharishi described this "transcendental consciousness" as a condition of "restful alertness." The idea of a fourth level of consciousness is at least as old as the Indian UPANISHADS (prior to 500 B.C.), but Western scientific awareness and studies of such a state are new. From 1970 on, many articles appeared describing the physiology of the "wakeful hypometabolic state" which TM produces and the benefits that result. According to those studies, the practice of TM neutralizes deep-rooted stress, accelerates cognitive growth in children, facilitates the development of moral reasoning in adolescents, and improves the test scores of adults in the areas of fluid intelligence, field independence, and perceptual flexibility. Studies of the elderly indicate that TM improves learning ability, cognitive flexibility, systolic blood pressure, and longevity.

The TM program and the TM-Siddhi program are part of the Maharishi Technology of the Unified Field, an integrated science of life which seeks to unify Vedic teachings with the ideas of modern science, especially unified field theories in physics. Another aspect of the Technology is Maharishi Aryuveda, a holistic system of medicine that emphasizes prevention, balance, and the restoration of harmony along with the development of consciousness. For social problems, Maharishi maintains that there is a collective consciousness which is ultimately based on the transcendental consciousness attained in TM. This transcendental consciousness in turn is a field of pure consciousness which is the unified field of natural law. According to this theory, one individual transcending to the unified field can influence the development of coherence and orderliness in the whole of society and the physical environment.

See Also: NEW RELIGIOUS MOVEMENTS; HINDUISM.

Bibliography: R. K. WALLACE, *The Maharishi Technology of the Unified Field* (Fairfield, Iowa 1986); *Modern Science and Vedic Science* 1 (January 1987), MAHARISHI MAHESH YOGI, *The Science of Being and Art of Living* (New York 1963). D. DENISTON, *The TM Book* (rev. ed. Fairfield, Iowa 1986).

[T. ANDERSON]

TRANSCENDENTAL METHOD

The transcendental method is that approach to philosophical reflection that has as its major concern the human being as primordial subject—that is, it centers its inquiry on those conditions in the knowing subject that make knowledge possible. It is properly theological whenever it provides critical reflection upon a given religious language. Whether or not explicitly theological, however, transcendental method affirms the subject's

self-transcendence as knower insofar as the act of judgment has absolute being and truth as its ultimate horizon.

By means of the transcendental method, theology attempts to explicate the central concepts of religious faith that are necessarily affirmed or denied by basic beliefs and understandings. In this sense, the transcendental method fulfills the need for a reflective discipline that is capable of accounting for all human experience and not simply for one or another aspect of experience.

The transcendental method in theology receives its basic formulation from Immanuel KANT who sought the "conditions for the possibility" of our existing or understanding anything at all. Thus, it acknowledges Kant's advance over his contemporaries and over classical philosophy in general through his critical analysis of the formal elements of consciousness. Kant's achievement was to shatter the philosophical ideal of "pure" reason and to prepare for significant attempts at making explicit the operations of the human mind. Hegel, for example, elaborated the notion of "dialectic" as a way of extending the Kantian critique to every abstraction. The neo-Kantians, such as Cassirer, Langer, Urban, and Wheelwright, broadened the critique by including cultural and symbolic forms. PHENOMENOLOGISTS, such as HUSSERL, HEIDEGGER, and RICOEUR, continued to present transcendental consciousness as an essential, but not necessarily exclusive, aspect of human existence.

Although it can be found to be implicitly present in most theological procedure, transcendental method enters Catholic theology explicitly with BLONDEL's reinterpretation of Kant and Hegel and through MARÉCHAL's reinterpretation of Aquinas by means of a Kantian analytic. RAHNER's "formal-fundamental" theology involves a modification of the reality designated in Kant's a priori, which for Rahner is being itself, most fully disclosed in the questioning of being. In the Anglo-American tradition, LONERGAN does not propose to reformulate the Kantian question as the German theologians do, but instead is interested in developing a transcendental method that provides "a normative pattern of related and recurrent operations yielding cumulative and progressive results." In the Protestant milieu, FICHTE and SCHELLING, and more recently Whitehead and Hartshorne, are concerned with overcoming Kant's distinction between pure and practical reason.

Bibliography: E. CORETH *Metaphysics* (New York 1968). J. DONCEEL, *Natural Theology* (New York 1962). J. G. FICHTE, *The Science of Knowledge,* tr. A. E. KROEGER (London 1889). M. HEIDEGGER, *Introduction to Metaphysics* (New Haven 1958); *Kant and the Problem of Metaphysics* (Bloomington, Ind. 1962). I. KANT, *Critique of Pure Reason,* ed. N. K. SMITH (New York 1965). B. LONERGAN, *Insight: A Study of Human Understanding* (New York 1956); *Method in Theology* (New York 1972). J. MARÉCHAL, *Le*

Point de depart de la metaphysique (Paris 1927–49). O. MUCK, *The Transcendental Method* (New York 1968). K. RAHNER, *Hearers of the Word* (New York 1968); *Spirit in the World* (New York 1968). J. M. SOMERVILLE, *Total Commitment: Blondel's "L'Action"* (Cleveland 1968). D. TRACY, *The Achievement of Bernard Lonergan* (New York 1970).

[M. GERHART]

TRANSCENDENTALISM

A form of epistemological IDEALISM that, besides rejecting the empirical aspect of human cognition, claims to find a foundation for absolute truths immanent in the human mind or soul. This foundation is variously named "reason," "the Ego," "Absolute Spirit," etc., and is often identified in some way with GOD. The transcendentalism of New England, while adopting some of the notions of the European idealists, made little use of the logical rigor that characterized the latter movement.

German Transcendentalism. In modern philosophy the term transcendentalism is traced to the attempt made by KANT to save universal and necessary truths after his philosophical CRITICISM had concluded that man's cognitive powers were incapable of attaining nonempirical objects. While Kant did not deny the reality of such objects, he said they transcended human cognition and were accessible to autonomous practical reason only by an act of faith [see CATEGORICAL IMPERATIVE; TRANSCENDENTAL (KANTIAN)]. Subsequent transcendentalists constructed elaborate systems in which all reality was deduced from a single principle attained by an INTUITION either of the knowing subject or of the act of cognition itself.

J. G. FICHTE replaced Kant's autonomous practical reason by the SELF, or EGO, taken as an absolute principle of both metaphysical truth and all reality. By systematic deduction he sought to demonstrate the procession of the nonself, that is, nature, from the practical ego as a necessary condition for moral striving. Thus, like Kant, he founded metaphysical reality upon the exigencies of morality. Reacting against this moralism, SCHELLING identified both consciousness and nature with the ABSOLUTE or God, while HEGEL attempted to describe in terms of dialectical triads—thesis-antithesis-synthesis—the necessary procession of nature and finite consciousness from the Absolute. Hegel sought to justify his theory by finding in the history of finite CONSCIOUSNESS (man) and nature conclusive evidence of the dialectical life of the Absolute SPIRIT. Here modern philosophy reached the ultimate in pantheistic MONISM (see PANTHEISM). Subsequent thinkers rebelled against such a closed system, which united RATIONALISM with idealism, and so rejected all METAPHYSICS as absurd speculation.

American Transcendentalism. Transcendentalism in New England flourished in the 1830s after several Unitarian clergymen discovered the writings of COLERIDGE. Coleridge's thought, while largely Romantic, had been influenced by Kant. The common notion of the transcendental philosophers, that God was somehow immanent in nature and in the human soul, was very welcome to men in revolt against the Calvinist concepts of a wrathful God and the total depravity of human nature (*see* UNITARIANS; CALVINISM.)

Prominent in the original group of "like-minded men"—first labeled transcendentalists by opponents—were William Ellery CHANNING, Ralph Waldo EMERSON, Theodore PARKER, Henry David THOREAU and Orestes A. BROWNSON. Differences in background, interests and temperament made disagreement and disunity among them inevitable. They agreed in asserting the IMMANENCE of divinity in man and in nature—leaving the terms vague—but each added whatever intellectual tradition he found congenial, while using their common assertion to promote his personally chosen mission in life.

Channing labored to prevent Unitarian theology from hardening into a rigid orthodoxy like the Calvinism against which it had rebelled. Advocating his "principle of essential sameness" of God and man, he appeared pantheistic in his efforts to uphold the spiritual dignity of human nature. Emerson was so inspired by the same vision of man's inalienable worth that he opposed any system that seemed to deny the natural adequacy of man to live as befitted a spiritual being; thus he broke with institutionalized Christianity as an antihuman supernaturalism. His seeming apotheosis of NATURE, both human and nonhuman, was offset by his Yankee practicality. His widespread popularity in America rested on the shrewd wisdom of his epigrams on self-culture rather than upon his metaphysical speculations, which were incomprehensible to most of his followers.

Parker espoused social reform, especially abolitionism, while Thoreau divorced himself from human society to become the spokesman for the world of nature.

Brownson's range of interests included religions and social reform as well as history and philosophical speculation. In seeking to justify "the divinity of man" both metaphysically and historically, he saw that the low state of humanity that had called forth the reforms of transcendentalism contradicted its basic assertion that the most sublime dignity of man was purely natural. He went on, not to deny the fact of man's godlike state, but to accept the traditional Christian doctrine that, through the INCARNATION, God had gratuitously elevated man to a sharing in the Divine Life. Historical research, soul searching and prayer led him to the step for which his transcendentalist friends never forgave him: he entered the Catholic Church.

New England transcendentalism illustrates well the interests and ideals of 19th-century America. For a consideration of the influence of New England transcendentalism on literature, culture and intellectual history in the United States, *see* TRANSCENDENTALISM, LITERARY.

Bibliography: German Transcendentalism. J. D. COLLINS, *History of Modern European Philosophy* (Milwaukee 1954). F. C. COPLESTON, *History of Philosophy* (Westminster, Md 1946–) v.3,4. American Transcendentalism. P. MILLER, *The Transcendentalists: An Anthology* (Cambridge, Mass. 1960). O. A. BROWNSON, *Works,* ed. H. F. BROWNSON, 20 v. (Detroit 1882–1907).

[J. E. DALY]

TRANSCENDENTALISM, LITERARY

Although New England TRANSCENDENTALISM was primarily a religious protest against rational conservatism and a mercantile civilization, its memory remains viable chiefly because of its contributions to U.S. literature. The works of the principal transcendentalists, EMERSON, THOREAU, and WHITMAN, have an assured place on any shelf of great books. But American literature's debt to transcendentalism merely begins with these authors. Many members of the transcendental fellowship were not themselves gifted creatively, yet they exercised wide influence as reformers and critics. In addition, several powerful works of the creative imagination owe their existence to animosities stirred in writers to whom transcendentalism was anathema. Literature's greatest debt to transcendentalism, however, lies beyond the perimeter drawn here. The transcendental insurgence bade the American genius renounce European influence and harken to the voice of Nature. Rallying to this gospel, American writers in all parts of the young nation found courage to choose their own themes and forms. Although the noonday of transcendentalism lasted little more than a dozen years (1836–50), by the end of the 19th century much critical and creative work in American literature was touched by the transcendental impulse.

Beginnings in the U.S. American recognition of transcendentalism began in 1833 with Frederick Henry Hedge's essay on Coleridge in *The Christian Examiner.* Further essays in this journal by Hedge, George Ripley, and Orestes BROWNSON, particularly Brownson's "New Views of Christianity, Society, and the Church" (1836), brought the movement to America. In 1836 the Transcendental Club was formed in Boston when the pioneers of the movement were joined by Emerson, Theodore PARKER, Amos Bronson Alcott, Margaret Fuller, and Elizabeth Peabody. That same year, with *Nature,* which

Walt Whitman.

explored the implications of transcendentalism with remarkable fecundity, Emerson established his primacy over the group and fixed its center at Concord village, where he lived. Emerson's "American Scholar Address" (1837) and "Divinity School Address" (1838), which amplified appeals made by the earlier transcendentalists for intellectual and spiritual independence, gave the movement the broad base from which it worked to create an authentic American culture. Emerson's prose recreates the transcendental experience of unheralded intuitions; his poetry is didactic but metrically precocious, a harbinger of new forms; his views on a transcendental aesthetic are given in "The Poet" and *The Conduct of Life.* "Poetry and Imagination" describes the transcendental doctrine of the symbol and reveals Emerson's decisive role in the development of symbolism in modern literature.

Thoreau's contemporaries said he was Emerson's literary shadow; Emerson said nothing to disabuse them. Yet posterity acknowledges Thoreau as the supreme artist of transcendentalism; his five speculative books of rural travels, a multivolume journal, several striking essays, most notably "Civil Disobedience" (1849) and "Life Without Principle" (1863), and above all *Walden* (1854) are his monument. In "Walking," the most articulate statement of transcendentalism's aims in literature, Thoreau insisted that more of the wildness of nature must

Amos Bronson Alcott, one of the pioneers of the Transcendental Movement.

enter into American literature. His own writings uphold his argument. His prose proclaims the vitality that experience and action give to style.

Spread of the Movement. The distinction of transmitting the transcendental view to America at large belonged to Parker, the master of 20 languages, who spoke to thousands from pulpit and lecture platform, and whose readership ran to hundreds of thousands. Among his contemporaries, Horace Greeley alone rivaled him in influence. Parker's "Discourse of the Transient and Permanent in Christianity" (1841) stands beside *Nature* as one of the two supreme articulations of transcendentalism. Scarcely less important was his pellucid "Discourse of Matters Pertaining to Religion" (1842), the principal route along which many, bewildered by Emerson's vagueness, passed to an understanding of transcendentalism. His essay on "The Position and Duties of the American Scholar" (1849) finds Parker at his characteristic best, persuading men by argument to accept views toward

which Emerson's wraithlike insights had already inclined them.

Two of the major transcendentalists, Alcott and the Yankee Minerva, Margaret Fuller, shone more in conversation than in letters. Alcott's huge journals abound with the epigrams from which *Orphic Sayings* (1840) and *Concord Days* (1872) were culled, but his inquisitive, unbiased mind served him best in his role as teacher; he was not a writer. Nonetheless, his *Conversations on the Gospels* (1836) joined Emerson's *Nature* and Brownson's "New Views" to spread the transcendentalist endeavor. *Woman in the Nineteenth Century* (1845), the one book for which Margaret Fuller is remembered, made courageous claims for woman's rights. Her *Papers on Literature and Art* (1846), compiled from her work as literary editor of Greeley's *Tribune,* discloses her real influence on literature. As able a critic as could be found in America in her day, she drew freely upon her firsthand knowledge of European literature to formulate demands for higher standards of achievement among American writers, urging upon them the fluent sense of life she found in Catholic countries.

Transcendentalism found in Brownson its boldest champion. His is the distinction of having convinced others that literature is an organic expression of the whole community. He was himself convinced that American literature's real affinities reposed in the literature of the Continent, and he propagated an interest in German philosophical IDEALISM and liberal French thought. This led to publication, under Ripley's editorship, of *Specimens of Foreign Standard Literature* (14 v., 1838–42), and Hedge's anthology, *Prose Writers of Germany* (1848). Both works not only made accessible seminal documents from which transcendentalism derived, but opened up a view of literature that assured continuance of unhampered receptivity to experience, a view that transcendentalism coveted.

Influence on Poetry. Despite heavy commitments to religion, ethics, and sociology, from the outset the transcendentalists regarded the creation of an American poetry as their chief task. The attempts of Thoreau, Hedge, William Ellery CHANNING, Alcott, and Margaret Fuller to court the muse produced only versified epistemology. Christopher Cranch's poem "Correspondences" is, except for Emerson's essays, the best statement transcendentalists made on epistemology; moreover Cranch brought to his poetry a penetrating and agile wit that gave it literary value. In the Boston locale, Jones Very was the only true poet among the transcendentalists; his *Essays and Poems* (1839), edited by Emerson, contains the best sonnets written in 19th-century America; his essays on epic poetry and Shakespeare have a sophistication not matched in their time. Elsewhere, at Brooklyn and Amherst, transcendental expectancy sponsored the poetic achievement of Whitman and Emily Dickinson. Whitman traveled to Boston to seek personal assurance from Emerson that the transcendental afflatus had descended upon him. Emily Dickinson, in seclusion at Amherst, after assessing Emerson's poems and essays (e.g., ''The Poet,'' ''Worship,'' and ''Compensation''), concluded that ''By intuition, Mightiest things Assert themselves'' and set down ''bulletins . . . From Immortality'' that proclaim her transcendentalism's rarest flower.

Journals to Promote the Movement. The transcendentalists made repeated attempts to launch a journal to propagate their views; none was successful. The first venture, *The Western Messenger* (1835–40), was published in Cincinnati by several exiled Bostonians, including Channing, Cranch, James Freeman Clarke, and William G. Eliot, grandfather of T. S. Eliot. It failed when, with commendable integrity, it boosted Brownson's ''Laboring Classes.'' Meanwhile, Brownson himself started the *Boston Quarterly Review* (1838–42), likewise short-lived, but the most spirited journal of its day. *The Dial* (1840–44), named by Alcott, published by Elizabeth Peabody, and edited by Ripley and Emerson with help from Margaret Fuller and Thoreau, gave many Transcendentalists, including Thoreau, their first chance to appear in print. When it failed, Ripley began at BROOK FARM his *Harbinger* (1845–49), a weekly with a socialist bias, but strong in criticism. Its contributors included Greeley, Lowell, Whittier, Albert Brisbane, Thomas Wentworth Higginson, Henry James, Sr., and Ripley's brilliant wife, Sophia, whose conversion to Catholicism followed that of Brownson, Isaac HECKER, and other Brook Farm associates. The *Harbinger* was discontinued when Ripley transferred his services to Greeley's *Tribune,* where, as literary editor, he did many excellent pieces. Parker's *Massachusetts Quarterly Review* (1847–50), though it carried perceptive reviews and a brilliant résumé of the literary creed of transcendentalism, fared no better than its predecessors. Elizabeth Peabody's *Aesthetic Papers* (1849), where Thoreau's ''Civil Disobedience'' first appeared, and William Henry Channing's *The Spirit of the Age* (1849–50) survived only for the publication of an issue or two.

Reactions against Transcendentalism. In *American Notes,* Charles Dickens says of his visit to Boston: ''I was given to understand that whatever was unintelligible would be certainly transcendental.'' This view of transcendentalism reflects a belief held by several eminent writers and is a reminder that transcendentalism goaded its detractors to greater creative efforts than it did it adherents. Hawthorne, himself a transcendentalist apostate, lampooned the movement in ''Earth's Holocaust,'' ''The Celestial Railroad,'' and *The Blithedale Romance* (1852), which contains abrasive fictional portraits of Brownson and Margaret Fuller. James Fenimore Cooper, despite the Leatherstocking's intimacy with nature, warns in *The Crater* (1847) against transcendental excess. Edgar Allan Poe's ''Never Bet the Devil Your Head'' enjoins the same caution. The defiant individualism of Herman Melville's Ahab discloses a hardy distaste for transcendentalism, which Melville indulges further in *Pierre* (1852), where Emerson and Thoreau, as Plinlimmon and Millthorpe, are gibed at, and in *The Confidence Man* (1857). Louisa May Alcott's *Silver Pitchers* (1876) and Henry James's *The Bostonians* (1886) attest to the durability of transcendentalism as an object of ridicule.

The afterglow of transcendentalism, however, flared in more than negations. Transcendentalism had established new tastes that raised the aims of American literature and assured its growth. Well might James Joyce's Finnegan regard ''Concord on the Merrymaking'' with soulful respect.

Bibliography: O. B. FROTHINGHAM, *Transcendentalism in New England: A History* (New York 1959). P. MILLER, ed., *The Transcendentalists: An Anthology* (Cambridge, Mass. 1960). G. F. WHICHER, ed., *The Transcendentalist Revolt against Materialism* (pa. Boston 1949).

[J. J. MCALEER]

TRANSCENDENTALS

The moving force behind all philosophical thought is the concept of being. Apart from this concept itself, the metaphysician gives detailed examination also to the properties that necessarily accompany being and thus are found with every being. The most common of these are unity, truth, and goodness. Because such concepts transcend the categories of Aristotle, scholastic philosophers generally refer to them as the transcendentals. The development of these concepts is considered here both historically and systematically.

Historical Development

In the history of philosophy, greatest attention was given to the transcendentals in the Greek, medieval, and modern periods. The following details the principal developments relevant to the analysis of this concept to be given later.

Greek Philosophy. PLATO traced earthly things to their ideas and, through ascending levels, to the highest idea. The ideas, however, are the ὄντως ὄν, the being or true beings, in which the real essence of being shines forth untarnished. Here, being shows itself to be unity as opposed to plurality, truth as opposed to appearance, and good as opposed to evil. Since visible being has a share in the ideas and thereby a share in being, it partakes of these properties even though they are found in it only imperfectly.

Aristotle treated expressly of the properties of being as such. He examines the true and the one in Books 6 and 10 of his *Metaphysics,* the good in Book 1 of the *Nicomachean Ethics,* and thereby lays the foundations for much of the scholastic teaching on transcendentals.

PLOTINUS, the main representative of NEOPLATONISM, saw the ultimate source of all things as the One and the Good. From this emanates the νοῦς (mind), which brings ideas to their perfection in thought; thus it also is the truth. The soul and all things participate in this, although the brightness of being and its properties grows dimmer and dimmer in descending degrees because of the influence of matter, which corresponds roughly to nonbeing.

Medieval Doctrine. During the patristic period, AUGUSTINE expressed the essence of being in the precise formulas: *Nihil autem est esse quam unum esse* (Being is nothing more than being one)—*Mor. Manich.* 2.6; *Verum mihi videtur esse id quod est* (The true appears to me to be that which is)—*Soliloq.* 2.5; *Inquantum est, quidquid est, bonum est* (Insofar as it is, whatever exists is good)— *Vera relig.* 11.21.

Among the scholastics, ALEXANDER OF HALES and ALBERT THE GREAT proposed the same three essential attributes of being, while the latter gave a clear systematic development. Albert also inquired whether THING (*res*) and otherness (*aliquid*) are to be enumerated among these properties; his answer was that thing is synonymous with being while otherness is already contained in the concept of unity. In this, one detects the influence of the Arabian commentator on Aristotle, Avicenna, who enumerated thing, being, and one (*res et ens et unum—Meta.* 1:6B) as attributes belonging to everything. Avicenna added that while being (*ens*) and thing (*res*) are two distinct determinants, being (*ens*) and otherness (*aliquid*) are synonymous (*ibid.* 6C).

With St. THOMAS AQUINAS one comes to the most advanced of the medieval theories on the basic attributes of being. In all, St. Thomas lists five properties as accompanying being, namely, thing, unity, otherness, truth, and goodness (*ens, res, unum, aliquid, verum, bonum—De ver.* 1.1; *De nat. gen.* 2). Admittedly in some texts he mentions only three attributes as essential to being, viz, unity, truth, and goodness (*De ver.* 21.1–3; *De pot.* 9.7 ad 6; *In 1 sent.* 8.1.3). St. Thomas does not include beauty in these enumerations. In other texts, however, he does

see beauty as closely related to the good (*Summa theologiae* 1a2ae, 27.1 ad 3), considers physical beauty as intimately connected with spiritual beauty (*Summa theologiae* 2a2ae, 145.2 and ad 3), and stresses that there is nothing that does not partake of beauty and the good (*In Dion. de div. nom.* 4.5; cf. *In 1 sent.* 31.2.1; *De ver.* 22.1 ad 12). On the basis of these texts some argue that St. Thomas regards beauty itself as coextensive with being.

With the renewal of scholasticism in the 16th century, F. SUÁREZ presented his doctrine of the basic attributes of being along systematic lines. Not wishing to multiply distinctions, he held that there are only three properties of being, namely, unity, truth, and goodness (*Disp. metaph.* 3.2.3); the other two attributes added by St. Thomas he considered in much the same way as did Albert the Great. The later scholastic development continued in the direction he inaugurated, and its influence was felt by the rationalistic philosophy of the 18th century, which flourished mainly through efforts of C. WOLFF.

Modern Thought. G. W. von LEIBNIZ was prominent in this development and actually contributed to it. His thinking culminated in the doctrine of monadology. Everything is there traced back to the MONAD, which presents itself as the original unity and which develops through perception and appetition, thereby also embracing truth and goodness. Briefly, Leibniz proclaims being as a monad and thus, implicitly, as unity, truth, and goodness.

A trace of the scholastic heritage is also to be found in Kant's *Critique of Pure Reason.* In the second edition, Kant discusses a ''cornerstone in the transcendentalist philosophy of the ancients'' that ''features the sentence so widely acclaimed among the scholastics: *quodlibet ens est unum, verum, bonum*'' (B 113). According to Kant, this sentence does not enumerate metaphysical attributes of being but merely logical conditions preliminary to the comprehension of any object; they are required to furnish a basis for categories of unity, plurality, and universality. [*See* TRANSCENDENTAL (KANTIAN).]

The way in which Kant elucidated this triad prepared the stage for the development of his ideas by G. W. F. HEGEL. The latter has resort to the metaphysical depths of being and to its properties as these manifest themselves in ''Logic.'' His dialectical movement, of course, ultimately leads to PANTHEISM.

In the second half of the 19th century only F. W. NIETZSCHE is noteworthy. He attempts, in *Wille zur Macht,* to overcome the absolute opposition between unity and plurality, truth and falsehood, goodness and evil. The essential attributes of being thus no longer have primacy over their opposites, but become identical with them, as expressed in the Dionysian coming-to-be, in the ''Will to Power,'' and the ''Everlasting Return.'' With this notion there is an accompanying destruction of metaphysics and, ultimately, of being.

The position of Nicolai HARTMANN is characteristic of nonscholastic thought in the 20th century. Hartmann takes the categories as actual determinants of being, and indeed as its principal and innermost determinants. Consequently the essential attributes of being are not superadded to the categories but are included among them. Rather than being differentiated from the categories, they become categories themselves. Behind this development is the restriction of philosophical thought to finite natural being. If the supernatural Infinite Being, God, is ruled out, then the basic determinants of being, as well as those of finite being (namely, the categories), coincide.

Systematic Analysis

The properties referred to as transcendentals necessarily accompany being; being manifests itself in them and reveals what it actually is. Just as being is never found without such properties, so these are inseparably bound up with one another in the sense that they include and interpenetrate each other. Consequently, according to the measure and manner in which a thing possesses being, it partakes of unity, truth and goodness; and conversely, according to the measure and manner in which a thing shares in these properties, it possesses being. This ultimately implies that subsistent being is also subsistent unity, truth, and goodness.

Properties of Being. Precisely as essentially given with being, these determinants are called its essential attributes; as transcending all particularities in the order of being, they are called transcendental; and as belonging to everything whatsoever, they are designated as the most common determinants of all things. Finally, their denomination as properties of being establishes their connection with the fourth of the PREDICABLES, *proprium,* with the following consequences:

1. These are not synonyms for being, but rather characteristics that add something to being and are of necessity found with it.

2. Neither are they accidents, such as properties usually are, but rather determinants that are formally identical with being. Thus they have the status of metaphysical properties.

3. These properties do not actually arise out of being; being is their foundation, and is otherwise identical with them. Being is not their principle, therefore, and certainly not their cause.

4. It follows from this that the distinction between being and its attributes is merely a conceptual one.

On the one hand this has a foundation in reality, because the attributes either manifest what being is or add something to it; on the other hand, this distinction is the least possible one, because it excludes every type of development or division, since it is made within being itself. Therefore, the attributes add nothing to being but merely predicate fully what being itself is. (*See* DISTINCTION, KINDS OF.)

5. Since the attributes are distinct from being as their foundation, one may speak of them, somewhat improperly, as a synthesis; since the attributes are all formally identical with being, however, this synthesis is a priori, or one that provides only an insight into an intrinsically necessary relationship. Such an a priori synthesis belongs to the metaphysical realm, and thus is essentially superior to Kant's synthesis, which is valid only for phenomena, i.e., for human knowledge.

As to the treatment of the individual transcendental attributes of being, all are agreed that unity, truth, and goodness are found in every being. We would add beauty to this, although those who regard beauty as pertaining essentially to sensible intuition do not follow us here. The four attributes named lend themselves to predication in either of two ways, depending on whether one emphasizes being itself (*esse*), or what has being (*ens*). The corresponding formulas read: (1) Being is unity, truth, goodness, and beauty, where the ''is'' expresses formal identity. (2) Every being, so far as existence comes to it, is one, true, good, and beautiful, all of which are implied by this formal identity.

Other attributes, some of which are ascribed to being, are either not actually transcendental, or are included under one of the attributes already named. Thus order and wholeness are not transcendental because they include multitude, which is not found in God. Duration and SIMILARITY can be reduced to unity, because duration is unity in time or surpassing time, while similarity implies a congruity or unity of various things in some substantial or accidental grouping.

Connection between the Transcendentals. The foregoing account of the transcendentals permits their intrinsic or essential connection to be seen. Through being, unity comes directly to an entity; it is given with being directly, without any intermediary, and for this reason can be referred to as a preoperative attribute of being. Truth and goodness build upon this; they are not merely reduced from the unity of being, but rather are given through a type of operation, and thus are referred to as operative attributes. Intrinsic to truth is a relevance to or conformity with a spiritual knower, and this comes to an entity in virtue of its being. In the same way, goodness implies a similar accessibility to or conformity with AP-PETITE, and this too comes to an entity in virtue of its being. Further, since in knowledge there is only an imperfect or still incomplete union of spirit with being, while in appetition or love this union is complete or perfect, truth is ontologically prior to goodness. What begins in truth, however, finds its completion in goodness. Beauty includes unity, truth, and goodness simultaneously, and in this sense is their completion and perfect harmony. Unity transforms an entity, making it a harmonious whole in which truth is so luminous that it is not merely grasped discursively, but is perceived directly. But the perception of truth also embraces goodness, which leads one from the disquiet of appetite to the quiet of pleasure or delightful enjoyment (*fruitio*).

The two further determinants that Thomas Aquinas, following Avicenna, names as attributes of being, namely, thing (*res*) and otherness (*aliquid*), although transcendental, do not, it appears, stand out as special attributes in contrast to the others, but rather are reducible to these as coconstituted with them. Thus *res* goes with *ens* because being bespeaks ''something'' that accompanies being; this ''something,'' or subject of being, is in fact exactly the same as thing or essence. In a similar manner unity includes otherness (*aliquid,* i.e., *aliud quid*), because what is undivided in itself is necessarily divided from everything else or separate, for which reason unity as separation is already implied in intrinsic unity.

Demonstration of Properties. Proofs that the properties of being are actually transcendental are here sketched in summary fashion.

Unity. Every being either has parts or has not, and therefore either is divisible or is not. The indivisible is secure in its being owing to its simplicity, because it cannot be destroyed by separation. The divisible, on the other hand, is continually robbed of its being through separation, so that it either ceases to exist or at least no longer exists as an undamaged whole. At the same time the hierarchy of being shows how intrinsic unity grows correspondingly with separation from other things. By reason of His perfect simplicity, God is the Absolute (*Absolutus*) when compared with creatures. Because the nonliving is least one in itself, it is also the least separated from others, or the least individual.

Truth. To the extent that the content of the CONCEPT is understood to penetrate to transcendental being as adding some type of determination, and thus as constituting such and such a being, it is capable of being known. In the JUDGMENT, on the other hand, a thing is capable of being grasped because it is seen as something to which being comes in this mode or that. Therefore, in virtue of the transcendental quality of being, everything that dif-

ferentiates itself from nothing is either being or something to which being is added; thus it has the basis of intelligibility within itself and is fully intelligible. Furthermore, everything is implicitly grasped by spirit in the concept of being because of its transcendental quality; therefore, everything is open to spirit, and nothing is heterogeneous or absolutely inaccessible to it. This applies to every entity as a whole, as well as to all considerations relating to such an entity, since these are always being. Yet the human mind, because of its finiteness, cannot convert all that it grasps implicitly into knowledge that is comprehended and known explicitly.

Goodness. A thing is desired and loved because (and inasmuch as) it has being; thus being manifests itself as the basis of desirableness or goodness. For this reason every entity, in virtue of its being, is good and consequently to be sought. More profoundly, being is good for itself insofar as its degree of participation in being corresponds to its natural strivings; and it is good for another insofar as it is able to fulfill this striving. Free will, which alone can freely choose between limited goods as material objects, goes deeper still, since it is ordered to the good itself as a formal object, and ultimately to limitless good (*summum bonum in genere*). It is evident here that goodness is not a limited aspect of being, but rather is as all-encompassing as being itself, and consequently transcendental. Because of this identification of being and goodness, evil and vice can exist only in the absence of being, namely in the lack of perfection demanded by a being's natural ordination, and without which the being suffers a privation.

Beauty. As a condition for the fulfilment and perfect harmony of the one, the true, and the good, beauty may be included with these three transcendentals. Since our analysis applies as much to the spiritually perceptible as to the sensibly visible, there is a purely spiritual beauty. In the physical order, however, we usually apply the term ''beautiful'' only to what is intensely experienced, because beauty shines brightly in it. Yet metaphysical analysis finds at least a rudimentary beauty in every being, because the complete destruction of harmonious wholeness, which makes contemplation and pleasure possible, is equivalent to the annihilation of being. The more this disintegration spreads through something, the uglier it becomes; yet even the ugly always contains a residue of beauty because, according to what has just been said, there can never be anything radically or absolutely ugly.

See Also: BEAUTY; BEING; FIRST PRINCIPLES; GOOD; THING; TRUTH; UNITY

Bibliography: J. E. TWOMEY, *The General Notion of the Transcendentals in the Metaphysics of Saint Thomas Aquinas* (Catholic University of America Philosophic Studies 195; Washington 1958).

"The Transfiguration," painting by Raphael. (AP/Wide World Photos)

A. B. WOLTER, *The Transcendentals and Their Function in the Metaphysics of Duns Scotus* (St. Bonaventure, N.Y. 1946). L. ELDERS, *Aristotle's Theory of the One* (Assen 1961). J. B. LOTZ, *Metaphysica operationis humanae* . . . (Analecta Gregoriana 94; 2d ed. Rome 1961); *Ontología* (Barcelona 1962). L. LACHANCE, *L'Être et ses propriétés* (Montréal-Ottawa 1950). H. KUHN, *Das Sein und das Gute* (Munich 1962). M. SAINT-PIERRE, *Beauté, bonté, vérité chez Hans Urs von Balthasar* (Paris 1998). J. A. AERTSEN, *Medieval Philosophy and the Transcendentals: The Case of Thomas Aquinas* (Leiden; New York 1996). S. MACDONALD, "The Metaphysics of Goodness and the Doctrine of the Transcendentals," *Being and Goodness* (Ithaca, N.Y. 1991) 31–55. N. KRETZMANN, "Trinity and Transcendentals," *Trinity, Incarnation, & Atonement,* ed. R. J. FEENSTRA and C. PLANTINGA JR. (Notre Dame, Ind. 1989) 79–109.

[J. B. LOTZ]

TRANSFIGURATION

This event, singular in that it is the only time during His mortal life when Jesus permitted His divine glory to shine through His humanity, is placed in the same sequence by the three Evangelists (Mt 17.1–8; Mk 9.1–7; Lk 9.28–36) who recorded it. The event, transmitted through the Gospels, holds a significant place in Christian theology, worship, and iconography.

Gospel Account. The Transfiguration took place about a week (six days in Mt 17.1; Mk 9.1; eight days in Lk 9.28) after the promise of the primacy to Peter. In parallel passages of the first three Evangelists, we are told that "Jesus took Peter, James, and his brother John," the three disciples closest to Our Lord, who were later to be the witnesses of the contrasting agony in the garden, to "a high mountain off by themselves." Luke, whose Gospel is often referred to as the gospel of prayer, adds that Jesus "went up the mountain to pray."

Place. The high mountain is not identified in the texts, although a tradition dating back to the fourth century places the Transfiguration on Mt. TABOR, where there is now a beautiful basilica commemorating this event. Some scholars prefer Mt. Hermon as the location; in its favor is the description of the mountain as "high." As God had appeared to Moses and to Elijah on a mountain (Ex 19.20–24; Dt 4.10–11; 1 Kgs 19.8–18), so now God in the flesh ascends a mountain to be met by these two representatives of the Old Testament, Moses the lawgiver, and Elijah the Prophet.

Manner. During the time of His prayer (Lk 9.29), Jesus "was transfigured before them," that is, the glory of His divinity of which He "had emptied himself" (Phil 2.7) shone through His countenance and His garments. The Evangelists are careful to use terms in the Greek that point out the nature of this transformation. It came from within and was due to an internal "metamorphosis." This was soon to pass away, for the permanent transfiguration and glorification could come only through His sufferings, the very topic of conversation between Jesus and the two heavenly visitors (Lk 9.31). This is stressed by St. Paul in Phil 2.5–11: Jesus was obedient unto death, and for this reason God has exalted Him. The Evangelists also seem to point out a connection between Christ's sufferings and His glorification, for the Transfiguration is placed in the context of the first prediction of the Passion and death and Resurrection (Mt 16.21–23; Mk 8.31–33; Lk 9.22).

Peter's Words. As it was Peter who was the central figure in the context (the promise of the primacy and in the prediction of the sufferings of Christ), so now it is he who speaks for himself and for the others. His comment is ambiguous, for it may mean that it is "good" for the Apostles to be there, or it could mean that it is "good" for Christ that the three are there, for they could set up three tents or booths, one for Christ, one for Moses, and one for Elijah. This reference to tents or booths has helped to give a probable date to this event in the life of Christ. It was during the Feast of BOOTHS (TABERNACLES), celebrated from the 15th to the 22d day of the seventh month (September–October), that the Israelites built booths or tents in their vineyards or other fields in memory of the time when their ancestors lived in tents in the desert (Nm 29.12–39). Peter's comment, then, may have had its origin in the proximity of this feast. A further corroboration is to be found in the radiance that came forth from Christ, as well as in the brightness of the cloud that came over them. For during this feast the Temple was ablaze with lights [*The Catholic Biblical Quarterly* 21 (1959) 24–38].

God's Words. The climax of the Transfiguration is the voice of God the Father as it was heard at the time of the BAPTISM OF THE LORD, so now it is heard: "This is my beloved Son, in whom I am well pleased; hear

him." God's presence is symbolized by the bright cloud, a standard part of an Old Testament THEOPHANY (Ex 19.16–18; 24.15–16; 1 Kgs 8.10–11). While God's Chosen People is called His son (Ex 4.22), Christ is God's beloved Son, the Only-Begotten One, united to Him in a special and unique way. Because this Son fulfills the divine will, He is pleasing to the Father. He is God's word (Jn 1.1), sent to give the word of God to men; men, therefore, have an obligation to listen to Him.

The reaction of the three Apostles is fear, the ordinary reaction so often recorded in the Bible when the Divinity presents itself in one form or another. It is only after Jesus comes to them and reassures them that they are able to overcome this emotion. To prevent a premature acceptance of Jesus as the Messiah by people who had hopes of a politically minded one, should this extraordinary event become known, Jesus cautions his Apostles to tell no one about it.

Theological Aspects. The context gives the scene of the Transfiguration its significance in the life of Christ and its fruitful implications in the life of the Christian.

Mystery Revealed Jesus here appears as the Lord, realizing the Scriptures (cf. Lk 24.44–48) and their prophecies about the Messiah, the Servant of Yahweh (*see* SUFFERING SERVANT, SONG OF THE), and the SON OF MAN. The glory overwhelms the Disciples with the tremendous awe-fear of the religious experience of man before the divine presence (cf. Lk 1.29–30). The experience provokes the suggestion of Peter, who expresses his joy before the glory of the one whom he has confessed to be the Messiah. At last God is going to dwell with His own people as the Prophets foretold He would in Messianic times. The glory here, however, is not that of the Last Day; rather, it illuminates only the face of Jesus and His vestments as it has already illumined the visage of Moses (Ex 34.29–35). It is the glory of Christ (Lk 9.32) who is the well-beloved Son, as the voice from the cloud proclaims Him. At the same time, this voice ratifies the revelation that Jesus has made to His Disciples and that is the topic of His conversation with Moses and Elijah. His death, the final Exodus of which Jerusalem is to be the point of departure (Lk 9.31), is the necessary passage to the new and eternal Alliance, the Alliance where all who hear the WORD made Flesh and believe in Him will see the glory of God [cf. Jn 1.14; *see* GLORY (IN THE BIBLE)].

Signification for Christ and the Church. The Transfiguration confirms the confession of Peter at CAESAREA PHILIPPI (Mt 16.16) and consecrates the revelation about Jesus, the Son of Man suffering and glorious, whose death-Resurrection fulfills the Scriptures. It reveals the Person of Jesus, the well-beloved Son who possesses the same glory as God the Father. It proclaims Jesus and His word as the New Law, while anticipating and prefiguring the paschal event that, by the pathway of the Cross, will introduce the Christ into the full development of His glory and the dignity of His sonship. This experience is also designed to sustain the Disciples during their own agony and participation in the mystery of the Cross.

In the SALVATION HISTORY of humanity, the Transfiguration is a prophetic sign, an apocalyptic event, that points to the future transfiguration of all Christians in Christ. Its mystery is also the mystery of the Christian's transfiguration—of the increasing hold of the Holy Spirit upon men, incarnate spirits, and through men, upon the entire universe. By the sacramental encounter with the Person of the Risen Lord, the Christian participates in the mystery of the death-Resurrection of the firstborn of every creature—the mystery prefigured by the Transfiguration. A Christian is a person called in the present to be always and ever increasingly transfigured by the action of the Spirit (2 Cor 3.18) in love-living expectation of the total transfiguration, the glorious universal resurrection at the Lord's Second Coming. In what may be called the sacrament of man's second regeneration, just as Baptism was his first (cf. *Summa theologiae* 3a, 45.4), the transfiguration of the Church, i.e., man's transfiguration, will complete the *pleroma,* bringing to Christ "a little fulfillment." "Father, I will that where I am, they also whom thou hast given me may be with me: in order that they may behold my glory" (Jn 17.24).

This total glory of final transfiguration will not, however, come magically. The Christian who recognizes the deep signification of the transfiguration does not deny the final judgment, the *dies irae.* He knows well that before ultimate glory, transfiguration with Christ, there must be configuration with Him. Indeed, living in the world is a forceful reminder of this—the place of suffering and the cross, and of Satan. However, the Christian hopes, fully confident that the work of the Holy Spirit will end in the triumphant glory of ultimate transfiguration.

For now, the Christian's life is hidden with Christ in God, but when Christ shall appear on the Last Day, then the Christian also shall appear with Him in glory, and God shall be all in all, and the Christian's whole being will be a praise of glory (*see* Col 3.3–4; 1 Cor 15.28; Eph 1.12).

Feast and Iconography. The importance of the Transfiguration is shown by the high rank given to its feast (first class) in the liturgy of the Church. The feast has been celebrated in the East since the fourth or fifth century, and locally in the West since at least the eighth century. It was extended to the universal Church by Pope Callistus III in 1457 in commemoration of the Christians' victory over the Turks at Belgrade on July 22, 1456.

News of this victory reached Rome on August 6, the traditional date of the Feast of the Transfiguration. Apparently this was the date of the consecration of a chapel in the fourth century on Mt. Tabor in honor of the Transfiguration.

The Transfiguration has been frequently represented in Christian art, beginning in the fourth century when, in the Christological disputes, the orthodox found this an excellent way to stress the divinity of Christ. However, the oldest preserved work of art showing this scene is the mosaic in the apse of the church at Mt. Sinai from the sixth century. Almost as old as this is the mosaic in the Church of St. Apollinaris in Classe at Ravenna. There Christ is represented only by a jeweled cross in a nimbus, with inscriptions. [*See* RAVENNA (ART OF).] The Transfiguration was a favorite subject in the art of the Renaissance—a relief on the bronze doors of the baptistry in Florence by Lorenzo Ghiberti, a fresco in the convent of St. Mark at Florence by Fra Angelico, and the well-known oil painting in the Vatican Museum by Raphael.

See Also: ASCENSION OF JESUS CHRIST; PAROUSIA; PASSION OF CHRIST; RESURRECTION OF CHRIST.

Bibliography: THOMAS AQUINAS, *Summe theologiae* 3a, 45. *Dictionnaire de théologie catholique,* ed. A. VACANT et al., (Paris 1903—50) Tables générales 2:2626. J. M. VOSTÉ, *De baptismo, tentatione et Transfiguratione Jesu Christi,* v.2 of *Studia Theologiae biblicae: Novi Testamenti,* 3 v. (Rome 1933–37). A. KENNY, "The Transfiguration and Agony in the Garden," *The Catholic Biblical Quarterly* 19 (1957) 444–452. C. E. CARLSTON, "Transfiguration and Resurrection," *Journal of Biblical Literature* 80 (1961) 233–240. *Encyclopedic Dictionary of the Bible,* tr. and adap. by L. HARTMAN (New York 1963) 2487–89. P. MIQUEL, "Le Mystère de la transfiguration," *Questions liturgiques et paroissiales* 42 (1961) 194–223, exceptional biblio., tr. and abr. *Theology Digest* 11 (1963) 159–164. X. LÉON-DUFOUR, ed., *Vocabulaire de théologie biblique* (Paris 1962) 1071. P. TEILHARD DE CHARDIN, *The Divine Milieu* (New York 1960). F. X. DURRWELL, *In the Redeeming Christ,* tr. R. SHEED (New York 1963). R. OTTO, *The Idea of the Holy,* tr. J. W. HARVEY (New York 1958).

[G. H. GUYOT/J. L. CYPRIANO]

TRANSMIGRATION OF SOULS

The supposed passing of the soul at death into another body is called transmigration of souls (REINCARNATION, METEMPSYCHOSIS). This doctrine, in its most developed form, as in Greece and India, involved three restrictions: the place where the soul and its new body dwell must be, at least in part, in this world; the new body must be acquired for more than a temporary period; and the soul must be that which creates an individual personality common to the several incarnations. More or less elaborate doctrines of transmigration have been widespread in the world, occurring in Asia, Africa, Australia, Oceania,

155

among North and South American Indians, and in parts of Europe. It is most unlikely that the doctrine spread from a common center; in fact, it could easily have been developed separately in these places in order to account for the resemblance of children to their parents or other relatives—as a pseudoscientific theory of heredity. This article deals almost exclusively with the idea of transmigration in Western European culture.

In ancient Greece, transmigration was a tenet of restricted groups and appeared first, so far as is known, at the end of the archaic period, in the 6th century B.C. It was probably a native development. The doctrine hardly occurred in Egyptian religion, though Herodotus (2.123) supposed that the Greeks learned of it in Egypt; moreover, there was no communication between Greece and India at this early date. Greece itself already had the basic beliefs upon which such a doctrine could be constructed (Nilsson 1:654–658). Greeks had entertained the idea that the soul of a dead man can pass into an animal (*ibid.,* 182–184), and the belief that the soul is divine, and therefore immortal and preexistent. This posed the question of where the soul comes from (*see* SOUL HUMAN).

Pythagoras. The Greek lexicon of Suidas (*c.* A.D. 1000) attributes the doctrine to Pherecydes, Pythagoras's supposed teacher. But PYTHAGORAS himself (late 6th century) is the earliest Greek to whom the doctrine can be assigned almost certainly, although he left no written works and became a legendary figure even in his own day, so that the task of delineating ''the real Pythagoras'' is complex (cf. K. von Fritz, ''Pythagoras,'' and H. Dörrie, ''Pythagoreer,'' *Paulys Realenzyklopädie der klassischen Altertumswissenschaft,* 24 [1963] 209–277). Later authors, beginning with Diodorus Siculus (5.28.5–6), were sure that Pythagoras taught transmigration; but there is an excellent early testimony also in a fragment of Xenophanes (H. Diels, *Die Fragmente der Vorsokratiker: Griechisch und Deutsch,* 21 B 7), a near contemporary of Pythagoras. Xenophanes wrote in a satirical poem that Pythagoras once ordered a man to stop beating a dog because he recognized the voice of a departed friend in the dog's howls. Another early testimony (Empedocles in Diels *op. cit.,* 31 B 129) alleges that Pythagoras, when he really exerted his mind, could recall the events of 10 and 20 human generations, i.e., over a millennium, on the normal system of reckoning generations.

Herodotus (2.123) also probably referred to Pythagoras and his followers by the phrase ''some earlier'' (οἱ μὲν πρότεροι). Herodotus wrote: ''The Egyptians were the first to enunciate the following doctrine: the human soul is immortal, and when the body perishes the soul enters one animal after another in succession, and when it

has made the rounds of all the land, sea and air creatures, it returns to a human body. The cycle requires 3000 years.'' The doctrine described here was very probably not Egyptian; it *may* have been Pythagorean. Whatever the details of Pythagoras's doctrine of transmigration were, they probably had ethical implications, for Pythagoras enjoyed a reputation among the Greeks as an inculcator of morality (e.g., Plato, *Rep.* 559B–600C).

Among the Orphics and Others before Plato. Transmigration is often said to have been introduced to Greece by the Orphic sect(s), but the doctrine was not ascribed to the Orphics in the early sources (Stettner, 86–88; Long, Appendix II). Some scholars have greatly emphasized the extent, importance, and organizational and philosophic unity of the Orphic movement. O. Kern (*Die Religion der Griechen* [Berlin 1935]) 2:144) and W. K. C. Guthrie (*Orpheus and Greek Religion* [London 1935]) insist on a unity for which I. M. Linforth (*The Arts of Orpheus* [Berkeley 1941]) finds little evidence in his methodical study of the ancient testimonies. (*See* ORPHISM.) Without becoming involved in the details of this controversy, it seems fair to state that, on the available evidence, transmigration seems to have been taught in Pythagorean circles and also, perhaps at the same time and certainly a little later, in other religious groups as well.

The existence of such groups is clearly implied in a passage of Pindar, who referred to the doctrine twice (*Olympian* 2.53–83 and Frg. 127 [ed. M. Bowra]). Since Pindar's usual view of the life after death was Homeric, it is likely that these two passages were composed to suit the beliefs of particular persons or groups, one of which was located in Sicily, for *Olympian 2* (476 B.C.) was written for Theron, tyrant of Acragas. Transmigration, as delineated in these passages, was a doctrine with obvious and emphatic ethical implications: sin must be punished; atonement is part of the very order of nature; the possibility of a blessed life in the other world is held out to men as an inducement to righteous living in this.

The philosopher Empedocles (*c.* 493–433 B.C.), another resident of western Greece, believed in transmigration (see Frgs. 117, 129, 146, 115, 126, 127, 120, 119, 121–3, in H. Diels, *Die Fragmente der Vorsokratiker: Griechisch und Deutsch,*). He taught that all souls are divine by nature, and originally enjoyed a divine status. Whenever any soul stains itself with sin it is condemned to wander for 30,000 seasons away from the company of the blessed and to assume all sorts of mortal forms (plant, animal, and human), retaining the memory of its previous incarnations.

Plato. The importance of transmigration in European thought is due in no small measure to PLATO's concern with the doctrine. He became interested in it after his first journey to western Greece (Long, 69–73), and described it in a number of striking passages (*Meno,* 81A–D: *Phaedo,* 70A–73B, 80A–84b; *Rep.* 10.614B–end; *Phaedrus,* 245C–256E; *Tim.* 41D–42E). These passages are fundamentally consistent, although there are variations of detail among them; the details are usually similar to or identical with those found in Herodotus, Pindar, and Empedocles (Long, 85). The purport of these passages is as follows: Human souls were originally created by the Demiurge out of Existence, Sameness, and Difference, and placed each upon a separate star, from which they were shown the nature of the universe and the laws of destiny. All of them are, at various times, incarnated as humans. They die, are judged, experience punishments or rewards for their deeds in life, and after 1,000 years are again incarnated. They choose their own new bodies, and this choice is of crucial importance; but it is governed partly by the necessities of their own nature. A soul that has kept itself free from bodily taint for three lives is released completely from the cycle of births; most souls must live ten earthly lives—spread over 10,000 years—and then they rise again to the region of the gods and a vision of Truth. According to the *Phaedo* (81E–82B), incarnation is possible into animals, birds, or even insects, but some Neoplatonists insisted that Plato was here speaking allegorically. Since the concept of orthodoxy scarcely existed in Greek religion, Plato or any other philosopher was free to borrow details of any doctrine from various sources, combining them to produce the sort of synthesis he wished. Plato gave us a doctrine of transmigration that is constructed to emphasize in particular the divine source and nature of the soul and that encourages righteousness to the end that the soul may return to its proper divine status.

From 300 B.C. to A.D. 200. In the Hellenistic and Roman period transmigration was accepted in at least some branches of NEO-PYTHAGOREANISM, as well as by some Stoics, who are thought to have been influenced by Posidonius or Varro. The normal Stoic doctrine was that the soul is actualized at the moment of birth by a process of cooling; but there seems no doubt that some Stoics did accept transmigration (see Vergil, *Aen.* 6.724–751, with Norden's introduction and notes *ad loc.;* Pseudo-Tibullus 4.1.206–212; Seneca, *Epist. Mor.* 65.20; 104.11; 108.19–21; and the passages quoted in H. Diels, *Doxographi Graeci* [Berlin 1929] 571–587; 614). Epicureans naturally opposed the doctrine: e.g., Lucretius 3.670–783. Platonic sources lie behind the speculations of Philo Judaeus (*De somniis* 1.133–149, in his interpretation of Jacob's dream) and of Plutarch (*De facie* 30; *De esu carn.* 996bc, 998c–f; *De gen. Soc.* 591c; *De ser. num. vind.* 565e–567f; and *De def. orac.* 431e). The doctrine

played a part also in the Mysteries of Mithra (see F. Cumont, *The Mysteries of Mithra,* Eng. tr. T. J. McCormack [New York 1956] 144).

Transmigration was so well known as a doctrine that it could become a literary theme. See, for example, Ennius's dream, *Annals* 2 Frgs. 4–14 (ed. E. H. Warmington), probably based on Callimachus (Frg. 191, verses 56–63 [ed. Pfeiffer]); Ovid, *Metamor.* 15.158–1721; and the jibes of Lucian (*Oneiros* 4, *Alexander* 43, *Gallus* 20).

In Neoplatonism. Transmigration was taught by many of the forerunners of NEOPLATONISM, such as Cronius, who wrote a monograph on it (not extant), Albinus, Numenius, Harpocration, and possibly Celsus, the general tenor of whose doctrines implies belief in transmigration (see O. Glöckner in *Philologus* 82 [1927] 336). It was a standard tenet of Neoplatonism, though members of the school did not agree whether transmigration into an animal was possible, and some of them taught that, while a human soul can be confined in an animal's body for punishment, it exists alongside of the animal's proper soul. The fullest extant discussion is that of PLOTINUS (*Enn.* 4.3.12–4.4 and 8), but the doctrine is also attested for Porphyry (see especially the Frgs. of *De regress animae,* quoted in St. Augustine [*Civ.* 10.9, 29, 30; 12.21, 27; 22.19, and elsewhere]), Iamblichus and his pupil Sallustius (ch. 19–21, *Sallustius Philosophus* ed. [Cambridge, Eng. 1926]), and the members of the later Athenian group: Theodorus of Asine, Hierocles of Athens, Syrianus, and Proclus. The doctrine became so widely held among pagans at this time that Nemesius, Bishop of Emesa (*c.* A.D. 400, περὶ φύσεως ἀνθρώπου 2.50) could write that all Greeks who believed in immortality at all believed in transmigration.

Later History. The doctrine was held by some Jewish sects (as the Karaites) and by some Muslims, as well as by Gnostic groups (cf. Tertullian, *De anima* 28–, esp. 34–35). Though flatly opposed to the Christian doctrine of redemption, it also found adherents among nominal Christians. Origen was accused of believing it by Theophilus (see St. Jerome, *Ep.* 98.10f), though his extant works, such as the *De principiis,* rather imply that the soul is variously embodied in successive worlds. The doctrine was held by the Manichaeans and, in the Middle Ages, by the groups known collectively as CATHARI. It was held also by Giordano BRUNO (chiefly in *Degli heroici furori*) and J. B. van Helmont. It interested Soame Jenyns (1704–1787), Goethe, Lessing, J. B. Fourier (1768–1830), and some of J. K. Lavater's (1741–1801) followers, among others, and it enjoyed a recrudescence in the 19th century under the influence of translated documents from the Far East. Hitherto the chief inspiration had come from Plato and Neoplatonism. At present the doctrine is studied seriously by Western adherents of the VEDANTA and other Oriental philosophies, and held in a more fantastic form by theosophists (see A. Besant, *La Réincarnation,* [Paris 1910]) and others.

Bibliography: H. VON GLASENAPP, *Die Religion in Geschichte und Gegenwart,* 7 v. (3d ed. Tübingen 1957–65) 5:1637–39. N. W. THOMAS et al., *Encyclopedia of Religion and Ethics,* ed. J. HASTINGS, 13 v. (Edinburgh 1908–27) 12:425–440. G. F. MOORE, *Metempsychosis* (Cambridge, Mass. 1914). M. P. NILSSON, *Geschichte der griechischen Religion,* 2 v. (2d ed. Munich 1955–61) 1:654–658, 663–664, 772–774. E. ROHDE, *Psyche,* ed. O. WEINREICH (9th and 10th ed. Tübingen 1925). W. STETTNER, *Die Seelenwanderung bei Griechen und Römern* (Stuttgart 1934). H. S. LONG, *A Study of the Doctrine of Metempsychosis in Greece from Pythagoras to Plato* (Princeton 1948). A. DÖRING, ''Die eschatologischen Mythen Platons,'' *Archiv für die Geschichte der Philosophie* 6 (1893) 475–490. J. A. STEWART, *The Myths of Plato* (London 1905). P. FRUTIGER, *Les Mythes de Platon* (Paris 1930). H. W. THOMAS, EIIEKEINA (Würzburg 1938).

[H. S. LONG]

TRANSUBSTANTIATION

Transubstantiation is the change or conversion of one substance into another. Its usage is confined to the Eucharistic rite, where it signifies the change of the entire substance or basic reality of the bread and wine into the body and blood of Jesus Christ, while the outward appearances (species, accidents) of the bread and wine are unaffected. The neologism was employed by Roland Bandinelli (the future Alexander III) before 1153; it rapidly gained currency and soon appeared in official documents of the Church. This article treats the history of the doctrine and theological analysis.

History of Doctrine

Although the term is neither Biblical nor patristic, the idea it expresses is as old as Christian revelation. The scriptural evidence (Mt 26.26–28; Mk 14.22–24; Lk 22.19–20; Jn 6.50–67; 1 Cor 11.23–25) requires that the bread cease to exist and that Christ's body be made present. The cessation of the bread is connected with the presence of Christ's body; that is, by divine omnipotence, the bread has been changed into Christ's body. On the other hand, no modification of the visible phenomena of the bread and wine took place before the eyes of the Apostles. Hence Christ's words express the conversion of the substances of bread and wine into Christ's body and blood, although in outward appearance no alteration whatever occurs.

Patristic Period. Much theological reflection was needed before the doctrine became explicit. In the 2nd century, Ignatius of Antioch (d. *c.* 117) simply points out

that the Eucharist is the Savior's flesh [*Epist. ad Smyrnaeos* 7.1; J. Quasten, ed. *Monumenta eucharista et liturgica vetustissima* (Bonn 1935–37) 336]. Justin (d. *c.* 165) remarks that Christians regard the Eucharist not as ordinary food but as Christ's flesh and blood (*Apologia* 1.66; *ibid.,* 18). According to Irenaeus (d. *c.* 202), the wine in the chalice and the bread that has been baked become the Eucharist of the Lord's blood and body (*Adversus haereses* 5.2.3; *ibid.,* 347).

By the 4th century, attention begins to focus more distinctly on the change itself. Gregory of Nyssa (d. 394) asserts that the bread, consecrated by God's word, is transmuted into the body of God the Word [*Oratio catech. magna* 37; *Patrologia Graeca,* ed. J. P. Migne, 161 v. (Paris 1857–66) 45:95]. After testifying that Christ Himself through His priest causes the bread and wine to be made His body and blood, John Chrysostom (d. 407) adds that the formula, ''This is my body,'' transforms the Eucharistic elements (*De proditione Iudae hom.* 1.6; *ibid.,* 49:380). A similar account is found in Ambrose (d. 397), who employs the term ''transfigure'' [*De fide ad Gratianum* 4.10.124; *Patrologia Latina,* ed. J. P. Migne, 217 v., indexes 4 v. (Paris 1878–90) 16:641], and in Cyril of Alexandria (d. 444), who uses the word ''transform'' [*In Matt. com.* 26.27; *Patrologia Graeca* 72:431]. By the end of the 7th century, the doctrine was understood throughout Christendom. John Damascene (d. *c.* 750) sums up the teaching of his predecessors. He explains that the bread and wine are transmuted or converted into the Lord's body and blood; the bread and wine are by no means mere figures but have been really ''changed'' into the body and blood (*De fide orthodoxa* 4.13; *ibid.,* 94:1146).

Medieval Period. A new epoch of reflection on the Eucharist opened up in the 9th century. The outstanding figure in this period was PASCHASIUS RADBERTUS (d. *c.* 859), who clearly set forth the Catholic teaching on transubstantiation. A further impetus to the clarification of the doctrine was provided by BERENGARIUS OF TOURS (d. 1086), who denied the Eucharistic conversion and advocated a purely spiritual and symbolic presence of Christ. Theologians of the time refuted his views by appealing to the ancient and universal faith, and the teaching authority of the Church condemned his errors in a number of regional synods. The most important of these was the Roman Council of 1079, which for the first time in an official document declared that the bread and wine were ''substantially changed'' into the body and blood of Jesus (*Enchiridion symbolorum,* 700). By the 13th century the doctrine had achieved an adequate formulation, well exemplified in the incisive summary of Thomas Aquinas: ''The whole substance of the bread is changed into the whole substance of Christ's body, and the whole substance of the wine into the whole substance of Christ's blood. Hence this conversion . . . may be designated by a name of its own, transubstantiation'' (*Summa theologiae,* 3a, 75.4).

From the 12th century on, ''transubstantiation'' and ''transubstantiate'' appear frequently in ecclesiastical documents. The Fourth LATERAN COUNCIL in 1215 (*Enchiridion symbolorum,* 802) and the Second Council of LYONS in 1274 (*ibid.,* 860) use the term in brief expositions of the doctrine. A more ample explanation is given by the Council of FLORENCE in 1439 (*ibid.,* 1321). But in spite of gains in precision, a new opposition set in with Luther's Eucharistic proposals.

Reformation Period. Martin Luther (d. 1546) admitted the Real Presence of Christ in the Eucharist. However, he repudiated transubstantiation and taught that the glorified body and blood of Christ are present ''in, with, and under'' the bread and wine (consubstantiation). By way of explanation, Luther himself and many of his followers appealed to the idea of ''ubiquity'': because of its union with the divine nature, Christ's human nature acquires the property of coexisting with other created objects. At the celebration of the Lord's Supper, He wills it to be present at the moment the participants receive the consecrated bread and wine. Other reformers, such as Andreas OSIANDER (d. 1552), preferred ''impanation'' (coined on the analogy of ''incarnation''). This theory affirms the presence of the substance of Christ's body and blood along with the bread and wine in a kind of hypostatic union. These ideas were opposed by the SACRAMENTARIANS, particularly H. Zwingli (d. 1531), who regarded the Sacraments as no more than visible symbols. In this view the Eucharist is only a figure or sign of Christ's presence; he who believes that the Lord's body and blood were given for us, may be said to eat His flesh and drink His blood spiritually. John Calvin (d. 1564), who attacked both transubstantiation and consubstantiation, contended that Christ's body and blood are present in the Eucharist virtually, that is, by a power emanating from them.

Teaching of the Magisterium. Confronted with such challenges, the Council of Trent issued an authoritative teaching on transubstantiation (Oct. 11, 1551). Chapter 4 of session 13 defines: ''It has always been the conviction of the Church of God, and this holy Council now again declares, that by the consecration of the bread and wine a change takes place in which the entire substance of the bread is changed into the substance of the body of Christ our Lord and the entire substance of the wine into the substance of His blood. This change the holy Catholic Church fittingly and properly calls transubstantiation'' (*Enchiridion symbolorum,* 1642). Canon 2

asserts that the substance of bread and wine do not remain together with the Lord's body and blood, and insists again on the ''marvelous and extraordinary change of the whole substance of the bread into Christ's body and the whole substance of the wine into his blood, so that only the species of bread and wine remain'' (*ibid.,* 1652).

Among the errors fostered by the Jansenist Synod of Pistoia (1786), Pius VI condemned proposition 29 for omitting mention of ''transubstantiation or the change of the whole substance of the bread into the body, and of the whole substance of wine into the blood'' of Christ, on the ground that such omission tends to suppress both an article of faith and a highly useful term consecrated by the Church (bull *Auctorem fidei* of 1794; *ibid.,* 2629). In the encyclical *Humani generis* (1950) Pius XII states that the doctrine of transubstantiation may not be distorted to mean that the Real Presence of Christ in the Eucharist is reduced to a symbolism whereby the consecrated species would be merely signs of Christ's spiritual presence (*ibid.,* 3891). Thus he rejects the suggestion that nothing changes except the religious entity of the bread and wine.

Theological Analysis

According to Trent, the substance of the bread and wine does not remain but is changed into Christ's body and blood; nothing persists of the bread and wine but their appearances or species. The term ''substance'' in conciliar decrees does not sanction any philosophical system, but indicates the basic reality by which bread and wine are what they are and not something else. In modern parlance we may say that substance is the existent that is grasped by the intellect, whereas species are the properties that manifest this existent on the level of sensorial and scientific experience. In the 13th century, theologians endeavored to clarify transubstantiation by exploiting the Aristotelian categories of substance and accident. But the dogma itself does not imply that the substance that is changed into Christ's body is the prime matter and substantial form of a piece of bread, or that the species are accidents in the strict scholastic sense.

Nature of Transubstantiation. Although the Church has defined the doctrine of transubstantiation, theologians disagree about its precise nature. Two general tendencies have emerged. According to the first, the substance of the bread and wine is destroyed, and the body and blood of Christ are either reproduced or adduced. According to the second tendency, the substance of the bread and wine does indeed cease, but is not simply annihilated, for it passes into the preexistent body and blood of the Savior.

Annihilation. In the period following the Council of Trent, some theologians thought that the substance of the bread, as an obstacle to the presence of Christ's body, must be removed by a sort of annihilation. This annihilation is required to make room for Christ's body, or else results from the fact that Christ's body expels the substance of the bread, which thereupon lapses into nothingness.

Reproduction. Theologians who favor some form of annihilation are divided when they come to explain positively how Christ's body becomes present. According to Francisco SUÁREZ (d. 1617), Leonard LESSIUS (d. 1623), and others down to modern times, the body of Christ is made present by a productive action, which is equivalent to creation, because it is powerful enough to create the body if it did not already exist. Since, however, Christ does exist before the consecration, the action is better called reproduction or replication, for it reproduces His body without compromising its numerical identity with the same body in heaven.

Adduction. Other theologians of the 17th century, with many followers in later ages, dismiss the idea of reproduction. Under the leadership of Robert BELLARMINE (d. 1621), they contend that Christ's preexisting body is made present by adduction, which brings the body under the species of bread in such a way that it does not leave heaven or undergo any local motion. John de Lugo (d. 1660) adds that the body of Christ succeeds the substance of bread in the function of sustaining the accidents of bread.

Conversion. Even if the theories of reproduction and adduction were metaphysically sound, which in the judgment of many critics is questionable, they advocate an exchange of substances rather than a true change of one substance into another. A growing number of theologians agree with L. Billot (d. 1931) that we must return to an explanation that they insist is common to Thomas Aquinas (*Summa theologiae,* 3a, 75.4) and the great medieval scholastics. Transubstantiation is not the destruction of one substance and the substitution of another in its place, but a single action by which God, who has power over all being, changes the entire substance of bread into the entire substance of Christ's body. The substance of bread ceases, not by way of annihilation, but by way of conversion into the body of Christ; and the species of bread that remain acquire a relationship to Christ's body that is like the relationship between a container and its contents.

See Also: EUCHARIST IN CONTEMPORARY CATHOLIC THOUGHT; SACRAMENTAL THEOLOGY

Bibliography: A. MICHEL, *Dictionnaire de théologie catholique,* ed. A. VACANT et al., 15 v. (Paris 1903–40; Tables générales 1951) 15.1:1396–1406. J. FILOGRASSI, *De Sanctissima Eucharistia* (Rome 1962) 156–235. A. PIOLANTI, *The Holy Eucharist,* tr. L. PENZO (New York 1961) 68–77, bibliography. F. J. LEEN-HARDT, "This is My Body," *Essays on the Lord's Supper,* tr. J. G. DAVIES (London 1958). F. SELVAGGI, "Realtà fisica e sostanza sensibile nella dottrina eucaristica," *Gregorianum* 37 (1956) 16–33. C. VOLLERT, "The Eucharist: Controversy on Transubstantiation," *Theological Studies* 22 (1961) 391–425.

[C. VOLLERT]

TRAPPISTS

The Cistercian Order of the Strict Observance (OCSO), popularly known as Trappists, originated in 1098, when SS. ROBERT OF MOLESME, Alberic, and STEPHEN HARDING led a group from the flourishing Benedictine Abbey at MOLESME to the wilds of CÎTEAUX in the Diocese of Chalon-sur-Saone (Dijon), France. These men were determined to seek God by following the Rule of St. Benedict in its fullness.

Early History. For the first 200 years of the order, Cistercian saints and writers played an important role in Christendom. Many abbots were called forth from their cloisters to be consecrated bishops, including Saint William of Bourges and Saint Amadeus of Lausanne. Saint Bernard of Clairvaux was the spiritual leader of the twelfth century; his spiritual son became Pope Eugene III. Saint Aelred of Reivaulx, Blessed Guerric of Igny and William of Saint Theirry, among other early Cistercian writers, are still popularly read today (*see* CISTERCIANS). But as monastic wealth increased, abbots and monks became more and more involved in secular affairs, and the original Cistercian spirit weakened. Extrinsic contributing factors were the Hundred Years' War, the Black Death, the Western Schism, and the *in commendam* system, whereby laymen were often granted the title and insignia of abbots with rights to all the revenues of abbeys (*see* COMMENDATION). These factors led to a neglect of general chapters, annual visitations, and discipline in general.

During the long period of decline various attempts at a stricter observance were made. The most noteworthy, since it actually brought about a split in observance that endures to this day, began at Charmoye, France, in 1598, when Abbot Octave Arnolphini reintroduced the traditional monastic practice of total abstinence from flesh meat. This movement toward a return to the early austerities of Cîteaux gained momentum in 1615 when Abbot Denis Largentier of CLAIRVAUX led a group of his monks back to more of the primitive observances. The abbot of Cîteaux approved this reform and gave it the name of the Congregation of St. Bernard of the Strict Observance. By 1660, 62 monasteries of men and seven of women were living this reform, though not without opposition from those who considered these "Abstainers" misguided enthusiasts who were disregarding higher authority that had approved a mitigated way of life.

In 1664 Alexander VII issued a brief *In Suprema,* which, while maintaining the unity of the order, acknowledged the existence of two observances: one called "Common," the other "Strict,".

Abbot Armand Jean de RANCÉ OF LA TRAPPE, was successful in restoring within his community silence, enclosure, manual labor, and seclusion from the world.

In 1791, just before the French Revolution closed the last Cistercian monastery in France, Augustine de Lestrange took 21 monks from La Trappe to a refuge in La Val Sainte, Switzerland. So many applicants flocked to this monastery that De Lestrange sent groups of monks to Spain, Belgium, England, and Italy. In approving this observance, Pius VI named it the Congregation of Trappists. Two years later Dom Augustine founded the first convent of Trappistines at Saint-Branchier, wherein women observed the same regulations as the monks.

When Napoleon invaded Switzerland (1798), Dom Augustine led his 244 charges on a "monastic Odyssey" through Germany, Bavaria, and Austria, into Russian Poland. In 1803 he sent a contingent to the U.S.

After the fall of Napoleon in 1815, the monks were able to return to France and repopulated La Trappe. A new fervor was experienced. Within a few years the Rancean regulations were being observed in 14 houses, while those of Cîteaux were being practiced in 20 houses. The Trappists in Belgium increased also, making five foundations. In 1888 Leo XIII invited the superiors to Rome. At this meeting he constituted the three observances as an autonomous order under the title of the Reformed Cistercians of Our Lady of La Trappe. Dom Sebastian Wyart, Abbot of Sept-Fons, was elected the first abbot general. In 1902 Leo XIII dropped La Trappe from the title and named the order the Reformed Cistercians, or Cistercians of the Strict Observance.

Rule and Constitutions. The order follows the Rule of St. Benedict. Its constitutions and statutes are based on Saint Stephen's *Charta Caritatis,* and the ancient usages and definitions of the general chapters of Cîteaux. Supreme authority resides in the general chapter, composed of abbots actually in office, titular priors, and provisional superiors of houses. The chapter meets every third year under the presidency of the abbot general. After Vatican Council II the abbesses were allowed to form a general chapter. This chapter usually meets at the same time as the monks' chapter and the two chapters meet together in a mixed general meeting to elect an abbot general. When the chapters are not in session the abbot general has the necessary authority to lead the Order with the aid of his council which is elected by the general chapter.

Graveyard of Trappist Monastery, Our Lady of Gethsemane, near Louisville, Kentucky. (©Hulton-Deutsch Collection/ CORBIS)

Following the prescriptions of the *Charta Caritatis,* the order is divided not into provinces, but into motherhouses and the houses founded from them, called daughterhouses. In recent years regional meetings have developed and are gradually taking on a more important role in the Order. Nonetheless each monastery is autonomous. The abbots of motherhouses visit the daughterhouses regularly to help each community maintain a high level of fervor and regularity. Thus a unity of spirit is maintained.

Like all other monastic orders, after Vatican Council II the Cistercian Order of the Strict Observance, as it is now named, undertook to write new constitutions and statutes, a work which was completed at Holyoke, Mass. in 1983. The Order has continued to grow and by the year 2000 had over 100 houses of men and almost 70 of women, with most of the new foundations being made in Africa and Latin America. The Order maintains its strictly contemplative orientation, while at the same time sharing its contemplative heritage through its guesthouses, associate programs, and the Contemplative Outreach as well as through its many writers, most notably Dom CHAUTARD, Father M. RAYMOND, Thomas MERTON, Thomas Keating, and M. Basil Pennington.

Trappists begin their day while it is still dark, at 3 or 4 in the morning, and end it around 7 or 8 in the evening. Several hours each day are devoted to the *Opus Dei* (the Divine Office or Liturgical Hours and Community Mass). Four to six hours are given to manual labor to enable them to be self-supporting. The rest of the 17-hour day is devoted to contemplative prayer, lectio divina, and study. The Trappists lead a strictly coenobitical life. Silence is held in high honor and prevails in their monasteries. A very simple diet excludes meat and encourages fasting. Simplicity, the Trappists' characteristic virtue, marks everything in their life, a hallmark of their beautiful abbeys.

After a two-year novitiate (usually preceded by a postulancy) the monks take simple vows for a period of three years or more, then solemn perpetual vows of obedience, stability, and the monastic way of life (conversatio morum). Some monks pursue further studies to prepare themselves to serve their community in the ministerial priesthood.

Trappists in America. The first group of Trappists arrived in Baltimore, Md., in 1803. Led by Dom Urban Guillet, who had been commissioned by Dom Augustine de Lestrange to find a refuge in the New World, these monks first established themselves at Pigeon Hill, near Hanover, Pa. Two years later, they established themselves on Casey Creek, Ky., where they enjoyed four years of relative prosperity. Despite their success, Dom Urban removed to Monks Mound, near Cahokia, Ill. Miseries of every sort then plagued them for almost four years until Dom Augustine summoned them to New York City where they set up a monastery on the Fifth Avenue site now occupied by St. Patrick's Cathedral. When Napoleon fell in 1814, the monks returned to France with the exception of Father Vincent de Paul Merle, who founded the monastery of Petit Clairvaux at Tracadie, Antigonish, Canada (1825). During a period of growth this community made a foundation in Quebec which in turn made a foundation in Old Monroe, Mo. in 1872. In 1900 the short-lived Tracadie community transferred to to Lonsdale, R.I, in the United States. After a fire in 1950, it moved to Spencer, Mass. and was renamed St. Joseph Abbey. By that time two other Cistercian houses had been in existence in the United States for more than 100 years.

The first of these was made in 1848 at Gethsemani, Ky., when a group from Melleray, France settled in Nelson County. The following year, Mt. Melleray in Ireland, a daughterhouse of Melleray in France, sent a band to Dubuque, Iowa, where the Abbey of New Melleray was established. For the most part these three houses had to struggle for their existence, but in the late 1930s, just before World War II, the tide changed, ushering in a period of steady growth and success.

In 1944 GETHSEMANI ABBEY made the first foundation from an American house by opening Our Lady of Holy Spirit Abbey at Conyers, Ga. Three years later it again established a daughterhouse, Our Lady of the Trinity, Huntsville, Utah. In 1949, it founded Our Lady of Mepkin, at Moncks Corner, S.C., and two years later that of Our Lady of the Genesee, at Piffard, N.Y. In 1955 it sent a group to Vina, Calif., to found Our Lady of New Clairvaux. Since 1947, when Saint Joseph's Abbey made a first foundation, that of Our Lady of Guadalupe, at Pecos, N. Mex. (later transferred to Lafayette, Ore.), it has made four other foundations— two in the United States (Holy Cross Abbey, Berryville, Va., in 1950, and St. Benedict's Monastery, Snowmass, Colo. in 1956) and the first Trappist monasteries in South America (Our Lady of the Angels, Argentina, in 1959 and Our Lady of the Andes, Chile, in 1960). In 1951 New Melleray Abbey sent a group to begin Assumption Abbey in Ava, Mo. For some years annexes existed in Oxford, South Carolina and Belleville, Miss.

In 1949 Saint Joseph's Abbey brought a group of Trappistine nuns from Glencarin in Ireland to establish Mount Saint Mary's Abbey in Wrentham, Massachusetts. This abbey in turn sent nuns to establish Our Lady of the Mississippi Abbey (1964) in Dubuque, Iowa; Santa Rita Abbey (1972) in Senoita, Ariz., and Our Lady of the Angels Abbey (1987) in Crozet, Va. In 1962 nuns came from Nazareth in Belgium to establish Redwoods Abbey in Whitethorn, Calif.

Bibliography: L. JANAUSCHEK, *Origines Cistercienses* v. 1 (Vienna 1877). J. M. CANIVEZ, ed., *Statuta capitulorum generalium Ordinis cisterciensis ab anno 1116 ad annum 1786,* 8 v. (Louvain 1933–41). H. SÉJALON, ed., *Nomasticon cisterciense* (Solesmes 1892). A. MANRIQUE, *Cisterciensium seu verius ecclesiasticorum annalium a condito Cistercio,* 4 v. (Lyons 1642–49). T. MERTON, *Waters of Siloe* (New York 1949). C. F. R. DE TRYON, COMTE DE MONTALEMBERT, *The Monks of the West From St. Benedict to St. Bernard,* 6 v. (New York 1896). M. HEIMBUCHER, *Die Orden und Kongregationen der katholischen Kirche,* 2 v. (Paderborn 1932–34) 1:363–373. Periodicals. *Collectanea Ordinis Cisterciensium Reformatorum* (1934-). *Cistercienser Chronik* (1889-). *Analecta Sacri Ordinis Cisterciensis* (Rome 1945-). BENEDICT OF NURSIA, *The Rule of St. Benedict 1980* (Collegeville, Minn., 1980). Cistercian Fathers Series, E. R. ELDER et al., ed. (Spencer, Mass./Kalamazoo 1970—). Cistercian Studies Series, E. R. ELDER et al., ed. (Spencer, Mass./Kalamazoo 1969—). C. CUMMINGS, *Monastic Practices* (Kalamazoo 1986). J. LECLERCQ, *Bernard of Clairvaux and the Cistercian Spirit* (Kalamazoo 1976). L. I. LEKAI, *The Cistercians. Ideals and Reality* (Kent, Ohio 1977). A. LOUF, *The Cistercian Way* (Kalamazoo 1980). T. MERTON, *The Waters of Siloe* (New York 1949). T. MERTON, trans. and ed., *The Spirit of Simplicity Characteristic of the Cistercian Order* (Trappist, Ky. 1948). M. B. PENNINGTON, *Bernard of Clairvaux. A Saint's Life in Word and Image* (Huntington, Ind. 1994). *The Cistercians* (Collegeville, Minn. 1992). *The Last of the Fathers. The Cistercian Fathers of the Twelfth Century. A Collection of Essays* (Still River, Mass. 1983).

[M. R. FLANAGAN/M. B. PENNINGTON]

TRAUBE, LUDWIG

Paleographer and medieval Latin philologist; b. Berlin, June 19, 1861; d. Munich, May 19, 1907. His father was a professor of medicine. At an early age Traube showed a distinct gift for textual emendation. Apart from one semester at Greifswald in 1881, he spent his entire university life as student and teacher in Munich, where he earned his doctorate in 1883 and habilitated in 1888 with his *Karolingische Dichtungen.* A new chair in medieval Latin philology was founded for him in 1902. An indefatigable scholar, he published, among many other works: the *Poetae Latini Aevi Carolini* (3 v., 1886–96) in *Monumenta Germaniae Historica,* of whose editorial board he became an important member; *Textgeschichte der Regula S. Benedicti* (1898), a model of textual criticism; and *Perrona Scottorum* (1900), a work opening new vistas in Latin PALEOGRAPHY. His final work, *Nomina Sacra* (1907), written after he was stricken by leukemia, is a monumental contribution to the history of Latin abbreviations. His influence in Latin paleography is second only to Jean MABILLON's, and his followers are found in every land. He was as rare a man as he was a scholar.

Bibliography: L. TRAUBE, *Vorlesungen und Abhandlungen von Ludwig Traube,* ed. F. BOLL, 3 v. (Munich 1909–20) with a biographical introduction.

[E. A. LOWE]

TRE FONTANE, ABBEY OF

Formerly Santi Vincenzo ed Anastasio (Latin, *Trium Fontium ad Aquas Salvias*), Trappist monastery in the suburbs of Rome. It was founded by Pope Honorius I in 625 near the site of St. Paul's martyrdom and was originally given to the BENEDICTINES. From the 7th to the 10th century Eastern monks used it as a refuge. It then belonged to CLUNY until Pope Innocent II transferred it to the CISTERCIANS in 1140. Monks came from CLAIRVAUX with Bernard Paganelli (later Pope Eugene III) as abbot. In 1449 Cardinal Brando was appointed the first commendatory abbot, but in 1519 Pope Leo X authorized the Cistercians to elect their own claustral prior. The abbey was suppressed in 1812. Franciscans held it from 1826 to 1868, when Cistercians from LATRAPPE took possession. The Italian government confiscated all church lands in 1870, but the TRAPPISTS remained at Tre Fontane, at first renting, then purchasing the lands (1886). This abbey, which has an abbot *nullius,* remains today in the hands of the Trappists.

Bibliography: F. UGHELLI, *Italia sacra,* ed. N. COLETI, 10 v. (Venice 1717–22) v.1. P. LE NAIN DE TILLEMONT, *Essai de l'histoire de l'ordre de Cîteaux,* 9 v. in 12 (Paris 1696–97). A. MANRIQUE, *Annales cistercienses,* 4 v. (Lyons 1642–59) v.3. L. JANAUSCHEK, *Origines Cistercienses,* v.1 (Vienna 1877). J. J. GAUME, *Les Trois Rome,* 4 v. (4th ed. 1876) v.3. L. H. COTTINEAU, *Répertoire topo-bibliographique des abbayes et prieurés,* 2 v. (Mâcon 1935–39) 2: 2503–04.

[M. B. MORRIS]

TREBNITZ, ABBEY OF

Cistercian abbey of nuns, near Breslau in Silesia, founded 1202 by Duke Henry I (the Bearded d. 1238) and his wife, St. HEDWIG (d. 1243). The first nuns, selected by Bp. Ekbert of Bamberg, brother of Hedwig, were ruled by Petrussa, the first abbess. She was succeeded by (Bl.) Gertrude, one of Hedwig's seven children. Trebnitz was placed under papal protection by Innocent III on Dec. 22, 1202, and in a few years it accepted the Cistercian rule and guidance of the nearby abbey of LEUBUS. It was richly endowed by Henry, and became the home of Hedwig after the duke's death in 1238. Up to the 15th century the abbesses were princesses of the Polish Piast House, but the character of the abbey was mostly German. From the 16th to the 18th century the Polish influence was dominant. Except for periods of famine and fire, the abbey flourished until the 30 Years' War (1618–48), when the nuns fled to Poland. They fled again when the Turks began the invasion of Silesia in 1663. The last abbess was Dominica von Giller, who died Aug. 17, 1810. Three months later, Trebnitz was suppressed, and after the Battle of Waterloo in 1815, the estates came to Prussian Field Marshal Gebhard Leberect von Blücher (1742–1819). For a while the buildings were used as a cloth factory, and in 1870 parts were transformed into a hospital by the Silesian Knights of Malta and entrusted to the care of the Sisters of Mercy of St. Borromeo. In 1889 they established their motherhouse there. The tombs of the founders are in the abbey church, which since the 18th century has been a distinctive Baroque edifice and is now the parish church.

Bibliography: L. H. COTTINEAU, *Répertoire topobibliographique des abbayes et prieurés,* 2 v. (Mâcon 1935–39) 2:3203. K. SCHMIDT, *Geschichte des Klosterstiftes Trebnitz* (Oppeln 1853). F. X. SEPPELT, *Lexikon für Theologie und Kirche,* ed. M. BUCHBERGER, 10 v. (Freiburg 1930–38) 10:266–267.

[E. D. MCSHANE]

TRECY, JEREMIAH

Missionary, colonizer; b. Drogheda, Ireland, *c.* 1824; d. St. Louis, Mo., March 5, 1888. After he was brought to the U.S. as a child, he studied at Mt. St. Mary's Seminary, Emmitsburg, Md. He was ordained by Bp. Mathias Loras at Dubuque, Iowa, in 1851. He then served in Iowa at Cascade, Independence, and Garryowen, where he was pastor from 1852 to 1856. To further Loras's Catholic colonization program, Trecy explored the Iowa-Nebraska border and surveyed native settlements and army installations within the Nebraska vicariate apostolic. After reporting his findings to Loras and consulting with Thomas D'Arcy McGee at the 1856 Catholic colonization convention at Buffalo, N.Y., Trecy selected a site near Sioux City, Iowa, and registered it as "St. John's City in St. Patrick's Colony, Nebraska Territory." In June 1856, a total of 25 families arrived from Garryowen to face grasshopper plagues, crop failures, severe winters, and threats from native tribes. Despite a reassuring report signed by 52 colonists early in 1857, the ensuing panic of that year, together with a premature government sale of lands and Trecy's frequent missionary absences, had caused dispersal of the population by 1860. Trecy then settled in Huntsville, Ala., for his health. In 1862 and 1863, he was regimental chaplain for Gen. William S. Rosecrans. After the Civil War he served again in the Mobile diocese until 1881, when he was incapacitated by a paralytic stroke.

Bibliography: Archives, Archdioceses of Dubuque and Omaha. H. W. CASPER, *History of the Catholic Church in Nebraska* (Milwaukee 1960—) v.1, *The Church on the Northern Plains 1838–1874.* G. HENDERSON, "An Epic of Early Iowa: Father Trecy's Colonization Scheme," *Iowa Catholic Historical Review* 3 (Spring 1931) 3–13. M. G. KELLY, *Catholic Immigrant Colonization Projects in the United States* 1815–1860 (New York 1939). R. M. MARTIN, *The Catholic Church on the Nebraska Frontier 1854–1885.* (*Catholic University of America Canon Law Studies; Studies in American Church History* 26; Washington 1937).

[M. G. KELLY]

TREE OF JESSE

A common iconographic subject in medieval and early Renaissance art, representing the royal genealogy of Christ from Jesse, father of David (Mt 1.1–17). The image of the tree was taken from Isaiah 11.1, "But a shoot shall sprout from the stump of Jesse, and from his roots a bud shall blossom." As early as Tertullian the Fathers interpreted the shoot (*virga*) as the Blessed Virgin (*virgo*), the blossom as Christ her Son. In the 11th century the subject makes its appearance in German miniature painting, after which it appears throughout Europe in manuscripts, stained glass, and sculpture. An Advent theme presented with wide variations, it generally represents the Prophet Jesse reclining on the ground with a tree rising from his side. The tree might carry any number of figures from the genealogy of Christ. Earlier representations show Christ at the summit in majesty; but from the beginning of the 13th century, with the rise of the Marian cult, Mary becomes the blossom holding the Christ Child

in her arms. Often the Virgin is enthroned, and sometimes she is surrounded with the seven gifts of the Holy Ghost mentioned in the same prophecy (Is 11.2). Iconologically the theme is a testimony of the true humanity of Christ. But it is also a testimony to the royalty of Christ, hence its popularity at Saint-Denis and CHARTRES.

See Also: MARY, BLESSED VIRGIN, ICONOGRAPHY OF.

Bibliography: A. WATSON, *The Early Iconography of the Tree of Jesse* (London 1934). L. RÉAU, *Iconographie de l'art chrétien,* 3 v. in 6 (Paris 1955–59) 2:129–140.

[J. R. JOHNSON]

TREE OF KNOWLEDGE

The tree in PARADISE whose fruit Adam and Eve were forbidden to eat. Like the TREE OF LIFE, this tree with the full name of the tree of the knowledge of good and evil (Gn 2.9, 17) was thus called from its effect: the eating of its fruit gave the knowledge of good and evil. The tree, the focal point in the narrative, is linked to bodily death, which is not to occur immediately after its fruit is eaten, but eventually (2.17; 3.3). However, the tree is linked also to the knowledge of good and evil, which, in context, is a liability to man and woman. The phrase, the knowledge of good and evil, occurs several times in the Old Testament, sometimes with reference to all knowledge that lies between the two extremes of good and evil (2 Sm 14.17, 20), and then it can mean "everything or anything" (Gn 31.24). But the phrase may refer also to a knowledge that judges what is authentically good, or evil, or both (2 Sm 19.36; 1 Kgs 3.9). This second notion seems to be present here. But it is not for man to decide lightly, arbitrarily, or in opposition to Yahweh what is right or wrong—as man has always tended to do, and was doing when the YAHWIST tradition took shape. The aptness, even though deceptive, of Gn 3.5 should be underscored; for man does become, by presumption, like *'Ĕlōhîm* (meaning either God or superior beings), as the SERPENT in Paradise had claimed he would and as Yahweh Himself admitted (3.5, 22). To eat of the tree is tantamount to insolence and open rebellion against God. The tree is a literary and pedagogical device not to be taken at face value, and yet implying a much deeper reality than any tree—a reality inherent in man's condition. The tree's identification as an apple tree is pure fancy, resting on Ct 8.5 (mistranslated and misunderstood), or on a Latin wordplay involving *malum,* or on a later meaning of *pomum.* The tree has no close analogy (as a tree) in ancient Near Eastern literature; but note *GILGAMESH EPIC* 11.29, 34 for a similarity in effect: "wisdom, broader understanding," and "like a god" (*see* J. B. Pritchard, *An-*

"Tree of Jesse," fresco painting, late 16th-early 17th century. (©Archivo Iconografico, S.A./CORBIS)

"God Warning Adam and Eve," from the *"Parable of the Good Samaritan,"* Lancet Window at Chartres Cathedral, France. (©Dean Conger/CORBIS)

cient *Near Eastern Texts Relating to the Old Testament* 75b).

Over and beyond what has been said, however, the phrase probably has a sexual implication already in such Old Testament texts as Dt 1.39 and 2 Sm 19.36. That the term as used in the Yahwist's story of the fall of man should have this additional connotation is borne out, too, by a usage of the phrase in the Qumran *Rule of the Congregation (Serek ha-ʿĒdâh),* 1.1.11, where "sexual maturity" has been suggested as an adequate translation for the Hebrew that is literally "the knowledge of good and evil." Such an interpretation fits in with what many scholars think about the serpent in Paradise.

Bibliography: *Encyclopedic Dictionary of the Bible,* translated and adapted by L. HARTMAN (New York, 1963) 1288–90. H. JUNKER, *Lexikon für Theologie und Kirche,* ed. J. HOFER and K. RAHNER, 10 v. (2d, new ed. Freiburg 1957–65); suppl., *Das ZweiteVatikanische Konzil: Dokumente und kommentare,* ed. H. S. BRECHTER et al., pt. 1 (1966) 2:67–68. L. F. HARTMAN, "Sin in Paradise," *The Catholic Biblical Quarterly* 20 (Washington 1958) 26–40. J. COPPENS, *La Connaisance du bien et du mal et le Péché du Paradis* (Louvain 1948) and review by R. DE VAUX, *Revue Biblique* 56 (1949) 300–308. B. J. LEFROIS, "The Forbidden Fruit," *American Ecclesiastical Review* 136 (1957) 175–183. H. RENCKENS, *Israel's Concept of the Beginning,* tr. C. NAPIER (New York 1964) 272–282.

[I. HUNT]

TREE OF LIFE

The tree in PARADISE that was to give unending life to Adam and Eve as long as they ate of its fruit. The tree of life is mentioned three times (Gn 2.9; 3.22, 24) in the deeply significant but symbolically expressed YAHWIST account of mankind's present condition and how it arose (Gn 2.4a–3.24). Since the writer composed this account about the 10th century B.C., the meaning of the tree of life can be better understood if viewed from that perspective. Under divine inspiration, he rightly assumed that some catastrophe had come upon mankind in the beginning that threw it into the state of ORIGINAL SIN. It is in this frame of reference that the story of mankind (both primeval and contemporary) is related. Most agree that the tree of life, named from its effect, symbolized the IMMORTALITY (at least bodily) that man lost through disobedience to God.

The Yahwist narrative shows signs of being composite, and its most original form may not have contained any reference to the tree of life; for Gn 3.22 and 3.24 may well be additions, and the statement in 3.3 conflicts with that in 2.9 (on the location of the tree). The bulk of the narrative, too, is concerned with the TREE OF KNOWLEDGE.

As the story goes, it is not certain whether man ever ate of the tree of life, speaking symbolically of course. Had he done so, instead of being attracted to the tree of knowledge, he would have been deprived of access to the tree.

The term tree of life occurs also in Prv 3.18; 11.30; 13.12; 15.4, but in a much wider context. The term reappears in Rv 2.7; 22.2, 14, 19 with reminiscences of the Eden narrative, though set in an apocalyptic and imagery-laden context.

The idea of a plant or tree of life must have been fairly prevalent in the ancient Near East; it turns up for somewhat lengthy, even though naïve, consideration in the *GILGAMESH EPIC* (*see* J. B. Pritchard, *Ancient Near Eastern Texts Relating to the Old Testament* 93–97), where the plant is obtained by Gilgamesh from Utnapishtim, only to be stolen by a serpent. Immortality plays a large part in the *Adapa Myth* (see *ibid.,* 101–103), though its fragmentary condition makes the presence of a tree uncertain. The Sumerians knew of a god called Ningishzidda, i.e., lord of the tree of life, and their art links tree and serpent together in a context of immortality.

Bibliography: *Encyclopedic Dictionary of the Bible,* translated and adapted by L. HARTMAN (New York, 1963) 2490–91. H. VORGRIMLER, *Lexikon für Theologie und Kirche,* ed. J. HOFER and K. RAHNER, 10 v. (2d, new ed. Freiburg 1957–65); suppl., *Das ZweiteVatikanische Konzil: Dokumente und kommentare,* ed. H. S. BRECHTER et al., pt. 1 (1966) 6:864–865. G. WIDENGREN, *The King and the Tree of Life* (Uppsala 1951). J. A. MACCULLOCH, ed., *The Mythology of All Races,* v.5, S. H. LANGDON, *Semitic* (Boston 1931) 177–179, with pertinent illus. B. VAWTER, *A Path through Genesis* (New York 1956). E. A. SPEISER, *Genesis* (Anchor Bible; Garden City, N.Y. 1964) 20–28.

[I. HUNT]

The Tree of Life, from 15th-century manuscript (Sloane MS 2471, fol. 102 v).

TREJO Y SANABRIA, FERNANDO DE

Bishop of Tucumán, founder of the University of Córdoba in Argentina; b. Biaza (formerly Paraguay, now Brazil), 1553; d. Córdoba, 1614. He was a Franciscan and served as custodian and provincial of his order in Peru, where he completed his studies. He was consecrated in Quito for the episcopal See of Tucumán and occupied this position from 1595. His two objectives were converting unbelievers and expanding culture. He was not against the *encomiendas,* but he condemned the abuses they initiated. For that purpose and others, he held three synods, which were attended by priests and laity. He established a seminary in Santiago del Estero, the student living quarters of San Javier, and the monastery of Santa Catalina in Córdoba. In 1612 he obtained the cooperation of the Jesuits in establishing a university, but it was not founded until ten years later. According to the Constitutions of the Jesuits, one was required to give a certain sum in order to be considered a founder. He promised that sum, but at the time of his death he had given only a third of the total. He is nevertheless considered the founder, because he proposed the plan and took the first steps toward that end, although the university was not established until 1622. A monument to this humble, dedicated man of extraordi-

Fernando de Trejo y Sanabria.

nary culture was erected at the entrance to the university in 1903.

Bibliography: G. FURLONG, "Fernando Trejo y Sanabria, O.F.M.: The Fourth Centenary of His Birth," *Americas* 9 (1952) 169–176.

[G. FURLONG]

TRENT, COUNCIL OF

The Nineteenth Ecumenical Council, which opened at Trent, Italy, on Dec. 13, 1545, and closed there on Dec. 4, 1563, having held 25 sessions. The council's objective was the order and clarification of Catholic doctrine, and legislation for a thorough reform of the Church.

The 25-Year Conflict over Its Convocation

On June 15, 1520, Pope LEO X had condemned 41 propositions from the writings of Martin LUTHER. But this condemnation had, in many quarters, not been accepted or regarded as the final, irrevocable decision of the Church, because the impression persisted, partly under the influence of the conciliar theory and partly because of the memory of the councils of the early centuries of the Church, that the final decision on controversies concerning the faith accrued to an ecumenical council. [*See* CONCILIARISM (HISTORY OF); CONCILIARISM (THEOLOGICAL ASPECT).]

Charles V and the Lutherans. Both the Catholic estates of the empire and those friendly to Luther de-

manded in the Diet of Nuremberg (1523) a "free, Christian Council on German soil" within a year. The Lutherans understood this to mean a council "free of the Pope," which would be summoned by pope and emperor in concert; "Christian" meant that the Bible alone would be the touchstone at that council and that the laity would be represented; "on German soil" meant within the boundaries of the empire, analogously to the ancient Christian councils that had been held where the controversies had erupted. The tenor of this Nuremberg formula explains why Pope CLEMENT VII was dilatory in his treatment of the demand for a council, which had the support of Emperor CHARLES V; besides, wars between the emperor and King Francis I of France (1521–29, 1536–38) made the convocation of a council in the empire virtually impossible. The Lutherans gained time to establish, with the support of the secular authorities, a new ecclesiastical organization and submitted a profession of faith at the Diet of Augsburg (1530). The emperor made an effort to reach agreement with the Lutherans at this Diet but without success. Thereupon, in accord with an agreement reached with Charles V in Bologna, Clement VII offered to summon a council. But the pope attached so many conditions to the proposal that nothing came of it.

Proposal of Paul III. Pope PAUL III was the first to make the council a part of his program; but the convocation agreed upon during Charles V's visit to Rome in April of 1536 came to nothing, because of the demand of the duke of Mantua for the provision of a strong papal guard for the council, which according to a previous agreement was to be brought to Mantua, at that time an imperial fief. The date of this convocation had been set for June 2, 1536; and when this effort failed, the council was transferred to Vicenza, to which city papal delegates journeyed to find that no bishops had appeared. The German Protestants and France refused to send delegates to the council. The emperor again made an effort to heal the breach at the Diet of Regensburg (1541) by direct negotiations with the Protestants, but in vain (*see* INTERIMS).

On May 22, 1542, the pope summoned the council to Trent, a site recommended by the emperor and approved by the estates. But a new war between Charles V and Francis I intervened, and seven months later there were only ten bishops present in Trent. The council had to be suspended; only after the Peace of Crépy (Sept. 18, 1544), in which the king of France assumed the obligation of sending delegates to the council, could the date March 15, 1545, be set for its convocation at Trent. The council was decreed by the bull *Laetare Jerusalem* (Nov. 19, 1544). The bull set three orders of business: healing of the confessional split, reform of the Church, and establishment of peace so that a defense against the Ottomans could be elaborated. On Feb. 22, 1545, the pope named

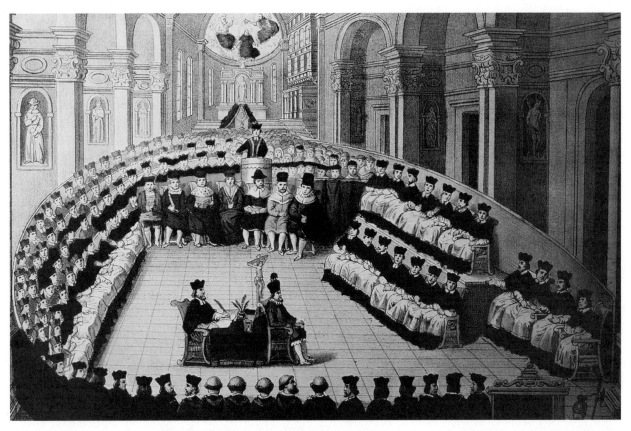

Council of Trent, 18th-century lithograph. (©Archivo Iconografico, S.A./CORBIS.)

Cardinals Giovanni Del Monte, Marcello Cervini, and Reginald Pole as his legates.

The Council Under Paul III and Julius III (1545–52)

This second convocation sent to Trent was successful primarily because the pope and the emperor had reached agreement on a common procedure against the German Protestants: First, their opposition to the council (and to the emperor) was to be broken with military force, and then they were to present themselves to the council and, if necessary, be compelled to submit to its decisions. Because no imperial campaign against the Schmalkaldic League materialized, and it seemed unwise to keep the bishops already in Trent waiting much longer, the pope ordered the council to open on Dec. 13, 1545, in the Cathedral of St. Vigilius, although there were only 34 participants present with the right to vote. Since there had not been sufficient preparatory work, the deliberations took almost two months to get into meaningful action; on Jan. 22, 1546, the decision was taken to treat dogma and reform side by side.

Scripture and tradition. The debates on dogmatic points by the council fathers with right to vote in the general congregations were prepared in theological congregations (the first held on Feb. 20, 1546). Since *Sola scriptura* (Scripture alone), was recognized by the Protestants as a rule of faith, this was the point first attacked. The decree on the sources of revelation published in session 4 (April 8, 1546) contained a list of the canonical Books of the Old Testament and New Testament [*see* CANON, BIBLICAL] and decreed that the apostolic traditions on faith and custom that "have been transmitted in some sense from generation to generation down to our times" were to be accepted "with as much reverence" (*pari pietatis affectu ac reverentia*) as Sacred Scripture. There is scarcely any doubt that the majority of the council fathers were thinking in terms of a material supplementation to Sacred Scripture when they proposed the principle of TRADITION. A second decree declared the Vulgate (*vetus et vulgata editio*) to be authentic, that is, apodictic when quoted in lectures, debates, and sermons. Criticism of this decree in Rome was answered by the council legates with the declaration that no suppression of the study of the original texts (Greek and Hebrew) was intended.

License for preaching. The proclamation of the Word of God in sermons presupposed a better training of priests. The council judged that it could content itself with the renewal and expansion of the decree promulgated at the Fourth Lateran Council on the establishment of lectorates in grammar and theology in the cathedral churches. Preaching on Sundays and holy days was made obligatory for all bishops and pastors; a controversy between bishops and exempt orders concerning the granting of the license to preach was resolved by a ruling that in the churches of exempt orders only the permission of the superiors of the order was required, whereas in all other churches, the license of the local ordinary was needed.

Original sin and justification. Also in session 5 (June 17, 1546), the council condemned in six canons both the Pelagian denial of ORIGINAL SIN and Luther's teaching that original sin is not entirely effaced by Baptism; the evil concupiscence remaining after Baptism was held to be not sin in the strict sense but was sometimes called sin (even by the Apostle Paul), because it came from sin and inclined to sin (*quia ex peccato est et ad peccatum inclinat*).

The ensuing debate on the doctrine of JUSTIFICATION lasted seven months because of the impossibility of resolving the question by recourse to the decisions of earlier councils and because of the desire to avoid definite statements on standing controversies within the Catholic schools of theology (Thomists, Scotists, Augustinians). Moreover, in July of 1546 the war against the Protestants began, and at times it approached so threateningly close to the city of Trent that consideration was given to a suspension or transferral of the council. The first draft of a decree on justification (submitted on July 28) had to be withdrawn since it encountered general disapproval; the second draft, commissioned by Cervini from the Augustinian general Girolamo SERIPANDO (submitted on August 23) was finally adopted after repeated revision in session 6 (Jan. 13, 1547). For the first time, 16 doctrinal chapters were prefaced to the 33 canons in order to present the Catholic doctrine in positive form. The council answered Luther's most ardent desire by affirming that God's grace is necessary for the entire process of justification, although the process does not exclude dispositions for grace or the collaboration of free will (*see* GRACE; FREE WILL AND GRACE). The essence of justification was declared to consist not in the remission of sins alone but rather in the "sanctification and renovation of the inner man" by supernatural charity. Faith is not the only condition of justification, although it is the "beginning, foundation and root"; no one can be certain that he is in a state of grace. The grace of justification increases through observance of the commandments of God, which is a duty imposed by God and not simply a sign of accomplished justification. The grace of justification can be lost as a result of mortal sin (not simply by loss of faith), and it can

be regained through the Sacrament of PENANCE. Eternal life in God is a grace, not merely a reward.

Residence and jurisdiction of bishops. The decree on justification was adopted almost unanimously, but the decree on obligatory residence for bishops and pastors, submitted on Jan. 7, 1547 in the general congregation, encountered strong opposition because it limited itself to enacting the punishment for the neglect of residence over a six-month period, that is, deprivation of revenue, without giving sufficient consideration to the reasons for nonresidence (*impedimenta residentiae*), which had already been submitted for consideration by many bishops in the summer of 1546: These were the trammeling of episcopal activities by the secular power, the Curia, the exempt cathedral chapters, and others. Only 28 of the 60 participants with the right to vote gave the decree their unconditional *placet* in this session, and only in the general congregation of February 25 could its adoption be established by taking account of the qualified *placet* votes. The legates felt compelled to consider the bishops' demands and expand their reform program. The reform decree adopted in session 7 (March 3, 1547) eliminated a number of abuses in the matter of rights of jurisdiction and ordination; the prerogatives of the bishops were extended to include the right to make visitations of exempt parochial benefices as well.

First deliberation on the sacraments. The same session, after a detailed debate that extended from February 8 to 22, determined the Catholic notion of a Sacrament and placed their number at seven. The Sacraments were defined as efficacious signs, bringing grace by the rite itself *ex opere operato* and not simply by reason of the faith of the recipient. The council also defined the doctrine on the Sacraments of Baptism and CONFIRMATION (*see* SACRAMENTAL, THEOLOGY).

Transfer to Bologna. An epidemic of typhus, probably brought in from the German war front, provided the opportunity to transfer the council from Trent, the sphere of the emperor's influence, to Bologna, which was under papal hegemony. The decree of transference, adopted in session 8 (March 11, 1547), was protested by a minority of 14 bishops, almost all of them subjects of the emperor; they remained in Trent. The majority attended the first session in Bologna, held on April 21, 1547. The ensuing months were spent in intensive treatment of the doctrine on the remaining Sacraments and on the Sacrifice of the Mass [*see* SACRIFICE, IV (IN CHRISTIAN THEOLOGY); EUCHARIST IN CONTEMPORARY CATHOLIC THOUGHT], PURGATORY, veneration of the saints, and monastic vows, both in the theological congregation and the general congregation. But not a single one of the decrees on these dogmatic matters and their corresponding abuses could be adopted, because the pope did not want to push to the breaking point the tension with the emperor, which resulted from the council's transfer. The pope, however, rejected Charles V's demand for a return to Trent. After the emperor had submitted a solemn protest both in Rome and Bologna against the change of the site of the council, Paul III decreed a suspension of its deliberations on February 16, 1548. The significance of the Bologna interval lay in its important preparatory work for later conciliar debates.

Return to Trent. After the death of Paul III, his successor, JULIUS III, yielded to the pressure of the emperor and on Nov. 14, 1550 transferred the council back to Trent. The only legate was Cardinal Marcello Crescenzio, with whom were associated as co-chairmen Bishop Sebastiano Pighino and Bishop Luigi Lippomano. The council opened punctually on May 1, 1551, but it did not begin its deliberations until late summer; yet, as a result of the work that had been done in Bologna, it managed as early as Oct. 11, 1551 (session 13) to finish with the important decree on the Eucharist, which defined the Real Presence of Christ (*vere, realiter et substantialiter*) in opposition chiefly to the doctrine of U. ZWINGLI, and the doctrine of TRANSUBSTANTIATION, as opposed to that of Luther. These definitions covered eight doctrinal chapters and 11 canons. On Nov. 25, 1551 (session 14), there followed the definition of the doctrine on Penance and Extreme Unction. [*See* ANOINTING OF THE SICK, I (THEOLOGY OF).] In the matter of the Sacrament of Penance, the council distinguished three elements: contrition, confession (at least of mortal sins), and reparation; the priestly absolution was defined to be a juridical act. In the matter of Extreme Unction, the main issue at stake was the sacramental nature of this action, which Luther had contested. The reform decrees of both sessions concerned the rights and duties of the bishops with respect to their clergy and regulated the procedure in church courts.

Meanwhile, ambassadors and theologians of several Protestant estates (Brandenburg, Württemberg, Strassburg) had appeared in Trent for the first and only time. They had indeed promised to attend the council of Trent; this promise had been given at the Diet of Augsburg in 1548 after the defeat of the Schmalkaldic League, but conditions had been attached that made any *rapprochement* difficult, if not impossible. These included a revision of the resolutions already taken by the council so as to base them solely on Scripture and the subordination of the pope to the council. The demand for an improved safe-conduct that would guarantee their safety in Trent was acceded to in session 15 (Jan. 25, 1552), but fulfillment of the other provisions was impossible. The debate on the Sacrament of HOLY ORDERS and the Sacrifice of the Mass, begun on Jan. 2, 1552, could not be concluded

because of the revolt against Charles by the German princes allied with France. This broke out in the spring and forced suspension of the council on April 28, 1552 (session 16).

Ten-year prorogation. The council's deliberations remained suspended for a decade, and thus far it had arrived only at fragmentary results: Its dogmatic definitions were incomplete, only a fraction of the controversies with the Protestants having been doctrinally resolved; still less satisfactory were its reform decrees, which left unanswered many urgent petitions of the bishops. In 1553 Julius III prepared an extensive reform bull to cope with the many unresolved practical problems, but he died before it could be published. PAUL IV, who had always been opposed to the council, summoned a papal reform assembly to Rome in 1556 as a substitute for the council, but this assembly was dissolved after a short time because of the pope's war against Spain.

The Council Under Pius IV (1562–63)

The reopening of the council under Paul IV's successor, PIUS IV, was occasioned by the advance of CALVINISM in France. As a result of the vacillating attitude of the regent CATHERINE DE MÉDICIS, Catholicism seemed to be so severely threatened in France that only a general council could rescue it. Should this be a new council, as France and Emperor Ferdinand I wished, or should it be a continuation of the previous sessions, as King PHILIP II OF SPAIN demanded? Although the bull of convocation, published on Nov. 29, 1560, evaded the controversial question, an answer was implicit when in the course of the negotiations opened at Trent on Jan. 18, 1563, with 113 Council fathers present with right to vote, it was decided to resume discussion of the agenda broken off in 1551 and 1552, namely, Communion under both species and the doctrine of the Sacrifice of the Mass.

Renewed deliberation on episcopal residence. Presiding as legates were Cardinals Ercole Gonzaga, Girolamo Seripando, Stanislaus HOSIUS, and Ludovico SIMONETTA; the pope's nephew, Cardinal Marcus Sitticus von Hohenems (Altemps), also named as legate, left the council after a short time. In order to avoid the politically tense question of whether this was a new council or a continuation of Trent, the legates on March 11, 1562, presented 12 reform articles, the first of which dealt with the yet unresolved problem of episcopal residence. The debate centered on whether the council should declare bishops to be obliged to reside in their dioceses by divine law. The supporters of the *ius divinum* were convinced that this was the only way to cure the neglectfulness of bishops who resided at court or elsewhere than the territory entrusted to their pastoral care; the opponents saw in such a declaration a threat to papal primacy. A vote taken on April 20 on whether the council should make a declaration on the *ius divinum* of the residence obligation yielded 67 *placets,* 35 *non-placets,* with 34 council fathers referring the decision to the pope. Thereupon Pius IV forbade a continuation of the debate. Cardinals Gonzaga and Seripando, who were reputed to be in favor of the *ius divinum* solution, fell into disfavor with the pope, and their recall was contemplated. The vehement reaction of the Spanish bishops, led by Archbishop Pedro Guarrero of Granada, and of the imperial bishops against the measure condemned the council to inactivity until Gonzaga promised in the general congregation of June 6 to continue the debate on the residence obligation when the Sacrament of Holy Orders would be discussed. The crisis was temporarily surmounted.

Communion under both species. The first fruit of the renewed deliberations was the decree of session 21 (July 16, 1562) on Communion under both species, which laid the dogmatic basis (expressed in the statement that under either species the whole and undivided Christ is received) for the resolution of the practical question of the granting of the chalice to the laity. The practical question itself, however, which had been raised by Emperor Ferdinand I and the duke of Bavaria, was postponed in view of the reservations expressed, especially by the Spaniards. In the following session, the regulation of the practical question was referred to the pope, who, after the conclusion of the council (April 16, 1564) authorized the chalice for the laity under certain conditions for several ecclesiastical provinces of Germany and the hereditary territories of the HAPSBURGS.

Sacrifice of the Mass. The nine canons and nine doctrinal chapters adopted in session 22 (Sept. 17, 1562) on the Sacrifice of the Mass are, together with the decree on justification, by far the most important definitions of the entire council. All the reformers had denied the sacrificial character of the Mass, and its abolition had always been the decisive step toward separation. For the Catholic Church the Mass is the center of the mystery of salvation, latreutic and Eucharistic but also propitiatory, a commemoration but also a rendering present of the sacrifice of the cross; the Mass in no way encroaches upon the uniqueness of the sacrifice of Calvary because the same sacrificial priest offers the same sacrificial gift, although in a different way (*eadem hostia, idem offerens, sola offerendi ratione diversa*). The council defined that the Sacrifice of the Mass may be offered in honor of the saints and for the faithful, living and dead. A simultaneous reform decree bound the bishops to eliminate abuses in its celebration. The claim that a contemplated ban on florid counterpoint was prevented by Giovanni Pierluigi da PALESTRINA's *Missa Papae Marcelli* is a legend that origi-

nated only in 1609; but there may be a grain of historical truth in it inasmuch as the council fathers were acquainted with the newly developing church music of Palestrina and Orlando di Lassus through the polyphonic conciliar prayers by the Dutch composer Jacobus de Kerle and through other compositions.

Ius Divinum of episcopal office. During the ensuing debate on the Sacrament of Holy Orders (October 13 to 20, November 3 to 10) and on the schema on the obligation of residence presented on December 10, the clash between the supporters of the *ius divinum* of the episcopal office and the "Zelanti" backed by the legate Simonetta broke out afresh. The former were reinforced by 12 French bishops led by Cardinal Charles Guise, who arrived in Trent on November 13. All the efforts of Gonzaga and Seripando to bring the two parties to agreement on the controversial canon 7 of the decree on Holy Orders were unsuccessful. The draft formula of Seripando to the effect that the bishops had "been established in the Church by Christ" but received their jurisdiction from the pope was rejected not only by the "Zelanti" but also in Rome; conversely, the French resisted the suggestion made by Rome that the Florentine council's definition of the primacy be adopted. Again the negotiations bogged down and the council seemed incapable of fruitful progress. Guise, now the undisputed leader of the opposition, went to Emperor Ferdinand I at Innsbruck and persuaded him to draw the attention of the pope in two letters written on March 3, 1563, to the seriousness of the situation; simultaneously a special ambassador of the king of Spain appeared in Rome with similar complaints. This intervention of the secular powers accented the full seriousness of the conciliar crisis.

It was surmounted only after the two senior legates, Gonzaga and Seripando, had died (March 2 and 17 respectively) and been replaced by Cardinals Giovanni MORONE and Bernardo Navagero. Morone, the best diplomat then available to the Curia, and possessing the full confidence of the pope, became the savior of the council. Soon after his arrival in Trent, he went to the emperor at Innsbruck and dissipated his fears that the pope wanted neither reform of the Church nor the council's continuation. The pope meanwhile assured the king of Spain in several personal letters that he was resolved to continue the council, to confirm and implement its decisions, in short "to do everything that a good pope and a good Christian can and must do." This put a stop to the intervention of the secular states in the affairs of the council. In Trent itself, Cardinal Morone's diplomatic skill managed to win over Cardinal Guise for a compromise involving a simple omission of the most important point of doctrinal controversy, the *ius divinum* of the episcopal office.

The decree on Holy Orders (4 chapters and 8 canons) adopted in session 23 (July 15, 1563) defined the sacramental character of sacerdotal ordination and the existence of an ecclesiastical hierarchy based on divine ordinance. The controversial canon 7, now become canon 8, condemned the contention that bishops named by the pope are not legal and true bishops. The simultaneously adopted decree on the residence obligation began with the words "it is a divine precept that the pastor know his flock," but refrained from any statement concerning the basis of the obligation of episcopal residence that was made specifically to include the cardinals.

Establishment of seminaries. Session 23 also ordered the establishment of episcopal seminaries for the training of priests (*De ref.* c. 18). Previously there had been neither binding norms nor appropriate institutions for the training and education of future priests; it had been left up to each individual candidate to acquire the training necessary for his priestly functions. There was practically no question of any spiritual formation. The council averted to certain examples of organized training already in existence in Verona and Granada, and noted the decree of the English National Synod (1556) that established cathedral schools as "nurseries" (*seminaria*) of the clergy and laid upon the bishops the obligation of erecting, with the financial assistance of their diocesan clergy, "colleges" for the training and education of future priests.

Reform petitions. The deepest reason for the two crises of the council was the suspicion of many non-Italian bishops that the pope and Curia wanted to avoid any consequential reform of the Church and preferred to settle for measures of little gravity. What the bishops judged was needed for reform they had committed to writing in reform memoranda. On April 6, 1562, the Spaniards had presented such a list to the legates; later the emperor and the French had proposed similar "reform petitions," but the council had not taken them up. Now Morone had these proposals sifted by the auditor of the Rota, Gabrielle Paleotti, and an extensive text was elaborated, taking account of curial traditions; its first portion was put up for debate on Sept. 3, 1563. Its basic thought was that the salvation of souls must be the supreme law. Therefore, in the selection of bishops, attention was to be paid to choosing only the more worthy (*digniores*), who would be able to function, on the model of Christ, as good shepherds and heralds of the gospel. The episcopal powers, hitherto exposed to many limitations, were *de facto* expanded; bishops were given, for instance, in their quality as delegates of the Holy See, the right of correction and punishment over all exempt orders and chapters, institutions and individuals insofar as any of these were engaged in pastoral work. Provincial synods were to be held every three years, diocesan synods every year; the exempt were also to appear at them and obey their enactments. Competition for pastoral appointments was introduced after the Spanish model, so as to discover the most qualified (*magis idoneus*) candidates.

Decrees on marriage. Session 24 (Nov. 11, 1563), which adopted this reform legislation, also enacted a dogmatic and a disciplinary decree on marriage. The former defended the sacramental character of marriage, from which derived the Church's right to establish impediments; it likewise proclaimed the unity and indissolubility of marriage. The second decree, usually called the Tametsi from its initial word, declared that secret marriages not solemnized *in facie ecclesiae* (*matrimonia clandestina*) were not only illicit, as the law then in force had declared, but invalid as well: It made the validity of a marriage dependent on the observance of the prescription regarding form, namely, that the marriage be solemnized before a competent pastor and two or three witnesses. The fact of the marriage is to be entered in a register. The *Tametsi* decree came into force only where it was promulgated.

Morone made every effort, in accord with Pius IV and his nephew Charles BORROMEO, who was responsible for the correspondence with the conciliar legates, to end the council before Christmas; the Spanish ambassador, Count Luna, with a small group of malcontents, tried to prolong it, but without success. The second part of the great reform text was debated in the general congregation. It was directed against excessive ostentation on the part of cardinals and bishops and reminded them that they ought to be models of holy humility (*sanctae humilitatis exempla*); in the interest of pastoral efficiency, many changes were made in the law governing ecclesiastical offices, with particular regard to patronage, union of benefices, and claims to benefices.

Regular clerics. The schema on reform of the regulars presented on November 20 limited itself to establishing certain definite principles concerning the novitiate, the making of profession and the *vita communis,* binding for all orders. It contained precautions to safeguard the freedom of action in making profession and a tightening of the enclosure for convents. The ban on awarding abbeys to secular priests, especially cardinals, as commendatories, was so vaguely worded as to be ineffectual. A minority of about 40 cardinals complained of its indefiniteness but to no avail, and this abuse was not entirely suppressed in the sequel.

Indulgences. Besides these reform decrees, there was on the agenda a declaration of the council on indulgences, against which Luther had previously composed his 95 Theses, on purgatory, and on the veneration of the saints, of their relics, and of images; this veneration of saints had been a great point of contention in the polemic with the Protestants. Since it proved impossible for lack of time to treat these articles of faith in detail with the same care as the others (in the theological and general congregations), Morone yielded to the insistence of Guise and formed three council committees to elaborate brief decrees that reproduced the essentials of Catholic doctrine on these points and also contained the reform measures necessary precisely in this area. The council stated that the Church has full power to grant indulgences; that there is a place of purification for the dead that is accessible to the intercession and sacrifice of the faithful; that it "is good and profitable to invoke the saints" and to venerate their relics; that it is permissible to place images of Christ and the saints in churches and to venerate them, because, as the seventh Ecumenical Council had defined: "the honor given them is directed to the originals whom they represent."

Close of the council. It was intended to publish these decrees and the last-mentioned reform decrees on December 9 and thus to conclude the council. But when during the night of November 30 and December 1 a courier brought the news from Rome that the pope was dangerously ill, session 25 was advanced to December 3. It lasted two days because the decrees from all the previous sessions were read again and approved and signed. The signatories were 6 cardinals, 3 patriarchs, 25 archbishops, 169 bishops, 19 proxies for absent bishops, and 7 generals of religious orders. At the conclusion of the session, Cardinal Guise acclaimed the reigning pope and his predecessors Paul III and Julius III, who had convoked and continued the council. All the council fathers then obligated themselves to confess the faith and doctrine contained in the dogmatic decrees and to observe the directives of the reform decrees.

Papal confirmation. In its final session the council had commissioned the legates to obtain papal confirmation of their work. This was given on Jan. 26, 1564; after this oral approval, the bull *Benedictus Deus* was prepared but was not published until June 30, 1564. All decrees were approved without alteration; the pope reserved the authentic interpretation to the Apostolic See and forbade the publication of commentaries and glosses without its approval. On Aug. 2, 1564, the authentic interpretation of the decrees was entrusted to a committee of cardinals from which developed the Sacred Congregation of the Council.

Supplementation. The council had also in its final session given over to the pope several pieces of business that it had not been able to dispatch itself. Accordingly, Pius IV published on March 24, 1564, the revised *Index of Forbidden Books;* Pius V, the *Roman Catechism for Pastors* (1566), the reformed *Roman Breviary* (1568), and the *Reformed Roman Missal* (1570). The revised edition of the Vulgate did not appear until 1592 (Sixto-Clementina). The reform of the offices of the Roman Curia, from which the council had abstained entirely, was mainly the work of Pius V and Sixtus V.

Implementation. Still more important than the supplementation of the decrees was their implementation. The official edition of the decrees printed by Paulus Manutius was sent to the bishops; in this way they also reached America and Africa (Congo). They were accepted and accommodated at provincial and diocesan synods. A crucial factor was the intervention of the popes on behalf of an implementation of the decrees; nuncios and apostolic visitors were commissioned to supervise this execution. In view of the still-intimate ties between Church and State, the papal representatives were also at pains to get the decrees accepted by the governments. The Italian states and Poland accepted them unconditionally; Spain, "without prejudice to the rights of the King." The decrees were not officially accepted by the secular power either in France or in the empire.

Historical significance. The Council of Trent was the Church's answer to the Protestant REFORMATION. It delimited Catholic doctrine sharply from Protestant doctrine and eliminated the disastrous obscurity as to what was an essential element of the faith and what was merely a subject for theological controversy. This Tridentine faith was briefly summarized in the *Professio fidei Tridentina,* prescribed on Nov. 13, 1564. This profession of faith has one striking lacuna: There is no definition of the Church or of the papal primacy, against which the attacks of the reformers had been concentrated. It is clear from the history of the council that this definition was impossible at that time because the opposing conceptions still in existence could not be reconciled.

The reform decrees of the council were a compromise between the radical reformers' wishes and the curial tradition, not an ideal solution but a serviceable one. Wherever implemented, they effected a renewal and strengthening of ecclesiastical life. The new Catholic piety and mysticism, the revival of scholastic theology, the emergence of positive theology, and the art and culture of the baroque age depend upon the Council of Trent or at least are inconceivable without it. It was no mere restoration of the Middle Ages; rather, it brought so many new features to the countenance of the Church that with it a new era of Church history begins. To the present-day reproach that the council deepened the split between Catholics and Protestants and imbued the Catholic Church for a century with an anti-Protestant attitude, the answer must be that there was an absolute need to delimit clearly the Catholic faith from the Protestant confessions. A resultant anti-Protestant posture was scarcely avoidable given the circumstances. The Council of Trent is not an insurmountable barrier for Christian reunion, as often alleged, for its doctrinal decrees, though not in need of revision, are capable of supplementation.

Bibliography: Sources. H. JEDIN, *Das Konzil von Trient: Ein Überlick über die Erforschung seiner Geschichte* (Rome 1948). *Canones et decreta S. . .Concilii Tridentini* (Rome 1564), the official standard ed. repr. many times; critical text now in G. ALBERIGO, *Conciliorum oeucumenicorum decreta* (New York 1962) 633–775. The oldest collection of the *Acta* was provided by J. LE PLAT, *Monumentorum ad historiam Concilii Tridentini potissimum illustrandam spectantium amplissima collectio,* 7 v. (Louvain 1781–87). Critical edition of all available sources, *Concilium Tridentinum,* containing: *Diaries,* ed. S. MERKLE, v. 1–3.1; *Acts,* ed. S. EHSES, v. 4, 5, 7.2, and 9, and T. FREUDENBERGER, v. 6.1 and 7.1; *Letters,* ed. G. BUSCHBELL, v. 10 and 11; *Treatises,* ed. V. SCHWEITZER, v. 12, and H. JEDIN, v. 13. The correspondence of the Legates during the last sessions in J. ŠUSTA, *Die Römische Kurie und das Konzil von Trient unter Pius IV,* 4 v. (Vienna 1904–14). S. KUTTNER, ed., *Decreta septem priorum sessionum Concilii Tridentini sub Paulo III P. M.* (Washington 1945), autograph of Council Secretary Massarelli reproduced in photostat copy with important introd. on the oldest printed eds. of the decrees. Narrative and interpretative works. General. P. SARPI, *Istoria del Concilio Tridentino* (London 1619), strongly antipapal, critical ed. by G. GAMBARIN, 3 v. (Bari 1935). P. S. PALLAVICINO, *Istoria del Concilio di Trento,* 3 v. (Rome 1656–57), best ed. by F. A. ZACCARIA, 6 v. (Faenza 1792–97), with H. JEDIN, *Der Quellenapparat der Konzilsgeschichte Pallavicinos* (Rome 1940). P. RICHARD, *Histoire du Concile de Trente,* 2 v. (Paris 1930–31). L. CRISTIANI, *L'Église à l'époque du concile de Trente* (Paris 1948). G. SCHREIBER, *Das Weltkonzil von Trient,* 2 v. (Freiburg 1951). H. JEDIN, *A History of the Council of Trent,* tr. E. GRAF, v. 1–2 (St. Louis 1957–60), v. 3 in prep. Participants in the Council. J. DE CASTRO, *Portugal no Concílio de Trento,* 6 v. (Lisbon 1944–46). C. GUTIÉRREZ, ed. and tr., *Españoles en Trento* (Valladolid 1951). A. WALZ, *I domenicani al Concilio di Trento* (Rome 1961). G. ALBERIGO, "Cataloghi dei partecipanti al Concilio di Trento editi durante il medesimo," *Rivista di storia della Chiesa iri Italia* 10 (1956) 345–373; 11 (1957) 49–94. I. ROGGER, *Le nazioni al Concilio di Trento durante la sua epoca imperiale, 1545–1552* (Rome 1952). Further bibliog. on participants from religious orders in H. JEDIN, *History of the Council of Trent,* tr. E. GRAF, v. 1–2 (St. Louis 1957–60) 2:60, also H. O. EVENNETT, "Three Benedictine Abbots at the Council of Trent, 1545–1547," *Studia monastica* 1 (1959) 343–377. The entire duration of the council, H. JEDIN, *Papal Legate at the Council of Trent: Cardinal Seripando,* tr. F. C. ECKHOFF (St. Louis 1947); "Rede- und Stimmfreiheit auf dem Konzil von Trient," *Historisches Jahrbuch der Görres- Gesellschaft* 75 (1956) 73–93. The council under Paul III and Julius III (1545–52). H. JEDIN, "Die Kosten des Konzils von Trient unter Paul III," *Münchener theologische Zeitschrift* 4 (1953) 119–132. G. ALBERIGO, *I vescovi italiani al Concilio di Trento 1545–47* (Florence 1959). Bibliog. of older writings on Scripture and tradition, H. JEDIN, *History of the Council of Trent,* tr. E. GRAF, v. 1–2 (St. Louis 1957–60) 2:52. The extensive literature that appeared during Vatican II: J. R. GEISELMANN, *Die Heilige Schrift und die Tradition* (Quaestiones disputatae 18; Freiburg 1962). The older opinion, held also by H. Jedin, on the sense of the *et-et* in F. LENNERZ, *Gregorianum* 40 (1959) 38–53, 624–635. W. KOCH, "Der authentische Charakter der Vulgata im Lichte der Trienter Konzilsverhandlungen," *Theologische Quartalschrift* 96 (1914) 401–422, 542–572; 97 (1915) 225–249, 529–549. R. DRAGUET, "Le Maître louvaniste Driedo inspirateur du décret de Trente sur la Vulgate," *Miscellanea historica in honorem A. de Meyer* (Louvain 1946) 836–854. S. EHSES, "Das Konzil von Trient und die Übersetzung der Bibel in die Landessprache," *Vereinsschrift der Görres-Gesellschaft, 1908* 3 (1908) 37–50. J. RAINER, "Entstehungsgeschichte des Trienter Predigtreformdekretes," *Zeitschrift für katholische Theologie* 39 (1915) 256–317, 465–523. Bibliog. on older works on original sin and decree of justification, H. JEDIN, *History of the Council of Trent,* (2d ed. Freiburg 1951) 2:146, 175–176, 178–179. J. OLAZARAN, *Documentos inéditos Tridentinos sobre la justificación* (Madrid 1957). A. MOBILIA, *Cornelio Musso e la prima forma del decreto sulla giustificazione* (Naples 1960). The doctrine of the sacraments in general. D. ITURRIOZ, *La definición del Concilio de Trento sobre la causalidad de los sacramentos* (Madrid 1951). Bologna sessions. L. CARCERERI, *Il Concilio di Trento dalla traslazione e Bologna alla sospensione* (Bologna 1910). T. FREUDENBERGER, "Der Kampf um die radikale Abschaffung der Stolgebühren während der Bologneser Periode des Trienter Konzils," *Münchener theologische Zeitschrift* 1 (1950) 40–53. H. JEDIN, "Il significato del periodo bolognese per le decisioni dogmatiche e l'opera di riforma del Concilio di Trento" in *Problemi di vita religiosa in Italia nel Cinquecento* (Padua 1960) 1–16; "Der kaiserliche Protest gegen die Translation des Konzils von Trient nach Bologna," *Historisches Jahrbuch der Görres-Gesellschaft* 71 (1952) 184–196. Sessions of 1551 and 1552. C. ERDMANN, "Die Wiedereröffnung des Trienter Konzils durch Julius III," *Quellen und Forschungen aus italienischen Archiven und Bibliotheken* 20 (1928–29) 238–317. J. BIRKNER, "Kardinal M. Crescentius," *Römische Quartalschrift für christliche Altertumskunde und für Kirchengeschichte* 43 (1935) 267–285. H. JEDIN, "Das Konzilstagebuch des Bischofs Julius Pflug von Naumburg 1551–1552," *ibid.* 50 (1955) 22–43; "Die Deutschen am Trienter Konzil 1551–1552," *Historische Zeitschrift* 188 (1959) 1–16. G. ALBERIGO, "Un informatore senese al Concilio di Trento 1551–1552," *Rivista di storia della Chiesa iri Italia* 12 (1958) 173–201. Protestant participation in the council. R. STUPPERICH, "Die Reformation und das Tridentinum," *Archiv für Reformationsgeschichte* 47 (1956) 20–63. R. E. MACNALLY, "The Council of Trent and the German Protestants," *Theological Studies* 25 (1964) 1–22. The council under Pius IV (1562–63). H. JEDIN, "Kirchenreform und Konzilsgedanke 1550–1559," *Historisches Jahrbuch der Görres-Gesellschaft* 54 (1934) 401–431. New sources for the history of the third period of sessions, which were not yet processed in *Concilium Tridentinum,* or in Šusta, have been adduced in G. DREI, "La corrispondenza del card. Ercole Gonzaga, presidente del Concilio di Trento," *Archivio storico per le provincie Parmensi* 17 (1917) 185–242; 18 (1918) 29–143. H. JEDIN, *Krisis und Wendepunkt des Trienter Konzils, 1562–1563* (Würzburg 1941). M. CALINI, *Lettere conciliari 1561–63,* ed. A. MARANI (Brescia 1963). J. I. TELLECHEA IDIGORAS, "Cartas y documentos tridentinos inéditos," *Hispania sacra* 16 (1963) 191–248. N. RODOLICO, A. D. Addario, *Osservatori Aoscani al C. di Trento* (Florence 1965). H. O. EVENNETT, *The Cardinal of Lorraine and the Council of Trent* (Cambridge, Eng. 1940). B. CHUDOBA, "Las relaciones de las dos cortes Absburgesas en la tercera asamblea del Concilio Tridentino," *Boletín de la Real Academia de la Historia* 103 (1933) 297–368. L. CASTANO, *Mons. Nicolò Sfrondati, vescovo di Cremona al Concilio di Trento, 1561–1563* (Turin 1939). L. PROSDOCIMI, "Il progetto di *reforma dei principi* al Concilio di Trento," *Aevum* 13 (1939) 3–64. P. PRODI, *Il cardinale G. Paleotti,* v. 1 (Uomi e dottrine 7; Rome 1959). H. JEDIN, "Das Gefolge der Trienter Konzilsprälaten im Jahre 1562," *Festschrift Franz Steinbach*

(Bonn 1960) 580–596. The fundamental work on the deliberations on Communion under both species for the laity is G. CONSTANT, *Concession à l'Allemagne de la communion sous les deux espèces,* 2 v. (Paris 1923). Debate on the Sacrifice of the Mass. É JAMOULLE, "Le Sacrifice eucharistique au Concile de Trente," *Nouvelle revue théolgique* 67 (1945) 513–531; *Ephemerides theologicae Louvanienses* 22 (1946) 34–69. O. URSPRUNG, "Palestrina und die tridentinische Reform der Kirchenmusik," *Monatshefte für katholische Kirchenmusik* 10 (1928) 210–219. J. A. O'DONOHOE, *Tridentine Seminary Legislation: Its Sources and Its Formation* (Louvain 1957). P. FRANSEN, "Ehescheidung bei Ehebruch," *Scholastik* 29 (1954) 537–560. H. JEDIN, "L'importanza del dectreto tridentino sui seminari nella vita della Chiesa," *Seminarium* 15 (1963) 396–412; "Das Konzil von Trient und die Anfänge der Kirchenmatrikeln," *Zeitschrift der Savigny-Stiftung für Rechtsgeschichte, Kanonistische* 32 (1943) 419–494; "Zur Vorgeschichte der Regularenreform Trid. Sess. XXV," *Römische Quartalschrift für christliche Altertumskunde und für Kirchengeschichte* 44 (1936) 231–281; "Entstehung und Tragweite des Trienter Dekrets über die Bilderverehrung," *Theologische Quartalschrift* 116 (1935) 143–188, 404–429; suppl. in *Zeitschrift für Kirchgeschichte* 74 (1963) 321–339; *Krisis und Abschluss des Trienter Konzils 1562–63* (Freiburg 1964), brief summary of third period of sessions. Confirmation, supplementation, and implementation of the council and its historical importance, Pastor v. 15–18. Excellent reports on latest literature, G. ALBERIGO, "Studi e problemi relativi all'applicazione del Concilio di Trento in Italia," *Rivisita storica italiana* 70 (1958) 239–298. S. KUTTNER, "The Reform of the Church and the Council of Trent," *Jurist* 22 (1962) 123–142. H. JEDIN, "Das Konzil von Trient und die Reform der liturgischen Bücher," *Ephemerides liturgicae* 59 (1945) 5–38. P. PASCHINI, in *Cinquecento Romano e riforma cattolica* (Rome 1958) 49–89, on the Roman Catechism. É MÂLE, *L'Art religieux de la fin du XVIᵉ siècle, du XVIIᵉ siècle et du XVIIIᵉ siècle: Étude sur l'iconographie après le concile de Trente* (2d ed. Paris 1951). P. PRODI, *Ricerche sulla teorica delle arti figurative nella Riforma cattolica* (Rome 1962). General estimate. H. JEDIN, "Il Concilio di Trento: Scopo, svolgimento e risultati," *Divinitas* 5 (1961) 345–360; "Ist das Konzil von Trient ein Hindernis der Wiedervereinigung?" *Ephemerides theologicae Louvanienses* 38 (1962) 841–855. N. MINNICH, "'Wie in dem Basilischen Concilie den Behemen Gescheen': The Status of the Protestants at the Council of Trent," *The Contentious Triangle* (Kirksville, Mo. 1999) 201–219. K. MCDONNELL, "Luther and Trent on Penance," *Lutheran Quarterly* ns 7 (1993) 261–276. D. N. POWER, "The Priestly Prayer: The Tridentine Theologians and the Roman Canon," *Fountain of Life,* ed. G. AUSTIN (Washington, D.C. 1991) 131–164. J. F. MCHUGH, "The Sacrifice of the Mass at the Council of Trent," *Sacrifice and Redemption,* ed S. W. SYKES (Cambridge 1991) 157–181. J. E. VERCRUYSSE, "Luther as Reformer within Christendom," *Studia Missionalia* 34 (1985) 351–371. R. A. KOLB, "The German Lutheran Reaction to the Third Period of the Council of Trent," *Lutherjahrbuch* (1984) 63–95.

[H. JEDIN]

TRESHAM

A prominent Northamptonshire Catholic family.

Thomas, speaker of the House of Commons; b. date unknown; d. May 6, 1471. Son of William and Isabel Vaux, he was raised in the household of Henry VI. Despite his father's Yorkist sympathies, Thomas supported Henry VI during the War of the Roses. He was knighted and made comptroller of Henry's household. Sir Thomas served as speaker of the Parliament that met at Coventry and attainted the Duke of York (1459). When the Yorkists triumphed, Tresham's lands were seized, and he was attainted of high treason. In 1464 he was pardoned, and his lands were restored in 1467. When Warwick and Queen Margaret of Anjou, Henry's wife, reasserted the Lancastrian claim, Sir Thomas was placed under precautionary arrest. Warwick freed him, and Tresham fought at Tewkesbury. A pardon offered by Edward IV was later withdrawn, and Sir Thomas was beheaded. Henry VII later (1485) restored his estates to his son, John Tresham.

Thomas, grand prior of England in the Order of Knights Hospitallers of St. John of Jerusalem; b. unknown; d. Rushton, Northamptonshire, March 8, 1559. Thomas, son of John Tresham, grandson of Sir Thomas Tresham, served four terms as sheriff of Northamptonshire (1524–26, 1539–40, 1548–49, and 1556–57). He served also in Parliament and on many local public commissions. He was knighted in 1530, and served Henry VIII, Edward VI, and Queen Mary with loyalty and devotion. He opposed rebellion and disorder. In 1553, he accompanied Mary on her entrance into London. A staunch Catholic, he was rewarded with Mary's appointment as grand prior of the Knights of St. John with its income of almost £ 1,500. He served in the House of Lords from 1557 to 1558. At his death, his lands were inherited by his grandson.

Thomas, prominent recusant; b. 1543?; d. Northamptonshire, Sept. 11, 1605. Young Thomas, son of John and grandson of Sir Thomas Tresham, was reared a Protestant by his guardians. He was knighted in 1570, and he served as sheriff of Northamptonshire in 1573–74. Robert Persons, SJ, converted (1580) him to Catholicism. Sir Thomas was arrested (1581) for harboring Edmund Campion. He was tried by the Star Chamber, and was confined to Fleet prison and his residence until 1588. He was fined annually for recusancy and was imprisoned again in 1597 and 1599. Tresham was the leader of those English Catholics who attempted a reconciliation between their religion and their duties to their sovereign. He loyally proclaimed James I as king and carefully avoided any pro-Spanish sentiments and plots throughout his life. He died a patriotic English Catholic.

Bibliography: A. F. POLLARD, *The Dictionary of National Biography from the Earliest Times to 1900* 19:1130–32. *Paston Letters,* ed. J. GAIRDNER, 6 v. (London 1904). E. WAUGH, *Edmund Campion* (New York 1935). W. R. TRIMBLE, *Catholic Laity in Elizabethan England* (Cambridge, Mass. 1964).

[P. S. MCGARRY]

TREVISA, JOHN

Translator, whose writings stimulated the translation of Holy Scripture into English; d. before May 1402. He was educated at Oxford, but it is not known when he became an M.A. He was a fellow at Exeter College, Oxford, *c.* 1362 to 1369. In 1369 he became a fellow of Queen's College, Oxford, but he was deprived of his fellowship about 1379. An acolyte in 1370, he became subdeacon, deacon, and priest during the same year. He is known to have rented rooms in Queen's College (1382–86 and 1394–96). From *c.* 1387 until his death, he was vicar of Berkeley, Gloucestershire, and chaplain to Thomas, Lord Berkeley, and from *c.* 1389 he was also canon and prebendary of Westbury on Severn, Gloucestershire. His main writings are his English translations of RALPH HIGDEN's *Polychronicon,* completed at Berkeley on April 18, 1387, and of BARTHOLOMAEUS ANGLICUS's *De proprietatibus rerum,* completed at the same place on Feb. 6, 1398. These translations are forerunners to William TYNDALE's English Bible. Trevisa's *Dialogus inter militem et clericum* throws interesting light on his outlook and ideas.

Bibliography: J. TREVISA, *Dialogus inter militem et clericum,* ed. A. J. PERRY (*Early English Text Society* 167; 1925). R. HIGDEN, *Polychronicon,* tr. J. TREVISA, ed. C. BABINGTON and J. R. LUMBY, 9 v. (London 1865–86). BARTHOLOMAEUS ANGLICUS, *De proprietatibus rerum,* tr. J. TREVISA (Westminster, Eng. 1495). C. L. KINGSFORD, *The Dictionary of National Biography from the Earliest Times to 1900,* 63 v. (London 1885–1900) 19:1139–40. M. DEANESLY, *The Lollard Bible and Other Medieval Biblical Versions* (Cambridge, Eng. 1920). A. B. EMDEN, *A Biographical Register of the Scholars of the University of Oxford to A.D. 1500,* 3 v. (Oxford 1957–59) 3:1903–04.

[R. WEISS]

TRIAGE

The metaphor ''triage'' (a French word meaning ''to pick or sort according to quality'') gained entry into medical parlance from a military context in which Napoleon's chief surgeon, Jean Larrey, found it necessary to categorize wounded soldiers needing treatment according to a utilitarian principle: those whose wounds, even if left untreated, were such as not to preclude a return to the battlefield; those sustaining mortal wounds for whom treatment would be futile; those needing immediate attention for whom there would be hope for survival and eventual return to active duty. Only the last group would be given medical attention when human, medicinal, and facility resources had to be rationed. Strategies for ''triaging'' in times of warfare, natural disasters (e.g., earthquakes, famines, etc.), and civil defense planning have marked the modern era. Similarly and more routinely, contempo-

rary health care practice necessitates the application of triage where patients must be sorted or prioritized because of restricted medical resources. Hospital emergency rooms often designate a triage nurse whose task it is to order those seeking treatment according to greatest need and best potential for benefit.

Medical Care. The highly technical nature of modern medicine has further contributed to the complexity of selecting patients for treatment. For example, advances in organ transplant technology utilizing both natural and artificial organs offer new hope to patients with life threatening vital organ failure, but the supply of transplantable organs remains limited and the selection of recipients presents an ethical as well as a logistical dilemma. In organ allocation the utilitarian questions of ''Who has greatest need?'' and ''Who might benefit most?'' are further complicated by possible considerations of social worth and equality of persons. Should younger patients with as yet untapped potential for social contribution be chosen over the retired, or those with disabling mental or physical handicap? If three patients are equal in need and in their potential to benefit from treatment, and there are resources for treating only one, what criteria or selection principle will accord with the traditional Christian belief in a fundamental obligation in justice to recognize the irreducible, inalienable equality of all persons?

Some ethicists (e.g., Joseph Fletcher), appealing to a pragmatic distributive or allocative justice, propose that we choose on the basis of the good of the greatest number or the social interest. Thus, a bank president and father of four children would be chosen to receive treatment over an unemployed single person or a prison inmate. Paul Ramsey, and most Roman Catholic moral theologians, espousing a principle of the absolute equality of persons (commutative justice), argues that selection among medically equal and suitable patients be by random choice (e.g., lottery, choosing straws, or ''first-come, first-served'') so as to avoid reducing the value of persons to their social worth. To do otherwise, it is argued, is to enter upon a ''slippery slope'' with implications unacceptable in a Christian ethic. Decisions based on social worth criteria are highly relative and rooted in a value system in which power and material things take precedence over persons. Further, the power entrusted to selected decision or policy makers, who would be calculating and evaluating the social value of another, raises disturbing ethical questions about who decides and who decides who decides.

The power at stake here is not just power *for* persons but power *over* persons. Ramsey and others object that there are some things we can do which we ought not to do, things which in the extended calculus hold potential for disproportionate harm to the *humanum* which is to be sustained by a Christian ethic. In a more positive vein, Ramsey observes that blind or lottery selection of persons to benefit from rationed medical resources emulates God's own indiscriminate care for us.

The social distribution of health care also invokes the ethical consideration of triage when a choice must be made between providing for a few patients whose need is critical and those for whom there is immediate, though limited, potential for benefit; expensive, even esoteric, treatments (e.g., the artificial heart); and supplying a large number of persons, especially the poor and underprivileged, with more routine medical care and preventive medicine (e.g., vaccines, dietary supplements). Many Christian ethicists maintain that in public policy concerning health care

> priority ought to be given to that kind of preventive medicine or treatment of acute disease which will raise the general standards of health, especially for the young, over elaborate modes of treatment for the aged or seriously handicapped (Ashley and O'Rourke, 240).

A factor in this position is a recognized distinction between Biblical justice and the justice prevalent in secular society. The latter is avowedly impartial and favors individualistic opportunism. Those who find access and the financial means to pay have a right to benefit. Biblical justice, on the other hand, is not impartial and individualistic, but biased in favor of the poor and decidedly social in its thrust (*see* OPTION FOR THE POOR).

Social Triage. The "lifeboat ethics" conundrum is yet another example of the metaphor of triage, here, social triage. The world population explosion, with attendant world hunger, confronts the developed nations with a disturbing specter: providing medical aid and food to underdeveloped countries will insure burgeoning population growth and, ultimately, increased starvation, unless such aid is contingent upon compulsory population control. Garrett Hardin (1980) argues for such contingencies in his "lifeboat ethics" proposal, cautioning the developed countries against lowering their own standards of living and health care lest their children, who ensure the future of the human race, become similarly deprived and lose their edge. Hardin contends that no amount of aid can reverse the plight of the underdeveloped nations. His utilitarian ethic effectively dictates that one save oneself even at the cost of sacrificing the other.

Hardin's assessment of the imminence of the overpopulation crisis is disputed by others who, nonetheless, do acknowledge a significant socio-economic and political problem confronting the world community. Some Catholic ethicists contend that

the advanced countries by introducing modern medicine [into underdeveloped nations] . . . upset the ecological balance and produced a rapid population growth, without at the same time producing the standard of living which in developed countries motivates and facilitates responsible parenthood (Ashley and O'Rourke, 241).

Rather than "sailing away," the developed nations are bound by principles of distributive and Biblical justice to restore the balance which they helped to destroy by raising the standards of living and education in the underdeveloped world. When resources are scarce those who stand to benefit most from enhanced opportunity are those whose need is greatest.

Bibliography: B. M. ASHLEY and K. D. O'ROURKE, *Health Care Ethics: A Theological Analysis* (rev. ed. St. Louis 1982). J. F. CHILDRESS, "Who Shall Live When Not All Can Live?" *Readings on Ethical and Social Issues in Biomedicine*, R. W. WERTZ, ed. (New Jersey 1973) 143–153. R. A. MCCORMICK, "Justice in Health Care," *Health and Medicine in the Catholic Tradition* (New York 1984) 75–85. G. OUTKA, "Social Justice and Equal Access to Health Care," *On Moral Medicine: Theological Perspectives in Medical Ethics*, S. LAMMERS and A. VERHEY, eds. (Michigan 1987) 632–642. A. VERHEY, "Sanctity and Scarcity: The Makings of Tragedy," *ibid.*, 653–657. P. RAMSEY, *The Patient as Person* (New Haven, 1970); *Ethics at the Edges of Life* (New Haven 1977).

[R. M. FRIDAY]

TRIAL OF JESUS

The legal proceeding by which Jesus was judged after His arrest and condemned to death, first by the Jewish Sanhedrin, then by Pontius Pilate, Roman Procurator of Judea. The account of the trial given by the Synoptic Gospels (Mk 14.53–15.15; Mt 26.57–27.26; Lk 22.54–23.25) differs considerably from that of the Gospel according to St. John (18.12–19.16), although all four are substantially in accord. Mark and Matthew describe the trial before the Sanhedrin in two phases, with Peter's denial between them; Luke places the denial before his uninterrupted account of a single Sanhedrin trial; John gives a description of the interview between Jesus and Annas, as well as of those between Jesus and Pilate, but he omits a description of the actual trial, except for a brief reference to CAIAPHAS, the actual high priest, and son-in-law of Annas. Only Matthew speaks of the wife of Pilate and her dream.

Chronology. The time sequence of the trial and execution of Jesus is difficult to determine because of the differences between the Synoptic and Johannine accounts and because of the complicated nature of astronomical calculations. The Synoptic account places the Last Supper, which was apparently the Passover meal of Jesus and

His Apostles, before the trial, i.e., on the 14th of the month of Nisan, and the death of Jesus on Friday the 15th of Nisan. John's account describes the reluctance of the accusers to enter the courtyard of Pilate's palace on the morning of the day of execution as caused by their desire to avoid contamination that would prevent their eating the Passover meal, which Jesus and His Apostles appear to have already had. Yet all four Gospels agree that Jesus died on a Friday, and that they had had the Supper before the arrest. If the Last Supper was for them the ritual Passover meal prescribed for the evening of the 14th of Nisan, then that day was Thursday and the following day, Friday, the day of Jesus' death, was the 15th of Nisan. The Johannine account, clearly divergent from this, indicates that Jesus' Last Supper was on the day before the Passover meal of the judges who condemned Him and that He died on the day that these judges considered the Preparation Day (παρασκευή) of the Passover, i.e., the 14th of Nisan. Although the question remains open, one solution is that of the two calendars whereby the Sadducees observed the Passover meal and feast (the 14th and the 15th of Nisan) on Friday and Saturday and the Pharisees kept the two days on Thursday and Friday. The Synoptic account is reconcilable with the Pharisee calendar; the Johannine, with that of the Sadducees. In either case, given the tenuous nature of the question, the date of the execution of Jesus must be a Friday, either the 14th or the 15th of Nisan, during the reign of Pilate (A.D. 26 to 36). Within this period the only possible dates for the 14th of Nisan are March 18, 29, and April 3, 33. Of these two dates, the former is incompatible with the date of the beginning of Jesus' public life in the 15th year of Tiberius Caesar (Lk 3.1), which was A.D. 29. The only possible dates for the 15th of Nisan are April 7, 30, and April 27, 31. According to the Synoptic account the two latter dates are possible; the Johannine narrative favors the A.D. 33 date.

Revision of the chronology of the entire Last Supper-Crucifixion sequence has been proposed (1957) on the basis of the material contained in the Dead Sea Scrolls and the apocryphal Books of Jubilees and Enoch. According to this proposal, which has been well received, Jesus and His Apostles followed the solar calendar that was used also by the QUMRAN COMMUNITY, according to which the Passover always fell on a Wednesday, so that the Passover meal was eaten on Tuesday evening. Although this ''chronology of three days'' for the trial of Jesus has much in its favor, including the approval of many reputable authorities, it still remains a minority opinion.

Trial before the Sanhedrin. With the substance of the Gospel accounts taken as historically reliable and with allowances made for the peculiarities of each Evangelist, a probable reconstruction of the course of events

Trial of Jesus of Nazareth before Pontius Pilate (seated above).

is as follows: Jesus was apprehended at night in the garden of Gethsemani by Jewish police (probably attached to the Jerusalem Temple guard) and taken first to Annas, who, although no longer acting high priest since his deposition in A.D. 15, nevertheless continued to retain the title and to wield decisive influence; five of his sons, as well as a son-in-law (Joseph Caiaphas, A.D. 18 to 37), and a grandson were successors in the pontificate. Annas's honorary but powerful position explains why Jesus was brought first to him. Only John (Jn 18.12–14; 19–23) records this interview, but not the one conducted by Caiaphas, to which he merely alludes (Jn 18.24), probably because he considers it sufficiently described in the Synoptics and also because it serves as a background to his account of Peter's denial, which he considers indispensable because it contains fulfillment of the denial prediction recorded in Jn 13.38. Annas's questioning of Jesus was most probably not of an official character, since he was no longer high priest, although he was undoubtedly familiar with the plot against Jesus (Jn 18.14).

If the narrative of John 18.19–23 refers to Annas, the preliminary examination failed to produce any evidence of secret activity on the part of Jesus against the Jewish or Roman authorities. In any case, Jesus manifested neither the guilty bearing of a criminal nor the servility typical of defendants. He was then taken before the

Sanhedrin and Caiphas, the reigning high priest and its president ex officio. Other members of the 71-man ruling council were CHIEF PRIESTS and leading elders, both of which groups were chiefly SADDUCEES and SCRIBES, the latter of the Pharisee caste. Although Flavius JOSEPHUS, the MISHNAH, and the TALMUD indicate that the regular meeting place of the Sanhedrin was either on the western slope of the Temple mount or in one of the halls of the Temple complex itself (some scholars speak of a meeting place on the Mount of Olives), still the Gospels clearly say that the preliminary planning for the arrest and conviction of Jesus, as well as the trial itself and the denial by Peter, all occurred in the house of the high priest. These indications are reconcilable with the tradition that both Annas and Caiphas lived in the same palace, near the CENACLE. This would also explain why Jesus was brought to Annas first.

The predetermined purpose of the trial was the condemnation to death of Jesus (Mt 26.3–5: Mk 14.1, 55; Lk 22.1–2; Jn 11.45–53). However, the testimony of the witnesses for the prosecution was legally invalid because their depositions, being fragmentary and confused, failed to agree in every detail, as was required by Deuteronomy 17.6; 19.5 (Mishnah *Sanh.* 4.1d). Jesus' refusal to defend Himself against these accusers (Mt 26.62) is an indication that He was aware of the futility of offering any defense against those whose purpose was obvious. Having failed to adduce damning evidence from competent witnesses, the Sanhedrists realized that other means were necessary in order to achieve the desired conviction. The high priest himself then demanded personally that Jesus state unequivocally whether He was the Messiah, the Son of God, i.e., the divinely appointed leader of national restoration and inaugurator of the messianic era described in the writings of the Prophets and more prominent in the expectations of later Judaism from the Machabean period onward. Just as directly, Jesus answered in the affirmative, arrogating to Himself the imagery of Daniel 7.13 and Psalms 109 (110).1, both of which passages vindicate the regal power of dominion to the legitimate representative (''son'') of God. Jesus' reply was His death warrant. His judges declared Him guilty of blasphemy and liable to the extreme penalty of death. [*See* BLASPHEMY (IN THE BIBLE).]

That the judgment of the Sanhedrin was a true death sentence is evident from Mark's use of the word κατέκριναν (14.64); the same word occurs in Mt 27.3, which describes Judas's remorse at learning that Jesus had been condemned (κατεκρίθη). The same verb, κατακρινοῦσιν (they will condemn), is used in Mk 10.33; Mt 20.18 concerning the action of the Sanhedrin in Jesus' third prediction of His Passion. These two latter statements, even if they are to be taken as predictions *post factum,* nevertheless are clear in their presentation of the nature of the verdict.

It is evident in the light of later Jewish history that the Sanhedrists who condemned Jesus did so, not on the basis of Mishnaic law, which only later became codified and generally applicable under Pharisaic auspices following the Synod of Jamnia (A.D. 90), but according to the broader and consequently less tolerant notion of blasphemy characteristic of the Sadducean legalists whose influence predominated within the Sanhedrin at the time of Jesus' trial. That this less benign view was current is evident from the earlier accusations of blasphemy which were leveled against Jesus in Mark 2.7 and John 10.33 (cf. also Acts 12.22; 14.14). Although the Old Testament does not define blasphemy, it does discuss it in general terms (Ex 22.27: Lev 24.11–16; Nm 15.30). Furthermore, the mutual antagonism of Jesus and the legalists perdured since the beginning of the Public Ministry (Mt 7.28: Mk 1.22; 2.6–8); occasionally it is described in the Gospels as open conflict, but more often it appeared in the form of incessant criticism of each other's attitude toward the prevailing interpretation of the Mosaic tradition. The plot against Jesus therefore was the culmination of a long period in which the dominant legal parties had observed Jesus' growing popularity and their proportionately diminishing influence (Mk 12.35–37; Lk 19.48). John presents the resuscitation of Lazarus as the last and decisive event of this conflict (Jn 12.9–11). In view of this long-continuing antagonism, it is not unlikely that at least some of the judges at Jesus' trial were less than completely impartial and were easily influenced by the decisive dialogue between Jesus and Caiphas to bring their attitude to definitive expression by a capital verdict.

Trial before Pilate's Tribunal. Under Roman rule, however, this sentence of the Sanhedrin was only declaratory; the execution of it was reserved to the procurator, who, as representative of the Roman imperial court, reserved to himself the *jus gladii.* It was therefore necessary to obtain from Pontius PILATE the confirmation of the sentence and its execution.

The procurators ordinarily resided in the port city of CAESAREA IN PALESTINE, but at festival times they were accustomed to stay in Jerusalem, establishing their court, or PRAETORIUM, in the palace of Herod. Although many maintain that Pilate's residence was in the fortress Antonia, overlooking the Temple complex, the more favored opinion is that Jesus was brought before Pilate in Herod's palace.

The Sanhedrists who had condemned Jesus to the death penalty on religious grounds of blasphemy, brought before Pilate charges against Jesus of a political nature. Obviously they could hope for no execution unless Jesus would be convicted of a capital violation of Roman law. The judges thus charged Jesus before Pilate of stirring up the people, forbidding payment of taxes to Caesar, and declaring Himself a king (Lk 23.1–2; cf. Mt 27.63, where after His death Jesus is called a deceiver).

Pilate's studied judgment was that Jesus was not guilty of any crime against Roman law. Upon the insistence of the accusers, he continued to consider the case, interviewing Jesus privately, sending Him to HEROD ANTIPAS (who, as tetrarch of Galilee and Perea since the death of his father Herod the Great in 4 B.C., might have jurisdiction over Jesus, a native of Nazareth), offering to release Him in virtue of the traditional Passover amnesty, and allowing Jesus to be scourged (a police punishment ordinarily meted out to agitators who were not Roman citizens, cf. Acts 22.22–29), in the hope that this limited punishment would placate the accusers and allow himself to be absolved of further involvement in the case. [*See* BARABBAS; FLAGELLATION (IN THE BIBLE).] Although in the course of private interviews with Pilate, Jesus had acknowledged His claim to the title of king, Pilate apparently saw in Jesus' insistence either a religious claim which he considered an internal affair of the Jews, or a delusion, but hardly a likely source of insurrection. Finally, however, Pilate submitted to a threat from the Jews that his releasing of Jesus would be reported to the imperial court in Rome as a failure to crush a possible sedition (*crimen laesae majestatis*), since Jesus' acknowledged claim was to the title of Messiah, King of the Jews (Jn 19.12–15). This threat, coupled with the insistence of the crowds, whom the Sanhedrists had incited to demand Jesus' death, finally led Pilate to dismiss the matter as quickly and easily as possible, i.e., by acquiescence. He therefore issued the condemnatory order, confirming the death sentence, and assigning CRUCIFIXION, the usual Roman form of execution for treason.

See Also: PASSION OF CHRIST, I (IN THE BIBLE).

Bibliography: J. BLINZLER, *The Trial of Jesus,* tr. I. and F. MCHUGH (Westminster, MD 1959). A. JAUBERT, *La Date de la Cène: Calendrier biblique et liturgie chrétienne (Études bibliques*; 1957) 116–33. J. A. O'FLYNN, ''The Date of the Last Supper,'' *The Irish Theological Quarterly* 25 (1958) 58–63. T. A. BURKILL, ''The Competence of the Sanhedrin,'' *Vigiliae christianae* 10 (1956) 80–96. P. WINTER, ''Marginal Notes on the Trial of Jesus,'' *Zeitschrift für die neutestamentliche Wissenschaft und die Kunde der älteren Kirche* 50 (1959) 14–33, 221–51. X. LÉON-DUFOUR, *Dictionnaire de la Bible,* suppl. ed. L. PIROT et al. (Paris 1928–) 6:1485–87. S. LÉGASSE, *The Trial of Jesus: Jesus' Vision of God* (Atlanta 1997). M. SABBE, ''The Trial of Jesus before Pilate in John and its Relation to the Synoptic Gospels,'' *John and the Synoptics,* ed. A. DENAUX (Leuven 1992), 341–85. F. MILLAR, ''Reflections on the Trial of Jesus,'' *A Tribute to Geza Vermes,* ed. P. R. DAVIES and R. T. WHITE (Sheffield, Eng 1990) 355–81. R. GORDIS, ed., ''Trial of Jesus in the Light of History: A Symposium,'' *Judaism* 20 (Winter 1971) 6–74.

[T. E. CRANE]

TRICHET, MARIE-LOUISE OF JESUS, BL.

Baptized Louise Trichet; co-foundress of the Daughters of Wisdom *(La Sagesse)*; b. Poitiers, France, May 7, 1684; d. Saint Laurent sur Sèvre, Vendée, France, April 28, 1759. Trichet was the fourth of eight children of devout, bourgeois parents, who ensured that she was baptized on the day of her birth. Her family life and the Christian education that she received endowed her with virtue and an awareness of the needs of others.

At age 17, the beautiful young woman met the already-esteemed LOUIS DE MONTFORT in the hospital of Poitiers and spontaneously offered her services, confiding to him her desire for religious life. Two years later she responded to his invitation to commit herself totally to working with the sick. Although her mother opposed her decision to follow ''this mad priest,'' she accepted the grey religious habit and the name Sister Marie-Louise of Jesus on February 2, 1703 and began her humble duty as a nurse.

Together with de Montfort, she founded the Daughters of Wisdom, the mainspring of whose spirituality was to be Jesus, the ''Eternal and Incarnate Wisdom.'' After de Montfort's departure, she worked alone until she met Catherine Brunet in 1714. The following year the two women, who had now been joined by two others, established the order's first community at La Rochelle (Charente) where they continued to help the children of the poor, the neglected sick (both in hospitals and homes), and others in need. The order continued to grow, and by the end of the twentieth century the Daughters of Wisdom had more than 2,361 members on five continents.

Pope John Paul II beatified her on May 16, 1993. Sister Marie-Louise of Jesus is buried next to the relics of St. Louis de Montfort in the parish church of Saint-Laurent, in Saint Laurent sur Sèvre, where both were venerated by Pope John Paul II during a visit September 19, 1996.

Feast: May 7.

Bibliography: R. LAURENTIN, *Petite vie de Marie-Louise Trichet* (Paris 1993). M. T. LE MOIGN-KLIPFFEL, *Les Filles de la Sagesse* (Paris 1947). B. PAPASOGLI, *Wisdom of the Heart: The Story of Marie Louis Trichet* (Bay Shore, N.Y. 1993). M. T. PIERCE, *Marie Louise of Jesus: De Montfort's Spiritual Daughter* (Dublin 1963). A. RICHOMME, *Marie-Louise Trichet* (Paris 1971).

[K. I. RABENSTEIN]

TRIDENTINE MASS

Named for the Council of TRENT (*Concilium Tridentinum*), the Roman-Rite form of celebrating the EUCHA-

RIST had been in obligatory use from 1570 until the 1969 publication of the Order of Mass reformed by decree of VATICAN COUNCIL II. In its 25th and final session in 1562 Trent left it to the Roman Pontiff to reform the Missal. Beginning in 1564, a commission under Pius IV and St. Pius V worked on the *Missale Romanum ex decreto SS. Concilii Tridentini restitutum, Pii V Pont. Max. iussu editum,* published in 1570 (last *editio typica,* 1962). A more accurate designation of the form of celebration proper to this Missal would be "the Mass of Pius V."

In current usage the designation "Tridentine Mass" may simply connote an Order distinct from that of the 1969 Order of Mass. Once the latter was promulgated, its use obligatorily replaced, first in Latin and then in the vernacular, the former Order of Mass. This was made clear by the Apostolic Constitution *Missale Romanum* (April 3, 1969) of Pope Paul VI, and implemented by the Congregation for Divine Worship in the Instruction *Constitutione Apostolica* (Oct. 20, 1969). The same document (no. 19) authorized Ordinaries to allow elderly priests to retain the 1962 Missal and its Order of Mass when celebrating without a congregation. These dispositions were repeated in the Notifications of the same Congregation *Instructione de Constitutione* of 1971 and *Conferentiarum Episcoporum* of 1974.

Controversy. The opponents of Vatican Council II intend by the name "Tridentine Mass" an orthodox continuity with the Eucharistic teaching of Trent alleged to be missing from the 1969 Order of Mass, which they impugn as invalid, even heretical. In a letter to Archbishop Marcel Lefebvre, leader of the most publicized recalcitrance, Pope Paul VI expressed the reason for the obligatory adoption of the new Order of Mass: the unity of the whole ecclesial community, of which the Order of Mass is a singular sign. Paul VI also stated and rejected the key point of the Lefebvre opposition that only the Tridentine Mass preserved the authentic sacrifice of the Mass and ministerial priesthood.

The issue of the Tridentine Mass took a new turn in 1984. A survey of all the bishops of the Church, reported in *Notitiae* in 1981, indicated little dissatisfaction with the reformed Missal and a minuscule interest in a return to the Latin liturgy. Apparently, however, there were some loyalists who wished to celebrate the Tridentine Mass. In their favor the Congregation for Divine Worship announced in 1984 an indult allowing petitioners to celebrate a Tridentine Mass in the letter "Quattor Abhinc Annos" (*Acta Apostolicae Sedis* no. 76 [1984]: 1088–1089). The concession can be made by the diocesan bishop to those known to have no ties with the opponents of the 1970 Roman Missal. The celebration must be in Latin, follow the *Missale Romanum* of 1962, without intermingling elements of the 1970 *Missale Romanum.* The bishop determines the day and place of celebration and limits participation to the petitioning priest and faithful.

In 1988 John Paul II issued the apostolic letter *Ecclesia Dei,* which called for a wider and more generous application of the directives for the Tridentine Mass. The Pontifical Commission *Ecclesia Dei* issued guidelines implementing the apostolic letter in 1991. The guidelines indicate that the celebration of the Tridentine Mass may be celebrated in parish churches, the regularity and frequency of which depends on the needs of the faithful. The guidelines grant faculties to the local ordinary to give permission for the use of the 1962 Missal. It calls for the celebrants of these Masses to emphasize their adherence to legislation of the universal Church and the juridical value of the liturgy of Vatican II in their preaching and contacts. It does grant, however, that the new lectionary in the vernacular could be used at these Masses, but cautions that pastors should take care not to impose it and thus impede the return of those who maintain the integrity of the former tradition.

Bibliography: International Commission on English in the Liturgy, *Documents on the Liturgy* (Collegeville, Minn. 1982) documents 59, 61 (on the Lefebvre case); 202, 313 (promulgation of the new Order of Mass); 209, 216 (on the use of the new Roman Missal). J. J. JUNGMANN, translated by F. A. BRUNNER, *The Mass of the Roman Rite,* reprint (Westminster, Md. 1986). "La Messe du toujours," *Notitiae* 6 (1970) 231–232. Pontifical Commission *Ecclesia Dei,* "Guidelines on the Tridentine Mass," *Origins* 21 (July 18, 1991) 144–145. For the inquiry on the use of Latin and of the so-called Tridentine Mass, see *Notitiae* 7 (1981) 589–609. For the 1984 indult, see *Notitiae* 11 (1985) 9–10.

[T. O'BRIEN/EDS.]

TRIDUUM

A Latin word meaning a space of three days, signifies in Catholic usage, a period of three consecutive days on which specified devotions are observed, determined prayers are said, or both, in order to obtain particular graces, to give thanks for special favors, to solemnize feasts, or to honor outstanding events as, for example, the election of a pope or the coronation of a king.

The choice of the number three for these devotions had its origin in a sacredness popularly attributed to it from pre–Christian times. In the OT, three–day periods were given particular importance (Tb 3.10; 6.16, 22; Jdt 12.6; Est 4.16; Dn 10.2–3; 2 Mc 13.12). In the NT, Our Lord referred to the three days Jonah spent in the whale's belly (Jn 2.1), and often spoke of the three days his own body would be in the tomb (Mt 17.22; 26.61; 27.40, 63; Mk 9.30).

View of the city of Trier, Germany, from across the Moselle River.

Christians, very early, adopted the practice of a two–or three–day fast, in remembrance of our Lord's sojourn in the tomb, at different seasons of the year. In time, this led to the establishment of the liturgical observance of EMBER DAYS, three days of fasting and special prayer, which were observed at the beginning of each of the four seasons. The days before Easter, namely, HOLY THURSDAY, GOOD FRIDAY, and Holy Saturday, came to be known as *Triduum sanctum,* the holy triduum, or more commonly, ''Easter Triduum.'' In early medieval times, a three–day period of prayer and fasting came to be associated with all the important events of Catholic life. There was a triduum in preparation for Baptism, for the election of a pope, even for the end of the carnival.

Bibliography: L. DUCHESNE, *Origines du culte chrétien* (5th ed. Paris 1925) 305–306. A. ANWANDER, *Wörterbuch der Religion* (2d ed. Würzburg 1962) 111–112.

[P. MULHERN]

TRIER

On the Moselle River between the Eifel and Hunsrück regions of Germany, a bishopric (*Trevirensis*) in the second century and a metropolitanate from the sixth century at the latest (with suffragans Metz, Toul, and Verdun until 1802); it has been a suffragan of COLOGNE since 1821.

Early History. Trier (Trèves), after AUGSBURG the oldest city on German soil, was a Roman base founded by AUGUSTUS among the Celtic-Germanic *Treveri* (*Augusta Treverorum*) *c.* 15 B.C., which because of its favorable location at the intersection of important military and commercial roads became the most important city in Gaul. DIOCLETIAN (*c.* 285) made it the capital of Gaul (the seat of the *Praetor Galliarum*) and an imperial residence, which Constantine Chlorus and his son CONSTANTINE THE GREAT developed.

Trier's monuments can be traced back, in part, to Roman buildings: the amphitheater of 30,000 seats, the Barbara baths, the Porta Nigra (north gate of the city with a 12th– to 19th–century double church), the Roman bridge, the ''Basilica'' (originally part of the imperial palace, today a Protestant church), the imperial baths, and the Roman basis of the present cathedral. Extensive early Christian tombs in series and tomb inscriptions, along with other items discovered, point to an early Christianization of the city and area.

This Christian community, founded in the second century primarily from south France, became in the third century a Christian center of influence in the Rhineland. The first known bishop, Eucharius, lived *c.* 250. His third successor, Agroecius, built a large double basilica (326–348) on the grounds of the imperial palace, out of which have grown the present cathedral (the oldest north of the Alps) and the adjoining church of Our Lady (1230–60, after the French Gothic). St. ATHANASIUS was in Trier during exile (335–337); St. AMBROSE was born there, and SS. JEROME, AUGUSTINE, and MARTIN OF TOURS, as well as Ausonius, visited it when it was a cultural center of VALENTINIAN I. By the year 400, Christianity had won out over paganism, but it took 300 years more to Christianize the countryside.

Trier declined in the fifth century when the praetorian prefect moved to ARLES, and the city was taken by the Franks *c.* 460. In the sixth century, the ecclesiastical province developed, and in the seventh and eighth, many monasteries were established, especially under Archbishop Ludwin (d. 711). The Benedictine Abbey of St. Maximin, suppressed in 1802, was favored by Merovingians and Carolingians and known for its nineth–century scriptorium; it helped found the abbeys of ECHTERNACH, TEGERNSEE, MARIA LAACH, and BRAUWEILER. In 843 Trier became part of LOTHAIR I's kingdom, and secular power passed into the hands of the archbishops until 1803 (except 1212–1308). A Norman pillage in 882 destroyed many buildings, but the archdiocese, divided into five archdeaneries in 910, spread east across the Moselle and the Rhine to Giessen and west across Luxembourg to Stenay. In the tenth (from *c.* 930) and 11th centuries, a secular territory formed around the city, but, being relatively weak, had no more than local importance, except for several powerful archbishops.

Medieval bishops of note are St. AUCTOR (*c.* 430), St. ABRUNCULUS (d. 527), the famous St. NICETIUS (527–566), St. MAGNERICUS (*c.* 570–596), and AMALARIUS (809–813). Archbishop Albero of Montreuil (1131–52) took part in imperial affairs and, as a friend of St. BERNARD OF CLAIRVAUX, encouraged the new orders of Cistercians (HIMMEROD), Premonstratensians, and Augustinians. Archbishop Baldwin of Luxembourg (1307–54), greatest of the Electors of Trier and brother of Emperor HENRY VII, expanded the territory by new acquisitions, reorganized his administration, and revived the religious life through the wise reforms that he introduced.

Modern History. In the Age of HUMANISM the University of Trier, modeled after that of Cologne, was founded (1454) at the request of Abp. James von Sierck (1439–56) and NICHOLAS OF CUSA; but the fall of Constantinople postponed its opening until 1473. Its influence was limited to the Electorate and to those parts of the archdiocese that remained Catholic until, in the year 1798, the leaders of the French Revolution closed it.

The Protestant Reformation did not enter the electorate, but in the east and south those parts of the archdiocese not part of the electorate became Protestant. Claims of Trier to be a free imperial city were successfully thwarted from the 13th to the 16th century, and an attempt at reformation in 1559 by Caspar Olevian, a Trier patrician, was suppressed. Archbishop John VI von der Leyen (1556–67) called in the Jesuits, who took charge of all education, including the theological faculty. Archbishop James III von Eltz (1567–81) guided the diocese decisively along the path of the COUNTER REFORMATION, which was completed under Archbishop John of Schönenberg (1581–99).

Just as the Electors of the 16th and 17th centuries came from the local nobility, so the right of reservation for the cathedral chapter in the 18th century served to staff the administration from princely German families. F. G. von SCHÖNBORN (1729–56) who, like his brothers, was renowned for artistic taste, had the fourth–century church of St. Paulinus (destroyed in 1674) rebuilt (1732–54) in magnificent rococo by B. Neumann. Under the last Elector, CLEMENS WENZESLAUS (1768–1802), a church reform emphasizing the claims of episcopalism and conciliarism [*see* CONCILIARISM (HISTORY OF)] was prepared and thought out by Auxiliary Bp. J. N. von HONTHEIM (1749–90), and gained considerable support in Germany (*see* FEBRONIANISM).

The Enactment of the Imperial Delegates of 1803 sealed the fate of the spiritual principality. Trier became politically a part of Prussia in 1815, and the diocese was made suffragan to Cologne in 1821. Bishop Joseph von Hommer (1824–36) carefully rebuilt the diocese in a tolerant and liturgically progressive manner. Bishops W. Arnoldi (1842–64) and the well-known preacher M. Eberhard (1867–76) had a conflict with the state during the Cologne mixed-marriage dispute and the KULTURKAMPF. The Alsatian M. F. Korum (1881–1921) emphasized purposeful and precise ecclesiastical care; he worked politically for the assignment of the Saar to Germany, as did his successors after World War II. Bishop F. R. Bornewasser (1921–51) showed the courage of Christian conviction during the reign of terror under National Socialism.

Since 1952 Matthias Wehr has been bishop. In 1950 the major seminary, established in 1773, became a pontifical institute (236 students and a good theological library). The liturgical institute that serves the German dioceses is located in Trier.

The cathedral has been redone frequently—Romanesque by Archbishop Poppo (1016–47), baroque in 1719, renovated 1891 to 1910. The Benedictine Abbey of Maria ad Martyres (seventh century) was suppressed by Napoleon I (1809); that of St. Martin, also on the Moselle, founded *c.* 587, was restored in 888 after the Norman sack. The Benedictine Abbey of St. Matthias, known in the 15th century for its school, scholarship, and historical work, has a Romanesque church consecrated in 1148 with the tomb of St. Eucharius and relics of St. Matthew (since 1127). The Abbey of PRÜM had ties with Trier.

The Holy Garment. Trier's claim to have the seamless robe of Christ (Jn 19.23), supposedly woven by the Blessed Virgin and discovered by St. HELENA, is favored over about 20 other such claims because of the city's late Roman and early Christian importance. The first sure notice dates from after 1000. The authors of the *Gesta Treverorum* after 1101 inserted a notice about its discovery in the older forged diploma attributed to Sylvester. Trier's Holy Garment was exhibited for the first time in 1512. After 1654 it was shown privately in the fortress Ehrenbreitstein. Since the 19th century it has been exhibited publicly in the cathedral of Trier. Public expositions (1,000,000 pilgrims between Aug. 18 and Oct. 6, 1844; 2,000,000 in 1933; 1,700,000 in 1959) have helped Catholic self-confidence and devotion to Christ; but an inadequate theological and critical foundation has given rise to denominational polemics and ecclesiastical rifts (*see* RONGE, JOHANN). Even though recent excavations (1943–54) point to the existence of an early Christian relic of the Savior in Trier, the authenticity of the Holy Garment cannot be scientifically proved. It has been associated with an early cloth relic that came into contact with Christ or some other relic of the Crusades that came to be regarded as the tunic of Christ. The propriety of the veneration, however, is independent of the question of authenticity. The cult is justifiable because veneration is shown to Christ through the symbol (St. Thomas, *Summa theologiae* 3a, 25.3, 4), which in this case represents undivided Christianity.

Bibliography: J. MARX, *Trevirensia: Literaturkunde zur Geschichte der Trierer Lande* (Trier 1909), bibliog. N. IRSCH, *Der Dom zu Trier* (Düsseldorf 1931). H. BUNJES et al., *Die kirchlichen Kunstdenkmäler der Stadt Trier* (Düsseldorf 1938). E. EWIG, *Trier im Merowingerreich* (Trier 1954). V. CONZEMIUS, *Jakob III von Eltz* (Wiesbaden 1956). N. KYLL, ''Siedlung, Christianisierung und kirchliche Organisation der Westeifel,'' *Rheinische Vierteljahrblätter* 26 (1961) 159–241. *Trierisches Jahrbuch* (Trier 1950–), annual. E. GOSE et al., *Die Religion in Geschichte und Gegenwart* (Tübingen 1957–65) 6:1018–21. E. ISERLOH, *Lexikon für Theologie und Kirche*, ed. J. HOFER and K. RAHNER (Freiberg 1957–65) 8:1348–50. ''Trier,'' ibid. v.10. *Annuario Pontificio* (Rome 1964) 457.

[V. CONZEMIUS]

TRIEST, ANTOINE

Bishop, protector of the first Jansenists; b. Beveren-Waas (Belgium), 1576; d. Ghent, May 28, 1657. Through his father be belonged to the family of the Barons of Auwegem; and through his mother, Marie Van Royen, to the Villain family of Ghent. Having received his licentiate in law at Louvain, he went to Rome to study theology. He was ordained on Sept. 2, 1602, and was successively chaplain at the court of the archdukes at Brussels, canon at Anderlecht and Ghent, archdeacon and dean of St. Baron in Ghent, member of the Estates of Flanders, bishop of Bruges (1616), bishop of Ghent (1620), and counselor to the Council of State. A very rich man, he was generous to the poor, to ecclesiastical institutions, to artists, and to horticulturists (whence his influence on the *Floralies* of Ghent). Imbued with the spirit of Catholic restoration, he administered his dioceses energetically, and made extensive visitations. He applied the Tridentine decrees, improving education and helping religious communities of men and women. His historical importance stems especially from his support of Jansenism in its early stages. Having known and esteemed his colleague Cornelius JANSEN (Jansenius), Bishop of Ypres, he always believed that Jansenius had been misunderstood and treated unfairly. That is why, together with Abp. Jacques BOONEN, he labored to obtain a revision of the matter in Rome; he eventually had the support of the King of Spain in so doing. His work *Raisons* (1647) was written in support of Jansenius. Rome misunderstood his views and imposed heavy censures upon him, but these were soon removed (1653).

Bibliography: *Biographie nationale de Belgique* 25:614–624. *Augustiniana* 13 (1963) 56.

[L. CEYSSENS]

TRIEST, PETER JOSEPH

Founder of four religious congregations; b. Brussels, Belgium, Aug. 31, 1760; d. Ghent, June 24, 1836. Triest, the ninth of 14 children, entered Louvain University (1780), then went to the seminary at Malines and was ordained (1789). As a seminarian he was noted for his devotion to the Sacred Heart and great compassion for the needy and sick. Soon after ordination Triest courageously ministered to those stricken in a typhoid epidemic and continued pastoral work during the French occupation, notwithstanding constant danger. In 1803, while a curate at Lovendegem, he founded the Sisters of Charity of Jesus and Mary (Ghent) to teach, and to care for orphans, the aged, and the infirm. In 1807 he founded the Brothers of CHARITY with similar aims. To nurse the sick at home

KANUNNIK P.J. TRIEST 1760-1836

BELGIE BELGIQUE 3 F

Peter Joseph Triest, from Belgian postage stamp.

he instituted the Brothers of St. John of God (1823). He founded also the Sisters of the Holy Childhood for the care and education of foundlings (1835). As a member of the Almshouses' Committee, he came to know intimately the miseries of Belgium's poor and sick after the French Revolution. For three decades he was so much the inspiration of the charitable works in Ghent and throughout the country that he was popularly known as the St. Vincent de Paul of Belgium; on three occasions he received from the king the highest civil decorations.

Bibliography: *P. J. Triest 1760–1960: A Brief Biography,* by a Sister and a Brother of Charity (Ghent 1960). CANON LOONTJENS, *Ontstaan en Spiritualiteit van de Religieuze Stichtingen van Kan. Triest* (Ghent 1961).

[L. C. DE BEUCKELAER]

TRIGAULT, NICOLAS

Jesuit missionary to China and publicist; b. Douai, Belgium, March 3, 1577; d. Hangzhou, China, Nov. 14, 1628. Trigault entered the Society of Jesus at Tournai on Nov. 9, 1594. After completing his studies, he embarked for the Far East (March 1607) and arrived in China shortly after the mission's founder, Matteo RICCI had died (1610). Two years later Ricci's successor, Nicolò Longobardo, dispatched the young missionary to Europe to promote a comprehensive program of Christian expansion. On the way Trigault translated Ricci's Italian memoirs into Latin, *De christiana expeditione apud Sinas,* publication of which in 1615 (with later editions and versions) met with extraordinary success and brought Chinese culture and the Jesuit penetration to the attention of the West. After he reached Rome (Oct. 11, 1614), one of his noteworthy achievements was to obtain from the Holy Office the substitution of literary Chinese for Latin in the Church's mission liturgy (March 26, 1615). To interest the Catholic secular and ecclesiastical princes in the promising China evangelization and to recruit numerous personnel, Trigault made two remarkable propaganda journeys through most of Continental Europe (1615, 1616–17), but opposition at home and the outbreak of persecution in the field hampered fulfillment of his projects. On his return to the Orient (Macau, July 22, 1619), he devoted himself mainly to literary tasks, editing the annual Jesuit relations and translating Chinese classics. In the rites controversy he was an outstanding spokesman for the Ricci interpretation (*see* CHINESE RITES CONTROVERSY), but excessive application to this and his other Sinological pursuits brought on a nervous breakdown that proved fatal.

Bibliography: M. RICCI, *China in the 16th Century,* tr. L. J. GALLAGHER (New York 1953), tr. of Trigault's *De christiana expeditione.* C. DEHAISNES, *Vie du Père Nicolas Trigault* (Tournai 1864), outdated but still useful. L. PFISTER, *Notices biographiques et bibliographiques sur les Jésuites de l'ancienne mission de Chine,* 2 v. (Shanghai 1932–34) 111–120, catalogue and description of T.'s works. E. LAMALLE, ''La Propagande du P. Nicolas Trigault en faveur des missions de Chine, 1616,'' *Archivum Historicum Societas Jesu* 9 (1940) 49–120, based on extensive archival research. *Bibliothèque de la Compagnie de Jésus* 8:237–244.

[F. ROULEAU]

TRINITARIANS

Also known as Holy Trinity Fathers; the Order of the Most Holy Trinity (Ordo Sanctissimae Trinitatis, O.SS.T.; Official Catholic Directory #1310) was founded by (St.) JOHN OF MATHA (d. 1213) and approved by Innocent III in 1198. Because of the lack of records, the early Trinitarian history is surrounded by difficulties. Although (St.) FELIX OF VALOIS has been traditionally considered as cofounder with John of Matha, recent critics have questioned the existence of Felix. Some, however, have sought to identify him with a certain Felix who was the minister (superior) of the Trinitarian house in Marseilles.

The order is dedicated primarily to promoting devotion to the Holy Trinity. In the beginning its unique apostolate was the redemption of Christians held captive by Muslims in Spain, North Africa, and the Near East. Later, the Trinitarians became engaged in teaching, serving in parishes, hospitals, and prisons, ministering to refugees and the homeless, and working for persecuted Christians.

Organization and Rule. The Trinitarians are an exempt MENDICANT ORDER, combining elements of both contemplative and active life. Besides the three solemn vows of poverty, chastity, and obedience, a fourth vow is taken, not to aspire after ecclesiastical dignities. The Trinitarians follow their own rule, which was included in the bull of approbation, Dec. 17, 1198. This rule, influenced by that of the monastery of Saint-Victor in Paris, provided a workable way of life for the friars who were to be both men of activity and men of prayer. Certain relaxations in prayer and fasting were permitted in conformity with the needs of the apostolate. According to this rule nearly all income was divided into three parts, with one third being devoted exclusively to ransoming captives. Although this division was a great aid in financing the redemptions, it proved a severe strain on the resources of the Trinitarians, so that they were not able to afford large libraries or even to further the causes of their members who were eligible for canonization. Although revised somewhat in the reform movement of the late 16th century, the original rule was kept virtually intact, except that the use of sandals was introduced. This rule, which is followed by Trinitarians today, is now supplemented by the revised constitutions of the order.

History. At the time of John of Matha, Muslims in North Africa, Palestine, and sections of Spain, held Christian captives who could be ransomed by individuals, families, or the Christian states. The Trinitarian Order was founded to systematize the ransoming procedure, to solicit the necessary funds and carry them to Muslim ports, and to provide released prisoners with spiritual, physical, and moral rehabilitation. The Trinitarians were one of the first religious orders to combine features of monasticism with an apostolate that was international in scope. The friars traveled extensively on their missions of redemption and thus established houses in most of Europe and in North Africa and Palestine. When John of Matra died in 1213, about 35 Trinitarian foundations had been made.

The order continued to grow in subsequent years, but by the end of the Middle Ages a decline had set in and the 16th century saw various reforms attempted. In France, the reformed Trinitarians, founded in 1578, introduced a strict observance. Later (1766), they separated themselves from the order and took the name Canons

Mosaic depicting Trinitarian seal, 13th century, over main door of Ospedale di S. Tommaso, Formis, Rome.

Regular of the Most Holy Trinity, following the Rule of St. Augustine. This branch became extinct toward the end of the last century. The reform in Spain was led by (Bl.) JOHN BAPTIST OF THE CONCEPTION who, in 1597, founded the Discalced Trinitarians and effected a return to the ancient observance. The influence of his group spread to other countries and in 1636 the discalced became autonomous under their own general superior. Of the three Trinitarian branches thus created—the original or unreformed friars, the French reformed, and the discalced—only the last has survived.

No accurate estimate can be given for the number of captives ransomed from the time of the first redemption in 1199 until the last one in 1855. For the discalced branch alone it is estimated that 9,692 captives were rescued between 1625 and 1855. A comprehensive figure, embracing the work of all the Trinitarians from the beginning, has been estimated to be as high as 140,000 captives ransomed.

American Foundation. Although the order did not appear in the U.S. until 1906, its work was known to Americans before that time. In 1787, Thomas Jefferson, as minister to France, appealed to the Trinitarian minister general to aid in redeeming 21 American seamen held captive by the Dey of Algiers for a ransom of $58,800.

Trinitarian Monastery, Adare, Ireland. (©Dave G. Houser/CORBIS)

The poet John Greenleaf Whittier saw in the work of the Trinitarians a subject for his antislavery polemic and in 1865 published his ballad ''The Mantle of St. John de Matha.''

The American beginnings date from the attempt of an Italian Trinitarian to open a parish in the U.S. in 1906. He was not successful, but five years later another Italian priest arrived, and in 1912 he took charge of a parish in Asbury Park, N.J. When more Trinitarians arrived, a novitiate was established at Bristol, Pa., in 1921. The first American Trinitarian ordained was an African-American convert, Augustine Derricks (d. 1927). The order has since established other parishes, and in 1931 was able to open a house for clerics in Hyattsville, Md., also the site of a new high school for boys in 1946. In 1948 a Diocesan Eucharistic Congress was held at Johnston City, Ill., in honor of the 750th anniversary of the papal approval of the order. The following year the novitiate was moved to Pikesville, Md., where the provincial headquarters and

a junior college are located. In 1950 the American foundations were made a separate province. The U.S. provincialate is in Baltimore, MD; the generalate is in Rome.

Bibliography: P. DESLANDRES, *L'Ordre des Trinitaires pour le rachat des captifs,* 2 v. (Toulouse 1903).

[A. T.WALSH/EDS.]

TRINITY, HOLY, ARTICLES ON

The major article on the Holy Trinity is TRINITY, HOLY. It is immediately followed by TRINITY, HOLY (IN THE BIBLE); TRINITY, HOLY, DEVOTION TO; TRINITY, HOLY, ICONOGRAPHY OF. Other articles take up particular concepts important in Trinitarian theology in general: PERSON, DIVINE; PERSON (IN THEOLOGY); NATURE; RELATIONS, TRINITARIAN; PROCESSIONS, TRINITARIAN; CIRCUMINCESSION; PROPERTIES, DIVINE PERSONAL; ACTS, NOTIONAL; APPROPRIATION; MISSIONS, DIVINE. There are articles on GOD (FATHER) (along with AGENNĒTOS; PATERNITY, DIVINE), GOD (SON) (along with CONSUBSTANTIALITY; FILIATION; GENERATION OF THE WORD; LOGOS; WORD, THE), and GOD (HOLY SPIRIT) (along with SPIRATION). There is a special article on TRINITY, HOLY, CONTROVERSIES ON, as well as individual articles on SUBORDINATIONISM; MODALISM; PATRIPASSIANISM; FILIOQUE, etc. The above list does not include articles on God in general (for which *see* GOD, ARTICLES ON); nor does the list include articles dealing with material ordinarily treated in Christology, for which *see* JESUS CHRIST, ARTICLES ON.

[G. F. LANAVE]

TRINITY, HOLY

Father, Son, and Holy Spirit; the one God in three Persons that is the object of the Christian confession concerning the deity. This article will look at how the doctrine of the Holy Trinity came to be articulated in the early Church, then consider the development of Trinitarian theology, and conclude with an examination of contemporary approaches to this central mystery of the faith.

Gradual Evolution of the Fourth-Century Dogma

It will be convenient first to trace the gradual development of a Trinitarian consciousness from the end of the NT period to the late 4th century and relate this evolution to the elemental Trinitarianism of the primitive sources.

History of doctrine to Constantinople I. If God is one but also three, it follows necessarily that the sense in which He is one differs from the sense in which He is three. Otherwise, there would be in God's self-revelation not only mystery, but contradiction. Historically, however, this is said in retrospect, looking back from the moment when Christian intelligence was at least well on the way toward a Trinitarian solution. But before there could be any question of solution, a Trinitarian problem had first to be put into focus, and even this required time.

To End of 2d Century. Among the Apostolic Fathers, CLEMENT OF ROME, for instance, writing to the Church of Corinth in the final decade of the 1st century, bears witness to God the Father, to the Son, to the Spirit, and mentions all three together (ch. 58, ch. 46). Some few years later, IGNATIUS OF ANTIOCH portrays in a famous passage (*Eph.* 9) the Christian's incorporation into the divine temple as becoming one with Christ in the Spirit unto sonship of the Father. Yet, neither Clement nor Ignatius nor any other writer of this most ancient period raises the question that would turn out to be decisive: precisely how are Son and Spirit related to the Godhead? Before the 2d century

had run its course, however, this question, and with it the Trinitarian problem, began to take form. It happened quite naturally.

With the Apostolic Fathers, Ignatius certainly, the center of gravity in the Christian message had ever been Christ; in this, if O. Cullmann is correct (*The Christology of the New Testament*), they did no more than preserve the authentic rhythm of the New Testament. With their successors, the great Apologists, however, the proclamation of Christ and the defense of the Christian gospel had first to contend with pagan polytheism. The God of the Christian, like the God of the Israelite, was unequivocally one. Nevertheless, if, as Justin notes (1 *Apol.* 13), Christians worship Christ in the second place and the Spirit in the third place, there is still no inconsistency; for Word and Spirit are not to be separated from the unique Godhead of the Father.

But why not? The apologists at least attempted a reply. For Justin, the Godhead was very clearly a *Triad,* though it was Theophilus (*Ad Autol.* 2.15) who first introduced this expression. For Justin, the Word is no less than *something numerically other* (*Dial.* 128) in relation to the Father, and also, though more loosely affirmed (e.g., 1 *Apol.* 60–63), to the Spirit. In the very same passages, however, neither Word nor Spirit, the former more explicitly, are to be separated from the Father, from the being of the Godhead, since both Word and Spirit are God.

To explain how this can be, to give at least an incipiently theological account of how the Word can be one with the Father but still other, Justin pictures the preexistent Word as the Father's rational consciousness (1 *Apol.* 46; 2 *Apol.* 13), as emerging, therefore, from the interiority of the Godhead while nevertheless remaining inseparable from the Godhead. Tatian employs much the same explanatory machinery (*Orat.* 5), likewise Theophilus (*Ad Autol.* 2.10; 2.22). So also does Athenagoras (*Legat.* 10), who extends the imagery to the third member and speaks of the Spirit here as God's effluence.

IRENAEUS, writing at the same time, presents a paradox. This great pastor of souls reflects indeed the theological heavy print of his day, but has far less confidence than the apologists in the mind's ability to explore the Godhead through finite analogies (e.g., *Adversus haereses* 2.28.6). On the other hand, with a better recognition of the Spirit's role in the economy of salvation, and a rather more emphatic insistence on the coeternity of the Word with the Father, it may well be, as J. N. D. Kelly suggests (*Early Christian Doctrines* 107), that Irenaeus's understanding is the most complete, and the most explicitly Trinitarian, before that of Tertullian.

"The Trinity of the Old Testament," icon by Andrea Rublyov. (©Dean Conger/CORBIS)

"Trinity With the Virgin Enthroned," fresco painting by Belisario Corenzio, 16th–17th century. (Archivo Iconografico, S.A./CORBIS)

To Eve of Nicaea I. In the last analysis, the 2d-century theological achievement was limited. The Trinitarian problem may have been clear: the relation of the Son and (at least nebulously) Spirit to the Godhead. But a Trinitarian solution was still in the future. The apologists spoke too haltingly of the Spirit; with a measure of anticipation, one might say too impersonally. The emerging-thought figure as employed by them to explain at once the unity and otherness of Father and Son was little more than suggestive. The device, in fact, closed only partially with the problem of otherness. The Word existed before all creatures. But the Word came forth within the Godhead as the Father's agent with a view to creation. Is the Word's distinct existence, then, unequivocally eternal?

A generation later, however, with Hippolytus of Rome and still more with his African contemporary Tertullian, the image would sharpen, and theological insight into the eternal plurality would make notable advances.

At the same time, to the carry-over from the apologists of the monotheistic emphasis would now be added the dialectical influence of an antipluralist reaction. The net result would be a synthesis of sorts, pointing the way toward the 4th-century dogma.

HIPPOLYTUS, in his refutation of Noetus and the exaggerated identification of Christ with the Father, insists that God was multiple from the beginning. Tertullian, combating the same attitude (*Adv. Prax.* 5), all but explicitly personalizes this eternal multiplicity. The Word stands forth and is other than the Father though still within the Godhead in the manner suggested by human reflection, as internal discourse is in some sense another, a second in addition to oneself, though yet within oneself.

Next, as both theologians, especially TERTULLIAN, shift their focus from the absolutely eternal moment to that in which the divine plurality becomes manifested in creation and redemption, the personalist idiom intensifies, though not without presenting a difficulty. The divine unity, Tertullian writes (*ibid.* 2), is "disposed [distributed] into trinity," the Latin expression *trinitas* being the term Tertullian has now come to use. From the same passage, it is clear that he thinks of the three as three individuals. Elsewhere, to designate the proper and distinct reality of both Son (*ibid.* 7) and Spirit (*ibid.* 11), he introduces the word "Person" explicitly. There is a problem, however. As Kelly (*Early Christian Doctrines* 114) observes, both Hippolytus and Tertullian recognized, on the one hand, that the plurality manifested in the salvific economy reached back, so to speak, into the immanent life of the Godhead. On the other hand, neither would apply at this primordial level the overtly personalist language. In fact, even Tertullian seems to think (*Adv. Hermog.* 3) that God is neither Son nor, in the strictly personal sense, Father until "after" the coming forth of the Word with a view to creation. Side remarks in his treatise against Praxeas show more conclusively still that a concept of truly eternal generation or nativity was not yet current.

Nevertheless, at least for a Trinitarianism of the economy or dispensation, Tertullian's grasp of the sense in which God is one and the sense in which God is three was impressively clear and systematic. On the one hand, against Sabellius's moralism and other extremes of monarchian ("unitarian") perspective (*see* MONARCHIANISM), the distinction is not of mere words, or aspects, or modalities. The Persons differ one from the other really; in fact (*ibid.* 2), they can be enumerated. On the other hand, as the painstaking qualifications in the same passage bring out, there is no tritheism here, no compromising of the divine unity. God is indeed three: in grade or order, in appearance or aspect, but with a realist connotation, and in manifestation; but in substance (granting an indecisiveness in Tertullian's use of the term), in status or condition of being, and in power, God is perfectly one. If (*ibid.* 9) in the Godhead there is distribution, distinction, there is yet no diversity, no division, certainly no separation.

By the middle of the 3d century, as one may see reflected in Novatian's treatise *De Trinitate,* the Roman Church, originally cool toward this stress on otherness and plurality, had come to incorporate Tertullian's main insights. Novatian, moreover, insists (ch. 31) quite frankly on the unequivocal eternity of fatherhood and sonship in the Godhead.

In the East, however, and closer in time of writing to Hippolytus and Tertullian, the theologians of the great school of Alexandria had incorporated a concept of eternal generation, one might say from the start, beginning with Clement (e.g., *Strom.* 7.2.2). ORIGEN, Clement's successor, envisioned the universe of being along Neoplatonist lines of hierarchical extrapolation. At the utterly transcendent apex, there is God the Father (*De princ.* 1.1.6.), alone source without source or, to use Origen's favorite term (e.g., *In Ioan.* 2.10.75), ungenerate (ἀγέννητος). But (*De princ.* 1.2.3) the Father has from all eternity generated a Son, and (*In Ioan.* 2.10.75) through this Son, the Word, He has brought forth the Holy Spirit.

The three, Origen maintains in the same passage, are three distinct individuals or HYPOSTASES. On the other hand (*Frag. in Hebr.*), with explicit reference here to Father and Son, they share together a "community of substance." For the Son, he adds a moment later, is "of the same substance" [HOMOOUSIOS (ὁμοούσιος)] as the Father.

At this point, however, a problem arises, and it sets the stage from a 100 years' distance for the decision at NICAEA I. For if Origen did not fail to include a oneness of substance, his emphasis was nevertheless on the otherness and plurality of the three as really distinct Persons or hypostases. The oneness of substance may even be subordinationist, may indicate that Word and Spirit, while not strictly creatures, are nevertheless separated from the Father by an essential inferiority (*see* SUBORDINATIONISM). For only the Father is "God from Himself" (αὐτόθεος: *In Ioan.* 2.2.17); and in Origen's mind (*C. Cels.* 5.39) Christians rightly refer to the Son as a "secondary" (δεύτερος) deity. Nor is affirmation of coeternity decisive, since Origen (e.g., in *De princ.* 1.2.10) postulated eternal creation. Still, theological idiom in the pre-Nicene period was far from established. Justin, to take but one example, had spoken similarly. The question can always be asked: is this the strictly subordinationist inferiority in quality, so to put it, of being, or merely an inferiority in order, anticipating later and orthodox processionalism?

In any case, the need for clarification soon began to be felt. By the middle of the century, Dionysius of Rome, locked in a controversial exchange with his namesake the bishop of Alexandria, demanded (*apud Athan., De decr. Nic. syn.* 26), and to some extent received (*apud Athan., De sent. Dion.* 14–18), assurances that the Origenist insistence on three hypostases neither implied separation nor compromised coeternity.

Final period: Nicaea I to Constantinople I. On the eve of Nicaea I, the Trinitarian problem raised more than a century earlier was still far from settled. It was the problem of plurality within the single, undivided Godhead. In what sense is God one? In what sense, a necessarily different sense, is God yet three?

The more serious half of the problem, it was now turning out to be, was the first: in what sense is God one? The proper designation of the divine unity had already been suggested: God is one in power, being, and community of substance. On hasty examination, it might appear that the dogmatic formulation arrived at toward the end of the 4th century did little more than sanction these same terms. In the meantime, however, a gap had been closed. With Nicaea I's determination of the divinity of the Son as CONSUBSTANTIALITY with the Father (ὁμοούσιον τῷ πατρί) and the extension by CONSTANTINOPLE I of the device to the divinity of the Spirit, the earlier terms would take on a far greater degree of theological precision. Historically, it was this twofold determination of codivinity that would prove decisive for the formulation of the Trinitarian dogma.

From the logical point of view, it could probably be said that the HERESIES of this time (perhaps of any time?) have as a common note oversimplification: the selection of a single alternative in despair of synthesis. ARIANISM was no exception. The plurality, the real otherness of Father, Son, and Spirit, was considered beyond challenge. But so also was the unique transcendence of God the Father. If Son and Spirit can be called ''God,'' it must be an improper sense; or to put it bluntly, they must be creatures.

The Father alone, Arius argued (*apud Athan., De syn.* 16), up to this point echoing the best Origenist tradition, is ungenerate, source without source, self-existent. Therefore the Father alone is truly eternal, all-wise, all-good. The divine being, moreover, utterly immaterial and indivisible, cannot be communicated. Hence it follows that whatever else has come into existence from this uniquely transcendent source, beginning with the Word, is necessarily made, created. In short, there was when He was not. And if He is yet to be called God (*apud Athan., Or. 1 C. Arian.* 6), this is in the improper, extended sense based on His extraordinary prerogatives of creation and grace.

This speculation was not original. Some of its more blatantly subordinationist features are found, for instance, in Eusebius of Caesarea (e.g., *Dem. evang.* 5.1, 20). But the popularization did much to spread disunity throughout the East and force the decision at Nicaea in 325.

The history of the council, the condemnation of Arius, and the endless controversies that were to follow can only be mentioned here. For what is of immediate pertinence is not the solemn declaration of Christ's unequivocal divinity, but rather the contribution of this decision to the slowly emerging Trinitarian dogma. In this connection, however, the NICENE CREED, preserved in a letter of the reluctant Eusebius (Eng. tr. Hardy, 338), must at least be looked at.

Subordinationist theology as it had come full turn in Arianism identified unbegotten (ungenerate) with self-existent, and emphatically asserted that consequently whatever was generated could not possibly be self-existent, but had to be creature. On this point, the reaction of the Fathers of Nicaea I could not have been more clear. It was the neat antithesis: the Son is indeed begotten, but begotten, not made; He is of the substance of the Father, true God of true God; He is uncreated, eternal, nor was there ever when He was not.

Against the sophisms of subordinationist speculation, the Fathers of the Council of Nicaea insisted that the message of the apostolic revelation, and particularly of the Johannine Prologue, be taken seriously. Yet, they went further. To preclude once and for all the Arian equivocation on the concept of true divinity, they introduced a speculation, an explanatory device, of their own. This was the famous ὁμοούσιον: the Word is truly God in the sense that He is *consubstantial,* that He is of the same substance as the Father. The expression (Tertullian's Latin, Origen's Greek) was not new; but it might just as well have been. For in historical context, with coeternity now unequivocally asserted, all manner of creaturehood definitively excluded, eternal generation firmly established, the term at least took on a far more precise significance and assumed in the process a new pregnancy.

From this juncture until the end of the 4th century, investigation into the origins of the Trinitarian dogma must weave its way through two closely interlocked questions. The first concerns the very meaning of the ὁμοούσιον formula on subjection to further critical and theological analysis. The second, more clearly marked by historical signposts and permitting of merely summary treatment here, refers to the longstanding resistance to the formula among Arians and orthodox alike.

Compared with the imprecision that had gone before, Nicaea I's ''of the same substance'' left little undecided. A difficulty remains, however. Is ''same'' used here in the generic or numerical sense? Is the Word of the same substance as the Father in the way that John is of the same substance as Paul—as both belong to the same species? Or is He of the same substance as the Father in the way that cannot be extended to John and Paul, or to any finite being, the way of simple identity? In terms of objective implication, of course, Nicaea I's ''sharing the same substance'' has to be the latter. The Godhead is not a species, nor a general class admitting distribution among individuals. Unless the Son possessed the entire Godhead, the (quasi-) numerically and identically same Godhead, as the Father, He would not be truly God; and to define His unequivocally true divinity was precisely Nicaea I's purpose. As Kelly (*Early Christian Doctrines* 233–237) argues, however—and he concedes that this is the minority view—it is more than possible that the Fathers of the council were not quite conscious of this implication and were content for the moment to affirm a looser, though still metaphysically serious, substantial oneness. B. Lonergan (*De Deo trino* 1.114) is of the same view, and his care not to overstate the objectively historical evidence at this crucial point is to be borne in mind if his nonetheless highly intellectualist interpretation of the Nicene achievement should give rise to a suspicion of reading a 4th-century text through the eyepiece of a much later scholasticism.

The ὁμοούσιον formula, in any event, and carrying the intention of at least specific identity, encountered so much opposition that more than once in the half century prior to its final reassertion at Constantinople I, in 381, it appeared close to being abandoned. To not a few even among the fiercest anti-Arians, introduction into the confession of faith of a non-biblical device, albeit to articulate a biblically inescapable conclusion, was for a long time unacceptable.

In the ensuing debacle, fortunes alternated, more often as a consequence of political shifts and civil patronage than theological argument. But the doctrinal issues were also clarified. Identity of substance was the emphasis in the formula (*apud Theod., Hist. eccl.* 2.8.37–52) drawn up by the Westerners at Sardica in 342 or 343. A still more theologically precise recognition of the fact that the same one divinity and being of the Father *is* the divinity and being of the Son became the urging of Athanasius (e.g., *C. Arian.* 1.61; 3.6; 3.41). And in his letter promulgating the Alexandrian synod of 362 (*Tom. ad Antioch.* 5, 6), Athanasius not only went far to reconcile conflicting terminologies, but for all practical purposes anticipated the definitive formula of Constantinople I: Father, Son, and Holy Spirit, one in being, three hypostases.

By this time, moreover, the irenic gestures of such avowed supporters of Nicaea I as Athanasius and Hilary of Poitiers toward the great compromise faction known as the Homoiousians had begun to bear results in the direction of a new unity. These men—Meletius of Antioch, Cyril of Jerusalem, Basil of Ancyra—were by no means Arians, but they were dissatisfied with the ὁμοούσιον. Instead of saying that the Son was of the *same* substance (ὁμοούσιον) as the Father, they preferred to say that the Son was of *like* substance (ὁμοιούσιον) to the Father. As Athanasius had the insight (*De syn.* 41) to realize, however, the position, once allowed to explain itself, was basically orthodox. On the other side, as a consequence, reluctance to accept Nicaea I's formula gradually dwindled; in another 20 years, this reluctance to accept the formula would have vanished.

The historian's access to what transpired at Constantinople I in 381 is unfortunately indirect—a summary of its doctrinal tome contained in a synodical letter of the following year, this letter itself preserved by Theodoret (*Hist. eccl.* 5.9.10–13; Eng. tr. Hardy, 343–345). Nicaea I's teaching was in any case solemnly re-enthroned. And this time, against Eunomians, so-called Macedonians, and others, some Arians some not, who made a creature of the Spirit (Pneumatomachians), it extended to define the true divinity of the Third Person as well.

The tome of Constantinople I expressed in sufficiently clear and simple language what would forever afterward stand as the Trinitarian dogma. What the formulation really amounted to was a solution to the problem of plurality within the unique, undivided Godhead. After so long a reflection and contest, the sense in which God is one had become fixed in the Christian consciousness: Father, Son, and Holy Spirit are consubstantial, one Godhead, one power, one substance, of equal dignity and majesty; but in three perfect hypostases or Persons. The other and different sense in which God is yet three had also become fixed by this time, due largely to Athanasius and the Cappadocians.

Further Development and Influence of the Dogma

Subsequent history of trinitarian doctrine. It is in the writings of the Cappadocian Fathers (BASIL, GREGORY OF NAZIANZUS, GREGORY OF NYSSA) that one can see already in motion the ideas of procession, property, and relation around which still further development was going to settle.

Concepts of Procession and the Filioque. The concept of procession was not entirely new. In Jn 8:42, for instance, there is the saying attributed to Jesus according to which He referred to Himself as having proceeded or come forth (ἐξῆλθον) from the Godhead of the Father. Taken in context with the later discourses in the same Fourth Gospel and Jesus' reference to the procession (verb ἐκπορεύεται) of the Paraclete in 15:26, the manner of speaking at least shows the primitive availability of such a concept to grasp the eternal origins of Son and Spirit. To this extent, procession was not the fruit of subsequent reflection, but part of the immediate NT teaching. Nevertheless, the notion would reenter now at a different, rather more technical or theological, level.

The Cappadocians, while defending identity of substance, put their main emphasis on the three distinct hypostases. This element of the composite dogma, moreover, they not merely affirmed, but endeavored to explore in theological understanding. What was distinctive, other, plural, hypostasis or Person in the Deity, the Cappadocians beginning with Basil (e.g., *Adv. Eunom.* 1.19) explained, was not what made Father and Son God, but what made Father precisely Father and Son precisely Son—the properties or marks of identification (ἰδιότητες) peculiar to each, ''ungenerateness'' and ''generateness.'' These properties, as Gregory of Nyssa (*Ad Ablab.* 133M; ed. Jaeger 3.1:55–56) brought out more clearly, were entirely a matter of origin or procession, of the unique way in which the undiminished Godhead was communicated from the Father to both Son and Spirit. In a later day, Thomas Aquinas would discover in a still more refined understanding of *immanent procession* the key, insofar as the human mind is capable of one, for penetrating into the mystery of the divine plurality. But even with the Cappadocians, origin or procession was not simply a statement of the truth of plurality, but an incipient explanation of the how.

Mention should also be made, at least briefly, of the long and painfully divisive controversy over the FILIO-QUE. Gregory of Nyssa, in the passage just cited, had spoken of the Son as proceeding directly from the Father, but of the Holy Spirit as proceeding from the Father through the Son as intermediary. From the Father *through* the Son became the accepted manner of conceiving the procession of the Spirit in the East. But from the Father *and* the Son (filioque) is the formula one sees becoming standard in the Western creeds, beginning at least as far back as the 5th-century *Quicumque* (H. Denzinger, *Enchiridion symbolorum* 75).

To Photius in the late 9th century, and to like-minded theologians of the East rather generally for several centuries following, filioque was a heretical addition splitting the second Trinitarian procession into two. Western theologians, however, felt that the Greek intention (if not words) was actually to exclude the Son and conceive the Spirit's procession as from the Father alone. At the two famous Councils of reunion, Lyons II (cf. *ibid.* 850) in 1274 and Florence (cf. bull *Laetentur caeli, ibid.* 1300–02) in 1439, an attempt was made to heal the wound, one side accepting filioque, the other concurring in explicit rejection of the split feared by Photius and in affirmation of the utter oneness of the Spirit's procession: from the Father and the Son, but as from a single source. Unfortunately, however, theological misunderstanding was neither the only nor the greatest obstacle to a lasting reunion.

Property and Relation. The concepts of property and relation rounded out Trinitarian doctrine. The dominating influence of the 4th-century dogma on later Trinitarian-ism is quickly recognizable in the fact that all subsequent doctrinal articulations of the triadic mystery were aimed at amplification and understanding precisely of the dogma ''one God in three Persons,'' and not of other elements in the Father-Son-Spirit revelation. The only serious exceptions would be the doctrine of the filioque just mentioned, and perhaps, but only with qualification, the doctrine of the missions to be discussed later in this article.

God is one in substance or being, three in Person or hypostasis. But why is this not a contradiction? The ''answer,'' the explanation eventually assimilated into Christian life and teaching and affixed, so to speak, to the dogma, was that whatever is distinct, other, personal in the Godhead is exclusively *proper* and *relative*. As noted above, this explanation was already operative in the Trinitarianism of the Cappadocians. It was, moreover, at least vaguely implicit in the decision of Constantinople I; otherwise, there would have been no point to the substance-Person distinction upon which the council's dogmatic formula pivots.

The divinity of the Son, as ATHANASIUS (*Or. 3 c. Arian.* 4) had written earlier, is the divinity of the Father, one and indivisible. Son differs from Father, therefore, not as God, but as He who is begotten, In Athanasius' thought, this is the only thing *special* about the Son. And on the other side, everything that can be said of the Father can be said also of the Son, the name Father alone excepted. For this name and what it implies is the only thing *special* about the Father. To differ from another as a distinct Divine Person, then, means to differ only in what is peculiar to oneself as being either the source from whom another originates (Father), or the one who originates (Son). With the Cappadocians, as already noted, the same line of reasoning was continued and extended. Thus came into being the doctrine of *relative properties* to explain in some measure the noncontradictory plurality of Persons in the one unique Godhead.

In the West, however, during roughly the first two decades of the 5th century, AUGUSTINE was putting together the treatise on the Trinity that was destined to control Trinitarian theology from then until the time of Aquinas. But this would seem to be the place to introduce an important observation. As elemental Trinitarianism of the NT period has to be distinguished carefully from the gradually emerging Trinitarian dogma, so must Trinitarian dogma (doctrine in the strictest sense) be distinguished carefully from Trinitarian theology. The dogma in its preparatory stages had been merely theology: efforts on the part of individuals and schools to interpret and understand revealed mystery. Then, as certain of these efforts became assimilated through authoritative decision into the teaching of the Church, some of what had heretofore been theology was from now on also DOGMA of faith. But note *some,* for much else—in Tertullian and Origen, Athanasius and the Cappadocians, Augustine, Anselm, Aquinas—would never receive such ratification, never attain such clear-cut status as Christian doctrine.

In the present account, it is not possible to examine minutely each point of Christian Trinitarianism and determine precisely what is dogma of faith, what is Church teaching in a lesser or modified sense, what deserves at least peculiar reverence as patristic tradition, what is verifiably a so-called theological consensus implying a measure of authoritative sanction, and what is, on the other hand, only theological understanding and synthesis. A good beginning, however, would be to look briefly at some of the creedal formulas extending from the late 4th century to the 15th century. In these formulas, one can see reflected assimilation into Church teaching of at least the basic features of the theology of property and relation as developed in the East by the Cappadocians and in the West by Augustine.

The doctrinal tome of Constantinople I in 381 had already declared against the Sabellian tendency to take away from the three Persons their distinguishing properties (ἰδιότητες). The language of the 5th-century *Quicumque* (H. Denzinger, *Enchiridion symbolorum* 75), and the 5th- or 6th-century *Clemens Trinitas* (*ibid.* 73), is at least suggestive of similar doctrinal consciousness. Letters of three 6th-century pontiffs, Hormisdas (*Inter ea quae. ibid.* 367), Vigilius (*Dum in sanctae, ibid.* 412–415), and Pelagius I (*Humani generis, ibid.* 441), explicitly inculcate the doctrine of personal distinction through personal properties. So likewise does the Trinitarian Preface of the Roman Missal, though this possibly 7th-century creation is not strictly a creedal formula. All of these documents at least infer, moreover, that what is significant about the personal property is the element of the relative. What is proper or characteristic of each Person is simply and exclusively the relationship each bears to the others in terms of eternal origin.

In 1215, the fourth LATERAN COUNCIL (*ibid.* 800) solemnly ratified the doctrine of personal properties. At the Council of Florence in 1442, in the bull *Cantate Domino* (*ibid.* 1330), the ratification was extended to the doctrine of relations. This did not mean, of course, that the entire and complex scholastic theology of the Trinitarian relations was incorporated into official Church teaching. It meant only that sanction was now given at least to the Anselmian dictum (*De proc. Sp. Sanc.* 1; ed. Schmitt 2:181) to the effect that whatever is other, distinct, plural, personal, and proper in the Godhead is exclusively a matter of relationship. Father, Son, and Spirit do not differ

as God, but in the way each is God with respect to the others. Each has and is the divine nature, but each has it differently: the Father from Himself, the Son from the Father, the Spirit from both the Father and the Son. God, then, is one in substance, three in Person; and what is significant about this distinction, what makes it noncontradictory, is that what is personal in the Godhead is not something absolute, but something purely relative.

Further exploration, synthesis of Aquinas. Space does not permit even a survey coverage of Trinitarian speculation and explanatory theory. And if a selection has to be made, there are good reasons why it should be in favor of the Thomist synthesis. First, this is the particular theological tradition that has been most influential until comparatively modern times. Second, this tradition continues to be spoken for by some leading contemporary theologians; hence it is the tradition most immediately involved in tension with today's return-to-the-sources movement mentioned at the beginning of this article.

In several respects, including the very ideal of theological understanding, it was Augustinian Trinitarianism that lighted the way for Aquinas's achievement. For Augustine, as even the introductory first two chapters of *De Trinitate* make evident, the starting place in Trinitarian theology is not the Father exactly, but the divine nature or essence. It is the very nature of God to be triune. Thomas will maintain and extend the same perspective. Again, to penetrate in some limited way into the mystery of this triune essence, Augustine (*ibid.* 9, 10, 14) appealed to ANALOGIES drawn from the spiritual operations of the human mind. With significant differences in the precise points of comparison, this too would become an essential feature, in fact *the* essential feature, of the Thomist synthesis.

Early in his career (*In Boeth. de Trin.* 1, 2, 6), Aquinas laid out the canons of his own ideal of rational or scientific theology. The object was not to demonstrate the truths of faith—he considered this impossible—nor even to corroborate what was known and had to be known only from revelation by means of some sort of purely rational flashback (the truth had to be revealed, but reason can then show that it is what one should have expected all along). The object was rather to accept the truths of faith, and with these same truths as basic premises, to discover what human intelligence, enlightened by faith, might conclude as to their further understanding.

Book 4 of *C. gent,* applies this ideal to the mystery of the Trinity. Aquinas begins with what he considers the biblical proclamation of generation, paternity, and sonship in God. But, he asks, how is this to be taken? How is it to be understood? Chapters 4 to 9 examine and reject all the classical heterodox understandings. Then in chapter 11 he offers what he believes to be the only under-standing of the matter reconcilable with revealed truth.

The Son is born of the Father, generated. The Son's eternal origin, therefore, is a mode of emanation, or com-ing forth. But is there in the universe of creatures, Aqui-nas asks, any comparison or analogy that might give some glimmer of understanding of this emanation? In the material, vegetable, and sensory worlds, really no. In the sphere of intellectual activity, however, yes. Men can and do think of their own minds; and when the human intel-lect reflects upon itself, understands itself, there comes forth within the intellect, in consequence of the act of un-derstanding, the concept or interior conceptualization of the intellect itself so understood. This, moreover, is the only type of generation or coming forth that is possible in the immaterial and infinite Godhead. As God under-stands Himself, there issues forth from *God Understand-ing* (the Father) *God Understood* (the Son). In terms of this psychological analogy, then, the three Persons are both immanent to the undivided Godhead and yet distinct as Persons—as *God Understood in God Understanding,* and as *God Beloved* (the Spirit, ch. 19) in *God Loving* (the Father and the Son as single source).

In Aquinas's theology, the ultimate reason, insofar as the mind is capable of determining one, for the divine plurality is immanent procession. The divine essence is utterly simple and immutable; nevertheless, theological understanding, guided by faith at every step of its analy-sis, is led to postulate in the divine essence the twofold activity and twofold procession of intellect and love. For such, the generalization can now (*Summa theologiae* 1a, 27.1) be made, is of the very nature of spiritual being, be-ginning with God Himself.

In *Summa theologiae* 1a, 27–43, then, St. THOMAS sets out to restructure and coordinate all the elements of Trinitarian revelation, doctrine, and theology in an im-pressively unified synthesis at the apex of which stands precisely this theological generalization. It is not that from this universal principle of immanent procession in spiritual reality, he will deduce the relations, the three distinct Persons, their terrestrial manifestation and activi-ty in the missions of Son and Spirit; it is rather that by understanding the total revelation as expanding from this principle and quasi-cause, he will attempt to give to the Trinitarian mystery some true measure of intelligent order and understanding. There is, first of all, procession in the Godhead; concretely, the two processions of intel-lect and love. Upon these two processions are grounded the real and subsistent relations. Finally, it is these subsis-tent relations that constitute the three distinct Persons, the three Persons whose salvific activity in the world of men is manifested through the Incarnation of the Son and the imparting of the Spirit.

In this way, the Trinitarian synthesis of the *Summa* returns to what had been immediate in the NT message. The detailed exposition of this message would occupy Thomas the theologian as Thomas the prolific biblical commentator. The movement of Aquinas's thought, therefore, is not further and further away from the sources of revelation. The movement is circular: from the sources through analysis to synthesis; then back again to the sources for a second and more theologically enlightened assimilation. Imitations of the Thomist approach, howev-er, would tend more and more to forget this all-important return. Today, and partly as a consequence, even the suc-cessful imitation is apt to be received with impatience.

Contemporary Approaches

Recent theology has attempted to recoup the doctrine of the Trinity, especially by adverting anew to its charac-ter as a mystery of salvation. Previously, the doctrine re-tained its august role in Christian thought but was handed on in an unquestioned way in a spirit of dogmatism, i.e., in terms of the dogmatic formula "three persons of one divine substance." The dogma expressed in propositional form overshadowed the revelation that was its source and whence came its salvific relevance for Christian life. Par-adoxically, this issued in both a fideism that confessed the doctrine in an unexamined way and a rationalism that de-ployed it as offering grounds for other beliefs logically derived from it. By the time of Friedrich Schleiermacher (d. 1834), the doctrine had been reduced to a mere appen-dix in his *The Christian Faith,* and Kant was able to re-mark that from it "taken literally, nothing whatsoever can be gained for practical purposes, even if one believed that one comprehended it."

Neo-modalism. After centuries of benign neglect, a new beginning was made to restore the doctrine to its tra-ditional place of primacy by the Reformed theologian Karl BARTH (d. 1968) in his *Church Dogmatics,* and on the Catholic side by Karl RAHNER (d. 1984). Barth con-ceived of God as event, that event which is revelation, whose very structure in turn is trinitarian: God is the sub-ject (Father), the content (Son), and the very happening (Spirit) of revelation. Rahner's version of this same in-sight conceives God as self-communicating and is encap-sulated in his axiom "the economic Trinity *is* the immanent Trinity." A major reservation on this achieve-ment is that it allows a *concept* of revelation to determine the understanding of God's inner reality. Its lasting gain, however, was in establishing that faith in God as a trinity was grounded in Christology, and not vice versa. Conse-quently, the point of departure for understanding God as triune is only the economy of salvation.

Rahner's axiom is misunderstood, however, if it be taken to imply an absolute identity, i.e., one that would reduce the immanent Trinity to the economic Trinity, or allow that the former could be deduced from the latter. What it does make clear is that in the historical Jesus, God Himself is present in the world as he is in His own inner divine reality; the immanent Trinity is present in a new way *in* the economy and not merely *behind* it. Still, the Barthian/Rahnerian approach seemingly reintroduces a modalistic understanding of the Trinity. God is ultimately grasped as uni-personal; the plural term ''persons'' (Greek: *hypostases*) in the confessional formula signifies ''three distinct modes of existing'' (Barth), or ''three distinct modes of subsisting'' (Rahner), of the one Godhead.

Neo-economic trinitarianism. Building on the works of Barth and Rahner, subsequent thinkers sought an advance over their implicit neo-modalism by moving beyond theories of revelation to the concrete historical events themselves as recounted in the New Testament. Eberhard Jüngel pioneered this approach—in which it is maintained that history ultimately is our history with God and His history with us—with the thesis that ''God's being is in becoming.'' The becoming in question is not that of a transition from potency to act within divinity, whereby God, in dependence upon the world, acquires something previously lacking to Him. But it does mean that God's being is intrinsically oriented to the world and involves His entrance into the order of temporality. Traditional notions of divine immutability and eternity are thus displaced in favor of God's self-revelation by way of a self-reiteration that is precisely the trinitarian event. This grounds God's being-for-us in God's being-for-himself. The ontological locus of God's being is thus in becoming, so that there is ''no being of God in-and-for-itself without man.'' There is no *Logos asarkos* in God, no Word other than the enfleshed Word; there is no *Pneuma* other than the Spirit at work in the community of believers. Incarnation and Pentecost constitute the *history* of God, i.e., His coming to man; the doctrine of the inner-divine Trinity constitutes God's *historicality,* i.e., His ''Being-in-coming.'' For Jüngel, the inner structure of God's being as a Trinity makes His relationship to time and humanity something intrinsic and essential to him. At the same time, Jüngel insists that God remains ontologically independent of the temporal order; in the inner divine processions God comes forth eternally from God. But God freely wills that this not be otherwise than in virtue of His coming into humankind's history. The Christian God cannot be conceived then except as Trinity, which means He cannot be conceived of apart from humanity. This in turn renders man intrinsic to the definition of God as He has manifested Himself in revelation. The unresolved problem that remains, however, is whether this explanation does not compromise God's freedom in choosing to become man.

This understanding of the Trinity was further radicalized by Jürgen Moltmann. Arguing that faith in God cannot be vindicated until the Eschaton, he contends that the focus of history is the Cross of Jesus, which means that God is with us in our suffering. That event, the death of God, is to be interpreted in a strictly trinitarian way. It is an inner-trinitarian mystery that transpires not between God and man but between God and God. The Father suffers in abandoning His Son, and the Son suffers that abandonment by the Father. Thus the Cross differentiates the Father and the Son eternally within the Godhead, but in function of the economy of salvation. This ''separation'' is then overcome by the Holy Spirit, who reunites Father and Son in raising Christ from the dead, and (because Christ has become one with all mankind in the Incarnation) brings back alienated humanity to the Father.

God thus enacts Himself, i.e., comes to the fullness of His divinity, in relationship to the world. This is not because God by nature needs the world over which He ever exercises sovereignty, but solely because out of uncreated love He chooses in absolute freedom to need the world in coming to Himself. He chooses not to be God apart from humankind: ''He does not will to be Himself in any other way than He is in this relationship [to mankind]'' (Jüngel, *The Doctrine of the Trinity,* 67). Moltmann calls the sending of the *Logos* (in creation and in the death on the Cross) ''seeking love'' and the sending of the *Pneuma* (in resurrection and sanctification) ''gathering love.'' God's reality is thus a trinitarian history, and the resurrection of Jesus is not the terminus of this history but its mid-point as a promise of what is to come in the future. What logically follows from this is that the consummation of the missions of Son and Spirit (when all is handed over to the Father in the achievement of the Kingdom) is not only the fulfillment of earthly history but simultaneously of that history constituting deity. God acquires something new, then, in the consummation of history which is ultimately an inner-trinitarian fulfillment. Traditional notions of divine immutability are thus jettisoned in favor of a panentheism in which God enters into composition with, and so dependence upon, creatures.

What is pivotal in Moltmann's thought, however, is that this is not something ontologically necessitated by God's nature but something freely willed by Him on no other motive than His uncreated love, which takes the suffering of the creature upon Himself to overcome it by transforming it within Himself. Operative here is an understanding of love as a freely chosen vulnerability to the evils that oppress the beloved. Only God offers a final answer to innocent suffering, but that awaits the Eschaton when God's sovereignty will assert itself—for now, His love demands a self-effacing impoverishment. But it can be asked in what sense God remains God if His will to create implies His being conditioned by the world and so diminished in His own being and Lordship. Creaturely love, of course, in its finitude is ultimately impotent in its attempts to overcome the suffering of the beloved and can only in the final analysis assume vicariously the evil by sharing it in genuine compassion. But is this true of uncreated love? If so, does it not call into question the truly redemptive power of divine love, and God's genuine lordship over evil? Christian theology has traditionally identified God's omnipotence precisely as love; it is because God is transcendent to evil (and thus ontically immune to suffering) that He is able to overcome it. Moltmann's thought is not entirely free of the implication that ultimately God himself is responsible for evil, and second that His transformation of it is part of a process of self-actualization.

Hans Urs von BALTHASAR represents a modified version of Moltmann's trinitarian thought from a Catholic standpoint. His strong endorsement of the doctrine of pre-existence safeguards him from introducing temporality into the Godhead and collapsing the immanent Trinity into the economic Trinity as Moltmann appears to do. Yet the identity of the Second Person in God is that of Son, of a filial relationship of obedience to the Father. And in the Incarnation, the humanity assumed is that of a sinful, alienated humanity. The suffering on the cross—caused by the evil already unleashed in the world by men and nowise attributable to God—is Jesus' obedience to the Father seeking to reconcile mankind to himself. As such, it is a reflection of the eternal Sonship within the Trinity. The temporal event of the Cross is in this sense a "separation" of Father and Son in the economy—a "separation," however, that is intelligible only in the context of their mutual love who is the Holy Spirit, the spirit who raises Jesus from the dead, thereby reuniting mankind and God.

Trinity as community. A quite different development begins with plurality in God as a given, simply confessing the Three who are revealed in the New Testament as there for us in the economy of salvation, and conceiving of them as relatively autonomous centers of divine consciousness. Initial probings in this direction came from Heribert Mühlen, who sought to exploit the "discourse situation" rooted in man's linguisticality as an analogy for understanding the Trinity in which the divine Persons are seen as constituting an "I-Thou-We" relationship. Later thinkers construed the unity, which is the divine nature, as logically subsequent to the Persons and constituted by their mutual self-surrender.

This trinitarian concept of the divine Persons as three independent subjects (which owes much to Hegel) does away with any notion of the divine unity as numerical in favor of an organic unity that results from "the co-workings of the three divine subjects" (Moltmann). Clearly, this is a social model of the Trinity, which unavoidably runs the risk of tritheism. Father, Son, and Spirit are three "non-interchangeable subjects" whose unity is rooted, not in an identity of substance, but in a common history. Moltmann appears to view traditional monotheism as inimical to trinitarianism, even suggesting that the former gives theological warrant to totalitarianism in the political order. Joseph Bracken argues boldly that the Persons "possess separate consciousnesses which nevertheless together form a single shared consciousness" (*The Triune Symbol,* 25). This extreme view should not be confused with the position that argues for three relatively distinct centers of a *single* divine consciousness identical with the one divine substance (cf. W. Hill, *The Three-Personed God* 1982). Bernard de Margerie (*The Christian Trinity in History* 1982) attempted to rehabilitate the familial model in which father/mother/child is seen as remotely analogous to Father/Son/Spirit (an analogy rejected by both Augustine and Aquinas on the grounds that then the individual would image, not the Trinity, but one of the divine Persons) by exploiting the value given to intersubjectivity in contemporary thought. This led him to explore also the ecclesial model in which baptismal generation is seen as analogous to the procession of the Word and communion of the faithful in love is analogous to the procession of the Spirit. In this ecclesial model "the reciprocal immanence of the Christians who are equal among themselves is the analogical image of the circuminsession of the divine Persons" (p. 295). Following the lead of Bernard LONERGAN, the psychological model, which remains basically *intra*subjective in Augustine and Aquinas, is recast by De Margerie in a psycho-social context and thereby given an *inter*subjective dimension.

"Persons" in God. Wolfhart Pannenberg has also called for reconceiving the meaning of "person" as predicated of God, and thus as a trinitarian category. He opposes any analogical transfer of human personality onto the divine where it becomes (as in the atheist claim) a mere anthropomorphic projection. An analogical transference of the I-Thou relationship between fellow humans to the relationship between God and man would attribute personhood to God only in a mythic sense. Rather, a religiously determined experience of reality issues in a conception of God, not as the ground of the cosmos, but as the free origin of contingent events. It is these events, in their contingency and non-manipulatableness, that are perceived as personal acts and explain how the power that determines all reality can be thought of as a person. Human personhood is derivative from this.

The trinitarian implication of this is that the unity and distinction between Jesus and the Father, which is personal, is established historically. But that relationship belongs as such to the divinity of God. The concern here is not with the relationship between divinity and humanity in Christ but with that between the Father and Jesus as His Word of revelation, which occurs as a dialectic within history. Jesus is thus no longer the preexistent *Logos* existing as a distinct hypostasis alongside the Father. As for the Spirit, He "shows himself to be personal reality by not extinguishing the personal character of human action through his activity" (*Jesus, God and Man,* 177). He is not to be conceived as a third preexistent and distinct hypostasis in God. Indeed, one cannot claim "a similar personal uniqueness for the Spirit from the personal uniqueness of the Son" (*ibid.,* 178).

Process trinitarianism. Attempts to adapt the philosophy of Alfred Whitehead with its markedly panentheistic world view in which God and world are correlates, each existing in dependence on the other, to Christian theology by such thinkers as Charles Hartshorne, John Cobb, Shubert Ogden, Lewis Ford, Langdon Gilkey, and a host of others, seemingly reduces the Trinity to a Dyad; trinitarianism becomes binitarianism. Here, God's being is at once absolute and relative, and this dipolarity prevails over the Christian notion of triunity.

Father is a symbol for God in His absoluteness; *Logos* and *Pneuma* rather express two distinct modes of His relationality to the cosmos. God is named Father as in His primordial nature He lures the world forward, making available to it values otherwise inaccessible. *Logos* symbolizes God as He is present within Jesus, supplying him with special initial aims so that He re-presents objectively God's purposes for the world. Jesus prehends not only these initial aims but their divine origin as well and that prehension forms the very center of His consciousness, constituting his unique personhood, on which basis He is called the Son of God. *Pneuma* conveys God's universal immanence in all actual entities, His direct relation to, and so presence in, everything—operative in a non-coercive way in the structures of both nature and history.

Filioque. Little progress of any efficacious kind has been made recently in resolving the question of whether the Holy Spirit proceeds from the Father alone as maintained in the Orthodox Church of the East, or from the Father "and the Son" (*FILIOQUE*) as professed in Christianity in the West. This seemingly minor doctrinal difference—originating in the different approaches of the Cappadaocians and Augustine in the late 4th and early 5th centuries, developing into bitter controversy with Photius in the 9th century, and assuming the formal status

of a schism in the 11th century—actually articulates major differences in soteriology and ecclesiology but especially in the concept of deity itself. In 1978, the Commission on Faith and Order of the World Council of Churches addressed the question at a conference of Eastern and Western theologians convened just outside Strasbourg, France. At its conclusion, two proposals were advanced: first, the *Filioque* was to be dropped from the official Nicene-Constantinople Creed because this had been added in the West without the acquiesence of the Eastern Churches for whom the clause continued to cause deep offense; second, this was not to be understood as an abandonment of the filioquist theology in favor of Eastern trinitarianism. Instead, the real intent of the *Filioque* was to be retained, namely that the Spirit was also the Spirit of Christ. This was to be secured with the formula that "the Spirit proceeds from the Father alone who is already the Father of the Son." This grants to the Son a role in the procession of the Spirit from the Father, one that cannot be understood only in terms of the temporal mission of the Spirit.

Some clarification of the theological difficulties that remain has come from disseminating the ideas of the renowned Orthodox theologian Paul Evdokimov (d. 1970). He has suggested that what is to be sought ecumenically is a unity of the three Churches (Catholic, Orthodox, and Protestant) that reflects the plurality within unity of the three divine Persons, a unity without confusion or subordination (*L'Esprit saint dans la tradition orthodoxe,* 111). Moreover, he sees the *Filioque* as entailing also a doctrine of *Spirituque* in which the Spirit plays a role in the generation of the Son—not only in the economy of salvation but within the immanent Trinity. This latter understanding is possible only if the relations between the divine Three are non-causal in kind. Undergirding this is the famous distinction of Gregory PALAMAS (d. 1359) between the divine essence and the uncreated divine "energies." The former cannot be shared by creatures, whereas the latter can because they are communicated hypostatically, i.e., they involve communion with God on the level of the threefold personhood. Obviously, the communion achieved here is not substantial as in the Incarnation but accidental as in sanctification by grace.

Pneumatology. Other developments have centered on recovering the forgotten Person, the Holy Spirit. Emphasis has shifted in soteriology from created grace to the gift of the Holy Spirit as co-founder of the Church (Yves Congar). Some theological speculation wishes to recognize the Spirit as the "person" of the believing community analogous to the way in which the Word is the person of Jesus' humanity (Heribert Mühlen). By this is meant something more than is conveyed in the doctrine of "appropriation"; indwelling the souls of the just is proper to the Spirit in his role, and indeed his hypostatic identity, as unitive love within the Trinity.

Last may be noted an increased recourse to the doctrine of the Trinity in ecumenical discussions on world religions, where the Trinity is "the juncture where the authentic spiritual dimensions of all religions meet" (Raimundo Panikkar). The Christian symbol of Father finds some resonance in the apophatic Absolute of Buddhism; that of Word is not entirely alien to the kataphatic God of Israel and Islam; and Spirit bespeaks some approximation to the All that is immanent in everything of Hinduism.

See Also: GOD, ARTICLES ON; TRINITY, HOLY, ARTICLES ON; TRINITARIAN CONTROVERSY; GOD (FATHER); PATERNITY, DIVINE; GOD (SON); WORD, THE; LOGOS; GENERATION OF THE WORD; GOD (HOLY SPIRIT); ACTS, NOTIONAL; CIRCUMINCESSION; MISSIONS, DIVINE; NATURE; PERSON (IN THEOLOGY); PERSON, DIVINE; PROCESSIONS, TRINITARIAN; PROPERTIES, DIVINE PERSONAL; RELATIONS, TRINITARIAN; SABELLIANISM.

Bibliography: Evolution of 4th-century dogma: history. G. BARDY, *Dictionnaire de théologie catholique,* ed. A. VACANT (Paris 1903–50) 15.2:1545–1702, still useful for systematically complete coverage; bibliog. 1699–1702 includes all important studies prior to 1939. H. DE LAVALETTE et al., *Lexikon für Theologie und Kirche,* ed. J. HOFER and K. RAHNER (Freiburg 1957–65) 3:543–560, a more recent but much briefer account of the hist. development. P. HUGHES, *The Church in Crisis* (Garden City, N.Y. 1961) and his more satisfactory *A History of the Church* (New York, v. 1–2, rev. 1949; v. 3, rev. 1947); v. 1 provides introd. hist. background. J. N. D. KELLY, *Early Christian Doctrines* (2d ed. New York 1960), a detailed account of the gradually emerging dogma. B. LONERGAN, *De Deo trino,* v. 1 (new ed. Rome 1964), presents the same material as Kelly in a more synthetically interpretative fashion. Many of Lonergan's central insights, in addition to the author's own, can be seen reflected in J. C. MURRAY, *The Problem of God* (New Haven, Conn. 1964) 31–76. B. ALTANER, *Patrology* (New York 1960) in notations on Fathers and documents of the early period, mentions what is of Trinitarian significance, supplying extensive references to the best texts and studies. Evolution of 4th-century dogma: question of continuity. On the pertinent material from the investigation of the primitive creedal forms, V. H. NEUFELD, *The Earliest Christian Confessions* (Grand Rapids 1963), with full bibliog. for the field. C. H. DODD, *The Apostolic Preaching and Its Developments* (London 1936; repr. 1963). O. CULLMANN, "Les Premières confessions de foi chrétiennes," *La Foi et le culte de l'église primitive* (Paris 1943; repr. 1963). J. N. D. KELLY, *Early Christian Creeds* (2d ed. New York 1960). On the theory of doctrinal development with respect to the primitive sources in this area, J. H. NEWMAN, *An Essay on the Development of Christian Doctrine,* ed. C. F. HARROLD (New York 1949); more recently, K. RAHNER, "The Development of Dogma," *Theological Investigations,* tr. C. ERNST, v. 1. (Baltimore, Md. 1961) 39–77. B. LONERGAN, *De Deo trino,* v. 2 (3d ed. Rome 1964) 7–64. From the perspective of biblical theology, A. W. WAINWRIGHT, *The Trinity in the New Testament* (Society for Promoting Christian Knowledge, London 1962). By way of important tangential comment, O. CULLMANN, *The Christology of the N. T.,* tr. S. C. GUTHRIE and C. A. M. HALL (rev. ed. Philadelphia, Pa. 1963). Further development and influence: subsequent history. A. MICHEL, *Dictionnaire de théologie catholique,* ed. A. VACANT (Paris 1903–50) 15.2:1702–1830, treats the early period from the focus of prescholastic Trinitarian theology. B. LONERGAN, *De Deo trino* (3d ed. Rome 1964) 1:178–215, analyzes the doctrinal development of properties and relations. Further development and influence: explorations, synthesis of Aquinas. For Augustine's specific contribution to the scholastic Trinitarian synthesis, reference is still made to M. SCHMAUS, *Die psychologische Trinitätslehre des hl. Augustinus* (Münster 1927). H. PAISSAC, *Théologie du Verbe: Saint Augustin et saint Thomas* (Paris 1951). For Anselm's role in the same tradition, R. PERINO, *La dottrina trinitaria di Sant'Anselmo* (Rome 1952). C. VAGAGGINI, "La Hantise des *rationes necessariae* de saint Anselme dans la théologie des processions trinitaires de saint Thomas," *Spicilegium Beccense* (Paris 1959) 103–139. For the Trinitarian theology of Aquinas, R. RICHARD, *The Problem of an Apologetical Perspective in the Trinitarian Theology of St. Thomas Aquinas* (Rome 1963), a different interpretation from Vagaggini's, perhaps useful as restating in Eng. the main lines of the Thomist Trinitarian synthesis. More thorough is *B.* LONERGAN *De Deo trino* (3d ed. Rome 1964) v. 2. Also valuable, P. VANIER, *Théologie trinitaire chez saint Thomas d'Aquin* (Montreal 1953). G. EMERY, *La Trinité créatrice: Trinité et création dans les commentaires aux Sentences de Thomas d'Aquin et de ses précurseurs Albert le Grand et Bonaventure* (Paris 1995). On the missions, B. LONERGAN, *De Deo trino* (3d ed. Rome 1964) 2:216–258. Contemporary approaches. K. RAHNER, "Bemerkungen zum dogmatischen Traktat *De Trinitate,*" *Schriften zur Theologie* (Einsiedeln 1954—) 4:103–133. W. J. HILL, *The Three-Personed God* (Washington, D.C. 1982). B. DE MARGERIE, *The Christian Trinity in History* (Still River, Mass. 1982). E. JÜNGEL, *The Doctrine of the Trinity* (Grand Rapids, Mich. 1976). J. MOLTMANN, *The Trinity and the Kingdom* (San Francisco 1981). J. J. O'DONNELL, *Trinity and Temporality* (Oxford 1983). J. A. BRACKEN, *The Triune Identity* (Philadelphia, Pa. 1982). G. H. TAVARD, *The Vision of the Trinity* (Lanham, Md. 1981). W. KASPER, *The God of Jesus Christ* (New York 1984). D. BROWN, *The Divine Trinity* (LaSalle, Ill. 1985). K. RAHNER, *The Trinity* (New York 1970). H. U. VON BALTHASAR and A. GRILLMEIER, "Le Mystère Pascal," *Mysterium Salutis,* v. 12 (Paris 1972). H. MÜHLEN, *Der Heilige Geist als Person* (2d ed. Münster 1966). W. PANNENBERG, "Die Subjektivität Gottes und die Trinitätslehre," *Kerygma und Dogma* 23 (1977) 199–213. R. PANIKKAR, *The Trinity and the Religious Experience of Man* (New York 1973). G. O'COLLINS, *The Tripersonal God: Understanding and Interpreting the Trinity* (New York 1999). C. LACUGNA, *God for Us: The Trinity and Christian Life* (San Francisco, Cal. 1991). E. JOHNSON, *She Who Is* (New York 1993). D. COFFEY, *Deus Trinitas: The Doctrine of the Triune God* (New York 2000).

[R. L. RICHARD/W. J. HILL/EDS.]

TRINITY, HOLY (IN THE BIBLE)

In a long tradition with roots in the early patristic period, Christian writers have identified certain revelations of God in the Old Testament (OT) as containing representations or foreshadowings of the Trinity. In the strict sense, however, God is not explicitly revealed as Trinity in the OT. In the New Testament (NT) the oldest evidence of this revelation is in the Pauline epistles, especially 2 Cor 13.13, and 1 Cor 12.4–6. In the Gospels much of the evidence of the Trinity has to do with the revelation of the relation between the Father and the Son. The only direct statement of Trinitarian revelation is the baptismal formula of Mt 28.19.

In the Old Testament. On account of the polytheistic religions of Israel's pagan neighbors, it was necessary for the teachers of Israel to stress the oneness of God. In many places of the OT, however, expressions are used in which some of the Fathers of the Church saw references or foreshadowings of the Trinity. The personified use of such terms as the Word of God [Ps 32(33).6] and the SPIRIT OF GOD (Is 63.14) reflects poetic license, though it does show a sense for a self-communication of God to the world in which the divine force is distinct from God, is not part of the world, and is not a being intermediate between God and the world. Such language shows that the minds of God's people were being prepared for the concepts that would be involved in the forthcoming revelation of the doctrine of the Trinity.

In the New Testament. The revelation of the truth of the triune life of God was first made in the NT, where the earliest references to it are in the Pauline Epistles. The doctrine is most easily seen in St. Paul's recurrent use of the terms God, Lord, and Spirit. What makes his use of these terms so significant is that they appear against a strictly monotheistic background.

In the Pauline Epistles. The clearest instance of this usage is found in 2 Cor 13.13, ''The grace of our Lord Jesus Christ, the love of God, and the fellowship of the Holy Spirit be with you all.'' This blessing is perhaps a quotation from the early Christian liturgy. The grammatical usage in this blessing, especially the subjective genitives τοῦ κυρίου Ἰησοῦ Χριστοῦ . . . τοῦ θεοῦ . . . τοῦ ἁγίου πνεύματος gives us a basis not only for the distinction of persons, but also for their equality inasmuch as all the benefits are to flow from the one Godhead.

Another example of Paul's probable reference to the Trinity by his use of the triad, Spirit, Lord, God, can be seen in 1 Cor 12.4–6. Here, in speaking of the spiritual gifts or charisms that are bestowed upon Christians, he says, ''Now there are varieties of gifts, but the same Spirit; and there are varieties of ministries, but the same Lord; and there are varieties of workings, but the same God, who works all things in all.'' This passage witnesses to the doctrine of the Trinity by ascribing the various charisms, viz, gifts, ministries, and workings, to the Spirit, the Lord (the Son), and God (the Father), respectively. Since all these charisms of their very nature demand a divine source, the three Persons are put on a par, thus clearly indicating their divine nature while at the same time maintaining the distinction of persons.

In the Gospels. The only place in the Gospels where the three divine Persons are explicitly mentioned together is in St. Matthew's account of Christ's last command to His Apostles, ''Go, therefore, and make disciples of all nations, baptizing them in the name of the Father, and of the Son, and of the Holy Spirit'' (Mt 28.19). In this commission Christ commands the Apostles to baptize all men ''in the name of'' the Father, Son, and Holy Spirit. The expression ''in the name of'' (εἰς τὸ ὄνομα, literally, ''into the name'') indicates a dedication or consecration to the one named. Thus Christian baptism is a dedication or consecration to God—Father, Son, and Holy Spirit. Since the Son and the Holy Spirit are mentioned here on a par with the Father, the passage clearly teaches that they are equally divine with the Father, who is obviously God. These words testify to the belief of the Apostolic Church in a doctrine of three Persons in one God.

The accounts of the BAPTISM OF THE LORD as described in Mt 3.13–17; Mk 1.9–11; Lk 3.21–22; Jn 1.32–34 have been understood by older scholars as indications of the doctrine of the Trinity. Modern scholars, however, see rather in these accounts references to the authoritative anointing of Jesus as the Messiah. Yet in the light of the fullness of revelation, the possibility is not to be excluded that the Evangelists had the doctrine of the Trinity in mind when they described this event.

See Also: JOHANNINE COMMA.

Bibliography: J. LEBRETON, ''La Révélation de la Sainte Trinité,'' *La Vie spirituelle* 74 (Paris 1946) 225–240. E. B. ALLO, *Saint Paul: Première epître aux Corinthiens* [*Études bibliques* (Paris 1956) 323]. J. SCHMID, *Das Evangelium nach Matthäus* (Regensburg 1956). K. RAHNER, ''Trinity, Divine,'' in *Sacramentum Mundi* v. 6, 295–297; ''Theos in the New Testament,'' *Theological Investigations* 1 (London 1961) 79–148. W. KASPER, *The God of Jesus Christ* (New York 1984). A. WAINWRIGHT, *The Trinity in the New Testament* (London 1962).

[C. DRAINA]

TRINITY, HOLY, CONTROVERSIES ON

The controversies that occasioned the early Councils stemmed partly from the difficulty of the subject—the Trinity and Christology—and partly from the lack of an accepted terminology. Today the catechism states that in God there are three Persons and one nature, and that in Jesus Christ there is one Person and two natures. This answer is the fruit of vast theological reflection. The Scriptures speak of the Father, Son, and Holy Spirit and record that the Word became flesh, but never use the terms ''person,'' ''nature,'' or ''substance.'' When the first ages of faith had passed, answers had to be found for such questions as: Are the Father, Son, and Holy Spirit distinct persons? Is the Son God? Is the Holy Spirit God? Is Jesus Christ God? Is He man? Is He a human person? How are the relations of nature and person to be expressed?

Terminology. In regard to terminology, the problem was to find Greek words for person and nature that would express the Christian doctrine of three Persons and one nature in God, one Person and two natures in Christ. Greek philosophy knew nothing of a rational nature that was not a person, and the Greek words *ousia, physis,* and *hypostasis* could and did mean either nature or person. When CYRIL OF ALEXANDRIA spoke of "one *physis* of the Incarnate Word" he meant "one Person of the Incarnate Word," but his statement could be taken in Antioch to mean "in the Incarnate Word there is only one nature" (*see* MONOPHYSITISM). There were similar difficulties about *ousia* and *hypostasis.* There were heretics, such as Sabellius and Arius, who denied Christian truths; but there were well-meaning bishops, priests, and people who unconsciously furthered heresy because they were genuinely confused about words.

A word formed from *ousia* played a key role in the first four Councils. The word was HOMOOUSIOS (of the same nature or substance). The Council of Nicaea (325) defined against Arius that the Son is homoousios Patri (of the same substance as the Father), but many bishops who would die for the belief that the Son is God abhorred the term homoousios because it conveyed to them the Monarchian heresy that the Son is the same Person as the Father. This misunderstanding plagued the Church for 50 years after Nicaea.

The passionate and even violent defense of their beliefs by Christian leaders may appear excessive in the 20th century, but it must be seen in its setting. Account must be taken not only of the fundamental doctrines involved, but of the more robust manners of the age and of the fact that first-class minds, often with immense resources of wealth and influence, were debating most abstruse areas of doctrine and at the same time were committed to maintaining the prestige of great sees.

Errors in regard to the Trinity took the form of (1) denying the real distinction of Persons (Monarchianism, Anti-Trinitarianism, and Unitarianism); (2) denying the divinity of the Second or Third Person (SUBORDINATIONISM); or (3) denying the unity of the divine nature (Tritheism). Early controversy concerned chiefly the first two.

Monarchianism. For Christians, committed as monotheists to holding the unity (*monarchia*) of God, the teaching of Scripture (Jn 10.30; 14.9–11, 16 ff.; Rom 9.5; Phil 2.6 ff.; 2 Peter 1.1) on a Person equal in power and glory to the Father posed a problem from the beginning.

The heresy of the Judaizers, underrating the dignity of Christ and the efficacy of His Redemption, contained the seeds of Subordinationism. Toward the end of the second century, the Gnostic theory of partly divine *aeons* to bridge the gap between God and creatures, to which St. Irenaeus opposed the traditional teaching of the Church handed down from the Apostles, caused a reaction in favor of an extreme form of Monotheism that resulted in Monarchianism—the denial of the Son's distinct personality.

The teaching and philosophizing of the APOLOGISTS on the Trinity, although orthodox, was often vague and couched in language that later standards would reject. It was not as clear to them as to their successors (and to Rome, cf. the letter of Pope Dionysius to Dionysius of Alexandria, 260) that equality of Son and Father had to be or could be maintained; that divinity does not admit of degrees; and that if the Word is divine, distinct, and begotten of the Father, He must be equal to the Father and His generation must be eternal.

ORIGEN, in spite of his formulation of the eternal generation of the Son, tended to Subordinationism, and others, too, used ambiguous terms in combating Monarchianism. To defend the equality and consubstantiality of Father and Son and to profess the Son's eternal generation seemed to make the refutation of Monarchianism well-nigh impossible; for how then were Father and Son to be distinguished? The Monarchians made the unity of God and the divinity of the Word their starting point, and as they could not deny either, they denied the distinct personality of the Son. To their opponents it seemed easier to deny the equality and consubstantiality of Father and Son at a time when the implications of divinity, eternal generation, and the Incarnation had not been fully worked out.

TERTULLIAN furnished a solution (*Adv. Praxeam*)—trinity of Persons, unity of nature—but appears to tend to Subordinationism in holding that they differ *gradu et forma* and that while the Father is the entire substance, the Son is *derivatio totius et portio.* DIONYSIUS OF ALEXANDRIA, in opposing Monarchianism (Sabellianism), exceeded orthodoxy and exposed himself to the charge of teaching Ditheism. Pope Dionysius intervened (262) and in a letter of "epoch-making significance" (Scheeben) condemned Sabellianism, Tritheism, and Subordinationism, while reproving Dionysius for his statement of doctrine. Dionysius readily submitted and pointed out that he had used ποίημα of the Son not in the sense of a created but of self-existent (against Sabellianism) being.

Subordinationism. In the condemnation of Monarchianism considerable progress had been made toward the formulation of the doctrine of three divine Persons distinct and equal, but early in the fourth century ARIUS fell into the heresy of Subordinationism. He accepted, against Sabellianism, three distinct Persons, but he denied the divinity and eternal generation of the Son. The Word, he taught, is a creature made freely by the Father out of nothing; not the Son of God by nature but by adoption only; not equal to God but a being intermediary between God and creation. When his bishop, Alexander, condemned him, Arius fled to Palestine and enlisted the aid of a friend, EUSEBIUS OF CAESAREA, who convened a council and requested Alexander to receive Arius back. The canvassing of support for and against Arius inflamed the whole East, and rioting broke out in the chief cities, eventually attracting the attention of CONSTANTINE I. Meanwhile, in Antioch the bishops in council condemned Arius, and councils followed in Alexandria and Nicomedia. It was felt that an assembly of the bishops of the world—the *oikoumene*—an ecumenical council should be summoned, and one was convened for Nicaea, May 325.

The problem was to find a formula that would exclude Sabellianism and Arianism. Athanasius, the outstanding theologian of the Council, pressed for the word homoousios, for a definition that the Son is consubstantial with the Father. Eusebius and many bishops, some orthodox, some semi-Arian, wished for a more vague term and reacted violently against homoousios, which suggested Sabellianism to them. Athanasius won his point; the term homoousios was used for the definition and became the test word of orthodoxy. It was defined that the Son is true God, begotten of the Father and consubstantial with Him—a definition that condemned also semi-Arianism, the *via media* refuge of those who rejected both Arianism and homoousios, admitting only that the Son is homoiousios, like in substance to the Father.

Immediately after Nicaea bishops began to organize support for Arius, who signed a compromise formula not containing homoousios. With imperial backing a terror campaign against the defenders of Nicaea began, and a series of councils was held in the East and West at which bishops unwittingly accepted ambiguous statements of doctrine, so that St. Jerome wrote after the Council of Ariminum (359): "the world groaned and marveled to find itself Arian." A Council held in Constantinople (381) repeated homoousios, named and condemned different forms of Arianism, and affirmed that there is one divine substance in three Persons in God and that the Second Person became man.

The Council also condemned Macedonianism, the teaching of the semi-Arian bishop of Constantinople, Macedonius (deposed 360). He, it is said, extended the heresy of Subordinationism to the Holy Spirit, teaching that the Holy Spirit is a creature made by the Son. The Holy Spirit is "great," the Son "greater," and the Father "greatest." The Council defined (indirectly) the divinity of the Holy Spirit by calling Him Lord and ascribing to Him divine attributes (giving of life, adoration and glory such as are due to Father and Son, and illumination of the Prophets). Also condemned at this council was the teaching of APOLLINARIS OF LAODICEA that Christ had no human soul, a heresy that was later the occasion of the Councils of Ephesus (431) and Chalcedon (451).

Tritheism. Tritheists deny God's unity and profess three essences or natures as well as three Persons in God. Their error is due to failure to distinguish between nature and person, so that to admit three Persons is to accept three divine natures.

John Philoponus (d. 565), Christian commentator on Aristotle, identified nature and person and supported Monophysitism (one nature in Christ). He taught that Father, Son, and Holy Spirit are three distinct individuals of the species "God," as Peter, Paul, and John are three of the species "man," three part substances in one common abstract substance. The three Persons share a specifically same, not numerically same, nature. He refused to admit the consequence—three Gods.

ROSCELIN OF COMPIÈGNE (d. *c.* 1120) taught that the Father, Son, and Holy Spirit are three distinct substances as three angels or three men, but are so completely in agreement of will and equal in power that they can be regarded as one. He was opposed by St. Anselm of Canterbury and his teaching was condemned at Soissons (1092).

The Abbot JOACHIM DA FIORE, Calabria (d. 1202), taught that Father, Son, and Holy Spirit have one essence, but in reality he denied the unity of divine nature because he conceived the oneness of the three Persons as a mere collective or generic unity, as many men are said to be a people. His teaching was condemned at the Fourth Lateran Council (1215).

Anton GÜNTHER (d. 1873) taught that the Absolute determined itself three times in a process of self-development, thesis, antithesis, and synthesis. The divine substance is trebled, and the three substances attracted to one another through consciousness make a formal unity. This was condemned by Pius IX (1857). Liberal Protestantism, while retaining the traditional terminology, regards the three Persons only as divine attributes, such as power, wisdom, and goodness.

See Also: ADOPTIONISM; MODALISM.

Bibliography: G. BARDY, *Dictionnaire de théologie catholique*, ed. A. VACANT et al., (Paris 1903—50) 15.2:1545–1702, bibliog. J. LEBRETON, *Histoire du dogme de la Trinité*, 2 v. (1927–28) v.1. A. D'ALÈS, *Gregorianum* 3 (1922) 420–446;

497–523; *Le dogme de Nicée* (Paris 1926). R. ARNOU, *Gregorianum* 15 (1934) 242–254. C. HAURET, *Comment le ''Defenseur de Nicée'' a-t-il compris le dogme de Nicée?* (Rome 1936). I. ORTIZ DE URBINA, *El símbolo niceno* (Madrid 1947). C. ZEDDA, ''La dottrina trinitaria di Lucifero di Cagliari,'' *Divus Thomas* (Piacenza 1924–) 52 (1949) 276–329.

[P. J. HAMELL]

TRINITY, HOLY, DEVOTION TO

There are few signs of devotion to the Trinity in the early Church, aside from the ritual use of the Trinitarian formula in the administration of the Sacraments. Doxologies of praise are found in the writings of St. Justin (d. 166) and Clement of Alexandria (d. 199). St. Basil (d. 397) cites a prayer used by Christians when lighting the evening lamps, ''We praise the Father, the Son, and the Holy Spirit'' (*De Spir. Sancto* 290.72). A number of early carvings, representing the Trinity or praising it, are dated as of the 4th century [cf. *Dictionnaire d'archéologie chrétienne et de liturgie,* ed. F. Cabrol, H. Leclercq, and H. I. Marrou, 15 v. (Paris 1907–53) 15:2787].

Devotion to the Trinity as it is known today seems to have begun in monasteries at Aniane and Tours, in the 8th century. St. Benedict of Aniane, who spread the devotion through his monastic reform, dedicated his abbey church to the Trinity in 872. And there are references to Masses in honor of the Trinity, at Tours and at Fulda in 796 and 804. A feast of the Trinity was introduced at Cluny in 1091, and at Canterbury by Thomas Becket in 1162. Rome resisted this observance, and it was not until 1331 that the Feast of the Trinity was approved by John XXII for the whole Church.

The revitalization by the early scholastics of the doctrine on the divine indwelling led to many works on the subject and to a devotion to the divine Persons that continues to modern times. SS. Thomas Aquinas and Bonaventure brought to light and refined the ancient teachings of the Fathers, especially of St. Augustine, on the personal presence of God in the souls of the just. The application of this doctrine, though interpreted differently by the various theological schools, has emphasized, in the practical order, the central part played by the Trinity in interior life. All spiritual writers since the Middle Ages insist that a living devotion to the Trinity is both an essential means and an accompaniment to true sanctity. This is reinforced by the encyclical of Leo XIII, *Divinum illud munus,* on the Holy Spirit (May 9, 1897).

Bibliography: F. L. B. CUNNINGHAM, *The Indwelling of the Trinity* (Dubuque 1955). B. FROGET, *The Indwelling of the Holy Spirit in the Souls of the Just,* tr. S. A. RAEMERS (Westminster, Md. 1950). H. LECLERCQ, *Dictionnaire d'archéologie chrétienne et de liturgie,* ed. F. CABROL, H. LECLERCQ, and H. I. MARROU, 15 v. (Paris 1907–53) 15.2:2787–92.

Trinity with Christ crucified, panel painting, ca. 1410. (©National Gallery Collection by kind permission of the Trust and the National Gallery, London/CORBIS)

[P. MULHERN]

TRINITY, HOLY, ICONOGRAPHY OF

Representation and symbolization of the Holy Trinity, based on the interpretation of Scripture and belief in the Trinity, is manifest in architecture and architectural decoration, painting, and manuscript illumination.

In Architecture. In early Christian architecture the Trinity was symbolized by the *ecclesia triplex* (three churches either within one enclosure or under a single roof). A Trinitarian symbolism still dominated the planning of certain 10th- and 11th-century churches: the triple church built at Saint-Bénigne (Dijon) by Abbot William of Volpiano; the three matutinal altars at Cluny II; and the three among the *quinque altaria principalia* dedicated in 1095 by Pope Urban II at Cluny III. The Delta plan, with a more exceptional Trinitarian connotation, was used to pattern the foundation of churches such as the Romanesque one of Planès in French Catalogne, and the baroque pilgrimage church, Die Kappel, near Waldsassen, begun by George Dientzenhofer in 1865.

The Etimasia. At the apex of the mosaics covering the triumphal arch of Saint Mary Major (Rome, 432–440), the Trinity is symbolized by the giant version of the *etimasia* (ἑτοιμασία): the empty throne (the same

"The Trinity," (1577–1579) by El Greco, Museo del Prado, Madrid, Spain. (©Archivo Iconografico, S.A./CORBIS)

throne that presided over the Council of Ephesus, 430–31), the book on a cushion and a purple veil, the dove and the *crux gemmata,* wreathed with the *aurun coronarium.* The book is sealed with the seven seals that are interpreted as Incarnation, Nativity, Passion, Harrowing of Hell, Resurrection, Ascension, and the Last Judgment.

The Three Men. The three men, seen by Abraham in the vale of Mamre, were interpreted by Saint Ambrose (*De Abraham, Patrologia Latina*, ed. J. P. Migne, 14:435) and Saint Augustine (*Contra Maximinum Arianum Episcopum, Patrolgia Latina* 42:809) as manifestations of the Godhead, one and triune. On a mosaic in the nave of Saint Mary Major the central figure of the three men adored by Abraham is circumscribed within an etheric *mandorla,* as if to translate in terms of light the formula of Saint Augustine: "et ipse Abraham tres vidit, unum adoravit." That iconography, well represented in Byzantine mosaics (S. Vitale, Ravenna, mid-6th century; Monreale, *c.* 1175) was transmitted through illuminated Greek manuscripts to icon painting. It was given the place of honor on the iconostasis (*see* ICON). The most famous "three angels" icon, symbolizing both the Trinity and the Eucharist, is the languid and graceful painting of Andreǐ RUBLËV, *c.* 1410, in the Historical Museum, Moscow. The Byzantine iconography of the Trinity influenced Romanesque and early Gothic art mainly through German illuminations copying Byzantine models. When it is found in the French Psalter of Queen Ingeburge, *c.* 1210 (Musée Condé, Chantilly, folio 10v), it is because the unknown artist who painted the Psalter was indebted to the antiquating and neo-Greek style propagated in northeastern France by the enameled works of the goldsmith Nicholas of Verdun.

Three Identical Figures. The representation of the Trinity as the figure, three times repeated, of the same divine person wearing the cruciform nimbus appeared on 10th-century English pen drawings (Pontifical from Sherborne, 992.5, in the Bibliothèque Nationale, Paris, Pat. 943, folio 5, 5v, 6). Such triple images, which may have been motivated by Carolingian and remote Coptic prototypes, were soon to be connected with the Trinity creating the world and, more specifically, shaping man into a microcosm made in the semblance of God (illumination in HERRAD OF LANDSBERG's *Hortus Deliciarum,* 1170–80).

In later medieval art the *Synthronos,* on which the three persons of the Trinity are seated, was to be given also a particular emphasis in connection with the last episode of the so-called *Drama of the Virtues* (cf. Psalm 84) in which the Virtues argued about the Incarnation. In the mystery plays (cf. *Le Pélerinage de Jésus-Christ* of Guillaume de Deguileville), Jesus, back from His pilgrimage on earth, is enthroned by God the Father on His right, among the chanting hosts of the entire paradise. Jean Fouquet painted that scene (*c.* 1450) in the Book of Hours of Étienne Chevalier (Musée Condé). The three Persons, all in white and alike, are seated on a bench with three separate canopies (as the *sedilia* from the Holy Chapel of Bourges, founded in 1391 by Jean, Duke of Berry). The Virgin, in Fouquet's illumination, occupies another throne, on the proper right of the triune Godhead. But the Virgin Theotokos, holding Jesus Incarnate and crowned by the dove, symbol of the Holy Spirit (as she is crowned by the dove in the *Belle Verrière* stained glass of Chartres Cathedral), had already been incorporated within the *mandorla,* with God the Father and God the Son, in an Anglo-Saxon drawing, dating between 1023 and 1035. The drawing that belongs to a manuscript from New Minster, Winchester, is the oldest illustration of the feast of the Trinity (British Museum, Cotton Manuscript. Titus D. 27, folio 75v).

The Ancient of Days. In Greek illuminated manuscripts of the 11th century (a lectionary of Mt. Athos, Dionysius 740 folio 3v; homilies of John Climacus, Vatican Library, MS. gr. 394 folio 7), the Theotokos of the *Sedes Sapientiae* is replaced by the Ancient of Days (Dn 7.9, 13, 22): God the Father, holding in His lap Christ-Emmanuel, the Logos, everlastingly engendered, "the only-begotten Son, who is in the bosom of the Father . . ." (Jn 1.18). The dove is in the lap of Christ. It flutters around in the *mandorla* in a miniature of a Weingarten manuscript, *c.* 1200 (Landesbibliotek, Fulda, Manuscript A 32 folio 170). Early imitations of the Trinitarian Byzantine type are met in the Bible of Saint-Bénigne, Dijon, and in an 11th-century Anglo-Saxon manuscript (British Musuem, Harley 603). The Nikopoia, variant of the *Sedes Sapientiae,* in which the Virgin holds Christ Emmanuel in an elongated shield or a round *clipeus,* was also transformed into a corresponding image of the Ancient of Days (cf. the Byzantinized image in an early 13th-century Bohemian psalter, the Codex Ostroviensis, Prague, Metropolitan Chapter, Manuscript A 57, 1 folio 83). In the *Liber Scivias* of the visionary Hildegard of Bingen, *c.* 1180, the Ancient of Days holds as an *imago clipeata* the Lamb bearing the Cross [cf. ed. and tr. of *Scivias* by Maura Bockeler (Salzburg 1954) 34]. In the Bohemian *Liber Viaticus* of John of Streda, Chancellor of Emperor Charles IV (*c.* 1360), Christ Logos is replaced in the medallion by the Man of Sorrows (National Museum, Prague, codex 13 A 12 folio 165). The admission of elements pertaining to the Passion of Christ in the symbol of the Trinity can be explained by a 12th-century creation of the utmost importance for the development of the representation of the Trinity in medieval art: the so-called throne of grace.

Throne of Grace and Passion Elements. The Throne of Grace is the Lutheran translation of what the King James version of the Old Testament rendered as the mercy seat. The mercy seat of gold was set in the ark, and in the ceremonies of atonement it was sprinkled with the blood of a bullock (Ex 25.21; Lv 16.14). Saint Paul referred to it as a symbol of propitiation through faith in the blood of Christ for the remission of sins (Rom 4.25; cf. Heb 4.16; 9.5). That symbol was expressed by 12th-century artists in the decoration of portable altars and in illuminations introducing the Canon of the Mass.

Christ crucified may be represented under the theophany of God the Father wearing the cruciform halo with the two Persons interconnected by the dove as shown on the Mauritius portable altar by Eilbertus of Cologne in Siegburg (*c.* 1150); or God the Father supports the cross in the *mandorla,* and His lips are put in communication with those of the crucified Son by the dove. This materializes the procession of the Third Person *per spirationem* from the Father and the Son (Missal in Cambrai, Bibliothèque Municipale, 234 folio 2). Abbot Suger adopted a similar iconography for the program of the Last Judgment portal of the abbey church of Saint-Denis (1137–40): the dove, carved at the apex of the outer archivolt, hovers above God, holding the Lamb bearing the cross, which is represented underneath on the keystone of the third archivolt (compare the tympanum relief of S. Domingo, Soria, *c.* 1150). On the tympanum, Christ, enthroned and crucified, proffers his stigmatized hands. An extraordinary painting, the Torún altar (1390) from the Franciscan church of Torún, Poland, kept in the National Museum, Warsaw, sums up the interpenetration of the divine Persons against the background of the Redemption. God the Father, surmounted by the dove, holds in His lap the child Christ and is seated on the apocalyptic rainbow, in *mandorla* and with the apparatus of a *Majestas Trinitatis.* The *mandorla* enframes the Tree of Life, on which Christ is crucified, but only His nailed hands and feet are seen. His head is concealed by the haloed head of the Father, and His body is hidden behind a double veil made of a patterned brocade. This veil represents, typologically, the veil in the Temple of Jerusalem, which, on the day of reconciliation, the High Priest sprinkled with blood. Mystically it represents the body of Christ as Priest opening on Calvary the way to the New Jerusalem [Hebrews 10.19, 20; Saint Anselm of Canterbury, *In Omnes Pauli Epistolas enarrationes* (Cologne 1545) 504].

Christ crucified held by His Father, or detached from the cross and supported by His Father, or lying as a corpse on the lap of His seated Father, are the main schemes representing the Trinity from the late Gothic period to the time of the Counter Reformation. The works of art after 1400 simplified the highly concentrated symbolism that obtained during the three previous centuries. The benefit of a clearer delineation and more dramatic grouping was had at the cost of the deepest theological implications.

Bibliography: A. N. DIDRON, *Iconographie chretienne. Histoire de Dieu* (Paris 1844). A. HACKEL, *Die Trinität in der Kunst* (Berlin 1931). A. HEIMANN, "L'Iconographie de la Trinité et son développement en Occident," *L'Art Chrétien* 1 (1934); "Trinitas Creator Mundi," *Journal of the Warburg and Courtauld Institutes* 2 (1938) 42–52. W. BRAUNFELS, *Die Heilige Dreifaltigkeit* (Düsseldorf 1954). T. DOBMZENIECKI, "The Torún Quinity in the National Museum in Warsaw," *Art Bulletin* 46 (1964) 380–88.

[P. VERDIER]

TRINITY, SISTERS OF THE MOST HOLY

(OSST, Official Catholic Directory #2060); a title that embraces various congregations of women religious who are affiliated with the TRINITARIANS through their common rule and tradition. The early history of the Trinitarian nuns, like that of the friars, is rather obscure because of the lack of sufficient historical records. A convent of nuns, pertaining to the Trinitarian second order, is known to have come into existence in 1236 in Avingania, a town in Aragon, Spain. Much later, in the early 17th century, a movement of reform of the cloistered Trinitarian nuns was directed in Madrid, Spain, by St. JOHN BAPTIST OF THE CONCEPTION. An influential figure among these discalced Trinitarians was Mother Angela Maria of the Immaculate Conception (1649–90). Convents of this branch of the order exist in Spain and in South America.

There are several groups of Trinitarian Sisters of the conventual third order. Motherhouses of congregations, some of them with papal approbation, have been founded in Rome, Italy; Valence and Sainte-Marthe (near Marseilles), in France; Madrid, Valencia, and Seville, in Spain; and Palma, on the island of Majorca. The Trinitarian Sisters of Valence were the largest of these congregations. Founded at Lyons, France, about 1660, the motherhouse was moved to Valence in 1685. Suppressed during the French Revolution, the community revived in 1824, and subsequently spread to England, Belgium, and Italy. The sisters are engaged in teaching and in hospital work.

The Trinitarian Sisters of Madrid are an autonomous branch of a congregation begun in Italy in the early 19th century and approved by the Holy See in 1828. It was from the Italian congregation that the Trinitarian Sisters came to the U.S. in 1920. At the request of Father Isidore Ienne, OSST, and with the approval of Dennis Dougherty, Archbishop, and later Cardinal, of Philadelphia, four sisters came to teach school in Bristol, PA. A few years later they took charge of a school in Cleveland, OH, where they also opened a novitiate. In 1952 the sisters purchased the shrine of Our Lady of Lourdes in Cleveland from the Sisters of Our Lady of Charity of the GOOD SHEPHERD. The U.S. provincialate is Euclid, OH; the generalate is in Rome.

[M. S. VILLELLA/EDS.]

TRISAGION

Trisagion (τρίς thrice, ἅγιος holy) is a doxology that is distinct from the *SANCTUS* concluding the Preface. The text of the Trisagion reads: ''Hagios ho Theos, hagios ischyros, hagios athanatos, eleison hymas'' [Holy God, holy and mighty, holy and immortal, have mercy on us]. The Trisagion was first mentioned in the 5th century as a devotional invocation that assumed a liturgical role in Eastern liturgies. For example, in the Byzantine Divine Liturgy of St. John Chrysostom, the Trisagion precedes the scriptural readings. From the East, it spread to the West, where it assumed a similar position in the eucharist of the ancient Gallican and Mozarabic rites. In the 11th century, the Trisagion appeared in the Roman rite for the liturgy of Good Friday, where it is sung alternately in Greek and Latin with the *IMPROPERIA* or Reproaches during the veneration of the cross.

Bibliography: J. HANSSENS, *Institutiones liturgicae de ritibus orientalibus*, 3 v. (Rome 1932) 3:883–931. J. QUASTEN, ''Oriental Influence in the Gallican Liturgy,'' *Traditio* 1 (1943) 55–78. L. BROU, ''Etudes sur la liturgie mozarabe: le Trisagion de la messe d'après les sources manuscrites,'' *Ephemerides liturgicae* 61 (1947) 309–84. J. MATEOS, ''Evolution historique de la liturgie de Saint Jean Chrysostome, II: Le chant du trisagion et la session à l'abside,'' *Proche-Orient chrétien* 17 (1967) 141–76. K. LEVY, ''The Trisagion in Byzantium and the West,'' *International Musicological Society: Congress Report* 11 (Copenhagen 1972) 761–65. S.P. BROCK, ''The Thrice-Holy Hymn in the Liturgy,'' *Sobornost* (incorporating *Eastern Churches Review*) NS 7:2 (1985) 24–34.

[E. J. GRATSCH/EDS.]

TRITHEMIUS, JOHANNES (TRITHEIM)

Benedictine scholar, spiritual writer, and abbot; b. Trittenheim on the Moselle, Feb. 1, 1462; d. Würzburg, Dec. 13, 1516. He entered the Benedictines at Sponheim, an abbey of the congregation of Bursfeld (*see* BURSFELD, ABBEY OF), at the age of 20 and the following year was elected to the office of abbot. In this position he strove vigorously to create a center of scholarly study and to re-

form monastic discipline. During the 23 years in which he was abbot he succeeded in gathering a collection of books that made the abbey library one of the most renowned in Europe at that time. Trithemius himself was highly regarded in the world of scholarship, and he counted among his friends men such as Conrad Celtis, Johann REUCHLIN, and Johann von DALBERG and enjoyed the favor and friendship of the Emperor Maximilian. His attempt at disciplinary reform, however, was resisted by malcontents in the community, and as time went on the opposition increased rather than diminished. In 1503 he resigned his abbacy and retired to seek peace and quiet at the small Scottish monastery of St. Jacob at Würzburg, where he was elected abbot in 1506. He gave much of his energy during the last ten years of his life to writing books. He wrote in all more than 80 works, only a portion of which appeared later in printed editions. Among his historical works were *Catalogus scriptorum ecclesiasticorum* (1494), *De viris illustribus Germaniae* (1495), *De viris illustribus Ordinis S. Benedicti,* and a number of volumes of annals and chronicles. A part of his historical writing was published by M. Freher under the title *Joannis Trithemii opera historica* (Frankfurt 1601). Some of his ascetical work was published by Johannes BUSAEUS under the title *Joannis Trithemii opera pia et spiritualia* (Mainz 1604) and is considered among the best devotional literature of the time. What he had written incidentally about the Immaculate Conception in his *De laudibus S. Annae* led to an attack by Wigand Wirt. Trithemius also took an interest in the occult and left works on witchcraft and cryptography.

Bibliography: N. SCHEID, *Catholic Encyclopedia* 15:62–63. P. LEHMANN, *Merkwürdigkeiten des Abtes Johannes Trithemus* (*Sitzungsberichte der Bayerischen Akademie der Wissenschaft zu München* 1961.2). Esp. for further biog. references, J. BECKMAN, *Lexikon für Theologie und Kirche* 1 10:296–298. H. BÜTTNER, *Die Religion in Geschichte und Gegenwart*3 6:1042–43.

[P. K. MEAGHER]

TRIUMPH, ROMAN

The sacred procession of a victorious general, culminating in his sacrifice to Jupiter on the Capitol. It was a solemn act of thanksgiving for victory. The procession comprised the *triumphator* himself, preceded by the magistrates, members of the Senate, the victorious troops, war captives in chains, war booty on wagons, and white oxen for sacrifice. The *triumphator,* dressed in an embroidered toga—the *toga picta*—wearing a crown and carrying a scepter in one hand and a spray of laurel in the other, rode in a chariot drawn by four horses. Beside him a slave kept repeating *Hominem te memento.* The laurel was placed on the lap of the god. Christianity, in adapting Roman military language to express its own religious concepts, employed *triumphus* and *triumphare* to signify victory over the Devil, the *hostis* of Christ and the Church.

Bibliography: A. MOMIGLIANO, *The Oxford Classical Dictionary,* ed. M. CARY (Oxford 1949) 926. W. EHLERS, *Paulys Realenzyklopädie der klassischen Altertumswissenschaft,* ed. G. WISSOWA, et al. (Stuttgart 1893–) 7A.1: 493–511. A. BLAISE, *Dictionnaire Latin-Français des auteurs chrétiens* (Paris 1954), *s.v.* "triumpho."

[M. R. P. MCGUIRE]

TRIUMPHALISM

In characterizing the proposed *schema* on the CHURCH at the first session of Vatican Council II, Bishop Émile J. M. De Smedt of Bruges used the word "triumphalism." This word describes a tendency to think of the Church as irresistibly conquering throughout the centuries, always receiving universal admiration for the words and deeds of its heads, and seemingly more interested in upholding its own rights and privileges than in promoting the SALVATION of all.

Yet the word can characterize a great truth. For Christ is triumphant; the Church in eschatological time will be perfectly triumphant; and even now the earthly Church shares in a restricted sense the triumph of its Master.

Christ is triumphant. He drove out devils (Mk 1.23–28, 5.1–13, 7.24–30). He overcame sin by forgiving it in others (Mk 2.1–12). He even triumphed over sickness and death by means of His miracles (Mk 5.24–34, 10.46–52, 5.35–43; Lk 7.11–17). Hence, before His death He said, "I have overcome the world" (Jn 16.33). These words anticipate the victory that is personally His by His Passion and Resurrection, as a result of which all power is given Him in heaven and on earth (Mt 28.18) and all creatures are made subject to Him (Phil 2.5–11). (*See* RESURRECTION OF CHRIST.)

The Church is destined to share Christ's total triumph. At the end of time it will live fully the risen life with Christ. It will be utterly subject to Him and through Him to the Father. All other authority and power will be destroyed that God may be all in all (1 Cor 15.22–28). And because of its union with God, all elements of defeat that now exist—sin, death, suffering—will be blotted out (Ap 21.1–8).

Even now the Church partially shares Christ's victory. He died for it (Eph 5.25–27) in order to deliver it "from the wickedness of this present world" (Gal 1.4) and to give its members a foretaste of the "powers of the world to come" (Heb 6.5). Hence, even now the Church

manifests aspects that anticipate the final triumph. It possesses the very Spirit of Christ, who was poured out at its Pentecostal birth. To it is entrusted the truth in such a way that it is called "the pillar and mainstay of the truth" (1 Tm 3.15). It is so firmly grounded in God that the powers of hell can never prevail against it (Mt 16.18). In its Sacraments, it daily overcomes the powers of sin; in the miracles that have always been a part of its life, it conquers the physical evils resulting from sin. With unshakable hope it awaits the irresistible victory of the last day.

Yet the Church of earth is primarily a weak, suffering Church. It is sinful in its members, at times ignorant, imprudent, ineffectual in its leadership. And like Christ it must suffer before entering into glory (Lk 24.26). For it to assume a "triumphalistic" attitude is entirely out of character. It is to re-present the lowly aspects of Christ's public life and in so doing to fill up what is lacking of the sufferings of Christ for the Redemption of all men.

Bibliography: PIUS XII, "Mystici Corporis Christi," *Acta Apostolicae Sedis* 35 (1943) 193–248; 22–23, 64–66, 92–93. PAUL VI, "Ecclesiam suam" (Encyclical, Aug. 6, 1964) 10–11, 41, 44–49, 54, in *Acta Apostolicae Sedis* 56 (1964) 611–612, 626–627, 628–631, 634. Vatican Council II, *Dogmatic Constitution on the Church* 7, 8, 48–51, *Acta Apostolicae Sedis,* 57 (1965) 9–12, 53–58; F. HOLBÖCK and T. SARTORY eds., *Mysterium Kirche in der Sicht der theologischen Disziplinen* (Salzburg 1962) 1:201–346.

[P. F. CHIRICO]

TRIVULZIO

One of the eight chief noble families in Milan. Important members of this family, which flourished from the 13th to the 20th century, were generals, cardinals, and bibliophiles. The most famous member, *Gian Giacomo the Great,* b. Milan, 1441; d. Chartres, France, 1518; served in the regency for Gian Galeazzo SFORZA. In 1476 he traveled to the Holy Land with two other Milanese, a journey rather usual for wealthy Milanese at the time. When he fell out of favor with Ludovico il Moro, he entered the service of Ferdinand II of Aragon in Naples. After the expedition of Charles VIII of France into Italy, Trivulzio went to France. He returned to Italy with King Louis XII, who rewarded him with the titles, marshal of France, marquis of Vigevano, and count of Mesocco and appointed him governor of Milan. The Swiss defeated Trivulzio at Novara (1513), but in 1515 he won a victory for France at Marignano. He was a patron of writers in Milan. He and his grandson were the first members of the family who were permitted to coin money. *Teodoro,* b. 1474, d. 1551, was another marshal of France. *Alessandro,* b. 1773, d. 1805, served under Napoleon.

Five members of the family became cardinals (the first date given being that of their cardinalate). *Antonio,*

1500, d. 1509, the brother of Teodoro, was elevated according to the wish of Louis XII. Their nephew, *Agostino*, 1517, d. 1548, served as legate to France for Pope PAUL III. *Scaramuzza*, 1517, d. 1527, nephew of Gian Giacomo, taught law at the universities of Pavia and Padua, acted as adviser for Louis XII, and lost all his income from Lombardy because he supported the French. His nephew, *Antonio*, 1557, d. 1559, noted for his learning, served as nuncio to France and Venice, and as legate to King Henry II of France in an attempt to bring about peace between France and Spain. *Teodoro* (or *Gian Giacomo Teodoro*), 1629, d. 1657, began his career as general for King Philip III of Spain. It was unusual for a Milanese to be trusted and given offices by Spain, but the cardinal served as King Philip IV's viceroy in Sicily and Sardinia, governor of Milan, and ambassador in Rome. Three titles were conferred on him: grandee of Spain, illustrious, and Prince of the Empire.

A strong tradition in the family was its interest in learning. Gian Giacomo the Great was no exception. Three inventories of books that minor members possessed before 1500 have been published. With books inherited and purchased, *Alessandro Teodoro*, b. 1694, d. 1763, founded a library; Abbé *Carlo*, b. 1715, d. 1789, his brother, assisted him. Succeeding generations added to the collection until it became one of the important private libraries in Europe. It contained manuscripts, incunabula, and other printed books. Among the incunabula were all the editions of the *Divine Comedy*; the only other library where these are complete is the British Museum. The Trivulzio had also 25 manuscript copies of the *Divine Comedy* and many original letters. In 1935 the city of Milan acquired the library, and it is now in the Sforza castle.

Bibliography: P. LITTA et al., *Famiglie celebri italiane* 14 v. (Milan 1819–99), v.14. C. DE ROSMINI, *Dell'istoria intorno alle militari imprese e alla vita di Gian Jacopo Trivulzio*, 2 v. (Milan 1815). F. A. GUALTERIO, ed., *Corrispondenza segreta di Giovanni Matteo Giberto, datario di Clemente VII col cardinale Agostino Trivulzio dell'anno 1527* (Turin 1845). G. MORONI, *Dizionario de erudizione storico-ecclesiastica* 81: 81–84. F. and E. GNECCHI, *Le monete dei Trivulzio* (Milan 1887). C. SANTORO, *Milano d'altri tempi* (Milan 1938) 113–174, about the Trivulzio library. *Storia di Milano* (Milan 1953–) 7:487–508; 8:3–222.

[M. L. SHAY]

TROARN, ABBEY OF

Former BENEDICTINE monastery of Saint-Martin in Troarn, Calvados, France, diocese of Bayeux. It was founded by Roger de Montgomery in place of a college of canons established by his father. The original monks were drawn from Conches *c.* 1050, and the first church was dedicated in 1059 under Abbot DURANDUS OF TROARN, poet, liturgist, and writer on the Eucharist. It secured freedom from secular control in 1190 and flourished considerably in its first three centuries, playing a vital part in regional economic life till the 16th century. In 1562 the Calvinists launched an iconoclastic attack on the monastery. This was used by the monastery's tenants as a cover for pillaging, and the monks were unable to reestablish their rights. During the 17th century it was in the hands of commendatory abbots (*see* COMMENDATION), and attempts to reform it in the 18th century achieved nothing. It was dispersed during the French Revolution (1790). Only a few ruins of the claustral buildings survive.

Bibliography: R. F. N. SAUVAGE, *Histoire et développement économique d'un monastère normand au moyen âge: L'abbaye de Saint-Martin de Troarn* (Caen 1911). L. H. COTTINEAU, *Répertoire topobibliographique des abbayes et prieurés,* 2 v. (Mâcon 1935–39) 2:3220.

[D. J. A. MATTHEW]

TROELTSCH, ERNST

German Protestant theologian and philosopher, known especially for his comprehensive historical presentation of Christian social teaching; b. Haustetten, near Augsburg, Feb. 17, 1865; d. Berlin, Feb. 1, 1923. Troeltsch began his academic career in theology at Göttingen in 1891, moved to Bonn in 1892, was appointed ordinary professor at Heidelberg in 1894, and was called to Berlin as professor of philosophy in 1915. After the collapse of the old regime, he was elected a representative to the Prussian Diet in 1919, served from 1919 to 1921 as undersecretary for evangelical affairs in the Prussian Kultusministerium, and became a deputy in the German Reichstag in 1921, as a member of the German Democratic Party.

Troeltsch's importance for a reexamination of the place of religion in society can scarcely be overrated. He exemplifies the conflict between appreciation of the variety and universality of the historical process and recognition of the independence of the religious idea with its demand for security, unity, and balance. His historicism has been called a non-skeptical relativism because he was striving for a firm stand on the ultimate ground of life, and found it in the commitment of the individual to fulfillment of his personal destiny (*in der Entschlossenheit zu einer persönlichen Lebenstat*). He feared man would fall into the trap of externalized faith and dogma, and thereby misinterpret the overwhelming manifestation of God in the great Prophets as a thought process or a system of social order instead of an expression of life and vital power. This made him particularly sensitive to the idea of finality in Christianity.

Troeltsch, however, saw the position of Christianity as unique and outstanding only within the framework of the European value system. He did not believe that a common spiritual denominator for all mankind could be found in any of the historical religions. The problem of reconciling the existence of absolute values with divergent and changing cultural orders (*Kulturkreise*) led him to write one of his most important essays, "Measuring Norms for the Evaluation of Historical Matters and their Relationship to an Actual Cultural Ideal." Slowly he developed the idea of *Europäismus* as a new culture synthesis illustrating the concept of historical individuality; he was concerned especially with the intimate nexus between the individualities of the European tradition and Christianity. But while he promoted a living Christian ethics, adaptable to social changes and never to be turned into a final system, he also tried to overcome dependence on history alone. His premature death cut off his attempt to find a solution beyond the conscience and personal determination of the individual. His works remain an inexhaustible source of knowledge and stimulation, but the relativism that he never succeeded in dissolving by rational means renders his philosophy sterile and unsatisfactory.

See Also: RELIGION, SOCIOLOGY OF.

Bibliography: *Gesammelte Schriften,* 4 v. (Tübingen 1912–25). v.1 is translated as *The Social Teaching of the Christian Churches,* tr. O. WYON, 2 v. (New York 1931). W. MÜLLER, "Troeltsch," *Staatslexikon,* ed. *Görres-Gesellschaft* (Freiburg 1957–63) 7:1045–47.

[R. E. MORRIS]

TROIANI, CATERINA, BL.

Baptized Costanza (Constance), known in religion as Mary Catherine of Saint Rose of Viterbo, Poor Clare, foundress of the Institute of Franciscan Missionary Sisters of the Immaculate Heart of Mary; b. Jan.19, 1813, at Giuliano (near Rome), Italy; d. May 6, 1887, at Cairo, Egypt.

Upon the death of her mother (1819), Costanza was entrusted to the Poor Clares at the convent in Ferentino near Frosinone, Campania, Italy. In the course of her decade living with the sisters, she came to love the Rule. At age 16, she became a novice and made her profession the following year. She and five other sisters responded to the call of Bishop Guasco, apostolic vicar of Egypt, for missionaries. Upon arriving in Cairo (September 14, 1859), the sisters established an elementary school that was open to all children. Troiani earned the affectionate title "mother of the poor" for her many acts of charity and her collaboration in the movement to emancipate slaves. In 1868, she founded the Sisters of the Immaculate Heart. Her poor house established in the Clot-Bey district became her headquarters; however, the generalate was later transferred to Rome and the sisters continue Troiani's work in Brazil, China, Egypt, France, Ghana, Iraq, Israel, Italy, Jordan, Lebanon, Malta, Morocco, Palestine, Syria, the United States, and West Africa.

Her relics were translated from Cairo to the congregation's generalate in Rome in 1967. In beatifying (April 14, 1985) Maria Caterina Troiani, Pope John Paul II praised her courage in using the faith to bridge cultural differences for the benefit of the young and needy.

Bibliography: *Acta Apostolicae Sedis:* 913–16. *L'Osservatore Romano,* English edition, no. 19: 6–8.

[K. I. RABENSTEIN]

TROITSKAYA LAURA (ZAGORSK MONASTERY)

Troitskaya Laura, a.k.a. Troitse-Sergieva Laura, or more popularly as Zagorsk Monastery is a Russian monastery founded in Zagorsk (northeast of Moscow), *c.* 1340 by St. SERGIUS OF RADONEZH, and called originally Sergiev Posad (Sergius's Foundation). The founder's illustrious character, sanctity, and political status and the monastery's strict cenobitic rule early made it a model for Russian monastic life. At the beginning of the 17th century the monastery waged a courageous fight against a Polish siege; this further enhanced its patriotic status. When order was restored, the monastery became an outstanding and unique center of pilgrimage for the faithful from all over Russia. In 1744 it was given the status of a Laura. It had extensive holdings and possessions and was consistently regarded as a national patriotic center, as well as a religious center. Although secularized in 1764, it nevertheless continued to be the richest monastery in Russia with 13 large stone churches containing precious treasures, including icons and vestments, and a library containing many ancient manuscripts. From 1814, the Moscow Theological Academy was located there. A century later, at the outbreak of World War I, the Troitskaya Laura numbered more than 400 monks and novices. It supported and managed its own hospital, orphanage, home for the aged, and asylum; it also had its own iconography school and printing press, which specialized in liturgical texts and religious publications. Its monks also made vestments. In 1920 the Laura was nationalized by the Soviet government and turned into a Museum of History; the churches were closed and the monks expelled. In the wake of J. Stalin's policy of *rapprochement* with the Orthodox Church during World War II and in gratitude for the patriotic solidarity of church leaders, the Troitskaya Laura was given back some churches and other buildings and became again a religious center for the faithful; a little later, its Theological Academy was reopened. In the post-communist era, the monastery is gradually regaining its preeminent role in Russian monasticism.

Bibliography: I. SMOLITSCH, *Russisches Mönchtum* (Würzburg 1953).

[A. G. GIBSON/EDS.]

TROMBELLI, JOHN CHRYSOSTOM

Theologian; b. Galeazza near Nonantola, March 5, 1697; d. Bologna, Italy, Jan. 7, 1784. Educated at Bologna, he joined the Canons Regular of the Most Holy Savior in 1713. He taught philosophy at Candiana (Padua) and, for 15 years, theology at Bologna. In 1746 he was named academician of the Bologna Institute of Sciences. In 1737 he was elected abbot and subsequently held the highest offices of his Congregation: superior in Bologna (1739), secretary to the abbot-general (1751), and abbottgeneral (1760). In 1740 he published the six-volume theological work, *De cultu sanctorum dissertationes decem* (Bologna), attacked by the Protestants and praised by Benedict XIV. In reply to the criticisms of the Protestant J. Kiesling, he published *Priorum quatuor de cultu sanctorum dissertationum vindiciae* (Bologna 1751). He has left numerous theological and historical works: *Trattato degli Angeli Custodi* (Bologna 1747), *Vita e culto di S. Giuseppe* (Bologna 1767), and *B.M.V. vita ac gesta,* 6 v. (Bologna 1761), reprinted in J. Migne, *Summa Aurea* (Paris 1866). He also wrote a history of his own institute, *Ricerche istoriche concernenti le due canoniche di S. Maria di Reno e di S. Salvatore* (Bologna 1752). The two-volume *Veterum Patrum Latinorum opuscula* (Bologna 1751), containing some doubtful and apocryphal writings, is characteristic of his interest in patristics.

Bibliography: *De vita J. C. Trombelli commentarius* [by V. GAROFALO] (Bologna 1788). H. HURTER, *Nomenclator literarius theologiae catholicae,* 5 v. in 6 (3d ed. Innsbruck 1903–13) 5.1:331–334.

[L. LOSCHIAVO]

TROMBETTA, ANTONIO

Known also as Tubeta; Franciscan philosopher and theologian; b. Padua, 1436; d. there, 1517. He was regent of the Conventual *studium generale* at Padua and from c. 1476 to 1511 was professor of Scotistic metaphysics at the university. For 18 years he was provincial minister; in 1511 he was elected bishop of Urbino; and he was one of eight bishops on a commission that prepared a decree for the Fifth Lateran Council in 1513 condemning the Averroist thesis on the mortality and unity of the human soul. A follower of DUNS SCOTUS, Trombetta edited one of the first editions of Scotus's *In I sententiarum* (Venice 1472). While defending Scotistic doctrine, he was frequently involved in debate with the occupant of the Thomistic chair at the university, particularly Tommaso de Vio CAJETAN, who bitterly attacked Trombetta in his commentary on *De ente et essentia.* Trombetta's principal works include his *Quaestiones metaphysicales* (Venice 1493), which reappeared in 1502 as a commentary on the 12 books of Aristotle's *Metaphysics; Sententia in tractatum formalitatum scoticarum* (Venice 1493); *Quaestio de animarum humanarum pluralitate* (Venice 1498); *Quaestio de efficientia primi principii, quod est Deus, ad mentem Aristotelis et de eius infinitate intensiva* (Venice 1513); and *De adulto non baptizato* (Venice 1513).

See Also: SCOTISM.

Bibliography: L. WADDING, *Scriptores Ordinis Minorum* (Rome 1650; 3d ed. 1906). J. H. SBARALEA, *Supplementum et castigatio ad scriptores trium ordinum S. Francisci a Waddingo,* 2 v. (Rome 1806; new ed. in 4 v. 1906–36) v.1. A. POPPI, "Lo scotista patavino A. Trombetta," *Il Santo* 2 (1962) 349–367; "L'anti-averroismo della scolastica padovana alla fine del secolo XV," *Studia Patavina* 11 (1964) 102–124.

[A. POPPI]

TRONSON, LOUIS

Third superior of the Society of St. Sulpice, important for his work in the formulation of the Sulpician Constitution and the development of the Sulpician method of mental prayer; b. Paris, Jan. 17, 1622; d. Paris, Feb. 26, 1700. As the son of Louis Tronson, secretary to the privy council of Louis XIII, he attended the College of Navarre and was awarded a licentiate in Canon Law, a rarity in those days. He was ordained in 1647 and was appointed chaplain to the king. In 1656, after resigning his chaplaincy, he entered the Sulpicians. In the society, he was director of the solitude (1656) and director of the seminary (1657) until he was elected superior of the society on July 1, 1676. In 1680 he edited the *Réglements de la Compagnie,* based on the rules outlined by its founder M. Olier. He fought Jansenism strenuously, defending the papal decisions. Tronson became involved in the quietist controversy when he was asked to participate in the Issy conferences of 1694 and in the evaluation of Fénelon's *Maxims of the Saints.* He was a staunch defender of the cause of orthodoxy against Gallicanism. He edited both the letters and the writings on the priesthood of M. Olier. Tronson's principal work is the *Examens particuliers sur divers sujets propres aux ecclésiastiques.*

Bibliography: *Oeuvres complètes,* 2 v. (Paris 1857). J. MONVAL, *Les Sulpiciens* (Paris 1934).

[J. A. LAUBACHER]

TROPE

A relatively free but appropriate musical text interpolated in the authorized liturgy of the Roman rite during the period between the ninth and 12th centuries. The interpolation, which may be purely melodic or a melody with a text, functions as an amplification, embellishment, or intercalation in the official text but in no way changes the identity of the text itself. Neither is the material of the addition, although a new creation in both text and music, capable of artistic existence separate from the liturgical text whose handmaid it was intended to be. Only the antiphonal texts of the Proper of the Mass (Introit, Offertory, Communion) and some choral chants of the Mass Ordinary (*Gloria, Sanctus, Agnus Dei*) normally received text interpolation of this kind. In this article the substantive "trope" (from the Greek τρόπος) will refer to an object, an end product of a process of liturgical adaptation, and the verb "to trope" will refer to the process of interpolating upon an official text of the liturgy in any way, musically or verbally. Among the processes used from the ninth to the 12th centuries the following may be listed: 1. Addition of melodic extensions to the end of each phrase of an official liturgical piece; 2. Addition of a preface to an extant chant; 3. Addition of new text and new melody to existing chants.

Essentially all these processes were generated by the poetic sentiment of the official text. When this text has been expanded as a result of a fresh dramatic or lyrical response, the new musical introduction or continuation may display artistic vocal declamation reminiscent of the classic period of Gregorian composition. Not concerned with the meaning and the representation of separate words, the composers of tropes expressed their lyrical or dramatic responses like their predecessors in shaped phrases that projected the idea of the whole in a single stream of melody. These shaped phrases of the trope reflect the same syntactical structure as plainsong.

At approximately the same period in the history of liturgy, and largely in the same centers in which the trope originated, another process of liturgical amplification was yielding a distinct and separate repertory of paraliturgical elaboration designated as SEQUENCE, *prosa* or *prosula.* This second process marked an opposite direction in artistic creation and yielded amplifications that should not be confused with the tropes. Creatively the trope artist moved from the defined sentiment of a canonical text to a new but dependent expression—the trope. In the sequence process the artist moved from an unarticulated musical sentiment to a new text that became an autonomous expression.

At a period in the history of Gregorian chant when the official repertory had already been fixed, many of the new pieces resulting from either sequence or trope process were recorded, if at all, in unofficial collections possessing the technical generic name *troper.* As supplements to the official books, these collections contain examples of all that has been preserved of the new developments in the music of the liturgy between the ninth and 12th centuries.

Two traditions. Music scientists normally divide the existing manuscripts of Latin liturgical books, whether official or unofficial, into two general categories: the French or West Frankish tradition and the German or East Frankish tradition. The official books contained the repertory of music and prayers imposed by the Church for the canonical celebration of the liturgy. Of these books only those pertaining to the Mass and the Divine Office (*see* LITURGY OF THE HOURS)—the *Gradual* and the *Antiphonale*—will concern us here. The unofficial books contained the music and poetry that medieval artists added to the fixed repertory of the official books. These latter artifacts, while indeed adapted to particular occasions and usages, never achieved canonical rank. The greatest concentration of manuscripts of the French tradition was stored in the Abbey of Saint Martial at Limoges in France, and that of the German tradition, in the Abbey of Saint Gall (SANKT GALLEN) in Switzerland. The terms "French" and "German" used here to characterize particular traditions are generic conveniences rather than geographical precisions. To the French provenance, for example, belong some tropers of English and perhaps Spanish origin; and to the German provenance, some tropers of Italian and perhaps eastern European origin.

The French group of manuscripts is often referred to as the St. Martial Repertory and some of the earliest manuscripts involved are the following: Paris, Bibliothèque Nationale fonds lat. 1240 (Limoges); Paris, B.N. fonds lat. 1120 (Limoges); Paris, B.N. fonds lat. 1121 (Limoges); Oxford, Bodl. 775 (Winchester); Paris, B.N. fonds lat. 1118 (Southern France). The German group of manuscripts containing the Saint Gall Repertory has been studied by SCHUBIGER, Gaultier and Van den Steinen.

Liturgical music quotation from an early trope "Introit of the Third Mass of Christmas."

Among early examples of this repertory are the following: St. Gall 484 (St. Gall); Vienna 1609 (St. Gall); London, British Museum Add. 19768 (Mainz?-St. Alban), St. Gall 381 (St. Gall). Whatever their origin or provenance, tropes in the early tropers have some traits in common. Whether melodic and textual or purely melodic additions, the style of both the poetry and the music suggests that they are new compositions. They function with the new text in such a way, however, that the integrity of the official text, as well as its musical and textual identity, is both preserved and artistically amplified in its new context.

Words and music. The poetry of the trope has been dealt with in several monumental editions. The editorial decision to give only *incipits* of the official texts in these editions has distorted the aesthetic impression. The economic consideration that likely prompted the decision is clear; the practice itself, however, tends either to deemphasize the official text by taking it for granted or to overemphasize the new text by suggesting that its aesthetic character is to function independently of the official text. The implied shift of emphasis in either direction thwarts the precise balance between the two extremes, which was the perfection of the trope in its classic moment. History testifies to the fact that when in practice this aesthetic of liturgical amplification and dependence upon the text was taken over by other musical practices in the liturgy (for example, polyphony), the trope as an aesthetic object in its classic sense ceased to exist. It left the liturgical ground and began to develop in an independent direction. In this attempt it failed. In its failure, however, the trope helped to solidify and stabilize its already existing and independent counterpart, the sequence and to develop a new independent form, the liturgical drama. In its independence, on the other hand, it was unable to retain its classic identity or to survive as an aesthetic object.

While an aural awareness of the aesthetic logic characterizing the trope is important for the text, it is more important for the music. The musical ear can test stylistic consistency, good continuation and a feeling for unity and diversity within the parts. As an object to be experienced through hearing, the trope was constructed to appeal to the listener. Inspired by the traditional texts and saturated with the atmosphere, artistry and technical sophistication of the original Gregorian melodies, trope composers produced genuine artifacts to meet the needs of the time. Their creations had aesthetic as well as human appeal. The tradition they enshrined with fresh lyricism acquired a value appreciated for its own sake by creator and listener. In remounting the familiar, composers created suspensions and anticipations in the new which they later resolved or fulfilled in the familiar. Didactic, persuasive, or instructional purposes of the traditional texts were so highlighted in their surroundings that their practical purpose was less noticed than their aesthetic quality.

The music of the trope provides a multiplicity of textures covering the entire spectrum of vocal possibilities from melismatic textless melodies on one extreme to syl-

labic melodies with text at the other. A striking preponderance of neumatic textures characterizes the trope of the classical period. The musical additions function always as integral musical units with the official text and the contextual relation between old and new are aural rather than visual. When examining some antiphonal chants of the Proper, one is struck by the classical balance between words and music. The texts are normally well-wrought sentences in shape and syntax, and the prevailing neumatic tune grows out of that sentence structure, describing the same line with amplitude of melody. The earliest tropes set to some of these antiphonal chants match this texture. During the late Middle Ages, amplifications that entered into artistic dialogue with traditional pieces preserved a dynamic relation to the poetic and musical artistry of the original. They achieved their own artistic value because they were forms appropriate to function with the original and to objectify tradition at the personal creative level. The character of the entire structure was given by the tradition, then continued, intensified, or brought into relief by the music and the poetry of the addition.

In a prevailingly syllabic official text the addition tends to be melismatic and vice versa. Since the antiphonal chants usually lie between these extremes, aesthetic unity seems to have directed the composer to choose a corresponding neumatic texture for the trope also. When, as frequently happens, the addition begins in a tonality different from the official text, it may come to a point of momentary arrival on a word of grammatical punctuation (for example, *dicentes, exclamantes*) and at a pitch level that functions as a pivotal tone between the two tonalities. At other times a seamless passage is achieved by avoiding all arrival points in the new. Introductory tropes, often deceptively extended beyond possible arrival points, delay the anticipated and heighten tension. The created tension of the new in these latter two cases is resolved in the flow of the traditional that follows. The trope *Hodie Cantandus,* for the third (*Puer Natus*) Mass of Christmas, may serve as an example of the first of these devices. The trope, prevailingly in the Dorian mode on D, cadences on the pitch G (*praedixit*), the tonal center both of the transposed Dorian and the Mixolydian mode, the mode in which the official chant continues. The musical example is printed in *Laudes festivae,* ed., B. Reiser (2d ed. Rome 1940) 206–207.

Two other examples from more recent publications may serve as objects to test other criteria here offered. The first is the trope *Invice nos Stephani,* for the *Etenim sederunt* Introit of St. Stephen.

> *Invice nos Stephani, Dominum pulsando canamus: Eia!*
> [Etenim sederunt princi]pes, Supra cathedram

malignis suffultam testimoniis.

[et adversum me loqueban] tur: Istic homo loqui blasphema numquam desinit in legem.

[et iniqui persecuti sunt] me: Ne morte quidem vel sepulchro communi dignum me ducentes.

[adjuva me, Domine Deus] meus, Qui solus es adiutor in tribulationis supremis.

[quia servus tuus exercebatur in tuis justificationibus].

[Ps. Beati immaculati in via: QUI AMBULANT IN LEGE] Domini. Quam iste adeo servavit ut morti pro ipsa succubuerit.

[v. Gloria Patri . . .]

[r. Sicut erat . . . saeculorum.] Amen. Cujus hic trinitatis assertor meruit coronam sanguine. [Weakland, 486–487]

Here is a graphic interplay of an official text in neumatic style garlanded by a trope that at times is purely syllabic and at times purely melismatic. Using the first letters of each of these words (N)eumatic, (S)yllabic, (M)elismatic, one can also visualize what is audible in performance—the balanced succession of contrasting style between syllabic and melismatic polarities.

S NSM NSM NSM NS M

The second is the trope *Cunctipotens dominator* for the Kyrie of Mass XIV in the Kyriale. Here the text has been replaced by a syllabic one. The piece has been transformed by a creative process that moves from text to melody, a direction opposite that of the trope that essentially finds its unity of style in heterogeneity. This, then, is actually a *prosula* rather than a trope.

For methodological convenience the editors of Anal Hymn (v. 47 and 49) grouped all text interpolations of Gradual chants into tropes of the Proper (*Tropi Graduales ad Proprium Missarum*) or tropes of the Ordinary (*Tropi Graduales ad Ordinarium Missae*). Only the interpolations to the Introit, Offertory and Communion Antiphons of the Proper were called tropes in the *Gradual* sources. So-called Ordinary tropes are designated by a variety of terms: *Prosae ad Kyrieleison; Versus super Sanctus; Laudes de Agnus Dei.* This variety suggests a common aesthetic movement, from melody to some kind of verbalization. By the end of the 11th century medieval artists had begun to choose other means of defining the relevance of contemporary feelings to the tradition of the Church. Both of the earlier aesthetics were changed, but whereas the independent sequence and *prosula* were reorganized, the dependent trope was replaced. Polyphony, like the trope, was a listener's art. As an embellishment that amplified the sound of the text yet depended upon the text for its musical character, polyphony was structured to appeal to the senses of the people in their own churches, which had emerged as cathedrals in the new parochial

schema. The trope, meanwhile divorced from its liturgical connection and failing to achieve aesthetic independence, continued to contribute to a number of independent forms, especially those that, like the drama, were related to the audience as listeners and viewers.

Bibliography: J. HANDSCHIN, ''Trope, Sequence, and Conductus,'' *New Oxford History of Music,* ed., J. A. WESTRUP, 11 v. (New York 1957–) 2:128–174. G. REESE, *Music in the Middle Ages,* (New York 1940). C. BLUME, *Tropen des Missale im Mittelalter,* 2 v. *Analecta hymnica,* 47, 49; 1905–06). J. CHAILLEY, *L'École musicale de St. Martial de Limoges* (Paris 1960). *The Winchester Troper,* ed., W. A. FRERE, (London 1894). L. GAUTIER, *Les Tropes,* v.1 of *Histoire de la poésie liturgique au moyen âge* (Paris 1886). A. SCHUBIGER, *Die Sängerschule St. Gallens* (Einsiedeln 1858). W. VON DEN STEINEN, *Notker der Dichter und seine geistige Welt,* 2 v. (Bern 1948). P. EVANS, ''Some Reflections on the Origin of the Trope,'' *Journal of the American Musicological Society* 14 (1961) 119–130. R. WEAKLAND, ''The Beginnings of Troping,'' *Musical Quarterly* 44 (1958) 477–488. B. STÄBLEIN, ''Die Unterlegung von Texten unter Melismen,'' *International Musicological Society: Report of the Eighth Congress,* 2 v. (Basel 1961) 1:12–29.

[E. LEAHY/EDS.]

TROY, JOHN THOMAS

Archbishop of Dublin; b. Porterstown, County Dublin, June 26, 1739; d. Dublin, May 10, 1823. His father, James Troy, was a Dublin merchant; his mother, Mary (Neville) Troy, was descended from an old County Wexford family. In 1754 he entered the DOMINICANS, and was sent to study at St. Clement's, Rome. After ordination (1762) he taught at St. Clement's, where he became regent of studies (1771) and prior (1772). In November 1776 he was named bishop of Ossory, Ireland. As bishop he sought to dispel the allegation, which was used to justify penal laws against Catholics, that Catholicism was in principle inimical to a Protestant government and constitution. He consistently denounced riots and civil disturbances as incompatible with the duty of obedience to established government. Troy was transferred to the archbishopric of Dublin (Nov. 27, 1786). Irish opinion strongly favored this appointment, especially after the competence and zeal that he had displayed during his brief tenure as administrator of the See of ARMAGH in trying circumstances (1782) and his tact in correcting abuses. Troy incurred considerable unpopularity, however, by opposing the spread of FRENCH REVOLUTION philosophy in Ireland after 1789. He denounced the Irish Rising of 1798 as stemming from this source, although he petitioned the government to protect the victims of the Orange outrages that accompanied the uprising. In return for assurances that measures would be taken to end bigotry, he supported the legislative union of Great Britain and Ireland (1801) and agreed that only candidates loyal to the government would be promoted to Irish bishoprics. Various plans to implement this principle as a condition of Catholic EMANCIPATION involved Troy in violent political controversy, despite his efforts to limit himself to the religious issues. These activities did not materially affect his pastoral labors, which fostered the foundation of new religious institutes and enriched Catholic life. For long periods during his episcopacy communication with Rome was impossible. During that time bishops in Ireland and elsewhere in the English-speaking world were guided by his actions and advice. He died in poverty and was buried in the procathedral, Dublin.

Bibliography: W. CARRIGAN, *The History and Antiquities of the Diocese of Ossory,* 4 v. (Dublin 1905). J. D'ALTON, *The Memoirs of the Archbishops of Dublin* (Dublin 1838). L. NOLAN, *The Irish Dominicans in Rome* (Rome 1913).

[H. E. PEEL]

TRUCHSESS VON WALDBURG, OTTO AND GEBHARD

Prominent ecclesiastics from a princely German family whose ancestral seat was the city of Ravensberg.

Otto. Cardinal, bishop of Augsburg, and leader in Tridentine reform; b. Scheer Castle, near Sigmaringen, Feb. 25, 1514; d. Rome, April 2, 1573. During his studies at the Universities of Tübingen, Padua, Pavia, and Bologna, he counted as his student friends Alessandro FARNESE, Cristofero MADRUZZO, and Stanislaus HOSIUS, themselves later figures in the movement for Church reform. Otto held benefices at Augsburg (1526), Speyer (1529), and Trent (1540), and rose in the diplomatic service, becoming papal chamberlain to Paul III (1540), councilor of Emperor Charles V (1541), and bishop of Augsburg (1543). The next year Paul III created him a cardinal priest with the title of St. Balbina. He initiated reforms in his diocese, held synods (1543, 1548, 1567), and founded an academy (later the university), and a seminary at Dillingen (1549), which he entrusted to the care of the Jesuits. His interest in the Society of Jesus and its place in Catholic reform led to his friendship with the Jesuits, Claude LE JAY (JAJUS), Robert BELLARMINE, and Peter CANISIUS. Although he failed to erect a Jesuit college at Augsburg, he became a patron of the establishment of the German College at Rome.

As imperial councilor, he championed Catholicism and opposed the SCHMALKALDIC LEAGUE (1531–47) and the articles of the Peace of Augsburg (1555). This position and his appointment as protector of the Empire by Charles V earned him the hostility of the Protestants and forced him to live mostly at Rome (1559–63; 1568 to his

death). In 1562 he was made bishop of Albano, and he succeeded to the sees of Sabina and Palestrina (1570). During the third period of the Council of Trent (1562–63) he was an ardent promoter of legislation for the erection of seminaries.

Gebhard. Archbishop of Cologne; b. Scheer Castle, Nov. 10, 1547; d. Strassburg, May 31, 1601. He was the nephew of Otto and destined for an ecclesiastical career. When 13 years old he held a benefice in the cathedral of Augsburg, later becoming a canon there (1567), at Cologne (1568), and at Strassburg (1574). On Dec. 5, 1577, amid tense political feeling, he was elected to the archbishopric of Cologne (12 votes to 10) against Ernest of Bavaria (1554–1612), youngest son of Albrecht of Bavaria. His choice was confirmed by Rome as well as by the imperial electoral college. It was hoped that Gebhard would plan a program of reform after the pattern of his uncle Otto, but after 1579 he kept a mistress, Countess Agnes von Mansfeld, and in an attempt to legalize this union, he sought the support of Johann Casimir, the Calvinistic Count Palatine. He married Agnes on March 2, 1583, and tried to secularize Cologne by making it a free religious city. Following his excommunication by Gregory XIII, April 1, 1583, a new election brought Ernest of Bavaria to the vacated see. Gebhard opposed the new archbishop's Bavarian troops with the aid of Johann Casimir and William of Orange (the Cologne War), but in 1589 he retired to Strassburg where he resided until his death.

Bibliography: OTTO. B. SCHWARZ, *Kardinal Otto, Truchsess v. Waldburg* (Hildesheim 1923). B. DUHR, ''Die Quellen zu einer Biographie des Kardinals Otto Truchsess von Weldburg,'' *Historisches Jahrbuch der Görres-Gesellschaft* 7 (1886) 177–209; 20 (1899) 71–74. H. JEDIN, *History of the Council of Trent,* tr. E. GRAF, v. 1–2 (St. Louis 1957–60), v.3; *Geschichte des Konzils von Trient,* 2 v. (Freiburg 1949–57; v.1, 2d ed. 1951) v.1. F. SIEBERT, *Lexikon für Theologie und Kirche,* ed. M. BUCHBERGER, 10 v. (Freiburg 1930–38) 10:723–725. L. PASTOR, *The History of the Popes from the Close of the Middle Ages,* 40 v. (London-St. Louis 1938–61) v.12–19, 20, 23. GEBHARD. M. LOSSEN, *Der kölnische Krieg . . .* (Gotha 1882). G. SCHREIBER, ed., *Das Weltkonzil von Trient,* 2 v. (Freiburg 1951) v.2. H. JEDIN, *History of the Council of Trent,* tr. E. GRAF, v. 1–2 (St. Louis 1957–60), v.3; *Geschichte des Konzils von Trient,* 2 v. (Freiburg 1949–57; v.1, 2d ed. 1951) v.2. L. PASTOR, *The History of the Popes from the Close of the Middle Ages,* 40 v. (London-St. Louis 1938–61) v.19, 20, 22.

[E. D. MCSHANE]

TRUDO OF BRABANT (TROND), ST.

Benedictine abbot, patron of the Hesbaye region of Brabant, Belgium; d. *c.* 698. An ardent youth, Trudo was sent by Bp. Remaclus of Maastrict to the school of St. Stephan-Protomartyr in Metz, there being no schools in the Low Countries at that time. Trudo founded a convent near Bruges and a monastery near Louvain, which took his name after his death (*see* SAINT TROND, ABBEY OF) and promoted his cult as a monk "who professed the rule of St. Benedict and lived it regularly." By the 11th century, Trudo was almost forgotten. However, his relics were translated to St. Stephen-Protomartyr in 1227.

Feast: Nov. 23.

Bibliography: *Monumenta Germaniae Historica: Scriptores rerum Merovingicarum* (Berlin 1826–) 6:264–298. A. M. ZIMMERMANN, *Kalendarium Benedictinum: Die Heiligen und Seligen des Benediktinerordens und seiner Zwiege,* 4. (Metten 1933–38) 3:346–348. J. L. BAUDOT and L. CHAUSSIN, *Vies des saints et des bienheureux selon l'ordre du calendrier avec l'historique des fêtes,* ed. by the Benedictines of Paris, 12 v. (Paris 1935–56); v. 13, suppl. and table générale (1959) 11:795–796. M. COENS, "Les Saints particulièrement honorés à l'Abbaye de Saint-Trond," *Analecta Bollandiana* 72 (Brussels 1954) 90–94, 98–100. A. BUTLER, *The Lives of the Saints,* rev. ed. H. THURSTON and D. ATTWATER, 4 v. (New York 1956) 4:413.

[R. BALCH]

TRUDPERT, ST.

German solitary in the Black Forest; d. *c.* 643. In the first half of the 7th century he established a cell in the Münstertal (Breisgau) in the southern part of the Black Forest of Germany. According to tradition he was murdered by his servants; later the Benedictine monastery of Sankt Trudpert (dissolved 1806) rose on the site. The traditional date of Trudpert's death, 607, is based on a 13th-century calculation and is probably incorrect; he may have died *c.* 643. The surviving sources for his career, dating from the 10th century and later, mingle fact and legend; very little credence can be placed in the traditions that make him an Irishman, a brother of St. RUPERT OF SALZBURG, and a relative of the Hapsburgs. His relics were elevated, i.e., his cult recognized, in 902.

Feast: April 26.

Bibliography: *Passio Thrudperti, Monumenta Germaniae Historica: Scriptores rerum Merovingicarum* (Berlin 1826–) 4:352–363. *Beiträge zur Geschichte von Sankt Trudpert,* ed. T. MAYER (Freiburg 1937).

[W. A. ERNEST]

TRUSTEEISM

In U.S. Catholic history, trusteeism was a form of insubordination in which lay parishioners, particularly lay parish trustees, on the basis of civil law claimed excessive parochial administrative powers and even the right to choose and dismiss pastors.

Lay intrusion into the temporal and temporal-spiritual affairs of the Catholic Church has a long history, and trusteeism has been its principal American episode. Although trustee troubles were far from universal, they occurred widely and sometimes intensely in nearly 20 states of the East, South, and near Middle West. The "trustee-mania" waned only when the hierarchy, through more adequate canonical and civil rulings, gained legal protection for their native right to manage church goods and appoint church personnel.

Roots of Trusteeism. An old American trustee system of parish administration, Protestant in origin and conception, invested lay trustees or churchwardens with wide control of parish temporalities, a control that in the Protestant context usually implied the right of patronage. Early state legislation favored the system, and where a state granted legal incorporation to a Catholic parish, it recognized the laity as the true administrators.

Lay parochial associates were not unknown in the Catholic Church where the existence of *fabricae,* or boards of lay managers, was recognized by the Council of Trent (Sess. 22, Cap. 9, de ref.). Committees of these churchwardens (*marguilliers*) were familiar in the parishes of France, and in the Rhineland, the home country of many early German Catholic immigrants to the U.S. But there was this difference between *marguillier* board and trustee board: the original *marguilliers* were essentially subject to the clergy; the trustees, essentially independent of them. Catholic trustees could, of course, interpret their civil powers in a Catholic light, even as a civilly divorced Catholic can repudiate his legal "right" to remarry. But too frequent abuse eventually turned the hierarchy against the old trustee system in principle.

Initial Period: 1785–1829. The state of New York was the first to enact a law of general incorporation for church congregations. The Act of April 6, 1784 (somewhat amended in 1813), allowed the male adults of a parish of any denomination to elect trustees, who thereby became a parochial corporation with wide administrative powers. While the law declared its intention not to disturb the "doctrine, discipline, or worship" of the incorporating denomination, its inadequate terminology gave parish suffrage even to lapsed Catholics, left clergy off trustee boards, and tolerated lay "right of patronage" [S. Jones and R. Varick, eds., *Laws of the State of New York* (New York 1789) 1:104–10; *Laws of the State of New York* (Albany 1813) 2:212–19]. Several states imitated the New York law; others made parallel provisions.

The first case of trusteeism occurred in New York City's pioneer Catholic parish while John Carroll was prefect apostolic of the U.S. The lay founders of St. Peter's chose to incorporate on June 10, 1785, under the

Act of 1784, as "The Trustees of the Roman Catholic Church of the City of New York." Carroll permitted the incorporation and granted faculties as rector to Irish-born Charles Whelan, OFMCap, and as assistant rector—some months later—to Irish-born Andrew Nugent, OFMCap. But before long the ambitious Nugent, abler than Whelan as a preacher, so influenced the trustees that in January 1786 they threatened to invoke civil law if Carroll did not at once discharge Whelan and replace him with Nugent. Dismayed by the trustees' un-Catholic appeal to their "civil rights" and by the partisan tumult they had caused in church, Carroll rejected their demand and pointed out that in Church law they enjoyed no right of patronage. Whelan chose to depart after intolerable harassment. Nugent, however, soon antagonized even the trustees by his misbehavior. Suspended by Carroll, he led his die-hard adherents into schism, declaring himself subject only to Christ and the civil officials of New York. The trustees had to bring suit to wrest from the unfortunate friar the church property that he had forcibly retained.

Most of the elements of trusteeism, including unruly priests, were present in this original case.

Soon national sensitivities also began to figure. Carroll's trouble with Holy Trinity in Philadelphia was largely one of German nationalism. At St. Mary's, Charleston, S.C., the Irish objected to French-born pastors. As a bishop, John Carroll met new complications in the Diocese of Louisiana when he was named its administrator in 1805. The *marguilliers,* recently installed by civil authority at St. Louis Cathedral in New Orleans, claimed the right in American civil law to elect church superiors, and therefore refused to accept the priest whom Carroll appointed as their vicar-general.

After the subdivision of the Diocese of Baltimore in 1808, trusteeism spread rather than subsided, largely for want of an organized stand against it. True, the bishops of Boston and Bardstown kept matters in hand throughout New England and the near Middle West, but there were grave disorders in the Diocese of New York, the Archdiocese of Baltimore, and the Diocese of Philadelphia. The factions dispersed at St. Peter's, New York, only after Rome, in 1821, ordered Bp. John Connolly to dismiss two troublesome clerics. The trustees of St. Mary's, Charleston, S.C., and the Gallican-minded trustees of St. Patrick's, Norfolk, Va., by incessant agitation coupled with the threat of a Jansenist schism, wrung from the Holy See the establishment of new dioceses centered at Charleston and Richmond, Va. In Philadelphia the aged Bp. Henry Conwell, after long withstanding the scandalous Hogan schism at St. Mary's Church, incurred the displeasure of Rome because of an ill-advised strategy, and had to yield his jurisdiction and its trustee problems into the hands of a coadjutor and administrator, Bp. Francis P. Kenrick.

One good effect of these conflicts was the issuance of two papal documents. Disturbed by the Hogan schism, Pius VII, in the brief *Non sine magno* (Aug. 24, 1822), reiterated to the American hierarchy the Catholic principle that church property is subject to hierarchical, not lay, control and branded trusteeist claims to the *jus patronatus* as "novum . . . ac plane inauditum" (novel . . . and quite unheard of) [R. De Martinis, *Juris Pontifici de Propaganda Fide* (Rome 1888–98), Pars Ia, 4:619–22]. Leo XII, in the *Quo longius,* addressed on Aug. 28, 1828, to Bp. Joseph Rosati, administrator of the Diocese of New Orleans, restated the warnings of the *Non sine magno* to the New Orleans Cathedral trustees (*ibid.,* 705–706).

Decisive Period: 1829 to 1884. As first bishop of Charleston, John England harnessed trusteeism with his ingenious diocesan "constitution" of 1823. The hierarchy in general at last found an effective weapon in the antitrusteeist legislation of the Councils of BALTIMORE. Decree 5 of the First Provincial Council (1829) urged bishops wherever possible to demand the property deed before dedicating any future church. Decree 6 denied the existence of any canonical *jus patronatus* in the province of Baltimore and declared that church benefactors did not acquire such a right by virtue of their donations. Decrees 7 and 8 instructed bishops to impose canonical penalties on refractory clerics and laymen. Amplified in subsequent Provincial Councils—the Third (1837), Fourth (1840), Fifth (1843), and Seventh (1847)—the legislation was extended to the whole country by Decrees 2, 15, 16, and 17 of the First Plenary Council of Baltimore (1852).

Applying the Baltimorean rules with all deference to civil law, the bishops gradually cured the old cases of trusteeism and checked its westward spread. The task was hardest in Louisiana, Pennsylvania, and New York.

When in 1846 Bp. Anthony Blanc of New Orleans vanquished the *marguilliers* of his cathedral, his hand was strengthened by a Louisiana supreme court decision and a letter from Gregory XVI (*Ecclesiae universae,* March 26, 1844: De Martinis, 5:331–32). But at Holy Trinity in Philadelphia and St. Louis in Buffalo the trusteeists stoutly withstood Abp. Gaetano BEDINI, whom the Holy See sent over in 1853 to examine their claims. Two years later a number of trusteeists, conspiring with newly elected state legislators of the anti-Catholic Know-Nothing Party (*see* KNOW-NOTHINGISM), procured in New York, Pennsylvania, and elsewhere laws intended to compel all Catholic parishes to adopt the odious trustee form of incorporation.

Except in Pennsylvania this discriminatory legislation was soon repealed and fairer regulations for property tenure were devised. The most influential was the New York State act of March 25, 1863, which framed a type of corporation aggregate quite acceptable to Catholics in that its board comprised the bishop, vicar-general, pastor, and two lay trustees chosen by the three [*Laws of the State of New York Passed in the Eighty-Sixth Session of the Legislature* (Albany 1863) 65–67; *McKinney's Consolidated Laws of New York Annotated* (Brooklyn 1952) 50:116–19, 120–22]. While *Titulus IV* of the Second Plenary Council of Baltimore (1866) indicated no preference regarding modes of property tenure, *Titulus IX* of the Third Plenary Council (1884) implicitly favored the aggregate corporation. On July 29, 1911, the Congregation of the Council officially ranked the corporation aggregate ahead of the corporation sole [Decree *Sacrorum Antistitum,* in *American Ecclesiastical Review,* 45 (1911) 585–86]. Precedents had meanwhile accumulated in civil courts tending to uphold the church authorities in litigation over church properties, e.g., *Watson v. Jones,* U.S. Supreme Court, 1871 [80 U.S., 679 (1872)].

Later Trusteeism. After 1884 trusteeism occurred mostly among Slavic immigrants from central and eastern Europe. Untutored like the earlier immigrants and faced with similar parish problems, the new immigrants likewise appealed to the un-Catholic ambiguities of civil law. The story of later trusteeism has yet to be investigated. A trusteeist mentality was certainly evident in the formation of the POLISH NATIONAL CATHOLIC CHURCH and the large schismatic movements among the Greek-rite Ruthenian Catholics, both Ukrainian and Russian.

Conclusion. The struggle with trusteeism was an important phase in the accommodation of the Catholic Church to the American milieu. Extreme doctrinaire trusteeists were few, were usually nominal Catholics, and maintained their brief leadership only in the face of a real or imagined grievance. It must be admitted, however, that the trustee system appealed to many worthy Catholics. Entranced by the democratic procedures of the U.S., they were eager to apply them even as their Protestant neighbors did, in the small republic of the parish. The battle against trusteeism was therefore a canonical, legal, and educational battle against an incipient Catholic congregationalism. Understandably, the campaign engendered in the American hierarchy a caution, sometimes even excessive, about delegating to laymen extensive authority over church temporalities.

Bibliography: P. J. DIGNAN, *A History of the Legal Incorporation of Catholic Church Property in the United States, 1784–1932* (Washington 1933). R. F. MCNAMARA, ''Trusteeism in the Atlantic States, 1785–1863,'' *American Catholic Historical Review* 30 (1944) 135–154. A. G. STRITCH, ''Trusteeism in the Old Northwest, 1800–1850,'' *ibid.* 155–164; and works cited by all three. For the *marguillier* tradition *see* R. BAUDIER, *The Catholic Church in Louisiana* (New Orleans 1939). G. PARÉ, *The Catholic Church in Detroit, 1701–1888* (Detroit 1951). See also recent histories of eastern and southern dioceses and M. J. CURLEY, *Venerable John Neumann, CSSR, Fourth Bishop of Philadelphia* (Washington 1952). V. J. FECHER, *A Study of the Movement for German National Parishes in Philadelphia and Baltimore, 1787–1802* (Rome 1955). H. J. NOLAN, *The Most Reverend Francis Patrick Kenrick, Third Bishop of Philadelphia, 1813–1886* in Catholic University of America, *Studies in American Church History,* 37 (Washington 1948). A. P. STOKES, *Church and State in the United States,* 3 v. (New York 1950). Slavic trusteeism is touched on in: T. ANDREWS, *The Polish National Catholic Church* (Society for Promoting Christian Knowledge, London 1953). S. GULOVICH, *Windows Westward: Rome, Russia, Reunion* (New York 1947); ''The Russian Exarchate in the United States,'' *The Eastern Churches Quarterly* 6 (1946) 459–486. A. SENYSHYN, ''The Ukrainian Catholics in the United States,'' *ibid.* 439–458.

[R. F. MCNAMARA]

TRUSZKOWSKA, ANGELA MARIA, BL.

Baptized Sophia (Zofia) Camille; foundress of the Felician Sisters; b. May 16, 1825, Kalisz, Poland; d. Oct. 10, 1899, Krakow, Poland.

Joseph Truszkowski, a judge, and his wife Josephine had the means to educate their frail daughter Sophia at home. She enrolled in Madame Guerin's academy when her family moved to Warsaw (1837), but tuberculosis forced her to continue her studies in her father's extensive library after she recovered in a Swiss sanitarium. She considered joining the Visitation Nuns, but she remained at home to assist her ailing father.

Sophia came to understand her vocation was serving the poor, not cloistered contemplation, during a trip to Cologne, Germany (1848). At first she answered the call as a member of the Society of Saint VINCENT DE PAUL. Later she became a lay Franciscan and took the name Angela. At age 29, she sought out and helped street children and the aged homeless in the Warsaw slums. Soon she and her cousin Clothilde were caring for six children in two attic rooms with the financial help of her father.

On Nov. 21, 1855, Sophia and Clothilde made private vows before the icon of Our Lady of Częstochowa. They attracted other volunteers to form a congregation in 1857, which responds to the needs of the Church in social service or catechetical centers. Mother Angela's name is inexorably linked with that of Blessed Honorat KOZMINSKI (1829–1916), who was appointed spiritual director for the new order. The congregation received its name—the Sisters of Saint Felix of Cantalice—because the sisters took their young charges to pray at the shrine of the patron of children.

After three successive terms as superior general of the Felician sisters, Mother Angela (age 44) stepped aside because of her increasing deafness. She served another 30 years as a simple sister, but did continue to guide the order and inspire new ministries, including their mission to the United States (1874). Towards the end of her life, Sister Angela suffered from deafness and cancer; the latter eventually claimed her life. Her remains were enshrined in the motherhouse chapel on Smolensk Street, Krakow.

In his homily at Bl. Angela's beatification (Apr. 18, 1993), Pope John Paul II, who had opened her cause as Cardinal Karol Wojtyła of Krakow, noted that ''Christ formed her spirit through great suffering, which she accepted with faith and truly heroic submission to his will: in seclusion and solitude, through a long, painful disease, and in the dark night of the soul.''

Feast: Oct. 10.

Bibliography: F. A. CEGIELKA, *The Pierced Heart* (Milwaukee 1955). M. WINOWSKA, *Go, Repair My House*, tr. C. QUINTAL (Lodi, NJ 1976). M. B. DMOWSKA, *Matka Maria Angela Truszkowska: Założycielka Zgromadzenia Sióstr Felicjanek* (Buffalo 1949). M. J. ZIOLKOWSKI, *The Felician Sisters of Livonia, Michigan: First Province in America* (Detroit, MI 1984).

[K. I. RABENSTEIN]

TRUTH

The accordance or conformity between what is asserted and what is, or the conformity of intellection with being. From the viewpoint of the intellect as consciously conformed to being, truth is called logical or epistemological; from the viewpoint of being as conformed to intellection, it is called ontological. This article deals first with the history of the notion of truth, then with truth as studied in EPISTEMOLOGY, and finally with truth as studied in ONTOLOGY.

HISTORY OF THE NOTION OF TRUTH

The historical development of the concept of truth may be divided into phases corresponding to the development of Greek, patristic and medieval, modern, and contemporary philosophy.

Greek origins. The problem of truth was implicitly treated at the dawn of Western philosophy (6th century B.C.), when men first sought principles that would explain the changing universe. It was explicitly treated by PARMENIDES; rejecting the doctrine of HERACLITUS, he distinguished the world of sense as the domain of appearance, change, multiplicity, and falsity from the world of thought as the world of the stable, the one, and the true.

The true, for Parmenides, is the object of thought or the intelligible, and the true or being is one. Multiplicity is appearance; it is the effect of the disintegrating influence of man's senses on being.

The SOPHISTS, holding that man cannot attain certainty and that the only truth he has is the contingent judgment of the senses, which differs from one individual to another, first posed the problem of necessary truth and of the subject-object relationship in the knowing process.

PLATO taught that on the occasion of sensation there is awakened in man a corresponding IDEA, which was dormant in the soul from its contemplation of the subsisting Ideas before its incarnation in the body. The Ideas are the universal, necessary, and immutable essences, the archetypes of the sensible reality that imitates and participates in them. The Ideas, existing in the intelligible world hierarchically under the supreme Idea of the Good, are more real than sensible reality. Necessary truth, therefore, is the conformity of man's thought to the Ideas. Contingent and changeable truth, or OPINION, is the conformity of his knowledge to the sensible world.

For ARISTOTLE, truth is primarily in the JUDGMENT. The judgment is true when it attributes a predicate to, or denies it of, a subject, according to what reality itself demands. Truth then is the adequation of the intellect to reality. Judgment guarantees the necessary truth of the FIRST PRINCIPLES, particularly that of contradiction, which are founded in being. The universal CONCEPT that functions in judgment is not had from an intuition of the subsisting Ideas, but is obtained by abstracting or dematerializing the formal notes of sensible reality (*see* ABSTRACTION). Aristotle even conceived God as Thought Thinking Itself (*Meta.* 1074b 15–1075a 11), and in this sense as subsisting Idea or Truth.

Patristic and Medieval thought. Christianity, as the revealed truth of God proposing the Second Person of the Holy Trinity as the Truth by whom all things that exist are made, opened up new vistas for philosophical speculation on the nature of truth. The greatest of the Church Fathers, St. AUGUSTINE, inspired by Plato (as interpreted and synthesized with Aristotle by PLOTINUS), made the idea of truth central in his philosophy (C. Boyer, *L'Idée de vérité dans la philosophie de saint Augustin,* 2nd ed. Paris 1947). Truth, as a property of knowledge, is the affirmation of that which is. Man knows immutable and eternal truths, e.g., the laws of number and essences, with certainty. By these truths he judges the sensible. These truths are not justified by sensible reality, but are a PARTICIPATION in man's intellect of the first and subsistent truth, which is God. Hence from necessary truth, such as two and two make four, one can prove the existence of God (*Lib. arb.* 2.8.20–24). Truth as applied to reality is the identity of the idea and reality. Reality is true when it fully verifies what is said of it, when it fully verifies the idea, and hence when it is the idea. Only God fully verifies the idea. He is truth. Finite beings are true insofar as they are imperfect imitations of the first Truth, of the Subsistent Idea, which is God.

St. THOMAS AQUINAS, who achieved the most perfect synthesis of Christian philosophy, unlike Aristotle treated truth explicitly as a transcendental property of being. Being as true is being as related to man's intellect (*De ver.* 1.1). Since being does not depend on man's intellect, the relation that truth adds to being is a relation of reason manifesting the intelligibility of being. This intelligibility is the dependence of being on its intelligent cause, God. Hence every being as intelligible presupposes its idea in the mind of God. God is identically subsisting Intellection and Being, or subsistent Truth. Knowing His essence as imitable, He forms the idea of every creature He can produce. Creating, God conforms to His intellect the reality produced, making it identically intelligible and existing (*Summa theologiae* 1a, 15). Man attains truth properly in the judgment. His direct judgment is the affirmation of the nature of sensible reality according to the norm of being.

Modern development. R. DESCARTES, the father of modern philosophy, was concerned primarily with CERTITUDE as this is found in mathematics. Hence, for him, truth is that which man conceives in a clear and distinct idea. Clear and distinct concepts, which are also innate and intuitive, represent reality exactly as it is in itself. Reality and the conceptual are identical. The analytical laws of connection of concepts are laws of reality. This is the principle of RATIONALISM. It led N. MALEBRANCHE to ONTOLOGISM, wherein man is proposed as having immediate intuition of the divine ideas. It led G. W. LEIBNIZ, complementing Cartesianism by DYNAMISM, to his doctrine of a pre-established harmony among the active elements of the universe, which he conceived as incapable of acting on each other. Rationalism found its logical conclusion in the absolute MONISM of B. SPINOZA: there is only one substance, God, of whose infinite modes man knows only two, namely, extension and cognition.

Diametrically opposed to rationalism is EMPIRICISM, which, prepared for by the NOMINALISM of WILLIAM OF OCKHAM and by the scientific method of Francis BACON, appeared in England under T. HOBBES, J. LOCKE, and G. BERKELEY, but found its full expression in D. HUME. With the exception of mathematics, which he saw as a logical analysis of identities, Hume reduced all valid knowledge to sense impressions and to images derived from sense impressions and associated by habit. Therefore, for him, the notions of causality, of substance, of

soul, etc., are invalid. Hence truth for man is the conformity of his knowing to sense impressions. B. RUSSELL and logical positivists such as A. J. Ayer (1910–89) follow Hume in making sense verifiability the norm of truth for all factual statements.

For I. KANT, who reacted against the extremes of rationalism and empiricism, truth is the conformity of thought to its object. The object of thought is not reality as it is in itself, however, but is the product of the a priori forms of the unity of consciousness, which synthesize the elements of sensation received from reality. Hence necessary and universal truth is founded not in being itself but in the forms of man's cognitive faculties. Since the knowing subject produces the formal elements of knowledge, this system is called transcendental IDEALISM.

The successors of Kant, J. G. FICHTE, F. W. J. SCHELLING, and G. W. F. HEGEL, sought to remove the opposition between the two sources of valid knowledge in Kant, namely, the a priori forms of the subject and the material elements from reality itself. Hence they explained knowledge by the knowing Ego alone, thus reducing being to knowing. The most complete statement of this form of idealism is Hegel's. For Hegel truth is dialectically (i.e., by a synthesis of oppositions) evolving reason, realizing itself first as external nature, then as the human spirit, and finally as the absolute idea of absolute truth. This necessary evolution of reason constitutes history. Hence in this non-relative sense truth is historical.

Contemporary directions. Existentialists such as S. A. KIERKEGAARD, K. JASPERS, G. MARCEL, and J. P. SARTRE, reacting to the impersonal nature of idealism, reject objective and universal truth as superficial and of no personal value (*see* EXISTENTIALISM). Truth in the real sense of the word is practical and subjective. Real truth reveals itself to man only in and as the exercise of his liberty of accepting himself in the authentic human situation. Hence real truth is personal truth: the truth by which one lives and to which one commits oneself.

M. Heidegger holds the truth of judgment, as the conformity of judgment to reality, to be truth only in a derived sense. Truth in the primary sense, which makes the truth of judgment possible, is the revelation through man's being of the ''to be'' of being as such. This revelation takes place historically under different forms, all of which are true. In this sense truth is historical (see M. Heidegger, *Vom Wesen der Wahrheit,* Frankfurt-am-Main 1943).

For pragmatists, such as C. S. PEIRCE, W. JAMES, and J. Dewey, a proposition is true when, once admitted, it leads to satisfactory results.

Marxism, the doctrine of K. MARX and F. ENGELS as developed by N. LENIN and J. Stalin, applies the dialectic of Hegel to matter. The only reality is matter, which evolves dialectically with historical necessity in function of economic factors toward a classless society. All man's thoughts, desires, and activity are a result of economic needs. Truth therefore is pragmatic; it is the conformity of knowing to that which here and now most promotes evolution toward the Communist society.

Bibliography: M. J. ADLER, ed., *The Great Ideas: A Syntopicon of Great Books of the Western World* (Chicago 1952) 2:915–938. R. EISLER, *Wörterbuch der philosophischen Begriffe* (Berlin 1927–30) 3:450–471. G. GAWLICK, *Die Religion in Geschichte und Gegenwart* (3d ed. Tübingen 1957–63) 6:1518–25. A. CARLINI, *Enciclopedia filosofica* 4:1549–60. A. FOSSATI, *ibid.* 4:1560–61. A. MICHEL, *Dictionnaire de théologie catholique* v. 15 (Paris 1950) 2:2675–87.

[F. P. O'FARRELL]

TRUTH IN EPISTEMOLOGY

EPISTEMOLOGY is concerned with the efforts of the human mind to attain true and certain knowledge; it seeks to establish and evaluate canons whereby such knowledge may be differentiated from the false and the dubious. Truth in human knowing is the concern also of logic, however, and thus, before analyzing truth from an epistemological point of view, it will be advantageous to explain how truth is treated in logic.

Truth in logic. As the science and the art that directs the mind in its reasoning process, LOGIC is concerned in some way with truth. In its instrumental role, however, logic considers the correctness of the thought processes by which man knows things and judges and reasons about them. Thus logic aims directly at formal truth alone and can assure only the correct form of the mind's constructions; the matter or content with which such constructions are concerned remain outside its scope. It is possible, for example, to argue correctly from premises to a conclusion, attaining in the process formal correctness, and yet to miss material truth because the premises are false in their content. The truth that logic seeks, therefore, is a truth of method rather than one of content. This is well illustrated in the treatment of truth functions in symbolic logic (*see* LOGIC, SYMBOLIC). In a complicated argument, logical relations may be seen more clearly and manipulated more easily and correctly if symbols, rather than involved verbal expressions, are used. Particularly is this so in verifying the investigations of the physical sciences, where mathematics is an important tool.

Truth of knowledge. The word truth (Lat. *veritas*, Gr. ἀλήθεια) means in general some kind of agreement between thought and its object, between knowledge and that which is known. It is sometimes applied to things, and a thing is said to be true in the sense of ontological truth. In reference to speech, truth is called veracity, or

moral truth, and is present when a person expresses what is in his mind. *See* TRUTHFULNESS (VERACITY). But the primary meaning of the word refers to the truth of the INTELLECT, the truth of thought as opposed to the derived notions of truth of being and truth of speech. St. Thomas Aquinas reminds his readers that Aristotle maintained that "the true is properly not in things but in the mind" (*C. gent.* 1.59; cf. *Meta.* 1027b 25) and accepts as a satisfactory definition of truth "the adequation of intellect and thing," a definition that some trace to ISAAC ISRAELI and others to AVICENNA. Whatever its source, it has come to be generally used and is the most frequently cited definition.

Apprehension and Sense Knowledge. Since truth in its most general sense is a conformity of knowledge with its object, it is possible to apply the term truth to any knowledge, including simple APPREHENSION and even SENSE KNOWLEDGE, insofar as these are in genuine conformity with their respective objects. The intuitive contact of the SENSES with their proper objects guarantees the validity of sensory knowledge and thus its truth. So, too, intellectual knowledge in its apprehensive dimension, i.e., simply knowing what a thing is, is impervious to falsity and must attain what it knows as it is; therefore it must attain truth. In other words, the kind of truth associated with apprehensive knowledge at both the sensory and intellectual levels is assured by the necessary relationship that exists between the powers of knowledge and their respective objects. Truth in this sense is necessary and unavoidable; it is built into the cognitive operations themselves; which may not be false. This type of truth, however, even though naturally guaranteed, is as imperfect as the apprehensive knowledge of which it is a necessary and infallible property.

Judgment. Truth in its full significance is found only in the second act of the mind, the JUDGMENT. St. Thomas implies this when he states: "Truth, therefore, may be in the sense or in the intellect knowing what a thing is, as in a true thing, but not as a thing known is in the knower, as the word truth implies; for the perfection of the intellect is the true as known" (*Summa theologiae* 1a, 16.2). To understand why St. Thomas holds that truth formally taken is found only in the judgment, one must recognize that in apprehension the human mind grasps only bits and snatches of the real. Through his ideas and concepts man appropriates to himself isolated elements of reality, or single aspects of the things he knows, without putting these aspects and isolated elements together as they are found in nature. Only through a series of judgments does he begin the process of unifying this knowledge to bring it into conformity with the constitution of things in the world. The real problem of truth arises in the process of putting unity into these isolated impressions. When the intellect makes the unification in a way that corresponds to the actual unity found in the object known, the mind enunciates a statement that is true. When the enunciation is at variance with the mode of being found in reality, the result is falsity. St. Thomas refers to this when he says: "Of all the types of intellectual discourse, the true and false exist only in enunciation, because only enunciation signifies absolutely the intellectual conception in which the true and the false exist (*In 1 perih.* 7.4).

Composition and Division. The meaning of truth becomes clearer if it is kept in mind that the very possibility of truth is implicit in the difference between the two intellectual functions of apprehension and judgment. In apprehension the mind simply grasps an object and represents it to itself conceptually. In this function of conception, the mind has no alternative to presenting the object that stimulates it to produce its own vital act of knowing. But in judgment, the act of composing or dividing apprehended concepts, the mind's function is different. Here, consequent upon apprehension, is a dynamic act in which the intellect does not simply report the things it knows but goes on to say something about them. The product of this operation, called enunciation, alone possesses the quality of being true or false. Here the mind no longer depends solely on the object represented but produces something new and original, i.e., a composition or division contributed by itself. It is this original element, a new unity, that opens up the possibility of truth or falsity. Truth is the property possessed by an enunciation that expresses a composition or division that is conformed to the real. FALSITY arises when the mind reassembles the aspects of the real in a way out of conformity with the actual mode that exists in reality.

Habits for attaining truth. "The true is the good of the intellect and the false its evil" (*C. gent.* 1.61). Thus the human mind is made to know truth, and "its ultimate perfection, according to the philosophers, is to have inscribed within it the entire order of the universe and its causes" (*De ver.* 2.2). Moreover, "although no man can attain to perfect apprehension of truth, yet no one is so completely deprived of it as not to know any at all. The knowledge of truth is easy in the sense that immediately known principles, by means of which we come to truth, are evident for all men" (*In 2 meta.* 1.275). Thus the pursuit of truth, the natural occupation of man, is not left to man's choice or inclination; there are certain basic truths that all men who begin to think must know. These are called FIRST PRINCIPLES and may be exemplified in the first principle of all, viz, "being cannot be nonbeing," and in the first principle of arithmetic, "a whole is equal to the sum of its parts." Self-evident principles of this type are the source of all science and wisdom. The human intellect does not learn them, nor does it assume them;

it arrives at them naturally and necessarily once it grasps the terms that make them up. The mind thus initially attains truth and certitude by knowing first principles; it then proceeds from these to conclusions. This does not mean that all knowledge can be deduced from these principles, but only that these principles must be admitted at least implicitly and then applied to experience before anything else can be deduced.

Understanding. The human intellect possesses a habit called UNDERSTANDING (*INTELLECTUS*) that is not properly innate but is gained by one act, the act by which it grasps the principle of CONTRADICTION. This act assures its first grasp of truth and necessitates its assent to immediate EVIDENCE. From further material supplied by the senses the intellect goes on to perceive other first principles that form the basis for each special field of knowledge. The precise way in which these primary judgments are formed is analyzed by St. Thomas at the very beginning of his treatise on truth (*De ver.* 1.1). These judgments are the primary mental assents at which the mind arrives in its inspection of reality, in terms of both the general modes of being common to all things, and the special modes of being proper to the different kinds of things encountered in experience. The judgments that relate to the general modes of being concern the TRANSCENDENTALS and are the source of all the principles and conclusions of METAPHYSICS. The judgments that relate to the special modes concern the CATEGORIES OF BEING and are the sources of the principles and conclusions of the special sciences. The ultimate test of any fact is always EXPERIENCE itself, but the ultimate test of the truth of any judgment is the analytic resolution of that judgment back to first principles (*see* ANALYSIS AND SYNTHESIS). St. Thomas states simply: "There is never falsity in the intellect if the resolution to first principles be rightly carried out" (*De ver.* 1.12).

There is, then, a minimum of truth that each man must possess, at least implicitly, and from which he may (though he need not) proceed to all other truths within the scope of his experience. In the speculative order, the habit by which this minimum is known is called understanding; in the practical order, the corresponding habit is referred to as SYNDERESIS. St. Thomas makes the distinction: "Just as there is a natural habit of the human soul through which it knows principles of the speculative sciences, which we call understanding, so too there is in the soul a natural habit of first principles of action which are the universal principles of the natural law. This habit pertains to synderesis" (*De ver.* 16.1).

Science and Wisdom. To assist man in the attainment of truth there are two other intellectual habits: one, called SCIENCE (*SCIENTIA*), provides skill in moving intellectually from principles to conclusions; the other, called WIS-DOM, disposes the intellect rightly to regard conclusions drawn from first principles and causes that are ultimate.

These two habits, themselves based on the habit of understanding, are indispensable for the proper operation of the intellect. Since they dispose the mind to attain truth, they are perfect qualities and therefore virtues (*see* VIRTUE). Science and wisdom do not differ as being opposed or as regarding entirely different objects; rather, wisdom includes science and adds something to it. Science proceeds from any cause whatever, whereas wisdom proceeds only from ultimate causes. The habit of science, moreover, is concerned only with conclusions, whereas the habit of wisdom is concerned with principles also. It explains and defends both its own principles and those of the other sciences. One of the supreme works of wisdom is to contemplate the order connecting all truths and to show how these are derived from the first truth.

Awareness of truth. Men have always been concerned with the question how anyone can know that his judgment is true. In fact, the motive prompting the study of epistemology or of the critique of knowledge is that men are generally aware of their proneness to error; they are conscious of the ease with which the false can be mistaken for the true.

Egocentric Predicament. The problem is further complicated by the fact that truth and error are relationships that exist between thought and reality. To examine these relationships critically one must have a simultaneous grasp of the enunciation and that to which the enunciation refers. This seemingly simple requirement lays a trap for the unwary, into which not a few epistemologists fall because of their impoverished conception of knowledge. In their view, the process of knowing resembles what occurs when a camera takes a picture; the test of truth, for them, consists of comparing the picture with the reality to see how closely the two correspond. The attempt to apply this photographic analysis to knowledge runs into difficulties, however, since knowledge is involved in the very act of comparison, there is no way of attaining to reality apart from the knowing act itself. This situation, frequently called the egocentric predicament, has often been alleged as a reason why some form of IDEALISM in epistemology is necessary. The difficulty here is actually the misconception of knowledge itself—the reduction of what is really a vital and immaterial action to mere mechanical copying. Such a misconception makes any satisfactory answer impossible because it raises only false problems. The real problem can be solved only in the context of a sound psychology of knowledge.

On this general problem St. Thomas observes: "There is truth and falsity only in the second operation of the mind, in which the intellect not only has the likeness of the thing understood but also reflects upon it, knowing it and judging it" (*In 6 meta.* 4.1236). Here are noted the basic elements that make up a judgment. First there is the likeness of the object, which in this case is complex, being made up of subject and predicate; second there is the reflection, the intellectual consideration of the mental content; and third there is the knowing of the conformity, i.e., the consciousness that what the mind has grasped in its act of composing or dividing corresponds to what exists in reality. Formal certitude can be present only when the intellect knows itself to be conformed to the real. This can come only from a process of reflection on the content grasped by the mind in its act of apprehension. Such reflection, which is really a resolution back to reality, is psychologically complex because of man's nature and his connatural mode of knowing. Ultimately, to recognize conformity or its absence involves returning reflectively to the phantasms from which the ideas were derived, and finally to the senses themselves, which are in direct contact with extramental reality. As St. Thomas notes: "All our knowledge in its origin consists in becoming aware of the first indemonstrable principles. Our knowledge of these arises from sense experience" (*De ver.* 10.6).

Known Conformity. The ultimate test of truth is thus the reflective resolution by which the mind goes back to the thing as it really is. And the element to be emphasized here is that there is a genuine *known* conformity between mind and object insofar as the conformity can be traced back to its origin in the object as originally known. All the data come from sense ultimately; not only are concepts derived from sense but the connection or nexus between them also is sense-derived. This connection is already present in the apprehension and the related PHANTASM. The function of the intellect in the process of judging is to assent or to deny the connection as being in accord with the objective structure of the object in reality, i.e., to pronounce: so it is, or so it is not. In this act of judging nothing quidditative is added to what was represented by the apprehension. What is contributed is an assertion about the mode of the thing's existence.

The truth value of the judgment is thus based on a known conformity, which means that the judgment not only represents the object as complex but enunciates the objectivity of the connection represented in the very complexity. This enunciation, itself the heart of the judgment, can exhibit a known conformity precisely because the mind is simultaneously aware both of the complex object and of itself in its ability to understand and encompass the thing as it exists in reality. Only on this basis can the mind pronounce the judgment. The mental act of composing or dividing does not simply affirm that the predicate belongs to the subject. This relationship has already been perceived in the simple apprehension. What the judgment asserts is the awareness of the mind that the complexity enunciated is conformed to the mode in which the object actually exists and that the intellect is aware of its ability to grasp things as they really are. Here is the crucial point the idealists miss. Here also is the existential element that is a necessary component of every judgment.

Objectivity and Existence. The dynamic assertion in the judgment differs from the representation of the object in simple apprehension in that, in the former, the reflective power of the mind simultaneously grasps the two poles of the process, i.e., itself knowing and the objective structure of the thing known. This reflective procedure is neither unusual nor something to which the mind has to force itself. It is rather a natural tendency of the intelligence, a natural curiosity that is stimulated whenever the intellect faces an object that is not completely or satisfactorily known. When the natural tendency of the mind is fulfilled in seeing and asserting a positive relationship between the two elements in the apprehended complexity, a positive judgment results. When the relationship is seen to be contradictory, a negative judgment is made, with the mind denying the objectivity of any positive nexus between the predicate and the subject because it sees that the connection is not there in reality. Finally, it is possible that the mind's tendency remain unactualized when intelligibility is absent. In this case no judgment occurs, even though a composite concept has presented the two elements together. But the mind sees that their relationship in reality is not intelligible, and therefore makes no judgment. What must be stressed is that, while the objectivity of the content is guaranteed by its derivation from sense experience, the motive for the intellectual affirmation is not the sense apprehension. The motive is rather the intelligibility of the connection seen in the object, and the simultaneous intuition of the intellect as a power able to understand and encompass the thing in its existence and objective structure. It is in this sense that the judgment is concerned with existence.

Every judgment, therefore, of its nature has an existential component, and because of this it has a guaranteed OBJECTIVITY. This does not mean that every judgment is automatically true. It happens frequently that the intellect misses part of the evidence, or mistakes partial evidence for total, or misconceives the significance of the evidence. Whenever such situations occur, the result is ERROR and the possibility of false judgment. Even though the mind of man was made for truth, except in the case of first principles it can fail in its efforts to attain truth. Yet the pursuit of truth can be successful in many areas. Proceeding from first principles, the mind of man can reach true conclusions, but not always immediately or easily. It is for this reason that it must be fortified by the habits of understanding, science, and wisdom.

Other theories of truth. Theories contradicting the view of truth presented here usually have their roots in metaphysical and psychological doctrines that deny the basic Thomistic theses concerning being, existence, the spirituality of man's soul, the immateriality of his intellect, etc. Only if this be kept in mind do any of these theories make sense in light of the foregoing.

Intellectualist Theories. Among the intellectualist theories may be noted those associated with R. DESCARTES and with H. SPENCER. Descartes maintained that after doubting everything he was finally unable to doubt his own existence, for he saw very clearly that in order to think he must exist. From this he derived the general rule that the things man conceives clearly and distinctly must be true. As far as this test goes it is correct, for the clearly perceived nature contained in the judgment is really the adequate ground for asserting its truth. It was Spencer's thought, on the other hand, that through an evolutionary process the intellectual dispositions of the human race have been so conditioned by gradually accumulated and inherited experiences that the mind is unable to conceive the opposite of that to which it has become accustomed. The evolutionary hypothesis aside, there is a partial truth in the theory of the inconceivability of the opposite, but it is stated in a negative and misleading way. One does not see judgments as true became he cannot conceive the opposite; rather he is unable to conceive the opposite because he sees his judgments to be necessarily true.

Another test of truth, offered by G. W. F. HEGEL and his followers, is the theory of coherence or consistency. Rooted in the metaphysics of idealistic MONISM, this view assumes that thought and thing, the real and the ideal, are all fundamentally identical in the ABSOLUTE. There is no genuine dualism and thus no extramental reality with which a judgment can be compared. Hence the truth of a proposition must be its coherence with the whole system of knowledge, that is, the harmony of all judgments with one another. The proponents of this theory are quite ready to admit that the mere consistency of one judgment with another does not necessarily bespeak truth and that it is possible to have even a conformity among a limited set of judgments without having truth. But they insist that truth consists in the wider conformity of the whole system of accepted judgments. Once this is recognized, they are willing even to accept the definition of truth as the conformity of the mind judging with the reality judged, since, for them, reality is nothing more than the whole system of judgments. Truth, then, consists in this coherence throughout the entire system, and the criterion of truth is the consistency of any judgment with the entire system.

This view without doubt contains a partial truth, but it also implies much that is false and inadequate. Consistency and coherence are certainly a negative criterion of truth in the sense that truth cannot contradict truth; of two contradictories, moreover, one at least must be false. But the fact remains that both may be false and that any series of judgments may be totally compatible and yet totally untrue. Besides this, it becomes clear on examination that consistency and coherence, even as a negative test, have no value apart from evidential being itself. For if a judgment be rejected as false because of its lack of compatibility with other judgments, this can occur only because the incompatibility is clearly seen, and thus one comes back to evidential being. Seeming incompatibility between a new judgment and a judgment already maintained can only be the cause of further reflection or of more complete investigation to discover which one is to be accepted. The only basis for a decision in any case will ultimately be the evidence available for either.

The theory of consistency maintains that a judgment is true if it conforms to other judgments. This CRITERION is rejected by those who insist that truth is more properly contained in a judgment that is conformed to reality. Reality itself is not to be identified with the sum total of judgments already known, for it may be that a particular reality is known solely through this individual judgment. It is true, of course, that any judgment based on mediate evidence will be in conformity with knowledge already possessed; yet this cannot be so for all judgments, and certainly not for those that are self-evident. Otherwise knowledge could never begin; it would always require a point of reference in other judgments. This theory, therefore, is as unsatisfactory as the idealistic monism in which it has its roots.

Anti-Intellectualist Theories. Contemporary pragmatism and INSTRUMENTALISM, which offer the best illustrations of anti-intellectualist theories of truth, are associated with the names of C. S. Peirce, W. James, and J. Dewey. Dewey's idea of truth is in harmony with his general notion that reality is in flux and is to be identified with becoming rather than with being. Truth in this view is something relative; it has reference to a changing reality. Things are never true in themselves but only in their application to existential situations. Since the only test here is experimental VERIFICATION, Dewey says that truth means verification, either actual or possible. His theory is one of correspondence—not a static but an operational correspondence.

Actually, in discussing truth and verification, Dewey uses the terms equivocally. In the Thomistic theory, truth is inseparable from being; if there is no being, there is no truth. In a world of pure becoming there can be no question of truth, for becoming without being is unintelligible. Thus, for the Thomist, Dewey's truth is unintelligible. Even the shift to verification does not help; for if truth consists in making sure experimentally, then there must be some standard of surety and ultimately some absolute. Without such a standard there is no possibility of verification: all that is possible is a series of guesses. In general, pragmatic epistemology shares in the inadequacy of pragmatic philosophy. Such a philosophy canonizes the empirical method, effects a reduction to SENSISM, and amounts to a denial of intellect. While supremely concerned with the practical, it neglects the speculative on which the practical is based, and offers no substantial base from which the changing and the ephemeral must ultimately be judged.

See Also: CERTITUDE; EPISTEMOLOGY; KNOWLEDGE.

Bibliography: THOMAS AQUINAS, *Truth,* tr. R. W. MULLIGAN et al., 3 v. (Chicago 1952–54). L. M. RÉGIS, *Epistemology,* tr. I. C. BYRNE (New York 1959). J. MARITAIN, *Distinguish to Unite; or, The Degrees of Knowledge,* tr. G. B. PHELAN (New York 1959). F. D. WILHELMSEN, *Man's Knowledge of Reality* (Englewood Cliffs, N.J. 1956). T. GILBY, *Phoenix and Turtle: The Unity of Knowing and Being* (New York 1950). L. ROUGIER, *Traité de Connaissance* (Paris 1955) 435–442. P. PRINI, *Enciclopedia filosofica* 2:813–840.

[G. C. REILLY]

TRUTH IN ONTOLOGY

The following analysis of ontological truth treats of intelligibility as a property of being, the intelligibility of finite beings as caused by God's creative intellect, the analogy of ontological truth, and Subsistent Truth as the origin of all truth, both epistemological and ontological.

Intelligibility as a property of being. The truth of man's intellection depends on being as such; it is caused by being. But being does not really depend on intellection. Being founds intellection; intellection does not found being. Hence intellection is really related to being in a relationship of conformity or of measure. Man cannot think his intellection as really related to being without by that very fact thinking being as related—by a relation of reason—to his intellect as intellect. Being as standing in relation of conformity to the intellect is being as true, as founding truth. A relation of conformity to the intellect is what is expressed by the word intelligible. Hence being as true, or the ontologically true, is being as intelligible. By the very fact that man thinks, he thinks being, and insofar as he thinks being, he affirms implicitly that being is necessarily intelligible. He affirms that being as such and the intelligible as such are really identical.

Since being as such and the intelligible as such are identical, the act of being (*esse*) and intelligibility or ontological truth are identical. Hence everything that possesses the act of being, insofar as it does, possesses intelligibility. Or everything that is, insofar as it is, is intelligible. Or every being as being is ontologically true. What is excluded from intelligibility is excluded from being (*see* INTELLIGIBILITY, PRINCIPLE OF).

Intelligibility caused by God's intellect. Being as such includes everything that is, a plurality of particular beings, each of which has its own act of being and exists with others in the one order of being. Hence each particular being has the same ultimate ontological explanation, i.e., the one Uncaused Cause of the act of being. This cause is the subsisting and therefore infinite act of being, God.

Every being therefore is because God has freely willed it to be. If it were not freely willed, God would depend on it and hence could not be infinite, nor God. Freely to will something to be presupposes the knowledge or idea of that which is so willed. Hence each particular being presupposes its idea in the mind of God. God, willing this or that reality to be, conforms this or that reality to the idea in His mind or realizes the idea in reality.

The example most helpful in understanding this creative action of God is that of the artist. When Michelangelo executed in the Sistine Chapel his painting of Adam, he wished to realize his conception, his idea of the newly created Adam. The painting of Adam exists because Michelangelo freely decided to paint it. The painting depended on the idea in Michelangelo's mind to be what it is; it has its intelligibility, therefore, from the mind of Michelangelo. It is essentially true by dependence on his mind and is the realization of his idea outside himself. When someone contemplates that painting of Adam, he conforms his mind to it and hence, through the medium of the painting, conforms his mind to Michelangelo's.

To apply this example to God's creative action, one must remove the imperfection that the example implies. The surface of the ceiling on which Michelangelo painted existed independently of him and so continued to exist when Michelangelo died. Hence the configuration or conformity to Michelangelo's mind, which the surface of the ceiling received from his brush, once received, no longer depended on him. But no matter exists prior to the creative activity of the divine Artist. His action reaches not only to the surface of reality, but to the whole of reality, in its innermost fibers and in all the details of its being. Exactly as it is, and in all that it is, and in its ordination to its proper activity, the created being is the realization of God's idea. If it ceased to depend on God's idea, it would, by that very fact, cease to be. If God ceased to think it, it would immediately cease to be.

Hence every being, insofar as it is, is conformed to God's intellect. Its total intelligibility is received from God's intellect. Its intelligibility is identified with its act of being: it *is* intelligible. Hence every created being depends essentially on God's creative intellect; and the ontological truth of such a being is measured by God's intellect.

The possible is a POSSIBILITY of being: only as a possibility of being is it intelligible. Why is the possible possible, i.e., why can God produce this form of being? Because God's act of being is imitable in this way or according to this mode of PARTICIPATION. Hence the intrinsic possibility of possibles, or the necessary truth of possibles, is founded in the necessity that God is. This necessity is the exclusion of nothingness or contradiction from being.

Again, contingent truth implies necessary truth. That James is, is true; but James need not have existed, had God not so willed. James's being denotes an ontological truth that need not have been and hence is contingent. Once he is, however, he is necessarily conformed to God's intellect and necessarily conformable to every other intellect. The contingent truth of James implies the necessary conformity of intellect and being. Further, when James is taking a stroll through the park, it is true to say that he is walking. When, however, he sits down to rest his limbs, it is no longer true to say that he is walking, but that he is sitting. The truth about James has changed in successive moments, not into falsehood, but into another truth (*De ver.* 1.6). Thus his truth is changeable insofar as his being is changeable. But his changeableness and the contingency of his truth imply once more the necessary conformity of being and intellect, without which James could neither be, nor be intelligible, nor even change. Hence no truth is so contingent that it does not presuppose and manifest necessary truth (ST 1a, 86.3).

Analogy of ontological truth. Every being, insofar as it is, is true by a relation of conformity or assimilation to the intellect. There are only three possible ways in which this assimilation of intellect and (finite) being can be brought about. Either one causes the other or another causes both, since a cause causing assimilates to itself. Hence either the intellect renders being similar to itself (God's creative knowledge); or being renders the intellect similar to itself (man's natural knowledge); or the intellect that renders being similar to itself, namely, God's, renders another intellect similar to being (angel's natural knowledge).

Practically considered, therefore, one can reduce to two the relationships of conformity to intellect that being as true denotes: the relationship to man's intellect and the relationship to God's. Being as true is being as actually conformed to God's intellect, on which it depends, and as conformable to man's intellect, on which it does not depend. The truth of being is constituted by God's intellect; it is manifested and not constituted by man's intellect. Being, therefore, is primarily true by relation to God's intellect, secondarily true in relation to man's intellect. Hence ontological truth, implying this secondary and primary sense, has a meaning that in the two cases is neither fully the same nor fully different; it has an analogical meaning (*see* ANALOGY).

Considering ontological truth as that which has relation to the intellect, or as the intelligible, it is analogical in another sense, namely, in the same way as being is analogical. In his proofs for the existence of God (ST 1a, 2.3), St. Thomas argues from things that are more and less true to a most true; and these degrees of truth are identically those of being. His argument, therefore, means that intelligibility is a perfection that is verified in some beings more perfectly, in others less perfectly. This fact implies a being that is pure or subsisting intelligibility (*see* GOD, PROOFS FOR THE EXISTENCE OF).

Subsistent truth. Because self-consciousness means CONSCIOUSNESS of oneself as one is or has being, self-consciousness depends on consciousness of being as such. If, as in man's case, the SELF is not identically the plenitude of being, there is an opposition, or nonidentity, between the knower and being, which expresses itself in the opposition of subject and object. As a result of this opposition, man's knowing being is not simply being; or, in other words, in his knowing as knowing being, ontological truth and epistemological truth are opposed.

Hence his way of knowing, by its imperfection, reveals itself as limited in being and hence as caused by another Being. Or, man's way of knowing presupposes and depends on a Being whose way of knowing is not limited, viz, God.

God is identically self-consciousness and consciousness of being, since He is PURE ACT of being, which is identically unlimited act of intellection. No other being except God is intelligibility (intelligibility is the act of being), and no other being except God is intellection (intellection is the act of knowing). Intelligibility is ontological truth; intellection is epistemological truth. Other beings besides God are ontologically true or have ontological truth, and in their cognition have epistemological truth. God alone is identically and unlimitedly ontological truth and epistemological truth. God, therefore, is subsisting truth: He is the self-thinking act of being.

From God as subsisting truth, as self-thinking act of being, all truth without exception is derived. Every finite being, insofar as it is, is caused by God; and insofar as it is, it is ontologically true. Hence all ontological truth is from God, who knowing Himself knows all that He can will to be, all that can be. Again, every finite being that is capable of intellection is as such created immediately by God, who fashions its intellect to know truth and thus ordains it and inclines it to the knowledge of truth as to its proper good. Hence its good, which is epistemological truth, is from God and is achieved under His inclination and cooperation (*De ver.* 1.8). Hence all epistemological truth is from God. God is the inner teacher without whose guidance and light no truth, even the most seemingly insignificant, would be discovered (*De ver.* 11.1).

See Also: DOUBLE TRUTH, THEORY OF.

Bibliography: B. J. F. LONERGAN, *Insight: A Study of Human Understanding* (New York 1957). L. DE RAEYMAEKER, *The Philosophy of Being,* tr. E. H. ZIEGELMEYER (St. Louis 1954). G. SMITH and L. KENDZIERSKI, *The Philosophy of Being: Metaphysics. 1* (New York 1961). A. D. SERTILLANGES, *St. Thomas Aquinas and His Work,* tr. G. ANSTRUTHER (London 1933). É. H. GILSON, *Being and Some Philosophers* (2nd ed. Toronto 1952). P. ROUSSELOT, *The Intellectualism of Saint Thomas,* tr. J. E. O'MAHONY (New York 1935). M. D. ROLAND-GOSSELIN, *Essai d'une étude critique de la connaissance* (Bibliothèque Thomiste 17; 1932). A. MARC, *Dialectic de l'affirmation: Essai de métaphysique réflexive* (Paris 1952). J. MARÉCHAL, *Le Point de départ de la métaphysique,* 5 v. (3rd ed. Paris 1944–49), v.5 (2nd ed.). J. DENINGER, *"Wahres Sein" in der Philosophie des Aristoteles* (Monographien zur philosophischen Forschung 25; Meisenheim am Glan 1961).

[F. P. O'FARRELL]

TRUTH, DIVINE

A relationship of conformity pertaining to God's intellect by which He is perfectly and truly Himself and determines the being of all things according to His idea of them (ontological truth); understands fully and accurately His own being and that of all other things (logical truth, only virtually in God); and sincerely manifests Himself to man in divine revelation (moral truth).

The OT word for truth is '*ĕmet,* which conveys not only the idea of truthfulness and fidelity to one's word but also of the firmness, steadiness, reliability, and objective accuracy of that word. It is related to the word AMEN ('*āmēn*), Israel's sure affirmation that a statement or revelation of God is certain. The word '*ĕmet* means that God as truth can be trusted, relied upon, that He and His utterances are a solid base or guide for directing one's own actions and give a guarantee of practical certitude. This theme runs through the entire OT. In this sense, God "renders" truth in 2 Sm 2.6. The prophets, too, have the certainty of truth in 1 Kgs 17.24 and Jer 23.28. God's words and law are '*ĕmet,* that is, a solid reality on which a man can base his life [cf. Psalm 118 (119); 26 (27).3; Jn 3.21]. And, in fact, God's truth (a certain way of life) demands a corresponding truth from man (observance of God's law, or morality).

In the OT *'ĕmet* goes with *ḥesed*. The word *ḥesed* means God's goodness, loyal devotedness, gracious kindness. These two notions of devotedness and fidelity, or truth, convey the fact that God is utterly faithful to His self-appointed responsibilities toward Israel, as well as that Israel has experienced this constancy: God is rich in devotedness and fidelity (Ex 34.6).

In the NT, with the Greek word ἀλήθεια certain Hellenistic overtones are added, particularly in the Gospel and Epistles of St. John and in St. Paul. Here truth suggests the manifestation of God's essence, or inner reality, which also casts light on the meaning of created things. God's truth thus delivers man from the blindness of falsehood that surrounds him (Jn 1.9; 8.37, 40, 45; 2 Jn 1–2; 1 Tm 2.4). Thus, history, creation, and the physical universe become a revelation of God Himself, not merely this or that doctrine. God unveils Himself, especially in manifesting throughout history His fidelity to His covenant and election of Israel, culminating in the Incarnation and Second Coming.

The Fathers and the magisterium of the Church speak of God as true, opposing this note to His supposed nonexistence or illusory character (see creeds and Vatican Council I, *Enchiridion symbolorum*, 3001, 3021). The Church also teaches that God is the font of every truth (*Enchiridion symbolorum*, 2811), that God is incapable of deceiving man (*Enchiridion symbolorum*, 3008).

St. Thomas Aquinas explores God as first truth. God is perfectly Himself as He must be because He is infinitely perfect (ontological truth). God knows Himself fully, exhaustively; for if knowledge is a union between knower and known, God is absolutely identified with His own being and with His own act of self-understanding (logical truth). Furthermore, God is the truth of all other things since they depend upon Him for the truth or perfection of their own being; His knowledge of them determines them.

This doctrine relates to the life of Christian contemplation, which seeks the fullness of truth, in that the Christian man, like the Biblical man of both Testaments, must come to perceive God's truth as manifested in things and see their relationship of dependence upon God. This use of the created universe in contemplation can lead the Christian to a heightened understanding and awareness of his intimate contact in this life with God's own being through FAITH, GRACE, the divine INDWELLING, and the gifts. It can also lead to a strengthening of

the contact itself to be brought to perfection in the immediacy of the BEATIFIC VISION.

In addition to theology's interest in the subject of divine truth, there is also a frequent concern of philosophy with many questions about knowing God and knowing Him as the true God, about reconciling natural and possible supernatural sources of truth, and about the objectivity of human knowledge.

See Also: GOD, ARTICLES ON; TRUTH; TRUTH (IN THE BIBLE); REVELATION, THEOLOGY OF.

Bibliography: A. GELIN, *Dictionnaire de théologie catholique*, ed. A. VACANT et al., 15 v. (Paris 1903–50; Tables générales 1951-), *Tables générales* 1:975–993. "Wahrheit," *Lexikon für Theologie und Kirche*, ed. J. HOFER and K. RAHNER, 10 v. (2d new ed. Freiburg 1957–65) v.10. *Encyclopedic Dictionary of the Bible*, tr. and adap. by L. HARTMAN (New York 1963) 2498–2502. J. J. VON ALLMEN, ed., *A Companion to the Bible* (New York 1958) 430–433. J. GUILLET, *Themes of the Bible*, tr. A. J. LAMOTHE (Notre Dame, Ind. 1960) 32–40. St. Thomas, *Summa theologiae* 1a, 16, 21; *De ver.*

[G. J. ROXBURGH]

TRUTHFULNESS (VERACITY)

Truthfulness, or veracity, is a virtue, allied to justice, by which its possessor is inclined to manifest himself not otherwise than he is. Plato (*Rep.* 381) recognized it as a divine characteristic, and he taunted polytheists with the question: ". . . can you imagine that God will be willing to lie, whether in word or deed, to put forth a phantom of himself?" Aristotle, after briefly portraying the habitually truthful person, is unequivocal in his evaluation of him. He says: "The man who loves truth, and is truthful where nothing is at stake will still more be truthful where something is at stake; he will avoid falsehood as something base, seeing that he avoided it even for its own sake; and such a man is worthy of praise." (*Eth. Nic.* 1127.) Praise for the truthful person has been unstinting and constant in Christian tradition, both by condemnations of its opposite, LYING, and by its association, in a theological context, with the most exalted of moral virtues, justice.

In other than a moral context, truth is a relationship, a formal identity or conformity, between what is in the mind and reality that exists apart from the mind. If the relationship is considered as emanating from an intellect, primarily divine, to the thing, then the truth is called ontological or metaphysical. If it is viewed from the thing to the intellect, so that the intellect is formed according to reality, then it is called logical. Truth, in a moral sense, exists where there is conformity between one's thought and one's speech. This is subject to voluntary control. Because there are various ways in which that conformity may be distorted, there is need for habituation of the will to a proper standard of conformity. That habituation is a virtue, the special virtue truthfulness or veracity.

The good action, which distinguishes the virtue of truthfulness from all others, is one ''whereby a man, both in life and in speech, shows himself to be such as he is, and other things not differently than they are in his regard, and neither greater nor less, than they are.'' (St. Thomas Aquinas, *Summa theologiae,* 2a2ae, 109.3 ad 3.)

The basic reason that a person is made good by being truthful is that he finds his own fulfillment in fulfilling his social responsibility. ''Since man is a social animal, one man naturally owes another whatever is necessary for the preservation of human society. Now it would be impossible for men to live together, unless they believed one another, as declaring the truth one to another. Hence the virtue of truth does in some sense regard the truth as something owed.'' (*Summa theologiae,* 2a2ae, 109.3 ad 1.)

Bibliography: THOMAS AQUINAS, *Summa theologiae,* 2a2ae, 109. J. A. MCHUGH and C. J. CALLAN, *Moral Theology,* 2 v. (New York 1958) 2:436–438. R. MIDDLETON, ''The Obligation of Veracity,'' *American Ecclesiastical Review* 19 (1898) 163–173.

[D. HUGHES]

TSCHIDERER ZU GLEIFHEIM, JOHANN NEOPMUK, BL.

Also known as John von (zu) Gleifheim or Giovanni Nepomuceno Tschiderer, bishop of Trent (Italy); b. April 15, 1777, Bolzano, South Tyrol, Italy; d. Dec. 3, 1860, Trent, Italy.

Tschiderer's family immigrated from the Grisons to the Tyrol in 1529 and was given a patent of nobility in 1620. He completed his secondary education under the Franciscans (1792), and then he rejoined his parents, Josef Joachim and Caterina de Giovanelli. They had moved to Innsbruck, Austria, where he studied philosophy and theology.

On July 27, 1800 he was ordained a priest by Emmanuel Count von Thun, bishop of Trent. After spending two years ministering in mountain parishes, he went for further training to Rome, where he was appointed Apostolic notary.

Upon his return north he took up pastoral work again in the German part of the Diocese of Trent, and from 1807 was professor of moral and pastoral theology at the seminary at Trent. In 1810 he was appointed pastor at Sarnthal (Sarentino) and in 1819 at Meran (Merano),

where he was also school inspector. In 1827 he was appointed as a canon of the Cathedral of St. Vigilius, Trent, and pro-vicar of the diocese. Wherever he went he gained a lasting reputation for zeal and charity.

On May 20, 1832, he was consecrated bishop of Heliopolis and auxiliary bishop of Bressanone and took up residence at Feldkirch. Two years later Emperor Francis I nominated him prince-bishop of Trent to replace Francis Xavier Luschin, who had been transferred to Lemberg (now Lviv, Ukraine) and named him as successor.

From May 1835 until his death, Tschiderer governed his diocese with the same apostolic zeal and charity he had demonstrated in earlier endeavors. He devoted a considerable part of his revenues and personal wealth for the building or restoration of more than 60 churches, and the purchasing of good books for parish rectories. He provided for the continuous formation of priests, Christian education for youth, and the generous care of the poor and sick. He used the third centenary of the opening of the Council of Trent (1545–63) to promote a religious revival through popular missions and other pastoral activities.

He intervened promptly and decisively to prevent the March 20, 1848 uprising from becoming a blood-bath; when his petition to the Austrians for clemency for 21 young members of the Franco-Italian forces was refused, he saw to their preparation for execution and Christian burial.

Bishop von Tschiderer lived in deep communion with God through long periods of prayer, the celebration of Mass, and meditation on Scripture, Magisterial teachings, and the rosary. During his 25-year episcopacy he was distinguished for the exercise of virtue and charity, and for intense zeal in the fulfillment of the duties of his episcopal office. He was exceedingly simple and abstinent in his personal habits. His charity to the poor and sick was carried so far that he was often left without a penny, because he had given away everything he had. Twice (1836 and 1855) cholera raged in his diocese and on these occasions he set a shining example of Christian courage before his clergy.

He left his property to the institution for the deaf and dumb at Trent and to the seminary that he had founded, which was named after him the Joanneum. Directly after his death he was honored, and the process for his beatification was initiated by his successor, Benedict Riccabona, in 1873. His body now lies in the north transept of Trent's cathedral.

Pope John Paul II beatified von Tschiderer during a pastoral visit to Trent (April 30, 1995), praising him as ''a man who transcended borders. . . . [He] was able to bridge the gap between various social classes, different languages and diverse mentalities, and bring them together. The new blessed indeed worked in the heart of Europe and was able to preserve these identities in the shining example of his person, while promoting a sense of community.''

Feast: Dec. 4.

Bibliography: *Acta Apostolicae Sedis,* 61 (1969) 121–125. *Mitteilungen über das Leben des . . . J. N. Tschiderer* (Bolzano 1876). *L'Osservatore Romano,* English edition, nos. 18 and 19 (1995). M. A. BUOL and V. BERENBERG, *Johann Nepomuk von Tschiderer und seine Zeit* (1934). A. COSTA, *I Vescovi di Trento* (1977) 238–248. J. MAYR, *Bischof Johann Nepomuk von Tschiderer* (Bozen 1998). A. TAIT, *Vita del Venerabile Servo di Dio Giovanni Nepomuceno di Tschiderer, Principe vescovo di Trento,* 2 v. (Venice 1904).

[K. I. RABENSTEIN]

TUAM, ABBEY OF

Former Celtic monastery at Tuam, County Galway, Ireland, which became the seat of the Archdiocese of Tuam (Irish, *Tuaim-dá-gualann*). The abbey was founded mid-6th century by St. Iarlaithe (Jarlath), who is said to have taught St. BRENDAN OF CLONFERT and whose relics were preserved until the Reformation in a church called Tempull na Scríne in Tuam. Obituaries of abbots from the 8th to the 11th century show that the monastery survived but was unimportant. Then in the 11th century the O'Connor Kings of Connaught transferred the center of their rule from Roscommon to the Tuam region, making the church at Tuam the object of their special favor. From 1121 to 1156 Toirdelbach O'Connor was the most powerful prince in Ireland, and Tuam came to be regarded as the chief church in the western kingdom. In 1152, at the Synod of Kells, Cardinal Paparo gave Tuam archiepiscopal status. Toirdelbach rebuilt the church in a style worthy of a cathedral, and it is this same King's name that appears on the High-Cross in the market place at Tuam and on the shaft of a second cross now in the Protestant cathedral at Tuam. Both crosses bear also the name of Aed O'hOisin (O'Hessian), who was abbot of Tuam from *c.* 1126 to 1150, when he became bishop, and then first archbishop of Tuam in 1152. It is likely that at this time the original monastery ceased to function as such and that its lands passed to the archbishop. Later, Tuam town had a house of CANONS REGULAR OF ST. AUGUSTINE (priory of St. John) and a house of PREMONSTRATENSIANS.

Bibliography: J. COLGAN, *Acta Sanctorum Hiberniae,* ed. B. JENNINGS (Louvain 1645; repr. Dublin 1948) 307–310. J. RYAN, *Irish Monasticism* (London 1931). E. A. D'ALTON, *History of the Archdiocese of Tuam,* 2 v. (Dublin 1928). *Annála Connacht: The Annals of Connacht, A. D. 1224–1544,* ed. and tr. A. M. FREEMAN (Dublin 1944). *The Annals of Loch Cé,* ed. and tr. W. M. HENNESSY, 2 v. (*Rerum Brittanicarum medii aevi scriptores* 54; 1871). *Annals of the Four Masters: Annals of the Kingdom of Ireland,* ed. and tr. J. O'DONOVAN, 7 v. (2d ed. Dublin 1856). R. A. S. MACALISTER, *Corpus inscriptionum insularum Celticarum* v.2 (Dublin 1949).

[J. RYAN]

TÜBINGEN, UNIVERSITY OF

An autonomous institution of higher learning under the jurisdiction of the ministry of education and financially supported by the state of Baden-Württemberg.

History. Founded in 1477 by Count Eberhard im Bart of Württemberg, Tübingen belongs to a series of German universities that owed their existence at the close of the Middle Ages to the growing independence of regional princes and the increasing needs of education. Following the bull of Sixtus IV authorizing the foundation of the new University, Eberhard transferred a chapter of Canons Regular with eight canonries to Tübingen and transformed its prebends into professorships. Their number was increased through the incorporation of several additional prebends. The university thus acquired 15 chairs: three in theology, five in law (three of these in Canon Law), two in medicine, and five in arts. Its constitution was modeled on that of the University of Basel, Switzerland, and as at Basel followed the two main tendencies in late medieval scholasticism, namely, the *Via antiqua* and the *Via moderna,* which were equally represented.

The most significant theologians of the first period were Joannes Heynlin de Lapide (Johann Stein), Conrad Summenhart, and especially Gabriel BIEL, whose famous commentary on the *Sentences* (*Collectorium*) had its origin in his Tübingen lectures. Among the numerous early students were J. ECK, J. Fabri, and J. von STAUPITZ, who in 1502 organized the University of Wittenberg on the model of Tübingen. Although humanism had influenced the compilation of a well-known world chronicle by J. NAUCLERUS, chancellor of the University, it could not be successfully established at Tübingen. J. REUCHLIN was a member of the university faculty for a short time before his death. In a circle of students whom he had previously gathered around him was P. MELANCHTHON, who in 1518 also went to Wittenberg. When the Reformation was introduced into Württemberg in 1534, the now Protestant theological faculty obtained the leading position at Tübingen and retained its position into the 19th century. The whole university was stamped with Lutheran orthodoxy. While it produced scholars of the caliber of the astronomer J. KEPLER, it resisted PIETISM and remained almost wholly closed against the influences of the ENLIGHTEN-

MENT that were pointing to the future. No significant change of attitude took place before the early 19th century.

Later Development. In 1806 Württemberg, which now included areas of heavy Catholic population, had become a kingdom. Accordingly, in 1817 two new faculties were created: Political Science, and Catholic Theology with five chairs. Here the so-called ''Catholic School of Tübingen'' was quickly formed, with J. A. Möhler (d. 1838) as its most outstanding representative. The combination of historical and speculative theology, which it developed under the influence of IDEALISM and ROMANTICISM, was of the greatest importance in the history of theological study and exercised an influence on other German universities. Among Möhler's distinguished successors at Tübingen were J. E. KUHN (d. 1887), and the church historians K. J. HEFELE (d. 1893 as bishop of Rottenburg), F. X. FUNK (d. 1907), and K. BIHLMEYER (d. 1942). Outstanding in the Evangelical Theological Faculty was F. C. BAUR (d. 1860), who, influenced by Hegel's philosophy, unaugurated the historico-critical theology that, along with a certain Biblicism, has characterized this Faculty through the 20th century. The most significant of Baur's successors were A. SCHLATTER (d. 1938) and K. Heim (d. 1958).

In view of its institutions and number of students, the University of Tübingen holds a high place among the universities of Germany. This is also true of its theological faculties. In the evangelical theological faculty, the historico-critical tendency is dominant. The *Zeitschrift für Theologie und Kirche* is published mainly by its professors. The *Theologische Wörterbuch zum Neuen Testament* had its beginning at Tübingen, which is also contributing to both the new edition of the *Biblia Hebraica* and the critical edition of the *Opera omnia* of Luther. Since the early 1960s, New Testament research at Tübingen has also exercised a marked influence on Protestant theology in the United States.

The Catholic theological faculty has remained true to its 19th-century inheritance. It still publishes the *Theologische Quartalschrift,* founded in 1819.

Bibliography: *Studienführer der Universität Tübingen* (Tübingen 1963). J. HALLER, *Die Anfänge der Universität (Tübingen, 1477–1537,* 2 v. (Stuttgart 1927–29). E. STOLZ, et al., ''Beiträge zur Geschichte der Universität, besonders der katholisch-theologischen Fakultät in Tübingen,'' *Theologische Quartalschrift* 108 (1927) 1–220. J. R. GEISELMANN, *Lebendiger Glaube aus geheiligter Überlieferung: Der Grundgedanke der Theologie Johann A. Möhlers und der katholischen Tübinger Schule* (Mainz 1942). E. VERMEIL, *Jean Adam Möhler et l'École catholique de Tubingue, 1815–40* (Paris 1913). C. VON WEIZSÄCKER, *Lehrer und Unterricht an der evangelisch-theologischen Facultät der Universität Tübingen von der Reformation bis zur Gegenwart* (Tübingen 1877).

[M. ELZE]

TÜBINGEN SCHOOL

A group of 19th-century Protestant theologians, whose main interest was the New Testament and the nature of Christianity as described therein. The school's founder was F. C. BAUR (1792–1860), who had been formed in the Lutheran orthodox tradition that had flourished until then at the University of Tübingen. The movement's first élan came seemingly from Baur's *Symbolik und Mythologie der Naturreligion des Altertums* (1824–25), written from a viewpoint produced by contact with the thought of SCHLEIERMACHER. The substance of the school's endeavors, however, consisted in the rigorous application of the ideas of HEGEL to the development to Christianity, especially that of the primitive Church. The thesis and antithesis, as conceived by Baur and his colleagues, were Petrine and Pauline Christianity, presented as radically opposed orientations. The Petrinists, according to this view, held a doctrine of justification by faith and the works of the Mosaic Law; while the Pauline faction insisted on justification by faith alone. Similar opposition existed in the area of church polity, according to the school, for the Petrine party wanted to model church government on the ''hierarchical'' structure of Judaism with the high priest at the summit; whereas the followers of St. Paul insisted on a synodal or presbyterian type of rule. According to this theory a synthesis (in the Hegelian sense) emerged gradually during the second and third centuries, when Catholicism came into existence.

The system further developed by sorting New Testament literature. Apostolic authenticity was denied to most books of the New Testament. St. Mark's Gospel was held to be the earliest of the Synoptics, although it was composed after the time of St. JUSTIN MARTYR. The criterion for such conclusions was the presence or absence of indications of compromise. Sharp polemic favoring the Petrine or the Pauline position was taken to indicate an early date. The most vigorous expression of this theorizing came from a member of the school, Albert Schwegler (1819–57), in his *Nachapostolische Zeitalter* (1846). David STRAUSS (1808–74) was another prominent representative. Meanwhile another colleague, Eduard Zeller, had founded an organ to propagate the school's ideas, the *Tübinger theologische Jahrbücher,* (1842–57). In 1858 Adolf Hilgenfeld (1823–1907) began editing a continuation, the *Zeitschrift für wissenschaftliche Theologie,* which appeared regularly until 1914. By that time Tübingen had been completely eclipsed. RITSCHL, one of its early adherents, founded a school of his own, and it became widely accepted that the simplistic Hegelian interpretation of ecclesiastical history does not conform with historic reality. After reaching its peak of popularity and influence in the decade preceding 1850, the school declined rapidly in prestige.

Bibliography: R. W. MACKAY, *The Tübingen School and its Antecedents* (Hertford 1863). F. L. CROSS, *The Oxford Dictionary of the Christian Church* (London 1957) 1379. M. ELZE, *Die Religion in Geschichte und Gegenwart* (Tübingen 1957–65) 6:1067–68. "Tübinger Schule," *Lexikon für Theologie und Kirche*, ed. J. HOFER and K. RAHNER (Freiberg 1957–65) v.10.

[M. B. SCHEPERS]

TUDESCHIS, NICOLAUS DE

Canonist; b. Catania, 1386; d. Palermo, 1445. He studied under Antonius de Butrio and Franciscus Zabarella, and taught from 1412 in Bologna, Parma, Sienna, and Florence. He was named an auditor general of the Camera Apostolica in 1421 and abbot of the Benedictine Abbey of Santa Maria de Maniaco in 1425 (thus his title abbas Siculus, abbas modernus). In 1434 he was nominated archbishop of Palermo by King Alfonso V of Aragon and Sicily, and was confirmed in this see in 1435 by Eugene IV (hence he was called also Panormitanus). In 1436 he was the ambassador of Alfonso V to the Council of Basel, where he played, with interruptions, a changing but always leading role. He was named a cardinal by the Basel antipope Felix V in 1440.

A sharp distinction is to be made between his juridico-dogmatic works and the polemical speeches occasioned by the ecclesiastical political quarrels of the time. The principal works of the first group are the extensive *Commentarium* begun in 1421 on the decretals of Gregory IX, a *Lectura* on the *Clementines,* 221 *Consilia,* and seven *Questiones.* The *Quaestio Episcopus et quidam rector curatus* reflects his moderate conciliar ideas stemming from the canonistic tradition. To the second group belong the many polemical addresses given in Basel and at the Frankfort Diets of 1438 and 1442. These speeches are to be used with caution as a source for his views on ecclesiastical constitutional law.

Bibliography: C. LEFEBVRE, *Dictionnaire de droit canonique,* ed. R. NAZ, 7 v. (Paris 1935–65) 6:1195–1215, excellent article. J. F. VON SCHULTE, *Die Geschichte der Quellen und der Literatur des kanonischen Rechts,* 3 v. in 4 pts. (Stuttgart 1875–80; repr. Graz 1956) 2:312–313. A. VAN HOVE, *Commentarium Lovaniense in Codicem iuris canonici 1,* v.1–5 (Mechlin 1928–); v.1, Prolegomena (2d ed. 1945) 1:466 and *passim.* J. SCHWEIZER, *Nicolaus de Tudeschi . . .: Seine Tätigkeit am Basler Konzil* (Strasbourg 1924). C. LEFEBVRE, "L'Enseignement de Nicolas de Tudeschis et l'autorité pontificale," *Ephemerides iuris canonici* 14 (1958) 312–339. K. W. NÖRR, *Kirche und Konzil bei Nicolaus de Tudeschis* (Cologne 1964).

[K. W. NÖRR]

TULSA, DIOCESE OF

In 1973 when the Diocese of Oklahoma City and Tulsa was divided, Oklahoma City was made an archdio-cese and the new Diocese of Tulsa, *Tulsensis,* one of the suffragan sees. The new diocese covers 36 counties in the eastern part of the state of Oklahoma. At the time it was established the area had a population of 1.1 million, 51,000 of whom were Catholic. In 2001, the total population was 1.5 million and the number of Catholics about 62,000.

The first bishop of the diocese of Tulsa was Monsignor Bernard J. Ganter, chancellor of the Galveston-Houston diocese. He would serve for four hectic years (1973–1977), creating the infrastructure of the new see, until he was transferred to Beaumont in his home state of Texas. A principal occurrence during his tenure was the arrival of thousands of Vietnamese refugees at nearby Fort Chaffee, Arkansas, following the end of the war in 1975. Bishop Ganter took the lead in resettling them and preparing them for life in the United States. Shortly before his departure, he ordained the first permanent deacons in Oklahoma. (Bishop Ganter died as Bishop of Beaumont, Texas, of cancer, on Oct. 9, 1993.)

Bishop Ganter's successor was Monsignor Eusebius J. Beltran, formerly vicar general of the Archdiocese of Atlanta, Georgia. His episcopal ordination took place in Tulsa on April 20, 1978. During the fifteen ensuing years, he brought to fruition many of the programs begun by his predecessor, especially in vocation recruitment—he ordained 32 priests and 47 permanent deacons—and in the creation of new parishes. He also expanded the system of Catholic Charities in the diocese and worked to preserve the parish schools, in two instances bringing them directly under diocesan control until they recovered sufficiently to continue on their own. Upon the retirement of Archbishop Salatka in Oklahoma City late in 1992, Bishop Beltran was appointed to replace him.

Tulsa's third ordinary, Edward J. Slattery, a priest of the archdiocese of Chicago had been president of the Catholic Church Extension Society. Pope JOHN PAUL II ordained him a bishop in Rome on Jan. 6, 1994. Among his principal concerns have been expanding the Church's ministry among Hispanics and codifying diocesan policies. To the latter end he has announced a synod for May 2002.

Bibliography: J. D. WHITE, *This Far by Faith: 125 Years of Catholic Life in Oklahoma, 1875–2000* (Strasbourg, France 2001).

[J. D. WHITE]

TUNISIA, THE CATHOLIC CHURCH IN

The Republic of Tunisia is located on the coast of North Africa, and is bordered on the north and east by the

> **Capital:** Tunis.
> **Size:** 59,664 sq. miles.
> **Population:** 9,593,402 in 2000.
> **Languages:** Arabic (official), French.
> **Religions:** 1,730 Catholics (.01%), 9,588,685 Muslims (99%), 1,887 Jews (.01%), 1,100 other.
> **Diocese:** Tunis, directly subject to the Holy See.

Mediterranean Sea, on the southeast by Libya and on the west by Algeria. The semi-forested hills of the north transition to salt marches under the hot, dry climate of the central region, while the south is a desert with few oasis. Natural resources include phosphate deposits in the central regions, as well as petroleum, iron ore, zinc, lead and natural gas deposits offshore. Agricultural production includes grains, olives, grapes, dates and citrus. Tourism is a mainstay of the Tunisian economy.

A French protectorate since the late 19th century, Tunisia gained its independence in 1955. Political upheaval in the early 1980s resulted in a coup that returned the country to multiparty politics. The country's neutrality during the Gulf War in the late 20th century cost it U.S. aid, although government efforts to privatize industry promised a stable economy in the early 21st century. Most Tunisians are ethnic Arabs.

History. A land of strategic importance in the ancient world, Tunisia was devastated by the VANDALS in the 5th century and invaded by the Muslims in the 7th century. Due to the presence of the slave trade along its coast, few Christians entered the region until after slavery had been suppressed in the early 19th century. Pope Gregory XVI made the Prefecture of Tunis into a vicariate in 1843. In 1881 Tunisia became a French protectorate. In that same year Archbishop, later Cardinal, C. M. A. LAVIGERIE of Algiers (d. 1892) was appointed administrator of the prefecture. Three years later, while retaining the See of Algiers, Monsignor Lavigerie also became archbishop of Carthage and primate of Africa, the Archdiocese of Carthage encompassing the whole of Tunisia. Much of Cardinal Lavigerie's energy during the last eight years of his life was devoted to restoring the ancient See of Carthage. In addition to providing for the spiritual needs of the 50,000 Europeans living in Tunisia, Lavigerie opened the College of St. Louis for the Muslim population, confiding it to the White Fathers.

The region declared its independence from France on March 20, 1956. During the following year, the bey (provincial governor) was overthrown and Tunisia was proclaimed a republic under the control of President Habib Bourguiba, with a new constitution announced on June 1, 1959. Along with some Italians, French Europe-

ans constituted the major Christian element in Tunisia, and when the country became independent, large numbers of them left the country, fearing reprisals. Relations with France deteriorated still further in the late 1950s, the result of skirmishes between Tunisian and French troops along the Algerian border and the retaliatory bombing of a Tunisian village by French military planes. The dispute lasted until October of 1963.

For the most part, those Catholics who remained in Tunisia following independence lived in towns, with the result that rural parishes fell into disuse. The number of priests proportionately diminished; among those priests remaining by the latter part of the 20th century were the White Fathers whose center for Arabic studies (Institut des Belles Lettres Arabes) was much appreciated by Muslim intellectuals for its pervading spirit of a deep, friendly and disinterested knowledge of the country.

An agreement of July 10, 1964, concluded between the Holy See and the Bourguiba government radically altered the situation of the Church in Tunisia. The Archdiocese of Carthage was suppressed and replaced by the Prelature of Tunis, which was made a diocese in 1995. Only seven churches, of which two were in Tunis, remained the property of the new prelature; more than 100 others, many of which had become vacant, were handed over, without compensation, to the Tunisian state, which converted them to civil uses. The cathedral of Carthage was transformed into a museum. Only Church-run educational and nursing institutes, including the hospital in Tunis, were allowed to carry on their activities.

Although the government of Tunisia strengthened its ties with the Arab world during the mid-1960s, the withdrawal of French financial aid from the region greatly harmed the economy. In 1987 a coup was staged against President Bourguiba, who was declared mentally unfit to fulfill his duties. Under a constitutional amendment, a multi-party system was established and free elections were held for the first time in 30 years in April of 1989. Zine el-Abidine ben Ali was elected president with no opposition, and under his administration the government began to gradually privatize local industries, encourage foreign trade and stabilize the nation's economy. Under the constitution, Islam was the state religion, although the Catholic Church was granted special status due to its formal recognition by the government.

By 2000 there were 13 parishes in Tunis, tended by 15 secular and 20 religious priests. The Church owned five churches and seven cultural centers. Religious included fewer than ten brothers and 175 sisters, who administered the nation's eight primary and five Catholic secondary schools, most of their students Muslims. The Church in Tunisia encouraged its faithful to live among the Muslim majority in a spirit of disinterested service, making what contribution they could toward creating a secure quality of life for all Tunisians. While Islamic fundamentalism began to gain a foothold in Tunisia during the early 1990s, the government responded by cracking down on all Muslim militants.

For the region's early ecclesiastical history, *see* CARTHAGE.

Bibliography: A. PONS, *La Nouvelle Église d'Afrique* (Tunis 1930). L. BAUNARD, *Le Cardinal Lavigerie*, 2 v. (Paris 1898). *Revue de l'Institut des belles lettres arabes (IBLA) des Pères Blancs* (Tunis 1937–). *Bilan du Monde* 2:857–863.

[J. CUOQ/EDS.]

TUNSTALL, CUTHBERT

English bishop, statesman, and humanist; b. Hackforth, Catterick, Yorkshire, 1474; d. London, Nov. 18, 1559. The natural son of a squire, Thomas Tunstall, and of a daughter of Sir John Conyers of Hornby Castle, Yorkshire (the parents were probably married in later years), he was educated at Oxford and Cambridge before taking a doctorate in Canon and Roman law at Padua. Ordained in 1511 and made bishop of London in 1522, he was translated to Durham in 1530. In the period from 1515 to 1526 he was employed several times by Henry VIII in negotiations with Emperor Charles V and Francis I of France. As bishop of Durham he served Henry on the Council of the North (1537) and in conferences with the Scots. Devout and chaste, he owed his ecclesiastical promotion primarily to the king; his learning won him the friendship of Erasmus and Thomas More. Tunstall was a decided opponent of the Protestant reformers, and reluctantly acquiesced in the religious changes of Henry's reign. He disliked using force in the suppression of heresy but showed less consideration for political offenders. Opposed to the introduction of Protestantism under Edward VI, he was imprisoned in 1550 and deprived of his bishopric in 1552. Restored by Mary, he assisted in the return of papal supremacy but adopted a passive attitude to her persecution of Protestants. For refusing to acknowledge the royal supremacy under Elizabeth he again lost his see and died a prisoner in Lambeth Palace. Tunstall wrote two important works: *De arte supputandi*, a treatise on arithmetic, and *De veritate corporis* . . . , a defense of the Real Presence.

Bibliography: C. STURGE, *Cuthbert Tunstal* (New York 1938). P. HUGHES, *The Reformation in England*, 3 v. in 1 (5th, rev. ed. New York 1963). L. B. SMITH, *Tudor Prelates and Politics, 1536–1558* (Princeton 1953). A. F. POLLARD, *The Dictionary of National Biography from the Earliest Times to 1900*, 63 v. (London 1885–1900) 19:1237–42.

[M. R. O'CONNELL]

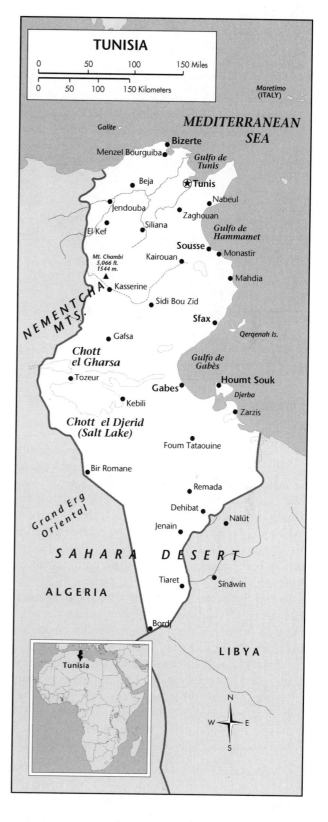

Corinthian columns of a church near the Winter Baths at the Roman site of Thuburbo Majus, a city that flourished in the 2nd and 3rd centuries A.D., Tunisia. (©Roger Wood/CORBIS)

TURKEY, THE CATHOLIC CHURCH IN

The Republic of Turkey is located in southeastern Europe, and comprises part of Kurdistan in the east, all the mountainous peninsula known as Asia Minor or Anatolia (Anadolu) and part of Thrace in the southeast extremity of Europe. With 95 percent of its land located in Asia, Turkey is bound on the north by the Black Sea, on the northeast by Georgia, Armenia and Azerbaijan, on the east by Iran, on the southeast by Iraq, on the south by Syria and the Mediterranean Sea, on the west by the Aegean Sea, and on the northwest by Greece and Bulgaria. The region is mountainous, particularly in the northeast and east, while the central area is plateau. Numerous lakes as well as rivers cross Turkey, and its coastline is extensive, although the country has claim to only a few nearby islands. Agricultural products include wheat, barley, corn, rice, olives and tobacco, while natural resources consist of coal, iron ore, chromium, copper and mercury. Of historic and economic importance, Turkey controls the straits linking the Black Sea and the Aegean.

As a bridge between East and West, Turkey is the site of one of the oldest civilized regions in the world; the massive ruins of the ancient Hittite Empire, for example, are still evident in the interior. Controlled by Ottomans for much of its recent history, Turkey gained independence in 1919 and was proclaimed a republic four years later. Although neutral during World War II, Turkey

joined NATO in 1951. Relations between Turkey and Greece continue to be strained following Turkey's invasion of Cyprus in 1974 to prevent a Greek takeover. Turkey is 80 percent ethnic Turkish, although a Kurdish minority lives in Kurdistan in the southeast, and various other ethnic groups still exist in the interior. The violence perpetrated by Kurdish nationalists continued to draw condemnation from human rights groups into 2000.

History to Ottoman Rule. Most of Asia Minor belonged to the Persian Empire, while Greek colonies were established along the coasts. Under Alexander the Great the area became Hellenized and Greek-speaking in varying degrees. During the 2d century B.C. it gradually came under the Romans, developing into a populous and prosperous part of the empire. Many Jewish colonies, in close contact with Jerusalem, facilitated the spread of Christianity by affording points of contact for the first missionaries, especially St. Paul, himself a native of Tarsus on the southeast coast. The Epistles of St. Paul; Acts of the Apostles; Revelation, addressed to the seven churches of Asia; the letters of St. IGNATIUS OF ANTIOCH; and other early Christian writings attested to the numerous Christian communities throughout the area. The region also became a home for early heresies: in the 2d century Montanism established itself in the interior; later it was the center for Christological heresies, for Manichaeism and for Iconoclasm. At the same time, it was the residence of many famous Fathers of the Church, the scene of the earliest councils and of a highly organized ecclesiastical structure: by the mid-7th century Asia Minor contained 33 metropolitan sees with about 440 suffragans.

Despite Muslim efforts to penetrate the area, Turkey remained in Roman (Byzantine) control through most of the early Middle Ages, although the eastern frontier was constantly shifting. By the time of the death of Basil II (1025) the entire region seemed securely in BYZANTINE possession, but civil strife and the incursions of the Seljuk Turks hastened its decline. The disastrous defeat of the Byzantines by the Turks at Manzikert in 1071 opened up the whole of Asia Minor, so that ten years later the capital of the Turkish Sultanate of Rum was established as far west as Nicaea (Iznik). In 1097, however, Nicaea was taken by the crusaders, who then advanced through Asia Minor, enabling the Byzantine emperor to recover much of his former domain. During the Latin occupation of Constantinople (1204–61), the emperors settled in Nicaea; on returning to Constantinople they became more and more involved in European politics to the detriment of their eastern defenses, and by 1300 the Turks controlled almost all of western Anatolia.

Under Ottoman Rule. The early 14th century saw the Seljuks decline, only to be replaced by a more militant group, the OTTOMAN TURKS. While continuing their eastern conquests, the Ottomans also crossed the Dardanelles to Gallipoli in 1354, and a decade later had Adrianople in their hands. In 1387 Thessalonica fell after a long siege, and the Balkans were then rapidly subdued. Finally, under Sultan Mohammed II, on May 29, 1453, they stormed Constantinople, which as Istanbul would remain their capital until 1923, when the capital was transferred to Ankara. In the course of the 15th and 16th centuries the borders of the Ottoman Empire expanded in all directions, reaching their greatest extent in about the mid-17th century. The Turkish Sultan ruled all of the Near East, North Africa as far as Algeria, all of the Balkans, Hungary and the Crimean area, advancing in the West to the walls of Vienna. But the same period also began Ottoman decline, a result of internal inefficiency and corruption and by external foes, chiefly Austria and later Russia.

During the 19th century most of the Balkan states recovered their freedom, and as a result of World War I, the Turks lost most of their Arab territories, reducing the country more or less to its present borders. A movement of national resurgence was led by Mustafa Kemal, who was also known as Atatürk; the sultanate was abolished on Nov. 22, 1922, and the republic proclaimed on Oct. 29, 1923. Atatürk introduced a series of revolutionary reforms designed to modernize the country: Islam was no longer the state religion; the civil code, the calendar and even the manner of dress were all Westernized. In 1928 the Latin alphabet was made obligatory.

Turkish Policy toward Christianity. The 11th-century Turkish establishment in Asia Minor initiated a gradual change from a predominantly Christian, Greek-speaking population to an Islamic Turkish one. Many Christians, particularly after 1453, chose to emigrate, while those who remained, largely Greek Orthodox and Armenian, were subjected to many restrictions, although allowed a certain autonomy as a *millet* (nation) under the rule of their patriarch. Protected by European powers, chiefly France, Catholic missionaries were able to work in the Ottoman Empire, particularly among the Eastern Christians in Syria, Iraq and Egypt. But in the 19th century, national revolutions in the Balkans accompanied by European interference led the Turks to take severe anti-Christian measures, culminating in a series of brutal massacres lasting well into the 20th century, in which the Armenians suffered the worst. The Treaty of Lausanne in 1923, which settled the Greco-Turkish war, exchanged the Greeks in Anatolia for the Muslims in Greece, with the exception of those in Thrace and the Greek community in Istanbul.

Into the 21st Century. Atatürk's reforms continued under his party's leadership until 1950, when the country

Capital: Ankara.
Size: 301,380 sq. miles.
Population: 65,666,677 in 2000.
Languages: Turkish; Kurdish, Arabic, Armenian, and Greek are also spoken in various regions.
Religions: 78,900 Catholics (.1%), 65,557,852 Muslims (99.85%), 5,125 Orthodox (.008%), 24,800 Jews (.04%).
Ecclesiastical organization: The Roman Catholic Church has an archdiocese in Izmir, with apostolic vicariates in Anatolia and Istanbul. Several Eastern Catholic churches also exist in Turkey, their administrations divided between Asia and Europe. The Armenian Orthodox Church in Asia is overseen by the Patriarchate of Cilicia who resides in Beirut, Lebanon, while the Church in Europe is subject to the Archeparchy of Istanbul. The Chaldean has an archeparchy in Diyarbakir. The Byzantine Church has an apostolic exarchate in Istanbul.

held free elections and brought to power the opposition. A decade later a military coup wrestled power for a short time, and although a military government would seize power again from 1971–73, Turkey found itself increasingly influenced by a religious revival sparked by conservative Islamic political factions who pushed traditional Muslim values as a means of stabilizing both society and the economy. The country's relationship with neighboring Greece as well as the world were strained during the Turkish invasion of Cyprus in 1974, although the situation normalized internationally by 1978. Meanwhile, diplomatic relations between Turkey and the Holy See had been established by Pope John XXIII in 1959, a move that did little to calm the growing hostility of Islamic fundamentalists desirous of making Turkey a Muslim state. In addition, ethnic tensions between Turks, Kurds and Armenians simmered, reaching a state of military emergency in the mid-1980s, as Kurds demanded an independent Kurdistan. Military action taken against Kurdish rebels in 1995 drew condemnation from human rights groups and resulted in the collapse of the moderate government and brought a pro-Islamic party to power. Into 2000 the balance of power in Turkey remained tenuous, as Islamic fundamentalists continued to agitate for the creation of a Muslim state, and its application for membership in the European Union remained on hold. However, under the leadership of Prime Minister Bulent Ecevit, economic reforms were underway that were viewed as stabilizing the economy and rebuilding the confidence of foreign investors.

By 2000 Turkey had 52 parishes, tended by 15 diocesan and 49 religious priests, as well as 12 brothers and 115 sisters. In addition to the Latin-rite and Eastern-rite Catholics, a Greek Orthodox community continued to reside in Istanbul under the jurisdiction of the patriarch of CONSTANTINOPLE, and a small Syriac Christian community remained in the southeast. Government attempts to

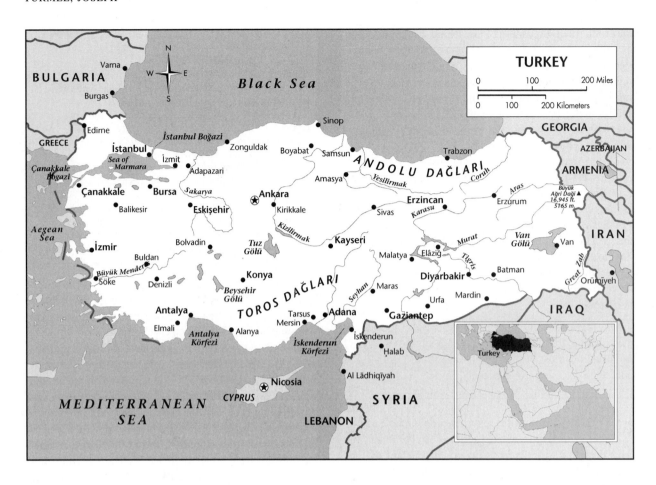

halt the rising Islamic influence included a ban on the wearing of religious head coverings in public buildings and a 1997 mandate that children attend eight years of public school before being allowed to attend religious academies. Scattered outbreaks of violence were directed by fundamentalists groups toward Christians, including a grenade thrown on the grounds of the Ecumenical Orthodox Patriarchate in Istanbul in 1996 and the bombing of a Greek Orthodox Church in 1998. The state-run Office of Foundations regulated the activities of religious minorities, and recognized only the three faiths covered in the 1923 Lausanne Treaty: Greek Orthodox, Armenian Orthodox and Jewish. Roman Catholics, as an "unrecognized minority," were confined to existing churches, classified as "diplomatic property." In 2001 Pope John Paul II encouraged Church leaders to develop closer relations with Turkey's Orthodox, commenting that "the Church of Christ must be truly involved in the life of Turkish society."

See Also: ARMENIAN CHRISTIANITY

Bibliography: W. M. RAMSAY, *The Historical Geography of Asia Minor* (London 1890); *The Cities and Bishoprics of Phrygia,* 2 v. (Oxford 1895–97). M. F. KÖPRÜLÜ, *Les Origines de l'empire ottoman* (Paris 1936). A. H. M. JONES, *The Cities of the Eastern Roman Provinces* (New York 1937). P. WITTEK, *The Rise of the Ottoman Empire* (London 1938). J. K. BIRGE, *A Guide to Turkish Area Study* (Washington 1949). D. MAGIE, *Roman Rule in Asia Minor,* 2 v. (Princeton, NJ 1950). F. BABINGER, *Mehmed der Eroberer* (Munich 1953). C. CAHEN, "Le Problème ethnique en Anatolie," *Journal of World History,* 2 (1954) 347–362. *A History of the Crusades,* ed. K. M. SETTON et al., (Philadelphia 1955–). F. TAESCHNER, *Encyclopedia of Islam,* ed. B. LEWIS et al. (2d ed. Leiden 1954–) 1:461–480. S. VRYONIS, *Problems in the History of Byzantine Anatolia* (Ankara 1963); *The Decline of Medieval Hellenism in Asia Minor and the Process of Islamization, 11th to 15th Centuries,* in preparation.

[G. T. DENNIS/EDS.]

TURMEL, JOSEPH

Modernist, historian of dogma; b. Rennes (Ille-et-Vilaine), France, Dec. 13, 1853; d. Rennes, Feb. 5, 1943. After ordination (1882), Turmel taught dogmatic theology at the seminary in Rennes from 1882 until his removal in 1892. He then acted as chaplain of the Little Sisters of the Poor for years, but continued his scientific research and writing. Turmel is one of the most enigmatic figures among the disciples of MODERNISM. Although he had early abandoned faith in the God of Christian revelation

(March 18, 1886, according to him), he decided to remain outwardly attached to the church and to fight it anonymously while in clerical garb. His extraordinary knowledge of early Christian theology, and particularly of St. Augustine, enabled him to become an esteemed contributor to the leading French theological journals. He supplied the historical chronicle for the *Revue du clergé; français* (1902–08). His two-volume *Histoire de la théologie positive* (1904–06) opened the series *Bibliothèque de théologie historique*, sponsored by the professors of the Paris Catholic Institute (Institut Catholique), and included well-known works by A. d' ALÈS and F. PRAT; but it was placed on the Index (1910–11). In 1909–10 his *L'eschatologie à la fin du IV siècle, Histoire du dogme du péché originel, Histoire du dogme de la papauté, Saint Jérome*, and *Tertullian* were also included on the Index. After these condemnations he began publishing, under 14 different pseudonyms, numerous attacks on Catholic doctrines from a radical, Modernistic–historical viewpoint. Fourteen other books by him under the names Louis Coulanges, Henri Delafosse, Antoine Dupin, Guillaume Herzog, Edmond Perrin, and André Lagarde (*The Latin Church in the Middle Ages*) can also be found in the Index of Forbidden Books. Not until 1929, after more than two decades of research, did Louis Saltet succeed in tracing the single authorship of these writings. In 1930 the Holy Office decreed Turmel's excommunication (*vitandus*) and his degradation from the priestly state. In the Modernist movement Turmel, along with LOISY and HOUTIN, represented the extreme radical wing. He claimed that scientific progress and advancing knowledge would lead to the disintegration of belief in Christian revelation.

Bibliography: F. SARTIAUX, *Joseph Turmel, prêtre, historien des dogmes* (Paris 1931), placed on Index April 6, 1932. J. BRUGERETTE, *Le Prêtre français et la société contemporaine*, 3 v. (Paris 1933–38) v.3. É. POULAT, *Histoire, dogme et critique dans la crise moderniste* (Paris 1962). ''Turmel,'' *Lexikon für Theologie und Kirche* 2 v.10.

[V. CONZEMIUS]

TURNER, ANTONY, BL.

Jesuit priest, martyr; b. 1628, Dalby Parva, Leicestershire, England; hanged, drawn, and quartered at Tyburn (London), June 20, 1679. As the son of a Protestant minister, Antony attended Cambridge. There both he and his brother Edward converted to Catholicism. Both entered the English College at Rome (1650), but Antony left for the Jesuit novitiate at Watten, Flanders, in April 1653, studied theology at Liège, and was ordained (1659). Thereafter he ministered for 18 years in the environs of Worchester (1661–78). In September 1678 the fictitious Oates Plot became public. Turner went to Lon-

Christian frescos decorate the interior of the St. Barbara Chapel at the Goreme Open-Air Museum in the Cappadocia region of Turkey. (©Richard T. Nowitz/CORBIS)

don to seek the means to escape to the Continent (January 1679). Finding no assistance, he gave away his last money and surrendered himself to the justice as an illegal priest. He was incarcerated at the Gatehouse, then at Newgate. He stood trial at the Old Bailey on the charge of conspiracy to assassinate the king and was convicted based on perjured testimony. On the gallows he declared his innocence in the Oates Plot, forgave those involved in his death, and asked for God's mercy. He was beatified by Pius XI on Dec. 15, 1929.

Feast of the English Martyrs: May 4 (England); December 1 (Jesuits).

See Also: ENGLAND, SCOTLAND, AND WALES, MARTYRS OF.

Bibliography: R. CHALLONER, *Memoirs of Missionary Priests,* ed. J. H. POLLEN (rev. ed. London 1924; repr. Farnborough 1969). J. H. POLLEN, *Acts of English Martyrs* (London 1891). J. N. TYLENDA, *Jesuit Saints & Martyrs* (Chicago 1998), a179–81.

[K. I. RABENSTEIN]

TURNER, CUTHBERT HAMILTON

Ecclesiastical historian and scholar; b. Paddington, July 7, 1860; d. Oxford, Oct. 10, 1930. He was educated

City walls stand in Istanbul, Turkey. The walls are the remains of the original city built in AD 324 by Constantine I of Rome. (©Adam Woolfitt/CORBIS)

in Winchester and at Oxford where he spent most of his adult life teaching and in positions of honor. In 1885 he was appointed lecturer in theology of St. John's College and in 1889 he became professor of ecclesiastical history. He was editor of the *Journal of Theological Studies* from 1899 to 1902. Since he was keenly interested in textual criticism he concentrated on the material of early Western canon law and New Testament studies. He is most noted for his *Ecclesiae occidentalis monumenta iuris antiquissima* (2 v. Oxford 1899–1913) and *Studies in Early Church History* (Oxford 1912).

Bibliography: H. N. BATE, *The Dictionary of National Biography from the Earliest Times to 1900,* suppl. (London 1922–30) 861–864.

[H. A. LARROQUE]

TURNER, THOMAS WYATT

Biologist, educator, pioneer leader of African American Catholics; b. March 16, 1877, Hughesville, Md.; d. April 21, 1978, Washington, D. C. In the preface to his unpublished autobiography, Thomas Wyatt Turner captured in simple language the meaning of a life which spanned more than a century: ''For me, my color was my earliest handicap. Doors would be closed, opportunities lacking, barriers erected because I was black. The American dream would be a dream only—to become a train engineer, a wealthy farmer, a storekeeper or whatever. But if I just had a chance, I would exert every effort to push open the door, tear down the barriers, seek every opportunity to become a man with dignity, respected for my personal worth.'' In May 1976 The Catholic University of America recognized that personal worth in bestowing an honorary doctor of science degree on this remarkable Catholic educator. The award came 75 years after Turner had left the University as a graduate student because of insufficient funds and more than 40 years after he had received an ironic letter of refusal to his appeal for the admission of African American students to the institution.

Poverty and racism were battles which Turner waged most of his life. He was born in a sharecropper's cabin in Charles Co., Southern Maryland, fifth of the nine children of Eli and Linnie (Gross) Turner. Baptized as an infant, he once remarked that he had ''remained baptized ever since.'' The phrase was fitting, for Turner discovered early in life that the color barrier existed in church as elsewhere. While sitting in the old slave gallery for

Kariye Camii in Istanbul: Parekklesion Dome. (©Archivo Iconografico, S.A./CORBIS)

Sunday Mass as a child, young Thomas vowed he would change such immoral practices. He received his early education in the county schools and in the fields as a sharecropper, completing his studies at an Episcopalian school in Charlotte Hall, Maryland. As graduation neared, this young student known as "Lawyer" was offered a college scholarship on the condition that he become an Episcopalian. Accepting the advice of a friendly Quaker woman, Turner chose to "stick with" his church instead. Shortly thereafter, he set out for Howard University in Washington, D. C., penniless but ambitious. Working his way through school, Turner obtained his B.A. degree in 1901. He accepted a scholarship for graduate study in science at Catholic University, but soon ran out of funds. About that time Turner received a request from Booker T. Washington to teach at Tuskegee Institute, which the young man eagerly accepted.

In 1902 Turner returned to Maryland to join the faculty of the Baltimore High and Training School, among the first African American teachers to staff African American schools in the state. He joined the fledgling NAACP as the first secretary of its Baltimore branch in 1910. Three years later he moved to Howard University as a biologist in the School of Education. Continuing his civil rights activities, he organized the first city–wide membership drive for the Washington NAACP in 1915.

At the same time Turner directed his attention to the racist practices in his own church. With fellow African–American Catholics he organized the Committee against the Extension of Race Prejudice in the Church, which wrote to bishops letters of protest against discrimination in churches, schools, hospitals, orphanages, and seminaries. Racism in seminaries and convents was a primary concern to the committee. Finally, in 1924 the group adopted a constitution; established a permanent organization, Federated Colored Catholics; and elected Turner its first president.

Catholic Church, Istanbul. (©Yann Arthus-Bertrand/CORBIS)

Although Turner saw the organization as representative of the interests of African American Catholics in America, he welcomed the support of all groups, including white priests. One of the earliest such advocates was John LaFarge, SJ, editor of *America* magazine. Another was William Markoe, SJ of St. Louis, who became editor of the Federation's official journal. For a time the three men worked harmoniously to keep the cause of racial justice before the American hierarchy through annual Federation conventions, letters to bishops, and local efforts at change. When William Markoe sought to transform the organization into a more "interracial" group, however, Turner balked. As an older African American Catholic who remembered stories of the earlier Afro American Catholic Congress movement (1889–94) and its demise because of militancy, Turner feared a white domination which would reduce the Federation to mere discussion. The controversy between Turner and Markoe (with La-Farge largely silent) was waged, often bitterly, in private correspondence, meetings, and the press from 1931 to 1932.

Finally, the organization split into two factions, with Turner as president of a small eastern group of Federation members. This organization functioned until 1952, with Turner often at the helm. Throughout this period the Federation president combined his church activities with a strenuous career as a professional educator. Receiving his master's degree from Howard in 1905 and his Ph.D. in botany from Cornell University in 1921, Turner served as acting dean of the School of Education at Howard (1914–20) and went to Hampton Institute in Virginia as first chairman of the biology department in 1924. He retired from that institution in 1945 after a distinguished career. The author of numerous published articles, he was the first African American man to present a paper before the Virginia Academy of Science and to serve as a research cytologist for the U. S. Department of Agriculture. He was honored by Hampton Institute in 1978 when its new natural sciences building was named Turner Hall. His pioneer work for equal rights in the church is memorialized in the Dr. Thomas Wyatt Turner Award, given yearly to a deserving individual by the Secretariat of the National Office of Black Catholics in Washington, D. C. Besides his unpublished autobiography Turner also left in manuscript a history of African American Catholicism.

Bibliography: M. W. NICKELS, ''The Federated Colored Catholics: A Study in the Variant Perspectives on Racial Justice as Represented by John LaFarge, William Markoe, and Thomas Turner'' (Ph.D. dissertation, Catholic University, 1975); ''Journey of a Black Catholic,'' *America* 135 (Jul. 1976) 6–8. M. W. NICKELS et al., ''NOBC Pioneer Dies in 102nd Year,'' *Impact!* 8 (Apr.–May 1978) 2–3.

[M. W. NICKELS]

TURNER, VICTOR

Professor of anthropology and religious studies; b. Glasgow, Scotland, May 28, 1920; d. Charlottesville, Va., Dec. 18, 1983. He received his doctoral degree in 1955 from Manchester University for research in the social organization and ritual of the Ndembu people of Zambia. In 1959 he became a member of the Catholic Church, and remained so until his death. He taught at the University of Manchester, Cornell University, the University of Chicago, and the University of Virginia. Turner was one of the foremost theorists of ritual and symbolism in the mid-20th century. He also influenced many other disciplines, notably social thought, history, medical anthropology, performance studies, and literature.

Symbol and Ritual. A major part of Turner's work developed from Van Gennep's discovery of rites of passage in world cultures (1910). A variety of rites which denoted and created cultural change contained a distinct phase in which the subject was withdrawn from an old status structure but not yet introduced into a new one. Turner pointed out that this intermediate liminal phase was characterized by ''antistructure and sentiments of *communitas*''—the undifferentiated free spirit of fellowship between comrades, brought about by the communication of sacra, ritual reversal, and the deconstruction and recombination of familiar cultural configurations. He set up analytical frameworks for the study of ritual symbols, which he used to explain their properties. The cross, for example, he held to be fired by its sensory character and corporeality, an element which in every symbol is indissolubly combined with its ideological meaning. Such an antithesis he called ''the polarization of a symbol.''

Social Theory. In his social theory Turner was process oriented. He argued, like SARTRE, that social structures are created by unstructured activity. Turner thus drew attention to the idea that religions, as well as systems of law and all objectified culture, derived from the living moments of human experience and activity—the study of which he later termed the anthropology of experience. Initially a Marxist convinced of the dynamic processual nature of human social existence, he became dissatisfied with the structuralist-functionalist approach and its argument that all social organization results from functional necessity and absolutely determines the character of culture. This did not seem to explain the curious symbolic and ritual phenomena he encountered in Africa. In 1962, exploring this theme further, he wrote *Chihamba, the White Spirit: A Ritual Drama of the Ndembu* [republished in *Revelation and Divination in Ndembu Ritual* (Ithaca, N.Y. 1975)] in which he borrowed Étienne GILSON's idea of ''the ungraspable act-of-being'' to describe the Ndembu's ungraspable spirit figure of Kavula, the thunder god. These were the terms of mysticism, not those of a reductionist anthropology.

In *The Ritual Process: Structure and Anti-Structure* (Chicago 1969) Turner introduced and expanded the themes of liminality and *communitas*. The fate of spontaneous *communitas* when it enters social history was exemplified by early Franciscanism. St. FRANCIS lived a spiritual life, in poverty. His thinking was concrete, personal, and imagist, characteristic of those in love with existential *communitas*. After his death problems emerged concerning the continuity of the order, and the Conventual system was developed. This insured the incorporation of permanent structural features into the order—a prime example of the movement from *communitas* to structure. In *Dramas, Fields, and Metaphors* (Ithaca, N.Y. 1974, pp. 275–294) Turner described how *communitas* may emerge within such an organization, and even exhibit itself as an oscillation with structure through time. He defended the archaic patterns of Church ritual and symbol that arose from the free space within liminality, and held that such patterns can become protective of future free spaces. He warned liturgiologists that structural-functionalism had little understanding of ritual liminality and should not be the basis for abolishing ancient liturgical traditions [''Passages, Margins and Poverty: Religious Symbols of *Communitas*,'' *Worship* 46 (1972) and ''Ritual, Tribal and Catholic,'' *Worship* 50 (1976)].

Turner regarded religious action as deeply connected to and rooted in social life, though not determined by it. He saw ritual in the early days of humankind arising in situations of sickness, life crisis, or the conflict of social drama—the latter consisting of four stages: breach of a norm; crisis; redress; followed either by reintegration or the recognition of irreparable schism. In the stage of redress, Turner held that ritual can effect a more comprehensive solution than law, because it can encompass the paradox of two irreconcilable goods.

Later Work. Turner applied his processualism and symbolic theory to the lives of St. Thomas Becket, Miguel Hidalgo, and many other historic figures, and he made use of literary examples such as the events and symbols in the Icelandic sagas and Dante's *Purgatorio*. In his monograph, *Image and Pilgrimage in Christian Culture: Anthropological Perspectives* (with E. Turner, New York 1978), he treated pilgrimage as a rite of passage, studying it as an important liminal phenomenon within the structured lives of the common people.

Shortly before he died, Turner began to use the findings of neuroscience to throw light on ritual. He became interested in the nonverbal right cerebral hemisphere, with its powers of holistic thinking. He realized that many of the problems of spiritual existence and human conflict found in his anthropological material were not resolved at the cognitive left-hemispheric level, but in the nonverbal noetic mode known as "ritual knowledge"—when the brain's instrument for religion, in both its hemispheres, was most fully engaged.

See Also: STRUCTURALISM.

Bibliography: H. B. PORTER, "Liminal Mysteries: Some Writings by Victor Turner," *Anglican Theological Review,* 57: 215–219. U. T. HOLMES, "Liminality and Liturgy," *Worship* 47: 386–397; "Ritual and Social Drama," *Worship* 51: 197–213. J. R. NICHOLS, "Worship as Anti-Structure: The Contribution of Victor Turner," *Theology Today* 41: 401–409. R. L. MOORE and F. E. REYNOLDS, eds., *Anthropology and the Study of Religion*, pt. 2, "The Work of Victor Turner" (Chicago 1984) 77–143.

[E. TURNER]

TURNER, WILLIAM

Sixth bishop of Buffalo, N.Y., educator, author; b. Killmalloch, County Limerick, Ireland, April 8, 1871; d. Buffalo, July 10, 1936. He attended national schools and the Jesuit college at Mungret, Limerick. In 1888, he received his B.A. from the Royal University of Ireland, and the S.T.D. in 1893 from the North American College in Rome, winning the Benemerenti medal of the Roman Academy of St. Thomas for proficiency in philosophy. He was ordained in Rome at 22 for the Diocese of St. Augustine, Fla., on Aug. 13, 1893. His services were obtained by Abp. John Ireland of St. Paul, Minn., who installed him in his archdiocesan seminary in 1895 as chairman of the philosophy department. After further studies in Europe, he was appointed in 1906 to the chair of philosophy at the Catholic University of America, Washington, D.C., also serving as librarian. Two widely used textbooks issued from his classroom experience:

History of Philosophy (1903), the first English textbook with a Catholic orientation on that subject, and *Lessons in Logic* (1911). He also wrote articles for the *Catholic Mind* and other publications, edited the *American Ecclesiastical Review* from 1914 to 1919, and was associate editor of the *Catholic Historical Review* from 1915 to 1918.

On March 10, 1919, he was chosen to succeed Bp. (later Cardinal) Dennis J. Dougherty as bishop of Buffalo. He was consecrated by Cardinal James Gibbons on March 29 and installed by Abp. (later Cardinal) Patrick Hayes on April 9. During his episcopacy he ordained 173 priests, created 30 new parishes, and was especially zealous in developing social services in his see. In 1923, he combined various charitable institutions, organizing the diocesan Catholic charities, which had raised several million dollars for the indigent by the time of his death. St. Vincent de Paul Society conferences were founded in all large parishes, as were numerous health facilities for undernourished children among his charges. He was honored in 1934 by the Italian government for his work among Italians in the U.S.

Bibliography: T. A. DONOHUE, *History: Diocese of Buffalo* (Buffalo 1930). "Death of Bishop Turner of Buffalo," *Catholic World* 143 (Aug. 1936) 619–620. C. BARRY, *The Catholic University of America, 1903–1909: The Rectorship of Denis J. O'Connell* (Washington 1949).

[I. F. MOGAVERO]

TURÓN, MARTYRS OF, SS.

Also known as Martyrs of the Asturias, Martyrs of the LaSallian Christian Brothers, Cirilo Bertrán and Companions; d. Oct. 9, 1934, Turón, Asturias, northern Spain; both beatified (April 29, 1990) and canonized (Nov. 21, 1999) by John Paul II. They are the first saints of the Spanish Civil War.

Most of the 6,832 modern Spanish martyrdoms occurred during the persecutions of the Civil War itself (July 18, 1936, to April 1, 1939). In 1931 a mild revolution overthrew Alfonso XIII, the last Bourbon, and instituted a republic. To combat the entrenched power of the Church, anticlerical legislation was enacted, generally removing education from the hands of the religious or forbidding religious education. The government tried to placate the peasantry through land reform, but not vigorously enough to satisfy the extremists. Dissatisfaction led to strikes and uprisings, especially in the mining areas of the Asturias, where the nine Martyrs of Turón died about two years before the July 1936 insurrection. During the 14 bloody days of this first test of the revolution, 10 diocesan priests, 13 religious, and 6 seminarians were killed, including the Martyrs of Turón. They were caught in this political upheaval that was then fomenting in Spain.

Eight of the Martyrs of Turón were followers of Saint John-Baptiste de la Salle. They ran the LaSallian Christian School of Our Lady of Covadonga College in Turón for the sons of local miners. The last was a Passionist priest. After withstanding a victorious attack with heavy artillery on the forces of the Second Republic, revolutionary authorities broke into the house of the brothers on the pretext that arms had been hidden there (Oct. 5, 1934). The nine were arrested and held in the ''People's House'' over the weekend without a trial. The Revolutionary Committee decided that they must die because of their influence over the children of the region. A witness at their sentencing reported that the martyrs heard their fate calmly. On the evening of October 9, they walked to the local cemetery under guard while softly praying. There they were executed by firing squad. The cause of Jaime Hilario Barbal Cosan was attached to that of the Martyrs of the Asturias, but it is dealt with separately in this volume because he was not martyred with this group.

The bodies of the LaSallian martyrs were buried in the cemetery of Bujedo near Burgos (Feb. 26, 1935), but that of Father Inocencio de la Immaculada, buried in the cemetery of Mieres, was destroyed in the bombings of 1936. Their cause for beatification began in the Diocese of Oviedo (Oct. 9, 1944, to June 22, 1945), and the decree of martyrdom was issued in Rome, May 16, 1989. At their beatification, Pope John Paul II stated: ''The Passionist priest met occasionally with the de la Salle Brothers. In that way God in his inscrutable providence wished to unite in martyrdom members of two congregations who worked in solidarity for the Church's one mission.'' The martyrs are:

Augusto Andrés, in the world Román Martín Fernández, LaSallian brother; b. May 6, 1910, Santander, Spain. An expressive child, Román joined the LaSallians after recovery from a grave illness (Aug. 8, 1922) and entered the novitiate (Feb. 3, 1926). After completing his formation (1929), he taught at Valladolid (1929–32), then completed his obligatory military service (1932–33) at Palencia. Brother Augusto was sent to Turón in 1933 when the school at Valladolid, to which he had returned following his military service, was closed by rebels.

Aniceto Adolfo, in the world Manuel Seco Gutiérrez, LaSallian brother, b. Oct. 4, 1912, Celada Marlantes (on the border between Cantabria and Castilla), Spain. The son of Pio Seco, Anceito is the youngest of the martyrs. He followed his eldest brother Maximino into the LaSallians at Bujedo, and he himself was followed by his younger brother Florencio. Manuel joined the house of studies (Sept. 6, 1926), then entered the novitiate (1928),

and received the habit together with the name Aniceto Adolfo (February 1929). He became known for his mercy and diligence. After finishing his studies at Bujedo, Aniceto Adolfo taught young children in Valladolid (August 1932–October 1933). He arrived in the mining town of Asturias to begin his new assignment in October 1933.

Benito de Jesús, in the world Héctor Valdivieso Sáez, LaSallian brother, first native Argentinian to be canonized; b. Oct. 31, 1910, Buenos Aires, Argentina. His parents, Benigno Valdivielso y Aurora Sáez, came from La Bureba near Burgos, Spain. When life in Argentina proved unsatisfactory, they returned to Briviesca, Spain, where Héctor was raised. Héctor attended the city school, then the school of the Daughters of Charity, until he discovered and entered the LaSallian school at Bujedo (August 1923). Because of his brilliance as a student, he was sent to the international house of studies at Lembecqles-Hall, Belgium, with three companions. He returned to Bujedo to begin his novitiate (Oct. 26, 1926). He began teaching at Astorga (Aug. 24, 1929), where he won acclaim from parents and students for his teaching methods. There he began to write as a means of propagating the faith, *La luz de Astorga* (*The Light of Astorga*). He also wrote beautifully about martyrdom in letters to his father, who had suffered in the recent persecutions in Mexico. He was sent to Turón in the summer of 1933.

Benjamín Julián, in the world Vicente Alonso Andrés, LaSallian brother; b. Oct. 27, 1908, Jaramillo de la Fuente near Burgos, Spain. Vicente's parents, Lesmes and Tomasina, were simple farmers who encouraged his vocation, evoked by a LaSallian brother who visited his school in 1919 to invite the students to become Christian educators. He was received at Bujedo (Oct. 7, 1920) at a much younger age (age 11) than usual because of his enthusiasm. He found his studies difficult because of his lack of preparation, but he persisted and entered the novitiate Feb. 2, 1924. He proved to be a masterful educator whose joy engaged his students in his first assignment at Santiago de Compostela (summer 1927). He was sent to Turón in the summer of 1933.

Cirilo Bertrán, in the world José Sanz Tejedor, LaSallian Christian brother; b. at Lerma near Burgos, Spain, March 20, 1888. Born of humble workers, José joined the order at Bujedo (July 12, 1905) and entered the novitiate (March 4, 1907). As Brother Cirilo Bertrán, he taught in Duesto near Bilbao (1909–10), the orphanage of the Sacred Heart of Jesus in Madrid (1910–11), Puente de Vallecas in Madrid (March–June 1911), Santa Susana in Madrid (June 1911–12), and many other places before making his final vows (1916). He served as director in Santander (1918, 1925), Riotuerto near La Cavada (1919, 1924), Valladolid (1930), and other places for 13 years.

In 1933, he began his assignment as director in Turón with a 30-day retreat. He defied the government by continuing religious instruction and urging attendance at Mass.

Inocencio de la Immaculada, in the world Manuel Canoure Arnau, Passionist priest; b. March 10, 1887, Santa Cecilia y San Acisclo del Valle de Oro (between Ferreira and Foz near Lugo), Galicia, Spain. After joining the Passionists (1902), he made his novitiate at Peñafiel, Valladolid, then Deusto in Vizcaya. Upon professing his first vows (July 26, 1905), Manuel became Inocencio de la Immaculada. He was ordained to the priesthood in 1913. In additional to his sacradotal duties, Innocencio taught philosophy, literature, and theology at various houses: Daimiel (Ciudad Real), Corella (Navarra), Peñaranda de Duero (Burgos), and three times at Mieres (Asturias), the last time in September 1934.

Julián Alfredo, in the world Vilfrido Fernández Zapico, LaSallian brother; b. Dec. 24, 1902, Cifuentes de Rueda on the Esla River near León. Born into a humble, pious family, Vilfrido's uncle, a priest, convinced him to join the Capuchins at León. He was about to begin his novitiate at the Capuchin house at Bilbao when he had to return home because of illness. After a second attempt and a second illness, he decided to enter the LaSallian novitiate at Bujedo, Feb. 4, 1926. Upon completing his studies, he began his first teaching assignment (Aug. 24, 1929) and was renowned for his joy in teaching children. He professed his perpetual vows during the summer of 1932. The following September (1933) he was assigned to Turón.

Marciano José, in the world Filomeno López y López, LaSallian brother; b. Nov. 15, 1900, El Pedregal near Molina de Aragón, Guadalajara, Spain. Filomeno's parents were farmers, but his uncle was Brother Gumersindo, infirmarian at Bujedo, who inspired the young man's vocation. Filomeno did well in his studies at Bujedo, but had to return home due to a serious ear infection that left him functionally deaf. Although he was unable to engage in teaching with this disability, he wanted to serve the brothers in other ways. He retuned to Bujedo, entered the novitiate (Sept. 20, 1916) and made his first vows (April 3, 1918). He served as gardener and housekeeper in Bujedo, and sacristan in the Premonstratensian church nearby. Thereafter he was sent as cook at Terán in Santander (May 28, 1928), then to Caborana (Asturias), Valladolid, Colunga (Asturias), Gallarta (Biscay), and Mieres (Asturias). Before he was sent to Turón (April 1934) to replace a brother who was afraid to stay because of the mounting tension, he wrote to his relatives that martyrdom was likely in the current situation—and he was willing to die. He could have saved himself simply by stating he was a cook and not revealing that he was also a brother religious.

Victoriano Pío, in the world Claudio Bernabé Cano, LaSallian brother, b. July 7, 1905, San Millan de Lara near Burgos, Spain. His parents were farmers. He began his studies at Bujedo (Aug. 26, 1918) and continued into the novitiate (Aug. 30, 1921). Brother Victoriano passed nearly ten years (1925–34) at the school in Palencia, where he used his musical talents to teach others, formed a choir, and used music to motivate slow learners. He arrived in Turón about a month before his martyrdom to replace another frightened brother.

Feast: Oct. 9.

Bibliography: V. CÁRCEL ORTÍ, *Martires españoles del siglo XX* (Madrid 1995). J. PÉREZ DE URBEL, *Catholic Martyrs of the Spanish Civil War,* tr. M. F. INGRAMS (Kansas City, Mo. 1993). L. SALM, *The Martyrs of Turón and Tarragona: The De La Salle Brothers in Spain* (Romeoville, Ill. 1990).

[K. I. RABENSTEIN]

TURPIN OF REIMS

Monk, at Saint-Denis (748 or 749), archbishop of Reims (753), famous, according to legend (*Chanson de Roland*), as one of the paladins of CHARLEMAGNE in his supposed crusade into Spain; d. 794. His death, also according to legend, occurred in Spain while he was ministering to Roland at Roncesvalles. Turpin (Tilpinus) participated with 11 other French bishops in a synod held at the Lateran by STEPHEN III in 769. To him is falsely attributed a Latin chronicle, *De vita et gesta Caroli Magni.* There also appears under his name, or rather under that of pseudo-Turpin, a *Liber s. Jacobi in Santiago de Compostela.* The work apparently stems from the mid-12th century. It appeared in many redactions in Old French, Provençal, and Celtic. An abridged or shortened version was made in the 12th century for the proceedings related to the canonization of Charlemagne. Some of the early chapters are also found in the *De sanctitate meritorum et gloria miraculorum beati Caroli Magni,* which was prepared at the request of Emperor FREDERICK I Barbarossa.

Bibliography: Sources. *Historia Karoli Magni et Rotholandi: Ou, Chronique du Pseudo-Turpin,* ed. C. MEREDITH-JONES (Paris 1936); *The Pseudo-Turpin,* ed. H. M. SMYSER (Cambridge, Mass. 1937). Literature. M. MANITIUS, *Geschichte der lateinischen Literatur des Mittelalters,* 3 v. (Munich 1911–31) 3:487–493. H. LECLERCQ, *Dictionnaire d'archéologie chrétienne et de liturgie,* ed. F. CABROL, H. LECLERCQ and H. I. MARROU, 15 v. (Paris 1907–53) 14.2:2239–40. A. HÄMEL, *Lexikon für Theologie und Kirche,* ed. M. BUCHBERGER, 10 v. (Freiburg 1930–38)[1] 10:339–340; *Speculum* 13 (1938) 248–252. R. N. WALPOLE, *Philip Mouskés and the Pseudo-Turpin Chronicle* (Berkeley 1947). P. G. FOOTE, *The Pseudo-Turpin*

Chronicle in Iceland: A Contribution to the Study of the Karla-magnús Saga (London 1959).

[P. KIBRE]

TURRETTINI

Family of Genevan Calvinist theologians, originating in Italy near Lucca. The Italian branch became extinct in the 18th century. The Geneva branch descended from Francesco (1547–1628), who left Italy for religious reasons and settled in Geneva (1592).

Benedict, son of Francesco; b. Zurich, Nov. 9, 1588; d. Geneva, March 4, 1631. He was responsible for introducing the decrees of the Synod of Dort (1618–19) into France. He wrote *Défense de la fidélité des traductions de la S. Bible faites à Genève,* 3 v. (Geneva 1618–20) in answer to Pierre COTON's *Genève plagiaire* (Paris 1618).

François, son of Benedict; b. Geneva, Oct. 17, 1623; d. Geneva, Sept. 28, 1687. He was educated at Geneva, Leyden, Utrecht, Paris, Saumur, Montauban, and Nîmes, and he served as pastor of the Italian congregation at Geneva (1647). He was a professor of theology at Geneva (1653), an ardent opponent of the theology of Saumur, and an equally ardent defender of the orthodoxy of the Synod of Dort, and one of the authors of the *Formula Consensus Helvetica* (1675).

Jean Alphonse, son of François; b. Geneva, Aug. 13, 1671; d. Geneva, May 1, 1737. After being educated at Geneva and Leyden he was received into the *Vénérable Compagnie des Pasteurs* of Geneva (1693). He became pastor of the Italian congregation (1693), professor of Church history (1697), and professor of theology (1705). An advocate of liberalization of the Geneva theology, he helped to abolish the *Formula Consensus Helvetica* and endeavored, without success, to unite all Protestants on the basis of a few fundamental doctrines.

See Also: CONFESSIONS OF FAITH, PROTESTANT.

Bibliography: F. TURRETTINI, *Notice biographique sur Bénédict Turrettini* (Geneva 1871). E. DE BUDÉ, *Vie de François Turrettini* (Lausanne 1871); *Vie de J. A. Turrettini* (Lausanne 1880). R. PFISTER, *Die Religion in Geschichte und Gegenwart,* 7 v. (3d ed. Tübingen 1957–65) 6:1089–90.

[C. J. BERSCHNEIDER]

TUSCULANI

An important Italian political family descending from Theophylactus; it reached the peak of its importance in the 11th century. The first member of the family to call

"Charlemagne Departing for Spanish Crusade with Roland and Archbishop Turpin of Reims," Charlemagne Lancet Window, Chartres Cathedral. (©Dean Conger/CORBIS.)

himself *De Tusculana* was *Gregory,* who, having become a partisan of the emperors, received the title and functions of *praefectus navalis* from Emperor OTTO III. Gregory had three sons: Alberic, Theophylactus, and Romanus. Alberic was made Count Palatine. Theophylactus was created cardinal in 1012, after an abbreviated ecclesiastical career. Through his imperial and aristocratic ties he became Pope BENEDICT VIII. Romanus became senator and thus temporal governor of Rome. Despite the opposition of the CRESCENTII (who defended Rome's independence), Romanus, backed by the Tusculani family, carried out imperial policy in Rome. In 1014 he was made PATRICIUS ROMANORUM. From this time on the Tusculani ruled Rome completely in both the ecclesiastical and temporal spheres. In 1024 Romanus succeeded his brother as Pope JOHN XIX; the family now considered the papacy as its own dominion. The last of the Tusculani popes was a nephew, BENEDICT IX (1032–45), who was "elected" by way of SIMONY. Although its ecclesiastical role in Rome diminished after this, the family still exercised an enormous political influence, which it used to oppose both the GREGORIAN REFORM and the restoration of papal independence. Only in 1170 did Pope ALEXANDER III succeed in regaining Tusculum (southeast of Rome) for the STATES OF THE CHURCH. From then on the family transferred its political sphere of influence to southern Italy, but it never regained its former importance.

Bibliography: P. FEDELE, ''Ricerche per la storia di Roma e del papato nel secolo X,'' *Archivio della Società romana di storia patria* 33 (1910) 177–247. R. L. POOLE, ''Benedict IX and Gregory VI,'' *Proceedings of the British Academy* 8 (1917–18) 199–235. J. GAY, *Les Papes du XIᵉ siècle et la chrétienté* (2d ed. Paris 1926) 69–120. W. KÖLMEL, *Rom und der Kirchenstaat im 10. und 11. Jahrhundert* (Berlin 1935). A. FLICHE and V. MARTIN, eds., *Histoire de l'église depuis les origines jusqu'à nos jours* (Paris 1935–) v.7, 8.

[W. M. PLÖCHL]

TUTIORISM

The moral system that taught that, in a doubt about the morality of a particular course of conduct, one must follow the safer side (the opinion for law) unless the likelihood that the law does not bind (the opinion for liberty) is most probable. The view was defended by the Louvain professor J. Opstraet (d.1720) after the condemnation of rigorism, and later by Cardinal Gerdil (d. 1802). In practice, this system does not differ much from rigorism; and, though it has never been formally condemned by the Church, it is now rejected by all theologians. For, if God had obliged man to follow the opinion for law unless the opinion for liberty were most probable, He would have imposed an intolerable burden on mankind and would have demanded of good persons a way of life open to innumerable anxieties.

See Also: MORALITY, SYSTEMS OF; RIGORISM; DOUBT, MORAL.

Bibliography: D. M. PRÜMMER, *Manuale theologiae moralis,* ed. E. M. MÜNCH, 3 v. (10th ed. Barcelona 1945–46) 1:339. J. AERINYS and C. A. DAMEN, *Theologia moralis,* 2 v. (16th ed. Marietti 1950) 1:101. M. ZALBA, *Theologiae moralis compendium,* 2 v. (Madrid 1958) 1:674.

[F. J. CONNELL]

TWELVE, THE

An expression used 39 times in the New Testament to designate the APOSTLES. Its frequent recurrence gives emphasis to the fact that the Twelve formed a distinct group, bound to one another and to Christ by a unity that was clearly discernible. The urgency manifested in the election of Matthias to fill the place left vacant by the defection and suicide of Judas stresses the importance of keeping the number intact (Acts 1.20–26). With the election of Matthias the college of Apostles was closed; it is significant that no further additions occurred.

Christ with the Twelve Apostles and attributes of the Four Evangelists, from ''Liber Chronicarum,'' compiled by Hartmann Schedel. (©Historical Picture Archive/CORBIS)

Aside from the fact that the number 12 served the purpose of Christ, it also contains an intentional symbolism. The Apostles are the 12 patriarchs of the New Israel (Mt 19.28; 21.10–15). In the Old Testament the 12 sons of Israel were the leaders of the 12 tribes of God's chosen people. Now that Israel as a nation was on the verge of rejecting the Messiah, God formed unto Himself a new people under the 12 spiritual heads of the New Testament. Their choice constituted a twofold memorial: one to the old covenant that was past, the other to the new covenant that was being inaugurated.

The earliest extant representations of the Twelve date back to the fourth century. They are rich in historical and doctrinal interest. In the universal unspoken language of symbolism, they give artistic expression to the reality of Christ's choice of the Twelve and to Christian belief in the existence of the apostolic college. The first purely symbolic representations of the Twelve depict them as 12 sheep grouped around Christ, the Good Shepherd, who either bears a lamb in His arms, or holds a cross; He stands on an eminence, a nimbus above His head, while the Twelve, represented by as many lambs, are grouped six to the right and six to the left of Him. Jesus, the Lamb of God, is usually represented as larger than the other sheep, an indication of Christ's transcendence and headship. Later, and less frequently, the Twelve are symbolized by doves.

Toward the end of the fourth century the Twelve are shown as men grouped in a semicircle around the Master, who is seated on a lecture chair holding a scroll (Apse of Lateran Basilica). At the time of Constantine, emphasis was placed on Christ as Lord; Christ is shown receiving the homage of the Twelve, or giving them their commission, against a backdrop of apocalyptic events. In the Middle Ages, when the Last Judgment was a favorite theme, the Twelve were represented as seated on 12 thrones and assisting Christ in the judgment of the nations (cf. Mt 19.28). In the consequent rapid evolution of the arts, the Twelve became one of the most popular themes used for pediments, choir-screens, triumphal arches, roods, reliquaries, and baptistries. (*See* APOSTLES, ICONOGRAPHY OF.)

Bibliography: F. J. FOAKES JACKSON and K. LAKE, eds., *The Beginnings of Christianity:* pt. 1, *Acts of the Apostoles* (London 1920–33) 5:37–59. A. LEGNER, *Lexikon für Theologie und Kirche*, ed. J. HOFER and K. RAHNER (Freiberg 1957–65) 1:739. V. TAYLOR, ed., *The Gospel According to St. Mark* (London 1952) 619–627. J. DUPONT, *Le Nom d'apôtres a-t-il été donné aux douze par Jesus?* (Bruges 1956); also appeared in *Orient Syrien* 1 (1956) 266–290, 425–444.

[M. L. HELD]

TWO WAYS

A method of paraenesis used in the DIDACHE and other church documents for purposes of moral catechesis. The *Didache* begins, "There are two ways, one of Life and one of Death," and proceeds to describe behaviors that foster life and excoriate conduct that leads to destruction and death. Another second-century work, the *Epistle of Barnabas*, using very similar language, speaks of "two ways of instruction," the way of light and the way of darkness. The first is "controlled by God's light- bringing angels, the other by angels of Satan" (c. 18). The dualism in this approach expounds in detail the "great difference between the two ways." This approach to moral teaching, a prominent theme in the Wisdom literature of the ancient world, is found in the earliest books of the Bible (Deut 30: 15–20). Citing Matthew (7: 13–14), the *Catechism of the Catholic Church* states, "The Gospel parable of the *two ways* remains ever present in the catechesis of the Church; it shows the importance of moral decisions for our salvation" (1696).

Bibliography: R. E. ALDRIDGE, "Peter and the 'Two Ways,'" *Vigilae Christianae*, v. 53 (1999), 233–264. B.B. BUTLER, "The 'Two Ways' in the *Didache*," *Journal of Theological Studies*, v. 12 (1961) n.s., 27–38. K. NIEDERWIMMER, *The Didache: A Commentary*, tr. L. MALONEY (Minneapolis, MN 1998). W. RORDORF, "Un Chapitre d'Éthique Judéo-Chrétienne: Les Deux Voies," *Recherches de Science Religieuse*, v. 60 (1972), 109–128. A. SEEBERG, *Die beiden Wege und das Aposteldekret* (Leipzig 1906). M. J. SUGGS, "The Christian Two Ways Tradition," in D. AUNE ed., *Studies in New Testament and Early Christian Literature: Essays in Honor of Allen P. Wikgren* (Leiden 1972), 60–74. J. VAN OORT, *Jerusalem and Babylon: A Study into Augustine's City of God and the Sources of His Doctrine of the Two Cities* (Leiden and New York 1991).

[P. J. HAYES]

TWOMEY, LOUIS J.

Pioneer in interracial and labor relations; b. Tampa, Fla., Oct. 5, 1905; d. New Orleans, La., Oct. 8, 1969. He graduated from Sacred Heart College (now known as Jesuit High School) in 1923, after which he attended Georgetown University, then entered the Society of Jesus at Grand Coteau, La. in 1926, His father's health led him to return home the following year, but he reentered the novitiate in 1929 and took vows there Feb. 2, 1931. He spent the next two years studying philosophy at St. Louis University; from 1933 to 1936 he taught at Spring Hill College (Mobile, Ala.), resuming his seminary studies in theology at St. Mary's College (St. Marys, Kan.), where he was ordained to the priesthood on June 21, 1939.

While at St. Mary's College, Twomey became vitally interested in social problems and published his first articles on the subject, drawing heavily from *Quadragesimo anno* and *Rerum novarum*. In 1945 he started working under the labor relations expert, Leo C. Brown, SJ, at St. Louis University's Institute of Social Order in 1945.

He returned to the South in 1947 to set up the Institute of Industrial Relations (later called Institute of Human Relations) at Loyola University in New Orleans. During the 1950s and 1960s, Twomey was in the vanguard of the movement toward interracial justice in the South. His Institute's direct focus was on social justice and much of its work dealt with trade unionism and management-labor relations. In the South, however, this meant the constant handling of racial issues.

Twomey was constantly at pains to demonstrate that Christian social justice was the most effective answer to Communism. He lectured on the subject continually, especially during the Summer School for Catholic Action sessions all over the U.S. and Canada, starting in 1947 and ending two decades later. In 1964 he established at

Loyola University an Inter-American Center "to train younger leadership groups in . . . building democratic, social institutions."

Much of Twomey's most effective work, however, was done in the press, in *Social Order* and other such journals. Perhaps most important, however, was *Christ's Blueprint of the South* (later titled *Blueprint for the Christian Reshaping of Society*), which he started in 1948 and wrote singlehandedly almost until his death. It started as a mimeographed letter to Southern Jesuits, but quickly became national and international. By 1958 it went out to 2,000 Jesuits in 44 countries and elicited a strong letter of approval from the Jesuit superior general, John Baptist Janssens, SJ. In 1967, Janssens' successor, Pedro ARRUPE, SJ, summoned Twomey to Rome to help prepare an official letter to all Jesuits "On the Interracial Apostolate." It is generally acknowledged that this letter, coupled with the monthly *Blueprint*, had most to do with shaping Jesuit social attitudes for a generation.

Bibliography: J. H. FICHTER, *One Man Research: Reminiscences of a Catholic Sociologist* (New York 1973). C. J. MCNASPY, *At Face Value: A Biography of Father Louis J. Twomey, SJ*, with a preface by W. Persy and afterword by D. A. Boileau (Institute of Human Relations, Loyola Univ. of New Orleans 1978). J. R. PAYNE, "A Jesuit Search for Social Justice: The Public Career of Louis J. Twomey, S.J." (Ph.D. dissertation, Univ. of Texas, 1976).

[C. J. MCNASPY]

TYE, CHRISTOPHER

Renaissance composer of Catholic and Anglican liturgical music; b. England, *c.* 1500; d. Doddington, *c.* 1573. Tye was possibly a chorister at King's College, Cambridge; he took the degrees of Mus.B. (1536) and Mus.D. (1545) there, and in 1548, received another music doctorate at Oxford. He was choirmaster at Ely Cathedral for 20 years from 1541, when it became Protestant. In 1560 he was ordained (Anglican), and he was rector at Doddington from 1561 to his death. His Latin works include three Masses and some Mass fragments, about 20 motets and Magnificats, and some instrumental pieces. His motets include psalm excerpts, which had begun to replace votive antiphons, and are often characterized by chromatic cross relations and elaborate polyphony. A simpler, more hymnlike style characterizes his English anthems and the famous *Acts of the Apostles,* a work dedicated to Edward VI and designed to popularize the vernacular Bible. (*See* PSALTER, METRICAL.) Tye was one of the chief composers of the instrumental settings called *In nomine's,* based on the antiphon *Gloria Tibi* (*see* TAVERNER, JOHN).

Bibliography: G. E. P. ARKWRIGHT et al., *Grove's Dictionary of Music and Musicians*, ed. E. BLOM 9 v. (5th ed. London 1954) 8:624–627. F. L. HARRISON, *Music in Medieval Britain* (New York 1958). G. REESE, *Music in the Renaissance* (rev. ed. New York 1959) 782–783. Y. ROKSETH, "The Instrumental Music of the Middle Ages and Early Sixteenth Century," *New Oxford History of Music*, ed. J. A. WESTRUP, 11 v. (New York 1957–) 3:458–464. D. STEVENS, *Die Musik in Geschichte und Gegenwart*, ed. F. BLUME (Kassel-Basel 1949–). P. DOE, "Christopher Tye" in *The New Grove Dictionary of Music and Musicians*, vol. 19, ed. S. SADIE (New York 1980) 297–300. D. M. RANDEL, ed., *The Harvard Biographical Dictionary of Music* (Cambridge 1996) 930–931. J. R. SATTERFIELD, JR., "The Latin Church Music of Christopher Tye" (Ph.D. diss. University of North Carolina, 1962). N. SLONIMSKY, ed., *Baker's Biographical Dictionary of Musicians*, Eighth Edition (New York 1992) 1917.

[S. W. KENNEY]

TYNDALE, WILLIAM

English reformer and biblical translator, b. Gloucestershire, *c.* 1491, d. Vilvoorde, near Brussels, Belgium, Oct. 6, 1536.

Early Life. On the eve of the Protestant Reformation, William Tyndale was ordained a Roman Catholic priest in London, Holy Saturday, 1515. Assuming he was then the canonical age of 24, we can place his birth *c.* 1491. Celebrations of his birth were held in 1994, however, because the relevant records were not discovered and published until 1996.

Raised in a yeoman family in Gloucestershire, Tyndale entered Magdalen Hall, later Hertford College, Oxford, where he earned his B.A in 1512 and his M.A. in 1515. According to John Foxe the Martyrologist, Tyndale pursued further studies at Cambridge, where Erasmus had recently taught Greek from 1511 to 1514. Erasmus was the first to publish a printed version of the Greek NT (Basel, 1516), and Martin Luther would use Erasmus' second edition (Basel, 1519) for his German NT.

In 1409 the Constitutions of Oxford had reacted to the Wycliffite translations of the Vulgate by requiring episcopal approval for English translations of the Bible. This permission was not given, even when vernacular Bibles began to be printed on the Continent (e.g. Strassburg, 1466; Venice, 1471; Lyons, *c.* 1477). Tyndale would be the first to translate the Scriptures from their original languages into English. In order to work freely, Tyndale left England in 1524, perhaps visiting Luther before moving to the Rhineland.

Biblical Translations. Tyndale translated the Greek NT from Erasmus's third edition (Basel, 1522) while consulting Luther's first German NT (Wittenberg, 1522). A quarto version of Tyndale's prologue and the Gospel of Matthew up to 22.12 was in press (Cologne, 1525) when the work was interrupted by Catholic authorities.

Tyndale escaped to publish the complete NT in octavo but without prologue and sidenotes (Worms, 1526). Later, Tyndale published octavo editions of his revised NT (Antwerp, 1534 and 1535). Tyndale would better show the influence of Semitic grammar on NT Greek after he had translated the Pentateuch. Tyndale's NT of 1534 were edited by N. Hardy Wallis in the original spelling (Cambridge, 1938) and by David Daniell in modern spelling (New Haven and London, 1989).

For the OT, Tyndale could have used printed editions of the Hebrew Bible (Venice, 1488, 1517) or the Polyglot Bible (Alcala, 1522). In Antwerp he published octavo editions of the Pentateuch in 1530, Jonah in 1531, and in 1534 a revised Genesis bound with reissues of Exodus, Leviticus, Numbers, and Deuteronomy. Although Tyndale's NT and Pentateuch had been banned by royal authority in June 1530, they were included in Coverdale's Bible (Zurich, 1535) commissioned by Thomas Cromwell, and in Matthew's Bible (Antwerp, 1537) licensed by Henry VIII. Tyndale's translations of Judges through 2 Chronicles were published posthumously in Matthew's Bible. All of Tyndale's biblical translations, except Jonah, were substantially incorporated into the Great Bible (1539), the Bishops' Bible (1568), and the King James Bible (1611). Tyndale's Pentateuch was edited by J.I. Mombert in the original spelling (Carbondale, Il, 1967). All of his OT translations (Pentateuch, Joshua to 2 Chronicles, and Jonah) were edited in modern spelling by David Daniell (New Haven and London, 1992).

Exegetical and Polemical Works. Tyndale devoted his best energies to his biblical translations, but these occasioned secondary works of exegesis and polemic. Four of his scriptural commentaries are expanded translations of works by Luther: *Introduction to Romans* (1526) from Luther's preface to the Epistle to the Romans in his 1522 NT; *Parable of the Wicked Mammon* (May 1528) from Luther's sermon for the Ninth Sunday after Trinity, 1522; *Exposition of Matthew 5, 6, 7* (1533) from Luther's *Commentary on the Sermon on the Mount*, 1532; *Pathway into the Holy Scripture* (1536?) from Luther's preface to his 1522 NT and revised from Tyndale's prologue to the aborted 1525 NT. Tyndale's brief *Exposition of 1 John* (September 1531) has no known source.

Although Luther and Tyndale both agree on the Reformation principles of *sola scriptura, sola fide, sola gratia*, they differ in their interpretation of the Law and of the Eucharist. Luther asserts that the Law condemns me and teaches me the impossibility of truly serving God. Tyndale affirms that God writes the Law on my heart to enable me to love it and therefore keep it (cf. Jer. 31.33). For Tyndale, faith in God's mercy brings forth true works of love (cf. Gal. 5.6), but these do not justify or merit a

William Tyndale.

reward (cf. *Answer to More* 195/21–197/4). Luther holds that Christ is corporally present in the Eucharist along with the bread and wine. Somewhat like Zwingli, Tyndale emphasizes the meaning of the signs of Christ's body and blood: to believe with a repenting heart in Christ's saving death for my sins (cf. *Answer to More* 178/11–180/7).

Tyndale's exegetical works glow with faith, but his polemical works flash with wit. Tyndale wrote his threefold treatise, *Obedience of a Christian Man* (October 1528), partly to argue that Gospel freedom was not a valid reason for the Peasants' Rebellion of 1525. The first section defines the duties of subjects and superiors in the household and state against the encroachments of the papacy. The second section argues that Baptism and the Eucharist are the only sacraments found in the Christian Scriptures. Tyndale devotes only one paragraph to the Eucharist but discusses Penance at length because he finds auricular confession a burden to scrupulous consciences. Sir Thomas More defends all seven sacraments in Bk. 1 of his *Confutation of Tyndale* (1532). In the *Brief Declaration of the Sacraments* (1548?), Tyndale will explain his position on sacraments as only signs, not causes of grace. The third section of *Obedience* affirms that the literal sense of the Scripture is spiritual, i.e., it gives life through faith in Christ.

Practice of Prelates (1530) is partially based on an anonymous Reformation tract about papal dealings with the Carolingian dynasty, *Vom alten und neuen Gott, Glauben und Lehre* (Basel, 1521). Then Tyndale attacks the excesses of Cardinal Wolsey and, alone among the English reformers, upholds Henry VIII's marriage to Catherine of Aragon.

In response to Sir Thomas More's *Dialogue Concerning Heresies* (June 1529, May 1531), Tyndale asserts six major theses in *Answer to More* (*c.* July 1531). The first two points (the validity of Tyndale's translation of ecclesiastical terms and the subordination of tradition to Scripture) are Tyndale's defence of his 1526 NT, criticized in Bk. 3 of More's *Dialogue*. The next three topics (predestination to heaven, the corruption of the papacy, and the inferiority of historical faith to feeling faith) express Tyndale's support of Luther, attacked in Bk. 4 of More's *Dialogue*. Tyndale's last issue (religious ceremonies) is More's first, expounded in Bk. 1–2 of More's *Dialogue*. More's *Confutation of Tyndale* (Bk. 1–3, 1532 and Bk. 4–8, 1533) argues against Tyndale's first five theses, but does not defend religious ceremonies because More had discussed them thoroughly in *Dialogue*. In length and importance *Answer to More* is second only to the *Obedience of a Christian Man* among Tyndale's independent works.

Henry Walter edited Tyndale's exegetical and polemical works in modern spelling with brief annotations for the Parker Society, vol. 42-44 (Cambridge, 1848–50). Anne M. O'Donnell, S.N.D. is directing a critical edition of these same works in five volumes for the Catholic University of America Press (Washington, D.C., 2000ff). Tyndale's independent works are noteworthy for their relation to Erasmus, More, and Luther, for their lively English, and for their heartfelt theology.

Imprisonment and Death. Arrested in May 1535, Tyndale was imprisoned near Brussels and interrogated by theologians from Louvain. He was condemned for upholding justification by faith alone, not for translating the Scriptures into English, which his judges probably could not read. Tyndale was garroted, and his corpse burnt in October 1536. He was executed before he could make English translations of the prophets and wisdom books, especially the Psalms. Because the King James Version largely follows Tyndale's translations of the NT from Greek and the historical books of the OT from Hebrew, his vivid diction and compelling syntax live on.

Bibliography: A. J. BROWN, *William Tyndale . . . New Light on His Early Career* (London 1996). D. DANIELL, *William Tyndale: A Biography* (New Haven and London 1994). J. F. MOZLEY, *William Tyndale* (Westport, Conn. 1971).

[A. M. O'DONNELL]

TYNEMOUTH, PRIORY OF

Former Benedictine foundation, Northumberland, England, Diocese of Durham (patrons, St. Mary and St. Oswin of Deira). (*See* DURHAM, ANCIENT SEE OF.) On the site of an abbey probably of the 7th century destroyed by Danes in 875, Tynemouth was refounded *c.* 1085 by Robert de Mowbray and given to the Abbey of ST. ALBANS. The latter retained Tynemouth as its foremost dependency despite claims by Durham Priory and the Crown and disputes with the bishop. The priory had coal, salt, and fishing interests, and was an important fortress against the Scots. It had a substantial early Gothic church with later chapels. The community numbered from 16 to 19. The house declined during the late 15th century; in 1535 its income was £397; it was suppressed in 1539.

Bibliography: Sources. W. DUGDALE, *Monasticon Anglicanum* (London 1655–73); best ed. by J. CALEY, et al., 6 v. (1817–30) 3:302–322. SIMEON OF DURHAM, *Symeonis monachi opera omnia,* ed. T. ARNOLD, 2 v. (*Rerum Brittanicarum medii aevi scriptores* 75; 1882–85). Literature. H. H. E. CRASTER, *The Parish of Tynemouth,* v.8 of *A History of Northumberland* (Newcastle 1907). L. H. COTTINEAU, *Répertoire topobibliographique des abbayes et prieurés,* 2 v. (Mâcon 1935–39) 2:3237. D. HAY, ''The Dissolution of the Monasteries in the Diocese of Durham,'' *Archaeologia Aeliana,* ser. 4, 15 (1938) 69–114.

[S. WOOD]

TYPE AND ANTITYPE

The word ''type'' is a transcription of the Greek word τύπος (from τύπτω, to strike), which means, first of all, a blow, and then the mark left by a blow or the application of pressure, e.g., the mark of the nails in Christ's hands (Jn 20.25). It can refer also to an image or model (a statue is the τύπος of the one represented) and is so used in the Septuagint (Am 5.26, where it refers to statues of false gods; see also Acts 7.43). But in its strictly Biblical sense it refers either to a moral lesson (the events of the Exodus are lessons, τύπτοι, for the Christian community; 1 Cor 10.6); or to some person, event, or institution of the Old Law related in some way to the new and definitive self-revelation of God in Christ. In this sense Adam is ''a type of the one to come'' (Rom 5.14).

In the Gospels. It is a basic supposition in all the sources of the Gospel tradition that Jesus fulfills the Old Law, and He Himself affirms this (Mt 5.17). Not only was Jesus seen as the climax of sacred history, but an ever deepening meditation gradually revealed hidden correspondences between the time of promise and that of fulfillment. Thus, while Mark has no mention of the sign of Jona (in Mk 8.12 Jesus refuses to give a sign), the Logia source (*see* SYNOPTIC GOSPELS) contained a well-developed form of it, though this has been variously transmitted (Mt 12.38–41; Lk 11.29–32) (*see* JONAH, SIGN OF).

In John this process is taken much further and no doubt owes a debt to the liturgical life of one or more early Christian communities. Structurally basic to this Gospel is the idea that Jesus fulfills what is implicit in the great Jewish feasts (*see* JOHN, GOSPEL ACCORDING TO ST.). The realities of the Old Testament are on a lower and representational level: the bronze serpent (Nm 21.4–9) prefigures Christ on the Cross (Jn 3.14); the water of Jacob's well and that of the rite of pouring water at the Feast of BOOTHS serve only as figures of the true life-giving water (Jn 4.10; 7.37–39). The MANNA in the desert points forward to the reality possessed by the antitype, the true Bread (Jn 6.32). A hidden correspondence is also traced between the Passion of Jesus and the Old Testament Passover (Jn 19.33–36; cf. Ex 12.46) (*see* PASSOVER, FEAST OF).

In the Epistles. St. Paul's typological actualization of the Old Testament was already prepared for in that of contemporary Judaism. This was true of Adam as type (*see* ADAM), though Paul's application in Rom 5.14 is certainly original [*see* W. D. Davies, *Paul and Rabbinical Judaism* (London 1958) 44] and can be compared with that of Philo's heavenly Adam who is stamped (τετύπωσθαι) with the divine image. Paul uses Exodus typology also (1 Cor 10.6–11) and speaks of the "allegory" of the two sons of Abraham (Gal 4.21–31), with a term that appears to have been first used by PHILO JUDAEUS and Flavius JOSEPHUS.

The typological correspondence is carried through more thoroughly in Hebrews than elsewhere in the New Testament and can be compared with the discourse of Stephen (Acts 7), in which the Old Testament is given a largely typological value. The contribution of Hebrews lies in a Platonic-Philonian distinction between the representational and real levels: Old Testament liturgy is but a copy and shadow (σκία: Heb 8.5) of the new, the "heavenly things" (9.23–24); the "earthly" sanctuary (9.1) points forward to the "true tent" (8.2). And, in particular, the entry of the High Priest into the inner sanctuary on the Day of ATONEMENT (Yom Kippur) is a figure (παραβολή: 9.9) that refers to the salvific entry of Jesus into heaven after His Resurrection.

It will be clear from the preceding that antitype is the correspondent in the New Testament to the Old Testament type as in 1 Pt 3.21 where Baptism is the ἀντίτυπος of the Flood. In Heb 9.24 the word is synonymous with type, but this is due to the different thought-context.

Conclusions. These correspondences between persons, events, and institutions of the Old Law and the new

reality in Christ show that the typological relation follows from the unity of SALVATION HISTORY and, at the same time, the uniqueness of the Christ-event, which, as the final and all-inclusive reality, is foreshadowed in the Old Testament. The discovery of such types may not, therefore, be an arbitrary process but must be based on the literal sense of the Scriptures and be guided by the primitive tradition. It is especially important to distinguish typology from allegory, which generally aims at a point-by-point correspondence and is not so controlled. Philo's allegorical methods left their mark on the Christian Alexandrian school (see F. Büchsel in G. Kittel, *Theologisches Wörterbuch zum Neuen Testament* 1:260–261), which, through the great prestige of ORIGEN, deeply influenced the West, as can be seen in the homilies of St. Augustine and St. Gregory the Great. This approach is still strong in the works of St. Thomas Aquinas and later writers; it led to a depreciation of the literal sense and of a genuine typology (*see* EXEGESIS, BIBLICAL, 5, 6, 7). Though a reaction had already set in with the Antiochean School, chiefly in the works of THEODORE OF MOPSUESTIA, it is only in the modern period that the balance has been restored.

The typological or spiritual sense of Scripture includes the identification of these types. It too must be based firmly on the literal sense (*see* DIVINO AFFLANTE SPIRITU; H. Denzinger, *Enchiridion symbolorum,* ed. A. Schönmetzer, 2293) but can have wider connotations: dogmatic (allegorical) referring to Christ and redemption; moral (tropological), to moral conduct; or eschatological (anagogical), to the realities of the future life.

Bibliography: É. AMANN, *Dictionnaire de théologie catholique,* ed. A. VACANT, 15 v. (Paris 1903–50; Tables générales 1951–) 15.2:1935–45. P. GRELOT, *Sens chrétien de l'Ancien Testament* (Tournai 1962). J. DANIÉLOU, *From Shadows to Reality: Studies in the Typology of the Fathers,* tr. W. HIBBERD (Westminster, MD 1960). H. DE LUBAC, "'Typologie' et 'allegorisme','' *Recherches de science religieuse* 34 (Paris 1947) 180–226. J. LEVIE, *The Bible: Word of God in Words of Men,* tr. S. H. TREMAN (New York 1962) 252–264. J. COPPENS, *Les Harmonies des deux Testaments* (new ed. Tournai 1949). On Origen, see J. DANIÉLOU, *Dictionnaire de la Bible,* suppl. ed. L. PIROT, et al. (Paris 1928–) 6:884–908 and H. DE LUBAC, *Histoire et Esprit: L'Intelligence de l'Écriture selon Origéne* (Paris 1950). For Protestant views, see H. H. ROWLEY, *The Unity of the Bible* (Philadelphia 1955); G. VON RAD, "Typological Interpretation of the Old Testament," *Interpretation* 15 (1961) 174–192; G. W. H. LAMPE and K. J. WOOLLCOMBE, *Essays in Typology* (Naperville, IL 1957).

[J. BLENKINSOPP]

TYPOS

The decree of Emperor CONSTANS II published in 648 to replace the *Ecthesis* of the Emperor HERACLIUS of

638. The Holy See, supported by many Byzantine and Latin Christians, had determinedly refused to accept the *Ecthesis* because of its Monothelite doctrine. Constans, who was faced with the necessity of restoring unity to a Christendom menaced by the Arabs, attempted to effect a compromise through the *Typos,* which forbade all discussions whatsoever on the subject of one or two wills, one or two operations in Christ. This implied a hidden support of MONOTHELITISM. Pope MARTIN I in the Lateran synod of 649 condemned both the *Typos* and the *Ecthesis.* He was arrested by order of the Emperor (654) and, after a mock trial and maltreatment in Constantinople, was banished to Cherson in the Crimea. The controversy continued under Martin's successors at Rome, and under Emperor CONSTANTINE IV, who ultimately summoned the ecumenical Council of CONSTANTINOPLE III (680), which finally condemned Monothelitism.

[C. TOUMANOFF]

TYRANNICIDE

The killing of a tyrant. The question to be dealt with here is whether such an action can ever be justified. The Greeks and Romans, and during the Christian Era John of Salisbury (d. 1180), Jean Petit (d. 1411), and the Protestant theologians Melanchthon, Zwingli, and Calvin, considered tyrannicide, whether executed by public or private authority, a lawful, patriotic, and praiseworthy deed.

Catholic theologians commonly distinguished between a tyrant by usurpation, i.e., one who is such by an illegitimate seizure of power, and a tyrant by oppression, i.e., one who, though legitimately enthroned, rules oppressively and is unjust in the exercise of his power. The killing of a tyrant by oppression has generally been considered unlawful by Catholic moralists when there is question of the deed being done by a private citizen acting on his own authority. The violent execution of justice is not the province of private citizens, and furthermore, it cannot be safely left to individuals to determine who is and who is not a tyrant.

According to St. Thomas Aquinas, "he who kills a tyrant (i.e., a usurper) to free his country is praised and rewarded" (*In 2 sent.* 44.2.2). Some have doubted whether in this text St. Thomas was expressing his own opinion or merely interpreting the words of Cicero. More probably, however, he was giving his own thought, and in any case the opinion is in accord with principles he enunciated elsewhere. It was the view taken by his faithful commentators, Cajetan, Vitoria, Billuart, and others. They added by way of clarification that the private citizen in

taking the life of a usurper acts with public authority just as a soldier does in time of war. The required conditions are that the killing be a necessary means to end the usurpation, that there be no higher authority able and willing to remove the usurper, and that there be no probability of bringing about greater evils by the assassination than would have to be faced in enduring the tyranny. St. Thomas held that no private citizen, acting on his own authority, can legitimately take the life of a tyrant by oppression. The community, however, could lawfully depose such a tyrant and probably would have the right to sentence him to death. F. Suárez was of the same opinion, although he went further than St. Thomas, and held that in some circumstances it would be permissible even for a private citizen to kill the tyrant, e.g., if he actually attacked a citizen, or jeopardized the state with the intention of destroying it and killing its citizens, or perpetrated similar evils. Moreover, the tyrant who, being deposed, does not step down, ceases to be a legitimate ruler and becomes a usurper, in which case the principles concerning the killing of a tyrant by usurpation become applicable.

Juan de MARIANA (d. 1624) was somewhat more liberal in his view of tyrannicide. His opinion, however, when stripped of certain unfortunate and inadmissible expressions used in the first edition of his book *De rege et regis institutione* (3 v. Toledo 1599), is that either type of tyrant may be slain, not only by the state, but also by a private citizen when there is no other way of defending the nation, and when the citizen knows that the act would meet with general approval. This thesis differs from that of Salisbury, for the individual in this case would act, so to speak, in the name of the community.

After the 17th century, Catholic moralists, influenced undoubtedly by the new revolutionary theories and their social and political consequences, abandoned the scholastic teaching regarding tyrannicide. St. Alphonsus Liguori (d. 1787) condemned any type of tyrannicide and rejected as false and pernicious the opinions of Suárez and other 16th–century theologians, as well as their democratic principle regarding the source of political power.

The Church has made no authoritative declaration upon the subject. The Council of Constance condemned a statement representing the position of Jean Petit, although he was not named by the Council (H. Denzinger, *Enchiridion symbolorum,* ed. A. Schönmetzer [Freiburg 1963] 1235). This decision of the Council never received papal approval, and, moreover, the statement is so convoluted and contains so many qualifications that it is impossible to say precisely what was anathematized. Proposition 63 of the *Syllabus* of Pius IX (*Enchiridion symbolorum,* 2963) has not the scope some authors have attached to it: it refers only to the withdrawal of obedience from legitimate rulers.

Bibliography: XENOPHON, *Hiero, Scripta Minora,* tr. E. C. MARCHANT (*Loeb Classical Library;* London-New York-Cambridge, Mass. 1925) 4. CICERO, *De officiis,* tr. W. MILLER (*Loeb Classical Library;* 1913) 3.4. JOHN OF SALISBURY, *Policraticus,* 3.15 in *Patrologia Latina,* ed. J. P. MIGNE (Paris 1878–90) 199:512. THOMAS AQUINAS, *In 2 sent.* 44.2.2.5; *De reg. princ.* 1.6. F. SUÁREZ, *De charitate,* disp. 13, sec. 8.2; *Defensio fidei* 6.4.7a. J. DE MARIANA, *The King and the Education of the King,* tr. G. A. MOORE (Washington 1948) 142–161. ALPHONSE LIGUORI, *Homo apostolicus* 8.2.13. L. TAPPARELLI D'AZEGLIO, *Saggio teoretico di Diritto naturale,* 2 v. (3d ed. Rome 1900) v.2. G. M. MANSER, *Angewandtes Naturrecht* (Freiburg 1947) 163. C. J. VON HEFELE, *Histoire des conciles d'après les documents originaux,* tr. and continued by H. LECLERCQ (Paris 1907–38) 7.1:287–296. A. BRIDE, *Dictionnaire de théologie catholique,* ed. A. VACANT et al. (Paris 1903—50) 15.2:1988–2016. C. GIACON, *La seconda scolastica,* 3 v. (Milan 1950) 3:249–274.

[F. ALLUNTIS]

TYRANNY

A form of government characterized by the deviation of political rulers from commonly accepted standards of moral and political behavior *or* by the illegitimate title to the exercise of power of the persons who actually rule. Government is the rule of men by men. But by what men, by what kind of rule? The concept of tyranny arose from early Greek experience. Originally, it had no pejorative connotation. The tyrant was a popular leader who arose either to combat external enemies or to represent the lower classes against oligarchy. As his rule became more permanent, it became also more oppressive, often being exercised against the citizens. For ARISTOTLE, tyranny was the degeneration of kingly rule into rule for the personal interest of the tyrant rather than for the common interest of the city.

The idea of tyranny has evolved along two lines. The more ancient line concerned the moral purpose of the exercise of power. Aristotle had established that rule had to be for the commonweal of the city. But how could this commonweal be recognized so that the citizens would know whether rule was in their interest or not? Three historical movements combined to give content to the public purpose. The first was the growth of the tradition of natural law associated with Cicero and the Stoics and later with the Christian theologians. This tradition held that there were certain principles of reason and life common to all men and that political rule would be tyrannical if it violated these principles. The second element was the acknowledgment of the primacy of the spiritual, best represented by Peter's response in the Sanhedrin: "We must obey God rather than men" (Acts 5.29). On this princi-

ple, when a political ruler acts against a man's religious obligations and beliefs, he is judged to be tyrannical. The third contribution came from the Germanic notion of immemorial custom. The natural law and the Christian dispensation were in many respects vague and abstract in daily life. In the Germanic tradition, law was concretized. It was made up of the customs and procedures of the people. To be just, political rule had to be in conformity with these particular customs that practically identified each people.

The second and more modern line along which the notion of tyranny has evolved had its origin in a more liberal and dynamic notion of the state in relation to the commonweal. Since the problem of just rule involves not only the objective criteria of the precise content of the public good but also the actual persons who exercise authority, the modern issue arising from tyranny is the constitutional one, the regular and legal designation of who is to rule, for how long, with what limits.

Traditional rulers needed to be judged by their actual ability to promote the public good. Therefore, the actual ruler of the people, to be legitimate, had to be one who was duly designated by the people or approved by them to rule in accordance with the public interest. The people always retained the right to choose new rulers at stated times and to review the policies of rulers in the light of the public good. In this context, tyranny came to mean rule that was acquired, retained, or carried on by other than legal, accepted means.

Although the classical notion of tyranny is not in vogue in modern thought, the basic elements associated with this kind of rule are still often present and operative. The frequency of forcible revolutions in many parts of the modern world, notably in Latin America, Asia, Africa, and the Middle East, is constant witness to the presence of the problem of tyranny. Current revolutions are always justified on the basis of one of the two elements that have been gradually subsumed into the notion of tyranny—violation of the objective content and promotion of the public good by present rulers, or the unjust title of these same rulers to office. Thus the problem of tyranny is still a significant political concept.

Bibliography: P. N. URE, *Origin of Tyranny* (Cambridge, England 1922). K. A. WITTFOGEL, *Oriental Despotisms* (New Haven 1957). F. M. WATKINS, *Encyclopaedia of the Social Sciences,* ed. E. R. SELIGMAN and A. JOHNSON (New York 1930–35) 8:135–137. A. BRIDE, *Dictionnaire de théologie catholique,* ed. A. VACANT, 15 v. (Paris 1903–50; Tables générales 1951–) 15:1948–88. W. PARSONS, "Medieval Theory of the Tyrant," *Review of Politics* 4 (Notre Dame, IN 1942) 129–143.

[J. V. SCHALL]

TYRIE, JAMES

Jesuit theologian; b. Drumkilbo, Scotland, 1543; d. Rome, 1597. He was educated at St. Andrew's University, but left Scotland in 1562. He reached Rome via Louvain, and joined the Society of Jesus in 1563. Tyrie, sent to Paris to help found the Jesuit Clermont College, June 1567, stayed there as professor of philosophy and theology, rector, and head of the Scottish Jesuit Mission from 1585 to 1590. A letter to persuade his brother David to return to the Catholic Church from the Scottish Kirk was sent to John KNOX for reply. When this was published (1572), each paragraph of Tyrie's letter was printed with Knox's answer. Tyrie at once published a refutation of Knox (Paris 1573), which was publicly burned. A further answer to Tyrie, by a committee appointed for that purpose, never materialized. In 1585 Tyrie was summoned to Rome to represent France on the Committee of Six to draw up the Jesuit General Acquaviva's first edition of the Ratio Studiorum. During the Siege of Paris, 1590, Tyrie was rector of Clermont and then returned to Rome. In December 1590, Tyrie was sent to the University of Pont-à-Mousson as professor of Scripture, and head of the Scots College. In May 1592 he went back to Rome as assistant for France and Germany in the sixth general congregation of the Society of Jesus (1593). In Rome, Tyrie was constantly consulted by Clement VIII and the Catholic Earls of Huntly, Erroll and Angus, in their efforts for papal subsidy to support an armed expedition against the Kirk (1594). He also helped restore the Scottish hospital in Rome, which became the present Scots College (1600). Tyrie earned high praise, even from his opponents, for his "singular modesty, gentleness and charity."

Bibliography: A. BELLESHEIM, *History of the Catholic Church of Scotland,* tr. D. O. HUNTER-BLAIR, 4 v. (Edinburgh 1887–90) v.2–3. W. F. LEITH, ed., *Narratives of Scottish Catholics under Mary Stuart and James VI* (Edinburgh 1885). H. FOLEY, ed., *Records of the English Province of the Society of Jesus,* 7 v. (London 1877–82) 3.2:726. H. FOUQUERAY, *Histoire de la Compagnie de Jésus en France,* 5 v. (Paris 1910–25). N. ABRAM, *L'Université de Pont-à-Mousson* (Paris 1870).

[G. ALBION]

TYRRELL, GEORGE

Modernist, writer; b. Dublin, Ireland, Feb. 6, 1861; d. Storrington, England, July 15, 1909. Tyrell, who assessed himself as melancholic, impatient, and restless, was born into a Low Church Anglican family and raised as a Calvinist, but in 1879 converted to Roman Catholicism in England. A year later he joined the English province of the Society of Jesus. Following ordination to the priesthood in 1891 he taught moral philosophy to Jesuit seminarians at Stonyhurst College, where he proved himself an enthusiastic follower of St. Thomas Aquinas (1894–96). He was assigned in 1896 as a writer for the English Jesuit review the *Month,* for which he wrote 39 articles over a period of seven years. While on the *Month's* staff, he was also a popular spiritual director and preacher of retreats.

Two important events in Tyrrell's life occurred in 1907: the publication of his first book of spiritual musings, *Nova et Vetera,* and the beginning of his long friendship and correspondence with Baron Friedrich von Hügel. The baron introduced Tyrrell to the works of authors from across the channel: Blondel, Laberthonniére, Bergson, Loisy, Troeltsch, Rudolf Eucken, and Paul Wernle. About this time Tyrrell began his close friendship with Henri Bremond. Others of Tyrrell's early works were: *Hard Sayings* (1898), a collection of spiritual conferences and meditations, and *External Religion* (1899), a series of instructions for Catholic undergraduates at Oxford. In 1899 his article "A Perverted Devotion" drew sharp criticism from Jesuit censors at Rome. Tyrrell was removed from the *Month's* staff in 1900 and assigned to a quiet parish in Richmond, where he remained until 1906. In 1900 he became a close friend of Maude D. Petre, who sympathized with the Modernist movement in the Catholic Church. During 1901 there appeared two volumes called *The Faith of the Millions,* composed mostly of articles that had originally appeared in the *Month.* When Tyrrell attempted that same year to publish a series of meditations in a book entitled *Oil and Wine,* he met opposition from English and Roman censors. He then proceeded to publish and circulate the work privately, not beyond the notice of his religious and ecclesiastical superiors. Now that he was under a cloud as a religious writer, he began to use pseudonyms. *Religion as a Factor of Life* appeared in 1902 under the name of Dr. Ernest Engels. In 1903 Tyrrell privately printed *The Church and the Future,* which he called a restatement of Catholicism, under the pseudonym Hilaire Bourdon. *Lex Orandi* (1904) attempted to show the relationship between prayer and creed; its sequel, *Lex Credendi,* appeared in 1906. An anonymous work by Tyrrell, *A Letter to a Professor of Anthropology,* which circulated privately in 1904, advised a "professor" whose identity remains obscure, to continue in the Church despite difficulties in reconciling Church teaching with the results of scientific research. After an Italian translation appeared in the *Corriere della Serra* of Milan in 1906, Father Martin, Jesuit Superior General, asked Tyrrell to repudiate publicly the doctrine in the Italian translation. When Tyrrell refused, he was dismissed from the order and suspended *a divinis* (1906). Unable to find a bishop who would accept him as a diocesan priest, Tyrrell finally settled at Storrington, England, on property owned by Maude Petre (1907). His literary activity continued. In 1907 he published his most famous book, *Through Scylla and Charybdis,* which stressed with characteristic bitterness his favorite themes: insistence on the importance of interior religious experience, anti-intellectualism, and the distinction between dogma and revelation, which for Tyrrell amounted to distinguishing between theology and revelation. Because of his public criticism of the condemnation of Modernism by Pius X in 1907, he was excommunicated, his case being reserved to the Holy See. Shortly afterward, he stopped assisting at Mass. In *Mediaevalism* (1908) he answered an attack against Modernism by Cardinal Mercier. Tyrrell died of Bright's disease shortly after receiving the Anointing of the Sick and conditional absolution. Because he had not publicly retracted his teachings, burial in a Catholic cemetery was forbidden. His old friend Abbé Henri Bremond recited prayers at a burial service in an Anglican cemetery at Storrington and was punished for this by the bishop of Southwark, who suspended him from priestly functions. This *suspensio a divinis* was later withdrawn.

Bibliography: *Autobiography and Life,* arr. M. D. PETRE, 2 v. (New York 1912); *Letters,* selected and ed. M. D. PETRE (London 1920). M. D. PETRE, *Von Hügel and Tyrrell* (New York 1938). E. F. SUTCLIFFE, comp., *Bibliography of the English Province of the Society of Jesus 1773–1953* (Roehampton 1957), this gives a list of Tyrrell's Jesuit writings. Works by those sympathetic to Modernism include A. LOISY, *George Tyrrell et Henri Brémond* (Paris 1936). R. GOUT, *L'Affair Tyrrell* (Paris 1910). See also H. EGERTON, *Father Tyrrell's Modernism* (London 1909). D. GRASSO, ''La Conversione e l'apostasia di George Tyrrell,'' *Gregorioanum* 38 (Rome 1957) 446–480, 593–629. D. G. SCHULTENOVER, *George Tyrell: In Search of Catholicism* (Shepherdstown 1981). E. LEONARD, *George Tyrell and the Catholic Tradition* (New York 1982).

[F. M. O'CONNOR]

U

UBALD D'ALENÇON

Capuchin historian, whose name in the world was Leo Louis Berson; b. Alençon, France, Dec. 22, 1872; d. Bry-sur-Marne, July 5, 1927. At the age of 19 (1891) he entered the Capuchins and made his profession of simple vows in November of the following year. He was ordained June 29, 1898. Chronic ill health kept him from the active mission apostolate, so he devoted his talents to the history of his order. Doing most of his research in Paris, he quickly acquired an acknowledged competency in his field. Despite continual illness, he turned out a large number of works and lectured at the *Institut Catholique de Paris* during the 1915–16 school year. Ubald was a frequent contributor to the *Études franciscaines,* the *Annales franciscaines,* the *Revue Sacerdotale,* the *Neerlandia franciscana,* and other periodicals.

His works include: *Les FF. Mineurs et l'Université d'Angers* (1901), *L'Obituaire et le nécrologe des Cordeliers d'Angers* (1902), *Catalogues des manuscrits de la bibliothèque franciscaine provinciale [des Capucins]* (Paris 1902), *Les Travaux des Capucins sur l'Ecriture Sainte aux XVII–XVIII siècle* (1902), *Mémoires et lettres du P. Timothée de la Flèche, O. Cap.* (1907), *Les Idées de St. François sur la pauvreté* (1909), *Les Idées de St. François sur la science* (1910), *Les FF. Mineurs et les débuts de la Réforme à Port Royal* (1911), *Des influences franciscaines sur l'auteur du "Combat Spirituel"* (1912), *L'Ame franciscaine* (Paris 1912, 1913), *Leçons d'histoire franciscaine* (1918), and *Le "Chemin de la Croix" dans l'histoire et dans l'art* (1923).

Bibliography: *Analecta Ordinis Fratrum Minorum Cappucinorum* 43 (1927) 267–268, Necrology. ÉDOUARD D'ALENÇON, *Bibliotheca Mariana Ord. FF. min. Cappucinorum* (Rome 1910) 71. JEAN DE DIEU, "Le Révérend Père Ubald D'Alençon," *Études Franciscaines* 39 (1927) 552–566. *Lexicon Capuccinum* (Rome 1951) 1756. H. LEMAITRE in *Revue d'histoire Franciscaine* 4 (1927) 652–655.

[D. LA GUARDIA]

UBALD OF GUBBIO, ST.

Bishop; b. Gubbio, Umbria, Italy, *ca.* 1080–85; d. there, May 16, 1160. Ubald Baldassini was born of Germanic parentage, but was early orphaned by the death of his father. He was educated and then accepted as a canon regular at the cathedral in Gubbio. Ordained in 1114, by 1117 he was prior of the cathedral chapter, which he reformed. While directing the reconstruction of the burned cathedral (1125), Ubald led a delegation to Pope Honorius II to seek a successor to Gubbio's late bishop. But he himself was consecrated (1129) and served as bishop for 31 years. After his death there was reputed evidence of his intervention, e.g., at the issue of the Commune (1135), the siege of the 11 allies (1153). This led to his canonization by Pope Celestine III on March 5, 1192. His body, which had been buried in the cathedral, was found incorrupt; it was translated Sept. 11, 1194, to Colle Ingino, where a chapel, which is still a place of pilgrimage, was built. Devotion to Ubald is found mainly in Umbria, especially at Gubbio. He is invoked as a patron against diabolic possession and other madnesses.

Feast: May 16.

Bibliography: *Acta Sanctorum* May 3:625–650. P. CENCI, "*La Vita beati Ubaldi,* scritta da Giordano di Città di Castello," *Archivio per la storia ecclesiastica dell'Umbria* 4 (1917–19) 70–136; *Vita di S. Uboldo* (Gubbio 1924). M. DEL NINNO, *Un rito e i suoi segni: La corsa dei ceri a Gubbio* (Urbino 1976). A. BUTLER, *The Lives of the Saints,* rev. ed. H. THURSTON and D. ATTWATER, 4v. (New York 1956) 2:325–326.

[J. F. MAHONEY]

UBERTINO OF CASALE

A leader of FRANCISCAN SPIRITUALS; b. Casale, near Vercelli, Italy, *c.* 1259 d. *c.* 1329 to 1341. He studied for nine years at Paris and then returned to Italy, where in the 1280s he came under the influence of the mystic ANGELA OF FOLIGNO, of (Bl.) JOHN OF PARMA, who imbued him

"St. Ubald of Gubbio with St. Sebastian and the Virgin and Child," painting on panel by Sinibaldo Ibi da Perugia, 1507, in the cathedral at Gubbio, Umbria, Italy.

with the ideas of JOACHIM OF FIORE, and especially of PETER JOHN OLIVI, the first of the major Spiritual leaders. For a considerable period in the 1290s and early 1300s Ubertino preached in Tuscany and Umbria and established his position as a leader among the Spirituals. In 1304 and 1305 he lived in enforced retirement at Alvernia (La Verna) and wrote his great book, the *Arbor vitae crucifixae Jesu*. In form it is an account of the life and Passion of Christ, followed by a commentary on the REVELATION. But it includes much else: autobiography, ecstatic meditations on St. FRANCIS and on poverty, and savage attacks on the laxity of the upper clergy in general and the majority of FRANCISCANS in particular. It is a large, diffuse book, revealing very vividly the author's intense religious devotion and his violence in argument. This work made him many enemies, and he spent much of his later life in strife.

Between 1309 and 1312 he was deeply engaged in the controversies on the future of the order, urging the Pope in a succession of skillful, indeed brilliant, pamphlets to authorize the division of the order (*see* POVERTY CONTROVERSY). Pope JOHN XXII at first treated Ubertino with respect; after failing to reconcile him to his order, he transferred him to the Benedictines. But good relations

between two such firebrands could not last indefinitely; in 1325 Ubertino fled from Avignon. Although he is known to have lived some years longer and to have preached against the Pope in Como in 1329, his last years are covered in mystery; legend has it that he died by violence.

Bibliography: Works. *Arbor vitae crucifixae Jesu* (Venice 1485). For pamphlets written during the poverty controversy (1309–12), H. DENIFLE and F. EHRLE, eds., *Archiv für Literatur- und Kirchengeschichte des Mittelalters*, 7 v. [(Berlin) Freiburg 1885–1900] 2:374–416; 3:48–137, 160–195. A. HEYSSE, "Ubertini de Casale opusculum *Super tribus sceleribus*," *Archivum Franciscanum historicum* 10 (1917) 103–174. É. BALUZE, "Responsio fratris U. de C. ordinis minorum circa quaestionem de paupertale Christi et Apostolorum, facta coram Iohanne XXII. . . ," in his *Miscellanea*, ed. J. D. MANSI (Lucca 1761) 2:279–280. **Literature.** D. L. DOUIE, *The Nature and the Effect of the Heresy of the Fraticelli* (Manchester 1932). F. L. CROSS, *The Oxford Dictionary of the Christian Church* (London 1957) 1385. P GODEFROY, *Dictionnaire de théologie catholique*, ed. A. VACANT et al., 15 v. (Paris 1903–50; Tables Générales 1951–) 15.2:2021–34. M. DAMIATA, *Pieta e storia nell'Arbor vitae di Ubertino da Casale* (Florence 1988). C. M. MARTÍNEZ RUÍZ, *De la dramatización de los acontecimientos de la Pascua a la Cristología: El cuarto libro del Arbor vitae crucifixae Iesu de Ubertino de Casale* (Rome 2000). G. POTESTÀ, *Storia ed escatologia in Ubertino da Casale* (Milan 1980). H. M. THOMAS, *Franziskanische Geschichtsvision und europäische Bildentfaltung: Die Gefährtenbeweging des hl. Franziskus, Ubertino da Casale, der "Lebensbaum," Giottos Fresken der Arenakapelle in Padua, die Meditationes vitae Christi Heilsspiegel und Armenbibel* (Wiesbaden 1989).

[R. B. BROOKE]

UBIARCO ROBLES, TRANQUILINO, ST.

Martyr, priest; b. July 8, 1899, Zapotlán el Grande, Jalisco, Diocese of Ciudad Guzmán, Mexico; d. Oct. 5, 1928, Guadalajara. During the Carrancista Revolution his seminary was closed and its buildings seized, but Tranquilino continued his studies in private while undertaking pastoral work. In 1920, at the invitation of the bishop, he went to Sinaloa, but returned when the bishop died soon after his arrival. He resumed his studies at Guadalajara's seminary and was ordained (August 1923). Thereafter Tranquilino taught catechism in study circles and founded a Christian newspaper. At the height of the persecution, he was named pastor of Tepatitlán's parish (Diocese of San Juan de los Lagos). For 15 months he ministered in private homes and established a public feeding center. While preparing to celebrate a nuptial Mass in a private home in Guadalajara on Oct. 5, 1928, soldiers arrived to arrest him. He was sentenced to death by hanging on the outskirts of the city. Tranquilino's mortal remains were transferred to the parish church. He was both beatified (Nov. 22, 1992) and canonized (May

21, 2000) with Cristobal MAGALLANES by Pope John Paul II.

Feast: May 25 (Mexico).

See Also: MEXICO, MODERN; GUADALAJARA (MEXICO), MARTYRS OF, SS.

Bibliography: J. CARDOSO, *Los mártires mexicanos* (Mexico City 1953). J. DÍAZ ESTRELLA, *El movimiento cristero: sociedad y conflicto en los Altos de Jalisco* (México, D.F. 1979).

[K. I. RABENSTEIN]

UBIQUITARIANISM

Ubiquitarianism is a theory peculiar to Lutheranism, according to which the body of Christ is, in some sense, omnipresent. This Lutheran position came as a reaction against the denial of the Real Presence of Christ's body and blood in the Eucharist by certain Reformers (SACRAMENTARIANS), a denial based ostensibly on the article of faith concerning Christ's sitting in majesty at the Father's right hand. Luther himself countered with arguments which led to the ubiquitarian position. He assumed as its basis the hypostatic union of the two natures in one Person. According to Luther, such a union gives a supernatural mode of being to Christ's human nature, such that omnipresence is not precluded as one of its properties.

Lutherans themselves were divided over the question in the 16th century. Philipp MELANCHTHON held a position more moderate than that of Luther; and the former's authority prevailed in northern Germany, given the assistance of Martin CHEMNITZ. In the south Johann BRENZ gained support for the doctrine of Luther.

The *Formula of Concord* (1577) presents the theory as follows: "[Christ's body] is able to be somewhere or other according to a divine and heavenly mode, since he is one person with God. . . . According to this . . . wonderful and sublime mode, he [is] in all creatures, so that they do not include, circumscribe or contain them; rather, he has them present to himself, and even circumscribes and contains them" [*Von heiligen Abendmahl,* in *Die Bekenntnisschriften der evangelisch–luterischen Kirche,* ed. *Der Deutsche Evangelische Kirchenausschuss* (Göttingen 1956) 1007].

After the period of Lutheran orthodoxy, interest in the question dwindled considerably. Still, the theory belongs to the Lutheran confessional tradition. More important, however, it stands as a monument to the nominalist influence upon Luther and his contemporaries; for the theory is ultimately founded on the notion of God's absolute power to do anything, without regard for whether or not, according to man's way of thinking, a contradiction is involved.

Bibliography: A. MICHEL, *Dictionnaire de théologie catholique,* ed. A. VACANT et al., 15 v. (Paris 1903–50; Tables générales 1951–) 15.2:2034–48.

[M. B. SCHEPERS]

UDO

Theologian at Paris after the middle of the 12th century, of whom nothing more is known than that he was the author of a *Summa super Sententias Petri Lombardi,* of great value for its treatment of some dogmatic questions. The *Summa* is not a commentary but a systematic work, a collection of *quaestiones* in four books, quoting, abbreviating, and elaborating upon the Lombard's work. It refers to a *magister* Odo (doubtless the chancellor of Paris, 1164–68) and borrows from the *Glossae super Sententias* of Pseudo-Peter of Poitiers. It was used in the Commentary on St. Paul's Epistles in manuscript Paris, Arsenal 534 (itself used by the *Allegoriae super Novum Testamentum* of Richard of Saint Victor), and at least 38 times by Peter of Poitiers in his *Sententiae.* Relative chronology suggests that the *Summa,* preserved in 15 manuscripts, be dated about 1165. An edition was in preparation in 1964.

Bibliography: O. LOTTIN, "Le Premier commentaire connu des Sentences de Pierre Lombard," *Recherches de théologie ancienne et médiévale* 11 (1939) 64–71; *Psychologie et morale aux XIIe et XIIIe siècles,* 6 v. in 8 (Louvain 1942–60) v.6. J. N. GARVIN, "Magister Udo: A Source of Peter of Poitiers' Sentences," *The New Scholasticism* 28 (1954) 285–298; "The Manuscripts of Udo's *Summa super Sententias Petri Lombardi,*" *Scriptorium* 16 (1962) 376. For further studies dealing with Udo and his doctrine see the indexes of *Bulletin de Théologie ancienne et médiévale* (Louvain 1929–).

[J. N. GARVIN]

UGANDA, MARTYRS OF, SS.

A group of 22 African youths put to death by the *kabaka* (ruler) of Buganda (Uganda), 1885–1887. The persecution occurred early in the reign of Mwanga, a vicious, perverse youth, after his Christian page boys refused to submit to his homosexual demands. Joseph Mukasa (or Mkasa), the majordomo of the royal household, died first, beheaded (Nov. 15, 1885) for encouraging the pages to remain chaste and protesting the massacre of the Anglican Bp. James Hannington (1885). He is the protomartyr of Bantu Africa. On May 25, 1886, Mwanga ordered slain the page Denis Sebuggwawo for

Pope Paul VI officiates at the altar of a Roman Catholic shrine to 22 Uganda martyrs in Kampala, August 2nd, 1969. The martyrs, Roman Catholic boys, were ritually put to death at Naumgongo in 1886 for refusing to renounce their faith. (©Bettmann/CORBIS)

instructing his favorite boy in the Christian faith. During the next few days others were put to death individually; a soldier, Pontian Ngondwe; the Catholic leaders Andrew Kaggwa (band master, chief of Kigoaw, and catechist; baptized 1881), Matthias Mulumba (a.k.a. Matthias Kalemba, a district judge; baptized 1881), and Noe Mawaggali (a potter); and the pages Athanasius Bazzeku-ketta (baptized 1885) and Gonzaga Gonza. On June 3, 1886, at Namugongo, 13 were burned to death: Charles Lwanga, who had charge of the pages; Ambrose Kibuka (baptized 1885), Anatole Kiriggwajjo (from a herding tribe), Achilles Kiwanuka (formerly a clerk), Mbaga-Tuzinde (adopted son of the chief executioner), Mugagga (apprentice to royal clothmaker), Mukasa Kiriwawanvu (served at the royal table), Adolphus Mukasa Ludigo (from a tribe of herdsmen), Gyavira (messenger), Kizi-to—all pages in their teens; Bruno Serunkuma (soldier baptized in 1885), James Buzabaliawo (soldier baptized in 1885), and Luke Banabakintu (baptized 1881). On Jan.

27, 1887, Jean Marie Muzeyi, age 30, a former page, was beheaded. The Martyrs of Uganda were beatified on June 6, 1920, by Benedict XV and canonized on Oct. 18, 1964, by Paul VI. A similar number of Protestants were put to death in the same persecution.

Feast: June 3.

Bibliography: M. ANDRÉ, *Les martyrs noirs de l'Ouganda* (Paris 1936). J. F. FAUPEL, *African Holocaust: The Story of the Uganda Martyrs* (Kampala 1984). D. KAVULU, *The Uganda Martyrs* (Kampala 1969). A. KERKVLIET, *The Martyrs of Uganda* (Bamenda, Uganda 1990). L. PIROUET, *Strong in the Faith: The Witness of the Uganda Martyrs* (Mukono, Uganda 1969). BR. TARCISIO, *The Blood of the Martyrs* (Masaka, Uganda 1969). J. P. THOONEN, *Black Martyrs* (London 1941). D. WOODING and R. BARNETT, *Uganda Holocaust* (Grand Rapids, MI 1980). *Acta Apostolicae Sedis* 56 (1964) 901–912.

[J. F. FAUPEL]

UGANDA, THE CATHOLIC CHURCH IN

The Republic of Uganda straddles the equator in East Africa, bordering Sudan on the north, Kenya on the east, Tanzania on the south, Rwanda on the southwest and the Democratic Republic of the Congo (formerly Zaire) on the west. Lake Victoria is located in the southeast corner of Uganda, and the waters of the Nile flow northward from there, beginning at the Rippon Falls and branching through several lakes in the central region on their way to Egypt. Mountains rise in the east and west, while a plateau region in the southwest is heavily forested at its western edge. A land of many lakes, approximately one-fifth of Uganda is covered by water. Agricultural crops include cotton, coffee, tea and sugar, while natural resources consist of copper, phosphates and salt. Coffee is the region's main export crop in this primarily agricultural nation.

Uganda was a British protectorate from 1894 until 1962, when it became a fully independent member of the British Commonwealth. Its inhabitants comprise four ethnic groups: Bantu, Nilotic, Nilo-Hamitic and Sudanic, divided into 36 tribes, with many different languages. The recipient of a large amount of foreign aid, Uganda was fortunate when Great Britain determined to cancel all monies owed it as part of the Jubilee 2000 goal of providing debt relief to developing nations. Tragically, Uganda was also one of the African nations hardest hit by the AIDS epidemic: by 2000 ten percent of the population was infected, leaving 1.7 million children orphaned.

History. Uganda witnessed some of its first Caucasian visitors in 1862 when British explorer John Speke crossed the region in his search for the source of the Nile. Four White Fathers began Catholic evangelization in 1879, nearly two years after the arrival of Anglican missionaries. The zeal of the early converts helped to spread Catholicity rapidly, although it also led to rivalry and factionalism. The persecution of 1885–87 produced the 22 UGANDA MARTYRS canonized in 1964. By 1888 Catholics numbered 8,500. Civil wars between Muslims and Christians, and later between the English (Protestants) and the French (Catholics) halted mission activity for some years, but by 1890 the region was under British control. In 1894 the MILL HILL MISSIONARIES took charge of eastern Uganda, and the Verona Fathers, the northern part. Their efforts were successful: In 1905 Catholics numbered 86,000, and in 1923, 375,000. Joseph Kiwanuka, consecrated in 1939, became the first native bishop of modern times. The hierarchy was created in 1953 with the Archdiocese of RUBAGA as sole metropolitan see.

On Oct. 9, 1962 Uganda was granted independence from Great Britain, implemented a republican constitu-

Capital: Kampala.
Size: 93,981 sq. miles.
Population: 23,317,560 in 2000.
Languages: English, Ganda; other tribal languages are spoken in various regions.
Religions: 10,026,550 Catholics (43%), 3,164,455 Muslims (14%), 7,461,619 Protestants (32%), 2,664,936 practice indigenous faiths.

tion in 1967, and briefly joined Kenya and Tanzania in the East African Community. However, a military coup staged in 1971 brought dictator Idi Amin to power, and with him a severe suppression of society and the Church. Over 300,000 individuals were killed under Amin's brutal regime, some of them Catholics. While Amin was deposed in early 1979, guerillas active in the north and southwest continued to disrupt the stability of Nigeria, and the death toll under the government of Milton Obote (1980–85) reached 100,000 lives. Church leaders were by now vigilant in their efforts to publicly address the government's disregard of human rights, and they were also forced to marshal their resources against a new devastation: the spread of AIDS, which was increasingly impacting the Ugandan population. In 1995 a new constitution was drafted and multiparty elections restored Lt. Gen. Yoweri Kaguta Museveni to the position he had held since a coup staged in January of 1986. Elected president with 74 percent of the vote, Museveni's administration was shadowed by allegations of fraud prompted by the revelation that there were more votes cast than were citizens. While successful in stabilizing the Ugandan economy, Museveni's government was accused of corruption, and his ability to sustain prosperity continued to be questioned into 2000.

By 2000 Uganda contained 384 parishes tended by 1,110 diocesan and 335 religious priests. Through the work of 455 brothers and 2,800 sisters, the Catholic mission maintained much-needed hospitals, dispensaries, leprosaria, a school for the blind and training centers for social workers. In 2001 the Holy See aided their efforts through its donation of $ 500,000 toward efforts to combat AIDS in Uganda. The Church maintained amicable relations with members of other faiths as well as with the state, although certain Christian ''fringe'' churches were forbidden by the government to operate under the suspicion that they were cults. The Church's efforts to reach out to the nation's warring tribal groups were encouraged by Pope John Paul II, who noted during a 1997 meeting with Ugandan bishops that ''Tribal rivalries and ethnic hostilities cannot have any place in the Church of God and among His holy people.'' The mission operated 3,350 Catholic primary schools and 425 secondary

Archdioceses	Suffragans
Gulu	Arua, Lira, Nebbi
Kampala	Kasana-Luweero, Kiyinda-Mityana, Lugazi, Masaka
Mbarara	Fort Portal, Hoima, Kabale, Kasese
Tororo	Jinja, Kotido, Moroto, Soroti.

There is also a military ordinariate located in the country.

schools within Uganda; religion was not taught in public-run educational facilities. Issues facing Church leaders into the 21st century included an effort by a Ugandan minister to legalize prostitution, the introduction of an abortion pill by the government and continued activities by several rebel forces that often focused on the Church. In June of 1999 the Catholic peace group Sant'Egidio was successful in its efforts to bring about a peace between the government and one insurgent group that had been holding 109 Catholic school students hostage for over a year.

Bibliography: K. INGHAM, *The Making of Modern Uganda* (London 1958). H. P. GALE, *Uganda and the Mill Hill Fathers* (London 1959). *Bilan du Monde* 2:655–661. *Catholic Directory of Eastern Africa 1965* (Tabora, Tanzania) biannual. *Annuario Pontificio* has annual statistics on all dioceses.

[J. F. FAUPEL/EDS.]

UGARIT

An ancient city whose ruins form the mound (65 feet high and covering *c.* 63 acres) of Ras Shamra on the Syrian coast eight miles north of modern Latakia. Excavations have been conducted at this site by C. F. A. Schaeffer for the French Académie des Inscriptions annually, except in war years, since 1929. Before the accidental discovery by a farmer of an ancient tomb, which prompted this archeological undertaking, W. F. Albright had already localized at the spot the scattered references in Egyptian, Hittite, and Akkadian documents to the city of Ugarit.

The Late Bronze Age City. Apart from minor Iron Age and Hellenistic settlements, the excavations have revealed five strata that indicate a relatively continuous occupation from the 6th millennium to *c.* 1200 B.C., when Ugarit was definitively destroyed by the Sea Peoples. The top stratum (*c.* 1550–1200 B.C.) is of permanent importance for Old Testament and ancient historical studies; the first half of this period represents the golden age of Ugarit.

Structures that have been excavated include: two temples dedicated to BAAL and DAGON, respectively; a temple library; the royal palace with 67 rooms and halls; two royal archive buildings and three private archives and libraries; royal stables; a warehouse containing numerous storage jars more than 40 inches high; hundreds of private homes, under many of which were found well-built tombs, often in Mycenaean style; and excellent drainage systems. The contents of the houses and tombs have been most diversified. Two gold bowls represent the finest examples of the Canaanite goldsmith's craft yet found. One bronze cache unearthed from beneath the floor of the high priest's house numbered 74 tools and weapons, five of which bore alphabetic cuneiform inscriptions showing they were the property of the high priest. Another cache included a large anvil and a double ax of Cretan style. In a goldsmith's house were found a number of weights and some molds for jewelry and ornaments. The king's palace, uncovered between 1950 and 1953, yielded a trumpet, two feet long, carved from a single elephant's tusk and bearing in relief and engraving, near the mouthpiece, a naked goddess guarded by sphinxes with outspread wings. This palace also contained the largest single ivory carving discovered in the Near East, a footboard 40 inches wide and 20 inches high, with 16 panels carved in a style mainly Egyptian. The central panel shows a standing goddess, probably Asherah, to judge from the literary mythological references; she is represented giving suck to two royal children standing in front of her. The pottery finds at Ras Shamra are among the most abundant and variegated in the Near East.

Languages and Literature at Ugarit. The most precious discoveries, however, are the thousands of clay tablets inscribed in seven different languages: Sumerian, Akkadian, Hurrian, Hittite, Egyptian, Cypro-Minoan Linear B, and Ugaritic. The Akkadian texts, which alone number in the thousands (texts in Akkadian and Ugaritic found in the 1959 campaign alone filled 30 cases) are mainly juridical, administrative, commercial, and epistolary in nature. Of unusual philological importance are a quadrilingual lexicon, found in 1958, listing words syllabically written, in Sumerian, Akkadian, Hurrian, and Ugaritic, and a Canaanite wisdom text, also written in Akkadian, which contains epigrams such as, "Where you put your wallet, tell not your wife."

The excavations of 1929 brought to light scores of clay tablets and fragments covered with a cuneiform script of Mesopotamian type, but differing in the form and number of the signs. This new script was deciphered within a year of the publication of the hand copies. The number of signs (30) led to an inference that the writing was alphabetic; the individual words, often separated by a word divider, generally contained three radicals, sometimes four, and rarely five. These observations, coupled with the fact that the tablets were discovered in Canaanite territory, prompted the hypothesis, fully confirmed in the decipherment, that the language was Semitic. H. L. Ginsberg labeled it Ugaritic. The precise linguistic classification of Ugaritic within the Semitic family has been continuously debated. The view that it is a Canaanite dialect—some prefer to call it a Northwest Semitic dialect—whose closest linguistic affinities are with the poetic sections of the Hebrew Bible seems to be the most reasonable. Religious texts, letters, diplomatic documents, recipes for curing ailing horses, administrative, statistical, and commercial documents, and several *a-b-c* tablets were written in this script, as well as literary texts in the strict sense. These last are of the greatest interest; they contain myths and legends of the Canaanites of the 2d millennium B.C., and enable the historian of religion to formulate the ethical ideals and the religious beliefs of the pre-Biblical Canaanites. The longest text, the *Baal Cycle,* a pure myth about the gods, is really a series of episodes narrating the contests between Baal, the god of the storm and fertility, and his two principal adversaries, Sea and Mōt (or Death, the god of aridity and sterility). The *Legend of Keret* tells about a just King Keret whose entire family is tragically wiped out. Through the counsel of El, the head of the Canaanite pantheon, who appears to him in a dream, Keret leads a military expedition to capture a wife who will bear him numerous offspring. *The Legend of Aqhat,* which is half myth and half legend, recounts how the childless King Daniel, through the intercession of Baal, is blessed with a son. This son, Aqhat, is later slain by the goddess Anat because he refuses to hand over to her a bow and some arrows given to him by the divine artisan Kothar. A curious composition, which seems to be a religious libretto, describes the birth of Shahar, the god of dawn, and Shalim, the god of evening, whom two wives bear to El. There is also a hymn that celebrates the marriage of the goddess Nikkal to the moon-god Yarikh.

Though the actual tablets discovered date to the period *c.* 1400 to 1350 B.C., the original composition of these myths and legends is considerably earlier; the *Baal Cycle* may go back even to the 3d millennium. Materials much more limited in quantity in a reduced cuneiform alphabet of 22 letters, corresponding to the standard Canaanite-Hebrew alphabet of the Iron Age, and attributable to the 13th century B.C., have also been found.

It is difficult to overestimate the importance of the Ugaritic discoveries. In 1937 R. Dussaud rated the Ugaritic tablets as the most important discovery ever made in the realm of Biblical studies. New excavations at the site and subsequent progress in the study of the contents

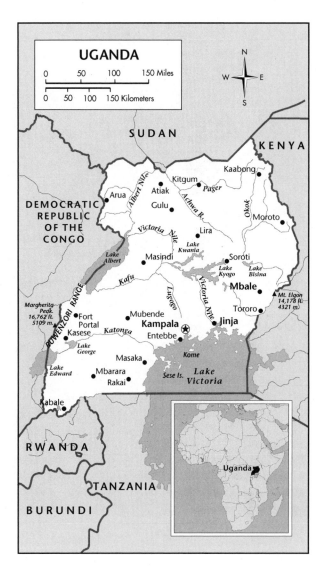

of the Ugaritic tablets fully bear out the accuracy of Dussaud's evaluation.

Bibliography: C. F. SCHAEFFER, *The Cuneiform Texts of Ras Shamra-Ugarit* (London 1939). C. H. GORDON, *Ugaritic Textbook* (Analecta Orientalia 38; Rome 1965), grammar, texts in transliteration, glossary; *Ugaritic Literature* (Rome 1949). H. L. GINSBERG, ''Ugaritic Myths, Epics, and Legends,'' J. B. PRITCHARD, *Ancient Near Eastern Texts Relating to the Old Testament* (Princeton 1955). T. H. GASTER, *Thespis* (rev. ed. New York 1961). G. R. DRIVER, *Canaanite Myths and Legends* (Edinburgh 1956). J. GRAY, *The Legacy of Canaan: The Ras Shamra Texts and Their Relevance to the Old Testament* (Vetus Testamentum Suppl 5; 2d ed. 1964).

[M. J. DAHOOD]

UGARITIC-CANAANITE RELIGION

This ancient Syro-Palestinian paganism is of more than antiquarian interest. It was the religion that the Isra-

Ruins of a fort constructed c. 1400 B.C. stand at Ugarit. (©Charles & Josette Lenars/CORBIS)

elites encountered when they entered the Promised Land, and which they imitated to a certain extent in the outward forms of their cult, and absorbed into their literature and popular lore. Israel's religion had behind it a background of the common culture of Canaan; while it had a character of its own, which it did not share with the Canaanites, it did express itself through shared forms and language. Though there were forms that could not be integrated into Yahwism, there were other forms, such as sacred poetry, music, and architecture, which were taken over and made the organ of Israelite religion. Both where the Old Testament incorporates them, and where it reacts against them, Canaanite religion and mythology continue to exert their impact upon us through the Bible.

Sources. Until the discoveries at Ugarit-Ras Shamra, little was known about Canaanite religion, and that little was based mainly on second-hand sources. To be sure, the Old Testament contained numerous allusions to Canaanite gods and practices, but these references were in-variably polemic and had to be interpreted accordingly. There were some references to Canaanite deities, and sometimes also to ritual implements and usages, in Egyptian and Mesopotamian texts, in the El Amarna letters, and in the Phoenician inscriptions of the 1st millennium, especially those from Karatepe discovered in 1946; but these could not yield a coherent summary of the religion. Greek writers, e.g., Lucian and PHILO OF BYBLOS, preserved accounts of Canaanite mythology and religion, which they claimed to have derived from native sources, but it was difficult to separate the genuine deposit from later accretions. Finally, excavations at such sites as Byblos, Megiddo, Hazor, Gezer, and Tell Beit Mirsim have yielded some temples, numerous altars, statues, figurines, incense-burners, bones of sacrificial animals and the like, which, while giving valuable information, permitted at best a tentative reconstruction.

Today, the Canaanites speak for themselves. In a series of remarkable discoveries at Ras Shamra (ancient

UGARIT) on the North Syrian coast near Latakia have come to light hundreds of clay tablets inscribed in a Canaanite dialect closely related to Biblical Hebrew. In addition to material that is not here relevant, these tablets contain a series of relatively long mythological poems and of shorter documents relating to the service of the sanctuary. There are lists of gods and sacrifices to be offered to them, classes of temple functionaries, and ritual texts mentioning animals for sacrifice. Discovery of non-literary materials includes remains of temples to Baal and to Dagon, two stelae with dedications to Dagon, stelae with carved reliefs representing El and Baal, and installations for the cult of the dead.

General Characteristics. Though Canaanite religion was substantially the same in all regions of Greater Syria, one must allow for local variations and peculiarities. It must not be taken for granted that each Canaanite town recognized the sum total of deities revealed to us in the texts. Religion among the Canaanites, however it may have varied from place to place, was also more a public institution than a private experience. Its rites were public exercises aimed primarily to secure fertility of man and land; and while it doubtless inspired feelings of individual piety—witness the numerous votive inscriptions in Phoenician—it was in essence an expression of communal economy. It was an approach to the world which was thought to establish an intimacy between the community and the personified forces of nature, and which, by the large place given to sympathetic magic and rites of fertility, made man a necessary agent in the continuous process of creation and revitalization.

The Pantheon. The importance of certain gods in the mythological texts does not necessarily correspond to their popularity among Canaanite worshippers. The reverse is also true: e.g., DAGON, whose place in the myths is limited to being described as the father of BAAL, appears to have been quite popular, to judge from the temple and two stelae dedicated to him at Ugarit.

The God El. In the extreme recesses of Mt. Sāphôn, the great mountain of assembly, the gods held session. In the Ugaritic texts the pantheon is called "the totality of the sons of El," "the totality of the gods," "the assembly (family) of the gods." The head of the pantheon is El, whose titles include "the Creator of Creatures," "the King," "the Bull El," and "the Father of Mankind." Though *regalitas* in the full sense is ascribed only to El, he was no more than titular head of the pantheon and part of the time he seems quite otiose, what anthropologists call a "remote high god." He resided in a distant cosmic spot known as "the Sources of the Two Deeps" where he received suppliants and sent instructions by messengers. El was conceived as a mild old man; one of his titles

is "El the Merciful" and the stress on this attribute, according to O. Eissfeldt [*Journal of Semitic Studies* 1 (1956) 37], may have served to moderate the Israelite concept of the severe Yahweh so as to stress more His paternal gentleness. The most probable etymology of the name El derives it from the root *'wl* "to be strong, leader"; the form would be that of a stative participle [W. F. Albright, *Archaeology and the Religion of Israel* (Baltimore 1946) 72].

Baal, the Sea, and Death. Practical dominion over the world was divided among the three powers who correspond roughly to Zeus, Poseidon, and Hades of the Greeks. The sky and the rains were under the control of Baal, the dominant figure of the Canaanite pantheon. His epithets include "the Rider of the Clouds," and "the Mighty One." When he gives forth his voice from the heavens the mountains rock, the earth shakes, and his enemies take to the forests. Since the word *ba'lu* simply meant "lord," it could be applied to different gods. In practice, however, from before the 15th century B.C., the Semitic storm-god Hadad, identified with Baal in the Ugaritic tablets, had become "the Lord" par excellence. As lord of the storm, Baal was the god of fertility, since in Syria-Palestine fertility depended in very large measure upon rainfall. In actual cult, the mythological figure of Baal was identified in each locality with the peculiar *genius loci;* hence one encounters him under such diverse titles as "Baal of Sidon," "Baal Ḥammôn," and "Baal Addîr." His most frequent title among later Phoenicians is "Baal Shamên" or "Lord of the Heavens." This is none other than the great storm-god of Ras Shamra. The problem of henotheism is in this connection quite academic since there is no evidence that the local Baal was less than cosmic in scope. The Canaanite Baals were all high gods in their own right.

The oceans, rivers, lakes, and subterranean springs were under the dominion of Yamm, "Sea." Each year Yamm sought to gain control of the earth by flooding it, but was invariably repelled by Baal after a fierce battle. Yamm was regarded as a seven-headed monster-dragon and bore the title Lôtan (Leviathan).

The nether world and the barren places were the realm of Môt, "Death," the genius of aridity and sterility. When he stalked the earth all life ceased among men, the earth became a desert. Even the great Baal was helpless before him, for, as one text describes it, "Baal became as a lamb in his mouth." The text that follows is important for comparative mythology, since it tells how the goddess Anath attacked Death with an avenging fury, "cutting him off with her sword, winnowing him with the sieve, burning him in the fire, grinding him with the handmill, sowing his remains in the field" (J. B. Pritchard, *An-*

cient Near Eastern Texts Relating to the Old Testament 140). The ritual was intended to revive the god of fertility by sympathetic action.

The three-cornered contest of Baal, Yamm, and Death for domination of the earth forms the central theme of one of the myths from Ras Shamra (*Ancient Near Eastern Texts Relating to the Old Testament* 138–39).

Minor Deities. A popular Canaanite god was Kôthar, whose nature was not understood until the Ugaritic data made it possible to interpret already available material. He was the Canaanite Hephaestus or Vulcan, the wise craftsman and inventor of tools and weapons, as well as of musical instruments. In the myths he supervises the building of Baal's palace, equips the sanctuaries of the gods, and makes the divine bows. His forge was located in *kptr,* Biblical Caphtor, which is probably Crete.

Another god whose attributes were unknown until 1935 was Hôron. In an Egyptian execration text from the 19th century B.C., two Palestinian princes bear the name *ḥauranu-abum* "Hôron is Father," and during the Nineteenth Dynasty in Egypt when there was considerable Canaanite influence on Egyptian religion, Hôron was identified with Horus. References to him in the Harris magical papyrus make it clear that he is the Canaanite equivalent of Babylonian Nergal, the god of the plague and the nether world. This may be inferred also from his name, which probably means "the One of the Pit." In a comminatory formula in the Legend of King Keret from Ras Shamra, he is invoked thus: "May Hôron break, O my son, may Hôron break your head, Astarte, name of Baal, your pate" (*Ancient Near Eastern Texts Relating to the Old Testament* 149).

The Canaanite god of pestilence, Resheph, has long been known through inscriptions from Cyprus and Zinjirli, and Cypriote bilingual texts identify him with Apollo. In El Amarna letter 35, *belia* "my lord" is considered the cause of a recent plague in Cyprus; clearly, Resheph is intended, since in the Legend of King Keret he is described as gathering to himself one-sixth of Keret's family. On the other hand, in the Karatepe inscriptions (*see* CANAAN AND CANAANITES) Resheph appears as a god of well-being and prosperity; he is thus a god of health as well as of the plague. These apparently irreconcilable attributes find their sharpest expression in the composite deity Resheph-Shalmon (W. F. Albright, *op. cit.* 79–80). In Canaanite religious belief and practice there was a strong tendency to bring opposites together. Polarities were felt to be the very essence of life. What could be more natural than to pray to the god of pestilence for healing from the disease that he controlled?

Goddesses. As the Canaanite judged that certain functions might be attributed more appropriately to the operation of a female principle, the male deities were supplemented by three principal goddesses: Asherah, Astarte, and Anath.

By reason of her position as consort of El, Asherah is sometimes simply called *'ilt* "the goddess." She is also styled "the progenitress of the gods," while, conversely, the gods are termed "the sons of Asherah." Her most frequent epithet, however, is "the one who walks in the sea." Asherah is the embodiment of matronly qualities, the wife and mother, the head of the home and family. Since in practical cult Baal tended to replace El as head of the pantheon, it is with Baal that Asherah is most frequently paired in the ritual texts from Ras Shamra and in the Old Testament (2 Kgs 18.19; 23.4). In the Bible, the common noun *asherah* meant a wooden cult object, which might be burned or cut down like a tree. Just what the cult object was we cannot determine with precision; some kind of wooden emblem, like contemporary Babylonian examples, has been proposed.

Astarte, whom late Greek writers describe as the personification of sexual passion, comparable to Aphrodite, often interchanges with Asherah in the Bible, where both are mentioned with Baal. On the other hand, an Egyptian text associated her with Anath as one of the "two great goddesses who conceive but do not bear," i.e., the goddesses who are perennially fruitful without ever losing virginity. Astarte was also the genius of warfare and combat, and it is in this role that she makes her rare appearances in Ugaritic literature. She helps Baal defeat his rival Yamm, and is thrice invoked with Hôron (see above) in a standard curse, to break the head of an enemy.

Though Anath is the best attested of the three main goddesses, it is not clear whether her original attributes were sensuality and fertility, or strength and martial ardor. The uncertainty stems from the general trend toward the virtual fusion, by Roman times, of all the West Asiatic goddesses into the one figure of *dea Syra,* whose principal traits were sensuality and fecundity. In Egypt, moreover, at a very early date Astarte and Anath borrowed one another's attributes, but the Egyptian papyrus Chester Beatty 7 does preserve a reminiscence of what is probably the original concept of Anath. She is there called "the strong goddess, the woman being a warrior, clothed as a man, dressed as a woman." In iconic representations she generally bears arms, only exceptionally fertility symbols. The Ugaritic texts regularly designate her "the virgin Anath," one "the maiden Anath," and several times, apparently, simply as "maiden." The Anath of the middle Bronze period was a beautiful, youthful, vigorous, bellicose, even vicious goddess, but not a voluptuous or reproductive one. She figures as a fighter in behalf of Baal (*Ancient Near Eastern Texts Re-*

lating to the Old Testament 137), indulges in an orgy of slaughter (*ibid.* 136), and acts as a wet nurse to offspring begotten by Baal, presumably for the purpose of imparting to the infants in question some of her martial spirit.

The Ugaritic myths mention other deities whose roles are quite minor. There is mention of Ashtar who is depicted as competing unsuccessfully with both Yamm and Baal for possession of the earth. Baal's three daughters Arsiya (goddess of the earth), Talliya (goddess of dew), and Pidraya (goddess of the clouds), and his two messengers "Vine" and "Field" are all personifications of natural phenomena closely associated with the operations of Baal as genius of rainfall and fertility.

Astral Deities and the King. Several heavenly bodies also were divinized, though their cult seems not to have been very popular among the Canaanites. The sun-goddess Shapsh is mentioned in the myths as "the torch of the gods" and "the illuminatrix of the heavens." The moon-god Yarikh figures only in the hymn to Nikkal and Ib where the lack of poetic parallelism has led some scholars to suspect that the hymn may be of Hurrian and not Canaanite origin. The birth of the two gods Shahar, "dawn," and Shalim, "sunset," begotten by El who seduced two women, forms the subject of a dramatic text that has been described as "a landmark in the prehistory of classical drama" (Gordon, *Mythologies,* 185).

An aura of divinity also surrounded the king. He was regarded as a nursling of the goddess Asherah, and an ivory panel from Ras Shamra shows two royal sucklings at the breasts of a goddess [C. H. Gordon, *Antiquity* 115 (1955) 147–49].

Cult. We have very little direct evidence regarding the nature of Canaanite ceremonial. Their sacrificial ritual was more diversified than the Israelites'; many more animals were employed as offerings. Sacrificial texts from Ugarit mention various bovines, especially bullocks, and small cattle (rams, ewes, lambs, kids, etc.), as well as small birds and doves. A mythological text adds wild bulls, stags, wild goats, and deer. The same picture emerges essentially from the sacrificial tariffs of Marseilles and Carthage from *c.* 4th century B.C.

Ugaritic administrative texts imply a highly developed cultic establishment with functions departmentalized among priests under the supervision of a chief priest, consecrated persons, singers, doorkeepers, etc. There were also numerous guilds that looked after the temple interests.

There is no evidence in the Ugaritic tablets of human sacrifice, though the practice was rampant among the Canaanites of the 1st millennium B.C. as is clear from frequent Biblical allusions, as well as from the fact, attested by many Roman witnesses, that the Carthaginians, who migrated from Phoenicia in the 9th and 8th century B.C., practiced human sacrifice on a large scale down to the fall of Carthage. The root of this practice in Punic religion is illustrated by the fact that it had not ceased by the 3d century A.D. despite repeated Roman efforts to wipe it out.

It is possible to reconstruct some of the details of Canaanite ritual from references in the Old Testament, e.g., 1 Kgs 18.23–40 describes the contest of Elijah with the prophets of Baal on the summit of Mt. Carmel. The latter are said to have "leaped about the altar" and to have "cut themselves after their manner with knives and lances till the blood gushed out upon them." The gashing with knives is found in the description of El's mourning for the dead Baal as well as in the writings of Lucian of Samosata, in the 2d century A.D., who states that the custom was characteristic of the ceremonial mourning for Adonis, which was performed annually at the Syrian sanctuary in Hierapolis.

Bibliography: W. F. ALBRIGHT, *From the Stone Age to Christianity* (2d ed. New York 1957); *Archaeology and the Religion of Israel* (Baltimore 1946; 2d rev. ed. 1953). T. H. GASTER, "The Religion of the Canaanites," *Forgotten Religions,* ed. V. FERM (New York 1950) 111–43; *Thespis* (rev. ed. New York 1961). C. H. GORDON, "Canaanite Mythology," *Mythologies of the Ancient World,* ed. S. N. KRAMER (New York 1961). J. GRAY, *The Legacy of Canaan: The Ras Shamra Texts and Their Relevance to the Old Testament* (Vetus Testamentum Supplement 5; 2d ed. Leiden 1964). R. DELANGHE, "Myth, Ritual, and Kingship in the Ras Shamra Tablets," *Myth, Ritual and Kingship,* ed. S. H. HOOKE (Oxford 1958) 122–48. M. H. POPE, *El in the Ugaritic Texts* (Vetus Testamentum Supplement 2; Leiden 1955).

[M. J. DAHOOD]

UGLINESS

Ugliness, a quality, in life or in art, related by negation to BEAUTY. Its exact nature has been a classical and much controverted subject in the history of AESTHETICS since Aristotle's *Poetics*. It is variously defined as the positive negation of beauty, that is, a radical failure in something trying to be, or expected to be, beautiful; a perversion of beauty; the perversion of the characteristic function of anything or anyone. The implication is that there is prototype of beauty or some expectation in mind, in terms of which the falling off produces shock. Much of the "ironic" nature of modern poetry, e.g., T.S. Eliot's *The Wasteland,* seems to depend on such a technique. A more radical probing of ugliness tends to consider it as the very material through which art and life move to accomplish their final triumphs. Special notice should also be given to the theory maintaining that the artist can produce beauty when by his craftsmanship he makes us recognize, with the enjoyment of recognition, the ugly in life. Thus theories about the comic can be closely related to theories about ugliness, and what deals with the ugly need not itself be ugly.

See Also: TRANSCENDENTALS.

Bibliography: E. AUERBACH, *Mimesis,* tr. W.R. TRASK (Princeton, N.J. 1953). K. ROSENKRANZ, *Aesthetik des Hasslichen* (Konigsberg 1853).

[W. F. LYNCH]

UGUZO, ST.

Popular saint in Lombardy; d. July 12, before 1200. He was, according to legend, a poor shepherd who lived near Cavargna and was extremely generous in dispensing his meager savings to the poor and needy. Suspecting that the shepherd was giving away his property, Uguzo's employer drove him away. Uguzo's subsequent employer prospered from the moment he hired him, to such an extent that hatred and envy drove the first employer to kill the unfortunate shepherd. The cult of Uguzo was authenticated as early as 1280 at Milan and has been honored by various popes. He is the patron of cheese-makers and is invoked in cases of cattle and eye diseases. He appears in iconography with a cheese-cutter and a cheese with a slice cut out of it.

Feast: July 12 and Aug. 16.

Bibliography: *Acta Sanctorum* July 3:296. A. MERCATI and A. PELZER, *Dizionario ecclesiastico* (Turin 1954–58) 3:1211. U. CHEVALIER, *Répertoire des sources historiques du moyen-age. Bio-bibliographie* (Paris 1905–07) 2:4585. E. F. J. MÜLLER, *Lexikon für Theologie und Kirche* (Freiburg 1930–38) 10:361.

[F. D. LAZENBY]

UKRAINE, THE CATHOLIC CHURCH IN

Located in southeastern Europe, Ukraine is bordered on the north by Belarus and Hungary, on the east by Russia, on the south by the Black Sea, Moldova and Romania, and on the west by Hungary, Slovakia and Poland. Predominately steppe, the southwest encompasses the Carpathian mountain chain while in the north forests are dotted with a number of lakes. The climate ranges from continental in the central region to Mediterranean near the southern coast. The southernmost region, Crimea, which divides the Black Sea and the Sea of Azov, declared independence from Ukraine in 1991 but was restored to the region in 1995. The region's wealth of natural resources include iron ore, coal, natural gas, pe-

troleum, graphite, titanium, magnesium, nickel and mercury. An additional resource is its black soil, and agricultural products consist of grains, sugar beets, sunflower seeds, vegetables, as well as livestock and dairy concerns. During the decades the region was part of the USSR, Ukraine was considered the agricultural heartland of the Soviet sphere.

Known as the Kievan Rus until the 16th century, after 1200 the region fell under the control of Lithuania, then Poland before being subsumed by Russia by the 19th century. A short period of independence after the Russian Revolution ended in 1920 when the Red Army subdued Kiev. As the Ukranian Soviet Socialist Republic it was a part of the USSR until the fall of communism in August of 1991. Devastated by both World War II and by widespread famine, as food stores were taken from the region by the Soviet state, Ukrainians also suffered through the 1986 Chernobyl nuclear power plant disaster. Following independence, the government attempted to liberalize the government, although most industries remained under state control. A close relationship with Russia continued, both militarily and economically. By the late 1990s inflation and rising unemployment sparked by Russia's economic woes, caused social instability in the region, although the election of a reformist prime minister in late 1999 was viewed optimistically.

Christianity of the Kievan Rus. Slavic/Rus tribes from the east settled the region by the second half of the 9th century, making Kiev a political and cultural center for much of eastern Europe. Vikings introduced Christianity, and an affiliation with the Byzantine Empire was the result. In 989 St. VLADIMIR (979–1015) made Christianity the state religion, ordering the baptism of his retinue and people. Many missionaries entered the region from the west, their work supplemented by the presences of monasteries such as that of the ascetic monks of the Caves near Kiev, which strongly influenced early Catholics in the practice of their faith. While Orthodoxy grew to encompass the region, because Byzantium was less zealous in teaching its daughter churches than was Rome in educating the West, a cultural lag developed between eastern and western Europe, between Orthodox and Roman Catholic.

The first known metropolitan of Kiev was Theopempt (1039), a Greek as were most of his successors, who were consecrated in Constantinople until the mid-15th century (*see* CONSTANTINOPLE, PATRIARCHATE OF). The metropolitan of Kiev covered the territory from Galicia (northeast of the Carpathian Mountains, in modern Poland and Ukraine), northeast to the Upper Volga and Oka Rivers (central Russia). With the invasion of the Mongols in 1240, Kiev was destroyed and replaced by new religious centers in Halicz, Novgorod, Vladimir, and later, Moscow and Lithuania. Maximus, metropolitan of Kiev from 1283–1305 left the region and moved to Moscow. Thereafter, Moscow became home of the metropolitan of Kiev, the spiritual heir of the ancient Rus. While Kievan Catholics remained in union with Rome following the schism in 1054, estrangement from the West was growing, and at the Council of FLORENCE in 1439 the separation was completed (*see* EASTERN SCHISM; ORTHODOX CHURCHES).

The Union of Brest and the Return to Rome. From the late 13th century through 1559 Ukraine was under the control of Lithuania and Poland, and its Orthodox were exposed to the Western Church. In 1436 Orthodox metropolitan ISIDORE OF KIEV—appointed by Constantinople—found acceptance among the Slavs of his region for union with Rome, and this union was supported at Florence. Basil II, the Great Prince of Moscow, rejected the union decreed at Florence and elected his own metropolitan in 1448, thus precipitating the break of the Russian Orthodox Church from Byzantium, the final break from Rome, and the division of the Slavic Church of Eastern Europe into two metropolitan areas: Kiev and Moscow. Kiev, then part of Lithuania, saw its metropolitans continue in union with Rome, although officially dependent on the patriarch of Constantinople, until 1517, after which they renounced the union of Florence. In 1569 the Ukraine became part of Poland, and the Orthodox church was oppressed and the people impoverished.

During the Protestant Reformation of the 16th century, many nobles in the region converted to CALVINISM, while brotherhoods formed in Lvov and set up schools. The Academy of Ostrog, established by the magnate Constantine Ostrozhski (d. 1608), provided higher education, while in that city the first complete Slavonic printed Bible was published in 1581. By 1555 the Jesuit-led COUNTER REFORMATION proved successful even among the nobles. Despite opposition from these nobles, in 1596 the Union of Brest proclaimed the union with Rome, of the ecclesiastical province of Kiev, as a means of preserving and protecting the Slavic traditions of the faith from the aggressions of the Moscow patriarchate and the westernizing influences of the Polish Roman Catholic Church. The Union of BREST created the Eastern-rite UKRAINIAN CATHOLIC CHURCH (later the Ukrainian Greek-rite Catholic Church). The new church found little support among the nobility, most of whom attended Jesuit colleges and adopted the Latin rite. The situation of the Eastern Church deteriorated further in 1620, when the patriarch of Jerusalem, Theophanes reestablished the dissident Ruthenian (Ukranian/Byleorussian) hierarchy under a new metropolitan of Kiev, Job Boretski (1620–33), dependent on the patriarch of Constantinople. The attempts

Capital: Kiev.
Size: 233,000 sq. miles.
Population: 49,153,030 in 2000.
Languages: Ukranian, Russian, Romanian, Polish, Hungarian.
Religions: 6,488,200 Catholics (13.2%), 1,130,520 Jews (2.3%), 37,356,400 Orthodox (76%), 4,177,910 practice other faiths or are without religious affiliation.
Ecclesiastical organizations: The Ukranian Greek-Catholic Church has a major archeparchy at Lvov, with suffragans Bučač, Ivano-Frankivsk, Klolmyia-Chernivtsi, Sambir-Drohobych, Sokal-Zhovkva, Stryj, Ternopil-Zbioriv. A Latin archdiocese at Lvov has suffragans Kamyanets-Podilskyi, Kyiv-Zhytomyr, and Lutsk. The Ruthenian Byzantine Church has an eparchy at Mukacheve that is directly subject to the Holy See. The Armenian Church has an archeparchy at Lvov. An apostolic administration is located in Zakarpattia.

of the newly consecrated metropolitan to wrest bishoprics from legitimate Catholic prelates led to deplorable events. King Vladyslav's constitution of 1632 legally restored the Eastern Church.

Greek-rite Catholics in the Ukraine were harassed by their Orthodox countrymen as traitors, yet received no help from Latin Catholics. Catholic prelates were excluded from the ecclesiastical class of the kingdom and consequently never obtained seats in the senate. The Union of Brest was in danger of being completely destroyed during the uprising of Bogdan Khmelnitsky and the prolonged Cossack and Swedish wars. However, on the strength of its religious, the Church survived and prospered during the reigns of Koribut Wiśniowetski (1669–73) and John Sobieski (1674–96). The Peace of Andrusovo (1667) ceded the anti-Catholic territory east of the Dnieper to Russia, allowing a renaissance *c.* 1700, when the last three dissident ordinaries joined the Ukrainian Greek-rite Catholic Church.

Despite its numerical strength, the Greek-rite Church was too weak to create an autonomous Catholic Byzantine-Slavonic culture, and Latin elements infiltrated its ecclesiastical life. The Catholic metropolitan of Kiev resided usually in Novogrudek in Lithuania. After the partition of Poland in the late 18th century (1772, 1793, 1795), the greater part of his ecclesiastical province was incorporated into Russia. With the death of Theodosius Rostotski (1805), the last Catholic metropolitan of Kiev disappeared.

Russian Rule and a Shifting Orthodoxy. In 1654 an agreement was made with RUSSIA that, while promising autonomy for the Ukrainian Orthodox Church, resulted in the weakening of Kiev as a center of Orthodox power. In 1680 the region was made part of Russia, and within five years the Orthodox metropolitan of Kiev lost

its independence when the patriarch of Moscow, without recourse to Constantinople, appointed the metropolitan of Kiev and assimilated the Ukranian Orthodox Church into the Moscow patriarchate. Where once Kiev's influence had extended through most of eastern Europe, after 1720 while a metropolitan continued to be appointed, his jurisdiction was limited to the city's territorial limits. Meanwhile, through the end of the 17th century, Ukrainian scholars, educated at Mogila Academy in Kiev, continued to exert a strong influence on Russian intellectual life. Among the pioneers were Epiphanius Slavinetski (d. 1675), representative of Greek-Slavonic culture; Simeon of Polotsk (d. 1680), familiar with Catholic theological thought; and his disciple Silvester Medvedev (d. 1691).

Following the break-up of Poland, western Ukraine fell under the control of Russia, along with Crimea, which before 1795 had remained under Ottoman rule. Latin- and Greek-rite Catholics living in the region became subjects of the Russian Empire, whereas those in the eastern region of Galicia came under Austrian rule.

In 1897 Emperor Francis I of Austria obtained from the Holy See the erection of the ecclesiastical province of Halicz with its seat in Lvov. Ukrainian-rite Catholics in Galicia and the Transcarpathian region of the Ukraine gained from Austria freedom of religion and rite, but were pressured by the patriarch of Budapest until 1918.

The Russian government also tolerated Catholics, but only those of the Latin rite, and those in ethnic groups that traditionally belonged to Catholic nations. Catholics of the Eastern rite were viewed as schismatic Orthodox and remained under heavy pressure from the Moscow patriarchate. The destruction of their union with Rome occurred during the reign of Nicholas I, whose motto ''Orthodoxy, Russianism, absolutism'' opposed the existence of the Ukranian Greek-rite Catholic Church. The plan to conscript these Eastern-rite Catholics into the official Orthodox Church was prepared by Joseph Semashko, a priest who, like most of his colleagues of both rites, was educated in the seminary at Vilna, where he imbibed the principles of GALLICANISM. Several legislative measures, and the death of the metropolitan-delegate Josaphat Bulhak (1817–38), a man devoted to the Holy See but too weak to offer resistance, brought about the final blow. In 1839 the Union of Brest was declared nonexistent, and the Greek-rite Catholics were subjected to the Holy Synod of the Moscow patriarchate. Opposition met harsh suppression, and was more easily subdued because many Ukrainian nobles had passed in earlier centuries to the Latin rite, and had aligned themselves with Poland, leaving the common people without leaders.

The Church under Communism. Following the Russian revolution of 1917, Ukraine declared independence on Jan. 28, 1918, but this effort was quickly suppressed by the communist forces now controlling the Soviet Union. In 1922 Ukraine became one of the first socialist republics to form the USSR, and its government began the first phase of communism: to break down the old order. As part of this objective, it encouraged the formation of sects, breakaway churches and the introduction of Protestantism, while attempting to disrupt the powerful Russian Orthodox infrastructure. Out of this atmosphere came the rebirth of the Ukrainian Orthodox Church as the Ukrainian Autocephalous Orthodox Church, which seceded from the Moscow patriarchate in 1921 with the blessings of the state and by 1924 claimed 3,000 parishes and upwards of four million faithful tended by 30 bishops and 1,500 priests.

In the relaxed atmosphere extended toward religion in the initial phase-in of communism, an effort was made by the Vatican to support Greek-rite Catholics in the region. In 1926 a papal commission set up nine administrative regions, one of which was Odessa, and appointed Bishop Frison as apostolic administrator to tend to the region's large Catholic population. Unfortunately, in 1929 the second phase of communism was enacted: namely the brutal repression of all religion, enforced via a religion law that promoted antireligious propaganda. Continued governmental oppression led to the imprisonment of the bishop, who was later shot. In its first phase, the communist government jailed hundreds of priests between 1929 and 1932, virtually destroying the Catholic Church organization. In 1930 the Ukrainian Autocephalous Orthodox Church that had been encouraged by the government less than a decade before was outlawed.

On March 15, 1939, the Carpathian Ukraine proclaimed its independence and on the same day elected Greek-rite priest Monsignor Augustine Vološyn as its president. The new country's life span was extremely brief, however; Hungarian troops began to occupy the region on the following day, forcing Vološyn into exile. The Transcarpathian Catholic Church retained a similar sense of independence from the Greek-rite Church in the rest of Ukraine, having its roots in the 1646 Union of Uzhhorod rather than the Union of Brest 50 years earlier.

Between 1946 and the fall of the Soviet state, Ukrainians were subjected to the greatest spiritual prohibitions in the communist sphere, as church properties were confiscated, schools and monasteries closed, and printed materials banned. The 1930s were also rough years for more temporal reasons, as enforced collectivized farming sparked peasant revolts that were put down through the confiscation of most of the region's agricultural production and the death of over five million Ukrainians due to starvation. During World War II the region was occupied by Germans, who turned a blind eye as the Greek-rite Church established a formal hierarchy in eastern Ukraine. While accusations later surfaced that the Greek-rite Catholic Church turned a blind eye to the mass deportation of Jews from the region under German occupation, Greek-rite metropolitan Andrei Sheptysts'kyi was arrested for his outspoken opposition to Nazi policies. In 1944, following the war during which seven million Ukrainians were killed, sections of Romania, eastern Poland and Slovakia were joined to the Ukraine, resulting in an increased persecution of Catholics, particularly the three and a half million Greek-rite Catholics living in eastern Poland. In 1945 Ukrainian Greek-rite Metropolitan Joseph Slipyj (1892–1984), four bishops and several priests were imprisoned and charged with collaboration with the Nazis; in March of 1946 a synod, that had no bishops in attendance, met in Lvov and under the ''protection'' of the Soviet secret police, proclaimed the Union of Brest annulled and the Ukrainian Greek-rite Catholic Church officially extinct. The Church's property was confiscated and given to the Russian Orthodox Church. While forcibly incorporated with the Orthodox Moscow patriarchate, many of the Ukranian Catholic clergy and laity refused to recognize the union. In Transcarpathian Ukraine, Monsignor Romzha, who headed the Church, was removed by a planned automobile accident in October of 1947. His successor, Monsignor Tschira, was imprisoned in 1948 and sent to a concentration camp, thereby forcing all remaining followers of the Greek-rite church underground. After 18 years in prison Slipyj left for the west and was created a cardinal in 1965. By the mid-1960s there were three Catholic churches remaining in Lvov, while Odessa, with several thousand Greek-rite Catholics, was without a priest. Despite the straitened circumstances of the Greek-rite Church, half of all churches still in existence in the USSR by independence were located in Ukraine.

An Independent Ukraine. During the 1980s, the rumblings of insurrection could be heard throughout the Soviet Union, and a growing nationalist movement was felt in the Ukraine and elsewhere. In the region the nationalist RUKH was vocal in its demands for cultural and linguistic traditions by 1989, and thousands of Greek-rite Catholics marched through the streets in Lvov, on September 17, demanding the restoration of their church. On Dec. 1, 1989, Soviet leader Mikhail Gorbachev, in an effort to stabilize a disintegrating union, promised the pope that legal status would be extended to the Greek-rite Church.

While for Catholics the fall of communism was viewed favorably, the impending break-up of the Soviet Union was seen as a threat by the Moscow patriarchate, which had benefited from its preferential treatment under communist dictator Josef Stalin and its receipt of many properties confiscated from other churches. In January of 1990 the Bishops' Council of the Russian Orthodox Church granted autonomy to the Ukranian Orthodox Church, which was made an exarchate of the Moscow patriarchate. However, the church demanded greater freedom, with the result that on Oct. 27, 1990 it was given autonomous status, its metropolitan, Major Archbishop Lubachivsky, retaining his membership in the Holy Synod of the Moscow patriarchate. The Soviet Union was officially dissolved on Dec. 25, 1991.

After Ukraine declared its independence on Aug. 24, 1991, multiparty elections were held and the region declared itself a nuclear-free zone in response to the Chernobyl disaster of only a few years ago. At independence, a religious forum was held by the new government, which vowed that there would be no ruling Church in Ukraine. The government also joined with Belarus and Russia in the Commonwealth of Independent States (CIS). While the new government attempted economic reforms, power struggles and disputes over the extent to which the region would remain involved with Russia continued to stall economic development, and violent disputes broke out in eastern Ukraine throughout 1992. On the religious front disputes existed as well, and efforts to create a national Orthodox church quickly fractionalized. In one such effort, recently appointed Metropolitan Filaret Denisenko attempted to seek complete separation of the Ukrainian Orthodox Church from Moscow, which had subjugated Kiev since the late 18th century. Continuing his efforts after his request was refused by the Russian Orthodox Bishop's Council in April of 1992, Filaret provolked matters to such a point that within a month the Moscow patriarchate had deposed him and appointed Metropolitan Vladimir Sabodan of Rostov as new metropolitan of the church. Subsequently, Filaret joined the non-canonical Ukrainian Autocephalous Church, which had been recreated in 1991, and gained a leadership position, ultimately becoming patriarchate. Although his presence caused the Autocephalous Church to fracture into two sections, the Filaret-led faction, the Ukrainian Orthodox Church (Kiev patriarchate), saw parishes in-

crease by one third due to the many Orthodox loyal to Filaret. Meanwhile, an anti-Filaret faction splintered from the former Ukrainian Autocephalous Church, retaining the old name and led by patriarch Dmytriy Yarema of Lvov.

By 2000 the four churches of historical foundation in Ukraine were the Ukrainian Orthodox Church (Moscow patriarchate), the Ukrainian Greek-rite Catholic Church, the Ukrainian Orthodox Church (Kievan patriarchate) and the Ukrainian Autocephalous Orthodox Church. Smaller Orthodox communities, such as the Old Believers, various Protestant evangelical groups, Lutherans, Jews and Muslims were among the other religious groups active in the country. In an effort to eliminate conflict among the faiths, the 1993 Balamand Accord prohibited Catholics and Orthodox from proselytization between them. As elsewhere across the former Soviet sphere, the issue of Church properties confiscated after 1946 under communist rule also surfaced, particularly with regard to the Greek-rite Church, which had been, at least on the surface, destroyed by the communist government. The Moscow patriarchate, which counted Catholic properties among the bulk of their current holdings, remained reluctant to discuss reparations, although it agreed to participate in a joint Catholic-Orthodox commission formed in December of 1999 to resolve property issues. In 2001 the Orthodox bishops aligned with the Moscow patriarchate, still concerned over competing Orthodox churches in the country, and discouraged Pope John Paul II from a visit to the country, citing his presence as a complication to continuing ecumenical relations in the Ukraine. Indeed, the pope was later criticized by Moscow for recognizing Kievan patriarch Filaret, which action, Russian Orthodox leaders maintained, furthered the efforts of this schismatic church. Following the pope's visit in June, the Autocephalous Orthodox Church and Filaret's Ukrainian Orthodox Church (Kieven patriarchate) were reported to have approached the ecumenical patriarch of Constantinople for official recognition as a single church.

Into the 21st Century. By 2000, in contrast to the over 10,500 Orthodox parishes in the country, there were approximately 3,400 Greek- and Latin-rite parishes in Ukraine, tended by 1,890 diocesan and 405 religious priests. Other religious included approximately 300 brothers and 925 sisters, who operated six theological schools, as well as Catholic primary and secondary schools in the country. By the late 1990s, due to the economic troubles that visited the area, Catholic leaders concentrated their efforts on dealing with the effects of poverty and homelessness among the faithful. As had been the tradition in the region, eastern and central Ukraine remained predominately Orthodox, while Greek-rite and Latin-rite Catholics resided in the eastern regions, where ethnic Poles predominated. While the Moscow patriarchate remained in control of the Orthodox in the region, it was seen as a vestige of Russian overlordship and many anticipated that Ukrainian Orthodox factions would ultimately merge into an independent church. Still others viewed the concept of a national church as inconsistent with a democratic nation comprising a variety of ethnicities and cultures.

Bibliography: F. DVORNIK, *The Slavs: Their Early History and Civilization* (Boston 1956); *The Slavs in European History and Civilization* (New Brunswick, NJ 1962). O. HALECKI, *From Florence to Brest (1439–1596)* (Rome 1958). T. WARE, *The Orthodox Church* (Baltimore, MD 1963). A. DAMI, *La Ruthénie subcarpathique* (Geneva 1944). F. NĚMEC, *The Soviet Seizure of Subcarpathian Ruthenia* (Toronto 1955). V. MARKUS, *L'Incorporation de l'Ukraine subcarpathique à l'Ukraine sovietique* (Louvain 1956). *Religion in the USSR,* ed. B. IWANOV, tr. J. LARKIN (Munich 1960). W. KOLARZ, *Religion in the Soviet Union* (New York 1961). C. DE GRUNWALD, *The Churches and the Soviet Union,* tr. G. J. ROBINSON-PASKEVSKY (New York 1962). N. STRUVE, *Les Chrétiens en URSS* (Paris 1963). *Eastern Christianity and Politics in the Twentieth Century,* ed. P. RAMET (Durham, NC 1988). S. P. RAMET, *Nihil Obstat: Religion, Politics, and Social Change in East-Central Europe and Russia* (Durham, NC 1998). A. WILSON, *The Ukraininians: Unexpected Nation* (New Haven, CT 2000).

[P. SHELTON]

UKRAINIAN CATHOLIC CHURCH (EASTERN CATHOLIC)

At the time of the Council of Nicaea (325) there was already a Church in the kingdom of the Bosporus on the north shores of the Black Sea. Arian Christianity was at that time spread among the Goths in Southern Ukraine. According to recent discoveries the first mission of Saints CYRIL and METHODIUS extended from the Black Sea to Kiev (*c.* 843–62). Photius stated that in 867 there was already a bishop in Rus. But official Christianization of Kievan-Rus, according to the mind of that time, took place when the ruler of the country, (Saint) Olga, was baptized in 955. Her grandson (Saint) Vladimir (baptized in Korsun, Crimea, 988) spread Christianity throughout the whole country.

Recent studies show that the immediate influence on that Church came not from Byzantium directly, but from Bulgaria. Just as the Bulgarian Church tried to have its own autonomous patriarch or at least an archbishop major, so did the Church in Kiev. The liturgical and canonical books also came from Bulgaria. There are Slavonic translations of Byzantine sources, such as the Nomocanon of Saint Methodius [Nomocanon (NC) of 50 titles—*Ustiuzhska Kormcha*], and even of the Nomocanon of 14 titles of the first (pre-Photian) redaction (*Ye-*

Ruthenian children in Sunday clothing, waiting for church, c. 1920, Tedevlja, Carpatho-Ukraine, USSR. (© Scheuffler Collection/CORBIS)

fremivska Kormcha). The relations between Church and State were based upon the Church Statutes issued by Prince (Saint) VLADIMIR and his son Yaroslav. Even if the origin of these documents is of a later time, the law they express was from the era of these princes. The first cathedral, built in Kiev by (Saint) Vladimir, was called the church of tithes (Desyatynna), because tithes were paid to it. The first metropolitan of Kiev, Ivan, appointed about 1008, was of Greek origin; the first metropolitan of Ukrainian origin was Ilarion (1051), author of *On the Law and Grace.*

After the Great Schism of 1054 (*see* EASTERN SCHISM), the Metropolitan See of Kiev changed hands between those friendly and those opposed to Rome. In the beginning of the 12th century Kievan metropolitans, mostly of Greek origin, alienated Kiev from Rome, but in neither the 12th century nor the 13th did the Church of Rus-Ukraine officially break off communion with the See of Rome.

The attack of the Tatars in eastern Europe brought the Ukraine nearer to the Apostolic See (e.g., the participation of the Metropolitan Peter in the Council of Lyons 1245; the mission of John Piano de Carpini 1245 to 1246; the coronation of King Daniel with a crown sent to him by Pope Innocent IV, 1253). Under the Tatars the Church was respected and its rights guaranteed by the decrees (*yarlycs*) of the Khans.

To restore the discipline broken under the yoke of the Tatars, Metropolitan Cyril III convoked a synod at

Exterior view of Ukrainian Catholic Church, Lexington, New York. (© Nik Wheeler/CORBIS)

Vladimir (1274), where the *Kormcha Knyha* was accepted as the official collection of the Slavic Nomocanon. The *Kormcha Knyha* was composed by the Serbian Archbishop Sava and came to the Ukraine from Bulgaria, through Prince Jacob Sviatoslavych, who was of Ukrainian origin. This canonical source underwent a double redaction, namely, Serbian and Ukrainian. The latter, with additions of sources of local origin [such as the constitution of Saint Vladimir, Niphonts' answers, some parts of *Pravda Ruska,* the *Pravylo* (rule) of Metropolitan Cyrill III], became the main canonical source for all Slavic Churches.

The fall of the first Ukrainian state (1349) brought chaos into the ecclesiastical situation in the UKRAINE, mostly because of an ardent propagandizing of Latin Catholicism emanating chiefly from the Latin metropolitanate. In the canonical field some new sources were obtained at this time: *Mirylo Pravednoie* (The Just Measure), a manual for judges composed of two parts, (1) instructions about just and unjust judgments, (2) 30 chapters taken mostly from the Ukrainian *Kormcha;* and the *Instructions,* which entered into the *Kormcha.*

Some hope for bringing order into Church relationships in the Ukraine was given by the Union of Florence (1439), in which the Kievan Metropolitan Isidore (1436–41) played a prominent part; this was an attempt to reconcile the Churches with due respect for the religious cultures of both. The immediate result of this union was the formation of the metropolitanate of Moscow (1448) and therefore, the division of the Kievan metropolitanate into two parts: the Kievan for the Ukraine and Byelorussia (1458), and the independent Muscovite, which also broke from Constantinople (1459). In the Polish-Lithuanian state the charter of King Ladislaus III (1443) acknowledged the Oriental clergy as equal to the Latin, but relations with Rome were terminated from the time of Metropolitan of Kiev, Joseph Bolharynovych (1501). His successor Jona abolished the decree against the Orthodox (1504). The next metropolitan, Joseph II Soltan (1507–21), wanted to introduce some reforms in the Ukrainian Orthodox Church at the synod of Wilno (1509), but they were never carried out. He also obtained from the Polish King a charter (1519) by which the rights of Kievan metropolitans over the whole Church, bishops, clergy, and monks, were acknowledged. This charter recalled the old constitutions of Kievan princes and was useful later for the Kievan Catholic metropolitans.

By right of patronage belonging to the Polish king, the highest spiritual posts were assigned to the laity, who were often unworthy. Monasticism fell into complete disorder and the secular clergy were uneducated. The Ukrainian Orthodox Church found itself under pressure from Latin Catholicism, as reformed by the Council of Trent, and from Protestantism. In the midst of this situation the leaders of the Ukrainian people came to the conclusion that the only feasible solution was communion with Rome. This was the origin of the Union of Brest Litovsk (1595–96). Prince Kostantin Ostrozhsky, with the papal legate Possevino, and Ipaty Potiy, with other bishops of the Metropolitanate of Kiev, had prepared the ground for this union. In 1594 in a secret meeting they decided to send to Rome Bps. Ipaty Potiy and Kyrylo Terletsky. In the autumn of 1595 these two legates, in the name of the Kievan Metropolitan Michael Rahoza and other bishops, submitted the Ecclesiastical Province of Kiev to the Roman pontiff. Pope Clement VIII issued two important documents at that time: the bull of union *Magnus Dominus,* Dec. 23, 1595, and the apostolic letter *Decet Romanum Pontificem,* Feb. 23, 1595. A concession was made to the Kievan metropolitans to appoint and consecrate bishops of the Kievan province without recourse to the Holy See. But the Pope wanted the formal act of union to be performed in the synod of bishops, which was held in Brest-Litovsk (1596). In the same ciity, at the same time, anothe synod was held by the opponents to the union, among whom were two bishops and Prince Ostrozhsky. This opposing faction then became the Orthodox Church in the Province of Kiev.

The History of Union (1596 to 1839). In this period of its history the Ukrainian Catholic Church was most expansive and had a rich canonical evolution, but it had many struggles. In 1620 the patriarch of Antioch, Theophanes, under the protection of Ukrainian Cossacks, consecrated Job Boretsky as the Orthodox metropolitan and consecrated also other bishops, among whom was Meletius Smotrytsky, learned and famous at that time. The Polish Catholics of the Latin Church were discouraged about even the possibility of the union; even Rome was in doubt. But the martyrdom of (Saint) Josaphat Kuntsevych, Bishop of Polotsk (1623), helped stabilize the union. In fact Bishop Meletius Smotrytsky became a Catholic (1624). At the end of that century the bishoprics of Galicia, Peremyshl in 1692 (led by Bishop Innocent Wynnytsky), and Lvov in 1700 (led by Bishop Joseph Shumlansky), as well as the bishopric of Lutsk in 1702 (led by Bishop Dionysius Zhabokrytsky), were reunited with Rome. Even in the Carpatho-Ukraine, a union was concluded in Uzhhorod (1646).

Along with the burden of expanding the union, the bishops were faced with the task of internal organization. The first two metropolitans, Rahoza and Potiy, were occupied primarily with defending the union; polemic literature of that time abounded. The real internal organization of the whole Church was the task of later metropolitans, among the most famous of whom was Joseph Velamin Rutsky.

Other metropolitans (as Sielava, Kolenda, Zhokhovsky) had to defend the union against the attacks of the Orthodox, especially during the Ukrainian people's insurrection for independence under Hetman Bohdan Khmelnytsky in 1648. The defeatist attitude of Polish Catholics concerning the future of the union was often the object of Polish political bargain. In those turbulent times the interior life of this Church was also in disorder. There were dissensions between the hierarchy and the Basilian Order, caused by the metropolitan's seeking to be elected protoarchimandrite of the order. The many letters and decrees of the Roman Curia sought to resolve these dissensions.

After all these troubles the union in the Ukraine and in White Ruthenia was strengthened internally, especially by the synod of Zamost (1720, approved in specific form by Pope Benedict XIII 1724), which became the common law for the whole Ukrainian (Ruthenian) rite. In general

the 18th century can be considered as the golden era of that union. Two-thirds of Ukrainian and Byelorussian people (about 11 million) were Catholic. West of the Dnieper River, union of the Orthodox Church with the Church of Rome was prevalent. In this expansion and development of the union the Basilians and their publications played a large part. The Basilian colleges, which rivaled those of the Jesuits and the Piarites, performed a great cultural mission to students from Russia, Moldavia, Rumenia, and Bulgaria.

Destruction of Union under Russia (1839). At the end of the 18th century the union in the Ukraine was endangered by the interference of RUSSIA in dismembering POLAND. Russia made use of the Haydamak Rebellion (1768), a social revolution, to persecute the union. To suppress the rebellion, the Russian armies invaded the Ukraine and carried out a purge against the union. The partitions of Poland (1772, 1793, 1795) placed under Russian rule all the parts of the Ukraine and White Ruthenia inhabited by Ukrainian Catholics, except Galicia, which passed under Austria and Carpatho-Ukraine. The suppression of the union under Russia was started by Empress CATHERINE II. Metropolitan Rostotsky was taken to Petersburg, other bishops were expelled from their sees, except the bishop of Polotsk, Heraclius Lisowsky, famous for his initiation of liturgical reforms (1785–95). After the death of Catherine II (1796), two Catholic eparchies were restored for the Ukrainians in Lutsk and Brest and in general an alleviation of persecution existed under Czar Paul I (1796–1801) and his successor ALEXANDER I (1801–25). A new and decisive suppression of the union in the Russian Empire was carried out by Czar NICHOLAS I (1825–55), using for this purpose three bishops, Siemashko, Luzhynsky, and Zubko, who formally transferred to the Russian Orthodox Church (1839). Under the rule of the czar there remained in union with Rome only the eparchy of Kholm, which was located in the territory of the autonomous Polish Kingdom; even this was suppressed in 1875 after the Polish revolt of 1863 to 1864.

The Ukrainian Metropolitanate of Galicia (1807 to 1946). In Galicia, which in the partition of Poland became a part of Austria (1772), the Ukrainian Catholic Church, whose membership comprised almost the total Ukrainian population, was highly developed. The metropolitan See of Halych-Lvov, reestablished by the bull of Pope Pius VII (Feb. 24, 1807), inspired a new life in this part of the Ukrainian Catholic Church. Outstanding metropolitans headed the reorganization and evolution of Catholic life, e.g., Cardinal Michael Levytsky (1816–58), Cardinal Sylvester Sembratovych (1882–99), Andrew Sheptytsky (1901–1944), and Joseph Slipyj, Archbishop Major (1944–). The Austrian government gave to the Ukrainian Catholics a special name, ''Greek Catholics,'' which is a misnomer. There were three eparchies (Lvov, Peremyshl, and Stanislaviv) and in 1934 the eparchy of Peremyshl was split in two parts by the erection of the Apostolic Administration of Lemkivshchyna. Each eparchy had its own major seminary, and in Lvov, Metropolitan A. Sheptytsky founded the Theological Academy (1928), directed by Joseph Slipyj. Even the chapters of canons were erected in each diocesan see in Austria. The Basilian Order (1882), renewed under Jesuit guidance, cooperated in the development of Catholic life in that province (both religous men and women). Missions, editorial work, and schools were administered by them. Studites (founded by Metropolitan A. Sheptytsky) as well as a Ukrainian branch of the Redemptorists were active. Several congregations of Sisters have been founded: Studites (1921); Servants of Mary Immaculate (1892); of the Holy Family (1912); of Saint Josaphat (1911); of Saint Joseph (1894); and Myrophores (1910).

Under the same Austro-Hungarian Empire, Carpatho Catholic life in Carpatho-Ukraine was concentrated in Uzhhorod, to which the bishopric see was transferred by Bishop Andrew Bachynsky (1772–1809). A theological seminary was founded there also. In 1816 in the western part of this diocese there was erected a separate Diocese of Pryashiv in Slovakia from the former separate vicariate.

In Hungary the Diocese of Hajdudorog (1912) for Hungarians and the Apostolic Exarchate in Miskolc (1923) for Carrpatho-Ukrainans were erected For Ukrainian emigrants, Croatians and Macedonians, the Diocese of Krizhevtsi (1777) was erected in Yugoslavia.

Destruction of Union in Galicia and Carpatho-Ukraine. Russia looked upon Galicia with hostile eyes even during World War I, and in the temporary occupation of Galicia in 1914 the Russians incarcerated Metropolitan A. Sheptytsky in a monastery of Suzdal (Russia).

In World War II the Communists, after final occupation of Galicia and Carpatho-Ukraine, determined to destroy completely the union in that area. In 1945 the Bolsheviks, after the death of Metropolitan A. Sheptytsky, arrested his successor Joseph Slipyj and all bishops ordinaries and auxiliaries: Hryhory Khomyshyn, Ordinary of Stanislaviv; Josaphat Kotsylovsky, Ordinary of Peremyshl; Nykyta Budka, Auxiliary of Lvov; Hryhory Lakota, Auxiliary of Peremyshl; and Mykola Charnetsky, Apostolic Visitor in Volynia. They all died except Slipyj who was liberated after 18 years of prison in Siberia and went to live in Rome (1963); he was elevated to the rank of cardinal by Pope Paul VI in February 1965. The clergy who refused to accept Orthodoxy were arrested and deported or shot. But even worse, the Communists called a mock synod at Lvov in 1946, composed of some terrorized priests, who proclaimed the union with Rome made in BrestLitovsk in 1596 null and void.

In a similar way the Communists destroyed the Catholic Church in Carpatho-Ukraine. Bishop Theodor Romzha of Mukachevo was killed in 1947, and Bishop Paul Goydych, a Basilian of Pryashiv, as well as his auxiliary, Bishop Basil Hopko, were imprisoned in Slovakia. P. Goydych died in prison in 1960. In both Galicia and Carpatho-Ukraine a new Orthodox hierarchy was imposed by the patriarch of Moscow. Not one Ukrainian Catholic bishop passed over to Orthodoxy. Whatever the role that the Moscow Patriarchate played in the suppression of the Ukrainian Catholic Church, relations between the Catholics and the Orthodox became highly poisoned. From 1945 to the 1980s, the Ukrainian Catholic Church survived as an underground church, their clergy and faithful harassed and persecuted for refusing to join the officially sanctioned Orthodox Church.

In the wake of the 1980s glasnost that President Gorbachev initiated, the Ukrainian Catholic Church emerged from the underground and were allowed to register as a church on Dec. 1, 1989. Their faith strengthened, many closet Ukrainian Catholics emerged and new churches were opened. In many places, after much persistence the Ukrainian Catholic Church managed to repossess some of their church properties, which had been handed over to the Orthodox Church. As the situation improved, the Major Archbishop of the Ukrainian Catholic Church, who was living in exile in Rome, was able to return to the archiepiscopal seat in Lviv. Since then, church life has grown by leaps and bounds. To cope with this growth, the Archepiscopal Exarchate of Kiev-Vyshhorod was established in April 1996, covering central and eastern Ukraine. The Ukrainian Catholic Church also received a big boost with the visit of Pope John Paul II to Ukraine in 2001.

Ukrainian Catholics in North America. There is a large Ukrainian Catholic diaspora in the United States, comprising four dioceses and 209 parishes. The Metropolitan See of Philadelphia is the principal Ukrainian Catholic See in the United States.

Bibliography: A. M. AMMANN, *Abriss der ostslawischen Kirchengeschichte* (Vienna 1950). A. BARAN, *Metropolia Kiovensis et Eparchia Mukačoviensis* (Analecta Ordinis S. Basilii Magni, ser.2, sec.1, v.10; 2d ed. Rome 1960). B. BOYSAK, *The Fate of the Holy Union in Carpatho-Ukraine* (New York 1963). T. HALUŠČYNSKYJ and M. M. WOJNAR, eds., *Acta Innocentii Pp. IV* (Sacra Congregazione Orientale, *Codificazione orientale, Fonti* (Rome 1930–), ser. 3, v. 4.1; 1962). M. HARASIEWICZ, *Annales ecclesiae Ruthenae* (Lvov 1862). E. HERMAN, *De fontibus iuris ecclesiastici Russorum* (*Codificazione orientale, Fonti*, ser. 2, fasc. 6; 1936). G. HOFMANN, *Die Wiedervereinigung der Ruthenen*, pt.1 of *Ruthenica*, 3 pts. (Oriontalia Christiana, v. 3.2, no.12; Rome 1925). H. D. HOLOVECK-YJ, *Fontes iuris canonici ecclesiae Ruthenae* (*Codificazione orien-*

tale, Fonti 8; 1932) 585–646. M. LACKO, "The Forced Liquidation of the Union of Uzhorod," *Slovak Studies* I, *Historica* 1 (1961) 145–85. J. PELESZ, *Geschichte der Union der ruthenischen Kirche mit Rom,* 2 v. (Vienna 1878–81). I. WLASOVSKY, *Outline of the History of the Ukrainian Church* (New York 1956–), in Ukrainian and English. I. PATRYLO, *Archiepiscopi-metropolitani Kievohalicienses* (Analecta Ordinis S. Basilii Magni, ser. 2, sec.1, v. 16; 2d ed. Rome 1962). B. PEKAR, *De erectione canonica eparchiae Mukačoviensis (an. 1717) (ibid.,* ser. 2, sec. 1, v. 7; 2d ed. 1956). S. TOMAŠIVSKYJ, *An Introduction to the History of the Church in the Ukraine (ibid.* v.4, fasc.1–2; 1931), in Ukrainian. A. G. WELYKYJ, *Documenta pontificum romanorum historiam Ucrainae illustrantia,* 2 v. *(ibid.* ser. 2, sec. 3, v.1–2; 1953–54). M. M. WOJNAR, *De regimine Basilianorum Ruthenorum a Metropolita J. V. Rutskyj instauratorum* (Rome 1949); "The Code of Oriental Canon Law *De Ritibus Orientalibus* and *De Personis,*" *Jurist* 19.4 (1959). R. ROBERSON, *The Eastern Christian Churches: A Brief Survey* (6th ed. Rome 1999).

[M. M. WOJNAR/EDS.]

ULFILAS

Fourth-century bishop and apostle of the Goths; b. probably Cappadocia, *c.* 311; d. Constantinople, 382 or 383. Of a Cappadocian Christian family captured by the GOTHS, Ulfilas (Gothic, Wulfila) was a lector in a Gothic community, and in 337 was sent as part of an embassy to Constantinople, where EUSEBIUS OF NICOMEDIA consecrated him as a missionary bishop. After seven years of activity north of the Danube (*c.* 341–348), he found refuge in the Roman Empire when a persecution of the Christians was inaugurated by the chieftain Athanaric. On his return to the Balkan mountain country, he served as both spiritual and civil leader for 30 years, exercising his missionary zeal on both sides of the imperial borders. He translated the Bible (probably only the New Testament) into the Gothic language. However, he had signed the Homoiousian (the Son is similar to the Father) symbol of Constantinople (360), and as his Confession of Faith (preserved by his biographer Auxentius of Dorostorum) indicates, he adhered to the Arian Creed and was thus a primary source of the Arian faith that characterized the Germanic and Gothic Christian peoples. He died during a synod to which he had been summoned by Theodosius I.

Bibliography: AUXENTIUS OF DOROSTORUM, "Epistola de Fide, vita et obitu Ulfilae," *Patrologiae cursus completus, series latina;* suppl., ed. A. HAMMAN, 1:703–727. G. FRIEDRICHSEN, *The Gothic Version of the Gospels* (London 1926). A. WILMART, "Les Évangiles gothiques," *Revue Biblique* 36 (1927) 46–61. J. MANSION, "Les Origines du christianisme chez les Gots," *Analecta Bollandiana* 33 (1914) 5–30. E. STEIN, *Histoire du Bas-Empire,* tr. J. R. PALANQUE, 2 v. in 3 (Paris 1949–59) 1:186. K. D. SCHMIDT, *Die Bekehrung der Ostgermanen zum Christentum* (Göttingen 1939). E. A. THOMPSON, "The Date of the Conversion of the Visigoths," *Journal of Ecclesiastical History* 7 (1956) 1–11. P. WACKWITZ, *Die*

William Bernard Ullathorne.

Religion in Geschichte und Gegenwart, 7 v. (3rd ed. Tübingen 1957–65) 6:1831.

[F. X. MURPHY]

ULLATHORNE, WILLIAM BERNARD

Benedictine monk and archbishop; b. Pocklington, Yorkshire, England, May 7, 1806; d. Oscott, Warwickshire, March 21, 1889. His family was one of yeoman farmers who remained Catholic throughout the period of penal laws. William traced his descent from St. THOMAS MORE. He was a cabin boy in his youth, but dissatisfaction with seafaring led to his entering the Benedictine priory at DOWNSIDE (1823), where he received the religious habit 12 months later. Following ordination in 1830 he taught for a short period before sailing in 1832 for AUSTRALIA as vicar-general to Bishop Morris, OSB. Here he worked assiduously among the colonists and convicts for ten years, with occasional visits to Rome, Ireland, and England on mission affairs. His pamphlet, *Horrors of Transportation,* is regarded as a classic indictment of the complacency of British government. After a breakdown in health, Ullathorne returned home and took charge of the mission at Coventry. His name was proposed as bishop, first of Hobart Town, then of Adelaide, and finally of

Perth, but he never returned to the Australian mission. In 1846 he was nominated vicar apostolic of the western district of England. Two years later he was transferred to the central district. In his autobiography, Ullathorne relates his early determination never to rest until the hierarchy was restored to England. Indeed, he was the leading protagonist of the cause at Rome. In 1850 he became the first bishop of Birmingham, where he resided until his resignation in 1888. He was then made titular archbishop of Cabasa. His role was a leading one in most of the social and religious movements of his day. He wrote many pamphlets on matters of moment, his *Döllingerites* and *Mr. Gladstone's Expostulation Unravelled* being especially noteworthy. His correspondence during attendance at VATICAN COUNCIL I proved an important historical source, utilized by Edward Cuthbert BUTLER as the backbone of his history of this synod.

Bibliography: W. B. ULLATHORNE, *From Cabin-boy to Archbishop* (London 1941), autobiography. E. C. BUTLER, *The Life and Times of Bishop Ullathorne, 1806–1889,* 2 v. (London 1926). M. F. GLANCEY, *Characteristics from the Writings of Archbishop Ullathorne* (London 1889).

[V. A. MCCLELLAND]

ULLERSTON, RICHARD

Theologian, conciliarist; b. Lancashire, England; d. Chilmark, Wiltshire, England, 1423. He was fellow of Queen's College, Oxford, 1391 to 1402; chancellor's commissary, 1407–08; canon of Salisbury and prebendary of Axford from 1416; rector of Chilmark from June 1423. In 1407–08, at the request of Robert HALLUM, bishop of Salisbury, he drew up 16 *Petitiones pro ecclesiae militantis reformatione,* which were the basis of the English bishops' reform movement at the Council of PISA. They were later used as a model for the Oxford Petitions to the Council of CONSTANCE, were quoted at Constance, and were used in the *Reformatoria.* He also wrote a treatise on knighthood, *De officio militari,* for Prince Henry of Monmouth, later Henry V, and the *Defensorium dotacionis ecclesiae,* against the attack of the LOLLARDS on Church endowments.

Bibliography: Sources. The fullest account to date, with sources, is A. B. EMDEN, *A Biographical Register of the Scholars of the University of Oxford to A.D. 1500,* 3 v. (Oxford 1957–59) 3:1928–29 and *Bodleian Library Record* 6 (1957–61) 685. *Petitiones,* ed. H. VON DER HARDT, *Magnum Oecumenicum Constantiense Concilium,* 7 v. (Berlin 1700) 1: 1126–70, and *Oxford Petitions* in D. WILKINS, *Concilia Magnae Britanniae et Hiberniae,* 4 v. (London 1737) 3:360–365. *Sermon on St. Osmund,* May 1416, ed. from Ullerston's holograph by A. R. MALDEN in *The Canonization of St. Osmond* (Salisbury 1901), appendix 2:236–242. **Literature.** E. F. JACOB, *Essays in the Conciliar Epoch* (2d ed. Manchester 1953); *The Fifteenth Century 1399–1485* (Oxford 1961).

[T. P. DUNNING]

ULRIC OF AUGSBURG, ST.

German bishop of the Ottonian Reform era; d. Augsburg, July 4, 973. A descendant of the Swabian noble family of Wittislinger, he attended the monastery school at SANKT GALLEN. He then entered the service of his uncle, Bp. Adalbert of Augsburg, who ordained him. After his uncle's death, Ulric administered the estates of his relatives for 15 years. Consecrated bishop in 924, he directed the Diocese of AUGSBURG for half a century. He encouraged liturgical reform in his church, founded (968) St. Stephen's monastery for canonesses, and rebuilt the cathedral, which had been destroyed by fire, and raised KEMPTEN and OTTOBEUREN to abbeys; he led a simple, pious, and charitable life. Ulric traveled to Rome three times on business matters. He was active in his role as an imperial prince and, in greatly aiding the successful defense of Augsburg in 955, contributed to the victory over the Hungarians, for which he was granted the title *Pater patriae,* and became the first German bishop to receive the right to mint coin, from Emperor OTTO I. He was buried in the crypt of the church of St. Afra. His was the first solemn CANONIZATION; it was held in 993 by Pope JOHN XV. His remains were transferred in 1187 to the newly constructed St. Ulric cathedral, where his grave is a pilgrimage site. He is patron saint of the city and Diocese of Augsburg, as well as of pilgrims, the dying, and weavers. He is invoked in many illnesses, and against rat and mouse plagues; an Ulric cross and Ulric waters were thought to protect the user. Ulric is usually portrayed with a fish.

Feast: July 4.

Bibliography: *Acta Sanctorum* July 2:73–135. *Monumenta Germaniae Historica* (Berlin 1826–) Scriptores 4:377–425. A. BIGELMAIR, *Lexikon für Theologie und Kirche,* ed. M. BUCHBERGER, 10 v. (Freiburg 1930–38) 10: 365–368. F. L. CROSS, *The Oxford Dictionary of the Christian Church* (London 1957) 1387. R. BAUERREISS, *Kirchengeschichte Bayerns* (2d ed. Munich 1958–) v.2. P. DÖRFLER, *St. Ulrich der grosse Bischof. . .*(2d ed. Augsburg 1955). F. ZOEPFL, *Das Bistum Augsburg und seine Bischöfe im Mittelalter* (Munich 1956). W. WOLF, *Von der Ulrichsvita zur Ulrichslegende* (Munich 1967). BERNO VON REICHENAU, *Das Leben des Heiligen Ulrich,* ed. K.–E. GEITH (Berlin 1971). W. PÖTZL, *Bischof Ulrich und seine Zeit* (Augsburg 1973). G. STEINBAUER, *St. Ulrich, Patron des Bistums Augsburg: Untersuchungen zur Ulrichslegende* (s.l. 1981).

[A. KRAUSE]

ULRIC OF STRASSBURG

Also Ulrich Engelberti, Dominican philosopher and theologian; b. early 13th century; d. Paris, 1278?. He studied at Cologne between 1248 and 1252 under ALBERT THE GREAT, with whom he had a close, filial relationship, as shown by his letters. At Strassburg he lectured for many years amid great literary activity. From 1272 to 1277 he was provincial of the German province. He was next sent to Paris to lecture on the *Sentences* and to obtain the degree of master, but it seems he died before achieving this.

Ulric's chief work is the *Summa theologiae* or *Summa de summo bono,* usually referred to as the *Summa de bono.* This is not devoted exclusively to the supreme good, but is a summary of theology and philosophy that dates from the same period as the *Summa* of THOMAS AQUINAS. While lacking the systematic unity of Aquinas's work, it shows progress over earlier *summae* in organization and plan. Projected in eight books, it was completed only to the fifth treatise of the sixth book. It has never been completely edited or printed; no manuscripts of the last two books exist, but there are indications they were written. The earlier books are largely a commentary on the *De divinis nominibus* and show Ulric's acquaintance with the principal Neoplatonic writings. They are of great interest to historians of thought and are especially noteworthy as a link between Albert and the later Rhineland mystics. The *Summa de bono* had great popularity in the 15th century.

Ulric also wrote commentaries on the *Sentences* and a book on meteors, but both are lost. Extant are a sermon in Old German and 25 letters, mostly of the period of his provincialate, and thus of value for Dominican history. A treatise on the soul is doubtfully ascribed to him, while a book on conscience is usually considered his.

Bibliography: É. H. GILSON, *History of Christian Philosophy in the Middle Ages.* P. GLORIEUX, *Répertoire des maîtres en théologie de Paris au XIIIe siècle* 1:148–151. L. THOMAS (C. J. FAGIN), "Ulrich of Strasbourg: His Doctrine of the Divine Ideas," *Modern Schoolman* 30 (November 1952) 21–32. C. PUTNAM, "Ulrich of Strasbourg and the Aristotelian Causes," *Studies in Philosophy and the History of Philosophy* 1 (1961) 139–159.

[J. F. HINNEBUSCH]

ULRIC OF ZELL, ST.

Cluniac monk; b. Regensburg, Germany, 1029; d. Zell, Germany, July 14, 1093. A godson of Emperor HENRY III, Ulric was trained and educated in the Abbey of SANKT EMMERAM, served in the court chapel of the emperor, and came to be archdeacon and provost in Freising. Ulric took part in the emperor's march on Rome (1046) and then made a pilgrimage to Palestine. On his return he disposed of all his possessions and, after a second visit to Rome, became a monk at CLUNY in 1061. After short terms of office as prior in three different monasteries, Ulric became in 1078 prior of the new foun-

dation in Grüningen near Freiburg im Breisgau. He moved this abbey, today known as Sankt Ulrich, to a more advantageous location at Zell (1087), and it is here that he was buried. His feast has been celebrated since 1139. Between 1079 and 1087, Ulric composed, at the suggestion of WILLIAM OF HIRSAU, the *Antiquiores consuetudines monasterii Cluniacensis* (*Patrologia Latina,* ed. J. P. Migne, 217 v., indexes 4 v. [Paris 1878–90] 149:635–778), which gives an important insight into the internal organization of the Abbey of Cluny during this period.

Feast: July 14.

Bibliography: *Acta Sanctorum* July 3:142–161. *Vita, Monumenta Germaniae Historica* (Berlin 1826–) Scriptores, 12:249–253. A. M. ZIMMERMANN, *Kalendarium Benedictinum: Die Heiligen und Seligen des Benediktinerorderns und seiner Zweige,* 4 v. (Metten 1933–38) 2:451–454. K. HALLINGER, *Gorze-Kluny,* 2 v. (*Studia anselmiana* [Rome 1933–] fasc. 22–25; 1950–51). A. ZIMMERMANN, *Lexikon für Theologie und Kirche,* ed. M. BUCHBERGER, 10 v. (Freiburg 1930–38) 10:370–371. A. BUTLER, *The Lives of the Saints,* rev. ed. H. THURSTON and D. ATTWATER, 4v. (New York 1956) 3:101.

[L. KURRAS]

ULTRAMONTANISM

A term created in the nineteenth century (jointly with its dialectic opponent Gallicanism) to describe the defenders of the Roman vision of the papacy (from the other side of the Alps) against the German or French national conception. In the Middle Ages, as papal claims to power and authority became more precise and also more extreme, they were backed by canonists and theologians from all countries who might well be called "proto-ultramontanes," but it is only in later controversies that this designation is fully operative, as they dealt not only with ecclesiological particulars but two visions of Catholicism. This "early ultramontanism" represented the concern to maintain or restore a strong Catholic identity by focusing on the Roman center and developing common features susceptible to reunite and expand Christendom. Therefore, to the defense of Roman prerogatives and pyramidal ecclesiology was associated a forceful missionary program. In this perspective there is a direct continuity between post-Tridentine "Romanism" and nineteenth-century Ultramontanism.

Romanism. Already in the later sessions of TRENT, a majority of bishops realized the necessity to quiet down their objections and fully support papal authority. At their request the reform movement that followed the council was clearly under the leadership of the popes and under the control of their reorganized administration; it could not but stress the bonds between the local church and the Apostolic See. This perspective was accepted by most, who saw in it a guarantee of unity and success. The impressive Catholic renewal that marked the seventeenth century was therefore inspired by a new attachment to the papacy. Especially in countries where Protestants were nearby, such as France and Germany, there was a tendency to stress the constitutive notes of the church including that of "romanitas." In France, the reforming prelates, Du Perron, La Rochefoucault, the reformers of old religious orders and the founders of new forms of apostolate, Bérulle, J. Eudes, V. DePaul, J. J. Olier, were all "Romans," in the sense that they emphasized the authority of the papacy and welcomed its intervention. Though this conviction was propagated by international religious orders, especially the Jesuits, in most cases it was accepted without any resistance. Far from being a bullwark of Gallicanism, the Faculty of Theology of Paris, where the elite of the French clergy was educated, represented a conflictual place, where an ultramontane majority confronted a Richerist or Gallican minority.

This "Romanism" has not been investigated in itself but only in the context of the growth of "GALLICANISM," which is understandable as it expressed itself mostly in these polemical circumstances. It was, however, an important and rather homogeneous movement, as its main features demonstrate.

A strong hierarchical system, that defends Roman prerogatives and strives to extend them [M. Mauclerc, *De Monarchia divina ecclesiastica* (Paris 1622)]. Papal primacy is clearly established, together with the exclusivity of doctrinal pronouncement. Papal INFALLIBILITY is also present, conceived more as a form of direct inspiration than protection from error. As a result of the Jansenist controversy, it has a great extension, including "dogmatic facts" [M. Grandin, *Opera theologica*, (Paris 1710–1712)]. On the other hand—this is the major difference with the Roman schools—there is no claim to direct or even indirect authority over the secular power. Thus the Gallican "distinction of powers" is tacitly admitted (Censure of Santarelli, 1626). The best presentation is in the *Tractatus de Libertatibus Ecclesiæ gallicanæ* by A. Charlas (Paris, 1682), a refutation of the Four Gallican Articles. It also develops important theological reflections, including the notion of dogmatic progress.

A clerical and authoritarian Catholicism that restrains access by the laity to the Bible or Liturgy. In adopting the *regulæ* of the Roman Index, it practically forbade any translation of normative texts: Scripture and Liturgy, but also philosophy (*Summa* of Th. Aquinas), or theology (including the documents of Trent). This attitude was directly in opposition to that of the Jansenists, who favored such an access.

A festive and sociable Catholicism. The clear differentiation between the tasks of the cleric and those of the layman is compensated by the involvement of all in the mission of the church. This is realized by the diverse associations or sodalities, such as the famous *Compagnie du Saint-Sacrement*, and the structuring of a religious life focused on the identity of the company: chapel, protector saint, specific pilgrimage.

A devotional and charitable Catholicism. This associative life is the starting point of a process of personal and collective sanctification at once educational, moralizing, and charitable. This aspect is better known through recent investigation of sodalities or *congrégations* in the *Europe of the Devouts* [L. Châtellier]. The features of "ultramontane piety" influenced by southern Europe, are clearly in evidence: an emotional and intense spirituality, attached to particular Marian devotions or devotions to the Sacred Heart.

An expansionist Catholicism. Another component of this attitude is a concurrent opposition to any religious toleration and a strong conversion venture. It is not a surprise that the first missionary endeavors of the time, associating clergy and laity, in close link with Rome's *Propaganda fide*, were born in this context (Missions Étrangères de Paris, 1658).

Though they did not openly express an ideology, all these components were specific enough to prepare its formulation. In addition, if the opposition raised in most Catholic countries by this vision forced its adherents to keep a low profile, it was never destroyed. It survived the suppression of the Society of Jesus and was able to resist and counter the Catholic Enlightenment in its various forms—a stand that the papacy started to acknowledge and encourage in the last decades of the 18th century. But it was undeniably the FRENCH REVOLUTION, both in its discrediting Gallicanism and in its reinforcing the spiritual authority of the pope, that allowed for an aggressive revival of Ultramontanism.

Ultramontanism. The advance of anti-Roman theories during the eighteenth century did not go without resistance, and, especially in Italy, the defenders of papal authority (Zaccharia, Cucagni, Marchetti, Anfossi, Ballerini, Cappelari) produced apologetic refutations that would become influential in the next century. The pope also prepared the future in the precise condemnations of every attack against his jurisdiction (Censures of Febronius, 1764; *Responsio super Nunciaturis,* 1789; *Auctorem Fidei* against the Synod of Pistoia, 1794). But it was in the new generations that new forms of Ultramontanism took shape. Rejecting the principles of the French Revolution in which they saw the realization of a process started by the Protestant Reformation and intensified by the Enlightenment, the "Traditionalists," de Bonald and de Maistre, stressed the necessity of an irrecusable authority, which they placed in the papacy. On the other side, it was because of Gallicanism's allegiance to liberal principles that Lamennais and his disciples rejected it and placed their hopes in a renewed papacy. Closer to early popular Ultramontanism, strengthened by the revolutionary trials, was the group lead by L. Veuillot, which expressed itself in the daily *L'Univers*. Lamennais' condemnation (1832) and the encyclical *Quanta Cura* (1864) detached from that movement the majority of the liberal Catholics, who joined a "neo-Gallican" episcopalist faction. The others (P. Guéranger) reinforced the Ultramontane party, bringing with them theological savvy and eager zeal. With more and more explicit support of Rome they launched a wide offensive against the remnants of Gallicanism: substituting diocesan liturgical books with Roman ones, correcting historical and theological class-books, soon replacing them with more adequate editions. The encyclical *Inter muliplices* (March 1853) marked a direct involvement of PIUS IX in favor of this centralizing effort. His intervention responded to the expectations of many, against the reservations of isolated bishops and theologians. It encouraged what has been called "neo-ultramontanism," to distinguish it from the doctrine proclaimed at Vatican I: an extreme exaltation of the Roman Pontiff, associated with a high interpretation of his infallibility, closer to direct inspiration than inerrancy. With interesting variations, it can be found in all Catholic countries, with the uncompromising and prejudiced traits well illustrated by *L'Univers*. The discussion of these themes at VATICAN I allowed for a beneficial reflection. The constitution *Pastor Aeternus* that resulted did affirm papal primacy and infallibility, but did not follow the more extreme Ultramontanes in their interpretation.

Four features appear constitutive of 19th-century Ultramontanism:

Ecclesiology. A rather weak theology that forsakes the supernatural and "mysterical" conception of the Roman School (Passaglia, Schrader, Franzelin, Perrone) in favor of a juridical interpretation. The church is founded upon the pope, principle of its unity.

Spirituality. The expression "Ultramontane piety" is used to define a popular and festive religion that accentuates the traits of baroque piety of the early centuries. It represents an integration of local traditions, formerly considered superstitious or pagan, an honoring of miraculous saints and relics, an evolution of the devotions to the Blessed Sacrament, the Sacred Heart, and the Virgin, into a more emotional and penitential type of piety. A great interest in the supernatural is generally evident, often associated with Marian apparitions (Lourdes 1858). Facilitated by new means of transportation, pilgrimages to old and new shrines are also very successful.

Moral theology. In direct opposition to "Jansenist" rigorism, the moral theology founded by St. ALPHONSUS LIGUORI became during the nineteenth century the official doctrine of the Church. This shift supported a more frequent use of penance and Eucharist, perceived as sources of spiritual strength and food of apostolate.

Apostolate. Under many diversified forms, lay and clerical men and women became involved in the apostolate of the church, thus manifesting both at home and in mission territories a perception of Roman Catholicism as a universal and expanding community.

After Vatican I, the concept of Ultramontanism is only analogical, for instance in the qualification of "integralist" perspectives that arose during the Modernist crisis, or of oppositions to the Vatican II doctrine of collegiality.

See Also: PAPACY; KETTELER, WILHELM EMMANUEL VON; LACORDAIRE, JEAN BAPTISTE HENRI; LAMENNAIS, HUGUES FÉLICITÉ ROBERT DE; MAISTRE, JOSEPH DE; MANNING, HENRY EDWARD; MONTALEMBERT, CHARLES FORBES RENÉ DE; VEUILLOT, LOUIS FRANÇOIS; WARD, WILLIAM GEORGE.

Bibliography: J. VIDAL, *Dans l'entourage de Caulet, III, Antoine Charlas directeur du séminaire et vicaire général de Pamiers, 1634–1698* (Castillon-de-Couserans 1943). A. G. MARTIMORT, *Le gallicanisme de Bossuet* (Paris 1953). J. ORCIBAL, "L'idée d'Église chez les catholiques du XVIIᵉ siècle," in *Études d'histoire et de littérature religieuses* (Paris 1997; org. pub. 1955). M. NÉDONCELLE, ed., *L'ecclésiologie au XIXᵉ siècle* (Paris 1960). H. RAAB, "Zur Geschichte und Bedeutung des Schlagswortes 'Ultramontan' im 18 und frühen 19. Jahrhundert," *Historisches Jahrbuch* 81 (1962), 59–173. J. GUERBER, *Le ralliement du clergé français à la morale liguorienne: l'abbé Gousset et ses précurseurs (1785–1832)* (Rome 1973). H. J. POTTMEYER, *Unfehlbarkeit und Souveränität: Die päpstliche Unfehlbarkeit der ultramonten Ekklesiologie des 19. Jahrhunderts* (Mayence 1975). R. F. COSTIGAN, *Rohrbacher and the Ecclesiology of Ultramontanism* (Rome 1980). U. HORST, *Unfehlbarkeit und Geschichte* (Mayence 1982). T. A. KSELMAN, *Miracles and Prophecies in Nineteenth Century France* (New Brunswick 1983). J. GADILLE, *Les Ultramontains Canadiens français* (Montréal 1985). A. GOUGH, *Paris and Rome: The Gallican Church and the Ultramontane Campaign, 1848–1853* (Oxford 1986). L. CHATELLIER, *Europe of the Devouts* (Cambridge 1989). K. GANZER, "Gallikanische und römische Primatauffassung im widerstreit. Zu den ekklesiologischen Auseinandersetzungen auf dem Konzil von Trient," *Historishe Jahrbuch* 109 (1989) 109–163. B. CHÉDOZEAU, *La Bible et la liturgie en français* (Paris 1990). K. SCHATZ, *Papal Primacy: From Its Origins to the Present* (Collegeville Minn. 1996). M. VÉNARD, "Ultramontane of Gallican? The French Episcopate at the End of the Sixteenth Century," *The Jurist* 52 (1992), 142–161. B. NEVEU, *L'erreur et son juge. Remarques sur les censures doctrinales à l'époque moderne* (Naples 1993). L. CHATELLIER, *The Reli-*

gion of the Poor (Cambridge 1997). J. VON ARX, ed., *Varieties of Ultramontanism* (Washington 1998). J. M. GRES-GAYER, *Le Gallicanisme de Sorbonne 1657–1688* (Paris 2001).

[J. M. GRES-GAYER]

UMAYYADS

Caliphs of the aristocratic Meccan clan of Banū Umayya, who came to power in Syria in 661 A.D., and began the first Islamic dynasty. Because they were unpopular with the pietist element among Muslims, they were destroyed in a general revolution in 750 (*see* 'ABBĀSIDS), but a prince of their house established himself in Spain, where they ruled until 1031A.D..

Rise. The Banū Umayya were the leaders of the pagan oligarchy at MECCA that had opposed the prophet Muḥammad. One of them however, 'Uthmān ibn 'Affān, was a prominent early convert to Islam. (*See* ALI.) After Muḥammad's triumph and the foundation of the Arab empire, 'Uthmān was elected CALIPH (644–656) and gave many of his kinsmen high places.

After 'Uthmān's assassination, his cousin Mu'āwiya ibn Abī Sufyān, the governor of Syria, asserted the right to vengeance and so adroitly directed his struggle against 'Alī that he emerged as caliph in 661. 'Alī's caliphate, important as it was, can thus be regarded as an interlude in events that made the Banū Umayya, former enemies of Muḥammad, his successors.

The base of Umayyad power was the formerly Byzantine Syria, where Mu'āwiya had the loyalty of the half-Christianized Syrian Arabs and the good will of the Syrian Christians, and where he had laid the foundations of Arab sea power in repeated campaigns against the Christian Byzantine Empire. An astute statesman and diplomat, more interested in governing than in religion, he drew heavily on the skills of the Syrian Christians in administering his realm. Iraq, 'Alī's former base, remained a seat of opposition. Mu'āwiya initiated the family policy of leaving the eastern provinces to be governed by determined, semiautonomous henchmen whose methods were not questioned so long as they kept order. Eventually this policy alienated Iraq and Iran from the dynasty.

Mu'āwiya's arrangements were crowned with the recognition of the right of his son to succeed him. This heir, the execrated Yazīd I (680–683), was unlucky enough to be responsible for the death of Husayn ibn 'Alī, the Prophet's surviving grandson. Husayn had tried to raise a rebellion in Iraq at Mu'āwiya's death and was killed in deplorable circumstances at Kerbela in 680 by the viceroy of Iraq. His "martyrdom" furnished the oc-

casion for the emergence of the SHĪ'ITES, and was a rallying point for all who distrusted the "irreligious" Umayyads. After Yazīd's premature death in 683, followed soon by that of his minor son, the Syrian tribes elected their aged cousin Marwān (684–685), the unpopular former secretary of 'Uthmān. His reign was spent in struggle with an anticaliph at MEDINA, son of the Prophet's companion Zubayr, who had once supported and then opposed 'Alī. Marwān's son 'Abd al-Malik (685–705) introduced a policy more Arab and Islamic, in conformity with Muslim public opinion, and discriminated against native Christians, who nevertheless remained influential. The eminent Doctor of the Greek Church, St. JOHN OF DAMASCUS, was reared at the Umayyad court and followed his family's tradition by acting as a high financial official perhaps as late as 726, before retiring to the Monastery of St. Sabas in Palestine.

Under Walīd ibn 'Abd al-Malik (705–715), the empire reached its greatest expansion; eastern Iran and Transoxania, Visigothic Spain and the lower valley of the Indus were conquered by Muslim armies, and the cities of the empire enriched with splendid sanctuaries worthy of an imperial destiny, in contrast to the rusticity of early Islam. Under his brother Sulaymān (715–717), a major attempt to take Constantinople failed.

Decline in the East. At first "Arab" and "Muslim" were synonymous. Converts were accepted often grudgingly, had an inferior status, and were expected to continue paying the tribute. The anti-Umayyad Shī'ites and Kharijites took up the cause of the new Muslims, and despite the objections of the Arab military class, orthodox pietists also insisted that Muslims of whatever origin must all receive equal treatment.

With the Umayyad 'Umar II, son of 'Abd al-'Azīz ibn Marwān, a man of pietist persuasion came to the throne (717–720). For expensive military expansion he substituted remission of the tribute for all converts, resulting in mass conversions, particularly in North Africa and the East. With his death, however, the old policies were resumed, and the now considerable convert element joined in opposition to the dynasty. Moreover, the caliphs had unwisely begun to take sides in the persistent feuds of the Arab tribal factions. The Arab character of the dynasty was always marked: they preferred the carefree life of desert residences to their capital of Damascus.

The fiscal policies of Hishām (724–743) brought local uprisings, and the profligacy of his nephew, Walīd II (743–744), pushed the dynasty into the abyss. A revolt of the Syrian Arabs cost Walīd his life; religious and tribal revolts broke out on every hand as a reflection of the family failure to adjust the simple patriarchal and tribal system they had inherited, either to the needs of the vast and cosmopolitan society growing up under them, or to ISLAM as a religion. Islam made universal claims and had gained in subtlety of expression through contacts with other creeds. It appeared briefly that a relative, the governor of Armenia, Marwān II (744–750), would restore order; but when he had exhausted himself in victories, a new general revolt engineered by the 'Abbāsids for "a leader of the Prophet's family" destroyed his power and his life, and a general extermination of the Umayyads followed.

Umayyads in Spain. A grandson of Hishām, 'Abd al-Raḥmān, managed to escape to the distant disorderly province of SPAIN, where he obtained military support and founded a flourishing kingdom. Under the Umayyads of Córdoba, Muslim Spain became the seat of a brilliant civilization, so that in 929 these princes were emboldened to fulfill their old dream of reclaiming the imperial title of the caliphate. This second caliphate collapsed in 1031 from internal weakness and civil wars.

Bibliography: J. WELLHAUSEN, *The Arab Kingdom and Its Fall,* tr. M. G. WEIR (Calcutta 1927). P. K. HITTI, *History of the Arabs* (6th ed. New York 1956). B. LEWIS, *The Arabs in History* (New York 1950). E. LÉVI-PROVENÇAL, *Encyclopedia of Islam,* ed. M. T. HOUTSMA et al. (Leiden 1913–38) 4:1052–66. R. ALTAMIRA, *Cambridge Medieval History* (London-New York 1911–36) 3, ch. 16.

[J. A. WILLIAMS/EDS.]

UNA SANCTA

This is a term that, in the broadest sense, refers to all efforts for church unity since the 16th century. More specifically, it applies to high-church tendencies within German Lutheranism, and a host of ecumenical activities since 1918 involving both Catholics and Protestants, including theological colloquia, institutes for ecumenical studies, and various discussion groups. In 1918 the high-church movement was founded by a group of Evangelical pastors in Berlin, Friedrich Heiler and F. Siegmund-Schultze being the chief leaders. This group emphasized development of a fuller sense of the visible Church, strengthening of the episcopal office, enrichment of divine liturgy, and discussion of doctrinal questions in an irenical framework. All this inevitably led to closer contacts and profitable discussions with Catholics. On the Catholic side the most prominent participating figure was Father Max Joseph Metzger (1887–1944), who founded the Weltfriedensbund vom weissen Kreuz (1917) and the Brüderschaft Una Sancta (1928), both of which groups functioned in close cooperation with Heiler's high-church movement. These developments received a temporary setback when the encyclical *Mortalium animos* (1928) disapproved "false irenicism."

With the rise of National Socialism, the need for confessional cooperation against the Hitler dictatorship gave new life to the Una Sancta movement. In this work Metzger was the guiding light until his execution (1944). In 1939 he established the Una Sancta Gesellschaft, which published the journal *Una Sancta.* After his death leadership passed to Dr. Matthias Laros, who organized a center for the coordination of ecumenical efforts at Mettingen (Augsburg), and to Thomas Sartory, OSB, of NIEDER-ALTAICH ABBEY, where the journal *Una Sancta* is edited. Distinguished members of the movement included such distinguished Germans as the church historian Joseph Lortz and the theologian Hugo Rahner, SJ. Although not directly affiliated with Una Sancta, many organizations have drawn their inspiration from its principles.

See Also: ECUMENICAL MOVEMENT.

Bibliography: G. A. DEISSMANN, *Una Sancta: Zum Geleit in das ökumenische Jahr 1937* (Gütersloh 1936). L. STEVENSON, *Max Josef Metzger, Priest and Martyr* (New York 1952). H. HERMELINK, *Katholizismus und Protestantismus im Gespräch zwischen den Konfessionen um die Una Sancta* (Stuttgart 1949). H. ASMUSSEN et al., *Katholische Reformation* (Stuttgart 1958). G. REIDICK, *Zur Una Sancta Bewegung* (Meitingen 1958). L. J. SWIDLER, *History of the Una Sancta Movement* (Pittsburgh 1965).

[S. J. T. MILLER/EDS.]

UNAM SANCTAM

A bull of BONIFACE VIII, issued Nov. 18, 1302, in which the unity of the Church and the spiritual authority of the papacy are proclaimed. Occasioned by the second major struggle between Boniface and Philip IV of France, yet addressed to the universal Church, the bull declares that there is one, holy, catholic, and apostolic church outside which there is neither salvation nor remission of sins. The Church represents the Mystical Body, whose head is Christ and in which there is one Lord, one faith, and one Baptism. Therefore, this one body, unlike a monster, has only one head, Christ and His vicar, Peter and his successors. Consequently, if anyone says that he has not been committed to Peter and his successors, he necessarily declares that he is not of Christ's sheep. In the power of the Church there are two swords, the spiritual and temporal, to be used by and for the Church. The first is in the hand of priests; the second is in the hand of kings and knights, but is to be used at the wish and permission of the priest. It is fitting that the temporal sword and power be subject to the spiritual since the latter excels the former in dignity and nobility as spiritual things are superior to temporal things. The spiritual power can establish the temporal power and judge it if it is not good. Consequently, if the temporal power should err, it will be judged by the spiritual; should a lesser spiritual power deviate, it will be judged by its superior; if, however, the supreme spiritual power errs, it will be judged not by man but by God alone. This authority, although given to men and exercised by them, is not human but divine. Therefore, whoever resists this power resists God's ordinance unless, like the heretical Manichaean, he argues for two original principles of power. Finally, in its only dogmatic definition the bull concludes: "We declare, state, and define that it is absolutely necessary for salvation that every human creature be subject to the Roman Pontiff." As a historical document, *Unam sanctam* must be set among the major events of the second crisis (1300–03) between Boniface and Philip IV and read as the culmination of the series of letters (*Recordare rex inclyte,* July 18, 1300; *Secundum divina, Salvator mundi, Ante promotionem nostram, AUSCULTA FILI*—and its French version, *Deum time,* Dec. 4–5, 1301, and *Nuper ad audientiam,* Aug.15, 1303) sent by Boniface to Philip. In its theological implications, *Unam sanctam* must be interpreted against the background of the dispute among theologians, canonists, and legalists over the nature of papal supremacy. Boniface denied that he intended to take over temporal jurisdiction; his purpose was to correct abuses *ratione peccati.* CLEMENT V, in his brief *Meruit,* informed Philip that the spiritual and temporal status of France was not changed by Boniface's bull. However, like its author, *Unam sanctam* has remained controversial.

Bibliography: H. DENZINGER, *Enchiridion symbolorum,* ed. A. SCHÖNMETZER, (Freiburg 1963) 870–875. G. H. TAVARD, "The Bull Unam Sanctam of Boniface VIII," in *Papal Primacy and the Universal Church,* eds. P. C. EMPIE and A. T. MURPHY (Minneapolis 1974) 105–119. W. ULLMANN, "Boniface VIII and His Contemporary Scholarship," *Journal of Theological Studies* 27 (1976) 58–87. D. E. LUSCOMBE, "*Lex divinitatis* in the Bull *Unam sanctam* Pope Boniface VIII," in C. N. L. BROOKE, *Church and Government in the Middle Ages* (Cambridge, Eng., 1976) 205–221. J. MULDOON, "Boniface VIII as Defender of Royal Power: Unam sanctam as a Basis for the Spanish Conquest of the Americas," in J. R. SWEENEY and S. CHODOROW, eds., *Popes, Teachers, and Canon Law in the Middle Ages* (Ithaca, NY 1989) 62–73.

[E. J. SMYTH]

UNAMUNO Y JUGO, MIGUEL DE

Spanish author and philosopher b. Bilbao, of Basque parentage, Sept. 29, 1864; d. Salamanca, Dec. 31, 1936. After graduating (1883) from the University of Madrid, he was first professor of Greek (1891) at the University of Salamanca, then rector (1901), a post he held until dismissed (1914) because of his criticism of King Alfonso XIII. In 1924 he was exiled to Fuerteventura in the Canary Islands because of his hostility to Premier Primo de Rivera. He escaped to Paris after a few months and remained in exile despite official offers of amnesty, settling in the Basque region of France and continuing his verbal attack upon the Spanish government.

When Rivera fell (1930), Unamuno returned to Spain. Alfonso abdicated in 1931, and the new Republican government reappointed Unamuno rector of Salamanca. He served as deputy to the Spanish Cortes from 1931 to 1933, but at the outbreak of the Civil War (1936) sided with General Franco's Nationalist movement. The Popular Front government of Manuel Azaña dismissed him from his rectorship, but in August 1936 he was quickly reappointed by the Nationalists. He soon quarreled with them also, and remained intensely critical of both sides until his death.

Unamuno's first novel, *Paz en la guerra* (1897), was inspired by childhood memories of the Second Carlist War, especially the bombardment of Bilbao in 1874. *Vida de Don Quijote y Sancho* (1905), a running commentary on Cervantes' great novel, is one of Unamuno's most important works. It is his contention that the two heroes, Don Quixote and Sancho Panza, soon developed their own individuality—or reality—in the novel and took over the story from Cervantes. Unamuno admires above all the knight's dedication to a life of struggle in accord with his ideals. *Niebla* (1914) centers on the idea that just as a flesh-and-blood man, once created, has a measure of free will, so an author can create a character, but in a sense may not completely control him, for the personage must follow his own inner logic and thus has autonomy to make his own decisions.

Unamuno once considered calling his novels *nivolas* because they are stripped of all nonessentials and concentrate on a few protagonists—or "agonists," as he would say—and their intimate passions and conflicts. A most successful use of this technique is manifest in *Abel Sanchez* (1917), a story of jealousy between two lifelong friends.

Unamuno's chief philosophical work, *Del sentimiento trágico de la vida* (1913), reveals strong influence by German Protestant theologians and wide familiarity with the work of Kant, Hegel, Schopenhauer, and Kierkegaard. But Unamuno's philosophy is highly personal and grows out of the clash between his strong desire to believe in immortality and his inability to find logical justification for it: "I need the immortality of my soul; the indefinite continuance of my individual consciousness I need; without it, without faith in this, I cannot live, and I am tormented by my doubt and inability to believe that I can attain it." On this inner torment Unamuno builds his philosophy of struggle, for he felt himself most alive when the conflict was strongest. Essential to his philosophy is his recognition of a moral imperative. He subscribes not only to the Christian concept of loving one's neighbor but also to the need for moral integrity.

In the short novel, *San Manuel Bueno y martir y historias más* (1933), Unamuno's thought seems to change. It is the story of a priest who, though utterly dedicated to his people, feels that he must protect them from his own conviction that there is no afterlife. The priest is still impelled to do good for his neighbor, but this includes the desire to spare the innocent the agony of his own doubt. Emmanuel is the embodiment of Unamuno's earlier expressed ideal: So live that men will say you deserved immortality even though you cannot expect to attain it. In Unamuno's thought, man is most real when striving, accomplishing, and influencing others, and this reality lasts as long as people are inspired by it. By this criterion Don Quixote is real and immortal, and to such ''immortality'' Don Miguel de Unamuno aspired. He always considered himself a Catholic. He was certainly unorthodox, but capable of strong religious fervor, as evident in his long poem, *El Cristo de Velazquez* (1920).

Bibliography: J. FERRATER MORA, *Unamuno: A Philosophy of Tragedy* (Berkeley 1962). J. MARÍAS AGUILERA, *Miguel de Unamuno* (Madrid 1943). J. B. TREND, *Unamuno* (Cambridge, Eng. 1951). M. DE UNAMUNO Y JUGO, *Obras completas* (Madrid 1950–).

[D. F. BROWN]

Miguel de Unamuno y Jugo.

UNCERTAINTY PRINCIPLE

The uncertainty principle in quantum mechanics states that the velocity and the position of a particle cannot be measured simultaneously with complete accuracy.

After the original ideas were laid down in 1927 by W. Heisenberg, a period followed in which the concepts of quantum mechanics were critically debated. The *Gedanken* experiments provided the primary intellectual ammunition in these discussions between physicists who believed that quantum mechanics was a closed structure free of internal contradictions and those who did not. (See, e.g., the discussions at the Solvay Congresses of 1927 and 1930.) The final word was the famous Niels Bohr paper that included details and examples of what became known as the ''Copenhagen Interpretation of Quantum Mechanics.'' Most physicists accept this interpretation, and modern textbooks treat it in an almost dogmatic fashion. The two important opponents of Bohr are Einstein and D. Bohm.

Philosophical Interpretations. Not all philosophers of science are agreed on the interpretation to be given to the uncertainty principle. The multiplicity of teachings can be separated into broad classes. (1) The first maintains that Heisenberg's uncertainty relations express subjective indeterminacies; i.e., they refer to man's imperfect knowledge of things, not to things themselves.

(2) The second holds that they express objective indeterminacies; i.e., they refer to something that characterizes matter or reality.

Epistemological Indeterminacy. The first type of interpretation, which is epistemological in character, subdivides into a variety of teachings. Some hold that the uncertainties arise from the inability of the human mind to comprehend the microcosm, an inability that necessitates the application of the concepts of particle dynamics to the description of wave phenomena (or vice versa), with a consequent loss of clarity. Others teach that the uncertainty arises from the coarseness of the measuring apparatus, which is very large compared to the thing being measured and thus leaves the result of the measurement indeterminate. Still others hold that the Heisenberg relations are exclusively a consequence of statistical methods of measurement and are independent of the perturbations caused by any measuring instrument. Yet others argue that the uncertainties refer to ''observables,'' but not to ''hidden variables,'' which have precise values at any given instant.

Particularly suited to this type of interpretation is the solution proposed by H. Reichenbach, who has developed a three-valued formal logic that permits questions about the microcosm to be answered with statements that are either true, false, or undecided. Also in accord with it are the solutions adopted by many logical positivists and linguistic philosophers, who hold generally that the complimentary and uncertainty principles refer not to objects but to ways in which words and concepts are used by contemporary physicists.

Ontological Indeterminacy. Among those who hold that Heisenberg's uncertainty relations express indeterminacies that are objective, or ontological in character, some propose these as ultimately reducible, others as irreducible. Those who claim that such indeterminacies are objective but reducible maintain that they arise from some lower level motion or sub-quantum state that is yet to be identified but nonetheless exists. Those who regard the indeterminacies as irreducible ascribe them either to the operation of absolute CHANCE at the subatomic level or to a basic indeterminacy that resides in some protomatter or substrate of which elementary particles are composed. Related to both views is that of those who see such indeterminacies as irreducible because of something "in the very nature of things" that prevents one ever from drawing a clear line of demarcation between subject and object at the subatomic level.

Philosophers in the Catholic or scholastic tradition recognize elements of truth in both the ontological and the epistemological interpretations of the uncertainty principle. In general they reject solutions that are antimetaphysical or antirealist in character; at the same time, they are wary of attempts to extrapolate interpretations relating to the substructure of matter to the domain of ethical or religious inquiry, e.g., proposing such theories as arguments for the existence of FREE WILL or God's influence in the world. Because of traditional teachings in the philosophy of nature, they are sympathetic to ontological interpretations that root quantum indeterminacy not in absolute chance, which they hold does not exist, but in the potency of primary matter (*see* MATTER AND FORM). Such interpretations have gained support from Heisenberg himself, who, in discussing the meaning of probability in quantum theory, states:

> The probability function combines objective and subjective elements. It contains statements about possibilities or better tendencies (*potentia* in Aristotelian philosophy), and these statements are completely objective, they do not depend on any observer; and it contains statements about our knowledge of the system, which of course are subjective in so far as they may be different for different observers. In ideal cases the subjective element in the probability function may be practically negligible as compared with the objective one [53].

If this is true, ontological and epistemological uncertainties do not bespeak incompatible interpretations but rather alternative ways of describing objective properties of matter and man's subjective limitations in comprehending them.

See Also: INDETERMINISM; SCIENCE, PHILOSOPHY OF.

Bibliography: H. REICHENBACH, *Philosophic Foundations of Quantum Mechanics* (Berkeley 1944). W. HEISENBERG, *Physics and Philosophy* (New York 1958). M. A. BUNGE, *Metascientific Queries* (Springfield, Ill. 1959). E. CASSIRER, *Determinism and Indeterminism in Modern Physics,* tr. O. T. BENFEY (New Haven, Conn. 1956). M. BORN, *Natural Philosophy of Cause and Chance* (Oxford 1949).

[W. A. WALLACE/P. H. E. MEIJER]

UNDA

Unda (Latin for "wave") is the international professional Catholic association for radio and television, the *Association Catholique Internationale pour la Radio et la Télévision*. Officially recognized by the Holy See, Unda began as the International Catholic Committee for Radio, founded in 1928 in Cologne, Germany. Unda's members internationally are not individuals but national and continental Catholic organizations which share Unda's objectives, while retaining responsibility for their own activities. Unda's headquarters are in Brussels.

Unda's objectives are: to help coordinate professional and apostolic activities of Catholics in radio and television; to promote collaboration among members, through conferences, publications, information exchanges, research; to represent internationally the interests of members; to help meet communications needs of members; to help meet communications needs of the Third World; and to collaborate with non-Catholic organizations having similar objectives.

At the continental and national levels, Unda conducts a variety of activities and programs suited to individual needs of each region. Development programs in broadcasting, planned, subsidized and executed under the auspices of Unda, are primarily in the Third World countries of Africa, Asia, Latin America, and Oceania. Projects prepared at the local level are presented to the Congregation for the Evangelization of Peoples in Rome and to other world funding agencies. In the past the Congregation has allotted through Unda more than two million U.S. dollars. Unda publishes a bimonthly newsletter (*Unda News*), in English and in French, and a documentation quarterly (*Educommunication News*).

Unda-USA. Unda-USA is a national professional Catholic Association for broadcasters and allied communicators. Organized in 1972, it succeeded the Catholic Broadcasters Association of America, which in 1948 had replaced the Catholic Forum of the Air, founded in 1939. Unda-USA's Board of Directors includes representatives of the United States Conference of Catholic Bishops (USCCB), Catholic Television Network, Association of Catholic Radio and Television Syndicators, and media and government.

Unda-USA's objectives are: to encourage cooperation among diocesan communications directors, religious program syndicators, instructional television personnel and the USCCB; to cooperate with all commercial and religious broadcasters whenever possible; to help develop a discerning audience for social communications; to assess the sources and influences of media; to be concerned with media government relations and the preservation of freedom of expression; to assess the impact of U.S. media upon other nations and peoples, and to help develop a sensitive awareness and mutual understanding among peoples of various cultures.

"Gabriel Awards" are made annually to national and local radio and TV programs in which commercial, educational, or religious broadcasters have best entertained, enriched, or informed with a vision of life reflecting basic religious principles. Awards are also given to a radio and TV station for consistently high quality programming, and to a person who has provided outstanding leadership in the field of national or local broadcasting.

Unda-USA annually holds a General Assembly for all members. A newsletter for members is published six times a year. Headquarters in the United States are in Dayton, OH.

[A. SCANNELL/EDS.]

UNDERHILL, EVELYN

(Mrs. Hubert Stuart Moore) Anglican authority on mystical theology, author, and spiritual director; b. Wolverhampton, England, Dec. 6, 1875; d. Hampstead, England, June 15, 1941. As the only daughter of a distinguished family of tolerant but agnostic outlook, Underhill was educated at King's College, London. A lifelong Anglican, she was attracted to Roman Catholic mystical experience as a result of a retreat at a Roman Catholic convent in 1907, but resigned herself to spiritual homelessness when the papal encyclical *Pascendi* condemned Modernism, with which she was in sympathy.

Underhill's spiritual struggles led to the 1911 publication of *Mysticism,* which, because of its comprehensive approach to religious experience, became a standard

work and established her as a foremost authority on the subject. A steady flow of smaller books blending scholarship and devotion followed. In 1936 her second work, the ecumenical classic *Worship,* was published; it is notable for its breadth of scope and depth of understanding of the nature and forms of Christian worship. In 1911 she came to know Baron Friedrich von HÜGEL, who became her spiritual director in 1921 and led her into full participation in the sacramental life of the Church of England. By that time she herself had begun to provide spiritual direction to others and to conduct retreats.

Although she was largely self-taught, she was the first woman to be invited to give a series of theological lectures at Oxford University (1921), the first woman Fellow of King's College, Cambridge (1928), and the first woman to serve as editor of the British religious journal, *Spectator.* She was also a prolific writer, producing 39 books on mysticism and spiritual life, and more than 350 articles and reviews. She received the degree of doctor of divinity from Aberdeen University in 1938. In her latter years she continued to write and conduct retreats, and some of her addresses were published. She was considered the foremost lay Anglican theologian of her time, and maintained a lifelong connection with Roman Catholicism.

Bibliography: (a) Underhill's Major Works: *Abba: Meditations on the Lord's Prayer* (London 1940), *Column of Dust* (London 1909), *The Golden Sequence* (London 1932), *Life of the Spirit and Life Today* (London 1922), *Lost World* (London 1907), *Mystery of the Sacrifice* (London 1938), *Mysticism* (12th edition, Oxford 1993), *Mystics of the Church* (London 1925), *Practical Mysticism* (New York 1915) and *Worship* (London 1936). **(b) Collections of Underhill's Principal Short Writings:** D. GREENE, ed., *Evelyn Underhill: Modern Guide to the Ancient Quest for the Holy* (Albany 1988), D. GREENE, ed., *Fragments from an Inner Life* (Harrisburg, PA 1993), C. WILLIAMS, ed., *The Letters of Evelyn Underhill* (London 1943), and L. MENZIES, ed., *Collected Papers* (New York 1946). **(c) Secondary Literature:** A. CALLAHAN, *Evelyn Underhill: Spirituality for Daily Living* (Lanham, MD 1997), M. CROPPER, *Life of Evelyn Underhill* (New York 1958), D. GREENE, *Evelyn Underhill: Artist of the Infinite Life* (New York 1990), and G.M. JANTZEN, "The Legacy of Evelyn Underhill," *Feminist Theology* 4 (1993) 79–100.

[J. T. L. JAMES/EDS.]

UNDERSTANDING (INTELLECTUS)

Understanding is a familiar occurrence in everyone's experience, but it is difficult to define philosophically. As D. HUME has said, "It is remarkable concerning the operations of the mind, that, though most intimately present to us, yet, whenever they become the object of reflexion, they seem involved in obscurity" (*An Enquiry concerning Human Understanding* [Oxford 1902] 13). The difficulty is accentuated when one tries to communicate his thought to another, for he cannot present his mental operation for inspection, and it becomes especially acute in crossing the barrier between modern language and medieval. This article therefore begins with modern philosophical usage in English and in German (on which English often depends), then gives a systematic exposition of the notion of understanding according to a modern writer, Father B. J. F. Lonergan, and concludes with a discussion of the Thomistic concept of *intellectus*.

Philosophical Usage. In modern usage, the substantive "understanding" may refer to the cognitional faculty (e.g., the understanding as opposed to the will), or to the developed state of the faculty (e.g., he showed great understanding), or to the content of the act of understanding (e.g., my understanding of the matter is . . .). But all these usages evidently derive from the verbal use, to understand, for which the *Oxford English Dictionary* gives as first definition: to comprehend, to apprehend the meaning or import of, to grasp the idea of. As the common man would say: to get the point, to catch on. Nor is there the slightest difficulty about this use of the word; everyone with a minimum of education knows what is meant by "I do not understand the question."

English. When the word enters English philosophy it has at first a rather vague sense. For John LOCKE, it is evidently interchangeable with mind (*Of Human Understanding,* The Epistle to the Reader, par. 1), and is defined as the faculty of perception, where the objects of perception are listed as: ideas in the mind, the meaning of signs, and the agreement or disagreement of ideas (*ibid.* 2.21.5). Elsewhere it is stated that the word "idea" comprehends "whatsoever is the object of the understanding" (1.1.8). Locke's work is more concerned, in fact, with ideas than with understanding, and ideas themselves are not sharply differentiated from other cognitional elements, including *"phantasm, notion, species,* or whatever it is which the mind can be employed about in thinking" (*ibid.*). Hume proposes "to enquire seriously into the nature of human understanding," to conduct "an exact analysis of its powers and capacity" (*op. cit.* 12), but he goes on to speak of "an accurate scrutiny into the powers and faculties of human nature" (13) and to state his hope of drawing "a mental geography, or delineation of the distinct parts and powers of the mind" (14); whence it appears that understanding for Hume is almost synonymous with what is most specific in human nature or with mind.

German. For nearly two centuries philosophical usage of the English word has had to reckon with the German counterpart, especially as used by I. Kant and W. DILTHEY. A direct concern with the faculty itself and its activity rather than with its objects appears in Kant who, moreover, sharply distinguishes *Verstand* and *Vernunft,* usually translated as "understanding" and "reason," respectively. Understanding is the power that forms concepts; it is the faculty of the rules ordering the intuitions of sense into the provisional unities of the categories; it is the faculty of the possible. Reason is the power that systematizes, the faculty of the principles ordering the less-inclusive rules into the absolute unities of the illusory transcendental ideas; it is the faculty of the necessary. Understanding clearly has an orientation to experience and the content of sense; reason tries to transcend experience. (See J. M. Baldwin, *Dictionary of Philosophy and Psychology* [3 v. New York 1901–05]; "Kant's Terminology" by J. R[oyce].)

With Dilthey understanding receives a still more restricted sense; confined by him to the human sciences, it corresponds to explanation (*Erklärung*) in the natural sciences, is distinguished from knowledge, and is closely linked with interpretation. Man knows what causes a rainbow, but he understands his friend's anxiety. Understanding is insight into the human mind, sympathetic entrance into the interior states of other persons, grasping the meaning in human institutions and in history.

For M. Heidegger's notions of existential understanding as projecting the possibilities of the subject and of interpretation as understanding becoming itself, see his *Being* and *Time,* tr. J. Macquarrie and E. Robinson (New York 1962) 182–195.

Lonergan's Exposition. The following more systematic exposition follows a work by B. J. F. Lonergan, *Insight. A Study of Human Understanding* (New York 1957).

Act of Understanding. Understanding, according to Father Lonergan, is the central and pivotal act in the human cognitional structure formed basically of experience, understanding, and judgment. Here experience has a very precise sense; it means the presentations of sense and the representations of imagination: what is seen, heard, imagined, etc. In this sense it is merely an animal activity, but in man there supervenes on mere experience the new factor of WONDER. Man expresses his wonder first in questions of the type, *Quid sit?* (What is it?). But wonder is not so much a question as the source of all questions, a dynamism and a need. The need is for understanding, for insight into the presented materials, for getting hold of the idea, grasping the QUIDDITY, finding the intelligibility immanent in the content of experience. Understanding, however, does not of itself satisfy the need of intellect, for its ideas are essentially hypothetical and what man seeks is the real. So there intervenes a second type of question, *An sit?* (Is it?). Is my idea correct? The reflective process that answers this question ends in judgment of existence, knowledge of the real. Thus, experience is explanatorily defined as what is presupposed and complemented by inquiry and understanding, understanding in turn as what is presupposed and complemented by REFLECTION and JUDGMENT (*Insight,* 333–334). The three levels form a dynamic structure with the two questions, *Quid sit?* and *An sit?* manifesting the dynamism that effects the shift from first level to second and from second to third.

On the second level itself, understanding is to be distinguished from DEFINITION, CONCEPT, hypothesis, THEORY, and system, i.e., from everything that expresses the content of the act of understanding. In short, understanding, as preconceptual, is distinguished from the formulation of understanding or, as St. Thomas Aquinas would say, from the *verbum incomplexum* that proceeds from it. The difference here is between the intelligibility grasped in the particular instance and the intelligibility disengaged from the particular instance and set free in the universal concept. In order to understand, man forms an image to think the matter out, or he constructs a model, or he draws a figure on paper, or he studies the data. The question is always put with regard to what man experiences; understanding always finds its primary object immanent in experience. "The act of understanding leaps forth when the sensible data are in a suitable constellation" (Lonergan, *Theological Studies* 7 [1946] 362). Thus understanding occurs with regard to an instance. The concept or formulation, on the contrary, is set free from the instance; it has become a universal. The difference between understanding and the explicit formulation of the universal is best epitomized in the contrast between artist and scientist. The artist certainly understands something but his understanding is tied to the sensible presentation (the work of art), nor has he full possession of his understanding: often enough he cannot tell just what his idea is. The scientist aims at disengaging the idea, taking possession of it, discovering its implications and applications, and drawing it into systematic relationship with other ideas.

Types of Understanding. Again, within understanding there occur various types, based not on specific differences in the object (physics, chemistry, etc.), but on different procedures in the subject. There is (1) commonsense understanding, which relates things to a person through his senses (the motion of the Sun as describing an arc over his head); (2) scientific understanding, which relates things to one another in abstraction from their relation to the observer as such (the motion of the Sun in relation to other bodies in the solar system); (3) heuristic understanding, which anticipates the idea by grasping the kind of activity through which it will occur; and (4) determinate understanding, which reaches the idea by carrying out the activity. These are four more important types of direct understanding; in contrast there is inverse understanding, which has as its object irrelevance as such; it grasps the irrelevance to direct understanding of the here and now, of constant velocity, of the nonsystematic in statistical laws, etc., and has fertile applications throughout empirical science, philosophy, and theology. Finally, the term is extended to judgmental activity on the third level of cognitional process; it is then called reflective understanding, again named in contrast to direct.

Differentiation from Other Notions. With respect then to Locke and Hume, Lonergan makes understanding in the strict sense a very specific activity; he distinguishes it from the level of sensation and image on one side, from the level of reflection and judgment on the other, and on its own level from the concepts that formulate it. With respect to Kant, Lonergan assigns understanding a more precise relationship to experience: it is indeed the power that forms concepts and subsumes instances under rule, but it does so because it is directly related to sensible materials through the question they raise; moreover, it is not restricted to a priori forms but is a ranging power, *potens omnia fieri.* With respect to Dilthey, Lonergan would admit the riches of meaning embedded in the data of the human sciences but would insist that these data are intelligible in the same way as other data, and that this intelligibility is in principle subject to formulation and its own scientific explanation. In short, understanding would "confer a basic yet startling unity" (*Insight,* ix) on all fields of human inquiry, those represented by Kant and Dilthey as well as others.

Thomistic Concept. For St. THOMAS AQUINAS, the term *intellectus* has many meanings (see L. Schütz, *Thomas-Lexikon* [2d ed. Paderborn 1895; repr. Stuttgart 1958] 406–413). (*See* ANGELS, THEOLOGY OF; INTELLECT.) In the context of modern discussions of the notion of understanding, however, two meanings assume particular significance, namely, that of understanding as a habit of first principles and that of understanding as a cognitional activity in some way related to reason.

Habit of First Principles. As a speculative habit of the intellect, understanding is to be distinguished from the habits of SCIENCE (*SCIENTIA*) and of WISDOM. The basis for this distinction is the following: "A speculative intellectual virtue perfects the speculative intellect in its consideration of truth, for this is its good. But truth can be attained in two ways: in one, as immediately (*per se*) grasped; in the other, as grasped through an intermediary (*per aliud*). What is grasped immediately has the status of a principle and is immediately perceived by the intellect. Thus the habit that perfects the intellect for this type of consideration of truth is called understanding; it is the habit of principles'' (*Summa theologiae* 1a2ae, 57.2). Explaining the nature of this habit in another place, St. Thomas notes: ''*Intellectus* is not here taken to mean the intellective power itself, but a particular habit by which man naturally knows indemonstrable principles in the light provided by the agent intellect. And the name is well chosen, for principles of this kind are known immediately once their terms are understood. As soon as one knows what a whole is and what a part is, he immediately recognizes that the whole is greater than the part. It is said to be intellectus from the fact that it reads within (*intus legit*) by grasping the essence of the thing'' (*In 6 eth.* 5.1179).

The habit of first principles in the speculative order, as thus explained, is called understanding in English usage; for a fuller explanation, *see* FIRST PRINCIPLES. Corresponding to these, there are also indemonstrable principles in the practical order; the habit of such principles may also be called understanding, though it is more frequently designated by the transliteration from the Greek συντήρησις (*see* SYNDERESIS); which came, by accident, to mean the light of conscience.

Ratio and Intellectus. Considerable discussion surrounds the significance of St. Thomas's usage of the term ''ratio'' as opposed to *intellectus*. Studies by P. ROUSSELOT, J. Peghaire, P. Hoenen, and Lonergan yield the following account: At the basis of all reasoning (*ratio*) is the simple act of understanding, the Thomist *intelligere* or the Aristotelian νοεῖν. It has its object in the image whence in English one speaks of ''insight into the phantasm.'' Thomas Aquinas could say that whenever man tries to understand (*intelligere*) he forms images (*phantasmata*) in which he, as it were, inspects (*inspiciat*) the solution (*Summa theologiae* 1a, 84.7), and Aristotle could assert that the noetic faculty (νοητικόν) understands (νοεῖ) the forms in images (ἐν τοῖς φαντάσμασι—*Anim.* 431b 2). But equally all reasoning has its term in understanding; man reasons in order to understand better, to develop his understanding. Understanding (*intelligere*), says St. Thomas, is the proper act of the human soul, perfectly demonstrating its power and nature (*Summa theologiae* 1a, 88.2 ad 3). But this does not eliminate *ratio* as the human characteristic, for *ratio* is the imperfect form of *intelligere* found in man: ''Human intellect is essentially intellect-in-process or reason'' (Lonergan, *Theological Studies* 7 [1946] 378; 8 [1947] 39–46).

The tendency found often enough in St. Thomas to distinguish *intellectus* and *ratio* more sharply can possibly be attributed to the predominance of the logical viewpoint he inherited. But he adverts also to a context that is not merely logical, that anticipates modern science to include empirical discovery and escape the confines of deduction (see Hoenen).

The effect of this analysis is to reduce the opposition between *ratio* and human *intellectus* to its proper proportion, to underline the basis in sense and imagination of every human concept (even man's concept of God), and to link Aristotle and Thomas Aquinas with what physics and other modern sciences are so obviously doing. It also gives a clear analogy for discussing both theological understanding and the understanding of mysteries (*donum intellectus*) that St. Thomas made a gift of the Holy Spirit (Lonergan, ''Theology and Understanding'').

Thomistic usage in this regard differs from that of modern philosophers. John Dewey, for example, makes understanding correspond to reason in the way conditional, reflective, mediate knowledge does to comprehensive, self-sufficing knowledge (Baldwin, *Dictionary . . . ,* ''Understanding and Reason''). K. Oehler agrees that the discursive faculty is διάνοια or *ratio,* the intuitive faculty νόησις or *intellectus.* In German usage up to Kant, *Vernunft* is *ratio* and *Verstand* is *intellectus;* but Kant reversed the usage, attributing to *Verstand* the constitution of the categories and to *Vernunft* the knowledge of ideas. This usage, except in A. SCHOPENHAUER and some others, prevailed in Germany, though in the mid-20th century there was concern about the arbitrary character of the choice and its lack of correspondence with the work of modern physics (see *Die Religion in Geschichte und Gegenwart,* 7 v. [3d ed. Tübingen 1957–65] 6:1364–65).

See Also: APPREHENSION, SIMPLE; INSIGHT; INTUITION; REASONING.

Bibliography: B. J. F. LONERGAN, ''The Concept of *Verbum* in the Writings of St. Thomas Aquinas,'' *Theological Studies* 7 (1946) 349–392; 8 (1947) 35–79, 404–444; 10 (1949) 3–40, 359–393; ''Theology and Understanding'' *Gregorianum* 35 (1954) 630–648. E. M. MACKINNON, ''Understanding according to Bernard J. F. Lonergan, S.J.,'' *Thomist* 28 (1964) 97–132; 338–372; 475–522. W. DILTHEY, *Meaning in History,* ed. H. P. RICKMAN (London 1961). H. G. GADAMER, *Die Religion in Geschichte und Gegenwart,* 7 v. (3d ed. Tübingen 1957–65) 6:1381–83. J. WACH, *Das Verstehen,* 3 v. (Tübingen 1926–33). M. MAGNUSSON, *Der Begriff ''Verstehen'' im exegetischen Zusammenhang . . .* (Lund 1954). D. DUBARLE, ''Esquisse du problème contemporain de la raison,'' in *La Crise de la raison dans la pensée contemporaine* (Paris 1960) 61–116. J. PEGHAIRE, *Intellectus et Ratio selon Saint Thomas d'Aquin* (Ottawa 1936). P. HOENEN, ''De origine primorum principiorum scientiae'' *Gregorianum* 14 (1933) 153–184. P. ROUSSELOT, *The Intellectualism of Saint Thomas,* tr. J. E. O'MAHONY (London 1935).

[F. E. CROWE]

UNDERSTANDING, GIFT OF

The gift of the Holy Spirit that perfects the virtue of faith by moving the intellect to penetrate revealed truths. Through the virtue of faith the mind has a knowledge of supernatural truths, but in a limited, human mode. Man's natural manner of knowing is discursive. Understanding provides a capacity for a penetration to the objects of faith that are beyond the discursive power of reason. Through it, the Holy Spirit elevates the intellect to act above its human mode and achieve a more profound penetration of the truth than is possible by faith alone. Perfected thus by the gift, faith can rise to an ever-greater intensity by a simple intuition of the divine truths. The influence of faith then tends to be extended to all the movements of the soul and all things are seen, increasingly, through faith. This gift, and its proper function, can best be understood by seeing it in its relation to the other gifts; for fuller explanation and additional bibliography, *see* HOLY SPIRIT, GIFTS OF.

Bibliography: A. ROYO, *The Theology of Christian Perfection,* ed. and tr. J. AUMANN (Dubuque, Iowa 1962) 370–377. R. CESSARIO, *Christian Faith and the Theological Life* (Washington, D.C. 1996). S. PINCKAERS, *The Sources of Christian Ethics,* tr. M. T. NOBLE (3d rev. ed.; Washington, D.C. 1995). THOMAS AQUINAS, *Summa theologiae* 2a2ae, q.68–69.

[P. MULHERN]

UNDSET, SIGRID

Norwegian novelist; b. Kalundborg, Denmark, May 20, 1882; d. Lillehammer, Norway, June 10, 1949. Undset' father, Ingvald, was a distinguished Norwegian archeologist and her mother was Danish. Straitened family circumstances curtailed her education, and she worked as a typist from 1898 to 1908. She was always keenly interested in her father's work and developed a fine sense of history, which was to give authenticity to her great historical novels.

Her first attempt at a novel was *Fru Marta Oulie* (1907), a picture of modern, everyday life in Oslo. After an excursion into the historical novel, *Gunnar's Daughter* (1909), she returned to studies of contemporary life, of which *Jenny* (1911) and *Spring* (1914) are perhaps the most representative. These are tinged with a spirit of the discontent of youth and reveal the agnosticism that was rife among members of her generation.

Gradually, and perhaps mainly, because of her interest in the Christian background of the Scandinavian countries as revealed by archeology, she discovered Christianity, and she was received into the Catholic Church in 1925. Her wide knowledge of the Middle Ages

Sigrid Undset. (AP/Wide World Photos)

laid the groundwork for the vast panorama she envisioned for the historical novels *Kristin Lavransdatter* (1920–22) and *Olav Audunsson* (1925–27). The basic motive of these masterpieces was a desire to make Christianity visible to modern man by showing how the light of revelation was carried to the heathen Nordic people as the supreme answer to the riddles of which humanity has always been aware. In her later works she turned to the spiritual crises of modern times, and although *The Wild Orchid* (1929), *The Burning Bush* (1930), *Ida Elisabeth* (1932), and *The Faithful Wife* (1936) do not have the sweep of her medieval themes, they are among the most penetrating of modern novels. Lesser, but by no means insignificant, are *The Longest Years* (1934), a charming recollection of her first 11 years; *Madame Dorothea* (1939), a picture of life in 18th-century Norway; and *Saga of Saints* (1935), in which she returned once again to the Middle Ages in studies of medieval sanctity.

When Norway was occupied by the Nazis, she came to the U.S. where she lectured extensively and published *Return to the Future* (1942) and *Happy Days in Norway* (1943). She had married the painter A. C. Svarstad in 1912 and had three children, but the marriage was dissolved in 1925. She was awarded the Nobel Prize for literature in 1928 for *Kristin Lavransdatter.* Her second son was killed by the Nazis in 1940, an event that inspired the anti-Nazi sentiments she expressed during her lectures in the U.S. She returned to Lillehammer in 1945, and in 1947 received the Grand Cross of the Order of St. Olaf, the first woman not of noble blood to be so honored.

Bibliography: S. UNDSET, *Artikler og taler fra krigstiden,* ed. A. H. WINSNES (Oslo 1952), a collection of her articles and speeches; *Middelalder-romaner,* 10 v. (3d ed. Oslo 1959), the medieval novels; *Nutridsfortellinger,* 9 v. (Oslo 1964–65), the modern novels. A. H. WINSNES, *Sigrid Undset: A Study in Christian Realism,* tr. P. G. FOOTE (New York 1953). E. STEEN, *Kristin Lavransdatter* (Oslo 1959). A. M. DE VOS, *Sigrid Undset* (Ghent 1953). C. A. BRADY, "An Appendix to the Sieridssaga," *Thought* 40 (1965) 73–130.

[A. H. WINSNES]

UNICITY OF GOD

The attribute of God by which He is one and unique, and thus set off from the multiplicity of His creatures. This article presents first the scriptural and patristic basis for this attribute and then some theological reflections on the concept of unicity, its attribution to God, and various ways in which it has been negated.

Scriptural and Patristic Basis. The primal truth conveyed by God to His people in primitive revelation is the uniqueness of God, a truth insisted upon as a corrective to the constant human tendency toward multiple deification. At least from the time of Moses on, the patriarchs were all monotheist, and their teaching set Israel apart from its neighbors. "Hear, O Israel the Lord our God is one Lord" (Dt 6.4); "See ye that I alone am and there is no other God besides me" (Dt 32.39). Moses was scandalized at the golden calf, for he saw this as an attempt to give place to another god (Ex 32.31). True enough, the full implications of this revelation were not grasped at once, and for a time the Israelites thought that other gods reigned over the peoples outside Israel. The henotheistic attitude, however, gradually gave way to absolute monotheism as the Prophets, especially Isaiah (Is 41–45), gave further clarity to the Word of God.

In the New Testament Christ explicitly repeated the monotheistic formula addressed by Yahweh to Israel (Mk 12.29). Only then did He manifest Himself as distinct in person from Father and Holy Spirit, and even this was done only against the background of understanding an identity of nature: "I and the Father am one" (Jn 10.30); "In the beginning. . . the Word was with God, and the Word was God" (Jn 1.1). St. John and St. Paul give clear confirmation to the truth: ". . . that they may know Thee, the only true God . . ." (Jn 17.3); ". . .one Lord, one faith, one baptism; one God and Father of all . . ." (Eph 4.6).

The understanding of the Fathers as to the uniqueness of God need not be insisted upon; it is evident and unanimous. The magisterium of the Church leaves no room for doubt in the earliest creed, "Credo in unum Deum" (H. Denzinger, *Enchiridion symbolorum,* ed. A. Schönmetzer [32d ed. Freiburg 1963] 150), and in many conciliar pronouncements, especially those of Lateran IV (ibid. 804–806), Florence (ibid. 1336–37), Trent (ibid. 1862), and Vatican I (ibid. 3001).

Concept of Unicity. The concept of unicity, or uniqueness, is but the ultimate and perfect realization of UNITY. The meaning of unity, in turn, can only be approached negatively as the denial of division and is immediately realized in two distinct orders, viz, the predicamental and the transcendental. Unity in the first sense is mathematical, the principle of number, and is the property of a thing precisely as quantified. Denial of matter and quantity to God renders impossible any attribution to Him of predicamental unity.

Transcendental unity belongs to the metaphysical order and is a property of being as such, really identified therewith. Everything, by the very fact that it is, is actually undivided in itself (whether simple or composed) and divided from all else not itself. Such oneness adds no determination or limitation to being; it *is* being conceived in its unity. The two notions (being and one) are not, however, equivalent (*see* TRANSCENDENTALS).

Such oneness is predicated of God, yet in so perfect a way that the unity of God is a unicity. God is so one as to include any other of like nature; He is unique. EXISTENCE is explanatory of all unity; a purely subsistent existence, one not the existence of an essence, demands unicity (*see* SUBSISTENCE).

Attribution to God. The affirmation of God's unicity is possible for unaided natural reason, and the lines of argumentation are varied. The multiplicity and complexity of creatures, though not themselves immediately implying the exclusiveness of God, leads to the recognition of God's simplicity, which is further discernible as a simplicity of infinite perfection. From these two prerogatives of God—simplicity and omniperfection—His unicity can be cogently demonstrated.

A plurality within a nature is possible only upon the assumption that the nature admit of composition. The nature, being common, can be differentiated into several individuals only by the addition thereto of distinct singularizing elements. Most obvious of these is the concrete act of existing, which must be entirely unique for each existent. A plurality of gods, then, demands a common divinity that is in a state of composition with other real and distinct principles accounting for its INDIVIDUATION. Granting the absolute simplicity of God, the hypothesis of several gods becomes untenable. (*See* SIMPLICITY OF GOD.)

God's infinity of perfection leads to the same conclusion. The hypothesis of several gods assumes that they differ in some fashion from one another, and such difference can only be in virtue of each possessing or being something that the others are not. Each god would then lack that which distinctly characterizes the others. And such lack is a denial of the divine prerogative of omniperfection; a denial in effect that the being in question is indeed God. (*See* PERFECTION, ONTOLOGICAL.)

Quite simply, the Act of Being in its absolute purity cannot involve any kind of plurality. Existence accounts for the unity of each thing; in God there is nothing besides pure existence; this is God not only One but Unique.

Negations of God's Unicity. Polytheism, acknowledging a plurality of gods, is an implicit negation of God's unity. It represents a primitive stage in the evolution of man's religious attitudes. The empirical investigative sciences, such as anthropology and paleontology, are inclined' to see primitive monotheism as the eventual refinement of an original polytheistic tendency. Catholic thought, on the other hand, relying on the Genesis account of creation, has tended almost entirely to conceive of the origins of polytheism in terms of the corruption of an initial revealed monotheism.

At any rate, the primitive forms of polytheism tend in time to give way to HENOTHEISM, i.e., the recognition of a single supreme god for each nation or people. Further refinements give rise to dualistic systems based largely on the polarities of matter and spirit and of evil and good. Historically, these range from the MANICHAEISM of the 3d century down to the teachings proposed by the ALBIGENSES of the 13th, and not a little of contemporary PANTHEISM offers a highly sophisticated form of the same ideology.

Finally the revelation that God's nature and life is triune affords, in the very depths of its mysteriousness, occasion for the error of tritheism. Avoidance of this lies in the indispensable understanding that the three Persons do not share a common nature; rather each Person *is* the divine nature in total identity.

Bibliography: THOMAS AQUINAS, *Summa theologiae* 1a, 11, Eng. tr. and comment. v.2., ed. T. MCDERMOTT (New York 1964–), 60 v. planned. JOHN OF ST. THOMAS, *Cursus theologicus* (ed. Solesmes; Paris 1931–) 2:101–119. R. GARRIGOU-LAGRANGE, *God: His Existence and His Nature*, tr. B. ROSE, 2 v. (St. Louis 1934–36) v.2. E. MANGENOT et al., *Dictionnaire de théologie catholique*, ed. A. VACANT et al., 15 v. (Paris 1903–50; Tables Générales 1951–) 4.1:948–1300. C. HARTSHORNE and W. L. REESE, eds., *Philosophers Speak of God* (Chicago 1953).

[W. J. HILL]

UNICITY OF THE CHURCH

Unicity means uniqueness; there is but one Church of Jesus Christ. This idea is closely related to the concept of the UNITY OF THE CHURCH, which signifies that the unique Church of Christ is organically one and undivided in itself. This article will consider the foundations of unicity as set forth in Scripture, and the varying ways in which Catholics and their separated brethren interpret this concept.

In the Bible. The evidence of the New Testament is abundant; all the elements that have always been associated with the Church are distinctly characterized as being one. In the Synoptic Gospels Christ is preoccupied with the formation of one group of disciples, the Apostles. In the Acts the early Christians of Jerusalem are conscious of their unity with one another (Acts 2.44–47; 4.32) and with the local Churches springing up elsewhere (Acts 9.31; 11.29); the authority of the leaders at Jerusalem extends even to the regulating of the Gentile Churches (Acts 15.1–29).

St. Paul and St. John underline the factor of unicity. For St. Paul there is but one Gospel (Gal 1.6–9; 2.1–2), "one body and one Spirit. . .in one hope. . .one Lord, one faith, one Baptism; one God and Father of all, Who is above all, and throughout all, and in us all" (Eph 4.4–6). And there is but one Eucharist which brings the many faithful into the one Body (1 Cor 10.17; *see* MYSTICAL BODY OF CHRIST). St. John is merely summing up this teaching of unity when he shows us Christ promising that "there shall be one fold and one shepherd" (Jn 10.16; cf. 17.20–23).

Today few Christians doubt that Christ willed but one Church. However, disagreement exists concerning the elements that constitute this one Church and the moment when this one Church has been or will be realized.

Catholic Teaching. The one Church of Christ from Pentecost on has always been that body of believers united to Christ in the power of the Holy Spirit who profess externally their internal unity in adhering to the successor of Peter (*see* PETER, APOSTLE, ST.) and the bishops united to him through obedience, profession of the same faith, and participation in the same sacramental worship (H. Denzinger, *Enchiridion symbolorum*, ed. A. Schönmetzer, 3300–10). According to this concept the essence of the one Church of Christ is composed of both visible and invisible elements that have been bestowed permanently by Christ upon the Church. The one Church exists fully only where these elements exist in an integral union, i.e., in the Catholic Church, although other Churches share in this fullness in varying degrees (Vatican Council II).

Furthermore, the oneness of the Church is not confined to a given moment of time, but spans all history. The one Church of Pentecostal times is the one Church of today and the one Church of all future time. All history represents but the various moments of existence of that growing divine-human organism founded and continuously sustained by Jesus Christ, destined to reach the perfection of its oneness on the last day.

The ultimate ground of this continuous oneness of the Church lies in the oneness of the divine plan of salvation in Jesus Christ. In the one Christ, in whom the divine and the human as well as the invisible and visible are wedded forever, God saves men; in the one Church, in which visible human elements are impregnated with an invisible divine power, this salvific work is signified and effected.

Other Views. The separated brethren reject such a concept of the one Church. Some propound the idea of unicity expressed by John HUS and rejected by the Council of Constance (*Enchiridion symbolorum* 1201); the one Church is a purely invisible entity composed of all those predestined to salvation. Others recognize visible elements in the one Church: the Church exists wherever the Word is rightly preached and the Sacraments correctly administered (many Lutherans); the one Church exists in three visible branches that have preserved the Apostolic succession—the Roman, the Orthodox, and the Anglican (for the Anglican view *see* BRANCH THEORY OF THE CHURCH); finally, there is a view that the one Church of Christ does not now exist but will exist in the future when the current scandal of divided Churches will be removed by visible union of those now separated.

Recent years have seen the emergence of two models for the organic union of the Church: that of a *conciliar fellowship,* gaining acceptance by members of the World Council of Churches and that of a *communion (communio) of Churches (typoi),* gaining acceptance in Roman Catholic circles.

Both models assume that the unity of the Church has been *given* by God in Jesus Christ and has had continuous existence, but that it must be constantly rediscovered and expressed anew in history. This unity is in need of being made visible where it has been obscured, recovered to the extent that it has been lost, maintained where it is threatened, and brought to full conformity with the will of Christ. The one Church of Christ subsists in the historical Churches in varying degrees.

The proposed models presuppose that the organically united Church has as constitutive elements both the *invisible* gifts of faith, grace, virtues, and charisms, and their *visible* expression in the proclamation of the Word,

celebration of the Sacraments, and in ministries for mission. Both the invisible gifts and their visible expression are to be *integrally united.* These two models accept the need for diversity-in-unity and unity-in-diversity as opposed to uniformity. Both models assume that there must be a visible unity of one faith expressed in a variety of forms, in worship and Eucharistic sharing, in common life in Christ, and in Christian witness and service to the world. Both models envision a universal communion (*communio*) or conciliar fellowship of local Churches united by a diversity of organizational patterns.

While the above comments stand in principle, the exact understanding of the elements varies from Church to Church. Such issues are debated as: the relationship between the local communities and the universal community; the meaning of ''local Church'' and ''conciliar fellowship''; authority; legitimate diversity; the relationship between Church and Eucharist; the nature of the Church and its mission; the place of experience vis-à-vis the sources of Revelation; and the relationship of the unity of the Church to the unity of mankind.

See Also: BROTHER IN CHRIST; CATHOLICITY; INCORPORATION IN CHRIST; SALVATION, NECESSITY OF THE CHURCH FOR; PEOPLE OF GOD; SOUL OF THE CHURCH; UNITY OF FAITH; VISIBILITY OF THE CHURCH.

Bibliography: LEO XIII, ''Satis cognitum'' (Encyclical letter, June 29, 1896) *Acta Sanctorum* 28 (1895–96) 708–39. H. DENZINGER, *Enchiridion symbolorum,* ed. A. SCHÖNMETZER (32 ed. Freiburg 1963) 3300–10. A. MICHEL, *Dictionnaire de théologie catholique,* ed. A. VACANT et al., 15 v. (Paris 1903–50) 15.2:2172–2230. H. VOLK, *Lexikon für Theologie und Kirche,* ed. J. HOFER and K. RAHNER, 10 v. (2d, new ed. Freiburg 1957–65) 3:750–56. J. A. MÖHLER, *Symbolism,* tr. J. B. ROBERTSON (London 1906). Y. CONGAR, *Divided Christendom,* tr. M. A. BOUSFIELD (London 1939). G. BAUM, *That They May Be One: A Study of Papal Doctrine (Leo XIII-Pius XII)* (Westminster, Maryland 1958). T. SARTORY, *The Ecumenical Movement and the Unity of the Church,* tr. H. GRAEF (Oxford 1963). Committee on Purposes and Goals of Ecumenism, Massachusetts Council of Churches, *Odyssey Toward Unity: Foundations and Functions of Ecumenism and Conciliarism* (Newburyport, Massachusetts 1977). Faith and Order, *What Kind of Unity?,* paper n. 69 (Geneva 1974); *Uniting in Hope,* paper n. 72 (Geneva 1974). E. LANNE, ''Pluralism and Unity: the Possibility of a Variety of 'Typologies' within the same Ecclesial Allegiance,'' *One-in-Christ* 6 (1970) 430–51; ''The Unity of the Church in the Work of Faith and Order,'' *One-in-Christ* 12 (1976) 34–57. J. MACQUARRIE *Christian Unity and Christian Diversity* (Philadelphia 1975). Roman Catholic/Presbyterian Reformed Consultation, U.S.A., Statement. *One-in-Christ* ''The Unity We Seek,'' 13 (1977) 258–79. J. WILLEBRANDS, ''Address in Cambridge, England,'' *Documents on Anglican/Roman Catholic Relations,* I (Washington, D.C. 1972) 32–41. JOHN PAUL II, encyclical letter *Ut Unum Sint* (Vatican City 1995).

[P. F. CHIRICO/A. LAUBENTHAL]

UNIFICATION CHURCH

The doctrines of the Unification Church derive from revelations provided to the Reverend Sun Myung Moon, a Korean-born charismatic figure whose followers number in the tens of thousands. He was born of converted Presbyterian parents in 1920, and at the age of 16, reported a vision in which Jesus charged him with the completion of the Messianic mission. Christ's mission was incomplete because he had been killed before he could generate a new human lineage and establish an earthly kingdom. Moon's teachings have been systematized by Young Oon Kim in the book *Divine Principle*, considered a sacred scripture of the church.

Although his formal education at Waseda University, Japan, prepared him for a career in electrical engineering, Moon began to preach his version of salvation history without seminary training, Biblical scholarship, or ministerial ordination. Gathering disciples first at Puson, he then moved to Seoul, the capitol of the Republic of Korea, and in 1954 established the Holy Spirit Association for the Unification of World Christianity. As the church grew in members it sent out missionaries, first to Japan in 1958, then to America in 1959. Eventually, it established missions in more than 100 countries. After the Rev. Moon took up permanent residence in the United States in 1972, the world headquarters was fixed in New York City.

Structures and Practices. In organizational polity the Church resembles a paternalistic kinship system, with the Rev. Moon as final authority and "true parent." There are no clergy in the Church, but governance is assisted by the spouses of the "36 blessed families" of the first mass wedding held in 1961. At the intermediary level are the "central figures," appointed as state and local leaders who direct the church's many missions and commercial enterprises. Loyalty at all levels is filial and familistic rather than hierarchical and ecclesial.

The Unification code of moral behavior emanates from the sanctity of the God-centered family. According to the teachings of Moon, the fall of Adam and Eve was due to sexual license and brought humanity under the spiritual and biological power of Satan. This power is to be broken by the blessings of marriage. Children born of the marriage union are a new and innocent race. Family stability and marital fidelity build on the key virtue of chastity, which is the absolute condition of membership. According to Moon, God's children "can attain divine perfection by becoming a family totally formed on God's principles, and can become dominant over the universe by means of biological reproduction." When members are matched by Rev. Moon for marriage they take on his lineage, become his spiritual children and spiritual siblings to fellow members.

Theology. The center of Unificationist theology is God, the Creator, who suffers as a result of the sins of his children. There is no place for the Trinity, because neither Jesus nor the Holy Spirit is acknowledged as divine. Human creatures pay some indemnity for human sinfulness, but the Father carries the greater share of this debt. The most marked contrast between the teachings of traditional Christianity and those of the Unification Church is the claim that "Jesus did not come to die, but to establish a God-centered family on earth." By his death and resurrection, Jesus paid indemnity for the spiritual redemption of humanity, but the restoration of a physical kingdom is still to be achieved.

With neither a sacramental nor a sacerdotal system, worship services are a simple liturgy patterned on the typical Protestant practices of congregational hymns, prayer, and preaching. The most solemn repetitive ritual is "The Pledge," a prayer recited in unison on Sundays and on the first day of each month. Personal meditation and prayer are the focus of spiritual training in seminars and retreats. All members are trained for public prayer and witnessing to prospective converts. In their ecumenical thrust, the Unificationists participate in the worship rituals of all Christian denominations.

The Rev. Moon's church has been widely described as a "cult." In a few celebrated cases, members have been stolen away by their parents and subsequently "deprogramed." In July 1982, the Rev. Moon was convicted of income tax evasion in the United States when a court rejected his claim that proceeds from the numerous commercial enterprises run by his followers should be exempted on religious grounds. Although many established Christian churches viewed the Unification Church with suspicion, they showed considerable support for Rev. Moon on the grounds that his trial violated the Constitutional separation of Church and State. The Supreme Court declined to hear his final appeal on May 14, 1984 (*Moon v. U.S.*).

Bibliography: J. H. FICHTER, *The Holy Family of Father Moon* (Kansas City 1985). Y. O. KIM, *Unification Theology* (New York 1980). T. MCGOWAN, "The Unification Church," *The Ecumenist* 17:2 (1979). F. SONTAG, *Sun Myung Moon and the Unification Church* (Nashville 1977). S. M. MOON, *Divine Principle* (New York 1973). E. BARKER, *The Making of a Moonie* (New York 1984).

[J. H. FICHTER/EDS.]

UNIFORMITY

Uniformity is the property of objects having one and the same form, or of a whole composed of similar parts, or of an agent always acting in the same way. In philosophy and science, the concept enters principally into the enunciation of the principle of uniformity in nature. According to this, nature acts in a uniform way, that is, the evolution of natural events always follows a determinate and constant order, and equal causes in identical circumstances produce equal effects.

PLATO considered uniformity as a property of the world of ideas, while ARISTOTLE applied it to the world of sensible things, wherein many individuals share in one and the same form or essence. St. THOMAS AQUINAS defines uniformity (*conformitas*) as "accordance in one form, and so it is the same as likeness caused by the unity of a quality" (*In 1 sent.* 48.1.1). Uniformity in essence and in the manner of acting signifies a perfection based upon a natural form and the finality of its nature; it signifies also the limitation of a material being that has no freedom. Aquinas thus notes that the will is a multiform principle, since it is related to opposites, whereas nature is a uniform principle, since it is determined to one genus (*De ver.* 5.2 ad 2).

Since the Renaissance, the principle of uniformity in nature has become the basis of SCIENCE and INDUCTION. It furnishes a precise indication of the existence of physical laws that are necessary and mathematically determined, and is equivalently enunciated as the principle of causality or physical DETERMINISM. It received explicit and systematic treatment from J. S. MILL in his logical teaching on induction (*System of Logic* 3.3). For Mill, it is an axiom related to the course of nature and to the order of the universe; its guarantee is the very success of science in determining physical laws. "In a world wherein similar events would not always recur in a uniform way, there would be no occasion for habitude and exercise, and, therefore, no place for inductive knowledge" [M. Schlick, *Allgemeine Erkenntnislehre* (Berlin 1918) 330]. Yet the purely empirical basis for the principle of uniformity in nature itself begs the principle. This principle should be the result of an induction, not its very beginning; it can have only a probable, heuristic, and pragmatic value, when not based upon the philosophical concept of nature that is urged by scholastic philosophers.

The results of quantum physics are cited against uniformity in nature: "The idea of uniformity of nature, so often claimed to be the ultimate result of science, cannot be extended to include the interphenomena of the world of quanta" [H. Reichenbach, *Philosophic Foundations of Quantum Mechanics* (Berkeley 1948) 39]. Yet the existence of statistical and probability laws is itself a confirmation of uniformity in nature beyond the limits of rigid determinism.

See Also: NATURE; PHILOSOPHY OF NATURE; FIRST PRINCIPLES; CAUSALITY, PRINCIPLE OF.

Bibliography: E. A. BURTT, *The Metaphysical Foundations of Modern Physical Science* (London 1956). R. HOOYKAAS, *The Principle of Uniformity in Geology, Biology and Theology* (Leiden 1963). W. C. SALMON, "The Uniformity of Nature," *Philosophy and Phenomenological Research* 14 (1953–54) 39–48. F. SELVAGGI, *Enciclopedia filosofica,* 4 v. (Venice–Rome 1957) 4:1391–93.

[F. SELVAGGI]

UNIFORMITY, ACTS OF

A series of statutes enacted to regulate the uniformity of public worship and the administration of the sacraments in the Church of England. The first statute enacted for such a purpose was 1 Edward VI, c. 1 (1547), which, after reciting the king's anxiety for religious concord, provided penalties for persons who should contemptuously revile the "Sacrament of the Altar" and enacted that it should be administered under both kinds. However, the first Act of Uniformity to be called by such a name was the act of 1548 (2 & 3 Edward VI, c. 1), which gave statutory authority to the prayer book of Edward VI (which was wholly in English) and prohibited all forms of worship not in accordance with that book; but prayers in Latin, Greek, or Hebrew were permitted to learned men and in universities. Shortly afterward certain alterations were made in the prayer book, and in its amended form it was given statutory authority by the Act of Uniformity of 1551–52 (5 & 6 Edward VI, c. 1). This act made attendance at public worship compulsory, prescribed the revised prayer book as the prayer book required by the act of 1548 to be used in all places of public worship, and imposed penalties for attendance at any unauthorized form of worship. On the accession of Queen Mary the foregoing acts were repealed by the statute 1 Mar., sess. 2, c. 2 (1554), and a further statute of 1555 (1 & 2 Phil. & Mar., c. 8) repealed all acts passed against the papacy since 1528, including the acts establishing the royal supremacy. With the accession of Elizabeth I, the royal supremacy was again imposed. The Elizabethan church settlement was founded upon the Acts of Supremacy (1 Elizabeth I, c. 1) and of Uniformity (1 Elizabeth I, c. 2) of 1559. The Act of Supremacy repealed Mary's repealing act of 1555 and revived a number of statutes of the reign of Henry VIII and the 1 Edward VI, c. 1. All foreign spiritual jurisdiction was abolished, and the royal supremacy reestablished. The Act of Uniformity repealed the repealing act of 1554, revived the repealed acts, and reimposed the second prayer book of Edward VI as modified by the act of 1559. Ministers were required to perform services in accordance with this prayer book, and every person was required to attend his parish church on Sundays and holy days; penalties were provided for failure to comply with the act. The act also provided that the ornaments of the church and its rites and ceremonies were to be regulated by the Queen and her ecclesiastical commissioners. The next statutory alteration was made in the reign of Charles II. On Oct. 25, 1660, the king issued a commission to certain bishops and divines to review the prayer book and to prepare such alterations and additions as they thought fit to offer. The work of this commission resulted in an altered and much expanded prayer book, which received statutory authority by the Act of Uniformity of 1662 (14 Car. II, c. 4) to which it was annexed (this act was one of the series of four statutes known as the Clarendon Code). The act required this prayer book to be used in all places of public worship, and required every beneficed minister to read in his church on some Sunday before Aug. 24, 1662, a prescribed declaration of assent to the prayer book and all its contents; failure to do so incurred the penalty of deprivation. The act prohibited the use of any form of ''common prayer, administration of sacraments, rites or ceremonies'' except those in the prayer book, and the heads of all colleges at Oxford and Cambridge, and of Westminster, Winchester, and Eton were required to subscribe the Thirty-nine Articles. It was provided, however, that the act should not extend to aliens of foreign reformed churches, and there were savings for Latin prayers in the college chapels of Oxford and Cambridge Universities and in the convocations of either province. The bishops of Hereford, St. David's, St. Asaph, and Bangor were required to cause the prayer book to be translated into Welsh. All former Acts of Uniformity were confirmed, and it was provided that they should stand in full force for all purposes for establishing and confirming the Book of Common Prayer authorized by the act of 1662. In 1663 there was passed a further statute (15 Car. II, c. 6) for the relief of those persons who, because of sickness or other impediment, were disabled from subscribing, within the time limited, the declaration required by the act of 1662, and clarifying certain parts of that act.

In 1791 some relief for Catholics from the penalties and disabilities to which they were subjected by the Acts of Uniformity and other acts was provided by the statute 31 Geo. III, c. 32 (given the short title ''The Roman Catholic Relief Act, 1791,'' by the Short Titles Act, 1896), but advantage could be taken of this act only by those who had subscribed the oath of allegiance and abjuration and a simple declaration prescribed by the act; this act was repealed, as to the taking and subscribing of any oath, by the Promissory Oaths Act, 1871 (34 & 35 Vict., c. 48). In 1846 the statute 9 & 10 Vict., c. 59 (given the short title ''The Religious Disabilities Act, 1846,'' by the Short Titles Act, 1896) provided further relief for all dissenters from the Church of England with respect to their religious opinions. This act repealed (in so far as such dissenters were affected) so much of the Act of Uniformity of 1551–52 as required all persons to resort to their parish church at the prescribed times, and so much of the Act of Supremacy of 1559 as made it punishable to defend a foreign ecclesiastical jurisdiction. (It may be noted, in passing, that attendance at public worship is still theoretically enforceable under the Act of 1551–52, except with regard to persons dissenting from the Church of England.) The Book of Common Prayer remained unaltered until the second half of the 19th century. In 1869 royal commissioners were appointed to consider, with a view to securing uniformity, the differences in practice that had arisen as a result of varying interpretations of the rubrics regulating public worship, and to consider the proper lessons to be read on the Sundays and holy days throughout the year. As a result of the reports of this commission two statutes were passed. The first, the Prayer Book (Table of Lessons) Act, 1871 (34 & 35 Vict., c. 37), substituted in the Book of Common Prayer a new Table of Proper Lessons in place of the existing table; and the second, the Act of Uniformity Amendment Act, 1872 (35 & 36 Vict., c. 35), amended the Act of Uniformity of 1662 (the term ''Act of Uniformity'' was defined as meaning the Act of 1662, and as including the enactments confirmed by that act and applied by it to the Book of COMMON PRAYER). The act of 1872 permitted the use of a shortened form of morning and evening prayer, the use of a special form of service approved by the ordinary on a special occasion, and additional services for Sundays and holy days. An alternative lectionary was provided by the Revised Table of Lessons Measure, 1922 (12 & 13 Geo. V., No. 3), and the Vestures of Ministers Measure, 1964 (1964, No. 7), regulating the vestures worn by the ministers of the Church of England, amended the Ornaments Rubric of the Prayer Book and s. 13 of the Act of Uniformity of 1559 (or 1558 as cited in the Measure). Finally, the Prayer Book (Alternative and Other Services) Measure, 1965 (1965, No. 1), authorized the experimental use of approved alternative services deviating from the Prayer Book annexed to the Act of 1662, and certain other forms of service not provided for therein. Meanwhile, in 1874 there had been passed the Public Worship Regulation Act, 1874 (37 & 38 Vict., c. 85), which established a unified procedure for enforcing the law relating to the form of services and ornaments as declared by or pursuant to the various Acts of Uniformity.

Bibliography: *Statutes of the Realm; Statutes at Large; Statutes Revised* (all published by authority).

[G. DE C. PARMITER]

UNIGENITUS

The bull of CLEMENT XI, dated Sept. 8, 1713, that condemns 101 propositions taken from *Nouveau Testa-*

ment avec des réflexions morales sur chaque verset by the Oratorian Pasquier QUESNEL. The first version of the work, which was much shorter, had appeared in 1671; the bull alludes to a much more developed text that the Archbishop of Paris, Cardinal L. de Noailles, had caused to be published in 1699 and in which he had introduced various corrections after having consulted Bossuet. The JANSENIST and Gallican leanings that are expressed in the *Réflexions morales* had already caused their being placed on the Index by the brief *Universi dominici gregis* of July 13, 1708. Many of the condemned propositions correspond to formulas in which the efficacy of grace is exalted to the point of seeming to destroy liberty; others seem to limit the Church to the predestined only. However, some seem at first sight very similar to formulas accepted by the orthodox Augustinians, which explains the painful controversies that followed the publication of the bull and led France to the brink of schism.

Bibliography: H. DENZINGER, *Enchiridion symbolorum,* ed. A. SCHÖNMETZER, (Freiburg 1963) 2400–2502. J. F. THOMAS, *La Querelle de l'Unigenitus* (Paris 1950). L. CEYSSENS, "Autour de la bulle 'Unigenitus': son acceptation par l'assemblée du clergé," *Revue d'Histoire Ecclesiastique* 80 (1985) 369–414 (Pt. I), 732–759 (Pt. II). J. M. GRES-GAYER, "The *Unigenitus* of Clement XI : A Fresh Look at the Issues," *Theological Studies* 49 (1988) 259–282; *Théologie et pouvoir en Sorbonne: la faculté de théologie de Paris et la bulle Unigenitus* (Paris 1991). L. CEYSSENS, *Le sort de la Bulle Unigenitus,* ed. M. LAMBERIGTS (Louvain, 1992).

[L. J. COGNET]

UNITARIAN UNIVERSALIST ASSOCIATION

Formed in May 1961 by a merger of the American Unitarian Association (1847) and the Universalist Church of America (1866).

Beginning about 1865, UNITARIANS and UNIVERSALISTS became conscious of each other as proponents of liberal religion, and efforts were initiated to bring the two denominations together. These attempts took three forms: higher councils, leaving the denominational bodies intact; increased cooperation; and organic union. A resolution, offered in 1865 in the American Unitarian Association calling for union with the Universalists, was defeated. Similar proposals were defeated in 1899 and 1931. Not until 1947 was a motion passed by both denominations to explore the possibility of church union. A joint commission was appointed and its report in 1949 laid the groundwork for federal union. In 1951 the joint commission presented a plan calling for federal union of religious education, publications, and public relations, and gradually a complete merger. The Council of Liberal Churches was created and a joint interim commission ap-

pointed to draft a constitution and bylaws. Meanwhile, Unitarian and Universalist youth, in joint convention, voted to dissolve their respective denominational youth organizations and formed the Liberal Religious Youth organization (1953). In the same year another joint interim commission was appointed to consider various departmental mergers; it recommended that delegates to the next biennial meetings should vote on whether or not the two denominations should sooner or later be merged. Efforts were renewed in 1955, and six years later union was finally achieved. Rev. Dr. Dana McLean Greeley, formerly Unitarian president, became first president of the new association.

Flexibility, freedom and autonomy are the principal hallmarks of the Unitarian Universalist Association (UUA). Both Unitarian and Universalist congregations are able to retain their respective distinctive theology and traditions within the setup of the UUA. The constitution of the UUA states, among other things, that no minister, member or congregation "shall be required to subscribe to any particular interpretation of religion, or to any particular religious belief or creed." Much of the work and a great part of the service programs of the UUA are carried forward through the work of the departments organized by the board and the administration. Its publishing house, Beacon Press is a well-respected publisher of mainstream religious books. The headquarters of the UUA is located in Boston.

Bibliography: H. H., CHEETHAM, *Unitarianism and Universalism* (Boston 1962). D. ROBINSON, *The Unitarians and the Universalists* (Westport, CT 1985). J. SIAS, *100 Questions That Nonmembers Ask about Unitarian Universalism* (Nashua, NH 1998). F.S. MEAD, S. S. HILL, and C. D. ATWOOD, eds., *Handbook of Denominations in the United States,* 11th ed (Nashville 2001).

[J. R. WILLIS/EDS.]

UNITARIANS

Those who reject the doctrine of the Trinity and favor the belief that there is no distinction of persons in God. They seek to demonstrate the possibility of creating a genuine and enduring religious community without requiring doctrinal conformity.

General Characteristics. "Deeds not creeds" expresses the Unitarian conviction that when doctrines are used as a test of entrance into the community, they beget hypocrisy; at best, they reduce religious belief to a matter of routine; at worst, they produce bigotry and persecution. Unitarians hold that religious beliefs are too often merely speculative statements about abstract and largely irrelevant questions instead of genuine personal commitments to real issues. Unitarian ministers must be dedicated to the building of the church as a religious community that shall be an indispensable medium for the fulfillment of individual and social life. Unitarian fellowship is one from which no one is excluded, except, as William Ellery CHANNING put it, ''by the death of goodness in his own breast.'' Unitarian churches do not reject all tradition, but they do not regard it as sacred simply because people immersed in that tradition believe it so. Their ideal is an openness that does not exclude anything that may be illuminating—from the Old Testament to today's newspaper. Truth cannot be reduced to a creed; indeed, creedal matters are purposely kept open. Differing opinions are not merely tolerated, but looked upon as the most likely source of new and better understanding.

Another characteristic of the Unitarian fellowship is its democratic form of church government, known in ecclesiastical circles as ''congregational polity.'' This means that a local congregation is a complete church, with all of the powers of a church; that its being and powers rest upon the free, deliberate consent of the individual members; and that all business is conducted within the church in accordance with accepted rules of order. Worship is generally of a nonliturgical character and consists of hymns; readings from Scriptures, both ancient and modern; prayer; a sermon, which is generally the high point of the worship service; and special music such as anthems, chorales, etc. Simplicity is the keynote; appurtenances such as vestments, a cross, religious pictures, surplices, and candles are seldom in evidence.

Origin and Historical Development. Although Unitarianism as now held originated in the period of the Protestant Reformation, there were examples in earlier centuries of those who consciously or unconsciously rejected the orthodox Catholic notions of a Triune God, original sin, predestination, redemption through Jesus Christ, the divine Redeemer, and a judgment of everlasting rewards or punishment. Among these were Michael SERVETUS, who was burned at the stake (1553) in Geneva for his antitrinitarian views. Although far from being a Unitarian by any modern standard of belief, he is rightfully considered one of its pioneers. The same may be said of Faustus Socinus (1539–1604) and his followers in Poland, and those of Franz DAVID (1510–79), who laid the foundation for the Unitarian Church in Transylvania (*see* SOCINIANISM). In England John BIDDLE (1615–62) is credited with being the father of Unitarianism, although no separate Unitarian denomination was formed there until the late 18th century, when T. Lindsey opened Essex Chapel in London (1774).

Origin in the U.S. In 17th-century America, Calvinistic theology and moral standards were planted in New England, and those who would not conform to their pat-

Clock tower atop First Unitarian Church, Providence, Rhode Island. (©Lee Snider/CORBIS.)

tern of belief and practice were invited to move elsewhere. In time, however, many refused to accept the stern inheritance of traditional Calvinism, with its doctrines of original sin, total depravity, and double predestination. Moreover, after the Revolutionary War the impact of deism, atheism, and skepticism led many liberal persons to reexamine the whole Puritan heritage. Matters came to a head in the celebrated Dedham Case of 1818, in which the voters of the parish in Dedham, Mass., who were predominantly Unitarian in sentiment, forced the appointment of a minister of Unitarian views, over the protest of the church, which was predominantly evangelical. A majority of the members of the church thereupon withdrew; and, claiming that they, rather than the minority that remained, constituted the First Church of Dedham, demanded the meetinghouse and property. The case, carried to the state supreme court, was decided against them: ''When the majority of the members of a Congregational Church separate from the majority of the parish, the members who remain, although a minority, constitute the church in such parish, and retain the rights and property thereto.'' In 1819 Channing preached his famous sermon on ''Unitarian Christianity'' at Baltimore, Md., and this, with some subsequent articles, constituted a platform of the Unitarian movement that eventuated (1825) in the organization of the American Unitarian Association. Another landmark statement of Unitarian principles was the Divinity School Address of Ralph Waldo Emerson (1838). This was followed three years later by Theodore Parker's ''The Transient and Permanent in Christianity,'' a sermon in defense of natural religion. Meanwhile, Unitarian activity on the frontier resulted in the Western Unitarian Conference of 1852 in Cincinnati, Ohio. This led to the National Conference of Unitarian Churches in 1865, the same year that a proposed resolution for union with the Universalists was defeated.

Later Modifications. By now the basic presuppositions of Calvinist theology were being severely challenged. Such dogmas as the depravity of man, the Trinity, the Atonement, the verbal inspiration of the Scriptures, and the ''sealed nature'' of Revelation were being liberally interpreted in the light of new ideas. God, instead of being conceived as a supernaturally all-powerful Being, was conceived as the force for goodness visible in the power and beauty of nature, the moral law, and noble human lives. Jesus was no longer considered the unique Son of God, the Redeemer, but a great spiritual genius in line with the Hebrew prophets. The religion *of* Jesus must be recaptured and replace the antiquated religion *about* Jesus. Christianity became just one of many possible roads to the divine, not the only religion of salvation. The Bible must be critically examined in light of modern science, and seen not to be a unique book, but as a work of man witnessing to his continual search for the meaning of life. In religion as in science, the new teaching was based on ''first hand experience'' and not upon blind acceptance of a supernaturally revealed dogma and moral code. Belief in the dignity of man, in the validity of the democratic processes, and in the oneness of the human family, as well as sensitivity to suffering and beauty, were seen to be a truer witness of religious growth than theological orthodoxy. The Western Unitarian Conference (1885) announced that it ''conditions its fellowship on no dogmatic tests, but welcomes all who wish to join it to help establish Truth, Righteousness and Love in the world.'' Forty-five years later the Tract Commission of the American Unitarian Association declared:''Unitarian churches are dedicated to the progressive transformation and ennoblement of individual and social life through religion, in accordance with the advancing knowledge and growing vision of mankind. Bound by this common purpose, and committed to freedom of belief, Unitarians hold in unity of spirit a diversity of convictions.'' Similar statements appeared in 1944 and again in 1958.

In 1902 the Beacon Press was established to broaden the book-publishing program, and some years later it began a series of pioneer publications in the field of religious education. By 1940 the number of Unitarians outside New England exceeded the number within New England. The Unitarian Service Committee was organized the same year, and in the following year, the United Unitarian Appeal, which marked the growing national awareness of Unitarianism. Meanwhile a *rapprochement* was taking place with the UNIVERSALISTS, and in 1953 the youth organizations of both denominations merged to form the Liberal Religious Youth. The same year saw an establishment of a joint commission on merger by the votes of the delegates at the joint biennial sessions, and eight years later the proposed merger achieved reality when the UNITARIAN UNIVERSALIST ASSOCIATION was given corporate status in May 1961 under special acts of legislature of the Commonwealth of Massachusetts and the State of New York.

Unitarians have long exerted an influence far greater than their numbers would indicate. Charles Beard, the American historian, noted that ''Jefferson, Paine, John Adams, Washington, Franklin, and many lesser lights were to be reckoned either among the Unitarians or the Deists,'' and such men as Channing, Emerson, and Parker exercised tremendous influence on the New England authors of the 19th century.

Bibliography: H. B. SCHOLEFIELD, ''Unitarian History: A Brief,'' *An Information Manual for the Use of Unitarian and Universalist Churches, Societies and Fellowships* (Wellesley Hills, Mass. 1958). J. H. ALLEN, *Historical Sketch of the Unitarian Movement since the Reformation* (New York 1894). C. WRIGHT, *The Beginnings of Unitarianism in America* (Boston 1955). D. B. PARKE, ed., *The Epic of Unitarianism* (Boston 1957). H. H. CHEETHAM, *Unitarianism and Universalism* (Boston 1962). C. WRIGHT, *The Liberal Christians; Essays on American Unitarian History* (Boston 1970). S. E. AHLSTROM and J. S. CAREY, *An American Reformation: A Documentary History of Unitarian Christianity* (Middletown, Conn. 1985). D. ROBINSON, *The Unitarians and the Universalists* (Westport, Conn. 1985). J. SIAS, *100 Questions that Non-members Ask about Unitarian Universalism* (Nashua, N.H. 1998).

[J. R. WILLIS/EDS.]

UNITED ARAB EMIRATES, THE CATHOLIC CHURCH IN

The United Arab Emirates is located on the Arabian Peninsula, and is bordered on the north by the Persian Gulf, on the east by Oman, and on the southwest and west by SAUDI ARABIA. Primarily desert, the region contains a flat western coastal plain that rises to rolling desert sands, with a mountainous region shared by Oman through a yet-undefined border. Cooler in the eastern mountains, most of the region remains hot throughout the year, and sand and dust storms are frequent. Fresh water is scarce, but desalination plants provide sufficient quantities for human needs and for the production of such agricultural crops as dates, vegetables and watermelons, and livestock and poultry raising. Natural resources are limited to petroleum and natural gas.

Formed through the 1971 merger of the seven Trucial States formed during the 19th century, the United Arab Emirates includes Abu Dhabi, 'Ajman, Al Mughayra, Ash Shâriqah, Dubayy, Umm al Qaywayn and Ra's al Khaymah, the last joining the federation in 1972. Aayid bin Sultan al Nuhayyan, emir of the state of Abu Dhabi, was made president, with other emirs assuming significant positions within the government. Officials are chosen from among the seven emirs, which meet four times a year; the position of president and vice president are reconsidered every five years.

History. Originally part of a Sumerian trade route, the region was converted to Islam in the 6th century. Portuguese traders entered the region in the 1500s, followed by the British East India Company a century later, although no mission activity followed. The sheikdoms of the region concluded a series of treaties banning maritime warfare with Great Britain, slave trading and arms trading beginning in the 1820s, and in 1892 they agreed to British control of their external affairs in exchange for military protection. From that point on they were known as the Trucial States. Massive oil reserves were discovered near Abu Dhabi in 1958.

On Dec. 2, 1971 the region ended its relationship with Great Britain through a treaty of friendship and proclaimed independence. The federation's constitution, drafted in 1971, was formally adopted in 1996. Islam was made the official religion throughout the federation, and Shari'a, Islamic law, guided the criminal and civil courts in each of the separate emirates. Unlike other Islamic states such as Saudi Arabia, the right to practice other faiths was tolerated by the state as long as such practice did not conflict with Shari'a; proselytization of Muslims was forbidden and marriage between a Muslim woman and a man outside her faith was punishable by the man's imprisonment. The Roman Catholic Church and the Eastern Orthodox Church were among the few religious groups recognized by the government, which considered them a legal entity.

Since 1973, when oil exportation was initiated, the region witnessed a marked improvement in its standard of living, and the government attempted to maintain the quality of life through an open economy and the implementation of economic reforms to supplement its reliance on oil exports. The immigration of foreign workers from

Capital: Abu Dhabi.
Size: 30,000 sq. miles.
Population: 2,369,155 in 2000.
Languages: Arabic, Persian, Hindi, English, Urdu.
Ethnic groups: Native Emirians constitute one fifth of the population; other groups include Arabs, South Asians, and Europeans, most of whom are not citizens of the Emirates.
Religions: 142,150 Catholics (6%), 1,826,860 Sunni Muslims (77%), 305,385 Shī'a Muslim (13%), 94,760 Protestants (4%).
Ecclesiastical organizations: The United Arab Emirates is the seat of the apostolic vicariate of Arabia, which oversees Bahrain, Oman, Qatar, Saudi Arabia, Yemen, and the United Arab Emirates from Abu-Dhabi.

Asia, Oceania and Africa to the region to work in the oil industry required that the Church provide places of worship. By 2000 the region was home to five parishes tended by three diocesan and 16 religious priests. Approximately 40 sisters aided the efforts of the Church through work in Catholic private schools, as well as in hospitals and orphanages. Christian churches and burial sites existed in many major cities, often on land donated by the local emir. Ash Shâriqah, saw the construction of a new Catholic church in 1997, and in another was under construction in Ra's al Khaymah in 2000, demonstrating an increase in the faith. Followers of the Armenian Orthodox Church and several Protestant faiths were also present and allowed to openly worship in the emirates. In 1999 the government sponsored a ecumenical meeting, ''Islam and the West'' in honor of a visit with British Prince Charles.

Bibliography: *A Century in 30 Years: Shaykh Zayed and the United Arab Emirates,* ed. J. A. KECHICHIAN (Middle East Policy Council 2000). R. SAID ZAHLAN *The Origins of the United Arab Emirates: A Political and Social History of the Trucial States.* F. HEARD-BEY, *From Trucial States to United Arab Emirates.*

[P. SHELTON]

UNITED BRETHREN

Officially styled Church of the United Brethren in Christ (Old Constitution), a minority group that seceded from the larger United Brethren Church in 1889, when it modified its ban against membership in secret societies. The parent body, United Brethren Church, had merged in 1946 with the Evangelical Church to form the EVANGELICAL UNITED BRETHREN Church (Eub), which in turn merged in 1968 with the Methodist Church to form the UNITED METHODIST CHURCH.

The United Brethren movement began with the evangelistic efforts of Philip William OTTERBEIN (1726–1813) and Martin BOEHM (1725–1813). Working

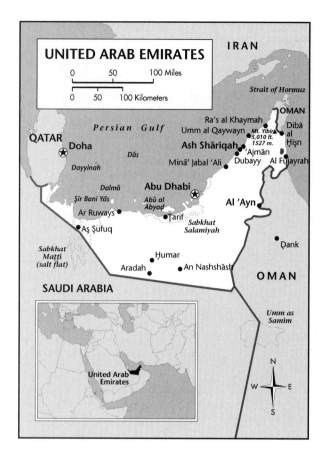

Bibliography: F. S. MEAD, S. S. HILL, and C. D. ATWOOD, eds., *Handbook of Denominations in the United States,* 11th ed (Nashville 2001).

[W. J. WHALEN]

UNITED CHURCH OF CHRIST

A Protestant denomination formed June 25, 1957, by the union of the EVANGELICAL AND REFORMED CHURCH and the General Council of the Congregational Christian Churches, the latter arose from a merger of the Congregational Churches and the Christian Church in 1931. It seeks to express more fully the oneness in Christ of the churches composing it, to make more effective their common witness to Him, and to serve His kingdom in the world. It acknowledges as its sole Head, Jesus Christ, the Son of God and the Savior of all, and it acknowledges as sisters and brothers in Christ all who share in their confession. It looks to the Word of God in the Scriptures, and to the presence and power of the Holy Spirit, to prosper its creative and redemptive work in the world. It claims as its own the faith of the historic church expressed in the ancient creeds and reclaimed in the basic insights of the Protestant Reformers.

Since both denominations were similar in belief, worship, and polity, their leaders began in the 1940s to explore the possibility of merger. A document called "The Basis of Union," outlining procedures and principles of church union, circulated through each denomination and was amended until it was acceptable to all. Both denominations independently gave official approval to this, thus leading to the uniting meeting of 1957.

The statement of faith of the United Church of Christ that was first adopted in 1959 includes the following:

> We believe in God, the Eternal Spirit, Father of our Lord Jesus Christ and our Father, and to his deeds we testify: He calls the worlds into being, creates man in his own image and sets before him the ways of life and death. He seeks in holy love to save all people from aimlessness and sin. He judges men and nations by his righteous will declared through prophets and apostles. In Jesus Christ, the man of Nazareth, our crucified and risen Lord, he has come to us and shared our common lot, conquering sin and death and reconciling the world to himself. He bestows upon us his Holy Spirit, creating and renewing the Church of Jesus Christ, binding in covenant faithful people of all ages, tongues, and races. He calls us into his Church to accept the cost and joy of discipleship, to be his servants in the service of men, to proclaim the gospel to all the world and resist the powers of evil, to share in Christ's baptism and eat

among the German settlers in Pennsylvania, they preached an Arminian theology and episcopal church polity almost identical with that of Methodism (*see* ARMINIANISM). Had the Methodist bishops been willing to accept the German-speaking congregations, the work of Otterbein and Boehm would not have resulted in a separate denomination. The United Brethren Church revealed traces also of the Lutheran, Mennonite, Dunkard, and Reformed heritages of its early leaders. The church's constitution of 1841 forbade affiliation with such societies as Freemasonry. In 1889 it was proposed that it apply this ban only to those secret societies "which infringe upon the rights of those outside their organization and whose principles and practices are injurious to the Christian character of their members." The dissenters understood this to mean toleration of membership in lodges and fraternities.

The United Brethren in Christ (Old Constitution) follow the same theology as the Methodist Churches. They are pacifists and must forswear alcohol, tobacco, and membership in lodges. Both men and women may be ordained to the ministry. The general conference of the church meets every four years and is composed of ministers, presiding elders, general church officials, and bishops.

at his table, to join him in his passion and victory. He promises to all who trust him forgiveness of sins and fullness of grace, courage in the struggle for justice and peace, his presence in trial and rejoicing, and eternal life in his kingdom which has no end.

The United Church of Christ affirms the responsibility of the church in each generation to make the faith of the historic church its own in purity of heart before God. It recognizes two sacraments: Baptism and the Lord's Supper, or Holy Communion.

Polity. The United Church of Christ is composed of local churches, associations, conferences, and the general synod. The basic unit of its life and organization is the local church, which is composed of persons who are organized for Christian worship, for the furtherance of Christian fellowship, and for the continuing work of Christian witness. Persons usually become church members by (1) Baptism and either confirmation or profession of faith in Jesus Christ as Lord and Savior; (2) reaffirmation or reprofession of faith; or (3) letter of transfer or certification from other Christian churches.

The United Church of Christ embodies both presbyterianism and congregationalism. It embraces: (1) the local churches of the Evangelical and Reformed Church; (2) the local churches of the Congregational Christian fellowship, which vote to become a part of the United Church of Christ, or approve its constitution; (3) any local congregational Christian church which, although it has not voted to become a part of the United Church of Christ, or to approve its constitution, votes to join later; and (4) local churches of any denomination that seek membership under mutually satisfactory provisions.

Local Church. The autonomy of the local church is inherent, and modifiable only by its own action. Nothing in the constitution and bylaws of the United Church of Christ destroys or limits the right of each local church to continue to operate in the way customary to it, or gives to the general synod, or to any conference or association, now or at any future time, the power to abridge or impair the autonomy of any local church in the management of its own affairs. These affairs include, but are not limited to, the right to retain or adopt its own methods of organization, worship, and education; to retain or secure its own charter or name; to adopt its own constitution and bylaws; to formulate its own covenants and confessions of faith; to admit members in its own way and to provide for their discipline or dismissal; to call or dismiss its pastor or pastors by such procedure as it shall determine; to acquire, own, manage, and dispose of property and funds; to control its own benevolences; and to withdraw by its own decision from the United Church of Christ at any time

without forfeiture of ownership or control of any real or personal property owned by it.

The privilege and responsibility of witnessing to the Gospel belong to every member of the church, which seeks to provide opportunities for teaching, evangelizing, healing, preaching, and administration; full-time service for various forms of ministry may be recognized by ordination, commissioning, or other appropriate services of dedication. Ordination is the rite whereby the United Church of Christ through an association, in cooperation with the local church, sets apart by prayer and laying on of hands those of its members whom God has called to the Christian ministry.

Association and Conference. An association is that body within a conference of the United Church of Christ which is composed of all local churches in a geographical area and of all ministers who have standing in that association. It may retain or secure its own charter and adopt its own constitution, bylaws, and other rules, which it deems essential to its own welfare and not inconsistent with the constitution and bylaws of the United Church of Christ. A conference is composed of all local churches in a geographical area and of all ministers who have standing in the associations of that conference or in the conference itself. The General Synod is the highest representative body of the United Church of Christ, comprising delegates chosen by the conferences, and of ex officio delegates; these constitute the voting delegates. The general synod has the following powers, provided, however, that no power vested in the general synod invades the autonomy of conferences, associations, and local churches, or impairs their right to acquire, own, manage, and dispose of property and funds: (1) it carries on—directly and through its executive council, instrumentalities, and other bodies—the work of the United Church of Christ, and provides for the financial support of this work; (2) it organizes as required for the transaction of business; (3) it nominates and elects officers chosen from its own membership; these, with the moderators, serve as officers of the general synod; (4) it establishes and maintains a national headquarters and central treasury; (5) it determines relationships with ecumenical organizations, world confessional bodies, and other interdenominational agencies; and (6) it looks to formal union with them when appropriate.

Areas of Concern. The United Church of Christ recognizes responsibilities at home and abroad for missions, fraternal aid and service, ecumenical relations, interchurch relations and Christian unity, education, publication, the ministry, ministerial pensions and relief, evangelism, stewardship, social action, health and welfare, and any other appropriate area of need or concern. The name in-

Saint George's United Methodist Church, built in 1769, Philadelphia, Pennsylvania. (©Lee Snider/CORBIS)

strumentalities is given to the boards and other organizations that serve as arms of the church.

The United Church of Christ is deeply concerned with Christian unity. It supports the WORLD COUNCIL OF CHURCHES, the NATIONAL COUNCIL OF THE CHURCHES OF CHRIST IN THE U.S.A., and also the CONSULTATION ON CHURCH UNION. It also established an ecumenical partnership with the Christian Churches (Disciples of Christ) in 1985. Its national headquarters are located in Cleveland, Ohio.

Bibliography: D. HORTON, *The United Church of Christ: Its Origins, Organization, and Role in the World Today* (New York 1962). F. S. MEAD, S. S. HILL, and C. D. ATWOOD, eds., *Handbook of Denominations in the United States,* 11th ed (Nashville 2001).

[J. R. WILLIS/EDS.]

UNITED METHODIST CHURCH

Two streams of American Protestantism, the Methodist Church and the EVANGELICAL UNITED BRETHREN CHURCH, merged on April 23, 1968 to form the United Methodist Church. Both of the former denominations emerged from or had strong ties with the Wesleyan movement which began in the American colonies of Maryland and New York through the preaching of Robert Strawbridge (probably 1764) and Philip Embury (1766). In 1769 John Wesley sent two of the English preachers to assist in the establishment of Methodist societies in the colonies. Two years later Francis Asbury was sent also by Wesley, and on Dec. 24, 1784, the Methodist Episcopal Church was organized, with Thomas Coke and Francis Asbury as joint superintendents. While not rigidly doctrinaire, the Methodist Episcopal Church took as its doctrinal standards the Twenty-five Articles of Religion, which Wesley had abbreviated from the Anglican Thirty-nine Articles, the Standard Sermons of Wesley, and Wesley's notes on the New Testament. The early Methodist movement was characterized by the emphases of its preachers on the universally available grace of God and the standards of moral holiness which the gospel of grace presents to persons who respond in repentance and faith.

The Methodist Episcopal Church experienced a division which in 1830 produced the Methodist Protestant Church. The controversy was not doctrinal but concerned polity, with the Methodist Reformers (Methodist Protestants) advocating less episcopal authority and wider lay participation in the church. The next serious breach occurred in 1845 when the Methodist Episcopal Church, South, was formed. Again the controversy was not doctrinal but centered on the issue of slavery. In 1939 these three Methodist bodies were reunited in the Methodist Church. The polity of the Methodist Church included bishops elected by six regional and one racial jurisdictions. Legislative and promotional work was effected through smaller regional conferences which met annually and a quadrennial general conference. The annual conference and the general conference sessions were to be composed of equal representation of clergy and laity.

The Evangelical United Brethren Church was formed in 1946 through a merger of the Evangelical Church and the Church of the United Brethren in Christ. These bodies originated in the late 18th and early 19th centuries, principally in the Middle Atlantic states of Maryland and Pennsylvania as chiefly German-speaking congregations. Their original leaders came from Reformed, Lutheran, and Mennonite backgrounds. The dominant influence, however, was Wesleyan theology, piety, and polity mediated through Francis Asbury and other early Methodist leaders.

Through the leadership of Philip William Otterbein, an ordained clergyman of the German Reformed Church, and Martin Boehm, Mennonite in background, evangelical work among the German-speaking population of Pennsylvania, Maryland, and Virginia spread until in 1800 an annual meeting of ministers under their direction was organized. Their influence spread into the Ohio Valley, and the name United Brethren in Christ designated their efforts.

The Evangelical Church arose through the efforts of Jacob Albright, whose conversion occurred in 1791. Albright's witnessing among the German-speaking people of Pennsylvania eventuated in a council called in 1803. In 1816 the name, the Evangelical Association, was adopted. A division within this group occurred in 1891 with the larger body taking the name, the United Evangelical Church. In 1922 the Evangelical Church was created as a result of the Evangelical Association and the United Evangelical Church coming together.

The Asbury group and the Otterbein-Boehm-Albright group had much in common. Their emphasis upon personal religious experience or personal salvation and their evangelical passion led them in similar directions, and frequently they were found working in close cooperation. Otterbein participated in the ordination of Asbury. When the book of Discipline for Asbury's Methodists was translated into German, it became the basis for the book of Discipline for the *Evangelische Gemeinschaft* of Albright. In some regions the Asbury group was called the "English Methodists" and the Otterbein-Boehm-Albright group was designated the "German Methodists" or the "Dutch Methodists." Conversations concerning union began as early as 1803. In 1871 the Evangelical Association by a narrow vote agreed to join the Methodists, but the union never occurred. The significant union of the United Brethren in Christ and the Evangelical Church in 1946 paved the way for the union of 1968 which resulted in the United Methodist Church.

The United Methodists are still characterized by their evangelical concerns, demonstrated by their extensive mission outreach in Asia, Africa, and Latin America. Their concern for social as well as personal morality is expressed in the Statement of Social Principles. The polity of the United Methodist Church remains essentially the same with episcopal leadership elected by jurisdictional conferences. Membership in annual conferences and the general conference is balanced between clergy and laity.

Bibliography: E. BUCK, ed., *History of American Methodism* (Nashville 1964). P. ELLER, *These Evangelical United Brethren* (Dayton, Ohio 1957). J. LEE, *A Short History of Methodism in the U.S.A.* (Baltimore 1810). W. W. SWEET, *Methodism in American History* (Nashville 1963). F.S. MEAD, S.S. HILL and C.D. ATWOOD, eds., *Handbook of Denominations in the United States,* 11th ed (Nashville 2001).

[J. C. LOGAN]

UNITED STATES CATHOLIC MISSION ASSOCIATION

The United States Catholic Mission Association (USCMA) unites and supports people committed to the global mission of Jesus in service to Church and world. Its membership includes mission-sending congregations and societies, diocesan mission offices, and individual missioners. The USCMA carries out its mandate through conferences and seminars, publications, and ongoing mission research. Its headquarters are in Washington, D.C.

Historically, the USCMA is linked both to the Mission Secretariat, which served mission-sending groups from 1949 to 1969, and to the U.S. Catholic Mission Council (USCMC) which existed from 1969 to 1981, when it was dissolved into the present association. The Mission Secretariat, an affiliate with the National Catholic Welfare Conference (NCWC), had a fourfold purpose: (i) to assist Catholic U.S.-based missionary communities by providing a convenient means of contact both among themselves and with governmental and private agencies; (ii) to facilitate information exchange for the various community headquarters and American missioners in the field; (iii) to help in the gathering of statistics and other information; and (iv) to provide Catholic agencies in the United States with a convenient means of contact with Catholic missionaries. Its successor, the USCMC emerged in response to the call for the establishment of a national mission council as recommended by the Missionary Decree, *Ad gentes* of Vatican II (art. 30). The USCMC consisted of five constituent committees, representing the National Conference of Catholic Bishops (NCCB), the Conference of Major Superiors of Men (CMSM), the Leadership Conference of Women Religious (LCWR), lay missionary groups and mission agencies. It provided a forum for exchange of ideas and information on mission issues, as well as enabled its members to collaborate on common projects. Since 1981, the USCMA continues the work of the USCMC in collaboration with the NCCB's Secretariat for Evangelization and Missions and U.S.-based mission sending societies.

Bibliography: R. RUSTEMEYER, "United States Catholic Mission Association: A Pastoral Perspective on Mission," *The Living Light* 34 (1998) 22–25.

[R. RUSTEMEYER]

UNITED STATES CONFERENCE OF CATHOLIC BISHOPS (USCCB)

General Background

The United States Conference of Catholic Bishops (USCCB) is a canonically established body which finds its charter in Vatican Council II's Decree on the Pastoral Office of Bishops in the Church, *Christus Dominus* (1965). In this decree, the Council declared that "it would be in the highest degree helpful if in all parts of the world the bishops of each country or region would meet regularly, so that by sharing their wisdom and experience and exchanging views they may jointly formulate a program for the common good of the Church" (#37).

The *motu proprio Ecclesiae Sanctae* (1966) of Pope Paul VI directed that episcopal conferences be established as soon as possible and that statutes be drawn up and approved by the Holy See. The initial statutes of the U.S. episcopal conference were approved on Dec. 19, 1970. Subsequent revisions were approved in 1976, 1981, 1988, and on Nov. 28, 2000.

The 1983 revised *Code of Canon Law* made the establishment of national and territorial episcopal conferences a matter of universal law. Canon 447 states, "A conference of bishops, a permanent institution, is a group of bishops of some nation or certain territory who jointly exercise certain pastoral functions for the Christian faithful of their territory in order to promote the greater good which the Church offers humanity, especially through forms and programs of the apostolate fittingly adapted to the circumstances of time and place, according to the norm of law."

The establishment of episcopal conferences gave rise to a lengthy discussion of their status, in particular, the extent to which they participate in the Church's teaching authority. The 1985 Extraordinary Assembly of the Synod of Bishops on the occasion of the twentieth anniversary of the conclusion of Vatican II made the clarification of the juridical status and the teaching authority of episcopal conferences a primary recommendation for action by the Holy See.

That clarification came in the *motu proprio Apostolos Suos* (1998) of Pope John Paul II which confirmed that an episcopal conference does exercise magisterial authority when teaching with unanimity "in communion with the head of the college [of bishops] and its members." If unanimity is lacking, a majority of the membership alone "cannot issue a declaration as authentic teaching to which all the faithful of the territory" must adhere unless it receives the subsequent *recognitio* (approval) by the Holy See which will be given only if the majority is "substantial" (#22).

Apostolos Suos made it clear that while the "collegial spirit" is given concrete application "when the bishops of a territory jointly exercise certain pastoral functions for the good of the faithful," this does not take on the "collegial nature" proper only to the entire college of bishops when acting in union with its head (#12). It also decreed several complementary norms with which every episcopal conference must be in conformity.

While the limitations placed on episcopal conferences in the Church's official documents are often emphasized, it must also be said that they have quickly assumed a regular role in the Church's life. In the 1983 revised *Code of Canon Law*, 84 canons call for or permit legislative action by the episcopal conference, through which the universal law is implemented in the conference's territory; liturgical adaptations and translations must be approved by the episcopal conference; and the Holy See, on an *ad hoc* basis, may ask a conference to devise norms to meet specific situations. Most of these steps require subsequent approval by the Holy See, but they demonstrate the utility of the episcopal conference both in providing a hierarchy with a unified voice and also in facilitating the Holy See's interaction with that hierarchy.

National Catholic Welfare Conference (NCWC), 1919–1966

The formal association of archbishops and bishops of the United States can be traced back to the 19th century and the Plenary Councils of Baltimore. After the Third Plenary Council of 1884, the U.S. hierarchy was not to meet again as whole until 1919, although the archbishops continued to meet annually.

More direct precedents for an episcopal conference in the United States are found in the National Catholic War Council and, especially, the National Catholic Welfare Conference (NCWC) whose activities were incorporated into the conference established in 1966 at the mandate of Vatican II.

In response to the first crisis of truly global proportions—the First World War—the National Catholic War Council was established as a wartime committee of the U.S. archbishops to coordinate the Catholic activities which had arisen in support of the war effort.

Such coordination was recommended in 1917 by Paulist Father John Burke, director of the Chaplains' Aid Association. With the support of Cardinal James Gibbons of Baltimore, Cardinal William O'Connell of Boston, and Cardinal John Farley of New York, Father Burke assembled a meeting of bishops, representatives of lay societies, and members of the Catholic press. As Burke's plan for coordination was discussed, fear that a new type of organization would usurp the work of existing societies was dispelled; and the delegates passed a resolution recommending the establishment of a national coordinating committee to be known as the National Catholic War Council.

Gibbons, quick to act on this resolution, wrote to the hierarchy proposing the formation of this Council, with all the U.S. archbishops as its administrative board and with a committee of four bishops to direct ordinary activities. After the hierarchy endorsed the plan, the committee of four bishops was appointed in December 1917. Burke was chosen to direct and coordinate the activities of the Council which quickly established a reputation for effectiveness. By the time the war drew to a close, the Council had clearly fulfilled its purpose and had also instilled in Catholics in the U.S. a consciousness of their resources and their responsibility.

In February 1919, the four bishops on the Council's Administrative Committee issued a far-reaching "Program for Social Reconstruction," saying that the only safeguard for the recently achieved peace was "social justice and a contented people." Yet with the armistice the previous November, the War Council faced an uncertain future. It was the intervention of Pope Benedict XV that ensured that its model of cooperative activity would continue. The papal representative at the golden jubilee of the episcopate of Cardinal Gibbons, which was celebrated that same February, told the large number of U.S. bishops gathered for the occasion that the pope wished them to join him in working for the cause of peace and social justice in the world. The bishops responded by resolving to meet annually and, by means of a continuing committee, to foster Christian principles, particularly in the fields of education and social justice. Benedict XV gave his approval of this resolve in a letter the following April. On September 24, the U.S. bishops met together formally for the first time in 35 years and approved the following resolution: "that an organization be formed of the Hierarchy to be known as the National Catholic Welfare Council and its duties and powers to be indicated by those present; and, that an Administrative Committee composed of seven members of the Hierarchy be elected by the National Catholic Welfare Council to transact all business between meetings of the National Catholic Welfare Council and to carry out the wishes of the National Catholic Welfare Council as expressed in the annual session." By secret ballot the seven members of the Administrative Committee were elected from a slate of 15, with Cardinal Gibbons as honorary chairman and Abp. Edward J. Hanna of San Francisco, Calif., as chairman.

The Administrative Committee foresaw that the mass of work involved would be too much for any bishop who also had the care of a diocese; so in December 1919, the committee took over the War Council and its staff, set up a national headquarters in Washington, DC, and unanimously elected its director, Father John Burke, to fill the post of NCWC executive secretary.

In its beginning stages, the NCWC had to face the question of its exact status in relation to a bishop in his own diocese. Some senior prelates saw it as an attempt at a new type of ecclesiastical jurisdiction which would impinge on the autonomy of a diocesan bishop. This point had been thrashed out at the first annual meeting of the bishops, and it was clear that they never intended for this to be the case. However, fears persisted and eventually affected Rome. In 1922, immediately after the election of the new pope, Pius XI, the Sacred Consistorial Congregation of the Roman Curia issued a decree suppressing the organization. Clarification was quickly sought by NCWC's Administrative Board. Through lengthy correspondence and personal representation in Rome, two fundamental points were established: first, the NCWC was a voluntary organization, depending for membership and support on the free choice of each bishop; second, the NCWC possessed no ecclesiastical jurisdiction or compulsory authority. Its only authority was the moral suasion it drew from the consensus of the U.S. bishops. With these clarifications, the Congregation issued instructions permitting the continued existence of the NCWC. Its name, however, was to be changed from "council" to avoid canonical implications; and "conference" was chosen. Thus began a development which brought the organization from a small staff and a budget of $145,000 at the time to a staff of 350 and total expenditures of $7.5 million in 1966.

Organization. Annually there was a meeting in Washington, DC, of all the U.S. bishops, diocesan, coadjutor, and auxiliary, who served the Church in the U.S., its territories, or possessions. At this meeting, the bishops elected ten of their number to serve one-year terms on the NCWC Administrative Board. The U.S. cardinals served on the Board *ex officio*. The Board acted on behalf of the bishops during the time between the annual meetings. It annually chose its own officers and designated from among its membership an episcopal chairman for each NCWC department.

In general, the Administrative Board acted as the executive agency in all matters referred to it at the bishops' annual meeting. In particular, the members of the board supervised the work of the departments, issued an annual report of their activities to each bishop prior to the annual meeting, and made recommendations to the body of bishops. The Board met in executive session twice a year, just prior to the annual meeting and immediately after Easter.

The chairman of the Board presided over the executive department, which supervised and coordinated the other departments' work. A general secretary served as the chief executive officer of the Board and was responsible for supervising the departments.

The bishops established the following NCWC departments in 1919, serving under the executive office: Education, Press and Literature, Social Action, Legal, Societies and Lay Activities—comprised of the National Council of Catholic Men (NCCM) and the National Council of Catholic Women (NCCW) — and the American Board of Missions, in support of both overseas and home missions. A department for immigration was founded in 1920, and one for youth in 1940. To these departments were added over the years offices and bureaus to deal with specialized fields of concern. Thus, the Family Life Bureau (1931) and the Bureau of Health and Hospitals (1948) were attached to the Social Action Department.

The Press and Literature Department included a news-gathering agency originally known as the NC (or National Catholic) News Service. By the 1960s, it had become the largest religious news service in the world, serving not only the Catholic press in the U.S. but also reaching over 60 countries. In 1941 the Press Department initiated *Noticias Catolicas*, a Spanish and Portuguese edition of the News Service for the Latin American press. Its operation moved to Lima, Peru, in 1964. In 1989, the NC News Service changed its name to the Catholic News Service in acknowledgment that its clientele was not solely within the U.S.

Other bureaus and offices within the permanent secretariat of the NCWC created as the need arose included: the Bureau of Information (1938); an Office for United Nations Affairs in New York (1945); a Foreign Visitors Office (1949) to assist the increasing number of visitors to the U.S. from other lands on student or government programs; and the Latin America Bureau (1960), in answer to a special plea from the Holy See to put at the disposal of the Pontifical Commission for Latin America the resources of the Church in the U.S.

Also operating under the aegis of the NCWC, but organized as a separate legal entity, was Catholic Relief Services (CRS), first established in 1943 to cope with war rehabilitation and continuing as the bishops' overseas relief agency.

Some committees were established by the general body of bishops and were directly subject to that body rather than to the Administrative Board. These were the Propagation of the Faith, the Confraternity of Christian Doctrine, and committees dealing with the liturgical movement, migrant workers, decent literature, and other specialized fields. Despite this different line of organization, these committees were an integral part of the NCWC.

Activities. In 1919, along with the resolution establishing the NCWC, the bishops issued an extensive pastoral letter on matters of concern to the Church and society. Throughout the following years, a variety of statements were issued to provide the Church in the U.S. with a voice on the concerns of the day—whether ecclesiastical or secular. Such statements dealt with the Depression, the persecution of the Church in Mexico, the Second World War, labor relations, indecent literature, aid to education, military service in peacetime, religious persecution behind the Iron Curtain, racial discrimination and bigotry, and liturgical renewal, among many other things. (Most of these can be found in the first three volumes of *Pastoral Letters of the United States Catholic Bishops*, published by the USCCB.)

An early instance of the NCWC coordinating a nationwide response to a problem occurred during the days of prohibition when, acting on the instruction of the Administrative Board, NCWC representatives met with federal officials to work out a generally acceptable procedure for obtaining wine for sacramental purposes. A delicate and controversial instance of NCWC activity was its participation, through its general secretary, in the negotiations to end the persecution of the Church in Mexico, involving officials of the Mexican and U.S. governments, the Mexican hierarchy, and the Holy See.

The NCWC was, in general, concerned about relations between Church and State, as evidenced by its commissioning a booklet on the subject entitled *The First Freedom*, published in 1948.

Through the establishment of an episcopal committee for motion pictures and the Legion of Decency (1934) and its successors, the National Catholic Office for Motion Pictures and the Office of Film and Broadcasting, the bishops had a substantial impact on the movie industry.

Committee chairmen and NCWC staff brought the public policy positions of the Bishops to the attention of the Federal government — Congress, the presidential administrations, and the executive regulatory agencies — through letters, testimony, and personal contact.

The NCWC also instituted several national collections in of support of important activities. Each bishop was free to have his diocese participate in these collections or not participate.

The NCWC's voluntary character and the complete freedom of every bishop to align himself or not with its programs and policies forced it to prove its own worth on the merits of the service that it rendered to the Church.

National Conference of Catholic Bishops (NCCB)/United States Catholic Conference (USCC), 1966–2001

In 1966, the bishops of the United States reorganized the NCWC, in response to the mandate of the Council, into the National Conference of Catholic Bishops (NCCB) and the United States Catholic Conference (USCC).

Even before the formal promulgation of the Vatican II decree, *Christus Dominus*, the U.S. Bishops had undertaken a review of the structure of the NCWC in light of the conciliar teaching. The NCWC was, after all, already a national assembly of bishops with approved statutes. What changes would now have to be made? A lengthy questionnaire was sent to the bishops in May 1965 seeking input about reorganizing the NCWC and revising its statutes. A report on the results was given at the Administrative Board meeting in November of that year; and the bishops authorized the establishment of two committees, one on reorganization and the other on the revision of the statutes and by-laws, the latter chaired by Archbishop (later Cardinal) John J. Krol of Philadelphia. Also crucial to this re-organization were Archbishop (later Cardinal) John F. Deaden of Detroit, the first NCCB/USCC president, and Atlanta Auxiliary Bishop (later Archbishop and Cardinal) Joseph L. Bernardin, its general secretary.

Organization. The membership of both the NCCB and the USCC was made up exclusively of U.S. bishops, but the exact relationship between the twin conferences was always difficult to describe precisely. The NCCB was not a civil corporation but rather an ecclesiastical association to preserve its character as a place where the Bishops could assemble, discuss, and act. As such, it was the U.S. Bishops' response to the mandate from the Council for an episcopal conference which would create the opportunity for some form of collegial pastoral action whose dimensions could not be fully foreseen. The USCC, on the other hand, a civil corporation operating under the nonprofit corporation statutes of the District of Columbia, continued the work of the NCWC whose activities had become well defined over a period of more than forty years. This dual structure also provided for the continued participation of the clergy, religious, and laity in the work of the bishops. So, for example, while, in the NCCB by-laws, its committees were to consist solely of bishops, USCC committees allowed for membership by non-bishops. However, this was at the committee level only. Actual membership in the USCC always belonged exclusively to bishops.

Another way of making a distinction between the two conferences was to describe the USCC as advancing the work of the Church in the area of public policy, while the NCCB was said to be more oriented to internal Church affairs. This distinction appeared in the NCCB/USCC Mission Statement, but it was never a sharp one. All the USCC committees dealt with internal church matters as well as with public policy issues. Alternatively, NCCB committees such as Migration and Pro-life Activities dealt with many public policy issues.

Adding to the difficulty in distinguishing the two was a complete overlap in the administration of the two conferences. The NCCB's Administrative Committee was identical to the USCC's Administrative Board; the officers of one conference were the officers of the other; and the chief executive officer—the general secretary—supervised the work of both.

The entire membership elected the twin conferences' four officers—president, vice-president, treasurer, and secretary—to three year terms. A tradition quickly grew-up, departed from only once, of electing the vice-president to the presidency. This made for significant continuity of administration.

The work of the NCCB/USCC, as with the NCWC, continued to be carried out through a structure of interlocked conference committees and departments staffed by full-time professionals. With the exception of "staff offices" such General Counsel and Government Liaison, which served the NCCB/USCC as a whole, every department was accountable to a conference standing committee. The chairmen of NCCB standing committees were bishops, usually elected by the entire membership of the conference. These chairmen, in turn, appointed the remaining committee membership in consultation with the conference president and general secretary. The membership usually consisted of the chairman and six additional bishops. Priests, religious and laity could serve as consultants to these committees. For the USCC "departmental committees," the equivalent of NCCB standing committees, the entire membership elected two bishops for each as chairman and as an "elected member" who, in consultation with the conference president and general secretary, appointed a membership consisting of an equal number of episcopal and non-episcopal members. The size of the USCC committees could range from 13 to 21 members.

The Administrative Committee/Board (usually called "the Permanent Council" in other episcopal conferences) consisted of the conference officers, the elected chairs of most of the NCCB standing committees and of the USCC departmental committees, the elected members of the USCC committees, and the president of the CRS board. In addition, the dioceses of the country were divided into 13 (originally 12) regions, the bishops of which elected a representative and an alternate to the Administrative Committee/Board. Each conference president also served on it for one year after the completion of his term. Unlike the NCWC, the U.S. cardinals were not automatically members of the Administrative Committee/Board.

There was also an Executive Committee consisting of the four officers and a fifth member elected by the Administrative Committee/Board from among its membership. Three other "executive committees" were chaired by the officers: Priorities and Plans by the president, Personnel by the vice president; and Budget and Finance by the treasurer.

The conference president, in conjunction with the Administrative Committee, could also appoint ad hoc committees and their chairs for periods of up to three years. If necessary, these committees could be renewed.

General meetings of the full body of bishops were held in the fall in Washington and in the spring originally in Chicago, but, later, in a variety of locations around the country. For several years in the early 1980s the spring business meeting was eliminated entirely. A custom also arose of replacing it every few years with a "special assembly" which was not a business meeting and which was long enough to offer time for spiritual and intellectual renewal. These occurred in 1982, 1986, 1990, 1994, and 1999.

The Administrative Committee/Board met in executive session three times a year, in the early spring and fall and the Saturday before the fall general meeting. Its main function was to set the agenda for the general meetings; but it also acted on the conferences' behalf, when necessary, in between general meetings, including issuing statements or authorizing committees to issue them.

As of 2001, the following comprised the NCCB standing committees: African American Catholics, American College of Louvain, Canonical Affairs, Church in Latin America, Consecrated Life, Diaconate, Doctrine, Ecumenical and Interreligious Affairs, Evangelization, Hispanic Affairs, Home Missions, Laity, Liturgy, Marriage and Family Life, Migration, North American College Rome, Pastoral Practices, Priestly Formation, Priestly Life and Ministry, Pro- life Activities, Relationship Between Eastern and Latin Catholic Churches, Science and Human Values, Vocations, Women in Society and in the Church, and World Mission. There were also committees for the American Bishops' Overseas Appeal, Boundaries of Dioceses and Provinces, and the Selection of Bishops chaired *ex officio* by the conference president.

The secretariats or departments whose work was overseen by the relevant committees were: African American Catholics; Church in Latin America; Diaconate; Doctrine and Pastoral Practices; Ecumenical and Interreligious Affairs; Evangelization; Family, Laity, Women and Youth; Hispanic Affairs; Liturgy; Migration and Refugee Services; Missions/ Science and Human Values; Priestly Formation/Vocations; Priestly Life and Ministry; and Pro- life Activities.

The USCC committees and departments were: Catholic Campaign for Human Development (CCHD), Communications, and Education, along with the Domestic Policy and International Policy Committees to which the Department for Social Development and World Peace was accountable.

A comparison between the committees and departments of the NCCB/USCC with those of the NCWC indicates both the continuity and also the increase in scope of concern of the NCCB/USCC.

In 1969, a council was set up to advise the Administrative Committee/Board about the conferences' proposed actions and to offer proposals of its own for action. Known as the National Advisory Council (NAC), it consists of about 60 members — bishops, priests, religious, and laity — selected in variety of ways, including two members elected from each of the 13 regions.

Successors to Cardinal Dearden as president were Cardinal John J. Krol of Philadelphia (1971–74), Archbishop Bernardin, then of Cincinnati (1974–1977), Archbishop John R. Quinn of San Francisco (1977–1980), Archbishop John R. Roach of St. Paul and Minneapolis (1980–1983), Bishop James W. Malone of Youngstown (1983–1986), Archbishop John L. May of St. Louis (1986–1989), Archbishop Daniel E. Pilarczyk of Cincinnati (1989–1992); Archbishop (later Cardinal) William H. Keeler of Baltimore (1992–1995), Bishop Anthony M. Pilla of Cleveland (1995–1998), and Bishop Joseph A. Fiorenza of Galveston-Houston (1998–2001).

Originally, the NCCB/USCC took over the headquarters of the National Catholic Welfare Conference on Massachusetts Avenue in Washington, DC, but in 1987 a cornerstone was laid for a new building near The Catholic University of America to house the conferences' headquarters and offices. The building was completed and the offices moved there in 1989.

Activities. Sources for the statements and activities of the NCCB/USCC over the years are the annual editions of the *Catholic Almanac, Origins*, published by the Catholic News Service, and the later volumes of the *Pastoral Letters of the United States Catholic Bishops*, published by the USCCB.

The bishops involved the clergy, religious, and laity of the U.S. in widespread consultations on a number of their efforts. Inspired by the national bicentennial, the bishops held hearings throughout the country to prepare a program for future social action. As with the NCWC, numerous statements gave voice to the bishops' concerns. Two major pastoral letters were developed over a number of years, through several drafts, in consultation with experts and church members. *The Challenge of Peace* (1983) dealt with issues surrounding peace and war and, especially, weapons of mass destruction. *Economic Justice for All* (1986) enunciated the social justice principles which should guide economic decisions. A third pastoral letter on the role of women in Church and society went through several drafts over nearly a decade, but it was never approved by the bishops due to a lack of consensus on some issues. Material and insights gathered in the process, however, contributed to the development of other documents.

The Challenge of Peace highlighted the impact that the statements of one episcopal conference can have on other conferences and on the Church universal. As a result, during its development, it became the subject of a formal consultation in Rome involving representatives of the NCCB/USCC, European episcopal conferences, and the Roman Curia.

The scope of their pastoral concerns can be read in the sheer variety of the matters with which the bishops dealt, including campus ministry, the Charismatic renewal, children and families, the conflict in the Middle East, domestic violence, evangelization, food and agricultural issues, health care, the laity, ministry to the Hispanic community, the moral life, persons with disabilities, racism, the relationship between bishops and theologians, and the third world debt.

The NCCB/USCC agenda also covered matters arising out of the reforms the Vatican II, especially those mandated by the Holy See for action by episcopal conferences with regard to liturgical renewal and the revision of the Code of Canon law.

Some of the major works of the NCCB/USCC have been the establishment of Campaign for Human Development (now the Catholic Campaign for Human Development) to strike at the root causes of poverty in the U.S.; the Catholic Communication Campaign in support of national and diocesan communications efforts in accord with NCCB/USCC goals; adoption of proposals on due process; endorsement of a "Program for Priestly Formation"; establishment of the permanent diaconate in the U.S.; coordination of pastoral visits of the Pope in the U.S.; 1993 celebration of World Youth Day in the U.S.; preparation and execution of plans for the celebration of the Great Jubilee of the Third Millennium of Christianity; and the implementation of the apostolic constitution on Catholic higher education, *Ex corde Ecclesiae.*

Church-state issues continued to occupy the bishops' attention. Within the first decade of its existence, the NCCB/USCC was put in a strongly confrontational position vis- a-vis the civil government. The U.S. Supreme Court decisions in 1973, *Roe v. Wade* and *Doe v. Bolton,* which resulted in the legalization of abortion on demand nationally, brought a quick response from the bishops who devised a Plan for Pro-Life Activities, which they supplemented regularly with numerous statements in defense of human life from conception to natural death. In a court case which lasted from 1980 to 1990, a group supporting legal abortion sued the Internal Revenue Service to remove the Catholic Church's tax exemption, claiming that the Church's pro-life efforts violated IRS regulations. The case ultimately failed but not before an attempt to force the NCCB/USCC to open up all of its files for discovery was turned back in an appeal to the Supreme Court.

As with the NCWC, committee chairmen and staff brought the public policy positions of the Bishops to the attention of the Congress, the administrations, and regulatory agencies. These efforts were facilitated by the Office of Government Liaison and the Office of General Counsel which also filed amicus briefs on behalf of the conferences in significant legal cases.

United States Conference of Catholic Bishops (USCCB), 2001–

In late 1991, an *ad hoc* Committee on Mission and Structure was appointed under the chairmanship of Cardinal Bernardin to examine the theological and canonical status of the NCCB/USCC, review the conferences' mission and goals, and propose modifications that would encourage greater participation by the bishops in the work of the conferences and enhance their sense of unity. (The committee did not involve itself with the internal operation of the secretariats and departments which underwent a separate review in 1991. They remain essentially as described above.) On the completion of its work, another *ad hoc* committee was set up in 1998, chaired by Archbishop Pilarczyk, to propose new statutes and by-laws, implementing the work of the Mission and Structure Committee and the complementary norms contained in the apostolic letter *Apostolos Suos.*

The revisions retain most of the structure of the NCCB/USCC as described above. However, the process provided an opportunity for a wide-ranging discussion of the nature and mission of the episcopal conference.

The principal proposed revisions dealt with the consolidation of the NCCB and the USCC into a single conference; the clarification of the episcopal nature of the conference by restricting membership on conference committees to bishops (as was already the case with the NCCB committees); the reorganization and reduction in the number of standing committees; and a change in the membership of the Administrative Committee by adding a second delegate from each region. The latter proposal was intended to promote participation by more bishops in the conference and to encourage them to use regional meetings to discuss the matters coming up at the general meetings.

The "single conference" recommendation and the limitation of all committee membership to bishops inspired a lengthy discussion about preserving the involvement of clergy, religious, and laity which had been a characteristic of the NCWC and the NCCB/USCC. Out of this emerged an affirmation that this involvement could continue through the service of consultants and advisers to the committees. Both these revisions were adopted by the full body of bishops and confirmed by the Holy See. The single conference was designated the United States Conference of Catholic Bishops (USCCB).

However, there was no consensus about reorganizing and reducing the number of standing committees, and they remained as they were. There seemed to be a consensus that the number of regional representatives on the Administrative Committee should be doubled to 26. Toward the end of the process, though, the argument prevailed that this would make its size too unwieldy for effective discussion; and the bishops voted to retain the 13 regional representatives.

The process of issuing statements was clarified to meet the concern that too many statements were issued which were not approved by the whole body and also that it was unclear to the public which statements should be attributed to the whole conference and which only to committees.

With regard to the complementary norms contained in *Apostolos Suos,* the statutes now include an article on "Authentic Magisterium" reflecting its teaching and legislation. Also in response to the letter's encouragement that episcopal conferences make more use of bishops *emeriti,* the USCCB by-laws now allow retired bishops to serve on standing and *ad hoc* committees. In addition, the revised by-laws indicate that the general secretary, as required by the Congregation of Bishops, "is to be a priest or a bishop." Another change made in response to the Congregation was a clarification of the territory of the USCCB as "an assembly of the Hierarchy of the United States and the U.S. Virgin Islands" (rather than "territories" as perviously).

The USCCB replaced the NCCB/USCC on July 1, 2001, the date the revised statutes and by-laws took effect.

[F. MANISCALCO]

UNITY

Unity, or oneness, is generally regarded as the attribute of a thing whereby it is undivided in itself and yet divided from others. Since it is an ultimate philosophical notion, it cannot be defined strictly, i.e., in terms that are better known; it is also somewhat ambiguous in meaning. As an abstract noun it refers to a property or character common to everything that can be said to be and in this sense is enumerated among the TRANSCENDENTALS; as a concrete noun it refers to *a* unity, i.e., to some one thing. The diversity of usage can be traced back to early Greek thought.

Among the pre-Socratics, PARMENIDES noted that the cosmos exists or simply is. He held that whatever *is* constitutes the realm of being, since he could not think that what is, is not. If all is being, there is nothing that is not being. Being becomes thus self-identical; it is one. A follower of Parmenides, ZENO OF ELEA, thereupon developed the paradoxes of the many. The "many," in his view, were also "ones" as parts or units of a quantitative whole, or as constitutive of plurality. The resulting positions, namely, that unity is a property of what is and that a unity is part of a whole, are respectively linked to the abstract and the concrete meaning. Although the parallel is not absolute, the abstract meaning envisages all being as participating in unity or as having the common character of unity, while the concrete meaning has reference to the parts of a whole.

In view of the influence of history on the development of this concept, we shall outline how unity is treated first in the works of Plato, Aristotle, and Plotinus; then in the medieval tradition as exemplified by St. Thomas Aquinas; and finally in modern thought, with particular emphasis on its role in recent mathematics.

Classical Thinkers. While aware of Parmenides's statement that whatever is, is one, PLATO understood "whatever is" as divided into *this* and *that* being. In his doctrine of forms (ἰδέαι), a form expresses being as a nature, a type; and forms are stable, necessary natures. Changing things are intelligible insofar as they participate in some form, or unchanging nature. Plato thus stresses a plurality of natures. He raises the question whether this "many" can be reduced to anything more ultimate, and suggests, in the *Republic,* a reduction to the GOOD. The Good, for him, is above natures or forms and is not strictly a form itself. Yet Plato makes no clear reduction of the Good to the One. His plurality of kinds of being, it should be noted, is not Zeno's plurality of units. Nor is his ''one'' a mathematical form, because Plato distinguishes mathematical forms from forms as natures. Forms as natures are of one specific kind, while there can be many instances of a mathematical form. Such instances resemble Zeno's idea of unity.

Stressing the origin of knowledge, Aristotle bases his theory of cognition on the plurality of sensible particulars. This plurality includes not only groups containing many instances of one kind, as many sheep, but also many classes or many different kinds, as men and animals. The Aristotelian view recognizes both the Platonic forms of nature and so the unity of BEING as self-identical, as well as Zeno's unity or part that is constitutive of a plurality (cf. *Meta.* 1001a ff., 1052a ff.).

The outstanding exponent of NEOPLATONISM, PLOTINUS, posits the principle that unity precedes multiplicity (*Enneades* 5.1.5). Thus, for him, all plurality must be reduced to the One. The One or Unity is consequently above being, and all else is one by participation. Plotinus's One expresses intense, unique perfection rather than the totality of the cosmos.

Thomistic Analysis. St. THOMAS AQUINAS further explains the unity of a nature or kind, and unity as one of many, through corresponding concepts associated with plurality or MULTITUDE: to the first corresponds transcendental multitude; to the second, numerical multitude.

Unity and Existence. Some Thomists maintain that St. Thomas gave new meaning to both unity and multitude by interpreting these concepts existentially (*see* EXISTENTIAL METAPHYSICS). When St. Thomas speaks of being, in this view, he means it primarily not as nature or intelligible content but as act of existence (*In 1 Sent.* 25.1.4; Summa theologiae 1a, 3.3–4). To say that a thing is, is to say that it is one; but it is one not primarily from what it is but rather through its act of existence. It is created to be a kind, and is not to be regarded as something that is already a kind and then given existence. As with both Plato and Aristotle, for St. Thomas unity does not add any reality to being; it is only the negation of division. Thus ''one'' means ''undivided being,'' and this in the sense of an existent or a possible existent (ST 1a, 11–14). To see the unity of a thing stemming from its manner of existence and not primarily from its nature as expressed through its definition allows such Thomists greater leeway in admitting unities of all sorts. For example, the parasitic plant is what it is only in a close conjunction with its host. Its unity taken from the point of view of its manner of existence includes this relationship, whereas from the point of view of ''ideas'' or definition it seems to exclude it.

St. Thomas contrasted unity with plurality in two ways: first, with different kinds of being, and secondly, with instances of the same kind. Among different kinds of being each could be said to be itself and not other. Each would be an existent individual. Unity here is not a property or characteristic of the thing in any accidental sense, but rather a transcendental property expressing the very *being* of the thing. Many such existents form a multitude, and here each being holds a determinate grade in being. St. Thomas refers to such a multitude as transcendental (ST 1a, 30.3); the best example is found in the realm of spiritual being. In this sense angel is not strictly a common noun, since there is nothing univocally common to Michael, Gabriel, Raphael, etc.

Unity and Number. Other instances occur in the material universe, which evidently is a quantitative whole constituted of many things as parts. It is this unity that St. Thomas considers the basis of number, for such parts or units are univocally alike, except for the fact that they are different parts of a whole or units of a group. They constitute a numerical multitude.

The first meaning of unity, as a transcendental property interchangeable with being, is not the basis of number, nor does it suggest any mathematical connotations. Like Plotinus, however, St. Thomas sees the necessity of reducing even transcendental multitude to unity. The many existents must be caused by the Pure Act of Existence that is Unique (*see* PURE ACT). The Unique is one only in an analogical sense.

The distinction between numerical and transcendental unity is important for guarding the distinction between METAPHYSICS and MATHEMATICS. For example, the principle of identity interpreted in metaphysical terms does not express a pure equality or a logical identity as in abstract mathematics (*see* IDENTITY, PRINCIPLE OF). The distinction also enables the theologian to eliminate all mathematical connotations from his analogical use of terms, as, for example, when he speaks of the Trinity as one God in three Divine Persons. Mystery as this is, it becomes absolutely contradictory if it is thought of strictly in mathematical terms.

Descartes and Leibniz. The revival of mathematics and of Platonic and Neoplatonic currents in the 17th century centered the attention of modern philosophy on unity. Primarily interested in mathematics and then in its philosophical foundations, R. DESCARTES sought not just the fundamental existent, the ego, but also clear and distinct ideas or simple natures as ultimates. He did not, however, clearly distinguish the unity of the ego in metaphysics from the unity studied in mathematics. His simple natures thus remain unclear. (Cf. *Regulae; Meditations.*)

For G. W. von LEIBNIZ, unity is the theme of his philosophy. His basic notion is the MONAD. "It is only indivisible substances and their different states which are absolutely real" (*Correspondence with Arnauld*). "If there were no true one, then every true being would be eliminated" (*Correspondence with De Volder*). The "true one" he likens to a spiritual soul. He was also a competent mathematician and a forerunner of much that is contemporary. While attempting to define unity and number in *The Art of Combination,* he says that unity is a notion abstracted from one being, whereas whole number is the idea of whole or totality formed by consideration of many unities—a description that suggests the notion of set or class as used in modern mathematics. Unity, he holds, is the simplest notion; while number is a more complex notion presupposing unity; and part or fraction is more complex than either since it presupposes both.

Unity in Mathematics. Modern mathematics begins with the notion of set as containing one or more members or as being null or empty; it also employs the idea of one set succeeding another. With these notions it defines the cardinal and ordinal numbers, including one. The procedure may be explained through the simple example of counting. If a shepherd wishes to count his sheep, he can match a stick or bead to each member of his flock and so establish a one-to-one correspondence between the units of the two groups, which indicates that both groups have the same number. The stick or bead can be refined to a stroke, or replaced by a symbol, or simply be considered as an element of a group or set, having the features of a unit with no character other than being matchable with other units or elements of another set or group. Since it is only after the operation of matching that both groups are said to have the same number, the idea of number is seen as subsequent to the idea of the unit-element.

Mathematicians, trying to define their basic terms logically, establish a distinction between "one" as a unit or member of a class and the "number one." They define the number one as the set of all those sets that contain only one member. This set of sets, however, is the result of the operation of forming a one-to-one correspondence among the member sets, and this operation presupposes "one" in the sense of unit or member. The last-named unit is what St. Thomas considered as the basis of his numerical multitude.

Since the number one presupposes an operation or relation established between sets and their unit members, the modern mathematician does not think in terms of substance, as does the philosopher, but rather in terms of RELATION. The result is that the notion of unity as employed in the mathematical sciences becomes even more distinct from unity as it is metaphysically understood.

Unity in Other Disciplines. Of the three fundamental ideas of unity, namely, that of number, that of unit-element of sets, and that of the existent, the last or transcendental notion of unity is the most important. This unity is exemplified for man, who does not have direct experience of the spiritual, in the unity of higher living organisms and especially in the living rational PERSON. Such organisms can be said to guard their unity as they guard their life.

The biological theory of organic evolution questions, for the modern mind, the concept of unity of natures. And as evolution has been extended to explain the entire material universe, the seeming progressive development from the simple to the complex modifies not only the unit-substance notion but also the concept of "this" being as distinct from "that" being. In fact, the very idea of SUBSTANCE seems to be negated by modern science. Perhaps this is an instance where the scientist intimates to the philosopher the importance of noting a particular manner of existence before making any attempt at definition. Even though the mode of existence of beings in evolution may have a strongly relational character, this does not eliminate the termini of such relations. From the outset these are the factors through whose interaction evolution comes about. As such their "unit" character is reexpressed whenever different, more or less stable levels are reached in the development through interaction. Since scientists study nature through its action and connections, their method does not lend itself to grasping substance in its unity. Moreover, since, as a general rule, they treat their data mathematically, relational aspects inevitably predominate in their analyses.

Analogous to the living organism with its integral coordination and functional unity is society, exemplified in the family or the nation. The Church is such a society, but one whose unity is so marked that it approximates the unity of a spiritual person. It is in this sense that unity is spoken of as one of the marks of the Church (*see* UNITY OF THE CHURCH).

See Also: INDIVIDUALITY; INDIVIDUATION; MONISM.

Bibliography: L. DE RAEYMAEKER, *The Philosophy of Being,* tr. E. H. ZIEGELMEYER (St. Louis 1954). *Enciclopedia filosofica,* 4 v. (Venice-Rome 1957) 4:1395–1406. P. FOULQUIÉ and R. SAINT-JEAN, *Dictionnaire de la langue philosophique* (Paris 1962). E. H. GILSON, *The Unity of Philosophical Experience* (New York 1937). R. EISLER, *Wörterbuch der philosophischen Begriffe,* 3 v. (4th ed. Berlin 1927–30) 1:307–313. J. R. NEWMAN, *The World of Mathematics,* 4 v. (New York 1956). R. A. DI NARDO, *The Unity of the Human Person* (CUA Philosophical Studies 199; Washington 1961). L. OEING-HANHOFF, *Ens et unum convertuntur* (*Beiträge zur Geschichte der Philosophie und Theologie des Mittelalters* [Münster 1891–] 37.3; Münster 1953).

[E. G. SALMON]

UNITY OF FAITH

The SUPERNATURAL bond that exists among all who adhere to the one divine revelation. This bond exists on two levels: the level of being, in that all participants in this unity share the same supernatural virtue of FAITH freely given them by God; and the level of conviction, in that these participants cling to the same revealed truth. Grounded in the oneness of God and of His plan of SALVATION, this bond admits of varying degrees of realization that culminate in the full-blown unity of faith that exists among the members of the Catholic Church.

A unity of faith exists because faith is the response to revelation, and revelation is one. Scripture says that there is one God and one mediator between God and men (1 Tm 2.5), one divine plan of salvation (Eph 1.3–14), one Church, one apostolic authority (Mt 16.13–19; 18.18; 28.19–20). The acceptance by men of this one God-revealed economy of salvation is what is called faith. And the unity resulting from the attachment of men to the one revealed divine order is the unity of faith.

Degrees. Unity of faith exists in varying degrees. First, there is a *basic* unity among all men who possess the virtue of faith, even at the minimal degree of those who have no conscious acceptance of the Christian revelation. Second, there is a *fundamental* Christian unity of faith among the baptized who by divine faith accept part, though not all, of the objective Christian revelation. Finally, there is the *integral* unity of faith that exists among the members of the Catholic Church.

Integral or Catholic unity of faith implies the acceptance by divine faith of the whole objective Christian revelation. Central to this concept is the recognition of the visible, divinely appointed, definitive indicator of revelation, the pope and the bishops, who constitute the authoritative teaching Church or magisterium. A Catholic, because of ignorance, may not explicitly accept some of the elements of divine revelation; yet, in adhering to the magisterium as part of the revealed economy and as the divinely assured teacher and interpreter of the whole of that economy, he implicitly adheres to all that God reveals. Hence, he participates in the fullness of the unity of faith. On the other hand, those rejecting—even in good faith—the magisterium, reject not only a part of the revealed economy but also the only means by which the total objective content of that economy can be ascertained.

Properties. Several properties characterize the integral Catholic unity of faith. First, it is ecclesiastical. Besides being an internal unity based upon the possession of the one supernatural virtue of faith and all the gifts of supernatural GRACE and CHARITY that normally accompany this virtue, it is also a unity expressed in the believing acceptance of a visible magisterium and whatever that magisterium indicates belongs to the economy of salvation. Therefore, it ultimately involves the acceptance of all the essential elements of the Church: its worship, its authority, its creed. Hence, to possess Catholic unity of faith is to be fully integrated into the Church; it is to be a member.

Second, the unity of faith is a rich and manifold organic unity. It is capable of an infinite variety of expressions—in worship, in the functioning of authority, in the verbal expression of belief—expressions that preserve the essence of the divine revelation while incorporating the distinct values of different ages and cultures.

Finally, the unity of faith is an eschatological unity. It will not reach its perfect expression until the last day when all the just will be perfectly united to God immediately and in Him to one another. Now, however, the various ministries in the Church work for the building up of the MYSTICAL BODY OF CHRIST so that finally ''all attain to the unity of the faith and of the deep knowledge of the Son of God, to perfect manhood, to the mature measure of the fullness of Christ'' (Eph 4.13). Thus, this unity is not only a current reality; it is a reality whose perfection is an ardent hope of the Church, a hope toward whose realization the Church is continuously obligated to strive.

See Also: BRANCH THEORY OF THE CHURCH; FAITHFUL; HERESY; INFIDEL; SOCIETY (THEOLOGY OF); VISIBILITY OF THE CHURCH.

Bibliography: *Dictionnaire de théologie catholique, Tables générales,* ed. A. VACANT (Paris 1951) 1:1537–71. O. KARRER, *Lexikon für Theologie und Kirche,* ed. J. HOFER and K. RAHNER (Freiburg 1957–65) 3:757–758. F. HOLBÖCK and T. SARTORY, eds., *Mysterium Kirche in der Sicht der theologischen Disziplinen* (Salzburg 1962) 1:201–346. LEO XIII, ''Satis cognitum,'' (Encyclical letter, June 29, 1896) *Acta Sanctorum* 28 (1895–96) 708–739. Y. CONGAR, *The Mystery of the Church,* tr. A. LITTLEDALE (Baltimore, Md. 1960) 58–96. T. SARTORY, *The Ecumenical Movement and the Unity of the Church,* tr. H. GRAEF (Westminster, Md. 1963).

[P. F. CHIRICO]

UNITY OF THE CHURCH

The fragmentation of Christianity is so evident a hindrance to its propagation that the unity of the Church might be sought solely on pragmatic grounds. Church unity would no doubt increase the effectiveness of the Church's mission, but even if it did not, it would still be necessary to strive for it. The Church's central purpose is to witness to God's unifying and reconciling love in Christ. Therefore the unity of all human beings and their communion with God is the goal towards which the

Church is directed (Vatican II, *Lumen gentium* 1). The Church's own unity, consequently, is an intrinsic necessity and, indeed, a given object of faith. Like other gifts of grace, it is also a never-ending task to utilize and manifest the gift of unity in the Church's life.

Two problems have commanded the most attention in recent years. The first arises over the choice of a starting point. Given the centrality of the Eucharistic celebration to the meaning of the word, "Church," should the unity be conceived primarily in terms of the local Church rather than of the Church universal? Then, what kind of diversity can and should be welcomed, and what sort of unity must be envisaged to make room for all the legitimate diversities of a truly catholic Church? (*See* CATHOLICITY.)

Cardinal Jan Willebrands, for example, noted that various existing "types" (traditions) of Church Bodies would not necessarily have to be abandoned in the event of union. The Presbyterian-Reformed/Roman Catholic Consultation in the U.S. has described the ecumenical goal as a "communion of communions"; each Communion would preserve its own traditions intact, as long as the latter remain vital and are compatible with the broader unity of the whole Church.

The International Lutheran/Roman Catholic Working Group is considering various "models of unity," elaborated on the basis of interconfessional experiences to date and of extrapolations therefrom. "Organic unity," for example, is the express ultimate goal of the Anglican/Roman Catholic conversations, although the model of "sister Churches in communion" also finds application. The World Council of Churches has put forth the strategy of working toward a "genuinely ecumenical council" to crown the ecumenical movement of the 20th century; the term "conciliar fellowship" describes this model. "Reconciled diversity" and "concord" are two further models. The latter, exemplified in the Continental Lutheran and Reformed Churches' Leuenberg Concord (Sept. 30, 1974; named for the Swiss Reformed academy where it was drafted in March, 1973; it is an agreement to full pulpit and altar fellowship), finds Churches healing their rifts by formally recognizing that their mutual condemnations of each other's doctrine in the past no longer have any relevance.

Bibliography: T. BACHMANN et al., on the Leuenberg Agreement. *Lutheran World* 21 (1974) 328–348. Y. CONGAR, "Die Einekirche," in J FEINER and M. LOHRER, eds., *Mysterium Salutis,* v. pt. I, (Einsiedeln 1972) 368–457. Consultation on Church Unity (COCU), "In Quest of a Church of Christ Uniting: A Statement of Emerging Theological Consensus," *Mid-Stream* 16 (1977) 49–92. N. EHRENSTROM, ed., *Confessions in Dialogue* (Geneva 1975) 196–211; *What Unity Requires* (Geneva 1976). E. LANNE, "The Unity of the Church in the Work of Faith and Order," *One-in-Christ* 12 (1976) 34–57. Secretariat for Promoting Christian Unity, *Information Service,* n. 31 (1976) (on Lutheran/Catholic Commission) 11–12. E. L. UNTERKOEFLER and A. HARSONYI eds., *The Unity We Seek: A Statement by the Roman Catholic/Presbyterian-Reformed Consultation* (New York 1977). J. WILLEBRANDS, "Moving Toward a Typology of Churches," *Catholic Mind* 68 (1970) 35–42; "Models for Reunion," *One-in-Christ* 7 (1971) 115–123.

[P. MISNER]

UNIVERSA LAUS

Literally, "Universal Praise" in Latin. International study group for liturgical singing and instrumental music, formally established at Lugano, Switzerland in April 1966 by a group of European liturgists and musicologists that had first started meeting in 1962 (though some of its members had been working together for a decade before that). The initial object was to support the work of those charged with presenting and then implementing the liturgical reforms of the Second Vatican Council; some of its members were in fact *periti* at the Council. The first trio of presidents were Joseph Gelineau (France), Erhard Quack (Germany) and Luigi Agustoni (Italian-speaking Switzerland). Other distinguished names present at the first formal meeting of the association included Helmut Hucke, Bernard Huijbers, David Julien and René Reboud.

Meetings are open to all, but membership is only granted after attendance at three international meetings (national section meetings are also regularly held in some countries). The organization has comprised members from many of the European countries, and meetings normally take place in one of those countries—England, France, Germany, Netherlands, Switzerland, Italy, occasionally Spain, Belgium. In the mid-1970s the first Australian member was admitted, in the early 1980s the first North American (there are currently a number of other U.S. members), and in the late 1990s two members from South America). The first U.S. meeting took place in Stamford, Connecticut in 1996, and a meeting in Montreal, Canada, followed in 2001. Membership is mostly Roman Catholic, though a small number of members has consistently come from other Christian churches (e.g. Lutheran), and includes both ordained pastors and lay people. Visitors have come to occasional meetings from much further afield (e.g. Africa, India). Participants from Eastern Europe arrived in the late 1990s and the first Russian participant was welcomed in 2000. The balance of liturgist-musicians, musicologists and pastoral musicians has varied over the course of time; but liturgical competence is assumed in all categories.

During the first period in the group's existence (1962–1968) work was concentrated on the ritual function of music in liturgy, and the relationship between form-function-signification. From 1969 to 1976, the group moved into a systematic study of the actual functioning of music in liturgy, and the impact of different cultural situations on worship. This led not only to two other triads (form-functioning-signification and music-rite-culture) but to cross-fertilization with other academic disciplines such as cultural anthropology, social psychology, semiology, and linguistics. In these first two periods, Universa Laus alternated between "working meetings," with 30 to 50 participants, and "congresses," numbering up to 200 to 300 and drawing in participants from the local region or country. These periods were also characterized by a massive but mostly unperceived influence on the post-conciliar liturgical reforms and their subsequent development through the large number of writings and teachings of the more prominent members of the association, and this influence continues to this day. In almost all cases these activities of Universa Laus members are not carried out under the Universa Laus banner, since most of the members already have high-profile national roles in their own countries. The principal journals in which Universa Laus papers can be found in English are *Music and Liturgy* (U.K.) and *Pastoral Music* (U.S.); and many other writings by Universa Laus authors will be found in these journals as well as in French, German, Italian and Dutch periodicals.

In addition to much mutual exchange of information about what is taking place in other countries, and the celebration of liturgies using the language and repertoire of those countries, substantial papers have been given on a wide variety of topics. From time to time over the past 25 years entire meetings have been devoted to working at a single theme—the Eucharistic Prayer, the litany form, the Fraction Rite, acclamation as a form, the Presentation of the Gifts, appropriate vocal production for liturgy, etc. The in-depth treatment from historical and different cultural viewpoints has been exceptionally beneficial.

In 1977, catalyzed by a public debate (and disagreement) over matters of fundamental principle between Joseph Gelineau and Bernard Huijbers, Universa Laus decided to commence work on a document which could at least express the beliefs that members held in common. The resulting Universa Laus document finally saw the light of day in 1980 under the title *Music in Christian Celebration*. Among other groundbreaking insights, it first proposed the notion of "Christian ritual music"—a more focused description than sacred music, or church music, or indeed liturgical music, and one which would be explored further in the ten-year report on the *Milwaukee Symposia for Church Composers* (1992). In 1988 a book-length exposition of the document by Claude Du-

chesneau and Michel Veuthey was published in French, translated into English as *Music and Liturgy—the Universa Laus Document and Commentary* (1992). In the mid-1990s, Universa Laus began to prepare a second document which would incorporate some of the insights and work carried out since the publication of the first document.

Bibliography: C. DUCHESNEAU and M. VEUTHEY, tr. P. INWOOD, *Music and Liturgy—the Universa Laus Document and Commentary* (Washington, D.C. 1992).

[P. INWOOD]

UNIVERSALISTS

Those who believe that it is the purpose of God, through the grace revealed in Our Lord Jesus Christ, to save every member of the human race from sin. Although the doctrine is old, no organized body of believers made it the distinctive feature of their church until modern times. In the 3d century some Christian Gnostics, including Origen and St. Clement of Alexandria, held that the punishment of devils and wicked men is temporary and that eventually they will be completely restored to their original state, but this point of view was condemned by the ninth canon of the Provincial Council of Constantinople (543). The idea, revived in Reformation times, appeared in a mystical universalism developed in Germany in the 17th and 18th centuries and was brought to Pennsylvania by Dr. George de Benneville. In England, James Relly opposed Calvinistic election and championed universal salvation in his book *Union*. This work profoundly influenced John Murray, who immigrated to America in 1770 and preached Universalism, leading to the establishment of the Independent Church of Gloucester, MA. In Philadelphia, PA., Dr. Joseph Priestly advocated Universalism, and it took form in New England in the Winchester Profession of Belief, adopted by New England Universalists. But the most influential force in the movement (*c.* 1796–1852) was Hosea Ballou, whose *Treatise on the Atonement* (1805), particularly his views on Christ's subordination to the Father, placed Universalists in a position very close to that of UNITARIANS.

At first, Universalism in America was a theological point of view that had its defenders and opponents in individual churches, but by 1840 a sense of denominational destiny had come to be felt. The General Convention of Universalists in the U.S., formed in 1833 with advisory powers only, had become by 1866 the Universalist General Convention, with unified, rational, and denominational policies. By 1890, statements of faith; pamphlets and magazines; extensive literary effort; the establishment of academies, colleges, and theological schools

(Tufts University, Medford, MA, 1852; Tufts Divinity School, 1861); the formation of a strong women's organization; and the establishment of a flourishing young people's movement were testimony to growing vitality. During the 19th century, under the impact of Darwinian evolution theories, the older individual salvation theories gave way to personal self-development and social improvement theories. The Boston statement of faith (1899) upheld the Bible as containing a revelation from God and the final harmony of all souls with God, but the Washington statement of faith (1935) asserted only its faith in the authority of truth, known or to be known, and the power of men of good will and sacrificial spirit to overcome all evil and progressively to establish the kingdom of God. The name Universalist General Convention was changed (1942) to the Universalist Church of America. In May 1961 it merged with the American Unitarian Association to form the UNITARIAN UNIVERSALIST ASSOCIATION.

Bibliography: M. A. KAPP, "Historical Sketch of Universalism," *An Information Manual of the American Unitarian Association and the Universalist Church of America* (Wellesley Hills, MA 1958). R. EDDY, *Universalism in America*, 2 v. (Boston 1884–86); "History of Universalism," *American Church History Series* 10 (New York 1894) 251–493. J. H. ALLEN, *An Historical Sketch of the Unitarian Movement since the Reformation* (New York 1894). H. H. CHEETHAM, *Unitarianism and Universalism* (Boston 1962). C. A. HOWE, *The Larger Faith : A Short History of American Universalism* (Boston 1993). E. CASSARA, *Universalism in America : A Documentary History of a Liberal Faith*, 3rd rev ed (Boston 1997). A.L. BRESSLER, *The Universalist Movement in America, 1770–1880* (New York 2001).

[J. R. WILLIS/EDS.]

UNIVERSALS

The term "universal," derived from the Latin *universalis* (*unum versus alia,* one against many), signifies a unity with reference to some plurality. Unlike the singular, which cannot be communicated, the universal is by definition something that is communicated or communicable to many.

In the history of thought the term is used in three distinct senses. In the context of being (*in essendo*), an ESSENCE is said to be universal when it is possessed or can be possessed by many individuals. In the context of CAUSALITY (*in causando*), a cause is said to be universal when it is capable of producing specifically different effects. In the context of thought (*in significando*), a CONCEPT, IDEA, or TERM is said to be universal when it signifies a certain plurality. This plurality is signified in two ways: by representing many (*in repraesentando*), e.g., many individual men are represented by a single term or concept; and by being predicable of many (*in praedicando*), e.g., the specific term "man" can be said univocally of many individual men. (*See* CATEGORIES OF BEING.)

Most properly, the universals are the five ways in which one term can be predicated univocally of another. These logical universals are second intentions that can be discussed as such, viz, genus, difference, species, property, and accident, or as applied to a particular nature known in first intentionality, e.g., man as species, animal as genus (*see* LOGIC; INTENTIONALITY).

More commonly, universals are taken to mean any intellectual concept obtained by ABSTRACTION. This use of the term in psychology presupposes the Aristotelian doctrine concerning abstraction, the agent intellect, and the immateriality of the INTELLECT (*see* KNOWLEDGE, PROCESS OF). In this psychological use of the term, every concept is universal, deriving its universality from the immateriality of the intellect.

The controversy over universals was a metaphysical discussion concerning the objective, ontological status of essences that are perceived universally by the intellect and that are seen to exist in many individuals. For PLATO and the extreme realist tradition, universal essences have, as such, some kind of reality independent of the mind. For ARISTOTLE and the moderate realist tradition, essences exist as individuals in reality, but these individuals possess a real basis in reality for the intellectual perception of universality (*see* REALISM). For NOMINALISM only words are universal, since one word can be applied to distinct individuals that appear to be similar, but have no ontological similarity in reality. For CONCEPTUALISM, universal terms signify universal concepts that are mentally constructed and correspond to nothing in reality.

The remainder of this article discusses the problem of universals in the Middle Ages and in modern thought.

Universals in the Middle Ages

Pioneer historians of medieval philosophy, despite some exaggerations, have had the merit of seeing the importance of the medieval controversy over universals. The first form in which the problem of the one and the many arose in the 12th century was in the context of logic, prior to the rediscovery of Aristotle. In the opening decades of the 14th century, the problem assumed deeper metaphysical significance.

Porphyry and Boethius. In his introduction to Aristotle's *Categories*, PORPHYRY had formulated a series of options on the ontological status of universals: "Do genera and species subsist or are they located in the naked understandings? If subsisting, are they corporeal or incorporeal? Are they separate from or located in sensibles?"

[*Isagoge,* ed. A. Busse, *Comment. in Arist. Graec.* (Berlin 1887) 4.1:1.9–13]. Porphyry thought these questions beyond the capacity of his readers, but BOETHIUS, commenting on Porphyry's *Isagoge,* made a formal attempt to answer them. His solution, expounded out of deference to Aristotle, was that "universals subsist in sensibles, although they are understood apart from bodies" (*In Isagogen Porph.* ed. 2, 1.11; *Corpus scriptorum ecclesiasticorum latinorum* 48.1:167). Yet the doctrine on universals contained in Boethius's personal works is not that of his commentaries on Porphyry and Aristotle. Boethius seems to have preferred the extreme realism of Plato and the Platonic tradition. GODFREY OF SAINT-VICTOR derided Boethius for his apparent inability to reach a definitive solution to the problem of universals (*Fons philosophiae* 233–236). Nevertheless, it was Boethius, translator of Aristotle's *logica vetus* and preserver of two ancient positions, who provoked the 12th-century controversy over universals.

Twelfth-Century Controversy. If no science is safe without a secure universal, it is not surprising that the first scientific theologians defended the objective reality of universals. All Christian theologians admitted God's eternal knowledge of things. Aristotle was content with essences that are realized only in concrete singulars, for an Aristotelian god is a thought that thinks itself alone, unconcerned with this world of generation and corruption and unaware of its existence. For Christians, all things are known eternally to the divine Intellect, are created in time, and are subject to divine providence.

Origins. St. AUGUSTINE had shown (*Divers. quaest.* 46.2) that Plato's Ideas might be taken as a philosophical statement of the Christian conviction that God knows eternally all that can come to be. St. ANSELM OF CANTERBURY, as was his custom, went one step beyond St. Augustine to claim that things enjoy a mode of existence in divine knowledge superior to that in created matter (*Monolog.* 36). He called those who made universals mere words (*voces*) "dialectically heretics" (*De fide trin.*). The most eminent of these was ROSCELIN OF COMPIÈGNE, who considered things so radically singular that he reduced the universal to "an emission of the voice" (*flatus vocis*), to the sound that is made in pronouncing a universal term. JOHN OF SALISBURY reports that the theory of Roscelin did not survive its author (*Metalog.* 2.17); one reason for this was the formidable opposition of Abelard.

Abelard. A "peripatetic," thanks to his mastery of the "old logic," Peter ABELARD boasted that he had humiliated Roscelin, while still his pupil, by establishing that his teacher had missed the point on universals. What was at stake, Abelard saw, was not the physical reality of the universal term, but the explanation of how a plurality of individuals can be signified by a term that remains one in meaning. More than "an emission of the voice," a universal has meaning, and meaning is the crux of the problem. At the Cathedral School of Notre Dame in Paris, Abelard heard the celebrated WILLIAM OF CHAMPEAUX describe the universal as "real" and "essentially common" to all the individuals of which it can be predicated. Only the "variety of accidents" differentiates individuals. Under pressure from his difficult pupil, William modified, or perhaps simply rephrased, the formulation of his view to the point of conceding that the real universal is but "indifferently common" to many individuals. This position seemed to Abelard only slightly better than the first.

All realist positions, Abelard thought, suffer from a fatal defect in that they attribute universality to things. Nor would it help to speak of a "collection" of things marked by substantial similitude. To be in agreement (*convenire*) with others was also inadequate, for how could "individual," which Abelard considered a sixth predicable, be predicated of only one subject if universality means having something in common with many? Neither one thing nor a collection of things can ever be predicated of many subjects taken one by one; but such predication is the essence of universality. Words, not things, said Abelard, are predicates. Universals must be words, but not words taken in their crude materiality, like Roscelin's *flatus vocis,* for not every grammatically correct combination of words is a logically acceptable proposition. Not a subsistent "humanity," but the state (*status*) of being, is the basis for predicating "man" of John and Peter.

Unacquainted with Aristotle's theory of abstraction, Abelard was forced to improvise a substitute. Using illustrations derived from man's memory of what he has seen, from his anticipation of what he has not yet seen, and from his dreams of what he shall never see, Abelard explained that exact and vivid representations apply to single individuals only, whereas weak and confused impressions of a whole class fit any and all members without restriction to any one of them. These conveniently vague conceptions, however, cannot be called "ideas." Individuals, anticipated but not experienced, and abstractions that lie beyond sensation, are the objects of "opinion" rather than intellection. In the last analysis, Abelard held that man has pragmatic knowledge of accidental artifacts and that God alone has universal concepts of the substantial natures that He alone creates. Pragmatic knowledge of individuals present to man is distinct from his confused grasp of the ultimate natures that only God truly knows.

Later Discussion. Going one step further, John of Salisbury dismissed universals as dreams (*somnia*) and monstrosities (*monstra*) and considered the problem of universals an obstacle to true learning (*Metalog.* 2.20). For him, what the theorizers had overlooked was that dialectic is a useful collaborator with every science; but, in his own pointed analogy, logic is philosophically barren unless impregnated by a source such as the real sciences (*Metalog.* 2.10).

AVICENNA provided the notion that the intellect adds determinations such as "universal," "accidental," "subject," or "predicate" to a metaphysically neutral common nature. Understood when a thing is understood, these "dispositions" have no reality apart from the understanding (*Meta.* 3.10). Before there can be either individual or universal, there must be a nature, of itself indifferent to both.

Thirteenth Century. For the masters of the 13th century, the truth about universals was a consequence of their metaphysical and psychological premises. Aristotelian premises made possible new explanations, rendering the controversy less conspicuous.

St. ALBERT THE GREAT taught that the universal is verified in three modes. Prior to the individual (*ante rem*), universals are forms that are the principles of things. In the individual (*in re*), universals are forms that exist in things, sources of their names and natures. Subsequent to the individual (*post rem*), they are forms that are separated through abstraction. Admitting the reality of universal Ideas in the Creator and a foundation in things for the universal that is abstracted from individuals, Albert held that "the intellect contrives universality." For Albert, as for Aristotle, the universality of human ideas comes by way of abstraction from matter (*De praedicab.* 2.3).

St. THOMAS AQUINAS was no less explicit in holding that "universals are not subsisting things, but have existence only in singulars" (*C. gent.* 1.65). Every existent is inevitably a singular: "What is common to many is not anything alongside the many, except by reason alone" (*ibid.* 1.26). Although Plato was wrong in positing subsisting, separate forms as immediate causes of forms in matter, he was right in saying that forms separated from matter are the model of those forms that actuate matter. They exist in God's intellect and cause inferior forms through the mediation of natural agencies (*ibid.* 3.24). Nevertheless, it is not in universals that God knows His creatures, but in individuals themselves. In human intellects alone, universal concepts are engendered through sense experience of many singulars, in which the intellect discerns similarity (*In 1 anal. post.* 42.7).

Fourteenth-Century Debate. Duns Scotus had no hesitation in granting reality and unity to absolute quiddi-

ties. This was far from committing the Subtle Doctor to a gross realism of actually existing separate forms. "The universal is intelligible of itself. The prime object of intellect, namely, essence (*quod quid est*), is understood under the formality (*sub ratione*) of universality. But that formality is not essentially identical with essence—rather it is an accidental mode. Therefore, the intellect can know the difference between its prime object and that mode" (*Sup. univ. Porphy.* 5). As "realist" as William of Champeaux but immeasurably more sophisticated, Scotus saw, with Avicenna, that of itself the absolute QUIDDITY is neither individual, as verified in the physical order, nor universal, as functioning in the logical order. The intellect is responsible for universality by its recognition that a common nature can be predicated of many. While the modality of universality is formally distinct from a common nature, the universal term signifies this nature determined by universality. Scotus knew that the term "universal" is sometimes used with less precision: "At times, however, 'universal' is taken for the reality (*pro re*) that underlies a second intention, that is, for the absolute quiddity of a thing, which is, of itself, neither universal nor singular, but of itself indifferent" (*De anim.* 17.14). The universal is "in the intellect as in its efficient cause and in the knower as known" (*Sup. univ. Porphy.* 9). The sensible encounter with singulars is a necessary condition of knowledge, since knowledge of singulars is a kind of "matter" from which the agent intellect forms universals. The unity of the real individual is not destroyed by its inner plurality because the graded forms—generic, specific, and accidental—are not "really," but only "formally," distinct. An individual is a galaxy of ever more determined forms, closed by an ultimate actuality, "thisness" (*haecceitas*), which, precisely because it is not a form, cannot be a universal.

WILLIAM OF OCKHAM was distressed to find that not only Scotus, but every writer he read on the problem, gave to universals some degree of reality in the extramental world (*In 1 sent.* 2.7). Since, for Ockham, the universal is strictly nothing, no degree of reality can be so slight as not to be too much. That creatures resemble each other was to him no evidence that universal natures are real. Things are similar to each other only because the omnipotent Creator has freely willed them to be so. Notwithstanding the rigor with which Ockham reduced the cosmos to a system of totally heterogeneous individuals (*In 1 sent.* 2.9), he held that science is "of universals" (*Expos. sup. physic,* prol.). Even when Ockham was willing to explain universals as figments (*ficta*), he held that they are not arbitrary, but natural signs of the individuals they represent in mental discourse (*In 1 sent.* 2.8). In this sense, science is reductively a knowledge of individual things; his theory of supposition shows how this is possible (*Summa tot. log.* 1.62–68). "Abstraction" is Ockham's term for the process by which a multiple experience of singulars results in universals and in second intentions generally, but it is not the abstraction of Aquinas and Albert, nor that of Aristotle himself (*Ordinatio,* prol. 1). The universal is as natural a consequence of man's exposure to sensibles as a groan is a natural result of pain (*Summa tot. log.* 1.14). For Ockham, the intellect conceives the universal by a natural spontaneity, and therefore the universal is nothing but the act of thus understanding the singular (*ibid.* 1.15). The universal is no more than an "intention of the soul, of such a nature as to be predicable of many" (*ibid.* 1.15).

Some authors designate Ockham's position as "conceptualist" or "conceptist" or "terminist." Still others, certain of his disciples among them, make him the founder of the "nominalist sect." One of his contemporaries declared that Ockham and his party "wish to save everything with concepts." But nothing was saved, and it would be difficult not to conclude that Ockham's attack on universals had a role in undermining philosophical certitude and so opened a path to a skepticism the Venerable Inceptor did not himself profess.

E. A. SYNAN

Position of Modern Thinkers

In modern thought, problems regarding universals continued to receive either a nominalist, conceptualist, realist, or moderate realist solution. From the 17th to the 20th centuries, all the classical positions have found ardent defenders. They have analyzed the problem of knowledge, the structure of meaning, and the relative merits of realism and idealism in ways unknown to medieval thinkers or, at least, not employed by them. Nevertheless, a philosopher's commitment to a particular solution of the problem of universals determines his entire philosophical system.

Seventeenth Century. Thomas HOBBES briskly stated his case for nominalism: "This word universal is never the name of anything existent in nature, nor of any idea or phantasm formed in the mind, but always the name of some word or name" (*De corpore,* 2.9). For Hobbes, names are universal because they stand for a multiplicity of individual images. Similarities between those images justifies limiting certain names solely to certain images.

René DESCARTES's analysis of the problem of universals is related to his efforts to destroy the scholastic philosophy of matter and form. The ideas of the real nature of "God, Mind, Body, Triangle and all true essences" come in no way through the senses but are dependent on God for their existence as objects in the mind (*Reply to Obj.* 5, *Meditations* 5). Each idea is known innately; each is the idea of a particular, immutable, external essence.

As J. Maritain aptly points out, each Cartesian innate idea is universal—not as a universal object of thought, nor as an abstract essence that has to be reflexively returned to the phantasm to know the singular—but as a means or instrument of grasping, from the same aspect, a number of individuals [*Three Reformers* (London 1928) 67]. In Descartes's words, "We form a certain idea which we call the idea of a triangle; and afterwards make use of it as a universal representing to ourselves all the figures having three sides" (*Principles of Philosophy,* 59).

Descartes has often been termed a conceptualist because he fashioned a functionally universal idea from what is the proper and immediate object of his knowledge—a singular innate idea. A more explicit conceptualism is found in John LOCKE, opponent of Hobbes's nominalism, Cartesian INNATISM, and the realism of the CAMBRIDGE PLATONISTS. For Locke, the internal constitution and real essences of things are unknown to man; yet he does fashion general, universal ideas. He does so by taking a particular idea, abstracting from its circumstances of time and place, and then considering it as a fixed meaning. Such an idea represents the plurality of individuals conforming to the abstracted idea. Its character of universality is a relation of representation "that by the mind of man is added to them"; it is an invention and creation of the understanding (*Essay Concerning Human Understanding* 3.3.11). Locke calls this mental construct a "nominal essence." Since the universal nominal essence is neither a word nor a name but a concept, Locke was neither a nominalist nor a realist but a conceptualist; for him, the universal, general idea corresponds to nothing in reality but is still the object of intuitive, general, and certain knowledge (*Essay* 4.3.31).

B. SPINOZA proposed three levels of knowing, each of which has a kind of universal proper to it: (1) Body sensations that are similar to each other correspond to vague, general, universal images in the mind, to which general names are given. (2) At the level of scientific reason one has adequate ideas of the universal properties of things as necessary characteristics of natures. (3) At the level of intuitive knowledge one fully knows finite, individual essences in the attributes of God (*Ethics* 2.40.2). Here the idea is universal in the sense that individuals are seen as modes within the infinite universal totality that is God. Spinoza presaged the concrete universal of Hegel, and, in a special sense, he was a realist, although in his pantheistic monism there is nothing real except God.

Eighteenth Century. Bishop George Berkeley's battle against MATERIALISM and SKEPTICISM centered upon the impossibility of separating the physical existence of an object from its existence in perception. BERKELEY rejected abstraction and Locke's abstract, general ideas without rejecting general ideas (*Principles of Human Knowledge,* Introd. 15). For him, a general non-abstract idea (image) is a particular idea possessing universality because it is used to signify other particulars of the same sort indifferently. Berkeley proposed resemblance as a justification for admitting a plurality of particulars. His was a conceptualist position wherein species are general ideas constructed by men's minds and words are universal designators of ideas.

Berkeley's stand on general ideas was considered by David HUME to be a most valuable discovery (*Treatise of Human Nature* 1.1.7). For Hume the idea in the mind designates a particular object used in reasoning as though it were universal. Hume adds to Berkeley's position what is called "the disposition theory": a word becomes universal or general when the particular idea basically associated with it is recalled and the imagination is disposed or alert to recall associated ideas. Given Hume's empiricist assumption that ideas that copy singular impressions of sensation or of reflection alone can exist, thinking deals with image-symbols. Insofar as the universal term has no real mental or nonmental referent, Hume can be termed a nominalist.

Immanuel KANT, an opponent of Hume's skepticism, nevertheless accepted Hume's basic empiricism and constructed an influential position on universals in the conceptualist tradition. Since, for Kant, mathematics and physics are composed of necessary and universal propositions while sensible experience lacks universality and necessity, the conditions of universality and necessity must, he believed, be imposed by the mind. "Understanding does not obtain its a priori laws from nature, it prescribes them to it" (*Prolegomena to any Future Metaphysics,* 2.36, 18–20). The universality and necessity of the object of scientific knowledge are thus fashioned by the understanding, not by the nature of what is given in sense experience (see *Critique of Pure Reason,* pref. to 2d ed.).

Nineteenth Century. The concrete universal of G. W. F. HEGEL testifies to Hegel's realism; for since the ideal is the real and the real the ideal, and since concepts are the way to reach absolute reality, concrete universal concepts do this best by including both the differences and the common aspects of things, their complete multiple relationships. For Hegel the concrete content of the concept possesses universal significance. All concrete concepts except one involve some abstractness; that one completely concrete universal is the Absolute Idea, Absolute Spirit in achieved self-possession (*Science of Logic,* 80).

The impact of Hume's nominalism was intensified by John Stuart MILL, for whom a universal term signified a totality of particular attributes or individuals. What some suppose to be essences, Mill claimed, are simply names conventionally applied to certain attributes (*A System of Logic* 1.5).

Twentieth Century. Henri BERGSON, a conceptualist, saw reality as constantly evolving duration. Universal concepts, therefore, are incapable of describing the real; nevertheless they are useful to indicate the practical attitude taken by a knower toward objects—an index of action rather than a means of knowing, for there can be no identical situations except in a conceptualized universe (*Évolution créatrice,* Paris 1907).

Realism. The early realism of Bertrand RUSSELL was tempered but not eliminated in his later life. For Russell, "a universal will be anything which may be shared by many particulars" [*Problems of Philosophy* (New York 1912) 93]. Russell was convinced that if the basic, nonformal elements of true propositions refer to nothing in the universe, then it is meaningless to speak of the truth of such propositions. But there are true propositions (e.g., "I [Russell] am in my room"), and a necessary condition for the existence of true propositions is that the irreducible, nonredundant factors of true propositions denote real universals that in some unexplained sense have being and are real (*ibid.* 90). Russell rejected the attempt of some nominalists to describe the world without the word "similar" or its equivalent; that is, for him, not every predicative expression can be successfully analyzed into nonpredicative expressions. Since nominalists cannot expunge the predicate of relation "is similar to," Russell saw no objection to keeping other universals as well ["Reply to Criticisms," *The Philosophy of Bertrand Russell,* ed. P. A. Schilpp (Evanston 1946) 688]. Vast metaphysical problems of participation were dismissed in Russell's gratuitous presupposition that every real universal may be exemplified by multitudes of particulars without losing its unity.

Also in the realist tradition is Alonzo Church, for whom a distinction must be made between (1) the proposition in the traditional sense, that is, a declarative sentence, judgment, or thought, together with its meaning, and (2) the proposition in the abstract sense, i.e., the objective content or meaning taken apart from the sentence as a purely syntactical entity. This meaning, common to the sentence and its translations into other languages, is thus common to many. In sense (2), propositions are universals. Without such postulated entities, the Church thinks that logical theory "would be intolerably complex if not impossible" (*Problem of Universals,* 9).

Nominalism. One of America's leading analytical philosophers, W. V. O. Quine (1908–) developed a nominalistic logical paraphernalia following on his position that the types of beings that are pragmatically justified are ordinary physical objects, "postulated entities which round out and simplify our account of the flux of experience . . ." (18). Just as physical objects are cultural posits or manners of speaking, so, for Quine, it may be useful to speak of universals as classes or attributes of physical objects, such as the class of red things: "the scattered total thing whose parts are all the red things" (72). Thus universals are culturally posited manners of speaking; classes or attributes of physical objects are as much myths as is the physicalistic conceptual scheme itself, when viewed from within the phenomenalistic conceptual scheme (17–19).

A personal intuition that paradoxes arise from the admission of any entitative reality for classes, attributes, meanings, modalities, etc., led Nelson Goodman (1906–) to reject those he considers Platonists (*Fact, Fiction and Forecast*, 37). Goodman's nominalism "consists specifically in the refusal to recognize classes" (*Problem of Universals*, 16). It is a description of the world as composed of individuals—a world made up of entities, no two of which break down into exactly the same entities. Where the Platonist admits classes of the minimal atomic elements, classes of classes, and so on, Goodman holds there can be no distinction of entities without a distinction of content, that is, that there cannot be different classes made up of the same entities. Where the Platonist admits the Class *K,* made of classes *a* and *b* and of classes *c* and *d,* and Class *L,* made of classes *a* and *c* and classes *b* and *d,* Goodman sees *K* and *L* as one individual, as a sum individual. In his view, different classes cannot be made up of the same entities, and clearly *K* and *L* break down into the same entities, not into different entities.

Linguistic Analysis. Some contemporary philosophers see universals as a problem not to be solved but to be dissolved. Many of these are linguistic analysts who infer, from the fact that one applies the same general, universal terms to different things, their basic presupposition, viz, that the recognition of natural classes is a fact to be noted, not explained. Since linguistic usage presupposes classes, this commitment to classes is not an explanation of general, universal terms, but merely a weakly elucidative and repetitive way of saying that there *are* meaningful classificatory terms (A. Quinton, 40–42). On the presupposition that they can never get outside language to discover what reality is independently of what ordinary linguistic usage says it is, some analysts hold that both realism and nominalism are circular explanations of universals—realism, because proposing that things are so named since they instantiate a certain universal; nominalism, because proposing that things are so named because they are similar, while the kind of similar-

ity can be specified only by reference to the name imposed because of the similarity (D. F. Pears, 53–57). Naming is held by analysts to be ultimate, because, for them, no explanation of naming is noncircular.

Moderate Realism. In contemporary philosophy, moderate realism is defended principally by Thomists, other scholastics, and dialectical materialists. Thomists, particularly after the middle of the 19th century, saw in moderate realism the basic commitment necessary for a sound philosophy of knowledge. Following St. Thomas Aquinas, they attribute true universality to intellectual knowledge alone and recognize in individuals a variable, proportional, and analogical foundation for the universal concept of SPECIES. Eclectic scholastics, influenced largely by St. Augustine, Avicenna, and Duns Scotus, defend a stronger realism that sees stable, specific common natures totally and absolutely present in each individual. While not all such scholastics defend the plurality of forms in an individual substance, all do concede a foundation for such a plurality.

Dialectical materialists, for vastly different reasons, also defend the universality of ideas in human consciousness and the individuality of events in nature. Ideas, being qualitatively different from animal images, are derived from singular events; they need to be verified and perfected in the dialectic of practical experience; and they reach an ultimate conformity with physical reality. Material individuals, on the other hand, manifest real qualitative differences in the dialectics of nature sufficient to provide a basis for universality of species both in nature and in consciousness.

Existentialism. EXISTENTIALISM, insisting on the absolute uniqueness of every event, considers universal concepts to be unrelated to life, even if such concepts can be granted. The universal, for existentialists, can be no more than an abstract category created by the mind without relevance to existential reality. Existentialism, therefore, is a realism of individual, personal experiences wherein the problem of universals is dismissed as irrelevant.

See Also: SCHOLASTICISM; PHILOSOPHY, HISTORY OF, 3; THOMISM; EPISTEMOLOGY; KNOWLEDGE; IDEALISM; MATERIALISM, DIALECTICAL AND HISTORICAL.

Bibliography: É. H. GILSON, *History of Christian Philosophy in the Middle Ages* (New York 1955). F. C. COPELSTON, *History of Philosophy* (Westminster, Md. 1946–) v. 2–3. C. CARBONARA, *Enciclopedia filosofica* (Venice-Rome 1957) 4:1408–12. M. H. CARRÉ, *Realists and Nominalists* (New York 1946). J. REINERS, *Der Aristotelische Realismus in der Frühscholastik* (Aachen 1907); "Der Nominalismus in der Frühscholastik," *Beiträge zur Geschichte der Philosophie und Theologie des Mittelalters* 8.5 (1910). J. MARITAIN, *The Degrees of Knowledge,* tr. G. B. PHELAN et al. (New

York 1959). É. H. GILSON, *The Unity of Philosophical Experience* (New York 1937). R. I. AARON, *The Theory of Universals* (Oxford 1952). B. BLANSHARD, *Reason and Analysis* (La Salle, Ill. 1962). H. H. PRICE, *Thinking and Experience* (Cambridge, Mass. 1953). I. M. BOCHEŃSKI et al., *The Problem of Universals: A Symposium* (Notre Dame, Ind. 1956). W. V. O. QUINE, *From a Logical Point of View* (Cambridge, Mass. 1953). N. GOODMAN, *Fact, Fiction and Forecast* (Cambridge, Mass. 1955). R. G. MILLER, "Realistic and Unrealistic Empiricisms," *The New Scholasticism* 35 (1961) 311–337; "Linguistic Analysis and Metaphysics," *American Catholic Philosophical Association Proceedings of the Annual Metting* 34 (1960) 80–109. D. F. PEARS, "Universals," *Logic and Language* (2d ser.), ed. A. G. N. FLEW (New York 1953) 51–64. A. QUINTON, "Properties and Causes," *Proceedings of the Aristotelian Society* (n.s. 58; 1958) 33–58.

[R. G. MILLER]

UNIVERSE, ORDER OF

The universe is here taken to mean the totality of created beings, both material and spiritual. The order of the universe is the complex of relationships joining them to one another and to God. The order of the universe can be considered from several points of view: scientific, purely philosophical, or theological. It is here considered from the theological point of view, i.e., relying not only on the evidence afforded by observation and reasoning, but especially on that coming from divine revelation. This consideration falls under two heads: a historical sketch of the idea in Western thought; and a doctrinal synthesis based chiefly on the writings of St. Thomas Aquinas, and indicating the use of this doctrine in theology.

Historical Development

Although the doctrine of the order of the universe was explained most fully by St. Thomas Aquinas in the 13th century, its roots go back 2,000 years before this to two widely separated cultures of the 6th century B.C.

Greek and Jewish Origins. Among the Greeks, PYTHAGORAS first explicitly formulated the idea of an ordered universe, calling the totality of things ὁ κόσμος the cosmos, i.e., the order or beauty [Aetius, *Placit.* 2.1.1, ed. H. Diels, *Doxographi Graeci,* 3d ed. (Berlin 1958) 327]. At approximately the same time a Jewish editor in exile at Babylon was giving the final form to the priestly account of the Mosaic teaching on creation in Genesis 1. Centuries of tradition and reflection were crystallized under divine inspiration in a description of all things as they were called into being and ordered by the creative word of Almighty God.

The Greek line of thought, oriented by Pythagoras, was continued through the 5th century by his followers, such as Philolaos, and became common in philosophical

poets such as Empedocles and PARMENIDES. In the 4th century PLATO wrote a magnificent description of the divine ordering of all things (*Tim.* 27A–34A). After this, Aristotle made the most important observation of antiquity about the good of the whole universe. This good is found in a twofold order, first between all the constitutive parts of the universe themselves, second between them and the external divine source of good. The first is on account of the second. The universe is like an army, where there is an order between various men and units, and where these are all ordered to the goal aimed at by the leader (*Meta.* 1075a 11–25). STOICISM, founded by Zeno at the end of the 4th century, regarded the whole multitude of existing things as constituting a unity, one living body [ed. H. von Arnim, *Stoicorum veterum fragmenta* (Leipzig 1903) 2:169f.]

The Greek and Jewish lines of thought, begun independently in the 6th century, met in Alexandria three centuries later. The Septuagint (LXX), whose earliest portions date from this period, makes frequent use of the word κόσμος, a use continued in later OT books, actually written in Greek (e.g., see Wis 7.18; 2 Mc 8.18). The Alexandrian PHILO JUDAEUS (20 B.C.–A.D. 60) used the Greek idea of the cosmos to help understand the universe and its relationship to God (see esp. *Op. mund.* and *Act. Mund.*). NT writers also use κόσμος to designate the universe created by God (e.g., Mt 24.21; Jn 17.5; Acts 17.24; 1 Cor 3.22).

Christian Era. For subsequent Christian writers God's work as an ordered universe is a frequent theme. Clement of Rome (*c.* A.D. 97) exhorts the disobedient Christians at Corinth to submission by proposing to them the divinely established order of the universe [1 Clem. 20, ed. F. X. Funk, *Patres Apostolici* (Tubingen 1891) 126]. The Apologists appealed to the order of the universe as evidence of the governing intelligence of the Creator (e.g., Theophilus of Antioch, *Ad Autol.* 1.6, *Patrologia Graeca*, ed. J. P. Migne, 6:1033; Tertullian, *Apol.* 17, *Corpus Christianorum. Series latina* (Turnhout, Belg. 1953–) 1:117).

Alexandria continued as a center of religious reflection upon the universe. CLEMENT OF ALEXANDRIA (*c.* A.D. 195) speaks of God as the true measure, containing and upholding the universe in balance [*Protrep.* 6, *Die griechischen christlichen Schriftsteller der ersten drei Jahrhunderte* (Leipzig 1897–) 12:52]. Origen argues against the polytheists from the manifest unity of the universe to the existence of only one God (*C. Cels.* 1.23, *Die griechischen christlichen Schriftsteller der ersten drei Jahrhunderte* 2:73). A group of non-Christian thinkers developed a doctrine on the order of the universe that combined ideas derived from Stoicism and from Gnostic theories of salvation [see *Herm.* 10; *Asclep.* 13; tr. W. Scott, *Hermetica* (Oxford 1924) 1:187–205, 311]. PLOTI-NUS also considered the universe and its order from the viewpoint of man's perfection and destiny (*Enn.* 1.2.1; 2.3.7; 3.2).

Patristic Period. Among the Latin writers after Tertullian, LACTANTIUS in the early 4th century saw the beauty and order of the universe as manifesting to all the existence of God [*Div. instit.* 1.2.5, *Corpus scriptorum ecclesiasticorum latinorum* (Vienna 1866–) 19:7]. A century later St. AUGUSTINE urged the goodness and beauty of the whole created universe against the Manichaean doctrine of the evil of matter (*Enchir.* 10, *Patrologia Latina,* ed. J. P. Migne, 40:236). Toward the close of the patristic age in the West, BOETHIUS taught a universal order of providence, embracing all things and drawing good even from evil (*Consolat. phil.* 4.6.52–53, *Corpus scriptorum ecclesiasticorum latinorum* 67:101).

Among the Greek Fathers, St. BASIL in the 4th century preached the manifestation of God's wisdom and beauty in the ordered arrangement of all things (see *Hom. in hexaem.,* esp. n. 6; *Patrologia Graeca* 29:117–48). In the following century, PSEUDO-DIONYSIUS produced four theological works expressing in the strongest way the ordered hierarchic structure of the universe (*Patrologia Graeca* 3). At the close of the patristic age in the 8th century St. JOHN DAMASCENE, summing up the traditions of Eastern Christianity, taught that the ordered unity of the universe, made up of various and opposing parts, offers manifest proof of the omnipotent power of the Creator, by whose will the cosmos holds together (*Fid. orthod.* 1.3, 2.29; *Patrologia Graeca* 94:796, 964).

Scholasticism. The doctrine of the order of the universe was directly introduced into the Christian thought of the early Middle Ages by Peter ABELARD (1079–1152). Citing the authority of Plato, he defended the position that the world of creatures is made and ordered by God in the best possible way (*In hexaem., de 6ᵃ die, Patrologia Latina* 178:766; *Theol. christ.* 20, *Patrologia Latina* 178:1141). HUGH OF SAINT-VICTOR (1096–1141) opposed him, saying God could make creatures better whether they be considered individually or as constituting a universe (*Summa sent.* 1.2.22, *Patrologia Latina* 176:69–70). This chapter of Hugh of Saint-Victor's work was reproduced almost word for word by PETER LOMBARD in his *Libri Sententiarum* (1.44). As this work became the standard theology text for centuries to come, all the great commentators on the *Sentences* treat at this point the question of the universe and its perfection: St. ALBERT THE GREAT, St. BONAVENTURE, St. THOMAS AQUINAS, Peter of Tarentaise (Bl. INNOCENT V), RICHARD OF MIDDLETON, GILES OF ROME, DURANDUS OF SAINT-POURÇAIN, and DENIS THE CARTHUSIAN. In the works of St. Thomas all the intellectual currents of the past on the order of the universe came together to receive a philosophical and theological exposition of unmatched precision and penetration (*C. gent.* 1.42, 78, 86; 2.42; 3.64, 112, 140; *Summa theologiae* 1a, 19–23; 47–50; 60–65; 103–05).

Recent Thought. Since St. Thomas very little has been added to the doctrine of the order of the universe, though scientific discoveries have revealed the staggering dimensions of this order on the material level. P. TEIL-HARD DE CHARDIN developed a religious concept of the universe that makes little use of traditional terminology [*The Divine Milieu* (New York 1960)]. Pope PIUS XII made the order of the universe the theme of his final Christmas message in 1957 [*Acta Apostolicae Sedis* 50 (1958) 5–24].

Thomistic Synthesis

The whole teaching of St. Thomas on the order of the universe is an elaboration of a basic insight derived from Aristotle: the order of the universe is twofold, of the parts of the universe to one another, and of the whole to God as end. The former order is on account of the latter. This statement has two different, complementary meanings. The first, a largely static meaning, is that the order of parts to one another flows from the ordination of all things to God as end. The second, a dynamic meaning, is that the order of parts to one another is aimed at promoting the movement of the whole universe toward God. These meanings are considered in turn.

Static Orientation. The universe with its order has its ultimate source in God's decree to create, to share His goodness and perfection with beings distinct from Himself. Now, when someone acts to produce something, the thing produced reflects in its purpose the intention of the one producing it. Since, then, God's intention to communicate His goodness is ultimately motivated by that goodness itself, the purpose of any individual creature has a double aspect: (1) to receive for itself a participation in the divine goodness, and (2) to act for the communication of the divine goodness to others. Both these aspects must be kept in mind or the inner meaning of the order of the universe does not emerge. The purpose of any individual creature is not adequately expressed by saying it is intended to share in the divine goodness, but rather in saying it is intended for the realization of God's intention to communicate His goodness. This second formulation makes each individual both a receiver and giver in the way proper to its nature. Thus, the order of each individual thing to God as end necessarily links it with all other things produced by God, according to their diverse capacities for mutually giving and receiving. Consequently, one has not only an order of individuals to God, but also an order of all things to one another.

This mutual ordering of all things to one another gives to the universe as a whole its own proper being, unity, truth, beauty, and goodness. The BEING of the universe comes from this order, because apart from it there is nothing objectively existing that can be called a universe, but only many isolated individual things. A mind might conceive of them as constituting some kind of a whole, but unless they are objectively linked no such whole would actually exist. Secondly, this internal ordering of all things to one another makes the universe one, a UNITY of order. All beings from the highest archangel to the most fleeting subatomic particle belong to this one same ordered universe. Further, the TRUTH of the universe, its inherent intelligibility as a whole comprising all created things, comes from this mutual ordering of its parts. Next, the BEAUTY of the universe, its power to delight the mind, is found in its all-embracing order where each thing is seen to fit in precisely where it belongs; hence the Greek name for the universe noted earlier, cosmos, meaning both order and beauty. Finally, and most important, the intrinsic GOOD of the universe is found in the order of its parts to one another. For this good is the common good of all created things. It is constituted by the contribution of every individual good and shared in by every individual creature. Now, that which gathers all individual goods into one, and at the same time enables all to share in the universal good, is the internal order linking all parts to one another according to their capacities to give and receive.

Dynamic Orientation. This leads to the dynamic meaning of the principle that the internal order of the universe is on account of the order to God as end. For, since God's intention to create many beings necessarily means the intention to create a universe whose parts cooperate for the good of each and all, it becomes evident that the creative intention of God should be conceived primarily as the intention to create the universe as such, viz, this unity whose ordered perfection is superior to every other created good. God wills individual things to exist in function of the perfection of the whole ordered to Himself as the end whose goodness is to be communicated and diffused. The universe, then, is God's proper effect, that to whose perfection and goodness His creative act chiefly tends. Thus, the internal order of the parts to one another is intended for the realization of the purpose of the whole universe in relation to God as end.

The purpose of any composite whole is what determines the order of its parts to one another. To understand, then, how this order within the universe promotes the purpose of the universe, it is necessary to ascertain precisely what purpose of the universe it is that requires for its attainment the order of parts actually given. There are two different but complementary ways of expressing this purpose: (1) God intends the universe to be a created likeness of His own goodness and perfection; and (2) God intends the whole universe to be united to Him through the beatific knowledge and love of intellectual creatures.

Created Likeness. If one considers the ultimate purpose of the universe as likeness to God, he can see why there must be a host of diverse beings, since the immense goodness and beauty of God could not otherwise be represented outside Himself. The diversity required is primarily a diversity of SPECIES rather than of individuals within the same species, since these have all essentially the same perfection. Furthermore, since the universe as such will always endure, inasmuch as it is willed immediately on account of God Himself, these things that belong to the essential perfection of the universe are imperishable. They include species, by reason of the unfailing succession of individuals; elements and first principles, since these are never wholly destroyed but only changed; and spiritual beings, in themselves naturally immortal. The internal order of the mutual sharing of goods is required for the universe to imitate God's act of diffusing His goodness. This involves a radical harmony between the basic tendencies of all created things, and establishes within the universe an order of ends, a subordination of lower to higher, all culminating in the similitude of each and all to God. Higher beings lead the lower to perfection, while the lower in turn serve the higher.

Beatific Union. Likeness to God by itself, however, is an insufficient explanation of the purpose of the universe. It is necessary to state further what God was intending in choosing to create this rather than any other possible universe. For uncounted universes were possible to God, each distinguished from the others by its own peculiar purpose, by its own special likeness to God. This leads to the consideration of the purpose of the universe as the activity of created intellectual beings seeing and loving God, an activity that terminates directly and immediately in the divine goodness itself. For intellectual beings are the highest in creation, and all other things are ordered to them, and through them are related to God as end. The universe is like an army where the activity of the weapons' maker is ordered to victory through the activity of the man using the weapon. The return of the universe to God is thus realized in spiritual activity, in the beatific vision and love of the saints.

The beatitude of the saints is not to be considered as a multitude of isolated acts of seeing and loving God. The unity of the order of the universe is found here, too, in the unity of a "We," wherein each speaks for all in praising and loving God. The perfection of the individual, considered precisely as his own subjective good, is subordinated to the perfection of the whole city of the blessed, but considered as joining him immediately to God, is superior to every created good, even the internal order of the universe. For here, in each case, is the order to the end that joins not only the individual to God, but also the whole ordered universe, of which the individual is a part.

But God did not create the universe in the state of ultimate perfection, joined to Him through the beatitude of the saints. He gave it an initial perfection in the completeness of its parts, and the universe, then, under the influence of God, moves from initial perfection to consummate perfection. For God wishes the blessed to be His friends, not mere puppets and slaves. They are to be with Him because they have freely accepted His offer of friendship, which they could not do if they were created in actual possession of the end. Their free response to His love is the essential movement of the universe to God. And all created beings cooperate to lead intellectual beings to the vision of God.

Thus to achieve His purpose God created angels, men, and nonintellectual beings. Angels, pure spirits, in one act make their total response to God, and afterward together assist men toward God by their inspirations and protection. Men, beings of spirit and matter, shape their total response to God through many acts governed by charity, and thereby simultaneously help one another. Nonintellectual beings, purely material, minister to man's needs both material and spiritual, by providing him with food, shelter, clothing, a field for the growth of knowledge, and a whole series of temporal situations in which charity and justice may develop.

Evil as Disorder. This harmonious structure apparently neglects one element: EVIL, the real disorder found in the universe. Evil is a failure in some particular being, the PRIVATION of an individual good. But God allows evil in some parts of the universe for the good of the whole. For He does what is best for the whole, whose perfection He primarily intends, but not always for the part, except in relation to the whole. Although beings not subject to failure are better in themselves than those that can fail, it is better that both kinds should exist in the universe than only the former. And if some beings exist that can fail, then sometimes they will fail, God so allowing it. He allows it in order not to cancel out the very natures He has made, nor to impede much good that is connected with such defects within the universe.

Kinds of Evil. Evil may be physical or moral. Physical evil is the privation of some good that pertains to the subjective well-being of a creature but has no direct, intrinsic reference to its ordination to God, e.g., poverty, disease, disgrace, death, which of themselves turn one neither to nor away from God. Since this sort of evil itself implies no disorder in the universe with respect to God as end, He may sometimes will it in connection with some good. In willing to nourish men and animals He wills to destroy some plants and animals. In willing to teach men patience and a true sense of values He may will them to be afflicted by some trial. At other times, however, He only permits physical evil, i.e., does not hinder its actual occurrence, since He can order its effects to good.

Moral evil or SIN, being a disorder with respect to God as end, is in no way intended by Him, but only permitted. He permits it so as not to destroy the FREEDOM of man's response to Him. He orders it to good either by repentance, patient endurance of its effects, and temporal afflictions, or if serious and finally unrepented, by eternal punishment. Through such punishment the order of justice manifests God's supreme worthiness to be loved and adored, a worthiness that unrepented sin continues to spurn. However, the order of the universe does not antecedently require for its perfection that anyone be punished eternally. Only those are finally disposed of in this way who by their obstinate refusal to love have freely rendered themselves unfit for anything else.

Remedy for Disorder. The ultimate remedy for the disorder of sin and the ultimate internal source of the universe's perfection is Christ, the Son of God made man. The movement of the universe toward God is supposed to be a created free response to God's loving initiative, not simply the passive reception and instrumental, necessary execution of His activity. Through the INCARNATION of the Word, a created nature was joined to a divine person as His own. Thus, a true man, freely accomplishing the divine will with an efficacy deriving from His personality as God, removed in principle the disorder of sin and linked the human race once more to its destiny in God. He freely entered into death, the ultimate purely physical evil consequent upon sin, and triumphed over it through His obedience and humility. Risen from the dead and exalted at the right hand of His Father, the man Christ Jesus continues to exercise His mediating function to restore all things, especially in and through the Church. And He awaits the day when at the command of His Father He will finally come to subject all things to Himself, even death by raising those who have believed in Him, and then hand over the universe to His Father as the kingdom He has won, the unfailing realization of divine wisdom and love. Thus the eternal kingdom o God, the beatitude of the saints, is the glory of Christ, wherein are manifested and adored His redeeming power and love. This is the final perfection of the order of the universe.

Order in Theology. St. Thomas uses the doctrine of the order of the universe to clarify more than 70 different questions in the *Summa theologiae* (see Wright, 194–212). Since the order of the universe is the complete plan of God for communicating His life and goodness, and includes both the natural disposition of things and the supernatural economy of grace in Christ, the universe as such is God's greatest created manifestation of Himself and can serve to illuminate almost every truth of faith. The individual themes that form the heart of this doctrine, such as CREATION, the twofold ordering of all things, the common good, beatitude, the permission of evil, and RE-DEMPTION are more fully understood when considered as parts of a whole to which they belong.

Furthermore, truths about GOD Himself can be more deeply penetrated by means of this doctrine. The being and unity and splendor of God are reflected in the beauty and unity of the whole universe. His detailed knowledge is manifested in the comprehensiveness of the order He has established. His wisdom and love are seen in the dynamic ordering of all things to Himself to share in His goodness. His mercy is seen in establishing and repairing this order; His justice, in maintaining it. The nature of His providence can be seen in the kind of created activity immediately establishing those relationships that are the order of the universe upheld by His providence. For creatures act not merely as puppets, but each with its own spontaneous part to play according to the nature it has received. The order of the universe even provides a dim analogy to help faith toward a deeper knowledge of the Holy TRINITY, which is an order of Divine Persons based on knowledge and love in the perfect and total communication of the divine nature.

Finally, other truths about creatures not directly required for stating the doctrine of the order of the universe can be integrated into it and thereby illuminated. For example, the solidarity of all men, implied in the doctrines of original sin and redemption, can best be grasped as an aspect of the solidarity of the whole universe. Mary as Mother of the Head of all creation is Queen of the universe. Sacred history is the movement of the universe to its final perfection. The CHURCH especially can be more fully appreciated. For the Church on earth is the essential anticipation and seed of the Church in heaven, the city of the blessed, which is the ultimate perfection of the universe. This makes clear the connection between Christ's headship of creation and of the Church, which St. Paul is concerned to emphasize (Col 1.15–20). The whole structure of the Church, its channels of authority in carrying on the mission it bears from Christ, its visible signs

of grace by which Christ's intention to redeem and sanctify is efficaciously applied to the world, its sacrifice in which Christ the Head unites all things to Himself as priest and victim in the movement of history toward God—this structure is set at the heart of the universe, the one supreme work of God.

See Also: ORDER; PROVIDENCE OF GOD; ANGELS; BEATIFIC VISION; PAROUSIA.

Bibliography: J. H. WRIGHT, *The Order of The Universe in the Theology of St. Thomas Aquinas* (Rome 1957); ''The Consummation of the Universe in Christ,'' *Gregorianum* 39 (1958) 285–94. B. COFFEY, ''The Notion of Order According to St. Thomas Aquinas,'' *The Modern Schoolman* 27 (1949) 1–18. J. DE FINANCE, ''La Finalité de l'être et le sens de l'univers,'' *Mélanges Joseph Maréchal,* 2 v. (Brussels 1950) 2:141–58. J. LEGRAND, *L'Univers et l'homme dans la philosophie de Saint Thomas,* 2 v. (Brussels 1946). M. J. ADLER, ed., *The Great Ideas: A Syntopicon of Great Books of the Western World,* 2 v. (Chicago 1952) 2:1132. G. GIANNINI, *Enciclopedia filosofica,* 4 v. (Venice-Rome 1957) 3:1061–68.

[J. H. WRIGHT]

UNLEAVENED BREAD (IN THE BIBLE)

Round, flat cakes of bread made from flour and water without yeast. The ordinary bread of nomadic peoples was unleavened (Hebrew *maṣṣâ*), as it still is today in the Near East, and was baked on hot coals or on a grill over an open fire. It can be quickly prepared, as there is no delay in waiting for the dough to rise; hence, it is mentioned in the Bible in cases where haste was required: Sarah baked unleavened bread for ''the three strangers'' (Gn 18.6), Lot did the same for the two angels (Gn 19.3), and the sorceress of Endor for Saul (1 Sm 28.24).

The legislation of the Pentateuchal PRIESTLY WRITERS prescribed the use of unleavened bread for various cultic offerings. However, this usage was much more ancient; it was probably for religious reasons that GIDEON provided unleavened bread with his sacrifice of a kid (Jgs 6.19), and the laws prohibiting the use of leavened bread with a sacrifice occurred as early as the BOOK OF THE COVENANT (Ex 23.18) and the ritual decalogue (Ex 34.25). The priestly legislation described the cereal offering (Hebrew *minḥâ*): when baked, it had to be unleavened and made with oil instead of water (Lv 2.4–10). The unleavened cakes accompanied a bloody sacrifice (Lv 7.12; 8.2; Nm 6.15).

The principal cultic use was for the Feast of Unleavened Bread (Ex 23.15; 34.18; Dt 16.16), which lasted seven days, during which all leaven was to be banished from homes and only unleavened bread eaten (Ex 12.15–20; 13.6–10; Nm 28.17). An agrarian feast, it marked the beginning of the barley harvest; probably it was borrowed from the Canaanites, though it early assumed distinctive Israelite characteristics. The feast fell in the month of Abib (near the spring equinox), but in ancient times the precise day depended upon the maturity of the crop. Since the Feast of PASSOVER was celebrated at the full moon of the same month and also required the eating of unleavened bread, the two feasts were combined shortly before the Exile, the Passover being fixed on the 14th of Abib (later called Nisan) and the Feast of Unleavened Bread from the 15th to the 21st of this month (Ez 45.21; Lv 23.5–8). The Feast of Unleavened Bread (ἡ ἑορτὴ τῶν ἀζύμων) is mentioned several times also in the New Testament (Mt 26.17; Mk 14.1, 12; Lk 22.1, 7; Acts 12.3, 20.6).

In a figurative sense, the Feast of Unleavened Bread provides a point of comparison in 1 Cor 5.6–8, where yeast stands for moral corruption, unleavened bread for newness of life in the risen Christ. Leaven is a symbol of corruption also in the saying of Jesus about the "leaven of the Pharisees" (Mk 8.15; Mt 16.6, 12; Lk 12.1). But there is no connection with Jewish ritual practice in the proverb quoted by Paul (Gal 5.9; 1 Cor 5.6) or in the parable that compares the kingdom of heaven to a small piece of yeast that leavens a whole mass of dough (Mt 13.33; Lk 13.21); in the latter case the leaven is not symbolic of corruption, but has a beneficial effect.

Piles of Matzo (unleavened bread). (©Hulton-Deutsch Collection/CORBIS)

Bibliography: *Encyclopedic Dictionary of the Bible,* translated and adapted by L. HARTMAN (New York, 1963) 2517–18. J. C. RYLAARSDAM, G. A. BUTTRICK, *The Interpreters' Dictionary of the Bible* (Nashville 1962) 4:734. H. WINDISCH, G. KITTEL, *Theologesches Wörterbuch zum Neuen Testament* (Stuttgart 1935) 2:904–908. J. THOMAS, *Dictionnaire de la Bible,* ed. F. VIGOUROUX, 5 v. (Paris 1895–1912) 1.2: 1311–14. R. DEVAUX, *Ancient Israel, Its Life and Institutions,* tr. J. MCHUGH (New York 1961) 470–473, 484–494.

[C. J. PEIFER]

UNNI OF HAMBURG, ST.

Monk of CORVEY, archbishop of Bremen-Hamburg, d. Björkä, Sweden, Sept. 17, 936. In 917 when Leidrad, who had been elected archbishop of Hamburg by the cathedral chapter, went to the royal court, Unni (or Wimo), who was then a simple monk, accompanied him. But it was Unni, rather than Leidrad, who actually received the high archiepiscopal dignity from King Conrad. Unni preserved the *status quo* of Christianity in the north through war against pagan Hungarians, Wends, and Danes. With the German victory over the Danes in Schleswig, Unni united under himself those Christians surviving in Denmark and Sweden who had been converted by ANSGAR and REMBERT. He gained the favor of Harold Bluetooth

of Denmark and his mother Thyra, though not that of the father, the fierce King Gorm, persecutor of Christians, who was defeated by Emperor Henry I. Harold, not yet baptized, granted Christians his protection; churches were given priests, and the number of Christians increased. Unni journeyed to the East Danish islands, and made mission trips among the Goths and Northmen; he died during his first missionary visit to the Swedish trading town of Björkä on Lake Mälar where he revived the old Christian communities. He was buried in Björkä but his head was brought back to St. Peter's church in Bremen. His relics are now at Corvey, where a statue was erected in his honor.

Feast: Sept. 17.

Bibliography: *Acta Sanctorum* Oct. 9:373–396. A. M. ZIMMERMANN, *Kalendarium Benedictinum: Die Heiligen und Seligen des Benediktinerordens und seiner Zweige,* 4 v. (Metten 1933–38) 3:64–68. ADAM OF BREMEN, *History of the Archbishops of Hamburg-Bremen,* tr. F. J. TSCHAN (New York 1959).

[G. SPAHR]

UNTERLINDEN, CONVENT OF

Former monastery of Dominican nuns, Colmar, France, formerly Diocese of Basel, today Diocese of Strasbourg. It was founded by Agnes of Mittelnheim and Agnes of Herkenheim at the suggestion of Walter, the Dominican prior of Strasbourg, and was moved in 1232 (perhaps the very year of its foundation) to Ufmühlen outside the city, but was finally returned to its original location in 1252. At first it probably followed the example of St. Mark's convent in Strasbourg and observed the constitutions of San Sisto in Rome. In 1245 Innocent IV incorporated Unterlinden into the Dominican Order (*see* DOMINICAN SISTERS). The spiritual direction was successively in the hands of the Dominicans of Basel (1234–68), Freiburg (1268–78), and finally Colmar. ALBERT THE GREAT consecrated the convent church in 1269. Until the mid-14th century Unterlinden was an important center of mysticism; it maintained close contact with Meister ECKHART, who stayed in Colmar in 1322, TAULER, HENRY SUSO, VENTURINO OF BERGAMO (d. 1346), and later, Otto of Passau. Catherine of Geberschweier (d. 1330), who had entered the convent *c.* 1260, described the virtues, visions, and ecstasies of 44 nuns of the convent's first two generations in her *Vitae sororum.* This chronicle of the mystical life in Unterlinden, in elegant Latin, became the model for man similar compositions written in the vernacular in southern Germany. Among the important figures in her Lives were the prioress Hedwig of Gundolsheim (d. 1281) and Adelaide of Rheinfelden, prioress *c.* 1285. In 1419, Unterlinden was reformed by Schönensteinbach (Alsace); in 1792 it was dissolved. The abbey church and Gothic cloister became the municipal library and museum in 1849.

Bibliography: J. ANCELET-HUSTACHE, "Les *Vitae Sororum* d'Unterlinden, edition critique. . . ," *Archives d'histoire doctrinale et littéraire du moyen-âge* 5 (1930) 317–509. H. GRUNDMANN, *Religiöse Bewegungen im Mittelalter* (Berlin 1935) 232–252. E. KREBS, W. STAMMLER and K. LANGOSCH, eds., *Die deutsche Literatur des Mittelalters: Verfasserlexikon,* 5 v. (Berlin-Leipzig 1933–55) 2:773–776. L. PFLEGER, *Lexikon für Theologie und Kirche,* ed. M. BUCHBERGER, 10 v. (Freiburg 1930–38) 10:423–424. M. BARTH, *Handbuch der elsässischen Kirchen im Mittelalter,* 3 v. (Archives de l'Église d'Alsace NS 11–13; Strasbourg 1960–63).

[A. A. SCHACHER]

UPANISHADS

Name of a class of texts in Indian literature that are appended to the *Brāhmaṇas* or treatises on the Vedic ritual and contain a more esoteric doctrine. Their teaching consists chiefly in setting up parallel series between ritual and nature or, more generally, between man and the world. Thus there are, according to the *Chandogya-Upanishad,* which is among the most interesting, not only three sacrificial fires, but five natural ones, called, respectively: "celestial world," from which Soma (the sacred liquor) is born; "thunderstorm," from which the rain comes; "earth," the source of food; "man," the source of *semen virile;* and "woman," from which comes the embryo. Such speculations are very old, for they have

their analogues in Iran. The chief single equation is that between the principle of the universe and an invisible principle inside man.

See Also: VEDAS; HINDUISM.

Bibliography: A. S. GEDEN and J. HASTINGS, ed., *Encyclopedia of Religion & Ethics,* 13 v. (Edinburgh 1908–27) 12:541–548.

[J. DUCHESNE-GUILLEMIN]

UR

Ancient city in southern Mesopotamia at a site now called Tell el-Muquaiyar, about 160 miles north of the present head of the Persian Gulf and almost ten miles west of the present Euphrates. The ancient city, however, which was called Urim in Sumerian and Uri in Akkadian, was situated right on the Euphrates and probably not far from the ancient head of the Persian Gulf.

According to the Hebrew text of Gn 11.28, 31 and Neh 9.7, Abraham's original home was in Ur of the Chaldees (Heb. *'ûr kaŝdîm*). It is usually assumed that this is the same city as the Sumerian-Babylonian city of Ur, even though there are certain difficulties in the identification. According to the Greek Septuagint, Abraham came not from Ur of the Chaldees, but "from the country of the Chaldees." Granted that the mention of the Chaldees [*see* CHALDEANS] is an anachronism, since this people did not appear in southern Mesopotamia until almost a millennium after the time of Abraham, there is still the difficulty that Biblical tradition did not connect the culture of the Patriarchs with that of southern Mesopotamia, as it did with that of Abraham's second reported home in Haran in northern Mesopotamia. On the other hand, it is remarkable that, after Ur, Haran was one of the most important centers of the worship of the moon-god Sin. It is therefore quite possible that Abraham's relatives, who were apparently devotees of this god in Haran, may have migrated northward from Ur after some destruction of this city.

Bibliography: C. L. WOOLLEY, *The Royal Cemetery* (London 1934) v.2, pts. 1 and 2 of *Ur Excavations* (London 1927–), Joint Expedition of the British Museum and Museum of University of Pennsylvania to Mesopotamia; *Ur of the Chaldees* (rev. ed. Baltimore 1954). *Encyclopedic Dictionary of the Bible,* translated and adapted by L. HARTMAN (New York, 1963) 2518–20.

[J. E. STEINMUELLER]

URBAN I, POPE, ST.

Pontificate: 222 to 230. Urban's pontificate, about which little is known, fell in the reign of Alexander Severus, who was favorably disposed toward Christians. Urban inherited from Calixtus the schism of HIPPOLYTUS, who by now had few followers. The Adoptionist students (*see* ADOPTIONISM) of Artemon and the Montanists of Proclus (*see* MONTANISM) seem also to have declined. The *Liber pontificalis* says, among other things, that Urban was a Roman, the son of Pontianus (the name of Urban's successor). It also errs in making him a martyr under Diocletian, buried in the cemetery of Praetextatus. This anachronism facilitated the association of Urban with St. CECILIA. He probably was buried in the cemetery of Calixtus, according to the report of the MARTYROLOGY OF ST. JEROME and the discoveries of G. B. de Rossi.

Feast: May 25.

Bibliography: EUSEBIUS, *Historia Ecclesiastca* 6:21, 23. G. B. DE ROSSI, *La Roma sotterranea cristiana,* 4 v. (Rome 1864–97) v.2. J.N.D. KELLY, *Oxford Dictionary of Popes* (New York 1997), 15–16.

[E. G. WELTIN]

Pope Urban II. (© Bettmann/CORBIS)

URBAN II, POPE, BL.

Pontificate: March 12, 1088 to July 29, 1099; b. Odo of Châtillon-sur-Marne *c.* 1035; d. Rome. Odo was educated and later was archdeacon at Rheims, then a monk and eventually prior at Cluny. In 1079/80 he was appointed by Pope Gregory VII as cardinal bishop of Ostia. Late in the year 1084, as Gregory found himself increasingly isolated, he entrusted Cardinal Odo with an important legation to Germany. Odo presided over a synod at Quedlinburg in which the antipope, Clement III, his followers and their orders, were condemned. Odo was still in the north when Pope Gregory died at Salerno in May 1085, and Gregory was followed by the brief pontificate of Abbot Desiderius of Monte Cassino as Victor III. But Victor's successor, elected at Terracina in March 1088, was Cardinal Odo, who took the name Urban II.

His reign can be divided into two parts. The first period, from 1088 to late 1093, was spent mainly in southern Italy, away from the forces of Clement III and Emperor Henry IV in Rome and the north. During these years Urban worked to undermine his enemies, to rally the fragmented Gregorian party, and to stabilize its support in both East and West. He was able to return to Rome at the end of 1093, and the remainder of his pontificate was characterized by visibility and activity throughout the Church (no pope since Leo IX travelled as widely as did Urban) and increasingly by vigorous pursuit of reforming goals, through correspondence, papal legates, and papal synods. Early on Urban had convened three councils in southern Italy, at Melfi (1089), Benevento (1091), and Troia (1093), which repromulgated many of

the reforming decrees of Gregory VII, including the prohibition against lay investiture of bishops and abbots (Melfi). But the councils over which Urban presided after returning north, especially those in 1095 at Piacenza and Clermont, renewed and amplified the Reform programs.

By the end of Urban II's pontificate the bleak prospects faced by the Gregorian party in the mid-1080s had been reversed, and the fortunes of Clement III and Henry IV diminished as Urban's support increased. The familiar notion of an 11th-century "Gregorian Reform" has been questioned by scholars in recent decades, and texts from Gregory VII are not especially visible in canon law books of the time. But from the beginning of the 12th century up to the time of the compilation of Gratian's *Decretum*—which marks a turning point in the collection of canon law from the first millennium of the Church—Urban II is a prominent source of law and papal authority. At times obscured by the spectacular political struggles which erupted during Gregory VII's pontificate, the contribution which Urban II made in rescuing and advancing the cause of papal reform, while also dealing with the concomitant political tensions that this movement generated, cannot be underestimated.

The preaching of the First Crusade must be seen in that larger context of papal leadership, and Urban's special concern for East-West relations. That concern already is visible during his early days in southern Italy, when he made contact with Constantinople, and sent legates there in 1089. Perhaps ambassadors from the Byzantine emperor, Alexius I, appeared in March, 1095, at the

Council of Piacenza, seeking military support for Alexius's battles against the Turks. Eight months later, at the Council of Clermont, Urban announced a great penitential pilgrimage/military expedition aimed both at helping the Greeks and capturing Jerusalem from Muslim control. In so doing he launched one of the most famous and multifaceted enterprises in Christian history. Crusading was an important element in Latin Christendom for centuries, yet Urban died in late July, 1099, no doubt without learning that Western armies had captured Jerusalem on July 15. A cult appeared soon after his death, and formal beatification was proclaimed by Leo XIII on July 14, 1881.

Feast: July 29 or 30.

Bibliography: *Patrologia Latina*, ed. J. P. MIGNE (Paris 1878–90) v.151. J. D. MANSI, *Sacrorum Conciliorum nova et amplissima collectio* v.20 (Paris 1889–1927, repr. Graz 1960—). P. JAFFÉ, *Regesta pontificum romanorum ab condita ecclesia ad annum post Christum natum 1198* (Graz 1956), ed. S. LÖWENFELD (882–1198) 1:657–701; 2:713, 752–753. *Liber pontificalis*, ed. L. DUCHESNE (Paris 1886–92) 2:293–295. C. J. VON HEFELE, *Histoire des conciles d'après les documents originaux*, tr. and continued by H. LECLERCQ (Paris 1907–38) 5.1:337–465. *Pontificum romanorum . . . vitae*, ed. J. M. WATTERICH, 2 v. (Leipzig 1862) 1:571–620. Literature. A. FLICHE and V. MARTIN, eds., *Histoire de l'église depuis les origines jusqu'à nos jours* (Paris 1935—) 8:199–337. F. X. SEPPELT, *Geschichte der Päpste von den Anfängen bis zur Mitte des 20. Jh.* v.3 (Munich 1956). A. BECKER, *Papst Urban II*, pt. 1–2 [Schriften der *Monumenta Germaniae Historica* 19.1–2 (Stuttgart 1988)]. F. KEMPF et al., *The Church in the Age of Feudalism* [*Handbook of Church History*, ed. H. JEDIN and J. DOLAN, III (New York 1969) 386–92]. R. SOMERVILLE (in collaboration with S. KUTTNER), *Pope Urban II, the Collectio Britannica, and the Council of Melfi (1089)* (Oxford 1996); "Clermont, 1095: Crusade and Canons," in *La primera cruzada, novecientos años después: El concilio de Clermont y los orígenes del movimiento cruzado*, ed. L. GARCÍA-GUIJARRO RAMOS (Madrid 1997) 63–77.

[R. SOMERVILLE]

URBAN III, POPE

Pontificate: Nov. 25, 1185 to Oct. 20, 1187; b. Uberto Crivelli, Milan; d. Ferrara. Urban, the former archbishop of Milan, was the unanimous choice of the cardinals gathered at Verona, but he was unable to enter Rome. In the Curia prior to his election, he had been one of the staunchest foes of the emperor FREDERICK BARBAROSSA. As pope he opposed Frederick's attempt to secure imperial coronation for his son, Henry, while the Emperor was still alive, and he was disturbed by Henry's coronation as King of Germany on Jan. 27, 1186. From Lucius III Urban had inherited the dispute over the Tuscan lands of the Countess Matilda (*see* MATILDA OF TUSCANY), long claimed by the Emperor. The disputed election of a new archbishop of Trier aggravated relations between pope

and emperor when Urban consecrated one of the contenders despite his promise to Frederick. These disagreements culminated in an invasion of Italy and the siege of the pope and Curia at Verona. Meanwhile, Barbarossa gained substantial support from the German bishops. Frustrated by the cautious Veronese in his attempts to excommunicate the emperor, Urban left for Venice. He died en route at Ferrara.

Bibliography: *Patrologia Latina*, ed. J. P. MIGNE (Paris 1878–90) 202:1329–1534. P. JAFFÉ, *Regesta pontificum romanorum ab condita ecclesia ad annum post Christum natum 1198*, ed. S. LÖWENFELD (repr. Graz 1956) 2:492–528, 726, 769–770. H. KAUFFMANN, *Die italienische Politik Kaiser Friedrichs I. nach dem Frieden von Constanz, 1183–1189* (Greifswald, Ger. 1933). É. JORDAN, *L'Allemagne et l'Italie aux XIIᵉ et XIIIᵉ siècles* (Paris 1939). M. C. DE FISCHER-REICHENBACH, *Urbain III et Barberousse* (Bern 1940). A. CASO, *I Crivelli. Una famiglia milanese tra politica, società ed economia nei secoli XII e XIII* (Rome 1994). R. CHALLET, "Quelques details sur la vie de Maître Humbert, cet archidacre [de Bourges] qui devint pape sous le nom d'Urbain III," *Bulletin des Amis du Musée Saint-Vic* 14 (1985) 11–27. G. FRANSEN, "Questions canoniques de la fin du douzième siècle (Milan, Ambrosiana, H 248 Inf., ff. 86–93)," *Aevum* 69 (Milano 1995) 373–87. V. MERTENS, "Der 'heisse Sommer' 1187 von Trier. Ein weiterer Erklärungsversuch zu Hausen MF 47, 38," *Zeitschrift für Deutsche Philologie* (1976) 346–56. J. N. D. KELLY, *Oxford Dictionary of Popes* (Oxford 1986) 181–82.

[J. M. POWELL]

URBAN IV, POPE

Pontificate: Aug. 29, 1261, to Oct. 2, 1264; b. Jacques Pantaléon, Troyes, France, *c.* 1200; d. Perugia, Italy. Although the son of a cobbler, he rose rapidly from priest and canon at Lyons, to bishop of Verdun (1253) and patriarch of Jerusalem (1255), to pope, being crowned at Viterbo. Participation at the Council of Lyons (1245), service as papal legate in Germany and Eastern Europe, as well as years spent in the Near East, gave him broad insight into political affairs. An able administrator, he reformed and strengthened his government in the Papal States. He reinforced the College of Cardinals by appointing new members, including six Frenchmen. Anarchy and wars in Rome forced him to reside at Viterbo and Orvieto. To arrest the growth in power of King Manfred of Naples and the allied Ghibelline party in Tuscany and Lombardy, which he held dangerous for the Church, Urban turned to France to find a candidate for the "vacant" Sicilian throne. King LOUIS IX refused the crown for himself and his sons, but did not object when Urban approached his brother, Charles of Anjou and Provence. Negotiations dragged on inconclusively and were even interrupted by attempts to come to terms with Manfred until he and the Ghibellines prepared a military offensive. Then the pope made all the concessions Charles requested. Although Urban died before the treaty was ratified, CLEMENT IV saw the project through. Urban's two Oriental plans, namely, the restoration of the Latin states on the Bosporus and in the Balkans, and the reunion with the Eastern Church, canceled each other. Moreover, for the latter an agreement with Emperor MICHAEL VIII Palaeologus would have been necessary, but Charles of Anjou, who wanted the empire for himself, would never have consented to this. Urban introduced the feast of CORPUS CHRISTI.

Bibliography: J. GUIRAUD, ed., *Les Registres d'Urbain IV, 1261–64* (Paris 1901–30). W. SIEVERT, ''Das Vorleben des Papstes Urban IV,'' *Römische Quartalschrift für christliche Altertumskunde und für Kirchengeschichte* 10 (Freiburg 1896) 451–505. K. HAMPE, *Urban IV und Manfred, 1261–64* (Heidelberg 1905). H. K. MANN, *The Lives of the Popes in the Early Middle Ages from 590 to 1304* 15 (London 1902–32). F. X. SEPPELT, *Geschichte der Päpste von den Anfängen bis zur Mitte des 20. Jh.*, 3 (Munich 1956). J. LONGNON, *L'Empire Latin de Constantinople et la principauté de Morée* (Paris 1949). A. FLICHE and V. MARTIN, eds. *Histoire de l'église depuis les origines jusqu'à nos jours* 10 (Paris 1950). Hallen 4. É. G. LÉONARD, *Les Angevins de Naples* (Paris 1954). S. RUNCIMAN, *The Sicilian Vespers* (Cambridge, Eng. 1958). F. BOCK, *Die Religion in Geschichte und Gegenwart* (Tübingen 1957–65) 6:1186. G. BERG, ''Manfred of Sicily and Urban IV: Negotiations of 1262,'' *Medieval Studies* 55 (Toronto 1993) 111–36. R. CAIELLI, *La bolla 'Transiturus' di Urbano IV e la sua fortuna lungo il Medio Evo* (Milano 1976). J. GARDENER, ''Cardinal Archer and the Piscina in Saint-Urbain at Troyes,'' *Architectural Studies in Memory of Richard Krautheimer* (Mainz 1996) 79–82. U. HORST, ''Thomas von Aquin. Professor und Consultor,'' *Münchener Theologische Zeitschrift* 48 (München 1997) 205–18. C. LE BRUN-GOUVANIC, ed. *Guillaume di Tocco. Ystoria sancti Thome de Aquino* (Toronto 1996). R. MATTICK, ''Eine Nürnberger Übertragung der Urbanregel für den Orden der heilge Klara und der ersten Regel der heilige Klara für die Armen Schwestern,'' *Franziskanische Studien* 69 (1987) 173–232. E. PÄSZTOR, ''Lettere di Urbano IV 'super negotio Regni Siciliae,''' *Onus Apostolicae Sedis. Curia romana e cardinalato nei secoli XI–XV* (Roma 1999) 229–44. R. E. REYNOLDS, ''Corpus Christi in Agnone,'' *Medieval Studies* 60 (Toronto 1998) 229–44. I. RODRÍGUEZ DE LAMA, *La documención pontificia de Urbano IV (1261–1264)* (Roma 1981). M. WILKS, ''Wycliff and the Great Persecution,'' *Prophecy and Eschatology* (Oxford 1994) 9–63.

[H. WIERUSZOWSKI]

URBAN V, POPE, BL.

Pontificate: Sept. 28, 1362 to Dec. 19, 1370; b. Guillaume de Grimoard, Grisac Lozère, France, *c.* 1310; d. Avignon. As a Benedictine monk, Guillaume studied law at Paris and Avignon, later teaching law at Montpellier and Avignon. In 1352, he became abbot of Saint-Germain in Auxerre; in 1361, abbot of SAINT-VICTOR IN MARSEILLES. By the time of the conclave following the death of INNOCENT VI (1362), Guillaume was a noted educator who had distinguished himself through his negoti-

Pope Urban VI. (© Bettmann/CORBIS)

ations with Giovanni Visconti over the vicariate of Bologna (1352) and through his legations to Italy. When dissension among the cardinals made the election of one of them impossible, their choice fell on Guillaume. He was crowned without pomp at Avignon, November 6 (*see* AVIGNON PAPACY).

As Urban V, he initiated a reform program in which he restrained the greed of the procurators and lawyers of the Avignon Curia, cut in half the tax of the tenth, curtailed the holding of a plurality of benefices, reorganized the APOSTOLIC CAMERA, and encouraged the convening of provincial councils despite the Hundred Years' War.

He agreed to the crusade plans of Peter of Lusignan, king of Cyprus, against the OTTOMAN TURKS who were threatening the Byzantine Empire. He hoped that the departure of the mercenary soldiers for the East would free Italy and France from their plundering. In preparation for this abortive crusade, he made peace with Bernabo Visconti (February 1364).

Urban determined to reestablish the seat of the papacy at Rome once Cardinal ALBORNOZ had reclaimed the STATES OF THE CHURCH. Despite violent objections from the French cardinals and contradictory pleadings from the king of France, but with the encouragement of Emperor Charles IV, Urban left Avignon, April 30, 1367, and disembarked at Corneto, Italy, June 3. Following a stay at Viterbo, he got through to Rome on October 15.

On Oct. 18, 1369, the Byzantine Emperor John V Palaeologus arrived in Rome, abjured the EASTERN SCHISM, and explicitly recognized the Roman papacy. However, at the magnificent ceremony at St. Peter's on October 21, the representatives of the Byzantine Church did not appear. Urban had compromised the desired union of the Eastern and Western Churches by his refusal to hold a Greco-Roman council—something he considered dangerous to the faith. Furthermore, Urban wanted to organize a Latin Church within the Byzantine Empire while the Greeks intended to retain their customary rites. Urban satisfied himself with sending missionaries, especially Franciscans, to the East.

By 1370, renewed hostilities in the States of the Church, a revolt in Perugia, and the massing of Bernabo Visconti's troops in Tuscany compelled the pope to seek refuge within the walls of Viterbo. Simultaneously, the desire to end the Hundred Years' War suggested his return to Avignon; he arrived in September 1370.

Urban's body, first buried at Notre-Dame-des-Doms in Avignon, was brought to the Abbey of Saint-Victor in Marseilles in June 1372. His personal virtue and goodness led to his beatification, March 10, 1870.

Feast: Dec. 19.

Bibliography: URBAN V, *Lettres secrètes et curiales du Pape Urbain V . . . se rapportant à la France,* ed. P. LECACHEUX and G. MOLLAT, 3 v. (Paris 1902–55); *Lettres communes,* ed. M. H. LAURENT (Paris 1954–). *Documenti Vaticani . . . Pontificato di Urbano V,* ed. T. LECCISOTTI (Monte Cassino 1952) publication of 59 bulls. G. MOLLAT, *Dictionnaire de théologie catholique,* ed. A. VACANT et al., (Paris 1903—50) 15.2:2295–2302; *The Popes at Avignon,* tr. J. LOVE from 9th French ed. (New York 1963). É. DELARUELLE, "La Translation des reliques de saint Thomas d'Aquin à Toulouse (1369) . . .," *Bulletin de Littérature Ecclésiastique* 56 (1955) 129–146. D. KNOWLES, *The Religious Orders in England* (Cambridge, Eng. 1948–60) v.2. M. BALMELLE, *Bibliographie du Gévaudan* (NS; Mende 1961–) v.2. J. MEYENDORFF, "Projets de concile oecuménique en 1367 . . .," *Dumbarton Oaks Papers,* Harvard University 14 (1960) 147–177. P. AMARGIER, *Urban V. Un homme. Une vie (1310–1370)* (Marseille 1987). F. R. CELSI, "I rapporti tra la Santa Sede e la Republica di Venezia attraverso a la lettere di Papa Urbano V al doge Lorenzo Celsi (1363–1365)," *Apollinaris* 65 (Roma 1992), 609–25. M. HARVEY, "Preaching in the Curia: Some Sermons by Thomas Brinton," *Archivum Historiae Pontificiae* 33 (Roma 1995), 299–301. A.-M. HAYEZ, ed., *Le terrier avignonnais de l'évêque Anglic Grimoard (1366–1368)* (Paris 1993); *Urbain V (1362–1370). Lettres communes analyées d'après les registres dits d'Avignon et du Vatican* (Rome 1985). J. KLOCZOWSKI, "Avignon et la Pologne à l'époque d'Urbain V et de Grégoire XI (1362–1378)," *La Pologne dans l'Eglise médiévale* 14 (Aldershot 1993). D. LE BLÉVEC, "L'aumône secrète de la papautè sous Urbain V," *Histoire et sociètè. Mèlanges offerts à George Duby* (Aix-en-Provence 1992) 209–19. D. LE BLÉVEC, "Urbain V et las Chartreux," *Die Ausbreitung karäusischen Lebens und Geistes im Mittelalter* (Salzburg 1991) 33–53. F. PETRARCA, *In difesa dell'Italia (Contra eum qui maledixit Italie)* (Venice 1995). N. G. M. VAN DOORNIK, *Katharina von Siena. Eine Frau, die in der Kirche nicht schwieg* (Freiburg 1980). L. VONES, *Urban V. (1362–1370): Kirchenreform zwischen Kardinalkollegium, Kurie und Klientel* (Stuttgart 1998). J. N. D. KELLY, *Oxford Dictionary of Popes* (New York 1986) 223.

[G. MOLLAT]

URBAN VI, POPE

Pontificate: April 8, 1378 to Oct. 15, 1389; b. Bartolomeo Prignano, Naples, *c.* 1318; d. Rome. He was archbishop of Acerenza (1363) and then of Bari (1377) and had proved himself an efficient and hardworking papal official as chancellor to GREGORY XI. In April 1378 the cardinals chose him pope in an enigmatic election. While it is certain that both Roman officials and the Roman populace exerted pressure on the cardinals to elect a Roman, or at least an Italian, as pope (*see* AVIGNON PAPACY), the cardinals were not sufficiently alarmed to summon the troops of the Church or to shelter themselves behind the walls of the Castel Sant' Angelo. In the summer of 1378, Urban rapidly alienated his electors and in full consistory made remarks that were so uncivil many considered him mentally deranged. This, combined with the circumstances of his election, encouraged the French cardinals to return to Avignon, where they declared Urban's election invalid and in September 1378, with the approval of the French king, Charles V, elected Robert of Geneva as antipope, CLEMENT VII, thus beginning the WESTERN SCHISM. Contemporaries were perplexed over the validity of Urban's, and hence of Clement's, elections; and all Europe was divided in its loyalty. Neither the Council of CONSTANCE nor MARTIN V pronounced sentence on the validity of the two elections. Opinions are still divergent.

Urban wasted little time in becoming embroiled in Italian quarrels; he excommunicated Clement's adherent, Queen Joanna of Sicily (1380), replacing her with Charles of Durazzo. Then, having learned of a plot by Charles and some of the cardinals to place him under some sort of council of regency, Urban preached a crusade against Charles (1385), revoked his title of royalty, and placed Naples under interdict. Urban was besieged by Charles's forces at Nocera, but was relieved by Urbanist forces and escaped with the guilty cardinals as prisoners. Five cardinals implicated in the plot died violent

Sarcophagus of Urban VI in the crypt, St. Peter's, Rome. (Alinari-Art Reference/Art Resource, NY)

deaths; the bishop of Aquila was dispatched by dagger. Urban refused to be reconciled with the house of Durazzo even after the death of Charles (1386) and moved successively to Lucca (1386), Perugia (1387), and finally to Rome (1388), where he died, perhaps as the result of poisoning. His pontificate was marked by anarchy in the STATES OF THE CHURCH and by the draining of the Church's treasury. He decreed a HOLY YEAR every 33 years and in 1389 extended the feast of the VISITATION OF MARY to the whole Church.

Bibliography: *Acta Urbani VI,* ed. K. KROFTA (Prague 1903–1905). THEODORICUS DE NIEM, *De scismate,* ed. G. ERLER (Leipzig 1890). H. V. SAUERLAND, ''Aktenstücke zur Geschichte des Papstes Urban VI,'' *Historisches Jahrbuch der Görres-Gesellschaft,* 14 (Munich 1893) 820–832. M. GIUSTI, *Studi e Testi,* 165 (Rome 1952) 417. P. SAQUELLA, *Papa U. VI, napoletano* (Naples 1894). N. VALOIS, *La France et le grand schisme d'Occident,* 4 v. (Paris 1896–1902) v.1, 2. H. FINKE, ''Über Schisma-Publikationen,'' *Historisches Jahrbuch der Görres-Gesellschaft,* 52 (Munich 1932) 457–464. E. PERROY, *L'Angleterre et le grand schisme d'Occident* (Paris 1934). M. DE BOÜARD, *Les Origines des guerres d'Italie: La France et l'Italie au temps du grand schisme d'Occident* (Paris 1936). L. PASTOR, *The History of the Popes from the Close of the Middle Ages* (London-St. Louis 1938–61) 1:117–137. M. SEIDLMAYER, *Die Anfänge des grossen abend-ländischen Schismas* (Münster 1940). W. ULLMANN, *The Origins of the Great Schism* (London 1967). L. MACFARLANE, ''An English Account of the Election of U. VI,'' *Bulletin of the Institute of Historical Research* 26 (1953) 75–85. O. PŘEROVSKÝ, *L'elezion di U. VI* (Rome 1960). *Suppliques et lettres d'Urbain VI,* ed. M. GASTOUT, *Analecta Vaticano-Belgica XXIX* (Rome 1976). *Repertorium Germanicum* 2, ed. G. TELLENBACH (Berlin 1961). K. A. FINK, ''Zur Beurteilung des grossen abendländischen Schismas,'' *Zeitschrift für Kirchengeschichte* 73 (1962) 335–343. J. FAVIER, *Les finances pontificales à lépoque du Grand Schisme d'Occident 1378–1409* (Paris 1966). W. BRANDMUELLER, ''Zur Frage nach der Gültigkeit der Wahl Urbans VI.,'' *Archivum Historiae Conciliorum* 6 (1974) 78–120. M. DYKMANS, ''La troisième élection du pape Urbain VI.,'' *Archivum Historiae Pontificiae* 15 (1977) 217–264.

[G. MOLLAT]

URBAN VII, POPE

Pontificate: Sept. 15, 1590, to Sept. 27, 1590; b. Giambattista Castagna, Rome, Aug. 4, 1521. Through his father, Cosimo, he descended from Genoese nobility; from his mother, Costanza, he traced his ancestry through the Roman families of the Ricci and Jacobazzi. After studies in Padua and Bologna he earned a doctorate *utriusque juris.* In 1551 he accompanied his uncle, Cardinal Girolamo Verallo, as auditor in the papal legation to Henry II, King of France. Two years later, Julius III made

"Monument of Pope Urban VII," sculpture by Ambrogio Bonvicino, located in S. Maria sopra Minerva, Rome. (Alinari-Art Reference/Art Resource, NY)

him referendary of the Segnatura di Giustizia and bishop of Rozzano. He became successively governor of Fano (1555) and of Perugia and Umbria (1559). During the third period of the Council of Trent (1562–63) he showed prudent leadership as president of several commissions. In a legation to Madrid, Castagna was in the service of Cardinal Ugo Boncompagni (later Gregory XIII), and remained as papal nuncio to the court of Philip II until 1572. In this capacity he represented the interests of the papacy in the formation of the Holy League against the Turks, which brought victory at Lepanto (1571). His appointment to the nunciature of Venice and then the governorship of Bologna (1577) followed his resignation of the See of Rozzano in 1573. He was again a papal legate at the peace negotiations at Cologne that ended the conflict between Philip II and the Low Countries (1578). Gregory XIII named him consultor of the Holy Office (1580) and created him a cardinal priest with the title of San Marcello al Corso on Dec. 12, 1583. The next year he was legate at Bologna; he held this post until 1590. Sixtus V appointed him inquisitor general of the Holy Office in November 1586.

His reputation for successful administration and Spanish support made him a likely choice of the conclave following the death of Sixtus V on Aug. 27, 1590. His election was accepted with popular acclaim. Urban's pontificate, though lasting for only 12 days, showed promise of an outstanding reign, particularly in the government of the Papal States. He encouraged public works to check unemployment, regulated the finances of the *MONTES PIETATIS* (lending houses), planned agencies for dispensing alms, and put the reform of the Datary into the hands of a commission comprised of Cardinals Gabriele Paleoto, Ippolito Aldobrandini (later Clement VIII), Scipione Lancelotti, and Antonio Facchinetti. He succumbed to malaria prior to his coronation. In his will left his patrimony of 30,000 scudi to the Confraternity of the Annunciation of S. Maria sopra Minerva, Rome, for the endowment of poor girls. In gratitude the Confraternity erected a statue by Ambrogio Bonvicino in their chapel.

Bibliography: L. PASTOR, *The History of the Popes from the Close of the Middle Ages* (London-St. Louis 1938–61) 22:313–333. C. EUBEL et al., *Hierarchia Catholica medii (et recentioris) aevi:* v. 3: 1503–1600 (2d. ed. Münster 1923) 54, 59. M. R. O'CONNELL, *The Counter-Reformation, 1559–1610* (New York 1974). M. A. MULLETT, *The Catholic Reformation* (New York 1999).

[E. D. MCSHANE]

URBAN VIII, POPE

Pontificate: Aug. 6, 1623, to July 29, 1644; b. Maffeo Barberini, Florence, Italy. This fifth son of a prominent, non-aristocratic family was born in April 1568. When he was three years old, his father died; as a child he was educated by the Jesuits in Florence according to the wishes of his mother. Later he went to Rome to live with his uncle, Francesco Barberini, Prothonotary Apostolic, and to study at the Roman College. In 1589 he obtained the degree of doctor of laws from the University of Pisa. After receiving his doctorate, Maffeo returned to Rome and filled various offices in the Church. In 1601 he was sent to France as papal legate to present Clement VIII's felicitations to King Henry IV on the birth of the Dauphin, the future King Louis XIII. Three years later he was appointed archbishop of Nazareth and sent as nuncio to France, where he became influential with the King. On Sept. 11, 1606, Maffeo became a cardinal with the titular church of S. Pietro in Montorio, which he exchanged on Sept. 6, 1610, for that of S. Onofrio. After being made bishop of Spoleto on Oct. 17, 1608, he convened a synod, completed the construction of one diocesan seminary, and built two others, at Visso and Spello. Paul V appointed him legate of Bologna and prefect of the Segnatura di Giustizia in 1617.

Election as Pope. On Aug. 6, 1623, he was elected Pope by 50 votes from 55 cardinals who had entered conclave on July 19 after the death of Gregory XV. On the very day of his election, Urban VIII issued the bulls of canonization of St. Ignatius Loyola, St. Francis Xavier, and St. Philip Neri, who had all been canonized by Gregory XV. During his pontificate he canonized St. Elizabeth of Portugal and St. Andrew Corsini, and beatified James of the Marches, a Minorite (Aug. 12, 1624); Francis Borgia, a Jesuit (Nov. 23, 1624); Andrew Avelino (June 10, 1625); Felix of Cantalice, a Minorite (Oct. 1, 1625); Mary Magdalen de'Pazzi (May 8, 1626); John of God (Sept. 21, 1630); and Josaphat Kuncevyč (May 16, 1643). The right of beatification was reserved during his reign to the Holy See. In 1642 Urban reduced the number of holy days of obligation to 34, not including Sundays, and introduced many new offices into the Roman BREVIARY. In 1631 he accepted and incorporated into the official 1632 edition of the Roman Breviary the recommendations of a committee appointed for its reform in 1629. Subsequent scholars have criticized these recommendations as ill advised and incomplete. Completed form was given to the famous bull *In Coena Domini* by Urban VIII in 1627. In 1628 he approved the Congregation of Our Saviour, a reformed branch of the Augustinian Canons founded by Peter Fourier in 1609; the Lazarists, or Priests of the Mission (Vincentians), founded by St. Vincent de Paul, were approved in 1632. During Urban VIII's reign, all ruling bishops, including cardinals, were instructed to adhere to the standards of episcopal residence as decreed by the Council of Trent.

Urban VIII was a strong supporter of the Church's global missionary activity. He formed dioceses and vicariates in various mission territories and encouraged missionaries by word and financial assistance. He enlarged the work of the Congregation for the PROPAGATION OF THE FAITH and in 1627 founded the Collegium Urbanum for the training of missionaries. In 1633 he opened China and Japan to all missionaries, nullifying the missionary monopoly that GREGORY XIII had awarded the Jesuits in 1585. Slavery of any kind among the natives of Brazil, Paraguay, and the entire West Indies was prohibited by a bull of April 22, 1639. The disturbed state of the realm, plus dissension between regulars and seculars over the question of whether the time was ripe for a bishop to be present in England, largely negated attempts to strengthen Catholicism in that country.

International Diplomacy. In his relations with the Catholic sovereigns of Europe, Urban VIII tried to follow a policy commensurate with his desire to work for the common benefit of the Church. Contrary to Leopold von Ranke and Ferdinand Gregorovius, he did not endeavor to humiliate the Hapsburgs during the period of the Thirty Years' War by favoring France. On the other hand, he was not blind to the threat that Hapsburg power posed re-

"Tomb of Pope Urban VIII" sculpture by Giovanni Lorenzo Bernini (Gianlorenzo), 1628–1647, located in the Basilica of St. Peter, Rome. (Alinari-Art Reference/Art Resource, NY)

garding the temporal sovereignty of the pope or to the anti-Hapsburg foundations of French policy in Europe. His position as the father of Christendom, however, prompted him to be unbiased. In an effort to be impartial he neglected to support the Catholic cause in Germany as strongly as he might have and in this way contributed to the making of the peace of WESTPHALIA, which was not approved by the papacy.

The weakness of Urban VIII's pontificate resided in his excessive nepotism and his failure to evaluate properly the new currents of intellectual energy that were increasing in importance during his reign. During his pontificate, his brother Antonio, a Capuchin, and two nephews, Francesco and Antonio, were created cardinals and given high offices in the Church. Carlo, the father of the two nephews, and his third son, Taddeo, were helped by Urban VIII to acquire property and titles. The wealth acquired by his nephews was so great that scruples induced the Pope twice to appoint special committees of theologians to investigate whether it was lawful for them to retain their possessions. On both occasions the committees reported favorably for the nephews. Over a question of protocol involving his nephews and Odoardo Farnese, the Duke of Parma, Urban VIII engaged in an unsuccessful war against the duke and his allies, Tuscany, Modena, and Venice. As part of his appreciation of the political and military situation, Urban VIII spent large sums on the production of armaments and the construction of fortifications for use by the papal government. His activities in this regard are countered by the support he gave to Giovanni Lorenzo Bernini and other artists in beautifying St. Peter's Basilica, the streets and piazzas of Rome, and other places. Urban VIII erected the Vatican Seminary as well as other religious and artistic edifices. During Urban VIII's long pontificate, the longest of the seventeenth century, there occurred the second trial and condemnation of Galileo by the Roman Inquisition. On March 6, 1642, the bull *In eminenti* condemning the *Augustinus* of Cornelius Jansenius was issued. Urban VIII's private life was above reproach; some of his poetical compositions were published during his pontificate. Use of the bronze girders of the Pantheon in the making of guns and the furthering of other projects by Urban VIII prompted the epigram "What the barbarians did not do the Barberini did."

Bibliography: A. NICOLETTI, *Vita di Papa Urbano VIII⁰. Storia del suo pontificato,* 9 v. (MSS in Vatican Library, Coll. Barberini). L. PASTOR, *The History of the Popes from the Close of the Middle Ages* (London-St. Louis 1938–61) v.28 and 29, see v.29, app. 584–590, for evaluation of Nicoletti's work. P. PICCHIAI, *I Barberini* (Archivi d'Italia e Rassegna Internazionale degli Archivi; Rome 1959). G. ALBION, *Charles I and the Court of Rome* (London 1935). A. LEMAN, *Urban VIII et la rivalité de la France et de la maison d'Autriche de 1631 à 1635* (Paris 1920). H. LIEBING, *Die Religion in Geschichte und Gegenwart,* 7 v. (3d ed. Tübingen 1957–65) 3 6:1187. G. MOLLAT, *Dictionnaire de théologie catholique,* ed. A. VACANT et al., 15 v. (Paris 1903–50; Tables générales 1951–) 15.2:2305–06. A. KRAUS, *Das päpstliche Staatssekretariat unter Urban VIII, 1623–1644* (Rome 1964). S. BORSI, *Roma di Urbano VIII* (Rome 1990). L. NUSSDORFER, *Civic Politics in the Rome of Urban VIII* (Princeton 1992). R. FELDHAY, *Galileo and the Church* (New York 1995). S. PIERALSI, *Urbano VIII e Galileo Galilei* (Rome 1875). P. REDONI, *Galileo Heretic,* trans. R. ROSENTHAL (Princeton 1987).

[V. PONKO, JR.]

URBS BEATA JERUSALEM DICTA PACIS VISIO

A nine-stanza office hymn that was historically prescribed for the dedication of a church. Authorship and date of origin are unknown, though it was probably written *c.* 700. The accentual trochaic tetrameter rhythm of the original was changed into quantitative iambic dimeter, and the beginning of the hymn changed to *Caelestis Urbs Jerusalem/Beata pacis visio* in the revision of office hymns under Pope Urban VIII. Many hymnologists think that this Scripture-filled hymn lost much of its strength and beauty when revised. There is another Latin version

of it, *Urbs beata, vera pacis visio Jerusalem* (Sens Breviary, 1726). Numerous translations exist of this hymn.

Bibliography: U. CHEVALIER, *Repertorium hymnologicum,* 6 v. (Louvain-Brussels 1892–1921) 2:695. *Analecta hymnica* (Leipzig 1886–1922) 51:110–112, text. J. JULIAN, ed., *A Dictionary of Hymnology,* 2 v. (2d ed. London 1907; repr. New York 1957) 2:1198–1200. A. S. WALPOLE, ed., *Early Latin Hymns* (Cambridge, Eng. 1922) 377–380. H. ASHWORTH, *Ephemerides liturgical* 70 (1956) 238–241. J. CONNELLY, *Hymns of the Roman Liturgy* (Westminster, Md. 1957) 158–161, Eng. tr. J. SZÖVÉRFFY, *Die Annalen der lateinischen Hymnendichtung. Ein Handbuch,* 2 v. (Berlin 1964–65) 1:151–153.

[G. E. CONWAY]

URDANETA, ANDRÉS DE

Augustinian priest, Spanish sailor, and cosmographer; b. Villafranca de Guipúzcoa, Spain, 1508; d. Mexico City, 1568. From 1525 to 1536 Urdaneta took part in García de Loaisa's expedition, thus acquiring a practical knowledge of the sea and of cosmography that he used later in discovering a return route from the Philippines to New Spain. In Valladolid he gave first an oral, then a written account of the expedition, after which he sailed to New Spain, where Viceroy Antonio de Mendoza entrusted him with important tasks in both war and peace time. On March 20, 1553, he made his religious profession at the Augustinian Convent in Mexico City.

Upon the recommendation of Viceroy Luis de Velasco, whom Urdaneta had convinced of the possibility of a safe return trip, Philip II instructed Urdaneta to organize, prepare, and direct the 1564 expedition to the Islas del Poniente. According to secret orders from the *audiencia* opened at sea, the expedition altered its destination to the Philippines and accomplished the conquest of those islands under the command of Legazpi, whom Urdaneta had chosen as head of the undertaking. The Spanish established a colony in Cebú, where they arrived on April 27, 1565. On June 1, Urdaneta started the return voyage; he successfully arrived in Acapulco Oct. 8, 1565, having discovered the route that was later used by the Manila fleet.

Bibliography: F. DE UNCILLA ARROITA-JÁUREGUI, *Urdaneta y la conquista de Filipinas* (San Sebastián 1907). A. VILLAREJO, "El fraile navegante P. Andrés de Urdaneta," *Peregrino, Revista de la Provincia Agustiniana de Chile* (1994) 12/20. I. RODRÍGUEZ, *Andrés de Urdaneta, agustino: En carreta sobre el Pacífico* (Valladolid 1994).

[L. MERINO]

URIBE VELASCO, DAVID, ST.

Martyr, pastor; b. Dec. 29, 1889, Buenavista de Cuéllar, Guerrero, Diocese of Chilapa, Mexico; d. Apr.

12, 1927, San José Vistahermosa Ranch, Chilapa-Chilpancingo, Morales, Diocese of Cuernavaca. He entered the seminary at age 14. During his third year of theology at Chilapa seminary, the bishop of Tabasco asked David to work with him. He was ordained priest (1913) and immediately served as assistant to the bishop. When persecution began in earnest the following year, both had to flee into hiding at Veracruz. Velasco returned to Chilapa, but soon left again for Guerrero because the situation was unstable. Finding conditions there intolerable, he went home again but was detained by the police en route, condemned to death, and released upon the petition of some of his parishioners. Thereafter David was the pastor of Iguala, Guerrero, a troubled area. Unable to remain safely, he fled to Mexico City. Upon returning, he was recognized, apprehended, and taken by train to Cuernavaca. He was offered his liberty if he accepted the laws and would be the bishop of the church to be created by the Republic. He refused and was shot in the nape of the neck. His relics are venerated in his hometown parish. Fr. Uribe was both beatified (Nov. 22, 1992) and canonized (May 21, 2000) with Cristobal MAGALLANES by Pope John Paul II.

Feast: May 25 (Mexico).

See Also: MEXICO, MODERN; GUADALAJARA (MEXICO), MARTYRS OF, SS.

Bibliography: J. CARDOSO, *Los mártires mexicanos* (Mexico City 1953).

[K. I. RABENSTEIN]

URIEL

The name given in some apocryphal Hebrew writings to a leading angel, listed sometimes with MICHAEL and GABRIEL, but never occurring as an angel's name in Sacred Scripture. In Hebrew the word means "God is my light," or "my fire." In certain Jewish traditions Uriel is variously an angel of thunder and earthquake, of fire, or of GEHENNA; he warns Lamech of the world's end (Henoch 10.1–2) and enlightens Ezra with visions (3 Ezra ch. 4–5). In medieval Jewish mysticism he became a symbol for the heat of the day in winter, for Sunday, first day of the week, and for daily good fortune. Christian tradition has paid little note to Uriel.

Bibliography: E. LOHSE, *Die Religion in Geschichte und Gegenwart,* 7 v. (3d ed. Tübingen 1957–65) 6:1193. O. GRAF, *Lexikon für Theologie und Kirche,* ed. M. BUCHBERGER, 10 v. (Freiburg 1930–38) 10:443–444.

[T. L. FALLON]

URIM AND THUMMIM

(Heb. *'ûrîm w^etummîm,* meaning uncertain). According to Ex 28.30 and Lv 8.8, the Urim and Thummim are two objects in the "breastpiece of decision" of the high priest used to ascertain God's decision. Aaron was to wear them in his breastpiece whenever he entered Yahweh's presence as a symbol of His decisions in favor of the Israelites (Ex 28.29–30). In 1 Sm 23.6–12 and 30.7–8 the EPHOD is described as an oracular tool and may have contained the Urim and Thummim. By restoring the Hebrew of 1 Sm 14.41 from the LXX, Old Latin and Vulgate, we have "If I or my son, Jonathan, are guilty of this sin, O Yahweh, God of Israel, give Urim; if your people Israel is guilty, give Thummim," as an example of their use. According to Dt 33.8,10 the tribe of Levi was entrusted with the divine decisions of the Thummim and Urim. Mention is made of the Urim, without Thummim but with other oracular means in 1 Sm 28.6: Yahweh did not answer Saul either by dreams or by Urim or by prophets. After the Babylonian Exile, the two oracular words appear in Ezr 2.63, which, translated literally, says: "and His Excellency forbade them to eat sacred food until a priest arose for the Urim and Thummim," meaning that the spurious priests could not act as priests until a high priest who had charge of the sacred lots was reinstalled and gave a decision on their case.

From the Biblical evidence we do not know clearly what these two objects were and how they operated. However, they appear to have been some sort of lots that could be distinguished only when fully seen. Perhaps the *'ûrîm* was inscribed with *'ālep,* the *tummîm* with *tāw,* the first and last letters of the Hebrew alphabet. One would mean "yes," and the other "no," and an affirmative or a negative answer could thus be given to a properly formulated question, for instance: "Shall I go and smite the Philistines?" (1 Sm 23.2); "Shall I pursue after these robbers, and shall I overtake them, or not?" (1 Sm 30.8; see also 23.12; 2 Sm 2.1; 5.19). These questions could be answered by a simple showing of either the Urim or the Thummim, much like the arrow divination of Ez 21.26–27. If, however, both objects came out together after being shaken, then, Yahweh's decision was withheld (1 Sm 28.6).

Bibliography: *Encyclopedic Dictionary of the Bible,* translated and adapted by L. HARTMAN (New York 1963) 2520–21. R. DE-VAUX, *Ancient Israel, Its Life and Institutions,* tr. J. MCHUGH (New York 1961) 349–353.

[J. E. STEINMUELLER]

URRÁBURU, JUAN JOSÉ

Spanish philosopher who contributed heavily to the textbook or manual tradition of contemporary SCHOLAS-

TICISM and THOMISM; b. Ceanuri, Spain, May 20, 1844; d. Burgos, Aug. 10, 1904. He entered the Society of Jesus on May 3, 1860, at Loyola, where after finishing his own studies, he taught rhetoric and humanities. He also taught philosophy and theology at Poyanne, France. In 1878, Urráburu was assigned to teach philosophy at the Gregorian University. After nine years he returned to Spain to assume administrative posts as rector successively of the College at Valladolid (1887–90), Colegio Maximo, Oña (1891–97), and the Jesuit seminary at Salamanca (1898–1902). During that period he published his famous manuals, *Institutiones philosophicae* (8 v. Valladolid 1890–1900), summarized later in his *Compendium philosophiae scholasticae* (5 v. Valladolid, 1902–04, 1924, 1927). These works assimilated to the scholastic tradition what he considered valuable in the rationalist and empiricist traditions and rejected what he found wanting. The influence of St. THOMAS AQUINAS and of F. SUÁREZ is dominant, although that of R. DESCARTES, C. WOLFF, and I. KANT is also noticeable.

Bibliography: J. L. PERRIER, *The Revival of Scholastic Philosophy in the Nineteenth Century* (New York 1909). C. EGUÍA RUIZ, "A propósito del centenario natal del P. Urráburu," *Estudios Eclesiásticos* 19 (1945) 45–59. A. NADAL, "La psicología del P. Urráburu," *Razón y Fe* 14 (1906) 314–330.

[N. J. WELLS]

URSICINUS OF RAVENNA, ST.

Bishop, martyr; d. Ravenna, April 537 or 538. Although there is an early Ursicinus of Ravenna, who was supposedly a physician martyred in the 2d century (feast, June 19), the saint considered here was archbishop of Ravenna, holding that see from 534 until his death. Very little is known of him. The BOLLANDIST Papebroch noted that his relics were preserved in a marble container in the altar of the basilica of San Vitale in Ravenna, that he was commonly entitled *sanctus* or *beatus,* but saw no other evidence of cult. In the 9th century, Agnellus the commendatory abbot gave an account of Ursicinus in his *Liber pontificalis ecclesiae Ravennatis* (*Patrologia Latina* 106:597–599), and noted that his relics were in the altar of San Vitale.

Feast: Sept. 5.

Bibliography: *Acta Sanctorum* Sept. 2 (Paris 1868) 535–536. PETER DAMIAN, *Carmina sacra et preces, Patrologia Latina*, ed. J. P. MIGNE, 217 v. (Paris 1878–90) 145:950. *Bibliotheca hagiographica latina antiquae et mediae aetatis,* 2 v. (Brussels 1898–1901; suppl. 1911) 2:8409. H. LECLERCQ, *Dictionnaire d'archéologie chrétienne et de liturgie,* ed. F. CABROL, H. LECLERQ, and H. I. MARROU, 15 v. (Paris 1907–53) 14.2:2083–84.

[W. A. JURGENS]

URSINUS, ANTIPOPE

Pontificate: Sept. 24, 366 to 367. Ursinus was a Roman deacon and a supporter of Pope LIBERIUS (352–366) in his struggles against the emperor CONSTANTIUS II (337–351) and the antipope FELIX (355–365). When Liberius died, his supporters elected Ursinus as his sucessor, and they took up a position in the Julian basilica. However, adherents of Felix and some other Roman clergy and lay people elected DAMASUS I (366–384) pope. The rivals' partisans engaged in bloody street battles, usually won by Damasus' men. When Damasus had sufficient strength, he got the city prefect to exile Ursinus and his chief followers. Ursinus successfully petitioned the emperor Valentinian I (364–375) for permission to return to Rome. He and his supporters triumphantly entered the city on Sept. 13, 367, but trouble broke out again, and regretting his earlier decision, Valentinian exiled Ursinus to Gaul. When his followers promised the government that they would maintain the peace with Damasus, the emperor released Ursinus from exile. He moved to northern Italy and immediately began plotting against Damasus. In 370 the Ursinians in Rome got a converted Jew named Isaac to accuse him of a "disgraceful" crime, apparently adultery. For a time Damasus found himself in a precarious position, but he soon extricated himself. The emperor decided that Ursinus simply could not be allowed to stay in Italy and so exiled him to Cologne. No one is sure what happened to him there, but some northern Italian bishops spoke of his machinations as late as 381. When Damasus died in 384, Ursinus let the Romans know of his availability for the papal office, but they chose Siricius (384–399). After that Ursinus disappeared from history.

Bibliography: H. JEDIN, ed., *History of the Church* (New York 1980) 2:250. J. N. D. KELLY, *Oxford Dictionary of Popes* (New York 1986) 35. C. PIETRI, *Roma Christiana* (Rome 1976) 408–418.

[J. F. KELLY]

URSINUS, ZACHARIAS

German Calvinist theologian; b. Breslau, July 18, 1534; d. Neustadt, June 3, 1583. He studied at Wittenberg from 1550 to 1557 and accompanied his teacher Philip MELANCHTHON to the disputation at Worms (1557), which was the last attempt on the part of the Empire to reconcile the religious differences. He then went to Geneva and studied under John CALVIN. He next obtained a chair in Breslau, but his strong Calvinist views brought about his dismissal. In 1561 he moved to Heidelberg where the first Calvinist academy in Germany had been established. There he lectured on dogma until the dissolution of his college and the triumph of Lutheranism at the university forced him to leave. He found a position at the Casimirianum College at Neustadt. With K. Olevian he compiled the HEIDELBERG CATECHISM in 1562. It was fundamentally Calvinist in its theology although modified by Lutheran tendencies. He was also active in the campaign against the Formula of Concord of 1577, which was the last of the classical Lutheran formulas of faith (*See* CONFESSIONS OF FAITH, PROTESTANT).

Bibliography: F. HAUSS, *Die Religion in Geschichte und Gegenwart,* 7 vol. (3rd ed. Tübingen 1957–65) 6:1204.

[T. S. BOKENKOTTER]

URSMAR, ST.

Missionary and abbot bishop of Lobbes; b. Floyon, near Avesnes, in northern France, *c.* 644; d. April 4, 713. He was appointed abbot of Lobbes by Pepin II of Heristal *c.* 690 to succeed St. LANDELIN (d. 686), and was consecrated bishop in 691. Ursmar preached the gospel in northern France and Flanders, founded monasteries, and consecrated the church of SS. Peter and Paul at Lobbes, Aug. 26, 697. He resigned in 711 or 712; he died after nine years of illness. His relics were burned in 1794 during the course of the French Revolution.

Feast: April 19.

Bibliography: *Vitae Ursmari . . . , Monumenta Germaniae Historica: Scriptores rerum Merovingicarum* 6:443–461. J. WARICHEZ, *L'Abbaye de Lobbes* (Tournai 1909). É. DE MOREAU, *Histoire de l'Église en Belgique* (2d ed. Brussels 1945-) v.1; *Lexikon für Theologie und Kirche,* (Freiburg 1930–38) 10:451. A. M. ZIMMERMANN, *Kalendarium Benedictinum: Die Heiligen und Seligen des Benediktinerordens und seiner Zweige* (Metten 1933–38) 2:68–71.

[P. BLECKER]

URSULA, ST.

Probably fourth-century virgin and martyr. In the church of St. Ursula at Cologne, Germany, there is a stone bearing a Latin inscription that dates probably back to the second half of the fourth century. It indicates that Clematius, a man of senatorial rank, rebuilt a ruined basilica in honor of certain virgins martyred on the spot. No authentic account identifying these virgins exists. Ursula was first nominated to their number in the ninth century. Some stories say there were 11 martyrs, others say 11,000. One Cologne version states that Ursula and her companions were British and that they were slain by the Huns in 451. The unearthing of presumed relics at Cologne in 1155 occasioned the embroidering of the story by inventing a litany of names for Ursula's companions. The original martyrs, of unknown name and origin, were put to death probably sometime in the beginning of the fourth century.

Feast: Oct. 21.

Bibliography: *Acta Sanctorum* (Antwerp 1643– ; Venice 1734– ; Paris 1863–) Oct. 9:73–303. *Ursula-Legenden im Kölner Druck,* ed. U. RAUTENBERG (Cologne 1992). C. M. KAUFFMANN, *The Legend of Saint Ursula* (London 1964). F. BARDON, *La peinture narrative de Carpaccio dans le cycle de Ste. Ursule* (Venice 1985). A. SCHNYDER, *Die Ursulabruderschaften des Spätmittelalters* (Bern 1986). I. KEHL, *Vittore Carpaccios Ursulalegendenzyklus der Scuola di Sant'Orsola in Venedig* (Worms 1992). *Hochgotischer Dialog: die Skulpturen der Hochaltäre von Marienstatt und Oberwesel im Vergleich,* ed. W. WILHELMY (Worms am Rhein 1993). V. CARPACCIO, *Carpaccio: storie di Sant'Orsola,* ed. G. NEPI SCIRÈ (Milan 2000). A. BUTLER, *The Lives of the Saints,* rev. ed. H. THURSTON and D. ATTWATER, 4 v. (New York 1956) 4:165–168.

[E. DAY]

URSULINA VENERII, BL.

B. Parma, 1375; d. Verona, April 7, 1410. She was the youngest of several women who attempted to end the WESTERN SCHISM. She claimed that a supernatural voice had urged her to intercede with CLEMENT VII, the antipope at Avignon, to renounce his claim to the papacy. Her efforts having proved fruitless, she similarly attempted to convince Pope BONIFACE IX in Rome. Boniface in turn encouraged her to undertake a second trip to Avignon. This time she was accused of sorcery and narrowly escaped a trial. In despair she undertook a perilous journey to the Holy Land. On her return she settled in Verona where, though an exile from her native town, she died peacefully, having devoted her last years to the task of reforming an enclosed monastery of nuns.

Feast: April 7.

Bibliography: *Acta Sanctorum* April 1:719–735. A. B. C. DUNBAR, *A Dictionary of Saintly Women,* 2 v. (London 1904–05) 2:282–283. A. M. GAROFANI, *Vita e viaggi della B. Orsolina di Parma* (Parma 1593; new ed. 1897).

[D. S. BUCZEK]

URSULINES

The Order of St. Ursula (OSU) was founded in 1535, at Brescia, Italy, by St. Angela MERICI for the education of girls. Known originally as the Company of St. Ursula, it became recognized later as a monastic order and spread throughout Europe and eventually to every continent. The title of Ursuline is claimed by religious institutes with varying constitutions, including independent monasteries of pontifical jurisdiction; unions, the largest of which is the Roman Union; and distinct convents of diocesan rite.

Foundations and Early History. Angela's plan for a religious society took a long time to evolve. Finally in

"The Martyrdom of Saint Ursula and the 11,000 Maidens," *17th-century Baroque Flemish oil on wood painting by Peter Paul Rubens.* (© Kimbell Art Museum/CORBIS)

1516, after many years at Desanzano on Lake Garda, where she sought to lead a life of Christian perfection and to attract others to follow her example, Angela settled in Brescia. There on Nov. 25, 1535, she and 28 companions formed the Company of St. Ursula to combat heresy by giving instruction in Christian doctrine and to oppose the widespread immorality of the time by their example. They placed themselves under the protection of St. URSULA, patroness of education, whose cult was popular in medieval Europe.

Among the writings Angela left to her daughters, the most important are her Testament, the Counsels, and her Primitive Rule, a document of 12 chapters in which the company was given a definite form. Necessary modifications were provided for in her Testament directive: ''If according to times and needs you should be obliged to make fresh rules and change certain things, do it with prudence and on good advice.'' By the end of the 16th century radical changes had taken place within the company. After the approval of the primitive rule by Paul III in 1544, the Ursulines spread rapidly throughout Italy. It was at Milan, whence they had gone in 1566, that the first major change in their organization was effected. Under the Brescian rule, the members of the company had lived with their families, but at the request of (St.) Charles BORROMEO, Milan's bishop, they began to live in community and to take simple vows publicly. A new rule entitled For Ursulines Desiring to Live in Community, dated 1585, was approved by Gregory XIII.

As early as 1574 there were Ursulines in France living under the primitive rule. The Avignon community was the first to adopt the Milan rule in 1596. Thereafter independent Ursuline communities modeled on those of St. Charles appeared throughout France, where the Order experienced its greatest growth and was raised to the monastic state. The bull of Paul V (June 16, 1612) elevating the community of Paris to the status of a religious Order was soon extended to Toulouse, Bordeaux, and other Ursuline monasteries. At the beginning of the 18th century, there were 350 monasteries in France, with about 9000 Ursulines, now officially termed nuns, living a strictly cloistered life under solemn vows (see NUN; SISTER, RELIGIOUS). During the French Revolution their numbers decreased; many religious were dispersed and about 35 Ursulines suffered martyrdom.

Missionary Expansion. The monasteries that were most important to the development of the Order were those of Paris and Bordeaux; many new foundations in France and other countries took their origin from them. In 1639 (Blessed) MARIE OF THE INCARNATION and two companions, the first Ursuline missionaries to the New World, left France for Canada. They had been invited by

''The Dream of St. Ursula,'' painting by Vittore Carpaccio.

the Jesuits to participate in the work of their newly founded mission to the Huron. Madame de la Peltrie, a wealthy widow of Alençon who had offered herself and her wealth for this venture, accompanied the pioneer Ursulines. The foundation made at Quebec was the first convent devoted to the instruction of girls in North America. Nearly a century passed before the next Ursuline foundation was made in the New World. In 1727, at the invitation of the Jesuits of Louisiana, 12 French Ursulines arrived at New Orleans and established their first school in what later became part of the United States. From the New Orleans convent, foundations were made in Cuba, Texas and Mexico. By the middle of the 19th century various other Ursuline missionaries from Europe had opened schools in the United States. But missionary activity was not confined to the New World, for during this period Holland sent nuns to Java, France sent them to Greece and Brazil, Belgium sent them to India and the Belgian Congo, and Germany sent nuns to Australia. In the 20th century missions were opened in Guinea, South Africa, China, Thailand, Alaska, Taiwan, and the Island of Flores in the Lesser Sundas, a province of Indonesia. Since Vatican II the Ursulines have continued their service to the Church by collaborating with the laity in works of parish ministry, in religious education and catechesis, in diocesan offices and marriage tribunals, and in volunteer work with the marginalized.

The Roman Union. In 1900 Leo XIII invited representatives of Ursuline convents throughout the world to convene in Rome to consider unification under one superior general. When 70 monasteries from nine countries

Orphanage run by the Ursulines of Tildonk. (©Rykoff Collection/CORBIS.)

responded and 63 of them voted for incorporation, the Pope, on Nov. 28, 1900, approved the Roman Union of the Order of St. Ursula. Mother St. Julian was elected first prioress general, and the motherhouse was permanently established in Rome. The Roman Union is international in character; the superior general exercises authority over the whole institute in the measure granted by the constitutions. She and her assistants, representatives of national groups, are elected every six years at a general chapter that convenes in Rome.

In 2000 the institute was composed of 30 provinces with 15 novitiates, where candidates for the Order spend several years of probation before they pronounce simple vows for a period of five years. During the period of temporary vows the sister continues her formation in the religious life and in the spirit of the Institute, and she also prepares for her active ministry in the Order. After the period of temporary vows, the religious pronounce simple perpetual vows. Approximately ten years after first profession, the sisters are given an opportunity for a year of

prayer and study. The tertianship of six months is made during this year, followed by a time for study and experience in a third-world country. The tertianship is usually spent at the Ursuline Generalate in Rome, Italy. In 2000 the Roman Union's 2600 members were distributed in 265 Communities in 37 countries and in 132 dioceses throughout the world.

UNITED STATES FOUNDATIONS

In 2000 there were about 3,600 professed Ursulines in the United States, including those belonging to independent houses and those of the Roman Union.

Roman Union Ursulines [#4110]. United States communities with membership in the Roman Union, the oldest of which is that at New Orleans (1727), are of varied origins. In the year 2000 there were about 500 professed members of the Roman Union in the United States, organized in four provinces and located in 44 communities. Their ministries are in the field of religious and academic education at all levels, in retreat work, and in varied pastoral and social services. These ministries are located in 18 states and the District of Columbia. One of these academic institutions, the College of NEW RO-CHELLE , New York, founded in 1904 by Mother Irene Gill, was the first Catholic college for women in New York State. The formation of the "Ursuline Associates" which consists of men and women who feel a personal response to the call of Ursulines in the modern world, was begun in the early 1990's. This group, numbering over 150 persons, shares the life and mission of the Ursulines through prayer, ministry, retreats, study, celebrations and bonds of friendship. Another group, "Companions in Mission," is a lay volunteer program that offers opportunities for temporary service in the Ursuline mission and ministry. Important branches of the Order not belonging to the Roman Union include those of Cincinnati, Cleveland, Toledo and Youngstown, Ohio; Paola, Kansas; Louisville and Owensboro, Kentucky; Belleville, Illinois; and Blue Point (Long Island), New York.

Ursulines of Cincinnati. [#4120–02] This pontifical community was founded in 1910, when 20 Ursulines, with the permission of Archbishop Henry Moeller, left the Brown County, Ohio, community to establish an autonomous convent in Cincinnati. Mother Fidelis Coleman was elected superior. Property was secured for a motherhouse and St. Ursula's Academy; soon after Rome approved the establishment of a novitiate. In 1961 a house of studies for junior nuns was opened at a 25-acre suburban site. The community gradually extended its apostolate to include teaching at the Archbishop's Choir School, at six Cincinnati and Dayton parish schools, and at three catechetical centers in suburban areas. Alert to Latin

American needs, the community gave residence and English instruction to 18 sisters of Spanish-speaking communities, exiled from Cuba.

Ursulines of Cleveland. [#4120–04] In 1850 at the request of Amadeus Rappe, first bishop of Cleveland, Ohio, a foundation of Ursuline nuns from Boulogne-sur-mer, France, was established in Cleveland by Mother Annunciation Beaumont and four companions. That September a boarding, day, and parochial school was opened on the convent property. Although the Ursulines were under a monastic rule and were cloistered, they obtained permission from Rome as early as 1853 to go out to teach in the parochial schools that were then beginning. The Cleveland convent established three foundations between 1854 and 1874 at Toledo, Tiffin, and Youngstown, Ohio; all became independent pontifical institutes.

In 1848 Rome, in approving new constitutions for the Cleveland Ursulines, whose only apostolate was teaching, granted them the privilege of the fourth vow of instruction. The nuns teach in 24 parochial schools and conduct 3 secondary academies and Ursuline College for women (1871), Cleveland. Beaumont School for Girls, operating under the original high school charter of the 1850s, is the second oldest secondary school in Cleveland. The Toledo Ursulines staff Mary Manse College for women (1873) in that city, as well as three boarding schools, 16 elementary schools, and five secondary schools. In the Diocese of Youngstown, the Ursulines teach in 16 parochial and two high schools. Aspirants make a year of postulancy, two years of novitiate, and three years under temporary vows prior to their final profession of vows.

Ursulines of Kentucky. Mother Salesia Reitmeiter, of Straubing, Bavaria, and two companions opened the first Ursuline school in Kentucky, St. Martin's Parochial School (1858) and later Ursuline Academy (1860). The academy building served as the first motherhouse of the Ursuline Nuns of the Immaculate Conception of Louisville, Kentucky, [#4120–03?] until a separate motherhouse was erected (1918). The community follows the Rule of St. AUGUSTINE and shares the general Ursuline ideal of the education of women and the custom of the Congregation of Paris in pronouncing a fourth vow, that of the instruction of youth. It amalgamated with Ursuline communities in Columbia, South Carolina (1937), and Pittsburgh, Pennsylvania (1956); in 1964 it had a total membership of 561. Two independent houses have branched from it, those at Paola, Kansas (1895), and Maple Mount, Kentucky (1912).

The Ursuline Nuns of Mt. St. Joseph, Maple Mount, Kentucky, [#4120–05] were founded from the Louisville house by Mother Aloysius Willett and her assistant,

Mother Agnes O'Flynn; they follow the rule and customs of the parent community.

Ursulines of Kansas City. [#4120–02] In 1895, led by Sisters Mary Jerome Schaub and Mary Maurice Albert, Ursulines from Louisville, Kentucky, arrived in Paola, Kansas, where they immediately opened schools under Bishop Louis M. Fink of the Leavenworth Diocese, which then comprised the entire state of Kansas.

Ursulines of Mt. Calvary. In 1838 Mother Theresia Schaefer and seven Bordeaux-Liège Ursulines transferred from the monastery in Montjoie near the French border to Mt. Calvary, Ahrweiler, Germany. Subsequently, these Ursulines founde several schools for women along the Rhine and Saar Rivers, among which were the colleges of Aix-la-Chapelle, Saarbrücken, and Koblenz, West Germany. In 1870 the motherhouse and five daughterhouses obtained permission from the Holy See to forgo papal enclosure and to form the first European congregation within the Ursuline Order. These Mt. Calvary Ursulines became leaders in elementary, secondary, and vocational schools; colleges; and normal schools. In 1910 at the call of Bishop Vincent Wehrle, OSB, of Bismarck, North Dakota, a group arrived in the United States and established their motherhouse at Kenmare, North Dakota, later transferring it to Belleville, Illinois (1945). The Mt. Calvary Ursulines also do catechetical work, summer mission work among the Native Americans and public school children in Montana and North Dakota. They have also undertaken the direction of youth clubs, sodalities, and adult groups.

Ursulines of Tildonk, Belgium (RU) [#4130]. A diocesan congregation founded in 1831 by John Corneille Martin Lambertz, parish priest of Tildonk; the group adopted the constitutions of the Bordeaux Ursulines. By 1869, when Lambertz died, 40 convents had been established and thereafter the congregation continued to spread in Belgium, Holland, England, the Transvaal, and Java. The first United States foundation was made in 1924 in Brooklyn, New York, and the American motherhouse, novitiate, and juniorate were located in Blue Point, New York. The generalate in Haecht, Belgium, exercised jurisdiction over all the congregation's houses. The members staffed schools, two hospitals (one each in Belgium and India), and nine dispensaries (seven in India and two in the Congo).

Ursuline Nuns of Quebec. In 1639 (Blessed) MARIE OF THE INCARNATION (Marie Guyard) left her monastery at Tours, France, to found a house in Canada. With Madame de la Peltrie and two religious companions, Mothers Saint Joseph and Sainte Croix, she landed at "Kebec" on August 1, and immediately opened a school for French and Indian girls in a small two-room house at

Lower Town, lent by the Company of the Hundred Associates. Two years later she erected the first monastery on Cape Diamond, site of the present convent. The first Ursulines of Quebec, like those of Tours, followed the rule of the Congregation of Bordeaux, but the arrival (1640) of nuns from the Paris convent brought about the problem of union. After various concessions on both sides, the Quebec Ursulines were affiliated to the Ursulines of Paris (1681). Twice burned to the ground, the Quebec monastery was rebuilt each time. In 1660 it temporarily became a fort against an Iroquois attack. A century later during the English siege, it sheltered both English and French wounded soldiers, and in 1760 became the headquarters of the military governor, General James Murray. During this time, the monastery had as superior a daughter of New England Puritans, Esther Wheelwright, Mother Mary of the Infant Jesus. As a child, Esther had been taken from her home during an Indian raid (1703) and brought to Canada by the Abenakis. Ransomed in 1708 by Governor Vaudreuil, she was sent with his own daughter to the Ursuline Convent and became a nun.

Since 1953, the Ursulines of Quebec have formed the Ursuline Union of Eastern Canada, and follow with a few modifications, the rule of Roman Union Ursulines, under a superior general residing at Quebec. In addition to the provinces of Quebec, Three Rivers, and Rimouski, the union embraces a vice-province in Japan with houses at Sendai and Hachinohe. A smaller mission in Aucayo, Peru, is under the Three Rivers Province. Mere Marie was declared "Blessed" by Pope John Paul II in Rome in 1980.

Bibliography: M. ARON, *The Ursulines,* tr. M. A. GRIFFIN (New York 1947). M. J. MCKIERNAN *The Order of Saint Ursula* (New Rochelle, New York 1945). M. M. BELLASIS, *Towards Unity: History of the Roman Union of the Order of Saint Ursula* (Exeter, England 1951) v.1. C. MONDESÉRT and H. DE LUBAC, "Spirituality," *The Ursulines of the Roman Union* (Lyon 1958) 43–59, sep. pub. (Lyon 1959). Archives, St. Ursula Content, Cincinnati, Ohio. Archives, Immaculate Heart of Mary Convent, St. Martin, Ohio. M. F. HEARON, *The Broad Highway: A History of the Ursuline Nuns in the Diocese of Cleveland, 1850–1950* (Cleveland 1951). Archives, Ursuline Nuns of the Immaculate Conception, Louisville, Kentucky. Archives, Ursuline Nuns of Mt. St. Joseph, Maple Mount, Kentucky. C. BATHILDE, *Die Ursulinen von Calvarienberg-Ahrweiler* (Trier 1940). M. H. PAGÉS, *Vexilla Regis: History of the Congregation of the Ursulines of Mount Calvary* (master's diss. St. Louis University 1951). Manuscript Archives, Ursulines of Quebec. M. DE ST. JEAN MARTIN, *The Spirit of St. Angela* (Rome 1950).

[D. DUNKERLEY/M. H. SANKER/M. W. CURRY/M. C. MCGRATH/M. C. FELHOELTER/M. H. PAGÉS/M. J. MCCARTHY/S. C. DAVIS]

URUGUAY, THE CATHOLIC CHURCH IN

The República Oriental del Uruguay is situated in South America, located between Brazil to the north and Argentina to the west, the Río de la Plata rounding the southern border and leading to the Atlantic Ocean along the east. Rolling hills predominate, dropping to fertile lowlands along the southern coast, and the warm, temperate climate is beneficial to the region' agriculture, although high winds are common. Although Uruguay has few mineral deposits, its resources include fisheries, hydropower and agricultural products that include wheat, rice, barley, corn and sorghum.

Once known as the Banda Oriental, Uruguay was part of the Spanish viceroyalty of Rio de la Plata until 1814 when its leaders broke with Argentina and gained independence. In 1820 the region began a five-year occupation by neighboring Brazil, and became a republic in 1825. Liberals and conservatives struggled for power during the next 50 years, followed by 86 years of liberal rule. Economic unrest during the mid-20th century was punctuated by military rule; civilian rule returned in 1985. About 90 percent of the population descended from Europeans, chiefly Spaniards and Italians. Uruguayans are considered among the most prosperous and literate people in all South America.

Church History. The territory was discovered in 1516 by Spanish navigator Juan Díaz de Solís, who claimed it for the crown of Castile. The few native tribes, which were believed to be ethnic Guaraní, included Charrúas, Chanaes, Bohanes, Yaros and Guenoas; these peoples either fled the region or were exterminated, the last surviving indigenous people being the warlike Charrúas, who were exterminated in 1832. The first missionaries who arrived from Buenos Aires were three Franciscans: Fray Bernardino de Guzmán, who founded the first reduction of Santo Domingo de Soriano and of whom it was said by a historian that "he must be considered as the originator of Uruguayan sociability, because he was able to wrench a whole tribe away from barbarity and relate it to the soil, establishing the habits of profitable and moralizing work''; Fray Villavicencio; and Fray Aldao. Later, Jesuits began their evangelical work, giving special attention to the teaching of the young.

Spanish authorities headquartered in Buenos Aires converted the area into pastoral lands and brought in 100 head of cattle, the basis of the prodigious cattle industry in the modern republic. Several small population centers sprang up: Soriano, Maldonado, Colonia and Montevideo, founded in 1726 by the Spanish governor of Buenos Aires, Bruno Mauricio de Zabala. During the Spanish period, Uruguayan colonists developed a flourishing society. Jesuits were expelled in 1767 as part of an effort to break their efforts to stop the enslavement of native people in South America. By 1800 Uruguay's merchant classes determined to cut ties with Spain. An uprising led by General José ARTIGAS in 1811, developed into a four-year battle for independence. In 1814, after defeats at Las Piedras and El Cerrito, the Spanish capitulated and left Uruguay. However, struggles against the nationalistic aspirations of Argentina, Portugal and Brazil continued to bloody the region for the next decade. The region declared independence on Aug. 27, 1828, although skirmishes with the government of Argentina continued.

Uruguay remained part of the diocese of Buenos Aires until 1824, when Dámaso Antonio Larrañaga was appointed vicar of the city of Montevideo and its province. The Church supported the political autonomy of Uruguay, and took an active part in the struggle for independence that achieved success on Aug. 14, 1832. At this point Larrañaga was elevated to vicar apostolic, and in 1878 Montevideo became a bishopric, its first bishop Jacinto VERA (1813–81), who had been acting vicar apostolic since 1859. Vera worked energetically to organize the Church in Uruguay, continuing the efforts of Larrañaga and of the vicars José Benito Lamas and Lorenzo Fernández. The Sisters of Our Lady of the Orchard, the first order of women to arrive, reached Uruguay about 1857, the same period that saw the return of the Jesuits. Other orders working in the country included Augustinians, Basilians, Regular Capuchins, Discalced Carmelites, Claretians, Dominicans, Black Franciscans, Vincentians, Maronites and Oblates of St. Francis de Sales. During the 19th and 20th centuries almost all priests were been foreigners, chiefly Italians and Spaniards. A lack of personnel and the limited financial resources continue to be obstacles to the propagation of the faith in Uruguay.

The Church after Independence. Following independence, Church leaders who had served as advisers to revolutionary leaders then acted as legislators. Among the most distinguished were Larrañaga, adviser to Artigas and founder of the National Library in 1816; José Benito Lamas, who was persecuted by Spanish governor Elío; Santiago Figueredo and then became rector of the University of Buenos Aires; Larrobla, president of the assembly that proclaimed the independence in Florida (1825); and Gadea, Pérez Castellano, Pelliza, Martínez, Peña and Gómez. The constitution of 1830 established Roman Catholicism as the religion of the State. The government subsidized the Church, made religious instruction obligatory and aided efforts to maintain missions for those native people remaining in Uruguay. However, political division between the Blancos (predominately Catholic conservatives) and the Colorados (liberals) sparked a se-

---

Capital: Montevideo.
Size: 72,162 sq. miles.
Population: 3,334,070 in 2000.
Languages: Spanish; Portunol/Brazilero is spoken on the frontier.
Religions: 1,733,720 Catholics (52%), 533,450 Protestants (16%), 33,500 Jews (1%), 1,033,400 follow other faiths or are without religious affiliation.
Archdiocese: Montevideo, with suffragans Canelones, Florida, Maldonado-Punta del Este, Melo, Mercedes, Minas, Salto, San José de Mayo, and Tcuarembó.

---

ries of civil wars that hampered the progress of the nation through the 19th century. The government remained in the hands of Colorados from 1872 to 1958, during which time the power of the Church declined, due predominately to the prevalence of anticlericalism. In 1904 the government of José Batlle y Ordóñez was installed and Uruguay entered a period of political and social stability.

Under the administration of Ordóñez, religious education in Uruguayan public schools was eliminated in 1909, and the constitution of 1917 created separation between Church and State, although it continued to grant tax exemption. After this point, the Church was supported completely by the contributions of the faithful and its financial resources declined substantially. Meanwhile, the government created a welfare state through social service programs and an economic infrastructure supported by legislations. The government of Gabriel Terra (1931–38) was unusually disposed to the Church, and during his term of office diplomatic relations with the Holy See, interrupted since 1911, were resumed.

In 1958 a conservative president came to power and the economy began to falter. In the late 1960s the Tupamaros, a Marxist guerilla force, began gaining political power and in 1973 they backed a military coup that gained control of the government. Within a year the military leaders had crushed the Tupamaros, but retained control of the state until 1985 when the country elected a civilian president. In 1989 amnesty was declared for political prisoners from the military regime. A coalition government elected in 1990 allowed the country to regain its social stability and traditionally high standard of living. In 1997 the Uruguayan bishops called on the president to reveal the fate of 150 citizens who disappeared during the military dictatorship, in order that they could be given a Christian burial.

By 2000 there were 384 parishes tended by 1,110 diocesan and 335 religious priests. Other religious included approximately 460 brothers and 2,800 sisters, many of whom were engaged in maintaining Uruguay's 170 pri-

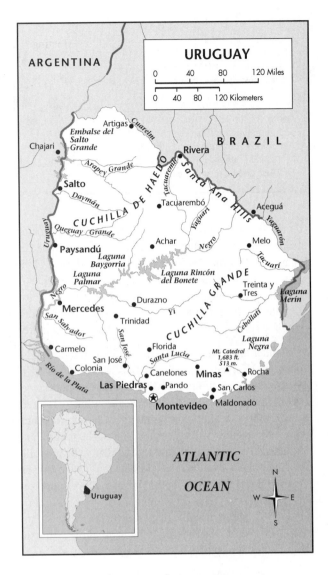

URUGUAY

thers to defend the cause of Protestantism. He became in turn professor of theology at Trinity College (1607), bishop of Meath (1620), and archbishop of Armagh (1624). He was always bitterly opposed to Catholicism, and in 1626 he succeeded in preventing Falkland, Viceroy of Ireland, from granting Irish Catholics some relief from the stringent Penal Laws. In 1629 he disapproved of Bp. William Bedell's proposal to revive the Irish language in religious worship. He helped draft the canons of the Church of Ireland (1634), and he defeated the attempt to make the Irish Church conform doctrinally in all points with the Church of England. While he was in England on scholarly research, the Great Rebellion of 1641, in which he lost his house and property in Armagh, broke out. He therefore remained in England, mostly in London, for the rest of his life, devoting his time to preaching and writing. By order of Cromwell he was buried in Westminster Abbey.

Among his many published writings (last complete edition, 17 v., Dublin 1847–64), the most influential was his *Annales Veteris et Novi Testamenti* (2 v., Dublin 1650–54), in which he propounded a Biblical chronology that was soon inserted in the marginal notes of the Authorized Version of the Bible and found its way later even into some editions of the Douay Bible. Using only the Biblical data for the early period of Biblical history, Ussher put the creation of the world at 4004 B.C. Although it was shown in the 19th century to be enormously wrong, Ussher's chronology continued to be printed in some editions of the Bible even in the 20th century.

Bibliography: J. A. CARR, *The Life and Times of James Ussher* (London 1895). W. B. WRIGHT, *The Ussher Memoirs* (London 1889), A. GORDON, *The Dictionary of National Biography from the Earliest Times to 1900,* 20:64–72.

[K. O'SULLIVAN]

mary and 90 secondary Catholic schools, as well as working in hospitals and sanatoriums, insane asylums and clinics.

Bibliography: *Annuario Pontificio* has information on all diocese.

[A. D. PIROTTO/EDS.]

USSHER, JAMES

Irish Protestant divine, now best known for his once widely held Biblical chronology; b. Dublin, Jan. 4, 1581; d. Reigate, England, March 20, 1656. After graduating from the newly founded University of Dublin in 1600, Ussher (also spelled Usher) became a fellow of Trinity College of this university and was ordained an Anglican clergyman (1601). Full of zeal for the Reformation, he engaged in an intense study of the Scriptures and the Fa-

USUARD

Martyrologist; fl. Saint-Germain-des-Prés, 838 to 875. When he first appeared in history in 838, he was already a monk and a priest. In 858 or 860, he and several companions made a journey to Spain in search of relics, returning in 863. For the edification of his brothers Usuard recounted stories he had heard of Spanish martyrs. Shortly thereafter, while he was a monk at SAINT-GERMAIN-DES-PRÉS in Paris (c. 875), he began compiling a martyrology (*Patrologia Latina,* ed. J. P. MIGNE 123:453–992; 124:1–860) at the order of Emperor Charles II the Bald. In this work he combined certain features of two types of MARTYROLOGIES then in vogue. The older models consisted of a simple listing of saints' names under appropriate feast days. But later compilers, notably ADO OF VIENNE, had begun to include information about each saint's life, thus providing the reader with inspirational material. Usuard combined both types, sometimes merely giving the saints' names, in other cases providing hagiographical material. His work borrowed heavily from that of Ado, as well as from St. JEROME, BEDE, and FLORUS OF LYONS. In some cases he inserted materials he himself had collected in Spain. His work became the model for every later Roman MARTYROLOGY.

Bibliography: H. QUENTIN, *Les Martyrologes historiques du moyen âge* (Paris 1908). É. AMANN, *Dictionnaire de théologie catholique,* ed. A. VACANT, 15 v. (Paris 1903–50; Tables générales 1951–) 15.2:2313–16.

[R. E. SULLIVAN]

USURY

From the Latin *usura,* usury originally meant a charge for the loan of a fungible, i.e., perishable, nonspecific good, whose use consisted of its consumption. Such a loan was called a *mutuum.* Money, considered to be "consumed" in the process of exchange for other goods, was classified as a fungible good. As a money loan became the most common form of loan of this type, usury came to signify a charge for the use of money. Only after repeal of the laws prohibiting interest (usury in the above sense) and the establishment of legal rates did usury assume its present meaning of a charge for a money loan that is exorbitant or exceeds the legal rate. The concept of interest underwent a similar metamorphosis. In Roman law interest was a title to compensation for loss suffered by the lender if the borrower failed to return a loan on time. This concept survived until the close of the Middle Ages, when the old concept of usury was superseded by the new one of interest, which now means the price of loanable funds. Hence, the former meaning of usury and the present meaning of INTEREST are practically identical.

Usury Controversy. There is hardly an older or keener dispute than that of the ethics of interest. Old Testament prohibitions of interest, based on exigencies of the times, include: (1) explicit prohibitions of interest on loans to the poor; (2) prohibitions referring only to loans to Jews, foreigners being specifically excepted; and (3) condemnations of greed, and the amassing of riches by oppressing the poor with usury. Greek law did not forbid, but often regulated, interest. The Greek philosophers vehemently attacked it. Plato condemned it as inimical to the welfare of the state, setting one class, poor borrowers, against another, wealthy lenders. Aristotle shared this contempt for the usurer, considering him guilty of injustice, pettiness, and illiberality. Going beyond its social effects, he attempted to prove that interest by its very nature violates justice. Money, he declared, is a barren thing, incapable of reproduction. Hence interest, in effecting the "birth of money from money," is contrary to nature and violates justice, which requires the exchange of two equal sums.

Roman philosophers like Cicero, Cato, and Seneca approved the Greeks' condemnation, but the attitude of Roman law, apart from its few unsuccessful attempts to forbid interest, was one of limited tolerance. The Law of the Twelve Tables (451–450 B.C.) and the *Lex Unciaria* (88 B.C.) set maximum legal rates of about 12 percent that remained in effect until the Code of Justinian (533 A.D.) differentiated the legal rate according to the status of the borrower. The New Testament makes no direct statement on the ethics of interest, referring with tolerance at least to the practice in the parable of the Talents. The pre-Nicene Fathers of the Church merely repeated the scriptural teaching that exacting usury of the poor is contrary to charity and mercy. On the other hand, the great Fathers vehemently denounced the exploitation and oppression of the poor by usury, contrasting with it the gospel precepts of charity and mercy. The later Fathers repeated these sentiments. Hence, for the Fathers of the Church the evil of usury lay in its origin and its effects. The lenders' greed resulted in exploitation and oppression, often driving the poor to despair, slavery, and even suicide. Nowhere do we find a discussion of the ethics of interest in general or of the morality of moderate rates of interest.

Early Scholastics. Although still considering isolated exchange rather than an organized market, scholastic philosophy changed the ethical criterion from the motive of the lender and the consequences of the loan to the intrinsic nature of interest by forging a tool of analysis intended for all debtor-creditor relationships. The bases of scholastic condemnation of interest as a violation of commutative justice were: (1) the classification of voluntary contracts as found in Roman law and (2) the Aristotelian condemnation of interest founded on the "sterility" of money. They argued that in the case of a *mutuum,* i.e., of a loan of a fungible or perishable or generic good (e.g., bread, grain, wine), it is unjust to demand, in addition to the return of the good, a charge for its use. For, unlike a horse or a house, its use consists of its consumption, i.e., of its immediate destruction. Money was considered a fungible good since, once it was exchanged for other goods, its use ceased to exist for the borrower. "Therefore," concluded Aquinas, "it is in itself illicit to accept a price for the use of money loaned, which is called usury." Although condemned on intrinsic grounds, i.e., the nature of the loan itself, interest was permitted on the basis of certain extrinsic titles, such as actual loss sustained or opportunities of profit forgone by the lender as a result of the loan. Hence until the close of the Middle

Ages and the growth of industry and commerce, the justification for interest lay in an increasingly liberal interpretation of the applicability of these extrinsic titles.

Later Scholastics. From the 16th century onward the usury controversy followed two main streams of thought, one of continuity with, and the other of departure from, traditional scholastic analysis. In the former are found some of the early reformers (Luther, Melanchthon, Zwingli) and most of the later scholastic writers (such as Biel, Eck, Major, Peter of Navarre, Medina, Gregory of Valencia, Molina, de Lugo, Lessius, and Laynez) who liberalized the application of the extrinsic titles, such as loss sustained, profit forgone, and risk of nonrepayment. Likewise in the latter school we find both Protestant writers (Calvin, Beza, Bucer, Bullinger, Molinaeus, Salmatius, Broedersen) and a growing number of Catholic moralists and economists (Pirot, Le Correur, Collet, Maffei, Galiani, Cardinal de Luzerne, Mastrofini, Lemkuhl, Antoine, Claudio-Jannet) who attacked the minor premise of the scholastic syllogism (the sterility of money) by distinguishing between loans for production and those for consumption, insisting that in the former case money capital was fertile or productive, or quasi-productive. Hence, interest could be justified on intrinsic as well as extrinsic grounds. To this some added that present and future sums of money of equal amount are not of equal present value. Interest serves to equalize the difference between present values of present and future sums of money.

Attitude of the Church. As for the official attitude of the Church, the taking of interest was forbidden to clerics by the 44th of the Apostolic Canons, by the first Council of Arles (314), by the first general Council of Nicea (325), and repeatedly in later councils. It was declared reprehensible also for laymen by the first Council of Carthage (345) and, in order to combat "the insatiable rapacity of usurers," strictly forbidden by the great general councils of the Middle Ages. These were the third Council of the Lateran (1179), the second Council of Lyons (1274), and the Council of Vienne (1311), the last declaring that anyone who maintained that the practice of usury is not sinful should be punished as a heretic. Yet nowhere is it stated that interest is in itself and under all conditions a violation of justice. Later canonists and theologians accepted the scholastic analysis, and from the 15th century popes and councils dealt for the most part with the licitness of new practices and institutions, such as the *contractus trinus, census,* and *societas, montes pietatis.* The scholastic doctrine was formally proclaimed in Benedict XIV's encyclical *Vix Pervenit,* 1745 (which was not an infallible decree), but this did not prevent subsequent confusion and divergence of policy among confessors that arose from the differences of opinion among moralists regarding the justification of interest. This dis-

quietude was ended by the issuance in the 19th century of some 14 decisions of the Congregations of the Holy Office, the Penitentiary, and the Propaganda stating that the faithful who lend money at moderate rates of interest are "not to be disturbed," provided that they are willing to abide by any future decisions of the Holy See. The practical problem settled, the theoretical question of how interest is justified remains open to discussion. While the Holy See now puts out its funds at interest and requires ecclesiastical administrators to do the same, the Church still provides in the Code of Canon Law (c.2354) severe penalties for those convicted of usury in the modern sense.

Interest in the Modern Economy. As for the theoretical question, although the justification of interest on either extrinsic or intrinsic grounds as surveyed above is compatible with recent decisions of the Church and c.1543 of the Code of Canon Law, neither analysis seems realistic or practical in the modern economy. Although the extrinsic titles of the scholastics served a useful purpose when, in the absence of an organized capital market, the rate of interest was determined by bargaining between individual lenders and borrowers, they seem to be irrelevant in the presence of a market rate of interest. In the case of exchanges between places or currencies, the scholastics declared that the equilibrium market price, determined by conditions of demand and supply in an open market, was acceptable as the criterion of the just price. It expressed the common estimate of the value of the good, in the presence of which there could be no exploitation. Why, then, cannot the market rate of interest be taken as the criterion of the just price in exchanges of money available today for money available later? It represents the common estimate of the price of loanable funds, the present values of goods available at different points of time. It constitutes a profit or gain only in that any consumer profits or gains when he values a commodity more highly than the price he has to pay for it. Otherwise, there would be no mutual advantage to buyer and seller, which Aristotle and Aquinas clearly recognized.

Though moralists have devoted their attention to interest almost exclusively as a problem of commutative justice, its role as an instrument of policy in the field of social justice should not be overlooked.

Bibliography: B. W. DEMPSEY, *Interest and Usury* (Washington 1943). T. F. DIVINE, *Interest: An Historical and Analytical Study in Economics and Modern Ethics* (Milwaukee 1959). J. T. NOONAN, *The Scholastic Analysis of Usury* (Cambridge, Mass. 1957). J. A. SCHUMPETER, *History of Economic Analysis,* ed. E. B. SCHUMPETER (New York 1954).

[T. F. DIVINE]

UT IN OMNIBUS GLORIFICETUR DEUS

Motto of the BENEDICTINES, found at the end of ch. 57 in the BENEDICTINE RULE. The quotation is originally taken from 1 Pt 4.11, where, however, the reading is *honorificetur*. The exhortation was originally intended for those who sold the monks' handiwork, reminding them that God should be glorified not only by the monks' labor, but also by the justice of the seller's transaction. However, it has been extended to mean that the labor of every monk should be undertaken in obedience, faith, penance, and prayer so that God might be glorified in all things according to the motto of the order.

Bibliography: *The Holy Rule of Our Most Holy Father Saint Benedict* (St. Meinrad, IN 1956). B. A. SAUSE, *The School of the Lord's Service,* 3 v. (St. Meinrad, IN 1948–51) 1:98–101. P. DELATTE, *The Rule of Saint Benedict: A Commentary,* tr. and notes J. MCCANN (Latrobe, PA 1950). O. L. KAPSNER, *A Benedictine Bibliography: An Author-Subject Union List,* 2 v. (2d ed. Collegeville, MN 1962): v.1 author part; v.2, subject part 2: 66–69.

[G. E. CONWAY]

UT QUEANT LAXIS RESONARE FIBRIS

A Carolingian hymn that was traditionally prescribed for the feast of John the Baptist. It was divided into three sections, for use at Vespers, Matins, and Lauds on the feast of the Baptist. The second and third divisions begin with *Antra deserti* and *O nimis felix*. In all it has 13 stanzas. Erroneously attributed to PAUL THE DEACON, it was in fact written by an anonymous poet, his contemporary. Its chief inspiration is the Bible (especially Luke 1.41–45 and 67–69, but cf. Mt 11.11 and 13.8). Several DOXOLOGIES are attached to this hymn and its divisions. It is written in the classical first sapphic meter, but displays some license. The poet closely follows Horace's Odes. After a brief introduction (first stanza), the hymn refers to various events of the saint's life, for example, the heavenly message about his birth, the Visitation, John in the desert, his mission as Christ's precursor, and Christ's baptism (stanzas 2–8). Stanza 8 refers also to Christ's words about John (Mt 11.11). The ninth stanza praises John's martyrdom. The next stanza alludes to Biblical passages about the heavenly reward of the Lord's followers. With reference to John's present glory, the poet asks for his intercession with God. The spirit of the CAROLINGIAN RENAISSANCE is reflected not only in the hymn's classical meter, but also in its style and terminology, e.g., the angel is called *nuntius celso veniens Olympo.* This hymn has left its mark on the history of music, since GUIDO OF AREZZO derived the names of the notes of the musical scale from the first syllables of the halflines in the first stanza (*ut* having been replaced by *do*).

Bibliography: Text. J. CONNELLY, *Hymns of the Roman Liturgy* (Westminster MD 1957) 200–202. *Analecta hymnica* 50–120–121. *Monumenta Germaniae Historica: Poetae* 1:83–84. Literature. F. J. E. RABY, *A History of Christian-Latin Poetry from the Beginnings to the Close of the Middle Ages* (Oxford 1953) 166–167. C. A. MOBERG, ''Die Musik in Guido von Arezzos Solmisationshymne,'' *Archiv für Musikwissenschaft* 16 (1959) 187–206. J. SZÖVÉRFFY, *Die Annalen der lateinischen Hymnendichtung* (Berlin 1964–65) 1:186–188.

[J. SZÖVÉRFFY]

UT UNUM SINT

Pope JOHN PAUL II's twelfth encyclical, issued May 25, 1995; reaffirms the ''impassioned commitment'' of the Second Vatican Council for the unity of the Church. In preparation for the Great Jubilee of the Incarnation, the letter recapitulates the progress the churches have made together in the last thirty years. The text lays out specific challenges for Catholics, and it offers a very concrete openness to the renewal of the papacy in service to the unity of the churches. The 103 paragraphs of the encyclical are divided into three sections.

The first section reiterates the centrality of the quest for unity in the identity of Catholics; the importance of conversion to Christ, the Church, and its unity; and the necessity of prayer. He introduces the ''martyrs of our century'' as ''the most powerful proof that every factor of division can be transcended'' (no. 1). In addition to resolving doctrinal divisions he also emphasizes the ''purification of past memories'' and the necessity ''to acknowledge with sincere and total objectivity the mistakes made'' (no. 2). The conversion and repentance are not only the duty of every Catholic, but also ''of the bishop of Rome as the successor of the apostle Peter'' (no. 4). The encyclical recalls that for the Catholic Church ecumenism is ''not just some sort of 'appendix''' but rather it is ''an organic part of her life and work, and consequently must pervade all that she is and does'' (no. 20). The letter outlines the centrality of dialogue, including the dialogue of love, of truth, of conversion, and of salvation as central in Catholic relationships with other Christians and in serving the journey to full communion.

The second section recapitulates the fruits of dialogue in the last three decades, which includes both cementing the real communion that exists among Christians and among churches as well as laying the basis for the full communion for which we pray. In this section the pope discusses the solidarity in service, mission, and social action. He outlines specific developments with the churches of the East and those that have emerged from the Reformation. Pope John Paul II's own personal experience of encounters in his many trips around the globe are recounted and celebrated. In this section the pope moves beyond the conciliar designation of ''separated brethren'' to speak of ''fellow Christians.'' He lifts up convergences in the sacramental life even though ''it is not yet possible to celebrate together the same eucharistic liturgy.'' He finds it ''a source of joy to note that Catholic ministers are able . . . to administer the sacraments of the eucharist, penance and anointing of the sick to Christians who are not in full communion with the Catholic Church'' (no. 45, 46).

These developments are seen not only in the context of the theological developments in the World Council of Churches and bilateral dialogues, but also in light of clarification of Catholic practice in the 1983 Code of Canon Law, the 1991 Code of Canons of the Eastern Churches, and the 1993 *Directory for the Application of Principles and Norms on Ecumenism.*

The third section outlines the future: the challenge of making the results of the dialogues ''a common heritage'' (no. 80, 81); the continued dialogue agenda: (1) Scripture and Tradition, (2) sacraments, (3) ordination, (4) authority and (5) Mary; prayer, collaboration, and common evangelization; and his willingness to enter into a ''patient and fraternal dialogue'' with ecumenical partners about how to exercise the papal office in a way to better serve the unity of the Church, even before full theological agreement is reached. He ends with an exhortation to ''implore from the Lord, with renewed enthusiasm . . . the grace to prepare ourselves'' for this unity (no. 102).

Bibliography: For the text of *Ut unum sint,* see: *Acta Apostolicae Sedis* 87 (1995): 921–982 (Latin). *Origins* 25, no. 4 (8 June 1995): 49–72 (English). *The Pope Speaks* 40 (1995): 295–343 (English).

[J. GROS]

UTAH, CATHOLIC CHURCH IN

Utah Catholicism emerged out of harsh frontier conditions and fractious cultural differences. Accordingly, Utah compiled a religious history marked by strife, played out against a background of mountains and valleys. As a result, the Catholic faithful of Utah took on characteristics often associated with the American West—hardy spirit and personal courage.

Early History. Utah, bordered by Idaho, Wyoming, Colorado (north and east), New Mexico, Arizona, and Nevada (south and west) came, as a political entity, to encompass 84,990 square miles of western land, much of it marked by the extremes of desert and mountain environments. But long before those political boundaries were drawn, native tribes—including the Ute, Southern Paiute, Gosiute, Shoshone, and Navajo—ranged widely across the area, claiming it as their homeland. These indigenous people followed the spiritual cadence of their own native religions, but each group drew the attention of various Christian denominations. Whether the Shoshone (located in the northern part of the state) and Navajos, Utes, and Southern Paiutes (commonly found in the eastern and southern regions) brushed against Catholicism through early trade with other tribes—those touched by French Catholics to the north or Spanish Catholics to the south—remains uncertain. Regardless, Catholicism officially entered Utah in the fall of 1776 with the religious and geographic expedition of two Spanish Franciscans, Francisco Atansasio Dominguez and Silvestre de Escalante, charged by their superiors with assessing possible Indian mission sites and marking a trail to California.

For several decades following the departure of these friars, whose explorations ended on an inconclusive note, Catholicism lacked permanence in Utah. While Catholic fur trappers, among them Kit Carson, Etienne Provost, and Thomas ''Broken Hand'' Fitzpatrick, drifted in and out of the region and while such mountain men on occasion married Native American women converts, it could not be said these individuals advanced the presence of the church. Their personal histories, which show them to be transients pursuing western profits as trappers and traders, do not suggest they promulgated the faith in any systematic or significant manner.

The 1847 arrival into this territory—over which a distant Mexico City claimed questionable control—of the first representatives of the Church of Jesus Christ of Latter-day Saints heralded dramatic changes for the religious legacy of Utah. Driven out of Nauvoo, Illinois, following escalating clashes with neighbors over several provocative issues and the murder of church-founder Joseph Smith, the Mormons, as they refer to themselves, proceeded under the leadership of Brigham YOUNG, to seek safety in the Far West. Young's site selection nestled along the Wasatch Front of the Rocky Mountains and close to the Great Salt Lake, eventually proved an excellent choice. Although the first years in Utah's Great Basin exacted bitter suffering from the settlers, as had their epic winter trek from Illinois, successful European proselytizing by LDS missionaries resulted in an influx of fresh workers. Many of the Mormon converts came from Scandinavia, bringing the farming and carpentry skills that facilitated community building, but also giving a northern

European flavor to the state that persists to the present day.

As they carved out their settlements—the principal one Salt Lake City—north and south along the spine of the Wasatch Mountains, the Mormons placed an indelible religious stamp on the region. Their vision for doing so mixed their secular and religious values into a tightly woven communal lifestyle that gained strength with each passing year. Scarred by the political events and physical dangers that had forced them from the United States, the Saints set about to transform their desert retreat into a self-sufficient, productive world, where they could practice their new religion, without interference.

To accomplish this goal of social, economic, and political independence, Brigham Young devised a plan of diversification that included both industrial and agricultural pursuits. Though industry—for example, iron manufacture—showed Mormon innovation, it was agriculture, based on an extensive system of irrigation, especially through the sugar beet crop, that set state-wide economic underpinnings, which continue into the 21st century. Mormon social and political initiatives centered on construction of tabernacles for civic and religious gatherings in small towns, while in Salt Lake City, building a temple, a replacement for the one lost in the tumultuous events at Nauvoo, focused community energies.

Though these newcomers to the Great Basin hoped to avoid interaction with non-church members, by 1848, the Mormons found themselves once again living under the American flag, a result of the U.S. acquisition of Mexican land through the Treaty of Guadalupe. The following year, the California gold rush dramatically altered the personal futures and economic goals of the nation's citizenry. Increasingly, migrants of every persuasion turned to the West, but looked to the national government for assistance and protection, especially in the form of the U.S. Army. Utah, once a barren non-welcoming desert, now, with its Mormon oasis of Salt Lake City, seemed an attractive path for miners, merchants, and pioneers headed for the gold fields and new settlements of the far West; it also became a camp site for military troops sent to secure U.S. sovereignty in Utah. For the Mormons, the speed of national events, alteration of East/West travel routes, and success of their own enterprise overtook them; "Gentiles," as they labeled everyone not of their faith, entered their "Zion in the Wilderness," and the resulting encounters were frequently contentious.

The burgeoning American West invaded Utah, bringing with it Roman Catholics, whose numbers, while few, continued to grow throughout the remainder of the century. The spiritual needs of those Catholics who lingered among the Mormons captured the attention of church administrators, but delivering the clerical personnel to provide religious leadership remained difficult. Bishops in all parts of the West struggled with the challenges created by great distances, limited numbers of clergy, and scant resources. In addition, missionary priests, typically recruited from beyond the United States, often found the physical exigencies of the American West overwhelming and begged for assignments in more salubrious climes. While some plunged into the West with a pioneer optimism that turned to love of the wilderness, others found the poverty and loneliness to be debilitating. In 1853, Joseph Sadoc Alemany, archbishop of San Francisco, accepted administrative oversight for Utah, but he could do little to secure a corps of mission priests, or change the circumstances of Catholics who continued to live surrounded by a hostile geography and a forceful counter religion.

The ongoing concern of Alemany and other clergy about missions for native people and the irregular adherence to the faith by Catholics saw successive fitful attempts, some colored by confusing disputes between frontier bishops, to carve out a manageable ecclesiastical space. The remoteness of the region remained only one of the problems, as the 19th-century Mormon community at large expressed its reluctance to welcome other religions; thus, success depended on courting favor with Brigham Young, who directed the secular and religious life of Utah. Mormon hesitation to embrace outsiders stemmed from the vitriolic attacks by civic and religious leaders concerning the practice of polygamy (correctly, polygyny—one husband with multiple wives), a custom that had caused public censure since the troubled days in Nauvoo; further, Mormon leaders, still stung by the economic drubbing taken in Illinois, determined their church would not again be vulnerable to "Gentile" business pressures. Individual priests visited this challenging arena on a sporadic basis, but it was not until 1866 that Father Edward Keller attempted to open the first Catholic chapel. Despite Keller's efforts, including careful negotiations with Brigham Young, Utah did not have its first permanent church until 1871, when Father Patrick Walsh oversaw completion of St. Mary Magdalene, the forerunner of the magnificent Salt Lake City Cathedral of the Madeline that stands today as a beacon for Utah Catholics.

The transformation of Utah Catholicism from missionary outpost to institutional church began with the 1873 appointment of Lawrence Scanlan, as priest for Utah. On his arrival, the Catholics in the two main municipalities, Ogden and Salt Lake City, numbered about 90. In 1879, Scanlan became vicar forane and in 1886 he was elevated to vicar bishop for the Vicariate of Utah; the Holy See named Salt Lake City a diocese, under the patronage of St. Mary Magdalene, and Scanlan as its bishop on Jan. 28, 1891, just less than five years before Utah entered the Union as the 45th state, on Jan. 4, 1896.

Lawrence Scanlan, who presided over the diocese until his death in 1915, built a legacy as the quintessential frontier priest. His travels took on a mantle of heroism, as he journeyed the breadth of his domain, establishing parishes and bringing Catholicism to the far reaches of Utah. A skilled diplomat who negotiated the Mormon terrain with grace, Scanlan sought not to supplant the LDS majority, but rather provide a Catholic sanctuary for the children of Rome. Growth of the railroads in the 1870s and expansion of the mining industry in the 1880s inflated the numbers of his scattered, beleaguered flock, as foreign Catholic laborers, especially Italians and Irish, moved into the eastern outlying industrial areas of Carbon, Sanpete, and Sevier counties. Often disadvantaged by low wages or language barriers, these immigrants encountered the usual volatile labor troubles associated with western industry. Scanlan perceived the needs of Utah Catholics as two-fold: monetary resources to build a Catholic infrastructure in the midst of poverty and human resources to nourish a spiritual life in the midst of isolation. While Scanlan used detailed, articulate annual reports to extract the former, financial support from the Society for the Propagation of the Faith, it was through his convincing efforts with religious congregations that he reached his far-flung, increasingly culturally diverse Catholics and set a solid spiritual foundation for the future.

Religious Men and Women. In 1875, four sisters of the Congregation of the Holy Cross from Indiana journeyed to Utah to open St. Mary's Academy and Holy Cross Hospital. Over the next 125 years, sisters from nearly two dozen congregations, including Sisters of Charity of the Incarnate Word, Daughters of Charity, Mexican Sisters of Perpetual Adoration, and Sisters of the Holy Family, answered the call to aid Utah's Catholic people. While nuns met opposition, often writing to a distant motherhouse about loneliness and withdrawing from extremely difficult venues, they were also welcomed by Catholics and non-Catholics, perhaps inspired by Brigham Young, who sent some of his daughters to St. Mary's Academy for schooling. Early occupations of the various communities centered on schools, hospitals, and orphanages, but as the role of sisters changed in the 20th century, so too did women's ministry. Their outreach embraced the Utah Hispanic community, included religious education and pastoral work, Native American affairs, care of the elderly and the handicapped. By 2001, the number of religious women in the state totaled fewer than 75, supporting one another through a diocesan sisters' council. In the post–World War II era, a small number of

religious brothers, including Dominicans, Jesuits, and Franciscans, brought their ministries to Utah, as did at least a dozen different communities of priests. In 1947, Trappist monks founded the Abbey of Our Lady of the Holy Trinity, in Huntsville, Utah, where currently approximately 30 men continue to live under the Cistercian rule. In 1952, four nuns of the Order of Discalced Carmelites moved from California and established a small cloister in Salt Lake City; over the next five decades, their number hovered between five and 13. Their courageous spirit was mirrored in 1998 when 11 Benedictine sisters, each with long service in the Beehive State, separated from their Minnesota abbey and opened, in an outpouring of public warmth, St. Benedict Monastery in Ogden, Utah.

Laity. Despite the commitment of these hard working religious men and women, the laity of Utah recognized the state would never see the army of religious found in other Catholic locations. Accordingly, lay Catholics responded in the manner typical of frontier people, becoming religious activists on their own behalf. Living and working amidst a powerful theocracy, with which relations would always be tempered by significant doctrinal differences, Utah Catholics have been notable for their strong spiritual family. In the late 19th century, Catholics families around the state routinely hosted visiting priests in their homes and prepared a place for the celebration of mass. In the early 20th century, small towns, like Helper, Utah, welcomed the Chicago-based Catholic Church Extension Society's St. Peter, a railroad car outfitted as a chapel, with altar, confessional, Stations of the Cross, and a ''circuit rider'' priest who brought sacraments and solace to rural people. With no permanent parish at hand, Utah Catholics have organized themselves into Bible study and prayer groups that gather in private homes. They have raised surprisingly large sums for the construction or renovation of mission stations and parishes and, following the example of Joseph the Carpenter, they have donated their labor to see these holy places become a reality. The rise in the 1970s of the permanent diaconate movement throughout the United States proved a boon to Utah, where deacons and their wives shouldered considerable responsibility for Catholic parish life.

The second bishop, Joseph Sarsfield Glass (1915–26) encouraged a close association between clergy and laity and, starting in 1899, promoted diocesan communication through the *Intermountain Catholic* newspaper. Men and women, together and in their own church organizations, have sustained Catholic action in this vast western region. The Knights of Columbus, Catholic Women's League, Legion of Mary, League of the Sacred Heart, Christian Family Movement, Diocesan Council of Catholic Women, Cana and Pre-Cana Conferences represent only a few of the organizations through which the laity infused the diocese with Catholic life. Children and youth were central to the initiatives of lay leaders, as seen in the Catholic Youth Organization, Confraternity of Christian Doctrine program, Catholic Big Brothers and Sisters, Salt Lake Chapter of Serra International for the promotion of vocations, and the state-wide college centered Newman Club, which in 2000 had almost 200 student members at Brigham Young University alone. Lay organizations—Cursillo, Ancient Order of Hibernians, Guadalupana Society, and the Utah Basque Club—point to the growing cultural diversity of Utah Catholics. Since 1976, Saint Jude's parish has served the Maronite Rite Lebanese Catholics throughout the Intermountain West. The growing Hispanic community brings greater attention to Spanish Catholic customs and more frequent occasions for dual language services.

As American Catholics face the challenges of the 21st century, Utahans are well acquainted with some of the dilemmas that concern the national church. They have long known the difficulties of stretched resources, human and monetary. Priests, brothers, sisters, and parishioners have always wrestled with the problems of building a spiritual network for people spread across a great expanse of rugged land. Yet, Utah Catholics, even the urban residents, are accustomed to the rhythms of rural life, they know how to extract the most from their spiritual opportunities, and they enjoy some unique advantages. While the modern diocese of Salt Lake City lacks the grand institutions—hospital, academy, college, or seminary—that are visual, public markers of large Catholic populations, it embraces an active and loyal constituency. The impact of living amidst an opposing religious majority, regardless of how well early differences have yielded to a modern ecumenical spirit, forged a deep bond between the Utah church and its members. With the Diocese of Salt Lake City supporting over 60 parishes and mission stations, with church membership approaching the 110,000 mark and with longstanding strategies in place for managing the peculiar demands of western space and cultural environment, Utah Catholics appear headed for a vibrant future in the 21st century.

Bibliography: L. J. ARRINGTON, *Great Basin Kingdom: Economic History of the Latter-Day Saints, 1830–1900* (Lincoln, Neb. 1958). A. M. BUTLER, M. E. ENGH, S.J., and T. W. SPALDING, C.F.X., eds., *The Frontiers and Catholic Identity* (Maryknoll 1999). A. M. BUTLER, "Western Spaces, Catholic Places," *U. S. Catholic Historian* (Fall 2000) 25–39. B. MCGLOIN, S.J., "Two Early Reports Concerning Roman Catholicism in Utah, 1876–1881," *Utah Historical Quarterly* 29 (October 1961) 33. B. M. MOONEY, *Salt of the Earth: History of the Catholic Diocese of Salt Lake City, 1776–1987* (Salt Lake City 1987).

[A. M. BUTLER]

UTHRED OF BOLDON

Oxford theologian censured for his doctrine of "clear vision"; b. Boldon, Durham, England, *c.* 1324; d. Finchdale, Durham, January 28, 1396. Though he was at Oxford by 1337, he interrupted his studies in 1342 to become a Benedictine at Durham. He returned to Oxford (Durham College) in 1347 and took his doctorate in theology in 1357. In disputations he rejected the mendicancy of the friars and defended the endowments of the Church. He opposed John WYCLIF. He developed a thesis that the soul, between life and death, has a clear vision of real truth and the choice between the acceptance or rejection of God, a doctrine that saw a revival in the 19th century. At the instigation of the friars this was examined for orthodoxy and censured by Abp. SIMON LANGHAM in 1368. Uthred had left Oxford in 1367 to become prior of Finchdale (a Durham dependency), and then subprior of Durham. He returned to Oxford for three years in 1383, but spent his last decade at Finchdale. His many theological treatises that defend the traditional views on the Eucharist and PREDESTINATION reveal his adoption of views associated with NICHOLAS OF AUTRECOURT. Other works treat the monastic ideal and discipline.

Bibliography: W. A. PANTIN, "Two Treatises of Uthred of Boldon on the Monastic Life," *Studies in Medieval History Presented to Frederick Maurice Powicke,* ed. R. W. HUNT et al. (Oxford 1948) 362–385, gives a list of Uthred's works. D. KNOWLES, *The Religious Orders in England,* 3 v. (Cambridge, England 1948–60) v.2. A. B. EMDEN, *A Biographical Register of the Scholars of the University of Oxford to A.D. 1500,* 3 v. (Oxford 1957–59) 1:212–213. D. KNOWLES, "The Censured Opinions of U. of B.," *Proceedings of the British Academy* 37 (1951) 305–342.

[F. D. BLACKLEY]

UTOPIA AND UTOPIANISM

"Utopia" denotes an imaginary perfect society or ideal political or social goal. The term was coined by St. Thomas MORE from the Greek words for "no" and "place" and titled his 1516 book about an island society that was a model of moral and political achievement. Utopia has since passed into almost universal usage. The adjectival form "utopian" is used both in a complimentary manner to describe perspectives that call for positive social change and in a derogatory manner to describe perspectives that are unrealistic and ultimately destructive in their social expectations. "Utopianism" is not an ideological system in and of itself but rather a quality attributed to other "-isms" (e.g., Marxism, Communism, Socialism) that promote an ideal social state.

The term "utopian" has taken on new life in contemporary discussion concerning liberation theology, political theology, and the social teaching of the Catholic Church. At issue is the extent to which the Christian tradition either supports or critiques a "utopian" social outlook. Individuals on both sides of the dispute lay claim to a long heritage of literature and political philosophy.

Historical Background. Utopian thought of one form or another can be found in virtually all cultures and all periods. Utopias have varied as to whether they are past or future, realizable or dreamlike, worldly or otherworldly. Historian of religion Mircea Eliade has claimed that premodern societies are characterized by a longing for a return to a mythical time of peace and harmony prior to the beginning of historical time. The Greek poet Hesiod, writing in the 8th century B.C., described a prior Golden Age in his *Works and Days.* In the OT, the story of the Garden of Eden reflects elements of earlier mythological stories that depict an original ideal state of life.

Plato's *Republic,* although not without predecessors, is the earliest extant utopian work that details how social institutions should work. Plato portrays an ideal society governed by communitarian philosopher-kings. Aristotle's *Politics,* in contrast with the *Republic,* is one of the earliest works that can be characterized as anti-utopian. Aristotle argues pragmatically in favor of a workable though imperfect social order based on private ownership. Both the *Republic* and the *Politics* are cornerstones of a long heritage. Although not without exception, utopian literature generally has emphasized idealism, community, egalitarianism, and human potential, whereas anti-utopian literature has stressed realism, individual rights, and human limitations.

The Old and the New Testaments provide a wealth of material for both utopian and anti-utopian mindsets to draw upon. On the one hand, a utopian dimension of the Scriptures is indicated by the communal stress in the Torah, the social critiques of the Prophets, the vision of the messianic age in Daniel, Jesus's preaching of the coming of the Kingdom of God, his warnings to the rich, the egalitarian elements of the early Christian communities evidenced in John, Acts, and Galatians, and the apocalypticism of Revelation.

On the other hand, an anti-utopian dimension in the Scriptures can be found in the pervading theme that the ideal society is not to be found in a final way in this world. In the OT, the creation is followed not long after by the fall from paradise. The people of Israel, despite their acceptance of kings, are never fully convinced that having an earthly ruler is in accordance with God's will. In the NT, Jesus's kingdom is both here and yet not of this world. The kingdom will not be simply the work of human beings building a better world but will be the work of God. Jesus did not propose a programmatic plan for social reconstruction. He counseled those who sought earthly glory instead to lift up their cross and follow him. Jesus's teaching to trust and hope in the Father and to take each day as it comes can also be interpreted as anti-utopian.

Some Christian utopias have reflected the ambivalence of the Scriptures. St. Augustine's *City of God* (426) combines an ideal vision of a humankind bound in peace, truth, and goodness in the love of God, with the recognition that in this world there is a coinciding bondage of a humankind that turns from God toward the love of bodily things. In the 13th century, the work of St. Thomas Aquinas, although it has much to say about the proper political order, is in line with the pragmatic realism of Aristotle rather than the utopian idealism of Plato.

With the Renaissance and the Reformation came a resurfacing of unambiguous utopian elements in Christianity and Western civilization. In the 15th century German philosopher Nicholas of Cusa manifested the Renaissance spirit by envisioning a globally unified and peaceful humankind. Thomas More's *Utopia* (1516) portrays the best possible social state that human beings could construct by their own doings, yet that society is still less than perfect because it lacks Christianity. Sixteenth century radical reformers such as the Anabaptist Thomas Munzer preached the need for a new social order and stirred the peasants of Germany to revolt. The radical branch of the Reformation spawned utopian communities such as the Hutterites and the Mennonites, and similar experimental communities proliferated in the New World.

The 17th century abounded in notable utopian works, most of which showed the influence of Plato and More. In *Christianopolis* (1619) by the Lutheran humanist Johann Valentin Andrea, an ideal Christian city was presented in warm, glowing colors. Social life revolved around the self-governing guilds, and education was universal. Some utopian literature combined the tendency toward the socialist and the egalitarian with a belief in progress through technological advances. One such work was *The City of the Sun* (1623), by Tommaso Campanella, an Italian Dominican friar suspected of heretical views. People of this quaint utopia lived by a combination of Gospel and astrology and were governed by a high priest selected from the better educated. The economic system, as often occurs in utopia, was communistic. Marriages were eugenically arranged by the state. Francis Bacon's fragmentary *The New Atlantis* (1627) is important for its description of Solomon's house, a scientific research institute. James Harrington's *Oceana* (1656) probably had a direct effect on the thinking of American 18th-century statesmen: it advocates a series of political checks and balances to prevent tyranny.

In the 20th century the outstanding utopian writer was perhaps H. G. Wells, notably in *A Modern Utopia* (1905) and *Men Like Gods* (1925). Wells tried harder than most utopians to make room for the individual and for personal quirks, though he could be stern enough about enforcing genetic controls and fostering the common good through reason and science. Wells was an intermittent utopian. Some of his stories were grim tales of hideous societies, e.g., *The Time Machine* (1895) and *The Shape of Things to Come* (1933). As the 20th century advanced, the hopeful mood of the preceding century darkened, and fewer major utopias have been written, though one should mention *Walden Two* (1947) by B. F. Skinner. It pictures a community kept happy and stable by psychological techniques.

In the modern world, utopian literature has often served to criticize what are taken to be advances in modern society. Denis Diderot implicitly satirized European society in his portrait of Tahitians in *The Supplement to Bougainville's Voyage* (1772). Karl Marx and Friedrich Engels in *The Communist Manifesto* (1848) directly critiqued the exploitation and alienation that had arisen in connection with the industrial revolution. Yet communitarian utopianism has throughout been balanced by pragmatic realism. Adam Smith's *An Inquiry into the Nature and Causes of the Wealth of Nations* (1776) is a mainstay of contemporary anti-utopian sentiment. Edward Bellamy's socialist novel *Looking Backward* (1888) won so large a public that Bellamy societies sprang up in Europe and America, yet it was countered by Theodore Hertzka's free-enterprise novel *Freeland* (1890). Works such as Aldous Huxley's *Brave New World* (1932), and George Orwell's *1984* (1949) augur a gruesome future for a humankind that tries to control its destiny through technology and totalitarian government.

The utopian outlook is rooted in the belief that human beings are perfectible, that the world would work properly if only it were arranged in the proper manner. The anti-utopian outlook is crystallized in the saying paraphrased from Voltaire's *Dictionnaire Philosophique* (1764): "Don't make the best the enemy of the good." That is, one should not trade an imperfect but tolerable situation for an intolerable situation by insisting upon unattainable perfection.

Contemporary Discussion. The term "utopian" was brought into the study of religion by the socialist Karl Mannheim in his *Ideology and Utopia* (1936). He used "utopian" to describe thinking that criticizes the existing order and promotes social change, in contrast with "ideological" thinking that serves to legitimate the prevailing social structures. The term was further developed by the Marxist philosopher Ernst Bloch. In *Das*

Prinzip der Hoffnung (1937–48), Bloch distinguished between "abstract" utopias that were unrealizable and "concrete" utopias that were sufficiently possible so as to lead to practical ideas for real social transformation. Theologian Gregory Baum draws upon these thinkers in his call for a "critical theology" that will examine the effect that Christian doctrine has on social practice and thereby foster religion that is "utopian" rather than "ideological."

Political theologians such as Jürgen Moltmann, Wolfhart Pannenberg, and Johannes Baptist Metz have stressed the traditionally utopian theme of the need to engage in the historical process by reforming existing institutions. In order to defend themselves from the appearance of an idealistic utopianism, however, they have relied heavily on a theistic version of Ernst Bloch's category of "hope" to make clear that they are not imposing a prepackaged idea of the future onto the present, but rather are trusting in God's eschatological promises.

Latin American liberation theologians, drawing upon the work of Karl Mannheim, have unabashedly promoted "utopia" as a positive and necessary category for Christian theology. Protestant Rubem Alves interprets third world liberation as a utopian movement extending what was begun in the Reformation. Leonardo Boff defines the "kingdom" taught by Jesus as "the utopia that is realized all over the world, the final good of the whole creation in God, completely liberated from all imperfection and penetrated by the Divine." A pervading theme of Latin American liberation theologians is that the social situation in which they find themselves is not simply imperfect but is humanly intolerable.

Gustavo Gutierrez has clarified the meaning of "utopia" in liberation theology by contrasting it with the idealistic usage of the term. Gutierrez argues in a detailed manner that "utopia" is not impractical but rather receives its verification in praxis, in the active creation of more human living conditions; "utopia" is not unrealistic but rational, accepting the findings of the empirical sciences and working in accordance with them. "Utopia" as used by Gutierrez is a technical category for uniting faith and political action:

> Utopia so understood, far from making the political struggler a dreamer, radicalizes one's commitment and helps one keep one's work from betraying one's purpose—which is to achieve a real encounter among human beings in the midst of a free society without social inequalities.

Contemporary utopian theology is not without its anti-utopian critics. Michael Novak draws upon the heritage of Aristotle and St. Thomas Aquinas in favoring patience and prudential wisdom over idealistic solutions.

Novak distinguishes between two approaches to the theology of political economy: the ''utopian'' and the ''realistic.'' According to Novak, both approaches have ideals, and both are directed to the future. The ''utopian'' approach, however, seeks an imagined social order that has never existed; it ''argues from abstractions about a future that has never been.'' The ''realistic'' approach uses practical judgement to compare what in fact has worked and what has not worked; it is ''concerned with concrete realities, proximate next steps, and comparisons based upon actual existents.'' According to Novak, the blanket condemnation of capitalism by liberation theologians, along with their acceptance of socialist principles, is based upon poor practical judgement concerning what has actually worked in concrete historical reality.

There is a need for utopian theologians and anti-utopian critics to come to terms. Gutierrez uses ''utopia'' in such a way that it is contrary to ''ideology''; Novak uses ''utopia'' as contrary to ''prudential wisdom.'' Gutierrez insists that ''utopia'' is supremely practical; Novak argues that it is impractical as long as it offers nothing but generalities about what the new society will be like. Gutierrez takes the position that thought is either ''utopian'' or it is not open to change; Novak holds that anti-utopian thought is not ideological in that it promotes reasonable and even dynamic change. The word ''utopia'' is used so differently that at this point it may inhibit rather than promote clear discussion.

Karl Rahner argued for a dynamic relationship between ''utopia'' and ''reality'': ''The Christian understanding of existence can be defined as the conviction that what appears as utopian is truly real and that what is called reality must be seen as highly relative and provisional.'' For Rahner, ''utopia'' refers not to the unreal but to whatever we should strive toward; human beings are to reach out to God without leaving so-called reality behind. Christians, therefore, are summoned to work toward ''utopia'' in concrete, practical ways in this world, ''even though attaining it is difficult, uncertain, or even impossible.''

The Christian ambivalence toward ''utopia'' is reflected in contemporary papal and episcopal social teaching. In *Populorum progressio* (1967), Pope Paul VI wrote that ''the Bible teaches us, from the first page on, that the whole of creation is for human beings, that it is our responsibility to develop it by intelligent effort and by means of our labor to perfect it, so to speak, for our use.'' In the same document, however, he cautioned that

> a revolutionary uprising—save where there is manifest, longstanding tyranny which would do great damage to fundamental personal rights and dangerous harm to the common good of the coun-
> try—produces new injustices, throws more elements out of balance, and brings on new disasters. A real evil should not be fought against at the cost of greater misery.

A similar dynamic can be found in the U.S. Catholic bishops pastoral letter, *Economic Justice for All* (1986). The bishops say that ''the life and words of Jesus and the teaching of his Church call us to serve those in need and to work actively for social and economic justice.'' At the same time, though, the bishops point out that

> the quest for economic and social justice will always combine hope and realism. . . . It involves diagnosing those situations that continue to alienate the world from God's creative love as well as presenting hopeful alternatives that arise from living in a new creation. . . . This hope is not a naïve optimism that imagines that simple formulas for creating a fully just society are ready at hand.

The discussion in contemporary theological circles thus reflects the polarity between the utopian and the anti-utopian that can be traced throughout the history of civilization. It seems to be an eternal struggle to strike a proper balance between the fulfillment of human potentiality and the acceptance of human limitations and sinfulness.

Bibliography: G. BAUM, *Religion and Alienation* (New York 1975). M. L. BERNERI, *Journey through Utopia* (Boston 1951). M. BUBER, *Paths in Utopia*, tr. R. F. HULL (New York 1950). J. CAREY, ed., *The Faber Book of Utopias* (London 1999). I. ELLACURIA, ''Utopia and Prophecy in Latin America,'' and J. B. LIBANIO, ''Hope, Utopia, Resurrection'' in *Mysterium Liberationis*, I. ELLACURIA and J. SOBRINO, eds., (New York 1990). R. GERBER, *Utopian Fantasy: A Study of English Utopian Fiction since the End of the Nineteenth Century* (London 1955). G. GUTIERREZ, *A Theology of Liberation* (Maryknoll, N.Y. 1973). O. HERTZLER, *The History of Utopian Thought* (New York 1926). K. MANNHEIM, *Ideologie und Utopie* (Bonn 1929), tr. L. WIRTH and E. SHILS as *Ideology and Utopia* (London 1936). F. E. MANUEL and F. P. MANUEL, *Utopian Thought in the Western World* (Cambridge, Mass. 1979). J. L. MUMFORD, *The Story of Utopias* (Gloucester, Mass. 1959). M. NOVAK, *Freedom with Justice* (San Francisco 1984); *Will It Liberate? Questions about Liberation Theology* (New York 1986). G. NEGLEY and P. J. MAX, eds., *The Quest for Utopia* (New York 1952). K. RAHNER ''Utopia and Reality,'' *Theology Digest* 32 (Summer 1985) 139–144. F. T. RUSSELL, *Touring Utopia: The Realm of Constructive Humanism* (New York 1932). C. WALSH, *From Utopia to Nightmare* (New York 1962).

[D. M. DOYLE/C. WALSH]

UTRAQUISTS

Utraquists are known also as Calixtines. They were a body of Hussites holding that the reception of Holy Communion under both species is indispensable for salvation. They had split into several sects, of whom the TA-

BORITES were the most radical; yet at the Synod of Prague (1418), they proclaimed their continuing membership in the Church, and retained only those beliefs and rituals in accord with the Bible. At the Diet of Prague (1419), the Hussite lords reconfirmed this stand, which was reflected in the *Four Articles of Prague* (July 1420). These *Articles,* containing the substance of Hussite belief, defined the creed of the Utraquists and, at the same time, established a basis for a dialogue with the Church.

Moreover, Konrad of Vechta, Archbishop of Prague, began a policy of compromise by signing an agreement (1421) favoring the *Articles,* a policy followed by the Diet of Čáslav and recommended to the Czech clergy at the general synod in Prague. Such action led to the Basel *Compact* by which the Council of BASEL (1433) recognized the Utraquists as true Christians. Nevertheless, their election of John Rokycana as archbishop of Prague (1435) was not recognized by Rome. Although the Utraquists developed into an independent national church unrecognized by Rome, it was dependent upon Roman bishops for the valid ordination of priests. This unique situation led to harmonious coexistence between the two groups. However, when the Lutherans, called Neo–Utraquists, who infiltrated and seized control of the Utraquist church, ended this tolerance, the Old Utraquists merged with Catholics following the restoration of a Catholic to the See of PRAGUE in 1561.

Bibliography: F. G. HEYMANN, "National Assembly of Čáslav," *Medievalie et humanistica* 8 (1954) 32-55; "John Rokycana: Church Reformer Between Hus and Luther," *Church History* 28 (1959) 240-280. L. NEMEC, *Church and State in Czechoslovakia* (New York 1955). F. SEIBT, "Communitas . . . Hegemonialpolitik hellip; hussitischen Revolution," *Historisches Jahrbuch der Görres–Gesellschaft* 81 (Munich 1962) 80-100.

[L. NEMEC]

UTRECHT, SCHISM OF

Arose early in the 18th century over the deposition of Pieter CODDE as vicar apostolic of Utrecht (1686–1704) because of his reputed JANSENISM. For a century previous to this the NETHERLANDS had shown a marked affinity to the theocentrism of BÉRULLE and the rigorism of PORT-ROYAL. Jansenism influenced the secular clergy especially through the Dutch College at Louvain, whose first rector was Cornelius JANSEN. The most prominent representative of this tendency was Johannes van NEERCASSEL, Vicar Apostolic of Utrecht (1663-86) and friend of ARNAULD, but also loyal to Rome. A far more important influence was the episcopalism of the Louvain canonist Van ESPEN. Both these tendencies, found mostly among the secular clergy, embittered rela-

tions between seculars and regulars, especially the JESUITS. Codde was not an impressive personality, and was strongly influenced by refugee Jansenists and Benedictines from France and by persons hostile to the Jesuits, all of whom he permitted to engage in pastoral work. In 1699 he was summoned to Rome to explain charges that he had taught Jansenistic doctrines and harbored such French Jansenists as QUESNEL and GERBERON. A commission of cardinals studied his case and decided to counteract Jansenistic tendencies among the Dutch clergy by requiring them to sign the formulary of ALEXANDER VII. When Codde refused, he was suspended (1702) and then dismissed as vicar apostolic (1704). The great majority of the secular and regular clergy sided with Codde. Led by J. C. van Erkel, one of Codde's provicars, and supported by the Protestant government, they refused to accept the new vicar apostolic of Utrecht, Theodorus de Cock.

Despite excommunication from Rome the rebellious clergy of the vicariate took Van Espen's advice and appointed, as archbishop of Utrecht, Cornelius Steenoven, who in 1724 was consecrated by a suspended French missionary bishop, Dominique Varlet. Juridical Jansenism, as distinct from preexisting theological and moral Jansenism, arose at this time with the formation of the Rooms-Katholieke Kerk der Oud-Bisschoppelijke Clerezie (OBC) as a schismatic church, which still exists; it then had 51 parishes, 47 Dutch priests, and 51 "appellant" priests from Belgium and France. Bishops were appointed also at Haarlem (1742) and Deventer (1758), and a seminary was started at Amersfoort (1724). During the remainder of the 18th century efforts continued to be made to reunite with Rome; but they were frustrated chiefly by divergent views concerning ecclesiastical law. At the Council of Utrecht (1763) the Little Church of Utrecht, as it came to be known popularly, rejected the extreme Jansenist teachings, and showed itself substantially one in doctrine with the Roman Church. Deep doctrinal cleavage appeared only in 1854 when Pius IX solemnly defined the dogma of the IMMACULATE CONCEPTION; it widened when VATICAN COUNCIL I defined papal primacy and infallibility (1870). Waning fervor led to a decline in the OBC after 1763.

The Church of Utrecht attracted other schismatic groups. Thus the PETITE ÉGLISE asked it for priests after 1832. In 1873 Bp. Herman Heykamp consecrated J. H. Reinkens, thereby supplying a bishop to the OLD CATHOLICS. The OBC was vigorous in its opposition to the restoration of the Dutch Catholic hierarchy (1853). Old Catholic influence induced the Utrecht group to enter into closer relations with Protestant churches after 1870.

Bibliography: L. J. ROGIER, *Geschiedenis van het katholicisme in Noord-Nederland,* 3 v. (Amsterdam 1945-47) v.2; *Henrie*

Grégoire en de Katholieken van Nederland (Hilversum 1964). B. VAN BILSEN, *Het schisma van Utrecht* (Utrecht 1949). J. Carreyre, *Dictionnaire de théologie catholique,* ed. A. VACANT, 15 v. (Paris 1903–50; Tables générales 1951–) 15.2:2390-2446. P. J. F. M. HARKX, *De oudbisschoppelijke cleresie en Rome: Contacten en vredespagingen, 1733-1749* (Helmond 1963).

[A. G. WEILER]

UTTO, BL.

Benedictine abbot also known as Otto, Othon, Odon; d. *c.* 800. He was baptized and reared by (Bl.) Gamelbert, priest(?) and lord of Michaelsbuch. Some time before 772 Utto founded the monastery of METTEN just north of Deggendorf in Lower Bavaria, on Gamelbert's property. Utto had possibly been a monk at REICHENAU, near Constance, for his first monks at Metten came from there. Legend says that Utto had a chance encounter with Charlemagne in the wood of Metten; Pope Leo III is supposed to have sent him an ivory crozier. His cult was authorized Aug. 25, 1909. The oldest likeness of him is in a pontifical (*c.* 1070) of Bl. GUNDECAR of Eichstätt. The figure on Utto's tomb in the abbey church is from the 14th century.

Feast: Oct. 3.

Bibliography: *Acta Sanctorum* Oct. 2:207-214. VITA GAMEL-BERTI, *Momumenta Germaniae Historica,* (Berlin 1826–), "Sriptores rerum Merovingicarum" 7.1:183-191. B. PONSCHAB, *Die heiligen Utto und Gamelbert* (Metten 1910). W. FINK, *Entwicklungsgeschichte der Benedictinerabtei Metten,* 3 v. (Munich 1926-30) 1:9-87; 2:9-24. J. BRAUN, *Tracht und Attribute der Heiligen in der deutschen Kunst* (Stuttgart 1943) 710-711.

[W. E. WILKIE]

V

VACANT, ALFRED

Theologian; b. Morfontaine, France Feb. 23, 1852; d. Nancy, April 2, 1901. He did his classical and philosophical studies at the minor and major seminary at Metz and studied theology at Saint Sulpice in Paris. He was ordained June 10, 1876, and received his licentiate in theology in 1879. He taught apologetics and dogmatic theology at the seminary in Nancy. Vacant wrote numerous scholarly articles on philosophy and contributed to Jaugey's *Dictionnaire apologétique*. He became well known for an important work, *Etudes théologiques sur les constitutions du Concile du Vatican d'après les Acres du Concile,* 2 v. (Paris 1895). He knew how to determine the sense of the apostolic constitution *Dei Filius* without exaggerating or minimizing the meaning of the text. Remaining above polemics, so frequent at the time, he exposed facts and ideas with exactness. He was one of the promoters in France of the historical method in theological studies. Most important of all, he was the founder and first director of the *Dictionnaire de Théologie Catholique.*

Bibliography: E. AMANN, *Dictionnaire de théologie catholique,* ed. A. VACANT et al., 15 v. (Paris 1903–50) 15.2447–62.

[J. DE VAULX]

VACARIUS

Glossator of Roman law, known as Master Vacarius; b. Lombardy *c.* 1115–1120; d. England, after 1198. Trained as a civilian at BOLOGNA, Vacarius came to England (between 1139 and 1145), invited to join the household of Abp. THEOBALD OF CANTERBURY. As a member of this distinguished *familia,* he was probably a cleric in minor orders. To him England owes the introduction into its schools of formal training in Roman law. His lectures, beginning in 1149, probably at OXFORD, would seem to push back the origin of that *studium generale* beyond the traditional 1167. He lectured also at Northampton. Tem-

porarily under a cloud during the reign of King STEPHEN, he entered the service of ROGER DE PONT L'ÉVÊQUE, Archbishop of YORK (1159), by whom he was made canon of Southwell and prebendary of Norwell before 1167. He seems to have been of the party, represented by Roger, opposed to the policies of THOMAS BECKET. During this controversy he served as Roger's agent to the papal court and later acted repeatedly as papal judge delegate. His bitter attack on GRATIAN, his lack of interest in canonistic science, and possibly also his adherence to the anti-Becket group suggest that Vacarius neither lectured on canon law nor was responsible for the introduction of the canonistic traditions of Bologna into England. His writings on law and juristic theology are the following: *Liber pauperum* (*c.* 1149); *Summa de matrimonio* (*c.* 1157-59); *De assumpto homine; Liber contra multiplices et varios errores* (1177).

Bibliography: T. E. HOLLAND, *The Dictionary of National Biography from the Earliest Times to 1900,* 20:80–81. F. DE ZULUETA, ed., *Liber pauperum of Vacarius* (Selden Society 44; London 1927). ILARINO DA MILANO, *L'eresia di Ugo Speroni nella confutazione del maestro Vacario* (Studi e Testi 115; 1945). J. DE GHELLINCK, "Magister Vacarius: Un juriste théologien peu aimable pour les canonistes," *Revue d'histoire ecclésiastique* 44 (1949) 173–178. S. KUTTNER and E. RATHBONE, "Anglo-Norman Canonists of the 12th Century," *Traditio* 7 (1949–51) 279–358. A. B. EMDEN, *A Biographical Register of the Scholars of the University of Oxford to A.D. 1500* 3:1939.

[O. J. BLUM]

VAGNOZZI, EGIDIO

Papal diplomat; b. Rome, Feb. 2, 1906; d. Dec. 26, 1986. Educated at the Lateran Pontifical Seminary, he obtained doctorates in philosophy, theology, and canon law from the Roman Seminary. He was ordained to the priesthood with a dispensation from age on Dec. 22, 1928, by Raffaele Cardinal Merry del Val. Following a period in the Vatican Secretariate of State (1930–32) he served in Washington, D.C., on the staff of the Apostolic Delegate as secretary (1932–35) and auditor (1935–42). Raised to the rank of counselor, he served on the staff of the Apostolic Nunciatures in Lisbon (1942–45) and later in Paris (1945–47), during the time that Archbishop Angelo Giuseppe Roncalli (later Pope John XXIII) was papal nuncio. In 1948, he was assigned to the Apostolic Delgation in India (1948–49).

Named a papal chamberlain in 1932 and a domestic prelate in 1945, Monsignor Vagnozzi was elevated to the titular archbishopric of Myra on March 14, 1949, and was consecrated on May 22 in the church of Santa Maria sopra Minerva. Archbishop Vagnozzi served as apostolic delegate in Manila (1949–51) and became the first papal nuncio to the Philippines (1951–58). Transferred to the United States, he was appointed seventh apostolic delegate in December 1958, by Pope John XXIII, a post he retained until May 1967, when Pope Paul VI created him Cardinal Deacon of San Giuseppe al Trionfale.

Cardinal Vagnozzi was a member of the Congregation for the Bishops and for Extraordinary Ecclesiastical Affairs. He was named Prefect of Economic Affairs of the Vatican in 1968, a position he retained until his death at the age of 75.

See Also: NUNCIO, APOSTOLIC.

[N. HALLIGAN]

VAINGLORY

Vainglory is the sin or vice of one who immoderately desires renown, prestige, or the praise and respect of others. The desire of these things is not necessarily sinful, but becomes so when it is immoderate and disordered. It is vitiated by immoderateness when glory is sought in wrong objects, from the wrong people, or in a wrong manner: in wrong objects, for example, when renown and esteem are desired for a perfection one does not truly possess or is not worthy of esteem; from the wrong people, when one glories in the esteem of those whose judgment is perverse or of little value; or in a wrong manner, when the glory is desired on its own account, as an end in itself, rather than as a means to a suitable goal such as the honor of God or the welfare of neighbor. When immoderate for one or another such reason, the desire is vain, or foolish.

The sinfulness of vainglory is clear from the Scriptures (e.g., Mt 6.1; 1 Cor 4.7; Phil 2.3) and from the constant teaching of the Fathers of the Church and theologians. It is directly opposed to the virtue of MAGNANIMITY, the potential part of FORTITUDE that prompts one to works worthy of honor and glory. Thus magnanimity should moderate or govern the desire for glory, and vainglory is directly opposed to this virtue. Of itself

vainglory is not mortally sinful, although in certain circumstances it can become such. One would, for example, sin seriously if he were to seek renown for a deed that was gravely sinful or if he were to prefer his glory to the commands of God or the good of his neighbor.

Vainglory is related to many other sins and vices. Some authors classify it as one of the sins that come from pride, a "daughter" of pride. Others, such as John Cassian and St. John Damascene, consider it an eighth capital sin. St. Thomas Aquinas, following St. Gregory the Great, thought that pride, because of its universal influence, transcended the category of capital sins, and in its place put vainglory as one of the seven sins that can most properly be classified as capital. The chief "daughters" of vainglory according to SS. Thomas and Gregory, are disobedience, boasting, hypocrisy, contention, stubbornness, and an inordinate love of novelty.

See Also: DEADLY SINS.

Bibliography: GREGORY I (the Great), *Moral,* 31.45.87–89, in *Patrologia Latina,* ed. J. P. MIGNE, 217 v., indexes 4 v. (Paris 1878–90) 76:620–622. THOMAS AQUINAS, *Summa theologiae,* 2a2ae, 132; *De malo* 9.1. FRANCIS DE SALES, *Introduction to the Devout Life,* 3.4,7. A. MICHEL, *Dictionnaire de théologie catholique,* ed. A. VACANT et al., 15 v. (Paris 1903–50; Tables générales 1951–) 6.2:1429–32.

[R. HENNESSEY]

VAISHNAVISM

A religious movement centered on the worship of Vishnu as the supreme God. It developed in India in the early centuries before Christ. Its characteristic is devotion (*bhakti*) to a personal God who manifests his love by his descent (*avatāra*) to save man. The *Bhagavad Gītā* is the classical expression of its doctrine and devotion. The cult was developed especially in South India from A.D. 500 to 1000 by poets known as *Ālvārs.* Its doctrine was developed by a number of masters of the *Vedānta,* from Rāmānuja in the 11th century to Vallabha in the 15th century. Its followers are now found all over India and are distinguished by the vertical lines in red or white that they paint on their foreheads.

Bibliography: W. CROOKE and J. HASTINGS, eds., *Encyclopedia of Religion & Ethics,* 13 v. (Edinburgh 1908–27) 12:570–572. *See* bibliography for HINDUISM.

[B. GRIFFITHS]

VAJRAYĀNA (DIAMOND VEHICLE)

The yoga, Śivaism, and polytheism of Pātañjali (*c.* 200 B.C.), systematized into tantric Buddhism by Asaṅga

(c. A.D. 500) and other Indian masters. It was introduced into China in 716 by Śubhakara (636–735) as a cult of a pantheon of patrons who were to be propitiated by spells. It was popularized by Vajrabodhi (671–741), developed by Amoghavajra (704–774), along with Samantabhadra's esoterism and the *Ullambana* (All Souls Suffrage, of Christian inspiration), and finally brought to Japan by Kūkai in 806.

The diamond element of the universe (*vajra*) is the wisdom of Vairocana (Great Sun) in its indestructibility and activity. It leads one to instant Buddhahood and wonderworking by spells (*dhāranī*), incantations (*mantra*), hand-poses as described in the esoteric scriptures (*tantra*), and meditation, and by the eightfold power to make one's body lighter, heavier, smaller, or larger than anything in the world, and to reach any place, take any shape, control any natural law, and make everything depend on one's will.

The Right Hand Vajrayāna was devoted to masculine divinities and strict asceticism, while the Left Hand Vajrayāna worshipped the wives of buddhas and bodhisattvas as female saviors (*tārā*), personifying the active aspects of their consorts. The initiated met secretly at night to recite spells and practice sexual promiscuity, to symbolize and effect the union of the phenomenal Means (*upāya*) with the noumenal Wisdom (*prajñā*) according to the philosophical doctrines of the Vijñānavāda and Mādhyamika schools.

Bibliography: Y. CHOU, ''Tantrism in China,'' *Harvard Journal of Asiatic Studies* 8 (1945) 241–332. S. DASGUPTA, *An Introduction to Tantric Buddhism* (2d ed. Calcutta 1958). R. TAJIMA, *Les deux grands mandalas et la doctrine de l'esotérisme Shingon* (Paris 1959). E. CONZE, *The Prajñāpāramitā Literature* (The Hague 1960). G. TUCCI, *The Theory and Practice of the Maṇḍala with Special Reference to the Modern Psychology of the Subconscious* (London 1961). G. E. CAIRNS, ''The Philosophy and Psychology of the Oriental Maṇḍala,'' *Philosophy East and West* 11 (1962) 219–229. A. WAYMAN, ''Buddhist Genesis and the Tantric Tradition,'' *Oriens Extremus* 9 (1962) 127–131. J. CHRISTIAN, ''Bouddhisme et Tantrisme,'' *France-Asie* N.S. 18 (1962) 314–319.

[A. S. ROSSO]

VAL-DES-ECOLIERS, MONASTERY OF

Or Grand Val, former monastery of CANONS REGULAR OF ST. AUGUSTINE, in Verbiesles, near Chaumont-en-Bassigny (Haute-Marne), France, Diocese of Langres. About 1200, the valley attracted an eminent doctor of the University of Paris, William the Englishman, and three colleagues anxious to flee the world. In 1212 Bp. William of Joinville granted them the property they occupied, and in 1215 officially approved their foundation. Meanwhile, others from the University of Paris had joined the founders who were living according to the Rule of St. AUGUSTINE, and whose constitutions had been inspired by the Abbey of SAINT-VICTOR. The monastery was consecrated to Our Lady and took the name of Val-des-Ecoliers (Latin, *Vallis scholarium*). In 1219 Pope Honorius III sanctioned the new order. Prodigious development forced it to expand and found other houses. The Val, as motherhouse, had as many as 22 daughter houses under its authority, and in 1469, was exempted from episcopal jurisdiction by Rome. It remained a PRIORY, however, until 1539 when Pope Paul III raised it to an ABBEY. The number and quality of its recruits allowed the abbey to retain a high level of spiritual and intellectual life; its members included important masters of the University of Paris. But with COMMENDATION came a period of decline, and in 1636, Abbot Laurent Michel, after trying in vain to reform his order, united it to the congregation of SAINTE-GENEVIÉVE. The abbey, which shortly after its foundation had moved two kilometers from its initial location, and which had suffered much during the 16th- and 17th-century wars, was rebuilt on a monumental scale; it included an outstanding library. It was almost totally destroyed during the French Revolution, and the remaining buildings are now part of a private home where General Pershing was headquartered during World War I.

Bibliography: *Gallia Christiana,* v.1–13 (Paris 1715–85), v.14–16 (Paris 1856–65) 4:777–795. C. F. ROUSSEL, *Le Diocèse de Langres,* 4 v. (Langres 1873-79) 2:114–117, list of priors and abbots. P. GLORIEUX, *Répertoire des maîtres en théologie de Paris au XIII siècle* (Paris 1933–34); 1:321; 2:275–281. J. LAURENT and F. CLAUDON, *Diocèses de Langres et de Dijon* (Archives de la France monastique 45; Liguge-Paris 1941) 386–391.

[J. C. DIDIER]

VALADÉS, DIEGO

Franciscan missionary, author, and artist; b. Mexico, 1533; d. Perugia?, 1579? He was the son of a conquistador and a Tlaxacaltec and thus one of the first mestizos in Mexico. When still very young, he entered the Franciscan Order and studied with Fray Pedro de Gante. He spoke several native languages, such as Nahuatl, Tarasco, and Otomí. In 1574, while in Seville, Spain, he published Juan Focher's *Itinerarium catholicum;* in 1579 in Perugia he published his own *Retórica christiana,* important as the first book published in Europe by a Mexican and for its introduction of the native Mexican culture. The *Retórica* has 26 illustrations, which provide some authentic details, such as the ornaments worn by the natives, their costumes (or nakedness), the reconstruction of temples, and their sacrificial ceremonies. However, many of the details are not authentic, and in some pictures the native Mexicans look more like Europeans. Valadés must also be considered a historian for having collected in his works many facts and observations at a time when very few histories had been written and published. He was one of the first to write a short treatise, as a chapter in the *Retórica,* on *Indorum republicae descriptio;* he described the work of the early friars and the spreading of the gospel. In 1587 Valentín Friccio, a German, translated portions of this treatise and incorporated the material in *Indianischer Religionstandt der gantzen Newen Welt.*

Bibliography: E. J. PALOMERA, *Fray Diego Valadés: El hombre y su época* (Mexico City 1963); *Fray Diego Valadés, O.F.M., evangelizador humanista de la Nueva España: Su obra* (Mexico City 1962). F. DE LA MEZA, *Fray Diego Valadés, escritor y grabador franciscano del siglo XVI* (Mexico City 1943).

[F. DE LA MAZA]

VALAMO, ABBEY OF

In Russian, *Valaam,* former Greek-Orthodox monastery on the Valamo islands in Lake Ladoga, in Karelia, a republic of Russia. It was founded by the holy hermits Sergios and Germanos and dedicated to the Transfiguration of Christ. According to legend the founders were supposed to have come from Athos in 1329. The monastery became a starting point for the missionary work in Novgorod Karelia. It was dissolved when Ladoga-Karelia was united with Sweden in 1618. In 1718 it was reestablished by Peter the Great and soon became a place of pilgrimage for the whole of northeastern Russia. After 1918 it was placed under the autonomous Greek Orthodox Church of Finland; but when the area was transferred to Russia after the Finnish Winter War (1940), the monks moved to Heinävesi in Finnish Karelia, where they are now living together with the displaced communities from Konevits and Petsamo. Before 1914 there were more than 400 monks, but their numbers have since diminished. The liturgical language of Valamo is Church Slavonic, and since 1926 the calendar has been Gregorian.

Bibliography: L. I. DENISOV, *Pravoslavnye monastyri rossijskoje imperii* (Moscow 1909). A. CHERAVIN, in *The Christian East* 8 (1927) 69–77. A. M. AMMANN, *Stimmen der Zeit* 132 (1936–37) 41–48. H. KIRKINEN, *Karjala idän kultuuripiirissä* (Helsinki 1963).

[J. GALLÉN]

VALDÉS, FERNANDO DE

Spanish archbishop and inquisitor general; b. Salas, Asturias, 1483; d. Madrid, Dec. 9, 1568. In 1512 he graduated from the Colegio de San Bartolomé de Cuenca in Salamanca, where he later served as professor of canon law. He soon became associated with the Spanish INQUISITION and was appointed dean of the cathedral of Oviedo. After serving on a mission to Portugal for Charles V he held successively the bishoprics of Huelva (1524), Orense (1529), Oviedo (1533), and Siqüenza (1539). In 1546 he was appointed archbishop of Seville and inquisitor general. He also held the title of president of the Royal Council of the Inquisition. His famous dispute with Bartolomé de CARRANZA, archbishop of Toledo, led to Carranza's arrest and trial on charges of heresy. Valdés was known for supporting marriage between Christians and Muslims. As inquisitor general he diligently promoted the work of the Inquisition. In 1558 a raid under his auspices resulted in the capture of the principal leaders of the Protestant movement. In 1561 he wrote *Instructions to the Holy Office,* which was published posthumously in 1612. In 1566 he was relieved of his role as inquisitor by Pius V.

Bibliography: M. MENÉNDEZ Y PELAYO, *Historia de los heterodoxos españoles,* 7 v. (2d ed. Madrid 1911–32) 5:1–73. *Enciclopedia de la Religión Católica,* ed. R. D. FERRERES et al., 7 v. (Barcelona 1950–56) 7:511.

[W. J. STEINER]

VALDÉS, JUAN DE

Humanist, religious leader, and theologian; b. Cuenca, Spain, 1490?; d. Naples, Italy, 1541. He was the son of a distinguished family of public servants. His elder brother, Alfonso de Valdés, became secretary for Latin letters to the Emperor Charles V. Juan belonged for some time to the household of Diego López Pacheco, Marqués de Villena, well known for his Erasmian and Alumbrado sympathies [*see* ALUMBRADOS (ILLUMINATI)]. Later he was a student at the new University of Alcalá de Henares, center of humanistic learning, where he probably learned his Greek and Hebrew. When the publication without his name of the *Diálogo de doctrina cristiana* (Alcalá 1529) provoked strong reactions for its Erasmian tendencies, he moved to Italy, spending his last years at Naples. He died there without ever being condemned by the Church. His contemporaries testify to his gentleness, distinguished manners, and irresistible charm.

Juan de Valdés never intended to start a religious movement, and the attempts to make him a Lutheran or an orthodox Catholic failed. However, he found himself the center and inspirer of a devoted group of followers, churchmen and aristocrats, who considered him as their spiritual leader. The most prominent was Giulia Gonzaga, for whom several of his writings were intended, particularly *Alfabeto cristiano* published posthumously in

Italian (1545) and the first nonrabbinical version in Spanish of the Book of Psalms. Other famous members of the cenacle of Valdés's friends in Naples were Bernardino OCHINO, PETER MARTYR VERMIGLI, Celio Secundo Curione, and the poet Marcantonio Flaminio, who translated into Italian the *Alfabeto* and possibly Valdés's main doctrinal work, *Le cento e dieci considerazioni. . .* (Basilea 1550). From this translation others in French and Dutch were made in the 16th century. The English, by Nicholas Ferrar of Little Gidding, was published in Oxford in 1638. Juan de Valdés wrote several shorter treatises and letters and translated and commented on the Gospel of St. Matthew and the Epistles of St. Paul to the Romans, and first Corinthians. The last two were published by Juan de Pineda in Switzerland from 1556 to 1557. In his writings three main influences can be detected: the Erasmian, already mentioned in connection with his *Diálogo de doctrina;* that of the Italian Renaissance, shown particularly in his well-known *Diálogo de la lengua;* and third, the extreme mystical trend of the Spanish Alumbrados. Erasmian influences can be found in his tendency to go back to the sources of Christianity; his evangelism and Paulinism; the spiritual interpretation of the Credo, Commandments, and Sacraments, as well as his belief in justification by faith. His Alumbrado tendencies were accentuated in his Italian period when he stressed his belief in personal inspiration and illumination as the sources of knowledge and action. He believed that the spiritual life should be strengthened by inward discipline rather than manifested by outward forms. The spiritual church is formed by those who are incorporated to the Mystical Body of Christ. Valdés' religion was more affective and volitive than intellectual. His strong sense of dependence upon the *Benefice of Christ* (1543), the title of a well-known book embodying his doctrine, makes his religion optimistic and euphoric.

Bibliography: J. C. NIETO, ed., *Juan de Valdes, Two Catechisms: "Dialogue on Christian Doctrine" and the "Christian Instruction for Children,"* trans. W. B. JONES and C. B. JONES (Lawrence, Ks. 1981). B. B. WIFFEN, *Life and Writings of Juan de Valdés. . .* (London 1865). E. BOEHMER, "Cenni biografici sui fratelli Giovanni e Alfonso Valdesso" in the Appendix to *Le cento e dieci divine considerazioni* (Halle 1860). M. MENÉNDEZ Y PELAYO, *Historia de los heterodoxos españoles,* 7 v. (2d ed. Madrid 1911–32), v.4 *passim.* E. CIONE, *Juan de Valdés, la sua vita e il suo pensiero religioso, con una completa bibliografia delle opere del Valdés e degli altri scritti intorno a lui* (Bari 1938). DOMINGO DE SANTA TERESA, *Juan de Valdés, su pensamiento religioso* (*Analecta Gregoriana* 85; Rome 1957), with bibliog. D. RICART, *Juan de Valdés y el pensamiento religioso europeo en los siglos XVI y XVII* (Mexico City 1958). R. KONETZKE, *Die Religion in Geschichte und Gegenwart,* 7 v. (3d ed. Tübingen 1957–65), 6:1224.

[D. RICART]

VALDIVIA, LUIS DE

Defender of the Araucanian people; b. Granada, Spain, 1561; d. Valladolid, Nov. 5, 1642. He became a Jesuit novice on April 2, 1581. He went to Peru in 1589 and taught philosophy and theology at Lima, where he was master of novices. In 1593 he was sent to Chile, where he was rector at Santiago the following year, and in 1597 he traveled through the Araucanian territory. In Lima, around 1602, he expounded his dual pacifist thesis: abolition of native personal service and reduction of the Araucanian war to a purely defensive one. Valdivia went personally to Araucanian territory, but failed in his peace efforts. In 1609 he returned to Spain and pleaded his ideas at court. As a result he was given religious jurisdiction in Arauco and, nominally, the bishopric of La Imperial. In 1612, named visitor general of Chile, he went to Arauco and assumed the direction of the war, but once again he failed. He returned to Spain in 1620. Upon the death of Philip III (1621), Valdivia had to retire to Valladolid. This powerful personality was also a distinguished linguist as demonstrated in his grammar, dictionary, catechism, and confessional in the Allentiac (Araucanian) language. Although an intrepid and zealous missionary, he was often imprudent and unrealistic, and would compromise the ecclesiastical cause in exchange for small temporary advantages.

Bibliography: P. HERNÁNDEZ, *El Padre Luis de Valdivia* (Santiago de Chile 1908). B. BLUM, "Luis de Valdivia, Defender of the Araucanians," *Mid-America* 24 (1942) 109–137.

[A. DE EGAÑA]

VALDIVIESO, RAFAEL VALENTÍN

Archbishop of Santiago, strong opponent of regalism in Chile; b. Santiago, Nov. 2, 1804; d. there, June 8, 1878. As the son of Manuel Joaquín de Valdivieso y Maciel and María Mercedes Zañartu, he witnessed during his youth the changing fortunes of the independence movement. He obtained the title of lawyer in 1825. In 1833, after performing some spiritual exercises, he decided to become a priest; he was ordained the following year. In the summer of 1835–36 he gave missions for four months in the archipelago of Chiloé and later (1841) in the province of Atacama. For several years he gave his efficient cooperation to the work of the kindly Archbishop VICUÑA LARRAÍN. In 1843 he was selected the first dean of theology in the University of Chile and director of the recently founded *Revista Católica.* As an energetic man with executive ability, he was archbishop of Santiago from 1845 on, organizing the see and defending the prerogatives of the church against the regalist state. This struggle assumed importance after the expulsion of a sacristan

(1856), who was defended by the *cabildo*, which gave two canons the opportunity to appeal to the Supreme Court of Justice. The court's verdict was against the archbishop, who began preparations for exile. A tremendous disturbance followed. Fortunately, as a result of pressure exerted by Joaquín Tocornal, the canons withdrew, but the struggle continued. In defense of the church, the archbishop established the St. Thomas of Canterbury Society. Valdivieso participated in the Vatican Council of 1870. He founded the seminaries of Talca and Valparaíso. Through a papal delegation, he intervened, with a firm and not always reliable hand, in the reform of the old religious orders.

Bibliography: R. VERGARA ANTÚNEZ, *Vide y obras del . . . Rafael Valentín Valdivieso* 2 v. (Santiago de Chile 1886–1906). C. ERRÁZURIZ, *Algo de lo que he visto* (Santiago de Chile 1934).

[A. M. ESCUDERO]

VALENCE, COUNCILS OF

Several notable Church assemblies were held at Valence, in southeastern France on the Rhone River. (1) In 374 an assembly of 22 bishops from Gaul approved four surviving disciplinary canons regulating the ordination of digamists (*see* DIGAMY), the penance of idolatrous and rebaptized Christians, and clerics who sought to be unfrocked under false pretenses. A conciliar letter covering the case that occasioned the last canon also has been preserved. (2) Suspicious of the doctrine of grace taught by CAESARIUS OF ARLES against Pelagianism (*see* PELAGIUS AND PELAGIANISM) and SEMI-PELAGIANISM, the bishops of Gaul summoned Caesarius to account at Valence *c.* 530. Pleading ill health, the saint did not appear but sent representatives and a written statement of his position; how these were received the sole source omits to tell, stating only that Pope BONIFACE II eventually confirmed Caesarius's position. It is uncertain how these events are related to the better-known Council of Orange (529); Valence may have occurred before or after it. (3) Shortly after HINCMAR OF REIMS' four propositions of QUIERCY (853) were condemned by Abp. REMIGIUS OF LYONS (854), the metropolitans of Lyons, Vienne, and Arles met at Valence to investigate certain charges against the bishop of that place. Once assembled in council, they promulgated 23 canons, the first six of which expounded the doctrine of Remigius, who was presiding. Pope NICHOLAS I may have approved these six anti-Hincmar canons; centuries later, the Jansenists (*see* JANSENISM) insisted that he did.

Bibliography: J. D. MANSI, *Sacrorum Conciliorum nova et amplissima collectio,* 31 v. (Florence-Venice 1757–98); reprinted and continued by L. PETIT and J. B. MARTIN, 53 v. in 60 (Paris 1889–1927; repr. Graz 1960–) 3:491–493; 8:723–726; 15:1–16. C. J. VON HEFELE, *Histoire des conciles d'après les documents originaux,* tr. and continued by H. LECLERCQ, 10 v. in 19 (Paris 1907–38) 1:982; 2:1108–10; 4:204–210, 1326, 1390–98. C. H. TURNER, ed., *Ecclesiae occidentalis monumenta iuris antiquissima. Canonum et conciliorum Graecorum interpretationes Latinae* (Oxford 1899–1939) 1:417–423 (for 374). *Vita s. Caesarii episcopi,* bk. 1, ch. 5, par. 46 in *Patrologia Latina,* 67:1023 (for *c.* 530).

[R. KAY]

VALENCIA, MARTÍN DE

Franciscan missionary, leader of the "Twelve Apostles of Mexico"; b. Valencia de Don Juan, near León, Spain, *c.* 1473; d. near Tlalmanalco, Mexico, March 21, 1534.

Although originally he joined the Franciscan Province of Santiago, Valencia was later attracted by the austere reform being fostered by Juan de Guadalupe in the Portuguese Province of La Piedad, and he transferred to that province. After the reformer's death in 1505, the friars from Santiago asked him to return, offering a separate house for the members of the reform; later six more houses joined the reform. In 1516 these were united with four Extremaduran houses of the Province of La Piedad to form the Custody of San Gabriel. On Aug. 14, 1520, the custody was made an independent province, and Valencia was elected its first provincial.

The Franciscan Minister General, Francisco de los Angeles QUIÑONES, commanded him to lead a select group of friars from his province to Mexico as the first formal Franciscan mission there. On Jan. 25, 1524, he sailed with eleven companions from Sanlucar de Barrameda. This group, known as the "Twelve Apostles of Mexico," arrived in Veracruz on May 12, 1524. In Mexico City on July 2, 1524, they organized their custody and elected Valencia as *custos*. By royal and papal appointment, he was now head of the infant Church in Mexico.

Valencia was of a retiring nature and in poor health, and he let other friars handle conflicts with the civil authorities. In the chapter of 1527 he was appointed guardian of Tlaxcala, where he built a friary called Madre de Dios. He was never able to master the native languages and instructed the indigenous people through interpreters. In January 1533 he led seven friars to Tehuantepec, intending to sail to new mission lands in the Far East. The expedition was unable to depart, and in July he returned to Mexico City for the election of a new *custos*. He then retired to Tlalmanalco.

Bibliography: T. MOTOLINÍA, *History of the Indians of New Spain,* tr. and ed. F. B. STECK (Washington 1951). S. ESCALANTE PLANCARTE, *Fray Martin de Valencia* (Mexico City 1945).

[F. B. WARREN]

VALENCIENNES, MARTYRS OF

A group of 11 beatified Ursuline sisters martyred during the FRENCH REVOLUTION. After the Ursuline convent in Valenciennes, northern France, was suppressed (September 1792), the community moved to the Ursuline house in Mons, Belgium, where it dwelt under Mother Clotilde Joseph de St. Borgia Poillot as superior. When the Austrian army occupied Valenciennes (1793), the sisters returned there and carried on their educational work, even after the Revolutionary forces recaptured the city (1794). Citizen Lacoste's commission discovered them in September and charged them with violating the law that decreed the death penalty for returned émigrés. Five sisters went on trial (Oct. 17, 1794), admitted their purpose in coming back to their homeland was to resume teaching the Catholic faith, and were sent to the guillotine the same day singing the Psalm *Miserere.* They were Mother Marie Natalie Joseph de St. Louis Vanot, Laurentine Joseph Reine de St. Stanislas Prin, Ursula Joseph de St. Bernardine Bourla, Louise Joseph de St. Francois Ducrez, Augustine Joseph du Sacré-Coeur de Jésus Dejardin. Six days later the superior, Mother Clotilde, suffered the same fate, with five companions: Scholastique Joseph de St. Jacques Leroux and her natural sister Anne Josephine Leroux, until recently a Poor Clare; two former Bridgettines Lievina Lecroix and Anne Marie Erraux; and the lay sister Cordule Joseph de St. Dominique Barré, who climbed into the tumbril carrying the others to execution in the market place after the commissioners overlooked her. The six went to death chanting the Ambrosian hymn and the Litany of the Blessed Virgin. Together with the martyrs of ARRAS they were beatified on June 13, 1920.

Feast: Oct. 17.

Bibliography: J. LORIDAN, *Les Bienheureuses Ursulines de Valenciennes* (2d ed. Paris 1920). A. BUTLER, *The Lives of the Saints,* ed. H. THURSTON and D. ATTWATER, 4 v. (New York 1956) 4:141–142. J. L. BAUDOT and L. CHAUSSIN, *Vies des saints et des bienheueux selon l'ordre du calendrier avec l'historique des fêtes,* ed. by The Benedictines of Paris, 12 v. (Paris 1935–56) 10:574–582.

[M. LAWLOR]

VALENS, ROMAN EMPEROR

Born in 364, Valens governed the East as colleague of his brother VALENTINIAN I. Indecisive and impressionable, he possessed administrative ability but little military competence. After a successful campaign against the Visigoths, 367–369, he allowed them to cross the Danube into Moesia as *foederati* in 376; but when they rebelled, he lost his life in a terrible defeat at Adrianople, Aug. 9, 378. The last Arian emperor, his religious policy was guided by Bishop Eudoxius of Constantinople until 370, and thereafter by Demophilus of Beroea. In 365 he ordered the expulsion of all (Catholic) bishops expelled by CONSTANTIUS II but reinstated by JULIAN THE APOSTATE. However, when faced with rebellion in Egypt after he exiled ATHANASIUS, he yielded; and BASIL OF CAESAREA overawed him. In 367 he blocked attempts of the semi–Arians to reunite with the Catholics; but he was about to moderate his program in the face of rising popular discontent when he died.

Bibliography: A. NAGL, *Paulys Realenzyklopädie der klassischen Altertumswissenschaft,* ed. G. WISSOWA et al. (Stuttgart 1893–) 7A.2:2097–2137. J. R. PALANQUE et al., *The Church in the Christian Roman Empire,* tr. E. C. MESSENGER (New York 1953–). E. STEIN, *Histoire du Bas-Empire,* tr. J. R. PALANQUE, 2 v. in 3 (Paris 1949–59).

[R. H. SCHMANDT]

VALENTINE, POPE

Pontificate: August 827 to September 827; b. Rome, date unknown; d. Rome. Trained in a noble Christian home of Rome, Valentine entered the Church at an early age. Pope PASCHAL I (817–824) made him the cardinal deacon of the Roman diaconate. When Pope EUGENE II died, August 27, 827, the Roman clergy and lay nobility sought young Valentine, found him at prayer in the church of St. Mary Major, led him to the Lateran Basilica, and there insisted that he accept the papacy. He was consecrated bishop and enthroned as pope at St. Peter's. This election showed the role played by the lay nobility and people in papal elections, despite previous conciliar regulations that denied them any participation (Roman Council, 796). During his short pontificate Valentine was noted for his piety, clemency, and liberality. He was buried at the Vatican.

Bibliography: L. JAFFÉ, *Regesta pontificum romanorum ab condita ecclesia ad annum post Christum natum 1198,* ed. P. EWALD 1:322–323. *Liber pontificalis,* ed. L. DUSHESNE (Paris 1958) 2:71–72. L. DUCHESNE, *The Beginnings of the Temporal Sovereignty of the Popes, A.D. 754–1073* (London 1908). H. K. MANN, *The Lives of the Popes in the Early Middle Ages from 590 to 1304* (London 1902–32) 2:183–186. É. AMANN, *Dictionnaire de théologie catholique,* ed. A. VACANT (Paris 1903–50; Tables générales 1951–) 15.2:2497. J. N. D. KELLY, *Oxford Dictionary of Popes* (New York 1986) 102.

[M. A. MULHOLLAND]

VALENTINE, ST.

The Roman Martyrology commemorates two martyrs named Valentine on February 14, indicating that both

Father Frank O'Gara kneels before shrine containing partial remains of Saint Valentine according to parchment by Pope Gregory XVI, Whitefriars Street Catholic Church, Dublin, Ireland. (AP/Wide World)

were beheaded on the Flaminian Way, one at Rome, the other at Terni some 60 miles from the capital. Valentine of Rome was a priest who is said to have died *c.* 269 during the persecution of Claudius the Goth. The other Valentine was allegedly bishop of Terni, and his death is attested to in the MARTYROLOGY OF ST. JEROME. Whether there were actually one or two Valentines is disputed. O. Marucchi held for two. H. Delehaye thought that Valentine of Terni may have been brought to Rome for execution and that two cults, one at Rome, another at Terni, sprang up to the same martyr. The late medieval custom of sending love notes on Saint Valentine's Day stems probably from the belief that it marked the mating season of birds.

According to the LIBERIAN CATALOGUE and the Liber pontificalis, Pope JULIUS I (336–356) built a basilica on the Via Flaminia, two miles from Rome, over the sepulcher of the martyr, a Valentine whose cult is attested to by fourth-century inscriptions. Remains of the *memoria* have recently been unearthed and indicate that an original three-nave church was rebuilt with colonnades substituted for walls, and that later a crypt and presbyterium were added. The *Notitia ecclesiarum* credits Pope Honorius I (625–638) with a reconstruction, whereas Popes Benedict II (684–685), Adrian I (772–795), Leo III (795–816), and Gregory IV (827–844) adorned and rebuilt the church. In 1060 Abbot Teubald restored the church and monastery. In 1905 fragments of an epigraph composed by Pope DAMASUS I and a marble sarcophagus adorned with a fourth-century representation of Christ before Pilate and two soldiers beneath a *crux invicta* were discovered. The body of the martyr seems to have been translated to the chapel of St. Zeno in Prassede in the 13th century.

Parts of a subterranean cemetery near the church of St. Valentine were discovered by P. Ugonio and A. Bosio in 1594, and in 1877 O. Marucchi rediscovered the site, which contained many archeological artifacts from A.D. 318 to 523, among them several fragments inscribed with the name of Valentine, and the decoration on a sarcophagus representing a ship called "Thecla" with Paul at the helm.

Feast: February 14.

Bibliography: *Acta Sanctorum* February 2:751–62. O. MARUCCHI, *Il cimitero e la basilica di S. Valentino* (Rome 1890); *Le Catacombe romane* (Rome 1932). H. DELEHAYE, *Les Origines du culte des martyrs* (2d ed. Brussels 1933) 270, 315–316. H. A. KELLY, *Chaucer and the Cult of Saint Valentine* (Leiden 1986). N. WILKINS, ed., *Two miracles: La nonne qui laissa son abbaie; [and] Saint Valentin* (New York 1973). R. SABUDA, *Saint Valentine* (New York 1992). C. C. F. HÜLSEN, *Le chiese di Roma* (Florence 1927). B. M. APOLLON J-GHETTI, *Rivista di archeologia cristiana* 25 (1949) 171–189.

[E. DAY]

VALENTINI, PIER FRANCESCO

Baroque composer and theorist; b. Rome, *c.* 1570; d. Rome, 1654. Little is known of his life except that he was a pupil of G. M. Nanino. He wrote a number of theoretical works and composed many motets, madrigals, spiritual songs, and litanies, all in the Roman style exemplified by the works of PALESTRINA. A remarkably skilled contrapuntalist, Valentini was best known in his time, and is chiefly remembered today, for his canon on the words of the *Salve Regina* "Illos tuos misericordes oculos ad nos converte" with resolutions in two, three, four, and six voices (1629). This canon had more than 2,000 possible resolutions, and became well known through Athanasius KIRCHER's publication of it in part one of his great work, *Musurgia universalis* (Rome 1650).

Bibliography: L. KUNZ, *Die Tonartenlehre des römischen Theoretikers und Komponisten P. F. Valentini* (Kassel 1937). G. CHOUQUET, *Grove's Dictionary of Music and Musicians*, ed. E. BLOM 9 v. (5th ed. London 1954) 8:654–655, contains theme of the Salve Regina Canon. G. GERBINO, review of *Institutional Patronage in Post-Tridentine Rome: Music at Santissima Trinità dei Pellegrini 1550–1650*, by N. O'REGAN, *Journal of Seventeenth-Century Music* 3 (1997), <http://www.sscm.harvard.edu/jscm/v3/no1/Gerbino.html>, par. 3.3. S. MARTINOTTI and A. ZIINO, ''Pier Francesco Valentini'' in *The New Grove Dictionary of Music and Musicians*, vol. 19, ed. S. SADIE, (New York 1980) 497–498. D. M. RANDEL, ed., *The Harvard Biographical Dictionary of Music* (Cambridge 1996) 937. N. SLONIMSKY, ed., *Baker's Biographical Dictionary of Musicians, Eighth Edition* (New York 1992) 1933.

[W. C. HOLMES]

VALENTINIAN I, ROMAN EMPEROR

Ruled 364–375; b. Pannonia. A career soldier elected by military and civil officials to succeed Jovian, he named his brother Valens co-emperor and resigned the East to him. Valentinian personally directed the war against the barbarians on the Rhine and Danube and tried unsuccessfully to prevent governmental corruption. Personally professing Catholicism, he proclaimed full freedom of religion and, to demonstrate his neutrality, successively confirmed the Arian Auxentius and the Catholic St. AMBROSE for the See of Milan. He repealed the apostate JULIAN's anti-Christian legislation but allowed pagan worship, except for bloody sacrifices. He enacted about 30 laws touching on the privileges of the Church and clergy, and clerical abuses. MARTIN OF TOURS visited his court at Trier and received many favors. Because of civil strife resulting from the disputed papal election of 366, Valentinian reluctantly intervened on behalf of Pope DAMASUS I and exiled antipope Ursinus. In 372, at Damasus' request, he confirmed the synodal decision that cleared the Pope of charges of immorality.

Bibliography: A. NAGL, *Paulys Realenzyklopädie der klassischen Altertumswissenschaft*, ed. G. WISSOWA, et al. (Stuttgart 1893–) 7a.2:2158–2204. J. R. PALANQUE et al., *The Church in the Christian Roman Empire*, tr. E. C. MESSENGER (New York 1953). E. STEIN and J. R. PALANQUE, *Histoire du bas-empire*, 2 v. (Paris 1949–59) v.1.

[R. H. SCHMANDT]

VALENTINIAN III, ROMAN EMPEROR

Reigned 424 to 455; Caesar, Oct. 23, 424; Augustus, Oct. 23, 425; b. son of Constantius III in Ravenna, July 2, 419; assassinated, Rome, March 16, 455. His mother and regent, Galla Placidia (d. November 450), successfully played off the Roman generals Felix, Boniface, and Aetius against one another. In 437 Valentinian went to Constantinople to marry Eudoxia, daughter of THEODOSIUS II. When he returned with his bride in 438, he brought the Theodosian Code to the West.

In 439 the Visigoths under Theodoric I defeated a Roman army near Toulouse and became sovereign. The Arian VANDALS, who with Donatist help (*see* DONATISM) sought to destroy Catholicism and Roman rule in Africa, captured Carthage and Mediterranean naval power in 439 and were recognized as sovereign in 442.

Despite the efforts of Valentinian's generals, the Romans withdrew from Britain in 442 and ties between Rome and the Church of St. PATRICK in Ireland were broken. Discontented *coloni* and slaves in Spain and Gaul rose against their masters *c.* 436 and again in 446. In 451 the HUNS under Attila invaded Gaul but were defeated by Aetius and the Visigoths, who returned to the status of *foederati*. When Attila died in 453 and Germanic troops again became available to the Empire, the value of Aetius declined and Valentinian assassinated him in the royal palace in Rome in September 454. The Emperor's campaign against Aetius's allies, the senatorial aristocracy, came to naught. He was killed on the Campus Martii by Aetius's cohorts.

Valentinian and his mother were probably influenced by Augustine's *City of God,* completed in 426, but their support of Pope LEO I's claims of primacy favored also the survival of a Roman tradition and a Roman administration, in the person of bishops, in an empire coming under barbarian rule. The unfavorable picture of Valentinian derives from writings of senatorial aristocrats. The laws he issued were part of a conscientious but futile struggle against the corruption, described by SALVIAN in 440, that was causing an enormous decline in imperial revenue. Valentinian was the last of the 91-year-old Theodosian dynasty, and after him no Western emperor reigned more than a few years or resided in Rome at any length.

Bibliography: W. ENSSLIN, *Paulys Realenzyklopädie der lkassischen Altertumswissenschaft*, ed. G. WISSOWA et al (Stuttgart 1893–) 7a.2 (1948) 2232–59. E. STEIN, *Histoire du Bas-Empire*, tr. J. R. PALANQUE, 2 v. in 3 (Paris 1949–59) 1:472–519. C. D. GORDON, *The Age of Attila* (Ann Arbor 1961). V. A. SIRAGO, *Galla Placidia e la trasformazione politica dell'Occidente* (Louvain 1961).

[E. P. COLBERT]

VALENTINUS

One of the outstanding Gnostic leaders, founder of a widespread sect in Rome in the second century. It is difficult to separate fact from legend among the few details of his life preserved by the ancient writers on heresies. Valentinus was born in Egypt and educated at Alexandria, where he first began to teach. Under Pope St. Hyginus (*c.* 136–140) he moved to Rome and flourished there for some 20 years. At Rome he broke with the Church because, according to Tertullian (*Adversus valentinus* 4), he was thwarted in his attempt to become bishop. Epiphanius (*Haereses* 31.7) states that he later left Rome for Cyprus. He wrote letters, homilies, and psalms of which only a few fragments are preserved in the *Stromata* of Clement of Alexandria and in other patristic sources. Irenaeus (*Adversus haereses* 3.11.9) mentions that he or his school composed a "gospel" called the *Gospel of Truth,* but bearing no resemblance whatever to the canonical Gospels. With this scholars now identify a writing of the same description in the *Codex Jung,* and some also attribute the *Letter to Rheginus* in the same codex to Valentinus. Though clearly Gnostic, the *Gospel of Truth* lacks the elaborate doctrines of the Aeons and the Demiurge; it may therefore represent an early stage of Valentinus' teaching, and is perhaps to be dated *c.* 140.

Apart from this source it is not easy to sketch the original teaching of Valentinus because his pupils developed his system considerably and branched out into two schools, the Italian and the Oriental, differing in their classification of the body of Jesus (Hippolytus, *Ref.* 6.35). The writers on heresies tended to describe and refute the followers rather than the founder. Under Platonic influence Valentinus distinguished a phenomenal world and a spiritual world, the Pleroma. In the latter there are a series of emanations from one Father (Hippolytus, *Ref.* 6.29) or from a primal pair (Irenaeus, *Adversus haereses* 1.1), forming a total of 30 Aeons in pairs or "syzygies." From the fall of the lowest of these, Sophia, into passion and disgrace, there resulted the emission of matter and the Demiurge, the God of the Old Testament, who shaped matter into our world. In the Pleroma the Holy Spirit and Christ emanated as Aeons. Christ united with the man, Jesus, who was conceived of in a purely Docetic sense, to effect the conquest of death and the salvation of mankind. Men are classified as pneumatics—the Valentinians themselves—saved by knowledge (gnosis); psychics, other Christians capable of intermediate salvation; and hylics, those of material nature, who are lost. Valentinus seems more of a mystic than a philosopher or theologian. His system, although clearly a Christian gnosis, is a caricature, however unconscious, of the message of the New Testament. His following was very large (Tertullian, *Adversus valentinus* 1) but the pure form of his teaching lasted only a few generations.

See Also: GNOSTICISM.

Bibliography: Texts. W. VÖLKER, ed., *Quellen zur Geschichte der christlichen Gnosis* (Tübingen 1932) 57–141. R. M. GRANT, *Gnosticism: A Sourcebook. . .* (New York 1961) 143–208. Studies. R. A. LIPSIUS, *A Dictionary of Christian Biography*, ed. W. SMITH and H. WACE, 4 v. (London 1877–87) 4:1076–99. W. FOERSTER, *Von Valentin zu Herakleon, Zeitschrift für die neutestamentliche Wissenschaft und die Kunde der älteren Kirche* 7 (1928). F. M. SAGNARD, *La Gnose valentinienne et le témoignage de saint Irénée* (Études de philosophic médiévale 36; Paris 1947). G. QUISPEL, "The Original Doctrine of Valentine," *Vigiliae christianea* 1 (1947) 43–73. G. BARDY, *Dictionnaire de théologie catholique*, ed. A. VACANT et al., 15 v. (Paris 1903–50; Tables Générales 1951–) 15.2:2497–2519. F. L. CROSS, ed., *The Jung Codex: Three Studies* (London 1955) H. JONAS, *The Gnostic Religion* (2d ed. Boston 1963) 174–205. R. M. WILSON, *The Gnostic Problem* (London 1958). J. DORESSE, *The Secret Books of the Egyptian Gnostics,* tr. P. MAIRET (New York 1960).

[G. W. MACRAE]

VALERIAN, ROMAN EMPEROR

Reigned 253 to 260; b. Publius Licinius Valerianus, before 200. He was a suffect consul in 238, and later held important posts under DECIUS and Trebonius Gallus. Valerian, hailed as emperor by his troops in Raetia, was accepted by the senate when Aemilianus was slain by his own soldiers; he appointed his son, Gallienus, as Augustus and coregent. While Gallienus undertook the defense of the West, Valerian set out to repel a Persian invasion in the East. After an initial success, his army was struck by a plague, and Valerian was himself captured by the Persian King Sapor, apparently in 259. He seems to have died in captivity the following year.

Under Decius, Valerian may have had charge of implementing the persecution of the Christians at Rome. During the first years of his own reign he proved to be tolerant, but after the empire had suffered a number of military reverses, he issued an edict in 257 ordering the Christians to observe the ceremonies of the state cult. At the same time he forbade their assembling or entering the cemeteries, which he confiscated along with other Christian properties. In 258 he issued another edict ordering "bishops, priests, and deacons to be executed at once; senators, high officials, and Roman knights to be deprived of their honors and possessions, and if after losing their position they continued to be Christians, to be executed; Christian women to be dispossessed of their property and banished; and the Caesariani (members of the imperial household) who earlier confessed, or who now confess themselves to be Christians, to be deprived of their goods and sent in chains to the imperial estates" (Cyprian, *Epist.* 80.1). Among the most celebrated martyrs of this era are SIXTUS II (put to death with four of his deacons in the cemetery of Calixtus), CYPRIAN OF CARTHAGE, and FRUCTUOSUS OF TARRAGONA.

Bibliography: P. J. HEALY, *The Valerian Persecution* (Boston 1905). U. WICKERT, *Paulys Realencyklopädie der klassischen Altertumswissenschaft*, ed. G. WISSOWA et al. 13.1 (1926) 488–495.

[M. J. COSTELLOE]

VALERIO OF BIERZO

Visigothic ascetic and author; fl. northwestern Spain, *c.* 675; d. after 695. He wrote three autobiographical accounts in decadent Latin, as well as several poems and religious treatises. In *Ordo querimoniae* Valerio recounted his retirement to a mountain solitude near Astorga where his rigorous life attracted disciples. In *Replicatio* and *Residuum* he further detailed his sufferings—many directly inflicted by Satan—in various hermitages. He resisted ordination as priest for a PROPRIETARY CHURCH, and thus is a witness to the existence of this institution in Spain. Valerio was connected in some way with the Abbey of San Pedro de Montes; he wrote for the monks there and was latter erroneously considered abbot. Of Valerio's other writings his *Vita et epistola beatissimae Egeriae* is important in helping to establish the spelling of Egeria's name (*see* EGERIA, ITINERARIUM OF). *De genere monachorum* vigorously condemns proprietary monasteries. Valerio also described in his writings three contemporary visions of heaven and hell. The BOLLANDISTS claim his cult is doubtful. His inscription, extant in the church of San Pedro, calls him "sanctus," then simply a title of honor. His various feast days have no sound authorization.

Bibliography: *Obras,* ed. R. FERNÁNDEZ POUSA (Madrid 1944). C. M. AHERNE, *Valerio of Bierzo, an Ascetic of the Late Visigothic Period* (Washington 1949). *Acta Sanctorum* Feb. 3:490.

[C. M. AHERNE]

VALFRÉ, SEBASTIAN, BL.

Italian Oratorian; b. Verduno, March 9, 1629; d. Turin, Jan. 30, 1710. Sebastian, of poor Piedmontese parents, studied in Turin and was ordained Feb. 24, 1652. The University of Turin, recognizing his learning, gave him an honorary doctorate in theology. In 1651 he joined an Oratorian priest working in Turin, and when others came, an Oratory was formed. Valfré was a devoted pastoral priest, preaching and teaching with winning good humor and simplicity. He was provost of the Oratory for many years, and tutor to the young Duke of Savoy, later Vittorio Amedeo II, to whom he dedicated a book, "The Art of Sanctifying War," recalling that only the most urgent reasons could ever justify war and that damage to noncombatants and all cruelty should be avoided. Valfré

wrote a treatise on Christian perfection. He ministered to many wretched Waldensian prisoners brought to Turin following Louis XIV's expedition against them (1685–86). When French troops besieged Turin for four months in 1706, Valfré helped encourage the inhabitants until the Duke relieved the city. Valfré died for punctuality. Hurrying to evening prayer, he arrived overheated, prayed in a cool room, and caught a fatal chill. He was beatified by Gregory XVI, Aug. 31, 1834.

Feast: Jan. 30.

Bibliography: P. CAPELLO, *Vita del beato Sebastiano Valfré* 2 v. (Turin 1872). A. KERR, *Life of the Blessed Sebastian Valfré* (London 1896). A. BUTLER, *The Lives of the Saints,* ed. H. THURSTON and D. ATTWATER, 4 v. (New York 1956) 1:207–208.

[J. C. CHALLENOR]

VALIGNANO, ALESSANDRO

Greatest organizer and superior of the Jesuit missions in the Middle and Far East since St. Francis Xavier; b. Chieti (Abruzzi), Italy, February 1539; d. Macau, Jan. 20, 1606. Members of his influential family had often served Chieti as chamberlains; his parents were friends of Gian Pietro Caraffa, Bishop of Chieti (1505–24), who became cardinal archbishop (1537–49) and Pope PAUL IV. After obtaining the degree of doctor of laws at Padua, probably in 1557, he expected promotion from Paul IV. He returned to Padua after Paul's death in 1559, and became involved in a law suit. After an imprisonment of 1½ years he was expelled from the territory of the Republic of Venice. Under Pius IV he was auditor of the Cardinal's nephew Mark Sittich of Hohenems (Altemps). In this period he underwent a profound spiritual experience (details as yet unknown), resulting in his entrance into the Society of Jesus at Rome in 1566. After studying philosophy and theology at the Collegium Romanum, he was ordained in St. John Lateran on March 25, 1570. The next year he was, for a short time, master of novices—one of the novices being Matteo RICCI—and from Sept. 1, 1572, rector of the college in Macerata.

Visitator. In the summer of 1573 he was called to Rome and appointed visitator of the East Indian Jesuit missions. He made his solemn profession at Rome (Sept. 8, 1573) and on March 21, 1574, departed from Lisbon with 41 other Jesuits; he arrived in Goa on Sept. 6, 1574. He was visitator of Asia (until October 1583), provincial of India (until September-October 1587), again visitator of Asia (until Sept. 24, 1595), and visitator of the Far East until his death.

Valignano gave a strong impetus to Jesuit missions and to the Church in general in many Asian countries. He visited Hither India (1574–77); made his first visit to the Far East from 1577 to 1583 (Japan 1579–82); was in charge of the province of Goa (1583–87); made his second visit to the Far East from 1588 to 1595 (Japan 1590–92); and was visitor of the Far East from 1595 until his death (third and last stay in Japan 1598–1603). He promoted the spiritual life among Jesuits in Asia by means of the Jesuit constitutions, retreats, etc., taking great care of the intellectual training of young Jesuit missionaries, reorganizing studies in St. Paul's College at Goa, founding a college at Funai (Ōita), Japan, and building (1593–94) the imposing structure of the college at Macau. Similar care was bestowed on the novitiates. In 1584 a magnificent Professed House was erected at Goa. Valignano tried to restore to the missions their original meaning of ''sending,'' and of performing pastoral work among Christians by radiating from large population centers. The missions were rigidly organized: there were annual visitations by superiors, frequent consultations with all missionary priests, careful reporting to the general of the Jesuits, to the pope, and to the king of Spain and Portugal. Valignano organized the first Japanese diplomatic mission to Europe (1582–90), a noteworthy contemporary event. He also knew how to find the material means for his large-scale activities, e.g., the papal ''Japan-Revenue'' first granted by Gregory XIII. An indirect participation of the Society of Jesus in the silk trade of Macau-Japan, taking the form of investments, was also approved by the Pope.

Missionary Adaptation. The basis of Valignano's missionary system was a far-reaching adaptation to national customs through the study of language and culture. Its high point was reached when the missionaries were fitted into the social structure of the country. To this end he composed a booklet of ceremonies for Japan (Bungo 1581). A native clergy was being trained, and the appointment of native bishops anticipated. His extant writings are collected by J. F. Schütte. English translations of these and other new sources are in preparation. Among the works already printed during the lifetime of Valignano are a catechism for Japan, and a report about the martyrdom of Rudolph Acquaviva and companions. His works and letters are a rich source of information for church history in Asian lands.

Bibliography: A. VALIGNANO, *Sumario de las cosas de Japón* (1583); *Adiciones del Sumario de Japón* (1592), ed. J. L. ALVAREZ-TALADRIZ (Tokyo 1954–); *Il cerimoniale per i missionari del Giappone*, ed. J. F. SCHÜTTE (Rome 1946). D. E. VALIGNANI, *Vita del Padre Alessandro Valignani della Compagnia di Giesù* (Rome 1698). I. NARDI, *Genealogia della famiglia Valignana* (Rome 1680). G. RAVIZZA, *Notizie biografiche che riguardano gli uomini illustri della Città di Chieti . . .* (Naples 1830); *Appendice alle notizie biografiche. . .* (Chieti 1834). J. F. SCHÜTTE, *Valignanos Missionsgrundsätze für Japan* (v.1.1–1.2 Rome 1951–58).

[J. F. SCHÜTTE]

VALLA, LORENZO

Italian humanist; b. Rome, 1407; d. Rome, 1457. After study in Rome, he taught eloquence at the University of Pavia (1429–33). He was ordained in 1431. In 1437 he became the secretary of King Alfonso V of Aragon and of Sicily, who eventually made good his claim to the throne of Naples also (1442). Finally, Valla was appointed apostolic secretary in 1448 under Pope NICHOLAS V. Valla belongs, essentially, to the second stage in the evolution of HUMANISM. C. SALUTATI, L. Bruni, and the other early followers of PETRARCH had already enthusiastically tested in their own works the basic principles of the new movement, mainly the belief that ancient literature was an invaluable help in the attainment of a moral and Christian life. The time had come to defend this new Christian culture against the many forms of opposition arising from traditional asceticism and from the late sterile scholasticism still prevailing in the schools. Valla brought to this battle a pugnacious character and a pride that often became arrogant and quarrelsome.

With the revival of classicism and the new appreciation for moral values, STOICISM seemed to be accepted with increasing favor by humanists. But Valla understood that Christian life consists of the pursuit of happiness, not of virtue as an end in itself, and he did not miss the occasion to set forth the apparently scandalous doctrine that EPICUREANISM, insofar as it asserts that man's goal is pleasure and that virtue is only a means to achieve happiness, is much more in agreement with Christian philosophy. And thus, in Valla's philosophical dialogue *De voluptate* (On Praise of Pleasure, 1431), L. Bruni and A. Beccadelli respectively are made to present the Stoic and Epicurean theses in their extreme forms. Then in the third book, N. Niccoli is made to enunciate the Christian doctrine that virtue expects a reward and that pleasure and happiness (*voluptas*) are the goals of human and Christian life. All three contrasting views are rather clumsily exaggerated by Valla's pen. But certainly there is no ground for attributing personally to Valla the views expressed by Beccadelli, and thus presenting the *De voluptate* as evidence for the centuries-old prejudice that the RENAISSANCE was steeped in paganism.

The true measure of Valla's ability is to be found in his philological and linguistic studies. His *Elegantiarum latinae linguae libri sex* (On the Beauties of the Latin Language, 1444) is one of the best expressions of the new sense of classicism that humanism was opposing to the corrupted taste and the arduous rhetorical technicalities of the Latin of Middle Ages. The same polemical spirit had earlier inspired Valla's *Dialecticae disputationes* (Dialectical Disputations, 1439). But in trying to attack the many abstract terms used in logic, such as ''being'' (*ens*), ''essence,'' or ''substance,'' Valla proved his knowledge of dialectics to be poor, for he stated that the term ''being'' is the same as ''thing'' (*res*) and that there is no difference between ''the-act-of-being'' (*esse*) and ''essence.'' By the same totally superficial deduction, Valla asserted that *persona* means ''property'' or ''quality'' and went on to argue that the three Persons of the Holy Trinity correspond to a ''triple divine quality'' (*triple qualitas divina*), a conclusion the Reformation was later to exploit. But these individual propositions should not be assumed to represent Valla's vital thinking: they were rather the result of a clumsy incursion into the field of dialectics. The same holds true for his treatise *De libero arbitrio* (On Free Will), in which Valla stressed (in opposition to Boethius and the scholastics) the transcendence of the divine Will; this work was later praised by Martin Luther because of its Pauline implications.

Valla's *Adnotationes in Novum Testamentum* (Notes on the New Testament), which found some favor among Protestants, has been considered by modern historians as one of the first manifestations of the free examination of Sacred Scripture. Valla made a collation of a limited number of good manuscripts (thus initiating textual criticism of the Bible in the Catholic Church) but despite the encouragement and help of such men as NICHOLAS OF CUSA and Cardinal BESSARION, the achievements of the collation were objectively rather slight. The author's tendency to correct the text according to a standard of classical style proved unprofitable in this case. The system itself and Valla's clear assertions prove that he was very far from aiming at establishing the principle of personal interpretation of Scripture, as has often been assumed.

On behalf of King Alfonso, Valla embarked on a bitter attack against Pope EUGENE IV, notably with his work *De falso credita et ementita Constantini donatione declamatio* (On the False DONATION OF CONSTANTINE, 1440), which demonstrated the spurious quality of that document, on which the Church had in large part based its claim to a temporal dominion (*see* STATES OF THE CHURCH). For centuries this work of Valla was taken as the manifesto of humanism's critical spirit of investigation; but in fact, it was only a professional plea in favor of Valla's protector as he struggled to gain Naples. As such, the attack was forgiven, and Pope Nicholas V made Valla apostolic secretary in 1448.

Bibliography: Works. *Opera* (Basel 1540); *De falso credita et ementita Constantini donatione,* ed. and tr. C. B. COLEMAN (New Haven 1922); *Adnotationes in New Testament,* ed. D. ERASMUS (Basil 1526); *De libero arbitrio,* ed. M. ANFOSSI (Florence 1934) and tr. C. E. TRINKAUS in E. CASSIRER et al., eds., *The Renaissance Philosophy of Man* (Chicago 1948; pa. 1956); *Historiarum Ferdinandi Regis Aragoniae libri tres* (Rome 1520); *Scritti filosofici e religiosi,* ed. G. RADETTI (Florence 1953). Literature. G. MANCINI, *Vita di L. Valla* (Florence 1891). R. SABBADINI, *Cronologia della vita del Panormita e del Valle* (Florence 1891). C. E. TRINKAUS, *Adversity's Noblemen: The Italian Humanists on Happiness* (New York 1940). E. GARIN, *L'Umanesimo italiano: Filosofia e vita civile nel Rinascimento* (Bari 1952). R. R. BOLGAR, *The Classical Heritage and Its Beneficiaries* (Cambridge, Eng. 1954). F. GAETA, *L. Valla: Filologia e storia nell'umanesimo italiano* (Naples 1955). R. MONTANO, ''L. Valla'' in *Letteratura italiana: I minori,* 2 v. (Milan 1961) 1:569–586. P. O. KRISTELLER, *Eight Philosophers of the Italian Renaissance* (Stanford 1964) 19–36.

[R. MONTANO]

VALLGORNERA, TOMAS DE

Theologian and spiritual writer; b. 1595?, Catalonia; d. Sept. 15, 1665. Vallgornera became a Dominican in Barcelona and became known for his piety and learning. He refused, on two occasions, to accept his election as provincial of Aragon. Under obedience he served as vicar-general of the Catalonian priories when that region joined France in 1642. In weak health during his last 20 years, he devoted himself to study and writing, publishing rosary meditations, *De Rosario B. Mariae Virginis;* and his major work, *Mystica theologia divi Thomae* (1662, enl. 1665). In this work he gathered and classified St. Thomas's ascetical and mystical doctrine. Written in a lucid and simple style, the volume, after a preliminary study of its subject, deals with the purgative, the illuminative, and the unitive ways. *Mystica theologia* was of significance in counteracting the ideas of the Alumbrados and is still much respected and studied.

Bibliography: T. DE VALLGORNERA, *Mystica theologia divi Thomae,* 2 v. (Turin 1924) 1:vii–x. J. QUÉTIF and J. ÉCHARD, *Scriptores Ordinis Praedicatorum* (New York 1959) 2.2:604. *Année Dominicaine* (Sept. 12, 1900) 523.

[B. PEÑA]

VALLISCAULIAN ORDER

A religious order of men deriving its name from the place of foundation, Vallis Caulium or Val-des-Choux (Valley of Cabbages), in Burgundy. In the 12th century, Viard, a lay brother in the Carthusian Priory of Loubigny in the diocese of Langres, secured permission to live as a hermit in the woods. His reputation for sanctity induced the Duke of Burdundy to build a church and a monastery on the site in fulfillment of a vow he had made before going into combat. On Nov. 2, 1193, this hermit became the first prior. The monks wore the Cistercian habit, but the constitution was based on Carthusian Rule. Pope Innocent III confirmed the order in 1205 in a rescript *Protectio apostolica.* The same year Duke Otto III of Burgundy gave a large tract of forest land around the priory to provide support for the monks. At its height Val-des-Choux had 30 dependent priories, of which the most important in France were Val-Croissant and Val-Benîte near Autun, and Saint-Lieu du petit Valdes-Choux in Dijon. A complete list exists of priors general from Viard, who died after 1213, to Dorothée Jallontz, the last grand prior, who was later abbot of the Cistercian SEPT-FONS MONASTERY. In 1230 monks from Val-des-Choux made three foundations in Scotland: St. John's Priory at Beauly in Inverness, PLUSCARDEN PRIORY, and ARDCHATTAN PRIORY on Loch Etive in Argyll. By the middle of the 18th century the Val-des-Choux Priory had dwindled to three monks since there had been no professions for 24 years. Gilbert, Bishop of Langres, advised union with a Cistercian monastery. With the approval of Pope Clement XIII and the ratification of the agreement by the Parlement of Burgundy, the Val-des-Choux Priory in 1764 was incorporated with the Cistercian Sept-Forts Monastery in the diocese of Moulins. For a quarter of a century Sept-Forts prospered, only to be swept away in the French Revolution, but restored again in 1845.

Bibliography: *Ordinale Conventus Vallis Caulium* (Lo, Belgium 1900); P. HÉLYOT, *Histoire des ordres monastiques . . . ,* 8 v. (Paris 1714–19), 6:15–21, 178–180. T. J. A. P. MIGNAUD, *Histoire des principales fondations religieuses . . . en Bourgogne* (Paris 1864). H. WOLTER, *Lexikon für Theologie und Kirche,* ed. J. HOFER and K. RAHNER, 10 v. (2d, new ed. Freiburg 1957–65); suppl., *Das ZweiteVatikanische Konzil: Dokumente und kommentare,* ed. H. S. BRECHTER et al., pt. 1 (1966) 6:95.

[G. M. GRAY]

VALLOMBROSA, ABBEY OF

Chief monastery of the VALLOMBROSANS, lies 300 feet up on the wooded slopes of Monte Secchieta in the Tuscan subApennines, 22 miles from Florence, Italy. There in 1039 a congregation of BENEDICTINE monks (*Congregatio Vallis Umbrosae ordinis sancti Benedicti*) was founded by the Florentine (St.) JOHN GUALBERT (d. 1073) in what was then a wild and inhospitable spot. The monks reclaimed the land, planting a forest of pines and firs and building a chapel and isolated wooden huts for themselves. The foundation gradually increased, receiving generous donations from Countess MATILDA OF TUSCANY and other benefactors, and had many daughterhouses in Tuscany and beyond, as can be seen from the "privileges" granted by various popes in the 11th and 12th centuries to the *Universa congregatio Vallis Umbrosana,* while the monks acquired fame for holiness and learning and for skill in miniature painting. The abbey buildings were constructed by Abbot Francesco Altoviti in the 15th century and subsequently enriched with many great works of art. In 1529 the abbey was

sacked by Charles V's army, and the library destroyed; a century later it was considerably enlarged by Abbot Averardo dei Niccolini, acquiring its present imposing appearance. Under NAPOLEON its lands were confiscated, and the abbey was suppresed in 1810. Reopened in 1817, it was again suppressed by the Italian government in 1866 and occupied by the National Forestry Institute until 1913. The abbey buildings have recently been restored to the monks, and it is now the residence of the abbot general of the Vallombrosans. An inscription on a nearby oratory recalls John Milton's visit to Vallombrosa, which he mentions in book two of *Paradise Lost.*

Bibliography: P. F. KEHR, *Regesta Pontificum Romanorum. Italia Pontificia,* 8 v. (Berlin 1906–35) 3:83–96. G. CAPPELLETTI, *Le Chiese d'Italia,* 21 v. (Venice 1844–70) v.17. E. REPETTI, *Dizionario geografico-fisico-storico della Toscana,* 6 v. (Florence 1833–46) v.5. B. ALBERS, ''Die aeltesten *consuetudines* von Vallumbrosa,'' *Rue Bénédictine* 28 (1911) 432–436. L. H. COTTINEAU, *Répertoire topobibliographique des abbayes et prieurés,* 2 v. (Mâcon 1935–39) 2:3286–87. P. LUGANO, ed., *L'Italia benedeltina* (Rome 1929). B. DOMENICHETTI, *Guida storica illustrata di Vallombrosa* (3d ed. Florence 1929). A. SALVINI, *Abbazia di Vallombrosa* (Florence 1960).

[S. OLIVIERI]

VALLOMBROSANS

Popular name for a congregation of monks, *Congregatio Vallisumbrosae Ordinis S. Benedicti* (CVUOSB), which takes its name from Vallombrosa, a solitary forest 16 miles southeast of Florence, Italy, 3300 feet above sea level. There, from 1035 to 1050, St. JOHN GUALBERT, a Benedictine monk, established a community with the intention of reviving in its integrity the BENEDICTINE RULE and of supporting openly the reform movement opposed to those guilty of SIMONY and Nicolaitanism (*see* CELIBACY, HISTORY OF). Characteristic of his institute was its stress on the spirit of poverty, evidenced by the tunic and cowl of coarse grey wool, its refusal to supply officials for churches and chapels, its extensive use of *conversi* for labors outside the monastery, its strictness in promoting to sacred orders, and the serious formation of clerics to be sent into various dioceses. The ordeal by fire successfully undertaken by the Vallombrosan Blessed Peter Igneus at the abbey of Settimo near Florence (February 1068) won for the new institute popular sympathy and papal protection.

The Vallombrosan constitutions, desired by the founder, and called the Bond of Charity (*Vinculum caritatis*), set up a congregation of monasteries, each one autonomous and governed by its abbot, who was to be elected by his community with the consent of the abbot of Vallombrosa, called the major abbot. The latter was to be elected by the abbots of the other monasteries. Annually all the abbots were to meet with true legislative power to handle all the congregation's affairs.

The abbeys numbered nine in 1073, when the founder died, 57 in 1155, and more than 80 in 1300. Each one had dependent on it hospices and churches in Tuscany, Lombardy, Emilia, Piedmont, and Sardinia. Many Vallombrosan characteristics were fully realized by the CISTERCIANS. Monasteries of nuns directly dependent on those of the monks started *c.* 1200.

In 1540, after suffering the evils of COMMENDATION, the Vallombrosan monks adopted the constitutions and customs, including the black garb, of the St. Justina, or Cassinese, Congregation. Thereafter abbots served three-year, rather than life terms. The superior general was no longer the abbot of Vallombrosa, but a titular abbot who remained in office four years with four definitors. All Vallombrosan houses were suppressed (1810) by the Napoleonic laws. Some were reopened in 1818. The Italian government was responsible for new expropriations in 1866 and 1870.

In Italy, the two principal Vallombrosan abbeys are at Montenero (Livorno) and at Vallombrosa (regained in 1961). The latter is also the official residence of the abbot general. Important Vallobrosan priories include S. Prassede in Rome, SS. Trinità in Florence, S. Apollinare in Classe in Ravenna, and S. M. Assunta in São Paulo, Brazil.

Among the many Vallombrosan saints and blesseds, the best known are the founder, St. Bernard of Uberti (d. 1133), St. Atto (d. 1154), St. Humility (d. 1322), and Blessed Peter Igneus.

Bibliography: F. TARANI, *L'ordine vallombrosano* (Florence 1921). M. HEIMBUCHER, *Die Orden und Kongregationen der katholischen Kirche*, 2 v. (3d ed. Paderborn 1932–34) 2:320–25. G. PENCO, *Storia del monachesimo in Italia* (Rome 1961) 230–37. B. QUILICI, *Giovanni Gualberto e la sua riforma monastica* (Florence 1943). D. MEADE, *The Constitutional Development of the Monastic Congregation of Vallombrosa from 1035 to 1484* (Rome 1960). N. VASATURO, ''L'espansione della Congregazione vallombrosana fino alla metà del secolo XII,'' *Rivista di storia della Chiesa in Italia* 16 (1962) 456–85. R. DUVERNAY, ''Cîteaux, Vallombreuse, et Étienne Harding,'' *Analecta Sacri Ordinis Cisterciensis* 8 (1952) 379–495. T. SALA, *Dizionario storico biografico di scrittori, letterati ed artisti dell'Ordine di Vallombrosa*, 2 v. (Florence 1929–37).

[E. BACCETTI/EDS.]

VALLS ESPÍ, CRESCENCIA, BL.

Lay martyr; b. June 9, 1863, Onteniente (or Ontinyent), Valencia, Spain; d. there, Sept. 20, 1936. Crescencia, daughter of Joaquin Valls and Francisca Espí, was baptized the day after her birth. She received her elementary education from the Vincentian Sisters.

Crescenis's profound piety was formed through daily Mass, Communion, and recitation of the Rosary with her family, and regular meetings with her spiritual director. She was a member of the Daughters of Mary, Apostleship of Prayer, St. Vincent de Paul Society, the Third Order of Carmelites, Catholic Action, and other religious groups. She exercised her lay apostolate by visiting the sick, seeking charitable contributions on behalf of the poor, and helping those in need.

After the Feb. 16, 1936 elections and the declaration of the Republic, Crescencia intensified her apostolic work and defended the Church. On Sept. 26, she and her sisters Concepción, Carmen, and Patrocinio were arrested by four militiamen just before noon. Twelve hours later they were taken to the stone quarry in Puerto de Ollería. All four sisters were shot. Crescencia pardoned her executioners and died shouting, ''Long live Christ the King.''

Her body was initially interred in Canals Cemetery in a common grave. After the revolution, the mummified cadaver was exhumed and identified by its personal effects and the wounds that caused her death. It was reburied in her hometown, then translated to Santa María Church. She was beatified by Pope John Paul II with José Aparicio Sanz and 232 companions on Mar. 11, 2001.

Feast: Sept. 22.

See Also: ABAD CASASEMPERE, AMALIA AND COMPANIONS, BB.

Bibliography: V. CÁRCEL ORTÍ, *Martires españoles del siglo XX* (Madrid 1995). W. H. CARROLL, *The Last Crusade* (Front Royal, VA 1996). J. PÉREZ DE URBEL, *Catholic Martyrs of the Spanish Civil War*, tr. M. F. INGRAMS (Kansas City, MO 1993). R. ROYAL, *The Catholic Martyrs of the Twentieth Century* (New York 2000). *L'Osservatore Romano*, Eng. no. 11 (Mar. 14, 2001), 1–4, 12.

[K. I. RABENSTEIN]

VALUE JUDGMENT

Contemporary discussions on value theory place great emphasis on the value JUDGMENT. The questions these discussions raise can basically be reduced to two: (1) Do values exist in some way apart from the person who makes the judgment? (2) If values exist in the thing itself, or in the situation, what faculty is used in forming value judgments, and how does it function?

Scholastic and realist philosophers, taking the position that GOOD, values, ideals, and norms reside in objects, hold that judgments of value, good, etc., are based on objective data. The judgment ''charity is worthwhile'' expresses an aspect of extramental reality; the value of charity is there to be known. Such value judgments are either true or false, complete or incomplete, insofar as they correspond to the way things are or ought to be. Such an approach to value judgment is based on the metaphysical conviction that an objective order of values exists independently of mind.

Some realists, such as Max SCHELER and W. M. Urban, think that the objective order of values is grasped by INTUITION. Others say that value judgments are made after an investigation and inquiry similar to that preceding judgments of other types. Scholastics see the COGITATIVE POWER as the internal faculty that apprehends the basic values of usefulness, convenience, or danger and furnishes the substratum of knowledge from which higher values, both moral and aesthetic, can be disengaged. An important functon of this internal sense is to make man aware of values as realized actually or potentially in individual situations. The values thus apprehended usually arouse DESIRE, interest, or emotional reaction on the part of the subject; it should be noted, however, that the value judgment may be made apart from any subjective feeling.

Value judgment is conceived quite differently by those who deny any objective status to values themselves. Divergent viewpoints are found among such subjectivists. Very often they see value judgments as expressions of the mental attitude a person takes toward an object or situation, such as expressions of interest (R. B. Perry), preference (D. HUME), desire (D. Parker), or pleasantness (G. SANTAYANA).

An extreme position toward value judgments is that taken by logical positivists, of whom M. Schlick and A. J. Ayer are representative. They hold that these are meaningless since they cannot be verified or justified by the empirical sciences. At best such judgments are expressions of emotion or attempts at persuasion; they are basically irrational. Such a stand makes any real theory of values an impossibility.

See Also: AXIOLOGY.

[R. R. KLINE]

VALVERDE, VICENTE DE

First bishop of Peru; b. Oropeza, Estremadura, Spain, date unknown; d. Puná Island, November 1541. He received the Dominican habit at S. Esteban monastery, Salamanca, in 1523 and finished his studies at S. Gregorio of Valladolid. In 1529 he sailed for Peru, along with other Dominican missionaries, and remained there alone to share the fate of his cousin Francisco Pizarro. He

assisted in the capture of Atahualpa in Cajamarca and instructed and baptized him before he died. In 1535 Valverde was informed of his elevation to the bishopric of Peru and called to the court to report on the conquest and to receive some instructions for the government. He returned to Peru in 1538 with supplies for the churches and missionaries for the doctrinas. According to royal orders, he surveyed the conquered territory and wrote a long report, pointing out the necessity of dividing the Peruvian lands into governmental districts and bishoprics. The civil war between the followers of Pizarro and Almagro prevented the organization of the vast Diocese of Peru. No sooner had Vaca de Castro arrived in Quito with the mission to set the boundaries of the Bishoprics of Cuzco, Lima, and Quito, than he received news of the death of Valverde.

Bibliography: A. M. TORRES, *El padre Valverde* (2d ed. Quito 1932). J. M. VARGAS, *Historia de la Iglesia en el Ecuador durante el patronato español* (Quito 1962) ch. 2.

[J. M. VARGAS]

VALVERDE TÉLLEZ, EMETERIO

Mexican bishop and bibliographer; b. Villa del Carbón, Mexico, March 1, 1864; d. León, Dec. 26, 1948. He was a seminarian in Mexico City from 1876 to 1887, and professor in the seminary (1882–90). After ordination in 1887, he contributed to many newspapers and journals. He became vicar-general in 1903. As bishop of León, Guanajuato (1909–48), he promoted the development of the seminary and of Catholic education of youth. He organized catechetical, missionary, sociological, and Eucharistic congresses, as well as congresses devoted to Our Lady of Guadalupe and to Christ the King. His 52 pastoral letters are a summary of the substance of his teaching and his episcopal work. Valverde's writings are numerous and varied; but his most noted ones are on philosophy, mystic theology, and bibliography. In philosophy three stand out: *Apuntaciones históricas sobre la filosofía en México, Crítica filosófica,* and *Bibliografía filosófica mexicana.* The principal value of these resides in the careful material contribution to the philosophical history of Mexico. Any future investigation in this field would have to start on this base. In mystical theology his *Poema del amor divino* is outstanding. According to his biographers, Valverde reveals in this work his own spirituality and the inner force that induced him to spread devotion to Christ the King and to erect a statue and a chapel to Him at the top of Cerro del Cubelete, at the geographic center of Mexican territory. Paul VI, as acting secretary of state to Pius XII, wrote to Valverde on Feb. 27, 1948, in the name of the pope, praising him for his devotion to

Christ the King. *Bio-bibliografía eclesiástica mexicana* (1821–1943), is his outstanding work on bibliography (3 v. Mexico City 1949). In this work Valverde refers only to writers (bishops and priests) of independent Mexico. The biographies are short; the bibliographies, on the other hand, are complete. In the preface of this posthumously published work, there is a 15-page bibliography of Valverde's published and unpublished works, including his pastoral letters and the names of the newspapers and journals to which he contributed, as well as a select number of publications in which Valverde and his works have been discussed.

[E. GÓMEZ-TAGLE]

VAN CALOEN, GERARD

Liturgist, bishop, missionary; b. Bruges, Belgium, March 12, 1853; d. Cap d'Antibes, France, Jan. 16, 1932. He was the son of Baron Charles and Savina de Gourcy-Serainchamps. He entered the Benedictine monastery of Beuron in 1872 and made his profession on May 25, 1874. After his ordination at Monte Cassino on Dec. 23, 1876, he was named prior of Maredsous. He was named rector of the abbey school in 1881, but the next year he was removed from the post because his pedagogy was considered too advanced and his ideas too original (he was the first to introduce dialogue Mass). At Tournai he edited the *Missel des fidèles,* the first French translation of the Roman Missal published in Belgium. The review that he started in 1884, *Messager des Fidèles* (later the learned *Revue Bénédictine*), aimed at supporting the liturgical movement.

At this time he proposed his ideal of a monastic apostolate. He wanted his order to take part in the evangelization of China and Africa, but his plans seemed radical to his superiors.

In 1886 he went to Rome as procurator for the Beuronese congregation; in 1893 he returned there, this time attached to the Collegio San Anselmo. His interest in the churches of the East then came to the fore; although the Pope approved, his project for a Benedictine congregation dedicated to the ecumenical endeavor was rejected by his superiors. When, two years later, Leo XIII asked Beuron to help the Brazilian congregation regain its former vitality, Van Caloen was designated for this task. Spending himself completely in Brazil from 1895 to 1919, he saved almost all of the abbeys there. In order to find sufficient personnel, he founded, near Bruges, what was to become the Abbey of St. André (1899).

He did not forget his dreams of a monastic apostolate. On Dec. 13, 1907, Pius X appointed him ordinary

Flavius Stilicho (right), (c. 365–408), son of a Vandal Chieftain, confers with three Goths, drawing by H. Leutemann. (©Bettmann/CORBIS)

of Rio Branco, and he was consecrated at Maredsous on Oct. 8, 1906. The difficulties he encountered—owing in part to his financial administration—forced him, on March 2, 1915, to resign his various responsibilities, with the exception of his mission at Rio Branco.

In 1919 he returned to Europe, and, while living at Cap d'Antibes near Nice, he published a little ecumenical review called *L'Union,* of which nine issues appeared between 1926 and 1928. He was buried in the Abbey of Saint-André-lez-Bruges.

Bibliography: G. LEFEBVRE, "Un Grand moine et apôtre au XXᵉ siècle," *Bulletin des Missions* 12 (1932). O. ROUSSEAU, "Un Grand apôtre belge, Mgr. van Caloen," *Revue générale belge* 89 (1953) 576–586. P. WEISSENBERGER, "Gérard van Caloen, Bischof und Erzabt der brasilianischen Kongregation," *Benediktinische Monatsschrift* 29 (1953) 121–125, 205–215. N. HUYGHEBAERT, *Biographie Nationale,* ed. L'Académie Royale de Belgique (Brussels 1866–) sup. 3.1 (1961) 152–162.

[N. HUYGHEBAERT]

VANDALS

A Germanic people, proceeding from the Baltic region, during the first century B.C. reached the plains of the Oder and the Vistula. The Gothic migrations of the second century A.D. divided the Vandals into two chief groups, the Silings and the Hasdings. They were reunited in the region north of the Rhine two centuries later, in company with the Alani and the Suevi. In 406 they forced their way across the Rhine near Mainz, pillaged Gaul, and in 409 entered Spain. The Hasdings and the Suevi accepted the northwest, or Galicia; the Silings conquered Baetica; and the Alani took the middle regions. In 416 the VISIGOTHS invaded Spain and wiped out the Silings. They inflicted such defeats upon the Alani that they united themselves to the Hasdings, and both peoples fled to the south of the peninsula, where in 425 their king, Guntharic, captured Carthagena and Seville from the Romans. Little is known about these years: Vandal skeletons cannot be distinguished from those of other Germanic peoples, and only three Vandalic words have been identified in local place names. The term *al-Andalus*, employed by the Arabs to designate Baetica after their conquest and later extended to the whole peninsula, seems to reflect the name of the Vandals, who made themselves masters of the Balearic Islands and looked longingly to the rich land of Africa a short distance across the strait.

The Invasion of Africa. In 428, on the death of Guntharic, his ruthless brother Geiseric became king and proved himself to be perhaps the outstanding Germanic ruler of his time. Civil war between Count Boniface (*comes Africae*) and a series of generals sent by Valentinian III's regent Galla Placidia greatly weakened Roman forces in Africa. Constant uprisings of the native Berbers, hostility of the Roman landowners to imperial fiscal exactions, and unrest among the lower classes also favored the Vandal invasion. Geiseric seized the opportunity to transport his people from the devastating barbarian wars of Europe to the prosperity and shelter of North Africa.

Sailing from Tarifa, Geiseric disembarked in the region of Tangier or that of Ceuta. With the Alani, Suevi, and a hodgepodge of other barbarians, Geiseric's subjects numbered about 80,000. Perhaps 15,000 of them were soldiers. They slaughtered, raped, pillaged and burned their way across North Africa to the gates of Hippo, where Boniface had taken refuge with the remnants of his Gothic auxiliaries. After the Vandals invested and blockaded Hippo for 14 months (during which St. AUGUSTINE died within its walls), Boniface quit the city and returned to Italy. In 431 Geiseric triumphantly entered Hippo, making it the seat of his power. Procopius reports that the Vandals defeated Roman forces in two battles, but it is doubtful than any major military confrontation ever took place. The Vandal conquest of Africa was singularly facilitated by the absence of any significant resistance. In 435 Geiseric signed a treaty with the western Roman government and received "permission" to occupy the three Mauretanias—Tingitana, Caesariensis, Sitifensis—and also part of Numidia. Geiseric used this treaty to dispel the suspicions of the Romans. In 439 he took Carthage by surprise and established himself therein. He developed a strong fleet, captured Lilybaeum in Sicily, and in 442

obtained a new treaty that gave the Vandals the best regions in Africa: Proconsularis, Byzacena, and part of Numidia. With the grain supply of Italy now at their mercy, the Vandals settled mainly in Proconsularis, chose the best lands for themselves, and declared them exempt from taxes. Roman landholders suffered a variety of fates: some were murdered, some enslaved, some exiled, and those allowed to retain their property were burdened with heavy taxes.

Vandal Religion. By the time they left Spain the Vandals had converted to Arianism. Geiseric's successor King Huneric (477 to 484), a vigorous opponent of Catholic Trinitarianism, confessed the same faith as the Arian councils of Ariminum and Seleucia. The Vandals derisively labeled Catholics as "*homousians*" and insisted that Christ was less than the Father. They forbade the celebration of *homousian* sacraments within their realm, demanded rebaptism upon conversion to Arianism, and sought to completely replace Catholicism with Arianism. Most of their efforts concentrated upon the bishops and clergy; the Vandals exiled or killed many bishops, and forbade the ordination of new ones. Church property was confiscated, destroyed, or handed over to the Arian clergy, who celebrated services in their native tongue. While there were occasional periods of toleration, prolonged persecution of the Catholic Church characterizes the Vandal reign and distinguishes the Vandals from other barbarians invading the Empire at this time. The Vandals truly were "the most Arian of all the barbarians."

Vandal Law. No body of Vandal laws has been preserved. The few sources that explain their institutions are contained in the works of VICTOR OF VITA and Procopius of Caesarea and in the so-called *Tablettes Albertini,* 45 wooden tablets, discovered near Tebessa (in northeast Algeria) in 1928, that cover 32 acts of property sales from 493 to 496.

Summit and Fall of Vandal Power. During the political disorders that followed the murder of Valentinian III in 455, Geiseric sailed for Italy. He entered Rome on June 2, and his armies pillaged the city for two weeks but refrained from slaughter and fire, as Pope Leo I had begged them to do. Geiseric's military and diplomatic skills made the Vandals temporarily the leading power in the West. Corsica and Sardinia were added to their empire, and their fleets ruled the Mediterranean. Under Geiseric (d. 477) they avoided or defeated several major imperial military expeditions sent against them, but their might gradually dwindled under his successors. Though King Gunthamund (484 to 496) gave more freedom to the Catholics, his successor, Thrasamund (496 to 523), exiled large numbers of bishops. Hilderic (523 to 530) was defeated decisively by the Berbers at Capsa. He was deposed in favor of Gelimer, who in turn was defeated and imprisoned by the Byzantine forces of JUSTINIAN I under Belisarius in 534 and brought in triumph to Constantinople. This marked the end of Vandal rule in Africa. Most of their soldiers were enslaved, their property was restored to the Romans, and their churches were returned to the Catholics. As a people they quickly disappeared.

Bibliography: J. MOORHEAD, *Victor of Vita: History of the Vandal Persecution* (Liverpool 1992). F. CLOVER, *The Late Roman West and the Vandals* (Brookfield 1993). A. ISOLA, *I cristiani dell'Africa vandalica nei Sermones del tempo (429–534)* (Milan 1990). F. B. MAPWAR, in *Cristianesimo e specificità regionali nel Mediterraneo latino (sec IV–VI)* ed. B. LUISELLI, et al., 189–213 (Rome 1994). H. WOLFRAM, *The Roman Empire and Its Germanic Peoples*, tr. T. DUNLAP. (Berkeley 1997). L. J. VAN DER LOF, *Zeitschrift für die neutestamentliche Wissenschaft und die Kunde der älteren Kirche* 64 (1973) 146–151. L. SCHMIDT, *Geschichte der Wandalen* (1942, repr. München 1970). C. COURTOIS, *Les Vandales et l'Afrique* (Paris 1955), fundamental; E. F. GAUTIER, *Genséric, roi des Vandales* (Paris 1951). C. COURTOIS et al., eds., *Tablettes Albertini: Actes privés de l'Époque vandale* (Paris 1952).

[J. J. GAVIGAN/D. VAN SLYKE]

VAN DEN BROEK, THEODORE

Missionary and colonizer of the Middle West; b. Holland, 1783; d. Little Chute, Wisconsin, Nov. 5, 1851. After serving as a Dominican priest in Holland, he immigrated to St. Rose, Washington County, Kentucky (1832), and soon went to the Dominican House at Somerset, Ohio, to prepare for work as an Indian missionary. On July 4, 1834, he arrived at Green Bay, Wisconsin, and for nearly ten years ministered to whites as well as to Indians in this area. He was particularly successful among the Chippewa and Menominee tribes of the Fox River Valley, converting 600 during his first eight years among them. From him they learned agricultural skills as well as those that made possible erection of St. John Nepomucene Church at Little Chute. Van den Broek returned to Holland (1847) and successfully recruited Catholic settlers for the Green Bay, DePere, and nearby regions of Wisconsin.

Bibliography: C. VERWYST, *The Life and Labors of Rt. Rev. Frederic Baraga: First Bishop of Marquette, Mich.* (Milwaukee 1900).

[T. O. HANLEY]

VAN DER SCHRIECK, LOUISE, SISTER

Pioneer U.S. educator, baptized Josephine; b. Bergenop-Zoom, Holland, Nov. 14, 1813; d. Cincinnati,

Ohio, Dec. 3, 1886. She was educated in Belgium, entered the Sisters of Notre Dame de Namur, and in 1840 came to the Diocese (now Archdiocese) of Cincinnati, the youngest of eight religious sent to inaugurate the work of her community in the New World. From 1848 until her death Sister Louise was superior of all Notre Dame houses east of the Rockies. She added 25 foundations to the two existing before her appointment, and extended the work to Boston, MA, in 1849; to Philadelphia, PA, in 1856; and to Washington, D.C., in 1873. Her foundations included several academies with secondary programs; nearly 50 elementary parochial schools were also staffed by her sisters.

In matters of religious discipline her outlook was traditionalist, but she was realistic about adapting educational policies and methods to existing needs. As early as 1867 she sent sisters to Cincinnati to staff a school for Negro children, and undertook the same work in Philadelphia in 1877. She opened night schools for adult Catholic immigrants in the principal cities where she had houses. In the continental tradition, however, she refused to accept schools for boys. In general, Sister Louise's administration, as religious superior and as an educational leader, was characterized by austerity, respect for the individual, and good sense. These qualities, together with unusual freedom from sentimental religious attitudes, formed the basis of the Notre Dame educational tradition in the U.S.

Bibliography: H. L. NUGENT, *Sister Louise* (Washington 1931).

[J. BLAND]

VAN DE VYVER, AUGUSTINE

Sixth bishop of Richmond, VA; b. Haesdonck, East Flanders, Belgium, Dec. 1, 1844; d. Richmond, Oct. 16, 1911. Following his graduation from the American College at Louvain, he was ordained at Brussels, July 24, 1870. He served as assistant at St. Peter's Cathedral, Richmond, pastor of St. Peter's Church, Harper's Ferry, WV, and vicar–general of the Richmond diocese from 1881 to 1889. On Oct. 20, 1889, he was consecrated bishop at St. Peter's Cathedral, succeeding John J. Keane. The Catholic population of his diocese more than doubled during Van de Vyver's episcopate. He founded 9 parishes; built 27 churches, including Sacred Heart Cathedral, Richmond; and founded two preparatory, four industrial, and four parochial schools. His resignation, submitted to the Holy See in 1908, was withdrawn upon the petition of his clergy and people.

Augustine Van De Vyver.

Bibliography: F. J. MAGRI, *The Catholic Church in the City and Diocese of Richmond* (Richmond 1906).

[J. H. BAILEY]

VANGADIZZA, ABBEY OF

Former BENEDICTINE MONASTERY, situated 15 miles from Rovigo, Italy, on the right bank of the River Adige, in the commune of Badia Polesine (pop. 12,000) to which it has given its name (Badia = abbey), in the province and Diocese of Rovigo. The church and monastery are mentioned in diplomas of Berengar II, King of Italy, and Adalbert (961), and in some charters (990s) of Hugh, Marquis of Tuscany, who gave it considerable endowments. Popes and emperors granted the abbey great privileges and large estates in the districts of Padua, Vicenza, Verona, Ferrara, and Bologna. In 1213 it passed from the Benedictines to the CAMALDOLESE who set up a school there and made it so famous that the abbot of Vangadizza held the third place after the abbot-general in the order's

general councils. It declined from its primitive splendor through the laxity of the monks, and in 1435 Pope Eugene IV transferred it *in commendam* (*see* COMMENDATION) under a prelate of the secular clergy who administered the property and provided for the monk's expenses. It was suppressed by governmental decree on April 25, 1810. Only the ruins of the outer walls of the abbey church remain, but there are still the fine Lady Chapel with valuable 16th-century stuccoes and frescoes, and the 13th-century bell tower. The monastery cloister, built soon after the first church (*c.* 1000) and restored at different periods, is in excellent condition.

The origin of the name Vangadizza is uncertain. It is believed that there was a spade (''vanga'') in the abbey coat of arms to indicate the work of land reclamation carried out by the monks in the Polestine district. There is an extant seal showing a spade between the letters A (Abbatia) and V (Vangadizza).

Bibliography: G. BRONZIERO, *Storia delle origini e condizioni de' luoghi principali del Polesine* (Venice 1747). F. R. A. GIURIATI, *De coenobio Vangaticiensi dissertatio epistolaris* (Ferrara 1758). G. B. MITTARELLI and A. COSTADONI, *Annales camaldulenses*, 9 v. (Venice 1755–73). A. E. BARUFFALDI, *Badia Polesine*, v.3 *La fine dell'abbazia della Vangadizza* (Padua 1906). P. F. KEHR, *Regesta Pontificum Romanorum. Italia Pontificia*, 8 v. (Berlin 1906–35) 5:193–197. L. H. COTTINEAU, *Répertoire topobibliographique des abbayes et prieurés*, 2 v. (Mâcon 1935–39) 2:3294.

[S. OLIVIERI]

VANN, GERALD

Dominican moralist and spiritual writer; b. St. Mary Cray (Kent), England, Aug. 24, 1906; d. Newcastle-upon-Tyne, July 14, 1963. He entered the Order of Preachers in 1923 and was ordained in 1929, and completed his theological studies at the Collegio Angelico (as it was then called) in Rome. After returning to England in 1931 he studied modern philosophy at Oxford for three years. In 1934 he was sent to Blackfriars School at Laxton (Northhamptonshire), where he taught until 1952, and during his last years of residence there was superior of the community and headmaster of the school. In 1938 he organized the Union of Prayer for Peace. From 1952 until his death he was occupied with writing, lecturing, and giving retreats, and was stationed successively at the Cambridge, Edinburgh, and Newcastle houses of his order. After World War II he made several visits to the U.S. to give lectures, and from 1959 to 1962 he lectured each second semester at The Catholic University of America in Washington, D.C.

Among his publications are *On Being Human* (1933), *Morals Makyth Man* (1937), *Morality and War*

(1939), *Of His Fullness* (1939), *St. Thomas Aquinas* (1940), *The Heart of Man* (1944), *The Divine Pity* (1945), *Eve and the Gryphon* (1946), *His Will is Our Peace* (1947), *The Pain of Christ* (1947), *Awake in Heaven* (1948), *The Two Trees* (1948), *The Seven Swords* (1950), *The High Green Hill* (1951), *The Water and the Fire* (1953), *The Temptations of Christ* (with P. K. Meagher, OP, 1957), *The Paradise Tree* (1959), *The Eagle's Word* (1961), and *Moral Dilemmas* (posthumous, 1963). His writings blend Thomistic philosophy and theology with the humanism current in the 1920s and 1930s when he was coming to maturity. He was deeply sensitive to human values and had a delicate and compassionate understanding of human problems.

[P. K. MEAGHER]

VANNINI, GIUSEPPINA, BL.

Josephine, baptized Giuditta Adelaides (Judith Adelaide); foundress of the Daughters of Saint Camillus; b. Rome, Italy, July 7, 1859; d. Rome, Feb. 23, 1911. Orphaned at age seven, Giuseppina was educated at the Torlonia orphanage at St. Onofrio until 1883. She joined the Daughters of Charity of St. Vincent de Paul (March 3, 1883), but after four years she was compelled to leave, mainly because of ill health. In 1891, she met Fr. Luigi Tezza, a Camillian priest, and at his suggestion she founded a congregation (Feb. 2, 1892). It followed the rule of St. Camillus de Lellis and aimed, like the Camillians, to care for the sick in hospitals, clinics, and rest homes. Giuseppina took her vows privately (1895), since her application for official ecclesiastical approval was at first rejected. Papal approval of the congregation came in 1909. She died peacefully and was interred in Rome, but later translated to Grottaferrata. She was beatified by Pope John Paul II on Oct. 16, 1994—during the ninth general assembly of the Synod of Bishops dealing with the consecrated life.

Feast: Oct. 16.

Bibliography: B. BRAZZAROLA, *Madre G. Vannini* (Rome 1956). G. SANDIGLIANO, *Madre G. Vannini* (Casale Monferrato 1925).

[F. G. SOTTOCORNOLA/EDS.]

VAN NOORT, GERARD

Theologian; b. Hageveld, Holland, May 10, 1861; d. Amsterdam, Sept. 15, 1946. He studied at Hageveld and Warmond. Following his ordination in 1884, he served as chaplain in Medemblik and Amsterdam. From 1892 to

Bl. Giuseppina Vannini.

1908 he was professor of dogmatic theology at the seminary of Warmond, and it was here that he completed his ten-volume manual of dogmatic theology, *Tractatus apologetici et dogmatici* (Leyden 1898–1908). It is a model of clarity and conciseness, with a judicious blend of positive and speculative theology. It is in use all over the world, and has gone through several editions. It was brought up to date by J. P. Verhaar, also of the Warmond faculty, and in an English edition (for the first three volumes) by John J. Castelot and William R. Murphy. In 1908 Van Noort left seminary work to become a pastor in Amsterdam, and in 1926 he was named a canon in the cathedral chapter of Haarlem. He received a Roman doctorate *honoris causa* in 1930 and in 1934 Pius XI appointed him a domestic prelate.

[J. J. CASTELOT]

VAN QUICKENBORNE, CHARLES FELIX

Missionary to the Native Americans, founder of the Missouri Jesuit province; b. Petergem, Belgium, Jan. 21, 1788; d. Portage des Sioux, MO, Aug. 17, 1837. Although ordained for the Diocese of Ghent, he entered the Society of Jesus on April 14, 1815, to follow a special call to the foreign missions. He arrived in the U.S. in 1817 and was named master of novices at the novitiate in Georgetown, Washington, D.C., but his inexperience as a Jesuit handicapped him, and in 1821 he asked to be sent to the native people missions. As early as 1814 Bp. Louis DUBOURG of Louisiana had sought help from the Maryland Jesuits. Because of financial and other difficulties, the Maryland novitiate at White Marsh, where it had been moved in 1819, was on the verge of dissolution. In 1823 Van Quickenborne led a group of Belgian recruits from White Marsh to Florissant, MO, where they founded the first house of the new mission that was to become the Missouri province. Here, besides governing the mission, he began his apostolate to the native peoples, being the first to make a missionary journey to the Osages. In 1828 Van Quickenborne had been the agent in the transfer of St. Louis College (University) from diocesan to Jesuit administration, and later directed the drive for money to construct the new school building. After nine years in Florissant, he spent some time on the upper Missouri River among the Kickapoo. In 1837 it was necessary to remove him from the Kickapoo mission because of his idiosyncrasies of temperament and despotic manner of government. His health was shattered by the hardships of his strenuous career and he died in his 50th year.

[E. R. VOLLMAR]

VAN ROSSUM, WILLEM MARINUS

Cardinal; b. Zwolle, Netherlands, Sept. 3, 1854; d. Maastricht, Aug. 30, 1932. After early education in an orphanage, he entered a seminary (1867), joined the REDEMPTORISTS (1874), and was ordained (1879). After being successively professor of dogmatic theology (1883–92) and rector (1893–95) at Wittem, he went to Rome (1895) and was appointed consultor to the Holy Office (1896) and to the Redemptorist superior general (1909). From 1904 to 1917 he was a member of the commission that prepared the Code of CANON LAW. Created cardinal (1911), he became a member of several Roman congregations and succeeded Cardinal RAMPOLLA as president of the PONTIFICAL BIBLICAL COMMISSION (1914). In 1918 he became prefect of the Congregation for the PROPAGATION OF THE FAITH (Propaganda), and titular archbishop of Caesarea in Mauritania. As head of Propaganda he played a key role in repairing the devastations of World War I in the missions and inaugurating a period of great mission activity. Vigorous and farsighted, he inspired the creation of native priesthoods and hierarchies, including the first seven Chinese bishops (1926) and the first Japanese bishop (1927). He was also responsible for founding several missionary seminaries, notably

the Collegium Urbanum at Rome (1928); creating 162 new missionary districts; and reassigning expelled German missionaries to new areas in South Africa and China. Centralized control of the missions from Rome was maintained by new apostolic delegations. The International Fides Service provided detailed information about mission territories. Van Rossum's inspiration was important in the appearance of the papal missionary encyclicals *Maximum illud* (1919) and *Rerum Ecclesiae* (1926). The cardinal was also largely instrumental in reorganizing and centralizing associations providing material aid to the missions. Through the *Unio cleri pro missionibus* he increased clerical participation in mission activities. Van Rossum acted as papal legate to the Eucharistic Congresses at Vienna (1912) and Amsterdam (1925). He also published theological and devotional works.

Bibliography: M. DE MEULEMEESTER et al., *Bibliographie générale des écrivains Rédemptoristes*, 3 v. (Louvain 1933–39) 2:444–447. J. M. DREHMANS, *Kardinaal van Rossum* (Roermond 1935). J. O. SMIT, *Wilhelmus Marinus kardinaal van Rossum* (Roermond 1955).

[A. G. WEILER]

VAN STEENBERGHEN, FERNAND

Philosopher, canon, member of the Royal Belgian Academy; b. Saint-Josse-ten-Noode (Brussels), Feb. 13, 1904. After completing his studies for the doctorate in philosophy at Louvain in 1923, Van Steenberghen studied theology there and was ordained in 1926. After spending some time working at the Vatican library, at Munich and at Oxford, he completed his magisterial study on the life and works of SIGER OF BRABANT: *Siger de Brabant d'après ses ouvres inédites*: v. I, *Les oeuvres inédites* (Louvain 1931). This work won for him at Louvain the still higher degree: *Maître-Agrégé de l'École Saint-Thomas d'Aquin* in 1931. Volume 2 was published at Louvain in 1942. Between the appearance of these two volumes he had completed his *Les oeuvres et la doctrine de Siger de Brabant* (Brussels 1938). This work was incorporated almost in whole into v. 2 of the above study.

Academic Career. His teaching career at Louvain began in 1931. The following year he was named *chargé de cours,* and became a professor in 1935. In 1939 he succeeded Maurice De Wulf in the chair of the history of medieval philosophy at Louvain. Since the early 1930s he had been collaborating with De Wulf, for instance on the sixth ed. of the latter's *Histoire de la philosophie médiévale* (3 v. 1934, 1936, 1947) and in directing the series *Les Philosophes Belges.*

In 1948 Van Steenberghen established the series *Philosophes médiévaux,* in which some 25 important contributions to the history of medieval philosophy have appeared. In 1956 he was involved in founding the De Wulf-Mansion Centre at Louvain, which has exercised considerable influence on the study of ancient and medieval philosophy. He also participated in the formation of the *Centre national de recherches d'histoire de la pensée médiévale* in 1959, and has served as its president. In 1966, together with his former student, Robert Bultot, he founded *l'Institut d'études médiévales* at Louvain.

His influence has extended far beyond the borders of Belgium, both through his writings and his lectures. Thus in 1950 he was a visiting professor at the Pontifical Institute of Mediaeval Studies in Toronto. After that he served as an exchange professor and lecturer in the United States, Canada, England, Ireland, Spain, Italy, The Netherlands, Germany, Switzerland, and France. In 1978 he received an honorary doctorate from The Catholic University of America in Wash., D.C., and on that occasion delivered three lectures, which were subsequently published under the title *Thomas Aquinas and Radical Aristotelianism* (Wash., D.C. 1980). On April 1, 1978, he received from the American Catholic Philosophical Association its highest award, the Aquinas Medal.

He retired from active teaching at Louvain in 1974, but his literary activity has continued without interruption. On that occasion his colleagues at Louvain presented him with a volume of choice selections drawn from some of his earlier articles: *Introduction à l'étude de la philosophie médiévale*, G. Van Riet, ed. (Louvain-Paris 1974). Included in that volume is a listing of his publications until that time—241 in number. A few of his many publications to appear since then will be mentioned below. Cited in that volume also are 78 licentiate and doctoral dissertations written under his direction.

Scholarly Focus. Van Steenberghen's scholarly publications fall into two broad fields: the history of medieval philosophy and speculative metaphysics. Already in the 1930s he proposed new and different ways of understanding the development of philosophical thought during the medieval period, especially during the 13th century. He has long been interested in the efforts of various medieval thinkers to work out the proper relationship between faith and reason, and since the 1930s has also participated in the debate concerning the appropriateness of referring to the philosophies developed by the medieval schoolmen as ''Christian philosophies.'' He acknowledges that this title may be applied when and only when the term philosophy is given a very broad interpretation (so as to be more or less equivalent to a general ''world-view'' [*Weltanschauung*]). But he has always denied that there was or is any such thing as Christian philosophy when the term philosophy is taken in the strict

Willem Marinus Van Rossum.

sense. So understood, philosophy is a purely rational discipline, not one based on data accepted on the strength of religious belief. At the same time, Van Steenberghen concurs with Thomas Aquinas in defending the fundamental harmony between faith rightly interpreted and reason rightly exercised.

In his study of BONAVENTURE, he has always refused to identify the philosophy of that Franciscan thinker as Augustinian rather than as Aristotelian. His views concerning this continue to be taken into account by the most recent discussions of that issue. In exposing the thought of THOMAS AQUINAS, Van Steenberghen has long recognized the importance of various Neoplatonic elements therein, along with the more generally acknowledged Aristotelian influences.

His name is associated especially with research concerning Siger of Brabant and the radical philosophical movement associated with the latter in the Arts Faculty at Paris in the 1260s and 1270s. Here Van Steenberghen's interpretation has been highly original. Thus in opposition to prevailing opinion at the time he first began to publish on Siger, Van Steenberghen has held that the 13th century Master of Arts underwent significant development in his views concerning the nature of the intellect and its relationship with individual human beings. If

Siger had begun by accepting the Averroistic doctrine of one separate possible intellect (and one separate agent intellect) for the entire human race, he eventually moved much closer to the position defended by Thomas Aquinas—each individual human being possesses his own agent and his own possible intellect. The authenticity of some of the alleged Sigerian writings on which Van Steenberghen originally built his case has been seriously challenged. But more recently he has enjoyed the good fortune of having his interpretation confirmed in striking fashion by the discovery and publication of one of Siger's previously unknown works, his Questions on the *Liber de causis,* A. Marlasca, ed. (Louvain-Paris 1972).

English-language readers have profited from Van Steenberghen's widely circulated *Aristotle in the West.* In this work, as in many of his original publications in French, Van Steenberghen combines his knowledge of the philosophical texts of the time with helpful information concerning the broader history of the medieval period, e.g., the rise of medieval universities, the transmission of Greek or Latin originals into medieval Latin, the role of the mendicant (Franciscan and Dominican) orders, etc. More recently he has drawn upon these two approaches—interpretation of philosophical texts and consultation of pertinent broader historical data—to produce a classical interpretation of 13th century philosophical thought—*La philosophie au XIIIe siècle* (Louvain 1966; rev. Ger. tr. 1977). And still more recently his decades of research on Siger of Brabant have been given definitive expression in his *Maître Siger de Brabant* (Louvain-Paris 1977).

Van Steenberghen has also long been interested in the pursuit of speculative metaphysics for its own sake. This is evident from the original interpretations he has offered of the metaphysical thought of various medieval thinkers. And it has been given special expression in his independent writings on epistemology, metaphysics, and natural theology, and in many articles dealing with such themes. While his treatment of metaphysics is usually ultimately inspired by the thought of Thomas Aquinas, he has often criticized what he regards as weaknesses or as lacunae in the latter's views. For instance, regarding Aquinas' argumentation for God's existence, Van Steenberghen has offered a number of critical and controverted analyses. More recently he has produced an important study of all of Thomas' arguments for God's existence: *Le problème de l'existence de Dieu dans les écrits de s. Thomas d'Aquin* (Louvain-la-Neuve 1980). In this book he combines precise historical presentation and interpretation of all the relevant texts with critical evaluations. Other independent presentations of his general views may be found in English translation in his *Ontology, Epistemology,* and *The Hidden God.*

In a number of recent publications he has challenged Aquinas's claim that purely natural reason cannot prove that the world began to be (*see,* for instance, Lecture 1 in his *Thomas Aquinas and Radical Aristotelianism*). On this point he prefers the position defended by St. Bonaventure—human reason can demonstrate that the world began to be. He also differs with Aquinas's explanation of divine knowledge of future contingents.

Bibliography: F. VAN STEENBERGHEN, *Aristote en Occident. Les origines de l'aristotélisme parisien* (Louvain 1946); Eng. tr. *Aristotle in the West. The Origins of Latin Aristotelianism* (Louvain 1955, 1970); *Directives pour la confection d'une monographie scientifique* (3d ed. Louvain 1961); *Épistémologie* (Louvain 1945; rev. eds. 1947, 1956; rev. ed. 1965); Eng. tr. of 2d ed: *Epistomology* (New York 1949), tr. 4th ed. (New York 1970); *Ontologie* (Louvain 1946; 2d ed., Louvain 1952: 3d ed., Louvain 1961; 4th ed., Louvain 1966); Eng. tr. of 2d ed.: *Ontology* (New York 1952); Eng. tr. of 4th ed. (Louvain-New York 1970); *Philosophie des Mittelalters* (Bern 1950); *Le XIIIe siècle,* A. FOREST, et al., eds., *Le mouvement doctrinal de IXe au XIVe siècle* (Paris 1951, 1956); *The Philosophical Movement in the Thirteenth Century* (Belfast 1955); *Dieu caché. Comment savons-nous que Dieu existe?* (Louvain 1961); Eng. tr.: *Hidden God. How Do We Know that God Exists?* (St. Louis 1966); *Histoire de la philosophie. Période chrétienne* (2d rev. ed. Louvain-Paris 1973); *La bibliothèque du philosophe mediéviste* (Louvain-Paris 1974), containing many of his book reviews; *Le thomisme* (Paris 1983); *Études philosophiques* (Longueil, Quebec 1985). Articles about Van Steenberghen. M. HOEHN, *Catholic Authors: Contemporary Biographical Sketches* (St. Mary's Abbey 1952) 607–609; C. A. GRAFF, *Enciclopedia filosofica* (2d ed. Florence 1967), v. 6, col. 841; J. F. WIPPEL, ''Presentation of the Aquinas Medal to Fernand Van Steenberghen,'' *Proceedings of the American Catholic Philosophical Association* 52 (1978) 213–215.

[J. F. WIPPEL]

VARDAN, MAMIKONIAN, ST.

Armenian noble and leader of Armenian uprising against the Persian Yazdgard II (440–457); b. Armenia, date unknown; d. Avarair, Armenia, June 2, 451 (feast, Thursday before Lent). Vardan, the son of Hamazasp and Sahaganoush, had two younger brothers, Hemaiak and Hamazaspian. From the days of TIRIDATES III (250–330?) the Mamikonians, who were descendants of Mancaeus, a native of China, had been outstanding in the nation, providing brave sparapets, or generals. Vardan had a thorough Christian education and excellent military training. He distinguished himself at the head of the Armenian cavalry in his own country and in Persia when the latter was an Armenian ally. Vardan was a member of the mission sent by Patriarch ISAAC THE GREAT to Emperor Marcian, on which occasion he was given the title of Stratelates.

He opposed Yazdgard II's efforts to impose Zoroastrianism on the Armenians. Imprisoned by Yazdgard, he unwillingly pretended to adore the sun at the insistence of his fellow prisoners, who were also of the nobility, in order to save his homeland from a gigantic invasion. He repented of this grave sin and desired to get away from his country. At the insistence of Prince Vahan Amaduni, however, Vardan accepted command of the Armenian armies. In the Synod of Shahabivan (450), Vardan was questioned, absolved, and declared "faithful in everything to the love of Christ."

Having freed Armenia of the armies and magi of Yazdgard II, he foresaw the vengeance that would be wreaked by this savage king and made a vain appeal to the Byzantine Emperor Marcian (450–457) for help. Mihr Narse, Yazdgard II's general, crossed the Araks River at the head of 300,000 soldiers equipped with assault elephants and thrust into the heartland of Armenia. Vardan met him with 60,000 men. The eve of the battle was a night of spiritual preparation: Mass was celebrated, all went to Communion, and many neophytes were baptized. Vardan explained to his troops the magnitude of the struggle and the ideal of martyrdom. The armies met on June 2, 451, near the hamlet of Avarair, on the banks of the Delmut (Akçay) River. Vardan fell bravely in battle together with the other princes. Despite the Persian victory the tenacity of the Armenians made Yazdgard II change his plans.

Bibliography: V. ELIŠE, *The History of Vartan and of the Battle of the Armenians,* tr. C. F. NEUMAN (London 1830). P'ARPEC 'I LAZAR, *Histoire d'Arménie,* Fr. tr. S. GHÉSARIAN in *Collection des historiens anciens et modernes de l'Arménie,* v.2, ed. V. LANGLOIS (Paris 1869) 253–368.

[N. M. SETIAN]

VARIN D'AINVILLE, JOSEPH DÉSIRÉ

Priest who influenced the religious renewal and the founding of religious congregations after the FRENCH REVOLUTION; b. Besançon, Feb. 7, 1769; d. Paris, April 19, 1850. Born of a wealthy family prominent in the government of Franche-Comté, he had received minor orders at Saint-Sulpice in Paris before the Revolution. In 1794, after two years in Condé's army, he joined several former fellow seminarians in the newly established Society of the SACRED HEART OF JESUS. He was its superior from 1797 until 1799 when the Society merged with the Paccanarists. Varin directed the Paccanarists in France from 1804 until their disbandment by Napoleon I in 1808. He joined the JESUITS upon their restoration (1814) and played a prominent role in rebuilding the order in France. Varin was largely instrumental in founding the Society of the SACRED HEART, the Sisters of NOTRE DAME DE NAMUR, the Sisters Faithful Companions of Jesus, and

other religious congregations of women, and continued to act as spiritual director to these groups and their foundresses. Militant, vigorous, and cheerful, he left his constantly reiterated "Courage and confidence!" as a family motto to the groups of religious whose formation was his most lasting accomplishment.

Bibliography: A. GUIDÉE, *Vie du R. P. Joseph Varin* (2d ed. Paris 1860). M. K. RICHARDSON, *Joseph Varin, Soldier* (London 1954). L. KOCH, *Jesuiten-Lexicon* (Paderborn 1934; Louvain-Heverlee 1962) 1794–95.

[C. E. MAGUIRE]

VATICAN

The present territory of the Vatican is only a small portion of the area that was known to the ancient Romans as *Vaticanum.* This territory extended on the right bank of the Tiber from Monte Mario to the Janiculum and embraced *mons Vaticanus,* the Vatican hill, *vallis Vaticana,* the Vatican valley, and *campus Vaticanus,* the Vatican plain, the broad surface of the "Prati." This was the last of 14 administrative regions into which Augustus divided the city of Rome.

EARLY HISTORY

In antiquity, the Vatican was valued for its many brickfields, notorious on account of its bitter wine but renowned also for several buildings. There stood the Naumachia (a stadium for aquatic sports); a kind of race course to which tradition has given the name of *Gaianum* (after Caligula); to the south of this, the sepulcher of the Emperor Hadrian and, in the neighborhood of the present St. Peter's, the *Phrygianum,* a sanctuary of the goddess Cybele. On the Janiculum towards the Tiber were Nero's gardens that took their origin from Agrippina, Caligula's mother.

Necropolis. During the rebuilding of St. Peter's at the end of the sixteenth century and the beginning of the seventh century, some pagan graves were discovered. However, it would not be until the twentieth century that discoveries would lead to extensive excavations. When the Annona (the store in Vatican City) was being constructed in 1930 some tombs were discovered below the surface. The inscriptions on the tombs were from the end of the first century and into the second century. Not far away but a little towards the West, a further cemetery was reached, and in part unearthed, during the preparatory work for a new building at the beginning of the same year. This time the burial places go back as far as the start of the first century and extend into the second. Two tombs of servants of the Roman Imperial house from the time of Nero were found.

Saint Peter's Interior, Vatican City. (©Susan Rock)

After the burial of Pius XI in 1939 work commenced on the grottos underneath ST. PETER'S BASILICA. In 1940 workmen uncovered a random series of marble and stone sarcophagi, some small and plain, other large and impressively ornamented. The tombs stretched in an East-West line on the slope of the Vatican hill and at one time they must have formed, as a whole, one of ancient Rome's largest cemeteries. The older row of mausoleums had its back wall so tightly against the hill on the northern side that only the upper part of the back of the wall was visible above the ground. The somewhat later series of mausoleums, separated from the former by a narrow pathway and running parallel with it to the south, had no lateral contact with the hill and rose free from the ground on every side. The northern mausoleums were originally arranged only for funeral urns. The southern mausoleums contained hollowed cavities for sarcophagi and tombs. The excavators used the Greek alphabet to identify the mausoleums. An important mausoleum is that of the Caetennii (F) with paintings of goblets, fruits, flowers, birds and gazelles, and mythological figures; there is also the image of the Christian Gorgonia holding a flask of fresh water, indicating eternal life. Another is the mausoleum M with its mosaic decorations; a pagan tomb that was used by Christians contains an image of Jonah, a fisherman with

line, and a Good Shepherd with sheep on either side. The mausoleum B is a purely Christian tomb that provides the most ancient mosaics discovered with a Christian subject, including the Christ-Helios. Finally the mausoleum of the Egyptians (Z) was erected at the end of the second century; old bones were displaced and then reverently collected in an ossarium and reburied. The mausoleums were used for 150–200 years.

The Tomb and Bones of Peter. A shrine was discovered under the high altar of St. Peter's Basilica that proved to be difficult to excavate. E. Kirschbaum describes how the excavators systematically made their way toward the area where St. Peter was believed to be buried. They broke through the walls of the Clementine chapel, which led to another wall at the time of Gregory the Great. An opening was made in this wall that revealed a white marble facade. The walls on either side were breached, which led to the Constantinian marble pavement. There was a red-colored wall (the Red Wall) that did not rest on the Constantinian pavement but went below. The Red Wall was part of a monument over a grave. A lamp and cross were discovered, which are described in the *Liber Pontificalis* as gifts from Constantine. The investigation continued on the rear side of the monument. After breaking through the Constantinian wall, a graffiti wall was discovered. This wall had scribble from pilgrims. Further excavation around the Red Wall revealed the "Tropaion" of Gaius, a pre-Constantinian monument. The Red Wall with two graveyards Q and P and a drainage canal were erected as a unified bloc between the already standing mausoleums R-R' and S. Five bricks were found stamped by the Emperor Marcus Aurelius about A.D.160, which gives the date of the Red Wall and the Tropaion. Human bones were found beneath the Red Wall. Pius XII was informed and he ordered testing. The bones (with no skull) were of a man between 65 and 70 years old and placed in a wooden box, and it was speculated that they might be the bones of St. Peter. The excavations ended in 1949.

A new stage began when the excavations were open to professionals in 1952. Dr. M. Guarducci deciphered the logogram PE discovered by A. Ferrua on the graffiti wall as "Peter is within"; another inscription was translated as "Christian men buried near your body." In 1956 Professor Correnti was asked to examine the bones. He discovered that the bones were of some animals and three people; there was no indication that any of the bones were of St. Peter. Correnti was asked to examine bones discovered in the courtyard and ones that were unknowingly removed in 1942 from the graffiti wall. He finished the examination of the courtyard bones in 1962; they were of four individuals. A year later he finished the examination the bones from the graffiti wall and determined that they were of one man between 60 and 70 years old. These bones were taken from the earth and wrapped in a purplish, gold-threaded cloth. Guarducci took the results of Correnti's study and developed a theory that demonstrated the likelihood that the bones were those of St. Peter. Guarducci published her report in 1965, which encountered criticism. She responded to her critics in a 1967 report. A troubling question was why the bones were removed from the grave and placed in a niche prior to the monument built by Constantine. Correspondence between Guarducci and Paul VI convinced the pope to announce in 1968 that the bones were of St. Peter. Most scholars accept that St. Peter was probably martyred within months after the fire of Rome in July of 64. In 1968 Guarducci proposed the date of Oct. 13, 64, because this is the anniversary of Nero's accession to the throne. J. E. Walsh reviewed the evidence in 1987 and became supportive of the Guarducci theory about the bones. He proposed that the bones were removed around 250 for security reasons during the persecutions of Emperor Valerian.

Constantine's Basilica. The basilica begun by Constantine *c.* 324 was completed by his son Constantius *c.* 354. It was a rectangular church whose central nave was

Monument to Pope Pius VII, sculpted by Pietro Tenarani, located in the Church of the Popes, St. Peter's Basilica. (AP/ Wide World Photos)

some 230 feet across and 40 feet long with a V-shaped wooden roof 131 feet high at its apex. Four rows of 22 columns each constituted the five aisles, the two central columns being 29 feet high. The top register of the clerestory was pierced by 11 windows, four on each side and three on the nave; and its walls were decorated with frescoes; those on the lowest level included the portraits of the popes commissioned by Liberius (352–366). The three middle sections of the clerestory contained representations of the Patriarchs, Prophets, and Apostles on the top story, and on each side of the nave, 46 scenes from the Old and New Testaments. The two aisles were some 29 feet wide and 62 feet high, while the outside aisles were 46 feet high and 29 feet wide. A triumphal mosaic arch dominated the central nave of the church with a scene in which Constantine was representing as presenting a model of the basilica to Christ.

In the center of the transept, which was 59 feet wide, the tomb of St. Peter formed the axis of the basilica. It was a block-shaped building made of blue-veined marble, boxed in by four porphyry columns and surmounted by an inverted ciborium supported by six white spiral columns. A votive crown with 50 lamps in the form of dolphins was suspended from the center of the umbrella like

Dutch Jesuit priest Brother Matthew Timmers and his colleague use the giant telescope in the Vatican's observatory at Castel Gandolfo. (©Hulton-Deutsch Collection/CORBIS)

chapels dedicated to the Holy Cross, St. John the Baptist, and St. John the Evangelist.

The Emperor Valentinian I, under Pope Sixtus III (432–440), had the facade of the tomb decorated with a representation of Christ flanked by the 12 Apostles standing before the 12 gates of Jerusalem. Pope Leo I (440–461) repaired the damages caused by an earthquake in 443, and restored the facade of the basilica with a mosaic of Christ, the Virgin Mary, St. Peter, the symbols of the Four Evangelists, and the 24 elders of the Apocalypse. The expenses were evidently borne by the consul Marinianus and his wife Anastasia.

Pelagius II (579–590) erected a pulpit in the sanctuary. Pope Gregory I (590–604) raised the level of the sanctuary and built a permanent altar directly over the tomb, leaving open a small window through which the eastern face of the Constantinian monument could be seen. He dismantled the original BALDACHINO, or pegola, used the six spiral columns to form a screen in front of the apse, and excavated behind the altar to form a semi-circular crypt giving access from the back. John VII (705–707) built a richly decorated chapel of the Virgin Mary, which was demolished in 1606. Gregory III (731–741) added six spiral columns to the screen in from of the altar, and succeeding popes took pride in adorning the basilica. Stephen II (732–757) erected a bell tower and enclosed one of the fountains in the atrium with an eight-column bronze cupola, while Leo III (795–816) enlarged the baptistery. Paschal I (817–824) built a chapel in honor of SS. Processus and Martianus.

Additions by Medieval Popes. Pillaged by the Saracens in 846, the basilica was repaired by Leo IV (847–855). Callistus II (1119–1124) enclosed the Gregorian altar in a boxlike construction and erected a new altar directly above it. In 1298 Cardinal James Stefaneschi had Giotto decorate the portico with a mosaic depicting Christ walking on the waters to calm the Apostles in the boat (Mt 14.22–33). This Mosaic, called the Navicella, was preserved, and today graces the ceiling of the atrium to the basilica. The basilica was neglected during the residence of the popes at Avignon; but Pope Benedict XII (1334–1342) repaired the roof; and Pope Eugene IV (1431–1441) had Antonio Averulino (Filarete) execute the door in bronze that today stands as the central portal of the modern basilica.

Vatican Monasteries. The early residence of the popes was in the Lateran palace, and the nearby Constaninian now known as the basilica of St. John Lateran served as the cathedral for the Bishop of Rome. St. Peter's was used as a station church and for special ceremonies.

covering. The details have been preserved on the facade of an ivory box found at Samagher, near Pola, Istria.

The Paradiso. Entrance to the basilica was provided by five doors called from right to left, the Porta Guidonea, Romana, Regia, Ravegnana, and Judicii. The last received its name from the fact that it was the door through which funerals passed; the others, probably from donors. Before the entrance was a garden with fountains called the Paradiso; it contained the pine-cone-shaped fountain admired by Dante and today decorating the courtyard of the Pigna. Entrance to this garden was provided by three bronze doors in a large portico supported by 46 columns and measuring some 203 feet by 184 feet. The platform in front was used for coronations and other ceremonials and was fronted by 35 steps.

Papal Ornamentation. The magnificence of this basilica on the side of a hill facing the city of Rome not only impressed the local citizenry, but it became a center of interest, and of pilgrimages from all over the Christian world. Pope Damasus I (366–384) erected a baptistery on the north transept of the basilica, using the water drained from the tomb area by his engineers; and Pope Symmachus (498–514) surrounded this area with three small

A document from the secret archives of the Vatican, which contains original letters and manuscripts by such historical figures as Galileo, Michaelangelo and Voltaire. (©Vittoriano Rastelli/CORBIS)

Leo I (*c.*450) seems to have erected a monastery dedicated to SS. John and Paul on the north side of the Vatican for the monks who served St. Peter's. A second monastery in honor of St. Martin was added on a spot now occupied by the pilaster supporting the cupola that contains the statue of St. Veronica; a third called St. Stephen Major, or *cata Galla Patricia,* stood behind the apse of the modern basilica; and a fourth, founded by Stephen IV on the site of the present sacristy, served later as a hospice for Hungarian pilgrims, but was demolished in 1776. A fifth monastery for nuns seems to have existed opposite the oratory of Symmachus during the early Middle Ages; and Pope Nicholas III (1277–1280) built a home for the canons of St. Peter on the south side of the basilica where the modern residence stands.

During the reign of Symmachus I (498–514), likewise, residences for the poor were constructed on the south side of the basilica; they were rebuilt under Sergius I (687–701), Gregory II (715–731), and Leo III, and baths were installed nearby. Five diaconiae, or offices, for the deacons who cared for the poor were established. The first, in honor of SS. Sergius and Baccus, was on the north side in the Palace of Charlemagne (palatium Caroli); a second, in honor of St. Mary, stood *in caput Portici,* or,

near the Portico of the basilica. Pope Stephen II built a hospice on the spot where the obelisk now stands in front of St. Peter's, and this housed the diaconia of St. Silvester in the 8th century. It was demolished by Pope Pius IV (1560–1565). A fourth diaconia stood near the Castel'Angelo and was first called the Hadrianum, later Santa Maria in Transpontina; it was destroyed in the 15th century. A fifth diaconia was also situated near the Portico, called St. Martino de Custina.

Scholae, or Hostels, for Pilgrims. Hostels were also founded for pilgrims from different nations. The oldest was erected by King Ine of Wessex (727–730), according to Matthew of Paris, whereas William of Malmesbury credits Offa of Mercia; it was called the *schola Saxonum* for the English, or Saxons. The *schola Francorum* with a chapel called S. Salvatore di Ferrione occupied a site on which the Holy Office now stands. The *schola Frisorum* for German and Flemish pilgrims stood on the present site of S. Maria in Campo Santo; while the *schola Langobadorum* is credited to Ansa, the wife of King Desiderius, and dates from *c.* 770. The chapel of SS. Michele e Magno, left of Bernini's colonnade, marks the foundation of the *schola Frisorum.* The Hungarian hospice was called ''de Aguila'' (needle) from the obelisk

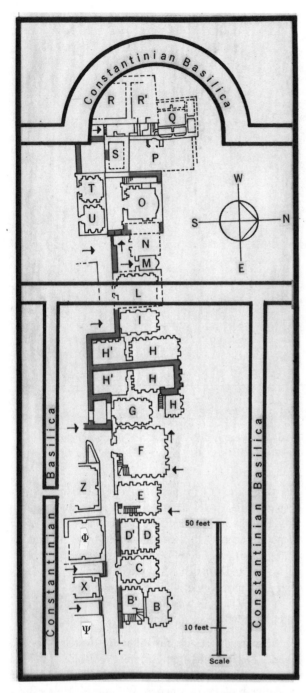

Architectural drawings of early Christian cemeteries excavated beneath the Constantinian Basilica. (The Catholic University of America)

that stood nearby; it was built over the old monastery of St. Stephen on the site of the present sacristy.

Leonine Wall. Pope Leo IV (847–855) built a wall around the Vatican using plans that originated with the Emperor Lothair after the sack of Rome by the Saracens in 846. Called the Leonine wall, it was two and one-

quarter Roman miles long and was pierced by 48 towers and three gates. Innocent III (1198–1216) built a fortified wall within the perimter of the older construction, and one of its towers, identified in 1947, was incorporated in the palace of Nicholas III (1277–1280).

Early Papal Palaces. In the 6th century Pope Symmachus I had built two small residences on either side of the basilica for brief stays connected with ceremonies or functions in St. Peter's; and Charlemagne constructed a palace (*palatium Caroli*) for his subjects during his stay in Rome (*c.* 800). Leo III, Eugene III (1153), and Innocent III reconstructed one of the Symmachan edifices that was further fortified with a wall by Leo IV. But it was Nicholas III who began the series of constructions known today as the papal palaces. Two of his decorated buildings were incorporated into the present palace, and their remains can be seen in the Sala dei Paramenti, Sala dei Pontifici, and Cubiculo di Niccolo V on the first floor, and in the halls of Chiaroscuro and of Constantine on the second floor. He also built a rectangular chapel that underlies the present Sistine Chapel; its gardens are occupied today by the court of the Belvedere.

THE RENAISSANCE

A new era of construction and decoration was introduced with the Renaissance. Nicholas V (1447–1455) added a fortified bastion to the north and west walls of the palace of Nicholas III. He built a chapel in which Fra Angelico (Giovanni di Fiesola) painted the pictures of SS. Stephen and Lawrence. Paul II (1458–1464) constructed the stairway from the courtyard at St. Damasus to that of the Pappagallo.

The New St. Peter's. The idea to construct a new St. Peter's basilica to replace the Constantinian one was first effectively broached under Pope Nicholas V when the architect Leon Battista Alberti discovered that the south wall had a list some five feet off perpendicular and that the frescoes of the south side of the central nave were some three-and-a-half feet off alignment. Nicholas commissioned Bernardo Rossellino in 1452 to construct a new apse for the basilica, to the west of the old one, but the work stopped on the pope's death. Paul II gave the project to Julian da Sangallo in 1470, and Sixtus IV (1471–1484) ordered the construction of a new baldachino over the altar.

Bramante. According to a plan submitted by Donato Bramante the new church was to be erected in the form of a Greek cross with a square area in the center surmounted by a dome and four smaller cupolas on the four corners. Julius II laid the cornerstone on April 18, 1506. The new church was to be constructed in two stages: the apse and altar of the old basilica were preserved from im-

The Piazza di San Pietro, detail of a fresco in the Vatican Library, 16th century.

mediate demolition; eventually under Antonio da Sangallo (1534–1546) they were shut off by a wall and served as a temporary church. Bramante tore down the nave of Constantine's church and without excavating dug emplacements for the four great pilasters upholding the new cupola. After Bramante's death in 1514 Leo X gave the project to the care of Raphael, Fra Giovanni Giocondo, and Julian da Sangallo, who changed the plan from a Greek to a Latin cross, constituted by a nave of three arches to be separated by pilasters.

Michelangelo. After the sack of Rome in 1527 Antonio da Sangallo assumed full charge under Paul III (1534–1549). The latter commissioned Michelangelo Buonarroti as architect in chief in 1546, and despite criticism of the changes he made in the original plans, Michelangelo was confirmed in this position by Julius II in 1552, and by Pius IV in 1561. Having almost completed the drum of the cupola before his death in 1564, Michelangelo was succeeded by Pirro Ligorio and Vignola (James Barozzi). The latter was placed in charge of the project by Gregory XIII (1572–1585), and the dome was completed under pressure from Sixtus V (1585–1590), who also had Domenico Fontana move the Egyptian obelisk from the spot near the sacristy to the center of the piazza in 1586.

Under Clement VIII (1592–1605) the old apse was pulled down and a new High Altar was constructed directly over the altar built by Callistus II. Likewise the pavement of the new basilica was laid some 15 feet above the level of the old Constantinian Church. Under Paul V (1605–1621) Carlo Maderno extended the eastern arm of the apse in such fashion as to emphasize the Latin-cross plan. Completed in 1615, the new edifice measured 613 feet in length; the facade was 377 feet in breadth and 151 feet high; the atrium was 233 feet long, 42 feet wide, and 65 feet high and decorated with Giotto's Navicella.

Giovanni Bernini. Paul V had a large area excavated in front of the main altar to constitute an open area or court with colored marble and bronze statues of Peter and Paul. It opens into the *Confessio* of St. Peter, which contained a window allowing objects to be lowered down to the Constantinian monument over the grave of St. Peter. After the election of Urban VIII (1623–1644), Giovanni Bernini undertook the construction of a new baldachino, or canopy, over the main altar. In gilded bronze, this canopy is 92 feet high and is held up by four pillars modeled on the original Constaninian columns were used to decorate the four loggias on the upper portions of the pilasters facing the altar, which were also decorated by Bernini.

The lower sections contain four niches filled by heroic-sized statues of SS. Longinus, Helena, Veronica, and Andrew the Apostle.

The marble decoration of the basilica's interior and the medallions representing the first 40 popes and 28 allegories of virtues were also the work of Bernini commissioned by Innocent X (1644–1655). Bernini designed the pavement of the basilica and the heroic statue of Constantine as well as the immense bronze cathedra at the base of the apse, which rests on the statues of the four great doctors of the Church, SS. Ambrose, Augustine, Athanasius, and John Chrysostom. Finally under Alexander VII (1655–1567) Bernini turned attention to the exterior, and between 1657 and 1663 erected the two semicircular sets of colonnades that enclasp the Piazza of St., Peter with four rows of 284 travertine columns on the balustrade, over which stand 140 heroic statutes of martyrs and confessors. In the piazza itself to the left of the obelisk he replaced the fountain of Innocent VIII; that on the right is the work of Carlo Fontana commissioned by Clement X in 1670.

Vatican Library and Archives. Independent of the construction of St. Peter's Sixtus IV renovated rooms and built other edifices. Though the idea to establish a place for a VATICAN LIBRARY was conceived by Nicholas in 1450, it was officially established by Sixtus IV by the papal bull, *Ad decorum militantis Ecclesiae* in 1475. He initially renovated three rooms, and later another one, on the ground floor of the Apostolic Palace to house the collection. Julius II (1503–1513) added rooms and Sixtus V had Domenico Fontana design a new building that divided the Belvedere courtyard from the Pigna courtyard. The top floor has a magnificent hall (184 feet long and 57 feet wide) that became known as the Sistine Library. In 1587, Sixtus V (1585–1590) moved the printing worked founded by Pius IV (1559–1565) in 1561. This act began the Vatican Press.

In 1612 Paul V created a separate archives section by bringing together materials from the library of Castel Sant'Angelo, the Apostolic Camera, and other official offices. This new section began the Vatican Secret Archives, located in rooms under the tower of Gregory XIII's observatory.

Sistine Chapel. Sixtus IV (1471–1484) commissioned Giovanni dei Dolci to erect the Sistine chapel on the site of the cappella magna built in the palace of Nicholas III (1277–1280) and used by the popes as a chapel until 1477. In 1481 Perugino, Botticelli, Ghirlandaio and Cosimo Rosselli signed a contract to paint ten biblical stories. The chapel was consecrated in 1483. Paul III (1534–1549) encouraged Michelangelo to decorate its ceiling with the magnificent story of Creation and the Last Judgment, completed between 1536 and 1541.

Other Developments. Under Julius II, Donato Bramante completed the north facade of the Belvedere palace, adding two loggias, and the extensive corridor holding the Chiaramonti galleries and Lapidaria, while Raphael supplied a third loggia. Raphael also painted the rooms of the *signatura,* the Heliodorus, and the loggias overlooking the courtyard of the Maresciallo.

Antonio de Sangallo built the Sala Regia for Paul III; it was decorated by Giorgio Vasari, Thaddeus Zuccaro, and the Della Portas. Sangallo also erected the Pauline chapel for the same Pope, who had it ornamented with scenes from the lives of SS. Peter and Paul by Michelangelo between 1542 and 1550. The corridor of the Belvedere was completed under Pius IV who erected the building known as the Casino of Pius IV in the Vatican Gardens. The chapels of SS. Stephen, Michael, and Peter were begun under the patronage of Pius V (1566–1672) and decorated with paintings by Vasari and stucco ornaments by James della Porta. Julius Mazzoni and Daniel della Volterra painted the chapel of the Swiss guards.

The famous Gallery of the Maps, containing the topography of the regions of Italy in the Dominican Ignatius Danti's designs, stems from the reign of Gregory XIII (1572–1585), who likewise commissioned the wing enclosing the courtyard of St. Damasus and the Tower of the Winds. Sixtus V (1585–1590) erected the present papal residence on the extreme eastern end of the court of Damasus, using Domenico Fontana as architect. He likewise cut the Belvedere courtyard in two with a new wing for the Vatican Library. Giovanni and Cherubino Alberti painted the Clementine hall under Clement VIII (1592–1605); and Paul Bril decorated the hall of Consistories. The new entrance to the papal palace with it s famous bronze doors was designed by Martin Ferrabosco and James Vasanzio.

The chapel of Countess Matilda decorated by Peter of Cortona was executed under Urban VIII (1623–1644); Alexander VII (1655–1667) had the Sala Regia united with the Sala Ducale; and Clement XII (1730–1740) added another wing to the Vatican Library. Benedict XIV (1740–1758) joined the Museum of Christian Antiquity, called the Museo Sacro, to the library, and Clement XIII built the Gallery of the Candelabra.

MODERN

The Nineteenth Century and the Vatican Museums. The modern Pio-Clementine Museum, on north side of Vatican City, consists of the Porch of the Four Doors, the Simonetti Staircase, Hall of the Greek Cross, Rotunda, Hall of the Muses, Hall of the Animals, Octagonal Courtyard, Cabinet of the Masks, and Room of the Busts, and is due to popes Clement XIV (1769–1774) and Pius

VI (1775–1799). Pius VII (1800–1823) commissioned the Chiaramonti Museum, and Gregory XIV (1823–1846) erected the Egyptian, Estruscan, and Gregorian Museums on the north side of the court of the Pigna. Pius IX (1846–1878) constructed the staircase leading to the Court of St. Damasus from the bronze doors of the papal palace on the right side of the Piazza of St. Peter's; he also built the Hall of the Immaculate Conception. Leo XIII (1878–1903) built the Gallery of the Chandeliers, and erected the Vatican Observatory on a height overlooking the Vatican Gardens. Leo XIII decreed in 1881 that the archives be open to researchers. Records are made available from the beginning until a pontificate has been catalogued. This will soon include the reign of Pius XI. Accessibility is also governed by standard archival norms.

The Twentieth Century. Pius X (1903–1914) made a passage from the corridor of Bramante to the gardens and a stairway from the Holy Office to the Viale del Belvedere. Pius XI (1922–1939) modernized the Vatican Library in 1928 by installing an elevator, electricity, and some temperature controls. More shelves were added by renovating the stables that were no longer needed with the advent of the automobile. A new entrance was constructed that opened into the Belvedere courtyard. After signing the Lateran Treaty (1929) he remodeled the papal summer palace at Castelgondolfo and moved the papal Observatory there. Giuseppe Momo, a friend of Pius XI, designed the Ethiopian College, the Palazzo del Governatorato (built in 1930), and the railway station (inaugurated in 1933). Between the Palazzo and the back of St. Peter's Basilica is the Vatican Gardens; there is a large flower arrangement of the coat of arms of the reigning pope. Pius XI also erected a post office (stamps have been issued by the Vatican since 1852); he constructed the buildings housing the tribunals, Annona store, and *L'Osservatore Romano* (the Vatican newspaper). Vatican Radio was established in 1931 with the assistance of Guglielmo Marconi; broadcasts are given in 34 languages. A new entrance to the Vatican Museums was completed in 1932.

Pius XII (1939–1958) restored the offices of the Secretariat of State and founded a television station together with a more powerful radio station near Santa Maria di Galleria in 1957. He authorized the excavation under St. Peter's, which led to the project for a resystematization of the sacred grottos underneath the present pavement of the basilica.

In 1960, during the reign of John XXIII (1958–1963), the entire territory of the Vatican was inscribed in the *International Register of Cultural Works under Special Protection in case of Armed Conflict* by the United Nations. The commencement of the Second Vatican Council involved intensive preparations, especially the installation of tiers of benches for the bishops on both sides of the main aisle of St. Peter's basilica and other provisions. John XXIII also renovated the tower containing the radio station and built a papal retreat in as second tower of the ancient Leonine wall on the north side of the gardens. John XXIII was the first pope to use the Vatican railway station for a pilgrimage to Assisi in 1962, a week before the Vatican Council began.

Paul VI (1963–1978) built the Museum of Modern Religious Art. He also constructed a modern audience hall that was completed in 1971 and holds over 9,000 people.

One of the first additions by John Paul II (1978–) was the Mater Ecclesiae mosaic on the exterior wall of the Apostolic Palace in 1981 that commemorated his survival from an assassination attempt in St. Peter's square. An extensive project was undertaken in the 1980s and completed in 1994 to clean the frescoes of the Sistine Chapel. John Paul II had a hospice built in 1989 at the request of MOTHER THERESA of Calcutta. The hospice, which houses over 70 women and provides evening meals to hundreds, is managed by the MISSIONARIES OF CHARITY. Some improvements were made in the Vatican in preparation for the Jubilee Year 2000, including renovations to the entrance of the Vatican museums in 1999 and cleaning the facade of the basilica of St. Peter's.

Bibliography: M. GUARDUCCI, ''La Data del Martirio di San Pietro,'' *La Parola del Passato* 23 (1968) 81–117; *Le Chiavi sulla Pietra* (Rome 1995). J. M. PACKARD, *Peter's Kingdom: Inside the Papal City* (New York 1985). A. M. STICKLER, *The Vatican Library: Its History and Treasures* (Vatican City 1989). J. E. WALSH, *The Bones of St. Peter* (Manila 1987). N. SUFFI, *St. Peter's* (Vatican City 1998).

[F. X. MURPHY/C. KOSANKE]

VATICAN ARCHIVES

The Vatican Archives began as the *Scrinium* (repository) of the popes, which served as both an archives and a library. This dual function continued until a separate custodian for the archives was appointed in 1612 by PAUL V (1605–1621). The nucleus of the material to establish the Vatican Archives came from the *Bibliotheca secreta* of Sixtus IV. Thus the prior history of the Vatican Secret Archives shares the same early history of the Vatican Library. The historical documentation of the Holy See is very complex because the Vatican Archives is not the only repository for records; other repositories include the Roman State Archives (*Archivio di Stato di Roma*) for the Papal States and those of some individual departments or congregations of the Curia; the several reforms of the Curia in the last few centuries has added to the complexity. The history and collection development can be viewed in three periods: the early church until the 16th century, the establishment of the Vatican Secret Archives, and the 19th century to the present.

History. *Apostolic Period to 16th Century.* There is no information on collections in the pre-Lateran period, probably because this was a period of persecution of the Christians, which did not allow for a specified location to house records. Certainly the Christians copied and distributed the Sacred Scriptures and copies of writings of the early Church Fathers that were probably kept in various places where the pope lived.

The Lateran Period. This period is dated from 313 to 1309. The Emperor Constantine gave Melchiades (311–14) the imperial residence on the Caelian Hill, named after the Lateran family. The Lateran Palace provided a location for the residence (including a library and archives) and central administration of the church for almost 1,000 years. Julian II (337–352) constituted the Holy Scrinium as a repository for literary and theological writings. St. Jerome mentioned the Scrinium in a 4th century letter. Gregory the Great (590–604) mentions that he placed his sermons at Lateran. The first listing of the documents of the papal administration occurred under Pope Innocent III (1198–1216), who created the important Regestes (registers); the first register is of John VIII (872–882) and the second of Gregory VII (1073–1085). This series of Registers is one of the principal sources for documents on the papacy from 872–1588. Innocent IV (1243–1254) brought some records from the archives to use at the Council of Lyon. Boniface VIII (1294–1303) became involved in conflicts when he attempted to assert his authority over the political leaders of Europe. Benedict XI (1303–1304) placed the archives in Perugia. The Lateran palace was destroyed by fire in 1308 and 1309. Clement V (1305–1314), fearing more attacks in 1310 from King Philip IV of France, transported 643 valuable codices to the sacristy of the monastery in Assisi. The monastery in Assisi was sacked in 1310. A section of the archives was also located at Carpentras.

The Avignon Period. The popes resided in Avignon from 1309 to 1377. Benedict XII (1334–1342) transferred the records from Assisi to Avignon in 1339. Documents, such as financial records and letters, continued to be collected during this period. This collection is known as the *Registra Avenionensia.*

Pre-Vatican Archives. Gregory XI returned to Rome in 1377 and died a year later. The archives remained in Avignon until the Great Schism ended with the election of Martin V (1417–1431). Martin V brought the archives

back to Rome (1419–1422), where they were temporarily housed in S. Maria Sopra Minerva, then established in his family palace (Colonna) in central Rome; though the Vatican Registers were returned to Rome during this time, the Avignon Registers were not brought to the Vatican until 1783. Eugene IV (1431–1447) brought some registers to use at the Council of Florence in 1435; these records traveled to Bologna (1437), Ferrara (1438) back to Florence (1440) and back to Rome (1443). The modern Vatican Secret Archives has its roots in the founding of the Vatican Library. Nicholas V (1447–1455) worked towards establishing a Vatican Library in preparation for the Holy Year in 1450. Sixtus IV (1471- 1484) established the Vatican Library in the modern sense of the term. On June 15, 1475, Sixtus IV issued the bull, *Ad decorum militantis Ecclesiae* that formally established the library and set a precedent for its good administration. Giovanni Andrea Bussi was appointed the librarian and was succeeded by Bartolomeo Platina in 1475, the first official librarian. The initial Library consisted of three rooms: *bibliotheca latina, bibliotheca graeca* and *bibliotheca secreta,* the latter being the predecessor to the Vatican Secret Archives. However, some records were placed in a special archive in Castel San'Angelo (*Archivum Arcis*). In 1483 an archives for the Roman Curia was formed at the founding of the College of Notaries. Julius II (1503–1513) sought to organize the archives of the apostolic Camera. In 1507 he mandated that all public and private writings belonging to the Camera be brought together at the Vatican. The Council of Trent was yet another church council that would influence the need and use of a central archives. Besides prescribing sacramental registers for parishes, Pius IV (1559–1565) announced that a central Archives would be set up in the Vatican Palace. Before his death in 1565 he ordered a search for all records and documents of his predecessors. Pius V continued the efforts of his forerunners to gather material for a central archives. He extended the decree on archives by Charles Borromeo at the Council of Milan in 1565 to the whole church a year later. Sixtus V (1585–1590) reformed the Roman Curia by establishing 15 permanent congregations. Inactive records from the previous bureaucratic structure as well as the records for the new administration were a growing concern. The Vatican Library was also concurrently growing.

Vatican Archives. As the Vatican Library developed as a center of research for scholars, the close access to government records and documents in the *Biblioteca secreta* became a security issue. In 1591 Gregory XIV forbid admittance to these records without his permission. Clement VIII began to move some material from the Library to a hall in Castel Sant'Angelo. He also prepared a bull in 1593 to have all the archives transferred. However, this course of action was cancelled because access to the documents by the Curia was deemed to be too inconvenient; only the most valuable records were kept in the castle. In 1612 Paul V (1605–21) created a separate central archives section by bringing together materials from the library of Castel Sant'Angelo, the Apostolic Camera, and other official offices. This new section, completed in 1630, was located in rooms under the tower of Gregory XIII's observatory; the reports from nuncios began to be sent in the same year. In 1656 Alexander VII (1655–1667) mandated that the records of the Secretary of State be kept in the archives. During this period records were placed in one of 80 cabinets (armaria) that constituted the central new archives; documents became classified by cabinet number. These records were only accessible to the Pope or Secretary of State or whom they gave permission. The resources for operating the archives have been provided by the Secretary of State.

19th and 20th Centuries. *Napoleonic Period.* The Emperor Napoleon Bonaparte created a central archive by having the archives of the European capitals brought together. The *Archivum Arcis*, transferred from Castel San'Angelo in 1798, was sent to Paris in 1799. Some other records went the following year. After the imprisonment of Pius VII (1800–1823) in 1809 Napoleon ordered that all the records in the Vatican Archives were to be brought to Paris. This transfer took place in 1810, 1811 and 1813. The Vatican Archives were returned to Rome after the defeat of Napoleon in 1814. From 1815 onwards countries such as Austria, Denmark, England, Hungry, Russia and Sweden were given permission to have copies made of sources relative to their history.

Papal States. In 1860 the armies of Pius IX (1846–1878) were defeated. When the Papal States were incorporated into the kingdom of Italy in 1870, many of the civil records were transferred to the new State Archives of Rome. Now another archives, separate from the Vatican, housed records that pertained to a period of the church's history.

Archives Opened. After some debate Leo XIII (1878–1903) decided in 1879 to open the Vatican Archives to researchers. He appointed an historian as the new Cardinal Librarian-Archivist; a year and half later, Jan. 1, 1881, the Vatican Archives was ready to receive scholars. Access to material in the Vatican Archives has been given in stages. Initially material was available until 1815. In 1920 access was granted to material until 1830 and later to 1846. This has since been extended to Jan. 22, 1922. Material is now made accessible according to the reign of a pope. The period of Pius XI (1922–1939) will soon be opened. Two general factors have currently determined the opening of a pontificate: completion of cataloging material during a respective reign, which can take several years, and sensitivity to material that pertains to people who may still be alive.

Collection. The records in the Vatican Archives are divided and organized according to the various functions of the Holy See. The arrangement of material has generally followed the bureaucratic structure that developed from the reforms of Sixtus V (1585–1590) in 1588 prior to the Archives being officially established. The archive section for the Roman Curia can become complicated as a result of reforms over the centuries. The divisions of the Vatican Archives include the College of Cardinals, the Papal Court (papal chapel and papal household), Roman Curia (congregations, offices, and tribunals), Apostolic Nunicatures, Internunciatures, Delegations (diplomatic records by country), the Papal States (found in the State Archives of Rome), and Permanent Commissions (Archeology, Biblical, Historical Sciences, etc.) and Miscellaneous collections (the Armaria, monasteries, convents, religious orders, confraternities, etc.).

The archives of the Holy See go beyond the Vatican Archives. The records of the Papal States are found in the State Archives of Rome. The archives for some departments and offices are kept at their respective location for convenience. Among them are: Congregation for the Doctrine of the Faith, Congregation for Worship and Sacraments, Congregation for the Evangelization of Peoples (Propagation of the Faith), Section for Relations with States (Secretary of State), Penitentiary, Pontifical Ceremonies, and the Fabbrica of St. Peter's Basilica.

Bibliography: M. A. AMBROSINI, *The Secret Archives of the Vatican* (Boston, 1969). L. E. BOYLE, *A Survey of the Vatican Archives and Its Medieval Holdings* (Toronto, 1972). O. CHADWICK, *Catholicism and History: The Opening of the Vatican Archives* (Cambridge, 1978). *L'Archivio Secreto Vaticano: Un secolo dalla sua apertura* 1881–1981 (Vatican City 1981). F. BLOUIN, *Vatican Archives: An Inventory and Guide to the Historical Documents of the Holy See* (New York 1997).

[C. KOSANKE]

VATICAN CITY, STATE OF

Lo Stato della Città del Vaticano is the official name of the independent state created in 1929 by the treaty in the LATERAN PACTS.

Geography. Vatican City is the smallest state in the world, occupying 108.7 acres, of which about one-third is covered with buildings. Trapezoidal in shape, it forms an enclave in the city of ROME, on the right side of the Tiber. Imposing walls, built during the Middle Ages and Renaissance, mark its boundaries except on the east, where the limits are the open edge of St. Peter's Square

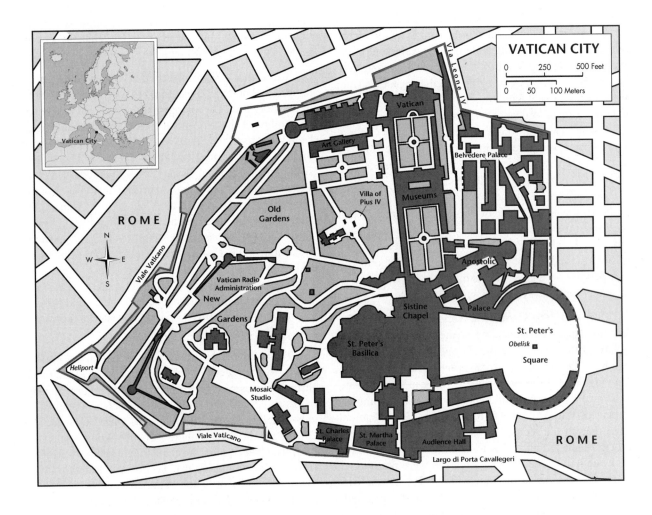

and the colonnade. Outside this area are other buildings and lands of the Holy See in or near Rome, which are part of the Republic of Italy, but whose permanent extraterritoriality, tax exemption, and freedom from expropriation are formally guaranteed. These include the basilicas of St. John Lateran, St. Mary Major, and St. Paul outside the Walls; the buildings of the Holy Office, Datary, Propaganda, Chancery, and Vicariate of Rome; the papal palace at CASTEL GANDOLFO; and the transmitting center of the Vatican radio station at Santa Maria di Galeria.

Origin. The seizure of the STATES OF THE CHURCH, which for several centuries had constituted the papal temporal domain, was completed in 1870; and the territory was annexed to the new Kingdom of Italy. Even after 1870 the Holy See continued to regard itself as a separate entity in international law, and was recognized as such by numerous states with which it retained normal diplomatic relations and active and passive legations. In virtue of this status the Holy See decisively rejected the unilateral solution to the ROMAN QUESTION proposed by the Law of GUARANTEES. After long discussions the Holy

See and Italy signed the Lateran Pacts (Feb. 11, 1929), which contained an international treaty in the accepted sense. In this treaty Italy recognized that the Holy See, the supreme directive organ of the Catholic Church, possesses sovereignty in the international field as an attribute inherent in its nature, conformed to its tradition and mission in the world. This treaty also established the bases of the new state of Vatican City, defining its limits and essential characteristics. The state was placed under the absolute sovereignty of the supreme pontiff, to the exclusion of all interference by the Italian government. The Republic of Italy reaffirmed its adherence to the Lateran Pacts in its constitution, which became effective in 1948. In 1984 a new concordat between the Italian republic and the Holy See reaffirmed the pope's sovereignty over the Vatican territories and further codified certain aspects of relations between the two states.

The Modern State. When the Lateran Treaty went into effect (June 7, 1929), Vatican City published a constitution. The juridical section, emanating from the pope, comprised the fundamental law, fonts of law, and regula-

Ruins of Hadrian's villa, Vatican City. (©Susan Rock)

tions on citizenship, residence, administration, public security, and economic, commercial, and professional controls. This complex of six laws remains the basis of the juridical and constitutional system of the Vatican State. Some later modifications occurred with the promulgation of the judicial regulation and code of civil procedure, approved by a motu proprio (May 1, 1946), and with the law on the right of authors (Jan. 12, 1960).

Vatican City is a state in the strict sense since it possesses all the necessary attributes and functions. This is widely admitted in the community of nations. It has territory, population, and sovereignty. This territory, limited as it is, suffices to guarantee the spiritual and temporal independence needed for the exercise of the Holy See's spiritual mission. Unlike other states the Holy See exercises not only sovereign rights over its entire territory but patrimonial rights as well. Vatican City has its own stamps, seal, flag, and coinage, which is interchangeable with Italian currency. Its official language is Italian, but that of the Holy See is Latin.

Citizenship and Population. Vatican citizenship is acquired by persons who reside permanently in Vatican City because of their work or dignity or because of papal authorization alone. The wife, children, parents, brothers, and sisters who are authorized to reside within the state in the home of a citizen also acquire citizenship. Curial cardinals also are citizens, even if they dwell outside Vatican City limits. Once a citizen ceases to fulfill these requirements, he loses citizenship. If he was previously an Italian citizen or a descendant of Italian citizens, he automatically becomes an Italian citizen. Those who were citizens of other countries or descendants of such citizens regain this citizenship if the laws of their respective countries permit dual citizenship; otherwise they become Italian citizens. Vatican citizenship is, therefore, one of the state's unusual features. Because of the manner in which it is gained or lost, the number of citizens tends to vary considerably, but in 2001 Vatican City had a population of just under 1,000.

Government. Sovereignty over Vatican City is exercised by the pope in his function as supreme head of the Catholic Church. The pope assumes this power at the moment of his canonical election to the Chair of St. Peter. In this exercise of power within Vatican City the pope is served by certain special organs delegated for this purpose, all of whose members are appointed and removed at will by him. The Papal Commission for Vatican City was established in 1939, composed initially of three car-

"Opening Procession of Vatican Council I" by Franklin McMahon. (©Franklin McMahon/CORBIS)

dinals and a secretary and later expanded to include seven cardinals and a lay delegate. After 1968, the commission also included 21 lay advisers. To it are delegated the pope's powers for the government of the state. The commission oversees a central council as well as the directors of the museums and other Vatican services.

Justice is administered by a tribunal of the first instance and in the higher stages by a court of appeals and a court of cassation. Recourse to the supreme tribunal of the Apostolic Signatura is also permitted. The lay tribunals of Vatican City do not handle matters that the Code of Canon Law reserves to ecclesiastical tribunals. Criminal matters are referred to the Italian courts.

Defense. For internal security, public order, and police work Vatican City maintains a security force under the Central Office of Security. There are also the SWISS GUARDS, whose full complement is 133 and who are under the supervision of the Pontifical Commission for the Vatican City. No armed forces in the usual acceptance of the term are maintained. Italian police normally patrol St. Peter's Square, which must be kept open to the public. The Holy See is bound to extradite to Italy persons charged with acts regarded as criminal in both states who take refuge in Vatican City or its extraterritorial possessions.

Communications. Vatican City maintains its own postal, telegraph, telephone, and railroad systems. There are seven radio stations broadcasting programs in over 30 languages. *L'Osservatore Romano,* the semi-official newspaper, is published daily, with weekly editions in English, Spanish, Portuguese, German, and French. The Vatican Television Center was founded in 1983 to produce and distribute religious programming.

International Relations. Vatican City is an effective member of the community of nations, maintaining diplomatic relations with some 166 countries, of which

69 maintain permanent resident diplomatic missions accredited to the Holy See in Rome. It has permanent observer status in the United Nations, maintains diplomatic relations with the European Union, and since 1997 has been a member of the World Trade Organization. Diplomatic relations are carried out through the secretariate of state, with the Secretary of the Section for Relations with States serving as the pope's foreign minister.

Relation to the Holy See. Vatican City and the HOLY SEE are distinct entities, both recognized internationally as such, and subjects of international law; but they are indissolubly united in the person of the pope, who is at once ruler of the state and head of the Catholic Church. Although the former is temporal in its purpose and the latter is spiritual, this intimate union prevents Vatican City's being restricted to purely political purposes. The Holy See exercises sovereignty over Vatican City, not for the advantage of the state itself, but for the higher interest of the Church. This state was created with temporal sovereignty primarily to assure independence of spiritual action to the Holy See. Vatican City is thus a means to a higher end, an instrument of another preexisting juridical subject, from which it cannot be separated. The close union with the Holy See imports to this miniscule state its great importance; it also makes it juridically and politically unique in the world.

See Also: ROME; VATICAN.

Bibliography: Juridical. M. MIELE, *Santa Sede e Città del Vaticano* (Pisa 1933); *La condizione giuridica internazionale della Santa Sede e della Città del Vaticano* (Milan 1937). M. FALCO, *The Legal Position of the Holy See before and after the Lateran Agreement,* tr. A. H. CAMPBELL (London 1935). P. D'AVACK, *Chiesa, Santa Sede e Città del Vaticano nel Jus publicum Ecclesiasticum* (Florence 1936). R. RAFFEL, *Die Rechtsstellung der Vatikanstadt* (Bonn 1961). I. CARDINALE, *Le Saint-Siège et la diplomatie* (Paris 1963). General. G. FALLANI and M. ESCOBAR, eds., *Vaticano* (Florence 1946). F. HAYWARD, *The Pope and Vatican City,* tr. B. WARD (Dublin 1950). J. NEUVECELLE, *The Vatican: Its Organization, Customs, and Way of Life,* tr. G. LIBAIRE (New York 1955). C. PALLENBERG, *Inside the Vatican* (New York 1960). R. NEVILLE, *The World of the Vatican* (New York 1962). G. BULL, *Inside the Vatican* (New York 1983). T. J. REESE, *Inside the Vatican: The Politics and Organization of the Catholic Church* (Cambridge, Mass. 1996).

[L. BARBARITO]

VATICAN COUNCIL I

The 20th of the general COUNCILS, and the first to be held in ST. PETER'S BASILICA, solemnly opened December 8, 1869, and suspended sessions September 1, 1870, after four solemn public sessions and 89 general congregations. About 800 cardinals, patriarchs, archbishops, bishops, abbots, and religious superiors general participated.

St. Peter's Basilica during beatification ceremony of Padre Pio, Italy's famous Capuchin monk, May 2, 1999. (AP/Wide World Photos)

It promulgated two doctrinal constitutions. *Dei Filius* (April 24, 1870) dealt with faith, reason and their interrelation; *Pastor aeternus* (July 18, 1870) defined the jurisdictional primacy and the infallibility of the pope.

Preparation. Pius IX announced (December 6, 1864) at a meeting of the Congregation of Rites that he intended to summon a general council to deal with the problems of the times. The cardinals in Rome approved the Pope's project; and further support came from a select group of about 40 bishops whose opinions were sought.

Preparatory Commissions. The first important preparatory step was the appointment (March 1865) of the Central Preparatory Commission, composed of one Bavarian, REISACH, and four Italian curial cardinals. Five more commissions were later added: Faith and Dogma, Politicoecclesiastical Relations, Eastern Churches and Missions, Ecclesiastical Discipline, and Religious Orders. These five subordinate commissions were assigned the task of preparing draft constitutions (*schemata*) in their various fields.

Following the plan proposed (March 9, 1865) by Cardinal Giuseppe Bizzarri, the commissions were built around members of the Roman Curia. Of the 96 consultors, or members, 61, mostly Italians, were regularly domiciled in Rome. Thirty-five theologians were invited from outside Italy. Almost all were well-known ultramontane sympathizers. John Henry NEWMAN was asked to come, but refused. At the request of the German bishops, however, several prominent figures from German universities were summoned, including HEFELE, but not DÖLLINGER. Only two English-speaking theologians participated in the preparatory phase: Dr. William Weathers, of England, and Dr. James A. CORCORAN of Charleston, South Carolina. Corcoran did not arrive in Rome until the end of 1868.

The preparatory commissions did not begin to function until the summer of 1867 because of the Austro-Prussian War, and the withdrawal of the French garrison from Rome. The dogmatic commission adopted (September 27, 1867) as its primary guide Pius IX's *QUANTA CURA* and the *SYLLABUS OF ERRORS*. As matters turned out, only *schemata* prepared by the dogmatic commission were ever brought to a final vote in the council. In the preparatory phase its consultors covered a wide range of topics, from Church-State relations, indifferentism, and latitudinarianism to the errors of semirationalists like GÜNTHER.

Infallibility Question. During the early months of 1869, this commission studied at length the possibility of a definition of papal infallibility. The need for a definition was strongly urged by upholders of ULTRAMONTANISM. Some Catholics believed that infallibility could not be defined as revealed doctrine or at least that the moment was not opportune for a definition. In Germany, Döllinger, writing under the pseudonym of ''Janus,'' strongly opposed the idea, but 5 days before the dogmatic commission began discussing the topic, *La Civiltà Cattolica* in Rome published an article (February 6, 1869) declaring that all true Catholics wanted infallibility defined by acclamation at the coming council.

Church-State Question. Another issue that occupied the commission was Church-State relations. Despite the efforts of Corcoran, the final *schema* reflected a preoccupation with medieval politicoecclesiastical concepts. The preparatory commissions did not complete their work until the end of 1869.

Convocation. Pius IX formally announced the convocation of the council to the nearly 500 bishops who attended the commemoration of the 18th centenary of the martyrdom of SS. Peter and Paul at Rome (June 29, 1867). Exactly a year later, the bull of convocation, *Aeterni Patris*, was published. Briefs were sent to the Eastern Orthodox patriarchs and to Protestant groups to announce the council, but no provision was made for their representation at its meeting. Unlike previous general councils, secular rulers were not invited to send representatives. The entire preparatory phase of Vatican I had been something new in conciliar history. Never before had a similar effort been made to prepare an agenda. The work had been done by theologians. No bishops shared in the work, except for curial officials.

The Council in Session. The world episcopate began to gather in Rome only in the late fall of 1869.

Membership. Approximately 1,050 were eligible to participate; of these, about 700 attended the first solemn session (December 8, 1869). Five hundred came from Europe. Most of the missionary bishops who represented Asia, Africa, and Oceania were also Europeans. The U.S. was represented by 48 archbishops and bishops, and one abbot.

Procedures. The parliamentary handbook of the gathering was the apostolic letter *Multiplices inter* (December 2, 1869). Five cardinals had already been named by the pope as council presidents. The apostolic letter reserved to the Pope the right of proposing questions for discussion, but it also provided for a special committee to entertain proposals from the fathers.

Two types of meetings were described: the ceremonial solemn sessions, and the general congregations in which the *schemata* prepared by the preliminary commissions would be debated. If the debates revealed that *schemata* had to be amended, this was to be done by one of four deputations to be elected by the council. These were the deputations on faith, ecclesiastical discipline, Eastern Churches, and religious orders. Each commission numbered 28 members. Every father had the right to speak in general congregations.

Voting. When a constitution was ready for a vote, a preliminary test occurred in general congregation. At this stage three votes were possible: *placet* (approval), *placet juxta modum* (conditional approval) and *non placet* (rejection). Members casting conditional ballots had to submit their reasons to the secretary, who transmitted them to the appropriate deputation. When a constitution was finally prepared, it was voted upon in solemn session, in the papal presence, with only a ''yes'' or a ''no'' ballot possible. Written ballots were allowed in the preliminary stage; the final vote was by roll call. The apostolic letter also commanded secrecy with regard to conciliar affairs but failed in practice to gain it. Members were also forbidden to depart from Rome without explicit permission.

Other Regulations. A second decree, *Apostolicis litteris* (February 20, 1870), later modified the rules and required that all amendments be submitted in writing; that discussion of *schemata* as a whole precede discussion of individual chapters; that deputation members be allowed to speak out of turn; and that cloture be imposed on a given debate by a simple majority vote. These procedures were intended to speed the activity of the council. Like the creation of the preparatory commissions they were an innovation in conciliar practice. Up to and including the Council of Trent, councils had prepared their own agenda and made their own rules.

Agenda. Of the 51 *schemata* prepared in advance, only six came before the council. Debates took place concerning bishops, vacant sees, the life and morals of the clergy, and the preparation of a universal primary catechism. Of these constitutions, only that on the catechism received even preliminary approval. A shortened version of the *schema* on faith and reason was approved as the constitution *Dei Filius*. The *schema* on the Church was replaced by one that defined the primacy and infallibility of the pope; it was promulgated as the constitution *Pastor aeternus*.

Choice of Commission. Business proceeded in four phases, after a preliminary organizational stage. The first general congregation met on December 10, 1869. The first order of business was the selection of deputation members and members of lesser commissions. With few exceptions, only fathers known to favor a definition of papal infallibility were chosen for the deputations. This was achieved by the activity of a self-appointed committee that included Cardinal Filippo de Angelis, Archbishop MANNING of Westminster, Archbishop Victor DECHAMPS of Mechelen, Bishop SENESTRÉY of Regensburg, and Auxiliary Bishop MERMILLOD of Lausanne and Geneva.

Opposing Groups. These prelates and others formed the nucleus of the ''infallibilist'' party. In opposition to them grew up the so-called ''international committee'' of the minority. The infallibilists represented about four-fifths of the fathers, although there were also small groups that tried to mediate between the opposing parties. Minority leaders were Archbishop DARBOY of Paris, Bishop DUPANLOUP of Orléans, Cardinal Jacques Mathieu of Besançon, Cardinal SCHWARZENBERG of Prague, Cardinal RAUSCHER of Vienna, Archbishops SIMOR and HAYNALD of Hungary, Bishop STROSSMAYER of Croatia, Archbishop Peter KENRICK of St. Louis, and Archbishop Thomas CONNOLLY of Halifax. Prominent among those who attempted to find a middle-of-the-road solution were Cardinal BONNECHOSE of Rouen and Archbishop Martin SPALDING of Baltimore. The minority

group objected to the way in which the deputation elections were handled. Both Archbishop Kenrick and Bishop Strossmayer presented protests at the first congregation. During the following several weeks other protests on procedural matters were made, but almost without exception they were disallowed.

Early Debates. The first phase of actual debate lasted from December 28, 1869, until January 10, 1870. The topic was the *schema* on Catholic faith, an 18-chapter document that condemned materialist, rationalist, and pantheistic errors and enunciated orthodox doctrine on the subjects of revelation, faith, motives of credibility, interrelation of faith and science, the Trinity, creation, the Incarnation, original justice, original sin, eternal punishment, and grace. Most of the fathers objected to the original draft of the constitution as too technical, too long and diffuse, too negative, too apodictic in matters hitherto left to free discussion among theologians, and lacking in pastoral tone. Among Americans who commented on it, Kenrick suggested that it be shortened; Vérot of Savannah asked that it be made more pastoral, less hostile to modern science, and Connolly suggested that it be ''buried with honor.'' The *schema*, largely the work of Johannes FRANZELIN, SJ, was returned to the deputation on faith for revision.

The next stage of the debate (January 10–February 22) considered *schemata* on bishops, vacant sees, clerical life, and the primary catechism. Discussion was inconclusive on all these matters save the last. Authorization for Roman authorities to compose such a catechism was asked, and granted (May 4) after further debate. The constitution, however, was never approved in solemn session.

The council recessed (February 22 to March 18) to allow acoustic modification of the council hall (the chapel of SS. Processus and Martinian in St. Peter's), and to permit the conciliar deputations to catch up on their work.

The prelates discussed (March 18 to April 24) a new and shorter version of the *schema* on Catholic faith that included only material from the first half of the document given them in December. This revision, the work of Joseph KLEUTGEN, SJ, was solemnly promulgated as the constitution *Dei Filius* on Low Sunday, April 24. The vote was 667 to 0. The council resumed debate (April 29 to May 4) on the elementary catechism, but by that time the attention of all was taken up with the major question of the council, that of papal infallibility.

Infallibility and Primacy. One of the chief issues dividing Catholics on the eve of the council was that of a possible definition of papal infallibility.

Preconciliar Views. Most Catholics favored it, but a good deal of confusion existed as to its exact meaning.

Overzealous partisans like William George WARD wanted all papal pronouncements considered infallible; bishops such as Manning and Mermillod spoke of the incarnation of the Holy Spirit, or of the Son of God in the pope. Manning confused infallibility with inspiration; Louis VEUILLOT revised the Breviary hymn of None so that it applied to Pius IX instead of to God.

On the other hand, in the U.S. papal infallibility had not been generally taught as a revealed doctrine. Among its bishops, John ENGLAND, John HUGHES, John PURCELL, and Michael DOMENEC had explicitly and publicly denied that it must be believed. In August 1869, Archbishop Spalding informed the Prefect of the Propaganda Congregation that he considered a definition inopportune.

Fourteen German bishops who met at Fulda (September 1869) sent a memorandum to the pope in the same sense. In France, the dean of the Paris theological faculty, Bishop MARET, opposed the definition strongly, while Dupanloup was an inopportunist. Similar opinions existed in other countries. Thus all the Hungarian hierarchy and most of the Austrian and German bishops were outright opponents or inopportunists. Among others present in Rome, Lord ACTON and the theologian of the Bavarian Cardinal Hohenlohe, Johann FRIEDRICH, strongly contested a definition. They supplied information to Döllinger that he used in the ''Quirinus'' letters, a running critique of the council.

Petitions and Counterpetitions. The first test of the relative strength of the opposing parties came early in January when the infallibilists mustered some 500 signatures to petitions for the definition. The opposition was able to get only 136 signers for its counterpetitions. On February 9, the congregation on petitions acceded to the majority request and asked that a chapter on infallibility be added to the *schema* on the Church. With papal approval, the text already drawn up by the preparatory commission was distributed to the fathers and they were asked for written comments (March 6). In March and April extraconciliar controversies enlivened the scene. Kenrick published two pamphlets attacking the definition. He and Purcell sided with Dupanloup in an epistolary exchange with Spalding. On the other side, Manning, Senestréy, and others had been successful in persuading the Pope to allow the question to be brought to the floor.

Conciliar Action. A new constitution incorporating definitions of the primacy and infallibility of the pope, was announced April 29. Debate on it followed (May 13 to July 13). Over 150 fathers spoke, most of them favoring the definitions. Opponents based their arguments mainly on historical difficulties and on the inopportuneness of raising the question. Finally, a formula proposed by Cardinal CULLEN of Dublin was accepted by a majori-

ty of the fathers for expressing the nature and extent of infallibility. In a test vote (July 13), 451 approved the two definitions, 88 rejected them, and 62 gave conditional approval. In the last group were some who wanted the definitions made stronger and others who wanted them somewhat attenuated. At the solemn session on July 18, with Pius IX presiding, the constitution *Pastor aeternus* was adopted, 433 to two.

Both bishops who voted negatively accepted the definitions immediately. They were Luigi Riccio of Caiazzo, Italy, and Edward FITZGERALD, of Little Rock, Ark. Sixty-one fathers had submitted written protests against the definitions and left Rome on the eve of the solemn session. All of them eventually gave their adherence, as did all bishops in the world. No bishop left the Church as a result of the council. Döllinger was excommunicated for refusing to accept infallibility. Friedrich, and others of his followers, formed the schismatic group called OLD CATHOLICS.

Nothing important was done in the three summer sessions attended by about 100 fathers after the above definitions. The 89th and final congregation was held on September 1. A week later the Italian invasion of the STATES OF THE CHURCH began. Rome surrendered on September 20. The Franco-Prussian War, which had erupted in July, distracted attention and cost the Pope possible French military support. Pius IX suspended the Council indefinitely on October 20. Sessions never resumed.

Results. Controversies continued, but they were not such as to disturb the Church greatly. Secular powers were too concerned with political problems to worry about theological issues. Within the Church the definitions of primacy and infallibility strengthened the spiritual power of the papacy at a time when it was losing the temporal authority it had held for a millennium. The council demolished the remnants of CONCILIARISM and GALLICANISM. These were its most important results. It also prepared the way for theological developments of the subsequent century by establishing the position of the pope firmly and unequivocally. Some questions were left unresolved, for example, the status of bishops in relation to the pope.

Bibliography: Sources. J. D. MANSI, *Sacrorum Conciliorum nova et amplissima collectio,* 31 v. (Florence-Venice 1757–98); reprinted and continued by L. PETIT and J. B. MARTIN, 53 v. in 60 (Paris 1889–1927; repr. Graz 1960–) v.40–53. *Collectio Lacensis: Acta et decreta sacrorum conciliorum recentiorum,* ed. JESUITS OF MARIA LAACH, (Freiburg 1870–90) v.7. J. FRIEDRICH, *Documenta ad illustrandum Concilium Vaticanum anni 1870* (Nördlingen 1871). *Conciliorum oecumenicorum decreta* (Bolgna-Freiburg 1962) 777–792. H. DENZINGER, *Enchiridion symolorum,* ed. A. SCHÖNMETZER (32d ed. Freiburg 1963) 3000–75. Literature. J.

FESSLER, *Das vatikanische Concilium* (Vienna 1871). L. VEUILLOT, *Rome pendant le Concile,* 2 v. (Paris 1872). E. OLLIVIER, *L'Église et l'état au Concile du Vatican,* 2 v. (Paris 1879). T. GRANDERATH, *Constitutiones dogmaticae Concilii Vaticani* (Freiburg 1892); *Geschichte des vatikanischen Konzils,* 3 v. (Freiburg 1903–06). J. GIBBONS, *A Retrospect of Fifty Years,* 2 v. (Baltimore 1916). F. MOURRET, *Le Concile du Vatican d'après des documents inédits* (Paris 1919). E. CAMPANA, *Il Concilio Vaticano,* 1 v. in 2 (Lugano 1926). C. BUTLER, *The Vatican Council,* 2 v. (New York 1930; abr. ed. Westminster, MD 1962). J. R. BEISER, *American Secular Newspapers and the Vatican Council* (Washington 1942). J. BRUGERETTE and É. AMANN, *Dictionnaire de théologie catholique,* ed. A. VACANT, 15 v. (Paris 1903–50; Tables générales 1951–)15.2:2536–86. R. AUBERT, *Le Pontificat de Pie IX* (Fliche-Martin 21; 2d ed., 1964). U. BETTI, *La costituzione dommatica "Pastor Aeternus" del Concilio Vaticano I* (Rome 1961). J. J. HENNESEY, *The First Council of the Vatican: The American Experience* (New York 1963).

[J. J. HENNESEY]

VATICAN COUNCIL II

On Jan. 25, 1959, less than 100 days after his election, in a speech in which he outlined the broad lines of his papacy, Pope JOHN XXIII told a group of cardinals gathered at St. Paul-Outside-the-Walls that he intended to revive two ancient forms for stating doctrine and ordering discipline: he would hold a diocesan synod for Rome and an ecumenical council for the universal Church, the two events to be followed by a reform of the Code of Canon Law. The announcement of a council surprised most Catholics. No ecumenical council had been held since the First Vatican Council, and some churchmen were of the view that its definitions of papal primacy and infallibility made further ecumenical councils superfluous. Both Pius XI and Pius XII had considered reconvening Vatican I, but although consultations were undertaken and some considerations of an agenda were begun, in the end both popes decided not to proceed.

In various speeches and messages over the next years, John XXIII set out three general purposes for the Council: he wished it to be an opportunity for a spiritual renewal and reinvigoration of the Church that would make it more faithful to Christ's will and for an updating (aggiornamento) of its pastoral attitudes, habits, and institutions to make them more effective in the changed conditions of the modern world; if these two goals could be achieved, the Council would also greatly promote the restoration of unity among Christians.

Preparatory Commissions. On Pentecost Sunday, May 17, 1959, the pope established an Antepreparatory Commission headed by Cardinal Tardini, with Msgr. Pericle Felici serving as secretary, and composed of ten clerics who held important posts in the Roman Curia. This commission's tasks were to consult the bishops of the world, the offices of the Curia, and the theological and canonical faculties of Catholic universities for their advice and suggestions about a conciliar agenda, to sketch the general lines of the topics to be discussed at the Council, and to suggest various bodies that would prepare the material for conciliar deliberation. The bishops and others consulted were left complete freedom to make suggestions in the areas of doctrine, discipline, pastoral activity, and contemporary problems. Over 75% of those invited responded; their responses filled 15 large tomes in four volumes. Proposals ranged in significance from the sublime to the trivial and reflected a very broad range of theological and pastoral perspectives; there were those who opposed any change and those who hoped the Council would be an opportunity for major reforms. If the majority of bishops were rather cautious and earth-bound in their suggestions, it could have been in part be because by the deadline for their submissions, and in part because it was not at all clear what Pope John himself wished the Council to be and to do.

In the vast material received the antepreparatory commission found no fewer than 9,338 suggestions which it organized for convenient reference according to the traditional divisions of dogmatic and moral theology and of the books and topics of the Code of Canon Law. The proposals received were placed under the seal of secrecy and could be consulted only by those officially engaged in the preparation of the Council. As the structure of the preparation took shape, the materials were divided once again, drastically reduced in number, and presented in the form of questions for further study.

On Pentecost, June 5, 1960, John XXIII announced the structure of the preparatory period. Ten commissions were established to draw up texts for the Council to consider: (1) the theological (for matters of faith and morals); (2) for bishops and the governance of dioceses; (3) for the discipline of the clergy and the Christian people; (4) for religious; (5) for the discipline of the sacraments; (6) for the liturgy; (7) for studies and seminaries; (8) for the eastern churches; (9) for the missions; (10) for the apostolate of the laity. In addition, the pope created two secretariats, one for the communications-media and the other for promoting the unity of Christians which, it was said, would enable non-Catholics to follow the work of the Council. A Central Commission was also established to supervise and coordinate the work of the other commissions, to review the texts they prepared and to recommend them to the pope for the conciliar agenda, and to draw up the rules that would govern the Council's work.

The ten commissions were chaired by the cardinal-heads of corresponding offices in the Roman Curia, with Curial figures also serving as secretaries on most of them.

The personnel of the commissions consisted of members and consultors, the former having voting rights, the latter offering advice when asked. Among the members and consultors, it was noted, were included some theologians who had been under suspicion or the subject of disciplinary measures during the previous decade, among them Yves Congar, Henri de Lubac, Bernhard Häring, and Karl Rahner. No women and no lay people were appointed to the preparatory commissions.

The commissions set to work on the basis of the questions proposed by the antepreparatory commission, although they were permitted to suggest additional questions. The work of preparation suffered from a lack of supervision and from the failure of the most of the commissions to collaborate on common or related problems. The Theological Commission, headed by Alfredo Cardinal Ottaviani, added to the problem by insisting that it had exclusive responsibility for doctrinal questions; as it would not enter into practical pastoral problems, so it expected all other commissions to submit to itself any and all matters of doctrine. In further expression of its conception of its own sovereignty, the Theological Commission refused to collaborate with other commissions and in particular with the Secretariat for Christian Unity. Compounding this lack of coordination, the pontifical secret that was supposed to surround the work of the commissions was widely understood to prohibit speaking about the work of one's own commission even with members of other commissions.

The commissions brought before the Central Commission a total of 75 texts which were later culled, some remanded to the postconciliar reform of canon law, some combined with others, so that a total of 22 Schemas were in the end considered fit for conciliar discussion. The texts prepared by the pastoral commissions generally flew very close to the ground; they did little more than recommend mostly minor changes in the Church's canonical and disciplinary norms; there was very little evidence that the commissions had considered the serious sociological and theological discussions of pastoral activity that had been going on for three decades. The one exception to this description was the Commission on the Sacred Liturgy whose members included many of the most important scholars in the liturgical movement; they decided to undertake serious historical and theological studies of the various topics they addressed and were therefore able to buttress with effective arguments their recommendations of significant liturgical reform.

The Theological Commission prepared eight texts: a new formula for the profession of faith, meant to be used at the opening of the Council, and seven constitutions: on the sources of revelation, on the moral order, on

defending the deposit of faith, on chastity, virginity, marriage and the family, on the Church, on the Blessed Virgin Mary, on the community of nations, and on the social order. In general, these texts were meant to confirm with the Council's high authority the orientations and emphases that had characterized the papal magisterium for the previous century and a half, and in particular as these had been expressed at Vatican I, in the anti-modernist documents, *Pascendi* and *Lamentabili*, and in the encyclical *Humani generis*. Their general tone was very defensive, suspicious of most of the recent movements of theological renewal in dogmatic and moral theology and in biblical studies, and at best indifferent to ecumenical implications.

During the preparatory period the Secretariat for Christian Unity, chaired by Cardinal Augustin Bea, represented a different notion of what the Council might do and how it might do it. Early on, it received permission from Pope John to prepare texts to alert the other commissions to the ecumenical dimensions of various subjects. When its efforts to collaborate with the Theological Commission were rebuffed, it began to prepare texts that the Pope said could eventually be brought to the Council itself. Some of the Secretariat's texts addressed questions being considered also by the Theological Commission, among them the Word of God, membership in the Church, hierarchical authority, and religious freedom. These texts were written with an eye to overcoming misunderstandings of Catholic doctrine on the part of other Christians, to exploring their views with sympathy, and to proposing ways of understanding and stating Christian doctrine that would go beyond polemical impasses.

All of the texts written by the preparatory commissions were brought for review before the Central Commission, which was composed of cardinals and archbishops from all over the world and which met in six meetings between June 12, 1961, and June 20, 1962. The members of this commission were not reluctant to criticize the prepared texts and to offer amendments. Had people been aware of the quality and vigor of the discussions within the Central Commission, the public might have anticipated the drama that unfolded when some of these texts reached the Council floor. The criticisms and proposed amendments were referred to a subcommission whose work was then to be reviewed by the whole Central Commission; time did not permit this last step and consequently the texts went before the Council as altered or not by the subcommission.

Rules and Procedures. By the motu proprio *Appropinquante concilio* (Aug. 6, 1962) John XXIII laid down the rules that were to govern to conduct of the Council. For the direction of the general congregations, in which the proposed decrees were to be discussed and voted on, he established a board of ten presidents, all cardinals, who were to supervise the debate and maintain discipline, one of them presiding each day. He also set up ten commissions, which were the same as those in the preparatory phase, although the first was now called the Commission for the Doctrine of Faith and Morals, and the last was now charged with matters pertaining not only to the apostolate of the laity but also to the mass media and entertainment. The Secretariat for Promoting Christan Unity, the Technical-Organizational Commission, and the Financial Secretariat were carried over, and at the last minute the Pope added a Secretariat for Extraordinary Affairs which would examine new questions proposed by the fathers. Besides the chairman, who was named by the pope, each conciliar commission consisted of 24 members, two-thirds of whom were elected by the fathers and the rest chosen by the pope; this represented a change from Vatican I where all the members of the conciliar commissions were elected by the assembly. Latin was to be used in the public sessions and general congregations; modern languages could also be used in commission meetings. The speeches of individual fathers were not to last more than ten minutes. The majority required for approval of all matters except elections consisted of two-thirds of those present and voting. Some of these provisions would be later modified in the light of the conciliar experience.

On July 23, 1962, the General Secretariat of the Council, with Archbishop Pericle Felici continuing at its head, sent the conciliar fathers a first volume containing the texts that would be discussed at the first session of the Second Vatican Council. It contained the following texts: drafts of dogmatic constitutions on the sources of revelation, on the defense of the deposit of faith, on the Christian moral order, on chastity, marriage, the family and virginity, drafts of constitutions on the sacred liturgy and on the mass media, and a draft of a decree on the unity of the Church (dealing with the Oriental Catholic Churches). Why out of the mass of material prepared these seven texts were chosen for the initial conciliar agenda is not known; that the draft of a dogmatic constitution on the Church and on the Blessed Virgin Mary was not included was explained by the fact that the final revisions and editing of these two texts were not completed when the Council opened; a second volume would be distributed to the fathers only early in November.

The ecumenical goal of the Council was reflected by invitations sent to the major Christian churches and communities. Their representatives were permitted to attend not only the public sessions but also the general congregations, but they did not have the right to vote or to speak; they would prove able, however, to make their views known to the commissions through the Secretariat for Christian Unity and through personal contacts with conciliar fathers. It was a great disappointment that most of the Orthodox Churches were not represented at the first session, but a decision made at a pan-Orthodox meeting in Rhodes in 1961 had decided upon a common response; on the very eve of the Council, however, the Moscow patriarchate broke with the rest and decided to send representatives. Representatives of the Patriarch of Constantinople would not attend the Council until the third session. Ecumenical representation at the Council increased from year to year; 17 Orthodox and Protestant denominations were represented by 35 delegate-observers and guests at the first period, while at the fourth 93 represented 28 groups.

The announcement of the Council and the years of its preparation had created widespread interest both within and without the Catholic Church. A spate of historical surveys and studies of the previous 20 ecumenical councils appeared, along with monographs on topics likely to be discussed at Vatican II, particularly in the areas of liturgy and ecclesiology. Surveys of the desires and wishes of Catholics with regard to the Council were published, and several authors published proposals for a reform agenda.

In the spring of 1962, several important members of the Central Commission, among them Cardinals Suenens (Archbishop of Malines-Brussels) and Léger (Archbishop of Montreal) and Archbishop Dennis Hurley (Durban, South Africa), wrote to Pope John to express their concern that the pastoral and ecumenical goals he had outlined for the Council were unlikely to be met on the basis of the texts the Central Commission had reviewed. Such fears spread as the character of the official texts became more widely known. There was some apprehension that the Council, which was not expected to last more than two sessions, would entail little more than rubber-stamping the documents placed before the fathers. As the bishops began to gather in Rome in the second week of October 1962, contrasting fears and hopes divided them.

Periods. The Second Vatican Council met in four periods: from Oct. 11 to Dec. 8, 1962; from Sept. 29 to Dec. 4, 1963; from Sept. 14 to Nov. 21, 1964; and from Sept. 14 to Dec. 8, 1965.

In the course of the four years of Vatican II, 3,058 fathers participated, by far the largest number in the history of the ecumenical councils. Besides the 129 superiors general of clerical religious orders, their numbers and the percentages of all those who attended, ranked by continent, are: Europe 1,060 (36%); South America 531 (18%); North America 416 (14%); Asia 408 (14%); Africa 351 (12%); Central America 89 (3%); and Oceania 74

(3%). Participation by those who had a right to attend fluctuated. It was the highest at the first (84.34%) and at the fourth (84.88%) periods; 82.34% attended the second and 80.23% the third. These numbers would have been higher had many bishops from countries under Communist domination been permitted to attend.

First Period. The most dramatic of the four periods of the Council opened with a solemn ceremony attended by representatives of 86 governments and international bodies. In his opening speech Pope John disagreed with "those prophets of doom who are always forecasting disaster" and recommended that the fathers instead consider whether God might not be providing new opportunities for the Church. He wanted the Council not only to defend the patrimony of the faith but to consider how to understand and present it to contemporaries; to this end he distinguished between the substance of the faith and the fashion in which it is articulated, and he urged a pastoral goal and the use of the methods of research and literary forms of modern thought. In the face of errors he advised the fathers to avoid condemnations and instead to give a positive demonstration of the validity of the Church's teaching. He emphasized the duty to work actively for the fulfillment of the mystery of unity with other Christians and with non-Christians. To those familiar with the preparatory material, it appeared that the pope was declaring his dissatisfaction with the official schemata and proposing that the Council adopt a different approach.

The first general congregation (Oct. 13, 1962) had permanent consequences for the Council, for instead of proceeding immediately, as had been planned, to electing the 16 members of each commission with only the lists of members and consultors of the defunct preparatory commissions to guide it, the Council, at the motion of Cardinal Achille Liénart, Bishop of Lille, and of Cardinal Josef Frings, Archbishop of Cologne, adjourned after a few minutes to allow more time for consultation among the bishops of the various countries or regions. Thereupon the national or regional episcopal conferences decided to recommend one or two candidates of their own number for each commission; and in the second general congregation (October 16), before the fathers cast their ballots, a composite list of all these nominees was distributed. In this way the commissions became more nearly representative of the whole assembly and did not merely perpetuate the mentality of the preparatory commissions, which had been largely dominated by curialists and could have been expected merely to defend texts which many fathers considered to be unacceptable. (Some continuity was assured, however, by the pope's appointment as presidents of the conciliar commissions of the same curial cardinals who had presided over the corresponding preparatory commissions.) The postponement of these elections was a first indication that the fathers were going to accept their responsibility for the Council, and the consultations undertaken established the importance for the Council of cooperation within and among the episcopal conferences.

In the course of this first period the Council discussed the schemata on the liturgy, on the sources of revelation, on mass media, on the unity of the Church, and on the Church. Lively discussions took place on the liturgical schema's proposals to allow greater use of vernacular languages, more common practice of communion under both kinds and concelebration, and greater authority in liturgical matters for episcopal conferences. The long debate came to a close with a vote on the general principles set out in the draft, and an overwhelming majority of the fathers (2,162 to 46) showed themselves ready to embark upon significant Church reform.

The second important debate concerned a schema on the sources of revelation which focused on two questions: the relationship between Scripture and Tradition and the value of modern historical critical methods in the interpretation of the Bible. The text was sharply criticized for its negative tone and lack of ecumenical and pastoral sensitivity, for prematurely settling the legitimately debated issue whether all revealed truths are found in the Scriptures, and for looking with such suspicion on the problems uncovered by modern biblical scholarship that it would prevent any fruitful Catholic contribution. Defenders of the text argued that the dogmatic issue had been settled at the Council of Trent and by subsequent common teaching and that the faith was being endangered by books and articles calling into question the historical character of both Old and New Testaments. A vote was taken on whether to discontinue the debate or to continue it with discussions of the individual chapters. Although the vote to discontinue (1,368 to 822) fell just short of the two-thirds majority required, the pope, to avoid prolonged and probably fruitless debate, intervened, halting the discussion and remanding the text to a special commission under the joint chairmanship of Cardinals Ottaviani and Bea to rewrite the text. It had become clear that a substantial majority of the fathers wished to compose texts different in orientation and purpose from those composed by the Theological Commission, and that the pope would back them up.

Now that the Council had clearly demonstrated its pastoral and doctrinal interests, the rest of the first period was somewhat anticlimactic. A few days were given at the end to a preliminary discussion of the schema on the Church, commonly considered the chief business and central theme of the whole Council. The official text was subjected to a by now familiar litany of complaints, and it was understood, even without a formal vote, that it too would have to be substantially revised. In fact, that would prove to be the fate of all the prepared schemata. On Dec. 6, 1962, it was announced that the Pope had appointed a Coordinating Commission, chaired by Cardinal Amleto Cicognani, whose task it would be to review the draft texts prepared for the Council and, in the light of the goals of the Council as stated by Pope John and ratified by the Council's votes, to decide which were to be retained on the conciliar agenda, which could be left for post-conciliar decisions, and what changes in content or in method and tone needed to be made. This "supercommission" rapidly reduced the texts to be retained to 17, the last of these being a new schema, championed in particular by Cardinal Suenens, to address the presence of the Church in the modern world. Throughout the intersession, the conciliar commissions undertook what has been called a "second preparation" of Vatican II.

The first period ended without its having approved a single schema, but the decisions made at it determined the orientation of the whole course of the Second Vatican Council. The people and the purposes that had largely dominated the preparation of the Council had been replaced; new leaders would now pursue goals largely ignored during the preparation.

With the death of John XXIII on June 3, 1963, the Council and all activities related to it were automatically suspended. But the day after his election (June 22), Pope Paul VI promised that the Council would be resumed and that it would pursue the goals set for it by his predecessor. Five days later he fixed the opening date of the second period for September 29.

Second Period. Before the fathers reconvened, Paul VI issued a revised edition of the *Ordo concilii . . .celebrandi* in order to correct some of the defects in organization and procedure manifested in the first period and to expedite the labors and ensure the freedom of the participants. He abolished the Secretariat for Extraordinary Affairs and enlarged to 12 members the board of presidents; it would be their duty to see that the rules were duly observed and to resolve any eventual doubts and remove difficulties. He also appointed four cardinals Agagianian, Prefect of the Congregation de Propaganda Fide; Giacomo Lercaro, Archbishop of Bologna; Julius Döpfner, Archbishop of Munich and Freising; and Leo Joseph Suenens, Archbishop of Malines-Brussels as moderators, who were to take turns in directing the discussions in the general congregations. The pope also made various changes in the procedural rules, such as reducing to 50 percent plus one the majority required for the rejection or deferment of a schema or a part of one, and permitting one father to speak in the name of others.

For the improvement and expansion of the news services, about which there had been many complaints during the first period, Paul VI appointed a Press Committee chaired by Abp. Martin J. O'Connor. The pope increased the number of non-Catholic Christian observers invited to the Council, and 31 more were present at the second period than at the first. John XXIII had invited one Catholic layman, Jean Guitton, to the latter part of the first period; Paul VI provided for the attendance of several lay auditors at the general congregations and for their assistance to the commissions; in addition to Guitton, ten other laymen from various countries, for the most part representing international Catholic organizations, were welcomed at the start of the new period.

At the public session which opened the second period on Sept. 29, 1963, Paul VI gave a memorable address in which he emphasized the pastoral nature of the assembly and specified its four purposes as: to define more fully the notion of the Church, especially with regard to the position of bishops; to renew the Church; to promote the restoration of unity among all Christians (he asked for non-Catholics to pardon Catholics for their faults in the schisms and condoned injuries done to Catholics); and to initiate a dialogue with the contemporary world.

The conciliar discussions began with the revised schema on the Church. Heated debate arose over the schema's discussion of the collegiality of bishops and its relation to the primacy of the pope defined at Vatican I. On October 30, the moderators, employing a procedure not envisaged in the *Ordo,* put to votes for the guidance of the Doctrinal Commission five propositions contained substantially in the schema's third chapter. Four of them concerned the sacramentality of the episcopate and its collegial character and authority; the fifth concerned the restoration of the diaconate as a permanent order. All five of the propositions received majorities of more than two-thirds, thus removing all doubts about the progressive tendency of the Council. But the "irregular" character of the votes would be evoked many times afterward to call into question their validity.

Also in connection with the schema on the Church, another division among the fathers appeared over the question whether the schema on the Blessed Virgin Mary should be a separate text or be incorporated into the schema on the Church. After an emotional debate, the question was put to a vote on October 29th, and by the narrowest margin in all the Council's deliberations (1,114 to 1,074) the assembly decided to incorporate it into the constitution on the Church.

During a discussion of the schema on bishops and the governance of dioceses (November 5–15), one of the Council's rare dramatic confrontations occurred when

Cardinal Frings frankly criticized the methods of the Holy Office and Cardinal Ottaviani, its secretary, vehemently defended them. The first three chapters of the schema on ecumenism were discussed (November 18-December 2) and were approved on condition of revision, but, to the consternation of many fathers, all action on the fourth chapter (on the Church's attitude toward non-Christians and especially the Jews) and on the fifth (on religious freedom) was deferred to the third period, allegedly because of lack of time for mature consideration.

On November 21 the pope announced that the number of members of each commission would be increased to 30. After the episcopal conferences again nominated candidates, the fathers elected the greater part of the new members on November 28, and the pope appointed the rest. The commissions then elected a new additional vice-chairman and secretary. The avowed purpose of these changes was to expedite the labors of the commissions, but they seem also to have been intended to help bring some recalcitrant commissions into greater harmony with the wishes of the conciliar majority.

During a ceremony commemorating the conclusion of the Council of Trent (December 3), Paul VI made known his *motu proprio Pastorale munus* (November 30), in which he either granted or declared to be restored (his language was ambiguous) to bishops certain faculties and privileges, many of which had been proposed in an appendix to the schema on bishops and the government of dioceses. The relatively insignificant character of many of these faculties or privileges underscored in the minds of many fathers and observers the degree to which the episcopate had in the past become dependent upon the papacy.

On December 4, the concluding public session of the second period was held. The fathers definitively passed the constitution on the liturgy by a vote of 2,147 to four and, by a vote of 1,980 to 164, the decree on the communications media. Against the latter opposition had been raised at the last minute on the grounds that it would not answer the expectation of Christians and would compromise the Council's authority, and the final vote in a general congregation on November 25 had seen over 500 bishops vote against it. The pope, using a formula that stressed his union with the other conciliar fathers, approved and promulgated the two texts, the first of the final documents of the Council. On Jan. 25, 1964, he issued the motu proprio *Sacram Liturgiam* by which he established a commission for the implementation of the liturgical constitution.

In his closing address Paul VI thanked those fathers who had contributed toward the expenses of the Council or had aided their needy brothers, remarked that the Council had been marked by assiduous labor and freedom of expression, expressed the hope that it could complete its work in a third period, and announced his forthcoming pilgrimage to the Holy Land.

During the interval between the second and third periods the fathers were again invited to submit further comments on the unfinished business, and with the help of this counsel the commissions continued to revise the schemata. At the direction of the Coordinating Commission and in accord with the pope's own desires, they reduced some of the topics, namely, those on priests, religious, education for the priesthood, missionary activity, marriage, and Catholic education, to a series of brief and basic principles on which the fathers would be expected to agree easily and quickly, and without public discussion, in the third period; the fuller articulation and implementation of these principles could be left to post-conciliar bodies. This reduction of the conciliar agenda, known as the "Döpfner plan," was designed to ensure that the Council could end its work with the third session, and in furtherance of this purpose changes were made also in the conciliar procedures to prevent repetitions and to expedite decisions.

Just before the third period was to open, the pope announced that women would now join the lay men as auditors of the Council. Among the increased number of observer-delegates, for the first time, were representatives of the Patriarchate of Constantinople.

Third Period. Pope Paul opened the third period on Sept. 14, 1964, with a public session at which he concelebrated Mass with 24 conciliar fathers, a first conciliar expression of the concrete reforms approved in the constitution on the liturgy at the end of the second period. The conciliar discussions began with chapters of the schema on the Church not yet approved in general and then with successive votes on the eight chapters as amended. In the discussion of the chapter on the Blessed Virgin Mary, debate focused on whether to accord her the titles "Mediatrix" and "Mother of the Church." Very great interest attended the votes on the third chapter, on the hierarchical constitution of the Church with special reference to bishops. The battle over the relationship between papal primacy and episcopal collegiality had not grown less fierce, and in fact on the very eve of the third period Paul VI had received a confidential note from prominent cardinals and heads of religious orders begging him not to allow the teaching of the chapter to be voted on and not very subtly implying that if he did not so act, he would be guilty of squandering the authority of his office. After four formal reports on the chapter were read out to the assembly, the voting did proceed and on the major issues under debate the votes were overwhelmingly favorable.

Discussions followed on the schema on the pastoral office of bishops whose progress, however, was impeded by the need to await the results of the voting on the schema on the Church. The schemas on religious freedom and on the Jews, which had originally been part of the schema on ecumenism, were now to become distinct documents; the debate on them was vigorous and was marked by concerns both theological and political. The text on religious freedom was criticized for departing from the Church's traditional insistence on the unique rights of the true religion; it was defended as reflecting the development of political realities, respecting the dignity and freedom of persons, and a prerequisite for any serious ecumenical or inter-religious dialogue. The schema on the Church's relationship with Jews continued to receive criticism because of the political consequences it was feared it would have for Christians in the Middle East. A revised text on divine revelation was also discussed as was a schema on the lay apostolate. Early in October the revised schema on ecumenism was put to a series of votes and approved.

Opposition to the Döpfner plan and to a premature closing of the Council grew during the early weeks of the third period and it was to show itself when the drastically reduced and so-called "minor schemas" came before the fathers. On October 12 a revised schema of 12 propositions "on the life and ministry of priests" was brought before the Council; it was attacked by many fathers as inadequate, superficial, jejune, and disappointing, and by a vote of 930 to 1,199 it was sent back to the competent commission to be completely recast. The discussion of the schema on the Church's missionary activity was initiated by Paul VI himself, but despite his favorable judgment of it, most of the speakers found it unsatisfactory because of its brevity and skeletal nature, and at the proposal of the commission the fathers by a vote of 1,601 to 311 remanded it to be completely rewritten. The schema of 19 propositions on the renewal of the religious life was also criticized but was accepted by a narrow margin (1,155 to 882) provided that it be extensively modified to take account of the thousands of reservations (*modi*) expressed. The schema of 22 propositions on education for the priesthood was more favorably received and was substantially adopted. The schema on Christian education, developed from the inadequate previous schema of propositions on Catholic schools, was substantially approved in spite of 419 negative votes. A brief document (*votum*) on the sacrament of marriage, intended for the guidance of the commission for revising the Code of Canon Law was discussed, and by vote the fathers accepted the moderators' proposal to submit the schema to the pope for his action in accord with their two-day discussion.

The Council also discussed the schema on the Oriental Catholic Churches and the long-awaited schema of a constitution on the Church in the world of today, commonly called Schema 13 from the number of its place on the agenda. The debate on the latter focused on the methodology of the schema, on whether it properly distinguished and related the realms of the natural and the supernatural, and on the appropriateness of a council addressing the very contingent questions discussed in appendices to the schema. The fathers were admonished to avoid the subject of artificial contraception, which the pope had reserved to the study of a special group of clerical and lay experts and to his own final judgment.

Four events in the last days of the third period were received so poorly by substantial numbers of the fathers that they spoke of "the black week." Because a minority persisted in its objections to the third chapter of the schema on the Church, the pope ordered that an "explanatory note" be prefaced to the Doctrinal Commission's explanation of the final revisions; drawn up to allay the minority's fears, this text was declared to provide the authoritative interpretation of the doctrine contained in the third chapter. Although the Council was never given an opportunity to discuss or to approve this note, it succeeded in its purpose and in a vote on November 17 only 47 out of 2,146 fathers were opposed to the text.

On November 20, the revised text on the Church's relationship with non-Christian religions was approved by the Council with the provision that recommended amendments would be taken into account. The revised schema on religious freedom suffered a different fate. It was distributed to the fathers on November 17 and, according to the moderators' decision was to be voted on two days later. Since the new schema differed considerably in structure, length, and argument from the text discussed earlier in the period, some fathers requested more time for study and consultation; to accommodate them, the moderators and presidents decided to take a preliminary vote to determine whether or not the fathers wished to proceed at once to the scheduled vote. But on the appointed day (November 19) Cardinal Tisserant in the name of the presidents announced that no vote would be taken in that period. Amid strong feelings of disappointment and resentment an urgent petition for an immediate vote, drawn up by U.S. bishops, was circulated in the council hall and was signed by 441 fathers (and later by hundreds more); it was then presented to Paul VI by Cardinals Albert Meyer, Archbishop of Chicago; Joseph Ritter, Archbishop of St. Louis; and Paul Léger, Archbishop of Montreal. The Pope upheld the decision to postpone the vote on the grounds that the *Ordo* required more time, but he promised that the schema on religious freedom would be the first item on the agenda of the fourth period.

On the same day, November 19, 19 modifications, which at the last minute had been introduced by papal mandate into the schema on ecumenism by the Secretariat for Christian Unity were distributed to the fathers; they were accepted by them the next day in the final vote on the whole schema, the alternative being rejection of the whole schema. The modifications were intended to clarify the text, but many of them were found offensive to and by Protestants.

At the public session that ended the third period, Paul VI concelebrated Mass with 24 priests having major Marian shrines in their territories. Then the fathers passed the constitution on the Church (2,151 to five), the decree on the Oriental Catholic Churches (2,110 to 39), and the decree on ecumenism (2,137 to 11), and the pope promulgated them. In his closing address the Pope, having expressed his pleasure at the doctrine concerning the episcopate and the Church in general, proclaimed on his own authority Mary to be the "Mother of the Church," that is, of all the faithful and all the pastors. The Council had followed the Doctrinal Commission's advice and declined to accord her this title explicitly and had contented itself with presenting the idea in equivalent terms. Many saw the pope's act as intended to reassert his own distinct papal authority.

Fourth Period. Paul VI opened the fourth and last period of the Council at a public session on Sept. 14, 1965, at which he again concelebrated Mass with 24 fathers. He announced that he was establishing (by the motu proprio *Apostolica sollicitudo*, dated September 15) a Synod of Bishops, as he had previously promised and as the fathers were requesting in the as yet unfinished schema on the pastoral office of bishops; in this way the close cooperation between the pope and the bishops could continue to benefit the Church even after the end of the Council.

Of the 16 final documents of Vatican II 11 were completed, approved, and promulgated at public sessions during the fourth period; five texts were promulgated on October 15, two on November 18, and four on December 7. The pace of developments was rapid, and to expedite matters opportunities for the bishops to intervene orally in the hall were reduced even more than during the third period.

As the pope had promised, the schema on religious freedom was the first discussed, and while opposition to it continued to be voiced, a preliminary vote on it taken on September 21 found that a majority of 1,997 to 224 had accepted it as the basis for a definitive text. This overwhelming success represented one of the high-points for the U.S. bishops and for their chief adviser on the issue, John Courtney Murray, S.J. Amended further, and with some last-minute changes from the pope, it was approved on October 15 by vote of 1,954 to 249.

The schema on the Church in the modern world had been greatly expanded by the inclusion of the appendices to the previous draft. Differences among progressives appeared with regard to this text with some fathers, particularly Germans, arguing that it was too positive, neglecting realities of sin, and confused the realms of the natural and the supernatural. The French-speaking bishops and theologians defended its incarnational approach. A rather evangelical approach, articulated by Cardinal Lercaro, was particularly upset that the text was not stronger in its section on war and peace. This section was criticized also, but on nearly opposite grounds, by some U.S. bishops on the grounds that it ignored the deterrent role played by nuclear weapons and implied criticism of the defense policies of the west. Some controversy also arose over the sections on marriage and the relationship among its ends and on the regulation of births. A large number of bishops were also upset that their plea for an explicit condemnation of communism was not seriously considered. On December 6 the schema was approved by a vote of 2,111 to 251.

The revised schema on divine revelation continued to be the subject of debate, particularly on the question of the relationship between scripture and tradition, on inerrancy, and on the historical character of the Gospels. Last-minute interventions of the pope once again reduced opposition, and the text was approved on October 29 by a vote of 2,081 to 27.

All the other texts went through the final stages of their redaction and approval without great controversy: the schemas on the pastoral office of bishops, on the renewal of the religious life, on priestly formation, on Christian education, on the Church's relation to non-Christian religions, on the apostolate of the laity, on the Church's missionary activity, and on the ministry and life of priests.

In a dramatic event on December 7, the day before the Council closed, Paul VI and Patriarch Athenagoras I, in order to remove the psychological barrier to reconciliation, expressed their regret for the mutual excommunications of the Roman See and Patriarchate of Constantinople in 1054 and for the offensive words, unfounded reproaches, and reprehensible gestures that accompanied those acts on both sides. They also expressed a desire to remove the memory of those events from the midst of the Church and committed them to oblivion. Finally, they deplored the preceding and subsequent untoward incidents, which, under the influence of various factors including lack of mutual understanding and trust, ultimately led to the effective rupture of ecclesiastical communion.

The last public session of the Council was held outdoors in front of St. Peter's Basilica on Dec. 8, 1965. After a Mass celebrated by the pope alone, a series of messages to the world, composed in French, were read out: to rulers, scholars, artists, women, workers, the poor and sick, and youth. The apostolic brief *In Spiritu Sancto* ordering the closure of the Council was then read by the secretary general and the acclamations traditional at ecumenical councils since the fifth century were chanted, and the fathers professed their obedience to the conciliar decrees.

To acquaint the faithful with the teachings of the Council and to stimulate them to acceptance of its decrees, to incite them to the desired spiritual renewal in their private, domestic, public, and social life and to gratitude to God for the Council, and to develop in them a feeling for and an awareness of the Church, Paul VI, by the apostolic constitution, *Mirificus eventus* (Dec. 7, 1965), proclaimed an extraordinary jubilee to be celebrated in all the dioceses of the world from Jan. 1 to May 29 (Pentecost), 1966. By the *motu proprio Integrae servandae* (Dec. 7, 1965) he changed the name of the Holy Office to the Congregation for the Doctrine of the Faith and altered its procedure. Then, by the motu proprio *Finis concilii* (Jan. 11, 1966) he established post-conciliar commissions for (1) bishops and the governance of dioceses, (2) religious, (3) the missions, (4) Christian education, and (5) the apostolate of the laity, all of which were composed of the same chairmen, members and secretaries as the corresponding conciliar commissions had been, and were to be assisted by experts chosen especially from among the conciliar *periti*. He established also a new central commission for the purpose of supervising the work of the other five commissions and of interpreting the documents of the Council. Finally, he confirmed the permanent existence of the three secretariats for promoting Christian Unity, for Non-Christian Religions, and for Non-Believers.

Pronouncements of the Council. The Council enacted four constitutions, nine decrees, and three declarations. Constitutions. These covered the Church, divine revelation, liturgy, and the Church in the modern world.

Dogmatic Constitution on the Church (Lumen gentium). In the fathers' discussion of this constitution the principal points centered on: Biblical figures for the Church; the Church as a mystery; the theological, spiritual, and juridical aspects of the Church; the relation between Christ's Church and the Roman Catholic Church; the position of separated Christians and of non- Christians vis-a-vis the Church; the authority of the body of bishops (collegiality) and its relations to the papal primacy; restoration of the permanent diaconate with or without celibacy; universal priesthood of the faithful; functions of the laity and their relation to the hierarchy; existence and role of charisms; the position of separated Christians and of non-Christians vis-a-vis the Church; balance between equality and authority; concern for the poor and the afflicted and for social justice; the missionary obligation of the Church; relations between Church and State; and the Blessed Virgin Mary as mediatrix of grace and as mother of the Church. The constitution has the following chapters: (1) "The Mystery of the Church," (2) "The People of God," (3) "The Hierarchical Structure of the Church and the Episcopate in Particular," (4) "The Laity," (5) "The Universal Call to Holiness in the Church," (6) "Religious," (7) "The Eschatological Nature of the Pilgrim Church and Its Union with the Church in Heaven," and (8) "The Blessed Virgin Mary, Mother of God, in the Mystery of Christ and of the Church."

Dogmatic Constitution on Divine Revelation (Dei verbum). The discussion centered on the nature of tradition and its relation to Scripture; whether all revelation is somehow contained in the Scriptures; inerrancy of the Bible; historicity of the Gospels; and reading, diffusion, and interpretation of the Bible. The chapters of the constitution are: (1) "Revelation Itself," (2) "The Handing on of Divine Revelation," (3) "Sacred Scripture," (4) "The Old Testament," (5) "The New Testament," and (6) "Sacred Scripture in the Life of the Church."

Constitution on the Sacred Liturgy (Sacrosanctum Concilium). The conciliar discussion touched on the Biblical, Christological, and ecclesiological foundations of the liturgy; its didactic value; liturgy as a unifying factor; the best ways to secure active and intelligent participation; simplification of rites; use of Latin and of modern languages; incorporation of local or national customs or traditions; making liturgy an effective influence in society; the competence of episcopal conferences and of individual bishops; concelebration of Mass; Communion under both kinds; Anointing of the Sick; and the length, language, and composition of the Breviary. In addition to an introduction, which states that the liturgy is the outstanding means whereby the faithful express in their lives and manifest to others the mystery of Christ and the real nature of the true Church, the constitution contains the following chapters: (1) "General Principles for the Restoration and Promotion of the Sacred Liturgy," (2) "The Most Sacred Mystery of the Eucharist," (3) "The Other Sacraments and the Sacramentals," (4) "The Divine Office," (5) "The Liturgical Year," (6) "Sacred Music," and (7) "Sacred Art and Sacred Furnishings." An appendix contains "A Declaration on the Revision of the Calendar."

Pastoral Constitution on the Church in the World of Today (Gaudium et spes). The fathers discussed the meaning and value of temporal activity; dignity of the human person; the conflict in the world between good and evil; the presence of sin; the role of women in society; racial discrimination; problems of the third world; world poverty and hunger; problems of emigration; atheism, Marxism, and communism; freedom and encouragement of scholarly research; the Church's influence on culture; Christian humanism and anthropology; the equality of all human beings; the necessity for Catholics to work with all men of good will; the solidarity of the Church with the world; the light shed by revelation on the mentality, problems, and forces of our age; the benefits of religion to civilization; the nature, ends, acts, and indissolubility of marriage; family life; abortion; economic production; the conditions of workers; relations between the Church and political society; the arms race; the possession and use of nuclear weapons; obligatory military service and conscientious objection; the obligations of nations toward an international authority; the growth of world population; aid to underdeveloped nations. The constitution contains an introductory statement on "The Situation of People in the Contemporary World." Part 1, entitled "The Church and the Human Person's Calling," consists of four chapters: "The Dignity of the Human Person," "The Community of Mankind," "Human Activity throughout the World," and "The Role of the Church in the Modern World." Part 2, entitled "Some Problems of Special Urgency," has five chapters: "Marriage and the Family," "Development of Culture," "Economic and Social Life," "Political Community," and "Peace and the Community of Nations." A concluding section states that the Church desires honest dialogue between her own members, with the separated brethren and communities, with all who acknowledge God, with those who cultivate the noble qualities of the human spirit without believing in God, and even with those who oppress the Church.

Decrees. The nine decrees consisted of the following:

Decree on the Pastoral Office of Bishops (Christus Dominus). The discussions centered on the bishop's office and the powers needed to exercise it; the Roman Curia and its relations with bishops; internationalization of the Curia; the powers needed for the proper discharge of bishops' duties; freedom in the appointment of bishops; compulsory retirement of bishops; the subjection of religious to the local ordinary; care for migrants; personal dioceses for people of a peculiar rite or nationality; powers of episcopal conferences; and a central organ of bishops to assist the pope in governing the Church.

Decree on Ecumenism (Unitatis redintegratio). Points of discussion included: the need of humility, chari-

ty, forgiveness, and the acknowledgment of errors and faults of all parties; assurance that unity does not mean uniformity; no simple "return" of the separated brethren; the meaning and use of the word "ecumenism"; the propriety of calling certain Protestant communities "churches"; the danger of engendering confusion and indifferentism in the minds of the faithful; participation in religious services with non-Catholic Christians; the validity of marriages celebrated before non-Catholic ministers; ways of conducting the dialogue; the desire for the restoration of unity among all followers of Christ. In conclusion the decree exhorts Catholics to refrain from superficiality and imprudent zeal, to be faithful to the truth received from the Apostles and Fathers of the Church, and to act in conjunction with the separated brethren so that no obstacle be put in the ways of divine Providence and no preconceived judgments impair the future inspirations of the Holy Spirit.

Decree on the Oriental Catholic Churches (Orientalium Ecclesiarum). The discussion treated structure of the Church; the rights and prerogatives of patriarchs; the evils of forced Latinization; determination of the rite of Oriental converts to the Catholic Church; the participation of Oriental Catholics in the religious services of Oriental non-Catholics and vice versa (*communicatio in sacris*); and marriages between Oriental Catholics and non-Catholics. The decree expresses the Catholic Church's esteem for the institutions, liturgical rites, ecclesiastical traditions, and the established standards of Christian life of Oriental Catholics.

Decree on the Ministry and Life of Priests (Presbyterorum ordinis). Central points of discussion included: the dignity and excellence of the priesthood; the spirituality and holiness of priests; the connection between their spiritual life and their ministry; their participation in Christ's priesthood; obedience and poverty; the importance of celibacy; life in common; associations of priests; their relations with bishops and laymen; an advisory council for the bishop; rights of priests; their duties toward non-Catholics; extraparochial apostolates; training in preaching; their intellectual activity and continued education in the ministry; the administration of the Sacrament of Penance; the missionary dimension of the priesthood; the equitable distribution of priests throughout the world; remuneration and financial equality of priests; abolition of the system of benefices and of honorary titles; and care for ill, aged, and fallen priests. The preface of the decree states that the decree applies to all priests.

Decree on Education for the Priesthood (Optatam totius). Points of discussion included: the notion of a vocation to the priesthood and means of fostering it; the nature and purpose of minor seminaries; adaptation of seminary discipline to modern times and to life in the world; organic unity in the spiritual, intellectual, and pastoral formation of candidates for the priesthood; sending them from other parts of the world to study in Europe; the place of scholasticism, especially Thomism, in the teaching of philosophy and theology; the need of natural, human virtues in candidates; the development of a missionary or apostolic spirit in them; isolation of seminarians from the world; a period for acquiring preliminary experience in the ministry or else a pastoral apprenticeship after ordination; and reform of the Congregation of Seminaries.

Decree on the Up-to-date Renewal of the Religious Life (Perfectae caritatis). Renewal according to the Gospel was discussed, as well as the attitude toward traditional practices; the theology of the vows; the role of contemplatives; the place of the apostolate in religious life; accommodation to contemporary needs; the spirituality of the active life; the recent decrease of vocations; and conferences of major superiors. The decree asserts that the adapted renewal includes both the constant return to the sources of all Christian life and to the original spirit of the institutes and their adaptation to changed conditions and the needs of the Church. The religious life is a state complete in itself and should be held in high esteem. The vows of chastity, poverty and obedience are related to dedication to the love and service of God and to the works of the apostolate. Priests and religious educators should foster religious vocations.

Decree on the Missionary Activity of the Church (Ad gentes). Conciliar discussion covered: the theology of the missions; the nature of the missionary vocation; flexibility and adaptation to other cultures with their own customs and values; creation of a central mission board; the new role of the Congregation for the Propagation of the Faith; the reason for missionary activity; the need of it for the salvation of non-Christians; dialogue with non-Christians; connection of missionary activity with ecumenism; extension of the mission area to other territories; the situation of the "new churches"; the status of prelatures *nullius;* the relations between missionary institutes and local ecclesiastical jurisdictions; the apostolic training of missionaries and catechists; borrowing of priests; lay missionaries; support of the missions; and twinning or pairing of an older diocese with a new jurisdiction.

Decree on the Apostolate of the Laity (postolicam actuositatem). Points discussed included: the dogmatic foundation of this apostolate and its objectives; lay spirituality; formation for the apostolate; relations with the hierarchy; Catholic Action; lay initiative and clericalism; the apostolate of youth; social action; cooperation with non-Catholics and non-Christians; and a secretariate in the Roman Curia.

Decree on the Media of Social Communication (Inter mirifica). The responsibility of the laity in this area was discussed, as well as the use of the media for evangelization; the need of concrete assistance in personnel and equipment in missionary countries; the formation of sound public opinion; institution of a special office in the Roman Curia or expansion of the then existing Pontifical Commission; and creation of an international Catholic news agency. The Council asks the pope to extend the duties and competence of the Secretariate for the Supervision of Publications and Entertainment to embrace all media, including the press, and to appoint to it experts from various countries, including laymen.

Declarations. The Council issued the following declarations:

Declaration on Religious Freedom (Dignitatis humanae). Points of discussion included: philosophical and juridical and/or dogmatic and theological arguments; connection between internal, personal freedom and external, social freedom; limitations; development of the Church's earlier teaching, especially of the doctrine of previous popes; effects on Catholic countries and on concordats; "rights of error"; danger of giving an excuse to antireligious governments; freedom or toleration; right of evangelization or of proselytism; danger of promoting indifferentism; rights of the Catholic Church; and application to predominantly non-Catholic countries and to those under Communist domination. Part 1 of the declaration, "The General Principles of Religious Freedom," states that the human person has a right to immunity from coercion on the part of individuals, social groups, or any human power. Government should respect and favor the religious life of the citizenry but should not command or inhibit religious acts; in preventing abuses, it must act according to juridical norms for the preservation of public order. Part 2, "Religious Freedom in the Light of Revelation," asserts that the human person's response to God in faith must be free. The Church must enjoy freedom and independence. The Council denounces and deplores the oppressive policies of some governments and emphasizes the necessity of religious freedom, which should everywhere be provided with an effective constitutional guarantee.

Declaration on the Church's Attitude toward Non-Christian Religions (Nostra aetate). The discussion covered: religious, not political, motives for a pronouncement in view of Arab opposition; the common religious patrimony of Christians and Jews; the alleged collective guilt of the Jewish people for the death of Christ (the accusation of deicide); their alleged rejection by God; the prediction of their eventual conversion to Christianity; the urgency of condemning anti-Semitism; and bonds with Islam and other world religions. The declaration affirms that all peoples have one community, origin, and goal. People ask the fundamental religious questions. The Church deplores hatred and persecution of the Jews and all displays of anti-Semitism and reproves any discrimination or harassment based on race, color, social status, or religion.

Declaration on Christian Education (*Gravissimum educationis*). The discussion covered: objectives; role of the family; obligations and limitations of the state; parents' right freely to choose schools; freedom within Catholic schools and freedom of research, especially in the sacred sciences; duties of the postconciliar commission. The declaration recognizes the importance of education for young people and adults amid present-day progress. All persons have a right to education; children have a right to moral instruction. The Church is obliged to educate its children, and it uses all suitable aids, such as catechetical instruction, but especially schools. In Catholic colleges and universities individual disciplines should be pursued according to their own principles and methods and with freedom of research, and there should be, if not a faculty, at least an institute or chair of theology with courses for lay students.

Bibliography: *Acta et Documenta Concilio Vaticano II Apparando,* Series I (*Antepraeparatoria*) (Vatican City 1960–61;; *Acta et Documenta Concilio Vaticano II Apparando,* Series II (*Praeparatoria*) (Vatican City 1964–69); *Acta Synodalia Sacrosancti Concilii Vaticani II* (Vatican City 1970–2000). *Acta congressus internationalis de theologia concilii Vaticani Secundi,* ed. A. SCHONMETZER (Vatican City 1968). *A la veille du Concile Vatican II: Vota et réactions en Europe et dans le catholicisme oriental,* ed. M. LAMBERIGTS and CL. SOETENS (Leuven 1992). *Commentary on the Documents of Vatican II,* ed. H. VORGRIMLER, 5 vols. (New York 1969). *Les commissions conciliaires à Vatican II,* ed. M. LAMBERIGTS et al. (Leuven 1996). *Der Beitrag der deutschsprachigen und osteuropäischen Länder zum Zwiten Vatikanischen Konzil,* ed. K. WITTSTADT and W. VERSCHOOTEN (Leuven 1996). *Le deuxième Concile du Vatican (1959–1965)* (Rome 1989). *L'Église canadienne et Vatican II,* ed. G. ROUTHIER (Québec 1997). *L'evento e le decisioni: Studi sulle dinamiche del concilio Vaticano II,* ed. M. T. FATTORI and A. MELLONI (Bologna 1997). *Experience, Organizations and Bodies at Vatican II,* ed. M. T. FATTORI and A. MELLONI (Leuven 1999). *Glaube im Prozess: Christsein nach dem II. Vatikanum,* ed. E. KLINGER and K. WITTSTADT (Freiburg 1984). JAN GROOTAERS, *I protagonisti del Vaticano II* (San Paolo 1994); *Actes et acteurs à Vatican II* (Leuven 1998). *History of Vatican II. Vol. I: Announcing and Preparing Vatican Council II: Toward a New Era in Catholicism,* ed. G. ALBERIGO and J. A. KOMONCHAK (Maryknoll/Leuven 1995); *Vol. II: The Formation of the Council's Identity: First Period and Intersession. October 1962–September 1963* (Maryknoll/Leuven 1997); *Vol. III: The Mature Council: Second Period and Intersession September 1963–September 1964* (Maryknoll/Leuven 2000). A. INDELICATO, *Difendere la dottrina o annunciare l'Evangelo: Il dibattito nella Commissione centrale preparatoria del Vaticano II* (Genoa 1992). J. H. MILLER, ed., *Vatican II: An Interfaith Appraisal* (Notre Dame 1966). *The Reception of Vatican II,* ed. G. ALBERIGO, J.-P. JOSSUA, and J.A. KOMONCHAK (Washington, D.C. 1987). *Per la storicizzazione del Vaticano II,* ed. G. ALBERIGO and A. MELLONI, *Cristianesimo nella Storia,* 13 (October 1992) 473–641. *Vatican II à Moscou: Actes du colloque de Moscou, 1995* (Leuven 1996). *Vatican II: Assessment and Perspectives Twenty-Five Years After (1962–1987),* ed. R. LATOURELLE, 3 vols. (New York 1988–89). *Vatican II commnence: Approches francophones,* ed. E. FOUILLOUX (Leuven 1993). *Vatican II et la Belgique,* ed. C. SOETENS (Ottignies 1996). *Vatican II Revisited by Those who Were There,* ed. A. STACPOOLE (Minneapolis 1986). *Vatican II: The Unfinished Agenda. A Look to the Future,* ed. L. R. et al. (New York 1987). *Il Vaticano II fra attese e celebrazione,* ed. G. ALBERIGO (Bologna 1995). *Vatikanum II und Modernisierung: Historische, theologische und soziologische Perspektiven,* ed. F. X. KAUFMANN and A. ZINGERLE (Paderborn 1996). *Verso il Concilio Vaticano II (1960–1962): Passaggi e problemi della preparazione conciliare,* ed. G. ALBERIGO and A. MELLONI (Genoa 1993). *Cristianismo e iglesias de América Latina en vìsperas del Vatican II,* ed. J.O. BEOZZO (San Jose, Costa Rica 1992). F. ANDERSON, *Council Daybook: Vatican II, Sessions 1 and 2; Session 3* (National Catholic Welfare Conference; Washington 1965). A. BERARD, tr., *Preparatory Reports, Second Vatican Council* (Philadelphia 1965). R. M. BROWN, *Observer in Rome: A Protestant Report on the Vatican Council* (Garden City, N.Y. 1964). R. CAPORALE, *Vatican II: Last of the Councils* (Baltimore 1964). G. CAPRILE, *Cronache del Concilio Vaticano II edite da "La Civiltà Cattolica,"* 5 v. (Rome 1965–66). Y. M. J. CONGAR, *Vatican II: Le Concile au jour le jour* (Paris 1963); *Deuxième session* (1964); *Troisième session* (1965). C. DOLLEN, *Vatican II: A Bibliography* (Metuchen, N.J.1969). H. FESQUET, *The Drama of Vatican II: The Ecumenical Council, January 1962–December 1965* (New York 1967). J. C. HAMPE, *Ende der Gegenreformation? Das Konzil: Dokumente und Deutung* (Stuttgart 1964). R. B. KAISER, *Pope, Council, and World: The Story of Vatican II* (New York 1963). W. KAMPE, *Das Konzil im Spiegel der Presse* (Würzburg 1963). H. KÜNG, *The Council in Action: Theological Reflections on the Second Vatican Council* (New York 1963); et al., eds., *Council Speeches of Vatican II* (Glen Rock, N.J. 1964). R. LAURENTIN, *L'Enjeu du Concile,* v.1 (Paris 1962); v.2 *Bilan de la première session* (1963); v.3 *Bilan de la deuxième session* (1964); v.4 *Bilan de la troisième session Bilan du Concile* (Paris 1966). M. NOVAK, *The Open Church: Vatican II, Act II* (New York 1964). J. RATZINGER, *Theological Highlights of Vatican II* (New York 1966). X. RYNNE (pseud.), *Letters from Vatican City: Vatican Council II (First Session): Background and Debates* (New York 1963); *The Second Session: The Debates and Decrees of Vatican Council II* (New York 1964); *The Third Session: The Debates and Decrees of Vatican Council II* (New York 1965); *The Fourth Session: The Debates and Decrees of Vatican Council II* (New York 1966). A. WENGER, *Vatican II: Première session* (Paris 1963); 2d ed. *Chronique de la première session* (1965); *Chronique de la deuxième session* (1964); *Chronique de la troisième session* (1965). RALPH M. WILTGEN, *The Rhine Flows into the Tiber: The Unknown Council* (New York 1967). V. A. YZERMANS, *A New Pentecost: Vatican Council II, Session 1* (Westminster, Md. 1963).

[R. F. TRISCO/J. A. KOMONCHAK]

VATICAN LIBRARY

The Vatican Library began as the Library of the popes, for since the beginning of papal times the popes

Scholars in reference room of the Vatican Library.

have collected archival documents. Using the place of residence of the popes and the locations of their collections as a basis for division, Nello Vian distinguishes five periods in the histories of the so-called libraries maintained by the popes: the pre-Lateran, when manuscripts were to be found in many different places; the Lateran period, when the archives were collected in the papal palace of the Lateran; the Avignon period, when the popes resided at AVIGNON; the pre-Vatican, the interim period when materials were being assembled in Rome; and the Vatican, from the middle of the fifteenth century to the present time. However, two general periods can be identified as the libraries of the popes prior to the Vatican Library and the Vatican Library.

Prior to the Vatican Library. There is no information on collections in the pre-Lateran period, probably because this was a period of persecution of the Christians, which did not allow for a specified location to house and maintain a collection of documents. Certainly the Christians copied and distributed the Sacred Scriptures and

copies of writings of the early Church Fathers that were kept in various places.

The Lateran period is dated from 313 to 1309. The Emperor Constantine gave Melchiades (311–14) the imperial residence on the Caelian Hill, named after the Lateran family. The Lateran Palace provided a location for the residence (including a library and archives) and central administration of the church for almost 1,000 years. Julian II (337–352) constituted the Holy Scrinium as a repository for literary and theological writings. St. Jerome (patron saint of librarians) mentioned the Scrinium in a 4th century letter. Gregory the Great (590–604) mentions that he placed his sermons at Lateran. The first listing of the documents of the papal administration occurred under Pope Innocent III (1198–1216), who created the important Regestes. The earliest extant catalogue (1295) identifies 443 items as belonging to the library of Boniface VIII (1294–1303). The papal collection of illuminated manuscripts had become of the most important in Europe. However, Boniface VIII initiated conflicts when he attempted to assert his authority over the political leaders of Europe. Clement V (1305–1314), fearing more attacks in 1310 from King Philip IV of France, transported 643 valuable codices to the sacristy of the monastery in Assisi. The Lateran palace was destroyed by fire in 1308 and 1309. The monastery in Assisi was sacked in 1310.

The popes resided in Avignon from 1309 to 1377. John XXII (1316–1334) not only bought manuscripts but had them copied at Avignon. Manuscripts were very frequently given to the popes, and through the exercise of the Law of Spoils the church fell heir to the possessions of the prelates. During the reign of Clement VI (1342–1352) the papal library achieved great distinction; the administration of the library was in the hands of the Sacristan of the Apostolic Palaces. The books themselves were located in the Tower of the Angels. In certain classes, for example, juridical literature, the papal library at Avignon surpassed even that of the Sorbonne. The library of the popes was open to those who had need of consulting it. A famous example is the request for a copy of Pliny in 1352 by Petrarch, who left his copy in Verona. Gregory XI returned to Rome in 1377 and died a year later. The Great Schism ended with the election of Martin V (1417–1431); he and his successor, Eugene IV (1431–1447) added to the library in Rome. However, unlike the Avignon period, the use of the library was limited to the private use of the popes and the Curia.

The Vatican Library A new period began with the election of Nicholas V (1447–1455), who wanted to make Rome a center of learning and culture. He conceived of a papal library that would be a great resource to all the world's scholars. Nicholas V began with over 340 manuscripts bequeathed by Eugene IV and sent men all over Europe to acquire more. Revenue from the Holy Year of 1450 provided the necessary resources. When CONSTANTINOPLE fell, the Imperial Library and the exiled Byzantine scholars came to the Vatican. At the time of Nicholas's death, the first catalogue indicated that there were between 1200 and 1500 volumes in the papal collection but no special depository for them.

Sixtus IV (1471–1484) established the Vatican Library in the modern sense of the term. Giovanni Andrea Bussi was appointed the librarian and was succeeded by Bartolomeo Platina in 1475, the first official librarian. On June 15, 1475, Sixtus IV issued the bull *Ad decorum militantis Ecclesiae,* formally establishing the library and setting a precedent for its good administration. The bull defined the function of the library, described the poor condition in which many of the volumes were found, provided for suitable quarters for the collection, officially appointed the librarian, insured employment of subordinate officials, and made certain that regular revenue be assigned to the library for the preservation, restoration, and

increase of the collection as well as support of its operating costs. The funds, moreover, were to be used for this purpose only, and a financial report of their use was to be made every January under pain of excommunication. The suitable quarters were the ground floor of the Vatican Palace, with the entrance to the Pappagallo courtyard. The initial library consisted of three rooms: the *bibliotheca latina, bibliotheca graeca* and *bibliotheca secreta;* later another room was added, the *bibliotheca pontificia.* On June 30, 1475, another papal bull was issued regarding the return of books. Platina's register of book charges for the years 1475 to 1485 is still available and includes the names of many noted humanists. Renowned artists were requisitioned to decorate the library: Domenico and David Ghirlandario, Melozzo da Forli, and Antoniazzo Romano. The catalogue of 1481 drawn up eight days before Sixtus's death indicates that the collection had grown to 3,499 items. The reputation of the Vatican Library was so great that scholars vied to be named librarian.

The acquisitions, space and prestige of the Vatican Library continued to grow in the 16th century. Julius II (1503'1513) added more rooms. Leo X (1513–1521) initiated a search for manuscripts all over Europe and the Orient by employing ''book hunters'' such as Johann Heitmers and Fausto Sabeo. He appointed well-known scholars to manage the library and to enforce the rules of Sixtus IV. Under Leo X the Vatican Library had 4070 items, making it the richest manuscript collection in the world. The growing influence of the library became reflected in new ecclesiastical titles. Paul III (1534–1549) appointed the first Cardinal Librarian. Julius III (1550–1555) changed the title of prefect to that of Bibliotecario di Santa Romana Chiesa, the official title that continues to be used. In order to accommodate the flood of new collections, Sixtus V (1585–1590) had Domenico Fontana design, between 1587 and 1589, a new building that divided the Belvedere courtyard from the Pigna courtyard. The top floor is a magnificent hall (184 feet long and 57 feet wide) that became known as the Sistine Library. In 1587, Sixtus V moved the printing works founded by Pius IV (1559–1565) in 1561. This act began the Vatican Press, the task of which was to publish the correct texts of the Scriptures, of the writings of the Church Fathers, of the decrees of the Council of TRENT, and of canonical laws. The council had underlined the importance of this work. By the end of the 16th century the Vatican Library had an arrangement of its collections.

The Vatican Library acquired many private collections in the 17th century. Though Gregory XIII (1572–1585) made arrangements in 1581 for acquiring the library of Fulvio Orisini, the library (413 manuscripts) remained in Orsini's possession until his death.

The Vatican acquired the collection in 1600. In 1612 Paul V (1605–21) created a separate archives section by bringing together materials from the library of Castel Sant'Angelo, the Apostolic Camera, and other official offices. This new section, completed in 1630, began the Vatican Secret Archives, located in rooms under the tower of Gregory XIII's observatory. Paul V also acquired the 28 precious codices from the monastery San Columbo in Bobbio. The Palatine Library of Heidelberg (3500 manuscripts and many printed works) was donated in 1622 to Gregory XV (1621–23). Until 1622 codices received at the Vatican Library were classified according to their contents, with special categories for Sacred Scripture, the Fathers of the Church, the Scholastics, liturgy, hagiography, homiletics, canon law, the classics, and the neo-Latin works. Afterwards a new system of classification was employed. The collections became known by their background (*Fondo*); the Vatican Library collection prior to 1622 became the Fondo Vaticano. In 1658, Alexander VII (1655–1667) received the important Fondo Urbinate (1767 Latin and Italian, 165 Greek and 128 Oriental manuscripts) established by the Duke of Urbino in the 15th century. In 1689 part of the Fondo Reginense (the collection of Queen Christina of Sweden) was sold to Alexander VIII (1689–1691). The entire collection (2,120 Latin manuscripts and 190 Greek manuscripts, plus 55 manuscripts from the library of Pius II) was later acquired by Benedict XIV (1740–1758).

The Vatican Library continued to receive important manuscript collections in the 18th century as well as important collections of antiquities. The Fondo Capponiano (288 codices) was bequeathed in 1746. Benedict XIV bought the Fondo Ottoboniano (3,394 Latin and 473 Greek manuscripts) in 1748. The Orientalists Joseph Simon Assemani and his nephew Stephan Evodius began an inventory of the Oriental manuscripts. The initial tome was published in 1756; the second in 1758; the third in 1759. The fourth tome was destroyed by fire in 1768. In 1738, the numismatic collection (*Medagliere*) was founded. The Museum of Sacred Art, with its artifacts from the early Christian era, was established in 1755. With the separation between sacred and secular arts came the founding of the Museum of Secular Art in 1767. (These museums are now part of the Vatican museums.)

There was little activity at the Vatican Library during most of the 19th century, probably due to the difficulties of using the library, such as a lack of indexes and inventories, and perhaps to restrictions caused by the political troubles of the time. From 1801 on each issue of the *Annuario pontificio* lists the *bibliotecario* of the library; the names of the *custody* and *scrittori* were also given. From 1814 to 1870 the Vatican Library and other major libraries in the area are listed in the annual under the heading *Biblioteche Pubbliche*. From 1820 to 1870 the list under this heading gave the location, staff, and hours of opening. During this time part of the Fondo Cicognara (4,300 volumes) was given to the library (1824) and the remainder in 1834. An inventory of the Latin manuscripts occurred during the period from 1852 to 1878. A renewal of life in the library took place under Leo XIII (1878–1903). In 1881 Leo removed all restrictions for research workers. His 1883 letter *Saepenumero*, on the importance of historical studies, formally decreed the Vatican Library open for historical research. Catalogues and descriptions of the library's collections became essential for access to the materials and were published in 1880, 1885, and 1886. In 1885 a reading room was opened; this later became the *sala di consultazione* or reference room. In 1888 the *motu proprio*, *Augustum sanctissimumque munus* was accompanied by the "Reglomento della Biblioteca Vaticana," which detailed the organization of personnel, administration, and service. In 1891 the Vatican Library received the Fondo Borghese with manuscripts from the Papal Library at Avignon. A catalogue of the Fondo Ottoboniano was completed in 1893. The process of cataloguing the Urbino collection began in 1895 and finished in 1921. A description of the manuscripts of the Fondo Capponiano was written in 1897.

The modernization of the Vatican Library generated by Leo XIII accelerated in the 20th century. A series called *Studi e Testi* was begun in 1900 by Father Francis Ehrle, S. J., the First Curator, to publish scholarship on the Vatican Library collections. (During Ehrle's time the role of First Curator changed to Prefect). In 1902 the library acquired the Fondo Borgiano (that was given to the Propaganda Fide in 1804) and the important Fondo Barberiniano (10,041 Latin manuscripts, 505 in Greek, 160 Oriental manuscripts and 36,049 printed volumes). The publication of the catalogues concerning the manuscripts *Vaticani latini* commenced in 1902 and was completed in 1931. The Fondo Rossiano (1,196 manuscripts, 6,000 rare prints and 2,500 incunabula) was added in 1921.

A significant stage in the modern development of the library occurred under Pius XI (1922–1939). The pope's special interest in the library was due to the fact that he was the prefect from 1914 to 1919. In 1923, the Italian state gave the library the Fondo Chigiano (3,916 manuscripts). The Fondo Ferrajoli (885 manuscripts and 100,000 autographs) was purchased in 1926. A project was quietly undertaken by the Carnegie Endowment for International Peace in 1928 to improve the Vatican Library for research.

An elevator was installed, which is still used today, and a new entrance was created. Electric lighting, temperature controls, and new steel books stacks were installed. An international committee, chaired by William Warner Bishop, provided technical assistance on indexing and cataloguing. One of the first steps taken under the reorganization plan was the adoption of the general principles and practices of the Library of Congress system of classification. This system was later abandoned. In 1934 a school of library science was established in connection with the library and staffed, primarily, by assistants who had had training and experience in the United States.

During the reign of Pius XII (1939–1958) many scholarly endeavors occurred. Catalogues were composed, including the Ferrajoli manuscripts (1939–1960), Coptic manuscripts (1947), Borghese manuscripts (1952), and Hebrew manuscripts (1956). Description of manuscripts were written, including the *Vaticani latini* (1947–61), Persian manuscripts (1948), *Vaticani greci* (1950), and Turkish manuscripts (1953). Due to the importance of the *Studi e Testi,* it was decided that from 1942 on every 100th volume would be an index volume with the table of contents, an analytic description of each volume, and a cumulative index of authors, by name and by subject, for the manuscripts and articles cited in these volumes. The first volume of tables and general indices was published in 1942 (for volumes 1–100), the second in 1959 (for volumes 101–200), the third in 1986 (for volumes 201–300); the fourth in 2002 (for volumes 301–400). During the reigns of John XXIII (1958–1963) and Paul VI (1963–1978) catalogues and descriptions of manuscripts continued a steady rate. A Sale di Riviste was opened in 1971; more than 1,000 journals are available there.

Major advances occurred under the reign of John Paul II (1978–). The American Friends of the Vatican Library was approved in a letter dated Oct. 9, 1981, to the prefect, Fr. (later Cardinal) Alfons M. Stickler, from the secretary of state, Cardinal Agostino Casaroli. This group raises funds for special projects for the library. A new subterranean storehouse was inaugurated in 1983. One of the most important projects of the 20th century in the library was the cataloguing of its 8,300 incunabula. Prior to this time only a handwritten list of 1,547 incunabula existed, compiled from 1853 to 1868. Some attempts at describing and cataloguing parts of the incunabula were made from 1927 to 1944, 1964, and 1983. The whole collection was finally inventoried from 1988 to 1997 and entered into a database (ISTC). The computerized Vatican catalogue (OPAC) is connected to the Roman network URBS. Its primary access is to books: 500,000 cards are accessible, which provide information about more than a million printed volumes. The electronic cataloguing of non-print material includes 150,000 manuscripts, more than 100,000 autographs, more than 300,000 coins and

medals, and over 100,000 prints and engravings. In 2001 a new reading room for periodicals was opened. An archives room was created underneath the prefect's office to properly house the volumes pertaining to the administration of the library. The *Guide to the Manuscript and Printed Book Collections and Numismatic Cabinet of the Vatican Library* was completed in 2002. This new guide provides more in depth information on the composition, the history, the means of cataloguing, and the bibliography for all the collections of the Vatican Library. There is no precedence to an undertaking of this kind, being based on the collaboration of dozens of specialists, both inside and outside of the Vatican, who edited hundreds of diverse entries. Improved security and atmospheric systems were being planned in 2002. Under the leadership of the librarian-archivist, Cardinal Jorge M. Mejía, and the prefect, Fr. Raffaele Farina, S.D.B., the Vatican Library continues to advance as a tremendous resource to scholars worldwide.

Bibliography: E. TISSERANT and T. W. KOCH, *The Vatican Library* (Jersey City, NJ 1929); *The Books Published by the Vatican Library* (Vatican City 1947). N. VIAN, *La Biblioteca Apostolica Vaticana* (Vatican City 1970). E. BOYLE, *A Survey of the Vatican Archives and Its Medieval Holdings* (Toronto 1972). C. CARLEN, ''The Popes and the Vatican Library'' in *Translatio Studii: Manuscript and Library Studies,* ed. J. G. PLANTE (Collegeville, MN 1973) 39–47. A. STICKLER, *Vatican Library: Its History and Treasures* (Vatican City 1989). *Bibliothecae Apostolicae Vaticanae Incunabula,* ed. W. SHEEHAN (Vatican City 1997). *Biblioteca Apostolica Vaticana* (Vatican City 2000).

[C. KOSANKE]

VAUGHAN, BERNARD JOHN

Jesuit preacher; b. Courtfield, Hertfordshire, England, Sept. 20, 1847; d. Roehampton, England, Oct. 31, 1922. His parents, Col. John F. Vaughan of Courtfield and Louisa Elizabeth (Rolls) Vaughan, a convert, gave to the Church six sons and five daughters, including Cardinal Herbert VAUGHAN and Abp. Roger VAUGHAN. After study at Stonyhurst College from 1859, Bernard entered the JESUITS (1866) and was ordained (1880). During his assignment to the Church of the Holy Name, Manchester, his participation in local controversies, formidable debating talents, unconventional preaching methods, excellent voice and delivery, and distinguished bearing soon attracted attention. He preached at Cannes, France (1898), where his sermons led to friendships with the British royal family and a transfer to the Jesuit church on Farm Street, London (1899). His series of sermons there on the ''Sins of Society'' (1906) firmly established his English reputation, which was extended by visits to Canada (1910), the U.S. (1911–13), the Far East (1913), and Africa (1922). The extensive publicity that he sought and received tended to conceal the basic simplicity of an obedient religious, who was most interested in work among the urban poor and efforts on behalf of social reform.

Bibliography: D. GWYNN, *The Dictionary of National Biography from the Earliest Times to 1900,* 63 v. (London 1885–1900; repr. With corrections, 21 v., 1908–09, 1921–22, 1938; suppl. 1901–) (1922–30) 867–868. C. C. MARTINDALE, *Bernard Vaughan, S.J.* (London 1923).

[D. MILBURN]

VAUGHAN, HERBERT ALFRED

Cardinal, third archbishop of WESTMINSTER; b. Gloucester, England, April 15, 1832; d. Mill Hill, London, June 19, 1903. Herbert was the eldest son of Col. John F. Vaughan of Courtfield and Louise Elizabeth (Rolls) Vaughan, a convert who gave six sons and five daughters to the Church, including Abp. Roger VAUGHAN and Bernard VAUGHAN, SJ. Educated at Stonyhurst and Downside in England, Brugelette in Belgium, and Rome, Herbert was ordained at Lucca, Italy (Oct. 28, 1854).

In 1855 he became vice president of St. Edmund's College, a seminary in Ware, England, and in 1857 he joined the OBLATES OF ST. CHARLES. Leaving St. Edmund's (1861), he traveled widely to collect money for an English college to train foreign missionaries (1863–65). The result was the establishment of St. Joseph's College, Mill Hill, which opened March 1, 1866. Vaughan was the founder of the MILL HILL MISSIONARIES, JOSEPHITE Fathers, and the FRANCISCAN Missionary Sisters of St. Joseph.

Largely through the influence of Cardinal MANNING, Vaughan became second bishop of Salford (1872). There he founded a pastoral seminary, and within 12 months he had established St. Bede's College in Manchester and begun his labors on behalf of poor Catholic children. He spent some time in Rome defending the claims of the English bishops against certain activities of the regular clergy.

Vaughan became archbishop of Westminster (March 1892) and cardinal (1893). Pursuing a different course than Manning, his predecessor, he closed the seminary at Hammersmith and became one of the seven bishops who sat on the board of control for the new common seminary at Oscott. He also persuaded the English hierarchy to request the Congregation of Propaganda to withdraw its admonition against Catholic attendance at the universities of Oxford and Cambridge. This petition was granted in 1895.

Vaughan was often involved in controversy, and in 1868 he bought the *Tablet* to propagate his ultramontane

Bernard John Vaughan. (The Catholic University of America)

views on papal infallibility. Between 1894 and 1897 he officially entered the discussion regarding Anglican orders. At his suggestion an international papal commission was formed, leading to Leo XIII's apostolic letter *Apostolicae curae* (1896), that denied the validity of Anglican orders. Vaughan also continued to campaign for the rights of denominational schools. The Education Act of 1902 recognized his fundamental principle that such schools merited government support.

Vaughan published many manuals of devotion and religious instruction whose simple style and direct thought contributed to their popularity. He is responsible for the present cathedral at Westminster—he envisioned it, engaged John F. Bentley as architect, and laid the foundation stone (June 29, 1895). The cathedral opened with his funeral service in 1903. Vaughan's impulsive and somewhat romantic nature found an appeal in bold enterprises. He was a natural leader, tall in appearance, but a seeming haughtiness and lack of sympathy lessened his attractiveness.

Bibliography: J. G. SNEAD-COX, *The Dictionary of National Biography from the Earliest Times to 1900* (London 1885–1900) (1901–11) 3:550–554; *The Life of Cardinal Vaughan,* 2 v. (London 1910; abr. ed. New York 1934); S. LESLIE, ed., *Letters of Herbert Cardinal Vaughan to Lady Herbert of Lea, 1867–1903* (London 1942).

[D. MILBURN]

VAUGHAN, ROGER WILLIAM BEDE

Second archbishop of Sydney, Australia; b. Courtfield, Herefordshire, England, Jan. 9, 1834; d. Ince Blundell Hall, Lancashire, Aug. 18, 1883. He was the brother of Cardinal Herbert VAUGHAN, and of Father Bernard VAUGHAN, SJ. Educated at DOWNSIDE ABBEY, he joined the BENEDICTINES (1854) and was ordained (1859). In 1873 he went to Australia from St. Michael's College, Herefordshire, where he had been a prior and professor. He was consecrated coadjutor with right of succession to Archbishop POLDING by Cardinal Wiseman, arrived in Sydney (December 1873), and succeeded to the see on Polding's death (1877). Recognizing that the Anglo-Benedictine community established by his predecessor was inadequate for the needs of the rapidly growing Irish-Australian population he developed a conventional diocesan structure, dispersed the Benedictine priests to parishes, and concentrated on recruiting missionary priests from Ireland. As a brilliant orator and writer, he led the Church in a losing struggle against the secularization of education and the withdrawal of State aid to Church schools that became law in New South Wales (1880), and was a prime mover in the decision of the Australian bishops to establish their own Catholic education system. In April 1883 he visited Europe to recruit religious teachers for the Catholic schools. Two days after reaching England he died. His remains were returned to Sydney in 1946 and rest in the crypt of St. Mary's Cathedral.

[J. G. MURTAGH]

VAUGHAN WILLIAMS, RALPH

Eminent 20th-century composer; b. Down Ampney (Gloucester), England, Oct. 12, 1872; d. London, Aug. 26, 1958. Of distinguished Welsh ancestry on his father's side and a descendant of Josiah Wedgwood and grandnephew of Charles DARWIN on his mother's, he grew up in the Wedgwood country seat in Surrey and studied with C. H. Parry and C. V. Stanford at the new Royal College of Music; with Charles Wood at Trinity College, Cambridge (B.Mus. 1894; Mus.D. 1901); and, for brief intervals, with Bruch in Berlin and Ravel in Paris. His creative vision found matter and form in the heritage of ancient English folk song, hymnody, and polyphony, in whose rediscovery he had energetically participated. His subsequent music broke ground for a new national expression, and together with his lectures and writings constitutes a declaration of English (and American) independence from a decadent European romanticism. In brief, he held that a musical style must be national before it can become international or "classic"; that the greatest music is only "an outward and visible sign of an inward and spiritual grace, rooted in an age-old tradition" (*The Making of Music,* 61). This comment reflects the nostalgic and paramystical temper of mind that pervades the whole varied range of his works from unison carol to ballet and film music (and a canon of nine symphonies, the last completed in his 85th year). Its ultimate utterance is found, however, in biblically oriented creations such as the cantatas *Sancta Civitas* and *Magnificat;* the *Te Deums;* the instrumental suite *Flos Campi;* the Anglican service music; and the Catholic Mass in G minor composed for Sir Richard Terry for use at Westminster Cathedral (1922). For this Mass he not only revived and extended the church modes but also invented a modal harmony to accompany them—an achievement at once refreshing and austerely contemplative in effect. As Terry wrote the composer, "In your individual and modern idiom, you have really captured the old liturgical spirit and atmosphere." The text has been translated for Anglican worship, and the Credo and Sanctus were sung during Queen Elizabeth II's coronation. In his three visits to the U.S., he appealed to American composers, as had DVOŘÁK before him, to look about them, as well as to Continental sources, for inspiration.

Bibliography: R. VAUGHAN WILLIAMS, *National Music* (New York 1934; repr. 1935), Bryn Mawr College lectures, 1932; *Some Thoughts on Beethoven's Choral Symphony* (New York 1953); *The Making of Music* (Ithaca, N.Y. 1955), Cornell U. lectures, 1954. R. VAUGHAN WILLIAMS and G. HOLST, *Heirs and Rebels,* ed. U. VAUGHAN WILLIAMS and I. HOLST (New York 1959). H. J. FOSS, *Ralph Vaughan Williams* (New York 1950). F. S. HOWES, *The Music of Ralph Vaughan Williams* (New York 1954). P. M. YOUNG, *Vaughan Williams* (London 1953). J. DAY, *Vaughan Williams* (Master Musicians Series; New York 1961). A. E. F. DICKINSON, *Vaughan Williams* (London 1963). M. KENNEDY, *The Works of Ralph Vaughan Williams* (New York 1964). U. VAUGHAN WILLIAMS, *Ralph Vaughan Williams* (New York 1964). P. M. YOUNG, *The Choral Tradition* (New York 1962). P. H. YOUNG and M. KENNEDY, *Die Musik in Geschichte und Gegenwart,* ed. F. BLUME (Kassel-Basel 1949–). J. DAY, "Hugh the Drover, or, Love in the Stocks" in *International Dictionary of Opera,* 2 v., ed. C. S. LARUE (Detroit 1993). J. ALLEN FELDMAN, "Riders To the Sea" ibid. L. FOREMAN, ed., *Ralph Vaughan Williams in Perspective: Studies of an English Composer* (Colchester 1998). A. FROGLEY, ed., *Vaughan Williams Studies* (Cambridge 1996). M. JAMESON, *Ralph Vaughan Williams: An Essential Guide to his Life and Works* (London 1997). C. LIVINGSTON, "The Christmas Fantasias of Vaughan Williams and Holst," *Journal of the British Music Society* 13 (1991) 59–66. A. MCFARLAND, "A Deconstruction of William Blake's Vision:

Vaughan Williams and *Job*," *International Journal of Musicology* 3 (1994) 339–71. W. MELLERS, *Vaughan Williams and the Vision of Albion* (London 1989). L. G. MUSSELWHITE, "Falstaff: Nationalism's Tie to Character Formation in *The Merry Wives of Windsor, Falstaff,* and *Sir John In Love.*" *The Opera Journal* 26/2 (1993) 27–29, 32–33.

[M. E. EVANS]

VAUX-DE-CERNAY, ABBEY OF

Former French Cistercian abbey present-day Diocese of Versailles. It was founded near Paris in 1118 by the reformed Benedictines of SAVIGNY. By 1137 it was able to found the abbey of Breuil-Benoît, near Evreux. Vaux-de-Cernay, as part of Savigny, joined the Cistercians in 1147. Abbot Guy (d. 1210), later Bishop of Carcassone, participated in the crusade against the ALBIGENSES, while his nephew, PETER OF VAUX-DE-CERNAY wrote an *Historia Albigensium*. The abbey reached its height under the great ascetic, THEOBALD OF VAUX-DE-CERNAY (d. 1247). The Hundred Years' War left Vaux-de-Cernay ruined and depopulated. Before the work of reconstruction could be completed, the abbey was lost to commendatory abbots. Early in the 17th century the community of 13 monks joined the Cistercian Strict Observance (*see* TRAPPISTS). The abbey regained a measure of its medieval reputation but was suppressed by the French Revolution in 1791. The remains of the 12th-century church and cloister are some of the finest monuments of early Cistercian Gothic.

Bibliography: L. MERLET and A. MOUTIÉ, eds., *Cartulaire de l'abbaye de Notre-Dame des Vaux de Cernay,* 3 v.(Paris 1857–58). L. MORIZE, *Étude archéologique sur l'abbaye de Notre-Dame des Vaux de Cernay* (Tours 1889). M. AUBERT, *L'Abbaye des Vaux de Cernay* (Paris 1934). U. CHEVALIER, *Répertoire des sources historiques du moyen–âge. Topobiobibliographie,* 2 v. (Paris 1894–1903) 2:3247–48. L. H. COTTINEAU, *Répertoire topobibliographique des abbayes et prieurés,* 2 v. (Mâcon 1935–39) 2:3308–09.

[L. J. LEKAI]

VAZ, JOSEPH, BL.

Priest of the Oratory of St. Philip Neri, apostle of Ceylon (Sri Lanka) and the country's first blessed; b. Benaulim, Province of Salcette, Goa, India, April 21, 1651; d. Kandy, Sri Lanka, January 16, 1711. Vaz, ordained in 1676, labored incessantly in his native Goa, although he desired to go to Ceylon where the Dutch denied religious freedom to Catholics. In 1681 he undertook a difficult missionary assignment in Kanara. He returned to Goa in 1685 convinced that the task in Ceylon could best be accomplished by a religious society. To-

Ralph Vaughan Williams. (©Hulton-Deutsch Collection/ CORBIS)

ward that end Vaz associated himself with a group of priests that under his leadership formed an Oratory of St. Philip Neri.

In the spring of 1686, accompanied by a lay brother, Vaz arrived in Ceylon. Because of the persecution, he disguised himself as a beggar. Although hunted as a criminal and forced to endure many hardships, he ministered to souls there who had been without a priest for more than three decades. Eventually he won the confidence of the king of Kandy through the working of a miracle, and religious liberty was restored.

In 1697, fellow Oratorians joined him. Under his supervision the territory was geographically divided, each Oratorian being responsible for an assigned area. Through his efforts, more than 70,000 openly professed the faith in Ceylon. Because of his success ecclesiastical authorities wanted to heap honors upon him, but he managed to resist.

By the time he died, he was revered for holiness. He was buried in the church he built in Kandy, which has since been destroyed and the relics lost. A shrine in his honor was inaugurated in Mangalore, February 6, 2000. Vaz's cause for beatification was opened in Ceylon in 1737; the necessary miracle attributed to his intercession

Vaux-de-Cernay Abbey. (©Dave Bartruff/Bettmann/CORBIS)

was approved July 6, 1993. Finally, Pope John Paul II beatified him, January 21, 1995, at Colomba, Sri Lanka. Bl. Joseph Vaz is the patron of Goa, India.

Feast: January 16.

Bibliography: P. COURTENAY, *History of Ceylon,* tr. M. G. FRANCIS, abridged translation (New Delhi 1999). C. GASBARRI, *A Saint for the New India* (Allahabad 1961). S. G. PERERA, *Life of the Venerable Father Joseph Vaz* (Galle, Ceylon 1953); *The Oratorian Mission in Ceylon* (Colombo, Ceylon 1936). W. L. A. DON PETER, *Star in the East* (Colombo, Sri Lanka 1995). G. SCHURHAMMER, *Lexikon für Theologie und Kirche,* first edition, 10:511.

[J. WAHL/EDS.]

VÁZQUEZ, FRANCISCO JAVIER

Peruvian Augustinian author; b. Cajamarca, Peru, 1703; d. Rome, Italy, Feb. 2, 1785. He joined the Augustinians in Lima, Peru, and completed his clerical education there. As a young priest, Vázquez accompanied his provincial to Rome, where he spent the greater part of his life, occupying various offices in the order. The prior general, Agostino Gioia, appointed him visitor to Mexico, but he was unable to carry out this mission because of the opposition of the Spanish government, whose displeasure

Vázquez had incurred by his vigorous defense of the teachings of Cardinal Henry NORIS, then under attack by the Spanish Inquisition. When Gioia died in 1751, Vázquez became vicar-general. Two years later the general chapter in Bologna elected him prior general for life. Noteworthy among the activities of his long rule were his promotion of studies and his enrichment of the valuable collection in the Biblioteca Angelica in Rome (*see* ROCCA, ANGELO). Vázquez was involved in conflict with the Dominicans and especially with the Jesuits. These conflicts had their basis in the theological controversies that arose in the wake of Jansenism. Vázquez collaborated closely with the enemies of the Jesuits, both in Spain and in Rome, to accomplish the suppression of the Society of Jesus (1773).

Bibliography: A. MERCATI and A. PELZER, *Dizionario ecclesiastico,* 3 v. (Turin 1954–58) 3:1273. *Analecta Augustiniana* 13 (1929–30) 84–119. G. DE SANTIAGO VELA, *Ensayo de una biblioteca ibero-americana de la orden de San Agustín,* 7 v. in 8 (Madrid 1913–31) 8:108–123. E. DAMMIG, *Il movimento giansenista a Roma nella seconda metà del secolo XVIII* (*Studi e Testi* 119; 1945).

[A. J. ENNIS]

VÁZQUEZ, GABRIEL

Theologian; b. Villaescusa de Haro, near Belmonte, Spain, June 18, 1549; d. Jesús del Monte, Alcalá, Sept. 30, 1604. He studied philosophy in Alcalá (1565–69) and joined the Society of Jesus in 1569. He taught philosophy while he pursued his theological studies in Alcalá (1571–75), and he later taught moral theology in Ocaña. He taught theology in Madrid from 1577 to 1579 and in Alcalá until 1585. He was then sent to Rome, where he replaced Francisco SUÁREZ at the Roman College until 1591. Because of national differences, he gave up his teaching position and returned to Alcalá where he dedicated two years to writing. In 1591, he followed Suárez as professor of theology in Alcalá until his death.

Vázquez was a man of solid virtue, especially in the observance of poverty, but at the same time he had a certain natural roughness and excessive vivacity. His whole life was dedicated to teaching and to spiritual direction.

Works. When they were edited in Alcalá from 1598 to 1616, his works filled ten volumes. Almost all his commentaries were on the *Summa* of St. Thomas. His treatises took the form, common enough at that time, of a brief explanation of the text of St. Thomas, followed by an ample discussion concerning the basis of the question. His last works were the *Paraphrasis et compendiosa expositio ad nonnullas epistolas S. Pauli* and *Opuscula moralia.* Before 1594 he had published *De cultu adorationis libri tres et disputationes contra errores Felicis et Elipandi,* inserting this in his commentaries on the third part of the *Summa.* Only the first three volumes were edited during his life; the others were published just as he had left them. In Madrid in 1617, Murcia de la Llana extracted the *Disputationes metaphysicae* from Vázquez' works; it was often reproduced, in whole or in part, outside of Spain. Other writings on various topics have not yet been edited.

Teaching. As a professor Vázquez attracted the admiration and enthusiasm of his students because of his brilliant and lively presentation and the subtlety and warmth of his academic discussions. His writings are famous for their clarity, conciseness, and elegant Latin.

Vázquez was renowned for his strong, sharp, and critical mind. His knowledge of the councils and the Fathers was extensive, especially of St. Augustine—he was called "Augustinus redivivus." He had a keen sense of history and philology, together with a metaphysical penetration, which, however, did not equal that of Suárez in breadth, depth, calmness, or comprehension. His many rivalries with the Doctor Eximius were proverbial.

The doctrine of Vázquez, which follows the teaching common among the Jesuits, cannot be compared to the greatness and equilibrium of that of his rival Suárez. He sustained pure MOLINISM, as opposed to CONGRUISM, but the notion of *scientia media* and the naturalness of divine concurrence were better explained by Suárez.

Vázquez' most controverted ideas are as follows: direct veneration of images is a purely external reverence; formal justification comes, not precisely through habitual grace, but through contrition (a doctrine that had to be suppressed in later editions); free will necessarily follows what is presented as a greater good; natural law is somewhat anterior to every act of the divine intellect and will. Other opinions of Vázquez are that the intuitive vision of God necessitates an impressed species; Anselm's ontological argument for the existence of God is valid; the generation of the Word is explained not only through an intellectual procession, but also by the concept of image; a good impulse, as grace, is required for every good work; the indwelling of the Holy Spirit consists in the production of grace; the real presence of Christ in the Eucharist is explained by adduction; the essence of the sacrifice of the Mass consists in a "mystical mactation" commemorative of the sacrifice of the Cross. In moral theology his probabilism is tainted with a certain tutiorism and admits of indifferent acts.

Bibliography: C. SOMMERVOGEL, *Bibliothèque de la Compagnie de Jésus,* 11 v. (Brussels-Paris 1890–1932) 8:513–519. J. HELLIN, *Dictionnaire de théologie catholique,* 15 v. (Paris 1903–50) 15:2601–2610. W. HENTRICH, *Lexikon für Theologie und Kirche,* ed. M. BUCHBERGER, 10 v. (Freiburg 1930–38) 10:511–513. A. ASTRAIN, *Historia de la Compañía de Jesús, en la asistencia de España* 7 v. (Madrid 1902–25) v. 4. M. SOLANA, *Los grandes escolásticos españoles de los siglos XVI y XVII* (Madrid 1928). X. M. LE BACHELET, *Prédestination et grâce efficace* 2 v. (Louvain 1931). F. STEGMÜLLER, *Beiträge zur Geschichte der Philosophie und Theologie des Mittelalters* suppl. 3.2 (1935): 1287–1311. F. CERECEDA, "Censuras y apologias del libro 'De adoratione' del P. Vasquez G.," *Estudios eclesiásticos* 14 (1935): 555–564. R. DE SCORRAILLE, *François Suarez de la Compagnie de Jésus* 2 v. (Paris 1912–13) 1:283–314.

[J. M. DALMAU]

VÁZQUEZ, PABLO

Mexican bishop and diplomat; b. Atlixco, Puebla, March 21, 1769; d. Cholula, Oct. 7, 1847. He started his ecclesiastical career at the Palafoxiano Seminary of Puebla in 1778. In 1790 he went to San Pablo in Mexico City where he eventually became a professor and rector. He received his doctor's degree in theology at the Royal Pontifical University of Mexico on Jan. 23, 1795. The following March he was ordained. In 1822 he was named minister plenipotentiary to the Holy See, but he did not receive his credentials until 1825. He then left for Europe and undertook the difficult mission of obtaining from the

Holy See recognition of Mexican independence and the appointment of bishops. Spain strongly opposed both. Although Mexico lacked an episcopacy because the bishops had either died or returned to Spain, the most the Pope would grant was that bishops for Mexico should be titular and vicars apostolic. This was unacceptable to Vázquez. With the accession of Gregory XVI he had more success. In the consistory of Feb. 28, 1831, the pope announced the first six bishops for independent Mexico, one of them being Vázquez for the See of Puebla. He was consecrated by Cardinal Odescalchi, March 6, 1831, in Rome, and returned to Mexico to take possession of his diocese on July 1. Immediately he reorganized the Mexican hierarchy, and in the following months consecrated the rest of the designated bishops. A learned priest, zealous pastor, and skillful diplomat, he was an exemplary bishop.

Bibliography: M. CUEVAS, *Historia de la Iglesia en México,* 5 v. (5th ed. Mexico City 1946–47). V. DE P. ANDRADE, *Los sumos pontífices romanos y la Iglesia mexicana* (Mexico City 1903).

[R. MONTEJANO Y AGUIÑAGA]

VÁZQUEZ DE ESPINOSA, ANTONIO

Spanish Discalced Carmelite writer; b. Jérez de la Frontera, *c.* 1570; d. Seville, 1630. Little is known of his life except details he inadvertently included in his writings. Wishing to save the souls of the American natives, Vázquez asked for and received permission to go to Spanish America; it is not known when he landed there. He was in Mexico in 1612 but must have arrived some time before, since by then he had already seen Puerto Rico, Cuba, Florida, and other Spanish areas. It is generally thought that he remained until 1622 and got as far south as Chiloé in Chile. The great flood at Potosí in 1626 is the latest event in his work that can be dated. Before leaving for America, he read the literature dealing with Spanish America. He visited almost all of the area. This, with his gift of great curiosity, his scientific and practical bent, and his objectivity of observation, made him well qualified to write one of the most important works on the Spanish-American empire at perhaps the height of its prosperity: *Compendio y descripción de las Indias Occidentales.* On his return to Spain, Vázquez began the printing of his work, but he died after completing only the first 80 pages. The manuscript was found in the Vatican Library in 1931 by Charles Upson Clark.

Botanists prize his descriptions of numerous plants. Among these is perhaps the first description of the quinaquina tree and the curative properties of quinine derived from it. His account of the mines is the fullest survey of early mining methods in Spanish America, and he gives an accurate eyewitness account of an auto-da-fé of the Inquisition. All the cities that he visited are fully described with exact details of the plans of the city, public buildings, and service institutions, such as hospitals, schools, and asylums. However, to quote Charles Upson Clark, "perhaps the greatest contribution lies neither in geography, botany, nor anthropology but in the field of Spanish colonial civil and ecclesiastical administration. Here his picture is so complete that the book will be required reading for any investigator into Spanish American history."

Bibliography: A. VÁZQUEZ DE ESPINOSA, *Compendium and Description of the West Indies,* tr. C. U. CLARK (Washington 1942).

[A. TIBESAR]

VÁZQUEZ DE HERRERA, FRANCISCO

Franciscan chronicler; b. Guatemala, Oct. 10, 1647; d. Guatemala, 1712?. As a young man, Vázquez studied in the local Jesuit college. Thereafter he served as secretary in the episcopal curia and in the offices of the audiencia. In 1662 he entered the Franciscan Order in his native city, and was ordained in 1670 in Ciudad Real de Chiapas. For some years, Vázquez was a teacher of theology, a censor for the Inquisition, and an examiner for the diocesan board of Guatemala. In 1681 the council of his province appointed him official chronicler of the province of the Most Holy Name of Jesus of Guatemala. The fulfillment of this task was to occupy the remaining years of his life, except for interludes because of his election in 1688 as vice provincial and the appointment in 1691 as guardian in Guatemala and in 1693 in San Salvador. From 1705 to 1707 he wrote his biography of Brother Pedro Betancur (first published in Guatemala in 1962 as *Vida y Virtudes del V. Hermano Pedro de San José Betancur*). Vázquez had no special training to fit him for his task of writing the official chronicle of his province. However, he was even-tempered, anxious to examine facts, and more given to peace than to disputes. Moreover, he was a direct descendant of the conquistador Antonio de Paredes. His Crónica was not published during his lifetime. Its style is frequently verbose, but Burrus considers it "an exceptionally good chronicle. It includes a wealth of details, with verbatim copies of numerous original documents."

Bibliography: F. VÁZQUEZ DE HERRERA, *Crónica de la provincia del Santísimo Nombre de Jesús. . . ,* ed. L. LAMADRID, 4 v. (2d ed. Guatemala City 1937–44). E. J. BURRUS, "Religious Chroniclers and Historians" (Washington 1963), a working paper of the Hispanic Foundation of the Library of Congress.

[L. LAMADRID]

VEDĀNTA

Meaning literally the "end" of the Vedas. The term originally applied to the Upanishads, the philosophical commentaries that come at the end of the Vedas, but later extended to include all philosophical systems based on the Vedas. The "triple foundation" of the *Vedānta* is the Upanishads, the *Brahma-sūtras* of *Bādarāyana,* written early in the Christian Era and consisting of short aphorisms summarizing the doctrine of the Upanishads, and the *Bhagavad Gītā.* The three principal systems of the *Vedānta* are the nondualism (advaita) of Śankara (8th century), the qualified nondualism (*vishiṣṭadvaita*) of Rāmānuja (11th–12th century), and the dualism (*dvaita*) of Madhva (13th century). Though based on revelation (ṣruti), they are strictly philosophical in their method and form one of the greatest metaphysical traditions in history.

See Also: INDIAN PHILOSOPHY; HINDUISM; and their bibliographies.

[B. GRIFFITHS]

VEDAS

Sacred books of Hinduism. The word Veda means "knowledge" or wisdom, and the Vedas are called *ṣruti* (that which has been heard) to signify that they were "revealed." Hindus regard them as "eternal" and not the work of man. They were originally handed down by word of mouth, and it is impossible to say when they took their present form. It is probable that the earliest collection of hymns, known as the Rig Veda, was completed by 900 B.C. A collection of verses from these hymns, arranged for chanting at the sacrifice, was added and was known as the Sāma Veda, and another collection containing prose formulas to be used in the ritual of sacrifice was added later and was known as the Yajur Veda. Finally at a much later date a further collection, known as the Atharva Veda, was made. It contained magic spells and incantations, chiefly derived from the cults of the non-Aryan population. To the original books of the Vedas there were added first the Brāhmaṇas, a kind of prose commentary explaining the significance of the rites, and then the Āraṇyakas (forest-books) and the Upanishads, in which a mystical interpretation of the rites was developed into profound and original philosophical speculation. Thus each Veda now consists of a Mantra (hymn), a Brāhmaṇa, an Āraṇyaka, and a Upanishad, and these together form the corpus of sacred scripture or ṣruti.

See Also: HINDUISM.

[B. GRIFFITHS]

VEDAST OF ARRAS, ST.

Bishop; b. probably Périgord in southwestern France; d. *ca.* 540. Information on Vedast (Eng., Foster, Gaston; Fr., Vaast) derives from two vitae, one ascribed (definitively, according to Krusch) to JONAS OF BOBBIO, the other written by ALCUIN (*ca.* 800). According to the vitae, Vedast, after living for some time as a recluse, was ordained for the Diocese of Toul. It was he who prepared CLOVIS for Baptism. Vedast then labored for a number of years at Reims under (St.) REMIGIUS, by whom he was consecrated bishop of Arras (*ca.* 500). To Arras the neighboring Cambrai was later added. In Arras Christianity was then virtually nonexistent. After 40 years of zealous episcopal effort, Vedast at his death left Arras a flourishing Christian community. The abbey of SAINT-VAAST was built to house his relics.

Feast: Feb. 6; July 15 (Arras); Oct. 1.

Bibliography: *Acta Sanctorum* February 1:782–815. *Monumenta Germaniae Historica: Scriptores rerum Merovingicarum* (Berlin 1826–) 3:399–427. *Patrologia Latina,* ed. J. P. MIGNE, 217 v. (Paris 1878–90) 101:663–682. L. VAN DER ESSEN, *Étude critique et littéraire sur les Vitae des saints mérovingiens de l'ancienne Belgique* (Louvain 1907) 211–219. E. GUILBERT, *S. Vaast: Fondateur de l'église d'Arras* (Arras 1928). J. L. BAUDOT and L. CHAUSSIN, *Vies des saints et des bienheureux selon l'ordre du calendrier avec l'historique des fêtes,* ed. by the Benedictines of Paris, 12 v. (Paris 1935–56); v. 13, suppl. and table générale (1959) 2:135–138. K. HOFMANN, *Lexikon für Theologie und Kirche,* ed. J. HOFER and K. RAHNER (Freiburg 1957–65) 10:515. A. BUTLER, *The Lives of the Saints,* rev. ed. H. THURSTON and D. ATTWATER, 4 v. (New York 1956) 1:262–263.

[G. M. COOK]

VEDRUNA DE MAS, JOAQUINA, ST.

Founder of the Carmelite Sisters of Charity; b. Barcelona, Spain, April 15, 1783; d. Barcelona, Aug. 28, 1854. Although attracted early in life toward the Carmelites, she married Teodoro de Mas (1799). After her husband's death (1816) she supervised the administration of her large inheritance and attended to the education of her nine sons for the next ten years. The Capuchin priest Esteban de Olot then guided her toward the active religious life of teaching and charity. Her congregation was launched when she and nine companions took the habit and vows in the presence of Bishop Corcuera of Vich, near Barcelona (Feb. 26, 1826). Despite many trials and difficulties, the institute soon spread to other areas. In 1850 it received canonical approval. In 1881 Vedruna de Mas's remains were transferred to Vich. She was beatified May 19, 1940, and canonized April 12, 1959.

Feast: May 22 (*see* CARMELITE SISTERS).

Bibliography: B. SANZ Y FORÈS, *Vida de la Madre Joaquina de Vedruna y de Mas* (2d ed. Vich 1930). E. FEDERICI, *Santa*

Gioachino de Vedruna (Rome 1958). J. A. BENACH, *Joaquina de Vedruna de Mas* (Barcelona 1959).

[I. BASTARRIKA]

VEGA, ANDREAS DE

Franciscan Observantine theologian; b. Segovia, Spain, 1498; d. Salamanca, Sept. 1549. He studied and taught at the University of Salamanca, and at the age of 40 became a Franciscan Observantine. He was sent by the emperor Charles V to the Council of Trent as theologian to Cardinal Pacheco, and was present at the first seven sessions of the council. Vega took a conspicuous part in the preliminary discussions on the canon of the Scriptures, and the decree promulgated in the fourth session adopted his opinion. He was also a leading participant in the preliminary discussions on the dogma of justification, and in these he engaged in debate with Domingo de SOTO. Vega wrote a defense of Catholic teaching on justification, *De iustificatione, gratia, fide, operibus et meritis* (Venice 1546), that antedated the decree of the council by one year. After the promulgation of the council's decree, he wrote in its defense *Tridentini decreti de iustificatione expositio et defensio libris XV distincta* (Venice 1548), the last two books of which were in refutation of Calvin's *Antidotum in acta Synodi Tridentinae.* Vega's two works on justification were regarded so highly by Peter CANISIUS that he had them printed together in one volume (Cologne 1572). Except for the posthumous *Commentaria in psalmos* (Alcalá de Henares, 1599), Vega's other writings have not been edited.

Bibliography: S. HORN, *Glaube und Rechtfertigung nack dem Konzilstheologen Andreas de Vega* (Paderborn 1972), bibliography, 293–302. H. RECLA, *Andreae Vega, OFM, Doctrina do Justificatione et Concilium Tridentinum* (Madrid 1966).

[P. K. MEAGHER]

VEGIUS, MAPHEUS

Churchman, humanist, educator, and scholar of the early Italian Renaissance; b. Lodi, Italy, 1406 or 1407; d. Rome, 1458. Born of distinguished parents, Vegius received his formal schooling at Milan where he studied the classics, particularly Virgil and Ovid. In 1422 he wrote his first volume of poems, *Pompeiana,* elegies and epigrams on country life. At his father's insistence he entered the University of Pavia at the age of 19 and studied philosophy and jurisprudence. He later devoted himself to his favorite study, poetry, and to Greek. On completing his studies he was made professor of poetry and law at Pavia. Ordained a secular priest, he went to Florence after

1431, where he became a member of the celebrated group of writers at the Medicean and papal courts. He was appointed secretary of papal briefs about 1433, and in 1442, apostolic datary. Named a canon of St. Peter's (1443) by Pope Eugene IV, Vegius remained in Rome, where he concentrated on philosophical and ecclesiastical studies. He gave his attention to Christian literature and history rather than to the classics, and eventually preferred Augustine to Virgil. After joining the Augustinians, he wrote several volumes, including *De educatione liberorum et eorum claris moribus (On the Education of Children and Their Moral Training)*—the most Christian in spirit of all humanistic educational treatises. In it he proposed St. Augustine and his mother, St. Monica, as models for Christian educators. Among its significant features, it urged the study of classical literature together with the study of the scripture and of the Church Fathers. It also provided for the education of girls, and emphasized the development of sound moral character as the chief end of education. Vegius wrote a total of about 50 works, including 38 poems. In 1907 the fifth centenary of Vegius's birth was celebrated at Lodi.

Bibliography: A. FRANZONI, *L'Opera pedagogica di Maffeo Vegio* (Lodi 1907). M. VEGIUS, *Maphei Vegii Laudensis de educatione liberorum et eorum claris moribus, libri sex: A Critical Text of Books 1–3* by M. W. FANNING (PHD Thesis CUA, Washington 1933); *Maphei Vegii Laudensis de educatione liberorum et eorum claris moribus, libri sex: A Critical Text of Books 4–6* by A. S. SULLIVAN (PHD Thesis CUA, Washington 1936). V. J. HORKAN, *Educational Theories and Principles of Maffeo Vegio* (Washington 1953).

[V. STAUDT SEXTON]

VELASCO, PEDRO DE

Mexican Jesuit missionary and spokesman for the society in the controversy with Bishop Palafox; b. Mexico City, 1581; d. there, Aug. 26, 1649. He entered the Society of Jesus on March 6, 1597; after being ordained in 1604, he was assigned to the missions in Sinaloa, a difficult post among poverty-stricken native peoples. Although his uncle the viceroy wanted him to return to Mexico City to teach philosophy, Velasco asked to be permitted to remain in Sinaloa, pleading that it was more for the glory of God to attend 1,600 baptized souls and baptize others than to teach 30 students. He was allowed to remain until 1631, when he was transferred to Tepotzotlán as rector and master of novices. He was chosen procurator of the province in 1637; on Feb. 21, 1646, he was elected provincial. That year he accepted from Don Nicolás Giustiniani the foundation of a *colegio* in Guatemala, where the Jesuits had been working for 40 years in extreme poverty. As provincial, he became involved in the legal controversy between the Jesuits and Bp. Juan de PALAFOX Y MENDOZA of Puebla. On learning of the difficult situation of the Jesuits in Puebla, he appointed several Dominicans as conservative judges. On Sept. 22, 1648, after accusations and counteraccusations, after both civil and ecclesiastical intervention, Velasco informed the viceroy that the Jesuits and Bishop Palafox had reached a peaceful agreement. Palafox was recalled to Spain and the Pope appointed a commission of four cardinals to investigate the unfortunate dispute that had caused much harm to the Church. The See of Puebla was left vacant until the appointment of Diego Osorio de Escobar y Llamas in 1656; but the Jesuits went back to work there at once as a result of Velasco's careful negotiations.

Bibliography: G. DECORME, *La obra de los Jesuitas mexicanos durante la época colonial, 1572–1767,* 2 v. (Mexico City 1941). F. J. ALEGRE, *Historia de la provincia de la Compañia de Jesús de Nueva España,* ed. E. J. BURRUS and F. ZUBILLAGA, 4 v. (new ed. Rome 1956–60).

[F. ZUBILLAGA]

VELITCHKOVSKY, PAISSY

Russian monastic founder and spiritual writer; b. Poltava, in the Ukraine, Dec. 2, 1722; d. Sekoul, Moldavia, 1794. He was attracted to the asceticism of the desert Fathers, and after attending the ecclesiastical academy of Kiev, tried monastic life at Lubetch near the Polish border, in the monastery of St. Nicholas in Moldavia, in the Pecherskaia Lavra of Kiev, and in the skete of St. Nicholas in Treisteny, Valachia. At 24 in 1746 he found his vocation as a hermit on Mt. ATHOS. His austerity attracted other Russian and Rumanian monks, and soon his monastery of St. Elias had grown so large that he was forced to transfer it to Moldavia. At Bukovin, near Dragomira, he organized a monastery along the lines of the Mt. Athos cenobitic rule of St. Basil and St. THEODORE the Studite. His community expanded into two monasteries, one at Sekoul with 300 monks, the other at Niametz with 700. For occupation he encouraged translators, copyists, and correctors to produce revisions and translations of the Greek and Latin Fathers. He translated the *Philocalia* of Macarius of Corinth and NICODEMUS the Hagiorite into Slavonic (1793) and called it *Dobrotoliubie,* i.e., love of the good. These hesychastic writings, dealing mostly with the JESUS PRAYER, formed a type of inward piety guided by spiritual devotion and provided, along with Holy Scripture, the spiritual food for monks and laity in Russia and other Slavic countries for two centuries. Through his writings and formation of disciples who became spiritual guides and monastic superiors in Russia and Rumania, Paissy Velitchkovsky started a spiritual revival that continued until the Russian Revolution in 1917

and that is still influential among the Startsy of the Optina Pustyn' tradition. He also passed on the Oriental spirituality of the Fathers of the desert, of the hesychastic writers of Mt. Sinai, Mt. Athos and of St. Nil Sorskii (d. 1508) to the Slav Christians.

Bibliography: K. ONASCH, *Die Religion in Geschichte und Gegenwart* ³ 6:1252. L. MÜLLER, *ibid.* 4:1664. E. KADLOUBOVSKY and G. H. PALMER, trs. and eds., *Early Fathers from the Philokalia* (London 1954), contains selections from the *Dobrotoliubie. La Prière de Jesus* (Collection Irénikon, NS 4; Chevetogne, Belg. 1951). V. V. ZEN'KOVSKII, *History of Russian Philosophy,* tr. G. L. KLINE, 2 v. (New York 1953) 1:63–64. V. LOSSKY, *The Mystical Theology of the Eastern Church* (London 1957).

[G. A. MALONEY]

VENANTIUS OF TOURS, ST.

B. near Bourges; d. Tours, 5th century. GREGORY OF TOURS (*Vitae patrum* 16; *De gloria confess.* 15) outlined his life. Venantius, renouncing marriage, left Bourges. In TOURS he was admitted to the monastery of the Abbot Silvius. On the death of Silvius, Venantius was elected abbot and led the monks in a life of discipline and prayer. He is credited with miracles during his life and after his death. His tomb is in the church of the monastery of St. Venantius near the basilica of St. MARTIN OF TOURS. St. Venantius is invoked against fevers.

Feast: Oct. 13.

Bibliography: *Acta Sanctorum* Oct. 6:211–221. *Gallia Christiana* 14:187–188. H. LECLERCQ, *Dictionnaire d'archéologie chrétienne et de liturgie,* ed. F. CABROL, H. LECLERCQ, and H. I. MARROU 15.2:2665.

[G. E. CONWAY]

VENANTIUS OF VIVIERS, ST.

Bishop of Viviers, date and place of birth and death unknown. He attended synods at Epaon in 517 and at Clermont in 535. According to an 11th- or 15th-century panegyric, not based on sources, he was the son of King St. SIGISMUND and became a monk, then bishop. The vita, composed perhaps for his feast, recounts his virtues with rhetorical embellishment.

Feast: Aug. 5.

Bibliography: *Vita, Acta Sanctorum* Aug. 2:107–110. *Monumenta Germaniae Historica: Concilia* (Berlin 1926) 1:30,70. *Bibliotheca hagiographica latina antiquae et mediae aetatis* (Brussels 1898–1901) 2:8528. *Histoire littéraire de la France* 8:473–474. P. H. MOLLIER, *Saints et pieux personnages du Vivarais* (Privas, Fr. 1895). L. DUCHESNE, *Fastes épiscopaux de l'ancienne Gaule* 1:238. G. ALLEMANG, *Lexikon für Theologie und Kirche* ed. M. BUCHBER-

GER (Freiburg 1930–38) 10:524–525. J. L. BAUDOT and L. CHAUS-SIN, *Vies des saints et des bienheureux selon l'ordre du calendrier avec l'historique des fêtes* (Paris 1935–56) 8:87.

[G. M. COOK]

VÉNARD, JEAN THÉOPHANE, ST.

Martyr; b. Saint-Loup-sur-Thouet (Poitou), France, Nov. 21, 1829; d. Hanoi, Vietnam, Feb. 2, 1861. Son of a village schoolmaster, Théophane studied for the priesthood first at Poitiers and then in the seminary of the PARIS FOREIGN MISSION SOCIETY, which he joined before his ordination (1852). He was sent first to Hong Kong. In 1854 he arrived secretly in Tonkin, where the Church had been experiencing violent persecution since 1848. Greatly impressed by the courage of the suffering Vietnamese Catholics, Théophane so dedicated himself to their spiritual needs as to endanger his own physical health and personal safety. When expelled from Namdinh (1856), he sought refuge in Hanoi, but the persecution reached there in 1858. Once again he was compelled to hide in caves, in the hulls of sampans, and in the homes of Catholics. On Nov. 30, 1860, at Kimbang, he was betrayed by a Christian. Carried in a bamboo cage, which remained his cell to the end, Théophane was brought to the mandarins of Hanoi, tried, and sentenced to beheading. In 1865, his mortal remains, except his head which was left in Vietnam, were translated to the Congregation's Church in Paris. He was beatified on May 2, 1909 and canonized with 116 other martyrs of Vietnam by Pope John Paul II on June 19, 1988.

See Also: VIETNAM, MARTYRS OF.

Feast: Feb. 2.

Bibliography: F. TROCHU, *Un Martyr français au XIXᵉ siècle: Le bx. T. Vénard* (Lyon 1929). J. NANTEUIL, *L'Épopée missionnaire de T. Vénard* (Paris 1950). J. L. BAUDOT and L. CHAUSSIN, *Vies des saints et des bienheueux selon l'ordre du calendrier avec l'historique des fêtes,* ed. by The Benedictines of Paris, 12 v. (Paris 1935–56) 2:56–58. A. BUTLER, *The Lives of the Saints,* ed. H. THURSTON and D. ATTWATER, 4 v. (New York 1956) 4:282–285. C. SIMONNET, *Théophane: Celui qui embellissait tout* (Paris 1983); *Théophane Vénard: A Martyr of Vietnam,* tr. C. SPLATT (San Francisco 1988).

[A. GÉLINAS]

VENCE, CHAPELLE DU ROSAIRE

Dominican convent oratory located outside Vence, about 25 miles from Nice in southern France; designed with all its appointments by the painter, Henri MATISSE. The cornerstone was laid Dec. 12, 1949 and the chapel consecrated June 25, 1951. Serving the nuns who conduct a convalescent home for girls, it stands almost opposite the villa where Matisse lived (1943–49).

Matisse considered this chapel a representative result of his "entire active life" and humbly presented it, considering it, "in spite of its imperfections," to be his "masterpiece" (message to Bp. Rémond on the day of dedication). His aims were clearly those of an artist; it was for him "the ultimate goal of a whole life of work" whose principal aim "was to balance a surface of light and color against a solid white wall covered with black drawings" (statement in *Chapelle du Rosaire . . . ,* 1951, as quoted in Barr, 288).

Sister Jacques, novice at Vence, who prior to religious life was nurse to Matisse at Nice, interested him in the project when she brought window designs for him to see; from his interest in the windows grew the idea that he design the chapel. Brother L. B. Rayssiguier, Dominican novice and architect who had come to Vence for his health, joined Matisse in his interest and supplied liturgical and architectural knowledge to the project; A. PERRET, the architect, became a consultant. Working for four years (1947–51) on models, drawings, and careful articulation of details, even the vestments, Matisse achieved a unique chapel, a kind of painter's architecture.

A nuns' choir, separate from the nave for the laity, required an L-shaped plan, with the altar at the intersection of the arms of the L, so that the celebrant might face diagonally toward both congregations. The chapel is small; nearly 17 feet high, and 50 feet long, and about 35 feet at its greatest width.

The decoration of the chapel is concentrated in the stained glass of the groups of full-length windows in the sanctuary and in the south wall of choir and nave, and in the large black-and-white glazed tile pictures on the walls opposite the windows. For the stained glass, Matisse was inspired by Revelation (21.19, 21): "And the foundations of the wall of the city were adorned with every precious stone . . . and the street of the city was pure gold, as it were transparent glass." His designs are based on a tree-of-life pattern, made up of brilliant yellow and blue leaves on a green ground rising at the top to a golden segment representing the sun. The tile pictures are drawn with the greatest economy of line: a huge St. Dominic towers above the altar, a Virgin and Child is set slightly off-center amid a decoration of flowerlike clouds, and on the end wall of the nave the Stations of the Cross are arranged in a narrative sequence, starting at the bottom and reading upward, recalling the medieval form of continuous representation, and rendered in a tense, nervous shorthand of jagged strokes. All the faces are left blank, so that the spectator is free to see the face of God, the Virgin, St. Dominic, Victim, mourners, and executioners, in his own imagination. Matisse also designed the elongated and simplified altar crucifix, several brilliantly colorful chasubles, and altar linen embroidered with fishes. The outside of the chapel is plain white, with blue tile decoration on the roof, which is crowned with a thin spirelike cross with a bell below it. In its simplicity, in the light and color glowing like jewels on the white of the walls and marble floor, in its insistence on meaning and content rather than on surface decoration, Vence joins RONCHAMP, ASSY, and COVENTRY as one of the few works of moving religious art created in this century.

Bibliography: A. H. BARR, *Matisse: His Art and His Public* (New York 1951) 279–288, 514–527. *Les Chapelles du Rosaire à Vence par Matisse et de Notre-Dame-du-Haut à Ronchamp par Le Corbusier,* ed. M. A. COUTURIER et al. (Paris 1955).

[L. MURRAY]

VENDÔME (SAINTE-TRINITÉ), ABBEY OF

Former Benedictine monastery of the Holy Trinity in Vendôme, Loir-et-Cher, France, on the banks of the Loire River (Latin, *Sancta Trinitas Vindocinensis*). It was founded by Geoffrey Martel, Count of Anjou, and Agnes of Burgundy; the first monks came from MARMOUTIER. The monastery was begun in 1032; the abbey church was consecrated, May 31, 1040. On May 8, 1063, Alexander II granted the abbot of Vendôme the Roman church of S. Prisca with the title of cardinal; from then on, the abbots of Vendôme enjoyed the dignity of cardinals. After 1579, the abbey entered the Congregation of the Exempts, and in 1621 it was incorporated into the Congregation of Saint-Maur (*see* MAURISTS). Only ten monks remained at the abbey in 1768. After the abbey was suppressed in the French Revolution, the abbey church, which today is a French national historical monument, became a parish church. Its great tower is a famous landmark. The abbey of Vendôme was famous for its reputed relic of the Holy Tear (a tear shed by the Lord over Lazarus), which had been brought back from the Holy Land by the founder. Several of its monks were renowned for their sanctity and their writings (e.g., GEOFFREY OF VENDÔME). It held a large number of dependent priories in the regions of Sarthe, Vendée, the Isle of Oléron, Mayenne, Indreet-Loire and Loir-et-Cher.

Bibliography: C. MÉTAIS, ed., *Cartulaire de l'abbaye cardinale de la Trinité de Vendôme,* 4 v. (Paris 1893–97). *Gallia Christiana,* v.1–13 (Paris 1715–85), v.14–16 (Paris 1856–65) 8: 1364–79. BEAUNIER, *Abbayes et prieurés de l'ancienne France,* ed. J. M. L. BESSE, 12 v. (Paris 1905–41) v.1. L. H. COTTINEAU, *Répertoire topobibliographique des abbayes et prieurés,* 2 v. (Mâcon 1935–39) 2: 3317–19. R. CROZET, ''Le Clocher de la Trinité de Vendôme,'' *Bulletin monumental* 119 (1961) 139–148, photos; ''Le Monument de la Sainte-Larme . . . ,'' *ibid.* 121 (1963) 171–180.

[J. DE LA C. BOUTON]

VENDRAMINI, ELISABETTA, BL.

Foundress of the Franciscan Tertiary Sisters of Saint Elizabeth of Hungary; b. Bassano del Grappa (near Treviso), Italy, April 9, 1790; d. Padua, April 2, 1860. Elisabetta was educated in an Augustinian convent where she was imbued with an intense spirituality. In 1917, Elisabetta broke off her six-year engagement on the evening before her wedding because she felt a strong, clear calling to dedicate herself to the poor. She cared for children in her hometown, then joined the staff of the Capuchin orphanage (1820). In 1821 she assumed the habit of the Third Order of St Francis. After moving to Padua (1827), she again worked with children and opened a tuition-free school at Padua with two friends (1829). She then founded the Sisters of St. Elizabeth, a religious institute to care for orphans, elderly women, and the sick (1830). The congregation's constitution, using the rule of the Third Order Regular of St. Francis, was completed October 4, 1830, and the first sisters were professed the following year. Elisabetta served as superior for more than three decades before her death. Pope John Paul II beatified her on Nov. 4, 1990.

Feast: April 2 (Franciscans).

Bibliography: *Madre Elisabetta Vendramini e la sua opera nella documentazione del tempo* (Padua 1972). *L'Osservatore Romano,* English edition, no. 6 (1990): 1.

[K. I. RABENSTEIN]

VENDVILLE, JEAN

Bishop and proponent of a central missionary seminary in Rome; b. Lille, June 24, 1527; d. Tournai, Oct. 15, 1592. After beginning the study of law at Paris, he received his doctorate at Louvain in 1553 and then became professor of canon law in the University of Douai. While still a layman, he journeyed to Rome in 1567 with his friend William ALLEN, an English priest who later became a cardinal. There he presented to Pius V memoranda proposing a missionary congregation and a seminary for the training of missionaries among non-Christians. Although unsuccessful in this petition, upon his return he gave considerable financial assistance to Allen in founding the famous English college at Douai, which trained priests for work in England under Elizabeth I. After the death of his wife, Vendville was ordained in the winter of 1580–81 and was made bishop of Tournai in 1588. In 1578 he put before Gregory XIII a concrete plan for a general Roman college for the propagation of the faith. Even though this Pope was zealous in establishing national seminaries in Rome, he did not act on the proposal of Vendville, who presented a similar petition to Sixtus

V on his *ad limina* visit in 1589 and again to Clement VIII. The deaths of these popes and the difficulties of the times prevented its realization. Although Vendville did not live to see it, his hopes were fulfilled by Urban VIII, who founded the College of the Propaganda in 1627 to train for the secular priesthood candidates from all nations who wished to dedicate themselves to the propagation and defense of the faith anywhere in the world. The memorandum presented by Vendville to the popes was published (1870) at Tournai by Prof. M. Reusens under the title *La première idée du Collège de la Propagande, ou mémoire présenté en 1589 par Jean Vendville, évêque de Tournai, au souverain pontife Sixte V.*

Bibliography: V. A. VON DESSEL, *Bibliotheca Belgica* (Brussels 1739) 744. R. STREIT and J. DINDINGER, *Bibliotheca missionum* 180, 1428. G. GOYAU, *L'Église en marche,* 4 v. (Paris 1930–34) 1:55–82. *A Literary and Biographical History or Bibliographical Dictionary of the English Catholics from 1534 to the Present time* 1:14–20.

[R. HOFFMANN]

VENEGAS DE LA TORRE, MARÍA DE JESÚS SACRAMENTADO, ST.

Baptized María Natividad; virgin, nurse, and foundress of the Congregation of Daughters of the Sacred Heart of Jesus; first female saint of Mexico; b. La Tapona near Zapotlanejo, Jalisco, Mexico, Sept. 8, 1868; d. Guadalajara, Mexico, July 30, 1959. When María was nineteen years old, her parents, both practicing Catholics, died and she was placed in the care of her paternal aunt and uncle. She had devotion for the Blessed Sacrament and participated in parish life.

Two years later she joined the flourishing Association of the Children of Mary (December 8, 1889) in her hometown. Following spiritual exercises in November 1905, she decided to enter the Daughters of the Sacred Heart of Jesus, a pious union originally founded by Guadalupe Villaseñor de Perez Veria to care for patients in Guadalajara's Sacred Heart Hospital, which had recently been founded by the future bishop Atenógenes Silva y Alvarez Tostado (Feb. 2, 1886). Sister María lived in the hospital from December 5, 1905, until her death at age ninety-one.

Her simplicity, tender love, and obedience to her superiors attracted others to her. In 1912, she was elected vicaress and maintained that position until January 25, 1921, when she was elected superior general. Because Mother María wrote the constitutions that gained canonical approval (1930) for the congregation, she is regarded as its foundress. Her cause for canonization was opened in 1978. Pope John Paul II both beatified (Nov. 22, 1992) and canonized (May 21, 2000) Mother María.

Feast: July 30.

Bibliography: *l'Osservatore Romano*: 22 (2000) 5-7. *Acta Apostolicae Sedis*: 1 (1992) 49.

[K. I. RABENSTEIN]

VENERABLE

The title allowed one whose cause for BEATIFICATION has been officially accepted by the Congregation for the Causes of Saints and who has been the subject of a special decree published in the name of the pope. This decree, issued within the course of the apostolic, or papal, process (as distinguished from the earlier one known as the ordinary, or diocesan, process) declares that the servant of God has practiced all the virtues in heroic degree. In the case of a martyr, it declares his martyrdom well proved. No public cult is allowed, though a private cult may exist, e.g., praising his virtues, praying to him.

See Also: CANONIZATION OF SAINTS (HISTORY AND PROCEDURE).

[A. E. GREEN/EDS.]

VENERINI SISTERS

(MPV); a congregation with papal approbation, founded Aug. 30, 1685, in Viterbo, Italy, by Bl. Rose Venerini (1656–1728; beatified 1952; feast: May 7) for the Christian education of young women, especially among the poorer classes. As a diocesan institute under the bishop of Viterbo, the congregation spread to other dioceses, especially to Montefiascone where St. Lucy FILIPPINI took up their work. At the death of Bl. Rose there were 40 houses in 17 dioceses. The sisters came to the United States in 1909, to a parochial school in Lawrence, Massachusetts. In 1914 they added a school in Providence, Rhode Island. Other foundations, usually in parishes of Italian immigrants, were established in Massachusetts, Rhode Island, and New York. In 1926, they opened their United States novitiate in Worcester, Massachusetts, where Venerini Academy is located. In parochial schools, day nurseries, and high schools, the sisters follow the method of their foundress, who was a pioneer in the education of young women. They hold frequent meetings of the mothers of their students, in order to coordinate the school with the family. In 1963 there were 82 professed sisters in the United States, and approximately 600 in the entire congregation.

Bibliography: G. V. GREMIGNI, *La beata Rosa Venerini* (Rome 1952).

[J. LAMBERT]

VENETO, PAOLO

Logician; b. Paolo Nicoletti, Udine, Italy, *c.* 1369; d. Padua, June 15, 1428. He joined the AUGUSTINIANS in Venice, and before ordination was sent to study at Oxford (1390–93). By 1408 he was a doctor of theology at Padua. In 1409 (or 1412) during the WESTERN SCHISM he was appointed general of the order (Roman obedience), but resigned after nine months. In 1413 he served as ambassador of Venice to Emperor SIGISMUND and King Ladislaus of Poland. He was banned from Venetian territory for reasons unknown in 1420. He then taught in Siena (1422), Bologna (1424), Perugia, and again Siena (1427), where he became rector of the university. From Oxford he had brought many books until then unknown in Italy. An outstanding professor, he introduced into Italy a type of logic that had flourished at Oxford during the 14th century, and that was still in vogue in Italy after 1500 (*see* LOGIC, HISTORY OF). His own widely read works on logic made him an authority no one dared contradict. The works include the *Logica parva* (Milan 1473), *Logica magna* (Venice 1481), *Summa totius philosophiae* (Milan 1476), and 10 commentaries on Aristotle. He leaned toward AVERROISM.

Bibliography: D. A. PERINI, *Bibliographia Augustiniana,* 4 v. (Florence 1929–38) 4:39–46. F. MOMIGLIANO, *Paolo Veneto e le correnti del pensiero religioso e filosofico nel suo tempo* (Turin 1907). C. VON PRANTL, *Geschichte der Logik im Abendlande,* 4 v. (Leipzig 1855–70; reprint Graz 1955) 4:118–140. B. NARDI, *Saggi sull'Aristotelismo Padovano dal secolo XIV al XVI* (Florence 1958). A. B. EMDEN, *A Biographical Register of the Scholars of the University of Oxford to A.D. 1500,* 3 v. (Oxford 1957–59) 3:1944–45.

[F. ROTH]

VENEZUELA, THE CATHOLIC CHURCH IN

Located in extreme northern South America, the Boliviarian Republic of Venezuela is bordered on the north by the Caribbean Sea, on the east by Guyana, on the southeast by Brazil and on the west by Columbia. The Andes Mountains of the north fall to the Maracaibo Lowlands at the northwest border and to the *llanos,* or central plains, while the Guiana Highlands characterize the southeast part of the country. Flooding, rock- and mudslides, and periodic droughts are visited upon the region. Venezuela, with its tropical climate moderating in the lowlands, produces corn, rice and some wheat; a variety of tubers; coffee, cacao, tropical fruits and vegetables. Next to oil, tobacco is the primary export crop; sugar, cotton and resinous plants, the basic industrial crops. Stock raising, which declined somewhat, together with the im-

---

Capital: Caracas.
Size: 352,143 sq. miles.
Population: 23,542,649 in 2000.
Languages: Spanish; Amerindian dialects are spoken in various regions.
Religions: 16,479,854 Catholics (70%), 6,827,368 Protestants (29%), 235,427 practice other religions.

---

mense resources of the sea and forests, are also a part of the national riches. Natural resources include petroleum, iron, gold, bauxite, diamonds and hydropower, with most petroleum produced in Zulia and Anzoátegui. Venezuela was the world's largest producer of petroleum by the 1920s; by 2000 it accounted for a third of the nation's gross domestic product.

History. Venezuela was seen for the first time by Christopher Columbus on Aug. 1, 1498. The region was named by Amerigo Vespucci, a companion of Alonso de Ojeda, Juan de la Cosa and Juan López Velasco, who discovered Lake Coquivocoa in 1499. Reminded of the city of Venice by the sight of native dwellings constructed on stilts atop the lake, he dubbed the region "Venetiola." New Cáadiz, the first Spanish settlement, was founded early in 1500 on the island of Cubagua, while on the mainland began the conquest and founding of cities such as Cumaná, which in 1520 was called New Toledo and later New Córdova, and Santa Ana de Coro, founded in 1527. Santa Ana de Coro became the starting point for the exploration and settling of the lands of what became in 1777 the Captaincy General of Venezuela.

In 1516 Cardinal Francisco Cisneros of Spain sent two royal decrees to the Hieronymite friars who governed Santo Domingo and its dependencies, requesting that they assist the Dominicans and Franciscans doing missionary work on the Gulf of Santa Fe, Chichirivichi and Cumaná. These documents referred to two missionaries killed by natives in reprisal for mistreatment by intruding conquerors. The missions established by the Church gradually evolved into towns, villages of converted natives and parishes with their own curates, and provided a means of freeing Venezuelan natives from the sadly famous *encomienda,* a kind of fief of the new Spanish masters.

Working in specified territories, groups of Observant Franciscans, Capuchins, Dominicans, Jesuits and to some extent Anchoritic Augustinians and Mercedarians each undertook missionary activities, the last two groups being established in the city of Caracas. The Observants worked for 160 years in the territory of New Barcelona, even going beyond the Orinoco River to the south. Founding hundreds of pueblos, the Capuchins evange-

Archdioceses	Suffragans
Barquisimeto	Carora, Guanare, San Filipe
Calabozo	San Fernando de Apure, Valle de la Pascua
Caracas	Guarenas, La Guaira, Los Teques
Ciudad Bolívar	Ciudad Guayana, Maturín
Coro	Punto Fijo
Cumaná	Barcelona, Carúpano, Margarita
Maraciabo	Cabimas, El Vigía-San Carolos del Zulia
Mérida	Barinas, San Cristóbal de Venezuela, Trujillo
Valencia en Venezuela	Maracay, Puerto Cabello, San Carlos en Venezuela

There are apostolic vicariates at Caroní, Machiques, Puerto Ayachucho, and Tucupita. There is a military ordinariate in Venezuela. The Greek Melkite Church also has an apostolic exarchate located in the country.

lized the llanos of Caracas, New Andalusia, Trinidad and Guayana as far as the Masaruni River to the east and as far as the Branco River to the south; also the upper Orinoco, the Meta, Maracaibo and the Guajira. The Dominicans were based at Apure and Barinas, where they founded 20 towns. The Jesuits were missionaries in the Orinoco region until their expulsion by Charles III. The cradle of those organized missions were La Concepción de Píritu and Santa Maria de los Angeles de Cocuisas in the mountainous regions of Guácharo. Indeed, no fewer than 347 towns owe their existence to the work of the missionaries, 54 missionaries giving up their lives for their faith between 1514 and 1817.

Development of Church Hierarchy. The first Venezuelan bishopric was created by Pope Clement VII on June 21, 1531, in the city of Coro. During the colonial period the development of the hierarchy was slow, and the see was raised to an archbishopric almost 300 years later, in 1803. The bishops not only organized the hierarchy in Venezuela and supervised ecclesiastical discipline but also contributed generally to the development of the country. González de Acuña, founder of the Tridentine Seminary in Caracas in 1673 (later renamed the Interdiocesano de Santa Rosa de Lima), introduced safe drinking water to the city. Diego de Baños y Sotomayor called the synod of 1686. Juan José Escalona y Calatayud estab-

lished the Royal Pontifical University in 1725. Pious Antonio Diez Madroñero was a zealous reformer. Mariano Martí, bishop of Puerto Rico, traveled over his extensive diocese in Venezuela from 1771 to 1784, becoming a pioneer in statistics, when he compiled his demographic analyses in the four-volume *Relación de la visita general.* Under the constitutions for the establishment of the Church organization in Venezuela, the first diocesan synod was held in Coro, on July 26, 1574, during the episcopate of Pedro de Agreda, a Dominican who governed the diocese from 1561 to 1579. The second synod was convoked in 1687 by Diego de Baños y Sotomayor, a Colombian, who governed the Diocese of Venezuela from 1683 to 1706.

Political Upheaval and Independence. The 19th century was characterized by political upheaval throughout much of South America. In 1806 the activities of Simon Bolívar and the Columbian Independence Movement resulted in the formation of Gran Colombia, an annexation of Venezuela, Colombia and Ecuador that resulted in Venezuela's declaration of independence from Spain on July 5, 1811. By 1829 this alliance had collapsed, and the following year the newly independent Venezuela elected General José Antonio Páez as its first president. While Páez provided stable leadership, such was not the case with future administrations, which saw a proliferation of political violence under a succession of dictators. A democratic government was installed in 1881 that encouraged the growth of the Venezuelan economy, but dictatorial policies resumed from 1899–1935. The discovery of oil in the early 1900s did little to help the lot of the average Venezuelan, providing as it did an even greater incentive for government corruption.

As a consequence of the succession of politically unstable dictatorships that followed independence, the missions declined during the mid-19th century, though not without first having made their contribution to almost all of the supplies that supported the liberating armies for two years. The Rifle Regiment, which earned glory for itself at Ayacucho, was recruited among the native peoples of the Capuchin Reductions. Responding to growing concerns over the restoration of Venezuelan missions, on March 4, 1922 Pius XI canonically established the Vicariate of Caroní. During the 20th century the Salesians, Daughters of Mary, Sisters of Charity of St. Anne, Franciscan Sisters of Venezuela, Capuchin Tertiaries, Dominican Sisters of Granada and Missionary Sisters of Mother Laura were active in the country. The Little Brothers of Jesus worked among the Makiritar of the upper Caura, a diocesan mission of the Archdiocese of Ciudad Bolívar.

In 1959 Rómulo Betancourt assumed the presidency, ushering in a democratic era that continued into the next

century. Among the reforms enacted under subsequent governments was the abolishment of the Ecclesiastical Patronage Law, a form of *patronato* that had been inherited from the Spanish crown. A pact of mutual understanding signed by President Raul Leoni on June 30, 1964 replaced the patronato. By virtue of this pact, bishops were named by the pope; the practice of coexistence with the government in all aspects of ecclesiastical administration was maintained: and the apportionment established by law remained a subsidy in exchange for the property and tithes of the Church that the government incorporated into the national treasury.

Modern Venezuela. Venezuela enjoyed a period of economic prosperity during the 1980s, the result of a rise in oil prices, but this was followed by a period of increasing inflation. In the 1990s the Church, as well as the gov-

ernment, was hard pressed to address the marked increase in violent crimes due to South American drug trafficking. Austerity measures imposed by the government of Carlos Andrés Pérez were met by riots and several unsuccessful military coups before Pérez was ousted on corruption charges. New elections were held in November of 1998 and on Dec. 30, 1999 a new, controversial, authoritarian constitution was implemented under the coalition government of Colonel Hugo Chavez, whose reform agenda was intended to counter an economic downturn and a rise in social problems. Under the new constitution, which was opposed by many Catholics due to its lack of a pro-life provision, the Directorate of Justice and Religion continued the longstanding policy of dispensing funds to the Catholic Church. However, public criticisms of certain government actions by members of the Church were met with an increasingly antagonistic response by mili-

Amerigo Vespucci.

tary intelligence by 2000. On his appointment as cardinal in 2001, Caracas Archbishop Ignacio Velasco vowed to continue his intervention in political matters, despite such government efforts. "I have decided to defend the Church's right to participate actively in the construction of a just, reconciled society," Cardinal Velasco promised. Venezuelan bishops followed suit, issuing statements critical of President Chavez' unwillingness to address the growth of crime and poverty within Venezuela. Under such provocation, Chavez attacked Church affluence and referred to some members of the clergy as "devils."

Into the 21st Century. Despite the escalation of tensions between the Church and a government attempting to battle a host of social and economic ills, Catholicism in Venezuela remained the faith of the majority. By 2000 there were 1,149 parishes within Venezuela, with 1,308 diocesan and 1,111 religious priests working among the citizenry. In addition, 324 brothers and 4,346 sisters tended to education, health and other humanitarian needs, particularly among the rural poor. Education remained among the Church's main goals, reflecting centuries of dedication to this effort. From the founding in 1514 of the first rudimentary boarding school for the Guaikerí Indians through the establishment of the Royal Pontifical University of Caracas between 1721 and 1725, to the es-

tablishment by ecclesiastical decree of Andrés Bello Catholic University, the academies of the religious as well as the primary and intermediary parochial schools reflected the desire of the Church to collaborate with the government's continued initiative to provide education to its citizens. In 1999 the government allocated $ 1.5 million to Church-run school and social programs.

The Church continued to demonstrate a strong commitment to social welfare through Caritas Nacional, affiliated with the international organization, specifically in the pastoral apostolate, where movements such as Catholic Action, the lay apostolate, the Legion of Mary, the Christian Family Movement, the Catholic Education Association of Venezuela, the Federation of Parents and Representatives of Catholic Students, workers' clubs, farmers' leagues and the Venezuelan Association of Catholic Doctors improved the quality of life for all Venezuelans. Through the efforts of such organizations, the country was able to recover from a devastating loss of over 30,000 lives due to severe rains that caused flooding and landslides along the northern coast in December of 1999.

Bibliography: M. WATTERS, *A History of the Church in Venezuela, 1810–1930* (Chapel Hill, NC 1933). L. MARRERO Y ARTILES, *Venezuela y sus recursos* (Caracas 1964), *Annuario Pontificio*.

[F. A. MALDONADO/EDS.]

VENGEANCE

Vengeance is here understood as punishment inflicted upon a person in retribution for an evil act that is injurious in some way to others. It is not to be confused with the violence employed against an unjust aggressor, which always supposes that the one defending himself is under present attack, and when this has ceased, further violence becomes unjustifiable on grounds of self-defense. The social order, however, requires the punishment of wrongdoers even after they have desisted from their aggression. Ultimate and perfect vengeance is exclusively the prerogative of God (Rom 12.19); only He can know perfectly what recompense is due to a man. An imperfect vengeance, however, must sometimes be taken upon those whose behavior is a threat to the common welfare. In this matter public authority, which is derived from God's own authority, "is God's minister, an avenger to execute wrath upon him who does evil" (Rom 13.4). For those in a position of authority the infliction of penalties upon violators of the law is therefore a strict duty in justice. Under ordinary circumstances private individuals are not obliged to take a personal part in securing the punishment of the guilty. Indeed, where personal injuries are concerned the Christian is counseled to pardon wrongs without seeking vengeance (Rom 12.18–20), although in some cases personal injuries are grievously dishonoring to God, or are damaging to the Church or to the civil community; in these circumstances an individual can be under strict obligation to take action against an offender.

Nevertheless, since the punishment of the wicked is a social good, the desire, even on the part of private individuals, that it should be effectively accomplished, whether in general or in particular, is reasonable and virtuous, provided that it stems from a concern for justice and not from malice, spite, an unwillingness to forgive, or the like. This desire, however, can easily get out of hand and become sinful by its excess or by the corruptness of its motives, and men are more familiar with its sinful exaggeration than its moderate exemplification, as is suggested by the unpleasant overtones conveyed by the terms ''vengeance'' and ''revenge.'' Vindicative justice, or vengeance (understood as a virtue) controls this desire and keeps it within legitimate bounds.

To be licit vengeance must be exercised under certain conditions. (1) The punishment of wrongdoers must be done by those vested with the proper authority. (2) It should be kept within the limits of justice, and should not be allowed to degenerate into cruelty by an excess of severity or to endanger the general welfare by its softness. Since the purpose of punishment is to protect the social order, the forms it takes should be such as serve effectively to restore injured persons to the enjoyment of their rights, to correct the delinquent and to discourage others who might be inclined to similar offenses. (3) It should aim at the putting down of wickedness, not at the injury or ruin of the sinner, toward whom charity obliges the Christian to retain an attitude of sincere benevolence.

See Also: PUNISHMENT; SANCTION; CLEMENCY.

Bibliography: THOMAS AQUINAS, *Summa theologiae* 2a2ae, 108. A. MICHEL, *Dictionnaire de théologie catholique,* ed., A. VACANT et al., 15 v. (Paris 1903–50) 15.2:2613–23.

[P. K. MEAGHER]

VENI CREATOR SPIRITUS

An office hymn addressed to the Holy Spirit. In the middle ages, it was prescribed for Terce and Vespers of Pentecost. It was also sung at ordination liturgies. This hymn of six Ambrosian stanzas is a deeply personal prayer. Stanzas two and three recall Who the Spirit is, and enumerate the titles under which He is invoked, while the last three stanzas elaborate the pleading imperatives *veni* (come), *visita* (visit), and *imple* (fill).

The oldest MS of the hymn is 10th century; its earliest recorded use is at the third session of the Council of

Simon Bolivar.

Reims (1049) when it was sung instead of the *Exaudi nos, Domine.* About this same time the hymn was incorporated into the ordination ritual. At various times the hymn has been attributed to St. AMBROSE and to St. GREGORY I the Great and with some apparent reason to CHARLEMAGNE and to RABANUS MAURUS. Charlemagne's supporters cite the emperor's devotion to the Holy Spirit, and his insistence on the double procession from the Father and the Son such as is reflected in line 23, ''Teque utriusque Spiritum credamus.'' Rabanus's claim rests on a 10th-century MS of Fulda, no longer extant. Because the MS attributed to him also certain hymns known definitely not to be his, this evidence is unreliable. However, the content of the *Veni Creator* parallels that of Rabanus's chapter on the Holy Spirit (*Patrologia Latina* ed. J. P. Migne (Paris 1878–90) 111:23–26). In any event, the true author remains unknown. He probably lived in the Frankish Empire in the late 9th century. This hymn has been widely translated into the vernacular and set to polyphony.

A single-story Roman Catholic church in the Venezuelan Los Roques islands, photograph by Paul Seheult. (©Eye Ubiquitous/ CORBIS)

Bibliography: S. G. PIMONT, *Les Hymnes du brévaire romain,* 3 v. (Paris 1874–87) 2:125–143. *Analecta hymnica* 50 (1907) 193–194, text. J. JULIAN, ed., *A Dictionary of Hymnology* (New York 1957) 2:1206–11, 1594. A. S. WALPOLE, ed., *Early Latin Hymns* (Cambridge, Eng. 1922) 373–376. A. WILMART, ''L'Hymne et la sequence du Saint-Esprit,'' *Auteurs spirituels et textes dévots du moyen-âge* (Paris 1932) 37–45. P. DORET, *Un Commentaire du Veni Creator Spiritus* (Brussels 1946). F. J. E. RABY, *A History of Christian-Latin Poetry from the Beginnings to the Close of the Middle Ages* (Oxford 1953) 183. J. SZÖVÉRFFY, *Die Annalen der lateinischen Hymnendichtung* (Berlin 1964–65) 1:120–121.

[M. I. J. ROUSSEAU]

VENI SANCTE SPIRITUS

The sequence that was traditionally assigned to PEN-TECOST. This sequence is also known as the ''Golden Sequence.'' It must be dated late 12th century, since its verse form is unknown before the middle of the 12th cen-tury; furthermore, whenever the sequence appears in ear-lier manuscripts it has obviously been inserted by a later hand. EKKEHARD V (*Acta Sanctorum* April 1:579–595), a monk of Sankt Gallen, says that Pope INNOCENT III is the author and that he gave the sequence to Ulric, Abbot of SANKT GALLEN, who was on a visit to Rome and who then introduced its use at Sankt Gallen. However, a con-temporary manuscript, *Distinctiones monasticae et mo-rales* (ed. Pitra, *Spicilegium Solesmense* 3:130), thought to be by an English Cistercian, cites the sequence as the work of STEPHEN LANGTON, Archbishop of Canterbury. Langton is known to have had close connections with the CISTERCIANS; and H. Thurston, having examined the whole MS, testifies that the unknown author is ''likely to be a well-informed and reliable witness,'' familiar both with English writers of the day and with Paris, where Langton had studied and taught for several decades, and where in fact he had been a friend and fellow student of the future Pope Innocent III. Moreover, evidence from

Two men costumed as devils at Corpus Christi ceremony, San Francisco de Yare, Caracas, Venezuela. (AP/Wide World Photos)

the manuscript tradition indicates the sequence spread from Paris rather than from Rome. Today scholars hold it probable or see little reason to doubt that Langton is probably the author of this sequence.

In form the *Veni Sancte Spiritus* represents the final evolution of the sequence. Its stanzas are homomorphic, its lines are all of the same length. The meter is accentual trochaic dimeter catalectic; the rhyme scheme is aabccb and every third line ends in *ium,* so that the antiphony is obscured by the use of the same final rhyme to all the strophes. The high technical skill of the versification is matched by a clarity of thought and expression and a deep religious feeling that deserve the high praise the poem receives.

Bibliography: N. GIHR, *Die Sequenzen des römischen Messbuches dogmatisch und ascetisch erklärt* (Freiburg 1887). *Analecta hymnica* 54:234–239, text. J. JULIAN, ed., *A Dictionary of Hymnology* (New York 1957) 2:1212–15. F. M. POWICKE, *Stephen Langton* (Oxford 1928). A. WILMART, *Auteurs spirituels et textes dévots du moyen âge latin* (Paris 1932). M. DULONG, ''Étienne Langton versificateur,'' *Mélanges Mandonnet,* 2 v. (Bibliothèque Thomiste 13–14; 1930) 2:183–190. F. J. E. RABY, *A History of Christian-Latin Poetry from the Beginnings to the Close of the Middle Ages* (Oxford 1953) 343–344. J. DE GHELLINCK, *L'Essor de la littérature latine au XIIe siècle* (Brussels-Paris 1946). H. THUSRSTON, *Familiar Prayers,* ed. P. GROSJEAN (Westminster, MD 1953). J. CONNELLY, *Hymns of the Roman Liturgy* (Westminster, MD 1957) 110–113, tr. J. SZÖVÉRFFY, *Die Annalen der lateinischen Hymnendichtung* (Berlin 1964–65).

[A. J. KINNEREY]

VENTURA DI RAULICA, GIOACCHINO

Preacher, writer, philosopher, publicist; b. Palermo, Sicily, Dec. 8, 1792; d. Versailles, France, Aug. 2, 1861. After completing classical studies under the JESUITS, he was a member of that order (1809–17), and then he joined

Gioacchino Ventura di Raulica.

the THEATINES (1818). His literary activity began at Naples with the publication of the periodical *Enciclopedia ecclesiastica e morale* (5 v. 1821–23), which often discussed the progress of the Church in the United States and published unedited correspondence of missionaries in Louisiana. He acted as press censor and member of the committee for public education. Ventura won renown as a preacher, particularly for his funeral eulogies, notably that for Pius VII. As a disciple of TRADITIONALISM, he translated and published the works of the French traditionalists. Ventura was the leading Italian follower of Hugues Félicité de LAMENNAIS, with whom he corresponded.

Transferred to Rome in 1824 as Theatine procurator general, he contributed to the *Giornale ecclesiastico,* and was appointed by Leo XII as professor of law at the *Sapienza.* His lectures exposing his theocratic theories were published in *De jure publico ecclesiastico commentaria* (1826). He attempted to give traditionalism a Thomistic basis in *De methodo philosophandi* (1828) and *Schiarimenti sulla questione della certezza . . .Osservazioni sulle dottrine dei De Bonald, De Maistre, De La Mennais e Laurentie* (1829).

As Theatine superior general (1831–33) Ventura improved the order's discipline, and he increased its activity with the addition of numerous members. During these years he became friendly with Emmanuel d'Alzon, whose studies he guided. He protested against the intemperance of *L'Avenir,* but when Lamennais and his fellow "pilgrims of liberty" came to Rome, he greeted them fraternally. For this he fell into disgrace with GREGORY XVI and retired to Modena, where he wrote (August–November 1833), but did not publish, *Dello spirito della rivoluzione e dei mezzi per farla cessare.* Reconciled with the pope, he returned to Rome and became examiner of the clergy, censor, consultor of the Congregation of Rites, and collaborator with Vincenzo PALLOTTI in the institution of services during the Epiphany octave, which led him to publish *Le bellezze della fede* (3 v. 1839–42). His book *La madre di Dio madre degli uomini* (1841) inaugurated modern literature on Mary's spiritual maternity. Between 1841 and 1848 he was on four occasions the Lenten preacher at St. Peter's basilica.

As friend and counselor of Pius IX (1846–78) at the beginning of the pontificate, Ventura championed politico-social reforms and popular democratic aspirations in the face of absolutist governments. His motto was "Church, people, liberty." His published discourse commemorating the death of Daniel O'CONNELL (1847) won applause; but another on the dead at Vienna was placed on the Index (May 30, 1849). In a series of writings in 1848 he supported Sicilian independence and alliance with the United States. As Sicilian diplomatic representative in Rome, he recognized as a *de facto* state the Roman Republic, whose inauguration in 1848 by Mazzini forced the exile of Pius IX to Gaeta. Together with ROSMINI-SERBATI, he proposed that Italy be united as a federation of states, with the pope as president. Foreseeing the imminent fall of the Roman Republic, he departed for France to spend the remainder of his life, going to Montpellier (1849) and then to Paris (1851). Soon he became one of France's leading pulpit orators, and even preached at the Tuileries before Napoleon III. The definitive elaboration of his philosophy, which also expressed his hopes for the revival of Scholasticism, appeared in *Essai sur l'origine des idées* (1853), *La Tradition et les semipélagiens de la philosophie* (1856), and *La philosophie chrétienne* (3 v. 1861). His system was traditionalism in its most mitigated form. Blameless in his private life, he died after receiving Pius IX's blessing, and he was buried in the Theatine church of St. Andrea della Valle in Rome, where his epitaph reads: *Defunctus adhuc loquitur.*

Bibliography: *Opere complete,* 31 v. (Milan-Venice 1852–63); also in 11 v. (Naples 1856–63); *Opere postume e inedite,* 3 v. (Venice 1863). P. CULTRERA, *Della vita e delle opere del P. G. Ventura* (Palermo 1877). A. RASTOUL, *Le P. Ventura* (Paris 1906). A. CRISTOFOLI, *Il pensiero religioso del P. G. Ventura* (Milan 1927). E. DI CARLO, "Gli opuscoli politici del P. V. nella rivoluzione del' 48," *Regnum Dei: Collectanea Theatina* 5 (1949):

134–137. F. ANDREU, "Il P. G. V.: Saggio biografico," *ibid.* 17 (1961): 1–161. R. COLAPIETRA, "L'insegnamento del V. alla Sapienza," *ibid.* 230–259. G. ALBINO, "Contributo del P. V. al rinascita del tomismo nel secolo 19," *ibid.* 260–268. Additional studies on V., *ibid.,* v. 19 (1963); v. 20 (1964), full bibliog. 148–210. P. SEJOURNÉ, *Dictionnaire de théologie catholique,* 15 v. (Paris 1903–50) 15.2:2635–39. J. GRISAR, *Lexikon für Theologie und Kirche,* ed. M. BUCHBERGER, 10 v. (Freiburg 1930–38) 10:534–535.

[F. ANDREU]

VENTURINO OF BERGAMO

Dominican preacher and religious leader, called also Venturino de Apibus; b. Bergamo, April 9, 1304; d. Smyrna, March 28, 1346. He entered the Dominicans at Bergamo and was ordained at Genoa (1328). Venturino joined the Dominican congregation of the Pilgrim Brothers and started for the Eastern missions, but was forced to remain teaching and preaching in Italy. He had a reputation for holiness and was involved in the political-religious problems of his times. He was emaciated and high-strung and spoke vividly in quick Latin or vernacular. His rich spiritual life, given expression in his treatise *De profectu spirituali,* suggests the mystical idea of penance propagated by St. Vincent Ferrer. He founded the monastery of nuns, St. Mary's in Bergamo. He led many pilgrims to Rome in penance, but was judged a hypocrite by Benedict XII in a letter from Avignon and exiled to France. After eight years he was cleared by Clement VI and given the crusader's flag. In the company of Henry II of the Dauphiné, and together with thousands of Italian recruits, he sailed in 1344 to Smyrna, where he died of fever two weeks after his arrival. There is a biographical-inspirational *Legend* concerning him. The title "Blessed" is sometimes given him, but he was never formally beatified.

Bibliography: G. CLEMENTI, *Il B. Venturino da Bergamo* (Rome 1904). P. A. GRION, "La *Legenda* del B. Venturino . . . ," *Bergomum* 30 (1956) 11–110. E. HOCEDEZ, "La Legende latine du B. Venturino da Bergamo," *Analecta Bollandiana* 25 (1906) 298–303.

[B. CAVANAUGH]

VERA, JACINTO

The first bishop of Uruguay; b. Brazil, July 3, 1813; d. Uruguay, May 6, 1881. His parents settled in Uruguay soon after his birth, so Vera studied at the Colegio San Ignacio in Buenos Aires. He was ordained in 1841 and then returned to Uruguay. In 1858 he was elected a deputy, but did not occupy his legislative seat. After the death of José Benito Lamas, Vera succeeded him as apostolic vicar. He carried out his duties with energy and zeal, touring the countryside, and giving organization and inspiration to the clergy of the nation. In 1862, as the result of a conflict with the government on the matter of competence, the Executive Power decreed "the expulsion of the priests Conde and Jacinto Vera from the territory of the Republic." The Holy See approved Vera's conduct. In 1863 the revolution of Gen. Venancio Flores occurred. The government ended Bishop Vera's exile, and he returned to Montevideo, where he was given a great welcome. He became bishop of Megara in 1864. He went to Rome in 1867 and again in 1869 to attend the Vatican Council. When the Diocese of Montevideo was established independent from that of Buenos Aires, Vera took the civil oath as first bishop of Uruguay, Jan. 8, 1879. His death occurred while he was on one of his customary missions. A virtuous priest of a strong character whose charity was evident in many different works, Bishop Vera achieved national prominence in Uruguay. The process for his canonization has been under way for some time.

Bibliography: L. A. PONS, *Biografía del ilmo. y revmo. señor don Jacinto Vera y Durán: Primer obispo de Montevideo* (Montevideo 1904).

[A. D. GONZÁLEZ]

VERA CRUZ, ALONSO DE LA, FRAY

Augustinian scholar linked with the beginninngs of philosophic thought an instruction in the Americas; b. Caspueñas, Toledo, 1504; d. Mexico, 1584. Fray Alonso studied the liberal arts and theology at the Universities of Alcalá and Salamanca, where he received the M.A. degree. While he was teaching the liberal arts at Salamanca, the university was famous as one of the centers of culture and learning of the early Renaissance.

The arrival in Spain of Fray Francisco de la Cruz, a prominent member of the Mexican Province of the mendicant Order of the Hermits of St. Augustine, proved decisive for Fray Alonso. The Augustinian Hermits of Mexico had founded a *studium generale* for their scholastics at Tiripitío, and Fray Francisco's journey to Spain had been undertaken to recruit additional coworkers and teachers. When Fray Alonso went to Vera Cruz in 1536, he had resolved to join the community of Augustinian Hermits.

For three years he was *magister novitiorum* in the Convento de México of Tiripitío. He subsequently taught philosophy and theology, and was temporarily in charge of diocesan administration. In 1545 he became prior of the monastery of Tacámbaro and, in 1548, provincial of the order. When in 1553 the Royal and Pontifical University of Mexico (the ancestor of the Universidad Nacional Autónoma de México) was founded, Fray Alonso was given the chair in Sacred Scripture and, later, in scholastic theology. Devoting himself exclusively to intellectual and apostolic work, he rejected the episcopates of Michoacán and of León de Nicaragua, as well as the position of commissioner general of New Spain, offered to him on the occasion of a visit to Spain in 1561.

Fray Alonso—often referred to as "the father of Mexican philosophy,"—was among the first to transplant the spirituality of Christian-Catholic civilization to the New World and established the tradition of Christian humanism in the Americas. Among his major works, the following deserve special mention: *Recognitio summularum* (a compendium of logic), *Dialectica resolutio* (a commentary on Aristotle's *Categories* and *Posterior Analytics*) and, above all, *Los libros del alma. Physica speculatio,* the original title, is indicative of an empirico-rational investigation, relating to the philosophy of nature.

A true disciple of the *philosophia perennis,* Fray Alonso achieved his philosophic synthesis by virtue of his openness to many sources of truth and to diverse modes of philosophic thought. While he shows his indebtedness to the Thomistic tradition, marked originality as well as a strongly Augustinian emphasis is evident in his extensive discussion of the passions and in his analysis of the active intellect. His epistemology is in essential agreement with that of Francisco de VITORIA.

Bibliography: A. DE LA VERA CRUZ, *Investigación filosófico-natural: Los libros del alma, libros I y II,* ed. O. ROBLES (Mexico City 1942); *De justo bello contra Indios* (bilingual ed.) (Madrid 1997). E. J. MCCARTHY, *The Augustinians in Primitive Mexico, 1533–1572* (Washington 1938). L. ORTIZ DEL CASTILLO, "La filosofía natural de los vivientes en Fray Alonso de la Vera Cruz," *Anuario de filosofía del seminario de investigaciones filosóficas* 1 (1943) 9–45. W. REDMOND and M. BEUCHOT, *Pensamiento y realidad en Fray Alonso de Vera Cruz, 1507–1584* (Mexico 1996).

[K. F. REINHARDT]

VERANUS OF CAVAILLON, ST.

Bishop of Cavaillon (now Département of Vaucluse, France); d. Nov. 11, after 589. GREGORY OF TOURS had a high opinion of Veranus whom he met in Cavaillon, and whom he ranked among the devotees of St. Martin. In fact, Veranus had been cured of a quartan fever as a result of a pilgrimage to the basilica dedicated to St. Martin in Cavaillon. Himself a wonder-worker, Veranus, adds Gregory of Tours, "was endowed with great powers so that often, by the grace of God, he would cure the sick with a sign of the cross." He attended the Council of

Mâcon (585) and the same year was sent by King Guntram, together with two other bishops, to hold an inquiry into the assassination of Pretextatus, Bishop of Rouen, victim of Fredegund. In 587 he baptized Thierry, son of Childebert, and in 589 sat on the episcopal commission charged with restoring order among the nuns of Holy Cross Monastery in Poitiers. An anonymous legend recounts his extraordinary life and especially the miracles he is supposed to have performed during a journey to Rome, but little confidence can be placed in this biography. His relics were translated to Jargeau, in the Diocese of Orléans. Veranus is honored in the whole southeast of France, at Paris, Orléans, and even in Italy, especially at St. Lawrence in Milan. He is often confused with a namesake; in addition the translators of Gregory of Tours compounded the confusion by writing Chalon (sur-Saône) instead of Cavaillon.

Feast: Oct. 19; Nov. 10 and 13.

Bibliography: GREGORY OF TOURS, *De virtutibus s. Martini,* bk. 3, ch. 60, ed. B. KRUSCH, *Monumenta Germaniae Historica: Scriptores rerum Merovingicarum* (Berlin 1826–) v.1; *The History of the Franks,* tr. O. M. DALTON, 2 v. (Oxford 1927). *Bibliotheca hagiographica latina antiquae et mediae aetatis,* 2 v. (Brussels 1898–1901; suppl. 1911) 2: 8536. *Acta Sanctorum* (Antwerp 1643–) Oct. 8:452–474. J. L. BAUDOT and L. CHAUSSIN, *Vies des saints et des bienheureux selon l'ordre du calendrier avec l'historique des fêtes,* ed. by the Benedictines of Paris, 12 v. (Paris 1935–56); v. 13, suppl. and table générale (1959) 10:629–631.

[J. DAOUST]

VERBIST, THEOPHILE

Founder of the Congregation of the IMMACULATE HEART OF MARY (Scheut Missionaries); b. Antwerp, Belgium, June 12, 1823; d. Lao-hu-kou, Inner Mongolia, Feb. 23, 1868. Of a middle-class family, he became a secular priest of the Archdiocese of Mechelen, ordained Sept. 18, 1846. He became successively subregent at the Mechelen minor seminary, chaplain at the École Militaire in Brussels, and national director of the Holy Childhood Association in 1860. He requested permission to establish a Belgian Mission in some port city of China and was urged by the Congregation for the Propagation of the Faith to establish a congregation of foreign missionaries. He became superior general of his congregation Nov. 28, 1862, and pronounced his vows Oct. 24, 1864, in the 15th-century chapel of Our Lady of Grace at Scheut, a suburb of Brussels. He became provicar apostolic of the Apostolic Vicariate of Mongolia, September 12, and arrived in Hsi-wan-tzu on Dec. 6, 1865. Verbist undertook the direction of the major seminary in Hsi-wan-tzu and within a year arranged the transfer of all mission stations in the vicariate from the Vincentians. During his 2½-year tenure as superior general and apostolic provicar he twice saw the arrival of a small group of his followers. He lost the cofounder of the congregation, Father Alois Van Segvelt, after two years. Verbist stressed the establishment of orphanages, thorough instruction of the few existing Catholics, and training of a native clergy. Preaching to the residents of Mongolia did not begin during his lifetime because of the missioners' unfamiliarity with the local language and customs. Verbist lamented his own failure to master Chinese thoroughly. During an inspection tour of his vicariate, he was taken ill, probably with typhus, and died in Lao-hu-kou. His remains were transferred to the enlarged chapel of Our Lady at Scheut (May 1931). Kindness and eagerness to help others were his most noted traits.

Bibliography: V. RONDELEZ, *Scheut, Congrégation missionnaire* (Brussels 1962).

[A. F. VERSTRAETE]

VERBUM SUPERNUM PRODIENS

The beginning of two famous hymns, a hymn on the Incarnation that was formerly sung at Matins in Advent, and a hymn that was historically sung at Lauds on the Feast of CORPUS CHRISTI and at the procession on that day. The first is thought to date variously from some time in the period between the 5th and the 8th centuries (Gaselee). Both the original and the revised form that was found in the Roman Breviary of 1632 consist of four verses, imitating the Ambrosian stanza. The *Verbum supernum* shows developed forms of assonance used in hymns from the 5th century on. The initial lines may have been influenced by a hymn of St. AMBROSE (*Intende, qui regis Israel*), and its last line, in turn, became a model of several later hymns (including one in honor of St. Dominic). Its second stanza displays affinities to the equally ancient *Iam lucis orto sidere* and to the Carolingian hymn *VENI CREATOR SPIRITUS*. The last two verses contain eschatological ideas, underlining the post-Ambrosian character of the hymn. The Biblical background (Mt 10.26–27; 24.29; Mk 13.24) is identical with that of the celebrated *DIES IRAE*, but is less elaborate. The author of the second hymn obviously chose as his model the older Incarnation hymn (above) and follows its first verse very closely, his choice being motivated perhaps by the fact that the Christmas preface serves also the Corpus Christi feast. The second stanza of the Corpus Christi hymn recalls the institution of the Holy Eucharist at the Last Supper. The third stresses the fact that the Eucharist was given under two species that correspond to the dual character of the nature of humanity. The fourth refers to the four stages of Redemption and Salvation. The fifth verse,

Theophile Verbist.

perhaps the most famous, calls upon the Eucharist to grant strength in war and among enemies. The hymn, part of the Corpus Christi office, is believed to be a poem of THOMAS AQUINAS (or of one of his co-workers); however, it differs somewhat from the other hymns for the same feast.

Bibliography: Text. For the Incarnation hymn. *Analecta hymnica* 51:48. A. S. WALPOLE, ed., *Early Latin Hymns* (Cambridge, Eng. 1922) 302–303. J. CONNELLY, *Hymns of the Roman Liturgy* (Westminster, MD 1957) 50–53. For the Corpus Christi hymn. *Analecta hymnica* 50:588–589. S. GASELEE, comp. *The Oxford Book of Medieval Latin Verse* (Oxford 1937) 144. J. CONNELLY, *Hymns of the Roman Liturgy* (Westminster, MD 1957) 122–124. Literature. A. S. WALPOLE, op. cit. 302–303. J. SZÖVÉRFFY, *Die Annalen der lateinischen Hymnendichtung* (Berlin 1964–65) 2:252. F. J. E. RABY, *A History of Christian-Latin Poetry from the Beginnings to the Close of the Middle Ages* (Oxford 1953) 409, on the possibility that Thomas Aquinas abridged and improved an earlier Cistercian hymn.

[J. SZÖVÉRFFY]

VERDI, GIUSEPPE

Distinguished opera composer; b. Le Roncole (near Busseto), Italy, Oct. 10, 1813 (baptized Fortunino Giuseppe Francesco); d. Milan, Jan. 27, 1901. Verdi was the son of a tavern keeper, and his musical education was al-

Giuseppe Verdi. (Archive Photos)

most entirely financed by Antonio Barezzi, a merchant. After studying composition privately under Vincenzo Lavigna, he was appointed *maestro di musica* at Busseto in 1835 and a year later married Barezzi's daughter. Two children born in 1838 and 1839 died within a year, and were followed by their mother in 1840. Verdi's first opera, *Oberto* (La Scala 1839), was sufficiently well received for him to resign his post at Busseto and devote himself to composition. *Nabucco* (1842) established his reputation in Italy; *I Lombardi* (1843) and *Ernani* (1844) brought him European fame. From 1848 he openly supported the cause of Italian unity and independence. *La battaglia di Legnano* (1849) aroused unprecedented enthusiasm at its Roman premiere by reason of its thinly veiled relevance to the *Risorgimento.* In 1849 he formed a permanent association with the singer Giuseppina Strepponi, and nine years later, married her. With the appearance of *Rigoletto* (1851), *Il Trovatore* (1853), and *La Traviata* (1853) Verdi was recognized as one of the greatest composers of the time. International renown brought him commissions from Paris (*The Sicilian Vespers,* 1855, and *Don Carlos,* 1867) and Egypt (*Aïda,* 1871). The Shakesperian operas of his old age, *Otello* (1887) and *Falstaff* (1893), are universally acknowledged to be his masterpieces.

In his youth and middle age Verdi was a freethinker. His return to religion in old age was probably delayed by political considerations: the apparent support of the *status quo* of a divided Italy by the Vatican and the incompetence and corruption displayed in the government of the Papal States were scandals that alienated many Italians. But for his last 30 years he was a practicing Catholic, as is evidenced by a letter from his wife to Archbishop Magnasco of Genoa, her confessor from 1871 to 1892: "There are those who wish to make believe that he is very different from what he really is, especially in certain matters concerning his intimate spiritual life. Verdi's soul, since several years ago, has changed much in this respect; not changed substantially, because there was no need, but formally and apparently. Much of this change is owing to the work of Abbé MERMILLOD—the most worthy priest who married us . . . who knew how to find the way to reach efficaciously his soul and his heart. If externally and for reasons concerning politics . . . Verdi does not appear that which in effect he is, one must not judge him solely by appearances. He is respectful towards religion, is a believer like me, and never fails to carry out those practices necessary for a good Christian, such as he wishes to be" (quoted in *Grove's Dictionary of Music and Musicians,* ed. E. Blom 9 v. (5th ed. London 1954); see Bibliography).

Verdi's early Masses and motets written at Busseto have not survived. His published religious music, none of which was intended for liturgical use, consists of a *Pater noster* for five-part chorus and *Ave Maria* for soprano and strings, both to texts by Dante (1880); a *Requiem* in memory of Manzoni for soloists, chorus, and orchestra; *Quattro Pezzi Sacri* (1898), including *Ave Maria* and *Laudi alla Vergine Maria* for unaccompanied choir, and *Stabat Mater* and *Te Deum* for chorus and orchestra. The *Requiem,* of oratorio dimensions, is undeniably operatic in style, but this is justified by the deep feeling for the words, the passionate sincerity, and overwhelming emotional effect of its dramatic approach. Technically and artistically it is one of Verdi's greatest achievements, and it has an unchallenged place in the concert hall beside Bach's B-minor Mass and Beethoven's *Missa solemnis.*

Bibliography: G. VERDI, *Verdi, the Man in His Letters,* ed. F. WERFEL and P. STEFAN, tr. E. DOWNES (New York 1942). F. ABBIATI, *Giuseppe Verdi,* 4 v. (Milan 1959). F. BONAVIA, *Verdi* (London 1930; repr. 1947). C. GATTI, *Verdi, the Man and His Music,* tr. E. ABBOTT (New York 1955). G. W. MARTIN, *Verdi: His Music, Life and Times* (New York 1963). F. TOYE, *Giuseppe Verdi* (London 1931; repr. New York 1946). F. WALKER, *The Man Verdi* (New York 1962). A. A. ABERT, *Die Musik in Geschichte und Gegenwart,* ed. F. BLUME (Kassel-Basel 1949–). M. CHUSID, ed. *Verdi's Middle Period (1849–1859), Source Studies, Analysis, and Performance Practice* (Chicago 1997). A. PARISINI, "La nuova via di Verdi: *Macbeth* e il meraviglioso nell'opera," *Rassegna Musicale Curci*

51 (1998) 22–26. R. PARKER, "'One Priest, One Candle, One Cross': Some Thoughts on Verdi and Religion," *The Opera Quarterly* 12/1 (1995) 27–34; *Leonora's Last Act: Essays in Verdian Discourse* (Princeton 1997). G. DE VAN, "La notion de *tinta:* mémoire confuse et affinités thématiques dans les opéras de Verdi," *Revue de Musicologie* 76 (1990) 187–98.

[A. MILNER]

VERDUN-SUR-MEUSE, ABBEY OF

Former Benedictine abbey, known also as Saint-Vanne of Verdun, France. The abbey was founded *c.* 951 by Bishop Berengar, on the site of the first church in Verdun (4th century) which had been built at the tomb of St. VITONUS. The church already had a community of canons. After an uncertain beginning, the Benedictine foundation took root under Abbot Richard (1004–46), a reformer whose activities and reputation spread far beyond Lorraine. The relics of St. Sanctinus, first bishop of Verdun, were brought from Meaux in 1032 and were kept at Saint-Vanne in great veneration. After 1552 the buildings of the abbey were enclosed by the walls of the citadel of Verdun, a famous French fortification. In 1604 the Abbey of Saint-Vanne was united to the Abbey of MOYENMOUTIER to form the Congregation of Saint-Vanne and Saint-Hydulphe, binding together more than 50 monasteries in Lorraine, Franche-Comté, and Champagne. Though it had given its name to the congregation, the Abbey of Saint-Vanne did not hold a special place in it. The whole congregation (Saint-Vanne especially) was penetrated by JANSENISM. The abbey was suppressed in 1791, after having been used for a time as a gathering place for the religious of the city of Verdun who wished to follow the COMMON LIFE after the French Revolution had suppressed their monasteries.

See Also: MAURISTS.

Bibliography: H. BLOCH, "Die älteren Urkunden des Klosters S. Vanne zu Verdun," *Jahrbuch der Gesellschaft für lothringische Geschichte und Altertumskunde* 10 (1898) 341–449; 14 (1902) 48–150. E. DIDIER-LAURENT, "Dom Didier de la cour et la réforme des Bénédictins de Lorraine," *Mémoires de la société d'archéologie Lorraine* 53 (1903) 265–502. H. DAUPHIN, *Le Bienheureux Richard, Abbé de Saint-Vanne de Verdun,†1046* (Louvain 1946). R. TAVENEAUX, *Le Jansénisme en Lorraine, 1640–1789* (Paris 1960). *Matricula religiosorum professorum . . . congregationis sanctorum Vitoni et Hydulphi* (new ed. Paris 1963).

[J. CHOUX]

VEREMUNDUS, ST.

Benedictine abbot; b. Arelbano, Navarre, Spain, *c.* 1020; d. abbey of Irache, March 8, 1092. He came to the Abbey of Irache as a youth of ten during the regime of his uncle, Abbot Munius. Shortly after the abbot's death, Veremundus was elected to succeed him (*c.* 1052). During his tenure, Irache reached the height of its fame, both spiritual and temporal; in recognition of its abbot's sanctity, it was the recipient of gifts and privileges from King Sancho Ramírez. Commissioned by ALEXANDER II to reform the Church in Spain, Veremundus was successful in promoting a liturgical renewal based on the texts and practices of his abbey. The discovery of the ancient image of Our Lady of Puy (1080) through the prayers of the abbot and his community led King Sancho to found the city of Estella on the site of the find. His relics, frequently translated (the latest in 1926), rest in the church of S. Juan de Estella; his cult was approved by Paul V in 1614.

Feast: March 8.

Bibliography: *Acta Sanctorum* March 1:793–798. J. PÉREZ DE URBEL, *Semblanzas benedictinas,* 2 v. (Madrid 1925–26) 1:95–99. P. RODRÍGUEZ GONZÁLEZ, *San Veremundo* (s.l. 1970). *Enciclopedia universal ilustrada Europeo-Americana,* 70 v. (Barcelona 1908–30; suppl. 1934–) 67:1480–81. A. M. ZIMMERMANN, *Kalendarium Benedictinum: Die Heiligen und Seligen des Benediktinerordens und seiner Zweige,* 4 v. (Metten 1933–38) 1:300, 302.

[O. J. BLUM]

VERGER, RAFAEL

Director of San Fernando Mission College during the establishment of missions in California; b. Santasy, Mallorca, Spain, Oct. 10, 1722; d. Monterrey, Mexico, July 4, 1790. He joined the Franciscans at 17 and was ordained Dec. 17, 1746. Later he was awarded a doctor's degree, and taught for some time at the University of Mallorca. In 1749 he volunteered for missionary work in the New World. He sailed from Spain in December of that year and reached San Fernando College, Mexico, the following April. There he again engaged in teaching, but was assigned to administrative positions after a few years. For six years he served as a member of the college council; and for six additional years, as guardian of the college, he was major superior of all the missionaries of the college. Verger's appointment to high office was opportune; by temperament he was cautious, practical, and painstaking, and the college at that time was assuming charge of a large mission territory. It was during his administration that the groundwork for the California mission system was laid; and although the chief credit for the success of the system is justly attributed to Junípero SERRA and his successors, without guidance, inspiration, and implementation on the part of Verger, little would have been achieved at that time. In 1783 he was made bishop of Nueva Leon. As bishop, Verger transferred his see city, Monterrey, to its present advantageous location.

Bibliography: L. G. CANEDO, ''Fray Rafael Verger en San Fernando de México'' *Humanitas* 3 (Monterrey, Mexico 1962) 551–575. C. PÉREZ-MALDONADO, *El Obispado* (Monterrey, Mexico 1947).

[F. KENNEALLY]

VERGERIO, PIER PAOLO

Italian humanist, educator, canonist, and statesman, remembered chiefly as the first and most influential of Italian Renaissance educational theorists; b. Capodistria, Italy, July 23, 1370; d. Budapest, Hungary, July 8, 1444 or 45. Vergerio studied at Padua, Florence, and Bologna. From 1390 to 1406 he taught rhetoric and logic at Padua and Florence and served as tutor for the Princes of Carrara at Padua. In 1392 or shortly after, Vergerio composed his famous treatise *On the Manners of a Gentleman and Liberal Studies* (*De ingenuis moribus*). This first of over a dozen Italian Renaissance educational treatises, and most influential of all of them, saw more than 20 editions by 1500, and more than 40 by 1600. In it, Vergerio advocates the extensive study of Latin literature as the core of the curriculum in general education; a revival of the study of Greek; the relegation of logic to a secondary status; and a broad curriculum, to include varied academic subjects, physical education, and military training. He gives primary importance to the careful inculcation of good habits and Christian morality. He especially praises the study of history as ''philosophy teaching by example'' and stresses the value of recreation and games of skill.

From 1406 to 1417 Vergerio served as papal secretary to INNOCENT VII and GREGORY XII, but following the Council of Constance (1414–18), he became secretary to SIGISMUND, Holy Roman Emperor. Vergerio was the author of several works, including a treatise *On Restoring Unity in the Church,* a *Life of Petrarch,* a *History of the Princes of Carrara,* numerous *Letters,* which have been printed, and several poems, comedies, and biographical works that are still in manuscript. His chief claim to fame, however, is his concise and comprehensive, balanced and discerning implementation of humanistic concepts in the field of pedagogy, which made him, according to W. H. Woodward, ''the true founder of the new education.''

Bibliography: W. H. WOODWARD, *Vittorino da Feltre and Other Humanist Educators: Essays and Versions* (Cambridge, Eng. 1921); *Studies in Education during the Age of the Renaissance,1400–1600* (Cambridge, Eng. 1924). C. BISCHOFF, *Studien zu P. P. Vergerio* (Berlin 1909). K. A. KOPP, ''Petrus Paulus Vergerius der aeltere: ein Beiträge zur Geschichte des beginnen Humanisus,'' *Historisches Jahrbuch des Görres-Gesellschaft* 18 (1897) 273–310, 533–571.

[D. D. MCGARRY]

VERGIL (PUBLIUS VERGILIUS MARO)

Greatest of the Latin poets and of major significance in Christian education and culture; b. Andes, near Mantua, 79 B.C.; d. Brundisium, 19 B.C., buried at Naples. The greatness of Vergil's *Eclogues, Georgics,* and *Aeneid* were recognized in his own lifetime. The few hostile critics, such as Carbilius Pictor with his *Aeneidomastix,* were soon forgotten. While owing much to the Greeks, and especially to Homer and Hesiod, Vergil put his own stamp on all his poetry. His *Aeneid* is truly a mature national epic whose language itself mirrors the majesty of Rome. But underlying the glorification of Rome, there is deep religio-philosophical reflection on peace, duty, and the lot of mankind that has universal appeal for all times and peoples.

Vergil's works immediately became a schoolbook in the Roman schools of grammar and rhetoric and has occupied a central position in the Latin curriculum ever since. Subsequent Latin poets and prose writers were thus deeply influenced by Vergilian episodes, thought, and diction. The Vergilian borrowings of Lucan, Statius, Silvus Italicus, Ausonius, and Claudian are well known. Latin Christians trained in the schools were likewise deeply influenced by Vergil. In this respect, the fourth *Eclogue* was important, because the mysterious reference to the birth of a child who would begin a new age was interpreted early as a pagan witness to the coming birth of Jesus. The familiarity of Lacantius, St. Ambrose, St. Jerome, St. Augustine, and above all of Prudentius, who was called the ''Christian Vergil,'' with Vergil has been established in detail by special philological studies. The allegorical interpretation of Vergil by Fabius Planciades Fulgentius helped to make him a source and symbol of wisdom.

Vergil's works and the scholarly commentaries on them by Servius and others were among the most precious and influential medieval inheritances from antiquity. The *Aeneid* was the most important pagan text employed in the school tradition of the Middle Ages, and it served as a standard model for the composition of Latin hexameters. The hexameter, either alone or in combination with the pentameter, was the most widely used Latin verse form throughout the medieval period.

L. Traube coined the happy phrase *aetas Vergiliana* to emphasize the role of Vergil in the 8th and 9th centuries; but despite the popularity of Ovid in the 11th and 12th centuries, Vergil continued to occupy the chief position, at least in the schools. Owing in part to the connection of his name in the form *Virgilius* with *virga* (wand), Vergil had a great vogue in medieval literature and folklore as the good magician. The medieval influence of Vergil culminates in DANTE, who makes him, as the symbol of human wisdom, his guide in the *Inferno* and *Purgatorio.*

The Renaissance inaugurated a new epoch in Vergilian study and influence. In Neo-Latin epic and pastoral poetry he was the supreme model, and his epic structure, content, and style have left their mark especially on the Romance and English literatures. Vergil has remained the favorite Latin poet of the school tradition from the rise of the new education of the Renaissance down to the present time. In 19th-century Germany, enthusiasm for Homer led to a temporary eclipse of Vergil in that country, but recent German scholarship has again recognized his full greatness in the history of poetry and in the classical tradition.

Bibliography: M. SCHANZ, C. HOSIUS, and G. KRÜGER, *Geschichte der römischen Literatur*, 4 v. in 5 (Munich 1914–35) 2:3 1–113, esp. 96–113. K. BÜCHNER, *Paulys Realenzyklopädie der klassischen Altertumswissenschaft*, ed. G. WISSOWA et al. (Stuttgart 1893–) 8A.2 (1958) 1265–1486, esp. 1463–86. R. R. BOLGAR, *The Classical Heritage and Its Beneficiaries* (Cambridge, Eng. 1954), *passim*, Index *s.v.* ''Vergil.'' Manitius, v.1–3, Indexes *s.v.* ''Vergilius.'' T. HAECKER, *Virgil: Father of the West*, tr. A. W. WHEEN (New York 1934). J. W. SPARGO, *Virgil the Necromancer* (Cambridge, Mass. 1934). G. HIGHET, *The Classical Tradition* (New York 1949), *passim,* Index *s.v.* ''Vergil.''

[M. R. P. MCGUIRE]

VERGIL, POLYDORE

Humanist and author of the first ''modern'' history of England; b. Urbino, Italy, *c.* 1470; d. Urbino, April 18, 1555. Vergil was educated at Padua, and by 1496 he had been ordained. Presumably, he spent some time in papal service. Under the patronage of Adriano Castelli, papal collector and cardinal, Vergil was sent to England as deputy collector in 1502.

He was already an author of note, having published a collection of adages, the *Prouerbiorum libellus* (1498) and a book on the originators of human institutions and activities, the *De rerum inuentoribus* (1499). Both books became best sellers and their reputation led Henry VII to invite Vergil to write a history of England. Vergil began writing this history around 1505, and a draft exists completed to 1513. He was rewarded with canonries in Lincoln, Hereford, and St. Paul's, and the archdeaconry of Wells (1508). Under HENRY VIII, Vergil enjoyed less favor at court and endured brief imprisonment in the Tower for intriguing against WOLSEY (1515). He later revenged himself in the *Anglica historia.*

This work first appeared at Basle in 1534 in 26 books that followed English history to the end of Henry VII's

Vergil (Publius Vergilius Maro). (Archive Photos, Inc.)

reign (1509). A revised version was published in 1546, and in 1555 the work appeared with an additional book continuing the history to 1537. A popular and important work, it was used as groundwork by later English historians, and thus influenced the picture of the English past found referenced in later works, such as Shakespeare's plays.

Besides his history of England, Vergil continued to publish revised and enlarged editions of his *Prouerbiorum libellus.* The even more successful *De rerum inuentoribus* was translated into English and other vernaculars. Originally, it had consisted of three books, to which Vergil, in 1521, added five more about the origins of ecclesiastical institutions and practices; it figures in early editions of the Index of Prohibited Books, and an expurgated version was published in Rome in 1576. Other works by Vergil are a brief commentary on the Lord's Prayer, a dialogue on prodigies, and other dialogues on patience, the perfect life, truth and falsehood.

Vergil played little part in the exciting ecclesiastical upheavels of the 1530s. Although he signed the renunciation of papal supremacy (1536) and the declaration for Communion under both species (1547), he made no secret of his sympathy for CATHERINE OF ARAGON and the old order, published in the last book of his history when he was safely out of England for the last time. He was bitterly attacked by chauvinist historians like Leland for his skeptical attitude to such British legends as Arthur; in defense of his position Vergil published (1525) an edition of GILDAS, the earliest British medieval text to be printed as such by a Renaissance scholar. As a stylist, Vergil is plain; as a scholar, he is methodical and reliable. His writings had considerable influence—more, perhaps, on the Continent than in England.

Bibliography: P. VERGIL, *Three Books of Polydore Vergil's English History,* ed. H. ELLIS (Camden Ser. 29; London 1844), the Tudor translation; *Anglica Historia,* ed. and tr. D. HAY (Camden 3d Ser. 74; London 1950), the early draft for 1485 to 1513 and the printed text thence to 1537. D. HAY, *Polydore Vergil: Renaissance Historian and Man of Letters* (Oxford 1952).

[D. HAY]

VERHAEGEN, PETER J.

First president of ST. LOUIS UNIVERSITY, St. Louis, Mo.; b. Haeght, Belgium, June 21, 1800; d. Grand Coteau, La., July 21, 1868. While a lay teacher at the minor seminary in Mechlin, Belgium, he was recruited by Rev. Charles Nerinckx for the American missions and entered the Jesuit novitiate in Maryland in 1821. Two years later he migrated with the Jesuit band that established a novitiate at Florissant, Mo. Before and after ordination (March 11, 1826), he instructed his companions in theology and Scripture.

Assigned first to the missions of St. Charles, Portage des Sioux, and three attached stations, in 1829 he was appointed head of St. Louis College (founded 1818), then newly placed under Jesuit supervision by Bp. Joseph Rosati. In 1832 he obtained a university charter, thus establishing the first university west of the Mississippi River. He remained its president until 1836 when he was appointed superior of the Jesuit Missouri mission. When the mission became a vice province, he was named vice provincial (1839). He established missions among the Potawatomi and Kickapoo tribes and assigned Pierre Jean de Smet to the Rocky Mountain and Oregon missions. He also filled the posts of vicar-general and administrator of the diocese while Bishop Rosati attended the Fourth Provincial Council of Baltimore (1840) and made his *ad limina* visit to Rome.

Under Verhaegen's leadership the Jesuits assumed control of St. Charles College, Grand Coteau, La., and St. Xavier College (now Xavier University), Cincinnati, Ohio. In 1845 he was appointed provincial of the Maryland province, and following this duty became the first president of St. Joseph's College, Bardstown, Ky. In 1851 he returned to St. Charles, leaving only for a brief interval to teach theology at the School of Divinity, St. Louis University.

Bibliography: Archives, Jesuit Province of Missouri. G. J. GARRAGHAN, *Jesuits in the Middle United States,* 3 v. (New York 1938).

[M. F. HASTING]

VERIFICATION

The term "verification" concerns statements or theories. Since a THEORY can be formulated as a conjunction of hypotheses, and therefore as a single statement, the considerations pertaining to statements are also valid for theories. This article considers only the case of statements. In a strict sense, to verify a statement is to recognize its TRUTH. But in the current theory of verification, the term is used in a broader sense: to verify a statement is to test its truth-value. A statement is said to be verifiable if a method can be given for its verification, at least in principle. The theory of verification concerns statements only in their cognitive meaning. And it has been developed only for purely logical and empirical statements (i.e., statements belonging to the empirical sciences). In the case of metaphysical statements, the conditions of their truth coincide with the validity of the methods that are used to establish them (e.g., metaphysical inference or reflexive analysis).

Logical statements. Purely logical statements are statements whose truth-value depends not on the content but only on the form, and more exactly on the meaning of the logical constants they contain. In the frame of a formalized language (for which the notion of consequence is defined), a statement is formally (or logically) true, or analytic, if it is a consequence of every class of statements; it is formally (or logically) false if every statement is a consequence of it. A tautology is a formally true statement containing only propositional connectives. The problem of verification for purely logical statements is the logical problem of decision. It can be solved for tautologies, but it cannot be solved, in the general case, for statements containing quantifiers (*see* LOGIC, SYMBOLIC).

Empirical statements and confirmation. The verification of an empirical statement can be direct or indirect. Direct verification is a confrontation between a statement and empirical observation. A statement *P* is indirectly verified as follows: from this statement, in conjunction with other statements that are already verified or analytic, a consequence *C* is deduced that can be directly verified. The falsification of a statement amounts to the verification of its negation. If *C* is verified, it cannot be concluded that *P* is true. If *C* is falsified, according to the case, either *P* or some other nonanalytic premise in the deduction is to be rejected. An empirical statement can thus never be considered as true or false in a definitive manner; it must always be treated as a hypothesis. (Even a directly verifiable statement can be treated in this manner to the extent that it admits of indirect verification.) It is therefore preferable to speak of confirmation rather than verification.

The confirmation of a statement is a test procedure accompanied by the specification of the conditions under which, according to the result obtained, this statement is considered as scientifically accepted or rejected. Confirmation may be direct or indirect. An empirical statement can never be considered as accepted or rejected in a definitive manner; it has only a certain degree of confirmation. Different criteria have been proposed to characterize this concept: probability, falsification of rival hypothesis, simplicity, and syntactical or metrical expression. The theory of confirmation is still in the process of development.

Verification and meaning. The concept of verification has been used by modern EMPIRICISM as a criterion of meaning: a statement is meaningful if and only if it is directly or indirectly verifiable. According to this criterion, metaphysical statements are meaningless. The verifiability criterion of meaningfulness has been criticized by many empiricists, and alternative criteria have been proposed—for example, translatability into an empiricist language or inclusion in a system that is partially interpretable in observational terms. C. G. Hempel has pointed out that the notion of cognitive significance can perhaps be attributed only to systems considered as wholes and that "cognitive significance in a system is a matter of degree."

The search for an empiricist criterion of meaning is linked with the empiricist principle according to which a statement has cognitive meaning only if it is logically true or false, or capable, at least potentially, of being tested by experiential evidence. And this principle in turn is based on the epistemological assumption that the only sources of knowledge are sense intuition and analysis. An abstractionist theory of concepts seems to be more apt to give account of the procedures of science; it is in any case indispensable, together with a theory of ANALOGY, to found the possibility of METAPHYSICS.

See Also: LOGICAL POSITIVISM; METAPHYSICS, VALIDITY OF; SEMANTICS.

Bibliography: A. PAP, *An Introduction to the Philosophy of Science* (Glencoe, Ill. 1962). C. G. HEMPEL, "The Concept of Cognitive Significance: A Reconsideration," *Proceedings of the American Academy of Arts and Sciences* 80 (1951) 61–77.

[J. A. LADRIÈRE]

VERITATIS SPLENDOR

Pope JOHN PAUL II's tenth encyclical, issued on the feast of the Transfiguration (August 6) in 1993. The purpose of the encyclical is to set forth "the principles of a moral teaching based upon Sacred Scripture and the living Apostolic Tradition" (no. 5). In the introduction, the pope notes that the Church's magisterial teaching, particularly in the past two centuries, has touched on many different questions concerning the moral life; in *Veritatis splendor* he intends rather "to reflect on the whole of the Church's moral teaching" (no. 4). The occasion for this reflection is the growth of a systematic questioning of this teaching, based on presuppositions that have "serious implications" for individual moral life, the communal life of the Church, and the just life of society. The immediate context for the encyclical is the publication of the *Catechism of the Catholic Church:* the fullness of the moral life, such as it is presented in the *Catechism* must be understood as the backdrop to the encyclical's concern with certain fundamental moral questions.

Veritatis splendor is divided into three parts. In the first, "Christ and the Answer to the Question about Morality," the pope uses the encounter between Jesus and the rich young man (Mt 19.16ff.) to show what is involved in moral teaching. The human heart naturally desires to know the full meaning of its life, and what it must do to achieve that meaning; this is why the rich young man comes to Christ. Christ's response highlights the fact that the moral life is a response to God's initiative—the "One who alone is good" alone makes the moral life possible. The commandments and the beatitudes are equally valid norms for the moral life, because they both point to the fullness of love to which every person is called. This life becomes possible in the following of Christ and the gift of the Spirit. Yet, though it is supernatural in origin, it is the norm for man in every time and place; and the role of the Church is to promote and preserve this life.

In part 2, "The Church and the Discernment of Certain Tendencies in Present-Day Moral Theology," the pope goes on to speak of a crisis in modern thought: freedom is opposed to natural law, conscience is presented as the ultimate arbiter of good and evil, and the Church's teaching on intrinsically evil acts is dismissed as irrelevant to moral evaluation. These tendencies are rooted in a denial of the dependence of freedom on truth. Rightful human autonomy does not involve the creation of one's own moral norms, but a recognition of human nature and the right order of creation through "participated theonomy," a participation in "the light of natural reason and of Divine Revelation" (no. 41). The natural law thus recognized contains both positive and negative precepts:

these are equally universal, but only the latter can be formulated as norms that oblige always and everywhere because "the commandment of love of God and neighbor does not have in its dynamic any higher limit, but it does have a lower limit, beneath which the commandment is broken" (no. 52). "Conscience" also cannot be rightly understood unless it is seen as a "practical judgment": that is, a judgment that does not establish the good, but identifies the good to be done in a particular situation in light of the natural law. The pope draws particularly attention to a tendency in moral theology to separate the "fundamental option" of a person from his particular, individual acts, locating moral assessment only in the former. He notes that the fundamental option is made real only through the exercise of freedom, and therefore only through particular acts—and by the same token, it can be revoked through particular acts. Therefore, the Church's teaching that particular acts can be mortal sins must be upheld. Finally, against a "teleologistic" moral theology that locates the moral quality of acts entirely in the intention of the person and the foreseeable consequences of the act, the pope emphasizes the importance of the object of the acting person. An act can be good only when its object is, by its nature, capable of being ordered to God; if the object is incapable of being so ordered, the act is "intrinsically evil."

Part 3, "Moral Good for the Life of the Church and of the World," draws out the pastoral conclusions of the previous analysis. The Church must witness to the dependence of freedom on truth. The Crucified Christ reveals that "freedom is acquired in love" (no. 87), and the martyrs continue to exemplify this truth. Only the recognition of certain universal moral norms guarantees just relations in society. The witness of the moral life is essential to the Church's task of evangelization and the fulfillment of her prophetic office. The pope also identifies the responsibilities of theologians and pastors for preserving and promoting this truth.

The encyclical ends with an invocation of Mary, the Mother of Mercy. Through her we learn of the possibility of the moral life lived in discipleship to Christ.

Bibliography: For the text of *Vertitatis splendor,* see: *Acta Apostolicae Sedis,* 85 (1993): 1134–1228 (Latin); *Origins* 23, no. 18 (Oct 14, 1993): 297–334 (English); *The Pope Speaks* 39 (1994) 6–63 (English). For commentaries and summaries of *Vertitatis splendor,* see: J. A. DINOIA and R. CESSARIO, eds., *Veritatis Splendor and the Renewal of Moral Theology* (Chicago 1999). M. E. ALLSOPP and J. O'KEEFE, *Veritatis Splendor: American Responses* (Kansas City 1995). J. A. SELLING and J. JANS, *The Splendor of Accuracy: An Examination of the Assertions Made by Veritatis Splendor* (Grand Rapids, MI 1995).

[G. F. LANAVE]

VERMEERSCH, ARTHUR

Jesuit moral theologian, canonist, and spiritual writeer; b. Ertvelde, East Flander (Belgium), Aug. 26, 1858; d. Eegenhoven, near Louvain, July 12, 1936. Vermeersch spent four years as a young boy in the diocesan seminary of Termonde and seven years in the Jesuit schools of Liège and Namur, after which he began studies at the University of Louvain, leading to the doctorate of civil law in political and administrative sciences. Upon the completion of these studies at the age of 21, he entered the Jesuit novitiate in Tronchiennes. He did his philosophical studies at Louvain and his theology at the Gregorian University in Rome. In December of 1893, he returned to the Jesuit college for theology in Louvain, and taught moral theology and Canon Law there for 25 years, publishing during this time a series of meditations on the Sacred Heart, the Blessed Virgin, and the nature of a religious vocation, as well as his *Miles Christi Jesu* (1914), a commentary on the Jesuit rule of life.

At the same time, Vermeersch's interest in social justice prompted him to write several books and articles on social legislation in Belgium, particularly in reference to the Belgian Congo, which he visited to study its racial problems firsthand. His views anticipated the mid-20th-century unrest in Africa and expressed the need for racial justice based on Christian principles as expressed in the Gospels and in several papal encyclicals.

Vermeersch also traveled to Canada and the U.S., and between 1908 and 1914 he contributed to the *Catholic Encyclopedia* 19 articles on moral theology and Canon Law, as well as the articles "Congo Independent State and Congo Missions" and "Modernism." During this time he also published the book *Tolerance* (1912), an analysis of the problem of religious freedom in civil society and of the relationship between Church and State. Lecturing extensively throughout Europe and frequently consulting with ecclesiastical authorities in Rome, he began collaboration in 1904 on the codification of Canon Law ordered by Pius X, especially on the section dealing with religious orders, and was later appointed consultor to three Roman Congregations: of the Council, of the Sacraments, and of Religious.

In 1918 Vermeersch was named successor to G. Bucceroni in the chair of moral theology at the Gregorian University. During the next 16 years of teaching, he founded and edited the journal *Periodica de re canonica et morali.* Together with J. Creusen, he published the first full commentary on the new Code (1918), and later the more definitive three-volume commentary, *Epitome juris canonici cum commentariis* (1921–23). Between 1922 and 1924 he completed his summation of moral theology, *Theologiae moralis principia, responsa, consilia* (4 v.

1922–24). During the last decade of his life, he published articles on the Lambeth Conference of the Anglican Church, the notion of social justice in the encyclical *Rerum novarum,* Christian marriage in connection with the encyclical *Casti connubii,* and social legislation in connection with the encyclical *Quadragesimo anno* (May 15, 1931) of Pope Pius XI.

Bibliography: J. CREUSEN, *Le Père Arthur Vermeersch: L'Homme et l'oeuvre* (Brussels 1947). J. DE GHELLINCK and G. GILLEMAN, *Dictionnaire de théologie catholique,* ed. A. VACANT et al., (Paris 1903–50) 15.2:2687–93, contains an excellent bibliog. and a list of his bks. and articles. *The Catholic Encyclopedia and Its Makers* (New York 1917) 178.

[J. M. UPTON]

VERMONT, CATHOLIC CHURCH IN

The history of Catholicism in Vermont began in July of 1609 with the arrival of Samuel de Champlain, who named the land for its green mountains ('' *Voilà les monts verts!*''). The Church developed slowly through three phases. The early period of evangelization and missionary activity planted the seed and set down roots. Catholicism in Vermont came of age with the establishment of the Diocese of Burlington in 1853. The third, contemporary phase began after about 1965 with efforts to implement the renewal of the Second Vatican Council.

Evangelization and Missionary Activity. The year before CHAMPLAIN arrived in Vermont, the explorer had engaged the Society of Jesus to evangelize the Native Americans in the new lands, but the Jesuits did not arrive until the year after his death. One of them was St. Isaac Jogues (1607–46) who passed through Vermont on at least four journeys between New York and Quebec in the years before his martyrdom. Among his stops as a captive was the little island on Lake Champlain where he was tortured and where later Jesuit missionaries offered Mass.

In fact, before Sieur de La Motte constructed a fort on the island that bears his name, Jesuits Simon Le Moyne crossed through Vermont on a diplomatic journey between Quebec and New York in September of 1654 and Pierre Raffeix stopped at the Shrine of St. Anne on the Isle La Motte, in May of 1666. Later Charles Albanel joined Raffeix there in September of that year in hearing confessions and saying Mass. And, in the summer of 1667, Jesuits Jacques Bruyas, Jacques Frémin, and Jean Pierron ministered to some three hundred soldiers on the island near the feast of St. Anne. Of these, Jacques Frémin (1628–91), famous for converting 10,000 Native Americans, was among the founders of the Isle La Motte.

At the time, Vermont came under the jurisdiction of Blessed François de Montmorency Laval (1623–1708),

Vicar Apostolic to New France, who arrived in North America in the summer of 1659. In 1668, before he became the Bishop of Quebec in 1674, Laval became the first prelate to visit the Shrine of St. Anne. As for the apostolate among the Native Americans in his diocese, Laval left this to the Jesuits.

A letter of Jesuit Jean Pierron, on Oct. 10, 1682, is evidence that Jesuits cared for the Abnakis at their various missions. They crisscrossed Vermont to help the Native Americans before the fall of Quebec in 1763 and until the suppression of the Society of Jesus in 1773. The association of the Jesuits with the Abenakis was known to New Englanders who raided their mission site on the Connecticut River. On Sept. 26, 1992, the Order of Alhambra, a Catholic fraternal organization with caravans at Rutland in 1912 and at Burlington in 1946 and devoted to marking historical sites, dedicated a plaque at Our Lady of Perpetual Help Church in Bradford commemorating the old mission at Koes. This was located near what is now Newbury before it was destroyed early in the 18th century.

Thereafter, missionary activities centered at what is now Swanton where the Jesuits had constructed their first church in Vermont. When the state celebrated its tercentenary, the people of Swanton dedicated a large granite shaft commemorating the site of that church on Missisquoi Bay. Peter Kalm, a Swiss naturalist, provided further evidence when, just before mid-18th century, he found the Jesuits in areas now known as Alburg, Chimney Point, and Ferrisburg. Through such contacts, the Jesuits taught the Abenakis the essentials of religion and of European culture.

When John Carroll (1736–1815), who had already visited Vermont in 1776, became the first American bishop in 1789, a Catholic community of French Canadians was flourishing. Vermont, not unlike other states in New England in discriminating against Catholics, repealed these measures in 1793. Although it was the only state in New England which he did not visit as its bishop, Carroll was influential in placing it in the new Diocese of Boston established in 1808.

Jean Lefebvre de Cheverus (1768–1836), First Bishop of Boston, who visited Vermont only on a trip to Montreal in 1821, left the care of Vermonters to the Bishop of Quebec. When Quebec was elevated to an archiepiscopal see in 1815, Joseph-Octave Plessis (1763–1825), the great grandson of Thomas French, a deacon of the Congregational Church in colonial Deerfield, Massachusetts, was instrumental in having Father François-Antoine Matignon (1753–1818), a Boston priest, set up a mission in Burlington with its hundred Catholics in 1815. In 1816, after the desecration of the Jesuit church on the St. Francis River in Canada by Rogers Rangers in 1759, a farmer in West Charleston discovered its candelabra. Before 1838, another Vermonter recovered, near the mouth of Lake Magog, a gilded image taken from that same church.

Some remarkable converts to Catholicism emerged during the 19th century. In 1807, Frances (Fanny) Margaret Allen (1784–1819), daughter of hero Ethan Allen became a Catholic and later the first woman of Vermont to become a nun. In 1818, Daniel Barber (1756–1834), an Episcopal minister who served Vermont from the border area of Claremont, New Hampshire, was accepted into the Catholic church by Cheverus. Later, Barber's sson, Virgil (1782–1847) who had converted in 1816 and was ordained a Jesuit priest on Dec. 3, 1822, established the first Catholic church and school near the site of his father's former church. One of its students was William B. Tyler (1806–49), a native of Derby, who became the First Catholic Bishop of Hartford, Connecticut, in 1844.

Benedict Joseph Fenwick (1782–1846), to whom Virgil Barber had brought his reservations about his faith, become the Bishop of Boston in 1825. On Barber's suggestion, the bishop climbed Mount Ascutney on June 5, 1826, in search of an appropriate site for a college, but Fenwick did not find it suitable. Though Barber won converts, the English-speaking Catholics of Vermont had no resident priest when he left Claremont in 1828. The faithful had to depend on James Fitton (1805–81), renowned in New England, until Fenwick sent Jeremiah O'Callaghan (d. 1861), a priest from County Kerry in Ireland, to Burlington as its first resident priest in 1830. With Bennington and Middlebury, Burlington, which numbered about a thousand Catholics, was one of three largest Catholic cities in the state.

Under O'Callaghan, "The Apostle of Vermont," the church grew for 25 years. When Fenwick dedicated St. Mary's in Burlington, on Sept. 9, 1832, it was the city's first Catholic church and was built on land donated by Colonel Archibald W. Hyde (1786–1847), a Protestant who eventually became a Catholic. Meanwhile, O'Callaghan had expanded the church into other areas like Vergennes, where the home of Mrs. Daniel Nichols (Mary Ann Booth) was the center of Catholic worship and where both Fenwick and O'Callaghan offered Mass. St. Peter's, the church later constructed in that town, did not open until 1854. Not unlike other Catholic priests in New England, O'Callaghan had to put up with anti-Catholics who destroyed St. Mary's in Burlington by fire on May 9, 1838. Still, the church continued when, on Oct. 31, 1841, Fenwick dedicated a new church, St. Peter's, on the corner of Cherry and St. Paul streets so that, before two more years passed, Catholics in Vermont numbered

close to 5,000, of which the district covering Swanton, St. Albans, and Fairfield had a total of about 2,000 Catholics when Fenwick went there for confirmations with his brother, George, on Oct. 5, 1841. In Swanton, a brick church constructed on land donated by James McNally was completed in 1847. And, Catholicism, due to O'Callaghan, expanded even into Bennington, Montpelier, Rutland, and Shelburne. In addition to O'Callaghan, there was John B. Daly (d. 1870), a Franciscan, who became famous as the president of the Catholic Total Abstinence Society in Vermont. In 1837, Daly was appointed resident priest in the area of Rutland and Middlebury to lighten O'Callaghan's burdens in the lower half of the state. Though Fitton had visited the Castleton area in 1828, Fenwick did not open a church there until 1836, in what became the parish of St. John the Baptist with about 150 Catholics. Then, Daly opened one in Middlebury in 1840, later Assumption Parish.

Perhaps the most famous convert in Vermont's history was Orestes Augustus Brownson (1803–76), a native of Stockbridge. Moving from one set of beliefs to another, he had also served for as a Universalist minister in Rutland, Windsor, and Windham. It was to John B. Fitzpatrick (1812–66), his coadjutor, that Bishop Fenwick entrusted Brownson for instructions in the Catholic faith. This intellectual ended his religious wanderings by becoming a Catholic on Oct. 20, 1844.

At Bellows Falls, Fitzpatrick, a faithful successor to Fenwick, ran into hostility against Catholics when they were refused the use of the Methodist church. Nevertheless, accompanied by Jesuits George Fenwick and Samuel A. Mulledy, the bishop had to settle for a pine grove on the west side of town where he conducted a confirmation ceremony, on Sept. 4, 1846, with a thousand people, including some Protestants who witnessed the episcopal visitation.

During Fitzpatrick's time, the first Mass was offered in Brattleboro, on Aug. 15, 1848. This took place when Father Joseph Coolidge Shaw (1821–51), a Jesuit priest who came from a prominent Boston family, was spending time in the area taking the water cure for his troubled leg. While the medicinal baths were producing their healing effects, Shaw offered Mass in a place called "the Wood farm" where Catholics later built a shed for Sunday Mass.

Under Fitzpatrick, two parishes were established in Vermont: Immaculate Conception in St. Albans in 1847 and St. Augustine's in Montpelier in 1850. With respect to the latter, General Dewitt Clinton Clarke (1812–70), a convert and a state legislator left the senate to attend Mass and his letter of Nov. 3, 1850 is the first record of Mass there. In Fitzpatrick's first year as Bishop of Boston, William Henry Hoyt (1813–83), an Episcopal minister, converted to Catholicism and eventually became a Catholic priest. Around this time, Francis P. Kenrick (1797–1863), Catholic Archbishop of Baltimore, was vindicating the Catholic faith against Vermont's Episcopal Bishop John Henry Hopkins, Sr. (1792–1868).

Given the proximity of French-speaking Catholics in Vermont to Canada, Fenwick had entrusted them to the care of Abbé Pierre-Marie Mignault (1784–1868). This abbé, who was memorialized in the old parish of Notre Dame des Victoires in St. Johnsbury, came from Chambly, Canada, and cared for that flock from the early 1820s until a new see was established at Burlington on July 29, 1853.

Establishment of the Diocese of Burlington. Catholicism in Vermont had come of age with the appointment of Louis De Goesbriand (1816–99) as the First Bishop of Burlington. A native of Saint-Urbain, France, he had been the vicar general in the Diocese of Cleveland, Ohio, and began his new diocese with about 20,000 Catholics, ten churches, and five priests. Following De Goesbriand's installation, priests from Ireland and France were accepted into the diocese so that there were at least 50 priests by the end of his episcopate. These helped to expand his diocese with at least 30 new parishes as Catholics continued to come into the state to build its public works, construct its railroads, excavate its quarries, produce its farm lands, and operate its factories.

In 1890, the Catholic population numbered 45,000, of which at least 33,000 were of French-Canadian background. Some of the increase was due to conversions like those, before the Civil War, of the three daughters (Helen, Debbie, and Anna) of Bradley Barlow (1814–89), one of the most prominent citizens in St. Albans. Yet, the growth was due more to the foreign-speaking Catholics for whom De Goesbriand, not unlike other Catholic bishops, opened up more national parishes, in addition to St. Joseph's in Burlington, which dates back to 1850 and is today the oldest Franco-American parish in New England.

When Bishop De Goesbriand died on Nov. 23, 1899, he was the oldest American bishop and had participated in the councils of Baltimore and in the First Vatican Council. With his retirement in 1893 to the orphanage which the Sisters of Charity had opened in 1854, his diocese came under John Stephen Michaud (1843–1908). A native of Vermont and of Canadian and Irish ancestry, he reflected the ethnic composition of the majority of the Catholics population and became the first Catholic bishop to receive an honorary degree from the University Vermont.

The diocese had grown to almost a hundred parishes and missions under Michaud with an equal number of priests, diocesan and religious. In 1898, the Knights of Columbus founded their first council in the state with Bennington Council, No. 307, and, in 1899, Michaud welcomed into Vermont the Society of St. Edmund which opened St. Michael's College in Winooski in 1904. Of his achievements, the establishment of Fanny Allen Hospital at Winooski Park was important in showing the strength of Catholic social action in Vermont.

Beyond Native Americans, Canadian Americans, and Irish Americans, Catholicism grew because of those other immigrants who came into Vermont near the turn of the century. If they did not come to work on the railroads or on the farm lands, they were in the quarries and or the woolen mills of the state. The Italians, coming in the last decade of the 19th century were concentrated around Barre where carvers and stonecutters helped to increase the granite and marble industry while the Poles, coming at the start of the 20th century, settled around West Rutland. Here, for example, Polish immigrants, drawn to the quarries, started in November of 1904 the Church of St. Stanislaus Kostka under the leadership of Father Valentin Michulka (d. 1969), their pastor for more than a half century.

Joseph J. Rice (1871–1938), a native of Leicester, Massachusetts, was ordained as the Third Bishop of Burlington, on April 14, 1910. While caring for the diocese, he was responsible for De Goesbriand Memorial Hospital which Rice placed under the Religious Hospitalers of St. Joseph in 1923. Rice showed himself a leader in education by opening up three high schools and by welcoming the Sisters of Mercy who opened Trinity College in 1925. During those days, bigotry manifested itself in Montpelier when, on Nov. 21, 1925, the Ku Klux Klan burned a cross on the steps of St. Augustine's Church.

Rice's successor in 1938 was Matthew F. Brady (1893–1959), a native of Waterbury, Connecticut, who strengthened the substructure of the diocese in various ways. Very much interested in the young people, he organized branches of the Boy Scouts and the Catholic Youth. His tenure also saw the construction of about a dozen new churches, at least half in towns like Fairfax, Gilman, North Troy, Orleans, and South Burlington which never had such parishes.

With Bishop Brady's transfer to Manchester in 1944, Edward F. Ryan (1879–1956), a native of Lynn, Massachusetts, became Burlington's fifth Catholic bishop in 1945, having served as a chaplain in the Second World War. Noteworthy in his tenure was the establishment of the first Carthusian monastery in the United States in the area of Whitingham (later at Arlington) in 1951, of the

Benedictine Priory at Weston in 1953, and of the College of St. Joseph the Provider by the Sisters of St. Joseph in Rutland in 1954. Responsible for almost two dozen new churches, Ryan also raised the people's consciousness of the importance of the Catholic press, especially by giving the diocese its own weekly, the *Vermont Catholic Tribune* in 1956. And, he showed the Church's ongoing concern for the welfare of the youth by providing a camp and a school for boys in Burlington area. Ryan also established Blessed Sacrament Church in Stowe. A native son Joseph Dutton (1843–1931) who, having converted to Catholicism in 1883 after serving in the Civil War, spent the rest of his life as a Sacred Hearts Brother carrying on the work of Father Damien (1840–89), ''Apostle of Molokai.'' More famous, certainly, was Maria von Trapp (1905–87) whose life inspired, ''The Sound of Music'' in 1959, and who made Stowe a tourist attraction with the 800-acre farm which the Trapp Family purchased as music camp in 1942.

Renewal and Reaction to the Second Vatican Council. Robert F. Joyce (1896–1990), a native of Proctor, who succeeded Ryan in 1957, directed the renewal of the Catholic church in an era inaugurated by the Second Vatican Council in 1962. A model for him in handling the reforms was Bernard J. Flanagan (1908–98), also a native of Proctor, and the Second Bishop of Worcester (1959–83) in Massachusetts. In 1958, Bishop Joyce completed, Rice Memorial High School, begun by his predecessor and, in the next year, set up Our Lady of Fatima in Wilmington, a parish that serves the ski area of Mount Snow. By sponsoring the Papal Volunteers for Latin America and reorganizing services for teaching religion and for children with disabilities, the Catholic Church was reaching out under Joyce. Indicative of the maturity of Catholicism was the elevation of Walter H. Cleary of Newport as the state's Chief Justice in 1958.

John A. Marshall (1928–94), a native of Worcester, Massachusetts, was the state's seventh Catholic bishop, from 1971 to 1991, before he was transferred to Springfield, Massachusetts. Coming to grips with new problems that confronted bishops after the Second Vatican Council, the church was forced to undergo retrenchment with a loss of vocations and the decline in church attendance. Consequently, the only parish founded was that of Our Lady of the Mountains in Shelburne in 1979. Paradoxically, the public face of Catholicism became more evident during Marshall's tenure. Thomas P. Salmon as the first Catholic to be elected governor of Vermont in 1972 and, two years later, Patrick Leahy was the first Catholic elected a U.S. senator. But, this coming of age of Catholics was not without its problems as a more active laity dealt with moral issues, as in the concern raised by Catholics for a Free Choice, chartered in 1989, with their first

issue of a newsletter, *Pro Conscience,* published in Middlebury. On Nov. 9, 1992, Bishop Kenneth A. Angell (b. 1930), a native of Providence, Rhode Island, was installed as the Burlington's eighth bishop. Having served for almost 20 years as an auxiliary bishop in Providence, he was familiar with the workings of a diocese and encountered challenges not unlike other American bishops in the lack of priests and the decline of attendance. These forced a consolidation of parishes like Sacred Heart and St. Francis de Sales in Bennington as well as St. Cecilia and St. Frances Cabrini in Washington, and closed Our Lady of the Lake in St. Albans. In the case of St. Francis de Sales, which began in 1830 and had a Gothic church constructed from the stone of Vermont's native quarries dating to 1889, the change was not easy. While his problems concerning the relation of the political order to the moral order were no different than most of the bishops in New England, Bishop Angell was the first to cope with a civil unions law that took effect in his diocese in July of 2000 legitimizing same-sex marriages.

By the start of the third millennium, the Diocese of Burlington was serving about 150,000 Catholics out of total population of almost 600,000. It had almost 90 active priests, more than 40 permanent deacons, and 225 sisters covering almost 80 parishes. At the same time, the diocese included 15 elementary schools, two high schools, and three colleges, not to mention a catechetical system with at least 240 lay teachers instructing almost 20,000 students. Given its special centers for social services and homes for the aged, it was assisting almost 9,000 people. Thus, while it reflected a church caring for the needs of its members on the intellectual, pastoral, and social levels of existence, the Diocese of Vermont was also engaged in eliminating debts, raising funds, and slashing budgets as it tried to consolidate its parishes and schools and cope with its retired clergy and religious.

Bibliography: J. N. COUTURE, ''The Catholic Clergy of Vermont'' (Typewritten Manuscript; St. Michael's College, Winooski, 1964). V. A. LAPOMARDA, *The Jesuit Heritage in New England* (Worcester 1977). W. L. LUCEY, ''The Diocese of Burlington, Vermont,'' *Records of the American Catholic Historical Society of Philadelphia,* LXIV, No. 3 (September 1953) 123–54, and No. 4 (December 1953), 213–35. V. B. MALONEY and J. K. DURICK eds., *1853–1953: One Hundred Years of Achievement by the Catholic Church in the Diocese of Burlington, Vermont* (Burlington 1953). J. S. MICHAUD, ''The Diocese of Burlington,'' in W. BYRNE and others, *History of the Catholic Church in the New England States,* 2 v. (Boston 1899), II, pp. 465–587. M. NEILL, *Fiery Crosses in the Green Mountains* (Randolph Center 1989). F. X. TALBOT, *Saint among Savages* (New York 1935).

[V. A. LAPOMARDA]

VERONICA

The Greek name Βερνίκη, Βερονίκη, *Beronica,* given from antiquity to a woman, variously identified in legend with persons mentioned in the New Testament, who was associated with an image of the face of Christ that was said to have been brought to Rome. This name was later applied by metonymy to the image itself, which in medieval times was sometimes referred to as a veronica. This provided some plausibility for the suggestion of GIRALDUS CAMBRENSIS in his *Speculum ecclesiae* that the word was derived from *vera icon* (true image), which in popular use became veronica and was appropriated as the proper name of the woman whom legend connected with the image.

There is evidence that a cloth with the image of the face of Christ was venerated at St. Peter's in Rome as early as the end of the 10th or the beginning of the 11th century, and there was a great devotion to it during the Middle Ages. It is still preserved among the major relics at St. Peter's, although what was depicted upon it has faded away or become indiscernible, or at any rate cannot be inspected or studied. Indications of its style, gathered from copies made in earlier times, suggest that the image was of a kind that had its prototype in the μανδύλιον of Edessa, brought to Constantinople in 944.

Various stories to account for the origin of the picture have been told. One of the earliest is an account given in the *Mors Pilati,* according to which a matron called Veronica, who desired to have a picture of Jesus to comfort her when He was away preaching, was taking a linen cloth to a painter to have a picture put upon it, when she happened to meet Jesus. He, upon hearing what she wished, took the cloth from her and caused his features to appear upon it [see M. R. James, tr., *The Apocryphal New Testament* (Oxford 1926)]. In later versions the image was caused by direct impression upon the face of Christ. At one time it was popularly believed that this occurred during the bloody sweat in the Garden. In the 14th century the story of a compassionate woman wiping the face of Christ on His way to Calvary began to find favor. There is no evidence that this event was a part of a popular belief in earlier times, and it was not pictured in art, so far as is known, before the 14th century. The woman, of course, was identified with the Veronica of earlier legend. She was venerated in various places as a saint and in some localities Mass and the Office were celebrated in her honor. St. Charles Borromeo suppressed these liturgical honors accorded to her in the Ambrosian Rite at Milan. The name Veronica is to be found in none of the early martyrologies, nor does it appear in the present Roman Martyrology in connection with this legendary woman. Veronica was venerated also under a number of variants of the name—Berenice, Bernice, Venice, Venisse, Vernice, Veronce, Verone, etc.

Bibliography: There is a very extensive Veronica literature, a guide to which can be found in the following sources. A. DEGERT, *The Catholic Encyclopedia,* ed. C. G. HERBERMANN, 16 v. (New York 1907–14; suppl. 1922) 15:362–366. *Acta Sanctorum* (Paris 1863–), February 1:454–463. H. LECLERCQ, *Dictionnaire d'archéologie chrétienne et de liturgie,* ed. F. CABROL, H. LECLERCQ and H. I. MARROU, 15 v. (Paris 1907–53) 15.2:2962–66. A. BUTLER, *The Lives of the Saints,* ed. H. THURSTON and D. ATTWATER, 4 v. (New York 1956) 3:82–83. L. RÉAU, *Iconographie de l'art chrétien,* 6 v. (Paris 1955–59) 3.3:1314–17.

[P. K. MEAGHER]

VEROT, JEAN PIERRE AUGUSTIN MARCELLIN

Third bishop of Savannah, Georgia, first bishop of St. Augustine, Florida; b. LePuy, France, May 23, 1805; d. St. Augustine, June 10, 1876. After ordination on Sept. 20, 1828, Verot joined the Society of the Priests of St. Sulpice at Paris. In 1830 he was sent to the U.S., where he taught mathematics and science at St. Mary's College, Baltimore, Maryland. From 1852 to 1858 he did pastoral work at Ellicott's Mills, Clarksville, Sykesville, and Doughoregan Manor, all in Maryland.

Verot was consecrated titular bishop of Danaba and vicar apostolic of Florida on April 25, 1858. As a new bishop, he participated in the Ninth Provincial Council of Baltimore (1858) before setting out for his vicariate. On arrival he found only three priests, two churches, and seven mission chapels. A year later the Sisters of Mercy arrived from Hartford, Connecticut, and six priests, four Christian Brothers, and additional nuns came from Europe to the vicariate. On July 16, 1861, Verot became the third bishop of Savannah, but he continued to administer the vicariate apostolic of Florida.

The Civil War brought widespread destruction of churches and institutions in Verot's diocese and vicariate, from Chattanooga, Tennessee, to the Florida Keys. To obtain needed money and priests, he preached in the North and sent written appeals to Europe. A Southern sympathizer during the war, Verot's celebrated sermon of 1861, "A Tract for the Times: Slavery and Abolitionism," condemned the slave trade and suggested a code of rights and duties for slaves and masters, but sustained the property rights of slave owners. Nevertheless, he supplied priests to, and personally worked among, Union soldiers imprisoned at Andersonville, Georgia. In a pastoral letter of Aug. 1, 1866, he rejoiced over the extinction of slavery, invited African-Americans to share the benefits of Catholic education, and inaugurated a cam-

"Saint Veronica," right wing of a diptych by Hans Memling c. 1483. (©Francis G. Mayer/CORBIS)

paign to remove prejudice against African-Americans. In the same year, he brought Sisters of St. Joseph from Le Puy, France, to work among the African-Americans of Florida and Georgia.

In addition to his numerous pastoral letters, Verot wrote articles in the *Pacificator,* edited by Leopold T. Blome and Patrick Walsh at Augusta, Georgia; a catechism of Christian doctrine, published in 1864; and frequent letters to the Lyons Society for the Propagation of the Faith, including the official letter for the Second Plenary Council of Baltimore in 1866. At Vatican Council I, he took an active part in the discussions, becoming known as *l'enfant terrible* of the gathering. He opposed the definition of papal infallibility, asked for a condemnation of the theory that people of color have no souls, and sought corrections in the Breviary. With 54 others, he absented himself from the final public vote on papal infallibility rather than vote *non placet.* However, he accepted the decision of the council without hesitation. In March 1870, Verot became the first bishop of St. Augustine, Florida, relinquishing his Savannah jurisdiction. He continued his efforts for African-Americans, the Seminole, and the progress of the Church until his death following a stroke.

Bibliography: L. BERTRAND, *Bibliothèque sulpicienne,* 3 v. (Paris 1900) v.2. C. G. HERBERMANN, *The Sulpicians in the United States* (New York 1916). M. V. GANNON, *Rebel Bishop: The Life and Era of Augustin Verot* (Milwaukee 1964).

[V. DE P. MCMURRY]

Jean Pierre Augustin Marcellin Verot.

VERSIGLIA, LUIGI, ST.

Also known as Aloysius of John Bosco, missionary bishop, Salesian protomartyr; b. June 5, 1873, Oliva Gessi (near Pavia), Italy; d. Feb. 25, 1930, Lin-Chow Tsieu, southern China. Versiglia studied at the oratory of St. John Bosco in Valdocco (1885–89), before joining the Salesians at age 16. He earned a doctorate in philosophy from the Gregorian University (1893), received presbyteral ordination in 1895 (with a dispensation because he was only 22), then served as the rector and the demanding, but idolized, novice master at the Genzano, Rome (1896 to 1905). On Jan. 7, 1906, he arrived in Macao as head of the first Salesian mission to the Far East. In the Portuguese colony he founded an orphanage, which later became the Salesian motherhouse in the Orient. After his consecration (Jan. 9, 1921) in Canton cathedral as vicar apostolic, he took up his work in Shiu Chow. All his many skills were engaged to found schools, a seminary, two leper colonies, and medical facilities; he served as printer, catechist, sacristan, gardener, builder, painter, and barber, in addition to his priestly duties. The turmoil following the 1902 overthrow of the last emperor permitted armed bands and pirates to roam the countryside. In 1930, the river boat on which Bishop Versiglia, Fr. Caravario, and four young teachers traveled to the Lin-Chow mission was ambushed. The bishop successfully intervened to save the female teachers. He pleaded for Caravario's life to be spared, but both bishop and priest were shot to death. Versiglia's body was enshrined at the cathedral of Lin Kong-How, which was vandalized by the Red Guards during the Cultural Revolution. John Paul II beatified (May 15, 1983) and canonized (Oct. 1, 2000) Bishop Versiglia.

Feast: Nov. 13 (Salesians).

Bibliography: *Acta Apostolicae Sedis* 78 (1986): 137–39. *L'Osservatore Romano,* English edition, no. 21 (1983): 1. G. BOSIO, *Monsignor Versiglia e Don Caravario* (Turin 1935); *Martiri in China* (Turin 1977). B. LARENO, *Assassinio di Mons. Luigi Versiglia e di Don Callisto Caravario* (Hong Kong 1933). T. LEWICKI, *"Ten kielich mam wypelniać krwią": opowiesc o pierwszych meczennikach salezjanskich* (Warsaw 1985). A. J. ORTAS, "Protomartiri Salesiani in missione," *Martirio e spiritualità apostolica* 12 (1983) 17–65. M. RASSIGA, *Blood on the River Bank,* tr. J. CARPELLA (Hong Kong 1980).

[K. I. RABENSTEIN]

VERSTEGAN, RICHARD (ROWLANDS)

Author, publisher, engraver, and agent for Catholic exiles; b. London, *c.* 1550; d. Antwerp, 1640. His father, John, of a Dutch immigrant family, was a cooper. Under the surname Rowland, a family Christian name, Richard entered Christ Church, Oxford, as a sizar in 1565, but since he was a Catholic he could not take a degree. About 1570 he returned to London, became a goldsmith, and acquired great skill as an engraver. He also gained experience at printing and was responsible for publishing a book on E. CAMPION'S MARTYRDOM in 1582. When this press was discovered, he had to flee to France. In Paris he continued as a Catholic publisher and engraver and he was arrested in 1583 at the instigation of the English ambassador, for publishing an illustrated account of the persecution in England; however Cardinal William ALLEN quickly secured his release. After visiting Rome and Paris he settled in Antwerp in 1587. For the next 20 or 30 years he was an important link of communication between leading Catholics at home and abroad, especially Allen, R. PERSONS, and H. GARNET, and he was the chief publisher and distributor of recusant books printed at Antwerp. For this service he was made a Spanish pensioner and obtained a license to import English cloth. In later years he was absorbed into the Dutch way of life, particularly after his second marriage, to Catharina de Sauchy, which took place in 1610.

His works, more than 30 in number and in four languages, include polemic tracts, epigrams, emblem verse, and many other forms. The controversial works include the martyrology, *Theatrum crudelitatum* (1587), two replies to the proclamation of November 1591, and part authorship of *A Conference about the Next Succession* (1595). Most successful among his devotional works are the *Primer or Office of the Blessed Virgin Marie* (1599)—the first in English and Latin—and the collection of sacred verse, *Odes* (1601). His outstanding nonreligious work is the scholarly *Restitution of Decayed Intelligence in Antiquities* (1605).

Bibliography: R. VERSTEGAN, "Letters and Despatches," ed. A. G. PETTI, *Publications of the Catholic Record Society* 52 (1959). E. ROMBAUTS, *Richard Verstegen, een Polemist der Contra-Reformatie* (Brussels 1933). A. G. PETTI, "A Bibliography of the Writings of Richard Verstegan," *Recusant History* 7 (1963) 82–103. *A Literary and Biographical History or Bibliographical Dictionary of the English Catholics from 1534 to the Present Time* 5:566–568.

[A. G. PETTI]

VERTIN, JOHN

Third bishop of Marquette, MI; b. Dobliče, Carniola, Austria, July 17, 1844; d. Marquette, Feb. 26, 1899. His family immigrated to Houghton, Michigan (1863), where his father established a business. Accepted by Bp. F. Baraga as a student for the diocese, Vettin continued his education first with the great missionary John Čebul and later at St. Francis Seminary, Milwaukee, Wisconsin. He was ordained Aug. 31, 1866, and successfully fulfilled pastorates at Houghton and Negaunee, Michigan, before his consecration Sept. 14, 1879. As a careful but liberal administrator, Vertin kept pace with the expanding needs of the Church in the Upper Peninsula during the great ore and lumber booms. He gave his own family wealth to aid this expansion and was especially generous in financing the construction of the second Cathedral of St. Peter at Marquette. Vertin convoked the diocese's first synod (1899) to implement the decrees of the Third Plenary Council of Baltimore. By determined effort, he was generally successful in avoiding the nationalist controversies that disturbed the American Church in his era. During the two decades of his administration, three Catholic high schools and four hospitals were established in the diocese, where the Catholic population increased to 65,000; the number of priests, to 52; and churches, to 58.

Bibliography: Archives, Diocese of Marquette, *Vertin Papers.* A. I. REZEK, *History of the Diocese of Sault Ste. Marie and Marquette,* 2 v. (Houghton, MI 1906–07).

[C. J. CARMODY]

VERUELA, ABBEY OF

Cistercian monastery in Saragossa province, Spain. It was suppressed in 1835, but since 1877 Jesuits have restored many of the buildings. Pedro de Atarés, who is buried in the church, in 1146 gave French monks from Scala Dei the site and surrounding land in return for perpetual prayers. The Romanesque church, consecrated in 1248, resembles CLAIRVAUX in having a main altar and five chapels, ambulatory, three naves, and transept. Abbots and the Dukes of Villahermosa are buried there. The late 13th-century Gothic cloister is decorated with designs of leaves, serpents, lions, and other animals, real and imaginary. The first 20 abbots are buried in the large severe chapter hall, noted for its Romanesque doorway. The monk A. J. Rodríguez (d. 1777), an advocate of the experimental method in the sciences, wrote treatises on respiration and hypodermics and a *Palestra críticomédica.*

Bibliography: J. M. LÓPEZ LANDA, *Estudio arquitectónico del monasterio de Veruela* (Lérida 1918). J. PÉREZ DE URBEL, *Las*

The Monastery of Veruela, founded in the 12th century, Tarazona, Spain. (©Manuel Bellver/CORBIS)

grandes abadías benedictinas (Madrid 1928). R. DEL ARCO, *El monasterio de Santa María de Veruela* (Zaragoza 1923). *Enciclopedia universal illustrada Europeo-Americana,* 70 v. (Barcelona 1908–30; suppl. 1934–) 68:145–156.

[J. PÉREZ DE URBEL]

VERWYST, CHRYSOSTOM ADRIAN

Franciscan missionary, linguist, historiographer; b. Uden, Netherlands, Nov. 23, 1841; d. Bayfield, WI, June 23, 1925. He went to the U.S. with his family in 1848 at the urging of Theodore Van den Broek, OP, a fellow countryman and a missionary. Lack of funds detained the family in New England until 1855, when the Verwysts joined the other Dutch who had settled near Lake Winnebago in Wisconsin. Verwyst studied at St. Francis Seminary, Milwaukee. Following his ordination on Nov. 5, 1865, he held pastorates at New London, Hudson, and Seneca, WI, and worked among the native peoples and whites on the southern shore of Lake Superior. After four years of itinerant preaching he joined the Franciscans at Teutopolis, Ill., and was assigned to Bayfield. Except for three years spent in Missouri and California for his health, he worked along Chequamegon Bay on Lake Superior until his death.

Verwyst acquired such proficiency in the Chippewa language that he issued a monthly magazine in it. He published *Chippewa Exercises: Being a Practical Introduction into the Study of the Chippewa Language* (Harbor Springs, MI 1901), and he spent seven more years compiling an (unpublished) native-language dictionary. Growing interested in the Jesuit missionaries who had been at Chequamegon Bay around 1640, he sought out Rev. Edward Jacker, who had excavated Marquette's grave at St. Ignace in 1877. Before long Verwyst published *Missionary Labors of Fathers Marquette, Menard, and Allouez in the Lake Superior Region* (Milwaukee 1886). After that he gathered material for another monograph, *Life and Labors of Rt. Rev. Frederic Baraga* (Milwaukee 1900). His "Reminiscences," published in the Wisconsin Historical Society's *Proceedings,* provide source material for the history of Wisconsin and of the Dutch in the New World.

Bibliography: B. J. BLIED, "The Rev. Chrysostom Verwyst, Early Alumnus and Historiographer," *Salesianum* 54 (July 1959) 91–99.

[B. J. BLIED]

VERZERI, TERESA EUSTOCHIO, ST.

The foundress of the Daughters of the SACRED HEART (Bergamo); b. Bergamo, Italy, July 31, 1801; d. Brescia, March 3, 1852. Her family was noble and very religious—her mother and three of her sisters joined her congregation; her brother Gerolamo became bishop of Brescia. Even as an adolescent Teresa aspired to the cloister. It was a much-disturbed period when new ideas were profoundly transforming the popular outlook. Democratic aspirations opened the door to a spirit of laicism, which often led to open Church and State conflicts. In this disorientation of values Teresa preserved complete devotion to the pope, and matured her vocation as educator. After entering the Benedictine convent of St. Grata on three different occasions, and then leaving it upon the advice of her spiritual director, Canon Giuseppe Benaglio, she founded in 1831, together with him, her own congregation. She was noted for her ability at governing and writing, and still more for her vigorous spirituality, strong faith, and balance between contemplation and action. As an educator she showed originality, particularly in her preventive method. She was beatified on Oct. 27, 1946 and canonized on June 10, 2001.

Feast: March 3.

Bibliography: Works. *Lettere,* 7 v. (Brescia 1874–78); *Libro dei doveri,* 3 v. (5th ed. Bergamo 1952). Literature. G. ARCANGELI, *Vita di Teresa Verzeri* (2d ed. Bergamo 1896). E. VALENTINI, *Il sistema preventivo della Beata Verzeri* (Turin 1952). D. T. DONADONI, *Teresa Verzeri* (Turin 1964).

[D. DONADONI]

VESPERS

The Church's evening prayer, one of the two main hours of the daily Office. The Latin word *vesper,* from which it takes its name, means evening and by transference evening star and evening meal. It was only natural then to use it also of evening prayer. *Lucernarium* (literally: lamp, lamplighting time) was another early name for Vespers. When the light of day faded, lamps were lighted. The Jews had a blessing prayer for this, and Christians continued the custom. Thus the *lucernarium,* a preliminary rite, lent its name to the prayer service that followed.

Vespers was also called the evening sacrifice, a counterpart of the sacrifice of incense offered every evening in the Temple at Jerusalem and alluded to in Ps 140.2: "Let my prayer come like incense before you; the lifting up of my hands, like the evening sacrifice." This Psalm became the favorite Vesper Psalm, in some places the only Psalm, and prompted the use of incense, at first

during its recitation and later during the MAGNIFICAT. The Fathers of the Church regarded burning and sweet-smelling incense as a symbol of the sacrifice of Christ on Calvary. They read the Psalm as a prayer of the crucified Lord who stretched out His arms on the cross and celebrated the first Vespers of the New Covenant at the hour of the evening sacrifice. Hence the Church made Vespers her evening sacrifice of praise and thanksgiving, commemorating Calvary and the Last Supper and offering thanks for all the benefits of creation and Redemption.

History. Scholars agree that by the end of the 4th century there did exist a public prayer of the Church in the sense in which we understand it today. This liturgical Office was the outcome of a long development going back to apostolic times. The Jews had a daily evening sacrifice, and in the last centuries before Christ they had a corresponding prayer service in their synagogues. The Essenes of Qumran prayed regularly at evening. It is practically certain, therefore, that the Jews had a long-standing tradition of prayer at this hour, whether public or private. Most scholars believe that the testimony to customary prayer three times a day in the late text, Dn 6.10 is to morning, noon, and evening prayer as specified in Ps 54.18, Enoch 26.1–3, and the Qumran *Manual of Discipline* (1QS 10.1–3, 9–11). The 1st-century Didache in its exhortation to pray the Our Father three times a day could well have been a Christianizing of this usage (8; *Ancient Christian Writers,* ed. J. Quasten et al., 6:19).

The 3d century provides the first clear and extensive evidence of a Christian evening prayer. Tertullian asserted that morning and evening prayer were prescribed, obligatory prayers (*De oratione* 25; *Corpus scriptorum ecclesiasticorum latinorum,* 20:198). Fifteen years or so later, the *Apostolic Tradition* described a common evening service that consisted of a *lucernarium,* psalmody, and an agape [25, 26; M. Bouquet, *Recueil des historiens des Gaules et de la France (Rerum gallicarum et francicarum scriptores)* 64–66]. The Alleluia Psalms it mentions are still among the group of Psalms reserved for Vespers.

The work of converting these primitive evening prayers into the set form of today's Vespers was done mainly in the 4th, 5th, and 6th centuries. Cathedral churches and monastic communities were chiefly responsible. The Office described in the Rule of St. Benedict (ch. 8–18) was basically the Roman Office of the 6th century. It shows that Vespers had then reached its present shape in all essentials.

Subsequent reforms of the Roman Office have affected Vespers but slightly. When the Breviary came into

Bishop and priests celebrating Pontifical Vespers. (©Dean Conger/CORBIS)

use in the 12th and 13th centuries, Vespers went untouched. In Trent's reform, only an introductory *Pater* and *Ave* were prescribed and the *Preces* limited to certain days. Pius X in 1911 ordered a new arrangement of the weekly Psalter. Vespers was the hour least affected. The reforms of 1955 and 1960 dropped the introductory *Pater* and *Ave,* limited First Vespers (Vespers of the previous evening) to Sundays and first class feasts, and radically reduced the practice of commemoration.

Content. In the revised Liturgy of the Hours (1972), Vespers begins with an introductory versicle and response, followed by a hymn, two psalms and one New Testament canticle, the *capitulum* (a short reading from Scripture), the Magnificat with its antiphon, the *Preces* or intercessory prayers, the Lord's Prayer, the closing prayer and concluding versicle. Hymns were introduced as early as the 4th century but not adopted by the Roman Office until the 12th. They either stress the festal theme or elaborate on a theme appropriate to the hour. Tradi-

tionally, the Psalms used at Vespers are those from 109 (a very fitting proclamation of Christ's triumph) to 144. The antiphons that accompany the Psalms are ordinarily taken from the Psalms themselves. Major feasts have proper antiphons to elaborate the festal theme. The *capitulum* was once of some length, but since the 6th century at least it has been very short. The Magnificat is the climax of the hour. In Mary's sublime words the Church loves to express her own thanks for the mighty and merciful works of God.

Bibliography: P. F. BRADSHAW, *Daily Prayer in the Early Church: A Study of the Origin and Early Development of the Divine Office* (London 1981). G. GUIVER, *Company of Voices: Daily Prayer and the People of God* (New York 1988). R. TAFT, *The Liturgy of the Hours in East and West: The Origins of the Divine Office and Its Meaning for Today* 2nd rev. ed. (Collegeville, Minn. 1993).

[G. E. SCHIDEL/EDS.]

Vestal virgin, fragment of a Roman statue, 1st century A.D., *in the Museo Nazionale, Rome.* (Alinari-Art Reference/Art Resource, NY)

VESTAL VIRGINS

The college of priestesses who were in charge of the worship of Vesta, the *numen* or power inherent in the fire of the hearth, one of the oldest, most famous, and most elevated of ancient cults. The vestals were the representatives of the girls, not yet old enough to work in the fields, who in primitive agricultural villages were charged with keeping fires alight. The sacred fire which they kept continually burning in the temple of Vesta symbolized the unbroken continuation of the life of the state. If the fire should become extinguished, they were required to relight it, not by flint and steel, but by the primitive method of the fire drill. The round temple of Vesta with its pointed roof recalled its primitive origin, and it contained no statue. Vesta more than any other Roman divinity reflected the early Roman concept of *numen.*

The vestals formed a college of six priestesses under the direction of the senior member, the *Vestalis maxima,* and lived in a house adjoining the temple of Vesta and near the *Regia,* the house of the *Pontifex Maximus,* the head of the state religion. They were selected, at the age of six to ten, by the *Pontifex Maximus* from families of noble condition. Both parents of each had to be living at the time and each girl had to be without physical blemish.

On being appointed, they were no longer under the tutelage of their parents, but came under the supervision of the *Pontifex Maximus.* They took a vow of chastity for 30 years. The first ten years were spent in learning their duties, the next ten in performing them, and the last ten in teaching the new members. They wore a sacred dress, with much symbolism attached to it, that otherwise was worn only by Roman brides. At the end of 30 years a vestal was free to leave the college and marry, but few did so. Vestals guilty of negligence in their duties were flogged by the *Pontifex Maximus.* The vestal who broke her vow of chastity was cursed and buried alive.

In addition to attending the sacred fire of Vesta, the vestals had charge of the *penus* or special storeroom containing sacred objects of direct concern to the welfare of the state. The precise nature of these objects was never revealed. The vestals celebrated the feast of Vesta, the *Vestalia,* on June 7 to 15, and participated in a number of other religious feasts, as the *Feralia* on February 13, the *Lupercalia* on February 15, the *Parilia* on April 21, and the *Consualia* and *Opalia* on August 21 and 25, respectively. Special seats were assigned to them at various functions at which they were permitted to be present, and they enjoyed universal public reverence and esteem. Their prayers were always regarded as being especially efficacious. Over a period of more than 1,000 years, the number of vestals accused of breaking the vow of chastity was very small. Following the defeat of the pagan usurper, Eugenius, the Emperor Theodosius suppressed the cult of Vesta, along with other pagan cults, in A.D. 394.

Bibliography: H. J. ROSE, *The Oxford Classical Dictionary,* ed. M. CARY et al. (Oxford 1949) 943–944. J. A. HILD, C. DAREMBERG and E. SAGLIO, *Dictionnaire des antiquités grecques et romaines d'après les textes et les monuments,* 5 v. in 9 (Graz 1962–63) 5:742–760. C. KOCH, *Paulys Realenzyklopädie der klassischen Altertumswissenschaft,* ed. G. WISSOWA, et al. (Stuttgart 1893–) 7A. 1:1717–76. G. WISSOWA, W. H. ROSCHER, ed., *Ausfürliches Lexikon der griechischen und römischen Mythologie* (Leipzig 1884–1937) 6:241–273.

[M. R. P. MCGUIRE]

VETANCURT, AGUSTÍN DE

Franciscan chronicler; b. Mexico City, 1620; d. there, 1700. While Fray Agustín spelled his name Vetancurt, it has been spelled in various ways as Vetancourt, Bethencourt, Betancourt, Betancurt. Very little is known about his life; nevertheless, he is well known through his writings, which are basic documents for students of the history of Mexico and the history of the Franciscan Order. While still very young, he joined the Franciscans and he was ordained in Puebla de los Angeles; the reason and date of his moving to that city are unknown. Later, for 40 years he held the office of pastor in the native parish of San José in Mexico City. He was a teacher of philosophy and theology, and also of Nahuatl, important at that time for communicating with the natives. He was appointed by the commissary general of the Indies as the chronicler of the province of the Holy Evangelist. As such, he wrote his monumental work, *Teatro mexicano,* which is divided into four parts. The first is a summary of the natural history of Mexico. The second deals with political and religious events in pre-Hispanic Mexico. The third covers the period from the discovery of America to the capture of Tenochtitlán by Cortés. The fourth part, published before the others, can be considered a separate work, owing to its theme and its length. It is called *Crónica de la Provincia del Santo Evangelio de México;* it contains the *Menelogio franciscano.* He produced many other writings in a clear pleasant style; unfortunately he usually failed to cite his sources.

Bibliography: J. M. BERISTAIN DE SOUZA, *Biblioteca hispano americana septentrional,* 5 v. in 2 (3d ed. Mexico City 1947). R. RICARD, *La conquista espiritual de México* (Mexico City 1947).

[A. M. BETANCOURT]

VEUILLOT, LOUIS FRANÇOIS

French Catholic journalist and writer; b. Boynes (Loiret), Oct. 11, 1813; d. Paris, Apr. 7, 1883. Son of a cooper, he received little formal education but succeeded by educating himself and acquiring a broad cultural knowledge. At age 13 he was a lawyer's clerk; at age 17 he became a journalist, wrote for *L'Écho de Rouen,* later for *Mémorial de la Dordogne,* and began to manifest his polemical talents. In Paris he contributed to *La Charte de 1830, La Paix,* and *Moniteur parisien.* In 1839 during a visit to Rome, he returned to practicing Catholicism, and later he retraced his spiritual odyssey in two works: *Pèlerinages en Suisse* (1839) and *Rome et Lorette* (1841). Thereafter he dedicated himself to defending ULTRAMONTANISM, even to extremes, in journalism. He began to contribute to *L'Univers* in 1840, and he became its chief editor in 1843. This newspaper, founded in 1833 by Abbé Migne, was then stagnating. Veuillot soon made it the leading French Catholic organ. He battled mainly to win freedom for Catholic education. So ardent were his polemics that he became involved in lawsuits, and he was even sent to prison. Catholics sometimes disliked his anti-liberal positions and his aggressiveness. On at least three occasions within seven years, RAVIGNAN, MONTALEMBERT, and DUPANLOUP tried in vain to found another newspaper to avoid identifying the Catholic cause with the spirit of *L'Univers.*

Veuillot accepted the Second French Republic (1848–52) in the hope that it would serve his ideal better

than had the July Monarchy (1830–48); but he did not adhere to the new regime as completely as did *L'Ère nouvelle,* inspired by LACORDAIRE, and he soon developed fears about the government's tendencies. His thought during this period was revealed in two works: *Les libres penseurs* (1848) and *Dialogues socialistes* (1848–52). He combatted the Falloux law (1850), which accorded freedom of teaching, because it seemed to him insufficient. It required the advice of Pope Pius IX to change his view.

After 1850 Catholics in France divided into two opposing groups. The "Romans" or ultramontanes were intransigent on doctrines and on total submission to papal directives, and looked especially to Bishop Pie of Poitiers for leadership. Veuillot supported them in *L'Univers.* He became a kind of director of conscience for an important segment of the French clergy, particularly the country priests. In the other camp were the Catholic liberals, more or less addicted to GALLICANISM, more reticent in regard to Rome, and desirous above all of having Catholic teachings accepted by contemporaries. Their leaders were Bishop Dupanloup of Orléans and Montalembert; their organ was *Le Correspondant.* Lively polemics engaged the two groups concerning such matters as the study of the pagan classics in schools, the *coup d'état* (1851), and the proclamation of the Second Empire (1852), which Veuillot supported with all his strength. So violent was his criticism of the bishop of Orléans that the latter induced the archbishop of Paris to suppress *L'Univers;* but Pius IX, who had complete confidence in Veuillot, intervened, and the journal reappeared. Veuillot did not turn against NAPOLEON III until the emperor's Italian policy favored the unification of Italy and menaced the STATES OF THE CHURCH. In 1860 Napoleon III suppressed *L'Univers,* which did not reappear until 1867.

Veuillot then collected his articles written between 1842 and 1860 in two series of *Mélanges* (1860–62), each in six volumes. On the ROMAN QUESTION he wrote: *Le Pape et la diplomatie* (1861) and *Le Guêpier italien* (1865); and on the Catholic liberals he wrote: *L'Illusion libérale* (1866), which was especially critical of Montalembert's speech at the Catholic congress in Mechelen (1863). In addition he wrote literary criticisms against Voltaire, Victor Hugo, and Émile Augier, among others. His mordant irony against adversaries appeared in other writings of this period, such as *Çà et Là* (2 v. 1859) and in two productions in verse, *Satires* (1863) and *Les Couleuvres* (1869). As a reply to the life of Christ by RENAN, he composed *Vie de Notre Seigneur Jésus-Christ* (1864). *Le Parfum de Rome* (1861) attested his loyalty to the Holy See, while *Les Odeurs de Paris* (1866) revived his battle against irreligion.

L'Univers was allowed back in print in 1867. Numerous articles, printed therein by Veuillot, were gathered in a third series of *Mélanges* (3 v. 1876). *Derniers Mélanges,* grouping later articles (1873–77), was published in four volumes by François Veuillot, a nephew, in 1908; they dwelt especially on VATICAN COUNCIL I, during whose sessions Veuillot resided in Rome, and combatted vigorously those opposed to the definition of papal infallibility. The same topic preoccupied Veuillot in *Rome pendant le Concile* (2 v. 1872). Meanwhile the Franco-Prussian War and the Commune gave him the opportunity to bolster French courage and hope through his articles. *Paris pendant les deux sièges* (1871) united his recent recollections and appeals. His pen then took up the Roman question, the pope's status after losing his temporal power, the construction of the basilica of *Sacré-Coeur* in Paris, and the struggle for Catholic liberty in higher education. He fell ill in 1877 and wrote no further articles for *L'Univers,* save for a final article in 1880 on Cardinal Pie, who had recently died.

Veuillot also wrote novels, such as *Pierre Saintive* (1840), *Agnès de Lauvens* (1845), *L'Honnête femme* (1844), and *Corbin et d'Aubecourt* (1850). His historical and biographical works include *Étude sur saint Vincent de Paul* (1854), *Vie de la bienheureuse Germaine Cousin, bergère* (1854), and *De quelques erreurs sur la papauté* (1859). *Molière et Bourdaloue* (1878) and *Oeuvres poétiques* (1878) belong among his literary productions. Many other writings, including 12 volumes of correspondence, appear in his collected works: *Oeuvres complètes de Louis Veuillot* (40 v. 1924–40).

Impelled by strong faith and ardent love for the Church and the pope, Veuillot vigorously faced the attacks of unbelievers and sustained Catholics in defense of their rights. His belligerence and satiric verve won him considerable influence, much less among the laity than the clergy, especially the lower clergy in rural districts. It was unfortunate, however, that his writings so often contained excessive, violent expressions that went beyond the limits of truth or offended against charity. Eager for the fray, he was not always sufficiently careful in making the necessary preparations, but his sincerity was beyond question. In several genres he merited renown as a true writer.

Bibliography: E. and F. VEUILLOT, *Louis Veuillot,* 4 v. (Paris 1899–1913), apologetic. E. TAVERNIER, *Louis Veuillot, l'homme, le lutteur, l'écrivain* (Paris 1913). P. FERNESSOLE, *Bio-bibliographie de la jeunesse de Louis Veuillot (1813–1843)* (Paris 1923). M. M. MACDEVITT, *Louis Veuillot d'après sa correspondance* (Paris 1935). F. VEUILLOT, *Louis Veuillot, sa vie, son âme, son oeuvre* (Paris 1937). E. GAUTHIER, *Le vrai Louis Veuillot* (Paris 1938); *Le Génie satirique de Louis Veuillot* (Lyon 1953). W. GURIAN, in *American Catholic Historical Review* 36 (1951): 385–414. P. H. SPENCER, *Politics of Belief in Nineteenth-Century France* (London 1954). A. DANSETTE, *Religious History of Modern France,* tr. J. DINGLE, 2 v. (New York 1961). J. MORIENVAL, *Louis Veuillot* (Paris 1941). É AMANN, *Dictionnaire de theologie catholique,* 15 v. (Paris 1903–50) 15.2:2799–2835.

[R. LIMOUZIN-LAMOTHE]

VEUSTER, JOSEPH DE (FR. DAMIEN), BL.

Picpus (SS.CC.) priest, missionary to lepers; b. Jan. 3, 1840, Tremeloo, Belgium; d. April 15, 1889, Molokai, Hawaii, USA.

Joseph, one of many children of prosperous farmers, was sent to college at Braine-le-Comte, to prepare for a commercial career, but he decided to follow his eldest brother, Auguste (later Fr. Pamphile), into the Congregation of the Sacred Hearts of Jesus and Mary (Picpus Fathers) at Louvain. He was professed on Oct. 7, 1860, taking the name Damien. When Fr. Pamphile was unable to sail for the missions, Damien received permission to go in his place. He arrived in Honolulu, Hawaii, on March 19, 1864, and was ordained May 21 in Our Lady of Peace Cathedral.

Damien served for eight years as a missionary on the island of Hawaii at Puna and Kohala. In 1873, when the vicar apostolic, Louis Maigret, decided to supply a priest for Kalaupapa, the Molokai leper settlement, Damien volunteered. On May 10, 1873, he went to Molokai and was subsequently given permission to remain there permanently. The colony's 800 lepers had only the clothing and food rations supplied by the government. Officially, Damien was the pastor of the Catholics in the colony, but actually he served as the lepers' physician, counselor, teacher, house-builder, sheriff, maker of musical instruments, gravedigger, and undertaker in order to transform their prison into a home. For ten of his 16 years with the lepers, he was without the companionship of other priests. He founded two orphanages at the leprosarium, and effectively fought the immorality, drunkenness, and lawlessness that he found among the adult lepers when he came. Most importantly he instilled in his flock a sense of their human dignity; he taught them to live rather than simply await death.

By 1884, when he had contracted leprosy (Hansen's disease), he wrote that he would not wish to he cured if the price of his cure involved leaving the island and giving up his work. He continued that work untiringly until the month before his death. He was buried next to the church he built, St. Philomena. In 1936 his relics were translated to Louvain, Belgium, where they were placed in a crypt of his congregation's church.

John Paul II beatified Fr. Damien on the Sacred Heart Basilica esplanade in the Koekelberg neighbor-

The grave of Father Damien on Molokai, Hawaii. Although Father Damien's remains were translated to Louvain, Belgium in 1936, his right hand was returned for reburial in the original plot on Molokai in 1995. (©Michael T. Sedam/CORBIS)

hood of Brussels, Belgium, Pentecost Sunday, June 4, 1995. After the beatification ceremony, Fr. Damien's right hand was returned to the Hawaiian people, who placed it in his original grave at Kalaupapa, Molokai. In 1965, his sacrifices were honored with the placement of a bronze statue of Damien in Statuary Hall in the U.S. Capitol to represent Hawaii. Less than two months after his death, a ''leprosy fund'' was established in London, the first such organized effort devoted to helping the victims of this disease.

Before and after his death, derogatory rumors circulated regarding Damien's morals, primarily because some held the mistaken notion that Hansen's disease was sexually transmitted. He was completely exonerated by a thorough investigation made shortly after he died. During his last years he also suffered from the misunderstanding of his superior and some fellow priests because of his fund raising efforts and invitation to a secular priest to join him. One attack upon Damien's reputation by a Protestant clergyman was answered by R. L. Stevenson in his *Open Letter to Dr. Hyde* (Boston 1900). He is the patron of lepers and those with incurable diseases, particularly AIDS.

Feast: April 15.

Bibliography: *Acta Apostolicae Sedis* (1995) 633–644. Archives, Hawaii Catholic Mission. P. BRADLEY, *Father Damien, SS.CC., Missionary* (Rome 1990). E. BRION, *Comme un arbre au bord des eaux. Le Pére Damien, apôtre des lépreux* (Paris 1994); *Un étrange bonheur. Lettres du Père Damien lépreux* (Paris 1988). M. R. BUNSON, *Father Damien: The Man and His Era* (Huntington, Ind. 1989). G. DAWS, *Holy Man. Father Damien of Molokai* (Honolulu 1984). H. EYNIKEL, *Het zieke paradijs. De biografie van Damiaan* (Antwerp 1994); *Molokai: The story of Father Damien*, tr. L. GILBERT (New York 1999). J. FARROW, *Damien the Leper* (New York 1999). J. GUNTZELMAN, *A retreat with Mother Teresa and Damien of Molokai* (Cincinnati, Ohio 1999). V. JOURDAN, *The Heart of Father Damien* tr. F. LARKIN and C. DAVENPORT, rev. ed. (New York 1960). *L'Osservatore Romano*, English edition, no. 23 (1995). L. DE REYES, *Damien De Veuster SSCC, un homme aux relations théologales* (Montréal 1989). R. STEWART, *Leper Priest of Molokai* (Honolulu 2000). D. THOMAS, *Crusaders for God* (New York 1952), 22–50. R. YZENDOORN, *History of the Catholic Mission in the Hawaiian Islands* (Honolulu 1927).

[R. E. CARSON]

VEXILLA REGIS PRODEUNT

A Latin hymn by Venantius FORTUNATUS (d. *c.* 610) celebrating the mystery of Christ triumphant on the cross. The original hymn consisted of eight stanzas, the first

Father Damien.

Monthly 38 (1935) 152–166. J. SZÖVÉRFFY, *Die Annalen der lateinischen Hymnendichtung* (Berlin 1964–65) 1:135–137.

[M. I. J. ROUSSEAU]

VEZZOSI, ANTONIO FRANCESCO

Theatine historian and theologian; b. Florence, Oct. 4, 1708; d. Rome, May 29, 1783. He joined the Theatine Order on Dec. 6, 1732, after graduating from the University of Florence. From 1736 to 1750 he held a professor's chair at the Rimini Seminary and the Theatine houses of studies in Bergamo and Rome. In 1751 Benedict XIV made him professor of Church history at the Sapienza and in 1756 named him bisbop's examiner. In this capacity he served on a panel that examined St. Alphonsus Liguori on June 11, 1762. During his two terms as general of the Theatines (1756–59 and 1774–77) he enriched the library of St. Sylvester at the Quirinale. The chronicles of the order relate that Clement XIII intended to make Vezzosi a cardinal but the machinations of the Pope's nephew blocked the appointment. On the night before his nomination, Vezzosi's name was withdrawn in favor of Lorenzo Ganganelli. The reversal did not disturb his equanimity. He published in critical edition the *Opera Omnia* of the Roman liturgist Cardinal Bl. Giuseppe TOMMASI (Rome 1749–69). For this work he received great praise, as he did also for his two-volume work *I Scrittori dei chierici regolari detti teatini* (Rome 1780).

Bibliography: B. ANDREU, ''Bibliografia tomasiana,'' *Regnum Dei* 5 (1949) 291–338.

[A. SAGRERA]

VIADANA, LODOVICO DA

Early baroque composer of the *concertato* style; b. Viadana, Italy, *c.* 1564 (family name, Grossi); d. Gualtieri, May 2, 1627 (Haberl) or 1645 (Parazzi). He was a pupil of C. Porta, and was chapelmaster at the Mantua cathedral 1590 to 1609, at Concordia (1609–12), and at Fano (1612). He had joined the Franciscan Order in 1596. His music, which consists of numerous Masses, Vesper psalms, and other church works, in addition to two books of canzonettas, falls in the transitional style between Renaissance and baroque. He was among the first to use *basso continuo* in church music, sometimes utilizing both this and older techniques within the same piece. The preface and musical content of his two-volume *Cento concerti ecclesiastici. . .Con il basso continuo per sonar nel'organo* (Venice 1602–07) became a well-known manual for the use of *basso continuo* in church music.

Bibliography: L. DA VIADANA, ''Cento concerti ecclesiastici: Preface,'' O. STRUNK, *Source Readings in Music History* (New

four describing Christ's Crucifixion; the second four devoted to the cross itself. A frequently quoted line in the third stanza, ''Regnavit a ligno Deus,'' is from Ps 95.10, following a reading well known in the early Church. The exceptionally beautiful plainsong melody has also been attributed to Fortunatus himself. The *Vexilla Regis* is further distinguished by the circumstances of its composition. Emperor JUSTIN II sent to Queen Radegunda a relic of the true cross for her convent in Poitiers. Processions from Tours and Poitiers converging at Migné accompanied the envoys from Constantinople back to Poitiers with the relic, singing the *Vexilla Regis* for the first time on Nov. 19, 569.

Until the reform of the Holy Week liturgies by Pius XII in 1955, this hymn was assigned as a processional hymn for Good Friday when the Blessed Sacrament was brought from the Altar of Repose. In the Divine Office, this hymn was historically prescribed as a Vesper hymn during Passiontide and for the feast of Triumph of the Cross. The hymn, modified for liturgical use, dropped the second strophe and has two new stanzas (*O crux ave* and a doxology) in place of the original seventh and eighth.

Bibliography: *Analecta hymnica* 50 (1907) 74–75. J. JULIAN, ed., *A Dictionary of Hymnology* (New York 1957). A. S. WALPOLE, ed., *Early Latin Hymns* (Cambridge, Eng. 1922) 173–177. B. M. PEEBLES, ''Fortunatus, Poet of the Holy Cross,'' *American Church*

York 1950) 419–423. L. G. PARAZZI, *Viadana* (Milan 1876). F. X. HABERL, *Kirchenmusikalisches Jahrbuch* 14 (1889) 44–67. *Musica sacra* 30 (1897) 267–268. R. HAAS, *Die Musik des Barocks* (Handbuch der Musikwissenschaft 3; New York 1928). R. EITNER, *Quellen-Lexikon der Musiker und Musikgelehrten* (Leipzig 1900–04; New York n.d. 1947) 10:72–75. R. L. POOLE and F. T. ARNOLD, *Grove's Dictionary of Music and Musicians*, ed. E. BLOM, (5th ed. London 1954) 8:760–761. F. MOMPELLIO, *Die Musik in Geschichte und Gegenwart*, ed. F. BLUME, (Kassel-Basel 1949–). G. REESE, *Music in the Renaissance* (rev. ed. New York 1959). M. F. BUKOFZER, *Music in the Baroque Era* (New York 1947). F. MOMPELLIO, ''Lodovico Viadana'' in *The New Grove Dictionary of Music and Musicians, vol. 19*, ed. S. SADIE (New York 1980) 692–693. D. M. RANDEL, ed., *The Harvard Biographical Dictionary of Music* (Cambridge, Massachusetts, 1996) 948. N. SLONIMSKY, ed. *Baker's Biographical Dictionary of Musicians*, Eighth Edition (New York 1992) 1959. J. J. SOLURI, ''The *Concerti ecclesiastici* of Lodovico Grossi de Viadana'' (Ph.D. diss. University of Michigan, 1967). L. DA VIADANA, ''Preface to 'One Hundred Sacred Concertos, op. 12'.'' In *Strunk's Source Readings in Music History, vol. 4: The Baroque Era*, rev. ed. L. TREITLER, (New York 1998) 109–113.

[J. G. DOMER]

VIALAR, ÉMILIE DE, ST.

Foundress of the Sisters of St. Joseph of the Apparition; b. Gaillac (Tarn), France, Sept. 12, 1797; d. Marseilles, Aug. 24, 1856. Vialar was the daughter of Augustin and Antoinette Émilie (de Portal) de Vialar, who belonged to the petty nobility. She studied at the Abbey-aux-Bois in Paris until her mother's death, after which she returned home to care for the household. Refusing a marriage arranged by her father, Vialar took a private vow of chastity and devoted herself to the sick and the poor. With the fortune inherited from her maternal grandfather, she established a house in Gaillac (Dec. 25, 1832), which marks the foundation of the Sisters of St. Joseph of the Apparition. Archbishop François de Gualy of Albi approved the new institute and received the vows of Vialar and her 17 companions (Dec. 16, 1835). From 1835 to 1840 the sisters labored in Algeria, where they won distinction for their heroic care of the afflicted during a cholera epidemic. When Vialar opposed Bishop Dupuch of Algiers in his attempt to render the congregation totally submissive to his aims, he excommunicated the sisters and dismissed them from his diocese. Rumors of these difficulties caused the congregation to move its headquarters from Gaillac to Toulouse (1847) and then to Marseilles (1852), although GREGORY XVI had praised their labors. By the time of Vialar's death, however, these losses were offset by the establishment of more than 40 houses in the Near East, Asia, and elsewhere. She was beatified June 18, 1939, and canonized June 24, 1951.

Feast: June 17.

Bibliography: G. BERNOVILLE, *Émilie de Vialar* (Paris 1953). P. DELOOZ, ''Sainte Émilie de Vialar,'' *Nouvelle revue théologique* 82 (1960) 716–717.

[V. A. LAPOMARDA]

VIANNEY, JEAN BAPTISTE MARIE, ST.

The Curé d'Ars; b. Dardilly near Lyons, France, May 8, 1786; d. Ars, Aug. 4, 1859. He was the fourth of six children of Matthieu and Marie (Beluse) Vianney. Because of the unsettled times of the French Revolution he received only a few months of formal education and was then sent to herd cattle. His family, except for a short time, remained loyal to the priests who refused to take the oath supporting the CIVIL CONSTITUTION OF THE CLERGY; and so Jean had to make, in secret, his first confession (1794) and first Communion (1796). At 18 he began to study privately for the priesthood with Abbé Bailey, pastor of Écully. Lacking natural ability and earlier schooling he found study, particularly of Latin, most difficult. The youth gained encouragement to pursue his vocation from a pilgrimage to the shrine of St. John Francis REGIS at La Louvesc (1806) and from the reception of Confirmation (1807). As an unregistered ecclesiastical student he was called for military service (1809). Illness prevented his departure with his unit for the Spanish campaign, and he failed to join a second unit at Roanne because he stopped to pray in a church. Trying to catch up with his detachment, Jean met another defaulter from military service, who led him to asylum in the remote mountain village of Les Noës. There he remained in hiding until a general amnesty was proclaimed (March 25, 1810). He then began the course in philosophy at the minor seminary in Varrieres (1811), and in theology at the major seminary in Lyons (1813). But his inability to understand the Latin lectures led to his dismissal (1814). Abbé Balley resumed private tutoring and won two special examinations for Vianney. The seminary officials were highly impressed by Jean's goodness and common sense, and he was ordained at Grenoble (Aug. 13,1815).

His first assignment was as assistant to his old friend and benefactor Balley at Écully. In 1818 he moved to Ars-en-Dombes, a village with 230 inhabitants. Jean had previously lived very ascetically, but in Ars he intensified his prayers and penances. For years he subsisted on little more than potatoes. The village was not notoriously immoral or malicious but was seriously lacking in a true sense of religion, especially in its profanation of the Lord's Day. Jean started by restoring the church, visiting every family, and teaching catechism. From the pulpit he upbraided his flock for drunkenness, blasphemy, profanity, obscenity, dancing, and working on Sunday. After eight years he had completely reformed the religious tone of Ars and, through guilds for men and women, had Christianized homes. In 1821 Ars became a parish with Vianney as first pastor. In 1824 with Catherine Lassagne and Benedicta Lardet he established a home for girls called La Providence.

Vianney's greatest fame came as a confessor. Owing to his apparent ability to read hearts, his reputation soon spread beyond the neighborhood of Ars. Beginning in 1827 penitents by the thousands came from afar to his confessional. Vianney regularly heard confessions from shortly after midnight until early evening, except for brief interruptions for his Breviary, meals, or special interviews.

He became an honorary canon of Belley and member of the Legion of Honor, but he sold the insignia of these honors to buy bread for the poor. For 30 years after 1824 he was disturbed by strange phenomena, such as nocturnal noise, cruel beatings and, once, a fire in his bed. These he attributed to the devil. His own austerity intruded into his preaching a rigorism that was severely criticized, sometimes justifiably, by other priests. His devotion to St. PHILOMENA was more trusting than modern hagiographical research permits. Exhausted by spiritual ministrations and penances, Vianney died at the age of 73. He was beatified (Jan. 8, 1905) and canonized (May 31, 1925). In 1929 the Holy See declared him heavenly patron of parish priests. Devotion to him has been particularly strong among the diocesan clergy throughout the world.

Feast: Aug. 4.

Bibliography: F. TROCHU, *The Curé d'Ars, St. Jean-Marie-Baptiste Vianney 1786–1859,* tr. E. GRAF (London 1927). H. GHÉON, *The Secret of the Curé d'Ars,* tr. F. J. SHEED (New York 1948). J. GENET, *L'Énigme des sermons du curé d'Ars* (Paris 1961). A. BUTLER, *The Lives of the Saints,* rev. ed. H. THURSTON and D. ATTWATER, 4 v. (New York 1956) 3:285–292. A. LAPERCHIN, *Satan and Saint: Chronicles of the Life of Saint Jean-Marie Baptiste Vianney* (Pittsburgh 1999). G. W. RUTLER, *Saint John Vianney: The Cure d'Ars Today* (San Francisco 1988).

[T. F. CASEY]

VIATICUM

A Latin word meaning provision for the journey, viaticum is the sacrament proper to the dying Christian, wherein the Eucharist is given to one in danger of death as the food for the passage through death to eternal life. The First Council of Nicaea (325), in an effort to comfort the dying and avoid rigorous attitudes, legislated that the dying were not to be deprived of "their last, most necessary viaticum." The biographies of holy people such as

St. Ambrose (ca. 339–97) and St. John Chrysostom (347–407) also attest to this practice of receiving holy communion just before death. Early ritual evidence of viaticum appears in *Ordo Romanus XLIX* (ca. 800), which states that "the holy sacrifice," will be the dying person's "defender and helper at the resurrection of the just." Given at the point of death, communion is a pledge or promise of resurrection and of everlasting life. As late as the thirteenth century, holy communion is still administered in close proximity to the commendation of the dying person. The rites for the dying in the thirteenth-century *Pontifical of the Roman Curia,* for instance, closely follow the monastic pattern for attending to the sick and the dying: caring for the sick, anointing with oil, administering holy communion, commending the dying person in the death agony, and providing funeral services that involve the waking, care, and burial of the body. However, in a departure from this pattern, the *Franciscan Ritual of the Last Sacraments* (1260) provides three distinct rites which are celebrated at different times: communion of the sick, anointing, and commendation of the soul. Here, communion given as viaticum is contained within the order of communion of the sick as a rite that is no longer associated with the hour of death, but is now given early in a grave illness. In addition, viaticum is further separated from the commendation rite by another distinct rite, anointing of the sick, which has been transformed by this time from a rite for the restoration of health to a rite for the spiritual preparation of death. The Franciscan ritual spread and perpetuated this separation of viaticum from the hour of death, a practice which is evident in two important sixteenth-century rituals, Alberto Castellano's *Liber Sacerdotalis* (1523) and Julius Santori's *Rituale Sacramentorum Romanum* (1602), and which is taken up and continued in the 1614 *Rituale Romanum.* The communion rite itself had become a penitential rite that emphasized the forgiveness of sins, deliverance from pain and punishment after death, and the need for protection against the enemy. These concerns are expressed in the formula that the 1614 *RR* uses when communicating the dying: "Receive brother, or sister, the food for your journey, the Body of our Lord Jesus Christ. May he preserve you from the wicked enemy, and lead you to everlasting life."

At the direction of the Second Vatican Council (1962–65), the rites of anointing and viaticum were to be revised, wherein viaticum was restored as the sacrament for the dying (*Pastoral Care of the Sick,* no. 174). In addition to retrieving the more ancient pattern of viaticum-commendation, the post-conciliar reforms restored viaticum as a sacrament of passage, in which the dying person, strengthened with the Body and Blood of Christ, passes through death with Christ, going from this world to the Father in the hope of the resurrection (*PCS*, nos. 26 and 175). The dying Christian should receive viaticum within Mass, but there is a celebration of this sacrament outside Mass and another within a continuous rite used in exceptional circumstances. A distinctive feature of the rite is the renewal of the baptismal profession of faith, which, in the context of viaticum, is a renewal and fulfillment of initiation into the Christian mysteries (*PCS*, no. 179). The sign of communion is more complete when received under both kinds because it expresses more fully and clearly the nature of the Eucharist as a meal, one which prepares all who take part in it for the heavenly banquet (*PCS*, no. 181).

Bibliography: Sources. M. ANDRIEU, *Ordo Romanus XLIX, in Les Ordines romani du haut moyen-âge: Les textes (Ordines XXXV–XLIX)* (Spicilegium Sacrum Lovaniense 28; Louvain 1956), 4:529–530. M. ANDRIEU, *Le pontifical de la curie romaine au XIIIe siècle*, vol. 2 (*Studi e Testi* 87; Vatican City 1940). *Sources of the Modern Roman Liturgy: The Ordinals by Haymo of Faversham and Related Documents (1243–1307)*, ed. S.J.P. VAN DIJK (Leiden 1963). A. CASTELLANO, *Liber Sacerdotalis* (Venice 1523; Paris 1973). J. A. CARDINAL SANTORI, *Rituale Sacramentorum Romanum Gregorii Papae XIII Pont. Max. iussu editum* (Rome: 1584–1602; Paris 1973). *Rituale Romanum Pauli V. Pont. Max. iussu editem* (Rome 1614; Paris 1973). *Ordo Unctionis infirmorum eorumque pastoralis curae*, Rituale Romanum ex decreto sacrosancti oecumenici Concilii Vaticani II instauratum auctoritate Pauli PP. VI promulgatum, editio typica (Rome 1972). *Pastoral Care of the Sick: Rites of Anointing and Viaticum*, the Roman Ritual Revised by Decree of the Second Vatican Ecumenical Council and Published by Authority of Pope Paul VI, Approved for Use in the Dioceses of the United States of America by the National Conference of Catholic Bishops and Confirmed by the Apostolic See, Prepared by the International Commission on English in the Liturgy: A Joint Commission of Catholic Bishops' Conferences (New York 1983). **Literature.** J. M. DONOHUE, ''The Rite for the Commendation of the Dying in the 1983 *Pastoral Care of the Sick: Rites of Anointing and Viaticum*,'' (Ph.D. diss., The Catholic University of America, 1999). F. S. PAXTON, *Christianizing Death: The Creation of a Ritual Process in Early Medieval Europe* (Ithaca, 1990). D. N. POWER, ''Commendation of the Dying and the Reading of the Passion,'' in *Rule of Prayer, Rule of Faith: Essays in Honor of Aidan Kavanagh, O.S.B.*, ed. N. MITCHELL and J. F. BALDOVIN (Collegeville, Minn. 1996): 281–302. A. C. RUSH, ''The Eucharist: The Sacrament of the Dying in Christian Antiquity,'' *The Jurist* 34 (1974): 10:35. D. SICARD, *La Liturgie de la mort dans l'église latine des origines à la réforme carolingienne* (Liturgiewissenschaftliche Quellen und Forschungen, vol. 63; Münster 1978).

[J. M. DONOHUE]

VIATORIANS

(CSV, Official Catholic Directory, #1320). The Clerics of St. Viator were founded in 1835 by Louis Joseph Querbes (1793–1859), pastor of Vourles, in the Archdiocese of Lyons, France. Since the French Revolution had plunged France into a state of religious illiteracy, Querbes assembled a group of young men dedicated to the task of teaching Christian doctrine and serving the altar. He chose as the patron of this community St. Viator, who, in the 4th century, had discharged similar functions as a lector in the cathedral church of Lyons. Three years later the statutes of the congregation were approved by Gregory XVI.

Under the generalship of Querbes, the membership increased so rapidly that before his death there existed three provinces of the society in France and Canada. The clerics not only taught in elementary schools and colleges, but also established a publishing house from which were issued a large number of practical school classics and educational magazines, such as *L'École et la famille* and *L'Ange gardien*, setting forth the necessity of cooperation between the home, Church, and school. After passage of the 1903 law, suppressing all religious schools in France, most of the Viatorians emigrated to Belgium and Canada. In 1847, Bp. Ignace BOURGET of Montreal obtained teachers from Querbes for a small college in Joliette, Canada. In subsequent years the Canadian Viatorians were divided into two provinces, Montreal and Joliette, and two subprovinces, Abitibi and Rimouski. In addition to their other teaching, the Viatorians have established several large schools for the deaf.

In 1842 they began their first mission in the U.S. at Carondelet, MO, but unfavorable circumstances led them to abandon the project in 1857. In 1865 the Viatorians from Canada were invited to open a school for boys in Bourbonnais, IL. Another was established at the Holy Name Cathedral in Chicago, IL, in 1884. The Viatorians taught there until the cathedral parish was divided in 1904; their school was made a parochial school for boys and girls under the direction of sisters. St. Viator College, Bourbonnais, IL, the principal foundation of the Viatorians in the U.S., was begun in 1868. It included under its administration not only the usual courses leading to the bachelor's degree, but also a seminary, a high school, and the upper elementary grades. To comply with new educational requirements, the last two mentioned were discontinued by the year 1929. The results of two disastrous fires (1906, 1926) and the financial crash of 1929 made the maintenance of St. Viator College impossible; it was closed in 1938.

In the U.S., the Viatorians take charge of schools and parishes; many work as teachers, administrators, chaplains, counselors, pastors, spiritual and retreat directors, and missionaries. The U.S. provincialate is in Arlington Heights, IL. The generalate is in Rome.

Bibliography: E. L. RIVARD, *St. Viator and the Viatorians* (Chicago 1916). A. BERNARD, *Histoire des clercs de Saint-Viateur au Canada. . .1807–1882* (Montreal 1947).

[E. V. CARDINAL/EDS.]

VICAR FORANE

A priest appointed by the bishop to supervise a section or district of the diocese (*Corpus iuris canonici*, 553–555). The office of vicar forane was introduced by St. Charles Borromeo in the first Provincial Council of Milan in 1565; it spread rapidly to other provinces of Italy and finally throughout the world. The regulations governing this office became general law in the 1917 Code of Canon Law, and were revised in the 1983 Code.

In the U.S. and some English-speaking countries, the vicar forane, formerly referred to as ''rural dean,'' is designated as regional vicar (dean). He is a priest, usually a pastor, who is appointed by the bishop after consultation with the priests who exercise their ministry in a designated area. Appointed for a determined period of time, he has the duty and office of vigilance and coordination over the apostolic and pastoral ministry of the clergy in his vicariate.

The vicar forane also has the duty of encouraging presbyters in his area to take part in educational opportunities offered to them, and may even be called upon to organize such gatherings. He is to further the spiritual development of the priests by encouraging them to attend days of recollection and retreats. He is to be vigilant and solicitous for their physical and material well-being, and in the defense of their rights. At the death of any priest in his vicariate, he is to take steps to safeguard the property and records of the parish.

The vicar forane makes sure that sacred functions are carried out according to established liturgical directives, and that the Blessed Sacrament is properly reserved in the churches of the vicariate. In many dioceses, where the vicar forane is an ex officio member of the Board of Diocesan Consultors, he is to be called to a diocesan synod (c. 463, §1, 7). The diocesan bishop is to hear his opinion when a new pastor is assigned (c. 524), or when a pastor is reassigned. Many vicars forane also serve as ex officio members of the Diocesan Presbyteral Council. In some circumstances, he may receive the faculty from his bishop to grant dispensations, such as those for mixed marriages and from disparity of cult.

The 1990 Code of Canon Law of the Eastern Churches (cc. 276–278) covers the office of the vicar forane under the title of protopresbyter.

Bibliography: M. CONTE, A CORONATA, *Institutiones iuris canonici*, 5 v. (4th ed. Turin-Rome 1950–56) 1:463–465. J. L. ZAPLONTNIK, *De vicariis foraneis* (Catholic University of America Canon Law Studies 47; Washington 1927).

[P. W. RICE/G. CARIE]

VICAR OF CHRIST

A title of the Roman PONTIFF expressing his claim to universal jurisdiction in virtue of Christ's words to St. Peter, ''Feed my lambs . . . Feed my sheep'' (Jn 21.16–17). It occurs in ecclesiastical writings as early as the 3d century, but until the 9th century it was used for the emperor as well as for bishops and popes. With INNOCENT III (1198–1216) it became the exclusive title of the pope and completely superseded the older titles ''Vicar of St. Peter,'' and ''Vicar of God,'' which had enjoyed preeminence before this time. This development, which was of particular importance in the contemporary discussion about papal jurisdiction, was effected in large part by the medieval DECRETALISTS, and grew out of their treatment of the problem of secular and spiritual power.

Bibliography: M. MACCARRONE, *Vicarius Christi: Storia del titolo papale* (Rome 1952). O. HAGENEDER, ''Studien zum Dekretale *Vergentis*,'' *Zeitschrift der Savigny-Stiftung für Rechtsgeschichte, Kanonistische Abteilung* 49 (1963) 138–173. J. A. WATT, ''The Theory of Papal Monarchy in the Thirteenth Century,'' *Traditio* 20 (1964).

[J. J. MUZAS]

VICARI, HERMANN VON

Archbishop of Freiburg im Breisgau (1842–68); b. Aulendorf (Württemberg), Germany, May 13, 1773; d. Freiburg, April 14, 1868. He came from a devout family of civil servants, was educated at the Abbey of WEINGARTEN and in Constance, and studied philosophy at St. Salvator in Augsburg (1790–91) and law in Vienna (1791–95). In 1797 he became doctor of canon and civil law at Dillingen, a priest (October 1), and canon of St. John's in Constance. From 1802 he was spiritual counselor and associate of Ignaz von WESSENBERG, vicar-general in Constance. After the suppression of this diocese (1821), he was the only person from Constance to become an official in the new Diocese of Freiburg, where he became a member of the cathedral chapter (1827), dean (1830), auxiliary bishop (1832), and archbishop (1842) after the government of Baden vetoed him as a choice (1836). His determined efforts to end State oppression of the Church were helped by general demands for freedom made in the Revolution of 1848. Three of his provincial synods (1851–53) had little success against the state, which imprisoned him for a week in 1854 after he had acted in accordance with ecclesiastical law. Negotiations led to a convention in 1859 that permitted the government a voice in appointments to benefices and joint Church-State administration of Church goods. Vicari did not survive a new struggle over compulsory nondenominational schools. After his death the see was vacant for

14 years. Vicari belongs among the leaders of the 19th-century German Catholic restoration.

Bibliography: L. H. MAAS, *Geschichte der katholischen Kirche im Grossherzogtum Baden* (Freiburg 1891). H. LAUER, *Geschichte der katholischen Kirche im Grossherzogtum Baden* (Freiburg 1908). L. A. VEIT, *Dictionnaire d'histoire et de géographie ecclésiastiques* 6:121–129. J. SAUER, *Lexikon für Theologie und Kirche*[1] 10:592–593. ''Vicari,'' *Lexikon für Theologie und Kirche* [2] v.10.

[W. MÜLLER]

VICE

Habitual degradation, the state of being given up to evil conduct. Just as virtue is a confirmed disposition to act rightly, so its opposite is a confirmed disposition to act evilly.

Just as virtue is a disposition of a person to act in accord with nature, so vice is a disposition to act contrary to nature. In this context nature is not to be understood in the sense of abstract nature, but rather in the sense of the integral nature that is actually born with all its possibilities and aptitudinal inclinations toward rational perfection, all the unfulfilled promise inherent in being human. Vice is the frustration of all such expectation.

The virtues are perfect dispositions of all the human powers for good. Prudence qualifies and conditions the practical reason so that it habitually chooses what is right. Justice perfects the will of man so that he spontaneously respects the rights of others. Fortitude and temperance channel the behavior of the lower appetites to follow smoothly the direction of right reason in the matter of animal fear and desire. These moral dispositions are built up by accumulated human experience. The vices are contrary to the moral virtues in the same sense that contrary qualities, for example, heat and cold, tend to exclude each other from the same subject.

Patterns of Vice. The moral virtues tend to coexist and develop with prudence since prudence provides the norm for the other virtues. There is no exact parallel to this in the realm of vice. The classical list of the capital sins is a list of the commonest patterns of moral failure. Scripture mentions pride, which is the obstacle to the growth and development of charity, as a ''reservoir of all sin, a source which runs over with vice'' (Sir 10.13). As inordinate self-love, pride provides the motivational impulse for the development of all other vices. St. Paul noted ''Covetousness is the root of all evil'' (1 Tm 6.10), which is true in the sense that the grasping man usually has the funds to finance a completely vicious life. In the sixth century, Gregory I pointed out that certain of the deadly sins initiated frequent patterns of moral dissolu-

tion. Sloth, or ACEDIA, for example, involves a certain torpor with regard to divine good; it is the opposite of the joy characteristic of charity. Unless there is enthusiasm for the divine good, an all-prevailing fear for the hardship involved in the development of the virtuous life sets in. In fleeing from the divine good, sloth abandons interest in supernatural beatitude, which is despair. Since the means to beatitude are arduous, sloth makes a man a coward. When others rebuke the slothful man for his neglect, rancor ensues along with malicious detestation for all the values that the slothful man's advisers esteem. Furthermore, the slothful man experiences lethargy regarding all the precepts of the law. Not finding delight in the things of the spirit, he compensates for this loss by transferring his interest to the readily available delights of the flesh.

As St. Thomas points out (ST 2a2ae, 153.5) there is only a given amount of psychic energy available, and the more man's energy is consumed in the vehement pursuit of fleshly delights in lust, the less he has left for the spiritual. The commonest failure following from lust is a weakening of the person's appreciation for the truly good things in life by a kind of mental blindness and a weakening by precipitous reactions of the will's ability to select appropriate means to goals. Normal careful judgment about appropriate means gives way to inconsideration, and firm capacity to command the self yields to inconstancy in decision and action. Disordered lower appetites are fertile ground for disorder in the will in which self-love abounds in reference to what is sinfully delightful, and, as Augustine pointed out, this leads to the sinner's despising God. Affection for the present delights of this world leads to despair for the spiritual delights of the world to come.

A similar series of reactions sets in with envy, which consists in sadness over the good of others. Envy impels the sinner to flee from his sadness or to abate it by murmuring about others, by actual detraction, by exulting in the calamities that befall others; and it culminates in actual hatred of others. These patterns of moral decay have always been familiar.

Just as the moral virtues are dispositions acquired by repeated good actions, so their contrasting vices are acquired by repeated evil acts. Faith, hope and charity, however, are infused gifts from God rather than acquired dispositions. The states of soul that are contrary to these gifts result from single acts of sin.

The list of vices is longer than the list of virtues since departure from the middle course that is typical of moral virtue comes about by either excess or defect. Specific vices can be described either in terms of the virtues to which they are contrary or in terms of the manner in which they depart from the middle course. Vices are specified also in terms of the objects of the actions to which they are related.

Moral Gravity. The concept of gravity is associated with a vice either in terms of the nobility of its opposite virtue or in terms of the object to which it is related. However, it must be kept in mind that the sinner is a free agent, and although he is disposed by habit to sin seriously he can in fact sin only venially.

Habitual degradation that comes about through a sinful life extends to the whole human person. Sanctifying grace, which resides in the soul itself, can be lost by any mortal sin and yield its place to a state called mortal sin that is a privative reality making the soul hateful in the sight of God; and that is human unfulfillment in the profoundest sense.

However, there are limits to this degradation. The habit of sanctifying grace can be lost along with virtue, but the natural goodness of the human faculties themselves remains intact. And the natural inclinations to virtue that are part of the integral nature of man also remain, although once sin has intervened they are more or less impeded in their development by contrary dispositions.

The Human Powers Affected. Since all vice is acquired by deliberate sin, the will also is involved in moral disintegration as the source of malice. In the human personality the will is the basic conative power, the ultimate spiritual capacity for love, desire and hate, the wellspring of human action. Malice involves not only corruption of the will but also guilt or estrangement from the approval of God and man. This volitional derangement applies not only to the will itself, which elicits voluntary responses, but also to the other powers of the soul and body, which are normally imperated by the will in the production of a vicious act—the imagination, the estimative power, the motor powers of the body, and the nervous system, and the neuromuscular patterns of response.

The dispositions of the sense powers of man, including those of the internal faculties of estimative sense and imagination and the concupiscible and irascible appetitive faculties, as well as those of the physical organs of the body that provide the concomitant bodily changes accompanying such things as fear and anger, can be a part of vice. Although this part of the human person is not properly the subject of voluntariness, it can and should be under the control of reason, and when it is not, it develops a tendency to function apart from reason and in response to impulses of a vicious nature. On this level of the human personality also, disintegrating behavior patterns are developed which are a part of the vicious man.

Man's reason also is involved in this dissolution. All sin involves a culpable error on the part of the intellect that enables it to view evil as apparently good. In some cases the evil man even deliberately wills to be ignorant of the moral law so that he will feel freer to sin without any compunction from conscience. Not infrequently the promptness with which practical judgment rejects the allure of a sinful object decreases, and morose delectation takes place in the process of dealing with temptations.

A mystery of iniquity lies within the human heart itself when it chooses evil from cold malice, that is, not from ignorance or the influence of passion, but with clear and deliberate choice of a temporal advantage with advertence to the loss of the divine good and the punishment of eternal damnation, especially when this becomes a habitual disposition so that it is, so to speak, a sinner's second nature. However, even in those whose utter malice is the complete antithesis of virtue, good actions are possible, since the evil agent is always free to behave out of character, with the special grace of God.

Bibliography: THOMAS AQUINAS, *Summa theologiae* 1a2ae, 71–89. A. MICHEL, *Dictionnaire de théologie catholique,* ed., A. VACANT et al., 15 v. (Paris 1903–50) 15.2:2858–62.

[J. D. FEARON]

VICELINUS OF OLDENBURG, ST.

Missionary bishop, apostle of the Wends; b. Hameln, Germany, *ca.* 1086; d. Neumünster monastery, Holstein, Germany, 1154. Vicelinus was a canon and teacher at Bremen and then a student for three years at Laon, France; he returned to Germany *ca.* 1126 and was ordained by NORBERT OF XANTEN. He immediately began his life's work: the evangelization of the Slavs of Holstein. His progress was closely dependent on German political and colonial penetration into this region. At Neumünster on the German-Wendish border, his customary residence, he established a house of CANONS REGULAR OF ST. AUGUSTINE where Helmold was one of his pupils. He made other foundations at Högersdorf and Segeburg. On Sept. 25, 1149, Vicelinus became bishop of Oldenburg, an abandoned see beyond the German frontier. Unable to take possession permanently, he labored instead in Bosau (Holstein) for two years, then returned to Neumünster where he died after a long illness. Despite his eloquence and zeal, his work enjoyed little apparent success.

Feast: Dec. 12.

Bibliography: HELMOLDUS, *The Chronicle of the Slavs,* tr. F. J. TSCHAN (New York 1935; repr. New York 1966). A. HAUCK, *Kirchengeschichte Deutschlands,* 5 v. (9th ed. Berlin-Leipzig 1958) v.4. F. DVORNIK, *The Slavs: Their Early History and Civilization* (Boston 1956).

[R. H. SCHMANDT]

VICENTINO, NICOLA

Important Renaissance composer and theorist; b. Vicenza, Italy, 1511; d. Rome, 1572. Vincentino was a disciple of the great musician A. WILLAERT, and after priestly studies and ordination he served as chapelmaster at the Ferrara court (to 1539), at Rome with Cardinal Ippolito II d'Este, at Vincenza, and at Milan. One of the leading innovators of the 16th century, he had a significant role in the development of monody and also of a new, expressive harmony further developed by C. de RORE and Gesualdo. In his madrigals he expanded tonality to include chromatic and enharmonic progressions, constructing two instruments, the archicembalo and archiorgano, to demonstrate their intervals. In his church music, notably his several books of motets, his style was that of *musica moderna.* He preferred free compositions to those using a liturgical *cantus firmus,* gave precedence to the text over the polyphonic structure, precipitated the question of *musica reservata,* and in certain of his concepts anticipated the departures of ZARLINO. It was a controversy with Lusitano (1551) that led to his treatise *L'Antica musica ridotta alla moderna prattica* [1555; microcarded by Eastman School of Music (Rochester 1954)]. In his writings he advocated the liberation of composition from established traditions and the reform of old-fashioned counterpoint and of stereotyped handling of church modes and their cadences.

Bibliography: *Collected Works,* ed. H. W. KAUFMANN (*Corpus mensurabilis musicae,* ed. American Institute of Musicology, 26; 1963). T. KROYER, *Die Anfänge der Chromatik* (Leipzig 1901). R. O. MORRIS, *Contrapuntal Technique in the 16th Century* (Oxford 1934). B. MEIER, "Reservata-Probleme," *Acta musicologica* 30 (1958) 77–89. G. REESE, *Music in the Renaissance* (rev. ed. New York 1959). H. W. KAUFMANN, *Die Musik in Geschichte und Gegenwart,* ed. F. BLUME (Kassel-Basel 1949–). P. R. BRINK, "The Archicembalo of Nicola Vicentino" (Ph.D. diss., Ohio State University, 1966). H. W. KAUFMANN, *The Life and Works of Nicola Vicentino (1511–c.1576)* (Rome 1966); "Nicola Vicentino" in *The New Grove Dictionary of Music and Musicians, vol. 19,* ed. S. SADIE (New York 1980) 699–701. C. NICK, "A Stylistic Analysis of the Music of Nicola Vicentino" (Ph.D. diss. Indiana University, 1967). D. M. RANDEL, ed., *The Harvard Biographical Dictionary of Music* (Cambridge 1996) 948. N. SLONIMSKY, ed. *Baker's Biographical Dictionary of Musicians,* Eighth Edition (New York 1992) 1960.

[K. G. FELLERER]

VICO, GIAMBATTISTA

Italian philosopher, historian, and jurisprudent; b. Naples, June 23, 1668; d. there, Jan. 23, 1744. His work *Scienza Nuova d'intorno alla comune natura delle Nazioni* (1744) opened a new epoch in the theory of history, of historiography, and of culture.

Giambattista Vico. (©Bettmann-CORBIS)

Early Work. Vico's first philosophical orientation was Cartesian, but his strongly humanistic formation led to an early dissociation from this current. In a literary sense, his criticism is linked to Descartes's animadversions on the humanistic disciplines in the *Discourse on Method;* Vico's corrective is his *De nostri temporis studiorum ratione* [1708; in G. B. Vico, *Orazioni inaugurali, De antiquissima Italorum sapientia, le Polemiche,* ed. G. Gentile and F. Nicolini (Bari 1914)], which gives the first intimation of his unification of philosophy and philology. In the doctrinal sense, his criticism of Cartesianism centers upon the *cogito,* which he considers without ontological force, and upon the clear and distinct idea, which he considers too narrowly evidential. His corrective is found in the *Liber metaphysicus* of the *De antiquissima,* which exhibits the first outlines of his doctrine of the human mind and of the philological method in philosophy, both elaborated later in the *Scienza Nuova.*

Vico's doctrine takes its greatest impetus from his studies in the history of law. He concluded that the codes of Roman law were subject, both in construction and interpretation, to the *boria degli dotti,* the illusion of the learned "who will have it that whatever they know is as old as the world" (*Scienza Nuova* 1.2.127; Bergin and Fisch, 55). That is, the laws so codified were considered to be the products of reason and will. Vico's vision is that they must be, rather, crystallizations of a vast body of historical experience, behind which lay not only the development of institutions but that of the human mind itself. The first results of his efforts in this direction appear in the *Diritto Universale* [1719–23, ed. F. Nicolini 3 v. (Bari 1936)]. In this document, however, the intellectualism against which his criticism is directed is only partially overcome. The fulfillment of this insight had to await the *Scienza Nuova* itself.

The New Science. The *Scienza Nuova* records Vico's two basic and profoundly revolutionary achievements: the reconstruction of human presence and, on this basis, the reconstruction, in principle, of historical social process. Though for purposes of exposition these achievements are best distinguished, in this document and in Vico's thought as a whole they are absolutely immanent to each other and to the concrete process of interpreting historical documents. On these two chief achievements depend all of the celebrated "discoveries" of the *New Science:* for example, the theory of poetry and myth, the poetic ages of man, and the theory of the class struggle as the basic dynamic of social change.

The "reconstruction of human presence" turns about the epistemological vindication of the senses and of the imagination, and an assertion of the practical effectiveness of the passions. In classical INTELLECTUALISM, the principle of consciousness had been reason; by contrast, sense and imagination had been assigned inferior cognitive roles. In like manner, the center of ethical force had been placed in the will, and the passions denigrated. Vico mitigates such intellectualism. Reason and will remain for him ultimately normative; yet he assigns to sense, imagination, and passion an autonomous validity. This validity is nevertheless subordinated, through the dialectic of spontaneity and reflection, to reason and will in the total economy of "human presence."

The second achievement documented in the *Scienza Nuova* is the reordering of human cultural history upon the basis of the moments of presence or "modifications of the human mind." In the classical tradition the distinctions and relations between these moments of presence had been purely formal. Above all, any time-existential relationship between them had been, if at all, only inchoately indicated. As a result, there had emerged various dualisms, such as that between the logical and the real; and history, regarded essentially as a logical process, had been assigned little value. Vico opposes this tradition. He deploys the moments of human presence through time, presenting the time process as generating the logical order, and not as incidental to it. For him, in fact, history is not merely a science, but the universal matrix of significant human discourse.

Vico maintains that the deployment of human presence through time is in the collective consciousness rather than in the individual. He does not, however, conceive this deployment along psychological lines. Rather, he places it in the document, which, for him, is not simply the written record; it is also, and even more, the living social process and the institution. Thus one can understand how, for Vico, the Roman law is *un serioso poema.* At the same time, the "course of nations" is the working out in time of the "eternal and ideal history," and these are entirely immanent to each other. Yet, between them appears a tension that leaves place for providence. For Vico, providence is the principle of rectification of the temporal course of nations in the direction of ideal and eternal history; the latter, moreover, is subject in its temporal manifestation to the law of *ricorsi* or eternal return. It is traversed anew by every nation and in every nation works itself out afresh.

These principles are applied in the substantive portion of the *New Science:* the history of "poetic wisdom." Poetic wisdom is the record of the spontaneous consciousness of early man in his literature, social institutions, and the like. The dimensions of this wisdom include poetic theology, poetic physics, and poetic politics. These Vico undertakes to reconstruct on the basis of the documents of early Mediterranean culture.

Bibliography: G. B. VICO, *The New Science . . .* , tr. T. G. BERGIN and M. H. FISCH from 3d ed., 1744 (Ithaca 1948); *The Autobiography . . .* , tr. M. H. FISCH and T. G. BERGIN (Ithaca 1944), important introd. F. AMERIO, *Enciclopedia filosofica,* 4 v. (Venice-Rome 1957) 4:1572–88. B. CROCE, *Bibliografia Vichiana,* ed. F. NICOLINI, 2 v. (Naples 1947–48). F. NICOLINI, *Saggi Vichiani* (Naples 1955–). A. R. CAPONIGRI, *Time and Idea: The Theory of History in Giambattista Vico* (London 1953). T. BERRY, *The Historical Theory of Giambattista Vico* (Washington 1949). A. CORSANO, *Giambattista Vico* (Bari 1956).

[A. R. CAPONIGRI]

VICTIMAE PASCHALI LAUDES

The SEQUENCE that was traditionally used during Easter Week. Its composition is traditionally assigned to WIPO (d. after 1046). One of the finest of the transitional Sequences, the *Victimae paschali laudes* or "Praise to the Paschal Victim bring," is in rhythmical prose of seven strophes; the first stanza is unpaired but the others—two and three, four and five, six and seven—form a strophe and antistrophe, with correspondence between the Sequence's literary structure and its music. The first strophe calls on Christians to praise the Paschal Victim. In stanzas two and three, Christ's redemptive work is pictured. The middle section, stanzas four and five, is a lively dialogue in which the faithful question Mary Magdalen, who delivers the message of Christ's triumph. Stanzas six and seven are an act of faith on the part of the Christian community and an address to Christ, now reigning gloriously. The 1570 reform of the Roman Missal dropped stanza six, ''Let us believe Mary''; thus stanza seven is now unpaired as is stanza one.

The poem falls into two distinct sections; stanzas one to three are of a lyrical nature showing varied assonances while stanzas four to seven form a dramatic section with dissyllabic rhyme. This has led some scholars to question Wipo's authorship and to ascribe the two sections to different backgrounds and authors. However, Wipo's ''Song of Lament for Emperor Conrad II'' shows these same characteristics, a fact which strengthens his claim.

Early in the 12th century, the Sequence, incorporated into many versions of the *Visitatio sepulchri,* played an important part in the foundation of liturgical drama.

Bibliography: J. JULIAN, ed., *A Dictionary of Hymnology* (New York 1957) 2:1222–24, for Eng. tr. *Die Werke Wipos,* ed. H. BRESSLAU, *Monumenta Germaniae Historica: Scriptore rerum Germanicum* 61. *Analecta hymnica* 54:12–13, text. K. YOUNG, *The Drama of the Medieval Church,* 2 v. (Oxford 1933) 1:273–288. F. J. E. RABY, *A History of Christian-Latin Poetry from the Beginnings to the Close of the Middle Ages* (Oxford 1953) 217–219. J. SZÖVÉRFFY, *Die Annalen der lateinischen Hymnendichtung* (Berlin 1964–65) 1:372–374.

[M. I. J. ROUSSEAU]

VICTOR, SS.

In their Lives of the Saints, the Benedictines of Paris have retained 40 SS. Victor, the majority of whom were martyrs in the early Church. Since the name fits the disciples of Christ as victors or conquerors of death through His resurrection, it is difficult to distinguish archeological and other evidence that may be providing an epithet rather than the true name of an otherwise unknown saint. Pope St. VICTOR (189–198) intervened in the controversy over the date of Easter and thus became well known in early Church history. In Africa the name Victor occurs frequently in the calendar and almost all the Victors are martyrs: a soldier martyred at Milan in 303 (Feast: May 8); a fifth-century bishop at Utica (Feast: Aug. 23); a martyr at Carthage in 259 (Feast: Feb. 24); martyrs at Caesarea in Mauritania (Feasts: Aug. 26, May 10, Sept. 10 and 14, Nov. 2, and Dec. 18, 28, and 29). Other Victors were martyred at Alexandria (Feasts: Jan. 31, May 17); Barcelona (Feast: April 4); Braga in the 4th century (Feast: April 12); Chalcedon (Feast: Sept. 10); Diospolis in 284 (Feast: Feb. 25); Gerone in 304 (Feast: Jan. 22); Mérida (Feast: July 24); Nicomedia (Feast: March 6, Dec. 3, and April 20); Ravenna (Feast: Nov. 13); Rome (Feast: Dec.

15); Solothurn (Feast: Sept. 30); Thessalonica in 304 (Feast: March 30). A Victor was one of the THEBAN LEGION (Feast: Sept. 22); another Victor was martyred at Marseilles *c.* 290 (Feast: July 21) and became famous because of the monastery founded there by John Cassian. A seventh-century solitary is honored as St. Victor (Feast: Aug. 29); so are Victor, Bishop of Capua (d. 554; Feast: April 2); a fourth-century bishop of Metz (Feast: June 22); and a fourth-century bishop of Piacenza (Feast: Dec. 7).

Bibliography: J. L. BAUDOT and L. CHAUSSIN, *Vies des saints et des bienheureux selon l'ordre du calendrier avec l'historique des fêtes.* ed. by the Benedictines of Paris (Paris 1935–56). H. QUENTIN, *Les Martyrologes historiques du moyen âge* (Paris 1908).

[P. ROCHE]

VICTOR I, POPE, ST.

Pontificate: 186 or 189 to 197 or 201. Most sources agree that Victor reigned ten years, although the LIBERIAN CATALOGUE assigns nine years. Eusebius begins his reign in 189. Under Victor, an African, the Latin element in Rome grew at the expense of the Greco-Oriental. In the EASTER CONTROVERSY Victor sought to impose the Roman tradition of observance of the feast on a Sunday over the Oriental QUARTODECIMAN observance on 14 Nisân. Earlier, Pope Anicetus and POLYCARP had discussed the differences without result. Upon Victor's initiative synods met throughout the Christian world, and the bishops all agreed with the Roman tradition, except those in Asia led by Polycrates of Ephesus. Victor threatened excommunication, but his fellow bishops, especially St. IRENAEUS, pointed out that the Quartodeciman tradition was an ancient one observed by illustrious churches, and that the dispute was not about a matter of essential importance. Victor's response to this is not known.

The Victor-Polycrates controversy provides the first evidence of a move by the Roman church to influence the affairs of foreign patriarchs. Victor's insistence on the primacy of Rome would shape much later papal history. That the Asians could ignore him with impunity and that Irenaeus could rebuke him, prove that his assertion of universal authority was not widely accepted outside Rome. Jerome (*Vir. ill.* 34) notes that Victor composed a work on the controversy, but his suggestion that Victor was the first ecclesiastical author to write in Latin is to be doubted.

Victor did excommunicate the Adoptionist Theodotus of Byzantium. Victor is the first bishop of Rome known to have dealt with the imperial household. He drew up a list of names of Christians suffering in the mines of Sardinia who were freed through the good offices of Marcia, the Christian concubine of Commodus. Victor is the last bishop reported by the *Liber pontificalis* to have been buried near Peter in the Vatican, but modern excavations do not confirm the report.

Feast: July 28.

Bibliography: EUSEBIUS, *Historia Ecclesiastica,* 5:22–24, 28. É. AMANN, *Dictionnaire de théologie catholique,* ed. A. VACANT et al., (Paris 1903–50) 15:2862–63. H. JEDIN, *Handbuch der Kirchengeschichte* (Freiburg 1962–) 1:411. E. FERGUSON, ed., *Encyclopedia of Early Christianity* (New York 1997), 2.1159. J. N. D. KELLY, *Oxford Dictionary of Popes* (New York 1986). CH. PIETRI, ''Les origines de la mission lyonnaise: remarques critiques'' *Christiana Respublica: Eléments d'une enquête sur le christianisme antique* (Rome 1997) 1165–85.

[E. G. WELTIN]

VICTOR II, POPE, BL.

Pontificate: April 13, 1055 to July 28, 1057; b. Gebhard, Swabia; d. Arezzo, Italy. Scion of a Swabian aristocratic lineage from which the later Counts of Calw descended, Gebhard was also related to the royal dynasty of the Salians. He appears to have been educated in the cathedral school of Regensburg and was a canon there under Bishop Gebhard III. At the bishop's suggestion, Emperor Henry III appointed Gebhard bishop of Eichstätt in 1042, despite the fact that the new prelate had not yet attained the canonically appropriate age. As bishop, Gebhard is said to have impressed contemporaries with his knowledge and skill in matters both divine and worldly. Apparently, he impressed Henry III as well. By 1050, Gebhard figured among the emperor's chief advisors. A near contemporary, emphasizing the esteem in which the prelate was held, describes him as ''second after the king.'' He was instrumental in obstructing aid for Pope Leo IX's campaign against the Normans in southern Italy and hence, contributed indirectly to the pope's humiliating defeat at Civitate (June 18, 1053). Following Duke Conrad's deposition, in 1053, Henry III appointed Gerhard regent for Bavaria.

Upon Leo IX's death, an embassy from Rome approached the emperor and requested the appointment of a successor. After much deliberation, the emperor designated Gebhard (Mainz, September 1054) who, however, refused to accept the nomination until March 1055. In the meantime, Gebhard received assurances that property taken from the Roman church would be returned and that he could retain his German bishopric. On April 13, 1055, in the basilica of St. Peter, he was enthroned as Pope Victor II. As with the other ''German popes'' appointed by

Henry III, Victor II's relations with the emperor were characterized by amicable cooperation in ecclesiastical matters, in protecting the papal patrimony, and in maintaining papal and imperial rights in southern Italy. Together pope and emperor presided over a synod in Florence (June 1055). If the accounts in later, undoubtedly biased sources can be believed, the synod took up more or less the same policies of ecclesiastical reform advocated by Leo IX; condemning clerical unchastity, simony, and the alienation of ecclesiastical property. Leo held other synods at Rome, in April 1057 and at Arezzo in July 1057. During Victor's reign, Hildebrand (Pope Gregory VII), acting as legate, presided over a synod that dealt with the eucharistic heresy of Berengar of Tours.

To support both papal and imperial interests against Duke Godfrey III of Upper Lotharingia and now also Marquis of Tuscany, Henry III gave Victor responsibility for administering the Duchy of Spoleto and the March of Fermo. In September 1056, pope and emperor met at Goslar to resolve their mutual problems in southern Italy. The emperor's death less than a month later (October 5) ensured that these plans came to naught. On his death bed, the emperor commended his minor son, the future Henry IV, to Pope Victor's protection. After seeing to the ruler's interment at Speyer, the pope secured the regency for the imperial widow, Empress Agnes, had Henry IV crowned at Aachen, and negotiated a peace with the monarchy's chief enemies, Count Balduin V of Flanders and Godfrey III. In February 1057, he returned to Italy, held synods at Rome and Arezzo (see above), and died on July 28. Although his entourage wished to return his body to Germany, for burial at Eichstätt, the populace of Ravenna instead seized it for burial in their own church of Santa Maria Rotunda (i.e. the tomb of Theodorich).

Bibliography: *Anonymous Haserensis de episcopis Eichstetensibus* ed. L. C. BETHMANN. *Monumenta Germaniae Historica: Scriptores,* 7 (Hanover 1846) 263–266. G. D. MANSI, *Sacroum conciliorum* (Paris 1901) 19, 833–862. S. WEINFURTER, *Die Geschichte der Eichstätter Bischöfe des Anonymous Haserensis* (Regensburg 1987) passim. G. FRECH, ''Die deutschen Päpste-Kontinuität und Wandel,'' in *Die Salier und Das Reich 3,* ed. S. WEINFURTER (Sigmaringen 1991) 303–332. G. TELLENBACH, *The Church in Western Europe from the Tenth to the Early Twelfth Century,* tr. T. REUTER (Cambridge 1993) 142–146, 192–193. G. MARTIN, ''Der Salische Herrscher als *Patricius Romanorum.* Zur Einflussnahme Heinrichs III und Heinrichs IV auf die Besetzung der *cathedra Petri,''* *Frühmittelalterliche Studien* 28 (1994) 257–295.

[D. A. WARNER]

VICTOR III, POPE

Pontificate: May 24, 1086 (election); May 9, 1087 (consecration), to Sept. 16, 1087 (at the abbey of Monte-

Pope Victor III as Abbot Desiderius of Monte Cassino, from the "Life of St. Benedict."

cassino); b. Dauferius/Daufari *c.* 1027 to a noble Beneventan family related to the Lombard dukes. Leaving an eremitical life, he became a Benedictine monk at the abbey of S. Sofia at Benevento (southern Italy), adopting the name Desiderius. With the approval of Pope Victor II he entered the abbey of Montecassino in 1055, where he was elected abbot in 1058 (April 10). Pope Nicholas II named him cardinal-priest of S. Cecilia in Rome in 1059. He participated in the Lateran council of that year subscribing its papal election decree and brought about the revolutionary alliance of the papacy with the Normans, concluded solemnly at the council of Melfi in August 1059. He supported the Gregorian reformers and was a frequent collaborator not only of Nicholas II but also of popes Alexander II and Gregory VII. In 1080 he reconciled the latter with Robert Guiscard, who although a vassal of the papacy had not ceased his attacks on papal territory but failed to bring about a reconciliation between Gregory and Emperor Henry IV, with whom he

met in 1082 provoking Gregory's anger. It is unlikely, however, that Gregory went so far to excommunicate the abbot who was among the few who surrounded the deathbed of the pope in exile at Salerno in May 1085 after having been Gregory's host at Montecassino during the papal flight from Rome in 1084. Although Gregory did not name him among possible successors, Desiderius was elected pope in May 1086. But he hesitated to assume the heavy burden—Wibert of Ravenna dominated as anti–pope Clement III—in part also because of ecclesiastical opposition to his election from Hugh of Die and his circle. He continued in his office as abbot of Montecassino, but was eventually consecrated and enthroned as Pope Victor III (May 1087) under the protection of Norman troops. During his brief papacy he celebrated a synod at Benevento (August 1087), excommunicating Hugh of Die and Wibert of Ravenna, but he apparently neither renewed the prohibition of investiture nor the excommunication of Henry IV. In contrast with his troubled papacy the almost 30 years of his abbacy at Montecassino were highly successful. The library holdings in all areas of study were vastly expanded; the property of the abbey increased and its basilica (consecrated by Pope Alexander II in 1071) and monastic buildings reconstructed. Victor himself wrote between 1076 and 1079 a work extolling the miracles of St. Benedict. Cardinal Deusdedit dedicated his *Collectio canonum* to him. His beatification was confirmed by Leo XIII on Sept. 23, 1887.

Bibliography: H. BLOCH, *Monte Cassino in the Middle Ages*, 3 v. (Cambridge, MA and Rome 1986). H. E. J. COWDREY, *The Age of Abbot Desiderius* (Oxford 1983). J. DEÉR, *Papsttum und Normannen* (Cologne-Vienna 1972). H. DORMEIER, *Montecassino und die Laien im 11. und 12. Jahrhundert* (Stuttgart 1979). G. A. LOUD, "Abbot Desiderius of Montecassino and the Gregorian Papacy," *Journal of Ecclesiastical History* 30 (1979) 305–326. *L'età dell'abate Desiderio*, 3 v., ed. F. AVAGLIANO and O. PECERE (Montecassino 1989–1992). M. GUDE, "Die 'fideles sancti Petri' im Streit um die Nachfolge Papst Gregors VII.," *Frühmittelalterliche Studien* 27 (1993) 290–316. R. HÜLS, *Kardinäle, Klerus und Kirchen Roms 1049–1130* (Tübingen 1977) 154–157. J. LAUDAGE, "Victor III," *Lexikon der Päpste und des Papsttums* (Freiburg-Basel-Vienna 2001) 400. W. D. MACCREADY, "The Incomplete 'Dialogues' of Desiderius of Montecassino," *Analecta Bollandiana* 116 (1998) 115–146; idem, "Dating the Dialogues' of Abbot Desiderius of Montecassino," *Revue bénédictine* 108 (1998) 145–168. R. SCHIEFFER, "Viktor III," *Lexikon des Mittelalters*, col. 1665f.

[U.-R. BLUMENTHAL]

VICTOR IV, ANTIPOPE

Pontificate: March to May 29, 1138. The date of his death is not known, but Gregory Conti was born at Ceccano (in Frosinone) and became cardinal priest of SS. Apostoli in 1110 under Pope Paschal II (1099–1118). From early in his career he was strongly opposed to the imperial position in the Investiture Controversy, and he bitterly protested Paschal's capitulation to Henry V (1106–25) in the Privilege of Ponte Mammolo (1111). Not surprisingly, in the irregular double election of 1130 Gregory was part of the majority of cardinals who voted for Antipope Anacletus II (1130–38) over Innocent II (1130–43). He remained loyal to Anacletus and was one of three representatives sent to Salerno to argue the antipope's case in front of Duke Roger II of Sicily (1095–1154). After Anacletus died, his followers elected Gregory as Victor IV. Notably, this was done with the approval of Duke Roger, even though Anacletus had clearly lost his case (and several of his remaining followers) at Salerno. There is no record of any actions by Victor as antipope, except that after only four months Bernard of Clairvaux presented him to Pope Innocent II, to whom he submitted. Innocent pardoned him and his few supporters. But the Second Lateran Council (April 1139) stripped Gregory of his cardinalate in spite of Innocent's

earlier promise to the contrary. Bernard was quite upset with Innocent for this betrayal. After this event, the historical record is silent about Gregory-Victor.

Bibliography: L. DUCHESNE, ed. *Liber Pontificalis* (Paris 1886–92; repr. 1955–57) 2.383; 3.138. J. D. MANSI, *Sacrorum conciliorum nova et amplissima collectio* (Florence and Venice 1759–98; repr. Graz 1960–61) 21.535. P. JAFFÉ, *Regesta pontificum Romanorum* (Leipzig 1885–88; repr. Graz 1956) 1.919. *Monumenta Germaniae historica, Constitutiones* 1.143, 573. BERNARD OF CLAIRVAUX, Letters 213 and 317, in J. LECLERCQ and H. M. ROCHAIS, eds. *Sancti Bernardi Opera*, v. 8 (Rome 1963); also *Patrologia Latina*, ed. J. P. MIGNE (Paris 1878–80) 182.378, 523. H. W. KLEWITZ, "Das Ende des Reformpapstums," *Deutsches Archiv für Erforschung des Mittelalters* 3 (1939) 376–77. F. X. SEPPELT, *Geschichte der Päpste von den Anfängen bis zur Mitte des zwanzigsten Jahrhunderts* (Munich 1954–59) 3.184. F. J. SCHMALE, *Studien zum Schisma des Jahres 1130* (Cologne 1961) 60–61, 175ff. J. N. D. KELLY, *The Oxford Dictionary of Popes* (New York 1986) 170.

[P. M. SAVAGE]

VICTOR IV, ANTIPOPE

Pontificate Sept. 7, 1159 to April 20, 1164. We do not know the date of his birth, but Octavian of Monticelli was born in the Sabina (north of Rome) to an aristocratic family related to the Crescentii, a powerful and influential Roman family. By 1138 he had been made cardinal deacon of St. Nicholas in Carcere Tulliano, and was promoted in 1151 to cardinal priest of St. Cecilia. He was an important member of the curia of Eugene III (1145–53), for whom he served as legate to Germany, where he met Frederick, Duke of Swabia, who would soon become the new emperor (i.e., FREDERICK I BARBAROSSA, 1152–90) and his supporter as antipope. Octavian was thus associated with those who supported imperial influence within the curia, and even served as a legate for Barbarossa. After the strongly anti-imperialist Pope Adrian IV died in 1159, two groups within the curia came to a sharp disagreement over his successor. Octavian's minority group was pro-imperialist, while the majority of cardinals favored an alliance with Norman Sicily to insure independence from the emperor. This difference resulted in a disputed election. At the conclave, the overwhelming majority of cardinals elected Cardinal Roland to be Alexander III (1159–81), while a group of no more than five imperialist cardinals, with the support of Barbarossa's ambassadors in Rome, would not acknowledge Alexander and maintained that they had elected Octavian, who took the name Victor IV (thus ignoring the four-month reign of Antipope Victor IV in 1138). At this point, confusion broke out when a Roman mob supporting Octavian broke into St. Peter's. Octavian and Roland fought over the papal mantle. According to most sources, Octavian managed to put it on, and the people proclaimed him pope. Roland was forced to flee but was soon consecrated as Pope Alexander III.

Frederick Barbarossa then called for a synod at Pavia (February 1160) and invited each rival to submit his claim. Since only 50 bishops attended, none from England or France, the synod was clearly intended to ratify Victor. Alexander would not come, since to do so would acknowledge the emperor's authority over the church, precisely the position his group opposed. Not surprisingly, the synod decided that Victor was the legitimate pope. It also excommunicated Alexander, who in turn excommunicated Victor, the emperor, and his advisors. Later, in October 1160, there was another meeting that included most of the other bishops, many monastic leaders, and kings Henry II of England (1154–89) and Louis VII of France (1137–79). This group determined that Alexander was the rightful pope, and thus began an 18-year schism that would pit three imperial antipopes (cf. Paschal III, 1164–68, and Callistus III, 1168–78) against the long-lived and politically astute Alexander.

Victor was never widely recognized in Europe. His support in Germany was significant only in those areas that supported Barbarossa, and his strength in northern Italy depended directly on the strength of the emperor. France, England, Spain, Hungary, and Ireland all sided with Alexander, and nothing Barbarossa did in the subsequent years altered the fact. Initially, as the emperor seemed to consolidate his control of northern Italy, Victor's prospects looked secure (Alexander was forced to live in France), but Alexander continued to gather support. On Sept. 7, 1162 Victor presided at a synod at Dôle where he renewed his excommunication of Alexander, but he was for the most part fighting a losing battle. He died suddenly on April 20, 1164 in Lucca while traveling with Rainald of Dassel, Frederick's chancellor to Italy and archbishop of Cologne (1159–67), who then oversaw the election of his successor, the antipope Paschal III.

Bibliography: L. DUCHESNE, ed. *Liber Pontificalis* (Paris 1886–92; repr. 1955–57) 2.397–410. P. JAFFÉ, *Regesta pontificum Romanorum* (Leipzig 1885–88; repr. Graz 1956) 2.418–26. *Boso's Life of Alexander III*, intro. PETER MUNZ (Totowa, NJ 1973). ALEXANDER III, Letter 1, in J. P. MIGNE, ed. *Patrologia latina* (Paris 1841–64) 200.69–70. P. F. KER, ''Zur Geschichte Viktors IV,'' *Neues Archiv der Gesellschaft für ältere deutsche Geschichtskunde* 46 (1926) 53–85. F. X. SEPPELT, *Geschichte der Päpste von den Anfängen bis zur Mitte des zwanzigsten Jahrhunderts* (Munich 1954–59) 3.232–48. H. JEDIN and J. DOLAN, eds. *Handbook of Church History* (New York 1965–81) 4.57–63. M. BALDWIN, *Alexander III and the Twelfth Century* (New York 1968) 43–84. H. M. SCHWARZMAIR, ''Zur Familie Viktors VI in der Sabina,'' *Quellen und Forschungen aus Italienischen Archiven und Bibliotheken* 48 (1968) 64–79. W. ULLMANN, *A Short History of the Papacy in the Middle Ages* (London 1972). T. REUTER, *The Papal Schism, the Empire and the West, 1159–69* (Diss. Exeter 1975). R. SOMERVILLE, *Pope Alexander III and the Council of Tours, 1163* (Berkeley 1977). J. N. D. KELLY, *The Oxford Dictionary of Popes* (New York 1986) 177–78. I. S. ROBINSON, *The Papacy 1073–1198: Continuity and Innovation* (Cambridge 1990). W. MALECZEK, *Lexikon des Mittelalters* (Munich 1997) 8.1666–67.

[P. M. SAVAGE]

VICTOR EMMANUEL II

Last king of Sardinia and first king of Italy; b. Turin, March 14, 1820; d. Rome, Jan. 9, 1878. Educated in the military tradition of the house of Savoy and in the devout atmosphere of the Piedmontese court, he retained throughout life the bluff manners of the soldier and a sincere if superficial religious faith, coupled with serious shortcomings in his private life. A shrewd judge of human nature, he chose able men to serve him. His sense of responsibility and duty and his personal bravery helped him to overcome the many crises of his reign and to gain popularity among his people. His public life began when his father, Charles Albert, defeated by the Austrians at Novara, abdicated in his favor (March 23, 1849). When he refused Austrian demands for a revocation of the liberal constitution granted by Charles Albert in 1848, his courage and determination were acclaimed throughout Italy and won him the soubriquet of ''re galantuomo'' (honest king). His association with CAVOUR began in 1852. Although Victor Emmanuel did not always agree with him, he recognized that Cavour's plan helped to strengthen the monarchy and to transform Piedmont-Sardinia into a modern state. At first much opposed to Cavour's ecclesiastical laws, the King signed them when convinced that they constituted an essential part of Cavour's economic and political reforms. This caused conflict with Pius IX.

As the revolutionary tactics of Mazzini failed, Italian nationalists looked more and more to the house of Savoy for leadership. Victor Emmanuel began playing an active and important role in the movement that resulted in the unification of the peninsula. He persuaded the republican and Mazzinian Garibaldi to support the monarchic cause. To gain French support against Austria he agreed to the marriage of his daughter Clothilde with the dissolute Prince Napoleon, cousin of Emperor Napoleon III, and promised to cede Nice and his ancestral province of Savoy to France. By 1860 most of the peninsula had rallied to his side after the Franco-Sardinian victory over Austria (1859), which inspired revolts in the small states in north central Italy. Garibaldi meanwhile had penetrated southern Italy.

Victor Emmanuel II esteemed Pius IX highly, and carried on a considerable correspondence with him, unknown to his ministers, in the hope of gaining the Pope's consent to the incorporation of the STATES OF THE CHURCH into the new Italy, with the pope as governor of the central portion. Pius IX refused to abdicate his sovereignty. In 1861 Victor Emmanuel was proclaimed king of a united Italy with Rome as its capital. This created the ROMAN QUESTION, which plagued Vatican-Italian relations until the Lateran Pacts (1929). The seizure of the States of the Church, completed in 1870, resulted in the King's excommunication. Victor Emmanuel hoped to reconcile Church-State relations, but the Law of GUARANTEES proved unacceptable to the Pope. Before death the King was reconciled with the Church and assured his chaplain that he "intended to die a good Catholic." When he was dying, Pius IX released him from all canonical censures, permitted him to receive the Last Rites, and imparted to him his blessing. As a constitutional monarch he sought to provide leadership in the very difficult early period of Italian nationhood.

Bibliography: C. S. FORESTER, *Victor Emmanuel II and the Union of Italy* (New York 1927). G. ARDAU, *Vittorio Emanuele II e i suoi tempi,* 2 v. (Milan 1939). F. COGNASSO, *Vittorio Emanuele II* (Turin 1946). D. MASSÈ, *Il caso di coscienza del risorgimento italiano dalle origini alla Conciliazione* (Rome 1961). P. PIRRI, ed., *Pio IX e Vittorio Emanuele dal loro carteggio privato,* 5 v. (Rome 1944–61).

[E. P. NOETHER]

VICTOR OF PLANCY, ST.

Hermit; b. Troyes, France; d. Plancy, sixth century. He was educated for the priesthood and ordained, and he served as a priest before becoming a hermit in Plancy (Arcis-sur-Aube, near Troyes). His prodigies attracted large crowds, including a king of France (Chilperic, Childeric, or Clotaire II), to his cell. He was buried in his cell; an oratory was built there and his cult spread under the name "St. Vittre." In 837 his remains were transferred to Moutier-Ramey in the Diocese of Troyes; in 1791, to Arcis. His cult was especially popular in the 12th century when BERNARD OF CLAIRVAUX composed an Office in his honor (*Patrologia Latina*, ed. J. P. Migne, 217 v., indexes 4 v. (Paris 1878–90) 183:775–780). His *vita,* written before 837 by an anonymous author, is of little value (*Acta Sanctorum* Feb. 3:665–667).

Feast: Feb. 26.

Bibliography: A. E. MOLINIER et al., *Les Sources de l'histoire de France,* 6 v. (Paris 1901–06) :300. A. ZIMMERMANN, *Lexikon für Theologie und Kirche,* ed. M. BUCHBERGER, 10 v. (Freiburg 1930–38) 10:618. J. L. BAUDOT and L. CHAUSSIN, *Vies des saints et des bienheureux selon l'ordre du calendrier avec l'historique des fêtes,* ed. by the Benedictines of Paris, 12 v. (Paris 1935–56); v. 13, suppl. and table générale (1959) 2:557. A. BUTLER, *The Lives of the Saints,* rev. ed. H. THURSTON and D. ATTWATER, 4v. (New York 1956) 1:426–427.

[É. BROUETTE]

VICTOR OF TUNNUNA

Historian, bishop of Tunnuna (near Carthage?); d. Constantinople, c. 567. He was imprisoned in the Balearics by JUSTINIAN I and exiled to Egypt in 555 for his defense of the THREE CHAPTERS. JUSTIN II imprisoned him and five other bishops in monasteries near Constantinople in 565 when they still refused to recant. In his last years Victor composed a chronicle from the Creation to 566, revising and continuing that of PROSPER OF AQUITAINE. The extant part of Victor's chronicle (443–566), like Prosper's, deals with religious controversies, beginning with Eutyches in 447. Victor records events in Rome, Carthage, and the Eastern patriarchates, and along the barbarian frontier. His chronology follows consular years until 563 when, with errors, he adopts imperial years. JOHN OF BICLARO continued his chronicle and MAXIMUS OF SARAGOSSA probably revised it. After Isidore of Seville it was neglected. Another Victor (of Cartenna) probably wrote the *Liber de paenitentia* (*Patrologia Latina,* ed. J. P. Migne 17:971–1004).

Bibliography: ISIDORE OF SEVILLE, *De viris illustribus,* ch. 38. T. MOMMSEN, *Monumenta Germaniae Auctores antiquissimi* (Berlin 1825–) 11:163–206. O. BARDENHEWER, *Geschichte der altkirchlichen Literatur,* 5 v. (Freiburg 1913–1932) 5:329–331. G. BARDY, *Dictionnaire de théologie catholique,* ed. A. VACANT, 15 v. (Paris 1903–50; Tables générales 1951–) 15.2:2880–81.

[E. P. COLBERT]

VICTOR OF VITA

A 5th-century African bishop and Church historian, bishop of Vita in the African province of Byzacene. Victor describes the persecution of the African Catholics by the Arian VANDALS in his *Historia persecutionis Africanae provinciae.* The critical edition of the work comprises three, not five books, the first of which describes the persecution under Gaiseric (428–477); the others, that under Hunneric (477–484). For the early years, Victor relies on the recollection of others, but he gives an eyewitness account of the later years and, though personally involved, supplies a basically trustworthy and unbiased history.

The history is important as witness to Hunneric's edicts of persecution; it certifies that Victor was bishop of Vita in 484, when he is listed as 17th out of 107 bishops in the province of Byzacene. Of value to theologians is the anti-Arian defense of Catholic doctrine contained in a confession of faith drawn up by Eugene, Archbishop of Carthage, for the Arian-Catholic conference held there on Feb. 1, 484. Many vivid scenes of heroic bravery under torture recall a glorious episode in the history of the Church, as Victor boasts of the saints hastening joyfully to the crown of martyrdom and bewails the cruelty of the Vandals who ordered the Christians to be buried in silence without the solemnity of Psalms and hymns.

A gruesome conclusion portrays the death of Hunneric in 484, but it is a later addition. The prologue was probably not written by Victor; nor is he the author of the *Passio septem monachorum,* even though he mentions the martyrdom of these seven monks.

Bibliography: C. HALM, ed., *Monumenta Germaniae Historica: Auctores antiquissimi* (Berlin 1826–) v.3. *Corpus scriptorum ecclesiasticorum latinorum* (Vienna 1866–) v. 7. E. DEKKERS, ed. *Clavis Patrum latinorum* (2d ed. Streenbrugge 1961) 708, 798–799. G. BARDY, *Dictionnaire de théologie catholique,* ed. A. VACANT et al. (Paris 1903–50) 5.2:2881. O. BARDENHEWER, *Geschichte der altkirchlichen Literatur,* 5 v. (Freiburg 1913–32) 4:550–552.

[A. C. RUSH]

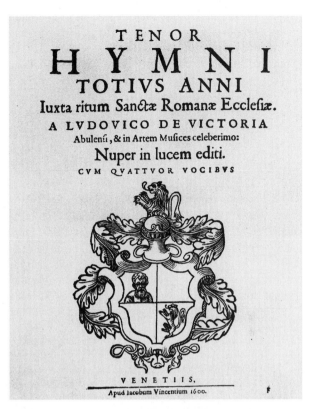

Title page from "Hymni otius anni," by Tomás Luis de Victoria, 1600, published in Venice.

VICTORIA, TOMÁS LUIS DE

Leading composer of the Spanish polyphonic school; b. Ávila, *c.* 1548; d. Madrid, Aug. 27, 1611. The composer's parents were Francisco Luis de Victoria and Francisca Suárez de la Concha of Segovia, and he was the seventh of their ten children who survived to maturity. When Tomás was only nine his father died, leaving the family to the guardianship of the boy's uncle, Juan Luis de Victoria, a priest in Ávila Diocese. Tomás received his first music instruction as a choirboy in the local cathedral, whose chapelmasters during the period were Gerónimo de Espinar (1550–58), Bernardino de Ribera (1559–63), and Juan Navarro, the last two reckoned as among the finest composers of 16th-century Spain. In 1565 Victoria enrolled for three years at the Jesuit Collegium Germanicum in Rome, whose principal benefactors were Philip II of Spain and Otto Cardinal TRUCHSESS VON WALDBURG, Archbishop of Augsburg. Truchsess early singled out Victoria for his special protection, and the supremely beautiful *Motecta* (Venice 1572), Victoria's first publication, were dedicated to Truchess.

From early 1569 until 1574 Victoria served as singer and organist in the Aragonese church of S. Maria di Monserrato, and from 1573 through 1582 he sang occasionally at the other Spanish church in Rome, S. Giacomo degli Spagnoli. In 1571 the Collegium Germanicum hired him as music instructor, and two years later he became *maestro di cappella* of the nearby Roman Seminary, a post occupied up to Sept. 25, 1571, by PALESTRINA, with whom Victoria had perhaps studied. After Gregory XIII gave the Collegium Germanicum new quarters in the jubilee year 1575, Victoria served simultaneously as *moderator musicae* of the college and chapelmaster of the college church, S. Apollinare. On March 6 and 13, 1575, Victoria received minor orders in the English church, St. Thomas of Canterbury, at the hands of Thomas Goldwell, exiled bishop of St. Asaph, who ordained him deacon and priest on August 25 and 28 of that same year. On June 8, 1578, he became a chaplain at S. Girolamo della Carità, seat of the new Congregation of the Oratory (*see* ORATORIANS). For the next several years, while in close association with (St.) Philip NERI, he published in lavish folio his *Cantica B. Virginis* (1581); *Hymni totius anni* (1581, dedicated to Gregory XIII); *Missarum Libri Duo* (1583, dedicated to Philip II); and in 1585 his sublime *Officium Hebdomadae Sanctae* and *Motecta Festorum Totius Anni.*

Again in Spain, from 1587 until her death in 1603, he was chaplain to the Dowager Empress Maria (who was living in retirement with her daughter Margaret at the Royal Convent of Discalced Clarist Nuns in Madrid). He also directed the priests' and boys' choir attached to the convent, and from 1604 to 1611 served by choice as convent organist. In 1592 he was in Rome to superintend publication of another folio—*Missae quatuor, quinque, sex et octo vocibus.* In Madrid (1600) he published in separate part-books a miscellany of Masses, Magnificats, motets, and psalms that look forward to the baroque with their frequent polychoralism, their organ scoring, and the pulsating intensity of such inclusions as the *Missa pro victoria* (nine voice-parts). To commemorate Empress Maria's death he published an *Officium Defunctorum* (1605), which returns to the unaccompanied Renaissance ideal.

By comparison with that of Palestrina or Lasso, Victoria's output of 180 compositions is small. Yet he has endeared himself to all posterity with his mystical fervor and the nobility of his musical concepts. Fortunate in his early contacts with German and English students who took his works home with them, he has inspired unending admiration in countries where Spanish music is otherwise unknown or ignored. Several spurious works have been repeatedly published as his (e.g., *Jesu dulcis memoria, Missa dominicalis*).

Bibliography: *Opera omnia,* ed. F. PEDRELL, 8 v. (Leipzig 1902–13). F. PEDRELL, *Tomás Luis de Victoria* (Valencia 1918), a separate biog. and bibliog. study extracted from the above. R. M. STEVENSON, *Spanish Cathedral Music in the Golden Age* (Berkeley 1961); *Die Musik in Geschichte und Gegenwart,* ed. F. BLUME (Kassel-Basel 1949–) v. 13. R. CASIMIRI, "Il Vittoria: Nuovi documenti," *Note d'archivio,* 11.2 (1934) 111–197. F. HERNÁNDEZ, "La cuna y la escuela de Tomás L. de Victoria," *Ritmo* 11.141 (1940) 27. J. PENA, *Diccionario de la música Labor,* ed. H. ANGLÈS, 2 v. (Barcelona 1954) 2:2218–24. *Enciclopedia universal ilustrada Europeo-Americana,* 70 v. (Barcelona 1908–30; suppl. 1934–) 68:622–628. E. C. CRAMER, The *Officium hebdomadae sanctae of Tomás Luis de Victoria: A Study of Selected Aspects and an Edition and Commentary* (Ph.D. diss. Boston University 1973). N. O'REGAN, "Victoria, Soto, and the Spanish Archconfraternity of the Resurrection in Rome," *Early Music* 22 (1994) 279–295; "Tomás Luis de Victoria's Roman Churches Revisited," *Early Music* 28 (2000) 403–418. R. STEVENSON, "Tomás Luis de Victoria," in *The New Grove Dictionary of Music and Musicians,* ed. S. SADIE, v. 19 (New York 1980) 703–709. J. V. GONZÁLEZ VALLE, "Recepción del *Officium Hebdomadae Sanctae* de T. L. de Victoria y edición de F. Pedrell," *Recerca Musicológica* 11/12 (1991/92) 133–155. L. WOJCICKA-HRUZA, "A Manuscript Source for Magnificats by Victoria," *Early Music* 25 (1997) 83–98.

[R. M. STEVENSON]

VICTORIA AND ANATOLIA, SS.

Virgin martyrs. Though the passio of St. Anatolia and St. Victoria is worthless, there seems to be reason enough to believe that the two saints existed. According to their acts, when Anatolia refused to marry her suitor, Aurelius, the young man asked her sister, Victoria, to plead his case. But Victoria was converted to her sister's Christian views on virginity and broke off her engagement to her fiancé, Eugenius. The two suitors then seized the girls and attempted to starve them into submission. Finally, denounced as Christians, Victoria and Anatolia were put to the sword. The martyrs enjoyed a cultus in several parts of Italy, but the facts concerning their martyrdom are unknown. The doctrine on marriage, as outlined in the passio, reflects the rigorous teaching of the Encratics rather than Christian teaching. St. ALDHELM of Sherborne (709) used the passio of St. Victoria for his *De laudibus virginitatis.*

Feast: Dec. 23.

Bibliography: P. PASCHINI, *La "Passio" delle martire Sabine Vittoria ed Anatolia* (Rome 1919). H. DELEHAYE, *Étude sur le légendier romain* (Brussels 1936) 59–60; ed., *Commentarius perpetuus in martyrologium Hieronymianum* (Acta Sanctorum; Paris 1863–] Nov. 2.2; 1931) 364, 654. A. BUTLER, *The Lives of the Saints,* rev. ed. H. THURSTON and D. ATTWATER, 4v. (New York 1956) 4:599–600.

[E. DAY]

VICTORINE SPIRITUALITY

Founded in 1108 by WILLIAM OF CHAMPEAUX, the Abbey of Saint-Victor, Paris, became one of the leading houses of Regular Canons in France in the 12th century. William was archdeacon of Paris and head of the cathedral school when he resigned in order to establish a small community of religious on the Left Bank of the Seine at a site dedicated to St. Victor of Marseilles. With urging from others, William soon resumed his teaching and attracted students to the new foundation. In 1113 William became bishop of Châlons. Leadership passed to Gilduin (d. 1155), who was named the first abbot of the community. Saint-Victor received gifts and endowments from King Louis VI and was known (like the Abbey of Saint-Denis) as a Royal Abbey. The Victorines followed the Rule of St. Augustine, developed on the basis of letters and writings of Augustine and used in the eleventh century and later as a vehicle for reforming cathedral clerics (canons) or as the rule of independent houses of religious (e.g. Premontré and Saint Victor). Most houses of Regular Canons combined the asceticism and prayer typical of monks with pastoral duties of priests. The Victorine *Liber ordinis* (written during Gilduin's abbacy) was a supplement to the Rule of St. Augustine and reveals much about organization and daily life, including the hierarchy of officials, ritualized behavior in chapter-house and church, a yearly cycle of daily readings in the refectory, the use of sign-language, books and the library, and the like. Saint-Victor was particularly significant in the history of twelfth-century thought because of the brilliant combination of biblical study, theological reflection, mystical writing, and liturgical observance that characterized writings of the leading thinkers in the community. Unfortunately, after Gilduin (1114–1155) and his successors Achard (1155–1161) and Gunther (1161–1162), the Abbey suffered financial problems and internal strife under the abbacy of Ernis (1162–1172), who was removed from office by Alexander III. In the thirteenth century the Abbey lost its grandeur as a center of learning, but it continued a significant role in the religious life of Paris, for the canons served as confessors for students in the schools, later the University. Saint- Victor gave rise to a number of other communities of Regular Canons in France, England, Ireland, Germany, Denmark, and Italy. The community was dispersed in the French Revolution and the buildings were destroyed. By 1813 the Abbey had disappeared from maps. Much of the medieval library of Saint-Victor remained intact and exists today in the Bibliothèque Nationale.

Although William of Champeaux's interests in theological questions and biblical exegesis no doubt shaped the early intellectual climate of Saint- Victor, the formative intellectual and spiritual leader from the 1120s was Hugh of Saint-Victor (d. 1141). Hugh was one of the leading biblical interpreters, theologians, and mystical writers of his generation and his combination of these fields in his own work placed a distinctive mark on Victorine thought for the next several generations. Hugh stressed the place of the historical meaning of scripture as the foundation of all further interpretation (e.g., allegory and tropology). His *De sacramentis christianae fidei* was the first of the *summae* of theology that would become so characteristic of medieval theology from the twelfth century onward. His mystical writings, especially *De arca Noe morali* and *Libellus de foramatione Arca* (also knows as *De arca Noe mysticis*) were among the foremost products of the revival of contemplative writing in the twelfth century and especially reflect the increasing desire to 'order' the stages of advance in asceticism/ prayer/mysticism. They are notable for their use of visual images of biblical origin to provide a "structure" for initiation into the mystical path. Andrew of Saint-Victor, who may have been a direct student of Hugh's, dedicated himself single-mindedly to the literal interpretation of the Hebrew Bible and (following Hugh's lead) turned to contemporary Jews to inform his search for the literal meaning of the text. Adam of Saint-Victor's contributions to twelfth-century religious life underscore the importance of the liturgy at Saint-Victor: he brought the medieval liturgical sequence to perfection and left a significant body of sequences composed for use at the Abbey. In the "second generation "of Victorines, Richard of Saint-Victor stands out particularly for the depth of his understanding

of the mystic way; his treatises *On the Twelve Patriarchs* (also known as *Benjamin minor*) and *On the Mystical Ark* (also known as *Benjamin major*) were major contributions to mystical literature and influenced thinkers as diverse as the Franciscan Bonaventure and the anonymous English author of *The Cloud of Unknowing*. In his poetry and prose, Godfrey of Saint-Victor continued the broad humanistic and spiritual vision of the founders, but the more narrow-minded Walter produced works violently opposed to the scholastic theology of the day and also to broad humanistic learning characteristic of Hugh, Richard, and Godfrey. Victorine thinkers also were instrumental in interpreting and spreading the writings and ideas of Dionysius the pseudo-Areopagite. Hugh wrote a commentary on Dionysius' work entitled *On the Celestial Hierarchy* (using the translation made by John Scotus Eriugena) and Richard incorporated Dionysian ideas in his mysticism. A thirteenth-century Victorine, Thomas Gallus (or Thomas of Vercelli—he helped to found the community of Regular Canons at the Abbey of St. Andrew in Vercelli, Italy) also incorporated Dionysian themes into his writings, which included commentaries on the Song of Songs and an extract of Dionysius' writings.

The particular "spirituality" of Saint-Victor would be the pattern life and attitude set out in the writings of Hugh and Richard in particular. Their combination of a biblical foundation for thought, clear and creative theological reflection, and profound mystical writing was influential far beyond the walls of Saint-Victor and can be found in thought of Bonaventure, the author of the *Cloud of Unknowing* and also the current of spirituality identified with the late-medieval Brethren of the Common Life and the Abbey of Regular Canons at Windesheim. Recent scholars, especially Caroline Bynum, have found in the phrase *docere verbo et exemplo* ("to teach by word and example") a possible defining characteristic of Regular Canons, as opposed to Benedictine monasticism. Canons seem to have seen themselves in a role of "teaching" others (inside or outside the community) "by word and example" while monks appear to have been more concerned with an individual's spiritual development.

Little is known about the actual lives of individual canons of Saint-Victor. They wrote almost nothing about themselves; no "lives" like those of contemporary Cistercians exist and later generations did not supply much in the way of an historical recollection of the founders or their followers.

Bibliography: F. BONNARD, *Histoire de l'abbaye royale et de l'ordre des chanoines réguliers de Saint-Victor de Paris*, 2 v. (Paris 1905–07). C. W. BYNUM, *Jesus as Mother: Studies in the Spirituality of the High Middle Ages* (Berkeley, Los Angeles, London 1982). J. CHÂTILLON, *Le mouvement canonial au Moyen Age. Réforme de* *l'Église, spiritualité et culture. Études réunies par Patrice Sicard,* Bibliotheca Victorina, 3 (Paris-Turnhout 1992); "De Guillaume de Champeaux à Thomas Gallus: Chronique d'histoire littéraire et doctrinale de l'école de Saint-Victor," *Revue du Moyen Âge Latin* 8 (1952) 139–62, 247–72. J. C. DICKINSON, *The Origins of the Austin Canons and their Introduction into England* (London 1950). L. JOCQUÉ and L. MILLIS, eds. *Liber ordinis Sancti Victoris Parisiensis,* Corpus Christianorum Continuatio Mediaevalis 61 (Turnhout 1984). G. LAWLESS, *Augustine of Hippo and His Monastic Rule* (Oxford 1987). J. LONGÈRE, ed. *L'abbaye parisienne de Saint-Victor au moyen âge* (Turnhout 1991). B. MCGINN, *The Growth of Mysticism,* v. 2 of *The Presence of God: A History of Western Christian Mysticism* (New York 1994) 363–418. G. OUY, et al. *Le catalogue de la bibliothèque de l'abbaye de Saint-Victor de Paris de Claude de Grandrue 1514* (Paris 1983). G. OUY, *Les manuscrits de l'Abbaye de Saint-Victor: Catalogue établi sur la base du répertoire de Claude de Grandrue (1514),* 2 v. Bibliotheca Victorina, 10 (Turnhout 1999). B. SMALLEY, *The Study of the Bible in the Middle Ages,* (3rd ed. Oxford 1983), chaps. 3 and 4. A. ZUMKELLER, *Augustine's Ideal of the Religious Life,* tr. E. COLLEDGE (New York 1980).

[G. A. ZINN]

VICTORINUS OF PETTAU, ST.

Fourth-century Latin exegete, bishop, and martyr; d. *ca.* 303. The little known of his life is provided by St. JEROME (*De viris ill.* 74). Victorinus, the first exegete to write in Latin, was bishop of Pettau in Styria (Austria), and was put to death during the persecution of Diocletian.

Victorinus commented on selected passages from Genesis, Exodus, Leviticus, Isaiah, Ezekiel, Habakkuk, Ecclesiastes, the Song of Songs, Matthew, and Revelation. The commentary on the last is the only one extant. His exegesis, influenced by MILLENARIANISM, was based on that of Papias of Hieropolis, IRENAEUS, HIPPOLYTUS OF ROME, and especially Origen.

The "Commentary on the Apocalypse," preserved in a 15th-century manuscript (Vat. Codex Ottobon. Latin. 3288A) is certainly a work of Victorinus. He is also credited with a "De fabrica mundi" of which a fragment is preserved in the ninth-century Lambeth Codex 414 edited by W. CAVE in 1688.

Jerome tells us that Victorinus wrote also a treatise "Against all Heresies." It is possible that this latter is the same as that work appended to Tertullian's "Prescription of Heretics." A. von Harnack believed in this identity but there is doubt on the matter. The Decretum Gelasianum condemned Victorinus's work as open to censure because of its millenarianism. There is no known cult to him except in Pettau, where it began officially in 1768. Eventually his relics were taken to Rome.

Feast: Aug. 7 (formerly Nov. 2).

Bibliography: *Opera,* ed. J. HAUSSLEITER (Corpus scriptorum ecclesiasticorum latinorum 49; Vienna 1916). J. QUASTEN, *Patrology,* 3 v. (Westminster, Md. 1950–) 2:411–413. G. BARDY, *Dictionnaire de théologie catholique,* ed. A. VACANT et al., (Paris 1903–50; Tables générales 1951–) 15.2:2882–87. B. ALTANER, *Patrology,* tr. H. GRAEF from 5th German ed. (New York 1960) 205. F. CROSS, *The Early Christian Fathers* (London 1960) 187. M. DULAEY, *Victorin de Poetovio, premier exégète latin* (Paris 1993). G. VAN HOOFF, *Acta Sanctorum* Nov. (Antwerp 1643–)1:432–443.

[P. W. LAWLER]

VICTRICIUS OF ROUEN, ST.

Bishop; b. *c.* 330; d. before 409. At 17 he enlisted in Roman military service, and later became a Christian. Upon renouncing military service he was flogged and sentenced to death, but was miraculously freed. Victricius then devoted himself to the study of philosophy and theology; he was chosen bishop of Rouen *c.* 380 while still a layman. He renewed ecclesiastical discipline, founded numerous parish churches in rural areas, promoted monastic life in his episcopal see, and acquired numerous relics for his cathedral from Italy. He met (St.) MARTIN OF TOURS and (St.) PAULINUS OF NOLA in 386 and again about 395 in Chartres. He preached among the heathen tribes of Gaul in Artois, western Flanders, Hainaut, and Brabant. When his orthodoxy was impugned groundlessly, he went to Rome late in 403 to clear himself. There he met Emperor HONORIUS and Pope INNOCENT I who sent him a famous decretal on disciplinary matters dated Feb. 15, 404. He must have died before 409, since St. Paulinus in a letter to St. AUGUSTINE in 409 named the eminent bishops of Gaul without mentioning Victricius. In 941 his relics were brought to the church of St. REMIGIUS in Braine (near Soissons). Here they were solemnly exalted in 1865.

Feast: Aug. 7.

Bibliography: E. VACANDARD. *Saint Victrice, évêque de Rouen, IVᵉ–Vᵉ s.* (Paris 1903). É. DE MOREAU, *Histoire de l'Église en Belgique,* v.1 (2d ed. Brussels 1945). P. GROSJEAN, *Analecta Bollandiana* 63 (1945) 94–99.

[P. VOLK]

VICTURIUS OF LE MANS, ST.

Bishop of Le Mans, France, known also as Victorius or Victor; b. before 450; d. Sept. 1, 490. He assisted at the synods of Angers (453) and Tours (461) and collaborated with fellow bishops in matters of church discipline. Soon after his death GREGORY OF TOURS alluded to him as "venerable confessor," described how he miraculously saved Le Mans from destruction by fire, and attributed to his sanctity cures that took place at his tomb. Since the 7th century he has been venerated at the basilica dedicated to him in Le Mans.

Feast: Sept. 1.

Bibliography: *Acta Sanctorum* Sept. 1:220–223. L. DUCHESNE, *Fastes épiscopaux de l'ancienne Gaule* (Paris 1907–15) 2:312–313, 336–337. GREGORY OF TOURS, *De gloria confessorum,* ch. 55, *Patrologia latina,* ed. J. P. MIGNE (Paris 1878–90) 71:868–869. A. LEDRU, *Les Premiers temps de l'église du Mans* (Le Mans 1913). *Bibliotheca hagiographica latina antiquae et mediae aetatis* 2:1243. *Analecta Bollandiana* 39 (1921) 93,100–101, 110.

[L. M. COFFEY]

VICUÑA, LAURA, BL.

Virgin, martyr; b. Apr. 5, 1891, Santiago, Chile; d. Jan. 22, 1904, Junín de los Andes (on the Rio Negro near Chile), Patagonia, Argentina.

Following the death in 1895 of her soldier father, José Domingo Vicuña, Laura's mother, Mercedes Piño, moved the family to Junín de los Andes. Because of the family's poverty and her inability to find work, Mercedes became the mistress of a local *hacendero,* Manuel Mora, on his ranch called Quilquihu near Neuquén. In Junín Laura and her younger sister Julia Amanda were accepted into the new school run by the Daughters of Mary Help of Christians (Jan. 21, 1900). Laura came to understand that her mother's illicit union endangered her soul. Laura pledged her life for her mother's conversion before her confessor. Laura fell ill during the winter of 1903, and Mercedes moved with her daughters into a small house near the parish church at Junín. Mora, enraged by the abandonment, sought out and began beating Mercedes. Laura intervened and received Mora's abuse as well. She died at age twelve from internal injuries inflicted by Manuel Mora during that final confrontation. After Laura admitted on her deathbed the promise she had made to God—her life for Mercedes' salvation—her mother returned to the Church. Vicuña's body rests in the María Auxiliadora Chapel.

Pope John Paul II called her the "Eucharistic flower of Junín de los Andes, whose life was a poem of purity, sacrifice, and filial love" (beatification homily, Sept. 3, 1988, Turin, Italy). Patron of Argentina.

Feast: Jan. 22 (Salesians).

Bibliography: A. AUFFRAY and A. SWIDA, *Pszeniczne klosy: opowiesc o niezwyklym zyciu trojga wychowanków salezjánskich,* 2nd ed. (Łodz 1982). J. M. BLANCO, *Laura, la flor del paraíso* (San José Costa Rica 1942). D. GRASSIANO, *Laura Vicuña* (2d. ed. V Rìme, Slovenia 1969).

[K. I. RABENSTEIN]

VICUÑA LARRAÍN, MANUEL

Chilean archbishop, known for his conciliatory spirit; b. Santiago, April 20, 1778; d. Valparaíso, 1843. Manuel, son of Francisco Vicuña Hidalgo and Carmen Larraín Salas, studied at the Convictorio Carolino and later at the University of San Felipe. He received a degree in theology in 1802 and was ordained in March 1803. He was assigned to the church that had belonged to the Jesuits, where with other priests he lived a common life. He gave spiritual retreats and conducted fruitful missions in the rural area. In 1828 Leo XII appointed him titular bishop and apostolic vicar in Santiago. Upon the death of RODRÍGUEZ ZORRILLA, Gregory XVI appointed Vicuña Larraín Bishop of Santiago (1832). In 1813, when the diocesan seminary became part of the Instituto Nacional, ecclesiastical students, secular as well as religious, preferred to study at the convents. Owing to Vicuña Larraín and to the minister, Joaquín Tocornal, the seminary was separated from the Instituto (1835). Santiago was raised to an archbishopric and the bishoprics of La Serena and Ancud were established during his episcopacy because of the Catholic tendencies of the government and of Vicuña Larraín's cooperative attitude (1840). From 1833 to 1836 he was also a councillor of state. From 1833 to 1838 he visited the diocese from the River Maule to Petorca. During his term of office, the Sacred Heart congregation was established in Chile, and the Jesuits returned. Vicuña Larraín also founded a retreat house in San José and a home for aged and infirm priests. P. de Leturia says that he was "the most prudent and able of all the Spanish-American bishops of his time."

Bibliography: L. F. PRIETO DEL RÍO, *Diccionario biográfico del clero secular de Chile* (Santiago de Chile 1922) 711–712. F. ARANEDA BRAVO, *Obispos, sacerdotes y frailes* (Santiago de Chile 1962).

[A. M. ESCUDERO]

VIDA, MARCO GIROLAMO

Italian humanist poet and Church reformer; b. Cremona *c.* 1485; d. Alba, Sept. 27, 1566. Of a noble though poor family, Vida received a classical education at Cremona and at Mantua, and studied philosophy, theology, and canon law in Rome, where he was ordained before 1510. Much of his earliest poetry has been lost. His poems on chess, *Scacchia ludus,* and the silkworm, *De bombyce,* won him the favor of Leo X, who commissioned him to write a great epic on the life of Christ. His interest in Vergil led him to compose *Poeticorum libri tres* (1527), which has had undue and unexpected influence in literary history; in fact he became known as the "Christian Vergil." The epic *Christiad* (1535), in six books, was a great success in its own time and long after. In 1533 Clement VII appointed Vida bishop of Alba in Lombardy, and there he devoted himself to religious, social, and political problems. Though forced to leave Alba by the alternating French and Spanish invaders, he nonetheless persevered in reform work. He took stern measures against Protestants and was sometimes overzealous in invoking the secular arm. He worked for the improvement of clerical standards, and urged this also on the popes and his fellow bishops. Vida participated in some sessions of the Council of Trent, but left at least once in protest of its inactivity (1545). In 1564 he was instrumental in organizing the synod of Milan under Abp. Charles Borromeo.

Vida was known throughout his long life for personal integrity and high ideals. His secular poetry remained extensively popular into the 19th century; the *Christiad* and the *Hymns* that he composed in the 1530s and 1540s influenced religious literature after Trent. His *Constitutiones synodales* (1562) were exemplary for Borromeo and others as paradigms of diocesan and clerical reform.

Bibliography: V. CICCHITELLI, *Sulle opere poetiche di M. G. Vida* (Naples 1904); *Sulle opere in prosa* (Naples 1909). M. DI CESARE, *Vida's Christiad and Vergilian Epic* (New York 1963). M. G. VIDA, *Sedici lettere inedite*, ed. F. NOVATI (Milan 1898).

[M. A. DI CESARE]

VIEBAN, ANTHONY

Sulpician, seminary professor; b. St. Pantaleonde-Lapleau, Tulle, France, Jan. 8, 1872; d. St. Petersburg, FL, Jan. 28, 1944. In 1891, after attending the ecclesiastical college of Theil, near Ussel, he entered the major seminary of Tulle; he was ordained on June 29, 1895. He then joined the Sulpicians and spent the next two years doing graduate work at L'Institut Catholique, Paris, receiving doctorates in theology and Canon Law (1897). After novitiate training at Issy, near Paris (1897–98), Vieban was sent to the U.S. Except for two years (1909–11) on the faculty of St. John's Seminary, Brighton, MA, he spent the next 20 years teaching dogmatic and pastoral theology, Canon Law, and Scripture at St. Mary's Seminary, Baltimore, MD. He contributed to Adolphe Tanquerey's *Synopsis of Dogmatic Theology* and to numerous ecclesiastical magazines. In 1917 he was transferred to Washington, DC, and became (1919) the superior of the Sulpician novitiate, first in Washington and then in Catonsville, MD, until his appointment as rector of the Theological College of The Catholic University of America, Washington, DC. During his 46 years in the U.S., he served his society as a member of the provincial council, twice secretary to the superior general of the Sulpicians, personal counselor to his provincial at the world chapter of his society in 1922, and an elected American representative to later chapters (1929, 1936). Although

thoroughly Americanized, Vieban always remained loyal to his native country and visited there whenever possible, preaching and giving parochial, seminary, and clerical retreats.

Bibliography: P. BOISARD, *Lettre circulair à l'occasion de la mort de M. Anthony Vieban* (Seminaire Saint Sulpice, Issy, 1944).

[C. M. CUYLER]

VIEIRA, ANTÔNIO

Portuguese theologian, spiritual and political adviser to the crown and court, pulpit orator, social critic, and man of letters; b. Lisbon, Feb. 6, 1608; d. Salvador, Bahia, Brazil, July 18, 1697. At the age of six he moved with his parents to Salvador, where he was educated in the Old World scholastic and humanistic tradition of the Jesuits. He entered the society in 1623 and was ordained in 1635. After returning to Lisbon in 1641, he so impressed King John IV with his political insight, poise, and eloquence in the pulpit, that the monarch appointed him preacher of the royal chapel (1644) and soon thereafter his adviser and emissary to European capitals. As a means of improving the newly restored monarchy, Vieira advocated the protection of the new Christians and Jews so that they might invest in Portuguese overseas enterprises.

For most of the decade 1651 to 1661 Vieira labored in Brazil as superior of the temporal and spiritual ministry to the native peoples of Maranhão and the Amazon; this apostolate was ill fated, but it deserves comparison with the civilizing mission of the earlier Jesuits ANCHIETA and NÓBREGA. The death of the King (1656) foreshadowed a series of bitter frustrations, which began with a revolt of the colonists against laws Vieira had instituted to better the lot of the native peoples. He was expelled from Maranhão in 1661, and, once more in Portugal, he was exiled to Pôrto by Alfonso VI for his part in a palace intrigue. The INQUISITION, long irritated at Vieira's influence, especially in royal policy affecting Jewish property, then denounced as heretical and judaistic one of his writings prophesying the resurrection of King John IV. From 1662 to 1668, Vieira underwent examination, imprisonment for more than two years, and sentence, including indefinite isolation and privation of speech; but these penalties were soon set aside. Vieira did not enjoy the political power he had expected when the regent Pedro was crowned King, and he left in 1669 for Rome, where the acclaim for his sermons in both Portuguese and Italian gave him an international reputation. With a papal brief (April 1675) granting him immunity from the Portuguese Inquisition, he returned to Portugal, ailing and old but pleased to have this measure of revenge upon his tormentors.

In 1681 Vieira voyaged to his province in Bahia, there to find solace in correspondence, in editing his sermons, and in writing what he considered his greatest work, the notable *Clavis Prophetarum,* on the consummation of Christ's kingdom on earth. It was left incomplete at his death and now survives only in fragments. His sermons, full of conceptual and theological subtleties but generally avoiding the cultist and the obscure, are the basis of a new-found importance in literary scholarship, after valuable studies by A. Sérgio, H. Cidade, E. Gomes, and, most recently, R. Cantel; they are important not only for their criticism of 17th-century man but also as examples of well-wrought baroque pulpit oratory, some of whose vividness is still moving. Vieira's letters appear in the edition of J. L. de Azevedo, who is his most discerning biographer. Vieira's basic writings on messianism and prophecy, *History of the Future, Portugal's Hopes and the Fifth Empire,* and the fragments of *Clavis Prophetarum* have been analyzed by H. Cidade and R. Cantel, the latter giving the newest vision of Vieira as Christian prophet and utopian.

Bibliography: A. VIEIRA, *Obras escolhidas,* ed. A. SÉRGIO and H. CIDADE, 12 v. (Lisbon 1951–54), scholarly sampling with notes and introductions and esp. valuable as no complete or critical ed. exists; *Cartas,* ed. J. L. D'AZEVEDO, 3 v. (Coimbra 1925–28); *Sermões,* 16 v. (Lisbon 1679–1748; facs. São Paulo 1944–45), all but the last 3 v. reworked from notes by Vieira, making this *editio princeps* the best even today. C. R. BOXER, *A Great Luso-Brazilian Figure: Padre Antônio Vieira, S. J., 1608–1697* (London 1957). J. L. D'AZEVEDO, *História de Antônio Vieira,* 2 v. (2d ed. Lisbon 1931), the basic biography. R. CANTEL, *Les Sermons de Vieira: Étude de style* (Paris 1959); *Prophétisme et messianisme dans l'oeuvre d'Antônio Vieira* (Paris 1960), constitutes, with the preceding, a good working bibliog. E. GOMES, "Antônio Vieira," in *A literatura no Brasil,* ed. A. COUTINHO (Rio de Janeiro 1955–) 1:323–360. I. MONTEIRO DE BARROS LINS, *Aspectos do Padre Antônio Vieira* (2d ed. Rio de Janeiro 1962). S. LEITE, *História da Companhia de Jesus no Brasil,* 10 v. (Lisbon 1938–50) 9:192–363.

[F. P. ELLISON]

VIEL, PLACIDA, BL.

Superior general of the Sisters of the CHRISTIAN SCHOOLS OF MERCY; b. ValValcher, Normandy, Sept. 26, 1815; d. Saint-Sauveurle-Vicomte (Manche), March 4, 1877. As a farmer's daughter she had seven years of elementary schooling and then worked at housekeeping in her home until 1833 when she entered religious life at Saint-Sauveur-le-Vicomte, and exchanged her given name, Victoria Eulalia Jacqueline, for that of Placida. After teaching for a few years, she became mistress of novices. She was also sent to the French court to raise funds, and entrusted with opening new houses. Upon the death of the foundress, St. Mary Magdalene POSTEL, in 1846, Placida succeeded her as superior general, an office

Antônio Vieira.

she retained until death. During this period the congregation increased its membership from 150 to more than 1,000, and its number of houses from 37 to 105. She was noted for a humble and retiring disposition, high intelligence and charm; but no great mystical graces or spiritual trials are recorded. She was beatified on May 6, 1951.

Feast: March 4.

Bibliography: *Blessed Placide Viel,* by S. C. (London 1951). A. BUTLER, *The Lives of the Saints,* ed. H. THURSTON and D. ATTWATER, 4 v. (New York 1956) 1:483–484.

[W. J. BATTERSBY]

VIENNE, COUNCIL OF

The Ecumenical Council of Vienne, in session from Oct. 16, 1311, to May 6, 1312, was convoked by CLEMENT V at a particularly critical period in the history of the Church. Its complete acts have been lost.

History. The trial of the Knights TEMPLARS played a dominant role in the convocation of the Council, but this serious affair was not the only problem facing the new Pope, the former archbishop of Bordeaux, upon his election (June 5, 1305). PHILIP IV the Fair, King of France, had brought pressure to bear on the new Pope to initiate a trial of the deceased BONIFACE VIII; the idea of a crusade to the Holy Land was again emergent, and it seemed generally clear that the Church was in serious need of internal reform. These were the reasons motivating the convocation of a general council; the bull *Regnans in caelis,* promulgated at Poitiers, Aug. 12, 1308, set the opening date as Oct. 1, 1310. Vienne (Department of Isère, France) was chosen as the site of the Council because it was easily accessible and especially because of its location in a province of the Empire, the Dauphiné de Viennois, a little state still practically independent; it was not acquired by the Kingdom of France until 1349.

The protracted trial of the Templars, however, delayed the Council, and on April 4, 1310, by the bull *Alma mater* a new opening date was fixed for Oct. 1, 1311. The sessions were held in the cathedral, and the number of prelates present included 20 cardinals, four patriarchs, 39 archbishops, 79 bishops, and 38 abbots. There were three sessions, in the course of which the Council examined the three points proposed by the Pope. These three points were the major preoccupation not only of the Pope but of the whole of Christendom.

The affair of the Templars had already been the subject of many provincial synods, both in France, where the proceedings had gone against the order, and in the other kingdoms of Europe, where the innocence of the knights had been accepted in the majority of cases. A plenary session of the special conciliar commission named to study the affair closed in December 1311 with a vote favorable to the order; but the arrival in Vienne on March 20, 1312, of Philip the Fair forced the Pope to pronounce a sentence, which had been prepared with the active participation of the archbishops of Reims, Sens, and Rouen and of William of Nogaret and Enguerrand of Marigny. On March 22 Clement V promulgated the bull *Vox in excelso* (*Conciliorum oecumenicorum decreta* (Bolgna-Freiburg 1962) 312–19), abolishing the Order of the Templars, not indeed *de jure* but *per viam provisionis.* This bull, given solemn reading at the second session, was followed by *Ad providam,* dated May 2, which handed over to the KNIGHTS OF MALTA the goods of the Templars; but the Pope on May 6 reserved to himself the judgment of the grand master of the Templars, JACQUES DE MOLAY. On the other hand, the Council refused to comply with the French King's demand to condemn the memory of Pope Boniface VIII.

An expedition to the Holy Land was discussed at the second and third sessions; the Kings of France, England, and Navarre promised to take part within a year. But the Council's consideration to the reform of the Church received greater attention and was the subject of protracted discussion. This reform was treated under two aspects:

(1) clerical morals and (2) protection of the freedoms of the Church. In each case there was a statement of the *GRAVAMINA,* i.e., of the injury to which the Church was being exposed, and a list of *remedia,* remedies to be applied. Debate on the various points followed the definitive vote on the affair of the Templars and occupied the last session of the Council. The decrees approved by the Council and the subsequent constitutions published by the Pope were collected by him into a volume published by his successor JOHN XXII in 1327 under the title, *CLEMENTINAE.* It was in this form that the proceedings and decisions of the council were known to its contemporaries. There is now a better knowledge of them from MS Paris Bib. nat. lat. 1450, which is a statement of the grievances presented by the prelates and examined by the commission presided over by Cardinals Nicholas of Fréauville and Napoleon Orsini. The grievances concerned especially the encroachments of the civil power on ecclesiastical jurisdiction and the statement of the remedies proposed.

Decrees. The decrees adopted at Vienne number 38(?) in all, of which only 19 were published in the *Clementinae.* They condemned the doctrine that the substance of the rational or intellectual soul is not *vere et per se* the form of the human body, attributed to PETER JOHN OLIVI, a leading figure of the Franciscan Spirituals, who was not, however, formally condemned. The decrees (c.37–38) further prepared the way for the reconciliation of the two opposing factions among the FRANCISCANS, the Spirituals and the Conventuals. They also defined the pastoral activities of the MENDICANT ORDERS in the Church (c.10), condemned the BEGUINES AND BEGHARDS (c.16, 28), who had become widespread in the Low Countries and in northern Germany and France, laid down rules for the operation of hospitals (c.17), ordered the creation of chairs of Hebrew, Arabic, and Chaldean at the universities of Bologna, Oxford, Paris, and Salamanca (c.24), and legislated (c.26) against the encroachments by inquisitors (*see* INQUISITION) by making more precise the rules to be followed for their designation. The decrees also curbed USURY (c.29) and violence committed against the person of clerics (c.33–34). The decrees of the Council's third session, whose number and text are unknown, were published May 6, 1312, by Clement V, who on May 2 had already left to return to Avignon.

Bibliography: J. HARDOUIN, *Acta conciliorum et epistolae decretales ac constitutiones summorum pontoficum (34–1714),* 11 v. in 12 (Paris 1715) v.7. J. D. MANSI, *Sacrorum Conciliorum nova et amplissima collectio,* 31 v. (Florence-Venice 1757–98); reprinted and continued by L. PETIT and J. B. MARTIN, 53 v. in 60 (Paris 1889–1927; repr. Graz 1960–) v.25. *Continuatio chronici Guillelmi de Nangis* in M. BOUQUET, *Recueil des historiens des Gaules et de la France (Rerum gallicarum et francicarum scriptores),* 24 v. (Paris 1738–1904) v.20. G. VILLANI, *Historie fiorentine,* L. A.

MURATORI, *Rerum italicarum scriptores, 500–1000*, 25 v. in 28 (Milan 1723–51); continued by G. M. TARTINI and N. G. MITTARELLI (1748–71) 13:454–55. C. BARONIUS, *Annales ecclesiastici*, ed. J. D. MANSI et al., 38 v. (Lucca 1738–59) v.23. F. EHRLE, "Zur Vorgeschichte des Concils von Vienne," H. DENIFLE and F. EHRLE, eds., *Archiv für Literatur- und Kirchengeschichte des Mittelalters*, 7 v. (Berlin Freiburg-1886) 353–416; "Ein Bruchstück der Acten des Concils von Vienne," *ibid.* 4 (1888) 361–470. G. LIZERAND, *Clément V et Philippe le Bel* (Paris 1911). C. J. VON HEFELE, *Histoire des conciles d'apreès les documents originaux*, tr. and continued by H. LECLERCQ, 10 v. in 19 (Paris 1907–38) 6.2:643–719. G. MOLLAT, *The Popes at Avignon, 1305–1378*, tr. J. LOVE (New York 1963). E. MÜLLER, *Das Konzil von Vienne, 1311–1312* (Münster 1934). H. J. SCHROEDER, *Disciplinary Decrees of the General Councils* (St. Louis 1937) 365–442. J. LECLERCQ, *Dictionnaire de théologie catholique*, ed. A. VACANT et al., 15 v. (Paris 1903–50) 15.2:2973–79. *Conciliorum oecumenicorum decreta* (Bologna-Freiburg 1962) 309–77, and bibliog. M. MOLLAT, *Le councile de Vienne: concordance, index, listes de frequence, tables comparatives* (Louvain-la-Neuve 1978).

[M. FRANÇOIS]

VIERNE, LOUIS VICTOR

Blind organist and composer; b. Poitiers, France, Oct. 8, 1870; d. Paris, June 2, 1937. After training in organ under César FRANCK, Guilmant, and WIDOR at the Paris Conservatory, he became in 1892 assistant to Widor at Saint-Sulpice; in 1894, professor at the Conservatory; and in 1900, organist at the cathedral of Notre Dame. In 1911 he joined the faculty of the D' Indy SCHOLA CANTORUM, where some of his disciples were Bonnet, Boulanger, Dupré, and Duruflé. Except for a period in Switzerland (1916–20), he divided his time between teaching in Paris and concert tours throughout Europe and America. He was stricken at the Notre Dame organ after introducing his own *Tryptique,* and died immediately. His music for organ, based on the Franck chromatic harmonies and carefully structured, idiomatic, and imaginative, includes organ symphonies, a Mass for two organs, and *24 Pièces en style libre.* He produced also chamber, choral, and orchestral works, and song cycles.

Bibliography: B. GAVOTY, *Louis Vierne* (Paris 1943). H. M. HENDERSON, "Personal Memories of Louis Vierne," *Diapason* 45.6 (May 1954) 5. H. RIEMANN, *Musik-lexicon*, ed. W. GURLITT, 3 v. (12th ed. Mainz 1958–) 2:1352. F. RAUGEL, *Die Musik in Geschichte und Gegenwart*, ed. F. BLUME (Kassel-Basel 1949–). X. DARASSE, "Louis Vierne" in *The New Grove Dictionary of Music and Musicians*, vol. 19, ed. S. SADIE (New York 1980) 743. D. M. RANDEL, ed., *The Harvard Biographical Dictionary of Music* (Cambridge 1996) 949. N. SLONIMSKY, ed., *Baker's Biographical Dictionary of Musicians*, Eighth Edition (New York 1992) 1962–1963. R. SMITH, *Louis Vierne: Organist of Notre Dame* (Hillsdale 2000).

[C. A. CARROLL]

VIETNAM, MARTYRS OF, SS.

A.k.a. Andrew Dũng-Lạ and 116 Companions, martyrs of Tonkin (in North Vietnam [Bắc Việt]); martyrs of Indo-China (Đông Dương); d. 18th-19th centuries. Canonized June 19, 1988 by Pope John Paul II.

This entry provides information on the 117 martyrs of Vietnam, comprising 96 Vietnamese, 11 Spanish Dominicans, and 10 French members of the Paris Foreign Mission Society. Of these 117 martyrs, 8 were bishops, 50 priests (15 Dominicans, 8 members of the Paris Foreign Mission Society, 27 seculars), 1 seminarian, and 58 lay people (9 Dominican tertiaries and 17 catechists). These martyrs were earlier beatified on four separate occasions: 64 in 1900 by Pope Leo XIII; 8 in 1906 by Pope Pius X (all Dominicans); 20 in 1909 also by Pius X; and 25 in 1951 by Pope Pius XII. On 19 June 1988, some 8,000 exiled Vietnamese Catholics participated in the canonization ceremony in Rome. They heard Pope John Paul II announce: "The Vietnamese Church, with its martyrs and its witness, has been able to proclaim its desire and resolve not to reject the cultural traditions and the legal institutions of the country; rather, it has declared and demonstrated that it wants to incarnate them in itself, in order to contribute faithfully to the true building up of the country."

The corporate feast of the saints is November 24. A personal feast day is shown only when it is not the *dies natalis.* This date is given to aid further research in older documents. For information on the historical background of Vietnam during this period, (*see* VIETNAM, CATHOLIC CHURCH IN).

Almato, Pedro (PhêrôAlmato Bình), Dominican priest; b. 1830 at Sassera (Vich), Spain; d. Nov. 1, 1861, at Hải Dủỏng, Tonkin. He was first sent to the Philippines upon his profession as a Dominican. Thereafter he was sent to Ximabara under Jerome Hermosilla, with whom he was beheaded. Beatified 1906.

Berrio-Ochoa, Valentín (Valentine Berriochoa, Valentinô Berrio-Ochoa Vinh), Dominican bishop of Central Tonkin; b. 1827 at Ellorio (Vitoria), Spain; d. Nov. 1, 1861 at Hải Dương, Tonkin. Following his profession in the Order of Preachers, he was sent to the Philippines, where he was known as an especially devout member of the order. In 1858, he was consecrated titular bishop of Tonkin and appointed vicar apostolic. Upon his arrival in Vietnam, he faced persecution by the government and worked in extremely difficult conditions. Like his Master, the bishop was betrayed by one of his own who had apostatized. In 1861, he was arrested, degraded, imprisoned, tortured, and beheaded with Bishop Hermosilla and Fr. Almato. For a time Valentine's cause was separated from the group because his intercession was credited with several miracles. Beatified 1906.

Bonnard, Jean-Louis (John Louis Bonnard Hương), priest; b. 1824 at Saint-Christo-em-Jarez, France; d. May 1, 1852 Nam Định, Tonkin. He was a attached to the MEP during his work in Annam (Vietnam). While awaiting execution, he wrote a letter of farewell to his family. He was beheaded at the age of 28. Beatified 1900.

Uy Van Bui, Domingo (Dominic Uy, Bùi, Văn Úy Đaminh), Dominican tertiary, lay catechist; b. 1813 in Tiên Mon, Thái Bình, Tonkin; d. Dec. 19, 1839, Cổ Mê, Tonkin. He was seized as a Christian with Thomas Đệ and strangled for refusing to abjure the faith. Beatified 1900.

Buong Viet Tong, Paul (Paul Doi Buong, Paul Tong Viet Buong, Phaolô Tống Viết Bường), soldier; b. in Phủ Cam, Huế (Trung Việt); d. Oct. 23, 1833, in Thủ Đức (Nam Việt) He was the captain of the Emperor Minh-Mạng's bodyguard. As a Christian he became attached to the MEP. He was arrested in 1832, degraded, and suffered for months before he was beheaded. Beatified 1900. Feast: Oct. 22.

Cam, Dominic (Đaminh Cẩm), priest, Dominican tertiary; b. at Cẩm Chương, Bắc Ninh, Tonkin; d. 3 March 1859, at Hưng Yên, Tonkin. Beatified 1951.

Can Nguyen, Francisco Javier (Francis Xavier Can, Phanxicô Xaviê Cần), lay catechist; b. 1803 at Sơn Miêng (Son-Mieng), Hà Đông, West Tonkin; d. Nov. 20, 1837, at Ô Cầu Giấy, Tonkin. He was a catechist for the fathers of the MEP. Strangled in prison. Beatified 1900.

Canh Luong Hoang, José (Joseph Canh, Giuse Hoàng Lương Cảnh), physician, Dominican Tertiary; b. ca. 1763–1765 at Làng Văn, Bắc Giang, Tonkin; d. Sept. 5, 1838, at Bắc Ninh, Tonkin. Beheaded. Beatified 1900.

Castadeda, Jacinto (Jacinto Castaneda Gia), Dominican priest; b. 1743 at Jávita (Valencia), Spain; d. Nov. 7, 1773 at Đồng Mơ, Tonkin. After his profession as a Dominican, he was sent to the Philippines. An extant account tells of the difficulties of their sailing across the Atlantic, their march across Mexico, and a difficult final voyage across the Pacific. When they finally arrived, Manila was in the hands of the English. After months of searching for his Dominican brothers, he located the community and was ordained. Thereafter he travelled by ship another 66 days to China, from where he was deported to Tonkin. His ministry lasted for only a very short time before he was arrested and imprisoned for three years. He was beheaded with Vincent Liêm. Beatified 1906.

Chieu van Do, Francisco (Francis Chieu, Francis Do van Chieu, Phanxicô Đỗ Văn Chiểu), Dominican tertiary,

lay catechist; b. ca. 1796–97 at Trung Lễ, Liên Thủy, Nam Định, Tonkin; d. June 12, 1838 at Nam Định. Francis aided the Dominican priests in their Vietnamese mission. He was captured in the village of Kiên-Lao with Bishop Dominic Henares, whom he was serving as catechist, and beheaded with him. His remains were also retrieved by Christians seeking their preservation. Beatified 1900. Feast: June 25.

Con, John Baptist (Gioan Baotixita Cỏn), married man, lay catechist; b. 1805 at Kẻ Bàng, Nam Định (near Hanoi, Tonkin); d. Nov. 8, 1840, at Bảy Mẫu, Tonkin. Beheaded. Beatified 1900. Feast: Nov. 7.

Cornay, Jean-Charles (John Cornay, John Corny, Jean-Charles Cornay Tân), priest; b. 1809 at Loudun (Poitiers), France; d. Sept. 20, 1837, at Sơn Tây (West Tonkin). Cornay worked in Annam (Vietnam) as a member of the MEP. He was arrested at Bản-no, Tonkin. He had been framed by the wife of a brigand chief, who had planted weapons in a plot of land that he cultivated. Thereafter Cornay was kept in a cage for three months and taken out only to be bound and brutally beaten. He was compelled to use his fine voice to sing to his captors. Beatified 1900. Feast: Feb. 8.

Cuénot, Étienne-Théodore (Stephen Cuénot, Étienne-Théodore Cuénot Thể), bishop, vicar apostolic; b. 1802 at Beaulieu, Besaňon, France; d. Nov. 14, 1861, at Bình Định, Cochin-China (Nam Việt). He was ordained, became a member of the MEP, and was sent to Annam (Vietnam). In 1833, he was appointed vicar apostolic of East Cochin-China and consecrated bishop in Singapore. He labored in the missions, establishing three vicarates during his 25-year episcopate. When the persecutions heightened he was safely hidden until he had to emerge for water at which time he was arrested. He died of dysentery just before the edict for his execution arrived. Beatified 1909. Feast: Feb. 8.

Dac Nguyen, Matthew (Matthew Nguyen van Phuong, Matthew Phung, Matthêô Nguyễn Văn Đắc (Phương), lay catechist; b. ca. 1801 at Kẻ Lai (Ke-lay), Quảng Bình (Trung Việt); d. May 26, 1861, near Đồng-Hới (Trung Việt). Like Andrew Dung-Lac, he used an alias. Beheaded. Beatified 1909.

Da, Peter (Peter Da, Phêrô Đa), lay catechist; b. at Ngọc Cục, Nam Định, Tonkin; d. June 17, 1862, in Nam Định. He was burnt alive in a bamboo hut with two Catholic fishermen. Beatified 1951.

Dat Dinh, Domingo Nicolás (Dominic Nicholas Dat, Đaminh Đinh Đạt), soldier; b. 1803 in Phú Nhai, Nam Định, Tonkin; d. 18 July1838, in Nam Định. When it was discovered that Dominic was a convert to Christianity, he was arrested, and stripped of his military position for embracing the faith. He may have been a Dominican tertiary. Strangled. Beatified 1900.

Dat, Juan (John Dat, Gioan Đạt), priest; b. ca. 1764 in Đông Chuối, Thanh Hóa (Trung Việt); d. Oct. 28, 1798, in West Tonkin. Đạt, described as a man of great serenity, was ordained to the priesthood in 1798. Following his arrest as an outlawed priest, he was held in captivity for three months, then beheaded. He and Emmanuel Triệu were the first Vietnamese diocesan priests for whose martyrdom a written account has been preserved. Beatified 1900.

De Van Nguyen, Tomás (Thomas De, Tôma Nguyễn Văn Đệ), tailor, Dominican tertiary; b. 1810, in Bồ Trang, Nam Định, Tonkin; d. 19 Dec. 1839, in Cổ Mê, Tonkin. He was strangled with four Dominic Uy, Francis Xavier Mậu, Stephen Vinh, and another companion for giving shelter to the missionaries. Beatified 1900.

Delgado y Cebrian, Ignacio (Ignatius Delgado, Clemente Ignatius Delgado, Clementé Ignaxiô Delgado Hy); Dominican bishop of East Tonkin; b. ca. 1761 at Villa Felice, Spain; d. July 21, 1838, at Nam Định, Tonkin. Most of the information on Delgado derives from the decree of condemnation. After professing himself as a Dominican, he was sent to the Tonkinese mission, where he labored for nearly 50 years and was appointed vicar apostolic of East Tonkin. He had been hidden in the village of Kien-Lao until he was betrayed through the artful questioning of a young boy. The bishop was locked in a cage. When questioned he answered truthfully about himself but would reveal nothing about other Christians. For this the 76-year-old bishop died of dysentery and hunger in a cage exposed to the summer sun. After his death soldiers cut off his head and tossed his remains into the river, where they were recovered by fishermen and honorably buried by Jerome Hermosilla. Beatified 1900. Feast: July 11.

Diaz Sanjurjo, José (Joseph Diaz, Giuse Maria Diaz Sanjuro An), Dominican bishop, vicar apostolic; b. 1818 at Santa Eulalia de Suegos, Lugo, Spain; d. July 20, 1857 in Nam Định, Tonkin. His parents had determined that he would have a successful career using his literary skills. He secretly entered the Dominicans at Ocada, Spain. There he was trained for the missions. He made his vows at Cadiz prior to undertaking the 120-day voyage to Manila, where he was assigned teaching duties at the University of Santo Tomás. After six months, he entered Tonkin with Melchoir Garcia-Sampedro under the cover of night disguised in native dress. Shortly thereafter, Diaz was appointed vicar apostolic of Central Tonkin with Garcia as his coadjutor. Although the Christian community tried to hide them as the persecution intensified. Sanjuro was arrested in a surprise raid and imprisoned for two months

during which he demonstrated his forgiveness of his betrayer. He was beheaded and his body thrown into the sea. Beatified 1951.

Dich Nguyen, Anthony (Anthony Nguyen Dich, Antôn Nguyễn Đích), farmer; b. in Chi Long, Nam Định, Tonkin; d. Aug. 12, 1838, Bảy Mẫu, Tonkin. Anthony used his wealth from agriculture generously to assist the work of the MEP. He was arrested for sheltering priests, including James Nam, who were fleeing government persecution. Beheaded. Beatified 1900.

Diem The Nguyen, Vincent (Vinh Sơn Nguyễn Thế Điểm), priest; b. 1761 at An Đô, Quảng Trị (Trung Việt); d. Nov., 28. 1838, at Đông Hới (Trung Việt). Beheaded. Beatified 1900.

Du Viet Dinh, Tomás (Thomas Du, Tôma Đinh Viết Dụ), priest, Dominican tertiary; b. 1774 at Nam Định, Tonkin; d. Nov. 26, 1839, at Bảy Mẫu, Tonkin. After his ordination Thomas worked in the Province of Nam-Định. He underwent horrible tortures before he was beheaded. Beatified 1900. Feast: May 31.

Due Van Vo, Bernardo (Bernard Vo van Due, Bênađô Võ Văn Duệ), priest; b. 1755 at Quần Anh, Nam Định, Tonkin; d. Nov. 26, 1838, at Ba Tòa, Tonkin. Bernard converted to the faith, studied in the seminary, and was ordained. After laboring for many years in the mission, Bernard retired. He was living quietly until he felt called to offer himself to the soldiers as a Christian priest. Beheaded at age 83. Beatified 1900. Feast: August 1.

Dumoulin-Borie, Pierre (Peter Dumoulin, Phêrô Dumoulin-Borie Cao), missionary priest of the MEP; b. 1808 at Cors (diocese of Tulle), France; d. Nov. 24, 1838, at Đông Hới (Trung Việt). Peter studied for the priesthood in Paris, was ordained in 1832, and sent to Tonkin. He was arrested in 1836. While in prison he was appointed vicar apostolic and titular bishop of Western Tonkin, but was never consecrated. Beatified 1900.

Dung Lac An Tran, Andrew (Anrê Trần An Dũng (Lạc), priest; b. ca. 1795 in Bắc Ninh, Tonkin; d. Dec. 21, 1839, Cầu Giấy, Tonkin. When Dũng An Trần was 12, his family moved to Hanoi (Hà-Nội) to find work. His non-Christian parents allowed their son to receive instruction from a lay catechist so that he might benefit from the education generally denied the poor. He was baptized Andrew at Vịnh-Tri. He studied Chinese and Latin, served as a catechist for ten years, and then was ordained to the priesthood in 1823. He was a tireless preacher—both by word and example—in several parishes until his arrest in 1835 as a Christian. His parishioners gathered the money needed to purchase his release. Thereafter, he changed his name from Dũng to Lạc in order to disguise his identity and went to another area to continue his ministry. On Nov. 10, 1839, he was again arrested with another Vietnamese priest, Peter Thi. Both were freed once ransom was paid on their behalf, but they were soon arrested again and taken to Hanoi, where priests of the MEP were singled out for especially harsh punishment. Beheaded. Beatified 1900. Feast formerly on December 26.

Dung Van Dinh, Peter (Phêrô Dũng), lay catechist; b. in Đồng Hào, Thái Bình, Tonkin; d. June 6, 1862, in Nam Định, Tonkin. Beatified 1951.

Duong, Paul (Paul Dong, Phalô Vũ Văn Dương (Đổng), layman; b. 1792 at Vực Đường, Hưng Yên, Tonkin; d. June 3, 1862, in Nam Định, Tonkin. Beatified 1951.

Duong Van Truong, Peter (Peter Truong Dang Duong, Phêrô Trương Văn Đường), lay catechist; b. 1808 at Kẻ Sở, Hà Nam, Tonkin; d. Dec. 18, 1838, at Sơn Tây (West Tonkin). He was strangled together with another catechist, Peter Truật. Beatified 1900.

Duong, Vincent (Vinh-sơn Dương), layman; b. in Doãn Trung, Thái Bình, Tonkin; d. June 6, 1862, at Nam Định, Tonkin. Beatified 1951.

Fernández, José (Joseph Fernández, Giuse Fernández Hiền), Dominican priest; b. 1775 at Ventosa de la Cueva, Spain; d. July 24, 1838 in Nam Định, Tonkin. After his profession as a Dominican friar, he studied in the seminary expressly to serve in the Vietnamese mission. In 1805, he was sent to Tonkin, where he was ordained. He was appointed provincial vicar there and arrested shortly thereafter. Beheaded. Beatified 1900. Feast: July 11.

Gagelin, François (Francis Isidore Gagelin, François-Isidore Gagelin Kính), priest; b. 1799 at Montperreux (Besañon), France; d. Oct. 17, 1833 in Bãi Dầu (Bồng Sơn). Belonged to the MEP. Sent to Cochin-China (Nam Việt) in 1822 (age 23), where he was ordained to the priesthood upon his arrival. He worked zealously until the outbreak of persecution, when he gave himself up to the mandarin of Bồng Sơn and was strangled. Beatified 1900.

Gam Van Le, Matthew (Matthew Le van Gam, Matthêô Lê Văn Gẫm), merchant; b. ca. 1812 in Gò Công, Biên Hòa, Cochin-China (Nam-Việt); d. May 11, 1847, in Chợ Đũi (Nam Việt). As a dedicated member of the MEP, he carried the missionaries in his fishing boat from Singapore to Annam (Vietnam). He was captured in this illegal act in 1846, imprisoned, tortured, and beheaded. Beatified 1900. Feast: May 26.

Garcia Sampedro, Melchoir (Melchior Garcia-Sampedro Xuyên), Dominican, vicar apostolic; b. 1821 at Cortes, Asturias, Spain; d. July 28, 1858, in Nam Định. Melchoir was born into a poor family that was unable to provide him with an education. He earned his way through school by teaching grammar to younger students. He opted to become a Dominican (1845) and was prepared for the missions at the novitiate at Ocada. He went to the Philippines, and then to Tonkin in an arduous journey (with José Diaz Sanjurjo). Shortly after their arrival Garcia was named coadjutor to Diaz, the vicar apostolic. While Gracia wanted to proclaim publically that he was a priest, the local Christian community convinced him that his presence with them was needed, and they kept him in hiding. Evenutally Garcia was found, arrested, and put in a cage with two native brothers. He was hacked to death, the brothers beheaded, and their remains were thrown into a ditch. Some of their relics were recovered. Beatified 1951.

Gil de Federich, Francisco (Francis Gil, Phanxicô Gil de Fedrich Tế), Dominican priest; b. 1702 in Tortosa, Cataluda, Spain; d. Jan. 22, 1745 at Thăng Long, Tonkin. Francis was educated in Barcelona and became a Dominican there before being sent to the Philippines. In 1732, he continued on to Tonkin, where he was arrested in 1742. During his confinement Gil directed a fruitful apostolate, then he was beheaded. He is the earliest martyr of whom there is substantial documentation. Beatified 1906. Feast: Jan. 29.

Hanh Van Nguyen, Domingo (Dominic Du, Dominic Nguyen van Hanh, Đaminh Nguyễn Văn Hạnh), Hạnh is his alias; his real name is Domingo Dụ, Dominican priest; b. 1772 in Năng A, Nghệ An (Trung Việt); d. Aug. 1, 1838, in Ba Tòa, Tonkin. He ministered as a priest to persecuted Christians for decades before his arrest and execution as a Christian at age 67. Beatified 1900.

Hanh, Paul (Phaolô Hạnh), layman; b. 1826 in Chợ Quán, Gia Định, Cochin-China; d. May 28, 1859 near Saigon (Ho-Chi-Minh City). He abandoned formal practice of his faith to join a band of outlaws, although he secretly assisted the Christian community. When he was arrested for his crimes, he professed his faith and, after torture, was beheaded. Beatified 1909.

Henares, Domingo (Dominic Henarez, Đaminh Henares Minh); Dominican auxiliary bishop; b. 1765 in Baena, Cordova, Spain; d. June 25, 1838, in Nam Định, Tonkin. He was appointed bishop-coadjutor (1803) to Ignatius Delgado, vicar apostolic of Tonkin. After working for about 50 years in Vietnam, Bishop Henares hid himself in the village of Kiên-Lao with his bishop during a renewed outbreak of persecution. He managed to escape immediate arrest by hiding himself in a fishing boat. The boatman betrayed him, and a detachment of 500 soldiers was sent to arrest Henares and his catechist Francis Chiểu. They were kept separate from Delgado and beheaded two weeks after their bishop's death. His body was recovered and buried by Hermosilla. Beatified 1900.

Hermosilla, Jeronimo (Jerome Hermosilla, Jêrônimô Hermosilla Liêm), Dominican bishop East Tonkin; b. 1880 at Santo Domingo de la Calzada, Old Castile, Spain; d. Nov. 1, 1861, Nam Định, Tonkin. After his profession as a Dominican, he was sent to Manila, where he was ordained. In 1828, he was appointed to the mission at East Tonkin. In April 1841, he succeeded Ignatius Delgado as vicar apostolic and consecrated bishop, which marked him for persecution. Nevertheless, he was able to serve his flock for 20 years. As his first episcopal task, he gathered the relics of his two predecessors and recorded the eyewitness accounts of their martyrdoms. After many trials and the loss of some of his finest supporters, Hermosilla was betrayed by an apostate. He and Berrio-Ochoa had been hidden aboard a ship that would take them to a group of Christians. They were captured, humiliated, and finally beheaded. Their bodies were guarded for several days to prevent Christians from rescuing the relics. Beatified 1906.

Hien Quang Do, José (Joseph Hien, Joseph Yen, Giuse Đỗ Quang Hiển), Dominican priest; b. 1775 in Đông Chuối, Ninh Bình, Tonkin; d. May 9, 1840, at Nam-Định, Tonkin. Beheaded. Beatified 1900. Feast: June 27.

Hieu Van Nguyen, Peter (Peter Nguyen van Hieu, Phêrô Nguyễn Văn Hiếu, lay catechist; b. 1783 in Đông Chuối, Ninh Bình, Tonkin; d. there on April 28, 1840. His attachment to the MEP led to his beheading during the persecution of Minh-Mạng. Beatified 1900.

Hoa Dac Phan, Simon (Simon Phan Dac Hoa, Simon Phan Dac Thu, Simon Phan Đắc Hòa), lay physician; b. 1778 in Mai Vĩnh, Thừa Thiên (Trung Việt); d. Dec. 12, 1840, in An Hòa (Trung Việt). In addition to serving his community as a doctor, Simon was mayor of his native village. A married man with 12 children, he also assisted the evangelization efforts of the MEP. He persisted in coming to the aid of the persecuted clergy, which led to his arrest, torture, and execution. Beatified 1909.

Hoan trinh Doan, John (John Doan trinh Hoan, Gioan Đoàn Trinh Hoan), priest; b. ca. 1790 at Kim-Long, Thừa Thiên (Trung Việt); d. May 26, 1861 near Đồng Hới (Trung Việt). He received his education from the missionaries ministering in his land, continued his education through the seminary, and was ordained. Beheaded under King Tự-Đức. Beatified 1909.

Huong Van Nguyen, Lawrence (Lorenzo Huong, Laurensô Nguyễn Văn Hưởng), priest; b. ca. 1802 in Kẻ

Sài, Hà Nội, Tonkin; d. Feb. 10, 1855 or 56, near Ninh-Bình, West Tonkin. Beatified 1909. Feast: April 27.

Huy Viet Phan, Augustin (Augustine Phan Viet Huy, Augustinô Phan Viết Huy), soldier; b. 1795 in Hạ Linh, Nam Định, Tonkin; d. June 12, 1838, Thừa Thiên (Trung Việt). Beatified 1900. Feast: June 13.

Huyen, Dominic (Đaminh Huyện), layman; b. 1817 in Đông Thành, Thái Bình, Tonkin; d. June 5, 1862, in Nam Định, Tonkin. Beatified 1951.

Hy-Dinh-Ho, Michael (Michael Ho dinh Hy, Micae Hồ Đình Hy), mandarin (high government official); b. ca. 1808 at Nhu Lâm (Nhu-lam); d. May 22, 1857 at An-Hòa near Huế (Trung Việt). Michael was born into a noble, Christian family. He became a great mandarin and superintendent of the royal silk mills. For a long time he did not practice his faith, but eventually he became a leader and protector of his fellow-Christians. Beheaded. Beatified 1909.

Jaccard, François (Francis Jaccard, Phanxicô Jaccard Phan), priest; b. 1799 at Onnion, Annecy, Savoy, France; d. Sept. 21, 1838, at Nhan Biểu (Trung Việt). He entered the seminary for MEP in Paris, was ordained, and was sent to Cochin-China (Nam Việt) in 1826. Strangled. Beatified 1900.

Kham Viet Pham, Dominic (Dominic An-Kham, Đaminh Phạm Viết Khảm), judge, Dominican tertiary; b. 1799 at Quần Cống, Nam Định ; d. Jan. 13, 1859 in Nam Định, Tonkin. He was a wealthy, respected member of the community, as well as the prior of the Dominican Confraternity. He died with his son and several other wealthy members of the Confraternity who were protecting missionaries. Beatified 1951.

Khang Duy Nguyen, Jose (Joseph Klang, Giuse Nguyen Duy Khang), servant, Dominican tertiary; b. 1832 at Trà Vi (Tra-vi), Nam-Định, Tonkin; d. Dec. 6, 1861, at Hải Dương, Tonkin. Joseph was Bishop Hermosilla's servant. While trying to rescue his master from prison, he was caught, tortured, and finally beheaded. Beatified 1906.

Khanh, Peter (Phêrô Khanh), priest; b. 1780 at Hòa Duệ, Nghệ An (Trung Việt); d. July 12, 1842, Hà Tĩnh (Trung Việt). Beheaded. Beatified 1909.

Khoan Khan Pham, Paul (Phaolô Phạm Khắc Khoan), priest; b. 1771 in Duyên Mậu, Ninh Bình, Tonkin; d. there, April 28, 1840. Paul studied with the MEP, was ordained, and labored with the missionaries for 40 years. He was imprisoned and tortured for two years prior to his decapitation. Beatified 1900. Feast: April 28.

Khuong, Thomas (Thomas Huong, Tôma Khuông), priest, Dominican tertiary; b. 1789 at Nam Hào, Hưng

Yên, Tonkin; d. there Jan. 30, 1860. Son of a mandarin, he suffered great tortures before his death. Beatified 1951.

Phung van Le, Emmanuel (Manuel Phung, Emmanuel Lê Văn Phụng), mandarin, catechist; b. 1796 at Đầu-Nước, Cù Lao Giêng (Nam Việt); d. July 31, 1859, near Châu Đốc (Nam Việt). Emmanuel was the father of a family. Garrotted. Beatified 1909.

Lenziniana, Mateo Alonzo (Matthew Leziniana, Matthew Liciniana, Matthêô Alonzo-Leciniana Đậu), Dominican priest; b. 1702 at Navas del Rey (Valladolid), Spain; d. Jan. 22, 1745, at Thăng Long, Tonkin. Matthew was sent to Philippines after his ordination, then to Tonkin. There he ministered furtively to the Christian community while dodging the authorities for 13 years. He was beheaded with Francisco Gil and is one of the earliest of the canonized martyrs of Vietnam. Beatified 1906.

Liem de la Paz, Vicente (Vincent Liem da Pace, Vinh-sơn Lê Quang Liêm), Dominican priest; b. 1732 in Trà Lũ, Nam Định, Tonkin; d. Nov. 7, 1773, in Đồng Mơ, Tonkin. Vincent was born into the nobility of Tonkin. He labored as a priest for 14 years with Dominican Bishop Hyacinth Casteđeda prior to his arrest and execution by decapitation. Liêm is the first Indo-Chinese Dominican known to be martyred for the faith. Beatified 1906. Feast: November 7.

Loan Ba Vu, Luke (Luke Vu Ba Loan, Luca Vũ Bá Loan), priest; b. 1756 in Trại Bút, Phú Đa, Tonkin; d. June 5, 1840, at Ô Cầu Giấy, Tonkin. Luke was raised in a Christian family. He ministered for decades to a people who revered him; beheaded for his priesthood. Beatified 1900. Feast: June 4.

Loc Van Le, Paul (Paul Lok, Paul Le van Loc, Phaolô Lê Văn Lộc), priest; b. ca. 1830 at An Nhơn, Gia Định; d. Feb. 13, 1859 at Gia Định (Saigon or Ho-Chi-Minh City). He served in the army prior to entering the seminary; beheaded shortly after his ordination to the priesthood. Beatified 1909.

Luu van Nguyen, Joseph (Joseph Nguyen van Luu, Giuse Nguyễn Văn Lựu), lay catechist; b. ca. 1790 at Cái-Nhum (Nam Việt); d. May 2, 1854 or 55, at Vĩnh-long (Nam Việt). He died in prison from torture and abuse. Beatified 1909.

Mao Trong Ha, Dominic (Dominic Mao, Đaminh Mạo), layman; b. 1818 in Ngọc Cục, Nam Định, Tonkin; d. June 16, 1862, in Làng Cốc, Tonkin. Beatified 1951.

Marchand, Joseph (Giuse Marchand Du), priest; b. 1803 at Passavant, Besançon, France; d. Nov. 30, 1835, in Thọ Đức near Saigon (Ho-Chi-Minh City). Joseph completed his theological studies at the seminary of MEP, was ordained, and sent to Annam (Vietnam). He was arrested at Saigon. Beatified 1900.

Mau, Dominic (Dominic Mau, Đaminh Mẫu), Dominican priest; b. 1808 in Phú Nhai, Nam Định, Tonkin; d. Nov. 5, 1858, in Hưng Yên, Tonkin. He died after a long torture. Beatified 1951.

Mau, Francisco Javier (Francis Xavier) (Phanxicô Xaviê Hà Trọng Mậu), Dominican tertiary, catechist; b. 1790, in Kẻ Điều, Thái Bình, Tonkin; d. Dec. 19, 1839, in Cổ Mê, Tonkin. He was strangled with four companions, including Stephen Vinh and Dominic Uy. Beatified 1900.

Moi Van Nguyen, Agustín (Augustine Moi, Augustinô Nguyễn Văn Mới), day-laborer, Dominican tertiary; b. 1806 at Phù Trang, Nam Định, Tonkin; d. Dec. 19, 1839, in Cổ Mê, Tonkin. Agustín was known for his piety and charity, though a poor man himself. Strangled. Beatified 1900. Feast: Dec. 18.

Minh Van Phan, Philip (Philip Phan van Minh, Philiphê Phan Văn Minh), priest; b. 1815 in Cái Mơn, Vĩnh Long (Caimon); d. July 3, 1853, at Đinh Khao. Philip joined the MEP and was ordained a priest for East Cochin-China (Miền Tây Nam Việt). Beheaded. Beatified 1900.

My Huy Nguyen, Michael (Michael Mi, Michael Nguyen Hủy My, Micae Nguyễn Huy Mỹ), married farmer; b. 1804 in Kẻ Vĩnh, Hà Nội, Tonkin; d. Aug. 12, 1838, in Bảy Mẫu, Tonkin. Michael had been mayor of Vĩnh-Tri, where several of the saints were arrested. He served the Church faithfully, but gave special assistance to Anthony Đích, his son-in-law, to protect the missionaries during the persecution. When Đích tried to hide Fr. James Năm in 1838, they were all arrested and beheaded. Beatified 1900.

My Van Nguyen, Paul (Paul Mi, Phaolô Nguyễn Văn Mỹ), layman; b. 1798 at Kẻ Non, Hà Nam, Tonkin; d. Dec. 18, 1838, at Sơn Tây. He was attached to the MEP. Strangled. Beatified 1900.

Nam, James (Jacob Nam, James Mai Nami, Giacôbê Đỗ Mai Năm), priest; b. 1781 in Đông Biên, Thanh Hóa (Trung Việt); d. Aug. 12, 1838, in Bảy Mẫu, Tonkin. James, a priest attached to the MEP, found refuge from persecution for a long period in the home of Anthony Đích. He was discovered and both were arrested together with Anthony's father-in-law, Michael Mỹ. Beheaded. Beatified 1900.

Néron, Pierre-François (Peter Francis Néron, Phêrô Phanxicô Néron Bắc), priest; b. 1818 at Bornay, Saint-Claude (Jura), France; d. Nov. 3, 1860, in Sơn Tây (West Tonkin). He entered the MEP in 1846, was ordained two years later (1848), and sent to Hong Kong. He labored in West Tonkin as director of the central seminary until his arrest and decapitation. Beatified 1909.

Ngan Nguyen, Paul (Phaolô Nguyễn Ngân), priest; b. 1771 in Kẻ Biên, Thanh Hóa (Trung Việt); d. Nov. 8, 1840, in Bảy Mẫu, Nam-Định, Tonkin. Beatified 1900.

Nghi, José (Joseph Nien Kim, Joseph Nguyen Dinh Nghi, Giuse Nguyễn Đình Nghi), priest; b. 1771 in Kẻ Vôi, Hà Nội, Tonkin; d. Nov. 8, 1840 in Bảy Mẫu, Tonkin. He was beheaded because he was a member of the MEP. Beatified 1900.

Ngon, Lorenzo (Lawrence Ngon, Laurensô Ngôn), layman; b. at Lục Thủy, Nam Định; d. May 22, 1862, in Nam Định. Beatified 1951.

Nguyen, Domingo (Dominic Nguyen, Đaminh Nguyện), layman; b. 1802 in Ngọc Cục, Nam Định, Tonkin; d. June 16, 1862, in Làng Cốc, Tonkin. Beatified 1951.

Nhi, Domingo (Dominic Nhi, Đaminh Nhi), layman; b. at Ngọc Cục, Nam Định, Tonkin; d. June 16, 1861, in Làng Cốc, Tonkin. Beatified 1951.

Ninh, Dominic (Đaminh Ninh), layman; b. 1835 in Trung Linh, Nam Định, Tonkin; d. June 2, 1862, at An Triêm. Beatified 1951.

Nguyen, Huu Nam Anthony (Anthony Quynh-Nam, Antôn Nguyễn Hữu Quỳnh), physician, lay catechist; b. 1768 in Mỹ Hương, Quảng Bình (Trung Việt); d. July 10, 1840, Đồng Hới (Trung Việt). He was arrested in 1838 because of his attachment to the MEP. During his two-year imprisonment he tended the inmates and endured tortures. Strangled. Beatified 1900. Feast: November 24.

Nguyễn Văn Lựu (Luu, Peter) Phêrô, priest; b. 1812 at Gò Vấp, Gia Định (Nam Việt); d. April 7, 1861, at Mỹ Tho (Nam Việt). Beatified 1909.

Nguyen, Van Vinh, Esteban (Stephen Vinh, Stephanô Nguyễn Văn Vinh), lay catechist, Dominican tertiary; b. 1814 in Phù Trang, Nam Định, Tonkin; d. Dec. 19, 1839, at Cổ Mê, Tonkin. Devout peasant; strangled with 4 companions, including Thomas Đệ. Beatified 1900.

Pham, Trong Ta Joseph (Joseph Cai Ta, Cai Tả, Giuse Phạm Trọng Tả), soldier; b. 1800 at Quần Cống, Nam Định, Tonkin; d. Jan. 13, 1859, in Nam Định. Tortured to death. Beatified 1951.

Quy Cong Doan, Pedro (Peter Qui, Phêrô Đoàn Công Quý), priest; b. 1826 in Búng, Gia Định (Nam Việt); d. July 31, 1859, in Châu Đốc (Nam Việt). Beheaded. Beatified 1909.

Schoeffler, Agustin (Augustine Schoeffler Đông), priest, Dominican tertiary; b. 1822 at Mittelbronn

(Nancy) Lorraine, France; d. May 1, 1851 in Sơn Tây (West Tonkin). Augustine joined the MEP and was sent to Vietnam in 1848. He labored in the missions for only a short time before his arrest and beheading. Beatified 1900.

Ta, Duc Thinh, Martin (Matthew Ta Duc Thinh, Martin Thinh, Martinô Tạ Đức Thịnh), priest; b. 1760 in Kẻ Sặt, Hà Nội, Tonkin; d. Nov. 8, 1840, in Bảy Mẫu, Tonkin. Martin, a member of the MEP, labored for decades as a priest to his own people. Beheaded with Martin Thọ. Beatified 1900.

Thanh Van Dinh, Juan-Baptist (John Baptist Thanh, Gioan B. Đinh Văn Thành), lay catechist; b. 1796 in Nộn Khê, Ninh Bình, Tonkin; d. April 28, 1840, Ninh Bình. He was beheaded with Peter Hiếu and Paul Khoan because of his attachment to the MEP. Beatified 1900.

Thanh Thi Le, Inés (Agnes De, Inê Lê Thị Thành [Bà Đe]), married woman; b. 1781 at Bái- Đền, West Tonkin; d. July 12, 1841, at Nam-Định. She was born into a Christian family and was the mother of six. She was caught carrying letters from the Christians in prison and arrested. Died in prison. Beatified 1909. Feast: Feb. 18.

Thé, Nicolás (Nicholas Duc Bui, Nicholas Bui Buc The, Nicôla Bùi Đức Thế), soldier, b. 1792 in Kiên Trung, Nam Định, Tonkin; d. June 12, 1838, at Thừa Thiên (Trung Việt). Beatified 1900. Feast: June 13.

Thi Dang Le, José (Joseph Le dang Thi, Giuse Lê Đăng Thi), soldier; b. 1825 at Kẻ Văn, Quảng Trị (Trung Việt); d. Oct. 25, 1860 at An-Hòa (Trung Việt). A captain in the army of King Tự-Đức. Once it was discovered that he was a Christian and he refused to deny his faith, he was garrotted. Beatified 1909. Feast: Oct. 24.

Thi Văn Truong, Pedro (Peter Pham Thi, Phêrô Trương Văn Thi), priest; b. 1763 at Kẻ Sở, Hà Nội, Tonkin; d. Dec. 21, 1839, at Ô Cầu Giấy, Tonkin. Beheaded. Beatified 1900. Feast: December 20.

Thien van Tran, Tomás (Thomas Tran Dien, Thomas Tran van Thien, Tôma Trần Văn Thiện), seminarian, lay catechist; b. 1820 at Trung Quán, Quảng Bình (Trung Việt); d. Sept. 21, 1838, in Nhan Biểu (Trung Việt). He was studying with MEP, preparing for ordination at the time of his arrest. After being scourged, he was strangled at the age of 18. Beatified 1900. Feast: September 21.

Thin Trong Pham, Luca (Lucius Cai Thin, Luca Phạm Trọng Thìn), layman; b. 1819 in Quần Cống, Nam Định ; d. Jan. 13, 1862, in Nam Định. Beatified 1951.

Tho, Martin (Martinô Thọ), tax collector; b. 1787 at Kẻ Bàng, Nam Định, Tonkin; d. Nov. 8, 1840, in Bảy Mẫu, Tonkin. Martin, the head of his parish council, was martyred with Martin Tinh, an 80-year-old native priest, and Joseph Nghi. Beatified 1900.

Thong Kim Nguyen, Andrew (Andrew Thong Kim Nguyen, Anrê Nguyễn Kim Thông (Năm Thuông), politician, lay catechist; b. ca. 1790 in Gò Thị, Bình Định (Trung Việt); d. July 15, 1855, in Mỹ Tho (Miền Tây Nam Việt). Andrew, the chief of his village, was exiled at the beginning of the persecution because of his devotion to the Catholic faith. He died from exhaustion and dehydration en route to exile at Mỹ-Tho. Beatified 1909. Feast: February 18.

Thuan, Peter (Phêrô Thuần), fisherman; b. at Đông Phú, Thái Bình, Tonkin; d. June 6, 1862, in Nam Định, Tonkin. Burnt alive with Peter Đa. Beatified 1951.

Tinh Bao Le, Paul (Paul Le Bao Tinh, Phaolô Lê Bảo Tịnh), priest; b. 1793 at Trinh-Hà, Tonkin; d. April 6, 1857 at Sơn Tây (West Tonkin). He wrote a letter to the seminary of Kẻ Vĩnh in 1843 detailing the sufferings of Christian prisoners. Beheaded. Beatified 1909. Feast: April 6.

Toai, Domingo (Dominic Toai, Đaminh Toái), fisherman; b. 1811 in Đông Thành, Thái Bình, Tonkin; d. June 5, 1862, in Nam Định, Tonkin. Burnt alive with Peter Đa and Peter Thuần. Beatified 1951.

Toan, Tomás (Thomas Toan, Tôma Toán), Dominican tertiary, lay catechist; b. 1767 in Cần Phan, Nam Định, Tonkin; d. June 27, 1840, in Nam Định. Although he was teaching the faith to others, Thomas's faith waivered. After showing signs of apostatizing, he repented. In consequence, he was tortured and starved to death. Beatified 1900.

Trach, Domingo (Dominic Doai, Đaminh Trạch (Đoài), priest, Dominican tertiary; b. 1792 in Ngoại Bồi, Nam Định, Tonkin; d. Sept. 18, 1840, at Bảy Mẫu, Tonkin. Dominic, a native Dominican priest, had labored to evangelize his own land until his arrest. The following year Dominic was given the choice to renounce the faith and go free or suffer death. He confessed and encouraged his friends before his own beheading. Beatified 1900.

Tran, van Tuan Joseph (Giuse Tuân), Dominican priest; b. 1821 in Trân Xá, Hưng Yên, Tonkin; d. there April 30, 1861, after a long torture. Beatified 1951.

Trieu van Nguyen, Manuel (Emmanuel Nguyen van-Trieu, Emmanuel Nguyễn Văn Triệu), priest; b. ca. 1756 in Saigon (Ho-Chi-Minh City), Phú Xuân, Huế; d. Sept. 17, 1798, in Bãi Dâu (Bồng Sơn). Emmanuel, who had been born into a Christian family, joined the army. Later he was ordained to the priesthood at Pong-King and worked with his brother priests in the Paris Foreign Mission Society. He was arrested while visiting his mother and beheaded, becoming one of the first Vietnamese diocesan priests to die for the faith. Beatified 1900.

Trong Van Tran, Andrew (Andrew Tran van Trong, Anrê Trần Văn Trông), soldier; b. 1817 in Kim Long, Huế (Trung Việt); d. Nov. 28, 1835 at An Hòa, Huế. Trong was a young native soldier or silk-weaver to the king of Annam (Việt Nam) and attached to the MEP. When this affiliation was discovered by the authorities in 1834, he was arrested, stripped of his military rank, and imprisoned. Beatified 1900. Feast: November 18.

Truat Van Vu, Peter (Peter Truat, Phêrô Vũ Văn Truật), lay catechist; b. 1816 in Kẻ Thiếc, Hà Nam, Tonkin; d. Dec. 18, 1838, in Sơn Tây (West Tonkin). Beatified 1900.

Trung Van Tran, Francisco (Francis Tran van Trung, Phanxicô Trần Văn Trung), soldier; b. 1825 in Phan-Xã; d. May 2, 1858, at An-Hòa (Trung Việt). Francis was a corporal in the army, who converted to Christianity. Beheaded. Beatified 1909. Feast: October 6.

Tu Khac Nguyen, Pedro (Peter Tu, Phêrô Nguyễn Khắc Tự), lay catechist; b. 1811 in Ninh Bình, Tonkin; d. July 10, 1840, in Đồng Hới (Trung Việt). Beheaded. Beatified 1900.

Tu Van Nguyen, Peter (Phêrô Nguyễn Văn Tự), Dominican priest; b. 1796 in Ninh Cường, Nam Định, Tonkin; d. Sept. 5, 1838, in Bắc Ninh, Tonkin. Beatified 1900.

Tuan, Joseph (Giuse Tuân), layman; b. 1825 in Nam Điền, Nam Định; d. Jan. 7, 1862, in Nam Định. Beatified 1951.

Tuan Ba Nguyen, Pedro (Peter Tu, Phêrô Nguyễn Bá Tuần), priest; b. 1766 in Ngọc Đồng, Hưng Yên, Tonkin; d. July 15, 1838, at Ninh Tai, Nam Định. Beatified 1900.

Tuc, Joseph (Giuse Túc), layman; b. 1852 in Hoàng Xá, Bắc Ninh, Tonkin; d. there on June 1, 1862. A child of 9 who was martyred for the faith. Beatified 1951.

Tuoc, Domingo (Dominic Tuoc, Đaminh Tước), priest; Dominican tertiary, b. 1775 in Trung Lao, Nam Định, Tonkin; d. April 2, 1839, in Nam Định. Dominic from wounds in prison. Beatified 1900.

Tuong, Andrew (Andrew Thuong, Anrê Tưởng), lay catechist; b. 1812 in Ngọc Cúc, Nam Định, Tonkin; d. June 16, 1862, in Làng Cốc, Tonkin. Beatified 1951.

Tuong, Vincent (Vincent Truong, Vinh-Sơn Tường), judge, layman; b. 1814 in Ngọc Cục, Nam Định, Tonkin; d. June 16, 1862, in Làng Cốc, Tonkin. Beatified 1951.

Tuy Le, Pedro (Peter Tu, Peter Le Tuy, Phêrô Lê Tùy), priest; b. 1773 in Bằng Sở, Hà Đông (West Tonkin); d. Oct. 11, 1833, in Quan Ban. Arrested after many years of ministry and beheaded. Beatified 1900.

Uyen Dinh Nguyen, José (Joseph Nguyen Dinh Uyen, Joseph Peter Uyen, Joseph Yuen, Joseph Uen,

Giuse Nguyễn Đình Uyển), Dominican tertiary, lay catechist; b. ca. 1775 in Ninh Cường, Nam Định, Tonkin; d. July 4, 1838 in Hưng Yên, Tonkin. After a year's tortuous imprisonment, he was strangled in his cell. Beatified 1900. Feast: July 3.

Van Van Doan, Peter (Peter Doan van Van, Phêrô Đoàn Văn Vân), lay catechist; b. ca. 1780 in Kẻ Bói, Hà Nam, Tonkin; d. May 25, 1857, at Sơn-Tây, West Tonkin. Beheaded. Beatified 1909.

Vénard, Jean-Théophane (Théophane Vénard, Giuse Theophanô Vénard Ven), priest; b. Nov. 21, 1829 in St.-Loup-sur-Thouet (Deux-Sèvres), Poitiers, France; d. Feb. 2, 1861, in Ô Cầu Giấy, Tonkin. This son of the village schoolmaster studied at the College of Doue-la-Fontaine, and at the seminaries at Montmorillon and Poitiers, where he was ordained subdeacon (1850). He transferred to the MEP (1851), was ordained priest on June 5, 1852, and departed for Hong Kong on September 19. After fifteen months studying Vietnamese at Hong Kong he arrived (1854) secretly at his mission in West Tonkin, where the Christians had recently been tried by a series of persecutions under Minh-Mạng. In 1856, he was expelled from Nam-Định and went to Hanoi. Shortly after Vénard's arrival a new royal edict was issued against Christians; bishops and priests were obliged to seek refuge in caves, dense woods, the hulls of sampans, and elsewhere. Vénard, whose constitution had always been delicate, suffered almost constantly, but continued to exercise his ministry at night, and, more boldly, in broad day because he was greatly impressed by the courage of the Vietnamese Catholics who had been suffering since 1848. On Nov. 30, 1860, he was betrayed by a Christian and captured at Kim Bàng. Tried before a mandarin, he refused to apostatize and was sentenced to be beheaded. While chained in a tiny bamboo cage, he wrote to his family beautiful and consoling letters.

Vien Dinh Dang, Joseph (Joseph Dang Dinh Vien, Joseph Nien, Giuse Đặng Đình Viên), Dominican tertiary, lay catechist; b. ca. 1786 in Tiên Chu, Hưng Yên, Tonkin; d. Aug. 21, 1838, in Bảy Mẫu, Tonkin. Beatified 1900.

Võ Dăng Khoa, Pedro (Peter Khoa), priest; b. 1790, in Thuận Nghĩa, Nghệ An (Trung Việt); d. Nov. 24, 1838 at Đồng-Hới. Strangled. Beatified 1900.

Xuyen Van Nguyen, Domingo (Dominic Doan, Dominic Xuyen, Đaminh Nguyễn Văn Xuyên), Dominican priest; b. ca. 1787 in Hưng Lập, Nam Định, Tonkin; d. Nov. 26, 1839, in Bảy Mẫu, Tonkin. Beheaded with Thomas Dụ. Beatified 1900. Feast: Oct. 26.

Yen Do, Vicente (Vincent Do Yen, Vinh Sơn Đỗ Yến), Dominican priest; b. ca. 1764 in Trà Lũ, Nam

Định, Tonkin; d. June 30, 1838, in Hải Dương, Tonkin. After becoming a Dominican in 1808, he labored in the mission field until his martyrdom. From the publication of the edict of persecution in 1832, he lived 6 years in hiding and continued to minister secretly. He was finally betrayed and beheaded. Beatified 1900.

Bibliography: B. BLOOMFIELD, *Martyrs of Vietnam* (London 1995). M. J. DORCY, *Saint Dominic's Family* (Dubuque, IA 1963) 498–99, 506–9, 511–13. V. GOMEZ, *Pedro Almato y Ribera, OP, Martir del Vietnam: Letters to Family and Friends* (Valencia 1987). *Kỷ Yếu Phong Thánh Tử' Đạo Việt Nam* (Canonization of The Vietnamese Martyrs), prepared by the Canonization Committee (Vatican City 1989). Mission Étrangères de Paris, *Le Clergé Annamite et ses Prêtres Martyrs* (Paris 1925). B. T. NGUYÊN *Les Martyrs de l'Annam,* (Hanoi 1937). V. T. TRẦN, *Histoire des Persecutions au Vietnam,* (Paris 1955). V. N. T. TRẦN, *Giáo Hội Việt Nam: Tập 1: Vụ Án Phong Thánh* (Vietnamese Church, Vol 1: Canonization Proceeding; Vietnam 1987). V. Y. TRỊNH, *Máu Tử Đạo Trên Đất Việt Nam* (Blood of the Martyrs in the Land of Vietnam; National Canonization Committee, U.S.A., 1987). *Witnesses of the Faith in the Orient* (Hong Kong 1989).

[THU BUI/K. I. RABENSTEIN]

VIETNAM, THE CATHOLIC CHURCH IN

Background

Early History. According to traditional mythology, Vietnamese history began with Lạc Long Quân (Dragon Lord Lạc) and his consort Âu Cơ, who gave birth to 100 sons. Lạc Long Quân led 50 sons with him to the sea and Âu Cơ took 50 with her to Mount Tản-viên, from which came the first of the Hùng kings who ruled over the Lạc (a.k.a. Đông-sơn) kingdom of Văn-lang, the earliest known Vietnamese kingdom. Archaeological excavations reveal that the Lạc society was sophisticated in its use of bronze implements and agronomic expertise. Their success in taming and farming the land attracted the Chinese, who moved in and attempted to control the area. Sporadic resistance to Chinese domination culminated in the celebrated rebellion of the two sisters Trưng Trắc and Trúng Nhị in 40 A.D., which resulted in a brief three-year independence for the Vietnamese. This brief independence was ruthlessly crushed by the Chinese General Ma Yuan, who imposed direct Chinese rule over the region. Chinese colonial rule lasted for almost 1,000 years, until the collapse of the Chinese T'ang dynasty in 939 paved the way for the establishment of the indigenous Lý dynasty in 1010. The Lý dynasty was succeeded in 1225 by the Trần dynasty, which was in turn succeeded by the Lê dynasty (1428–1788).

European Influence. The arrival of European explorers in the early sixteenth century coincided with the

Capital: Hà Nội.
Size: 332,600 sq. km. (128,400 sq. mi.).
Population: About 85% of its population are ethnic Vietnamese, with small but significant ethnic Chinese and tribal (Muong, Tho, Tai, Meo, Khmer, Man, Nung and Cham) minorities. Ethnic Chinese are found predominantly in the Cho Lon district of Hồ Chí Minh City.
Languages: Vietnamese (official); Chinese, English, French, Khmer, tribal languages (Mon-Khmer and Malayo-Polynesian) are also spoken.
Religions: About two-thirds of Vietnamese observe an eclectic mix of Confucianism, Taoism and Buddhism, while some 5% of the population are drawn to the indigenous religions of Cao Dai and Hoa Hao. Christians number close to one-tenth of the population. Catholics outnumber Protestants by almost nine-to-one.

near-collapse of the weak and decadent Lê dynasty. Two feuding clans, the Trịnh in the north and the Nguyễn in the south, fought for political control throughout much of the next two centuries, resulting in much general unrest. Capitalizing on the peasants' discontent, three brothers, Nguyễn Nhạc, Nguyễn Lữ and Nguyễn Huệ led a peasant revolt that overthrew the Lê dynasty, crushed the power of the Trịnh and Nguyễn clans, and established the Tây-Sơn dynasty in 1788. Defeated but not vanquished, Nguyễn Phú Ánh from the southern Nguyễn clan overthrew the Tây-Sơn dynasty with French military assistance, and declared himself Emperor Gia Long of the Nguyễn dynasty in 1802. Taking advantage of subsequent Nguyễn rulers' persecution of foreign missionaries and Vietnamese Christians, the French military conquered the southern region (Nam Việt) in 1862, which became French Cochinchina. Moving northward, they gained control of the northern region (Bắc Việt), which they called Tonkin, and by 1883 they gained control of the central region (Trung Việt), which they named Annam. In 1887, the French combined French Cochinchina, Tonkin and Annam with Cambodia (and ten years later, Laos) to form the French Indochinese Union.

Political Upheavals. The twentieth century witnessed the sporadic attempts of Vietnamese nationalist groups to regain independence for Vietnam. The Japanese occupation of Vietnam during World War II severely weakened French control, enabling the Việt-Minh, a broad coalition of anti-French nationalists and communists, to drive the French out of the northern region. From their southern bases, the French fought a losing war to regain control of the north. After suffering a humiliating defeat in Điện Biên Phủ, the French and the communists signed the 1954 Geneva Accord which divided the country at the 17th parallel: communist North Vietnam (com-

prising the former French Tonkin and northern part of Annam) and non-communist South Vietnam (comprising the former French Cochinchina and southern part of Annam). Ignoring the Geneva Accord, North Vietnam invaded the South, drawing the United States into a bloody war. In 1973, the warring parties with their respective sponsors met at Geneva and signed a cease-fire agreement which led to the withdrawal of American troops. The North then invaded the South in 1974, and with the fall of Saigon on April 30, 1975, the country was reunified under communist rule.

[V.T. PHAM]

History of the Catholic Church in Vietnam

Origins. Christianity was first introduced in Vietnam in 1533 by Inigo, a European missionary on his way to China. Two Jesuits fleeing persecution in Japan, Francesco Buzomi and Diego Carvalho, established the first permanent mission in 1615 at Đà Nẵng in central Vietnam (Trung Việt). Full-scale missionary activity commenced with the arrival of another contingent of Jesuits in 1624. Leading this contingent was Alexander de RHODES, SJ (1593–1660), the "apostle of Vietnam." De Rhodes made his way to Hà Nội in 1627, where he encountered extraordinary success, baptizing the king's sister and about 6,700 Vietnamese in three years. In 1630, he was expelled and the first Christian (unnamed) was beheaded for the faith. De Rhodes returned to Vietnam in 1639, reporting that there were now 100,000 Vietnamese Catholics. The influx of new missionaries from the PARIS FOREIGN MISSION SOCIETY (Société des Mission Étrangères de Paris) led to a period of swift growth. By 1658, there were 300,000 Catholics in Bắc Việt alone. In 1659, the burgeoning mission was divided at the Giang River into two vicariates apostolic: Bắc Việt in the north and Nam Việt in the south. The first seminary opened in 1666, and the first two native priests were ordained in 1668. In 1670, Pierre LAMBERT DE LA MOTTE, a missionary priest of the Paris Foreign Society, founded the first indigenous religious congregation of women, the LOVERS OF THE HOLY CROSS (Dòng Mến Thánh Giá).

Persecution. The first major persecution erupted in 1698, the culmination of sporadic persecutions in preceding decades. Others followed (notably 1712, 1723, and 1750) during which at least 100,000 Christians, including the first of the canonized (Gil and Lenziniana, 1745), were martyred. Persecutions ceased temporarily in 1787 when the local vicar apostolic, Pierre Pigneau de Behaine, MEP, arranged a treaty between the French government and the ambitious southern provincial lord who later became Emperor Gia Long (1802–1820). Persecution resumed with increased intensity during the reign of his fourth son and successor, Emperor Minh Mạng (1820–1841). A strict Confucian, Emperor Minh Mạng feared that Christianity was undermining the Confucian foundation of Vietnamese socio-political life, doubting Vietnamese Christians' absolute fealty to and veneration of him as the "son of heaven." In 1825, he barred new foreign missionaries from entry. When rebellion broke out in 1833 and rebels sought help from Christian missionaries, the enraged emperor responded with a ferocious persecution campaign, expelling all remaining foreign missionaries and forcing Vietnamese Christians to apostatize by trampling a crucifix underfoot. Under the reign of his son, Emperor Thiệu Trị (1841–1847), persecutions abated somewhat, with sporadic executions and expulsions.

The final and worst wave of persecution resumed in 1847 with the ascension of Emperor Tự Đức (1847–1883) to the throne. Cruel, insecure and intransigent, the emperor distrusted foreign missionaries and Vietnamese Christians, suspecting them of instigating and participating in sporadic rebellions against his rule. Foreign missionaries were executed, and Vietnamese Christians were marked on their faces with the words "tả đạo" ("false religion"). Families were forcibly separated and tortured to elicit recantations. The ferocity of Tự Đức's persecution reached such proportions that French emissaries lodged a formal protest at his court in 1856. The decapitation of Bishop José María Díaz in 1857 was the last straw. The French seized upon it as an excuse to invade Vietnam, occupying Đà Nẵng in 1858 and moving southward. By a treaty with the French in 1862, Tự Đức agreed to grant freedom of religion to his subjects and to cede the southern region (Nam Việt) to the French. The interpretation of the terms of the 1862 treaty became a point of contention between Tự Đức and the French, who openly sided with his rivals. The French captured Hà Nội in 1873 and seized control of the northern region (Bắc Việt). Tự Đức's plea to China for help to drive out the French went unheeded, and by his death in 1883 the French had extended their grip over the whole of Vietnam.

During the 19th century, a total of almost 300,000 Christians suffered for their faith. Catholic resistance, shown notably in hiding priests, was heroic. In the five years between 1857 and 1862, it is estimated that more than 5,000 faithful were martyred in addition to 215 native priests and nuns, and about 40,000 Catholics were dispossessed and exiled from their home regions. Although the records of most who suffered have been destroyed, a total of 117 martyrs, comprising 96 Vietnamese, 11 Spanish Dominicans, and 10 French members of the Paris Foreign Mission Society, were later beatified on four different occasions (64 on May 27,

Archdioceses	Suffragans
Hà Nội	Bắc Ninh, Bùi Chu, Hải Phòng, Hưng Hoá, Lạng Sơn & Cao Bằng, Phát Diệm, Thái Bình, Thanh Hoá, Vinh
Huế	Ban Mê Thuột, Đà Nẵng, Kon Tum, Nha Trang, Quy Nhơn
Thành-Phô Hồ Chí Minh (Hồ Chí Minh City)	Cần Thơ, Đà Lạt, Long Xuyên, Mỹ Tho, Phan Thiết, Phú Cường, Vinh Long, Xuân Lộc

1900, 8 on April 20, 1906, 20 on May 2, 1909 and 25 on April 29, 1951). Of these 117, 8 were bishops, 50 priests (15 Dominicans, 8 members of the Paris Foreign Mission Society, 27 seculars), 1 seminarian, and 58 lay people (9 Dominican tertiaries and 17 catechists). On June 19, 1988, Pope John Paul II canonized these 117 Martyrs of Vietnam (*see* VIETNAM, MARTYRS OF, SS.)

[J. Y. TAN]

The Catholic Church in Present-Day Vietnam

The Church in the North. Cut off from the Church in the south and the Church of Rome for almost 21 years (1954–75), persecuted by the Communist government, and devastated by the departure of more than half a million laity and clergy in the 1954 exodus, the Church in the north barely survived with only slightly more than half of the Catholic population remaining. Several dioceses in the north lost more than half of their members in the 1954 migration, and all but two lost more than half of the clergy (see Table 3: Decimation of the Northern Church, 1954). After 1954 the Communist government confiscated the Church's social and cultural institutions, and confined the clergy and religious to strictly religious activities. Bishops and priests were practically under house arrest. Sick people had to be carried to the priest's house for the sacrament of anointing; a pastor could not celebrate Mass outside of his parish without the special permission of local authorities. In the aftermath of the Communist victory over the south in 1975, there was another massive exodus. More than 1.5 million Vietnamese fled to foreign countries, especially to the United States.

After 1986, when the government began a policy of liberalization, Church life improved significantly. Liturgical reforms mandated by the Second Vatican Council were slowly implemented. The new Roman Missal in a revised translation came into use. Bibles, catechisms, and liturgical books no longer needed to be smuggled to the north at great personal risk as "counterrevolutionary pro-

Diocese	Catholics who stayed	Catholics who left	Priests who stayed	Priests who left
Hà Nội	155,000	60,000	54	112
Lang Sơn	2,500	2,500	4	13
Hải Phòng	54,000	60,000	8	75
Bắc Ninh	35,423	38,000	7	56
Hưng Hoá	70,181	7,000	34	23
Thái Bình	88,652	80,000	13	79
Bùi Chu	165,000	150,000	30	165
Phát Diệm	58,000	80,000	26	139
Thanh Hoá	47,000	18,500	27	58
Vinh	156,195	57,080	124	67
TOTAL	**831,568**	**553,080**	**327**	**787**

Decimation of the northern Church, 1954.

paganda.'' Notable were a new translation of the Bible by Joseph Cardinal Trịnh Văn Căn and the multivolumed work on spirituality Bước Đường Hành Hương (On Pilgrimage) by Bishop Francis Xavier Nguyễn Văn Sang. The Catholic magazine Người Công Giáo Việt Nam (Vietnamese Catholics) is held suspect by many because it is published by a group regarded as friendly to the government.

Church activities are mostly limited to sacramental celebrations and pious devotions, without much impact on the socio-political and cultural order. Religious education consists mainly in teaching prayers and question-and-answer catechism class in preparation for first communion and confirmation. Instruction is most often given by the elders in the parish who, deprived of all opportunities for religious training since 1954, have not had access to the documents of the Second Vatican Council. Catechetical textbooks such as Bổn đồng ấu and Thánh giáo thuyết minh, written by Bishop Hồ Ngọc Cẩn in 1939, are still in common use. Despite these handicaps, the Catholic population in the north has grown steadily. Christian faith is nourished predominantly by the family with its practice of the daily recitation of morning and evening prayers. Prayers most often include the rosary, litanies, prayers to the patron saints (especially St. Joseph), the Miserere (Psalm 51) for the ancestors, and the acts of faith, hope, and charity. When a priest visits the parish church, bells toll to announce the Mass.

In the 1990s the government signaled a more open policy regarding the Church. It allowed seminaries to open in the archdiocese of Hà Nội and in the dioceses of Vinh and Thanh Hoá. In 1994 the government permitted the transfer of Bishop Bartholomew Nguyễn Sơn Lâm, formerly bishop of Đà Lạt (in the south), to the diocese of Thanh Hoá that had been sede vacante since February 1990.

The Church in the South. Compared with the Church in the north, the Church in the south is in a far more favorable situation. Not only did it benefit from the massive influx of Catholics in 1954, it also enjoyed twenty years of freedom (1955–75) which coincided with a period of radical renewal in the Catholic Church. After 1975 it was the policy of the government that all religious organizations must be under its control. As a consequence almost all Catholic organizations were disbanded, from the committees of the Vietnamese Episcopal Conference to parish councils. Even the Development Fund, which was administered by the Episcopal Development Committee in 870 parishes, vanished. Catholic students who wanted to enroll in universities encountered difficulties because of their Catholic identity. A government decree, issued Nov. 11, 1977, declared that permission of city, county, and province authorities was required for religious activities with numerous participants. Christmas celebrations, catechism classes, priests' retreats, visits by bishops for confirmation, in short, anything out of the ordinary needed special permits or a least had to be reported to local authorities.

Generally speaking, the government relaxed some of its controls after 1988. A decree issued on March 21, 1991, stated that religious activities such as prayer meetings, liturgical celebrations, preaching, and religious education that were in accord with local religious tradition and had been listed in the annual programs registered with the government no longer required permission. In practice, there exists greater freedom in big cities, whereas in areas the government still considers unsafe, such as the western mountainous region, difficulties persist. Despite the government control and restrictions, the Church in south has continued to grow in numbers and influence in the two ecclesiastical provinces in the south, Huế and Hồ Chí Minh, although the percentage of Catholics relative to overall population has decreased.

Bishops. The first indigenous Vietnamese bishop, Nguyễn Bá Tòng was appointed in 1933. By 1964 the entire hierarchy in North and South Vietnam was indigenous Vietnamese except for two French-born missionary (MEP) prelates. From the 1970s onward, all Vietnamese bishops were indigenous. The Vietnamese government's policy of seeking to control all religious organizations had resulted in much tension with the Holy See on the issue of episcopal appointments, especially in Hồ Chí Minh City (Saigon). The Holy See had appointed the then Archbishop Nguyễn Văn Thuận as coadjutor with right of succession in 1975. However, the Vietnamese government refused to recognize him and imprisoned him as a collaborator. Upon his release, he went into exile. Pope John Paul II appointed him the President of the Pontifical Commission on Peace and Justice and in 2001, made him a cardinal. Hùynh Công Nghi, bishop of Phan Thiết diocese, was appointed apostolic administrator of the archdiocese in August 1993 but was prevented by the government to assume office. In effect, the archdiocese was *sede impedita*; it was administered in limited capacity by auxiliary bishop Phạm Văn Nẫm. The impasse was finally resolved 23 years later when the Vietnamese government agreed to the recognize the Holy See's appointment of Archbishop Phạm Minh Mẫn in 1998.

Vietnamese Episcopal Conference. The two vicariates apostolic of 1659 increased to 17 in 1957. In 1960, the Holy See formally established the Vietnamese hierarchy with three archdioceses and 18 suffragan sees. Before 1975 the Vietnamese Episcopal Conference, which, though called Vietnamese, in fact consisted only of the two ecclesiastical provinces of the south, (Huế and Hồ Chí Minh City) held annual meetings regularly. After national unification in 1976, the conference temporarily suspended its activities. In May 1980, the conference met officially for the first time in Hà Nội, and by September of 1994 there had been seven such meetings. Each meeting and its location required permission of the government. Of the seven meetings, only the sixth was held in Hồ Chí Minh City; the others were in Hà Nội. The bishops issued two pastoral letters.

To judge the effectiveness of the Vietnamese Episcopal Conference, account must be taken of the extraordinary circumstances under which it has had to operate. All religious activities, including those of Buddhism, Protestantism, Caodaism, and Islam, must be conducted within the legal constraints of a socialist-Communist government. Besides having to follow the directions of the Holy See, which negotiates common agreements with the government, the conference must abide by the laws and customs of the country. For instance, at the beginning of the sixth meeting in Hồ Chí Minh City (Oct. 18-26, 1993), Trương Tấn Sang, head of the City People's Committee,

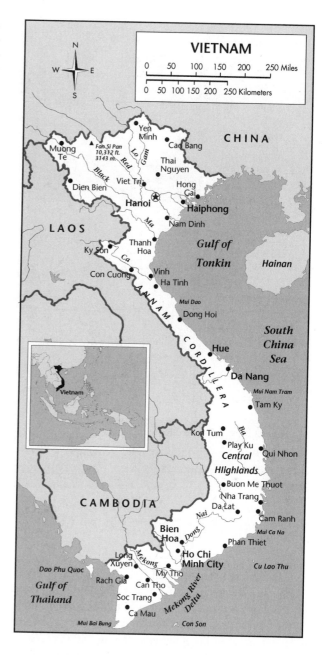

welcomed the attending bishops, and at its close, Bishop Lê Phong Thuận, secretary of the Conference, sent to Vũ Quang, head of the Government Committee on Religious Affairs, a report on the procedures and contents of the meeting. The twenty-six bishops attending the seventh meeting in Hà Nội (Sept. 5–12, 1994) were received by General Secretary Đỗ Mười and by Prime Minister Võ Văn Kiệt. The conference has one president, two vice-presidents, one general secretary, three associate secretaries, three chairmen of three standing committees (on worship; on priests, religious and seminarians; and on the laity).

Celebration of Christmas Mass in the Notre Dame de Saigon Cathedral, Ho Chi Minh City, Vietnam. (©Nevada Wier/ CORBIS)

In a memorandum dated Oct. 26, 1993 to Võ Văn Kiệt, the Vietnamese Episcopal Conference requested that bishops and priests be allowed to move about freely in their territories, without need of permission, to perform their ministry. In his communication no. 46 CV/TGCP, Vũ Quang, head of the Government Committee on Religious Affairs, affirmed that the government would create favorable conditions for bishops and priests to move about without need of permission in their territories to perform their ministry. Permission to travel to Rome or abroad for *ad limina* visits or for conferences was subsequently granted with greater frequency and ease, though bishops who were still not considered "good citizens" experienced delays in obtaining travel documents. The government also permitted Cardinal Paul Joseph Phạm Đình Tụng of Hà Nội and seven Vietnamese bishops to attend the 1998 Asian Synod in Rome.

Clergy. Since 1975 priestly ordinations have required permission of the government. Bishops must pro-

vide city and county authorities with a detailed dossier on the candidate who will be interviewed several times by the police and other local authorities to assess his suitability for ordination. Most dioceses have celebrated priestly ordinations annually. The diocese of Huế is an exception. Before the ordination of five priests on Sept. 1, 1994, no one had been ordained for the diocese in 19 years. Since 1954, the ten northern dioceses have suffered a severe shortage of priests. Despite unification of the country, the government does not allow priests of the south to serve in the dioceses of the north. Annual retreats for the clergy have been organized with the permission of the government to whom the name of the preacher and those of the participants must be submitted in advance.

A number of priests actively participate in the Committee for the Unification of Vietnamese Catholics (Ủy ban Đoàn Kết Công giào Việt Nam), known until 1990 as the Committee for the Unification of National Vietnamese Catholics. The bishops of five dioceses (Xuân Lộc, Phú Cường, Long Xuyên, Kon Tum, and Mỹ Tho) sent letters of congratulation to the organization on the occasion of its second general assembly in October 1990, attended by 133 priests, 17 religious, and 151 laypeople. Because this organization is part of the Vietnamese National Front, it is held suspect by some who regard it as an instrument of the government. To others it plays a useful role of liaison between the government and the Church under current political circumstances. All the priests, religious, and laypeople of this organization are in good standing with and faithful to the Church.

On May 20, 1992, Angelo Cardinal Sodano, the Vatican secretary of state, sent a communication to Bishop Nguyễn Minh Nhật, president of the Vietnamese Episcopal Conference, stating that no priest is permitted to take part in the Committee for the Unification of the Vietnamese Catholics. In June 1992, a government representative protested this ruling of the Vatican as contrary to the Vietnamese constitution concerning the human and civil rights of the Vietnamese people and as violating the accord between the Vatican and the government of Vietnam on the necessity of holding prior discussion with each other about any measure to be taken with regard to the Church. On Aug. 20, 1992, a representative of the Vatican officially responded that it falls within the competency of the Church to admonish its priests regarding participation in political organizations. It was added, however, that such participation is voluntary and that priests must observe the laws of their country. In light of this, a number of priests continue to be active in the committee, and its weekly magazine, *Công giáo và Dân toc* (*The Catholic Church and the People*) continues to be regularly published.

Bo trees flank Catholic Church, Bien Hoa, Vietnam. (©Tim Page/CORBIS)

Seminarians and Seminaries. After 1975 all major seminaries were shut down, and the seminary property was confiscated by the government. In 1986, some seminaries were allowed to reopen. By the end of 1994 seminaries were in operation in six dioceses: Hà Nội, Vinh-Thanh, Nha Trang, Hồ Chí Minh, Cần Thơ, and Huế. The number of seminarians grew so large that in the October 1993 the Vietnamese Episcopal Conference requested the opening of two more seminaries in the dioceses of Xuân Lộc and Thái Bình. The conference asked further that the buildings of St. Pius X Pontifical Institute be returned to the Church for the use of theological training. In its response, dated Jan. 17, 1994, the government Committee on Religious Affairs made no mention of the request to open two more seminaries, but in paragraph 9 it stated that the buildings of St. Pius X Pontifical Institute were being used for nuclear research and that the request that they be returned to the Church would be taken into consideration in the future.

Besides these official seminaries, there are several underground centers where thousands of seminarians are being trained. The lack of qualified professors is severe, and the level of academic preparation is far from satisfactory. In general, since 1954 in the north, and since 1975 in the south, there has been little serious intellectual formation for the clergy. The government has permitted a few priests to go to France, Rome and the United States for advanced studies.

Religious. All religious institutions were confiscated after 1975. Religious were dispersed into small communities in new "economic zones" and forced to engage in various activities beside ministry to eke out a meager existence. Life was especially hard for female religious and those not belonging to international orders. Nonetheless, enthusiasm for and commitment to consecrated life flourished. Several religious orders, especially female ones, even went to the north and secretly recruited vocations and brought them to the south for formation. As a consequence, the police would search a religious community in the dead of night to look for "illegal residents." In general, however, after 1986 life for religious improved significantly. They were then able to move from place to place and community to community. Some were permitted to go abroad for studies, and religious superiors were allowed to attend general assemblies of their orders in other countries. The government has permitted Archbishop Nguyễn Văn Bình of Hồ Chí Minh City to sponsor theological classes for religious: one session for female religious (a two-year program, full time, with 70 religious); a second session for female religious (a five-year program, one month per year, with 400 religious, some of whom came from the north); one session for male religious (a six-year program, with 70 religious preparing for ordination).

In many places women religious conduct kindergartens. A secular religious society in Thủ Đức runs a boarding school with nearly 1,000 students, from the sixth to the twelfth grade. Religious are working in hospitals, leprosaria, and retirement homes. Many are enrolled at state universities. A large number teach reading, catechism, and health care among the moutain tribes in the highlands. Some female religious orders have quietly sent missionaries to Cambodia and Laos.

Catholic Publications and Intellectual Life. With the victory of the Communists in 1975, all important Catholic educational institutions were either nationalized or shut down. The Catholic University in Đà Lạt was closed. Many books, documents, archives in libraries, diocesan chanceries, religious houses, and private homes were burnt for fear of harboring incriminating evidence. The library of the Vietnamese Episcopal Conference located in Hồ Chí Minh City was as good as destroyed. Fortunately, the libraries of St. Pius X Pontifical Faculty in Đà Lạt and of St. Joseph Seminary of the Hồ Chí Minh Archdiocese have been preserved in a relatively good condition.

Pre-1975 Catholic periodicals and magazines which no longer exist include *Thăng Tiến (Progress), Phụng Vụ (Liturgy), Nhà Chúa (God's House), Tông Đồ (Apostolate), Sống Đạo (Christian Living), Phương Đông (The Orient), Trái Tim Đức Mẹ (Mary's Heart), Công Lý Hòa Bình (Justice and Peace), Đức Mẹ Hằng Cứu Giúp (Our Lady of Perpetual Help)*, and *Linh Mục Nguyệt San (Priest's Monthly Magazine)*. Diocesan weekly or monthly newspapers also disappeared. Only the Catholic *ordo* was permitted publication. The well-known bookstore Khai-Trí in Hồ Chí Minh City was confiscated, and its owner sent to re-education camp. On May 3, 1977, a decree of the Information and Culture Department published the names of 857 authors whose works were forbidden circulation. In December 1980, the Jesuit educational Alexandre de Rhodes Center with its central library of more than 100,000 volumes was confiscated.

This does not mean that all publication and circulation of Catholic writings ceased. An underground press ran a brisk business thanks to computer and photocopying technologies. Foreign books on the Bible, theology, spirituality, and canon law were smuggled into the country and quickly translated into Vietnamese and widely distributed. Sometimes the original volumes were disassembled and photocopied, and the copies bound with gilded letters on the cover and publicly sold at much-reduced prices in bookstores such as those of the chancery of the Hồ Chí Minh archdiocese, of the Redemptorists, and of Fatima Church at Bình Triệu. At times, the police would confiscate the books and impose fines, but distributors would usually resume their trade.

Since the late 1980s restrictions on publication of religious works have been eased. Works on the Bible, theology, spirituality, liturgy, and liturgical music have appeared. Of special note are new translations of the Liturgy of the Hours and the Roman Missal (the new version has been in use throughout the country since 1992). Deserving the highest praise is a modern translation of the New Testament with scholarly introduction and notes, the fruit of 20 years of labor by a team of 14 translators. Thirty thousand copies of this 1,299-page volume, published in August 1994, were sold out immediately. The translation of the Old Testament has also been completed.

A new set of forty-five laws regulating publication, promulgated on July 7, 1993, by Nông Đức Mạnh, the president of the National Assembly, relaxes government control of publication. Article 18, which deals with religious publications, stipulates that the government will create favorable conditions for the publication of catechisms, prayer books, and other religious works. On Oct. 26, 1993, Bishop Nguyễn Minh Nhật, the president of the Vietnamese Episcopal Conference, sent a memorandum to Prime Minister Võ Văn Kiệt requesting, among other things, the establishment of a Catholic publishing house for Catholic books and of an official Catholic magazine.

The Twenty-First Century. Despite external difficulties, the Vietnamese Catholic Church is vibrant and dynamic. With regard to percentages, Vietnam has the third largest number of Catholics in Asia, after the Philippines and East Timor. This fact testifies to the truth of Tertullian's statement that the blood of martyrs is the seed of Christians. Such vibrancy and vitality are all the more remarkable given the hostile conditions under which the Church has had to operate, first in the north, then in the south. Even with the recent policies of liberalization, religious freedom is still under threat. At any rate, there is no danger whatsoever of a Vietnamese "national church" comparable to the Chinese Church in Communist China, even with the Committee for the Unification of Vietnamese Catholics, both because the government itself has no wish to institute such a thing and because the Vietnamese Catholic Church is strongly united with Rome and the universal Church.

It is the conviction of many Vietnamese, both at home and abroad, that the Communist regime will sooner or later topple, not necessarily by means of external military intervention, but because of its internal weaknesses. There is a basic contradiction between the Communist ideology and the profound religious ethos of the Vietnamese culture. The grip of the Communist government, unless strengthened by repression and violence, is bound to be pried open unless it begins to relax, as it has attempted to do so since the late 1980s.

Paradoxically, the greatest danger to the Vietnamese Catholic Church is not communism —it might be argued that communism has been a purifying fire for the Church—but unbridled capitalism that is now being viewed as the panacea of all social ills. In this context one of the urgent tasks of the Church seems to be disseminating the entire body of Catholic social teaching, especially that of John Paul II. Connected with this must be a decisive ''option for the poor,'' which the Vietnamese hierarchy has consistently urged upon Church members in its pastoral letters. Another immediate task is the training or, as the case may be, re-training of the clergy and religious, and through them, the laity in all aspects of theology and ministry. It is easy to be seduced by external achievements such as the building of churches and other structures. Far more important is the building of the Church by means of what a Vietnamese archbishop calls the ''living bricks'' of personnel.

[P. C. PHAN]

Bibliography: Vietnamese History. *Ðại Việt sử ký toàn thư (The Complete Book of the Historical Records of Ðại Việt).* 4 volumes (Hanoi 1967). N. L. JAMIESON, *Understanding Vietnam* (Berkeley 1993). A. LAUNAY, *Histoire ancienne et moderne de l'Annam, Tong-King et Cochinchine* (Paris 1884). LÊ THÀNH KHÔI, *Le Việt-Nam: Histoire et civilisation* (Paris 1955). K.W. TAYLOR, *The Birth of Vietnam* (Berkeley 1983). Christianity in Vietnam. *Mission de la Cochinchine et du Tonkin* (Paris 1858). *Histoire générale de la Société des Missions Étrangères,* 3 v. (Paris 1894). *Histoire de la Mission de Cochinchine 1625–1823: Documents historiques* (Paris 1920). *Histoire de la Mission de Tonkin: Documents Historiques* (Paris 1927). J. VŨ-KHÁNH TƯỜNG, *Les Missions jésuites avant les Missions Étrangères au Vietnam, 1615–1666* (Paris 1956). T. N. K. BUI, ''Religious Life in Vietnam: Opportunity and Challenge,'' *Tripod* 49 (1989) 62–68. S. B. DOELY, ed., ''Catholicism and Contemporary Vietnam,'' *IDOC Internazionale* 42 (1972) 3–96. P. GHEDDO, ''Vietnam: Der Leidensweg einer Kirche,'' *Internationale Katholische Zeitschrift (Communio)* 16 (1987) 122–31. P. X. HO, ''Church-State Relations in Vietnam,'' *Transformation* 6 (1989) 21–26. G. JACKSON, ''An Assessment of Church Life in Vietnam,'' *Religion in Communist Lands* 10 (1982) 54–68. B. MATTHEWS, ''The Place of Religion in Vietnam Today,'' *Buddhist Christian Studies* 12 (1992) 65–74. J. M. MEP, ''Church-State Relations in Vietnam,'' *Pro Mundi Vita Dossiers (Europe/North America)* 32 (1985) 1–35. P. C. PHAN, *Mission and Catechesis: Alexandre de Rhodes and Inculturation in 17th Century Vietnam* (Maryknoll, NY 1998). R. REIMER, ''The Church in Vietnam,'' *Transformation* 4 (1987) 20–28.

VIGERIO, MARCO

Cardinal bishop; b. Savona, 1446; d. Rome, July 18, 1516. He became a Franciscan, prompted by his great uncle, Francesco Della Rovere, who was general of the order in 1464. Vigerio taught theology in Padua and, after Francesco became Pope Sixtus IV in 1471, lectured at the Sapienza in Rome. He was made bishop of Senigallia in 1476 and was given administrative assignments by Sixtus IV, Innocent VIII, and Alexander VI. Under Julius II, a Franciscan and a relative, he was governor of Castel Sant'Angelo. In December 1505 he was made a cardinal and protector of the Franciscan order. In 1506 he returned to his studies but was taken away from them and put in command of the papal troops that beseiged and captured Mirandola in 1511. He defended Julius II against the irregular council of Pisa, was made cardinal bishop of Palestrina, and attended the Fifth LATERAN COUNCIL in 1512. In 1513, on the death of Julius, he resigned the See of Senigallia to his nephew. His writings show him more a learned humanist than a theologian. He was a precursor of the 16th-century cult of St. Joseph, and the *Decachordum,* his best known work, can be viewed as a treatise of asceticism based on the virtues of the Holy Family. He wrote two works on the life and the rule of St. FRANCIS OF PAOLA, whose patron he had been. Vigerio's sermons, reputedly of value, seem to be lost.

Bibliography: A. AUBERY, *Histoire géérale des cardinaux,* 5 v. (Paris 1642–49) 3:93–95. P. GODEFROY, *Dictionnaire de théologie catholique,* ed. A. VACANT, 15 v. (Paris 1903–50; Tables générales 1951–) 15.2:2988–92. P. RIDOLFI DA TOSSIGNANO, *Historiarum seraphicae religionis libri tres* (Venice 1586). A. CHACON, *Vitae, et res gestae pontificum romanorum et S. R. E. cardinalium ab initio nascentis ecclesiae usque ad Clementem IX,* 4 v. (Rome 1677).

[D. R. CAMPBELL]

VIGIL, FRANCISCO DE PAULA GONZÁLEZ

Peruvian priest, politician, and writer against the Church; b. Tacna, Sept. 13, 1792; d. Lima, June 9, 1875. In 1803 Vigil began his studies in the seminary of Arequipa, founded by the liberal Bishop Pedro José CHAVES DE LA ROSA. At the seminary Vigil met Francisco Javier LUNA PIZARRO, then a professor there and later one of the outstanding parliamentarians of the country and archbishop of Lima. The acquaintance did not lead to friendship but rather to a lifelong rivalry between the two men. Vigil's seminary studies were completed in 1812, but instead of receiving Sacred Orders, he returned to his home in Tacna, apparently motivated by personal scruples. In 1818, however, he returned to Arequipa and was or-

Francisco de Paula González Vigil.

dained. Even then he refused the care of souls and instead devoted himself to teaching in the Colegio de Independencia, of which he became vice rector.

In 1825 the people of his native city elected him their deputy to the Congress of Lima. There he met Francisco Javier Mariátegui and Benito Laso, and soon the three were united in a strong bond of shared interests. All three were at that time strong regalists, convinced republicans, and democrats. As such they helped to defeat the dictatorial ambitions of Bolívar and to fasten the yoke of subjection to the State on the Peruvian Church. In 1833 Vigil, still deputy for Tacna, condemned President Gamarra as a tyrant in a speech that won him acclaim for the first time outside Peru. His dislike for the Peruvian-Bolivian Confederation of Santa Cruz caused him to desert the Congress and to return to Tacna in 1835, but in 1836 he was called back to Lima to become director of the National Library. He lost this post for a time in 1839, when he was exiled, but in 1845 he was reinstated in the position, which he held until four days before his death. As director of the library, Vigil had the opportunity and the leisure to devote himself to study and also to encourage the young men of the country in their literary and scholarly endeavors.

In 1846 he completed the work begun in 1836 entitled *Defensa de la autoridad de los gobiernos contra las pretensiones de la Curia Romana,* 6 v. (1848–49). A second part, *Defensa de la autoridad de los obispos contra las pretensiones de la Curia Romana,* was printed later in four volumes. Each part was then reprinted in a single summary volume, so that the entire work occupied 12 volumes. In addition, Vigil wrote numerous pamphlets in answer to the condemnation of the work by Rome. Archbishop Luna Pizarro tried to find some Peruvian priest to answer this work, but none was eager to enter a direct challenge. Finally Fray Pedro GUAL undertook the thankless task. At this time Vigil was still a Catholic professing reverence and obedience to the Holy Father. However, in his two *defensas* he limited the power of the pope substantially to strictly spiritual interests. The civil government was given the right to regulate all civil matters and even those so-called mixed obligations, that is, those that are partly spiritual and partly civil, such as impediments for marriage, the erection of dioceses, the naming of bishops, and clerical celibacy. Vigil's reverence for the spiritual power of the pope came to an end when Pius IX condemned this work in 1851. He wrote an impudent letter to the Holy Father, denying his authority to condemn books, stating that this was the prerogative of the state. The papal condemnation was circulated, but the Peruvian Congress refused to grant the *pase,* for Vigil was then a senator. The publication of the *defensas* marked the beginning of Vigil's career as a writer. In the field of religion he gradually became increasingly radical, until in his later works, such as *Manual de derecho público eclesiástico* and *Diálogos sobre la existencia de Dios,* one can scarcely call him even a Christian in the traditional meaning of that term. He also ceased to function as a priest and instead called himself a "lay priest." On the other hand, many of his nonreligious works of this later period espoused valuable social causes, such as the abolition of the death penalty, the outlawing of war, a true confederation of the Americas, the development of cooperatives, and universal popular education.

Today relatively few read Vigil. Probably this was true even during his lifetime in regard to his complete works, but the shorter editions of his works were widely subscribed to and quoted. Unfortunately, his style is pedestrian, and the pace of the narrative is slowed by overly long quotations and frequent repetitions. Erudition fills every page of his books until it becomes almost overwhelming for the ordinary reader. However, during his life this aspect won him the admiration of his fellows in Peru and even in some circles in Europe. This, coupled with the singular purity and nobility of his private life, gave him such influence that no Peruvian government dared inaugurate direct relations with the Holy See during his lifetime. He refused the Sacraments before his death, as did his friend Mariátegui.

Bibliography: C. A. GONZÁLEZ MARÍN, *Francisco de Paula González Vigil* (Lima 1961). J. BASADRE, *Historia de la República del Perú* (5th ed. Lima 1961).

[A. S. TIBESAR]

VIGILIUS, POPE

Pontificate: March 29, 537 to June 7, 555; b. Rome, before 500; d. Syracuse, Sicily, June 7, 555. Vigilius was a Roman deacon, son of John, the consul and Pretorian prefect under Theodoric, and brother of the Senator Reparatus. Boniface II chose him as his successor in a Roman synod (*c.* 531); but this designation had to be rescinded under pressure of the Roman clergy and Senate in a second synod.

Deposition of Silverius. Nothing is known of the involvement of Vigilius in the simoniacal intrigue that surrounded the election of John II (late December 532), reported by King Athalaric (Cassiodorus, *Vivarium* 9.15) or of the part he may have played under Pope AGAPETUS I (elected May 13, 535) in pacifying the Roman clerical factions. He was with Agapetus in Constantinople (March 536) and on that Pope's death (April 22, 536) he entered into an agreement with the Empress THEODORA (1) in which he implied he would modify Western intransigence toward the Monophysites. On his return to Rome with the body of Agapetus he found SILVERIUS had been elected Pope (June 536) with the aid of the Gothic King Theodatus. In the fall the Goths evacuated Rome, and the Byzantine General BELISARIUS took control. Silverius was accused of treason and deposed, and Vigilius was enthroned as pope by the Byzantines (April or May 537). Silverius appealed to the Emperor JUSTINIAN I and was returned to Rome for trial, but Vigilius, now pope, arranged for a second exile during which Silverius died (December of 537). While extremely complicated, contemporary evidence points to Vigilius' involvement in the deposition of his predecessor and his own election.

Vigilius as Pope. As pope Vigilius set about rebuilding the city of Rome, devastated in the recent wars; he restored the aqueducts, reconstructed churches and buildings, and reopened the cemeteries. He dealt efficiently with Western affairs. He referred the request concerning penance for bigamy received from the Frankish King Theudibert to CAESARIUS OF ARLES and on the latter's death (August 27, 543) supported Auxanius of Arles as papal representative (*noster vicarius*) in Gaul. He charged Auxanius with presiding over territorial synods, as well as with regulating episcopal travel and the use of the pallium, and he cautioned against too rapid advancement of the laity in orders. To Aurelian, successor to Auxanius, he cautioned that the bishop's first duty was

to provide for the peace of the Church, and had him caution King Childebert not to be disturbed by false rumors regarding the Pope's difficulties with Constantinople. Vigilius wrote to Profuturus of Braga (March 29, 538), settling problems that had arisen concerning Baptism, Penance, and the reconsecration of churches.

Justinian and the Three Chapters. In his dealings with Eastern Church affairs, Vigilius insisted on two principles: a faithful upholding of the decrees of Chalcedon, and Rome as the final arbiter of what constitutes the faith, but, as Justinian learned, he could be intimidated away from those principles.

In 541 Vigilius accepted a dogmatic edict condemning ORIGEN, which had been suggested to the Emperor Justinian by the papal *apocrisiarius* Pelagius, who was replaced in Constantinople (542) by the deacon Stephen. But when in 544 Justinian condemned the THREE CHAPTERS, the Pope reacted by censuring not the emperor but the Patriarchs of Constantinople, Alexandria, and Antioch, who had signed the document, though under protest. During the preparations for the siege of Rome by Totila an imperial official arrived in the Eternal City and on November 25, 545, took Pope Vigilius in custody with orders to transport him to Constantinople. The party departed at once for Sicily, but the Pope was forced to stay in Catania until the summer of 546. There he received emissaries from the African bishops exiled in Sardinia, Bishop Dacius of Milan, the north Italian ambassador in Constantinople, and a messenger from Zoilus, Patriarch of Alexandria, who advised against his acceding to the condemnation of the Three Chapters. Stopping at Patras and Thessalonica in his journey through Illyricum and Greece, Vigilius received further support in favor of the Three Chapters.

Vigilius was greeted with esteem by Justinian. Although he excommunicated the Patriarch MENNAS for accepting the edict against the Three Chapters, he himself signed two secret agreements with Justinian and Theodora stating that he would undertake to convince the Western bishops that the Three Chapters should be condemned. He held a consultation of seventy bishops on this problem; but when FACUNDUS OF HERMIANE offered proof that Ibas of Edessa had not been condemned at Chalcedon, Vigilius clotured the synod and asked for written opinions.

Judicatum. On April 11, 548, he sent to the Patriarch Mennas his *Judicatum*, in which he now condemned the Three Chapters but protected the validity of the Chalcedonian decisions. Following the death of Theodora (June 28, 548) he received complaints from Dalmatia, Arles, and Tomi in Scythia, and news of his condemnation by a council in Africa until he should retract. He did not, and in 550 the African bishops excommunicated him. Trouble was also brewing in Rome itself. His nephew the deacon Rusticus and another deacon Sebastian rudely repudiated the papal decision on Christmas day 549, and early in 550 he excommunicated them.

Ceding to the Pope's importuning, Justinian returned the *Judicatum* for cancellation. An agreement was made between Pope and Emperor that no further discussion of the Three Chapters would be tolerated until a council could be convoked to settle the matter, and in August 550 Justinian extracted from Vigilius a third secret promise, that he would exert every effort to have the condemnation of the Three Chapters accepted in the West. With the aid of THEODORE ASCIDAS of Caesarea, Theodora's protégé, who dwelt in Constantinople and had great influence on the Emperor, Justinian broke the truce and affixed a condemnatory edict to the church doors of Constantinople in July 551. But when Ascidas and the imperial officials approached the Pope for his signature, they were rebuffed. Surrounded by Dacius of Milan, the deacon Pelagius, and several Western bishops, the Pope prepared a condemnation of the Patriarch Mennas, Bishop Ascidas, and his associates (August 14, 551), which was published only six months later. Then he fled to the rather symbolic basilica of SS. Peter and Paul for asylum and together with his court was subjected to the indignity of an attempted arrest by the praetorian prefect.

Vigilius Assaulted. Vigilius returned to the palace of Placidia upon an imperial guarantee of safety but was subjected to such harassment that on December 23, 551, together with his household he fled across the Bosphorus and sought asylum in another symbolically important church, of St. Euphemia, site of the Council of Chalcedon. Approached once more by Belisarius the Pope reacted by writing an encyclical letter to all the Christian people, in which he described the indignities to which he and his entourage had been subjected (February 5, 552). Justinian replied by ordering his arrest, and imperial officers attempted unsuccessfully to accomplish this task. The Pope was physically maltreated but clung to the columns of the altar until the people rescued him. The next day he had the document condemning Mennas, Ascidas, and their supporters affixed to the church doors of Constantinople.

In the early summer Justinian changed his policy and sent Mennas, Ascidas, and their entourage to the Pope in the basilica of Euphemia to make an act of submission, in which they expressed respect for Chalcedon, agreed to cancel all that had been written about the Three Chapters since the agreement of 550 between Pope and Emperor for a moratorium on discussion of the Three Chapters, and begged the Pope's pardon for the misdeeds to which he had been subjected.

Council of Constantinople II. Vigilius returned to the palace of Placidia on June 26, 552, was honored by the Emperor, and shortly thereafter was rejoined by the deacon Pelagius. In March 552 he had lost the support of Bishop Dacius of Milan, and in late August Mennas died and was replaced as patriarch by Eutyches of Amasea. In December 552 Eustachius was consecrated as the new patriarch of Alexandria and given instructions to curb the Origenistic monks in Egypt. Orders had also been issued convoking a general council for the early summer of 553, and on January 6 the patriarchs of Constantinople, Antioch, and Jerusalem met with Vigilius, presented him with a profession of faith based on Chalcedonian doctrine, and invited him to the council. The Pope sent them a written document signifying his willingness to attend but suggested that it be held in the West or at least preceded by a synod in Italy or Sicily. Justinian denied these requests but asked for the names of Western bishops who should be invited to the council.

Constitutum I. To offset the lack of Western representation Vigilius proposed a commission of himself and three Western bishops to meet with the three Eastern patriarchs to prepare for the council. When the emperor also turned this down the pope decided he would not attend the council, but instead would submit his judgment in writing. He prepared a document called the *Constitutum I*, dated May 24, which he tried to submit to the Emperor. The Pope condemned the doctrines ascribed to Theodore of Mopsuestia and Theodoret of Cyr *prout sonant,* as they read, in the florilegia of texts submitted to him, and appended five anathemas; but he refused to condemn these theologians as heretics since they died in peace with the Church. He exonerated Ibas of Edessa. The document was rejected by Justinian as "either useless, because it agreed with the Council; or condemnable because it disagreed."

Constitutum II. Meanwhile, in its seventh session, acting on orders from the Emperor, who supplied it with the secret documents signed by Vigilius in 547 and 550, the Council condemned Vigilius until he should repent; but they made it clear to the Emperor that they were breaking communion not with the See of Rome but the one occupying it—*non sedem sed sedentem.* Justinian delayed publication of the Council's edict against the Pope until July 14, 553, then began a series of harassments that by December brought the Pope into subjection. On December 8, Vigilius directed a letter to the Patriarch Eutychius in which he confessed that Satan had deceived him into separating from his fellow bishops. Appealing to the example of Augustine's *Retractations,* he condemned the Three Chapters and explicitly canceled his previous *Constitutum I.* Early in 554 he was persuaded to compose a second *Constitutum* in which he officially condemned the

Three Chapters and all who dared to defend them: "whatever is brought forward or anywhere discovered in my name in defense of the Three Chapters is now nullified." This document was published on February 23, 554. Six months later (August 13, 554) Vigilius was given a pragmatic sanction meant to regulate civil affairs in Rome and Italy. He tarried in Constantinople until the spring of 555, probably for reasons of health, and died in Syracuse on the way home.

Judgment regarding the Pope's career and turnabout in the matter of the Three Chapters is most difficult. Apparently to accommodate the pontiff after his retraction, Justinian had omitted the section of the seventh session of the Acts of the Council in which Vigilius was condemned; and this longer text was only discovered by S. Baluzius and published in 1683 (Mansi 9:163–658). Though retained only in the Latin version, it appears that the acts are basically authentic.

The problem presented to the theologians of a pope retracting decisions regarding doctrinal matters has been needlessly complicated. Vigilius was dealing with factual statements of doctrine, not defining revealed truth as such; besides, his final decision was made under duress. While he did receive aid from the deacon Pelagius and his entourage in preparing *Constitutum I*, that document is mainly his own work, and it is one of the finest theological tracts produced in the sixth century. As for the character of the Pope, it is certainly difficult to judge; but it is impossible to exonerate Vigilius from possible collusion in the deposition of Silverius, or changing his mind in a doctrinal dispute. His own retraction speaks for itself.

Bibliography: É. AMANN, *Dictionnaire de théologie catholique*, ed. A. VACANT et al., (Paris 1903–50; Tables générales 1951–) 15.2:1868–1924, 2994–3005. *Acta conciliorum oecumenicorum* 4.2:138–168. PELAGIUS I, *Pelagii diaconi ecclesiae romance in defensione trium capitulorum*, ed. R. DEVREESSE (Studi e Testi 57). H. M. DIEPIN, *Douze dialogues de christologie ancienne* (Rome 1960). L. DAVIS, S.J., *First Seven Ecumenical Councils* (Wilmington, Del., 1983), 235–243. G.EVERY, "Was Vigilius a Victim or an Ally of Justinian," *Heythrop Journal* 20: 257–266. E. FERGUSON, ed., *Encyclopedia of Early Christianity* (New York 1997) 2:1161. H. JEDIN, *History of the Church* (New York 1980) 2:450–455, 627–628. J. N. D. KELLY, *Oxford Dictionary of Popes* (New York 1986) 60–62. J. RICHARDS, *Popes and Papacy the Early Middle Ages* (London 1979) 129–133, 141–160. C. SOTINEL, "Autorité pontificale et pourvoir impériale sour le règne Justinien: le pape Vigile," *Mélanges d'archéologie d'histoire de l'lécole française de Rome* 104 (1992) 439–463. C. ALZATI, "'Pro sancta, fide, pro dogma patrum'. La tradizione dogmatica delle Chiese italiane di fronte alla questione dei Tre Capitoli. Caratteri dottrinali e implicazioni ecclesiologiche dello scisma," in *Atti del Convegno. Como e Aquileia. Per una storia della Società Comasca (612–1751)* (Como 1991) 49–82. D. J. CONSTANELOS, "Justinian and the Three Chapters Controversy," *Studies in Early Christianity* 7 (1993) 217–240.

[F. X. MURPHY]

VIGILIUS OF AUXERRE, ST.

Bishop; d. 684 or 689. He was born of a noble family noted for its sanctity. As bishop, Vigilius built a monastery on the outskirts of Auxerre dedicated to the Mother of God. He endowed it richly. In the editions of the document of its foundation, MABILLON states (*Annales OSB*, appendix 1:694) that the monastery was later given to CANONS REGULAR OF ST. AUGUSTINE and ultimately to the PREMONSTRATENSIANS. Beyond these several facts not much is certain. Vigilius is credited with establishing a hospital for the poor near the monastery. His death strikingly resembles that of LEODEGAR OF AUTUN; like Leodegar, Vigilius was murdered in a forest (*Cotia silva*, or *Coatia silva*, near Compiègne?) by Warato, (Waratto, Warado), successor as mayor of the palace to Ebroin, Leodegar's assassin. An account by one Saussauis blames Ebroin for both murders. *Mirabilia* attended Vigilius's death: his body was returned to Auxerre, and as it passed a prison in Sens, chains fell from all the prisoners and they were freed. The chains were then attached to Vigilius's coffin for all to see. His episcopate had lasted for 25 years and five months. His remains, kept in a silver reliquary, were scattered by the Calvinists (1567) but were recovered and enshrined anew in 1589.

Feast: March 11.

Bibliography: *Acta Sanctorum* (Antwerp 1643–) March 2:71–72. *Gallia Christiana*, v. 1–13 (Paris 1715–85), v. 14–16 (Paris 1856–65) 12:269. L. DUCHESNE, *Fastes épiscopaux de l'ancienne Gaule*, 3 v. (2d ed. Paris 1907–15) 2:427–446. G. ALLEMANG, *Lexikon für Theologie und Kirche*, ed. M. BUCHBERGER, 10 v. (Freiburg 1930–38) 10:608. A. MERCATI and A. PELZER, *Dizionario ecclesiastico*, 3 v. (Turin 1954–58)3:1321.

[C. M. AHERNE]

VIGNIER, JÉRÔME

French Oratorian scholar; b. Blois, 1606; d. Saint-Magloire, Nov. 14, 1661. Vignier, the son of a Calvinist minister, became a lawyer. While doing historical research, he met the bishop of Orléans, who occasioned his conversion to Catholicism. He joined the Bérullian Oratory at Blois (1630) and became a priest. He studied Greek, Hebrew, and Scripture, and also genealogy and numismatics. From 1648 he taught at the seminary at Saint-Magloire. He published the *Véritable Origine des Maisons d'Alsace, de Lorraine, et d'Autriche* (Paris 1649), a relevant contribution to the complex dynastic politics of the period. He edited (1654) St. Augustine's *Contra Julianum, Opus Imperfectum* (a second treatise against Julian; four of the six books hitherto unpublished). Relationships between this and Cornelius Otto JANSEN's *Augustinus* caused some to allege the books were spurious, thus delaying publication for a time. Friendship with Cardinal Jean de RETZ brought Vignier into political disgrace, and he had to hide in the house of the bishop of Châlons until the cardinal was reconciled to the court. Vignier then resumed work at Saint-Magloire, but he died soon afterward. His *Endiatessaron, Histoire et Harmonie de l'Evangile* (Paris 1662), the best concordance then available, did not appear until after his death.

Bibliography: H. HURTER, *Nomenclator literarius theologiae catholicae,* 5 v. in 6 (3d ed. Innsbruck 1903–1913); v.1 (4th ed. 1926) 1:461. H. RAHNER, *Lexikon für Theologie und Kirche,* ed. M. BUCHBERGER, 10 v. (Freiburg 1930–38) 10:611.

[J. C. CHALLENOR]

VIGOUROUX, FULCRAN GRÉGOIRE

Exegete; b. Nant, France, Feb. 13, 1837; d. Paris, Feb. 21, 1915. After his ordination (Dec. 21, 1861) he entered the Society of Saint-Sulpice. He taught philosophy to seminarians at Autun (1862–64) and Issy (1864–68) before being called to Saint-Sulpice in Paris to begin his life of teaching Scripture. In 1890 he became professor of Scripture at the Institut Catholique of Paris. After the establishment of the PONTIFICAL BIBLICAL COMMISSION in 1902, he was appointed its first secretary. Much of the rest of his life was spent at Rome, where he served in the formulation of the decrees of this Commission that were issued between 1905 and 1912. Shortly after his return to Paris (1913) he was struck with paralysis.

Vigouroux was one of the key figures in the Catholic Scripture revival. His most significant contribution was his editorship of the *Dictionnaire de la Bible* (1895–1912). Among his other works are: *La Bible et les Découvertes modernes en Égypte et en Assyrie* (6th ed. 1896), *Le Nouveau Testament et les Découvertes archéologiques modernes* (2d ed. 1896), and *Les Livres Saints et la critique rationaliste* (5th ed. 1901–02). His *Manuel biblique ou cours d'Écriture Sainte a l'usage des séminaires: Ancien Testament,* first published in 1879–80, went through numerous editions and translations and became a classic in French seminaries. The bulk of his work was apologetical, largely concerned with defending the Bible's historicity. Conservative in temperament, he was yet open to the new currents in Biblical studies.

Bibliography: E. LÉVESQUE, ''M. Vigouroux et ses écrits,'' *Revue Biblique* 12 (1915) 183–216.

[P. F. CHIRICO]

VIKTRING, ABBEY OF

Former CISTERCIAN ABBEY in Carinthia, Austria, Diocese of Gurk. Viktring (Victoria) was founded by Count Bernhard of Sponheim in 1142 and was colonized from Villers-Betnach in Lotharingia. In 1202 the three-naved, Romanesque, pillared basilica with barrel vaults was consecrated. The three tracery windows of the early-14th-century rib-vaulted apse contain what is probably Austria's most famous Gothic stained glass (1380–90). The abbey's high altar (dating from 1447) is in St. Stephen's Cathedral in Vienna today. Viktring's fame was enhanced by its abbot John of Viktring (1312–45?), a notable historian. Emperor Joseph II of Austria suppressed the abbey in 1786. In 1847 half of the nave of the abbey church was torn down, and the remaining church was used as a parish church. The extensive late-baroque monastic buildings (front, 427 feet long) with two courtyards still exist (now used as a factory).

Bibliography: K. HAID, ''Zur Kenntnis Johanns von Viktring,'' *Cistercienser-Chronik* 18 (1906) 161–167. M. ROSCHER, *Geschichte der Cist. Abtei V.* (unpub. diss. Vienna 1954). JOHANN VON VIKTRING, *Cronica Romanorum,* ed. A. LHOTSKY (Klagenfurt 1960). K. GINHART, *Viktring* (Salzburg 1962).

[A. SCHNEIDER]

VILAR DAVID, VICENTE, BL.

Martyr, married layman, and industrial engineer; b. Manises, Valencia, Spain, June 28, 1889; d. Manises, Feb.14, 1937. Vicente, husband of Isabel Rodes Reig (d. 1993), was the youngest of eight children of a family that owned a ceramics factory. He received his initial education from the PIARISTS, then studied industrial engineering in Valencia. While working in his family's business, Vicente undertook charitable work among the poor, involved himself in parish activities, and enacted some of the Church's social teaching during his tenure in several municipal positions. Beginning in 1931, he openly and courageously offered refuge to persecuted religious during the surge of anti-ecclesial sentiment and refused to moderate his own religious practices. He was killed ''in odium fidei''; shot in the street a few yards from his home. Pope John Paul II beatified him on Oct.1, 1995.

Feast: Feb. 24.

Bibliography: V. CÁRCEL ORTÍ, *Martires españoles del siglo XX* (Madrid 1995). J. PÉREZ DE URBEL, *Catholic Martyrs of the Spanish Civil War, 1936-1939,* tr. M. F. INGRAMS (Kansas City, Mo. 1993). *Acta Apostolicae Sedis* 19 (1995): 923–26. *L'Osservatore Romano,* English edition, no. 40 (1995): 1–3.

[K. I. RABENSTEIN]

VILARRASA, FRANCIS SADOC

Founder of the Dominican Order in California; b. La Pobla de Lillet, Spain, Aug. 9, 1814; d. Benicia, Calif., March 17, 1888. After profession at the monastery of St. Catherine, Barcelona, Spain, Sept. 25, 1830, Vilarrasa studied there until the building was burned down by antireligious rioters in July 1835. He then transferred to the La Quercia priory near Viterbo, then in the Papal States. There he was ordained, probably on May 17, 1837, and remained as assistant to the novice master for two years. At Santa Maria sopra Minerva, Rome, he took his lectorate in sacred theology in 1841. After his return to La Quercia, he volunteered for the missions and was assigned to the U.S. In January 1845 he arrived at St. Joseph's Priory near Somerset, Ohio, where he was chosen prior before the year's end. In 1849, as definitor of the province of St. Joseph, he accompanied Joseph S. ALEMANY, then U.S. provincial, to Europe on Dominican business. At Rome Alemany was named bishop of Monterey, Calif., and shortly afterward, Vilarrasa was appointed commissary general of the Dominicans in California, with the authority of a provincial superior.

Vilarrasa and his bishop arrived in San Francisco on Dec. 6, 1850, accompanied by Sister Mary of the Cross Goemare, OP, who opened the state's first convent and girls' school in Monterey. On Feb. 4, 1852, in Monterey, Vilarrasa formally erected the first Dominican foundation in California and gave the Dominican habit to six young men from Catalonia, Spain. The community was transferred to Benicia, then the state capital, on March 31, 1854. During these early years Vilarrasa served as local superior, parish priest, novice master, and professor of all ecclesiastical disciplines. Under his administration the foundation came to include a priory in San Francisco, eight mission stations, and a community of more than 40 members. From this nucleus grew Holy Name province, created in 1912 with headquarters in San Francisco.

Bibliography: P. M. STARRS, "The California Chronicle of Francis Sadoc Vilarrasa, O.P. 1850–1884," *Catholic Historical Review* 37 (1952) 415–436. V. F. O'DANIEL, *The Dominican Province of St. Joseph* (New York 1942).

[P. M. STARRS]

VILLA-LOBOS, HEITOR

Important South American composer and music educator; b. Rio de Janeiro, March 5, 1887; d. there, Nov. 17, 1959. After music studies with his father, an amateur cellist, and later at the National Institute of Music, he made his mark first on the concert stage; but several folklorist expeditions into the Brazilian interior, however, fired his

Heitor Villa-Lobos.

ambition to create the "musical image" of his country. A government grant for composition study in Paris (1923–26) intensified his awareness of his role, and he returned to Brazil "still more Brazilian." Undertaking an intensive campaign of "musicalization of the masses," he was appointed director of public school music in São Paulo (1930) and Rio de Janeiro (1932). To implement his work with children he turned out innumerable teaching aids—rounds, cradle songs, folk song arrangements, practical exercises—in addition to his adult compositions.

His total output was more than 2,000 works, placing him among the most prolific composers on record. Inevitably some of his music has only its spontaneity to redeem it; at its best it is virtuoso work—vital and imaginative, in content evocative of the ethnic sentiment and idiom of his environment, and always expertly crafted. Among his most original works are the *Bachianas brasileiras*—nine inventions in which Brazilian themes are grafted on to Bach-like counterpoint; 14 elaborations of the Brazilian dance-song form, *chôros;* and the symphonic poems. His Mass dedicated to St. Sebastian and incorporating animist liturgies; his suites entitled *Descobrimento do Brasil* (Discovery of Brazil), a vast fresco of the Christianization of the native people; his spiritual motets, and the *Magnificat-Alleluia* commissioned by the Vatican dominate his tribute to religion. Among his "absolute" writings are 11 symphonies, 11 concertos (six for piano), 17 quartets, and many experimental works. Although a nationalist to the extent that his music echoes the indigenous rhythms and nostalgic melismas, the spatial vistas of his homeland, he was never a propagandist, but sought rather in each problem to deduce the formula of equilibrium between native atmosphere and universal artistic values. He was also a noted conductor, and introduced both Beethoven's *Missa solemnis* and J. S. Bach's B-minor Mass to Brazil.

Bibliography: V. MARIZ, *Heitor Villa-Lobos* (Rio de Janeiro 1949), condensed tr. with same title pub. Gainesville. Fla. 1963. A. MURICY, "Villa-Lobos," *Pan American Union. Bulletin* 79.1 (1945) 1–10. O. L. FERNÂNDEZ, "A contribuição harmônica de Villa-Lobos," *Boletín Latino-americano de música* 6 (1946) 283–300. N. SLONIMSKY, Music of Latin America (New York 1945; rev. 1949). *Baker's Biographical Dictionary of Musicians*, ed. N. SLONIMSKY (5th, rev. ed. New York 1958) 1710–12. N. FRASER, *Grove's Dictionary of Music and Musicians*, ed. E. BLOM 9 v. (5th ed. London 1954) 8:792–797. L. H. CORRÊA BE AZEVEDO *Die Musik in Geschichte und Gegenwart*, ed. F. BLUME (Kassel-Basel 1949–). GERARD BÉHAGUE, *Heitor Villa-Lobos: The Search for Brazil's Musical Soul* (Austin 1994). L. M. PEPPERCORN, *The World of Villa-Lobos in Pictures and Documents* (Aldershot 1996); "H. Villa-Lobos in Paris," *Latin American Music Review* 6 (1985) 235–48. G. RICKARDS, "Heitor Villa-Lobos" in *International Dictionary of Opera* 2 v., ed. C. S. LARUE (Detroit 1993); "Yerma" *ibid.* E. STORNI, *Villa-Lobos* (Madrid 1988). S. WRIGHT, *Villa-Lobos* (Oxford 1992).

[M. BEAUFILS]

VILLANI, GIOVANNI

Florentine chronicler; b. Florence, *c.* 1275; d. Florence, 1348. Villani joined the business firm of the Peruzzi as a young man, and traveled first on its behalf to Rome, where he witnessed the HOLY YEAR of 1300, and later to France and Flanders. Business affairs kept him in northern Europe from 1302 to 1308, when he returned to Italy. He continued in the employ of the Peruzzi for another year, after which he settled in FLORENCE, taking an active part in political life. In 1316 he was elected prior for the first time, and subsequently he held many public offices. The failure in 1345 of the Bardi and Bonaccorsi firms, in whose affairs he was involved, led to his brief imprisonment as a debtor. He died during the epidemic of the plague of 1348. The 12 books of Villani's *Florentine Chronicle* are medieval in form; Florentine events are not separated from universal history. Villani begins with an account of the tower of Babel, and only in books seven to twelve does he write specifically about Florence, covering the period from 1266 to 1348. In discussing the society and economic life of his native city he proves to be an excellent observer, writing with freshness and perception, going beyond his predecessors in scope and detail.

Bibliography: No complete tr. of the *Chronicle* into English exists, but see G. VILLANI, *Chronicle: Selections from the First Nine Books of the Croniche Florentine*, ed. P. H. WICKSTEED, tr. R. E. SELFE (London 1906). E. MEHL, *Die Weltanschauung des Giovanni Villani* (Leipzig 1927). E. FIUMI, "Economia e vita privata dei fiorentini nelle rilevazioni statistiche di G. V.," *Archivio-storico italiano* 111 (1953) 207–241.

[E. G. GLEASON]

VILLANOVA UNIVERSITY

Villanova University was founded by the Augustinian Order in 1842. It traces its origins to old St. Augustine's Church in Philadelphia, which the Augustinians founded in 1796, and to the parish school, St. Augustine's Academy, established in 1811. The university is located outside of Philadelphia on the site of the "Belle Air" estate of John Rudolph, whose wife, Jane Lloyd Rudolph, was a close friend of the Augustinians. A few years after John Rudolph's death, in 1838, Jane Rudolph generously agreed to sell the estate to the Augustinians for $18,000, well below its reported worth of $40,000. The college was placed under the patronage of St. Thomas of Villanova, a sixteenth-century Augustinian theologian, educator, and bishop of Valencia, Spain, and called the "Augustinian College of Villanova." The college came to be known simply as Villanova and gave its name to the town that eventually grew up around it.

The college opened on Sept. 18, 1843 with an entering class of thirteen students, but its beginnings were uncertain. The anti-Catholic, "Know Nothing" riots in Philadelphia resulted in the burning of St. Augustine's Church in 1844, causing a financial crisis for the Augustinians. As a result, the College was forced to close on February 20, 1845. It reopened in September of 1846, with a student enrollment of twenty-four, and the first commencement took place on July 21, 1847. On March 10, 1848, the Governor of Pennsylvania, Francis R. Shunk, signed the Act of Legislature incorporating "The Augustinian College of Villanova in the State of Pennsylvania," giving it "the power to grant and confirm such degrees in the Arts and Sciences."

During its first fifty years, the college concentrated exclusively on the liberal arts but remained open to the changes in the curriculum that were required to meet students' needs and the demands for specialization. The School of Technology, later, the College of Engineering, was established in 1905 and, in 1915 a two-year premedical program was established. In 1926, a four-year pre-medical program and the B.S. in biology were established. The College of Commerce and Finance was founded in 1922.

In 1918, the college began to offer programs to women religious, in large part to assist in their preparation to teach in the parochial school system, aa well as to laywomen. The first degree was granted to a laywoman in 1938. The College of Engineering admitted its first female student in 1958, and the other academic divisions were allowed to admit women as commuters. Finally in 1968, Villanova became fully coeducational.

In 1953, the College of Nursing was established, the first of its kind under Catholic auspices in Pennsylvania. That same year, the School of Law was established and distinguished itself as the first law school under Catholic auspices to be awarded a chapter of the Order of Coif, a national honor society devoted to the encouragement of high standards of legal scholarship. In recognition of its enhanced academic programs and reputation, Villanova achieved university status on Nov. 18, 1953. The university's 1979 Mission Statement reaffirmed Villanova's Catholic, Augustinian character and commitment to the liberal arts.

Falvey Memorial Library holds over 800,000 volumes, 5,600 current serial subscriptions, approximately two hundred and fifty electronic databases, nearly ten thousand full-text electronic journals, and extensive microfilm and audiovisual collections. The Special Collections Department has incunabula, early Catholic Americana, the Augustiniana Collection, and the Joseph McGarrity collection of approximately 10,000 items that have an Irish and/or Irish-American focus. Other publications emanating from the university include the *Journal for Peace and Justice Studies, Journal of South Asian and Middle Eastern Studies*, and *Horizons.*

Bibliography: A. J. ENNIS, *No Easy Road: The Early Years of the Augustinians in the United States, 1796–1874* (New York 1993). D. R. CONTOSTA, *Villanova University 1842–1992, American-Catholic-Augustinian* (University Park, Penn. 1995). *A Future of Promise, A Future of Excellence, The Comprehensive Academic and Administrative Plan of Villanova University* (Villanova 1995).

[K. ELLIS]

VILLARROEL, GASPAR DE

Augustinian bishop, writer, and defender of the royal prerogatives in the Spanish Empire; b. Quito, Ecuador, *c.* 1590; d. Charcas (La Plata or, more recently, Sucre), Bolivia, Oct. 12, 1665. His parents, though living in poverty, were born of aristocratic colonial families. His father, Gaspar de Villarroel y Coruña of Guatemala City, Guatemala, was a lawyer who had studied at Bologna, Italy, and who became a priest after the death of his wife. About 1591 the family moved to Lima, Peru, where Villarroel joined the Augustinians and made his religious profession in October 1608. After ordination he taught in the monastery of San Agustín, in the Colegio San Ildefonso, and at the University of San Marcos, where he obtained the doctorate in theology (*c.* 1620). He held several offices in his order, acquired fame as a gifted preacher, and in the late 1620s went to Madrid, Spain, as the procurator of the province of Peru. While in Spain, Villarroel began publication of his several works—the first two (a short book of sermons and a commentary on the Gospels) appeared at Lisbon in 1631. Appointed as court preacher to Philip IV and to the Council of the Indies, he became well known in official circles. In 1637 he was chosen to be bishop of Santiago de Chile, at that time a remote and difficult see. Having acquitted himself well in that post, he was advanced first to the See of Arequipa, Peru, in 1651, and then to the Archbishopric of Charcas, which he ruled from 1660 until his death. Villarroel proved himself a model bishop, one who governed wisely and who was devoted to the interests of his people.

His most notable work is the *Gobierno eclesiástico-pacífico y unión de los dos cuchillos pontificio y regio,* written at Santiago in 1646 and published in two volumes at Madrid (1656–57; repr. 1738). It is primarily a collection, explanation, and justification of the royal cedulas pertaining to ecclesiastical affairs, but it contains also much information about political and social life in the Spanish colonies. In its defense of the so-called royal vicariate, this work is particularly significant in that it was written by a member of the hierarchy (*see* PATRONATO REAL). In defending the powers of the King, Villarroel cited the regalist opinions of his friend Juan de Solórzano Pereira. Another of Villarroel's works is his *Historias sagradas y eclesiásticas* (Madrid 1660), three volumes of stories and legends about the Blessed Mother.

Bibliography: G. DE SANTIAGO VELA, *Ensayo de una biblioteca ibero-americana de la orden de San Agustín,* 7 v. in 8 (Madrid 1913–31) 8:303–314. A. DE EGAÑA, *La teoría del Regio Vicariato Español en Indias,* in *Analecta Gregoriana* 95 (1958) 156–162. A. J. GONZÁLEZ DE ZUMÁRRAGA, "Fray Gaspar de Villarroel, O.S.A., Obispo de Santiago de Chile," *Anuario de estudios americanos* 14 (1957) 201–240.

[A. J. ENNIS]

VILLENEUVE, JEAN MARIE RODRIGUE

Cardinal archbishop of Quebec, Canada; b. Montreal, Canada, Nov. 2, 1883; d. Alhambra, Calif., Jan. 17, 1947. Born of an old (nine generation) Canadian family, Villeneuve studied at Mont-St.-Louis, Montreal. He entered the novitiate of the Oblates of Mary Immaculate at Lachine, took his vows Aug. 15, 1902, and after study at the University of Ottawa was ordained May 27, 1907. From 1907 to 1919 he taught at the university; obtained doctorates in philosophy, theology, and Canon Law; and was outstanding in the religious, social, and literary worlds of Canada, taking part in the Semaines sociales and the Canadian Academy of St. Thomas Aquinas, and initiating closed retreats in Ottawa. Named superior of the Oblate scholasticate (1920), he directed the formation of his young colleagues until his nomination as first bishop of Gravelburg, Saskatchewan (1930). He was consecrated at Ottawa on September 11 and set about organizing his diocese, where he founded a major seminary. A year later the Holy See recalled him east as archbishop of Quebec. He was installed there Feb. 24, 1932, and created a cardinal March 13, 1933.

His active apostolate, particularly in preaching and writing, made him well known nationally and internationally. He preached often during Advent and Lent in the Cathedral of Quebec, published many of his discourses, was the author of *Quelques pierres de doctrine* (Montreal 1938), and contributed frequently to newspapers and periodicals. His pastoral letters and charges alone fill three volumes of the collection of *Mandements des Evêques de Québec*. During his 15-year reign he consecrated several churches and many bishops and, as far as possible, insisted on ordaining all priests. During World War II he took keen interest in visiting Canadian soldiers even on the battlefield. He was the recipient of numerous religious and other honors, including Knight of the Grand Cross of the Order of the Holy Sepulchre (1932), Grand Cross of the National Order of the Legion of Honor (1934), member of the Roman Academy of St. Thomas Aquinas (1935), honorary member of the Royal Society of Canada (1942), and numerous honorary doctorates from universities in Canada and elsewhere. The high points of his career were the three papal appointments as legate *a latere* to the first National Eucharistic Congress of Quebec (1938), of which he was the guiding spirit; the dedication of the Basilica of St. Joan of Arc at Domrémy, France, (1939); and the crowning of the Virgin of Guadalupe in Mexico (1945).

Cares and hardships prematurely weakened the cardinal's health; in June 1946, while returning from a tiring trip to the Oblate missions of Northwest Canada, he suffered his first heart attack. Despite rest cures at l'Hôtel-Dieu of Quebec, his country home in Neuville, a New York hospital, and finally in California, he suffered his final attack in a sisters' convent at Alhambra. On Jan. 24, 1947, after simple obsequies in his cathedral, his remains were interred in the crypt of bishops of Quebec.

Bibliography: L. M. LEJEUNE, *Dictionnaire général . . . du Canada,* 2 v. (Ottawa 1931) v.2. *Semaine Religieuse de Québec* 59 (Jan. 23, 1947).

[H. PROVOST]

VILLENEUVE-BARGEMONT, JEAN PAUL ALBAN DE

A forerunner of the Catholic social movement in France; b. Saint-Auban (Var), Aug. 8, 1784; d. Paris, June 8, 1850. After having participated in the prefectorial administration of the Empire and the Restoration, he became councilor of state in 1828, but in 1830 he refused to take the oath to the government of Louis-Philippe. He was a deputy in 1830 and 1831 and from 1840 to 1848 held a seat among the legitimists. In 1832 when the Duchess of Berri was planning to land in Provence, he accepted from her the commission of royal commissary in the Var, but he soon returned to Paris to devote himself chiefly to studies in political economy. In 1848 he was appointed a member of the Académie des Sciences Morales. He was impressed with the importance of the SOCIAL QUESTION when he visited Lille, where the 32,000 paupers constituted nearly half the population of the city. The idea of combating pauperism was thenceforth in his mind. As a deputy he was one of the foremost authors of the law of 1841 limiting child labor; this law, for the first time in France, embodied the principle of legal protection for laborers. He was instrumental in securing the amendment of the fiscal law of 1847 to dispense the marriage of the poor and the legitimation of their children from stamp taxes and registration fees. As an economist he stood apart from the classical school represented by Adam SMITH and Jean Baptiste Say, whom he regarded as materialists. He considered that political economy should be concerned less with the production of wealth than with its distribution and the general diffusion of well-being, and he believed that the state ought to intervene to protect the weak against the "new feudalism of patrons." In his *Livre des affliges* (Paris 1841) he depicted a bishop complaining with equal bitterness of industrial proprietors who thought only of increasing their gains and of legislators who were concerned solely with enacting penal prohibitions against labor organizations. He held to the concept of a "vital and family salary" sufficient to sustain both the workman and his family, and he believed that an employer should receive a profit only after the payment of this salary. Among other writings in which his ideas are set forth are the *Économie politique chrétienne, ou recherches sur la nature et les causes du paupérisme en France et en Europe, et sur les moyens de le soulager et de le prévenir* (Paris 1834); *Histoire de l'économie politique, ou Études historiques, philo-*

sophiques et religieuses sur l'économie politique des peuples anciens et modernes (Paris 1841).

Bibliography: M. I. RING, *Villeneuve-Bargemont: Catholic Social Protagonist* (Milwaukee 1935). A. THÉRY, *Un Précurseur du catholicisme social: Le Vicomte de Villeneuve-Bargemont* (Lille 1911).

[C. J. NUESSE]

VILLENEUVE-LES-AVIGNON, ABBEY OF

Or Abbey of Saint-André of Villeneuve-les-Avignon, on the Rhone, facing Avignon, France, a former Benedictine monastery under the patronage of SS. Andrew and Martin and of St. Caesarius, a recluse who died at this spot on the hill of Andaon in 586 (Latin, *Andoanense* or *Avenionense*). The earliest origins of this monastery can no longer be traced, but Bp. Garnerius of Avignon established monks at the site in 976. In 1024 a basilica in honor of St. Martin was built over the sanctuary dedicated to St. Andrew. From 1063 to 1087 St. Pons was abbot there. The 12th and 13th centuries were a prosperous era for the monastery and were marked by many gifts from the Counts of Toulouse; in 1118 Pope Gelasius II consecrated the new abbey church; Abbot Raymond II rebuilt the monastery buildings *c.* 1171 to 1175. In 1226 the King authorized the monks to build a town around their monastery, but it was not until 1292, under King Philip IV the Fair, that the city of Villeneuve came into being. Fortified by the kings, it was separated only by the Rhone from the papal domain, the VENAISSIN. In the 16th century, Abbot François de Castellane restored the monastic buildings and published a Breviary according to the usage of Saint-André. A successor, François Brancas (1573–98) was a Jewish convert, familiar with 22 languages. Jean Sicard rebuilt the cloister in 1604, and the monastery was amalgamated with the Congregation of the Exempt. In 1635, however, Abbot du Rouvre called in the MAURISTS. Prior Perreciot built a new dormitory and refectory. In 1768 only ten monks remained in the abbey, and these were dispersed by the Revolution. Fort-Saint-Andrew, a vast enclosure built by the King of France (1362–68) to face AVIGNON and encompassing the monastery and village of Saint-André, still stands. Inside is the Romanesque chapel of Our Lady of Belvéset, admirable for the purity of its lines.

Bibliography: *Gallia Christiana*, v.1–13 (Paris 1715–85), v.14–16 (Paris 1856–65) 1:871–885. M. MÉRITAN, *Étude sur les abbés et le monastère de Saint-André de Villeneuve-lez-Avignon* (Avignon 1898). L. H. LABANDE, *Le Palais des papes et les monuments d'Avignon . . . ,* 2 v. (Marseille 1925). F. BENOÎT, *Villeneuve-lez-Avignon* (Paris 1930). L. H. COTTINEAU, *Répertoire topobibliographique des abbayes et prieurés,* 2 v. (Mâcon 1935–39) 2: 3393–94.

[J. DAOUST]

VILLERS, ABBEY OF

Ancient Cistercian abbey (*Villarium*) in Belgium (Brabant), Diocese of Namur, founded in 1146, suppressed in 1796.

Villers was founded by Clairvaux, and reached its peak in the 13th century with 100 monks and 300 lay brothers. It established two other houses in Belgium, Grandpré (1231) and Saint-Bernard-sur-l'Escaut (1235), and its jurisdiction was extended over a number of Cistercian nunneries. In the Middle Ages Villers was noted for mysticism, piety, and generosity toward the poor, and more than 60 of its monks were venerated locally. The abbey suffered during the wars of the 16th and 17th centuries, but the 18th brought a new era of prosperity, in which magnificent rebuilding and expansion took place. The French Revolution, secularizing in its wake all monasteries, brought an abrupt end to it. The ruins of the 13th-century Gothic church are the most remarkable monuments of Cistercian architecture in Belgium.

Bibliography: L. H. COTTINEAU, *Répertoire topobibliographique des abbayes et prieurés,* 2 v. (Mâcon 1935–39) 2:3395-97. K. HOFMANN, *Lexikon für Theologie und Kirche,* ed. M. BUCHBERGER, 10 v. (Freiburg 1930–38) 10:626–627. U. CHEVALIER, *Répertoire des sources historiques du moyen-âge. Topobiobibliographie,* 2 v. (Paris 1894–1903) 2:3309.

[L. J. LEKAI]

VILLOT, JEAN

Cardinal, Vatican Secretary of State; b. Clermont-Ferrand, France, 1905 (possibly 1906); d. Rome, Italy, March 9, 1979. Villot was tall, gangling, chain-smoking, and exasperatingly courteous in the French manner. Little in his previous career prepared him for the top post in Vatican diplomacy. He was a theology professor at Clermont-Ferrand and the Institut Catholique of Lyons. From 1950 to 1959 he was secretary of the French episcopal conference, which led to his being appointed as the French-language secretary when Vatican II started in 1962. This brought him to the attention of Paul VI who made him a cardinal in 1965 and brought him from Lyons to Rome in 1967 as Prefect of the Congregation of the Clergy. In May 1969 he was advanced to Secretary of State.

This was a crucial time in the pontificate of Pope Paul VI. The anti-authority mood of 1968 affected the

Church and led to intense criticism of *Humanae vitae.* Pope Paul needed someone to steady the ship. The surprise was not so much that Pope Paul had appointed a non-Italian Secretary of State for the first time, but that he had persisted with the aged Cicognani for so long—he was 86 before he was forced to retire.

Paul also wanted Villot to carry through the reform of the Roman Curia. It had been done "on paper" with *Regimini ecclesiae* (Aug. 15, 1967), but to be made effective, it needed strong leadership. Villot could bring a fresh mind to this task, and flanked by the dynamic Giovanni BENELLI as *sostituto,* he would perform that function of co-ordination which Paul VI saw as the main role of the Secretariat of State.

Villot was energetic, methodical, and pastorally-minded. He tried to rationalize the working methods of the Secretariat of State, insisting on shorter hours and fewer time-wasting procedures. The bureaucrats were reminded that they were priests, and he set an example for them by hearing confessions, visiting hospitals, and preaching on Sundays. The Villa Barberini near Castelgandolfo had been fitted out as the summer residence of the Secretary of State; yet no previous Secretary of State had actually lived there. Villot spent his summers there in order to be close to Paul VI. Although the Pope remained alone with the burden of his office, Villot shouldered some of the load.

Villot often had difficulties with Giovanni Benelli. Benelli specialized in Italian affairs about which Villot was deemed ignorant. Villot thought that the Church would expose itself to humiliation if it fought the divorce reform proposal of May 12, 1974; he was later proven correct. Benelli, who had been secretary to Monsignor Montini from 1947 to 1950, had known the Pope far longer than Villot had, and had access to him whenever he liked. This rankled Villot, but it was Benelli who left in June of 1977.

Villot played a crucial role as *camerlengo* responsible for organizing the two conclaves of 1978. Pope John Paul I immediately named him his Secretary of State. An ill-informed writer later claimed that Villot had joined in a plot to murder the Pope because he was about to be removed from office, but Villot had no desire to retain his position and wished to resign. After John Paul I's death and the subsequent election of John Paul II on Oct. 18, 1978, Villot was forced to remain in the Vatican as Secretary of State. The unique combination of a non-Italian pope and a non-Italian Secretary of State was short lived. Villot died a few months later at the age of 73.

Bibliography: P. HEBBLETHWAITE, *The Year of Three Popes* (1978). H. DENIS, Eglise, *qu'as tu fait de ton concile?* (Paris 1985).

[P. HEBBLETHWAITE]

VINCENT DE PAUL, ST.

Apostle of charity and founder of the Congregation of the Mission (*see* VINCENTIANS) and of the Daughters of CHARITY; b. Pouy (now called Saint-Vincent de Paul), Landes, France, April 1581; d. Paris, Sept. 27, 1660. Vincent was the third of six children born in a peasant family. He studied the humanities at Dax from 1595 to 1597, then went to Toulouse for theology. After his ordination (1600) he earned the baccalaureate in theology at Toulouse (1604). His whereabouts from 1605 to 1607 are uncertain; one version has it that he was captured at sea and enslaved by the Muslims of Barbary, then made an adventurous escape by ship. It is certain that he was at Avignon and Rome in 1607–08.

The Conversion of an Apostle. In 1608 he arrived in Paris and there met Pierre de BÉRULLE who later, exercised a profound influence on his life. The gradual conversion of Vincent from a seeker of benefices to a seeker of God began probably about this time; it seems to have been completed at the latest by about 1620. During the years immediately after conversion Vincent was almoner (1610) to Queen Marguerite of Valois (repudiated wife of Henry IV); pastor (1612–26) of the parish of Clichy near Paris; and chaplain (1613 to *c.* 1625) to the family of Philippe-Emmanuel de Gondi, who was general of the galleys of France, brother of Henri de Gondi (first cardinal de Retz), and father of Jean François Paul de Gondi (second cardinal de RETZ).

From about 1611, Vincent endured a three- or four-year temptation against faith; the trial left him after he resolved to devote his life to the service of the poor. As chaplain, he not only looked after the spiritual needs of the Gondi family and their household staff, but also felt himself responsible for the peasants on the vast Gondi estates. The deathbed repentance (1617) of an apparently good-living peasant opened his eyes to the spiritual misery of the peasantry. A sermon on general confession preached with great fruit on Jan. 25, 1617, in Folleville, near Amiens, was considered by the chaplain as the first of his mission. For a brief period in 1617, Vincent was pastor of Chatillon-les-Dombes near Lyons, where he founded the first Confraternity of Charity, an association of pious laywomen who helped the poor and the sick. Having returned to the Gondis in December 1617, he drew up plans to evangelize all their lands; thus his principal work from 1618 to 1624 was preaching missions and establishing the Confraternity of Charity on the Gondi territories. As chaplain general of the galleys from 1619, Vincent did all in his power to alleviate the corporal and spiritual woes of the galley slaves.

His friendship with (St.) FRANCIS DE SALES and (St.) Jane Frances de CHANTAL began in the winter of

1618–1619. In 1622 Francis de Sales appointed him superior of the Visitation convents in Paris; at this time Vincent also undertook the spiritual direction of Mme. de Chantal. Vincent became principal of the Collège des Bons-Enfants in Paris in 1624; that same year Bérulle introduced him to Jean Duvergier de Hauranne, later known as the Abbé de Saint-Cyran. Vincent and Jean became very close at this time, even sharing a common purse. When Duvergier's Jansenistic convictions became more pronounced, however, their friendship cooled considerably, and in 1648 Vincent took an active stand in opposing JANSENISM. The defeat of the movement in France is due in great measure to his work and influence in the subsequent years.

Apostolic Foundations. On April 17, 1625, the Gondis founded the Congregation of the Mission (known also as Vincentians and Lazarists) for the purpose of preaching missions to poor country people. The congregation was approved by the archbishop of Paris April 24, 1626, and soon after, the first missionaries banded together in formal union around Vincent. Royal ratification in May 1627 gave the congregation legal status in France, but in 1628 Rome twice refused its approval. In Paris in 1632, Vincent took possession of the priory of Saint-Lazare, which became the motherhouse of the congregation until the Revolution, and from which the name Lazarists is derived. Urban VIII finally approved the community in the bull *Salvatoris nostri* (1633).

Vincent had met LOUISE DE MARILLAC, his collaborator in many charitable works, in 1625. The Daughters of Charity were formed (1633) from a group of girls who had been assisting her and had gathered together in her home. Vincent composed their rule, gave them conferences, and governed as superior general. They in turn rendered him invaluable assistance in his charitable works, e.g., the care of foundlings, which they undertook in 1638 and in which they continued long after his death.

In 1626 in Beauvais, Vincent initiated the retreats for ordinands, a 10-day period of training in moral theology and Holy Orders for those about to be ordained. These retreats spread quickly over France and into Italy and Poland. Until 1642 they were the most successful form of clerical training in the whole of France, and they became the inspiration and basis for the later seminaries of ordinands. Vincent also organized (1633) the Tuesday Conferences, a select group of clerics who had made the retreats for ordinands and who wished to meet together for their own benefit and for that of the apostolate. In 1636, following the norms of the Council of Trent, he founded a seminary for young boys at Bons-Enfants. In 1642 he added to it a seminary of ordinands, the first of 18 such institutions conducted by his congregation during

Saint Vincent de Paul. (Archive Photos)

his lifetime. In 1645 Vincent moved the conciliar seminary from Bons-Enfants to Saint-Lazare and renamed it the Seminary of Saint-Charles; an utter failure as a Tridentine seminary, it proved a success as a minor seminary. The seminary of ordinands at Bons-Enfants meanwhile gradually developed into a major seminary.

Vincent sent ten priests to serve as chaplains with the French army in 1636, and beginning in 1639 he organized relief for Lorraine and other provinces devastated during the Wars of Religion. Several times he acted as mediator in attempting to restore peace to a divided France. Vincent assisted Louis XIII on his deathbed in 1643 and became a member of the Council of Conscience, a committee formed to advise the King on religious matters. He kept this post until 1653, when opposition to Mazarin forced him to quit the office.

Years of Fulfillment. The last period of his life was not one of many new undertakings, but rather one in which his earlier works (Congregation of the Mission, Daughters of Charity, missions, seminaries, charities) spread throughout France and beyond it. He completed and distributed the rules of his congregation to his disciples in 1658. The death of Louise de Marillac early in 1660 saddened him, and Vincent himself died peacefully in that year. His body lies at the motherhouse of the Parisian province of the Congregation of the Mission.

Although acclaimed a saint by his contemporaries, Vincent was not formally beatified until 1729. In 1737 he was canonized by Clement XII and in 1885 he was named patron of all works of charity of which he is in any way the inspiration. Vincent de Paul was neither a profound nor an original thinker; yet few have accomplished as much. His success was a result of natural talents and of a tremendous amount of work, but above all of a profound spiritual life. In this he was deeply influenced by Bérulle and Francis de Sales, but he modified their ideas according to his own insights. The piety that he practiced and taught was simple, nonmystical, Christocentric and oriented toward action.

Feast: July 19.

Bibliography: Works. *Correspondance, entretiens, documents*, ed. P. COSTE, 14 v. (Paris 1920–25), v.11 and 12 rev. and ed. A. DODIN as *Entretiens spirituels aux Missionnaires* (Paris 1960); *Letters,* ed. and tr. J. LEONARD (London 1937); *Conferences . . . to the Sisters of Charity,* tr. J. LEONARD, 4 v. (Westminster, Md. 1952); *V. de P. and Louise de Marillac: Rules, Conferences, and Writings*, ed. F. RYAN and J. E. RYBOLT (New York 1995); *Correspondence, Conferences, Documents,* tr. P. COSTE (Brooklyn, N.Y. 1985). Literature. L. ABELLY, *Vie du vénérable serviteur de Dieu, V. de P.,* 3 v. (Paris 1664); *The Life of the Venerable Servant of God Vincent de Paul,* ed. J. E. RYBOLT (New Rochelle, N.Y. 1993). G. ARNAUD D'AGNEL, *Saint V. de P., A Guide for Priests,* tr. J. LEONARD (London 1932). G. L. COLUCCIA, *Spiritualità vincenziana* (Rome 1978, 1980). P. COSTE, *The Life and Works of St. V. de P.,* tr. J. LEONARD, 3 v. (Westminster, Md. 1952). L. CRISTIANI, *Saint V. de P.,* tr. J. R. GREGOLI (Boston 1977). H. DANIEL-ROPS, *Monsieur Vincent,* tr. J. KERNAN (New York 1961), picture album. J. DELARUE, *L'Idéal Missionnaire du prêtre d'après saint Vincent* (Paris 1947); *Ce que croyait Monsieur Vincent* (Paris 1974). A. DODIN, *Saint V. de P. et la Charité* (Paris 1960), tr. as *V. de P. and charity,* tr. J. M. SMITH and D. SAUNDERS, ed. H. O'DONNELL and M. G. HORNSTEIN (New Rochelle, NY 1993); *L'esprit vincentien* (Paris 1981); *Monsieur Vincent parle à ceux qui souffrent. Suivi de La prière de Blaise Pascal, pour demander Dieu le bon usage des maladies* (Paris 1981); *En prière avec Monsieur Vincent* (Paris 1982); *François de Sales, V. de P.* (Paris 1984); *La légende et l'histoire de Monsieur Depaul à saint V. de P.* (Paris 1985); *Initiation à saint V. de P.* (Paris 1993). P. GUILHAUME, *Saint V. de P.: l'ambassadeur des pauvres* (Monte Carlo 1988). J. M. IBÁÑEZ, *Vicente de Paúl y los pobres de su tiempo* (Salamanca 1977); *Vicente de Paúl: realismo y encarnación* (Salamanca 1982). A. L. MCLAUGHLIN, *St. V. de P., Servant of the Poor* (Milwaukee 1965). R. P. MALONEY, *The Way of V. de P.: A Contemporary Spirituality in the Service of the Poor* (Brooklyn, N.Y. 1992); *He Hears the Cry of the Poor* (Hyde Park, NY 1995). M. U. MAYNARD, *Virtues and Spiritual Doctrine of Saint V. de P.,* rev. C. A. PRINDEVILLE (St. Louis 1961). P. MIQUEL, *Vincent de Paul* (Paris 1996). J. M. MUNETA, *V. de P.: animador del culto* (Salamanca 1974). B. PUJO, *V. de P.: le précurseur* (Paris 1998). M. PURCELL, *The world of Monsieur Vincent* (Chicago 1989). L. ROBINEAU, *Monsieur Vincent, raconté par son secrétaire* (Paris 1991). M. ROCHE, *Saint V. de P. and the Formation of Clerics* (Fribourg 1964). Y.-M. SALEM-CARRIÈRE, *Saint V. de P. et l'armée* (Paris 1975). *Saint Vincent de Paul et la Révolution française* (Bouère 1989).

[M. A. ROCHE]

VINCENT FERRER, ST.

Dominican apostolic preacher called the "Angel of the Judgment"; b. Valencia, Spain, Jan. 23, 1350; d. Vannes, Brittany, France, April 5, 1419. He was the fourth child of William Ferrer and Constance Miguel, who early decided on a Church career for him. He was a brilliant dialectician at the age of 15 and, despite parental opposition, he entered the Order of Preachers in his native city, making profession on Feb. 6, 1368. He studied at Tarragona for two years and then taught logic at Lerida. It was during these years that he wrote the treatises *De suppositionibus dialecticis* and *De natura universalis.* In 1373 he began his theological studies at the Biblical Studium of the order at Barcelona, where for a time he taught the natural sciences. In 1379 he completed his formal studies at Toulouse. As he described his early life, "study followed prayer, and prayer study." He was ordained at Barcelona in 1379 by Cardinal Pedro de Luna.

In Vincent growth in holiness paralleled intellectual development. From his earliest years he had cultivated a fervent devotion to Our Lord and His blessed Mother. He embraced and practiced the austerities of his order with all the ardor of his passionate nature. Marvels accompanied his prayers even during his formative years. Such indeed was his prominence that almost immediately after his ordination he was chosen prior of the convent in his native Valencia. It was probably while governing his brethren that he wrote his brief but admirable treatise *De vita spirituali.* He resigned as prior, however, in 1384 to teach theology in the cathedral school at Valencia. In 1389 he was made master of theology.

The Schism. But it was not as professor he was to do his most distinguished work. The evils that afflicted society after the Black Death (1347–50) were aggravated and intensified by the Western Schism. All Christendom was divided in its allegiance. Vincent had early espoused the cause of Clement VII, the Avignonese claimant to the throne of St. Peter, convinced that the election of the Roman pontiff, Urban VI, had been invalidated by fear. In support of Clement, Vincent had addressed his impassioned *De moderno Ecclesiae schismate* to Pedro IV, king of Aragon. About the same time St. CATHERINE OF SIENA was laboring in behalf of Urban.

In the service of his compatriot Cardinal de Luna (1390–94), Vincent made use of all his eloquence and learning to persuade the clergy, kings, princes, and people of nearly the whole of the Iberian peninsula to give their allegiance to Clement. So far as his official duties permitted, he also devoted himself to preaching, administering the Sacraments, settling disputes, and protecting and converting the Jews. He was then convinced that the effective revival of Christian life and morals depended primarily upon the healing of the Schism. Yet it was by his preaching that he rose to the height of his power and influence.

Upon the death of Clement in 1394, Vincent was called to Avignon by his learned and admired friend Cardinal de Luna, who had been elected to succeed the Avignonese pope and who took the name of Benedict XIII. At the papal court, as apostolic penitentiary and Master of the Sacred Palace, Vincent was indefatigable in his efforts to bring an end to the Schism; but he declined all honors, even the cardinalate. He had expected that Benedict would, in fulfillment of the oath taken by all the cardinals in the conclave that elected him, arrange with the pope for a double resignation, thus opening the way for the election of an undisputed successor. But Benedict remained obdurate, even after he had been deserted by the French king and nearly all his cardinals.

Apostolic Preaching. Vincent was disillusioned; he became gravely ill. In a vision, he was commissioned by the Lord, who was accompanied by St. Dominic and St. Francis, "to go through the world preaching Christ." After a year had passed Benedict permitted him to go. In November 1399, therefore, he set forth from Avignon and spent 20 years in apostolic preaching. As the spirit moved him or as he was requested, he visited and revisited places throughout Spain, southern France, Lombardy, Switzerland, northern France, and the Low Countries. With fiery eloquence he preached the need of repentance and the coming of the Judgment. He seldom remained in any place for more than a day, and then only when the people had been long neglected or when heresy or paganism was rife. Miracles in the order of nature and of grace accompanied his steps. He had with him fellow priests to assist in instructing the ignorant and in reconciling sinners. Flagellants joined his suite—both men and women whom he had inspired to make public atonement. These he organized into what was called "The Company of Master Vincent" to assist in the apostolate. By his personal influence and constant direction he was able to prevent enthusiasm from degenerating into fanaticism, for no reproach was ever leveled against his select group.

Repudiation of Benedict XIII. Despite his incessant journeyings and his unique apostolate, Vincent never forgot the sad plight of the Church in schism, though he had now come to look upon the Schism as a symptom rather than a cause of the frightful evils against which he preached. Twice (in 1408 and again in 1415) he sought to persuade Benedict that he should resign in the interest of unity. But in vain. In his last effort he became convinced that the obstinate Benedict was not the true pope. Once again, close to death, he suddenly recovered his strength, mounted the pulpit, and, in dramatic fashion be-

fore an enormous assembly over which Benedict was presiding, thundered his denunciation. Benedict fled for his life, abandoned by those who had previously supported him. He took refuge on the fortified isle of Peniscola where, tragically, he lived out what was left of his life.

Vincent had no part in the Council of Constance, which brought an end to the Schism. He resumed his preaching with renewed vigor. His relics are preserved at Vannes in Brittany where he died. He was canonized by Calixtus III, June 3, 1455; however, the formal Bull was issued by Pius II, 1458.

Feast: April 5.

Bibliography: M. M. GORCE, *Dictionaire de théologie catholique,* ed. A. VACANT et al. (Paris 1903–50) 15.2:3033–45; *St. Vincent Ferrier* (Paris 1924). P. FAGES, *Histoire de S. Vincent Ferrier,* 2 v. (Louvain 1901). H. GHÉON, *St. Vincent Ferrer,* tr. F. J. SHEED (New York 1939). M. CATHERINE, *Angel of the Judgment: Life of Vincent Ferrer* (Notre Dame, Ind. 1954). M. H. ALLIES, *Three Catholic Reformers of the Fifteenth Century* (Freeport, N.Y. 1972). G. SCHIB, *Vocabulari de Sant Vicent Ferrer* (Barcelona 1977). U. TOMARELLI, *San Vincenzo Ferreri: apostolo e taumaturgo* (Bologna 1990). J. A. GARCÍA CUADRADO, *Hacia una semántica realista* (Pamplona 1994). R. CHABÁS Y LLORENS, *Opúsculos* (Valencia 1995). P. M. CÁTEDRA, *Sermón, sociedad y literatura en la Edad Media: San Vicente Ferrer en Castilla* (Valladolid 1994).

[J. B. WALKER]

VINCENT MADELGARIUS, ST.

Married man, abbot of Soignies (Hainaut, Belgium); d. *c.* 687. Madelgarius or Mauger married WALDETRUD, also called Waudru or Valtrude, daughter of a count of Hainaut; they had four children who are all regarded as saints, but to lead a more perfect life, separated and both entered religious life. While Waudru (*c.* 650) was establishing at Mons a convent, which later bore her name and which was to continue in existence until 1792 as a noble chapter of canonesses, Madelgarius, tonsured by St. Aubert, Bishop of Cambrai, founded a monastery at Hautmont and there became a monk about 653. Soon Madelgarius, longing for still greater solitude, changed his name to Vincent and retired to his own estate of Soignies, there building a monastery of which he became abbot. Shortly before his death, he entrusted the monastery to his son (St.) Landry, later said to have become bishop of Meaux. The biography of Vincent Madelgarius seems suspect to more than one historian: the oldest *Vita* of this saint goes back no further than the 11th century, and the first mention of the Abbey of Soignies dates only from 870. Nevertheless the saint's relics are venerated in the collegiate church of Soignies dedicated to him (choir dating from about 1000; nave, 12th century; remodeled 15th to 17th century). Every Pentecost Monday a great procession in his honor marches with elaborate pageantry around the city.

Feast: Sept. 20 (formerly July 14).

Bibliography: B. DE GAIFFIER, *Analecta Bollandiana* 12 (1893) 422–440, 11th-century *vita*. J. MABILLON, *Acta sanctorum ordinis S. Benedicti*, 9 v. (Paris 1668–1701; 2d ed. Venice 1733–40) 2:643–645, 760. *Acta Sanctorum* July 3:629–659. *Acta sanctorum Belgii*, ed. J. H. GHESQUIÈRE et al., 6 v. (Brussels 1783–94) 4:3–38, 12th-century *vita*. U. BERLIÉRE, *Monasticon belge*, v.1 (Bruges 1890) 315. É. DE MOREAU, *Histoire de l'Église en Belgique*, v.1 (2d ed. Brussels 1945) 145. J. L. BAUDOT and L. CHAUSSIN, *Vies des saints et des bienheureux selon l'ordre du calendrier avec l'historique des fêtes*, ed. by the Benedictines of Paris, 12 v. (Paris 1935–56); v. 13, suppl. and table générale (1959) 7:312–313. A. M. ZIMMERMANN, *Kalendarium Benedictinum: Die Heiligen und Seligen des Benediktinerordens und seiner Zweige*, 4 v. (Metten 1933–38) 2:450–451, 453. È. MICHEL, *Abbayes et monastères de Belgique* (Brussels 1923).

[J. DAOUST]

VINCENT OF BEAUVAIS

French Dominican encyclopedist and theoretician, called Bellovacensis; b. Beauvais, Oise, between 1190 and 1200; d. Beauvais, probably 1264. While a student at the University of Paris, he entered the DOMINICANS at Saint-Jacques, Paris, *c.* 1220. During his assignment to the priory in Beauvais (established 1228), he became intimately acquainted with the nearby Cistercian Abbey of Royaumont which was founded by LOUIS IX in 1228 and with its first abbot, Ralph. Observing the multiplicity, and the frequent inaccessibility and inaccuracy of copies of works by learned authors, he planned to compile a systematic, encyclopedic *Speculum maius* that would make readily accessible the wisdom of others. His original vast collection of quotations, classified into *naturale* and *historiale*, came to the attention of King Louis *c.* 1244 through Abbot Ralph (Oursel 253, 257). Desirous of a copy, the king offered necessary financial aid. After verifying, correcting, and completing all the quotations, Vincent sent a volume (Dijon manuscript 568) containing the first half of the second part, *Historiale*, explaining that the rest still needed to be fully checked and that the prologue to the *Historiale* summarized the entire first part. Vincent was anxious that learned and sympathetic men, such as the bishops of Cambrai (Guidardus of Laon, d. 1247) and Paris (WILLIAM OF AUVERGNE, d. 1248) be the critics. In its final form the *Speculum historiale* was a history of mankind from creation to 1254. The finished *Naturale* was a gigantic encyclopedia of nature, the six days of creation, of elements and properties, and of the first man, his Fall and Redemption through the Sacraments and virtues. Extensive remaining material inaugurated a third part, *Speculum doctrinale,* summarizing all learned arts: liberal, mechanical, and practical (moral philosophy and medicine).

The *Speculum maius,* Vincent's major work, claiming no originality for itself, was the most extensive encyclopedic venture until modern times; it required considerable financial and secretarial assistance as well as patience. A spurious *Speculum morale,* drawn mainly from THOMAS AQUINAS, was added between 1310 and 1325. The *Historiale,* being most popular, often circulated separately, and it was translated into French (*c.* 1328), Catalan, and Dutch verse in the fourteenth century (Ullman 323). The *Speculum maius* was printed seven times: Strassburg (1473–76); Basel (1481, *Naturale* and *Morale*); Nuremberg (1473–86); Venice (1484, 1494, 1591); Douai (4 v. 1624). QUÉTIF, Échard, and B. L. Ullman have demonstrated fully that none of these editions is reliable, all being contaminated by numerous editorial interpolations, rearrangements, and falsifications.

Having acquired the admiration of Louis IX and the Cistercians, Vincent was given the office of lector at the abbey of Royaumont (*c.* 1250), appointed lector at the royal court (*lector regis*), and became a lifelong friend of the king, although never tutor to the royal children. Upon the death of the dauphin, Louis, on Jan. 13, 1260, Vincent wrote a moving letter, *Epistola consolatoria super morte filii.* At the request of Queen Marguerite, Vincent, still lector at the abbey, laid aside an *opus quoddam universale* requested by the king to write a treatise for the tutors of Prince Philip on the manner of educating princes, *De eruditione filiorum nobilium* (1260–61). Through the Dominican master general, HUMBERT OF ROMANS, both Louis IX and King Theobald of Navarre exerted pressure on Vincent to complete his *opus universale* concerning royal governance. Pleading overwork, although no longer lector in the abbey, he sent the first part (*primus libellus*), entitled *De morali principis institutione* before Pentecost of 1263. Need for a second part eventually produced *De eruditione principum* by William Peraldus, which was long ascribed to Thomas Aquinas (Berges 308–313). Other works sometimes ascribed to him are of less significance and insufficiently established as authentic.

The probability that Vincent died in 1264 rests on the explicit statement of Luis of Valladolid (d. 1436), a historian familiar with the archives of Saint-Jacques, and on an enigmatic epitaph, reasonably interpreted by Quétif and Échard.

Bibliography: J. QUÉTIF and J. ÉCHARD, *Scriptores Ordinis Praedicatorum* 5 v. (Paris 1719–23) 1.1:212–240. U. CHEVALIER, *Répertoire des sources historiques du moyen-âge. Bibliographie,* 2 v. (2d ed. Paris 1905–07) 2: 4683–4684. L. THORNDIKE, *A History of Magic and Experimental Science,* 8 v. (New York 1923–58) 2:457–476. C. OURSEL, ''Un Exemplaire du *Speculum Majus* de Vincent de Beauvais provenant de la bibliothèque de saint Louis,''

Page from the 15th-century manuscript "Miroir Historial," written by Vincent of Beauvais, translated by Jean du Vignai.

Bibliothèque de l'École des Chartres 85 (1924): 251–262. L. LIESER, *Vinzenz von Beauvais als Kompilator und Philosoph* (Leipzig 1928). B. L. ULLMAN, "A Project for a New Edition of Vincent of Beauvais," *Speculum* 8 (1933): 312–326. VINCENT OF BEAUVAIS, *De eruditione filiorum nobilium,* ed. A. STEINER (Cambridge, Mass. 1938). W. BERGES, *Die Fürstenspiegel des hohen und späten Mittelaliers* (Leipzig 1938; repr. 1952). H. PELTIER, *Dictionnaire de théologie catholique,* 15 v. (Paris 1903–50) 15.2:3026–3333. F. STEGMÜLLER, *Repertorium biblicum medii aevi,* 7 v. (Madrid 1949–61) 5:8304-8306.

[J. A. WEISHEIPL]

VINCENT OF LÉRINS, ST.

Fifth-century monk and theologian; d. before 450. Gennadius describes Vincent as Gallic by birth, a priest of wide learning at the monastery of Lérins, author of an *Adversus haereticos* under the pseudonym of Peregrinus (Pilgrim), whose death occurred in the reign of Theodosius II and Valentinian III between 425 and 450 (*De vir. ill.* 65). That Vincent served as tutor to Eucherius's son, Salonius, is known from Eucherius of Lyons (*Instruct.* 1, pref.); while Vincent's own *Commonitoria* (ch. 1) suggests that he had undertaken military service before coming to Lérins.

Of Vincent's works, the heresiography mentioned by Gennadius is now called the *Commonitoria* (from a term in ch. 1, 27, 28) and has been frequently edited. The first part (ch. 1–28) exists in its original form, but the second (ch. 29–33) is a compendium of what had been two books. This recapitulation dates from A.D. 434 (*c.* 29).

The recently discovered *Excerpta Vincentii Lirinensis* proves to be a florilegium of texts taken from St. AUGUSTINE with preface and epilogus by Vincent and is plausibly dated 434–440 (see *Commonit.*, ch. 16 for the design). It is marked by strong Augustinian sympathies, which call into question the assumption of many scholars that Vincent displays an anti-Augustinianism. That there is a link between the *Excerpta* and the creed *Quicumque vult* seems to have been demonstrated by J. Madoz. Hence the possibility that Vincent may be the author of some, at least, of the creedal formulas must be considered, though critical opinion on this creed is not concordant. A no longer extant *Objectiones Vincentianae* is presupposed by the *Pro Augustino responsiones* which PROSPER OF AQUITAINE composed *c.* 431–434. In 1673 the future cardinal Henri Noris suggested that Vincent was the originator of the *Objectiones,* a view which has also been espoused by H. Koch. On the contrary L. de Tillemont is of the opinion that the author is that Vincent cited by Gennadius (*De vir. ill.* 81)

The mark of Lérins's true importance lies in his position on tradition and the development of Christian doctrine described in the *Commonitoria.* Whether this treatise is to be interpreted as a veiled polemic against St. Augustine or as composed quite apart from the Semi-Pelagian controversy, its theologizing marks an epoch in the understanding of the Catholic faith.

According to *Commonit.* (ch. 2, 29) it is the double authority of the Scriptures and of the Church's tradition which distinguishes Catholic truth from heretical falsity. Though the canon of the Scriptures is a sufficient norm for truth, the very existence of variant interpretations shows the need for recourse to a standard outside the Scriptures (ch. 2: "secundum ecclesiastici et catholici sensus normam"; also ch. 27). In this case, stress is to be laid upon what has been believed everywhere, always and by all; this is the famed Vincentian canon, marked by the notes of universality, antiquity, and consent (ch. 2: "quod ubique, quod semper, quod ab omnibus creditum est"; ch. 27, 29). Since Vincent places peculiar doctrinal force upon the judgments of the Roman See (ch. 6, 32, 33) and of ecumenical councils (ch. 23, 28, 29, 30), it is clear that his concept of tradition makes room both for a deposit of truth and for authoritative organs to proclaim the truth. Doctrinal development (*profectus religionis*) is legitimate and necessary when it is true unfoldment and not change (ch. 23). It deepens the understanding of the Faith on the part of the entire Church as well as of individuals and is likened to the growth of the human body, to the process whence seed becomes plant, to the polishing of metal (ch. 23). While the Church ever guards the truths committed to her, what was at first simply believed achieves sharper delineation as authoritative decrees define the ancient Faith in new formulas (ch. 23).

Modern theologians, e.g., Cardinal Franzelin, consider the Vincentian canon true in the affirmative but not in the exclusive sense, i.e., whatever is universal, ancient, and the object of Catholic consensus is certainly true, yet precisely because legitimate development has been at work there are truths securely Catholic today which have not ever, everywhere, and by all been explicitly believed in the past. A phrase from *Commonitorium* (ch. 23) is cited by Vatican Council I, sess. III, cap. 4 (Denzinger, 3020).

Feast: May 24.

Bibliography: VINCENT OF LÉRINS, *Commonitories,* tr. R. E. MORRIS (The Fathers of the Church: A New Translation, ed. R. J. DEFERRARI et al. 7; New York 1949) 257–332. B. ALTANER, *Patrology,* tr. H. GRAEF from 5th German ed. (New York 1960) 540–541; *Tradition et progrès: Le Commonitorium,* tr. P. DE LABRIOLLE (Paris 1978). J. MADOZ, *Excerpta Vincentii Lirinensis* (Madrid 1940); *El Concepto de la tradición en s. Vincente de Lérins* (Analecta Gregoriana 5; Rome 1933); *Gregorianum* 21 (Rome 1940) 75–94; *Recherches de science religieuse* 39 (Paris 1951) 461–471. H. KOCH, *Vincenz von Lérins und Gennadius* (Texte und Untersuchungen zur Geschichte der altchristlichen Literatur 31; Berlin 1907) 39–58. G. MORAN, *Scripture and Tradition* (New York 1963). É. GRIFFE, *Bulletin de littérature ecclésiastique* 62 (1961) 26–31.

[H. G. J. BECK]

VINCENT OF SPAIN

A native of the Iberian Peninsula; b. date and place unknown; d. sometime after 1234. He arrived in Bologna as a student about 1200, and from 1210 to 1215, already a cleric, he was teaching Canon Law there and writing most of his works. There is no evidence of his teaching civil law, although his works show that he knew it well. In all likelihood Silvester was his professor of Canon Law, and perhaps also LAWRENCE OF SPAIN and JOHN OF WALES; in civil law he studied under Azo (not Accursius, as it has been alleged frequently). The terms *bonus* and *hilaris* are added to his sigla in one manuscript. Among his disciples were BERNARD OF PARMA and Sinibaldo Fieschi (later Pope INNOCENT IV). Soon after 1220 Vincent left Bologna. He was a bishop, but it is disputed whether his see was Saragossa (Spain) or Idanha (Portugal): if the former, then Vincent was a Cistercian monk of the monastery of Veruela; if the latter, he may be identified with a certain official of the King of Portugal.

The following works, all in manuscript, are known: (1) Glosses on the *Decretum* of GRATIAN; (2, 3) *Apparatus* to *Compilationes* I and III, on which he worked simultaneously between 1210 and 1215; (4) Glosses on *Compilatio* II (there is no indication that he ever commented on *Compilatio* IV); (5) *Apparatus* to the decrees of the Fourth Lateran Council of 1215, of which two recensions, both written before 1220, are extant; (6) Glosses on the trees of consanguinity and affinity; (7) *Apparatus* or *Lectura* to the Decretals of GREGORY IX; (8) *Casus* respecting *Compilatio* III (covering only a few isolated titles); (9) *Casus* in respect of the Decretals of Gregory IX; (10) *Summula* or *quaestiones de exceptionibus;* and (11) *De discordia testium et de consonantia et qualiter debeant repelli.* The attribution to Vincent of writings (10) and (11) still requires further study. Writings (3), (5), and (6) will be published in *Monumenta Iuris Canonici* of the Institute of Medieval Canon Law. The most extensive and important works are (2), (3), (5), and (7). He exerted great influence on his contemporaries through his teaching and writings, and today is considered one of the most important medieval canonists.

See Also: DECRETISTS; QUINQUE COMPILATIONES ANTIQUAE.

Bibliography: G. POST, ''*Blessed Lady Spain:* Vincentius Hispanus and Spanish National Imperialism in the 13th Century,'' *Speculum* 29 (1954) 198–209. J. OCHOA SANZ, *Vincentius Hispanus* (Rome 1960), with bibliog. S. KUTTNER, ''Notes on Manuscripts,'' *Traditio* 17 (1961) 537–541. R. WEIGAND, *Die bedingte Eheschliessung im kanonischen Recht* (Münchener Theologische Studien, Kanonistische Abteilung 16; Munich 1963).

[A. GARCÍA]

VINCENTIAN (VIANCE), ST.

Hermit; b. Anjou; d. Jan. 2, 672? According to legend he lost his parents as a very young child and was brought up by Berald, duke of Aquitaine, who gave him to Bp. DESIDERIUS OF CAHORS so that he might study for the priesthood. When Berald died, however, his successor discontinued Vincentian's studies and put him in charge of the stables. After much abuse, Vincentian ran away and became a hermit in Limousin. His life was marked by miracles; a vision foretold his death. His *vita* (*Monumenta Germaniae Historica: Scriptores rerum Merovingicarum* 5:112–128) was supposedly written by a deacon, Hermenbert, who was Vincentian's tutor, but evidence now indicates that the *vita* is a later 11th-century work and is highly untrustworthy. Except for his cult in the Diocese of Toul, there is no solid evidence that Vincentian ever existed.

Feast: Jan. 2.

Bibliography: B. KRUSCH, *Neues Archiv der Gesellschaft für ältere deutsche Geschichtskunde* 18 (Hanover 1893) 549–649, esp. 561. J. L. BAUDOT and L. CHAUSSIN, *Vies des saints et des bienheureux selon l'ordre du calendrier avec l'historique des fêtes,* ed. by the Benedictines of Paris, 12 v. (Paris 1935–56); v. 13, suppl. and table générale (1959) 1:35. A. BUTLER, *The Lives of the Saints,* rev. ed. H. THURSTON and D. ATTWATER, 4 v. (New York 1956) 1:22.

[G. J. DONNELLY]

Felix de Andreis, first superior of the Vincentians in the United States.

VINCENTIANS

Lazarists and Paúles are other popular names for the members of the Congregation of the Mission (CM), a community of priests and brothers. Founded by St. VINCENT DE PAUL (c. 1581–1660), they and the Daughters of Charity constitute the ''Double Family of St. Vincent,'' under one superior general. The aims of the congregation, besides personal sanctification of its members, are parish administration, chaplaincies, foreign missions, pastoral ministries, social outreach, and academic and seminary education.

Foundation and Organization. The congregation derives its origin from Vincent's awareness of the lack of religious instruction among the peasants on the estates of Count Philip Emmanuel de Gondi, whose chaplain and almoner he was. Vincent's sermon at Folleville, Jan. 25, 1617, is regarded as the beginning of the congregation, although it was not formally organized until April 17, 1625, when Vincent and his first disciple, Antoine Portail (1590–1660), pledged themselves to preach missions on a permanent basis. Endowed by the Count de Gondi, and authorized by the count's brother, the archbishop of Paris, they took up residence at the Parisian Collège des Bons Enfants. On Sept. 4, 1626, Vincent de Paul, with

St. Mary's, Vincentian major seminary in Perryville, Missouri.

Portail and two other priests, legally signified their intention to live in community, an act that received episcopal and royal approbation and, ultimately, confirmation by Urban VIII, Jan. 12, 1632. Vincent then took possession of the former priory of St. Lazare at Paris, whence the Vincentians came to be known in France as Lazarists. From this headquarters 550 missions were organized between 1632 and 1660. To obviate friction between regular and secular clergy, Vincent desired that his missionaries partake of the nature of both: they were to be secular priests living in community according to a rule.

Early Expansion. During Vincent's lifetime the congregation grew to 500 members, located mainly in 23 houses and 15 seminaries in France. Not only was the original purpose of country missions diligently pursued, but many projects of clerical training evolved from the first clergy retreat given at Beauvais in 1628. Retreats for ordinands began in 1631; presently five or six per year

were given at Paris. From 1633 to the French Revolution the renowned ''Tuesday Conferences'' at St. Lazare attracted many earnest ecclesiastics; among them were the Sulpician founder Jean Jacques OLIER and the future Bishop Jacques Bénigne BOSSUET. The Collège des Bons Enfants began to function as a seminary in 1636.

Negotiations with the Papal Curia required the presence of Vincentians at Rome where a house was permanently established in 1642. By papal directive all ordinands in Rome were obliged to make a retreat with the Vincentians. Foundations in Italy multiplied: at Genoa (1645), Turin (1654), and Naples (1668). The advent of a French queen in Poland led to the opening of a Vincentian house at Warsaw in 1651. Vincentian missionaries exposed themselves to savage reprisals in Ireland and Scotland between 1646 and 1679; the cleric Thady Lee became the Vincentian protomartyr in 1651. French diplomatic relations with the Muslim world contributed to establishing a chaplaincy to the consulate at

Algiers with a Vincentian often serving as interim consul. Alhough missionary opportunities were limited, 1,200 Christians were ransomed from the Moors. Jean Le Vacher was slain at this perilous post in 1683. Vincent's disciples also responded to the summons of the Holy See to evangelize Madagascar, but 17th-century tropical Africa proved uninhabitable for Europeans; disease or unfriendly natives claimed the lives of 31 priests and ten brothers between 1648 and 1674. Nevertheless the field was reopened in 1896.

European Development: 1660–1800. Vincent de Paul's successor as superior general, René Alméras (1661–72), presided over a general assembly in 1668 that drew up the basic constitutions. His successors were Edmond Jolly (1673–97), Nicolas Pierron (1697–1703), François Watel (1703–10), Jean Bonnet (1711–35), Jean Couty (1736–46), Louis De Bras (1747–61), Antoine Jacquier (1762–87), and Felix Cayla de la Garde (1788–1800). Missions given gratuitously preserved Vincent's "Little Method" of simple instruction in contrast to contemporary baroque norms. Any parishes or chaplaincies that the congregation accepted were usually bases for such missions. Vincentians in Marseilles continued to care for some 10,000 galley prisoners, while those of Les Invalides looked after pensioned soldiers. As the Tridentine reforms were introduced into France, more prelates erected seminaries. On the eve of the French Revolution, Vincentians directed 60 of these in France and 30 more in Italy, Poland, and the Spanish Peninsula. Prelates who favored GALLICANISM or JANSENISM sometimes tried to dictate the content of seminary instruction, but the Vincentian assemblies and superiors firmly purged the congregation of the disaffected, and in 1724 the general assembly exacted an oath in support of the papal pronouncements against Jansenism.

Vincentian instruction strove to stress traditional solidity rather than novelty. Pierre Collet (1693–1770), who achieved distinction as a theologian, also compiled *Meditations* long in use in the congregation. Victor Soardi (1713–52) upheld papal primacy, and (B1.) Louis Francois (1751–92) issued pamphlets against the schismatic CIVIL CONSTITUTION OF THE CLERGY. Francois Brunet (1731–1806) was a pioneer in comparative religion. The foreign missions were served by the Malagasy grammar of Philippe Caulier, the Chinese dictionary of Joaquín Gonçalvez, the Turkish primer of Pierre Viguier, and Jean Coulbeau's Ethiopic Missal.

The French Revolution inflicted heavy material losses on the 78 Vincentian houses, but revealed spiritual resources. Cayla led the majority of 824 French Vincentians in refusing the schismatic oath to the Civil Constitution. Louis Francois, superior of St. Firmin Seminary—the old Bons Enfants—was martyred during the September Massacres along with (B1.) Henri Gruyer (1734–92) and 75 inmates or refugees. St. Lazare was plundered and then confiscated; the general and his subjects had to flee abroad or go underground. (B1.) René Rogue (1758–96) and scores of other Vincentians were executed or imprisoned down to the cessation of the persecution in 1799.

European Revival in the 19th century. One of the consequences of the concordat with the Holy See (1802) was the decree of 1804 legalizing the Congregation of the Mission anew in France. Yet so disrupted was Vincentian government that for 25 years after Cayla's death in Rome (1800) there were two provisional vicarsgeneral, one residing at Rome, the other at Paris. Finally Leo XII named Pierre de Wailly sole superior general (1827–28), and he took up residence in the new Parisian motherhouse, the former Hotel des Lorges, 95 rue de Sèvres, that housed only 14 survivors of St. Lazare. The new chapel was blessed by Archbishop de Quelen of Paris, Nov. 1, 1827, and here St. Vincent's relics were solemnly reinterred, Eastertide 1830. Later the same year the Blessed Virgin commended the MIRACULOUS MEDAL to St. Vincent's Double Family in apparitions to the Daughter of Charity, (St.) Catherine LABOURÉ, at nearby Rue du Bac.

Vincentians participated in the great Catholic revival in France during the early 19th century. New seminaries were confided to them, and prior to the dissolution of the concordat in 1906 they possessed some 50 establishments. Confiscation by the state then seriously hampered their educational activities, although with the waning of anticlericalism new foundations have since been made. The congregation revived in Poland, Italy, Spain, and Portugal, and promising new provinces were organized in Belgium and Holland. Vincentians also returned to Germany and Austria-Hungary, although they suffered during Bismarck's Kulturkampf. In the 20th century they have shared the protracted ordeal of communism. The Spanish Civil War (1936–39) claimed the lives of 37 priests, 20 brothers, and 30 Daughters of Charity, while the Polish, Hungarian, Czechoslovakian, and Yugoslavian provinces were veiled by the Iron Curtain from 1945–1989. These losses have been compensated to some degree by growth in other areas; during the 20th century Irish Vincentians extended their missions successfully into England, Scotland, Australia, and New Zealand.

Foreign Missions. French interests within Muslim territories continued to give Vincentian missionaries a foothold in Tunis and Algiers, but ministrations had to be confined largely to French colonists. Pierre Viguier initiated Vincentian residence at Constantinople in 1782 and shortly thereafter a promising Bulgarian mission was launched. Vincentians, entering Syria in 1784, founded schools and parishes, and by 1838 a Near East province could be formed. Eugene Boré (1809–78), later superior general, had come to Persia as a lay Oriental scholar, and in 1840 he obtained entry for Vincentian missionaries. At the invitation of the Congregation for the Propagation of the Faith, the Italian Vincentian (Bl.) Giustino de JACO-BIS (1800–60) went to Alexandria, Egypt, whence he penetrated into Ethiopia and established a promising mission. In 1958 Stephen Sidarouss became Catholic Coptic Patriarch of Alexandria.

Following the suppression of the Jesuits, Nicolas Raux (1754–1801) led a group of Vincentian replacements to the missions of the Far East. They soon encountered persecutions in China that claimed the lives of many, including Francois Clet (1748–1820) and Jean Perboyre (1802–40). The missionaries were driven from Peking, but Joseph Mouly (1807–68), vicar apostolic of Chil-li, was able to return there in 1860. One of his successors, Bp. Alphonse FAVIER (1837–1905), was at Beijing during the Boxer massacres (1900). Noted Vincentians in the China area were: Évariste HUC (1813–60), Tibetan explorer; Joaquín Gongalvez (1781–1844), sinologist; Armand DAVID (1826–1900), naturalist: and Vincent LEBBE (d. 1940), influential in establishing a native clergy. When China became communist in 1949, there were many native Chinese Vincentians besides the missionaries from France, Italy, Holland, Poland, and the U.S. After their expulsion from mainland China, many of the refugee missionaries went to Taiwan.

Vincentians in the U.S. The purchase of Louisiana from France by the U.S. in 1803 was the occasion for Vincentian entry into America. Frequent changes of administration had retarded growth in this area, and Bp. Louis DUBOURG of New Orleans, La., was in desperate need of priests. On his visit to Rome for episcopal consecration, he secured the services of Italian Vincentians for his immense diocese. The pioneers were Felix De Andreis (1778–1820), superior of the band; Joseph ROSATI, later bishop of St. Louis, Mo.; John Acquaroni; and Brother Martin Blanka. Disembarking at Baltimore, Md., July 26, 1816, they set out for St. Louis, but broke their journey at Bardstown, Ky., where they assisted for some time as professors in the existing seminary. On their arrival at St. Louis, January 1818, Bishop Dubourg named De Andreis his vicar-general for the Upper Mississippi district. A temporary novitiate was opened at St. Louis, and before the end of the year Father Andrew Ferari and the subdeacons F. X. Dahmen and Joseph Tichitoli became the first Vincentian recruits for the U.S. The donation of 640 acres of land 80 miles south of St. Louis by Catholic families of the "Barrens," Perryville, Mo., laid

the foundations in 1818 for the Vincentian American motherhouse. By 1820 a log rectory-seminary had been built and missionary work was begun in the neighborhood. De Andreis's delicate constitution succumbed to unstinted exertions; he died Oct. 15, 1820.

Rosati succeeded him as superior and continued to exercise this charge until 1830, although in 1824 he was consecrated bishop, serving first as coadjutor to Bishop Dubourg, and later as the first ordinary of St. Louis (1827–43). When Dubourg resigned his see, he was succeeded at New Orleans by another Vincentian, Leo De Neckere (1829–33). The original foundations at St. Louis and Perryville became an American St. Lazare, parent to many parishes, mission centers, and seminaries. St. Mary's Seminary, begun in 1820, was empowered to grant degrees in 1830. In 1835 the American foundations became a province with the native Pennsylvanian John TIMON as first visitor (provincial) from 1835 to 1847.

From the beginning Vincentian missionaries had worked out of Perryville and St. Louis, preaching, catechizing, and administering the Sacraments through Missouri, Arkansas, Mississippi, Illinois, and Indiana. Following a canonical visitation of Texas, instituted on the authority of the Holy See and conducted by John Timon and John Mary ODIN (1801–70), the latter was named vicar apostolic of Texas in 1842. Odin later became first bishop of Galveston, Texas, and archbishop of New Orleans. For a while Vincentians staffed diocesan seminaries for New Orleans, New York, and Philadelphia until the recall of missionaries on loan from Europe obliged them to relinquish these posts. Timon, who, in 1845, introduced into the U.S. the ST. VINCENT DE PAUL SOCIETY, was named bishop of Buffalo, N.Y. (1847–67), and induced his confreres to open Our Lady of Angels Seminary at Niagara (1856). The founder, John Joseph Lynch, was subsequently archbishop of Toronto, Canada.

After the provincial headquarters were moved from Perryville to St. Louis in 1847, the office of visitor was held successively by Mariano Maller (1847–50), Anthony Penco (1851–55), John Masnou (1855–56), and Stephen Vincent Ryan (1857–68). The Vincentians took charge of St. Joseph's parish at Emmitsburg, Md., in 1850, the same year that Mother Elizabeth Seton's Sisters of Charity were united with the Daughters of Charity of St. Vincent. Michael DOMENEC, later bishop of Pittsburgh, established St. Vincent's parish at Germantown, Philadelphia, in 1851. Soon after (1853) the rector of St. Charles Seminary, Philadelphia, Thaddeus AMAT, having become bishop of Monterey, Calif., introduced the Vincentians and the Daughters of Charity to the West Coast. Stephen Ryan guided the community during the difficult days of the Civil War and all 11 Vincentian houses escaped harm. At this time there were 57 priests, 40 brothers, ten scholastics, and seven novices.

During 1867–68 Ryan transferred the provincial headquarters to Germantown, where St. Vincent's Seminary was opened to care for students and novices from the Perryville seminary, damaged by fire in 1866. When Ryan was consecrated bishop of Buffalo in 1868, he was succeeded as visitor by John Hayden (1868–72), James Rolando (1872–78), and Thomas Smith (1879–1905). In 1868 St. John's parish and college opened at Brooklyn, N.Y. This became the nucleus of St. John's University, which grew from 42 students in 1870 to over 10,000 when it expanded to Jamaica, Long Island, in 1958. At Chicago, Ill., the founding of St. Vincent's parish in 1875 provided for the later development of St. Vincent's College and De Paul University. In 1883, moreover, the college previously established at Niagara attained university rank.

In 1888 the American Vincentian province was divided. The eastern province continued to have headquarters at Germantown, moving subsequently to Philadelphia. Vincentians in the east established centers at Springfield, Mass. (1903); Opelika, Ala. (1910); Bangor, Pa. (1914); Groveport, Ohio (1932); Toronto, Canada (1933); and Spring Lake, Mich. (1952). Similar work was done by the Central Association of the MIRACULOUS MEDAL founded by Joseph Skelly in 1915. The Vincentian Thomas JUDGE founded two new religious communities for missionary work in the South. The Vincentians themselves opened parochial centers in Alabama, North Carolina, and Maryland, besides founding new parishes, schools. and seminaries in several of the Northern states.

With its headquarters at St. Louis, the western province (later, the Midwest Province) continued under Thomas Smith as visitor from 1888 to 1905. Administration of the province—which comprised two-thirds of the U.S.—was facilitated in 1958 by the creating of two vice provinces: one at Los Angeles and the other at New Orleans. In 1975, these two vice-provinces were elevated to the status of full provinces—the Province of the West with its headquarters in Los Angeles, CA and the Southern Province with its headquarters in Dallas, TX. A new province—the New England Province was also established in 1975, with its headquarters in Manchester, CT.

Bibliography: CM, Official Catholic Directory #1330. R. BAYARD, *Lone-Star Vanguard: The Catholic Reoccupation of Texas, 1838–1848* (St. Louis 1945). P. COSTE, *The Life and Works of St. Vincent de Paul,* tr. J. LEONARD, 3 v. (Westminster, Md. 1952); *La Congrégation de la Mission* (Paris 1927). S. DELACROIX, ed. *Histoire universelle des missions catholiques,* 4 v. (Paris 1956–59) v. 2. F. J. EASTERLY, *Life of Rt. Rev. Joseph Rosati* (Washington 1942); "The Vincentian Fathers: A Survey," *Thought Patterns* 9 (1961) 120–157. J. CALVET, *St. Vincent de Paul,* tr. L. C. SHEPPARD (New York 1952).

[N. C. EBERHARDT/EDS.]

VINDICIANUS OF CAMBRAI-ARRAS, ST.

Early bishop in the Low Countries; b. Bullecourt, near Bapaume, Pas-de-Calais, France, *ca.* 620; d. Brussels, 712? Elected to succeed Bp. Aubert of Cambrai-Arras (*ca.* 668), he supervised the translation of the relics of St. Maxellendis to Caudry, France, in 673. He blessed the abbey for nuns at Honnecourt (673). In 675 he consecrated the abbey church at Hasnon, and in 686 dedicated the abbey church at Hamaye (Hamage) and witnessed the elevation of its former Abbesses EUSEBIA OF HAMAY and Rictrude. He made donations to several monasteries, e.g., in 675 to Maroilles (made famous by St. HUMBERT OF MAROILLES). About 682 he completed the Abbey of SAINT-VAAST (ARRAS) begun by his predecessor, and appointed Hatto its abbot (685). He entrusted its temporalities to the protection of Theodoric III, King of Neustria (673–698). When rebuked by Vindicianus for the wanton murder of Bp. LEODEGAR OF AUTUN by Ebroin, his mayor of the palace, Theodoric repented and made reparation—so the legend goes—by richly endowing Saint-Vaast. Vindicianus tried (681) to secure Leodegar's remains for his diocese but was forestalled by Bp. Ansoald of Poitiers. Vindicianus would frequently retire for prayer to Saint-Vaast or to Mont Saint-Eloi, where he asked to be buried. After numerous translations (the first in 1030 by Bp. GERARD, to Cambrai), his remains now rest in the cathedral of Arras (since 1601).

Feast: March 11.

Bibliography: *Acta sanctorum Belgii,* ed. J. H. GHESQUIÈRE et al., 6 v. (Brussels 1783–94) 503–533. L. VAN DER ESSEN, *Étude critique et littéraire sur les Vitae des saints mérovingiens de l'ancienne Belgique* (Louvain 1907) 276–277. A. PONCELET, *Analecta Bollandiana* (Brussels 1882–)27:384–390. A. BUTLER, *The Lives of the Saints,* rev. ed. H. THURSTON and D. ATTWATER, 4 v. (New York 1956) 1:558–559.

[C. M. AHERNE]

VINET, ALEXANDRE RODOLPHE

Swiss liberal Protestant apologist; b. Lausanne, Switzerland, June 17, 1797; d. Lausanne, May 5, 1847. He studied French literature and theology at Lausanne and Basel. After teaching French literature and doing some pastoral work in Basel, he became professor of practical theology at Lausanne (1838). His thought was influenced by Wilhelm De Wette, a disciple of SCHLEIER-MACHER, and by the Scottish Calvinist, Thomas Erskine. Vinet was particularly interested in the psychological aspects of the doctrine of grace. He participated in the current revival of Protestantism, and became more and more attached to theological LIBERALISM. Dissatisfied with Protestantism in his own sect, he repudiated the Helvetic Confession of Faith, and established a liberal church at Lausanne. Vinet's movement spread, especially among Protestants in the French-speaking cantons. He also supported liberalism of a political kind, and championed the separation of Church and State. His chief significance to Protestant theology, however, rested on his formulation, at least in bare outline, of a theology of experience. In this he anticipated the later theories of Louis Auguste SABA-TIER and Modernism. Four volumes of his correspondence and twenty-four volumes of his works have been published in the definitive edition since 1908.

Bibliography: L. M. LANE, *The Life and Writings of Alexander Vinet* (Edinburgh 1890). P. BRIDEL, *La Pensée de Vinet* (Lausanne 1944). P. A. ROBERT, *La Flamme sur l'autel: Le Crise religieuse de Vinet* (Lausanne 1948). H. MEYLAN, *Die Religion in Geschichte und Gegenwart,* 7 v. (3rd ed. Tübingen 1957–65) 6:1405–06. ''Vinet,'' *Lexikon für Theologie und Kirche,* ed. J. HOFER and K. RAHNER, 10 v. (2d, new ed. Freiburg 1957–65) v.10.

[M. B. SCHEPERS]

VIOLENCE

From the Latin *violentia,* itself from *vis,* force (Gr. βία), usually denotes great force, excessive force, or constraint. The first two meanings are taken from the standpoint of an agent's activity, though the second also implies a norm; the third is taken from that of a passive principle affected adversely by the activity of the agent. The Aristotelian definition of violence, used by St. Thomas Aquinas throughout his works, is an explication of the third and stricter meaning: that is violent of which the principle is extrinsic, the thing suffering the violence contributing nothing (Aristotle, *Eth. Nic.* 1110b 15, cf. 1110a 2; for a discussion of violent movement, see *Phys.* 230a 18–231a 20, 255a 1–256a 4, *Cael.* 269a 7–269b 17, 300a 21–301b 32). This article elaborates the above definition and briefly considers the problem raised by modern physical science regarding violence. (For the moral treatment of violence, *see* FORCE AND MORAL RESPONSIBILITY.)

Definition. Involved in violence are two principles: the constraining and the constrained; the latter, though always passive relative to the AGENT inflicting violence, may suffer violence either as an active or as a passive PRINCIPLE. If it is an active principle, it suffers violence when, by an extrinsic agent, it is forced to act contrary to its own inclination or prevented from acting according to it. This inclination is the intrinsic source of activity: will for rational life, sensory desire for sentient life, the tendency of the form or nature in the case of both vegetative life and the spontaneous, non-vital activities of bodies. If it is a passive principle (i.e., one that requires an external agent to bring it into act), it suffers violence when it is moved to an ACT (i.e., a FORM or determination) opposed to the one to which it is naturally, though passively, inclined; or when it is prevented from receiving, from a corresponding natural agent, its proper act to which it has a natural passive inclination. Such a natural passive inclination would be found in primary matter already disposed for a certain act or in the secondary receptive principles of any natural substance. The agent or patient to which violence is done contributes nothing, since there is opposition to the intrinsic, voluntary or natural, active or passive inclination. Since inclination necessarily involves END, violence, in this strict sense, cannot be understood without reference to FINAL CAUSALITY. Violent movement in the natural world is incomprehensible unless NATURE implies an intrinsic principle of activity or passivity relative to certain determinate ends.

It is to be noted that in inanimate nature, since purpose is not always clearly discernible, the distinction between natural and violent movements becomes much less sharp than in the sphere of human activity or even of living beings in general. Also, the distinction is less easily seen in the case of a passive than in the case of an active principle. It is sometimes only with reference to the order of the universe as a whole that the activities and the corresponding receptivities of inanimate nature can be seen as contributing in some way to a purpose. Note also that what is violent in one respect could be natural in another, e.g., corruption, though violent for the individual, is within the intention of universal nature (*see* GENERATION-CORRUPTION).

Modern Science. Modern physics, because it interprets movement in terms of mathematical equations, abstracts from any consideration of teleology and hence ignores any distinction between natural and violent movements. To disregard certain facets of nature is not only a legitimate procedure for science, it is necessitated by its method, and is certainly justified by the results. It must be pointed out, however, that mathematical physics, as such, can neither affirm nor deny the existence of things that, by its very nature, it must exclude from its consideration.

See Also: ACTION AND PASSION; IMPETUS; NATURE.

Bibliography: G. SANTONASTASO, *Enciclopedia filosofica*, 4 v. (Venice-Rome 1957) 4:1597–98. V. E. SMITH, *The General Science of Nature* (Milwaukee 1958).

[S. O'FLYNN BRENNAN]

VIRET, PIERRE

Reformation figure; b. Orbe, Pays de Vaud, 1511; d. Orthez, France, May 1, 1571. From Marc Romain at Orbe he acquired an eagerness for New Testament study before attending the Collège de Montaigu, Paris (1528–31). There he embraced the Reformation, possibly under the influence of Guillaume FAREL, who in May 1531 inducted him into a preaching ministry at Orbe. A gifted preacher, he was called to serve rising Reformed congregations at Payerne, Neuchâtel, and Lausanne; in 1534 he joined Farel in Geneva, where violence and a poisoning attempt damaged his health. Having returned to Neuchâtel, he was recalled to Lausanne in March 1536; he was instrumental in establishing the Reformation there, and also founded a flourishing academy. His work there was ended through the opposition of Bern to his discipline (1559). Calvin's trusted friend and correspondent, Viret was associated with him at the Lausanne Disputation of 1536 and in Geneva (1541–42, 1559–61). Seeking medical treatment at Montpellier, Viret transferred his activities to southern France. At Lyons he presided at a Reformed national synod in 1563. His many books are brilliant, but unoriginal. Best known is his *Instruction chrestienne en la doctrine de la loi et l'Evangile* (3 v. Geneva 1564).

Bibliography: J. BARNAUD, *Pierre Viret: Sa vie et son oeuvre, 1511–1571* (Saint Amans, France 1911). H. VUILLEUMIER, *Histoire de l'Église Réformée du Pays de Vaud* 4 v. (Lausanne 1927–33) v.1–2.

[J. T. MC NEIL]

VIRGILIUS OF ARLES, ST.

Early archbishop of Arles; b. Gascony, mid-sixth century; d. *ca.* 610. He was educated in the monastery of LÉRINS, and was called to be abbot of Saint-Symphorien by Syagrius, bishop of Autun. During the pontificate of Gregory I (590–604). Virgilius received the PALLIUM as archbishop of ARLES and was later appointed apostolic vicar to the court of Childeric II, a position of great influence in the Frankish Church. Venerable BEDE mentions that AUGUSTINE OF CANTERBURY resided with Virgilius for a short time and probably was consecrated by him. Virgilius was extraordinary in some of the measures he espoused in governing his see in Arles; e.g., he was repri-

manded by GREGORY I for his excessive zeal in advocating the forcible conversion of Jews to Christianity. Virgilius is the subject of numerous legends and fables concerning his supposed encounters with devils and fiends. His *vita* states that he lived a life of personal austerity, which included the wearing of a hair shirt. A sizable correspondence between Gregory I and Virgilius on matters ranging from questions of simony to the protection of monasteries belonging to the Holy See has been preserved. The churches of St. Honoratus and St. Saviour, and the basilica of St. Stephen in Arles owe their existence to him.

Feast: March 5.

Bibliography: *Acta Sanctorum* March 2:397–402. GREGORY I, *Epistolae, Patrologia Latina*, ed. J. P. MIGNE, 217 v., indexes 4 v. (Paris 1878–90) 77:510–511, 782–785, 1028–33, 1042–45. *Gallia Christiana*, v. 1–13 (Paris 1715–85), v. 14–16 (Paris 1856–65) 1:540–541. L. DUCHESNE, *Fastes épiscopaux de l'ancienne Gaule*, 3 v. (2d ed. Paris 1907–15) 1:252.

[B. F. SCHERER]

VIRGILIUS (FERGAL OR FEIRGIL) OF SALZBURG, ST.

Abbot and bishop; also spelled Fergal, Feirgil, Ferghil, Vergil, etc.; b. perhaps on the Irish colonized island of Heth, West Scotland, *ca.* 710; d. Salzburg Austria, Nov. 27, 784. As abbot of Aghaboe near Dublin, he was known as the "Geometer," because of his knowledge of geography. In 743 he went to the court of PEPIN III at Quierzy with Dobdagrecus (Dub-dá-chrich) and Sidonius, later bishop of Passau. In 745 Pepin forced Duke Odilo of Bavaria, who had just been defeated, to accept Virgilius as the abbot bishop of Salzburg. As abbot of SANKT PETER, he administered the diocese according to Irish custom, while Dobdagrecus performed the episcopal acts, until Virgilius had himself consecrated June 15, 767, supposedly to satisfy the request of the "people." Virgilius's most celebrated deed as bishop was the conversion of the Alpine Slavs, which, despite reverses he accomplished in 772 by taking advantage of the situation that found the inhabitants of Carinthia seeking protection in the West from the Avars.

On Sept. 24, 774, Virgilius dedicated the first Salzburg cathedral to St. RUPERT OF SALZBURG. This celebrated church, praised by ALCUIN, has only recently been properly appreciated. The discovery of Virgilius's grave, resulting from the destruction of the cathedral by fire in 1181, occasioned the start of his canonization process, completed by Gregory IX, June 18, 1233. In 1288 Virgilius was honored with an altar in the new Romanesque cathedral. As the patron of Salzburg, he is depicted in sacred art as a bishop with a double-towered Romanesque church.

At the beginning of his career he was twice involved in controversies with (St.) BONIFACE, who in 739 had installed the Anglo-Saxon John as bishop of Salzburg, whereas the Irishman Virgilius had been sent directly by the Frankish mayor of the palace. Boniface demanded the rebaptism of those who had been christened with the grammatically inaccurate formula: *Ego te baptizo in nomine patria et filia et spiritus sancti* (*Monumenta Germaniae Historica, Epistolae* 3:336). Virgilius and Sidonius refused, and upon appealing to Pope Zachary they were upheld. In 748 Boniface complained to Rome that Virgilius held heretical views about the spherical shape of the earth and about the antipodes. Nothing is known about a condemnation or recantation supposedly made by Virgilius. In any case, under the pseudonym *Aethicus Ister,* he wrote a fictitious cosmography that had great influence on later works. This piece claims the authority of St. Jerome and, with its subtle hints, may only have poked fun at his unquestionably less gifted adversaries. To the extant original of the *Liber confraternitatum* of the Salzburg church Virgilius added "a liturgical note, which has the value of an historical monument."

Feast: Nov. 27.

Bibliography: Sources. *Conversio Bagoariorum et Carantanorum,* ed. M. KOS (Laibach 1936), also in 11:1–15. *Monumenta Germaniae Historica, Scriptores* (Berlin 1826–) 3:744. *Monumenta Germaniae Historica, Epistolae selectae* (Berlin 1826–) 1:300. *Monumenta Germaniae Historica, Necrologia* (Berlin 1826–) 2:18. W. HAUTHALER and F. MARTIN, eds., *Salzburger Urkundenbuch* (Salzburg 1898) 1:16; 2:8–18, app. Literature. P. KARNER, *Die Heiligen und Seligen Salzburgs* (Austria Sancta 12; Vienna 1913). H. LÖWE, "Ein literarischer Widersacher des Bonifatius," *Abhandlungen der geistes- und sozialwissenschaftlichen Klasse der Mainzer Akademie der Wissenschaften* 11 (1951) 908–988. A. LHOTSKY, *Quellenkunde zur mittelalterlichen Geschichte Österreichs* (Graz 1963). *Virgil von Salzburg, Missionar und Gelehrter,* proceedings of intl. symposium, Salzburg, 21–24 September 1984, ed. H. DOPSCH and R. JUFFINGER (Salzburg 1985).

[H. WOLFRAM]

VIRGIN BIRTH

The perpetual virginity of the Blessed Virgin Mary is a dogma of the Catholic Church and has been so recognized explicitly since the 5th century. Three points are included in the dogma: the virginal conception of Jesus by Mary without any human father, the virginal birth of the child from the womb of His mother without injury to the bodily integrity of Mary, and Mary's observance of virginity afterward throughout her earthly life. The three points are treated in that order in the present article.

It is important to keep this dogma in its proper theological perspective. The theological significance of Mary's virginity must never be obscured by physiological or biological considerations. Mary's virginity is indeed a physical and real fact; and the Church rejected, from the very beginning, the heresy of DOCETISM, which held that Christ's body was a mere appearance. Nevertheless the theological and spiritual significance of VIRGINITY is an integral part of the Catholic belief. Its significance is seen first of all as totally relative to her divine Son and to the special nature of her dedication to the unique world event of the REDEMPTION. Hence the Fathers of the Church, with true insight, have exalted the "new birth" and its miraculous character less as a privilege of Mary than as a glory of Christ and the beginning of the regenerated human race. Her dignity as MOTHER OF GOD is her supreme privilege; and once the dignity of her relationship of maternity to the Son of God is profoundly recognized, wonder at corollary privileges, such as her virginity, tends to fade. Belief in Christ's divinity furnishes an antecedent basis for expecting sublime and wonderful privileges regarding the manner of His entry into the world and the unique human instrument He chose to be His mother.

It is important also for theological perspective to appreciate the development of these beliefs from the first seeds of doctrine sown in the original deposit of revelation, to the full flowering of belief in the Church under the guidance of the Holy Spirit. Belief in the virginal conception of Jesus did enjoy fully explicit formulation in the catechesis of the Church from the time of the redaction of the Gospels of Matthew and Luke. But belief in the virginal parturition of Mary and the preservation of her virginity ever after did not achieve universal recognition in the writings of the Fathers until the end of the 4th century and the beginning of the 5th.

Virginity in Conception. The doctrine that Jesus was born of the Virgin Mary without any human father entered early and without incident into the public teaching of the Church.

Teaching of the Church. The doctrine was proclaimed by the earliest Fathers: Ignatius, Justin, Irenaeus, Aristides. It also appears in the early Roman baptismal profession of faith as attested in Hippolytus's *Apostolic Tradition* (c. 215), which probably reflects even earlier professions of the 1st century [P. Palmer, *Mary in the Documents of the Church* (Westminster, Md. 1952) 4].

This doctrine was never in dispute in the Catholic Church. The belief, when attacked from outside, found capable defenders in Justin, Irenaeus, and Origen; and its denial was considered from the beginning as heresy. By the 4th century the doctrine is found in the creed of Constantinople I. It was taught in the authoritative letter of St. Leo to the Council of Chalcedon, held in 451, and it was defined by the great regional Council of the Lateran in 649, the acts of which were accepted by Constantinople III in 681. From its universal proposition in the creeds of the Church ever since, it is clear that, although it has never been expressly defined by a general council, it is in every sense of the word a dogma of the faith in virtue of the ordinary and universal teaching authority of the Church. [See A. Van Hove, ''Is Maria's maagdelijkkeid een eigenlijk geloofsdogma?'' *Coll. Mechl.* 45 (1960) 283–287.]

Fathers. St. Ignatius of Antioch repeatedly proclaims the virginal conception of Jesus as an undoubted truth of the faith. ''And the Prince of this world was in ignorance of the virginity of Mary and her childbearing and also of the death of the Lord—three mysteries loudly proclaimed to the world, though accomplished in the stillness of God'' [*Eph.* 19.1; *Ancient Christian Writers* ed. J. Quasten et al. (Westminster, Md.–London 1946) 1:67]. Aristides of Athens (*c.* 125), the first Apologist, wrote to the Emperor Hadrian, professing the virginal conception as an article of Christian belief (*Apol.* 2). Justin Martyr, a generation later, interpreted Is 7.14 of the virginal conception (*Patrologia Graeca* 6:381). Irenaeus proclaimed it a doctrine of the Church received from the Apostles (*Adv. haer.* 3.21.3–4; *Patrologia Graeca* 7:945). Origen defended it against the supposedly Jewish calumny of the conception of Jesus through adultery (*C. Celsum* 1.32; *Patrologia Latina* 11:720–721). Tertullian, who denied the virginal childbirth and the virginity of Mary after Bethlehem, held the virginal conception as a truth of faith (*Corpus scriptorum ecclesiasticorum latinorum* 70:17–18). It would be superfluous to cite further, since the witness of the Fathers to the virginal conception is unanimous and unquestioned.

Sacred Scripture. There seems to be no doubt that the infancy narratives of Matthew and Luke were later additions to the original body of the apostolic catechesis, the content of which began with the advent of John the Baptist and ended with the Ascension. But this fact in no way hinders the genuineness and authenticity of the place of these narratives in the written Gospels of Matthew and Luke. External and internal criticism render their authenticity certain. The written Gospels were undoubtedly intended to begin with the infancy narratives.

Matthew teaches the supernatural and virginal conception of Jesus by bluntly stating in 1.18 that after betrothal Mary was found pregnant and that her pregnancy was due to the supernatural intervention of the Holy Spirit. Matthew goes on to reaffirm this fact and to establish the legal paternity of Jesus the MESSIAH as SON OF DAVID

''The Virgin and Child,'' by Luca della Robbia, 15th century, Florence, Italy. (©David Lees/CORBIS)

through the medium of Joseph's difficulty arising from the discovery of the pregnancy of his betrothed, in which he had had no part. He is freed from the anguish of his mind by the command of the angel to accept Mary as his wife and thus to establish the legal paternity of Jesus as Son of David by imposing on Him the name Jesus. He receives the assurance of the angel that Mary's conception is the work of the Holy Spirit. ''Do not be afraid, Joseph, son of David, to take to thee Mary thy wife, for that which is begotten in her is of the Holy Spirit. And she shall bring forth a son, and thou shalt call his name Jesus; for he shall save his people from their sins'' (Mt 1.20–21). One of the problems in Matthew's narrative is the use of Is 7.14 as a prophecy of the virginal conception. Modern opinion tends to the view that Matthew saw the true meaning of the prophecy only in the light of its fulfillment. The rabbinic interpretation of the prophecy in the era immediately before Christ gives no evidence that a virginal conception of the Messiah was expected, even though the Septuagint (LXX) had rendered the Hebrew *'almâ* (*see* ALMA) by παρθένος, the technical word in Greek for virgin. Recent exegesis of the strictly literal sense of the text and comparison with Ugaritic writing tend to confirm this view. It is also confirmed by the fact that much of the early Jewish opposition to Christianity centered on the Virgin Birth. When Matthew sees here the fulfillment of the prophecy, this might possibly be explained on the basis of the somewhat loose rabbinic usage of the term fulfillment.

St. Luke's treatment of the virginal conception is presented in the form of a Midrash, that is, in the form of a meditation on the SALVATION HISTORY against a background of the ideas and terms of the OT. Mary is the culmination of the long line of the devout, humble poor of Israel, the true remnant. She is the handmaid of the Lord, exalting God and exalted by Him because of her humble submission. It is her stupendous privilege to become the true sanctuary of the presence of God in Israel, the true Ark of the Covenant, the mother of the true Emmanuel. God has already shown His power and mercy to the lowly in the miraculous conception of John the Baptist by Elizabeth in her old age. Mary, in the ANNUNCIATION scene, is greeted by the angel with the joyous proclamation that she is to be the mother of the Messiah. Her reaction poses the problem of her mind. "How shall this happen, since I do not know man?" (Lk 1.34) There is no doubt at all about the meaning of the angel's answer (Lk 1.35). It is that the omnipotence of God will cause the conception of her child and that the conception will therefore be virginal, without any human father.

Theological Reflection. When, after the fact, one looks for reasons, he finds the Fathers of the Church pointing out analogies with the eternal birth of the SON OF GOD before all ages. St. Thomas Aquinas, summing up their thought, sees in the virginal human conception a distant reflection of the immaculate purity of the eternal generation of the divine WORD and a safeguard of the exclusive character of the divine paternity (*Summa theologiae* 3a, 28.1–3). The avoidance of the transmission of ORIGINAL SIN has also been invoked, but the validity of this reason seems open to question.

Virginity in Parturition. The doctrine that Mary remained a virgin in giving birth to Jesus involves the preservation of her bodily virginal integrity intact and her exemption from the ordinary pangs of childbirth. Both features are strongly attested in tradition and are presented as miraculous. The element of the preservation was predominant among the Western Fathers. The element of joy and freedom from the pangs of childbirth was more accentuated in the East. The preservation of bodily integrity is more strongly attested in tradition as a whole. In regard to the manner of preservation, many of the Fathers represent the birth as taking place from the closed womb without its being opened. They use the expression "closed and sealed womb," using the scriptural illustration of the enclosed garden, the sealed fountain (Ct 4.12), and the closed door (Ez 44.1–2). They illustrate it by comparison with the emergence of Christ from the closed sepulcher and His entry into the upper room through closed doors.

Teaching of the Church. The first explicit formulation is found in the letter of the Synod of Milan to Pope Siricius in 390:

> But if they do not believe the teaching of the priests let them believe the oracles of Christ, let them believe the admonitions of the angels saying: "For nothing is impossible with God" [Lk 1.37]. Let them believe the Apostles' Creed which the Church of Rome ever guards and preserves inviolate. . . . This is the virgin who conceived in her womb and as a virgin bore a son. For thus it is written: "Behold a virgin shall conceive in the womb and shall bear a son" [Is 7.14]. He has said not only that a virgin shall conceive but also that a virgin shall give birth. Now, who is that gate of the temple, that outer gate toward the east, which remains closed "and no-one," he says, "shall pass through it, except the God of Israel alone" [Ez 44.2]? Is not Mary this portal through which the Redeemer entered into this world? . . . This portal is the blessed Mary of whom it is written that "the Lord shall pass through it and it shall be closed" [Ez 44.2] after birth, because a virgin did conceive and give birth. What then is there impossible of belief if, contrary to the natural way of birth, Mary has given birth and remained a virgin, when contrary to the course of nature, "the sea looked and fled and the waters of the Jordan turned back towards their source" [Ps 113A(114).3]? [St. Ambrose, *Epist.* 42.4; *Patrologia Latina* 16:1125–26]

The letter represents the teaching of Ambrose and his suffragans, who signed the letter. It is noteworthy for its references to the Scriptures and to the faith of the Roman Church as expressed in the Apostles' Creed concerning Mary's virginity in parturition.

About 50 years later, in 449, St. Leo the Great, in his letter to Flavian, Archbishop of Constantinople, in preparation for the Council of Chalcedon, stated: ". . . she brought Him forth without the loss of virginity, even as she conceived Him without its loss. . . . [Jesus Christ was] born from the virgin's womb, because it was a miraculous birth . . ." (H. Denzinger, *Enchiridion symbolorum* 291, 294). The authoritative statement of the pope and the wholehearted reception of his teaching by the Council manifests the secure acceptance of the belief at that time in both the East and West.

In 649 the Lateran synod, apparently without discussion, included the virginal parturition in its definition of the maternity of Mary:

> If anyone does not, in accord with the holy Fathers, acknowledge . . . that Mary is the holy mother of God, ever virgin and without stain, inasmuch as she specially and truly conceived of the

Holy Ghost, without seed, in the fullness of time God the Word Himself, who was born of God the Father before all ages, and without corruption brought Him forth, her virginity remaining intact also after His birth, let him be condemned. (H. Denzinger, *Enchiridion symbolorum* 503)

In 1555 Paul IV condemned the denial of the virginity of Mary in, during, and after the birth of Jesus (H. Denzinger, *Enchiridion symbolorum* 1880).

Mary's virginity in giving birth is proposed in the Church's liturgy in both the East and the West (J. B. Carol, ed., *Mariology* 1:200, 208, 236, 260, 278). In the Roman liturgy the Preface of the feasts of the Blessed Virgin proclaimed that she "both conceived her only-begotten Son by the overshadowing of the Holy Spirit, and, with the glory of her virginity remaining, brought forth into the world the eternal light, Jesus Christ." The doctrine is proposed in some of the major catechisms, such as the Catechism of the Council of Trent.

Tradition. The teaching of the Fathers in both East and West achieved universality and unanimity on this point *c.* 375 to 425, the period between the decline of Arianism and the outbreak of NESTORIANISM. Their concordant witness is impressive. Zeno of Verona (d. *c.* 375) uses the triple formula affirming Mary's virginity before, in, and after the birth of Jesus (*Patrologia Latina* 11:303, 414–415). Ambrose has been cited above. Augustine strongly attests the doctrine (*Patrologia Latina* 38:1010, 999, 1008, 1019); Peter Chrysologus uses the triple formula (*Patrologia Latina* 52:521); St. Leo the Great's testimony has been already mentioned. In the East, Proclus, Archbishop of Constantinople (*Patrologia Graeca* 65: 693), Cyril of Alexandria (*Patrologia Graeca* 76: 1129), John Chrysostom, (*Patrologia Graeca* 56:390), Theodoret (under Cyril's name in Migne, *Patrologia Graeca* 75:1460–61), and Ephrem of Syria in his Hymns on Blessed Mary (*Hymni de beata Maria,* ed. Lamy 2:567), offer abundant witness to the doctrine. Two centuries earlier, the doctrine had not achieved this obligatory character. Tertullian denied it (*Corpus scriptorum ecclesiasticorum latinorum* 70: 246–247), and perhaps also Origen (see J. B. Carol, ed., *Mariology* 2:270–271), while Clement of Alexandria affirmed the doctrine, though not as binding. This early state of the doctrine helps to explain why St. Jerome in his time, in his *Adversus Helvidium* (*Patrologia Latina* 23:201), described Christ's birth in terms similar to Tertullian's. However, virginity in birth was not the point at issue, and the passage is possibly hypothetical. Jerome's position has remained enigmatic, despite the fact that at the end of his career, in his *Dialogus adversus Pelagianos* (*Patrologia Latina* 23:538) and in his letter to Pammachius (*Patrologia Latina* 22:510), he gives some evidence of

rejoining the concord of the Fathers in affirming Mary's virginity in childbirth.

To understand this situation one must remember that Tertullian's denial was an exaggeration of his zeal in defense of the reality of Christ's body against the Docetists. Jovinian's denial was a repercussion of his excessive zeal in exalting marriage to the level of virginity in order to combat the ascetic movement of the time. In regard to the present dogma, the process was completed by the time of the Council of EPHESUS in 431. The turning point had been the denial of Jovinian, which occasioned the vigorous defense by St. Ambrose.

Patristic evidence for the belief in the earlier centuries is sparse. Clement of Alexandria clearly held the doctrine, though apparently in dependence on the Apocryphals and not as necessary to orthodoxy (*Strom.* 7.16; *Die griechischen christlichen Schriftsteller der ersten drei Jahrhunderte* Clem. 3:66). Irenaeus has an allusion to the belief in his *Proof of the Apostolic Preaching* (*Ancient Christian Writers* 16:83), in his explanation of Is 66.7, and a possible allusion in his phrase "Purus, pure puram aperiens vulvam" ("the Pure One, purely opening the pure womb") in *Adv. haer.* 4.33.11 (*Patrologia Graeca* 7: 1080). Before Irenaeus there is only the faintly possible allusion in Ignatius's letter to the Ephesians: "the virginity of Mary and her childbearing and also of the death of the Lord—three mysteries loudly proclaimed to the world, though accomplished in the stillness of God" (*Ancient Christian Writers* 1:67).

It would be helpful if one could fill the gap in early tradition by the Apocryphals—the *Protoevangelium of James,* the *Odes of Solomon,* and the *Vision of Isaia*—which recount the story of Mary's virginity in childbirth in great but legendary detail. But they are not patristic testimony. J. C. Plumpe, though recognizing that they are not patristic teaching but evidence of the trends of the Christian piety of the times, nevertheless attaches considerable importance to them as a chain of witnesses for the period between Irenaeus and Ignatius [*Theological Studies* 9 (1948) 567]. Laurentin, however, considers their influence on the development of the dogma in the 4th century to be negligible. Hence, instead of seeking in vain to fill the gaps in the historical record, it seems better to conclude with Laurentin that the corporal virginity, like the Assumption of the Virgin, is part of a mystery the implications of which are gradually discovered by the intuition of faith.

Sacred Scripture. There is no clear text of Sacred Scripture concerning Mary's virginity in childbirth. G. Jouassard remarks that Anastasius the Sinaite had noted this in the 8th century (Du Manoir 1:138). Ambrose interpreted Is 7.14 to mean virginity in birth as well as in conception. Modern scriptural opinion fails to see this meaning in the literal sense of the text. Consequently, if there is a scriptural basis here, it must be sought in a typical or plenary sense as discerned by tradition. This has not yet been adequately established. The Fathers have rather worked out the privilege as one of Christ's, an anticipation of His Resurrection freedom from subjection to the laws of the corporal world. Mary, too, as the new Eve, blessed among women (Lk 1.28) in contrast with the malediction of the first Eve, is seen by the Fathers as free from the punishments of Gn 3.16, which include the pangs of childbirth. They strongly assert that the birth of Christ, like His conception, was miraculous. There are therefore indications of a basis in Scripture for the belief, but no direct statements. The suggestions that Luke was hinting at the Virgin Birth by mentioning that Mary herself wrapped the child in swaddling clothes and laid Him in a manger (Lk 2.7) are not too convincing. The patristic references to the closed door of Ez 44.1–2 and the sealed fountain of Sg 4.12 are more commonly considered to be no more than accommodations of Sacred Scripture.

Theological Significance. The virginal birth of Christ in the perspective of the Fathers has its primary significance as a privilege of Christ Himself. It reflects the glory of His eternal birth, and it is an anticipated eschatological realization of the new birth of humanity begun in Him. From the standpoint of Mary, it is a privilege of her role as the new Eve, exempt from the curse and sorrows of the first Eve. It is part of her full and intimate sharing in the triumph of her Son over sin and its consequences. It is one of the ways in which she is blessed among women and contrasted with the maledictions of Eve. The perfect preservation of Mary's virginity is also involved in her role as model of virgins, a title with which the Church has saluted her from the early centuries. It is viewed as miraculous, and the ultimate reason for it is not to be sought in natural explanations but in the power of God. The tendency to seek a natural explanation of the parturition has appeared at various times in the history of the dogma. Paschasius Radbertus in the 9th century refuted an error that stated that the birth of Christ had to, and did, take place in the ordinary way of all mothers in order that the birth of Christ might be called a true birth. Durandus, in the 14th century, to bolster his theory of the impossibility of the compenetration of two bodies, explained the birth by a miraculous dilation of the membranes without any loss of corporal integrity. His view was severely censured by many theologians. In the middle of the 20th century, Albert Mitterer, in his *Dogma und Biologie der heiligen Familie,* took the position that the opening of the womb and its consequences pertain not to virginity but to maternity. The denial of them would seem to derogate from the true maternity of Mary. In so doing, he seems to empty

the virginity in parturition of any specific content. Mitterer put forth his views for the consideration of theologians, while recognizing that the definitive word on the matter must be sought in tradition. His views received a sympathetic reception from many theologians but sharp criticism from others.

A similar controversy took place in the United States in 1953–54, in regard to the permissibility of solutions akin to that of Durandus. The reaction to such a suggestion seems to have been preponderantly unfavorable [*Homiletic and Pastoral Review* 54 (1953) 219–223, 446–447, 636–638; *American Ecclesiastical Review* 130 (1954) 46–53].

In the course of these controversies more than one writer saw fit to deplore the tendency of abandoning the theological level for the biological. The Holy Office seems to have had this partly in mind when it issued an instruction to the superiors general of religious institutes (July 27, 1960), mentioning that "several theological studies have been published in which the delicate problem of Mary's virginity *in partu* is dealt with in unbecoming terms and, what is worse, in a manner that is clearly opposed to the traditional doctrine of the Church and to the devotional sense of the faithful."

A number of studies of tradition on this matter, since made, have confirmed abundantly the dogmatic data of the preservation of the bodily integrity and the absence of the pangs of childbirth. Apparently the investigation of the binding dogmatic character of the manner of birth, namely, from the closed womb, has not been so decisive, even though it is the only one proposed by the Fathers and is very frequent in their writings, not only in the 5th century but from then to the end of the patristic age.

Virginity after the Birth of Christ. The meaning of this part of the dogma is that Mary had no conjugal relations or any other voluntary use of the generative faculties after the birth of Christ. Joined to this, in the Catholic concept of the perpetual virginity, though not explicitly part of the dogma as defined, is the "virginity of mind," the motivation and resolve by which virginity is freely chosen for the love and service of God.

Teaching of the Church. This dogma has never been made the object of a direct definition by a general council. However, St. Leo the Great set forth this teaching in his dogmatic letter to Flavian, and it was accepted by the Council of Chalcedon in 451. The Lateran Council of 649 included this belief in its definition of the divine maternity. Although not ecumenical in the strict sense, the Council gave a clear manifestation of the magisterium's ordinary teaching under Pope Martin I. It attested the doctrine of the East and of the West and found acceptance without question in Constantinople III in 681. By that time, the belief had been in possession for two and a half centuries. Subsequent expression of the dogma is found in the profession of faith of Nicephorus of Constantinople, made to Pope Leo II in 811, and in the condemnation of the Unitarian error on this subject in 1555, which repeated the teaching of the Lateran Council.

Fathers. Patristic testimony to this belief appeared earlier than that for Mary's virginity in childbirth, but showed the same overall pattern of development. The doctrine was apparently denied by Tertullian (*Corpus scriptorum ecclesiasticorum latinorum* 47.393; 70:208–212). Also in the first half of the 3rd century, however, Origen showed the sentiment of the Church in Egypt and Palestine by his statement to the effect that sound doctrine in regard to Mary would not claim that she had any other son than Jesus. Both Origen and Clement of Alexandria explained the ''brethren of the Lord'' as children of Joseph by a previous marriage, at least in the sense that this was a current opinion of their time. Origen stated that those who held this opinion wished to protect the perpetual virginity of Mary (*Die griechischen christlichen Schriftsteller der ersten drei Jahrhunderte* 10:21–22). A century later, Hilary of Poitiers characterized adversaries of the perpetual virginity as ''irreligious and very far removed from spiritual teaching'' (*Patrologia Latina* 9:921–922). Basil the Great, replying to the denial of the belief by Eunomius, the Arian Bishop of Cyzicus, said that although only Mary's virginity in conception was a binding dogma, nevertheless: ''The friends of Christ refuse to admit that the Mother of God ever ceased to be a virgin'' (*Patrologia Graeca* 31:1468). Epiphanius in his *Panarion* stigmatized the denial of this belief as ''unheard of insanity and preposterous novelty'' (*Patrologia Graeca* 42:705). Gregory of Nyssa defended the belief with an appeal to Lk 1.34, which he interpreted as involving the intention of perpetual virginity (*Patrologia Graeca* 46:1140–41). Zeno of Verona in the same period used the triple formula: ''Mary conceived as a virgin incorrupt; after conception she gave birth as a virgin; after childbirth she remained a virgin'' (*Patrologia Latina* 11:414–415).

In the middle of the 4th century the term ''ever virgin'' was in use and spread rapidly. When Helvidius denied the belief in support of his contention of the equality of marriage and virginity, Jerome replied in his treatise *Adversus Helvidium* (383), effectively demolishing the arguments of his opponent and solving the objections from Sacred Scripture (*Patrologia Latina* 23:183–206). When Bonosus, Bishop of Naissus (*c.* 390), renewed the denial, St. Ambrose defended the belief in his *De institutione virginis* and was influential in securing the condemnation of Bonosus by the bishops of Illyria. From the close of the 4th century, belief in the perpetual virginity of Mary is recognized as obligatory by the concordant teaching of the Fathers. The triple formula of Mary's virginity before, in, and after the birth of Jesus is standard usage in Augustine (*Patrologia Latina* 38:1008), Peter Chrysologus (*Patrologia Latina* 52:521), and Leo the Great (*Patrologia Latina* 54:195). In the process of this development the influence of the ascetic movement, in the times of both Origen and Jerome, undoubtedly helped to form a climate favorable to the consideration of the perpetual virginity of Mary. The Fathers first saw her virginity after Bethlehem as a belief in consonance with their whole picture of the Mother of Christ. Only later came the increasing penetration that linked it to the other truths of faith as a binding belief. St. Jerome utilized the Scriptures in defense of it. St. Augustine and perhaps St. Gregory of Nyssa saw an implication in Lk 1.34, Mary's reply to the angel: ''How shall this happen, since I do not know man?'' Augustine was convinced that Mary would not have spoken thus unless she had previously dedicated her virginity to God. This view, though it received somewhat slim patristic support, encountered no denial and received universal acceptance by theologians in the Middle Ages. Cajetan's opinion excepted, it remained the common opinion. That this conviction has a valid basis in the text of Luke, one has Lagrange's statement: ''The immense majority of Catholic exegetes has always understood οὐ γινώσκω (''I know not'') in an absolute sense, excluding the future as well as the present'' (*Évangile selon saint Luc,* 7th ed., 33). Even Alfred Loisy, the Modernist, recognized the implication in Luke: ''Luke represents Joseph and Mary as having the dispositions of two Christian spouses who preserve their continence in marriage'' [*Les Évangiles synoptiques* (Ceffonds 1907) 1:291]. Among recent Catholic exegetes, R. Laurentin contends that, short of twisting the text, such an interpretation is inescapable. A number of Protestant exegetes, though in the minority, agree with the Catholic interpretation (J. B. Carol, ed., *Mariology* 2:237).

In more recent years the question has come under discussion among Catholics for the first time since Cajetan. Quite a number of Catholic scholars have come to reject the use of Lk 1.34 as implying such a resolution of virginity. There is no intention of impugning the fact of such a resolution on the part of Mary, simultaneous with, or consequent upon, the Annunciation; but there is simply a refusal to see such a resolution implied in Mary's question. No ecclesiastical censure has been imposed on their views, and attention has been called to the fact that the encyclical of Pius XII on virginity [*Acta Apostolicae Sedis* 46 (1954) 162] has no reference to such a vow in spite of its exaltation of Mary as model of virgins.

The implication of Mary's intention of virginity in Lk 1.34 is the most commonly utilized basis in the sources for the dogma of Mary's perpetual virginity; but it can hardly be the whole basis, since it refers to the intention of virginity, and does not state the fulfillment. Other indications, such as the title virgin, twice used by Luke in the same context, along with the virginal character of Mary in the new-Eve parallel of tradition, are other probable sources of the doctrine.

Recent Discussions. Certain aspects concerning the mystery have been the special subject of theological discussion during recent years. Difficulties have been raised by biblical scholars, Roman Catholic exegetes among them, regarding the historicity of the virginal conception of Christ as recorded in the infancy narratives of Matthew and Luke. New theories have been proposed about the interpretation of Mary's virginity in parturition, of her "vow" to remain a virgin throughout life. Some important developments have also taken place in the Christological symbolism and spiritual significance of Mary's virginity.

Historicity. The problems regarding the historicity of Mary's virginal conception center around three main issues: (1) the dubious historical status of the infancy narratives in general; (2) the fact that the rest of the NT is silent in the matter; and (3) the implication in virginal conception of a "high" Christology, since knowledge that he had no human father would have meant a premature realization of his divine origins, a diminution of his humanness according to modern Christological theories. Consequently it has been proposed that the virginal conception is a theologoumenon, i.e. a theological symbol, to support the later Christological belief that Jesus was God's Son from the moment of his conception.

Other Catholic exegetes and theologians have responded to such difficulties in accord with such lines of argumentation as the following. In principle historicity is compatible with any literary genre and the evangelists indeed record the virginal conception as a fact. If Joseph were the human father of Jesus, this certainly would have been made clear in a *Jewish* narrative which attaches great importance to paternity. Likewise, the silence in the rest of the NT is to be interpreted in favor of the virginal conception's being a fact because reference is never made to Joseph but only to Mary as the parent of Jesus. Further, to exegete the virginal conception as a Christological theologoumenon invented by the early Christians and evangelists is to create the even greater problems of determining whence they derived the notion and how they would reconcile it with their belief that Jesus as the Messiah must be "of the seed of David."

Virgin In Partu. Concerning the virginity of Mary in giving birth to Christ, more recent theologizing avoids the concrete details of birth pangs, etc., as quite irrelevant to the religious meaning of the revealed mystery. Rather, the emphasis is upon Mary as the subject of a unique act of childbearing. She bore her Son as the virginal Mother of God (*theotokos*) and the immaculate woman of faith filled with divine grace and free from the influence of any sin and concupiscence. Such an interpretation of the Fathers' sayings about the genetic details represents a development of the dogma. Similarly there is a growing tendency to interpret Lk 1.34, "And Mary said to the angel, 'How can this be, since I have no husband?'," as a Lucan literary device to give Gabriel an opening for the second part of his message, that Mary's conception will be virginal. Unlike these who hold the traditional theory that Mary had vowed to remain a virgin all her life prior to the Annunciation, an increasing number of exegetes are of the opinion that she realized only after it that God willed her perpetual virginity as a total consecration to the service of his Son. Thus Mary is the first person in salvation history, and her spouse Joseph is the second, to choose lifelong virginity out of love for Jesus.

Symbolism of the Virgin Birth. The interpretation of Mary's virginity as a historical reality is in complete conformity with its rich symbolic value, especially in relation to Christ. The theological tradition from Augustine through Aquinas abounds with such reasons of fittingness for Mary's virginity as Christ's having but one Father in heaven and that his members are born of a virgin Church through the spiritual regeneration of Baptism. This Christocentric and ecclesio-typical emphasis is characteristic of contemporary Mariology. Concerning Mary's virginity it helps preclude any interpretation of it as a negative attitude toward sexual love in marriage. At the same time the religious significance of her virginal Motherhood of God is being developed to deepen the Christian doctrines of grace revealed in the complete gratuitousness of the Incarnation and of the eschatological value of consecrated virginity for the sake of God's reign.

See Also: MARY, BLESSED VIRGIN, ARTICLES ON.

Bibliography: K. SCHELKLE and O. SEMMELROTH, *Handbuch theologischer Grundbegriffe,* ed. H. FRIES (Munich 1962–63) 2:111–122. J. B. CAROL, *Mariology,* 3 v. (Milwaukee 1954–61). J. G. MACHEN, *The Virgin Birth of Christ* (New York 1930). R. LAURENTIN, *Structure et théologie du Luc I–II* (Études bibliques 1957); *Court traié de théologie mariale* (4th ed. Paris 1959); "Le Mystère de la naissance virginale," *Ephemerides Mariologicae* 10 (1960) 345–373. D'H. DU MANOIR, ed., *Maria,* 6 v. (Paris 1949–61). A. MITTERER, *Dogma und Biologie der heiligen Familie* (Vienna 1952). M. J. SCHEEBEN, *Mariology,* tr. T. L. GEUKERS, 2 v. (St. Louis 1946–47). J. J. COLLINS, "Our Lady's Vow of Virginity," *The Catholic Biblical Quarterly* 5 (1943) 371–380. P. GAECHTER, "The Chronology from Mary's Betrothal to the Birth of Christ," *Theological Studies* 2 (1941) 145–170, 347–368. E. P. NUGENT, "The Closed Womb of the Mother of God," *Ephemerides Mariologicae* 8 (1958) 249–270. *Estudios Marianos* 21 (1960). *Marian Studies*

7 (1956); 12 (1961). [L. G. OWENS] R. E. BROWN, *The Virginal Conception and Bodily Resurrection of Jesus* (New York 1973). R. E. BROWN et al., *Mary in the New Testament* (New York, Philadelphia, Toronto 1978). J. F. CRAGHAN, "The Gospel Witness to Mary's 'Ante Partum' Virginity" *Marian Studies* 21 (1970) 28–68. J. A. FITZMYER, "The Virginal Conception of Jesus in the New Testament," *Theological Studies* 34 (1973) 541–575. F. M. JELLY, "Mary's Virginity in the Symbols and Councils," *Marian Studies* 21 (1970) 69–93. J. MCHUGH, *The Mother of Jesus in the New Testament* (New York 1975). M. MIGUENS, *The Virgin Birth: An Evaluation of Scriptural Evidence* (Westminister, Md. 1975). K RAHNER, "*Virginitas in Partu:* A Contribution to the Problem of the Development of Dogma and of Tradition," *Theological Investigations* 4, tr. K. SMYTH (Baltimore 1966) 134–162.

[L. G. OWENS/F. M. JELLY]

VIRGINES SUBINTRODUCTAE

Latin term, corresponding to the Greek παρθένοι συνείσακτοι [virgins brought in with (a man)] given to the virgins or widows who were referred to as ἀγαπηταί or beloved and lived with a man dedicated to celibacy to care for his domestic needs. The term *virgines subintroductae* appears in the 3d century in a pejorative sense and is the result of the accusation that such virgins or widows considered themselves united to the ascetic in a spiritual marriage for mutual assistance in achieving a high spirituality. In the 5th century the term was applied almost indiscriminately to women, whether relatives or not, who lived as domestics in the houses of ecclesiastics.

In the New Testament. It is uncertain whether the words of St. Paul in 1 Cor 7.36–38 can be understood as referring to this or a similar custom. The passage is difficult. The Apostle is applying to a particular case his teaching on the superiority of celibacy and virginity over marriage in the Christian dispensation. Someone must decide whether this virgin should get married or continue a virgin. The main difficulty is to determine the relationship to the virgin of the man who must make the decision. Is he her father or a man who can marry her? The traditional exegesis, which was unquestioned until the close of the 19th century, understands Paul to be referring to the father (or guardian) of a virgin daughter (or ward) who is fully of an age to marry. Should he give her in marriage or keep her a virgin? The difficulties to this interpretation are the plural γαμείτωσαν (let them get married: v. 36) and the terms by which the Apostle designates the man and maid, τις (anyone) and παρθένος (virgin). The subject of the plural "let them get married" can only be a man and a woman who may licitly become man and wife. The τις would, consequently, be the girl's fiancée. It was probably in order to obviate this difficulty that the Western text, followed by the Vulgate, changed the plural verb to a singular, γαμείτω (let her get married), *si nubat* (if she get married) in the Vulgate. Neither the Church Fathers who condemned the συνείσακτοι nor the συνείσακτοι themselves ever appealed to this text of Paul. Apart from the obscure passage of 1 Cor 7.36–38, there is no evidence for the existence of any such custom in the 1st-century Church. Consequently very few exegetes would read the custom into the text of Paul. But a growing number of exegetes do see in the passage a case analogous to the later *Virgines subintroductae.* A betrothed Christian couple, inspired by Paul's teaching on celibacy, must make a difficult decision: should they get married or continue simply as betrothed? This interpretation, however, which is adopted by the Revised Standard Version, has its own difficulties. The adjective ὑπέρακμος (v. 36) and the participle γαμίζων (twice in v. 38) are given unusual meaning. The adjective is taken as a masculine modifying τις and describing the sex urge of the man: "If anyone . . . if his passions are strong." But usage hardly supports such a meaning. The adjective ὑπέρακμος should mean, etymologically, beyond the ἀκμή (high point, i.e., prime of life). In this passage it would be made to mean, therefore, sexually well developed or fully of an age to marry; it could, indeed, refer to the maiden as well as to the man. The participle γαμίζων (from γαμίζω) would normally mean giving in marriage, so that it would seem to indicate that the τις who must make the decision is the girl's father or guardian. The fiancé interpretation can be maintained only on the supposition that γαμίζων is here a synonym for γαμῶν (from γαμέω) in the sense of take in marriage.

Bibliography: *Encyclopedic Dictionary of the Bible,* translated and adapted by L. HARTMAN (New York, 1963) 2547–48. R. KUGELMAN, "1 Cor 7:36–38," *The Catholic Biblical Quarterly* 10 (Washington 1948) 63–71. J. J. O'ROURKE, "Hypotheses regarding 1 Cor 7:36–38," *ibid.* 20 (1958) 292–298. W. G. KÜMMEL, "Verlobung und Heirat bei Paulus," *Beiheft zur Zeitschrift für die Neutestamentliche Wissenschaft* 21 (Berlin 1954) 275–295. R. H. A. SEBOLDT, "Spiritual Marriage in the Early Church: A Suggested Interpretation of 1 Cor 7:36–38," *Concordia Theological Monthly* 30 (1959) 103–119.

[R. KUGELMAN]

In the Primitive Church. There is almost no evidence for this practice in the primitive Church despite apparent references in the Shepherd of HERMAS (ch. 9), the DIDACHE (11.11), IRENAEUS (*Adv. Haer.* 1.6.3), and TERTULLIAN (*De exhort. cast.* 12). Later attempts to justify the practice by St. Paul's reference to a woman companion (1 Cor 9.5) were offset by his cautions: *adolescentiores viduas devita* (1 Tim 5.11–13). The custom is known mainly through condemnations by the Fathers and councils, which indicate that this system, without being general, had a considerable diffusion particularly in connection with the Gnostic sects. It is explicitly referred to by St. CYPRIAN OF CARTHAGE (*Epist.* 4), the synod of Antioch, which condemned PAUL OF SAMOSATA and his companions in 268 (Eusebius, *Ecclesiatical History* 7.30.12), the Pseudo-Clementine *Epistula ad Virgines,* Jerome (*Epist.* 22), and in the synods of ELVIRA 306 (c.27), Ancyra 314 (c.19), and Nicaea 325 (c.3), which discouraged spiritual marriages.

With the condemnation of the practice by JOHN CHRYSOSTOM in two pastoral letters written shortly after he became patriarch of Constantinople (*Patrologia Graeca,* ed. J. P. Migne 47:495–532) and the prevalence of clerical celibacy particularly in the West, many councils prohibited the custom outright: Orléans in 549 (c.3), Tours in 567 (c.11), and Toledo IV in 633 (c.42). The Council of Bordeaux in 663 or 675 (c.3) seems to be the only Merovingian synod to speak of the practice by name. Justinian I legislated against it (*Novel.* 123.29) as did Gregory I in a letter to the bishop of Spoleto (*Epist.* 13.39).

In Celtic countries during the 5th and early 6th centuries monks and nuns lived in separate buildings but within the same monastery walls (*see* MONASTERIES, DOUBLE). There seems to be a reference to the designation of *virgines subintroductae* in the so-called Synod of Bishops Patrick, Auxilius, and Isnerius *c.* 459 (c.9), and in Armorican Brittany in the early 6th century these virgins and widows, referred to as *conhospitae,* assisted the priest in the celebration of Mass and in presenting the chalice to communicants, a practice that horrified certain Gallican bishops. There is evidence for a similar practice among the Syrian Nestorians in the early 6th century.

Bibliography: J. SCHMID and D. MISONNE, *Lexikon für Theologie und Kirche,* ed. J. HOFER and K. RAHNER, 10 v. (2d, new ed. Freiburg 1957–65); suppl., *Das Zweite Vatikanische Konzil: Dokumente und kommentare,* ed. H. S. BRECHTER et al., pt. 1 (1966) 9:1229–31. A. ADAM, *Die Religion in Geschichte und Gegenwart,* 7 v. (3d ed. Tübingen 1957–65) 6:560–561. H. ACHELIS, *Virgines subintroductae* (Leipzig 1902). P. DE LABRIOLLE, *Revue Historique* 137 (Paris 1921) 204–225, spiritual marriage. G. MORIN, *Revue Bénédictine* 47 (Maredsous 1935) 101–113. E. KÄHLER, *Die Frau in den paulinischen Briefen* (Zürich 1960) 38–41, 215–218.

[F. X. MURPHY]

VIRGINIA, CATHOLIC CHURCH IN

The first of the thirteen colonies, one of the four commonwealths in the U.S., bordered on the north by Maryland and West Virginia, on the south by North Carolina and Tennessee, on the east by Maryland and the Atlantic Ocean, and on the west by Kentucky and West Virginia. Richmond is the capital and Norfolk the largest city. The two Catholic dioceses in Virginia, Richmond (1820) and Arlington (1974) are suffragan of the Archdiocese of Baltimore. In 2001 Catholics numbered some eight percent of the total state population of 6.9 million.

Early History. Colonial Virginia was not a friendly place for Catholics. In 1570 eight Spanish Jesuits from Florida established a mission near the future Jamestown, but were betrayed by their Native American guide and massacred. When the Virginia colony was founded at Jamestown in 1607, its charter from James I stated: "We should be loath that any person should be permitted to pass, that we suspected to affect the superstitions of the Church of Rome." Nominally, the Church of England was officially established. In 1634 hostility toward Catholicism increased with the settlement of Maryland under Catholic auspices. In 1642 Virginia enacted laws banning priests and prohibiting the exercise of Catholicism. Despite these restrictions, in 1651 Giles Brent, a Catholic, and his family, moved from Maryland and settled in Stafford County, between the Potomac and Rappahannaock Rivers. Throughout the colonial period, the Brents remained loyal to the Church, and some held public office. Two sisters of John Carroll, the future bishop, married Brents. In 1784 Carroll was named superior of the American mission. In his first report to the Congregation of Propaganda Fide, the missionary arm of the pope, he stated that "there are not more than 200 [Catholics] in Virginia who are visited four or five times a year by a priest."

In 1789 Carroll was named the first bishop of Baltimore with jurisdiction over the entire nation, including Virginia; in 1808, he was named archbishop. By the 1790s Catholics had settled in Alexandria, part of the District of Columbia until 1846, and in Norfolk. In 1791 Jean Dubois said Mass for a small congregation in Norfolk, but then moved to Richmond where he taught school for over a year and established friendships with leading Protestants, including Patrick Henry. Once in Richmond, he received a request from Colonel John Fitzgerald, George Washington's aide-de-camp, to say Mass in Alexandria from time to time. While he never visited Alexandria, he did go at Carroll's request to Emmitsburg, Maryland, where he was one of the founders of Mt. St. Mary's College before becoming the third Bishop of New York. The church in Alexandria was then served—and owned—by former Jesuits, suppressed as an order in 1773 and restored in the U.S. in 1805.

By 1817 lay trusteeism had arisen in Norfolk. Though most of the congregation were Irish, a Portuguese physician, Oliviera Fernandez, was their leader. In a series of long, learned, and tedious broadsides, he rejected the authority of Father James Lucas, appointed to Norfolk by Archbishop Leonard NEALE, Carroll's successor, and refused to accept the jurisdiction of Carroll's second successor, the French-born Archbishop Ambrose MARECHAL. He argued that the trustees were the heirs to the *patronato real* and that, just as the pope signed a concordat with a king in a monarchy allowing him to appoint bishops and pastors, he should sign one with the people in a democracy—arguments that could scarcely be persuasive in Rome, which had witnessed the devastating effects on the Church of the French Revolution and its form of democracy. Sending a delegation to Rome, he claimed there was no pastor, and then called Thomas Carbry, OP, to take charge of the church he had built. What exacerbated trusteeism was Virginia's law prohibiting the incorporation of church property, which was therefore held either by lay trustees or by the priest or bishop in his own name—a situation that continued to cause confusion well into the twentieth century.

In 1820, contrary to Marechal's advice, Propaganda established the Diocese of Richmond, which comprised all of Virginia, including the present state of West Virginia, but excluding Alexandria, still subject to the Archdiocese of Baltimore. The first bishop, Patrick Kelly, came from Ireland, but received an icy welcome from Marechal in Baltimore. In Norfolk, he mollified the trustees, but then removed Father Lucas' faculties. Without ever getting to Richmond, he remained in Norfolk and supported himself by teaching school. After less than a year, he returned to Ireland to become the Bishop of Waterford and Lismore. The Diocese of Richmond now fell under the administration of the Archbishop of Baltimore.

In September of 1822, Kelly submitted his final report to Propaganda. Out of a total Virginia population of over a million, he wrote, there were about 1,000 Catholics, served by five priests in three principal regions: Norfolk, Richmond, and the northwestern section around Martinsburg and Harpers Ferry. The congregations in each region would develop in different ways. Norfolk, a seaport, remained the principal Catholic center as Irish immigrants arrived to work there and in the shipyard at nearby Portsmouth, which soon became a separate parish. For some time, a priest from Norfolk also journeyed to Richmond, where the original Catholic congregation was comprised of several wealthy Frenchmen. One Catholic citizen, Joseph Gallego, left a sum of money and a lot for a church to the congregation. Because of Virginia's laws, the bequest remained in litigation for many years.

Richmond's Catholic congregation gained stability only with the arrival in 1832 of Father Timothy O'Brien. Determined to make the Catholic presence visible in the city, he built St. Peter's Church, near the capitol. In 1834 he also succeeded in having the Sisters—later named the Daughters—of Charity open St. Joseph's orphanage and, later, a school, the first of numerous institutions the order would staff in Virginia. Richmond lay at the beginning of the James River and Kanawah Canal, which soon drew Irish and later German laborers. O'Brien used it to travel

to Lynchburg, which had a resident priest by the 1840s. Lynchburg gradually became a center from which priests rode circuit and founded parishes in Wytheville in the west and in Lexington and Staunton in the Shenandoah Valley. Martinsburg, a small farming town, had a small Catholic congregation by 1794, but it then evolved into first a center for the C&O canal and then for the B&O railroad. It also served as the headquarters for priests riding circuit to Harpers Ferry, Winchester in the northern Shenandoah Valley, and Bath (now Berkeley Springs, WV).

In 1841 Richard Vincent Whelan, the pastor in Martinsburg, became the second bishop of Richmond. In his see city he opened a short-lived seminary, but, in 1846, moved to Wheeling, where he unsuccessfully attempted to have the Jesuits open a college. To gain priests for his poor diocese, he begged from other dioceses and then became the first southern bishop to recruit from All Hallows College, outside of Dublin. Irish priests were soon working with Irish immigrant laborers on the railroads, particularly around Harpers Ferry and the Shenandoah Valley.

In 1851 at Whelan's request, the Holy See established the new diocese of Wheeling for the section of Virginia west of the Allegheny Mountains and transferred Whelan there. John McGill, a priest of Louisville, then became the third Bishop of Richmond. Within a week of arriving, he had a dispute with Father O'Brien, who held property in his own name until its debt was paid. After nineteen years of service, O'Brien left Richmond. Unlike the North, Virginia never attracted large numbers of immigrants. Many of the Irish who came to Richmond and Norfolk in the 1830s belonged to the merchant or professional classes. A smaller number of Germans also settled in Richmond, where in 1848 they founded the only strictly national parish in the diocese. Austrian Jesuits, who had fled from the revolution of 1848 to the United States, had charge of it until 1860, when Benedictines from Latrobe took over.

In the 1830s and 1840s there were also significant conversions, including the three daughters, wife, and son of Governor John R. Floyd, Sr. These converts and the Irish middle class helped gain acceptance for the Church with Virginia's Protestant establishment. While during the 1850s, therefore, the North was wracked with Nativism and the KNOW-NOTHINGS, the Church in Virginia was largely spared the tumult, except in the western part of the state and the port areas around Norfolk. In 1855, moreover, Catholics were heroic during the yellow fever epidemic in Norfolk and Portsmouth and won Protestant admiration. Father Matthew O'Keefe of St. Patrick's Church in Norfolk formed a pact with a Protestant minister to remain in the city and, if either died, the other would have the funeral. He was twice stricken by the fever, but recovered—years later, he did bury his Protestant friend. The Daughters of Charity, already operating a school and orphanage in Norfolk, now began nursing the victims. The following year they opened St. Vincent's Hospital (now De Paul Medical Center), the result of a bequest of Anne Behan Plum Herron, a wealthy Irish immigrant who died while nursing the victims. Yet, such Catholic heroism did not completely overcome Protestant prejudice. At midnight on Dec. 7, 1856, arsonists burned O'Keefe's church. O'Keefe made almost weekly trips to the northeast to raise money for a new church, which was dedicated in 1858 as St. Mary of the Immaculate Conception. In 1991 it was elevated to the rank of a minor basilica, the only one in Virginia.

One price of accommodation to the predominantly Protestant culture was that Virginia Catholics, though few were slave owners, opposed abolition. They supported the Confederate cause and many served in the army. Both McGill in Richmond and Whelan in Wheeling supported secession, but, while McGill's see city became the capital of the Confederacy, Whelan found himself in the capital of West Virginia which seceded from Virginia. The diocesan boundaries now crossed state lines.

After the war, McGill was still plagued with a shortage of priests. To supplement his own clergy diminished by death or departures from the diocese, he recruited from the American College in Louvain. One of his first recruits was Francis Janssens, who, after service in Virginia, was successively Bishop of Natchez and Archbishop of New Orleans. Another Louvain recruit was Augustine van de Vyver, who became Bishop of Richmond and recruited both his nephew and great nephew from Louvain for the diocese. In 1866, moreover, Sisters of the Visitation arrived in Richmond from Baltimore to open Monte Maria Monastery and Academy for girls— they later closed the school and later still moved to a more rural location.

As Reconstruction ended in Virginia in 1870, service in the Confederate Army provided the credentials for Catholics to assume prominent positions. In 1870 Anthony J. Keiley, born of Irish parents in New Jersey, but raised in Petersburg, became mayor of Richmond, served for many years as the President of the Irish Catholic Benevolent Union, and later became a judge of the international court in Cairo. James Dooley, son of an Irish merchant in Richmond, served in the state legislature, became a millionaire through railroad and land speculation, and, at his death in 1921, left three million dollars for St. Joseph's Villa to replace the existing orphanage for girls run by the Daughters of Charity in Richmond. Others in

high office also had Catholic connections. John W. Johnston served two terms in the U.S. Senate. His wife, Niketti Floyd, was a convert and their children were all Catholic.

In 1872 McGill died. James GIBBONS, the fourth bishop of Richmond, was a Baltimore native who in 1868 was appointed the first Vicar Apostolic of North Carolina, jurisdiction over which he and his successor in Richmond retained until 1881. In 1875 Gibbons thwarted the efforts of Bishop John J. Kain of Wheeling, a Martinsburg native, to have Rome realign the dioceses of Wheeling and Richmond to coincide with the new state lines, for, he said, this would take away the area around Martinsburg, then the most prosperous section of his diocese. Gibbons also initiated work among the freed African Americans, few of whom were Catholic.

In 1877 Gibbons became coadjutor Archbishop of Baltimore and was named a cardinal in 1886. John J. KEANE, the fifth bishop, was Irish-born, the first foreign-born bishop of Richmond since Kelly, and had served as a pastor in Washington. Influenced by Isaac HECKER, the founder of the PAULISTS, he sought to nourish the spiritual development of his clergy through semi-annual conferences and monthly regional meetings and promoted parish missions for the laity. In the 1880s the southern Shenandoah Valley experienced the greatest Catholic development. In 1882 Roanoke had been founded as a railroad center, but by 1892 it had a school and orphanage staffed by the Sisters of Charity of Nazareth. Moreover, in 1883 the Josephites opened their first parish for African Americans in Richmond. In 1888 Keane was named the first rector of The CATHOLIC UNIVERSITY OF AMERICA, established by the Third Plenary Council in 1884.

The succession to Keane was fraught with the undertones of the ethnic tension characteristic of the American Church elsewhere. Van de Vyver, then the vicar general, was the first choice of both the Richmond priests eligible to nominate and the bishops of the province of Baltimore, but Gibbons sought to gain the appointment of Denis J. O'CONNELL, a priest of Richmond, who had been named rector of the American College in Rome in 1885 and who appeared only on the bishops' list. After Leo XIII rejected O'Connell's appointment because of his service in Rome, Gibbons and Keane tried to prevent the appointment of van de Vyver, who was, however, named bishop in 1889.

In the 1890s, Gibbons, Keane, and O'Connell, together with Archbishop John Ireland of St. Paul, took leading roles in the controversies that divided the hierarchy and in the crisis of AMERICANISM, condemned in 1899, but van de Vyver remained aloof and concentrated on the internal development of the diocese. During his episcopate the Josephites expanded their work with African Americans to Norfolk, Lynchburg, and Alexandria. In addition, Louise D. Morrell and her sister, Saint Katherine DREXEL, in 1895 and 1896, respectively, opened high schools for African American boys and girls at Rock Castle. The diocese also received another major benefaction from Mr. and Mrs. Thomas Fortune Ryan, who built the Cathedral of the Sacred Heart, dedicated in 1906. When van de Vyver died in 1911, O'Connell, then auxiliary bishop of San Francisco, was finally named to Richmond.

World War I brought the first major increase in the state's Catholic population as the U.S. Navy established the Norfolk Naval Operating Station, and the government located other installations in Northern Virginia. The end of the war temporarily stifled Virginia's Catholic growth, as the United States retreated into isolationism, but these two regions were poised for the growth that followed World War II, when the United States became a super power. In the early 1920s, however, anti-Catholicism also had a resurgence, but the old style of Virginia Catholicism's accommodation with the political establishment initially held fast. In 1920 O'Connell advised against forming a Catholic Laymen's Association, similar to those in other states, since friendly Protestant legislators had prevented the passage of such bills as convent-inspection laws. But in 1924 the Ku Klux Klan launched a vociferous but unsuccessful campaign against the reelection of the incumbent state treasurer, John Purcell, a Catholic. In 1925, in what would later be called ecumenism, the Episcopal Diocese of Virginia donated land to the Catholics to build a church at Baileys Crossroads in northern Virginia. But the Al Smith campaign of 1928 evoked more anti-Catholicism, after which the diocese formed a Laymen's League to defend Catholic rights.

Forced by ill health to resign in 1925, O'Connell died the following year. His successor, Andrew J. Brennan, formerly auxiliary bishop of Scranton, restructured the diocese along the lines of those in the north. The Bureau of Catholic Charities, which had begun in 1922, was expanded. In 1931, St. Joseph's Villa, a model orphanage for girls made possible by Dooley's bequest, opened with a vast display of the Catholic presence in Virginia—Brennan planned the event just before the annual bishops' meeting in Washington, so as many bishops as possible could attend. But the Depression placed a greater burden on Brennan. In 1934 he suffered a massive stroke that left him unable to speak. In 1935 Peter Leo Ireton, a priest of Baltimore, became coadjutor bishop and, in 1945, succeeded as ordinary when Brennan formally resigned—Brennan died in 1956. While Ireton left much of the diocesan administration to a series of able chancellors, he followed Brennan in modeling his diocese on the

larger ones in the north. He actively promoted the Conference of Jews and Christians—later renamed the Conference of Christians and Jews—and established several urban parishes for African Americans. World War II and the postwar years ushered in the period of greatest growth in Catholic population.

In 1936 Ireton reported that the native Virginians moved out of the state far outnumbered those who had moved in. A decade later the situation had changed. Northern Virginia, long a rural outpost of the diocese, rapidly developed into a suburb of Washington. By 1941 one sixth of Virginia's Catholic population was in the area, a percentage that would rapidly increase. In the Norfolk area, military expansion and new housing turned Virginia Beach into one of the state's largest cities. What canals and railroads had been in the nineteenth and early twentieth century, the automobile became in the postwar years. Interstates and highways determined the location of new suburban parishes.

Ireton died in 1958 and was succeeded by John Russell, the Bishop of Charleston and a native of Baltimore. Under Russell, the diocese realized a long-time dream and opened St. John Vianney minor seminary in 1961, only to have it close a decade later. In the name of integration, Russell closed many of the Black parishes Ireton had opened. He actively participated in the SECOND VATICAN COUNCIL and immediately sought to implement its decrees. He established an ecumenical commission, the second in the U.S., and promoted racial justice. Although only one Virginia priest took part in the March on Selma in 1965, Russell defended the participants. At his retirement in 1973, Walter F. Sullivan, the auxiliary bishop, was appointed administrator. In 1974 Sullivan became the bishop, and, a short time later, the new diocese of Arlington, consisting of twenty-one counties in northern Virginia, was established. Thomas Welch was the first bishop—in 1983, he was transferred to Allentown and was replaced in Arlington by Thomas R. Keating, who died in 1998. In 1999 Paul Loverde, former Bishop of Ogdensburg, became the third Bishop of Arlington. Those counties of West Virginia that had belonged to the Richmond diocese were transferred to Wheeling, while the counties of southwest Virginia, formerly in Wheeling, and the counties on the Delmarva Peninsula, formerly belonging to the Diocese of Wilmington, were ceded to Richmond.

As a result, the dioceses of both Richmond and Arlington coincide with the state boundaries. In 2001 the Catholic population of the Diocese of Richmond was 200,342 out of a total population of 4,555,139; Arlington had 353,367 Catholics in a population of 2,317,773, with the Catholic population in at least three counties in the Washington suburbs exceeding 25 percent.

Bibliography: J. H. BAILEY, *A History of the Diocese of Richmond, the Formative Years* (Richmond 1956). G. P. FOGARTY, SJ, *Commonwealth Catholicism: A History of the Catholic Church in Virginia* (Notre Dame, IN 2001).

[G. P. FOGARTY]

VIRGINIS PROLES OPIFEXQUE MATRIS

The hymn in the Divine Office that was historically assigned for Matins of the Common of a virgin-martyr. It has five stanzas each of which has three sapphic and one adonic verse. Stanzas one, four, and five are used also in the Common of a virgin; stanzas four and five, in the Common of a non-virgin. The author is unknown. Its inclusion in a 9th-century hymnal suggests the 8th century as the time of its origin. The fact that it is found in increasingly numerous manuscripts after the 9th century attests its merit. Its graceful sapphic strophes originally had an end syllable rhyme in the 3d and 4th verses, but in the revision of the hymns under Pope URBAN VIII the rhyme disappeared. Several phrases and lines also were revised, but on the whole the hymn did not suffer radical change.

Bibliography: M. BRITT, *The Hymns of the Breviary and Missal* (new ed. New York 1948) 376–378.

[G. E. CONWAY/EDS.]

VIRGINITY

In the most general sense of the word, virginity is the state of one who has not had sexual relations and has not experienced voluntary carnal pleasures involving grave sin. It may therefore be attributed to men as well as to women. Apart from considerations of religion and virtue, however, it has generally been more highly honored in women than in men. Its existence in women is a verifiable fact, so far as physical integrity is concerned; also, the purity of blood lines and the authenticity of family relationships depend more upon the virtue of the woman than of the man. The optimum of chastity, which is virginity, is therefore given more attention in the case of a woman than of a man, and the term is, in fact, rarely used in reference to a man.

In Non-Christian Religion. The virginity of a young woman is considered with esteem and respect, for it appears in her as a symbol of freshness and purity, and a sort of youthful integrity of the forces of life. Primitive and ancient religions sometimes attach to virginity a religious significance; thus a certain sexual purity was required for particular ritual and magical rites, perhaps because of an intuition that the integrity of natural forces permitted magical or mystical union with cosmic forces. Similarly, in Greco-Roman antiquity the cult of the virgin goddesses (Artemis, Athena) attributed to the virginity of a goddess a magic power of strength and blessedness. It also demanded continence or even virginity, at least temporarily, in priests and priestesses of certain cults. Such was the case with the vestals in Rome: the immaterial purity of sacred fire had to be attended only by virgin priestesses (Ovid, *Fasti,* 6, 291–294), and a miraculous power was attributed to the prayer of the vestals (Pliny, *Hist. Nat.* 28, 2). The practice of castration for certain priests was not unrelated to this same regard for the religious value of continence (γάλλοι). Dualist philosophical speculation, for example that of the Pythagoreans, Platonists, and Neoplatonists, tended to encourage abstention from carnal pleasures, but this was advocated more to encourage contemplation and the pursuit of wisdom than because any properly religious value was attributed to continence or virginity.

In the Bible. In the Old Testament, virginity as a permanent state in life for religious motives was quite unknown. Marriage was regarded as the normal state for all adult men and women in Israel, but premarital virginity was expected in women. According to the older law in Ex 22.16–17, a man who seduced a virgin who was not yet betrothed had, at the decision of her father, either to pay her marriage price and marry her, or to pay "the customary marriage price for virgins" without marrying her (*see* MATRIMONY). According to a later law in Dt 22.28–29, such a man must pay the girl's father 50 silver shekels and take her as his wife without the right of ever divorcing her. This later law (Dt 22.23–24) also decreed the death penalty by stoning for a betrothed maiden who consented to intercourse with a man other than her future husband; the crime was considered ADULTERY. The Law of Holiness (*see* HOLINESS, LAW OF) ordained that "a priest may not marry a woman who has been a prostitute, or has lost her honor, or has been divorced by her husband" (Lv 21.7). Ezekiel (Ez 44.22) forbade a priest to marry a widow unless she was the widow of another priest. Ordinarily, therefore, the bride of a priest would be a virgin. The Law of Holiness also decrees that "a priest's daughter who loses her honor by committing fornication . . . shall be burned to death" (Lv 21.9). These laws were based on the taboos that surrounded the sacredness of the Old Testament priesthood.

Although the evidence is not conclusive, it seems that most of the ESSENES and the members of the QUMRAN COMMUNITY were celibates, primarily because of their apocalyptic, eschatological preoccupations.

In the New Testament, virginity, not in itself, but as practiced for supernatural motives, is placed on a higher level than marriage. Jesus praises those who remain voluntary "eunuchs," i.e., celibates, "for the sake of the kingdom of heaven" (Mt 19.10–12), so that, freed from the burdens of married life, they may more easily be His intimate followers in seeking the kingdom of God. St. Paul, while making it clear that all Christians may marry (1 Cor 7.25), recommends that the unmarried remain as they are because of the nearness of the PAROUSIA (1 Cor 7.25–31) and because of the greater freedom they have to serve the Lord (1 Cor 7.32–35). At the time he wrote these words, the Apostle himself was not married (1 Cor 7.7). He may have been a widower, since, as an ardent Pharisee in early life, he would hardly have violated the almost universal Jewish custom of marrying. St. Peter certainly was married (Mt 8.14; 1 Cor 9.5), and probably the other Apostles were also, though St. John, "the disciple whom Jesus loved," has been traditionally regarded as a virgin. A married clergy was taken for granted in the early Church, but the prescription that a bishop, priest, or deacon must be μιᾶς γυναικὸς ἄνδρα, literally "one woman's husband" (1 Tim 3.2.12; Ti 1.6), does not mean that he must necessarily marry; it merely means that, if his wife died, he could not marry a second time. (*See* VIRGINES SUBINTRODUCTAE.)

First Centuries—Patristic Era. From the end of the 1st century and the beginning of the 2d, one finds allusions to ascetics who lived continently "in honor of the flesh of Christ" (Ignatius, *Pol.* 5.2; cf. 1 *Clem.* 38, 2). From these words we may conclude that the imitation of the virginity of Christ had become by that time a motive for continence. Perfect continence, along with voluntary poverty and austerity of life, was a constitutive element of the ascetical life that began to develop in the 2d century, and of which Origen, in the following century, was to be an illustrious example (Eusebius *Hist. Eccl.* 6, 3, 9–10; 8, 1–3).

The state of men practicing continence and asceticism soon evolved into monasticism, and ultimately into ecclesiastical celibacy, and the word "virgins" came in time to be reserved especially for women who gave themselves to perfect chastity.

In effect, it would seem that from the beginning of the 2d century, a state or a profession of virginity was recognized in the Church, which granted those who practiced it a place apart, comparable to that of a widow (Ignatius, *Magn.* 13.1, thus speaks of virgins "called widows"). After the 3d century there are abundant texts that attest to the place, increasingly important, that "the holy virgins," *virgines sanctae,* assume in the life of the Church. From Africa comes the important testimony of Tertullian (*De virginibus velandis*), and of Cyprian (*De habitu virginum*): virgins are "the most illustrious por-

tion of the flock of Christ" (Cyprian, *op. cit.,* 3); they are "the spouses of Christ" (Tertullian, *De virg. vel.* 16; *De resurrectione carnis* 61; cf. *De oratione,* 22), and the violation of their purpose of virginity is considered adultery (Cyprian, *Ep.* 4, 2; *De habitu virg.* 20).

Tertullian and St. Cyprian use words in this connection that seem to suggest a kind of vow (Tertullian, *De orat.* 22; Cyprian, *De habitu virg.* 4) but it is still no more than a private vow, a *continentiae propositum* (Cyprian, *Ep.* 55, 21). One does not find evidence that this purpose of chastity was consecrated and solemnized by a liturgical rite, or sanctioned by ecclesiastical legislation. The council of Elvira in Spain (*c.* 306) was the first to impose canonical sanctions against virgins "who have consecrated themselves to God" and who have been unfaithful to their "pact of virginity": they are excommunicated, and even if they repent, they are allowed to receive communion only at the end of their lives (c.13): moreover, the text clearly distinguishes between consecrated virgins, and women guilty of misconduct before marriage (c. 14). At about the same time the council of Ancyra (314) condemns virgins who have married as guilty of bigamy (c.19): a virgin is the spouse of Christ and thus must not contract other marriages. A little later, civil legislation sanctioned these decrees, and went to the extent of punishing by death anyone who married a consecrated virgin (Valens, 364, in *Cod. Theod.* 9, 25, 2).

In the 4th century, the writings of the Fathers who exalted virginity were numerous; they emphatically recommended it and elaborated upon its spiritual value. In the East, Methodius of Olympus, even in the 3d century, wrote of virginity in a lyrical dialogue inspired by Plato's *Banquet.* In the same manner, SS. Athanasius, Basil, Gregory of Nazianzus, Gregory of Nyssa especially, and John Chrysostom wrote of virginity with enthusiasm.

In the West, St. Ambrose has no less than four treatises dedicated to virginity: *De virginibus, De virginirate, De institutione virginis,* and *Exhortatio virginitatis;* he also wrote a treatise addressed to widows, *De viduis.* He insisted especially on the example of the Virgin Mary; he is the great Marian Doctor as well as the preacher of virginity. St. Jerome wrote to the virgins of whom he had become spiritual director (*Ep.* 22 to Eustochium, 130 to Demetrias) and engaged in vigorous polemic against the adversaries of asceticism and virginity: *Adversus Helvidium de Mariae virginirate perpetua, Adversus Jovinianum,* and *Contra Vigilantium.* St. Augustine also wrote an eloquent treatise, *On Holy Virginity.*

These exhortations to virgins were composed with a view to the condition of virgins living in the world, in their own familial menage, where they sometimes made up little communities that were still characterized by considerable personal freedom. Such were the holy women, widows, and virgins, who were disciples of St. Jerome. Little by little these groups organized themselves and settled according to a monastic or cenobitic way of life; they used Rules established by virgins living in true monastic communities, for example, the *Regula ad virgines* of St. Caesarius of Arles (534).

We must note here a strange practice that existed in antiquity, in the West as well as in the East—the cohabitation of clerics and monks with virgins (*syneisaktoi, virgines subintroductae, agapetae*). Under the pretext of assisting and protecting them, clerics or monks shared the houses and the lives of the virgins. This questionable sort of cohabitation and the abuses to which it could lead set off a sharp reaction on the part of bishops and preachers (St. John Chrysostom), and led to disciplinary measures on the part of the councils. In this way ecclesiastical legislation was developed and established to preserve the virtue of virgins still living in the world, and to guarantee their fidelity to the commitments they had assumed. These prescriptions parallel those which govern female monasticism, which began to be developed and organized at the same time. The history of consecrated virginity mingles with that of religious life for women, and even at the present time one finds numerous women who choose to lead lives of consecrated virginity in the world (*see* SECULAR INSTITUTES).

Rite of Consecration. There is no indication before the 4th century of a liturgical ceremony of consecration. It does not seem that the celebrated fresco in the catacomb of Priscilla (3d century) represents the taking of the veil by a virgin: it appears rather to represent the *velatio conjugalis* in the Christian marriage ceremony. In Rome, in the middle of the 4th century, the solemn rite of the consecration of virgins consisted essentially in taking the veil. Marcellina, the sister of St. Ambrose, made her profession between 352 and 354 before Pope Liberius, who gave her a veil of somber color (*De Virg.* 3.1.1; cf. Jerome, *Ep.* 24, 3). The imposition of the veil on virgins is found first in Africa, then in Milan, where it was accompanied by the blessing of the bishop (Ambrose, *Ep.* 19, 7). At the end of the 4th century, this rite had passed to Rome and Gaul. One can thus distinguish between virgins who have promised to live in their proposed virginity, but who have not received the sacred veil, and those who have made public profession of chastity and have received the veil from the bishop, with a long prayer of blessing (Siricius, *Ep.* 10, 3.4, to the bishops of Gaul; Innocent I, *Ep.* 2, 15, to Victricius of Rouen). This veiling, borrowed from the Roman marriage ceremonies, symbolized the mystical marriage of the virgin with Christ. The veiling was accompanied by a long preface of consecration that, with the exception of some clauses added in the

Gelasian Sacramentary and reproduced in later versions, goes back to the *Leonine Sacramentary*. The rite of imposition of the veil upon virgins is not found in the East in antiquity. Other ceremonies also symbolized the mystical marriage between Christ and the newly consecrated virgin. In the Middle Ages it became customary to give the virgins a ring and a crown that, like the veil, were traditional symbols of marriage.

Theology and Spirituality. Moral theology distinguishes a triple element in virginity: physical integrity; the absence of all voluntary and complete venereal pleasure in the past; and, as regards the future, a determination to abstain perpetually from such pleasure. This determination, so to speak, is the formal element of virginity; inexperience of voluntary carnal pleasure is the material element; integrity of the flesh is no more than an accidental element. Such is the teaching of St. Thomas Aquinas (*Summa theologiae* 2a2ae, 152.1), who adheres closely to the doctrine of St. Augustine (*De sancta virginitate,* 8; cf. *De Civ. Dei* 1.18). St. Bonaventure makes the same distinction, though less formally; he speaks of virginity of the flesh, virginity of the spirit, and virginity of flesh and of spirit. For this reason the accidental and involuntary loss of physical integrity (e.g., by accident, surgical operation, rape) leaves virginity, which is most essentially in the will, intact.

Theologians also show the eminent value of virginity, which abstains not only from all disordered and culpable carnal pleasure, but absolutely from all carnal delectation, no matter what it is, and applies itself to divine things, and particularly to the contemplation of divine truth (*Summa theologiae* 2a2ae, 152.2–3). Moreover, although it is not the highest of the virtues (*ibid.* a.5), it is more excellent than marriage, since it has as its object a superior good. Marriage is ordered to the multiplication of the human race, but virginity is ordered to a divine good, and enjoys a completely spiritual fecundity (*ibid.* a.4; cf. St. Augustine, *loc. cit*).

The Council of Trent defined against Luther, who had repudiated the religious vows, that "the conjugal state is not to be preferred to the state of virginity, and it is better and more felicitous to remain in virginity or celibacy than to be bound by marriage" (H. Denzinger, *Enchiridion symbolorum,* ed. A. Schönmetzer [32d ed. Freiburg 1963] 1810). In the 20th century Pope Pius XII, in reaction against a tendency to exalt beyond measure the dignity and greatness of marriage at the expense of consecrated virginity, reminded us of the excellence of the latter; he reminded us equally that celibacy and virginity are not an obstacle to the development and flowering of the person ("SACRA VIRGINITAS," March 25, 1954; *Acta Apostolicae Sedis,* 46 [1954] 161–191. Cf.

"Allocutions to the International Congress of Superiors General of Orders and Congregations of Women," Sept. 15, 1952; 44 [1952] 824).

Here the true value of virginity becomes apparent: it is not only simple abstention, even virtuous, from carnal relations; still less is it a timorous refusal of sexual experience. Rather it is a voluntary and perpetual choice, "for the kingdom of Heaven" (Mt 19.12; cf. Lk 18.29). It is a sign of a greater love, and of a will determined to seek God alone and to belong to Him exclusively (I Cor 7.34). Thus, as a special virtue, it implies the consecration of a vow, which expresses and confirms the determination to follow Christ irrevocably (*Summa theologiae* 2a2ae, 186.6 ad 1).

As a matter of fact, certain Fathers of the Church, in order to exalt and commend virginity, show a tendency to depreciate sexual activity and to exaggerate the inconveniences of marriage (so with certain of the Greek Fathers, St. Gregory of Nyssa, or Basil of Ancyra; or among the Latins, St. Jerome). In this tendency they are victims of a Platonic mentality that disdains the "flesh," or the sense order, to exalt the "spirit," or the "intelligible"; or they indulge in rhetorical exaggeration. But this is not the true sense of Christian virginity, the intention and orientation of which are properly religious, and the motive inspired exclusively by charity.

In the teaching of the Fathers and of masters of the spiritual life, one should remember several important features that enable us to grasp the spirituality of virginity: Virginity is inspired above all by charity. The virgin vows to Christ an exclusive love that admits of no sharing, and because of this she may call herself spouse, according to a theme already used in the Canticle of Canticles and by the Prophets, and which is adopted and developed in the whole of monastic and spiritual tradition. In this there is no element of unhealthy compensation for a grudgingly accepted chastity or for repressed sexuality. All must be raised to the level of the spirit and of charity. Without an increasingly limpid and pure charity, virginity would in fact involve a risk of repression, or dessication of the heart. With charity, which it requires and develops, it is an occasion of growth, and brings about a remarkable equilibrium of the affections. Moreover, inspired by charity, virginity disposes toward a mystical union, which is the supreme fruit of charity.

Because of this we are enabled to understand better the superiority of virginity to marriage. If Christian marriage is the sacred sign (*sacramentum*) of the union of Christ and the Church, consecrated virgins attain to something beyond the sign and are in immediate contact with the holy reality, of which marriage is the sign. In them is realized the nuptial union of Christ and the Church. This doctrine is expressed with exactness in the preface of the consecration of virgins in the Roman Pontifical, which employs the terms of the Leonine Sacramentary alluded to above.

Thus the ecclesial significance of consecrated virginity is clear. We would demean it if we were to consider it only under its utilitarian aspect, and see the virgin as renouncing marriage simply to devote herself more efficaciously to charitable or apostolic works. Virginity is best seen in the mystery of the Church, which is at the same time virgin and spouse (cf. 2 Cor 11.2; Eph 5.25–27). In the Church, the virgin spouse of Christ is the visible sign of this mystery. This is the most profound meaning of consecrated virginity in the Church, and through it, the virgin participates in maternal fecundity of the Church (St. Augustine).

Virginity has also an eschatological significance: it is, in a sense, a present experience of future life in the kingdom of heaven, where "they will neither marry nor be given in marriage" (Mt 22.30); it is the living now of the life of angels in heaven (*ibid.* cf. St. Augustine *De Sancta Virg.* 12); and in this sense virginity, like monastic life, may be qualified as an "angelic" life. The integrity of the flesh, conserved in virginity, assumes a particular significance: it represents in some way the state of the creature in the Garden, as it came intact from the hands of the Creator; and it is the state of the creature in heaven, restored to his primitive integrity. This also is the eschatological significance of monastic life. It represents a return to Paradise and an anticipation of heaven. This helps us to understand also the profound meaning of the perpetual virginity of the Blessed Virgin Mother, who in her absolute integrity is the first of creatures.

Furthermore, we should note that virginity is oriented toward contemplation. It realizes in a special way the beatitude concerning the "pure of heart," who "will see God." The essential element is purity of heart, i.e., purity in the profound center of intention and desire. Even the legitimate and holy use of the pleasures of marriage involves the risk of keeping the soul captive to the "flesh," causing it to lose something of its spiritual purity and its readiness to open itself to the mystery of God. Perfect chastity, on the contrary, allows a total freedom of spirit, which nothing will hinder in its inclination toward the contemplation of the light of God (Gregory of Nyssa, *De Virg.* 2; Basil of Ancyra, *De Virg.* 66).

The practice and the guarding of virginity require a careful asceticism. Mortification of the flesh is necessary, and spiritual authors insist very particularly upon fasting as well as upon modesty; restraint; and prudence in bearing, dress, diversions, and relations with the world— especially where men are concerned. Custody of the eyes is the necessary condition for protecting the heart. In modern times these precautions continue to be necessary. Humility is a point insisted upon by St. Augustine, who made much of its necessity to virginity. Humble spouses "follow the Lamb" more easily than pious virgins (*De Sancta Virg.* 52). In fact, whatever strengthens and nourishes Christian life, and particularly the life of faith, is especially necessary for consecrated virgins: reading of holy books, prayers, etc.

Finally, it can be stated that a sane and balanced psychology is required for virginity to be chosen and accepted in its full light, not as timidity or repression but as the opening up of a generous love and of affections wholly rectified and transformed by agape.

See Also: CHASTITY.

Bibliography: R. GUARDINI, ed., *Ehe und Jungfräulichkeit* (Mainz 1926). G. DELLING, G. KITTEL, *Theologisches Wörterbuch zum Neuen Testament* (Stuttgart 1935–) 4:824–835. J. MAYER, ed., *Monumenta de viduis, diaconissis virginibusque tractantia* (*Florilegium Patristicum,* ed. J. ZELLINGER et al. 42; Bonn 1938). J. DILLERSBERGER, *Wer es fassen kann* (Salzburg 1932). T. CAMELOT, *Virgines Christi* (Paris 1944). F. VIZAMANOS, *Las virgines cristianas de la Iglesia primitiva* (Madrid 1949). *Congrès International de Psychologie Religieuse,* 7th ed., 1950, "Mystique et continence" (Études Carmélitaines 31a; Bruges 1952). F. BOURASSA, *La Virginité chrétienne* (Montreal 1952). J. M. PERRIN, *Virginity,* tr. K. GORDON (Westminster, Md. 1956). L. MÜNSTER, *Hochzeit des Lammes* (Düsseldoff 1955). M. VILLER and K. RAHNER, *Aszese und Mystik in der Väterzeit* (Freiburg 1939). D. VON HILDEBRAND, *In Defense of Purity* (New York 1931; repr. Baltimore 1962).

[P. T. CAMELOT]

VIRTUE

A habitual, well-established, readiness or disposition of man's powers directing them to some specific goodness of act.

Scripture. There is no Hebrew term in the Old Testament (OT) that expresses the general notion of virtue. The word ṣᵉdāqā is used in reference to a righteous act (Gn 15.6; Dt 6.25; 24.13; Ps 106.13). In the Septuagint the Greek term ἀρετή, which like the Latin *virtus,* denotes manliness, is found in 2 Mc 6.3; 10,28; 15.12, 17 having the sense of valor or constancy. In Wisdom it is used in reference to virtue generally (4.1; 5.13) and is applied to temperance, prudence, justice, and courage (8.7). In the New Testament (NT) ἀρετή signifies virtue as moral goodness in Phil 4.8 and 2 Pt 1.5.

In the OT use of justice-judgment (ṣedeq-mišpāt), fidelity-goodness ('ĕmet-ḥesed), goodness-tenderness (ḥesed-raḥămîm), there is progress from legalistic righteousness in actions to interior moral attitudes [see J. Guillet, *Themes of the Bible* (Notre Dame, IN 1960) ch. 2–3]. The NT instructions on the virtues of the Christian life manifest the morality of the New Law as interior above all, springing from interior grace and charity and other God-given sources of life according to the gospel (L. Pirot, *Dictionnaire de la Bible,* "Grace").

Fathers. While the apologists spoke of various Christian virtues (Aristides, *Patrologia Graeca,* 96:1121; Theophilus of Antioch, *Patrologia Graeca,* 6:1141; Minucius Felix, *Patrologia Latina,* 3:337,349; Tertullian *Patrologia Latina,* 1:307, 456–459, 471, 534; Origen, *Patrologia Graeca,* 11:957), Lactantius was the first to formulate a general concept of Christian virtue. He adopted the etymology of Cicero, deriving *virtus* from *vir,* and showed against the Stoics that it consists not in mere knowledge but in the willing of good *Patrologia Latina* (6:650–651). St. Ambrose designated as cardinal the four virtues already singled out by Plato, Aristotle, and Cicero, namely, prudence, justice, courage, and temperance (*Patrologia Latina,* 14:280–282). He also stressed the connection of the virtues (*ibid.*).

St. Augustine's contribution to the development of the concept was of major importance. He gave two principal definitions of virtue. One was from Cicero—*virtus est animi habitus, naturae modo et rationi consentaneus* (*De Inventione* 2.53); so conceived, virtue is a fixed disposition of soul, making connatural the response to what is right (PL 40:20). According to the second definition, virtue is the art of living rightly and in a proper manner, and this is a frequently recurrent thought in St. Augustine (e.g., *Patrologia Latina* 41:128; 42:1267). Rectitude of life, however, is to be conceived in reference to eternal happiness (*Patrologia Latina* 42: 1267). True virtue must be supernatural in its finality (*Patrologia Latina* 41:656; 33:670), and against the Pelagians, St. Augustine made it clear that virtue comes only with God's grace (*Patrologia Latina* 41:656; 44: 762; 32:1267; 32:598). He enumerated the four cardinal virtues (*Patrologia Latina* 41:127; 40:20–21) and called attention to the connection of the virtues (*Patrologia Latina* 42:927).

St. Gregory the Great assigned preeminent places among the virtues to faith, hope, and charity (*Patrologia Latina* 75:544, 594) and made them the foundations of the spiritual life (*Patrologia Latina* 76:1068–69), without which salvation is impossible (*Patrologia Latina* 76:975). He also pointed to the four cardinal virtues and their connection (*Patrologia Latina* 75:692; 76:808–809). And his emphasis on humility in the practical life of virtue is noteworthy (*Patrologia Latina* 75:100–103, 27, 76–78, 443–444).

From these indications it is evident that in Christian thought virtue came to be understood as a stable disposition of soul. Christian virtues are an endowment coming from God with his grace and are in strict dependence on charity. The primacy of faith, hope, and charity; the cardinal virtues; and the connection of the virtues are universally accepted points of doctrine.

Scholastics. The scholastic milieu sheds light on the significance of St. Thomas Aquinas's development of the notion of virtue. Two principal streams of thought, from which gradually more precise notions emerged, have been discerned (*see* O. Lottin, *Psychologie et morale*, 3.2:99–150). The first of these was Augustinian. Out of St. Augustine's treatment of virtue, Peter Lombard formulated the following definition: *Bona qualitas mentis, qua recte vivitur et qua nullus male utitur, quam Deus in homine operetur.* (*4 Sent.* 1.2.27.2–3; ed. Quaracchi, 1:444–445). By this he meant only supernatural virtue and the virtues he held to be identical with grace. They were exclusively the work of God moving the will through them as forms supernaturalizing man's actions.

The other stream was Aristotelian. Through the commentaries of Boethius (*In Categ. Aristotle; Patrologia Latina* 24: 242–243) Aristotle's notion of virtue as a fixed disposition of soul, a habit of choosing that observes the just mean in actions, was introduced. Boethius himself principally stressed the notion of habit as a deep-rooted condition (ἕξις), rather than a simple disposition readily subject to change (διάθεσις). Abelard relied on this in his definition of virtue as *habitus animi optimus* (*Patrologia Latina* 188:1651). From the interplay of this with the Lombardian definition certain important problems and distinctions emerged.

In the teaching of both Simon of Tournai and William of Auxerre the difference between natural and supernatural virtue was elaborated in the light of the two earlier definitions. For the first, the definition of virtue applied to both ''political virtues'' and ''catholic virtues'' (see Lottin, *opere citato* 374–375). William of Auxerre, surpassing his predecessors in his systematization of virtue, stated that the last phrase of the Lombardian definition distinguished supernatural virtues—he called them ''theological''—from natural or political virtues. The first God alone causes in man; the second are caused by man's own actions [*Summa Aurea* (ed. Pads 1550) fol. 128v–129r].

St. Thomas Aquinas. By the time of St. Thomas, then, the process of Christian thought had applied the concept of habit in the analysis of the nature of virtue. This made it possible to distinguish clearly between natural and supernatural virtues. Aided by the possession of the complete text of Aristotle's *Ethics*, St. Thomas proceeded to elaborate a complete synthesis of virtue. According to his definition, virtue is a good operative habit, or a habit that is good and productive of good (*Summa Theologiae* 1a2ae, 56.1–3). The English ''habit'' does not give satisfactory expression to the meaning of the Latin *habitus*, and is acceptable only when understood as a transliteration retaining the sense of the Latin term. As habit, virtue is the adaptation of those faculties involved in actions under the control of man's deliberative will. Involved in the notion of habit is its employability at will (cf. *Summa Theologiae* 1a2ae, 50.5), and this is important. Thus understood, habits are called ''operative''; they are modifications of man's powers by which these are readied and adapted to specifically human action. On the one hand, human powers are not identical with their activities or their objectives; they are potential and perfectible. On the other, these powers are under man's control and can be directed. He has choices to make and must shape his activities toward his chosen objectives. Operative habits are the set or modification given to his powers that make possible the ready and easy performance of actions leading to those objectives. Virtue as habit, then, is not the approval given an action after it has been performed, but the source of action, a modification over and above the unqualified faculty, inclining it toward its full realization in action.

Virtue is a good habit. Because man directs his activities toward objectives to be realized, and these objectives are in conformity or opposition with the authentic finality of his nature, his actions can be good or bad. But just as his objectives measure the moral value of his activities, so they measure the value of the habits that are the sources of his actions. If these habits give a bent toward truly human goals, then they are good and are called virtues; otherwise they are bad, and are called vices.

Distinction of Virtues. Besides differing from evil habits, virtues differ also among themselves. The powers of man that are perfected by virtuous habits all have their proper spheres of operation. A habit perfecting one operative power differs from a habit perfecting another. But differentiation is possible also within the same general sphere of operation. Differences of object call for differences of adaptation in a power. Any action is obviously what it is, and is distinguished from other kinds of action, because of its reference to some particular object. Thus actions are said to be ''specified'' by their objects. For the same reason, the virtues, as habits ordered to operation, are specified by the diversity of their objects. When there are different objects, different human values, specific kinds or dimensions of goodness, to be realized in human action, a diversity of virtue is necessary to equip man to achieve them.

Subject of Virtue. The power or faculty that is perfected by a virtue is called its subject. Those powers whose activities are fixed and determined by nature are not susceptible to development by habit. They have no need to be adapted to their proper activity. Thus the powers exercised in the purely biological processes of physical life and the sensory powers, which react spontaneously to their proper stimuli, provide no scope for virtue. Only those powers in which originates activity that is the expression of man's controlled self-realization—activity that is humanly determinable—can be the subjects of virtue. The emotive powers, the sensitive appetites, are thus determinable. Although they are concerned with what is agreeable or disagreeable to man's bodily nature, the emotions and the emotive faculties are subject to control by reason and will. One has some choice as to whether he reacts in a purely instinctual way or in a manner consonant with his total welfare as man. This determinability makes virtue necessary if the faculty is to respond regularly and dependably as it should.

Because they correspond to the spiritual nature of the soul, intelligence and will have an orientation that is not determined to a single objective but to truth and goodness in general. However, these powers are perfected by being properly determined with respect to the concrete objects of understanding and volition. The modifications of mind and will effected in the process are virtues if they do in fact relate man reasonably to reality. The idea of virtue is realized only imperfectly in the arts and sciences, whose subject is the intelligence, because through them a man becomes learned or skilled, but not necessarily a better man; they make a man good, but only in a qualified sense. The intellectual virtue of prudence, however, is a virtue in the full sense, because it has as its subject matter the acts of the moral virtues; and through its association with these it becomes a readiness not only to judge soundly but also to act rightly. The will has no need to be regulated by virtue so far as the pursuit of its own good is concerned. Its inherent and innate direction is sufficient to assure that. However, a man's will is less satisfactorily disposed by nature to pursue goods not immediately and obviously identifiable with his own or to pursue a good that transcends the natural order of things. For these effects the will needs to be perfected by the virtue of justice and its allied virtues and by the supernatural and infused virtues.

Acquired Virtues. Virtues are not natural in the sense that they are innate. Inbred characteristics of temperament, even of body, may favor the development of virtue, but they may also lead to vice. Virtue in the natural order can exist only in consequence of deliberate, human activity. In the basic orientation of the mind toward truth and of the will toward the good, there is a certain inclination in the direction of virtue, but it is only

through activity that virtue actually comes into being. Human or moral action inevitably results in the formation either of virtue or of vice. Acting modifies the powers of action. The original indetermination of the operative faculties is affected by the kind of activities exercised. Habits are generated and developed, and these are either good or bad, virtues or vices, depending on the kind of action that brings them into being. The development of virtue, then, is not incidental to human activity, but one of two necessary alternatives. But the dynamics of the development of virtue and vice differ in one important respect. Just as a man cannot perform a good act without intending its moral goodness, so neither can he develop virtues without intending this. On the other hand, just as one sins without intending the moral evil as such, but simply by failing to attend to the true human value in a given situation, so he acquires vice not by setting out to do so, but by failing to develop his powers according to their interrelated human value.

Infused Virtues. That certain permanent principles of actions are divinely infused as a concomitant endowment of grace is Catholic teaching. In addition to the scriptural evidence already cited, the gradual pronouncements of the Church are worthy of note. The letter of Innocent III, *Majores Ecclesiae causas*, to the bishop of Arles in 1201 recognized the distinction between having the virtues of faith, hope and charity and putting them to actual use (H. Denzinger, *Enchiridion symolorum* 780). This position was developed from the doctrine of Peter Lombard and by the middle of the 13th century was commonly accepted by theologians (cf. A. Michel, *Dictionnaire de théologie catholique,* 15:276162). The Council of Vienne in 1312 stated as more probable the opinion that Baptism confers on both adults and infants "informing grace and the virtues" (*Enchiridion symolorum* 904). More positively, it is clear from the Council of Trent that justification includes the reception of grace and gifts, righteousness brings with it faith, hope, and charity. These are said to be "infused"; with respect to charity especially the terms "diffused" and "inhering" are used (*Enchiridion symolorum* 1529–30; 1561). The preparatory discussions reveal that although there was reluctance to employ the technical term habit, there was nevertheless an intention of indicating through the terms used that the gifts bestowed are not passing acts but permanent endowments. Faith's character as an abiding interior gift is brought out by the teaching that it remains even when grace is lost (*Enchiridion symolorum* 1579). Finally, Vatican Council I explicitly described faith as a supernatural virtue (*Enchiridion symolorum* 3008).

That these infused endowments are best described as true virtues is theologically certain. There is not, however, unanimity of opinion with regard to the identification of the infused virtues: some theologians include moral virtues among their number, and some do not. The most notable dissent from the more common opinion that there are infused moral virtues was that of Duns Scotus (*Quaestiones in Librum III Sententiarum*, 36.28; ed. Vivès, 15.701). He insisted that through charity and faith the acquired moral virtues receives a direction as to mode, mean, and end that makes infused moral virtues superfluous. This position has its modern defenders [P. De Voogt, "Y-a-t-il des vertus morales infuses?" *Ephemerides Theologicae Lovanienses* 10 (1933) 3:232–242; O. Lottin, *Principes de morale* 2 (Louvain 1947) 213–225].

In Thomistic thought the supernatural life that man enjoys by grace, while transcending the forces of his nature, is not to be conceived as something alien. It does not consist in a transient and periodic divine intervention; rather the soul and its powers receive abiding sources for living the new life of grace. The soul itself is elevated and transformed by sanctifying grace, so as to become a partaker in God's own nature. Just as in its natural vitality the soul is the source of activity, but through the mediation of its powers, so the activities of the supernatural life come from sanctifying grace through the mediation of the infused virtues. These virtues enable a man to walk in a way corresponding to the life of grace" (*Summa Theologiae* 1a2ae, 110.3). The parallel with man's natural dynamism is extended with regard to the infused virtues in particular. As the natural virtues are rooted in the natural orientation toward human fulfillment, so the theological virtues emanate from grace as adaptations of man toward his supernatural destiny. Parallel to the primary truths of reason in the natural order, there is faith putting man's mind in contact with the truth of his supernatural end. The will is naturally the appetite for perfection; the will is oriented toward eternal life by hope pointing it toward God, and by charity transforming it so that the love of God becomes connatural (*Summa Theologiae* 1a2ae, 62.3). The acquired moral virtues are developed by acts conformed to the direction included in man's primitive natural knowledge and the natural bent of the will. Similarly, God causes moral virtues corresponding to the new life bestowed by grace and the theological virtues. For even as the life of grace is from God, so the sources of a proportionate right conduct can come only from God. These moral virtues, then, are also infused.

Comparison of Natural and Supernatural Virtues. The term virtue is analogical when applied to natural and supernatural habits. Acquired virtues, developed by repeated acts, are modifications of the innate resources of man's faculties, making it second nature for the powers to operate in the most fruitful way. When they are deeply ingrained the possibility of deflection from the best use of the powers is diminished, but is not entirely removed. The infused virtues, however, have a different history. They are immediately caused by God. In this they resemble undeveloped powers of action, conferring simply the capacity, the *posse*, for supernatural activity. Yet they are habits because through them the powers are true principles of a new kind of activity. The infused virtues do not from the outset bestow the facility characteristic of the acquired virtues, nor do they remove dispositions contrary to their own direction. Yet in themselves, because they are graces, they are sufficient principles for virtuous action at all times, not just most of the time, as is the case with the acquired virtues (St. Thomas, *De virt. in comm* 10 ad 14). Further, the acquired virtues make man good in regard to his natural fulfillment; the infused, with regard to his supernatural destiny. Thus the notion of virtue as a habit making man good is diversely verified of each. Only the infused virtues perfect man in regard to the actual goal of human life, which is eternal happiness, and thus they only make man good in an unqualified sense, for supernatural happiness is the actual purpose of all human life (cf. St. Thomas, *Summa Theologiae* 1a2ae, 65.2).

There is further diversity, which is obvious if the acquired virtues are compared with the theological. None of the acquired virtues has the transcendent direction of the theological virtues, which unite man to God as an object known in the knower and an object loved in the lover (cf. *Summa Theologiae* 1a, 8.2). Through faith, hope, and charity man literally shares in God's own knowledge and love of Himself (*Summa Theologiae* 1a2ae, 110.4). Thus they totally transcend all human virtue and belong to man as he is a partaker in the divine life (*Summa Theologiae* 1a2ae, 58.3 ad 3). The rejection of the uniqueness of this order to God apparently led L. Molina (*Concordia* 38) and in later times L. Billot [*De virtutibus infusis* (Rome 1928) 5057] to speak of acquired habits of faith, hope, and charity, supernaturalized only by the influence of actual grace.

The difference between acquired and infused moral virtues is less immediately evident. The general sphere of human conduct, their "matter," is the same for both. But the kind of action appropriate to a man transformed by grace is quite different from what would be expected of him on a purely natural plane. The activities of his emotive powers, his relationships with other men, even his moral decisions have not only a higher purpose but an inherently diverse specification, a proper value. The dimension of goodness specifying the acquired virtues is, in general, the "operability" of actions and emotions by man simply as human; in the case of the infused virtues, it is their operability in reference to man as made a son of God by divine grace. As the moral values differ, so too do the virtues specified by them.

Interrelation of Natural and Infused Virtues. It has been noted that some have denied the necessity of infused moral virtues. The opposite extreme of opinion holds that man in sanctifying grace has no natural but only infused virtues [cf. È. H. Gilson, *The Christian Philosophy of St. Thomas Aquinas* (New York 1956) 337–348]. For those who take the commoner view that there is a place for both natural and infused virtues in the man in grace, the interrelation of the two is developed particularly in connection with the explanation of what happens when there is an increase in facility in the practice of the infused virtues. [See A. F. Coerver, *The Quality of Facility in the Moral Virtues* (Washington 1946) 35–72; J. Harvey, ''The Nature of the Infused Moral Virtues,'' *Proceedings of the Catholic Theological Society of America* (1955) 172–217; G. Klubertanz, ''*Une théorie sur les vertus morales naturelles et surnaturelles,*'' *Revue Thomiste* 59 (Paris 1959) 565–575].

It was to men without grace that the medieval authom, St. Thomas included, ascribed natural virtues. Aquinas held that such virtues do not perfect a man simply speaking, but only with reference to ends in some particular sphere (*Summa Theologiae* 1a2ae, 65.2). In view of his complete teaching on the need for grace for total and effective moral rectification even with respect to natural moral goods (cf. *Summa Theologiae* 1a2ae, 109.2–4, 8), it would seem impossible for man without grace to acquire all the moral virtues. The good habits developed in some particular area would be accompanied by moral deviation in other areas. The fundamental moral choice of God the author of creation as supreme end would lie beyond the range of man's natural abilities. His good habits, then, would not be virtues simply speaking.

It has been suggested that man in grace has need of acquired moral virtues to regulate himself with respect to natural moral values, such, for example, as the payment of debts of justice. But to see acquired virtues as necessary for this purpose seems to imply an artificial dichotomy between the natural and the supernatural life. In every concrete human act the ultimate end of charity itself is in fact involved, and that not merely as directing extrinsically an act of acquired virtue to its own end. The interior value of any act is modified, and its object determined, in accord with charity. When a debt of justice is paid, for example, it is an act measured by the exigencies not only of ''right reason,'' but of charity as well. It is significant that St. Thomas, seeing a specific moral value in the objects of human activity consequent upon the supernatural life of grace, required supernatural moral virtues proportionate to those values. That such activity is commanded

by charity and directed by faith is not enough. The powers proximately engaged must also be rightly disposed to respond to the supernatural dimensions of their objects (*De virt. in comm.* 10. ad 5, ad 10). It does not seem reasonable, therefore, either to allow the acquired virtues to supplant the infused or to see them as functioning in unrelated coordination, as though attending to moral values not accounted for by infused virtues.

The infused virtues are like powers or faculties in that they bestow the basic capacity for their acts; yet they are habits because the powers of man operate through them. In the man in grace, these virtues are the sole principles by which his faculties function in the good moral life. There are no moral virtues acquired from activities based on purely natural sources and motivation. The action of a man in grace through the infused virtues does two things. It merits an increase of the virtue. This increase comes directly from God, and it corresponds to the increase in charity; it takes the form of a fuller possession of the virtues in their essential nature as formal principles of supernatural activity. The other result of virtuous activity is a modification of the faculties themselves. By the repetition of acts the faculties become psychologically accustomed to them. The autonomous response of the faculties to their own unqualified objects is lessened; impediments to their acting in accord with the life of grace are diminished; they become more amenable to what is required by the infused virtues. These dispositions are not the product of the natural energies of the faculties, but are strictly the effect of the supernatural actions produced through the infused virtues. They can be termed simply the increased subjection of the faculties to the infused virtues. As long as man remains in grace, they belong to the infused virtues as their secondary element. If grace is lost, and with it the virtues, the modifications remain, but separated from the formal principles of supernatural action. But they do not become acquired virtues in a proper sense of the term, because they were not acquired by natural activity.

Connection of the Virtues. Even in the sphere of their own activities the moral virtues are interconnected. Prudence is the link that binds them together. The virtues of the will and the emotive powers are exercised in the making of concrete moral choices. Although the virtues themselves dispose the appetitive faculties to seek true moral values in their own sphere, the actual choices depend upon the concrete determination of what the good is in each case. The determination of what should be chosen is the work of PRUDENCE, and hence if prudence is defective a man cannot be perfectly just, temperate, or courageous. On the other hand, prudence presupposes a satisfactory disposition of the appetites with regard to the goals of human conduct, because man's moral decisions involve affective knowledge; they are judgments to which assent is given on the basis of appetitive dispositions. Thus, unless a man's appetites are rectified by the moral virtues, prudence cannot make right moral decisions (*Summa Theologiae* 1a2ae, 65.1).

The moral virtues are also connected in charity. Right moral decisions cannot be made unless the will is habitually conformed to God as loved above all by charity. Nor is it on prudence alone that charity exercises its influence. The totality of charity's love for God also measures the moral values in all other areas of human concern (cf. *Summa Theologiae* 2a2ae, 23.7,8; 24.12), so that upon charity depends the very specification of the infused moral virtues. This is seen most clearly in such virtues as patience (*Summa Theologiae* 2a2ae, 136.3), humility (ibid. 161), virginity (*ibid.* 152), Christian magnanimity (*ibid.* 129), but it is also verified in so primary a virtue as temperance (*Summa Theologiae* 1a2ae, 63.4 and ad 2). The objects of all the infused moral virtues are measured according to the totality of charity's act of the love of God (*Summa Theologiae* 2a2ae, 24.12; 1a2ae, 71.4).

As to the connection of the theological virtues, it is Catholic teaching, declared by the Council of Trent, that even with the loss of grace through mortal sin, faith may remain (H. Denzinger, *Enchiridion symolorum* 1578). It is the common teaching of theologians that hope may remain as well. But if grace and charity are lost, neither faith nor hope remain as perfect virtues. The perfect work of faith requires the right adherence of the will to the object of assent, and this adherence is by charity. Faith without love is called "unformed" (*informis*); it is neither salutary nor effective of true Christian living. Hope aspires to eternal life, but with God's help to enable man to merit it, and this presuppose charity, the source of meritorious activity (*Summa Theologiae* 1a2ae, 65.4). Charity itself presupposes faith and hope; faith, to put before man's mind the object of charity's love; hope, to bestow upon man the will to enter charity's union of friendship with God (*Summa Theologiae* 1a2ae, 65.6).

Right Mean of Virtue. Virtues are sources of actions in conformity with the true objectives of human life. These objectives are thus the measure according to which an act is good or bad. Deviations can be by way of excess or defect, and hence conformity is said to be a "mean" between extremes. All the virtues consist in a mean in the sense that all are causative of acts that are good and thus conform to their measure. Among the moral virtues, prudence achieves this mean by directing toward concrete, balanced choice; the other moral virtues, by being the habitual conformity of the appetites toward the mean dictated by prudence. As sources of good actions, some virtues are themselves essentially midway between two vices of

excess and defect, but this is not always the case. Virtue's mean may be simply a "mean of reason," as when the moral good in an object is determined simply in reference to the subjective dispositions of the virtuous person. In the sphere of justice, however, the mean of virtue demands also that the real reference of actions to other persons be respected. Thus the mean of virtue here includes a "real mean," that is determined by objective and exterior considerations. The acts of the theological virtues have God as their object and measure, and these acts are more perfect according as they tend toward a more complete and intense union with Him. Thus one cannot love God, or believe Him, or trust in Him, too much. Only in the sense that the acts of these virtues may be exercised in unsuitable circumstances, or are directed to what is not properly embraced in the object of the virtue, can they be said to be excessive. Thus presumption appears to be an excess of hope. But it is not; the presumptuous man does not put his trust in God or rely upon His promises; on the contrary, he puts his trust in what God has not promised.

Bibliography: Basic works. THOMAS AQUINAS, *Summa Theologiae* 1a2ae,4970, see esp. tr. by R. BERNARD, *La Vertu*, 2 v. (Paris 1933–35); *De virt. in comm.; De virt. card.; De carit.; De spe; In 2 eth; La Prudence* (*Summa Theologiae* 2a2ae, 47–56), tr. and ed. T. H. DEMAN (2d ed. Paris 1949). P. BONNETAIN, *Dictionnaire de la Bible,* suppl. ed. L. PIROT, et al. (Paris 1928–) 3:7011319. T. DEMAN and F. DE LANVERSIN, *Dictionnaire de spiritualité ascétique et mystique. Doctrine et histoire,* ed., M. VILLER et al. (Paris 1932) 1:137166. A. MICHEL, *Dictionnaire de théologie catholique,* ed. A. VACANT, 15 v. (Paris 1903–50; Tables générales 1951–) 15.2:2739–99. **Hist. works.** A. LANDGRAF, "Die Erkenntnis der heiligmachenden Gnade in der Früh- scholastik," *Scholastik* 3 (1928) 28–64; "Studien zur Erkenntnis des Übernatürlichen in der Frühscholastik," *ibid.* 4 (1929) 1–37, 189–220, 352–389. O. LOTTIN, "Les Premières définitions et classifications des vertus au moyen âge," *Psychologie et morale aux XIIe et XIIIe siècles,* 6 v. in 8 (Louvain 1942–60) 3.1:99–150; "Les Vertus cardinales et leurs ramifications chez les théologiens de 1230 à 1250," *ibid.* 3.1:153–194; "La Connexion des vertus chez Saint Thomas d'Aquin et ses prédécesseurs," *ibid.* 3.1:197–252; "Les Vertus morales infuses pendent la séconde moitié du XIIIe siècle," *ibid.* 3.2:459–535; "La Connexion des vertus morales acquises de Saint Thomas d'Aquin à Jean Duns Scot, *ibid.* 4.2:552–663; "Les Vertus morales infuses au début du XIVe siècle," *ibid.* 4.2:739–807. **Doctrinal works.** L. BILLOT, *De virtutibus infusis* (5th ed. Rome 1928). BONAVENTURE, *Commentarius in 2 libri sententiarum* 27, dubium 2, in *Opera omnia,* ed. D. FLEMING, 10 v. (Quaracchi-Florence 1882–1902) 2:670–671. G. BULLET, *Vertus morales infuses et vertus morales acquises selon Saint Thomas d'Aquin* (Fribourg 1958). R. F. COERVER, *The Quality of Facility in the Moral Virtues* (Washington 1946). R. A. GAUTHIER, *Magnanimité* (Paris 1951). T. GRAF, *De subiecto psychico gratiae et virtutum secundum doctrinam scholasticorum usque at medium saeculum XIV,* 2 v. (St. Anselm 2, 3, 4; Rome 1934–35). A. GRAHAM, *The Love of God* (New York 1939). A. M. HENRY, ed., *Man and His Happiness,* tr. C. MILTNER (Theology Library 3; Chicago 1956). R. GARRIGOU-LAGRANGE, *Christian Perfection and Contemplation,* tr. T. DOYLE (St. Louis 1937); *The Three Ages of the Interior Life,* tr. M. T. DOYLE, 2 v. (St. Louis 1947–48). O. LOTTIN, *Principes de morale,* 2 v. (Louvain 1947) v.2. P. LUMBRERAS, *De habitibus et virtutibus in communi*

(Rome 1950); "Notes on the Connexion of the Virtues," *Thomist* 11 (1948) 218–240. C. MAZZELLA, *De virtutibus infusis* (3d ed. Rome 1884). J. M. PARENT, "Les Venus morales infuses dans la vie chrétienne," *Theologie* (Ottawa-Montreal 1944) 179–223. P. P. PARENTE, *The Ascetical Life* (rev. ed. St. Louis 1955). A. ROYO, *The Theology of Christian Perfection,* ed. and tr. J. AUMANN (Dubuque 1962). C. SHEEDY, *The Christian Virtues* (2d ed. Notre Dame, IN 1956). G. C. MEILAENDER, *The Theory and Practice of Virtue* (Notre Dame 1984). A. C. MACINTYRE, *After Virtue: A Study in Moral Theory* (Notre Dame 1981); *Dependent Rational Animals: Why Human Beings Need the Virtues* (Chicago 1999). J. PORTER, *The Recovery of Virtue: The Relevance of Aquinas for Christian Ethics* (Louisville 1990). R. CESSARIO, *Moral Virtue and Theological Ethics* (Notre Dame 1991). S. PINCKAERS, *The Sources of Christian Ethics,* tr. M. T. NOBLE (Washington, DC 1995)

[T. C. O'BRIEN]

VIRTUE, HEROIC

A term first used by Aristotle in the *Nicomachean Ethics* where he spoke of "superhuman virtue," or moral virtue on a heroic or godlike scale (1145a 15–30). Through St. Albert the Great and St. Thomas Aquinas, who borrowed it from Aristotle, the term found its way into scholastic and later ascetico-mystical use. In its adoption by Christianity the term became rich with Christian meaning. It was applied to Christian perfection, the concept of which, drawn from the Scriptures, had been elaborately developed in the writings of the Fathers, in monastic literature, spiritual biographies, and treatises on the spiritual life.

The martyr was the first to be venerated as a "saint," but Clement of Alexandria, Origen, Cyprian, and others likened the intense effort to grow in virtue to martyrdom. Thus the type of the holy "confessor" came to be recognized, for which a basis of extraordinary virtue was understood to be requisite. [See L. V. Hertling, "Der mittelalterliche Heiligentypus nach den Tugendkatalogen," *Zeitschrift für Aszese und Mystik* (Würzburg 1933) 8, 260–268.] The strict inquiry into the holiness of a servant of God, according to the scheme of the three theological and the four cardinal virtues, was first made in the process of canonization for St. Bonaventure in 1482. By the time of the Renaissance, heroic virtue had become a technical term for the holiness necessary for beatification or canonization.

In Beatification and Canonization. Prospero Lambertini (later BENEDICT XIV) was the first to organize and evaluate the theological and juridical thought of his own and earlier times upon the subject in his five-volume work *De beatificatione Servorum Dei et de Beatorum canonizatione* (Bologna 1734–38). This became and remained the classical study of the subject. The norms it laid down have been applied consistently by the Congregation of Rites in passing judgment upon heroic virtue. According to Lambertini, the attainment of a heroic degree of natural virtue of one kind or another was theoretically possible to nature unaided by grace, though it was rarely, if ever, actually so attained. This was an achievement reserved to the people of God under the Old Law and to the Church under the law of grace. Moreover, with the aid of grace, a heroic degree of the supernatural or infused virtues, theological and moral, was attainable.

They are called heroic when their exercise exceeds what is ordinary even among those who live virtuously. The heroic degree is, in fact, simply the perfection of virtue. It does not differ in kind from ordinary virtue, but only in the excellence of its act and the intensity of the habit from which it comes. Heroic virtue is based upon the intensity of charity. Although the counsels are ordered to charity, perfection does not consist in these, but primarily and per se in the fulfillment of the precepts of the law, and particularly of the precept of charity. Hence it is not necessary to heroic virtue that its act should be of counsel rather than of precept. Moreover, a few heroic acts do not suffice as evidence of heroic virtue. They must be numerous in proportion to the opportunities for action, and examples of heroism must be shown in the exercise of the different virtues. Perfect virtues are interconnected, so that a person who has one will also have the others. Still, their perfection is manifest through their interconnection, and consequently proof is necessary that a servant of God possessed them all. The existence of venial sin, even if committed deliberately and after a person has attained the level of heroic virtue, does not exclude him from beatification, provided satisfaction was made for the sin and precautions taken against its recurrence. One must have lived for a certain extended period of time in the state of heroic virtue, but the length of this time cannot be precisely determined, for in some cases a person can be raised to a height of holiness that will compensate for the relative shortness of its duration. No proof of infused contemplation is necessary for beatification. CHARISMS, such as the gift of prophecy, ecstasy, or visions, by themselves are not satisfactory evidence of the heroic virtue necessary for beatification (*see* MYSTICAL PHENOMENA). Neither are miracles wrought during a servant of God's lifetime.

Modern Emphasis. In later times, Benedict XV insisted upon the connection between heroic virtue and the duties of a person's state of life: heroicity consists in the faithful and constant fulfillment of the duties and obligations of one's state [*Acta Apostolicae Sedis* 14 (Rome 1922) 23; *ibid.,* 12 (Rome 1920) 170–174]. So also Pius XI declared that heroic virtue was to be sought in the ordinary things of daily life [*Discorsi di Pio XI* (Turin 1960) 1:73–74, 759–760]. The Church's judgment upon a person's heroic virtue involves no judgment upon the supernatural character of the extraordinary phenomena, such as visions or stigmata, that may have marked his life.

Reasons for Caution. One of the reasons for the care taken by the Church in passing formal judgment upon a person's holiness is that a psychopathological counterfeit of heroic virtue is possible. The Christian ought indeed to strive for perfection and thus give glory to God. But this striving can, in subtle and almost unconscious ways, be perverted by egoistic ambition. Such a distortion can have its roots in a person's neurotic need for prestige and admiration, or in an unwillingness to accept gracefully limitations or a want of success in other aspects of life. In such circumstances an individual can be drawn to externalize the idea that he has of holiness, and may want to appear conspicuously humble, charitable, and zealous. He acts the part of a ''saint,'' and may permit himself to be treated as a ''saint.'' Unfortunately, this kind of veneration may be readily forthcoming, for there is often no dearth of misguided souls who seek miracles and other wonders by associating themselves with such a ''saint'' and by propagating his reputation for holiness.

See Also: VIRTUE; PERFECTION, SPIRITUAL; CANONIZATION OF SAINTS.

Bibliography: A. RADEMACHER, *Das Seelenleben der Heiligen*, 4 v. (4th and 5th ed. Paderborn 1923). H. DELEHAYE, *Sanctus: Essai sur le culte des saints dans l'antiquité* (Subsida hagiographica 17; Brussels 1927). GABRIEL DE STE. MARIE-MADELEINÉ, ''Normes actuelles de la sainteté,'' *Études Carmélitaines* 28 (1949) 175–188. K. RAHNER, ''Die Kirche der Heiligen.'' *Schriften zur Theologie*, 3 v. (Einsiedeln 1954–56) 3:111–126, English tr. v.1, 1962. R. HOFMANN, *Die heroische Tugend: Geschichte und Inhalt eines theologischen Begriffes* (Munich 1933).

[K. V. TRUHLAR]

VIRTUES AND VICES, ICONOGRAPHY OF

The personification of virtues and vices, extant in medieval manuscript illumination and sculptural decoration, occurs early in Christian literature.

Early Literary Formulation. Its formulation is found first in Tertullian's *De spectaculis* (29), where the vices and virtues are personified as two armies contending for the soul. This antagonism of the virtues and vices as expressing various moral conflicts within the soul received its epic imagery later in the *Psychomachia,* an allegorical poem written by the Christian poet, A. C. PRUDENTIUS (348–after 405). In the poem of Prudentius

the seven conflicting pairs personified (to be submitted later to considerable variations or additions or both) are: Worship of the Ancient Gods (*Vetera cultura deorum*) and Faith (*Fides*), Lust (*Libido*) and Modesty (*Pudicitia*), Anger (*Ira*) and Patience (*Patientia*), Pride (*Superbia*) and Humility (*Mens Humilis*), Avarice (*Avaritia*) and works of Charity (*Operatio,* with the assistance of *Ratio*), Harmony (*Concordia*) and Discord (*Discordia*). At the end of the struggle, the victorious virtues erect a temple to Wisdom.

Visual Representation. Already in a fresco of the S. Gennaro catacombs (Naples) three virtues were depicted completing a tower symbolizing the church. Sixteen illuminated manuscripts of Prudentius's *Psychomachia* bear witness to the channeling of the theme into Christian art. They date from the 9th century to 1298. The illustrated prototypes are lost. In them, as well as in the pattern books that circulated from one scriptorium to another, the fight of the virtues against the vices was originally represented as battle scenes themselves copied after sculptured groups of warriors and battle scenes of late Roman art. From the 9th century on, the complex and dynamic story of the battle depicted in the narrative style was superseded by a sequence of duels between two opposed enemies: a virtue and its contrary, the corresponding vice. Impersonal allegorical figures were replaced by characters dressed in contemporary costume or by demons. Apart from the *Psychomachia,* the whole drama is seen in the *Gospels* of Henry the Lion (by Hermann of Helmarshausen, *c.* 1175) and, with the addition of supplementary figures of virtues, in the ivory front cover of the Melisenda Psalter (British Museum, *c.* 1131–44). In the *Hortus Deliciarum* of Herrad von Landsberg (*c.* 1185) the three theological virtues, clad as knights, followed by the four cardinal virtues, are arrayed phalanx-like behind the leading Humility. They hold a sword symbolizing the Word of God while Faith carries the cross staff and Temperance a vase whose contents are pouring into a mixing bowl. That distribution, which opposed Humility and her companions to Superbia and her suite, derives from the *De fructibus carnis et spiritus,* a treatise attributed to Hugh of Saint-Victor.

The very triumph of the virtues was pregnant with a more static theme in those formulations where they stand over the vices. The immobile imagery that one may detect also in Prudentius's *Peristephanon* was influenced by imperial iconography in which the ruler, after his victory, crushes underfoot his defeated enemy (exemplified in late Roman coinage, and on a Carolingian ivory book cover in the National Museum, Florence), as well as by that of Christ trampling the monsters [Ps 90(91).13]. Types of specific virtues in the Old Testament became associated with their embodiments in the Bamberg Apoca-

The cycle of the Virtues and Vices, Last Judgement Portal, Notre Dame, Paris, c. 1210. (Alinari-Art Reference/Art Resource, NY)

lypse (1001–02): Abraham with Obedience, Moses with Purity, David with Penitence, Job with Patience. During the 12th century in Mosan enamels and in an illumination of a copy of Conrad of Hirsau's *Speculum Virginum* (British Museum, second quarter of the 12th century), the emphasis was laid on the victory of Humility as the root of all virtues, over Superbia as root of all vices. In a drawing illustrating an allegorizing tract written in Ratisbon (*c.* 1170–85), the cross on which Christ is crucified transfixes the four monsters mentioned in Psalm 90 while Humility stabs Pride (Munich, Bayerische Staatsbibliothek, Cod. Pat. 14159 fol. 5).

Incorporation in Sculptural Ornamentation. The *Psychomachia* in its static formulation met an extraordinary fortune in Romanesque sculpture of Western France, a region where painted representations survive also (for instance in the crypt of the church at Tavant). The figures of Prudentius's virtues standing over the vices were carved along the archivolts of tympanumless

portals or blind arcades. The *Psychomachia* was also incorporated into the iconographical program of the Last Judgment through the parable of the wise and foolish virgins (Saint-Gilles's portal at Argenton-Château, *c.* 1135). The elongated figures of virtues, covered by oval pointed shields, enframing a window in the south transept of the church of Saint-Pierre, Aulnay (*c.* 1130), reappeared along the jambs of the Porte Mantile of Tournai cathedral, *c.* 1170. In the cycle of the west front of the cathedral of Strasbourg (*c.* 1280), both the virtues triumphant and the virgins of the Last Judgment parable are standing figures, no longer allegorized, but represented as attractive women. Toward the close of the 12th century, the *Psychomachia* was given an archivolt over the Magi portal in the west front of the cathedral of Laon, side by side with the types of the Virgin in the Old Testament. The psychomachy archivolt in the north porch of Chartres cathedral, in the early 13th century, was connected, in the same manner as at Laon, with a program dedicated to the life and glorification of the Virgin.

Reflecting the allegorized theology of the 12th century and anticipating the logical disquisitions of the 13th-century scholastic *Summae,* 12 pairs of virtues and vices were set up on the plinths, left and right of the Last Judgment portal of the west front of the cathedral of Paris, *c.* 1210. In the upper rows of each side the virtues were exquisitely carved in relief under trefoils. On the right side are: Humility, Prudence, Chastity, Charity, Hope, and Faith; and, on the other side: Fortitude, Patience, Gentleness, Harmony, Obedience, and Perseverance. Each holds her proper emblem in a disc: dove, serpent, the fabulous bird *charista* (which, without igniting, hovers above a blazing mountain), lamb, banner, cross and chalice, lion, ox, sheep, olive branch, camel, and crown of life. The virtues are allegorically treated and engage only in a few gestures (Charity distributes clothing, Hope reaches for a crown, and Fortitude holds a sword upright). The vices, represented below them in a lower relief and sunk in roundels, allude to instances of sinful life: the falling rider (Pride) followed by a fool; a harlot looking at herself in a mirror; a miserly woman; a suicide; an idolator; a knight fleeing from a hare; a lord threatening a monk; a master kicking a servant; a brawl; an altercation between a bishop and a layman; and a monk eloping from his abbey.

Many iconographical features appear to have been inspired by law treatises (*Decreta*) and manuals of penitence (*Poenitentialia*). The 12 pairs illustrating the conceptual contest between the virtues and the vices occupied a place on the jambs of the Paris Notre Dame portal under the 12 statues of the Apostles, who assist Christ on Last Judgment day. Medallions of the virtues and vices were added also, as warning footnotes to the Last Judgment, in the western stained glass rose window of the same Paris cathedral. This occurs also on the plinths of the jambs under the Apostles of the central portal of Amiens Cathedral (*c.* 1230) and on the central piers, south porch of Chartres cathedral (*c.* 1240).

Bibliography: R. STETTINER, *Die illustrierten Prudentius Handschriften* (Berlin 1905). P. DESCHAMPS, "Le Combat des vertus et des vices sur les portails romans de la Saintonge et du Poitou," *Congrès Archéologique de France . . . à Reims en 1911,* 2 v. (Paris 1912) 2:309. A. E. M. KATZENELLENBOGEN, *Allegories of the Virtues and Vices in Mediaeval Art* (London 1939).

[P. VERDIER]

VISCH, CHARLES DE

Cistercian historian; b. Bulscamp (Flanders), *c.* 1600; d. Les Dunes, April 11, 1666. He joined the Cistercian community of Les Dunes near Bruges and was professed in 1618. During the first phase of the Thirty Years' War, the monks were dispersed and Visch sought refuge in several German monasteries, including Eberbach where, from 1628 on, he was professor of theology. Later he acted as chaplain of the Cistercian nuns of Val Céleste. Meanwhile Visch copied and collected a large number of Cistercian manuscripts. In 1646 he became prior of Les Dunes and devoted the rest of his life to the composition and publication of his great and still indispensable bio-bibliographical work: *Bibliotheca scriptorum S. Ordinis Cisterciensis* (1st ed. Douai 1649; 2d corrected and augmented ed. Cologne 1656). Further additions remained in manuscript form until they were edited by J. M. Canivez, "Auctarium D. Caroli de Visch ad Bibliothecam Scriptorum S.O. Cisterciensis," *Cisterciencer-Chronik* 38–39 (1926–27, serial; offprint, Bregenz 1927).

Bibliography: P. A. FRUYTIER, "Namenliste der Religiosen von Eberbach aus dem Jahre 1631 von Karl De Visch," *Cisterciencer-Chronik* 26 (1914) 267–272. J. MERCIER, *Dictionnaire de théologie catholique,* ed. A. VACANT, 15 v. (Paris 1903–50; Tables générales 1951–) 15.2:3098–99.

[L. J. LEKAI]

VISDELOU, CLAUDE DE

Sinologist and opponent of the CHINESE RITES; b. Château de Bienassis, Pléneuf, France, Aug. 22, 1656; d. Pondicherry, French India, Nov. 11, 1737. He entered the Society of Jesus on Sept. 5, 1673, and was sent to China in 1685. Although he laid the foundations for the celebrated French Beijing mission, he is more renowned as a Sinologist than as an active missionary. When Charles de TOURNON, papal legate for Clement XI, arrived in Canton, April 8, 1705, Visdelou was the sole Jesuit adverse to the adoption of the Chinese rites. Tournon, who had banned the Malabar rites in India on June 23, 1704, was banished from Beijing by Emperor K'ang-hi for attempting a similar prohibition in China. The legate traveled to Nanjing and there issued a decree on Jan. 25, 1707, obliging all missionaries under pain of excommunication to abolish the rites. He also made Visdelou vicar apostolic of Guiyang with the title of bishop of Claudiopolis. Against the opposition of his Jesuit superiors, Visdelou was consecrated at Macao on Feb. 12, 1708, and in June of that year moved to Pondicherry. There he lived in retirement with the Capuchins until his death. During these 28 years he wrote on the rites, and composed a chronology of Chinese history, a life of Confucius, and the valuable *Histoire de Tartarie.*

Bibliography: C. SOMMERVOGEL, *Bibliotèque de la Compagnie de Jésus,* 11 v. (Brussels-Paris 1890–1932) 8:838–843.

[E. D. MCSHANE]

The ten avatars of the Hindu god Vishnu. (Archive Photos)

VISHNU

Now one of the two principal gods of HINDUISM, but originally a solar deity of no great importance in the Vedas. Later he was identified with Vāsudeva, a non-Aryan hero, and with Nārāyana, a cosmic deity, and came to be worshipped as the Supreme God, the Creator and Preserver of the world. He is represented sleeping in the primeval ocean on the thousand-headed snake Śeṣa, while Brahmā, the demiurge, is born from a lotus that springs from his navel. He is usually depicted as four-armed, bearing in his hands the conch, the discus, the mace, and the lotus, which are his emblems, and riding on the eagle, Garuḍa. His spouse, Lakṣmī, is the goddess of wealth. Vishnu is believed to have manifested himself by his descent (*avatāra*) in different forms to save mankind. His descent in the form of Krishna is celebrated in the *Bhagavad Gītā* and later in the Vishnu and *Bhāgavata Purāṇas*.

[B. GRIFFITHS]

VISIBILITY OF THE CHURCH

Scripture clearly shows that the Church must appear visibly in the world. Yet Catholics and their separated brethren are split on the precise way in which the visibility of the Church is related to its essence as well as upon the precise nature of the elements that necessarily belong to the Church's visible side. To understand the gulf separating the two points of view it is necessary to investigate the extension of the visibility of the Church, its ultimate foundation, and its final perfection.

"The Church is visible because it is a Body" (H. Denzinger, *Enchiridion symbolorum* 3300). This affirmation of Pope Leo XIII reflects the scriptural designations of the Church as the "body of Christ" (1 Cor 12.27; Eph 4.12), the "people of God" (Heb 4.9; 1 Pt 2.10), the "house of God" (Heb 10.21; cf. 1 Pt 4.17), the "city of the living God" (Heb 12.22; cf. Rv 3.12). It reflects, too, the constant mention in the m of visibly determinable local Churches—Churches to which St. Paul wrote his various letters.

However, it is not the existence but the precise nature of this visibility that divides Catholic and Protestant. For most Protestants the Church is essentially invisible. Its visible elements are necessary for the presence and spread of the invisible Church but are not to be completely identified with it. The visible elements are not so united to the invisible elements that together they constitute but one Church in a manner analogous to the way that the invisible soul and the visible body constitute a single man.

In the Catholic concept, however, visibility belongs to the very essence of the Church. In the Church Christ does work through the Spirit (*see* SOUL OF THE CHURCH) to bind the members together in an invisible union through the possession of common supernatural virtues and gifts. But at the same time the Church also has a Christ-instituted visible side. In its teaching authority and ruling authority, in its discernible priestly office and sacramental ministry, in the whole Body of its membership that is identified by BAPTISM and the acceptance of a common faith and a common ruling authority, Christ also works through the Holy Spirit. And the whole organism—both in its invisible and visible aspects—constitutes but one Church. Thus, visibility is an essential component of the mystery of the Church, and the profession of belief in the Church made in the Creeds is a profession of belief in the Church in its total extension, visible and invisible.

The ultimate ground for the compenetration of the visible and invisible, the divine and the human, in the Church is the divine plan of salvation that culminates in Christ. Throughout the OT period the invisible God carried on His salvific purpose through visible men. In Christ (*see* JESUS CHRIST, ARTICLES ON) this process reached its climax; in Him the divine became so immersed in the human and the visible that the acts of One who walked on earth in visible form became the cause of universal eternal salvation (*see* INCARNATION). It is this salvific work that is continued in the Church by a union of the divine power and visible human elements that is analogous to the union of the divine and human in Christ.

This does not mean that the visible element in the Church is now perfect as is the human element in Christ. Only on the last day (*see* PAROUSIA), when all creation will be utterly subjected to the rule of the Spirit and the definitive reign of God over things invisible and visible is established—only then will the visible element in the Church be perfect. Until then the Church's visible aspect will remain a blend of the imperfect and the perfect: imperfect in the prudential judgments of its leaders, in the lives of all its members; perfect (at least in a limited sense) in the efficacy of its Sacraments, in the infallibility of its teaching office. Through these latter perfect elements the Church points to and anticipates the perfection of the last days.

See Also: MIRACLE, MORAL (THE CHURCH); MARKS OF THE CHURCH; MYSTICAL BODY OF CHRIST; CHURCH, ARTICLES ON.

Bibliography: J. B. WALZ, *Die Sichtbarkeit der Kirche* (Würzburg 1924). E. DUBLANCHY, *Dictionnaire de théologie catholique,* ed. A. VACANT et al. (Paris 1903–50) 4.2:2138–45, Tables générales 1:1115–16. C. JOURNET, *L'Église du verbe incarné,* 2 v. (2d ed. Bruges 1954–62) v. 2. B. C. BUTLER, *The Idea of the Church* (Baltimore 1962). M. SCHMAUS, *Katholische Dogmatik,* 5 v. in 8 (5th ed. Munich 1953–59; 6th ed. 1960) 3.1:391–409, with full bibliog.

[P. F. CHIRICO]

Pelayo leads the Visigoths against the Moors. (Archive Photos)

VISIGOTHS

An east Germanic tribe, part of the Gothic peoples who migrated in the first century B.C. from southern Sweden (Gotland) to the mouth of the Vistula and at the end of the second century A.D. to the Black Sea coast of southern Russia. They split in the mid-third century into Ostrogoths and Visigoths.

The Visigoths expanded their territory north of the Danube to the west (Dacia). After thrusts to the Bithynian Black Sea coast (258), Ephesus (262), and Cappadocia (*c.* 264), the Visigoths launched a largescale expedition against Greece that ended (269) in an annihilating defeat for them near Naissus. They did not risk substantial inroads on the territories of the Roman Empire until Constantine's clash with Licinius offered them an opportunity of invading in the direction of Moesia and Thrace. Emperor CONSTANTINE I made them *foederati* of the Roman Empire in 332 and bound them to defense of the Danube frontier for annual subsidies.

Christianity was first brought to the Goths by Christians taken as prisoners from Cappadocia and by the native populace of the Crimean Peninsula and Dacia. Bishop Theophilus of Gothia took part in the Council of Nicaea I (325), but the key figure was ULFILAS, consecrated bishop of the Goths by EUSEBIUS OF NICOMEDIA in Constantinople (probably 341); Ulfilas was a Homoiousian Arian. Upon the outbreak of a persecution of the Christians in 348 among the Danubean Goths, Ulfilas and the majority of his fellow believers fled; they were settled (most probably 348 or 349) by CONSTANTIUS II near Nicopolis (Lower Moesia). While Athanaric was implementing a bloody persecution of Christians. (*c.* 370), his rival Fritigern became a convert to Arian Christianity in order to win the Roman Emperor VALENS to his side.

At Fritigern's invitation, Ulfilas preached the gospel to the Visigoths north of the Danube. The Hunnic tide drove the portion of the Visigoths led by Fritigern across the Danube (376). Valens settled them as *foederati* on crown land (Thrace), but soon they began marching on Constantinople. In a furious battle near Adrianople, Valens was beaten and killed Aug. 9, 378. This defeat was a turning point in the fortunes of the Roman Empire.

THEODOSIUS I settled the Visigoths in Thrace and Moesia in 382, but he was unsuccessful in his efforts to bring the Visigoths to accept Niceanism after the return of the Imperial Church to Orthodoxy (381). The Visigoths, on the contrary, brought their Arian faith to the Ostrogoths, Burgundians, and Vandals, who were thus split off in religion from the orthodox population of the empire. In 395 the Visigoths left Thrace under King Alaric and crossed Macedonia and the whole of Greece. In 401 Alaric led his people to Italy, besieged Rome (408–409), and took the city in August 410. The population and the churches were spared in the ensuing pillage, but the Romans suffered a severe trauma from the fall of Rome (Augustine, *Civ.*).

Alaric's brother-in-law, King Athaulf (410–415) led the Visigoths to Gaul and married Galla Placida. Under his brother Wallia (415–418), the Visigoths were settled as *foederati* between the Loire and Garonne, but Theodoric I (419–451) made himself independent of the Emperor. In 419 the Tolosan Kingdom of the Visigoths with its capital at Toulouse began; it attained its greatest extent under Euric (466–484); Spain and Gaul to the Loire were

in the hands of the Visigoths. Although Goths and native provincials were divided by difference of religious confession and by marriage, an assimilation of Roman and Germanic customs and laws (*Codex Euricianus*) followed. The Visigoths were tolerant toward the Catholic population; Euric, however, made efforts to eliminate the Catholic hierarchy, that was opposed to the Arian foreign rule; so did Alaric II (485–507) temporarily, because of the conspiratorial liaison between the episcopate and the Frankish King CLOVIS who had become a Catholic. The king of the Franks attacked the Visigoths, for their alleged heretical beliefs; Alaric fell in the battle of Vouillé (507) and the Visigothic kingdom was thenceforth limited to Spain (with the exception of Galicia, ruled by the Suevi) and a coastal strip in Gaul reaching to the Rhone.

The latent tension between Catholic Romans and Arian Visigoths in the Spanish Visigoth kingdom with its capital at Toledo, was exacerbated under Agila (d. 554) into a conflict, and when the southeast coast of Spain had been reconquered for the Byzantine Empire (*see* JUSTINIAN I, BYZANTINE EMPEROR), Leovigild (568–586) began open warfare, exiling bishops, facilitating conversion to Arianism, and having his Catholic son Hermenegild, who was allied with Byzantium, put to death in 585.

With the acceptance of the Catholic faith by Reccared (king since 586), the end came for Arianism in Spain; and Arius was anathematized in 589 at the Synod of Toledo. The King summoned royal synods mainly in Toledo, which dealt equally with ecclesiastical and state affairs. These assemblies witness to the intimate contact between the State and the Church; the latter, despite its pronounced autonomy, maintained its contact with Rome. LEANDER and ISIDORE OF SEVILLE were pioneers and representatives of ecclesiastical flowering and cultural advance. The fact that the Code of Recceswind (654) introduced a single law for all citizens was a proof of the total fusion of all the tribes in the Visigoth kingdom. Later the kingdom was weakened in proportion to the loss of harmony between Church and State. The Visigothic kingdom was destroyed in 711 by the Arabs in the battle of Xeres de la Fontera.

Bibliography: L. SCHMIDT, *Die Ostgermanen,* v.1 of *Geschichte der deutschen Stämme* (2d ed. Munich 1941). *Cambridge Medieval History* (London-New York 1911–36) 1:183–217, 250–292. E. STEIN, *Histoire du Bas-Empire,* tr. J. R. PALANQUE (Paris 1949–59) v.1. R. MENÉNDEZ PIDAL, ed., *Historia de España,* v.3 (Madrid 1940). K. F. STROHEKER, *Eurich* (Stuttgart 1937); "Leowigild," *Die Welt als Geschichte* 5 (1939) 446–485. H. HELBLING, *Goten und Wandalen* (Zurich 1954). E. A. THOMPSON, "The Visigoths from Fritigern to Euric," *Historia* 12 (1963) 105–126. A. K. ZIEGLER, *Church and State in Visigothic Spain* (Washington 1930). H. E. GIESECKE, *Die Ostgermanen und der Arianismus* (Berlin 1939). A. LIPPOLD, *Paulys Realenzyklopädie der klassischen Al-*

tertumswissenschaft, ed. G. WISSOWA et al. (Stuttgart 1893–) 9A (1961) 512–532.

[K. H. SCHWARTE]

VISINTAINER, AMABILE LUCIA, BL.

Religious name: Mother Paulina of the Agonizing Heart of Jesus (Paolina del Cuore Agonizzante di Gesú); foundress of the Daughters of the Immaculate Conception (*Irmazinhas da Imaculada Conceiçao*); b. Vigolo Vattaro, Trentino, Italy (then Austria) Dec.16, 1865; d. Sao Paolo, Brazil, July 9, 1942. For two years before emigrating to Brazil with her family (1875), Amabile, the daughter of Antonio Napoleone Visintainer and Anna Pianezzer, worked in the local silk mill. With other immigrants they established the village of Vigolo (now part of Nova Trento, sixty miles from Florianópolis) in Santa Catarina Province. Upon her mother's death in 1886, Amabile assumed household responsibilities and cared for her twelve siblings.

When her father remarried, Amabile was free to respond to her recurring dream of religious life. Together with Virginia Nicolodi and Teresa Maoli, Amabile pronounced religious vows on Dec. 7, 1895, before Bishop José de Camargo Barros of Curitaiba, and assumed the name Paolina. The bishop approved the religious order that began in 1890 with Amabile and Virginia nursing a woman with cancer in an abandoned shack.

The Sisters of the Immaculate Conception soon spread to nearby towns and to Sao Paolo where they directed hospitals and asylums and assisted the recently emancipated slaves. In 1909, after difficult internal conflicts in the order, Mother Paolina accepted her removal from the office of mother general "ad vitam" by the archbishop, Duarte Leopoldo da Silva.

For the next ten years she humbly served her sisters at Santa Casa de Bragança Paulista and remained assiduous in prayer. Although she never reclaimed her office as superior, Mother Paolina's reputation was rehabilitated, and she was venerated during her lifetime as the congregation's founder. Beginning in 1938, she suffered complications from illness and cancer that lead to her death.

Upon her beatification (Oct. 18, 1991) by Pope John Paul II at Florianópolis, Sao Paulo, Brazil, she became the first Brazilian citizen to be raised to the altars. On July 7, 2001, Pope John Paul II approved the miracle necessary for canonization.

Feast: July 9 (Bolzano).

Bibliography: F. A. FARACE, *Love's Harvest: The Life of Blessed Pauline,* ed. J. KINDEL and B. LEWIS (Milford, Ohio 1994). *L'Osservatore Romano,* English edition, no. 19 (1995): 6.

[K. I. RABENSTEIN]

VISION (DREAM) LITERATURE

Many writings of the ancients, the Bible, and early and late Christian and pagan records contain dreams and visions that purport to be revelations from the divinity: warnings, omens, instructions, prophecies. Fascinated by the phenomenon, man has speculated about the nature of dreams, their cause, classification, and meaning (*see* DREAM; VISIONS.)

The term vision or dream literature is applied generally to narrations that use dreams or visions as an artistic device. All attempts to classify the many kinds of literary dreams or visions seem unsuccessful; those that are religious and those that are profane, those occurring in sleep and those in waking hours, those that are clearly didactic, and those that are playfully fanciful are all known as dreams, visions, or dream visions. In such a general way Cicero's *Somnium Scipionis, The Dream of the Rood,* the *Divina commedia, Le Roman de la Rose,* and Joyce's *Finnegans Wake* all fall in the category of dream or vision literature. The most typical poetic convention of 18th-century Irish Gaelic literature was the *Aisling* (vision poem).

An author may use a dream as the frame for his entire work, or he may narrate a dream within a larger, different context. The dream may be introduced abruptly and succinctly or more circuitously and artfully. "I will declare the best of the dreams I dreamt" is sufficient transition from the world of reality to the dream world for one author, while another may approach the dream by elaborate descriptions of circumstances that led to it. The recounted dreams or visions serve various purposes. Many, especially in the early Christian tradition, were eschatological; the dream section in the *Shepherd* of HERMAS may perhaps be instanced. Some attempt to inculcate moral truths; *PIERS PLOWMAN* is an example. Others are apocalyptic; Cardinal Newman's *The Dream of Gerontius* (1866) falls in this category. In dreams recounted in secular literature, fashionable social conventions are depicted, utopias are proposed, man's shortcomings are satirized, allegories enacted, and fantasies enjoyed.

When dreams are only incidental to the main literary work, they may be alleged as the source of inspiration for the composition or they may be fitted into the action to advance the plot, to whet the interest of the reader, to point a moral, to heighten suspense by forecasting events, to achieve atmosphere, or to accommodate the writer who wishes to make use of the dream as a flashback.

Not a few literary visions spring from a form of mysticism, as in BLAKE'S fantasies, or are rooted in genuine supernatural experiences (*see* MYSTICISM IN LITERATURE; MYSTICS, ENGLISH).

Bibliography: W. S. MESSER, *The Dream in Homer and Greek Tragedy* (New York 1918). J. B. STEARNS, *Studies of the Dream as a Technical Device in Latin Epic and Drama* (Lancaster, PA 1927). M. DODS, *Forerunners of Dante* (Edinburgh 1903). W. O. SYPHERD, *Studies in Chaucer's House of Fame* (London 1907). R. L. WOODS, ed., *The World of Dreams: An Anthology* (New York 1947).

[G. M. LIEGEY]

VISIONS

A supernatural vision is a CHARISM (*gratia gratis data*) through which an individual perceives some object that is naturally invisible to man. The term "supernatural" is used to distinguish true visions from illusions or hallucinations caused by pathological mental states or diabolical influence. The term "charismatic" is used to exclude the illuminations that ordinarily accompany mystical activity (cf. St. John of the Cross, *Ascent of Mount Carmel*, bk. 2, ch. 11, 17, 24; St. Teresa of Avila, *The Life*, ch. 28–29; *Interior Castle*, 6th Mansions ch. 9). St. Augustine, and after him, St. John of the Cross, St. Teresa of Avila, and St. Thomas Aquinas, divided visions into corporeal, imaginative, and intellectual.

In a corporeal vision, also called an apparition, the eyes perceive an object that is normally invisible to the sense of sight. This may be caused by an external object or by some power impressing an image directly on the sense of sight. A corporeal vision could be caused directly by God or mediately through an angelic power. It could also be caused by the devil or be a purely natural phenomenon (optical illusion). Imaginative vision is a phantasm supernaturally caused in the imagination without the aid of the sense of sight. It may occur during sleep, or in waking hours when it is usually accompanied by ecstasy. The vision may be symbolic (the ladder in Jacob's dream), personal (vision of the Sacred Heart to St. Margaret Mary), or dramatic (the vision during the mystical espousal of St. Catherine of Siena). Signs of the supernatural origin of imaginative visions are that they produce greater virtue in the soul; they cannot be produced or dismissed at will; they leave the soul in great peace (cf. St. Teresa of Avila, *Interior Castle*, 6th Mansions, ch. 10; J. G. Arintero, *The Mystical Evolution*, v. 2, ch. 7). Imaginative visions can proceed also from diabolical influence or purely natural causes. In an intellectual vision a simple intuitive knowledge is produced supernaturally without the aid of any impressed species in the internal or external senses (*see* SPECIES, INTENTIONAL). The impression may last for hours or days, unlike the lower types of vision, which are usually transitory. It may occur during sleep or in waking hours, but only God can produce it, since only God has access to the human intellect. It gives remarkable certitude to the visionary. The vision is often a simple mental intuition of some truth or mystery that is seen by the intellect without any form or image (cf. St. Teresa of Avila, *The Life*, ch. 27; *Interior Castle* 6th Mansions, ch. 8).

Apparitions of Christ, Mary, and the blessed are to be considered as representations effected through the instrumentality of angels (cf. St. Thomas, *In 4 sent.* 44 sol. 3 ad 4). Visions of the divine essence are to be considered as "some kind of representation" (cf. St. Teresa of Avila, *Interior Castle,* 7th Mansions, ch. 1) and not an intuitive vision of the divine essence, although some theologians admit the possibility of a transitory beatific vision in this life (cf. St. Thomas, *Summa theologiae* 2a2ae, 175.3). Angels or demons could be permitted by God to assume some material form, as of a cloud, vapor, or rays of light. The same explanation can be offered for the appearance of those who are dead, for the separated human soul is a purely spiritual substance (cf. St. Thomas, *ibid.* 1a, 51.2 ad 2; Suppl. 69.3). The appearance of persons still living on earth is an apparent BILOCATION and is to be judged accordingly (*see* MYSTICAL PHENOMENA).

Like charisms, visions are primarily for the good of others. They are not proofs of sanctity and are not to be sought or desired, since they are not necessary for salvation or sanctity. On the other hand, illuminations that are concomitant with the mystical state are primarily for the benefit of the mystic who receives them and they may be desired.

The word of a visionary cannot be taken as certain proof that a vision was supernatural in origin. It could have been the result of diabolical intervention or the pathological state of the individual. Even in devout souls it is possible for the subliminal activity of the subconscious to influence the conscious mind so that the individual is unwittingly a victim of illusion. In such instances the most that can be granted is a negative approval, namely, that there is nothing in the vision contrary to faith and morals.

Bibliography: JOHN OF THE CROSS, *Ascent of Mount Carmel,* bk 2, v.1 of *Complete Works,* ed. P. SILVERIO DE SANTA TERESA and E. A. PEERS, 3 v. (Westminster, Md. 1953). TERESA OF AVILA, *Complete Works,* ed. P. SILVERIO DE SANTA TERESA and E. A. PEERS, 3 v. (New York 1946), v.1 *The Life,* 10–300; v.2 *Interior Castle,* 199–351. THOMAS AQUINAS, *Summa theologiae* 2a2ae, 171–175. J. G. ARINTERO, *The Mystical Evolution in the Development and Vitality of the Church,* tr. J. AUMANN, 2 v. (St. Louis 1949–51) 2:304–333. A. ROYO and J. AUMANN, *The Theology of Christian Perfection* (Dubuque, IA 1962) 655–658. R. GARRIGOU-LAGRANGE,

The Three Ages of the Interior Life, tr. T. DOYLE, 2 v. (St. Louis 1947–48) 2:280-288. A. F. POULAIN, *The Graces of Interior Prayer*, tr. L. L. SMITH (6th ed. St. Louis 1950) 266–297.

[J. AUMANN]

VISITATION NUNS

(VHM; Official Catholic Directory #4190) Founded June 6, 1610, at Annecy, France, by St. FRANCIS DE SALES and St. Jane Frances de CHANTAL, who wished to form a simple congregation, contemplative but not cloistered, devoted to the apostolate of visiting the sick poor in their homes. For five years the Visitandines fulfilled this purpose at Annecy. However, after the second foundation was made at Lyons, the archbishop of that see, Cardinal de Marquemont, insisted that the congregation be raised to the status of a religious order with solemn vows and strict enclosure. Francis de Sales yielded to this request, but held to his plan of admitting widows, those in delicate health, and women of advanced age, as well as young girls. The Rule of St. Augustine was adopted and enforced by constitutions that successive popes praised for their ''wisdom and discretion.'' Interior mortification replaced the corporal austerities characteristic of other orders founded at that time. Exact observance of the daily order as prescribed in the Spiritual Directory was designed to foster an atmosphere of prayer, a spirit of dependence, and union with God. Humility before God and meekness toward one's neighbor constitute the spirit of the order. The nuns chant the Little Office of the Blessed Virgin, adding hymns and prayers from the Breviary for Sundays and designated feasts.

Expansion and Government. When Francis de Sales died in 1622 there were 13 monasteries; in 1641, the year of Jane de Chantal's death, the number had increased to 85. By 1700 the order was established in Italy, Switzerland, Belgium, Germany, and Poland. During the 18th century it spread to England, Austria, Syria, Spain, and Portugal; in the 19th century, to the U.S., South America, and Czechoslovakia. It also reappeared in France, where all monasteries had been suppressed during the French Revolution. During the 20th century foundations were made in Mexico, Canada, Hungary, and Ireland.

Visitation monasteries are grouped according to regional federations. Each federation is governed by a regional superior. The monasteries remain autonomous. Papal enclosure, either major or minor, is enforced throughout the institute. In the U.S. monasteries were grouped into two federations: the First Federation of North America and the Second Federation of North America.

Apostolate. Although Francis de Sales did not intend the teaching apostolate for the Visitation nuns, they nevertheless conducted private academies to combat heresy even before 1641. When monasteries were reestablished in France after the Revolution, schools were reopened. In the U.S. the GEORGETOWN VISITATION foundation at Washington, D.C., was made in 1799 under Bp. Leonard Neale, SJ, of Baltimore, Md., who sponsored the community and gave them the Rule of the Visitation. In 1815 Pius VII, at Neale's request, granted the foundation the rights and privileges of the Visitation order. This foundation and the 13 that branched from it conduct academies. In 1853 a foundation from Montluel, France, was made in Keokuk, Iowa; from this developed five others, of which three survived: Georgetown, Ky.; Rock Island, Ill.; and Tacoma, Wash. All conducted academies. The Keokuk community transferred to Wilmington, Del., in 1868, closed their school in 1893, and reverted to the strictly contemplative life. During the next 50 years the same change was made by monasteries descended from the Georgetown foundation, in New York; Washington, D.C.; Richmond, Va.; and Philadelphia, Pa. In 1915 the Georgetown nuns founded a strictly contemplative monastery in Toledo, Ohio, from which the monastery of Atlanta, Ga., was founded in 1954, bringing the number of strictly contemplative monasteries in the U.S. to seven. The monasteries with schools include those in Georgetown, D.C.; St. Louis, Mo.; Baltimore, Frederick, and Catonsville, Md.; Wheeling and Parkersburg, W. Va.; Brooklyn, N.Y.; Rock Island and Springfield, Ill.; St. Paul, Minn.; and Georgetown, Ky. The monasteries of Mobile, Ala., and Tacoma, Wash., engage in retreat work. The unifying apostolate of the Visitation nuns is the spread of devotion to the Sacred Heart, which became distinctive after the revelations of the Sacred Heart to St. Margaret Mary ALACOQUE at Paray-le-Monial, France, between 1673 and 1675. The apostolate found new expression in the Confraternity of the Guard of Honor of the Sacred Heart, established at the monastery of Bourg, France, in 1863; the organization was raised to an archcon-fraternity by the Holy See in 1878.

Bibliography: É. BOUGAUD, *The Life of St. Chantal and the Foundation of the Visitation*, 2 v. (New York 1895). FRANCIS DE SALES, *The Interior Spirit of the Religious of the Visitation of Holy Mary* (Cork, Ire. 1943). G. P. and R. H. LATHROP, *A Study of Courage: Annals of the Georgetown Convent of the Visitation* (Cambridge, Mass. 1895). M. L. LYNN, *The Silver is Mine: A Brief History of St. Joseph's Monastery of the Visitation 1853–1953* (Wilmington, Del. 1953).

[M. L. LYNN/EDS.]

VISITATION OF MARY

The Gospel account of Mary's journey and visit to St. ELIZABETH. It forms part of the Lucan INFANCY GOSPEL and so should be interpreted against the broader background of the theology of Luke ch. 1–2. The incident follows immediately upon the ANNUNCIATION, on which occasion Mary learned that her cousin Elizabeth had conceived a child (Lk 1.36).

Gospel Account. Mary went in haste, (or possibly, as C. Stuhlmueller suggests, "in deep thought") to the hill country of Judea to the house of Zachary (1.39). There is no certainty as to the exact location of the town, but since the 6th century, tradition has located it about six miles west of Jerusalem (see C. Kopp, 90–96).

The incident is related very simply. Mary entered the house and greeted Elizabeth. As soon as Elizabeth heard Mary's greeting the infant in her womb leapt for joy, and Elizabeth was filled with the Holy Spirit (1.40–41). Joy and the outpouring of the Spirit were two signs of the advent of the messianic era. Elizabeth cried out: "Blessed art thou among women [i.e., beyond any other woman; cf. Jdt 13.23] and blessed is the fruit of thy womb! How have I deserved that the mother of my Lord should come to me? For the moment that the sound of thy greeting came to my ears, the babe in my womb leapt for joy" (Lk 1.42–44). Then Elizabeth praised Mary's faith, which is here set in relief (Lk 1.45). Mary was not called blessed because of the future accomplishment of that which was proposed for her faith, but because of her faith itself (M. J. Lagrange). Elizabeth exalts Mary as later her son, JOHN THE BAPTIST, will exalt the Son of Mary. The praise of Mary's faith recalls a very important messianic theme of the Old Testament that was underlined by Isaiah, who received his call to faith immediately before his oracle concerning EMMANUEL (Is 7.14).

Mary answered Elizabeth with her MAGNIFICAT. She remained with her cousin for three months. Although at first glance the text seems to indicate that Mary left the house of Zachary before the birth of John (Lk 1.56), this would have been unlikely, since she had gone to assist her cousin. Luke had a stylistic habit of finishing one incident before beginning the narrative of another.

Theology. The allusive use of Old Testament texts to communicate a deeper theological meaning is evident here. Mary, the Virgin Daughter of ZION, the dwelling place of Yahweh, and the perfect eschatological personification of Israel, is presented in the Visitation account as the new ark of the covenant. There is a marked literary dependence on 2 Sm 6.9–15, which tells the story of the bringing of the ark to Jerusalem by David. As David and his people rejoiced in the presence of the ark (2 Sm 6.12–15), so did Elizabeth and her unborn child in the presence of Mary. As David leapt for joy before the ark (2 Sm 6.14), so did John in his mother's womb (Lk 1.44). The cry of David, "How shall the ark of the Lord come to me?" (2 Sm 6.9), is echoed by that of Elizabeth, "How have I deserved that the mother of my Lord should come to me?" (Lk 1.43), which is probably a paraphrase of David's words. As the ark remained for three months in the house of Obededom (2 Sm 6.11), so did Mary remain for three months in the house of Zachary (Lk 1.56).

The person of Mary is put into prominent relief throughout the whole account. It is Mary who greets Elizabeth, and it is after hearing the greeting of Mary that Elizabeth hails her as the Mother of her Lord. Honor comes to Elizabeth because it is the visit of the Mother of the Lord.

In Liturgy and Art. The Feast of the Visitation, of medieval origin, had been kept by the Franciscan Order before it was extended to the universal Church by Urban VI in 1389. The date of celebration was fixed on July 2 by the Council of Basel in 1441. The present liturgical texts date from the reform of Clement VIII (1592–1605). In thanksgiving for his safe return to the Papal States in 1850, Pius IX elevated the feast to a higher rank.

There is no trace of the representation of the Visitation in the Catacombs. The first representations date from the 5th and 6th centuries. The Visitation has been a popular subject in art from the late Middle Ages to modern times, but particularly in the 15th and 16th centuries. While secondary scenes in the story, such as Mary traveling over the mountains, assisting at the birth of John, or back at Nazareth after her journey, are occasionally portrayed, most frequent are representations of the meeting of the two women. In some 16th-century paintings the two infants are actually portrayed in visible form in their mother's wombs.

Bibliography: R. LAURENTIN, *Structure et théologie de Luc I–II ÉtBibl* (Paris 1957). M. J. LAGRANGE, *Évangile selon Saint Luc* (Paris 1927). C. STUHLMUELLER, *The Gospel of St. Luke* (Collegeville, MN 1960). *Encyclopedic Dictionary of the Bible*, translated and adapted by L. HARTMAN (New York, 1963) 1059–61. L. RÉAU, *Iconographie de l'art chrétien*, 6 v. (Paris 1955–59) 2.2:195–210. C. KOPP, *The Holy Places of the Gospels*, tr. R. WALLS (New York 1963) 90–96.

[M. E. MC IVER]

VISITATION SISTERS, MARTYRS OF, BB.

Maria Gabriela de Hinojosa Naveros, and six other members of the Order of the Visitation of Holy Mary; b.

"The Visitation" of the Virgin Mary to her cousin Elizabeth (the mother of St. John the Baptist), ca. 1200. (©Archivo Iconografico, S.A/CORBIS)

Alhama, Granada, Spain, July 24, 1872; d. Nov. 18, 1936. Five of her sister companions died with her: Josefa Maria Barrera Izaguirre, b. El Ferrol, La Coruna May 23, 1881; Teresa Maria Cavestany y Anduaga, b. Puerto Real, Cadiz, July 30, 1888; Maria Angela Olaizola Garagarza, b. Azpeitia, Guipuzcoa, Nov. 12, 1893; Maria Engracia Lecuona Aramburu, b. Oyarzun, Guipuzcoa, July 2, 1897; and Maria Ines Zudaire Galdeano, b. Echavarri, Navarra, Jan. 28, 1900. Maria Cecilia Cendoya Araquistain (b. Azpeita, Guipuzcoa, Jan. 10, 1910) escaped execution with the rest, but was martyred five days later, Nov. 23, 1936. They were beatified May 10, 1998 by John Paul II.

All of the nuns had been brought up in deeply Christian families, but they represented varying social and economic backgrounds. They were bonded in their vocation to the Order of the Visitation, in their communal and contemplative prayer, and in the value they placed on life lived in community, where they performed the ordinary tasks of daily life with great love and fidelity.

The religious persecution marking the Spanish civil war intensified during the first months of 1936, and convents and churches were looted and burned. The Sisters of the Visitation realized that it was too dangerous for their community—numbering more than 80 sisters—to stay in Madrid and decided to move to Oronoz, a small town in Navarra. However, they felt called to maintain a presence in the capital, where the monastery church was one of the few still open for worship; thus seven nuns were asked to remain. Before leaving, the superior of the community rented a basement apartment nearby to serve as a shelter if the sisters who were to stay ever needed a place of refuge. S. Maria Gabriela de Hinojosa was given charge of the group.

The sisters were able to continue in the monastery for only one month. On July 13, 1936 they moved to the apartment, but spent their days in the monastery—ringing the bells, trying to give the impression that it was lived in. The situation deteriorated, however, and by the end of July it was impossible for the sisters to leave the apartment. Occasionally a priest slipped in and celebrated Mass, and the extern sisters attempted to do errands, but it was dangerous: S. Maria Angela was arrested, booked, and warned. The sisters could be seen from the street as they moved about, and friends warned them to apply to foreign consulates for refuge. The Visitandines were convinced that the neighbors who had seen them in the interior courtyard respected them and would keep their secret. They refused to consider separating. However, they were reported and both they and those who had helped them were denounced.

On August 14 the apartment was searched and soldiers carried off their belongings. After this, the community became entirely dependent on others for provisions. The house was searched again; S. Teresa Maria Cavestany was taken captive and S. Josefa Maria Barrera, who had previously declared herself fearful now bravely offered to accompany her. The police detained both nuns for 24 hours.

The militia searched the apartment yet again on November 17, remarking as they left that they would return the following day. S. Maria Gabriela called the sisters together and offered them a chance to seek refuge in foreign consulates, but they refused. They spent that night in prayer, preparing themselves for death. On the evening of November 18, a patrol of the Iberian Anarchist Federation broke into the apartment. They ordered the sisters out. A mob gathered in the street, demanding that they be shot immediately. Each had made the sign of the cross as she entered a waiting van—an act of defiance in the eyes of the government. They were driven to a vacant lot on Lopez de Hoyos Street in Madrid. As the nuns emerged two by two, clasping hands to support one another, a barrage of gunfire shattered their bodies.

S. Maria Cecilia, 26 years old, felt S. Maria Gabriela fall next to her and dropped her hand. She took off running, fleeing instinctively. A short time later she surrendered herself to the militiamen, declaring that she too was a nun and wanted to die as her sisters had. She was held in a crowded cell for five days before being shot against the wall of the cemetery in Vallecas in the outskirts of Madrid. S. Maria Cecilia's cross, worn over her heart as a sign of her religious profession, was retrieved, pierced by a bullet. Because of S. Maria Cecilia's incarceration, the story of the sisters' martyrdom became public. Prisoners held in the same cell with her later shared her story with others.

Speaking of the Visitation Martyrs at their beatification, Pope John Paul II emphasized their fidelity to their own charism of gentleness and nonviolence. "I beg God that the marvelous example of these women who shed their blood for Christ, pardoning from their hearts their executioners . . . may succeed in softening the hearts of those who today use terror and violence to impose their will upon others."

Feast: Nov. 18.

Bibliography: JOHN PAUL II, "Allocution" (Remarks at the End of the Mass and Rite of Beatification of Visitation Martyrs and Others) May 10, 1998.

[M. GELL]

VISSER'T HOOFT, WILLEM ADOLF

Internationally recognized leader of the modern ecumenical movement; b. Haarlem, Netherlands, Sept. 20,

1900; d. Geneva, Switzerland, July 4, 1985. Visser't Hooft did his doctoral studies at the University of Leiden writing his thesis on ''The Background of the Social Gospel in America.'' He married Jetty Boddaert in 1924, the same year he became secretary of the World Committee of the Young Men's Christian Association (YMCA). As its youngest participant, Visser't Hooft was present at the 1925 Stockholm conference on Life and Work. In 1931 he was elected general secretary of the World's Student Christian Federation.

At the World Conference on Life and Work held in Oxford, 1937, he served as chairperson of the subsection on ''The Church and War.'' He was present, too, at the Second World Conference on Faith and Order in Edinburgh, Scotland, that same year. Each of these consultations voted for the creation of the World Council of Churches to carry on the pioneering programs of Faith and Order and Life and Work in one organization. At Utrecht in 1938 Visser't Hooft was elected general secretary of the Provisional Committee for the World Council of Churches (in Process of Formation). He carried that responsibility until the inauguration of the World Council of Churches at its first Assembly in Amsterdam in 1948. He there assumed the post of the first general secretary of the new ecumenical organization, a position he held until 1966.

In Amsterdam in 1939, Visser't Hooft chaired the Steering Committee of the World Conference of Christian youth. When World War II broke out and hostilities intensified around Switzerland, he remained in Geneva to assist refugees from Nazi Germany and to act as a communications link between churches in occupied territories and the rest of the world.

The year of his retirement, 1966, saw a virtual flood of expressions of recognition and honor for his long and distinguished ecumenical career. He remained active after his retirement. Nearly to the time of his death he continued to visit the Ecumenical Center in Geneva to work and to consult with staff and visitors over tea. He also carried on a series of informal discussion sessions in his Geneva home on the history of the ecumenical movement. He produced five major books after his retirement, including his *Memoirs* which appeared first in Dutch in 1971. His beloved wife and colleague died in 1968.

In addition to his autobiography, Visser't Hooft's books include: *Anglo-Catholicism and Orthodoxy* (1933); *No Other Gods* (1937); *The Church and its Function in Society* (with J. H. Oldham 1937); *The Wretchedness and Greatness of the Church* (1944); *The Struggle of the Dutch Church* (1946); *The Kingship of Christ* (1948); *The Meaning of Ecumenical* (1953); *The Renewal of the Church* (1956); *The Pressure of Our Common Calling* (1959); *No Other Name: The Choice between Syncretism and Christian Universalism* (1963); *Peace amongst Christians* (1967); *Has the Ecumenical Movement a Future?* (1974); *Genesis and Formation of the World Council of Churches* (1982); and *The Fatherhood of God in an Age of Emancipation* (1982).

Johannes Cardinal Willebrands, president of the Vatican Secretariat for Promoting Christian Unity, observed at the time of Visser't Hooft's death that their friendship embodied more than a personal relationship. He said that Visser't Hooft's perceptive mind made him aware of the importance of the participation of the Roman Catholic Church in the ecumenical movement, and the problems it created. Visser't Hooft's relationship with the Roman Catholic Church directly, or through close friends such as Cardinal Bea, was always marked by a love for and in Christ, which lies at the heart of ecumenism.

Bibliography: Ecumenical Press Service (July 6–10,1985) 52:24. W. A. VISSER'T HOOFT, *Memoirs* (Philadelphia 1973). H. BERKHOF, ''Visser't Hooft as Ecumenical Theologian,'' EcumRev 38 (April 1986) 203–208. A.J. VAND DER BENT, ed. *Voices of Unity: Essays in Honour of Willem Adolf Visser't Hooft on the Occasion of His Eightieth Birthday* (Geneva 1981).

[D. F. MARTENSEN]

VITAL DU FOUR

Otherwise known as Vidal or Vitalis de Furno, Franciscan philosopher and theologian; b. Bazas, near Bordeaux, *c.* 1260; d. Avignon, Aug. 16, 1327. He studied theology at Paris (1285–91) under Jacques du Quesnoy and Raymond Rigaut, then taught at his order's *studium generale* at Montpellier from 1292 to 1296 and at Toulouse from 1296 to 1307. From 1307 to 1312 he served as minister provincial of Aquitaine. Created cardinal in 1312, he was consecrated bishop of Albano in 1321. He served in various capacities at the papal court of Clement V and John XXII. During the controversies arising at the universities and in the Franciscan Order concerning the doctrine of PETER JOHN OLIVI, he was appointed to the board of examiners studying the propositions submitted for condemnation. Pope John XXII assigned him to help in the composition of the papal bull against Bonagratia of Bergamo in his dispute concerning the poverty of Christ. He took sides with the Franciscan Spirituals on the question of apostolic poverty, thus incurring the disfavor of the Pope. Among his numerous works is a commentary on the four books of the *Sentences,* several quodlibets, the *Speculum morale totius sacrae scripturae* (Lyons 1513), sermons, and disputed questions. The *De rerum principio,* edited erroneously under the name of

DUNS SCOTUS (Quaracchi 1910), contains at least 15 of his disputed questions. F. Delorme has edited "Le Cardinal Vital du Four: Huit questions disputées sur le problème de la connaissance" [*Archives d'histoire doctrinale et littéraire du moyen-âge* 2 (1927) 157–337], and *Vitalis de Furno SRE. Card. Quodlibeta tria* (Rome 1947).

Vital belongs to the pre-Scotistic Franciscan school, holding many doctrines in common with MATTHEW OF AQUASPARTA, JOHN PECKHAM, GILES OF ROME, and ROGER MARSTON. His later doctrines show the influence of HENRY OF GHENT. He taught that the essence of real beings is identical with their existence, admitting only an intentional distinction in the individual. Existence is essence itself as related to its efficient cause. Actual existence is the principle of individuation. Of particular interest is his theory of special intellectual illumination by which he interprets the operation of eternal reasons. Natural understanding, aided by the general concursus of God, is capable of direct cognition of concepts. To discover the ultimate foundation of truth (*sincera veritas*), an extraordinary intervention by God in the form of an efficient special illumination is necessary. This divine illumination is conceived as an intimate union of the soul with the light of God. Though not always faithful to his school, Vital does, nevertheless, follow the main Bonaventurian doctrines, e.g., the intellectual cognition of the singular, the direct and intuitive self-knowledge of the soul as to its existence and essence, and the plurality of forms in the soul.

Bibliography: F. X. PUTALLAZ, "La Connaissance de Soi au Moyen Age: Vital du Four," in *Mèlanges Bèrubè: Ètudes de Philosophie et Thèologie Mèdièvales Offertes a Camille Bèrubè, OFM-Cap pour son 80e anniversaire,* ed., V. CRISCOLO (Rome 1991). J. LYNCH, *The Theory of Knowledge of Vital du Four* (St. Bonaventure, N.Y. 1972), bibliography.

[M. J. GRAJEWSKI]

VITALIAN, POPE, ST.

Pontificate: July 30, 657 to Jan. 27, 672; b. Segni, near Rome; buried in St. Peter's. At his election, Vitalian notified the Emperor CONSTANS II and his son, Constantine IV Pogonatus, by a synodical letter; in it Vitalian did not mention the TYPOS by which Constans II forbade the discussion of MONOTHELITISM. This omission was considered a conciliatory gesture as was his letter to Peter, patriarch of Constantinople. Probably the burning issues were simply not discussed. The emperor confirmed Vitalian's election, renewed the privileges of the Roman See, and sent rich presents. The schism ended and Vitalian's name was inscribed in the dipitychs at Constantinople; he was the first pope to be thus recognized after HONORIUS I (d. 638).

Constans II, fearing for Africa, Italy, and Sicily, terribly threatened by Muslim naval supremacy in the Mediterranean, visited Rome in July 663. Royally received by Vitalian, Constans visited the major churches, bestowing rich gifts but stripping St. Mary of the Martyrs (the Pantheon) of its bronze tile roof. After an unsuccessful attempt to check the Lombards of Benevento, he returned to Syracuse, where he remained until his death by assassination (668). Constans had oppressed his subjects with taxes, considered exorbitant, but probably necessary in the desperate military emergency.

Over Vitalian's protest Constans approved the rejection of Rome's metropolitan control by Maurus, the rebellious archbishop of Ravenna, thereby making Ravenna "autocephalous." In 666 Vitalian protested also against obstacles that Archbishop Paul of Crete placed in the way of Bishop John of Lappa's appeal to Rome, where John received justice and redress.

Deeply interested in the development of the Anglo-Saxon Church, Vitalian supported the efforts of Oswy, king of Northumbria, after the Synod of WHITBY (664) to establish Roman usage regarding tonsure and the date of Easter. For this purpose he consecrated Theodore of Tarsus (March 26, 668), a Greek monk living in Rome, as archbishop of Canterbury with full powers over the English Church (*see* THEODORE OF CANTERBURY). Wulfhere, king of Mercia, endowed PETERBOROUGH monastery, placing it immediately under Vitalian, an early example of a monastery under papal protection.

Feast: Jan. 27.

Bibliography: *Regesta pontificum romanorum ab condita ecclesia ad annum post Christum natum 1198,* ed. P. EWALD (Graz 1956) 1:235–237; 2:699, 740. *Liber pontificalis,* ed. L. DUCHESNE (Paris 1886–92) 1:343–345. C. J. VON HEFELE, *Histoire des conciles d'après les documents originaux,* tr. and continued by H. LECLERCQ (Paris 1907–38) 3.1:472–475. H. K. MANN, *The Lives of the Popes in the Early Middle Ages from 590 to 1304* (London 1902–32) 1.2:1–16. A. FLICHE and V. MARTIN, *Histoire de l'église depuis les origines jusqu'à nos jours* (Paris 1935—) 5:176–179, 403. É. AMANN, *Dictionnaire de théologie catholique,* ed. A. VACANT et al., (Paris 1903–50) 15.2:3115–17. R. ABELS, "The Council of Whitby: A Study in Early Anglo-Saxon Politics," *Journal of British Studies* 23 (Chicago, IL 1983/1984) 1: 1–25. P. CLEMOES, ed., *Anglo-Saxon England* (Cambridge 1979). P. FELICI, "San Vitaliano papa, assertore dell'unità con l'Oriente," *Oikoumenikon* 12 (Rome 1972), 2, 394–400. B. S. NAVARRA, "Musica e musicisti a Segni," *Lunario* 15 (Rome 1986) 51–66. B. S. NAVARRA, "Vitaliano," *La Storia di Segni* 2 (1998) 47–60. E. PULSFORT, *Biographisch-Bibliographisches Kirchenlexikon,* 12 (Herzberg 1997) s.v. "Vitalian, Papst." V. R. STALBAUMER, "The Canterbury School of Theodore and Hadrian," *American Benedictine Review* (Collegeville, MN 1971) 46–63. A. N. STATOS, "Expédition de l'empereur Constantin III surnommé Constant en Italie," in *Bisanzio e l'Italia. Raccolta di studi in memoria di Agostino Pertusi* (Milan 1982) 348–57. J. N. D. KELLY, *Oxford Dictionary of Popes* (New York 1986) 75.

[C. M. AHERNE]

VITALIS, ST.

Benedictine hermit; d. S. Maria delle Viole, near Assisi, Italy, probably May 31, 1370. Vitalis, an outlaw in his early life, turned to a life of asceticism. The Benedictines of Monte Subasio received him and assigned him the hermitage connected with the chapel of S. Maria delle Viole. There he lived 20 years in severe mortification. His example led to the foundation of a society of laymen, dedicated to the care of the sick and needy, which existed until the 17th century. His body was buried in the chapel of S. Maria until 1587, when it was transferred to the cathedral at Assisi. He was honored as a saint there as early as 1377. His feast day was first celebrated by the Cobblers Guild on January 7; then on May 31, on which day a procession, displaying his relics, is held.

Feast: May 31; Sept. 22 (translation).

Bibliography: *Acta Sanctorum* May 7:467. A. M. ZIMMERMANN, *Kalendarium Benedictinum: Die Heiligen und Seligen des Benediktinerorderns und seiner Zweige,* 4 v. (Metten 1933–38) 2:252–253.

[J. J. SMITH]

VITALIS OF SALZBURG, ST.

Abbot-bishop of SANKT PETERS; d. Oct. 20, *c.* 730. Although the *Liber vitae* (*Verbrüderungsbuch*) lists him as the third, the *Conversio* calls him the immediate successor of RUPERT OF SALZBURG and also *seminator verbi Dei.* Supported by this evidence and by the fact that the bondmen of St. Peter's in Pinzgau annually paid a rent of bread and cheese on October 20, the feast and probable date of the saint's death, the legend of his missionary activity in Pinzgau has spread. Authentic sources are not extant. The cult of Vitalis, popular since the late Middle Ages, was approved for the abbey in 1519 and for the archdiocese of Salzburg in 1628; the canonization process, begun in 1459, was never completed. Vitalis is portrayed as a bishop with a white lily growing out of his heart.

Feast: Oct. 20.

Bibliography: *Conversio Bagoariorum et Carantanorum,* ed. M. KOS (Laibach 1936) 128. *Monumenta Germaniae Historica* (Berlin 1826–), Necrologia 2:18. P. KARNER, *Die Heiligen und Seligen Salzburgs* (Austria Sancta 12; Vienna 1913). M. SHELLHORN, *Lexikon für Theologie und Kirche,* ed. M. BUCHBERGER, 10 v. (Freiburg 1930–38) 10:653, uncritical.

[H. WOLFRAM]

VITALIS OF SAVIGNY, BL.

Abbot; b. Tierceville, near Bayeux, France, 1060–65; d. Savigny, Sept. 16, 1122. He was the founder of the Benedictine Congregation of SAVIGNY. About 1082 he became a chaplain to Robert, count of Mortain, the Conqueror's brother. After 1095 he lived as a hermit in the forest of Craon with other ascetics, including ROBERT OF ARBRISSEL. Even then his fame as a preacher spread, and he visited England several times. Sometime after 1105 he went to the forest of Savigny where a number of disciples joined him. Their abbey was established most likely in 1112 and its rule seems to have been consciously modeled upon that of CÎTEAUX, stressing agricultural work, lay brothers, visitation, and general chapters. Savigny influenced both English and Norman monasticism for a quarter century after its founder's death—until the congregation merged with the CISTERCIANS in 1147.

Feast: Sept. 16 and Jan. 7.

Bibliography: *Acta Sanctorum* (Antwerp 1643– ; Venice 1734– ; Paris 1863–) Jan 1:389–390. *Vitae BB. Vitalis et Gaufridi,* ed. E. P. SAUVAGE, B. DE GAIFFIER, *Analecta Bollandiana* (Brussels 1882–) 1:355–390. C. AUVRY and A. LAVEILLE, *Histoire de la congrégation de Savigny,* 3 v. (Paris 1896–98). *Rouleau mortuaire du bx. Vital, abbé de Savigne* (Paris 1909). D. KNOWLES, *The Monastic Order in England,* 943–1216 (2d ed. Cambridge, Eng. 1962) 202, 227.

[E. J. KEALEY]

VITELLESCHI, MUTIUS

Sixth general of the Society of Jesus; b. Rome, Dec. 2, 1563; d. there, Feb. 9, 1645. After his entrance into the novitiate in 1583, he pursued ecclesiastical studies, taught philosophy and theology, and in 1593 was made rector of the English College. He served as provincial of the Roman and Neopolitan provinces, became assistant for Italy in 1608, and was elected general on Nov. 15, 1615, by the seventh general congregation, in spite of the Spanish opposition, which tried to regain control of the society. Under Vitelleschi, the society experienced constant expansion in Europe and the missions, and at his death there were more than 16,000 members, 35 provinces, three vice provinces, 521 colleges, 49 seminaries, and more than 360 residences throughout the world. He has been criticized by L. von Ranke and H. Boehmer for his mild rule and his allowing a growing bureaucracy of Roman professors. He approved A. Santarelli's ultramontanist *De haeresi. . .et de potestate romani pontificis,* which provoked political difficulties with Richelieu. His approbation of PROBABILISM, and the condemnation of the *MONITA SECRETA,* a forgery attributed to the society, were other matters that belied the easygoing *monotone de bonheur* with which Crétineau-Joly described his generalate.

Bibliography: J. CRÉTINEAU-JOLY, *Histoire religieuse, politique et littéraire de la Compagnie de Jésus,* 6 v. (Paris 1844–46) v.3. C. SOMMERVOGEL, *Bibliotèque de la Compagnie de Jésus,* 11 v. (Brussels-Paris 1890–1932) 8:848–852. L. KOCH, *Jesuiten-Lexikon: Die Gesellschaft Jesu einst und jetzt* (Paderborn 1934); photoduplicated with rev. and suppl., 2 v. (Louvain-Heverlee 1962) 1822–23.

[P. J. GODA]

VITONUS (VANNE), ST.

Bishop of Verdun; d. *c.* 529? According to legend, Vitonus succeeded St. FIRMIN in the see of Verdun, by appointment of CLOVIS. His episcopate lasted for some 25 years at the beginning of the sixth century. In the episcopal list for Verdun preserved in the 12th-century chartulary of the Abbey of QUIMPERLÉ, however, the name of Vitonus does not appear. Despite the obscurity of his life, Vitonus left behind him a well-established reputation for sanctity, given permanence by the Benedictine Abbey of Saint-Vanne at VERDUN-SUR-MEUSE and by the Benedictine congregation that for centuries bore his name.

Feast: Nov. 9.

Bibliography: BERTARIUS, *De gestis episcoporum Virdunensium, Patrologia Latina,* ed. J. P. MIGNE, 217 v. (Paris 1878–90) 132:509–510. RICHARD, *Libellus de vita et miraculis s. Vitoni episcopi,* J. MABILLON, *Acta sanctorum ordinis S. Benedicti,* 9 v. (Paris 1668–1701; 2d ed. Venice 1733–40) 8:496–500. *Bibliotheca hagiographica latina antiquae et mediae aetatis,* 2 v. (Brussels 1898–1901; suppl. 1911) 2:8708–10. *Gallia Christiana,* v. 1–13 (Paris 1715–85), v. 14–16 (Paris 1856–65) 13:1165–66. L. DUCHESNE, *Fastes épiscopaux de l'ancienne Gaule,* 3 v. (2d ed. Paris 1907–15) 3:70. G. ALLEMANG, *Lexikon für Theologie und Kirche,* ed. M. BUCHBERGER, 10 v. (Freiburg 1930–38) 10:656. H. LECLERCQ, *Dictionnaire d'archéologie chrétienne et de liturgie,* ed. F. CABROL, H. LECLERQ, and H. I. MARROU, 15 v. (Paris 1907–53) 15.2:2913–14. J. L. BAUDOT and L. CHAUSSIN, *Vies des saints et des bienheureux selon l'ordre du calendrier avec l'historique des fêtes,* ed. by the Benedictines of Paris, 12 v. (Paris 1935–56); v. 13, suppl. and table générale (1959) 11:296–299. A. BUTLER, *The Lives of the Saints,* rev. ed. H. THURSTON and D. ATTWATER, 4 v. (New York 1956) 4:304.

[G. M. COOK]

VITORIA, FRANCISCO DE

Dominican theologian and international jurist; b. Vitoria, Old Castile, *c.* 1483; d. Salamanca, Aug. 12, 1546. While still very young he entered the Order of Preachers at the convent of St. Paul in Burgos. After completing his novitiate and the required course of philosophy and theology, he was assigned for further study to the convent of Saint-Jacques in Paris, then the principal house of studies in the order. He remained there, first as a student and then as a professor, for 18 years, during which time he became acquainted with Erasmus of Rotterdam, Juan Luis Vives, and other leading humanists of the period.

Vitoria's success at Paris prompted his superiors to appoint him regent of studies and professor of theology at the College of San Gregorio in Valladolid, a post he filled for three years. In 1526 the principal chair of theology at the University of Salamanca became vacant, and in accordance with the custom of the period it had to be filled by election. Vitoria was chosen by the students, who cast their votes after attending for some time the lectures of the various candidates. The University of Salamanca was at the time chief seat of learning in Spain and, after the Reformation, was the theological center of Catholic Europe. Here Vitoria introduced the *Summa theologiae* of St. Thomas Aquinas as a classroom text supplanting the *Sententiae* of Peter Lombard, and thus gave impetus to the practice that later became general.

Among the students of Vitoria during his professorship at Salamanca were Melchior CANO, Pedro de SOTO, Bartolomé de MEDINA, and Domingo BÁÑEZ, whose division of the history of Spanish theology into two epochs, before and after Vitoria, is evidence of the esteem in which he was held by his students. He was frequently consulted by Charles V on delicate matters of state. Charles sought his opinion on the validity of the arguments of Henry VIII of England in the latter's attempt to secure the nullification of his marriage to Catherine of Aragon, who was the Emperor's aunt.

The Relectiones. For 20 years, at the beginning of each formal opening of the university, Vitoria delivered a public address in which he discussed important current world problems. Although he did not publish these lectures himself, the notes of 12 of them were subsequently published and several have become famous. It is particularly upon the basis of the two *relectiones,* as they were called, *De Indis* and *De jure belli Hispanorum in barbaros,* that Vitoria was later acclaimed as founder of modern international law. These lectures were occasioned by the discovery of the New World and the consequent discussions among leaders on the rights of the Spaniards to colonize the new lands and to trade with and Christianize the natives.

Vitoria justified his consideration of these matters, which as legal problems seemed to be outside his field of competence, on the grounds that no argument, no discussion, no text is unrelated to theology. The law was to be respected and observed, but the law also must be evaluated in terms of morality.

In *De Indis* he considered the true and false titles the Spaniards might advance to justify their domination in the New World. *De jure belli* was supplementary to *De Indis,* but the two taken together constitute the first treatise of the law of peace and war. A third lecture, *De potestate civili,* set forth his theory of the state and of civil power. This work too was complemented by another, *De potestate ecclesiae*. His political philosophy was further elaborated in his commentaries on the *Prima secundae* and the *Secunda secundae* of the *Summa theologiae* of Thomas Aquinas. Some of these commentaries have yet to be edited.

The State. In Vitoria's day the unity of Christendom was being challenged by new and powerful forces of nationalism. Consequently the whole question of civil government, the authority of the ruler and the origin of sovereignty, was contested between popes and emperors in the dispute about investiture. It was vigorously debated in academic circles and among religious and civil leaders.

For Vitoria, the state (*respublica*) alone is the juridically perfect civil society, because the state alone is capable of fulfilling all the necessities of life. He accepted the Aristotelian concept that man as a social and political animal must live in an organized society. Only in society could the individual achieve the fullness of his nature. The perfect state must be intrinsically complete in itself, that is, not part of another state. It must be self-sufficient, have its own laws, its own councils, and its own magistrates. The state was the natural outgrowth of society; it was essential to it. Since God alone is the Author of the natural law, He alone is the immediate efficient cause of public power. But once the political community is constituted, power (*potestas*) is immediately inherent in that society. The mode of the regime and the particular individuals who exercise authority are left to the free determination of the people. The primacy of the common good is the dominant note in Vitoria's political philosophy.

His doctrine of citizenship was far ahead of his time. He has been called a prophet in the matter of nationality, for his ideas on the subject have been put into practice by every country of the Western world. He held that citizenship was dependent primarily upon place of origin rather than upon nationality of parents; in technical terms, he held for *jus soli* rather than *jus sanguinis*. He admitted, however, the possibility of expatriation and the right of adopted citizenship, or naturalization, by statute. This was to be the same for all peoples, and those who accepted the privilege were also to share equally in the burdens of the state.

International Theories. In the *De Indis* Vitoria considered the rights of the Spaniards with regard to the recently discovered lands of the New World and their relationship with the aborigines. He asked: (1) by what right the native peoples had come under Spanish domination; (2) what rights the Spanish sovereigns obtained over them in temporal and civil matters; and (3) what rights the Spanish civil authorities or the Church obtained over them in spiritual matters.

Vitoria was a stanch advocate of the rights of the native peoples. He maintained that they had been in peaceful possession of their property, both publicly and privately, and that they must be considered as possessing true ownership, except in cases in which the contrary was evident. He admitted in one passage that the government of backward peoples, such as the native peoples appeared to be, might be taken over by a more enlightened state, in this case the Spaniards, provided it was for the welfare and in the interests of the former and not merely for the profit of the latter. This was the principle of the system of mandates that was established after World War I.

It was in this same *relectio* that Vitoria first defined international law. He stated its source and the way in which it was enlarged to meet the world's changing condition and how it bound every state of the international community and the individuals who, taken together, composed the states of the world.

In discussing the rights of the Spaniards in the New World he based these rights on the "law of nations that is natural law and derived from natural law." Then taking a statement of Gaius as given in the Institutes of Justinian, he substituted the word "nations" (*nationes*) for the word "peoples" (*gentes*) and declared: "What natural reason has established among all nations is called the law of nations."

Vitoria not only defined international law, but he also stated the relationship of states to one another. He visualized an international society constituting one integral political order. His contribution was twofold: (1) he applied the principles of Thomas Aquinas to the concept of the new national, sovereign, independent states; (2) he built a theory of international society on the basis of Thomistic social and political principles by preserving the thoroughly objective and theological character of society, and authority, and law. It is too much to expect that Vitoria, a pioneer in the field of international relations, living at the beginning of the modern era, should have elaborated a complete and detailed doctrine of international society; yet he did give in principle an outline of world organization based on the equality of states.

In Vitoria's mind, humanity constitutes a universal society, and it needed a law by which to be governed. This law was the law of nations. In *De potestate civili*, Vitoria wrote: "International law has not only the force of a pact and agreement among men, but also the force of a law; for the world as a whole, being in some sense a single state, has the power to create laws that are just and fitting for all persons, as are rules of international law." He held that the world could create an organ of authority to govern the international community. "Just as the majority of the members of a state may set up a king over the whole state, although other members are unwilling, so the majority of Christians could, in spite of the opposition of some, lawfully create a monarch whom all princes and provinces would be under obligation to obey.'' He thus envisioned a community of nations endowed with greater power and authority than that of the League of Nations after World War I or the United Nations after World War II.

Vitoria's doctrine on the law of war can be found under the heading of Origins of the Just War Theory in the article WAR, MORALITY OF.

Bibliography: F. DE VITORIA, *Relectiones theologicae* (Lyons 1587); *Relecciones teológicos del Maestro Fray Francisco de Vitoria,* ed. L. G. ALONSO GETINO, 3 v. (Madrid 1933–36), critical ed.; *Comentarios a la Secunda secundae de Santo Tomás,* ed. V. BELTRAN DE HEREDIA, 5 v. (Salamanca 1932–35); *De Indis et de iure bello relectiones,* ed. and tr. E. NYS et al., v. 7 of *Classics of International Law,* ed. J. B. SCOTT (Washington 1917), text and tr. J. T. DELOS, *La Societé internationale et les principes du droit public* (Paris 1929); ''Christian Principles and International Relations,'' tr. M. LANGFORD, in *International Relations from a Catholic Standpoint,* ed. S. J. BROWN (Dublin 1932); ''Political Causes of International Disorder,'' in *The Foundations of International Order* (Catholic Congress on International Peace; Oxford 1938). J. B. SCOTT, *The Spanish Origin of International Law* (Washington 1928); *The Spanish Origin of International Law: Francisco de Vitoria and His Law of Nations* (Oxford 1934). C. H. MCKENNA, ''Francisco de Vitoria: Father of International Law,'' *Studies* 21 (1932) 635–648. G. F. BENKERT, *The Thomistic Conception of an International Society* (Washington 1942). S. J. REIDY, *Civil Authority according to Francis de Vitoria* (River Forest, Ill. 1959). H. MÚNOZ, ''The International Community according to Francisco de Vitoria,'' *Thomist* 10 (1947) 1–55. H. F. WRIGHT, *Catholic Founders of Modern International Law* (Washington 1934). E. NYS, *Les Origines de droit international* (Brussels 1894). Y. DE LA BRIÈRE, *La Conception du droit international chez les théologiens catholiques* (Paris 1930).

[C. H. MCKENNA]

VITRY, PHILIPPE DE

Medieval composer and theorist of great originality (also spelled Vitri); b. Vitry (Champagne), France, Oct. 31, 1291; d. Meaux, June 2, 1361. In addition to writing, Vitry served for some time as secretary to Charles IV and Philip VI of France, held several canonries, and eventually became bishop of Meaux. His praises were sung by PETRARCH and others, yet little of his music has been preserved in comparison with what we have of his near-contemporary, MACHAUT. Vitry's treatise, *Ars Nova* (Paris *c.* 1320), deals with then-current problems of rhythm in a way that characterizes its author as a musician's theorist. His compositions not only bear out his theories but also present the epigrammatic medieval *ordo,* or rhythmic pattern, in a new and more spacious guise, which in modern times has come to be known as

isorhythm. Vitry's motets are not liturgical: the political scene held his interest when he had leisure to compose, so that texts are found on such subjects as the struggle between the Angevins and the Aragonese for possession of Sicily (*O canenda vulgo/Rex quem metrorum*).

Bibliography: E. DANNEMANN, *Grove's Dictionary of Music and Musicians,* ed. E. BLOM (London 1954) 9:24–25. H. RIEMANN, *History of Music Theory,* tr. and ed. R. H. HAGGH (Lincoln, Nebr. 1962). G. REESE, *Music in the Middle Ages* (New York 1940). L. SCHRADE, ''Philippe de Vitry: Some New Discoveries,'' *Musical Quarterly* 42 (New York 1956) 330–354. D. J. LEECH-WILKINSON, ''Compositional Procedure in the Four-Part Isorhythmic Works of Philippe de Vitry and His Contemporaries'' (Ph.D. diss. Cambridge University, 1983); ''The Emergence of *ars nova,*'' *The Journal of Musicology* 13 (1995), 285–317. D. M. RANDEL, ed., *The Harvard Biographical Dictionary of Music* 953 (Cambridge, Massachusetts 1996). E. H. SANDERS, ''Philippe de Vitry'' in *The New Grove Dictionary of Music and Musicians,* vol. 20, ed. S. SADIE (New York 1980) 22–28. N. SLONIMSKY, ed., *Baker's Biographical Dictionary of Musicians,* Eighth Edition (New York 1992) 1970. A. WATHEY, ''The motet texts of Philippe de Vitry in German humanist manuscripts of the fifteenth century,'' in *Music in the German Renaissance: Sources, Styles, and Contexts,* ed. J. KMETZ (Cambridge 1994) 195–201.

[D. STEVENS]

VITTORINO DA FELTRE

Also known as Vittorino de' Rambaldoni; Humanist, scholar, and educator; b. Feltre, Italy, 1378; d. Mantua, 1446. In 1396 Vittorino entered the University of Padua, an institution famed not only in Italy, but beyond the Alps. He was associated with Padua as student and teacher for nearly 20 years. During this period, he studied grammar and Latin letters with Gasparino Barzizza, the greatest Latin scholar of the age, as well as dialectic, philosophy, rhetoric, and Canon Law. After receiving his doctorate, he obtained private instruction in mathematics and Greek, and soon became known for his knowledge of mathematical and literary subjects. His attractive personality made him one of the outstanding scholars in Padua. As his fame grew steadily, his teaching was much in demand. A competent scholar and an exemplary Catholic layman, he continually tried to harmonize Christian principles with ancient learning. More than any other humanist, he helped to systematize the new studies.

Vittorino opened a private school in Padua and, in 1422, accepted the chair of rhetoric at the University. The following year he resigned either because of the immorality of the university city or because of his inability to control the students. His experience at Padua convinced him that the critical adolescent years demand close supervision and guidance. In 1423 he went to Venice where he organized a school. That same year he accepted the invitation of Gianfrancesco Gonzaga to come to Mantua and assume charge of his children's education. Vittorino continued in the service of the Gonzaga family for until his death many years later.

At Mantua Vittorino established a court school, Casa Giocosa (pleasant house), that offered instruction not only to the Gonzaga family and to the sons of the leading Mantuan families, but also to the promising sons of indigent parents. The spirit, curriculum, and method that characterized the Casa Giocosa made it the first great school of the Renaissance and an outstanding model school of the humanities. The pupils learned mathematics, music, philosophy, Latin, and Greek. The favorite writers of Vittorino, the schoolmaster, were Virgil and Livy in Latin; Homer, Demosthenes, and Aeschylus in Greek; and he introduced St. Chrysostom and St. Augustine from among the Church Fathers. He included physical training, which he regarded as an integral part of a complete education.

Vittorino concerned himself seriously with his pupils' work, welfare, interests, abilities, personalities, and character, and gave them personal, educational, and vocational guidance. In his opinion, the chief purpose of education was to train young men to serve God and state in whatever position they would be called upon to assume. The same humanistic education was offered to both girls and boys—one of the most cultured women of the 15th century, Cecilia Gonzaga, studied at the court school. Vittorino left no educational treatises, but at Casa Giocosa trained many who later became prominent teachers, ecclesiastics, scholars, and statesmen.

Bibliography: P. J. MCCORMICK, *Vittorino da Feltre and Guarino de Verona: An Educational Study of the Fifteenth Century* (Washington 1906). W. H. WOODWARD, *Vittorino da Feltre and Other Humanist Educators: Essays and Versions* (Cambridge, England 1897; repr. 1921).

[V. STAUDT SEXTON]

VITUS, MODESTUS, AND CRESCENTIA, SS.

Martyrs. They appear to be victims of the persecution of Diocletian and are mentioned in the MARTYROLOGY OF ST. JEROME. Vitus appears in the old Sacramentarium Gelasianum, while Modestus and Crescentia were added in the Roman Missal (Milan 1474). Various copies of the *passio* do not merit credence, but according to them Vitus was born in Sicily or Lucania. His Christian nurse was Crescentia and her husband, Modestus. Since the fifth century churches were dedicated to St. Vitus in Rome, Sicily, and Sardinia. In the Mid-

dle Ages his cult spread, especially among Germans and Slavs, for his miraculous power against epilepsy, which was called "St. Vitus dance"; and for this reason he was enumerated among the "auxiliary saints" or 14 Holy Helpers. St. Vitus's relics were first taken to Saint Denis in Paris (*c.* 750), then to Corvey in Saxony (836); the head was taken from Pavia to Prague in 1355 by the Emperor Charles IV. Vitus is usually represented as immersed in a burning cauldron, or as holding a small one in his hand and a dog on a leash.

Feast: June 15.

Bibliography: *Acta Sanctorum* June 2:1013–42. *Bibliotheca hagiographica latina antiquae et mediae aetatis*, 2 v. (Brussels 1898–1901; suppl. 1911) 8711–23. J. BRAUN, *Tracht und Attribute der Heiligen in der deutschen Kunst* (Stuttgart 1943) 728–738. P. BRUYLANTS, *Les Oraisons du Missel Romain*, 2 v. (Louvain 1952) 1:107. A. PANER, *Swiety Wit* (Gdansk 1995).

[E. HOADE]

VIVA, DOMENICO

Jesuit theological writer; b. Lecce in southeast Italy, Oct. 19, 1648; d. July 5, 1726. After entering the Naples province of the Society of Jesus on May 12, 1663, he spent the major part of his active life as a teacher. His subjects ranged from the humanities and Greek in his early years, to philosophy for nine years and moral and dogmatic theology for eight years each. The latter part of his life was spent in administration. He was prefect of studies for two years, rector of the College of Naples, and then provincial. His writings include *Enchiridion*, primarily concerned with indulgences and published in connection with the Holy Year jubilee (Naples, 1699). He also wrote three books for students: a dogmatic theology text, compiled from his lectures at the College of Naples; *Opuscula theologico-moralia;* and a textbook for moral theology. These latter are highly regarded and are quoted by such men as St. Alphonsus Liguori and Claude Lacroix. Viva's most well-known work, *Damnatae theses ab Alexandro VII. . .* , was published in three volumes (Naples 1708). These list propositions condemned by three 17th-century popes: 45 by Alexander VII, 65 by Innocent XI, 39 by Alexander VIII, and five propositions from the *Augustinus* of Jansenius. An additional volume, *Trutina theologica thesium Quesnellianarum,* was published in Naples in 1716–17. This contained a study and refutation of the 101 propositions which were condemned in 1713 by the bull *Unigenitus* of Clement XI.

Bibliography: *Opera omnia theologica-moralia,* 8 v. (Ferrara 1757). C. SOMMERVOGEL, *Bibliotèque de la Compagnie de Jésus,* 11 v. (Brussels-Paris 1890–1932) 8:859–866. F. X. DE FELLER, *Dictionnaire historique,* 8 v. (3d ed. Liège 1816) 8:681–682.

[P. K. CLARK]

VIVALD (UBALD), BL.

Franciscan tertiary; d. Boscotondo, Italy, May 1, 1320. Vivald was a pious and charitable man, converted by Bl. Bartolus Bompedoni, a leprous priest. He became, like Bartolus, a Franciscan tertiary and renounced all worldly possessions. After the latter's death in December 1300, Vivald withdrew to a forest near Camporena, eight miles from San Gimignano to devote himself to prayer and fasting. He died in a humble cell at Boscotondo and immediately the bells of Montaione, almost five miles to the northeast, began to chime. A huntsman discovered the hermit's body and sounded the alarm. Crowds of people came, miracles occurred, and a small church to Our Lady as built on the spot. Over a period of 13 years in the early 16th century Cherubim Conzi of Florence directed the erection of the church and convent of San Vivaldo. Vivald was beatified in 1908.

Feast: May 21 (formerly May 1).

Bibliography: *Acta Sanctorum* May 1:163–167. C. PALAEO-TUS and F. GHILARDI, *Archivum Franciscanum historicum* (Quaracchi-Florence 1909–) 1 (1908) 521–535. M. DE FLORENTIA, *ibid.* d (1909) 627. F. GHILARDI, ''San Vivaldo e la sua iconografia,'' *ibid.* 9 (1916) 42–50; *San Vivaldo* in Toscana (Florence 1895). J. L. BAUDOT and L. CHAUSSIN, *Vies des saints et des bienheureux selon l'ordre du calendrier avec l'historique des fêtes,* ed. by the Benedictines of Paris, 12 v. (Paris 1935–56); v. 13, suppl. and table générale (1959) 5:8.

[J. CAMBELL]

VIVALDI, ANTONIO

Illustrious baroque composer and violinist; b. Venice, *c.* 1675; d. Vienna, July 1741. The son of a violinist at St. Mark's, Venice, Vivaldi achieved fame as an executant while still quite young. In 1693 he received the first of the minor orders of priesthood, and in 1703 was ordained. In the following year he set about his duties as violin teacher and player at the Venice Ospedale della Pietà, whose chorus and orchestra of orphaned girls he soon molded into an ensemble of world-renowned excellence. In 1716 he was named *maestro de concerti,* a position he held until 1740, except for extensive travels with his friend and patron the Marchese BENTIVOGLIO. He was welcomed in every city except Ferrara, whose ecclesiastical authorities forbade a proposed visit on the grounds that he did not say Mass. In a letter to Bentivoglio, Vivaldi explained that although he said Mass for a little longer than a year after his ordination, he was compelled to give it up on account of an illness he described as a severe pain and constriction in the chest. On leaving Venice he went to Vienna, probably with the hope of writing operas with his compatriots Zeno and Metastasio, but he died within that year.

Vivaldi's contract with the orphanage bound him to write two concertos a month for the orchestra, but he also composed much religious music during this period. Since the church music was not published in his lifetime—the best of his concertos were—his European fame rested upon his amazing skill in making the most of contemporary instrumental fashion (J. S. BACH modeled his own concerto style on Vivaldi's concertos and transcribed six of them) and his ability to write at great speed: it was said that he could compose music faster than a copyist could copy it. While his church music is still largely unknown, the few available works indicate that he was equally conversant with vocal and instrumental style, and capable of massive and brilliant effects (as in the oratorio *Juditha triumphans*) as well as of texture of a more intimate nature (the *Magnificat* for solo voices and small orchestra). He wrote also an oratorio on the subject of Moses, a *Kyrie,* a paired *Gloria* and *Credo,* 14 settings of Vespers, and various psalms and motets; and much of his instrumental music was intended for use in church.

Bibliography: *Opere* (Milan 1947–). M. PINCHERLE, *Antonio Vivaldi et la musique instrumentale,* 2 v. (Paris 1948); *Vivaldi: Genius of the Baroque,* tr. C. HATCH (New York 1957). M. F. BUKOFZER, *Music in the Baroque Era* (New York 1947). P. H. LÁNG, *Music in Western Civilization* (New York 1941). R. ELLER, *Die Musik in Geschichte und Gegenwart,* ed. F. BLUME (Kassel-Basel 1949–). C. FERTONANI, *La musica strumentale di Antonio Vivaldi* (Florence 1998). P. HURLEY, ''The Vivaldi Lute Music,'' *Lute Society of America, Inc. Quarterly* 31:2 (1996) 4–11. J. PARSONS, *Orlando,* in *International Dictionary of Opera* 2 v., ed. C. S. LARUE (Detroit 1993). F. RICCI, ''Il *Concerto Funebre* de Antonio Vivaldi: Alcune ipotesi storiche,'' *Esercizi: Musica e Spettacolo* 12 (1993) 31–45. M. TALBOT, *The Sacred Vocal Music of Antonio Vivaldi* (Florence 1995).

[D. STEVENS]

VIVENTIOLUS, ST.

Twenty-fourth bishop of Lyons; d. *c.* 523–524. A monk and teacher at St. Croyland, or Condet, he was elected bishop of Lyons (*c.* 514) on the recommendation of AVITUS, Archbishop of Vienne. He was present at the Fifth Council of Lyons (*c.* 516) and at the Council of Epaon (517). He presided at the sixth Council of Lyons (*c.* 518), which dealt with a number of disciplinary matters. Avitus praises his zeal and affection in the five extant letters he wrote to him. Fragments of the extant works of Viventiolus are available in Migne (*Patrologia Latina* 67:994–996).

Feast: July 12.

Bibliography: *Acta Sanctorum* July 3:290–291. G. W. DANIELL, *A Dictionary of Christian Biography,* ed. W. SMITH and H. WACE 4:1166. H. LECLERQ, *Dictionnaire d'archéologie chrétienne* *et de liturgie*, ed. F. CABROL, H. LECLERCQ, and H. I. MARROU 10.1:201–203.

[M. R. P. MCGUIRE]

VIVES, JUAN BAUTISTA

Zealous promoter of missionary education; b. Valencia, Spain, May 3, 1545; d. Rome, Feb. 22, 1632. He was of the same family as the humanist philosopher and scholar Juan Luis Vives. Juan Bautista went to Rome in 1588 after obtaining his doctorate in both civil and Canon Law. He was ordained subdeacon in 1591 but deferred his ordination to the priesthood until 1609. Under Sixtus V, Clement VIII, Gregory XV, and Urban VIII, he held various offices in the Roman Curia. He also was Roman agent for the Spanish Inquisition, and served as ambassador for the Kingdom of Congo. In 1622 when Gregory XV formally established the Congregation for the Propagation of the Faith, Vives was one of the prelates appointed to it.

Throughout his career Vives was active in promoting the education of ecclesiastics and especially those destined for missionary work. In 1591 he founded a school in the house in which he was then living in the Piazza del Populo; and later, with the cooperation of St. John LEONARDI, he changed this into a missionary college in the care of a missionary congregation of clerks regular that he and Leonardi established. However, neither of these enterprises prospered. He acquired the Palazzo Ferratini and about 1625 offered it, together with certain revenues for its maintenance, to the THEATINES for a college to train secular priests for the missionary apostolate. This plan failed also, and Vives then offered the palace, and with it sufficient income to support 12 students, to Urban VIII and his successors with the proviso that it was to be used as a college for secular priests and clerics from all nations preparing themselves for work on the missions in any part of the world. With the impetus given to the establishment of seminaries by the Council of Trent, various national colleges had been erected in Rome; but it seemed desirable that there should also be an international college for the training of prospective missionaries not only from countries that had no national college but from all nations. An international center devoted exclusively to the preparation of missionaries could give a specific direction to ecclesiastical studies that was much needed to fit the young men for their work. At the request of the Congregation for the Propagation of the Faith, Vives drew up a rule and statutes for the proposed institution. These proved satisfactory, and the Pope accepted the gift and its terms, and in his bull *Immortalis Dei Filius* of Aug. 1, 1627, established the Urban Pontifical College,

Antonio Vivaldi. (Archive Photos/Damiano)

sometimes known simply as the Urban College, or the College of the Propaganda. Since the motu proprio *Fidei propagandae* of John XXIII (Oct. 1, 1962), the official name of the institution has been the *Pontificia Università Urbaniana.*

[P. K. MEAGHER]

VIZCARDÓ, JUAN PABLO

Jesuit precursor of Latin American independence; b. Pampacolca, Peru, June 26, 1748; d. London, February 1798. Vizcardó was a member of a wealthy and socially prominent family of the valley of Arequipa in southern Peru. Juan Pablo and an older brother, Anselmo, studied with the Jesuits in Cuzco. In about 1760, their father, Gaspar, died, and their mother, Manuela de Zea, wished them to return home. Instead, they joined the society in Cuzco on May 24, 1761, although they had not reached canonical age for the reception of vows.

The profession was invalid, and soon the two young men were requesting an official declaration to that effect. The edict for the expulsion of the Jesuits overtook them on Sept. 7, 1767, in Cuzco before this question had been cleared up. So on March 15, 1768, the two brothers were among the Peruvian Jesuits who were embarked in Lima for Cádiz. There they accepted the option offered by the Crown to leave the society in the hope that they would be permitted to return to Peru. In this they were disillusioned because the Crown continued to treat them in the same fashion as it did those who persevered in the society.

By 1771 Juan Pablo and Anselmo were in Massacarrara, Italy. Neither one was ever to be ordained. Both unremittingly petitioned the Spanish royal officials to be allowed to return to Peru or, at least, to be permitted to share in the inheritance of their father and uncle. In 1781, probably aroused by the news of the revolution of Tupac Amaru II in Peru and Bolivia, Juan Pablo contacted the English diplomatic agents in Leghorn and Genoa with a plan for an English fleet to land in South America to help the rebels against Spain. The English found his suggestions interesting and by the spring of 1782, Juan Pablo was in London living in Soho on an English agent's salary. However, by the time of his arrival, the English were on the verge of making peace with Spain, and so Juan Pablo's plans were filed.

Next the French Revolution seems to have inspired him with hope that this government would heed his suggestions. By late 1791 Juan Pablo was in France, where he composed his *Lettre aux Espagnols-Américains,* a call to his fellow Creoles to rebel against Spain. It is thought that this letter was not published at that time. In 1795 Vizcardó was back in London, again on the payroll of the British Foreign Office and there he died.

In life, Vizcardó had never met the outstanding Spanish American conspirator of the epoch, General Miranda. However, Rufus King, U.S. Minister in London, to whom Vizcardó willed his papers, called the attention of Miranda to the documents. It was Miranda who made use of the *Lettre.* In preparation for his own attack on Venezuela in 1806, Miranda had the French manuscript text translated into Spanish as *Carta Dirijida a los Españoles Americanos* and printed in London (1801). There are 42 pages in the Spanish text and 41 in the French text, printed in 1799 by an unknown printer in Philadelphia, Pennsylvania. A careful reading of the *Carta* shows that it is full of errors and exaggerations and possesses little that would reflect on Vizcardó's nobility of purpose. Miranda, however, wanted to give his conspiracy ostensible Jesuit support, and thus gain an advantage among the simple believers of South America.

Bibliography: M. BATLLORI, *El abate Viscardo* (Caracas 1953). P. DE LETÚRIA in *Archiv Historicum Societatis Jesu* 23 (1954) 181–184, bk. rev. of Batllori's vol. R. VARGAS UGARTE, *La carta a los españoles americanos de Don Juan Pablo Vizcardo y Guzmán* (Lima 1954).

[A. S. TIBESAR]

VLADIMIR, ST.

Grand Duke of Kiev (980–1015), first Christian ruler of Russia; b. 956. The youngest son of Sviatoslav of Kiev (964–972) and a great-grandson of Rurik (mid-9th century), the traditional founder of the Rurikid dynasty and of the Russian state, Vladimir was made Prince of Novgorod in 970. Then in 972, at the death of Sviatoslav, a fierce struggle broke out among his sons Yaropolk, Oleg, and Vladimir. Oleg was slain, and Vladimir was forced to flee to Scandinavia. Vladimir returned with Scandinavian auxiliaries, seized Novgorod and Kiev, slew Yaropolk, and made himself master of the entire Russian realm in 980. He was eminently successful in his military campaigns and expanded Russian control over the vast area from southeastern Poland to the Volga Valley. He built fortresses along the southern and eastern borders of his Kievan Russia against the inroads of the nomadic Patzinaks. Under Vladimir, Christianity was officially introduced among the Eastern SLAVS, and the Church was established in Russia. St. OLGA, Vladimir's grandmother, was a Christian, and there had been a church of St. Elias in Kiev as early as 945.

By the late 10th century the influence of the neighboring Christian states had become too strong to disregard, and Vladimir, having accomplished the consolidation of all the Eastern Slavs under the rule of the Rurikid dynasty of Kiev, decided to bring his people within the community of Christian nations. In 988 he dispatched military aid to the Byzantine Emperor BASIL II, who was menaced by Bardas Phocas's revolt, requesting in return the hand of the Emperor's sister Anna. The Emperor agreed, provided that Vladimir became a Christian, and Vladimir was baptized the same year. The subsequent Byzantine reluctance to meet their obligation led to Vladimir's attack on the Byzantine Crimea and the capture of Cherson in July 989. Thus Princess Anna became the wife of Vladimir. After the conversion of Vladimir and his family, the Christianization of Kievan Russia proceeded rapidly, and an ecclesiastical organization headed by the archbishop metropolitan of Kiev was established. The Russian Church remained under the jurisdiction of Constantinople, but Vladimir and his successors remained close and friendly to the West. Vladimir is venerated as a saint by both Byzantine Catholics and the Russian Orthodox.

Feast: July 15.

Bibliography: B. LEIB, *Rome, Kiev et Byzance à la fin du XIe siècle* (Paris 1924). A. FLICHE and V. MARTIN, *Histoire de l'église depuis les origines jusqu'à nos jours* (Paris 1935–) v.7. F. DVORNIK, *The Slavs: Their Early History and Civilization* (Boston 1956). S. H. CROSS and O. P. SHERBOWITZ-WETZOR, ed. and tr., *The Russian Primary Chronicle* (Cambridge, Mass. 1953). *The Legacy of St.*

Vladimir: Byzantium, Russia, America, ed J. BRECK, J. MEYENDOR-FF, and E. SILK (Crestwood, NY 1990).

[O. P. SHERBOWITZ-WETZOR]

VOID

Used as an adjective, the term void means empty, unoccupied or vacant; as a noun, it means that which is void and particularly an empty SPACE. In the latter sense it admits of various meanings: (1) geometrical space or pure EXTENSION (of one or two or more dimensions) that is the object of geometry; (2) psychological space, considered as infinitely extended and empty, the indispensable receptacle of bodies and absolutely penetrable by them; and (3) physical space, conceived as the basis for real spatial relations between bodies and as the referential system for their position and motion.

History. The Greek philosopher PARMENIDES (*c.* 540–*c.* 475 B.C.) formulated the so-called Eleatic principle: ''Being is, non-being is not.'' This principle was challenged by the Greek atomists (*c.* 400 B.C.), who claimed that nonbeing (the vacuum or void) exists, just as being (the plenum or ''full'') exists; in other words, they accepted the real existence of empty space or of the void. Medieval and scholastic philosophers, following ARISTOTLE, generally equated the void with nonbeing and thus rejected its real existence.

Among modern philosophers, R. DESCARTES (1596–1650), for whom extension constituted the essence of material bodies, regarded an extended void as contradiction and an absurdity. Yet his contemporary, P. GASSENDI (1592–1655), accepted the existence of an eternal and infinite space in which God created the finite world. Isaac Newton (1642–1727) and Samuel Clarke (1675–1729) admitted the reality of absolute space in which ordinary bodies are located and move; as opposed to this, G.W. LEIBNIZ (1646–1716) rejected the reality of an independently existing space because of the contradictions it implied. For rather different reasons I. KANT (1724–1804) denied that real space and time have an independent existence and accepted them only as a priori forms of intuition. Many scientists of recent times verbally admit the existence of a void as well as of ACTION at a distance, but implicitly contradict themselves when they subsequently attribute properties and activities to this empty space.

Reality. Does anything real correspond to the void or empty space conceived by the imagination? If the void is considered as the general receptacle of bodies, it would appear that this empty space is infinitely extended; for example, it must function as the receptacle of any new bodies that could be added to those that already exist, and this can be conceived as going on ad infinitum. It is difficult to attribute reality to such an infinitely extended space, particularly when its only function is to serve as a receptacle for perceptible bodies and when it is in no way involved in their existence and activities. The difficulty becomes more acute when one considers that the same argument that requires this space to be real also demands another real container as the receptacle of this real space, followed by a third container, and so on. The result is an infinite series of spaces, which is itself absurd. Thus void understood in this sense cannot be a real being.

Nevertheless the void so conceived does exist in the imagination and can be termed a being of reason with a foundation in reality. This expression means that the term void can be used in meaningful sentences that state a judgment concerning reality. For example, it is meaningful to speak of a void existing between celestial bodies in the sense that the universe is not filled with such bodies in a continuous fashion. Likewise, one can say that the void extends to infinity in the sense that the existing cosmos can expand indefinitely. It is meaningful also to state that this void is three dimensional, understanding this to mean that the bodies in the universe are three dimensional. It should be noted, however, that the space created by the imagination is not empty in the strict sense; rather it is a kind of obscure three–dimensional CONTINUUM in which different parts can be distinguished, and wherein positions and motions can be attributed to the imagined bodies.

Bibliography: V.E. SMITH, *The General Science of Nature* (Milwaukee 1958). P. HOENEN, *Cosmologia* (4th ed. Rome 1949). P.H. VAN LAER, *Actio in distans en aether* (Utrecht 1947).

[P. H. VAN LER]

VOLPICELLI, CATERINA, BL.

Foundress of the Servants of the Sacred Heart; b. Naples, Italy, Jan. 21, 1839; d. there, Dec. 28, 1894. Born into an upper middle-class family, Caterina received an excellent education at the Royal College of S. Marcellino under the tutelage of Marguerita Salatino. She became the spiritual mother to Bl. Bartolo LONGO after meeting him in the home of her brother-in-law, Marchese Francesco Imperiali in 1854. She sought entrance into the Adorers of the Blessed Sacrament (May 28, 1859), but was forced to leave the community due to illness. Upon her recovery she was active in promoting the Apostleship of Prayer. On July 20, 1861, she received approval from Cardinal Sisto Riario Sforza to promote holy hours for the conversion of sinners. In addition to founding the Servants of the Sacred Heart in Naples with the Third Rule

Voltaire.

of St. Francis (July 1, 1874), Caterina instituted the Daughters of Mary, opened an orphanage, established a lending library, and participated in the national Eucharistic conference in Naples (Nov. 19–22, 1891).

The congregation, which includes both cloistered nuns as well as married and single oblates, tended to the sick during a cholera epidemic (1884). The constitution was approved in 1911.

The diocesan process for Volpicelli's beatification was completed 1896–1902 and officially presented to the Congregation for the Causes of Saints on Jan. 11, 1911. She was declared venerable by Pope Pius XII (March 25, 1945) and beatified by John Paul II, April 29, 2001, for being "prophetically oriented to the promotion of the laity and new forms of consecrated life."

Feast: Dec. 28.

Bibliography: *L'Osservatore Romano,* Eng. Ed. 18 (2001), 1, 6–8; 19 (2001), 7, 10.

[K. I. RABENSTEIN]

VOLTAIRE

French writer and philosopher; b. François Marie Arouet, Paris, Nov. 21, 1691; d. there, May 30, 1778. He received a classical education at the Collège Louis-le-Grand, directed by the Jesuits, but he was initiated into the immorality prevalent during the Regency in the libertine milieu of the Société du Temple. He was imprisoned in the Bastille for the first time (1717–18) for an epigram against the Regent Duke of Orléans, and for the second time (1726) after a dispute with the Duke of Rohan. When sentenced to a period of exile, he chose to go to England where he spent three fruitful years (1726–29). In 1734, Voltaire was once more forced to flee Paris after condemnation of his *Lettres Philosophiques.* He accepted the hospitality of Mme. du Châtelet in her castle of Cirey, near Lorraine, where he resided off and on until 1749. This was a period of intense literary and scientific activity: Voltaire studied physics and chemistry and wrote *Eléments de la philosophie de Newton* (1738). After the death of Mme. du Châtelet, Voltaire went to Berlin at the urging of Frederick II, King of Prussia, with whom he had corresponded since 1734.

The sojourn in Prussia, however, was embittered by Voltaire's rivalry with Maupertuis, whom Frederick had appointed president of his Academy of Sciences, and by difficulties with the King himself. Voltaire, disillusioned, left Berlin in 1753 and spent two years wandering in Alsace (1753–55). Finally, in 1755, he bought a property near Geneva, "Les Délices," where he lived until he moved to Ferney in 1760. There, amid a large household directed by his niece, Mme. Denis, Voltaire played munificently the role of lord of the village. His influence was felt all over Europe, through his innumerable writings, mainly brochures on philosophical subjects, and an enormous correspondence, amounting to more than 6,000 letters for that period alone, with kings, statesmen, philosophers, and disciples.

Through his gift of remarkable business sense, Voltaire transformed Ferney into a prosperous village of 1,200 people, with a watch factory and a silk-stocking mill. In 1778, he returned to Paris, where he was received in triumph. He died shortly thereafter without renouncing any of his ideas. He was buried secretly near Troyes in the Abbey of Scellières, of which his nephew was abbot. In 1791, his remains were transferred to the Panthéon next to those of his bitter enemy, Jean Jacques ROUSSEAU.

Dramatic and Historical Work. Voltaire's name is commonly associated with a philosophy of revolt against tradition and authority, but his fertile genius was employed in many fields. His first and greatest love, which reveals the lasting influence of his classical formation, was for the theater. From *Oedipe* (1718) to *Irène* (1778), he wrote more than 20 plays. His discovery of Shakespeare led him to widen the narrow field from which the classic authors chose their subjects. Voltaire's literary criticism, as expressed in *Le Temple du Goût* (1733), in his *Commentaire sur Corneille* (1764), and in numerous prefaces to his tragedies, reflect the same classical taste and principles.

Voltaire was original, and even an innovator, in historiography. Up to his time, history had been concerned mainly with kings, wars, and treaties. Voltaire extended it to include the history of the people, of customs, religion, commerce, literature, and the arts. His theory of history, inspired in part by FÉNELON's *Lettre à l'Académie,* called for exact and exhaustive documentation, critical analysis of the information thus uncovered, and absolute impartiality.

Wide Historical Vision. In Voltaire's first history, *Histoire de Charles XII* (1731), the center is still the epic character of the King of Sweden, but in the *Siècle de Louis XIV* (1751), his scope widens. Louis XIV is still, of course, the dominant figure and his actions are minutely recorded, but Voltaire writes in this book the history of a nation in its manifold manifestations. Many chapters are devoted to the laws, the administration of justice, the army, the navy, finances, religious life, great men of letters, and artists. Both works are based on extensive and careful oral and written documentation. Voltaire was able to consult important personages, ministers, ambassadors, and generals, who had played a role in the still recent events of the reigns of Louis XIV and Charles XII.

Antireligious Slant. The admirable presentation of the *Siècle de Louis XIV* is often marred, however, by Voltaire's antireligious bias, expressed in snide remarks against those who indulged in religious practices. Voltaire failed to recognize the prominent role of the Church in the 17th century, and the impartiality in writing history that he advocated is glaringly absent. This defect is still more evident in *L'Essai sur les Moeurs* (1756), a work as much philosophy as history, which Voltaire intended to be a refutation of BOSSUET's *Discours sur l'Histoire universelle*. The *Essai* proper begins where Bossuet's *Discours* ends—that is, with the reign of Charlemagne—but it is preceded by an extended introduction that summarizes the history of the world before Charlemagne. It takes issue specifically with the theory of Providence at work in history, the basic principle of Bossuet's philosophy.

Rejection of the Supernatural. Voltaire rejects any supernatural influences on the development of history and attributes all events solely to chance or to necessary causes that determine the course of men and empires. He paints a dark tableau of the entire period before the ENLIGHTENMENT, seeing "superstition" and "intolerance" as the harsh masters of credulous people. He attacks the teaching of the Church and traditional apologetics. Al-

though these defects are serious, the *Essai* is nevertheless a grandiose survey of the slow progress of civilization. Nations, such as China, unknown to previous historians, in it assume their rightful place in world history, owing in great part to the impressive documentation Voltaire amassed concerning them.

Philosophical Work. Philosophy in the 18th century, especially in connection with Voltaire, must be understood in a very general sense. Voltaire is not an original and systematic philosopher. His philosophy does embody a set of ideas, even if they are often repetitious and contradictory; but it consists much more in an attitude of general skepticism, of disrespect, of rebellion against received ideas, particularly religious dogmas. His rationalism, more practical than metaphysical, is directed against the very notion of the supernatural, against miracles, against "superstition," by which he means any and all revelation. At the same time, he detested equally as much atheists such as Paul d'Holbach, whose *Le Christianisme dévoilé* (1761) roused Voltaire's indignation.

Deistic Stance. Like Rousseau, Voltaire is a deist, but while Rousseau reaches God through his heart, Voltaire asserts His existence through reason (*see* DEISM). He believes in God as creator of the universe, in a Providence that has established the eternal and immutable laws of the physical world. But Voltaire's God has no relation to the world He has created; He can receive no glory from men, and no prayer can move Him. Strictly speaking, man has no duty toward such a remote God. To maintain fear among the common people, and hence social stability, Voltaire preaches also a revengeful God as remunerator, a teaching quite inconsistent with his denial of an immortal soul.

Inconsistency of His Thought. Voltaire's philosophical ideas are spread throughout his works, in the form of rapid attacks, clever insinuations, or lengthy exposés. The *Lettres Philosophiques* (1734), which exploded on the French scene like a bombshell, are mainly an account of Voltaire's experience in England (the original title was *Lettres sur les Anglais*). The 24 letters deal with many subjects: the variety of religions in England, Parliament, political institutions, Newton, Shakespeare, Addison, Pope, Swift, and Locke. In an extraneous 25th letter, Voltaire vented his animosity against PASCAL, an attack to which he returned in *Remarques sur les Pensées de Pascal* (1742) and in *Dernières Remarques* (1777). The *Traité de métaphysique* (1734) contains Voltaire's speculative philosophy, based on an experimental observation on the nature of man, expressed in simple terms, which the layman can comprehend.

The *Dictionnaire philosophique portatif* (1764), which in its final form included 614 articles, is the summary of Voltaire's entire philosophy presented in alphabetical order. He was influenced by many thinkers— Montaigne, Bayle, Condillac, Locke, Collins, and the English deists—and his thought is gravely inconsistent on fundamental points. Voltaire, an optimist in the Cirey period (e.g., *Le Mondain,* 1736, and *Discours en vers sur l'homme,* 1738), turned into a bitter cynic and pessimist in the *Poème sur le désastre de la Ville de Lisbonne* (1756) and in *Candide* (1759). In a similar *volte-face,* the defender of free will in the *Traité de métaphysique* and in a correspondence with Frederick beginning in 1734, became the apologist of determinism in *Le Philosophe ignorant* (1755) and in the *Dictionnaire philosophique* (s.v. ''Liberté'').

Voltaire's *Contes de Guillaume Vadé* (1764), masterpieces of satire, cynicism, irony, and wit, are practical and amusing demonstrations of philosophical themes. *Zadig* (1747), showing the vagaries of human destiny and the trials of a just man, is, in spite of the conclusion, an attack against Providence. *Candide* (1759) is a more overt denunciation of the optimism of POPE and of LEIBNIZ and again of Providence. Candide pursues his beloved Cunégonde throughout Europe and parts of America, but meets only with disappointments, cruelty, injustice, and stupidity in a long series of unbelievable adventures. In a genre imitative of Swift, his *Micromégas* (1752) introduces two travelers from the planet Sirius who, judging the affairs of men from the point of view of giants, find everything ridiculously small and unimportant. *L'Ingénu* (1764) shows the difficulties a good Huron Indian encounters in adapting himself to civilized society; under this guise Voltaire ridiculed religion and denounced social abuses.

Overt Attacks on the Church. Fearful of the civil authority that had condemned many of his works, Voltaire waited until he enjoyed a relative security in Ferney to launch his open attacks against the Church and her dogmas. In dozens of brochures, starting with the *Sermon des Cinquante* (1755), he mocked the inspiration of the Bible, the notion of a chosen people, the Sacraments, and the institution of the Church. (Some 39 of his works were placed on the Index.) Even in Voltaire's time learned exegetes, such as the Abbé Guénée, had refuted his assertions, but they were no match for him in popular style, and their scholarly vindication of the truth never reached large audiences.

Influence on Social Problems. Voltaire's fight against intolerance was carried into the field of legislation when he became the champion of CALAS and Sirven. Calas and Sirven, both Protestants, had been unjustly, it was thought, condemned by the Parliament of Toulouse for having murdered a son and a daughter, respectively,

because they had embraced Catholicism. Voltaire obtained the rehabilitation of both and described Calas's case in his *Traité sur la Tolérance* (1763). In *Commentaire sur les délits et les peines* (1766) he advocated the principle that punishment should be commensurate with the offense. He berated the various provincial parliaments for their abuses of power and denounced the varieties of laws in different jurisdictions. He demanded an equitable assessment of taxes and the suppression of many imposts that paralyzed commerce. In this field of social and legal reform, Voltaire's ideas are sound; they paved the way for many improvements.

Voltaire may rightly be called the father of RATIONALISM in the 19th century and even in the 20th. The successive waves of anticlericalism that swept first through the French *bourgeoisie* and then through the masses, and the harsh measures taken against the Church may possibly be traced to his influence. The weakness and the incoherence of his philosophy have been established by modern critics, but none has denied him his place as an inimitable master of style and one of the greatest writers in French literature.

Bibliography: G. L. DESNOIRESTERRES, *Voltaire et la société française au XVIIIe siècle,* 8 v. (Paris 1867–76). G. LANSON, *Voltaire* (2d ed. Paris 1910). R. NAVES, *Voltaire: L'Homme et l'oeuvre* (Paris 1942). A. NOYES, *Voltaire* (New York 1936). N. L. TORREY, *The Spirit of Voltaire* (New York 1938). F. VIAL, *Voltaire: Sa vie, son oeuvre* (Paris 1953). F. M. A. VOLTAIRE, *Oeuvres complètes,* ed. L. MOLAND, 52 v. (rev. ed. Paris 1877–85); *The Works of Voltaire,* with critique and biog. by J. MORLEY, notes by T. SMOLLETT, new tr. W. F. FLEMING and introd. by O. H. G. LEIGH, 42 v. (New York 1901–03). M. M. BARR, *A Century of Voltaire Study: A Bibliography of Writings on Voltaire, 1825–1925* (New York 1929). D. C. CABEEN, ed., *A Critical Bibliography of French Literature,* v. 4 *The Eighteenth Century,* ed., G. R. HAVENS and D. F. BOND (Syracuse 1951).

[F. VIAL]

VOLUNTARISM

From the Latin *voluntas,* meaning will, ''voluntarism'' is used in two senses in philosophy and theology. For scholastics, the term is applied to any theory that gives prominence to will as opposed to intellect; whereas among modern thinkers, the term designates any theory that explains the universe as emanating ultimately from Will itself. In the former sense, the philosophies of St. AUGUSTINE, St. ANSELM OF CANTERBURY, WILLIAM OF OCKHAM, and John DUNS SCOTUS may be styled voluntarist. Among the moderns, the principal voluntarists include Blaise PASCAL, Immanuel KANT, and Arthur SCHOPENHAUER.

Patristic and Medieval Voluntarism. Christian thinkers of the patristic and medieval period are usually classified as voluntarists, not because they grant an exclusive primacy to will, since God is also Truth, but because they approach existential truth by a subjective involvement, by choices based upon love.

Augustinian Theory. The philosophy of St. Augustine, for example, is characterized by a burning search for the beatifying Good. For him, the spirit can rest in a saturating joy only if it is free from all doubt and uncertainty. While admitting that the mind attains unchanging and necessary truths, St. Augustine inquires how it would perceive these truths if it were not illumined by God. He holds that, in the order of means, knowledge seems to be first, but its function is only mediative; in the order of the end or perfection, love is primordial. Man does not have to acknowledge the truth passively; such a truth does not beatify; it must be desired, willed, and loved. God is more than an idea, He is a presence; He is more than an imposing need, He is an attracting and exalting love. "God is charity."

Yet nowhere does Augustine subordinate intellect to will. The Neoplatonism that underlies the whole of his philosophical speculation makes such an attitude impossible. Although his doctrine of grace and of providence supposes a definite and characteristic psychology of will, in the metaphysical order Augustine always conceives God as essentially intelligence. God is the "Father of Truth." On this is based a proof of God's existence that occurs several times in his works and is peculiarly Augustinian in tone (*Div. daem.* 53.2 [*Patrologia Latina,* ed. J. P. Migne, 271 v., indexes 4 v. (Paris 1878–90) 40:35]; *Lib. arb.* 2.7–33 [*Patrologia Latina* 32:1243–63]). God is "the sun of the soul," Himself performing the functions that scholastics ascribed to the *intellectus agens* (*Gen. ad litt.* 12.31.59 [*Patrologia Latina* 34:479]). Faith, too, with St. Augustine as with St. Anselm, involves intelligence. For both, the principle *intelligo ut credam* is no less true than the principle *credo ut intelligam* (*In psalm.* 118.18.3 [*Patrologia Latina* 37:1552]; *Serm.* 43.7.9 [*Patrologia Latina* 38:258]).

Scotus's Voluntarism. The philosophy of John Duns Scotus is more distinctly voluntaristic. On the freedom of the will he is particularly clear and emphatic. He insists that the will itself, and nothing but the will, is the total cause of its volitions. It is not determined by another, but determines itself *contingenter,* not *inevitabiliter,* to one of the alternatives that are before it (*In 2 sent.* 25). This is freedom, an attribute that is essential to all higher forms of will, and consequently is not suspended or annulled in the beatific vision (*In 4 sent.* 49.4). Because the will holds sway over all other faculties, and again because to it pertains that charity which is the greatest of the virtues, will is a more noble attribute of man than is

intelligence. Will supposes intelligence, but the former is *posterior generatione,* and it is therefore the more perfect (*In 4 sent.* 49.4).

Modern Theories of Will. Among modern philosophers for whom voluntarism is basic, the general attempt is to approach being, not through thought and necessity, but through will and freedom.

Pascal's Voluntarism. In the 17th century, the voluntaristic Christianity of Blaise Pascal was set in opposition to the rationalistic humanism of René DESCARTES. According to Pascal, the mathematical method is not the only method permitting one to attain the truth; he therefore draws a sharp distinction between the spirit of geometry and the spirit of refinement. The heart has reasons that reason does not know; the heart, rather than reason, experiences God.

For Pascal, if man is to attain belief in God, he must arouse his desire, eliminate the obstacles, and jolt himself from his torpor. The desire for happiness haunts and disturbs man's heart. God is vastly desirable and infinitely lovable; it is tragic not to seek Him.

Kant's Theory. The voluntarism of Immanuel Kant arises from the fact that he perceives only the structural element of intellectual knowledge, without its existential aspect. He explains knowledge by the determinism of the datum and the forms of sensitivity, the categories of the spirit and pure apperception, the term of which is a purely ideal Absolute. From his analysis of knowledge, he concludes that, since understanding has no intuition proper to it, metaphysics lacks ontological import.

Yet one more easily renounces the truth than the good. Despite his agnosticism, Kant seeks, at any price, to maintain the absolute value of the moral act. For this purpose, he separates this act from God, since the mind cannot know His existence with certitude, as well as from interest and sentiment, which would make this value relative. The moral precept is categorical and universal (*see* CATEGORICAL IMPERATIVE). One must perform one's duty, not because it is pleasing or interesting, or because one seeks to attain God, but only because it is a duty. Since the law obliges absolutely, and no one is held to the impossible, Kant concludes that human freedom is apodictically certain.

The ETHICAL FORMALISM of Kantian morality results from a dualism that separates the will from the instincts, goodness from truth, and man from God. This is a nonexistent formalism, since, if the will must take account of universal precepts, it should also be concrete, under the penalty of being whimsical and unreal. It is an idolatrous formalism, since this law must be adored although it arises from human subjectivity and does not beatify. Kant's moralism tolls the knell of morality.

Schopenhauer's Quietism. Arthur Schopenhauer, a disciple of Kant, adopted Kantian agnosticism and accentuated it. Nevertheless, although Kant held that NOUMENA were unknowable, he did not want to eliminate them. How can one explain the presence of noumena in consciousness other than by a faculty concerned with the absolute? According to Schopenhauer, this faculty of the absolute constituting the substance of being is the will. The will is the only substance, the ultimate reality, the sole, indestructible producer of existence. Yet, in man, the will, which is one, infinite, and unchangeable in itself, is individualized and limited by its relation with the body, and misled by knowledge, which deceives it by empty delusions. Because of this fact, man's will-to-live, which is temporal, is illusory, impotent, and forever doomed to misfortune. How can man be freed from misfortune? The philosopher or sage has intuition about the worthlessness of the will-to-live; he is healed from illusion; freed from desire and fear, need and regret. Renouncing the principle of individuation, he identifies himself with that impersonal and cosmic will which constitutes Being. QUIETISM, a radical will ostracizing the world and annihilating the self, is the supreme wisdom. This is a curious metaphysics, since, having exalted the will and isolated knowledge, it states that the will is basically impotent and constrains it not to will any more and to undergo an impersonal Destiny.

Nietzsche and the Will. Schopenhauer said that the will is the substance of being; in order to be, he renounced existence. According to Nietzsche, the mischievous phantasmagoria of the noumena must be renounced; the only existents are the PHENOMENA, the free acts of the will. The act of the will is absolute in itself, not ordered to something beyond it, whether it is a matter of the values claimed by the moralists, the paradise of the Christians, the nirvana of the Buddhists, or the happiness dreamed by Schopenhauer. One must forget to act ''for,'' ''for the sake of,'' or ''because.'' These expressions are sacrilegious, since they divest the will of what belongs to it and make it dependent, whereas it is absolutely good in itself. Centuries of logic, morality, and religion have debased the will, which, of itself, is free and sovereign. There are those who have spoken of necessary truths, necessary laws, absolute certainties, and religious duties. Man subjected himself to these false teachers and became corrupt. He must become free from this subjection. Morality is a crutch for the crippled, religion a hospice for the sick. Superman emancipates himself by an act of revolt, he seeks the death of God. Being completely free, he feels joyful in this act of complete emancipation. This, however, is a purely formal, fictitious, and nonexistent freedom, since, for Nietzsche as for Schopenhauer, the will, lacking all power of accomplishment, remains impotent and is imprisoned in the immutable cycle of the eternal return.

Pragmatism and Value Philosophies. Although voluntaristic, other modern philosophies such as PRAGMATISM and the many philosophies of value are not so negative. William JAMES, basically an empiricist, reacts against positive scientism. One thinks, not for the pleasure of thinking, but to live. Whether scientific or philosophical, every thought arises from a need and corresponds to an interest. Every judgment, then, is an act of faith. A true judgment is specified and determined, not by the nature of the object, but by the finality of the subject. Its criterion, then, is subjective. Thereby James justifies belief in freedom, assuring more than one value for man's action, and belief in God, provided that God gives him help and thereby strengthens him.

The point of departure for Kantian morality is the categorical and universal imperative, which is the source of the identical character in the moral duties imposed upon all men. The point of departure for contemporary moralities is not an a priori reality, namely, law, but the subject who desires, wills, projects, who is situated in such a milieu at such a time, who uses such a resource or suffers such a weakness. Each person's duty must be defined, and the ideal line of his progress must be traced, from the aspect of this concrete situation. Duty is defined, not only by the moral law, but even more so by vocation, that is, the singular call resounding in each conscience and simultaneously taking account of its effective reality and the universal values inciting this call.

For Kant, the aim of the will is the law; for the pragmatist, the will is finalized by values. A value is what is desirable, what makes a thing good, a principle of existentiality. Values are surely multiple: economic and spiritual values, esthetic and moral values, profane and religious values. Is a subordination among these possible? Some place them in a hierarchical order, since some values are relative, others absolute; some are hypothetical, others unconditional. There is an a priori order of the heart as well as an a priori order of reason. At the top of all these values there appears the Value par excellence, a living God, who actualizes and infinitely prolongs human activity. Very often this God is no longer the God of philosophers, but the God of Christians.

Critique. In opposition to the determinism of the intellectualism philosophers, modern voluntarists overemphasize the fact of freedom and analyze it as something intrinsically constituting being. On the basis that man's conduct is not predetermined like that of the animal, they go to the extreme position of holding that man should make himself exist, that, to exist and make the world exist, man must recognize self-imposing subjective attitudes. The pitfalls of intellectualism and voluntarism seem to be present throughout the history of human thought. As two extreme philosophical attitudes, they are oversimplified attempts to arrive at the truth, as well as oversimplified means of combating patent error.

See Also: EXISTENTIALISM; INTELLECTUALISM; IRRATIONALISM; WILL.

Bibliography: H. J. MARROU and A. M. LA BONNARDIÈRE, *S. Augustin et l'Augustinisme* (Paris 1955). J. LAPORTE, *Le Coeur et la raison d'après Pascal* (Paris 1950). E. BOUTROUX, *La Philosophie de Kant* (Paris 1926). J. WAHL, *Études Kierkegaardiennes* (Paris 1938). F. COPLESTON, *Arthur Schopenhauer* (London 1946). W. A. KAUFMANN, *Nietzsche* (Princeton 1950). J. ROYCE, *William James and Other Essays* (New York 1911). P. ORTEGAT, *Religion et Intuition,* 2 v. (Gembloux 1948). R. EISLER, *Wörterbuch der philosophischen Begriffe,* 3 v. (4th ed. Berlin 1927–30) 3:429–435. A. COLOMBO, *Enciclopedia filosofica,* 4 v. (Venice-Rome 1957) 4:1691–94. A. MICHEL, *Dictionnaire de théologie catholique,* ed. A. VACANT et al., 15 v. (Paris 1903–50; Tables générales 1951–) 15.2:3301–22.

[P. ORTEGAT/L. J. WALKER]

VOLUNTARITY

The character of a HUMAN ACT that is free, i.e., performed with adequate knowledge of the circumstances and without necessitation from external forces. As with human FREEDOM or FREE WILL, the concept of voluntarity includes both cognitive and appetitive factors. This article provides an explanation of the concept from the viewpoint of Aristotelian-Thomistic psychology and moral philosophy; for other views, *see* VOLUNTARISM; WILL; CHOICE; DETERMINISM.

End of the Human Act. The specifically human act is one that proceeds from antecedent deliberation and without necessitation by forces outside the AGENT. As in the case of deliberation, choice bears formally on means rather than on ends. Some goods, it may be noted, are means from one perspective and ends from another; yet there is an overall good of human action, an ultimate end, that is only an END and must be loved and sought for itself alone. With respect to this end man is in one sense necessitated and in another sense not.

Each human APPETITE has the GOOD for its end. This statement is true by definition. The good may be nominally defined as that which all things seek as perfective of themselves. Any good is sought or pursued as making up some lack or lacuna in the agent. Every human agent, insofar as to be a human agent implies having a mind and a will, cannot not seek its good. Aristotle held that verbal agreement could be achieved concerning the comprehensive good sought by man; for him, all men seek happi-

ness. This is intended to be a purely factual or descriptive statement: to be a human agent is to direct oneself toward some end as perfective and as constitutive of happiness.

Unanimity is not so complete, however concerning where human happiness is to be found. Aristotle grouped these differences under three general headings, speaking of a life lived for pleasure, the political life, and the contemplative life. So too S. A. Kierkegaard attempted a classification of the goals that *de facto* define human lives in his notion of spheres of existence: the aesthetic, the ethical, and the religious. In either case, attention is directed to the fact that men live their lives in many ways, that some men seek happiness in ends that differ from those sought by others. From this it would appear that, though no man is free not to intend *some* ultimate goal of action, men are free to choose what ultimate end they will.

This is not exactly true. Speaking generally and from the vantage point of philosophy, there is only one ultimate end that truly perfects the human agent. Aristotle's search for, and definition of, this end is classic and provides the basis for the following analysis (*see* MAN, NATURAL END OF).

Only a good commensurate with the agent can be perfective of the agent. For this reason the human good, human happiness, cannot consist in the activity of the vegetative faculties or in that of the sensitive faculties as such (*see* FACULTIES OF THE SOUL). The specifically human function (ἔργον) is rational activity, and the human good consists in the excellence (ἀρετή) of that activity. Consequently, Aristotle observes, the human good must consist in excellent, or virtuous, rational activity. And since "rational activity" is ambiguous, covering both the activity of reason itself and the acts of other faculties insofar as they can be brought under the sway of reason, the excellences, or virtues, that constitute the good perfective of the human agent are either intellectual or moral.

To employ the schema of the cardinal virtues, man is not free to choose whether or not his happiness or perfection consists in prudence, justice, temperance, and fortitude. These can be considered as so many articulations of the end that, in the natural dispensation, is given man as alone perfective of him as a human agent. Deliberation and choice bear on the means to achieve, or realize, this end in particular acts. It is to this arena of deliberative choice that the concept of voluntarity applies.

The Voluntary Act. The concept of voluntarity arises when one asks, and this not simply theoretically but on the basis of experience, what is required if man is successfully to direct himself to the end that is naturally his. Once more man is not free to choose just any end as perfective of the kind of agent he is, anymore than he can constitute his own nature otherwise than as it is. But, unlike other cosmic agents, man must direct himself to the end he recognizes as his. He must choose, in the various and fluctuating circumstances in which he finds himself, the way in which he can achieve his good, or perfection. In order so to choose, he must be aware of his circumstances so that, given these, he can deliberate about and assess the best way to act here and now. The voluntary act is one that proceeds from such deliberation and involves a choice that is not necessitated by any external force.

The voluntary act is deliberate, flowing knowingly from a principle intrinsic to the agent. Since voluntary activity involves acting for an end, and since many animals obviously act for an end and with knowledge, the question can arise whether brutes are capable of voluntary activity. St. THOMAS AQUINAS, by distinguishing between a full, or perfect, knowledge of the end and an imperfect knowledge of the end, is able to distinguish between the perfect and imperfect voluntary act.

> The voluntary in the full sense follows on a perfect knowledge of the end which is had insofar as one is able, once the end has been apprehended, to deliberate concerning the end and the means of achieving it and to direct or not direct himself to the end. A lesser sense of the voluntary follows on the imperfect knowledge of the end, which is had when the agent apprehends the end but does not deliberate, being immediately moved toward it. Hence the voluntary in the full sense belongs only to rational agents, while brute animals may be said to act voluntarily in a lesser sense of the term. [*Summa theologiae* 1a2ae, 6.2.]

Aquinas indeed maintains that every agent, whether cognitive or noncognitive, acts for an end (*see* FINALITY, PRINCIPLE OF). Yet it is the knowing agent who deliberates about the way to achieve the end, in his view, who has voluntarity in the full sense. One may dispute at length concerning the degree of, or approximation to, deliberation present in brutes, but for present purposes it suffices to note that voluntary activity is obviously found in the human agent.

A further point about the voluntary act can be made in terms of the traditional distinction between the elicited and commanded acts of the WILL. As the very term suggests, an elicited act is the act of the will itself, whereas the commanded act is the activity of a faculty other than the will that comes under the sway of will. Thus, just as acts can be rational either essentially or by way of participation, so too acts can be denominated voluntary either essentially or by way of participation.

Furthermore, it can be pointed out in the interest of clarification that sometimes inaction or not willing is said to be voluntary. A mark of the voluntary agent is that he has it within his power both to act and not to act; and although it is the positive action that first comes to mind when one speaks of the voluntary, the refusal to act, the refusal to will, can be praiseworthy or culpable—itself a sign that not acting too is sometimes voluntary.

Privations of Voluntarity. The nature of the voluntary act can better be seen by examining cases in which the voluntarity of an act is seemingly or really, wholly or partially, impeded, and thereby gives rise to what is known as INVOLUNTARITY.

Violence. The most manifest privation of voluntarity is had when a human agent is subject to VIOLENCE. Thus, if a person is taken forcibly where he does not wish to go, his going can hardly be described as voluntary. His activity proceeds not from his own inner powers but from outside forces. One can say that Igor went to Siberia; but, if one knows the circumstances, he may regard it as odd to attribute the trip to Igor without qualification. The whole thing may have been forced upon him and thus is not something he brought about; in this event, Igor has been reduced to the status of a thing.

Fear. Another privation of voluntarity, one to which Aristotle pays particular attention, is found in actions done through FEAR.

> But with regard to the things that are done from fear of greater evils or for some noble object (e.g. if a tyrant were to order one to do something base, having one's parents and children in his power, and if one did the action they were to be saved, but otherwise would be put to death), it may be debated whether such actions are involuntary or voluntary. Something of the sort happens also with regard to the throwing of goods overboard in a storm; for in the abstract no one throws goods away voluntarily, but on condition of its securing the safety of himself and his crew any sensible man does so. [*Eth. Nic.* 1110a 4–11.]

The very nature of the first case indicates that the assertion that human acts are voluntary cannot be equated with the unrealistic view that human action is easy. A man who acts treasonably because of a threat to loved ones in hostage may be performing an act that, in the abstract, he finds reprehensible and immoral; yet, in the given circumstances, he acts under a kind of suasion that is difficult to resist. One can, however, as Aristotle suggests, allow that there is an element of the involuntary in what he does, since by committing treason he is doing something that goes contrary to what he wills. On the other hand, since he is not powerless to act otherwise than as he does, it does not seem right to say that his action is unqualifiedly involuntary. Indeed, considered concretely, the action can be judged voluntary. In the case of the captain, one might say that he does not wish to throw his cargo overboard, and yet, in the concrete circumstances, this is just what he deliberately and voluntarily does. He is acting out of fear, and yet he chooses to do what he does.

The seeming harshness of this conclusion is alleviated when one takes account of the fact that fear may be so intense as to be productive of severe psychic disorder and that acts performed in such a state, whether of long or short duration, whether temporary or permanent, do not fully qualify as human acts. Even without this addendum, Aristotle notes that it is not easy to lay down rules for deciding which of two alternatives (voluntary or involuntary) is to be chosen, since particular cases do differ widely (cf. *ibid.* 1110b 1–8). When one takes into account fuller knowledge of the mountains of the mind, "frightful, sheer, no-man-fathomed," the difficulties of laying down rigid rules for, or boundaries of, the voluntary increase enormously. However, and this must be insisted upon, the difficulties could not even be defined if one did not have certitude that there are human acts, and these by far the majority, that are unquestionably voluntary.

Ignorance and Nonvoluntarity. The human act proceeds from the deliberative will of the agent. In the case of violence or fear the agent is aware of what is going on; but his will is either utterly contrary to what is happening, or he is acting in conflict with what he wishes because of fear. Voluntarity can be absent from action because of ignorance as well. The following is Aristotle's analysis.

> Everything that is done by reason of ignorance is *non*-voluntary; it is only what produces pain and repentance that is *in*voluntary. For the man who has done something owing to ignorance, and feels not the least vexation at his action, has not acted voluntarily, since he did not know what he was doing, nor yet involuntarily, since he is not pained. Of people, then, who act by reason of ignorance he who repents is thought an involuntary agent, and the man who does not repent may, since he is different, be called a nonvoluntary agent; for, since he differs from the other, it is better that he should have a name of his own. [*Eth. Nic.* 1110b 18–24.]

Pain and repentance are introduced here as signs of the involuntary, since for Aristotle they indicate that what has happened is actually contrary to what the agent wills. Something done without awareness and that, when recognized, does not cause pain and regret cannot be said to be contrary to the wishes of the agent. Nevertheless, because the agent did not know what he was doing, his act cannot be called voluntary either. So Aristotle suggests that one call such a man a nonvoluntary agent to indicate the negation of deliberative action but not the privation of his desires.

Culpable Ignorance. Aristotle raises the question whether, since violent activity is such that its cause is wholly outside the agent without any assent being given by the agent, one may say that the pleasurable object does violence to the agent and thus that actions performed under its influence are involuntary. The objection is hardly serious, but it becomes the occasion for introducing a necessary distinction with respect to the way in which one can act without knowledge. "Acting by reason of ignorance seems also to be different from acting *in* ignorance; for the man who is drunk or in a rage is thought to act as a result not of ignorance but of one of the causes mentioned, yet not knowingly but in ignorance" (*ibid.* 1110b 25–30). Aristotle goes on to say that wicked men in general are ignorant of what they ought to do; one must here be aware of his variation on the Socratic contention that to know the right thing is to do it and that, consequently, not to do the right thing is to be ignorant.

Aquinas adds somewhat to Aristotle's reasoning:

> One who like the incontinent man acts because of concupiscence loses sight of his original desire, which would repudiate what he now desires, since he has changed and now desires what earlier he would have repudiated. Therefore, what is done out of fear is in a certain sense involuntary, but that which is done because of concupiscence is in no way so. For the incontinent man, under the influence of concupiscence, acts contrary to what he at first wished but not contrary to what he wishes now. [*Summa theologiae* 1a2ae, 6.6 ad 2.]

A man who, because of moral weakness, does something contrary to what he earlier and generally knew he ought to do ignores the knowledge he has when he acts. In that sense he is acting through ignorance, an induced ignorance thanks to which he does not actually consider what he ought to do in this particular case. In short, in every instance of wrongdoing there is a failure of knowledge; and, in the case of the incontinent man, this failure is a result of concupiscence. But the ignorance involved is responsible and culpable; moreover, because at the moment of choice nothing contrary to the will of the agent is involved, such acts can scarcely qualify as involuntary.

Innocent Ignorance. What kind of ignorance, then, makes an act involuntary? It is useful at this point to invoke the Aristotelian analysis of FORTUNE, or CHANCE, because it is possible to link the involuntary act resulting from ignorance and bad fortune, on the one hand, and the nonvoluntary act and good fortune on the other. One says that something has come about by fortune, or luck, when an agent who is acting to achieve a given goal unwittingly brings about an effect he did not intend, which is accidentally connected with what he intends and which relates to him as good or evil. Thus, a man who digs a well and discovers a buried treasure has come upon something he did not expect to find, which he cannot count on finding when he digs a well and which, being found, puts him in a state of high elation. In short, the example is one of good luck. Since the man in the example did not set out to find the treasure, his finding of the treasure can hardly be called voluntary. However, since the finding of it does not go contrary to his wishes, one cannot say he acted involuntarily. Consequently, one can apply to the agent who luckily brings about a beneficent result Aristotle's notion of nonvoluntary agent. In the case of bad luck, however, it is more appropriate to speak of the agent as acting involuntarily. Thus, one who drives home with caution and circumspection and hits a child who darts into the street brings about a result he did not intend, which is rare and unexpected and exceedingly painful to him. This is not the sort of thing he wants to do. Since it goes contrary to his will, this act must be classified as involuntary (cf. *Summa theologiae* 1a2ae, 76.3). Thus, not every instance of acting *in* ignorance is a case of the involuntary act due to ignorance, but only one bringing about a painful or evil effect that is contrary to the wishes of the agent.

Human Responses to Voluntarity. It is useful, in speaking of types of voluntarity, to consider human responses to the acts involved, for these are often signs of the differences one seeks to explicate. In the case of acts performed in fear, people praise the man who, despite his fear of painful consequences, does the right thing. In the case of a man who, out of fear, does the wrong thing, and this does not outweigh to any great degree the harm he fears, their tendency is to forgive and pardon. However, if the evil done is completely out of proportion to the evil he fears, they are more severe and, in many cases, condemn the act outright. Pity they reserve, Aristotle suggests, for a man caught in the plight of the tragic hero. Such a one unwittingly brings about a tremendous evil, one that goes massively contrary to his wishes. The tragic consequence, though not intended, though proceeding from no culpable defect of knowledge, is so great that the man involved may feel the need to make expiation. The witness can only pity such a man. He will feel, as Aristotle puts it in the *Poetics*, pity *and* fear. The fear arises from the recognition that men are all subject to such eventualities, that their occurrence illuminates something essential about the human situation.

There is, as already noted, a range of deeds that are responsible and voluntary; it is extremely important to insist on this. But at the same time that one asserts that man is, within the range of such deeds, the master of his destiny, a free agent, one must also take into account that there is an encompassing darkness, a perpetual possibility of results of choice that man can neither foresee nor intend. In many cases such unintended effects introduce surprise and joy into men's lives; in many other cases they cause sorrow and pain, evils that escape the canons of morality because the actions in question are involuntary. Grievous misfortune is one example of the limit-situations of which Karl Jaspers speaks. It is when, in lived experience, men are brought face to face with the limitations on their freedom and responsibility that they find their attention inescapably drawn to ultimate questions.

See Also: MORALITY; CIRCUMSTANCES, MORAL; HABIT.

Bibliography: M. J. ADLER, ed., *The Great Ideas: A Syntopicon of Great Books of the Western World*, 2 v. (Chicago 1952) 2:1071–1101. A. CARLINI, *Enciclopedia filosofica*, 4 v. (Venice-Rome 1957) 4:1687–91. A. MICHEL, *Dictionnaire de théologie catholique*, ed. A. VACANT et al., 15 v. (Paris 1903–50) 15.2:3300–09. J. A. OESTERLE, *Ethics: The Introduction to Moral Science* (Englewood Cliffs, N.J. 1957). R. ZAVALLONI, *Experience of Voluntary Activity* (Milan 1955).

[R. M. MCINERNY]

VOLUSENUS, FLORENTIUS

Also Florence Wilson, Scottish humanist; b. Morayshire, Scotland, c. 1500; d. c. 1557. He studied at Aberdeen under ERASMUS's friend, Hector Boece, before moving to Paris, where about 1526 he became tutor to Thomas Wolsey's son. Thus introduced to English affairs, and supported by Thomas Cromwell, he played a minor role in Henry VIII's divorce negotiations. After teaching in the school founded by SADOLETO at Carpentras (1535) he eventually settled in Lyons, where he was still active in 1551.

Volusenus's *Scholia in Somnium Scipionis* (1529) shows a cautious taste for the Christian Platonism of Ficino, while commentaries on Psalms 15 and 50 (1531–32) associate him with the scholars around J. LEFÈVRE d'Étaples. In these, enthusiasm for Hebrew and patristic studies was clearly opposed to the Sorbonne dialectictans who "lack the fire and force of speech that stirs the mind to love." This pastoral concern was reflected in his *Commentatio theologica* (1539), where the spirit of the DEVOTIO MODERNA was clothed in Ciceronian eloquence; yet he admired St. Thomas Aquinas and censured Erasmus's ignorance of philosophy.

Like his friend Thomas Starkey, Volusenus supported the English schism in its early years; but in 1536, the year of Reginald POLE's *Defence*, he left the country for the last time. The works of his Lyons years show no departure from orthodox doctrine; and his teaching on justification, described as Lutheran, was basically anti-Pelagian, and indebted to St. John FISHER. Certainly his sympathies were wide: his friends included Protestant and Catholic martyrs, while his writings dealt with the inner life and shunned polemic. The lengthy dialogue *De animi tranquillitate* (1543) rehearsed pagan wisdom before arriving at a Pauline vision of the cross, true seat of inner peace. Volusenus's final work, it ran through six editions and was admired in settings as diverse as Renaissance Siena and Boswell's Edinburgh.

Bibliography: J. DURKAN, "The Beginnings of Humanism in Scotland," *Innes Review* 4 (1953) 11–13. *Musa Latina Aberdonensis,* ed. W. D. GEDDES (Aberdeen 1910) 3:449–455. F. BUISSON, *Sébastien Castellion,* 2 v. (Paris 1892) 1:35–36.

[D. BAKER-SMITH]

VOLUSIANUS OF TOURS, ST.

Eighth bishop of Tours; d. Toulouse, France, *c.* 498. Of senatorial rank, married and related to his two predecessors, PERPETUUS and Eustochius, he occupied the see from 488 to 496. A letter to him from Ruricius, Bishop of Limoges, makes reference to his bad-tempered wife, and Gregory of Tours reported that, suspected of sympathy for the Franks, Volusianus was exiled to Toulouse by the Visigoths and died there, possibly martyred by decapitation. His relics were brought to Foix, where a celebrated Augustinian church was erected in his honor.

Feast: Jan. 18.

Bibliography: *Acta Sanctorum* Jan. 2:558–559. GREGORY OF TOURS, *The History of the Franks,* ed. and tr. O. M. DALTON, 2 v. (Oxford 1927) 2:65, 473. L. DUCHESNE, *Fastes épiscopaux de l'ancienne Gaule,* 3 v. (2d ed. Paris 1907–15) 2:301–304. A. BUTLER, *The Lives of the Saints,* rev. ed. H. THURSTON and D. ATTWATER, 4v. (New York 1956) 1: 116. P. DE LA COUDRE, *La Vie de St. Volusien* (2d ed. Foix 1893). A. MERCATI and A. PELZER, *Dizionario ecclesiastico,* 3 v. (Turin 1954–58) 3:1358.

[L. M. COFFEY]

VONIER, ANSCAR

Benedictine, theologian; b. Ringschnait, Württemberg, Nov. 15, 1875; d. Buckfast Abbey, Dec. 26, 1938. Vonier entered Buckfast Abbey as a boy, and after his ordination in 1898 was sent to the College of S. Anselmo, Rome, for his doctorate in philosophy. En route from Barcelona to Niño Dios, Argentina, the "Sirio" in which Vonier and his abbot were sailing was wrecked off Cartagena, and Abbot Natter was among the many who were drowned. Dom Anscar was rescued and six weeks later was elected second abbot of Buckfast. Convinced that he had been spared for some special work, he immediately began the rebuilding of the abbey church on its ancient foundations. This was a huge undertaking, for the work was carried out exclusively by the monks, and its completion took 32 years. Besides this achievement Abbot Vonier gained prominence as a theologian. His *The Human Soul* (1913) and *A Key to the Doctrine of the Eucharist* (1925) soon became classics. *The Personality of Christ* (1915), *The Christian Mind* (1921), *Christianus* (1933) were also well received and have been widely read not only in English but in translations. The posthumous *Sketches and Studies in Theology* (1940) also deserves mention. In 1952 Burns & Oates, London, published his *Collected Works.* Abbot Vonier possessed the gift of expounding abstruse questions so as to make them intelligible not only to professional theologians but to intelligent lay readers as well.

Bibliography: E. GRAF, *Anscar Vonier: Abbot of Buckfast* (Westminster, Md. 1957).

[J. STÉPHAN]

VOODOO

A set of beliefs and rites, African in origin but closely interwoven with practices borrowed from the Roman Catholic Church, constituting the living religion of both the rural and urban masses of the Republic of HAITI. Its followers expect from it what every man has always expected from his religion, a remedy for his ills, the satisfaction of his needs, and the hope that at least part of him will survive death.

Voodoo was able to grow strong roots in Haiti because of the long "schism" or separation from Rome (1804–60). The Catholic cult never ceased but it had fallen into unworthy hands. A black legend of voodoo, fostered in colonial times by hatred and fear, was strengthened in the 19th century by Spencer St. John's report of a court case of cannibalism and other stories of doubtful veracity; its almost perfect expression is found in W. B. Seabrook's *The Magic Island* (New York 1929).

Voodoo worshipers believe in one supreme God, too good to get angry, and in numerous spirits to whom a cult is offered: the *lwa,* the *marasa* or twins, and the dead. Many *lwa* are African deities; others are local spirits. Communication between voodooists and the supernatural world is effected through possession. The individual becomes the instrument, the "horse" of a spirit, and displays in his new personality a behavior that has sometimes been characterized as hysteric.

There are undeniable affiliations between Dahomean and Haitian mythologies, but the tradition has been impoverished and only insignificant remnants are left of the functions and attributes of the major Dahomean gods. The ritual has suffered from its uprooting much less than the system of beliefs; the *kanzo* or initiation, for example, still reproduces the scheme of its Dahomean prototype.

MAGIC and WITCHCRAFT have proliferated in the shadow of voodoo. One can still find suspicious objects at the crossroads, discover traces of mysterious ceremonies in the cemeteries, ponder over "werewolf passports" or hear about weird crimes, which prove that, although many stories of bewitchment and poisoning are the product of wild imagination, black magic is practiced. Moreover, if there are wizards, societies of witches, and "werewolves" who do not belong to the voodoo cult, there are also *houngans* (voodoo priests) who "serve with both hands," that is to say, are at the same time sorcerers. In fact a good *houngan* is expected to know everything about witchcraft (a mixed product of African and French medieval magic) in order to fight it.

Numerous similarities between voodoo and ancient Mediterranean orgiastic cults have been pointed out: groups centered on sanctuaries, dances followed by possessions, and initiation rites; but it should not be forgotten that voodoo deities move also in the industrialized modern world and form a part of modern civilization. Contributions to voodoo tax heavily the poor man's income; on the other hand, in many regions voodoo songs and dances are the only recreation and *houngans* the only healers. As a religious system, voodoo has lost nothing of its creative power; the faith of its followers is as deep as ever and its ritual and mythology are in constant growth. Two trends, however, favor an impending decay. First, the campaign of the Roman Catholic Church against superstition has made the peasant conscious of the opposition between voodoo and Christianity and of the evil in his use of Catholic liturgy in a pagan cult. Second, the commercialization of voodoo, favored in Port-au-Prince by the development of tourism, is bringing into the ritual changes that displease the majority.

Bibliography: A. MÉTRAUX, *Le Vaudou haïtien* (Paris 1958), tr. H. CHARTERIS (Oxford 1959). J. G. LEYBURN, *The Haitian People* (New Haven 1941) 131–142. J. L. COMHAIRE, "The Haitian Schism: 1804–1860," *Anthropological Quarterly* 29 (1956) 1–10. S. and J. COMHAIRE-SYLVAIN, "Survivances africaines dans le vocabulaire religieux d'Haïti," *Études dahoméennes* 10 (1955) 8–20. M. DEREN, *Divine Horsemen: The Living Gods of Haiti* (New York 1953). M. J. HERSKOVITS, *Life in a Haitian Valley* (New York 1937) 205–218; *The Myth of the Negro Past* (New York 1941) 33–53. M. LEIRIS, "Note sur l'usage des chromolithographies par les vodouisants d'Haïti," in *Les Afro-Américains* (Dakar 1953). L. DENIS and F. DUVALIER, "L'Evolution stadiale du vodou," *Bulletin du Bureau d'ethnologie, Haiti* 3 (February 1944) 9–32. L. MARS, *La Crise de possession dans le vaudou: Essais de psychiatrie comparée* (Port-au-Prince 1946). L. MAXIMILIEN, *Le Voudou haïtien: Rite radakanzo* (Port-au-Prince 1945). O. MENNESSON-RIGAUD, "Étude sur le culte des marassa en Haïti," *Zaire* (1952) 597–621. C. E. PETERS, *Le Service des loas* (Port-au-Prince 1956). M. RIGAUD, *La Tradition voudoo et le voudoo haïtien* (Paris 1953). J. ROUMAIN, *Le Sacrifice du tambour assotor* (Publication du Bureau d'ethnologie, Haiti, No. 2; Port-au-Prince 1943). G. E. SIMPSON, "Magical Practices in Northern Haiti," *Journal of American Folklore* 67 (1954) 395–403.

[S. COMHAIRE-SYLVAIN]

VORAU, MONASTERY OF

Belonging to the Austrian congregation of Canons Regular of St. Augustine, in the diocese of Graz-Seckau. In 1163 Margrave Ottokar III of Traungau gave his lands of Vorau to Abp. Eberhard I of Salzburg to found a cloister as a pastoral center in northeast Styria. The monastery flourished for a long time before the Reformation and after the Council of Trent. The Romanesque church, built after a fire in 1237 in which Provost Bernhard II died saving MSS, and later made Gothic, was rebuilt in 1660 by Domenico Sciassia and so richly decorated (1696–1758) that it is the most splendid baroque church in Styria. Walled and fortified from 1458, Vorau was a bulwark against the Turks for 300 years. Its library, whose hall, built in 1731, is one of the most beautiful in Austria, has 35,000 volumes, 206 incunabula, and 415 MSS, including codex 276 (*c.* 1190), the oldest collection of Middle High German poems. Vorau's history is in great part that of its provosts.

Bibliography: P. FANK, *Catalogus Voraviensis* (Graz 1936); *Das Augustiner-Chorherrenstift Vorau* (2d ed. Vorau 1959); *Lexikon für Theologie und Kirche,* ed. M. BUCHBERGER, 10 v. (Freiburg 1930–38) 10:692–693. R. KOHLBACH, *Die Stifte Steiermarks* (Graz 1953).

[P. FANK]

VOSTÉ, JACQUES MARIE

Scripture scholar, b. Bruges, Belgium, May 3, 1883; d. Rome, Feb. 24, 1949. He entered the Dominican Order in 1900 and was ordained in 1906. After studying under Ladeuze and Van Hoonacker at Louvain, he went (1909) to the ÉCOLE BIBLIQUE in Jerusalem. Upon obtaining the licentiate in Scripture in 1911, he was appointed to the faculty of the Angelicum (Rome). In 1929 he became a member of the Biblical Commission and was also consultor to several Oriental Congregations. An excellent pedagogue and endowed with great linguistic ability, he wrote on a wide variety of scriptural subjects. A *Festschrift in his honor* [*Angelicum* 20 (1943)] features a bibliography of his works complete up to that year; it covers 158 items. Best known are his *De Scripturarum veritate* (1924), *De synopticorum mutua relatione et dependentia* (1928), *Studia Ioannea* (2d ed. 1930), *Studia Paulina* (2d ed. 1941), *De Passione et morte Iesu Christi* (1937), and two volumes of *Parabolae selectae* (2d ed. 1933). In 1939 he was named Secretary of the Biblical Commission. The three outstanding events that occurred during his term of office were the encyclical *DIVINO AFFLANTE SPIRITU* (1943), the new translation of the Psalter (1945), and his own *Letter to Cardinal Suhard* (Jan. 16, 1948) concerning the Pentateuch and the literary forms of Genesis 1 to 11. He also edited two volumes of a Syriac text of Theodore of Mopsuestia in CSCO (1940).

Bibliography: R. T. A. MURPHY, ''The Very Reverend James Vosté, OP,'' *The Catholic Biblical Quarterly* 11 (1949) 121–125; ''James Marie Vosté, OP, STM, SScrD,'' *Homiletic and Pastoral Review* 49.2 (1949) 526–528.

[R. T. A. MURPHY]

VOTIVE OFFERINGS

A rather imprecise term denoting many different objects dedicated to deities, religious dignitaries, or institutions.

General Use. Votive offerings are more or less distinguishable from sacrifices: (1) by the fact that they are not prescribed in a formal, regular way; (2) by the greater degree of permanence of the object that is dedicated, (temple, altar, priestly utensil, etc.); (3) by the manner in which the gift is linked with a vow or wish (Lat. *votum*) of the giver, whether in the case of a thanksgiving offering made for a blessing bestowed on the giver, in the case of an offering meant to guarantee a deity's help for some future undertaking or therapy, or in the case of a gift of submission sealing the giver's transition to a new state of life.

Even when clearly related to a vow or wish, votive offerings can be manifold. Well known are the sculptured legs, feet, etc., or abandoned crutches—as in ancient temples of Asclepius or in certain Catholic shrines—of grateful devotees, cured of deformities or disease in their legs or other parts of their bodies. Although much superstition must have been associated with votive offering at all times, the religious sense of these gifts is to be seen at the two poles of the offering transaction, viz, the giver, dedicating himself through his offering, and the deity, to whom or in whose name the gift is made. A telling example of a votive offering with a strong emphasis on the sacrificial vow and self-dedication is provided by Tacitus (*Germania* 31). The Teutonic tribe of the Chatti used to let their hair and beards grow and did not cut them until an enemy was killed. Another illustration of this aspect is the ceremony of *devotio,* in which the ancient Roman general vowed destruction to himself, and the army of his enemy with him, in order that his side might be given the victory by the gods. Again, temple precincts of the god Aiyanar in South India are often filled with clay. models of horses, the god's favored animal, which are gifts of grateful devotees seeking the god's assistance. The custom of presenting symbols proper to the deity whose help is invoked, or images of that diety, itself is indicated from Mycenaean times in Greece. The reason is undoubtedly to be found in the basic symbolism of each religious structure; the god who is worshiped can ultimately be given only himself. This symbolism is continued in the prayers of devotion to God in Judaism and Christianity: the offerings of prayer find in God not only their goal but their origin as well.

Bibliography: G. VAN DER LEEUW, *Religion in Essence and Manifestation,* tr. J. E. TURNER, 2 v. (London 1938; 2 v. New York 1963). M. P. NILSSON, *Geschichte der griechschen Religion* (Munich 1955–61), *passim.* S. EITREM, *The Oxford Classical Dictionary,* ed. MARY CARY et al. (Oxford 1949) 954–955. W. H. D ROUSE, *Greek Votive Offerings* (Cambridge, England 1902); J. HASTINGS, ed., *Encyclopedia of Religion & Ethics,* 13 v. (Edinburgh 1908–27) 12:641–643. H. WHITEHEAD, *The Village Gods of South India* (New York 1921).

[K. W. BOLLE]

In the Bible. In the Old Testament, a votive offering was a voluntary offering vowed to God but not required by the Law. The technical term in Hebrew for such an offering is *neder* (vow). The only legislation prescribed for votive offerings regulated the place where they were to be made (Dt 12.5–6, 11).

The purpose of such a vowed offering was to give force to the prayer offered by the Israelite, and the formula in which the vow was couched contained either a positive or negative condition—negative, if the promise was to be fulfilled before the favor was granted, e.g., abstaining from wine for a certain period of time in order to gain God's blessing (1 Sm 14.24), and positive, if the Israelite promised to do something after Yahweh granted the favor. The positive vow always had as its object a cultic action. The Psalms contain frequent references to votive sacrifices that were publicly celebrated in the Temple at Jerusalem as a result of Yahweh's having granted a favor [Ps 21(22).26; 49.(50).14; 55 (56). 13]. Nowhere is there any mention of good works or charity as the thing being vowed.

Abuses made their appearance later when vows were made too easily. This resulted in the lessening of their binding force and opened the way to the practice of allowing payment of a price to substitute for the object vowed to God. Thus the uniquely religious significance of the vow was depreciated. [*See* VOW (IN THE BIBLE)].

In the New Testament there is no direct evidence that the early Christians carried over the Jewish practice of votive offerings.

Bibliography: R. DEVAUX, *Ancient Israel, Its Life and Institutions,* tr. J. MCHUGH (New York 1961) 417–418. *Encyclopedic Dictionary of the Bible,* translated and adapted by L. HARTMAN (New York, 1963) 2552–2554.

[R. J. FLYNN]

VOTUM

A word (from Lat. *voveo,* I desire) used in the technical description of a doctrine elaborated to show that God's salvific will embraces those who inculpably cannot actually use the indispensable sociosacramental means of SALVATION, i.e., the Church and the Church's Sacraments (specifically Baptism, Eucharist, and Penance). Concretely, this qualified *votum* is the intention (not necessarily explicit) to use the divinely appointed means when feasible to do so, an intention that is contained in SUPERNATURAL ''FAITH which works through charity'' (Gal 5.6). God accepts this *votum* as a surrogate for actual Church membership and for actual sacramental use. See Trent: Denz 1524, 1543, 1604, 1677; Pius XII: Denz 3821, 3866–72. Vatican II's *Gaudium et Spes* teaches that ''since Christ died for everyone, and since all are in fact called to one and the same destiny, which is divine, we must hold that the Holy Spirit offers to all the possibility of being made partners, in a way known to God, in the paschal mystery.'' (22) The *votum* can be understood as the human response to this divine offer.

See Also: SALVATION, NECESSITY OF THE CHURCH FOR.

Bibliography: G. VODOPIVEC, ''Membri *in re* ed appartenenza *in voto* alla Chiesa di Cristo,'' *Euntes Docete* 10 (1957) 65–104. F. SULLIVAN, *Salvation outside the Church? Tracing the History of the Catholic Response* (New York 1992).

[F. X. LAWLOR/D. M. DOYLE]

VOW (IN THE BIBLE)

The practice of making vows or solemn promises to God deliberately and freely to perform some good work was ancient among the Israelites. Ordinarily a vow consisted in a promise to offer a sacrifice, if God would give some assistance in a difficulty; hence, the Hebrew word *neder* means both vow and VOTIVE OFFERING. No directive in the Mosaic Law obliged man to make vows or votive offerings; but it specified where they were to be carried out (Dt 12.5–6), and it regulated and stressed their fulfillment (Dt 23.22–24), since there was an evident tendency among the Israelites to promise frequently but lightly (Dt 22.21–23; Nm 30.2–16; Na 2.1; Eccl 5.1–6; Sir 18.22–23). Every Israelite could consecrate himself in a particular manner to God by vow for a limited period or for life. Such persons were called NAZIRITES. They bound themselves to abstain from all products of the grapevine, from contact with a corpse, and from cutting or shaving their hair (Nm 6.1–8).

The legislation of the Pentateuchal PRIESTLY WRITERS permitted the commutation of certain vows or votive offerings, but specified the amount of money to be paid in each case (Lv 27.1–25). The vows of unmarried women were subject to the approval of their fathers (Nm 30.4–6); those of married women to that of their husbands (Nm 30.7–9, 11–16). Vows of widows and divorced women were automatically valid (Nm 30.10), since they were no longer subject to husbands.

Frequently a vow was accompanied by an oath invoking a curse if the vow was broken (1 Sm 14.24). When a vow was fulfilled, God's praises were sung [Ps 65 (66); 66(67); 115 (116B); etc.]. Vows of destruction (Lv 27.28–29), a particular kind of consecration known as ban or anathema (Hebrew ḥērem), were curses by which persons or things were dedicated, wholly or in part, to the exclusive service of God and, if the ban was by God's decrees, consigned to destruction. Jephthah vow to sacrifice to God the first person whom he should meet on his victorious return from battle (it proved to be his daughter) is a singular incident relative to vows in the Bible (Jgs 11.29–31). There can be no doubt that he intended to offer a human sacrifice. Jephthah's act may be excused in the light of customs of the time; moreover, the story may be in part etiological to explain the ancient Israelite custom of annual mourning of women for maidens who died before they became mothers (Jgs 11.37–40).

Because of the denunciations of abuses concerning vows found so frequently in the Prophets, it has been wrongly argued that the taking of vows was merely an OT custom that ceased to have justification with the coming of Christianity. The contrary is evident from the practice of primitive Christianity. Christ, although He spoke in repudiation of the abuses connected with certain vows, such as the CORBAN vow (Mk 7.9–13), never denounced them as such. St. Paul shaved his head at Cenchrae in fulfillment of his Nazirite vow (Acts 18.18), and on his last journey to Jerusalem he took a temporary Nazirite vow (Acts 21.22–26).

Bibliography: *Encyclopedic Dictionary of the Bible,* translated and adapted by L. HARTMAN (New York, 1963) 2552–54. *Catholic Bible Encyclopedia,* ed. J. E. STEINMUELLER and K. SULLIVAN (New York 1956), Old Testament (1956)1118–19, New Testament (1950) 661. H. GROSS, *Lexikon für Theologie und Kirche,* ed. J. HOFER and K. RAHNER, 10 v. (2d, new ed. Freiburg 1957–65) 4:640. A. WENDEL and J. JEREMIAS, *Die Religion in Geschichte und Gegenwart,* 7 v. (3d ed. Tübingen 1957–65) 2:1322–24.

[M. R. E. MASTERMAN]

VULGATE

Latin translation of the Bible made almost entirely by St. JEROME and declared the official (*authentica*) edition of the Bible for the Latin Church. The word Vulgate comes from the Latin term *versio vulgata* meaning the popular, widespread version. This term was used by the early Fathers of the Church, particularly by St. Jerome, to designate the SEPTUAGINT version of the Bible, both in its Greek form and in its Latin translation that is now commonly called the Old Latin Version (*Vetus Latina*). But in the early Middle Ages, when Jerome's version had everywhere supplanted the pre-Jerome version, the former began to be called the Vulgate. The Council of TRENT decreed that, among the various Latin versions then (1546) in circulation, the Vulgate (of Jerome) was to be received as the official one (*pro authentica habeatur*), and referred to it as the *vetus et vulgata editio* (old and widespread edition).

Old Latin Versions

These versions consist of the Latin texts of the Bible that precede those revisions and fresh translations, largely produced by St. Jerome, that form the complete Latin Bible known for centuries as the Vulgate. In broad terms, then, the Old Latin Bible is the pre-Hieronymian Latin Bible—the body of the Latin Scripture that first came into being when the Church spread among people who were not at home in Greek. In the New Testament the Old Latin presents translations from the Greek original; in the Old Testament, retranslations of Greek versions of Semitic originals.

Origin. The following statement made in 1963 by the scholar perhaps best qualified to speak, Pater Bonifatius Fischer of Beuron, summarizes certain essential points: ''The Old Latin translation of the Bible came into being little by little during the 2d century, perhaps in Africa, perhaps in Rome or Gaul, probably in different places, in any event not in one effort and not as the work of one single translator. It underwent rapid and extensive development and differentiation.''

Characteristics. A number of characteristic features stand out in the Old Latin texts, with their abundant richness of forms, generated by a freedom of approach to the Scriptures that readily permitted adaptations, modifications, or changes. The language itself is peculiar, reflecting Greek syntax, and expecially the Latin coinages produced to represent in neo-Latin form the Greek words that the translator saw before him (thus, e.g., *salvator, sanctifico, glorifico*), coupled with the transliterations from the Greek (e.g., *apostolus, baptizo, parabolor*). The vulgar and colloquial flavor in the Old Latin versions makes clear that they were prepared not for a cultured elite but for the ill-educated. The widespread influence of this Old Latin Biblical text has naturally been felt in subsequent writings, the effect being sometimes direct, sometimes through the absorption of Old Latin readings into the Vulgate, and quite regularly through quotations in patristic texts.

The Vulgate

Typically, the production of the Old Latin text of the Bible is the work of unknown writers (even though certain of the Fathers produced their own renderings as occasion demanded and Augustine in particular came to revise a large portion of the Latin Scriptures).

Work of St. Jerome. The production of the body of renderings that are called the Vulgate, however, is dominated by one individual, St. JEROME (d. 420), Father and Doctor of the Church, acting as reviser, acting as translator, and in some instances refusing to act at all. If these distinctions are made one may with reasonable accuracy call the Vulgate his work. It is providential that what was to become the standard Bible of the Latin Church reflects in so large a measure the religious conviction, the critical acumen, the learning and scholarship, and the writing skill of such a man.

Revision of Old Latin Gospels. Jerome's production of the Latin Bible text extends over a period of some 22 of his middle years, from 383 to 405. Most of it took place in the first two decades of his long, final residence in Bethlehem; but it began during the nearly three years that he spent in Rome in his late 30s, largely occupied as secretary to Pope St. Damasus. According to Jerome, it was the Pope himself who directed him to the most impressive of these Roman achievements, the correction of an Old Latin text of the Gospels against the Greek in order to erect a standard of correctness among a welter of widely divergent and often faulty copies. In acceding to the Pope's invitation—official commission it hardly can have been—Jerome produced what is now known as the Vulgate Gospels, the four texts that in due course became and still remain official in the Latin Church.

Partial Revision of Old Latin Old Testament. Settled in Bethlehem, Jerome found in the library of nearby CAE-

SAREA IN PALESTINE the stupendous work of Biblical erudition that Origen achieved in his *Hexapla.* The fifth of the six columns in this massive assemblage contained Origen's own edition of the Septuagint (LXX), with its spits (*obeli*) and asterisks to mark redundancies or deficiencies in the LXX. It would seem that Jerome felt impelled to translate the whole of this into Latin or at least to revise existing Latin in the light of it, continuing his Roman procedures but now using an authoritative and critical Greek text. Some modern scholars hold that he fully achieved this exacting task, even if little now remains of it; others, that his Hexaplaric recension was applied only to 1 and 2 Chronicles, the so-called books of Solomon (Proverbs, Ecclesiastes, and the Song of Songs), Job, and the Psalms. In these four cases the evidence is compelling. The text of the Hexaplaric 1 and 2 Chronicles is lost, but the preface that Jerome prefixed to it is preserved.

Gallican Psalter. The most fruitful result of Jerome's concern with Origen's *Hexapla* was the Psalter that he based on it—Jerome's second (*Vat. Vulg.*). This was the Psalter that gradually achieved an ascendancy even over Jerome's own direct translation from the Hebrew. It was probably introduced in the liturgy in Gaul before Alcuin, who was led by this fact to adopt it for his recension of the Bible. It thus won its place in the typical Bible of the Middle Ages, and was absorbed into the Roman Breviary, where it reigned supreme until the coming of the New Latin Psalter in 1945. (The term Gallican applied to it came from the popularity the Psalter received in Gaul in the early Middle Ages.) As the Vulgate Psalter par excellence, this Hexaplaric Psalter was retained by the Benedictines of S. Girolamo to form part of the Vatican Vulgate, where it appeared in 1953 as v.10, furnished with Origenic critical signs such as Jerome had noted down in Caesarea. For all its popularity the Gallican Psalter contains a large number of verses that trouble readers. Some of these readings resist comprehension because they are faulty translations; others are hard to understand either because they are slavish translations or because of difficulties inherent in the original Hebrew or because of the reader's lack of familiarity with Biblical locutions or Christian Latin vocabulary. Pius XII's new Psalter of 1945 came into being partly for the purpose that those who recited the Psalter might have an intelligible text in every verse. There were many who thought that its editors had gone much too far, showing little tendency to conserve the excellencies of Jerome's work. Consequently, in 1961, at Clervaux, Dom Robert Weber, OSB, brought out *pro manuscripto* a "new recension" of the Gallican Psalter (*Psalterii secundum Vulgatam Bibliorum Versionem nova recensio*) in which only those verses are reworded that required it for intelligibility.

New Version of Old Testament Protocanonical Books. While he was still occupied with his revisions according to the *Hexapla,* Jerome had entered upon the most important phase in his provision of Latin Bible text, the translation from the Hebrew itself. His awareness of the apologetic value of presenting the *Hebraica veritas* directly, bypassing even Origen's Septuagint, is found in a letter (*Ep.* 32.1) written before he left Rome, where he seems to have had at his disposal at least the greater part of the Hebrew text of the Bible, and it is elsewhere explicit [see *Praef. in Isa., Patrologia Latina*, ed. J. P. Migne 28:774 (828): *Adv. Rufin.* 3.25, *Patrologia Latina* 23:476 (498)]. At Bethlehem he provided himself with Hebrew teachers, especially a certain Baranina (*Ep.* 84.3).

The basic chronology of Jerome's activity is reasonably clear. If ch. 134 of the *De viris illustribus* of 392–393 is a later addition of the author and hence does not prove that Jerome had already by then completed the Psalms and the Prophets (less Baruch), it at least groups these books together as occupying the translator in the first stages. What prompted the order in which Jerome proceeded was less the scheme of any Biblical canon than the promptings of friends eager to have one or another book translated. If one adopts the chronology determined by F. Cavallera, 1 and 2 Samuel, 1 and 2 Kings, and Job were grouped with the Psalter and the Prophets in the early period from 389 to 392. Ezra and Nehemiah followed in 394; 1 and 2 Chronicles, two years later. In 398 the three books of Solomon were rendered in eight days, but Jerome was busy also at the Octateuch, which was completed by 405. The prefaces and dedicatory letters that accompanied Jerome's translations show that most frequently the unit of publication was the single book (the four Major Prophets separately, the Psalms, Job, Ezra and Nehemiah, 1 and 2 Chronicles, Tobit, Judith, and Esther), but in some cases the books were published in groups, as had been the Gospels at Rome (1 and 2 Samuel with 1 and 2 Kings, the Minor Prophets, the books of Solomon, the Pentateuch, Joshua with Judges and Ruth).

New Version of Some of the Old Testament Deuterocanonical Books. Having done so much, Jerome regarded his work on the Old Testament text as complete, for he declined to issue translations of five books that had a place in the canon of the Greek-speaking Jews but were lacking in the Palestinian—Wisdom, Ecclesiasticus (Sirach), Baruch, and 1 and 2 Maccabees. These books, consequently, came into the Latin Bible only in Old Latin texts that had received not even revisory attention from Jerome. To Tobias (Tobit) and Judith, which were in the same position, he was more receptive, for he produced Latin versions from Aramaic sources available to him. If Jerome is to be taken literally in what he says in his preface to Tobias, he had the Aramaic text of that book translated to him orally by a person who knew both Aramaic and Hebrew, and both prefaces stress the rapidity with which he worked at these two versions. Jerome was similarly receptive toward certain sections of Daniel and Esther that were not to be found in the Hebrew. For the well-known passages in Daniel—the Song of the Three Youths in the fiery furnace and the stories of Susanna and of Bel and the Dragon (Dn 3.24–90; 13.1–14.42)—Jerome drew upon the Greek of the so-called Theodotion recension (presumably as found in the sixth column of Origen's *Hexapla*), as he himself tells us in notes before 3.24, after 3.90, and after 12.13. The parts of Esther that Jerome found present in the LXX Greek but wanting in the Latin he set out after 10.3 with full notes accompanying the several excerpts to indicate the places from which they had been assembled.

Books of the New Testament after the Gospels. To the evolving complete Latin Bible that was eventually to become known as the Vulgate, all three periods of Jerome's application to the sacred text contributed. From the triennium at Rome came the Gospels: from the earlier years at Bethlehem, with their special dedication to Origen's *Hexapla,* came the Psalms (the Gallican Psalter); from Jerome's continued residence there, centered in rendering the *Hebraica veritas,* came all the Old Testament except the five deuterocanonical books, which he declined to translate or revise. The Vulgate was thus complete except for the second half of the New Testament—the Acts, the Epistles, and Revelation. What is the origin of the Vulgate text of these books? There is no consensus on this question. The common opinion has been that these books, showing in any event a correction of Old Latin text from the Greek, received this treatment from Jerome himself, who would have continued in their case the process he began with the Gospels. This position is consistent with, but not proved by, Jerome's twice uttered declaration that he had indeed revised the New Testament after the Greek. A strong denial to Jerome of the Vulgate Pauline Epistles made by D. De Bruyne in the early decades of the 20th century still has its effect and tends moreover to involve the other Epistles and the Acts and Apocalypse as well. De Bruyne held that the Vulgate text of St. Paul goes back to Pelagius. However, the editor of Ephesians in the *Vetus Latina,* H. J. Frede, has shown that, although Pelagius was the first to use the Vulgate St. Paul, he did not compose it—and neither did Jerome. Among Frede's positive conclusions are these (*Vet. Lat.* 24.36*): "The Vulgate text of St. Paul's letters came into being in the last years of the 4th century at the latest. . . . Its author is unknown, although he is identical with the man who gave to the Vulgate at least the Catholic Epistles and perhaps the whole of the New Testament outside of the Gospels."

Psalterium Romanum. It remains here to return briefly to the Psalter that Jerome produced at Rome *c.* 384. The common opinion is an attractive one: that this Psalter is the *Psalterium Romanum,* whose use, once widely extended, is now virtually limited to the canons of St. Peter's Basilica in Rome, but which was the source of many of the older chants (Introits, etc.) of the Roman Missal. Once again it was Dom De Bruyne who in recent times (1930) most effectively contested the tradition. Studies made or reported by Vaccari (*Scritti* 1:211–221) have modified De Bruyne's conclusions and give reason to believe that the *Romanum,* while indeed not Jerome's work, was used and studied by him and ought to be regarded as the text on which he based his now long lost, first rapid correction and revision of the Psalms.

Transmission of the Vulgate Text. The universal use that St. Jerome's new versions and revisions would ultimately receive could hardly have been predicted from the person-to-person basis in which he issued his works one by one as he executed them or from the reactions of influential contemporaries. In one quarter were the objections collected by RUFINUS and answered by Jerome in his *Contra Rufinum* [2.24–35, *Patrologia Latina* 23:447 (468)]; and in another was St. Augustine, with his loyalty to the LXX, who first showed himself disturbed by the new venture (*Epist.* 71.4–5; 82.35; *Corpus scriptorum ecclesiasticorum latinorum* 34.2: 252, 386) and only gradually changed his position (*Doctr. christ.* 4.15, *Patrologia Latina* 34:96; *Civ.* 18.43, *Corpus Christianorum. Series latina* 47:638). In one of his letters (*Epist.* 71.5) Augustine tells Jerome of the tumult aroused at Oea (present-day Tripoli in North Africa) when passages from the new version were used in public worship.

Gradual Acceptance. Enthusiasts, however, were not lacking; one of them, Jerome's friend Sophronius of Bethlehem (d. after 392), rendered part of the new translation into Greek. Possibly the staunchest supporters of Jerome's versions in the 5th century were the disciples of Pelagius (notably, JULIAN OF ECLANUM); it is in works of Pelagians that the earliest witness to the Vulgate text of certain of the New Testament Epistles is to be had. In the Gaul of the 5th and 6th centuries a selective use of the Vulgate was made by John CASSIAN, St. EUCHERIUS OF LYONS, Salonius (d. after 451), St. AVITUS OF VIENNE, and St. GREGORY OF TOURS.

Early Pandects. As an effective agent in the dissemination of Vulgate text, Gaul was surpassed in the 5th, 6th, and 7th centuries by Italy. The ecclesiastical writers, in their quotations from Scripture, furnish important evidence, but not a little is based on what has been shown—especially by B. Fischer—of the origins of early editions of the Bible, whether these present single books (or groups of books) or the whole Bible in one volume (pandect). Fifth-century Italy was probably the source of an edition of the Vulgate 1 and 2 Samuel that carried in its margins 114 Old Latin readings. No portion of the original still exists, but few subsequent Vulgate manuscripts of these books are free of its influence. The Spanish Bishop Peregrinus produced in the 5th century an edition of the letters of Paul that was based in part on a Vulgate text of Italian origin. To northern Italy of the 7th century probably belongs the source of the two-volume 9th-century Bible known complete to Robert ESTIENNE at St. Germain-des-Prés in Paris in the early 16th century but now reduced to its second volume (B.N. lat. 11553). Among all Bibles this *Sangermanensis* has been found by Fischer to give a "reasonably accurate reproduction of an ancient pandect." From CASSIODORUS (d. *c.* 580) comes the earliest-known evidence of such Latin pandects; but as will at once be clear, his copies have not themselves survived or, in their text, been reproduced in later codices. Important as being preserved in its original form is a New Testament produced under the direction of Bishop Victor of Capua (d. 554) in Campania and completed in 547, a volume that has been at Fulda since St. BONIFACE owned it there. In this book the Gospels are represented only in a harmony, based, it seems, on an Old Latin form of Tatian's Diatessaron. Only in the Gospel harmony did Victor's New Testament exercise discernible influence, becoming in time the model for the first Biblical translations into Old High German and Italian.

Italy, north and south, was not unique in this early period in owning pandects of the Vulgate. Spain also had them, but only one has thus far been identified—one in the underscript of 82 leaves of a manuscript (15) of the León Cathedral chapter (Lowe 11:1636), these forming less than one-eighth of the 7th-century original. Certain later Spanish Bibles of the 9th and 10th centuries may well reflect more or less faithfully models close in date to the León fragments.

Supplanting of the Old Latin. While none of these Spanish Bibles has been satisfactorily linked with St. ISIDORE OF SEVILLE, this influential bishop (600–636) handed down more than one strong commendation of the Vulgate. He declared Jerome's translation "justly preferred to all others" (*Etym.* 6.4.5), stating his reasons in the very language—as Dom Gribomont has noted—used by St. Augustine (*Doctr. christ.* 2.22, *Patrologia Latina* 34:46) in praise of the "Itala." The tone Isidore employed elsewhere (*De ecclesiasticis officiis* 1.12.8, *Patrologia Latina* 83:748C) in commending Jerome's version for liturgical use suggests approbation of the *status quo* rather than a newly proposed position. And, indeed, a generation earlier St. GREGORY I at Rome had given strong support to the Vulgate Old Testament

through his prevailing use of it in his commentaries. Farther to the north—in Ireland and England—the Vulgate had long before penetrated, in some cases in the best texts of southern Italy. The liturgical agreements reached in the synod of Clovesho (747) tended to terminate local Celtic usages in favor of the Roman—the beginning of a reform that would, in turn, through the missionaries, affect both Germany and Gaul. The insular shift in Bible text may be seen in the writings, on the one hand, of Saints PATRICK and COLUMBAN, who still used the Old Latin, and on the other, in the *De excidio,* attributed to St. GILDAS, where a mixed Biblical text shows strong Vulgate infusion. Wax tablets of *c.* 600 found in an Irish bog and reported on by D. H. Wright in 1962 show Psalms 30–32 in a basically Gallican text.

Such diversity in the Biblical text found in ecclesiastical writers comes about in more than one way but partly reflects the Bible manuscripts themselves, to which the crosscurrents of transmission often brought a pattern of mixture. Thus, in a single volume a set of the Prophets may show Jeremia in St. Jerome's translation along with the others in the Old Latin; or the canticles that are scattered through the books of the Bible may appear as Old Latin set in a Vulgate context.

The supremacy of the Vulgate, which had begun to be quite clear in the 6th and 7th centuries, was by the 8th established beyond question, and Italian books had played the major part in it.

Alcuin. The reign of CHARLEMAGNE was eventful and, in at least one point, decisive for the editing and copying of the Vulgate Bible. Attention commonly focuses here upon ALCUIN of York, who migrated to France in 793 and died there in 804; he was abbot of St. Martin's, Tours, from 796 on and for more than 20 years was a close associate of Charlemagne. In a letter for Easter 800 Alcuin declared himself occupied in the "emendation of the Old and New Testaments" at the "king's instruction [*praeceptum*]" (*Monumenta Germaniae Historica: Epistolae* 4.322–323), but the Biblical manuscripts associated with him carry no foreword or title page to mark them as officially sponsored.

The manuscript on which Gutenberg was to draw some 650 years later was little more than a somewhat debased descendant of the Alcuin Bible. The Alcuin text, Vulgate throughout, was not formed with very great care. In correctness and orthography, the books from Alcuin's own time in particular are deficient and lag behind the Bibles of Maurdramn and Angilramnus; but some improvement appeared under Alcuin's successors at St. Martin's.

The Alcuin Bible was not based upon a preexisting pandect. Like the *Amiatinus,* it was a composite of different texts assembled into one. A distinctive component was its Psalter—Jerome's revision after Origen's Hexapla, not his translation from the Hebrew. The preference in Charlemagne's realm for the Psalter that thereafter was to be called "Gallican" may have been initially independent of Alcuin. However, the Alcuin Bible put the seal upon the choice and, in the Latin rite, determined the near universality of the Gallican Psalter for a millennium.

Theodulf. One subject and adviser of Charlemagne who withstood the preference for the Gallican Psalter—choosing rather Jerome's rendering from the Hebrew—was THEODULF, Bishop of Orléans (d. 821) and Abbot of the nearby monasteries of Fleury and Micy. From him have come down a series of six or eight Bibles, small in format and written in small script. Equipped with additional texts to assist the interpretation of the Scripture and beautifully transcribed, these Bibles are at once works of art and truly scientific editions of the sacred text. Characteristic are the variants set in the margin with indication of source. With the help of a baptized Jew, Theodulf went back to the Hebrew and dared to improve upon Jerome.

The 10th to the 15th Century. The long period that falls between the reign of Charlemagne and the stabilization of the Vulgate text through the use of printing has its special importance for the prescholastic and scholastic interpretation (*see* EXEGESIS, BIBLICAL) but is less significant for the study of the text, since recension leading to the recovery of the archetype can draw but little from these six and a half centuries. Only certain salient matters from this period will be touched on here.

First in a succession of revisers is St. PETER DAMIAN. LANFRANC, too, is declared to have taken pains to correct both Testaments and also the "writings of the Holy Fathers . . . in accordance with the orthodox faith" (see E. Mangenot, *Dictionnaire de la Bible,* ed. F. Vigouroux, 5:2478). St. STEPHEN HARDING prepared a Bible at Cîteaux as a model for Cistercian use. Not long afterward another Cistercian, Nicholas Maniacoria (d. *c.* 1145), worked at the text of all three principal Latin Psalters.

In the central stream of the tradition lay the study of Scripture in the schools and universities and especially that study as practiced in the University of Paris. It was here around 1225 that the present usual system of chapter division in the Bible, introduced by STEPHEN LANGTON, came into being.

Vulgate Manuscripts. In listing here the principal manuscripts of the Vulgate—a few out of the thousands that exist—those will be selected that have been found by recent editors to be the most important for establishing the text.

Genesis through Esther. For the Old Testament the report will be confined largely to the well-advanced but still unfinished Benedictine revision (*Vat. Vulg.*) of the Vulgate. Here an average of 30 manuscripts are reported for each Biblical book, but generally the text chosen depends on a very small number—in the typical case, and especially in the Octateuch (Genesis through Ruth), the three that represent as many families (Quentin, *Mémoire,* 453–456).

Psalter and Protocanonical Wisdom Books. With the Psalter (the Gallican), the manuscripts in the top rank are entirely new, partly because a number of the familiar manuscript Bibles, notably the *Amiatinus,* show as Psalter not the Gallican but Jerome's *Iuxta Hebraeos.*

Deuterocanonical Books. With the deuterocanonical books Wisdom and Sirach, the Vulgate offers its first non-Hieronymian elements.

Gospels. The 30 manuscripts used by Wordsworth and White (WW) in their critical edition of the Gospels are divided into three classes: (1) the old, uninterpolated manuscripts (with texts written in Italy or traceable thereto); (2) those whose text shows clear local characteristics (three groups: Celtic, Irish-Gallic, and Spanish); (3) those that supply the recensions (Theodulfian, Alcuinian), plus a Salisbury Bible of 1254 (W) as an example of a scholastic text.

Acts. In the Acts WW used 17 manuscripts (aside from the ten with Old Latin text), of which ten were used for the Gospels and seven were new. In respect of their textual value, four classes are indicated: the principal witnesses, the derivative witnesses, the recensions, and again W. the medieval manuscript from Salisbury.

Epistles and Apocalypse. The manuscripts used by WW for the Epistles (Pauline and Canonical) and the Apocalypse were mainly those already drawn on in editing the Gospel and the Acts.

Printed Editions. The first book of importance to be produced with movable type, the 42-line Bible printed at Mainz between the years 1452 and 1455 by Johann Gutenberg, had as its model a typical Bible of the University of Paris; no manuscript closer to this presumably lost model has been found than *Mainz Stadtbibl. II 67* (14th century). The editions that appeared up to 1511 all derived from this Gutenberg Bible except one printed at Vicenza in 1476. From this period the printed Bibles may be reduced, in terms of text recension, to the 42-line Bible of Mainz.

Early Attempts at Critical Editions. The first attempts at criticism in the printed Bibles begin in 1511; that year, under the editorship of Albert Castellano, OP, there appeared at Venice a Bible with a system of marginal variants. Up to this point corrections brought into the text were not assigned to their source, and frequently none had been used. A new period, however, began with the scholar-printer of Paris and Geneva Robert Estienne (Étienne), whose Bibles run from 1528 to 1556–57. Some of these show a variety of critical signs, and that of 1540 shows in the margin readings from 20 identifiable manuscripts and editions. One of Estienne's Bibles, printed by Badius in Geneva in 1555, is celebrated as being the first to carry the numbered division of verses within the chapters (those of Stephen Langton) that is still in use.

Having in mind criticisms of the Vulgate voiced as early as Lorenzo VALLA, then by ERASMUS, and in turn by the Reformers, the Council of Trent in 1546 issued a decree that assigned to that Bible the character of "authenticity" and called for the printing of a carefully corrected text.

Sistine Edition. The work of revision called for by the fathers of Trent—introduced by extensive and minute collations made under now unknown auspices by the Benedictines of Monte Cassino in the period 1550–69—was carried out through three pontifical commissions, appointed, in turn, by Pius IV, Pius V, and Sixtus V. The first of these was not specialized to the Vulgate and left nothing of importance for it. The commission of PIUS V, which had the revision of the Vulgate as its sole objective, began its work April 28, 1569 and lasted into December 1569; it came to little. Under Gregory XIII, who succeeded to Pius V, more was done for the Septuagint than for the Vulgate. The leader of the Septuagint project, Cardinal Antonio CARAFA, was named by Gregory's successor, SIXTUS V, as president of the third commission concerned with the Vulgate. This held its first session on Nov. 28, 1586.

By November 1588 Pope Sixtus had become impatient with what he regarded as the slow progress of the commission, and, having himself practiced the critical art earlier on the works of St. Ambrose, he took personal charge of the edition, thus beginning a sorrowful chapter in the history of the Vulgate text. In his quite energetic, personal, and often arbitrary corrections, Sixtus only rarely followed the recommendations of his own commission. After hardly more than 6 months of work the near septuaginarian had completed his almost single-handed work of correction. With less than six months consumed at the presses, the printing was complete on Nov. 25, 1589.

Clementine Edition. The bull *Aeternus ille caelestium* that introduced the folio volume is dated March 1, 1590. On August 27 came the sudden death of the Pope, occurring when only the first copies had been distributed. In view of the criticism that had been raised against the edition even in Sixtus's lifetime and that was to become

more intense thereafter, the cardinals, hardly a week after the Pope's death, suspended the new Bible. Many of the changes that the Pope had made were in opposition to the manuscripts. Hence the edition was considered likely to have a disturbing effect among Catholics and to have propaganda value for the heretics. Sixtus's successor, Gregory XIV, taking counsel from St. Robert BELLARMINE, decided, therefore, to have a new revision made in which the faulty changes of the Sistine text might be removed and the Bible republished, still under Sixtus's name. After Gregory's death in the next October and the two-month pontificate of Innocent IX it was upon CLEMENT VIII, elected Jan. 30, 1592, that the task of publishing the revised Bible fell. In the mid-autumn of 1592 the new Bible appeared. It was not until 1604 that the now regular form *Biblia Sacra Vulgatae Editionis Sixti V Pont. Max. iussu recognita et Clementis VIII auctoritate edita* is found, and even then it did not at once displace the original shorter title. But there were in fact some 4,900 differences between the two editions, many, of course, all but negligible yet forming a mass of divergence large enough to arouse among Protestant controversialists such a work as the satirically entitled *Bellum Papale* of Thomas James (London 1600). Official printings of 1593 and 1598 brought in numerous largely mechanical improvements, to produce what remained, in its successive reappearances, the official Vulgate of the Church until 1979 with the issue of the Neo-Vulgate under Pope John Paul II.

Council of Trent and the Vulgate. On April 8, 1546, after more than a month of deliberation, the Fathers of the Council of TRENT issued two decrees on Sacred Scripture. The second of them, called *Insuper* from its opening word and inspired in no small part by a work published in 1533 by the Louvain theologian J. Driedo [d. 1535; see R. Draguet, "Le maître louvaniste Driedo inspirateur du décret de Trent sur la Vulgate," *Miscellanea historica in honorem Alberti De Meyer* (Louvain and Brussels 1946) 836–854], declares that of the then circulating Latin editions of the sacred books, "precisely the ancient and widely current [*vulgata*] edition that had been approved by long use within the Church for so many centuries . . . should be held as authentic"; it also determined that that edition "should be printed in as correct a form as possible" (H. Denzinger, *Enchiridion symbolorum*, ed. A. Schönmetzer 1506, 1508; *Encyclopedia biblica*, ed. T. K. Cheyne and J. S. Black 61, 63). If effective action toward the production of a correct edition of the Vulgate came only slowly—with the Sisto-Clementine Bible of 1592 and, definitively, with the Neo-Vulgate, in 1979—there was an immediate critical response toward the declaration of authenticity, as there already had been toward reports of the council's preliminary deliberations on the point. The criticisms introduced from the Roman Curia and reflected and enlarged in controversies that flourished in the 16th and 17th centuries, especially in Catholic Spain but in Protestant circles as well (a treatise from MELANCHTHON appeared in the very year of the decree), embraced many elements, some of them grounded in misconceptions—e.g., did not the decree debase the scriptural originals and ignore the manifest faults of the Vulgate? [See B. Emmi, "Il Decreto Tridentino sulla Volgata nei commenti della prima (seconda) polemica protestanticocattolica," *Angelicum* 30 (1953) 107–130, 228–272.] A dissertation by St. Robert Bellarmine published posthumously in 1749 largely anticipated the now clear, official interpretation but could not check the continuing criticism of the council's action.

As recently as 1941 a long letter had to be addressed by the PONTIFICAL BIBLICAL COMMISSION to the archbishops and bishops of Italy to put them on their guard against an anonymous attack, made earlier in the year, upon the scientific study of Scripture, that claimed justification in the Tridentine decree *Insuper* (*Enchiridion symbolorum* 3794; *Encyclopedia biblica* 526). This letter, issued under the authority of Pope Pius XII, and especially two paragraphs of the same Pontiff's encyclical of September 1943, *DIVINO AFFLANTE SPIRITU* (par. 21–22; *Enchiridion symbolorum* 3825; *Encyclopedia biblica* 549), state plainly the meaning of the council's use of the term "authentic": that the decree applied only to the Latin Church and to its public use of the Scriptures; that it diminished in no way the authority and value of the original texts, Hebrew or Greek; that the decree in effect affirmed that the Vulgate was free from any error whatever in matters of faith and morals and so could be quoted with complete authority in disputations, lectures, and preaching—that, in short, the term had been used primarily in a juridical rather than a critical sense; and that there had been no intention to prohibit the making of vernacular versions from the original texts rather than from the Vulgate.

Critical Studies. The Vulgate of the 1590s was not, then, the carefully amended recension prescribed by the Council of Trent. It remained for PIUS X, in 1907, to impose the task that would in fact bring this edition into being—a Vatican Vulgate. Much in the intervening three centuries had taken place in the world of scholarship that would help the 20th-century project toward its success. Only a few of these events can be mentioned here.

As early as 1618 there were the *Romanae correctiones* of the Lucas of Bruges. The Maurists A. Pouget and J. Martianay, in editing (1693) the works of St. Jerome, produced a new text of the Vulgate, largely based on the Theodulfian recension. Lacking a certain balance,

therefore, this edition was not worthy to replace the Clementine and, fortunately, did not do so (in D. Vallarsi's reediting it occupies *Patrologia Latina* v.28, 29). Monumental work on the Old Latin text was done in the early 18th century by another Maurist, Pierre Sabatier. In England Richard BENTLEY and J. Walker projected a New Testament (Greek and Latin). Although their plan did not mature, their extensive collections were preserved at Cambridge and proved useful to later scholars. At Leipzig in 1850, Konstantin von TISCHENDORF, known also in Latin Biblical scholarship for editions of more than one Old Latin text, printed that of the *Amiatinus*. In 1873 he produced also an Old Testament begun by T. Heyse, in which the Clementine text was divided according to the *cola et commata* of the *Amiatinus* (also, the *capitula* of that manuscript were printed here). In 1893 Samuel Berger, a young Protestant pastor, encouraged to studies in the Latin Bible by Léopold V. Delisle (d. 1910), produced his invaluable *Histoire de la Vulgate pendant les premiers siècles du moyen âge* (Paris 1893). Near at hand was the professorship at Munich of Ludwig TRAUBE (d. 1907), pregnant with blessing for those paleographical and historical studies in "the age of photography" that brought about and made fruitful the vast collections of facsimiles of manuscripts on which so much of 20th-century Biblical scholarship depends.

New Testament of Wordsworth and White. This rapid survey may serve to introduce a brief account of the two projects in the critical editing of Latin Vulgate text that are here called for—the Oxford edition of the New Testament of Wordsworth-White-Sparks (WWS) and the Benedictine work at Rome on the whole of the Vulgate Latin Bible (*Vat. Vulg.*). Three scholars, helped indeed by many friends and assistants (among them Baron Von HÜGEL), were the makers of this edition. Its first leader, John Wordsworth, when made Anglican bishop of Salisbury, found an able collaborator in another Oxford scholar, Henry J. White, at whose death (1934) yet a third Oxonian, H. F. D. Sparks, brought to completion in 1954 what had been started in 1889 and dedicated then to Queen Victoria. As the three-volume work progressed, the attention given by the editors to the Old Latin sources became greater, so much so that in the second and third volumes WWS goes far toward replacing Sabatier. Valuable supplements to the edition itself are the seven volumes (1883–1923) of *Old-Latin Biblical Texts.* In his assessment of WWS, Fischer (*op. cit.*) pointed out various ways in which advances must still be made in editing the Vulgate New Testament.

Benedictine Edition. The stimulus to the Benedictine revision of the Vulgate came with a letter addressed by Pope Pius X on April 30, 1907, to the abbot primate asking the united efforts of the Benedictines of the Confederated Congregations toward realizing the truly adequate edition of the Vulgate that the Council of Trent had entrusted to the Holy See. A commission was set up under the direction of Dom Aidan (Francis Neil) GASQUET (d. 1929), the well-known historian. Among the members of the commission were Dom De Bruyne and Dom Henri QUENTIN (d. 1935). Publication began in 1913 with a series of *Collectanea Biblica Latina*. The sixth in this series is of outstanding importance, Dom Quentin's *Mémoire sur l'établissement du texte de la Vulgate,* providing conclusions and directives valid for all the future work of revision, and describing a method for classifying the manuscripts that, though not without its partisans, embroiled scholars on both sides of the Atlantic and has for the most part been rejected. In 1926 came the first volume of the new revision, presenting the text of Genesis. The form of presentation there adopted has continued throughout the dozen volumes that appeared. Horizontally the page is divided into four parts: at the top is the text in double columns, underneath is a triple apparatus. The first part of the latter presents the reading of the key manuscripts, whose relations generally determine the choice of reading; next, below, comes the full apparatus of variants, in double columns; the apparatus at the bottom presents from selected manuscripts the evidence for the *cola et commata* divisions of the text. Edited with no less diligence than the Scripture itself are the prologues or prefaces (especially those of St. Jerome) found in the manuscripts reported and the various sets of chapter headings or summaries (ten series in the case of the Book Genesis, which are subdivisible into 18 types).

New Editions of the Vulgate. In 1959, from the publishing house of Marietti in Rome, appeared a new Vulgate, noteworthy on several counts. One novelty is the generous provision of Psalter texts. The customary Gallicanum is joined in parallel columns not only by the New Psalter of Pius XII (1945; see below) but also by St. Jerome's *Iuxta Hebraeos* in the text of Dom H. de Sainte-Marie [*Coll. Bibl. Lat.* 11 (Vatican City 1954)]. More remarkable, the Marietti edition presents, in a critical apparatus attributed to the monks of S. Girolamo, the significant differences between the Clementine text and that of the Oxford New Testament, that of the *Vat. Vulg.* (through v.11: Proverbs, Ecclesiastes, and the Song of Songs), and Dom De Bruyne's edition of the Maccabees (Vulgate column). The appearance of such an assembly of variants in an official edition of the Vulgate is noted by S. Garofalo in his preface as a first occurrence, permitted under a declaration of the Pontifical Biblical Commission of Nov. 17, 1921. These critical studies of the Vulgate gave impetus to the creation of the Neo-Vulgate, or New Vulgate, which became in 1979 the edition authorized by the Church. The New Vulgate replaced the Sisto-Clementine edition, which had prevailed since the Council of Trent.

New Vulgate. At the close of the Second Vatican Council, on Nov. 29, 1965, Pope Paul VI established the Pontifical Commission for the Neo-Vulgate, ''an edition made desirable by the progress of biblical studies and the necessity of giving the Church and the world a new and authoritative text of Holy Scripture.'' (Paul VI in *L'Ossservatore Romano*, Dec. 8, 1977). Paul VI did not intend a new Latin translation but rather a restoration of St. Jerome's Vulgate, corrected in light of the ''healthy critical requirements of our times.'' A team of exegetes and textual critics, working for just over 12 years, corrected the text on the basis of the original Hebrew, Aramaic, and Greek manuscripts witnesses, supplemented by comparison with recent critical editions (including that of R. Weber, Stuttgart, 1969). The New Testament of the New Vulgate was published in three volumes in 1970–71 and the Old Testament in four volumes in 1976–77. Although the work came to a close in 1977 under Paul VI, it was Pope John Paul II, on April 25, 1979, who formally decreed and promulgated the new edition in an apostolic constitution *Scripturarum Thesaurus* (The Treasury of Scriptures). The New Vulgate would be the editio typica, the normative edition of the Church, serving as the text for liturgical books and official documents. The Sacred Congregation for Divine Worship first incorporated the psalms of the New Vulgate into the Liturgy of the Hours in 1971; the New Vulgate again served as the editio typica for the Liturgy of the Hours in 1985. In 1983 the New Vulgate supplied the Latin text for the Greek-Latin bilingual edition of Nestle-Aland's New Testament (Nestle-Aland, *Novum Testamentum Graece et Latine*, ed. 26. Deutsche Bibelgesellschaft, Stuttgart, 1983). The New Vulgate's status as the editio typica for the Church had thus been established; it is presupposed by the recent church document *Liturgiam Authenticam* (2001) which advises that Sacred Scriptures for liturgical use follow the Church's approved translation.

Bibliography: New work on the Latin Bible annually reported in the *Année philologique* (s.v. ''Testamenta, -um'') and in *Biblica* (in the ''Elenchus bibliographicus biblicus,'' III, 5 and 6). Critical reports on the yield of successive periods of years in the ''Bulletin d'ancienne littérature latine chrétienne'' (supplement to *Revue Bénédictine*), in the section ''Bulletin de la Bible Latine''; latest installment (M. BOGAERT's report on 298 items) published with *Revue Bénédictine* 74 (1964) and 75 (1965). See also B. M. METZGER, *Annotated Bibliography of the Textual Criticism of the New Testament 1914–1939* (Copenhagen 1955) 30–45 (nos. 352–527); *cf. New Testament Studies* 2 (1955–56) 3–5; ''Latin Versions,'' *New Testament Manuscript Studies,* ed. M. M. PARVIS and A. P. WIKREN (Chicago 1950) 51–61. **Latin Bible in general.** K. T. SCHÄFER, *Lexikon für Theologie und Kirche*, ed. J. HOFER and K. RAHNER, 10 v. (2d, new ed. 1957–65) 2:380–384. W. THIELE, *Die Religion in Geschichte und Gegenwart*, 7 v. (3d ed. Tübingen

1957–65) 1:1196–97. A. ROBERT and A. TRICOT, *Guide to the Bible*, tr. E. P. ARBEZ and M. P. MCGUIRE, 2 v. (Tournai-New York 1951–55; v.1 revised and enlarged 1960) 1:637–664, 674–676 (includes references on Biblical Latinity). A. ALLGEIER, "Haec vetus et vulgata editio," *Biblica* 29 (1948) 353–390. "Prooemium," *Biblia Polyglotta Matritensia* (Madrid 1957). L. BIELER, *The Grammarian's Craft: An Introduction to Textual Criticism* (Worcester, Massachusetts 1964) 21–27 (on Quentin's method), reprinted from *(Classical) Folia* 10.2 (1958) 13–19. L. BROU, ed., *The Psalter Collects from V–VIth Century Sources . . . from the Papers of the Late Dom André Wilmart* (Henry Bradshaw Society 83; 1949). D. DE BRUYNE and B. SODAR, eds., *Les Anciennes traductions latines des Machabées* (Anecdota Maredsolana 4; Maredsous 1932). *Clavis Patrum latinorum*, ed. E. DEKKERS (2d ed. Steenbrugge 1961), Nos. 1947–94 (on Lectionaries), with Elenchus codicum, 462–467. O. EISSFELDT, *Einleitung in das Alte Testament* (3d ed. Tübingen 1964) 973–977. B. FISCHER, "Die Bibel im Abendland," *Vetus Latina: Arbeitsbericht* 4 (1955) 12–23; "Bibelausgaben des frühen Mittelalters," *La Bibbia nell'alto medioevo* (Settimane di studio del Centro di studi sull'alto medioevo 10; Spoleto 1963) 519–600, 685–704; abr. in *Vetus Latina: Arbeitsbericht* 12 (1963) 10–38; "Codex Amiatinus und Cassiodor," *Biblische Zeitschrift* 6 (1962) 57–79. H. J. FREDE, *Die lateinischen Texte des 1. Petrusbriefes* (Vetus Latina: Aus der Geschichte der lateinischen Bibel 5; Freiburg 1965); *Pelagius, der irische Paulustext, Sedulius Scottus* (ibid. 3; 1961). J. GRIBOMONT, "Conscience philologique chez les scribes du haut moyen âge," *La Bibbia nell'alto medioevo, op. cit.* 601–630, 705–714; "L'Église et les versions bibliques," *Maison-Dieu* 62 (1960) 41–68. F. G. KENYON, *Our Bible and the Ancient Manuscripts,* 5th ed. rev. A. W. ADAMS (New York 1958) 138–144, 238–264. M. J. LAGRANGE, *Introduction à l'étude du N.T.,* pt. 2: *Critique textuelle* 2: *La Critique rationelle* (2d ed. *Études bibliques*; 1935) 240–312, 421–441, 488–515, 539–568, 598–616. E. A. LOWE, *Codices latini antiquiores. A Palaeographical Guide to Latin Manuscripts Prior to the Ninth Century* (Oxford 1934–). E. A. LOWE, *English Uncial* (Oxford 1960); "Codices rescripti," *Mélanges E. Tisserant* (Studi e Testi 5; 1964) 67–113, with six plates. P. MCGURK, *Latin Gospel Books from A.D. 400 to A.D. 800* (Les Publications de Scriptorium 5; Paris 1961). A. MERK, ed., *Novum Testamentum Graece et Latinum* (9th ed. Rome 1964). B. M. METZGER, *The Text of the New Testament* (New York 1964) 72–79 and (on Quentin's method) 163–165. *Richesses et déficiences des anciens psautiers latins* (Collectanea Biblica Latina 13; Vatican City 1959). P. SALMON, *Les "Tituli Psalmorum" des manuscrits latins* (ibid. 12; 1959). H. RÖNSCH, *Itala und Vulgata* (2d ed. Marburg 1875). H. ROST, *Die Bibel im Mittelalter: Beiträge zur Geschichte und Bibliographie der Bibel* (Augsburg 1939); *Die Bibel in den ersten Jahrhunderten* (Westheim bei Augsburg 1946). K. T. SCHÄFER, "Pelagius und die Vulgata," *New Testament Studies* 9 (1962–63) 361–366. B. SMALLEY, *The Study of the Bible in the Middle Ages* (2d ed. New York 1952; repr. Notre Dame, Indiana 1964). F. STEGMÜLLER, *Repertorium biblicum medii aevi,* 7 v. (Madrid 1949–61), especially v.1. O. STEGMÜLLER, in *Geschichte der Textüberlieferung der antiken und mittelalterlichen Literatur,* ed. H. HUNGER et al., 2 v. (Zurich 1961–64) 1:190–194. F. STUMMER, *Einführung in die lateinische Bibel* (Paderborn 1928). E. F. SUTCLIFFE, "The Name *Vulgate*," *Biblica* 29 (1948) 345–352. W. THIELE, *Wortschatzuntersuchungen zu den lateinischen Texten der Johannesbriefe* (Vetus Latina: Aus der Geschichte der lateinischen Bibel 2; 1958). A. VACCARI, *Scritti di erudizione e filologia,* 2 v. (Rome 1952–58). H. J. VOGELS, ed., *Codicum Novi Testamenti specimina* (Bonn 1929), plates 19–41, 50, 52–54; *Handbuch der Textkritik des NT* (2d ed. Bonn 1955) 78–110. A. VÖÖBUS, *Early Versions of the New Testament: Manuscript Studies* (Stockholm 1954) 33–65. W.

WIKENHAUSER, *New Testament Introduction,* tr. J. CUNNINGHAM (New York 1958) 93–108. **Old Latin.** B. BOTTE, *Dictionnaire de la Bible,* supplemental ed. L. PIROT, et al. 5:334–347. L. MÉCHINEAU, *Dictionnaire de la Bible,* ed. F. VIGOUROUX (Paris 1895–1912) 4:97–123. *Vetus Latina: Die Reste der altlateinischen Bibel nach Petrus Sabatier neu gesammelt und herausgegeben von der Erzabtei Beuron,* ed. B. FISCHER et al. (Freiburg 1949–) v.1, Verzeichnis der Sigel; v.1.1 (2d ed. 1963, with suppls.); v.2, Genesis; v.24.1–5, Ephesians; v.26.1–3, James, 1 and 2 Peter. *Vetus Latina: Arbeitsbericht* 1 (1951–52) and annually thereafter. A. JÜLICHER et al, eds., *Itala: Das Neue Testament in altlateinischer Überlieferung,* 4 v. (Berlin 1938–63). T. AYUSO MARAZUELA, ed., *Psalterium Visigothicum-Mozarabicum* (Biblia Polyglotta Matritensia 7, L.21; Madrid 1957); *La Vetus Latina Hispana: Prolegómenos* (Madrid 1953); v.5 in three parts, *El Salterio* (Madrid 1962). D. DE BRUYNE, "Le Problème du psautier romain," *Revue Bénédictine* 42 (1930) 101–126; "Saint Augustin réviseur de la Bible," *Miscellanea Agostiniana* 2 (Rome 1931) 521–606; *Revue Bénédictine* 45 (1933) 20–28. H. J. FREDE, *Altlateinische Paulus-Handschriften* (Vetus Latina: Aus der Geschichte der lateinischen Bibel 4; 1964). J. GRIBOMONT, "Le Calendrier en latin du Sinaï," *Analecta Bollandiana* 75 (1957) 110, with nn. 1 and 2. J. SCHILDENBERGER, "Die Itala des hl. Augustinus," *Colligere fragmenta: Festschrift A. Dold* (Beuron 1952) 84–102. A. VACCARI, "St. Augustin, St. Ambroise und Aquila," *Augustinus Magister* 3 (Paris 1955) 471–482. R. WEBER, *Les Anciennes versions latines du deuxième livre des Paralipomènes* (Collectanea Biblica Latina 8; Vatican City 1945); ed., *Le Psautier romain et les autres psautiers latins* (ibid. 10; 1953). Vulgate. E. MANGENOT, *Dictionnaire de la Bible* 5:2456–2500. *Biblia sacra iuxta Latinam vulgatam versionem ad codicum fidem . . . cura et studio monachorum (Sancti Benedicti) edita. . .* (Rome 1926–) v.1–12 embrace Genesis through Sirach. J. WORDSWORTH et al., eds., *Novum Testamentum Domini Nostri Iesu Christi Latine secundum editionem Sancti Hieronymi,* 3 v. (Oxford 1889–1954); see review by B. FISCHER, *Zeitschrift für die neutestamentliche Wissenchaft und die Kunde der älteren Kirche* 46 (1955) 178–196. *L'attività della Santa Sede,* v.12– (1950–), annual reports on the work of the S. Girolamo Vulgate. T. AYUSO MARAZUELA, ed., *Psalterium S. Hieronymi de Hebraica veritate interpretatum* (Biblia Polyglotta Matritensia 8, L.21; Madrid 1960). S. BERGER, *Histoire de la Vulgate pendant les premiers siècles du moyen âge* (Paris 1893; repr. New York 1958); see review by P. CORSSEN, *Göttingische gelehrte Anzeigen* (1894) 855–875. T. J. BROWN and R. L. S. BRUCE-MITFORD, *The Lindisfarne Gospels: A Complete Facsimile . . .,* 2 v. (Olten-Lausanne 1956–60) 2:3–104, 281–295. F. CAVALLERA, *Saint Jérôme: Sa vie et son oeuvre,* 2 v. (Spicilegium sacrum Lovaniense 1, 2; 1922). L. COTTINEAU, "Chronologie des versions bibliques de Saint Jérôme," *Miscellanea Geronimiana* (Rome 1920) 43–68. D. DE BRUYNE, "Étude sur les origines de notre texte latin de Saint Paul," *Revue biblique* 12 (1915) 358–392; "La Reconstitution du psautier hexaplaire latin," *Revue Bénédictine* 41 (1929) 297–324, especially 299 on the name "Gallican." H. DE SAINTE-MARIE, ed., *Sancti Hieronymi Psalterium iuxta Hebraeos* (Collectanea Biblica Latina 11; Vatican City 1954). B. FISCHER, *Die Alkuin-Bibel* (Vetus Latina: Aus der Geschichte der lateinischen Bibel 1; 1957); "Bibeltext und Bibelreform unter Karl dem Grossen," in *Karl der Grosse: Werk und Wirkung,* ed. W. BRAUNFELS, v.1, *Das geistige Leben,* ed. B. BISCHOFF (Düsseldorf 1965) 156–216. E. B. GARRISON, "Notes on the History of Certain Twelfth-Century Central Italian Manuscripts of Importance for the History of Printing," *La Bibliofilia* 54 (1952) 1–34; *Studies in the History of Mediaeval Italian Painting,* 4 v. (Florence 1953–60). H. H. GLUNZ, *History of the Vulgate in England from Alcuin to Roger Bacon* (Cambridge, England 1933). J. GRIBO-

MONT, "Les Éditions critiques de la Vulgate," *Studi medievali*, 3d set., 2 (1961) 363–377. *Libri Iudicum capitula selecta* [10.1–12.15] *iuxta Latinam Vulgatam versionem ad codicum fidem* (Vatican City 1939), useful guide to the new Vatican Vulgate, with valuable *adnotationes* on the text and apparatus. R. LOEWE, "The Mediaeval Christian Hebraists of England," *Hebrew Union College Annual* 28 (1957) 205–252. G. MORIN, "Saint Jérôme et ses maîtres hébreux," *Revue Bénédictine* 46 (1934) 145–164. M. B. OGLE, "The Way of All Flesh," *Harvard Theological Review* 31 (1938) 41–51; "Bible Text or Liturgy," *ibid.* 33 (1940) 191–224. W. E. PLATER and H. J. WHITE, *A Grammar of the Vulgate* (Oxford 1926). H. QUENTIN, *Essais de critique textuelle* (Paris 1926); *Mémoire sur l'établissement du texte de la Vulgate* (Collectanea Biblica Latina 6; Rome-Paris 1922). F. ROSENTHAL, *Christian Hebraists of Western Europe: The Hebrew Scriptures in Christian Learning from the Time of the Vulgate of Jerome to the "Opus Grammaticum" of Münster* (University of Pittsburgh Bulletin 42.1; 1946). J. O. SMIT, *De Vulgaat . . .* (Roermond 1948), rich in illustrations especially of manuscripts and the working materials of the Benedictine Vulgate project. D. H. WRIGHT, *American Journal of Archaeology* 67 (1963) 219, on the Springmont Bog Psalter tablets. **New Vulgate.** JOHN PAUL II, "Letter to Biblical Symposium: From Revelation the Church Draws Faith and Rule of Life," *L'Osservatore Romano* 41 (Oct. 14, 1985) 10. T. STRAMARE, "The Neo-Vulgate: an Extraordinary Historical Event," *L'Osservatore Romano* 49 (Dec. 8, 1977) 9–10, 12. T. STRAMARE, "The Second Edition Typical of the New Vulgate," *L'Osservatore Romano* 51–52 (Dec. 22 to 29, 1986) 16, 12.

[L. F. HARTMAN/B. F. PEEBLES/M. STEVENSON]

VULPES, ANGELO

Theologian and Mariologist; b. Montepiloso in the kingdom of Naples (exact date not known); d. Naples, April 19, 1647. He entered the Order of Friars Minor Conventual at an early age. In 1614 his superiors sent him to St. Bonaventure College in Rome. After a brief stay in Assisi where he taught sacred theology, he was sent to Naples as regent of the Collegio di San Lorenzo, an office he held for 25 years, during which he expounded the *Books of Sentences* of Duns Scotus. Besides other works he wrote a summa of theology entitled *Sacrae Theologiae Summa Ioannis Duns Scoti . . . et Commentaria quibus eius doctrina elucidatur, comprobatur, defenditur*. It is an immense work [12 v. in folio (Naples 1622–46)] patterned after the order and method of St. Thomas. Christ and the Immaculate Virgin Mary are the two beacons that, as it were, shine throughout the summa and illumine his teaching. An ardent Scotist, he is at odds with the Angelic Doctor on the traditional Franciscan theses (*see* SCOTISM; THOMISM). The esteem and authority that Vulpes enjoyed suffered greatly in the 18th century, for despite an imposing array of prominent names of popes, cardinals, and theologians who directly or indi-

rectly attested the orthodoxy of his summa, his work was placed on the Index. He is buried at the convent of San Lorenzo in Naples.

Bibliography: L. WADDING, *Scriptores Ordinis Minorum* (Rome 1650; 3d ed. 1906) 22. J. H. SBARALEA, *Supplementum et castigatio ad scriptores trium ordinum S. Francisci a Waddingo*, 2 v. (Rome 1806; new ed. in 4 v. 1906–36) 48. P. APOLLINAIRE, *Dictionnaire de théologie catholique*, ed. A. VACANT, 15 v. (Paris 1903–50; Tables générales 1951–) 15.2:3492–94. G. FRANCHINI, *Bibliosofia e memorie letterarie di scrittori francescani conventuali* (Modena 1693) 52–57.

[G. M. GRABKA]

VYSHENSKY, IVAN

Orthodox monk and polemicist; d. Mt. Athos, after 1621. Originally from Sodova Wyshnia, near Lvov, Vyshensky lived at Lutsk in his youth and had some connection with the Orthodox champion Prince Constantine Ostrogsky. He entered MOUNT ATHOS, *c.* 1600, where, after passing through several monasteries, he became a solitary in a grotto. He followed the religious controversies in the Ukraine through correspondence with friends and polemical exchanges with the unionists. Early in 1600 he returned to the Ukraine and visited the monk Job Kniahynycky and the confraternity of Lvov, but in 1607 he returned to Mt. Athos. In a letter of 1633 to the confraternity at Lvov, Leontius speaks of Vyshensky as deceased.

Vyshensky defended Orthodoxy frequently and with vehemence in popular, uncouth, but colorful language. The frankness with which he railed against religious and social abuses and against union with Rome did not meet with universal approval among the Orthodox, hence his writings were neglected until discovered by S. Solov'ev in 1858 and published in part by M. Kostomoriev in 1865.

Sixteen of his works written between 1597 and 1601 are known. His *Book for the Alerting of Orthodox Christians* is a mélange in 10 chapters, with recommendations for detachment and piety (ch. 1, 3), and open letters against Roman–minded unionists and reformers, the Jesuits, and the nobility (ch. 2, 4–9). His other writings are polemical pieces mainly against Piotr SKARGA, the political union of Lublin (1569), and the religious union of Brest (1596).

Bibliography: J. MIRTSHUK, *Lexikon für Theologie und Kirche*[1] 10:706.

[V. MALANCZUK]

W

WAAL, ANTON MARIA DE

Noted German prelate and archeologist; b. Emmerich, May 5, 1836; d. Rome, Feb. 23, 1917. After ordination at Münster on Oct. 11, 1862, he was first a teacher in the seminary of Gaesdonck, was sent to Rome in 1868 for a doctorate in theology (1869), and finally became rector of the Teutonic College of Santa Maria in Camposanto (1873), which he reorganized as a hospice for priests engaged in scholarly study. He provided it with statutes approved by Pope Pius IX on Nov. 21, 1876. He played a part in the spiritual life of Germans in Rome and other parts of Italy and founded a refuge for youth, Marienheim (1887); an association for assistance to women, Liebfrauenverein (1874); and a pension for the aged and infirm, Antoniusheim (1912). To his archeological interests are due the explorations under the basilica of St. Sebastian on the Via Appia in 1892 and 1893. These were continued in 1915 with the aid of P. Styger and O. Fasiolo and resulted in the discovery there of the famous third–century *Triclia,* or *Memoria Apostolorum,* which had originally served as a place for Eucharistic or other worship. He founded a library for archeological research and started the periodicals *Römische Quartatschrift* (1887) and *Oriens Christianus* (1901), which were devoted to the study of Christian antiquity. He published many monographs, including *Die Nationalstiftungen des deutschen Volkes in Rom* (Frankfurt 1880); *Die Apostelgruft ad catacumbas* (Freiburg 1894); *Roma Sacra* (Munich 1926); 12 editions of *Die Walfahrt zu den Sieben Hauptkirchen zu Rom* (Freiburg 1870–1925); and biographies of contemporary pontiffs, including Leo XII (Münster 1878), *Papst Pius X Lebensbild* (Munich 1903), and Benedict XV (1915). He is buried in the cemetery of the Teutonic College in Camposanto.

Bibliography: A. DE WAAL, *Prälat Dr. Anton de Waal* (Karlsruhe 1937). J. SAUER, *Lexikon für Theologie und Kirche*[1] 10:706–707.

[F. CHIOVARO]

WACH, JOACHIM

Protestant scholar in the science of religion; b. Chemnïtz, Germany, Jan. 25, 1898; d. Orselina, Switzerland, Aug. 27, 1955. On being relieved of his professorship in the history of religion at the University of Leipzig in 1935 by the Nazi government, he came to the United States and served as a professor in his field at Brown University (1935–45), and then at the University of Chicago (1945 to his death). He taught courses in the history of religion, but he was especially recognized for his work in the sociology of religion. In the latter field he was distinguished for his profound knowledge, unusual breadth of view, and effective use of an empirical–humanistic method. His major works were *Religionswissenschaft: Prolegomena zu ihrer wissenschaftstheoretischen Grundlegung* (Leipzig 1924), *Das Verstehen. Grundzüge einer Geschichte der hermeneutischen Theorie im 19. Jahrhundert* (3 v., Tübingen 1926–33), *Sociology of Religion* (Chicago 1944), *Types of Religious Experience* (Chicago 1951), and *Comparative Study of Religions* (New York 1958).

Bibliography: F. HELLER et al., ''Mémorial Joachim Wach,'' *Archives de sociologie des religions* (1956) 19–69, with complete bibliog. of Wach's publications 64–69.

[A. HOLL]

WADDING, LUKE

Franciscan historian and Scotist scholar; b. Waterford, Oct. 16, 1588; d. Rome, Nov. 18, 1657. Wadding, from a family profoundly Catholic and prolific in vocations, in 1603 entered the Irish College, Lisbon, and in 1604 became a Franciscan at Matozinhos. After studying philosophy at Leiria and theology in Lisbon and at Coimbra University, he was ordained at Vizeu, Portugal (1613). He then studied theology at Salamanca. In 1618 he went to Rome as theologian on the special Spanish mission requesting the dogmatic definition of the Immaculate Conception. Its work has been recorded in his *Lega-*

Luke Wadding.

tio Philippi 111 et IV. In 1625 Wadding took over the new friary of St. Isidore, Rome, which he developed into a college for Irish Franciscans. The establishment of the Ludovisian College for Irish secular clerics came in 1627. A novitiate for Irish Franciscans was founded by him at Capranica in 1656. He served as consultor at the Congregation of Rites and also at the Holy Office and the Index, where he became involved in the contemporary Jansenist disputes. His work for his order in Rome included a short period as its vice procurator-general and another as its vice commissary. Besides benefitting from his two new foundations in Italy, the Irish province availed itself to no small extent of his advice and his position at the Roman Curia. His services were in demand at the new Congregation de Propaganda Fide, where he helped considerably to forward the cause of the Catholic reorganization in Ireland. He corresponded regularly with many Irish clerics, especially the bishops, to whom he was guide, counselor, and in some cases procurator. After the 1641 revolt in Ireland he persuaded many influential cardinals and others, and eventually the Pope, to interest themselves in the Irish Catholic confederation. He personally obtained papal approval, financial aid, and ships and arms for the Irish cause and secured the sending of the papal nuncio, Giovanni Battista RINUCCINI. Wadding himself became the confederation's accredited agent at Rome. The con-

federation split, largely on racial lines, because of the Ormond peace and the Inchiquin truce; despite all he had done, Wadding was then blamed by the Old Irish for being partisan, even for furthering Anglo-Irish interests by cunning deception and shameless scheming. But from an impartial historical analysis of the facts, his reputation as a noble, disinterested patriot emerges untarnished and even enhanced. Devoid of ambition, he resisted all efforts to promote him to the episcopate or the cardinalate. Of the many writers that the Franciscan order has produced, Wadding was one of the most prolific, scholarly, and profound. His interest in writing can be traced to his student days in the Iberian Peninsula. It was then that he conceived that deep love, so evident in his later writings, for things Franciscan and for the Franciscan doctor John DUNS SCOTUS. His first publication was an edition of the writings of St. Francis, which he had begun when a student in Portugal. Between 1625 and 1654 he published the *Annales Minorum,* a monumental history (8 v.) of the Franciscan Order from the birth of St. Francis to 1540. This work, perhaps his greatest literary achievement, won him an international reputation as a historian. An equally ambitious project was realized in 1639 with the publication of the first critical edition of the *opera omnia* of Scotus. This edition and the school of Scotist studies organized by Wadding at St. Isidore's initiated a new epoch in the history of Scotism. His Franciscan bibliography, *Scriptores Ordinis Minorum,* appeared in 1650. Though defective and unwieldy by modern bibliographical standards, it has proved itself an invaluable work. He published many other scholarly volumes and had many others on hand, in various stages of completion, when he died. His memory is held in benediction not merely because of his saintly life but also because of his constructive, unselfish work for the Irish Church and nation and his formidable scholarship in the domains of history and theology.

Bibliography: L. EYSSENS, "Les Cinq Propositions de Jansenius a Rome," *Revue-d'Histoire Ecclesiastique* 66, no. 2 (1971) 449–501. FRANCISCAN FATHERS (PROVINCE OF IRELAND), *Father Luke Wadding: Commemorative Volume* (Dublin 1957). P. J. CORISH, "Father Luke Wadding and the Irish Nation," *The Irish Ecclesiastical Record* 88 (1957) 377–395. C. MOONEY, "The Letters of Luke Wadding," *The Irish Ecclesiastical Record* 88 (1957) 396–409. C. MURPHY, "The Wexford Catholic Community in the Later Seventeenth Century," in *Religion, Conflict, and Coexistence in Ireland* (Dublin 1990) 78–98. "The Writings of Father Luke Wadding, O.F.M.," *Franciscan Studies* 18 (1958) 225–239.

[B. MILLETT]

WADHAMS, EDGAR PHILIP

Bishop of Ogdensburg, NY; b. Essex County, NY, May 17, 1817; d. Ogdensburg, Dec. 5, 1891. Son of

Luman and Lucy (Bostick) Wadhams, Edgar, a Presbyterian, became an Episcopalian while attending Middlebury College, VT. In 1838 he entered the General Theological Seminary, New York, and there became a close friend of Arthur Carey, an American follower of Cardinal Newman. As an ordained deacon he began ministerial work in northern New York; but, influenced by the Oxford Movement and doubting the validity of Anglican orders, he resigned his post and entered the Church in 1846. He studied for the priesthood at St. Mary's Seminary, Baltimore, MD, and was ordained for the Diocese of Albany, Jan. 5, 1850, by Bp. John McCloskey (later cardinal–archbishop of New York). After two years on the cathedral staff he was named its rector and vicar–general of the diocese. When the Diocese of Ogdensburg was created in 1872, Wadhams was appointed first bishop and was consecrated by McCloskey on May 5, 1872. With characteristic energy and a thorough knowledge of the territory, he set about organizing the upper New York counties into a thriving see, greatly increasing the number of priests, sisters, churches, chapels, and schools; founding a hospital, orphan home, and aged people's home; and enlarging St. Mary's Cathedral, in whose crypt his body was interred after his death 20 years later. He held three diocesan synods and attended the New York Provincial Council of 1883 and the Third Plenary Council of Baltimore in 1884.

Bibliography: C. A. WALWORTH, *Reminiscences of Edgar P. Wadhams* (New York 1893). J. T. SMITH, *History of the Diocese of Ogdensburg* (New York n.d.).

[V. F. HOLDEN]

Richard Wagner.

CATI and A. PELZER, *Dizionario ecclesiatico* (Turin 1954–58) 3:1364. *Acta Apostolae Sedis* 66 [1974] 373–375. *L'Osservatore Romano* (Eng) 1974, n. 15, 4–5.

[F. D. S. BORAN]

WAGNER, LIBORIUS, BL.

Martyr, convert, and priest; b. Mülhausen, Thuringia, Germany, 1593; d. Schonungen, Germany, December 9, 1631. He studied at Leipzig, Gotha, Strasbourg, and Würzburg, where he was converted to Catholicism by the Jesuits. He was ordained in 1625, was chaplain in Hardheim, and in 1626 became pastor in Altenmünster, near Schweinfurt, devoting himself to regaining Catholics who had become Protestants. During the Thirty Years' War, when the Swedes invaded Germany, Liborius hid, but he was betrayed and imprisoned. For refusing to apostatize he was tortured for five days and then killed. His body was thrown into the Main but recovered. It has been in Klosterheidenfeld since 1803. At Wagner's beatification on March 24, 1974, Pope Paul VI cited him as a model in the cause of ecumenism and unity.

Feast: Dec. 9.

Bibliography: K. HOFMANN, *Lexicon für Theologie und Kirche*, ed. M. BUCHBERGER (Freiburg 19307–38) 10:711–712. A. MER-

WAGNER, RICHARD

Composer and theorist of the "music-drama" (symphonic opera); b. Leipzig, May 22, 1813 (baptized Wilhelm Richard); d. Venice, Feb. 13, 1883. His putative father, Karl F. Wagner, a police court actuary, died when Richard was six months old, whereupon his mother, Johanna (Paetz) Wagner, married Ludwig Geyer, an actor, who died when the boy was eight. His music training progressed by uneasy stages (at 14 he composed his first opera, to a tragedy he had written) until discovery of Beethoven's symphonies liberated his creative forces. After a prentice period ending with *Rienzi* (1842) and *The Flying Dutchman* (1841) he delivered *Tannhäuser* (1845) and *Lohengrin* (1847), conventional "grand" operas, albeit suggestive of the break to come. Then came the masterpieces of the new "music-drama" style: *Tristan und Isolde* (1859); the "Ring" tetralogy [*Das Rheingold* (1854), *Die Walküre* (1856), *Siegfried* (1871), and *Götterdämmerung* (1872)]; and his self-styled "sacred dramatic festival,'' *Parsifal* (1882), after a chauvinistic indulgence in *Die Meistersinger* (1867), Wagner's only national (i.e., German) or comic opera.

Wagner was the supreme egoist, living luxuriously off his friends' largesse, intriguing against his opponents, dallying with inaccessible women (his three children were born to LISZT'S daughter Mrs. Cosima von Bülow, whom he later married). At the same time, in his pseudophilosophic writings (mainly a rationale for his aesthetic departures), as in his librettos, he posited a dream-world populated by a purified, redeemed humanity (his *Volk*), unfettered by law or religious dogma—a Faustian distillation of all the influences he had absorbed from the romanticist *Zeitgeist:* from Feuerbach's sensualist Hegelianism, Schopenhauer's pessimism, ''Father'' Jahn's ''German Jacobinism,'' Nietzsche's will to power (Wagner was actually the model for superman), and the anarchism of Bakunin, his fellow revolutionary in the 1849 Dresden insurrection. In his dramaturgy, erected on the Teutonic or Celtic counterparts of Greek mythology, this redemption takes as many forms as there are music-dramas: in the ''Ring,'' a ''nuclear'' liberation, in the self-destruction of humanity; in *Tristan*, a Manichaean escape into divinization of erotic passion; in *Parsifal,* a para-Christian type, in the hero's compassion for all suffering (the ''vegetarian'' Eucharistic interpretation being simply bizarre). Wagner's allusions to Christianity range from aloof, quasi-nostalgic tolerance to virtual hatred of the ''Catholic God'' (as in his letter apropos Liszt's *Dante* symphony). In his texts he bends Christian truth to his narcissistic mentality; thus the Jesus in his projected opera of that subject ''wills his death because he knows that the world is not worthy of him'' (P. Bekker)—which is how Wagner felt about his world. Yet Christian notes do serve his dramatic ends, e.g., the ''Dresden Amen'' of J. G. Naumann (1741–80), featured in *Parsifal*. Wagner's one ''religious'' work, *Das Liebesmahl der Apostel* (1843), a commissioned cantata that he included on his ''list of uninspired compositions,'' begins simply and reverently but grows increasingly theatrical, and is cited now only as rehearsing the Grail effects in *Parsifal*.

On the other hand, thanks to Liszt's inspiration and the publication of the first anthologies of 16th-century polyphony, as well as to his own unerring artistic taste, Wagner lent his weight to the incipient church-music reform (*see* CAECILIAN MOVEMENT); and his memorandum, ''Plan of Organisation of a German National Theatre'' (1849), contains a devastating commentary on current Catholic music based on his six-year (1843–49) experience as Dresden Hofkapellmeister (see Prose Works 7:319–60). He embraced PALESTRINA's polyphony as the ideal of tonal purity, and, by way of promoting the return of true *A CAPPELLA* church music, he ''arranged'' Palestrina's *Stabat Mater* and conducted it on March 8, 1848, at a subscription concert at the royal chapel. While his efforts went ''for nought,'' as he said, the shimmering incandescence of *Parsifal's* best passages reveals his debt to Palestrina's harmonies. Moreover, he encouraged church-music reform in a practical way through his abandonment of ''set,'' symmetrical numbers—arias, duets, and other ensembles—which were cluttering the concerted Masses as much as the opera of the period, in favor of primacy of the word. And if his *Gesamtkunstwerk*—a construct in which music and the space arts would selflessly, anonymously subserve the drama's exigencies—was unthinkable in the theater, it had already been realized in the sacred-art synthesis of the Christian past, and may be realized anew in the art of the liturgical renaissance.

Bibliography: *Gesammelte Schriften und Dichtungen,* ed. R. WAGNER, 10 v. in 5 (Leipzig 1871–83), Eng. *Richard Wagner's Prose Works,* tr. W. A. ELLIS, 8 v. (London 1893–99): *Mein Leben,* 2 v. (Leipzig 1911; rev. ed. W. ALTMANN 1923), authorized Eng. tr. *My Life* (New York 1911); *Letters,* selected and ed. W. ALTMANN, tr. M. M. BOZMAN, 2 v. (New York 1927; repr. 1936); *Letters: The Burrell Collection,* ed. J. N. BURK, tr. H. ABRAHAM et al. (New York 1950); *Wagner on Music and Drama,* ed. A. GOLDMAN and E. SPRINCHORN, tr. W. A. ELLIS (New York 1964). O. STRUNK, ed., *Source Readings in Music History* (New York 1950) 874–903. E. NEWMAN, *The Life of Richard Wagner,* 4 v. (New York 1933–46); *Wagner as Man and Artist* (New York 1924; repr. 1937); *The Wagner Operas* (New York 1949; repr. 1963). P. BEKKER, *Richard Wagner: His Life in His Work,* tr. M. M. BOZMAN (New York 1931). M. BEAUFILS, *Wagner et le wagnérisme* (Paris 1946). J. HATZFELD-SANDEBECK, ''Richard Wagner und die katholische Kirchenmusik,'' *Musica sacra* 46 (1913) 126–134, 154–165, 179–184. J. M. STEIN, *Richard Wagner and the Synthesis of the Arts* (Detroit 1960). D. DE ROUGEMONT, *Love in the Western World,* tr. M. BELGION (rev. ed. New York 1956). P. R. E. VIERECK, *Metapolitics* (rev. ed. New York 1961). *La Rassegna musicale* 31.3 (1961), special Wagner number. A. EINSTEIN, *Music in the Romantic Era* (New York 1947). P. H. LÁNG, *Music in Western Civilization* (New York 1941). C. VON WESTERNHAGEN and G. STROBEL, *Die Musik in Geschichte und Gegenwart,* ed. F. BLUME (Kassel-Basel 1949–). R. BAILEY, ''Romantic Encounter: Is *Der Fliegende Holländer* the Ultimate German Romantic Opera?,'' *Opera News* 65 (2000) 30–35. R. DELAGE, ''Chabrier et Wagner,'' *Revue de Musicologie* 82 (1996) 167–79. J. F. FULCHER, ''A Political Barometer of Twentieth-Century France: Wagner as Jew or Anti-Semite,'' *The Musical Quarterly* 84 (2000) 41–57. L. GOEHR, *The Quest for Voice: Music, Politics, and the Limits of Philosophy* (Los Angeles 1998). W. KIRSCH, ''Richard Wagners Biblische Scene *Das Liebesmahl der Apostel, Hamburger Jahrbuch für Musikwissenschaft* 8 (1985) 157–84. D. J. LEVIN, *Richard Wagner, Fritz Land, and the Nibelungen: The Dramaturgy of Disavowal* (Princeton 1998). S. MCCLATCHIE, *Analyzing Wagner's Operas: Alfred Lorenz and German Nationalist Ideology* (Rochester 1998).

[M. BEAUFILS; M. E. EVANS]

WAHHĀBIS

Members of a puritanical Islamic movement founded in Nejd in the mid-18th century by Muḥammad ibn-'Abd-al-Wahhāb (1703–93), who began his career as a jurist of the ultraconservative school of the Syrian theologian ibn-Taymīyah (d. 1328). After journeying in neighboring lands the young reformer returned home convinced that Islam had deviated from the original path and determined to restore it to the golden age of the Prophet. All innovations (sing. *bid'ah*), including past attempts at adapting the religion to changing conditions, were to be abandoned. The cult of saints, veneration of tombs, and visitation of shrines compromised the unity of God and savored of polytheism (*shirk*), if not idolatry. Idolatry was *kufr*, punishable by death. Even Muḥammmad's intercession was condemned. The Wahhābi name for themselves was *Muwaḥḥidūn* (''unitarians''). The Prophet's mosque in MEDINA had no minaret, no mosaic or gilded decoration, therefore Muslim MOSQUES were to follow suit. Not only drinking and gambling, prohibited by the Qur'ān, were proscribed, but smoking, silken apparel, and all forms of luxury in living and self-indulgence were forbidden.

Such reforms could win no sizable number of adherents until a Nejdi chieftain, Muḥammad ibn-Saud (Su'ūd, d. 1765), espoused their cause. In addition, he married the reformer's daughter. This was not the first time religion and the sword in ISLAM marched together to victory. Converts flocked to the new movement, prompted more by convenience than conviction. Riyadh (al-Riyāḍ), the future Wahhābi-Saudi capital, was captured in 1773. The drive eastward netted the entire area to the Persian Gulf. Northward the raids reached (in 1801) the two most sacred shrines of the Shī'ah, Kerbela (Karbalā') and al-Najaf (in the Iraq desert) commemorating the burial places of Ḥusayn and his father ALI. Both were pillaged and stripped of their treasures that had been accumulated as votive offerings. Masters of central and eastern Arabia, Wahhābi warriors moved against Mecca and Medina and subjected them to a purge (1803–04). The road was open to Damascus, which was attacked. Thus did the Wahhābi realm in about 30 years extend itself from Hejaz to al-Hasa and in the north from Palmyra to Kerbela.

Alarmed, Sultan Maḥmūd II directed his Egyptian viceroy Muḥammad 'Ali to check the rising menace to the Ottoman Empire. In a series of campaigns in the Arabian peninsula, ending in 1818, the Wahhābi power was broken. Later even Nejd fell under a rival dynasty, al-Rashīd's of Jabal Shammar in northern Nejd.

The revival of Saudi-Wahhābi power was initiated by a young refugee in al-Kuwayt (KUWAIT), 'Abd-al-'Azīz ibn-Saud. In a surprise attack 'Abd-al-'Azīz seized Riyadh (1901), consolidated his ancestral realm in Nejd and in 1913 added al-Ḥasa. Fifteen years later he drove King Ḥusayn (Hussein) out of Mecca and occupied it together with Medina. In 1932 he declared himself head of the newly created Kingdom of SAUDI ARABIA. He maintained an army with a core of the Wahhābi fraternity (*Ikhwān*), recruited mostly from Bedouins, but settled in agricultural colonies; these were trained and disciplined warriors as well as active propagandists of the faith. Though limited today largely to the Arabian peninsula, Wahhābis still exercise appreciable influence on Islam, especially in many parts of Pakistan and Afghanistan.

Bibliography: A. F. RIHANI, *Maker of Modern Arabia* (Boston 1926). K. WILLIAMS, *Ibn Sa'ud: The Puritan King of Arabia* (New York 1933). H. ST. JOHN B. PHILBY, *Arabia* (New York 1930); *Arabia of the Wahhabis* (New York 1930).

[P. K. HITTI/EDS.]

WALA, ST.

Statesman, Benedictine abbot; b. *c.* 755; d. Bobbio, Italy, Aug. 31, 836. Wala, a member of a Carolingian family, was the brother of Abbot ADALARD and of (St.) IDA OF HERZFELD. He was educated at the palace school. He served under CHARLEMAGNE and for a time under Louis the Pious, and then entered the Abbey of CORBIE, where he held various offices. He later (*c.* 815) helped in the foundation of CORVEY and Herford. Wala accompanied LOTHAIR I to Rome (822–825). He was made abbot of Corbie in 826 and worked to restore monastic discipline. Because of his opposition to the Empress Judith, he was exiled (830–833); but GREGORY IV asked him to help resolve the discord in the imperial family shortly thereafter. The *Epitaphium Arsenii seu vita Walae,* probably by PASCHASIUS RADBERTUS, shows the difficult political role Wala had to play in these family crises. Wala was abbot of Bobbio when he died.

Feast: Aug. 31.

Bibliography: L. WEINRICH, *Wala, Graf, Mönch und Rebell* (Lubeck 1963). PASCHASIUS RADBERTUS, *Charlemagne's Cousins; Contemporary Lives of Adalard and Wala,* tr. A. CABANISS (Syracuse, N.Y. 1967). *Bibliotheca hagiographica latina antiquae et mediae aetatis*, 2 v. (Brussels 1898–1901; suppl. 1911) 2:8761. *Patrologia Latina*, ed. J. P. MIGNE, 217 v., indexes 4 v. (Paris 1878–90) 120:1557–1650. *Monumenta Germaniae Historica* (Berlin 1826–), *Scriptores* 2:533–569. A. M. ZIMMERMANN, *Kalendarium Benedictinum: Die Heiligen und Seligen des Benediktinerorderns und seiner Zweige*, 4 v. (Metten 1933–38) 3:4–8. H. PELTIER, *Dictionnaire de théologie catholique*, ed. A. VACANT et al., 15 v. (Paris 1903–50; Tables générals 1951–) 13.2:1628.

[G. J. DONNELLY]

WALAFRID STRABO

The "Squinter" abbot, CAROLINGIAN RENAISSANCE scholar; b. *c.* 808; d. Aug. 18, 849. Born of a poor Swabian family, he was educated at REICHENAU under Tatto, Wettin, and Grimaldus, and later at Fulda under RABANUS MAURUS. He thus received a thorough foundation in secular and religious learning. From 829 to 838 he was tutor of Charles the Bald, son of Emperor Louis the Pious. As a reward, he was made abbot of Reichenau in 838. Although expelled from Reichenau in 840 by Louis the German for supporting Emperor LOTHAIR I after the death of Louis the Pious, he was reinstated in 842. He died on an embassy from Louis the German to his former pupil, Charles the Bald.

The long poem in hexameters, *Visio Wettinis,* composed when Walafrid was 18, records visions of hell, purgatory, and paradise that anticipate those of Dante. In a delightfully charming and simple manner that marks Walafrid as ALCUIN's worthy successor in Latin lyric, the *De cultura hortorum* (better known as *Hortulus*), his most famous poem, describes 23 herbs or flowers, their mythological or Christian associations, and their healing properties. Two hagiographies in verse (of St. Blaitmaïc and St. Mamas), as well as poems in praise of the Empress Judith, Louis the Pious (*De imagine Tetrici*), and other important personages, reveal Walafrid's mastery of intricate lyric meters, his use of alliteration, assonance, end and internal rhyme, and his skill at acrostics. His best known theological work is the *Liber de exordiis et incrementis quarundam in observationibus ecclesiasticis rerum* (*c.* 841), which gives considerable insight into contemporary liturgical rites and customs. The *Glossa ordinaria* of the Bible, a compilation of exegetical excerpts from patristic sources that remained in use throughout the Middle Ages, is now generally thought to be only partially—if at all—the work of Walafrid. He revised EINHARD's *Life of Charlemagne,* Thegan's life of Louis the Pious, perhaps Wettin's life of St. GALL, and Gozbert's life of St. OTHMAR.

See Also: MEDIEVAL LATIN LITERATURE.

Bibliography: Complete works, *Patrologia Latina,* ed. J. P. MIGNE, 217 v., indexes 4 v., (Paris 1878–90) 113–114. Poems, *Monumenta Germaniae Historica: Poetae* (Berlin 1826–) 2:259–473. W. STRABO, *Hortulus; vom Gartenbau,* tr. W. NÄF and M. GABATHULER (2d ed., St. Gallen 1957), bibliog. M. MANITIUS *Geschichte der lateinischen Literatur des Mittelalters,* 3 v. (Munich 1911–31) 1:302–314. H. PELTIER, *Dictionnaire de Théologie catholique,* ed. A. VACANT et al., 15 v. (Paris 1903–50; Tables générales 1951–) 15.2:3498–3505. A. HAUCK, *Kirchengeschichte Deutschlands,* 5 v. (9th ed. Berlin–Leipzig 1958) 2:674–677. F. L. CROSS, *The Oxford Dictionary of the Christian Church* (London 1957) 1434, bibliog. W. KOSCH, *Deutsches Literatur-Lexikon,* ed. B. BERGER in 1 v. (Bern 1963) 468, bibliog.

[M. F. MCCARTHY]

WALARICH (VALÉRY, WALERIC), ST.

Hermit; b. Auvergne, France, toward the middle of the sixth century; d. April 1, 619. His attraction to monastic chant led him to seek admission to the monastery of Automnon. Later he went to the monastery of Saint-Germain d'Auxerre, stayed for a while at LUXEUIL with COLUMBAN, and after the latter's departure, governed the abbey. Next he went to the court of Clotaire, king of Neustria, who gave him the land of Leuconay on the Somme. At the place where his hermitage had stood, a monastery, nucleus of the city of Saint-Valéry, was later built. His life was written by Raimbert, abbot of Leuconay. In Normandy he is the patron saint of boatsmen. The translation of his relics in 981 from Sithiu (Saint-Bertin) to Saint-Valéry is commemorated at Amiens.

Feast: April 1; Dec. 12 (translation).

Bibliography: *Vita, Monumenta Germaniae Historica* (Berlin 1826–), *Scriptores rerum Merovingicarum* 4:157–175. *Acta Sanctorum* April 1:14–30. A. M. ZIMMERMANN, *Kalendarium Benedictinum: Die Heiligen und Seligen des Benediktinerordens und seiner Zweige,* 4 v. (Metten 1933–38) 2:4. J. L. BAUDOT and L. CHAUSSIN, *Vies des saints et des bienheureux selon l'ordre du calendrier avec l'historique des fêtes,* ed. by the Benedictines of Paris, 12 v. (Paris 1935–56); v. 13, suppl. and table générale (1959) 4:9–14.

[É. BROUETTE]

WALBURGA OF HEIDENHEIM, ST.

Benedictine abbess, sister of SS. WILLIBALD OF EICHSTÄTT and WINNEBALD; b. *c.* 710; d. Heidenheim, Germany, Feb. 25, 779. It is not certain whether Walburga's (Waldburg, Walpurgis, Vaubourg) father's name was Richard, but he was definitely not royal. After education at WIMBORNE in Dorsetshire, she went with St. LIOBA as a missionary to Tauberbischofsheim, Germany, at the request of St. BONIFACE. About 751 she entered the double monastery in Heidenheim, which had been founded by her brothers according to Anglo-Saxon models. After Winnebald's death, she became abbess and, like Lioba, favored the education of German women. Between 870 and 879 her remains were brought to the convent in EICHSTÄTT, later called St. Walpurg. Unlike the cult of other women saints in early German history, veneration of Walburga as a patroness against hunger and plague exceeded by far the radius of her activities. Her relics were sent to Monheim (Bavaria) and to Furness, which became the center of her cult in Flanders and northern France. Already in the ninth century "Walburga's oil" had become a sacramental (as evidenced in *Monumenta Germaniae Historica Scriptores rerum Germanicarum* 15:541). The oil, a deposit on the stone slab near her relics, still flows from October 12 to February 25 each year and is collected into small—often artistic—bottles and sent to many places, to be used in various forms of illness.

Feast: Feb. 25; May 1 (translation), Sept. 24 (translation at Zutphen), Oct. 12 (translation at Eichstatt).

Bibliography: *Acta Sanctorum* Feb. 3:516–577. *Bibliotheca hagiographica latina antiquae et mediae aetatis,* 2 v. (Brussels 1898–1901; suppl. 1911) 2:8765–74. F. L. CROSS, *The Oxford Dictionary of the Christian Church* (London 1957) 1434. A. MERCATI and A. PELZER, *Dizionario ecclesiastico,* 3 v. (Turin 1954–58) 3:1257. A. ZIMMERMANN, *Lexikon für Theologie und Kirche,* ed. M. BUCHBERGER, 10 v. (Freiburg 1930–38) 10:726–727. A. M. ZIMMERMANN, *Kalendarium Benedictinum: Die Heiligen und Seligen des Benediktinerorderns und seiner Zweige,* 4 v. (Metten 1933–38) 1:251–252. R. BAUERREISS, *Kirchengeschichte Bayerns* (2d ed. St. Ottilien 1958–) v.1. T. SCHIEFFER, *Winfrid-Bonifatius und die christliche Grundlegung Europas* (Freiburg 1954) 166, 277; *Encyclopaedia Britannica,* 24 v. (New York 1929–), with continuing rev. (1965) 23:313. J. PIHAN, *Sainte Walburge* (Vesly 1979). H. HOLZBAUER, *Mittelalterliche Heiligenverehrung; Heilige Walpurgis* (Kevelaer 1972).

[H. V. REDLICH]

WALDENSES

Members of a movement, founded by Valdes of Lyons, which was inspired by the ideal of evangelical poverty and later deviated into an antisacerdotal heresy.

Evangelical Movement. Disregarding the legendary accounts that have obscured the movement, the origins of Waldensianism are easy to discern. Valdes (Valdesius), a merchant of Lyons who had amassed a great fortune, renounced his possessions in 1173, and having decided to observe the ideal of poverty, began to preach to the people. He employed two clerics to translate the Gospels and other texts for his use. The name Peter, which appears only in 1368, was attributed to him with symbolical overtones. Valdes and his disciples went to Rome on the occasion of the Third LATERAN COUNCIL (1179). ALEXANDER III received them favorably, approved their vow of poverty, but reminded them that laymen were forbidden to preach without authorization. The pope's entourage, however, was much less gracious and ridiculed their doctrinal ignorance. It was at this time that Valdes made a profession of faith, accepting Catholic dogmas in their entirety, renewed his vow of poverty, and pledged himself to accept only such alms as were sufficient for the needs of each day.

In the beginning, Archbishop Guichard of Lyons had tended to be favorable to the newly formed fraternity. But his successor, John Bellesmains (1182–93), expelled them from Lyons probably over the issue of preaching,

Manuscript page consultation between Inquisitor William of Valence, OP, and his colleagues, and the prior of the Dominicans of Avignon and his lawyers, concerning the Waldenses, 1235.

and denounced them to the pope. At the Council of Verona (1184), LUCIUS III condemned the Waldenses, also known as the Poor of Lyons, as heretics. After his condemnation, Valdes's later career is unknown. A contemporary group, called the Humiliati, an evangelical movement among the wool workers of Milan, were also condemned at Verona. The followers of this movement joined the Waldenses to form the sect of the Poor Lombards.

Heresy. The Poor Lombards and the Poor of Lyons found it impossible to live in harmony, and in 1205 the two groups separated. Although a conference of the two groups was held at Bergamo in 1218, the Poor of Lyons and the Lombards were unable to reconcile their points of view regarding the respect due to Valdes and the subject of the Eucharist, on which the Poor of Lyons held that only a priest could consecrate.

Certain Waldenses had remained close to the traditional beliefs. After a contradictory meeting in Languedoc (1207), Durandus of Huesca and his companions sought to return to the Catholic faith and to achieve recognition of their rule with its common life and absolute poverty. INNOCENT III reconciled them (December 1208), then took the Poor Catholics of Durandus under his protection (1212). The Lombard Bernard Prim also subscribed to a profession of faith, joined to a vow of poverty (June 1210), and became the head of a community of reconciled Poor Lombards. Durandus of Huesca and his companion, Ermengaudus, wrote polemical works against the CATHARI (Dondaine, *Durand,* 233–239, 257–259). Prim took part also in these controversies in Languedoc.

Despite internal divisions, the heresy spread rapidly through the cities of Provence, the Dauphiné, Burgundy, the Franche-Comté, Lorraine, Alsace, Switzerland, Bavaria, Austria, Bohemia, and the Midi. The Waldenses, however, were always far less numerous than the Cathari. At the beginning of the 14th century, Waldenses from the Diocese of Vienne sought refuge in Languedoc. They moved also into the Alpine valleys of the Dauphiné and Piedmont (*c.* 1330), where they converted the inhabitants.

Organization. The hierarchy, described by the inquisitor BERNARD GUI, seems to have been an exceptional case. At the head were bishops or maiorales, who administered the Sacraments of Penance and the Holy Eucharist; then came the priests who preached and heard confessions; and finally the deacons who gave material help to the bishops and priests. No mention of this organization is to be found in other texts. In the Dauphiné, all the ministers, the "masters," were called *barbes* (uncles) to indicate that they were considered venerable. They were generally men of little education and of humble condition, who lived an itinerant life, preaching in secret, hearing the confessions of the faithful, and imposing fasts and the recitation of the Our Father as their penance. The faithful were to keep from doing evil and from harming their neighbor.

At the end of the 12th century, the Waldenses were rebuked for usurping the office of preaching and rejecting the authority of unworthy priests, for wearing sandals, refusing to take oaths, and for categorically forbidding the killing of any man. But contempt for the power of the Church, which was the basis of the heresy, led the Waldenses into a much more radical attitude. In their view, priests of the Roman Church had lost their authority; churches were useless; religious chants, superfluous; and it was futile to observe the feasts of the saints and to pray to them. They also violently attacked the doctrine of purgatory and its consequences, and scoffed at indulgences.

Later Development. The Waldenses continued to form a compact and homogenous group in the valleys of the Piedmont and the Briançonnais. In 1403, VINCENT FERRER preached effectively among them for three months. The Waldenses, pursued by the INQUISITION, were subjected especially to confiscations and fines. Though protected in the reign of Louis XI (1461–83), they were the object of the crusade of 1487–88, but by 1509 were allowed to live in peace. Later, however, they were again severely persecuted at the instigation of civil authorities (1545, 1555–59). The French Waldenses, reduced in numbers, transferred allegiance to the Reformation churches. The Waldenses of the Piedmont, however, stood their ground, and their history included the insurrection of 1655. In 1848, the act of emancipation granted them equality with Catholics. Torre Pellice, in the province of Turin, became the center of their activities; a Waldensian university, established in Florence in 1860, was transferred to Rome in 1922.

Bibliography: A. A. HUGON and G. GONNET, *Bibliografia Valdese* (Torre Pellice 1953). EMILIO COMBA, *Histoire des Vaudois,* 2 v. (Paris 1898–1901). ERNESTO COMBA, *Storia dei Valdesi* (Torre Pellice 1923). J. GUIRAUD, *Histoire de l'inquisition au moyen âge,* 2 v. (Paris 1935–38) v.1. K. MÜLLER, *Die Waldenser und ihre einzelnen Gruppen bis zum Anfang des 14. Jahrhunderts* (Gotha 1886). G. GONNET, "Waldensia," *Revue d'histoire et de philosophie religieuses* 33 (1953) 202–254. P. POUZET, "Les Origines lyonnaises de la secte des vaudois," *Revue d'histoire de l'Église de France* 22 (1936) 5–37. A. DONDAINE, "Aux origines du Valéisme: Une Profession de foi de Valdès," *Archivum Fratrum Praedicatorum* 16 (1946) 191–235; "Durand de Huesca et la polémique anti-cathare," *ibid.,* 29 (1959) 228–276. Y. DOSSAT, "Les Débuts de l'Inquisition à Montpellier et en Provence," *Bulletin philologique et historique* (1961) 561–579. BERNARDUS GUIDONIS, *Manuel de l'inquisiteur,* ed. and tr. G. MOLLAT, 2 v. (Paris 1926–27). J. MARX, *L'Inquisition en Dauphiné* (Paris 1914). W. L. WAKEFIELD, *Heresy, Crusade, and Inquisition in Southern France, 1100–1250* (Berkeley, Calif. 1974). E. CAMERON, *The Reformation of the Heretics: The Waldenses of the Alps, 1480–1580* (Oxford 1984). G. AUDISIO, *The Waldensian Dissent: Persecution and Survival, c. 1170–c. 1570* (Cambridge, England 1999). E. CAMERON, *Waldenses: Rejections of Holy Church in Medieval Europe* (Oxford 2000). P. BILLER, *The Waldenses, 1170–1530: Between a Religious Order and a Church* (Aldershot 2001).

[Y. DOSSAT/EDS.]

WALDETRUD, ST.

Benedictine abbess; b. Cousolre, Belgium, 628?; d. April 9, 688? Her family is remarkable for its sanctity; her parents were St. Bertilia and St. Walbert (Count of Hainaut); her sister St. Aldegund, foundress-abbess of Maubeuge. Waldetrud married the nobleman St. VINCENT MADELGARIUS, and became the mother of four who became saints: LANDRY, Dentilinus, Madelberta, and ALDETRUDE. She persuaded her husband to retire to Hautmont

Abbey, which he had founded. Two years later Waldetrud herself withdrew as a recluse to a site called *Castrilocus in Monte,* around which the abbey and city of Mons (Belgium) developed. Her relics are kept in a rich shrine, the head in a special reliquary, and are carried through the city of Mons each year on the Monday after Trinity Sunday.

Feasts: April 9 (death); Feb. 3 (translation); Nov. 2 (canonization); Aug. 12 (separation of head from body, 1250).

Bibliography: E. REUSENS et al., eds., *Analectes pour servir à l'histoire ecclésiastique de la Belgique* 4 (1867) 218–231, oldest known *vita,* 11th-century MS of 8th–9th-century work. *Acta Sanctorum* April 1:826–833. J. L. BAUDOT and L. CHAUSSIN, *Vies des saints et des bienheureux selon l'ordre du calendrier avec l'historique des fêtes,* ed. by the Benedictines of Paris, 12 v. (Paris 1935–56); v. 13, suppl. and table générale (1959) 4:213–216. A. BUTLER, *The Lives of the Saints,* rev. ed. H. THURSTON and D. ATTWATER, 4v. (New York 1956) 2:58–59. L. VAN DER ESSEN, *Étude critique et littéraire sur les vitae des saints mérovingiens de l'ancienne Belgique* (Louvain 1907) 231–237.

[H. E. AIKINS]

WALDRON, JOHN A.

Marianist educator, author, editor; b. Cleveland, OH, June 20, 1859; d. St. Louis, MO, Nov. 9, 1937. He received his B.A. from the University of Dayton, OH (1881), and his licentiate from Stanislaus College, Paris, France (1885). While teaching in diocesan and Marianist schools, he contributed numerous articles to the Catholic Educational Association (CEA, after 1927 National Catholic Educational Association, NCEA) *Bulletin* (1906–1107 22). He was a member of the general executive board of the CEA (1909), member of its advisory board (1912); and general secretary (1914). He supplied resolutions, topics, and materials for meetings of the CEA, and advised members of the U.S. hierarchy, especially Bp. Francis Howard, of Covington, KY, and Cardinal John Glennon, of St. Louis, MO. When the National Catholic Welfare Conference (NCWC) was organized (1919), he served on the executive committee of its Department of Education. In addition to his work on the editorial board of the *Catholic School Journal* (1929–37) and the St. Louis diocesan school board (1916–24), he contributed to *America, Apostle of Mary,* and the *Catholic Educational Review.*

Bibliography: P. C. GOELZ, *John A. Waldron* (Master's diss. unpub. U. of Dayton 1945).

[G. J. RUPPEL]

WALDSASSEN, ABBEY OF

In the Diocese of Regensburg, Bavaria, Germany; the 100th Cistercian abbey according to the abbots catalogue of CÎTEAUX. Founded *c.* 1133 by Margrave Diepold III of Vohburg with monks from Volkenrode in Thuringia (1131–1540), it was favored by German rulers and gained the royal protection of Conrad III and imperial immunity in 1147. From the 15th century the abbots, first called prince in a charter of Emperor SIGISMUND in 1434, had an important place in imperial diets. The kings of Bohemia, especially the Przemyslids, smoothed the way for Waldassen to colonize and found new houses in Bohemia: Sedletz (*c.* 1143–1783) and Ossegg (1194–1945); German Christian culture was then consolidated around Cheb (CZECH REPUBLIC). Protestant in 1559 and secularized in 1571, the abbey flourished anew after its restoration by Fürstenfeld Abbey in 1669, although without its former privileges. When suppressed in 1803 it had 62 members and its lands comprised 13 square miles with 20,000 persons. Cistercian nuns from Seligenthal in Landshut (founded 1232 from TREBNITZ and an abbey since 1925) purchased the bright and famous cloister buildings in 1863. Waldsassen became independent again in 1894 and an abbey in 1925; it is known for its elementary and secondary girls' schools. The library has famous portraits, and the splendid church interior (1681–1704), with later rococo decoration, is the work of Italian, Bohemian, and South German masters.

Bibliography: L. H. COTTINEAU, *Répertoire topobibliographique des abbayes et prieurés,* 2 v. (Mâcon 1935–39) 2:3428–29. E. KRAUSEN, *Die Klöster des Zisterzienserordens in Bayern* (Munich 1953). *Catalogus generalis . . . S. O. Cist.* (Rome 1954). H. HAHN, *Die frühe Kirchenbaukunst der Zisterzienser* (Berlin 1957). ''Waldsassen,'' *Lexikon für Theologie und Kirche,* ed. J. HOFER and K. RAHNER, 10 v. (2d, new ed. Freiburg 1957–65) v. 10.

[C. SPAHR]

WALES, THE CATHOLIC CHURCH IN

Located on the island of Great Britain, the principality of Wales is located west of England. Bounded on the north by the Irish Sea and Ireland, on the south by the Bristol Channel, and on the west by St. George's Channel, Wales comprises the upland region known as the Cambrian Mountains. Its northern and southern coasts are largely industrialized, but its mountainous interior is pastoral and sparsely settled.

Wales (''Cymru'' in the Welsh language) has been politically integrated with England since 1536, and is now part of the United Kingdom of Great Britain and

Capital: Cardiff.
Size: 8,016 sq. miles.
Population: 3,065,805 in 2000.
Languages: Welsh, English.
Religions: 153,290 Catholics (5%), 1,379,612 Anglicans (45%), 551,844 Methodists (18%), 214,606 other (7%), 766,453 without religious affiliation.
Metropolitan See: Cardiff, with suffragans Menevia and Wrexham.

Northern Ireland. Despite its political links to England, the region retains many distinctive cultural characteristics. About 30 percent of the inhabitants speak Welsh, along with English. Welsh literature originated in the 5th century and is one of the important European Catholic literatures.

Early and Medieval Christianity. Wales was originally inhabited by a Celtic people, the Cymric. According to Tertullian and Origen, Christianity had entered the region by the 2d century, in conjunction with the Roman occupation. Another indication of the early introduction of Christianity is the rough coincidence between the territories of the ancient Dioceses of Saint Davids, SAINT ASAPH, BANGOR, and LLANDAFF and those of the four pre-Roman tribes. Since three British bishops attended the Council of ARLES (314), an ecclesiastical organization must have existed then.

Celtic missionaries completely christianized Wales by the end of the 6th century. The end of Roman rule (406) exposed Britain to raids by pagan Saxons, particularly in eastern sections of the island. In western Britain (modern Wales), St. Elen, disciple of MARTIN OF TOURS before 400, inaugurated Celtic monasticism, which transcended the enervated, urbanized Catholicism of the Roman occupation. Welsh Christianity received its distinctive form during the age of the saints (sancti). The saints were Christians, trained in the ascetical discipline of the Egyptian DESERT FATHERS, who lived in a fraternity (clas). Among the best-remembered figures are DAVID (patron of Wales), ILLTUD, Teilo, Dyfrig, Beuno, and Samson. Monastic colleges at Llantwit Major, Glamorgan, and elsewhere gathered students from other lands.

In 597 AUGUSTINE OF CANTERBURY, personal emissary of Pope GREGORY I to the English, requested of Welsh and Celtic bishops personal submission to him and modification of certain customs that had evolved in Wales and other Celtic lands because of their isolation from the continental Church. Inferring that this would substitute submission of the Welsh Church to Canterbury for their direct allegiance to Rome, the bishops refused; they also rejected Augustine's requests for abolition of the Celtic tonsure, readjustment of the date of Easter to Continental usage (see EASTER CONTROVERSY), and uniformity in the baptismal rite. This event, of traumatic importance in Welsh ecclesiastical history, was reflected in the hatred between Christian Welsh and pagan English that can be found in contemporary Welsh literature. The disputed points were conceded in 768 to Elfodd, a young Welsh bishop. (See CELTIC RITE.)

The 6th century climaxed the age of the saints, and British coastal islands still bear evidence of their settlements. Records of the 8th to 11th centuries are meager. Despite the struggle against Norse raiders, Christian society progressed, and in 950 emerged the laws of Wales, codified by Prince Hywel the Good with monastic aid; they revealed a Christian stamp on the social order. By the time of the reign of Prince Owain in North Wales (1137–69), Norman infiltration had begun. In 1143 the Norman Gilbert became bishop of Saint Asaph. The Welsh hierarchy came increasingly under the control of Canterbury. Welsh arguments against this were so cogent that Bernard, first Norman bishop of Saint Davids, the primatial see, carried the Welsh case to Rome; but his attempt proved unsuccessful. The key interpreter of this struggle was GIRALDUS CAMBRENSIS, of Welsh and Norman princely birth, archdeacon of Saint Davids (1176) who fought for and lost the case at Rome for an independent Welsh hierarchy. Until the death of Llywellyn (1282), last prince of Wales, the Welsh princes opposed foreign administration of Welsh dioceses, because it deflected their direct allegiance to Rome, and did so by royal violence, not by papal authority. Llywellyn's death also ended Welsh formal diplomatic contacts at Rome. Later popes, however, sought to strengthen the Welsh Church against increasing political erosion by England.

The imposition of Norman ecclesiastical organization increased the difficulties. The Celtic structure, derived from monastic origins, consisted of mother churches served by daughter churches over wide areas. The Norman pattern of territorially defined dioceses required a century to establish. Archdeacons, assisted by rural deans, became pivotal men. Roman canons of discipline and ecclesiastical courts were introduced. Three issues proved insoluble: hereditary succession to ecclesiastical office, clerical celibacy, and marriage within prohibited degrees. Of the religious orders, the CANONS REGULAR OF ST. AUGUSTINE were established earliest; but the CISTERCIANS, whose arrival was independent of all political association, were the most loved. They cultivated desolate lands and were learned in native tradition; and therefore they recalled the age of the sancti. During the 13th century, the newly established mendicant orders of

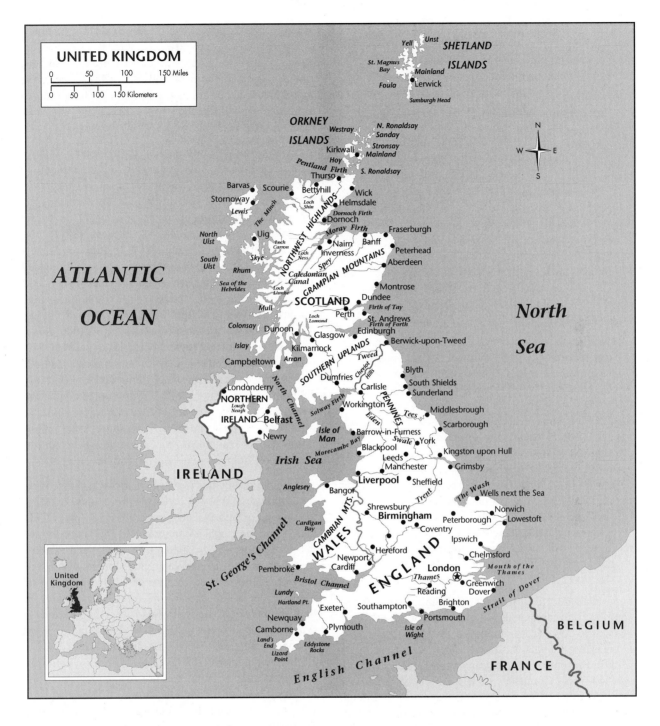

FRANCISCANS, DOMINICANS, and CARMELITES came to Wales. They were superior in contemporary learning to monks and secular clergy, but the latter continued to maintain traditions of scholarship. Following the decrees of the Fourth LATERAN COUNCIL in 1215 the type of theology popularized by the Dominicans began to appear. Augustinian theology, mediating through the Victorine school (*see* SAINT-VICTOR, MONASTERY OF), and varied trends in scholastic theology coming from Oxford and Paris were reflected in contemporary literature.

In 1284, two years after the death of Welsh King Llewellan, Edward I of England completed the conquest of Wales, and the region became an English principality. Cultural differences remained between Wales and England, however, and by 1400 these differences had sparked a national rebellion, which lasted ten years. It was led by Owain Glyndwr, who supported the Avignon claimant to the papacy (*see* WESTERN SCHISM) and destroyed all church property held by incumbent agents of

English expansion. Seculars, Cistercians, and Franciscans supported Glyndwr's unsuccessful uprising. In addition to causing enormous material loss to the Church, Glyndwr's rebellion did little to aid in the Church's transition to a diocesan, rather than monastic structure.

Introduction of Protestantism. From the mid-14th to the mid-15th century the Church's structure became increasingly unstable. The practice of farming out Church land led to a preponderance of lay control, while abbots became privileged landowners. Welsh sees were staffed by politically appointed Englishmen en route to preferment in England. Yet social recovery in the years after the rebellions was rapid and beneficial to the Church, since the faithful remained loyal. As Welsh literature testifies, Pope Nicholas V's jubilee in 1450 revived pilgrimages to Rome, SANTIAGO DE COMPOSTELA, and elsewhere, while Cistercian monastic discipline tightened under the reform of John de Cireyo of Cîteaux (1467–1503).

While Church ritual and hierarchical organization became increasingly stable, lay control continued to be a source of grave abuses. Clerical celibacy was enforced briefly by Queen MARY TUDOR. In 1536, when Henry VIII suppressed all monasteries in England following his break with Rome and his divorce from Catherine of Aragon, the loss of the 47 Welsh religious houses was a grievous blow in a land of so few institutions. Formal grammar and bardic schooling ended, while the persecution of Catholics began. The persecution would last for the next 150 years, causing many ordinary folk to suffer heroically. Between 1557 and 1680, 91 Welsh Catholics sacrificed their lives publicly for the faith, and hundreds more testified in obscurity (*see* REFORMATION, PROTESTANT IN THE BRITISH ISLES; ENGLAND, SCOTLAND, AND WALES, MARTYRS OF).

Meanwhile, illustrious Welsh Catholic exiles abroad contributed to the Counter Reformation with translations and original works for circulation in Wales. Perceiving the need for literacy, Gruffydd Robert, confessor to St. Charles Borromeo in Milan, produced his famous *Grammadeg* (Welsh Grammar). Later his *Y Drych Cristionogawl* (Mirror of Christianity) was printed in a cliffside cave near Llandudno. Throughout the period of the PENAL LAWS, numerous Welsh aspirants to the priesthood left for continental seminaries. Up to the Civil War (1642) more than 25 percent of British clerical students in continental seminaries were from North Wales. It was not persecution that caused Catholicism to yield, but the PURITANS, whose preachers came in the wake of the Civil War and supplied the spiritually starved Welsh with religious nourishment.

The OATES PLOT (1678–81) definitively ended the old Catholicism in Wales as in England. Movements dissenting from the formalism of Anglicanism kept multiplying. By 1750 Methodism, Calvinistic or Wesleyan, prevailed in Wales. There developed a different religious culture, based on literacy and the ability to read the Welsh Bible, translated in 1588 by Bp. William Morgan at the command of Elizabeth I. Welsh religion was henceforth presented entirely in the Welsh vernacular.

The Catholic Church after 1800. Modern Catholicism came to Wales early in the 19th century, brought by immigrants from Ireland who were attracted by the industrial revolution. From 1688 to 1840 the few Catholics living in Wales were under the jurisdiction of the vicars apostolic of the Western District, resident in Bath, England. In 1801 the population of the counties of Glamorgan and Monmouthshire, which combined totaled 126,000, included only two Catholics, in Cardiff. Within the entire region, there were only 1,000 Catholics and a few private Catholic chapels. But within 40 years industrialism would increase the population to 305,000. About 1847 famine in Ireland forced thousands of destitute Irish to this Nonconformist milieu where numerous Catholic missions took root. Msgr. Peter Bernardine Collingridge, OSF, became vicar apostolic. Priests worked among impoverished exiles; frequently they had to contend also with strong opposition from Nonconformists. Catholic EMANCIPATION came in 1829. In that year Peter BAINES succeeded Collingridge as vicar apostolic.

In 1840, when the Western District was divided into two vicariates, Wales (including the county of Monmouthshire, which is sometimes considered part of England) and the English county of Herefordshire formed one of them. When the hierarchy was restored in 1850, the six counties of South Wales plus Monmouthshire and Herefordshire became the Diocese of Newport and Menevia; and the six counties of North Wales, part of the English Diocese of Shrewsbury. In 1895 the Vicariate of Wales was created by uniting all Welsh counties except Glamorganshire and Monmouthshire, and from 1898 to 1916 this area formed the Diocese of Menevia, suffragan to Westminster. Glamorganshire, Monmouthshire, and Herefordshire constituted the Diocese of Newport from 1896 to 1916, when the name was changed to Cardiff. Since 1916 Wales has been a separate ecclesiastical province with the Archdiocese of CARDIFF as metropolitan and Menevia and Wrexham as its suffragans. The county system was redrawn in 1974, and by 2000 Wales was politically divided into eight counties.

Oblates of Mary Immaculate came from Brittany in 1900, and maintained a mission in the Conway Valley in North Wales until World War I. A Welsh seminary, founded at Holywell in 1904, lasted until 1933. After the Anglican monastic community on Caldey Island, South

Pembrokeshire, was converted to Catholicism in 1913, it functioned as a Benedictine community until 1928, when French Cistercians obtained Caldey, and the previous occupants moved to PRINKNASH ABBEY.

Into the Twenty-First Century. In 2000 Wales boasted 153,286 Catholics, 89 churches and chapels, 2 bishops, and 258 priests. There were 187 parish churches in the principality. Because of their relatively small numbers, Welsh Catholics have organized few religious-based organizations. Wales traditionally joined England in its Conference of Bishops.

Bibliography: C. GROSS, *Sources and Literature of English History . . . to 1485* (2d ed. New York 1915; repr. 1952). C. READ, ed., *Bibliography of British History: Tudor Period, 1485–1603* (2d ed. New York 1959). G. DAVIES, ed., *Bibliography of British History, Stuart Period, 1603–1714* (Oxford 1928). S. MACC. PARGELLIS and D. J. MEDLEY, eds., *Bibliography of British History, 1714–89* (Oxford 1951). A. W. W. EVANS, *Welsh Christian Origins* (Oxford 1934). G. WILLIAMS, *The Welsh Church from Conquest to Reformation* (Cardiff 1962). D. ATTWATER, *The Catholic Church in Modern Wales* (London 1935). K. S. LATOURETTE, *Christianity in a Revolutionary Age: A History of Christianity in the 19th and 20th Centuries* (New York 1958–62). v.2, 4. *Bilan du Monde* 2:752–766. *CathDir* (London 1838—). *Annuarai Pontifico.*

[C. M. DANIEL/EDS.]

WALFRID, ST.

Also known as Galfrido, Gualfredus, founder, first abbot of the Benedictine Abbey of St. Peter, Palazzuolo; b. Pisa, Italy; d. Feb. 15, *c.* 765. Walfrid, who was of the noble family of Gherardesca, and his wife, Thesia, decided to become religious under monastic discipline. Consequently he withdrew from secular life and with the aid of a kinsman, Gundualld, and a Corsican, Fortis, established a monastery for men (754) near Monte Verde, in Tuscany. A little later he made another foundation, some 18 miles away, for the wives of those who had become monks. There his wife and a daughter (Rattruda) took the veil. The Abbey of Palazzuolo flourished and later enjoyed the favor of the German Emperor and of the popes. Walfrid's priest son Ginfred, who had once defected from the monastery but returned penitent, succeeded his father as abbot. Gundualld's only son, Andrew, became the third abbot and wrote Walfrid's biography (*Acta Sanctorum* Feb. 2:843–847). Walfrid's cult was approved in 1861.

Feast: Feb. 15.

Bibliography: P. F. KEHR, *Regesta Pontificum Romanorum. Italia Pontificia,* 8 v. (Berlin 1906–35) 3:274–276. A. M. ZIMMERMANN, *Kalendarium Benedictinum: Die Heiligen und Seligen des Benediktinerordens und seiner Zweige,* 4 v. (Metten 1933–38) 1:215–217. L. H. COTTINEAU, *Répertoire topobibliographique des abbayes et prieurés,* 2 v. (Mâcon 1935–39) 2:2176. J. L. BAUDOT and L. CHAUSSIN, *Vies des saints et des bienheureux selon l'ordre du calendrier avec l'historique des fêtes,* ed. by the Benedictines of Paris, 12 v. (Paris 1935–56); v. 13, suppl. and table générale (1959) 2:349. A. BUTLER, *The Lives of the Saints,* rev. ed. H. THURSTON and D. ATTWATER, 4 v. (New York 1956) 1:341–342. J. H. ZEDLER, *Grosses vollständiges Universal-Lexikon,* 64 v. (Halle 1732–50; repr. Graz 1961–) 52: 1593. *Vita Walfredi und Kloster Monteverdi,* ed. K. SCHMID (Tübingen 1991).

[M. J. KISHPAUGH]

WALL, JOHN, ST.

English martyr; b. Chingle Hall?, Lancashire, 1620; d. Worcester, Aug. 22, 1679. The son of William Wall of Aldeby, Norfolk, he was baptized by Edmund ARROWSMITH, and at the age of 13, he was sent to Douai. There he spent eight years before entering the English College, Rome, for his ecclesiastical studies on May 11, 1642, under the name of Marsh. He was followed there by his brother William, who because of ill health had failed to persevere as a Carthusian at Nieuport in Flanders and later became a Benedictine monk of Lambspring in Germany. John, ordained on Dec. 3, 1645, after higher studies, left for England (1648); on the way there he stayed at the Franciscan friary of St. Bonaventure, Douai, where he sought to join the Friars Minor. After a year in England he returned to St. Bonaventure's, and was clothed as a novice on Jan. 1, 1651, taking the name of Brother Joachim of St. Anne. In 1656 he was again sent to England, and under the name of Mr. Webb, worked mainly in Warwickshire for 23 years. Wall's name is commonly associated with Harvington Hall, the seat of a Catholic branch of the Talbot family. At the outbreak of the violence caused by the OATES PLOT, Wall was in London for a Franciscan provincial chapter. In defiance of the proclamation ordering all priests to leave the kingdom, he returned to Worcestershire. About a month later, at Rushock Court, he was arrested and taken to Worcester Castle, where he received into the Church a number of his fellow prisoners; then in May 1679 he was taken to London to be questioned concerning the Oates Plot. When his examination before the Privy Council emphasized his innoçence, he was confined in Newgate (where his brother, now Dom Cuthbert, a fellow prisoner, was not permitted to see him) and then sent back to Worcester. At the summer assizes in the city he was condemned for his priesthood (Aug. 17, 1679), and he was executed five days later. Wall was beatified by Pius XI on Dec. 15, 1929 and canonized by Paul VI in 1970. His head, which was secured after his execution by a fellow Franciscan, John Baptist Leveson, was preserved at Douai until the French Revolution, when it was lost. (*See* ENGLAND, SCOTLAND, AND WALES, MARTYRS OF.)

Feast: Aug. 26.

Bibliography: F. DAVEY, *Blessed John Wall* (Postulation Pamphlet; London 1961). A. BUTLER, *The Lives of the Saints,* rev. ed. H. THURSTON and D. ATTWATER, 4 v. (New York 1956) 3:409–410. R. CHALLONER, *Memoirs of Missionary Priests,* ed. J. H. POLLEN (rev. ed. London 1924).

[G. FITZHERBERT]

WALLENSTEIN, ALBRECHT EUSEBIUS WENZEL VON

Duke of Friedland, Sagan, and Mecklenburg; b. Hermanice, Bohemia, Sept. 24, 1583; d. Eger, Bohemia, Feb. 25, 1634. Wallenstein, a member of the noble, but not rich, Waldstein family, was sent by his uncle, Heinrich von Slavata, to the Jesuit college at Olmütz where he converted to Roman Catholicism. After studying also at Altdorf, Bologna, and Padua, where he acquired his lifelong interest in astrology, Wallenstein joined the army of George Basta, an imperialist general of Rudolph II. Wallenstein's bravery in the Hungarian campaign against the Turks won him command of a company (1605). After returning to Bohemia, he married (1609) an elderly Moravian widow, Lucretia von Vičkov, whose estates he inherited at her death in 1614. The independently wealthy Wallenstein fought for the Emperor against the Venetians and, after the outbreak of the THIRTY YEARS' WAR, against the Bohemian rebels. It was he who delivered the treasury of the Moravian Estates to Vienna, later using the money to raise a regiment in the imperial cause. He fought against Bethlen Gabor, the Transylvanian ally of the rebels, and against Count Ernst Mansfeld, and consequently was not present at White Mountain (November 1620), the crucial defeat of the Bohemian cause. Wallenstein proceeded to amalgamate his estates with his conquests, and some purchases from Emperor FERDINAND II. He was appointed imperial count palatine (1622), prince (1623), and then duke of Friedland (1624); he quickly won favor at court and with the army. Wallenstein married Isabella Harrach, the wealthy daughter of a close imperial advisor, and used his riches to lend money to the Emperor and to extend his influence. He seems also to have been a firm ruler and capable administrator who took a sincere interest in the welfare of his subjects.

When Christian IV of Denmark declared war on Ferdinand II, Wallenstein joined forces with Johann Tserclaes of Tilly, general of the Catholic League, against the Danes. An army of more than 20,000 men flocked to Wallenstein's banner, attracted by his reputation and the promise of spoils. The campaigns of 1625, 1626, and 1627 witnessed Wallenstein's defeat of Mansfeld, and Gabor, and the conquest of Silesia and Mecklenburg. He was granted the latter in 1628, and named hereditary duke of Mecklenburg in June 1629. His siege of Stralsund was unsuccessful and his effort to extend Hapsburg power to the Baltic was thwarted. Eventually, Wallenstein urged Ferdinand II to sign a treaty with the Danes and at that time also expressed his opposition to the Edict of RESTITUTION (1629). Wallenstein's ambition made enemies for him at court and among the princes of the Catholic League. On Aug. 13, 1630, Ferdinand II dismissed Wallenstein from the imperial service. Upon returning to Friedland, Wallenstein quietly negotiated with Gustavus II Adolphus, King of Sweden and new leader of the Protestant cause. The Swedish victories at Breitenfeld (1631) and Lech (1632), as well as the death of Tilly, forced Ferdinand to recall Wallenstein. Reluctantly, Wallenstein returned, but eventually he launched a full-scale campaign against the Protestants. Wallenstein's victories at Prague and Nuremberg were followed by his defeat at Lützen, (November 1632). King Gustavus was killed in the battle, however, and the Swedes were demoralized. Wallenstein failed to attack the Swedes, preferring negotiations with Saxony, France, Brandenburg, and Sweden to fighting against them. It would appear that he was contemplating desertion of the imperial cause, and preparing a personal coup, which portended some reorganization of the Empire. By October 1633, however, these negotiations were broken off and Wallenstein renewed his campaign against the Saxons.

By this time, Ferdinand II, influenced by the Spanish ambassador and by Wallenstein's enemies, was determined to dismiss him. In January 1634, the Emperor signed a secret patent removing him. On February 18, Wallenstein was accused of high treason. While on his way to an intended meeting with Duke Benhard of Saxe-Weimar, Wallenstein was murdered by some Irish and Scots officers in the imperial army who were led by Col. Walter Butler and Capt. Walter Devereux. Haughty, boastful, and ambitious, Wallenstein was a skillful strategist, a brave soldier, and a clever diplomat. Sharp controversy over his motives and principles still rages among historians. Sometimes called a traitor to Catholicism, he has been hailed by others as a herald of German nationalism, by still others as a ruthless and calculating *condottiere.* As Friedrich Schiller wrote in his dramatic *Wallensteins Tod,* "his portrait fluctuates in history."

Bibliography: J. PEKAR, *Wallenstein 1630–1634: Tragödie einer Verschwörung,* 2 v. (Berlin 1937). C. V. WEDGWOOD, *The Thirty Years' War* (New Haven 1939). H. VON SRBIK, *Wallensteins Ende* (Vienna 1920). F. WATSON, *Wallenstein: Soldier under Saturn* (London 1938). C. J. FRIEDRICH, *The Age of the Baroque, 1610–1660* (New York 1952). W. PICKEL, *Gustav Adolf und Wallenstein in der Schlacht an der Alten Veste bei Nürnberg, 1632* (Nuremberg 1926). G. MANN, *Wallenstein,* ed., C. KESSLER (New York 1976). H. DIWALD, *Wallenstein* (Munich 1969).

[P. S. MCGARRY]

WALLINGFORD, WILLIAM

English Benedictine abbot; d. May 19, 1492. Possibly educated at Oxford, Wallingford became a Benedictine monk at SAINT ALBANS Abbey where he was called *officiarius generalis* because of the many offices he held (1445–54). He served as prior and kitchener (1464–76) and finally became abbot (1476–92), being appointed visitor to the Benedictine houses of the diocese of Lincoln in 1480.

As early as 1454 Wallingford was accused of fraud in handling the abbey's money by Abbot John Whethamstede; Wallingford must have persisted in such questionable monetary practices during his term as abbot, because chancery proceedings were later brought against him at the King's Bench (1483) and by the prioress of Sopwell at the Court of ARCHES (*c.* 1485). Wallingford failed in his efforts to secure from Rome episcopal EXEMPTION for his abbey (1487). In February 1490, however, he procured a papal bull commanding Abp. John Morton of Canterbury to protect existing abbatial privileges. In July of 1490, however, the archbishop warned Wallingford that if certain abuses were not eradicated (simony, usury, the selling of abbey goods, and consorting with nuns of Pres are specified), he would make an official VISITATION of the abbey. Morton was upheld by Pope INNOCENT VIII against the abbot's appeal, but whether the archbishop used his permission to visit is not known. Wallingford contributed a fine reredos to the abbey church and carried out various building projects at the abbey at an estimated expense of £8600. He is thought to be buried there.

Bibliography: *Registra Johannis Whetharnstede . . . et Witlelmi Walingforde, abbatum monasterii S. Albani,* ed. H. T. RILEY, 2 v. (*Rerum Britannicarum medii aevi scriptores* 28; London 1872–73) 1:109–124, 476–479, and *passim;* 2:140–291. D. WILKINS, *Concilia Magnae Britanniae et Hiberniae,* 4 v. (London 1737) 3:630–632. V. H. GALBRAITH, *The Abbey of St. Albans* (Oxford 1911) 55–61. 33–74. *The Victoria History of the County of Hertford,* ed. W. PAGE, 4 v. (Westminster, Eng. 1902–14) 2:495; 4:403–408. D. D. KNOWLES, "The Case of St. Albans Abbey in 1490," *The Journal of Ecclesiastical History* 3 (1952) 144–158. A. B. EMDEN, *A Biographical Register of the University of Oxford to A. D. 1500* (Oxford 1957–59) 3:1967–68.

[V. I. J. FLINT]

WALPOLE, HENRY, ST.

Jesuit priest, martyr; b. Docking, near Sandringham, Norfolk, England, 1558; d. York, England, Apr. 7, 1595. As the eldest son of Christopher Walpole, he was educated at Norwich Grammar School (1567–74), Peterhouse, Cambridge, and Gray's Inn, London. He is said to have been converted to the faith when he witnessed, on Dec. 1, 1581, the execution of St. Edmund CAMPION, in whose

St. Henry Walpole.

honor he wrote a long narrative poem, secretly printed and offensive to the government. Crossing to Paris, he went on to Rheims, where he entered the English seminary on July 7, 1582. On April 28, 1583, he was admitted into the English College, Rome. He entered the Society of Jesus in 1584 and, to benefit his poor health, continued his studies for the priesthood at the Scots College, Pont-á-Mousson. After his ordination at Paris, Dec. 17, 1588, he acted as chaplain to the Spanish army in the Netherlands, and was caught and imprisoned for a year by the English at Flushing. He was then sent to teach in the English seminaries at Seville and Valladolid. Under Father Robert PERSONS'S direction he visited Philip II and from him obtained a charter for the erection of an English school at Saint-Omer. He was sent to England in November 1593 and took ship at Dunkirk. Since the ports of southern England were closed as a result of the plague, he embarked with his brother Thomas and an English soldier, Edward Lingham, in a convoy of three warships sailing for Scotland.

On the night of December 6, after ten stormy days at sea, he was put ashore north of Bridlinton, Yorkshire. At Kelham, ten miles inland on the road to York, while resting for the night at an inn, he was arrested on suspicion of being a priest. He had, in fact, been betrayed by a Scottish soldier who had landed three days earlier. At

York he was frequently examined, first by Lord Huntingdon, the president of the Council of the North, then by Richard Topcliffe, sent for that purpose from London. In late February 1594, he was transferred to the Tower of London, where he was examined ten times between April and June and submitted to torture fourteen times; he completely lost the use of his fingers. The reports of his examinations, partially forged, were not used in evidence against him in the York trial in the spring of 1595. Indicted under the Act (27 Eliz, cap. 2) that made it high treason for a native Englishman ordained overseas to minister as a priest in England, he pleaded that he had been arrested before the 36 hours' grace, allowed by the statute, had expired. Nevertheless, he was condemned and executed at the York gallows.

Walpole was beatified by Pius XI on Dec. 15, 1929, and canonized by Paul VI on Oct. 25, 1970 as one of the Forty Martyrs of England and Wales.

Feast: April 7; Oct. 25 (Feast of the 40 Martyrs of England and Wales); May 4 (Feast of the English Martyrs in England); Dec. 1 (Jesuits).

See Also: ENGLAND, SCOTLAND, AND WALES, MARTYRS OF.

Bibliography: A. JESSOP, *One Generation of a Norfolk House . . .* (London 1879). P. CARAMAN, *Henry Garnet* (London 1964). J. GERARD, *Autobiography of a Hunted Priest,* ed. and tr. P. CARAMAN (New York 1952). R. CHALLONER, *Memoirs of Missionary Priests,* ed. J. H. POLLEN (rev. ed. London 1924; repr. Farnborough 1969) 223–32. A. BUTLER, *The Lives of the Saints,* ed. H. THURSTON and D. ATTWATER (New York 1956) 2:50–51. J. N. TYLENDA, *Jesuit Saints & Martyrs* (Chicago 1998) 88–90.

[G. FITZHERBERT]

WALRAM OF NAUMBERG

Bishop; d. April 12, 1111. He was consecrated bishop in 1091 and was a supporter of the Emperor HENRY IV in the INVESTITURE STRUGGLE. Some of his letters giving evidence of this support have survived (*Monumenta Germaniae Historica: Libelli de lite,* 2:286–91). He is not the author, however, of the *De unitate ecclesiae conservanda* (*Ibid.* 2:182–284), or of the *Tractatus de investitura* (*Ibid.* 2:498–504). In later years, under the irenic efforts of PASCHAL II, Walram was reconciled with Rome. He is mentioned in several undated letters of ANSELM OF CANTERBURY.

Bibliography: M. MANITIUS, *Geschichte der lateinischen Literatur des Mittelalters,* 3 v. (Munich 1911–31) 3:44. W. DEINHARDT, *Lexikon für Theologie und Kirche,* ed. J. HOFER and K. RAHNER, 10 v. (2d, new ed. Freiburg 1957–65) 10:740.

[S. WILLIAMS]

WALSH, EDMUND ALOYSIUS

Educator and author; b. South Boston, Massachusetts, Oct. 10, 1885; d. Washington, D.C., Oct. 31, 1956. Walsh was the son of John Francis and Catherine J. (Noonan) Walsh. After entering the Jesuit novitiate at Frederick, Maryland, in 1902, he taught English at Georgetown University, Washington, D.C., from 1909 to 1911. He went abroad for graduate work in Dublin and London and theological studies at the University of Innsbruck, Austria, before being ordained by Cardinal James Gibbons at Woodstock College, Maryland, in 1916. He became dean of Georgetown University and was given additional appointments in 1918 as assistant educational director of the Jesuits' New England colleges and member of the coordinating board of the Students' Army Training Corps. He founded the Georgetown University School of Foreign Service in 1919 and served as its first director and regent.

Walsh, having been appointed in 1922 as director of the Papal Relief Mission in Russia, recovered from Moscow the relics of St. Andrew Bobola and had them transferred to Rome. This assignment, and his selection as president of the Catholic Near East Welfare Association in 1927, inaugurated a series of international experiences that made him an authority on foreign affairs. He published his first book on Russia, *The Fall of the Russian Empire,* in 1928, and this was followed by *The Last Stand* (1931), *Ships and National Safety* (1934), *Total Power* (1948), and *Total Empire* (1951).

In 1929 Walsh was sent as Vatican representative to Mexico where he served with Dwight Morrow and Miguel Cruchaga on a commission that sought to reconcile the Mexican government with the Church. Two years later he was dispatched as Vatican legate to Iraq where he negotiated for the establishment of Baghdad College. Following service as visiting lecturer (1935, 1939) at the Academy of International Law, The Hague, and acting president (1937) of Georgetown University, Walsh became lecturer and consultant for the U.S. Department of War in 1942. After World War II, he was a civilian consultant to the U.S. chief of counsel at the Nuremberg war crimes trials. In 1947–48 he went to Japan as visitor general in order to reorganize the Society of Jesus there. In 1949 he was named to presidential commissions on universal military training and on religious needs in the Armed Forces. That same year he founded the Institute of Languages and Linguistics at Georgetown. Walsh was honored when the Edmund A. Walsh School of Foreign Service of Georgetown University was renamed for him on Oct. 13, 1958. He also received two honorary doctorates and was made a knight of the Spanish Order of Isabella La Católica.

[L. J. GALLAGHER]

WALSH, FRANCIS AUGUSTINE

Philosopher, author, and one of the founders of St. Anselm's Priory; b. near Cincinnati, March 21, 1884; d. Washington, D.C., Aug. 12, 1938. Walsh's parents were Thomas and Mary (Comerford) Walsh, from Ireland. He received his A.B. in 1903 and his Ph.D. in 1922 from Xavier University, Cincinnati, Ohio. He attended Mt. St. Mary's Seminary of the West, Norwood, Ohio, and Capranica College in Rome, and was ordained in 1907. After four years in parish work he joined Mt. St. Mary's faculty and was professor of philosophy and vice rector from 1914 to 1921, except for a period as chaplain during World War I. In 1923, while pastor of St. Andrew's Parish in Cincinnati, he joined the Benedictines and went to St. Benedict's Abbey, Fort Augustus, Scotland, for his novitiate.

A professed Benedictine with the name of Augustine, he returned to Washington in 1924 to help establish St. Anselm's Priory (now Abbey) near The Catholic University of America. He taught philosophy at Catholic University and at Trinity College, Washington, D.C., published several books on the spiritual life and philosophy, and wrote pamphlets and articles for Catholic journals. He also edited six *Benedictine Historical Monographs* (1926–31); the *Placidian* (1924–30), a quarterly review (both published at St. Anselm's Priory); and the *New Roman Missal* (1937). He was associate editor of *Studies in Psychology and Psychiatry* (1926–38), sponsored by Catholic University, and president of the American Catholic Philosophical Association (1933–34) and editor of its review *New Scholasticism* (1936–38).

Dom Augustine promoted the liturgical awakening in the Church in the U.S. and worked vigorously in the early 1930s to improve the lot of African-Americans, founding and directing the Clergy Conference on Negro Welfare (1933–38) and the Newman Club at Howard University, Washington, D.C. He was the first national director of the Confraternity of Christian Doctrine (1933–38), and a member of a special advisory committee of the National Catholic Educational Association (1928–38).

[J. FARRELLY]

WALSH, JAMES ANTHONY

Cofounder and first superior general of the Catholic Foreign Mission Society of America (MARYKNOLL FATHERS AND BROTHERS); titular bishop of Siene; b. Cambridge, Mass., Feb. 24, 1867; d. Maryknoll, N.Y., Apr. 14, 1936. He was born of modestly affluent Irish immigrant parents, James Walsh and Hannah Shea. He attend-

ed Boston College, and for a year was a special student at Harvard University. He completed his studies for the priesthood at St. John's Seminary, Brighton, Mass., and was ordained for the Archdiocese of Boston on May 20, 1892. After serving ten years as an assistant in St. Mary's Parish, Roxbury, he was named, in 1903, archdiocesan director of the Society for the Propagation of the Faith, a position he held for eight years.

Promoting Foreign Missions. In 1904, at a meeting in Washington, D.C. of priests engaged in missionary activity in the United States, Walsh expressed his conviction that the home missionary spirit in the United States would be strengthened if the urgency of foreign missions were likewise promoted. Among his hearers was Fr. Thomas F. Price, the organizer of a small mission group in Raleigh, North Carolina. Price offered his support for Walsh's proposal in his national Catholic magazine *Truth*. In 1906 Walsh, with three other priests, established in Boston a "Catholic Foreign Mission Bureau" for the purpose of publishing a magazine to inform U.S. Catholics about the Church's worldwide missions and to urge the establishment of a foreign mission seminary for U.S. diocesan priests. *The Field Afar* appeared in 1907. Assisting Walsh in the editing was Mary Josephine Rogers, the future foundress of the Maryknoll Sisters.

Cofounder of Maryknoll. In 1911 Walsh and Price met again by chance at a Eucharistic Congress in Montreal. Price was convinced that the time had come for them to unite their efforts to found a foreign mission seminary and society. Walsh readily accepted the challenge. Price was instrumental in securing the release of Walsh from the Boston archdiocese and in obtaining the support of Cardinal James Gibbons and the apostolic delegate, Diomede Falconio. Approval of the project was given by the U.S. archbishops at their national meeting in Washington, D.C. on April 27, 1911. Walsh and Price then proceeded to Rome where, on June 29, 1911 the Congregation for the Propagation of the Faith authorized the project. The following day, Pope Pius X received Walsh and Price and gave them and the project his blessing.

Upon their return to the United States, Price asked Walsh to assume the office of superior. While Price devoted much of his time to fundraising and vocation promotion, Walsh directed the administration and supervised the formation of the candidates. Assisted by Mary Rogers and other volunteer laywomen, he also edited *The Field Afar*, which then became the publication of The Catholic Foreign Mission Society of America. In 1912 Walsh selected the hilltop site near Ossining, N.Y, henceforth named "Maryknoll," as the permanent home of the society.

In 1917 Walsh journeyed to East Asia to secure mission territory for the young society. Throughout the next 25 years of his life he annually commissioned new missionaries to the society's missions in China, Korea, Japan, the Philippines, and Hawaii. He likewise encouraged the founding and development of the Maryknoll Sisters under the leadership of Mother Mary Joseph Rogers. As early as 1922 he urged the incorporation of lay missionaries into overseas mission work. He was a strong supporter of The Catholic University and gave encouragement to Michael Williams, founder of the *Commonweal* and to Maurice Lavanoux, founder of the Liturgical Arts Society. He felt that it was important for missionaries not to be narrow in their attitudes. "Be big," he insisted to Maryknollers, "bigger than your own Society, as big as the Church." (Discourses, p. 361)

In 1933, Pope Pius XI, in recognition of Walsh's achievement in promoting mission interest in the United States, named him titular bishop of Siene. He was ordained in Rome by Cardinal Fumasoni Biondi, prefect of the Congregation for the Propagation of the Faith. He chose as his episcopal motto words that he had made the motto of the society, "Seek first the kingdom of God." A prolific writer, his major works include *Thoughts from Modern Martyrs* (Boston, Catholic Foreign Mission Bureau, 1906); *A Modern Martyr: Blessed Theophane Venard* (Maryknoll, N.Y./Ossining, Catholic Foreign Mission Society, 1913); *Observations in the Orient* (Ossining, N.Y., Catholic Foreign Mission Society of America, 1919); and *In the Homes of the Martyrs* (Maryknoll, N.Y.: Catholic Foreign Mission Society, 1922).

Bibliography: *Discourses of James Anthony Walsh, M.M. (1890–1936)*, comp. R. E. SHERIDAN (Maryknoll, N.Y. 1981). A. DRIES, "The Foreign Mission Impulse of the American Catholic Church, 1893–1925," *International Bulletin of Missionary Research* 15:2 (April 1991): 61–66. R. A. LANE, *The Early Days of Maryknoll* (New York 1951). G. C. POWERS, *The Maryknoll Movement* (Maryknoll, N.Y. 1926). D. SARGENT, *All the Day Long: James Anthony Walsh, Cofounder of Maryknoll* (New York 1941). R.E. SHERIDAN, *The Founders of Maryknoll: Historical Reflections*, rev. ed. (Maryknoll, N.Y. 1981).

[W. D. MCCARTHY]

WALSH, JAMES EDWARD

Maryknoll Missioner and bishop; b. Cumberland, Md., Apr. 30, 1891; d. Maryknoll, N.Y., July 29, 1981. His parents were William Walsh, an Irish immigrant and lawyer, and Mary Concannon. After studies at Mount St. Mary's College, Emmitsburg, Md., and employment at the U.S. Rail steel mill in Cumberland, he entered the Maryknoll Seminary near Ossining, N.Y. in 1912; he was ordained there on Dec. 7, 1915. In 1917 he was assigned

with three other Maryknoll priests to open Maryknoll's first mission, in Jiangmen (Kongmoon) in southern China. In 1919, upon the death of Fr. Thomas F. PRICE, a Maryknoll cofounder, Walsh became the superior of the Jiangmen mission. In 1927 he was named vicar apostolic of Jiangmen, and he was ordained bishop at the shrine of St. Francis Xavier on Shangchuan (Sancian) Island on May 22, 1927. Committed to developing a self-sufficient Chinese church, Walsh founded Little Flower minor seminary in 1926 and a Congregation of Sisters of the Immaculate Heart of Mary in 1927. It was during these years that he began recording his personal reflections on missionary spirituality, which he later incorporated in *The Maryknoll Spiritual Directory*. His prayerful commitment to the poor, "Shine on Farmer Boy," became a classic of inspiration among Maryknollers.

Superior General. Following the death in 1936 of Maryknoll cofounder, Bishop James A. WALSH, Bishop James E. Walsh was elected to succeed him as the society's second superior general. His ten-year term (1936–1946) spanned the difficult years of World War II. During 1940–1941, at the request of Japanese authorities and the acceptance of the U.S. State Department, Walsh and his vicar general, Fr. James Drought, gave their services as an unofficial channel for negotiations in the interests of avoiding war between the two powers. Though the effort failed, as did all other efforts, Walsh defended it as an expression of Christian responsibility in working for peace.

Under Walsh's direction, Maryknoll made the decision to work in Africa (1946), and it was he who visited Latin America (1942) to lay the groundwork for sending Maryknoll missionaries. Addressing those whom the society was sending to Latin America, he affirmed: "We are going to South America as missioners, but we are not going as exponents of any so-called North American civilization. We will endeavor to preach the Catholic faith in areas where priests are scarce and mission work is needed; but as regards the elements of true civilization, we expect to receive as much as we have to give."(*Maryknoll*, May 1942, p. 3)

Return to China; Imprisonment. In 1947 Walsh returned to China at the invitation of the Chinese bishops to serve as executive secretary of their newly organized Catholic Central Bureau in Shanghai. The project was short lived. In 1951 the communist government closed the bureau and placed Walsh and his associates under continual surveillance. Though prodded to leave China, he determined he should stay, expressing his view in the article "Why the Missionaries Remain," (Hong Kong 1951). In 1958 Walsh was arrested and charged with a currency violation and of being a spy for the United

States. For a year and a half he was subjected to daily interrogations and in 1960 was finally sentenced to 20 years imprisonment and interned in Ward Road Prison in Shanghai. The only visitor permitted him was that of his brother William in 1960. In July of 1970 he was abruptly released and deported to Hong Kong. Walsh spent his final 11 years at Maryknoll, N.Y. To his death, he remained strongly devoted to the Chinese people. "I have no bitterness," he said, "toward those who tried and condemned me. I could just never feel angry with any Chinese. I felt that way almost from the day I set foot in China in 1918 and it has grown stronger with the years, even during my imprisonment. I love the Chinese people."

A prolific writer, Walsh's major works include *Mission Manual of the Vicariate of Kongmoon* [Jiangmen., southern China] (Hong Kong: Nazareth Press, 1937); his inspirational classic "Shine On Farmer Boy," *Maryknoll,* (July–August, 1942) 12; "Description of a Missioner by One," *Worldmission* 6 (Winter 1955): 402–416; *Blueprint of the Missionary Vocation.* (World Horizon Report no. 19) (Maryknoll, N.Y.: Maryknoll Publications, n.d. [about 1953]); *The Church's World Wide Mission* (New York: Benziger, 1948); *Zeal for Your House,* ed. R. E. Sheridan (Huntington, Ind.: Our Sunday Visitor Press, 1976), which includes his famous plea "Why the Missionaries Remain" (1951), and the text of press conference on his release following 12 years of imprisonment in China (1970). Walsh was also the compiler of *Maryknoll Spiritual Directory* (Maryknoll, N.Y.: Field Afar Press, 1947).

Bibliography: R. J. C. BUTOW, *The John Doe Associates: Backdoor Diplomacy for Peace, 1941* (Stanford, Calif. 1974). R. KERRISON, *Bishop Walsh of Maryknoll: A Biography* (New York 1962). R. E. SHERIDAN, *Bishop James E. Walsh As I Knew Him* (Maryknoll, N.Y. 1981). J. P. WIEST, *Maryknoll in China: A History 1918–1955* (2d ed. Maryknoll, N.Y. 1997); "The Spiritual Legacy of Bishop James E. Walsh of Maryknoll" *Tripod* 3 (1989): 56–69.

[W. D. MCCARTHY]

WALSH, JOHN

Archbishop; b. Mooncoin, Kilkenny, Ireland, May 23, 1830; d. Toronto, Ontario, Canada, July 31, 1898. He was the son of James and Ellen (MacDonald) Walsh, and he studied for the priesthood at St. John's College, Waterford, Ireland. In 1852 he immigrated to Canada to study for the Diocese of Toronto at the Grand Seminary of Montreal. He was ordained Nov. 1, 1854, at Toronto, where he worked for many years as a missionary and parish priest. He was appointed vicar-general on Apr. 20, 1862. In May of the following year he attended the Third

Provincial Council of Quebec as personal theologian to the bishop of Toronto. He was consecrated bishop of Sandwich, Ontario, Nov. 10, 1867, and in January of 1868 he removed the episcopal residence to London. He did not attend Vatican Council I (1869–70) because of ill health; nevertheless, he wrote several pastorals on the subjects under discussion. In the fall of 1884 Walsh, by special invitation, assisted at the Third Plenary Council of Baltimore. In December 1889 he was installed as archbishop of Toronto and directed the expansion of the Church there. He was noted as a writer and preacher and encouraged the organization of the Irish Race Convention (1896).

Bibliography: *Jubilee Volume: The Archdiocese of Toronto* (Toronto 1892).

[J. T. FLYNN]

WALSH, MARY ROSALIA

Religious educator, author, and lecturer; b. April 26, 1896; d. Jan. 21, 1982. Baptized Josephine Mary, but better known by her religious name, Sister Rosalia (sister of Bishop James WALSH of Maryknoll), she entered the Mission Helpers of the Sacred Heart (MHSH) in 1916. Sister Rosalia was the chief author and promoter of the Adaptive Way Method of teaching religion, a program which greatly influenced elementary religion curriculum development in the United States. She received an M.A. from Fordham University in 1963 at the age of 67.

Her first work, *Child Psychology and Religion* (New York), a collection of talks on method, was published anonymously in 1937. She wrote an elementary religion course in 1939, entitled *The Adaptive Way Course of Religious Instruction for Catholic Children Attending Public Schools*, and in 1944 a methods text, *Teaching Confraternity Classes, The Adaptive Way* (Chicago). The method stressed adapting all religion teaching to the student's particular needs and to the circumstances under which students were taught. It was a concentric approach which divided lessons into units and encouraged graded classes. Walsh wrote over 30 articles on the subject between the years 1939 and 1959.

In 1947 the National Center for the CONFRATERNITY OF CHRISTIAN DOCTRINE asked Walsh to head a committee to revise their *School Year Religious Instruction Manual,* making her the first Sister to chair a committee of the National Center. The result was *The Confraternity School Year Religion Course, The Adaptive Way (SYCR)* (Wash., D.C.), published between 1949 and 1953. Walsh spoke at Catechetical Congresses sponsored by the National Center, and taught CCD methods courses around the country, including at The Catholic University of America in the Catholic Action Institute from 1947 to 1957.

An early and chief supporter of the CCD in the United States, Sister Rosalia has had a lasting influence on Catholic religious education through the Adaptive Way.

[M. E. SPELLACY]

WALSH, PETER

Franciscan priest and theologian of church-state relations in Ireland; b. Moortown, County Kildare, *c.* 1615; d. London, March 15, 1688. He studied as a Franciscan cleric in St. Anthony's College, Louvain. On returning to Ireland (1639), he was appointed to teach philosophy and later (1647) theology in Kilkenny, the seat of the Catholic Confederation. In 1647 he was suspended from preaching and disciplined for supporting Nuncio Giovanni Battista RINUCCINI's opponents. In 1648, after the Inchiquin Truce, he sided openly with those bishops and priests who resisted Rinuccini's censure. When the schism resulting from Redmond CARON's visitation of the Irish Franciscans ended in 1650 with the submission of Caron and his supporters (Walsh's followers), Walsh himself did not submit. Having lived in hiding in England during the Puritan rule, in January 1661 he was named London procurator of the Irish clergy. He was sent the Remonstrance formulated in Dublin in December 1661 by a group of mostly lay Anglo-Irish Catholics to present to Charles II and James Butler, 12th Earl and 1st Duke of Ormond. This Remonstrance contained a formal statement of grievances, a protestation of allegiance (the part generally known as the Remonstrance), and a petition for protection from persecution. The protestation of allegiance was objectionable because it was disrespectful to the pope and Holy See, and it repudiated the indirect power of the pope in the temporal realm. At Ormond's insistence, Walsh spent the next five years in an intensive but unsuccessful campaign, involving a national synod (1666), to persuade the Irish clergy to sign the Remonstrance. He was excommunicated in 1670 when, despite frequent warnings, he went too far. The remainder of his life was spent in England, devoting much time to writing books and pamphlets in defense of the Remonstrance. He did not embrace Protestantism. On March 13, 1688, shortly before his death, he signed a recantation and submission to the Holy See. He was a well-educated man of keen intellect, and a fluent speaker given to loquacity—he was born for political intrigue. He was not ambitious or immoral in the accepted sense. His writings are egotistical, and his pride and stubbornness explain his insubordination. His most valuable publication is *The History and Vindication of the Loyal Formulary or Irish Remonstrance.*

Bibliography: R. BAGWELL, *The Dictionary of National Biography from the Earliest Times to 1900,* 63 v. (London 1885–1900; repr. with corrections, 21 v., 1908–09, 1921–22, 1938; suppl. 1901–) 20:675–681. B. MILLETT, *The Irish Franciscans, 1651–1665* (Rome 1964), 418–463, 502–503. *Father Luke Wadding: Commemorative Volume* (Dublin 1957) 190–191, 200, 201–223. J. WARE, *The History and Antiquities of Ireland . . . with the History of the Writers of Ireland,* ed. W. HARRIS, 2 v. in 1 (Dublin 1764) 195–198. D. G. WING, *Short-title Catalogue of Books Printed in England . . . 1641–1700* 3 v. (New York 1945–51) 3:447–448. M. J. HYNES, *The Mission of Rinuccini* (Dublin 1932). *Collectanea Hibernica* 1 (1958) 117, 119, 124:3 (1960) *passim;* 6 (1963) *passim;* 7 (1964) *passim. Archivium Hibernicum* 24 (1961) 173–183, 194; 25 (1962) *passim;* 26 (1963) 36. J. BRENNAN, "A Gallican Interlude in Ireland: The Irish Remonstrance of 1661" *The Irish Thrological Quarterly* 24 (1957) 219–237, 283–309.

[B. MILLETT]

WALSH, WILLIAM

Chaplain to Cardinal Pole, bishop of Meath; b. Dunboyne, County Meath, Ireland, 1512; d. Alcalà de Henares, Spain, Jan. 4, 1577. Walsh joined the CISTERCIANS at Bective in Meath. After receiving a doctorate in divinity at Oxford, Walsh was forced to flee abroad because of Thomas Cromwell's suppression of Bective in 1537. He was appointed chaplain to Cardinal Reginald POLE in Rome, and obtained a papal dispensation allowing him to transfer to the AUGUSTINIANS. Pole as papal legate appointed Walsh bishop of Meath (1554) when Catholicism was restored under MARY I. The bishop served on several ecclesiastical commissions during Mary's reign. At ELIZABETH I's accession (1558) Walsh refused the oath of supremacy and opposed the introduction of the Elizabethan liturgy and the BOOK OF COMMON PRAYER. He was placed in custody, and he and his episcopal status were challenged; the case was brought to Rome where Pole's earlier use of legatine power to appoint bishops was declared void. After being reappointed by PIUS IV in 1564, Walsh was imprisoned in Dublin Castle (1565–72) by royal commission. He managed to escape to France and then to Spain, where he served as suffragan to the archbishop of Toledo.

See Also: IRISH CONFESSORS AND MARTYRS.

Bibliography: A. COGAN, *The Diocese of Meath . . . ,* 3 v. (Dublin 1862–70). W. M. BRADY, *The Episcopal Succession in England, Scotland, and Ireland, A.D. 1400–1875,* 3 v. (Rome 1876–77).

[M. B. MACCURTAIN]

WALSH, WILLIAM JOSEPH

Archbishop of Dublin, theologian, and Irish patriot; b. Dublin, Jan. 30, 1841; d. Dublin, April 9, 1921. William, son of Ralph and Mary Walsh, shared his father's enthusiasm for Irish national and political independence. He attended the Catholic University of Dublin during NEWMAN's rectorship, and entered St. Patrick's College, MAYNOOTH (1858). After ordination (1867) he continued at Maynooth as professor of theology, becoming vice president (1878) and president (1880). Walsh was drawn into the agitation for land tenure reform. His testimony before the Bessborough commission of 1880, which had been appointed by Gladstone to inquire into the Irish land system, was decisive in exposing the most flagrant abuses of the landlords, and influenced the drafting of the Land Act of 1881. Despite the British government's strong objection, Walsh was archbishop of Dublin (1885). Quickly he became the most influential Irish bishop and usually served as spokesman for the hierarchy. His nationalism was more temperate than that of Thomas CROKE, Archbishop of Armagh. He never attempted to defy governmental authority but firmly supported the Home Rule movement. During the Parnell scandal (1890) he preserved silence publicly until his private urging that Parnell retire as leader of the Irish parliamentary party was ignored. Then he publicly warned that the Irish bishops could no longer support such discredited leadership. Many blamed Walsh for the ensuing party split.

Walsh's most lasting achievement was in national education. As a member of the Catholic Headmasters' Committee he promoted reform of secondary education. As archbishop he served as a commissioner of primary (1895–1901) and intermediate (1892–1909) education. As early as 1883 his book *The Queen's Colleges and the Royal University of Ireland* challenged the Irish system of higher education. In his later works, *Statement of the Chief Grievances of Irish Catholics in the Matter of Education* (1890) and *The Irish University Question* (1897), he demanded that Catholic training colleges be supported by public funds and that a Catholic college on an equal footing with the Protestant Trinity College be substituted for the Queen's Colleges. But Walsh welcomed the establishment of the National University of Ireland and was elected its first chancellor (1908).

Walsh was temperamentally aloof, but deeply sympathetic toward the Irish peasants. He was thoroughly democratic and believed firmly in representative government. He was never close to the lord lieutenant of Ireland or to Castle society. He advocated bimetallism, trade unions, woman suffrage, and the admission of women to the university and to the professions. As a scholar Walsh was primarily a theologian, but he exerted his greatest influence in interpreting to Roman officials complicated economic questions, such as land tenure in Ireland or Henry George's single-tax. In his declining years he withdrew from public questions until the rise of the Sinn Fein. He objected to the Irish Government Bill of 1912

Priory garden with archway, Little Walsingham Priory, Norfolk, England. (©Robert Estall/CORBIS)

and opposed the leadership of John Redmond and John Dillon of the Irish parliamentary party. He publically denounced the partition of Ireland, and during the 1919 elections, supported the Sinn Fein. Although he supported the establishment of the illegal Irish Parliament, he participated in efforts to bring the Sinn Fein and Lloyd George's government together for negotiations. He vigorously condemned violence.

Bibliography: P. J. WALSH, *Life of William J. Walsh: Archbishop of Dublin* (Dublin 1928). M. CURRAN. ''The Late Archbishop of Dublin, 1841–1921,'' *Dublin Review* 169 (1921) 93–107.

[T. JOYCE]

WALSINGHAM, MONASTERY OF

Little Walsingham, a small town in northern Norfolk, became famous as the center of the major shrine of Our Lady in medieval England. The origin of the cult there is not quite clear, but certainly belongs to the days after the Norman Conquest. About 1120 Richelde de Fervaques, widow of a local magnate, built at Walsingham a copy of the Holy House at Nazareth. In 1153 her son Geoffrey established at the same site a small priory of CANONS REGULAR OF ST. AUGUSTINE, to whose care the house was committed. But the establishment had little more than local importance until the time of King Henry III (1216–72) and his son Edward I (1272–1307), both of whom visited the place frequently. The latter had a great veneration for a statue of Our Lady there (probably of 12th century date), and this in the 14th and 15th centuries attracted considerable numbers of pilgrims from the British Isles (including a very high proportion of the contemporary kings and queens of England) and some from neighboring parts of the Continent. By the early 16th century, Walsingham's shrine seems to have been the most popular place of pilgrimage (*see* PILGRIMAGES, 3) in England, and had attracted considerable benefactions, though its attendant priory was never large. Among the last royal pilgrims were HENRY VIII and his wife Catherine of Aragon. In 1535 the monastery's annual net income was estimated at £652 4s. 11d. (about $32,600) of which £250 1s, (about $12,500) came from offerings at the shrine; it was by now the second richest monastery in Norfolk. Evidently in July 1538 the shrine was despoiled of its wealth, the statute of Our Lady being sent up to London where it was burnt. In August the priory, which had about 22 brethren, was dissolved after an uneventful history.

Of the medieval buildings the principal remains are the eastern gable and base of the west tower of the church, much of the refectory and also part of the prior's lodging, which is now incorporated in a later house. The site of the shrine, which adjoined the north side of the priory church, was excavated in 1855 and in 1955. In recent times pilgrimages to Walsingham have been revived.

Bibliography: J. L. WARNER, ''Walsingham Priory . . . ,'' *Archaeological Journal* 13 (1856) 115–133. J. C. DICKINSON, *Shrine of Our Lady of Walsingham* (New York 1956). H. A. BOND, ''Walsingham Topography,'' *Norfolk Archaeology* 31 (1955–57) 359–366.

[J. C. DICKINSON]

WALSINGHAM, THOMAS

Monk and historian of SAINT ALBANS Abbey, England; d. *c.* 1422. Walsingham first came to notice in 1380 when he compiled the Book of Benefactors of his house (London, Brit. Mus., Cotton, Nero D.VIII). In that year he described himself as *precentor et scriptorarius* of St. Albans. During the next 14 years he continued MATTHEW PARIS's Great Chronicle with his own *Chronica maiora;* wrote the *Gesta abbatum;* and, according to V. H. Galbraith, compiled a second Book of Benefactors and a St. Albans Chartulary, now at Chatsworth.

In 1394 Walsingham was made prior of the cell of Wymondham, where he wrote a short history, actually ''a

condensation of the *Chronica maiora*'' (Galbraith). Six years later he returned to St. Albans. It has been suggested (Galbraith) that during his years away he had become a finished Latin scholar, improving upon the mythological chronicle known as the *Dictys Cretensis* in an elaborate later medieval diction that can be recognized in the flowery style of younger disciples in the SCRIPTORIUM, one of the most important being the future abbot John Whethamstede.

Upon his return to St. Albans he undertook his biggest work, the *St. Albans Chronicle,* in which his section from Matthew Paris (1259) to the Good Parliament (1376) is a pure compilation from various sources. The narrative after 1376 is Walsingham's own work, but it is the section from 1392 to 1422 that is the original chronicle of events that Walsingham noted as a contemporary. The part from 1406 to 1420 (Oxford, Bodl. 462) has now been edited by Galbraith. This section of the Chronicle is notable for the information it gives on the reign of King Henry IV (particularly on the relation of Prince Henry to his father), on the LOLLARDS, and on the WESTERN SCHISM.

Bibliography: T. WALSINGHAM, *Historia Anglicana*, ed. H. T. RILEY, 2 v. (*Rerum Britannicarum medii aevi scriptores* 28.1; London 1863–64); *Ypodigma Neustriae*, ed. H. T. RILEY (*Rerum Britannicarum medii aevi scriptores* 28.7; 1876); *St. Alban's Chronicle, 1406–1420*, ed. V. H. GALBRAITH (Oxford 1937); *comp., Gesta abbatum monasterii Sancti Albani*, ed. H. T. RILEY, 3 v. (*Rerum Britannicarum medii aevi scriptores* 28.4; 1867–69). C. JENKINS, *The Monastic Chronicler and the Early School of St. Albans* (Society for Promoting Christian Knowledge 1922), for Matthew Paris.

[E. F. JACOB]

WALTER BURLEY

English secular scholastic, called *Doctor planus* and *Doctor perspicuus;* b. Yorkshire, 1275; d. after 1344. He was master of arts of Oxford by 1301 and fellow of Merton College from 1301 to 1305. Ordained in June 1309, he studied theology in Paris under Thomas of Wilton by 1310, becoming a master in theology around 1322. While traveling on the king's business, he held a disputation *de quolibet* at Toulouse in 1327 and another at Bologna in 1341. From 1309 until his death he held, with dispensation, a plurality of benefices, including a canonry at York and another at Salisbury. Associated with the highest ranks of English society, he was sent in 1327 as envoy of King Edward III to the Papal Curia for the canonization of Thomas, Earl of Lancaster (d. 1322); according to Holinshed's *Chronicles,* he was almoner to Philippa of Hainault at her marriage to Edward III in 1328 and tutor to the Black Prince (1330–76). Around 1333 he was one of the clerks in the household of RICHARD OF BURY, Bishop of Durham, and in 1336 he was a clerk in the King's household. When "certain of his rivals" had him imprisoned for having two oak trees cut in Sherwood Forest, Richard of Bury secured his pardon, and he was again abroad on king's business in 1338. In November 1343 he was at Avignon where he presented a copy of his *Expositio librorum politicorum* to CLEMENT VI.

From at least 1301 until 1337 he wrote commentaries on Aristotle's logic, making successive revisions of his works; *notabilia;* treatises on the *Parva logicalia;* and original works, notably *De puritate artis logicae* (two versions) and *De suppositionibus.* The closing part of his *Tractatus de universalibus realibus* contains probably the earliest indication of his antagonism to the nominalism of WILLIAM OF OCKHAM, whom he strongly refuted in later works. He wrote also commentaries on Aristotle's *Ethics* and the *Libri naturales* in the form of both questions and exposition. Many of his original works deal with problems of natural philosophy: *De intensione et remissione formarum, De potentiis animac, De substantia orbis,* and *De materia et forma.* His most popular work was *De vitis et moribus philosophorum,* the first treatise of its kind in the Middle Ages, dealing with the lives and anecdotes of philosophers.

Perhaps the first to make syllogistics a subdivision of consequences, Burley anticipated later developments in his treatment of negation and in his conception of the formal character of logic. In his treatment of UNIVERSALS, he was an Aristotelian realist.

Bibliography: A. B. EMDEN, *A Biographical Register of the University of Oxford to A. D. 1500,* 3 v. (Oxford 1957–59) 1:312–314. C. MARTIN, "Walter Burley," *Oxford Studies Presented to Daniel Callus* (Oxford 1964). P. M. M. DUHEM, *Le Système du monde: Histoire des doctrines cosmologiques de Platon à Copernic* (5 v. Paris 1913–17; repr. 10 v. 1954–59) 6:678–680; *Études sur Léonard de Vinci,* 3 v. (Paris 1906–13; repr. 1955). P. BÖHNER, *Medieval Logic* (Chicago 1952). A. N. PRIOR, "On Some Consequentiae in Walter Burleigh," *New Scholasticism* 27 (1953) 433–446. S. H. THOMPSON, "Walter Burley's Commentary on the *Politics* of Aristotle," *Mélanges Auguste Pelzer* (Louvain 1947) 557–578.

[E. A. SYNAN]

WALTER DE GRAY (GREY)

Chancellor of England and archbishop of YORK; b. probably Rotherfield in Oxfordshire, date unknown; d. Fulham, May 1, 1255. He was the son of John and Hawisia Gray and the nephew of Bp. JOHN DE GREY. He studied at Oxford and heard EDMUND OF ABINGDON lecture. He was chancellor from 1205 to 1213 and again in 1214. He was twice elected bishop of COVENTRY and Lichfield, but unconfirmed; in 1214 successfully elected bishop of Worcester; and in 1215 elected archbishop of York through the influence of King JOHN and INNOCENT III. He was translated to York in 1216. Much involved in royal business, he was present at the granting of MAGNA CARTA in 1215. After John's death he supported the legate against the French. In later life he acted once as royal regent and often presided at occasions of high ceremony. He was an active diocesan at York (where he was bored and longed for news of the court). He was a builder; he translated the relics of St. WILFRID OF YORK. He made Bishopthorpe an archiepiscopal manor, and he bought York Place in London. Fresh from King John's record-keeping government, he kept the rolls that are the first registers at York.

Bibliography: *The Register, or Rolls, of Walter Gray, Archbishop of York,* ed. J. RAINE (Durham 1872). W. H. DIXON, *Fasti eboracenses. Lives of the Archbishops of York,* ed. J. RAINE (London 1863). C. A. F. MEEKINGS, "Six Letters Concerning the Eyres of 1226–28," *English Historical Review* 65 (1950) 492–504. A. B. EMDEN, *A Biographical Register of the University of Oxford to A.D. 1500* 2: 807–808.

[R. BRENTANO]

WALTER DE STAPELDON

Bishop, lord treasurer; b. Annery, Devon, England, Feb. 1, *c.* 1261; d. London, Oct. 15, 1326. Stapeldon was a professor of Canon Law at Oxford and then papal chaplain. On Oct. 13, 1308, he was consecrated bishop of EXETER. As bishop he rebuilt a large part of the cathedral, including the choir screen, and founded Stapeldon Hall, later Exeter College, at Oxford and projected an episcopal grammar school in Exeter in connection with it. In 1316 he joined the Middle party and in 1320 became lord treasurer for Edward II. His administrative reforms in this office ensured the preservation of all exchequer records up to 1323. He arranged for a complete classification and catalogue of the archives of the exchequer and wardrobe. Stapeldon's calendar was printed by F. Palgrave, *Ancient Kalendars and Inventories*; the contemporary Gascon calendar of 1322 by Henry of Canterbury has been edited by G. P. Cuttino. The mob supporting the Queen beheaded Stapeldon as one of the instruments of Edward II's misgovernment, while he was trying to reach sanctuary in St. Paul's.

Bibliography: *The Register of Walter de Stapeldon, Bishop of Exeter, A.D. 1307–1326,* ed. F. C. HINGESTON-RANDOLPH. F. C. HINGESTON-RANDOLPH, *The Dictionary of National Biography from the Earliest Times to 1900* 18:979980. T. F. TOUT, *The Place of the Reign of Edward II in English History,* ed. H. JOHNSTONE (2d ed. Manchester 1936). M. MCKISACK, *The Fourteenth Century* (Oxford 1959). F. L. CROSS, *The Oxford Dictionary of the Christian Church* 1286. A. B. EMDEN, *A Biographical Register of the University of Oxford to A.D. 1500* 3:176465.

[N. DENHOLM-YOUNG]

WALTER GIFFARD

Bishop of BATH AND WELLS and later archbishop of York; place and date of birth unknown; d. York, England, April 24 or 25, 1279. He was the son of Hugh and Sybil Giffard of Boyton in Wiltshire and the brother of GODFREY GIFFARD, bishop of Worcester. He was educated at Oxford and like his brother represents an interesting combination of aristocrat, scholar, and serious bishop. He was elected bishop of Bath and Wells on May 22, 1264, and provided to the archbishopric of York in November 1266. In 1265 he became chancellor of England; his brother succeeded him in that office in March 1267. Giffard revived the long-standing dispute between YORK and CANTERBURY.

Bibliography: *The Register of Walter Giffard, Lord Archbishop of York, 1266–1279,* ed. W. BROWN (Durham 1904); *The Registers of Walter Giffard . . . and of Henry Bowett . . . ,* ed. T. S. HOLMES (London 1899). W. H. DIXON, *Fast eboracenses. Lives of the Archbishops of York,* ed. J. RAINE (London 1863). A. B. EMDEN, *A Biographical Register of the University of Oxford to A.D. 1500* 2:762–763.

[R. BRENTANO]

WALTER JORZ

Also Jorse, Jorsz, Joyce, English DOMINICAN, archbishop of Armagh; b. Nottinghamshire, England; d. Lincoln, February 1321. The brother of Cardinal THOMAS JORZ, he received faculties in 1300 for the Diocese of Lincoln. He subsequently won renown at Oxford by his teaching and writing. On Aug. 6, 1307, Walter Jorz was appointed to the Irish primatial See of ARMAGH by Pope Clement V. After Jorz's consecration, King Edward II forced him to renounce certain clauses in the papal brief of appointment deemed prejudicial to the royal rights. Jorz's brief tenure at Armagh was marked by frequent difficulties with secular officials. In 1310 he successfully fought a law excluding native Irishmen from religious orders, but in 1311 he resigned from his archdiocese. His brother Roland, also a Dominican, succeeded him. From September 1319, Jorz was auxiliary bishop of Lincoln. Among the works attributed to him, none of which seem to have survived, are *Promptuarium theologiae, de peccatis in genere,* and *Quaestiones variae.*

Bibliography: J. QUÉTIF and J. ÉCHARD, *Scriptores Ordinis Praedicatorum* (New York 1959) 1.2:513–514. M. H. MACINERNY, *A History of the Irish Dominicans* (Dublin 1916). A. B. EMDEN, *A Biographical Register of the University of Oxford to A.D. 1500* (Oxford 1957–59) 2:1023–24.

[A. B. WILLIAMS]

WALTER MAP

Satirical writer; b. *c.* 1140; d. April 1, 1209 or 1210. Although a resident of Herefordshire, England, Map spoke of the Welsh as his fellow countrymen. He studied at Paris, where Girard la Pucelle was one of his teachers. Map's parents had been of service to HENRY II of England, and he himself frequented the King's court until Henry's death, being familiar also with Henry the Young King, Louis VII of France, and Henry of Champagne. Henry II often employed him as justice in eyre and sent him as envoy to Pope Alexander III, who assigned him to argue against the representatives of the WALDENSES at the Third LATERAN COUNCIL (1179). Map was chancellor of Lincoln by 1186; canon of Saint Paul's Cathedral, London, 1192; archdeacon of Oxford from 1197; and canon of Hereford and unsuccessful candidate for bishop of Hereford, 1199.

His only surviving work, *De nugis curialium* (ed. T. Wright, Camden Society, 1850; Eng. tr. M. R. James with historical notes by J. E. Lloyd, ed. E. S. Hartland, Cymmrodorion Record Series, 1923), is a miscellaneous collection of legends, gossip, anecdotes, reminiscences, and historical information. Directing sharp satire at King and court, at secular and regular clergy, and at the Welsh people, it exhibits Map's ability as a storyteller and his learning in theology and literature. It is an important source for the early history of the CISTERCIANS, the CARTHUSIANS, the Order of GRANDMONT, the GILBERTINES, the TEMPLARS, the HOSPITALLERS, the Waldenses, and the English court both before and during Map's lifetime. His supposed authorship of Arthurian legend and Goliardic verse has not been substantiated. Most information about Walter Map comes from himself, but some can be found in Gitaldus Cambrensis, *Opera,* v.1 3–5 (*Rerum Britannicarum medii aevi scriptores;* London 1861–91).

Bibliography: C. L. KINGSFORD, *The Dictionary of National Biography from the Earliest Times to 1900* (London 1885–1900) 12:994–997. R. E. BENNETT, "Walter Map's *Sadius and Galo,*" *Speculum* 16 (1941) 34–56. F. SEIBT, "Über den Plan der Schrift *De nugis curalium* des Magisters Walter Map," *Archiv für Kulturgeschichte* 37 (1955) 183–203. A. B. EMDEN, *A Biographical Register of the University of Oxford to A. D. 1500* (Oxford 1957–59) 2:1219.

[R. W. HAYS]

WALTER OF BIRBECK, BL.

Cistercian monk; b. Birbeck (Birbach), in the Brabant, between 1154 and 1160; d. Himmerod Abbey, *c.* 1206. A relative of Duke Henry the Lion, he entered the Abbey of HIMMEROD *c.* 1182. He was noted for his devotion to Mary. His personality gave rise to numerous legends, and in the Middle Ages he was publicly venerated at Himmerod.

Feast: Jan. 22.

Bibliography: *Acta Sanctorum* Jan. 2:60–63. CAESARIUS OF HEISTERBACH, *The Dialogue on Miracles* 7.38, tr. H. VON E. SCOTT and C. C. S. BLAND, 2 v. (London 1929). M. GLONING, *Cistercienser-Chronik* 9 (1897) 170–174. A. M. ZIMMERMANN, *Kalendarium Benedictinum: Die Heiligen und Seligen des Benediktinerorderns und seiner Zweige,* 4 v. (Metten 1933–38) 1:115–117. E. MÜLLER, in *Unsere Liebe Frau von Himmerod* 31 (1961) 51–55, 85–89.

[A. SCHNEIDER]

WALTER OF BRUGES

Franciscan philosopher and theologian; b. Zande, near Dixmuide, *c.* 1225; d. Poitiers, Jan. 21, 1307. Walter entered the order *c.* 1240 at Bruges and was sent to Paris for his theological studies, which he completed under BONAVENTURE. He became regent at Paris *c.* 1267 to 1269. Elected minister provincial of the French Province, he served from 1269 to 1279. He was consecrated Bishop of Poitiers in 1279 and remained in the diocese until he retired because of ill health in 1306. The final year of his life was spent with the Franciscans at Poitiers. Among his writings are a commentary on the first, second, and fourth books of the *Sentences* composed between 1261 and 1265 and as yet unpublished; 36 disputed questions edited by E. Longpré under the title *Quaestiones disputatae du B. Gauthier de Bruges* (Louvain 1928); a *Tabula originalium;* and some sermons.

Walter held to the main theses of the Bonaventurian school. He taught the hylomorphic composition of spiritual substances (souls and angels), in which he distinguished form and spiritual or intelligible matter. The faculties of the soul, for him, are not accidents but in-here in the soul substantially or essentially. In his doctrine on the will, which he elaborated at great length, he stressed its radical independence and upheld its primacy over the intellect. He held that the proposition "God exists" is *per se nota;* he admitted the use of a posteriori proofs for God's existence, but sought their foundation in the habitual, innate knowledge of God possessed by the soul. Other doctrines held by Walter include the divine illumination theory, the subservience of philosophy to theology, and the intellectual knowledge of the singular.

Bibliography: É. H. GILSON, *History of Christian Philosophy in the Middle Ages* (New York 1955). P. GLORIEUX, *Répertoire des maîtres en théologie de Paris au XIIIe siècle* (Paris 1933–34) 2:84–86. G. BONAFEDE, *Enciclopedia filosofica* (Venice-Rome 1957) 2:922–923.

[M. J. GRAJEWSKI]

WALTER OF CANTELUPE

Bishop, ecclesiastical administrator, political reformer; d. Blockley, Worcester, England, Feb. 4, 1266. Walter was second son of William, first Baron Cantelupe and steward of the royal household; he probably studied at Oxford. He was elected bishop of WORCESTER in 1236 and consecrated in 1237. Living during the reign of King HENRY III, Cantelupe was a member of the committee appointed to draw up proposals for constitutional reform in 1244, and was a consistent supporter of SIMON DE MONT-FORT's baronial plan of reform between 1258 and 1265. During this period he was the leading spokesman of the bishops favoring reform. Although he had spoken in favor of pluralism in 1237, Cantelupe was a notable ecclesiastical reformer, as is evidenced by his diocesan statutes of 1240. These statutes were wide in their scope and detailed, including sections on the administration of the Sacraments, on the life and conduct of the clergy (arranged ingeniously under the titles of the seven deadly sins), and on archdeacons' visitations. They provided much material for the diocesan statutes of the next generation.

In 1245 he attended the Council of LYONS, where he supported Bp. ROBERT GROSSETESTE on taxation of clergy. Cantelupe had a local reputation for sanctity, and after his death miracles were said to have been worked at his tomb. Proposals for his canonization may have been made.

Bibliography: H. R. LUARD, *The Dictionary of National Biography from the Earliest Times to 1900* (London 1885–1900) 3:904–906. C. R. CHENEY, *English Synodalia of the 13th Century* (Oxford 1941). F. M. POWICKE, *King Henry III and the Lord Edward,* 2 v. (New York 1947). A. B. EMDEN, *A Biographical Register of the Scholars of the University of Oxford to A.D. 1500* 1:349–350. M. GIBBS and J. LANG, *Bishops and Reform, 1215–1272* (London 1934; repr. 1962).

[H. MAYR-HARTING]

WALTER OF CHÂTILLON

Humanist poet of the 12th century; b. Ronchin, near Lille, France, *c.* 1135; d. Amiens. Because Walter was born at Lille, JOHN OF SALISBURY called him *ab Insula* or *de Insulis.* He studied at Paris and at Reims. He taught at Laon and later at Châtillon-sur-Marne (hence the surname *de Castellione*); he was a canon at Reims (hence the name *Remensis*). His career included service for King HENRY II of England and a mission to England but he seems to have resigned from Henry's chancellery over the BECKET affair. His travels encompassed study at Bologna and a visit to Rome. He was later in the service of Abp. William (Guillelmus) of Reims (1176–1201), whom he served as *notarius* and *orator.*

Perhaps his greatest claim to fame is his epic poem, the *Alexandreis* (*Patrologia Latina* 209:463–572), with its 5,464 hexameter verses. After some five years of work (*c.* 1178 to 1182) it was published in 1184. The epic comprised 10 books just as the Latin name of his good friend, Abp. William, had 10 letters; the plan called for each of the books to begin with a successive letter of that name. The work owes much to Quintus Curtius's history of Alexander the Great, with borrowings from other sources such as Justinus and Josephus, and Isidore's *Etymologies*. Both its prosody and its rhyme have been admired. Walter's moral and satirical works, which form the bulk of his lyrical verse, and which are noted for their attacks on the upper clergy of his day, had considerable influence on contemporary Latin writers.

He wrote also a *Tractatus contra Judaeos* consisting of a prologue and three books presented as a dialogue between Walter himself and Canon Baldwin of Valenciennes. A work under the Vergilian title of *Georgica* has in the past been attributed to Walter but this attribution is now seriously doubted. Walter's familiarity with the poets of antiquity is well established; his place among the more distinguished of medieval versifiers is securely fixed.

Bibliography: WALTER OF CHÂTILLON, *Die Lieder W. von C. in der Handschrift 351 von St. Omer*, ed. K. STRECKER (Berlin 1925); *Moralisch-satirische Gedichte W. von C.*, ed. K. STRECKER (Heidelberg 1929). M. MANITIUS, *Geschichte der lateinischen Literatur des Mittelalters*, 3 v. (Munich 1911–31) 3:920–936. A. WILMART, "Poèmes de Gauthier de Châtillon . . .," *Revue Bénédictine* 49 (1937) 322–365. J. DE GHELLINCK, *L'Essor de la littérature latine au XIIe siècle*, 2 v. (Brussels-Paris 1946) *passim.* F. CHÂTILLON, "Flagello . . . Contribution à l'étude des mauvais traitements infligés à Gauthier . . .," *Revue du moyen-âge latin* 7 (1951) 151–174. R. A. GAUTHIER, "Pour l'attribution à Gauthier . . . du *Moralium* . . .," *ibid.* 19–64; "Les Deux recensions du *Moralium* . . .," *ibid.* 9 (1953) 171–260. P. DELHAYE, *Gauthier de Châtillon est–il l'auteur du "Moralium dogma"?* (Namur 1952). F. J. E. RABY, *A History of Secular Latin Poetry in the Middle Ages*, 2 v. 2d ed. (Oxford 1957) 2:72–80, 190–214.

[W. C. KORFMACHER]

WALTER OF CHATTON

English Franciscan scholastic variously designated as of Catton, Caton, Cepton, Schaton, etc. b. Chatton, Northumbria, *c.* 1285; d. Avignon, 1343. Entering the order as a young boy [*Archivum Franciscanum historicum* 19 (1926) 866], he was ordained a subdeacon in 1307 by John of Halton, bishop of Carlisle. He commented on the *Sentences* (1322 to 1323) at Oxford, and possibly a second time, likely in England. He was in Oxford again in 1330, as 53rd regent, then in Assisi in the summer of 1332, apparently in the company of Gerard

Odonis (Guiral Ot), Minister General [*Archivum Franciscanum historicum* 48 (1955) 292]. Next found at the papal court of Avignon in 1333, he was an active opponent of the English Dominican THOMAS WALEYS, on trial there for doctrinal errors. So notable was his role that the Dominican considered him a leader among his adversaries [T. Käpelli, *Le Procès contre Thomas Waleys OP* (Rome 1936), 60–63, 118, 241–246]. In September Walter was named one of the examiners of the works of DURANDUS OF SAINT-POURÇAIN as well as of the writings of Waleys [*Chartularium universitatis Parisiensis,* ed. H. Denifle and E. Chatelain, 4 v. (Paris 1889–97), 2:418–423, n.975]. Chatton was one of the 16 theologians summoned by BENEDICT XII in 1335 to examine the pontiff's tract "On the State of Souls Before the General Judgment" and to discuss the theological problems involved (*ibid.* 2:453, n.995). The following year his name is mentioned among those who had helped the pope frame new constitutions for the Friars Minor [*Archivum Franciscanum historicum* 30 (1937) 309–390, esp. 334]. In 1341 he was made a papal penitentiary for English-speaking visitors at Avignon; two years later he is mentioned as having given counsel in a dispute between Benedictines and Franciscans. In the same year CLEMENT VI conferred on him the Welsh See of St. Asaph, under the impression that the incumbent, David of Blethyn, had died. Walter never took possession of the see, since he died at Avignon before David, in late 1343 or early 1344 [C. Eubel et al., *Hierarchia Catholica medii (et recentioris) aevi* 1:112].

Of Walter's scholastic writings, his *Sentences* have come down in two *reportationes*. The texts are so different as to imply that he lectured twice, at least on the prologue and part of the first book. Both the first version of 1322 to 1323 (Paris BN lat. 15887; Florence Bibl. Naz. Cod. Conv. Sopp. C.5.357) and the second (Paris BN lat. 15886) reveal that Walter was one of the first to oppose the doctrines of WILLIAM OF OCKHAM. Although his master was DUNS SCOTUS, there are few Ockhamist theses that he does not consider in detail. In addition, Chatton cites PETER AUREOLI, RICHARD OF CAMPSALL, HENRY OF HARCLAY, and others. His own position is that of a conservative Scotist. He merited the attention of Ockham in his *Quodlibeta* and a rebuttal by ADAM WODHAM of a lost work on indivisibles. Before he left England, Walter became interested in the controversy over poverty and wrote a *Tract on Evangelical Poverty* [*Archivum Franciscanum historicum* 24 (1931) 343–346; 25 (1932) 36–58; 210–240; cf. *ibid.* 11 (1918) 251–269]. Other works attributed to him have not been identified.

See Also: SCOTISM; POVERTY CONTROVERSY.

Bibliography: L. ELDREDGE, "Walter of Chatillon and the Drectum of Gratian: An Analysis of Propter Zion non Tacebo"

Studies in Medieval Culture 3 (Kalamazoo, Mich. 1970). G. ETZ-KORN, "Walter Chatton and the Controversy on the Absolute Necessity of Grace," *Franciscan Studies, Annual XV*, 32–65. N. FITZPATRICK, "Walter Chatton on the Univocity of Being: A Reaction to Peter Aureoli and William Ockham," *Franciscan Studies*, 31, 88–177. E. KARGER, "William of Ockham, Walter Chatton and Adam Wodeham on the Objects of Knowledge and Belief," *Vivarium* 33 (1995), 176–196. A. MCGRADE, "Enjoyment at Oxford after Ockham: Philosophy, Psychology, and the Love of God," *From Ockham to Wyclif* (Oxford 1987) 63–88.

[I. C. BRADY]

WALTER OF COINCY

Vernacular poet; b. Coincy, near Fère-en-Tardenois, Aisne, France, 1177 or 1178; d. Saint-Médard, Soissons, Sept. 25, 1236. Walter entered the Abbey of Saint-Médard in 1193, became prior of Vic-sur-Aisne in August 1214, and returned to Saint-Médard as grand prior on June 19, 1233. He wrote his main work, the two-volume *Miracles Nostre Dame* while at Vic-sur-Aisne, specifically between 1218 and 1227. It first appeared as a single volume, but after substantial revision by Walter it consisted of two volumes, each having a prologue; opening chansons; a number of *miracles,*—miraculous events told in verse; and a few lyric poems. In all, it contains about 60 miracles in 30,000 verses. The miracles were generally taken from Latin prose sources and recast by Walter into French vernacular verse. They were in no particular order and through the years have been rearranged. Those commonly numbered 12 and 13 concern St. Leocadia and the miraculous recovery of her reliquary from the river; though there were only 115 verses in the first redaction, they were extended to 2,342 verses in Walter's final version. Marian miracle collections were much in vogue in the 12th and 13th centuries; Walter's collection for Soissons proved one of the most popular.

Besides the *Miracles* he wrote a life of St. Christine in 1221 (ed. A. C. Ott, Erlangen 1922). The only other work credited to Walter with any degree of certainty that is not an integral part of the *Miracles* is the long moral poem *De la chastée as nonains* (ed. T. Nurmela, Helsinki 1938), written between 1223 and 1227, a sermon in verse to the nuns of Notre-Dame in Soissons. It usually appears in the *Miracles* MSS after the miracle *De la bonne empereris.* Some also claim separate existence for the moral poem *De la doutance de la mort* (ed. Poquet) likewise included in the final edition of the *Miracles* at the end of the second volume. A poem of 810 verses in the first redaction it was augmented by 2,000 verses in its final version.

Bibliography: *Chronicon S. Medardi Suessionensis*, ed. L. D'ARCHERY, *Spicilegium*, 3 v. (Paris 1723) 2:489–491. A. P. DUCROT-GRANDERYE, *Études sur les "Miracles Nostre Dame" de Gautier de Coincy* (Helsinki 1932). Partial eds, A. E. POQUET (Paris 1857). E. BOMAN (Paris 1935), A. LÅNGFORS (Helsinki 1937), E. VON KRAEMER (Helsinki 1950, 1953, 1960). Critical ed., V. F. KOENIG, *Les "Miracles de Nostre Dame" par Gautier de C.* (v.1 Geneva 1955; v.2 1961), 5 v. projected.

[M. J. HAMILTON]

WALTER OF MERTON

Bishop, chancellor, founder of Merton College, Oxford; d. Rochester, Oct. 27, 1277. His parents came from Basingstoke, Hampshire, where Walter established a hospital in their honor. He was probably educated first at the famous Austin priory of Merton, Surrey, and then at Mauger Hall, Oxford, where he made the acquaintance of ADAM MARSH and Bp. ROBERT GROSSETESTE. He became a clerk in the royal chancery and as such took part in negotiating the grant of Sicily to Edmund Crouchback. For this and other services to King Henry III he received many ecclesiastical offices and, in 1261, the chancellorship of England. A keen supporter of the king in the Baronial Wars, Merton lost the chancellorship (1263) when the barons were in the ascendant, recovered it only in 1272 and retained it until 1274, when he was elected bishop of ROCHESTER. The liberality and learning that a contemporary attributed to Merton is symbolized in Merton College, Oxford, which he endowed and organized between 1261 and 1274, when he drew up its finished statutes. The collegiate system he thus established has served as a model for universities ever since.

Bibliography: C. L. KINGSFORD, *The Dictionary of National Biography From the Earliest Times to 1900* (London 1885–1900) 13:297–299. F. M. POWICKE, *The 13th Century* (2d ed. Oxford 1962). J. WELLS, *Oxford and Its Colleges* (9th ed. London 1910).

[D. NICHOLL]

WALTER OF MORTAGNE

Lat. Gualterus de Mauretania, theologian and bishop; b. Mortagne, Flanders, *c.* 1090; d. Laon, France, July 14 or 16, 1174. Son of the feudal lord of Tournai and Mortagne, Walter went to Reims with the future abbot, Hugh of Marchiennes (1102–58), and attended the school of Alberic (d. 1141), who had been a disciple of ANSELM OF LAON. Walter frequently embarassed his plodding teacher and, in competition with him, set up a school at the monastery of Saint-Rémy. This experiment seems to have been brief; about 1120 Walter was in Laon, where he conducted a school "with an iron rod," and those who "studied under him either acted well or were expelled from school." A remark by JOHN OF SALISBURY (*Met-*

alog. 2.17) has led some historians to think that Walter taught for a short time at the school of Sainte-Geneviève in Paris. About 1150 he was dean of the cathedral at Laon, and in 1155 he was consecrated bishop of that diocese.

His writings include *Liber de Trinitate* (*Patrologia Latina* 209:575–590); *De conjugio* (*Patrologia Latina* 176:153–174), which early found its way into the *Summa sententiarum,* formerly attributed to HUGH OF SAINT-VICTOR; and 10 letters: (1) to William, a monk, on the efficacy of baptism administered by heretics, (2) on the meaning of *assumptus homo est deus,* ''the man assumed is God,'' (3) to Master Theodoric on the nature of divine omnipresence, (4) to Master Alberic on the sadness and trepidation of Christ before His death, (5) to Peter ABELARD, courteously, but pointedly, requesting clarification on reports that his dialectics attempted to remove all mystery from the faith, (6 and 7) to Alberic on the legal effect of a promise to marry, (8) to Master Gilbert, probably Gilbertus Universalis (d. 1134, as bishop of London) discussing the effect of vows on the right to marry, (9) to Master Chrysanthus on various theological questions, and (10) to Hugh of Saint-Victor on the problem of knowledge in the soul of Christ.

Bibliography: Letters. 1 in *Patrologia Latina*. ed. J. P. MIGNE (Paris 1878–90) 186:1052–54; 4 in E. MARTÈNE, *Veterum scriptorum et monumentorum ecclesiasticorum et dogmaticorum amplisima collectio* (Paris 1724–33) 1:834–848; 5 in *Spicilegium . . . Opera et studio,* ed. L. D'ACHERY, 13 v. (Paris 1655–77) 2:459–479 (1723 ed., 3 v.) 3:520–526. Literature. L. OTT, ''Untersuchungen zur theologischen Briefliteratur der Frühscholastik,'' *Beiträge zur Geschichte der Philosophie und Theologie des Mittlealters* 34.2 (1937) 126–347. J. C. DIDIER, *Catholicisme* 4:1784–85. *Dictionnaire de théologie catholique,* ed. A. VACANT et al., (Paris 1903–50), Tables générales 1:1781.

[E. A. SYNAN]

WALTER OF PONTOISE, ST.

Walter of Pontoise was b. Andainville, Picardy, *c.* 1025; d. Pontoise, Normandy, 1095 or 1099. Walter became a monk in the monastery at Rebais-en-Brie in the Diocese of Meaux. The lack of any knowledge of his early life together with his reputation for learning suggests he entered upon a monastic career at an early age. In 1069 he was appointed the first abbot of the newly founded monastery at Pontoise, known at first as St. Germain and later as St. Martins after Walter had built a chapel to his honor. He reportedly introduced the Rule of St. Benedict into the monastery. Although he was admired and loved by his monks and by the laity, his desire for a life of solitude is cleary evidenced by several attempts to escape from the responsibilities of his office.

In 1072 he left the monastery and went secretly to CLUNY, then directed by the great HUGH. His identity, however, was soon discovered and at the command of John of Bayeux, archbishop of Rouen, he returned to Pontoise. He left the monastery a second time and lived for a time anonymously on an island in the Loire near Tours. Again his identity was discovered and he was persuaded by his own monks to return to the monastery. His final attempt to be rid of his responsibilities was made during a visit to Rome when he unsuccessfully pleaded with Pope GREGORY VII to be allowed to resign and seek out a life of solitude and prayer. He returned to Pontoise on the pope's orders and remained there as abbot till his death. Two contemporary biographers stress his learning and the austerity of his life. He was involved in the controversy over clerical CELIBACY, and his efforts to encourage obedience to the GREGORIAN REFORM brought him into conflict with court circles. A charming story is told of him in his early days as a novice in the monastery at Rebais. It seems that he took pity on an inmate of the monastic prison confined for some unnamed crime; he not only fed him but engineered his escape, for which Walter has been named, presumably without consultation with prison authorities, patron saint of prisoners.

Feast: April 8.

Bibliography: *Acta Sanctorum* (Paris 1863—) 1:749764. I. HESS, *Studien u. Mitteilungen aus dem Benediktiner- u. dem Zisterzienserorden* 20 297406, a critical ed. of first and older of two biographies in *Acta Sanctorum*. A. BUTLER, *The Lives of the Saints*, rev. ed. H. THURSTON and D. ATTWATER (New York 1956) 2:5354.

[H. MACKINNON]

WALTER OF SAINT-VICTOR

Prior of the Parisian Abbey of Saint-Victor between 1173 and his death *c.* 1190. Some 30 of his sermons have been preserved, eloquent witnesses to his lack of intellectual breadth and originality. He confined himself to copying, rather artlessly at that, texts preserved in the abbeys library, especially those of RICHARD OF SAINT-VICTOR, whom he succeeded as prior. Shortly after taking office, Walter began to take public part in contemporary theological controversies. He attacked the Christological teaching of PETER LOMBARD, making heavy use of an anonymous work, the *Apologia pro Verbo Incarnato*. This first attempt was later inserted in an extended expos of heresies and their refutation entitled *Contra quattuor labyrinthos Franciae*. Within the four labyrinths, in Walters view, lie hidden the four minotaurs who seek to devour the Christian faith: Peter Lombard, ABELARD, PETER OF POITIERS, and GILBERT DE LA PORREE. One is forced to recognize, along with P. Glorieux, the worthless character of this treatise. Under the pretext of defending orthodoxy, Walter gave it regrettable service. In the belief that he was attacking rationalism, which was then called dialectics, he did in fact attack reason itself, along with its legitimate activity.

See Also: DIALECTICS IN THE MIDDLE AGES.

Bibliography: P. GLORIEUX, ed., Le *Contra quattuor labyrinthos Franciae* de Gauthier de Saint-Victor, *Archives d'histoire doctrinale et littéraire du moyan-âge* (Paris 1926–) 27 187–335; Mauvaise action et mauvais travail. Le *Contra, Recherches de théologie ancienne et médiévale* (Louvaine 1929–) 21 179–193. R. STUDENY, W. of S. V. and the *Apologia de Verbo Incarnato, Gregorianum* (Rome 1920–) 18 579–585.

[P. MICHAUD-QUANTIN]

WALTER OF SKIRLAW

Bishop of Durham; b. South Skirlaugh, Swine, Yorkshire, England; d. Howden manor, Yorkshire, March 24, 1406. He studied Canon and civil law at Oxford, becoming a bachelor of civil law (by 1358) and then a doctor of Canon Law (by 1373). As early as 1359 he was secretary to JOHN of Thoresby, Archbishop of York. He became an experienced diplomat and canon lawyer, high in favor with the pope, and consequently was frequently out of England. A follower of King RICHARD II in the early 1380s, he was keeper of the privy seal from Aug. 9, 1382, to Oct. 24, 1386. Skirlaw was successively bishop of Coventry and Lichfield (1386), and bishop of Bath and Wells (1386), and was then made bishop of DURHAM (1388) as recompense for joining the appellants before they entered the lists with the king in the parliament of the same year. He supported the revolution of 1399 and the new king, Henry IV. While bishop, he examined the LOLLARD Richard Wyche on a charge of preaching heresy in the diocese of Durham (*c.* 1401). He gave book gifts to University College and New College, Oxford. He is buried in Durham cathedral between two pillars on the north side of the choir.

Bibliography: J. TAIT, *The Dictionary of National Biography from the Earliest Times to 1900,* 63 v. (London 1885–1900) 18:357–358. F. D. MATTHEW, ''The Trial of Richard Wyche,'' *English Historical Review* 5 (1890) 530–544. T. F. TOUT, *Chapters in the Administrative History of Mediaeval England,* 6 v. (New York 1920–33). A. B. STEEL, *Richard II* (Cambridge, Eng. 1941). A. B. EMDEN, *A Biographical Register of the Scholars of the University of Oxford to A.D. 1500,* 3 v. (Oxford 1957–59) 3:1708–10.

[V. MUDROCH]

WALTER REYNOLDS

Archbishop of Canterbury; b. Windsor, Berkshire; d. Mortlake, Surrey, England, Nov. 16, 1327. The son of a baker, Reynolds played a prominent role in affairs of state in the early years of the reign of King Edward II. Very early in life he found his way into the royal service and, doubtless, was trained in a royal department. His rise in ecclesiastical and secular offices can be traced to his close association, during the reign of Edward I, with the Prince of Wales, becoming keeper of his wardrobe in 1301. When the Prince acceded to the throne as Edward II in 1307, Reynolds soon found himself bishop of WORCESTER and treasurer of England. In 1310 Edward made him his chancellor, which office he held almost uninterruptedly until 1314, when he surrendered it in the changes following the English defeat at Bannockburn. When the See of Canterbury fell vacant at the death of the saintly ROBERT OF WINCHELSEA in 1313, the king secured—by suitable subventions, it was rumored—Reynolds appointment by Pope Clement V, who quashed the election of THOMAS OF COBHAM by the Canterbury monks. Weak in character and limited in intelligence, Reynolds must be numbered among the least qualified archbishops of Canterbury. Politically, he exerted no effective force in the waning years of Edward II's reign and, at length and tardily, gave his support to the Queen and the revolution that culminated in the crowning of Edward III. His body rests in the south choir aisle of Canterbury cathedral.

Bibliography: His register as bishop of Worcester has been pub. by the Dugdale Society, v.9, and by the Worcestershire Historical Society, v.39, ed. R. A. WILSON. W. F. HOOK, *Lives of the Archbishops of Canterbury,* 12 v. (London 1860–84) v.3. T. F. TOUT, *The Dictionary of National Biography from the Earliest Times to 1900* (London 1885–1900) 16:963–966. W. E. L. SMITH, *Episcopal Appointments and Patronage in the Reign of Edward II* (Chicago 1938). K. EDWARDS, ''The Political Importance of the English Bishops during the Reign of Edward II,'' *English Historical Review* 59 311–347.

[F. D. LOGAN]

WALTHAM, MONASTERY OF

Former house of Austin canons, in the county of Essex and the ancient See of London, England. The original foundation of the landowner Tovi was enlarged in 1060 by Earl Harold of Wessex who believed he had been miraculously cured of palsy there. After its destruction by Geoffrey de Mandeville in 1144, King Henry II reendowed the house as part of his penance for the murder of BECKET, replacing the secular canons with CANONS REGULAR OF ST. AUGUSTINE. It was elevated to the status of an abbey in 1184 under Walter de Gant and was the most important house of Augustinian canons in England. It was the last monastery to be suppressed by King HENRY VIII; the abbot and 17 canons were then pensioned. The nave of the church remained in use as a parish church.

Waltham Abbey, founded in 1060 by King Harold, who was buried here after the Battle of Hastings in 1066. (©Angelo Hornak/CORBIS)

Bibliography: *The Foundation of Waltham Abbey,* ed. W. STUBBS (Oxford 1861). *The Victoria History of the County of Essex,* ed. H. A. DOUBLEDAY et al. (Westminster, Eng. 1903–) v.2 J. C. DICKINSON, *The Origins of the Austin Canons and Their Introduction into England* (London 1950).

[F. R. JOHNSTON]

WALTHEOF, ST.

Cistercian abbot, second son of Simon of Saint-Liz, earl of Northampton and Huntingdon; d. Aug. 3, 1159. Waltheof (Waldef, Walden, or Wallevus) He was educated at the court of his stepfather, King DAVID OF SCOTLAND, where AELRED OF RIEVAULX was his companion. He became a canon regular at the priory of Nostell, *c.* 1130, and about three years later was elected prior of Kirkham. In 1143 he joined with Cistercians in protest at Rome against the election of WILLIAM FITZHERBERT to the archbishopric of York; shortly afterward he became a Cistercian at Wardon. Waltheof retired to RIEVAULX to avoid the displeasure of his brother, Simon, earl of Northampton, and in 1148 was elected abbot of MELROSE, SCOTLAND. He refused the bishopric of Glasgow shortly before his death. Miracles at his tomb caused his incorrupt body to be transferred to a new marble sarcophagus in 1171; in 1240 it was moved to the east part of the chapter house.

Feast: Aug. 6.

Bibliography: JOCELIN OF FURNESS, *Vita S. Waltheni abbatis, Acta Sanctorum* (Paris 1863—) 1:249277. *Chronicle of Melrose,* ed. and tr. J. STEVENSON (London 1936). W. E. RHODES, *The Dictionary of National Biography From the Earliest Times to 1900* (London 1938) 20:724725. WALTER DANIEL, *The Life of Ailred of Rievaulx,* ed. and tr. F. M. POWICKE (New York 1950).

[C. H. TALBOT]

WALTHER, CARL FERDINAND WILLIAM

Lutheran theologian, founder of the Missouri Synod; b. Langenchursdorf, Germany, Oct. 25, 1811; d. St. Louis, Mo., May 7, 1887. He was the son of a Lutheran pastor. After attending the University of Leipzig, he accepted a call in 1836 as pastor at Braeunsdorf, Saxony, and was ordained there on Jan. 15, 1837. The following year he joined a large number of Saxon Lutherans who migrated to America rather than accept a union with the Reformed Church. Walther settled in Perry County, MO, where he established a Gymnasium that eventually grew into Concordia Seminary, St. Louis. In 1841 he accepted a call to Trinity Church, St. Louis, and in 1844 established *Der Lutheraner,* a religious periodical. In 1846 Walther began a series of meetings with Lutheran leaders that resulted in the formation of the Missouri Synod. He was chosen its first president at Chicago, IL; he also served as professor of theology at Concordia from 1850 until his death.

Walther's theological writings appeared chiefly in the quarterly *Lehre und Wehre,* which he founded at Concordia in 1855, and in his textbook, *Pastoral Theology.* He advocated traditional Lutheran doctrine, with emphasis on the binding force of Lutheran confessions and divine predilection as the cause of faith. His controversy with Adolph Grabau resulted in the union of the Missouri and Buffalo Synods in 1867, but the Ohio and Norwegian Synods separated from Missouri in 1881–82 over Walther's doctrine of predestination. In addition to his conservative impact on the Missouri Synods doctrinal position, Walther helped to shape its parochial school system, securing educational provisions for English–speaking Lutherans at the Synodal Conference of 1872.

Bibliography: D. H. STEFFENS, *Dr. Carl Ferdinand Wilhelm Walther.* W. G. POLACK, *The Story of C. F. W. Walther.* A. WENTZ, *A Basic History of Lutheranism in America* (Philadelphia 1955) bibliog.

[R. K. MACMASTER]

WALTMAN OF ANTWERP, BL.

Premonstratensian abbot also known as Gualtmannus; d. Antwerp, April 15, 1138. When TANCHELM proved effective in spreading his new heretical movement in Antwerp, the local bishop, Burchard of Cambrai, sought the help of NORBERT OF XANTEN and the newly formed PREMONSTRATENSIANS in combating the heresy. Norbert's success over Tanchelm (commemorated in a stained glass window of the cathedral) led the canons of historic St. Michaels in Antwerp to move to Notre-Dame and give St. Michaels to Norbert as the site of the first Premonstratensian foundation in Antwerp. Waltman, one of Norbert's talented helpers in Antwerp, became first abbot. During his 14 years in that office Waltman made St. Michaels the center of reestablished religious unity in Antwerp. He also founded as daughter-houses the Premonstratensian abbeys of Averbode and TONGERLOO, both of which still exist today, though St. Michaels was suppressed during the French Revolution.

Feast: April 11.

Bibliography: *Acta Sanctorum* June 1:797–845. J. LE PAIGE, *Bibliotheca praemonstratensis ordinis.* C. J. KIRKFLEET, *History of Saint Norbert.* G. MADELAINE, *Histoire de saint Norbert*, 2 v. (3d ed. Tongerloo Abbey, Belg. 1928). N. BACKMUND, *Monasticon Praemonstratense* 2:265–269, 600. A. BUTLER, *The Lives of the Saints* 2:73. J. L. BAUDOT and L. CHAUSSIN, *Vies des saints et des bienheureux selon l'ordre du calendrier avec l'historique des fêtes* 4:356.

[L. L. RUMMEL]

WALWORTH, CLARENCE AUGUSTUS

Missionary and writer; b. Plattsburg, New York, May 30, 1820; d. Albany, New York, Sept. 19, 1900. Walworth's father, Reuben H. Walworth, a Presbyterian, was a judge, congressman, and last chancellor of New York State; his mother was Mary K. Walworth. He graduated from Union College, Schenectady, New York, in 1838, was admitted to the bar in 1841, and practiced law for a year in Rochester, New York. He spent three years studying for the ministry at General Theological Seminary, New York City, during the agitation over Tractarianism, which he later described in his book *The Oxford Movement in America.* He entered the Catholic Church in 1845, was received into the Congregation of the Most Holy Redeemer, and was ordained at the Redemptorist college in Wittem, Holland, Aug. 27, 1848.

After his return to the U.S. in 1851, he preached for seven years with the mission band led by Isaac HECKER. He withdrew from the group a few weeks before they formed the Missionary Priests of St. Paul the Apostle in 1858 because he disagreed with their plan for community life without formal vows. He was received into the Albany, New York, diocese and stationed at St. Peters Church in Troy, New York, until 1861 when he was reunited with his Paulist associates. In 1865, however, overwork and malaria forced him to leave the new community, and he became pastor of St. Mary's Church, Albany. There he vigorously opposed industrial abuses and political corruption, promoted the temperance cause, and worked for better conditions at St. Regis Indian reservation.

He wrote *The Gentle Skeptic, The Doctrine of Hell, Andiatorocte and Other Poems, Reminiscences of Edgar P. Wadhams, The Walworths in America*, and many pamphlets and tracts. His verse paraphrase of the *Te Deum*, "Holy God, We Praise Thy Name," became one of the foremost hymns of English-speaking Catholics.

Bibliography: V. F. HOLDEN, *The Yankee Paul: Isaac Thomas Hecker.* J. MCSORLEY, *Father Hecker and His Friends* (2d ed. St. Louis 1953). E. H. WALWORTH, *Life Sketches of Father Walworth.* W. ELLIOT, "Father Walworth: A Character Sketch," *Catholic World* 73 (1901) 320–337.

[J. P. FLYNN]

WANDERING JEW, LEGEND OF THE

A development of a more ancient legend dealing with a man's insensibility of Jesus' plight while He was on His way to Calvary. As a result of his action, the subject of this legend is destined to remain alive until the time of the second coming of Christ. The origin of the legend may possibly be similar to the misunderstanding of a saying of Jesus that occasioned the explanation of Jn 21.22–23. In this passage, it is denied that the beloved disciple was granted any privilege of remaining alive until the second coming of Christ.

From the notion of a privilege of remaining until the second coming, the idea developed into that of the subjects being forced to remain as a curse provoked by a cruel rejection of Jesus. In this form the legend is recorded in the *Flores Historiarum* of Roger of Wendover, a monk of St. Albans in England. It is contained also in the *Historia Majora* of MATTHEW PARIS, dating from the same period. It recounts how a doorkeeper of Pontius Pilate named Cartaphilus, not necessarily a Jew, struck

Jesus as He carried His cross on the way to Calvary, saying, "Go faster, Jesus, what are you waiting for?" Jesus answered, "I am going, but you shall wait until I return." Thus, Cartaphilus became immortal. He repeatedly ages and is rejuvenated, while he wanders everywhere, seeking death. He has become a Christian and taken the name of Joseph. In Italy the legend has some variations; the wanderer is called Joanes Buttadeus or Malchus.

The first mention of this legend with the identification of the wanderer as a Jew is in a pamphlet entitled *Kurze Beschreibung und Erzählung von einem Juden mit Namen Ahasuerus* that was circulated in Germany at the beginning of the 17th century. This Ahasuerus is presented as a former shoemaker of Jerusalem who had angrily opposed Jesus and had been condemned by Him to wander eternally. In haggadic literature the name Ahasuerus is commonly applied to a wicked fool.

The story became very popular throughout Europe, perhaps reflecting popular prejudices of the time. L. Neubaur records various German, Flemish, Danish, and Swedish versions. A. Yarmolinsky adds to this list several Slavonic, Polish, and Russian versions. In all these there are some variations, but the basic theme remains the same. It is often used in art and literature; some examples are: O. Henry, *The Door of Unrest*; Lew Wallace, *The Prince of India*; E. Temple Thurston, *The Wandering Jew*.

The legend is looked upon with disfavor by Jewish people today since it is considered to be an instrument that has been used to foster anti-Semitism.

Bibliography: L. NEUBAUR, *Die Sage vom ewigen Juden* (2d ed. Leipzig 1893). A. YARMOLINSKY, "The Wandering Jew," *Studies in Jewish Bibliography and Related Subjects in Memory of Abraham S. Freidus* (New York 1928) 319–328. S. COHEN, *Universal Jewish Encyclopedia* 10:448–449.

[S. M. POLAN]

WANDRILLE (WANDREGISILUS), ST.

Benedictine, founder of the Abbey of FONTENELLE; b. near Verdun, France, *c.* 600; d. Abbey of Fontenelle, July 22, 663. Wandrille came of a noble Frankish family, possibly related to Merovingian royalty, and served at the court of Dagobert I (d. 639) as *comes palatii*. By parental arrangement he married a young noblewoman, from whom, however, he separated by mutual agreement; he then entered the monastery of Montfauçon near Verdun. After a period of ascetical observance in this house, he moved on to live as a hermit. His restless spirit led him to BOBBIO, where the Celtic monastic practices of the rule of St. COLUMBAN seemed to satisfy his need for the peni-

tential life. Still unfulfilled, he went to live at the Abbey of ROMAINMÔTIER, and finally moved to ROUEN. There Bishop OUEN ordained him a subdeacon, later promoting him to the diaconate, and enlisted him in pastoral activity. Ordained a priest by St. OMER, he then founded Fontenelle (also known as Saint-Wandrille), March 1, 649. As its first abbot he also established a thriving monastic school; he continued to direct the abbey until his death.

Feast: July 22; March 3 (translation).

Bibliography: *Vita Wandregisili, Monumenta Germaniae Historica: Scriptores rerum Merovingicarum* (Berlin 1826—) 5:13–24. *Acta Sanctorum* (Paris 1863—) 5:253–302. *Monumenta Germaniae Historica: Scriptores* (Berlin 1826—) 30.2:814–820. E. VACANDARD, *Vie de saint Ouen* (Paris 1902). A. M. ZIMMERMAN, *Kalendarium Benedictinum: Die Heiligen und Seligen des Benediktinerordens und seiner Zweige* (Metten 1933–38) 2:486–488. J. LAPORTE, *Histoire de St-Wandrille* (St-Wandrille 1936). L. DAVID, *L'Abbaye St-Wandrille de Fontenelle* (Saint-Wandrille 1957).

[O. J. BLUM]

WANG ERMAN, PETER, ST.

Cook, lay martyr ; b. 1864, Guchengyin Cun, Taiyuan Xian, Shangxi, China; d. July 9, 1900, Taiyüan, Shanxi Province. When Peter Wang Erman (given also as Wang Erh-man or Wang-Oi-Man) came of age, he worked in the same orphanage at Kolao-Kou that cared for him in his youth. Prior to being captured by the Boxers and beheaded, he worked in a print shop, served as footman to two priests, and for two years was cook for the Franciscan seminary at Taiyüan. He was beatified by Pope Pius XII (Nov. 24, 1946) and canonized (Oct. 1, 2000) by Pope John Paul II with Augustine Zhao Rong and companions.

Feast: July 4.

Bibliography: L. M. BALCONI, *Le Martiri di Taiyuen* (Milan 1945). *Acta Apostolicae Sedis* 47 (1955) 381–388; *Vita del b. A. Crescitelli* (Milan 1950). M. T. DE BLARER, *Les Bse Marie Hermine de Jésus et ses compagnes, franciscaines missionnaires de Marie, massacrées le 9 juillet 1900 à Tai-Yuan-Fou, Chine* (Paris 1947). *Les Vingt-neuf martyrs de Chine, massacrés en 1900, béatifiés par Sa Sainteté Pie XII, le 24 novembre, 1946* (Rome 1946). L. MINER, *China's Book of Martyrs: A Record of Heroic Martyrdoms and Marvelous Deliverances of Chinese Christians during the Summer of 1900* (Ann Arbor 1994). J. SIMON, *Sous le sabre des Boxers* (Lille 1955). C. TESTORE, *Sangue e palme sul fiume giallo. I beati martiri cinesi nella persecuzione della Boxe Celi Sud-Est, 1900* (Rome 1955). *L'Osservatore Romano*, Eng. Ed. 40 (2000): 1–2, 10.

[K. I. RABENSTEIN]

WANG LI, MARY, ST.

Lay martyr; b. 1851, Wei County, Hebei (Hopeh) Province, China; d. 1900 Daning, Hebei. Mary Wang Li

(Li-Shih or Li-Cheu) was captured by the Boxers as she tried to escape the persecution with her two children. Although her neighbors tried to persuade her captors that she was not a Christian and, therefore, should be spared, Mary stated simply, ''Please, do not beg them for my life. I am certainly one of the faithful and my family has been for generations.'' Thereupon she was beheaded. Mary was among the 2,072 killed between June and August 1900 whose causes were submitted to the Vatican. Of these, 56, including Mary Wang Li, were beatified by Pope Pius XII (April 17, 1955) and canonized (Oct. 1, 2000) by Pope John Paul II with Augustine Zhao Rong and companions.

Feast: July 20.

Bibliography: L. MINER, *China's Book of Martyrs: A Record of Heroic Martyrdoms and Marvelous Deliverances of Chinese Christians during the Summer of 1900* (Ann Arbor 1994). J. SIMON, *Sous le sabre des Boxers* (Lille 1955). C. TESTORE, *Sangue e palme sul fiume giallo. I beati martiri cinesi nella persecuzione della Boxe Celi Sud-Est, 1900* (Rome 1955). *L'Osservatore Romano,* Eng. ed. 40 (2000): 1–2, 10.

[K. I. RABENSTEIN]

WANG RUI, JOHN, ST.

Franciscan seminarian, martyr; b. Feb. 26, 1885, Xinli, Wenshui Xian, Shanxi Province; d. July 9, 1900, Taiyüan, Shanxi Province, China. John Wang Rui (or Van) was the eldest of the three children of Joseph Wang Daxing and Cecilia Liu, who were pious Christians. He began his studies in the minor seminary of Dongergou in 1895. The 10-year-old became a quick favorite because of his good nature and beautiful singing voice. While he was studying at Taiyüan's major seminary, he was chosen to travel with Bp. Francesco FOGOLLA to the 1897 International Exhibition in Turin, Italy. Although the bishop suggested that all the seminarians flee the persecution anticipated by the Boxers, John remained, saying: ''I shall be a martyr for God.'' He was among the dozens of Christians captured in the Taiyüan cathedral and executed. John was beatified by Pope Pius XII (Nov. 24, 1946) and canonized (Oct. 1, 2000) by Pope John Paul II with Augustine Zhao Rong and companions.

Feast: July 4.

Bibliography: L. M. BALCONI, *Le Martiri di Taiyuen* (Milan 1945). *Acta Apostolicae Sedis* 47 (1955) 381–388; *Vita del b. A. Crescitelli* (Milan 1950). M. T. DE BLARER, *Les Bse Marie Hermine de Jésus et ses compagnes, franciscaines missionnaires de Marie, massacrées le 9 juillet 1900 à Tai-Yuan-Fou, Chine* (Paris 1947). *Les Vingt-neuf martyrs de Chine, massacrés en 1900, béatifiés par Sa Sainteté Pie XII, le 24 novembre, 1946* (Rome 1946). L. MINER, *China's Book of Martyrs: A Record of Heroic Martyrdoms and Marvelous Deliverances of Chinese Christians during the Summer*

of 1900 (Ann Arbor 1994). J. SIMON, *Sous le sabre des Boxers* (Lille 1955). C. TESTORE, *Sangue e palme sul fiume giallo. I beati martiri cinesi nella persecuzione della Boxe Celi Sud-Est, 1900* (Rome 1955). *L'Osservatore Romano,* Eng. Ed. 40 (2000): 1–2, 10.

[K. I. RABENSTEIN]

WANG YUMEI, JOSEPH, ST.

Lay martyr; b. 1823, Majiazhuang, Wei County, Hebei (Hopeh) Province, China; d. there, July 21, 1900. Sixty-eight-year-old Joseph Wang Yumei (spelled otherwise Yü-mei or Jou-Mei) was arrested by the Boxers and immediately killed because he was the village leader of the Catholics. The others, including SS. Anna Wang, Lucy Wang, and Andrew Wang Tianqing were martyred the following day. He was among the 2,072 killed between June and August 1900 whose causes were submitted to the Vatican. Of these, 56, including Joseph, were beatified by Pope Pius XII (April 17, 1955) and canonized (Oct. 1, 2000) by Pope John Paul II with Augustine Zhao Rong and companions.

Feast: July 20.

Bibliography: L. MINER, *China's Book of Martyrs: A Record of Heroic Martyrdoms and Marvelous Deliverances of Chinese Christians during the Summer of 1900* (Ann Arbor 1994). J. SIMON, *Sous le sabre des Boxers* (Lille 1955). C. TESTORE, *Sangue e palme sul fiume giallo. I beati martiri cinesi nella persecuzione della Boxe Celi Sud-Est, 1900* (Rome 1955). *L'Osservatore Romano,* Eng. ed. 40 (2000): 1–2, 10.

[K. I. RABENSTEIN]

WANINGUS, ST.

Founder of the abbey of Fécamp and patron of the monastery of Ham in Picardy; b. Rouen: d. Fécamp, *c.* 688. Waningus (Vaneng) was count of the district of Caux, a royal chase, adviser at the court of Queen BATHILDIS, and tutor of Clotaire III. Renouncing court life, he bequeathed land holdings for the erection of monasteries, and assisted (St.) WANDRILLE in the founding of FONTENELLE (March 1, 649), which he also helped endow. He entrusted his son, Desideratus, to Wandrille to be educated as a Benedictine monk. In 658 after recovery from a severe illness he built a convent at FÉCAMP. There, under the administration of Wandrille and (St.) OUEN, 366 nuns were soon collected, with Childemarcha as abbess. (St.) LEODEGAR, mutilated and expelled from his diocese, was placed in the custody of Waningus and cared for at Fécamp. Waningus is depicted clothed in armour, with a mantle of red emblazoned with a fleur-de-lis, and holding a sword in one hand and a church in the other. His relics (a small portion of the bones) may still be seen in the church of Ham.

"David Punishing Ammonites." (Bettmann/CORBIS)

Feast: Jan. 9.

Bibliography: O. L. KAPSNER, *A Benedictine Bibliography: An Author-Subject Union List*, (Collegeville, MN 1962) 2:3370–72, 4004–13, 7276–82. A. ZIMMERMANN, *Lexikon für Theologie und Kirche* (Freiburg 1957–65) 10:750. P. COUSIN in *L'Abbaye bénédictine de Fécamp*, 4 v. (Fécamp 1959–63) 1:23–44.

[M. J. STALLINGS]

WAR (IN THE BIBLE)

From the serpent's hostility to God in the Garden of Eden (Gn 3.1, 14–15) to his absolute and everlasting defeat in the final apocalyptic struggle (Rv 12.9; 20.9–10), there is in SALVATION HISTORY an underlying, unifying, multicolored theme of warfare between God and his enemies. This article treats in order: holy war in the Old Testament, the technical aspects of Old Testament war, and war terminology in the New Testament.

Holy War in the Old Testament. In Old Testament history Yahweh, the God of Israel, fights His own and Israel's enemies in holy war, the terminology of which takes on in the Prophets' "DAY OF THE LORD" an eschatological significance. Israel's pagan neighbors looked upon war as having a sacred character; it was the war of its god, undertaken and accomplished according to religious prescription. In the MESHA INSCRIPTION, the king of Moab says that Chamos, the God of the Moabites, commanded him to wage war against Israel (see J. B. Pritchard, *Ancient Near Eastern Texts Relating to the Old Testament* [Princeton 1955] 320). In Israel, holy war had similar characteristics: it was Yahweh's war against His enemies (1 Sm 18.17; 25.18; see also Nm 21.14 where mention is made of the "Book of Wars of Yahweh"), Yahweh commanding what was to be done, fighting as a *gibbôr,* "warrior" [Dt 10.17; Jer 32.18; Ps 23(24).8; see also Ex 15.3; Nm 32.20–21; 2 Sm 22.35; Jos 10.14, 42; Dt 20.4], and gaining the victory (Nm 10.35); the warriors were volunteers inspired by faith in Yahweh (Jos 8.1; 10.25; Jgs 5.14), led by a charismatic leader (Jgs 6.34); they were consecrated (Is 13.3; Jos 3.5); they observed the laws of ritual purity (Dt 23.10–15), entered battle carrying the sacred ark (Jos 6.6; 2 Sm 11.11), and gave the prescribed shout, *terû'â* (1 Sm 4.5–6; 10.35–36). When the weakhearted had been sent back home (Dt 20.8), the warriors were convinced that victory was certain; with Yahweh present there was no fear, for, if necessary, He could call the elements to fight for Israel (Jos 10.11; 24.7; Jgs 5.20; 1 Sm 7.10), throwing the enemy into sudden fright (1 Sm 14.15), defeat (Jgs 5.31; Dt 32.29), and total destruction, *herem* (Dt 7.2; Jos 8.2; 1 Sm 15.3).

Under the monarchy the ideals of holy war were more or less lost sight of. The king, now a hereditary leader, relying on his professional army and foreign allies, and with less stress on Yahweh's aid, led his armies to battle; it was his war, no longer Yahweh's (1 Sm 8.20). The wars of the Maccabees, although intensely religious, were not ''holy wars''; Yahweh, considered more in a transcendent sense, did not fight as a *gibbôr* for Israel; Judas prays that God may send His angel (2 Mc 15.23).

The terminology of holy war, appropriated by the Prophets for their conception of the ''day of Yahweh,'' later took on an ever more eschatological significance.

Technical Aspects of Old Testament War. The wars mentioned in the book of Joshua were wars of conquest aimed at occupying the promised land. During the period of the Judges (*c.* 1200–1025 B.C.), the Israelites fought mostly defensive wars against marauding Canaanites, Midianites, Moabites, Edomites, and Philistines. Open warfare began under David (*c.* 1000–961 B.C.), whose army consisted entirely of infantry. Solomon (*c.* 961–922 B.C.) introduced cavalry and the chariot corps in Israel (1 Kgs 4.26; 10.26). During the Maccabean wars (*c.* 166–134 B.C.), the Jewish rebels successfully employed guerrilla tactics against the powerful Greek cavalry and elephant corps (2 Mc 13.2, 15).

War usually began in the spring (2 Sm 11.1) after spies had provided intelligence reports about the enemy (Nm 13.1–33). Battles consisted mostly in fierce hand-to-hand fighting in surprise attacks, with the Israelite warriors outmaneuvering the enemy by dividing into two or three separate companies (Jgs 7.16; 9.43).

Sources of information concerning the arms of Israelite soldiers are vague, for no technical description of Israelite weapons is given in the Bible, nor is the precise meaning of the Hebrew words describing military equipment known. Present evidence indicates that shields, bucklers, helmets, and breastplates were used as protective armor. Clubs, battle-axes, and maces were used for crushing the skull; daggers, lances, and swords were effective in hand-to-hand combat. Missiles included darts, spears, and javelins, and later on, slings, catapults, and bows and arrows were used in long range fighting.

War Terminology in the New Testament. The New Testament usage of war terminology falls roughly into three patterns describing the warfare between Christ and the devil (Gospels), the individual and the devil (St. Paul), and the final eschatological struggle between good and evil (Revelation). The Synoptic Gospels, more in the theme than the terminology, present Christ's mission as a warfare against the kingdom of Satan (Lk 4.1–13). Christ has come to dispossess Satan of his kingdom (Mk 3.27); He conquers him by casting out devils (Mk 1.23–27), healing (Mk 1.31–34), preaching (Mk 1.15), founding His Church (Mt 16.18), and undergoing His Passion (Mk 8.31–33; 9.31; 10.32–34, 38; Lk 24.26).

St. Paul, mixing military and theological terminology, describes the spiritual life as a warfare between the Christian, armed like a soldier with his virtues, and the devil, the adversary, with his allied powers of darkness. The faithful must be spiritually armed (Rom 6.13; 13.12; 2 Cor 6.7; 10.4; 1 Thes 5.8) and must put on God's armor when battling with the powers of darkness. This armor includes the breastplate of justice, the shield of faith, the helmet of salvation, the sword of the spirit, as well as belt and military boots (Eph 6.10–17; cf. Wis 5.17–22). Paul looks on apostolic workers such as Timothy (2 Tm 2.3), Epaphroditus (Phil 2.25) and Archippus (Phlm 2) as fellow soldiers in the army of Christ. Revelation, following the literary tradition of the later Prophets who in the Old Testament spoke of the ''day of Yahweh'' as the decisive day of salvation, describes with warlike phantasmagoria the final eschatological war between good and evil as occurring on ''the great day of God almighty'' (16.14; 20.7–10).

Bibliography: R. DE VAUX, *Ancient Israel, Its Life and Institutions,* tr. J. MCHUGH (New York 1961) 213–267. Y. YADIN, *The Art of Warfare in Biblical Lands in the Light of Archaeological Study,* tr. M. PEARLMAN, 2 v. (New York 1963). J. W. WEVERS, ed. G. A. BUTTRICK, *The Interpreters' Dictionary of the Bible* (Nashville 1962) 4:820–825. W. CORSWANT, *A Dictionary of Life in Bible Times,* tr. A. HEATHCOTE (New York 1960) 35–36, 292–294. G. T. MONTAGUE, *Growth in Christ, a Study in Saint Paul's Theology of Progress* (Kirkwood, Mo. 1961).

[F. J. MONTALBANO]

WAR, MORALITY OF

The history of Catholic attitudes toward war is varied and complex. Evangelical commitments to nonviolence and love of enemies mingle with recognition of the state's duty to uphold justice and defend the peace. The New Testament commands love of enemies, blesses peacemakers, and repeatedly urges forgiveness, but it also urges respect for authority and regards political authority, with its duty to repress evildoers, as coming from God. Early Christians seemed to have avoided military service because it involved sacrifice to Roman deities and allegiance to the divine figure of the emperor as well as the shedding of blood. As long as military service consisted mostly of police work, many Christians could be found serving in the military, with the numbers growing as the Empire grew more Christian. With the increase of warfare with the barbarians, many Christians, such as the so-called Moorish Legion, were martyred for their unwillingness to draw blood. The first nonmartyr saint, Martin of Tours, was a soldier-convert who was about to be executed, but won release when he successfully spoke with the enemy who then surrendered and asked for baptism.

History

Late Antiquity. In the Western Roman Empire, Christian attitudes toward war evolved under pressure from the barbarian invasions. On the one hand, the barbarian attacks on the Christian imperial heartland led St. AUGUSTINE to articulate, in a series of occasional writings, the classic bases for Christian just-war thinking. On the other hand, the "conversion" of the Germanic tribes led to Christianity's inculturation into warrior societies where, except largely for monastic foundations, the nonviolence of the early Church was forgotten. In the Eastern Empire, where there was a close relation between church and state, formalized just-war thinking did not take hold. At the same time, monks and bishops adhered to nonviolence, even at times mounting campaigns of nonviolent resistance to imperial Byzantine policy.

The Middle Ages. In the West, during the Middle Ages, efforts were made to curb the savagery of the warrior culture. Monastic and popular movements of nonviolence, like the PEACE OF GOD, especially in French territory, and later the Truce of God, and massive grassroots peace movements, such as the Bianchi in Italy, attempted to restrict the opportunities for warfare and pacify the warrior culture. Meanwhile, codes of chivalry, the penitential rules for confessors, and the development of just-war thinking attempted to limit, control, and refine the martial spirit.

The Just-War Tradition. Under the influence of reforming canonists, Christian just-war thinking developed gradually during the Middle Ages. St. Augustine had laid out the foundations for this tradition, arguing that a just war required a just cause, legitimate authority, and a right

intention. Later canonists and moral theologians would articulate other norms as well.

THOMAS AQUINAS adopted Augustine's three criteria for a just war, but adapted them to fit the circumstances of his own day. In the context of conflict in the Italian city-states, for example, he had to accommodate wider participation in politics than existed in Augustine's day. Accordingly, whereas Augustine would have regarded authority as coming directly from God, Aquinas identified service of the common good as a norm for judging the legitimacy of a ruler or ruling party, forbade government by faction, and allowed rebellion when the people rose as one.

Christians regarded the just-war tradition as essentially a set of rules regulating conflict among Christian nations. With the European discovery of the Americas and East Asia, questions arose about the application of just-war norms to wars with non-Christian peoples. The Spanish conquest had been particularly brutal in its treatment of natives in the Americas. The detailed reports of Bartolomeo de las Casas on the atrocities of the conquistadors inspired the Spanish scholastics, especially Francisco de Vitoria, to argue for the extension of the norms of conflict to native peoples, laying the foundations for modern international law.

By the time of the rise of the modern nation-state, the just-war doctrine had become the prevailing doctrine in western Christendom. Protestant reformers, like LUTHER and CALVIN, embraced the idea. Except for the ANABAPTISTS and FREE CHURCH movements, like the Quakers, Christian nonviolence was in eclipse until the 20th century.

It was in the 16th and 17th centuries that the spirit and thought of Augustine and Thomas were transcribed and expanded into a fully developed theory of the just war, especially by VITORIA (1487?–1546) and SUÁREZ (1548–1617). Hostile actions are divided by Vitoria and Suárez into two kinds: (1) armed attack upon a peaceful people, and (2) injurious actions (those generally involving an infringement of a right). Armed response to the first type of hostile action was regarded as a defensive war. This was conceived as different in type from armed response to injurious action. The collective and intentional effecting of death and destruction in response to "injurious action" of other kinds was "offensive" or "aggressive" war and was seen as a completely different undertaking. In the thinking of Vitoria and Suárez, the defensive war required no special moral justification. It appeared to them rather as "an involuntary act" forced upon a peaceful community, which need not then justify its response. Taking up arms, however, in response to "injurious action" appeared to them to require special moral justification. Since in this case, the injurious action to which war was the response would *not* involve destruction and death, how could the Christian voluntarily elect war as a means of responding to it? It was in connection with such offensive war that they applied conditions for a just war. The problem for them was the reconciliation of the will's love of peace with the voluntary procurement of death and destruction. The conditions of the just war were intended to depict ranges of response in such a way as to preserve the Christian's adherence to God and peace.

World War II, the Vietnam War, and the nuclear debates of the Cold War gradually saw an increased acceptance of nonviolence on the part of Christians. At the same time there was an appropriation of the just-war tradition to the realities of contemporary warfare. The return to biblical foundations in moral theology urged by VATICAN COUNCIL II, as well as ecumenical dialogue, also contributed to more sympathetic understanding in Catholic circles of the nonviolent tradition as well as to critical use of the just-war doctrine.

The extended public debate over the 1983 United States Bishops' pastoral letter on nuclear war and deterrence, *The Challenge of Peace: God's Promise and Our Response*, led to broad public awareness of just-war norms. The letter had actually called for public engagement in the debate over U.S. nuclear policy, an area heretofore reserved for a small elite. The just-war categories became so well known that in the months leading up to the Persian Gulf War (1990–91), the U.S. public, and even the U.S. Congress, debated the coming conflict in just-war terms.

The Presumption against War. A significant development in late 20th-century Catholic just-war teaching was the presumption against the use of force. The U.S. Catholic bishops in *The Challenge of Peace* taught that the just-war doctrine shares with Christian nonviolence "a presumption against war and for the peaceful settlement of disputes" which is "binding on all." The function of the *ad bellum* norms is to determine when that presumption may be overridden.

Some critics charge that this presumption is an innovation in the tradition of just-war thinking. It overlooks, they assert, the inherent duty of the state to defend the peace, it makes avoiding war a greater priority than correcting injustice, and it attributes too great a weight to the destructiveness of modern warfare. Defenders argue that Christian thinkers, including St. Augustine, have articulated such a proviso before, that the critics make war too automatic a response to injustice, and that they underestimate the potentially greater injustice that can be perpetrated by resorting to force before exhausting alternative methods of dispute resolution.

Just-War Principles

The term "just war" is employed to refer in a shorthand way to the set of norms or criteria for assessing whether a government's recourse to force is morally justified. The just-war tradition is expressed in many forms: in international law, in the codes of conduct of national military forces, in moral philosophy and theology, in church teaching. The just-war norms embrace two sets of criteria. One, the *ius ad bellum*, identifies criteria for judging whether the resort to force is justified. These are sometimes called the "war-decision" rules. The second set of criteria, *ius in bello*, regulates and limits the use of force in combat. These are sometimes called the "war-conduct" rules.

Ius ad bellum. The *ius ad bellum* contains six (or seven) criteria to determine whether resort to force is justified. They are: (1) just cause, (2) competent authority, (3) right intention, (4) last resort, (5) probability of success, and (6) proportionality. To these is sometimes added the criterion of comparative justice, which assesses which of two adversaries is "sufficiently 'right'" to override a presumption against the use of force.

Just Cause. According to *The Challenge of Peace*, "War is permissible only to confront 'a real and certain danger,' i.e., to protect innocent life, to preserve conditions necessary for decent human existence, and to secure basic human rights."

Defense against Aggression. For much of the 20th century, the sole justification for war was taken to be defense against aggression. That definition, however, proved too narrow to deal with a variety of conflicts that emerged in the late 20th century, especially guerrilla warfare, terrorism and counter-terrorist campaigns, and ethnic cleansing.

During the Persian Gulf War, the Vatican made an attempt to narrow the definition to defense against "an aggression in progress," a formula that would have precluded a Coalition attack against Iraq and would have allowed that country to retain the fruits of its aggression in Kuwait. In the wake of the terror attacks against the United States on Sept. 11, 2001, while repeatedly warning against a war of religions and urging forgiveness, Pope John Paul II declared that there is "a right to defend oneself against terrorism, a right which as always must be exercised with respect for moral and legal limits in the choice of means and ends" ("World Day of Peace Message," Jan. 1, 2002).

Humanitarian Intervention. The ethnic cleansing that accompanied the breakup of the former Yugoslavia and the wars in Croatia (1991–92), Bosnia (1992–96), and Kosovo (1999) led to the emergence of "humanitarian intervention'' as a new criterion of just cause. According to this norm, the international community or, as a last resort, any nation with the capacity has ''the right and the duty'' to intervene militarily where, in the words of Pope John Paul II, ''the survival of populations and entire ethnic groups are seriously compromised.'' Though humanitarian intervention entailed overriding the established international legal principles of national sovereignty and nonintervention, in a short time Pope John Paul II's declaration that ''states no longer have a 'right to indifference''' prevailed. Humanitarian intervention became in practice a recognized, though not unquestioned, just cause.

Competent Authority. According to Catholic teaching, war must be declared by public authorities charged with maintaining the peace, not by private groups or individuals. Establishing competent authority is a complicated issue in the modern world. The simplest case, that of defense against aggression, places the burden squarely on the shoulders of national governments.

United Nations. The United Nations Charter, however, also makes aggression a matter for U.N. action. When there is aggression, and especially where an outside response to a regional or internal conflict is demanded, the United Nations Security Council stands *de jure* as the constituted authority. As a matter of practice, the council has devised or acquiesced to a variety of ad hoc arrangements to undertake necessary military action. When the council is immobilized by divisions among its members, the question of competent authority is made more difficult. In general, official Catholic pronouncements tend to emphasize multilateral responses and discourage unilateral actions. In the case of humanitarian intervention, however, failure to act, or delay on the part of the international community to act, has led to pleas for any national political authority or alliance with the capacity to intervene.

Guerrilla/Civil War. Customarily, the criterion of competent authority stood as a barrier to guerrilla and civil war. Following World War II, wars of national liberation and guerrilla wars, particularly in Latin America, opened new questions about the applicability of the norm. In the 13th century, Thomas Aquinas had provided for the overthrow of predatory regimes by granting that rebellion was permissible if the people rose up ''as one.'' While a unified popular uprising might have been feasible in the city-states of northern Italy, it is much less so in the larger nation-state of today, and it is no remedy for repressed minorities. Contemporary international practice has provided revolutionary movements with a step toward legitimacy by permitting the International Committee of the Red Cross to establish relations with rebel movements when rebels are in control of a defined territory.

Pope Paul VI in his encyclical letter, *POPULORUM PROGRESSIO*, admitted, ''There are certainly situations whose injustices cry to heaven.'' He continued, ''We know, however, that a revolutionary uprising—save where there is manifest, long-standing tyranny which do great damage to fundamental personal rights and dangerous harm to the common good of the country—produces new injustices, throws more elements out of balance and brings on new disasters.'' The proviso about ''manifest, long-standing tyranny'' tends to allow revolution. On the whole, however, the burden of Pope Paul's teaching was reformist and opposed to revolution. His prudential judgement was that ''a real evil should not be fought against at the price of greater misery.'' After the first wave of national wars of independence following World War II, popular revolutionary movements in many countries led either to decades of conflict and failed government, as in Angola, Colombia and Afghanistan, or to meager improvements for the oppressed, as in El Salvador and Guatemala. On the whole, however, as the U.S. bishops observed in *The Challenge of Peace*, ''Insufficient analytical attention has been given to the moral issues of revolutionary warfare.''

Right Intention. Right intention is the last of three criteria (along with just cause and proper authority) that St. Augustine stipulated as conditions for a just war. For Augustine, as for later generations, right intention consisted in aiming at the restoration of peace, correcting the injustice that constituted a breach of the peace, and, in some circumstances, punishing the offender. The aim of the war, therefore, must be narrowly construed. Accordingly, right intention excludes the taking of territory and wreaking vengeance as war aims. It likewise requires reestablishing peaceful relations when the armed conflict is ended. Right intention also governs *in bello* acts, prohibiting ''unnecessarily destructive acts'' and individually criminal acts such as random killings, massacre, rape, and pillage.

Some contemporary ethicists put special emphasis on these first three criteria (just cause, competent authority, and right intention) on the grounds that they are (1) deontological, that is, exceptionless moral principles, and (2) they are legitimating, that is, they undergird the exercise of the state's war powers. While compared with principles that came into use in later periods, such as last resort, success, and proportionality, these three principles appear to require less calculation; they nonetheless require sophisticated and evolving judgements. In the last century even the understanding of as evident a matter as just cause has shifted markedly, thereby impairing the notion of self-evident morality attached to a deontological ethic. Similarly, if right intention includes avoiding indiscriminately destructive acts, judgments based on calculations of more or less will be necessary obviating the distinction between the allegedly deonotological and the calculative (or proportional) judgments. As to the legitimating function of just-war reasoning, the legitimation is conditional. Even established authority needs a just cause, must resort to force out of necessity, and must refrain from indiscriminate killing and destruction. Distinguishing between the legitimating and limiting functions of the just-war system, therefore, brings only a dubious clarity.

Last Resort. Last resort corresponds to the traditional Augustinian idea of "necessity," that is, that the decision to go to war is forced on political authorities when all peaceful alternatives have been tried. In the 19th and early 20th centuries, this criterion fit easily with the diplomatic practice of exchanging memorandums, issuing ultimatums, and making declarations of war. It has been more difficult to apply in the modern period, since the collapse of the Soviet Union (1991) and the rise of the United States as the world's single remaining superpower.

Some Vatican criticism over the Persian Gulf War arose out of the sense that negotiation was not seriously attempted and that economic sanctions, rather than being seriously employed as an alternative to war, were utilized instead as a prelude to and later as an extension of war, causing enormous harm to the Iraqi people. Both the Holy See and the U.S. Catholic bishops were critics of economic sanctions as illegitimate forms of coercive diplomacy violating the principle of civilian immunity.

Probability of Success. Political and military leaders must make an assessment of whether a war is winnable or not. Probability of success stands guard both against irrational resort to force, whether risking wreaking havoc on one's own country or employing disproportionate measures to achieve victory over the enemy, and against futile resistance in an unwinnable cause. *The Challenge of Peace*, however, adds that at times part of the calculation may be that "defense of key values, even against great odds, may be a 'proportionate' witness."

Proportionality. Probability of success and proportionality are closely related. In *ad bellum* terms, proportionality means that the damage to be inflicted and the costs incurred by armed conflict must be weighed in relation to the good to be gained (or re-established) by resorting to force. *The Challenge of Peace* set a high standard for proportionality, in the context of nuclear war, that in today's interdependent world, "a nation cannot justly go to war . . . without considering the effect of its action on the international community."

Proportionality is not static. It may change throughout the conduct of a war, so that a war may be judged *in medias res* as disproportionate and so unjustifiable. Such was the case with the U.S. bishops' judgment in 1971 that the U.S. involvement in Vietnam could no longer be sustained because of the destruction done to Vietnam and the moral and political divisions that the war had stimulated in the United States.

Ius in bello. The *ius in bello* or war-conduct criteria are two: noncombatant immunity and proportionality. Both are connected to a third term, "discrimination," which means military action must aim narrowly at attaining specific military objectives, excluding direct attack on civilians and other noncombatants and limiting collateral damage to persons and property.

Noncombatant Immunity. In the Catholic tradition, noncombatant immunity rests on a pervasive overall respect for life, the Decalogue's prohibition against killing, and the New Testament's call to love of enemies. A state of war permits the application of force only against those actively threatening the innocent (literally 'the unarmed' or 'nonthreatening'). While civilians, including enemy civilians, make up the bulk of the innocent, the category also includes others who are unarmed and nonthreatening, e.g., prisoners, the wounded, and medical personnel.

Noncombatant immunity has become, perhaps, the most prominent criterion in the application of just-war analysis in the last 50 years. Historically, concerns were aroused in the 1950s and 1960s by the strategic doctrine of mutually assured destruction in which the Soviet Union and the United States and its allies held one another's populations hostage to reciprocal nuclear terror. Beginning with the Vietnam War, however, concerns were also stirred about the rising number of civilian casualties in conventional conflicts. During World War II, civilian casualties amounted to 45 percent of casualties. By the time of Vietnam, they counted for 65 percent of the total. By the 1990s, they constituted more than 90 percent.

Much of the increase in noncombatant, civilian casualties was due to the rise in guerrilla warfare, civil wars, terrorism and counter-terrorism, and ethnic cleansing. A significant portion, however, was also attributable to shifts in the war-fighting styles of developed countries' militaries, especially that of the United States. The growing lethality of conventional weapons, strategies like air dominance and the use of overwhelming and decisive force, as well as the practice of force protection (giving primacy to guarding the safety of one's own troops), contributed to this trend in civilian vulnerability. For example, during the U.S.'s short incursion into Panama in 1990 (a small and conventional military action), unofficial estimates of the ratio of civilian to military casualties ranged from ten to one to 100 to one. The proposed strategy of using air-power "to break civilian will" is a serious violation of the norm of civilian immunity.

In light of the alarming rise in civilian casualties, the U.S. bishops in their 1993 pastoral statement, *The Harvest of Justice*, added to the usual injunction that "civilians may not be the object of direct attack" the further requirement that "military personnel must take due care to avoid and minimize indirect harm to civilians."

Such restraints on military action are regarded by some critics as placing excessive limits on military policymaking. It is alleged that the restrictive application and refinement of just-war norms amounts to just-war pacifism. Rather, it must be said that there are more or less stringent schools of just-war thinking, and official Catholic thinking tends to the stringent side. It is committed to the idea that just-war thinking, especially as compatible with Christian premises, is intended not only to 'enable' or permit war in a just cause but also to limit the harm done by the recourse to force.

In the Christian understanding, a just war is undertaken in defense of the innocent. On such a premise, the deliberate killing of innocents to defend other innocents is not justifiable. Some secular just-war theorists, proceeding from premises of state interest, may be less anxious about the killing of innocents in war-time than church officials and moral theologians. In any case, arguments defending collateral killing on grounds of "double effect" have grown infrequent and the exhortation to honor noncombatant, especially civilian, immunity has grown in recent years along with public criticism of the military for violations of the norm. Some military authorities argue that the use of so-called "smart weapons" will contribute to a future decline in civilian casualties.

Proportionality. The *in bello* criteria attempt to restrain the violence of a war in progress. Customarily, proportionality was determined in relation to the military notion of "necessity." The norm dictated that no more force be used than "necessary" to attain a military objective. It also excluded excessive destruction. The most notable controversy concerning proportionality in a recent conflict related to the bombing of the Iraqi infrastructure (electricity and water supply) during the Persian Gulf War. Critics charged that the bombing severely undercut the bases of civilian life. Defenders contended that the infrastructure was "dual use," supplying both military and civilian purposes, and for that reason a legitimate military target. A problematic effect of the destruction of the infrastructure was that the burden of the economic sanctions against Iraq was increased, so that there was increased civilian suffering after hostilities had ended.

Applying Just-War Norms. While some elements of the just-war analysis, especially proportionality and prospect of success, require a greater degree of prudential judgment and even calculation, the just-war norms provide neither a mere checklist nor some sort of moral calculus for assessing the morality of the use of force. The *ad bellum* norms, in particular, ought to be taken as a whole, but without necessarily giving equal weight to every norm.

While much just-war analysis is done in an academic context or in policy oriented settings, moral judgment based on the just-war tradition requires that the reasoning be informed by a life of virtue. "Moral reflection on the use of force calls for a spirit of moderation rare in contemporary political culture," wrote the U.S. bishops in 1993. "The increasing violence in our society, its growing insensitivity to the sacredness of life, and the glorification of the technology of destruction in popular culture," they concluded, "could inevitably impair our society's ability to apply just-war criteria honestly and effectively in time of crisis."

Contemporary Developments

Vatican II. The Second Vatican Council marked the beginning of a significant shift in official Catholic teaching on issues of war and peace. The council, in its own words, felt compelled to undertake "an evaluation of war with an entirely new attitude." Drawing on the experience of World War II, the Holocaust and the Cold War, the council's Pastoral Constitution on the Church in the Modern World, *Gaudium et spes*, censured the notion of "total war," understood as counter-population warfare. "Any act of war aimed indiscriminately at the destruction of entire cities or of extensive areas along with their population is a crime against God and man himself. It merits unequivocal and unhesitating condemnation."

Behind the condemnation lay the Nazi blitz against London, the Allied firebombing of Hamburg and Dresden, the firebombing of Tokyo, and the atomic bombing of Hiroshima and Nagasaki. Already in a landmark 1944 article in *Theological Studies*, John Ford, S.J., had documented the Allied practice of "obliteration bombing" and the numerous condemnations made by church officials of the Allied air strategy. In addition, the council fathers had in mind the strategic nuclear balance between the United States and the Soviet Union built on the threat of "mutually assured destruction." The council noted that the occasion for perpetrating abominable acts is provided by "the possession of modern scientific weapons" and by a kind of technological reasoning which "urge men on to the most atrocious decisions."

The council, likewise, condemned genocide, described as "acts designed for the methodical extermination of an entire people, nation, or ethnic minority." Such actions "must be vehemently condemned as horrendous crimes." To build a barrier against such war-borne atrocities the council appeals to "the permanent binding force of universal natural law and its all-embracing principles." Linking these principles to the call of conscience, the council described as criminal orders that contravene the moral law, denounced the notion of "blind obedience" to immoral orders, and offered "supreme commendation" to those who resisted such orders.

In keeping with this stress on conscience, the council also advised that legal provision be made for conscientious objection. This last recommendation marked a break with the pastoral practice that had existed through the Second World War under which Catholics were denied Church support for conscientious refusal to bear arms.

Even more remarkable, again in keeping with the council's reliance on personal conscience, was its praise for the practitioners of nonviolence. "We cannot fail to praise those who renounce the use of violence in the vindication of their rights and who resort to methods of defense which are otherwise available to weaker parties too, provided that can be done without injury to the rights and duties of others or of the community itself." This endorsement of "nonviolent direct action" marked another departure in modern Catholic social teaching. The passage established a common norm for both nonviolent action and the state's justified resort to arms, namely, the vindication of rights. The praise of nonviolence begins to disclose an underlying premise of contemporary Catholic teaching about public order, namely, whether by nonviolent means or by the justified and legitimate use of force, Catholics are obligated to resist grave offenses against human rights and other serious public evils. The council's reliance on conscience as a bulwark against the evils of war, therefore, entailed not only notions of opposition to immoral orders and legal allowance for conscientious objection, but also revealed an underlying obligation of resistance to grievous public injustices shared by nonviolent activists and just warriors alike. As the United States bishops wrote in 1983, "The Christian has no choice but to defend peace against aggression. This is an inalienable obligation. It is the *how* of defending peace which offers moral options."

At the same time as it attempted to mitigate the evils of modern war and provide moral space for objectors and resisters, the council continued to recognize the need for states to provide for the legitimate defense of their people. With a note of realism the council fathers wrote, "As long as the danger of war remains, and there is no competent and sufficiently powerful authority at the international level, governments cannot be denied the right to legitimate defense once every means of peaceful settlement has been exhausted." Thus, the Church continued to recognize the right and the duty of governments to protect their people under the evolving canons of the just war.

Three observations are in order concerning the conciliar warrant of the state's war powers. First, it is conditioned on the lack of adequate international authority. Modern Catholic teaching (PACEM IN TERRIS, *Gaudium et spes*, CENTESIMUS ANNUS) has been strong in its support for the establishment of transnational authorities for the avoidance of war and the advancement of the universal common good. Critical of all forms of totalitarianism, the Church has nonetheless regarded the creation of international authority as a key factor in helping reduce the occasions for war.

Second, recourse to force is also conditioned by the exhaustion of all peaceful alternatives. Particularly during the pontificate of Pope John Paul II, and most notably during the Persian Gulf War, failure to pursue alternative means or half-hearted employment of them was a repeated theme of papal interventions and commentary on diplomacy.

Third, the council's warrant for a governments' use of force is made in a cautionary mode. After warning against military action for the subjugation of other nations, the council remarks, "Nor does the possession of war potential make every military or political use of it lawful. Neither does the mere fact that war has unhappily begun, mean that all is fair between the warring parties." In the late 20th century, Catholic teaching on war had grown cautious, even skeptical, of the moral use of force as a tool of politics.

Having given renewed, though conditional, sanction for just war, the council went on to offer words of encouragement for the military. "Those who are pledged to the service of their own country as members of its armed forces should regard themselves as agents of security and freedom on the behalf of their people. As long as they fulfill this role properly, they are making a genuine contribution to the establishment of peace." Thus, the council continued to affirm that military personnel possess a legitimate place in the life of the Christian community. That traditional position is informed, however, by renewed appreciation of the moral principles pertaining to warfare, by support for the exercise of conscience, and even encouragement for the right to resist immoral orders.

Rejection of Nuclear War. *Gaudium et spes* was drafted in the shadow of the Cuban Missile Crisis (1962). The threat of a nuclear holocaust had inspired Pope John XXIII to issue his last encyclical letter, *Pacem in terris* (1963), which laid out a positive vision of peace built on the promotion and defense of human rights. Pope John called for an end to the arms race, cuts in arms stockpiles, the banning of nuclear weapons, and disarmament. "[I]n an age such as ours," the pope wrote, "which prides itself on atomic energy, it is contrary to reason to hold that war is now a suitable way to restore rights which have been violated."

For its part, the council contemplated a scenario in which the strategic doctrine of mutually assured destruction would be played out to its catastrophic end and concluded that "an almost total and altogether reciprocal slaughter of each side by the other would follow." Acts of war, it argued, "inflicting such massive and indiscriminate destruction [would far exceed] the limits of legitimate defense." Accordingly, the council condemned the nuclear arms race and lent its support to efforts for disarmament and the avoidance of war, pending the establishment of some "universal public authority" that would make the banning of war feasible.

In 1983 the U.S. bishops' pastoral letter, *The Challenge of Peace*, condemned nuclear warfare and offered a morally conditioned acceptance of nuclear deterrence. In the years since World War II, especially in the ethical debates over nuclear strategy in the 1960s and 1970s, the *in bello* just-war norm of noncombatant immunity had become a near-absolute moral principle. Arguments made to allow collateral damage in conventional warfare on grounds of DOUBLE EFFECT were simply inapplicable in the case of the prevailing policies for nuclear-war fighting. The collateral effects of nuclear blasts were too extensive and too damaging. The prevailing doctrine of deterrence, namely, mutually assured destruction, moreover, took direct aim at the adversary's major population centers in contravention of the Second Vatican Council's condemnation of acts of "total war." The bishops' condemnation extended to "the retaliatory use of weapons striking enemy cities after our own have been struck."

The bishops also laid down the same moral strictures, though in somewhat muted language, against the initiation of nuclear conflict. "We do not perceive any situation," they wrote, admitting a small margin of uncertainty, "in which the deliberate initiation of nuclear warfare, on however a restricted scale, can be morally justified. Non-nuclear attacks by another state must be resisted by other than nuclear means." Thus, they ruled out the use of so-called theater nuclear weapons, then contemplated as a response to a massive Soviet conventional invasion, and possible nuclear (preventative or retaliatory) attacks against chemical or biological attacks by so-called rogue states. A principal reason for this opposition to first use was the bishops' "extreme skepticism about the prospects for controlling a nuclear exchange, however limited the first strike might be." Arguing that policymakers should be wary of "crossing boundary from the conventional to the nuclear arena in any form," they urged political leaders to "resist the notion that nuclear conflict can be limited, contained, or won in any traditional sense."

The bishops also took up the morally perplexing issue of nuclear deterrence. On the one hand, deterrence sustained the danger of nuclear war and contributed enormously to the arms race. On the other hand, the nuclear shield guarded "the independence and freedom of nations and entire peoples." It assured "a peace of a sort," but at risk of enormous miscalculation. Accordingly, following a proposal of Pope John Paul II, the bishops argued for a morally conditioned acceptance of deterrence "as a step on the way to progressive disarmament."

Holding to this baseline, the bishops offered three criteria for evaluation of deterrence policy: (1) prevention, (2) sufficiency, and (3) disarmament.

Deterrence. A deterrent force exists solely for the purposes of preventing the use of nuclear weapons by others. Accordingly, planning for prolonged periods of repeated nuclear strikes and counterstrikes or 'prevailing' in nuclear war are unacceptable.

Sufficiency. Concerning the size and quality of a deterrent, 'sufficiency' to deter an enemy attack is an adequate policy. Calls for nuclear superiority must be rejected.

Disarmament. Deterrence is permitted only as a step toward further disarmament. For that reason, every change in the nuclear arsenal must be assessed in terms of "whether it will render further steps toward 'progressive disarmament' more or less likely." The bishops summarized their position with a single word: "we must continually say 'no' to the idea of nuclear war."

In 1993, looking at the nuclear issue following the dissolution of the Soviet Union and the end of the Cold War, the bishops proposed that abolition of nuclear weapons should be the deliberate aim of public policy.

A New Look at Nonviolence. Vatican II praised nonviolent activists and legitimated CONSCIENTIOUS OBJECTION. In *The Challenge of Peace*, the U.S. bishops placed nonviolence in the broad sweep of the Catholic social teaching. The bishops regarded "the just-war teaching and nonviolence as distinct but interrelated methods of evaluating warfare. While the two positions may diverge on specific conclusions, they share a common presumption against the use of force as a means of settling disputes.'' *The Challenge of Peace* endorsed the development of nonviolent means of defending against aggression and for promoting conflict resolution. On the whole, however, it treated nonviolence as a religious matter of personal vocation. The bishops recognized that modern weapons made nonviolence (and PACIFISM) urgently necessary, but at the same time they did not regard nonviolence as adequate to guide public policy in an age when power remained divided among contending states. In the public realm, the state ethic for the moral limitation of conflict remained the just-war tradition.

Events, however, were moving ahead. In 1986, a nonviolent, ''people-power'' revolution overthrew the longstanding Marcos dictatorship in the Philippines. In 1989, one after another, the Communist governments of the eastern European Soviet satellite states fell, mostly nonviolently. The one exception was Rumania, where the Ceaucescu regime fought a short-lived resistance and the victors took vengeance on their former rulers. Above all, in 1991, the Soviet Union itself dissolved. Pope John Paul II had been an active participant in the broader transformation in eastern Europe, first as a mentor to the Polish Solidarity labor movement, later as an international mediator fostering a nonviolent transition throughout the region. In three-way communication with Soviet president Mikhail Gorbachev and Polish president Wojciech Jaruzelski, the Polish-born pontiff argued successfully against the introduction of Soviet troops to suppress the uprisings as they had in 1956 and 1968.

In 1991, John Paul commented on the collapse of the Communist states in his encyclical, *Centesimus annus*, laying the success of the revolts to nonviolence. Pope John Paul attributed the victory to ''the Gospel spirit'' and a repudiation of the sort of ''political realism'' which '''wishes' to banish law and morality from the public arena.'' The European order established by the Yalta Agreements was, he wrote, ''overcome by the nonviolent commitment of people who, while always refusing to yield to the force of power, succeeded time after time in finding effective ways of bearing witness to the truth.'' According to the Holy Father, the nonviolent activists had a moral clarity not possessed by those who trust in force, because ''by joining their sufferings for the sake of truth and freedom to the sufferings of Christ on the Cross,'' they were ''in a position to discern the often narrow path between the cowardice which gives in to evil and the violence which, under the illusion of fighting evil, only makes it worse.'' Accordingly, he prayed that others would follow their example ''[fighting] for justice without violence, renouncing class struggle in their internal disputes, and war in international ones.''

In 1993, writing on the tenth anniversary of *The Challenge of Peace*, the United States bishops, taking their cue from Pope John Paul II, asked ''in light of recent history, whether nonviolence should be restricted to personal commitments or whether it should have a place in the public order with the tradition of justified and limited force.'' Their pastoral statement, *The Harvest of Justice Is Sown in Peace*, laid on national leaders the obligation to consider seriously nonviolent alternatives for dealing with conflicts, and urged exploration and improvement of new styles of preventative diplomacy and conflict resolution. While these obligations to nonviolence ''do not detract from the state's right and duty to defend against aggression,'' they wrote, ''they do raise the threshold for the recourse to force.'' In just-war terms, the obligation of the state to develop and employ nonviolent alternatives to the resolution of conflict should move back the point at which a government or nation reaches the condition of ''last resort.'' *The Harvest of Justice*, like *The Challenge of Peace*, acknowledged legitimate diversity among Catholics concerning the place of nonviolence and just war in relation to the conduct of war and their place in the Christian life. Each document also distinguished between Church teaching on matters of principle and the prudential applications of those principles by governments, opinion leaders, and the public.

In keeping with the teaching of the Second Vatican Council and his predecessors, John XXIII and Paul VI, Pope John Paul II has called for ''a concerted worldwide effort to promote development'' as a positive contribution to peace and a remedy for the causes of war. The duty to promote development for the poor is as grave an obligation, in his teaching, as the duty to avoid war. ''Another name for peace,'' he wrote in *Centesimus annus*, ''is development.'' This is not a plea for 'charity' in the pejorative sense of indiscriminate aid. Rather, development is intended to provide the poor with opportunities ''to improve their condition through work or to make a positive contribution to economic prosperity.'' A second theme of recent papal teaching has been the importance of international law. The international legal order is seen as providing a framework for the prevention of conflict through establishment of more equitable relations between peoples and nations, establishing procedures for nonviolent resolution of conflict, and creating structures and practices capable of promoting the universal common good. A third contribution of Pope John Paul II has been, by teaching and personal witness, to hold up the importance of forgiveness in the resolution of conflict. His numerous statements of apology for offenses committed in the name of the Church culminated during the Great

Jubilee with the Day of Pardon, his visits to Yad Vashem and the Wailing Wall (2000), and his embrace of Greek Orthodox Archbishop Christodoulos (2001). In his "World Day of Peace Message" for 2002 ("No Peace without Justice, No Justice without Forgiveness"), the pontiff applied his teaching on forgiveness to the international order. Writing explicitly in the context of the U.S.-led war against terrorism, he wrote, "Families, groups, societies, states and the international community itself need forgiveness in order to renew ties that have been sundered, go beyond sterile situations of mutual condemnation and overcome the temptation to discriminate against others without appeal. The ability to forgive," he concluded, "lies at the very basis of a future society marked by justice and solidarity."

Bibliography: E. ABRAMS, ed., *Close Calls: Intervention, Terrorism, Missile Defense, and 'Just War' Today* (Washington, DC 1998). D. CHRISTIANSEN, "Afterword: A Roman Catholic Response," in J. H. YODER, *When War Is Unjust: Being Honest in Just-War Thinking*, rev. ed. (Maryknoll, NY 1996) 102–117; "Peacemaking and the Use of Force: Behind the Pope's Stringent Just War Teaching," *America* 180:17 (May 17, 1999) 13–18. R. DOUGHERTY, ed., *The Just War: The Relevance of Just War Theory in the Modern Age*, forthcoming. J. FINNIS, J. BOYLE, JR., and G. GRISEZ, *Nuclear Deterrence, Morality and Realism* (Oxford 1987). J. B. EL-SHTAIN, et al., *But Is It Just?: Reflections on the Morality of the Persian Gulf War*, with an appendix from *Civilta Catolica*, tr. P. HEINEGG, ed. D. DE COSSE (New York 1992). D. HOLLENBACH, *Nuclear Ethics: A Christian Moral Argument* (Maryknoll, NY 1983). P. J. MURNION, ed., *Catholics and Nuclear War: A Commentary on "The Challenge of Peace,"* foreword by T. M. HESBURGH (New York 1983). R. MUSTO, *The Catholic Peace Tradition* (Maryknoll, NY 1988). W. V. O'BRIEN and J. LANGAN, eds., *The Nuclear Dilemma and the Just War Tradition* (Lexington, MA 1986). G. POWERS, et al., eds., *Peacemaking: Moral and Policy Challenges for a New World* (Washington, DC 1984). T. A. SHANNON, ed., *War or Peace? The Search for New Answers* (Maryknoll, NY 1980).

[R. A. MCCORMICK/D. CHRISTIANSEN]

WARD, BARBARA (JACKSON)

British political economist, writer, lecturer; b. York, England, May 23, 1914; d. Lodsworth, England, May 31, 1981. The daughter of lawyer Walter Ward, a Quaker, and Teresa Mary Burge, a Roman Catholic, she attended Jesus and Mary Convent School, Felixstowe, Suffolk, the Lycée Molière and the Sorbonne in Paris, and returned after a year's study in Germany to Somerville College, Oxford, where she received a B.A. in 1935 with first class honors in "Modern Greats." She began her lecturing career at Cambridge University, England, in the University extension program (1936–39).

In 1939, Ward became a writer for the London *Economist*, and during and after World War II (1940–50), was foreign affairs editor, acting as contributing editor after 1950. Other wartime activities included work for the British Broadcasting Corporation's *Brains Trust*, a discussion program, and membership in the Sword of the Spirit, a Catholic social action movement. She was also a council member of the Royal Institute of International Affairs (1943–44), and governor of both Sadlers Wells Old Vic Trust (1944–53) and the BBC (1946–50).

In 1950 she married Australian-born Robert Gillman Allen Jackson (later Sir Robert Jackson), an international development expert who worked in Ghana and Asia and was Assistant Secretary General of the United Nations. They would later have a son, Robert. During the next two decades her husband's work took the couple to Australia, West Africa, and Asia, and Ward (the name she used professionally) continued her interest in international affairs, particularly in the developing third world nations. During this period, she lectured widely in Canada, England, and the United States. From 1959 to 1968, she spent her winters as a Carnegie Fellow at Harvard University where she lectured and held seminars on economic development.

During the 1960s she was to influence or be influenced by some of the most powerful personalities of the times. She became an advisor on international economics to United Nations Secretary General U Thant. She knew John F. Kennedy as both senator and president. Walt Rostow said that "of those outside government . . . only Jean Monnet ranked in the same class as Barbara among those whose advice Kennedy was pleased to receive" (*The Economist,* June 6, 1981). According to *Time* (Sept. 3, 1965), Ward was an "influential if unofficial advisor" to the Lyndon Johnson administration. Two days before he left office in 1969, Johnson sent a note to Ward in which he said, "You have given me much more than your priceless friendship. You have brought wisdom and inspiration . . ." (*Economist,* June 6, 1981). Ward was also a friend of Adlai Stevenson, Robert McNamara, and John Kenneth Galbraith.

In the same decade, Ward was impressed with the interest of Popes John XXIII and Paul VI in problems of world poverty and in 1967 she was named to the first Pontifical Commission for Studies of Justice and Peace, and took an active part in the World Congress of Roman Catholic Laity in October. Named Albert Schweitzer Professor of International Economic Development at Columbia University in December 1967, she held the professorship until her resignation in 1973. From 1973 to 1980, she was president of the International Institute for Environment and Development in London and continued to attend many conferences worldwide on those topics. In 1976, when Harold Wilson retired as prime minister, Ward, a lifelong Labour Party member, was on his list to be conferred a life peerage with the title Baroness Jackson of Lodsworth by Queen Elizabeth II.

Writings. Her writing has been variously described as "prolific," "simplistic," "persuasive although not original," and she has been called a generalist, an optimist, and, by Paul Lewis, "a synthesizer and propagandist." In *Nationalism and Ideology* (1966), she summarized what she considered to be "our needs—for political cooperation (rather than nationalism), for economic generosity, for faith in man," and those words were generally the topics for her facile pen beginning with her first book, *The International Share–Out* (1938) on colonial problems, and continuing with *The West at Bay* (1948), *Policy for the West* (1951), *Faith and Freedom* (1954), *Interplay of East and West: Points of Conflict and Cooperation* (1957), and *Five Ideas that Changed the World* (1959), with a foreword by Kwame Nkrumah, prime minister of Ghana. The five ideas she singled out were nationalism, industrialism, colonialism, communism, and internationalism. She continued her earlier theme that the industrialized Western countries must help the newly developed countries in *The Rich Nations and the Poor Nations* (1962), *Spaceship Earth* (1966), and *The Lopsided World* (1968).

Many of her books were the result of lectures given at McGill University in Montreal, the Canadian Broadcasting Corporation, Carleton University in Ottawa, Johns Hopkins University, and the University of Ghana. She won three Christopher Literary Awards and was awarded numerous honorary degrees. Other awards she received included the Order of the British Empire (1974) and the Jawarharlal Nehru Memorial Award for International Understanding (1980).

Bibliography: *Contemporary Authors*, New Revision Series, v. 6 (1982). *Current Biography* (1977). *The New York Times Biographical Service* (June 1981).

[M. H. MAHONEY]

WARD, BERNARD

Bishop, ecclesiastical historian; b. Ware, Hertfordshire, England, Feb. 4, 1857; d. Brentwood, Jan. 21, 1920. His father, William George WARD, was closely associated with the OXFORD MOVEMENT. After studying at St. Edmund's College in Ware, where his father lectured on theology, and at Oscott, Ward was ordained in 1882. Returning to St. Edmund's, he acted as prefect (1882–85), vice president (1890–92), and president (1892–1916). As president he set out to revive its fortunes; he extended accommodations, doubled the enrollment, and reorganized the program of studies. After

resigning to become missionary rector at Brook Green, he was soon appointed administrator apostolic of the new Diocese of Brentwood, and consecrated as its first bishop (Apr. 10, 1917). He saw the Catholic population of his diocese increase from 26,000 to 40,000 and the number of priests from 78 to 90, by 1920.

After publishing the *History of St. Edmund's College* (1893), Ward took the suggestion offered by the bishop of Clifton and began research on the history of British Catholicism during its most neglected period. His resultant seven–volume masterpiece, *The Dawn of the Catholic Revival in England 1781–1803* (2 v. 1909), *The Eve of Catholic Emancipation, 1803–1829* (3 v. 1911–12), and *The Sequel to Catholic Emancipation, 1830–1850* (2 v. 1915), has become the standard authority, notable for its wealth of information, literary skill, and balanced judgment. Ward wrote also *Catholic London A Century Ago* (1905) and *The Priestly Vocation* (1913), a contribution to the Westminster Library for Priests and Students, of which he was the joint editor.

Bibliography: *Tablet* (London) 135 (1920) 117–120. M. WARD, *The Wilfrid Wards and the Transition,* 2 v. (New York 1934–37).

[D. MILBURN]

WARD, CORNELIUS

Irish Franciscan missionary; b. Ulster, date unknown; d. probably at the Franciscan friary of Donegal, 1641. Of Ward's early life nothing is known with certainty. It is likely that he studied for the priesthood at Salamanca, Spain. He was at St. Anthony's College, Louvain, in 1623, and toward the end of that year was chosen with three other members of the community for the mission to the Western Highlands and Isles of Scotland, where the Irish Franciscans had arrived a few years earlier. He made many hundreds of converts and brought thousands back to the faith. On two occasions (1626, 1629) he visited the nuncio at Brussels to promote the interests of the mission. While passing through London from Belgium toward the end of 1629, he was arrested, tortured and then imprisoned for two years. On obtaining his freedom through the intervention of the Polish ambassador, Ward traveled to Danzig and eventually reached Rome, where he pleaded the cause of the mission. In November 1635 he returned to Scotland, and he labored there till August 1637. In September 1640, because of ill health, he retired permanently from the mission. Besides conducting his mission work in the Irish language, Ward wrote some poetry in that tongue.

Bibliography: C. GIBLIN, ed., *Irish Franciscan Mission to Scotland, 1619–1646* (Dublin 1964), *passim.* L. WADDING, *Scrip-*

tores Ordinis Minorum 26 (1623–27) 122, 449–450, 545; 27 (1628–32) 65, 140, 259; 28 (1633–40) 173–174, 405, 529, 581. *Archivium Hibernicum* 12 (1946) 115–117, 118–119, 126–127, 148–149, 190–192, 193–195.

[C. GIBLIN]

WARD, HUGH

Irish Franciscan historian: b. Ulster, *c.* 1593; d. Louvain, Belgium, Nov. 8, 1635. Ward belonged to a family noted for its poets and chroniclers. The chief family residence was at Lettermac-Bhaird in County Donegal. Ward studied humanities for six years in Ireland under different masters. He then went abroad, and registered as a student at the university of Salamanca, Jan. 15, 1612. While there, he came under the influence of Luke WADDING, OFM, and joined the Franciscan Order at Salamanca in 1616.

Ward left for Paris in 1623, and on his way, as well as in Paris, he sought out manuscripts containing lives of Irish saints, a collection of which he intended to publish. In the same year Patrick FLEMING, OFM, who was also gathering Irish hagiographical material, met Ward in Paris. They decided to collaborate. In the autumn of 1623 Ward went to Louvain, visiting libraries at Rouen, Harfleur, and Nantes in search of manuscripts. He was made lector of theology at St. Anthony's College and on April 26, 1626, was chosen guardian. Through his influence Brother Michael O'Clery was sent to Ireland in 1626 to gather documents in the Irish language from the old books that had escaped destruction.

Ward planned the publication of the acts of the principal Irish saints in several volumes with appendices and notes; the remaining history of Ireland was to be prefixed to the whole work by way of prolegomena. He sent the plan of these prolegomena to Luke Wadding at Rome and sought his help in the undertaking. Among other works planned by Ward was a disquisition on the ancient names of Ireland, and an Hiberno-Latin martyrology. At the request of the archbishop of Malines he wrote a life of St. Rumold. In 1633 Ward acted as visitator of the Franciscan houses of the province of St. Andrew in Belgium. He died before any of his work appeared in print. His life of St. Rumold was published in 1662, and his work on the Irish saints whose feastdays fell in January, February, and March was the basis of John Colgan's *Acta Sanctorum,* which appeared in 1645.

Bibliography: B. JENNINGS, *Michael O'Cléirigh, Chief of the Four Masters, and His Associates* (Dublin 1936), *passim;* ed., *Wadding Papers, 1614–1638* (Dublin 1953) 189, 294, 299, 386–388, 414. F. O'BRIEN, "Irish Franciscan Historians of St. Anthony's College, Louvain: Father Hugh Ward," *The Irish Ecclesiastical Record* 32 (1928) 113–129. *Archivium Hibernicum* 2 (1913) 29.

[C. GIBLIN]

WARD, JUSTINE BAYARD CUTTING

Musician and educator; b. Aug. 7, 1879, Morristown, New Jersey; daughter of William Bayard and Olivia Murray Cutting; d. Nov. 27, 1975, Washington, D.C. After her conversion to Roman Catholicism in 1904, she devoted herself to the cause of church music, inspired by the motu proprio, *Tra le sollecitudini,* on sacred music of Pius X (1903), which called for a revival of interest in GREGORIAN CHANT and classic polyphony.

Ward was convinced that any reform in church music had to begin at the earliest stages of the child's education with proper training in music. In 1910 Dean Thomas E. Shields of Sisters' College, the Catholic University of America asked her to prepare a music curriculum for the parochial schools. With the collaboration of J. Young, SJ she published *Music First Year* of the Ward Method in 1916. That same year she introduced her method in the Annunication School, in New York, assisted by Mother G. Stevens, a religious of the Sacred Heart, and in 1917 she endowed a Pius X Chair of Liturgical Music at Manhattanville College. This later became known as the PIUS X SCHOOL OF LITURGICAL MUSIC. For many years, Ward taught at Sisters' College as well as at the Pius X School.

In 1920, Ward, secretary of the Auxiliary Committee for the Pontifical School of Sacred Music, Rome, joined forces with the St. Gregory Society of America to organize an International Congress of Gregorian Chant in New York. Dom André Mocquereau and Dom Augustin Gatard, Benedictine monks of the Solesmes Congregation, conducted the services at St. Patrick's Cathedral where hundreds of adults and children trained in the Ward Method sang the Gregorian chants. She was responsible, too, for the 1922 summer session at Manhattanville, where Dom Mocquereau taught the chant and Dom Hebert Desrocquettes, Gregorian accompaniment, both courses according to the principles of Solesmes.

The Ward Method spread quickly throughout the world. In particular, Ward reached a wide audience with her lectures on the chant illustrated with examples sung by the Pius X Choir, whose training she carefully supervised. In the early 1930s the partnership of Mother Stevens and Ward was dissolved, but both continued to work zealously for the reform of church music.

In 1929 Ward established the Dom Mocquereau *Schola Cantorum* Foundation for the teaching and the dissemination of Gregorian Chant and in 1930, she founded a *schola cantorum* at Catholic University. For her long service to church music Ward received many honors: decorations from the Italian and Dutch governments: the *Croce di Benemerenza*, Order of Malta: the Cross, *Pro Ecclesia et pontifice* from Pius XII; honorary degrees from the Pontifical School of Sacred Music and Catholic University. The liturgical reforms of Vatican II with the emphasis on the vernacular de-emphasized plainchant but Ward, until her death, continued to support Solesmes in its research and study of Gregorian chant.

Bibliography: J. B. WARD, "The Reform in Church Music," *Atlantic Monthly* 97 (1906) 455–463; "Music in the Parochial Schools," *Catholic Choirmaster* 2 (Apr. 1916) 6–8; "School Music in Its Relation to Church Music," *Catholic Choirmaster* 4 (Jan. 1918) 2–9; *Hymnal* (Washington, D.C. 1918 rev. ed. 1930); *Gregorian Chant*, v. 1 and 2, Catholic Education Series (Washington, D.C. 1923 and 1949); "Ex ore infantium," *Commonweal* 2 (1925) 450–451; *That All May Sing* (Washington, D.C. 1956, rev. ed. New York 1976).

[C. A. CARROLL]

WARD, MAISIE

Author, publisher; b. Shanklin, Isle of Wight, England, Jan. 4, 1889; d. New York City, Jan. 28, 1975. Maisie Ward was the daughter of Wilfrid WARD, and granddaughter of William George ("Ideal") WARD. Her mother was Josephine Mary Ward, the novelist, daughter of James Robert Hope-Scott of Abbotsford. Maisie's education was entrusted to governesses and later to the Mary Ward nuns at Cambridge until 1907. She grew up in a family with many eminent friends and visitors, among them Chesterton, Belloc, George Windham, and the Baron von Hügel. During World War I Ward served as a Red Cross nurse. After the war she became a charter member of the Catholic Evidence Guild; she and a scrubwoman were its first two women speakers. In 1926 she married Frank SHEED, a young Australian with whom she had worked at the Guild. Together they founded the publishing house, Sheed & Ward, and they were parents of two children, Wilfrid Sheed, the novelist and critic, and Rosemary Sheed Middleton, the columnist and translator.

Sheed & Ward brought a fresh and bracing spirit, considerable excitement, style, and wit to Catholic publishing, a hitherto rather heavy and unimaginative business. In the first number of their house organ, *The Trumpet*, was the notice: "In answer to many inquiries, we do not sell crucifixes, statues, rosary beads or medals; we sell books." Their goal was to lift the awareness of Catholic readers. They aimed, they said, "just above the middle of the brow," and introduced to readers not only new works in English, but such continental writers as

Claudel, Karl Adam, Henri Ghéon, François Mauriac and others, up to and including Hans Küng. By 1933 the firm had opened a branch in New York City and Ward and her husband "commuted" from London. In 1939 the couple moved to the U. S. and Frank Sheed "commuted" the other way. The London office was completely destroyed in the World War II bombings; Sheed, in London at the time, rented a new office the following day. In 1960 Christopher Dawson remarked that the foundation of Sheed & Ward marked "an epoch in the history of English Catholicism," and "had changed the whole climate." The venture continued into the early 1970s and was then sold. It had belonged to an era between the final conflicts and agonies of Modernism and Vatican Council II. During those years Sheed & Ward helped many Catholics keep their minds open and their hopes up.

Besides being a lecturer and publisher, Ward was the author of a number of books. Possibly the most important were *The Wilfrid Wards and the Transition* (1934) and *Insurrection and Resurrection* (1937). "Transition" in the first title refers to what her father, the eminent editor of the DUBLIN REVIEW, saw as the shift of the church from a 19th–century state of siege and its accompanying siege mentality to an opening to the world outside the church. "Insurrection" in the second title was the Modernist revolt, and "Resurrection," the survival and renewed life of the church after the crisis had passed. Both books are livened by the author's own recollections of many of the principals involved in that history. Other works of hers were a full biography, *Gilbert Keith Chesterton* (1943) and her own favorite, *Young Mr. Newman* (1948).

Ward was also actively interested in such humane projects as the Catholic Housing Aid Society, the Grail, and the Catholic Worker. She was a person of remarkable energy, intellectual vigor, wit, and humanity.

Bibliography: M. HOEHN, ed., *Catholic Authors: Contemporary Biographical Sketches: 1930–1947* (Newark, N.J. 1948). C. MORITZ, ed., *Current Biography Yearbook: 1966* (New York 1966). W. ROMIG, ed., *The Book of Catholic Authors* (4th Series) (Grosse Pointe, Mich. 1948). M. WARD, *Unfinished Business* (New York 1964); *To and Fro on the Earth* (New York 1974).

[E. D. CUFFE]

WARD, MARGARET, ST.

English martyr; b. Congleton, Cheshire, date unknown; d. Tyburn, Aug. 30, 1588. Nothing is known of her early life except that she was in the service of the Whittles, a Catholic family living in London at the time of her arrest. There is much divergence in the contemporary accounts of the episode that led up to it. It seems that after several visits to William Watson, confined in Bridewell prison, she succeeded in smuggling a rope into his cell. At 2:00 or 3:00 A.M., Margaret together with an Irish boatman, John Roche (alias Neale), waited in the street below, while the priest made his escape over the tiles of the roof. Misjudging the distance, Watson doubled the rope and was forced to jump before he was half way down. Though injured he was concealed by Roche and escaped. The rope, left dangling from a cornice of the roof, was traced to Margaret, who was arrested the following day. Robert SOUTHWELL wrote to the Jesuit General, Claudius ACQUAVIVA, "She was flogged and hung up by the wrists, the tips of her toes just touching the ground, for so long a time that she was crippled and paralyzed . . . ." She refused to reveal Watson's whereabouts when charged with assisting at his escape. She also refused the liberty offered to her if she would attend a Protestant service. On August 29 she was tried at the Old Bailey and executed the following day. With her suffered four Catholic laymen, including John Roche, and Richard Leigh, a secular priest. She was beatified by Pius XI on Dec. 15, 1929 and and canonized by Paul VI on Oct. 25, 1970 (*see* ENGLAND, SCOTLAND, AND WALES, MARTYRS OF).

Feast: Aug. 20.

Bibliography: L. E. WHATMORE, *Blessed Margaret Ward* (Postulation pamphlet; London 1961). A. BUTLER, *The Lives of the Saints*, rev. ed. H. THURSTON and D. ATTWATER (New York 1956) 3:437–438.

[G. FITZHERBERT]

WARD, MARY

Lay apostle, founder of the Institute of Mary; b. Mulwith, Yorkshire, Feb. 2, 1586 (N.S.; Jan. 23, 1585, O.S.); d. Hewarth, Yorkshire, Jan. 30, 1646 (N.S.; Jan. 20, 1645, O.S.). Ward's parents, Marmaduke and Ursula Wright Ward, were from wealthy, established, Catholic families. Ward's girlhood was placid in spite of the penal laws and reverberations of the ARCHPRIEST CONTROVERSY, a quarrel between the secular clergy and the Jesuits, which plagued her life's work.

In 1606, on the advice of Jesuits at St. Omer, Ward entered a Belgian convent of Poor Clares. A difficult year as a lay sister terminated in Ward's founding and entering at Gravelines a new Poor Clare convent for Englishwomen. Ward's conviction of a still different vocation compelled her to return to England in 1609. Her practicality, zeal, and charm made her a remarkable lay apostle.

At St. Omer again, Ward and a few companions opened a free school for English girls. The Institute started with a modified Poor Clare rule, but Ward soon chose to adopt the rules of the Society of Jesus. She wanted a group of uncloistered nuns without any distinctive habit, bound together by their vows and their rule, and under a superior general with authority to transfer the sisters. Ward's ideas were regarded as dangerously novel, and their Ignatian spirit aroused the anti-Jesuits. Nevertheless, Ward secured approbation of Bp. James Blaise of St. Omer in 1612, and within three years opened an affiliation in England. She sent to Paul V in 1616 the "Scheme of the Institute," which was favorably received but not formally approved. Optimistically, the community opened new houses in Germany and Italy. Growth brought more attacks. Ward pleaded her cause before an unrelenting Particular Congregation of Cardinals; but five months later, on Sept. 30, 1629, the Congregation of the Propaganda suppressed the "Jesuitesses." Publication of the decree to the various nuncios was neither simultaneous nor clear, and Ward's attempt to steady the confidence of her sisters was considered rebellion. She was imprisoned for a short time in the Anger convent in Munich but was released after a personal appeal to the pope.

Although the definitive suppression was handed down on Jan. 13, 1631, Ward obtained permission for some of her sisters to continue their apostolate while living in community under private vows. Ward returned to England in 1639, stayed in London until the Civil War, and then transferred to Hewarth Hall where she died. She was buried in Osbaldwick Churchyard, near York.

Ward's institute received final papal approbation only in 1877; meanwhile modern congregations patterned their rule upon hers. Pius XII spoke of Ward to the First International Congress of the Lay Apostolate, 1951 as "cette femme incomparable" and ranked her with St. Vincent de Paul as promoter of the lay apostolate. The Grail community honors her as a precursor.

Bibliography: *Publications of the Catholic Record Society* 10 (1911) 397–398; 22 (1921) 132–186; 41 (1948) 97–150, documentary sources. M. C. E. CHAMBERS, *The Life of Mary Ward*, 2 v. (London 1882–85), appendices contain documents *in extenso*. M. O'CONNOR, *That Incomparable Woman* (Montreal 1962).

[M. P. TRAUTH]

WARD, WILFRID PHILIP

British author and Catholic apologist; b. Ware, Hertfordshire, England, Jan. 2, 1856; d. London, April 9, 1916. Ward's father, William George WARD, was one of the leaders of the the OXFORD MOVEMENT. Wilfrid attended Ushaw College, Durham, and the Gregorian University in Rome before being appointed lecturer in philosophy (1890) at Ushaw and a member of the royal commission on Irish university education (1901). In 1906 he was named editor of the *DUBLIN REVIEW,* which thereafter carried influential discussions of Catholic ideas and national events. Ward visited the U.S. in 1913 and 1915 to deliver the Lowell lectures in Boston, and to tour the country lecturing on Cardinal John Henry Newman, Cardinal Herbert Vaughn, and Alfred Tennyson. Ward was buried on the Isle of Wight, where his family had long been landed gentry. His widow was Josephine Mary Hope-Scott, whom he had married in 1887.

Ward was equally noted for his biographical studies and his interpretations of contemporary British Catholicism. Among his works were a two-volume biography of his father, *William George Ward and the Oxford Movement* (1889) and *William George Ward and the Catholic Revival* (1893), *The Life and Times of Cardinal Wiseman* (1897), and *Aubrey de Vere* (1904). Ward's most important book was his monumental two-volume *Life of Newman* (1912), a product of seven years' research that helped win wider acceptance of Newman's thought.

In addition to recreating the Oxford Movement in these biographies, Ward exerted a moderating influence in the midst of the contemporary controversy over Modernism. Attributing past rigidity of thought to the ''state of siege'' that had prevailed in the English church since the Reformation, he argued that it was now possible to incorporate new theories into Scholasticism. Relying heavily on Newman's theory of development, Ward's ideas afforded an alternative to Modernism that proved attractive, even to non-Catholic intellectuals. Ward capitalized upon this and his wide-ranging friendships to found (1896) the Synthetic Society to promote dialogue by Catholics with Anglicans and Nonconformists.

Bibliography: M. WARD, *The Wilfrid Wards and the Transition* (New York 1934). S. LESLIE, *The Dictionary of National Biography From the Earliest Times to 1900* (London 1912–21) 552–553.

[J. L. MORRISON]

WARD, WILLIAM, BL.

Priest, martyr; *vere* Webster; b. c. 1560, Thornby (Thrimby), Westmorland, England; hanged, drawn, and quartered at Tyburn (London), July 26, 1641. Little is known of the first four decades of his life. He had already reached his 40th birthday before undertaking seminary studies at Douai (1604–08), where he received priestly ordination on June 1, 1608. He labored in the English mission for 33 years—20 of which were spent in prison. He was arrested in Scotland shortly after his arrival from the Continent in October 1608. Three years later he was

William George Ward.

released and continued to England. Throughout his ministry he was known for his zeal, devotion to hearing confessions and providing spiritual direction, and his personal austerity. He refused to leave England after the Parliamentary proclamation banishing all priests (April 7, 1641). He was arrested in his nephew's home (July 15), tried at the Old Bailey, and condemned to death (July 23). His portrait hangs at St. Edmund's College, Old Hall. He was beatified by Pius XI on Dec. 15, 1929.

Feast of the English Martyrs: May 4 (England).

See Also: ENGLAND, SCOTLAND, AND WALES, MARTYRS OF.

Bibliography: R. CHALLONER, *Memoirs of Missionary Priests,* ed. J. H. POLLEN (rev. ed. London 1924; repr. Farnborough 1969). J. H. POLLEN, *Acts of English Martyrs* (London 1891).

[K. I. RABENSTEIN]

WARD, WILLIAM GEORGE

Theologian and author; b. London, England, March 21, 1812; d. there, July 6, 1882. He was educated privately in part and at Winchester College, where he won the gold medal for Latin prose. At Oxford he was first a commoner of Christ Church, then a scholar at Lincoln, and finally (1834) a fellow of Balliol, when he took minor orders in the Anglican church. He had early manifested great ability in mathematics and made positive contributions to the science of logarithms, but he had as well a keen aptitude for philosophy. He took a leading part in debate in the Oxford Union and became its president in 1832. At Balliol he showed a zest for controversy, his chief opponent being Archibald Campbell Tait, later archbishop of Canterbury. Ward became the close friend of Benjamin Jowett, a fellow tutor; Arthur Stanley, later dean of Westminster; and Arthur Hugh Clough, the poet. Ward was one of the strongest opponents of the Evangelicals (Low Church Anglicans); but he was equally opposed to the new Broad Church, represented by Jowett, Richard Whately, and Thomas Arnold, being progressively convinced of the importance of ecclesiastical authority. He was ordained in 1840, but his pamphlets in support of John Henry Newman resulted in deprivation of his lectureship and tutorial position in Balliol (1841), though he was allowed to continue as bursar.

Ward began to frequent Catholic seminaries and colleges, where he felt instinctively at home. He published *The Ideal of a Christian Church, Considered in Comparison with Existing Practice* (1844), which gained him the nickname "Ideal" Ward. He was summoned before university authorities; and when he refused to disavow the work or even parts of it, the book was formally censored and Ward was degraded by the vote of a large majority of convocation. He then resigned his fellowship, settled near Oxford, and was received into the Roman church on Sept. 5, 1845, just ahead of Newman. The following year he began to lecture in philosophy at St. Edmund's College, the seminary at Ware, Hertfordshire, and six years later, under Cardinal Nicholas WISEMAN'S sponsorship, was appointed professor of theology, a unique position for a layman. He published his lectures as a book, *On Nature and Grace* (1858), only part of a more ambitious work he had planned. The same year he resigned his lectureship and retired to his inherited estates in the Isle of Wight.

Ward continued his intellectual activity and became a great opponent of liberal Catholics such as Johannes DÖLLINGER, Charles MONTALEMBERT, and J. E. ACTON; in 1861 he left the Isle of Wight, settled near St. Edmund's College, and became editor of the *Dublin Review* (1863), which he made highly influential between 1863 and 1878. He defended Pius IX's SYLLABUS OF ERRORS and espoused an extreme ULTRAMONTANISM, which was congenial to Abp. Henry Edward MANNING, his friend and protector. Deeply upset at the influence of the moderate party at VATICAN COUNCIL I, Ward was further distressed when the all-embracing definition of papal infallibility that he hoped was not forthcoming. He sided with Manning against Newman in holding that Catholics should not be exposed to the "corrupting influences" of Oxford and Cambridge, and was instrumental in the foundation of the Metaphysical Society in 1869.

Despite the vehement expression of his extreme views, Ward was singularly good-tempered and managed to retain friendship even with his most vigorous adversaries. He was a stout, genial, easy man, though it was said he did not care to see anything of his children until they were old enough to argue with him. He retired in his later years to the Isle of Wight, where he was the neighbor and close friend of Tennyson; but he came to Hampstead for the musical entertainment that London offered. There he had other friends, particularly Richard Holt Hutton, editor of the *Spectator,* and Baron Friedrich von HÜGEL. He was buried in the Isle of Wight where he had a large property.

Bibliography: W. P. WARD, *William George Ward and the Oxford Movement* (New York 1889); *William George Ward and the Catholic Revival* (New York 1893). M. WARD, *The Wilfred Wards and the Transition,* 2 v. (New York 1934–37). D. MCELRATH, *The Syllabus of Pius IX: Some Reactions in England* (Louvain 1964).

[D. WOODRUFF]

WARDE, MARY FRANCES XAVIER, MOTHER

Foundress of the Sisters of Mercy in the U.S.; b. Mountrath, Ireland, 1810; d. Manchester, NH, Sept. 17, 1884. As the daughter of John and Jane (Maher) Warde, Frances Teresa was a Dublin socialite until she met Catherine MCAULEY and began work at her Baggot Street center for children and needy women. When Mother McAuley founded the SISTERS OF MERCY in 1831, Frances was her first postulant and was indispensable in consolidating the new community. In 1837 Sister Frances Xavier was sent to Carlow, Ireland, to establish a Mercy foundation. While there she also founded houses at Naas, Wexford, and Westport. In 1843 she responded to Bp. Michael O'Connor's call by leading six young Carlow sisters to Pittsburgh, PA. They were the first Sisters of Mercy in the U.S. Although typhus and tuberculosis decimated the community at first, it soon was able to establish parish schools, two academies, a House of Mercy for the protection and training of young women, an orphanage, and the first hospital in western Pennsylvania. During her six years as superior, Mother Warde founded convents in Chicago, IL (1846), and Loretto, PA (1848). In 1850 she was appointed superior of the mission to Providence, RI. Despite threats stemming from the Know–Nothing Movement, the sisters prospered there and Mother Warde led new foundations to Hartford and New Haven, CT

(1852), and Rochester and Buffalo, NY (1857). Release from the Providence superiorship in 1858 allowed her to go to Manchester, NH, where she was superior for 26 years. There she promoted night schools for young mill hands and dispatched foundations to seven states.

Bibliography: M. T. A. CARROLL, *Leaves from the Annals of the Sisters of Mercy,* 4 v. (New York 1881–95). SISTERS OF MERCY, Manchester, *Reverend Mother Mary Xavier Warde* (Boston 1902).

[M. T. A. CARROLL]

WARDLAW, HENRY DE

Scottish bishop, founder of the University of Saint Andrews; b Wilton, Roxburghshire, Scotland, *c.* 1365; d. Saint Andrews, Scotland, April 6, 1440. Henry, the son of the laird of Wilton, and nephew of Cardinal Wardlaw, studied arts and law at the universities of Oxford, Paris, Orléans and Avignon, and was archdeacon and precentor of Glasgow and a canon of Aberdeen and Moray before being provided to the See of Saint Andrews, Sept. 10, 1403. Gifted and widely traveled, Wardlaw clearly understood the needs of his war–torn and impoverished country, and he strove for political stability, peace with England, the encouragement of learning, and clerical reform. As loyal counselor of King Robert III and tutor to his son James I, he was able to exercise a moderating and constructive influence on the Crown at a crucial time. His greatest achievement, however, was the erection in 1412 of the University of Saint Andrews, the first in Scotland, by which he was able to provide for the Long–term needs of the Scottish clergy and laity.

Bibliography: J. C. GIBSON, *Henry Wardlaw, Founder of St. Andrews University* (privately pr.; Stirling 1911). J. H. BAXTER, ''H. W., Bishop of St. Andrews,'' *Scots Magazine* NS 33 (1940) 5–14. A. B. EMDEN, *A Biographical Register of the University of Oxford to A.D. 1500* 3:1983–84.

[L. MACFARLANE]

WARFIELD, BENJAMIN BRECKINRIDGE

American Presbyterian theologian whose writings influenced both the fundamentalist and neo-orthodox movements in American theology; b. Lexington, Kentucky, Nov. 5, 1851; d. Princeton, New Jersey, Feb. 17, 1921. Warfield was the son of a wealthy planter and prepared for college under private tutors. He graduated from Princeton in 1871 and studied at Edinburgh, Scotland, and Heidelberg, Germany, until 1873. His early interests were chiefly scientific, and he was considerably influenced by the writings of C. R. DARWIN. Warfield entered Princeton Theological Seminary (1873), then dominated by the Old School tradition of Charles HODGE; he graduated in 1876 and spent an additional year in studies at Leipzig, Germany. After a brief pastorate in Baltimore, Maryland, he was called to Western Theological Seminary, Allegheny, Pennsylvania, as professor of New Testament literature (1878). Nine years later he accepted the chair of systematic theology at Princeton Seminary and held that post until his death.

At Western, he published *An Introduction to the Textual Criticism of the New Testament* (1886). During his years at Princeton, he contributed numerous articles to the *Princeton Theological Review* and published *The Gospel of the Incarnation* (1893) and *The Right of Systematic Theology* (1897), both directed against the spreading Modernism in the Presbyterian Church. Warfield had a profound knowledge of patristics, ecclesiastical history, and Reformed theology, and he was abreast of critical scholarship in the study of the Scriptures. He understood the Bible as not merely a record of the events of salvation history, but the authoritative interpretation of them, and he held that Christianity is constituted by these understood in one specific manner

His theology was orthodox CALVINISM, taught in a conservative and even authoritarian manner in the light of Scripture and the WESTMINSTER CONFESSION. In apologetics, he taught that faith is a conviction grounded on evidence, and he opposed any shadow of irrationalism. In *Two Studies in the History of Doctrine* (1897), he taught Calvinistic predestination, but moderated the orthodox view to allow for the salvation of infants by a special providence. Among his later publications, *Counterfeit Miracles* (1918) rejected all post-Apostolic miracles. A selection of Warfield's many articles and monographs was published in nine volumes (1929–32). A new edition of his collected writings was begun in 1952.

Bibliography: B. B. WARFIELD, *Biblical and Theological Studies,* ed. S. CRAIG (Philadelphia 1952), contains a brief biog.

[R. K. MACMASTER]

WARHAM, WILLIAM

Archbishop of Canterbury and lord chancellor of England; b. Church Oakley, Hampshire, England, 1450; d. Hackington, near Canterbury, Aug. 22, 1532. Warham was educated at Winchester and Oxford. After a variety of services to the crown, he was appointed bishop of London in 1501; two years later he was translated to Canterbury. In 1504 he became lord chancellor, and for the next 11 years he, together with Bishop Richard Fox, was one

William Warham.

of the two most powerful men in the kingdom headed by Henry VII and his son HENRY VIII. In late 1515, Warham terminated his chancellorship and virtually retired, but despite the buffeting he received from Cardinal Thomas WOLSEY, his successor, Warham lived on; it was Wolsey who predeceased Warham. By 1530 the old archbishop had been recalled to the forefront of affairs by Henry's divorce and the first stages of the English Reformation.

Initially Warham supported Henry. For reasons unknown he had always been uneasy about the legitimacy of the King's marriage, and Henry now pinned much hope on him, but with remarkable courage Warham later turned against the King and condemned, at least, his methods. Furthermore (in early 1532), he denounced all that had recently been done against Rome and his see. The King replied to this double offense with a praemunire charge—for having consecrated the bishop of St. Asaph's without royal permission 14 years previously. Warham braced himself to fight, as a magnificent speech in self-defense, still extant, shows. Then suddenly, it seems, he broke.

In May 1532 he acquiesced in the English clergy's surrender of their legislative independence to the King. Three months after Henry had won this victory, Warham died a natural death. He was a slow, forthright man, a

generous friend of ERASMUS, and the subject of a masterpiece by Holbein. He was an upright archbishop who was jealous of his authority and remarkably devoted to St. Thomas BECKET.

Bibliography: J. GAIRDNER, *The Dictionary of National Biography from the Earliest Times to 1900* (London 1885–1900) 20:835–840. P. HUGHES, *The Reformation in England* (New York 1963). H. M. SMITH, *Henry VIII and the Reformation* (New York 1962). W. F. HOOK, *Lives of the Archbishops of Canterbury,* 12 v. (London 1860–84) 6:155–421.

[J. J. SCARISBRICK]

WARIN, BL.

Benedictine abbot; d. 856. Warin was a member of a Carolingian family and seems to have been the son of the Saxon Count Eckbert and St. IDA OF HERZFELD. During his early years he belonged to the imperial court, but he later entered the Abbey of CORBIE, where he was a disciple of PASCHASIUS RADBERTUS, who called him Placidus Varinus. In 822 Warin was sent to the new Abbey of CORVEY and in 826 became abbot after the death of ADALARD. At the same time Louis the Pious gave him the Abbey of Rebais. Corvey flourished during his administration. At Warin's request Radbertus wrote the *De corpore et sanguine Domini* (831) for the instruction of the recently Christianized Saxon monks at Corvey who were still poorly versed in doctrine. For his novices, Warin had Radbertus write the *De fide, spe, et caritate*. Warin accepted the missionary fields of Meppen (834) and Visbek (855) for Corvey, thus beginning the mission among the Germans of the North. HILDUIN OF SAINT-DENIS sent him the relic of St. Vitus in 836.

Feast: Sept. 26.

Bibliography: H. PELTIER, *Dictionnaire de théologie catholique* 13.2:1630–31. A. M. ZIMMERMANN, *Kalendarium Benedictinum: Die Heiligen und Seligen des Benediktinerorderns und seiner Zweige* v.3. H. J. WURM, *Lexikon für Theologie und Kirche*[1] 10:754.

[G. J. DONNELLY]

WARMUND OF IVREA, BL.

Bishop; alive in 1006; died between 1010 and 1014. Warmund (Varmondo, Veremundus) was named bishop of Ivrea by Emperor OTTO I in 969. His public life was part of the conflict between civil and ecclesiastical powers for control of the city of Ivrea, in Piedmont, Italy. His main antagonist was King Arduin of Italy whom he twice excommunicated between 997 and 999. A poet and a craftsman, Warmund restored the cultural arts to subalpine Italy by his building projects, which included the cathedral of Ivrea, and by introducing Carolingian bookhands into the SCRIPTORIUM of his episcopal school. Many of his poems are extant, as are manuscripts done under his supervision. Pius IX confirmed his cult in 1857.

Feast: Aug. 9.

Bibliography: L. G. PROVANA DEL SABBIONE, *Studi critici sovra la storia d'Italia a' tempi del re Ardoino* (Turin 1844), for sources. F. SAVIO, *Gli antichi vescovi d'Italia dalle origini al* 1300, 4 v. (1898–1932) v.1.

[N. M. RIEHLE]

WARTENBERG, FRANZ WILHELM VON

Cardinal; b. Munich, Mar. 1, 1593; d. Regensburg, Dec. 1, 1661. He was educated at Ingolstadt and Rome. Wartenberg became political administrator for the Elector Ferdinand of Cologne in the early years of the THIRTY YEARS' WAR (1621). On Oct. 26, 1625, he was elected bishop of Osnabrück, then in Protestant hands, but he did not take up residence until March 1628, when he entered the city with the aid of Johann TILLY, general of the forces of the Catholic League. During the next five years, until Osnabrück was captured by the Swedes, Wartenberg energetically reestablished the Church in religious, political, and educational matters. In addition, he was responsible for administering the Edict of RESTITUTION (1629) in Lower Saxony; he became also the bishop of Verden (1630) and of Minden (1631). With the advent of the Swedes in 1633, Wartenberg took refuge in Regensburg, where he was ordained priest (1636), and appointed vicar apostolic to Bremen (1645), and bishop of Regensburg (1649).

After the Peace of WESTPHALIA (1648), during the negotiations of which he served as a representative of the Catholic imperial electors, Wartenberg returned to Osnabrück. Bremen and Verden had been transferred to Sweden, and Minden to Prussia, although he nominally retained spiritual authority there. In April 1661, eight months before his death, he was created a cardinal priest.

Bibliography: G. SCHWAIGER, *Kardinal Franz Wilhelm von Wartenberg als Bischof von Regensburg, 1649–1661* (Munich 1950). H. LÜNENBORG, *Lexikon für Theologie und Kirche*[1] 10:757.

[T. T. HELDE]

WASHING OF THE FEET

The liturgical rite of the washing of the feet on Holy Thursday takes its inspiration from the Last Supper, where Jesus first washed the feet of his apostles and commanded them to do likewise (see Jn 13:4-14). As a liturgical rite for Holy Thursday it is first found in the canons of the 17th Synod of Toledo in Spain (694). Evidently, however, it was even older, for the synod recommends its restoration (C. J. von Hefele, *Histoire des conciles d'après les documents originaux* 3:586). It made its way to Rome by the 11th century; the pope washed the feet of 12 subdeacons at the end of the evening Mass on Holy Thursday. When the other Holy Thursday rites were moved to the morning hours during the 14th century, the Mandatum remained a separate service to be held in the afternoon. Pius XII's Holy Week Ordinal places it during the evening Mass of the Lord's Supper immediately after the Gospel and homily. It has remained in this position in the liturgical books promulgated in the wake of the Second Vatican Council. Accompanying the washing of feet is the beautiful hymn *Ubi caritas et amor* ("Where charity and love prevails").

Bibliography: N. M. HARING, "Historical Notes on the Interpretation of John 13:10," *Catholic Biblical Quarterly* 13 (1951) 355–380. H. WEISS, "Foot Washing in the Johannine community," *Novum Testamentum* 21 (1979), p. 298–325. S. M. SCHNEIDERS, "The Foot Washing (John 13:1–20): An Experiment in Hermeneutics," *Catholic Biblical Quarterly* 43 (1981) 76–92. *Abendmahl und Fusswaschung* (Hamburg 1991) C. NIEMAND, *Die Fusswaschungserzählung des Johannesevangeliums: Untersuchungen zu ihrer Entstehung und Überlieferung im Urchristentum* (Rome 1993). J. C. THOMAS, *Footwashing in John 13 and the Johannine Community* (Sheffield, England 1991). P. JEFFERY, *A New Commandment : Toward a Renewed Rite for the Washing of Feet* (Collegeville, MN 1992). D. TRIPP, "Meanings of the Foot-Washing: John 13 and Oxyrhynchus Papyrus 840," *Expository Times* 103 (1992) 237–239.

[J. A. FISCHER/W. J. O'SHEA/EDS.]

WASHINGTON, CATHOLIC CHURCH IN

Bounded by British Columbia, including Vancouver Island, on the north, the Pacific Ocean on the west, Oregon on the south, and Idaho on the east, the "Evergreen State" was admitted to the Union on Nov. 11, 1889, as the 42nd state. Originally part of the Oregon Territory, Washington Territory was separated from it in March 1853, and reduced to its current boundaries with the formation of the Idaho Territory in 1863. At the beginning of the third millennium, the majority of Washington's 5,894,121 people are of Euro-American descent. Other ethnic populations include Hispanics/Latino, 441,509 (7.5%), Asians, 322,335 (5.5%), Blacks/African Americans, 190,267 (3.2%), Native Americans and Alaska Natives, 93,301, (1.6%), and Native Hawaiians and other Pacific Islanders, 23,953 (0.4%). The bulk of the popula-

Archdiocese/Diocese	Year Created
Archdiocese of Seattle	1951
Diocese of Spokane	1913
Diocese of Yakima	1951

tion resides on Puget Sound from Everett to Olympia. To the east the population centers are Spokane, Yakima, and the Tri-cities area of Richland, Pasco, and Kennewick.

Washington is among the least churched and most religiously diverse states in the United States. Roughly 30 percent of the state's population is churched. Between 10 and 17 percent are adamantly disinterested in religion in any form. Approximately 15 percent attend church on any given weekend. Catholics make up about 12 percent of the state's population, followed by Lutherans (3.6%), Latter-Day Saints (3.1%), United Methodists (1.8%) and Assemblies of God (1.7%). The Catholic Church is the largest religious body in a state where all social institutions are relatively weak. Geographic space, high population mobility, the absence of large, stable ethnic communities, fluid class lines, and limited personnel and financial resources have created a context where committed Catholics from all parts of the Americas, Asia, and Europe, have worked to build and sustain their church. There are three dioceses; in addition to the Archdiocese of Seattle (diocese, 1907; archdiocese, 1951), the metropolitan see, there are its suffragan sees of Spokane (1914) and Yakima (1951).

Catholic Presence. On July 14, 1775, a Franciscan priest with the Spanish Heceta and Bodega y Cuandra expedition erected a cross at today's Point Grenville. Permanent Catholic presence began with the French-Canadian Metis (persons of mixed French-Canadian and Native American descent), and Native Americans involved in the fur trade in the Oregon Country. Even before trappers turned farmers petitioned Bishop Joseph Signay of Quebec for priests in 1834, they had secured a separate Catholic cemetery at the Hudson's Bay Company's Fort Vancouver. In November, 1838, two French-Canadian priests, Francis Norbert BLANCHET (1795–1883 [1843–1880]) and Modeste Demers (1809–1871) arrived. They immediately began pastoral work among the French and Metis and engaged in evangelistic work among Native Americans, using the Catholic Ladder, a pictorial representation of salvation history. They appointed Native Americans and other lay catechists to lead emerging Catholic communities in prayer and provide basic instruction. By 1842, Fr. John Baptiste Bolduc (1818–1889) had arrived and Jesuits from St. Louis, most

notably Pierre DE SMET S.J. (1801–1873), were active in the eastern portion of the region.

The region changed rapidly between 1840 and 1880. In 1843, Pope Gregory XVI erected an apostolic vicariate that included the area from the Pacific to the Rockies and Russian Alaska to California. In 1846, less than six weeks after the U.S. took control of the land below the 49th parallel as a result of the Oregon Treaty, the apostolic vicariate was elevated to the Ecclesiastical Province of Oregon City, the second in the United States. Blanchet was appointed to the metropolitan see, Modeste Demers to the diocese of Vancouver Island, and the archbishop's brother, Augustin Magliore Blanchet (1797–1887 [1846–1879]), to the diocese of Walla Walla, the first diocese in what was to become the state of Washington. The entire province had 6,000 Catholics, over 5,000 of whom were Native Americans. One of the 5,000 was Chief Seattle (1786–1866) of the Suquamish and Duwamish tribes of Puget Sound, after whom the city of Seattle was named.

Bishop Augustin Magliore Blanchet traveled to Walla Walla over the Oregon Trail in 1847, accompanied by his vicar general, John Baptist Abraham Brouillet (1813–1884), and members of the Oblates of Mary Immaculate. Brouillet, a tireless advocate for Native Americans, became the first director of the Catholic Bureau of Indian Affairs in the 1880s. Fathers Eugene Casimir Chirouse, O.M.I. (1821–1892) and Charles Pandosy, O.M.I. (1824–1891), the first priests ordained in Washington, spent most of their active ministries among Native Americans in the state.

Blanchet arrived at Fort Walla Walla, in September 1847. In November the Whitman Massacre occurred, sparking the Cayuse War, exacerbating tensions between Catholic and Protestant missionaries, and forcing closure of the Walla Walla mission. The California Gold Rush emptied much of the Euro-American population from the region. In 1850 Blanchet was transferred from Walla Walla to the newly erected Diocese of Nesqually, with Vancouver as the see city. In 1853, Walla Walla was suppressed and the Washington territory came under the jurisdiction of Nesqually.

Blanchet depended on the Societies for the Propagation of the Faith in Lyons and Paris and the Leopoldine Society in Vienna for financial support, and on Montreal for personnel. In 1856 Mother Joseph of the Sacred Heart (1823–1902), who would come to be known as the Pacific Northwest's first architect, and four other Sisters of Providence began work in health care and education. By 1864, 31 Providence Sisters, five Jesuits, two Oblate missionaries, and seven diocesan priests served in the diocese. Though Irish and German Catholic populations grew steadily, the Church in Washington retained a French Canadian, Metis, and Native American orientation into the 1880s.

Institutional Growth. The construction of the transcontinental railroad to Washington brought Irish and Chinese laborers to the state. Once completed in 1883, the state became a destination point for immigrants. Between 1880 and 1895, the Euro-American population of the diocese increased from 75,000 to nearly 400,000, the Catholic population from 12,000 to 30,000. Churches and public chapels increased from 22 to 46, diocesan clergy from 15 to 37, and religious priests, including Jesuits, Benedictines, and Redemptorists, to 20. Women religious increased from 60 to 286. Sisters of Providence and Sisters of the Holy Names of Jesus and Mary from Montreal predominated, but many other communities would serve in the state over the next 150 years, among them Benedictines, Sisters of St. Francis of Philadelphia, and Sisters of St. Dominic.

Bishop Augustin Blanchet resigned in 1879. His successor, Aegidius Junger (1879–1895), a Belgian who had served the diocese since ordination in 1864, like Blanchet was a missionary bishop oriented toward and dependent on Quebec and Europe. The third, Edward J. O'Dea (1896–1932), the first westerner raised to the episcopacy, transformed Nesqually from an immigrant, frontier missionary diocese, into a diocese of the U.S. Catholic Church, the Diocese of Seattle. During his long tenure, the state's population quadrupled from nearly 400,000 to 1,600,000. He led the diocese through the turmoil that ensued after the Panic of 1893, the economic disruption of the 1898 Alaska gold rush, massive immigration, World War I, anti-Catholic agitation in the 1920s, and the beginnings of the Great Depression. O'Dea moved his see from Vancouver to Seattle in 1903, began construction of a cathedral in 1905, and at the dedication of the cathedral in 1907 announced the change of the name of the diocese from Nesqually to Seattle.

Increases in population generated a need for more educational and health-care institutions. In 1891, the Jesuits began Seattle College, which became one of the first co-educational colleges in the United States. German Benedictines established St. Martin's College in Lacey in 1895. Between 1903 and 1915, Mother (later Saint) Frances Xavier Cabrini (1850–1917) and the Missionary Sisters of the Sacred Heart came to Puget Sound to minister to Italian immigrants with an orphanage, school and hospital. An official diocesan newspaper, *The Catholic Northwest Progress*, appeared in 1911.

Lay organizations aimed at spiritual growth, support of the church, mutual support, and social activities, burgeoned between 1880 and 1932, including expanded altar societies, the Young Men's Institute (1890s), the KNIGHTS OF COLUMBUS (1902), the Young Ladies' Institute (1905), the Holy Name Society (1909) and Catholic Daughters of America (1910). In the 1920s the Diocesan Council of Catholic Women supported the Newman Club at the University of Washington. The Society of St. Vincent de Paul officially organized in January 1920, successor to the Immaculate Conception Association of Charity, active in Seattle since 1893. The National Council of Catholic Men provided monetary support for the Catholic Filipino Club in Seattle.

The Knights of Columbus began the Laymen's retreat in 1918. A women's retreat movement followed in the 1920s. By 1930, the Holy Angels Society, Boys Sanctuary, Children of St. Mary, Sodality of Mary, and League of the Sacred Heart were present in Washington. Annual parish missions were a regular feature. In 1934 Catholic businessmen founded the Serra Club to provide spiritual and financial assistance for priestly vocations.

Even as Catholics participated in the progressive agenda of the 1920s through work in social welfare, including the Catholic Social Betterment League, they faced increasing nativist hostility during the post World War I years. It reached a peak in 1924 when the Ku Klux Klan supported initiative No. 49, designed to eliminate private schools. The initiative was defeated, in large part because prominent Catholic laymen like William Pigott (1860–1929), helped organize a religiously ecumenical, civic, and business-oriented opposition.

Maryknoll priests and sisters arrived in the state in 1920 to work among the growing Asian population on Puget Sound, especially Japanese and Filipinos. The mission grew out of a proposal in 1916 by a nucleus of Seattle Japanese Catholics, two of whom, Mr. Akashi and Mr. Hirata, traced their Catholicism back to the Nagasaki Martyrs. Sisters Teresa and Gemma opened a kindergarten for Japanese children. By 1925, Our Lady Queen of Martyrs Parish was a thriving Japanese-Filipino national parish that carried on a vibrant, intercultural ministry until the internment of the Japanese in 1942. Maryknoll Father Leopold H. Tibesar, pastor from 1935, accompanied parishioners to the camps.

Late in 1913, on O'Dea's recommendation, Rome created a new diocese. The diocese of Spokane comprised of half the territory of the state, and Augustine Schinner was appointed the first bishop (1914–1925). He was succeeded by Charles D. White (1926–1954), who was followed by Bernard J. Topel (1955–1978), and Lawrence Welsh (1978–1990). Catholicism in Spokane was rooted in the efforts of Jesuits, including de Smet, Joseph Joset (1810–1910), and Joseph Cataldo (1837–1928), and diocesan priests Toussaint Mesplie

(1824–1895), Emile Kauten (d. 1912), and Peter Poaps (d. 1890). The Sisters of Providence and Sisters of the Holy Names early had established educational and health care ministries to Native Americans and Euro-Americans there. Jesuits worked with Native Americans; in 1887 they established Gonzaga College in Spokane. The Sisters of the Holy Names opened a college, later Fort Wright College, in 1907, that operated until 1981. Bishop White Seminary was built in 1956.

The Seattle Province. After Pearl Harbor was bombed on Dec. 7, 1941, Seattle's Bishop Gerald SHAUGHNESSY, S.M. (1933–1950), spoke out publicly against hatred of Japanese and Japanese Americans, the first western bishop to do so. Washington's dioceses cooperated in the war effort through establishing clubs for soldiers and war workers, curtailing building projects, and adjusting liturgies to comply with dimout regulations.

The war brought tens of thousands of soldiers, workers, and their families into the state. Among them were large numbers of African Americans taking advantage of access to industrial and clerical jobs that the labor shortage provided. Some were from families with centuries-long histories as Catholics. After the war, the Knights St. Peter Claver and Ladies Auxiliary became the major African American Catholic parish organization in the state. Bishop Thomas J. Connolly (1950–1975) of Seattle established the St. Peter Claver Interracial Center to provide social services to the city's growing African American community. He also worked actively for open housing during the 1960s. Black lay Catholics such as Clayton Pitrie and Walter Hubbard, became leaders in the state and nationally with the National Black Catholic Lay Caucus. In the 1970s, the first two African American priests in the state were ordained, Fathers Joseph McGowan, S.J. and John Cornelius.

Washington's Hispanic/Latino began growing rapidly beginning in the 1930s, with people who lost their farms in Colorado during the Great Depression seeking work. The influx of population caused by the construction of the Grand Coulee Dam, the Columbia Basin irrigation project, and the war effort transformed all of eastern Washington, especially the Yakima Valley and Tri-cities. In response, Bishop Connolly proposed another diocese. Yakima was erected in June 1951, for an area with a Catholic presence dating back to the 1850s and ministry by the Jesuits, Oblates, Sisters of Providence and Sisters of St. Dominic. The new bishop, Joseph P. Dougherty (1951–1969), quickly began building churches, schools, social services, and an extensive ministry to Spanish-speaking Catholics. Continued growth through the rest of the century made Hispanics a major presence throughout the state. By the beginning of the 21st century, one-half of the Catholic population of the diocese of Yakima was Hispanic/Latino. Bishop Dougherty attended to the Yakima Indian Reservation mission, one of the oldest in the state, and elevated it to the status of parish with a resident pastor in 1958. In 1981, Heritage College, successor to the Holy Names Sisters' Fort Wright College, opened. Cornelius M. Power (1969–1974) succeeded Dougherty, to be followed by Nicholas E. Walsh (1974–1976) and William S. Skylstad (1977–1988).

Seattle became an archdiocese in 1951 amidst the post-war boom. Confraternity of Christian Doctrine, present in the state since the 1930s, expanded to serve Catholic students in public schools. Adults joined Catholic Action and discussion clubs. Seattle became the third diocese in the nation to have a Knights of Columbus Religious Information Bureau, which operated under the guidance of William Treacy (b. 1919), a diocesan priest who came to Seattle from Ireland in 1945. The archdiocese opened St. Thomas Seminary, which was staffed by the Sulpicians and operated until 1977. The Catholic Youth Organization facilitated athletics, camping, and other programs for adolescents. Catholic Charities broadened its focus to include housing and a range of social services for the poor, the elderly, and ethnic minorities. Refugee programs were initiated for Hungarians and Koreans in the 1950s, Southeast Asians in the 1960s, and Central Americans in the 1980s.

Vatican II into the 21st Century. In 1962 the Catholic Church in Washington was institutionally stable and successful. That year the Archdiocese of Seattle hosted the 47th annual Liturgical Conference, its contribution to the Seattle World's Fair. Among the liturgical leaders in attendance was Msgr. H. A. Reinhold (1897–1968), who had been incardinated in the Archdiocese of Seattle and later served as curate and pastor (1944–1956) in Sunnyside in the diocese of Yakima.

In the wake of Vatican Council II, the archdiocese participated in an ecumenical discussion program on KOMO television, Challenge. For over a decade its weekly 300,000 viewers saw Fr. William Treacy in conversation with Rabbi Raphael Levine (1901–1985) and a Protestant minister.

Seattle University and the archdiocese initiated new education and training for catechists and lay leaders. Across the state parish councils were formed, liturgical renewal initiated, social justice ministries expanded, and pastoral ministries oriented toward diverse ethnic populations. New lay organizations formed, focused around professional, liturgical, educational, and justice issues. Seattle's Fr. James Dunning (1937–1995) gained national prominence as head of the North American Forum on the Catechumenate.

In 1970 the Washington State Catholic Conference was established in order to provide a more effective public voice for the Catholic Church in the state with regard to public policy issues. When Archbishop Connolly retired in 1975 (d. April 18, 1991), he was succeeded by the bishop of Helena, Mont., Raymond G. Hunthausen. Having attended all the sessions of Vatican II, he set about instilling in the archdiocese a vision of service and participation on the part of the laity. He vigorously promoted ecumenical collaboration but alienated goodly numbers in the government and the local church because of his stance opposing nuclear weapons. Hunthausen retired in 1991, and the Most Reverend Thomas J. Murphy, who since 1987 had been coadjutor archbishop, succeeded him. Archbishop Murphy's episcopacy (1991–1997), was cut short by leukemia, and Alex J. Brunett became archbishop of Seattle in 1997. The Archdiocese of Seattle transformed Catholic Charities into Catholic Community Services of Western Washington in 1988 in order to provide better social services to the poor and elderly.

In the 1990s change continued to characterize the church in Washington, beginning with its leadership. Bishop Welsh of Spokane was succeeded by William S. Skylstad (1990–); Skylstad's replacement in Yakima was Francis E. George, O.M.I. (1990–1996), succeeded by Carlos A. Sevilla, S.J. (1997–). The number of lay church professionals increased across the state as priests and vowed religious declined as a proportion of the Catholic population. Seattle University and the archdiocese cooperatively established the Institute for Theological Studies to train pastoral ministers for the church in western Washington. Gonzaga University expanded its pastoral education offerings for the eastern part of the state. Women's religious communities initiated new spirituality and social justice ministries. The Church continued to welcome immigrants, engage in pastoral care, and struggle with issues of justice in a state economically influenced by globalization, species extinction, and other forces. Entering the 21st century, the state's episcopacy cooperated with archbishops and bishops in Oregon, Idaho, Montana, and British Columbia, on a joint pastoral letter, "The Columbia River Watershed: Caring for Creation and the Common Good." This letter has inspired bishops in other parts of North America to look at care of the environment as a major pastoral issue.

As a new century began, thousands of lay professionals and volunteers joined with clergy and religious in carrying on the Church's extensive social service programs, and the health-care, spiritual, educational, and social service ministries to all the people of Washington.

Bibliography: D. BUERGE and J. ROCHESTER, *Roots and Branches* (Seattle 1988). M. DUNTLEY, "Japanese and Filipino Together: The Transethnic Vision of Our Lady Queen of Martyrs Parish," *U.S. Catholic Historian* 18/1 (Winter 2000) 74–98. R. E. FICKEN and C. LEWARNE, *Washington: A Centennial History* (Seattle 1988). P. O'CONNELL KILLEN, "The Geography of a Minority Religion: Roman Catholicism in the Pacific Northwest," *U.S. Catholic Historian* 18/3 (Summer 2000): 51–72. W. SCHOENBERG, *A History of the Catholic Church in the Pacific Northwest, 1743–1983* (Washington, D.C. 1987). C. A. SCHWANTES, *The Pacific Northwest: An Interpretive History* (Lincoln 1996). C. TAYLOR, ed., *Abundance of Grace: A History of the Archdiocese of Seattle 1850–2000* (Strasbourg 2000).

[P. O'CONNELL KILLEN]

WASHINGTON, D.C., ARCHDIOCESE OF

The archdiocese of Washington, D.C. (*Washingtonensis*), was erected by Pius XII on July 22, 1939, and united with the Archdiocese of BALTIMORE, Md., on equal status, under Michael J. CURLEY, tenth archbishop of Baltimore, whose title was changed to archbishop of Baltimore and Washington. On Nov. 27, 1947, the Federal District of Columbia, and Montgomery, Prince Georges, St. Mary's, Calvert, and Charles Counties of the state of Maryland, an area of 2,104 square miles, were separated from the See of Baltimore and their administration entrusted to Patrick A. O'BOYLE (1896–1987) as archbishop of Washington. Like approximately 40 other archiepiscopal sees, Washington, until 1965, had no metropolitan jurisdiction over suffragan sees. However, in 1965, it was given metropolitan status, with the prelature *nullius* of the Virgin Islands as a suffragan see.

Catholic beginnings. It was in St. Mary's County that the original settlers of colonial Maryland landed from the *Ark* and the *Dove* on March 25, 1634, under the leadership of Leonard Calvert, brother of the lord proprietor, Cecilius Calvert, second baron of Baltimore. Accompanying this group of approximately 150 Englishmen, the majority of whom were Protestants, were three English Jesuits, Fathers Andrew WHITE and John Altham and Brother Thomas Gervase. From the Jesuits' headquarters in St. Mary's City, the first colonial capital, came an unbroken succession of priests from whose number the first bishop of the United States was chosen 155 years later in the person of John CARROLL. There, too, the general assembly of the colony, composed of both Catholic and Protestant members, enacted in April of 1649 the famous act of religious TOLERATION, unique in the English-speaking world of that time, which stated that no one "professing to believe in Jesus Christ, shall from henceforth bee any waies troubled, Molested or discountenanced for or in respect of his or her religion nor in the free exercise thereof within this Province. . ."

(Ellis, *Documents,* 116). After the Protestant triumph in England in 1688, however, the Maryland Catholics were subjected to a penal code that was in effect for the better part of a century. But with the American Revolution there ensued a radical change, and on Nov. 11, 1776, Maryland's assembly adopted a Declaration of Rights that guaranteed religious liberty, giving Maryland's Catholics a new start.

The Federal district and the five counties of Maryland, which today constitute the archdiocese, have shared in the rule of the archbishops of Baltimore, who, beginning with Carroll, numbered men such as Francis Patrick KENRICK (1851–63), Martin John SPALDING (1864–72), James Roosevelt BAYLEY (1872–77), and James GIBBONS (1877–1921). With the rise of the United States to a world power in the late 19th century, attention was focused on its national capital, and the suggestion was made that in keeping with its dignity it should be made an episcopal see. Gibbons, who was strongly opposed to the separation of Washington from Baltimore, made a trip to Rome in May of 1914, expressly to prevent the rumored separation. However, he was ready to second the suggestion of Giovanni Bonzano, apostolic delegate to the United States, to the effect that the name of Washington be added to that of Baltimore in the title of the see. But Gibbons had been dead 18 years before the Holy See took the first step by erecting the Archdiocese of Washington and putting it under the administration of the same prelate who ruled the Archdiocese of Baltimore. The complete separation of the two sees occurred six months after the death of Archbishop Curley, Gibbons' successor.

Independent Jurisdiction. Patrick A. O'Boyle, a priest of the Archdiocese of New York, was installed as the second archbishop of Washington at St. Matthew's Cathedral on Jan. 21, 1948. During his 25-year tenure, the archdiocese experienced tremendous growth. The size of its Catholic population more than doubled, reaching a total of 389,000 in 1973. The number of Catholic institutions also greatly increased, with the number of parishes growing by 50% (to 122) at the time of O'Boyle's retirement.

It was also under O'Boyle that events in the Archdiocese of Washington became the focus of media attention. The first of these events was the archdiocese's successful integration of its parishes and schools prior to the Supreme Court decision of 1954 striking down the legality of racial segregation. In recognition of his efforts as a progressive leader in the area of race relations, as well as of his other accomplishments, O'Boyle was elevated to the College of Cardinals in 1967. The following year, the archdiocese became the focus of world-wide attention

when Cardinal O'Boyle withdrew the ministerial faculties of numerous priests who publicly opposed Pope Paul VI's encyclical *HUMANE VITAE* (cf. entry on Cardinal O'Boyle). Cardinal O'Boyle retired in 1973 and died in 1987.

William W. Baum, bishop of the Diocese of Springfield–Cape Girardeau and a national voice on ecumenism, was consecrated the third archbishop of Washington in May of 1973 and created a cardinal in 1976. Six more parishes were established in the archdiocese during Baum's tenure in order to meet the needs of Washington's ever-expanding suburbs, and new organizations were established to minister to African American and Hispanic Catholics. One of the highlights of Cardinal Baum's service as the archbishop of Washington was the historic visit of Pope John Paul II to the nation's capital in the fall of 1979. The following year the same pope named Cardinal Baum prefect of the Congregation for Catholic Education. At the time of Cardinal Baum's departure for Rome, the Catholic population of the Archdiocese had reached 396,000. The fourth archbishop of Washington, James A. Hickey, formerly bishop of Cleveland, was installed on Aug. 5, 1980 and elected to the College of Cardinals in 1988. During Cardinal Hickey's 20-year tenure, the Archdiocese of Washington met new challenges posed by the changing demographics of the Washington region. The suburbanization of once rural areas necessitated the erection of new parishes in the Maryland counties, with the total number of parishes reaching 141 in the year 2000. Concurrently, the declining population of the city of Washington required a new commitment to and the consolidation of its Catholic elementary and secondary schools. The arrival of thousands of immigrant Catholics from the Caribbean, Asia, and most especially Latin America, since the 1980s, has brought a great racial and ethnic richness to the local Church as well as pastoral challenges.

On Jan. 3, 2001, Archbishop Theodore E. McCarrick of Newark was installed as the fifth archbishop of Washington. Shortly thereafter, on Feb. 21, 2001, he too was elevated to the College of Cardinals, at a time when the archdiocese had 141 parishes, 109 schools and some 320 priests serving over 500,000 Catholics.

The archdiocese of Washington has a unique place within the Catholic Church in America, being home to numerous national Catholic institutions. Among these are the United States Conference of Catholic Bishops, the Archdiocese of the Military Services, the CATHOLIC UNIVERSITY OF AMERICA (1887), Trinity College (1897), GEORGETOWN UNIVERSITY (1789), Mt. St. Sepulchre (the Franciscan Monastery, 1899), and the Basilica of the NATIONAL SHRINE OF THE IMMACULATE CONCEPTION. The archdiocese is also honored to be the residence of the Apostolic Nuncio to the United States.

Bibliography: R. T. CONLEY, *The Truth in Charity: A History of the Archdiocese of Washington* (Paris 2001). M. J. MACGREGOR, *A Parish for the Federal City: St. Patrick's in Washington, 1794–1994* (Washington, D.C. 1994). T. W. SPALDING, *The Premier See: A History of the Archdiocese of Baltimore, 1789–1989* (Baltimore, Md. 1989). W. W. WARNER, *At Peace with All Their Neighbors: Catholics and Catholicism in the National Capital 1787–1860* (Washington, D.C. 1994). An additional source of information on the archdiocese is The Catholic Historical Society of Washington, which was established in 1976.

[J. T. ELLIS/R. T. CONLEY]

WASHINGTON THEOLOGICAL UNION

The Washington Theological Union, located in metropolitan Washington, DC, is a Roman Catholic School for ministry and graduate theological studies owned and operated by several religious communities. Incorporated as the Washington Theological Coalition in 1969, the school was accredited in 1972 by the Maryland State Board of Education, the Commission of Higher Education of the Middle States Association, and by the Association of Theological Schools, to offer masters degrees in theology. In 1977 the school changed its name to the Washington Theological Union (WTU) in recognition of the reality that it was not a temporary alliance, but a unified and stable educational institution.

The Union was formed from several of the Roman Catholic seminaries in the Washington area that functioned independently before the Second Vatican Council. In 1968, in the aftermath of the Council, several leaders of those schools worked out a collaborative arrangement, which they first named the Coalition of Religious Seminaries. Their aim was to draw upon the resources of all of the schools, faculty, students, libraries, and classrooms, and pool them for more effective theological education, but maintain their independence as institutions. Their focus was on religious candidates for the priesthood, but they were open to others preparing for ministry in the church.

The interchange was successful and matured into a joint effort under the vigorous leadership of the first president, Conan Gallagher, ST. The trustees were the superiors of the six founding religious communities: Augustinians, Carmelites, Franciscans, Missionary Servants, Oblates of St. Francis de Sales, and Viatorians. Over the ensuing years several communities departed as corporate members, and others joined, e.g., Sacred Hearts of Jesus and Mary, Conventual Franciscans, and Redemptorists. Other religious communities of women and of men send their students to the school.

Robert Welch, OSA, former president of Villanova University, became president in 1972 and solidified the school's governance structures and academic procedures. At the time, the enrollment was 278 students, and non-ordinational candidates, including women students, were officially welcomed. The full-time faculty numbered twenty-nine. Over the years the student enrollment remained between 210 and 280, with about 20 full-time faculty. Both faculty and students include lay persons as well as religious men and women. Under the third president, Vincent Cushing, OFM, lay persons joined the board of trustees, and WTU initiated a development program and established an endowment.

From the outset the Union stressed ecumenical engagement. It helped to found the Washington Theological Consortium, the grouping of all the theological schools in the Washington area, and remains a full and active partner in its activities. The Union's ethos, programs, and theology were strongly influenced by the spirit and teachings of the Second Vatican Council. The school has worked to read and respond to the ministerial needs of the contemporary church, adapting its theological and pastoral programs in view of "the signs of the times." Its offerings include the Master of Divinity, Master of Arts in Pastoral Studies, and Master of Arts in Theology degrees, as well as certificate and sabbatical programs.

[J. A. CORIDEN]

WASMANN, ERICH

Jesuit entomologist and philosopher of science; b. May 29, 1859, Meran, Austria; d. Valkenburg, Holland, Feb. 27, 1931. He was the son of an artist, and was raised in the Tyrolese Alps. Wasmann early showed intense interest in nature. His early training was in public and Catholic schools, and in the Jesuit college at Feldkirch. Not until the early 1890s, however, as a Jesuit priest, did he receive his graduate training in zoology at the universities of Vienna and Prague. The University of Freiburg awarded him an honorary doctorate in 1921.

In 1875, he joined the Jesuits at Exaten, Holland. Thenceforth, he devoted his entire life to writing, lecturing, research, and religious duties. He was a pioneer in symphilology, the involved ecology of termites and ants. His theistically oriented psychology and evolution were well developed and militantly expressed. He saw interspecific mutualism, harmony, and evolution as manifestations of teleology. More than 100 lectures (especially from 1910 to 1921) and about 750 publications bespeak his physical and intellectual activity, despite his delicate health. Most of his lectures were delivered to scholars at

Erich Wasmann.

Swiss, German, and Austrian universities, but his famous Berlin series, written in counter–action to Haeckel's atheistic evolution and MONISM, were given before great public throngs (1907).

Wasmann's entomological papers, which included bionomics, systematics, mimicry, symphilology, and psychology, were well received by his scientific colleagues. On his 70th birthday an entire issue of the foremost zoological journal in Germany was dedicated to him. Two of his most famous books are *Comparative Studies in the Psychology of Ants and of Higher Animals* (St. Louis 1905) and *The Berlin Discussions of the Problem of Evolution* (St. Louis 1912).

Bibliography: C. J. WIDEMAN, "Erich Wasmann, S.J.," *The Wasmann Collector* 5.2 (1942) 41–46.

[L. P. COONEN]

WATER, LITURGICAL USE OF

Symbolism. The natural symbolism of water led to its liturgical use. Water, of course, serves to cleanse from filth and impurity; consequently, washing is an apt symbol of interior cleanliness and purification. Water is nec-

essary for the existence of all living things humans, animals and plants; it is therefore a symbol of life. The mobility of water, with its property of evaporating (resembling human breathing), increases this vital symbolism. The force of water rushing in a wadi after a rain storm was for the people of the Near East a symbol of the majesty and power of the divinity. An abundance of water was, and still is, for the peoples of parched lands a symbol of happiness and divine blessing. On the other hand, the raging sea tossing ships helplessly about and striking terror into the hearts of sailors is a symbol of any terrible danger. However, water was employed in Christian liturgy primarily as a symbol of purification and life.

Water in the Old Testament. In the Old Testament, water was used in rites of purification. Purification with water might be accomplished in different ways. Sometimes the subject to be purified was sprinkled with lustral water. The Book of Numbers (19.1–22) gives minute instructions for the preparation and use of lustral water in which the ashes of a red heifer were mixed. This water was used to remove legal uncleanness. Sometimes the subject of purification was required to wash his hands and feet or some other part of the body. Thus Aaron and his sons had to purify themselves before entering the tabernacle (Ex 30.18–20). Solomon made a large vessel of cast bronze, the "molten sea" (1 Kgs 7.23). According to 2 Chr 4.6, "the sea was for the priests to wash in." In certain circumstances, objects such as garments had to be washed completely (Lv 6.20; 11.28, 32, 40; 13.6; 14.8, 9, 47; 15.5–11, 13, 21–22). In connection with the Feast of Tabernacles, at the morning service on each of the seven days of the feast, water from the pool of Siloam was carried in procession to the temple. Subsequently, the water and also wine were poured out simultaneously as libations.

Water in the New Testament. In the New Testament, John the Baptist prepared the way for the Savior by baptizing with water. The rite of baptizing was employed by several Jewish sects of the period, for example, the Essenes. Thus John was not an innovator in this respect. Following the command of Christ (Mt 28:18–20), the Church in every age and place has sought to baptize those who have embraced the Gospel of Jesus Christ. Baptism may be administered in the ancient manner by immersion, or by sprinkling or pouring water on the subject. At the Last Supper, Jesus "poured water into a basin and began to wash the feet of the disciples" (Jn 13.5). (*See* WASHING OF THE FEET.) The example of Jesus on this occasion led to the introduction of the washing of the feet into the liturgy.

Blessing of Baptismal Water. It is uncertain when baptismal water first began to be blessed. The *Didache*

(90–100) and Justin Martyr (d. *c.* 165), for example, say nothing of the consecration of baptismal water. The first mention of such a consecration seems to come from the African Church. Cyprian (d. 258) says: "It is required then that the water should first be cleansed and sanctified by the priest, that it may wash away by its Baptism the sins of the man who is baptized" [*Epist.* (70.1) *Synodica ad Januarium;* J. D. Mansi, *Scarorum Conciliorum nova et amplissima collectio* 1:923]. The *Apostolic Constitutions* (*c.* 400) contains a prayer that God may sanctify the water of Baptism that it may accomplish its spiritual effect (7.43; J. Quasten, ed., *Monumenta eucharista et liturgica vetusissima* 192–94). The first written formula for blessing baptismal water is found in the *Euchologion* of Serapion (d. 392): "King and Lord . . . look upon these waters and fill them with the Holy Spirit . . . that those who are being baptized may be no longer flesh and blood but spiritual" (19; F. X. Funk, ed., *Didascalia et constitutiones apostolorum* 2:181–83).

Today in the Eastern Churches it is customary to bless baptismal water immediately before the administration of the Sacrament. Part of the rite is to pour blessed oil or chrism into the water. In the Roman Rite, baptismal water is solemnly blessed at the EASTER VIGIL service. The blessing consists of an introductory oration, a preface accompanied by such actions as dipping the paschal candle into it. The Roman Ritual, however, contains formulas for blessing baptismal water apart from the Easter Vigil. The contemporary rite of consecrating baptismal water is based on such documents as the Gelasian Sacramentary, the Gregorian Sacramentary, and the 11th Roman Ordinal.

Blessing of Holy Water. Holy water is blessed by a bishop or priest who solemnly implores God's blessing upon those who use it. As a sacramental, holy water obtains favors from God through the prayers of the Church offered for those who make use of it and through the devotion it inspires. The most ancient testimony about the use of blessed water is found in the apocryphal Acts of Peter (2d century). These acts report that a Christian sanctified his home in which Simon Magus had lived by sprinkling it and invoking the name of Jesus [R. A. Lipsius and M. Bonnet, *Acta Apostolorum Apocrypha* (Leipzig 1891) 1:59, 66]. The *Euchologion* of Serapion (representing Egyptian practices of the 3d and 4th centuries) contains a formula for blessing oil or water for the benefit of the sick (17; *Didascalia et constitutiones apostolorum* 2:179–181). In the *Apostolic Constitutions* there is a blessing of water that is supposed to stem from the Apostle Matthias (8.29; *Didascalia et constitutiones apostolorum* 1:533).

The first document representative of the Latin Church is the *Liber pontificalis* (6th century), which as-cribes to Alexander I (d. *c.* 116) a prescription about blessing water mixed with salt for blessing homes (*Liber pontificalis*, ed. L. Duchesne, 1:127). The ascription is not based on fact, but it probably does reflect a Latin practice of the 6th century. The modern Roman formula of blessing holy water, found in the Roman Ritual and Roman Missal, is based upon the supplement of Alcuin (d. 804) to the Gregorian Sacramentary and even earlier documents. The use of holy water for blessing persons and objects is most frequent. Its use upon entering a church is meant to recall one's baptism.

The Asperges. The Asperges is the liturgical rite of sprinkling altar, clergy, and people with holy water on Sundays, so-named after the antiphon *Asperges me* (but during Paschal time, *Vidi aquam*) which accompanies the sprinkling. Pope Leo IV (d. 885) decreed that each priest should bless water every Sunday in his own church and sprinkle the people with it (*Patrologia Latina*, ed. J. P. Migne, 115:679). At the same time Hincmar (d. 882), Archbishop of Reims, made a similar disposition for his diocese:

> Every Sunday, before the celebration of Mass, the priest shall bless water in his church; and, for this holy purpose, he shall use a clean and suitable vessel. The people, when entering the church, are to be sprinkled with this water; and those who desire may carry some away in clean vessels so as to sprinkle their houses, fields, vineyards, and cattle, and the provender with which these last are fed, as also to throw over their own food. (*Capitula synodica* 5; *Patrologia Latina* 125:774)

Other Uses of Water in the Mass. In the Mass, water is added to the wine in accordance with a Greek practice observed in Palestine in Christ's time. Justin Martyr mentions the practice in the 2d century (*Apol.* 1.65, 67). The Church Fathers attached great meaning to the addition of this water. In the Roman liturgy a little water is added to the wine in the chalice at the preparation of gifts. In the Byzantine liturgical tradition, warm water (in Greek, *zeon*) is poured into the chalice of wine. The Roman Rite of the Mass also calls for the washing of hands (in Latin, *lavabo*) or liturgical vessels, either for actual cleansing (e.g., the cleansing of liturgical vessels) or symbolic purification (as is the case with the *lavabo*).

Bibliography: P. REYMOND, *L'Eau: Sa Vie et sa signification dans l'ancien Testament* (Vetus Testamentum Suppl. 6; Leiden 1958). J. QUASTEN, *Monumenta eucharistica et liturgica vetustissima* (Florilegium Patristicum 7; Bonn 1935–37). A. FRANZ, *Die kirchlichen Benediktionen im Mittelalter*, 2 v. (Graz 1960). H. SCHMIDT, *Hebdomada Sancta*, 2 v. (Rome 1956). B. NEUNHEUSER, "De benedictione aquae baptismalis," *Ephemerides liturgicae* 44 (1930) 194–207, 258–81, 369–412, 455–92. C. GOEB, "Asperges," *Orate Fratres* 2 (1927–28) 338–42. J. A. JUNGMANN, *The Mass of* *the Roman Rite,* tr. F. A. BRUNNER, 2 v. (New York 1951–55) 2:38–44.

[E. J. GRATSCH/EDS.]

WATERSON, EDWARD, BL.

Priest, martyr; b. London, England; hanged, drawn, and quartered at Newcastle-on-Tyne, England, Jan. 7, 1594 (new calendar). As a young Protestant, Edward Waterson traveled to Turkey in the company of English merchants. There he attracted the attention of a wealthy man who offered Waterson his daughter in marriage, if the young man would embrace Islam. Edward rejected the offer. In returning to Europe, he traveled through Italy and was converted to Catholicism (1588) by the future Bp. Richard Smith of Chalcedon. He studied theology at the English College in Rheims (1589–93), where he was ordained March 11, 1593. Full of zeal for the care of souls, he returned to England (June 24), where he was arrested mid-summer. Throughout his torture he remained humble and accepting of trials. It is related that several miraculous events tried to prevent his execution: the horses refused to drag his hurdle to the scaffold and the ladder there was mysteriously agitated by invisible means until the martyr signed it with the cross. He was beatified by Pius XI on Dec. 15, 1929.

Feast: Feast of the English Martyrs, May 4 (England).

See Also: ENGLAND, SCOTLAND, AND WALES, MARTYRS OF.

Bibliography: R. CHALLONER, *Memoirs of Missionary Priests,* ed. J. H. POLLEN (rev. ed. London 1924; repr. Farnborough 1969). J. H. POLLEN, *Acts of English Martyrs* (London 1891).

[K. I. RABENSTEIN]

WATKINSON, THOMAS, BL.

Lay martyr; b. at Hemingborough or Menthrope, Yorkshire, England; d. May 31, 1591, hanged at York. He was a Catholic of the lesser nobility who is described as a widower with a family and as cleric; he may have been in minor orders. Watkinson lived a solitary life and assisted the seminary priests out of his devotion to Christ. He was arrested when Bl. Robert THORPE was discovered in his home on Palm Sunday 1595. He was charged with harboring a priest, but was offered clemency if he would worship in the state church. He refused and was executed. He was beatified by Pope John Paul II on Nov. 22, 1987 with George Haydock and companions.

Feast of the English Martyrs: May 4 (England).

See Also: ENGLAND, SCOTLAND, AND WALES, MARTYRS OF.

Bibliography: R. CHALLONER, *Memoirs of Missionary Priests,* ed. J. H. POLLEN (rev. ed. London 1924). J. H. POLLEN, *Acts of English Martyrs* (London 1891).

[K. I. RABENSTEIN]

WATTSON, PAUL JAMES FRANCES

Founder of the Society of the ATONEMENT; b. Millington, MD, Jan. 16, 1863; d. Garrison, NY, Feb. 8, 1940. He was baptized Lewis Thomas Wattson. In 1882, having studied at St. Mary's Hall, Burlington, NJ, and St. Stephen's (now Bard) College, Annandale, NY, he entered General Theological Seminary, New York City. After his ordination for the Episcopal Church in 1886, he began to work for reunion with the Holy See. In December 1898, with Mother Mary Lurana White, an Episcopal nun, he founded at Graymoor, NY, the Society of the Atonement, comprising Franciscan friars and Franciscan sisters of the Atonement who worked and prayed for this objective. Following a year's novitiate under the Anglican Fathers of the Holy Cross at Westminster, MD, he received the habit of the friars of the Atonement (1900) and took the name, Paul James. In 1903 he began publishing *The Lamp,* in which he defended papal infallibility and urged all Anglicans to return to Rome. To this end, in 1909 he inaugurated an eight-day period of prayer called the Church Unity Octave. Under Catholic auspices this became the Chair of Unity Octave, held each year January 18 to 25, and observed by non-Catholic bodies as the Universal Week of Prayer for Christian Unity.

The Graymoor community of 17 friars, sisters, and laymen was received corporately into the Catholic Church in 1909. After theological studies at St. Joseph's Seminary, Dunwoodie, NY, Wattson was ordained in 1910 by Abp. John M. Farley. Besides directing his society, he founded St. Christopher's Inn, a refuge for homeless men at Graymoor; organized the Graymoor Press and the "Ave Maria Hour" on radio; established a major seminary in Washington, DC; and collaborated with Richard Barry Doyle to found the CATHOLIC NEAR EAST WELFARE ASSOCIATION, which was incorporated in 1924 with his Union-That-Nothing-Be-Lost, initiated in 1904.

Bibliography: T. CRANNY, *Father Paul, Apostle of Unity* (Peekskill, NY 1955). D. GANNON, *Father Paul of Graymoor* (New York 1951).

[D. GANNON]

WAUGH, EVELYN

English novelist; b. Hampstead, England, Oct. 28, 1903; d. Combe Florey House, near Taunton, April 10, 1966. Arthur Evelyn St. John Waugh's father was managing director of Chapman and Hall publishing company; his brother Alex (b. 1898) was a prolific author. At Lancing College and Hertford College, Oxford, Waugh distinguished himself as journalist, cartoonist, and debater. After desultory attendance at art and carpentry schools and a brief career as schoolmaster, as well as revels with the ''Bright Young People'' portrayed in his novel *Vile Bodies* (1930), he entered ''the family trade of literature'' and in 1928 published a biography (*Rossetti*) and his first novel, *Decline and Fall*. He also married Evelyn Gardner. They were divorced in 1930; later that year Waugh became a Catholic. The marriage was annulled in 1936, and a year later he married Laura Herbert, with whom he had six children. The eldest son, Auberon, was a novelist and journalist.

Professional writer as well as novelist, Waugh read and traveled widely, interspersing novels with reviews, travel books, and journalism about the Mediterranean and Egypt, Africa, Abyssina and the Italian-Abyssinian War, and British Guiana and Mexico. During World War II he served with the Royal Marines, the commandos, and the British mission to Yugoslavia, drawing upon these experiences for a trilogy of novels collected as *Sword of Honour* (1965). His interest in English Catholicism led to biographies of Edmund CAMPION (1935) and of Msgr. Ronald Knox (1959). His autobiography, *A Little Learning* (1964), deals with his life to 1925. In his last years he spoke out against the effects, especially on liturgy, of the Second VATICAN COUNCIL.

Waugh's reputation as stylist and satirist, considerable in his lifetime, has grown since his death. Known in the 1930s for his detached, hard-minded satiric vision in such novels as *Black Mischief* (1932) and, what many think his best, *A Handful of Dust* (1934), Waugh did not use explicitly Catholic themes until *Brideshead Revisited* (1945), a panoramic view of England in the decades between world wars which focused on the decline of an aristocratic Catholic family. The novel brought him widespread recognition in America, but it was frequently criticized for sectarian partisanship and excessively lush prose. Some of these same charges were made of the subsequent novel *Sword of Honour,* (1965), but it nevertheless came to be regarded as his most important postwar work and probably the best English novel about World War II. It traces the progress of Guy Crouchback, member of an old Catholic family, from social isolation and moral paralysis, through superficial enthusiasm for military life, to an acceptance of his involvement with and responsibilities toward God and man.

Evelyn Waugh.

Bibliography: R. DAVIS, P. DOYLE, H. KOSOK, C. LINCK, *Evelyn Waugh: A Checklist of Primary and Secondary Material* (Troy, NY 1972). B. ULANOV, ''The Ordeal of Evelyn Waugh'' in *The Vision Obscured: Perceptions of Some Twentieth-Century Catholics,* ed. M. FRIEDMAN (New York 1970). J. F. CARENS, *The Satiric Art of Evelyn Waugh* (Seattle 1966). D. L. PATEY, *The Life of Evelyn Waugh: A Critical Biography* (Oxford 1998).

[R. DAVIS]

WAVERLEY, ABBEY OF

First Cistercian monastery in England, founded near Farnham (Surrey) in 1128, by Bp. William Giffard of Winchester, and colonized from Aûmone. In spite of material difficulties, it founded Garendon (1133), Ford (1136), Thame (1137), Bruerne (1147), Combe (1150), and Grâce Dieu (1226). In 1187, it had 70 choir monks and 120 lay brothers. Its seniority in England, though disputed by Furness until 1232, gave Waverley precedence and the task of defending the privileges of the order. Waverley was one of the few abbeys successfully to oppose the royal privilege of assigning corodies. Historical material concerning life at Waverley is ample for the period covered by the chronicle, but much less is known of its later history. Although never a wealthy monastery, it managed to survive many material disasters, including floods, but when it was suppressed in 1536, there were only 13 monks. Of the buildings, little remains today on a site that now lies within a private estate.

Bibliography: *Annales Monastici*, ed. H. R. LUARD, 5 v. (*Rerum Brittanicarum medii aevi scriptores* 36) v.2. *A History of Hampshire and the Isle of Wight*, 5 v. (Westminster-London 1900–12). H. BRAKSPEAR, *Waverley Abbey* (London 1905). L. H. COTTINEAU, *Répertoire topobibliographique des abbayes et prieurés*, 2 v. (Mâcon 1935–39) 2:3435–36. D. KNOWLES and R. N. HADCOCK, *Medieval Religious Houses: England and Wales* (New York 1953) 117. D. KNOWLES, *The Monastic Order in England, 943–1216* (2d ed. Cambridge, England 1962).

[S. F. HOCKEY]

WAY, WILLIAM, BL.

Priest, martyr; *alias* May, Flower; b. 1531, Exeter, England; hanged, drawn, and quartered at Kingston-on-Thames, Sept. 23, 1588. Following his ordination at Laon, France (Sept. 18, 1586), Fr. Way returned to England. He was arrested within six months (June 1587) and committed to the Clink. He was indicted for his priesthood at Newgate (September 1588), but declined to be tried by a secular judge. When he also refused to acknowledge the legitimacy of the bishop of London and the supremacy of Queen Elizabeth in Church matters, he was condemned. He joyfully prepared for his martyrdom with fasting and mortification. Way was beatified by Pius XI on Dec. 15, 1929.

Feast: Feast of the English Martyrs, May 4 (England).

See Also: ENGLAND, SCOTLAND, AND WALES, MARTYRS OF.

Bibliography: R. CHALLONER, *Memoirs of Missionary Priests*, ed. J. H. POLLEN (rev. ed. London 1924; repr. Farnborough 1969), I, 60. J. MORRIS, ed., *The Troubles of Our Catholic Forefathers Related by Themselves*, 3 v. (London 1872–77), II, 234; III, 38. J. H. POLLEN, *Acts of English Martyrs* (London 1891) 287, 307.

[K. I. RABENSTEIN]

WAYNFLETE, WILLIAM

Bishop, chancellor of England; b. Wainfleet, Lincolnshire, *c.* 1394; d. South Waltham, Hampshire, Aug. 11, 1486. Having studied at OXFORD, he was made headmaster of Winchester College (1429–42) and provost of Henry VI's new school at Eton, (1442–47). Henry's great regard for him led to his promotion to the See of WINCHESTER by papal provision (May 10, 1447) and his appointment as chancellor of England, October 1456 to July 1460. A peace-loving man, he tried to mediate in the civil strife of Henry's later years, and despite his Lancastrian connections, enjoyed the confidence of the Yorkist kings. As a considerable patron of education, he obtained a license to found an Oxford hall for the study of theology and philosophy in May 1448; this foundation was later transformed (1457–58) into his college of Magdalen, Oxford. His statutes for Magdalen pointed the way to future developments in collegiate education. His belief in the need for a thorough grounding in language led him to establish a grammar school in Oxford beside his college (1478). He founded another school in his native village of Wainfleet (1459) and completed the building of Eton College largely at his own expense.

Bibliography: R. CHANDLER, *Life of William Waynliete* (London 1811). H. A. WILSON, *Magdalen College* (London 1899). A. B. EMDEN, *A Biographical Register of the University of Oxford to A.D. 1500* 3:2001–03.

[C. D. ROSS]

WAZO OF LIÈGE

Bishop, theologian, and leading theoretician of the 11th-century GREGORIAN REFORM; b. in the region of Lobbes or Namur, 980 or 990; d. Liège, July 14, 1048. After studies at LOBBES and in the cathedral school of Liège, Wazo became one of the disciples of the celebrated master, FULBERT OF CHARTRES. He returned to Liège (1008), succeeding NOTKER OF LIÈGE as master of the cathedral school, and thereafter rose rapidly in the Church. In 1042 he was unanimously elected bishop of LIÈGE, but this office made him a temporal prince as well, and as such he took an active part in imperial politics. Generally loyal to Emperor HENRY III, he challenged the caesaropapist tendencies of the Emperor (*see* INVESTITURE STRUGGLE), especially on the occasion of the deposition of Pope GREGORY VI by the Council of SUTRI (1046). At this time he enunciated the basic Gregorian principle, that the sovereign pontiff may be judged by no one but God. Wazo probably helped to formulate the Church's position on the repression of heresy, because in his response to an inquiry from the bishop of Châlons, Wazo replied that Christianity demands toleration of heretics, and although Christians may seek to combat heresy, it must be done by Christian conversion rather than by spilling blood.

Bibliography: *Monumenta Germaniae Historica: Scriptores* (Berlin 1826–) 7:210–234. A. FLICHE, *La Réforme grégorienne*, 3 v. (Louvain 1924–37) 1:113–123. R. H. A. HUYSMANS, *Wazo van Luik* (Nijmegen 1932). J. CLOSON, "Wazon, évêque de Liège, 1042–1048," *Chronique archéologique du pays de Liège* 28 (1937) 57–70. H. GLAESENER, "Les Démêles de Godefroid le Barbu avec Henri III et l'évêque Wazon," *Revue d'histoire ecclésiastique* 40 (1944–45) 141–170. É. DE MOREAU, *Histoire de l'église en Belgique* (2d ed. Brussels 1945) 2:34–52. É. AMANN, *Dictionnaire de* *théologie catholique,* ed. A. VACANT et al., (Paris 1903–50) 15.2:3520–24. E. HOERSCHELMANN, *Bischof W. von Lüttich und seine Bedeutung für den Beginn des Investiturstreites* (Düsseldorf 1955).

[D. S. BUCZEK]

WEARMOUTH, ABBEY OF

Former Benedictine monastery in Northumbria, England, on the Wear River. The abbey was founded in 674 by BENEDICT BISCOP on land given by King Egfrid of Northumbria and was dedicated to the Apostle Peter. Eight years later, in 682, Benedict Biscop founded the sisterhouse of JARROW, on the Tyne River, some six or seven miles away, and dedicated it to the Apostle Paul. These two abbeys, always intimately associated with each other and usually ruled by the same abbot, were frequently thought of as constituting one double monastery. They rapidly became a center of learning and Christian culture for the early English Church. Benedict Biscop, the first abbot, and his successor CEOLFRID compiled the basis of an impressive library through their collections of MSS in the course of their numerous Italian travels. This library, as well as the famous SCRIPTORIUM, made possible Wearmouth's renowned monastic school, of which Venerable BEDE was both the most celebrated product and the most outstanding master. As a result of the scholarly work of this school and scriptorium, a group of Northumbrian MSS with obviously common features is extant; of these the *Codex Amiatinus* of the Vulgate is the best-known example; it mentions Abbot Ceolfrid by name and comes probably from Wearmouth. The *Codex Fuldensis* of the New Testament seems to have been preserved for a time at Jarrow. After two centuries of brilliant contributions to Anglo-Saxon intellectual and cultural life, both abbeys were destroyed during the Danish invasions of 867–870. Although reconstructed by Aldwin of Winchcombe *c.* 1074, they never again attained their earlier importance; they became cells of DURHAM, on which they remained dependent until their dissolution in 1539. Today a parish church occupies part of the site of Wearmouth at Sunderland, Durham, England.

Bibliography: BEDE, *Historia abbatum* in *Opera historica,* ed. C. PLUMMER (2d ed. Oxford 1956) 364–387. W. DUGDALE, *Monasticon Anglicanum* (London 1655–73); best ed. by J. CALEY, et al., 6 v. (1817–30) 1:501–504. J. RAINE, ed., *The Inventories and Account Rolls of the Benedictine Houses or Cells of Jarrow and Monk-Wearmouth* (Surtees Society 29; Durham 1854). F. M. STENTON, *Anglo-Saxon England* (2d ed. Oxford 1947). D. KNOWLES and R. N. HADCOCK, *Medieval Religious Houses: England and Wales* (New York 1953). D. KNOWLES, *The Monastic Order in England, 943–1216* (2d ed. Cambridge, England 1962) 168–171.

[J. BRÜCKMANN]

WEBB, BENEDICT JOSEPH

Pioneer publisher, editor, and historian; b. Bardstown, KY, Feb. 25, 1814; d. Louisville, KY, Aug. 2, 1897. He was the son of Nehemiah, a native of Pennsylvania and convert from Quakerism, and Clotilda (Edelin) Webb, of a Maryland Catholic family. Known as Ben J. Webb (sometimes erroneously called Benjamin Joseph), he was educated at St. Joseph's College, Bardstown (1821–28). A printer by trade, Webb early promoted the *Catholic Advocate,* Kentucky's first Catholic newspaper, for which he was publisher (1836–48). Later (1858–62) he was chief editor of the *Guardian,* the local organ of the St. Vincent de Paul Society, and then editor of the revived *Catholic Advocate* (1869–72). In 1854 he attracted notice during the Know-Nothing (*see* KNOW-NOTHINGISM) troubles by a series of public letters defending Catholicism against George D. Prentice, editor of the *Louisville Journal;* the whole series was published as *Letters of a Kentucky Catholic* (1856). From 1867 to 1875 Webb served in the Kentucky Legislature as senator from the Louisville area. In 1884 he published *The Centenary of Catholicity in Kentucky,* a basic historical work, which demonstrates his personal acquaintance with the pioneer Church in Kentucky and with many of its clerical and lay leaders. Webb's close association with the early bishops and clergy of the Bardstown-Louisville diocese and his initiative in Catholic journalism and charitable organizations provided an example of lay leadership unusual in the rising American Church of the 19th century.

Bibliography: B. J. WEBB, *The Centenary of Catholicity in Kentucky* (Louisville 1884). J. S. JOHNSTON, "B. J. W., Kentucky Historian," *The Filson Club Historical Quarterly* 6 (1932) 205–207.

[D. RECKTENWALD]

WEBER, ANSELM

Missionary; b. New Salem, MI, Nov. 10, 1862; d. Rochester, MN, March 7, 1921. He was the son of Peter and Anna (Pfeiffer) Weber. He entered the Franciscan novitiate at Oldenburg, IN (1882), and later studied at St. Francis College, Cincinnati, Ohio, where he was ordained in 1889. He taught at the college until his health failed in 1898. He then embarked upon his missionary career in St. Michael's, AZ. At the outset Weber recognized that linguistic inadequacies represented the most serious hindrance to the Christianization of the Navahos. For 12 years he worked to help correct these deficiencies, and in 1912 his two-volume *English-Navaho and Navaho-English Dictionary* was published. During the time he was working on his dictionary, Weber traveled widely on mission assignments and established day schools at Chin

Medallion featuring Carl Maria von Weber.

Lee, AZ, and at Lukachukai on the Arizona–New Mexico border. From 1913 to his death Weber devoted himself to the editorship of the *Franciscan Missions of the Southwest,* an annual magazine.

Bibliography: R. L. WILKIN, *Anselm Weber, O.F.M.* (Milwaukee 1955).

[J. L. MORRISON]

WEBER, CARL MARIA VON

Founder of German romantic opera; b. Eutin (near Lübeck), Germany, Nov. 18, 1786; d. London, June 5, 1826. He was a son of Franz Anton von Weber, an unstable musician with a spurious claim to noble rank, and his second wife Genofeva von Brenner, a talented singer with whom he led an itinerant theatrical troupe. His father, determined to produce a child prodigy such as his nephew MOZART, taught him piano and voice, but Carl's genius unfolded at its own tempo under professional training in several towns, including Salzburg, where he studied briefly with M. HAYDN, and Vienna, where at 17 he came under the intensive tutelage of G. J. Vogler. From then until he became, at 30, conductor of German opera at the Dresden court and married the singer Caroline Brandt, his career was one of harrowing frustration but also one of solid creative growth toward his ideal of a national operatic style, realized in 1821 with the opera *Der Freischütz.* This work synthesized the finest aspirations of the German folk soul in music of universal charm, shattered the monopoly of Italian opera, and pro-

vided a starting point for Richard WAGNER and the opera of the future. Besides nine other operas (notably, *Euryanthe* and *Oberon*), Weber composed many ingratiating concert works, as well as three Masses and two Offertoria in his floridly romantic, hence liturgically inappropriate, vein. A self-schooled thinker and writer, he also published a quantity of serious music criticism. He kept the Catholic faith of his fathers, which sustained him in adversity if it played little part in his artistic development. After his lonely death, his body was interred at Moorfields Chapel (St. Mary's Catholic church), London, but was reinterred in 1844, with much pomp and a peroration and choral composition by Wagner, in the Inner Catholic Cemetery, Dresden.

Bibliography: *Musikalische Werke,* ed. H. J. MOSER (Augsburg 1926–); *Sämtliche Schriften,* ed. G. KAISER (Berlin 1908); *Ein Brevier,* ed. H. DÜNNEBEIL (Berlin 1949); *Ausgewählte Schriften,* ed. W. ALTMANN (Regensburg 1937). O. STRUNK, ed., *Source Readings in Music History* (New York 1950) 802–807. M. M. VON WEBER, *Carl Maria von Weber,* 3 v. (Leipzig 1864–66), new ed. by R. PECHEL (Berlin 1912); unsatisfactory adaptation by J. P. SIMPSON, *The Life of an Artist,* 2 v. (Boston 1865). E. KROLL, *Weber* (Potsdam 1934). H. ALLEKOTTE, *C. M. v. Webers Messen* (Bonn 1913). L. P. and R. P. STEBBINS, *Enchanted Wanderer* (New York 1940), original research, with exhaustive bibliog. A. A. ABERT et al., *Die Musik in Geschichte und Gegenwart,* ed. F. BLUME (Kassel-Basel 1949–) v.13 (in press). P. SPITTA, *Grove's Dictionary of Music and Musicians,* ed. E. BLOM 9 v. (5th ed. London 1954) 9:195–222. K. G. FELLERER, *The History of Catholic Church Music,* tr. F. A. BRUNNER (Baltimore 1961). D. J. GROUT, *A Short History of Opera,* 2 v. (2d, rev. and enl. ed. New York 1965). M. S. COLE, "*Der Freischütz,*" In *International Dictionary of Opera* 2 v., ed. C. S. LARUE, (Detroit 1993) 466–468. K. DITZLER, "The Motif of the Forest in Weber's *Silvana* and *Der Freischütz,*" *The Opera Journal* 31/2and3 (1998) 35–49. M. F. DOERNER, "German Romantic Opera? A Critical Reappraisal of *Undine* and *Der Freischütz,*" *The Opera Quarterly* 10/2 (1993/1994) 10–26. N. GUBKINA, "Carl Maria von Webers *Waldmädchen:* Ein wiedergefundenes Jugendwerk," *Die Musikforschung* 53 (2000) 57–59. C. HEADINGTON, "*Oberon*" in *International Dictionary of Opera* 2 v., ed. C. S. LARUE (Detroit 1993) 950; "*Euryanthe*" in *International Dictionary of Opera* 2 v., ed. C. S. LARUE (Detroit 1993) 399–400. A. HOUTCHENS, "Carl Maria von Weber in Mozart's Prague," *The Opera Journal* 27/2 (1994) 2–11.

[M. E. EVANS]

WEBER, MAX

Jurist, political economist, sociologist; b. Erfurt, Germany, April 21, 1864; d. Munich, June 14, 1920. A precocious child, Weber began the study of history and philosophy at an early age. In 1882 he enrolled in the juridical faculty at Heidelberg and later transferred to Göttingen and Berlin where he studied law, history, and theology. He passed his bar examination in 1887; then, while practicing law in Berlin, he obtained a doctorate in 1889, with a thesis on the history of medieval commercial associations. In 1891 he qualified as a university lecturer in Roman and commercial law with a masterful work on the history of agrarian institutions in Rome. A study on the conditions of agrarian workers in East Prussia, published in 1892, established his reputation as a social scientist. He was called to Freiburg as professor of economics in 1894. In 1896 he moved to Heidelberg to succeed Karl Knies. Brilliant lecturer and great conversationalist though he was, his leadership as an academician was cut short by a severe nervous breakdown in 1898. For four years he was virtually incapacitated physically and mentally. He never fully recovered. Although he had to give up teaching, he resumed scholarly activities and in 1919 accepted a chair of sociology at Munich, where soon afterward he succumbed to influenza.

In 1903 Weber became associate editor of the *Archivs für Sozialwissenschaft und Sozialpolitik,* in which all his scholarly writings were published. There was a posthumous edition of his collected works. He visited the U.S. in 1904 and spent several months collecting material on American Protestant sects. The trip greatly improved his mental health and on his return to Germany he plunged into intensive work. In the period from 1905 to 1914 he wrote his major essays on the nature of social science and on the sociology of religion. He undertook several empirical investigations, produced his classic study on agrarian conditions in antiquity, and prepared the manuscript of his magnum opus, *Wirtschaft und Gesellschaft* (Tubingen 1922). In 1908 Weber and Georg Simmel organized the German Sociological Society.

During World War I Weber served for a year as a captain in charge of a field hospital. He foresaw the eventual defeat of Germany. In editorials written for the *Frankfurter Zeitung* he tried to forestall the event by advocating peace without annexation, abandonment of unrestricted submarine warfare, and democratic government. After the war Weber helped draft the Weimar Constitution.

Religion and Society. Weber's most original contribution to sociology is his analysis of the relation between religion and social organization. His basic work on the subject is *The Protestant Ethic and the Spirit of Capitalism* (New York 1958), devoted to the appearance at the end of the 17th century of an unprecedented set of norms regulating the conduct of business in western European societies. According to these norms, business is a calling (*Beruf*), work is a way, not a means, of living, and its fruits are not to be enjoyed, but to be held in temporary stewardship. This "spirit of capitalism" involved a break with traditional norms and, according to Weber, it coincided with the propagation of a new conception of life preached by Protestant reformers like Calvin, and by the

Max Weber.

Puritans. Weber concluded that the "ethos of ascetic Protestantism" exerted a determining influence because the majority of middle class merchants of the 17th and early 18th centuries were ardent members of the new evangelical sects. Since Weber's thesis has often been misinterpreted, it should be noted that the "spirit of capitalism" refers only to the professional ethics of entrepreneurs, not to the form of economic organization. The thesis has nothing to do with the origin or function of the capitalist system as such.

After completing his study of Protestant ethics, Weber made a systematic analysis of other religions: Judaism, Confucianism, Taoism, Hinduism, and Buddhism. These studies support the general proposition that there exists a meaningful congruence between the religious ethos of a culture and its prevailing norms of conduct. They also show that there is no equivalent to Protestant asceticism in other religions, and this is taken as one possible reason for the fact that capitalism in other cultures did not evolve the characteristic forms. In *The Sociology of Religion* (Boston 1963), Weber analyzed the evolution of religion and showed it to have been a dynamic factor in social change.

Method of Social Science. Weber's sociopolitical studies of charismatic leadership and bureaucracy were

Anton von Webern. (©Bettmann/CORBIS)

as clearly an innovation as his studies of religion. The development of a set of concepts and general rules, called ideal-types, designed to serve as tools for the establishment of causal explanations of concrete and culturally significant phenomena, was an important methodological contribution to social science.

Weber defined social science as the attempt to apply the methods and techniques of scientific inquiry to the study of concrete situations, events, or conditions that directly influence social goals and values. He claimed that in this respect social science differs from physical science, since the latter aims to discover universal laws that are independent of human motivations and evaluations.

Bibliography: R. BENDIX, *Max Weber: An Intellectual Portrait* (Garden City, N.Y. 1962). T. PARSONS, *The Structure of Social Action* (New York 1937). T. ABEL, *Systematic Sociology in Germany* (New York 1929). H. S. HUGHES, *Consciousness and Society* (New York 1961) 278–335. M. WEBER, *Max Weber: Ein Lebensbild* (Heidelberg 1950), contains a full bibliography of his writings.

[T. ABEL]

WEBERN, ANTON VON

Renowned composer of the 12-tone method; b. Vienna, Austria, Dec. 3, 1883; d. Mittersill, Austria, Sept. 15, 1945, when accidentally shot by an American occupation serviceman. In 1904 he began studying with Arnold SCHOENBERG and soon mastered the "ultra-short" form in which Schoenberg excelled. Good examples of this are his *Six Bagatelles for String Quartet* (Op. 9), of which Schoenberg wrote, ". . . such concentration can only be present in proportion to the absence of self-pity." Webern was a Catholic of deep, simple faith, and his religious feeling appears in his choice of texts for the following songs and choral works: *Five Spiritual Songs* (Op. 15); *Five Canons* (Op. 16): (*Christus factus est pro nobis, Dormi Jesu, Crux fidelis, Asperges me, Crucem tuam adoramus*); *Three Folk Texts* (Op. 17); *Ave, Regina Coelorum* (from Op. 18); *Three Songs* (Op. 23) from Hildegard Jone's *Viae inviae; Das Augenlicht* (Op. 26); and two cantatas (Op. 29 and 31), also to Jone texts. After 1924 he adopted Schoenberg's 12-tone (serial) method, and the resulting works foreshadow many present-day compositional experiments. Webern dropped the prefix of nobility (von) in later years.

Bibliography: A. VON WEBERN, *Briefe an Hildegard Jone und Josef Humplik,* ed. J. POLNAUER (Vienna 1959). "Anton Webern," tr. L. BLACK and E. SMITH, *Die Reihe* 2 (1955; Bryn Mawr 1958), entire issue devoted to Webern. W. KOLNEDER, *Anton Webern* (Rodenkirchen, Ger. 1961). H. MOLDENHAUER, *The Death of Anton Webern* (New York 1961). R. LEIBOWITZ, *Schoenberg and His School,* tr. D. NEWLIN (New York 1949). H. F. REDLICH, *Die Musik in Geschichte und Gegenwart,* ed. F. BLUME (Kassel-Basel 1949–). M. HAYES, *Anton von Webern* (London 1995). J. NOLLER, "Weberns Innerlichkeit und das Theater," *Österreichische Musik Zeitschrift* 47 (1992) 502–13. S. RODE, "Anton Webern und Karl Kraus: Aspekte einer ungewöhnlichen Kraus-Rezeption," *Österreichische Musik Zeitschrift* 46 (1991) 313–24. A. C. SHREFFLER, *Webern and the Lyric Impulse: Songs and Fragments on Poems of Georg Trakl* (Oxford 1994). B. ZUBER, "Bei Goethe überall zu lesn . . . Anton Webern und der Monismus," *Österreichische Musik Zeitschrift* 50 (1995) 369–78.

[D. NEWLIN]

WEBLEY, HENRY, BL.

Lay martyr; b. ca. 1558 at Gloucester, England; d. Aug. 28, 1588, hanged at Mile's End Green, London. He was arrested at Chichester Harbour in 1586 and condemned for assisting Bl. William DEAN, a seminary priest. Webley was beatified by Pope John Paul II on Nov. 22, 1987 with George Haydock and companions.

Feast of the English Martyrs: May 4 (England).

See Also: ENGLAND, SCOTLAND, AND WALES, MARTYRS OF.

Bibliography: R. CHALLONER, *Memoirs of Missionary Priests,* ed. J. H. POLLEN (rev. ed. London 1924). J. H. POLLEN, *Acts of English Martyrs* (London 1891).

[K. I. RABENSTEIN]

WEBSTER, AUGUSTINE, ST.

Carthusian martyr; b. unknown; d. Tyburn, London, England, May 4, 1535. He received his B.A. degree from Cambridge in 1510 and his M.A. three years later. Thomas Cranmer, his exact contemporary at Cambridge, described him as a learned man who did not originally believe in the papal primacy. He entered the Charterhouse at Sheen and was chosen as prior of Axholme in Lincolnshire not before 1531. In a decree of Feb. 15, 1535, Henry VIII assumed the title of Supreme Head of the English Church. Webster came to London to consult St. John HOUGHTON, prior of the London Charterhouse, on this issue. He accompanied Houghton and St. Robert LAWRENCE, prior of Beauvale, in a plea to Thomas Cromwell for a form of the oath suitable to their conscience. They were imprisoned in the Tower together with St. Richard REYNOLDS, a Bridgettine of Syon. They were examined by royal commissioners on April 20 and stood trial in Westminster Hall. They pleaded not guilty since they did not seditiously oppose the king's supremacy. The jury hesitated for two days but through pressure of Cromwell they entered a verdict of guilty. On May 4 together with Bl. John Haile, the aged vicar of Isleworth, these protomartyrs were drawn from the Tower to Tyburn. There they suffered the penalty for treason by being hanged, cut down while still alive, drawn, and quartered. Webster was beatified by Leo XIII, and canonized by Paul VI on Oct. 25, 1970 as one of the Forty Martyrs of England and Wales.

Feast: May 4; October 25 (Feast of the 40 Martyrs of England and Wales); May 4 (Feast of the English Martyrs in England).

See Also: ENGLAND, SCOTLAND, AND WALES, MARTYRS OF.

Bibliography: A contemporary account in M. CHAUNCY, "De B.B. Martyribus Carthusiensibus in Anglia," ed. F. VAN ORTROY, *Analecta Bollandiana* 14 (1895) 268–283; "Martyrum Monachorum Carthusianorum in Anglia Passio minor," ed. F. VAN ORTROY, *ibid.* 22 (1903) 51–78; *Passion and Martyrdom of the Holy English Carthusian Fathers,* tr. A. F. RADCLIFFE (New York 1936). L. HENDRIKS, *London Charterhouse, Its Monks and Its Martyrs* (London 1889). E. M. THOMPSON, *The Carthusian Order in England* (New York 1930). L. E. WHATMORE, *Blessed Carthusian Martyrs* (London 1962).

[L. E. WHATMORE]

WEHRLE, VINCENT DE PAUL

Missionary, monastic founder, and bishop; b. Berg, Saint-Gallen, Switzerland, Dec. 19, 1855; d. Bismarck, ND, Nov. 2, 1941. After his ordination at the Benedictine Abbey of Einsiedeln in 1882, he spent four years as a

Vincent de Paul Wehrle.

missionary in Arkansas and Indiana before going to Yankton, Dakota Territory, in 1886. While caring for the settlers along 275 miles of the Great Northern Railroad (1888–99), he founded St. Gall's Monastery at Devils Lake (1893). His apostolic concern for the German-speaking immigrants flocking to southwestern North Dakota led him to relocate his monastery in Richardton in 1899. The extensive spiritual and educational care that he and his monks gave to the settlers merited for him the title "Apostle of the German-Russians and German-Hungarians"—the people who formed the majority of the Catholic population in western North Dakota. Both as abbot (1904–15) and as the first bishop of the Diocese of BISMARCK (1910–39), he did much to preserve and deepen the faith of the settlers by personal mission preaching, circuit visitation of parishes and missions, and building churches and parochial schools. Worn out by his vigorous activities, he resigned as bishop in 1939.

[L. PFALLER]

WEIGEL, GUSTAVE

Theologian and ecumenist; b. Buffalo, New York, Jan. 15, 1906; d. New York City, Jan. 3, 1964. Weigel entered the Society of Jesus (1922); made his philosophical and theological studies at Woodstock College, Maryland, where he was ordained (1933); and pursued doctoral studies in theology at the Gregorian University, Rome (1935–37), receiving his degree in 1938. He was professor of dogmatic theology at the Universidad Católica de Chile (1937–48), dean of its faculty of theology (1942–48), and professor of ecclesiology at Woodstock College (1948–64).

Weigel wrote 11 books: *Faustus of Riez* (Philadelphia 1938); *El cristianismo oriental* (Buenos Aires 1945); *La psicología de la religión* (Santiago de Chile 1945); *A Catholic Primer on the Ecumenical Movement* (Westminster, Md. 1957); *Faith and Understanding in America* (New York 1959); *American Dialogue,* with Robert McAfee Brown (New York 1960); *Churches in North America* (Baltimore 1961); *Catholic Theology in Dialogue* (New York 1961); *Knowledge: Its Values and Limits* and *Religion and Knowledge of God,* both with Arthur Madden (Englewood Cliffs, N.J. 1961); and *The Modern God* (New York 1963). He wrote numerous articles in journals, books, and encyclopedias; lectured incessantly on college and university campuses throughout the U.S.; was State Department intellectual exchange lecturer in Germany (1953) and in Chile and Colombia (1956); and was a Catholic consultant for the *Encyclopaedia Britannica.*

Weigel's theological activity ultimately centered on ecclesiology and, especially in the last decade of his life, was focused on the ecumenical movement, in which he was a Catholic pioneer in the U.S. Surely the most significant, active, and respected Catholic ecumenist in America, he wedded wide knowledge of Protestantism and Eastern Orthodoxy to rich personal relationships with non-Catholic scholars, a warm love transcending creedal limits, an uncommon openness to alien viewpoints, and the unsparing gift of himself to others. He was a consulting member of the Secretariat for Promoting Christian Unity and an official of Vatican Council II, where, during the first two sessions, he was English translator for the non-Catholic observers.

Weigel's theological and ecumenical significance was recognized in honorary degrees from the Universidad Católica de Chile (1956), the University of Vermont (1960), Georgetown University (1962), Yale University (1962), Alfred University (1963), and St. Mary's College, Winona, Minnesota (1963).

[W. J. BURGHARDT]

WEIGHTS AND MEASURES (IN THE BIBLE)

The Israelites did not invent their own system of metrology, but were content to use the commonly accepted weights and measures. The pastoral patriarchs continued to use the Mesopotamian measures of their ancient homeland in their mutual interchange and readily adapted themselves to the weights and measures of the foreigners with whom they bartered. With the conquest of Canaan, the Israelites, as they became sedentary and urbanized, adopted the so-called Phoenician measures. When they in turn were conquered, variations in their metrology were necessitated for their dealings with their overlords. Thus there was flux and variation in Biblical weights and measures. Nor has archeology supplied us with sufficient data to warrant precise conclusions about metrology during the various epochs of Israel's existence. Hence we must be satisfied with approximations.

Linear Measures. In linear measurements the nomenclature was derived principally from the parts of the arm and hand used by the artisan in making his calculations. Thus the cubit was the length from the elbow to the tip of the extended middle finger; the span, the width of the spread from the tip of the thumb to the tip of the little finger; the palm, the width of the hand at the base of the fingers; and the finger, the width of the thumb. Although the Bible does not indicate the interrelation or proportion of the measurements, they probably followed the actual proportion of the hand and arm. Thus one cubit equaled two spans, six palms, or 24 fingers. The ordinary cubit, however, was distinct from the great or royal cubit, the equivalent of seven palms or 28 fingers. The absolute length, therefore, of the cubit remains uncertain; nor do the apparently precise statistics in the SILOAM INSCRIPTION lead to an exact evaluation, since round numbers were used in them. For rough estimation the ordinary cubit may be taken as about 18 inches; the royal, about 21 inches. The Greek cubit of the New Testament measures was about 18 inches.

Distances were generally given empirically, e.g., a three-day journey. Later notations in stadia are difficult to evaluate because of the variant values of the Greek stadium (from 194 to 210 yards). A fathom is six feet, and a Roman mile is 1,618 yards.

Measures of Capacity. Both solid and liquid measures varied during the different epochs of Israel's history, two different systems being discernible: a decimal system and a sexagesimal one. The combination of the two systems and the table of proportions given here are hypothetical and represent the post-Exilic period at the earliest. The dry measures are: homor (ass load) = 10 ephas = (30 $s^e\hat{a}$) = 100 gomors ('$\bar{o}mer$) = 180 qābs. Sexagesimal proportions are here enclosed in parentheses. R. de Vaux maintains that it is impossible to give the equivalents in modern measures. Estimations for the homor run from 6.77 bushels to 11.43 bushels. The kor, equal to the homor in Ez 45.14, may actually have equaled two homors.

The liquid measures are: one kor or one homor = ten baths = 60 hin = 720 logs. The bath contained about five gallons, but some archeological evidence suggests the existence of a royal bath of about ten gallons.

Weights. These were used to measure precious stones and metals, the basic unit being the shekel, i.e., "weight." The Bible mentions royal weights, sanctuary weights, and merchant's weights. The royal shekel was probably double the ordinary shekel. The value of premonarchical weights and the original sanctuary shekel have not been determined. The shekel's multiples were the mina and the talent. The Mesopotamian mina equaled 60 shekels, but the Phoenician only 50 shekels. The Israelites of the 12th to the 6th century B.C. apparently used the Phoenician system, but the earlier and later Israelites followed the Mesopotamian system. The proportions are: one talent = 60 minas = 3,000 (or 3,600) shekels = 6,000 becas = 72,000 geras.

Archeology has supplied us with about 50 stamped weights, leading to the estimation of the common shekel as the equivalent of 11 to 12 grams, with an average of 11.5 grams or 0.41 ounces. Thus, a talent of 3,000 (or 3,600) shekels equaled about 76 pounds (or about 91 pounds).

In the Hellenistic period, the Seleucid Dynasty adopted Attic standards for weights. ANTIOCHUS IV EPIPHANES, however, devalued the Attic drachma from 4.35 grams to 4.20 grams, and Tryphon further debased it to 4.0 grams. The following are equivalent Grecian weights: 1 talent = 60 minas = 6,000 drachmas = 36,000 obols.

Bibliography: *Encyclopedic Dictionary of the Bible,* translated and adapted by L. HARTMAN (New York, 1963) 2572–75, 1487–91, 405–407. R. DEVAUX, *Ancient Israel, Its Life and Institutions,* tr. J. MCHUGH (New York 1961) 195–209. D. DIRINGER, "The Royal Jar-Handle Stamps of Ancient Judah," *The Biblical Archeologist* 12 (New Haven 1949) 70–86. H. LEWY, "Assyro-Babylonian and Israelite Measures of Capacity and Rates of Seeding," *The Journal of the American Oriental Society* 64 (New Haven 1944) 65–73. A. SEGRE, "A Documentary Analysis of Ancient Palestine Unit of Measure." *Journal of Biblical Literature* 64 (Boston 1945) 357–375. C. C. WYLIE, "On King Solomon's Molten Sea," *The Biblical Archeologist* 12 (New Haven 1949) 86–90.

[J. A. PIERCE]

WEIL, SIMONE

French-Jewish writer, a radical in her social and political thinking, but drawn toward Catholicism (pseudonym Emile Novis); b. Paris, 1909; d. Ashford, England, Aug. 24, 1943. Weil was the daughter of a physician of the Parisian bourgeois milieu. Her childhood was happy, but World War I sharpened precociously her sensitivity to the miseries of man. The genius of her brother, Andrew ("his childhood was comparable to that of Pascal") stimulated her passion for the truth. She was attracted from her ninth year to Bolshevism, became an anarchist, and helped Trotsky. Simone was a student of Alain (Emile Chartier, 1868–1951), entered the Ecole Normale Supérieure, and earned the agrégée in philosophy. Weil taught at Le Puy, Roanne, Bourges, and then, obtaining leave, became a worker, and took part in the social movements and strikes of 1936. After that she involved herself with anarchists in the civil war in Spain.

Her position was strictly agnostic and anticlerical in 1938, when, on a visit to Solesmes, "Christ took hold of her." From then on she believed in His love and divinity and discovered the meaning of the Passion. Anti-Semitic decrees brought her to Provence where she met Father J. M. Perrin and worked as an agricultural laborer while a guest of G. Thibon. Then she discovered the relation of prayer to God and the Eucharist, but, beset by tormenting intellectual problems, did not enter the Church. She remained "waiting for God."

With her parents, she went to the U. S. to join her brother in the summer of 1942. She then returned to Free France and went to London in November. She obstinately shared the privations of the war and died the following August in a state of exhaustion.

Weil had an ardent compassion for the unfortunate, a great desire for the truth, and an eagerness to search out the will of God. Spiritually, she was torn by the conflict she felt between the attraction of Christ, of the Eucharist, and of the Gospel, on the one hand; and, on the other, the social, philosophical, and historical objections that oppressed her. In these the major lacunae in her knowledge are evident.

Bibliography: J. M. PERRIN and G. THIBON, *Simone Weil as We Knew Her,* tr. E. CRAUFURD (London 1953). G. FIORI, *Simone Weil: An Intellectual Biography,* tr. J. R. BERRIGAN (Athens, Ga. 1989). R. H. BELL, *Simone Weil: The Way of Justice as Compassion* (Lanham, Md. 1998). M. VETÖ *The Religious Metaphysics of Simone Weil,* tr. J. DARGAN (Albany, N.Y. 1994).

[J. M. PERRIN]

WEINGARTEN, ABBEY OF

Benedictine, in Württemberg, Germany. After 934 Count Henry, father of St. CONRAD OF CONSTANCE, founded a cloister of nuns, who in 1056 moved to Altomünster in Freising, while monks from there came to Weingarten. The imperial abbey, established by Welf IV and his wife Judith, followed the customs of HIRSAU (after 1088), joined the Swabian congregation of Benedictines (1603) and the Salzburg confederation (1653), was suppressed (1803) and restored (1922) with monks from ERDINGTON and BEURON. Bequests from GUELFS of Altdorf-Weingarten (990–1126) who are buried in Weingarten and from Hohenstaufen, as well as purchases by the abbey contributed to the endowment that in 1802 amounted to 124 square miles with 10,000 inhabitants and 1,200 farms. The 271-foot-long basilica and the cloister (Romanesque, late Gothic, and Renaissance), both built after 1123, are still standing. Rebuilding begun in 1685 is incomplete. The 335-foot-long baroque church (1715–24), the largest in Germany, has choir stalls by J. A. Feuchtmayer and two organs (77 and 46 registers) by Joseph Gabler (1737–50). A relic of the PRECIOUS BLOOD occasions a feast and cavalcade the Friday after Ascension Thursday. Freising, England, and Normandy, homelands of the monks and of the foundress Judith, influenced the scriptorium, which produced the most important Romanesque miniature painting in south Germany. In 1630 the library of the cathedral of Constance was purchased. Today the abbey is noted for music, history, translations from English, its school or *Progymnasium,* and its parish apostolate. (For illustrations, see following page.)

Bibliography: L. H. COTTINEAU, *Répertoire topobibliographique des abbayes et prieurés,* 2 v. (Mâcon 1935–39) 2:3437–39. G. SPAHR, ed., *Weingarten 1056–1956: Festschrift zur 900 Jahrfeier des Klosters* (Weingarten 1956). W. ELLERHORST, *Lexikon für Theologie und Kirche,* ed. M. BUCHBERGER, 10 v. (Freiburg 1930–38) 10:787–789. "Weingarten," *Lexikon für Theologie und Kirche,* ed. J. HOFER and K. RAHNER, 10 v. (2d, new ed. Freiburg 1957–65) v.10.

[G. SPAHR]

WEISHEIPL, JAMES ATHANASIUS

American DOMINICAN philosopher, author, editor; b. Oshkosh, Wis., July 3, 1923; d. Saskatoon, Saskatchewan, Dec. 3, 1985. Receiving his early education in his native city of Oshkosh, Father Weisheipl pursued higher studies in the Dominican Order, in which, after a novitiate year, he was first professed in 1943. In 1946 he received his licentiate in philosophy, and a year after his ordination in 1949, his lectorate in theology. After lecturing in England on natural philosophy, for which he always had a strong love, he pursued further studies in Rome, earning a doctorate in philosophy in 1953 from the Angelicum, the international university of the order.

Teaching and research dominated the remainder of Father Weisheipl's life. From 1957 to 1965 he taught the history of medieval philosophy at the Dominican House of Studies in River Forest, Ill., where he himself had been a student. In 1964, he began his long association with the Pontifical Institute of Medieval Studies, specializing in the history of medieval science. At the same time, he was a member of the graduate Centre for Medieval Studies, the Department of Philosophy, and the Institute for the History and the Philosophy of Science and Technology of the University of Toronto. Among numerous achievements should be mentioned his founding in 1965 and early direction of the American section of the Leonine Commission, which is producing the definitive critical edition of the works of St. THOMAS AQUINAS; his work as contributing editor of the *New Catholic Encyclopedia*; a year as visiting fellow of Corpus Christi College at Oxford; and his term as president of the American Catholic Philosophical Association from 1963 to 1964. But the recognition which he most cherished was the degree of Master of Sacred Theology which the Dominican Order awarded him in 1978.

Father Weisheipl was always very much a traditional Thomist, though certain convictions distinguished his own thought. One was his view of the new mathematical natural science of the modern age as largely constituted by theoretical constructs for the purpose of "saving appearances," and standing sharply against the philosophical penetration of nature by ARISTOTLE and Thomas. Another was the belief that philosophers must be seen in their historical contexts; his own work was largely an effort to marry systematic with historical expertise.

Especially noteworthy among his works— illustrating this penchant for joining the systematic and the historical—are his doctoral dissertation, *Nature and Gravitation*, his historical study, *The Development of Physical Theory in the Middle Ages*, and his biography of St. Thomas, *Friar Thomas d'Aquino.* The last–named work sums up and goes beyond previous lives of Thomas, and should help to keep the spirit of Thomas vigorously alive for the next generation of students.

Father Weisheipl was a very hard worker and his zeal and enthusiasm were extraordinary, as those who were fortunate to have him as a teacher can attest. He burned the candle at both ends in order to serve his generous response to his vocation. Though his health suffered, he continued until his death to exert himself to the fullest in the furthering of science and learning. His dedication to the intellectual life should not obscure his great pastoral concern for students and others. He was, in all that he did, not merely an intellectual but a Dominican priest with a very warm heart.

Bibliography: A. MAURER, ''James A. Weisheipl. O.P.,'' *Medieval Studies* 47 (1985) xii–xix.

[N. E. FENTON]

WEISS, ALBERT MARIA

Theologian; b. Indersdorf, Bavaria, Apr. 22, 1844; d. Fribourg, Switzerland, Aug. 15, 1925. He was ordained in 1867, and after studies in Würzburg, Mainz, Bonn, Tübingen, and Cologne, he received the doctorate in theology at the University of Munich in 1870. While teaching at Freising (1872–76), he collaborated on the second edition of the *Kirchenlexikon.* In Graz, where he joined the Dominican Order in 1876, and in Vienna, he prompted a Catholic social movement. In 1883 he was appointed to the Roman commission for editing St. Thomas's works, but sickness caused him to leave Rome. In 1884 he taught at the Dominican Studium at Vienna; he taught sociology (1890–92) and fundamental theology (1895–1919) at the University of Fribourg. His teaching anticipated the encyclical *Rerum novarum* (1891). His principal works are: *Die altkirchliche Pädagogik* (Freiburg 1869), *Gesetze für Kapitalzins u. Arbeitslohn* (Freiburg 1883), *Apologie des Christentums vom Standpunkt der Sitte u. der Kultur,* 5 v. (Freiburg 1878–89, 4th ed. 1904–08), *Lebens–u. Gewissensfragen der Gegenwart,* 2 v. (Freiburg 1911), *Liberalismus u. Christentum* (Trier 1914), *Lutherpsychologie* (Mainz 1906).

Bibliography: R. FEI, *Memorie Domenicane* 47 (1930) 47–59. S. SZABÓ, *Analecta Sacri Ordinis Praedicatorum* 17 (1925–26) 603–614. G. HÄFELE, *Theologische-praktische Quartalschrift* 79 (1926) 281–296, 552–567, 774–784.

[A. M. WALZ]

WEISS, LIBERAT

Franciscan missionary to Ethiopia and martyr; b. Konnersreuth, Bavaria, Jan. 4, 1675; d. Abbo, near Gondar, Ethiopia, March 3, 1716. He became a friar Oct. 13, 1693, at Graz, Austria; was ordained Sept. 14, 1698, at Vienna; and joined the Upper Egypt–Ethiopia mission, headed by Prefect Joseph of Jerusalem, OFM, in 1704 at Rome. On its way to Ethiopia, the party reached Sennar, Sudan, May 21, 1705, and was halted by a rupture of relations between the courts of Sennar and Gondar (Ethiopia's capital). Among unspeakable hardships, Weiss was named vice prefect by the dying prefect (May 29, 1709),

and returned to Cairo to plan a fresh start. Impressed by the heroic efforts of the missionaries, the Holy See determined to open the Ethiopian mission, and named Weiss prefect (April 20, 1711). In the fifth Franciscan attempt since 1632, when the Portuguese Jesuits and garrison fell victims of a dreadful persecution, the new prefect and confreres Michele Pio Fasoli and Samuele Marzorati left Cairo for Gondar by way of the Red Sea (Nov. 3, 1711). From Veinahaila, Tigrai, Weiss sent messengers with a letter to Abbot Gregory Tarara, a Basilian who had been converted by him at Sennar and was at that time attached to the Gondar court, to introduce the friars to King Yustos (1712–16). On July 20, 1712, the friars reached Gondar and were warmly welcomed by the king and Abbot Gregory. The king supported the friars against the Monophysite monks, who charged them as infidels, upholding two natures in Christ, uncircumcised, and irreverent to the cross and the Blessed Mother's icons.

While waiting for papal briefs for the king and church dignitaries, the friars studied both the vernacular Amhara and the scriptural Tigrai, and prudently did some pastoral work. To help Yustos curb disloyalty and revolt, on Nov. 20, 1713, Weiss wrote Clement XI and Charles VI to dispatch some 5,000 soldiers to act as royal bodyguards and to restore internal peace, a request that was to bring him a stern reprimand (May 11, 1716). By April 29, 1714, intrepid Father Giacomo Negro reached Gondar with aid, mail, and comfort for his confreres; he returned to Cairo 13 months later to organize steady support for the new mission. On May 9, Clement XI wrote King Yustos and Abbot Gregory letters of appreciation for their assistance to the missionaries. As the revolt mounted, on Sept. 30, 1715, the king sent the friars into hiding but soon afterward fell critically ill. One of his brothers seized the throne on Feb. 12, 1716, as David III. After Yustos's untimely death (Feb. 16, 1716), David had the friars brought back to the capital. On Saturday, February 29, the friars were put on trial and questioned on charges of heresy, uncircumcision, lack of reverence to the Virgin Mary, and refusal to accept the Monophysite Eucharist. After being questioned again on March 2, they were sentenced to be stoned to death the next day at Abbo, but would be pardoned by the king if they would recant and conform. Put in chains, they spent the night in prayer. On March 3, questioned for the third time and found unshakable in their faith, Fathers Weiss, Michele Pio, and Samuele were taken naked two miles (2,000 meters) south of Gondar to Abbo lying about 300 meters east of Agareb stream. There, led by the Armenian monk who headed the revolt, the people stoned the friars to death, thus ending a promising mission for which the Holy See had entertained high hopes and made great efforts. With the informative process for his beatification begun on

July 25, 1933, Weiss is now venerated as a Servant of God.

Bibliography: C. BECCARI, *Notizia e saggi di opere e documenti inediti riguardanti la storia di Etiopia durante i secoli XVI, XVII e XVIII* (Rome 1903). C. OTHMER, "P. Liberatus Weiss, O.F.M., seine Missionstätigkeit und sein Martyrium," *Archivum Franciscanum historicum* 20 (1927) 336–355; "Series documentorum ad vitam, missionem ac martyrium P. Liberati Weiss. . .," *ibid.* 31 (1938) 127–153. 440–457; *P. Liberat Weiss: Ein österreichischer Franziskaner Apostolischer Missionär und Blutzeuge* (2d ed. Vienna 1933). G. M. MONTANO, "Etiopia Francescana nei documenti dei secoli XVII–XVIII," *Biblioteca bio-bibliografica della Terra Santa. . . ,* ser. 3, v.2, ed. G. ZANELLA (Quaracchi–Florence 1948). M. A. HABIG, *The Franciscan Book of Saints* (Chicago 1959). P. M. SEVESI, *L'Ordine dei Frati Minori* (Milan 1960) 2.2:39 G. MANFREDI, *La figura del "Praefectus Missionum". . .ai Frati Minori, 1630–1792* (Studia Orientalia Cristiana Collectanea 3; Cairo 1958). G. GIAMBERARDINI, ed., *Itinerario in Oriente (1701–1718) del P. Giacomo Negro da Oleggio (ibid.* 6; 1961) 265–304; "I Viaggiatori Francescani attraverso la Nubia dal 1698 al 1710," (*ibid.* 8; 1963) 361–437; *"Historia" della missione Francescana in Alto Egitto–Fungi–Etiopia, 1686–1720, scritta dal P. Giacomo d'Albano* (Cairo 1961).

[A. S. ROSSO]

WEISSENAU, MONASTERY OF

Imperial Premonstratensian abbey near Ravensburg, Baden-Württemberg, Germany (Lat. *Augia minor, Augia candida*). In 1145 the Guelf nobleman Gebizo founded the monastery on his own estate and settled it with monks from Rot an der Rot. In 1164, Emperor FREDERICK I took the independent house under his protection, and in 1257 it was raised to the rank of an abbey. Emperor Rudolf I donated to the abbey the relic of the Precious Blood, still venerated in Weissenau. After the miseries and pillaging of the PEASANTS' WAR and the THIRTY YEARS' WAR, the present baroque edifice was erected, beginning in 1708. The monastery was secularized (1802–03) and subsequently bought in 1815 by the state of Württemberg; its buildings have since 1892 served as an insane asylum.

Bibliography: "Acta s. Petri in Augia," *Zeitschrift für die Geschichte des Oberrheins* 29 (1877) 1–128; 42 (1890) 359–373. M. MILLER, *Lexikon für Theologie und Kirche,* ed. M. BUCHBERGER, 10 v. (Freiburg 1930–38) 10:804. N. BACKMUND, *Monasticon Praemonstratense,* 3 v. (Straubing 1949–56). K. WILLER, *Württembergische Kirchengeschichte bis zum Ende der Stauferzeit* (Stuttgart 1936). P. LEHMANN, *Erforschung des Mittelalters,* 4 v. (2d ed. Stuttgart 1959–61) 3:110–120; 4:40–82.

[L. KURRAS]

WEISSENBURG, ABBEY OF

Or in French, Wissembourg Abbey, former BENEDICTINE monastery in Alsace, present-day France. It was founded between 620 and 630, was richly endowed, and became an important cultural center in the later eighth century. The so-called "Catechism of Weissenburg" (before 800) is the oldest known work reflecting CHARLEMAGNE's order (*see* CAROLINGIAN REFORM) to translate the essential texts of the faith into the vernacular; it contains an Old High German translation and explanation of the Our Father, a Latin-German list of principal sins, and translations of the Apostles' Creed, the Athanasian Creed, and the Gloria. Otfrid of Weissenburg's OHG life of Christ, completed between 863 and 871, was Weissenburg's greatest contribution to Carolingian missionary efforts. Weissenburg reached its cultural peak after Emperor OTTO I made it a free imperial abbey (973) and gave it privileges that matched those of FULDA, REICHENAU, and PRÜM. Abbot Adalbert (d. 981), formerly a monk of St. Maximin in Trier, later the first archbishop of Magdeburg, completed his *Continuatio Reginonis* at Weissenburg. From 957 to 1097, the abbey followed the customs of GORZE, except under Abbot Folmar (1031–43) who imposed the *consuetudo* of POPPO OF STAVELOT. Louis of Hirsau, who became abbot in 1097, introduced the customs of HIRSAU. In the late Middle Ages, after the abbey had suffered depredation by the town and surrounding nobility, an attempt at reform through union with the Congregation of BURSFELD failed (1482). Pope Clement VII transformed the abbey into a house of secular canons (1524), which was incorporated into the diocese of Speyer in 1548, the bishop of Speyer serving as provost of Weissenburg. Before Weissenburg passed to France (1697), most of its manuscripts were taken to Wolfenbüttel. The house was dissolved in 1789 during the French Revolution. The Gothic abbey church (13–14th century, with 11th-century tower) now serves as a parish church.

Bibliography: C. WOLFF, *Lexikon für Theologie und Kirche,* ed. M. BUCHBERGER, 10 v. (Freiburg 1930–38) 10:804–805. K. GLÖCKNER, "Eine Weissenburger Urkunde und der erste Karlingische König," *Elsass-Lothringisches Jahrbuch* 20 (1942) 1–9. F. HIMLY, "Les Plus anciennes charles et les origines de l'abbaye de Wissembourg. . .," *Bibliothèque de l'École des Chartes* 100 (1939) 281–294. A. BURG, *Histoire de l'Église d'Alsace* (Colmar 1946) 45. W. WATTENBACH, *Deutschlands Geschichtsquellen im Mittelalter. Vorzeit und Karolinger,* Hefte 1–4, ed. W. LEVISON and H. LÖWE (Weimar 1952–63) 2:166–170. A. DECKER, "Die Gründungszeit des Benediktinerklosters Weissenburg im Elsass," *Historisches Jahrbuch der Görres-Gesellschaft* 70 (1951) 42–52. M. BARTH, *Handbuch der elsässichen Kitchen im Mittelalter,* 3 v. (Archives de l'Église d'Alsace NS 11–13; Strasbourg 1960–63).

[A. A. SCHACHER]

WELBOURNE, THOMAS, BL.

Martyr; b. Hutton Bushel (then Kitenbushel), North Riding, Yorkshire, England; d. hanged, drawn, and quartered at York, Aug. 1, 1605. Little is known of this martyr beyond Bp. Challoner's record that he and John Fulthering "being zealous Catholics, and industrious in exhorting some of their neighbors to embrace the Catholic faith, were upon that account arraigned and condemned to suffer as in cases of high treason (II, 12). Welbourne was beatified by Pius XI on Dec. 15, 1929.

Feast of the English Martyrs: May 4 (England).

See Also: ENGLAND, SCOTLAND, AND WALES, MARTYRS OF.

Bibliography: R. CHALLONER, *Memoirs of Missionary Priests,* ed. J. H. POLLEN (rev. ed. London 1924; repr. Farnborough 1969). J. H. POLLEN, *Acts of English Martyrs* (London 1891).

[K. I. RABENSTEIN]

WELCH, SIDNEY

Journalist, lecturer, and historian of southern Africa; b. of South African parents (either in Japan or at sea en route to South Africa), 1871; d. Sea Point, Cape Providence, Sept. 2, 1956. Welch attended the Marist Brothers College in Cape Town and the Propaganda Fide College in Rome (now the Propaganda University) where he was ordained in 1894. After returning to South Africa, he collaborated with Frederick KOLBE in apologetic lecturing and work to improve Catholic education, and contributed frequently to the *South African Catholic Magazine,* founded by Kolbe in 1891.

Welch succeeded as editor in 1909 and, both in the magazine and on the public platform, frequently spoke out on controversial topics. From 1907 on he advocated a gradual political and social integration of the Bantus into the "European" community, and during World War I he campaigned for moderation and acceptance of the papal peace plan. After 1918 he vigorously criticized the terms of the Versailles Treaty. Most South African Catholics either disagreed with his positions or simply were disinterested; as a result, the magazine ceased publication in March of 1924.

Welch thereafter devoted himself almost exclusively to historical writing. His extensive research into the early Portuguese and Dutch colonization of southern Africa led him to the Vatican Archives and the Portuguese government archives in Lisbon. In 1954 the Portuguese government awarded him its Camões literature prize for *The Portuguese and Dutch in South Africa.* Most of his priestly life was spent at St. Mary's Cathedral in Cape Town, where he was administrator from 1909 to 1925. He was pastor of St. James parish, Cape Town, from 1925 until his retirement to a monastery at Sea Point in 1944.

Dr. Welch's historical works are: *Some Unpublished Documents Relating to the History of South and East Af-*

Thomas Weld.

rica (1930), *Europe's Discovery of South Africa* (1935), *South Africa under King Manuel, 1495–1521* (1946), *South Africa under John III, 1521–1557* (1949), *South Africa under King Sebastian and the Cardinal, 1557–1580* (1949), *Portuguese Rule and Spanish Crown in South Africa, 1581–1640* (1950), and *Portuguese and Dutch in South Africa, 1641–1806* (1951).

Bibliography: W. BROWN, *The Catholic Church in South Africa from its Origins to the Present Day,* ed. M. DERRICK (New York 1960).

[J. A. BELL]

WELD, THOMAS

Cardinal; b. London, Jan. 22, 1773; d. Rome, April 19, 1837. He was the son of Thomas Weld of Lullworth Castle, Dorset, head of an ancient Catholic family. The Welds offered shelter to members of religious orders, emigrés of the FRENCH REVOLUTION, gave homes to communities of Cistercian and Poor Clare nuns, and presented their house at Stonyhurst to the Jesuits. Weld married in 1796, but after the death of his wife (1815) and his daughter's marriage (1818), he made over his estates to his brother, was ordained by the archbishop of Paris (1821), and served in London until 1826, when he was consecrated as coadjutor to the bishop of Kingston, Canada. Poor health kept him in London, however, and led him to move to Italy where he was created cardinal (1830). Weld advised the pope on matters relating to England but otherwise took little part in the affairs of the Sacred College.

Bibliography: C. S. ISAACSON, *The Story of the English Cardinals* (London 1907) J. GILLOW, *A Literary and Biographical History or Bibliographical Dictionary of the English Catholics from 1534 to the Present Time,* 5 v. (London–New York 1885–1902; repr. New York 1961) 5:576. T. COOPER, *The Dictionary of National Biography from the Earliest Times to 1900,* 63 v. (London 1885–1900; repr. with corrections, 21 v., 1908–09, 1921–22, 1938; suppl. 1901–) 20:1072–73.

[B. FOTHERGILL]

WELLHAUSEN, JULIUS

Orientalist and Biblical scholar remembered chiefly for his contributions to the documentary theory on the composition of the Hexateuch; b. Hameln, Germany, May 17, 1844; d. Göttingen, Jan. 7, 1918. His studies in theology were made under the celebrated G. H. A. EWALD at Göttingen, where he also taught for two years (1870–72). In 1872 he became professor of theology at the University of Greifswald. In 1882 he resigned his post, because his views on Biblical inspiration conflicted with those accepted at the university. Subsequently he taught at Halle and Marburg (1882–85). In 1892 he transferred to Göttingen, where he remained until his death.

His *Prolegomena* and *Komposition des Hexateuchs* became standard works in critical Biblical studies, to the extent that the theories he developed came to be considered the "orthodox" view in most non-Catholic Biblical circles. A culmination of his influence may be seen in P. Haupt's "Rainbow Bible." Although later scholarship, e.g., that of the "Scandinavian School," has considerably modified Wellhausen's documentary theories, his influence on Biblical criticism in Catholic as well as non-Catholic scholarship has been established.

The following are among his more important works: *Pharisärer und Sadduzäer* (1874); *Prolegomena zur Geschichte Israels* (6th ed. 1905); *Die Komposition des Hexateuchs und der historischen Bücher des alten Testaments* (3d ed. 1899); *Israelitische und Jüdische Geschichte* (4th ed. 1901); *Reste arabischen Heidentums* (2d ed. 1897); *Das Evangelium Marci* (1903), *Matthäi* (1904), *Lucae* (1904), and *Johannis* (1908).

Bibliography: *Lexikon für Theologie und Kirche*[2], v.10. O. EISSFELDT, *Die Religion in geschichte und Gegenwart,* third ed. 6:1594–95.

[C. A. REHWINKEL]

WELLS, SWITHUN, ST.

Married lay martyr, one of the London martyrs of 1591; b. Bambridge, near Winchester, England, *c.* 1536; d. London, Dec. 10, 1591. As the son of a country gentleman, Thomas Wells, Swithun was well educated and traveled abroad in his early life. He was a linguist, musician, poet, and keen sportsman. Before his marriage he served as tutor in the household of the Earl of Southampton, and later set up his own school at Monkton Farleigh near Bath. It was probably to obtain the necessary license to teach that he conformed to the public observances of the Anglican Communion. Until 1582 he apparently led a quiet and peaceful life as one of the English gentry. However, he came under suspicion for popish tendencies, and he abandoned teaching and actively supported the Roman Church. Though he was subsequently impoverished, he devoted himself to the service of seminary priests, organizing their progress, and ensuring their safety and entertainment; frequently, he acted as their guide.

Early in 1586 Wells and his wife took a house at Grays Inn Fields, London, the better to serve in the missionary endeavor. He was twice arrested and interrogated, but each time released for lack of evidence. In November 1591, when he was absent, Mrs. Wells offered hospitality to two priests, Edmund GENNINGS and Polydore PLASDEN. They were apprehended in the house while Mass was being said, and Mrs. Wells, the priests, and six worshippers were taken to prison. Shortly after, Swithun was arrested, and the group was brought to trial at Westminster. The priests were charged with high treason and sentenced accordingly. Mr. and Mrs. Wells and two servants were found guilty of harboring the priests and were condemned to death. Alice Wells, who was later reprieved, spent the rest of her life, 10 years, in prison. Wells approached his death with tranquility and fortitude; his last words were forgiveness and a prayer for his executioners. He was beatified by Pius XI on Dec. 15, 1929 and canonized by Paul VI on Oct. 25, 1970 as one of the Forty Martyrs of England and Wales.

Feast: Oct. 25 (Feast of the 40 Martyrs of England and Wales); May 4 (Feast of the English Martyrs in England).

See Also: ENGLAND, SCOTLAND, AND WALES, MARTYRS OF.

Bibliography: R. CHALLONER, *Memoirs of Missionary Priests,* ed. J. H. POLLEN (rev. ed. London 1924; repr. Farnborough 1969), 169–85. J. GENNINGS, *Life and Death of Ven. Edmund Gennings* (London 1887). *Publications of the Catholic Record Society* 5:131–133, 204–208. A. BUTLER, *The Lives of the Saints,* ed. H. THURSTON and D. ATTWATER 4:532–534.

[A. M. FORSTER]

WELTANSCHAUUNG

Weltanschauung is an expression, used already by I. KANT in 1790, that came into common usage particularly in German romanticism from the mid-19th century onward. Weltanschauung (world view) denotes an image in which a person blends the multiplicity of beings, values, and duties, particularly through the concept of beginning, that explains the existence of the universe, and through the concept of supreme value, to which the universe tends as to its end and from which it derives its meaning. This image can be unconscious and latent; it can be expressed in mythical narratives or in more or less scientifically developed theories. From a cosmological viewpoint, the Weltanschauung may be qualified as skeptical, atheistic, pantheistic, theistic, etc.; from an axiological viewpoint, the Weltanschauung may be classified as hedonistic, humanistic, religious, etc.

Those philosophers who maintain that value is beyond the reach of rational knowledge (H. Lotze, M. SCHELER, N. HARTMANN) must admit that a Weltanschauung is a philosophical system—there exist two irreducible ways of conceiving the universe. If, on the contrary, one admits the intimate coherence of being and value, one must affirm that a metaphysical system is a scientifically elaborated Weltanschauung.

Historicism (W. DILTHEY) usually judges the various Weltanschauungs with reference only to physiological and psychological qualities, individual and collective experiences, the needs and conditions of the individual and of society. A Weltanschauung, according to HISTORICISM, is correct if it permits the individual or society to conceive the world coherently with its own subjective dispositions. In fact, the criterion of the validity of a Weltanschauung is its veracity, that is, its conformity with objective reality. Nevertheless, the same truths can be united in varied syntheses according to the diverse points of view from which they are considered. In this sense there are, in fact, various true Weltanschauungs, which are complementary and not contradictory.

In theology, the question arises concerning the relationship between Weltanschauung and FAITH. Protestants, for the most part, believe that faith does not include any judgment concerning the existence or value of beings; they are, therefore, inclined to admit that the Christian religion can coexist among the faithful with various contradictory Weltanschauungs. For Catholics, faith consists in a total submission of intellect and will to God the revealer: therefore the acceptance of the Catholic religion implies the rejection of a Weltanschauung that is contradictory to the revealed image of the world.

See Also: MAN; RELATIVISM.

Bibliography: R. EISLER, *Wörterbuch der philosophischen Begriffe,* 3 v. (4th ed. Berlin 1927–30) 3:505–507. L. GIUSSO, *Enciclopedia filosofica,* 4 v. (Venice–Rome 1957) 4:1742–43. A. E. WILHELM et al., *Evangelisches Kirchenlexicon: Kirchlich–theologisches Handwöterbuch,* ed. H. BRUNOTTE and O. WEBER, 4 v. (Göttingern 1956–61) 3:1761–73. "Weltanschauung," *Lexikon für Theologie und Kirche,* ed. J. HOFER and K. RAHNER, 10 v. (2d, new ed. Freiburg 1957–65) v.10. J. KLEIN, *Die Religion in Geschichte und Gegenwart,* 7 v. (3d ed. Tübingen 1957–65) 6:1603–06. P. LIPPERT, *Die Weltanschauung des Kathotizismus* (Leipzig 1927).

[Z. ALSZEGHY]

WENAILUS, ST.

Abbot; b. Brittany; d. *c.* 580–590. Wenailus (Guenael, Guenél, Guénaël) became a disciple of St. WINWALOË, whom he succeeded as abbot of Landevennec. After 540 he spent some years in Ireland, founding or reforming a number of monasteries there, and then returned (*c.* 547) to Landevennec, where he died. His relics were brought to Paris (*c.* 950) during the Norman invasions and were later transferred to the Abbey of Corbeil.

Feast: Nov. 3.

Bibliography: *Acta Sanctorum* (Paris 1863—) 1:669–679. J. L. BAUDOT and L. CHAUSSIN, *Vies des saints et des bienheureux selon l'ordre du calendrier avec l'historique des fêtes,* ed. by the Benedictines of Paris (Paris 1935–56) 11:97–98. G. A. LOBINEAU, *Les Vies des saints de Bretagne* (Rouen 1725). J. LOTH, *Les Noms des saints bretons* (Paris 1910). F. MORVANNOU, *Saint Guénaë: études et documents* (Brest 1997).

[O. L. KAPSNER]

WENCESLAUS, ST.

Duke of Bohemia, patron of the CZECH REPUBLIC; b. Stochov, near Prague, Czechoslovakia; d. Stara Boleslav, Sept. 28, 929. After the death of his Christian father, Duke Ratislav of Bohemia (d. *c.* 920), his mother, Drahomira, who was still practically a pagan, became regent for the young Wenceslaus (Vaclav). Earlier Wenceslaus had been entrusted to his grandmother, (St.) LUDMILLA, the wife of the first Christian duke of Bohemia, for his education. His mother resented the influence of Ludmilla and instigated her murder in 921. This, coupled with other intrigues of Drahomira, led Wenceslaus to take over the government himself in 922 in an attempt to end the internal struggles between the Christian and non-Christian factions in the country and to block (successfully) the invasion of Bohemia by Arnulf, duke of Bavaria. In 929 Bohemia faced the onslaught of German armies, and Wenceslaus decided to submit and recognize King Henry I as overlord rather than have his country devastated by a superior force. This policy of Bohemian compro-

St. Wenceslaus.

mise with Germany was the genesis of the "St. Wenceslaus Tradition." Wenceslaus brought the relic of St. Virus to Prague. Although successful as a ruler and effective in his foreign policy, Wenceslaus was not able to end the rivalry of the non-Christian party within Bohemia. But it was his brother, Boleslav, resentful at losing his chance at succession when Wenceslaus's son was born, who invited Wenceslaus to Stara Boleslav where he was murdered on his way to church. Canonized, he became the patron of Bohemia. His political activity and his Christian soul, are both part of the tradition reflected in the popular 19th-century Christmas carol "Good King Wenceslaus."

Feast: Sept. 28.

Bibliography: J. PEKAŘ, *Die Wenzels- und Ludmilla- Legenden . . .* (Prague 1906). P. PEETERS, *Analecta Bollandiana* 48 (Brussels 1930) 218–221. F. DVORNIK, *The Life of Saint Wenceslas* (Prague 1929); *The Making of Central and Eastern Europe* (London 1949). A. BUTLER, *The Lives of the Saints*, rev. ed. H. THURSTON and D. ATTWATER (New York 1956) 3:663–664. J. HOSNA, *Kníže Václav v obrazu legend* (Prague 1986). H. KØLLN, *Der Bericht über den Dänenkönig in den St.-Wenzels-Biographien des 13. und 14. Jahrhunderts* (Copenhagen 1986). K. OTAVSKY, *Die Sankt Wenzel- skrone im Prager Domschatz und die Frage der Kunstauffassung am Hofe Kaiser Karls IV* (Bern 1992). P. OBRAZOVÁ, *Svatý kníze Václav: Major Gloria* (Prague 1994). V. TATÍCEK, *Boleslavské atentáty* (Prague 1999). CHARLES IV, Holy Roman Emperor, *Karoli IV Imperatoris Romanorum vita ab eo ipso conscripta; et, Hystoria nova de Sancto Wenceslao Martyre* (*Autobiography of Emperor Charles IV; and, His Legend of St. Wenceslas*), ed. B. NAGY and F. SCHAER (New York 2001).

[J. PAPIN]

WENCESLAUS IV, KING OF BOHEMIA

Reigned 1378 to Aug. 16, 1419; German king, 1378 to 1410; b. Nuremberg, Germany, Feb. 2, 1361; d. Prague. The son of Emperor Charles IV, he was crowned king of Bohemia when three years old. He was elected king of the Romans in 1376, and after his father's death in 1378, German king. Despite Charles's attempt to prepare him for his royal duties, Wenceslaus further complicated the social, political, and religious problems of Bohemia by his unstable and violent temper. He was sympathetic to the townsmen and lower nobility, often appointing them to high offices, but he alienated the nobles. Wenceslaus made some attempts to enforce general peace, but the civil strife continued until the Bavarian cities were defeated by the lords in 1388 and the town leagues were dissolved. However, the public peace proclaimed at the *Reichstag* in Cheb (1389) gave the townsmen equal participation in the government with the nobles.

Wenceslaus ruined the good church-state relationship in Bohemia by his clashes with Abp. John of Jenštein, especially over his own desire to found a new bishopric. Further, he had John's vicar-general, (St.) JOHN OF NEPOMUC, drowned in the River Moldau (1393) for defending the archbishop. The dissatisfied nobles, organized into the League of the Lords, allied with the archbishop; and when Wenceslaus refused the League's demands, he was imprisoned (1394), although later rescued by his brother John, Duke of Görlitz. However, the archbishop failed to obtain the backing of Boniface IX and abdicated, retiring to Rome.

On the international scene, which was then complicated by the Hundred Years' War and the WESTERN SCHISM, Wenceslaus abandoned the alliance with France, forming instead one with the king of England, Richard II, an alliance sealed by Richard's marriage to Wenceslaus' sister, Anne (1382). As for the church, Wenceslaus was a faithful supporter of the popes in Rome, namely, URBAN VI and BONIFACE IX, against the Avignon antipope

CLEMENT VII. In an attempt to end the schism he urged French King Charles IV to convoke a general council for the purpose of electing a new pope. This angered Boniface IX who then allied himself with the king's enemies in Germany, and subsequently the princes deposed Wenceslaus, three ecclesiastical electors choosing Rupert in his place (1400). Encouraged by this defeat of Wenceslaus in Germany, the Bohemian lords renewed the civil war against him. In an attempt to defend his rights, Wenceslaus invited his brother SIGISMUND to Prague, offering him the coregency of Bohemia. But in 1402 Sigismund imprisoned Wenceslaus and appointed the bishop of Litomyšl regent of Bohemia. Wenceslaus escaped from Vienna to Prague, where he resumed full sovereignty over his lands (1404). After Rupert's death in 1410 Wenceslaus retained his title of king of the Romans but resigned his claims to the imperial dignity in favor of Sigismund, who was then elected to the German throne. When Sigismund convoked the Council at CONSTANCE (1414–18), Wenceslaus remained secluded in Bohemia trying in vain to resolve its political and religious problems. Meanwhile the HUSSITES were growing stronger there. Wenceslaus died of apoplexy.

Bibliography: K. KNEEBUSCH, *Die Politik König Wenzels* (Dortmund 1889). R. HELMKE, *König Wenzel und seine bömischen Günstlinge im Reiche* (Diss. Halle 1913). P. KLUCKHOHN, *Wenzels Jungenjahre . . .* (Diss. Halle 1914). S. STEINHERZ, *Ein Fürstenspiegel Karls IV* (Prague 1925). I. HLAVÁČEK, ''Studien zur Diplomatik König Wenzels,'' *Mitteilungen des Instituts für österreichische Geschichtsforschung* 69 (1961) 292–330. P. DE VOOGHT, *L'Hérésie de Jean Huss* (Louvain 1960); *Hussiana* (Louvain 1960).

[J. PAPIN]

WENDELIN, ST.

Died *c.* 617. Although little definite is known of him, he was among the most popular saints during the Middle Ages, especially in the Rhineland and Switzerland. According to a 14th-century legend he was born in Ireland about 554, the son of a Scottish king. During a pious pilgrimage he came to the area of Trier, Germany, where he lived for many years as a hermit and tended swine. The pilgrimages to his shrine gave origin to the town of St. Wendel in the Diocese of Trier. That he was abbot of the Benedictine Abbey of Tholey, only a few miles from St. Wendel, is probably legendary. In popular cult and art he is variously pictured as a pilgrim, shepherd, monk, abbot, patron of peasants and herdsmen, and patron against pestilence.

Feast: Oct. 20, 21, 22, 23.

Bibliography: *Acta Sanctorum* (Paris 1863—) 9:342–351. J. L. BAUDOT and L. CHAUSSIN, *Vies des saints et des bienheureux selon l'ordre du calendrier avec l'historique des fêtes,* ed. by the Benedictines of Paris (Paris 1935–56) 10:744–745. A. SELZER, *Sankt Wendel* (Saarbrücken 1936). A. M. ZIMMERMANN, *Kalendarium Benedictinum: Die Heiligen und Seligen des Benediktinerorderns und seiner Zweige,* 3:203–204 (Mettem 1933–38).

[O. L. KAPSNER]

WENINGER, FRANCIS XAVIER

Missionary and author; b. Styria, Austria, Oct. 31, 1805; d. Cincinnati, Ohio, June 29, 1888. Under the patronage of the Empress Carolina Augusta of Austria, Weninger studied at the University of Vienna, where he was ordained and received a doctorate in divinity in 1830. He was appointed to the theological faculty of the University of Graz, but resigned in 1832 to enter the Society of Jesus. Weninger then taught theology (notably at Innsbruck, 1834–48), published many books, and gained fame as a preacher of parish missions. When the Jesuits were suppressed in Austria during the Revolution of 1848, he volunteered for the U.S. and was assigned to Cincinnati, Ohio. There he preached missions in German-speaking parishes and soon achieved a nationwide and enduring reputation. So remarkable was his influence with German-Americans that his mission in St. Louis Church, Buffalo, New York, ended the schism that had previously defeated the efforts of Abps. John HUGHES and Gaetano BEDINI and Bp. John TIMON. For a generation, he was in constant demand and traveled continuously throughout the U.S., preaching missions in German, French, and broken English. It is estimated that by 1880 he had traveled over 200,000 miles, given more than 800 parish missions, and preached 30,000 times.

Prolific in writing as well as in preaching, Weninger considered his books more important than his missions and published works on catechetics, apologetics, and the liturgy; handbooks for the clergy; advice for the laity; and collections of his sermons. Carlos Sommervogel, Jesuit bibliographer, lists 56 titles—written in Latin, German, and English, many multi-volumed, many often reprinted, some translated into Italian and French—that in Weninger's day were both useful and popular. Although advancing age curtailed his activities, Weninger was still preaching parish missions at the age of 80.

Bibliography: G. J. GARRAGHAN, *Jesuits in the the Middle United States,* 3 v. (New York 1938) v.2. ''Father Francis Xavier Weninger,'' *Woodstock Letters* 18 (1889) 43–68. C. SOMMERVOGEL et al., *Bibliothéque de la Compagnie de Jésus* (Brussels-Paris 1890–1932) 8:1065–71.

[F. X. CURRAN]

WENLOCK, ABBEY OF

Or Much Wenlock, former Benedictine abbey in the county of Shropshire, ancient Diocese of HEREFORD, England. About 1080, at the request of Roger of Montgomery, CLUNIAC REFORM monks from La CHARITÉ-SUR-LOIRE came to occupy the site of a Saxon double monastery that had been founded by St. Milburga but destroyed by the Danes. The abbey in turn set up dependent houses at Dudley, St. Helens (Isle of Wight), and Preen. After having its property sequestrated as that of aliens in 1380, the community was granted denization in 1385 and complete independence of La Charité in 1494. In the early 16th century several monks, including William Corfill, the sacristan, were skilled craftsmen in metal. When the abbey was suppressed in 1539 under Henry VIII, most of the 14 monks obtained clerical appointments. Some of the buildings remain.

Bibliography: W. DUGDALE, *Monasticon Anglicanum* (London 1655–73); best ed. by J. CALEY, et al., 6 v. (1817–30) 5:72–82. R. GRAHAM, *English Ecclesiastical Studies* (New York 1929) 125–145. D. KNOWLES and R. N. HADCOCK, *Medieval Religious Houses: England and Wales* (New York 1953).

[F. R. JOHNSTON]

WENRICH OF TRIER

Pamphleteer; d. Sept. 30, 1081, or 1082. The few certain facts preserved about Wenrich may be stated briefly. Nothing is known of his place of origin or birth, nor is there information on his intellectual or ecclesiastical formation. He is, however, known to have been a canon of Verdun and to have later moved to Trier, where he was head of the cathedral school. While serving in this capacity in the period between Oct. 15, 1080, and August 1081, he composed the letter or tract for which he is remembered. There are indications that he was named bishop of Vercelli by the Emperor HENRY IV, but there is no certainty that he was consecrated or installed, although SIGEBERT OF GEMBLOUX and the Necrology of St. Vito give him the episcopal title. *Dietrich, Bishop of Verdun, To Hildebrand the Pope* is the title of Wenrich's influential pamphlet (*Monumenta Germaniae Historica: Libelli de lite* 1:280–299). It begins, perhaps sincerely, by lamenting the sorrow caused by Pope GREGORY VII's too great haste and injustice. Henry IV ought to have been heard before his excommunication. Gregory's attacks on clerical marriage and on married priests' Masses subvert ecclesiastical discipline. Royal investiture (*see* INVESTITURE STRUGGLE) is sanctioned by Holy Scripture and by the Fathers. Clearly, the royal cause had found a stout champion in the Trier schoolmaster (*see* GREGORIAN REFORM).

Bibliography: A. FLICHE, *La Réforme grégorienne*, 3 v. (Louvain 1924–37), Index. É. AMANN, *Dictionnaire de théologie catholique* 15.2:3528–29. A. HAUCK, *Kirchengeschichte Deutschlands* 3:828, 852.

[S. WILLIAMS]

WERBURGA, ST.

Abbess; daughter of King Wulfhere of Mercia and of St. Erminilda; d. Trentham (Threckingham, Lincolnshire), England, 699. On her mother's side Werburga (Werburh, Werbyrgh) was the granddaughter of St. Sexburga and grandniece of St. ETHELREDA, abbess of ELY. When she came to marriageable age, Werburga, who according to legend was beautiful and much sought after, dismissed her suitors and after having gained the consent of her reluctant father was received at Ely by Ethelreda. After Wulfhere's death in 675, Werburga's mother entered the same monastery.

Wulfhere's brother, Ethelred, who succeeded him as king, placed Werburga in charge of discipline in the houses of religious women in Mercia. He apparently made over to her the royal house at Weedon, which she made her headquarters. She supervised houses in Hanbury, Staffordshire, and Trentham. She died in Trentham and at her own request was buried in Hanbury. Her reputation for sanctity was such that during the Danish invasions (*c.* 875) her still incorrupt body was transferred to CHESTER. Legend has it that on the journey her body disintegrated into ashes. Her remains were enshrined at Chester where according to Cambden, Leofric (d. 1057) built a church in her honor. It is undoubtedly because her shrine early became a place of pilgrimage that the many legends recorded by Goscelin (fl. *c.* 1100), her first biographer, grew up about her. What remained of her shrine, desecrated under HENRY VIII, was converted into the throne of the bishops of Chester, which still displays the carved images of Werburga's royal ancestors.

Feast: Feb. 3; June 21 (translation, Chester).

Bibliography: *Acta Sanctorum* (Paris 1863—) 1:388–394, life and legends by Goscelin. S. BARING-GOULD, *Lives of the Saints*, v.2 (Edinburgh 1914) 52–56. A. BUTLER, *The Lives of the Saints*, rev. ed. H. THURSTON and D. ATTWATER (New York 1956) 1:241–242. A. ZIMMERMANN, *Lexikon für Theologie und Kirche*, ed. M. BUCHBERGER (Freiburg 1930–38) 10:825. J. TAIT, ed., *The Chartulary or Register of the Abbey of Saint Werburgh, Chester*, 2 v. (Manchester 1920–23) v.1. H. BRADSHAW, *The Life of Saint Werburge of Chester,* Ed. C. HORSTMANN (Millwood, NY 1988).

[M. E. COLLINS]

WERDEN, ABBEY OF

Former Benedictine monastery in the Ruhr (Rhineland), Germany; founded *c.* 800 by (St.) LUDGER as a base for his Saxon mission. In 887? it was given immunity and royal protection, and in 974, coinage and market rights; from the 12th century it came directly under imperial control. Eminent abbots of the early period were St. HILDIGRIM, who founded the abbey of Helmstedt, and St. BARDO. Helmstedt remained in personal union with Werden until secularization. The advocates were the counts of Mark and in the last period, electors of Brandenburg. Strong secularizing tendencies developed under the lay Abbot Conrad of Gleichen (1454–74); at the instigation of Pope and Emperor, Werden joined the Bursfeld Reform in 1478 and played a significant part in this reform movement. Fourteen general chapters met in Werden from 1524 to 1754, and four of Werden's abbots were presidents of the Bursfeld Union. Werden produced such scholars as Altfrid, Uffing, John Cincinnius, Abbot Duden, and the two brothers Gregory and Adolph Overham. The *Codex argenteus* of ULFILAS's translation of the Bible belonged to Werden at one time; it is now in the library of the university of Uppsala. The author of the *HELIAND* is also supposed to have lived there. The abbey came under Prussian control in 1803, but the monastic school continued to exist as a Latin school (*Rektoratsschule*) until 1881.

Bibliography: A. FUCHS, *Lexikon für Theologie und Kirche*, ed. M. BUCHBERGER, 10 v. (Freiburg 1930–38) 10:825–826. L. H. COTTINEAU, *Répertoire topobibliographique des abbayes et prieurés*, 2 v. (Mâcon 1935–39) 2:3443–44. P. VOLK, *Die Generalkapitel der Bursfelder Benediktiner Kongregation* (Münster 1928). D. P. BLOK, *De oudste particuliere oorkonden van het klooster Werden* (Assen 1960).

[P. VOLK]

WERENFRID, ST.

Anglo-Saxon missionary in the Netherlands; d. Westervoort, near Arnhem, Netherlands, *c.* 726. He was a Northumbrian, one of the companions of SS. WILLIBRORD and SWITHBERT. He preached to the pagan Frisians in Holland and Gelderland. He seems to have made one journey to France, and then returned to die in the mission field. He was venerated particularly at Elst in Gelderland, where he was buried. Since 1664 his relics have been at the Jesuit church in Emmerich, Germany.

Feast: Aug. 14 or 27.

Bibliography: *Acta Sanctorum* (Paris 1863—) 6:100–105. R. STANTON, *A Menology of England and Wales* (London 1887) 393–394. A. M. ZIMMERMANN, *Kalendarium Benedictinum: Die Heiligen und Seligen des Benediktinerordens und seiner Zweige* (Metten 1933–38) 2:572–573. W. LEVISON, *England and the Continent in the 8th Century* (Oxford 1946) 61.

[J. L. DRUSE]

WERNER OF OBERWESEL, ST.

Patron of winegrowers, martyr also known as Vernier or Verny; b. Womrath (Rhineland), *c.* 1273; d. 1287. The legend, based on testimony at hearings for his canonization in 1426, states that Werner, formerly a vineyard worker, was employed by a Jew at Oberwesel. After having received his Easter Communion, the boy was martyred; allegedly the Jews tied him to a pillar, head down, opened his arteries, and let him bleed to death. Persecution of the Jews set in, and only the intervention of Rudolf of Hapsburg ended it. Veneration of Werner sprang up quickly; a chapel over his grave in Bacharach, consecrated in 1293 (now a noteworthy Gothic ruin), was once an important place of pilgrimage. Under the name of St. Vernier he is venerated by the winegrowers of Auvergne, Burgundy, and Franche-Comté; his relics have been honored since 1548 in the collegiate church of St. Mary Magdalene in Besançon despite the lack of recognition from Rome. His cultus was suppressed by the Second Vatican Council and local dioceses.

Feast: April 18 or 19 (formerly).

Bibliography: T. VUY, *Geschichte des Trechirgaues und von Oberwesel* (Leipzig 1885) 155–159. J. MOHR, *Die Heiligen der Diözese Trier* (Trier 1892) 88–90. P. KANDELS, ''Der heilige Werner,'' *Pastor Bonus* 24 (1912) 393–400.

[D. ANDREINI]

WERNER OF TEGERNSEE

Date and place of birth unknown; d. June 15, after 1195. A monk at TEGERNSEE, once exiled to Salzburg, he later became head of the school at Tegernsee, hence his surname SCHOLASTICUS. In striving for a purer Latin, Werner took the classical authors as models for his students. He drew a map of the world, and he began a botanical garden. There is no proof for P. Lindner's suggestion that Werner and Metellus, the author of the *Quirinalia*, were the same person; nor is there any certain knowledge of his alleged activity as an illuminator or author of a *BIBLIA PAUPERUM*. The prose *Passio s. Quirini*, sometimes attributed to him, is the work of a monk by the name of Henry. Werner considerably increased his monastery's library. His hand can be recognized in codices Clm 18523b, 18527a, 18646, 18769, where he wrote part of the *Annales Tegernseenses* [*Monumenta Germaniae Historica: Scriptores* (Berlin 1826–) 24:58], and in Clm 19164, with its colophon: *W. diaconus et monachus patravit*. His hand also appears in Clm 19488, fol. 119b. His share in the writing of Clm 19411—if he can be identified with hand D—is the cause for his fame, rightful or undeserved. At the beginning of the 19th century, Docen believed hand D to be the same as that found in fragment B of the Priest Werner's *Driu liet von der maget,* the greatest religious poem in 12th–century German literature. Since Docen accepted fragment B as an autograph, a chain of speculations ensued, developing a whole literary myth. Werner Scholasticus was believed to be the author of this Marian poem—actually written by a secular priest in Augsburg in 1172—and of almost every piece in Clm 19411. This manuscript contains, e.g., the famous *Ludus de antichristo,* as well as a poem on the voices of birds and other animals. Yet hand D did not write these parts. The oldest section of the manuscript contained the *Breviarium de dictamine* of Alberic of Monte Cassino and parts of the *Praecepta dictaminum* of Adalbertus Samaritanus, both epistolary treatises; the model letters of Henricus Francigena; and a collection of model love letters. This "schoolbook" was enlarged in a number of different hands between 1178 and 1186 by the addition of the *Ludus* and other poetic and historical texts, but mainly by 306 letters drawn from the monastery's correspondence. Of this latter section, hand D—the teacher's—did the main work. It is in this hand that the three love letters (nos. 9–11) are written; these were added to the model collection in Tegernsee, and possibly composed in Tegernsee. Number 10 ends with the famous German love poem beginning with the line: "Dû bist mîn, ich bin dîn." Did Werner add to the Latin model letter this verse inspired by Ovid (*Her.* 6.134)? Plechl's complete research on this manuscript and his promised editions of the collection of letters and (with Groll) of the love letters will clarify the portrait of Werner, the monk and the teacher.

Bibliography: O. MAUSSER, *Allgemeine deutsche Biographie* 55:48–53. V. REDLICH, *Lexikon für Theologie und Kirche,* ed. J. HOFER and K. RAHNER, 10 v. (2d, new ed. Freiburg 1957–65) 10:829; 9:1338–39. R. BAUERREISS, *Kirchengeschichte Bayerns* (St. Ottilien 1949–55; 2d ed. 1958–) v.3 H. PLECHL, "Studien zur Tegernseer Briefsammlung des 12. Jahrhunderts," *Deutsches Archiv für Erforschung des Mittelalters* 13 (1957) 35–114; "Die Tegernseer Handschrift Clm 19411. Beschreibung und Inhalt," *ibid.* 18 (1962) 418–501.

[A. A. SCHACHER]

WESLEY, CHARLES

A founder of Methodism and a hymn writer; b. Epworth, Lincolnshire, Dec. 18, 1707; d. London, March 29, 1788. He was the 18th of the 19 children of Susanna and Reverend Samuel Wesley. In April 1716 he entered Westminster School and in June 1726, Christ Church, Oxford, from which he received his B.A. (1730). A pious student, he formed a Holy Club (1729), which was converted into a society by his older brother John WESLEY.

Charles was an excellent scholar and Latinist and took his M.A. in 1733. After being ordained an Anglican priest in 1735, he accompanied James Edward Oglethorpe (1696–1785) to Georgia, but partly because of ill health he returned to England (July 26, 1736). He met Nikolaus von ZINZENDORF, the celebrated Moravian evangelist in January 1737. After his "conversion" on May 21, 1738, he resumed preaching in London churches, ministered to felons, and, imitating George WHITEFIELD, preached in the fields. He and his brother John formed a partnership for itinerant missions and for ministering to the Methodist societies in Bristol and London. For 18 years he preached in many parts of England, visiting Ireland twice, and enduring persecution. But he was completely overshadowed by his more famous brother. As Charles saw it, the Methodist societies were wholly within the Anglican church. John's ordination of two ministers for America angered Charles, who regarded it as defiance of the church. Personal and religious differences tended to draw the devoted brothers apart in later years. But like John, Charles was Arminian in his theological views, and hostile to the doctrine of salvation of the Calvinistic Methodists. In 1749 he married Sarah (Sally) Gwynne (1726–1822), who bore him eight children. In 1771 Wesley removed his family to London, where he continued his labors on behalf of the Methodists to the end of his life. Although he was a great preacher, his fame today rests on his hymns. He published 4,430 hymns and left 2,840 in manuscript. The most famous collection was the joint work of John and Charles, *Hymns for the Use of the People Called Methodists* (1779). The hymns deeply influenced the English and helped diffuse the teachings of the Bible, which was the inspiration of the hymns.

Bibliography: T. JACKSON, *Life of the Rev. Charles Wesley,* 2 v. (London 1841). M. L. EDWARDS, *Sons to Samuel* (London 1961). F. BAKER, *Charles Wesley as Revealed by His Letters* (London 1948). J. E. RATTENBURY, *The Evangelical Doctrines of Charles Wesley's Hymns* (London 1941). C. W. FLINT, *Charles Wesley* (Washington 1957). R. A. KNOX, *Enthusiasm* (New York 1961). A. GORDON, *The Dictionary of National Biography from the Earliest Times to 1900,* 63 v. (London 1885–1900) 20:1209–13. M. SCHMIDT, *Die Religion in Geschichte und Gegenwart,* 7 v. (3d ed. Tübingen 1957–65) 6:1655–56. F. L. CROSS, *The Oxford Dictionary of the Christian Church* (London 1957) 1445–46.

[G. L. VINCITORIO]

WESLEY, JOHN

The founder of Methodism; b. Epworth Rectory, Lincolnshire, June 27, 1703; d. City Road, London, March 2, 1791. He was the 15th of 19 children of Rev. Samuel Wesley (1662–1735), Vicar of Epworth, and Susanna Annesley Wesley (1669–1742), who came from nonconformist stock but who were themselves high churchmen. The vicar's ardent ARMINIANISM deeply affected his children. Susanna was a pious and well-educated woman, devoted to her children's education and welfare. In 1714 John was sent to Charterhouse School, London, and in 1720, to Oxford. As a collegian he led a strict life and arose at 4 A.M., a habit he retained until his death. Wesley received his B.A. in 1724 and M.A. in 1727. A year later he was ordained an Anglican priest, and in 1729 he assumed his duties as fellow and tutor at Oxford. There he led the Holy Club, established by his younger brother Charles, whose members prayed, fasted, and received communion frequently, and engaged in philanthropic and evangelical work. The period of "Oxford Methodism" ended with the dispersal of the club in 1735.

John and Charles left for Georgia upon the invitation of James Oglethorpe in 1736. John did not achieve his goal of converting Native Americans and of ministering to the colonists, who resented his high-church services and insistence on puritanical conduct. He had to leave Georgia hurriedly to escape a suit brought against him by an angry husband for defamation of character of his wife. The young clergyman arrived in London Feb. 1, 1738.

Origins of Methodism. The Georgia Moravians influenced him on his trip to America, and following his return, he met a disciple of Count Nikolaus von Zinzendorf, Peter Böhler, who convinced him that Christ had died for *him*. Wesley adhered to a Moravian-inspired Society in Fetter Lane and, on May 24, 1738, "at a quarter to nine," experienced "conversion." But Wesley came to object to the Moravian doctrines of justification by faith *alone* and of the instantaneous effects of the New Birth. After being excluded from the pulpit in Fetter Lane, he took his followers and formed a society at the Foundry (July 1740) that was completely under his control, and by 1743 he had established two more chapels in London.

Wesley was one of the evangelicals in the Church of England. His fame rests in part on his extraordinary preaching and missionary tours. Following the example of George Whitefield, he preached in the fields or wherever he might assemble an audience. He and his brother Charles formed a partnership for sharing the work of ministering to their followers in London and Bristol and of evangelical tours of the British Isles. John's travels on horseback covered about 225,000 miles, and he gave more than 40,000 sermons. His message was simple: salvation is through Jesus Christ. A new life awaits every man who loves Jesus, believes in the Atonement, repents his sins, and lives according to His law. His audiences were frequently deeply moved and reacted emotionally. Although Methodist preaching affected some of the country's leaders, through Selina Hastings, Countess of

John Wesley.

Huntingdon, its appeal was primarily to the poor and the uneducated.

The partnership of the brothers was weakened by personal and religious differences. Charles opposed John's marriage to a widow, Mrs. Mary (Molly) Vazeille (1710–81); it proved an unhappy marriage. John's ordination of ministers for America also angered Charles because he regarded it as defiance of the revered Church of England. Much of their mutual affection and joint efforts on behalf of Methodism remained unaffected, however.

Wesley's great gift was not only for preaching but for organizing Methodist Societies everywhere in the British Isles. He adopted the idea of having members make one-penny weekly contributions. Leaders of the "classes" not only collected the contributions but inquired into personal behavior and could thus ferret out "disorderly walkers." Wesley was the driving spirit and inspiration of the Societies. Through the Deed of Declaration (1784), he named 100 preachers to constitute the legal body of the "people called Methodists," which he continued to lead until his death.

Teachings and Doctrine. In view of the fact that he did not want to create a sect, Wesley hoped that other evangelical-minded clergymen of the Church of England would help him shepherd the Methodist flocks. He enjoined his followers to attend services in their parishes and receive communion monthly. At the close of his life, he could say, "I live and die a member of the Church of England." Some of his utterances and actions, however, severed the fragile ties to Anglicanism. The Methodist movement appealed to many who did not conform, and these Wesley wished to reach. "Church or no church," he said, "we must attend to the work of saving souls." He opposed the parochial system because no one clergyman could minister to a congregation, which needed a change of teacher. As for himself, "the world was his parish." His employment of lay preachers and his ordinations of preachers further alienated him from the church. It was his conviction that bishops and presbyters were of the same order. In 1784 he "set apart as a superintendent" (bishop) the Rev. Thomas Coke for the American missions. He ordained preachers for America in 1784; for Scotland, in the following year; for Ireland, in 1786; and for England, in 1789. After his death, the churches divided into national units.

Wesley did not seek doctrinal innovation. In preaching justification by faith, he rejected Calvinistic predestination. In assigning a role to free will, he differed from George Whitefield and the Calvinistic Methodists. He believed that the reconciled sinner experiences real inward changes; for completely eradicating inward sin, a man must experience a second change or a New Birth, which he called "the great work which God does in us, in renewing our fallen nature." According to Father M. Piette (436), the pivot around which all Wesley's doctrine revolves is experience of the love of God: faith as it is lived, felt, and experienced. As for some of Wesley's other ideas, the rule of faith was "the Law and the Testimony," which meant his interpretation of the Bible. He believed in special providential dispensation, and he often opened the Bible at random to find a clue concerning the action he should take.

During his long journeys he read and wrote extensively. He translated German hymns; collaborated with Charles in writing hymns; published his sermons; produced 50 volumes of English practical divinity; compiled a dictionary; abridged Milton; and wrote manuals of history, philology, and medicine which were widely read. He kept a *Journal* and wrote numerous *Letters* (ed. J. Telford, 8 v. London 1931). Critics aver that his writings reached persons who had never read before; but because they were dedicated only to moral reform, they were utilitarian and at times Philistine.

In politics he was royalist and a stanch advocate of law and order. He denounced the inequities of political representation and the slave trade, yet opposed toleration of Roman Catholics. "I wish them well," but "I dare not trust them." Ironically, he was frequently charged with being a Roman instrument of subverting Anglicanism.

Bibliography: J. WESLEY, *The Journal . . .*, ed. N. CURNOCK, 8 v. (London 1909–16). M. PIETTE, *John Wesley in the Evolution of Protestantism*, tr. J. B. HOWARD (New York 1937). R. SOUTHEY, *The Life of Wesley and the Rise and Progress of Methodism*, ed. M. H. FITZGERALD, 2 v. (London 1925). R. A. KNOX, *Enthusiasm* (New York 1950). N. SYKES, *Church and State in England in the XVIIIth Century* (Cambridge, Eng. 1934). W. J. TOWNSEND et al., eds., *A New History of Methodism*, 2 v. (London 1909). R. N. STROMBERG, *Religious Liberalism in Eighteenth–Century England* (London 1954). M. L. EDWARDS, *Methodism and England* (London 1943). H. E. LUCCOCK and P. HUTCHINSON, *Story of Methodism* (New York 1949). J. S. SIMON, *John Wesley, the Master Builder* (London 1927). D. D. THOMPSON, *John Wesley as a Social Reformer* (New York 1898). A. B. LAWSON, *John Wesley and the Christian Ministry* (London 1963). M. SCHMIDT, *John Wesley: A Theological Biography*, v.1 *From 17th June, 1703 until 24th May, 1738*, tr. N. P. GOLDHAWK (Nashville 1962). A. C. OUTER, *John Wesley* (New York 1964).

[G. L. VINCITORIO]

WESSENBERG, IGNAZ HEINRICH VON

German ecclesiastic; b. Dresden, Nov. 4, 1774; d. Constance, Aug. 9, 1860. He came from a noble family. He studied at Dillingen from 1792; at Würzburg from 1794, where he came into contact with Karl von DALBERG and other supporters of the ENLIGHTENMENT; then at Vienna (1796–97). From 1792 he accumulated benefices as cathedral canon at Augsburg, Basel, and Constance. While a subdeacon he became vicar–general of the Diocese of Constance (1802); he was not ordained until 1812. Dalberg sought to have him made coadjutor bishop of Constance (1814), but Rome refused recognition. He was vicar of the cathedral chapter and administrator of the Diocese of Constance from 1817 despite the strong objection of Pius VII, who suppressed the see in 1821. The pope also disapproved the selection of Wessenberg as bishop of Freiburg and Rottenburg (1822).

Wessenberg's wide range of studies had not included special theological training, but he possessed deep insight into the practical needs of souls and suggested valuable pastoral and liturgical reforms that were far ahead of his time. He also labored zealously and effectively to aid persons in moral danger or in physical suffering. Commendably he urged such improvements as clergy conferences to continue clerical education after ordination, scripture reading in families, and better understanding of the Mass by the faithful. On the other hand, he disapproved pilgrimages, processions, and other external manifestations of piety, Marian devotions, the Rosary, numerous holy days, dogmas, monasteries, and mendicant orders. He exceeded his authority in dispensing from religious vows and the obligations of the Breviary for slight reasons. Wessenberg's pastoral and social labors evinced a certain loftiness of character. Less admirable was his attitude toward the pope and the Roman Curia, which developed from his own unpleasant experiences and from the currently widespread influences of FEBRONIANISM, JOSEPHINISM, and Episcopalism; yet he retained a fundamental loyalty to Rome.

Wessenberg was also a Catholic humanist well versed in politics, philosophy, pedagogy, music, and poetry. He sought to bridge the cultural gap between the church and the contemporary world, and cultivated close relations with outstanding Protestant intellectuals and scholars. His principal writings were: *Uber die Folgen der Säcularisation* (1801); *Coup d'oeil sur la situation actuelle et les vrais intérêts de l'église catholique* (1825); and *Die Grossen Kirchenversammlungen d. 15 u. 16 Jahrhunderts* (4 v. 1840). Two of his works are listed in the Index: *Die Stellung des römischen Stuhls gegenüber dem Geiste des 19. Jahrhunderts* (1833) and *Die Bisthums–Synode und die Erfordernisse und Bedingungen einer heilsamen Herstellung derselben* (1849).

Bibliography: C. GRÖBER, *Lexikon für Theologie und Kirche,* ed. J. HOFER and K. RAHNER, 10 v. (2d, new ed. Freiburg 1957–65) 10:835–839 K. ALAND, ''Wessenberg–Studien,'' *Zeitschrift für die Geschichte des Oberrheins* 95 (1943) 550–620; 96 (1948) 450–567; 105 (1957) 475–511. E. REINHARD, ''Briefe des . . . I. von Wessenberg an den Grafen F. A. von Spiegel,'' *ibid.* 105 (1957) 225–264. W. MÜLLER, ''Wessenberg in heutiger Sicht'' *Zeitschrift für schweizerische Kirchengeschichte* 58 (1964) 293–308.

[V. CONZEMIUS]

WESSOBRUNN, ABBEY OF

Former Benedictine monastery of SS. Peter and Paul, Upper Bavaria, Diocese of Augsburg. According to a tradition, it was founded in 753 by Duke Tassilo III, but its origins probably are associated with the important Huosi family, founders of BENEDIKTBEUERN. It soon became an imperial abbey. In the 9th century, when it colonized the wastelands between the Ammer and Lech Rivers, a monk wrote the famous Wessobrunn Prayer, one of the oldest and best examples of Old High German literature. In 955 Hungarians destroyed the monastery, whose lands were ruled by provosts until 1065, when Benedictines returned from SANKT EMMERAM in Regensburg and established a double monastery. One of the nuns, Diemud, *c.* 1150 excelled as a poet and calligrapher (45 MSS). Romanesque stone sculpture of the 12th–13th century discovered in Wessobrunn belongs among the

German masterpieces of the period. The abbey joined the reforms of HIRSAU and MELK (1438). In 1414 Abbot Ulrich Höhenkirchner was mitered. Under Leonhard Weiss (1671–96) began a period of glory, as Wessobrunn became a center of scholarship and baroque art with its famous school of stucco artists and painters. In the 18th century 30 monks taught at Salzburg University and at other Benedictine schools of higher learning. Wessobrunn monks compiled a Bible concordance that became a standard exegetic work. Three-fourths of the buildings, including the Romanesque church, were demolished after suppression of the abbey in 1803. Only the hostelry, with stuccoed and painted floors and halls, still stands. The grounds are owned by the archabbey of St. Ottilien; the buildings of Wessobrunn are occupied by the Missionary Benedictine Sisters of Tutzing.

Bibliography: P. LINDNER, *Professbuch von Wessobrunn* (Kempten 1909). G. HAGER, ''Die Bautätigkeit und Kunstpflege im Kloster Wessobrunn,'' *Oberbayerisches Archiv für vaterländische Geschichte* 48 (1892) 195–521. P. F. KEHR, *Regesta Pontificum Romanorum. Germania Pontificia,* ed. A. BRACKMANN, 3 v. (Berlin 1911–) 2: 64–68. L. H. COTTINEAU, *Répertoire topobibliographique des abbayes et prieurés,* 2 v. (Mâcon 1935–39) 2:3446. P. RUF, *Bistum Augsburg,* v.3.1 of *Mittelalterliche Bibliothekskataloge Deutschlands* (Munich 1932) 172–191. J. HEMMERLE, *Die Benediktinerklöster in Bayern* (Munich 1951) 139–141. ''Wessobrunn,'' *Lexikon für Theologie und Kirche,* ed. J. HOFER and K. RAHNER, 10 v. (2d, new ed. Freiburg 1957–65) v. 10.

[N. BACKMUND]

WEST, MORRIS L.

Novelist; b. April 26, 1916, Melbourne, Australia; d. Oct. 9, 1999, Sydney, Australia. At age fourteen West entered the order of the Christian Brothers, leaving nine years later on the eve of his scheduled final vows. As a Christian Brother he completed an undergraduate degree and taught for six years in the Australian schools of the order, both lower grades and high school. World War II drew him into military intelligence, where he also wrote and published his first novel, notable especially for its autobiographical detail.

By 1954, having left the military and worked successfully for ten years in Australian radio, West had suffered a failed marriage and an emotional collapse. A year of total bed-rest left him recovered and committed to a life of letters. In 1959, following a period of European travel, a second marriage, and the publication of a handful of undistinguished novels, West gained world attention and a prodigious readership with *The Devil's Advocate.* The surface story of the Church's investigation into the possible sainthood of a villager in wartime Italy is thickened by the political and procedural intricacies of

Morris L. West. (AP/Wide World Photos)

Vatican bureaucracy and subtle psychological layering of moral discernment. Thereafter, for nearly forty years, West's almost annual publications commanded wide critical and popular interest, interest centered within but not confined to denominational boundaries.

The Shoes of the Fisherman, written in 1963, projects much of the euphoric spirit of the Second Vatican Council while following the early papal career of an Eastern-bloc prelate. Kiril I spent years of his young life in a Soviet gulag, an experience that both toughened and humanized him in ways quite different from the usual clerical career path. His jailor, his personal persecutor, eventually becomes the Soviet premier; together they form a secret partnership to moderate East-West tensions. Both of these novels were immensely popular and both were recreated in film. Although West chafed at the label "Catholic novelist," which he carried throughout his publishing career, these two works, like many other novels he wrote, are fully immersed in a Catholic ecclesial context. Two titles with a similar intramural accent are *The Clowns of God* (1981), a futurist novel of a pope forced into abdication whose visions of the end of the world are feared as potential incitement to world crisis; and *Eminence* (1998), his final published work, which explores the possible direction of the papacy and Church after Pope John Paul II.

Equally characteristic of West's fictional style are his use of highly topical settings, which bring often powerful thrusts to his narrative momentum. In addition to Rome and the council, he uses, for example, Saigon during the Vietnam War (*The Ambassador* [1963]), and the Middle East in the midst of Jewish-Arab tensions (*The Tower of Babel* [1968]). The former title claimed wide interest for its insider's depiction of American complicity in the ouster and murder of a fictional President Diem. Students of West found in the novel a deepening interest in Eastern religion, especially Buddhism.

West's abiding interest in deeply spiritual encounters, explored within an explicitly Catholic context and idiom, combined with an ability to project his stories onto a stage framed by global ideological strife, caused him to be compared with Graham GREENE. A half-generation younger than Greene and the other heroes of the Catholic literary revival, West differs most significantly for having caught the wave of hope released by Vatican II. Thus although his moral landscapes project shadowy, often ambiguous pathways toward awareness and the good, they are far less bleak, their protagonists far less abject. Instead one finds West's stories imbued with a powerfully rising tone of personal renewal and spiritual possibility.

The comparison with Greene was costly to his critical reputation. But there were other reasons why West was considered an author of the second level. His plots are masterfully crafted and instantly engaging, but they often crowded the border of melodrama. And the chronic complaint about religious literature that the penetration of the divine into the secular is achieved more by "magic" than by a sure sacramentalism haunted the reviews of his novels. Nevertheless, even his critics honored him for his dogged persistence in searching out those narrow passages in life when the challenge of the cross is faced.

In 1996 West wrote a loosely connected but engaging retrospective of his life, *A View from the Ridge.* In it he reflected upon the refusal of the marriage court of his Australian archdiocese to annul his first marriage in 1951, and he declared that the spiritual crisis it provoked was a decisive moment for both his life and his art. "It forced me," he wrote, "to examine the roots and meaning of my unexamined beliefs I had held and taught for so long." Thereafter and to the end of his life, West remained outside the sacramental gates of the Church. But many vestiges of his public and professional life testify to a profound loyalty and commitment to the faith community of his birth. And his literary interpretation of Catholic Christianity during the latter half of the twentieth century will serve the interests of historians for many years to come. He died in his home in Sydney Australia on Oct. 9, 1999.

Bibliography: M. L. WEST,*The Devil's Advocate* (New York 1959); *The Shoes of the Fisherman* (New York 1963); *The Ambassador* (New York 1965); *A View from the Ridge* (San Francisco 1996); ''Testimony of a Twentieth Century Catholic,'' *America* 117 (Dec. 2, 1967): 678–681.

[P. MESSBARGER]

WEST VIRGINIA, CATHOLIC CHURCH IN

Catholic Beginnings. The first significant Catholic presence in West Virginia can be established in the years immediately following the American Revolution. The pioneer Catholic families are believed to have settled in the lower Shenandoah Valley, a region of West Virginia that is known as the Eastern Panhandle. Although Catholics had been settling on the Maryland/Pennsylvania side of the border of what was then western Virginia since the first part of the 18th century, few had crossed over into the lower Shenandoah Valley. The initial reluctance of Catholics to settle in Virginia can be directly related to the anti-Catholic laws enacted there during colonial times, when the practice of their religion was declared illegal and behavior towards Catholics was openly hostile. Catholic advance into Virginia appears to begin after the restrictions on their religion had been removed by the state legislature with the 1786 Act for Establishing Religious Freedom.

Priests from Maryland and Pennsylvania visited the Catholics who had settled in the Eastern Panhandle during these initial years. A letter written by a Reverend Denis Cahill in 1795 tells of the conditions he encountered in western Virginia. Based in Hagerstown, Maryland, Cahill traveled into western Virginia, getting as far as Cumberland, Maryland, a distance of some 70 miles. He ministered to the Catholic families he encountered, organizing them into formal missions, and initiating the building of churches. He reported finding Catholics throughout the Eastern Panhandle, including the towns of Harper's Ferry, Martinsburg, and Shepherdstown.

The Eastern Panhandle remained the center of Catholic activities until the second decade of the 19th century when a small community was formed in the city of Wheeling, located in the region of western Virginia known as the Northern Panhandle. Although a Catholic presence had been established there in the early part of the 19th century, it was not until an influx of immigrants around 1818 that their numbers were large enough to form a parish. Many of these immigrants were Irish laborers who had worked on the National Road project. They were soon joined by a number of Germans who were drawn to the city for its opportunities in the skilled trades.

With the exception of the Catholic communities in the Eastern and Northern Panhandles, western Virginia was described at this time as an ''unorganized spiritual wilderness.'' In Preston County, a small community of German immigrants had settled near what is now Howesville, built a church for the families to worship in, and arranged for a priest to come and visit them. Their experience, however, remained the exception. Most Catholics who settled in western Virginia during this period arrived on their own and settled at great distances from one another. Religious communities such as the Jesuits and Redemptorists sent missionaries into this region where they attempted to locate the Catholic families that had settled there. Priests from neighboring dioceses also traveled into western Virginia to say Mass and minister to the Catholic families, but their visits were all too infrequent and their numbers too few to visit the region regularly.

The turning point in the history of Catholicism in western Virginia came with the arrival of the Baltimore and Ohio Railroad project in the mid-1840s. Just as the National Road project brought Catholics to the Northern Panhandle, so the B&O Railroad brought Catholics to the undeveloped interior region of western Virginia. Stretching from Cumberland, Maryland, to Wheeling, Virginia, the location of Catholic families in this territory can be easily established. The laborers and their families founded new communities along the path followed by the railroad. The affordable prices of western Virginia's land persuaded many laborers to give up their itinerant lives and begin anew as farmers.

Establishment of the Diocese of Wheeling. Encouraged by the increase in the number of Catholics settling in western Virginia as well as the region's promising future, the bishop of Richmond, Richard V. Whelan, petitioned the Holy See for the creation of a new diocese. Until that time, the Catholics of western Virginia had been under the spiritual care of the Diocese of Richmond, which encompassed the entire state of Virginia. On July 19, 1850, Pope Pius IX established the Diocese of Wheeling, naming Whelan its first ordinary. At the time there were just four churches within its borders (St. James, Wheeling; St. Patrick, Weston; St. Mary, Wytheville; St. John, Summersville); one chapel, the German Settlement in Preston County; and a Catholic population of about five thousand.

The Allegheny Mountains were used to set the initial boundaries of the new diocese. At its founding in 1850, the diocese had both a different name and borders from the ones it possesses today. The eight counties of the Eastern Panhandle remained with the Diocese of Richmond and 17 and a half counties of southwestern Virginia constituted the Diocese of Wheeling. The outbreak of the Civil War and the creation of the new state of West Virginia in 1863 meant that diocesan and state boundaries were distinct from one another for over 100 years. It was not until a 1974 decree, promulgated by Pope Paul VI, that the diocesan borders were realigned to accord with those of the state. The 17 and a half counties in Virginia that had initially been part of the Diocese were transferred to the Diocese of Richmond, as were the eight counties of the Eastern Panhandle incorporated into the Diocese of Wheeling. The name of the diocese was also redesignated at this time to the Diocese of Wheeling-Charleston.

Bishop Whelan devoted the remainder of his life to the building up of the Catholic Church in West Virginia. At his death in 1874, the diocese claimed 46 churches, seven chapels, nine schools, one seminary, one hospital, 31 priests, and 109 women religious with a Catholic population estimated at 18,000.

John J. Kain (1840–1903) was appointed to succeed Bishop Whelan in 1875. Bishop Kain's years in the diocese were devoted to meeting the needs of the newly arrived immigrants who came in search of labor in West Virginia's mines and factories. He continued his predecessor's efforts of constructing the churches and schools, and remained in Wheeling until his appointment as archbishop of St. Louis in 1893.

A Church of Immigrants. As was true for much of the U.S. Catholic Church, West Virginia Catholicism was an immigrant church. At the time the diocese was founded in 1850, immigration was dominated by the Irish and Germans, who were brought into the region as laborers on the great public and private works projects of the 19th century. Others were attracted by the region's affordable land and Wheeling's prospects as a vital commercial center. Within 50 years, however, the Irish and Germans were outnumbered by their co-religionists from such countries as Russia, Italy, and the Austro-Hungarian Empire, when the diocese experienced its largest influx of immigrants, the majority of whom were employed as unskilled laborers in the emerging industries of the age: coal, steel, oil, natural gas, and timber.

Patrick J. Donahue (1849–1922) was bishop of the diocese during its greatest period of growth. In the 28 years he served as bishop, the Catholic population more than tripled, rising from approximately 20,000 when he was appointed in 1894 to over 62,000 at his death in 1922. Much of this growth took place in the decade between 1900 and 1910 when the Catholic population increased by over 20,000, and half of the nearly 150 parishes and missions that were founded during Donahue's reign were established.

To serve the growing Catholic population, Donahue invited religious communities to send priests, brothers, and sisters to serve, some of which continue to maintain a presence in the diocese, including the Marist Fathers, the Sisters of Our Lady of Charity, the Ursuline Sisters, the Dominican Sisters, and the Sisters of the Poor Child of Jesus. He also appealed to the missionary colleges in Ireland to send priests, and he made several trips to Europe to recruit priests who could speak in the native languages of the immigrants who were arriving in the diocese. By 1922 the number of priests serving in the diocese had more than tripled, increasing from 36 to 115, and the number of women religious had more than doubled from 143 to 340.

Donahue was succeeded by Bishop John J. SWINT (1879–1962), who had been appointed his auxiliary earlier that year. Swint was a native of Pickens, Randolph County, the son of immigrants who were among the first Catholics to settle in central West Virginia. He came to office during the period of "brick-and-mortar Catholicism." It was a time when the attention of the Catholic community was turned from meeting the immediate needs of arriving immigrants to establishing an institutional infrastructure to serve them.

When Swint died on Nov. 23, 1962, he had been bishop of the diocese for 40 years. During this period, the Catholic population had almost doubled, from over 62,000 Catholics in 1922 to nearly 110,000 in 1962. He devoted much of his energy to meeting the material needs of the Catholics in the diocese, through the building of churches and schools, and by promoting the development of the Catholic health care system and social outreach programs. At his death close to 100 churches, a new cathedral, one college, 52 elementary and high schools, and five hospitals had been established under his leadership. The title of "Archbishop ad personam" was conferred on him by Pius XII in recognition of his contributions to the development of the Church in West Virginia.

Bishop Joseph H. Hodges (1911–85) succeeded Archbishop Swint as the fifth bishop of the diocese in 1962. His participation in the Second Vatican Council would prove to be a defining moment in his life and lead to his becoming a major source of renewal and reform for the diocese. He dedicated his episcopacy to implementing the reforms of the council, which encompassed all aspects of Church life and led to new initiatives in the areas of social justice, evangelization, and ecumenism. He was a leader in the state's ecumenical movement and an outspoken advocate in the cause of social justice for all West Virginians. He was a driving force behind the 1975 pastoral letter issued jointly by the Roman Catholic bishops of Appalachia, "This Land Is Home to Me," which addressed the issues of economic and political powerlessness among the people of the region. He died on Jan. 27, 1985, after serving as bishop of the diocese for 23 years.

Contributions of Religious Orders. The arrival of the first religious preceded the founding of the Diocese. The Visitation Nuns came to Wheeling in 1848 to open an academy for young women at the invitation of Bishop Richard V. Whelan. Wheeling Female Academy (Mount de Chantal Visitation Academy) opened on April 10, 1848, with 30 students enrolled. It was the first of three academies established by the order in the diocese [De Sales Heights Academy, Parkersburg, and Villa Maria Academy, Abingdon (later Wytheville)]. Originally located near the cathedral, the academy and convent relocated outside of Wheeling in 1865, where it continues to operate. The Visitation Nuns also established St. Joseph's Benevolent School (Wheeling Catholic Elementary School) for the children of St. James Parish in 1848. The school continues to serve the children of Wheeling's inner city, and the Sisters of St. Joseph of Wheeling have maintained a presence at the school since 1865.

Concern over the staffing and administration of Wheeling Hospital, founded by Bishop Whelan and Dr. Simon Hullihen in 1850, brought a second religious order to the diocese in 1853. Whelan had petitioned the Sisters of St. Joseph of Carondelet, Missouri, in 1852, to found a convent in the diocese. Their decision to accept his invitation would have tremendous implications for the development of the diocese. Shortly after their arrival the Sisters of St. Joseph expanded their ministry to include education and social ministries. Over the course of their history in the diocese, the sisters have administered four hospitals (Wheeling Hospital, St. Mary Hospital, Clarksburg, St. Joseph Hospital, Parkersburg, and St. Francis Hospital, Charleston), two orphanages, over 60 parish schools, and numerous catechism and social outreach programs.

An effort to reorganize the governance of the Sisters of St. Joseph of Carondelet in the United States led to the members of the Wheeling convent establishing an independent motherhouse in 1860, and calling themselves the Congregation of the Sisters of St. Joseph of Wheeling. Membership in the community peaked in the 1960s with close to 300 Sisters. At the end of the 20th century, however, the community comprised about 100. The Sisters of St. Joseph of Wheeling are the only religious order to be incorporated in the diocese.

The Capuchin Friars were the first men's religious order to serve the diocese. Bishop Kain first invited the Friars to administer the diocese's German national parish, St. Alphonsus, Wheeling, in 1884. Through their work at St. Alphonsus, the Capuchins established an important apostolate among the German community and ministered to German-speaking immigrants throughout the Northern Panhandle. In 1900, they expanded their mission by taking over Sacred Heart Parish in Charleston and the missions it was responsible for in the Kanawha Valley. Today, the parishes that stand as witness to their labors include St. Francis of Assisi Parish, St. Albans, Christ the King Parish, Dunbar, and Our Lady of the Hills Parish, Elkview. Although the order has withdrawn from both Sacred Heart Co-Cathedral and St. Alphonsus, they continue to administer St. Anthony in Charleston, which now serves as the main residence of the Friars in southern West Virginia.

The Marist Fathers are another religious community with longstanding service in the diocese. Bishop Donahue first invited the Marist Fathers in 1898 to administer the newly founded St. Michael's in Wheeling. Their ministry was soon expanded when they agreed to take responsibility for the diocesan parishes and missions in central West Virginia. Holy Rosary, Buckhannon; St. Anne, Webster Springs; and Holy Family, Richwood are among the parishes that the Marist Fathers founded during their labors in this region. They continue to serve in Wheeling and central West Virginia. They are assisted in their work by diocesan priests, the Divine Word Missionary Fathers, the Sisters of St. Anne, the Sisters of Charity, and the Sisters of St. Joseph.

The Marist Fathers were also responsible for bringing the Pallottine Missionary Sisters into the diocese in 1912. Together they built and staffed the first Catholic schools and hospitals in central West Virginia. The hospitals at Richwood and Buckhannon were the first of four established by the Pallottine Missionary Sisters in the diocese. The Pallottine Missionary Sisters expanded their ministry in 1923 when they agreed to establish a hospital in Huntington. St. Mary's Hospital has since distinguished itself as one of the finest medical facilities in the state. The sisters also maintained their commitment to education when they arrived in Huntington by staffing parish schools in the southern region of the diocese.

The Sisters of Our Lady of Charity of Refuge, a Canadian congregation of women religious now known as the North American Union of the Sisters of Our Lady of Charity, were invited to establish a community in Wheeling by Bishop Donahue in 1899. Good Shepherd Home for Young Ladies was founded by the Sisters in order to care for young women who were at risk or in need of financial and emotional support. Over its history, Good Shepherd Home took in over 10,000 young women from across the state and surrounding communities, without regard to religious affiliation. Our Lady of the Valley School, as it came to be known, was closed in 1972. The

Sisters transferred the property to the diocese at this time and the building was converted into Good Shepherd Home for the Aged, through a financial bequest from Miss Clara Welty. The Sisters continue to maintain a presence at the home.

Other religious congregations that have made significant contributions in West Virginia include the Sisters of Divine Providence, Sisters Auxiliaries of the Apostolate, Daughters of Charity, Ursuline Sisters, Dominican Sisters, Passionist Fathers, Jesuit Fathers, and Marist Brothers.

Catholic Contributions in West Virginia. The Catholics of West Virginia have made tremendous contributions to the communities in which they live. They have been engaged in many charitable activities, including the establishment of hospitals and orphanages to care for the most vulnerable members of society. The diocese has become the second largest provider of social services in the state, operating 16 programs, ranging from disaster and emergency relief to pregnancy and parenting classes, with offices established in every region of the state.

The Catholic school system in West Virginia, which includes eight high schools and 27 elementary schools in addition to a number of preschool and day care programs, began in 1838 and is the largest privately run school system in the state. It provides education in the Catholic tradition for all students in a nurturing, Christ-centered environment.

In 1955 the diocese's only Catholic college was founded. The Jesuit Fathers accepted Archbishop John J. Swint's invitation to administer the college and within four years it became a reality. Wheeling College (now Wheeling Jesuit University) was established as a coeducational liberal arts college in the Jesuit tradition. It is located on 60 acres of property that was purchased by the diocese from the Visitation Nuns of Mount de Chantal Visitation Academy. Ground was broken for the first building on Nov. 23, 1953, and the college was dedicated two years later, on Oct. 23, 1955, with 90 students enrolled in its first class. The diocese financed the construction of the college's first three buildings, which were named after the three Bishops most closely associated with its founding: Richard V. Whelan, Patrick J. Donahue, and John J. Swint. The first women's dormitory, completed in 1959, was dedicated to Miss Sara Tracy in recognition of her significant contributions to the college. In the over 45 years of Wheeling Jesuit University's existence, the Jesuit traditions of educational excellence and service to others have guided all of its programs. The university has an enrollment of close to 1,900 students, offering degrees in 28 majors.

From Wheeling Hospital, recognized to be the first hospital founded in West Virginia, to the Children's Health Care Clinic in Pineville, the Catholic health care system has benefited tens of thousands of the state's citizens and has provided the people of West Virginia not only with quality health care for the past 150 years, but with a ministry of healing rooted in Catholic tradition that embraces the spiritual values of compassion, hospitality, and reverence for the sanctity of human life.

Bibliography: M. B. BRADLEY et al., ''State Summary, Table 3: Churches and Church Membership by State and Denomination, 1990,'' *Churches and Church Membership in the U.S., 1990* (Atlanta 1992) p. 35.

[T. T. PYNE]

WESTCOTT, BROOKE FOSS

Anglican scripturist and bishop; b. near Birmingham, England, Jan. 12, 1827; d. Auckland Castle, July 27, 1901. He studied at King Edward VI School and at Trinity College, Cambridge, receiving his degree in 1848. In the same year he was ordained to the ministry; four years later he became assistant master of Harrow, and in 1868 examining chaplain of Bp. Connor Magee of Peterborough. He was elected regius professor of divinity at Cambridge in 1870, appointed by the crown to a canonry at Westminster in 1883, then made examining chaplain to Archbishop Benson. In 1890 he succeeded J. B. LIGHTFOOT as bishop of Durham, where, during the decade of his episcopacy, he successfully met the different social questions he encountered. A prolific writer, he published about 20 books and many tracts and articles. As a scripturist, his most significant work was his collaboration with F. J. A. Hort on a critical edition of the Greek NT (1881). His *History of the NT Canon* (1855) long remained a standard work.

Bibliography: A. WESTCOTT, *Life and Letters of Brooke Foss Westcott,* 2 v. (New York 1903), includes bibliog. V. H. STANTON, *The Dictionary of National Biography from the Earliest Times to 1900* (1901–11) 635–641.

[B. VEROSTKO]

WESTERN SAHARA, THE CHURCH IN

An arid region located on the northwest coast of AFRICA, the territory of Western Sahara is bordered on the west by the Atlantic Ocean, on the north by MOROCCO, on the northeast by ALGERIA, and on the east and south by MAURITANIA. Consisting of low, flat, desert, the region is hot and dry, although it's brief annual rainy season draws thousands of nomads from neighboring countries. Coastal fishing, agriculture and some livestock raising provide a basic livelihood for most Saharan nomads, although the exploitation by Spain of phosphates and iron ore has traditionally employed many people living in the region.

The Portuguese explored the coastal area in the 15th century although no effort was made to colonize it. Because of its location near the Canary Islands, Spain officially claimed a protectorate over the region in 1884, but did not occupy it until 1934 due to resistance by nomadic natives. In 1954 the Prefecture Apostolic of Spanish Sahara and IFNI was created out of the Vicariate Apostolic of Ghardaia in Algeria, and entrusted to the Spanish province of the OBLATES OF MARY IMMACULATE. Four years later, as the Spanish Sahara, the region became an integral province of Spain. Infi was later removed to another ecclesiastical jurisdiction.

In the mid-1950s the Western Sahara was discovered to contain rich phosphate deposits, prompting native Saharan's to develop a sense of nationalism. Within two decades the region became the focus of a territorial dispute, as the three surrounding nations attempted to gain total control of the region following Spain's decision to terminate its claim in 1976. In the midst of secret negotiations between Morocco, Algeria and Mauritania, a nationalist faction known as the Polisaro Front proclaimed itself the government-in-exile of the region, and dubbed the region the Sahrawi Arab Democratic Republic. Through guerilla violence, the Polisaro deterred Mauritania from pursuing its territorial claims. Meanwhile, the International Court of Justice, meeting in The Hague, rejected Morocco's claim for total sovereignty. Morocco ignored this decision, as well as a mediated U.N. referendum following a cease-fire in 1991, and continued to press its claim into the 21st century.

By 2000 the territory of the Western Sahara contained two parishes administered by three religious priests; the Catholic population consisted mainly of Spaniards and members of the U.N. Interposition Force. Contact with the Muslim majority was limited to educational and cultural matters, which served as a vehicle for dialogue between the two faiths. Most Saharans were ethnic Arabs or Berbers. Morocco retained administrative control of the territory through 2000.

Bibliography: *Annuario Pontificio,* (1964) 786.

[J. A. BELL/EDS.]

WESTERN SCHISM

The period (1378–1417) in which Western Christendom was divided between two, and later three, papal obediences, and which was brought to an end by the Council of CONSTANCE.

Origins. The death of GREGORY XI on March 27, 1378, in Rome made it necessary to proceed forthwith to the election of a new pontiff. Gregory was the last pope of the AVIGNON PAPACY and had actually transferred the Curia from AVIGNON to Rome, where no election of a pope had taken place for 75 years. Although it cannot be said that the situation in Rome was conducive to an orderly and quiet election, and although the election itself exhibited some irregular features, there can be no doubt that it was canonical. At any rate, the result was the election on April 8, 1378, of the archbishop of Bari as URBAN VI, the last pope chosen from outside the College of Cardinals. At the time he seemed a very intelligent choice. Neapolitan by birth and upbringing, French in cultural outlook, he had been a curialist at Avignon, highly efficient and hardworking. It was thought that he would overcome the tensions between Italians and Frenchmen within the College of Cardinals. The cardinals, however, soon came to realize that the man they had elected was far from suitable for his office. Urban developed a domineering personality, was impervious to all counsel and advice, and showed signs of insanity. Above all, he wished to restore the proper monarchic function of the pope vis-à-vis the cardinals. At Avignon the cardinals had assumed ever greater powers which, in their aggregate, approached the form of oligarchic government—the very thing Urban wished to abolish. When the cardinals came to realize the pope's intentions, they withdrew one by one to Anagni, and on Sept. 20, 1378 elected one of themselves, Cardinal Robert of Geneva, as CLEMENT VII (antipope), ostensibly claiming that the election of Urban had been forced upon them by the unruly Roman mob. Urban's election, despite some irregularities, cannot be called uncanonical. In fact, for several months the cardinals had acknowledged Urban as pope, and the thesis of an enforced election emerged only gradually as they came to experience Urban's type of government. But their assertion that they had been subjected to force, however little this contention was supported by facts, offered their only means of impugning the election and presenting it as uncanonical.

Soon after the election, Clement and all the cardinals took up residence at Avignon, so that Latin Christendom

MOROCCO & WESTERN SAHARA

now had one pope, Urban VI, reigning in Rome, with a new College of Cardinals, and another, Clement VII, ruling from Avignon. The election of Clement was significant in two ways: (1) one and the same College had elected two popes; (2) such action starkly demonstrated a serious defect in the law of the Church, which provided no constitutional means of dealing with an obviously unsuitable pope. Once elected, a pope who had become insane, imbecile, or for any other reason unfit to govern, could not be removed. The cardinals were thus forced to resort to the one canonical regulation which left some sort of loophole, viz, the allegation that the election of the pope had not been free. From the strictly legal point of view their subsequent election was uncanonical, though there has never been an official papal pronouncement on the question of legality or illegality of the Roman or Avignonese lines of popes.

Effects. The results of this double headship were disastrous. The followers of each pope grouped themselves along rather clearly defined national lines. Among the adherents of Urban were the Holy Roman Empire, England, Hungary, Scandinavia, and most of Italy; while France, Naples, Savoy, Scotland, Spain, and Sicily adhered to Clement. Each pope anathematized his rival and all his rival's followers, so that the whole of Western Christendom found itself, at least in theory, excommunicated. It is obvious that the spectacle of two popes attacking each other in a most unseemly manner produced doubt and confusion where there had been unquestioned certainty before. The division likewise entailed for the papacy a heavy loss of dignity and authority. Matters were made worse by the frequently occurring division among cathedral chapters and religious institutions where, in one body, both Urbanist and Clementine followers could be found, with the result that whole orders were split into two camps. This division affected even parishes, where Urbanist and Clementine parish priests contended. Moreover, the expenses of the two curial households, each with its own College of Cardinals and retainers, as well as the costs of the political designs entertained by them, had to be met with an increase in taxes levied upon the clergy. Heretical movements received a particular stimulus, and it is no exaggeration to say that the result was utter chaos during the period of the schism.

Proposals for Ending the Schism. The means to end this disaster presented themselves in the movement called CONCILIARISM, according to which a general council was to decide the issue and henceforth was to be the supreme ecclesiastical authority, to which even the pope was to be subjected. Proposed primarily by the University of PARIS, this idea in course of time gained more and more adherents. The popes themselves were, of course, adamant in their opposition to conciliarism, and when Urban died, his College of Cardinals elected BONIFACE IX, who did little to heal the division of Christendom. No more did Clement's successor BENEDICT XIII (antipope), the fiery Peter de Luna, although discussions and negotiations between the two camps continued. In the same year in which Benedict was elected, the University of Paris put forward three concrete proposals for ending the Schism: (1) the *via cessionis,* that both popes should voluntarily resign; (2) the *via compromissi,* that an independent tribunal be empowered to decide which pope should resign; (3) the *via concilii,* that a decision be made by a general council. The university itself favored the first proposal. Benedict's stubbornness persuaded France and Spain to withdraw their obedience from him in 1398, resulting in the resignation of all but five cardinals. French troops besieged the papal palace at Avignon and kept Benedict a prisoner for four years. France had not, however, recognized Boniface, and the confusion became so great that a meeting of French lay and ecclesiastical princes in 1403 suggested resumption of relations with Benedict. Meanwhile, most universities proposed means of ending the schism, but every effort was nullified by the recalcitrancy of the popes. In the Roman line GREGORY XII succeeded Boniface in 1406 and initially was eager to terminate the conflict. However, when a meeting of the two popes was arranged for September 1407 at Savona near Genoa, Gregory changed his mind and refused to meet his rival. The scandal had reached such dimensions that a number of cardinals from both obediences arranged a council at Pisa, after France had declared its neutrality in the papal schism (1408). The Council of PISA began on March 25, 1409. It consisted of 24 cardinals, numerous archbishops and bishops, and doctors of theology and Canon Law, assisted by legations from many secular governments. It summoned both popes, but neither appeared, holding that the council was uncanonical; and on June 26, 1409, the council elected the third pope, ALEXANDER V, the former Peter of Candia, cardinal archbishop of Milan. On the death of Alexander in the following year the Pisan curia elected JOHN XXIII (antipope), formerly Cardinal Balthasar Cossa. It was through the instrumentality and persuasive efforts of the Emperor SIGISMUND that John convoked the Council of Constance for Nov. 1, 1414. Here he was formally deposed on March 29, 1415, while the nonagenarian Gregory resigned on July 4, 1415. Benedict, however, had fled to Perpignan, categorically refusing to entertain any thought of resignation; he remained ''pope'' until his death in 1423. With the election of MARTIN V on Nov. 11, 1417, the schism formally ended.

List of Popes During the Schism.

1. Roman obedience:
Urban VI (April 8, 1378, to Oct. 15, 1389)
Boniface IX (Nov. 2, 1389, to Oct. 1, 1404)
Innocent VII (Oct. 17, 1404, to Nov. 6, 1406)
Gregory XII (Nov. 30, 1406, to July 4, 1415)
2. Avignonese obedience:
Clement VII (Sept. 20, 1378, to Sept. 16, 1394)
Benedict XIII (Sept. 28, 1394, to May 23, 1423)
3. Pisan obedience:
Alexander V (June 26, 1409, to May 3, 1410)
John XXIII (May 17, 1410, to March 29, 1415)

Bibliography: N. VALOIS, *La France et le grand schisme,* 4 v. (Paris 1896–1902). E. PERROY, *L'Angleterre et e grand schisme d'Occident* (Paris 1934). M. DE BOÜARD, *La France et l'Italie au temps de grand schisme d'Occident* (Paris 1936). M. SEIDLMAYER, *Die Anfänge des grossen abendländischen Schismas* (Münster i.W. 1940). W. ULLMANN, *The Origins of the Great Schism* (London 1948; Reprint 1967); ''The University of Cambridge and the Great Schism,'' *Journal of Theological Studies* 8 (1958) 53–77. J. B. VILLIGER, *Lexikon für Theologie und Kirche,* ed. J. HOFER and K. RAHNER (Freiburg 1957–65) 1:21–26. O. PŘEROVSKÝ, *L'elezione di*

Westminster Abbey. (©Michael Nicholson/CORBIS)

Urbano VI e l'insorgere dello scisma d'Occidente (Rome 1960). E. DELARUELLE, E. R. LABANDE, and P. OURLIAC,*Histoire de l'Eglise depuis les origines jusqu'à nos jours,* ed. A. FLICHE and V. MARTIN (Paris 1962) v. 14. H. KAMINSKY, *Simon de Cramaud and the Great Schism* (New Brunswick, NJ 1983). R. N. SWANSON, *Universities, Academies and the Great Schism* (Cambridge 1979). P. H. STUMP, *The Reforms of the Council of Constance, 1414–1418* (Leiden and New York 1994).

[W. ULLMANN]

WESTMINSTER ABBEY

Former Benedictine abbey; present-day Collegiate Church of St. Peter's; on Thorney Island by the Thames, Middlesex, England, London Diocese (patron, St. Peter). Though traditionally founded in 616, it is not mentioned by Bede, and its early charters are dubious. It was founded or refounded by St. DUNSTAN OF CANTERBURY with 12 Benedictines (958–970) and lavishly endowed, rebuilt, and put under papal protection by EDWARD THE CONFESSOR (1042–65). Its exemption from episcopal jurisdiction was disputed from 1135 to 1175 and confirmed in 1222. The Confessor's church, with 12th-century Norman extensions, was totally replaced: the eastern part in contemporary French Gothic (1245–69) by King Henry III, the western part in consistent style (1375–c.1505). The Lady Chapel was completed in 1519. The western towers, originally designed by Christopher WREN, were completed between 1740 and 1750.

The first great abbot, GILBERT CRISPIN (1085–1117), left the abbey with 80 monks and three dependent prio-

ries. He established a high standard of learning, exemplified by Osbert of Clare (prior after 1136), advocate of the Immaculate Conception and of Edward the Confessor's canonization. In later centuries Westminster was not distinguished for learning, though monks were sent to Gloucester College, Oxford. Little is known of the library. The later 12th- and 13th-century scriptorium produced important manuscripts. Westminster was a meeting place of parliaments, and the coronation church and burial place of English kings. It was enriched with relics, works of art and war trophies by Henry III and Edward I. Though its abbots (1246–1307) had successful public careers, morale was not high after the later 13th century: there were internal disputes, a destructive fire (1298), and an unsolved burglary (1303). About half the community of 50 to 60 died of the Black Death (1349). SIMON LANGHAM (abbot 1349–62), later archbishop of Canterbury, restored concord, discipline, and solvency, and left a fortune for building the new nave. Numbers after this time were between 40 and 50. From the 13th to mid-15th century provision was regularly made for one monk to live as a recluse.

Both Abbot John Islip (1500–32) and his successor, William Boston, supported King HENRY VIII. In 1539 the monastery was suppressed (with income valued in 1535 at £3,470) and a collegiate church was founded with Boston as first dean. In 1556 the Queen, MARY TUDOR, refounded the Benedictine monastery under the resolutely orthodox JOHN OF FECKENHAM; in 1559 Queen ELIZABETH I dissolved it. One long-lived monk provided a link with the English Benedictines established in France (1606–15), through whom the Abbey of AMPLEFORTH traces its roots to Westminster. Westminster remains the place for the coronation of the English sovereign, in which the dean has a special part.

Bibliography: Sources. W. DUGDALE, *Monasticon Anglicanum,* 1:265–330 (London 1817–30). J. FLETE, *The History of Westminster Abbey,* ed. J. A. ROBINSON (Cambridge, Eng. 1909). G. R. C. DAVIS, *Medieval Cartularies . . .* (London 1958). Literature. H. F. WESTLAKE, *Westminster Abbey,* 2 v. (London 1921). *Inventory of the Historical Monuments in London* (London 1924) v.1. J. MCCANN and C. CARYELWES, *Ampleforth and Its Origins* (London 1952). P. BRIEGER, *English Art 1216–1307* (Oxford 1957) 106–134, 183–226. F. L. CROSS, *The Oxford Dictionary of the Christian Church,* 1449–50 (London 1957). D. KNOWLES, *The Monastic Order in England, 943–1216* (2nd ed. Cambridge, Eng. 1962); D. KNOWLES, *The Religious Orders in England,* 3 v. (Cambridge, Eng. 1948–60); and their bibliographies.

[S. WOOD]

WESTMINSTER CONFESSION

The historic doctrinal ''standard'' for English-speaking PRESBYTERIANISM was the product of the Westminster Assembly (so named from its sessions in the abbey precincts) that was convoked by the Long Parliament in June 1643 to reform the Church of England. The dominant Puritan party intended at first simply to revise the THIRTY-NINE ARTICLES, the basic formulary of the Elizabethan Establishment, along the lines of the Lambeth Articles of 1595 and the Irish Articles of 1615. When, however, the Solemn League and Covenant with Scotland was enacted in September 1643, Parliament ordered a new Confession of Faith for all three kingdoms of the British Isles, ''according to the Word of God and the example of the best reformed churches.'' Working simultaneously on a Directory of Public Worship (to replace the BOOK OF COMMON PRAYER) and two Catechisms, the Assembly submitted the Confession to Parliament in December 1646; it was published the next year. With some revisions it became the official formulary for England until the Restoration, while for Scotland and Ulster it became the subordinate standard that it has ever since remained. Even outside the direct Presbyterian tradition, its influence on later Congregationalist and Baptist confessions has been considerable.

In 33 chapters the Westminster Confession presents a comprehensive yet compact outline of the Calvinist faith. The characteristic doctrines of divine sovereignty and predestination and of human depravity and covenant are enunciated in a stately prose reminiscent of the Authorized Version of the Bible. Appealing always to a scriptural warrant, the Confession manifests a reserve regarding such problems in Puritan polemic as the freedom of the will and the visibility of the church, which sets it apart from most 16th- and 17th-century formularies and commends it to the appreciation of less fervid subsequent times.

Although the Confession has been amended by both of the leading Presbyterian bodies in the United States— by the addition, in 1903 and 1942, of two chapters (on the Holy Spirit and on the Gospel) and by the substitution, in 1959, of one (on Marriage)—it has been increasingly criticized for its excessively juridical and individualistic emphasis. The adoption of a new formulary, ''The Confession of 1967,'' and the subsequent issuance of a Book of Confessions comprised of all the major Reformed statements of faith have challenged the Westminster Confession's pre-eminence within the denomination. It is doubtful, though, that any other confession will ever assume the venerable prestige of the Westminster as the dominant statement of Reformed faith.

See Also: CONFESSIONS OF FAITH, 2: PROTESTANT.

Bibliography: S. W. CARRUTHERS, *The Everyday Work of the Westminster Assembly* (London 1943); *The Westminster Confession of Faith* (Manchester 1937). G. S. HENDRY, *The Westminster Confession for Today* (Richmond, VA 1960). E. W. SMITH, *The Creed of Presbyterians* (rev. ed. Richmond 1941). *Book of Confessions* (Knoxvile, TN 2000).

[R. I. BRADLEY/P. SOERGEL]

WESTON, WILLIAM

Jesuit priest; b. Trimworth Manor, Crundale, near Maidstone, Kent, 1551; d. Valladolid, April 9, 1615. He was educated at King's School, Canterbury, Christ's Church, Oxford, and Lincoln's Inn, London. In 1571 he studied at Paris, then for three years at the English College, Douai. On Nov. 5, 1575, he entered the Jesuit novitiate at Sant'Andrea, Rome. After being ordained in Spain (1579), he taught Hebrew and other ecclesiastical subjects at San Lucar and Seville. At Easter 1584 he left the latter city for the English mission, landing south of Yarmouth, Norfolk, on September 10 of the same year; his companion, Brother Ralph Emerson, was arrested in London within ten days. For the next two years Weston was the only Jesuit at liberty in England. During this time he became the chief organizer of the Catholic resistance; he also received into the Church, (St.) Philip HOWARD, the principal English nobleman. In July 1586 he was joined by (St.) Robert SOUTHWELL and Henry GARNET, but as soon as he initiated them into their work he himself was arrested (Aug. 3, 1586). The efforts of the Council to implicate him in the Babington plot failed: his stature as a priest and his innocence made them reluctant to bring him to trial. For the next 18 years he was kept in prison, first in the Clink (1586–88), then at Wisbech (1588–98), and finally in the Tower (1598–1603). From Wisbech he exercised much influence in the neighboring countryside. In the prison itself he became the reluctant spiritual guide of a group of fellow priests who bound themselves into a confraternity, thus causing resentment among the others; hence the Wisbech Stirs. For five years in the Tower he was in the most absolute solitary confinement.

On the accession of James I, Weston, broken in health, half blind, and prematurely old, was exiled. During his long imprisonment he had become a symbol of Catholic resistance: the popular saying ran: ''If I spoke with the tongue of Father Campion and wrote with the pen of Father Persons and led the austere life of Father Weston and yet had not charity, it would avail me nothing.'' When on May 13, 1603, he set out from the Tower wharf on his journey to the continent, the Catholics of London gathered to pay their tribute to a man they all regarded as a saint. After convalescing at Saint-Omer (1603–05) he returned to Seville. In June 1614 he was appointed rector of the English College, Valladolid, where he later died.

Bibliography: W. WESTON, *The Autobiography of an Elizabethan,* tr. P. CARAMAN (New York 1955). P. RENOLD, ed., *The Wisbech Stirs* (CathRecSoc 51; London 1958).

[P. CARAMAN]

WESTPHALIA, PEACE OF

The general settlement comprising the two treaties ending the THIRTY YEARS' WAR, signed Oct. 24, 1648. Throughout the many-sided conflict that had engaged nearly all the powers of Western Europe from Sweden to Spain, several efforts were made to establish peace. At Hamburg and Ratisbon in 1637–38, and again at Vienna and Hamburg in 1640–41, preliminary negotiations had been started. The Hamburg meetings of 1641 finally resulted in the summoning of a peace congress. It was not until after Rocroy (1643), that the Hapsburgs and their allies opened negotiations with the Swedes at Osnabrück and with the Dutch and French at Münster. Peace was not to be declared. however, until both meetings arrived at agreements. Exhausted by war, alarmed by the rising power of France and by the changes wrought in the balance of power, the remaining belligerents joined the major powers in the arranging of the negotiations. The choice of two different sites for the peace talks was dictated by the unusual dynastic, constitutional, religious, and national problems that had to be discussed. Hence, the negotiations were not only involved but often awkward and prolonged. States like Venice and Portugal that were not engaged in the fighting had to be consulted because the decisions of the negotiators impinged on their national interests. For the five years during which the peace conversations continued, hostilities were maintained, thereby prolonging the horror of war and influencing the bargaining of the negotiators. The imperial emissaries were Count Trauttmansdorf and Dr. Volmar, while France was represented by Count d'Avaux and Count Servien. Count John Oxenstierna, son of the Swedish chancellor, and Baron John Salvius guarded Swedish interests. Fabio Chigi, later Alexander VII, spoke for the papacy while numerous diplomats represented other powers.

The political, territorial, and religious provisions of the treaties arranged the following: (1) Sweden received western Pomerania and secured control of the mouths of the Weser, Elbe, and Oder Rivers. The archbishopric of Bremen (but not the city), the bishopric of Verden, the city of Wismar, and an indemnity of 5,000,000 Reichstalers were granted to the Swedes. (2) France retained the bishoprics and cities of Metz, Toul, and Verdun. Pignerol, Breisach, Upper and Lower Alsace including 10 imperial cities (but not Strasbourg) were acquired by France also. (3) The United Provinces and Switzerland, formerly dependencies of the Empire, acquired full sovereignty. (4) Brandenburg, beginning her significant expansion, gained eastern Pomerania and the bishoprics of Minden, Kammin, and Halberstadt as secular principalities, and was promised the archbishopric of Magdeburg after the death of its administrator. As a result of these and other minor changes, the Emperor Ferdinand III lost jurisdiction over 40,000 square miles of territory.

Politically, a general amnesty returned affairs to the conditions that had prevailed in 1618; the Bavarian retention of the electorate (granted in 1623) and the creation of a new electorate for the Palatinate were accomplished also. The religious settlement extended the provisions of the Peace of AUGSBURG to the Calvinists and guaranteed Protestant and Catholic states equality within the Empire. The imperial Edict of RESTITUTION (1629) was superseded and January 1, 1624, was selected as the date for determining proprietorship of ecclesiastical lands and religious practice. The imperial court (Reichskammergericht) was restored also with an equal number of Protestant and Catholic judges. Pope Innocent X denounced a number of the religious provisions and the papacy never formally lifted its condemnation. Although France and Spain continued their struggle until 1659, the Peace of Westphalia did restore peace to the Empire. Divided into 300 states and principalities the Empire survived until its dissolution by Napoleon in 1806. It remains an open question as to whether the Empire was politically effective in the wake of the Peace of Westphalia. Some have seen it as dangerously unstable, disunited and racked by petty rivalries. More recently, though, some scholars have stressed its efficiency as a confederation that ruled and kept the peace in a large, ethnically and religiously diverse portion of Central Europe.

Bibliography: C. V. WEDGWOOD, *The Thirty Years War* (New Haven 1939). C. J. FRIEDRICH, *The Age of the Baroque, 1610–1660* (New York 1952). F. A. SIX, ed., *Der Westfälische Friede von 1648* (3d ed. Berlin 1942) text. F. C. DAHLMANN and G. WAITZ, *Quellenkunde der deutschen Geschichte* (9th ed. Leipzig 1932) 667–707. G. BENECKE, *Society and Politics in Germany, 1500–1750* (London 1974). K. BUSSMANN and H. SCHILLING, eds., *1648, War and Peace in Europe* (Münster 1999). R. KONRAD, *Der westfälische Frieden* (Opladen 1999). *Book of Confessions* (Knoxville TN 2000).

[P. S. MCGARRY/P. SOERGEL]

WETTINGEN-MEHRERAU, ABBEY OF

Cistercian abbey *nullius* (*Maris stella*) in the Diocese of Basel, Aargau canton, Switzerland. It was founded in 1227 by Count Henry of Rapperswil with monks from Salem, a daughter-house (1134) of Gross Lützel, filiation of MORIMOND. Because it held many papal and imperial privileges as well as lands in Uri, Basel, and Zurich, it became a miniature state in the Limmat Valley. Although the abbey fell under the HAPSBURGS in the 14th century, it continued to govern its own lands and, as a consistorial abbey of confederated lands in the 15th century, lasted as a relic of bygone spiritual jurisdiction until 1798. *Pontificalia* were obtained in 1439 for Abbot Rudolph and his successors, and the abbots held visitation rights over ten convents. Threatened with collapse during the Reformation when most of the monks left in 1529, the abbey recovered under Catholic protection after the battle of Kappel (1531). It flourished anew under Abbot Peter II Schmid (1594–1633), one of the founders of the South German Congregation. The next abbot, Christopher II Bachmann, died after a saintly life. Nicholas, a descendant of St. NICHOLAS OF FLÜE, was known for theological and musical learning. Refugee monks from the French Revolution came under the excellent discipline and administration of Abbot Sebastian Steinegger, who in 1790 assumed the direction of Swiss and Alsatian abbeys; and the Swiss congregation developed under Wettingen in 1806. The abbey was suppressed in 1841; the monks moved to MEHRERAU in 1854, Wettingen becoming a teachers college. The basilica (three naves, flat roof, pillars) has a partly Gothic transept with famous stained glass, Renaissance choir stalls, baroque altars, and many tombs of abbots and nobles (especially Hapsburgs); King Albert I was buried in Wettingen (1308–09) until he was moved to Speyer.

Bibliography: L. H. COTTINEAU, *Répertoire topobibliographique des abbayes et prieurés,* 2 v. (Mâcon 1935–39) 2:1807–08, 3449–50. F. WERNLI, *Beitäge zur Geschichte des Klosters Wettingen* (Kaltbrunn 1948). A. BUGMANN, *Zürich und die Abtei Wettingen zur Zeit der Reformation und der Gegenreformation* (Zurich 1949). K. SPAHR, ''Der sogenannte Wettinger Stifterkelch,'' *Mehrerauer Grüsse* NS 9 (1958) 1–16. A. KOTTMANN, *Die Cistercienser-Abtei Wettingen 1768–1803* (Aargau 1959), with copious bibliog. *Wettingen gestern und heute,* ed. H. MENG (Wettingen 1959). A. DIETRICH, *Lexikon für Theologie und Kirche,* ed. M. BUCHBERGER, 10 v. (Freiburg 1930–38) 10:850–851. ''Wettingen,'' *Lexikon für Theologie und Kirche,* ed. J. HOFER and K. RAHNER, 10 v. (2d, new ed. Freiburg 1957–65) v.10.

[C. SPAHR]

WHARTON, CHRISTOPHER, BL.

Priest, martyr; b. ca. 1540 at Middleton, Yorkshire, England; hanged, drawn, and quartered Nov. 28, 1600 at York. The second son of Henry Wharton and Agnes Warcop, he received the master's degree from Trinity College, Oxford (1564), then became a fellow. In February 1583, he began seminary studies at Rheims. He continued his studies for two years after ordination (1584) before returning to England in the company of Bl. Edward BURDEN. After 13 years of labor in difficult circumstances, he was arrested with the widow Eleanor Hunt in her home and incarcerated in York Castle. They were tried at the Lenten assizes in 1600, condemned, and refused life in exchange for conformity to the state church. Hunt died in prison while Wharton heroically suffered the fate of those convicted of treason. Wharton was known for his humility and charity. He was beatified by Pope John Paul II on Nov. 22, 1987 with George Haydock and companions.

Feast of the English Martyrs: May 4 (England).

See Also: ENGLAND, SCOTLAND, AND WALES, MARTYRS OF.

Bibliography: R. CHALLONER, *Memoirs of Missionary Priests,* ed. J. H. POLLEN (rev. ed. London 1924). J. MORRIS, ed., *The Troubles of Our Catholic Forefathers Related by Themselves,* 3 v. (London 1872–77), III, 462. J. H. POLLEN, *Acts of English Martyrs* (London 1891).

[K. I. RABENSTEIN]

WHATELY, RICHARD

Anglican archbishop of Dublin; b. London, Feb. 1, 1787; d. Dublin. Oct. 1, 1863. He was the son of Joseph Whately, prebendary of Bristol. Educated at Oriel College, Oxford, and elected fellow of Oriel in 1811, he belonged to the brilliant Oxford circle, including Edward Hawkins and Edward Copleston, who criticized the traditional tenets of ANGLICANISM. His *Historic Doubts Relative to Napoleon Bonaparte* (1819) attacked exaggerated historical criticism, while his *Elements of Logic* (1826) enjoyed many editions. John Henry NEWMAN, his vice principal at St. Alban Hall, was influenced by Whately's anti-ERASTIANISM, but Whately opposed the OXFORD MOVEMENT and urged the condemnation of Newman's *Tract 90.* Appointed archbishop of Dublin in 1831, Whately collaborated with the Catholic archbishop to produce a religion course for the national schools that would satisfy both Catholics and Anglicans. He took an active interest in social reform.

See Also: IRELAND, CHURCH OF.

Bibliography: W. J. FITZPATRICK, *Memoirs of Richard Whately,* 2 v. (London 1864). E. J. WHATELY, *Life and Correspondence of Richard Whately,* 2 v. (London 1866). J. M. RIGG, *The Dictionary of National Biography from the Earliest Times to 1900* 20:1334–40.

[T. S. BOKENKOTTER]

WHEALON, JOHN FRANCIS

Second archbishop of Hartford; b. Barberton, Ohio, Jan. 15, 1921; d. Hartford, Connecticut, Aug. 2, 1991. Whealon was the son of Dr. John and Mary (Zanders) Whealon. After graduating from St. Charles preparatory seminary in Catonsville, Maryland, he completed his studies for the priesthood at St. Mary Seminary, Cleveland, Ohio, and was ordained there on May 26, 1945.

After ordination Whealon earned a licentiate degree in sacred theology from the University of Ottawa, Canada (1946) and a licentiate degree in sacred scripture from Pontifical Biblical Institute in Rome (1950). He taught scripture at St. Mary Seminary, Cleveland, until 1953, when he was appointed founding rector of a new minor seminary for the diocese of Cleveland. Pope John XXIII appointed Whealon as titular bishop of Andrapa and auxiliary to the bishop of Cleveland (July 1961). Whealon attended all the session of the second VATICAN COUNCIL between 1962 and 1965. On Nov. 30, 1966 he was named the sixth bishop of Erie, Pennsylvania, by Pope Paul VI and installed as bishop of Erie on March 7, 1967.

To the surprise of many and the consternation of some, on Dec. 28, 1968 Whealon was named the second archbishop of Hartford by Pope Paul VI.

A tireless worker, Whealon wrote weekly columns for the diocesan newspaper and daily radio programs for station WJMJ (which he founded). He was known to be a traditionalist on points of Church doctrine but was innovative and willing to experiment in pastoral practice. In addition to strong support for the development of the permanent diaconate and lay ministry within the archdiocese, Archbishop Whealon also introduced team ministry, developed collaborative ministry among priests and other members of the Christian faithful in parish administration, and promoted the role of women in the Church, appointing the first woman chancellor in the archdiocese.

Whealon's interests and scholarship were also recognized on the national level. Always an active participant in the activities of the National Conference of Catholic Bishops, he was chairman of several important committees and projects during the years he was in Hartford, including the committees on doctrine and on ecumenism, the development of the National Catechetical Directory, the New American Bible Revision, and Biblical Fundamentalism Projects. He was co-chairman of the Anglican-Roman Catholic dialogue.

Whealon's ecumenical interests were also applied in Connecticut. He was a founding member and sometime president of the Christian Conference of Connecticut. At the time of his death he was serving as both secretary and was co-chair of the faith and order commission of that organization.

In an editorial on the occasion of his death, *The Catholic Transcript* expressed what many had come to know during his 22 years as archbishop: "What he tried to convey in words, he achieved in action through a simple life style."

Bibliography: *Catholic Transcript,* March 19, 1969; *Catholic Transcript,* August 16, 1991.

[E.G. PFNAUSCH]

WHELAN, CHARLES MAURICE

Pioneer American missionary; b. Ballycommon, Ireland, 1741; d. Bohemia Manor, Md., March 21, 1806. In 1770 Whelan entered the Irish Capuchin novitiate, then located at Bar-sur-Aube, France, because of the Irish penal laws. He received the name Maurice and was professed there in 1771. After ordination he served as vicar of the Barsur-Aube friary, provincial secretary, and novice-master. When Louis XVI asked for volunteer chaplains to accompany the French fleet to America during the American Revolution, Whelan was accepted and assigned to the "Jason." The fleet arrived at Newport, R.I., in 1780 and a year later joined the fleet of Admiral François de Grasse in Chesapeake Bay. When De Grasse was defeated in the West Indies, Whelan was imprisoned for 13 months in Jamaica, where he ministered to some 7,000 French prisoners.

In 1784 he entered upon missionary work in New York City under Prefect Apostolic (later Bishop) John Carroll, and early in 1785 he began building St. Peter's Church on Barclay Street. Another Irish Capuchin, Andrew Nugent, arrived that year and stirred up such discord among the trustees that shortly before the dedication of the church in November 1786 Whelan withdrew to Johnston, N.Y., one of the first victims of lay TRUSTEEISM in the U.S. In 1787 Carroll sent him to Kentucky, where, in Carroll's words, he "not only . . . kept alive the spirit of religion amongst the Catholics but in addition he has gained a great increase for the Church of Jesus Christ." He returned to Johnston in 1790 and in 1799 was named rector at White Clay Creek, Pa., from which he visited numerous missions in Pennsylvania, Delaware, and Maryland, until retiring to the Jesuits' Bohemia Manor in 1805.

Bibliography: M. R. MATTINGLY, *The Catholic Church on the Kentucky Frontier, 1785–1812* (Catholic University of America Studies in American Church History 25; Washington 1936) 38–41, 55. L. R. RYAN, *Old St. Peter's, the Mother Church of Catholic New York, 1785–1935* (United States Catholic Historical Society 15;

New York 1935). N. H. MILLER, ''Pioneer Capuchin Missionaries in the United States, 1784–1816,'' *Historical Records and Studies of the U. S. Catholic Historical Society of New York* 21 (1932) 176–201.

[N. MILLER]

WHITAKER, THOMAS, BL.

Priest, martyr; *alias* Starkie; b. *c.* 1611–14 at Burnley, Lancashire; d. Aug. 7, 1646, at Lancaster under Charles I. He received his first education at the school where his father, Thomas Whitaker, was master. Through the influence of the Towneley family, he received his seminary education at the English College at Valladolid, Spain. Following his ordination (1638), he returned to England, where he ministered in Lancashire for five years. He was arrested once during this period, but escaped while being transferred to Lancaster Castle. On Aug. 7, 1643, he was seized at Place Hall, Goosenargh, and confined to Lancaster Castle. During his three-year imprisonment he became known for his spirit of continual prayer and his charity to fellow inmates. Before his trial he made a month's retreat in preparation for death. He was beatified by Pope John Paul II on Nov. 22, 1987 with George Haydock and companions.

Feast of the English Martyrs: May 4 (England).

See Also: ENGLAND, SCOTLAND, AND WALES, MARTYRS OF.

Bibliography: R. CHALLONER, *Memoirs of Missionary Priests,* ed. J. H. POLLEN (rev. ed. London 1924). J. H. POLLEN, *Acts of English Martyrs* (London 1891).

[K. I. RABENSTEIN]

WHITBREAD, THOMAS, BL.

Jesuit provincial and martyr; *alias* Harcourt and Harcott; b. Essex, 1618; d. hanged, drawn, and quartered at Tyburn (London), June 20, 1679. In order to maintain his Catholic identity, Whitbread's parents educated him at home until he attended the Jesuit college at St-Omer, Flanders (*c.* 1630–35). Upon completion of his studies there, he joined the English Jesuits at their novitiate in Watten, (now in Belgium). He was ordained abroad (1645), contrary to the law of England, but returned to his homeland two years later to begin a three-decade apostolate in the eastern counties of the English mission. During this time he was Jesuit superior in Suffolk, then Lincolnshire, and finally English provincial (1678).

In the course of his visitation of Continental seminaries, Whitbread met the infamous Titus Oates, a former Anglican minister who had allegedly converted to Catholicism and was studying for the priesthood. As provincial, Whitbread refused to admit Oates to the Order because of his irregular history and odd behavior. Rebuffed and seeking revenge, Oates joined forces with the paranoid Israel Tonge to convince King Charles II that Jesuits were planning his assassination.

Fr. Whitbread was placed under house arrest in London on Michaelmas Day, Sept. 29, 1678. He was so ill from the plague contracted in Antwerp that the Spanish ambassador intervened to prevent his transfer to Newgate Prison for three months. Whitbread was first indicted at the Old Bailey, Dec. 17, 1678, but the evidence against him and his companions was contradictory. Unwilling to allow the release of the Jesuit provincial, the trial was suspended and Whitbread returned to prison.

On June 13, 1679, Stephen Dugdale, a convicted embezzler, Oates, and William Bedloe provided false testimony leading to Whitbread's conviction despite evidence proving perjury. Whitbread was condemned to execution together with BB. John FENWICK, John GAVAN, William HARCOURT, and Anthony TURNER.

Just before his execution, Whitbread pronounced his innocence of the charges and forgave those who falsely accused him. A pardon was granted by the king as they stood on the gallows on the condition that they admit the conspiracy. Refusing to lie, they thanked the king and again protested their innocence. All five were permitted to hang until dead before the completion of the sentence of disembowelment and quartering. Their remains were buried in the churchyard of St. Giles's in the Fields. All five Jesuits were beatified by Pius XI on Dec. 15, 1929.

Feast of the English Martyrs: May 4 (England); Dec. 1 (Jesuits).

See Also: ENGLAND, SCOTLAND, AND WALES, MARTYRS OF.

Bibliography: T. WHITBREAD, *The Remonstrance of Piety and Innocence* (London 1683). *The Tryals and Condemnation of Thomas White, alias Whitebread . . . for High Treason in Conspiring the Death of the King . . .* (London 1679). R. CHALLONER, *Memoirs of Missionary Priests,* ed. J. H. POLLEN (rev. ed. London 1924; repr. Farnborough 1969). H. FOLEY, *Records of the English Province of the Society of Jesus* (London 1879–83) V, VII. J. H. POLLEN, *Acts of English Martyrs* (London 1891). J. N. TYLENDA, *Jesuit Saints & Martyrs* (Chicago 1998) 175–78.

[K. I. RABENSTEIN]

WHITBY, ABBEY OF

On the Northumbrian coast of England (now Whitby, Yorkshire) HILDA, Abbess of Hartlepool and member

The sandstone ruins of Whitby Abbey, founded in 657 by Saint Hilda and once the meeting place of the Synod of Whitby. The Abbey was rebuilt in 1078 after being sacked by the Danes. The existing abbey buildings date from the 13th century. (©Patrick Ward/ CORBIS)

of the royal house, founded the double MONASTERY of Streoneshalh (later called Whitby by the Danes) in 657. Here King Oswy summoned the synod of 664 (less probably 663) to unite the Celtic (*see* CELTIC RITE) and Roman churches of his realm. Not only did Oswy and his queen celebrate Easter on different days, but the two Northumbrian royal houses were identified with different churches, Bernicia with the Celtic and Deira with the Roman. At this decisive council the Iro-Celtic church was represented by Oswy, Bp. COLMAN of Lindisfarne, Hilda, and Bp. CEDD of the East Saxons, and Rome by Oswy's son, Alchfrith, Bp. Agilbert of Wessex, Abbot Wilfrid of Ripon, and James the Deacon. Of the differences separating the two churches, apparently only one, the subject of the EASTER CONTROVERSY, was discussed. Colman claimed the authority of St. John the Apostle, Anatolius of Laodicea, and COLUMBA OF IONA. Wilfrid, Rome's spokesman since the Frankish-born Agilbert spoke English poorly, denied that Anatolius supported the Celtic position, spoke disparagingly of Columba, and asserted the authority of Peter. Colman admitted Peter's preeminence, and King Oswy, "smiling," refused to disobey the gatekeeper of Heaven and decided for Roman usage. His decision opened the way for the ecclesiastical unity of England, since the south had already accepted Roman obedience. Colman resigned his see and went to Iona, although Celtic usage did not end immediately in Britain.

Whitby became the greatest house in northeast England, a noted center of learning, and a royal burial place; there lived CAEDMON (d. 680), "the father of English poetry." Hilda died in 680 and was succeeded by Aelfflaed, Oswy's daughter. Whitby perished in the Danish onslaught (*c.* 867) and was a desolate site when refounded as a PRIORY after the Norman Conquest, with Reinfrid as first prior; *c.* 1078 it established a daughterhouse, St.

Mary's, York. Whitby became an abbey under Henry I. Its later history was relatively calm, disturbed only by occasional pirate raids and a struggle between its abbots and the town. Henry VIII suppressed Whitby (Dec. 14, 1543), its abbot having resigned to avoid surrendering it.

Excavations have partly uncovered the Anglo-Saxon foundation, showing Celtic-type cells and houses in an enclosure. The present monastic ruins, following the collapse of much of the nave (1763) and the tower (1830), include portions of the Early English choir, the north transept, and the decorated nave.

Bibliography: Sources. BEDE, *Ecclesiastical History* 3.25. EDDIUS, *The Life of Bishop Wilfrid,* ed. and tr. B. COLGRAVE (Cambridge, Eng. 1927). SIMEON OF DURHAM, *Historia regum,* v. 2 of *Symeonis monachi opera omnia,* ed. T. ARNOLD, 2 v. in *Rerum Britannicarum medii aevi scriptores,* 244 v. (New York 1964–) 75; 1882–85). *Cartularium Abbathiae de Whiteby,* ed. J. C. ATKINSON, 2 v. (Surtees Society 69, 72; Newcastle 1879). Literature. G. YOUNG, *A History of Whitby and Streoneshalh Abbey,* 2 v. (Whitby 1817). C. PEERS and C. A. RALEGH RADFORD, "The Saxon Monastery of Whitby," *Archaeologia* 89 (1943) 27–88. M. DEANESLY, *The Pre–Conquest Church in England* (New York 1961). D. KNOWLES, *The Monastic Order in England, 943–1216* (Cambridge, Eng. 1962). D. KNOWLES and R. N. HADCOCK, *Medieval Religious Houses: England and Wales* (New York 1953).

[W. A. CHANEY]

WHITE, ANDREW

Missionary, "Apostle of Maryland"; b. London, England, 1579; d. near London, Dec. 27, 1656. White attended English refugee colleges on the Continent and was ordained at Douai, France (*c.* 1605). He then worked on the English mission until his banishment (1606), with 44 other priests, following the Gunpowder Plot turmoil. In 1607 he entered the novitiate of the Society of Jesus at Louvain, Belgium. He taught theology at Lisbon, Portugal, and Louvain and Liège, Belgium, but his inflexible Thomistic views and ultraconservatism led to difficulties. As a consequence he was several times relieved of his professorship and finally sent to the English mission, where he served in Suffolk, Middlesex, Devonshire, and Hampshire.

He was at St. Thomas, Hants., when he was selected for the North American mission. With Father John Gravener (alias Altham) and Brother Thomas Gervase, White joined Lord Baltimore's expedition to Maryland, landing on St. Clement's Island, March 25, 1634. For ten years he served the settlers and the Piscataway, Patuxent, Potomac, and Anacostan tribes of the surrounding area. When the Civil War in England disrupted the American missions, Maryland was attacked by Puritan insurrectionists from Virginia; White and Thomas Fisher (alias Cop-

ley), SJ, were captured (1664) and sent in chains to England to be tried for treason. Although they were acquitted on the plea that they had returned to England under force, they were ordered to depart from the realm. White went to Belgium, but soon returned to his own country and, failing in his attempts to return to Maryland, spent his remaining years as a missionary in southern England.

White's pamphlet, "Declaratio Coloniae Domini Baronis de Baltimore," was written to attract settlers for the New World enterprise, and his "Relatio Itineris in Marilandiam" was an account of the first expedition to Maryland. He also compiled a grammar, a dictionary, and a catechism.

Bibliography: E. I. DEVITT, "History of the Maryland-New York Province," *Woodstock Letters* 60 (1931) 199–226. T. HUGHES, *The History of the Society of Jesus in North America: Colonial and Federal* (Texts and Documents) 4 v. (New York 1907–17). A. WHITE, "Declaratio Coloniae Domini Baronis de Baltimore," *Woodstock Letters* 1 (1872) 12–21; "Relatio Itineris In Marilandiam," *ibid.* 1 (1872) 22–24, 71–80, 145–155; 2 (1873) 1–13. "An Historical Sketch of Father Andrew White, S.J., the Apostle of Maryland," *ibid.* 1 (1872) 1–11.

[F. G. MCMANAMIN]

WHITE, CHARLES IGNATIUS

Editor, author; b. Baltimore, Maryland, Feb. 1, 1807; d. Washington, D.C., April 1, 1878. White was the son of John and Nancy (Coombs) White. After graduation from Mt. St. Mary's College, Emmitsburg, Maryland, he studied theology at Saint-Sulpice, Paris. He was ordained in Paris at Notre Dame on June 5, 1830. Shortly after ordination, he was assigned (1833–43) to the Baltimore Cathedral, where he had access to important sources of ecclesiastical history. From 1843 to 1845 he served as professor of moral theology at St. Mary's Seminary, Baltimore. He attended several Provincial and Plenary Councils of Baltimore as secretary or theologian. From 1857 until his death, he was pastor of St. Matthew's Church (later Cathedral), Washington, D.C. There he built a church, a school, and a home for aged African-Americans. He also founded and established the St. Vincent de Paul Society in the District.

As an editor, White was responsible for the annual Catholic directory (1834–57) and for Baltimore's archdiocesan weekly, the *Catholic Mirror* (1850–55). He was cofounder (1842) of the *Religious Cabinet,* a monthly periodical, that was renamed the *United States Catholic Magazine* (1843–48) and revived in 1853 as the *Metropolitan Magazine.* Besides translating Chateaubriand's *The Genius of Christianity* (1856) and Charles Sainte-

Foi's *Mission and Duties of Young Women* (1858), White wrote two significant studies. His *Life of Mrs. Eliza A. Seton, Foundress and First Superior of the Sisters of Charity in the United States* (1853) was the first full-length biography of Mother Seton. Its scholarship was lacking in White's essay, "Sketch of the Origin and Progress of the Catholic Church in the United States of America," which appeared in an English translation of Joseph E. Darras's *General History of the Catholic Church* (1866). This popular historical sketch propagated many enduring legends about Abp. John CARROLL and played a large part in forming Protestant opinion of American Catholicism prior to the work of John Gilmary SHEA.

Bibliography: J. P. CADDEN, *The Historiography of the American Catholic Church: 1785–1943* (Washington 1944). A. T. ENGLISH, "The Historiography of American Catholic History (1785–1884)," *American Catholic Historical Review* 11 (1926) 561–598.

[R. J. CUNNINGHAM]

WHITE, EUSTACE, ST.

Priest, martyr; b. Louth, Lincolnshire, England, 1560 or 1561; d. Tyburn (London), Dec. 10, 1591. He came of a prominent Protestant family, became a Catholic about 1584, and went abroad. In October 1586 he entered the English College in Rome, took the College Oath in February 1588, was ordained deacon Apr. 16, 1589, and was a priest when he returned to England by way of Rheims in October. En route to the West country where his ministry was, he was captured near Blandford in Dorset, informed on by someone he had mistaken for a Catholic. After a successful theological disputation with a local divine, he was taken to London and imprisoned in Bridewell under harsh conditions. The Privy Council, apprehensive of a fresh attack by Spain, ordered his examination under torture, hoping for information about his associates and movements. Of his trial nothing is recorded, except that he was condemned for his priesthood and sentenced to be hanged, drawn, and quartered. He was executed with Edmund GENNINGS, Swithun WELLS, Polydore PLASDEN, Brian Lacey, John Mason, and Sidney Hodgson. White was beatified by Pius XI on Dec. 15, 1929, and canonized by Paul VI on Oct. 25, 1970 as one of the Forty Martyrs of England and Wales.

Feast: Dec. 10; October 25 (Feast of the 40 Martyrs of England and Wales); May 4 (Feast of the English Martyrs in England).

See Also: ENGLAND, SCOTLAND, AND WALES, MARTYRS OF.

Bibliography: R. CHALLONER, *Memoirs of Missionary Priests,* ed. J. H. POLLEN (rev. ed. London 1924; repr. Farnborough 1969), 169–85. J. H. POLLEN, *Acts of English Martyrs* (London 1891). A. BUTLER, *The Lives of the Saints,* ed. H. THURSTON and D. ATTWATER 4:533.

[A. M. C. FORSTER]

WHITE, STEPHEN

Distinguished 17th–century Jesuit scholar; b. Clonmel, Ireland, 1575; d. Galway, *c.* 1647. He graduated from Trinity College, Dublin, and the Jesuit College in Salamanca, Spain. White perhaps did more for Irish historical research and learning in the first half of the 17th century than any other Irish Catholic scholar studying on the Continent. He was a renowned teacher in Germany for many years, a prolific student and writer on Irish manuscripts, a universally acknowledged chronologist, and at one time the rector of the College at Cassel. Not only Germany, but Austria, Switzerland, and more than a dozen other European countries felt the influence of his scholarship in schools and colleges. Although often at odds, in matters theological, with the Calvinistic James Ussher, archbishop of Armagh, White corresponded frequently with him; and the two men worked together in Irish hagiography while the respect one had for the other's learning was outstanding. He contributed much to the collectanea of other Irish scholars of his generation, especially in manuscripts on Patrick, Brigid, Columba, and other Irish saints. Following a long academic career on the Continent, Father White returned to Ireland in the 1630s and collaborated with Ussher and other scholars, Irish and British, Protestant and Catholic. In Ireland he taught at a number of Jesuit colleges, especially in Dublin and Waterford. Of Father White the learned Dr. Reeves says: "It was he who opened that rich mine of Irish literature on the Continent, which has ever since yielded such valuable returns." White copied many manuscrips in German monasteries, including lives of St. Colman, St. Erhard, and St. Patrick.

Bibliography: R. BAGWELL, *The Dictionary of National Biography from the Earliest Times to 1900* 21:75–76. J. S. CRONE, *Concise Dictionary of Irish Biography* (Dublin 1937). W. REEVES, *Ecclesiastical Antiquities of Down, Connor and Dromore* (Dublin 1847). J. USSHER, *A Discourse of the Religion Anciently Professed by the Irish and British* (4th ed. enl. London 1687).

[E. J. MURRAY]

WHITE, THOMAS

Alias Blacklo or Blacklow, Vitus, Albius, and Anglus; theologian, controversialist, and party leader; b. Essex, 1593; d. London, July 6, 1676. White was a grandson of Edmund PLOWDEN, the prominent Elizabethan jurist and recusant. He was initiated early into a promising clerical career. From the various English colleges in Spain and the Netherlands, he became acquainted with the leading recusant exiles and their conflicting plans for restoring the Church in England. After his ordination and assignment to teach philosophy at Douai in 1617, he became actively engaged in pursuing a policy more or less identified with the Chapter, an advisory body of secular priests instituted by the first vicar apostolic in 1623 and constituting the *de facto* government of the Church after the retirement to France in 1631 of the second vicar apostolic, Richard Smith. In 1633 Blacklo returned to England after successive sojourns in Paris, Rome, and Lisbon; and through the next decade ''Blackloism'' began to emerge. This radically antiprobabilist and antipapal teaching was a kind of English Jansenism. For the next 30 years, sometimes in England but more often on the Continent, Blacklo personified the scientism, the antiquarianism, and the factionalism that characterized the followers of St. Cyran. The Chapter itself was never wholly Blackloist, especially after the Restoration had discredited his Cromwellian intrigues. Blacklo, undaunted by this reaction and by Rome's repeated condemnations of his writings, continued his controversies through some 40 works and constantly maintained both his certitudes and his Catholicism. His last years were said to have been spent, significantly enough, arguing with Thomas Hobbes.

Bibliography: J. GILLOW, *A Literary and Biographical History or Bibliographical Dictionary of the English Catholics from 1534 to the Present Time* 5:578–81. T. COOPER, *The Dictionary of National Biography from the Earliest Times to 1900* 21:79–81.

[R. I. BRADLEY]

WHITEFIELD, GEORGE

Anglican clergyman, leader of the GREAT AWAKENING; b. Gloucester, England, Dec. 16, 1714; d. Newburyport, Massachusetts, Sept. 30, 1770. Whitefield's parents were innkeepers and, after grammar school studies, he worked in the inn. At the age of 18 he obtained a position as a servitor at Pembroke College, Oxford, working as a domestic to pay his lecture fees. Here he became acquainted with John and Charles Wesley and in 1735 experienced a religious conversion. He obtained his B.A. degree and became a deacon in 1736. After doing missionary work in Georgia, he returned to England and was ordained in 1739.

While on a preaching tour of England, Scotland, and Wales, Whitefield became aware that working people were not attending church services. He began field preaching in a coal-mining town in 1739, and open-air

George Whitefield. (Archive Photos, Inc.)

preaching was his rule thereafter. Returning to America that year, he met William and Gilbert Tennent and Theodore Frelinghuysen, who were beginning a religious revival in the colonies. Whitefield's preaching tours (1739–41) began the Great Awakening in America. After another extended American visit (1744–48), he made four more colonial preaching tours (1751–52, 1754–55, 1763–65, 1769–70). Whitefield had the cooperation of many Congregationalist, Presbyterian, and Reformed clergymen, but was usually turned away by his Anglican colleagues. He supported many charitable causes, establishing (1740) his Savannah orphanage and a school for African-Americans in Georgia and helping to found (1769) Dartmouth College, Hanover, New Hampshire, for the education of Native Americans.

In England Whitefield was closely associated with Howell Harris, and in 1743 he was chosen to be moderator for life of the Calvinistic Welsh Methodists. He remained on friendly terms with the Wesleys and attended Methodist Conferences as late as 1767. His Calvinistic theology differed from Wesley's Arminian views on unconditional election, irresistible grace, final perseverance, and nonreprobation. In 1765 he became chaplain to Selina, Countess of Huntingdon, whose followers shared his theological views.

Alfred North Whitehead. (AP/Wide World Photos)

Bibliography: T. ROBERT, *A Narrative of the Life of George Whitefield* (London 1771). L. TYERMAN, *The Life of the Rev. George Whitefield,* 2 v. (New York 1877). S. C. HENRY, *George Whitefield: Wayfaring Witness* (Nashville 1957).

[R. K. MACMASTER]

WHITEHEAD, ALFRED NORTH

Mathematician and philosopher; b. Ramsgate, the Isle of Thanet, Kent, Feb. 15, 1861; d. Cambridge, Mass., Dec. 30, 1947.

Life. In three successive periods of his life, he made major contributions to symbolic logic, the philosophy of science, and metaphysics. In the first period, at Trinity College, Cambridge, as student and lecturer in mathematics, he acquired extensive knowledge of literature and philosophy. This led him to explore the foundations of mathematics and to pioneer in the development of symbolic logic. As a result he and B. RUSSELL wrote the *Principia Mathematica* (3 v., Cambridge, Eng. 1910–13). Study of the principles of mathematics drew his attention, in turn, to problems in the philosophy of science. In 1910 he went to London, where he held various posts at University College and a professorship at the Imperial College of Science and Technology. In this, his middle

period, he sought to formulate a philosophy of science that would replace scientific materialism, which he thought inadequate to the needs of science. He still avoided metaphysics, calling it dynamite that would blow up the entire arena. However, his attempt to give the widest possible generalization to the notions of science made him aware of the limitations of Hume's theory of knowledge.

In 1924, at the age of 63, he began his third period. As professor of philosophy at Harvard University, he had the opportunity to develop a metaphysics. Under the influence of Berkeley's "mind," Wordsworth's nature *in solido,* and progress within science, he had come to realize that scientific materialism involved "the fallacy of misplaced concreteness"; it had taken the abstractions of Newtonian physics to be concrete actuality. Whitehead felt that a metaphysics was needed to provide a critique of the cosmology of scientific materialism and to furnish an adequate and coherent grasp of the world of lived experience. With the use of abstractions he had no quarrel; he insisted only that they should not be mistaken for the real. Again, he agreed with Bergson's view that man in conceiving reality tends to spatialize. He denied, however, that such a tendency necessarily proceeds from the nature of the intellect, and held that it could be overcome in a metaphysics that took time seriously. Such a metaphysics was his philosophy of organism, formulated in *Process and Reality: An Essay in Cosmology* (Cambridge, Mass. 1929).

Philosophy of Organism. Whitehead's philosophy belongs to the philosophical tradition stemming from PLATO and ARISTOTLE. In it he sought to provide a metaphysics of experience by stressing the interconnectedness and continuity of things. To accentuate his determination not to take abstractions for reality, he substituted the term "actual entity" for the traditional "being." Entity means potentiality for process; the word actual adds the meaning of "decision," in the root sense of "cutting off." In his metaphysical scheme, to encompass the universe, he included the actual entities of the temporal world and their formative elements: eternal objects, God, and creativity.

Knowledge. Whitehead's revision of the Cartesian heritage led to his own Copernican revolution in epistemology. In experience he made the primitive stage of discrimination not, "I see a red blur," but "This-My-Self, That Other, The Whole." Experience included the totality of the actual fact, which comprised its own internality and the externality of the many facts. Accordingly, the starting point for metaphysics was a vague sense of the self-creative moment of one's self as a decision for the future. In this experience, the many are one, and the one includes the many. Whitehead's theory of knowledge rested, not on Hume's clear-cut atoms of sense-data, but on man's vague experience of interaction with a world that is composed of intertwined individual entities.

From this experience Whitehead learned that inherent in actuality is value; that every aspect of experience must therefore be judged in terms of its place in, and contribution to, what is credible, reliable, and humanly important.

Process. Whitehead judged that Plato had formulated the general notions necessary for metaphysics: ideas, physical elements, psyche, eros, harmony, mathematical relations, and the receptacle. In adapting these Platonic notions, Whitehead transformed the receptacle into "creativity." Creativity is the ultimate principle by which the many (the universe disjunctively) become the one actual entity (the universe conjunctively). Creativity is Whitehead's matrix for all becoming, whose essence is process in which connectedness is retained. The actual world, which is relative to each actual entity, so conditions creativity that each actual entity is a unique synthesis of the world. By limiting creativity, the past provides an element of continuity for each actual occasion. Both creativity and past actual occasions are real, but are nonbeing. Together they constitute the real potentiality for the process of self-creation. The many self-creating entities proceeding from the past into the future make up the one world process.

Eternal Objects. Closely tied to Whitehead's theory of knowledge was his conception of metaphysics as the search for the forms within the facts. These forms are "eternal objects," similar to Plato's ideas. They explain how actual entities can be related to one another. Together with creativity they constitute the abstract possibility of the interrelationship of actual entities. The forms do not exist apart from actual entities because, according to Whitehead's "ontological principle," there is nothing, either in fact or efficacy, outside of them. The search for intelligibility is limited.

Within the temporal process, however, there is order and harmony, and so, eternal objects have for each actual occasion a relevance that is prior to time. To account, therefore, for the order experienced in the world, there must be a nontemporal actual entity.

God. The timeless source of order answers man's finest religious intuitions, and in this sense may be called "God." On one point Whitehead compared this source to Aristotle's First Mover, for, in one respect, God's immanence in the world is an urge toward the future based upon an appetite in the present. However, since Aristotle tended to fashion God in the image of a metaphysical principle, Whitehead found the Stagirite's notion of God to be inadequate. He was even more strongly opposed to joining Aristotle's image of God with the image of God as an imperial ruler, or as a personification of moral energy.

Whitehead's God, then, was not the exception to all metaphysical principles but rather their chief exemplification. Like all actual entities, God has two rationally distinct aspects, or poles: one, conceptual; the other, physical. The conceptual aspect accounts for order in the temporal process; the physical aspect is God's experience of the world, integrated into an aesthetic unity by His own decision. Accordingly, God is in process, acquiring new perfections in time. Whitehead believed that his notion of God, since it stressed the tender elements of God at work in the world in quietness and in love, was in accord with Christianity.

Critique. Whitehead resisted too ready a submission to Greek thought and consciously assimilated Christian perspectives. This was especially true in his conception of God. He thought that man must begin his approach to God with man's creating himself by appropriating the past and realizing his own unique value in his free decisions for the future. Whitehead was led to this position because he rejected the reduction of experience to abstract concepts. This, in turn, is why he opposed the notion of God as a remote and abstract Unmoved Mover. Instead, Whitehead held that God must be within the actuality of this world; and since all actual entities—even God—are on the same level, God must be finite. God, for him, is no exception to metaphysical principles, but must be in an absolutely univocal way their chief exemplification. For Whitehead, therefore, man's experience becomes in effect the measure of reality. As opposed to this, however, theistic realism maintains that man's experience of cause enables him to reason to what transcends the bounds of his own finite nature and to know God as the Infinite. Also, in Whitehead's doctrine of process, man's experience of self as an enduring subject of change is almost obliterated.

Positively, philosophy is richer for Whitehead's awareness of the interrelatedness of things. His realization of God at work in the world in time can add dimensions to natural theology. And, in a world fascinated by positivism, he has helped restore interest in questions that are properly metaphysical.

See Also: PANENTHEISM; PROCESS PHILOSOPHY.

Bibliography: V. LOWE, *Understanding Whitehead* (Baltimore 1962). I. LECLERC, *Whitehead's Metaphysics* (New York 1958). D. M. EMMET, *Whitehead's Philosophy of Organism* (London 1932). P. A. SCHILPP, ed., *The Philosophy of Alfred North Whitehead* (2d ed. New York 1951). W. E. STOKES, "A Select and Annotated Bibliography of Alfred North Whitehead," *the Modern Schoolman*

39 (1962) 135–151; ''Recent Interpretations of Whitehead's Creativity,'' *ibid.* 303–333. R. M. PALTER, *Whitehead's Philosophy of Science* (Chicago 1960). W. A. CHRISTIAN, *An Interpretation of Whitehead's Metaphysics* (New Haven 1959). J. D. COLLINS, *God in Modern Philosophy* (Chicago 1959).

[W. E. STOKES]

WHITFIELD, JAMES

Fourth archbishop of Baltimore and originator of its provincial councils; b. Liverpool, England, Nov. 3, 1770; d. Baltimore, Md., Oct. 19, 1834. Born into the merchant class, James took over the family business when his father died in 1787; he then moved his mother to Leghorn, Italy, for her health's sake. They were returning to England in 1803 when at Lyons, France, they found further travel impossible because of the Napoleonic wars. Here he met Ambrose (later archbishop) Maréchal, SS, rector of St. Irenaeus Seminary, and the two became lifelong friends. Whitfield entered St. Irenaeus and was ordained July 24, 1809. After his mother's death two years later, he became a Jesuit novice at Stonyhurst, England, but soon left and was given charge of a small community of Catholics at Little Crosby near Liverpool. Maréchal had become coadjutor to Archbishop Neale of Baltimore, and was administering the see after Neale's death in June 1817. Whitfield joined him that year on Sept. 8, and was assigned to St. Peter's procathedral staff. After Maréchal's consecration as archbishop, he was appointed first rector of the Cathedral (now Basilica) of the Assumption at its dedication on May 31, 1821. The doctorate in sacred theology was conferred by St. Mary's Seminary, Baltimore, on him and two other priests—the first such degrees given to Catholic priests in America—on Jan. 25, 1824.

Whitfield was named coadjutor to Maréchal and titular bishop of Apollonia on Jan. 8, 1828; Maéchal, whose almost inseparable companion he was, died three weeks later, and on May 25, Whitfield was consecrated archbishop of Baltimore by Bishop Flaget of Bardstown, Ky. After a careful visitation of his see and that of Richmond, he convened the first of the historic provincial councils of Baltimore on Oct. 4, 1829. The same day he received the pallium from Bp. Benedict Fenwick of Boston. He convened a second council in 1833, which like the first was to deal with the problems confronting the growing American church (*see* BALTIMORE, COUNCILS OF). Besides being, as Maréchal described him, ''distinguished for tender piety, zeal, moving eloquence, exacting discipline,'' he devoted his considerable fortune to the building of his see. A south tower was added to the cathedral, and the archbishop's house and St. James Church were also erected at this time. On July 31, 1831, he laid the cor-

nerstone of St. Charles College, Ellicott City, Md., on a tract donated by Charles Carroll. He had petitioned for a coadjutor in 1834 and on Sept. 14 he consecrated his successor, Samuel ECCLESTON, then president of St. Mary's College, Baltimore. His brief but eventful episcopate ended a month later.

Bibliography: B. D. CESTELLO, *James Whitfield, Fourth Archbishop of Baltimore: The Early Years, 1770–1828* (Washington 1957).

[C. J. NOONAN]

WHITFORD, RICHARD

English author of devotional books; place and date of birth unknown; d. before the end of Queen Mary's reign (1559). He was of an ancient Flintshire family, was admitted to Queen's College, Cambridge, in 1498, held various offices (dean of the chapel, bursar) there, and was appointed chaplain to Bp. Richard Foxe of Winchester *c.* 1504. About 1507 he entered the Bridgittine monastery of Syon at Isleworth, Middlesex (*see* BRIGITTINE SISTERS), remaining there until its dissolution in 1539, when he retired on a pension to the household of the Mountjoys. He had accompanied William Blount, Lord Mountjoy, on a five–year study period in Europe, where he made the acquaintance of Erasmus. He was a friend of Thomas MORE, whom he is reputed to have encouraged in resisting Henry VIII's demands. Whitford bravely withstood the suppressive activities of T. Bedyll when that royal agent visited the monastery in 1535.

No less than 19 works have been attributed to Whitford. These, which he often refers to as being written by ''the Wretch of Syon,'' run from *The fruyte of redempscion* (1514) to *Of Detraction* (1541), and include the famous *Jesus Psalter* (*see* PRAYER BOOKS; PSALTER). His most famous work, however, is his translation (*c.* 1531) of the IMITATION OF CHRIST, under the title *The folowyng of Cryste*. This is the earliest English version and in many ways the most stylistically beautiful of all versions. Its edition by E. J. Klein (New York 1943) marked a new epoch in studies of the great book and its authorship.

Bibliography: A. B. EMDEN, *Biographical Register of the Scholars of the University of Cambridge before 1500* 635. J. GILLOW, *A Literary and Biographical History or Bibliographical Dictionary of the English Catholics from 1534 to the Present Time* 5:581–582. THOMAS À KEMPIS, *The Imitation of Christ*, ed. H. C. GARDINER (New York 1955), modernized version of Whitford's tr. with introd. treating Kempis and Whitford.

[H. C. GARDINER]

WHITGIFT, JOHN

Anglican divine; b. Lincolnshire, 1532; d. London, 1604. While still young, Whitgift embraced the principles of the Reformation and was strengthened in these convictions as a student at Cambridge during the Edwardian regime. Unlike many Anglicans, he did not flee to the Continent during the reign of Mary Tudor but unobtrusively continued his studies. He was ordained after Elizabeth I came to the throne, and within a few years he was made Regius professor of divinity and master of Trinity College, Cambridge. Whitgift, faced with financial difficulties and the turbulence caused by Puritanism, rewrote the University statutes and was singularly successful in administering the finances and discipline of his college.

His success in this difficult situation and firm opposition to Thomas CARTWRIGHT, the Puritan leader, brought him to the attention of the queen and her advisors. In 1577 he became bishop of Worcester and in 1583 succeeded the ineffective Grindal at Canterbury. His adherence to the Elizabethan settlement involved persecuting Catholics, but his chief concern was the threat of Puritanism within the Church of England. The Puritans, influenced by Geneva, encouraged by prominent laymen, and tolerated by many bishops, attempted to presbyterianize Anglican polity and worship. Although his doctrinal position was basically Calvinist, Whitgift rejected the *jure divino* claims made for the Genevan system and enforced conformity to the episcopate and Prayer Book. With the active support of the queen, he deprived those who would not conform and prevented the Puritans from abolishing the episcopate and liturgy in the Church of England.

Bibliography: P. M. DAWLEY, *John Whitgift and the English Reformation* (New York 1954). V. J. K. BROOK, *Whitgift and the English Church* (New York 1957). P. HUGHES, *The Reformation in England* 3 v. in 1 (5th ed. New York 1963) 3.

[R. H. GREENFIELD]

WHITHORN, PRIORY OF

Former Premonstratensian priory at Whithorn, Wigtownshire, Scotland. The Romanesque cathedral (now in ruins) of the Diocese of Galloway at Whithorn (Latin, *Candida Casa*) was begun by Bishop Gilla-Aldan (1125–?54) and continued by his successor Christian (1154–86), with the help of Fergus, Lord of Galloway (d. 1161). It was built on the site of the most important and hallowed Celtic monastery and bishop's see in Scotland, that founded by St. NINIAN *c.* 400. The Celtic foundation had declined during the period of Viking rule and Fergus was consciously attempting to reestablish it. Bishop Christian replaced the existing cathedral clergy with PRE-

MONSTRATENSIANS in 1177, thus founding Whithorn Priory. For centuries a place of pilgrimage, it was richly endowed, and after the death of its last prior in 1569, its revenues were appropriated by the crown and given to the reformed bishops of Galloway.

Bibliography: G. DONALDSON, "The Bishops and Priors of Whithorn," *Transactions of the Dumfriesshire and Galloway Natural History and Antiquarian Society,* 3d ser. 27 (1950) 127–154. C. A. R. RADFORD and G. DONALDSON, *Whithorn and Kirkmadrine, Wigtownshire* (Edinburgh 1953). D. E. EASSON, *Medieval Religious Houses: Scotland* (London 1957) 88.

[L. MACFARLANE]

WHITING, RICHARD, BL.

Last abbot of Glastonbury, martyr; b. unknown; hanged, drawn, and quartered Nov. 15, 1539, on Tor Hill, Glastonbury, England. He probably received his education and training at Glastonbury, where he later became a monk under Abbot Richard Bere. Former published statements that he graduated M.A. from Cambridge in 1483 and D.D. in 1505 have been proved erroneous. He was ordained Mar. 7, 1501, in Wells Cathedral, and held subsequently the office of chamberlain of Glastonbury. On the death of Abbot Bere, February 1525, the monks invited Cardinal Wolsey to choose the successor. Wolsey, at the suggestion of John Islip, Abbot of Westminster, in the chapel at York Place, Mar. 3, 1525, nominated Richard Whiting, a selection formally witnessed by Thomas More. The highly respected Abbot Whiting was warmly regarded by John Leland, the antiquary, and later, by Cromwell's visitor, Robert Layton (for which indiscretion Layton was reprimanded by Cromwell). As abbot, Whiting was a member of the House of Lords, and thus immediately involved in the King's divorce proceedings. Though privately unsympathetic, he prudently took no stand either in Parliament or in his abbey. He and his 51 monks subscribed to the Oath of Supremacy Sept. 19, 1534. Whiting endeavored to keep royal favor by a number of gifts and offers to Henry VIII and Cromwell. The first visitation to Glastonbury by Layton in August 1535 found such good discipline that Glastonbury was left for the most part unmolested, except that the jurisdiction of the abbey over the town was suspended. In succeeding years the property of the abbey was constantly being granted on leases to courtiers, while Cromwell continued to reassure the abbot there would be no suppression. Sensing trouble, Whiting pleaded illness in his nonattendance at the Parliament of 1539 that sealed the fate of monasteries still unsuppressed. On Sept. 19, 1539, the royal commissioners, headed by Layton, Pollard, and Moyle, arrived without warning at Glastonbury. Their interrogation of the weak and sickly old abbot showed them

his "cankered and traitorous heart"—the phrase used in government for independence of speech—and he was brought to the Tower to be examined by Cromwell himself. The search of Glastonbury revealed rich hidden treasures of gold plate and other costly items. It would seem that the original intention to accuse Whiting of treason was, as a result, abandoned in favor of the rather ironic charge of robbery. Despite older opinions to the contrary, there can be little doubt that Whiting at his trial at Wells was charged and convicted of robbery, not treason. He was arraigned at Wells, Friday, Nov. 14, and executed the following day. Two of his monks, John Thorne (treasurer) and Roger James were executed with him. He accepted his sufferings patiently and at the end asked pardon of God and his King. His limbs were exposed at Wells, Bath, Ilchester, and Bridgewater and his head set up over the gateway of the abbey. He was beatified by Leo XIII in 1896.

Feast: Dec. 1.

See Also: ENGLAND, SCOTLAND, AND WALES, MARTYRS OF.

Bibliography: J. S. BREWER et al., eds., *Letters and Papers . . . of the Reign of Henry VIII,* 22 v. (London 1862–1932). D. KNOWLES, *The Religious Orders in England,* v.3, bibliog. F. A. GASQUET, *The Last Abbot of Glastonbury* (London 1934; repr. Freeport, NY 1970). A. WATKIN, ed., *Dean Cosyn and Wells Cathedral: Miscellanea* (Somerset Record Society 56; London 1941); "Glastonbury, 1538–39, as Shown by Its Account Rolls," *Downside Review* 67 (1949) 437–450. T. WRIGHT, ed., *Three Chapters of Letters Relating to the Suppression of Monasteries* (Camden Society 26; London 1843). P. HUGHES, *The Reformation in England* (New York 1963). A. BUTLER, *The Lives of the Saints,* ed. H. THURSTON and D. ATTWATER 4:461–462.

[J. D. HANLON]

WHOLE

Things are said to be or to constitute a whole in various ways. That which is complete and entire, having all that belongs to it without deficiency, is called a whole in the sense of a totality. Such a whole is either a unit or a union of many in one (*see* UNITY). In this sense of totality the universe is called the whole, sometimes understood as a unit (monism) or as a union of many in one (pluralism). In this sense also particular individuals and particular unions are called wholes, each in itself complete and without deficiency.

Universal and Quantitative Wholes. Again, that which contains many in such a way that they are one is called a whole. A whole in this sense is either a universal or something continuous. In the case of a universal, the whole is one, and each of the inferiors contained in it as

parts in the whole is also one, whether these are actual or merely potential (*see* UNIVERSALS). Thus the human species is one, and each individual of the species is also one. In like manner each GENUS is one and each SPECIES contained in a genus is one. On the other hand, the continuous whole is one and unbroken, but contains many parts into which it is divisible, which themselves are either in potency or in act. Thus a drop of water contains many droplets in potency, whereas a quantity such as a line or a surface contains many parts in act, which are distinct from each other but conjoined, not separated. In the case of a continuous whole, many come from one by division of the whole, but in the case of a universal whole, many come from one by additional determination of unit differences, as the genus is determined by the specific difference or a number by the addition of units.

Furthermore, a quantity that has a beginning, middle and an end is called a whole, particularly when the position of the parts makes a difference, as in a geometric figure or in an organism. If the position of the parts makes a difference in the form or composition but not in the matter, the thing is called a whole with respect to the form, but one speaks of *all* with respect to the matter, as all the bricks in the wall, but the whole wall. When the parts are considered in potency, the whole is designated by the singular, as a heap of sand; when the parts are considered in act, the plural is employed, as the sands on the shore. A whole is the sum of its parts when considered as the result of addition, and the amount of the whole is the result reached by the accumulation of particular parts. In the order of division of a whole into its parts, the whole is prior to its parts; but in the order of becoming or composing a whole from its parts, these are prior to the whole. In a homogeneous whole, the parts are of the same essence or nature as the whole, and the essence of the whole remains in the part. In a heterogeneous whole, the essential nature is not in each part separately, but in all the parts jointly or conjoined, as in a compound or organism.

Potential Wholes. A whole that has various perfections or powers according to which parts can be distinguished that do not include the full perfection of the whole is called a potential whole, and the parts are called virtual parts. For example, an animal has both vegetative and sensitive powers, and it is a natural body that is a genuine being or substance. The perfections of vegetative and sensitive life in the whole are distinguishable, as are the perfections of body, sensible matter, and substantial being. The whole essence of one thing is included in each virtual part, but not wholly, that is, not according to its full power or perfection. Likewise, the human soul is a potential whole distinguishable according to virtual parts that include the whole but not its full power, as the sensitive part of the soul and the rational part. In like manner also the subjects of the various theoretical sciences are distinguishable according to the virtual parts of the sensible substance. This is the reality immediately evident to man, and it permits of scientific elaboration through irreducibly different basic principles. Thus natural philosophy is the science of sensible or natural being understood through the principles and causes of sensible change; mathematics is the science of quantity or corporeal being, whether discrete (arithmetic) or continuous (geometry) with its own proper principles, such as the unit, point and line; metaphysics is the science of being, whether sensible and material or immaterial, understood through the first principles and causes of being as such (*see* SCIENCES, CLASSIFICATION OF).

Thomists and Scotists differ in their explanations of how the virtual parts are present in a whole that has various powers and perfections. Scotists maintain that the perfections or formalities the mind can distinguish are somehow actually distinct in the whole itself, prior to the consideration of the mind, whereas Thomists hold that these formalities are merely distinguishable by the mind but are really identical and in no way actually distinct in the whole itself. According to this view the elements in a compound such as water are not formally and actually distinct in the water, but virtually distinct, that is, distinguishable by the mind; and the virtual parts of the soul are really identical with each other and with the whole although distinguishable by the mind. In the case of TRANSCENDENTALS such as being and goodness, whether in creatures or in God, the formalities are not perfectly distinguishable by the mind but are mutually inclusive and implicitly contain one another (*see* DISTINCTION, KINDS OF).

See Also: PART; ELEMENT; COMMUNITY; FACULTIES OF THE SOUL; PERFECTION, ONTOLOGICAL.

Bibliography: ARISTOTLE *Meta.* 1023b 26–1024a 10. L. SCHÜTZ, *Thomas-Lexikon* (Paderborn 1895; photo offprint Stuttgart 1958) 814–815. E. BETTONI, *Duns Scotus: The Basic Principles of His Philosophy,* tr. and ed. B. BONANSEA (Washington 1961) 78–81. *The Great Ideas: a Syntopicon of Great Books of the Western World,* ed. M. J. ADLER 2 v. (Chicago 1952) 2:282–302. R. EISLER, *Wörterbuch der philosophischen Begriffe,* 3 v. (4th ed. Berlin 1927–30) 1:452–454.

[W. H. KANE]

WIAUX, MUTIEN-MARIE, ST.

Baptized Louis Joseph Wiaux; religious of the Institute of the Brothers of the Christian Schools; b. Mellet (near Gosselies) Belgium, March 20, 1841; d. Malonne, Belgium, Jan. 29, 1917. Louis was the third of the six children of a blacksmith and his wife who ran a small

café in their home. After attending the village school, he unsuccessfully undertook an apprenticeship in his father's forge. On July 1, 1865 he joined the Brothers of the Christian Schools who had just arrived in the area. Following his novitiate at Namur, he made his profession, took the name Mutien-Marie, and taught for three years (1856–58) in parish schools at Chimay and Brussels. For the next fifty-eight years he taught art and music at St. Bertuin's at Malonne and served as parish catechist during his free time. Soon after the death of the man called by his students ''the brother who is always praying,'' miracles were attributed to his intercession. His tomb, moved into St. Bertuin's in Malonne, draws many pilgrims. In 1923, Bishop Heylen of Namur opened his cause, and he was beatified in 1977 by Paul VI. Mutien-Marie was canonized (Dec. 10, 1989) by John Paul II, not for great works, but for his transformation of the routine into moments of devotion.

Feast: Jan. 30 (De la Salle Brothers).

Bibliography: *L'Osservatore Romano,* English edition, no. 45 (1977): 8–9. L. SALM, *Brother Mutien-Marie Wiaux, FSC: Sanctity in Simplicity* (Romeoville, Ill. 1989).

[K. I. RABENSTEIN]

WIBALD OF STAVELOT

Monk, humanist, and statesman exemplifying the dynamic character of the 12th century; b. 1098; d. Bitolj, Macedonia, en route from Constantinople, July 19, 1158. He was probably the son of *ministeriales* of Stavelot, and there began his broad education, which took him to Liège, Waulsort, and back to Stavelot for Holy Orders. In 1122, when the Concordat of WORMS was being negotiated, Wibald was at work in the imperial chancellery. There he became acquainted with cardinals later elected pope as Lucius II and Anastasius IV. The monks of STAVELOT and its sister monastery, MALMEDY, elected Wibald abbot in 1130, and the next April he was invested by King Lothair. The monastery profited from having this renowned abbot who regained lost properties through the aid of his great patrons. Impelled by his devotion to copying and decorating books and his desire to embellish church furnishings, Wibald made his houses recognized art centers. He commanded a fleet off Naples for LOTHAIR III, and had full charge of the royal son, Henry, as well as of the Empire while Conrad III (1138–52) was on the Second Crusade. He continued as adviser and ambassador during the opening of the reign of FREDERICK I. Wibald's policy—criticized as being too Rome-oriented—worked for continued cooperation between the Empire and Constantinople. His correspondence is a capital source of historical information for the period 1125 to 1155.

Bibliography: É DE MOREAU, *Histoire de l'Église en Belgique* (2d ed. Brussels 1945) 2:353–354; 3:41–58. K. HOFMANN, *Lexikon für Theologie und Kirche*² 10:854–856. M. MANITIUS, *Geschichte der lateinischen Literatur des Mittelalters* 3:289–292.

[S. WILLIAMS]

WIBORADA, ST.

A recluse known also as Guiborat, Weibrath; b. Klingau, Aargau, Switzerland; d. SANKT GALLEN, May 2, 926. Having been a recluse at St. George from *c.* 912 to 916, she then went to Sankt Gallen and lived as a recluse near the church of St. Magnus. She worked as a bookbinder for the monks of Sankt Gallen (among whom was her brother, Hatto). Among the young ladies she gathered about her as students was (Bl.) Rachilde, also a recluse. From her cell Wiborada gained renown as a kind of prophetess. It was probably at Sankt Gallen that she met (St.) ULRIC, later bishop of Augsburg, to whom she gave counsel that was decisive in his career. When the Hungarians invaded the area on May 1, 926, Wiborada was fatally wounded and died the next day. Her first anniversary was celebrated with great honor, and her relics were discovered by Abbot Craloh (942–958). Wiborada was canonized by CLEMENT II in 1047; she is portrayed most often as a nun with a book and an axe.

Feast: May 2.

Bibliography: *Acta Sanctorum* (Paris 1863—) 1:287–313. A. ZIMMERMANN, *Lexikon für Theologie und Kirche*, ed. M. BUCHBERGER (Freiburg 1930–38) 10:858. E. SCHLUMPF, in *Zeitschrift für Schweizerische Kirchengeschichte* 19 (1925) 230–234; 20 (1926) 161–167; 21 (1927) 72–75, 22 (1928)142–151; 67–72. A. FÄH, *Die hl. Wiborada*, 2 v. (Sankt Gallen 1926). A. BUTLER, *The Lives of the Saints*, ed. H. THURSTON and D. ATTWATER (New York 1956) 2:218–219. E. IRBLICH, *Die Vitae sanctae Wiboradeae* (St. Gallen 1970). *Vitae Sanctae Wiboradae*, tr. W. BERSCHIN (St. Gallen 1983).

[M. J. STALLINGS]

WICCA

Wicca, a self-professed return to WITCHCRAFT that takes its name from the Old English word for witch, is also known by its adherents as the "Craft of the Wise" and the "Old Religion." They claim that Wicca is based on pre-Christian religious ideas and rituals that have survived despite attempts to eliminate them. Adherents augment the shamanistic core of this "Old Religion" tradition with elements from other traditions such as Christianity, the NEW AGE MOVEMENT, and classical paganism. Wicca places a special emphasis on the feminine aspect of divinity, on the role of the priestess in cultic activity, on the lunar and solar cycles, and on the magical and healing properties of various natural substances such as herbs. Organized groups of practitioners are called covens. The principal deities are the Goddess and her consort, the Horned God; its principle tenet, the "Wiccan Rede," is stated as "An it harm none, do as ye will." Holidays include the four "great Sabbats" of Imbolc (Feb. 2), Beltane (May 1), Lammas (Aug. 1), and Samhain (Oct. 31) and the four "lesser Sabbats" of the spring and autumn equinoxes and the summer and winter solstices. Esbats are the regular coven gatherings during the full moon where ritual activities take place.

The modern resurgence of Wicca has been heavily influenced by Gerald B. Gardner (1884–1964), a British amateur anthropologist who claimed to have been initiated in 1939 into a coven of witches that traced its lineage through covens founded by George Pickingill (1816–1909) to Julia Brandon, an 11th century witch. Gardner's books, *The Book of Shadows* and *Witchcraft Today*, became guides for those who subsequently formed covens across Europe and the United States. Gardner wrote that the witches of this coven considered their "craft of the wise" as the indigenous religion of Britain, yet the practices that he recounted have been described as an amalgam of shamanistic ritual, Masonry, Rosicrucianism, pagan folklore, ancient mythology and nudism. Gardnerian Wiccans undergo formal initiation into covens, with three degrees of advancement. Their worship gives primacy to the Goddess and emphasizes the role of the priestess in ritual activity, which is often performed "skyclad" (i.e., nude). Adherents claim that ecstatic dancing and other shamanistic techniques raise power from their bodies which can then be directed to magical effect. Other strands of contemporary Wicca include those that trace their origins to pre-Christian or medieval customs and myths (e.g. Celtic and Teutonic) and others that originated in the 1960s and 1970s as variations of Gardnerian Wicca or as eclectic combinations of elements from various traditions of witchcraft, Christianity, New Age, animism, and mythology.

Bibliography: M. ADLER, *Drawing down the Moon* (Boston 1986). R. HUTTON, *The Triumph of the Moon: A History of Modern Pagan Witchcraft* (New York 1999). L. ORION, *Never Again the Burning Times: Paganism Revived* (Prospect Heights, Ill. 1995). STARHAWK, *The Spiral Dance: A Rebirth of the Ancient Religion of the Great Goddess*, 10th anniversary edition with a new introduction and commentary (San Francisco 1989).

[L. HARRINGTON]

WICHITA, DIOCESE OF

Comprising 25 counties in southeastern and south central Kansas, an area of 20,021 square miles, the Diocese of Wichita (Wichitensis) was erected Aug. 2, 1887. The diocese had originally occupied the southern half of the state, until the Diocese of Dodge City was created in 1951, and it was a suffragan see of the Archdiocese of St. Louis, Missouri, until the creation of the new Metropolitan See of Kansas City in Kansas in 1952. At the beginning of the 21st century, Catholics comprised about 12% of the total population.

Franciscan Friar Juan de PADILLA (c1490–1542) was probably the first to bring the faith to this territory, making two journeys to evangelize the Quivira in 1541 and 1542. It is believed that he became the protomartyr of the United States near Saint Rose's Church, Council Grove. Fr. Charles de la Croix (1792–1869) made the next attempt to evangelize southeast Kansas, traveling to the Neosho River and converting many of the Osage (1822). In 1846, the Jesuits established a mission for soldiers at Fort Scott, and in 1847, Fathers John Schoenmakers, S.J. (1807–1883) and John Bax, S.J. (1817–1852), along with three lay brothers, established Osage Mission at St. Paul, with Saint Ann's Academy for girls, run by the Sisters of Loretto from Kentucky. Between 1851 and 1889, Fr. Paul Ponziglione, S.J. (1818–1900), expanded the mission to the Colorado border. In 1887, the Holy See divided the Diocese of Leavenworth, thus forming the dioceses of Concordia, in northwest Kansas, and Wichita. James O'Reilly (b. 1887), nominated the first bishop of Wichita, died before his installation and was replaced by John Joseph Hennessy (1888–1897). Saint Aloysius Church was designated the pro-cathedral until the dedication of the Cathedral of the Immaculate Conception (1912). Vast territory and rapidly changing populations due to immigration made early evangelization difficult.

The airline industry radically reshaped the diocese. Beginning in 1916, the creation of assembly lines and the establishment of McConnell Air Force Base (1951) brought rapid growth to the city of Wichita, which peaked during World War II. Workers came from surrounding rural areas and other states, thus giving the diocese a stronger urban concentration.

It was during the episcopate of Bishop Carroll that Father Emil Kapaun (1916–1951), a native of Pilsen, Kans., brought the diocese national attention by his service and death in the Korean Conflict. Having already distinguished himself as an army chaplain in World War II, Kapaun petitioned Carroll to release him for service in Korea in 1948. After being sent to Japan in 1949, he was transferred to Korea in July 1950. He frequently risked his life to celebrate the sacraments and minister to men of all faiths, who referred to him simply as "Father," and to enemy soldiers as well. After his capture on Nov. 2, 1950 he continued leading the men in prayer de-spite harassment from the guards and would often sneak out of the prisoner of war camp at night and return with food for the starving men. Sick with dysentery and denied medication, he died May 23, 1951 in a hospital. The Archdiocese for Military Services opened his cause for canonization in 1993.

In 1991 the pro-life organization Operation Rescue organized the ''Summer of Mercy,'' a six-week series of demonstrations, rallies, and protests, strengthening the pro-life movement in Wichita, throughout the state, and other parts of the country. The diocese has seen lasting effects as the pro-life issue has remained a source of unity, drawing adults, and especially youth, to greater participation in the life of the Church.

The Sisters of the Sorrowful Mother of the Third Order of Saint Francis, who started Saint Francis Hospital in Wichita in 1889, have been leaders in Catholic health care. By 1969, with 860 beds, Saint Francis had become the second largest Catholic hospital in the nation. In 1995, it merged with Saint Joseph's Hospital, for which the Sister's of Saint Joseph had assumed responsibility in 1925, forming the Via Christi Regional Medical Center.

Bishop Eugene J. Gerber (1983–2001), a native son of the diocese and bishop of Dodge City, was named bishop of Wichita in December of 1982 and served until his resignation in 2001. He led the diocese into the third Christian millennium by creating the Spiritual Life Center, which includes a retirement center for lay people and priests, a large retreat center, the Bishop's Residence, and plans for a Discalced Carmelite monastery; by fostering Eucharistic adoration, strengthening stewardship among the laity, and encouraging vocations to the priesthood and the religious life; and by preparing for the third diocesan synod (2002). Bishop Thomas J. Olmsted, formerly a priest of the diocese of Lincoln and rector of the Pontifical College Josephinum, succeeded him as Bishop of Wichita Oct. 4, 2001, having been named coadjutor in 1999.

Bibliography: J. M. MOEDER, *History of the Diocese of Wichita*, 1963. I. J. STRECKER, *The Church in Kansas 1850-1905: ''A Family Story,''* (Kansas 1990). A. TONNE, *The Story of Chaplain Kapaun: Patriot Priest of the Korean Conflict* (Emporia, Kans. 1954).

[D. MARSTALL]

WICHMANN OF ARNSTEIN, BL.

Premonstratenisan, later Dominican; d. Neuruppin, Germany, Nov. 2, 1270. He was born of a noble family, entered the Order of Prémontré, and became provost of the church of Our Lady in Magdeburg in 1210. He was elected bishop of Brandenburg in 1221, but the election was never confirmed. Instrumental in having the Dominicans established in Magdeburg in 1224, he later entered the order there. He was prior in Erfurt, in Eisenach, and finally in Neuruppin, where a house had been founded in 1246 by his brother, Count Gebhard of Arnstein. It was there that the legend concerning Wichmann developed. It is filled with accounts of miracles and visions related to the building of the convent, but it contains also some bits of historical information. His letters of spiritual direction, written between 1252 and 1270 testify to his own profound interior life.

Bibliography: W. WATTENBACH, *Deutschlands Geschichtsquellen im Mittelalter bis zur Mitte des 13. Jh.,* (7th ed. Stuttgart-Berlin 1904), v. 2 (6th ed. Berlin 1894) 2:350–351. G. LÖHR, *Lexikon für Theologie und Kirche,* ed. M. BUCHBERGER, 10 v. (Freiburg 1930–38) 10: 859.

[P. M. STARRS]

WIDMERPOOL, ROBERT, BL.

Lay martyr; b. Widmerpool, Nottinghamshire, England; hanged at Canterbury, Oct. 1, 1588. After completing his education at Gloucester Hall, Oxford, Widmerpool was tutor to the sons of Henry, ninth Earl of Northumberland, then a schoolmaster. He was arrested for helping an illegal priest find refuge in the home of the countess of Northumberland, imprisoned at the Marshalsea, and condemned to die with the priests (BB.) Robert WILCOX, Edward CAMPION, and Christopher BUXTON. After the executioner put the rope of the gallows around his neck, Widmerpool thanked God for the glory of martyrdom in Canterbury for the cause for which St. Thomas died. He was beatified by Pius XI on Dec. 15, 1929.

Feast of the English Martyrs: May 4 (England).

See Also: ENGLAND, SCOTLAND, AND WALES, MARTYRS OF.

Bibliography: R. CHALLONER, *Memoirs of Missionary Priests,* ed. J. H. POLLEN (rev. ed. London 1924; repr. Farnborough 1969) I, 61–63. H. FOLEY, *Records of the English Province of the Society of Jesus* (London 1877–82) I, 478, 481. J. MORRIS, ed., *The Troubles of Our Catholic Forefathers Related by Themselves,* 3 v. (London 1872–77) III, 39. J. H. POLLEN, *Acts of English Martyrs* (London 1891) 327.

[K. I. RABENSTEIN]

WIDOR, CHARLES MARIE

Organist, composer, critic; b. Lyons, Feb. 21, 1844; d. Paris, March 12, 1937. He was the pupil of his organist father and later of J. N. Lemmens and FÉTIS at Brussels Conservatory. He achieved fame at Sainte-Sulpice (1870–1934) for his organ technique and masterly improvisations. He succeeded César FRANCK as professor of organ at the Paris Conservatory (1891–1905), where he developed such masters as VIERNE, Dupré, and Schweitzer. He was also critic for *L'Estafette,* member of the Institute (1910), permanent secretary of the Académie des Beaux Arts (1914), reformer of the organ-building art with Cavaillé-Coll, and promoter of the Bach cult in recital hall and church. Most representative of his many compositions are the ten *Organ Symphonies* (suites), idiomatic music exploring the tonal and technical resources of the modern organ in modified Franck harmonic style. There are also symphonies, concerti, chamber and choral works, and operas, besides important scholarly products, e.g., the Widor-Schweitzer edition of Bach, and *La Musique grecque et les chants de l'église latine* (1895).

Bibliography: I. PHILIPP, *Musical Quarterly* 30 (1944) 125–133. H. GRACE, *Grove's Dictionary of Music and Musicians,* ed. E. BLOM 9 v. (5th ed. London 1954) 9:284–285. *Baker's Biographical Dictionary of Musicians,* ed. N. SLONIMSKY (5th, rev. ed. New York 1958) 1792. J. J. ANTHONY, *Charles-Marie Widor's Symphonies pour orgue: Their Artistic Context and Cultural Antecedents* (D.M.A., diss. University of Rochester, 1986). L. ARCHBOLD, ''Widor's *Symphonie romane,*'' *French Organ Music from the Revolution to Franck and Widor,* ed. L. ARCHBOLD and W. J. PETERSON, (Rochester 1995) 249-274. O. OCHSE, ''Widor as Teacher'' *Organists and Organ Playing in Nineteenth-Century France and Belgium* (Bloomington and Indianapolis 1994) 183-194. F. RAUGEL, ''Charles-Marie(-Jean-Albert) Widor'', *The New Grove Dictionary of Music and Musicians, vol. 20,* ed. S. SADIE (New York 1980) 398-399. N. SLONIMSKY, ed., *Baker's Biographical Dictionary of Musicians, Eighth Edition* (New York 1992) 2046. A. THOMSON, *The Life and Times of Charles-Marie Widor, 1844–1937* (Oxford 1987).

[C. A. CARROLL]

WIDOW (IN THE BIBLE)

This article will discuss the widow in the Old Testament, her status, legal protection, admonitions against mistreatment of her, God's compassion for her, and the symbolic use of the term. Then the article will treat of the widow in the New Testament, warnings against circumvention of her, and her place in the early Church.

In the Old Testament. Although some widows were comparatively wealthy by inheritance (Jdt 8.7), the lot of the majority, as reflected in the Old Testament, was one of penury (1 Kgs 17.8–15; 2 Kgs 4.1–7). Israelite belief that death before old age was a punishment for sin probably accounts for the reproach attached to the state of widowhood (Is 54.4; Ru 1.13). Priests were also forbidden to marry widows (Lv 21.14).

LEVIRATE MARRIAGE gave the widow a measure of security. If she remained childless after it she could remain a part of her husband's family or return to her parents (Gn 38.11; Lv 22.13; Ru 1.8). She could also look forward to another marriage outside her dead husband's family (Ru 1.9, 13; I Sm 25.42).

Old Testament warnings against mistreatment of widows are numerous [Ex 22.21–23; Is 1.17, 23; Jb 22.9; 31.16; Ps 93(94).6; Zec 7.10]. That the injustices visited upon them were common is attested by the repeated threat of prompt action against oppressors on the Day of the Lord (Mal 3.5).

God commanded that the widow be considered part of the covenantal community. The people of God must extend to her the same merciful protection that they bestow on orphans and defenseless aliens (Dt 14.29;16.11, 14). They are not to exact her clothing or other property in payment of a debt (Dt 24.17); at the harvest a portion of grain, some fruit of the olive tree, and grapes in the vineyard are to be left for her sustenance (Dt 24.19–21; Ru 2.2–12); she must also be made the beneficiary of additional gifts (Dt 26.12; 2 Mc 3.10; 8.28, 30).

God pledged Himself to sustain the widow who hopes in Him (Jer 49.11). He will preserve her inheritance (Prv 15.25) and be Himself her protector [Ps 67(68).5; 145(146) 9].

Deutero-Isaia symbolically compares Babylon to a widow left solitary in her desolation (Is 47.9). Israel is encouraged to forget the disgrace of her widowhood (Is 54.4–6) because Yahweh has taken her back as His spouse to enter into a holier and more fruitful alliance with her. The author of Lamentations makes a similar reference to Jerusalem. After the destruction of the city and the burning of the temple by the Babylonians, Jerusalem, ''the widow,'' in poignant distress, will call on God and men for pity (Lam 1.1; 5.3–4).

In the New Testament. Biblical emphasis on the lot of the widow continues into the New Testament, with frequent reference to her indigence. In the apostolic era this led to the appointment of the first seven DEACONS whose duty required them to care for the widows whom Hellenistic Jewish converts in Jerusalem accused the Hebrew-speaking Christians of neglecting in the distribution of alms (Acts 6.1). At Jaffa (Joppe), widows grieved so deeply over the death of Tabitha, who had supplied their needs by her industry, that Peter raised her to life that she might continue her works of charity to them (Acts 9.36–41).

Under pretense of offering long prayers for widows, the Scribes and Pharisees, whose avarice Jesus condemned (Mt 23.14), enriched themselves by ''devouring

Charles Widor. (©Hulton-Deutsch Collection/CORBIS)

the substance'' of these defenseless women (Mk 12.40; Lk 20.47).

St. Paul's advice that widows should remain unmarried was not binding (1 Cor 7.8–9, 39–40); later he preferred that they should remarry if their loneliness tended to lead them to conduct that disedified the Church and non-Christians. But he approved of an official body of widows that was highly honored in the early Church. To belong to this group widows had to meet the following requirements: be at least 60 years old, give themselves to prayer day and night, have no intention of remarrying, serve ''the saints,'' show hospitality, and help the indigent (1 Tm 5.3–16).

Bibliography: *Encyclopedic Dictionary of the Bible,* translated and adapted by L. HARTMAN (New York, 1963) 1456–60, 2577–78. R. DEVAUX, *Ancient Israel, Its Life and Institutions,* tr. J. MCHUGH (New York 1961) 39–40.

[M. L. HELD]

WIDOW (IN THE EARLY CHURCH)

The expectations of an imminent PAROUSIA, a closed group mentality fostered by the paralegal status of Christians, and the absence of centralized legislative institutions in the ancient Church led to the early evolution of a special, and possibly quasi-clerical, status for widows. Exact trustworthy documentary evidence on the postapostolic evolution of the status of widows is lacking for the West. Evidence in the East is unclear, but it seems probable that widows were regularly chosen as deaconesses, although the distinction between the two was not very great in respect to duties. However, deaconesses received the "laying on of hands" (*Const. Apost.* 8.19), whereas widows did not (*ibid.* 8.25). The institution of widows, at least as a rank (*tagma*), certainly survived the public recognition of the Church under CONSTANTINE I. Canon 11 of the Council of Laodicea (Mansi 2.565–566) suppressed institution of *presbytides,* apparently, precisely that higher rank of widows who had been chosen as deaconesses, but the lower rank of simple widows was not affected by this canon. The institution began to decline as an independent class with the 5th-century rise of female monasticism and the elimination of the need of providing financial and religions security for these precariously situated Christians.

Bibliography: F. L. CROSS, *The Oxford Dictionary of the Christian Church* (London 1957) 1457–58. K. PIEPER, *Lexikon für Theologie und Kirche,* ed. M. BUCHBERGER, 10 v. (Freiburg 1930–38) 10: 950–951. J. MAYER, ed., *Monumenta de viduis diaconissis virginibusque tractantia* (*Florilegium Patristicum,* ed. J. ZELLINGER 42; Bonn 1938). A. ROSAMBERT, *La Veuve en droit canonique jusqu'au XIVᵉ siècle* (Paris 1923). L. BOPP, *Das Witwentum als organische Gliedschaft im Gemeinschaftsleben der alten Kirche* (Mannheim 1950). P. H. LAFONTANE, *Les Conditions positives de l'accession aux ordres dans la premiere législation ecclésiastique, 300–492* (Ottawa 1963). C. H. TURNER, "Ministries of Women in the Primitive Church," in *Catholic and Apostolic,* ed. H. BATE (London 1931) 316–351.

[A. G. GIBSON]

WIDUKIND OF CORVEY

Saxon chronicler; b. *c.* 925; d. after 976. Widukind, a Saxon, became a monk of the aristocratic Benedictine Abbey of CORVEY *c.* 940. There he began his literary career by writing the lives of St. Paul the Hermit and St. Thecla, works that are no longer extant. His major and only surviving work is *The Deeds of the Saxons* in three books. It is dedicated to OTTO I the Great's daughter, Princess Matilda, later first abbess of QUEDLINBURG, for whom Widukind's *The Deeds of the Saxons* is an important source for the history of 10th-century Germany. Although Widukind was not a member of the royal court, as is sometimes alleged, he was extremely well informed about imperial politics. His information probably derived from imperial officers who visited Corvey.

Bibliography: WIDUKIND OF CORVEY, *Rerum gestarum Saxonicarum libri tres, Monumenta Germaniae Historica: Scriptores rerum Germanicarum* v.56; German tr. P. HIRSCH (Leipzig 1931).

W. WATTENBACH, *Deutschlands Geschichtsquellen im Mittelalter. Deutsche Kaiserzeit,* ed. R. HOLTSMANN 1.1:25–34. H. BEUMANN, *Widukind von Korvei* (Weimar 1950). J. A. BRUNDAGE, "W. of C. and the 'Non–Roman' Imperial Idea," *Mediaeval Studies* 22 (1960) 15–26.

[J. A. BRUNDAGE]

WIGBERT OF HERSFELD, ST.

Anglo-Saxon abbot and missionary in Germany; d. Fritzlar, Germany, *c.* 746. An English monk of renowned sanctity, he was invited (*c.* 734) by BONIFACE to assist in the evangelization of Germany. His peculiar talents being monastic, Boniface placed him as abbot of the old monastery of Fritzlar, in Hesse, to reform discipline there. STURMI was one of his students in the abbey school. Later he was sent on to Ohrdruf in Thuringia for the same purpose. Worn out by his efforts, he returned to Fritzlar, where he died. He was famous for his severe penances and fasts; his grave became a shrine. In 780 his relics were transferred to the abbey of HERSFELD, where they were lost in the fire of 1761. In ecclesiastical art he is represented as holding a bunch of grapes that he had pressed into a chalice.

Feast: Aug. 13.

Bibliography: LUPUS OF FERRIÈRES, *Vita* in *Monumenta Germaniae Historica: Scriptores* (Berlin 1826—) 15.1:37–43. C. HOLE, *A Dictionary of Christian Biography,* ed. W. SMITH and H. WACE (London 1877–87) 4:1176. A. M. ZIMMERMANN, *Kalendarium Benedictinum: Die Heiligen und Seligen des Benediktinerorderns und seiner Zweige* (Metten 1933–38) 2:567–569. W. LEVISON, *England and the Continent in the 8th Century* (Oxford 1946) 235–236. H. WUNDER, *Die Wigberttradition in Hersfeld und Fritzlar* (Erlangen 1969).

[J. L. DRUSE]

WIGGER, WINAND MICHAEL

Third bishop of Newark; b. New York City, Dec. 9, 1841; d. Newark, N.J., Jan. 5, 1901. Michael was the second of four sons of John Joseph and Elizabeth (Strucke) Wigger, successful German immigrants from Westphalia who settled in St. Francis of Assisi parish, New York City. After graduating from the College of St. Francis Xavier, New York City, in 1860, he was rejected as a seminarian in New York for poor health, but was accepted in the Diocese (now Archdiocese) of NEWARK. He began his studies at the seminary at Seton Hall College, South Orange, N.J.; entered Brignole-Sale Seminary, Genoa, Italy, in 1862; and was ordained there on June 20, 1865. Four years later, following his first assignment to St. Patrick's Cathedral, Newark, he received a doctor of divinity degree from the University of Rome. For the next 12 years he was pastor successively at St. Vincent's, Madison; St. John's, Orange; St. Teresa's, Summit; and again at Madison, all in New Jersey. Although first on the list of nominees for the new Diocese of Trenton, he was appointed third bishop of Newark, and was consecrated by Abp. Michael Corrigan at the Newark cathedral on Oct. 18, 1881.

Wigger was an advocate of temperance and included incorrigible drunkards among public sinners to be denied Christian burial. Although he opposed appointment of an apostolic delegate and disapproved of some of Abp. (later Cardinal) Francesco Satolli's early decisions, he applauded Leo XIII's letter *Testem benevolentiae* on ''Americanism.'' He did not approve of convoking the Third Plenary Council of Baltimore (1884); he did attend, however, and promptly implemented its legislation in his diocese. He ardently favored parochial schools, and in 1893 resisted the legislation, proposed by some Catholics and approved by the apostolic delegate, that would have allowed New Jersey parochial schools to be incorporated into the public school system and receive state funds.

Wigger was first president of the U.S. branch of the St. Raphael Society, which cared for German immigrants, and was one of the founders of Leo House, New York City, a Catholic hostel for immigrants. Although his German descent, associations, and alleged sympathy were criticized by some of his clergy, he made every effort to provide for all immigrants, especially the Italians. His fluency in German, Italian, and French made possible direct communication with most of his people. Although never robust, Wigger carried a heavy burden of pastoral work and was an able financial administrator.

Bibliography: C. J. BARRY, *The Catholic Church and German Americans* (Milwaukee 1953). J. M. FLYNN, *The Catholic Church in New Jersey* (Morristown, N.J. 1904). C. D. HINRICHSEN, *The History of the Diocese of Newark, 1873–1901* (Doctoral diss. unpub. Catholic U. 1963). C. G. HERBERMANN, *Historical Records and Studies of the U.S. Catholic Hisotrical Society of New York* 2 (1900) 292–320.

[C. D. HINRICHSEN]

WIKTERP, ST.

Bishop and confessor; b. Epfach, near Landsberg, fl. 738; d. 749? Wikterp, the first historically certain bishop of Augsburg, rebuilt the church of St. Afra destroyed by the Huns. Attributed to him are the foundation of numerous important monasteries, e.g., Füssen, BENEDIKTBEUERN, WESSOBRÜNN, ELLWANGEN, Polling, OTTOBEUREN, KEMPTEN. He participated with (St.) BONIFACE in synods that introduced the Roman diocesan structure into the Church in Germany, hitherto organized around monasteries. He was buried at Epfach; his relics were translated in 1489 to the church of SS. Afra and Ulric in Augsburg. He is not to be confused with other Wikterps (e.g., of Regensburg, Tours).

Feast: April 18.

Bibliography: C. STENGEL, *Vita s. Wicterpi episcopi Augustani et confessoris* (Augsburg 1607). *Acta Sanctorum* (Paris 1863—) 2:545–549. A. HAUCK, *Kirchengeschichte Deutschlands* (Berlin-Leipzig 1958) 1:465, 502. A. BIGELMAIR, *Lexikon für Theologie und Kirche*, ed. M. BUCHBERGER (Freiburg 1930–38) 10:884. J. L. BAUDOT and L. CHAUSSIN, *Vies des saints et des bienheureux selon l'ordre du calendrier avec l'historique des fêtes*, ed. by the Benedictines of Paris (Paris 1935–56) 4:435. A. M. ZIMMERMANN, *Kalendarium Benedictinum: Die Heiligen und Seligen des Benediktinerordens und seiner Zweige* (Metten 1933–38) 2:72–73.

[H. E. AIKINS]

WILBERFORCE, BERTRAND

Dominican preacher and spiritual director; b. Lavington-with-Graffham, Sussex, Mar. 14, 1839; d. London, Dec. 14, 1904. His baptismal name was Arthur. His grandfather was William Wilberforce, famous for his advocacy in Parliament of the abolition of slavery. His father was Henry William WILBERFORCE. In 1850, Arthur was received into the Church at the same time as his father. In 1853 he went to school at Ushaw, where in 1856 he decided to become a priest. After being ordained deacon he determined to enter the Dominican order. In April 1864 he therefore went to the Dominican priory at Woodchester, was ordained on May 1 and clothed as a novice on May 7. He made his simple profession in 1865 and took solemn vows in 1868. After this he was assigned successively to various houses of the order in England. From 1872 to 1875 he was prior at St. Dominics in London, and in 1877 and 1878 he served as chaplain to the nuns at Stone, with whom he remained closely associated. From 1878 he was almost continuously occupied with preaching missions, retreats, and special sermons, and acquired a considerable reputation as a confessor and spiritual director. He was a person of outstanding gifts: of holiness, wisdom, charm, and eloquence. His published works included: *Dominican Missions and Martyrs in Japan*; *Life of St. Lewis Bertrand*; *Memoir of Mother Francis Raphael Drane*; translations of Blosius, and several pamphlets, the most popular being *Mental Prayer* (Catholic Truth Society, London 1884).

Bibliography: W. GUMBLEY, *Obituary Notices of the English Dominicans from 1555 to 1952* (London 1955). H. M. CAPES, *The Life and Letters of Father Bertrand Wilberforce* (London 1906).

[S. BULLOUGH]

WILBERFORCE, HENRY WILLIAM

Journalist and historian; b. Clapham, England, Sept. 22, 1807; d. Stroud, Gloucestershire, April 23, 1873. Henry, the youngest son of the famous William WILBERFORCE, attended Oriel College, Oxford, where he became president of the Oxford Union and a favorite pupil of J. H. NEWMAN, under whose influence he forsook the idea of a career in the law and took Holy Orders. He had livings in Kent, where he finally succeeded his elder brother, Bp. Robert Isaac Wilberforce, as the rector of East Farleigh, near Maidstone. Henry and his wife were received into the Church at Brussels, the same year as Henry MANNING. Mrs. Wilberforce was a daughter of Rev. J. Sargent, another of whose daughters married Bishop Wilberforce, Henry's brother, and a third who, though she died young, had been Dr. Manning's wife when he was an Anglican archdeacon. After his conversion, Wilberforce turned to Catholic journalism, becoming proprietor of a weekly, the *Catholic Standard,* which he renamed the *Weekly Register.* He became also secretary of the Catholic Defence Association, which had been founded in Dublin, and he published a number of works, e.g., *Reasons for Submitting to the Catholic Church,* and *Proselytism in Ireland*, the correspondence between himself and an Irish Church minister. He later wrote Essay on Some Events Preparatory to the English Reformation for a volume edited by Manning, and *The Church and the Empires,* a textbook of Church history published the year after his death, with a memoir by Newman. He was buried in the new Dominican foundation of Woodchester in Gloucestershire near his home.

[D. WOODRUFF]

WILBERFORCE, WILLIAM

Antislavery leader and philanthropist; b. Hull, England, Aug. 24, 1759; d. London, July 29, 1833. Wilberforce was educated at Cambridge where he began a lifelong friendship with William Pitt, later prime minister. Both entered parliament in 1780. At Pitt's suggestion, Wilberforce became leader of the antislavery campaign. He continued to champion this cause in and out of parliament until SLAVERY was completely abolished in the British Empire—just a few weeks before his death. He was buried in Westminster Abbey.

Although famous chiefly as an emancipator of slaves, Wilberforce also exercised a profound religious influence. As a young man in London he moved in the privileged circles, light-hearted and self-satisfied, that dominated social and political life. After an intensive study of the New Testament, he was converted to Evangelicalism, abandoned worldly ambitions, and devoted himself to philanthropic works. His *Practical View of the Prevailing Religious System of Professed Christians* won wide popularity, and argued convincingly that reform of society must begin with individual sanctification. His famous diary shows how sincerely he applied this to himself.

As leader of the Evangelical and antislavery movements, Wilberforce linked these two causes. With great skill he used Evangelicalism to help wage the antislavery campaign. At the same time, the Evangelical movement raised the debased public morality of the 18th century to the higher standards of the Victorian Age. After his death, the Evangelical movement began to lose ground, but it had contributed to the abolition of slavery and raised moral standards under Wilberforce's guidance.

During the OXFORD MOVEMENT a generation later, three of Wilberforce's four sons were among the many followers of NEWMAN who entered the Catholic Church.

Bibliography: R. I. and S. WILBERFORCE, *The Life of William Wilberforce,* 5 v. R. COUPLAND, *Wilberforce.* F. H. BROWN, *Fathers of the Victorians: The Age of Wilberforce.* A. and H. LAWSON, *The Man Who Freed the Slaves* (London 1962).

[R. WILBERFORCE]

WILCOX, ROBERT, BL.

Priest martyr; b. Chester, England; hanged, drawn, and quartered at Canterbury, Oct. 1, 1588. Wilcox studied for the priesthood at Rheims and was ordained April 20, 1585. Within months of arriving (Jan. 7, 1586) in England, he was arrested while ministering in Kent. Following internment in the Marshalsea with BB. Edward CAMPION, Christopher BUXTON, and Robert Widmerpool, he was executed as a traitor under 27 Elizabeth cap. 2. He was beatified by Pius XI on Dec. 15, 1929.

Feast of the English Martyrs: May 4 (England).

See Also: ENGLAND, SCOTLAND, AND WALES, MARTYRS OF.

Bibliography: R. CHALLONER, *Memoirs of Missionary Priests,* ed. J. H. POLLEN (rev. ed. London 1924; repr. Farnborough 1969) I, 61–63. H. FOLEY, *Records of the English Province of the Society of Jesus* (London 1877–82) I, 478, 481. J. MORRIS, ed., *The Troubles of Our Catholic Forefathers Related by Themselves,* 3 v. (London 1872–77) III, 39. J. H. POLLEN, *Acts of English Martyrs* (London 1891) 327.

[K. I. RABENSTEIN]

WILFRID OF YORK, ST.

Anglo-Saxon monk, bishop of York; b. 634; d. monastery at Oundle, April 24, 709 or 710. Born of noble stock, he was sent as a boy of 14 years to the royal court of Northumbria, but Queen Eanfled, realizing his true bent, sent him to the Celtic-oriented Abbey of LINDIS-FARNE to be trained as a monk. Wilfrid longed to visit Rome, and so when he was 18, Eanfled sent him to Kent, whence after a year's wait he set out with BENEDICT BIS-COP, a fellow Northumbrian. On reaching Lyons they were received kindly by the archbishop, while the count, his brother, offered Wilfrid a large estate and his own daughter as wife, but Wilfrid refused. Benedict pressed on by himself to Rome while Wilfrid, after some months in Lyons, reached Rome in 654. There he visited many shrines and was instructed in the Scriptures and in Roman ecclesiastical discipline by Archdeacon Boniface. He returned to Lyons, and during his three years there was tonsured, and narrowly escaped death when his patron, the archbishop, was martyred. On returning to Northumbria where he was made abbot of RIPON, he imbued Alhfrith, King Oswius's son, with his own enthusiasm for Roman ways. After being ordained a priest by a visiting bishop, Agilbert, he took a prominent part in the Council of WHITBY at which the Northumbrian Church was reconciled to Rome and Roman liturgical use. As a result, the Irish bishop COLMAN of Lindisfarne resigned, and Wilfrid took his place as bishop of YORK. Refusing to be consecrated by Celtic bishops, he went to Gaul for the ceremony and on returning nearly two years later found that King Oswiu had appointed CHAD bishop in his place. However, in 669 he was restored to York by Abp. THEODORE OF CANTERBURY, and for nine years he ruled over the see, building great new churches at HEXHAM and Ripon, of which the crypts survive in each place. He introduced the BENEDICTINE Rule to Northumbria and made many improvements in the Church services. When Archbishop Theodore sought to divide the See of York in 678, Wilfrid objected and went to Rome to appeal to the pope. Although Wilfrid was successful in Rome, Ecgfrith, King Oswius's successor, refused to accept the pope's decision and after imprisoning Wilfrid, drove him into exile. During his six-year exile Wilfrid converted the pagan south Saxons, establishing a monastery at Selsey. In 687 Theodore, having made peace with Wilfrid, persuaded King Alhfrith, Ecgfrith's successor in Northumbria, to restore Wilfrid to his see, but in 703 he was again driven out, and he again personally appealed to the pope. Although vindicated in Rome, he resigned York to JOHN OF BEVERLEY on his return and accepted instead the newly created bishopric of Hexham, retaining also his monastery at Ripon. After his death at Oundle his relics were taken to Ripon and thence to Canterbury, but were restored to Ripon in 1226. Most of the information about Wilfrid is derived from a *Life* written before 720 by his disciple, Eddius Stephanus, edited and translated by B. Colgrave. BEDE [*Histoire ecclesiastique* 5.19, ed. C.

William Wilberforce.

Plummer (Oxford 1896)] used this *Life*, but added a little fresh information.

Feast: Oct. 12; April 24 (translation).

Bibliography: W. HUNT, *The Dictionary of National Biography From the Earliest Times to 1900* (London 1938) 21:238242. W. LEVISON, *England and the Continent, in the Eighth Century* 278–279. F. M. STENTON, *Anglo-Saxon England* (Oxford 1947). E. S. DUCKETT, *Anglo-Saxon Saints and Scholars* (Hamden, Conn. 1967). *The Age of Bede*, tr. J. F. WEBB, ed. D. H. FARMER (Harmondsworth, Middlesex, England 1983). S. EDDIUS, *The Life of Bishop Wilfrid*, tr. B. COLGRAVE (Cambridge 1985). W. T. FOLEY, *Images of Sanctity in Eddius Stephanus' Life of Bishop Wilfrid, An Early English Saint's Life* (Lewiston, N.Y. 1992).

[B. COLGRAVE]

WILGIS, ST.

Anglo-Saxon monk, father of St. WILLIBRORD; d. *c.* 700. A Northumbrian, he established a chapel dedicated to St. Andrew on the banks of the Humber and lived as

The rococo interior of the Abbey Church at Wilhering, near Linz, in Upper Austria. The church was founded in the 12th century but rebuilt following a fire in 1733. (©Adam Woolfitt/ CORBIS)

a hermit nearby in his later years. A community gathered about the spot, attracted by the reputation of his sanctity. Wilgis was buried in the chapel. ALCUIN at one time was prior of ST. ANDREWS Abbey, which derived from the chapel.

Feast: Jan. 31.

Bibliography: *Monumenta Germaniae Historica: Scriptores rerum Merovingicarum* (Berlin 1826—) 7.1:116–118. R. STANTON, *A Menology of England and Wales* (London 1887). A. M. ZIMMERMANN, *Kalendarium Benedictinum: Die Heiligen und Seligen des Benediktinerorderns und seiner Zweige* (Metten 1933–38) 7:152.

[J. L. DRUSE]

WILHERING, ABBEY OF

Cistercian house (Latin *Hilaria*, Gothic *Wilja hari*, Village of the Lord Wille) near Linz, Upper Austria. It was founded in 1146 by the brothers Ulric and Cholo of the Wilhering family with monks from Reun in Styria (founded 1129), but Reun later yielded its rights to its own motherhouse, EBRACH in Franconia. Wilhering founded three daughterhouses: Hohenfurt (1259), Engel-szell (1293–1786, 1925–), and Säusenstein (1334–1789); but it suffered greatly in the Turkish wars and almost collapsed in the Reformation. Able abbots revived the abbey, which survived a burning to the ground in 1733, Joseph II's decree of suppression and JOSEPHINISM's harm to monastic life, and the ravages of the Napoleonic wars. Abbot Theobald Grasböck (1892–1915) began another revival that was impeded by World Wars I and II and suppression under National Socialism. Material and spiritual reconstruction has taken place since 1945. Traces of the 12th-century church and cloister remain, and medieval inscriptions and frescoes were discovered in 1939. The abbey has a splendid 18th-century baroque church, elaborate guest rooms in the prelates' wing, a painting gallery with the best of Austrian baroque, a beautiful garden, a library with valuable MSS and incunabula, and good archives. It cares for a liberal arts school, nine parishes, and a mission station in Bolivia.

Bibliography: L. H. COTTINEAU, *Répertoire topobibliographique des abbayes et prieurés,* 2 v. (Mâcon 1935–39) 2:3454–55. *Catalogus generalis S. O. Cist.* (Rome 1954). J. OSWALD, ed., *Alte Klöster in Passau und Umgebung* (2d ed. Passau 1954). H. HAHN, *Die frühe Kirchenbaukunst der Zisterzienser* (Berlin 1957). S. BIRNGRUBER, in *Österreichische Ordensstifte (Notring-Jahrbuch;* Vienna 1961) 90ff. "Wilhering," *Lexikon für Theologie und Kirche,* ed. J. HOFER and K. RAHNER, 10 v. (2d, new ed. Freiburg 1957–65); suppl., *Das Zweite Vatikanische Konzil: Dokumente und kommentare,* ed. H. S. BRECHTER et al., pt. 1 (1966) v.10.

[C. SPAHR]

WILIGELMO DA MODENA

First important sculptor of the Romanesque period, active at Modena cathedral, *c.* 1099 to *c.* 1110. An inscription on a tablet supported by the prophets Enoch and Elias on the façade of Modena cathedral gives the date of the cathedral's foundation in 1099 and names Wiligelmo as the chief sculptor. That some part of the Modena sculpture was completed by 1106 is indicated by a similar relief at Cremona cathedral, dated 1107, which was directly influenced by Wiligelmo. The "Portale Maggiore" of the west façade at Modena includes reliefs of 12 Prophets; inhabited rinceaux carried by atlantes on the jambs; a series of four large reliefs, each with three episodes from Genesis, from the "Creation of Man" to "Noah's Ark"; winged genii; and capitals. The short, bulky figures with large heads and hands are arranged in friezelike compositions beneath an arcade; their drapery falls in long straight folds or is indicated by raised ridges between parallel incised lines. Although the structure of the Modena door is derived from the slightly earlier portal of S. Ambrogio, no direct prototypes for the figural style or the sculptural program exist in earlier Lombard art. The winged genii prove Wiligelmo's dependence on provincial Roman sarcophagi and funerary steles. The ''Portale dei Principi'' and ''Portale della Pescheria'' of Modena cathedral are by his workshop; his influence is apparent also at Cremona, Nonantola, and Quarantola. Wiligelmo's highly original portal ensemble is a possible source for the west façade of Saint-Denis, north of Paris (*c.* 1137–40) and for an early manifestation of the widespread revival of monumental stone sculpture in 12th-century Europe.

Bibliography: R. SALVINI, *Wiligelmo e le origini della scultura romanica* (Milan 1956).

[M. SCHAEFER]

WILL

Will is a capacity (or action or product) whereby a person is psychically attracted to some object that is apprehended as GOOD, or is psychically repelled by some object apprehended as EVIL. Willing is usually (but not always) distinguished from knowing, in that willing involves some sort of affective approach to what is cognitively present to consciousness. Psychic activities such as loving, intending, desiring, consenting, choosing, using, enjoying (and their contraries) are considered as examples of willing. Freedom, in the sense of the capacity for self-determination (the ability to ''make up one's mind''), is associated with the meaning of will. Writers in the Thomistic tradition regard will (Lat., *voluntas*) as the potency, function, or resultant of rational APPETITE (*see* FACULTIES OF THE SOUL). On the other hand, other Catholic writers follow the usage of St. Augustine, in which human will means the whole soul as active in any manner; this usage may still be found in prayers, works of piety, and spiritual exercises. In either case, will is an important constituent of personality, for it represents the seat of an intelligent commitment to some value or of a rejection of some disvalue. God, angels, and human persons are possessed of will in this broad sense; thus the term should not be limited to merely human activities.

This article presents a systematic analysis of the concept of will, with an accent on Catholic thought, and then furnishes a historical survey of other theories of willing.

Will and Willing: Systematic Analysis

The main points treated in this analysis are the existence of the will in man, the nature of the human will, man's various acts of willing, and the role of habituation in the training of the will.

Existence of the Will. That man is capable of willing may be shown from a study of one's personal experience and from observation of the behavior of other persons. In one's own consciousness, there are moments of decision, of commitment to some ideal or principle, of conscious choosing to do or not to do some action. These critical activities can be explained only by concluding that man is endowed with a special ability, a power, to make such decisions and choices. Similarly, one sees others in the course of deliberating and coming to decisions, and then acting as a result of such volitional processes. It is not that anyone directly observes the inner working of another's will: this he cannot do. Rather, the simplest and most reasonable explanation of certain affective and appetitive features of human conduct lies in granting that each person has his own power of willing.

Actually, there is not a great deal of opposition to the contention that each man is able to will for himself. Many would deny the existence of a special ''faculty'' of will, if faculty were taken to mean an agency separate from the basic substance of man. Thus, the British empirical philosophers from Hobbes to the present tend to interpret human will as a function of the person rather than as a distinct power. The suggestion that will is a rational appetite is frequently criticized by those who see no difference between sense perception and reasoning (*see* SENSISM). Much of this disagreement stems from terminological misunderstandings that arise between members of different schools of philosophy. Most philosophers think that the individual man is able, at least in part, to determine his actions under his own control. This capacity for self-determination is generally admitted to be will. Yet there are many variations in the detailed philosophical theories of willing (see below).

Nature of the Will. As rational appetite, man's will is a tendential power capable of inclining toward any object that is intellectually presented as a good. The nature of the will, then, is discoverable from a study of the kind of volitional actions that are performed by man. Clearly, the will is not a bodily power, like the ability to move the body in walking or talking, for willing is directed to an intelligible object that is known on a level above that of bodily activity. The will is an incorporeal power. Since it is quite real and not a mere abstraction, this immaterial power may also be called spiritual.

Some thinkers have regarded man's will as a power superior to his INTELLECT. In the late 13th century, for instance, PETER JOHN OLIVI wrote that the very possibility of understanding is due to a will act (see Bourke, 83–84). This exaltation of will over intellect is psychological VOLUNTARISM. The contrary view would be INTELLECTUALISM. A reasonable position maintains that intellect and will are equally important in the psychological constitution of man.

Human freedom—the capacity for self-determination, for personally controlling some of one's actions and omissions—is intimately associated with the functioning of the will. Here again, one may argue from his personal experience of desiring, choosing, and refraining from possible actions, to freedom's being evident in some of man's volitional functions. People who deny that man is free usually do so on two bases. (1) Some philosophers (Thomas HOBBES is the best example) have thought that man is nothing but a body and that he has no spiritual powers or activities. If this were true, then all human actions would be mechanically produced and man would not be free. However, Hobbes was wrong; man is able to perform immaterial actions (understanding and willing), and freedom is a prime characteristic of such functions (see SOUL, HUMAN; SPIRIT). The very fact that men are held responsible, morally and at law, for certain of their actions, is enough to indicate how eccentric it is to deny personal freedom. (2) Other philosophers have interpreted "free" to mean completely uncaused; as a consequence they have asserted that no free activity is possible to man. This is not what free means. The acts of man that are free are not caused by agencies external to man; they are caused by agencies within man. In other words, man's capacity for self-determination is the root of his personal FREEDOM. (See FREE WILL.)

Acts of the Will. Every positive willing is a tending toward a good. Negative volition is a tending away from some object that is apprehended as evil. The most basic act of will is loving; volitional love means affective approval of an intelligible good. All other positive acts of will may be regarded as variants of the fundamental action of loving. Similarly, negative acts of volition are variants of hating. (See LOVE.)

Where the good that is cognitively presented to the will is complete and unmixed with evil, the will is powerless to withhold its love of such an object (see GOOD, THE SUPREME). So, the volitional response to the universal good (for example, man's ultimate happiness, or God as the perfect good) is called a natural and necessary volition. It is an act of will as nature. However, where the object is presented as a particular good of limited appeal, the volitional response is called deliberate volition and it is free.

In traditional Catholic psychology, volitional acts are divided also into elicited and commanded (or imperated) actions. The latter are activities performed in some other power of man under the direction or use of will: thus, to walk or talk in a self-controlled manner is to perform a commanded act. Elicited acts of will are functions of the will itself as a power, e.g., wishing, intending, consenting (St. Thomas Aquinas, *Summa*

theologiae, 1a2ae,1.1 ad 2; 6 *prol.*). St. Thomas described six sorts of elicited action of human will (*ibid.,* 1a2ae, 8–17), and CAJETAN, in his commentary, systematized this teaching in the following outline relating the volitional acts to the respective intellectual activities (*see* HUMAN ACT).

Two points should be emphasized concerning this: (1) The analysis is not to be understood as if will and intellect were two separate agents: man is the agent who wills and understands; (2) The order in which these acts are listed is not necessarily the order of their occurrence in time.

1. In relation to an end.
   a. Wishing (*velle*): a will act of simple affective approval of something apprehended as a good in itself; the parallel intellectual act is the apprehension of an end.
   b. Intending (*intendere*): a will act of inclining toward the attainment of an end; associated with the intellectual judgment of the attainability of the end.
2. In relation to means.
   a. Consenting (*consentire*) to means: a will act of accepting a plural number of means as possible; associated with intellectual deliberation on the available means.
   b. Choosing (*eligere*): a will act of selecting the one means to be used, or of deciding to act or not to act; associated with the intellectual act of preferential judgment.
3. In relation to execution.
   a. Using (*uti*): a will act of applying other powers of the agent to their commanded actions; associated with the intellectual act of commanding.
   b. Enjoying (*frui*): a will act of taking satisfaction in the end attained; associated with the intellectual judgment of the suitability of what is accomplished.

An important feature of will activity is motivation. There is a "reason why" (*propter quod*) a person wills in one way rather than another: this is the MOTIVE for willing. A positive motive is the fact that some object is viewed by the agent as good. This "goodness" may be real or apparent; as long as it is apprehended as attractive it may motivate the will. On the other hand, an object regarded as evil motivates negative volitions: acts of dislike, refusal, and disagreement. A volitional motive does not move the agent from outside, but stimulates from within his own consciousness; thus motivation does not reduce freedom.

Habituation and Training of Will. Habit formation is possible in any psychic power whose activity is capable of being improved with use. Such a potency must be open to being actuated in several ways, and not wholly determined by its nature to but one way of operating. Although this is the case in regard to certain acts of human willing, it is not so in regard to other acts. Man's will is by nature wholly in favor, as it were, of the good that is loved, desired, chosen, for the sake of the possessor of the will. No habit can be formed, or is needed, to improve such self-directed volitions. It is not so natural to will the good for another person; effort and repeated practice are required to perform acts of altruistic volition. Volitional habits enabling one to seek the good for other persons are various modifications of the moral virtue of JUSTICE. Another area of volition that is open to improvement by habit formation is that in which one tries to love other persons because they are God's creatures. This is the domain of CHARITY, a supernatural habit of the will. In its highest sense, HOPE may also be a volitional habit. Many Catholic moralists, using a broad Augustinian meaning of will, would say that all moral virtues are good habits in the will. Aquinas taught that the above-mentioned moral virtues are habits in the will as subject, whereas various kinds of TEMPERANCE are in the concupiscible appetite as subject, habits related to FORTITUDE are in the irascible appetite, and habits of PRUDENCE are in the practical intellect. Of course, Aquinas thought that the will is involved in the exercise of the acts of all the moral virtues. (*See* VIRTUE; HABIT.)

As to the notion of "training" the will, this usually implies a dynamic power interpretation. As studied by Catholic psychologists such as J. Lindworsky, this popular view that one may increase the degree of strength of will power by certain exercises has not been confirmed. So-called strength of will is mostly a matter of attentiveness, of being able to maintain concentration on some objective that is regarded as desirable. Attention is more important than "strong" will. (*See* WILL POWER.)

Historical Survey of Theories of Will

The wide variety of theories dealing with the will precludes an exhaustive treatment. In what follows, the main lines of development in Western thought are sketched, with summary treatments of Greek, patristic, medieval, and modern contributions to this subject.

Greek Origins. Pre-Christian Greek philosophy did not stress the function of willing. In fact, it is difficult to identify the term that means, for Plato or Aristotle, what will does today. Plato divides man's soul into three parts: rational (τὸ λογιστικόν), desiderative (τὸ ἐπιθυμητικόν), and competitive (τὸ θυμοειδής); the second and third gave rise to appetitive function that only remotely resemble willing (*Rep.* 435E–442; *Tim.* 69B–72D). In the

Phaedrus (246–248) these appetites are compared to two wild horses that may be regulated by reason. Aristotle's psychology has a general theory of human desire (ὄρεξις) and some discussion of rational choice (προίρεσις) and wishing (βούλησις). The treatment of these functions (*Anim.* 433a 10b–30) does not lead to the postulation of a power that would be equivalent to will (*voluntas*) in the scholastic sense. Rational choice is hesitantly called (*Eth. Nic.* 1139b 3) intellective appetition or appetitive intellection. Aristotle does not clearly describe a power of will.

Among pre-Christian philosophers, the Stoics came closest to a concept of willing as distinctive of the person. Thus, Cicero says: "Wherefore, as soon as anything that has the appearance of good presents itself, nature incites us to endeavor to obtain it. Now, where the strong desire is consistent and founded on prudence, it is by the Stoics called βούλησις, and the name which we give it is will (*voluntas*)" [*Tusc. disp.* 4.6; tr. C. D. Yonge (London 1853) 403]. PLOTINUS (3rd century A.D.) discusses some functions of willing under the term βούλησις, and also uses the word θέλησις, which is adopted by some of the Greek Fathers (*Ennead.* 6.8.1–21).

Patristic Teaching. With the Christian emphasis on the dignity of the human person and on the concept of personal salvation and moral responsibility stressed in the Bible and early Christian writings, more attention came to be directed to the will and its acts. The well-developed psychology of St. AUGUSTINE distinguishes three main functions of the soul: knowing, remembering, and willing (*Trin.* 10.11.17). In this triadic view, will (*voluntas*) means the whole soul as active (*Retract.* 1.15.3; *De duab. anim.* 11.15). The Augustinian will is not a faculty but the soul itself as loving: indeed, will is but love in its strongest form (*Trin.* 15.21.41). Nor are there powers of sensory appetition, distinct from will, for St. Augustine: *cupiditas* (sensual desire) and *libido* (lust) are simply perverse movements of will (*Civ.* 14.6–7). Man's will, while essentially free to turn toward the good or away from it, is not, by itself, able to accomplish man's salvation; for that, divine grace is required (*Retract.* 1.9.5). The Will of God, according to Augustine, is identical with God as supreme cause and ruler of all things (cf. *Conf.* 12. 15.18).

St. JOHN DAMASCENE (8th century) introduced into Christian psychology an analysis of volition that differs from Augustine's theory and leads to the notion of a faculty of appetition. The third part of Damascene's *Source of Knowledge* (*Patrologia Graeca,* ed. J. P. Migne, 94:944–945) describes man's power of will (θέλησις) as a natural and rational appetite whose act is willing (βούλησις) an end. Rational deliberation makes possible a judgment regarding means, from which the will makes its choice (προαίρεσις). Thus are the seeds of Aristotelian and late Stoic (e.g., that of NEMESIUS OF EMESA) appetitive and faculty theories combined in Damascene and transmitted to later scholasticism.

Medieval Theories. In the 12th century, St. BERNARD OF CLAIRVAUX stressed will as the seat of spiritual love, and even knowledge, in the soul [*De diligendo Deo*, tr. T. Connolly, ed. A. C. Pegis, *Wisdom of Catholicism* (New York 1949) 230–268]. This emphasis continues in 13th-century Franciscan psychology (i.e., that of St. BONAVENTURE, JOHN OF LA ROCHELLE, and Peter John Olivi) where the human will is not distinguished from the general power of the soul, which reaches its fulfillment in the love of God in heaven.

With the adoption of an Aristotelian psychology by St. ALBERT THE GREAT and St. THOMAS AQUINAS, a theory of really distinct potencies of the soul was developed. It was not long before some of the views of Augustine and John Damascene were combined with this faculty psychology in such a way as to distinguish the two highest powers in man: intellect and will. The result was a new way of looking at the human will, viz, as the intellectual or rational appetite in man (see studies by Verbeke, Klubertanz, and Bourke).

Thomistic Teaching. Aquinas's explanation of human willing is central in his theory of human nature. He begins with a radical distinction between the generic functions of cognition and appetition (*Summa theologiae*, 1a, 80.1). To know is to take in and immanently react to information from the world of reality. To will is to incline toward, or away from, union with a known object. Cognition is ingoing; appetition is outgoing. Aquinas further distinguishes the cognition of individual aspects of bodily things (sensing) from the cognition of universal meanings. Two lower powers of sensory appetition (concupiscibility and irascibility) enable man to incline toward, or away from, sensory objects. These two sense appetites are powers that are really distinct from will. The intellectual appetite (will) is a third and higher appetitive power through which man inclines toward, or away from, universal aspects of things known as appealing or repulsive. Thus the Thomistic will is stimulated to its appetitive response through the intellectual presentation of some universal good or evil. (If one desires to eat an apple, simply because he likes the taste, then his appetitive response is not a will-act but a movement of the concupiscible appetite. If he also desires this apple because he thinks that its eating promotes good health, then his appetitive response to this universal good is an act of intellectual desire in his will.) Many of man's functions, according to Aquinas, are joint movements of sensory plus intellectual appetites.

As intellectual appetite, in the Thomistic theory, the will inclines without deliberation—an intellectual process of weighing the appeal of various apprehended goods—and so naturally, toward the good-in-general. Since such an object contains nothing repulsive, the will is naturally and wholly attracted to it (*Summa theologiae*, 1a, 82.1; *De malo* 6.1). Perfect happiness, for instance, cannot be volitionally rejected by man, although he may fail to will it by consciously rejecting all intellectual consideration of it. This first type of will movement is not free: it is a natural volition (*voluntas ut natura*). Second, man may think over, take counsel with himself, and deliberate on, the respective values of several intellectually known goods. If he responds to a deliberated judgment in a movement of will—which he does not have to do, because goods that can be deliberated on must be limited in appeal—then his will act is free. This kind of volitional act is called a deliberated volition (*voluntas deliberata*). It is most clearly exemplified in choices of means. Freedom of choice (*liberum arbitrium*) is not a function of will alone, for Thomists, but is a joint activity pertaining formally to intellect, and materially or substantially to will (*Summa theologiae*, 1a, 83.1; *De ver.* 24.1–2). It is man who is free, not his will or his intellect as powers.

Later Scholastic Views. In the 14th century there was much diversity of teaching concerning will. Some Oxford theologians held that the will performs cognitive functions (see study by Michalski). John Duns Scotus reacted against certain features of Thomism that he regarded as intellectualistic; so, he stressed the point that nothing moves the will except will itself—God, of course, excepted (*Op. Oxon.* 2.24–25). While Scotus retained the distinction of natural and deliberated volition, he tended to identify will with an essentially free power [*voluntas quae est potentia libera per essentiam*—*Ordinatio* 1.17.1–2; ed. Balić, (Vatican City 1950) 5:169]. He also adopted the notion of indifference from Franciscan discussions (e.g., those of Olivi), and used it to define volitional freedom. Other features of Scotus's teaching on will are: treatment of volition under efficient rather than final causality; strong emphasis on terminology of elicited and imperated acts of will, because all moral activity (*praxis*) is either immediately or mediately an action of will (*Ordinatio*, prol. 5.1; ed. Balić, 1:156). Much of later scholastic teaching on the human will fuses SCOTISM with THOMISM.

WILLIAM OF OCKHAM emphasized the essential freedom of will more than did Scotus. Ockham did not grant to the intellect any real influence on the will's activity: the human will is a wholly active power that is absolutely free [*In 1 sent.* 1.6 P-T (Lyons 1495)]. Ockham is very much interested in the Will of God, stressing the complete omnipotence of divine will [*De sacramento altaris*, ed. T. B. Birch (Burlington, Ia. 1930) 330]. Will is superior to understanding, both in man and in God (*In 1 sent.* 1.2 K).

There is considerable Ockhamist influence on the volitional theory of Francisco SUÁREZ (1548–1617), who was one of the most influential of the later schoolmen (*De anima,* 5; *Disp. meta.* 19). Final causality, for him, becomes a metaphor and volition is the work of an efficient power. The human will is completely and essentially free with the liberty of indifference (*De concursu motione et auxilio Dei* 1.8).

Modern Philosophy. In modern philosophy, dozens of different meanings have been given to will and volition. For purposes of convenience, these can be reduced to eight different views, according as will means (1) intellectual preference, (2) rational appetite, (3) the faculty of freedom, (4) dynamic power, (5) the seat of love, (6) popular conviction, (7) the source of law, and (8) basic reality. A brief explanation of each view follows.

Intellectual Preference. This view reduces volition to an almost purely cognitive function of judging. B. SPINOZA implies this when he says: "Only individual volitions exist, that is to say, this and that affirmation and this and that negation" (*Ethica* 1.49.2).

Rational Appetite. This is St. Thomas's view, as described above. G. W. LEIBNIZ is the modern thinker who is closest to this theory; he is very critical of Descartes's use of the liberty of indifference and of Spinoza's intellectualism.

Faculty of Freedom. This view is shared by many Catholic thinkers and is best represented in modern times by F. Suárez. It takes will as a power of self-determination whose every action is somewhat free. Perhaps MAINE DE BIRAN (a Catholic but not a scholastic philosopher) and later French "philosophers of the spirit" are the most prominent recent supporters of this view. Some existentialists (e.g., G. Marcel) share it.

Dynamic Power. Here will is considered as the efficient cause of activities of various sorts, either material or immaterial. Modern dynamic power theories take two forms: (1) Will power is regarded as physical energy, the capacity to move the human body (taught by Thomas Hobbes, in the 17th century, and by U.S. faculty psychologists such as Asa Burton and Jeremiah Day, in the 19th century); and (2) will power is mental energy, the capacity to generate ideas or new states of CONSCIOUSNESS [see Josiah Royce, *Conception of God* (New York 1897) 187–192].

Seat of Love. According to this theory, loving is made the key act of personality, and will expresses itself in various forms of affection. Friedrich SCHLEGEL popularized this view in German romantic philosophy. Love is regarded as the highest integration of human personality and even as the bond of all that is good in reality. Much the same notion is found in F. W. J. SCHELLING's works dealing with this subject.

Popular Conviction. This is a theory of volition as a group activity. Those with this view speak much of the "will of the people" or "general will." It was advocated by J. J. ROUSSEAU, who argued that the general will is an infallible arbiter of right and wrong. Modern democratic theory, with its reliance on popular elections, may owe something to this theory of will. Edmund BURKE strongly criticized this notion of will.

Source of Law. According to this interpretation, the most important product of willing is legislation. Immanuel KANT identified his legislative will with practical reason and saw it as the source of moral law (*see* CATEGORICAL IMPERATIVE).

Basic Reality. In this view, all existing being is of the nature of will. This makes will a metaphysical principle. Arthur SCHOPENHAUER is the most famous metaphysical voluntarist (*see* PESSIMISM).

See Also: APPETITE.

Bibliography: A. ALEXANDER, *Theories of Will in the History of Philosophy* (New York 1898). V. J. BOURKE, *Will in Western Thought* (New York 1964). R. P. SULLIVAN, *The Thomistic Concept of Natural Necessitation of the Human Will* (River Forest, Ill. 1952). G. GUSTAFSON, *The Theory of Natural Appetency in St. Thomas* (Washington 1944). G. VERBEKE, "Le Développement de la vie volitive d'après s. Thomas," *Revue philosophique de Louvain,* 56 (1958) 5–34. F. CROWE, "Complacency and Concern in the Thought of St. Thomas," *Theological Studies,* 20 (1959) 1–39, 198–230, 343–395. G. KLUBERTANZ, "The Root of Freedom in St. Thomas's Later Works," *Gregorianum* 42 (1961) 701–724. M. SCHMAUS, *Die psychologische Trinitätslehre des hl. Augustinus* (Münster i.W. 1927). O. LOTTIN, *La Théorie du libre arbitre depuis S. Anselme jusqu'à S. Thomas d'Aquin* (Louvain 1929). A. SAN CRISTÓBAL-SEBASTIÀN, *Controversias acerca de la voluntad desde 1270 a 1300* (Madrid 1958). K. MICHALSKI, "Le Problème de la volonté à Oxford et à Paris au XIVᵉ siècle," *Studia Philosophica* 2 (1937) 233–365. T. MULLANEY, *Suarez on Human Freedom* (Baltimore 1950). E. TEGEN, *Moderne Willenstheorien,* 2 v. (Uppsala 1924–28). J. DONCEEL, "The Psychology of the Will," *Mélanges Joseph Maréchal,* 2 v. (Brussels 1950) 2:223–232. J. LINDWORSKY, *The Training of the Will,* tr. A. STEINER and E. A. FITZPATRICK (Milwaukee 1955).

[V. J. BOURKE]

WILL OF GOD

The Existence of Divine Will: From Revelation. That God wills, and thus possesses a will, is evident within the Bible. Within the first creation story everything comes to be by the will of God. "Let there be light. . . . Let us make man in our image, after our likeness" (Gn 1:3–26). God wills to give the Promised Land to Abraham and to his descendants (Gn 2:13–15). The Psalmist delights to do the will of God (Ps 39/40:8), and prays that God would teach him to do his will (Ps 142/143:10). The Israelites are permitted to do things according to the will of God (Ez 7:18).

In the Gospels Jesus wills to do the will of his Father (Mt 26:39; Jn 5:30; 6:38). In the Lord's Prayer Jesus teaches his disciples to pray that they would do the will of the Father (Mt 6:10). Paul is apostle by the will of God (1 Cor 1:1, 2 Cor 1:1, Eph 1:1, Col 1:1, 2 Tim 1:1). Paul desires to visit the Romans in accordance with God's will (Rom 1:10; 15:32). The Holy Spirit allows Christians to know the will of God (Rom 8:27) and through the renewal of their minds are able to do God's will (Rom 12:2). Jesus delivered himself up for our salvation according to God's will (Gal 1:4). God wills our sanctification (1 Thes 4:3), and we are to give thanks in all circumstances for such is God's will (1 Thes 5:18). God equally wills all to be saved and to come to the knowledge of the truth (1 Tm 2:4). By doing the will of God, Christians silence the foolish (1 Pt 2:15), and it is better to suffer if such is God's will (1 Pt 3:17, 4:19). Christians must not live by the flesh but by the willl of God (1 Pt 4:2). While the world with its lusts passes away, the person who does the will of God abides forever (1 Jn 2:17).

The Existence of the Will of God: Christian Tradition. The Fathers of the Church acknowledged, in accordance with scripture, that all things are done in conformity to God's will and that human beings are morally obliged to obey the will of God. For example, Clement of Rome states that the sending of Christ and of the apostles "originate from the will of God" (*Ad Cor.*, 42.2). The Council of the Lateran (649) in defending the divinity of the three persons professes that the Father, the Son, and the Holy Spirit equally possess "the same Godhead . . . [and] will (H. Denzinger, *Enchiridion symbolorum*, ed. A. Schönmetzer, 501). Moreover, while condemning the Monothelite heresy, which held that Christ possessed only a divine will, the church professed that he possessed both a divine and a human will (*see* MONOTHELITISM) (*Enchiridion symbolorum* 487, 556). In such Church teaching we have the first official acknowledgement of the divine will. This tradition persists, and while not explicitly defined, is clearly implied in the teaching of Vatican I: "The Holy . . . Catholic Church believes and professes that there is one true and living God . . . infinite in intelligence and will and every perfection" (*Enchiridion symbolorum* 3001).

The Christian theological tradition has also emphasized that the Father, the Son and the Holy Spirit possess one divine will in conformity with their being the one God (Augustine, *De Trin* 5, 9–11; Aquinas, *Summa Theologiae* 1a, 39.3). Nonetheless, since the one God is a trinity of persons, each person, in oneness with the others, possesses the one divine will in accordance with the distinct and unique identity of each person. Thus the Father wills as Father, the Son as Son and the Holy Spirit as Holy Spirit. Thus Paul could write that Christians are inspired "by one and the same Spirit, who apportions to each one individually as he wills" (1 Cor 12:11).

The Existence of the Divine Will: From Reason. The Christian tradition has further argued that reason demands that God possesses a divine will. Aquinas taught that the divine will follows upon the divine intellect (*Summa Theologiae* 1a, 19.1; *Summa Contra Gentiles* I.72). Human beings seek and so desire to possess, through their intelligence, what is good. God, as intelligent, must also then possess will. However, because God is pure act, and as such possesses all perfections fully in act, so his will is fully in act for it possesses all good (*Summa Theologiae* 1a, 19.2). Just as God's intellect is one with his perfect existence so is his will.

Thus, the divine will differs in three ways from the human will. (1) The human will seeks the good it lacks. To this there is no divine counterpart, because God lacks nothing that is good. (2) The human will enjoys what limited good it possesses. Similarly, the divine continuously enjoys what it possesses, but this is infinite good, for the fullness of goodness in the divine essence is always actually possessed. (3) The human will, with its restless hunger for what is good which is ultimately God himself, must be "moved" by an object outside itself. The same is true of the intellect, for to understand something it must be "moved" from the capacity to know to actual knowledge. But the object of God's will is the supreme good of his own essence. Thus the divine will is not moved by anything outside itself. Rather, God's will is said to move itself. His will necessarily delights in his essence just as man's will necessarily desires happiness.

Freedom of the Divine Will. If God's will is fully actualized in accordance with his unchangeable perfect nature, is he truly free? Man's will must constantly seek things precisely as they relate, or seem to relate, to his happiness, for man's whole being desires happiness. However, God lacks nothing. Thus only God can suffice for God and so God "necessarily" wills to love himself. This is not a form of egoism, but the mere recognition that there is no greater good for God to love than himself. This doctrine can be explained in Trinitarian terms as follows. The Father completely gives himself in begetting his Son in the love of the Spirit. Thus the Father wills to glorify the Son (Jn 17). The Son completely gives himself to the Father in the same love of the Spirit. Thus the Son wills to glorify the Father (Jn 17). The Spirit completely gives himself as love to the Father and to the Son and so conforms them mutually to love, and so glorify, one another. Augustine states that "if any person in the Trinity is to be distinctively called the will of God, this name like charity fits the Holy Spirit more than the others. What else after all is charity but the will?" (*De Trin.* 15.38; see Aquinas, *Summa Theologiae* 1a, 27.3).

God's will extends beyond himself to embrace all of his creatures. Though the self-diffusive nature of God's infinite goodness is satisfied only in the communion of the Trinity (i.e., only in the infinite giving possible in a communion of infinite persons), God wills to diffuse his goodness in the creation of finite creatures, and in the case of human beings to create them so as to share ultimately in his own divine goodness. God freely creates purely out of his divine benevolent goodness and not from any necessity on his part (*Summa Theologiae* 1a, 32.1.ad3). Vatican I states: "If anyone shall say that. . .God created not by his will, free from all necessity, but by a necessity equal to that necessity whereby he love himself, let him be anathema" (*Enchiridion symbolorum* 3025).

God freely wills all things in his goodness by one single eternal act, just as he understands all things in his essence by one single eternal act. "Many are the plans in the mind of a man, but the will of the Lord abides forever (Prv 19:21). This does not mean that all acts that God wills are performed by God. God creates such that secondary causes bring about the ends he wills. For example, God wills that the gospel be preached, but such preaching is accomplished through the ministry of the Church. Or, God wills our holiness, but such is achieved through faith, repentance, prayer and the sacraments by which we receive the grace of the Holy Spirit. Thus, God often freely wills to work through the free actions of human beings.

God's Will and Evil. Because God is perfectly good and wills all that is good, it would seem that there should not be any evil. Yet evil does exist, and if God in no way willed it, then it could never arise. God willed to create human beings in his image and likeness and thus with freedom. God intended that such human freedom would be used to perform divine-like actions—love, kindness, generosity, courage. Yet, in giving freedom to human beings God allowed them to misuse their freedom. It is in this sense that he willed evil: not directly, but by creating a situation where sin and evil were possible (*Summa Theologiae* 1a, 19.9). Moreover, it must be noted that evil is the privation of some good and so can only exist in something that is good; for example, deformities exist in

bodies or in things and sin exist only in sinners. God freely created only what is good. Biblically the privation of good is primarily the effect of human sin—suffering due to sin, as well as sickness, death, and even disorders within nature. Even when human beings will to sin they do so under the guise that such sin is good. The thief steals not because stealing is evil but because possessing what is stolen is perceived as a good. Because moral evil is contrary to all that God is in his perfect goodness, love, and holiness, sinners cannot abide with God not by a free arbitrary act of God, but because sin itself effects a separation. Thus God is said to hate sin and punish sinners, not because he does not love sinners, but because sinners have freely disassociated themselves from God and so reap the punishment that such free actions effect, ultimately hell, that is, a life separated from God. God freely sanctions the punishment that sinful free acts impose. Nonetheless, God always wills what is good for human beings and ultimately wills their salvation in Jesus Christ, yet God equally wills that human beings remain free and so allows them to refuse the good he intends for them. Thus, while God's grace is always prior to and empowers every good action a human being performs, yet such grace does not overpower human freedom so as to make it void.

Bibliography: THOMAS AQUINAS, *Summa Theologiae* 1a, 19, 39; *Summa Contra Gentiles* I.72–90. B. DAVIES, *The Thought of Thomas Aquinas* (Oxford 1992). H. J. M. J. GORIS, *Free Creatures of an Eternal God* (Nijmegen 1996).

[T. C. DONLAN/T. G. WEINANDY]

WILL POWER

The WILL is a spiritual faculty whereby man freely selects something good. This freedom, while basic, is influenced in various degrees by emotions, physical health, mental states, and environment (*see* FREE WILL). Thus the expression "will power" usually designates a person's ability to do two things: (1) to make a choice when this is difficulty in view of divergent circumstances; (2) to effect externally what has been chosen, although execution may be more difficult than making the choice (*see* HUMAN ACT).

Training the Will. Since both intellect and will are faculties of individual souls, no two persons are born with the same intellectual abilities or volitional powers. In addition, physical dispositions, which usually vary during one's lifetime, can affect an individual's will power. Beyond this, each individual person, by his own responsible activity, can strengthen his will both in choosing and carrying out its choices. When he does so, he is said to acquire will power.

This is possible because man is influenced by habitual patters of activity (*see* HABIT). If his deliberate choices consistently tend toward actions that are good, he builds up within himself the moral virtues (*see* VIRTUE). These aid the will in different ways. Prudence gives a power to the will to choose deliberately and to select the best means of carrying out its choice (*see* PRUDENCE). Justice enables the will to be strong in protecting the rights of others in spite of the apparent disadvantage to oneself (*see* JUSTICE). Temperance and fortitude are personal regulators of conduct, the first enabling the will to resist attractive but only apparent goods, the second strengthening the will's resolve to surmount obstacles (*see* TEMPERANCE, VIRTUE OF; FORTITUDE, VIRTUE OF).

Related Concepts. Apathy and torpor are states opposed to the healthy and vigorous conditions of an active will. Apathy is a state of disinterest where the will is not attracted by any course of action, or if it is, cannot reach a decision except with struggle. Torpor inclines a person to avoid making choices and to follow the path of least resistance.

Will power is to be distinguished from the "will to power" of Friedrich NIETZSCHE and the "will to believe" of William JAMES. Nietzsche placed in his "superman" the vital instinct that irresistibly urges him to dominate other men as much as possible. The superman's will rejects so–called inferior men and is an evolvement of his pragmatism. Man wills to believe in a god because of the practical advantages such a belief affords him. According to this theory, the existence of a supreme being is postulated because of the psychological needs of man. As opposed to both of these concepts, will power basically means an individual's ability to fashion his own destiny, and to do this with some degree of ease.

[J. A. BURROUGHS]

WILLAERT, ADRIAN

Franco-Flemish composer who founded the "Venetian School"; b. Bruges, *c.* 1480; d. Venice, Dec. 7, 1562. After completing his musical studies in Paris with the Franco-Flemish master, Jean Mouton, he sojourned in Rome, then served as choir director to Duke Alfonso I d'Este at Ferrara (1522–25). In 1527 he was appointed choir director of St. Mark's in Venice, and he retained this important post for his remaining 35 years of life, training many illustrious composers who comprise the Venetian school. Willaert grafted northern polyphony onto the simple Italian madrigal, raising it to the level of the imitative motet; at the same time he continued to write uncomplicated native forms such as the *villanesca.*

His experiments in chromaticism were to influence such students as VICENTINO, while another pupil, ZARLINO, derived from his polyphonic achievements the most complete analysis of late 16th-century counterpoint. Willaert's collection of polychoral psalms (1550) popularized this already existent style of composition and influenced later composers such as Andreae and Giovanni GABRIELI to such a degree that the older master was even credited until recently with the invention of *chori spezzati* (scoring for two antiphonal choirs).

Bibliography: *Opera Omnia,* ed. H. ZENCK and W. GERSTENBERG. *Corpus mensurabilis musicae,* ed. American Institute of Musicology 3; Rome 1950–. A. CARAPETYAN, "The *Musica Nova* of A. Willaert," *Journal of Renaissance and Baroque Music* 1 (1946) 200–221. A. EINSTEIN, *The Italian Madrigal,* tr. A. H. KRAPPE et al., 3 v. (Princeton 1949) 1:318–339. G. REESE, *Music in the Renaissance* (rev. ed. New York 1959). *Histoire de la musique* ed. ROLAND-MANUEL, 2 v. (Paris 1960–63); v.9, 16 of *Encyclopédie de la Pléiade* v.1 *passim.* P. H. LÁNG, *Music in Western Civilization* (New York 1941). B. BUJIC, "Palestrina, Willaert, Arcadelt, and the art of imitation," *Recercare* 10 (1998) 105–131. R. FREEDMAN, "Claude Le Jeune, Adrian Willaert, and the Art of Musical Translation," in *Early Music History 13: Studies in Medieval and Early Modern Music,* ed. I. FENLON, (Cambridge 1994) 123–148. D. KÄMPER, "Willaerts *Quid non ebrietas,*" *Analecta Musicologica* 10 (1970) 91–93. G. M. LANFRANCO, "Miscellaneous Letters: Giovanni Maria Lanfranco to Adrian Willaert, 20, October 1531," in *A Correspondence of Renaissance Musicians,* ed. B. J. BLACKBURN, E. E. LOWINSKY, and C. A. MILLER (Oxford 1991) 957–971. A. SMITH, "Willaert motets and mode," *Basler Jahrbuch für Historische Musikpraxis* 16 (1992) 117–165. A. WATHEY, "The Motet Texts of Philippe de Vitry in German Humanist Manuscripts of the Fifteenth Century," in *Music in the German Renaissance: Sources, Styles, and Contexts,* ed. J. KMETZ (Cambridge 1994) 195–201.

[E. R. LERNER]

WILLAIK, ST.

Benedictine abbot; d. *c.* 725. Willaik, whose country of origin is uncertain, was a fellow worker of SWITHBERT, whom he succeeded in 713 as abbot of Kaiserswerth. His relics were rediscovered in 1626 in Swithbert's shrine at Kaiserswerth. His head, however, has been preserved in St. Lambert's in Düsseldorf since 1403.

Feast: March 7 or 8.

Bibliography: *Acta Sanctorum* (Paris 1863—) 1:148–150. R. STANTON, *A Menology of England and Wales* (London 1887). A. M. ZIMMERMANN, *Kalendarium Benedictinum: Die Heiligen und Seligen des Benediktineroderns und seiner Zweige* (Metten 1933–38) 1:274–275.

[J. L. DRUSE]

WILLEBOLD, BL.

Pilgrim; d. 1230. Nothing is known of his origin or his life, though it is suggested he might have been of the family of the counts of Calw. Miraculous happenings called attention to the death of this otherwise unknown pilgrim at Berkheim, in the Illertal (Swabia). Veneration began immediately, and his grave became a place of pilgrimage, where many sought and obtained his intercession. His relics were translated in 1273 to the parish church at Berkheim. He is the secondary patron of Berkheim and the patron of the Illertal, where his veneration continues today. Materials are now being gathered at Berkheim to determine the possibility of obtaining ecclesiastical confirmation of his cult.

Feast: July 25 or 27.

Bibliography: *Acta Sanctorum* July 2:453. A. SCHÜTTE, *Handbuch der deutschen Heiligen* (Cologne 1941) 352. A. KALBRECHT, *Der selige Willebold vole Berkheim* (9th ed. Munich 1957). J. TORSY, ed., *Lexikon der deutschen Heiligen, Seligen, Ehrwürdigen und Gottseligen* (Cologne 1959) 568.

[D. ANDREINI]

WILLEBRANDS, JOHANNES GERARDUS MARIA

Cardinal, president of the Pontifical Council for Promoting Christian Unity, archbishop of Utrecht and primate of Holland; b. Sept. 4, 1909, Bovenkarspel, Netherlands. Willebrands studied in the seminary of Warmond and was ordained a priest May 26, 1934. He earned a doctorate in philosophy at the University of St. Thomas Aquinas (Angelicum), Rome, in 1937 with a dissertation entitled ''The Illative Sense in the Thought of John Henry Newman.'' Back in Holland he taught at Warmond, becoming rector of the seminary in 1945.

In 1946 Willebrands accepted the presidency of the St. Willebrord Association, a group devoted to promoting Catholic apologetics. Through his efforts it developed into an instrument for promoting ecumenism in the Netherlands. Even more significant was his cooperation with a priest friend, Frans Thijssen, in founding the Catholic Conference for Ecumenical Questions. This unofficial group of Catholic scholars became, with the knowledge of the Dutch bishops and the Holy See, a kind of informal contact from within the Catholic Church with Orthodox, Anglican, and Protestant ecumenists and leaders. It contributed notably to the coming into being and operation of the Pontifical Council for Promoting Christian Unity.

In 1960 Pope John XXIII chose Monsignor Willebrands to be the secretary of the preparatory commission on ecumenism for the Second VATICAN COUNCIL, under the presidency of Cardinal Augustin BEA, S.J. In 1962 Willebrands visited Orthodox leaders, secretaries of world confessional families (e.g. Lutheran World Federa-

Adrian Willaert.

tion, World Alliance of Reformed Churches, etc.), and the World Council of Churches to explain the new ecumenical outreach on the part of the Catholic Church. This prepared the ground for other confessions to send observers to the council and, in the long run, led to the bilateral theological dialogues that began after the council and were to be central in the Catholic ecumenical enterprise.

Working with a number of scholars who had been in the Catholic Conference, Willebrands produced the text that was the basis for the conciliar Decree on Ecumenism, *Unitatis Redintegratio.* Willebrands also had major responsibility for the Declaration on Religious Liberty (*Dignitatis humanae*), the Declaration on the Relations of the Church to Non-Christian Religions (*Nostra Aetate*), and a substantial part of the Constitution on Divine Revelation (*Dei Verbum*).

Pope Paul VI consecrated Monsignor Willebrands titular bishop of Mauritania in 1964. Before the council ended, the preparatory commission for ecumenism was declared a permanent organ of the Roman Curia with the title of Secretariat for Promoting Christian Unity. (In 1988 it was renamed the Pontifical Council for Promoting Christian Unity.) After Cardinal Bea died in 1968 Willebrands was named president of the new dicastery and created cardinal deacon of Saints Cosmas and Damian.

Johannes Cardinal Willebrands. (©Bettmann-CORBIS)

Under his guidance the secretariat produced a Directory on Ecumenism and initiated a series of international bilateral theological dialogues with major Christian confessions (as of the year 2000 there are nine of these) as well as a cooperative relationship with the World Council of Churches, especially its Faith and Order Commission. To promote reception of the ecumenical stance of Vatican II within the Catholic Church, Willebrands encouraged the establishment of ecumenical commissions in bishops' conferences and began to have occasional meetings of their representatives in Rome. In 1974 Willebrands established within the secretariat the Commission for Religious Relations with Judaism, based on Vatican II's *Nostra Aetate 4.* He guided it carefully to focus on questions of doctrine, pastoral practice, and religious formation, avoiding complicated political questions. This approach bore visible and striking results with the visit of Pope John Paul II to the Rome synagogue in 1986 and ultimately to the more spectacular papal visit to Israel in 2000.

In 1975 Pope Paul VI asked Cardinal Willebrands to become archbishop of Utrecht and primate of Holland while remaining president of the secretariat. This meant living in Utrecht but coming to Rome at regular intervals. These visits became less frequent as he dealt with a Church whose institutions had been deconstructed by postconciliar polarization and by secularization. Using his sympathetic style and human relations skills he was able to win respect for his leadership and establish some sort of equilibrium without being able fully to recuperate the forces of the Church. It was a relief in 1983 to hand over the archdiocese to a successor whose way he had prepared. He returned to Rome at an important moment as several of the relationships and ecumenical dialogues were reaching new maturity. His collaboration with Pope John Paul II became closer and ever more fruitful. He provided leadership in such events as the 1986 Assisi World Day of Prayer for Peace and responded to the crisis in relations with the Anglican Communion and with the Orthodox Churches, as well as encouraged the ever-more promising theological developments with the Lutheran World Federation and with the Faith and Order Commission of the World Council of Churches.

When Willebrands reached the statutory age of retirement at seventy-five, John Paul asked him to continue in office; he did so until his eightieth birthday in 1989, at which time he became president emeritus of the Pontifical Council for Promoting Christian Unity and the Commission for Religious Relations with the Jews. Willem Visser't Hooft, the founding secretary of the World Council of Churches, described Cardinal Willebrands as "a man with a fine combination of vision and realism." That quality enabled him to give a stamp and direction to Catholic participation in the ecumenical movement. For the communications media, he never became the iconic figure that Cardinal Bea was. Yet Willebrands has been the architect of the current Catholic official ecumenical engagement, which has had Pope John Paul II as its immensely talented entrepreneur.

Bibliography: The Pontifical Council for Promoting Christian Unity: Information Service, nos: 1–101 (1966 to 2000) contains most major addresses, letters and articles by Cardinal Willebrands. Number 101 is devoted to him and includes biographical material, a selection of his writings and speeches and an evaluation of the present ecumenical situation. J. GROOTAERS, "Jan Cardinal Willebrands: The Recognition of Ecumenism in the Roman Catholic Church," *One in Christ* 6, no. 1 (1970): 23–44. J. WILLEBRANDS, "The Future of Ecumenism," *One in Christ* 11, no. 4 (1975): 310–323.

[B. MEEKING]

WILLEHAD OF BREMEN, ST.

Missionary bishop of Bremen; b. Northumbria, England, *c.* 735; d. Blexen, Germany, Nov. 8, 789. An Anglo-Saxon, he worked from *c.* 765 as a missionary in Frisia and from 780 in the region of the lower Weser on commission from CHARLEMAGNE. Expelled as a result of the Saxon uprising of 782, he went to Rome to report on his work and then retired into the monastery of ECH-TERNACH. After the subjection and baptism of WIDUKIND, Willehad returned to his Saxon mission area, and in 787 he was made bishop of Bremen. He is buried in the cathedral, which he consecrated shortly before his death. His vita was written after 838 in Echternach; but it was wrongly ascribed by Adam of Bremen to ANSGAR, author of the *Miracula Willehadi.*

Feast: Nov. 8.

Bibliography: *Acta Sanctorum* (Paris 1863—) 3:835–851. J. METZLER, *Lexikon für Theologie und Kirche,* ed. M. BUCHBERGER (Freiburg 1930–38) 10:917–918. C. E. CARSTENS, *Allgemeine deutsche Biographie* (Leipzig 1875–1910) 43:262–263. H. LÖWE, *Die Religion in Geschichte und Gegenwart* (Tübingen 1957–65) 6:1719. H. WIEDEMANN, *Die Sachsenbekehrung* (Münster 1932). G. NIEMEYER, ''Die Herkunft der *Vita Willehadi,*'' *Deutsches Archiv für Erforschung des Mittelalters* (Cologne-Graz 1956) 17–35. U. CHEVALIER, *Répertoire des sources historique du moyen-âge* 2:4771–72. *The Lives of the Saints,* rev. ed. H. THURSTON and D. ATTWATER (New York 1956) 4:297–298.

[L. KURRAS]

WILLIAM I, KING OF ENGLAND

Reigned 1066 to Sept. 9, 1087; the Conqueror, crowned first Norman king of England, Dec. 25, 1066; b. Falaise, probably 1028; d. Saint-Gervais, France. William, the illegitimate son of Robert II of Normandy and Herleve, became Duke of Normandy in 1035. In *c.* 1050–53 he married Matilda, daughter of Baldwin V of Flanders. William was the father of four sons, viz, Robert, Duke of Normandy; Richard; Kings WILLIAM II and HENRY I; and of six daughters. William's pre-Conquest Norman rule progressed through three main stages: his minority years of feudal disorder, ending in victory at Val-ès-Dunes in 1047; a phase of growing mastery and almost ceaseless warfare, with defeat for the French and Angevins at Mortemer in 1054 and Varaville in 1057; the years of consolidation to 1066, with Maine secured in 1063 and Brittany in 1064. Designated by EDWARD THE CONFESSOR in 1051 as heir to the English kingdom, a decision accepted by Harold Godwineson in 1064, William defeated the latter at Hastings, Oct. 14, 1066, and by five years of intermittent campaigning subjected the English kingdom to his will. The Scottish king submitted in 1072, Maine in 1073, and the disaffected earls in 1075. William's position was later weakened by the hostility of Robert, his son, and Odo of Bayeux, and by troubles in Brittany, from Scotland, and in his continental lands. A Danish threat led to ''The Salisbury Oath'' of 1086, binding the greater lords more closely to him. William died of a mortal injury received at Mantes in 1087; he was buried at Caen.

William I, King of England.

The Norman church early attained a distinguished reputation under William's guidance: a deeply penetrating monastic revival achieved its best expression at BEC; canonical reform was made effective through conciliar legislation. William was master of the Norman church, but no province reflected more closely the reforming spirit of the time, or more justly enjoyed resulting papal favor. William's irregular marriage was legalized by NICHOLAS II in 1059; his invasion of England in 1066 was supported by ALEXANDER II and Hildebrand (later GREGORY VII). The pre-Conquest English church was clearly touched by the same reforming spirit, and the Conquest coincided in time with the advance of the GREGORIAN REFORM; but, with LANFRANC at Canterbury from 1070, after the excommunicated Stigand's deposition, ecclesiastical, monastic, and canonical revival made decisive headway with crucial results for the future. William brought to England a tradition of effective secular control in church affairs: a barrier to the two-way traffic between England and the papal Curia was firmly erected, papal claims to feudal overlordship were unambiguously rejected; the INVESTITURE STRUGGLE found no expression in England in William's reign. Recognizing the merits and strength of William's policies, Gregory acted with prudence and circumspection.

William stressed his legality as Edward's successor. The legal and administrative achievements of the English kings were still further developed. But greater vitality and power of direction increased the monarchy's strength and resources; an alien feudal nobility now composed the ruling element in society; the DOMESDAY BOOK provides a striking insight into the condition of England at and after William's conquest. A vigorous, ruthless, clear-sighted, severe ruler, temperate and pious according to his fashion, William effected a point of departure in Norman and English history, and by his influence helped to shape the history of the western church.

Bibliography: Z. N. BROOKE, *The English Church and the Papacy* (Cambridge, Eng. 1931). F. M. STENTON, *Anglo-Saxon England* (2d ed. Oxford 1947). D. KNOWLES, *The Monastic Order in England, 943–1216* (2d ed. Cambridge, Eng. 1962). R. R. DARLINGTON, *The Norman Conquest* (London 1963). F. BARLOW, *The English Church 1000–1066: A Constitutional History* (Hamden, Conn. 1963). D. C. DOUGLAS, *William the Conqueror* (Berkeley, Calif. 1964). C. DUGGAN, "From the Conquest to the Death of John," in *The English Church and the Papacy in the Middle Ages,* ed. C. H. LAWRENCE (London 1965). S. KÖRNER, *The Battle of Hastings: England and Europe, 1035–1066* (Lund 1964). H. R. LOYN, *The Norman Conquest* (London 1965).

[C. DUGGAN]

WILLIAM II RUFUS, KING OF ENGLAND

Reigned from Sept. 26, 1087, to Aug. 2, 1100; b. 1056. William Rufus, as he was called, was the third son of WILLIAM I the Conqueror. It is possible, but not certain that he was raised and educated in Lanfranc's care; although he may have received some religious training, he later went in another direction. Inheriting the kingdom of England (but not Normandy) at his father's will, he thwarted a general conspiracy in 1087–88, and another in 1095. On his accession in 1087, Lanfranc forced him to promise better laws and redress of grievances, and to care for the Church. But on Lanfranc's death in 1089, Rufus began his repression and almost a systematic looting of the English Church. He left abbacies and bishoprics vacant and collected their revenues for the royal treasury, leaving the monks barely enough to live on. Indeed, he even dispersed some of the monks from the abbeys lacking abbots. Most grievous of all was his exploitation of Canterbury during its vacancy, and Rufus's refusal to appoint a new archbishop for four years. It was only in the midst of a serious illness, when he thought he was on his deathbed, that the king appointed Anselm of Bec to the archbishopric of Canterbury. After unsuccessfully trying to extort a simoniacal payment from Anselm, Rufus then attempted to bribe Pope

Urban II to hand Anselm's pallium over to the king for conferral on the archbishop—a precedent that would have spelled disaster for Canterbury's future. Anselm thwarted the king and received the pallium from the altar of Canterbury "as if from the hand of St. Peter." When William's brother, Robert Curthose, duke of Normandy, pledged the duchy to Rufus for 10,000 marks in 1096 to finance his journey on the First Crusade, Rufus had gained all the dominions of his father. When in autumn 1097 Anselm pressed the king to hold a reforming, kingdom-wide Council, and to enforce reforms within the English Church, Rufus refused, and the archbishop concluded that the king would never acquiesce in the reform of the Church. Thus, when Anselm determined to set out for Rome to consult the pope, Rufus confiscated the archbishopric and drove Anselm, penniless, into exile. Rufus was about to receive Aquitaine in pawn from Count William IX, who also wished to participate in the First Crusade, when suddenly he died in a hunting accident in the New Forest. Although there was later much talk of a conspiracy and murder, chiefly because his brother, HENRY I, galloped to Winchester and seized the treasury and the crown, it has been argued persuasively that Henry was not responsible for his brother's death. Rufus died unmarried and without issue. He received much criticism from the monastic chroniclers for his anti-religious manner and clear disrespect of and exploitation of the Church; but during his reign important administrative progress was made.

Bibliography: F. BARLOW, *William Rufus* (Berkeley 1983). R. W. SOUTHERN, *St. Anselm and his Biographer* (New York 1963). S. N. VAUGHN, *Anselm of Bec and Robert of Meulan* (Berkeley 1981). R. W. SOUTHERN, *Saint Anselm: A Portrait in a Landscape* (Cambridge 1990). C. W. HOLLISTER, *Henry I* (New Haven 2001). O. VITALIS, *The Ecclesiastical History of Orderic Vitalis,* ed. tr. M. CHIBNALL 6 v. (Oxford 1969–1980). EADMER, *Historia Novorum in Anglia,* ed. M. RULE [*Rerum Britannicarum medii aevi scriptores* 81 (London 1884)]. EADMER, *The Life of St. Anselm by Eadmer,* ed. tr. R. W. SOUTHERN (Oxford 1972). *The Letters of Saint Anselm of Canterbury,* tr. W. FRÖLICH 3 v. (Kalamazoo 1990–94)

[S. VAUGHN]

WILLIAM IV OF BAVARIA

Opponent of Lutheranism; b. Munich, Oct. 13, 1493; d. there, March 7, 1550. He was the son of Albert IV, surnamed "the Wise," and Kunigunde, the daughter of the Emperor Frederick III. When his father died in March 1508, William inherited the duchy of Bavaria. However, he was unable to prevent his brother Louis from gaining a strong voice in government in 1516. This situation was to continue throughout the greater part of William's reign until Louis died in 1545. In the best tradition of the house of Wittelsbach, William continued the anti–Hapsburg policies of his predecessors during the first half of his reign. Then in 1534 he settled his outstanding grievances with Ferdinand of Hapsburg, and strengthened that tie in 1546 with an alliance with the Emperor Charles V that bound him to the SCHMALKALDIC LEAGUE. William followed a domestic policy that was anti–Lutheran and was chiefly responsible for keeping Bavaria in union with Rome. With extensive powers given him by Pope Paul III, William was able to exercise far–reaching control over the bishops and abbots of his duchy, and to take energetic measures to suppress the reform teachings that had started to take hold in Bavaria. He invited the Jesuits to his duchy in 1542, and they soon made their headquarters for Germany at the Bavarian university of Ingolstadt.

Bibliography: S. VON RIEZLER, *Geschichte Bayerns,* 6 v. (Gotha 1878–1903). J. JANSSEN, *History of the German People at the Close of the Middle Ages,* tr. M. A. MITCHELL and A. M. CHRISTIE, 17 v. (London 1896–1925). J. LORTZ, *Die Reformation in Deutschland,* 2 v. (Freiburg 1939–40). R. BAUERREISS, *Kirchengeschichte Bayerns* (2d ed. Munich 1958–). B. HUBENSTEINER, *Bayerische Geschichte* (Munich 1955). H. HOLBORN, *A History of Modern Germany: The Reformation* (New York 1959). F. ZOEPFL, *Lexikon für Theologie und Kirche*[1] 10:892.

[J. G. GALLAHER]

WILLIAM ARNAUD, BL.

Dominican inquisitor, martyr; d. 1242. Little is known of him before 1234 when Pope Gregory IX appointed him inquisitor (*see* INQUISITION) for the dioceses of Toulouse, ALBI, Carcassonne, and Agen. He was evidently a native of Montpellier and had a reputation for canonical learning. His activity in the repression of heresy stirred up such hostility that he was banished from Toulouse, although he is also said to have effected many conversions by his ''sweetness and charity.'' On May 29, 1242, Raymond of Alfare, the bailiff of Count Raymond VII of Toulouse, pretending friendship, lured William and 11 associates to his castle at Avignonet, where he attacked and killed them. Miracles and cures reported at the time of their death and afterward gave rise to a cultus, which was confirmed by Pius IX on Oct. 6, 1866.

Feast: May 29.

Bibliography: *Monumenta Ordinis Fratrum Praedicatorum historica,* ed. B. M. REICHERT (Rome–Stuttgart–Paris 1896–) 1:231ff. *Acta Sanctorum* May 7:177–179. A. BUTLER, *The Lives of the Saints,* rev. ed. H. THURSTON and D. ATTWATER, 4 v. (New York 1956) 2:421.

[P. M. STARRS]

WILLIAM DE GAYNESBURGH

12th provincial minister of the Friars Minor in England, bishop of WORCESTER (1302–07); date of birth un-

King William II of England. (©Historical Picture Archive/ CORBIS.)

known; d. Beauvais, France, Sept. 17, 1307. He was elected provincial of the Franciscans Sept. 8, 1285, and served until *c.* 1292; he was then lector, i.e., regent master in theology, to the Franciscans at Oxford *c.* 1292 to 1294. A member of the king's council in 1295, he was from 1292 to 1300 employed by EDWARD I on various diplomatic missions of which the most important was the negotiation of the peace treaty with PHILIP IV of France, 1295 to 1298. In 1300 he was summoned by BONIFACE VIII to lecture in theology at the university of the papal Curia. Appointed to the See of Worcester by papal provision on Oct. 24, 1302, he was consecrated at Rome Nov. 25, 1302, and enthroned June 9, 1303. The king continued to use him as an envoy, and he was on a royal mission to the papal Curia when he died at Beauvais, where he was buried. J. Leland lists *Quaestiones* as William's, but neither these nor any other scholastic writings of his have been traced.

Bibliography: A. B. EMDEN, *A Biographical Register of the University of Oxford to A.D. 1500* 2:750–751. A. G. LITTLE and F.

PELSTER, *Oxford Theology and Theologians, c. A.D. 1282–1302* (Oxford 1934) 185–186. A. G. LITTLE, *Franciscan Papers, Lists, and Documents* (Manchester 1943) 193–194. *The Register of William de Geynesborough,* ed. J. W. WILLIS BUND, 2 v. (Oxford 1907–29).

[C. H. LAWRENCE]

WILLIAM DE GRENEFIELD

Archbishop of York and chancellor of England; b. possibly in Devon, date unknown; d. Cawood Castle, Yorkshire, Dec. 6, 1315. His relatives WALTER GIFFARD, Archbishop of York (1266–79), and GODFREY GIFFARD, Bishop of Worcester (1268–1302), smoothed the way for his advance in ecclesiastical and secular offices. Archbishop Giffard maintained him as a student at Oxford, where he probably began his studies in 1269, and later at Paris about 1271. By 1287 Grenefield was doctor of Roman law, and he later gained the doctorate in Canon Law and possibly studied theology. In 1297 he was ordained deacon and, later, priest. Ecclesiastical preferment easily came his way, and in 1297 he became dean of Chichester. During the 1290s he was frequently used by EDWARD I on diplomatic missions, and in 1302 the king made him his chancellor, petitioning a papal indult of nonresidence on his behalf. Two years later when the metropolitan See of YORK fell vacant, Grenefield was elected, but his consecration was delayed for two years during the interregnum before the election of CLEMENT V. Whereupon, he gave up the Great Seal, resided in the north, and devoted his considerable talents to the manifold needs of his far-flung diocese in a region of the country under hostile harassment from the Scots. With a sensitive and humane regard for the plight of the Knights TEMPLARS Grenefield oversaw the dissolution of their order. His body rests in the north transept of York Minster.

Bibliography: W. H. DIXON, *Fasti eboracenses. Lives of the Archbishops of York,* ed. J. RAINE (London 1863). T. F. TOUT, *The Dictionary of National Biography from the Earliest Times to 1900* 8:517–519. K. EDWARDS, "Bishops and Learning in the Reign of Edward II," *Church Quarterly Review* v. 138 (1944) 57–86. A. B. EMDEN, *A Biographical Register of the University of Oxford to A.D. 1500* 2:820–821.

[F. D. LOGAN]

WILLIAM DE HOTHUM

William Houghton, English Dominican theologian, archbishop of Dublin; b. probably Yorkshire; d. Dijon, France, Aug. 27, 1298. After having studied at the friary of Saint-Jacques in Paris, he taught theology at Oxford (c. 1269), acted as one of the DOMINICAN representatives in the mendicant controversy, lectured at Paris (c. 1275), became a doctor of theology, and was regent master at the University of Paris (1280). The general chapter of Vienne (1282) made him Dominican provincial of England, and he then publicly defended the Thomistic doctrine of the unity of forms (1284). When he was relieved of his office by the next chapter (Bordeaux 1287) and appointed to teach theology at Saint-Jacques, William, by then a trusted adviser of King Edward I of England and a busy royal diplomat, refused to comply; he was reproved, ineffectually, by the next chapter (Lucca 1288). Reelected provincial in 1290, he refused to accept the see of Llandaff from Pope NICHOLAS IV, but did accept the archbishopric of Dublin, which Edward had requested for him. He was consecrated at Ghent by Anthony BEK, bishop of Durham, in August or September 1297. Acting as emissary between the quarreling Edward and King Philip IV of France, he drew up a two-year treaty that he took to Rome for Pope BONIFACE VIII to arbitrate. He died on the way home, and his body, at Edward's command, was carried to Blackfriar's Church, London, for burial. Attributed to him are *Commentarii in IV sententiarum libros, De immediata visione Dei tractatus, De unitate formarum tractatus, Lectuare scholasticae,* and a speech defending the English king's rights. *In tres libros de anima* and *Questiones quodlibetales* also are possibly his.

Bibliography: M. H. MACINERNY, *A History of the Irish Dominicans* (Dublin 1916), only v.1 pub. A. G. LITTLE and F. PELSTER, *Oxford Theology and Theologians, c. A.D. 1282–1302* (Oxford 1934) 83. A. B. EMDEN, *A Biographical Register of the University of Oxford to A.D. 1500* (Oxford 1957–59) 2:970.

[B. CAVANAUGH]

WILLIAM DE LA MARE

Franciscan theologian and biblical scholar; b. England (place and date unknown); d. c. 1290. "He was certainly an Englishman, but until more is known of him, it is not safe to claim him as an Oxonian" [A. G. Little, *Archivum Franciscanum historicum* 19 (1926) 865]. De La Mare studied at Paris and became master of theology in 1274 or 1275. A fervent follower of St. BONAVENTURE, he commented on his master's commentary on the *Sentences.* To his teaching period belong his *Quaestiones disputatae,* and probably one *Quodlibet* (incomplete), that show the trend of his thought and foreshadow the conflict between Aristotelian psychology and the old school. His discourse is generally calm and reserved, yet a certain impatience and aggressiveness are noticeable in the crucial points of controversy.

On his return to England he preached at Lincoln, and, to prevent the influence of THOMISM among members of his order, wrote *Correctorium Fratris Thomae,* (1278) which gave rise to a number of Dominican replies, or *CORRECTORIA.* William meticulously examined, criticized, and censured 118 theses drawn from various writings of St. THOMAS AQUINAS that were, in his opinion, theologically unsound because they were in opposition to Holy Scripture and the Fathers, particularly St. AUGUSTINE, and were included, or implied, in the lists of reproved errors. This *Correctorium* received a quasiofficial approval in the General Chapter of Strasbourg (1282) when the Franciscan Minister General Bonagratia forbade the study of Aquinas's *Summa theologiae,* allowing it only to the most learned lectors if accompanied by William's *Declarationes.* Later, before 1284, William revised his first edition, adding new theses, supplementing the evidence, and improving the whole work. The so-called *Ur-Correctorium,* discovered and edited by F. Pelster (*Declarationes dde variis sententiis S. Thoma Aquinatis,* Münster 1956), is not William's first edition of the *Correctorium,* as Pelster believed [*Gregorianum* 28 (1947) 220–235], but rather a later anonymous compilation of 60 propositions extracted from William's revised recension [see D. A. Callus, *Blackfriars* 40 (1959) 39–41].

William's contribution to biblical studies is of greater importance. His *Correctio textus Bibliae* (*Correct.* D) was regarded by H. Denifle as the most learned and scientific of the biblical *Correctoria.* Moreover, he compiled an aid to students, *De Hebraeis et Graecis vocabulis glossarum Bibliae,* instructing them in Hebrew and Greek grammar, and explaining Hebrew and Greek words mentioned in the biblical glosses. These two works mark him as one of the great 13th-century biblical scholars.

Bibliography: F. X. PUTALLAZ, "Measures Prises par l'Ordre de Freres Mineurs Guillame de la Mare et Jean Peckham," in *Figures Franciscaines: De Bonaventure a Duns Scot* (Paris 1997) 37–50, bibliography. M. HOENEN, "The Literary Reception of Thomas Aquinas' view on the Probability of the Eternity of the World in De La Mare's Correctorium (1278–9) and the Correctoria Corruporii," in *Eternity of the World* (Leiden 1990) 39–68. L. J. ELDERS, *Die Metaphysik Des Thomas von Aquin in Historischer Perspektive* (Salzburg 1985) 197–213.

[D. A. CALLUS]

WILLIAM DE MELTON

Archbishop of York and treasurer of England; b. Melton, near Hull, in Yorkshire, date unknown; d. April 5, 1340. Probably because of the influence of Anthony Bek, Bishop of Durham, he came as a boy of humble parentage to the service of Edward Carnarvon, Prince of Wales, who shaped his political and ecclesiastical ca-

reers. After ordination Melton began to receive ecclesiastical preferment by 1299. When Edward came to the throne in 1307, Melton was appointed keeper of his privy seal; from 1314 to 1316 he was keeper of the wardrobe. Upon the death of Archbishop Grenefield, Edward II secured Melton's election to York in 1316, although papal provision was delayed until 1317 by a protracted interregnum. Melton supported the "Middle party" from 1318 to 1320 and held the treasurership of the realm from 1325 to 1326 and again in 1330. The northern barons and bishops rallied around him against the Scottish menace, although his forces were defeated at Myton–on–Swale in 1319. Melton retained his loyalty to Edward II and refused to attend the coronation of EDWARD III (1327) but officiated at his marriage the following year. In 1330 he was acquitted of cooperation in the abortive intrigues of the Earl of Kent. One of York's greatest pastors, Melton earned a contemporary reputation as a man of prayer and pastoral zeal. He used the financial resources at his disposal to grant gifts and loans on a wide scale. His body lies in the north aisle of York Minster.

Bibliography: W. H. DIXON, *Fasti eboracenses. Lives of the Archbishops of York,* ed. J. RAINE (London 1863). C. L. KINGSFORD, *The Dictionary of National Biography from the Earliest Times to 1900* 13:227–229, L. H. BUTLER, "Archbishop Melton, his Neighbours and his Kinsmen, 1317–1340," *The Journal of Ecclesiastical History* 2 (1951) 54–68.

[F. D. LOGAN]

WILLIAM DE MONTIBUS

Theologian and chancellor of Lincoln; d. MELROSE Abbey, 1213. During his lifetime he made the schools at Lincoln the most famous in England after Oxford, but he did not establish a lasting center of studies there. Between 1170 and 1180 he studied and taught in Paris, where GIRALDUS CAMBRENSIS and ALEXANDER NECKHAM were among those who attended his lectures on the Mont SAINTE-GENEVIÈVE. Through the influence of Bp. HUGH OF LINCOLN, he became canon and prebendary of the See of LINCOLN between 1186 and 1189, and was chancellor there from *c.* 1191 till his death. His lectures drew large numbers of students to Lincoln. He was not so much an original thinker as an able popularizer who simplified theological learning and provided practical manuals for the instruction of the less-educated parochial clergy. His influence was strongest in the East Midlands of England. Some of his sermons and manuals as well as a work on number symbolism, the *Arithmologia* or *Numerale,* survive in manuscript, but many works ascribed to him have not been positively identified.

Bibliography: G. LACOMBE and B. SMALLEY, "Lombard's Commentary on Isaiah and Other Fragments," *The New Scholasti-*

cism 5 (1931) 123–162, esp. 141–142, 148–150. R. W. HUNT, "English Learning in the Late Twelfth Century," *Transactions of the Royal Historical Society,* 4th ser. 19 (1936) 19–35, esp. 21–22. J. C. RUSSELL, *Dictionary of Writers of Thirteenth Century England* (New York 1936) 196–197. K. EDWARDS, *The English Secular Cathedrals in the Middle Ages* (Manchester, Eng. 1949) 189. A. B. EMDEN, *A Biographical Register of the University of Oxford to A.D. 1500* 12:1298–99.

[M. M. CHIBNALL]

WILLIAM FIRMATUS, ST.

Nobleman, priest, hermit, and possibly bishop; b. Tours; d. Mantilly, Normandy, April 24, *c.* 1095. He was educated at Tours, became a canon there, and acquired fame and wealth as a virtuous scholar, soldier, and physician. He then gave up all his possessions and withdrew to the wilderness with his widowed mother. After her death, he lived in several places in France and visited the Holy Land. Shortly after his death, his body was moved from Mantilly to the church of SAINT-EVROULT-D'OUCHE in nearby Mortain. Among the miracles credited to him was the freeing from prison of Count BALDWIN of Boulogne, later king of Jerusalem. William's life was written by Stephen of Fougères (d. 1178), bishop of Rennes [*Acta Sanctorum* (Paris 1863—) 3:334–342].

Feast: April 24.

Bibliography: A. BUTLER, *The Lives of the Saints*, rev. ed. H. THURSTON and D. ATTWATER (New York 1956) 2:158–159. G. MORIN, "Un Traité inédit de Guillaume Firmat sur l'amour du cloître et les saintes lectures," *Revue Bénédictine* 31 (Maredsous 1914–19) 244–249. J. LECLERCQ, "L'Exhortation de Guillaume Firmat," *Analecta Monastica* ser. 2 [*Studia anselmiana*, 31 (Rome 1953) 28–44].

[J. C. MOORE]

WILLIAM FITZHERBERT, ST.

Archbishop of York; d. York, June 8, 1154. His disputed election to the archbishopric was a *cause célèbre* of 12th-century ecclesiastical politics. William, the son of Herbert of Winchester and Emma, an illegitimate half sister of King Stephen of England, was treasurer of York Cathedral before 1114. Early in 1142 he was elected to the archbishopric as Stephen's candidate. But his election aroused violent opposition from the Yorkshire CISTERCIANS, who secured a powerful ally during their numerous appeals to Rome in BERNARD, Cistercian abbot of Clairvaux. None of the charges against Fitzherbert, except perhaps that of intrusion into the see, were convincing. He was consecrated in 1143, but deposed in 1147 through Bernard's influence with the Cistercian pope, EU-

GENE III, and the cardinals who favored the new monastic orders. Bernard referred to William (now his fellow saint) as "rotten from the soles of his feet to the crown of his head." More recently, Fitzherbert has been described as "amiable and generous, though unused to exertion of any kind" (Knowles). After the death of the Cistercian archbishop, HENRY MURDAC, who replaced him, Fitzherbert returned to York (May 1154), but he died a month later—of poison, it was suspected. He was canonized in 1226 through the memory of his patient sufferings, the miracles reported at his tomb, and the desire of the canons of YORK to rival RIPON as a center of pilgrimage.

Feast: June 8.

Bibliography: JOHN OF HEXHAM'S continuation of *Historia regum*, v.2 of *Symeonis monachi opera omnia*, ed. T. ARNOLD, 2 v. [*Rerum Britannicarum medii aevi scriptores*, 75 (London 1882–85) 306–332]. Two early sources now considered untrustworthy are *Life . . .* and *Miracles of St. William* in *The Historians of the Church of York*, ed. J. RAINE, 3 v. [*Rerum Britannicarum medii aevi scriptores* 71 (London 1879–94) 2:270–291, 531–543]. T. F. TOUT, *The Dictionary of National Biography From the Earliest Times to 1900* (London 1938) 7:173–176. R. L. POOLE, "The Appointment and Deprivation of St. W., Archbishop of York," *English Historical Review* 45 (London 1930) 273–281. D. KNOWLES, "The Case of St. W. of York," *Cambridge Historical Journal* 5 (Cambridge, Eng. 1935–37) 162–177, bibliog. 212–214. C. H. TALBOT, "New Documents in the Case of Saint W. of York," *ibid.* 10 (1950–52) 1–15. W. G. WHEELER, *Saint William of York* (London 1976). C. WILSON, *The shrines of St. William of York* (York 1977).

[H. MAYR-HARTING]

WILLIAM LA ZOUCHE

Archbishop of York; d. Cawood, Yorkshire, England, July 19, 1352. He was probably son of the first Baron La Zouche of Harringworth, Northamptonshire. By 1330 he had taken orders, and by 1335 had obtained, possibly at Oxford, the degrees of master of arts and bachelor in Canon Law. A king's clerk as early as 1328, La Zouche became keeper of the wardrobe in 1329, controller of the wardrobe in 1334, keeper of the privy seal in 1335, and treasurer of England in 1337. Ecclesiastical preferment kept pace with his advance in the royal service, leading to the deanship of York in 1335. His election to the See of YORK in 1340 ran counter to the wishes of Edward III, who favored William Kilsby, then keeper of his privy seal. A personal journey by La Zouche to AVIGNON, marked by his abduction and ransom at Geneva, gained for him papal confirmation; he was consecrated by CLEMENT VI at Avignon in 1342. Henceforth, his attention was centered almost wholly on problems facing the north of England, in particular the shortage of clergy following the plague, and the continuing menace of the Scots. La Zouche, in fact, commanded one of the three victorious English divisions at Neville's Cross in 1346. His resistance to a papal appointment to the deanship of York led to his excommunication in 1349. Otherwise, his was a comparatively quiet tenure of office, free from internal discord. He is buried in York Minster before St. Edward's altar.

Bibliography: W. H. DIXON, *Fasti eboracenses. Lives of the Archbishops of York,* ed. J. RAINE (London 1863). T. F. TOUT, *The Dictionary of National Biography from the Earliest Times to 1900* 21:1335–38. J. R. L. HIGHFIELD, "The English Hierarchy in the Reign of Edward III," *Transactions of the Royal Historical Society,* 5th ser., 6 (1956) 115–138. A. B. EMDEN, *A Biographical Register of the University of Oxford to A.D. 1500* 2:1115–16.

[F. D. LOGAN]

WILLIAM OF AEBELHOLT, ST.

Danish abbot; b. Paris, *c.* 1127; d. Aebelholt, Denmark, April 6, 1203. He was born of a noble family and was educated in France, becoming a Canon Regular at SAINTE-GENEVIÈVE-DE-PARIS. He was called to Denmark by ABSALON OF LUND, at that time bishop of Roskilde, to reform the house of canons on Eskilsø. Later, as first abbot of Aebelholt (founded 1175), he had great influence as churchman, writer, and teacher, and was an important intermediary between French and Scandinavian culture. His political activities in connection with the unsuccessful marriage between King PHILIP II AUGUSTUS and Ingeborg, a Danish princess, were a complete failure. His sanctity was revealed by numerous miracles shortly after his death, and he was canonized Jan. 21, 1224. His body was placed in the newly built church in Aebelholt in 1238.

Feast: April 6; June 16 (translation).

Bibliography: *Vitae sanctorum Danorum,* ed. M. C. GERTZ (Copenhagen 1908–12) 285–386. H. OLRIK, *Abbed Vilheim af Aebelholt* (Copenhagen 1912). *Dansk biografisk leksikon* 25:592–594.

[H. BEKKER-NIELSEN]

WILLIAM OF ALNWICK

Franciscan theologian, philosopher and bishop; b. Alnwick, Northumbria; d. Avignon, March 1333. William was the 42nd master of the Franciscan house at Oxford, (*c.* 1316); previously he had been at Paris as well as Oxford, and had studied under DUNS SCOTUS. The extent to which he collaborated with Scotus in preparing the latter's *Ordinatio* is still to be determined. Following the years at Paris and Oxford, he taught at Montpellier, Bologna, and Naples. In 1322, he participated in the Franciscan general chapter of Perugia and signed a document,

De paupertate Christi, against Pope JOHN XXII (*see* POVERTY CONTROVERSY). In the following year the bishops of Bologna and Ferrara were ordered by the pope to proceed against "William the Englishman" as a result of this. This perhaps necessitated his departure to Naples, where he became a friend of Robert of Sicily. Sometime shortly before July 31, 1330, he was made bishop of Giovinazzo. Nothing survives of his episcopate with the exception of a single sermon.

William seems to have produced three redactions (one incomplete) on the first book of the *Sentences* and two on the second; the fourth is incomplete in the one copy extant (Assisi cod. 172). In addition, he has left innumerable *Quaestiones,* some of which are important for the interpretation of Duns Scotus and other contemporary thinkers. At least one manuscript (Vat. lat. 876, fol. 310va), credits him with the so-called *Additiones magnae* to the first two books of Duns Scotus' commentary on the *Sentences.*

In his writings William shows himself familiar with the outstanding doctors of his day as with those of the past. Above all, it is Scotus who is both master and model for William and often the object of severe criticism. Thus he criticizes, abandons or modifies positions that were considered fundamental to SCOTISM, e.g., the formal distinction between the divine essence and perfections, the univocity of being, *haecceitas,* and Scotus' stand on the immortality of the soul (*see* IMMORTALITY). William's *De esse intelligibili* (*c.* 1316) investigates the degree of being an idea possesses in itself as a distinct object of divine knowledge. In his later *Determinations* composed at Bologna, several questions reflect the presence of Latin AVERROISM in that university; others show a growing interest in problems of physics. William of Alnwick was opposed by WILLIAM OF OCKHAM, PETER THOMAE, and perhaps by WALTER OF CHATTON.

Bibliography: É. H. GILSON, *History of Christian Philosophy in the Middle Ages* (New York 1955), 768. T. KÄPPELI, "Predigten am Päpstlichen Hof von Avignon," *Archivum Fratrum Praedicatorum* 19 (1949) 388–393. A. MAIER, "Wilhelm von Alnwicks Bologneser Quaestiones gegen den Averroismus," *Gregorianum* 30 (1949) 265–308; "Das Problem des Kontinuums in der Philosophie des 13. und 14. Jahrhunderts," *Antonianum* 20 (1945) 331–368. T. NOONE, "La Distinction Formelle dans l'Ecole Scotiste," *Revue des Siences Philosophiques et Theologiques* 83 (Ja 1999), 53–72. A. WOLTER, "Alnwick on Scotus and Divine Occurrence," in *Greek and Medieval Studies in Honor of Leo Sweeney, SJ.* (New York 1995), 255–283. J. M. M. H. THIJSSEN, "The Response to Thomas Aquinas in the Early Fourteenth Century: Eternity and Infinity in the Works of Henry of Harclay, Thomas of Wilton and William of Alnwick, OFM," in *The Eternity of the World,* J. B. M. WISSINK, ed. (Leiden and New York 1990), bibliography.

[I. C. BRADY]

WILLIAM OF AQUITAINE, ST.

Count of Toulouse, founder of Gellone; b. *c.* 755; d. Gellone Abbey, May 28, 812. He was the son of Count Thierry and his wife, Aldana, kinswoman of CHARLEMAGNE. In 790 Charlemagne appointed William the count of Toulouse and the protector of his son, Louis the Pious, king of Aquitaine. William campaigned against the Moors in Spain, and in 803 captured Barcelona from them. In 804 he founded a monastery at Gellone, which he placed under the authority of his friend, BENEDICT OF ANIANE. William himself was professed at Gellone in 806 and later died there. He was canonized by Pope Alexander II in 1066. His relics were at Saint-Sernin, Toulouse, and at Gellone (later known as SAINT-GUILHEM-DU-DÉSERT). In several *chansons de geste* he appears as William *au court-nez*, William Firebrace, and William of Orange. The chief biographical material on William is an 11th-century addition to *Ardonis vita Benedicti abbatis Anianensis et Indensis* [*Monumenta Germaniae Historica: Scriptores* (Berlin 1826—) 15:211–213; *Acta Sanctorum* (Paris 1863—) 6:811–820].

Feast: May 28.

Bibliography: L. CLARUS, *Herzog Wilhelm von Aquitanien* (Münster 1865). J. CALMETTE, "La Famille de saint Guilhem," *Annales du Midi* 18 (1906) 145–165. P. A. BECKER, *Die altfranzösische Wilhelmsage* (Halle 1896). G. MORIN, "L'Écrivain carolingien Hemmon et sa collection d'extraits des pères pour Saint Guillaume de Gellone," *Revue Charlemagne* 2 (1912) 116–126. "Wilhelm v. Aquitanien," *Lexikon für Theologie und Kirche*, ed. J. HOFER and K. RAHNER, v.10 (Freiburg 1957–65). F. SUARD, *Guillaume d'Orange: étude du roman en prose* (Paris 1979). *Guillaume d'Orange and the chanson de geste*, eds. W. VAN EMDEN and P. E. BENNETT (Reading 1984). B. GUIDOT, *Recherches sur la chanson de geste au XIIIe siècle, d'après certaines oeuvres du cycle de Guillaume d'Orange* (Aix-en-Provence 1986).

[B. HAMILTON]

WILLIAM OF AUVERGNE (OF PARIS)

Lat. Guilielmus Arvernus or Alvernus; b. Aurillac (Cantal), shortly before 1190; d. Paris, March 30, 1249. He became master of theology in 1223 and professor in 1225. In 1228 he was named bishop of Paris; Nicholas Cantor had already been named, but William objected so strongly against Nicholas that he was rejected and William named bishop in his place. Twice, in 1229 and 1237, Pope Gregory IX intervened to prevent William's undue meddling in affairs of the University of Paris. William began his monumental work, the *Magisterium divinale, c.* 1223; it is composed of seven main parts: (1) *De Trinitate* or *De primo principio*, (2) *Cur Deus homo*, (3) *De sacramentis in specie et in genere*, (4) *De fide et legibus*, (5) *De meritis et retributionibus*, (6) *De universo*, and (7) *De anima*. In addition to the *Magisterium divinale*, he wrote 20 other treatises, of which *De Immortalitate animae*, *De rhetorica divina*, and the *De bono et malo* are the most important. Many of these treatises are still unedited. Although William wrote many sermons, those found in the printed editions of the works of William of Auvergne belong rather to the Dominican William Perrauld.

The structure of William's thought is consistent. He begins in the *De Trinitate* to elaborate a doctrine of being that is the core of his system and has consequences for his teaching on truth, knowledge, and good. Only God is truly being and therefore only He is truly good and really true. The main sources of William's teachings are St. AUGUSTINE, BOETHIUS, the School of Chartres, and AVICENNA. Although William mentions Plato and Aristotle often and uses Avicenna, he criticizes them sharply, especially when their teaching is opposed to Christian doctrine on such topics as the divine liberty, providence, and the soul. William's influence on later writers can be seen in Augustinian EXEMPLARISM and in a doctrine of BEING that St. THOMAS AQUINAS found it necessary to combat energetically.

See Also: AUGUSTINIANISM; SCHOLASTICISM, 1.

Bibliography: *Opera omnia*, 2 v. (Paris 1674; repr. Frankfurt a. M. 1963). J. R. O'DONNELL, "Tractatus magistri Guillelmi Alvernensis *De bono et malo*," *Mediaeval Studies* (1946) 245–299; 16 (1954) 219–271. A. LANDGRAF, "Der Traktat *De errore Pelagii* . . .," *Speculum* 5 (1930) 168–180. G. BÜLOW, "De immortalitate animae," *Beiträge zur Geschichte der Philosophie und Theologie des Mittelalters* 2.3 (1897), app. É. H. GILSON *History of Christian Philosophy in the Middle Ages* (New York 1955) 250–258, 658–660. A. FOREST, "Guillaume d'Auvergne, critique d'Aristote," *Études médiévales offertes à m. le doyen A. Fliche* (Montpellier 1954). P. ANCIAUX, "Le Sacrement de Pénitence chez Guillaume d'Auvergne," *Ephemerides theologicae Lovanienses* 24 (1948) 98–118. P. GLORIEUX, "Le *Tractatus novus de poenitentia* de Guillaume d'Auvergne," *Miscellanea moralia A. Janssen* (Louvain 1948) 551–565. K. ZIESCHÉ, "Die Sakramentenlehre des Wilhelms von Auvergne," *Weidenauer Studien* 4 (1911) 149–226. J. LINGENHEIM, *L'Art de prier de Guillaume d'Auvergne* (Lyon 1934). T. M. CHARLAND, *Artes praedicandi* (Ottawa 1936) 39–42.

[J. R. O'DONNELL]

WILLIAM OF AUXERRE

Scholastic theologian; b. Auxerre (Lat. *Altissiodorensis*), *c.* 1150; d. Rome, Nov. 3, 1231. By 1189 he was renowned in Paris as a master in theology. Some believe that he was a disciple of RICHARD OF SAINT–VICTOR. During the pontificate of HONORIUS III (1216–27), he was archdeacon of Beauvais and proctor of the University of

Paris at the Roman Curia (*see* PARIS, UNIVERSITY OF). In February 1230 Blanche of Castile sent him as royal envoy to Pope GREGORY IX, who retained him as advisor concerning a serious dissension between the University of Paris and the citizens. On April 23, 1231, Gregory appointed him to a committee of three to correct the works of ARISTOTLE, and on May 6 he urged the king of France to restore William to his teaching position at the university so that he and Godfrey of Poitiers might reorganize the studies. William fell ill and died before he could leave Rome to collaborate in the correction of Aristotle's works.

His fame rests largely on the *Summa aurea,* written between 1215 and 1220 and published many times (Paris, n.d.; 1500; 1518; Venice 1591). Inspired by the *Sentences* of PETER LOMBARD, it discusses many problems neglected by the Lombard and passes over others. It is divided into four books: the One and Triune God (bk. 1); creation, angels, and man (bk. 2); Christ and the virtues (bk. 3); Sacraments and the four last things (bk. 4). The *Summa aurea* had extraordinary influence on contemporary authors, such as ALEXANDER OF HALES and HUGH OF SAINT–CHER, and on later scholastics, such as St. ALBERT THE GREAT, St. THOMAS AQUINAS, and St. BONAVENTURE. He wrote also a *Summa de officiis ecclesiasticis,* dealing with the Divine Office, Mass, temporal and sanctoral cycle, and liturgical vestments, that influenced the *Rationale divinorum officiorum* of William DURANTI THE ELDER.

Preceding as he did the Aristotelian revival, William was largely influenced by St. AUGUSTINE, St. ANSELM OF CANTERBURY, Richard and HUGH OF SAINT–VICTOR, and AVICENNA. He is considered the first medieval theologian to develop a systematic treatise on free will, the virtues, and the natural law.

Bibliography: J. RIBAILLIER, ed., *Magistri Guillelmi Altissiodorensis Summa aurea,* 7 vols. (Paris 1980–1987). É. H. GILSON, *History of Christian Philosophy in the Middle Ages* (New York 1955) 656–657. P. GLORIEUX, *Répertoire des maîtres en théologie de Paris au XIIIe siècle* (Paris 1933–34); v. 17–18 of *Bibliothèque Thomiste* (Le Saulchoir 1921–) 1:293–294. C. OTTAVIANO, *Guglielmo d'Auxerre . . . .: La vita, le opere, il pensiero* (Rome 1929). R. M. MARTINEAU, "Le Plan de la Summa aurea de Guillaume d'Auxerre," *Études et recherches d'Ottawa* 1 (1937) 79–114. J. VANWIJNSBERGHE, "De biechtleer van Willem van Auxerre in het licht der vroegscholastiek," *Studia catholica* 27 (1952) 289–308. G. BONAFEDE, *Enciclopedia filosofica,* 4 v. (Venice–Rome 1957) 2:934–935.

[G. GÁL]

WILLIAM OF BOURGES, ST.

Archbishop of Bourges; b. Arthel, France, 1150; d. Bourges, Jan. 10, 1209. William de Donjeon, member of a noble family of Nevers, became a canon of Soissons and then of Paris. He soon retired into the monastery of GRANDMONT, which he subsequently left as a result of serious disagreements between the choir monks and lay brothers. He entered the CISTERCIANS at PONTIGNY in 1167. In 1184 he became abbot of Fontaine Saint-Jean, then of Châlis in 1187. On Nov. 23, 1200, he was named archbishop of Bourges, but he accepted only on the insistence of his religious superiors. In his bishopric he lived with strictest regularity and austerity. He incurred the wrath of PHILIP II AUGUSTUS for carrying out the interdict of Pope INNOCENT III against Philip for having divorced Queen Ingeburg. William died while preparing to participate in a crusade against the ALBIGENSES and was buried in his cathedral. His body was enshrined in 1217, and many miracles have been attributed to his intercession. Pope HONORIUS III canonized him on May 17, 1218.

Feast: Jan. 10.

Bibliography: "Wilhelm v. Bourges," *Lexikon für Theologie und Kirche,* ed. J. HOFER and K. RAHNER, v.10 (Freiburg 1957–65). *Acta Sanctorum* (Paris 1863—) 1:627–639. *Histoire littéraire de la France (Paris),* ed. Académie des Inscriptions et Belles-Lettres (1814–1941) 21:575–576. M. B. BRARD, *Catholicisme. Hier, aujourd'hui et demain,* ed. G. JACQUEMET (Paris 1947—) 5:377. *Gallia Christiana* (Paris 1715–85) 2:60–63. *Analecta Bollandiana* (Brussels 1882—) 3:271–361. A. BUTLER, *The Lives of the Saints,* rev. ed. H. THURSTON and D. ATTWATER (New York 1956) 1:65–66.

[F. D. LAZENBY]

WILLIAM OF CHAMPEAUX

Theologian, philosopher, bishop; b. Champeaux, near Melun, France, *c.* 1070; d. Châlons-sur-Marne, 1122. William, a disciple of ANSELM OF LAON and possibly of MANEGOLD OF LAUTENBACH in Paris and of ROSCELIN in Compiègne, lectured for many years on dialectics and theology in the cathedral school of Paris. About 1100 he was archdeacon of Paris and head of the renowned school. Among his pupils was Peter ABELARD, who strongly objected to his doctrine of UNIVERSALS and forced him to change his opinion. Abandoning teaching in 1108, he retired to the hermitage of Saint-Victor outside the walls of Paris. Reorganizing the hermitage according to the new rule of Canons Regular of St. Augustine, he opened a school of theology at the abbey and again had Abelard as a bothersome pupil. In principle, the Canons Regular of Saint-Victor tried to bridge the chasm that had developed between the schoolmen (*scholares*) and the religious (*claustrales*). Under the inspiration of William, the Abbey of Saint-Victor flourished during the first half of the 12th century. In 1113 he was consecrated bishop of Châlons-sur-Marne and immediately began a reform of the clergy. His archdeacons and canons were obliged to accept the common life, to attend Divine Office, and to frequent his theology lectures in the cathedral school. A close friend of the Cistercians, he ordained St. BERNARD OF CLAIRVAUX to the priesthood toward the end of 1115. As bishop he fought for clerical celibacy and ecclesiastical investiture of the clergy as well as for religious reform.

Only a few of William's writings are extant. Among the authentic writings are the fragmentary theological *Sententiae vel quaestiones* 47, published by G. Lefèvre (Lille 1898); *De essentia et substantia Dei et de tribus eius personis,* published by V. Cousin (Paris 1865); and the fragment *De sacramento altaris* (*Patrologia Latina,* ed. J. P. Migne [Paris 1878–90] 163:1039–40), where mention is made of Communion under two species. The authenticity of *De origine animae* (*Patrologia Latina* 163:1043–44) and *Dialogus de fide catholica* (*Patrologia Latina* 163:1045–72) is commonly doubted.

Although none of his logical works are extant, he was for a long time known almost exclusively as a logician. His views on universals were reported by Abelard (*Historia calamitatum* 2). William, rejecting Roscelin's view restricting universality to vocal sounds, originally taught an extreme realism. He maintained that the identical essential nature is wholly present in each individual of the species. Thus, individuals within a species differ from one another not substantially, but by variation of accidents, while specific natures are numerically one and identical in all individuals. Against this "theory of identity," which was not original with William, Abelard raised serious objections, pointing out the absurd consequences that would follow from it. Thus, if humanity is substantially and totally present in each man, then it is wholly in Socrates, who is in Rome, and wholly in Plato, who is in Athens. Accordingly, Socrates would have to be Plato and be present simultaneously in two places. Furthermore, Abelard added, this view leads to pantheism, since, in the last analysis, all substances would be identical with the divine substance. The force of Abelard's criticism induced William to change this view for a "theory of indifference," maintaining that individuals of a species are not the same essentially (*essentialiter*), but indifferently (*indifferenter*). In this view, the essential nature is indifferently common to many individuals so that no one individual exhausts the possibility of other individuals of the "same" species. Abelard did not consider this view to be a substantial departure from the original realism espoused by William.

In theology William followed the teaching of his master, Anselm of Laon. His *Sententiae,* inspired by the school of Laon, is among the earliest attempts to systematize theological doctrine based on the Fathers of the Church. The apparent lack of originality in William's writing makes it difficult to distinguish his work from that of the Laon writers.

Bibliography: G. LEFÈVRE, *Les Variations de Guillaume de Champeaux et la question des universaux* (Lille 1898). É. H. GILSON, *History of Christian Philosophy in the Middle Ages* (New York 1955) 154–155, 626. F. C. COPLESTON, *History of Philosophy* (Westminster, Md. 1946–1963) 2:146–148. P. DELHAYE, *Catholicisme. Hier, aujourd'hui et demain* (Paris 1947–) 5:391–393. S. VANNI-ROVIGHI, *Enciclopedia filosofica* (Venice-Rome 1957) 2:935–936.

[B. M. BONANSEA]

WILLIAM OF CONCHES

Teacher, philosopher, theologian, natural scientist, and grammarian of Chartres; b. Normandy, *c.* 1090; d. *c.* 1155. William was a leading figure of what has come to be known as the 12th-century renaissance.

Life. From the scant biographical information, we ascertain that William was born in Conches, Normandy "in a country of mutton-heads under the dense sky of Normandy" (*Dragmaticon VI.i.i.*). John of Salisbury, one of his students and later bishop of Chartres, tells us that William studied under Master Bernard of Chartres most probably at the Cathedral school at Chartres, before taking up his own teaching duties around 1125, probably at Chartres and at Paris. There remains some scholarly disagreement as to where he taught. He was renowned as a teacher of grammar, although his writings reveal that he was equally adept in the natural sciences, philosophy, and, to a lesser extent, medicine. At some point in the ensuing 20 years William left teaching, at least in part because of a conflict with the Cornificians—a group of education reformists who sought to decrease the scope of those subjects required by the schools and the length of time spent studying them—and because of bitter attacks by William of St. Thierry, who denounced the Chartrian as a heretic (*De erroribus Guilielmi de Conchis ad sactum Bernardum,* ed. Leclercq, *Revue Bénédictine* LXXXIX [1969] 375–91). William found employment, and perhaps protection, in his native Normandy at the court of Geoffrey Plantagenet, the duke of Normandy and count of Anjou. Here, from around 1144–1151, William was entrusted, at least in part, with the education of the duke's sons, including the future king of England, Henry II (b. 1133). Of William's last years we know little. Alberic of Trois-Fontaines mentions William in his chronicle of 1154 indicating that "Master William of Conches was regarded as a philosopher of great fame" (*Monumenta Germaniae historica, Scriptores,* vol. 23, ed. Scheffer-Boichorst [Berlin 1874] 842). No futher mention is made o him, and he seems to have died soon after, around 1155–56. His writings were widely copied after his death.

Works. To William's youth are ascribed his glosses on Macrobius, Boethius, and two on Priscian. His gloss on Plato's Timaeus, is a more mature work and it appears, like the others, to have gone through several revisions. These commentaries did not merely repeat the words and ideas of the authors. Rather, William used his unique style of glossing both to probe the depths of the texts' meanings and to use them as vehicles to present his own ideas. To the list of his early works belongs his *Philosophia mundi*, wrongly assigned by Migne to St. Bede (*Patrologia Latina*, ed. J. P. Migne [Paris 1878–90] 90 1127–78) and Honorius of Autun (*Patrologia Latina* 172:39–102). Here William presents philosophy as the study of everything both visible and invisible. The text opens with a brief sketch of the Trinity, the angels, chaos, and the fundamental elements of creation. William argues that the Genesis account of creation is compatible with his beloved Timaeus and with contemporary scientific studies. The middle section of the text discusses astronomy, eclipses, and meteorology. The book concludes with an examination of the earth itself. William first expounds on geological and biological sciences, and he culminates with a portrait of humanity as the microcosm of the universe, covering all aspects of human development from the process of conception, development in the womb, menstruation, to memory loss in old age.

The *Philosophia* gives us a clear picture of the understanding of the natural sciences in the first quarter of the 12th century. When it is compared with William's final work, the *Dragmaticon*, written around 1148, the reader can see the extensive development that had taken place because of the transmission of Greek and Islamic sciences to the West. Although William's major source for *Dragmaticon* is Constantinus of Africa, he shows familiarity with the works of Adelard of Bath, and perhaps the medical texts of the Salernitan school.

The *Dragmaticon*, long thought to have been a mere updating of the earlier *Philosophia*, now has been revealed as a substantial independent. William writes it in the form of a dialogue. The character of the "Duke"—Geoffrey Plantagenet—asks questions and the "philosopher"—William—answers them. After opening with a perhaps insincere recantation of the "errors of his youth," William clarifies points made earlier in his writings and demonstrates his familiarity with the new learning and his willingness to change in light of new information. However, the integration of the newly arrived Aristotle with William's Platonic worldview proved most difficult.

The attribution of authorship to William of the compendium of moral maxims titled *Moralium dogma philosophorum* remains questionable. The *Glosae super Martianum* has not been preserved, if it was ever completed, and both the *Compendium philosophiae*, and the *Glosae in Juvenalem*, are no longer attributed to William. The extensive transmission of William's works, and what appears to have been his constant revisions, has made it difficult to distinguish William's writing's from those of his students and redactors.

Thought. William was a natural philosopher, a Platonist, and a staunch supporter of the liberal arts, human reason, and the dignity of humanity. He sought to comprehend the world in rational terms, but he understood that knowledge of creation led to knowledge of the creator. He was critical of contemporaries and mistrusted rational explanations of phenomena and of events in Scripture. In addition to classical Latin authors, Church Fathers, Plato, and Neoplatonists, William studied Constantinus of Africa, Abu Ma 'shar, Adelard of Bath, and new translations of Greek authors such as Ptolemy, Euclid, Nemesius, Galen, and Hippocrates.

Throughout his life, William remained a metaphysician whose writings were deeply influenced by Plato's Timaeus and such Neoplatonic sources as Boethius, Macrobius, Martianus Capella, and Chalcidius. Though not a theologian in the sense of his contemporaries Thierry of Chartres and Gilbert of Poitiers, he does speak a great deal about God, and he is not hesitant to expound on Scripture. William believed that humanity has the ability to know the Creator by studying the creation. William believed that "pagan" authors and the cosmos itself serve as a veiled source of divinely inspired truth. The role of the philosopher is to use the tools of reason and integument—pulling back the layers of metaphor and coloring—to reveal the kernel inside things. He felt that the contemplation of the natural world could lead humanity to know the nature of things in their corporeal reality and to knowledge of the eternal ideas that resided in the eternal exemplar who is the Son and through whom God the Father created the cosmos. All existence has its eternal being in God. In turn God, exists in things exemplaristically as the core of their being. This exemplarism is an interpretative lens by which he viewed the world.

To his exemplarism must be added William's understanding of the Platonic idea of the World Soul. In his early writings William argues that the power which Plato assigns to the World Soul can be none other than that which Christians call the Holy Spirit. William saw the World Soul as a metaphor or integument, for understanding how God, in the Person of the Holy Spirit, is present in the world. The World Soul is the natural energy by which some things move, others grow, others sense, others think.

The identification of the World Soul with the Holy Spirit, as it was thought to have been held by Peter Abelard, was condemned by the Council of Sens in 1141, the same year of William of St. Thierry's attack on the Chartrian. This seems to have had an effect on William, since in his last work, the *Dragmaticon*, the topic of the world soul is dropped. However, it is not explicitly denied, as are several other perceived "errors." William only refers to the errors of his *Philosophia* and makes no mention of his other works, most of which contain substantial commentary on the world soul. In what appears to be his later revisions of his glosses, William does not mention the connection between the Holy Spirit with the World Soul, and instead refers to the inherent power of God in the world as divine love and goodness. William tells us that it is divine love which moves humanity, the stars, and the planets towards God.

William's influence can be gleamed from the transmission of his works. There are numerous copies of his commentaries, and his two systematic works can be found in over 70 manuscripts.

Bibliography: Sources: *Philosophia mundi*, ed. G. MAURACH (Pretoria 1980). *Glosae super Platonem*, ed. E. JEAUNEAU (Paris 1965); "Deux redactions des gloses de Guillaume de Conches sur Priscian" *RTAM* 27, 1960: 212–47. *Glosae super Pricianum* (Paris, B.N. MS lat 15130). *Dragmaticon*, ed. I. RONCA (Turnhout 1997). *Glosae super Boethium*, ed. L. NAUTA (Turnhout 1999). *Glosse super Macrobium* (in preparation) ed. H. RODNITE LEMAY. Literature: T. GREGORY, *Anima mundi: la filosofia di Guglielmo di Conches e la scuola di Chartres* (Florence 1955); *Platonismo medievale* (Rome 1958). J. M. PARENT, *La doctrine de la création dans l' école de Chartres* (Paris 1938). J. A. CLERVAL, *Les écoles de Chartres au moyen Age du V siécle au XVI siécle* (Paris 1895). H. FLATTEN, *Die Philosophie des Wilhelm von Conches* (Koblenz 1929). E. JEAUNEAU, "L'usage de la notion d'integumentum a travers les gloses de Guillaume de Conches." *AHDLMA* 24 (1957), 35–100); "Macrobe, source du platonisme Chartrain" *Studi Medievali* 3rd. ser.1, 1960: 3–24. P. DRONKE, *Fabula: Explorations into the Uses of Myth in Medieval Platonism* (Leiden 1974). See as well the introductions to the critical editions mentioned above.

[P. ELLARD]

WILLIAM OF CREMONA

Also thought to be of Villana, Augustinian bishop and theologian; b. Cremona, Italy, *c.* 1270; d. Novara, Jan. 29, 1356. A doctor and professor of theology at Paris from at least 1320, William became prior general of his order in 1326 and held that office without interruption until appointed bishop of Novara in 1342. In the work *Reprobatio errorum* (pub. in part by R. Scholz), he misguidedly presented the Church and State theory of GILES OF ROME in refutation of the errors of MARSILIUS OF PADUA and JOHN OF JANDUN. Of his other works, only the *Reprobatio errorum Fraticellorum*, the *De jure monarchiae*, and a few official documents are extant.

Bibliography: *Analecta Augustiniana*, 4 (1911–12), *passim.* R. SCHOLZ, *Unbekannte kirchenpolitische Streitschriften aus der Zeit Ludwigs des Bayern, 1327–1354*, 2 v. (Rome 1911–14) 1:13–22; 2:16–28. JORDAN OF QUEDLINGBURG, *Jordani de Saxonia . . . Liber vitasfratrum*, ed. R. ARBESMANN and W. HÜMPFNER (New York 1943) 43–44, 62–67, 447. U. MARIANI, *Scrittori politici agostiniani del secolo XIV* (Florence 1927); *Bollettino storico agostiniano*, 11 (1934–35) 143–147; 12 (1935–36) 10–13, 46–52, 80–82. D. A. PERINI, *Bibliographia Augustiniana*, 4 v. (Florence 1929–38) 1:28–32. B. PIAIA, "Marsilio da Padova, Guglielmo Amidani e l'idea di Sovranita popolare," *Veritas,* 38 (1993) 297–304.

[J. E. BRESNAHAN]

WILLIAM OF DROGHEDA

Foremost canonist of his time in England; b. no earlier than 1200 (probably neither Irish nor of an Anglo-Irish family); d. at the hand of his valet in 1245 at his Oxford home, now Drawda Hall. Educated at Oxford, William was teaching law there by 1239. About that year he wrote but left unfinished the *Summa aurea,* a copious treatise on procedure in ecclesiastical courts. A work of high originality, this practitioner's book circulated in England and on the Continent, where it came to the favorable attention of JOANNES ANDREAE.

Bibliography: *Summa aurea,* in *Quellen zur Geschichte des römisch-kanonischen Processes im Mittelalter,* ed. L. WAHRMUND, 5 v. (Innsbruck 1905–31) v.2. F. W. MAITLAND, "William of Drogheda and the Universal Ordinary," *Roman Canon Law in the Church of England* (London 1898) 100–131. F. DE ZULUETA, "William of Drogheda," *Mélanges de droit romain dédiés à Georges Cornil,* 2 v. (Ghent 1926) 2:639–657. J. C. RUSSELL, *Dictionary of Writers of Thirteenth Century England* (New York 1936) 186–187. H. G. RICHARDSON, "Azo, Drogheda, and Bracton," *English Historical Review* 59 (1944) 22–47. A. B. EMDEN, *A Biographical Register of the University of Oxford to A.D. 1500* 1:594–598.

[F. D. LOGAN]

WILLIAM OF EDYNDON

Bishop, chancellor of England; b. Edington, Wiltshire, England; d. Oct. 1366. He had probably studied at Oxford before joining the household of Bp. ADAM OF ORLETON (1332). His royal offices included that of keeper of the wardrobe (1341), treasurer of the exchequer (1344), and then chancellor of England (1356–63). He is remembered for providing new windows in the clerestory of the nave in the church of the Hospital of St. Cross, Winchester, and for spending £1,000 on restoration of the hospital buildings and improvement of the condition of the almsmen while he was master there (1334–46). At the request of King EDWARD III he was made bishop of WINCHESTER in 1346. Under him the west end of the nave of Winchester cathedral, the two west bays on the north side, and one west bay on the south side were rebuilt and the construction of the presbytery was completed. He built a church in his birthplace and established there a college for a warden and secular priests, which he converted into a convent for *Bonshommes,* under a rector.

Bibliography: D. KNOWLES and R. N. HADCOCK, *Medieval Religious Houses: England and Wales* 179. R. L. POOLE, *The Dictionary of National Biography from the Earliest Times to 1900* 6:386–387. T. F. TOUT, *Chapters in the Administrative History of Mediaeval England* 6 v. (New York 1920–33). A. B. EMDEN, *A Biographical Register of the University of Oxford to A.D. 1500* 1:629–630. M. MCKISACK, *The Fourteenth Century, 1307–1399* (Oxford 1959).

[V. MUDROCH]

WILLIAM OF HECHAM

First known master of the Augustinian Order at the University of Oxford (also known as William of Hegham, or Heigham). By 1292, only five years after GILES OF ROME became the first of the AUGUSTINIANS (Austins) to obtain the magisterium at Paris, William had been made master regent at Oxford. Hecham's promotion to the magisterium in England enabled the English province to found a *studium generale* for the order. William helped to settle a dispute between the Abbey of Wellow and the Austin friary in Grimsby, whereupon Bp. John Dalderby of Lincoln lifted the ban against the Austins (1300). Two of William's university sermons are extant. The library of St. Augustine's Abbey, Canterbury, formerly had his *Quaestiones disputatae.*

Bibliography: A. B. LITTLE and F. PELSTER, *Oxford Theology and Theologians* (Oxford 1935) 186–187, 265–266. F. ROTH, *History of English Austin Friars,* 2 v. (New York 1961) 1:48, 150. A. B. EMDEN *A Biographical Register of the University of Oxford to A.D. 1500,* 3 v. (Oxford 1957–59) 2:899.

[F. ROTH]

WILLIAM OF HEYTESBURY

Scholastic, logician, chancellor of the University of Oxford (also known as Hentisbury, Hesberi, Tisbery); b. most likely in Wiltshire, England, *c.* 1313; d. December 1372, or January 1373. He became a fellow of Merton College, Oxford, by 1330, when THOMAS BRADWARDINE, Simon Bredon, and THOMAS OF BUCKINGHAM were already members. Merton had been founded by Bp. WALTER OF MERTON primarily as a residence for theological students, although young masters in arts were allowed to complete their regency before enrolling in the faculty of theology. By February 1340, Heytesbury was already a student of theology, for he was named one of the foundation fellows of Queen's College, which was restricted to theological students. He returned shortly to Merton,

where he remained at least until 1348, and where he was ordained, April 15, 1346. By July 1348, he was a "doctor in theology," but the date of his inception is unknown. He retained numerous benefices until his death, among them the rectorship of St. John's in Ickham, Kent (1354). In a university roll for papal graces, compiled before February 1363, Heytesbury is called "late Chancellor of the University." If this title is correct, he must have held office from 1353 to 1354, the only period for which no chancellor is known, or else he merely served temporarily between two chancellorships. According to another document, he was again chancellor on Nov. 9, 1371; hence the conjecture that Heytesbury held office from Pentecost 1370 until Pentecost 1372.

Heytesbury accepted the fundamental ideas of WILLIAM OF OCKHAM, particularly on logical supposition, substance, quantity, motion, and time. He also favored the new kinematic theorem of Thomas Bradwardine and attempted to apply it to the intension and remission of all qualitative forms, including knowledge and doubt. His works in LOGIC, probably written between 1331 and 1339, were popular aids to young "sophisters" in the university for responses and determination; and his beginners' text, *Natural Terms (Termini naturales),* contained the standard definitions needed in natural philosophy. His widely used *Logic,* or *Rules for Solving Sophismata (Regulae solvendi sophismata),* "given at Oxford in 1335," was addressed to first–year students of logic; the equivocal terms involved include various types of motion, knowing and doubting, beginning and ceasing, maximum and minimum, and relatives. The *Proofs of Conclusions (Probationes conclusionum),* attributed to him, involves the same equivocal terms and contains the first known proof of the theorem of mean speed. These works, together with his *Sophismata XXXII, De sensu composito et diviso,* and a famous *Treatise on Consequences,* served as textbooks in the universities of Vienna, Erfurt, Padua, and other continental schools as late as the 16th century. Nothing is known of his theological views.

Bibliography: P. M. M. DUHEM, *Études sur Léonard de Vinci,* 3 v. (Paris 1955) 3:405–409, 493–510. G. SARTON, *Introduction to the History of Science,* 3 v. in 5 (Baltimore 1927–48) 3.1:565–566. C. WILSON, *William Heytesbury: Medieval Logic and the Rise of Mathematical Physics* (Madison, Wis. 1956). A. B. EMDEN, *A Biographical Register of the Universtiy of Oxford to A. D. 1500,* 3 v. (Oxford 1957–59) 2:927–928. M. CLAGETT, *Science of Mechanics in the Middle Ages* (Madison, Wis. 1959) 235–242; 263–289 and *passim.*

[J. A. WEISHEIPL]

WILLIAM OF HIRSAU, BL.

Reforming abbot; b. Bavaria; d. Abbey of Hirsau, July 4, 1091. He was a child oblate at SANKT EMMERAM in Regensburg. In 1069 he was appointed abbot of the Benedictine Abbey of HIRSAU, although he refused to take office before the death of his predecessor, Abbot Frederick (1071), who he thought had been unjustly deposed. He received full EXEMPTION for his monastery from Pope GREGORY VII in 1075, and became a zealous supporter of the Hildebrandine cause within the Empire during the INVESTITURE STRUGGLE.

Between 1076 and 1078 William introduced at Hirsau the practice of professing monastic servants, who were known as *fratres exteriores*. This practice became widespread and was adopted at Cluny, probably at the end of the century. It marks an important step toward the development in the Benedictine tradition of *fratres CONVERSI*. Then, in 1079, Pope Gregory's legate Bernard, Abbot of SAINT-VICTOR in Marseilles, and ULRIC OF ZELL came to Hirsau and persuaded William to adopt the customs of CLUNY for his abbey. Abbot HUGH OF CLUNY then caused an adaptation of the customs to be made, and these—combined with customs from Sankt Emmeram—were implemented at Hirsau shortly before William's death, as the *Constitutiones Hirsaugienses* (*Patrologia Latina* 150:927–1146).

William attracted so many vocations that it became necessary to build a second monastery at Hirsau (1083–92), and colonies were sent to promote the work of reform in Styria and Carinthia, and at Magdeburg and Erfurt. Over 100 eventually came to observe the *Constitutiones Hirsaugienses*. William had sought to make Hirsau a learned community, and was himself the author of a work on musical theory (*Patrologia Latina* 50:1147–78) and one on astronomy (*Patrologia Latina,* 150:1639–42). His life was written by his disciple, Prior Haymo of Hirsau, who died in 1107 (*Monumenta Germaniae Historica: Scriptores* 12:209–225).

Feast: July 5.

Bibliography: P. GISEKE, *Die Hirschauer während des Investiturstreites* (Gotha 1883). M. FISCHER, *Studien zur Entstehung der Hirsauer Konstitutionen* (Stuttgart 1910). A. BRACKMANN, ''Die Anfänge von Hirsau,'' in *Papsttum und Kaisertum* (Munich 1926) 215–232. M. MANITIUS, *Geschichte der lateinischen Literatur des Mittelalters,* 3 v. (Munich 1911–31) 3:220–226. P. SCHMITZ, *Histoire de l'Ordre de Saint-Benoît,* 7 v. (Maredsous, Bel. 1942–56) 1:202–203, 289; 2:250. K. G. FELLERER, ''Zum Musiktraktat des W. von H.,'' *Festschrift Wilhelm Fischer zum 70. Geb.* (Vienna 1956) 61–70. M. A. SCHMIDT, *Die Religion in Geschichte und Gegenwart,* 7 v. (3d ed. Tübingen 1957–65) 6:1714.

[B. HAMILTON]

WILLIAM OF KILKENNY

English bishop, royal chancellor; d. Spain, Sept. 21, 1256. He was perhaps of a Durham family, though probably of Irish descent; he studied Canon and civil law at Oxford. He was elected to the See of Ossory, Ireland, in 1231, but resigned before consecration in 1232. By 1247 he was archdeacon of Coventry. He was elected bishop of ELY in 1254 and consecrated in 1255, one example of the many who rose to bishoprics through royal service in the 13th century. A clerk for King Henry III by 1232, he acted as king's proctor in Rome (1234–38), in which capacity he took part in various negotiations. From 1249 to 1252 he was controller of the king's wardrobe. In 1250 he was appointed keeper of the great seal, or acting chancellor, with Peter of Rivaux. From 1253 to 1255 he was sole keeper with the title of chancellor, and during Henry's absence in Gascony (1253–54) he was actual head of the administration with Richard of Cornwall. He was an envoy to Alphonso X of Castile (1256).

Bibliography: C. L. KINGSFORD, *The Dictionary of National Biography from Earliest Times to 1900* 11:104–105. T. F. TOUT, *Chapters in the Administrative History of Mediaeval England* 6 v. (New York 1920–33) v.1. A. B. EMDEN, *A Biographical Register of the University of Oxford to A.D. 1500* 2:1048–49. M. GIBBS and J. LANG, *Bishops and Reform* 1215–1272 (London 1934; repr. 1962).

[H. MAYR–HARTING]

WILLIAM OF MACCLESFELD

Dominican theologian; b. Coventry, England; d. Canterbury, between May and December 1303. Probably a member of the priory of Chester, he was a master of theology at the University of OXFORD, distinguished by prudence and brilliant theological works. Macclesfeld studied at St. Jacques, Paris, where he earned his bachelor of theology degree, and was probably the Willielmus Anglicus who preached university sermons in Paris (1293–94). He returned to England, was promoted as master, and served as regent of studies at Blackfriars. In 1302 with THOMAS JORZ and John de Cesterlade, he acted as arbiter in a dispute between Exeter priory and the dean and chapter of Exeter. The provincial chapter of 1302 chose Macclesfeld as definitor for the general chapter to be held in Besançon (1303). He died while returning from the chapter and was buried in London. Meanwhile, Pope Benedict XI, unaware of Macclesfeld's death, created him cardinal priest of St. Sabina (Dec. 18, 1303). His death is noted in the acts of the general chapter of 1304.

The following works are attributed to Macclesfeld: *Postillae in sacra biblia, In evangelium de decem virginibus, Quaestiones de angelis, Quaestiones ordinariae, Contra Henricum de Gandavo in quibus impugnat s. Tho-*

mam de Aquino, De unitate formarum, De comparatione statuum, Orationes ad clerum, and Varia problemata. Macclesfeld is held by some to have been the author of the Correctorium corruptorii Sciendum, one of the Dominican replies to the Correctorium fratris Thomae of the Franciscan WILLIAM DE LA MARE [P. Glorieux, ''Le Correctorum Corruptorii Sciendum,'' Bibliothèque Thomiste 31 (1956) 19]. This question, however, is still open [see L. J. Bataillon, Bulletin Thomiste, 10 (1957–59) 583–594].

Bibliography: J. QUÉTIF and J. ÉCHARD, Scriptores Ordinis Praedicatorum 1.2:493–494. A.B. EMDEN, A Biogrqaphical Register of the University of Oxford to A.D. 1500 2:1200–1201.

[B. PEÑA]

WILLIAM OF MALEVAL, ST.

Founder of the Hermits of St. William (Gulielmites); d. Maleval (Malavalla), near Siena, Italy, Feb. 10, 1157. After making a pilgrimage to Santiago de Compostela, he began to live as a hermit in 1153, first in a forest near Pisa, then on Mt. Pruno, where some disciples joined him. In 1155 he moved alone to the desert valley of Maleval (Stabulum Rodis), near Siena. After some time a companion, Albert, joined him, and, shortly before his death, a doctor named Renaldo. Thus was formed a religious community, called the Hermits of St. William (see WILLIAMITES; AUGUSTINIANS), who eventually established themselves throughout Europe. A life of William was written by his companion, Albert, but it has survived only in an expanded form edited by a certain Theobald [Acta Sanctorum (Paris 1863—) 2:450–473]; the first part of this biography is unreliable. William was canonized by Innocent III in 1202.

Feast: Feb. 10.

Bibliography: Bibliotheca hagiographica latina antiquae et mediae aetatis (Brussels 1898–1901) 2:8922–23. S. DE LA HAYE, De veritate vitae et ordinis s. Guillelmi (Paris 1587). M. HEIMBUCHER, Die Orden und Kongregationen der katholischen Kirche (Paderborn 1932–34) 1:539. R. GAZEAU, Catholicisme. Hier, aujourd'hui et demain, ed. G. JACQUEMET (Paris 1947—) 5:379–380. K. ELM, Beiträge zur Geschichte des Wilhelmitenordens (Cologne 1962).

[M. A. HABIG]

WILLIAM OF MALMESBURY

Benedictine monk, scholar, and writer; b. southwest England, c. 1090; d. 1143. William was of mixed Norman and Anglo-Saxon parentage and was educated and professed at MALMESBURY, where ALDHELM had been abbot

and DUNSTAN had reestablished monastic life. Because of the fine library there, and his own unremitting diligence and travel, William, though largely self-taught, achieved his ambition to become the most notable English historian since BEDE. His chief work, the Gesta regum, begun in 1118, was a history of England from the ANGLO-SAXON period till his own times. Its scale, perspective, and proportion raised it above most writings of the time; its vivid, but biting portraiture and elegant style make it enjoyable reading today. Its companion volume, the Gesta pontificum, about the English bishops, sees, and monasteries of the same period, was completed in 1125.

The Historia novella, describing the civil war of the reign of King Stephen of England, was unfinished at William's death. His devotional works included a commentary on Lamentations, lives of St. Dunstan and St. WULFSTAN, excerpts from St. Gregory, an abbreviation of AMALARIUS's De divinis officiis, and collections of St. ANSELM's works and of Miracles of the Virgin. William knew Cicero, Seneca's letters, and the Attic Nights of Aulus Gellius. He made a collection of works on Roman history and civil law and another on ancient Canon Law. He was precentor and librarian of his abbey, and claimed that he could have been elected abbot in 1140. Several of his autograph MSS survive. His wide achievements make him the most notable monastic example of the 12th–century renaissance in England.

Bibliography: Gesta regum, ed. with fine introduction by W. STUBBS, 2 v. (Rerum Britannicarum medii aevi scriptores 90); Gesta pontificum anglorum, ed. N. E. S. A. HAMILTON (Rerum Britannicarum medii aevi scriptores 52); The Historia Novella, tr. K. R. POTTER (New York 1955); The Vita Wulfstani, ed. R. R. DARLINGTON (London 1928). M. R. JAMES, Two Ancient English Scholars: St. Aldhelm and William of Malmesbury (Glasgow 1931). H. FARMER, ''William of Malmesbury's Life and Works,'' The Journal of Ecclesiastical History 13 (1962) 39–54; ''William of Malmesbury's Commentary on Lamentations,'' Studia Monastica 4 (1962) 283–311.

[H. FARMER]

WILLIAM OF MELITONA (MIDDLETON)

Franciscan theologian variously listed as de Mideltoun or de Militona; b. Middleton(?), England; d. 1260 or before. In 1245 he was in Paris in the company of ALEXANDER OF HALES and JOHN OF LA ROCHELLE. By 1248 he was certainly a master in theology and in that capacity was part of the commission that proposed the condemnation of the Talmud (see Chartularium universitatis Parisiensis, ed. H. Denifle and E. Chatelain, 4 v. (Paris 1889–97) 1:209). Some time later he was charged with completing, in collaboration with other friars, the Summa *theologica* of Alexander of Hales, left unfinished at the death of its author in 1245. William was also part of a commission of five friars that studied the rule proposed by (Bl.) Isabella, sister of (St.) Louis IX, King of France, for a monastery she intended to found at Longchamp, near Paris. The last certain mention of William is at the general chapter of the Friars Minor held at Narbonne on May 23, 1260, when suffrages were requested for him and for others who had died since the last general chapter held in Rome in February 1257. William was distinguished not only for his knowledge but also for his holiness and is listed in the *Martyrologium Franciscanum* under date of September 15.

William's principal work is the *Quaestiones de sacramentis* composed between 1245 and 1249. It is divided into six parts: *De sacramentis in genere* (69 qq.), *De sacramento baptismi* (52 qq.), *De sacramento confirmationis* (15 qq.), *De sacramento altaris* (75 qq.), *De poenitentia virtute* (34 qq.), and *De poenitentia sacramento* (25 qq.). It is the most extensive and the most important work written on the sacraments before those of BONAVENTURE and THOMAS AQUINAS. It had great influence on two anonymous compilations, one in Brussels (Bibl. Regia, cod. 1542) and the other in Assisi (Bibl. Comunale, cod. 182), and Bonaventure himself used it. Rearranged, modified, and often noticeably enlarged, it was also incorporated in the fourth book of the *Summa Halesiana* that William had been assigned to complete. He also compiled the *Opusculum super missam* [ed. A. Van Dijk, *Ephemerides liturgicae* (Rome 1887–) 53 (1939) 311–349], which explains the meaning of clerical tonsure, of liturgical garments, of the altar, of canonical hours, and of the Mass. Twenty-four of his *Quaestiones disputatae,* dealing primarily with theological and moral problems, have been discovered; with the exception of a fragment here or there, they are all unpublished. The manuscript codices attribute to William a long series of commentaries or marginalia on the scriptures (*see* F. Stegmüller, *Repertorium commentariorum in Sententias Petri Lombardi,* 2 v. [Würzburg 1947], nn. 2927–66), but the authenticity of these is not certain; they may be the work of a Dominican contemporary, William of Alton.

Bibliography: Introduction, *Quaestiones de sacramentis,* ed. C. PIANA and G. GÁL (*Bibliotheca Franciscana scholastica medii aevi* 22–23; 1961) 5*–33*. V. NATALINI, "Natura della grazia sacramentale nelle *Quaestiones de sacramentis* di Guglielmo de Militona," *Studi Francescani* 58 (1961) 62–92.

[G. GÁL]

WILLIAM OF MOERBEKE

Dominican archbishop, translator; b. Moerbeke, Belgium, *c.* 1215; d. Corinth, 1286. Although he is some-

times described as a native of Flanders or Brabant, because of the border town in which he was born, he belonged to the Dominican priory of Ghent. He studied at Cologne, possibly under Albert the Great. By 1260 he had been sent to the priory in Thebes, Greece, and later went to Nicea. From the pontificate of Clement IV (1265–68) until 1278 he was chaplain and confessor to several popes. Well known as a translator of Greek works, he translated certain writings "at the request of Friar Thomas Aquinas," whom he knew intimately at Viterbo and Orvieto. As an enthusiastic promoter of reunion between Greek and Latin churches, and as personal advisor of GREGORY X, he participated in the Council of Lyons (1274). On April 9, 1278, he was appointed archbishop of Corinth by NICHOLAS III and was given the pallium by Giacomo Savelli (later HONORIUS IV). He resided in Corinth until his death, presumably in 1286, when a successor was appointed. The Greek village of Merbeke is named after him.

The most eminent and prolific translator of the 13th century, he gave Latin scholars a careful, literal version of Aristotle, Proclus, many Greek commentators, Archimedes, Eutochius, and certain books of Ptolemy, Hero, Galen, and Hippocrates, which remained standard until the 16th century. Roger Bacon called these literal translations "barbaric," but their fidelity allowed St. Thomas to grasp Aristotle's exact meaning, and they enable modern scholars to reconstruct Greek originals, many of which are lost. Besides revising earlier translations of Aristotle, he introduced *De caelo* 3–4 (c. 1260), *Meteorological* 1–3 (1260), *Metaphysics* 11, *Politics* 3–8, *Rhetoric, De animalibus* 1–21, and *Poetics* (1278). All of William's versions are published in *Aristoteles Latinus.* Among the more important commentators translated by him are Ammonius on *Perihermeneias* (1268), Simplicius on *Praedicamenta* (1266) and *De caelo* (1271), Alexander of Aphrodisias on *Metaphysics* (1260), Themistius on *De anima* (c. 1268), and John Philoponus on *De anima,* 3 (1268, possibly two versions). These are published in the *Corpus Latinum Commentariorum in Artist. Graecorum* of Louvain. His translation of the *Elementatio theologica* of Proclus (Viterbo May 18, 1268) revealed to St. Thomas the true nature of the *Liber de Causis,* previously considered Aristotelian. This and other translations by William gave great impetus to NEOPLATONISM in the late Middle Ages. Neoplatonists, such as Witelo and Henry Bate, accepted his friendship and dedications, as did the physician Rosello of Arezzo and the mathematician John Campanus. Through his translations he contributed not only to a precise and embracing Thomism but also to an interesting Platonism in the Middle Ages.

Bibliography: M. GRABMANN, *Guglielmo di Moerbeke, O.P., il traduttore delle opere di Aristotele, (Miscellanea Historiae Pon-*

tificiae 11; Rome 1946). P. GLORIEUX, *Répertoire des maîtres en théologie de Paris au XIIIe siècle* (Paris 1934) 1:119–122. J. QUÉTIF and J. ÉCHARD, *Scriptores Ordinis Praedicatorum* (New York 1959) 1:388b–391a. L. MINIO-PALUELLO, "Guglielmo di Moerbeke traduttore della *Poetica* di Aristotele," *Rivista di filosofia neoscolastica* 39 (1947) 1–17; "Note sull'Aristotele Latino Medievale," *ibid.*, 44 (1952) 389–411. G. VERBEKE, "Guillaume de Moerbeke: traducteur de Proclus," *Revue philosophique de Louvain* 51 (1953) 349–373.

[J. C. VANSTEENKISTE]

WILLIAM OF NEWBURGH

Austin canon, historian, and theologian; b. near Bridlington, Yorkshire, England, 1136; d. probably 1198, certainly by 1201. William, one of the most outstanding historians of his day and a competent theologian, was educated by the canons of Newburgh and may have spent the whole of his life there, but probably he is to be identified with William, son of Elyas and brother of Bernard, prior of Newburgh, who acquired estates in Oxfordshire by marriage *c.* 1160 with Emma de Peri, who subsequently left his wife and children to become a CANON REGULAR OF ST. AUGUSTINE at Newburgh.

The writings to which William of Newburgh owes his reputation belong to the last decade of the century. He composed his *Historia rerum Anglicarum* at the request of Ernald, abbot of nearby RIEVAULX, probably between 1196 and 1198. This work, which extends from 1066 to May 8, 1198, is remarkable, less for the originality of the material it contains, than for its clarity of thought, its display of an unusually keen sense of historical criticism, and its attack on commonly accepted fables such as those of GEOFFREY OF MONMOUTH. William's chief theological work was a commentary on the SONG OF SONGS, composed before 1196 at the request of Roger, Cistercian abbot of Byland; it embodies the ideas of many earlier writers harmoniously, but without great originality of thought.

Bibliography: *Historia rerum Anglicarum,* v.1–2 of *Chronicles of the Reigns of Stephen, Henry II, and Richard I,* ed. R. HOWLETT, 4 v. (*Rerum Britannicarum medii aevi scriptores* 82.1–2; London 1884–85); ed. with three sermons by T. HEARNE, 3 v. (Oxford 1719); tr. J. STEVENSON, 2 v. (London 1856); *Explanatio Sacri Epithalamii in Matrem Sponsi: A Commentary on the Canticle of Canticles,* ed. J. C. GORMAN (Fribourg 1960), with biography. K. NORGATE, "The Date of Composition of W. of N.'s History," *English Historical Review* 19 (1904) 288–297. H. E. SALTER, "W. of N.," *ibid.* 22 (1907) 510–514. R. JAHNCKE, *Guilelmus Neubrigensis: Ein pragmatischer Geschichtsschreiber des zwölften Jahrhunderts* (Bonn 1912).

[M. M. CHIBNALL]

WILLIAM OF NORWICH, ST.

Supposed victim of a ritual murder; b. 1132; d. Mar. 22, 1144. According to Thomas of Monmouth, William, a 12-year-old tanner's apprentice, was enticed from his home and on Tuesday of Holy Week 1144 was last seen entering the house of a Norwich Jew. On Holy Saturday his mutilated body was found hanging on a tree in Mousehold Wood near the town. The boy's uncle, a priest named Godwin Sturt, claimed in a diocesan synod held a few days later that the Jews had murdered his nephew and offered to undergo the ORDEAL to prove his charge. The sheriff of Norwich protected the Jews and declared the case to be under civil, not ecclesiastical, jurisdiction.

William's body was meanwhile moved from Thorpe Wood to the cathedral monks' cemetery. Although a few miracles were reported at the grave, interest in the youth apparently waned until 1149, when certain Christians were brought to trial for murdering a Jew. The bishop of NORWICH now demanded that William's death be reinvestigated, but a verdict was never delivered. Thomas of Monmouth, a monk of Norwich, the only contemporary source for this episode, reported that the Jews had bribed King Stephen to postpone the case. In 1150 William's body was moved to the chapter house, a year later to the cathedral itself, and in 1154 was finally translated to a special chapel in the cathedral. More miracles were reported from this time forward. William thus became a popular saint and an attraction for the once debt-encumbered monastery and cathedral. Among those whom Thomas of Monmouth questioned regarding this murder were a Christian serving woman who claimed to have seen William's body in her Jewish master's home, and, more significantly, a converted Jew named Theobold who declared that every year in some part of the world Jews must sacrifice a Christian to obtain deliverance of their people. This is the earliest known example of blood accusation or of accusation of ritual murder against the Jews in England. In 1759 Cardinal Lorenzo Ganganelli (later CLEMENT XIV) refuted the legend, and the existence of this practice has been thoroughly disproved. Moreover, since contemporary authorities took no action in William's case, other parts of Monmouth's own account also seem to be open to suspicion.

Feast at Norwich: March 26.

See Also: MEDIEVAL BOY MARTYRS.

Bibliography: *Acta Sanctorum* March 3:586–588. THOMAS OF MONMOUTH, *The Life and Miracles of St. William of Norwich,* ed. and tr. A. JESSOPP and M. R. JAMES (Cambridge, England 1896). CLEMENT XIV, *The Ritual Murder Libel and the Jew,* ed. and tr. C. ROTH (London 1935). C. ROTH, *A History of the Jews in England* (Oxford 1941). A. BUTLER, *The Lives of the Saints,* ed. H. THURSTON and D. ATTWATER 1:672. J. TRACHTENBERG, *The Devil and the*

Jews: The Medieval Conception of the Jew and Its Relation to Modern Antisemitism (New Haven 1943). M. D. ANDERSON, *A Saint at Stake* (London 1964). W. HOLSTEN, *Die Religion in Geschichte und Gegenwart* 5:1127.

[E. J. KEALEY]

WILLIAM OF NOTINGHAM

Franciscan theologian; d. Oct. 5, 1336. A student at Oxford by 1290, he lectured on the *Sentences* (Gonv. and Caius, Cambr. MS 3:00) *c.* 1310. He became the 39th lector in the Oxford friary *c.* 1312–14. As an enthusiastic Biblical scholar, he, and not his 13th-century namesake as commonly thought, wrote the well-known commentary on the *Concordia evangelistarum* of Clement of Lanthony. He was 17th minister provincial of England from Sept. 8, 1316, until *c.* 1330. At the general chapter of Perugia, 1322, he added his name to the letter of protest against the decrees of JOHN XXII concerning evangelical poverty; he also attended the general chapter of Lyons, 1325. He was buried at Leicester.

Bibliography: C. KINGSFORD, *The Grey Friars of London* (Aberdeen 1965). P. HERMANN, trans, *The XIIIth-Century Chronicles* (Chicago 1961). M. SCHMAUS, "Guillelmi de Nottingham O.F.M. doctrina de aeternitate mundi," *Antonianum* 7 (1932) 139–166. B. SMALLEY, "Which William of Nottingham?" *Mediaeval and Renaissance Studies* 3 (1954) 200–238.

[J. A. WEISHEIPL]

WILLIAM OF NOTRE DAME DE L'OLIVE, ST.

Hermit; b. Flemish Brabant, Belgium; d. Feb. 10, 1240. At first he was a baker. He went to live at Thenaillies, a Premonstratensian monastery in Aisne, France, but soon left. Touched by divine grace, he lived as a hermit at Mariemont (Hainaut, Belgium) on land belonging to Eustace, lord of Roeulx. John of Nivelles, a canon of Oignies, persuaded him to study and become a priest. Between 1226 and 1233 William founded at Mariemont, Notre Dame de l'Olive, an abbey for nuns that became affiliated with CÎTEAUX. Its first nuns came from Fontenelle and from Moustier-sur-Sambre. William's tomb, in the church of l'Olive, disappeared when the monastery was burned in July 1554 by the troops of King Henry II of France. He has a local cult.

Feast: Feb. 10.

Bibliography: *Acta Sanctorum* (Paris 1863—) 2:493–500. *Gallia Christiana* (Paris 1715–85) 3:189. U. BERLIÈRE, *Monasticon belge* (Bruges 1890–97) 1.2:372–377. ABBÉ VAN GORP, *L'Abbaye de l'Olive* (Charleroi 19:13). J. M. CANIVEZ, *L'Ordre de Cîteaux en*

Belgique (Forges-lez-Chimay, Belg. 1926). L. H. COTTINEAU, *Répertoire topobibliographique des abbayes et prieurés* (Mâcon 1935–39) 2:2127.

[É. BROUETTE]

WILLIAM OF OCKHAM

Franciscan philosopher, theologian, and political writer, called *Venerabilis inceptor* (also, occasionally, *Doctor invincibilis* and *Doctor singularis*), the most outstanding representative of the "modern way"; b. Ockham, Surrey, *c.* 1285; d. Munich, April 10, 1347.

Life. The first certain date of his life is Feb. 26, 1306, when he was ordained subdeacon of Southwart, in the diocese of Winchester (hence not yet a resident of Oxford). On June 19, 1318, he was presented to the bishop of Lincoln for license to hear confessions. He studied theology at Oxford, but was not a disciple of Duns Scotus. From 1317 to 1319, as a *baccalarius sententiarum,* he commented on the *Sentences* of Peter Lombard. During the following two years, now as *baccalarius formatus,* he fulfilled the remaining scholastic requirement for the title of master of theology and probably also held his *principium* or *inceptio* (hence the name Inceptor), but he never became regent master. This was due almost certainly to the opposition of JOHN LUTTERELL (chancellor of Oxford University from October 1317 until September 1322), who in 1323 went to Avignon and denounced Ockham as a heretic, substantiating his accusation with a list of 56 propositions extracted from the writings of Ockham.

John XXII summoned Ockham to Avignon and appointed a commission of six theologians (among them the same Lutterell and DURANDUS OF SAINT-POURÇAIN) to examine the incriminating propositions. In 1326 the commission presented 51 propositions as open to censure, but no formal condemnation was pronounced by the pope. Nevertheless, Ockham was not allowed to leave Avignon. At this time MICHAEL OF CESENA, the minister general of the Friars Minor, at variance with the pope about the interpretation of Franciscan poverty, was summoned to and detained in Avignon (December 1327). Prompted by his general, Ockham undertook the study of the papal constitutions concerning the Franciscan rule and became firmly convinced that the pope, by contradicting the Gospels and the constitutions of his predecessors, had fallen into heresy and had forfeited his right to the Chair of Peter. The personal views of John XXII about the BEATIFIC VISION, expressed in 1332, only added fuel to the fire. On May 26, 1328, after having composed and signed an appellation against the pope, Michael of Cesena and Ockham, with two other friars, escaped to Italy, as a result of which they were excommunicated.

In September they joined at Pisa the archenemy of the pope, Louis of Bavaria, whose election as emperor of the Holy Roman Empire John XXII did not recognize. In 1330 they journeyed with him to Munich and, remaining under his protection, by their counsel and writings aided him in his struggle against John XXII (d. Dec. 4, 1334) and his successors, BENEDICT XII and CLEMENT VI. During all this time Ockham professed himself a faithful Catholic, willing to submit to the *legitimate* authorities of both the Church and the Franciscan Order. He died at Munich April 10, 1347 (according to his epitaph), and was buried in the choir of the Franciscan church. The opinion that places the date of his death in 1349, after a tentative reconciliation with the Church and his order, lacks solid foundation, as was shown by C. K. Brampton.

Teaching. The principal doctrines of Ockham may be conveniently summarized under the headings of knowledge, logic, nature and man, being and cause, and theology.

Knowledge. One of the basic tenets of Ockham's philosophy is that whatever exists, by its very existence, is singular and individual. There are no universal ideas in the divine mind, as patterns of creation; much less are there UNIVERSALS or common natures in things. The universal concept itself in the mind is singular; it is universal only inasmuch as it can be predicated of many singulars by reason of their similarity. Accordingly, the first step to knowledge is INTUITION, the appropriate way to the cognition of singular things, which enables man to know whether a thing exists or not. Ordinarily it presupposes the presence of an object that immediately becomes present to the senses in sense intuition or to the mind in intellective intuition. Also, the contents of the mind (intellection, volition, desires, etc.) are objects of direct intuition. Abstractive cognition of a singular thing presupposes the intuitive knowledge of the same, but it is not proper knowledge of a singular thing. It abstracts from existence or nonexistence and from all contingent conditions. Both forms of cognition can be sufficiently explained without species, either sensible or intelligible; therefore they must be eliminated (*see* SPECIES, INTENTIONAL). This is required by the frequently invoked principle of economy (Ockham's razor), which forbids positing a plurality of entities without necessity. On the same principle Ockham also suppresses the distinction between the agent and possible INTELLECT. Intuitive cognition of nonexistent but possible things he regarded as possible on the constantly invoked principle that God can produce the proper effects of all secondary causes without the aid of the secondary causes.

In an earlier period Ockham was inclined to hold that the universal concept is a thought-object, formed or fashioned (*fictum*) by the mind as a likeness of the object outside the mind; later he inclined to the opinion that it is the same as the act of intellect, which by its very nature (*signum naturale*) stands for the actual thing to which it refers. Though the proper name of this position is CONCEPTUALISM, Ockham generally became labeled as nominalist and was called *Princeps nominalium.*

Science, for him, is either speculative or practical, real or rational, and is concerned with propositions. In the strictest Aristotelian sense of the word, SCIENCE (*SCIENTIA*) means an "evident cognition of some necessary truth caused by the evident cognition of necessary premises and a process of syllogistic reasoning" [P. Boehner, *Ockham, Philosophical Writings* (Edinburgh 1957) 5]. Whenever Ockham says that a proposition cannot be proved (*demonstrari*), he has in mind this kind of DEMONSTRATION, which obviously has a very limited possibility of application. He does not mean that experimental knowledge, dialectical proofs (*ratio probabilis, persuasio*), or authority are conducive only to doubts; on the contrary, they often yield a high degree of certitude.

Logic. Ockham's most valid contribution was to logic. He commented on the *Isagoge* of Porphyry and on the *Praedicamenta, De interpretatione,* and *De sophisticis elenchis* of Aristotle, attempting to show that these do not imply any form of REALISM. He wrote three treatises on logic (one long and two compendiums) dealing with terms, propositions, syllogisms, demonstrations, consequences, and fallacies. His theorems on consequences reveal a knowledge of the laws that now pass under the name of A. DE MORGAN.

Since the distinctive trait of the "modern way" was the logic of terms (hence the name terminism), special attention should be given to Ockham's doctrine on the SUPPOSITION of terms (*suppositio terminorum*). The difference between logic and the real sciences is that the latter are about terms (not things) that stand (*supponunt*) for things; logic, on the other hand, is about terms or mental contents (*intentiones animae*) that stand for other terms or mental contents. Hence the capital importance of the doctrine on the supposition of terms. Supposition is either personal, simple, or material. Personal supposition obtains when a term of a proposition stands for what it signifies and is used in its significative function; in simple supposition the term stands for a mental content but is not used in its significative function; material supposition occurs when a term does not stand for what it signifies but for a vocal or written sign, as in the proposition: "Man" is a noun (Boehner, *op. cit.* 65–67).

Nature and Man. The science of nature, according to Ockham, is about mental contents that are common to corruptible and movable things and that stand precisely for such things (Boehner, *op. cit.* 11). Its more appropriate method is INDUCTION, which starts from the more known, and—through observation, experience, and reasoning—ascends from effects to causes. Of the generally admitted three natural principles, matter, form, and privation, he eliminates PRIVATION as superfluous; it means only that something lacks something (*see* MATTER AND FORM). Primary matter is not pure potentiality but a positive entity; it is the same (*eiusdem rationis*) in all composite physical bodies, heavenly as well as terrestrial. Matter and form are sufficient to explain the composite; no principle of INDIVIDUATION is required apart from the efficient cause. The form of the whole (*forma totius*) is nothing more than the united parts. Scotus's formal distinction he rejected. Ockham's razor was in full swing: of the Aristotelian categories only substance and quality were recognized as absolute entities; quantity, motion, place, time, relation, etc., he regarded as in no way different from the bodies concerned. This becomes clear, he thought, when one replaces these terms with their definition or uses verbs instead of nouns. He rejected also the theory of IMPETUS, claiming that the movement and the moving body are identical.

Concerning man, Ockham held it reasonable to admit that the intellective soul is the form of the body, though it cannot be demonstrated in the strict sense. Man has, by experience, evident knowledge of free will, but this defies a priori demonstration—one of many instances in which the impossibility of a priori demonstration is compatible with absolute certainty. There is no distinction, either real or formal, between the soul and its faculties, but it is likely that the sensitive soul is different from the intellective soul and perishable. It is also reasonable to assume a form of corporeity for the body (*forma corporeitatis*), distinct from the soul.

Being and Cause. Being, in Ockham's words, "is associated with a concept which is common to all things and can be predicated of all things in the manner of quiddity" (Boehner, *op. cit.* 90). In its broadest sense it does not imply any likeness, either substantial or accidental, in the things of which it is predicated, and in this sense it is univocal to God and creatures. Man would not be able to know God at all in this life unless he knew Him in a concept common to Him and other things. There is no "being as such" outside the mind in which all things "participate." For the same reason there is no distinction between essence and existence; both signify exactly the same thing (*see* ESSENCE AND EXISTENCE). Nevertheless, the difference between God and creatures is a radical one. It is the difference between infinite and finite, necessary and contingent, *a se* and *ab alio* beings.

Cause is a positive entity, distinct from what is caused by it. Ockham retains the fourfold Aristotelian di-

vision. The exemplar can be called a cause only in a metaphorical sense. Efficient cause is that which, having been posited, the effect follows and, having been removed (all other circumstances remaining the same), the effect does not follow. Hence it is by experience that man knows that one thing is the cause of another. Nevertheless, since God can supply for the causality of any secondary cause, one cannot prove that a given effect is caused by a secondary cause and not by God alone (*In 2 sent.* 4–5).

The existence of a first efficient cause cannot be sufficiently proved from production, because the impossibility of an infinite regress is difficult to prove against the philosophers; but it can be proved from conservation, because it presupposes the simultaneous existence of all conserving causes and an infinite number of actually existing beings is impossible. To this cause nothing is prior or superior in perfection, but since one cannot prove that it is more noble and more perfect than every other being, neither God's unicity nor its opposite can be evidently and demonstratively proved (Boehner, *op. cit.* 122–126).

Theology. Theology, according to Ockham, is not a science in the Aristotelian sense of the word, because its principles are not evident but accepted from revelation. Nevertheless, it is the highest and firmest knowledge and the sciences are its handmaids. It is partly speculative, partly practical. As a theologian, Ockham rigorously applied his terminist logic to man's knowledge of God and His attributes and of the Holy Trinity (man knows nothing but propositions; man's knowledge of God is terminated in a concept that is not God, etc.). He applied also his idea of God's absolute power to grace and justification (God can forgive sin without grace, etc.), and his notion of ACCIDENT to the Holy Eucharist (quantity is not a distinct entity apart from substance and qualities). It is not surprising, then, that Lutterell and the papal commission charged with the examination of his teaching felt that he was turning both theology and philosophy upside down. [For the list of the censured articles and their qualification, see J. Koch, "Neue Aktenstücke zu dem gegen Wilhelm Ockham in Avignon geführten Prozess," *Recherches de théologie ancienne et médiévale* (Louvain 1929–) 7 (1935) 353–380; 8 (1936) 79–83, 168–197].

A characteristic feature of Ockham's theology is the constant recourse to the distinction between God's ordained and absolute power. By this he wished to emphasize that the present order of nature and salvation is not necessary but has been freely established by God, who could have established a different order (and acted according to it) as long as it did not involve contradiction. The ultimate foundation of the moral order and of the distinction between good and evil is also the will of God.

He considered the Church (but neither the pope nor general councils) infallible, and never intended to say or write anything contrary to its teaching. In his polemical writing, he insisted that the pope had no power in political matters, except in case of emergency. The Empire is from God through the people and not from the pope. The emperor has the right and the duty to depose a heretical pope. It was these extremely daring views (considering the circumstances) and his open rebellion (and not his philosophical or theological teaching) that brought upon him the wrath of John XXII. His doctrine has never been officially condemned by the Church. For its influence, *see* OCKHAMISM.

Appreciation. Ockham's teaching cannot be correctly understood unless one takes into account all of the multiple and subtle distinctions he employs in defining the precise meaning of the terms he uses. Since this is extremely difficult, he usually receives a fairer treatment from those who have studied his writings thoroughly (E. Moody, L. Baudry, P. BOEHNER, etc.) than from authors of scholastic handbooks. In the latter he has been called a skeptic, an agnostic, a fideist, etc., the one who paved the way for Luther, who professed himself an Ockhamist. It can hardly be contested that, with his critical attitude, he contributed to the disintegration of scholastic philosophy and theology as it was understood in the 13th century. But it is also true that by his interest in singulars rather than universals, intuition rather than abstraction, and induction rather than deduction, he prepared the ground for a more scientific approach to reality.

Works. Ockham was a very prolific writer. He composed his philosophical and theological works in Oxford (*c.* 1317–23) and in Avignon (1324–28), and his polemical and political treatises in Munich (1330–47). For a detailed and reasoned description of these works, *see* Boehner, *op. cit.* lii–lix. The following is a simple enumeration:

On logic: (1) *In Porphyrium,* (2) *In praedicamenta,* (3) *In perihermenias,* (4) *In duos libros elenchorum,* (5) *Summa logicae,* (6) *Compendium logicae,* (7) *Elementarium logicae.*

On physics: (1) *Expositio in libros physicorum,* (2) *Summulae in libros physicorum,* (3) *Quaestiones in libros physicorum.*

On theology: (1) *Ordinatio* or *In 1 sententiarum,* (2) *Reportatio* or *In 2–3 sententiarum,* (3) *Quodlibeta septem,* (4) *Tractatus de corpore Christi* or *Primus tractatus de quantitate,* (5) *Tractatus de sacramento altaris* or *Secundus tractatus de quantitate,* (6) *Tractatus de praedestinatione et de praescientia Dei et de futuris contingentibus,* (7) *Quaestiones variae.*

Political and polemical writings: (1) *Opus nonaginta dierum,* (2) *De dogmatibus papae Ioannis XXII,* (3) *Contra Ioannem XXII,* (4) *Compendium errorum papae Ioannis XXII,* (5) *Tractatus ostendens (contra Benedictum XII),* (6) *Allegationes de potestate imperiali,* (7) *Octo quaestiones super potestate et dignitate papali,* (8) *An rex Angliae,* (9) *Consultatio de causa matrimoniali,* (10) *Dialogus,* (11) *Breviloquium de principatu tyrannico,* (12) *Tractatus de imperatorum et pontificum potestate.*

With few exceptions Ockham's works are available in 15th- and 16th-century editions and in facsimile reproductions, along with some recent publications. A critical edition of the philosophical and theological works is under the care of the Franciscan Institute at St. Bonaventure University, St. Bonaventure, N.Y. Of the political and polemical treatises three volumes have appeared in a critical edition at Manchester University, viz., v. 1, ed. J. G. Sikes, 1940; v. 2, ed. R. F. Bennett and H. S. Offler, 1963; v. 3, ed. H. S. Offler, 1956.

See Also: SCHOLASTICISM; NOMINALISM; OCKHAMISM; PHILOSOPHY, HISTORY OF, 3. MEDIEVAL.

Bibliography: C. K. BRAMPTON, ''Traditions Relating to the Death of William of Ockham,'' *Archivum Franciscanum historicum* (1960) 442–49. J. P. BECKMAN, *Wilhelm von Ockham* (Munich 1995); *Ockham-Bibliographie* (Hamburg 1992). A. A. MAURER, *The Philosophy of William of Ockham in the Light of Its Principles* (Toronto 1999). W. OCKHAM, *Quodlibetal Questions,* trans. A. FREDDOSO, and F. KELLEY (New Haven 1991). K. B. OSBORNE, ed., *A History of Franciscan Theology* (St. Bonaventure 1994). C. PANACCIO, *Les mots, les concepts, et les choses: La semantique de Guillaume d' Occam et le nominalisme d'aujourd'hui* (Montreal 1992). P. V. SPADE, ed., *The Cambridge Companion to Ockham* (Cambridge 1999).

[G. GÁL]

WILLIAM OF PAGULA (POUL)

Canon lawyer, a native of Paull (Pagula), Yorkshire, and perpetual vicar of Winkfield, near Windsor, Berkshire (1314–32); d. *c.* 1332. He was a doctor of Canon Law of Oxford by 1319. Between then and 1332, he wrote five works, all of which, with the exception of the last, are still in manuscript form: the *Oculus sacerdotis,* the most influential pastoral manual of 14th- and 15th-century England, some 60 manuscripts of which are extant (e.g., New College, Oxford, MS 292; Ohio State University, MS Lat. 1); *Summa summarum,* a compilation of Canon Law and theology for all grades of ecclesiastics, 13 manuscripts of which still survive (e.g., Oxford, MS Bodley 293; Huntingdon Library, MS EL. 9, H.3); *Speculum praelatorum,* a combination of the two previous works, of which only one manuscript is known; *Speculum religiosorum,* the first known tractate *De religiosis,* now extant in 10 manuscripts; and the *Epistola ad regem Edwardum,* an open letter to EDWARD III about excesses of royal retainers in the forest and area of Windsor.

Bibliography: J. MOISANT, *De speculo regis Edwardi III* (Paris 1891), who prints the *Epistola* at pp. 83–123 as a work of Simon Islip. L. BOYLE, ''The *Oculus sacerdotis . . .* of William of Pagula,'' *Transactions of the Royal Historical Society,* 5th ser., 5 (1955) 81–110. W. A. PANTIN, *The English Church in the Fourteenth Century* (Cambridge, Eng. 1955). A. B. EMDEN, *A Biographical Register of the University of Oxford to A.D. 1500* 3:1436–37.

[L. E. BOYLE]

WILLIAM OF PETER OF GODIN

French Dominican theologian; b. Bayonne *c.* 1260; d. Avignon, June 14, 1326. After entering the order at a very early age at Bayonne, he dedicated himself to: study philosophy at Beziers (1279–81), lector in various *studia naturalium* (1281–84), study theology at Montpellier (1284–87), lector in theology at various *studia* (1287–92), then higher studies at the University of Paris (1292–98), where he became bachelor in theology. He was provincial of Provence from July 21, 1301, until the division of the province, when he became provincial of the new province of Toulouse September 28, 1303. When relieved of this obligation, he was sent to Paris to obtain his doctorate and to teach in the Dominican chair for foreigners (1304–06). He was called by Clement V to be lector of the Sacred Palace at Avignon (1306–12), and was involved in great controversies of the time concerning Bernard Délicieux (1303), PETER JOHN OLIVI, the spirituals of Provence (1310–11), and UBERTINO OF CASALE. He was created cardinal of Saint-Cecilia by Clement V in December 1312, and made cardinal bishop of Santa Sabina by John XXII December 12, 1317. His major work, *Lectura Thomasina* (1296–98), is a commentary on the *Sentences* that incorporates the fundamental doctrines and texts of St. THOMAS AQUINAS. He probably wrote *De causa immediata ecclesiasticae potestatis,* published under the name of PETER OF LA PALU (Paris 1506).

Bibliography: É. H. GILSON, *History of Christian Philosophy in the Middle Ages,* (New York 1955) 746. P. GLORIEUX, *Répertoire des maîtres en théologie de Paris au XIIIᵉ siècle* (Paris 1933–34) 1:187–188. J. C. DIDIER, *Dictionnaire de théologie catholique,* ed. A. VACANT et al., 15 v., Tables générales (Paris 2000). M. GRABMANN, *Mittelalterliches Geistesleben,* 3 v. (Munich 1925–56) 2:559–576. F. J. ROENSCH, *Early Thomistic School* (Dubuque 1964).

[P. GLORIEUX]

WILLIAM OF RUISBROEK (RUYSBROECK)

(Ruysbroeck), Franciscan pioneer missionary and diplomat; fl. mid–13th century. Having heard rumors that Sartach, a Mongol ruler in the Volga region, was a Christian, William set out from Constantinople in 1253, accompanied by Bartholomew of Cremona, a fellow Franciscan, and three or four others, intending to establish a mission in Sartach's kingdom. When he had presented his credentials, including a letter from King LOUIS IX of France, at Sartach's court (July 21, 1253), he was obliged to proceed first to the headquarters of Batu, Sartach's father, and thence, accompanied only by Bartholomew, two Nestorian priests, and a guide, to the court of the great Khan Mangu at Karakoram (December 1253–January 1254). At Karakoram William found a colony of Europeans, mostly captives and artisans, that included the Parisian goldsmith William Boucher and his wife, and many Hungarians, as well as Russians, Alans, Georgians, and Armenians. Although his vehemence once disturbed the Khan, the friar was permitted to preach occasionally and he baptized some 60 persons. William left in August 1254, and in May 1255 he reached Acre, whence he sent his report to King Louis. He was a careful observer of persons and places, and his detailed account of his travels added much to Europe's knowledge of Asia and contained suggestions for further missionary endeavor.

Bibliography: *The Journey of William of Rubruck . . . ,* ed. W. W. ROCKHILL (London 1900). *Sinica franciscana,* ed. A. VAN DEN WYNGAERT, 5 v. (Quaracchi–Florence 1929–54) v.1. C. DAWSON, ed., *The Mongol Mission* (New York 1955). C. SCHOLLMEYER, ''Die Missionsfahrt Bruder Wilhelms von Rubruk,'' *Zeitschrift für Missionswissenschaft und Religionswissenschaft* 40 (1956) 200–205.

[M. W. BALDWIN]

WILLIAM OF SAINT-AMOUR

Secular theologian, opponent of the mendicant orders; b. Saint-Amour (Jura), France, *c.* 1200; d. there, Sept. 13, 1272. He was a master of arts of Paris by 1228, studied canon law, and received his doctorate before November 1238. In that year he was also canon of Beauvais and rector of the church of Guerville. In 1247, at the request of the bishop of Tarentaise and the Count of Savoy, he was given the care of souls in Granville, in the Diocese of Coutances, although he was only a subdeacon and student of theology at Paris. Upon becoming regent master in theology around 1250, he took a violent dislike to the new MENDICANT ORDERS and led the opposition against their masters in the university, particularly St. BONAVEN-

TURE and St. THOMAS AQUINAS. At his instigation, the university declared the Dominican masters suspended and excommunicated on Feb. 4, 1254, for not having participated in the suspension of classes the previous year (*see* PARIS, UNIVERSITY OF). As head of a university delegation that year, he was at the Papal Curia in Anagni, seeking condemnation of the Joachite *Introductorius in evangelium aeternum* by the Franciscan, Gerard of Borgo San Donnino. His efforts at the Curia were successful. On July 4, 1254, Innocent IV issued the bull *Quociens pro communi,* officially recognizing the university statutes of 1252, limiting chairs one to an order, although the Dominicans already had two. By the bull *Etsi animarum* of Nov. 21, 1254, Innocent rescinded certain privileges of mendicants to preach, hear confessions, administer sacraments, and bury the faithful, but on December 7 he died. Alexander IV, more sympathetic to the mendicants, abrogated his predecessor's restrictions on December 22, and on April 4, 1255, ordered the masters of Paris to receive the Dominicans back into the university by the bull *Quasi lignum vitae.* William not only organized passive resistance to the pope's decrees, but continued to attack the legitimacy of mendicant orders in sermons, disputations, and treatises, notably, *Liber de antichristo et eiusdem ministris,* in which he attempted to show that the Dominicans were precursors of antichrist (E. Martène, *Veterum scriptorum et monumentorum ecclesiasticorum et dogmaticorum amplissima collectio,* 9 v. [Paris 1724–33] 9:1213–1446). Alexander requested the bishops of Auxerre and Orléans to examine William's case against the mendicants on Dec.10, 1255. In June of the following year, Alexander deprived William and his followers of all benefices and requested King Louis to expel them from France. Ordered to appear before the bishops of Sens and Reims on July 31, 1256, William promised to revoke or correct anything found in his teaching that might be contrary to the decrees of the church. Meanwhile, between March and September 1256, with the cooperation of other Parisian masters, he prepared a scathing denunciation of the mendicant orders, *De periculis novissimorum temporum,* a copy of which was sent to the Papal Curia by King Louis. This work was condemned by Alexander on Oct. 5, 1256 (*Chartularium universitatis Parisiensis,* ed. H. Denifle and E. Chatelain, 4 v. [Paris 1889–97] 1:331–333). Arriving late at the Papal Curia toward the end of 1256 or the beginning of 1257, he presented his defense, *Casus et articuli super quibus accusatus fuit magister Guillelmus de Sancto Amore* (Faral, 340–361). Nevertheless, the condemnation of *De periculis* was repeated on Nov. 10, 1256, and on March 30, 1257. Forbidden to teach or preach, on Aug. 9, 1257, he was also exiled from France by order of the king. His friends at the university sent a delegation to the pope to seek a restoration of his position and privileges, but their request

Manuscript page from "Collections catholicae et canonicae scripturae," 14th-century manuscript by William of Saint-Amour, written by Wuberch.

was denied on Aug. 11, 1259; an appeal to the king to recall him from exile was refused also. While in exile, William wrote *Collectiones catholicae et canonicae scripturae,* which he sent to Pope Clement IV. In acknowledging its receipt on Oct. 18, 1266, the pope noted that its contents were substantially the same as those of *De periculis* (*Chartularium universitatis Parisiensis,* 1:459). Allowed to return from exile, William chose to live in his native village. Although forbidden by the Holy See, he continued correspondence with his faithful disciples at Paris, GERARD OF ABBEVILLE and Nicholas of Lisieux, who revived the antimendicant polemic before their master's death.

Bibliography: *Opera omnia* (Constance 1632). É. AMANN, *Dictionnaire de théologie catholique,* ed. A. VACANT et al., 15 v. (Paris 1903–50; Tables générales 1951–) 14.1:756–763. P. DELHAYE, *Catholicisme. Hier, aujourd'hui et demain* (Paris 1947–) 5:406–407. P. GLORIEUX, *Répertoire des maâitres en théologie de Paris au XIIIe siècle* (Paris 1933–34); v. 17–18 of *Bibliothèque Thomiste* (Le Saulchoir 1921–) 1:343–346. "Le *Contra Impugnantes* de S. Thomas," *Mélanges Mandonnet,* 2 v. (*Bibliothèque Thomiste* 13, 14; 1930) 1:51–81. E. FARAL, "Les *Responsiones* de Guillaume de Saint–Amour: Texte et commentaire," *Archives d' doctrinale et littéraire du moyen–âge* 18 (1950–51) 337–394. D. L.

DOUIE, *The Conflict between the Seculars and the Mendicants at the University of Paris in the Thirteenth Century* (London 1954).

[A. J. HEIMAN]

MARILIER, *Catholicisme. Hier, aujourd'hui et demain*, ed. G. JAC-QUEMET (Paris 1947—) 5:384–385.

[B. HAMILTON]

WILLIAM OF SAINT-BÉNIGNE OF DIJON, ST.

A reform abbot; b. Isola S. Giulio d'Orta, Novara, Italy, 962; d. Abbey of Fécamp, Jan. 1, 1031. The son of Robert, count of Volpiano, William was given as a child oblaté to the BENEDICTINE monastery of San Genuario at Locedio, near Vercelli, and was later professed there. He studied at Vercelli and at Pavia, and in 987 met Abbot MAJOLUS OF CLUNY, with whom he returned to CLUNY. In 988 Majolus entrusted him with the reform of Saint-Saurin, Avignon, and in 989 with the reform of the Abbey of Saint-Bénigne of Dijon. In 990 the community of Saint-Bénigne elected him abbot; at the same time he was ordained priest by Bruno, bishop of Dijon.

William was an ardent proponent of the CLUNIAC REFORM, and he founded (1001–03) the Abbey of FRUTTUARIA in Lombardy with the help of his brothers and of his uncle, King Arduin of Italy. This became a center of Cluniac influence in northern Italy, and in the mid-11th century the reforms of Fruttuaria were adopted at Siegburg and SANKT BLASIEN, and spread thence into Germany. In 1001 Richard II of Normandy replaced the secular canons of La Trinité Fécamp with monks from Dijon, and FÉCAMP became a center for monastic reform in Normandy. Among other monasteries there, William reformed JUMIÈGES and MONT SAINT-MICHEL. The observance of Dijon was introduced into Poland by Anastasius (or Astrik) of Hungary, a disciple of Bp. ADALBERT OF PRAGUE, who became first abbot of Meseritz in 996–997. By the time of his death William ruled 40 monasteries, and in all the houses reformed by him he had attempted to establish a tradition of learning. He also promoted the spread of Romanesque architecture in France, and rebuilt the abbey church of Saint-Bénigne. He was never canonized, but he is commemorated in the Benedictine martyrology. His biography was written by his contemporary, Rodulphus Glaber [*Patrologia Latina*, ed. J. P. Migne (Paris 1878–90) 142:697–720].

Feast: Jan. 1.

Bibliography: L. É. GOUGAUD, ed., *Chronique de l' abbaye de Saint-Bénigne de Dijon* (Dijon 1875), with a life. *Patrologia Latina*, ed. J. P. MIGNE (Paris 1878–90) 141:869–872, 1155–57. G. CHEVALLIER, *Le Vénérable Guillaume, abbé de Saint-Bénigne de Dijon . . .* (Paris 1875), with seven sermons and a tract attributed to William. W. WILLIAMS, "William of Dijon," *Monastic Studies* (Manchester, Eng. 1938) 99–120. P. SCHMITZ, *Histoire de l' Ordre de Saint-Benoît*, 7 v. (Maredsous, Bel. 1942–56) v.1, *passim*. J.

WILLIAM OF SAINT-BRIEUC, ST.

Bishop; b. St. Alban, in Brittany, France, *c.* 1175; d. Saint-Brieuc, July 29, 1234. He was ordained early in the 13th century, and served as secretary to three bishops of Saint-Brieuc and became bishop himself in 1220. William was a great friend of the poor and was noted for his charity. He staunchly defended the rights of the Church and its bishops against Peter Mauclerc, duke of Brittany (d. 1250), who in revenge expelled William from Saint-Brieuc. For two years he took refuge at Poitiers, where he assisted its ailing bishop. In 1230 Peter Mauclerc submitted himself to the Holy See, and William was able to return to his diocese, where he continued the construction of the cathedral. When he died, he left behind a great reputation for sanctity. Numerous miracles were performed at his tomb in the cathedral, and he was canonized by Pope INNOCENT IV in 1247.

Feast: July 29.

Bibliography: *Acta Sanctorum* (Paris 1863—) 7:131–138. J. TEMPLÉ, *Catholicisme. Hier, aujourd'hui et demain*, ed. G. JACQUEMET (Paris 1947—) 5:386–387. "Wilhelm v. St-Brieuc," *Lexikon für Theologie und Kirche*, ed. J. HOFER and K. RAHNER, 10 v. (Freiburg 1957–65). J. ARNAULT, *S. Guillaume: Évêque de Saint-Brieuc* (Saint-Brieuc 1934). A. BUTLER, *The Lives of the Saints*, rev. ed. H. THURSTON and D. ATTWATER (New York 1956) 3:212.

[F. D. LAZENBY]

WILLIAM OF SAINT-THIERRY

Twelfth-century theologian and mystic, Benedictine abbot of SAINT-THIERRY and later Cistercian monk of Signy; b. Liège, *c.* 1085; d. probably Sept. 8, 1148.

Life and Writings. William was born of a noble family, studied along with a certain Simon (his brother?), probably at Laon, under Anselm, disciple of St. Anselm, the abbot of Bec. In 1113 William entered the Benedictine Abbey of Saint-Nicasius at Reims, where he became thoroughly versed in the scriptures and the Fathers.

In the years 1116 to 1118 he made the acquaintance of St. Bernard of Clairvaux, with whom he formed a lasting friendship. In 1119 he was elected abbot of Saint–Thierry near Reims. In the next three years he wrote his first two works, *De Natura et dignitate amoris* and *De contemplando Deo*. Feeling little inclined to administrative work and preferring the life of silence and contemplation, he sought to enter Clairvaux, a desire that Bernard resolutely opposed. During the 1120s when the conflict between the Cluniacs and the Cistercians arose, William urged St. Bernard to defend the order of Cîteaux, and this resulted in Bernard's famous *Apologia* (1124), dedicated to William. Again in 1128 it was to William that Bernard dedicated his *De Gratia et libero arbitrio,* and William in turn dedicated to him in that same year his work *De Sacramento altaris.* During the years 1128 to 1135 William compiled a number of treatises drawn from the teachings of the Fathers: an exposition of the Canticle of Canticles drawn from SS. Gregory the Great and Ambrose that shows the influence of Origen; *De Natura Animae et corporis,* in which he synthesizes the teachings of East and West; an exposition on the Epistle to the Romans, drawn from St. Augustine, Origen, and Gregory of Nyssa. His *Meditativae orationes* (1130–45) reflect his ardent soul much in the same manner as the *Confessions* did that of St. Augustine.

In 1130 he took part in the first general chapter of Benedictines of the Reims province, held at the Abbey of St. Medard near Soissons. However, in 1135, seeking a more contemplative life, he resigned his office of abbot of Saint–Thierry and entered the recently established Cistercian foundation of Signy. Here he spent his time reading and in contemplation and prepared other treatises on the spiritual life and the problem of faith: *Speculum fidei* and *Aenigma fidei* (1140–44). Here too he urged Bernard to take up his pen against Peter Abelard, and William himself wrote his *Disputatio adversus Abelardum* and one entitled *De Erroribus Guillielmi de Conchis* (between 1135–40). In 1144 after a visit to the charterhouse of Mont-Dieu, near Reims, he wrote his *Epistola ad fratres de Monte Dei,* or the "Golden Epistle" as it is called, a work for many years attributed to Bernard. About this same time he wrote part of the life of Bernard known to us as the *Vita prima Bernardi.*

Doctrine. William's spiritual doctrine is an elaboration of his conception of the ascent of the soul toward God. His synthesis is rooted in the 12th–century theology of the image of God in man and is Trinitarian in character. Man, separated from God by sin, is destined to make his life a return to God that is realized in successive stages. In his early work, *De Natura et dignitate amoris,* William outlines the three degrees of love in which this image is restored. Love is the gift of God that is made to man through Jesus Christ in the Spirit; it is a possession of God and a participation in His life. Asceticism prepares the soul for this gift. By degrees, man passes from "animal" to "rational" and finally to "spiritual" life, in which he realizes union with God in the Spirit, a state that is an anticipation effected through contemplation here upon earth of the life of eternity. As the soul ascends

through these stages, it experiences a gradual liberation: from the obedience of "necessity," it passes on to "loving" obedience, and finally reaches a "unitive" obedience. Contemplation flowers into an experimental knowledge expressed in the formula *amor ipse intellectus est* by a participation in the life of the Spirit. The whole of the spiritual life is Trinitarian. William's conception of the image is related directly to the Trinity and exhibits the influence of St. Augustine and the Greek Fathers. For William, the image is dynamic and, by its essential constitution, impels the soul toward its archetype in the Trinity. The image is not merely the capacity for resemblance but the very process of actualization up through the three stages of animal, rational, and spiritual life. William places *memoria* in relation to the Father, *ratio* to the Son, and *amor* to the Spirit. Hence the three Persons are conceived of as raising man to a life superior to himself by supernaturalizing the dynamism of the image in man that from his creation has impelled him toward God.

Bibliography: WILLIAM OF SAINT–THIERRY, *Un Traité de la vie solitaire: Epistola ad fratres de Monte Dei,* crit. ed. M. M. DAVY, 2 v. (Paris 1940); *Deux traités de l'amour de Dieu: De la contemplation de Dieu, De la nature et de la dignité de l' amour,* ed. and tr. M. M. DAVY (Paris 1953); *De la contemplation de Dieu, l'oraison de Dom Guillaume,* ed. and tr. J. HOURLIER (*Sources Chrétiennes,* 61; Paris 1959); *Deux traités sur la foi: Le Miroir de la foi, L'Énigme de la foi,* ed. and tr. M. M. DAVY (Paris 1959); *Le Miroir de la foi,* ed. and tr. J. M. DÉCHANET (Bruges 1946); Eng. *The Mirror of Faith,* tr. G. WEBB and A. WALKER (London 1959); *Commentaire sur le Cantique des cantiques,* ed. and tr. M. M. DAVY (Paris 1958); *Exposé sur le Cantique des cantiques,* tr. M. DUMONTIER (*Sources Chrétiennes* 82; Paris 1962), Lat. text, introd. and nn. J. M. DÉCHANET; *Méditations et prières,* ed. and tr. J. M. DÉCHANET (Brussels 1945); *The Meditations of William of St. Thierry,* tr. A RELIGIOUS OF CSMV (New York 1954); *Oeuvres choisies,* ed. and tr. J. M. DÉCHANET (Paris 1944); *Lettre d'or aux frères du Mont-Dieu,* ed. and tr. J. M. DÉCHANET (Paris 1956); *The Golden Epistle of Abbot William of St. Thierry to the Carthusians of Mont-Dieu,* tr. W. SHEWRING, ed. J. MCCANN (London 1930). O. BROOKE, "The Trinitarian Aspect of the Ascent of the Soul to God in the Theology of William of St. Thierry," *Recherches de théologie ancienne et médiévale* 26 (1959) 85–127; "The Speculative Development of the Trinitarian Theology of William of St. Thierry in the *Aenigma Fidei,*" ibid. 27 (1960) 193–211; 28 (1961) 25–58; "William of St.–Thierry's Doctrine of Ascent to God by Faith," *ibid.* 30 (1963) 181–204. J. M. DÉCHANET, "Amor ipse intellectus est: La Doctrine de l'amour intellection chez G. de St.–Th.," *Revue du moyen–âge latin* 1 (1945) 349–374; *Aux sources de la spiritualité de G. de St.–Th.* (Bruges 1940); *G. de St.–Th.: L'Homme et son oeuvre* (Bruges 1942). T. KOEHLER, "Thème et vocabulaire de la *fruition divine* chez G. de St.–Th.," *Revue d'ascétique et de mystique* 40 (1964) 139–160. J. LECLERCQ et al., "G. de St.–Th. et la mystique trinitaire," *La Spiritualité du moyen âge,* v.2 of L. BOUYER et al., *Histoire de la spiritualité chrétienne* (Paris 1961) 249–254. L. MALVEZ, "La Doctrine de l'image et de la connaisance mystique chez G. de St.–Th.," *Recherches de science religieuse* 22 (1932) 178–205, 257–279. L. BOUYER, *The Cistercian Heritage,* tr. E. A. LIVINGSTONE (Westminster, Md. 1958) 67–124. P. GODET, *Diction-*

naire de théologie catholique, ed. A. VACANT et al., 15 v. (Paris 1903–50; Tables générales 1951–) 6.2:1981–82.

[B. LOHR]

WILLIAM OF SANDWICH, CHRONICLE OF

Account of the spread of the CARMELITES in the 13th century through the East and to Europe. Although presented as an eyewitness record, it was actually composed along with other unauthentic works *c.* 1380. The editor and probable author of the collection was the Carmelite Philip Ribot.

Bibliography: Sources. Ribot Collection. *Ghent Manuscript* (Karmelietenklooster, Boxmeer, Netherlands); *Codex Avila* (Collegio Sant'Alberto, Rome); Trier, Stadbibliothek, Manuscript 155; Munich Staatsbibliothek, Manuscript. Latin 471. Texts of Sandwich. G. WESSELS, *Analecta Ordinis Carmelitarum Calceatorum* 3 (Rome 1914–16) 302–315. Translations. J. CATTELONA, *Sword* 3 (1939) 365–368, 479–487. François de Sainte Marie, ed., *Les Plus vieux textes du Carmel* (2d ed. Paris 1961) 183–214, see p. 184 for other manuscripts, eds., and literature. Studies. R. HENDRIKS, "La Succession héréditaire," *Élie le prophète,* 2 v. in *Études Carmélitaines* 35 (1956) 2:69–70. A. STARING, "Notes on a List of Carmelite Houses in Medieval France," *Carmelus* 11 (1964) 153.

[K. J. EGAN]

WILLIAM OF SHERWOOD (SHYRESWOOD)

Treasurer of Lincoln cathedral from *c.* 1254 till his death (after 1267); to be distinguished from William de Monte, chancellor of Lincoln (d. 1213) and William of Durham (d. 1249), with both of whom he has often been confused. It is unproved that he taught Peter of Spain (Pope JOHN XXI) in Paris, but his *Introductiones in logicam* are comparable in scope with Peter's more famous *Summulae logicales;* they seem to be earlier (first half of 13th century), and, like William's *Syncategoremata,* bear a trace of Paris. ROGER BACON esteemed him as "far wiser" than Albert the Great in respect of *philosophia communis,* i.e., logic (*Op. tertium* 2). No other works can be certainly ascribed to William, but M. Grabmann has conjectured that the treatises *De insolubilibus, Obligationes,* and *Petitiones contrariorum* that follow the former two in Cod. Lat. 16617 of the Bibliothèque Nationale are also his. This body of work, and even the assured part of it, gives clear witness to the fact that medieval logic had already received its characteristic form by the middle of the 13th century. W. and M. Kneale have discussed William's theory of SUPPOSITION in some detail and in its historical context.

See Also: LOGIC, HISTORY OF.

Bibliography: M. GRABMANN, *Die Introductiones in logicam des Wilhelm von Shryeswood* in *Sitzungsberichte der Bayerischen Akademie der Wissenschaften zu München* (Munich 1937) Heft 10. J. R. O'DONNEL, ed., "The Syncategoremata of William of Sherwood," *Mediaeval Studies* 3 (1944) 46–93. W. and M. KNEALE, *The Development of Logic* (Oxford 1962).

[I. THOMAS]

WILLIAM OF TOULOUSE, ST.

Theologian and mystic; b. Toulouse 1297; d. May 18, 1369. He entered the Augustinian Order at about 19, was sent to the University of Paris for studies, and became a lecturer of theology. Effective as a preacher and spiritual adviser, he promoted especially prayers for the souls in purgatory. He read the lives of the saints frequently and sought to model his life according to their example. He overcame many temptations in his effort to attain perfection in the monastic virtues. God exalted him for his great humility through various wonders. A local cult was authorized 50 days after his death; miracles occurred; his cult was confirmed in 1893.

Feast: May 18.

Bibliography: *Acta Sanctorum* (Paris 1863—) 4:196–202. N. MATTIOLI, *B. Guglielmo da Tolosa dell'Ordine romitano di S. Agostino* (Rome 1894). T. BAURENS DE MOLINIER, *Le Missionnaire moderne . . . Suivi de la terrible vision des peines de' l'enfer, du B. Guillaume de Toulouse . . .* (Paris 1896).

[D. ANDREINI]

WILLIAM OF TRIPOLI

Dominican missionary and author; b. Tripoli? (modern Tarabulus, Lebanon), *c.* 1220; d. after 1273. Ordained at Acre, he converted many Muslims by preaching "without benefit of arms or philosophical argument." He may have accompanied ANDREW OF LONGJUMEAU on an embassy from (St.) LOUIS IX to the Mongol Khan (1249–51), and certainly represented Urban IV before Louis IX, the archbishop of Tyre, and the Count of Haifa. Gregory X, before leaving Acre for Rome, named him and Nicholas of Vicenza as his representatives with the Polos on their journey to China (1271–95); but the two left the embassy in Cilicia, on news of Sultan Baybars' attack on Armenia, to seek safety with the TEMPLARS in Acre. William's objective *Tractatus de statu Saracenorum et de Mahumeti pseudopropheta* [ed. H. Prutz, *Kulturgeschichte der Kreuzzüge* (1883) 575–598], done in 1273 at the request of Gregory X, depends on several Arabic sources, on Eastern chronicles through WILLIAM OF TYRE, and on his personal experience, which was unique in his day. It deals with Muhammad, the spread of Islam, and the Islamic doctrine and law as expounded in the Qu'ran.

Bibliography: J. QUÉTIF and J. ÉCHARD, *Scriptores Ordinis Praedicatorum* (New York 1959) 1.1:264–265. U. MONNERET DE VILLARD, *Lo studio dell'Islam in Europa nel XII e nel XIII secolo* (Vatican City 1944). M. VOERZIO, ''Fra Guglielmo da Tripoli orientalista domenicano,'' *Memorie Domenicane* 71 (1954) 73–113, 141–170, 209–250; 72 (1955) 127–148. A. DUVAL, *Catholicisme* 5:407–408.

[J. F. HINNEBUSCH]

WILLIAM OF TURBEVILLE

Bishop of Norwich, loyal partisan of Thomas BECKET; b. *c.* 1095; d. Norwich, Jan. 1174. William was educated in the Benedictine cathedral priory of NORWICH, where he was subsequently teacher and prior. In 1144, credulously accepting the unsubstantiated charges of the ''ritual murder'' of 12-year-old WILLIAM OF NORWICH by the Norwich Jewish community, he became the promoter of the ''boy martyr's'' cult. When he was elected bishop in 1146, he urged the monk Thomas of Monmouth to set down in writing the unreliable details of William's legend, thus instigating the first of an infamous series of ritual murder accusations against the Jews of Europe. Moreover, Bishop William moved the body of the boy to a place of high honor in Norwich cathedral and made his tomb a pilgrim attraction. Throughout the Becket controversy William gave the archbishop a unique and unfaltering loyalty.

Bibliography: THOMAS OF MONMOUTH, *The Life and Miracles of St. William of Norwich,* ed. and tr. A. JESSOPP and M. R. JAMES (Cambridge, Eng. 1896). D. KNOWLES, *Abp. Thomas Becket: A Character Study* (British Academy, London Proceedings, 1949, v.35; London 1952); *The Episcopal Colleagues of Archbishop Thomas Becket* (Cambridge, Eng. 1951). C. ROTH, *A History of the Jews in England* (Oxford 1941) 9, 13.

[A. R. HOGUE]

WILLIAM OF TYRE

Historian, diplomat, and polyglot (Latin, Greek, French, Arabic); b. Jerusalem, *c.* 1130; d. *c.* 1187. He was of a European merchant family in the Holy Land, and returned to Europe *c.* 1145, where for 20 years he pursued his studies: arts and theology in France, civil law and canon law in Bologna. Among his teachers were PETER LOMBARD and Hugh de Porta Ravennata. Having been ordained before 1161, he returned to the Holy Land in 1165. He became archdeacon in 1167, and was consecrated archbishop of Tyre, June 6, 1175. He has to his credit diplomatic missions to Constantinople and Rome (1169). In 1170, William was appointed tutor to Baldwin, the son of Amalric (Amaury), king of Jersualem (1163–74). In 1174, he became chancellor of the Latin Kingdom of JE-

RUSALEM. William represented his church at the Third LATERAN COUNCIL in 1179. When he failed to secure the patriarchate of Jerusalem in 1183, he retired from public life to spend his remaining years completing his history.

After 1169, at the request of Almaric, William had begun his *Historia rerum in partibus transmarinis gestarum,* covering crusading events from 1095 to 1184. It was translated into French in the 13th century and printed in Basel as early as 1549. His lost works include the *Gesta orientalium principum,* on the Arabs, and a treatise on the Third Lateran Council. William was familiar with the writings of Albert of Aachen (Aix), Fulcher of Chartres, and Balderic of Bourgueil, as well as with certain versions of the *Gesta Francorum.* The *Historia* is one of the most important works of medieval historiography, especially of the period after 1127, when its author became the primary witness. After *c.* 1144, it is a contemporary record. Though confused at times in its chronology, the *Historia* is an honest judgment of men and events, viewed by its author from the threefold aspect of religion, morality, and politics. His judgment of the Christian military effort in the Middle East is rather severe. The prologue to his work, written in 1184, is a brilliant statement of the author's determination to achieve objectivity, despite his association with the events he describes.

Bibliography: Editions. *Patrologia Latina,* ed. J. P. MIGNE, 217 v., indexes 4 v. (Paris 1878–90) 201; *Recueil des historiens des croisades: Historiens occidentaux* 1 (Paris 1844); Eng. *A History of Deeds Done beyond the Sea,* ed. and tr. E. A. BABCOCK and A. C. KREY, 2 v. (New York 1943). Literature. A. C. KREY, ''William of Tyre, The Making of an Historian in the Middle Ages,'' *Speculum* 16 (1941) 149–166. H. E. MAYER, ''Zum Tode Wilhelms von Tyrus,'' *Archiv für Diplomatik* 5–6 (1959–60) 182–201; *Deutsches Archiv für Erforschung des Mittelalters* 19.1 (1963) 240–241. R. B. C. HUYGENS, ''Guillaume de Tyr étudiant,'' *Latomus* 21 (1962) 811–829.

[B. LACROIX]

WILLIAM OF VAUROUILLON

Franciscan philosopher and theologian; b. Vauruellan (variants: de Valle Ruillonis, Vorillon, etc.) near Dinant, *c.* 1390; d. Rome, Jan. 22, 1463; some lists identify William as *Doctor Brevis.* In his youth he joined the Franciscans at Dinant. Though sent to the University of Paris in 1427, he did not begin his commentary on the *Sentences* before September 1429. Apparently because he refused to take part in the trial of Joan of Arc (February 1431), William left the University after completing only the first three books. He returned to Paris in 1447, becoming licentiate and master of theology in 1448 (cf. *Chartularium universitatis Parisiensis,* ed. H. Denifle and E. Chatelain [Paris 1889–97] 4:677–678, N. 2625).

Like others from Paris, he may have migrated in 1431 to the new university at Poitiers. He seems to have commented on the *Sentences* in some university before returning to Paris, and his *Vademecum* antedates the published text of the fourth book [*In 4 sent.* 11.2 (ed. 1502) fol. 238vb]. His *Liber de anima* was probably written during a later sojourn at Poitiers, after 1448. He remarks that during the years 1431 to 1447 he lived at Chateauroux and Dijon, and that he had been in Genoa, Germany, and at the Council of Basel (*ibid.,* fol. 274va, 281vb, 239ra). He served as minister provincial of the Touraine Conventuals from 1449–50 to 1461. In 1462, he was summoned to Rome because of a sermon he had preached, and there became involved in the famous controversy on the Precious Blood. He died soon after and was buried in Aracoeli.

As a scholastic, Vaurouillon is known primarily as a Scotist; he constantly refers to other great scholastics, however, and is a witness to the existence of a Franciscan school. In particular, his *Liber de anima* is a modernization of the *Summa de anima* of JOHN OF LA ROCHELLE, with influences from BONAVENTURE and DUNS SCOTUS.

See Also: SCOTISM.

Bibliography: I. C. BRADY, "The *Liber de anima* of William of Vaurouillon, O.F.M.," *Mediaeval Studies* 10 (1948) 225–297; 11 (1949) 247–307; "William of Vaurouillon († 1463): A Biographical Essay," in *Miscellanea Melchor de Pobladura*, v.1 (Rome 1964) 291–315.

[I. C. BRADY]

WILLIAM OF VERCELLI, ST.

Abbot; b. Vercelli, Piedmont, 1085; d. monastery of S. Salvatore at Goleto (or, Guglieto), near Nusco, Italy, June 25, 1142. He was the founder of the now extinct congregation of Benedictine monks called WILLIAMITES (1119) and of the celebrated abbey and shrine of Our Lady of Monte Vergine, near Avellino, southern Italy. At 14 he gave up his inheritance and made a pilgrimage to Santiago de Compostela, Spain. Upon returning to Italy in 1106, he began to live as a hermit. Some time later he built a cell on a mountain in the Partenio range, which he renamed Monte Vergine, and here he built the shrine to Our Lady, 1124. His first companions joined him in 1118 and 1119. When disagreements arose over alms received, William with five others moved to another mountain called Serra Cognata. Subsequently, he founded other monasteries, including the double monastery (*see* MONASTERY, DOUBLE) near Nusco, in southern Italy where he died at the age of 57. A Latin life of William by Felix Renda was published in Naples (1581), and another by Joannes Jacobus also at Naples (1643). His cultus was confirmed in 1728 and 1785.

Feast: June 25; Sept. 2 (translation).

Bibliography: *Acta Sanctorum*, June V (1744), 112ff. C. MERCURO, "Una leggenda medioevale di S. Guglielmo da Vercelli," *Rivista Storica Benedettina* 1 (1906) 321–333; 2 (1907) 74–100, 345–370. M. HEIMBUCHER, *Die Orden und Kongregationen der katholischen Kirche* (Paderborn 1932–34) 1:201. A. M. ZIMMERMANN, *Kalendarium Benedictinum: Die Heiligen und Seligen des Benediktinerorderns und seiner Zweige* (Metten 1933–38) 2:358–361. A. BUTLER, *The Lives of the Saints*, rev. ed. H. THURSTON and D. ATTWATER (New York 1956) 2:635–637.

[M. A. HABIG]

WILLIAM OF WARE

Listed variously as of Garo, Guarro, Varro, etc. (*see* A. B. Emden, *A Biographical Register of the University of Oxford to A.D. 1500*), English Franciscan honored as *Doctor fundatus, praeclarus*, and *acutus*; b. Ware, Hertfordshire, c. 1255–60; d. unknown. He entered the order early and studied at Oxford, where he commented on the *Sentences* c. 1292 to 1294, and possibly a second and third time also (c. 1300, c. 1305). He was an *inceptor* at Oxford; it is disputed whether he was ever at Paris, but some hold he was a *magister regens* there. An early tradition also maintains that he was the teacher of John DUNS SCOTUS.

Of his works, only his commentary on the *Sentences*, consisting of some 230 questions, is known, and of these only 25 have been published. Some 55 manuscripts contain distinct (probably three) redactions, *reportationes*, and abbreviations. Martin of Alnwick seems to have had a hand in the second redaction. William's commentary deals with many opinions of predecessors and contemporaries, especially of the Oxford milieu, and its critical attitude undoubtedly influenced Scotus and WILLIAM OF OCKHAM. An eclectic, Ware often stands at the midpoint between AUGUSTINIANISM and ARISTOTELIANISM, yet proposes many original views. In philosophy, he rejects the theory of ILLUMINATION and accepts the Aristotelian theory of knowledge, but with some emendations. He posits a formal distinction between essence and existence; between entity, truth, and goodness; and between the soul and its faculties. Primary matter is a positive entity in itself, and there are only two substantial forms, the intellective soul and the form of corporeity. William recognizes the primacy of the will and attaches to it an absolute autodeterminism.

Theology is not a strict science, since its principles, the articles of faith, are not evident. It is not a speculative, practical, or affective discipline, but a contemplative one. Its object is God "under the aspect of the good," whom man cannot know comprehensively, but only to some extent "under the notion of the infinite." The unicity of God is demonstrable by faith alone, a thesis that influenced Ockham and others. In the doctrine of the Trinity, William follows the psychological explanation proposed by HENRY OF GHENT. His Christology teaches the absolute primacy of Christ, and he was undoubtedly the first to introduce and positively defend the Immaculate Conception in university schools.

Bibliography: F. X. PUTALLAZ, "Measures prises par l'odre de Freres Mineurs (Guillame de la Mare et Jean Peckham)," in *Figures franciscaines: De Bonaventure a Duns Scot* (Paris 1997) 37–50, bibliography. G. GAL, ed., "Guilelmi de Ware OFM Doctrina Philosiphica per Summa Capita Proposita," *Franciscan Studies* 14 (1954)155–180; 265–292.

[A. EMMEN]

WILLIAM WICKWANE

Archbishop of York; place and date of birth unknown; d. PONTIGNY, August 1285. William appears to have come from the village of Child's Wickham in Gloucestershire, England. He was a university-educated *magister,* but there is no record of him before January 1264, when he was instituted to the church of Ivinghoe in the Diocese of Lincoln and in the gift of the bishop of Winchester. At that time he was already chancellor of York. Wickwane was elected archbishop of York, June 22, 1279, after the death of Abp. WALTER GIFFARD. His election was quashed, but he was then provided by NICHOLAS III and was consecrated at Viterbo in September of 1279. He was harrassed by Abp. JOHN PECKHAM of Canterbury on his way back to York.

An extremely conscientious diocesan, he devoted five years to the meticulous care of his province. His most ambitious project was the visitation of DURHAM, which he attempted when that see was both occupied and vacant. He was attacked both physically and legally, and the ensuing lawsuit survived Wickwane. As a result of his troubles, he left England for the Roman Curia, but stopped at the Cistercian abbey of Pontigny as had BECKET, STEPHEN LANGTON, and EDMUND OF ABINGDON. There he died of fever and was buried with a ring of gold on which was inscribed *Ave Maria gracia plena.* Wickwane sacrificed comfort and dignity for the principle of metropolitan jurisdiction and for the integrity of the church of York. He is a strong example of the 13th–century English type of pastoral bishop. His supposed work, the *Memoriale,* is not extant, but his register and a collection of his letters as chancellor survive.

Bibliography: *The Register of William Wickwane, Lord Archbishop of York, 1279–1285,* ed. W. BROWN (Durham 1907). W. H. DIXON, *Fasti eboracenses. Lives of the Archbishops of York,* ed.

J. RAINE (London 1863). W. HUNT, *The Dictionary of National Biography from the Earliest Times to 1900* (London 1885–1900) 21:178–179. C. R. CHENEY, "Letters of W. W., Chancellor of York, 1266–1268," *English Historical Review* 47 (1932) 626–642. R. BRENTANO, *York Metropolitan Jurisdiction and Papal Judges Delegate, 1279–1296* (Berkeley 1959).

[R. BRENTANO]

WILLIAM WOODFORD

Oxford Franciscan scholar, opponent of Wyclif, (fl. 1351-*c.* 1400). He was a Franciscan by 1351, and a doctor of theology by 1373. Woodford (Wodeford, Wydford) concentrated on scriptural studies. His apologetic works, however, were written to combat the views of his Oxford contemporary, John WYCLIF. The two men were on friendly terms during the 1370s and exchanged lecture notes on the *Sentences* of Peter Lombard. But as early as 1374 Woodford had become critical of Wyclif's teaching on dominion and suspicious of his views on the Eucharist. Because of their continuing friendship Woodford's treatises provide the best insight into the evolution of Wyclif's thought. In 1381, when Wyclif boldly attacked the doctrine of transubstantiation, Woodford wrote *De sacramento altaris or LXXII Questiones,* which indicated the various phases through which Wyclif's views had passed before his open confession of heresy. In 1389 Woodford was regent and master of theology among the Franciscans at Oxford, but after he was appointed vicar of the provincial minister he resided in London. He summed up his views on Wyclif's errors in the treatise *De causis condempnacionis articulorum 18 dampnatorum Johannis Wyclif.* Some place Woodford's death in 1397, others in 1411.

Bibliography: A. F. POLLARD, *The Dictionary of National Biography from the Earliest Times to 1900* 21:867–868. A. G. LITTLE, *The Grey Friars in Oxford* (Oxford 1892). A. B. EMDEN, *A Biographical Register of the University of Oxford to A.D. 1500* 3:2081–82. J. A. ROBSON, *Wyclif and the Oxford Schools* (Cambridge, Eng. 1961).

[J. E. HEALEY]

WILLIAMITES

A name used to designate three religious orders and three sects, none of which is in existence today.

The Benedictine congregation for both monks and nuns, founded by WILLIAM OF VERCELLI, continued to grow under his successors, receiving formal papal approbation in 1197. In 1611 the congregation of monks comprised 26 larger and 19 smaller monasteries. Today, Benedictines of the Congregation of Monte Cassino hold the abbey *nullius* of Monte Vergine and care for its Marian shrine. The Williamite convents of Benedictine nuns at one time numbered 50, but only two or three remained at the beginning of the 18th century.

The Hermits of St. William, named for WILLIAM OF MALEVAL but founded by his two companions, Albert and Renaldo, spread throughout Italy, France, Belgium, Germany, and Hungary. They were divided into two congregations when, in the 13th century, some monasteries accepted the BENEDICTINE RULE and others adopted the Rule of St. AUGUSTINE. Some of the latter were reincorporated into the order as Benedictines, but the motherhouse at Maleval became a house of AUGUSTINIANS. Most of the Benedictine monasteries that survived into the 17th century were absorbed by other branches of the Benedictine order.

The Williamite Order of Knights, which William the Pious, Duke of Aquitaine, is supposed to have founded in 887, never existed. However, an earlier Duke WILLIAM OF AQUITAINE (d. 812) had founded a Benedictine monastery for men and another for women at Gellone in Languedoc in 804. He entered the former; his two sisters, the latter. The Monastery of the Holy Cross (or of St. William) at Gellone existed until 1783.

The name of "Williamites" was sometimes given to the followers of WILLIAM OF SAINT-AMOUR (d. 1272), the adversary of the Dominicans and Franciscans at the University of Paris.

Wilhelmine of Milan (d. 1282) and her followers, both men and women, formed a secret heretical sect, the Williamites, which was discovered and suppressed only after her death. She had claimed to be the incarnation of the Holy Spirit.

In the late 14th century, Aegidius Cantoris, a layman of Brussels, who called himself the "Savior of Men," led a heretical sect, which William of Hildernisse, a Carmelite priest, was accused of supporting. For this reason his followers were called Williamites.

Bibliography: G. HENSCHEN, *Commentarius hist. de ordine eremit. S. Guilielmi, Acta Sanctorum* (Paris 1863–) February 2:473–486. M. HEIMBUCHER, *Die Order und Kongregationen der Katholischen Kirche,* 2 v. (3 ed. Paderborn 1932–34) 1:179, 201, 302, 539. K. ELM, *Beiträge zur Geschichte des Wilhelmitenordens* (Cologne 1962).

[M. A. HABIG]

WILLIAMS, JOHN JOSEPH

Fourth bishop and first archbishop of Boston; b. Boston, Mass., April 27, 1822; d. there Aug. 30, 1907. The son of Michael and Ann (Egan) Williams, Irish immigrants, John attended Boston's cathedral school, then went to the Sulpician college in Montreal and the Sulpician seminary in Paris. After ordination there on May 17, 1845, he was assigned first to the Holy Cross Cathedral in Boston, and returned there as rector in 1856. In 1857 he was appointed pastor of St. James Church, and later that year vicar-general of the diocese under Bp. J. B. Fitzpatrick. When Fitzpatrick's health declined, he selected Williams as auxiliary bishop. The bulls for the bishop-elect arrived from Rome on Feb. 9, 1866, and Fitzpatrick died four days later. Williams was consecrated fourth bishop of Boston on March 11, 1866, by Cardinal John MCCLOSKEY of New York. When the rapidly expanding diocese became difficult to administer, the Dioceses of Springfield and Providence were created from it (1870 and 1872, respectively). In February 1875 Boston was raised to a metropolitan see and Williams was appointed its first archbishop, receiving the pallium on May 2. He received John Brady as auxiliary bishop in 1891, but only in 1904, when he was 82, did he submit to the appointment of William Henry (later Cardinal) O'CONNELL as coadjutor.

Williams is assessed as a pastoral bishop rather than a national or international church statesman. His initial tasks were to acquire priests and religious orders, and to erect churches, schools, hospitals, charitable institutions, and a seminary. He considered construction of the new cathedral, which he dedicated Dec. 8, 1875, and St. John's Seminary (opened at nearby Brighton in September 1884) two of his most important projects. He attended the Second Plenary Council of Baltimore (1866) and Vatican Council I three years later, but at both he played a minor role. In the late 1800s the Catholics of New England were severely harassed, but the archbishop made every effort to mitigate these attacks, counseling prudence on the part of the Catholics—no easy task when his flock included rising political leaders and vociferous journalists. When some of his people faced financial ruin following the fire and panic of 1872–73, he embarked on a program, as a coproprietor of the *Pilot* with John Boyle O'REILLY, to help victims of business failure. He founded the first conference of the St. Vincent de Paul Society in New England and established the Catholic Union of Boston, a laymen's organization providing for participation in the spiritual and secular affairs of the diocese. On the national scene he was regarded variously as too conciliatory or too conservative. He aligned himself with so-called liberals among the hierarchy on such issues as the KNIGHTS OF LABOR and the Abbelen Memorial, while on others, such as the school debate, he took a conservative stand. His closest friend among the hierarchy was conservative Bp. Bernard J. MCQUAID of Rochester.

Bibliography: J. T. ELLIS, *The Life of James Cardinal Gibbons,* 2 v. (Milwaukee 1952). R. H. LORD et al., *History of the Archdiocese of Boston. . .1604 to 1943,* 3 v. (New York 1944). F. G. MCMANAMIN, *The American Years of John Boyle O'Reilly, 1870–1890* (Washington 1959).

[F. G. MCMANAMIN]

Bibliography: S. J. KUNITZ and H. HAYCRAFT, eds., *Twentieth Century Authors* (New York 1942) 1523.

[G. N. SHUSTER]

WILLIAMS, MICHAEL

Writer and founding editor of the *COMMONWEAL;* b. Halifax, Canada, Feb. 5, 1877; d. Westport, Connecticut, Oct. 12, 1950. One of six children born to Michael and Ann (Colston) Williams, Michael studied at St. Joseph's College, New Brunswick, Canada, until his father's death, when he found work in a warehouse. About this time he gave up the practice of his religion. A penniless young man, he sought his fortune in Boston, Massachusetts, as a writer of stories and verse under the pseudonym "The Quietist." Befriended by Philip Hale of the *Boston Journal,* he became a reporter on the *Boston Post,* then on the *New York World* and *Evening Telegram.*

He next went West, and had just been named city editor of the *San Francisco Examiner* when the 1906 earthquake and fire devastated the city. He subsequently joined Upton Sinclair's colony at Englewood, New Jersey, and with that author wrote *Good Health . . .* (1909). He reentered the Church in 1912 at Carmel, California, where he had settled to write. *The Book of the High Romance* (1918), a colorfully written account of his life and conversion, brought him a measure of fame.

Back in New York, he organized the Calvert Associates to promote the idea of a Catholic intellectual weekly to be edited by laymen with some non-Catholic collaborators (among them was the architect Ralph Adams Cram). The *Commonweal,* the realization of his idea, was launched in 1924 and was edited by Williams until 1937 when a new group of editors assumed responsibility. He thereafter contributed a column,"Views and Reviews," concerned especially with issues affecting the Church and Christianity—the rise of totalitarianism, the Calles persecutions in Mexico, anti-Semitic and anti-Catholic prejudice, the cause of African-Americans, and secularism. He married Margaret Olmstead and had two children, one of whom became Mother Margaret Williams, RSCJ.

His other published works are *American Catholics in the War* (1921), the fruit of his work with the National Catholic War Council of World War I; *The Little Flower of Carmel* (1926); *Catholicism and the Modern Mind* (1928); *The Shadow of the Pope* (1932); and *The Catholic Church in Action* (1935).

WILLIAMS, ROGER

American theologian and founder of the Rhode Island colony, whose writings opposed the union of church and state and argued for religious tolerance; b. London, England, *c.* 1603; d. Providence, R.I., *c.* March 1683. He was the son of a well-to-do merchant tailor of London. As the protégé of Sir Edward Coke, Williams was admitted to the Charterhouse School (1621) and entered Pembroke Hall, Cambridge (1623), on a scholarship from the Charterhouse. He received his A.B. degree in 1627, signing an acknowledgement of his belief in the THIRTY–NINE ARTICLES and the BOOK OF COMMON PRAYER. He continued to study at Pembroke until 1629, when he was ordained and settled as chaplain in the household of Sir William Masham, a leader of the PURITANS. In 1630 Williams and his bride left England for Massachusetts. On his arrival, he refused a call to the Boston church "as he durst not officiate to an unseparated people" and, after a brief stay at Salem, was accepted as assistant pastor by the separatists at Plymouth. Difference of opinion between Williams and his congregation ended this pastorate in 1633, when he accepted a call to Salem.

During this period he was a center of controversy because of his views on separation from the Church of England, his insistence that civil magistrates could not enforce divine worship because such laws offered a false motive for religion, and his argument that only purchase from the native peoples, and not royal grants, could give valid title to colonial lands. Underlying these specific points was his rejection of New England's claim to be a new Israel and his determined effort to make the New England churches communities of the regenerate. A lengthy series of discussions in the summer of 1635 between Williams and the Massachusetts authorities clarified his own position and led directly to his banishment from the colony on Jan. 11, 1636. He fled to the Narragansett country beyond the boundaries of the Massachusetts patent, where he purchased land from the native peoples and, with a group of his followers, formed the colony of Providence Plantations (1636). Williams was a theologian rather than a political theorist. His simplistic frame of government and land tenure provided grounds for lengthy controversies in early Rhode Island history and allowed less scrupulous followers to profit at his expense. His insistence that no settler be troubled for his conscience, however, made the colony a haven for victims of Massachusetts intolerance. In 1638 the loose fellowship envisioned in the original compact was more formally organized as a township; lands were divided among a company of proprietors; and Williams renounced both property and political power. At first he had served as the spiritual leader of the group; with the coming of the BAPTISTS (1639) he attended their services for a time without formally joining them, but then he cast off all church fellowship. In this step he was perfectly consistent. Throughout his life Williams was an orthodox Calvinist, teaching the same doctrines as his opponents and firmly holding to the absolute authority of the Bible. His difficulty was to find "a true Christian church, whose matter must not only be living stones, but also separated from the rubbish of Antichristian confusions and desolations." Both his appeals for religious tolerance and disestablishment and his bitter invective against the Quakers stemmed from the same source (*see* FRIENDS, RELIGIOUS SOCIETY OF). He believed "that some come nearer to the first primitive churches and the institutions and appointments of Christ Jesus than others" but "among so many pretenders to be the true Christian army" he was "in doubt unto which to associate himself."

His most important writings, composed on a visit to London in 1643 to secure confirmation of the Rhode Island claims, include *A Key into the Language of America* (1643), a native-language word book with theological overtones, and *Queries of Highest Consideration* (1644), on the separation of church and state and general tolerance. He elaborated on these ideas in *Mr. Cotton's Letter, Lately Printed, Examined and Answered,* where he rejected New England's application of the covenant theology, and in *The Bloudy Tenent, of Persecution, for Cause of Conscience* (1644) where he resumed his argument with Cotton and showed that the idea that men could be forced by law to accept Christ was in opposition to Christian teaching. Returning in 1644 with his charter, Williams found bitter opposition to his "pretended authority" in Rhode Island. The creation of a General Assembly in 1647 did little to halt the spread of disaffection. In 1651 he took his problems to Parliament, availing himself of the opportunity to publish a spirited plea for disestablishment and the abolition of tithes in England in *The Hireling Ministry None of Christ's* (1652). In *The Bloudy Tenent Yet More Bloudy* (1651) he answered Cotton's reply to his earlier pamphlet point by point. Cromwell's influence restored Williams's authority in Rhode Island, although opposition was by no means crushed. His policies made the colony a Quaker refuge after 1657 and Quakers became numerous enough to control the assembly in 1672. In that year, he engaged in public disputation with several Quaker preachers on doctrinal issues, publishing an account of the debate in *George Fox Digg'd Out of his Burrows* (1676). The *Complete Writings of Roger Williams* was issued in seven volumes at New York in 1963.

Bibliography: J. E. ERNST, *Roger Williams* (New York 1932). P. MILLER, *Roger Williams* (New York 1953). O. E. WINSLOW, *Master Roger Williams* (New York 1957). M. CALAMANDREI, "Neglected Aspects of Roger Williams' Thought," *Church History* 21 (1952) 239–258.

[R. K. MACMASTER]

WILLIAMS, WILLIAM

Welsh theologian and religious poet, commonly known as Pantycelyn; b. Cefncoed, Carmarthenshire, 1717; d. Pantycelyn, Jan. 2, 1791. Williams was the son of a prosperous farmer, and at 21 was converted to Methodism. He abandoned his medical studies and was ordained deacon (1740), but did not go on to full orders. The Methodist Revival, then stirring in Wales, was the result of long impatience with the formalism of the state church. The need for a personal, living response to grace gave birth, at first within the established church, to a group of great preachers whose sermons initiated a revival of religion.

Williams finally identified himself with Methodism as a system functioning independently of Church jurisdiction. Williams realized the necessity for the interiorization of Christian doctrine as a spiritual experience and early instituted weekly meetings of societies for the faithful for public confession of sin, discussion of spiritual experience, and mutual help to lead the Christian life. His natural aptitude as a psychologist, reinforced by his experience of spiritual diagnosis in the societies, enabled him to describe in his *Theomemphus* the soul's progress in union with Christ. This poem has been called by the Welsh critic Saunders Lewis "the first great romantic poem in European literature."

Williams is best known, however, for his hymns. Hundreds of them are still sung and some are included in the Welsh Catholic hymnal. Many deal with the transience of created things and the burden of man's earthly pilgrimage, but, above all, with the saving merits of Christ. They remain the true prayer of Nonconformity. Williams's great work was the definition of a structure within which Nonconformist spirituality developed. His voluminous output as theologian, poet, and preacher, and his extensive travels in supervising the societies, were all directed to this end. At his death the spiritual foundations of Methodism had been secured for the next 200 years.

Bibliography: G. M. ROBERTS, in *Dictionary of Welsh Biography down to 1940* (London 1959) 1077–78. S. LEWIS, *Williams Pantycelyn* (London 1927).

[C. DANIEL]

WILLIBALD OF EICHSTÄTT, ST.

Anglo-Saxon monk, missionary to Germany, bishop; b. Wessex, 700; d. Eichstätt, July 7, 781. Of noble birth, Willibald was the son of (St.) ''Richard'' (feast, February 7), and the brother of (St.) WINNEBALD and (St.) WALBURGA OF HEIDENHEIM. He was a kinsman of (St.) BONIFACE. At the age of five he was sent by his parents to the monastery of Bishop's Waltham. When grown up he determined to make a pilgrimage to Rome and persuaded his father and his brother, Winnebald, to accompany him. They all set out from Southampton in the summer of 721 and landed at Rouen. Thence they journeyed as far as Lucca, where their father died; around him there grew up a cult supported by a mass of legend. The two brothers arrived in Rome in the autumn and both fell victims to an intermittent fever; but since the bouts never coincided, each could nurse the other. Soon after recovery Willibald set out for Palestine with an Englishman named Tidberht. Leaving Rome in 722, they went by way of Naples to Sicily, Greece, Asia Minor, and Cyprus. Thence they sailed to Syria, where the Saracens imprisoned them; however, they were helped by a friendly merchant who provided them with dinner and supper every day and had them taken out for a bath each Wednesday and Saturday. They were soon liberated and passed on through Damascus to the Holy Land, wandering from site to site and paying four separate visits to Jerusalem. Altogether their journeyings lasted seven years, including two years in Constantinople. The full record of their wanderings, often called the *Hodoeporicon*, is the earliest English travel book. It is based directly on the pilgrim's own words, having survived in Willibald's biography written while he was still alive, by an English nun at Heidenheim, named Hugeburc or Hygeburh [*Monumenta Germaniae Historica: Scriptores* 15.1:86–106; Eng. tr. W.R.B. Brownlow (Berlin 1891)]. In 730 the two travelers went to Mone Cassino, where Willibald remained for ten years, until the abbot sent him to Rome. From there Pope GREGORY III sent him on to assist Boniface, who ordained him priest (741) and 12 months later consecrated him first bishop of the new Diocese of Eichstätt, in Bavaria. Willibald and Winnebald founded a double MONASTERY at Heidenheim (Württemberg), where their sister, Walburga, succeeded as abbess. Willibald's relics are still in Eichstätt cathedral.

Feast: July 7.

Bibliography: C. H. TALBOT, ed. and tr. *The Anglo-Saxon Missionaries in Germany* (New York 1954) 153–177. A. M. COOKE, *The Dictionary of National Biography From the Earliest Times to 1900* (London 1938) 21:483–484. M. COENS, ''Légende et miracles du Roi S. Richard,'' *Analecta Bollandiana* 49 (Brussels 1931) 353–397. W. LEVISON, *England and the Continent in the Eighth Century* (Oxford 1946). B. APPEL, E. BRAUN, and S. HOFMANN, eds., *Hl. Willibald* (Eichstätt 1987). H. DICKERHOF, E. REITER and S. WEINFURTER, eds., *Der Hl. Willibald—Klosterbischof oder Bistumsgründer?* (Regensburg 1990).

[B. COLGRAVE]

WILLIBRORD OF UTRECHT, ST.

Anglo-Saxon bishop and missionary, apostle of the Frisians; b. Northumbria, England, 658; d. Echternach, Luxembourg, Nov. 7, 739. Willibrord was the son of St. WILGIS; ALCUIN was his near relative. At an early age Willibrord entered the BENEDICTINES at RIPON under WILLRID OF YORK. About 678 he went to Rathmelsigi in Ireland to be the disciple of the renowned EGBERT OF IONA. He was ordained in 688, and in 690 Egbert dispatched him with 11 companions, including SWITHBERT, as a missionary to Frisia, where he established a mission at Wiltaburg and then one at Utrecht. His labors seemed fruitless, and he sought support at the court of Pepin of Heristal, who sent him on to Rome to seek the specific authorization of the pope. He returned, with papal authority and relics, to undertake the evangelization of north Brabant. During another trip to Rome in 695, he was consecrated archbishop of the Frisians in St. Cecilia's Church by Pope Sergius I, who gave him the Latin name Clement. He returned to the Netherlands with full pontifical authority and established his cathedral seat at Utrecht, where he was visited by Wilfrid. From there he made a series of extensive journeys: in 698 he established the Abbey of ECHTERNACH on land given him by the Frankish Princess, IRMINA; and he set out to Christianize Denmark. He returned from this journey with 30 young Danes to educate as Christians, pausing at Heligoland and Walcheren, in both islands boldly attacking the local pagan shrines. In the ensuing years the early Carolingians (*see* CAROLINGIAN DYNASTY) came to rely on his support, as he did on theirs, and in 714 he baptized PEPIN III, later the first Carolingian king of the FRANKS. The following year the mission in Frisia suffered its worst setback: the pagan Frisian King Radbod, taking advantage of the death of Pepin of Heristal, killed missionaries and destroyed churches, expelling Willibrord. When Radbod died (719), Willibrord, aided by CHARLES MARTEL, returned to Frisia. There he labored to reestablish his missions, and for some time he was aided by BONIFACE. In his later years he retired to his favorite spot, the Abbey of Echternach, where he died and was buried.

He was the first of the great series of Anglo-Saxon missionaries to the Continent who played a large part in strengthening the bonds between the local Frankish churches and the Holy See. The name Clement granted him indicates his affiliation with the Roman community, and it is no accident that the cathedral churches of Rome, Canterbury, and Utrecht all bore the name St. Savior. His reception of the pallium was the first papal grant to an archbishop on the Continent. His first trip to Rome seems to have initiated direct relationships between the papacy and the rising Carolingian dynasty. Extant writings of Willibrord are few. [There is a group of charters and confirmations (*Patrologia Latina* 89:535–556); his testament is printed and examined in *Analecta Bollandiana* 25:163–176 by A. Poncelot; the Calendar of St. Willibrord, reprinted in facsimile by the Henry Bradshaw Society, 55 (1918), appears to have some notes in Willibrord's handwriting]. He is represented in art as a bishop plunging the shaft of his crosier into a cask.

Feast: Nov. 7; Nov. 10 (translation).

Bibliography: ALCUIN, *Vita* bk. 1 *Acta Sanctorum* (Paris 1863—) 3:435–451; bk. 2, *Monumenta Germaniae Historica: Poetae* 1:207–220. C. H. TALBOT, ed. and tr., *The Anglo-Saxon Missionaries in Germany* (New York 1954) 3–22. M. TOUT, *The Dictionary of National Biography From the Earliest Times to 1900* (London 1938) 21:484–486. W. LEVISON, *England and the Continent in the 8th Century* (Oxford 1946). C. W. WAMPACH, *Sankt Willibrord* (Luxembourg 1953). P. VAN MOORSEL, *Willibrord en Bonifatius* (Bussum 1968); *Over Willibrord gesproken* (Ann Arbor 1989). G. KIESEL, *Der heilige Willibrord im Zeugnis der bildenden Kunst; Ikonographie des Apostels der Niederlande mit Beiträgen zu seiner Kultgeschichte* (Luxembourg 1969). H.-J. REISCHMANN, tr. and ed., *Willibrord, Apostel der Friesen* (Sigmaringendorf 1989). L. J. M. NOUWEN, *Willibrord: een heilige diplomaat of een diplomatieke heilige* (2d ed. Tielt 1993). L. VON PADBERG, *Heilige und Familie: Studien zur Bedeutung familiengebundener Aspekte in den Viten des Verwandten- und Schülerkreises um Willibrord, Bonifatius, und Liudger* (Mainz 1997).

[J. L. DRUSE]

WILLIGIS OF MAINZ, ST.

Archbishop, influential supporter of the imperial Saxon dynasty; b. Schoningen, Germany; d. Mainz, Germany, Feb. 23, 1011. Of Saxon birth, and possibly of unfree status, Willigis was educated by Prince Otto's tutor, Volkold, who introduced him to the court of OTTO I, where Willigis became chancellor in 971. In 975 OTTO II appointed him archbishop of Mainz as well as archchancellor. Although always politically active, Willigis reached the peak of his influence during OTTO III's minority when he saved the throne for Otto and served as principal adviser to the regents, Theophano and Adelaide. Willigis's decisive action helped HENRY II succeed to the German crown after Otto's early death, 1002. As archbishop, Willigis allowed extensive freedom to his 12 suffragans, who were predominantly his personal choices because of his intimacy with the royal court. They included men such as BURCHARD OF WORMS. Twice, however,

in 992 and 996, Willigis exerted his authority to induce Bp. ADALBERT OF PRAGUE to return to Bohemia from Rome. He engaged in a bitter controversy with Bp. BERNWARD OF HILDESHEIM over the convent of GANDERSHEIM, which was on the boundary of their sees. In 987 Willigis first asserted jurisdiction over this convent. Thirteen years later the dispute became acute when a Roman synod (1001) denied Willigis's claims and he defied its decision and the emperor's wishes. The papal legate of SYLVESTER II declared him deposed from his see, but could not enforce the sentence. Finally, in 1006, Henry II persuaded Willigis to abandon his claims. He then cooperated with Henry in restoring the Diocese of Merseburg and in founding the See of Bamberg, both dependent on Mainz.

Willigis encouraged the contemporary monastic reform movement, founded monasteries and parishes, and gained renown for his artistic patronage. His cathedral, after 30 years of construction, burned to the ground on its dedication day, Aug. 30, 1009, but Willigis promptly began to rebuild. Though interested in education, he was more a man of action than of scholarship. Little information survives about his personal or spiritual life.

Feast: Feb. 23.

Bibliography: J. F. BÖHMER and C. WILL, eds., *Regesta archiepiscoporum Moguntinensium*, 2 v. (Innsbruck 1877–86) v.1. H. BÖHMER, *Willigis von Mainz* (Leipzig 1895). E. N. JOHNSON, *The Secular Activities of the German Episcopate, 919–1024* (Lincoln, NE 1932). A. HAUCK, *Kirchengeschichte Deutschlands* (Berlin-Leipzig) 3:268–270, 414–418. W. KLENKE, "Die Gebeine . . . Willigis," *Mainzer Zeitschrift* 56–57 (1961–62) 137–145. *Willigis und sein Dom*, ed. A. PH. BRÜCK (Mainz 1975). *1000 Jahre St. Stephan in Mainz: Festschrift*, ed. H. HINKEL (Mainz 1990).

[R. H. SCHMANDT]

WILLMANN, OTTO

Philosopher and educator who pioneered in the theory of modern Catholic social education; b. Lissa, near Posen, Poland, April 24, 1839; d. Leitmeritz, Czechoslovakia, July 1, 1920. He was educated in the Comenius gymnasium of Lissa, and studied at Breslau, Poland, and Berlin, Germany, under H. Steinthal and A. Trendelenburg, taking his doctorate in 1862 with the thesis *De Figuris grammaticis*. In 1873 he began his study of education at Leipzig, Germany, under T. Ziller and became one of the foremost authorities on Herbartian pedagogy. Although Willmann is noted as a philosopher, and as the author of *Geschichte des Idealismus,* his educational theories greatly influenced European thought.

Willmann taught for four years at the Pädagogium in Vienna, Austria, and in 1872 was named professor of philosophy and pedagogy at the German University of Prague, a position he held until 1905. He became the leading German Catholic scholar in education, and an outstanding interpreter of German education. Willmann found fault with German pedagogy on several counts. Because of idealism, it had lost touch with reality; because of realism, it overemphasized methodology and stressed soulless techniques and organization. Theories of individualism overlooked the social nature of education, while theories of socialism threatened to absorb the individual into the group without regard for his personal destiny. Willmann undertook to review the whole area of pedagogy, trying to combine in a single synthesis the ideas of the thinkers of the past and the contributions of modern theorists.

He defined education as "the solicitous, formative, and directive action of adults on the development of the young, which aims at making them participate in the goods which are the bases of our social institutions." It embraces six fundamental elements: solicitude, formation, direction, discipline, ideal goods, and social institutions. Each has subordinate aspects. "Formation," for example, refers to the formation of the whole man, both his moral and spiritual perfection, and his social and personal development. Although any sound system should provide for all six, Willmann held that only Catholic philosophy could take every aspect into account. He particularly emphasized the social nature of education as the essential element that constantly renews the life of the group, while allowing for individual development.

Willmann maintained that although education, as a practical subject, should concern itself with methods, reforms, and adaptation, there was also need for broad historical understanding. Both practice and history, he felt, must be supported by reasonable theory lest they be sterile. He concluded that only a genuinely Catholic philosophy and concept of education fulfilled all requirements. Willmann, a devout Catholic, declared that the church had been his greatest teacher. His chief educational work is the *Didaktitk als Bildungslehre*.

Bibliography: F. DE HOVRE, *Philosophy and Education* (New York 1931). G. GREISSL, *Otto Willmann als Pädagog und seine Entwicklung* (Paderborn 1916). J. B. SEIDENBERGER, *Otto Willmann: Eine Einführung in seine Pädagogik und Philosophie* (Paderborn 1923).

[A. J. CLARK]

WILLSON, ROBERT WILLIAM

Bishop, Church leader, advocate of prison and hospital reforms; b. Lincoln, England, 1794; d. Nottingham, June 30, 1866. He was the son of William Willson, a builder, and Clarissa Tenney. He studied at Oscott and was ordained by Bishop MILNER Dec. 16, 1824. Having been for 18 years pastor of Nottingham, where his gifts of leadership won universal recognition, Willson was appointed first bishop of Hobart, Tasmania, Britain's main penal colony until 1853. For 10 years the bishop devoted his services almost entirely to the welfare of convicts, the insane, and orphans. He fought for and won many reforms and had much to do with ending the system of transporting convicts. Churches, schools, and parishes with resident clergy appeared in all the populated areas of the diocese, which embraced the whole of Tasmania. Sir W. Denison, the governor, and public bodies associated with charitable and philanthropic movements paid frequent tributes to the bishop's services to religion and the state.

Bibliography: W. B. ULLATHORNE, "Bishop Willson," *Dublin Review* 3d ser. 18 (1887) 1–26. Hobart Church Archives.

[J. H. CULLEN]

WILMART, ANDRÉ

Benedictine historian of Christian Latin literature, patristic and medieval; b. Orléans, France, Jan. 28, 1876; d. Paris, April 21, 1941. While a student in Paris (1893–96) Wilmart was guided by Pierre BATIFFOL to turn from philology to ecclesiastical erudition and to direct himself to the priesthood. Visits to Solesmes led to his profession there in 1901. After ordination at Appuldurcombe (Isle of Wight) in 1906, he was enrolled in another colony of the expatriated Solesmes monks, the Abbey of Farnborough in Hampshire, where he maintained his monastic stability until his death. There were, however, frequent *voyages littéraires*—in England, Belgium, and France, and later in Italy and Switzerland—without which his researches, regularly based upon direct study of manuscripts, would have been impossible. For a little more than a decade (1929–40), Wilmart resided mainly in Rome, occupied chiefly with the official catalogue of the *codices Reginenses latini* of the Vatican Library (the first 500 of these were covered in two magisterial volumes, the second of which was published posthumously). Upon Italy's entrance into World War II, Wilmart returned to France. There, amidst the rigors of wartime Paris, he spent his last working days describing Latin manuscripts of the Bibliothèque Nationale.

Wilmart's scholarly production (at least 377 books and articles and 87 reviews) centered first upon Latin patristic literature (notably Gregory of Elvira and St. Hilary) and, in part through intimate collaboration with Edmund Bishop, upon the Latin liturgy (outstanding studies on the Bobbio Missal, the Mone Masses, the

Pseudo-St. Germain of Paris). Wilmart's discovery (1916–17) of the genuine prayers of St. Anselm led him into the field of medieval spiritual literature and medieval poetry. His contributions to the study, not only of St. Anselm, but of John of Fécamp, St. Bernard, the two Guigos of the Grande Chartreuse, and Hildebert, were especially fruitful. A selection of papers in this field, prompted by H. Brémond, *Auteurs spirituels et textes dévots du moyen âge latin* (Paris 1932) well illustrates Wilmart's consummate mastery in research and presentation.

Bibliography: A. WILMART, *Lettres de jeunesse et lettres d'amitié* (Rome 1963–). J. BIGNAMIODIER et al., *Bibliographie sommaire des travaux du Père A. Wilmart* (Rome 1953), contains indispensable autobiog. sketches. N. ABERCROMBIE, *The Life and Work of Edmund Bishop* (London 1959).

[B. M. PEEBLES]

WILMINGTON, DIOCESE OF

When the diocese of Wilmington (*Wilmingtoniensis*) was erected March 3, 1868, it was made a suffragan see of the archdiocese of Baltimore. At the time it comprised the state of Delaware which had been part of diocese of PHILADELPHIA) and the counties of Maryland and Virginia east of Chesapeake Bay which had been parts of the dioceses of BALTIMORE and RICHMOND, respectively). In all it covered an area of 6,211 square miles.

Early History. When the bishops of the Second Plenary Council of Baltimore, 1866, petitioned the Holy See to unite under a single jurisdiction the three outlying districts, which together constituted geographically the so-called Delmarva Peninsula, the area had a total Catholic population of 5,000. Of these, 3,000 were in the city of Wilmington and vicinity where Catholics had been located from at least the second quarter of the 18th century. The remainder were scattered mostly along the Maryland Eastern Shore where their forefathers had persevered stubbornly in the faith since shortly after the founding of the Maryland colony in 1634. Maryland Jesuits, who maintained missions on the Eastern Shore continuously for over 260 years (1639–1898), ministered to the Catholics of this peninsula. Mass was first offered in what is now the diocese on Kent Island, Md., in 1639. Outstanding establishments included St. Francis Xavier (1704), also called "Old Bohemia," in Cecil County, Md.; St. Joseph (1765), Talbot County, Md.; and in New Castle County, Del., St. Mary (before 1772), known as "Coffee Run." During the tenure (1804–40) of Rev. Patrick Kenny, Coffee Run became the foundation stone of the Church in the see city area. From that time on the Catholic population came to be concentrated there first because of Irish, then for a while French, and much later, German,

Polish, and Italian immigration. In 1816 Kenny built the first Catholic church in the city of Wilmington, St. Peter's, now the cathedral. The Franciscans and Benedictines also served the area in the last quarter of the 17th century; the Sulpicians and Augustinians, in the last decade of the 18th century; and the Redemptorists, in the third quarter of the 19th century; the Daughters of Charity have been there since 1830.

First Bishops. When the first bishop of Wilmington, Thomas Andrew BECKER, of Richmond, was consecrated Aug. 16, 1868, there were eight priests, 18 churches, and an orphanage and school for girls conducted by the Daughters of Charity within his jurisdiction. Becker increased the number of priests almost threefold and doubled the number of churches, building especially in the rural areas. He founded an orphanage and school for boys, an academy for girls, and two parochial schools, admitting to the diocese the Visitandines, the Glen Riddle Franciscans, the Dominicans, and also the Benedictines expressly to found a church for the Germans, who had been entering the diocese in increasing numbers since 1857. The Catholic population rose to 18,000.

When Becker was transferred to Savannah, Ga., in 1886, Alfred Allen CURTIS of Baltimore was appointed second bishop and consecrated Nov. 14, 1886. Curtis liquidated completely the debts of the country parishes, at the same time successfully obtaining legislation in Delaware, Maryland, and Virginia to have all church properties incorporated individually. He asked the Benedictines to organize a church for the Polish, who had entered the diocese in 1883. The Josephites soon erected a church, orphanage, elementary school, and industrial school. During this time the Benedictine sisters came to the diocese, locating their motherhouse in Ridgely, Md., where they also opened an academy for girls. In 1893 the Ursulines took over the academy of the Visitandines, who returned to their primitive rule as cloistered choir nuns. Curtis convened the second diocesan synod and held regular clergy conferences. When he resigned for reasons of health June 10, 1896, the diocese was well established: there were 30 priests caring for 22 parishes and 18 missions; 12 seminarians; eight religious communities; three academies; nine parochial schools; three orphanages; and a monastery, for a Catholic population of 25,000.

Later Bishops. Curtis remained as administrator apostolic until the election of his successor, John James Monaghan, of Charleston, S.C., who was consecrated May 9, 1897. Monaghan established seven new parishes and seven missions, and opened eight new schools. He held the third diocesan synod in 1898. In 1903 the Little Sisters of the Poor established a home for the aged, and the Oblates of St. Francis de Sales opened a school (Salesianum) that for many years was the only secondary school for boys in the diocese. In 1924 the Oblates established a church and school for the Italians; earlier Bp. Stephan S. Ortynski, of Philadelphia, opened two parishes and an orphanage for Ukrainian Greek Catholics. St. Francis Hospital and nurses' training school were built and placed under the care of the Sisters of St. Francis of Glen Riddle. When illness caused Monaghan to resign, July 10, 1925, John Edmond FitzMaurice, of Philadelphia, was appointed fourth bishop and consecrated Nov. 30, 1925. The period of his episcopacy was characterized by a considerable growth in population and industrial development in the suburban and rural areas. The Catholic population of the diocese rose from 34,000 to 85,000. Eighteen new parishes were founded, eight in the country and nine in the suburbs of Wilmington, as well as eight missions. Nineteen elementary and nine secondary parochial schools were started, located in almost every section of the diocese. Three academies were begun: Archmere (Norbertines), secondary school for boys (1932); Padua (Franciscans), secondary school for girls (1957); and St. Edmond's Academy (Brothers of Holy Cross), primary school for boys (1959). Located in Cambridge, Md., the Mission Helpers of the Sacred Heart organized a visitation and catechetical instruction program for the Eastern Shore parishes where there were no parochial schools. Nine new religious communities came into the diocese, among them the Irish Capuchins who founded St. Patrick's Monastery near the city of Wilmington. FitzMaurice also directed the founding of a Catholic charities and child welfare program (1932), the Society for the Propagation of the Faith, the Confraternity of Christian Doctrine, an effective religious vocation program, the Catholic Forum of the Air, the Catholic Youth Organization, and the Catholic Educational Guild; the Knights of Columbus councils increased from one to ten. At his retirement, March 2, 1960, he became titular archbishop of Tomi, and Michael William Hyle, of Baltimore, who had been consecrated Sept. 24, 1958, as coadjutor with right of succession, succeeded to the see March 2, 1969.

Bishop Hyle was an exponent of civil rights, and during his tenure a new inner city program was developed in Wilmington. In 1964 he initiated the Diocesan Development Program, which provided for the building of St. Mark Diocesan High School. Hyle was present in Rome for Vatican Council II, attending the entire first, second, and third sessions, and upon his return, he demonstrated an eagerness to implement the new directions given to the church by the council. He established the diocesan newspaper, *The Dialog*, in 1965, and a Newman Center was established at the University of Delaware in 1962.

The sixth Bishop of Wilmington, Thomas J. Mardaga, was installed on April 6, 1968. He too concentrated on the reforms required by Vatican Council II, participating fully in efforts toward Christian unity, implementing liturgical reforms, and establishing parish councils. He created a diocesan Department of Finance, completed the building of St. Mark High School, and initiated a ministry for migrant workers. He founded several new parishes, among them: Elizabeth Ann Seton in Bear (1971), St. Ann in Bethany Beach (1972), and Holy Family in Ogletown (1979).

Mardaga was succeeded by Bishop Robert E. Mulvee, who was installed April 11, 1985. During his ten-year tenure the Catholic population increased to 165,000. He founded three new missions, including Mary Mother of Peace in Millsboro (1986), conducted a five-year planning process, called "A Church To Serve," and emphasized collegiality in ecclesiastical dealings.

The eighth Bishop of Wilmington, Michael A. Saltarelli, was appointed on Nov. 21, 1995. Among many priorities, he has promoted pastoral ministry to Hispanics and an increase of church vocations. In 1998 he established St. Thomas More High School in Magnolia, and in 1999 he founded a new parish, St. Margaret of Scotland in Glasgow. Through a diocesan-wide Capital Campaign, he planned to add new churches and schools to accommodate a rapidly increasing membership. In 2000 the population of Delaware was 783,600, of which 18 percent (205,000) was Catholic.

Bibliography: D. DEVINE, "Beginnings of the Catholic Church of Wilmington, Delaware" *Delaware History,* 28 (1999–2000): 323–344. C. A. H. ESLING, "Catholicity in the Three Lower Counties, or Planting of the Church in Delaware." *Records of the American Catholic Historical Society 1* (March 1886): 117–60. T. J. PETERMAN, *Catholics in Colonial Delmarva* (Devon, Penn. 1996); *The Cutting Edge of Life of Thomas Andrew Becker, the First Catholic Bishop of Wilmington, Delaware and Sixth Bishop of Savannah, Georgia, 1831–1899* (Devon, Penn. 1982); *Catholic Priests of the Diocese of Wilmington, A Jubilee Year 2000 Commemoration* (Devon, Penn. 2000). R. E. QUIGLEY, "Catholic Beginnings of the Delaware Valley," *History of the Archdiocese of Philadelphia,* J. E. CONNELLY, ed. (Philadelphia 1976). P. J. SCHIERSE, *Laws of the State of Delaware Affecting Church Property* (Catholic University of America Canon Law Studies 428 (Washington 1961).

[E. B. CARLEY/T. J. PETERMAN]

WILPERT, JOSEPH

Authority on the catacombs and churches of ancient Rome; b. Eiglau (Silesia), Aug. 22, 1857; d. Rome, Feb. 13, 1944. Wilpert was ordained at Innsbruck (July 2, 1883) and dedicated himself to the study of Christian antiquity. Arriving in Rome (Oct. 10, 1884), he stayed in the German hospice at Campo Santo; through the hospitality and support of its rector, Msgr. Anton de WAAL, he was introduced to Giovanni Battista de ROSSI who guided his early researches in the catacombs. He was successively appointed papal prelate (1897), member of the Pontifical Commission of Sacred Archaeology (1903), and apostolic prothonotary (1903). During World War I he lived at Freiburg im Breisgau and returned to Rome only in October of 1919. A professor of Christian iconography at the Pontifical Institute of Christian Archaeology (1926) and dean of apostolic prothonotaries (1930), he was chosen a member of the Institut de France in 1935.

Wilpert not only discovered unknown art treasures in the catacombs and ancient churches of Rome, but also brought new precision to the study of known frescoes and sarcophagi. He stressed the use of photography and the direct consultation of the art works themselves, rather than reliance upon artists' copies, sometimes inaccurate in important details.

A prolific author, his first scholarly publications appeared in 1886. His works include *Die Malereien der Katakomben Roms* (2 v. Freiburg im Breisgau 1903), *Die römischen Mosaiken und Malereien der kirchlichen Bauten vom iv. bis xiii. Jahrhundert* (4 v. Freiburg im Breisgau 1916), and *I sarcofagi cristiani antichi* (3 v. Rome 1929–36). In 1930 he published his memoirs, *Erlebnisse und Ergebnisse im Dienste der christlichen Archäologie* (Freiburg im Breisgau 1930), a series of lectures that he had prepared for delivery at Harvard University in 1928, although poor health prevented him from crossing the Atlantic. He contributed extensively to scholarly journals and his achievements earned him the personal title of ''Eccellenza,'' bestowed by Pius XI, and honorary doctorates from the Universities of Münster and Innsbruck.

Bibliography: *Rivista di archeologia cristiana* 15 (1938) 6–16, bibliog. J. SAUER, *Münster* 1 (1947) 118–122.

[W. E. KAEGI, JR.]

WILTON ABBEY

Wiltshire, England, established in 773 by Egbert, King of the East Saxons, as a college for priests. St. Alburga, sister of King Egbert, and first abbess, converted it to a Benedictine nunnery for 12 companions *c.* 800. Seventy years later ALFRED THE GREAT restored it to house 26 nuns. Its most famous member, St. Edith (d. 984), daughter of King EDGAR, was a friend of DUNSTAN and ETHELWOLD. Another Edith, wife of EDWARD THE CONFESSOR, replaced the wooden structure with a stone building. Royal benefactions increased its importance; King Stephen fortified it in 1143. The abbess ranked as baroness, a distinction shared by only the abbesses of

Shaftesbury, BARKING, and Winchester. Cecily Bodenham, the last abbess, surrendered the house to Henry VIII on March 25, 1539, and nothing now remains of the original buildings.

Bibliography: W. DUGDALE, *Monasticon Anglicanum* (London 1655–73); best ed. by J. CALEY, et al., 6 v. (1817–30) 2:315–332. L. H. COTTINEAU, *Répertoire topobibliographique des abbayes et prieurés,* 2 v. (Mâcon 1935–39) 2:3456–57. D. KNOWLES, *The Monastic Order in England, 943–1216* (2d ed. Cambridge, England 1962) 136–138, 270.

[F. CORRIGAN]

WILTRUDE, BL.

Widow, abbess; d. *c.* 990. She is supposed to have been the niece of Emperor Otto I (936–973) and the wife of Berthold, duke of Bavaria, who defeated the Hungarians in 943. Widowed in 947, she founded the Benedictine abbey of Bergen (diocese of Eichstätt) sometime after 976, and became its first abbess. Because of her piety she was known as Pia. She gave the cathedral of Eichstätt precious vestments made by her own hand. Today Bergen (near Neuberg, Bavaria) is a place of pilgrimage in honor of the Holy Cross.

Feast: Jan. 6.

Bibliography: R. BAUERREISS, *Kirchengeschichte Bayerns* (2d ed. St. Ottilien 1958–). A. HAUCK, *Kirchengeschichte Deutschlands,* 5 v. (9th ed. Berlin-Leipzig 1958) 3:1016. O. WIMMER, *Handbuch der Namen und Heiligen, mit einer Geschichte des christlichen Kalenders* (Innsbruck 1956) 467. J. TORSY, ed., *Lexikon der deutschen Heiligen, Seligen, Ehrwürdigen und Gottseligen* (Cologne 1959) 570.

[S. A. SCHULZ]

WIMBORNE ABBEY

Dorsetshire, England; founded *c.* 713, by King Ine's sister St. CUTHBERGA, who had been trained by HILDELIDE at BARKING ABBEY. In 748, BONIFACE wrote to Abbess Tetta, sister and successor of Cuthberga, begging for nuns to aid him in the evangelization of Germany. Under the leadership of LIOBA, Boniface's learned cousin, 30 missionary nuns crossed to Mainz. These included St. THECLA, future abbess of Kitzingen, and St. WALBURGA, sister of SS. WILLIBALD OF EICHSTÄTT and WINNEBALD, and later abbess of Heidenheim, whose tomb at Eichstätt is famous to this day for its flow of miraculous oil. Lioba and her companions erected innumerable foundations throughout Germany. The abbey of Wimborne was destroyed probably by the Danes; even its site is unknown. Wimborne Minster, now the Anglican parish church, dates posssibly from the time of the Confessor who there established a house of secular canons.

Bibliography: W. DUGDALE, *Monasticon Anglicanum* (London 1655–73); best ed. by J. CALEY, et al., 6 v. (1817–30) 2:88–89; 6.3:1452. L. H. COTTINEAU, *Répertoire topobibliographique des abbayes et prieurés,* 2 v. (Mâcon 1935–39) 2:3457. D. KNOWLES and R. N. HADCOCK, *Medieval Religious Houses: England and Wales* (New York 1953) 345.

[F. CORRIGAN]

WIMMER, BONIFACE

Archabbot, founder of the first U.S. Benedictine community; b. Thalmassing, Bavaria, Jan. 14, 1809; d. ST. VINCENT ARCHABBEY, Latrobe, Pennsylvania, Dec. 8, 1887. Baptized Sebastian, Wimmer was the son of Peter and Elizabeth (Lang) Wimmer. After making his classical and theological studies in Munich and Regensburg, Germany, he was ordained on July 31, 1831, for the Diocese of Regensburg. He served as curate at Altötting, a popular Marian shrine, and then entered the recently restored Benedictine Abbey of Metten, where he was professed on Dec. 27, 1833. During the next decade he held various posts in Bavaria. While stationed as prefect in a Munich boarding school, he became interested in the missions, particularly among German immigrants in the U.S.

With a group of candidates for the Benedictine priesthood and brotherhood he arrived in New York on Sept. 16, 1846. In October the community moved to the Diocese of Pittsburgh, Pennsylvania, where Wimmer received some farm land in St. Vincent de Paul parish near Latrobe from Bp. Michael O'Connor. Despite difficulties in adjusting an autonomous monastic institution to the ecclesiastical regimen then prevailing in the U.S. (*see* BENEDICTINES), this first Benedictine foundation gradually evolved into St. Vincent Archabbey, College, and Seminary. Wimmer established parishes and new Benedictine foundations in several states, receiving support for them from Ludwig I of Bavaria, the Ludwig Missionsverein, and confreres and friends in Bavaria. At the time of his death, five of his foundations had become independent abbeys. He attended the Provincial and Plenary Councils of Baltimore and Vatican Council I, and was influential in carrying out the wish of Leo XIII to unite all the Benedictine houses into a single international confederation.

Bibliography: C. J. BARRY, *Worship and Work: St. John's Abbey, and University, 1856–1956* (Collegeville, Minn. 1956). F. J. FELLNER, ''Archabbot Boniface Wimmer as an Educator,'' *National Benedictine Educational Association Bulletin* 25 (1942) 85–114.

[O. L. KAPSNER]

WIMPINA, KONRAD KOCH

Theologian; b. Wimpfen-on-the-Neckar, Germany, *c.* 1460; d. Amorbach, June 16, 1531. He called himself

Konrad Koch Wimpina.

Wimpina after his birthplace. Shortly after his birth the family moved to Buchen (Odenwald). Wimpina received the master's degree at the University of Leipzig in 1485. After studying theology at the same university, he received the doctorate in 1503. During this time he served as rector (1494), dean of arts (1494–95), and vice-chancellor of the university (1498–1502). He was ordained subdeacon (1495) and priest in Würzburg (1500?). During a long polemic against his former teacher, M. Polich, over the primacy of theology, he showed himself enthusiastic for scholastic theology, although he was more intent on amassing authoritative opinions than reaching original conclusions from the sources. He left Leipzig in 1505 to exert a decisive influence on the newly founded University of Frankfurt on the Oder. Three times he served as rector, and for many years he was dean of the theological faculty.

In the indulgence controversy, he opposed Luther by drafting 122 (95) theses, which J. TETZEL defended on Jan. 20, 1518. In the theses some debated theological opinions were presented as dogma, for example, that the state of grace is not necessary to gain indulgences for the dead. His disputations and essays against Luther, *Anacep halaeosis,* appeared at Frankfurt in 1528. Here he depicted Lutheranism as a collection of the sects and errors of all times, but the book was too cumbersome to be effective. In 1530 Wimpina accompanied Prince Joachim of Brandenburg to Augsburg where, together with J. Mensing and others, he wrote a refutation of Luther's 17 Schwabach Theses and took part in drafting the *Confutatio* against the Augsburg Confession. With J. Eck and J. Cochlaeus, he was on the commission that strove in vain from August 16 to 19 to achieve unity. His shorter writings appeared at Cologne in 1531 under the title *Farrago miscellaneorum.*

Bibliography: L. CRISTIANI, *Dictionnaire de théologie catholique.* ed. A. VACANT et al., (Paris 1903–50) 15.2:3549–53.

[E. ISERLOH]

WINCHESTER, ANCIENT SEE OF

One of the chief sees of medieval ENGLAND, from an early date ranking second in the southern province only to the archiepiscopal See of Canterbury. It was important for three reasons: its position in what was effectively the capital of Wessex (the greatest of the Anglo-Saxon kingdoms of England), its close contact with the Continent, and, above all, its wealth (a result chiefly of the munificence of Anglo-Saxon kings, e.g., ALFRED THE GREAT). The see was held to be richer than that of Canterbury, e.g., Bp. WILLIAM OF EDYNDON (d. 1366) refused translation to the latter, claiming "Canterbury had the higher rack, but Winchester had the deepest manger." In view of its importance and the paucity of archiepiscopal sees in medieval England, it would not have been surprising if Winchester had become the head of a province. This did not happen, though a scheme to this effect devised by Bp. HENRY OF BLOIS (1129–71) did come near to success.

The first bishop of Winchester (named, oddly enough, Wini) was consecrated in 664, at a time when England was a collection of small kingdoms of which Wessex was the chief. The conversion of Wessex had been effectively begun by St. BIRINUS, whose see was fixed at Dorchester (635), Wini's consecration seems to have been a step toward dividing this huge area into two dioceses. The division was long delayed, although western parts of the area were made into the Diocese of Sherborne, whose first bishop was consecrated in 705. Two centuries later an area covering roughly Wiltshire and Berkshire was made into the Diocese of Ramsbury (909), while Oxfordshire and Buckinghamshire passed to the revived See of Dorchester. This reduced the Diocese of Winchester to what was to become substantially its traditional extent, i.e., Hampshire, Surrey, and the Isle of Wight. In 1499 the Channel Isles were added to the diocese.

Before the Norman Conquest a number of the bishops of Winchester were BENEDICTINES, e.g., St. SWITHIN

(852–62), whose reputation for sanctity was very considerable; St. ALPHEGE OF WINCHESTER (d. 951); St. ETHELWOLD (963–84); and St. ALPHEGE OF CANTERBURY (984–1005). In later times the wealth and importance of the see, along with the control that the English monarchy had over episcopal appointments, resulted in a number of members of the royal family or high royal servants being made bishops. These, however, not infrequently used wealth to good purpose. Bp. Henry of Blois, brother of King Stephen, founded the important hospital of St. Cross, which still exists, while no less than three of the older colleges of OXFORD owe their existence to bishops of Winchester: New College, to Bp. William of WYKEHAM, who also founded Winchester College in his cathedral city; Magdalen College, to Bp. William WAYNFLETE; and Corpus Christi College, to Bp. Richard FOXE. Henry BEAUFORT was bishop of Winchester from 1404 to 1447.

By the 12th century, Archdeaconries of Surrey and Winchester had been formed, the former having three deaneries, the latter, nine. The cathedral chapter was originally formed of secular canons, but in 964 it was made Benedictine and so remained down to the REFORMATION when the last prior became the first dean; Stephen GARDINER succeeded as bishop. Recent excavations have revealed remains of a seventh-century church and of a large church of Ethelwold's era. The present cathedral was built on a new site in the Norman style in the late 11th century. Although the Norman transepts remain, the rest of the cathedral was gradually transformed to Gothic.

Bibliography: S. H. CASSAN, *The Lives of the Bishops of Winchester,* 2 v. (London 1827) v.1. G. HILL, *English Dioceses* (London 1900). F. BUSSBY, *Winchester Cathedral, 1079–1979* (Southampton 1979) R. WILLIS, *The Architectural History of Winchester Cathedral* (Winchester 1984) J. CROOK, *Winchester Cathedral: Nine Hundred Years, 1093–1993* (Chichester, West Sussex 1993).

[J. C. DICKINSON/EDS.]

WINDESHEIM, MONASTERY OF

The Monastery of Windesheim is the former foundation of CANONS REGULAR OF ST. AUGUSTINE, west of Zwolle, the Netherlands. It was founded in 1386 (the cloister and brick church being built in 1387) by six pupils of Gerard GROOTE (d. 1384) with FLORENTIUS RADEWIJNS and Radulf de Rivo, the champion of the Old Roman liturgy and rector of Cologne University, as advisers. The leader of the founders was Johann Goswini Vos, who became the second prior (1391–1424). All six were advocates of the DEVOTIO MODERNA and might have written or inspired the *IMITATION OF CHRIST* (*see* THOMAS À KEMPIS). Via the monastery of Emstein, near Dordrecht, founded in 1382, Windesheim also absorbed

King Canute and his wife, Queen Aelfgyfu (Emma) placing a gold cross upon the altar at Winchester, illustration in a registry/martyrology from Winchester, c. 1016-1020.

the tradition of Groenendals (near Brussels) and therewith much of the spirituality of Jan van RUYSBROECK, who lived near Groenendals. The Windesheim congregation was established in 1393 by the amalgamation of three other Dutch monasteries with Windesheim. The congregation's constitutions, drafted in 1402, were confirmed by Pope MARTIN V at Constance. They called for strict enclosure (many monasteries assuming the CARTHUSIAN enclosure), choir obligation, nocturnal chant, fast and abstinence four times a week, and systematic meditation. The congregation was promoted by Bp. Friedrich von Blankenheim of Utrecht (d. 1423), by the general chapter that was usually held on the second Sunday after Easter every year, and also by John Busch (b. Zwolle 1399; d. Hildesheim 1479), who reformed monasteries in north Germany in 1429, 1435, and 1450, with Cardinal NICHOLAS OF CUSA. It spread along the Rhine from Holland to Switzerland, and by 1430 encompassed 45 monasteries; by 1500 there were 97. Its way of life was a model for numerous houses of other orders, for the secular clergy (e.g., the Böddeken Reform), and also for the laity in its demand for Eucharistic devotion and intellectual training. Windesheim monasteries were located over the countryside, but kept in contact with universities; thus, e.g., Gabriel BIEL (d. 1495), the last of the scholastics in Germany and dean of Sankt Peter at Einsiedeln, near Tübingen, was a professor of the university there. Windesheim's monastic life called for manual labor, such as stonemasonry, carpentry, and stonecutting; for copying and writing books; for manuscript illumination; for correction of Biblical texts; for editions of the Fathers and translation of Latin writings into German; and for conducting a circulating library. But it did not include regular pastoral work in parishes. The congregation's decline in the 16th century was the result of the Reformation and the Revolt of the Netherlands. Windesheim itself was dissolved in 1581, its goods going to a Protestant divinity college and orphanage. The congregation was reorganized in 1573 by a bull of Gregory XIII. Headed by a prior general, it continued in Belgium and in Catholic areas of Germany until 1802. In 1728 it included 32 monasteries; today it has only one in Uden, the Netherlands. (*See* BRETHREN OF THE COMMON LIFE.)

Bibliography: *Acta capituli Windeshemensis, 1387–1611,* ed. S. VAN DER WOUDE (The Hague 1953). M. HEIMBUCHER, *Die Orden und Kongregationen der katholischen Kirche,* 2 v. (Paderborn 1932–34) 1:424–428. L. H. COTTINEAU, *Répertoire topobibliographique des abbayes et prieurés,* 2 v. (Mâcon 1935–39) 2:3459. F. RÜTTEN, *Lexikon für Theologie und Kirche*[1], ed. M. BUCHBERGER 10 v. (Freiburg 1930–38) 10:933–934. E. ISERLOH, *Lexikon für Theologie und Kirche* [2], ed. J. HOFER and K. RAHNER (Freiburg 1957–65) 7:762–764. E. BARNIKOL, *Die Religion in Geschichte und Gegenwart*[3] 7 v. (Tübingen 1957–65) 6:1731–32.

[G. SPAHR]

WINDS, WORSHIP OF THE

As is evident from the *Rig Veda* and *Avesta* as well as from Homer and Hesiod, the winds were worshipped by the Indo-Europeans as powers of nature. In the *Theogony* of Hesiod, they are mentioned formally as among the oldest beings. This fact, however, does not necessarily indicate that they occupied a relatively high position in religion—at least among the Greeks. Aeolus was not considered a wind god; he was simply a lower divinity who had the task of keeping the winds confined in his cave. In art, the winds often exhibit satyr-like features and are represented with unkempt and streaming hair. Complete plastic representation is rare. The worship of the winds in the classical world was restricted to specific circumstances. Thus, the Greeks instituted a cult of the winds following the destruction of the Persian fleet off Mt. Athos; L. Cornelius Scipio erected a temple to the *Tempestates* (Winds) at Porta Capena in 259 B.C. in thanksgiving for deliverance from disaster at sea; the Emperor Vespasian built a similar temple at Antioch.

At this late date it is hardly possible that belief in the winds as personal powers of nature was prevalent. Meteorology had already been long and eagerly studied as a science, and interest in it had led to the development of several theories on the origin of the winds. The winds went higher in the scale of importance with the rise of astral religion. Their task was to lead souls to higher realms. At the same time the evil spirits of vengeance, the Harpies, were given a new significance as attendant punishing angels. A plastic emphasis on the new function of the winds is noticeable, naturally, in the later funerary art. Moreover, several Mithraic monuments have representations of the winds, usually in the corners of reliefs. Since their scenes are predominantly of a cosmogonic nature, the inclusion of the winds is understandable.

Bibliography: F. CUMONT, "L'Atmosphère séjour des âmes," *Recherches sur le symbolisme funéraire des Romains* (Paris 1942) 104–176. H. STEUDING, "Windgötter," W. H. ROSCHER, ed. *Ausführliches Lexikon der griechischen und römischen Mythologie,* 6 v. (Leipzig 1884–1937) 6:511–517. E. ROEDER, "Wind." *ibid.,* 6:500–511. H. SEELIGER, "Weltschöpfung," *ibid.,* 6:430–505, especially sec. 4, "αἰθήρ, ἀήρ, Wolken und Winde," 470–473. H. GUNDEL and R. BÖKER, "Winde," *Paulys Realenzyklopädie der klassischen Altertumswissenschaft,* ed. G. WISSOWA, et al. 8A.2 (1958) 2211–2387.

[K. PRÜMM]

WINDTHORST, LUDWIG

German Catholic CENTER PARTY leader; b. Osterkappeln, Hanover, Jan. 17, 1812; d. Berlin, March 14, 1891. After studying law at Göttingen and Heidelberg, he became a successful attorney near Osnabruck. Elected president of the Hanoverian chamber of deputies (1851), he was minister of justice (1851–53, 1863–65), the only Catholic cabinet member ever in this predominantly Protestant state. Windhorst's political views coincided essentially with those of most contemporary middle-class Catholics. He favored constitutional government, judicial reform, free enterprise, the crown's right to formulate policy, and the influence of the various churches in lower education. He also upheld Catholic Austria's primacy in the German Confederation and states' rights. Although distressed by Prussia's annexation of Hanover and by Austria's withdrawal from Germany after the war of 1866, he accepted the situation. He entered the new North German parliament and the legislature of Prussia in 1867 and the new German parliament in 1871, and he voted against the North German and German constitutions for granting too much power to the central government.

Loyalty to the deposed Hanoverian king led Windthorst initially to shun the limelight in the new Germany, but after Hermann von Mallinckrodt's death (1874) he emerged as the Center party's leader. He continued the Center's policy of defending the church by purely constitutional means when the KULTURKAMPF reached its high point (1874–77), and he felt vindicated when Bismarck eased the struggle (1879). Despite the decision of LEO XIII to exclude him from peace negotiations with Prussia in the 1880s, Windthorst frustrated Bismarck's attempts to influence the Center through the Vatican. Largely because of Windthorst, Bismarck's successors considered the Center an indispensable ally in the Reichstag after 1890.

Windthorst was a rarely gifted party leader and parliamentarian, the ablest representative of modern political Catholicism, but not a political theorist. He excelled Bismarck in concern for moral values in government, but as a statesman he was inferior to the Iron Chancellor, whose hatred left room for esteem for the only competent party leader in the Reichstag. Notable too was Windthorst's defense of the constitutional rights of all groups and parties, even those of the Social Democrats, whose rise he feared.

Bibliography: C. BACHEM, *Vorgeschichte, Geschichte und Politik der deutschen Zentrumspartei,* 9 v. (Cologne 1927–32). T. P. NEILL, *They Lived the Faith* (Milwaukee 1951). G. G. WINDELL, *The Catholics and German Unity, 1866–1871* (Minneapolis 1954). A. ROSENBERG, *The Birth of the German Republic,* tr. I. MORROW (New York 1962). R. MORSEY, *Staatslexikon,* ed. GÖRRES-GESELLSCHAFT, 8 v. (6th, new and enl. ed. Freiburg 1957–63) 8:711–714.

[J. K. ZEENDER]

Ludwig Windthorst.

WINE, LITURGICAL USE OF

Wine, the fermented juice of the grape, first appears as a drink in the early civilizations of the Near East, from which it spread to the Middle East and to the West. In Egypt and Mesopotamia beer was the more common fermented beverage, but in Palestine, Syria, Greece, and Italy wine was and remained supreme. Through its widespread use as a liquid exhibiting mysterious power as a source of strength and joy, as a medicine, and especially as an intoxicant, it acquired a central place in public and private religion, being used in solemn petitions to divinities, in thanksgivings, in expiation rites, and in offerings to the dead. Among the Greeks, especially at Athens, the worship of Dionysus, or Bacchus, the god of wine, was a very influential cult, and it became popular also in Italy. The vintage festivals connected with the harvesting of the grapes and the making of wine were religious in character, but, in keeping with the spirit of fertility rites, these festivals condoned or even encouraged drunkenness and sexual license.

The observation of the physical and mental effects produced by drunkenness suggested the metaphorical employment of intoxication as a symbol of spiritual contemplation or ecstasy. Hence, in Philo of Alexandria, in Plotinus, and in the Fathers of the Church, there is an

John Cardinal Krol, Archbishop of Philadelphia, celebrating communion. (©James L. Amos/CORBIS)

elaborate development of the oxymoron ''sober intoxication'' (*sobria ebrietas*).

Wine is never referred to in the Jewish Scriptures as an independent sacrificial offering, but always as a libation accompanying the sacrifice of a lamb, a ram, or a bullock (Ex 29.40–41; Nm 15.7, 15.10). It was also poured out at the foot of the altar of holocausts (Sir 10.15). Officiating priests, however, had to abstain from wine and other fermented drinks (Lv 10.8–11), and NAZIRITES were bound by a like prohibition during their period of consecration (Nm 6.1–21). The Rechabites abstained from wine permanently. In later Judaism, wine was drunk according to a prescribed ritual at the Passover meal. It reached its supreme religious significance at the Last Supper, when Jesus used bread and wine in the institution of the Eucharist.

In the Eucharist. At the Preparation of Gifts in the Roman Rite of the Mass, a small quantity of water is mixed with wine. Irenaeus (*Adv. haer.* 5.3) and Cyprian (*Epist.* 63) were among the first to see in this the union of Christians with God Ambrose (*De sacr.* 5.1, 4) saw in this the symbol also of the blood and water that flowed from Christ's side on Calvary. The shedding of Christ's blood for the remission of sins is recalled, moreover, in the words of the consecration of the wine. For an explanation of the custom of dropping a particle of the consecrated bread into the consecrated wine, *see* COMMINGLING.

Requirements. The General Instruction of the Roman Missal states that ''the wine for the eucharist must be natural and pure, from the fruit of the vine,'' and ''should not be mixed with any foreign substance.'' (n. 284). The wine may be either red or white. Altar wine is not valid material for Mass if a notable part (more than a third) has become vinegar, or if added substances make up a notable part of it; such wine would be corrupted or not natural. Altar wine which has begun to turn to vinegar or to which significant additions have been made is illicit; it may be used only in an emergency.

Bibliography: H. LEWY, "Sobria Ebrietas: Untersuchungen zur Geschichte der Antiken Mystik," *Zeitschrift für die neutestamentliche Wissenschaft und die Kunde der älteren Kirche,* Beihefte 9 (1929). J. A. JUNGMANN, *The Mass of the Roman Rite,* tr. F. A. BRUNNER (rev. ed. New York 1959); *Public Worship,* tr. C. HOWELL (Collegeville, Minn. 1957). J. J. FARRAHER and T. D. TERRY, "Altar Wine," *American Ecclesiastical Review* 146 (1962) 73–88.

[M. R. P. MCGUIRE/T. D. TERRY/EDS.]

WINNEBALD, ST.

Anglo-Saxon missionary to Germany, abbot; b. Wessex, 702; d. Heidenheim monastery, (Württemberg), Dec. 18, 761. Of noble birth, he was the son of St. "Richard" (feast, Feb. 7) and the brother of SS. WILLIBALD and WALBURGA. He traveled to Rome with his father and brother in 721. After staying there seven years he returned to Britain but revisited Rome in 730 taking another brother with him. Later he joined his kinsman, St. BONIFACE, in Germany. He was ordained in Thuringia, served seven churches, and apparently spent three years in Bavaria. He rejoined Boniface at Mainz (*c.* 747) but, desiring the contemplative life, he founded and became first abbot of a double MONASTERY at Heidenheim to which his sister and other English nuns came. He died after three years' illness. After his death Hugeburc or Hygeburh, an Englishwoman, came to Heidenheim and there wrote his life.

Feast: Dec. 18.

Bibliography: *Monumenta Germaniae Historica: Scriptores* (Berlin 1826—) 15.1:106–117. W. LEVISON, *England and the Continent in the 8th Century* (Oxford 1946), passim. E. S. DUCKETT, *Anglo-Saxon Saints and Scholars* (New York 1947).

[B. COLGRAVE]

WINNING, THOMAS JOSEPH

Cardinal and archbishop of Glasgow, Scotland; b. Wishaw, Lanarkshire, Scotland, June 3, 1925; d. June 17, 2001. Winning was the only son of Thomas Winning and Agnes (née Canning). He began his studies for the priesthood at St. Mary's College, Blairs (1941–1943), where he studied philosophy. His theological studies started at St. Peter's College Glasgow, and continued, once peace was restored in Europe, at the newly reopened Pontifical Scots College in Rome and the Gregorian University, from which he obtained his licence in Sacred Theology. Although he had been accepted as a student for the archdiocese of Glasgow, he was ordained to the priesthood

Dec. 18, 1948 for the newly created suffragan diocese of Motherwell. Following a brief curacy at Chapelhall (1949–1950), he returned to the Scots College in Rome and received a doctorate *cum laude* in canon law at the Gregorian University in 1953.

Following his return to Scotland, he served in several pastoral assignments, and was diocesan secretary from 1956 to 1961. In 1961, he was appointed as spiritual director at the Scots College, and returned to Rome (1961–1966). While there, he was appointed an advocate of the Sacred Roman Rota (1965). On his return to Scotland, he became parish priest at St. Luke's, Motherwell, and also *Officialis* and Vicar Episcopal of the Motherwell diocese. In 1970, the Scottish hierarchy established a National Scottish Marriage Tribunal, and Winning was appointed its first president.

On Oct. 22, 1971 Winning was nominated titular bishop of Louth and appointed auxiliary bishop of Glasgow, receiving episcopal ordination from the archbishop of Glasgow on November 30, the Feast of St. Andrew. Following the death of Archbishop Scanlan, he was translated to Glasgow as archbishop in 1974. Twenty years later, Pope John Paul II created him cardinal priest (Nov. 26, 1994), with the title of S. Andrea delle Fratte. The only Scottish cardinal, he was a prominent spokesman for the church. In 1997 he attracted national attention for offering spiritual, personal, and financial help to any woman faced with the possibility of an unwanted pregnancy; those who felt that abortion was the only option would receive financial support from the Church to enable them to have their children. The same year, he was appointed special papal envoy to the celebration of the 14th centenary of the death of St. Columba. Winning died on June 17, 2001. His remains were interred with his predecessors in the crypt of St. Andrew's Cathedral, Glasgow.

[M. PURCELL/EDS.]

WINNOC, ST.

Monk of Wormhoudt, near Dunkirk, French Flanders; d. Nov. 6, *c.* 715. A vita written *c.* 900, valuable for the details it furnishes on St. OMER, bishop of Thérouanne (d. *c.* 670), St. BERTINUS, abbot of Sithiu (d. *c.* 698), and St. Winnoc (Winox, Vinox), describes how four youths, Britons or Bretons, one day presented themselves at the Sithiu monastery; their names were Quadanocus, Ingenocus, Madocus, and Winnocus. At the request of Bertinus, they later built a tiny monastery, a *cella,* in the countryside of Thérouanne and there devoted themselves to the poor and to the practice of hospitality. At the death of his three companions, Winnoc directed the house. Legend tells that out of pity for the old superior, God caused the mill stone to turn of itself, explaining how Winnoc became the patron of millers. A young monk, whose excessive curiosity urged him to discover the miracle by a trick, was struck blind; he recovered his sight through Winnoc's prayers. Winnoc died and was interred in his monastery, but *c.* 900 his remains were transferred to Bergues, where an abbey was built in his honor. Until 1746, it was customary to immerse his reliquary in the waters of the Colme in memory of a drowned child he was held to have brought back to life. In 1900 his relics were placed in a new reliquary.

Feast: Nov. 6; Sept. 18 (translation).

Bibliography: *Vita* in *Monumenta Germaniae Historica: Scriptores rerum Merovingicarum* (Berlin 1826—) 5:735–736, 769–775, 780–786. *Bibliotheca hagiographica latina antiquae et mediae aetatis* (Brussels 1898–1901) 1:1292; Suppl. (1911) 1289b. *Acta Sanctorum* (Paris 1863—) 3:253–289. P. BAYART, ''Les Offices de saint Winnoc . . . ,'' *Annales du Comité flamand de France* 35 (1926). C. DE CROOCQ in *ibid.* 44 (1944). J. L. BAUDOT and L. CHAUSSIN, *Vies des saints et des bienheureux selon l'ordre du calendrier avec l'historique des fêtes* (Paris 1935–56) 11:198–199. A. M. ZIMMERMAN, *Kalendarium Benedictinum: Die Heiligen und Seligen des Benediktinerorderns und seiner Zweige* (Metten 1933–38) 3:265–267.

[J. DAOUST]

WINONA, DIOCESE OF

The Diocese of Winona (*Winonensis*) was established Nov. 26, 1889, when 20 counties extending across southern Minnesota from the Mississippi River to South Dakota were separated from the Archdiocese of St.Paul.

The early history of the Winona diocese is closely associated with that of the archdioceses of Dubuque and St. Paul. In 1683 the Jesuit missionary Joseph Marist worked among the Sioux natives near the site of Wabasha in southeastern Minnesota, where a trading post had been established. More than a century and a half later, in 1839, Bp. Mathias Loras of Dubuque passed the future site of Winona while on a pastoral visit to an early Catholic settlement at Mendota. In 1856 the Rev. Joseph Cretin, the pioneer bishop of St. Paul and founder of many parishes in the diocese, visited Winona and organized the town's first parish.

In the 1860s there was an influx of German, Irish, and Polish immigrants into the growing industries along the Mississippi River and the rich agricultural lands of Southern Minnesota. Many new missions and parishes were established. A few decades later Abp. John IRELAND of St. Paul carried out an extensive colonization program

in southwestern Minnesota, laying the foundation there for many flourishing parishes. At the time of its incorporation, the Winona diocese had 45 parishes, 31 mission churches, 18 parish schools, 49 priests, and a Catholic population of approximately 38,000.

The Rev. Joseph Cotter was the first the bishop of the Winona diocese from the time of his appointment late in 1889 until his death June 28, 1909. His successors were Patrick Heffron (1910–27) and Francis Kelly (1928–49). From 1942 to 1949, Leo Binz was the coadjutor to Kelly and the apostolic administrator of the diocese. Following Bp. Binz were Edward Fitzgerald (1950–68), Loras Watters (1969–87), John Vlazy (1987–97), and Bernard Harrington (1999–). In 2001 there were 118 parishes and 79 active priests serving the dioceses' 148,400 Catholics.

Throughout its history, the Winona diocese has provided Catholic education at all levels of instruction. In 2001 it had 33 elementary schools, 4 high schools, and St. Mary University of Minnesota, sponsored by the Brothers of the Christian Schools of the Midwest District. St. Teresa College, a liberal arts college for women established in 1912, administered by the Sisters of Saint Francis of Rochester, MN, closed in 1989. Newman Centers serve the Catholic populations at Winona State University and Mankato State University. The diocese has a history of thriving parish religious education and youth ministry programs for young people. More recently the diocese has implemented extensive lay leadership formation programs and a deaconate preparation program. Immaculate Heart of Mary, a diocesan seminary built in 1950 by Bp. Fitzgerald on the campus of St. Mary University, serves pre-theology seminary preparation for 11 dioceses and 1 abbey in the Midwest. St. Mary's Press, an apostolate of the Brothers of the Christian School of the Midwest District, is located in Winona. The press is a prominent publisher of religious education materials for Catholic schools and parishes throughout the English-speaking world and for Catholic Hispanic youth in the United States. The *Courier*, a diocesan newspaper that began as a weekly in 1910, continues to be published as a monthly.

The diocese is home to two Catholic hospitals, St. Mary's in Rochester, the location of the world renowned Mayo Clinic, and St. Elizabeth's in Wabasha, a number of nursing homes, hospices and a retirement community.

Within the diocese, Mankato is the provincial center for the School Sisters of Notre Dame, and the administrative and retirement center for the Sisters of Saint Francis of the Congregation of Our Lady of Lourdes is in Rochester. There are five retreat houses in the diocese as well as a hermitage under the direction of the contemplative sisters, the Hermits of St. Mary of Carmel (Carmelites).

[G. H. SPELTZ/R. P. STAMSCHROR]

WINSTONE, HAROLD E.

Liturgical scholar, writer, translator; b. London, 1917; d. April 19, 1987. He was a parish priest of the archdiocese of Westminster and canon of the chapter of Westminster Cathedral. He was ordained a priest in 1943 and later took a classics degree at Cambridge University. At the time of his death he was parish priest of Saint Thomas More, Knebworth.

With a solid background in Latin and Greek, Winstone was also completely at home in German and French. This fitted him for work in translation and, combined with his liturgical and pastoral expertise, led to his principal contributions to the church in countries where English is spoken. Before the Second Vatican Council, he was widely known as translator of papal encyclicals and other documents and especially as translator of major books of liturgical scholarship and popularization, including works of Josef Jungmann and *The Liturgy of the Mass* by the Austrian Pius PARSCH.

In 1961 Father Winstone translated the proper chants of the Mass for *The Layman's Missal, Prayer Book, and Ritual*, the English edition of the immensely popular *Missel quotidien des fidèles* (the Feder missal). This work gives the key to his later contribution to liturgical translations. The intended goal was "to find a direct and dignified style of English that avoids as far as possible the aridities of conventional 'devotional language', and . . . acceptable to people of the 20th century without archaism, artificiality or avoidable obscurity." This stated purpose was equally the goal of the INTERNATIONAL COMMISSION ON ENGLISH IN THE LITURGY (ICEL), with which he was closely associated from its beginnings.

In 1964 Winstone was appointed by the ICEL committee of bishops as a member of its first Advisory Committee. He chaired this coordinating body from 1968 to 1975, while it directed the preparation of official English versions of the revised Latin missal, ritual, pontifical, and liturgy of the hours. He was also co–chairman of the (ecumenical) INTERNATIONAL CONSULTATION ON ENGLISH TEXTS (ICET), which prepared English versions of the chief texts in common liturgical use in the churches today.

As a priest always engaged in an intense and effective parish ministry, Harold Winstone employed his scholarly background in popular writing and lecturing in the fields of pastoral liturgy and music. He served as president of the Society of Saint Gregory and as a member of the National Liturgical Commission of England and Wales and of the (ecumenical) Joint Liturgical Group. In 1969, in conjunction with his appointment to establish a new parish in Manor House, London, Winstone founded the Saint Thomas More Centre for Pastoral Liturgy with the support of Cardinal John Carmel Heenan and directed it until 1983. Although the center directly serves the archdiocese of Westminster, it has had a much wider impact through its publications and conferences in pastoral liturgy, music, and special areas such as liturgies with children. Through this center Canon Winstone strongly influenced the post-conciliar generation of liturgical promoters, in addition to his part in ICEL and ICET, which has left an enduring and invaluable mark on English used in liturgical celebrations throughout the world.

[F. R. MCMANUS]

WINTHIR, ST.

Popular Bavarian saint of the 8th century, whose birth and origins are unknown. He seems to have been a wandering ascetic from the north, who was also a muleteer and was probably never a member of any religious order. He is supposed to have settled in Neuhausen (now in the northwest section of Munich), which claims him as patron and where he is buried in St. Nicholas church. He is invoked for good weather and against cattle plague.

Feast: Dec. 29.

Bibliography: M. RADER, *Bavaria sancta*, 2 v. (Munich 1615–28) 1:43–45. J. E. STADLER and F. J. HEIM, *Vollständiges Heiligen-Lexikon*, 5 v. (Augsburg 1858–82). F. DOYÉ, *Heilige und Selige der römisch-katholischen Kirche*, 2 v. (Leipzig 1930) 2:561. R. BAUERREISS, *Lexikon für Theologie und Kirche*, ed. J. HOFER and K. RAHNER (Freiburg 1957–65) 10:940.

[W. E. WILKIE]

WINWALOE, ST.

Abbot, confessor; Latin: Guengualoeus, in France called Guénolé; b. *c.* 461; d. March 3, *c.* 532. Winwaloe's father, Fracan, a British chieftain, migrated with his family to Armorica (Brittany), where Winwaloe was born. When 15 years old, he entered the monastic life under (St.) Budoc, on the island of Lauré (Istevert). With 11 monks, he spent several austere years on the island of Tibidi. He settled, *c.* 485, at LANDÉVENNEC, near Brest. His relics were translated to Montreuil-sur-Mer and elsewhere, in 914 and 926, by monks fleeing from Normans who destroyed the abbey in 914. Rebuilt by the Benedictines, it was again destroyed during the French Revolution, then reopened in 1958 by monks from nearby Kérbénst. Winwaloe is commemorated also in Britain, especially in Cornwall.

Feast: March 3 (deposition); April 28 (translation).

Bibliography: *Acta Sanctorum* (Paris 1863—) 1:243–259. R. LATOUCHE, *Mélanges d'histoire de Cornouaille, V ᵉ–XIᵉ siècle* (Paris 1911) 47–82, 97–112, Latin life of Winwaloe by 9th-century Abbot of Landévennec, Gourdisten. J. L. BAUDOT and L. CHAUSSIN, *Vies des saints et des bienheureux selon l'ordre de calendrier avec l'historique des fêtes* (Paris 1935–56) 3:52–57. A. ZIMMERMANN, *Lexikon für Theologie und Kirche,* ed. M. BUCHBERGER (Freiburg 1930–38) 10:940–941. A. BUTLER, *The Lives of the Saints,* rev. ed. H. THURSTON and D. ATTWATER (New York 1956) 1:469–470. P. DE LA HAYE, *Saint Guénolé de Landévennec* (Châteaulin 1973). M. SIMON, *L'abbaye de Landévennec de saint Guénolé à nos jours* (Rennes 1985).

[H. E. AIKINS]

WIRCEBURGENSES

The name given to those members of the Company of Jesus who, from 1766 on, as professors at the University of Würzburg, published the *Theologia Wirceburgensis.* The name refers, then, to its origin and not to a definite theological trend. This theological series bears the title *RR. PP. Societatis Jesu Theologia dogmatica, polemica, scholastica et moralis, praelectionibus publicis in alma Universitate Wirceburgensi accommodata* (14 v. Würzburg 1766–71). The work was slightly altered when it was republished in ten volumes (Paris 1852), and still a third time (Paris 1879–80). The authors were Ignaz Neubauer, Heinrich Kilber, Thomas Holzklau, and Ulrich Munier. The work was actually begun when in 1749 they were asked by Karl Philipp von Greiffenklau, the prince-bishop and duke of the Franks, to produce it. The duke disapproved of "dictation" in theological lectures and wanted printed works used. The undertaking, then, grew out of the lectures given to theological students and was conceived as an aid for both the lectures themselves and personal study. The series contained all the theological disciplines commonly studied at the time and hence is a comprehensive handbook. It is of great importance for the history of 18th-century theological faculties and a valuable source for knowledge of the general history of theology. Its procedure is scholastic and speculative; yet it gives indications of the historico-critical method developing in the 18th century. Thus, although the work belongs to a former age, it stands on the line of demarcation between the old and the new, closing the doors on one era of theology and prudently opening them to another. A synthesis of tradition and progress with a stronger emphasis on tradition is characteristic of the work's theology. All in all, it belonged to the genuine achievements of Catholic theology in the 18th century and was, as the new editions showed, still useful to later times.

I. Neubauer (d. 1795) taught philosophy in Bamberg and Würzburg, oriental languages at Heidelberg, and dogmatic and moral theology at Würzburg. His apologetics were original enough and are found in *Vera religio,* volume 2 of the series.

H. Kilber (d. 1782), the most important of the four Wirceburgenses, taught exegesis and dogmatic theology in Heidelberg and Würzburg. In 1764 he accepted the chair of Holy Scripture that had been specially created for him. After the suppression of the society, he became rector of the Seminary of St. Charles and assessor of the faculty of theology in Heidelberg. His principal work is *Novi Testamenti pars prima seu historica complectens historiam dominicam concordia evangeliorum concinnatam* (Würzburg 1765; 2d ed. 1792). There followed an *Analysis biblica* (Heidelberg 1773).

T. Holzklau (d. 1783), in many respects more original than Kilber, taught philosophy in Würzburg, theology in Mainz, and dogmatic theology and exegesis in Würzburg. He published a chronology and history of the Book of Judith (Würzburg 1772), a work on Assuerus from the Book of Esther (Würzburg 1772), and the *Prodromus complectens prolegomena in Scripturam s. Universam* (Würzburg 1775), conceived as an introduction to a larger work, *Institutiones Scripturisticae,* which was not continued because of objections raised against it by E. KLÜPFEL.

U. Munier (originally Müller; d. 1759) taught the humanities in Erfurt, Worms, Baden, and Mannheim; philosophy in Aschaffenburg and Würzburg; Oriental languages in Heidelberg; and theology in Molsheim, Fulda, and Würzburg. His specialties were exegesis and dogmatic theology. His essays *De incarnatione* and *De jure et justitia* (Würzburg 1749) were not included in the *Theologia Wirceburgensis.*

The Würzburg theological collection was not a group project in the strict sense of the word; each author was alone responsible for that part written by him. They also made part of the collection individual sections of works published by other Jesuit theologians or added their own already edited works.

The following is the arrangement of the ten-volume Paris edition. Book 1 contains Kilber's *Principia theologica ad usum candidatorum theologiae* (already published in 1862, then included in the complete series). Book 2 contains Neubauer's *Tractatus de religione.* In book 3 are Kilber's *De Deo uno et trino, De angelis,* and *De Deo creatore.* The Incarnation is covered in book 4 by Holzklau. In book 5 Neubauer treats *De beatitudine, De actibus humanis,* and *De legibus.* Book 6 contains Holzklau's *De jure et justitia* and the tract *De virtute* from Lessius's work *De justitia et jure.* Book 7 contains Kilber's treatises: *De peccato, De gratia, De justificatione,* and *De merito.* Book 8 contains *De virtutibus theologicis* by Kilber with an appendix *De virtutibus cardinalibus* from the above-mentioned work of Lessius. Book 9 contains Holzklau's treatises: *De sacramentis in genere, De baptismo,* and *De confirmatione et eucharistia;* appended to this book is Holzklau's attempt to establish the authenticity of Pseudo-Dionysius's works. Book 10 offers the treatises *De poenitentia et extrema unctione* by Munier and *De ordine et matrimonio* by Holzklau. Lacking are special treatises on the Last Things and Mariology.

Bibliography: C. SOMMERVOGEL et al., *Bibliothèque de la Compagnie de Jésus* (Brussels-Paris 1890–32) 4:437–441 (Holzklau), 1038–41 (Kilber); 5:1435–37 (Munier), 1638–41 (Neubauer). M. GRABMANN, *Die Geschichte der katholischen Theologie* (Freiburg 1933) 196. H. RONDET, *Dictionnaire de théologie catholique,* ed. A. VACANT (Paris 1903–50) 15.2:3556–61.

[M. SCHMAUS]

WIRNT, BL.

Benedictine abbot; d. March 10, 1127. Very little is known of the actual events of his life until 1108, when he became the second abbot of Formbach. This was a Benedictine abbey near Passau, founded in 1040 by Himiltrude, daughter of Count Henry of Vornbach. Wirnt proved himself to be a remarkable combination of the strict ascetic and the good administrator, and he was widely known for numerous miraculous cures of the sick. However, the author (GERHOH OF REICHERSBERG) of the extant vita was imbued with a superstition excessive even for his time and recorded little beyond miracles that are, in some cases, difficult to believe.

Feast: March 10.

Bibliography: ''Wirnt(o)'' *Lexikon für Theologie und Kirche,* ed. J. HOFER and K. RAHNER, 10 v. (2d, new ed. Freiburg 1957–65); suppl., *Das Zweite Vatikanische Konzil: Dokumente und Kommentare,* ed. H. S. BRECHTER et al., pt. 1 (1966) v.10. *Momumenta Germaniae Historica,* (Berlin 1826–) ''Scriptores'' 15:1126–35, ed. O. HOLDER-EGGER. *Patrolgia Latina,* ed. J. P. MIGNE, 217 v., indexes 4 v. (Paris 1878–90) 194:1425–44, the vita is attributed to Gerhoh of Reichersberg (d. 1169), but Riezler [*Forschungen zur deutschen Geschichte* 18 (1878) 547] shows that it could not have been written before 1181. *Bibliothec hagiographica latina antiquae et mediae aetatis,* 2 v. (Brussels 1898–1901; suppl. 1911) 2:8972. U. CHEVALIER, *Répertoire des sources historiques du moyen-âge. Biobibliographie,* 2 v. (2d ed. Paris 1905–07) 2:4782. A. M. ZIMMERMANN, *Kalendarium Benedictinum: Die Heiligen und Seligen des Benediktinerorderns und seiner Zweige,* 4 v. (Metten 1933–38) 3:231–233.

[F. D. LAZENBY]

WIRT, WIGAND

Theologian, known also as Martin, nicknamed Caupo (innkeeper); b. Frankfort am Main 1460; d. Steyer, June 30, 1519. He entered the DOMINICAN Order at Frankfort. Because of his activity and acrimonious polemics against the doctrine of the Immaculate Conception, the University of Cologne (where he was professor, 1495–96) demanded a retraction from him. Earlier, in 1494, he had written a polemic against the *De laudibus S. Annae* of John Trithemius under the pseudonym Frater Pensans-manus (Weig-Hand, Wigand). The subsequent dispute was resolved Sept. 12, 1495, when a reconciliation between Wirt and Trithemius was effected; but the controversy flared up anew at a public disputation with John Spenglar, OFM, preacher and lector at Heidelberg, June 18, 1501. Conrad Hensel opposed Wirt and his order in a two-year process before the bishop of Strassburg. Hensel won the verdict in 1503. Wirt answered Sebastian Brant's *Pro virginalis conceptionis defensione* (1498) with the *Defensio bullae Sixtinae* by which Sixtus IV in 1483 forbade opponents in this matter to call each other heretics. Wirt wrote the *Dialogus apologeticus contra wesalianicam perfidiam* (1504) against the *Concordia curatorum et fratrum mendicantium* of Wigand Trebellius. John Spenglar and his fellow Franciscans (Observant) prevailed upon the archbishop of Mainz to proscribe the *Dialogus* in 1506. Wirt, now prior at Stuttgart, posted a public accusation of heresy against his opponents on his church door. The Franciscans took the case to Rome, where the *Dialogus* was condemned, Oct. 22, 1512. On Feb. 24, 1513, Wirt read his submission from the pulpit of Holy Spirit Church, Heidelberg, and was heard from no more. Although his name is often connected with the Jetzer Case, 1509, he was not involved.

Bibliography: *Wetzer und Welte's Kirchenlexikon,* 12 v. (2d ed. Freiburg 1882–1901; index 1903) 12:1708–10. G. LOHR, *Lexikon für Theologie und Kirche,* ed. M. BUCHBERGER (Freiburg 1930–38) 10:942. H. HURTER, *Nomenclator literarius theologiae catholicae* (Innsbruck 1903–13) 2:1113–14.

[B. CAVANAUGH]

WISCONSIN, CATHOLIC CHURCH IN

A state in the North Central U.S., embracing 56,154 sq. miles including 1,449 sq. miles of inland water surface. It was admitted to the Union on May 28, 1848. Mad-

Archdiocese/Diocese	Year Created
Archdiocese of Milwaukee	1875
Diocese of Green Bay	1907
Diocese of La Crosse	1905
Diocese of Madison	1946
Diocese of Superior	1905

ison is its capital; Milwaukee, its largest city. By 2001 the population of Wisconsin reached 5.2 million of whom 1.6 million, or about 31% were Catholic. There were five Catholic dioceses in the state, the Archdiocese of Milwaukee (established as a diocese in 1843, made an archdiocese in 1875), and four suffragan sees: Green Bay (1868), La Crosse (1868), Superior (1905), and Madison (1946).

Early History and Missionary Activity. Widely scattered Native American mounds give evidence of a primitive culture that goes back 10,000 years. The oldest tools were fashioned out of copper by Woodland and Hopewell natives, who were at home in the middle and upper Mississippi Valley. Clay was used for making pottery and stone, for arrowheads, knives, and beads. Aztalan, a Wisconsin native settlement, reveals the influence of Mexican Aztecs. Water routes and barriers afforded by Lakes Michigan and Superior, and by the Mississippi, made Wisconsin the center of the native population in the Middle West and the goal of French explorers, traders, and missionaries. In 1634 French explorer Jean Nicolet landed at Redbanks near Green Bay where he was greeted by the Winnebagoes. After the Iroquois wars of the 1640s, missionaries returned to the Great Lakes seeking souls in the wake of Nicolet. Traders like M. C. des Groseilliers and P. E. de Radisson arrived in 1656; the latter wrote the first detailed account of Wisconsin natives and geography.

Fr. René Ménard, S.J., accompanied a band of Ottawa and wintered on the Keweenaw Bay in 1660 only to proceed the next year farther west to Chequamegon Bay. Wishing to minister to the remnants of Huronia, he traveled inland and became separated from his party some days southeast of Lac Court Oreilles. He was never seen again. Fr. Claude ALLOUEZ, S.J., the ''Francis Xavier'' of the western missions, followed to serve the French and the natives at Chequamegon Bay, establishing the mission of the Holy Spirit across from La Pointe in 1665. Returning from a visit to Quebec, some Potawatomi convinced Allouez to travel with them from Saulte Ste. Marie and visit their settlement in Green Bay. On Dec. 3, 1669, the feast day of Francis Xavier, he dedicated a mission to that priest near De Pere. Allouez's successor

at Chequamegon Bay, Fr. Jacques MARQUETTE, S.J., fled the area in 1671 with his flock after some of them had killed a Sioux leader and justly feared a reprisal. The Holy Spirit mission was next visited by Fr. Frederic BARAGA in 1835 who built a church and after eight years of ministry was serving about 700 native converts. Marquette became even more famous when he and explorer, Louis Joliet, traversed the Wisconsin River to the Mississippi and traveled down it in 1673.

In 1679 Fr. Louis HENNEPIN, with two other Recollects, accompanied the sieur de La Salle aboard the *Griffin* arriving at Green Bay. They continued down the Wisconsin coast in canoes until they reached the St. Joseph River in southwest Michigan. The Fox War of 1682, Cadillac's establishment of a trading post and fort at Detroit in 1701 as part of the English and French struggle for control of the area, and the devastations of the liquor trade all led to a general hiatus of missionary activity in the Wisconsin area. In fact, there was no regular priestly service from 1728 to 1823, when the pastor of St. Anne's in Detroit began a church in Green Bay, completed two years later by another Detroit priest, Vincent Badin. Meanwhile, on the southwestern edge of Wisconsin, the St. Louis Trappist, Marie Joseph Dunand, served the Catholics at Prarie du Chien in 1816 and in one decade there were 700 Catholics.

Ecclesiastically, the mission territory fell under the Diocese of Quebec until the victory of the American colonists over Britain and the establishment of the Diocese of Baltimore in 1789. The Diocese of Bardstown was given control of the entire Northwest Territory after 1808 and then the Diocese of Cincinnati assumed control in 1821, whose Bishop Fenwick was the first bishop to visit Wisconsin (Green Bay, March 27, 1829). Wisconsin was transferred to the Diocese of DETROIT at its creation in 1833. Finally, with the erection of the Diocese of MILWAUKEE in 1843, the Territory of Wisconsin (1836) now had its own diocese. Wisconsin became the 30th state in the Union in 1848.

In 1828, Samuel MAZZUCHELLI, O.P., (b. Milan, 1806) answered the call of Fr. Frederick Rese (1828) to serve the Diocese of Cincinnati and its Dominican Bishop Fenwick. After ordination in Cincinnati in 1830, Mazzuchelli was soon roaming over the northern Michigan and Wisconsin areas ministering to natives and western settlers. He opened a school in 1834 in Green Bay for the Menominees. He used native languages and teachers and did not separate the native children from their parents. He published a Winnebago prayer book in 1833. By 1835 he was ministering to the newly arrived Irish lead miners along the western Wisconsin-Iowa border. After a respite in Milan, he returned to the Wisconsin missions where he established courthouses, as well as 40 parishes and nine schools, furthering the immigration of even more Catholics to these sites. He opened St. Thomas College for men at Sinsinawa Mound in 1846 (ceased after the Civil War). At the same site in 1847, he gathered women interested in becoming teachers, and there laid the foundation of the community of Dominican sisters. He died in Boston in 1864 and is buried in St. Patrick Parish, Benton, WI.

While Mazzuchelli centered his work in the southwestern portion of Wisconsin, his colleague, the Swiss-born Fr. Martin KUNDIG (1805–79), ministered to Catholics around Milwuakee. Like the Italian Dominican Kundig, a friend, John Henni, responded to Rese's call for aid to the church in Cincinnati. Kundig and Henni were ordained together in 1829, the year before Mazzuchelli. When Rese was named bishop of Detroit in 1833, he brought Kundig with him. He left Michigan in 1842 with Bishop Peter Paul Lefevere, coadjutor of Detroit, to care for the missions in the Milwaukee area of Wisconsin. Kundig set to work helping to found, in addition to Catholic schools, the first public school supported by taxes in Wisconsin in 1845 in the basement of St. Mark's church in Kenosha. In addition to his many other labors, Kundig founded the Palestrina Society at St. Peter parish, utilizing his own formidable singing skills.

Diocesan Development. Responding to the petition of the Fifth Provincial Council of Baltimore in 1843, Rome made Milwaukee a diocese, and Kundig's Swiss compatriot, John Martin HENNI (1843–1881), was consecrated the first bishop on March 19, 1844. He arrived in Milwaukee with Fr. Michael Heiss, a friend from Cincinnati, ready to serve the 19,000 Catholics and 19 priests in the territory. The largest ethnic group was and would remain German-speaking people. Henni was credited with the phrase, ''Language saves faith,'' and his successors encouraged that Germanic culture. In 1857 Henni, along with Lefevere in Michigan, ceded pastoral care of the northern native tribes to Bishop Frederic Baraga of Saulte Ste. Marie. Henni made several attempts to start a seminary and finally the cornerstone of St. Francis de Sales was laid on July 15, 1855, and the seminary opened in January 1856 with Heiss as rector. The school opened to laity in 1972. Henni had Archbishop Gaetano Bedini, nuncio to Brazil, dedicate the new St. John the Evangelist Cathedral (1853); held the first diocesan synod to implement the Baltimore legislation (1847); and established the first St. Vincent de Paul conference (1849) to support the local orphanages. He also recruited several communities, including the Sisters of Charity of Emmitsburg who established St. Rose Orphan Asylum (1848); the Blessed Virgin Mary Sisters of Dubuque (1848); the Franciscan Sisters of Penance and Charity (1849; founded St. Clare

The Holy Church of the Gesu at Marquette University, Milwaukee, was built in 1893 and modeled after Chartres Cathedral. (©Lee Snider; Lee Snider/CORBIS)

College in 1932, later moved to Milwaukee as Cardinal Stritch College); the School Sisters of Notre Dame under Mother Karoline Friess (1850); the Jesuits of St. Louis (1855); Capuchins for work with the natives (1857); the Sisters of St. Agnes (1858 at Barton; founded Marian College in 1936 at Fond du Lac); the German Dominican Sisters (eventually at Racine) under Mother Benedicta Bauer (1863; founded St. Albertus College in 1935, later named Dominican College); the Franciscan Sisters of Christian Charity (founded Holy Family College at Manitowoc in 1869); the School Sisters of St. Francis (1871; founded St. Joseph's Teaching College in 1936); and German Franciscans to minister in the northern Native-American missions (1878). The bishop traveled to Europe to recruit clergy and raise mission funds; began a German language paper to counter anti-Catholicism, *Der Seebote*, (1850s) and encouraged an English paper in 1871 which became the *Catholic Vindicator* (1874; changed to the *Catholic Citizen* in 1878 and by 1880 being edited by a lawyer, Humphrey J. Desmond, who later helped found the Catholic Press Association); and opened a church music school under the layman, John Singenberger (1848–1924). The Capuchins began a Latin School at Mt. Calvary in 1860, adding the College of Lawrence of Brindisi four years later. The Jesuits began Marquette College in 1881. Holy Hill was dedicated as a Shrine to Mary in 1858 (Discalced Carmelite Friars took charge in 1906).

Upon the recommendation of the Second Plenary Council of Baltimore (1866), Rome approved the erection of the Dioceses of Green Bay and La Crosse on March 3, 1868. Henni became the first archbishop of Milwaukee in 1875 with these two new dioceses and Marquette, MI, as the three suffragan sees. With this change, Henni took on a more public posture on the national scene and often became the object of Irish-American episcopal concerns regarding the effective Americanization of the immigrant population. This became especially noteworthy when Henni requested Rome to name his good friend, Michael Heiss (now the first bishop of La Crosse), as his coadjutor bishop. After two years of a German-Irish struggle over this matter among some Milwaukee priests and United States bishops, Heiss became coadjutor in April 1880. Henni died the next year.

The tall, dignified Michael HEISS (1818–1890) was the first bishop consecrated in Wisconsin on Sept. 6, 1868, to serve the 30,000 Catholics and 15 priests of the La Crosse diocese. He brought with him from Milwaukee the Sisters of the Third Order of St. Francis who became the Franciscan Sisters of Perpetual Adoration. He dedicated the Church of St. Joseph as his cathedral in 1870, increased the number of schools from two to 24 and saw the number of priests rise to nearly 60. Heiss held the first diocesan synod at Prairie du Chien in July 1871 and would later convoke the first Milwaukee provincial council in March 1886, demonstrating the unity of the bishops in Wisconsin. Heiss also took over the care of the native missions in the north, inviting the Fathers of the Sacred Heart, St. Louis to serve there in 1878. He helped found St. John's College (later Sacred Heart College) in Prairie du Chien in 1871, with the help of John Lawler and the Christian Brothers.

The first bishop of Green Bay was the Austrian-born Joseph Melcher (1807–1873), who was consecrated in his diocese of St. Louis on July 12, 1868. Melcher began with 40,000 Catholics and 26 priests. He was succeeded by the Bavarian, Francis Xavier Krautbauer (1824–1885), who was consecrated in Milwaukee on June 29, 1875. The third bishop of Green Bay was the Austrian, Frederick Xavier KATZER (1844–1903), his predecessor's secretary since 1878. He was consecrated on Sept. 21,

1886 in Milwaukee. Katzer was transferred to Milwaukee in 1891. He was followed by the Swiss-born, Catholic University of America canon lawyer Sebastian Gebhart MESSMER (1847–1930), who was consecrated in Newark, NJ, on March 27, 1892 (transferred to Milwaukee in 1903). Messmer welcomed the Canons Regular of Premontre who began St. Norbert's College in De Pere in 1893 and promoted other educational activities while continuing his own scholarship. Succeeding Messmer was Joseph Fox (1855–1915), consecrated on July 25, 1904.

Ethnicity and Catholic Schools. In Milwaukee, Heiss strongly supported the German heritage of the state and faced the growing opposition of Irish and Polish Catholics. The first Polish parish in Milwaukee was St. Stanislaus, founded in 1866. Michael Kruszka's *Kuryer Polski* (''Polish Crier'') established in 1888, both criticized German control of the church in Milwaukee and agitated for Polish rights in the church. This became so pronounced that some of the bishops of Wisconsin, including Heiss's successor, Sebastian MESSMER, banned the reading of the paper by Catholics. Kruszka's lawsuit against this action was later dismissed. Messmer also fought with Kruszka's brother, Wenceslaus, one of his priests. Polish parish indebtedness and diocesan taxation of these parishes nearly led to a schism. Poles in Wisconsin felt accommodated, after the brief tenure (1914–1915) of the Milwaukee auxiliary bishop, Edward Kozlowski (1860–1915), and when Peter Paul Rhode (1871–1945) was named bishop of Green Bay in 1915. Poles succeeded to this post until the Most Reverend Robert Banks, auxiliary bishop in Boston, was named to the see in 1990. At the same time German Catholics were fighting for their own rights in the face of an Irish dominated American hierarchy. It was a Milwaukee priest, Fr. Peter Abbelen, whose 1886 memorial to Pope Leo XIII calling for better care of German immigrants triggered a hot contest between the German and Irish bishops in the Americanist dispute. In addition, all the German bishops in Wisconsin strongly supported and expanded the Catholic school system, often with the teaching in German, which ran counter to the Americanist's efforts to have education be an assimilating experience.

The Wisconsin bishops strongly opposed the Bennett Law of 1889 that required students be taught their major subjects in English and attend school in their own districts. Bishop Kilian Flasch of La Crosse voiced the official Catholic opposition in March 1890: ''We have never received one single cent of state help for our schools—we want no state interference with them, either'' (Fisher, 48). Lay Catholics were mustered into the battle and there was great cooperation with the Lutherans of Wisconsin. Candidates who opposed the legislation were elected in 1890 and they repealed the law in 1891.

When Katzer became the third archbishop of Milwaukee in January 1891, he strongly opposed the Americanist party in the American hierarchy. Thus he formally thanked Pope Leo XIII for his letter, *Testem benevolentiae* (1899), which took to task possible aberrations of the Americanist program. At the time, Katzer's colleagues in the hierarchy were claiming the letter had no application within the United States. Katzer witnessed the organization of the first Knights of Columbus Wisconsin council in 1900.

In the meantime, Catholic numbers in Wisconsin were growing. From 1870 to 1910 the number of priests increased from 197 to 837, serving 250,000 Catholics at the beginning of the period and 532,000 at the end. Katzer welcomed the Servites, Order of Servants of Mary, who opened a novitiate Mount St. Philip, at Granville Center in 1893 (closed in 1963).

Kilian Caspar Flasch (1831–1891), the rector of St. Francis Seminary in Milwaukee, was named the second bishop of La Crosse and was consecrated on Aug. 24, 1881. His service at the Third Plenary Council of Baltimore on the committee for schools expressed his lifelong interest. Allied with the German bishops and some others in the Midwest he wanted the conciliar fathers to be stronger in their education legislation, demanding that parents send their children to Catholic schools under pain of mortal sin. Flasch's successor, James Schwebach (1847–1927), was consecrated on Feb. 25, 1892, at St. Joseph Cathedral. He and his fellow Wisconsin bishops continued their support of Catholic schools to such an extent that the percentage of parishes in Wisconsin with schools was higher than anywhere else in the nation.

Further Growth and Development. On May 3, 1905, Rome established the Diocese of Superior. Augustine Francis Schinner (1863–1937), the vicar general of the Archdiocese of Milwaukee was named the first bishop. Fear that the first bishop might be a Pole led Archbishop Messmer of Milwaukee (1847–1930) to write these strange words to Cardinal Gibbons of Baltimore, ''The longer I think over it the more it seems to me a dangerous experiment. The Polish are not yet American enough and keep aloof too much from the rest of us,'' (Barry, 275). Nothing more than this indicates the transformation that had quickly taken place in the German community and its assimilation to the American project. Schinner resigned in 1913.

Messmer's leadership in Milwaukee (1903–1930) marked a time of bureaucratization and centralizing control of the diocese. This was seen especially in his organi-

zation of the Catholic schools under an archdiocesan superintendant, Fr. Joseph Barbian. Like his colleagues, he also encouraged sodalities, the Holy Name Society, and conferences of Catholic men and women. He also confronted the rise of socialism in the early part of the century and muted his pro-German stance, along with many of his compatriots after World War I. In 1911 the Redemptorists began Immaculate Conception Seminary in Oconomowoc (closed 1987) and the Priests of the Sacred Heart established a novitiate in Hales Corners in 1929 leading to a Major Seminary in 1932. Messmer also established an official diocesan paper, the *Catholic Herald*, in 1922. In the midst of the Depression, his successor, Samuel STRITCH (1887–1958), organized an emergency fund drive in 1934, which was so successful that it became an annual diocesan appeal. Stritch had been transferred from the Diocese of Toledo to Milwaukee in 1930. Like his predecessors, Stritch supported education and especially the professional training of the sisters as teachers. He too held down diocesan expenditures during the Depression, refusing to rebuild his cathedral burned in 1935. Imitating structures in the National Catholic Welfare Conference, he established in 1937 a Secretariat for Catholic Action which coordinated youth, athletic, educational, devotional, and women's organizations. In 1935 he merged the *Catholic Herald* with the independent *Catholic Citizen*, under the leadership of Humphrey E. Desmond and Msgr. Franklyn Kennedy, and greatly increased its subscription rate. By 1981 the name was changed to the *Catholic Herald*. In 1940 Stritch was transferred to Chicago, and in 1946 he was created a cardinal.

Moses Elias Kiley (1876–1953), after serving as the spiritual director of the North American College (1926–1934) and bishop of Trenton (1934–1940), was named to Milwaukee. He has been described as the most autocratic of Milwaukee's archbishops. He also made great strides in recovering from the hiatus in building during the Depression. The cathedral was restored by 1943. He expanded St. Francis Seminary in 1956, creating separate high school and college seminaries by 1962. Kiley's time saw the development of the lay Cardign Movement in the diocese, the formation of the Catholic Family Life Bureau (1948) (which promoted the Cana Conferences and later Marriage Encounter), the beginnings of the Legion of Mary in Milwaukee (1946), and the arrival of the Ladies of Charity in 1956 to help needy children.

Wisconsin produced some significant priest-economists signaling a coming of age for the Church in this area; people like Francis J. HAAS (1889–1953), who advised President Roosevelt and was heavily involved in labor mediation and in 1943 became bishop of Grand Rapids; Aloysius J. MUENCH (1889–1962), who challenged the Rev. Charles COUGHLIN's monetary views during the Depression; and Peter DIETZ (1878–1947), who was involved in Catholic social justice issues and enjoyed the support of Archbishop Messmer.

Albert Gregory MEYER (1903–1965) was transferred from Superior to Milwaukee in September 1953. He led the diocese on a building resurgence, especially with new schools trying to meet the growing suburbanization of Milwaukee's Catholics. In 1958 he was transferred to Chicago.

Alexander J. McGavick (1863–1948), an auxiliary bishop in Chicago, was named to La Crosse on Nov. 21, 1921. His greatest contribution was his support of the farmers. He appointed Fr. Urban Baer in 1936 to the Diocesan Rural Life Board. He also instituted the Confraternity of Christian Doctrine in all parishes in 1935. The Depression hit the churches as hard as other institutions and the bishop successfully prodded most of his parishes to pay off their debts. This frugality, however, prevented a raise in priests' salaries from 1928 to 1966. McGavick began a La Crosse edition of *The Register* in 1936 (which became independent as the *Times Review* in 1958). McGavick's old age gained him an auxiliary bishop, William Griffin (1881–1944), an old friend from Chicago, who was consecrated in Chicago on May 1, 1935. He was a strong arm for the bishop, especially in his relations with the priests, and was most noted for bringing the Catholic Youth Organization program from Chicago to La Crosse. By 1945, McGavick was 82 years old and thus needed the assistance of coadjutor John P. Treacy of Cleveland (1891–1964), who was consecrated in Cleveland on Oct. 2, 1945. The next year, Archbishop Cicognani, the apostolic delegate in Washington, DC, had to pressure McGavick into letting Treacy be of assistance. In fact, McGavick handed over the governance to him that year.

Treacy, after a very successful 1947 fund drive, began a seminary program that fall, and dedicated Holy Cross Seminary in October 1951 with 152 high school seminarians. He established the Brothers of Pius X in 1952 for various apostolates in the diocese, including the seminary. Treacy also built other high schools for the diocese, held the third diocesan synod (1955), and dedicated the new Cathedral of St. Joseph the Workman in May 1962.

Peter Paul Rhode, an auxiliary of Chicago, was transferred to Green Bay on July 5, 1915, serving that diocese for 30 years, dying on March 3, 1945. Like his colleagues, he centralized much of the diocesan bureaucracy, especially the education and social service agencies. He also encouraged the develoment of sodalities for the laity. He was succeeded by Stanislaus Bona (1888–1967), transferred from Grand Island, NE, on Dec. 2, 1944, as coadjutor. Bona began a Green Bay edition of *The Register* in 1956. Bona also built a minor seminary during his tenure. Bona received the first auxiliary bishop for Green Bay in the person of John B. Grellinger (1899–1984), who was consecrated on May 16, 1949.

The Superior diocese saw a series of bishops in this time of growth. Schinner was succeeded by Joseph M. KOUDELKA (1852–1921), an auxiliary of Cleveland, on Aug. 6, 1913, who worked to increase the number of parishes, missions, schools, and priests. Joseph Pinten (1867–1945) served as the third bishop from 1922 to 1926. He built a new cathedral for the diocese thus incurring a large debt with which his successor, Theodore Reverman (1877–1941), had to contend during the Depression. Next came William P. O'Connor (1886–1973), who served from 1941 until his transfer to the new diocese of Madison in 1946. He had been a chaplain in World War I and been awarded the Croix de Guerre for bravery. After the war, Albert Gregory Meyer (1903–1965), the rector of St. Francis Seminary and a very shy man, was named the sixth bishop of Superior in 1946. He spent his energy trying to create a sense of unity among the priests and parishes of this somewhat isolated diocese, and he established a diocesan paper to meet this goal. He was transferred to Milwaukee in 1953. While the diocese was established in anticipation of the growth of the port industry on Lake Superior, that growth never took place.

On Jan. 15, 1946, the Diocese of Madison was created from La Crosse and Milwaukee. The former semi-pro baseball player and current bishop of Superior, William P. O'Connor, was transferred on Feb. 22, 1946, to Madison. Like his brother bishops in Wisconsin, he rapidly expanded the educational opportunities of his people, brought in religious orders, enlarged the Cathedral of St. Raphael (1955), and held the first diocesan synod (1956), which served to unite the two sections of his diocese. O'Connor opened Holy Name Seminary in the fall of 1964 for high school seminarians, a culmination of the post-World War II Catholic confidence. After the Second Vatican Council, in another sign of the times, he organized one of the first Priest Senates on Sept. 21, 1966. On Sept. 3, 1963, O'Connor's secretary, Jerome Hastrich (1914–1995), was consecrated the first auxiliary bishop of the diocese. He spent most of his energies working with the poor, minorities, and migrants, establishing the Latin American Mission Program (1964) before his 1969 transfer to Gallup, NM.

Church in Change. The Dioceses of Wisconsin were very active in their implementation of the reforms of the Second Vatican Council. This positive thrust was countered by the loss of priests and religious and the closing of numerous schools during the rest of the century. Social issues also caused some discord. Fr. James Groppi (1930–1985), a Milwaukee priest, participated in voter registration and anti-racism movements in the mid-1960s, and led an open-housing battle in Milwaukee in 1967 and 1968, leading to his frequent arrest and finally the passage of the ordinance. He was excommunicated when he married in 1976 and he continued to agitate for a married clergy and equal rights for women in the Catholic Church.

In La Crosse, Frederick W. Freking (1913–1998), having been transferred from Salina on Feb. 24, 1965, inaugurated a Priests' Senate in 1968 increasing the consultation with the clergy. He retired on May 10, 1983 and was succeeded by John J. Paul (b. 1918), an auxiliary of La Crosse since 1977, on Oct. 18, 1983. On Paul's retirement (Dec. 10, 1994), Raymond L. Burke (b. 1948) was consecrated the next bishop of La Crosse on Jan. 6, 1995.

Cletus F. O'Donnell (1917–1992), an auxiliary of Chicago, was named to Madison on Feb. 22, 1967, from which diocese he retired on April 18, 1992. He sought to implement the Vatican Council legislation, especially establishing a priests' council, Office of Marriage and Family Life, and a divorce support group. He also established a Board of Education. He obtained an auxiliary bishop, George Wirz (b. 1929), in 1978. William H. Bullock (b. 1927) was transferred from Des Moines to Madison on April 13, 1993. In his first year in office, he wrote a pastoral letter on euthanasia, suicide, and the right to life. He also conducted a feasibility study of the seminary (1995) which concluded with the closing of the institution due to the number of priests needed to run it. Instead it has been turned into a diocesan center.

Joseph J. Annabring (1900–1959) succeeded Meyer in Superior (1954–1960). George A. Hammes (1911–1993) was consecrated for Superior on May 24, 1960, and retired on June 27, 1985, and was succeeded on that day by Raphael M. Fliss (b. 1930), who had been consecrated as coadjutor on Dec. 20, 1979.

In Green Bay, Aloysius J. Wycislo (b. 1908), an auxiliary of Chicago, was appointed on March 8, 1968 to succeed Stanislaus Bona. He retired on May 10, 1983, and was followed by Adam J. Maida (b. 1930), who was consecrated for Green Bay on Jan. 25, 1984. He was transferred to Detroit on June 12, 1990. His temperament was to see difficulties as challenges rather than problems and so he approached the governance of Green Bay in a very optimistic spirit. He held a diocesan synod in April 1988 which engaged some 400 delegates including ecumenical observers. He completed an educational endowment, the Lumen Christi Fund, of over $10 million, along with merging some schools and parishes and tightening

the finances of the diocese. Robert J. Banks (b. 1928), an auxiliary of Boston, was appointed to Green Bay on Oct. 16, 1990, seen by some as a counter to his metropolitan's progressivism.

William Cousins (1902–1988), the bishop of Peoria, was transferred to Milwaukee on Dec. 18, 1958 and retired Sept. 20, 1977. He was followed by the Benedictine, Rembert G. Weakland (b. 1927), who was consecrated on Nov. 8, 1977. In 1979 he closed the preparatory seminary, opened by his predecessor in 1963, turning it into diocesan offices and a clergy retirement home. Weakland continued Wisconsin's service to various ethnic groups by establishing the first urban parish for Native Americans in 1989, as well as the ministering to the Hmong and Lao refugees during the 1980s. One of Weakland's last major undertakings was an extensive remodeling of the Cathedral of St. John the Evangelist. Bishops from throughout Wisconsin, priests and representatives from each parish in the archdiocese, attended the Dedication Mass on Feb. 9, 2002.

In 1969 the bishops of Wisconsin, taking the cue from Vatican II that called upon the Church to be more involved in the world, established the Wisconsin Catholic Conference. The conference offered a forum where information and discussions are shared by the dioceses. It also coordinates the bishops' response, based on Catholic social teaching, to matters and issues of public policy that are of concern to the Church.

Catholic Institutions of Higher Learning. There are nine Catholic colleges and universities in the state, enrolling 37,000 students of all ages, races, and religions. Foremost of these is the Jesuit-administered Marquette University in Milwaukee. Established in 1881 as an all-male college, Marquette obtained a university charter from the State of Wisconsin in 1907. Two years later, in 1909, Marquette became the first Jesuit university in the world to officially admit women as students. In the 1960s, doctoral programs in religious studies, the sciences and humanities were introduced at Marquette. Other universities and colleges include Cardinal Stritch University in Milwaukee (sponsored by the Sisters of St. Francis), Alverno College in Milwaukee (an all-women liberal arts college, established in 1887 by the Sisters of St. Francis), Edgewood college in Madison (sponsored by the Dominican Sisters, Sinsinawa), Marian College of Fond du Lac (sponsored by the Congregation of the Sisters of St. Agnes), Mount Mary College in Milwaukee (sponsored by the Sisters of Notre Dame), St. Nobert College in De Pere (established 1898, by the Nobertines), Silver Lake College of the Holy Family in Manitowoc (established 1935 by the Franciscan Sisters of Christian Charity), and Viterbo College in La Crosse (established by the Franciscan Sisters of Perpetual Adoration in 1890).

Bibliography: H. R. AUSTIN, *The Wisconsin Story* (Milwaukee 1957). W. F. RANEY, *Wisconsin* (New York 1940). C. BARRY, *The Catholic Church and German Americans* (Milwaukee 1953). W. K. BROPHY, ed. *Commemorative History, Catholic Diocese of Madison: Building our Future in Faith* (Dallas 1997). P. L. P. JOHNSON, *Crosier on the Frontier: A Life of John Martin Henni* (Madison, WI 1959). A. J. KUZNIEWSKI, *Faith and Fatherland: The Polish Church War in Wisconsin, 1896–1918* (Notre Dame 1980). M. L. ROMAN and E. M. GINTOFT, eds. "Catholic Herald Special: 150th Anniversary Commemorative Edition," Nov. 18, 1993. L. RUMMEL, *History of the Catholic Church in Wisconsin* (Madison 1976).

[P. L. JOHNSON/E. BOYEA]

WISDOM

Wisdom in every culture, pagan or Judeo-Christian, suggests a kind of intellectual perfection. It may be given speculative or practical emphasis or even special religious value, but it always implies a type of knowing and usually a capacity to judge. In Christianity the roots of wisdom doctrine are to be found in the twin sources of her culture, Israel and Greece; thus, before analyzing the nature of wisdom as understood in later Christianity, this article gives a historical conspectus of the development of the concept.

Historical Conspectus

The main stages in the evolution of the notion of wisdom are found in pagan cultures, biblical literature, patristic writings, medieval thought, the Renaissance, and modern and contemporary thought.

Pagan Cultures. In the Egyptian, Babylonian, and Chinese cultures of the past, wisdom was considered as something distinctly practical, embracing both moral value and good sense. The wise man was seen as one who knows the principles of right living and who can instruct his fellows. In the literature of these civilizations the maxim or proverb was the ordinary form of wisdom writing. India and Greece, however, gradually gave to wisdom a purely intellectual cast. India's classic literature, its wisdom literature, is called Veda (meaning knowledge), a term that undoubtedly shares the etymology of the Latin *videre,* to see (*see* VEDAS).

In Greece wisdom (σοφία) enjoyed a varied usage before being given its primarily speculative overtones by ARISTOTLE. It was attributed to those possessing a *savoir-vivre* in general, to men of artistic ability, to religious men respecting the gods; even the dialectic of the SOPHISTS was thought to be wisdom. Before SOCRATES, PLATO, and Aristotle, Homer, Sophocles, Phidias, and Policlitus were the heroes of wisdom (cf. Aristotle, *Ethica Nicomachea* 1141a 9–15).

In the tradition of Socrates and Plato, wisdom was thought to be knowledge of self and of one's own ignorance. It also became identified with the ordering of one's conduct and then with the whole complex movement toward contemplation of the beautiful. In this Platonic tradition wisdom suggests a unified view of ends and means, resulting from an examination of the various arts (τέχναι). Hence the maxim that "it belongs to the wise men to order."

The early Aristotle continues the Platonic heritage wherein wisdom (σοφία) is not really distinguished from prudence (φρόνησις). But as he moves from the *Eudaemonean Ethics* (1215b 1–2) to the *Nicomachean Ethics* (1141a 9–114lb 8) and the *Metaphysics* (981b 25–983a 23), Aristotle is more careful in making this distinction and in characterizing wisdom ultimately as a disinterested, nonpragmatic type of knowledge. For the later Aristotle, only first philosophy, or metaphysics, meets the requisites of true wisdom. As a speculative knowledge of highest causes, wisdom grants a certain omniscience, involving the knowing of difficult things beyond the ordinary mind. It is most certain, eminently teachable, and, as above, disinterested—all of which grants to metaphysics the right to be called wisdom.

Biblical Literature. Within ancient literature the other important source of traditional Christianity's wisdom doctrine is the sapiential literature of the Old Testament. Although commentators on Israelitic wisdom may differ, two currents of thought seem to be discernible. From the secular, aristocratic milieu of the surrounding cultures Israel inherited an interest in a wisdom born of good sense, experience, and observation—something essentially rational and practical. The so-called wisdom schools developed in this tradition, dedicated as they were to teaching the rules for a happy, successful life. At the same time, within the more immediately religious context of Jewish cult and culture, another wisdom appeared. Born of faith, this is a gift of God, sought in prayer and bestowed upon man by a special grace. On the one hand, one finds an acquired *savoir-faire,* the subject of the didactic, moralistic poetry of wisdom. On the other, there is the mysterious wisdom of divine origin, personifying an attribute of God and sometimes God's own spirit, the source of knowledge and happiness and immortality, of all good things. But throughout the wisdom literature of the Old Testament, even in the more sublime poetry describing divine wisdom as personified, there is an accent that is distinctly moral and practical. The stress is rarely speculative, as it had been in the golden age of Greek writing.

Moving beyond the profane wisdom of philosophical speculation and the Old Testament portrait of wisdom as good sense linked with obedience to the Law, but in direct contrast to the verbal wisdom of the Sophists, St.

Paul presents the wisdom of Christianity as radically Christocentric: "to the Jews indeed a stumbling-block and to Gentiles foolishness, but to those who are called, both Jews and Greeks, Christ, the power of God and the wisdom of God" (1 Cor 1.23–24). New Testament wisdom is, first of all, the divine Logos, Christ, and second, man's taking on the "mind of Christ." The spiritual man is able to judge all things, because his union with Christ in the Spirit gives to him the very thought of Christ. In a context thoroughly existential, i.e., the emphasis is not on abstract essences and laws but on the concrete and personal, wisdom is salvation—as person and as participation. (*See* WISDOM [IN THE BIBLE].)

Patristic Writing. Among the Fathers, St. AUGUS-TINE added significantly to what had already been written. The Eastern tradition does not seem really to differ from his all-embracing idea (see, e.g., T. Spidlik, *La Sophiologie de S. Basile* [Rome 1961]). Augustine combines the Platonic ascent to contemplation and St. Paul's insistence on accepting the folly of the Cross. In a context of Christian contemplation, Augustine sees wisdom as understanding, but understanding based in love: "no good can be perfectly known unless it is perfectly loved" (*Divers. quaest.* 35.2). This insight seems to prompt the identification of wisdom with holiness:"Hominis sapientia pietas est" (*Enchir.* 1.2; *Civ.* 14.28; *Spir. et litt.* 13.22) Ultimately, for Augustine there is very little that wisdom is not. It embraces all the Christian values, intellectual as well as moral, and implies a state of perfection in which the soul is anchored in love, enjoying interior peace and habitual joy in God. Although Augustine does make much of a distinction between science and wisdom based upon their respective objects—science is of human things, wisdom of divine (*Trin.* 14.1.3)—wisdom remains for him deeply affective in character, conditioned throughout by the influence of happiness and love.

Medieval Thought. The transition from St. Augustine to St. THOMAS AQUINAS moved through eight centuries of emphasis on the affective aspect of wisdom; after all, *sapientia* finds its etymological roots in *sapor* (taste), and this must indicate affectivity of some kind. From St. Anselm's *FIDES QUAERENS INTELLECTUM* (faith seeking understanding), a faithful echo of St. Augustine's thought at the beginning of SCHOLASTICISM, to the writings of St. BONAVENTURE, St. ALBERT THE GREAT, and ROBERT KIL-WARDBY, the doctrine on wisdom was cast in a distinctly affective mold. This is evidenced by the consistent characterization of theology as primarily affective.

When the established religion of philosophical PLA-TONISM was challenged by the introduction of Aristotle in the West, however, the primacy of wisdom's speculative value was reasserted. It was St. Thomas Aquinas,

who, accepting Aristotle's teaching on the intellectual virtues, brought into focus again the speculative dimension of wisdom (see *In 1 meta.* 1–3; *Summa theologiae* 1a2ae, 57.2). Together with this reevaluation of speculative excellence, he introduced the distinctions separating metaphysics formally from theology and these two acquired wisdoms from the gift of the Holy Spirit. Yet these apparently extreme departures from Augustinian tradition were really not as extreme as a cursory reading of historical and doctrinal commentaries might lead one to believe. This will become evident in the doctrinal analysis below.

Renaissance. The writers of the 14th to the 16th centuries, when not simply repeating St. Augustine or St. Thomas or more directly the writers of pagan Greece, witness an evolution toward a radical SKEPTICISM coupled with an emphasis upon wisdom as moral virtue. The *docta pietas* of F. Petrarch and the *docta ignorantia* of NICHOLAS OF CUSA set the stage for the avowal of P. CHARRON, at the height of humanism's ascendancy, that wisdom is realized only in intellectual skepticism. The latter's *De la sagesse* marks the end of this period, as it combines within wisdom a complex of moralism, humanism, secularism, and skepticism.

Modern and Contemporary Thought. In R. DES-CARTES (*Princ. phil.*, praef., 12) wisdom continued to be given a distinctly moral cast, also noticeable in the so-called moral INTELLECTUALISM of G. W. von LEIBNIZ, B. SPINOZA, and G. W. F. HEGEL, and especially in the ethico-pragmatic doctrine of Kantian VOLUNTARISM. Then, at the dawn of the contemporary period, S. A. KIERKE-GAARD reacted in claiming that all ethics is worldly—the only true wisdom is "existential anxiety," which should force one into the presence of God. And although the word wisdom rarely appears, the thirst for "authentic existence" in M. HEIDEGGER, the "ultimate concern" of Paul TILLICH's writings, and similar positions reflect this attitude in the writers of the 20th century.

Doctrinal Analysis

Throughout the literature, wisdom as a perfection in man appears as a special kind of knowing, open to religious meaning, and therefore of ultimate value to the person who possesses it. Most simply, whether the emphasis be speculative, affective, or practical, wisdom suggests immediately or by implication a knowledge of God. For Aristotle it is the grasp of highest causes; for Old Testament writers it involves knowing God in the Law; for St. Paul and St. John it is knowing God in Christ. SS. Basil and Augustine see wisdom in all human knowing crowned by love of God in purity of heart, and for St. Thomas wisdom is open to three realizations—one based in reason (metaphysics), one based in faith and reason (theology), and finally the gift of the Holy Spirit (mystical wisdom). (*See* WISDOM, GIFT OF.)

As a knowledge of God, who is at once supremely knowable and supremely lovable—He is the first truth and the highest good—wisdom becomes truly contemplative. One might say that wisdom's primary act is *divina amata contemplari*—to contemplate divine things (persons) loved. Only in wisdom is the object known capable of evoking the personal surrender implied in genuine CONTEMPLATION.

Besides contemplation in this higher sense, there are other acts proper to wisdom. They involve its relationship to other sciences, its concern for and defense of its own principles, its direction of man's practical or moral life. But an examination of these various acts demands distinct analyses of metaphysics and theology.

Metaphysics. The study of BEING leads the metaphysician ultimately to affirm GOD. Confronted by the limited, contingent being in human existence, the philosophically wise man sees in reason's light the necessity of an unlimited ground of that being. And this ground of being is not merely the source, but the end and goal as well, of all existence.

With the awareness of God as principle and end, as ground and goal, of all things, the true metaphysician must recognize that the infinitely desirable Person of God is also his own proper end. He cannot remain indifferent. Here the object itself as the ultimate end and happiness of the individual can and should evoke an affective response. The truly wise man, the perfect metaphysician, cannot remain in detached disinterestedness. He is immediately engaged, involved, committed. As person confronts Person and the identification of infinite truth and supreme goodness is discovered, metaphysics becomes contemplative. One might argue that in metaphysics God is not fully discoverable as a ''Thou'' who calls for a personal response and that this awareness must await God's revelation from within. It is true that God as Person becomes more evident through the Judeo-Christian record of SALVATION HISTORY, above all, in His personal self-gift proclaimed in the New Testament; but this does not preclude the possibility of discovering God in the created universe as one who knows and loves and cares.

Besides contemplating God as the personal ground and goal of all being, the metaphysician reaches deep into the interior of being. This grants to reason's wise man the prerogative and obligation to judge, order, and defend the FIRST PRINCIPLES of being and knowing—contradiction, causality, and others—all of which depend upon being for their existence and meaning (see *Summa theologiae*

1a2ae, 66.5 ad 4). The examination of these first principles adds an important characteristic to metaphysical wisdom, for science as such cannot discourse about its principles; it must simply accept them.

A final privilege of metaphysical wisdom based on its concern for ultimates is its architectonic function regarding other sciences. Only the broader view of wisdom makes possible the ordering and using of less universal disciplines: ''The ultimate perfection of the human intellect is divine truth; other truths perfect the intellect as ordered toward divine truth'' (*Summa theologiae* 2a2ae, 18.04 ad 4). Yet if it belongs to wisdom to order and to use other sciences, the autonomy of the latter must always be carefully protected.

In metaphysical wisdom, God is attained not in Himself but as reflected in creation, and therefore He remains unknown from within. The contemplative act of metaphysics, though true knowledge, is plunged in mystery and best expressed in negation; for the infinite cannot be contained in finite concepts. It thus creates a longing for a more adequate knowledge of God, another and more perfect wisdom. (*See* CHRISTIAN PHILOSOPHY; THEOLOGY, NATURAL.)

Theology. God has graciously made such a wisdom possible. He has revealed himself to man in the Judeo-Christian tradition, climaxed in the gift of His Son, His Word, Jesus Christ. Man responds to this Word of God by FAITH, that complex personal commitment that involves obedience, trust, and repentance, as well as assent. But the faith by which man responds is not yet wisdom, or is only inchoatively so. The assent of faith lacks the order necessary to be a conceptual wisdom, and its affectivity is too elemental to qualify it as affective wisdom. Faith remains open both to reason in the quest for intelligibility and to CHARITY in the thirst for union, that is, to theological and to mystical wisdom (see *Summa theologiae* 1a, 1.6 ad 3; 2a2ae, 45.2).

Since God's truth is received on authority and not by vision, the natural WONDER of the human mind remains unsatisfied and prompts the quest for UNDERSTANDING. From this encounter of faith and wonder is born a new wisdom called theology.

In the genesis of theological wisdom two levels of reason's effort are distinguishable but not really separable. First, the believing Christian must discover what is revealed. This is ''faith seeking documentation''; its concern is the investigation of the authoritative documents—the constitutive, declarative, and corroborative sources of revelation (Scripture, magisterium, liturgy, Fathers, theologians). Second, the theologian seeks to grasp the intelligibility of God's revelation, essentially and existentially, in the order of being and the order of action. This complex task is "faith seeking understanding" in the Anselmian phrase; but lest this be understood as too abstract, it might be called "faith seeking relevance." On both levels theology is ultimately concerned with God and all else as related to God. This concern eminently qualifies it as wisdom.

Theology as wisdom, however, differs from metaphysics on two important counts. First, the theologian contemplates God not just as the One Who Is, but *as* He is, i.e., as a Love-Community. This deeply personalist dimension of theology—God reveals Himself as Father, Son, and Spirit—makes possible a degree of affectivity impossible in metaphysics. Faith itself begins *in affectione* (*De ver.* 14.2 ad 10), which gives an affective cast to all theology whose principles are held in faith. Here, especially, one can say with St. Thomas that "the ultimate perfection of the contemplative life is realized: that divine truth not only be known, but that it be also loved" (*Summa theologiae* 2a2ae, 180.7 ad 1). This is the act par excellence of genuine wisdom, "to contemplate divine things [persons] loved" (*In 3 sent.* 35.2.1.3).

The other significant aspect of theological wisdom distinguishing it from metaphysics is that theology realizes the traditional adage *sapientis est ordinare* (it belongs to the wise man to order), in the practical as well as in the speculative domain. Revelation presents the mystery of a God who is Love not merely for man's intellectual assent but, above all, for his life. And theology, as man's attempt to grasp the mystery in all its intelligibility, must examine the moral principles of Christian living together with the doctrines of Christian belief. To what degree holiness of life is itself required in the theologian is debated. But if theology is indeed a practical wisdom, its integral, if not its essential, perfection demands application of the knowledge (*De ver.* 14.4). Theology can in no sense be isolated from the spiritual life of the individual theologian.

This ordination to contemplation and to life can be understood only in the context of theology's concern for its principles. These reveal the unique God who relates to man as a self-manifesting, self-offering Love-Community of Persons. The theologian, reflecting upon the saving events of God proclaimed in Scripture and celebrated within the Christian community, is a man forever concerned with that mystery of Person and Love communicated to him in faith. Herein are discovered the principles of theology. And just as metaphysical wisdom is privileged and indeed obliged to judge, order, and defend the principles whose source is being, theology must judge, order, and defend the principles whose source is God. Further, as a rational enterprise concerned with rev-

elation's intelligibility, theology, like all SCIENCE (*SCIENTIA*), makes use of all the resources of reason—from the inductive search for meaning to the conclusiveness of DEMONSTRATION.

Theological wisdom also shares with its philosophical counterpart the prerogative of judgment, defense, and use of other disciplines. Without being in any way doctrinaire, theology must confront the world of human knowledge to serve it and to be aided by it. Only in this way can this wisdom of "faith seeking understanding" be made truly relevant to a contemporary world.

Finally, the wisdom of theology, like that of metaphysics, must also end in desire. The mediate knowledge of faith guards the mystery of God in conceptual chains that bind the theologian. In this opaque world, where vision is impossible, the wise man desires to be freed from his conceptual bonds to enjoy a more immediate knowledge of God, a more perfect contemplation, a higher wisdom.

See Also: DOGMATIC THEOLOGY; MORAL THEOLOGY; PHILOSOPHY; SPIRITUAL THEOLOGY.

Bibliography: General. K. CONLEY, *A Theology of Wisdom* (Dubuque 1963), comprehensive bibliog. M. J. ADLER, ed., *The Great Ideas: A Syntopicon of Great Books of the Western World,* 2 v. (Chicago 1952); v. 2, 3 of *Great Books of the Western World* 2:1102–18. M. J. CONGAR, *Dictionnaire de théologie catholique,* ed. A. VACANT et al., 15 v. (Paris 1903–50; Tables générales 1951–) 15.1:346–502. J. MARITAIN, *Science and Wisdom,* tr. B. WALL (London 1940). Ancient Wisdom. A. R. GORDON, *Encyclopedia of Religion and Ethics,* ed. J. HASTINGS, 13 v. (Edinburgh 1908–27) 12:742–747. A. M. J. FESTUGIÉRE, *Contemplation et vie contemplative selon Platon* (2d ed. Paris 1950). M. D. PHILIPPE, "La Sagesse selon Aristote," *Nova et vetera* 20 (1945) 325–374. Biblical Concept. R. E. MURPHY, *Seven Books of Wisdom* (Milwaukee 1960). M. NOTH and D. W. THOMAS, eds., *Wisdom in Israel and in the Ancient Near East* (Vetus Testamentum [Leiden 1951–] Suppl 3; 1955). E. B. ALLO, "Sagesse et pneuma dans la première épitre aux Corinthiens," *Revue biblique* 43 (1934) 321–346. A. FEUILLET, "Jésus et la sagesse divine après les évangiles synoptiques," *ibid.* 62 (1955) 161–196. J. DE FINANCE, "La ΣΟΦΙΑ chez s. Paul," *Recherches de science religieuse* 25 (1935) 385–417. St. Augustine. F. CAYRÉ, *La Contemplation augustinenne* (Bruges 1954). H. I. MARROU, *Saint Augustin et la fin de la culture antique* (4th ed. Paris 1958). E. PORTALIÉ, *Dictionnaire de théologie catholique,* ed. A. VACANT et al., 15 v. (Paris 1903–50; Tables générales 1951–) 1.2:2268–472. St. Thomas. C. JOURNET, *The Wisdom of the Faith,* tr. R. F. SMITH (Westminster, Md. 1952). J. LENZ, "Thomistische Philosophie als Lebensweisheit," *Pastor Bonus* 49 (1938) 323–337. F. P. MUÑIZ, *The Work of Theology,* tr. J. P. REID (Washington 1953). Modern Concepts. E. F. RICE, *The Renaissance Idea of Wisdom* (Cambridge, Mass. 1958). S. PIGNAGNOLI, *Enciclopedia filosofica,* 4 v. (Venice-Rome 1957) 4:275–277.

[K. CONLEY]

WISDOM (IN THE BIBLE)

The subject will be treated under these main headings: wisdom in the OT, extra-biblical wisdom literature, concept of wisdom, and wisdom in the NT.

Wisdom in the Old Testament

The concept of wisdom in the Bible must be delineated against the background of the so-called SAPIENTIAL BOOKS, which are the fruit of the wisdom movement in Israel.

Origins and Development. The origins of the wisdom literature are probably to be sought in the Israelite court. This does not deny that a great fund of popular wisdom and practical insight derived from the common people and the family; but the general impetus to the movement was provided by the court. This assumption is based upon a similar movement in Egypt. Just as Israel imitated its neighbors, especially Egypt, in establishing a kingdom (1 Sm 8.5), it also found here a tradition for the training of its courtiers. There are extant pieces of Egyptian wisdom literature covering a period of some 2,500 years, and many of these bear close resemblance to the teaching of the OT sages (see extra-biblical parallels below). The bureaucracy and demands of court life required a trained personnel, and the counsels of the elders were handed down for this purpose.

Confirmation of these royal origins is found in the description of Solomon in 1 Kgs 4.29–34 (Mt 5.9–14): His wisdom surpassed that of "all the people of the East and all the wisdom of Egypt." Wisdom is now recognized to have been an international possession. The standards were those set by ancient sages, such as the Egyptians. Solomon became the patron, or "author" of whatever passed for wisdom; hence the attribution of Proverbs, Ecclesiastes, and Wisdom to him; he was the prototype of the sages or *ḥăkāmîm,* who arose in Israel. During the monarchical period these men seem not to have been important in Israel's religious development. Thus, Isaiah's reference to them in 29.14 is harsh: When the Lord destroys Israel, their wisdom shall perish (perhaps they were the king's faulty advisers). But his words concerning the Egyptian sages are also threatening (19.11–12). Israel's wise men are described by Jeremiah as opposed to the preaching of the Prophets (8.8–9; cf. 18.18).

The paradox of the wisdom movement in Israel is that it reaches its climax when the kingdom no longer exists. All the OT sapiential literature was written in the postexilic period, with the exception of parts of Proverbs ch. 10–29 and perhaps a few wisdom Psalms. During this time the sage was a more markedly religious figure, a teacher with a school (Qoheleth, Eccl 12.9–11; Sirach, Sir 51.23), and "fear of the Lord" was the sapiential commonplace. The author of Proverbs 1–9 exemplifies this mentality: there is a more clear-cut orientation of the traditional "practical" wisdom to religious ends. The older proverbs had emphasized the solid virtues of diligence, integrity, honesty, and correct social conduct; these still had an important role to play in molding the character of young men, as the sages realized. If they were not always directly relevant to moral decision, they prepared a young man for the crises that involved such decisions. What are the effects of jealousy (Prv 14.30), of pride (Prv 29.23)? To what dangers should one be alerted in social relationships (Sir 8.1–9.16)? Thus the hard-headed, experiential lessons were put to the service of morality.

Characteristics. The style of the postexilic sages has been aptly characterized by A. Robert as "anthological composition," i.e., they were so permeated with the language of the earlier biblical writings that they borrowed even their very expressions. The process was often unconscious, but sometimes there were deliberate allusions. This style is characteristic of Proverbs 1–9, Sirach, and Wisdom (which, being written in Greek, depends on the Septuagint).

It is not possible to sum up adequately the wide range of topics that are treated in OT wisdom literature. The emphasis is on the practical: how to act, or not to act, in various situations: *savoir faire, savoir vivre.* Most often the lesson is founded upon experience. As G. von Rad has pointed out, the proverb is an attempt to master reality (and this includes the mysterious ways of God), to grasp the laws operating in nature and human society and in man himself. And both the popular wisdom and the "educated," stylized insight of the court sage are at one in this.

Retribution. There is a continuing dialogue in one particular area of this literature: retribution and the justice of God. The doctrine in Proverbs and Sirach is frozen: God rewards the good and punishes the evil. This is the traditional theory of the sages, and can be illustrated from almost any chapter of Proverbs (10.4; 11.5, etc.). The sages were aware that this belief was not always easy to accept. In the face of the prosperity of the wicked, they counseled against envy (Prv 3.31; Psalm 36 [37]), and they pointed out the pitfalls awaiting the wicked, all of them in this life, since after death SHEOL awaited both the good and evil. There was a brave way of interpreting the suffering of the virtuous man: it was the "discipline of the Lord" and not to be disdained, "for whom the Lord loves, he reproves" (Prv 3.11–12). But the tradition tended to a mechanical view: suffering was punishment for sin, prosperity was reward for virtue. The author of JOB wrote his work to demolish this rigid position, yet without himself escaping the traditional framework. ECCLESIASTES denied that there exist any clear signs of divine approval or disapproval in the government of the world (8.5–15). The author of Psalm 72(73) seemed to have reached a solution; he nearly slipped away from his faith, so great was his scandal at the prosperity of the wicked. But he saw that their end is not to be compared with the fate of the virtuous who will always be with God. In other words, man's true good is determined by his relationship with God. The Book of WISDOM finally spells this out: justice is immortal (1.15; cf. 3.1–4; 5.1–5).

Extra-Biblical Wisdom Literature

The international character of wisdom literature has already been suggested by the court origins of the movement. Proverbs (30.1; 31.1) refers to collections by Agur and Lemuel who were not Jews, and Job is described as an Arab from the land of Us (Jb 1.1). "Wisdom literature," however, is a term vague enough to include both the OT sapiential writings and the related literature of Israel's neighbors, since these are less oriented to religion. Here, what is common to ancient Near Eastern wisdom is pointed out.

Egypt. There are about a dozen extant examples of Egyptian "teaching" (*Sebayit*), from the early instruction of Hor-dedef (27th century B.C.) down to the Insinger papyrus of the Ptolemaic period (see J. B. Pritchard, *Ancient Near Eastern Texts relating to the Old Testament* "2d, rev. ed. Princeton 1955" 405–410; 412–424, etc.). These are teachings communicated in "father to son" style, and are designed to prepare the son for his duties in life, especially in the court. The Egyptian is concerned with *Maat*, or justice, which is the order or truth established by God; man's life must be in agreement with *Maat*. The advice handed down covers a wide range of situations: conduct at table, dealings with superiors and inferiors, friendship, evil women, honesty and reliability, diligence, self-control, etc. The wisdom of Amen-em-Ope bears a striking similarity to Prv 22.17–23.11, and it is probable (against E. Drioton) that the Israelite author modeled his 30 sayings on the 30 chapters of Amen-em-Ope. Besides these works of practical wisdom, Egypt produced "onomastica," systematic lists of persons and things in the world of nature. This sort of thing may have been the antecedent of the "nature-wisdom" that is ascribed to Solomon (1 Kgs 4.33; see also A. Alt, *Kleine Schriften* 2.89–99). The problem of the suffering of the righteous man finds a precedent in the Egyptian "Dispute over Suicide" and the "Protest of the Eloquent Peasant," but neither of these is as acute as the Hebrew or Mesopotamian works on the same theme.

Mesopotamia. The studies of S. N. Kramer, J. van Dijk, and E. Gordon have discovered the riches of wisdom literature in ancient Sumer, especially the collections of proverbs (see E. Gordon in *Bibliotheca orientalis* 17 [1960] 122–153). There is little evidence, however, for the royal associations of the wisdom literature in Sumer, except for the "Instructions of Shuruppak," which are the advice of a king to his son (fragments in W. Lambert, *Babylonian Wisdom Literature* [Oxford 1960] 92–94). The Babylonian "Counsels of Wisdom" are in the tradition of the Egyptian *Sebayit*, the admonitions of a vizier to his son. The story of AHIKAR is another famous wisdom tale, which originated in Mesopotamia. The theme of Job also is expressed in several works, such as the poem "I will praise the God of Wisdom" (J. B. Pritchard, *Ancient Near Eastern Texts relating to the Old Testament* [2d, rev. ed. Princeton 1955] 434–437), and the "Dialogue of Pessimism" (*ibid.* 439–440) has been compared to Ecclesiastes. While the biblical works are independent of these Mesopotamian writings, they follow in the same tradition, in the same world of thought.

Canaan. Although strong claims for Canaanite sources of Hebrew wisdom have been made (W. F. Albright [*Vetus Testamentum* Suppl 3; 1955] 1–15), not very much evidence has as yet been published. Nevertheless, the poetic forms (types of parallelism) and even the phraseology of Ugaritic literature are echoed in Proverbs and elsewhere, and there is some evidence of "Canaanitisms" in Proverbs (see Albright, *ibid.*), Job, and some Psalms. The contention of M. Dahood concerning the Phoenician origin and background of Ecclesiastes remains problematical.

Concept of Wisdom

OT wisdom (Heb. *ḥokmâ*) is not a univocal concept, nor can its ramifications be schematized. At best one can indicate the wide area within which wisdom is applied at various points in the OT. It describes the ability of an artisan (Ex 36.1–2), a professional mourner (Jer 9.17), a sailor (Ps 106 [107].27), as well as the royal adviser (Jer 50.35) or the astute matriarch (2 Sm 20.16). Animals (ants, in Prv 30.24) as well as humans are included. But the preferred area is human conduct, the ability to cope with life in all its situations (Proverbs, Sirach, *passim*), especially correct moral life, for "fear of the Lord is the beginning [i.e., the chief point] of wisdom" (Prv 1.7; cf. 3.7). From this point of view, the wise man is the pious man, equipped with all the moral virtues, and even with a great deal of practical *savoir faire*. His opposite is the "fool," whose folly is primarily moral, not intellectual. Proverbs is characterized by the moral contrast between the just man and the wicked, between wisdom and folly.

Divine Wisdom. Wisdom is applied to God also, but only rarely and in later books, as M. Noth has pointed out (*Vetus Testamentum* Suppl 3; [1955] 225–237). For some indefinable reason wisdom belongs to the human sphere. Although Yahweh "makes wise," and "gives wisdom," much as He "makes rich" or "gives riches," both of these values belong on the human level. Perhaps there were some early associations about wisdom to prevent Israel from affirming it of God. But eventually it becomes His prerogative (Jb 12.13; Dn 2.20) and is manifest in His creative work (Ps 103 [104].24; Jb 38.37; Prv 3.19). Once this occurs, the pendulum swings to the opposite and wisdom becomes divine.

The "theologizing" or divinization of wisdom is a striking fact in the wisdom movement of Israel. The first significant step is the recognition of the inaccessibility of wisdom. This is paradoxical, in view of the urging of the sages to obtain wisdom (Prv 2.1; etc.). Chapter 28 of Job warns us that wisdom is hid from the eyes of any man: "God knows the way to it" (28.23). Ecclesiastes admits that man cannot discover wisdom (8.16–17). God's exclusive knowledge of wisdom is affirmed also in Bar 3.15–22 and Sir 1.5–7. Wisdom's inaccessibility is due to the fact that she is with God.

Wisdom Personified. Secondly, wisdom is described as a person (feminine), who is born of God, before creation, in which she herself took part as "craftsman" (Prv 8.30, interpreted by others as "nursling" or "little child"). Such is the picture emerging from Prv 8.22–31; Sir 24.3–12; Wis 7.25–26. The personification of wisdom as a woman may be due to several factors, among them the fact that *ḥokmâ* is a feminine noun. She remains a personification, not a person, just as her opposite is personified as Dame Folly (Prv 9.13–18). Her divine origins are shrouded in mystery, for she was begotten before anything was created. The sages struggle for words to express this unique relationship; she is "poured forth." Pseudo-Solomon makes her a consort at God's throne (9.4), a "pure effusion of the glory of the Almighty," "the refulgence of eternal light" (Wis 7.25–26). It should be noted that wisdom is eventually identified by Sirach as the Torah, the Law (Sir 24.8; Bar 4.1). It was by this law—properly observed—that Israel was to give evidence of its wisdom to the nations who would be compelled to say, "This great nation is a truly wise and intelligent people" (Dt 4.6). The Church Fathers identified this wisdom with the Divine Word, but this point of view is too facile and too much of an oversimplification. The figure of wisdom is not meant to indicate a plurality of persons in God; this is a strictly NT revelation. But it does prepare for the Christian message in that it underlines that God does communicate Himself in some way. The supreme communication, in the NT view, is Christ, whom Paul calls the "wisdom of God" (1 Cor 1.24).

There are other important aspects of the personified wisdom developed by the sages: she leads to life, she is a spouse, and she is associated with the divine spirit. The relationship of wisdom and life is a commonplace in Proverbs ("he who finds me finds life": 8.35). While it is true that the "life" envisioned by the sages was length of days and earthly well-being, the notion of life was something that could develop—into the "eternal life" of Wisdom and John. It is not surprising then, that wisdom can be viewed as a spouse. Pseudo-Solomon, in particular, describes his courtship of wisdom: "I sought to take her for my bride and was enamored of her beauty" (Wis 8.2; cf. Sir 51.21).

Already in Job there is a certain kinship between wisdom and spirit. Elihu (Jb 32.7–9) says that wisdom is due to a certain spirit or breath in man. Sirach speaks of the spirit of understanding that God gives to a man who will then "pour forth his words of wisdom" (39.6). Pseudo-Solomon identifies God's "holy spirit" with wisdom in Wis 9.17 (cf. 1.6–7; 7.7, 22). Hence if the spirit (or breath) of God played an active role in creation (Ps 32[33].6; 103 [104].30), so also did wisdom (Prv 3.19; 8.22–31; Wis 7.22; 8.5). Indeed, Pseudo-Solomon describes wisdom as "the holy spirit of discipline," "kindly spirit," and finally as "the spirit of the Lord which fills the world" (Wis 1.5–7). Finally, the place of wisdom in the messianic era should be noted: the messianic King is to be endowed with "a spirit of wisdom and of understanding" (Is 11.2, the attributes of Yahweh in Jb 12.13–14; cf. Is 7.14).

Wisdom in the New Testament

In the NT a certain continuation of the OT wisdom movement may be detected. There are no sapiential books, in the strict sense, although the Epistle of James is in that general tradition. But more importantly, Jesus Himself appears as a wisdom teacher.

Jesus as Wisdom Teacher. In Lk 11.49 and Mt 23.34 it is indicated that Jesus is the "wisdom of God." The sending of prophets, wise men, and scribes is attributed to Jesus ("I" in Matthew), who is identified as the "wisdom of God" (Lk 21.15). Similarly, Jesus and John the Baptist appear as sages in Mt 11.16–19 (cf. Lk 7.31–35): their work is treated lightly by the evil generation that rejects them. The supreme comparison is between Jesus and Solomon, the sage par excellence of the OT (Mt 12.42; Lk 11.31): if the Queen of the South came from the ends of the earth to hear Solomon's wisdom, "behold, a greater than Solomon is here."

This portrayal of Jesus as a sage finds support in many of His sayings that have a sapiential coloring, such as, "Come to me, all you who labor and are burdened, and I will give you rest. Take my yoke upon you and learn from me" (Mt 11.28–29). R. Bultmann analyzes several wisdom sayings of Jesus in *The History of the Synoptic Tradition* ([Oxford 1962] 69–108), where he treats of "Jesus as a wisdom teacher." Despite his skepticism about attributing many of the *logia* to Christ, the sapiential style of Jesus' sayings is readily admitted by most scholars.

Wisdom in Paul, John, and James. Wisdom plays an important role and assumes various meanings in St. Paul's letters. The most typical Jewish usage is in Rom 11.33–34, where "the depth of the riches of the wisdom and the knowledge of God" are praised (cf. "the manifold wisdom of God": Eph 3.10). It is the divine plan of salvation that is meant, by which God has had mercy upon all (Rom 11.32). In 1 Corinthians he is polemicizing against the "wisdom of men" (2.4) that would do away with the cross of Christ (1.17). Whatever be the precise connotation of the Corinthians' wisdom, Paul will have no part of it; he came to them preaching Christ crucified—not with lofty words of wisdom—so that their faith might rest in "the power of God" and not "in the wisdom of men" (2.1–5). But, paradoxically, this Christ is the "wisdom of God" (1.24).

In Colossians the Pauline understanding of wisdom is different. Here he uses wisdom in an exalted sense, praying that the Colossians "be filled with the knowledge of His [God's] will in all spiritual wisdom and understanding" (1.9). He himself, "teaching every man in all wisdom" (1.28), preaches Christ "in whom are hidden all the treasures of wisdom and knowledge" (2.3).

In Revelation wisdom appears as one of the characteristics of the eschatological age, to be received by the Lamb along with power and wealth (5.12; cf. 7.12). But it is also the gift of insight (13.18), such as is enjoyed by an OT Joseph (Gn 40.8; 41.12–13) or Daniel (Dn 2.19–30), both of whom interpret dreams in virtue of a power from God.

The Epistle of James is the only single NT writing that can be said to approximate the OT sapiential books. He begins by considering the trials that Christians meet (cf. the attitude of the sage in Prv 3.12), and in 1.5 he urges those who lack wisdom to ask it of God (as in Prv 2.3–6; Wis 9.4, Sir 51.14). The entire epistle is didactic and hortatory. In 3.13–18 he distinguishes between a wisdom that is "earthly, sensual, devilish" and true wisdom that "is from above." The former is characterized by disorder and strife; but true wisdom is pure, peaceable, etc. There is a completely ethical and practical turn to James's doctrine on wisdom.

Finally, the Johannine development of the theme of Jesus as the wisdom of God should be noted, although it is subtle. The prologue to the Fourth Gospel presents so many contacts with OT wisdom that one can hardly doubt that the Evangelist was rethinking much of the traditional sapiential heritage in presenting Jesus as the LOGOS, or Word. A convenient list of parallels has been drawn up by C. H. Dodd (*The Interpretation of the Fourth Gospel* [Cambridge 1953] 274–275), and he remarks that one can hardly doubt that "the idea of the immanence of Wisdom in men, making them friends of God, provides a kind of matrix in which the idea of incarnation might be shaped." M. Boismard (*Saint John's Prologue* [Westminster, Md. 1957] 74–76) has pointed out that the sequence of thought in Jn 1.1–18 follows the pattern found in the OT description of personified wisdom. In Proverbs 8 and Sirach 24 wisdom describes herself in this order: as close to God, as playing a role in creation, as dwelling among men, and as bestowing benefits upon men. The same order is reflected in John's prologue: Jn 1.1 (the Word was God), 1.3 (everything was made by the Word), 1.9–14 (the Word came into the world), and 1.12–18 (the Word brought the grace of sonship, and grace and truth).

John 6, the discourse on the Bread of Life, is also reminiscent of OT wisdom themes, as A. Feuillet and R. Dillon (*Catholic Biblical Quarterly* 24 [1962] 268–296) have pointed out. Jesus interprets the miracle of the loaves in a manner that recalls the interpretation of the manna miracle in Wis 16.20–26. In both, the bread from heaven is the word of God sent from above, which believers eat as a divine nourishment in contrast to those who would understand the bread of heaven as merely bodily food. Moreover, the banquet offered by wisdom (Sir 24.18–21; 15.3) is akin to the nourishment offered by the Johannine Christ. In the Cana story also the bread and wine of wisdom's banquet are the background for the Johannine symbolism.

Bibliography: Old Testament. J. L. CRENSHAW, *Old Testament Wisdom* (Atlanta 1981); ed., *Studies in Ancient Israelite Wisdom* (New York 1976). C. R. FONTAINE, *Traditional Sayings in the Old Testament* (Sheffield 1982). R. E. MURPHY, "Wisdom Literature," *Forms of Old Testament Literature* (Grand Rapids 1981). G. T. SHEPPARD, "Wisdom as a Hermeneutical Construct," *Beibefte zur Zeitschrift für die Alttestamentliche Wissenschaft* 151 (Berlin 1980). P. W. SKEHAN, *Studies in Israelite Poetry and Wisdom*, Catholic Biblical Quarterly Monograph Series 1 (Washington 1971). G. VON RAD, *Wisdom in Israel* (Nashville 1972). R. N. WHYBRAY, "The Intellectual Tradition in the Old Testament," *Beibefte zur Zeitschrift für die Alttestamentliche Wissenschaft* 135 (Berlin 1974). J. WILLIAMS, *Those Who Ponder Proverbs* (Sheffield 1981). Extra-Biblical Literature. B. ALSTER, *The Instructions of Suruppak* (Copenhagen 1975). R. BRAUN, "Kohelet und die frühhellenistische Popular-Philosophie," *Beibefte zur Zeitschrift für die Alttestamentliche Wissenschaft* 130 (Berlin 1973). C. LARCHER, "Études sur le livre de la Sagesse," *Études bibliques* (Paris 1969). M. LICHTHEIM, *Ancient Egyptian Literature* 3 v. (Berkeley 1975–80). J.

REESE, *Hellenistic Influence on the Book of Wisdom and Its Consequences, Analecta biblica* 41 (Rome 1970). New Testament. W. BEARDSLEE, *Literary Criticism of the New Testament* (Philadelphia 1970). J. D. CROSSAN, *Cliffs of Fall* (New York 1980); *In Fragments* (New York 1983). P. PERKINS, *Hearing the Parables of Jesus* (New York 1981). B. SCOTT, *Jesus, Symbol-Maker for the Kingdom* (Philadelphia 1981). In general, see *The Jerome Biblical Commentary,* ed. R. E. BROWN et al. (Englewood Cliffs, N.J. 1968). Full surveys and bibliography are available in R. E. MURPHY, ''Hebrew Wisdom,'' *Journal of the American Oriental Society* 101 (1981) 21–34, and in J. L. CRENSHAW, ''The Wisdom Literature,'' *The New Hebrew Bible and Its Modern Interpreters,* eds. D. A. KNIGHT and G. M. TUCKER (Philadelphia 1985).

[R. E. MURPHY]

WISDOM, BOOK OF

Biblical book written when Judaism faced a serious crisis in the 2d and 1st centuries B.C. because of its failure to enter the mainstream of Greek wisdom. Defense of the Jewish way of life is the objective of this book.

Background and Nature. The Book of Wisdom was written in Greek for Greek-speaking Jews. The large colony in Alexandria was probably the immediate audience. The political persecution and oppression suffered there inspired an anonymous Jew of deep religious spirit to defend Judaism from the attacks leveled against it and to encourage his coreligionists to fidelity to that wisdom that gives meaning to life. Proselytism, however, is not outside his intention (Wis 18.4). The author writes in the name of King SOLOMON. This is a literary fiction intended to give the book authority. Addressing those ''who judge the earth'' (1.1) and ''kings'' (6.1) is part of the same literary device. The kings are really those who embrace divine wisdom; this leads to a kingdom (6.1). *See* WISDOM (IN THE BIBLE).

The author's acquaintance with Greek philosophy is apparent in his use of some of its terms. Alexandria, where Greek wisdom flourished, could well have provided the philosophical knowledge. The Egyptian background—preoccupation with Egyptian idolatry and Israel's slavery prior to the Exodus—points also to Alexandria. The Greek original reveals an author capable of writing according to the rhetorical standards of Alexandria. The book was written *c.* 100 B.C. or at least sometime shortly thereafter.

Literary Form and Organization. The Book of Wisdom is an exhortation in meditative form. The reflection follows different lines, as is seen in the various approaches found in the distinct parts of the book. Chapters 1–9 make a case for Hebrew wisdom by the method called anthological (borrowing thoughts and phrases from Biblical books and setting them in a sapiential con-

text). The pattern of thought remains entirely Jewish even though there is a real attempt to use whatever Greek thought had to offer. The result is not a systematic theology, but a theology that strings together whatever earlier Scriptures could contribute to the subject matter. Chapters 10–12 and 16–19 are haggadic MIDRASH. The Exodus narrative is exploited and given meaning for the author's contemporaries. Midrash does not merely copy the older Scripture, but gives a commentary. It handles the data freely, adding, subtracting, and exaggerating, to give it new life. The deliverance of the Jews from Egyptian slavery in the past was admirably suited to the author's purpose. Chapters 13–15 form a distinct literary piece. They are parenthetical and constitute a satire on idolatry. Ridicule and irony are effectively used to disarm the religion of Hellenism.

The book's unity has been questioned. Despite the variety in forms and, to an extent, in language, the unity is generally upheld. Some suggest that the same writer composed ch. 11–19 separately (perhaps as a Passover HAGGADAH, the commentary for a Passover meal) and later added it to his anthological reflection on wisdom. Chapter 10 does form a neat transition between the two parts.

Content and Teaching. The book is often divided into three parts to outline its content. After an introduction exhorting the reader to embrace wisdom (1.1–15), the desirability of striving for it is established by referring to the end to which wisdom leads (1.16–5.23), its nature (ch. 6–9), and its historical justification in the lives of Israel's heroes and the life of the nation (ch. 10–19).

Life, union with God, is the lot of the just (2.23). Death, separation from God, is the lot of the wicked (1.16; 2.24). Traditional views on retribution are swept aside. Numerous offspring (3.10–4.6) and a long life (4.7–19) are not necessarily signs of God's favor; moreover, virtue is what God rewards. The manner of life with God is not defined. Neither the immateriality of the soul nor the RESURRECTION OF THE DEAD enters into the perspective of the future life. Eternal life is envisioned as an entering of God's court, joining the ''SONS OF GOD'' (5.5).

Chapters 6–9 explore the nature of wisdom. Personified wisdom is said to come forth as an emanation from God to communicate herself in the physical and moral order (7.25–8.1). Her greatest activity is in the souls of men, whom she makes friends of God (7.27). This personification is literary and is not a revelation of wisdom as a person distinct from God.

Chapters 10–12 and 16–19 show the special providence of God in Israel's history. A sevenfold antithesis makes up the midrash on Exodus. The historical reflection specifies God's ways with man. Thus God uses one and the same thing now for helping man, now for punishing him (11.5); God punishes man by the very things through which man sins (11.16); God is merciful in punishment (12.1); the universe fights in behalf of the just (16.17).

The parenthetical development of ch. 13–15 analyzes different forms of idolatry. The powerless, lifeless gods of the pagan world are no match for the living God of Israel. In 13.1–9 is a beautiful summary of creation's role in bringing men to a knowledge of God.

Christian Use. The Book of Wisdom has been called the bridge between the Old Testament and the New Testament. The Church's use of the book from apostolic times makes the title accurate. John and Paul found no better source to express the new revelation of God's Son than the pages of this book. The Word made flesh, the highest communication of divine wisdom to the world, was presented in terms of the poem of 7.22–8.1. The spirit of God of which the book speaks (1.7, 9.17) was then seen clearly also as a divine person manifesting the power and the life of God. The great popularity of this book among Christians played its part in the Jewish refusal to admit it into the canon. But its language and late origin also were factors in this judgment.

See Also: SAPIENTIAL BOOKS.

Bibliography: *Encyclopedic Dictionary of the Bible,* translated and adapted by L. HARTMAN (New York, 1963) 2589–91. J. FICHTNER, *Die Religion in Geschichte und Gegenwart,* 7 v. (3d ed. Tübingen 1957–65) 5:1343–44. J. REIDER, *The Book of Wisdom: An English Translation with Introduction and Commentary* (New York 1957). É. OSTY, *Le Livre de la Sagesse* (BJ 20; 1950). J. FISCHER, *Das Buch der Weisheit (Echter Bibel: Altes Testament,* ed. F. NÖTSCHER 1950). P. W. SKEHAN, ''Isaias and the Teaching of the Book of Wisdom,'' *The Catholic Biblical Quarterly* 2 (Washington, DC 1940) 289–299; ''Borrowings from the Psalms in the Book of Wisdom,'' *ibid.* 10 (1948) 384–397. R. T. SIEBENECK, ''The Midrash of Wisdom—10–19,'' *ibid.* 22 (1960) 176–182. J. P. WEISENGOFF, ''Death and Immortality in the Book of Wisdom,'' *ibid.* 3 (1941) 104–133. M. DELCOR, ''L'Immortalité de l'âme dans le Livre de la Sagesse et dans les documents de Qumrân,'' *Nouvelle revue théologique* 77 (Tournai-Louvain-Paris 1955) 614–630. A. M. DUBARLE, ''Une Source du Livre de la Sagesse,'' *Revue des sciences philosophiques et théologiques* 37 (Paris 1953) 425–443. G. ZIENER, ''Weisheitsbuch und Johannesevangelium,'' *Biblica* 38 (1957) 396–418; 39 (1958) 37–60.

[R. T. SIEBENECK]

WISDOM, DAUGHTERS OF

(DW, Official Catholic Directory #0960); a congregation founded at Poitiers in France by (St.) Louis Marie GRIGNION DE MONTFORT on Feb. 2, 1703, when he gave the religious habit to Louise Trichet, known in religion as Sister Marie-Louise of Jesus. She was to be the leader of this new congregation founded to work among the neglected sick in hospitals and among the children of the poor. At the founder's death in 1716, the Daughters of Wisdom (DW) numbered only four sisters, but it grew rapidly thereafter. Despite the persecution during the French Revolution in which 34 sisters gave their lives for the faith, the membership of the community had increased by 1846 to 1,400 sisters. In 1810, at the call of Napoleon, the sisters left French soil for the first time to nurse wounded soldiers at Antwerp, Belgium. At the beginning of the 20th century the anticlerical laws of France occasioned the founding of houses in the United States. Having decided to maintain their religious habit even at the price of exile, numerous Daughters of Wisdom left France and settled in Maine and New York in 1904. The sisters have since established schools, hospitals, clinics and orphanages.

The congregation, which is a pontifical institute, has its generalate in St. Laurent-sur-Sevre, Vendee, France. The United States provincialate is in Islip, New York.

[M. C. KANE/EDS.]

WISDOM, GIFT OF

Often called the gift of the Holy Spirit par excellence. By this gift, one is made receptive to the divine motion that moves him to savor the things of God. Through a knowledge of God that is experimental rather than conceptual—a loving knowledge of God—the soul, under the influence of wisdom, is prompted to judge all things in their relationship to God. This operation of the gift perfects the theological virtue of charity by elevating it above the rule of reason that is the norm of all the virtues. Because of the divine modality, which replaces the human modality of reason, wisdom develops in the soul a kind of connaturality, or sympathy, for the divine. Thus, wisdom becomes both speculative and practical; it contemplates the divine truth and then directs human actions according to that truth. For a fuller explanation of this as compared with the other gifts, and for additional bibliography, *see* HOLY SPIRIT, GIFTS OF.

Bibliography: A. ROYO, *The Theology of Christian Perfection,* ed. and tr. J. AUMANN (Dubuque, Iowa 1962) 418–421. R. CESSARIO, *Christian Faith and the Theological Life* (Washington, D.C. 1996). S. PINCKAERS, *The Sources of Christian Ethics,* tr. M. T. NOBLE (3d rev. ed.; Washington, D.C. 1995). THOMAS AQUINAS, *Summa theologiae* 2a2ae, q.45.

[P. MULHERN]

WISDOM OF BEN SIRA

Among the earliest of the deuterocanonical books of the OT, the Wisdom of Ben Sira, also known as the Book of Sirach, contains the most comprehensive sample of wisdom literature preserved in the Bible. This literature also includes the Books of Job, Proverbs, Qoheleth or Ecclesiastes, the Wisdom of Solomon, and several so-called Wisdom Psalms. The book offers moral, cultic, and ethical aphorisms, folk proverbs, psalms of praise and lament, theological and philosophical thoughts, homiletic urging, and pointed comments about life and customs of the day. Hence it has been popular with both Jews and Christians, leaving its impact on the proverbial literature of the West. The following points will be treated: author, date of composition, and canonicity; nature of the book and contents; and history of the text.

Author, Date of Composition, and Canonicity. The Wisdom of Ben Sira is one of the few books of the OT to give the name of its author: "yēšûa‘ [Greek:’Ιησους, Jesus], son of Eleazar, son of sîrā’ [Greek: Σειραχ, Sirach]," in Sir 50.27. Hence, the author is commonly known today as Ben (son of) Sira. The Latin title of the book is ECCLESIASTICUS. Ben Sira, a devoted student of the OT (see the prologue of the book) and a professional scribe, i.e., wise man (cf. 38.24–39.11), says of himself, "Not for myself only have I labored, but for all who seek instruction" (33.18; see also 50.27). He lived in Jerusalem [as 50.27 of the Greek text tells us] but traveled widely, gaining much experience (34.10–12). He taught in what may be called an academy or school (51.23) where he imparted wisdom to young men, as we see from his frequent use of the Hebrew term běnî, "my son" at the beginning of many of his aphorisms. Ben Sira wrote his book in Hebrew c. 180 B.C.; his grandson translated it into Greek sometime between 132 and 117 and then published it after 117 B.C. [see A. A. Di Lella in Skehan and Di Lella, *The Wisdom of Ben Sira* (AB 39, 134–135)]. Though it was written in Hebrew and certainly had a Palestinian origin and was employed in the ancient synagogue liturgy, the Deuterocanonical Wisdom of Ben Sira was omitted from the Jewish (hence also from the Protestant) Canon, most likely because of the sectarianism of the Pharisees who defined this canon c. A.D. 95.

Nature of the Book and Contents. The Wisdom of Ben Sira is a collection of poems praising Wisdom as well as a kind of handbook of moral theology. It shows us what pious Jews of the 2nd century B.C. believed and how they should behave. Since there is no particular order in the book (except for ch. 44–50, a section in Cairo Geniza Hebrew MS B [see below] entitled "Praise of the Ancestors of Old"), only a topical outline, with some unavoidable overlapping of certain subjects, can convey an adequate impression of its contents and scope.

I. Wisdom and the Wise Man (1.1–43.33): "The beginning of wisdom is to fear the Lord," 1.14— 1.1–30; 4.11–19; 6.18–37; 16.24–17.23; 19.20–30; 24.1–31; 25.3–6, 10–11; 37.16–26.

A. Praise of Wisdom's Author: 39.12–35; 42.15–43.33.

B. Service of God and True Glory for Human Beings: 2.1–18; 7.29–31; 10.19–11,6; 17.24–18.14; 23.27; 32.14–33.15; 34.14–35.26.

C. Prayer for God's People: 36.1–22.

D. Autobiographical References: 24.30–34; 33.16–18; 34.12–13; most of the conclusion of the book, 50.25–51.30.

E. The Wise: 3.29; 14.20–15.10; 20.1–31; 21.11–24; 38.24–39.11.

  1. Wisdom applied to spiritual and personal life.

    a. Humility—3.17–24; 4.8; 7.16–17; 10. 26–28.

    b. Charity—3.30–4.6, 8–10; 7.32–36; 12.1–7; 29.8–13.

    c. Virtues and vices of the tongue— 5.9–6.1; 7.13; 19.5–17; 20.5–8, 13, 16–20, 24–31; 22.6, 27–23.4, 7–15; 27.4–7; 28.12–26.

    d. Pride, folly, sin (in general)—3.26–28; 10.6–18; 11.6; 16.5–23; 20.2–31; 21.1–22.2, 18; 25.2; 27.12–15, 28; 33.5; 35.22–24; 41.10.

    e. Anger, malice, vengeance—1.22–24; 27.22–28.11.

    f. Evil desire—6.2–4; 18.30–19.4; 23.5–6, 16–26.

    g. Other virtues and vices——4.20–31; 5.1–8; 7.1–15; 8.1–19; 9.11–10.5, 29; 11.7–22; 15.11–20; 18.15–29; 25.1, 7–11; 27.8–21; 34.1–8.

  2. Wisdom applied to practical life.

    a. Parents—3.1–16; 7.27–28; 23.14; 41.17.

    b. Children—7.23–25; 16.1–4; 22.3–4; 25.7; 30.1–13; 41.5–10.

    c. Women (including wife and daughters)—7.19, 24-26; 9.1–9; 19.2–4; 22.3–5; 23. 22–26; 25.1, 8, 13–26.18, 20-27; 28.15; 33.20; 36.26–31; 40.19, 23; 42.6, 9–14.

    d. Friends and associates—6.5–17; 7.18; 9.10; 11.29–34; 12.8–13.23; 22.19–26; 27.16–21; 33.6; 36.23–25; 37.1–15.

    e. Wealth—10.30–31; 11.10–11, 14, 18–19, 23–28; 13.15–14.10; 25.2–3; 26.28–27.3; 31.1–11.

    f. Poverty—10.30–11.6, 14; 13.18–14.2; 25.2–3.

g. Enjoyment of life—14.11–19.

h. Loans—29.1–7, 14–20.

i. Frugality—29.21–28.

j. Health and doctors—30.14–20; 38.1–15.

k. Death—38.16–23; 41.1–4.

l. Joy and pleasure—30.21–27; 40.1–27.

m. Table manners and self-control —31.12–32.13; 37.27–31.

n. Household management—7.20–22; 33.19–33.

o. The value of travel—34.9–12.

p. Begging—40.28–30.

q. The lasting treasure of a good name— 41.11–13.

r. The right and wrong kinds of shame— 41.14–42.8.

II. Praise of the Ancestors (44.1–50.21): "Now will I praise those godly people, our ancestors" (44.1).

III. Conclusion (50.22–51.30).

  A. Epilogue: 50.22–29.

  B. Song of Praise: 51.1–12.

  C. Alphabetic Canticle: 51.13–30.

From this outline one can see that Ben Sira discusses virtually every significant topic regarding religious and secular wisdom as well as the behavior expected of the faithful Jew. Some of the sage's observations and aphorisms may appear to today's reader as utterly pragmatic or self-serving rather than as spiritually enlightening:

> Moderate eating ensures sound slumber
> and a clear mind next day on rising.
> The distress of sleeplessness and of nausea
> and colic are with the glutton!
> If you have eaten too much,
> get up to vomit and you will have relief. (Sir 31.20–21)

But Ben Sira's statements are in keeping with what we read in other Wisdom authors. And for him this advice is practical wisdom both for the glutton and for the one who unintentionally eats too much. For other examples of such advice see Sir 9.1–9; 42.9–11; and Prv 23.29–35.

History of the Text. For centuries, the original Hebrew text of Ben Sira had been lost. Knowledge of the book came chiefly from two ancient versions translated directly from the Hebrew: the Greek (or the SEPTUAGINT) and the Syriac PESHITTA from which all other versions were made. Then, from 1896 to 1900 and again in 1931, 1958, and 1960, portions of five different MSS (A, B, C, D, and E), containing more than two-thirds of the Hebrew text of the Wisdom of Ben Sira, were found among the vast materials recovered from the GENIZA of the Karaite Synagogue in Old Cairo. In 1965 Y. Yadin published a fragmentary scroll that had been recovered from the ruins of Masada. In 1982 a sixth MS was discovered by A. Scheiber who had been examining the Cambridge collections of Geniza fragments; he mistakenly called it a leaf of MS D. Later the leaf was correctly identified and published by A. A. Di Lella (*Bib* 69 [1988] 226–238), who named it MS F. Despite the misgivings of a few scholars (e.g., D. S. Margoliouth, C. C. Torrey, and H. L. Ginsberg), the Geniza MSS—dating from the 9th to the 12th century—offer a text that is substantially genuine, even though it is disfigured by glosses, scribal errors, and occasional retranslations from the Peshitta. Among other reasons, because a 1st-century B.C. Hebrew fragment of Sir 6.20–31 found among the DEAD SEA SCROLLS of cave 2Q and the Masada scroll, also of the same date, basically match the wording of Geniza MSS A and B, respectively, some scholars believe that the basic text of the Geniza MSS was derived from exemplars that also date from the beginning of the Christian Era; for detailed evidence, see Di Lella in Skehan and Di Lella, *The Wisdom of Ben Sira*, ch. 8. The Greek version poses its own problems because there are two texts: the primary, represented by the uncials and many cursives; and the secondary, represented by Codex 248 but also by other cursives. The 248 text-type—reflected also in the Old Latin version and the Syro-Hexaplar—has some 150 distichs not found in the primary text; see R. Smend, *Die Weisheit des Jesus Ben Sira erklärt,* lxii–cxviii for further information.

Bibliography: General. D. S. MARGOLIOUTH, *The Origin of the 'Original Hebrew' of Ecclesiasticus* (London 1899). I. LÉVI, *L'Ecclésiastique, ou la Sagesse de Jésus, fils de Sira,* 2 v. (Paris 1898–1901). R. SMEND, *Die Weisheit des Jesus Sirach erklärt* (Berlin 1906). N. PETERS, *Das Buch Jesus Sirach oder Ecclesiasticus* (Exegetisches Handbuch zum Alten Testament 25, Münster 1913). G. H. BOX and W. O. E. OESTERLEY, "The Book of Sirach," *The Apocrypha and Pseudepigrapha of the Old Testament,* ed. R. H. CHARLES (Oxford 1913) 1:268–517. C. C. TORREY, "The Hebrew of the Geniza Sirach," *Alexander Marx Jubilee Volume,* ed. S. LIEBERMAN (New York 1950) 585–602. H. L. GINSBERG, "The Original Hebrew of Ben Sira 12.10–14," *Journal of Biblical Literature* 74 (1955) 93–95. L. F. HARTMAN, "Sirach in Hebrew and in Greek," *The Catholic Biblical Quarterly* 23 (1961) 443–451. A. A. DI LELLA, *The Hebrew Text of Sirach: A Text-Critical and Historical Study (The Hague 1965), with complete bibliography to 1963.* H. DUESBERG and I. FRANSEN, *Ecclesiastico* (La Sacra Bibbia, ed. G. RINALDI; Turin 1966). D. BARTHÉLEMY and O. RICKENBACHER, *Konkordanz zum hebräischen Sirach* (Göttingen 1973). P. W. SKEHAN and A. A. DI LELLA, *The Wisdom of Ben Sira* (AB 39; New York 1987). A. A. DI LELLA, "Wisdom of Ben-Sira," *ABD* 6 (New York 1992) 931–945. Idem, "The Wisdom of Ben Sira: Resources and Recent Research," *Currents in Research: Biblical Studies* 4 (1996) 161–181. P. C. BEENTJES, ed., *The Book of Ben Sira in Modern Research: Proceedings of the First International Ben Sira Conference, 28–31 July, Soesterberg, Netherlands* (BZAW 255; Berlin/New York 1997). N. CALDUCH-BENAGES and J. VERMEYLEN, eds., *Treasures of Wisdom: Studies in Ben Sira and the Book of Wisdom* (Festschrift M. Gilbert) (BETL 143; Louvain 1999). **Editions.** *Facsimiles of the Fragments Hitherto Recovered of the Book of Ecclesiasticus in Hebrew* (Oxford-Cambridge 1901). R. SMEND, *Die*

Weisheit des Jesus Sirach, hebräisch und deutsch (Berlin 1906), still the most reliable ed. of the fragments available at that time. M. H. SEGAL, *Sēper ben- Sîrā' ha-šālēm* (2d ed. Jerusalem, Israel 1958). M. BAILLET et al., *Les 'Petites grottes' de Qumrân* (*Discoveries in the Judean Desert* 3; 1962) 75–77 and pl. XV. *Biblia Sacra iuxta latinam vulgatam versionem, 12: Sapientia Salomonis, Liber Hiesu filii Sirach* (Rome 1964). A. A. DI LELLA, "The Recently Identified Leaves of Sirach in Hebrew," *Biblica* 45 (1964) 153–167, the 1958 and 1960 fragments. Y. YADIN, *The Ben Sira Scroll from Masada with Introduction, Emendations and Commentary* (Jerusalem 1965). J. A. SANDERS,*The Psalms Scroll of Qumrân Cave 11* (11QPs^a [containing Sir 51,13–20, 30b]) (DJD 4; Oxford 1965). F. VATTIONI, *Ecclesiastico: Testo ebraico con apparato critico e versioni greca, latina e siriaca* (Pubblicazioni del Seminario di Semitistica, Testi 1; Naples, 1968). Z. BEN HAYYIM (ed.), *The Book of Ben Sira: Text, Concordance and an Analysis of the Vocabulary* (Jerusalem 1973). J. ZIEGLER, *Sapientia Iesu Filii Sirach* (2d ed.; Septuaginta 12/2; Göttingen 1980). A. A. DI LELLA, "The Newly Discovered Sixth Manuscript of Ben Sira from the Cairo Geniza," *Bib* 69 (1988) 226–238. P. C. BEENTJES, *The Book of Ben Sira in Hebrew: A Text Edition of All Extant Hebrew Manuscripts and a Synopsis of All Parallel Hebrew Ben Sira Texts* (VTSup 68; Leiden/New York/Cologne 1997).

[A. A. DI LELLA]

WISEMAN, NICHOLAS PATRICK

Cardinal, archbishop of Westminster; b. Seville, Spain, Aug. 3, 1802; d. London, Feb. 15, 1865. The family returned to Ireland after the death of Wiseman's father (1804), and the boy was sent to school at Waterford, Ireland. In March 1810 he entered Ushaw College, Durham, and studied under the historian John LINGARD, who became his lifelong friend and counselor. In 1818 Wiseman was among the first students to attend the reopened English College in Rome, where he obtained a doctorate (1824), acquired a wide knowledge of the arts, and engaged in theological and linguistic researches. He published, in 1827, an exposition of a Syrian version of the Old Testament, *Horae Syriacae,* which won him an international reputation as an Oriental scholar and an appointment as professor in Oriental languages in the Roman University.

Catholic Revival. In 1828 Wiseman was named rector of the English College, Rome, a post in which he was called upon to act as the Roman representative of the English bishops. The arrival of George Spencer, a recent convert, as a student at the English College brought the OXFORD MOVEMENT to Wiseman's attention and led him to believe that a Catholic revival in England was imminent. This belief was strengthened when John Henry NEWMAN, still an Anglican, and Richard Hurrell FROUDE visited him (1832). Wiseman abandoned academic pursuits to encourage this revival, although he was able to deliver an influential course of lectures on *The Connection between Science and Revealed Religion* (1835). In

1835 he visited London, where he gave a successful series of lectures on aspects of the Catholic faith, published as *Lectures on the Principal Doctrines and Practices of the Catholic Church* (1836). They received a favorable review from Newman in the *British Critic,* and they mark the beginning of the Catholic revival. Before returning to Rome, Wiseman helped to found the DUBLIN REVIEW (*Wiseman Review* 1961–1965) as a literary quarterly presenting the Catholic viewpoint.

Wiseman devoted his remaining years in Rome to the restoration of the English hierarchy. As a preliminary step Rome increased the number of vicariates apostolic from four to eight (1840). At the same time, Wiseman was named coadjutor bishop to the vicar apostolic of the central district of England and president of Oscott College, Birmingham. Before leaving Rome Wiseman wrote for the *Dublin Review* an article on the Donatists, which drew a parallel between Donatism and Anglicanism. This essay profoundly affected Newman, then reaching the crisis of his Anglican career. Observing the Oxford Movement from nearby Oscott, Wiseman entertained high hopes for England's proximate conversion. He was oversanguine, because Newman delayed his conversion another four years, and the number of Anglicans who imitated Newman proved smaller than Wiseman had expected.

Restoration of English Hierarchy. At the request of the English bishops, Wiseman visited Rome in 1847 to present their case to the new Pope Pius IX (1846–78). Bishop ULLATHORNE soon replaced Wiseman, whom the Pope sent back to England to persuade the British government to resist Austria's ambitions against the STATES OF THE CHURCH. This diplomatic venture resulted in the mission of Lord Minto to Rome. Upon the death of the vicar apostolic for London, Wiseman was named to the post (1848). In September 1850 the Holy See decreed the restoration of the hierarchy. Wiseman became a cardinal and archbishop of WESTMINSTER, the sole metropolitan see, with 12 suffragans.

English Protestants bitterly resented his new title, and the British press denounced the restored hierarchy as "the papal aggression." Wiseman's publication of a jubilant but tactlessly phrased pastoral letter, *From out of the Flaminian Gate* (October 7), excited the public to further demonstrations on Guy Fawkes's Day, during which pope and cardinal were burned in effigy. The cardinal helped to calm fears by his published defense of the hierarchy, *Appeal to the Reason and Good Feeling of the English People,* but Protestants remained suspicious, as priests and laymen belonging to old Catholic families continued to assail Wiseman in signed and anonymous attacks. Wiseman was accused, not without foundation, of needlessly arousing the public by his pomposity, love of display, and desire for complete control over church properties and charitable bequests. Parliament in 1851 enacted the Ecclesiastical Titles Bill, which forbade Catholic clergymen to assume an English territorial title, and made those who did so liable to a fine of £100. The government did not enforce this law and repealed it in 1871; yet the furor that Wiseman stirred up over his title cost him the confidence of the British government and the public.

Archbishop of Westminster. Wiseman's period at Westminster was one of tremendous Catholic growth in England, largely because of Irish immigration. Anglican conversions continued. In 1850 Wiseman received into the church Henry MANNING, who succeeded him as archbishop. To adjust to the new conditions, Wiseman encouraged religious orders to establish houses in the country. He also convened the first provincial synod (1852); during it Newman preached his famous sermon on the ''Second Spring.'' As anti-Catholicism subsided, the cardinal frequently delivered lectures to very receptive audiences. He published one of his most popular lecture series as *Recollections of the Last Four Popes* (1858). Wiseman's best-known book, the extremely popular novel *Fabiola,* appeared in 1854.

Dr. George Errington became coadjutor bishop of Westminster in 1855. Since he and Wiseman differed widely in temperament and outlook, their association became increasingly unworkable. Errington's outlook was that of the old Catholic families who distrusted the cardinal's ULTRAMONTANISM and his promotion of converts such as Manning, who became a provost of the cathedral chapter in 1857. Serious misunderstandings arose between the archbishop and his coadjutor. In 1860 Pius IX removed Errington from office; he did not replace him during Wiseman's lifetime.

Wiseman was tall, generously proportioned, genial, and dignified. His intellectual and literary talents did much to increase Catholic prestige and to overcome the hostility that marked his appointment in 1850. His funeral was the occasion for numerous manifestations of popular interest and respect. Wiseman may be regarded as the architect of the English Catholic revival.

Bibliography: W. P. WARD, *The Life and Times of Cardinal Wiseman,* 2 v. (London 1897). D. GWYNN, *Cardinal Wiseman* (Dublin 1950). B. FOTHERGILL, *Nicholas Wiseman* (London 1963).

[B. FOTHERGILL]

Nicholas Patrick Wiseman, chalk drawing attributed to Henry Edward Doyle.

WISHART, GEORGE

Protestant reformer; b. *c.* 1510; d. St. Andrews, March 28, 1545 or 1546. Nothing is known with certainty of the parentage and early life of Wishart. He is probably the ''George Wishart of St. Andrews'' who was promoted in arts at the Château College of Louvain in 1532. In 1534 he was schoolmaster in Montrose, but, when summoned by John Hepburn, Bishop of Brechin, to answer a charge of heresy, he fled to England (1538). At Bristol he was accused of preaching against the worship and mediation of Our Lady and made public recantation in the church of St. Nicholas (1539). He spent the next two years in Germany and Switzerland. During this time he translated into English the Swiss Confession of Faith, drawn up at Basel in 1536; however, it remained unpublished until after his death. By 1543 Wishart had returned to England and was resident at Corpus Christi College, Cambridge, where his pupil, Emery Tylney, describes him as a man of scholarly, earnest, and frugal life.

Wishart seems to have returned to Scotland in 1543 and is possibly to be identified with ''a Scotishman called Wyshart,'' who was the bearer of letters between disaffected Scots nobles and Henry VIII of England, concerning a plot to assassinate Cardinal David Beaton. Protestant historians reject this identification, claiming that it is out of keeping with the character of Wishart, whom J. Knox describes as ''an innocent lamb.'' The destruction of altars and other furnishings of churches, associated with the violent phase of the Scottish Reformation, started seriously only with the arrival of George Wishart. During the years from 1543 to 1545, wherever he preached under the protection of local Protestant lairds, in Ayrshire, Angus, and elsewhere, he left a trail of pillaged churches. On Jan. 16, 1546, he was arrested at the house of the laird of Ormiston in East Lothian and was tried, convicted, and burned for heresy in front of the archiepiscopal castle of St. Andrew's. Within three months, partly in revenge for Wishart and partly for political reasons, Cardinal David Beaton was assassinated, and the castle of St. Andrew's was occupied by his murderers.

Bibliography: D. MCROBERTS, ed., *Essays on the Scottish Reformation, 1513–1625* (Glasgow 1962). C. ROGERS, *Life of George Wishart. . .* (Edinburgh 1876). J. KNOX, *Works,* ed. D. LAING, 6 v. (Edinburgh 1846–64); *History of the Reformation in Scotland,* ed. W. C. DICKINSON, 2 v. (New York 1949). M. SCHMIDT, *Die Religion in Geschichte und Gegenwart* (Tübingen 1957–65) 6:1775–76. A. J. G. MACKAY, *The Dictionary of National Biography from the Earliest Times to 1900* (London 1885–1900) 21:719–722.

[D. MCROBERTS]

WITCHCRAFT

Witchcraft (*magia, maleficium, incantatio*) may be defined as the practice of black magic, sorcery, or intercourse with evil spirits or demons in order, through supernatural aid, to accomplish evil of various kinds. Belief in the existence of demons and witches is deeply embedded in the mythology of antiquity and of the early Germans, and it received concrete expression in the acceptance of hobgoblins and vampires as actual creatures. The concept of the witch was later applied especially to women who, with the help of demons or the devil, wrought harm to men, animals, and property. The Mosaic Law had already condemned witchcraft as a crime to be punished by stoning to death.

The Witch. The German word *Hexe* occurs from the 13th century and is found first in the Alemanic area. The earliest Germanic words, *hagazussa,* Old English *haegtesse* (hedge woman), and Old High German *zunrîte* (mod. German, *Zaunreiterin,* fence rider) have been interpreted as taboo terms by scholars. While anthropophagy, according to Carolingian legislation [*capitulatio de partibus Saxoniae* (an. 785) 6; *Monumenta Germaniae Historica: Capitularia* (Berlin 1826) 1.26], was a characteristic trait of the *striga* and *furia,* the *herbaria* occupied herself with mixing poisons. The Germans ascribed to witches the power of causing storms and tempests. On the other hand, Italian witches seem to have occupied themselves rather with love spells. The complex image of the witch clearly bore the stamp of Oriental, Arabic, and Germanic ideas and rites. To this image was added the charge

of heresy after people had been converted to Christianity and attacks against orthodoxy were associated with MAGIC and witchcraft.

The Church and Witchcraft. Finally, in the eyes of the Church, witchcraft and soothsaying (*divinatio, necromantia, sortilegium*) were regarded without distinction as constituting SUPERSTITION (*superstitio*). From the 9th to the 13th century the Church prosecuted witchcraft exclusively by means of ecclesiastical penalties. Meanwhile, it remained customary on the basis of synodal decrees going back to the 6th century to excommunicate magicians [*Corpus iuris canonici,* ed. E. Friedberg, (Graz 1955) C.26 q. 5 cc.6.9]. The Church originally, however, rejected completely the whole idea of the existence of witches (e.g., *Canon episcopi,* Abbot Regino of Prüm). Bishop BURCHARD OF WORMS, in his penitential *Corrector et medicus* (*Patrologia latina,* 140), labeled witches' riding, flying demons, and the ability of witches to turn into animals (e.g., cats and wolves) as superstitious notions. But after the idea of the reality of the demon world had won general recognition, and magic, because of its association with heterodoxy, was no longer treated as a *delictum sui generis* but was brought under the formal heading of heresy, a change in the attitude toward witchcraft became evident.

In the 13th century witchcraft became a crime that was associated with intercourse with the DEVIL. The *crimen magiae* was now prosecuted also by secular law. In the course of the further development of procedure the papal INQUISITION formulated legal principles that became basic in the markedly increasing number of witch trials in the late Middle Ages. Through the punishment of witchcraft, in accord with both ecclesiastical and civil legislation, the offense in question and its punishment constituted an actual *delictum mixti fori*. Magic or witchcraft was prosecuted for the first time under German imperial law by the *Treuga Heinrici* (King HENRY VII, 1220–35) of 1224, and its punishment was placed at the discretion of the judge: *heretici, incantatores, malefici . . . ad arbitrium iudicis pena debita punientur* [*Monumenta Germaniae Historica: Constitutiones* (Berlin 1826) 2.284]. The German law books of the 13th century demanded the death penalty for magicians. The *Sachsenspiegel* of Eike of Repgow (*c.* 1225) and the *Schwabenspiegel* composed by an unknown Franciscan (*c.* 1275) threatened Christian magicians with burning at the stake.

The Witchcraft Delusion. At all levels of European society the witch obsession grew steadily stronger, especially since almost everywhere it found new support. The records of French witch trials in the 13th and 14th centuries already list many victims. Italian statutes of the 14th and 15th centuries prescribed fines, banishment, and fire for magicians and witches. When belief in demons began to assume truly epidemic proportions, Pope Innocent VIII (1482–92) issued his bull against witches, *Summis desiderantes affectibus* (1484), and ordered the Inquisition to investigate persons accused of practicing witchcraft. The Dominicans Henry Institoris and James Sprenger, making use of inquisitorial writings for the purpose (that of Nicholas Eymericus, 1320–99, among others), composed a commentary for court procedure, the notorious ''Hammer of Witches'' (*Malleus maleficarum*) of 1487. This work exercised a long and marked influence on forensic practice. Denunciation and torture governed procedure. Ordeals, witches' trials, and sympathetic measures were all employed to obtain evidence. For the penal treatment of witchcraft in the Holy Roman Empire of the German nation the *Constitutio criminalis Carolina* (CCC) of the Emperor Charles V in 1532 was decisive (art. 109). However, it still restricted burning at the stake as a penalty; it was to be used only for the practice of harmful or black magic.

The great witch prosecutions increased rapidly in the first half of the 15th century, reached their climax in the first third of the 16th, and petered out *c*. 1700. No one was safe from prosecution. Witchcraft came to embrace a wide field, and interpretation favored the accuser. Catholic territories emulated Evangelical areas in putting down the presumed crime. Even the leading Reformers were not immune to belief in witches. The witch craze and witch burning were not limited to a single religion, or to any one nationality, or to Europe. The mixed clerical-secular criminal trials manifest themselves rather as phenomena typical of their age in the general history of law.

Moreover, well-defined centers of witch prosecution arose. During the entire 15th century France was in the grip of the witch plague. The French victims of the late 16th century often confessed that they were guilty of lycanthropy. In 1641 ordeal by water was abolished on order of the Parlement of Paris, but even in 1670 there were severe witch prosecutions in Rouen and Normandy. In Spain the burning of witches did not begin prior to the 16th century, but in the 17th century the tribunal of Toledo alone handled 151 witch cases. Condemnation to the galleys or imprisonment for life were frequent penalties. In the magic and ASTROLOGY of the Iberian Peninsula, Arabic ideas were especially active beside the ancient traditions. Italian trials of the 15th and 16th centuries frequently ended with the imposition of the death penalty on the accused. In England the witch trials and condemnations in Essex (1576) aroused the whole country. Parliament in 1604 passed the famous English statute against witches. Even as late as 1716 a woman was executed as a witch at Huntingdon; in Scotland the last execution on this charge took place in 1722. Under Calvin's influence

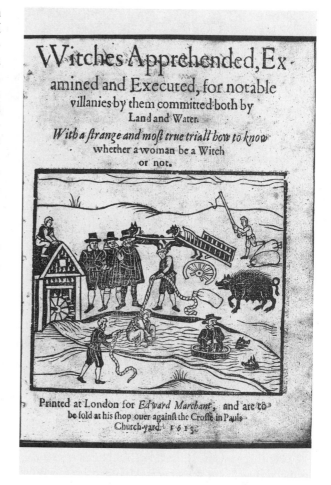

Title page from ''Witches Apprehended, Examined and Executed, for notable villanies by them committed both by Land and Water.'' 1613.

the persecution of witches spread first through the Romansch cantons of Switzerland. In Russia the death penalty and mutilation for witchcraft were still practically unknown in the 11th century, but belief in witches developed rapidly there later. Even in the 19th century Russian peasants murdered supposed witches. The Polish Parliament forbade witch trials in 1776. In Denmark there were numerous witch trials between 1572 and 1652; in 1670 in the Danish area of Mora alone 22 death sentences were imposed on women. Distant Iceland burned a man at the stake for magic in 1685. The witch craze reached America toward the end of the 17th century and a number of persons were executed for witchcraft, especially at Salem, Massachusetts.

In 1623 Pope Gregory XV (1621–23), by his constitution *Omnipotentis,* commanded that persons who had made a pact with the devil (*pactum cum diabolo*) or who had practiced malicious or black magic (*maleficium*) that had caused the death of another, should be surrendered

Salem Witch Trial, lithograph by George H. Walker. (©Bettmann/CORBIS)

to the secular court (*curia secularis*) and be given the death penalty. If the action of the evildoer did not result in the death of another, he should atone for his crime by imprisonment for life. In Germany, where there was much suffering from witch persecutions, especially during the Thirty Years' War, the last witch trials were conducted at Würzburg in 1749, at Endingen in 1751, and at Kempten in 1775. Leading advocates of witch prosecution were Jean Bodin, Peter Binsfeld, and Benedikt CARPZOV. Among the chief opponents were the Catholics Adam TANNER, Paulus LAYMANN, Ferdinand STERZINGER, Nicolas MALEBRANCHE, and, above all, the Jesuit Friedrich von SPEE [*Cautio criminalis contra sagas* (Rintelen 1631)], and the Protestants Balthasar Bekker, Lambert Daneau, and Christian Thomasius.

Evaluation. The witch trial was clearly a typical legal procedure in which torture was employed to prevail over the demons or ghosts who had taken possession of the accused. The prosecution or persecution of witches cannot be evaluated correctly on the basis of dramatic and tendentious literature on the theme. The phenomenon must be judged exclusively from the perspective of men afflicted with superstition and in the light of its concrete historical environment. The critic should not ignore the important fact that, despite great progress in the natural sciences, a propensity for the occult has not been completely excluded from the mind of contemporary man.

Bibliography: J. HANSEN, *Quellen und Untersuchungen zur Geschichte des Hexenwahns und der Hexenverfolgung im Mittelalter* (Bonn 1901); *Zauberwahn, Inquisition und Hexenprozess im Mittelalter und die Entstehung der grossen Hexenverfolgung* (Munich 1900). W. G. SOLDAN, *Geschichte der Hexenprozesse*, ed. H. HEPPE and M. BAUER, 2 v. (Munich 1912). S. J. D. SEYMOUR, *Irish Witchcraft and Demonology* (Dublin 1913). M. A. MURRAY, *The Witch-cult in Western Europe* (Oxford 1921). G. L. KITTREDGE, *Witchcraft in Old and New England* (Cambridge, Mass. 1929). M. O. HOWEY, *The Cat in the Mysteries of Religion and Magic* (London 1930). A. MAYER, *Erdmutter und Hexe* (Freising 1936). E. BLUM, *Das staatliche und kirchliche Recht des Frankenreichs in seiner Stellung zum Dämonen-, Zauber- und Hexenwesen* (Paderborn 1936). S. A. NULLI, *I processi delle streghe* (Turin 1939). G. R. SCOTT, *The History of Torture Throughout the Ages* (London 1940). S. CIRAC ESTOPAÑÁN, *Los procesos de hechicerías en la Inquisición de Castilla la Nueva* (Madrid 1942). G. BADER, *Die Hexenprozesse in der Schweiz* (Affoltern am Albis 1945). J. BRUNSMAND, *Køge huskors* (Copenhagen 1953). H. ZWETSLOOT, *Friedrich Spee und die Hexenprozesse* (Trier 1954). F. BAVOUX, *La Sorcellerie en Franche-Comté* (Monaco 1954). M. SUMMERS, *The History of Witchcraft and Demonology* (New York 1956). F. MERZBACHER, *Die Hexenprozesse in Franken* (Munich 1957); *Lexikon für Theologie und Kirche*², ed. J. HOFER and K. RAHNER (Freiburg 1957–65) 5:316–319. J. PALOU, *La Sorcellerie* (Paris 1957). E. ROSENFELD, *Friedrich Spee von Langenfeld* (Berlin 1958). M.

BOUTEILLER, *Sorciers et jeteurs de sort* (Paris 1958). E. DE MARTINO, *Sud e magia* (Milan 1959). J. SCHRITTENLOHER, "Aus der Gutachter- und Urteilstätigkeit der Ingolstädter Juristenfakultät im Zeitalter der Hexenverfolgungen," *Jahrbuch für Fränkische Landesforschung* 23 (1963) 315–353. W. KRÄMER, *Kurtrierische Hexenprozesse im 16. und 17. Jahrhundert, vornehmlich an der unteren Mosel* (Munich 1959).

[F. MERZBACHER]

WITELO

Diminutive of Wito or Wido (Guido), Renaissance Lat. Vitello, Polish philosopher and mathematician; b. Silesia (then a part of Poland) between 1220 and 1230; d. after 1278. He studied arts at Paris and Canon Law at Padua, but his major interest was mathematics and physics. In 1269 at the papal court in Viterbo he met the Dominican WILLIAM OF MOERBEKE, who translated scientific writings of Archimedes and Hero of Alexandria for his use. About 1274 Witelo finished his major work, *Perspectiva* (Nuremberg 1535, 1551), dedicating it to William. Later this was combined with the writings of Alhazen and republished in the *Opticae thesaurus* (Basel 1572), a work that served as the principal textbook of optics in the West until the 17th century. Witelo wrote also treatises *De primaria causa poenitentiae* and *De natura daemonum,* as yet unpublished; a work *De intelligentiis,* first ascribed to him by C. Baeumker, was later shown by the same historian to be the work of ADAM PULCHRAE MULIERIS.

In philosophy Witelo subscribed to the metaphysics of light, holding that God is the first light who irradiates spiritual forms that are then reflected in matter and bring about an influx of sensible forms. He had a mathematical conception of the structure of the universe not unlike that of ROBERT GROSSETESTE and ROGER BACON. In optics, Witelo proposed a theory of vision that took into account the anatomy of the eye and attempted to explain how a single object is seen with two eyes. He experimented with a parabolic mirror that would concentrate the sun's rays at a single focal point. He also improved on Alhazen's techniques by measuring the angles of refraction at the surfaces between air and water, air and glass, and glass and water. He taught, though not in correct detail, that the rainbow is seen both by reflection and by refraction, and recorded having seen as many as four concentric bows at one time. *See* SCIENCE (IN THE MIDDLE AGES).

Bibliography: C. BAEUMKER, *Witelo, Beiträge zur Geschichte der Philosophie und Theologie des Mittlalters* 3.2 (Münster 1908). A. C. CROMBIE, *Robert Grosseteste and the Origins of Experimental Science* (Oxford 1953) 213–232. L. THORNDIKE, *A History of Magic and Experimental Science,* 8 v. (New York 1923–58) 2:454–456; 3:431, 439, 441. B. NARDI, *Enciclopedia filosofica,* 4 v. (Venice-Rome 1957). F. UEBERWEG, *Grundriss der Geschichte der Philosophie,* ed. K. PRAECHTER (Berlin 1923–28) 2:474–77, 732, 761.

[W. A. WALLACE]

WITHAM CHARTERHOUSE

England's first Carthusian foundation, situated near Frome, Somerset, founded *c.* 1178 by HENRY II as part of his expiation for the death of St. Thomas BECKET. Two priors, daunted by foreign conditions and insufficient resources, returned to the motherhouse, the Grande Chartreuse. From 1180 St. Hugh of Avalon was prior. The house prospered in temporal and spiritual matters so that it became known for its fervor and attracted several monks and canons to join it, among whom was Adam of Dryburgh (*see* ADAM SCOTUS), who wrote there his *De quadripertito exercitio cellae* on CARTHUSIAN SPIRITUALITY. In 1186 St. HUGH became bishop of Lincoln but retained jurisdiction over Witham, where he returned for a month's retreat each year until his death in 1200, when the permanent buildings were almost complete.

Never large nor rich, Witham continued in its chosen obscurity, founding Hinton nearby in 1227. Its income came from cattle and sheep. It was involved in litigation with Maiden Bradley and the king's foresters in the 13th century, and it was exempted by its poverty from contributing to papal subsidies. In the 15th century the number of laybrothers, here as elsewhere, diminished. The library was increased notably by 68 books given by John BLACKMAN, some of which survive in Lambeth palace library.

Witham accepted the royal supremacy in 1535 and was suppressed in 1539, with an income of £215 15s. The laybrothers' church, built by St. Hugh but very much altered since, suvives as Witham parish church, but there is no trace of monastic buildings.

Bibliography: ADAM OF EYNSHAM, *Magna vita Sancti Hugonis,* ed. D. L. DOUIE and H. FARMER, 2 v. (London 1961–62). E. M. THOMPSON, *A History of the Somerset Carthusians* (London 1895); *The Carthusian Order in England* (New York 1930). A. WILMART, "Maître Adam chanoine Prémontré devenu chartreux à Witham," *Analecta Praemonstratensia* 9 (Tongerloo-Saint-Norbert, Belgium 1933) 209–232. D. KNOWLES, *The Monastic Order in England, 943–1216* (2d ed. Cambridge, England 1962) 375–391. M. J. HAMILTON, *Adam of Dryburgh: The Six Christmas Sermons* (Doctoral diss. microfilm; CUA 1964).

[H. FARMER]

WITHBURGA (WITBURH), ST.

Anglo-Saxon abbess, mid-7th century. The youngest daughter of Anna, king of the East Angles, she was a sister of (SS.) ETHELDREDA and ETHELBURGA. Her father was killed in battle *c.* 650, and she chose to become a nun. Her monastic career is obscure, and there are no contemporary records of her life. Tradition placed her at East Dereham, and it is thought she was abbess there, although another tradition says she was a solitary. The lands of the abbey of East Dereham passed to the monks of ELY in the 11th century, and Withburga's body was translated to Ely in 974 by the first reformed abbot, Brithnoth.

Feast: March 17; July 8 (translation); April 18 (Cambridge).

Bibliography: *Acta Sanctorum* (Paris 1863—) 2:603–607. A. M. ZIMMERMANN, *Kalendarium Benedictinum: Die Heiligen und Seligen des Benediktinerordens und Seligen des Benediktinerorderns und seiner Zweige* (Metten 1933–38) 1:339–340. F. M. STENTON, ''The East Anglian Kings,'' *The Anglo-Saxons*, ed. P. CLEMOES (London 1959) 43–52.

[E. JOHN]

WITHERSPOON, JOHN

Presbyterian minister, president of Princeton University, N.J.; b. Yester, Scotland, Feb. 5, 1723; d. Princeton, Nov. 15, 1794. He was the son of a Presbyterian clergyman. Educated at Haddington Grammar School and the University of Edinburgh, he was ordained in 1754. Witherspoon resisted every effort to modify the doctrine and polity of his church, publishing *Ecclesiastical Characteristics* (1755) and *Essay on the Doctrine of Justice* (1756) to combat innovators. He accepted a call to be president of Princeton and came to the U.S. in 1768. He was a signer of the Declaration of Independence and served in the Continental Congress from 1776 to 1782. After the American Revolution, he succeeded in organizing the Presbyterian Church on a national basis and was the first moderator of its General Assembly.

Bibliography: Works, 4 v. (2d ed. rev. Philadelphia 1802). V. L. COLLINS, *President Witherspoon*, 2 v. (Princeton 1925), with bibliog. L. H. BUTTERFIELD, *John Witherspoon Comes to America* (Princeton 1953).

[R. K. MAC MASTER]

WITNESS, CHRISTIAN

A witness is a person who calls attention to something other than himself, one who is called upon to give—or to be—evidence of something. He gives—or is—witness. All true religious witness is an exteriorization of inner COMMITMENT; it transmits truth to others in a living way. A witness is a person totally *given* to God and his fellow men. There are three elements in this Christian witness: message, signs to convince, divine helps to awaken and draw others to God.

Christ. ''The faithful and true witness'' to the Father is Christ (Rv 3.14). He is the great Witness. He came into the world precisely ''to bear witness to the truth'' (Jn 18.37), which He had received from the Father (Jn 8.26), to call attention not to Himself, but to the Father. And since He is God the Son as well as man, the witness He gives must be identical with that of the Father. All three elements of Christian witness are obviously verified in Christ.

Apostles, Primary Witnesses to Christ. JOHN THE BAPTIST ''came as a witness, to bear witness concerning the light'' (Jn 1.7), and he represents all witnesses who preceded Christ. But Jesus specifically asks His APOSTLES to be His witnesses even to the ends of the earth (Acts 1.8). They are the special eye- and ear-witnesses to Christ, testifying to the historical and saving events (Jn 3.11; 1 Jn 1.1–5; Lk 24.48). The primary object of their testimony was the RESURRECTION OF CHRIST (Acts 1.22; 4.33), but this soon broadened to include the whole earthly life of Jesus—particularly His PASSION, death, and Resurrection, and its effects on man: CONVERSION, FORGIVENESS OF SIN, and judgment (Acts 5.31; 10.42).

Message, convincing signs, and GRACE are evident in apostolic witness. The Apostle PAUL, for example, is a totally committed man. The commitment is expressed with the enthusiasm characteristic of him. His faithfulness, love, contagious conviction, and compelling words are elements of his witness to Christ, as is, finally, his MARTYRDOM. The Greek word for MARTYR, μάρτυς, from which the English is derived, means witness. A martyr is a witness to Christ and the faith even to death (cf. Acts 22.20).

Church as Witness to Christ. What is true of the Apostles as primary witnesses to Christ, is true of the CHURCH as the permanent witness. Its mission is to continue Christ and His saving work in the world. It must not only preach the gospel, then, but bear convincing witness to it. It is for this reason that the signs of its divine origin will always be evident in the Church (despite any failures of its members). And God by His graces and internal helps adapts these signs to the individual recipient (cf. H. Denzinger, *Enchiridion symolorum*, ed. A. Schönmetzer 3013–14).

Individual Witness to the Faith. The committed Christian finds God and His truth present and meaningful to his whole life. He lives the Christian message, in order to possess it authentically. And in living it, he is thereby a witness, for witness is but the necessary overflow and externalization of true commitment to the faith. Normally, Christian truth must make itself known through a Christian person: message, convincing signs, and grace must come in dependency upon individuals. ''You shall be my witnesses'' is applied not only to the Apostles, but to every Christian. God is not restricted. Yet just as the signs of credibility are not separable from the first Witness who is Christ, and just as they are not separable from the permanent witness which is the Church, so they usually are not separable from the individual Christian witness.

Thus the role of the witness is to realize a presence within himself and to transmit a call. Witnessing to Christ is so important that it constitutes the Christian's primary vocation. His first calling is to live and transmit Christ, through his second calling or role in life. The special Sacrament of Christian witness is CONFIRMATION. And because this demands the full commitment of a person, Confirmation is also the Sacrament of Christian maturity. The Holy Spirit offers to make a person a strong, docile, committed believer. Witnessing is first of all a question of what one is, rather than what one does. To be a Christian wholly given to Christ is, by that very fact, to bear eloquent witness to the faith. This is to let one's light shine among men. Christianity needs witnesses. It has to be ''caught'' rather than taught. And it is normally caught only from someone already ''caught up'' by it.

See Also: PROFESSION OF FAITH; CONFESSION OF FAITH.

Bibliography: ''Zeugnis,'' *Lexikon für Theologie und Kirche,* ed. J. HOFER and K. RAHNER, 10 v. (2d, new ed. Freiburg 1957–65); suppl., *Das ZweiteVatikanische Konzil: Dokumente und kommentare,* ed. H. S. BRECHTER et al., pt. 1 (1966) v.10. N. BROX, H. FRIES, ed., *Handbuch theologischer Grundbegriffe,* 2 v. (Munich 1962–63) 2:903–911. *Encyclopedic Dictionary of the Bible,* translated and adapted by L. HARTMAN (New York, 1963) 2591–94. J. MOUROUX, *I Believe,* tr. M. TURNER (New York 1959). D. GRASSO, ''The Catechist as Witness,'' *Worship* 38 (1964) 157–164. W. YEOMANS, ''You Shall Be My Witnesses,'' *Way* 4 (1964) 24–32.

[W. F. DEWAN]

WITTA, ST.

Latin, *Albinus,* or Albuin, possibly Old English for ''wise man''; d. *c.* 760. Most of the information about Witta, an Anglo-Saxon monk and missionary companion to (St.) BONIFACE, is gleaned from lives of the latter, from that of St. WILLIBALD OF EICHSTÄTT and from mention in other historical documents. In 741 when Boniface assigned four bishops to the new mission field in what is now central Germany, he appointed Witta first bishop of Hesse, designating the castle at Buraburg as his see since it was well fortified and near the previously established monastery at Fritzlar. On October 22 of the same year, with his fellow bishop, Burchard, Witta was coconsecrator of Willibald. His name is recorded as a participant in

two synods: the *Concilium Germanicum,* called by Charlemagne April 21, 742, and the *Synodus Liftinensis* in 743.

Feast: Oct. 26, Feb. 15.

Bibliography: *Acta Sanctorum* (Paris 1863—) 11:947–960. A. HAUCK, *Kirchengeschichte Deutschlands* (Berlin-Leipzig 1958) 1:477, 485 n.1, 498. *Lexikon der deutschen Heiligen, Seligen, Ehrwürdigen und Gottseligen,* ed. J. TORSY (Cologne 1959) 571. A. ZIMMERMANN, *Lexikon für Theologie und Kirche,* ed. M. BUCHBERGER (Freiburg 1930–38) 10:946. C. H. TALBOT, ed. and tr., *The Anglo-Saxon Missionaries in Germany* (New York 1954). A. M. ZIMMERMANN, *Kalendarium Benedictinum: Die Heiligen und Seligen des Benediktinerordens und seiner Zweige* (Metten 1933–38) 3:222.

[M. E. COLLINS]

WITTENBERG

Important university town in Electoral Saxony, home of the Ascanier line until 1422, and a trading post settled by Wendish and Flemish peoples as early as A.D. 1174. Albert the Bear gave the Wittenberg region to his son Bernhard, who attached to it his title of Duke of Saxony bestowed at Gelnhausen in 1180 by Emperor FREDERICK I BARBAROSSA. By 1266 his descendant, Albert II, had moved the royal house to Wittenberg, where it resided until a tragic collapse of the castle at Schweinitz wiped out the male line and the House of Wettin succeeded. By the time of the Reformation Wittenberg had a new castle and castle church (1490–1509), a beautiful Gothic structure, prized by Frederick the Wise, the reigning Prince. This richly endowed *Stiftskirche* at one time supported 81 clergymen. It was also one of the great relic centers of the North, attracting pilgrims from far and near, especially for the festival of All Saints Day on November 1. It was later to fall prey to artillery fire in the Seven Years' War. Near the castle was the residence and art school of Lucas Cranach, and in the town square stood the *Rathaus* and town church. Parts of the latter structure date to 1180.

In 1502 Frederick the Wise, although residing in Torgau, founded Wittenberg University, and the town became famous as an educational center. This institution became the key to the German Reformation; for during the tenure of Martin LUTHER and Philipp MELANCHTHON, more than 20,000 students matriculated there from all over Europe. Whereas the early university had been typically Catholic, between 1512 and 1533 it became a Lutheran institution with a Protestant system of education; it later merged with the university of Halle (1817). Wittenberg in the 16th century was a walled city, completely surrounded by a deep moat and well guarded day and night. Entry to the town was by three gates from west, south, and east. Although not large by today's standards, its permanent population of between 2,100 and 2,400 was about average for that day, and that number was doubled by the student population that lived in the town and its suburbs. In the eastern end of town the principal university buildings were the Black Cloister (Luther's home after 1524), the Melanchthon House (1541), the Old and New Friderici Colleges, and several small dormitories. Law College classes were in the castle at the western edge of town in rooms beautifully frescoed with Greek and Roman court scenes. The castle housed also the university library, and the castle church was the scene of university convocations and academic promotions. This entire complex was entered by way of a large door in the north side of the castle church. This door was also the university bulletin board for posting announcements, and it was here that the young professor, Martin Luther, might have nailed his 95 theses on October 31, 1517 to notify the crowds who would have visited the church on All Saints' Day. Whether Luther posted the theses there has more recently been called into doubt (Iserloh) and it remains an open question as to whether Luther's intentions were to present his attack upon indulgences to such a broad audience as early as October 1517. Luther and Melanchthon are buried in the restored castle church.

Bibliography: E. G. SCHWIEBERT, *Luther and His Times* (St. Louis 1950). O. THULIN, *Die Religion in Geschichte und Gegenwart,* 7 v. (3d ed. Tübingen 1957–65) 6:1782–84. W. FRIEDENSBURG, *Geschichte der Universität Wittenberg* (Halle 1917). M. BRECHT, *Martin Luther. His Road to Reformation 1483–1521,* J. L. SCHAAF, trans. (Philadelphia 1985). E. ISERLOH, *The Theses Were Not Posted,* J. WICKS, trans. (London 1968). H. OBERMAN, *Masters of the Reformation,* D. MARTIN, trans. (Cambridge 1981). E. G. RUPP and B. DREWERY, eds. *Martin Luther* (New York 1971).

[E. G. SCHWIEBERT]

WITTGENSTEIN, LUDWIG

Austrian philosopher who exerted considerable influence on both LOGICAL POSITIVISM and linguistic analysis, although he was an adherent of neither; b. Vienna, April 26, 1889; d. Cambridge, England, April 29, 1951.

Life. Wittgenstein's family was rich and cultured, Jewish by descent, Christian by religion. Educated privately and at a *Realschule* in Linz, he studied engineering at Charlottenburg and aeronautics at Manchester. Becoming interested in the foundations of mathematics, he had discussions with G. Frege and frequent and mutually profitable contact (1912–14) with B. RUSSELL. His war service did not interrupt his work, and he completed his *Tractatus Logico-Philosophicus* in an Italian prison camp in 1919. Giving away his money, he worked as a gardener, a village schoolmaster, and an architect. Returning to Cambridge in 1929, he soon became the chief philosophical influence there, though he usually repudiated the forms in which his new ideas were propagated. During World War II he did medical work and delayed his assumption of a Cambridge professorship. Ill health forced him to retire early, but he continued his writing. A man of fierce integrity, demanding much from his friends and even more from himself, he did not practice religion but respected it and felt contempt for any facile rejection of it.

Teaching. The *Tractatus* attempted to solve all the problems of philosophy with the help of logic, which shows the features that language (and hence any describable world) must possess. Propositions are not names for complexes (which would have to exist for the propositions to have sense) but are, like pictures, self-explanatory. The world must therefore consist of atomic states of affairs composed of indestructible elements designated by proper names. Any informative proposition depends for its truth on the truth of elementary propositions consisting of such names. (This was argued a priori: no such propositions could be produced.) Logical propositions, being unconditionally true, are not genuine propositions; nor are ethical or metaphysical propositions, since they are not truth–functions of elementary propositions. Indeed, his own propositions, since they describe the relation of language to the world, are an attempt to say what can only be shown and form some sort of ladder that one must kick down once he has climbed up it. Apart from natural science, all that is left is the inexpressible mystical feeling of the world as a whole, a world that, as it were, expands and contracts for the happy and the unhappy man: this feeling owed much to L. N. TOLSTOI and A. SCHOPENHAUER. Wittgenstein rejected the axiomatic method of the *Principia Mathematica:* all the propositions of logic are equally self-evident. Any axioms that are not self-evident must be dropped. The theory of types, since it involves attributing a type to symbols, is either a redundant or a nonsensical project.

Wittgenstein's canonization of natural science was welcomed by the Viennese logical positivists, but most of them rejected the book's professed inexpressibility and its mysticism. In later conversations with M. Schlick and F. Watsmann, Wittgenstein formulated the principle that the sense of a proposition was the method of its VERIFICATION, but he subsequently denied that he had held a general theory of this kind.

In his later work, published posthumously, Wittgenstein saw linguistic activities as essentially part of a way of life. For most purposes the meaning of a word is the role that it plays in life. Being the name of something is only one such role, and a more complicated role than the

Tractatus assumed, requiring some background such as a practice of manipulating things when their names are called. To investigate a concept Wittgenstein constructed "language games,"—i.e., fragmentary languages and customs embodying primitive forms of it. Games indeed exhibit an enormous variety (parallel to the multiplicity of operations possible with language): there is no one feature common to them all; at best they have a "family resemblance." The notion of following a rule (as in a game) also fascinated him: nothing *dictates* the next step of a man following a rule; yet in fact men agree in their interpretations of rules. Hence Wittgenstein's view of mathematics: each step in a calculation or proof involves a fresh decision.

In the philosophy of mind, Wittgenstein rejected the idea that man's sensations are inner objects fully known only to himself. Reports of sensations are not the naming of such objects: their role is more akin to that of spontaneous evincings of sensations. The aim of philosophy is still the dissolution of problems, but Wittgenstein ceased to believe in a permanent exorcism. Some Catholic philosophers, such as A. J. Kenny, have seen his work as a liberation from Cartesian prejudices.

Bibliography: Works. *Tractatus logico–philosophicus* (New York 1922), Ger. and Eng. (New York 1961), Ger. with new Eng. tr. D. F. PEARS and B. F. MCGUINNESS; *Philosophical Investigations,* tr. G. E. M. ANSCOMBE (2d ed. Oxford 1958), Ger. and Eng.; *Remarks on the Foundations of Mathematics,* ed. G. H. VON WRIGHT et al., tr. G. E. M. ANSCOMBE (New York 1956), Ger. and Eng. Studies. G. P. PITCHER, *The Philosophy of Wittgenstein* (Englewood Cliffs, N.J. 1964). M. BLACK, *A Companion to Wittgenstein's Tractatus* (Ithaca, N.Y. 1964). N. MALCOLM, *Ludwig Wittgenstein, A Memoir* (New York 1958), with a biog. sketch by G. H. VON WRIGHT. A. KENNY, "Aquinas and Wittgenstein," *Downside Review* 77 (1959) 217–235.

[B. F. MCGUINNESS]

WITZEL, GEORG (WICELIUS)

Theologian, liturgist, irenicist, generally recognized as the most representative of the "expectants" or those who followed a *via media* in hoping to reform the church along Erasmian and humanistic lines; b. Vacha, Germany, 1501; d. Mainz, Feb. 16, 1573. Witzel was among the most prolific publicists of the Catholic party during the century of the reform and was author of more than 130 published works. He wished to reform and reunite the church of the 16th century by a return to the practices of the primitive and postapostolic church. He was educated at the universities of Erfurt and Wittenberg, where he had M. LUTHER, A. KARLSTADT, and P. MELANCHTHON as masters. Bishop Adolph of Merseburg ordained him in 1521. Soon thereafter Witzel joined the Lutheran move-

ment, holding a number of pastorates in Vacha, Fulda, Neimegk, and Eisenach. He abandoned the Protestant party after the Confession of Augsburg (1530), and he was appointed consultant for religious affairs of the court of George of Saxony. With Christopher Carlowitz (1507–78) he represented the Catholic party at the Colloquy of Leipzig in 1539; and in collaboration with Martin BUCER he worked out a formula of reform that influenced the later religious colloquies of Hagenau and Regensburg. The reform program envisioned a return to the ancient liturgies based on the account of Justin Martyr; a modified interpretation of the *sola fide;* a reduction of feast days; Mass in the vernacular; and the chalice for the laity. Witzel prepared also a number of church ordinances (*Kirchenordnungen*) in Brandenburg, Meissen, Fulda, Cleve, and Strassburg. He was active at the diets of Regensburg in 1542 and 1544 and again at Augsburg in 1555, where he provided Emperor Ferdinand I with a formula of concord (*Pro concordia Ecclesiae repurgandae ac restituendae*). He was author of the first Catholic catechism published in the German language (1535), and he was the first to use an abbreviated Bible history for instructional purposes. It is, however, as a liturgist that Witzel exerted his greatest influence. He translated the Latin Mass into German and published a number of Eastern liturgies, including the Mass of St. Chrysostom and the Liturgy of St. Basil. He was a strong opponent of the Council of Trent until the time of his death. His conciliatory works, especially his *Via Regia* (1564) and his *Methodus Concordiae Ecclesiasticae* (1532), were used by the 17th-century ecumenists G. CALIXTUS, H. Conring, (1606–81), and H. GROTIUS.

Bibliography: G. RICHTER, *Die Schriften Georg Witzels . . .* (Fulda 1913), bibliog. W. TRUSEN, *Um Die Reform und Einheit der Kirche* (Münster 1957). J. P. DOLAN, "Witzel et Erasme à propos des sacrements," *Revue d'histoire ecclésiastique* 54:129–142; *The Influence of Erasmus, Witzel and Cassander in the Church Ordinances . . . of the Duchees of Cleve during the Middle Decades of the 16th Century* (Münster 1957). R. JAUERNIG, *Die Religion in Geschichte und Gegenwart,* 7 v. (3d ed. Tübingen 1957–65) 6:1787–88. È. AMANN, *Dictionnaire de théologie catholique,* ed. A. VACANT et al., 15 v. (Paris 1903–50; Tables générales 1951–) 15.2:3577–82.

[J. P. DOLAN]

WIWINA, ST.

Benedictine prioress (Wivina); b. Flanders; d. Dec. 17, 1170. At the age of 15 she had already determined to forsake the world. However, she was renowned for her beauty and sought in marriage by a young nobleman named Richard, who found favor in the eyes of her parents. When rejected by her, he became ill to the point of death. Whereupon Wiwina prayed and fasted for him until he was miraculously restored to health. At the age of 23, she went to live a hermit's life in a wood near Brussels. Here Count Godfrey of Brabant established the convent of Le Grand Bigard for her in 1120. Acting as prioress she put it under the direction of the abbot of AFFLIGEM and labored diligently to maintain the true religious life there. After her death she was glorified by many miracles. Her relics are now in Notre Dame du Sablon at Brussels. Her cultus was confirmed by Urban VII in 1625; a Mass and Office was approved in 1903.

Feast: Dec. 19 (formerly Dec. 17); Dec. 16 (Benedictines); Sept. 25 (translation).

Bibliography: *Acta Sanctorum* (Paris 1863—) 17:590. A. ZIMMERMANN, *Lexikon für Theologie und Kirche*, ed. M. BUCHBERGER (Freiburg 1930–38) 10:952–953. *Monumenta Germaniae Historica: Scriptores* (Berlin 1826—) 25:525. J. GIELEMANS, *Anecdota ex codicibus hagiographicis* (Brussels 1895) 57–79. L. H. COTTINEAU, *Répertoire topobibliographique des abbayes et prieurés* (Mâcon 1935–39) 1:379. U. CHEVALIER, *Répertoire des sources historiques du moyen-âge. Biobibliographie* (Paris 1905–07) 2:4712. A. BUTLER, *The Lives of the Saints*, rev. ed. H. THURSTON and D. ATTWATER (New York 1956) 4:580–581. A. M. ZIMMERMANN, *Kalendarium Benedictinum: Die Heiligen und Seligen des Benediktinerordens und seiner Zweige* (Metten 1933–38) 3:439–442.

[F. D. LAZENBY]

WOLFF, CHRISTIAN

German philosopher and mathematician, name sometimes spelled Wolf (Lat. Wolfius), best known for his systematization of scholastic philosophy; b. Breslau, Jan. 24, 1679; d. Halle, April 9, 1754. His father, a tanner, hoped that Christian would enter the ministry, and his early studies at the Magdalenen Gymnasium were so directed. In 1699 he entered the University of Jena where mathematics, physics, and philosophy became his predominant interests. He qualified as a *Privatdocent* at the University of Leipzig in 1703 with a treatise entitled *De philosophia practica universali methodo mathematica conscripta.* The title of this work indicated what was to become his lifelong goal, i.e., the attainment of certitude and the reorganization of knowledge by means of the mathematical method.

Academic Career. Upon the recommendation of LEIBNIZ in 1706, he was appointed professor of mathematics at the University of Halle. During the ensuing years his lecturing and writing, including numerous articles in *Acta Eruditorum,* Germany's first learned journal, gained him an ever-broadening reputation as a scholar. However, his increasing involvement with philosophical and moral issues brought him into conflict with the pietistic movement centered in Halle. The Lutheran theologians, led by Joachim Lange, accused him of teaching determinism and of making excessive claims for the abilities of reason in moral matters. In 1721 the dispute reached a climax with Wolff's lecture *De Sinarum philosophia practica* in which he concluded that the maxims of Confucius prove the power of unaided reason in the attainment of the good moral life. The argument became famous with hundreds of pamphlets and challenges for debate issued by many people on both sides. Finally Frederick William I was persuaded that Wolff's teachings were dangerous, and on Nov. 8, 1723, a royal proclamation ordered Wolff to leave Halle within 48 hours under pain of death.

Sympathy for his cause and respect for his reputation brought Wolff many attractive academic offers, and he finally settled in Marburg under the protection of the landgrave of Hesse. His years at Marburg were very productive, adding considerably to his already wide reknown. To reach a broader audience he began to write his major treatises in Latin rather than German. By the late 1730s the atmosphere in Prussia had changed but Wolff was unwilling to return. However, in 1740 Frederick the Great, a patron of learning and a friend of scholars, succeeded his authoritarian father, and one of his first acts was to invite Wolff back to Halle as vice-chancellor of the university. Wolff returned in triumph. In 1743 he became chancellor and in 1745 was made a baron. During these last years he wrote primarily on moral and political philosophy, but his popularity as a lecturer gradually began to decline.

Major Writings. Wolff was an unusually prolific writer, and only his major works can be indicated here. Most of his more important mathematical and physical treatises are collected together under the title *Elementa matheseos universae,* 4 volumes. Between 1713 and 1725 he published a series of seven works, the title of each beginning with the expression *Vernünfftige Gedanken von . . . ,* which are devoted to philosophy, morality, and physics. Of this group the *Vernünfftige Gedanken von Gott, der Welt und der Seele der Menschen, auch allen Dingen überhaupt* (1719) is a basic presentation of his metaphysics and methodology. The volumes of his Latin series in systematic philosophy include (abridged titles): *Philosophia rationalis sive logica* (1728) to which is prefaced the *Discursus praeliminaris de philosophia in genere, Philosophia prima sive ontologia* (1730); *Cosmologia generalis* (1731); *Psychologia empirica* (1732); *Psychologia rationalis* (1734); *Theologia naturalis* (Pars prior, 1736; Pars posterior, 1737); and *Philosophia practica* (Pars prior, 1738; Pars posterior, 1739). The second Halle period produced *Jus naturae* (8 v., 1740–48), *Jus gentium* (1749), *Institutiones juris naturae et gentium*

(1750), and *Philosophia moralis sive ethica* (5 v., 1750–53).

Nature and Division of Philosophy. Wolff's chief contribution to the history of thought has often been characterized as the introduction of the spirit of thoroughness and detailed organization into German philosophy. Not an unusually original thinker himself, he was heavily influenced by Leibniz, and in many ways he helped prepare the atmosphere from which KANT broke in the late 1760s. But as Wolff himself insisted, his philosophy is not simply a systematization of the ideas of Leibniz. Rather in Wolff one finds the meeting ground and attempted reconciliation of three earlier and often opposing traditions: (1) Cartesian-Leibnizian RATIONALISM with its stress on clear ideas and the power of reason, (2) Newtonian science with its foundations in experience and experimentation, and (3) the Aristotelian-scholastic school tradition which emphasized the primacy of METAPHYSICS. Wolff's synthesis was based on a rigorous application of the mathematico-deductive method to all the sciences, tempered by an inductive appeal to the facts of experience. As a result he organized each science into a strict, deductive pattern and then placed all the sciences into a hierarchical order built on the same principles.

Classification of the Sciences. His influential theory of the division of the sciences constituted the details of this program. All natural human knowledge falls under one of three headings: (1) history (knowledge of facts), (2) philosophy (knowledge of the reason of the facts), and (3) mathematics (knowledge of quantity). Philosophy receives its experiential foundation from history and its fullness of certitude from mathematical method. He distinguished the parts of philosophy on the basis of differences in subject matter. Theoretical philosophy was divided into ONTOLOGY (being in general), natural THEOLOGY (God), rational psychology (human souls), general COSMOLOGY (world in general), and dogmatic physics (material bodies). The first four taken together constitute metaphysics. Ontology was given the top position in the deductive hierarchy of the sciences. Because of the wealth and complexity of the factual information relating to man and the physical world, Wolff added the special disciplines of empirical psychology and experimental physics as inductive preparations for the principles in these areas. Practical philosophy followed the traditional divisions into cognitive, appetitive, and productive branches.

First Principles. Philosophy, defined as the science of the possibles insofar as they can be, was ultimately governed by the two great principles of CONTRADICTION and SUFFICIENT REASON, with the latter derived from the former. These two principles provided the starting points

Christian Wolff.

for the mathematically-modeled structuring of philosophy. The component elements (*essentialia*) of a possible must be mutually compatible. This consistency is regulated and judged by the principle of contradiction. But to be possible is not to be in ACT. Hence an explanation must be provided, according to Wolff, as to why the particular objects and events of the given world are actual in preference to the myriad of other possible objects and events. This explanation is what is demanded by the principle of sufficient reason, understanding by ''sufficient reason'' that which explains why something is. The Wolffian ontology developed from these principles was thoroughly essentialistic, with EXISTENCE being defined as the final complement in the order of possibility. In natural theology Wolff looked upon GOD as the sufficient reason of both His own existence and the existence of the contingent world. The possibles were ultimately grounded in the Divine Intellect, but the sufficient reasons motivating the Divine Will to create remain inscrutably hidden from human knowledge.

Man and the State. Wolff's conception of man shows an unmistakable debt to DESCARTES and Leibniz. Our consciousness of ourselves and of external things provides the foundation for his argument for the existence of the SOUL, with the Cartesian *cogito ergo sum* cast into syllogistic format. For Wolff the soul is an independent substance distinct from the body, and he shows little awareness of the Aristotelian doctrine of the soul and the body as incomplete principles of one substantial unity. As a result he was burdened with the soul-body DUALISM of classical rationalism. Although there must be a natural sufficient reason for the harmonious cooperation of soul and body, Wolff was unable to find it, and he concluded that Leibniz's doctrine of preestablished harmony is the most probable of the available hypotheses relating to the soul-body problem.

Wolff also held a representational theory of knowledge (*see* KNOWLEDGE, THEORIES OF). Perception is an unconscious mechanical process which produces our ideas. When apperception or consciousness arising from within the soul is brought to bear on our ideas, then knowledge results. What we know are our ideas as representative of external objects. Thus he defined the soul as consisting in the force of representing the universe (*vis repraesentativa universi*), which is reminiscent of Leibniz's view of the MONAD as a mirror of the world.

The moral ideal for Wolff was the attainment of self-perfection. This goal involved for him a complicated balance between the internal needs and demands of human nature, a proper and sufficient disposition of material goods, and involvement in social and political life. He stresses the values of education in producing a clear notion of these elements and their interrelations in the moral life.

Wolff's views on political theory were progressive for the 18th century. He argued that many duties, and therefore rights, are innate to human nature, and in this respect all men are by nature equal. No man can usurp the freedom of action of another. However to obtain a wider range of good and protection than the individual can attain by himself, the state is formed by implicit or explicit contract. The function of the state is to promote the common welfare with a minimum of interference with personal FREEDOM. Thus the root of governmental power is the consent of the people, although they may transfer this power to a monarch. But an absolute ruler may never dictate anything contrary to the laws of nature and society. Relations between nations are similar to relations between individuals. Hence Wolff advocated the development of a *jus voluntarium,* i.e., a society of nations formed by mutual consent devoted to the promotion and protection of the welfare of mankind in general.

Wolffian School. Because of their strict deductive format, the writings of Wolff appear dry, rigorous, and unimaginative to the modern reader. However, this was not the reaction of many of his contemporaries. During his own lifetime Wolff and his writings became very popular, and his teachings were widely adopted in the universities, especially in Germany. A Wolffian school of considerable influence soon developed, the members of which published numerous reformulations, compendia, and abridgments of the works of Wolff designed for use as textbooks. Notable among these supporters of Wolff were L. Thümmig, G. Bilfinger, J. Gottsched, A. Baumgarten, G. Maier, M. Knutzen (a teacher of Kant), and F. Baumeister. But Wolff was not without his critics, especially J. Lange, C. Crusius, and A. Ruediger. By the middle of the 18th century the Wolffian system predominated at the German universities, and it was in this atmosphere that Kant spent his early days as a student and teacher.

Another significant consequence of the work of Wolff was its effect on the development of scholastic philosophy. His theory of the division of the sciences and his emphasis on the principle of sufficient reason were the chief doctrines incorporated gradually into the scholastic manual tradition, and traces of these influences can still be seen in many 20th century textbooks of scholastic philosophy.

The first volume (*Ontologia*) of a 20-volume reprint of the works of Wolff, edited by J. Ecole and H. Arndt, was published in 1962 by Georg Olms Verlagsbuchhandlung, Hildesheim.

See Also: DYNAMISM; SCHOLASTICISM; ONTOLOGY; THEODICY.

Bibliography: C. WOLFF, *Jus gentium methodo scientifica pertractum,* 2 v. text and tr. J. H. DRAKE (Classics of International Law 13; Oxford 1934); *Preliminary Discourse on Philosophy in General,* tr. R. BLACKWELL (New York 1963). Secondary studies. M. CAMPO, *Cristiano Wolff e il razionalismo precritico,* 2 v. (Milan 1939). H. PICHLER, *Über Christian Wolffs Ontologie* (Leipzig 1910). M. WUNDT, *Die deutsche Schulphilosophie im Zeitalter der Aufklärung* (Tübingen 1945). J. GURR, *The Principle of Sufficient Reason in Some Scholastic Systems, 1750–1900* (Milwaukee 1959).

[R. J. BLACKWELL]

WOLFF, GEORGE DERING

Editor; b. Martinsburg, WV, Aug. 25, 1822; d. Norristown, PA, Jan. 29, 1894. His father was Rev. Bernard C. Wolff, professor at the German Reformed Theological Seminary, Mercersburg, PA. After reading law in Easton, PA, and being admitted to practice, Wolff studied theology at Mercersburg and was ordained in the Reformed Church. Both he and his father were strongly influenced by John Williamson NEVIN, leader of the Mercersburg movement, a development in the German Reformed Church paralleling the Tractarian movement in England (*see* MERCERSBURG THEOLOGY). After holding pastorates at Tiffin, OH, and at Norristown, Wolff left the active ministry to become principal of the Norristown high school. In 1871, together with three other Reformed clergymen, he was received into the Catholic Church at the old mission at Goshenhoppen, PA. That same year he became editor of the Baltimore, MD *Catholic Mirror*. In 1872 he transferred to the Philadelphia *Catholic Standard* as general editor, holding this position until his death. In 1876, with Rev. (later Bp.) James O'Connor and Msgr. James CORCORAN, he founded the *American Catholic Quarterly Review*. His writings reflect an interest in apologetics and in social philosophy.

Bibliography: G. D. WOLFF, ''The Mercersburg Movement,'' *American Catholic Quarterly Review* 3 (1898) 151–176. *Ibid.* 19 (1894) 433. *Records of the American Catholic Historical Society of Philadelphia* 20 (1909) 244–247.

[B. F. FAIR]

WOLFGANG OF REGENSBURG, ST.

Bishop, patron saint of Regensburg, popular saint in southern Germany during the late Middle Ages; b. probably in Pfullingen (Swabia), Germany, *c.* 924; d. Pupping (near Linz, Upper Austria), Oct. 31, 994. He was educated in REICHENAU with Henry, brother of Bp. Poppo of Würzburg, and went to Würzburg with him to study under the Italian grammarian Stephen. When Henry became archbishop of Trier (956), he made Wolfgang dean and head of the cathedral school. After Henry's death (964), Wolfgang became a monk in EINSIEDELN and was ordained by ULRIC OF AUGSBURG (968). His missionary activity in Hungary was cut short when Bp. PILGRIM OF PASSAU had him named bishop of Regensburg (972). There, Wolfgang became the teacher of the future Emperor Henry II, and Gisela, later wife of STEPHEN I of Hungary, as well as of several future archbishops and bishops. The Diocese of Prague, formed from his diocese (973–975), had as its first resident bishop (St.) ADALBERT OF PRAGUE (983–997), Wolfgang's disciple in Trier. Wolfgang loyally supported Emperors OTTO II and OTTO III. His greatest merits, however, lay in his pastoral care. He separated the bishop's office from that of abbot of SANKT EMMERAM, calling on his friend, Ramwold of St. Maximin in Trier to introduce GORZE customs there. Abbots Ramwold (975–1000) and Godehard of NIEDER-ALTAICH proved his best helpers in renewing the spiritual life in monasteries throughout his diocese. The Regensburg convent for nuns, Mittelmünster, founded by him *c.*

974, became the model for his reform of the convent of Obermünster. His reform spread to other Bavarian dioceses; he reformed also Mondsee (*c.* 976) in the Diocese of Salzburg (but property of Regensburg) and lived there as a hermit during the duke of Bavaria's rebellion aginst Otto II. Hence arose the legend that he had lived on the Abersee, now called Sankt Wolfgangsee in Upper Austria. He was buried in Sankt Emmeram and was canonized by Leo IX (1052).

Feast: Oct. 31.

Bibliography: A. ZIMMERMAN, *Lexikon für Theologie und Kirche*, ed. M. BUCHBERGER (Freiburg 1930–38) 10:960–962. W. WATTENBACH, *Deutschlands Geschichtsquellen im Mittelalter. Deutsche Kaiserzeit*, ed. R. HOLTZMANN (Tübingen 1948) 1.2:265–268. R. BAUERREISS, *Kirchengeschichte Bayerns*, 5 v. (St. Ottilien 1949–55) v.2. A. BURKHARD, *The St Wolfgang Altar of Michael Pacher* (Munich 1971). *Regensburg und Böhmen. Festschrift zur Tausendjahrfeier des Regierungsantrittes Bischof Wolfgangs von Regensburg*, ed. G. SCHWAIGER and J. STABER (Regensburg 1972). *Auf den Spuren des Heiligen Wolfgang* (Kallmünz 1973). R. ZINNHOBLER, *Der heilige Wolfgang: Leben, Legende, Kult* (Linz 1975). *Das Leben des heiligen Wolfgang*, ed. H. BLEIBRUNNER (Landshut 1976). *Der Hl. Wolfgang in Geschichte, Kunst und Kult*, ed. M. MOHR (Linz 1976). *Das Sakramentar-Pontifikale des Bischofs Wolfgang von Regensburg*, eds. K. GAMBER and S. REHLE (Regensburg 1985). *Liturgie zur Zeit des Hl. Wolfgang*, proceedings of Bistumspatrons St. Wolfgang in der Bischöflichen Zentralbibliothek Regensburg, June 17 to Sept. 16, 1994, ed. S. ACHT, (Regensburg 1994). W. PREISS-JOHN, *Wolfgang von Pfullingen: Bischof im Mönchsgewand* (Ostfildern 1994). M. KOLLER, *Der Flügelaltar von Michael Pacher in St. Wolfgang* (Vienna 1998).

[A. A. SCHACHER]

WOLFHARD OF VERONA, ST.

Camaldolese recluse; b. Augsburg, Germany; d. Verona, Italy, April 30, 1127. The account of his life has to be based on a contemporary but chiefly legendary vita. Wolfhard (called also Gualfard) trained as a saddlemaker in Augsburg, and already known for his piety, went to Verona as a journeyman in 1097 and worked at his trade. He soon decided to retire from the world, and he lived for 20 years as a recluse in a forest on the Adige River. He was prevailed upon by admirers of his piety and miracles to return to Verona. He entered the CAMALDOLESE monastery of San Salvatore as a recluse and died there. In 1507 the brotherhood of saddlers chose him as their patron and erected an altar in his honor in the church of San Salvatore. In 1602 some of his relics were taken to Augsburg where they are preserved in the church of St. Sebastian. The feast of October 27 commemorates this translation of his relics.

Feast: April 30 (Camaldolese); May 11 (Verona); Oct. 27 (Augsburg).

Bibliography: *Acta Sanctorum* (Paris 1863—) 3:836–841. A. M. ZIMMERMANN, *Kalendarium Benedictinum: Die Heiligen und*

Seligen des Benediktinerorderns und seiner Zweige (Metten 1933–38) 2:127–129.

[M. R. P. MCGUIRE]

WOLFHELM, BL.

Abbot and theologian; d. April 22, 1091. A BENEDIC-TINE monk, he was abbot of the monastery at BRAU-WEILER from 1065 until his death. His biography, composed by Konrad of Brauweiler between 1110 and 1123 (*Monumenta Germaniae Historica: Scriptores* 12:180–195), relates that he had two sisters, one of whom, Bertha, was abbess of Vilich *c.* 1030. According to the same source, he attended the cathedral school in Cologne, where his industry soon earned him the position of assistant teacher. Having become a monk in the monastery of Sankt Maximin in Trier, he returned for a brief time to Cologne and was then assigned successively to monasteries in Gladbach, Siegburg, and finally, Brauweiler. His involvement in the doctrinal disputes of the period is attested by his letter, written between 1076 and 1079 and included as chapter 11 in Conrad's biography; it is addressed to Abbot Meginhard of Gladbach, and expresses Wolfhelm's opposition to the views on the Eucharist held by BERENGARIUS OF TOURS. MANEGOLD OF LAUTENBACH, in a tract written after 1085, attacked Wolfhelm's view that the teachings of pagan philosophers could be reconciled with Christian dogma. A brief verse by Wolfhelm urging the reading of the Bible also has been preserved (at end of Konrad's vita as reprinted in *Patrologia Latina* 154:403–434).

Feast: April 22.

Bibliography: *Acta Sanctorum* Apr. 3:77–89. *Bibliotheca hagiographica latina antiquae et mediae aetatis* 2:8987–89. W. WATTENBACH, *Deutschlands Geschichtsquellen im Mittelalter bis zur Mitte des 13. Jh.* 2:139–140. M. MANITIUS, *Geschichte der lateinischen Literatur des Mittelalters* 2:119; 3:27–28, 584–586. A. MANSER, *Lexikon für Theologie und Kirche* 10:963. A. M. ZIMMER-MANN, *Kalendarium Benedictinum: Die Heiligen und Seligen des Benediktinerorderns und seiner Zweige* 2:91–94. KONRAD VON BRAUWEILER, *Vita Wolfhelmi*, tr. H. E. STIENE.

[C. J. ERMATINGER]

WOLSEY, THOMAS

Cardinal archbishop of York and lord chancellor of England; b. Ipswich, England, *c.* 1473; d. Leicester Abbey, Nov. 29, 1530. Following his education at Magdalen College, Oxford, he entered royal service at the end of Henry VII's reign. After the accession of HENRY VIII (1509), he became royal almoner and councillor, and he finally established himself by his able handling of the campaign in France (1513). He was appointed bishop of Lincoln in early 1514 and archbishop of York later that year. In 1515 he acquired a red hat and then began pressing the Pope to appoint him legate *a latere.* LEO X did so in 1518, whereupon Wolsey had the appointment repeatedly renewed and expanded until it was conferred on him for life (1524). After late 1515 he was chancellor, and thus, as chief officer of a king not given to sustained hard work, and as primate, cardinal, and legate of a papacy that exercised reduced influence over English church life, Wolsey dominated secular and ecclesiastical affairs as perhaps no other ever has.

Wolsey's Career. He has been heavily censured by history as the would-be reformer who did not reform himself first, as one who frittered away wealth and energy on foolish diplomacy, as the "author of the schism," and above all as the man who wasted vast powers. Much of this is true. He was greedy for power and money; he was a glaring pluralist and absentee (holding the abbacy of St. Alban's and, successively, the Sees of Bath and Wells, Durham, and Winchester, at the same time that he held York); he neglected his vow of chastity and openly showered preferment on his son; he lorded it over his fellow bishops, William WARHAM, Archbishop of Canterbury, in particular; he was unscrupulous, vainglorious and vindictive; he was not only personally unfit to carry out the renewal that the church in England needed so much, but probably scarcely understood what, fundamentally, was wrong; his head-on collision with Parliament in 1523 and his subsequent attempts to raise loans and the so-called Amicable Grant revealed ineptitude and unpopularity; finally, when he fell, there was nothing to show for 15 years of incessant diplomacy. It was therefore not surprising that within a few weeks of his fall when the Reformation Parliament met, the lay estate should have unleashed violent pent-up anticlericalism against the church of which Wolsey had so long been leader.

But there is another side to all this. Wolsey was a man endowed with a wonderfully swift mind and accurate memory; he was loyal and extraordinarily energetic. He breathed intense life into Star Chamber, making it a court that delivered quick, sure justice, and he reveled in administering "the new law of Star Chamber," as he called it. He was probably a remarkable lord chancellor, giving to his post that decisively legal bent it has retained. He was sincerely concerned with the poor and, as his servant and biographer, George Cavendish, testifies, won the affection of the commons. If his pluralism was shocking by English standards it was not so by Continental ones, while his legacy was no more capacious than that acquired by several contemporaries. This was an age of mighty cardinal legates to whom wide powers were delegated by Rome, and Wolsey was not the worst of them.

It is probably not true that he seriously aspired to the papacy or that, because of this ambition, his whole foreign policy was tied to Rome.

Wolsey's Policies. In the notable treaty of London of 1518 Wolsey first attempted to achieve his purpose—the key to his subsequent diplomacy—to bring concord to Europe. His own (and Henry's) appetite for the spectacular led him into a "forward" European policy, but he came to Europe to help, not to harm. His policy failed. Though it had left him little time to tackle the problems of the church in England, he did try to improve the life of the Black Monks (only to be repulsed by them). The clerical appointments that he sponsored often show a marked sense of responsibility. It is very difficult to believe that his union of spiritual and temporal authority taught Henry VIII a lesson; and it is not true that Wolsey first suggested to his king that he should rid himself of Catherine of Aragon. Wolsey in fact disliked the divorce for diplomatic reasons, though he gave all his energy and talents to securing it, and came near to doing so when he and Cardinal Lorenzo CAMPEGGIO held their legatine court at Blackfriars in the summer of 1529. He founded a school at Ipswich and a college at Oxford (Cardinal's College, now Christchurch), both of which showed a keen awareness of the educational ideals of humanism; the medallions on the gateways of his residence at Hampton Court are among the first bits of Renaissance art to be seen on an English building. There was more of the Renaissance in Wolsey than one might suppose, more perhaps than there was in Henry.

Wolsey's Decline. In late 1529 he fell victim of a king whose divorce he had failed to procure and of an aristocratic counterattack against an upstart cleric whose monopoly of power and haughty ways had long been resented. He was indicted on a praemunire charge in the king's bench for having misused his legatine powers and was found guilty. Stripped of his secular office, he went north in April 1530 to visit his archbishopric for the first time. But he was not entirely forgiven or trusted, and, moreover, he was apparently trying to recover power. In early November 1530 he was arrested. His guard was to bring him to London, presumably to trial. But on November 29, while on his way there, Wolsey, now a man much changed and wearing a hair shirt, died at Leicester Abbey and was buried there.

Bibliography: J. GAIRDNER, *The Dictionary of National Biography from the Earliest Times to 1900,* 63 v. (London 1885–1900; repr. with corrections, 21 v., 1908–09, 1921–22, 1938; suppl. 1901–) 21:796–814. G. CAVENDISH, *The Life and Death of Cardinal Wolsey,* ed. R. S. SYLVESTER (Early English Text Society; London 1959). A. F. POLLARD, *Wolsey* (New York 1929). C. W. FERGUSON, *Naked to Mine Enemies: The Life of Cardinal Wolsey* (Boston 1958). P. HUGHES, *The Reformation in England,* 3 v. in 1 (5th, rev. ed. New York 1963). H. MAYNARD SMITH, *Henry VIII and the Reformation* (London 1948).

Thomas Wolsey. (Archive Photos)

[J. J. SCARISBRICK]

WOLTER, MAURUS

Spiritual writer, Benedictine founder; b. Bonn, Germany, June 4, 1825; d. Beuron, Germany, July 8, 1890. Maurus, whose baptismal name was Rudolf, came of a devout, middle-class family, his mother being a convert from Lutheranism in 1852. He received his Ph.D. at Bonn (1849), studied at the seminary in Cologne, and was ordained (1850). After directing a secondary school in Julich and the cathedral school in Aachen, he joined his brother, Placid, as a member of the BENEDICTINES at the Abbey of SAINT PAUL-OUTSIDE-THE-WALLS IN ROME (1856) and was professed (1857). In 1860 he and his brother returned to Prussia, where he founded a monastery in 1863 after acquiring the former Augustinian house at BEURON, which later became an archabbey. As its first abbot, Wolter promoted the liturgy, Gregorian chant, art, science, and parochial work, modeling his efforts on those of Dom GUÉRANGER at SOLESMES. Between 1871 and 1890 Wolter published a five-volume explanation of the Psalms, *Psallite sapienter*. His views on monastic life, together with his ideas on Benedictine unity, appeared (1880) in *Praecipua Ordinis Monastici Elementa* (Eng. tr. *The Principles of Monasticism*, 1962). Wolter started the Beuronese Benedictine Congregation and founded houses in MAREDSOUS, Belgium (1872); Erdington, in the Birmingham diocese, England (1876); Prague (1880); and Seckau, in Styria (1883). He also drew up the congregation's constitutions, which were approved by the Holy See (1884).

Bibliography: S. MAYER, *Beuroner Bibliographie, 1863–1963* (Beuron 1963). *Beuron 1863–1963: Festschrift* (Beuron 1963). *Maurus Wolter, dem Gründer Beurons zum 100. Geburtstag*, ed. J. UTTENWEILER (Beuron 1925). J. UTTENWEILER, *Lexikon für Theologie und Kirche*, ed. M. BUCHBERGER (Freiburg 1930–38) 10:966–967. "Wolter, Maurus," *Lexikon für Theologie und Kirche*, ed. K. RAHNER and J. HOFER v.10 (Freiburg 1957–65).

[V. FIALA]

WOMAN

Transcendentally considered, a woman's basic role in any society is to perfect herself. She is to perfect herself physically, emotionally, intellectually, morally, and religiously. A woman is called in union with man to represent humanity and to develop both herself and humanity in as complete a manner as possible. Her role in society ideally includes the actualization of all of her talents to the fullest possible extent.

There are likewise existential considerations. When inquiring into the role of woman in society, one must ask, "Which woman?" and "Which society?" Which woman?—for her role will differ according to whether she is young or old, educated or uneducated, rich or poor, single or married, with no children or with many children, with a husband present or absent, participating in a domestic or commercial career, etc. Which society?—primitive or modern, rural or urban, agricultural or industrial, underpopulated or overpopulated, at peace or at war, in an era of penury or affluence, of social chaos or order, with a family system that is patriarchal or egalitarian, in which women are of low or high status? Each of these variables, and many others, affect a woman's role in society.

In these transcendental and existential considerations of the role of woman in society there are two valid and mutually supplemental emphases: (1) the natural law principles that are incorporated in and elevated by Christian teaching, manifesting the self-identity of every human being as an image of God, and the divergent but complementary natures of male and female social roles; (2) the changing sociocultural circumstances. The first of these emphases represents the unique permanent contribution made by the Christian evaluation of the status and role of woman' the second suggests that a stereotype of social-sexual roles derived from one culture can quickly become antiquarian in interest and applicability, since specific roles must be constantly reanalyzed in relation to existing circumstances.

Nature of Woman

Reason teaches that the identical human nature appears in the male and female in two different forms. Moreover, Scripture affirms, "God created man in his image. In the image of God he created him. Male and female he created them" (Gn 1.27). It follows that woman is in possession of full human nature and perfectly equal with man in moral value and status before the Creator. It is, therefore, not reasonable to take one sex as the ideal and standard of value for the other. Aristotle's and Freud's designation of woman as an incomplete or mutilated man must be rejected [*Gen. animal.* 737a 25,767a 35, b 65, 775a 15; *New Introductory Lectures on Psychoanalysis* tr. W. J. H. Sprott (New York 1933) 153–173]. St. Thomas's acceptance of Aristotle's evaluation results in the same masculocentrism (*Summa theologiae* 1a, 92.1 ad 1).

As a sovereign human being, a woman has as her prime role that of perfecting herself with the aid of divine grace and thus saving her soul. Every other role in her life is subordinate to this one. In terms of this absolute, woman is no more subordinate to man than man is to woman. A mature and single woman is as free and independent an agent as a mature and single man. Within the context of marriage on the other hand, both man and woman subordinate themselves to the principles of a suprapersonal moral and physical union. Woman's basic role as a sovereign human being may not be violated even in marriage. Her individual moral independence and responsibility may not be replaced or superseded by the interposition or superordination of any other agent, male or female.

Physical Characteristics. The physical differences associated with reproduction are obvious. The sexual life of the female moves sequentially and rhythmically through complex changes that have no close counterpart in the male. Her earlier maturation, her greater vulnerability, her inescapable biological suitability for motherhood cannot be ignored. Menstruation is a factor in woman's life from about age 13 to about age 48 in 21st century America. Pregnancy, childbirth, lactation, and menopause, with their varied and critical glandular and hormonal adjustments, are differences between male and female that are not without psychic and social import.

Less obvious but equally relevant is the fact that every cell of a female's body is distinguishable from every cell of a male's body because of differential chromosomal content. Modern findings show the differential functioning of hormones associated with the male and female body in influencing behavior. Woman's blood has a greater white corpuscle content with consequently greater self-healing capacities. The greater viability of the female is evident at every age of life, from the fetal stage to old age; it is offset by a sex ratio at birth of roughly 105 male to 100 female births. Woman's metabolism is anabolic rather than catabolic, thus differing from the male's. Her total nervous system is of greater sensitivity, excepting the nerve centers in the genitals. The fact that a woman possesses about one-half the oxygen capacity, one-half the muscular capacity, and a less rugged bone structure than a man tends to place a woman at a disadvantage in physical activities. Consideration of skeletal and muscular structure, skin and hair texture, subcutaneous disposition of fat, rate of bodily growth, or any other of the gross secondary characteristics of the sexes makes it apparent that women differ from men physically in more than reproductive mechanisms.

Psychological Attributes. There is no inherent disparity of intellectual capacity between men and women. There are, however, in every culture, male-female dichotomies of psychic, emotional, and temperamental orientations. These cannot be appraised adequately without consideration of the particular cultures in which they originate and take shape. In every culture, women must come to terms psychologically with themselves as women just as men must come to terms psychologically with themselves as men. Prof. Morris Zelditch observes that in every society, the husband role has certain distinctive attributes, and the wife role has other psychic and emotional characteristics. He maintains that most commonly the husband's role can be described as that of ''instrumental leader'' and the wife's role most commonly is that of ''expressive leader.'' Expressive leadership has to do with nurture—feeding the family members, caring for the children, keeping house—and with the emotional and psychological concomitants of these tasks. Instrumental leadership is expressed in the making of important decisions, being the ultimate disciplinarian, and taking the responsibility for the family's economic security. [''Role Differentiation in the Nuclear Family: A Comparative Study,'' in T. Parsons and R. F. Bales, *Family, Socialization and Interaction Process* (Glencoe, Ill. 1955) ch. 6].

Woman in History

Whatever validity there may be in occasional references to prehistoric matriarchies, the dominance of the human male at the beginning of the historic era is clear. The available evidence indicates that the status of woman was all but universally low. A comprehensive study of 500 primitive societies revealed female equality in only eight, and in each of these there was a notable shortage of women [L. T. Hobhouse, *Morals in Evolution* (New York 1919)]. Permitted polygyny was found to be standard; the owning of many women, like the owning of many cattle, was but a matter of wealth. The mother right (not to be confused with the mythical matriarchate) and matrilineal descent in no way implied a high position of the female. The common conclusion concerning the status of the sexes among primitives was: ''Woman is almost universally considered property''[G. May, *Social Control of Sex Expression* (New York 1931) 186].

Traditional India. The status of woman in non-Christian traditional civilizations was that of a person who lacks inalienable rights. The family system of India is a prototype of the traditional extended kinship system and is associated with the oldest organized religion in the world (*see* HINDUISM). The classical Indian family consists of a plurality of married couples and their children, who live together as a joint family in the same household or compound. All the men are related by blood. The senior male, usually the father or grandfather, is the patriarch. The males are by law the owners of the property; the women have only the right to maintenance. The legal framework of this type of joint family was crystallized in about the 11th century in the Mitakshara, one of the many commentaries on the Indian sacred scriptures that stretch back 3,500 years. Although these sources contain not a few passages eulogizing women, they likewise fix the female's status as radically inferior. The bearing of a male child was the only valid initiation rite, so much so that an orthodox Hindu beggar would not accept alms from a barren woman. The widespread incidence of child marriage is due in part to this religious belief that it is necessary to bear a legitimate son at the earliest possible moment.

Polygyny was permitted in India, but it was seldom practiced except when a first wife had not become the mother of a son or sons. Female infanticide has roots in the fact that daughters have often been considered of little value. Until the beginning of the 20th century, 99 percent of the women were illiterate; a generation later it was reported that only one out of every 100 girls received an elementary education and one out of every 1,000 a secondary education. The double standard of morality, the absolute subordination of women to men, the suttee or burning of widows on the funeral pyre of their husbands, the purdah or veiled seclusion of women, limn in clear outline the traditional status of woman in India.

Ancient China. In another Oriental civilization, Confucianism for more than 2,000 years stereotyped a social system revolving about a father-son axis and held in theological equilibrium by family worship of ancestral males (*see* CONFUCIANISM AND NEO-CONFUCIANISM). Within its sociojuridical system one could find polygyny, unilateral divorce for the male, and the relegation of woman to a secondary role. Women were without the right to immovable property and were not entitled to formal education since their activities were confined to the home. They were subject to their fathers before marriage, to their husbands after marriage, and to their sons should they become widowed. A husband could kill his wife if she were taken in adultery; his adultery was taken as a matter of course. He could strike her; she received 100 blows for striking him. He could sell his wife; she had no legal recourse. Traditional Chinese marriage was solely by agreement of the couple's parents, contracted possibly even before the birth of the prospective life partners. A married woman's duty was above all to her parents-in-law just as a married man's was above all to his parents. A man who suppressed his wife because of his father or mother and a woman who neglected her husband because of his father were equally praiseworthy.

Ancient Greece. It is an irony of history that the ancient Western society that most uniquely idealized beauty and first formalized scientific thought was the one that reduced woman's status to a lower level than in any other major civilization. Moderns find it difficult to comprehend that the Golden Age of Greek classical civilization permitted not only slavery but a male monosexual mania. The faithful and tender love that in Christian tradition is realized fully only by a married couple, the classical Greeks assumed could be fulfilled between two men. If not more common than heterosexuality, homosexuality was at least more idealized. The *Oration Against Neaera,* ascribed to Demosthenes, sheds light upon the roles of women in classical Greece: "Mistresses we keep for the sake of pleasure, concubines for the daily care of our persons, but wives to bear us legitimate children and to be faithful guardians of our households" (59.122).

Ancient Rome. Under the ancient Roman trustee family system, the most conspicuous rule in relations of the sexes was that of the *patria potestas* that gave the male head in the family the power of life and death not only over his wife but over his children and other members of his patriarchal domain. He had the rights of chief executive, legislator, judge, and priest. The father had the right to accept or reject a child at birth, to give his daughter in marriage irrespective of her wishes, and to name a guardian for his wife and children. Legally, women and children were not citizens. Public justice existed only through the male, and he alone was responsible for the crimes committed by his family. Her adultery was punishable by death, her husband's taken for granted. She

was a perpetual minor, a form of property in a patriarchal, patrilineal, patrilocal, male civilization.

Nevertheless, since the civilization was centered in family mores, she had great dignity in her roles as mistress of the home, wife, and mother. She had the security derived from social ideals of family continuity. It was once Rome's boast that for over 500 years, from the mythical founding of the city (753 B.C.) to the Punic Wars (264–202 B.C.), there had not been a divorce, and the security of woman was as certain as the marriage bond. It is misleading to speak of the "emancipation" of woman in the declining centuries of the Roman Empire. It was a period of general decline in the power of the family over all of its members. Woman remained legally subject to the absolute power—the *manus*—of the male even when the historical circumstance that had given rise to this power had long vanished.

Christian Revolution. The birth of Jesus was the turning point in the history of woman. Previous civilizations had held woman to be essentially inferior to the male. Christianity denied the basis for a sexual caste system and proclaimed a spiritual unity that integrated all human differences in a higher supernatural principle: "There is neither Jew nor Greek; there is neither slave nor freeman; there is neither male nor female. For you are all one in Christ Jesus" (Gal 3.28). No previous civilization had maintained that men, women, and children had inalienable rights. Christ insisted that both male and female were made in the image and likeness of God and that these divine composites could not be violated without offense to their Maker. By accenting the sovereignty of the individual within unity of all human persons, Christ made untenable the slavery that was part of all pre-Christian civilizations and that had inevitably undermined the status of woman.

Every major civilization before the time of Christ had permitted polygyny with its demeaning effects upon the self-image and integrity of women. Christ reestablished the basic divine pattern of monogamy at the same time that He sacramentalized it: "This is a great mystery—I mean in reference to Christ and to the Church" (Eph 5.32). Christ reaffirmed that marriage was of divine, not only human origin: "What therefore God has joined together, let no man put asunder" (Mk 10.9). [*See* MATRIMONY (SACRAMENT OF).]

Previous civilizations had made the patriarchal extended family, clan, and tribe the basis of social organization. When Christ stated that "a man shall leave his father and mother, and cleave to his wife" (Mk 10.7), He shifted the axis of society toward the nuclear family. The male had had complete authority in regard to the female; the female had no juridical authority in regard to the male. Christianity recognized the need for centralized domestic authority, but it established a binuclear familial pattern adjustable within limits to democratic processes: "Be subject to one another in the fear of Christ" (Eph 5.21). "The wife has not authority over her body, but the husband; the husband likewise has not authority over his body, but the wife" (1 Cor 7.4). The marriage of a young woman in traditional societies depended upon the decision of the family irrespective of the will of the bride. In Christianity the agreement of the spouses themselves was recognized as the bond of marriage; consequently without the free assent of the woman there could be no valid marriage.

The double standard of morality had characterized discrimination against woman from time immemorial. Christ held it to be null; what was wrong for woman was wrong for man: "Whoever puts away his wife and marries another, commits adultery against her; and if the wife puts away her husband, and marries another, she commits adultery" (Mk 10.11–12). The single standard would weigh more heavily upon the man: "But I say to you that anyone who so much as looks with lust at a woman has already committed adultery with her in his heart" (Mt 5.28).

Infanticide, especially female infanticide, had been an accepted practice. Christ declared the child—male or female—to be a model, an angelically guarded deputy: "for of such is the kingdom of God" (Mk 10.14), "for I tell you, their angels in heaven always behold the face of My Father in heaven" (Mt 18.10), "And whoever receives one such little child for my sake, receives me" (Mt 18.5).

In previous civilizations, the doors of formal education and religious membership were regularly closed to women. A devoted band of female followers gathered about Christ and His mother during His lifetime. Within the primitive Christian Church the status of female teachers and auxiliary workers was recognized as of ecclesiastical importance [see DEACONESS; WIDOW (IN THE EARLY CHURCH)]. Whereas no previous civilization had held out a dignified alternative to marriage for woman, Christ established life in virginity undertaken for spiritual reasons as meriting "a hundred-fold, and . . . life everlasting" (Mt 19.29). The portals of learning, teaching, and social service were opened to women as well as to men.

Historical religions had been male-centered and male-oriented, with masculine ideals. Christianity provided for the first time ideal models of both male and female. From a human viewpoint, Jesus presented an ego ideal for fishermen, laborers, artisans, soldiers; Mary, His mother, presented a more immediate model to women, whether virgins or mothers. In making purity, gentleness,

humility, care of others, love, and the traditional "feminine" virtues primary Christian ideals, Christ in effect idealized the whole of womankind.

It is sometimes asserted that Christianity introduced a spate of misogynist writings. St. Paul, Tertullian, and St. Jerome are held to be the prime offenders. The misapprehension springs partly from failure to understand that Christ expanded woman's self-concept and social functions by setting up an alternative to the traditional roles of wife and mother, namely, dedication to contemplation and social service undertaken for the kingdom of God's sake. In seeking to establish the ideal of virginity ("spiritual fertility") and the monastic ideal, authors such as Tertullian and St. Jerome made some incautious statements within the historical context of a sex-saturated society. Their statements were tempered, however, by the Christian dominance of love, sacramentality of marriage, personal sovereignty of the individual woman, and the single moral norm for both male and female. Although he did not approve the conduct of his protégé and friend Fabiola, who had abandoned her philandering husband and remarried, St. Jerome repudiated society's double standard that would countenance certain behaviors on the part of a husband that it would not condone on the part of a wife. "With us Christians what is unlawful from women is equally unlawful for men, and as both serve the same God both are bound by the same obligations" (Letter 77).

The irony of accusing the early Church of antifeminism is that there was a curious and powerful force in the world, outside and in opposition to historical Christianity, that was undoubtedly antisexual, antifeminine, and antifamilial. This was Manichaeism; it was an element in practically every one of the major Christian heresies of the first five centuries. Woman's status was not elevated immediately by Christ's coming any more than slavery was abolished immediately or is even abolished completely today. Christ's mission was and is spiritual. He did not establish a women's rights movement. But Christian doctrine and sacramental life contained the dynamic truth that was destined to revolutionize the status of woman.

End of the Roman Empire. From the 4th to the 6th centuries of the Christian Era, peoples from the North overran the empire of the Caesars. The Vandals, Visigoths, Franks, Burgundians, Alemanni, East Goths, Angles, Jutes, and Saxons influenced the family system. Whereas the Romans reckoned kinship from the common ancestor through males only (the system of agnation), the invading tribes reckoned kinship through both male and female lines. This tended to deemphasize the male domination in the traditional Roman family and to accent the binuclear family system. This was a juridical gain for the status of woman.

Middle Ages. It was feudalism that held society together after the fall of the Roman Empire. With the collapse of law and order and the self-protective regrouping of families around the strongest local lords, Western Europe became a vast network of fiefs or landed estates held on condition of service to an overlord in return for his protection of lands and persons. The effects of this social system were profound. Insofar as it was a military system dependent upon a succession of male heirs, the status of woman was depressed. Insofar as it was Christian and monogamic, women were secure under a noble and presumably single standard of morality. Insofar as it was an economic system promoting self-sufficiency, men, women, and children were integrated into a communality of labor that had little reference to stereotypes of "man's work" and "woman's work" except when requirements of muscularity or maternity occasioned their distinctness. Insofar as it was a system of inheritance and interlocking marriages, calculating families continued the ancient practice of promising their young sons and daughters in opportunistic marriages, so that the institutionalization of extramarital romantic alliances became inevitable.

Throughout the Middle Ages the convents and monasteries were the centers of formal education. The available evidence indicates that there were more convents than monasteries and that on occasion an abbess would be the religious superior of men as well as of women. It is likewise quite probable that more women than men received what formal education was given. With the men dedicating themselves to war, chivalry, and husbandry, reading and writing were quite frequently thought of as the work of clerics and women. The Crusades led to the further involvement and predominance of women in domestic economies and industries. The guilds generally did not exclude women. The growth of towns, international trade, universities, and the amazing development of church architecture were all liberalizing influences in male-female relationships. Women were not only students but likewise, in not rare instances, professors at the universities, especially in Italy and Germany. In summarizing the relative position of women in the period, a severe critic has concluded that "women in the Middle Ages probably enjoyed more equality with men than most of the time since" [A. W. Calhoun, *A Social History of the American Family,* v. 1 (Cleveland 1917) 15].

Reformation. The social forces culminating in the Protestant Reformation brought a sharp change. Granted that innumerable factors were involved in the widespread revolt from the authority of the Catholic Church—such as corruption, avarice, chicanery, ignorance, and perfidy in and out of the Church—the Reformation was a religious revolution. It renewed many evangelical family virtues: godliness, obedience, hard work, frugality, chastity, sobriety, faithfulness, honesty, instruction in the Scriptures, etc.

In denying that marriage was a sacrament, the reformers intentionally placed its control in the hands of the State. The immediate result was not without many direct and indirect benefits. Among the latter were the many needed reforms concerning lay spirituality, marriage legislation, and the regularization of clerical and conventual life achieved by the Counter Reformation. The long-range results of the secularization of marriage and governmental control were, however, dysfunctional to both the state of marriage and the status of woman. The denial of Christ's establishment of dedicated virginity as a superior way of life restricted woman's role to its pre-Christian categories of wife and mother. The closing of convents wherever the Protestant reformers gained control meant the suppression of the only schools that were regularly available to the public and a setback to the education of women that was not remedied for two centuries. The accentuation of the OT in place of the NT revived its patriarchal obediential rigidity rather than evangelical egalitarian love.

Although the Reformation, especially in its Puritan form, was marked by rigidly dogmatic and authoritarian control of society in general and of women in particular, the eventual historical result was a liberalization of controls throughout society. The survivor of the internecine religious warfare of the next few centuries was the spirit of democracy. Women eventually gained suffrage and greater control over their own destinies.

The legal development from the English Protestant tradition was remarkably infelicitous, however. Sir William Blackstone's *Commentaries on the Laws of England* (1765) crystallized it and became the standard textbook for the training of lawyers in both England and the United States for more than a century. Its classic statement of the legal position of married women was as follows:

> By marriage, the husband and wife are one person in law; that is, the very being or legal existence of the woman is suspended during the marriage, or at least is incorporated and consolidated into that of the husband. . . . Upon this principle, of a union of person in husband and wife, depend almost all the legal rights, duties, and disabilities, that either of them acquire by the marriage. . . . For this reason, a man cannot grant any thing to his wife, or enter into covenant with her: for the grant would be to suppose her separate existence; and to covenant with her, would be only to cove-

nant with himself: and therefore it is also generally true, that all compacts made between husband and wife, when single, are voided by the intermarriage. [21st ed. (London 1862) 1.441]

Even the wife's clothes and objects of personal adornment had become legally the husband's. The children were regarded as having but one guardian: the father. The OT paternal power, strengthened by Pauline texts on the seeming absolute subjection of woman to man, and fortified by Puritan beliefs in the evil of human nature and play as the agent of the devil, made the Puritan father of England and New England no ineffectual figure for women and children.

Contemporary Trends

A pen picture of the traditional "valiant woman" contained in Prv (31.10–31) was reputedly written by King Solomon ten centuries before Christ [see WOMAN (IN THE BIBLE)]. It has been applicable even in its details from the dawn of history to modern times in farm communities, in underdeveloped areas, and wherever an agricultural handicraft economy has not been rendered obsolete by the Industrial Revolution. Central to the biblical concept is the manufacturing role of the woman within the household economy. Charm, beauty, virtue, and the roles of wife and mother receive much less emphasis than this. But her activities are not confined to food preparation, textile processing, care of the extended family, or education of children. "She picks out a field to purchase; out of her earnings she plants a vineyard. . . . She enjoys the success of her dealings. . . . She reaches out her hands to the poor. . . . She makes garments and sells them, and stocks the merchants with belts. . . . Let her works praise her at the city gates." Thus, the "worthy wife" is above all a worker: industrious, thrifty, enterprising, competent, a good manager, a wise counselor, a competent educator, a capable homemaker, a woman who earns her own way and advances to a remarkable extent the livelihood of her family. She works hand in hand with her husband to keep the farm and domestic industries solvent. Isolation of her role as that of child-rearer and his as that of breadwinner would have been a luxury that the society could not afford. The whole family was a relatively homogeneous economic unit. The biblical picture of woman as breadwinner, wife, and mother within the home was the ideal of woman's role from the beginning of human history until the advent of the Industrial Revolution.

Industrial Revolution. A revolutionary series of inventions took manufacturing out of the home and located it in the factory. Woman's daily partner in production and child-rearing was now claimed by the factory. She was left with the children. She became the domestic "child-rearer" and he became the non-domestic "breadwinner." It was this revolutionary separation of male and female roles that women came to resent. As manufacturing has taken over more and more of woman's work by prefabricating clothes, premixing foods, and preparing in advance all types of domestic services from housecleaning to social entertaining, women's feelings of noninvolvement and nonfulfillment have been deepened. Both economic and psychological needs have forced women to follow men into industry.

As the industrial revolution has spread beyond the West, it has stimulated a "revolution of rising expectations" within the non-industrialized countries and thus aggravated international tensions by dividing the world into the affluent "have" and the indigent "have not" nations. In all these developments, woman's role in modern society is a central issue.

Domestic Revolution. The Industrial Revolution precipitated a domestic revolution. It was not just a matter of removing industry from the home. Other traditional functions were removed at least in part to other social agencies: the functions of status-giving, protection, health, religion, recreation, and education. However, although the roles of women within the home were minimized in these areas, there were several in which they were maximized. Whereas formerly male and female kinfolk to the third and fourth generations assisted in child-rearing functions, the mother in the relatively isolated family now became the prime socializing agent. Whereas the many jobs in the home had formerly made social control of children and stabilization of adult personalities relatively easy, the abandonment of domestic manufacturing made the mother the predominant agent in accomplishing such control and stabilization. Woman's role was thus maximized in personal relations and minimized in economic relations. The wedge driven by the industrial revolution into the home divided woman's reproductive role from her productive role and her domestic career from her commercial career. Modern society has not yet been able to solve the problems introduced by this revolution in the female role.

Medical Revolution. A more recent historical development may be termed a "medical revolution." For eons early marriage and continued childbearing were the complements of high mortality. No people could survive unless religion, tradition, and custom reinforced the economic and biologically necessary role of woman as the bearer and rearer of numerous children. The tradition was more accurately one of abundant rather than of completed child-rearing, for few children survived. The medical advances of contemporary civilization have changed this.

Widespread improvements in sanitation have so reduced mortality and prolonged the life span that woman's unrestricted fertility is no longer the ideal that it was in traditional society. This social fact challenges the view—never the Christian one—that woman's role must be confined to childbearing and the home. As the Industrial Revolution minimized woman's productive role, so the medical revolution minimized her reproductive role. The reunion of these careers is the task of the present era.

International Dimensions. The extent of the revolution of women's rights that occurred in the 20th century is evident from a consideration that whereas at the turn of the century women could take part in the government of their countries in but a few instances, by 1945, when the United Nations Charter was signed, about 50 percent of the sovereign states of the world had recognized the right of women to vote and to stand for public office. At the end of the 20th century, women had the right to vote in nearly every country; however, they are still underrepresented in political institutions. In 1994 women held only ten percent of seats in parliamentary bodies and only slightly more than five percent of ministerial posts (*United Nations 1997 Report on the World Social Situation, Part II: Core Issues,* ch. VII, 38).

Little protective occupational legislation for women was provided until well into the 20th century. There had been sporadic attempts earlier to minimize some of the outrageous effects of laissez-faire policy. England in 1847 limited the working hours of women in textile factories by its Ten Hour Act. France in the following year passed legislation that presumably limited the working day to 12 hours for both men and women, but it was another quarter of a century before inspectors were provided to see that the 12-hour limit was operative. In the United States, protective state legislation affecting women workers dates from the 1870s, but it was not until the New Deal legislation of the 1930s and the wartime conditions of the 1940s that a general federal standard of minimum wages, hours, and conditions was accepted. On the international scene, advancement has been achieved by the UN Commission on the Status of Women and the International Labor Organization. Catholic effort is represented by the World Union of Catholic Women's Organizations and voluntary groups like the St. Joan's International Alliance.

Several UN documents uphold "equal rights of men and women." In various countries the promotion of equal rights legislation has had a mixed reception. Advocates insist that women are still so extensively deprived of personal property, family, and other rights by law that their status is distinctly inferior to that of men, and that this situation can be effectively remedied only by equal rights legislation. Opponents maintain that such measures might destroy hard-won legislation designed to protect women and would upset the existing body of law governing family relationships and property; they claim that there are fundamental differences between the sexes that require differential treatment in law. In spite of generally improving conditions internationally, the lack of appreciation of the importance of women's work in and out of the home, the continued concentration of women upon early marriage with its resulting lack of education, prejudice, and apathy—primarily of women themselves—prevent women from accepting their full responsibility in civic, political, and social life.

Catholic Interpretations. The Catholic Church is a participant in and not a mere observer of the revolutionary changes in the status of woman. A distinction may be made between the teachings of the Church that are unchanging and those that change in accord with historical evolution. Among the unchanging teachings are those concerning the sovereignty of the individual, the equality of dignity and goals of the male and the female, the single standard of morality, the indissolubility and sacramentality of Christian marriage, the denial that woman's role in society is exhausted by her role of wife and mother, the selective exaltation of virginity dedicated to contemplation and social service, the recognition of the characteristic qualities and virtues of man and woman, the invalidity of any marriage not characterized by the free choice of both partners, the promotion of education for women, and the provision of institutionalized care for the disadvantaged and derelicts of all types.

The new emphases in the teaching of the Church are chiefly those precipitated by the Industrial Revolution. Instances of these new orientations are especially evident in the remarkable series of encyclicals and papal addresses beginning with Leo XIII (*see* SOCIAL THOUGHT, PAPAL). Insistence upon social justice for both men and women, equal payment for equal work, special precautions for women workers, women's obligation to vote and participate in public life, encouragement of women to utilize their leisure in social service and professional careers, counsel to the growing number of women forced by circumstances to remain unmarried, the inclusion of physical education in the training of young women, the encouragement of capable women who show "great ability in every sphere of public life," the advice to women not to slight their mission as wives and mothers for unnecessary commercial careers, and allusions to the mother's authority as well as to the father's are examples of these new or changing emphases. The prevalence of democracy and the reallocation of functions to agencies outside the home have brought about a reorientation concerning authority within the home. The sentence in St.

Paul's Epistle that states: "Let wives be subject to their husbands as to the Lord" (Eph 5.22) is less frequently separated from the injunction immediately preceding: "Be subject to one another in the fear of Christ" (Eph 5.21). As modern social science emphasizes the man's instrumental leadership and the woman's expressive leadership, so modern Catholic theology stresses the husband's primacy in matters of ultimate administration and the wife's primacy—not mere equality—in matters pertaining to love. In the words of Pius XI, "For as the man is the head, the woman is the heart, and as he occupies the chief place in ruling, so she may and ought to claim for herself the chief place in love" [*Casti connubi* in *Acta Apostolicae Sedis* 22 (1930) 549].

In the mid-twentieth century, Pius XII attempted to unify and apply Catholic teaching on the status of woman: "This is your hour, Catholic women and Catholic girls. Public life needs you. . . . The fortunes of the family, the fortunes of human society, are at stake; and they are in your hands. Therefore every woman without exception is under an obligation—a strict obligation of conscience, mind you!—not to remain aloof; every woman must go into action, each in her own way, and join in stemming the tides which threaten to engulf the home, in fighting the doctrines which undermine its foundations, in preparing, organizing, and completing its restoration. . . . A wide field is opened to woman's activity, an activity primarily intellectual or primarily practical, according to the capabilities and qualities of each individual." [*Questa grande vostra adunata,* in *Acta Apostolicae Sedis* 37 (1945) 288–291.]

At the end of the century, John Paul II, following the trajectory set by John XXIII, the Second Vatican Council, and Paul VI, also recognized the "sign of the times" of women's greater participation in every sphere of human endeavor. His homilies, letters, and encyclicals emphasize the equal human dignity of men and women, calling for an end to the obstacles to their full development as human persons. In *Mulieris Dignitatem* he wrote, "The biblical text Gen 2:23 provides sufficient bases for recognizing the essential equality of man and woman from the point of view of their humanity. From the very beginning, both are persons, unlike the other living beings in the world about them. The woman is another 'I' in a common humanity" (*Mulieris Dignitatem* 6). He wrote further: "The moral and spiritual strength of a woman is joined to her awareness that God entrusts the human being to her in a special way. . . . This awareness and this fundamental vocation speak to women of the dignity which they receive from God himself. . . . In our own time, the successes of science and technology make it possible to attain material well being to a degree hitherto unknown. While this favors some, it pushes oth-

ers to the margins of society. In this way, unilateral progress can also lead to a gradual loss of sensitivity for . . . what is essentially human. In this sense, our time in particular awaits the manifestation of that 'genius' which belongs to women, and which can ensure sensitivity for human beings in every circumstance: because they are human!'' (*Mulieris Dignitatem* 30).

See Also: FEMINISM; SEX; WOMEN AND PAPAL TEACHING.

Bibliography: American Assoc. of University Women, *Adventures in Freedom: Status of Women Handbook* (Washington, D.C. 1955). P. ALLEN, *The Concept of Woman, Vol. 1: The Aristotelian Revolution, 750 B.C.–A.D. 1250* (Grand Rapids, Mich. 1992). P. ALLEN, *The Concept of Woman, Vol. 2: The Early Humanist Reformation, 1250–1500* (Grand Rapids, Mich. 2001). R. N. ANSHEN, ed., *The Family: Its Function and Destiny* (rev. ed. New York 1959). M. BEARD, *Woman As Force in History* (New York 1946). E. W. BURGESS, et al., *The Family: From Institution to Companionship* (3d ed. New York 1963). O. D. DAVID, ed., *The Education of Women: Signs for the Future* (Washington, D.C. 1959). P. EVDOKIMOV, *Woman and the Salvation of the World: A Christian Anthropology on the Charisms of Women* (Crestwood, N.Y. 1994). M. L. FRANKLIN, *The Case of Woman Suffrage: A Bibliography* (New York 1913). W. GOODSELL, *A History of Marriage and the Family* (rev. ed. New York 1934). A. O'HARA GRAFF, ed., *In the Embrace of God: Feminist Approaches to Theological Anthropology* (Maryknoll, NY 1995). JOHN PAUL II, *Mulieris Dignitatem: Apostolic Letter on the Dignity and Vocation of Women on the Occasion of the Marian Year* (1988). JOHN PAUL II, *The Theology of the Body: Human Love in the Divine Plan* (Boston, Mass. 1997). R. KELSO, *Doctrine for the Lady of the Renaissance* (Urbana, Ill. 1956). J. MARTOS and P. HÉGY, *Equal at the Creation: Sexism, Society, and Christian Thought* (Toronto, Ont. 1998). H. SVEISTRUP and A. VON ZAHN-HARNACK, eds., *Die Frauenfrage in Deutschland* (Burg b.M., Germany 1934) 800-page bibliog. listing books and articles written on woman's problems in Germany from 1790 to 1930. M. J. CHOMBART DE LAUWE et al., "Images of Women in Society," *International Social Science Journal* 14 (1962) 7–174. L. M. YOUNG, ed., "Women's Opportunities and Responsibilities," *Annals of the American Academy of Political and Social Science* 251 (1947) 1–185. C. C. ZIMMERMAN, *Family and Civilization* (New York 1947). C. C. ZIMMERMAN and L. F. CERVANTES, *Marriage and the Family* (Chicago, Ill. 1956).

[L. F. CERVANTES/L. HARRINGTON]

WOMAN, CANON LAW ON

The Second Vatican Council effected a notable shift in the ecclesial perspective of woman and major changes in her canonical status in the universal law of the Church. Biblical and theological insights, the concept of the Church as *COMMUNIO*, conciliar regard for significant human values such as the human dignity and social advancement of persons, resulted in a significant change in the Church's attitude toward woman. This gradual evolution can be traced through the antepreparatory and preparatory documents, conciliar discussions, and the definitive texts of the council. Pope John XXIII in *Pacem in terris* addressed the social progress of woman and decried the deprivation of her fundamental rights in many parts of the world. Conciliar documents, particularly *Lumen gentium* 32, *Gaudium et spes* 9, 29, 60 and *Perfectae caritatis* 15, addressed woman's dignity as person, her equality with man, and corresponding rights and responsibilities in the mission of Christ.

The 1967 ordinary assembly of the Synod of Bishops affirmed the fundamental equality of all the Christian faithful. Discussions during the various ordinary assemblies of the Synod of Bishops reflected in the apostolic exhortations on ministry, justice, evangelization, and catechetics challenged the inferior ecclesial status of woman evidenced in the 1917 Code of Canon Law. The sixth principle of the Pontifical Commission for the Revision of the Code of Canon Law ordered that the fundamental equality of all persons regardless of their functional and ministerial diversity be protected in the revised code.

With few exceptions, the Christian faithful share a common juridic status in the 1,752 canons of the 1983 Code of Canon Law. Women are recognized in law as members of the Christian faithful, baptized in Christ, incorporated into the Church, and constituted persons with duties and rights proper to Christians in accord with their condition (c. 96). Consonant with baptism, each of the faithful in accord with his or her own proper condition participates in the priestly, prophetic, and kingly functions of Christ (c. 204). All of the Christian faithful enjoy a true equality and dignity and cooperate in building up the Body of Christ in accord with their condition and function (c. 208). Women are members of the laity (c. 207 §1) or consecrated to God through the profession of the evangelical counsels by means of vows or other sacred bonds recognized and sanctioned by the Church (c. 207 §2). Women as members of the Christian faithful share with men the rights and obligations set forth in the canons (cc. 208–223). Likewise, lay women share rights and obligations with lay men (cc. 224–231). Women enjoy an equal status with men in the determination of domicile (c. 104), in changing rite at the time of marriage (c. 112 §1, 2°), in establishing associations of the faithful (c. 299 §1) or joining them (c. 298), and in choosing a place of Christian burial (c. 1177).

Teaching Function. Canon 766 provides that lay persons can be permitted to preach in a church or oratory if necessity requires it, or it seems advantageous in particular cases in accord with the prescripts of the conference of bishops without prejudice to the prescriptions for the homily (c. 767 §1). When sacred ministers are not available and the needs of the Church require it, lay people,

though neither lectors nor acolytes, can supply certain of their functions. In such cases, both lay men and women can exercise the ministry of the word, preside over liturgical prayers, confer baptism, and distribute holy communion in accord with the provisions of law (c. 230 §3). Parents have the primary right and obligation for the education of their children (c. 793). Canon 830 §1 includes the laity among the censors chosen by local ordinaries or submitted on a list made available to diocesan curias by the conference of bishops for judging books.

Sanctifying Function. Canon 861 §2 provides that when an ordinary minister is absent or impeded, a catechist or some other person deputed by the local ordinary, or indeed any person in case of necessity, who has the right intention may lawfully confer baptism. In accord with canon 230 §2, a lay person can receive a temporary deputation as lector in liturgical actions. The norm also provides that the laity can exercise the roles of commentator, cantor, or other liturgical services in accord with law. In 1992, the Pontifical Council for the Interpretation of Legislative Texts gave an affirmative reply to the question of female altar servers. This authentic interpretation of canon 230 §2 was followed by a letter, dated April 12, 1994, from the Congregation for Divine Worship and the Discipline of the Sacraments advising presidents of conferences of bishops of the decision, and providing that each diocesan bishop, having heard the opinion of the episcopal conference, would make a prudential judgment on the matter in his own diocese in accord with the development of liturgical life. In the absence of sacred ministers, a lay person can serve as an extraordinary minister of holy communion (cc. 230 §3, 910 §2). In the absence of priests and deacons, the diocesan bishop can delegate lay persons to assist at marriages if the bishops' conference has voted favorably and the diocesan bishop has obtained permission from the Holy See (c. 1112). Laity who possess the appropriate qualities can, with the permission of the local ordinary, administer certain sacramentals in accord with the prescribed liturgical books (c. 1168).

Governing Function. Suitable lay persons are capable of being admitted by sacred pastors to those ecclesiastical offices and functions which, in accord with the provisions of law, they can discharge (c. 228 §1). In accord with their knowledge, prudence, and integrity, qualified lay persons can assist pastors as experts and advisors even in councils according to the norms of law (c. 228 §2). Lay persons may be appointed as chancellors or vice-chancellors in the diocesan curias (c. 482). Lay persons may be appointed as diocesan notaries (cc. 482 §3; 483 §1). The conference of bishops can permit a lay person of good repute and possessing a doctorate or at least a licentiate in canon law to be appointed as a judge in a collegiate tribunal (c. 1421 §2 §3). In any trial a sole judge can employ two assessors as advisors who can be lay persons of good repute (c. 1424). A bishop can approve lay persons outstanding for their good character, prudence, and doctrine for the function of auditor (c. 1428 §1, §2). The presiding judge may designate a lay judge of the collegiate tribunal as *ponens* or *relator* in order to present the case at the meeting of the judges and set out the judgment in writing (c. 1429). A lay person may be appointed as a promoter of justice (c. 1430) or defender of the bond in a diocese (c. 1432). The laity may participate in a particular council with a consultative vote (c. 443 §3, 2 degree, §4 §5). Lay persons may be designated by the diocesan bishop to participate in a pastoral council (c. 512 §1). Lay persons can be part of the parish council presided over by the parish priest (c. 536 §1). Lay persons can be members of the parish finance committee assisting the parish priest in the administration of the goods of the parish (c. 537). Due to a shortage of priests, the diocesan bishop can entrust a lay person or a community of persons a share in the pastoral care of a parish (c. 517 §2). The bishop can appoint a lay person as diocesan financial officer (c. 494). Lay persons can be appointed by the ordinary as administrators of public juridic persons subject to him (c. 1279 §2). A lay person may be designated to represent the Apostolic See as a delegate or observer at international councils, conferences, or meetings (c. 363 §2).

Discriminatory Canons. While the present legislation shows a marked improvement and places women in an enhanced juridic condition vis-à-vis the former code, there remain a few discriminatory norms. Only laymen (*viri laici*) can be formally installed as lectors or acolytes (c. 230 §1). This norm seems clearly inconsistent and discriminatory toward women, inasmuch as Pope Paul VI in his *motu proprio Ministeria quaedam* of August 15, 1972 proclaimed the functions of lector and acolyte to be lay ministries in the Church. A few norms in the code's section on consecrated life reflect a discriminatory stance toward women religious. Nuns (women religious professing solemn vows) who live a life totally dedicated to contemplation do not have equality with monks with regard to cloistral regulations (c. 667 §2 §3 §4). While male religious in various monasteries can order their cloister in accord with their constitutions (c. 667 §2), nuns are subject to papal norms on cloister prescribed in canon 667 §3 and the instruction *Verbi sponsa*. These norms endure despite the directive principle of the *coetus* on consecrated life and the provision of canon 606 which state that the norms for institutes of consecrated life and societies of apostolic life be applied equally to both sexes, unless determined otherwise from the context or from the nature of things. Undoubtedly, the predominant issue in the ongoing discussion of the legal condition of

women is their exclusion from ordained ministry (c. 1024), which precludes their capacity for the care of souls and the exercise of ecclesiastical power of GOVERNANCE (c. 129 §1). These latter powers (orders and jurisdiction) distinguish clerics by divine institution (*divina institutione*) from the laity (c. 207 §1). Ecclesiastical authorities, biblical scholars, theologians, and historians have addressed the issue of women's ordination at length over the last 30 years. On May 22, 1994, Pope John Paul II, in his apostolic letter *Ordinatio sacerdotalis*, stated that the Church is not able to ordain women to the priesthood.

Code of Canons of the Eastern Churches (CCEO). The common law for the Eastern churches likewise reflects conciliar and postconciliar teachings on the fundamental equality and dignity of persons. A review of the canons shows that women share an equal juridical status with laymen with few exceptions. While a wife is free to transfer to the church of her husband at the celebration of or during the marriage and can freely return to the original church when the marriage has ended, there is no mention in the norm of the husband transferring to the church of his wife (c. 33). A chancellor in the CCEO is to be a presbyter or a deacon (c. 252 §1), and there is no provision in the code for a layperson assuming the pastoral care of a parish (c. 287 §2). While the Latin code provides that no valid marriage can take place between a woman and the man who abducted or at least detained her for the purpose of entering marriage (c. 1089), the Eastern code recognizes the abduction or detention of a person (man or woman) by another for the purpose of marriage as an invalidating impediment to marriage (c. 806).

[R. MCDERMOTT]

WOMAN CLOTHED WITH THE SUN

In a passage full of reminiscences of the Old Testament, John describes the vision of a "great sign" in the sky: the futile attempt of Satan, the "great red dragon," to destroy the male child to whom a "woman clothed with the sun," with the moon under her feet and a crown of 12 stars on her head (cf. Gn 37.9), gives painful birth; the child is snatched up to the throne of God, while the woman flees to the desert, to "a place prepared by God" (Rv 12.1–6).

Identity of the Woman. The description is based on the PROTO-EVANGELIUM (Gn 3.15), which should be taken as the starting point for a correct understanding of Rv 12.1-6. The identity of the "male child" born of the woman is certain: the Messiah, Jesus Christ, not only individually, but also collectively, as united with the

Church; this is clear from the context and from the terms and Biblical allusions used in describing him. Almost certainly it is not the birth of Jesus at Bethlehem that John had in mind. Since immediately after his ''birth'' the child is ''caught up to God and to his throne'' (12.5), Christ's redemptive death, followed by His Resurrection and Ascension, is meant. The birth pangs, then, would be metaphorical for the sufferings of the passion, experienced by the nascent Church in the person of the Apostles (cf. Jn 16.19–22).

That the woman is a collective, the Church of God of both the Old and the New Covenants, is recognized by practically all theologians. This view best accounts for all the data of the vision; it harmonizes with Gn 3.15 and it is familiar to the mentality of Biblical authors, evidenced in the personification of Zion or Israel as a woman (e.g., Is 66.7–11) or the Church as a bride (2 Cor 11.2; Eph 5.23–27; Rv 21.2, 9).

Mariological Importance. In what way, then, does the text refer to Mary? The words of Rv 12.1 are used as the Introit verse of the new Mass of the Assumption and are cited in the apostolic constitution *Munificentissimus Deus* of Nov. 1, 1950 [*Acta Apostolicae Sedis* 42 (1950) 763]. Patristic evidence can be traced as far back as St. IRENAEUS [Adv. *haer.* 3.22.7; *see* F. M. Braun, ''La Femme vêtue du soleil (Apoc. xii),'' *Revue Thomiste* 55 (Paris 1955) 639–669, esp. 642], but a Mariological interpretation was far from unanimous among the Fathers. In post-Reformation exegesis the ecclesial interpretation predominated. Today many scholars see a double reference intended by the author: the Church and Mary, the mother of Christ and of the Christian people (Rv 12.17); moreover, the text suggests that Mary is the type of the Church. These double references are frequent in John's Gospel, in Revelation, and in other apocalyptic literature.

In Christian Art. The iconography of the woman clothed with the sun goes back to 9th-century illuminations in the Apocalypses from Treves and Cambrai, in which the woman, or the Virgin-Church, is represented without her child and praying for protection against the dragon. An Apocalypse from Bamberg of the 11th century portrays the woman with an enormous diadem made up of the sun and 12 stars, protecting her son from the seven-headed dragon. Later depictions introduce other elements of the Apocalypse vision, including the man-child's escape to heaven, the flight from the dragon, and the angel giving wings to the woman (Rv 12.13–17). Albrecht Dürer emphasizes the monstrosity of the dragon in his engraving of the scene and reduces the woman to a small figure with wings and a crown of stars. The banner of the Carmelite Order, which depicts the immaculate Virgin standing upon a crescent moon, served to popularize the woman of the Apocalypse.

See Also: MARY, BLESSED VIRGIN, ICONOGRAPHY OF.

Bibliography: B. J. LE FROIS, *The Woman Clothed with the Sun (Rv 12) Individual or Collective?* (Rome 1954). P. PRIGENT, *Revelation 12: Histoire de l'exégèse* (Beiträge zur Geschichte der biblischen Exegesis 2; Tübingen 1959). L. RÉAU, *Iconographie de l'art chrétien,* 6 v. (Paris 1955–59) 2.2:708–711.

[E. F. SIEGMAN]

WOMANIST THEOLOGY

The term ''womanist'' in the phrase ''womanist theology'' signals a perspective or approach that places the differentiated (e.g., religious, personal, cultural, social, psychological, biological) experience of African American women at the hermeneutical center of theological inquiry and research, reflection and judgment.

History and Origin of the Term. In the early 1980s, already as doctoral students, African-American women theologians and ethicists began to question the marginalization of African-American women's perspectives and experiences within academic religious discourse as well as within black and FEMINIST theologies. They argued that the differentiated experience of black women provided necessary data for theological reflection. In order to distinguish this work from that of African-American male and white female theologians, they named it ''womanist.''

The term womanist was coined by novelist Alice Walker and derived from the African-American cultural epithet *womanish* (*In Search of Our Mother's Garden's* [1983]). Walker described a womanist as a black feminist or feminist of color. Thus, she affirmed attempts by activists and thinkers, such as Sojourner Truth and Anna Julia Cooper in the 19th century and Frances Beale, Audre Lorde, and Bell Hooks in the 20th century, to correct the myth of feminism as a white woman's issue. Use of the term womanist raises awareness of the ideology and practice of sexism within the African American community and exposes the uncritical complicity of women and men in the structures of patriarchy. Walker's definition explicitly encouraged black women to embrace and to love their embodied selves in the midst of a religious, aesthetic, and social environment that is frequently hostile to women's intellectual creativity, emotional flexibility, and sexuality.

In Christian Theology and Scholarship. Although scarcely twenty years old at the end of the 20th century, womanist religious scholarship proved remarkably generative in identifying and coming to terms with the biased ways in which black women have been and are perceived, not only in white, but black religious, cultural, and interpersonal contexts. Womanist theologians, ethicists, and exegetes are Protestant and Catholic, and form no single, uniform school of thought. Despite the specificity of their starting point, these scholars share a fundamental, practical, intellectual commitment to advocate for the survival and wholeness of an entire people, male and female and, thus, refuse to set black women against black men.

Critical analysis of the interlocking and mutually conditioning forces of sexism, rampant acquisitive materialism, and anti-black racism stand at the core of womanist reflection and religious scholarship. The understandings gained from this inquiry contribute to rethinking the content and method of Christian theology, ethics, and biblical exegesis.

Theology. With regard to the doctrine of christology, womanist analysis contests the bleaching of Jesus Christ (Grant 1989). With regard to the doctrine of SOTERIOLOGY, womanist analysis uncovers tendencies to spiritualize slavery and overlook the enslaved peoples' experience of commodification and brutality (Grant 1993). With regard to the doctrine of ECCLESIOLOGY, womanist analysis has focused on INCULTURATION as communion and liberation (Phelps 1998). With regard to the doctrine of theological anthropology, womanist analysis exposes the sexual and commercial objectification and commodification of black bodies and hence takes the body and sexuality seriously (Eugene 1994, Copeland 1993, Brown Douglas, 1999). With regard to the notion of Christian hope, womanist analysis emphasize the healthy and whole in African American communities (Boyd 1997, Thomas 1997, Hayes 1997).

Ethics. With regard to sin and evil, womanist analysis puts forward both fundamental (Townes 1993; Cannon 1996) and practical-political ethical responses to social injustices (Townes 1998; Cannon 1996; Ross 1997). In theological and ethical method, womanists advance strategies to debunk, unmask and disentangle religious, cultural and social situations, in order to promote and sustain the moral agency of black women (Cannon 1996; Gilkes 2001). In retrieving black women's history, womanist interrogation furthers the vitality of the category of memory (Higginbotham 1993, Baker-Fletcher 1994, Riggs 1997).

Biblical Scholarship. Womanists work discloses putatively innocent readings of 'dangerous' texts and enlarges the scope of HERMENEUTICS to meet the exigencies of black life (Martin 1991; Weems 1995).

As a body, African American women theologians, ethicists, and scholars participate in the American Academy of Religion (AAR), and have attained the status of a Group. Womanists have identified the mentoring of newer black female scholars a priority, and each year since 1995 have conducted a consultation for the presentation of papers, exchange of syllabi and information on teaching and research.

Bibliography: K. BAKER FLETCHER, *A Singing Something: Womanist Reflections on Anna Julia Cooper* (New York 1994); *Sisters of Dust, Sisters of Spirit : Womanist Wordings on God and Creation* (Minneapolis 1998). K. BROWN DOUGLAS, *Sexuality and the Black Church: A Womanist Perspective* (Maryknoll, N.Y. 1999). K. G. CANNON, *Black Womanist Ethics* (Atlanta 1988); *Katie's Cannon: Womanism and the Soul of the Black Community* (New York 1996). C. T. GILKES, ''*If It Wasn't for the Women . . .*'' *Black Women's Experience and Womanist Culture in Church and Community* (Maryknoll, N.Y. 2001). J. GRANT, *White Women's Christ, Black Women's Jesus: White Feminist Christology and Womanist Response* (Atlanta 1989). D. L. HAYES and C. DAVIS, eds., *Taking Down Our Harps: Black Catholics in the United States* (Maryknoll, N.Y. 1998). J. T. PHELPS, ed. *Black and Catholic: The Challenge and Gift of Black Folk: Contributions of African American Experience and Thought to Catholic Theology* (Milwaukee 1998). E. M. TOWNES, *Womanist Justice, Womanist Hope* (Atlanta 1993); *In a Blaze of Glory: Womanist Spirituality as Social Witness* (Nashville 1995). E. M. TOWNES, ed., *A Troubling in My Soul: Womanist Perspectives on Evil and Suffering* (Maryknoll, N.Y. 1993). R. J. WEEMS, *Battered Love: Marriage, Sex, and Violence in the Hebrew Prophets* (Minneapolis 1995). D. S. WILLIAMS, *Sisters in the Wilderness: The Challenge of Womanist God-Talk* (Maryknoll, N.Y. 1993).

[M. S. COPELAND]

WOMEN AND PAPAL TEACHING

The ''woman question'' has emerged with urgency in the contemporary world. From the late 1800s through the twentieth century, momentous changes in Western society shaped the context for church teaching on women. Rapid industrialization, advancement of political rights, especially the drive for women's suffrage, two world wars with an intervening economic depression, scientific advances affecting everything from life expectancy to reproduction, efforts toward universal education, the rise of communism, feminist movements, social science research on the nature of sex and gender, new participation by women in church ministry and theological education—all of these affected what women did, how they were viewed, and how they viewed themselves. Thus this period saw an unprecedented attention to women in papal and other official teachings. These teachings evidenced the church's desire to speak to the needs of women in modern society in light of Christian faith, and its call to Catholics to address social issues in new and creative ways.

A review of these teachings on women shows an uneven but noticeable progression from initial reservations

Young girls carry shrine to St. Rocco at St. Joachim's Church, on Roosevelt Street, New York City, 1933. (©Bettmann/CORBIS)

and resistance toward increasingly active promotion for the equal involvement of women with men in all dimensions of society: access to opportunities for work, protection from violence and other exploitation, political participation, and the shaping of culture. Simultaneously, the church insisted that women fulfill what it presents as their distinctive and vital role in the home, especially in the rearing of children, with an analogous form of participation in society. This vocation has been continually presented in terms of ''complementarity'': the anthropological and theological conviction that women and men, while equal in dignity before God, have qualities and functions rooted in their nature that complement one another.

Leo XIII through Pius XII (1878–1958). Women increasingly took jobs outside the home during this period due to personal and family economic necessity, the need to keep national economies functioning as men went off to war, and for personal fulfillment. Popes both de-

cried this phenomenon and sought to place limits on it in accord with their understanding of women's primary role in the home. LEO XIII (1878–1903), while speaking strongly for workers' rights in the 1891 encyclical *Rerum novarum,* argued against women's presence in unsuitable jobs and for their domestic vocation: ''Women, again, are not suited to certain trades; for a woman is by nature fitted for home work, and it is that which is best adapted at once to preserve her modesty, and to promote the good bringing up of children and the well-being of the family'' (33). PIUS XI (1922–1939), echoed by several later popes, supported the concept of a ''family wage,'' i.e., a wage sufficient for supporting a family. Paying this for the labor of husbands would eliminate the need for wives to take jobs outside the home (*Quadragesimo anno* [1931], 71).

While Church teaching in this era reflected a concern for women's safety and purity of character were they to engage too deeply in worldly affairs, over time the popes often affirmed the participation of women in social movements congenial with church concerns. Women's efforts were lauded in the twentieth-century expansion of church-related social apostolates, especially Catholic Action, a priority for PIUS XI. They were seen as particularly suited to revitalize religious values through, for example, fostering the Christian education of girls and women, encouraging modesty and restoring the family. Such work, however, should not detract from fulfillment of their own domestic responsibilities, and in fact is best pursued by women who are not responsible for rearing children. PIUS XII (1939–58) also pointed to the long history of women's religious congregations as a constant and church-sanctioned opportunity for women to work for the betterment of society (''Women's Duties'' [1945], 707).

As countries in the West adopted female suffrage into law, papal teaching eventually accepted political participation by women. The first explicit endorsement of women's right to vote came with Pius XII, in the context of church concern over the spread of communism in Europe. He repeatedly spoke to Catholic women regarding the use of their franchise to uphold the family against forces seeking to destroy it. Church teachings repeatedly affirmed the sacredness of marriage and the unique relationship of husband and wife. Leo XIII charged socialists with seeking to break the indissoluble bond of marriage (*Quod apostolici muneris* [1878], 8) and thus to undermine the family. In the marriage relationship, Leo XIII stated that ''The husband is the chief of the family and the head of the wife. The woman, because she is flesh of his flesh, and bone of his bone, must be subject to her husband and obey him; not, indeed, as a servant, but as a companion, so that her obedience shall be wanting in neither honor nor dignity'' (*Arcanum divinae* [1880], 11). Ephesians 5:21–33 was regularly cited in discussions of this subjection, with the corresponding reminder that the ruling function of the man is always to be exercised in love rather than domination (see *Casti connubii* [1930], 26–28). Subsequent popes echoed this focus on the domestic sphere as the setting for the woman's fulfillment of her distinctive vocation as wife, mother, and companion.

Most significantly, the popes insisted that the dignity of women would only be fully understood in relation to God, not through the arguments of liberalism, FEMINISM, Marxism, and other secular movements. In *CASTI CONNUBII*, Pius XI denounced feminist demands for equality in the ordering of family affairs and in child rearing as those of ''false teachers'' and the ''false liberty and unnatural equality'' they advocated as detrimental to woman, who would then descend ''from her truly regal throne to which she has been raised within the walls of the home by means of the Gospel'' to ''become as

amongst the pagans the mere instrument of man'' (75). Instead, as articulated by Pius XII (1939–58), the dignity of women is apparent in the church's teaching that women are equal to men as created by God, redeemed in Christ, and sharing the same eternal destiny.

Pius XII is notable for a sustained discussion of the prominent themes raised by previous popes, and in arguing forcefully for women's full participation in society in accord with their distinctive qualities. Women are differentiated from men in possessing particular physical and psychological characteristics that fit them to be mothers: for example, women are characterized by warm self-giving to God and neighbor, while men's giving may be more impersonal. ''So we have an absolute equality in personal and fundamental values, but different functions which are complementary and superbly equivalent, and from them arise the various rights and duties of the one and the other'' (''The Dignity of Woman'' [1957]: 370).

While women's vocation normally will be fulfilled in marriage and motherhood, Pius XII also strongly supported the call to consecrated virginity of vowed women religious. Likewise, he affirmed the status of single women as a de facto state (rather than choosing to be single to pursue a career), and encouraged these women to enter professions that would draw on their motherly qualities, such as education, child care, social service, and political activity on behalf of families. Regardless of her state in life, ''Every woman is made to be a mother: a mother in the physical meaning of the word or in the more spiritual and exalted but no less real sense'' (''Woman's Duties,'' 708).

The Popes of the Second Vatican Council, Conciliar and Post-Conciliar Teachings (1958–1978). The teachings of the church on women during the pontificates of John XXIII and Paul VI occurred in the context of the Vatican II determination to read the ''signs of the times'' (*Gaudium et spes* 4). In *Pacem in terris* (1963), John XXIII cited the fact that ''women are now taking part in public life'' as one of the ''distinctive characteristics'' of the present day, and ''they will not tolerate being treated as mere material instruments, but demand rights befitting a human person both in domestic and in public life'' (41). *Gaudium et spes* notes that as part of the ''broader desires'' of humanity in the present time, women are claiming ''an equity with men before the law and in fact'' (9). Such developments are supported by the church as part of its overall concern for full human development in social, political, economic, and cultural dimensions.

The tone and direction of church teachings further sought to promote the apostolate of the laity in the secular realm. Already an important concern of the twentieth century church, it gained ecclesiological depth through the characterization of the laity, women and men alike, as participating in the "universal call to holiness" (*Lumen gentium*, especially 30–42) and the mission of the church through their efforts in the world.

At the same time, the papal teachings continued to caution that woman's participation in these realms must be distinctive to her special calling, and should not detract from the fulfillment of her indispensable role in the home. Thus, John XXIII, in addressing a congress on the theme of woman in the family and at work, warned that the irreplaceable role of the mother in the family was threatened by a woman's outside employment, both because she would have less time and energy to provide a warm and nurturing home for her family and because her constant exposure to the corruptions of the world placed her "open and delicate spirit" in jeopardy ("The Woman of Today" [1961]: 172).

While such discussion of women's "frailty" and "delicacy" began to disappear from church teaching, the sense of a distinctive nature was continually reaffirmed in these years. Thus *Gaudium et spes* states, in regard to cultural life, that "It is appropriate that [women] should be able to assume their full proper role in accordance with their own nature" (60). And in the closing address to the Second Vatican Council (1965), Paul VI exhorted woman to use her growing influence to help restrain the hand of man, who might destroy civilization through technology ("Closing Address," 733). Women who are mothers should raise up generations of children able to meet the enormous demands of the future; unmarried women should assist families; consecrated virgins should be "guardians of purity, unselfishness, and piety"; and women suffering trials should do so patiently while encouraging men in their vital undertakings (ibid.). Despite the arguments of secular feminism, women should not seek a "false equality which would deny the distinctions laid down by the Creator himself and which would be in contradiction with women's proper role, which is of such capital importance, at the heart of the family as well as within society" (Paul VI, *Octogesima adveniens* [1971], 13).

The 1976 Congregation for the Doctrine of the Faith instruction *Inter insignores* addressed the question of the reservation of priestly ordination to men, increasingly raised within the church in this period. The document, along with subsequent explanations, stressed women's equal dignity with men as created by God and in the "objective order of grace" (Paul VI, "Women in the Plan of God" [1977]: 125), but at the same time insisted that the church is not authorized to ordain women due to Christ's having limited the role to men in the calling of his twelve apostles, and to women's inability to image Christ fully

(see *Inter insignores*, 24–28). "[W]hen Christ's role in the Eucharist is to be expressed sacramentally, there would not be this 'natural resemblance' which must exist between Christ and his minister if the role of Christ were not taken by a man: in such a case it would be difficult to see in the minister the image of Christ. For Christ himself was and remains a man" (*Inter insignores*, 27).

John Paul II (1978–). John Paul II addressed specific concerns regarding women in his 1981 encyclical on the nature and dignity of human work, *Laborem exercens*. Cognizant and supportive of women's legitimate aspirations for advancement in many occupations, he called for a "social re-evaluation" of how their irreplaceable role in the rearing of children may be exercised without loss of opportunities for gainful and fulfilling work. "Having to abandon these [child-rearing] tasks in order to take up paid work outside the home is wrong from the point of view of the good of society and of the family when it contradicts or hinders these primary goals of the mission of a mother" (19). Thus society, and not only individual mothers, bears a responsibility to address this problem. The "family wage" is one possibility.

In *Christifideles laici* (1988), John Paul II affirmed that the family continues to be the fundamental context for nurturing a community committed to mission in church and the world, the "domestic church" (62; see *Familiaris consortio* [1981], 21). Through women's intervention, men can be more fully involved in parenting as a mutual endeavor, and can better understand and practice the interpersonal communion of family life (*Christifideles laici*, 49).

The 1988 apostolic letter *Mulieris dignitatem,* Pope John Paul II's major contribution to the Church teachings on women and the most extensive treatment by any modern pope warrants extended review. In this lengthy work, which he characterizes as a "meditation" written to close the Marian Year, John Paul maintains that the role of women can only be understood in terms of their essential dignity and vocation, which in turn must be explicated through a discussion of their anthropological and theological bases, with particular reference to Mary. The result is a thoroughgoing presentation of complementarity.

The Role of Mary, Mother of God. As THEOTOKOS, Mary is the essential "horizon" for reflection on women (5). At the Annunciation we see her as the biblical "woman" who represents all people's humanity, yet has a unique dignity (3–4). In her acceptance of God's will she acts as a free human subject, makes possible God's new covenant with humanity (the only occasion in Scripture where a covenant begins with a woman), and returns "woman" to her original state of goodness in creation. As both virgin and mother she shows the full meaning of each of these "two particular dimensions of the fulfillment of the female personality," which "explain and complete each other" (17). Women, through physical motherhood in marriage or the "spiritual motherhood" of consecrated virginity and marriage to Christ, find fulfillment of the "naturally spousal predisposition of the feminine personality" (20).

Women and Men Created in the Image and Likeness of God. The pope develops the first account of the creation of humans as male and female in Genesis 1:26–27 as the basis of all CHRISTIAN ANTHROPOLOGY. Created in the image of God, "Man is a person, man and woman equally so . . ." (6), from the beginning. The second creation account in Genesis 2:18–25 reinforces this truth, as man cannot live alone and may only exist in unity with another human person. The mutuality of man and woman mirrors that of the Trinity, "the communion of love that is in God, through which the Three Persons love each other in the intimate mystery of the one divine life" (7). The dignity and vocation of women and men "result from [their] specific diversity and personal originality"; women must not appropriate characteristics opposed to their feminine originality, or they may lose their "essential richness" (10). "The personal resources of femininity are certainly no less than the resources of masculinity: they are merely different" (10). Patriarchal domination of women by men does not reflect God's will, but is rather a consequence of original sin, disturbing their fundamental equality (10).

Jesus' Treatment of Women and Their Redemption in Christ. John Paul II points to the gospel accounts to show how Christ consistently promoted the dignity and vocation of women in ways that countered the usual discrimination toward them in his culture and times. Jesus heals women; he speaks with them publicly; they appear in parables to help reveal the nature of the kingdom of God; they accompany and provide for him and his disciples; they themselves become disciples; they are the first witnesses of the resurrection (see 12–16). In honoring women he reflects the divine plan of redemption that he will fulfill: "Jesus of Nazareth confirms this dignity [of women], recalls it, renews it, and makes it a part of the Gospel and of the Redemption for which he is sent into the world. Every word and gesture of Christ about women must therefore be brought into the dimension of the Paschal Mystery. In this way everything is completely explained" (13).

The Church as Bride of Christ and Women's Particular Role in This Reality. As taught in *Lumen gentium* (10), all the faithful participate in the universal priesthood of Christ and are united as his Body. This full participation of Christian men and women in Christ's spiritual sac-

rifice is also expressed through the Bride and Bridegroom images of Ephesians. This symbolism receives a sustained treatment by John Paul II as another foundation for complementarity. The church is the Bride, called to respond to the full, self-giving and redeeming love of Christ the Bridegroom. In this understanding, "'being the bride,' and thus the 'feminine' element, becomes a symbol of all that is 'human'" (25). While the Bride role applies to both men and women as the church, Christ became incarnate as a human male, and the Bridegroom symbol is masculine. "This masculine symbol represents the human aspect of the divine love which God has for Israel, for the Church, and for all people. . . . Precisely because Christ's divine love is the love of a Bridegroom, it is the model and pattern of all human love, men's love in particular" (25). Thus the pope concludes that the "feminine" role of the Bride in returning the love given by the Bridegroom is the universal role of women, whether married or not: "woman can only find herself by giving love to others" (30).

In this context the pope also reconfirms the authoritative teaching of *Inter insignores* (and again reiterates it in his 1994 apostolic letter, *Ordinatio sacerdotalis*) that priestly ordination is reserved to men alone. Christ's calling of twelve male apostles is a "free and sovereign" act and should not be seen as conformity to prevailing customs; his freedom here is consistent with his treatment of women with dignity despite the norms of his society. The Eucharist, instituted by Christ in explicit connection to the priestly service of the Twelve, "expresses the redemptive act of Christ the Bridegroom towards the Church the Bride. This is clear and unambiguous when the sacramental ministry of the Eucharist, in which the priest acts 'in persona Christi,' is performed by a man" (26).

Special note should also be taken of John Paul II's use of Ephesians 5. Rather than enjoining a wife's subjection to a loving husband, he stresses verse 21 and "mutual subjection out of reverence for Christ" (24) as the basis for the relationship of husband and wife. The *Catechism of the Catholic Church* echoes this in naming each partner as the "helpmate" of the other, "for they are equal as persons . . . and complementary as masculine and feminine" (372).

Toward the Future. The teachings of John Paul II on women will undoubtedly be a continuing point of focus as church teaching and theological reflection continue into the twenty-first century. In particular, as women's role in church and society continues to evolve and as scholarship in various theological disciplines engages with the "signs of the times" and Christian tradition, alternative models to a male-female complementarity are being proposed. Concurrently, the Jubilee Year reconciliation efforts by John Paul II have included repentance for past sins against the dignity of women by members of the church. While lamenting the prior failings of Christians and the ongoing domination of women in many aspects of human relationships, the church upholds a vision of the future in which inequality and discrimination will be no more, and the dignity and vocation of women, as well as men, may be fully realized.

Bibliography: R. CAMP, ''From Passive Subordination to Complementary Partnership: The Papal Conception of a Woman's Place in Church and Society Since 1878,'' *Catholic Historical Review* 76, no. 3 (1990): 506–525. A. CARR and E. SCHÜSSLER FIOREN-ZA, eds. *The Special Nature of Women?* Concilium 6 (London 1991). W. FAHERTY, *The Destiny of Modern Woman in the Light of Papal Teaching* (Westminster, Md. 1950). JOHN XXIII, ''The Woman of Today: At Home and at Work,'' address to the Italian Center for Women, 7 December 1960, *The Pope Speaks* 7, no. 2 (1961): 169–174. JOHN PAUL II, ''Service at St. Peter's Basilica Requesting Pardon.'' *Origins* 29, no. 40 (23 March 2000). PAUL VI, ''Women in the Plan of God,'' remarks of Pope Paul VI before the Sunday Angelus, 30 January 1977, *The Pope Speaks* 22, no. 2 (1977): 124–125. L. PORTER, ''Gender in Theology: The Example of John Paul II's *Mulieris Dignitatem*,'' *Gregorianum* 77, no. 1 (1996): 97–131. R. LEONARD, *Beloved Daughters: 100 Years of Papal Teaching on Women* (Ottawa 1995). PIUS XII, ''The Dignity of Woman,'' address of Pope Pius XII to a pilgrimage sponsored by the Federation of Italian Women, 14 October 1956, *The Pope Speaks* 3, no. 4 (Spring 1957): 367–375. PIUS XII, ''Woman's Duties in Social and Political Life,'' delivered by Pope Pius XII to Italian women, 21 October 1945, *The Catholic Mind* 43, no. 996 (December 1945): 705–716. G. TAVARD, *Woman in Christian Tradition* (Notre Dame 1973).

[M. R. O'BRIEN]

WOMEN IN THE BIBLE

Old Testament

The biblical understanding of woman is grounded in the traditions embodied in the narrative accounts of CREATION (Gn 1–2). In the first account the woman is depicted, with the man, as created in the image of God with both privilege and responsibility (Gn 1.26–28). In the second account she is said to be his *'ēzer*, his ''suitable partner'' (Gn 2.18–20). Despite their fundamental goodness, the first couple sinned and were subsequently punished. Their relationship with God was altered and the harmony that they had originally enjoyed with each other and with the rest of the world was gravely disrupted. The subsequent biblical portraits of the woman and the man, as well as the social and religious roles that each plays in the narratives, must be understood against this basic anthropological/theological point of view. These portraits suggest that the prevailing situation is not what was intended at the beginning.

There is one principal Hebrew word, *'iššâ*, that translates as ''woman.'' The linguistic relationship between *'iššâ* and *'îš* (man or husband) is most likely based on the similarity of sound rather than on linguistic etymology. Because the word means woman in contrast to man, it is sometimes translated ''wife.'' Unlike the word for female (*neqēbâ*), which merely denotes gender, this word connotes relationship between the woman and her man. However, the word itself does not indicate the nature of this relationship. The social groups do that.

Family Relationships. Because of the patriarchal nature and androcentric structure of ancient society, the roles the woman played in the family were secondary to corresponding roles played by the man. The wife was subservient to her husband (Gn 3.16). In one version of the decalogue she was even listed among his possessions (Ex 20.17). The mother was subordinate to the father; sisters were dependent on brothers (Gn 34); widows were among the most vulnerable members of the society because they had severed ties with their own family and were bereft of a male protector among the husband's kin (Dt 26.12).

Israelite women were expected to marry and thus pass from the control of their fathers or brothers to that of their husbands and fathers-in-law. Since only through them would their husband's bloodline be transmitted, it was imperative that the women be virgins at the time of marriage and faithful to their husbands ever after. Wives were valued primarily for their reproductive powers. (Exceptions to this can be found in Gn 29.18 and 1 Sm 1.8.) Since children, specifically sons, carried forward the family name and ensured possession of the family property, the fertility of the wife was of utmost importance not only to the husband but also to the entire family, clan, or tribe. The tensions between Sarah and Hagar (Gn 16.4–6), Rachel and Leah (Gn 30.1–2), and Hannah and Peninnah (1 Sm 1.2–8) were due to the barrenness of the former woman and the fruitfulness of the latter. The stories about the earliest ancestresses recount how often, to circumvent their own inability to provide their husbands with heirs, they offered them their maidservants as surrogates. Thus Hagar became Abram's concubine and bore him a son (Gn 16), and Bilhah, the maidservant of Rachel, and Zilpah, the maidservant of Leah, augmented the family of Jacob in the same way (Gn 30.3–14).

Despite the fact that in the patriarchal family the mother was subordinate to the father, the law dictated that respect and love be given to her as well as to the father (Ex 20.12; 21.15, 17; Lv 19.3; 20.9; Dt 5.16; 21.18–20; 27.16). The plight of the WIDOW was a matter of public concern. If her husband died and left her without children, his family might provide her with a levirate marriage. In this situation, a brother or nearest male relative of the deceased was obliged to act as surrogate husband of the widow. The child born of this union was considered the legal heir of the deceased man, assuming his name and inheriting his property (Dt 25.5–10; see also Gn 38.6–11; Ru 4.1–12). Although the practice was concerned primarily with the perpetuation of the name and property rights of the deceased, it afforded the widow considerable security.

Social and Religious Status. Marriage itself was a social arrangement wherein women were exchanged, that is, given over for some monetary or property return by fathers (Gn 29.14b–30) or brothers (Gn 24.29–54). These men were responsible for devising arrangements that would enhance the economic status of the family. This was done through the exchange of property which constituted an integral element of the marriage. The women brought a dowry and the man paid a bride price or bridewealth (*mōhar*, Gn 34.12). The dowry served as the woman's portion of the family inheritance. It was administered by her husband and might significantly alter his economic status, but it did not by right belong to him. It offered the woman some degree of protection against domestic abuse, since it had to be returned to her family in the event of divorce. The bridewealth, on the other hand, was a sample of the man's productive ability (Jacob worked seven years for each of his two wives [Gn 29.18; 27]). It compensated the woman's family for the loss of her reproductive capacity.

In patriarchal societies, rape was seldom regarded as a violation of the woman, but rather of her husband, father, or brother. Since it jeopardized the patriarchal bloodline, rape undercut the economic advantage that the woman's family might have realized through a substantial bridewealth.

It appears that Israelite society did not accept its king's wife as ruler in her own right. However, it did recognize her as a regent or temporary care-taker monarch (2 Kgs 11). Even when women appear to have exercised a certain amount of authority and responsibility, they did so as an exception to the patriarchal norm, in the absence of a man, or with the consent of the men of that social group. Daughters were valued in as much as they might augment the family resources by commanding substantial bridewealth. They could inherit only in the absence of a male heir, and even then, when they would marry, they were required to do so within the father's tribe in order to ensure the tribal possession of the father's property (Nm 27.1–11; 36.1–9). A notable exception to this inheritance custom is found in the epilogue of the Book of Job, where his three daughters receive a share of the estate along with their brothers (Jb 42.13–15).

The priesthood was closed to Israelite women, most likely because of the mysterious reproductive powers of the female body as well as the blood taboo. Despite this restriction, women still participated in the cultic life of the people. They served at the entrance of the meeting tent (Ex 38.8; 1 Sm 2.22) and as singers in the postexilic community (Ez 2.65; Neh 7.67). Furthermore, the people did endorse the prophetic activity of Deborah (Jgs 4.4), Miriam (Ex 15.20), Huldah (2 Kgs 22.14), Noadiah (Neh 6.14) and the wife of Isaiah (Is 8.3). Finally, the David saga includes accounts of two different wise women who were able to influence the lives of their respective communities and, thereby, save them from disaster (2 Sm 14.1–20; 20.14–22). Unlike the roles of monarch and priest, which were fixed institutions, the roles of prophet and sage were more charismatic and, thus, open. This may explain why women were more easily accepted in some roles than in others.

[D. BERGANT]

New Testament

In the New Testament women appear in the genealogy of Jesus, are healed and forgiven by him, become his disciples, and exercise a variety of ministries. Women are featured in sayings and parables of Jesus and in Pauline and Deuteropauline teachings. In the Book of Revelation female figures are used symbolically. The stories and sayings about women in the NT give only a partial picture of their life in the apostolic church. Moreover, while it is possible that some of the biblical traditions have come from circles of women, the Bible has been written, for the most part, by men and for men, and told from a male perspective. For a fuller retrieval of the place of women in early Christian communities and for interpreting the biblical traditions about women it is necessary to engage the tools of FEMINIST HERMENEUTICS.

The Greek word *thēlus,* ''female,'' appears at Mt 19.4; Mk 10.6; Gal 3.28, texts that allude to Gn 1.27. In one other instance it is found in a vice list (Rom 1.26–27). Otherwise the term is *gynē,* which means both ''woman'' and ''wife.'' Sometimes it is not possible to know which is intended, e.g., 1 Cor 9.5, where it is not clear whether Paul speaks of his right to take along on mission a Christian woman or a believing wife (*adelphēn gynaika*). In several NT passages ''woman'' is a direct address on the lips of Jesus (Mt 15.28; Lk 22.57; Jn 2.4; 4.21; 19.26; 20.13, 15). This does not convey disrespect, but reflects his patriarchal world in which a woman's identity is embedded in that of her father, husband, and sons. Thus many biblical women are unnamed.

Women in the Genealogy of Jesus. In Matthew's version of the genealogy of Jesus (1.1–17 cf. Lk 3.23–38) the names of four women, Tamar, Rahab, Ruth, and Uriah's wife, disrupt the stylized pattern that features 39 male ancestors. Each is noted for acting in an unconventional manner that furthered God's purposes for Israel. This prepares for the unusual circumstances surrounding the birth of Jesus to MARY. The Gospel of Luke gives the most extended treatment to Mary, the mother of Jesus. Her story is intertwined with that of Elizabeth, as their stories of annunciation, visitation, and birth of their sons replicate the births of other saving figures of Israel's past (Lk 1–2). Elizabeth is portrayed as upright and faithful (1.6), reliably naming God's grace despite opposition (1.57–66). Mary is grace-filled, favored one (1.28, 30), who assents to God's will (1.38) and continues to ponder God's ways (2.19, 51). The MAGNIFICAT (1.46–55), an early Christian hymn, is placed on her lips, casting her like Hannah (1 Sm 2.1–10), and prefiguring the mission of Jesus (4.18–19). Upon presenting her newborn son in the Temple, she encounters the prophet Anna who never left the Temple, fasting and praying day and night and speaking about the child to all who were looking for the redemption of Israel (Lk 2.36–38). Mary is mentioned briefly in two other episodes (Mk 3.31–33; Mt 12.46–50; Lk 8.19–21) and reappears at Acts 1.14 with the disciples awaiting the coming of the Spirit. In the Gospel of John she is the catalyst for the beginning of Jesus' public ministry (2.1–12) and is a witness to the crucifixion of her son (19.25–27). There she and the Beloved Disciple are entrusted to one another. Paul only once alludes to Mary, when he speaks of God's Son having been born of a woman (Gal 4.4).

Women Fed, Healed, and Forgiven. Each of the gospels relays accounts of women who have saving encounters with Jesus during his Galilean ministry. The mother-in-law of Simon is healed of a fever and immediately ministers (*diēkonei*) to Jesus (Mk 1.29–31; Mt 8.14–15; Lk 4.38–39). A woman with a hemorrhage is healed and the daughter of Jairus is resuscitated (Mk 5.21–43; Mt 9.18–26; Lk 8.40–56). A persistent Gentile woman of exemplary faith pleads with Jesus to heal her daughter (Mt 15.21–28; Mk 7.24–30). A woman who had been bent over for eighteen years is freed from her infirmity (Lk 13.10–17). A widow from Nain who had lost her only son receives him back when Jesus restores him to life (Lk 7.11–17). A woman caught in adultery is freed from her accusers and her sin (Jn 8.1–11). In the Matthean versions of the feeding of the multitudes, women and children are explicitly mentioned as having been fed along with the men (Mt 14.21; 15.38; cf. Mk 6.30–44; 8.9; Lk 9.10–17; Jn 6.1–14). In the Gospel of Matthew, Pilate's wife has been affected by her encounter with Jesus, so that she dreams of him and urges her husband to have nothing more to do with him (27.19).

Women in Parables and Sayings. Four gospel parables center on women characters. In Mt 13.33 and Lk 13.20–21 a woman hiding yeast in a mass of dough is a metaphor for the reign of God. Luke depicts God's costly search for the lost as a woman who sweeps the house looking for a stray coin (15.8–10). He also tells of a widow who takes on a corrupt judge and achieves justice by her persistence (18.1–8). Matthew likens the need for preparedness for the second coming of Christ to that of ten virgins awaiting the arrival of a bridegroom (25.1–13). A saying about watchfulness for the end time concerns two women grinding, only one of whom will be taken (Mt 24.41; Lk 17.35). A request from the mother of the sons of Zebedee (Mk 10.35–45; Mt 20.20–23) prompts sayings from Jesus about his passion. As his passion approaches, Jesus tells his disciples that their pain at his death will be forgotten for the joy of new life, as a woman no longer remembers labor pains after she has given birth (Jn 16.20–22). Similarly, Paul compares the onset of the end time to the sudden labor pains of a pregnant woman (1 Thes 5.31). In one instance he likens his ministry to that of a nursing mother (1 Thes 2.7). Paul uses the story of Sarah and Hagar in an extended allegory to illustrate to the Galatians their movement from slavery to the Law toward freedom in Christ (Gal 4.21–5.1).

The New Family. A number of sayings of Jesus in the gospels concern the effect of discipleship on the patriarchal family structure. There will be conflicts between family members, including mothers, daughters, and daughters-in-law (Mt 10.34–39; Mk 10.34–36; Lk 12.51–53). Disciples may leave their mothers, wives, and sisters (Mt 19.29; Mk 10.29; Lk 14.26–27; 18.29). Jesus declares that his mother, brothers and sisters are those who hear and do the will of God (Mk 3.31–35; Mt 12.46–50; Lk 8.19–21; 11.27–28). As for sexual relations, Jesus warns against adultery and lust (Mt 5.27–28) and takes a negative stance on divorce (Mt 5.31–32; 19.9; Mk 10.11; Lk 16.18), a position with which Paul concurs (1 Cor 7.10–14), though he allows separation when one member is a non-believer and does not wish to remain with the Christian (1 Cor 7.15–16). He prefers, in view of the impending parousia, that Christians remain unmarried (1 Cor 7.8). Paul uses an analogy from marriage (Rom 7.1–6) to illustrate how as a woman is not bound to her husband after his death and is free to marry another, so Christians are no longer bound to the Law and are freed by belonging to Christ. A growing appreciation of the value of celibacy is reflected in texts such as 1 Cor 7.25–40 and Rv 14.4. In the resurrection there will not be the present order of patriarchal marriage (Mk 12.18; Mt 22.23–33; Lk 20.27–40).

Women Disciples and Ministers. The four gospels are unanimous in telling that there were a number of women disciples of Jesus from Galilee who followed him to Jerusalem, witnessed the crucifixion (Mt 27.55; Mk 15.40–41; Lk 23.49), saw where he was buried (Mt 27.6; Mk 15.47; Lk 23.55–56), and were the ones who found the tomb empty (Mt 28.1–10; Mk 16.1–8; Lk 24.1–12; Jn 20. 1–2; 11–18). In the Gospels of Matthew and John they are also the first to encounter the risen Christ. Each of the gospels gives a slightly different version. The names of the women vary and the accounts of what happened after they found the empty tomb differ. Mark tells that the women fled from the tomb in terror and amazement and said nothing to anyone because they were afraid (16.8). In the Gospel of Luke Mary Magdalene, Joanna, Mary the mother of James, and the other women with them tell what they have seen and heard to the apostles but they are not believed (24.10–11). Matthew says that the risen Christ appeared to Mary Magdalene and ''the other Mary'' while they were on their way to tell the others (28.9–10). He reiterates the instructions to tell the other disciples to go to Galilee, which they obey (28.16). In the Gospel of John Mary Magdalene goes to the tomb alone, is the first to encounter the risen Christ, and reports to the others what Jesus says to her (20.1–2, 11–18). She is portrayed as apostle to the apostles, much as the Samaritan woman is also cast by the Fourth Evangelist as apostle to her entire town (Jn 4.4–42).

While all four Gospels tell of the Galilean women who followed Jesus to Jerusalem, only Luke notes their discipleship during the Galilean ministry. Mary Magdalene, Joanna, Susanna, and other women who had been healed of illnesses, ministered (*diēkonoun*) to Jesus and the twelve out of their monetary resources (Lk 8.1–3). Luke also tells of Mary who takes the attentive position of a disciple at Jesus' feet and her sister Martha who voices her ministerial concerns (*pollēn diakonian*) to Jesus (10.38–42). John also preserves traditions about these two sisters. Martha proclaims her belief in Jesus as the Messiah, the Son of God, the One coming into the world (11.27). Mary anoints Jesus for burial (12.1–12). In the Gospels of Mark (14.3–9) and Matthew (26.6–13) the woman who performs this prophetic anointing is anonymous. A similar tradition is found in Luke 7.36–50. There the woman is also anonymous and performs this lavish demonstration of love after having experienced great forgiveness. A similarly extravagant gift to which Jesus calls the attention of his disciples is that of a widow who gives to the Temple treasury all she had to live on (Mk 12.41–44; Lk 21.1–4).

In the Acts of the Apostles the Spirit fills both women and men disciples (1.14; 2.18). Luke explicitly mentions both women and men who became believers (Acts 5.14; 8.12; 17.4, 12), one of whom was named Damaris (17.34), another being Timothy's mother (16.1).

Her name, Eunice, is given at 2 Tm 1.5, where she and Timothy's grandmother, Lois, are extolled for passing on their sincere faith to him. Dorcas, also known as Tabitha, is a disciple who engaged in charitable ministries with other widows (9.36–43). Women are among those dragged off to prison by Paul (Acts 8.3; 9.2; 22.4). Negatively, women are among those who became incited against Paul and Barnabas in Pisidian Antioch (13.50). A tragic story of a disciple who is struck dead is that of Sapphira, who is complicit in her husband's lie to the community (Acts 5.1–11). Several minor female characters appear in Acts: the slave girl who prophesied in Philippi (16.16–18), the maid Rhoda (12.13), Philip's four unmarried daughters who were prophets (21.9), Bernice, sister of Agrippa II (25.13, 23; 26.30), and Drusilla, the wife of Felix, the Roman procurator (24.24).

In the Pauline letters, the apostle does not list the Galilean women among the witnesses to the resurrection (1 Cor 15.5–8) but he does name many women who ministered in the early church. Among them are Phoebe, deacon of the church at Cenchreae and patron of Paul and many others (Rom 16.1–2), Junia, ''notable among the apostles'' (Rom 16.7), PRISCA, who with her husband Aquila was a coworker, risked her neck for Paul, and was head of a house church (Rom 16.3–5; 1 Cor 16.19). She and Aquila explained the Way of God more accurately to Apollos, an eloquent preacher from Alexandria (Acts 18.26). Other women heads of house churches are Nympha (Col 4.15), Mary, the mother of John Mark (Acts 12.12), Lydia (Acts 16.40), and perhaps Chloe who reported to Paul about divisions in Corinth (1 Cor 1.11), Martha who welcomed Jesus into her home (Lk 10.38), and the ''elect lady'' (a person or a community) to whom 2 John is addressed. Other women coworkers named by Paul are Euodia and Syntyche, who struggled at Paul's side in promoting the gospel (Phil 4.3), Mary (Rom 16.6), Tryphaena, Tryphosa, and Persis (Rom 16.12). Three other women are greeted by Paul, about whom little more is known: Rufus' mother (Rom 16.13), Julia, and Nereus' sister (Rom 16.15). The letter to Philemon is addressed as well to Apphia, ''our sister'' (Phlm 2). The term *adelphē* (''sister''), used also of Phoebe (Rom 16.1) may have been a title with ministerial connotations beyond the usual address of Christians toward female members of the community. In the Pastoral letters are listed qualifications for women deacons (1 Tm 3.11) and for ministering widows (1 Tm 5.3–16). There are instructions to treat older women as mothers and younger ones as sisters (1 Tm 5.2) as well as directions regarding their comportment (Ti 2.3–5). There are warnings about the vulnerability of women to false teachers (2 Tm 3.6).

Apocalypse. In the Book of Revelation female figures are used symbolically. Most notable is the personification of virtue and vice as a good woman versus an evil woman, a device found in other ancient literature, urging the reader to choose the former. In 12.1–6 a woman clothed with the sun gives birth to a child, which a dragon stands ready to devour. She symbolizes either the persecuted church or Mary giving birth to Jesus. The antithesis is the great harlot, "Babylon" (17.1–6), which stands for Rome, cast as idolatrous in contrast to the people of God. Similarly, in the message to the church at Thyatira, Christians are warned against a false prophet, "Jezebel," recalling the wife of Ahab, who led Israel into idolatry (2 Kgs 9.22). In the concluding vision of the multitude in heaven, the church is symbolized as a bride adorned for her wedding to the victorious Lamb, Christ (9.7; see also Eph 5.21–32; 2 Cor 11.2).

The portrait of women in the NT is mixed. There are passages such as Galatians 3.28 where distinctions between male and female are said to be made irrelevant by baptism into Christ, but there are also passages (Col 3.18–4.1; Eph 5.21–33; 1 Pt 3.1–7), where subordination of women in patriarchal households is upheld—a pattern that is replicated in the faith communities, who saw themselves as the "household of God" (Eph 2.19; 1 Tm 3.5). Some of the biblical authors appear to highlight and approve women's exercise of leadership in ministerial roles in the Christian communities (e.g., Jn 20.1–2, 11–18) and others advocate restriction of such. Passages such as 1 Cor 14.34–36 and 1 Tm 2.11–14 proscribe women from speaking in the gathered assembly or from teaching men. The author of 1 Timothy bases his reasoning on an interpretation of the creation story in Genesis that is quite opposite that of Paul, who alludes to this text in 1 Cor 11.8–12 when addressing a matter concerning Corinthian women prophets. The theological ANTHROPOLOGY of the Genesis accounts is also invoked in the gospel sayings about not divorcing (Mt 19.3–9; Mk 10.2–12).

Bibliography: A. O. BELLINS, *Helpmates, Harlots, Heroes: Women's Stories in the Hebrew Bible* (Louisville 1994). A. BRENNER, *The Israelite Woman: Social Role and Literary Type in Biblical Narrative* (Sheffield 1985). A. BRENNER and C. FONTAINE, *A Feminist Companion to Reading the Bible: Approaches, Methods and Strategies. Sheffield* (Sheffield 1997). P. DAY, ed. *Gender and Difference in Ancient Israel* (Minneapolis 1989). C. MEYERS, *Discovering Eve: Ancient Israelite Women in Context* (New York 1988). C. MEYERS, ed. *Women in Scripture: A Dictionary of Named and Unnamed Women in the Hebrew Bible, the Apocryphal/Deuterocanonical Books, and the New Testament* (Boston 2000). C. B. MILLET, *In God's Image: Archetypes of Women in Scripture* (San Diego 1991). C. NEWSOM and S. RINGE, eds., *The Women's Bible Commentary* (rev. ed. Louisville 1998). I. NOWELL, *Women in the Old Testament* (Collegeville, MN 1997). C. OSIEK and D. BALCH, *Families in the New Testament World* (Louisville 1997). I. PARDES, *Countertraditions in the Bible: A Feminist Approach* (Cambridge 1992). B. E. REID, *Choosing the Better Part? Women in the Gospel of Luke* (Collegeville, MN 1996). I. RICHTER REIMER, *Women in the Acts of the Apostles. A Feminist Liberation Perspective* (Minneapolis 1995). S. SCHNEIDERS, "Women in the Fourth Gospel and the Role of Women in the Contemporary Church," BTB 12 (1982) 35–45. E. SCHÜSSLER FIORENZA, *In Memory of Her: A Feminist Theological Reconstruction of Christian Origins* (New York 1984); *Searching the Scriptures* (2 vols. New York 1993, 1994); *But She Said: Feminist Practices of Biblical Interpretation* (Boston 1992). T. KARLSEN SEIM, *The Double Message: Patterns of Gender in Luke-Acts* (Nashville 1994). B. THURSTON, *Women in the New Testament* (New York 1998).

[B. E. REID]

WONDER

A state of mind excited by the perception of novelty or of something strange or not well understood. Both PLATO and ARISTOTLE speak of wonder as the point of origin for philosophy. In the *Theaetetus,* Socrates is recorded as saying, "Wonder is the feeling of a philosopher, and philosophy begins in wonder" (155D). Similarly, Aristotle refers to earlier philosophers when showing that wisdom is a speculative rather than a practical science: "It is owing to their wonder that men both now begin and at first began to philosophize. . . . And a man who is puzzled and wonders thinks himself ignorant . . . . Since they philosophized in order to escape from ignorance, evidently they were pursuing science in order to know, and not for any utilitarian end" (*Metaphysics* 982b 11–21).

The Greek verb used in these texts is θαυμάζειν, which can be translated by "wonder at" or "be astonished at," although the latter is perhaps too passive a sense to designate the origin of philosophical inquiry. St. THOMAS AQUINAS translates the Greek with the Latin *admirari,* a word that means "to regard with wonder." As is the case with many words referring to KNOWLEDGE, wonder involves a reference to the sense of sight. One's attention is arrested by something, he fixes his gaze upon it and undertakes to grasp it well. Yet wonder implies the intervention of INTELLECT in the process of knowing; it has a contemplative aspect not associated with animal knowing.

Kinds. Wonder sometimes signifies a feeling of reverence or awe appropriately referred to the divine. In Is 9.5 "a child is born to us" who is given the title "Wonderful" (or "Wonder-Counselor"); the Hebrew word used here is elsewhere attributed only to the marvelous works of God. This is a sense of wonder that has for its object a good that is admired for its greatness and beauty—something precious in the sight of men.

Another sense of wonder is the wonder caused by IGNORANCE. St. Thomas, in commenting on the text of Aristotle cited above, indicates that wonder (*admiratio*) comes from ignorance, because when one sees effects whose cause is hidden from him, he then wonders at the cause (*In 1 meta.* 3.55). Such an object may surpass the knower's powers or at least be new or unusual to him. While it is ignorance that is the cause of wonder, a search for the truth is its result. This sense of wonder, then, is referred to knowledge.

The wonder of awe is concerned with the greatness of its object, while the wonder caused by ignorance is concerned with the hidden cause of something regarded as extraordinary. The immediate effect of the first is praise, but of the second it is inquiry. Both kinds of wonder yield a certain pleasure, but the pleasure of the wonder of awe comes from contemplating a splendid object, whereas the pleasure of the other comes from the exercise of the power of REASONING, an activity connatural to man, as well as from the hope of achieving the good of the intellect.

Wonder and Truth. St. Thomas makes a perceptive analysis of man's experience of the wonder associated with an inquiry after TRUTH (*Summa theologiae* 1a2ae, 41.4 ad 5; 32.8). With ignorance its starting point and science its goal, a kind of tension is set up between these two terms. There is on the one hand a fear of ignorance and on the other a desire for and a hope of attaining knowledge. A desire for knowledge is in a general way natural to man, and a desire to know a particular object is stimulated when it is seen as unexplained. But when one recognizes his own ignorance of the object, he is thereby acknowledging an evil for his own intellect. Since he does not know the reason for what he sees, he fears to commit himself because of the danger of being wrong. His desire for knowledge will be frustrated if his ignorance persists; he will be deprived of the goal of knowledge. However, the very possibility, difficult though it may be, of discovering the hidden cause for what he has observed is what gives rise to HOPE. The very hope of discovery, which is an element of wonder, makes wonder a source of PLEASURE. Hope is, in fact, the element that impels the inquirer to pursue his search for the truth. It is wonder that makes the natural desire to know effective. The moral virtue that guides the good exercise of wonder is STUDIOUSNESS (*Summa theologiae* 2a2ae, 166, 167, 182; on intellectual dispositions, see Aristotle, *Metaphysics* 995a 1–18).

See Also: DOUBT; OPINION; APORIA.

Bibliography: J. M. BALDWIN, ed., *Dictionary of Philosophy and Psychology,* 3 v. in 4 (New York 1901–05; repr. Gloucester 1949–57) 2:820–821. L. M. RÉGIS, *Epistemology,* tr. I. C. BYRNE (New York 1959). G. GODIN, "La notion d'admiration," *Laval théologique et philosophique* 17 (1961) 35–75; "L'Admiration, principe de la recherche philosophique," *ibid.* 213–242.

[H. J. DU LAC]

WOODCOCK, JOHN, BL.

Franciscan priest, martyr; *alias* John Faringdon or Thompson; in religion, Martin of St. Felix; b. 1603 at Clayton-le-Woods (near Preston), Lancashire, England; hanged, drawn, and quartered Aug. 7, 1646 at Lancaster under Charles I. He was born into a middle class family headed by his Protestant father, Thomas, and his Catholic mother, Dorothy. He himself confessed Catholicism ca. 1622. Thereafter he studied for a year at St. Omer, then entered the English College at Rome (Oct. 1629). In May 1630, he entered the Capuchin friary in Paris, but the following year he joined the exiled English Franciscans at St. Bonaventure, Douai. There he received the habit from Bl. Henry HEATH (1631), was professed by Bl. Arthur BELL (1632), and was ordained (1634). He served as chaplain at Arras, Flanders, until he was sent to England in 1640. After working zealously for two years, he retired to a friary on the Continent. Late in 1643 or early 1644, he returned to England via Newcastle-on-Tyne and was arrested his first night in Lancashire. After a two-year imprisonment, he was tried with BB. Edward BAMBER and Thomas WHITAKER. All confessed to their priesthood and were therefore condemned. The Franciscan nuns at Taunton possess an arm-bone of the martyr, who was beatified by Pope John Paul II on Nov. 22, 1987 with George Haydock and Companions.

Feast of the English Martyrs: May 4 (England).

See Also: ENGLAND, SCOTLAND, AND WALES, MARTYRS OF.

Bibliography: R. CHALLONER, *Memoirs of Missionary Priests,* ed. J. H. POLLEN (rev. ed. London 1924), II, no. 185. J. H. POLLEN, *Acts of English Martyrs* (London 1891). M. STANTON, *Menology of England and Wales* (London, 1887) 383–84. J. THADDEUS, *The Franciscans in England 1600–1859,* 15 v. (London, 1898).

[K. I. RABENSTEIN]

WOODFEN, NICHOLAS, BL.

Priest, martyr; *alias* Nicholas Wheeler; *vere* Wheeler; arraigned as Nicholas Devereux; b. *c.* 1550 at Leominster, Herefordshire, England; hanged, drawn, and quartered Jan. 27, 1586 at Tyburn (London). He studied at Douai and Rheims, where he was ordained (1581). Thereafter he immediately began his ministry in London, especially among the barristers of the Inns of Court. He was caught by pursuivants and convicted for his priesthood. Fr. Nicholas was beatified by Pope John Paul II on Nov. 22, 1987, with George Haydock and companions.

Feast of the English Martyrs: May 4 (England).

See Also: ENGLAND, SCOTLAND, AND WALES, MARTYRS OF.

Bibliography: R. CHALLONER, *Memoirs of Missionary Priests,* ed. J. H. POLLEN (rev. ed. London 1924). J. H. POLLEN, *Acts of English Martyrs* (London 1891).

[K. I. RABENSTEIN]

WOODHOUSE, THOMAS, BL.

Elizabethan clerical protomartyr; b. *c.* 1535, place unknown; d. Tyburn, June 19, 1573. Woodhouse, ordained shortly before 1558, was dissatisfied with the Elizabethan religious settlement. He resigned his pastorate in Lincolnshire and took a position as tutor to the children of a Welsh gentleman. Religious beliefs again proved a source of difficulty, and Woodhouse soon resigned from his post. Arrested while celebrating Mass, he was imprisoned on May 14, 1561. In Fleet prison from 1561 to 1563, he continued to say Mass and to seek converts. A plague in 1563 forced the jailers to move the Fleet prisoners to Cambridgeshire. Sometime after returning to his London prison, Woodhouse requested entrance into the Jesuit Society (1572). His acceptance into the society seems to have partially inspired his appeal to William Cecil, Lord Burghley, that he advise Elizabeth I to submit to the pope. Woodhouse also wrote a number of pamphlets urging Englishmen to adhere to the true faith. His novel way of distributing them was to attach them to stones that he threw from his prison window. Cecil ordered his trial, and on June 16, 1573, Woodhouse was tried and convicted of high treason at the Guildhall, London. Three days later he was taken from Newgate prison to Tyburn, where he became the first priest executed for high treason on strictly religious grounds during the reign of Elizabeth I. He was beatified by Leo XIII on Dec. 9, 1886.

Feast: Dec. 1 (Jesuits).

See Also: ENGLAND, SCOTLAND, AND WALES, MARTYRS OF.

Bibliography: E. I. CARLYLE, *The Dictionary of National Biography from the Earliest Times to 1900* 21:873–874. B. CAMM, ed., *Lives of the English Martyrs Declared Blessed by Pope Leo XIII in 1886 and 1895,* 2 v. (New York 1904–14). H. FOLEY, ed., *Records of the English Province of the Society of Jesus,* 7 v. (London 1877–82) 7.3:859–861, 967; 7.4:1257–67. J. H. POLLEN, *Acts of the English Martyrs* (London 1891). J. N. TYLENDA, *Jesuit Saints & Martyrs* (Chicago 1998), 189–90.

[P. S. MCGARRY]

WOODSTOCK THEOLOGICAL CENTER

The mission of the Woodstock Theological Center, located on the campus of Georgetown University in Washington, D.C., is to reflect on the Roman Catholic theological tradition and bring it into to dialogue with other traditions and other disciplines. It takes its name from the Woodstock College and Seminary established by the Society of Jesus on a large tract of land in Woodstock, Maryland, in 1869.

In the beginning the Woodstock scholasticate served as the house of studies for both philosophy and theology for the Jesuits in the entire United States. Angelo M. Paresce, SJ (1817–79), who as provincial of the Maryland Province purchased the land, was named the first rector. The faculty consisted of mostly Italian professors who had been driven from their homeland because of revolution and persecution. The college's first prefect of studies (or dean) was Camillo Mazzella, SJ (1833–1900); he was named a cardinal in 1886. In addition to philosophy and theology, the course of studies included languages (classical and modern), literature, history, mathematics, and science. After World War II, with an increased number of vocations to the society, the philosophy faculty and students moved (1952) to Bellarmine College in Plattsburgh, New York, and subsequently (1957) to Loyola Seminary in Shrub Oak, New York. With the departure of the philosophers, Woodstock became exclusively a theologate. In 1969, prompted by a desire to do theology in an urban setting, Woodstock College, after celebrating the centenary of its founding in Maryland, moved to Morningside Heights, New York City, where it entered into a collaborative relationship with Union Theological Seminary and the Jewish Theological School.

Renowned Faculty. During the college's more than a century in existence, many of its faculty gained international reputations, and their manuals, originally written for Woodstock students, were often used as textbooks in other seminaries. Among these Jesuit professors were Benedict Sestini (1816–90), mathematician/astronomer; Aemilius M. De AUGUSTINIS (1829–98), dogmatic theologian; Aloysius Sabetti (1839–98), moral theologian; Gustave WEIGEL (1906–64), ecumenist; John Courtney MURRAY (1904–67), dogmatic theologian; Avery Dulles (1918–), ecclesiologist; Walter J. Burghardt (1914–), patristic scholar; and Joseph A. Fitzmyer (1920–), biblical scholar.

Method of Reflection. With the reconfiguration of Jesuit seminaries in 1974, Woodstock College was closed. The library—one of the finest Catholic theological libraries in the United States—was moved to Georgetown University, and the Woodstock Theological Center was established. The center's method of theological reflection is rooted in the spirituality of discernment and decision making of St. Ignatius of Loyola. The cognitional theory and theological method of Bernard LONERGAN, SJ, gives a contemporary philosophical foundation to Woodstock's Ignatian process of theological reflection. The Center engages in research and conducts conferences and seminars. It publishes books and articles on a variety of topics and issues, e.g., national and world justice, power, population, environment, consumerism, etc. *The Woodstock Report*, a quarterly newsletter, covers Woodstock activities, programs, and public education events.

[J. L. CONNOR]

WOOLMAN, JOHN

American Quaker preacher; b. Rancocas, N.J., Oct. 19, 1720; d. York, England, Oct. 7, 1772. He was a tailor by trade and lived in Mount Holly, N.J., during most of his life. In 1743 he experienced a call to the Quaker ministry and traveled throughout the colonies as a preaching Friend. A visit to Virginia in 1746 intensified his opposition to African-American slavery, and he devoted the rest of his life to attacking this institution. In addition to his sermons on slavery, Woolman published *Some Considerations on the Keeping of Negroes* (1754). His famed *Journal* (1773) is a record of his spiritual experience on his preaching tours. He died on an antislavery mission to England.

Bibliography: J. WHITNEY, *John Woolman: American Quaker* (Boston 1942). T. E. DRAKE, *Quakers and Slavery in America* (New Haven 1950).

[R. K. MACMASTER]

WORCESTER, ANCIENT SEE OF

Lat. *Wigorniensis,* diocese established some time before 680 by Abp. THEODORE OF CANTERBURY, as part of his reorganization of the Church in England and the division of dioceses, e.g., Lichfield, that were too large. The first bishop-elect was Tatfrid, a monk of WHITBY, who died before consecration; the first bishop to be consecrated was Bosel, who was replaced *c.* 691 by Oftfor, another monk of Whitby. The see included the territory of the lower Severn Valley inhabited by a mixed Anglian and Saxon people called the Hwicce, viz, the later counties of Worcestershire, Gloucestershire, and part of Warwickshire. The original cathedral was dedicated to St. Peter; the cathedral completed in 983 was dedicated to both St. Peter and the Bl. Virgin Mary by St. OSWALD OF YORK (961–991), who replaced the secular canons with Benedictine monks; and the present cathedral, begun in 1084 by St. WULFSTAN (1062–95) and often rebuilt because of fires or structural collapse, was rededicated in 1218 to the Bl. Virgin Mary, St. Peter, and the Holy Confessors Oswald and Wulfstan. King JOHN was buried here in 1216. The monastery was suppressed in 1540. CLEMENT VII, before his election, had been bishop of Worcester; under Hugh LATIMER the see became a diocese of the Church of England.

Bibliography: BEDE, *Eccl. Hist.* 4.23. W. DUGDALE, *Monasticon Anglicanum* 1:567–622. HEMINGUS, *Chartularium ecclesiae Wigorniensis,* ed. T. HEARNE, 2 v. (Oxford 1723), *passim.*. V. NOAKE, *The Cathedral Church of Worcester* (Worcester 1951). H. LUBIN, *The Worcester Pilgrim* (Worcester 1990) P. BARKER et. al., *A Short Architectural History of Worcester Cathedral* (Worcester 1994) U. ENGEL, *Die Kathedrale von Worcester* (Munich 2000).

[R. S. HOYT/EDS.]

WORCESTER, DIOCESE OF

The diocese of Worcester (Wigorniensis) is the suffragan of the metropolitan See of BOSTON, comprising Worcester County, the central section of Massachusetts, an area of 1,532 square miles. It was detached from the SPRINGFIELD diocese Jan. 28, 1950, and John Joseph Wright, auxiliary bishop of Boston became the first residential bishop. When Wright was transferred to Pittsburgh, Pa., Jan. 23, 1959, Bp. Bernard Joseph Flanagan, of Norwich, Conn., was named to Worcester Aug. 12 and installed Sept. 24, 1959.

Organized parish life in Worcester County was more than a century old when the diocese was erected. The city of Worcester, second largest in the state, was from the start a center of Catholic life. There Christ Church, later St. John's, was built in 1836 by Rev. James FITTON. A remarkable succession of spiritual leaders were associated with St. John's and the growth of Catholicism in city and county: Matthew W. Gibson, the builder of the pioneer churches in the county; John Boyce, whose novels under the pen name of Paul Peppergrass gave the Catholics a feeling of importance; Patrick T. O'Reilly, the first bishop of Springfield; and Thomas Griffin, who spent his entire priestly life from 1867 to 1910 at St. John's and saw Catholics emerge from the Civil War as a respected minority. Signs of the improved status were the publication in Worcester of the *Catholic Messenger,* a weekly, in 1887, and the *Catholic School and Home Magazine,* a monthly edited (1892–97) by Rev. Thomas J. CONATY, until he was appointed rector of The Catholic University of America, Washington, D.C.

Worcester County has a high percentage of Catholics of diverse national origins. The pioneer Irish were augmented by a steady influx of more Irish; a large immigration of French-Canadians; and at the end of the 19th century by the arrival of Poles, Lithuanians, Italians, Slovaks, and Syrians. When the diocese was established, there were 16 French parishes, six Polish, four Italian, three Lithuanian, one Syrian, and one Slovakian.

During the diocese's first decade, the Church became an integral part of the local community, and the national groups, while retaining their parish life, became more unified through diocesan organizations. Following the tenure of Bishop Flanagan, Timothy J. Harrington (1983–94) and Daniel Reilly (1994–) have served as ordinaries of the Worcester diocese that encompasses 127 parishes and 196 priests. A diocesan weekly, the *Catholic Free Press,* began publication May 4, 1951. In 1964 there were three Catholic colleges in the diocese, Holy Cross (1843) and Assumption (1904) for men, both located in Worcester, and Anna Maria (1946), in Paxton, for women.

Bibliography: J. J. MCCOY, *History of the Catholic Church in the Diocese of Springfield* (Boston 1900). J. G. DEEDY, JR., *The Church in Worcester, New England* (Worcester, Mass. 1956). R. L. REYNOLDS, ''Worcester: A New Diocese on the New England Scene,'' *Jubilee,* 3 (Feb. 1956) 6–17.

[W. L. LUCEY/EDS.]

WORD

Most broadly considered, a word is an expression of thought. Even for pre-Christian philosophers, and most emphatically with Christians, the term ''word'' had three main applications: (1) the external sound that communicates an idea, (2) the internal thought or concept itself, (3) supramundane reason (*see* WORD, THE).

Heraclitus's all-inclusive fire, the universal reason, is called Λόγος. The Stoics posited a reason-containing-the-germ-of-all-things (λόγος σπερματικός) which was the primal fire, the origin of all processes of condensation and rarefaction. The logos of Philo is both an aggregate of ideas in the Divine Mind and an all-pervading world soul [cf. F. C. Copleston, *History of Philosophy* (Westminster, Md. 1946–1975) 1:43, 389, 459]. Christian philosophers were always keenly aware that the LOGOS of the prologue to St. John's Gospel was the Second Person of the Trinity.

From ARISTOTLE we have a succinct statement regarding the relation between exterior and interior words: ''Spoken words are the symbols of mental experience and written words are the symbols of spoken words'' (*Interp.* 16a 3). St. THOMAS AQUINAS further observes that since the exterior word is better known to us because of its sensibility, it is called a word ''according to the imposition of the name.'' However, the interior word is prior in nature, because it is the ''efficient and final cause of the exterior word'' (*De vet.* 4.1).

With regard to the interior word or CONCEPT there is a slight but typical difference between St. AUGUSTINE and St. Thomas. St. Augustine's psychology can no more be cut off from its theological roots than his theology can be cut off from its psychological roots. Augustine starts from the premise that man is an image of God; God is triune and consubstantial, hence man must be in some way a reflection of that trinity and consubstantiality. Therefore he holds that when the mind, prompted by desire, conceives a word in knowledge, love embraces this mental offspring and unites it to its begetter. The word, for Augustine, is not only knowledge but knowledge which is linked inseparably with love (*verbum est igitur. . . cum amore notitia*). Thus he can see in man an image of the Trinity [*Trin.* 9.10–12; *Patrologia Latina,* ed. J. P. Migne, 2217 v. indexes 4 v. (Paris 1878–90) 42:969–970].

Aquinas's psychology is less intertwined with his theology. He holds that just as we convey our thoughts of objects to others by exterior words, so we express knowledge to ourselves by means of interior words or concepts (*De pot.* 9.5). The exterior word is an instrumental and conventional SIGN of the interior word. The interior word is not an instrumental but a formal sign of the object known. As such, it is not itself known as an object but fulfills a purely mediatorial role. It leads directly and immediately to a knowledge of what it signifies.

See Also: TERM (LOGIC).

Bibliography: J. MARITAIN, *Distinguish to Unite or the Degrees of Knowledge,* tr. G. B. PHELAN from 4th French ed. (New York 1959). E. H. GILSON, *The Christian Philosophy of Saint Augustine,* tr. L. E. M. LYNCH (New York 1960). B. J. F. LONERGAN, ''The Concept of *Verbum* in the Writings of St. Thomas Aquinas,'' *Theological Studies* 7 (1946) 349–392; 8 (1947) 35–79, 404–444; 10 (1949) 3–40, 359–393.

[J. F. PEIFER]

WORD, THE

To understand the role and importance of the Word in Trinitarian theology, one must consider the Biblical theme that is its background, that is, the word of God to man in SALVATION HISTORY.

Old Testament. Many passages in the Old Testament depict God as communicating with man by means of words (Gn 2.16–17; 6.13–21; 13.14–17; 26.2–5; Jos 3.7–8; Is 6.9–10). If it is He who takes the initiative on such occasions, in so doing He inaugurates an interpersonal exchange between man and Himself (Gn 12.1–3; 15.1–11; 35.1, 9–15; Ex ch. 3–4). Between the two extremes involved in these encounters, His word mediates; divine in origin, it is decidedly human in destination-reception (Ex 4.10–17). From man's point of view, that word has a function that is both instructive and transformative (Gn 17.5, 15; Jer 1.4–10; Ez 2.2–5). These characteristics come as no surprise when one considers the Speaker and the content of the message imparted. For in these words it is God Himself who manifests His saving good pleasure toward man. This cannot but be informative with regard to the divine attitude; what is more, it does not leave the human condition or situation unaltered. When God manifests by a word His intent to save, this is of itself sufficient to put that intention into execution.

New Testament. Particularly in its Johannine corpus, the New Testament develops the details of the interpersonal context in which God's word was found in the Old (cf. Sir 24.5–16; Prv 8.22–30; 1 Cor 1.24). Connected with personality in the men to whom it is addressed and in its source, the Father, or ὁ θεός, that Word is now presented as personal in itself as well. For if it is by a word that God the Father fashioned the universe (Heb 11.3), this came about through the Son (Heb 1.2), who by His own word sustains it (Heb 1.3). Jesus is that preexisting Son (Jn 1.17–18), or Word (Jn 1.14), through whom all things were made (Jn 1.1–3). This Word does not begin when it is heard in time. Still its prior relation to the Father is a reality as far as man is concerned only because it is continued in an earthly utterance where the eternal Word of God is God's historical Word-to-man. If Yahweh's word through the Prophets was at once instructive, transformative, and salvific, so is the word of God's Word-made-flesh, who has all things in common with the Father (Mt 9.5–7; Mk 2.1–12; Lk 5.18–26; Jn 6.63; 10.28; 11.25–26; 12.48–50; 14.6–7; 17.10; 1 Jn 1.1–4).

Subsequent Dogmatic and Theological Development. As the formulation of Christological doctrine took place in the postapostolic Church, a gradual but definite change of emphasis occurred. The transient interpersonalism of the New Testament (Theos—Word-made-flesh—men) was in no way denied; still, a great deal more attention was focused on the immanent relationship within the Godhead between Word and Theos. This did not happen without concomitant efforts on the part of apologists to link the origin of God's Word with the divine command effecting creation [see Justin, *1 Apologies* 6; *Patrologia Graeca*, ed. J. P. Migne, 161 v. (Paris 1857–66) 6:453]. In the Arian controversy of the 4th century, as the condemnation issued by Nicaea I indicates (H. Denzinger, *Enchiridion symbolorum*, ed. A. Schönmetzer [32d ed. Freiburg 1963 126]), a central point of dispute was the pretemporal utterance of the Word. After the latter's oneness with the Father had been authentically expressed in terms of CONSUBSTANTIALITY, their dis-

tinction was explained by the Cappadocians as arising from mutually opposed relations within the same Godhead [see Gregory of Nazianzus, *Oration* 29.16; *Patrologia Graeca*, 36:96; Basil, *Adversus Eunomium* 2.9; *Patrologia Graeca*, 29:588].

In the scholastic theology of the Middle Ages, attempts were made to achieve a limited but real understanding of the faith professed in the Trinitarian dogma. That in knowledge and love human psychology provides natural analogues for the divine processions of Word and Spirit was accepted and seen as connected with the belief that man is the IMAGE OF GOD (Thomas Aquinas, *Summa theologiae* 1a, 93.7). The procession of a mental word within the intelligence of man was likened to the utterance of the Word by the Father (*Summa theologiae* 1a, 27.2–4).

Contemporary Catholic theology has sought to place the doctrine of the Word in the context of salvation history more explicitly again by showing its continuity with God's word in the Old Testament. This has been done in studies taking the form of a phenomenology of the divine word to men. The result is a description of the conditions and implications noted in its historical utterance throughout the Scriptures [R. Latourelle, *Théologie de la révélation* (Bruges 1963)]. It has been pointed out that this perspective offers a clear point of contact with Trinitarian theology for the fact that it places within God's conscious life the origin of a word spoken to man in time [S. Moore, "The Word of God: Kerygma and Theorem, a Note," *Heythrop Journal* 5 (1964) 268–275].

There has taken place as well a renewal of interest in the question of consciousness within the Trinity. The latter is proposed as having a role to play in explaining the unique relation between the Word and His humanity. For a survey of a number of Catholic opinions, see P. De Letter, "The Theology of God's Self-Gift," *Theological Studies*, 24 (1963) 402–422.

Similarly, it has been suggested that belief in a Word and Spirit proceeding within the Deity should occasion a rethinking and further elaboration in the Christian's concept of God's perfection. To complement the notion of PURE ACT realized in the divine essence, that of unity of order (constituted by the society of Divine Persons in their conscious giving and taking origin) is a necessity [*see* B. Lonergan, *De Deo trino,* v.2 (Rome 1964) 208–215].

See Also: FILIATION; GENERATION OF THE WORD; LOGOS; MISSIONS, DIVINE; PROCESSIONS, TRINITARIAN; TRINITY, HOLY ARTICLES ON.

Bibliography: A. MICHEL, *Dictionnaire de théologie catholique*, ed. A. VACANT et al., 15 v. (Paris 1903–50; Tables Générales 1951–) 15.2:2639–72. R. SCHNACKENBURG and C. HUBER, *Lexikon für Theologie und Kirche,* ed. J. HOFER and K. RAHNER, 10 v. (2d, new ed. Freiburg 1957–65); suppl., *Das Zweite Vatikanische Konzil: Dokumente und Kommentare,* ed. H. S. BRECHTER et al., pt. 1 (1966) 6:1122–28. G. KITTEL, *Theologisches Wörterbuch zum Neuen Testament* (Stuttgart 1935–) 4:126–140. O. CULLMANN, *The Christology of the New Testament,* tr. S. C. GUTHRIE and C. A. M. HALL (rev. ed. Philadelphia 1963). J. L. MCKENZIE, "The Word of God in the OT," *Theological Studies,* 21 (1960) 183–206.

[C. J. PETER]

WORKER PRIESTS

From 1944 to 1954 a small number of priests in France and Belgium shared the life of the working class. Never more than 100 in number, these priests were little known until their suppression in March 1954. Their existence posed certain problems, and their suppression left other serious problems unsolved. These included, along with the question of the evangelization of the working classes then largely estranged from the Church, the question of the relation of the Church in the world, the theology of the priesthood, and the relationship between the priest and the layman.

The phenomenon cannot be understood outside its historical context. The 20th century in France began in an atmosphere of struggle and misunderstanding. Church and State were separated by the abrogation of the Napoleonic concordat; the religious orders were expelled. After World War I laicism was less hostile, but the French working class was already profoundly de-Christianized. Class structures of the industrial era became a sign of religious division. The *bourgeoisie,* unbelieving a century earlier, rallied to religion as a force of social stability, and the Church was reduced almost to the status of a fief of the middle classes. Socialist movements hostile to the Church presented a promise of hope to the working classes. In 1927 Plus XI said to the Abbé CARDIJN, founder of the Jocists (*see* JOCISM), that the great scandal of the Church in the 19th century was that she had in fact lost the working classes.

Although there was a realization that the working classes were drifting away from religion, there was not at the time a consciousness of the extent of their de-Christianization, or of its causes and consequences. The traditional practice of baptism maintained the illusion that France was a Catholic nation. A minority of Christian workers formed a separate labor union, and CATHOLIC ACTION, born with the Jocists, led youth, lay and clerical, to new engagements in the events preceding World War II: the general strikes of June 1936, the Popular Front, the wars in Spain and Ethiopia, and the rise of Fascism and Nazism. An important intellectual movement was astir.

J. Meritain, E. Mounier (*Esprit*), the *Vie Intellectuelle, Sept,* and other forces hastened the awareness of the "wall" (to use the expression of Cardinal SUHARD) between the Christian and the modern world.

The disrupting influence of the war and the occupation of France affected the situation of the workers as well as that of the Church. French youth were deported to the factories of Germany, and the bishops appealed to young priests to join them secretly as workers. Nearly all were discovered, imprisoned, and sent to concentration camps or forcibly repatriated. One of these, Henri Pertin, OP, published on his return *Prêtre-ouvrier en Allemagne* (Paris 1945; English tr. *Priest-Workman in Germany,* New York 1947).

The experience of these priests confirmed that of others who were prisoners or engaged in the Resistance and the maquis. All discovered during those difficult years the real religious situation of the working-class world, and the value of their presence in a proletarian milieu.

In 1942 Father Augros founded the seminary of the Mission de Paris in Lisieux, and in 1943–44 the Abbé H. Godin began the Mission de Paris. The latter's report, *France pays de mission?,* appeared in September 1943 and sold 100,000 copies. Like the rest of the French Church, Cardinal Suhard was deeply impressed by Godin's book.

Although Godin's book did not formally propose the experiment of the worker priest, it nevertheless opened the way for it. France, which had given thousands of foreign missionaries to the Church, had itself become a missionary country. Missionary adaptation was a familiar idea since Gregory the Great. Was this not simply a new way of reaching non-Christians where they were to be found? It seemed important that the Church should not be conceived as something cut off from the world to which it must bring the message of Christ. To make its presence felt, it was proposed that priests should mingle with the workers in factories and on construction sites and docks. They would be workers like the rest, with no special privileges. Being diocesan and religious priests, they would live alone or in small communities of two or three, and work to form small groups of laymen to give witness to the faith. They were to live by their labor and to share the problems of their fellow workers. The expectation that they should join labor unions posed a problem, because of the variety of unions from which to chose. Generally they chose the union whose operations appeared to be the most efficacious. They shared in various manifestations of solidarity in the struggles and hopes of their fellows in such matters as housing, antiracism, and peace. They did not regard their engagement as a temporary thing, but rather as a vocation consciously entered upon for life. It was no concerted or structured movement created by a founder. Rather it was a current emerging from various sources, a missionary awakening of the Church centered on the point where the separation between the Church and the world was most in evidence—the working class.

Rome intervened in 1953–54 to stop the experiment. Later, in September 1959, the possibility of working was further restricted, leading to the demise of the vocation.

Bibliography: G. SIEFER, *La Mission des Prêtres-ouvriers: Les faits et conséquences,* tr. M. DEVIGNOT and J. ERNEST (Paris 1963). *Les Prêtres ouvriers* (Paris 1954). H. PERRIN, *Itinéraire d'Henri Perrin, prêtre ouvrier 1914–1954* (Paris 1958). D. L. EDWARDS, ed., *Priests and Workers: An Anglo-French Discussion* (London 1961).

[D. ROBERT]

WORKS OF GOD

Biblical expression denoting both the acts in history that God performed and the objects in nature made by Him. The theme is common to both the Old Testament and the New Testament.

In the early Old Testament literature, especially the YAHWIST traditions of the Pentateuch, God is presented anthropomorphically, as if He worked in a human way. Thus, He molds man out of clay (Gn 2.7), forms woman from the man's rib (Gn 2.21–22), makes skin garments (Gn 3.21), "comes down" to confuse men's speech (Gn 11.7), and writes the Decalogue with His finger (Ex 31.18).

Since the Israelites' experience of God was an experience of salvation, their consciousness was first directed to His "mighty works" in history, performed with "strong hand and outstretched arm" (Dt 4.34; 5.15; etc.). The "wonderful works of God" were primarily the escape from Egypt, crossing of the Red Sea, journey through the desert, Sinai covenant, and occupation of the promised land. These historical deeds of God were ceaselessly celebrated in the prophetic literature (Hos 11.1–3; Is 12.4; Jer 2.2–7) and in the hymns of the Psalter [Ps 104(105); 134(135).8–14; 135(136).10–24]. The Prophets denounced the people for their failure to recognize God's continued working in the present (Is 5.12; Jgs 2.7, 10), and they proclaimed that His work in the future would constitute a judgment on their infidelity (Is 10.12; 28.21; Hab 1.5).

While the idea of creation was already latent in early times (Jgs 5.20), it became explicit only through reflection upon God's saving acts in history. If Yahweh was master not only of Israel but of all nations, it was but a step further to regard Him as artisan and master of the universe, so that His "works" were extended to embrace all of nature. Jeremiah referred to God's work of creation (Jer 5.22; 27.2; 31.35–36), and it became a common theme after the Exile, especially in Deutero-Isaiah (Is 40.12–13, 28; 42.5; etc.) and in the hymns of the Psalter [Ps 8; 18(19); 28(29); 32(33); 103 (104); 148]. The Lord of history is also God of nature [Ps 144(145).4, 9, 10, 17].

In the New Testament God's work is the salvation of mankind, begun in the Old Testament but fulfilled in the work of Christ (Acts 2.22). The theme occurs especially in St. John: the works of Jesus are the works of God Himself (Jn 4.34), which the Father has shown Him (5.20), the proof of His mission (5.36) and of God's continued activity among men (9.3–4). For St. Paul, God's continuing work is the building up of the Church (Rom 14.20); hence, the apostolate is the Apostle's work for God (1 Cor 9.1;16.10), but more profoundly the work of God in him (1 Cor 15.58; Phil 1.6).

Bibliography: *Encyclopedic Dictionary of the Bible,* translated and adapted by L. HARTMAN (New York, 1963) 2603–04. C. R. NORTH and G. A. BUTTRICK, *The Interpreter's Bible* (Nashville 1962) 4:872–873. G. KITTEL, *Theologisches Wörterbuch zum Neuen Testament* (Stuttgart 1935) 2:633–640. G. E. WRIGHT, *God Who Acts* (Studies in Biblical Theology 8; Chicago 1952). F. MICHAÉLI, *Dieu à l'image de l'homme* (Neuchâtel 1950). J. L. MCKENZIE, "God and Nature in the Old Testament," *The Catholic Biblical Quarterly* 14 (Washington, DC 1952) 18–39, 124–145.

[C. J. PEIFER]

WORLD (IN THE BIBLE)

In the Old Testament there is no special Hebrew word for world in the sense of the ordered universe that the Greeks called the cosmos (κόσμος). The author of Genesis states that God created "the heavens and the earth" (*haššāmayim wᵉhā'āreṣ:* Gn 1.1). Elsewhere the universe is considered as consisting of the heavens, the earth, and the sea (Ex 20.4), or the heavens, the nether world, the earth, and the sea (Jb 11.8–9). For the Israelites the earth was the center of the universe, and the words *tēbel* and *'ereṣ,* both meaning earth, are often translated as "world" [Ps 9A.9; 17(18).16; 18 (19).5]. Also, the terms *hakkōl,* "everything" [Jer 10.16; Ps 102(103).19] or *kōl,* "all" (poetic, as in Is 44.24; Ps 8.7) are sometimes synonymous with world. The physical world was described by the Israelites according to the appearances of things, resembling those notions of the universe common to the West-Semitic milieu of the 2d and 1st millennia B.C.; for details, *see* COSMOGONY (IN THE BIBLE).

In the deutero-canonical books of the Old Testament that were originally written in Greek and in Jewish centers influenced by Hellenistic philosophy, the word κόσμος (world) in the sense of universe often occurs, replacing the phrase "the heavens and the earth" of Gn 1.1 (Wis 7.17; 9.9; 11.17, 22; 13.2; 16.17; 2 Mc 7.23; 8.18; 13.14).

In the New Testament the word κόσμος (world) occurs frequently in the sense of the material universe created by God (Mt 25.34; Jn 17.5, 24; Acts 17.24; Rom 1.20; Eph 1.4). In Heb 11.3 the Greek word αἰών (AEON, period of time, age) refers to the material world; the corresponding Hebrew word 'ôlām was sometimes used of the material world in post-Biblical Hebrew.

In many passages "the world" is the earth, the dwelling place of mankind (Mk 14.9; Jn 12.25; 16.21; 1 Cor 5.10; 1 Tm 6.7), in contrast to heaven, the dwelling place of God, whence Christ came (Jn 1.9; 3.17; 6.14; 10.36; 13.1; 1 Tm 1.15; 3.16; Heb 10.5). *See* HEAVEN (IN THE BIBLE). The things of "this world" are often contrasted with those of heaven (Mt 16.26; Mk 8.36; Lk 9.25; 1 Cor 7.31, 33), and what are earthly or worldly realities with heavenly or spiritual ones (Mt 16.26; Mk 8.36; Lk 9.25; Jn 3.31; 1 Cor 7.31, 33; Heb 8.5; 9.1, 23; 1 Jn 2.15; 3.17; Ti 2.12). In Lk 12.30 the phrase "the nations of the world" refers to the Gentiles or the non-Jewish world (Rom 11.12, 15). Sometimes "the world" means mankind itself (Mt 5.14; 18.7; Jn 1.29; 3.17; Rom 3.6, 19; 1 Cor 1.27), especially those who are the objects of God's love (Jn 3.16; 6.33, 51; 12.47).

Finally, in the Johannine and Pauline writings a new moral significance of this word developed, whereby "the world," i.e., mankind, becomes involved in God's plan of salvation. In this sense "the world" often stands for all that is hostile to God and His salvific plan.

In the Johannine writings, "the world," i.e., "mankind," is indeed generally presented as the object of Christ's saving mission rather than as opposed to His Kingdom; God loves it (Jn 3.16) and sent His Son to save it (Jn 3.17); Christ is the light who has come into the world (Jn 3.19) as its Savior (Jn 4.42). Yet, according to the prologue of John's Gospel, the Light is rejected (Jn 1.5, 10), and from chapter six onward (and especially from 13.2 to the end of chapter 17), Christ and His disciples are presented more and more in opposition to "the prince of the world," i.e., SATAN (Jn 12.31; 14.30; 16.11; 8.44–45) and his followers; in 7.7, "the world" hates Jesus; in 8.23, the non-believing Jews are of "this world," but Jesus is not; in 9.39 and 12.31, Christ has come to judge "the world." The sin of "the world" and the cause of its rejection is its refusal to believe in the Son (Jn 8.44–45; 9.39–41; 16.9; 1 Jn 2.15–17; 5.4–5).

In the Pauline writings "the world" may mean mankind in general, as opposed to the followers of Christ (1 Cor 5.20; 2 Cor 5.19), or the earth with its material goods in contrast to "the things of the Lord" (1 Cor 7.32; *see also* 1 Cor 2.12; 7.29; Col 3.1–2). "The spirit of the world," in contrast to "the Spirit that is of God," is characterized by a refusal to recognize the primacy of God (1 Cor 2.6, 12). "The Prince" of the world and its personified "powers" that are opposed to Christ's rule have been overcome by His salvific work (Eph 2.2; Col 2.15; *See Also* Jas 1.27; 4.4; 2 Pt 2.20).

In both the Johannine and Pauline writings, however, "the world" is regarded also as the possession of Christ by virtue of its creation and the Redemption. The original unity of the world, of the entire cosmic universe, was created by and for Him who is "the image of the invisible God" (Col 1.15–16; Jn 1.3). By His redemptive sacrifice, Christ has resumed Lordship of "the world" (Phil 2.10; Jn 12.32) and restored the whole cosmos to unity under Himself. God's purpose is "to re-establish all things in Christ" (Eph 1.10). The Church, which is the body of Christ in the new and definitive world order inaugurated by the risen Lord, continues His work in this present "world" (Col 1.18; 3.1–4; Eph 1.20–21; Jn 16.33; 17.20–23).

Bibliography: *Encyclopedic Dictionary of the Bible,* translated and adapted by L. HARTMAN (New York, 1963) 2604–06. H. SASSE, G. KITTEL, *Theologisches Wörterbuch zum Neuen Testament* (Stuttgart 1935) 3:867–896. H. W. HERTZBERG and E. DINKLER, *Die Religion in Geschichte und Gegenwart,* 7 v. (3d ed. Tübingen 1957–65) 6:1615–21. L. CERFAUX, *Christ in the Theology of St. Paul,* tr. G. WEBB and A. WALKER (New York 1959) 419–438. O. CULLMANN, *Christ and Time,* tr. F. V. FILSON (rev. ed. Philadelphia 1964). R. H. LIGHTFOOT, *St. John's Gospel: A Commentary,* ed. C. F. EVANS (Oxford 1956). R. SCHNACKENBURG, *God's Rule and Kingdom,* tr. J. MURRAY (New York 1963).

[J. L. RONAN]

WORLD COUNCIL OF CHURCHES

This article treats the origins, basis, membership, purposes, and organization of the World Council of Churches (WCC).

Origins. The WCC is the organized expression of three streams of ecumenical life. Two of these—LIFE AND WORK and FAITH AND ORDER—merged at the constituting assembly of the Council at Amsterdam (1948). The third stream, the missionary movement, organized in the INTERNATIONAL MISSIONARY COUNCIL, had its confluence with the WCC at the assembly at New Delhi (1961).

In a sense the modern ECUMENICAL MOVEMENT received its chief inspiration and impetus in the World Missionary Conference at Edinburgh (1910). As a result, a network of interdenominational councils in a score of countries was established in the succeeding decade, while many of the pioneers of the WCC were recruited from the missionary movement.

The institution of the WCC resulted from the decisions of the leaders of two ecumenical organizations. The Life and Work movement, associated especially with the name of Archbishop Nathan SÖDERBLOM, had called the churches to manifest Jesus Christ as Lord not only of the individual but of every realm of social, economic, and political life, and provided an international means for them to do so. The Faith and Order movement, associated especially with the name of Bishop Charles BRENT, provided an organization in which the separated bodies of Christendom could come together to study the areas of doctrinal and ecclesiological agreement and difference in the conviction that the churches have an essential unity in Christ. By 1937 it was becoming clear that Life and Work could not go forward without dealing with the theological issues of Christian unity, and that Faith and Order could not progress unless the churches began to work together in those areas in which they had found that there was a substantial measure of agreement.

On the eve of their conferences at Oxford and Edinburgh in 1937, representatives of the two movements met and proposed combining the two in a world council of churches, and recommended the establishing of a Committee of Fourteen to work out a plan for such a council. The conferences accepted the proposals. A conference at Utrecht (1938) agreed on the questions of basis and authority of the proposed world council, and completed interim arrangements that would serve until the council could be formally constituted at an assembly. The Committee of Fourteen approved the proposals, including one to establish a Provisional Committee for the WCC in process of formation. The International Missionary Council meeting in 1938 at Madras agreed to negotiate with the proposed WCC.

The second meeting of the Provisional Committee (January 1939) planned to hold the first assembly of the WCC in August 1941, but World War II intervened. Although no full Provisional Committee met between 1940 and 1946, the members gathered in geographical groups in the United States, and Great Britain, and Europe (Geneva).

When the Provisional Committee met in February 1946 it was discovered that World War II had furthered the formation of the WCC.

Basis of Membership. The First Assembly at Amsterdam, declared: "The World Council of Churches is a fellowship of churches which accept the Lord Jesus Christ as God and Saviour." This was the formula on

which the original invitation had been issued; by the time of the meeting of the Provisional Committee in Geneva, 1946, it had been accepted by 95 churches. At the time of the First Assembly 145 churches accepted membership on this basis. Soon the formulation of the basis gave rise to questions, inquiries, and requests for a clearer definition of its Christocentricity, a more explicit expression of Trinitarian belief, and a specific reference to the Holy Scriptures. The result was the formulation adopted by the Third Assembly at New Delhi (1961) stating: "The World Council of Churches is a fellowship of churches which confess the Lord Jesus Christ as God and Saviour according to the Scriptures and therefore seek to fulfil together their common calling to the glory of the one God, Father, Son and Holy Spirit."

Membership. The First Assembly was constituted by invitation, but since then membership of the WCC has been by application. The assembly and the central committee have from time to time formulated criteria of membership other than acceptance of the basis. These criteria include autonomy, stability, size, and relationship with other churches. The Third Assembly decided that as a rule no church with an inclusive membership of less than 10,000 should be admitted, and authorized the creation of a special category of associated churches for churches that satisfy the criteria except the one concerning size.

The WCC enters into working relationship with national and regional councils that accept its basis and invites such councils to send fraternal delegates to the assembly and representatives to the central committee. The WCC also maintains relationships with such world confessional bodies as may be designated by the central committee, and bodies so designated are invited to send fraternal delegates to the assembly and advisers to the central committee.

Purposes. The WCC is a council of Churches. It has no legislative authority over members. It exists to facilitate common action by the churches, to promote cooperation in study, to stimulate the growth of ecumenical and missionary consciousness in all the churches, to support the churches in their missionary and evangelistic task, to maintain relations with national and regional councils, world confessional bodies and other ecumenical organizations, and to call world conferences on specific subjects as occasion may require.

This formal list of functions does not adequately reveal the rich and full life that the WCC increasingly enjoys, or the variety and scope of its tasks. The council exists to serve the churches and to help them view their task as a part of the task of the whole Church in the whole world. It provides a forum for the churches to share theological insights and experiences of renewal. They thus receive correction from each other, learn to speak and act together on vital issues, and are prepared for that deeper unity that they seek.

As custodian of the tradition of faith and order, the WCC seeks "to proclaim the essential oneness of the Church of Christ and to keep prominently before the churches the obligation to manifest that unity and its urgency for the work of evangelism." As guardian of the tradition of life and work and of the International Missionary Council it holds continually before the churches the concern for unity understood in the context of the total calling of the Church. In providing the means whereby the churches may fulfil their common calling, the council seeks increasingly to be an instrument of the Holy Spirit for Church renewal.

The integration of the International Missionary Council into the WCC meant that the churches now see their task in mission and evangelism within a total ecumenical context. In this setting questions such as proselytism and religious liberty, the missionary task on all six continents, and confrontation with men of other faiths and no faith have gained a wholly new connotation.

Organization. The WCC has legislative and executive committees and officers.

The principle authority is that of the assembly, which is composed of official representatives appointed by the churches or groups of churches that make up the council. Seats in the assembly are allocated by the central committee to the member churches with regard for such factors as numerical size, adequate confessional representation, and geographical distribution. The members of the assembly are both clerical and lay, men and women.

The main committee of the assembly is the central committee, elected by the assembly from among its delegates. It normally meets annually in different parts of the world and acts in lieu of the assembly. The central committee appoints an executive committee, which normally meets twice a year. The chairman and vice chairman of the Central Committee, together with the general secretary of the WCC, are the recognized officers of the council.

The WCC experienced a significant growth in the first 25 years of its existence, growing from 145 churches in 1948 to more than 260, including all the major Orthodox and most of the larger Protestant churches. The entrance into membership of the WCC of the majority of the Orthodox Churches strengthened the WCC as an instrument of the ecumenical movement. Orthodoxy has played an important role from the very beginning of the WCC, especially in Faith and Order. The situation of

many of these churches, their openness in giving to and receiving from their fellow member churches, means that no aspect of the WCC's life is uninfluenced by their tradition, experience, and understanding of the Christian faith.

From the late 1960s onwards, the WCC broadened its constituency, with the admission in 1969 of the Kimbanguists of Zaire (now Democratic Republic of Congo) its first member from the native African churches. Admitted at the same time was the Evangelical Pentecostal church "Brazil for Christ," strengthening Pentecostal participation significantly, though two Pentecostal churches of Chile had joined earlier. This would be followed by other such churches.

Third World Issues. The growth of Third World participation in the WCC also led to a greater influence in its leadership. Philip Potter, a black Methodist from the Caribbean, became general secretary in 1972, succeeding Eugene Carson Blake, an American who had become general secretary in 1966. In 1968 M. M. Thomas of India became chairman of the central committee, succeeding Franklin Clark Fry, also of the United States.

From the 1970s onwards, tensions began to emerge in the WCC. Many of the tensions were the result of its increased emphasis on Third World issues, a trend first given impetus by a 1966 Church and Society conference in Geneva. In 1973 Potter told the central committee that the shift to Third World emphases had brought problems: U.S. churches feeling less involved; European churches charging a decrease in WCC theological and churchly concern; Orthodox Churches criticizing decreased emphasis on Christian unity while attention was focused on overcoming war, racism, economic injustice, and other evils blocking unity of the whole human community. The central committee received a message from the Moscow patriarchate charging that a 1973 conference on Salvation Today, sponsored by the WCC Commission on World Mission and Evangelism, showed insufficient concern with salvation as eternal life in God. A message from Patriarch Demetrios of Istanbul warned against letting social and political concerns overshadow religious goals. Many of these tensions remained through the next two decades. Several Orthodox Churches threatened to leave the WCC if things did not improve.

Conclusion. To the question "What is the World Council of Churches?" the answer has been given by the first general secretary of the council, Dr. W. A. VISSER'T HOOFT, in his address to the First Assembly: "We are a Council of Churches, not *the* Council of the one undivided Church. Our name indicates our weakness and our shame before God, for there can be and is finally only one Church of Christ on earth. But our name indicates that we are aware of that situation, that we do not accept it passively, that we move forward towards the manifestation of the one Holy Church. Our Council represents therefore an emergency solution—a stage on the road—a body living between the time of complete isolation of the churches from each other and the time—on earth as in heaven—when it will be visibly true that there is one shepherd and one flock.''

As the WCC entered the third Christian millennium, it counted on its membership rolls 342 churches, an increase from the 145 member churches at its founding. The WCC represented over 450 million Christians in more than 115 countries. These churches belonged to the following traditions: Anglican (34), Eastern Orthodox (15), Oriental Orthodox (6), Old Catholic (5), and Protestant (235); among these were Uniting and United (23), Pentecostal (7), and African Instituted churches (10). While the Roman Catholic Church maintained observer status at the WCC, it was a full member of the Faith and Order Commission, and served in a consultative capacity on the Mission & Evangelism board. The headquarters of the WCC is in Geneva, Switzerland.

Bibliography: R. ROUSE and S. C. NEILL, eds., *A History of the Ecumenical Movement, 1517–1948* (London 1954). N. GOODALL, *The Ecumenical Movement* (2d ed. London 1964). WORLD COUNCIL OF CHURCHES, *The First Assembly of the World Council of Churches: The Official Report,* ed. W. A. VISSER 'T HOOFT, v. 5 of *Man's Disorder and God's Design,* 5 v. in 2 (New York 1949); *The Evanston Report: The Second Assembly of the World Council of Churches, 1954,* ed. W. A. VISSER 'T HOOFT (New York 1955); *The New Delhi Report,* ed. W. A. VISSER 'T HOOFT (New York 1962), contains constitution and rules of the World Council of Churches; *The World Council of Churches: Its Process of Formation* (Geneva 1946); *The First Six Years* (Geneva 1954); *Evanston to New Delhi, 1954–1961* (Geneva 1961). *Ecumenical Review* (Geneva 1948–). E. DUFF, *The Social Thought of the World Council of Churches* (New York 1956). N. GODALL, ed., *The Uppsala Report, 1968* (Geneva 1968).

[W. A. VISSER'T HOOFT/L. E. COOKE/T. EARLY/EDS.]

WORLD SOUL (ANIMA MUNDI)

A principle regarded by some as animating the universe much as the human soul animates man's body. The notion of an organic and living world ruled by spiritual forces rather than by mechanical laws is not peculiar to primitive minds; it is found in the writings of early philosophers. The expression ''world soul'' or *anima mundi* (Gr. τοῦ κόσμου ψυχή) was apparently first used by Greek commentators to explain the hylozoic doctrines of the Pre-Socratics (*see* HYLOZOISM; GREEK PHILOSOPHY). The concept was further developed by the Socratics, enjoyed some currency in the Neoplatonic tradition, and reappeared again in various forms in Renaissance and modern thought.

Greek Thought. The world soul occupies a central position in the poetic-religious cosmogony of the *Ti-maeus.* There PLATO states that the *anima mundi* is a compound of three elements, an indivisible and unchangeable substance, a substance that is divisible and generated by material bodies, and a third and intermediate kind of substance partaking of the nature of both the indivisible and the divisible. The Demiurge placed the world soul ''in a mean between the indivisible, and the divisible and material'' (*Tim.* 35A). Even in such poetic and unprecise language as that of the *Timaeus,* it seems evident that the world soul plays an intermediary role between the forms and the material world. The soul is the principle of order and life that rules over the material world, which it excels in origin and nobility; it presides over the movement of heaven and the stars, and from it the Demiurge derives individual human souls (*Tim.* 41D–42).

The Platonic doctrine of the world soul was rejected by ARISTOTLE. The Aristotelian corpus, nonetheless, reflects some inspiration from the *Timaeus,* for the fragmentary dialogue on philosophy, Περὶ φιλοσοφίας, mentions such doctrines as the animation of the heavens and the existence of principles of eternal and regular movement. In works of undoubted authenticity, moreover, Aristotle speaks of heat as the principle of life in the sun; in living beings this becomes the vital breath or πνεῦμα that, together with ether, is the most noble and divine among the elements (*Gen. animal.* 736b 33–737a 7).

With the Stoics the πνεῦμα is the physical and rational principle of order and generation in the world (Cicero, *De natura deorum* 2.7.19), sustained as it is by a force (*vis*) that they call *animum mundi* and identify with God. From this principle are derived the *animantia principia* or λόγοι σπερματικοί (*see* STOICISM).

Patristic and Medieval Thought. For Neoplatonists such as PLOTINUS, the world soul becomes once more the connecting link between the suprasensual world and the sensual world, i.e., between the Nous and matter. In its superior part it looks upward to the Nous, while in its inferior part it looks downward toward the world of nature, which it creates according to the ideas contemplated in the Nous (*Enneads* 3.8.4).

This conception of a universe that is alive and pervaded by a soul or by rational and divine forces is presupposed in the religious contemplation of the universe that forms an essential part of Hellenistic culture. In the first centuries of Christian literature one finds copious references to these animistic doctrines; they furnish, as it were, the background for Christian teaching on God's omnipresence and paternity. Thus, it is the spirit of God that, in the words of Gn 1.2, ''moved over the waters.'' St. Paul had already made use of a famous Stoic verse to remind the Greeks that even their poets had felt the paternity of God (Acts 17.28). The Greek Fathers resort quite frequently to the Neoplatonic doctrine of the three hypostases to explain the mystery of the Holy Trinity, wherein the Holy Spirit is often likened to the *anima mundi*. (*See* NEOPLATONISM.)

The attitude of the Latin Fathers, however, is basically different. They are more concerned with the nature of the relationship among the three Divine Persons than with the kind of relationship existing between the Holy Trinity and the world through creation. Accordingly, they are not so eager to compare the *anima mundi* to the Holy Spirit. A typical example of this attitude is that of St. Augustine, who considers the problem of the world soul a *"magna atque abdita quaestio"* (Cons. Evang. 1.23.35) and never identifies the *anima mundi* with a Divine Person. Indeed, he seems uncertain as to whether one can properly speak of a world soul and an animated universe (*Retract.* 1.11.4).

The Middle Ages came to know the doctrine of the world soul mainly through Plato's *Timaeus* in its partial translation and commentary by CALCIDIUS, the commentary on the *Somnium Scipionis* by MACROBIUS, and the *De consolatione philosophiae* of BOETHIUS. In general, the scholastics rejected the doctrine of the *anima mundi* as a profane doctrine opposed to Christian theology. Yet with the 12th-century revival of Platonism centered around the School of Chartres, the doctrine of the world soul became once more an important item of speculation that was not without some reference to the mystery of the Holy Trinity (cf. William of Conches, *Philosophia mundi* 1.15; *Patrologia Latina* 172:46, 90:1130). One of Abelard's propositions condemned at Sens states precisely that the world soul is the Holy Spirit, but it is questionable whether this accurately represented Abelard's thought.

Renaissance Revival. When Platonic natural philosophy was replaced by peripatetic physics between the 12th and 13th centuries, the belief in the world soul began gradually to disappear, not to be revived until the Renaissance. It is with M. FICINO that the doctrine of the *anima mundi* again came into prominence. The idea of a "cosmic soul" as an active and autonomous principle of nature was treated with keen interest by men of wide reputation such as Agrippa of Nettesheim, Paracelsus, and B. TELESIO, while F. Patrizi adapted the theme of the *anima mundi* to his panpsychic conception of the universe. In the same vein, although with different philosophical implications, G. BRUNO described the "universal soul" as a large mirror in which the divine image is reflected and infinitely fragmentized. T. CAMPANELLA made the doctrine of the world soul an important part of his system of philosophy. He conceived the world as a huge animal with an extremely refined soul that surpasses in excellence the souls of all men, as well as the angels. In the *De sensu rerum et magia* he describes the world soul as a common nature created by God and infused into the universe; he calls it "the first instrument of the primary Wisdom" and says that it is through it that Divine Wisdom produces the abundant richness of life, the great variety of species and genera, and the endless series of individuals. (*See* PANPSYCHISM; RENAISSANCE PHILOSOPHY.)

Modern Currents. In the 17th century, the doctrine of the world soul was held by many thinkers throughout Europe, where it became the object of heated discussions.

Germany. In Germany J. COMENIUS laid the foundations of a physico-cosmological theory based on the notion that the *spiritus mundi* is "life itself infused into the world in order to operate in all things" (*Physicae synopsis,* 1643). According to him and his followers, God does not move natural bodies immediately, but through an invisible and spiritual substance that has the power to produce changes in things. A similar doctrine is also to be found in the writings of Johannes Bayer (*Ostium vel atrium naturae,* 1662), C. Axelson (*Physica et ethica mosaica,* 1613), and A. Bachimius (*Pansophia enchiretica,* 1682), all of whom invoke Biblical texts to support their teaching. Other representatives of this trend of thought were H. Nolle (*Physica hermetica,* 1619); D. van der Becke (Rechenberg), the author of a work entitled *De mundi anima;* Marcus Marci von Kronland; Hieronymus von Hirenheim; and the famous J. Sturm, who in his *Epistola* to Henry More (1685) showed his approval of the latter's panvitalism. For C. THOMASIUS (*Versuch vom Wesen des Geistes,* 1709) the spirit, conceived as a material principle, is a power that moves, molds, and animates matter. In his *Historia critica philosophiae* (1767), J. Brucker discusses at great length the doctrine of the world soul as it is found in Plato, the Stoics, Empedocles, and Plotinus, while J. G. HERDER speaks of a *Geist der Natur,* a theme that recurs again and again in the natural philosophy of romanticism and is developed, although from a somewhat different point of view, by F. W. J. SCHELLING (*Von der Weltseele,* 1798) and G. W. F. HEGEL.

England. In England the doctrine of a universal soul as an independent principle found its adherents mainly among the CAMBRIDGE PLATONISTS. Henry More speaks of a spirit of nature as an incorporeal substance that is the source of life and the physical laws of motion [*Opera omnia* (London 1679) 1:222], while Ralph Cudworth treats of the *anima mundi* in connection with Aristotle and Plato [*The Intellectual System of the Universe* (London 1678)]. C. Blount also published a work entitled *Anima mundi* in 1679. For R. Burthogge [*Essay upon Reason and the Nature of Spirits* (London 1694)], as for others, spirit, light, and world soul are equivalent terms. Even Sir Isaac Newton presupposed a certain relationship between ether and spirit, while G. BERKELEY in his last work, *Siris,* 1744, gave a somewhat favorable account of Platonic and Neoplatonic doctrines of the spirit of the world, light, fire, and heat as moving and vivifying forces.

France. In France M. Mersenne showed a certain leaning toward the doctrine of the world soul [*Impiété des déistes* (Paris 1624) 2:402–419]; his disciple G. de Launay is credited with an essay on this subject (*Essais physiques,* 1667). P. GASSENDI attributed the idea of the world soul—which he rejects though not wholeheartedly—to the Pythagoreans, Plato, the Stoics, the Cabalists, and even Aristotle and his Arabian disciples [*Opera omnia* (Lyons 1658) 1:155].

A favorable environment for the diffusion of the doctrine of the world soul on an international level was the circle of alchemists, chemists, and physiologists. The alchemists conceived the world soul as some kind of ether or heat (fire) and as a universal principle of change; chemists and physiologists represented it as an igneous substance, distinct, at least for some of them, from the spiritual and immortal soul.

Holland. In Holland J. B. van Helmont again took up Paracelsus' principle of the *arché,* while the chemists, Boerhaave and Homberg, followed by Nieuwentyt, made sulphur-fire the only active principle of the universe. Boerhaave taught also that a *spiritus rector* or *quinta essentia,* which is of a material nature, directs the growth of plants. The *natura naturans* of Spinoza was interpreted as meaning the world soul by P. BAYLE (*Dictionnaire,* under ''Spinoza''), by Yvon (Diderot's *Encyclopédie,* under ''Ame''), and by J. B. R. Robinet [*De la nature* (Amsterdam 1761–66) 2:366].

Italy. In Italy the doctrine of the world soul, popularized by Campanella, was reasserted by men like Di Capua, D'Andrea, Doria, and even by G. VICO in his youth, each in his own way and according to the principles of his particular system.

See Also: EMANATIONISM; MONISM.

Bibliography: T. GREGORY, *Anima Mundi* (Florence 1955); *Platonismo medievale* (Rome 1958). F. C. COPLESTON, *History of Philosophy* (Westminster, Md. 1946–) 2:30, 170, 189, 202; 3:242–243, 248, 251, 259, 261, 265–266, 271. *Enciclopedia filosofica* (Venice-Rome 1957) 1:246–247. R. EISLER, *Wörterbuch der philosophischen Bergriffe* (Berlin 1927–30) 3:509–511. A. J. FESTUGIÈRE, *La Révélation d'Hermès Trismégiste,* 4 v. (Paris 1944–54) v.2, *Le Dieu cosmique* (1949). J. MOREAU, *L'Âme du monde de Platon aux Stoïciens* (Paris 1939). G. VERBEKE, *L'évolution de la doctrine du pneuma du Stoicisme à S. Augustin* (Louvain 1945).

[T. GREGORY/G. TONELLI]

WORLD YOUTH DAY

The observance of a World Youth Day grew out of the United Nations International Youth Year in 1985. Pope John Paul II encouraged its annual observance by Roman Catholics. In most countries of the Catholic world, the observance is held on Palm Sunday, but in the United States it is customarily set for the last Sunday in October. Every second year, at the bidding of Pope John Paul, the Vatican Council for the Laity in collaboration with the bishops of the host country has organized an international gathering. Young adults and youth, 13 to 30, from all over the world come together to witness, proclaim, and celebrate their Christian faith. The 1987 assembly met in Buenos Aires, Argentina; in 1989, in Santiago de Compostela, Spain; in 1991, in Częstochowa, Poland; in 1993, in Denver, Colorado; and in 1995, in Manila, Philippines. John Paul II was present at these gatherings, attended in each case by several hundred thousand young people. The pope addressed a crowd of over two million at the fifteenth international World Youth Day, celebrated in Rome, Aug. 14–18, 2000, during the Jubilee year.

Bibliography: Bibliography: C. VAN DER PLANCKE, ''La rencontre mondiale des jeunes Częstochowa et la construction de l'Europe,'' *Lumen Vitae* 47 (1992) 61–66. *L'Osservatore Romano,* English edition (Aug. 23, 2000).

[B. L. MARTHALER]

WORLD'S PARLIAMENT OF RELIGION

The 1893 and 1993 World's Parliaments of Religion met, respectively, in conjunction with the year-long (1892–93) World's Columbian Exposition in Chicago, and from August 28 to September 5 in Chicago 100 years later. The suggestion of incorporating a major interfaith dialogue into the exposition came from a lay Swedenborgian, Charles C. Bonney. The Parliament, chaired by John Henry Barrows, a Presbyterian, included representatives from 41 denominations. Several thousand participants gathered to mark this first modern interfaith dialogue. Catholic representatives at the Parliament included James Cardinal Gibbons, the archbishop of Baltimore, Archbishops Patrick Feehan of Chicago and Thomas Ryan of Philadelphia, and Bishop John Keane, rector of the Catholic University of America.

The 1993 World Youth Day gathering. (Catholic News Service)

The objectives of the Parliament included reciprocal teaching and learning (with a focus on both common and distinctive beliefs and practices), defending theistic religion against 19th-century secularism, amplifying the spiritual bonds and cooperation between different faith communities, and engaging religious communities in current social problems and institutions, including the movement toward international peace. These objectives were articulated by an organizing committee composed of Protestants, Catholics, and Jews. The explicit evangelical agendas of some Christian participants were downplayed. Catholic involvement in the 1893 Parliament led to some controversy within the Church about the legitimacy and purpose of such gatherings, and the development of Catholic positions on interreligious dialogue were to some extent shaped by this debate.

The Parliament had the effect of drawing Catholicism, as well as Judaism, into the mainstream of American religious traditions. It also introduced some Eastern traditions into North America. Notably, the participation of Shaku Sōen (1859–1919), Angārika Dharmapāla (1864–1993), and Swami Vivekananda (1863–1902) played a significant role in bringing Buddhist and Hindu influences to North America, and provided impetus to the development of comparative studies of religion in North America.

The 1993 Parliament was designed to encourage interfaith dialogue through the commemoration of the centenary of the 1893 World's Parliament of Religion. With the involvement of the Institute for 21st-Century Studies, special attention was given to critical social problems confronting a global people preparing for the 21st century. Mutual understanding and respect in addressing the social crisis facing all participants was emphasized. Among the issues addressed were ecology, science, technology, business, social inequality, violence, community, health and healing, the media, pluralism, and women's issues. The Parliament brought together more than 8,000 registrants representing over 125 religions from 56 nations.

The 1993 Parliament included a relatively small section of academic papers and a very wide variety of dialogue media that emphasized informal discussion and praxis. These involved: festivals and performances of dance, music, song, drama, and poetry; exhibits, seminars, and workshops; symposia and panel discussions; slide, video, and film presentations; as well as a wide assortment of exercise, meditation, and prayer groups.

Moreover, the venue included Chicago area museums and local religious and cultural centers.

The varied program of over 600 scheduled entries was highlighted by plenary sessions and major presentations by secular, religious, and spiritual leaders and dignitaries. Also, noted academics and other personalities represented an eclectic range of churches, societies, missions, movements, and organizations. Some 119 groups from around the world sponsored the event.

As in the 1893 World's Parliament, Roman Catholic participation occurred at various levels of the 1993 Parliament: planning, presentations, panels, symposia, workshops, and the private Assembly of Religious and Spiritual Leaders. Official Catholic representatives included Joseph Cardinal Bernardin, archbishop of Chicago, and Archbishop Francesco Gioa of the Pontifical Council for Interreligious Dialogue. Thomas Baima, the director of the Chicago Office of Ecumenical and Interreligious Affairs, and Placido Rodriguez, auxiliary bishop of Chicago, were on the Parliament's Board of Trustees.

A Declaration of a Global Ethic. Hans Küng of the University of Tübingen drafted the basic formulation of "A Declaration of a Global Ethic." Remarkably, this 5,000-word document was signed, after Board debate and minor modifications, by 95 percent of the religious leaders in attendance. The document closely echoes many themes of the 1993 Parliament mandate and issues a direct and candid critique of current exploitive attitudes, institutions, and social structures.

The document begins with the premises of contemporary economic, ecological, and political crises. It clearly articulates a common foundational religious ethic based on the teachings of the world religions. The Declaration argues that this set of core values must be internalized in a transformation of consciousness if the current crises are to be overcome. "Irrevocable directives" of the Global Ethic are: 1) non-violence, respect, and justice towards humanity and the ecosystem as whole; 2) a condemnation of economic exploitation and an equitable restructuring of the world economy; 3) tolerance and truthfulness, especially in reference to politics, economics, the professions, and the mass media; and 4) an affirmation of respect and love, especially as this pertains to the equality of the sexes.

Future Interfaith Plans. Cited as an agenda for future dialogue, the Global Ethic is supported by the Metropolitan Interreligious Task Force. Directed initially by Dirk Ficca, this is a Chicago area organization representing 13 religious groups. This organization was created to carry on themes of the 1993 Parliament through enhancing interfaith education and community relations, including the promotion of public policy and advocacy.

Bibliography: J.H. BARROWS, *The World's Parliament of Religions* (Chicago 1893); "Results of the Parliament of Religions," *Forum* XVIII (September 1894). *Council for a Parliament of the World's Religions Journal* (Chicago, IL). R.S. ELLWOOD, "World's Parliament of Religions," in M. ELIADE, ed., *The Encyclopedia of Religion*, v. 15, 444–445. E. FELDMAN, "Americam Ecumenism: Chicago's World's Parliament of Religions of 1893," *Journal of Church and State* 9:2 (1967) 180–199. G.S. GODSPEED, ed., *The World's First Parliament of Religions* (Chicago 1895). W.R. HOUGHTON, ed., *Neely's History of the Parliament of Religions and Religious Congresses at the World's Columbian Exposition* (Chicago 1893). J.M. KITIGAWA, "The 1893 World's Parliament of Religions and Its Legacy" (Chicago 1983). M. STOEBER, "From Proclamation to Interreligious Dialogue: The Parliaments of Religion," *The Living Light* 30:1 (1993) 32–41. D.S. TOOLAN, "Chicago's Parliament of the World's Religions," *America* (Sept. 25, 1993) 3–4.

[M. STOEBER]

WORLDWIDE CHURCH OF GOD

Founded by Herbert W. Armstrong, the Worldwide Church of God was originally known as the Radio Church of God. It took its name and many of its basic tenets from the Church of God movement.

Armstrong, a former advertizing man, was ordained in 1931 in the Oregon Conference of the Church of God (Seventh-Day), a small splinter group which had broken off from the General Conference. In 1934 he began an independent radio ministry, the Radio Church of God; it was built around the weekly broadcast "The World Tomorrow," and *Plain Truth*, a free monthly publication. Broadcasting first from a small station in Eugene, Oregon, his following grew slowly but steadily. After World War II he moved his headquarters to Pasadena, California, and in 1947 founded Ambassador College. By the 1960s Armstrong and his son, Garner Ted Armstrong, were heard on hundreds of local radio stations, and at that time they began television broadcasts. In 1968 the name of the Radio Church of God was changed to Worldwide Church of God. The circulation of *Plain Truth* grew from 500,000 to 7.5 million between the 1960s and the 1970s.

Teaching and Turmoil. Originally, Armstrong denied the Christian teaching on the Holy Trinity, neither accepting Jesus Christ as a divine being nor acknowledging the Holy Spirit as a unique, divine person. During his tenure, the Church insisted on strict adherence to Old Testament ordinances, particularly with regard to dietary laws, Sabbath observance, and festivals. At that time, the WCG observed all seven Old Testament feasts: Passover and the Days of Unleavened Bread, Pentecost, Trumpets, Atonement, Tabernacles, the Last Great Day, and the

First Day of the Sacred Year, and regarded Christmas and Easter as pagan. Members were obliged to "triple tithe"; every year they were to give the WCG 10% of their income; another 10% was set aside for the Feast of the Tabernacles, their main festival; and every third year, members were required to give another 10% to the church for the maintenance of widows and orphans.

The most controversial of Armstrong's positions is his teaching of Anglo-Israelitism, a doctrine that affirms that England (Ephraim) and the United States (Manasseh) are what is left of the ten lost tribes of Israel. The racial overtones of the teaching were reflected in the Church's pattern of growth throughout the white world.

The 1970s were a difficult time for the WCG. It experienced internal discord and schism as a result of a reorganization of the ministerial staff, theological debate over a number of issues, including the dating of the feast of Pentecost, the question of divorce and remarriage among members, and scandal. In 1974 Garner Ted Armstrong broke with his father and was disfellowshipped. The younger Armstrong eventually founded the Church of God International. When the elder Armstrong died in 1986, Joseph Tkach became the Minister General, succeeded by his son, Joseph W. Tkach, Jr.

As schism developed in 1974, a number of former WCG members established a national fellowship, the Associated Churches of God, with headquarters in Columbia, Maryland. They issued a doctrinal statement that reaffirmed many of the principal teachings of the Worldwide Church of God, but rejected tithing in favor of freewill offering and outlined a form of congregational governance in place of the theocratic organization of the original WCG.

Under the leadership of Joseph W. Tkach, Jr., the WCG abandoned many of Armstrong's controversial positions, apologizing for its theological errors, and moving from a fringe group to a mainstream evangelical Protestant church. This included the affirmation of the doctrine of the Trinity (1993) and the renunciation of the Old Testament ordinances (1994). In 1997 the WCG joined the NATIONAL ASSOCIATION OF EVANGELICALS.

Bibliography: H. W. ARMSTRONG, *The United States and British Commonwealth in Prophecy* (Pasadena 1980); *This Is the Worldwide Church of God* (Pasadena 1971); *The Autobiography* (Pasadena 1967); *Mystery of the Ages* (Pasadena 1985). J. HOPKINS, *The Armstrong Empire* (Grand Rapids, Mich. 1974). D. ROBINSON, *Herbert Armstrong's Tangled Web* (Tulsa, OK 1980). *Fundamental Beliefs of the Associated Churches of God* (Columbia, MD 1974). F. S. MEAD, S. S. HILL, and C. D. ATWOOD, eds., *Handbook of Denominations in the United States*, 11th ed (Nashville 2001).

[A. PEDERSEN/EDS.]

WORLDWIDE MARRIAGE ENCOUNTER

Worldwide Marriage Encounter emerged from the leadership group of MARRIAGE ENCOUNTER within the Diocese of Rockville Centre, New York. As Charles Gallagher, SJ and the team couples became sensitive to the capacity for the Marriage Encounter weekend to renew the Church, no longer could they confine themselves to the area of metropolitan New York. Marriage Encounter has presented the weekend to well over a million couples, spreading through North America as well as into scores of foreign countries. As affiliates of Worldwide Marriage Encounter, other different faith traditions offer the same weekend, with their own theology of marriage and Church. Among Catholics, Worldwide Marriage Encounter weekends are presented by three couples and a priest. Because the sacraments of reconciliation and eucharist are an integral part of the Catholic experience of Marriage Encounter, no weekend can be conducted without the presence of a priest. The Mission and Vision Statement approved in 1995 states: "Worldwide Marriage Encounters Mission of renewal in the church and change in the world is to assist couples and priests to live fully intimate and responsible relationships by providing them with a Catholic 'experience' and ongoing community support for such a lifestyle."

The leadership group of Worldwide Marriage Encounter is comprised of a national board, with geographical representation from 19 sections in the United States— 13 English speaking, five Hispanic speaking, and one Korean speaking sections—and an executive secretariat team comprising one couple and a priest who are selected from the national board membership.

See Also: MARRIAGE ENCOUNTER.

[F. L. GUTHRIE/J. J. KAISING]

WORLOCK, DEREK JOHN HARFORD

Roman Catholic archbishop of Liverpool; b. Feb. 4, 1920, London; d. Feb. 8, 1996, Liverpool. Worlock was the elder of twins; he also had an older brother, Peter, killed early in World War II. Both his father, Harford, and mother, Dora, were converts to Catholicism before their marriage in 1913; his extended family was largely Anglican. Dora was active in the Women's Suffrage Movement, while his father's career embraced journalism, the civil service and, from 1929, the post of agent for the Conservative party in Winchester. It was in Winchester that Worlock spent much of his childhood, being educated at an Anglican school, Winton House. He early decided he had a vocation for the priesthood, but his own bishop would not accept him because he was not of Irish descent. In January of 1934, he entered the seminary of the diocese of Westminster, St. Edmund's College, Ware. In the seminary he joined the Young Christian Workers after an initial rebuff because he was considered to be too middle class. He was ordained to the priesthood in Westminster Cathedral on June 3, 1944, being posted to a church in Kensington, London. In the summer of 1945 he was appointed undersecretary to the new archbishop of Westminster, Bernard GRIFFIN, becoming secretary two years later, and remaining in that post under subsequent archbishops until 1964.

The first part of Worlock's period as secretary involved him in a number of political issues. The Church had a considerable interest in the new education legislation introduced in 1944 and in the welfare reforms under the postwar Labour government. Worlock was a facilitator in the negotiations between the government and Archbishop Griffin. Griffin was also a vigorous campaigner on behalf of the oppressed churches of Eastern Europe, especially those of Poland. Worlock attended the Second VATICAN COUNCIL first as secretary and later as a *peritus* with an especial interest in the lay apostolate. He helped to draft part of the Constitution on the Church in the Modern World.

In March of 1964 he was made parish priest in Stepney, in the East End in London. Just before setting out for the final session of Vatican II, he was told he had been appointed bishop of Portsmouth; he was consecrated on Dec. 21, 1965. The parish program for the implementation of Vatican II he had envisaged for Stepney he now transferred to a diocese with an emphasis on social action wherever possible, in collaboration with other churches. He was particularly concerned to see liturgical changes introduced, and he oversaw the reordering of the sanctuary of almost every church in his diocese. He served on the Vatican's Council for the Laity, and the Committee on the Family. He was regularly a member of the Synod of Bishops representing the Conference of Bishops of England and Wales, and he acted as the conference's liaison with the clergy when the National Conference of Priests was established. He also took a special interest in the creation of the Episcopal Conference's Media Office.

Upon the death of Cardinal Heenan in 1975, Worlock expected to be translated to Westminster, but instead was installed on March 16, 1976 as archbishop of Liverpool. His failure to be appointed to the (unofficial) primatial see rankled, yet Liverpool proved to be a great success. There he forged a powerful collaboration with the Anglican bishop, David Sheppard. It was in part because of their close liaison that it became possible to dissolve the British Council of Churches, which did not have Roman Catholic membership, and establish the Council of Churches for Britain and Ireland, which did. The two prelates were also active in attempting to moderate during the clashes between the people of Liverpool and the Conservative government during the early 1980s. Their collaboration produced two books: *Better Together* (1988) and *With Hope in Our Hearts* (1994).

Following a proposal by the National Conference of Priests, a National Pastoral Congress of English and Welsh Catholics took place in Liverpool in 1980. Archbishop Worlock was closely involved, from its inception to the writing of the final document and the response of the Episcopal Conference, The Easter People. Handing over this document to John Paul II, Worlock and Cardinal HUME invited the pope to visit Britain. In 1981, just before the visit took place, Britain and Argentina went to war over the Falkland Isles; the pope's visit still took place, largely due to Worlock's efforts. The negotiations led to considerable tension between himself and the more pro-war Hume.

Worlock's publications also include two anthologies: *Take One at Bedtime* (1962) and *Turn and Turn Again* (1971). His broadcasts on the English-language service of Vatican Radio appeared as *English Bishops at the Council* (1965) and his concern for implementing the council is reflected in *Parish Councils: In or Out?* (1974). He also published two other small books: *Give Me Your Hand* (1977) and *Bread Upon the Waters* (1991). For the Bible Reading Fellowship he produced with David Sheppard *With Christ in the Wilderness* (1990).

Bibliography: J. FURNIVAL and A. KNOWLES, *Archbishop Derek Worlock: His Personal Journey* (London 1998). C. LONGLEY, *The Worlock Archive* (London 2000).

[M. WALSH]

WORMS, CONCORDAT OF

Also called the *Pactum Calixtinum* (Sept. 23, 1122), it ended the INVESTITURE STRUGGLE. After two weeks of negotiation between the Emperor HENRY V and legates of CALLISTUS II, each side issued a formal concession in favor of the other. To the Church, the emperor conceded the right to invest any bishop or abbot with ring and crozier, symbols of the prelate's spiritual authority. Everywhere in the empire, election was to be canonical and consecration free. Callistus, on his part, conceded to Henry personally the privilege of having elections to *German* bishoprics and abbeys held in his presence. Moreover, if the electing chapter divided between two candidates, the emperor was to settle the dispute in favor of the *sanior pars.* Before consecration, the electee was to receive his temporalities (*REGALIA*) from the emperor, who invested him with a scepter. In Italy and Burgundy, election was to be local and investiture automatic within six months *after* consecration. The settlement was thus a compromise effected to end the hostilities honorably for both sides.

Bibliography: *Monumenta Germaniae Constitutiones* (Berlin 1826–) 1.1:159–161, for the text, ed. L. WEILAND. B. GEBHARDT, *Handbuch der deutschen Geschichte,* ed. H. GRUNDMANN (Stuttgart 1954–60) 1:278–280. A. HOFMEISTER, ''Das Wormser Konkordat: Zum Streit um seine Bedeutung,'' *Forschungen und Versuche zur Geschichte des Mittelalters und der Neuzeit: Festschrift Dietrich Schäfer* (Jena 1915) 64–148. G. BARRACLOUGH, tr., *Mediaeval Germany, 911–1250: Essays by German Historians,* 2 v. (Oxford 1938) 1:98–102.

[R. KAY]

WORMS, COUNCILS OF

CHARLEMAGNE and his successors frequently held conferences at Worms that have been termed *diètes synodales* or *concilia mixta.* Such meetings occurred in 770, 772, 776, 781, 786, 787, *c.* 790, 829, 836, and 857. Since in no instance is their ecclesiastical character certain, without evidence to the contrary, they must be regarded simply as *Reichstagen.* However, the meeting held in 868 to legislate for the lands of Louis the German was, without doubt, an ecclesiastical synod. Its principal business, other than the promulgation of about 80 statutes, was to approve a lengthy statement defending the Latin Church's position in the *FILIOQUE* controversy with the Greeks. Under the emperor HENRY IV a council convoked to meet in Worms at Christmas 1059 was never held. The city was the scene of the famous German diet and council of 1076, which opened the struggle between Pope and Emperor. GREGORY VII had sent a letter to Henry IV enumerating instances of his disobedience, especially of the new decree (1075) against lay INVESTITURE, and urging him to submission. The King's reply was to summon the German bishops to Worms, where they declared that they no longer recognized Gregory as pope. Thereupon, Henry wrote to ''Brother Hildebrand'' and the Roman people, announcing the decision. Rome replied with excommunication, and the INVESTITURE STRUGGLE was joined. The controversy was settled in 1122 at the very place it began, in a legatine council that concluded the Concordat of Worms. Two papal legates deposed the archbishop of Mainz at Worms 1153, even though St. Bernard himself defended the man.

Bibliography: C. J. VON HEFELE, *Histoire des conciles d'après les documents originaux,* tr. and continued by H. LECLERCQ, 10 v. in 19 (Paris 1907–38) 3.2:956, 976, 982, 994, 998, 1034; 4.1:76–78, 100, 213 (for meetings before 868), 458–465 (for 868); 4.2:1210–12 (for 1059); 5.1:151–156 (for 1076); 5.2:863 (for 1153); 6.1:77 (for a diocesan synod of Richard, bishop 1247–57); 8.1:198, 788 (for the diet of 1495), 215 (for the *Synodale* of 1496). *Monumenta Germaniae Constitutiones* (Berlin 1826–) 1.1:106–110, documents for 1076. B. GEBHARDT, *Handbuch der deutschen Geschichte,* ed. H. GRUNDMANN, 4 v. (8th ed. Stuttgart 1954–60) 1:256–258. A. WERMINGHOFF, ''Verzeichnis der Akten fränkischer Synoden von 742–843,'' *Neues Archiv der Gesellschaft für ältere deutsche Geschichtskunde* 24 (1899) 457–502.

[R. KAY]

WORSHIP

In Anglo-Saxon, ''weorð-scipe'' meant ''worthship,'' in which ''worth'' is to be understood in the sense of value or honor. Worship, therefore, originally meant the state of worth, the quality of being valuable or worthy. In the course of time, the word, both as a noun and as a verb, acquired a considerable variety of meanings, and at present almost defies definition. In general it may be said, however, that in the present usage of the word, worship has less to do with the state that commands respect or adoration than with the attitude or act of adoring. In a very general way, ''worship'' expresses the response of religious man to the Holy as he apprehends it: his attitude of submission, devotion, respect, and veneration, and the acts prompted by this attitude, his ''Godward'' dispositions and activities. The Holy is experienced by *homo religiosus* as an invitation, an address, an *Anspruch;* his response to it, internally as well as externally, in private as well as in public manifestation, in a free and spontaneous expression, as well as in the form of a rigidly fixed ritual, is worship. One could say, therefore, that worship is basically religion itself, in as far as it stresses the conscious involvement or devotion of man. It is the virtue of religion and its exteriorization in religious acts.

The function of worship is, in the first place, to make the Sacred present in the awareness of the worshiper or the worshiping community, as the power of being that safeguards, preserves, renews, or rejuvenates existence, not only in man, society, and mankind, but also in nature and the universe. By making the Holy present, or by recognizing and celebrating the reality of its presence in the world, worship is instrumental also in maintaining the cosmic order as the *conditio sine qua non* of life and salvation. By establishing his relation with the Holy, by acknowledging his total dependence on it, the worshiper participates in the Sacred; he recognizes himself as *homo religiosus;* he integrates himself in the sacredness of the cosmos; he lives in the powerful presence of the gods; and, in this state of communion, he is restored to his right relation to the universe. Even where the totally other character of the Holy is emphasized to such an extent that there is no awareness of possible communication with this Transcendence, the function of worship as a spiritual enrichment of man remains. A typical example is that of the Jains; they venerate the *Tirthankaras,* who are so far above all earthly things that they can neither perceive nor reward the acts of worship shown them. Nevertheless, the Jains continue to worship them, believing that it purifies their hearts and so brings them closer to their object. But it is not only the individual worshiper who finds a force of integration in worship; public worship likewise binds together those who share the same religious experience and serves to integrate the group. One might even say that, at least in archaic societies—in primitive cultures as well as higher civilizations—worship is the primary integrating factor of the group.

Object and Objects of Worship. Worship is bound up with the belief that there is a Transcendent Reality, and with at least implicit acknowledgment that man is meaningfully related to this Reality as to the end to which he aspires or should aspire. Thus Transcendence can be the only object of authentic worship. Its personal or impersonal character need not be treated here. However, the Transcendent, or the Holy, can become the object of worship only by manifesting itself or by being manifested: the necessary locus and focus of worship is the hierophany. Only by some sort of embodiment can the Holy become accessible. There is an immense variety of hierophanies—cosmic, biological, local, and symbolic—because absolutely everything that exists is a potential manifestation of the Sacred, and can, therefore, somewhere at some time become a hierophany, or be transfigured into one.

The error of popular theories about fetishism, nature worship, worship of stones, etc., results from a failure to understand the instrumentality of these hierophanies. Objects that become hierophanies are venerated, not because of what they are in themselves, but only because and insofar as they reveal what they are not; insofar as they point beyond themselves to the ''wholly other'' of which they are but a manifestation. Either by their appearance—novelty, unusual shape, unusual circumstances under which they appear, strength, beauty, monstrosity, etc.—or by consecration, they embody the Holy for the worshiper. They are transparent for their sacred meaning. Idolatry, the act directly opposed to worship with regard to the object, is precisely a misapprehension of a hierophany: an object that should be only instrumental in worship, because it is related to the Holy it reveals, becomes the end of veneration itself. Anything less than supremacy is fundamentally disqualified as an object of authentic worship. A holy statue, for example, may be worshiped only insofar as it is precisely a statue, i.e., a representa-

tion of the Sacred. The danger of idolatry looms when the hierophanic nature of the object becomes dimmed in the religious awareness of the believers. An idol frequently is such a outworn survival of a hierophany; it is no longer transparent, it blocks the view.

In a wider sense one may call objects of worship those things also that are in some way connected with worship, such as vestments or ceremonial attire, cult tools, and musical instruments. Entering the sphere of the Holy, these acquire the qualities of the Sacred either by a consecration *ad hoc,* or simply by being used in sacred activities; they are set apart, and may not be used by unqualified persons or for profane purposes. They share in the ambivalence, and consequently also in the taboos, of the Sacred. They belong to a different ontological level than other objects that are the same materially. In this way, they may in their turn stand for the Holy as full-fledged hierophanies.

Attitude and Act of Worship. Worship can be an attitude as well as an act, inward as well as outward. As an attitude it is a state of consciousness in which the presence of the Holy is experienced, or in which the Holy is experienced as present. As an act it is an attempt to establish contact or communication with the Holy, or a celebration of its presence. Attitude and act have a reciprocal influence: the attitude of worship inspires and prompts the acts, but devotional acts also create and foster the attitude proper to worship. Very often such acts succeed in making the Sacred present in the awareness of the worshiper, and in so doing they elicit the responsive attitude of religious man. Because of the ambivalent nature of the Holy, which, as R. OTTO has shown, is a simultaneity of *mysterium tremendum* and *mysterium fascinans,* the attitude of worship is equally ambivalent and characterized, in various degrees of amalgamation, by both awe, culminating in terror, and attraction, culminating in intimate communion or even ecstatic identification with the Holy.

Fundamentally opposed to the attitude of worship is that of magic. The attitude of worship, indeed, is an unequivocal and submissive acknowledgment of a transcendent power, whereas the attitude of magic is rather an attempt to dominate and manipulate power. Magic ceremonies, therefore, although they may look very much like acts of worship, are intrinsically opposed to them because they are expressions of a different underlying attitude. In practice, however, it is often very difficult to determine where worship ends and magic begins, or where the boundary is between the ἱερὸς λόγος of an authentic act of religion and the magic formula or incantation. This difficulty can exist not only because of a superficial and extrinsic similarity, but also because, even in the so-called higher religions, magic and superstition frequently accompany true worship. The difficulty of distinguishing between the respective attitudes of worship and magic is increased also by the fact that worship, although essentially submissive, does not necessarily exclude an often legitimate self-esteem, and that magic, although essentially dominating its object, does not exclude at all the awe-like terror that the power it attempts to manipulate may not be entirely under control. Magic very often is an outgrowth of an exaggerated fixation or ritualization of worship; the formula or the rite is then no longer the expression of a religious experience, but rather a substitute for it. A certain temptation to magic seems, in all religions, to be inherent in a misapprehension of the relation between attitude and act in worship.

An important distinction, in respect to the attitude of worship, is the classical one between the *do ut des* and the *do ut abeas* attitudes underlying sacrifices or offerings. They obviously correspond to the ambivalent nature of the Sacred, the object of worship; the exchange of gifts expresses the desire to establish communication with the *fascinosum,* while the apotropaic rites express the *horror sacer* for the *tremendum.* However much the Sacred is the Absolute for the believer, nevertheless its supernatural and superhuman character may be felt as a menace to the limitations of created and fallen existence. *Homo religiosus* worships with awareness that the object of his worship can be auspicious or harmful, even dangerous. In fact, it is always dangerous if he is not duly prepared for this encounter with the totally other.

Another important distinction is that made by L. Frobenius, between *Ausdruck,* the spontaneous expression of a personal experience, and *Anwendung,* the faithful execution of certain prescriptions, usually with a well-defined purpose. There seems to be a dialectical movement in process between both types: the spontaneous *Ausdruck* type, especially in its social aspects of public worship, has a tendency to change into an *Anwendung* type. However, the multiplication of ritual stipulations and prescriptions—and one needs only to think of the Vedic sacrifice of the horse, which required a careful preparation of up to two years—provokes a new reaction in the form of a ''worship in spirit and truth'' (Jn 4.24). On the one hand, there is a permanent danger that the ritual, which tends to overemphasize the importance of a fixed traditional form, may smother the inwardness of personal attitude and the spontaneity of individual expression. On the other hand, because of his very nature as a social being, man cannot escape the necessity of an embodiment of his worship in the visible and historical institutions of a worshiping community: in commonly accepted symbols, established rites, and concerted action. This dialectic movement between opposite poles is a necessary constituent of worship.

Individual spontaneity and sincerity must inspire and permeate communal worship, but the devotion of a cult community must provide the individual worshiper with a new dimension that not only responds to the social aspect of his religious nature, but also sustains and revitalizes his personal relation to the Sacred, making the Sacred more forcefully present to him than it usually is in the individual expression. E. Durkheim certainly went too far in making the collective self the object of worship, which in turn is of its very nature the expression of the collectivity. But the importance of corporate worship should not be underestimated. There is a reciprocal influence between society and worship. Society creates communal forms of contact with the Holy, but worship also integrates society and creates specific cult associations, which have their initiation ceremonies and from which strangers are excluded.

Forms of Worship. The forms of worship are extremely diversified because religion is a dimension of man's existential situation itself. Although there is a basic human mode-of-being-in-the-world as such, nevertheless the existential situation is modified profoundly by the concrete circumstances of time, place, cultural background, basic type of economy, sociological system of family and kinship, political organization, and many other factors. The worship of the desert is different from that of the city; the worship of primitives, from that in higher civilizations; the worship of planters, from that of hunters or pastoral nomads; the worship of a matriarchal people, from that of a patriarchal society; the worship of a small sib-type community of pygmies, from that of a strongly organized and dynastic state; the worship of a secret society, from the public cult in the same tribe; strict monotheism, from the worship of a religion in which a plurality of gods, and often other supernatural beings, are venerated; and the worship of a people with a highly developed priesthood and liturgical books, from that in which the head of the family or the clan conducts the cult activities according to oral traditions. Very often open and esoteric cults are found within the same religion. Age, sex, and position in society may command particular forms of worship; so also important events in human existence, such as birth, puberty, marriage, and death. Always, however, there are certain basic structures of worship.

Prayer. The typical form of individual worship is PRAYER; the typical form of social or public worship is cult, or ritual. However, the term ''cult'' is sometimes taken in a wider sense to include prayer, and in this case cult and worship are practically synonymous. The division adopted here seems to be the most convenient for a general classification of worship, but should not be applied too strictly. In fact, prayer may be, on the one hand, a social expression of worship and it may be associated with certain embryonic rites, such as the gestures (raising or folding of the hands), appropriate poses of the body (standing, kneeling, stooping, prostration), musical accompaniment, dance, and similar actions. On the other hand, prayer may be included in cult also as the ἱερὸς λόγος, interpreting and co-realizing the ritual. In this case, prayer (λεγόμενα) and ritual (δρώμενα) are complementary aspects of one act of worship. Prayer in its private or individaul form can be the most immediate and most flexible expression of the attitude of worship; sometimes it does not even need formulation, and becomes holy silence, a prayerful state of consciousness. While naturally remaining within the general function of worship, prayer still admits a variety of purposes, from the humble prayer of petition (an implicit acknowledgment at least of the submissive relation of the worshiper to the Transcendent), to that of praise (a disinterested affirmation of the reality and supremacy of the Holy) or to that of quiet union. Where prayer enters public worship, it inevitably becomes subject to a process of fixation, and, like the ritual, the symbolism of ceremonials and the objects and tools of cult, it assumes more and more a traditional and archaic character. Occasionally even a sacred language may develop. This conservatism of religious expression in general is often justified by the professed desire to imitate faithfully the holy deeds of the gods. When the process of estrangement between attitude and expression is completed, the formula or rite, no longer understood, may even become a new hierophany, since its otherness manifests the Sacred. This hieratic character of worship, together with the great emotional impact of religious manifestations, explains also the marked influence of worship on art, especially on poetry, music, and dance.

Cult. Cult is the socially recognized or institutional embodiment of worship in patterns of ceremonial acts, and may be sacrificial or sacramental. Here again the distinction is not absolute; there are intermediary types, and both basic forms may be intricately combined in the same act of worship. Sacrifice is, in the first place, an offering, a gift of man to the gods, and expresses the acknowledgment that the thing offered, or what it stands for, belongs to them. In fact, the thing offered is always in some way a substitution for the offering person: he acknowledges his own belonging to the deity and gives himself in and with his offering. The supreme sacrifice, therefore, even in non-Christian religions, is self-oblation, which, in some religions, may take the form even of self-immolation or ritual suicide. The *do ut des* formula, explicitly or implicitly connected with many sacrifices, does not necessarily indicate a commercial type of exchange or a bribing of the gods, but rather an establish-ment of communion by means of a ceremonial exchange of gifts. It is the binding force of mutual gifts that is important in this case.

Sacrificial and Sacramental Forms of Worship. Sacrifice is also essentially a consecration of the offered gift, by which, usually through some sort of transformation or destruction, the gift is totally withdrawn from profane use and assimilated to the Holy. Whether sacrifice means etymologically ''to make sacred'' or, rather, ''to do the sacred,'' this element is clearly essential to sacrifice: the gift is endowed with a new nature.

Here there is to be noted also a transition from the sacrificial to the sacramental sphere, because consecration is strictly speaking sacramental; it is an act that symbolically effects the communion with the Holy. The act is human, but the activity is divine. The same holds true for the sacrifice of a supernatural being and for the frequently ensuing sacrificial meal. Again, the activity is really divine, and it is by repeating or reenacting the deeds of the gods that man is able to effect communion with the Sacred: his acts are absorbed in the holy activity of the gods. This imitative aspect of cult is evident in the great cult dramas and mystery rituals of the higher religions, but it can be recognized also in the initiation ceremonies of primitive peoples and in such universal phenomena as the dance, e.g., the cosmic dance that repeats the movements of celestial bodies, or the great majority of animal dances. It is very likely, for that matter, that procession, dance, and drama are related expressions, and sometimes various stages of the same ritual reenactment of the great mythical events on the occasion of their celebration in festivals: the origin of nutritive plants, the reproduction of game animals, the coming of the rains, the investiture of the king who represents and safeguards cosmic order, and similar events. To the sacramental forms of worship belong the ritual celebration also of the common, ordinary activities of man, such as eating, drinking, and sexual intercourse. These activities are given their true dimension by being related to the prototypical deeds of the gods. It is significant that these forms (sacred meal and ritual intercourse), as well as many other ordinary rites (touch, kiss, etc.), nearly always symbolize communion with the deity. Cult really is the encounter with the gods in the celebration of their mysterious salvific presence.

Importance of Purification Rites in Worship. Precisely because of this communion with the Sacred in cult, purification rites have an essential importance in the life of worship. The Sacred is *mysterium tremendum* and has to be approached carefully. It is taboo for those who are unprepared. Purification frequently takes the form of washing in water, blood, or the urine of sacred animals, but includes also confession, exorcism, expiation, abstinence from sexual relations or from certain foods, beating, removal of shoes, ritual nakedness, and other practices. Fire, too, is a common and potent purifying substance.

Places and Times of Worship. The object of worship implies the necessity of places and times of worship. If the Transcendent really manifests itself to religious man, it must do so, of necessity, somewhere and at some time. For religious man, there is a holy ground. He has a consciousness of the sacred character of certain peculiar places, where the Holy is manifest to him in some special way, and where, consequently, he attempts to come in contact with it through worship. The place of the hierophany is the natural place of worship. It is qualitatively different from the surrounding space, and beyond its threshold is the meeting place with the gods. There are certain given places of worship, such as forests, rivers, mountains, caves, and springs. Other places are indicated by a theophany or by some sort of an oracle, e.g., or by some extraordinary event's taking place in them and interpreted as a god-sent sign of their holiness. Still other places of worship are manmade: the hearth for the family cult, the tomb (in particular the tombs of holy men), and the house devoted to cult. In this case the hierophanic nature of the place usually is the result of a consecration in which man repeats ritually the cosmogonic act of the gods: he creates his world. For this reason the holy place becomes for religious man the navel of the earth, the center of his world, to which everything else is oriented. It is the cosmos as opposed to chaos.

Cosmic Symbolism of the House of Worship. The cosmic symbolism of the house, and especially of the house of worship, is in many religions very striking: it is an *imago mundi.* Quite often the opening toward the world of the gods is symbolically represented, e.g., in the roof. Because the sanctuary is the dwelling place of the gods, religious man yearns to live there, and certain acts of worship express this desire in precise fashion, such as pilgrimage and orientation toward the holy place in prayer. Specially consecrated persons may even live in the temple. On the other hand, the sanctuary is also a *locus terribilis,* and purification rites are connected with the crossing of the threshold. Sometimes certain precincts of the sanctuary may even be all but inaccessible; only the initiated, the priest or the priest-king, may enter this most sacred place of divine presence.

Sacred Time. The sacred time is the era of the gods, the time of the beginning, the *illud tempus.* In time, as religious man knows it, certain periods mark a beginning: midnight, sunrise, new moon, the start of rains, the equinox. In his own life there are beginnings: birth, coming of age, marriage, even death as a transition to another mode of being. There are beginnings likewise in his social and economic activity: the founding of a village, the investiture of a king, sowing, the opening of hunting or harvesting seasons, the start of a war. Time is not continuous in his experience; it has a rhythm, it is a cycle of birth, growth, decay, death, and regeneration. In this process he recognizes and acknowledges the order instituted by the gods, and he aims at preserving this order because his existence and salvation depend on it.

His worship, therefore, is characterized by a celebration of the active and saving presence of the Holy in time, by his concern to co-realize the repetition of the work of the gods, by his effort to sanctify the great moments of his human existence, and, in general, by his desire to become contemporary with the gods. Worship is rhythmical and cyclical; particular rites mark the sacred moments of the day, the holy days of the week and the month, the holy periods of the year. The well-known ''rites of passage'' accompany the great events of his life. The calendar points out carefully the precise dates and times for feasts and festivals. The desire to reenact the deeds of the gods in these celebrations is evident, not only from the symbolism of the rites, but also quite frequently from the recitation of the myth that narrates these deeds, as the ἱερὸς λόγος of the ritual. Certain rites, such as fasts or vigils, may be required to prepare man for the sacredness of the time of worship.

Ministers of Worship. In the public forms of worship, one or a few members of the worshiping community direct the ritual. Certain acts are their prerogative. In simple religious ceremonies of natural groups, the ministers of the cult are the heads of families or clans, the chiefs or elders of the tribe. But as the cult becomes more elaborate and complicated and thus requires ritual of liturgical competence, specially qualified or specially traine persons—medicine men, shamans, priests—emerge to take charge. They may be elected to this office, assume it by mystical vocation, or receive it through hereditary transmission. They may be a natural choice because of certain talents or psychophysiological qualities, or they may acquire ritual competence only by long training. Their function is to communicate with the Sacred as mediators for the worshiping community. They guarantee the right fulfillment of all ritual prescriptions and the observance of the traditional feasts. Frequently they are the representatives of the gods—in the case of divine kingship, even their incarnations. They are the protagonists in the cult drama, ritually imitating the gestures of the gods, wearing the masks or other symbols—beard, hairdress, vestments—of the gods they represent, or, in ecstasy, acting under their possession. In coming into close contact with the Holy, the minister has to observe strict taboos and purifications: chastity, celibacy, and other austerities. But on entering the realm of the Sacred, and anointed, he becomes taboo himself, especially during the performance of his sacred functions.

In most religions the ministers of the cult are men, but women may occasionally have important functions, especially in agricultural societies and in the worship of female deities. It is customary for a priest to don vestments of the opposite sex in the worship of androgynous or bisexual deities. A special case is sacred prostitution, where girls or women perform ritual intercourse in the sanctuary of vegetation and fertility deities, sometimes on certain occasions with the minister of the cult, sometimes also on a more or less permanent basis with other worshipers. Both types are reenactments of the hierogamic union between heaven and earth and therefore are ritual acts.

See Also: EPIPHANY; FERTILITY AND VEGETATION CULTS; MAGIC; MYTH AND MYTHOLOGY; PRAYER; PROSTITUTION (SACRED); PURIFICATION; SACRED AND PROFANE; STONES, SACRED.

Bibliography: R. WILL, *Le Culte*, 3 v. (Paris 1925–35). J. CAZENEUVE, *Les Rites et la condition humaine d'après des documents ethnographiques* (Paris 1958). S. O. MOWINCKEL *Religion und Kultus* (Göttingen 1953); *Die Religion in Geschichte und Gegenwart*, 7 v. (3d ed. Tübingen 1957–65) 4:120–26. E. UNDERHILL, *Worship* (New York 1937). A. BERTHOLET, *Der Sinn des kultischen Opfers* (*Abhandlungen der Deutschen (Preussischen, to 1944) Akademie der Wissenschaften zu Berlin* 1942); *Grundformen der Erscheinungswelt der Gottesverehrung* (Tübingen 1953). L. BOUYER, *Rite and Man: Natural Sacredness and Christian Liturgy*, tr. M. J. COSTELLOE (Notre Dame, Indiana 1963). A. E. JENSEN, *Myth and Cult among Primitive Peoples*, tr. M. T. CHOLDIN and W. WEISSLEDER (Chicago 1963). J. G. FRAZER, *The Worship of Nature* (London 1926). A. BRUNNER, *Die Religion* (Freiburg 1956). M. ELIADE, *Patterns in Comparative Religion*, tr. R. SHEED (New York 1958). F. HEILER, *Erscheinungsformen und Wesen der Religion* (Stuttgart 1961). G. VAN DER LEEUW, *Religion in Essence and Manifestation*, tr. J. E. TURNER (London 1938; 2 v. Torchbooks New York 1963). A. S. HERBERT, *Worship in Ancient Israel* (Richmond 1959). V. P. GRØNBECH, *Essay on Ritual Drama* (London 1931). S. H. HOOKE, ed., *Myth and Ritual* (Oxford 1933). K. KERÉNYI, "Vom Wesen des Festes," *Paideuma* 1 (1938) 59–74. *Les Danses sacrées* (Sources Orientales 6; Paris 1963). A. VORBICHLER, *Das Opfer auf den uns heute noch erreichbaren ältesten Stufen der Menscheitsgeschichte* (Mödling 1956). H. HUBERT and M. MAUS in *Mélanges d'histoire des religions* (Paris 1909), English *Sacrifice: Its Name and Function*, tr. W. D. HALLS (Chicago 1964). C. L. ALBANESE, *Nature Religion in America: From the Algonkian Indians to the New Age* (Chicago 1990). E. HORNUNG, *Akhenaten and the Religion of Light* (Ithaca 1999). C. L. ALBANESE, *Reconsidering Nature Religion* (Harrisburg, Pennsylvania 2002).

[F. DE GRAEVE/EDS.]

WORSHIP (IN THE BIBLE)

The common Hebrew word in the Old Testament for cultic service or rite is *'ăbōdâ* (Ex 12.25; 13.5). The related verb *'ābad* (to work, to serve) frequently has the sense "to worship," but the specific verb meaning to perform a rite, especially by ministering at the sanctuary, is more commonly *šērēt* (Ex 28.35, 43). The Septuagint translates *'ābōdâ* and *'ābad* by λατρεία, "worship" and λατρεύειν, "to worship" (Ex 12.25; Jos 22.27) but also by λειτουργία and even the more general ἔργον, "work" and κάτεργον, "service." The New Testament uses λατρεία and λειτουργία almost synonymously, though the noun λειτουργία occurs more often (Rom 9.4; Acts 24.14; Lk 1.23; Heb 10.11). In addition to the technical sense of ritually serving God these terms may be employed also with the more general meaning of noncultic worship.

Worship in the Ancient Israelite Society. Practically everything related to rites and worship in the Old Testament bears the stamp of official religion. Expressions of popular piety are occasionally found archaeologically in votive objects and in inscriptions. Of interest for the religious and cultural background of rites and worship in Israel is the mention of "YAHWEH and his asherah" in recently found inscriptions of the 9th or 8th century B.C. at Kuntillat 'Ajrūd in the eastern Sinai peninsula and of the 8th century at Khirbet el-Qōm. In the Old Testament itself, Asherah is at times the name of a goddess, the consort of Baal, and at times an asherah is a cultic object, evidently of wood, perhaps with symbols of the goddess carved into it. In the newly found inscriptions, the word probably designates the goddess. Her association with Yahweh in them has led some to suspect that the worship of Asherah may have been acceptable in the Jahwistic religious practice of the early monarchical period, in popular piety if not officially, and that Asherah in the worship of that time may have been associated not only with Baal but also with Yahweh, perhaps as his consort, and perhaps as a component in the figure of Wisdom personified in Proverbs 1–9.

The revision of interpretative assessments of the attitudes towards rites and worship held in various sectors of Israelite society has continued. The view, widespread in the 19th and early 20th centuries, that the prophetic writings of the Old Testament canon represent an emphasis on the word of God opposed to, and superior to, sacrifice and ritual has been significantly modified, but recently there has also been some revision of the view, equally widespread, that the wisdom literature of the Old Testament was produced by persons who took a rather negative view of cultic practices. L. G. Perdue, without denying the lack of interest in matters of worship among the authors of the wisdom literature, or the occasional cynicism about public worship and ritual piety expressed in Ecclesiastes, has argued that persons with the attitudes expressed in the wisdom literature of Israel and of the Ancient Near East considered worship an integral and important part of rightly ordered society.

Sanctuaries. Much of the new information on sanctuaries where the ancient Israelites worshiped has been provided by archaeologists. Remains of sanctuaries of the monarchical period in Israel itself have at last come to light, for comparison with pre-Israelite Palestinian sanctuaries, with contemporary sanctuaries of the Iron Age outside Palestine, and above all with the information on holy places which can be drawn from the Old Testament. A sanctuary discovered in the excavations of Arad in the south included a small temple building with benches along its interior walls and with a niche in the wall opposite the entrance. In the niche, a sort of holy of holies, was a stele representing the divine presence. In the open space in front of the building was a sacrificial altar, which eventually went out of use, as did the niche with the stele somewhat later. If the benches along the interior served as places for food offerings, they are analogous to the table for the offerings of bread in the Temple of Jerusalem. The stele in the niche confirms the numinous sense of the Ark or of the "mercy-seat" (the *kappōret*) as the focus of God's presence in the holy of holies in Jerusalem. As the historical accuracy of the tradition, found in the Pentateuchal D and P, that the Ark contained the tables of the Law has been questioned, it has been proposed that the Ark originally contained some object like the sculptured stone stele found at Arad, to represent the presence of Yahweh. The sanctuary of Arad shows that Israelite sacrificial worship at sanctuaries with a house of God distinct from that in Jerusalem actually took place in the early monarchical period, until the religious reforms associated with the Judean kings Hezekiah and Josiah succeeded in abolishing such worship outside the Temple of Jerusalem. Those reforms probably explain why the altar of Arad, and then the holy of holies there, went out of use.

Comparison of the Israelite sanctuary found at Arad with the different kind of sanctuary found at Dan in far northern Israel has led to some new discussion of the nature of the high place (*bāmâ*) in early Israel. The sanctuary at Dan, like a similar sanctuary reported still more recently at Tell es-Sebac, had a sacrificial altar which once stood before a raised platform on which no building of the monarchical period has been discovered. It is now widely agreed that this was a typical high place, an open-air sanctuary with an altar and a raised platform, but with no building to serve as the house of God. But the sanctuary of Arad, even though it does have a temple building,

has itself been interpreted as a high place, and the building itself has been interpreted as an example of what is called a *bêt bāmâ* ("house of a high place") in Biblical texts; this remains disputed. So far, no positive archaeological evidence has been produced for or against W. F. Albright's thesis that worship at high places was associated with commemoration of the dead.

Sacrifices. It is perhaps in the study of sacrifices that the refinement of perceptions has been most productive. It was already known that the sacrifice which in the Old Testament is called the *zebaḥ šelāmîm* was a coalition of two originally distinct types of sacrifice: the *zebaḥ* (generally translated simply as "sacrifice"), which was originally a sacrifice of individuals or of families, with a common meal an important component (a type of sacrifice retained in the Passover ritual), and the *šelāmîm* (which has been translated as "peace offering" or "sacrifice of communion"). R. Rendtorff, and then B. A. Levine, have refined our understanding of the *šelāmîm* as a sacrifice originally considered a gift to God, apt for gaining or retaining his favor, made on solemn inaugural occasions like that of the dedication of a sanctuary, or in fulfilling a vow, or in making a covenant. Levine has encouraged us to accept without embarrassment the rather evident presence of an apotropaic element, somewhat magical in intent, in Israelite rites of sacrifice and purification.

The distinction between the function and purpose of the *'āšām* (often translated "guilt offering") and those of the *ḥaṭṭā't* (generally translated "sin offering") remains a difficult problem, because their distinction seems to have been blurred already when the Biblical texts dealing with them were compiled. In this problematic matter B. A. Levine and J. Milgrom, separately, have offered new insights and new solutions. For Levine, the *'āšām* was the result of a commutation of an offering of silver or other objects of value into a sacrifice, while the *ḥaṭṭā't* was originally two distinct types of sacrifice: one, eaten by priests, meant to expiate the guilt resulting from certain offenses of the people and their leaders, and another, burned but not eaten, meant to keep the holy place (the sanctuary) and holy persons (the priests) from contamination by what was unholy or impure. For Milgrom, the *'āšām* was a sacrifice to be made originally when someone had violated an oath, its use eventually extended to any situation in which someone had violated a stipulation of the Law, while the *ḥaṭṭā't* was essentially not a "sin offering" but a "sacrifice of purification," intended to purify sacred spaces and objects.

Milgrom sees not two but three species of "sacrifice of purification," applied against three degrees of contamination of the holy by the unholy or ritually impure: the *ḥaṭṭā't* eaten by the priests, by which the altar in the courtyard of the Temple was purified from impurity by inadvertent acts of an individual other than the high priest: the *ḥaṭṭā't* not eaten but burned, by which the large room (the *hêkāl*) inside the Temple building was purified from a greater degree of impurity caused by inadvertent acts of the high priest or of the people as a whole; and the *ḥaṭṭā't* offered once a year, one the Day of Atonement, by which the *kappōret* (the "mercy-seat") in the Holy of Holies, the entire Temple building, and the altar in the courtyard were all purified from the greatest degree of impurity, which was caused by deliberate sins.

Phenomena of the Holy and the Unholy. Both Levine and Milgrom perceive that, for the ancient Israelites, the holy or ritually pure as well as the profane or ritually impure could spread by contagion, and that human acts violating the holiness of God's ethical and cultic requirements could, and did, contaminate the sacred spaces of the Temple and the sacred altar, focal points of God's presence, even when such acts were committed at some distance from the sanctuary.

Levine and Milgrom, and M. Haran, have also perceived an applied concept of degrees of holiness. The people of Israel, as Yahweh's own people, was a holy people distinct from its profane neighbors; within the holy people the priests enjoyed a greater degree of holiness, while the highest degree of all was that of the high priest. Spatially, the outer courtyard of the Temple for which Ezekiel 40–48 provided was a space holy to a minor degree, while the holiness of the courtyard in front of the Temple building was greater, the holiness of the Altar which stood in that courtyard and of the interior of the Temple building was still greater, and the holiest space of all was the holy of holies at the far end of the Temple's interior. Corresponding to the various degrees of holiness of these spaces were various taboos. Awareness of these gradations in holiness, with their interdictions and taboos, has made it easier to understand why in Ezekiel's plan Israelites, but not heathens, might enter the outer courtyard of the Temple, while priests and Levites (and, in P, ordinary Israelites also, but only to slaughter a victim they were offering) might enter the inner courtyard, but, according to both Ezekiel and to P, only priests could approach the altar of sacrifice in that courtyard or enter the Temple building, and the high priest alone was allowed to enter the holy of holies.

Feasts and Ritual Occasions. The hypotheses of earlier decades whose gradual revision is most evident, in the study of ritual and worship, tend to be those engendered by an interest in feasts and ritual occasions on which certain elements of Israel's religious or historical awareness would have been specifically commemorated, or which served as settings in which certain Old Testament texts, particularly psalms of certain genres, would have been used. S. Mowinckel's postulation, in *Psalmenstudien* 2 (Kristiania 1922), of an autumnal new year festival in Israel of the monarchial celebrated as a feast of Yahweh's enthronement (with a ritual mime of his victory over chaos at the time of creation performed in order to renew annually the forces of creation, with the earthly king profoundly involved, and with a rite of enthronement of Yahweh as the festival climax) has seen its day, but not all of Mowinckel's imaginative ideas on the matter have been rejected. Assyriologists have pointed out that the Babylonian New Year Festival which served Mowinckel and others after him as a model was neither a feast of the Babylonian god Marduk's enthronement nor an explicitly royal festival, and scholars have been increasingly skeptical about the postulated transfer of the Babylonian mime of Marduk's victory over the gods of chaos to the ritual practice of the Israelites worshiping Yahweh.

The excess of some who came after Mowinckel and expanded his ideas yet further—particularly those of S. H. Hooke and the "Myth and Ritual School"—have now been discredited, both by Assyriologists and by biblicists. Nevertheless, there is now a certain quiet openness to the possibility that a new year festival in Israel of the monarchical period, when the new year began in the autumnal month of Tishri, may have existed as a festival on which Yahweh's kingship was commemorated, although not specifically as a festival of his enthronement. This might account for some passing allusions to an unspecified autumnal festival preserved in the Old Testament, and it would make it easier to understand why much later, in the second century A.D., when the Jewish new year had been placed in the autumn once more, after the year had begun in the springtime in the post-Exilic period, the Mishna associated the post-Biblical new year festival, *Rō'š haššānâ*, with the theme of Yahweh's kingship. That ideas of Yahweh's kingship were current in ancient Israel, and that his kingship and its effects in the universe are extolled in several psalms, are undeniable.

In the years when interest in covenant as a key concept for interpreting the thought and practice of ancient Israel was high, some scholars, like A. Weiser and H. J. Kraus, accepted the thesis of an autumnal new year festival in the monarchical period but interpreted it as a feast on which covenant with Yahweh was celebrated and renewed. Enthusiasm for that line of interpretation has waned in recent years, and Kraus himself proposed it with less conviction after he first enunciated it in 1951. The existence of a feast on which covenant was renewed has been denied altogether by F. E. Wilms, *Das jahwistische Bundesbuch in Exodus 34* (Munich 1973), as far as the Old Testament period is concerned. For New Testament times, however, an examination of the *targumim* of Exodus 19–20, Jewish festive readings, and related Old Testament passages has led J. Potin to the conclusion that by the Rabbinic period, at least, the Jewish Pentecost, i.e., the ancient Feast of Weeks which was originally a feast of thanksgiving for the spring harvest, had become an occasion for commemorating the covenant of Sinai and the giving of the Law.

The interest in ritual occasions as vital settings for various genres of psalms, stimulated by H. Gunkel at the turn of the century, continues, but its alliance with other interests has shifted slightly away from comparative religion of the Ancient Near East towards sociology of religion. An example is E. S. Gerstenberger's effort to reconstruct the vital setting of those psalms which have since Gunkel's days been called "songs of lamentation" (*Klagelieder*). For Gerstenberger, they should be called "songs of rogation" or "of entreaty" (*Bittlieder*). In his attempt at reconstruction of the vital setting in which they may have been used, he adduces some comparative material from Mesopotamia, but his sociological techniques lead him out of the Temple to secular spaces like river banks, or the roofs of houses, or the spaces just inside city gates, as places where the ritual may have taken place. A sociological interest in personal piety distinguished from official religion has led R. Albertz to see the "songs of lamentation of the individual" in the Psalter as expressions of personal piety, and the "songs of lamentation of the people" as expressions of the piety of Israelite society at large.

The theological rediscovery of the early Christian concept of sacramental rites as memorials of a saving action of the past with effects produced in the present has encouraged a moderate amount of interest in memorial as it is found in the context of feasts and ritual moments of ancient Israel and Judaism, with that Christian concept in mind. This may produce fresh insights into the concept of memorial in certain Old Testament texts, studied for their own sake and on their own terms.

New Directions. The most extensive work published recently on ancient Israelite rites, their material contexts, and the cultic persons responsible for them is M. Haran's *Temples and Temple-Service in Ancient Israel.* Many of the insights and ideas which it contains had, in fact, already appeared in articles which Haran published, often in Modern Hebrew, in the quarter of a century preceding. His view of the cultic part of the Pentateuchal P, in which so much of the pertinent Biblical material is to be found, is not that of a collection of originally independent *libelli* containing cultic prescriptions, but rather that of a consistently unified codification of prescriptions achieved long

before the Babylonian Exile, and indeed old enough to have served as the inspiration for the cultic reforms of Hezekiah *c.* 700 B.C.

Although such a view of P is not popular among Biblical scholars, it has found its supporters, especially among Israeli scholars. (It was basically the position of Haran's teacher, Y. Kaufmann.) Although some of the details in Haran's work go beyond the available evidence, and he dismisses at times too readily the arguments of those whose positions differ from his, his knowledge of the rites and the cultic institutions of ancient Israel is impressive, and his theses are well argued. Against P's having served as the inspiration of Hezekiah's reforms it has been objected that, of the relatively little we know of those reforms, some—most notably, the centralization of worship—are not concerns found in P. For Haran, the tradition of the Tabernacle is based on a cultic tent which existed in Shilo and which was really distinct from the "tent of meeting" which he sees as a place for oracular consultation. He has painstakingly distinguished the functions of a sanctuary with a temple building from those of an open-air sanctuary, and he has carefully worked out the concept of holiness as one admitting degrees, reflected in prescriptions for sacrifice, for roles of sacral persons, for distinctions of sacred space.

Haran's dating of P and its cultic material is an example of a tendency, visible perhaps especially in the United States, to move away from positions on the evolution of tradition and of Israel's religious institutions for which a general consensus has existed, with some significant modifications, since the work of J. Wellhausen. An important element in the systematic constructions elaborated by Wellhausen and his immediate followers was the application of views of the evolution of rites, feasts, and especially priesthood to the relative dating of sources. Both Haran and F. M. Cross, in expressing new answers to questions of historical development in priesthood, take pains to disavow Wellhausen, while A. Cody is content to remain basically within the general consensus in his relative dating of the evidence.

Prolongation into New Testament Times. The rites and worship of ancient Israel continued to evolve into New Testament times, until the Roman destruction of Jerusalem in A.D. 70 led to the radical interruption of all that was reserved to the Temple alone, but not of other forms of Jewish worship. J. H. Charlesworth, after summarizing major research on the Jewish background of the hymns and prayers in the New Testament particularly, has drawn conclusions of his own in which he is attentive to the need to make distinctions. H. J. Klauck has examined the background to early Christian house churches both in Judaism and in Hellenistic civilization, to move on to interesting reflections on the appearance of priests, of sacrificial concepts, and of buildings for strictly religious use as signs of an early Christian absorption both of Old Testament models and of Hellenistic religious culture. S. Safrai's work on pilgrimage to Jerusalem from the early post-Exilic period until the destruction of the Temple is fairly exhaustive, but it shows a lack of interest in critical evaluation of sources and a failure to be alert to distinctions of time and place.

In general, the view of an earlier generation that rites and worship in early Christianity moved from those of contemporary Judaism to a ritually austere evangelical worship and then on to a less evangelical "early Catholicism" is fading. New impulses arising from the study of Jewish sectarianism like that of Qumran and from the religious sociology of the Hellenistic world have opened scholarly eyes to the presence of diverse lines of development, of an early Christian urge to set out on new paths, with some signs of movement here and there back toward Jewish forms and interpretations. J. Heinemann's and J. Petuchowski's recent studies of prayer and worship in a Jewish synagogue have made it clear that the synagogue was more than a place of assembly and of Biblical reading with homiletic commentary. They have thus made it easier to see the synagogue in the background of the Christian hours of prayer. The synagogue was not a sacred place on Jewish terms, but when the Christian Eucharist came to be interpreted in an overtly sacrificial manner, the places where it was celebrated came to be sensed as sacred places, and those who presided at its celebration came to be identified as priests.

Several studies have appeared on the question whether the Berakoth said at meals of pious Jews provided a direct or indirect model for the structure of Christian anaphoras. Apart from that, interest in emphasizing the Eucharist as a meal in the attitudes of 20th-century Christians has made itself felt in recent studies on eucharistic origins. It is the thesis of W. Bösen that the original Jewish background of the Eucharist as meal lay not in the Passover meal but in the Jewish non-cultic farewell meal, and that the Eucharist only later became a cultic memorial, a dramatic representation of what happened at the Last Supper, ritualized still later. X. Léon-Dufour sees in the New Testament writing two traditions of eucharistic origins: one a cultic tradition, and the other a "testamentary" tradition of the Eucharist as farewell meal, both being meant to sustain a link between Christ's saving actions in the past and ourselves in the present—the cultic tradition doing so by presenting the Eucharist as memorial, the testamentary tradition by presenting it as fulfillment of the Lord's instructions.

Bibliography: R. ALBERTZ, *Persönliche Frömmigkeit und offizielle Religion* (Stuttgart 1978). A. BIRAN, ed., *Temples and High Places in Biblical Times* (Jerusalem 1981). W. BÖSEN, *Jesusmahl-Eucharistisches Mahl-Endzeitmahl* (Stuttgart 1980). T. BUSINK, *Der Tempel von Jerusalem von Salomo bis Herodes,* 2 v. (Leiden 1970–80). J. H. CHARLESWORTH, "A Prolegomenon to a New Study of the Jewish Background of the Hymns and Prayers in the New Testament," *Journal of Jewish Studies* 33 (1982) 265–85. A. CODY, *A History of Old Testament Priesthood* (Rome 1969). F. M. CROSS, *Canaanite Myth and Hebrew Epic* (Cambridge, Massachusetts 1973). J. A. EMERTON, "New Light on Israelite Religion: The Implications of the Inscriptions from Kuntillat 'Ajrud," *Zeitschrift für die alttestamentliche Wissenschaft* 94 (1982) 1–20. V. FRITZ, *Tempel und Zelt* (Neukirchen 1980). J. GUTMANN, ed., *Ancient Synagogues* (Chico, California 1981). M. HARAN. *Temples and Temple-Service in Ancient Israel* (Winona Lake, Indiana 1985). J. HEINEMANN, *Prayer in the Talmud: Forms and Patterns* (Berlin 1977). H. J. KLAUCK, *Hausgemeinde und Hauskirche im frühen Christentum* (Stuttgart 1981). X. LÉON-DUFOUR, *Sharing the Eucharistic Bread,* tr. M. J. O'CONNELL (New York/Mahwah 1987). B. A. LEVINE, *In the Presence of the Lord* (Leiden 1974). J. MILGROM, *Cult and Conscience* (Leiden 1976); *Studies in Cultic Theology and Terminology,* (Leiden 1983). J. PETUCHOWSKI, "The Liturgy of the Synagogue: History, Structure, and Contents," W. S. GRÉEN, ed., *Approaches to Ancient Judaism,* v. 4 (Chico, California 1983) 1–64. L. G. PERDUE, *Wisdom and Cult* (Missoula, Montana 1977). J. POTIN, *La fête juive de la Pentecôte,* 2 v. (Paris 1971). R. RENDTORFF, *Studien zur Geschichte des Opfers im Alten Israel* (Neukirchen 1967). S. SAFRAI, *Die Wallfahrt im Zeitalter des Zweiten Tempels* (Neukirchen 1981). M. S. SMITH, "God Male and Female in the Old Testament: Yahweh and his 'Asherah'," *Theological Studies* 48 (1987) 333–40. T. J. TALLEY. "The Eucharistic Prayer, Tradition and Development," K. STEVENSON, ed., *Liturgy Reshaped* (London 1982) 48–64.

[J. L. RONAN/A. CODY/EDS.]

WORTHINGTON, THOMAS

A leader in the English seminary movement; b. Blanscough Hall, Wigam, 1549; d. Biddulph Hall, Staffordshire, 1627. He was born of a staunchly Catholic Lancashire family, educated at Oxford and Douai College, and ordained in 1577. He departed for the English mission the following year. He was captured in 1584 and banished from the realm in 1585. For the next 28 years his main work was the English seminary in Reims and Douai. In 1589 he was named vice president of Douai and in 1599 succeeded Richard Barrett there as the third president. Despite a praiseworthy administration, he was plagued with ever-present financial difficulties, declining student morale, and the unfortunate quarrels that divided the English clergy during these years. In 1613 Dr. Worthington was summoned to Rome, and Matthew Kellison succeeded him as president. By 1616 he was again on the mission, working in London and Staffordshire, where he organized a sodality or association among his fellow priests for their mutual spiritual comfort and financial assistance. He was the author of several controversial and devotional works and did many of the annotations of the Douai Old Testament.

Bibliography: P. GUILDAY, *The English Catholic Refugees on the Continent* (London 1914). T. FITZHERBERT, *Letters,* ed. L. HICKS, *Publications of the Catholic Record Society* 41 (London 1948).

[T. H. CLANCY]

WOUNDS OF OUR LORD, DEVOTION TO

Consists in honoring the wounds in Christ's hands, feet, and side as the channels through which flowed His precious blood in his sacrificial death on the cross. "In him we have redemption through his blood, the remission of sins, according to the riches of his grace" (Eph 1.7). After the Resurrection Our Lord retained the marks of His wounds as badges of triumph. "Jesus came, the doors being closed, and stood in their midst, and said, 'Peace be to you!' Then he said to Thomas, 'Bring here thy finger, and see my hands; and bring here thy hand, and put it into my side; and be not unbelieving, but believing'" (Jn 20.26–27).

As the signs of His love in His Passion and death the sacred wounds of Christ were naturally invitations to devotion and imitation to all Christians pondering the Scriptures. St. John Chrysostom, for example, in his homilies on the Gospel of St. John points to Our Lord's deportment in His Passion as motive and model for his congregation (*see Homily* 83; Jn 18.1–36). With the Crusades there was a new impetus to devotion to the Passion of Christ. St. Bernard of Clairvaux set the trend, and with his preaching and prestige powerfully promoted special devotion to the five wounds of Our Lord. (*See* SACRED HUMANITY, DEVOTION TO THE.)

In the Middle Ages many different practices were employed in honoring the wounds of Christ, e.g., offices, hymns, the recitation of the Lord's Prayer every day, even the use of a corona of the five wounds. Many devotional manuals listed prayers and pious activities for private or public use in honor of Our Lord's Passion in general or specifically in honor of His sacred wounds. Usually devotion to the wounds was concerned only with the wounds in His hands, feet, and sacred side. However, in the medieval era there were devout attempts to list all the injuries inflicted on Jesus in the Passion by the crowning with thorns and the scourging, some number greater than 5,000 ordinarily being offered as the total. Obviously, the mathematics of the matter is arbitrary and of small importance, the point being the devout awareness of the reality of Christ's Passion. Various Offices and Masses in honor of the wounds of Our Lord were composed and celebrated locally in different places after the 14th century; none of these was ever extended to the whole Church.

Bibliography: F. PRAT, *Jesus Christ: His Life, His Teaching, and His Work,* tr. J. J. HEENAN, 2 v. (Milwaukee 1950) v.2, bk. 4, ch. 10–11; *The Theology, of St. Paul,* tr. J. L. STODDARD, 2 v. (London 1926–27; repr. Westminster, MD 1958) v.2, bk. 4, ch. 2.

[J. P. BRUNI/EDS.]

WOYWOD, STANISLAUS

Authority on the 1917 Code of Canon Law; b. Guttstadt, Germany, Aug. 10, 1880; d. New York, NY, Sept. 19, 1941. He took his preparatory seminary training in Holland before coming to the U.S. in 1897, then entered the Franciscan novitiate, Paterson, NJ, in 1899, and was ordained June 4, 1906. Three years later he received the lectorate in both theology and Canon Law at the Atheneum Antonianum, the Franciscan international college in Rome. Following his return to the U.S., he was professor of Canon Law in several Franciscan houses and at St. Bonaventure's Seminary, Allegany, NY. In 1930 he was named first superior of Holy Name College, his province's theological house of studies in Washington, DC. During these same years he was editor of *St. Anthony's Almanac* (now the *National Catholic Almanac*) and author of many articles for the *American Ecclesiastical Review.* In 1918 he published *The New Canon Law,* a paraphrase of the Code of Canon Law promulgated the year before. This volume, together with *A Practical Commentary on the Code of Canon Law* (New York 1925), did much to familiarize the English-speaking public with the new legislation. From 1918 until early 1941 his articles and answers to questions on Canon Law and moral and pastoral theology were a standard feature of the *Homiletic and Pastoral Review.* He prepared constitutions for a number of religious institutes of women in the U.S. and from 1927 to 1930 was vice postulator of the cause of Leo Heinrichs, OFM.

Bibliography: J. P. DONOVAN, "Code and the Homiletic These Thirty–One Years," *Homiletic and Pastoral Review* 50 (Oct. 1949) 38–44. FRANCISCAN PROVINCE OF THE MOST HOLY NAME, *Provincial Annals* 3 (October 1941) 177–179.

[B. C. GERHARDT]

WRENNO, ROGER, BL.

Lay martyr; b. *c.* 1576 at Chorley, Lancashire, England; d. March 18, 1616, hanged at Lancaster under James I. A devout layman, Wrenno was imprisoned with other Catholics in Lancaster Castle but escaped with Bl. John Thules one evening before the Lenten assizes. They were recaptured the following day. Wrenno refused to exchange the oath of supremacy for his life and was hanged just after Fr. Thules. He was beatified by Pope John Paul

II on Nov. 22, 1987 with George Haydock and companions.

Feast of the English Martyrs: May 4 (England).

See Also: ENGLAND, SCOTLAND, AND WALES, MARTYRS OF.

Bibliography: R. CHALLONER, *Memoirs of Missionary Priests,* ed. J. H. POLLEN (rev. ed. London 1924). J. H. POLLEN, *Acts of English Martyrs* (London 1891).

[K. I. RABENSTEIN]

WRIGHT, JOHN JOSEPH

American church leader, cardinal, preacher and theologian; b. Boston, Mass, July 18, 1909, of John Joseph and Harriet (Cokely) Wright; d. Aug. 1979. He was educated at Boston College (B.A. 1931) and the Gregorian University, Rome (S.T.L. 1936; S.T.D. 1939). While engaged in studies at North American College, Wright was ordained to the priesthood on Dec. 8, 1935. Wright returned to his native Archdiocese of Boston after completing his studies and was assigned to teach at St. John's Seminary in Brighton until 1945, when he was named secretary to Cardinal William O'Connell, the archbishop of Boston. On June 30, 1947, Wright was consecrated titular bishop of Aegea and auxiliary bishop of Boston, where he served until his installation as the first bishop of Worcester, Mass. on March 7, 1950. On March 18, 1959 Wright was installed as the eighth bishop of PITTSBURGH.

He served as bishop of Pittsburgh until his creation as a cardinal priest on April 28, 1969, with the titular church of Jesus the Divine Teacher. Wright served in various capacities at the National Conference of Catholic Bishops and was chairman of the drafting committee for the first two postconciliar collective pastoral letters of the American bishops, *The Church in Our Day* (1967) and *Human Life in Our Day* (1968). He was also elected by the American hierarchy as a delegate to the first two synods of bishops in 1967 and 1969. On April 23, 1969, Wright was appointed the prefect of the Congregation for the Clergy by Pope Paul VI, and in 1971 the pope designated him one of three presidents of the Second General Assembly of the Synod of Bishops. He was also appointed to two subsequent synods in 1974 on evangelization and 1977 on catechetics.

During the time of preparation for the Second VATICAN COUNCIL, Bishop Wright was named a member of the Theological Commission of the Preparatory Commission of the Council. He later noted that the most lasting fruits of the commissions' work included the "seed-ideas" contained in the chapters on collegiality, the laity,

and the Blessed Virgin in the *Constitution of the Church in the Modern World,* as well as in the sections on the person, Christian anthropology, dialogue with atheism, marriage, and peace and war. Bishop Wright was chairman of the subcommission that drafted the chapter on the laity in the *Dogmatic Constitution on the Church.* He also served on other subcommittees responsible for the chapters "Marriage and the Family," "The Signs of the Times," and "The Church of the Poor." Among Wright's most memorable interventions during the council was his address on the question "of religious liberty and its exercise" and its relationship to the question of "the common good."

During his tenure as head of the Congregation for the Clergy, the office issued the *Circular Letter on Priest Councils* (1969) mandating diocesan priest councils, the *General Catechetical Directory* (1971), and the *Circular Letter on Pastoral Councils* (1973), which was a landmark for practical lay involvement in the life and ministry of the local churches.

Cardinal Wright was urbane and witty and enjoyed a reputation, particularly in Europe, as an intellectual and theologian of considerable ability. He stressed in his teaching and preaching the need for theological clarity and continuity with the teaching tradition of the Church. In social issues he was one of the leading experts on Catholic social teaching and was a forceful and visible proponent of Catholic involvement in social justice and peace concerns. He was also one of the early leaders of the ecumenical movement in the United States.

In Rome, in addition to his responsibilities as head of the clergy office, Wright was also a member of various congregations including those for the doctrine of the faith, bishops, education, and evangelization, as well as a member of the Council for the Public Affairs of the Church, the Commission for the Revision of the Code of Canon Law and the commission for Vatican City. In the latter years of his life, Wright became increasingly outspoken against what he saw as an abuse and misapplication or misinterpretation of the teaching of the Second Vatican Council and called for a period of consolidation.

Cardinal Wright left his noted collection of material on St. Joan of Arc to the Boston Public Library, material which, in his interest and devotion, he had collected over a lifetime. His collection of books and material on both the Second Vatican Council and the subsequent five synods of bishops is housed at Duquesne University, Pittsburgh. The collected talks of Cardinal Wright covering his years in Boston, Worcester, Pittsburgh, and Rome are published in three volumes entitled *Resonare Christum.*

Bibliography: J. J. WRIGHT, *National Patriotism in Papal Teaching* (Boston 1942); *The Christian and the Law: Selected Red*

Mass Sermons (Notre Dame, Ind. 1962); *Meditations of the Church, Based on the Constitution of the Church* (New York 1967); *The Church: Hope of the World*, ed. D. W. WUERL (Kenosha, Wis. 1972).

[D. W. WUERL]

WRIGHT, PETER, BL.

Jesuit priest and martyr; b. Slipton, Northamptonshire, England, 1603; d. hanged at Tyburn (London), May 19, 1651. Following the death of his Catholic father, Peter worked for a local solicitor to help support his 11 siblings. Eventually he apostatized to Anglicanism under the influence of the firm's clients. He joined the English army to fight in the Netherlands, but deserted after a month's service. Soon thereafter he visited the English Jesuits in Liège and was reconciled to the Church. After two years (1627–29) studying at the Jesuit college in Ghent, he entered the novitiate at Watten, completed his seminary studies at Liège, and was ordained (1639). Thereafter he served at the English College in Saint-Omer and as military chaplain to Sir Henry Gage's English regiment in the service of Spain in Flanders. He returned to England with Gage in the spring of 1644, and was present at the relief of Basing House, the seat of John, fifth Marquis of Wincheser. On Gage's death (Jan. 13, 1645), at which he was present, Wright became the marquis's chaplain in Hampton, then at his London house, where he was arrested on Candlemas Day (Feb. 2) 1651. Committed to Newgate, he was condemned at the Old Bailey under 27 Eliz., c. 2, on May 17, 1651. His execution on Whit Monday was witnessed by over 20,000 spectators. Mercifully, he was allowed to hang until he was dead. His relics can be found at the Jesuit college in Liège. He was beatified by Pius XI on Dec. 15, 1929.

Feast of the English Martyrs: May 4 (England); December 1 (Jesuits).

See Also: ENGLAND, SCOTLAND, AND WALES, MARTYRS OF.

Bibliography: R. CHALLONER, *Memoirs of Missionary Priests,* ed. J. H. POLLEN (rev. ed. London 1924; repr. Farnborough 1969) II, 189. H. FOLEY, *Records of the English Province of the Society of Jesus* (London 1877–82) II, 506–65, VII, 870. J. H. POLLEN, *Acts of English Martyrs* (London 1891). M. STANTON, *Menology of England and Wales* (London, 1887) 218. J. N. TYLENDA, *Jesuit Saints & Martyrs* (Chicago 1998) 138–40.

[K. I. RABENSTEIN]

WRIGHT, WILLIAM

Jesuit; b. York, England, 1563; d. Leicestershire, England, Jan. 18, 1639. Wright was the son of John Wright, apothecary of York, a noted recusant; the Marian priest Dr. John Wright was probably an uncle. William, like his elder brother Thomas, was educated at York. He went to Reims and then to Rome, where he entered the English College (1581). Wright joined the Society of Jesus (1581) while still a student. For several years Wright taught theology at the Jesuit colleges at Vienna and Graz. Proceeding to the English Mission (1606), he was captured and imprisoned soon after arrival, but escaped (1607) and concealed himself in Leicestershire. He founded the Leicestershire mission of the society and was for many years its superior. He appears to have lived and worked in the county until his death. He published several substantial works against the English Protestants.

Bibliography: T. COOPER, *The Dictionary of National Biography from the Earliest Times to 1900* (London 1885–1900) 21:1050–51. H. FOLEY, ed., *Records of the English Province of the Society of Jesus,* 7 v. (London 1877–82) 2.2:275–286; 7.3:871–874. *Publications of the Catholic Record Society* (London 1905–) v.37. A. F. ALLISON and D. M. ROGERS, *A Catalogue of Catholic Books in English. . .1558–1640,* 2 v. (London 1956). C. SOMMERVOGEL et al., *Bibliothéque de la Compagnie de Jésus* (Brussels–Paris 1890–1932) 8:1223–24. J. GILLOW, *A Literary and Biographical History or Bibliographical Dictionary of the English Catholics from 1534 to the Present Time* (London-New York 1885–1902) 5:596–598.

[A. F. ALLISON]

WU ANBANG, PETER, ST.

Lay martyr, catechist, writer, member of the Third Order of St. Francis; b. 1860, ; d. July 9, 1900, Taiyüan, Shanxi Province, China. Peter Wu Anbang (Wu An-pan or U- Ngan-Pan), born into a Catholic family headed by Wu Gende, studied in the Franciscan seminary at Taiyüan, but was never ordained after determining that he had no priestly vocation. Nevertheless he served the community in the priests' refectory, as footman to Fr. Elias Facchini, as a catechist, and as copyist for Bp. Gregorio GRASSI. Peter wrote a booklet entitled *Veneration of the Sacred Heart of Jesus*, as well as poetry. Because he was a professed Catholic and refused to deny the faith, he was beaten and hanged from a beam by soldiers when he attempted to take money to priests hiding in the village of Changgou (June 28, 1900). He was released when he promised not to continue working for foreigners. Peter was among the several dozen Christians trapped inside the Taiyuan cathedral, arrested by the Boxers on July 5, 1900, and beheaded four days later. He was beatified by Pope Pius XII (Nov. 24, 1946) and canonized (Oct. 1, 2000) by Pope John Paul II with Augustine Zhao Rong and companions.

Feast: July 4.

Bibliography: L. M. BALCONI, *Le Martiri di Taiyuen* (Milan 1945). *Acta Apostolicae Sedis* 47 (1955) 381–388; *Vita del b. A. Crescitelli* (Milan 1950). M. T. DE BLARER, *Les Bse Marie Hermine de Jésus et ses compagnes, franciscaines missionnaires de Marie, massacrées le 9 juillet 1900 à Tai-Yuan-Fou, Chine* (Paris 1947). *Les Vingt-neuf martyrs de Chine, massacrés en 1900, béatifiés par Sa Sainteté Pie XII, le 24 novembre, 1946* (Rome 1946). L. MINER, *China's Book of Martyrs: A Record of Heroic Martyrdoms and Marvelous Deliverances of Chinese Christians during the Summer of 1900* (Ann Arbor 1994). J. SIMON, *Sous le sabre des Boxers* (Lille 1955). C. TESTORE, *Sangue e palme sul fiume giallo. I beati martiri cinesi nella persecuzione della Boxe Celi Sud-Est, 1900* (Rome 1955). *L'Osservatore Romano*, Eng. Ed. 40 (2000): 1–2, 10.

[K. I. RABENSTEIN]

WU LI

Chinese priest and artist; b. district of Changshu, Jiangsu, 1631; d. Shanghai, 1718. In his early days he studied painting, and soon won fame as both an artist and a poet. His native district was one of the centers of missionary activity and he must have had frequent communication with the Jesuit missionaries. He was baptized Simon Xavier shortly after 1675, and in 1688 adopted the surname A Cunha. After his mother and his wife had died, he entered the Jesuit novitiate at Macau in 1682 at the age of 50. He was ordained six years later by the first Chinese bishop, Mgr. Lo Wen-tsao, OP (1614–91), known to Westerners as Gregory Lopez. Wu Li had 30 years of fruitful ministry before his death.

Wu Li was one of the greatest painters in the Ch'ing period, and is said to have grasped the spirit of his Sung and Yüan masters. He has left a number of paintings that are still treasured by collectors. His poetic work, *Mo-ching shih-ch'ao,* was published (1719) by a disciple, together with a collection of his colophons on paintings.

His poems are graceful and limpid, especially those of his later years, which couch Catholic thought in exquisite style; he was perhaps the first in China to find a poetic vehicle for Christian doctrine. His poems manifest his devout life and his admiration of the scientific achievements of the early Jesuits. His religious and philosophical sayings were recorded under the title *K'ou-to.* Only the second series, dealing with the years 1695 to 1697, is extant. It was published in 1909, together with the *Mo-ching shih–ch'ao* and the *San-pachi,* another collection of poems. The *San-yü-chi* (90 additional poems) were first published in the *Shang-chiao tsa-chih* (*Revue Catholique Shanghai*) in 1937 on the occasion of the 250th anniversary of his ordination.

Bibliography: FANG CHAO–YING, *Eminent Chinese of the Ch'ing Period (1644–1912),* ed. A. W. HUMMEL, 2 v. (Washington 1943) v.2. M. CHANG and P. DE PRUNELÉ, *Le Père Simon A Cunha,* SJ (Variétés sinologiques 37; Shanghai 1914). L. PFISTER, *Notices biographiques et bibliographiques sur les Jésuites de l'ancienne mission de la Chine 1552–1773,* 2 v. (Variétés sinologiques 59–60; Shanghai 1932) v.1. J. and A. H. BURLING, "Wu Li: The Great Chinese Christian Painter," *China Journal* 34 (1941) 161–167. G. DUNNE, *Generation of Giants* (Notre Dame, Ind, 1962). CH'EN YÜAN, "In Commemoration of the 250th Anniversary of Wu Li's Ordination to the Priesthood," in *Fu–jen hsüleh–chin* 5.1–2 (Peiping 1939), in Chinese.

[A. CHAN]

WULFLAICUS, ST.

Also known as Vulfilaic, Wulphy, Walfroy; d. *c.* 594. GREGORY OF TOURS, who met him *c.* 585, described him as a holy hermit living near Yvois (Carignan near Sedan). Of Lombard stock, he came under the influence of (St.) AREDIUS OF ATTANE. After a pilgrimage to the tomb of St. MARTIN OF TOURS, he became the saint's ardent disciple. He built a hermitage near Yvois and won the inhabitants from the worship of Diana to Christianity, reportedly working miracles for them through the intercession of St. Martin. The neighboring bishops cut short his attempt to do penance on a pillar in the manner of St. Simon STYLITES. On July 7, 979, his relics were translated to Yvois. He should probably not be identified with Waltfrid (also Walfroy) in the calendar of Trier.

Feast: Oct. 21.

Bibliography: *Acta Sanctorum* (Paris 1863—) 2:478–481. GREGORY OF TOURS, *Historia Francorum,* ed. W. ARNDT, *Monumenta Germania Historica: Scriptores rerum Merovingicarum;* Eng. *The History of the Franks,* tr. O. M. DALTON, 2 v. (Oxford 1927). J. L. BAUDOT and L. CHAUSSIN, *Vies des saints et des bienheureux selon l'ordre du calendrier avec l'historique des fêtes,* ed. by the Benedictines of Paris (Paris 1935–56) 10:721–725. A. M. ZIMMERMANN, *Kalendarium Benedictinum: Die Heiligen und Seligen des Benediktinerorderns und seiner Zweige* (Metten 1933–38) 2:417; 3:207. A. ZIMMERMANN, *Lexikon für Theologie und Kirche,* ed. M. BUCHBERGER (Freiburg 1930–38) 10:979.

[M. C. MCCARTHY]

WULFRAM OF SENS, ST.

Latin, Wulframnus, also known as Wolfram; Merovingian bishop, missionary; b. Milly-er-Gâtinais, France; d. Fontenelle, March 20, either 695? (Laporte) or *c.* 700 (Boilandists). Convinced that his life at the royal court was endangering his soul, he gave his lands to the Abbey of FONTENELLE. Unanimously elected bishop of Sens (682?), he stabilized his diocesan government and then left, with several monks from Fontenelle, to evangelize the Frisians. It is said that just before this he resigned his bishopric of Sens because the legitimate Bishop Amatus, although exiled, was still living at the time of his election. The Frisian apostolate (known only through the Fontenelle tradition) apparently was a success. His cult followed the translations of his relics: in the first translation (704) the bodies of SS. WANDRILLE, ANSBERT, and Wulfram were exhumed and placed in the church of Saint-Peter (commemorated, March 31); the second translation of these relics (944) removed them to the Abbey Mont-Blandin near Ghent; in the 11th century a third translation placed Wulfram's relics at Abbeville (some hold that his body had reposed only at Fontenelle prior to this translation), where a chapter of canons and a parish were established in his honor (he is also patron saint of the town); in a fourth translation (May 21, 1662), the bishop of Amiens had his well-preserved bones transferred to a new shrine. A. Legris [*Analecta Bollandiana* (1898) 265–306] holds that the shorter vita of Wulfram is the older; W. Levison [*Neues Archiv der Gesellschaft für ältere deutsche Geschichtskunde* (1900) 593] claims this distinction for the longer life (*Monumenta Germaniae Historica: Scriptores* 5:657–673).

Feast: March 20; Oct. 15 (translation).

Bibliography: *Inventio et miracula s. Vulfranni*, ed. J. LAPORTE (Rouen 1938). *Martyrologium Romanum*, ed. H. DELEHAYE (Brussels 1940) 105. A. BUTLER, *The Lives of the Saints*, rev. ed. H. THURSTON and D. ATTWATER (New York 1956) 1:642–643.

[P. COUSIN]

WULFSTAN OF WORCESTER, ST.

Benedictine monk, bishop of Worcester; b. Little Itchington, near Warwick, England, *c.* 1008; d. Jan. 18, 1095. He was educated in the Benedictine Abbeys of EVESHAM and PETERBOROUGH and became a monk of the cathedral monastery of Worcester, where he was schoolmaster, and then prior, and was finally elected bishop in 1062 with the approval of the witenagemot. Since the See of WORCESTER was claimed by the Province of York before its affiliation as a suffragan of Canterbury in 1070 (it had even been occupied directly by archbishops of York on occasion), Wulfstan was consecrated at York—after some reluctance to accept the office at all. As bishop he rapidly became famous for his continued monastic asceticism and for his personal sanctity. Even though he had earlier been sympathetic to Harold of Wessex, he was among those who made their submission to King WILLIAM I, the Conqueror, at Berkhamstead in 1066. He therefore retained his see and even became one of the most trusted of William's advisers and administrators. He assisted in the compilation of the DOMESDAY BOOK, supported William against the rebellious barons in 1075, and remained loyal even to King WILLIAM II RUFUS. In ecclesiastical

politics he was frequently at odds with both Archbishop LANFRANC and the archbishop of York, THOMAS OF BAYEUX, without, however, suffering any loss in prestige or in reputation for holiness. As a pastor his greatest achievement was to stop the merchants of Bristol from their customary capture and sale of English slaves. Wulfstan is buried in the cathedral at Worcester, which he rebuilt. Pope Innocent III canonized him in 1203. He became one of the patron saints of his See of Worcester; more recently he became a patron saint of Worcester, MA, USA. His biography was written by Hemming and FLORENCE OF WORCESTER (ed. H. Whaton, *Anglia sacra*, 1691) and WILLIAM OF MALMESBURY (ed. R. R. Darlington, Camden Soc. 40, 1928; tr. J. H. F. Peile, Oxford 1934).

Feast: Jan. 19.

Bibliography: F. M. STENTON, *Anglo-Saxon England* (Oxford 1947). F. BARLOW, *The English Church 1000–1066: A Constitutional History* (Hamden, CT 1963). D. KNOWLES, *The Monastic Order in England, 943–1216* (Cambridge, Eng. 1962) 74–78, 159–163.

[J. BRÜCKMANN]

WULMAR, ST.

Also known as Vulmar; hermit and abbot; b. near Boulogne (Pas-de-Calais), France; d. July 20, *c.* 710. When his marriage was annulled in its first years because of his wife's earlier betrothal to a noble Frank, he became a monk at Hautmont, where he received his education. When ordained, he obtained permission to retire to a hermitage in his native Picardy. He abandoned this life to found two monasteries: one for women at Wière-au-Bois, the other for men at *Silvacius* (later known as Saint-Vulmer, or -Samer), where he was abbot until his death. He was buried there. His relics were translated to Boulogne, then Ghent. His *Vita 1a* dates from the middle of the 9th century and is of historical value. His *Vita 2a*, written during the 12th century, is only an amplification of the first.

Feast: July 20; June 17 (translation).

Bibliography: *Acta Sanctorum* (Paris 1863—) 5:84–89. *Analecta Bollandiana* 3 (Brussels 1884) 450–454; 17 (1898) 250–251. F. A. LEFEBVRE, *Saint Vulmer* (Boulogne-sur-Mer 1894). L. VAN DER ESSEN, *Étude critique . . . des saints mérovingiens* (Louvain 1907) 412–414. A. M. ZIMMERMANN, *Kalendarium Benedictinum: Die Heiligen und Seligen des Benediktinerordens und seiner Zweige* (Metten 1933–38) 2:478–480. J. L. BAUDOT, *Vies des saints et des bienheureux selon l'ordre du calendrier avec l'historique des fêtes*, ed. by the Benedictines of Paris (Paris 1935–56) 7:501–502.

[É. BROUETTE]

WULPHILDA, ST.

English Benedictine abbess; d. 980. Wulphilda (Wulfhilda, Wilfrida, Vulfride, Wolfhilda, etc.) was apparently the daughter of one Wulfhelmi, count of the West Saxons. She founded the Abbey of Horton in Dorsetshire and was also the abbess of BARKING in Exeter. She seems to have ruled both houses at the same time. Possibly because of the awkward spelling of her name, contemporary chroniclers and later scholars have often confused her with another holy woman of that era named Wulfhilda, who was the wife of the Saxon king, EDGAR the Peaceful, and mother of St. Edith. This woman apparently retired to a convent in her later years and died at WILTON *c.* 987. This confused information resulted in the tale of King Edgar's stealing Wulphilda from her monastery, violating her, and then reinstating her in the convent.

Feast: Sept. 9.

Bibliography: *Acta Sanctorum* (Paris 1863—) 3:454–460. A. M. ZIMMERMANN, *Kalendarium Benedictinum: Die Heiligen und Seligen des Benediktinerorderns und seiner Zweige* (Metten 1933–38) 3:33–37.

[E. J. KEALEY]

WYCLIF, JOHN

Oxford scholar, reformer; b. Yorkshire, *c.* 1330; d. Lutterworth, 1384. A son of the lower gentry, he entered OXFORD about 1345, received his doctorate in theology probably in 1372, and for most of his life remained associated with the University. About 1361 he was ordained for the See of Lincoln, later held a number of benefices, and on one occasion was reprimanded by his ordinary for failure to provide a vicar for one of his parishes. Such carelessness was a common failing with Oxford clerks of the fourteenth century.

Wyclif's first office, that of warden of Canterbury Hall (1365–67), ended abruptly when Abp. SIMON LANGHAM ordered the hall restricted to the use of the regular clergy. It is not certain whether John Wyclif or some other Wyclif served as warden; this and many other questions concerning the views and career of Wyclif remain unanswered.

In 1372 Wyclif entered the service of the crown and two years later was appointed to a commission to treat with a papal delegation at Bruges over the problem of papal provisions. No one knows what part he took in the negotiations and why he was not re-appointed the following year. One wonders, too, whether Wyclif's failure in 1375 to secure the rich prebend of Caistor, which he had sought, did not contribute to his hostility toward the papacy. Until his death, his most important provision remained the living of Lutterworth, which the King had given him in 1374.

Association with Gaunt. In September 1376 John of Gaunt (Duke of Lancaster), the son of EDWARD III, summoned Wyclif to the court. Wyclif served the Duke in the capacity of clerical advisor for the next two years. Because of the imminence of the deaths of his father and his older brother (Black Prince), Gaunt had assumed the direction of the government; he ruled as *de facto* regent until the emergence of Richard II from his minority shortly after 1381. For this reason, the nature of Gaunt's attitude toward Wyclif is a matter of considerable importance. The theory that it was Wyclif's anticlerical views that attracted Gaunt's attention rests upon the questionable testimony of the chronicler Thomas WALSINGHAM. The true relationship between the two men must be emphasized: Gaunt was the wealthiest and most influential man in England; Wyclif was but another clerk in the court's employ, entitled to the duke's protection.

The association between Gaunt and Wyclif became evident in February 1377 when Wyclif appeared in the duke's entourage before a group of bishops and theologians at St. Paul's, London, to answer to charges of heresy. According to Walsingham, certain suffragan bishops, notably the aristocratic Bishop of London, William COURTENAY, had finally prevailed upon the reluctant Abp. SIMON OF SUDBURY to take steps to silence Wyclif.

Wyclif's summons was probably precipitated by views that he had expressed in his treatises on dominion, several of which had already appeared. According to Wyclif, dominion, i.e., the right to exercise authority and, indirectly, to hold property, is held from God and is a right that God limits to those in sanctifying grace. Unworthy priests, therefore, forfeited this right, and lay lords might deprive them of their benefices. On the other hand, these same lay lords need not fear incurring the sentence of excommunication in return, since such a censure could be validly employed only for a strictly spiritual offense. Wyclif had earlier attacked the possessions of the monks, though he commended the friars for their desire to practice the poverty of Christ.

The meeting at St. Paul's accomplished nothing. A large crowd had gathered in the church, and the duke's party, which included Henry Percy, the king's marshal, had difficulty forcing its way through. When Percy peremptorily ordered the people to make way, Bishop Courtenay, who was coming down the aisle to meet the duke's party, warned the marshal not to presume to exercise his magisterial rights within the church. Harsh words followed, principally between the duke and the bishop, and the meeting broke up in a riot when the people, who hated

Gaunt, rose up in defense of their bishop. Wyclif departed unmolested.

Bulls of Gregory XI. In May 1377, unaware of the incident at St. Paul's, Pope GREGORY XI issued five bulls against Wyclif: three addressed to Sudbury and Courtenay, one to the King, and one to Oxford. He rebuked the bishops for their failure to silence Wyclif; he cautioned the King about the threat to both Church and State implicit in Wyclif's views; he warned the University to suppress heretical teaching and to hand Wyclif over to the hierarchy. The papal bulls included a list of 19 propositions attributed to Wyclif upon which the bishops were to examine him. These propositions, like those that had produced the meeting at St. Paul's, were drawn for the most part from Wyclif's treatises on dominion.

In accordance with the instructions received from Sudbury, Wyclif presented himself at the archiepiscopal palace at Lambeth some time in March 1378. An emissary from the Queen Mother, Joan of Kent, also introduced himself and produced an order forbidding the prelates to pass formal judgment against Wyclif. Consequently, after questioning Wyclif on the 19 propositions and receiving qualifying answers from him on several points, the bishops dismissed him and forbade him to discuss or preach his views. It is probable that it was again the duke who, although he was willing to have his ward silenced, interposed to save Wyclif from disciplining; for it was about this time that the great council ordered Wyclif to cease his attacks on the Church. Some time later Gaunt himself journeyed to Oxford to caution Wyclif to abide by a decision of a commission of Oxford scholars that had forbidden discussion of two of his views on transubstantiation.

Controversy over Transubstantiation. Wyclif's attack on TRANSUBSTANTIATION in his *De eucharistia* proved a turning point in his career. So long as he limited his attack to abuses, the wealth of the Church, and the "Caesarean clergy," he could expect at least tacit support from members of both the clergy (friars) and aristocracy. Once he attacked transubstantiation (*c.* 1380), his orthodoxy could no longer be defended. Two further developments cost him favor: the WESTERN SCHISM of 1378, which served to strengthen English ties with Pope URBAN VI and the Roman Curia, and the Peasant Revolt of 1381. Wyclif was not directly involved in the revolt, but it is not surprising that contemporary opinion, in its horror of the uprising, should have condemned his revolutionary views and the "poor priests" who were his agents.

Wyclif probably left Oxford about this time for he was no longer resident there in 1382 when Archbishop Courtenay forced his adherents at the University to re-

tract their Wyclifite views or flee. Wyclifite sentiment had continued strong at Oxford despite ecclesiastical hostility, and it was only after Courtenay had secured the formal condemnation by a council of theologians of 24 propositions attributed to Wyclif, as well as an ordinance from the King in support of this judgment, that the archbishop undertook its suppression.

Last Years. Wyclif's last years are shrouded in darkness, and his death, which followed a stroke suffered while hearing Mass, is scarcely noted by the chroniclers. Late in life he received a summons from Pope URBAN VI, but pleaded illness for his failure to comply. The Council of CONSTANCE condemned Wyclif's writings and ordered his books burned and his body removed from consecrated ground. This last order was confirmed by Pope MARTIN V and carried out in 1428.

Writings. Wyclif was a voluminous writer; few orthodox medieval theologians have left so large a store of books. His writings reveal a cold, rationalistic mind, a dull, prolix style, and a presentation of ideas frequently lacking in lucidity and consistency. There appears little question that Wyclif was not ready to proclaim views logically demanded by his premises. That a council of Oxford doctors in 1378 adjudged his propositions "ill-sounding though not erroneous" suggests the obscure manner in which he often expressed himself. Wyclif never ceased writing like a university sententiary, and an element of the academic and unreal hovers about his assertions. Despite his patent unorthodoxy, he repeatedly declared his willingness to submit his opinions to the judgment of the Church, even of the pope.

Perhaps Wyclif exerted his greatest influence in an area where he did little actual work himself, that is, in the translation of the Bible. Two complete versions of the Vulgate are associated with his name, although his actual contribution is not clear. Moderate opinion believes he encouraged his disciples at Oxford to do the work. Yet while no part of the Wyclifite Bibles may be his, he has been called the first and chief "deviser" of the English Bible because of his influence upon Nicholas HEREFORD, John PURVEY, and others.

Wyclif's English works are his least important, and their value is further impaired by the question of genuineness. Many of his 300 sermons were intended for others to present. They add little to our understanding of the man, although they declare the importance he attached to preaching.

Wyclif's reputation as a theologian rests squarely upon his Latin works. These establish him as a leading scholastic of the late Middle Ages. In keeping with his character as an Oxford sententiary, his earliest works deal principally with logical and metaphysical subjects and reflect deep dependence upon THOMAS BRADWARDINE and RICHARD FITZRALPH. Above all others, he himself acknowledged a great debt to St. Augustine. The *Summa de ente,* his first major philosophical work, reveals his extreme realism, and it may have been this attempt to apply principles founded upon realist metaphysics to the realm of faith and morals, as much as clerical corruption, that led him to tread the path of reformer and heretic. Furthermore, had Oxford not been at low ebb intellectually during his years there, it is possible that contemporary scholars might have been able to prevent his deviation into unorthodox ways.

Wyclif's best-known treatises concern dominion, but these are the least original of his works. In other writings he attacked the papal claims to compulsive authority, vows and religious orders, endowments and clerical wealth, indulgences, the liturgy, and the sacramental system: in general, whatever he believed was not directly founded upon the Bible. He considered the Bible to be God's most authoritative statement. His position on transubstantiation is not clearly drawn but suggests similarity to the consubstantiation of LUTHER. His political views are neither particularly original nor revolutionary. While he advocated expropriation of the wealth of unworthy priests, he was willing to grant the clergy the right to declare forfeit the goods of sinful laymen. And though he would force the "Caesarean clergy" out of politics, he thought the ruler had need of clerical advisors to guide him in his efforts to rule justly. The *Trialogus,* which he left unfinished at his death, is his best-known and most highly regarded work. In this he attempted a systematic study of theology.

Influence. Wyclif's voluminous writings brought him much posthumous fame, but his influence upon contemporary politics, even upon the reformers of the 16th century, was negligible. His connection with the Reformation is through the Bohemian students who attended Oxford in the late 14th century and through John HUS, although Hus's principal work, the *Ecclesia,* reveals little indebtedness to him. His associations with Lollardy remain in doubt. The LOLLARDS hailed him as their inspiration and endorsed his anticlericalism; but for his part, Wyclif could scarcely have stomached their social and economic program. Perhaps the most astonishing facet of the enigma that is "Wyclif" is the small niche he carved for himself in his own age and in the 16th century, despite the fact that his writings embodied the substance of the attack made on the Church by the later Reformers, who either knew nothing of his writings or ignored them.

Bibliography: **Sources.** Latin works ed. by Wyclif Society (London 1883–); 36 v. published to 1964. Not yet included in this ed.: *Tractatus de officio pastorali,* ed. G. V. LECHLER (Leipzig 1863); *Trialogus cum supplemento Trialogi, id.* (Oxford 1869); *De Christo et suo adversario antichristo,* ed. R. BUDDENSIEG (Gotha 1880); *Select English Works of John Wyclif,* ed. T. ARNOLD, 3 v. (Oxford 1869–71); *The English Works of Wyclif, Hitherto Unprinted,* ed. F. D. MATTHEW (*Early English Text Society*74; London 1880). *On Simony,* trans. T. A. MCVEIGH (New York 1992). **Literature.** H. B. WORKMAN, *John Wyclif,* 2 v. (Oxford 1926). B. L. MANNING, *Cambridge Medieval History,* 8 v. (London-New York 1911–36) 7:486–507. K. B. MCFARLANE, *John Wycliffe and the Beginnings of English Nonconformity* (New York 1953). J. H. DAHMUS, *The Prosecution of John Wyclyf* (New Haven 1952); "John Wyclif and the English Government," *Speculum* 35 (1960) 51–68. F. L. CROSS, *The Oxford Dictionary of the Christian Church* (London 1957) 1480–81. A. B. EMDEN, *A Biographical Register of the Scholars of the University of Oxford to A.D. 1500,* 3 v. (Oxford 1957–59) 3:2103–46. J. A. ROBSON, *Wyclif and the Oxford Schools* (Cambridge, England 1961). L. J. DALY, *The Political Theory of John Wyclif* (Chicago 1962). M. SCHMIDT, *Die Religion in Geschichte und Gegenwart,* 7 v. (3d ed. Tübingen 1957–65) 6:1849–51.

[J. DAHMUS]

WYKEHAM, WILLIAM OF

Bishop, chancellor, and founder of New College (Oxford) and Winchester grammar school; b. Wickham, Hampshire, 1324; d. Sept. 27, 1404. Wykeham's mother was perhaps of gentle birth. After some schooling at Winchester, he became an official, eventually in royal employ, serving mostly as a surveyor and works clerk. In 1363, he became keeper of the privy seal at which time Froissart said that he controlled the administration. The King had given him so much ecclesiastical preferment that URBAN V was reluctant to make him bishop of WINCHESTER, to which see he was elected in 1366. After much pressure was exerted by Edward III upon a number of cardinals at the Curia, Wykeham was provided in 1367. In that year he became chancellor of England, but in 1371 he was forced to resign by an anticlerical group, probably headed by John of Gaunt. At the Good Parliament of 1376, Wykeham assisted in the overthrow of Gaunt's ruling clique; when Parliament broke up, Wykeham was charged with improper conduct as chancellor and lost his temporalities. Back in favor on the accession of Richard II, he acted as a political moderate and was again chancellor from 1389 to 1391.

As a churchman, Wykeham was too lay-minded to make a mark, although he supported the measures against the LOLLARDS. His principal fame comes from his foundation, beginning in 1378 and 1380, of the two separate, but related, St. Mary Winton colleges, one at Oxford (New College) and one at Winchester (Winchester grammar school). Both marked a break with the past—the former was designed primarily for undergraduates in arts who had been trained in grammar at the latter, which became the first English "public school."

John Joseph Wynne. (The Catholic University of America)

Bibliography: G. C. HESELTINE, *William of Wykeham: A Commentary* (London 1932). G. H. MOBERLY, *Life of William of Wykeham* (2d ed. Winchester 1893). R. LOWTH, *The Life of William of Wykeham* (3d ed. Oxford 1777). J. R. L. HIGHFIELD, "The Promotion of William of Wickham to the See of Winchester," *The Journal of Ecclesiastical History* 4 (1953) 37–54. A. H. M. JONES, in *The Victoria History of The County of Oxford,* ed. L. F. SALZMAN et al., 7 v. (Oxford 1907–62) 3:144–162.

[F. D. BLACKLEY]

WYNNE, JOHN JOSEPH

Editor, author; b. New York, N.Y., Sept. 30, 1859; d. there, Nov. 30, 1948. He completed his early education at St. Francis Xavier's High School in New York City in 1870, and received his B.A. from the College of the same institution in 1876. He entered the Jesuit novitiate at West Park, N.Y., on July 30, 1876, and studied philosophy at Woodstock College, Md. (1879–82). He taught science and classics at his alma mater in New York (1882–86) and mathematics at Boston College (1886–87). He re-

turned to Woodstock for theological studies in 1887 and was ordained Aug. 24, 1890, by Cardinal James Gibbons. In 1891 Wynne joined the staff of the *Messenger of the Sacred Heart* (New York) and was its editor for the next 17 years. In the same period he was director of the Apostleship of Prayer, raising the number of centers from 1,600 to more than 8,000; director of the Shrine of the Jesuit NORTH AMERICAN MARTYRS at Auriesville, N.Y., and promoter of the beatification of those martyrs; editor of the *Pilgrim of Our Lady of Martyrs;* originator of the HOLY HOUR movement; and assistant in the revitalization of the Holy Name Society. Seeing the need for "a magazine of general Catholic interest," Wynne transformed the *Messenger of the Sacred Heart* into such a publication in 1897, and published a supplement as the official periodical of the Apostleship. In 1902 the magazine took the title of the *Messenger,* and the *Messenger of the Sacred Heart* resumed its link with the Apostleship of Prayer. The *Messenger* changed its name and editorial offices in 1909 to become the new weekly review *America,* and Wynne served as its editor for one year. He resigned to continue his work, begun in 1905, as associate editor of the *Catholic Encyclopedia.* From 1914 to 1917 he edited *Anno Domini,* the organ of the League of Daily Mass. He was author of *The Jesuit Martyrs of North America* (1925), editor of *The Great Encyclicals of Leo XIII* (1903), and coeditor (with Condé PALLEN) of *The New Catholic Dictionary* (1927). In 1923 Wynne was appointed vice-postulator of the causes of the North American Martyrs and Kateri TEKAKWITHA, and carried on this work until the martyrs' beatification in 1925 and canonization in 1929. The Catholic University of America (Washington, D.C.) awarded him the honorary degree of S.T.D. (1926), as "an outstanding apologist of our faith and life." His office was moved to Fordham University, New York, in 1929. Selecting a site in 1946 on Lake George for a statue of St. Isaac Jogues was Wynne's last service to the church.

Bibliography: XAVIER ALUMNI SODALITY, *Fifty Years in Conflict and Triumph* (New York 1927), autobiography and tributes from others.

[E. G. RYAN]

WYOMING, CATHOLIC CHURCH IN

The name "Wyoming" is said to mean "mountains with large plains between." The American historian Bancroft preferred, "Fontana," as the source of so many rivers. The landscape of Wyoming is big, "tremendious," to use a favorite word of Lewis and Clark. Astride the continental divide the region was part of three annexations to the United States—the Louisiana purchase

(1803), the Oregon country (1846), and the Mexican cession (1848)—reflecting historic European claims defined by the major western watersheds—the Missouri-Mississippi, the Snake-Columbia, and the Green-Colorado. The Rocky Mountains break up into several distinct ranges, providing openings, the easiest by way of the Oregon-California trail over the well-watered South pass or of the more direct Overland trail through the great divide basin, the route followed by the Union Pacific railroad, which brought settlement.

Before 1867 Wyoming was still largely *terra incognita,* having no definite name, no clear political organization, and no permanent population. The territory of Wyoming was organized in 1868, with newly founded Cheyenne the capital of a squared-off area of 100,000 square miles, exactly defined by the 104th and 111th meridians of longitude and the 41st and 45th parallels of north latitude. In 1869, the first Wyoming territorial legislature established legal equality for women, giving them the right to vote and hold office, hence the appellation "Equality State." The creation of the first national park, Yellowstone, in 1872, brought more national notice. Wyoming was admitted to the Union in 1890 as the 44th state.

On July 5, 1840, the Jesuit Father Pierre-Jean DE SMET had "the consolation of celebrating the holy sacrifice of the Mass," the first such documented in what became Wyoming. DeSmet, coming from St. Louis with the American Fur Company's expedition to the Rendezvous on the Green River near present-day Daniel, was travelling to the Flathead in answer to their request for "blackrobes," perhaps inspired by Catholic Iroquois who had drifted west. The Flathead delegation, with some Nez Percé and Shoshone, mountain men, and traders made up the congregation. DeSmet wrote: "It was a spectacle truly moving to the heart of a missionary, to behold an assembly composed of so many different nations, who all assisted at our holy mysteries with great satisfaction. The Canadians sang hymns in French and Latin, and the Indians [sic] in their native tongue. It was truly a Catholic worship . . . . This place has been called since that time, by the French Canadians, *la prairie de la Messe* " (Chittenden, I, 262).

In 1850, Wyoming east of the continental divide was included in the vicariate apostolic of the Indian Territory; Wyoming west of the divide was a practically inaccessible part of the province of Oregon City (established 1846). The first vicar apostolic was a John Baptist MIÈGE, S.J., (1850–59), a Savoyard newly arrived from Rome, who established a residence in Leavenworth, Kansas, and then, in consultation with Father DeSmet, worked to divide the vicariate, unmanageable because of its size. The

Sacred Congregation for the Propagation of the Faith detached the northern part by creating the vicariate apostolic of Nebraska in 1857. Bishop Miège continued as administrator until a vicar apostolic could be found. The first vicar apostolic of Nebraska (1859–74) was a Trappist monk, James Miles O'Gorman, born in Tipperary and prior of New Melleray abbey near Dubuque. Bishop O'Gorman established his residence in Omaha, the starting point of the Union Pacific railroad. In 1867 Bishop O'Gorman entrusted to Father William Kelly the first "parish" in Wyoming, a parish which included the whole length of the state along the railroad extending from Sidney, Nebraska, to the Wasatch Mountains in Utah (about 500 miles). When the railroad was completed in 1869, Bishop O'Gorman took it and became the first Catholic bishop to visit Wyoming. James O'Connor, a native of Ireland and priest of Philadelphia, was second vicar apostolic of Nebraska (1875–85) and first bishop of Omaha (1885–90). In 1877 Bishop O'Connor made a three-month visitation of the Catholic communities, the first towns and parishes in Wyoming having grown up around railroad supply points, about 100 miles apart, and around the coal mines constructed to fuel the trains.

In 1884, the Jesuits founded St. Stephen's Mission on the Wind River reservation shared by the Shoshone and the Northern Arapahoe. The Society of Jesus responded to Bishop O'Connor's petition by sending from the German house in Buffalo, New York, John Jutz, S.J., and Brother Ursus Nunlist, S.J., who immediately started building near the confluence of the Little and Big Wind rivers. Jesuits, at least 59 of them through 2000, three or four at a time, came from several provinces of the Society of Jesus in turn: the German (Buffalo, New York, 1884–86), Missouri (St. Louis, 1886–91), an Italian (California Rocky Mountain Mission, 1891–1912), again Missouri (St. Louis, 1912–92), and then Wisconsin (Milwaukee, since 1992). St. Stephen's school was first attended by the Sisters of Charity of Leavenworth (1888–90), then the Sisters of St. Joseph of Concordia, Kansas (1891–92), and finally Franciscan Sisters from Philadelphia came in 1892 and have remained to date. Fortunately, it happened that Bishop O'Connor was the spiritual director of Miss, later Mother Katharine M. Drexel, heiress and foundress of the Sisters of the Blessed Sacrament, who was ever ready to assist generously with funds at the foundation of St. Stephen's and at several critical times thereafter, most notably in 1928 when fire destroyed many mission buildings.

The Diocese of Cheyenne (*Cheyennensis*), coterminous with the state of Wyoming, was erected by Pope Leo XIII on Aug. 2, 1887, as suffragan of St. Louis. Maurice Francis Burke, born in Ireland and a priest of Chicago, was the first bishop of Cheyenne (1887–93). Upon his arrival in Wyoming, Bishop Burke found a diocese about the size of Great Britain, with four diocesan priests, a Jesuit priest and brother, eight churches and 28 missions (soon to be 43), for about 450 families, or 7,500 widely scattered Catholics. There were 21 religious women: Sisters of the Holy Child Jesus, who conducted an academy and school in Cheyenne, and Sisters of Charity of Leavenworth, who staffed a hospital and school in Laramie. Bishop Burke faced attacks against the Catholic Church by members of the American Protective Association (''Know Nothings''), whose hostility eventually obliged the Sisters of Charity to leave Laramie. Bishop Burke concluded that the diocese ought to be suppressed; but Rome rejected this proposal. In 1893 the diocese of Cheyenne was attached to the ecclesiastical province of Dubuque and Bishop Burke was transferred to the see of St. Joseph, Missouri. Fr. Hugh Cummiskey, pastor in Laramie, was appointed administrator of the diocese (1893–97).

Thomas Mathias Lenihan (1897–1901), Bishop Burke's successor appointed after almost four years, was born in Ireland and a priest of Dubuque, whose poor health, exacerbated by the high altitude and dryness, severely restricted his activity and finally compelled him to return to Iowa where he died. Fr. Cummiskey was again appointed administrator (1901–02).

James John Keane, third bishop of Cheyenne (1902–11), raised in Minnesota and a priest of St. Paul, came to Wyoming at a time when economic conditions were rapidly improving after a decade of depression. Population increased 60 percent between 1900 and 1910. Newly opened irrigated lands and new methods of dry farming, increased coal and iron mining, timber cutting, and exploration of vast oil and natural gas reserves, attracted immigrants. Bishop Keane undertook the task of bringing order to the diocesan administration and incorporated the diocese according to the laws of the state of Wyoming. Pastors were instructed to incorporate the parishes, each to have a board, which included the bishop, the pastor and two lay trustees. Soon after its foundation in 1905 Bishop Keane appealed to the Catholic Church Extension Society which became a generous and never failing channel of funds for the benefit of the Church in Wyoming. Bishop Keane directed the building of a residence and a cathedral in Cheyenne, laying the cornerstone of the cathedral July 7, 1907. On Aug. 11, 1911 Bishop Keane was named archbishop of Dubuque.

Conventual Franciscans (Order of Friars Minor Conventual), sometimes called Black Franciscans because of the color of their habit, came to Wyoming in 1909 at the invitation of Bishop Keane. Originally, these friars were from the province of the Immaculate Conception (New York), then, after 1926, from the province of Our Lady of Consolation (Indiana). Fr. Ignatius Berna was the first to arrive. On Dec. 15, 1910, Bishop Keane formally entrusted to him and the order the spiritual care of the parish of St. James in Douglas, together with churches and missions, founded and to be founded, in four counties of eastern Wyoming—Converse, Niobrara, Goshen, and Platte—an area of more than 11,000 square miles, about one-tenth of the state, making it one of the largest territorial parishes in the United States. The Sacred Congregation of Religious confirmed this action Dec. 1, 1911. St. James friary in Douglas was the center for 13 missions serving ranchers, farmers, miners, and oil-field workers. The friars usually traveled by rail until Bishop McGovern bought them an automobile in 1935. 49 Franciscans served at St. James friary for a half-century. Then, because of commitments elsewhere, the Conventual Franciscans withdrew from Wyoming, formally relinquishing their remaining churches on Sept. 15, 1960, the act confirmed Nov. 28, 1960, by the Sacred Congregation of Religious.

Patrick Aloysius McGovern (1912–51), the austere and formidable fourth bishop of Cheyenne, was a native and priest of Omaha. Bishop McGovern held two synods, one at the beginning of his administration (1913) in order to introduce himself to the priests, and one at the end (1948) to introduce the new coadjutor bishop, Hubert Newell. The further purpose of both synods, which included only priests, was to provide for the orderly government of clergy and people and to promote ecclesiastical discipline. At the 1913 synod, Bishop McGovern promulgated the decrees of the plenary councils of Baltimore and the statutes of the first synod of the diocese of Omaha in order to place the governance of the diocese on a regular juridical foundation. Similarly, the 1948 synod passed regulations regarding the conduct and duties of priests, administration of sacraments, conduct of liturgy, preaching and giving instructions, and the care of temporalities, all to accord with the 1917 code of Canon Law. Himself an orphan, Bishop McGovern was very much concerned about the plight of orphans in Wyoming, and worked tirelessly to establish St. Joseph's Children's Home (1930) and to obtain Sisters to care for the orphans, eventually welcoming Franciscans Sisters from Wisconsin. By 1990 St. Joseph's had become a home for troubled children and had a lay administration. In 1941 the diocese of Cheyenne became suffragan of the newly created metropolitan province of Denver.

Hubert Michael Newell (1951–78), native and a priest of Denver, was named coadjutor bishop of Cheyenne, with the right of succession, on Aug. 2, 1947, and he succeeded to the office of ordinary at the death of his predecessor on Nov. 8, 1951. Bishop Newell began publication of the *Wyoming Catholic Register* (April 11, 1952). In 1953, he persuaded the ladies of the long-existing altar and rosary societies to form the Wyoming Council of Catholic Women, a chapter of the national organization, with similar aims and functions as the Knights of Columbus. Bishop Newell promoted the Catholic Youth Organization, holding in 1959 its first state convention. He attended all the sessions of the Second Vatican Council convened by Pope John XXIII in 1962, and after the Council quickly mandated the prescribed liturgical changes, and in 1974 began commissioning men and women as lay ministers of the Eucharist. In 1972, the diocesan presbyteral council recommended that there be a mandatory retirement of pastors and that the tenure of pastors and assistants be limited to a defined term, recommendations which, when put into effect, ended an era during which pastors remained in the same place for life. Bishop Newell set up a diocesan pastoral council and a board for Catholic education, the members of both elected by their deaneries. Hubert Joseph Hart came to Cheyenne as auxiliary bishop in 1976, and in 1978 Bishop Newell resigned as ordinary, but remained as apostolic administrator until a successor was named.

Joseph Hart, born in Missouri and a priest of Kansas City–St. Joseph, was installed as sixth bishop of Cheyenne, on June 12, 1978, after an unprecedented consultative poll of the Catholics in Wyoming, directed by the diocesan pastoral council. Bishop Hart began immediately to ordain married men as deacons. Benedictine nuns of Perpetual Adoration, from Clyde, Missouri (Maria-Rickenbach, near Engleberg, Switzerland), founded a monastery in Wyoming in 1983.

Bishop Hart continued the post–Vatican II process of encouraging lay consultation. After 1980, he saw to the establishment of parish pastoral councils and, after 1985, parish finance councils throughout the diocese. In 1993, Bishop Hart invited the laity, prepared by a three-year spiritual renewal program, to participate in the third diocesan synod, whom he invited ''to dance out to the edge of possibility'' in finding and solving problems together, in an ongoing process. In answer to Bishop Hart's petition for a successor, the Holy See appointed David Laurin Ricken, born in Kansas and a priest of Pueblo, and on Jan. 6, 2000, Pope John Paul II ordained him coadjutor bishop of Cheyenne.

The increase in population in Wyoming was steady, if at times slow, advancing from about 9,000 in 1870 to about 330,000 in 1950, to nearly 500,000 in 2000, of which ten to fifteen percent were Catholics. The number of priests increased from four in 1887 to 14 in 1912, to 70 in 1972. In 2000 there were 51 diocesan priests, of whom 34 were active, and ten religious priests, assisted by ten permanent deacons, one religious brother and 24 sisters serving 36 parishes, 42 missions, and six parochial schools.

Bibliography: P. J. DESMET, S.J., *Life, Letters and Travels*, eds., H. M. CHITTENDEN and A. T. RICHARDSON (New York 1905). H. H. BANCROFT, *History of Nevada, Colorado, and Wyoming, 1540–1888* (San Francisco 1890). H. W. CASPER, S.J., *History of the Catholic Church in Nebraska*, 2 v. (Milwaukee 1960–66). P. A. MC-GOVERN, *History of the Diocese of Cheyenne* (Cheyenne 1941). H. M. NEWELL, ''Diocese of Cheyenne'' article in *New Catholic Encyclopedia* (1964). W. E. MULLEN, ''Wyoming'' article in *Catholic Encyclopedia* (1912). G. S. CARLSON, *A Brief History of the Diocese of Cheyenne* (Cheyenne 1993).

[J. J. SANTICH]

WYSZYŃSKI, CASIMIR, VEN.

Procurator-general of the Marian Fathers; b. Jeziora Wielka, near Warsaw, Poland, Aug. 19, 1700; d. Balsamão, near Bragança, Portugal, Oct. 21, 1755. Wyszyński attended the Piarist colleges in Góra Kalwaria and in Warsaw. After completing his studies, to comply with his father's wishes, he entered upon a civil service career. About 1722 he undertook a pilgrimage to Santiago de Compostela, Spain, in fulfillment of a vow. Near the Spanish border, overcome by an illness resulting from the adverse climate, he had to give up the remainder of his pilgrimage. In Rome, he obtained papal dispensation from his vow and entered the Marian Fathers (1723), receiving the religious name Casimir of St. Joseph. He returned to Poland and made his novitiate, and a year after his solemn profession he was ordained (1726). He held with distinction the offices of master of novices, local superior, superior general (1737–41; 1747–50), and procurator general in Rome (1750–53).

By wise direction and example he brought about a spiritual renewal of the order. He tirelessly promoted the beatification cause of Stanislaus PAPCZYŃSKI, founder of the Marian Fathers. In 1754 he established the first foundation of the Marians in Portugal at Balsamão, where he died. His body is buried in the monastery church. His beatification cause was started in 1763, introduced upon the apostolic forum in 1780, interrupted after the ''de non cultu'' decree in 1782, and resumed in 1953. His life of S. Papcznski, *Vita S. D. Stanislai Congr. P.P. Marianorum Fundatoris,* is extant only in the Portuguese translation by J. Teixeira, *Vida do Ven. Servo de Deos, o Padre Estanisláo de Jesus Maria* (Lisbon 1757).

Bibliography: A. J. DE S. A VARGAS, ''C. V. P. Casimiro vem a Portugal,'' *Memoria Acerca de Balsamão* (Bragança, Port. 1859) 100–120. M. ALVES, in *Memórias Arqueológico-Historicas do distrito de Bragança* (Porto, Port. 1931) v.7. J. DE CASTRO, ''Convento

Stefan Cardinal Wyszyński, Primate of Poland, kissing the hands of Pope John Paul II during papal investure ceremony in St. Peter's Square, Vatican City, Rome, Italy, 1978. (©Bettmann/ CORBIS)

de Balsamão, in *Bragança e Miranda* (Porto, Port. 1947) 2:257–273.

[C. J. KRZYŻANOWSKI]

WYSZYŃSKI, STEFAN

Cardinal, archbishop of Gniezno and Warsaw, Poland; b. Aug. 3, 1901 in the village of Zuzela on the River Bug (then in the Russian Empire, now in Poland), son of a church organist; d. in Warsaw, May 28, 1981.

Wyszyński's mother died when he was nine, and her last words were taken to mean that Stefan should become a priest, a vocation he remained certain of throughout his young adulthood. After finishing his secondary education at several different schools due to the adverse conditions of World War I, he studied theology and philosophy at the Włocławek Major Seminary and, despite ill-health, was ordained priest August 5, 1926.

After his recovery, he was appointed priest of the Włocławek Cathedral and editor of the diocesan newspaper. From 1925 to 1929, he studied law and Catholic social theory at the Catholic University of Lublin, writing a doctoral thesis on church-state relations and family rights as concerns education. He published prolifically on the subject of Catholic social teachings and their application in concrete social reform throughout the 1930s, and became actively involved in ministry to working-class youths, as well as in supporting the Christian trade union movement.

Targeted for arrest by the Gestapo after the Nazi invasion of Poland in 1939, he spent most of the years of World War II in hiding, during which time he variously ministered to the blind and served as a chaplain to the Polish underground resistance movement.

On March 25, 1946, he was named bishop of Lublin, and consecrated in Częstochowa on May 5 of that year. On Nov. 12, 1948, he was named archbishop of Gniezno and Warsaw, and Primate of Poland; he was named cardinal of Sancta Maria trans Tiberim by Pius XII on Jan. 12, 1953. It thus fell to him to lead the Polish church through the difficult years in which Poland was subjected to intense Stalinization. Wyszyński prudentially saw that although the church could not compromise its basic independence, it should also avoid, whenever possible, open confrontation with the Communist authorities. This did not stop the regime from imprisoning many priests, nuns, and bishops, or even Wyszyński himself (from Sept. 25, 1953 to Oct. 26, 1956), but it did spare the Polish clergy, already depleted by Nazi persecution, from another potential bloodbath. As a result of the ''Polish October'' civil disturbances of 1956, he was released from prison by the Communist authorities and appealed for public calm, thus helping to avoid a possible Soviet invasion of Poland.

In the next decade he devoted himself to encouraging the faithful to prepare spiritually for the great celebration marking the 1000th anniversary of Poland baptism in 1966, which, among other things, promoted Poland's strong tradition of Marian devotion, all as a way of strengthening the Polish church in the face of continuing attempts by the authorities to undermine it. He also took part in the Second Vatican Council.

Although in 1980 he proved slow to recognize at first the importance of the Solidarity workers' movement, in the last months of his life he gave it important and judicious moral support. A man of impressive charisma and charity, he was widely mourned at his passing. His case for beatification was begun in 1989.

Bibliography: A. MICEWSKI, *Cardinal Wyszyński: A Biography* (San Diego 1984). *Człowiek niezwykłej miary. Ojciec Święty*

Jan Paweł II o Kardynale Stefanie Wyszyńskim, Kardynał Wyszyński o sobie, Kardynał Józef Glemp o Kardynale Stefanie Wyszyńskim, M. PLASKARZ, et al, eds. (Warsaw 1984). S. WYSZYŃSKI, *A Freedom Within: The Prison Notes of Stefan Cardinal Wyszyński* (San Diego 1982); *All You Who Labor: Work and the Sanctification of Daily Life.* (Manchester, NH, 1985).

[P. RADZILOWSKI]

X

XAINCTONGE, ANNE DE, VEN.

Foundress of the Society of St. Ursula of the Blessed Virgin; b. Dijon, France, Nov. 21, 1567; d. Dôle, June 8, 1621. Her father, Jean, gave her an education usually reserved for the son of such a brilliant lawyer. The Xainctonge home adjoined the Jesuit College of Godran, and Anne yearned to provide girls with a training similar to the Jesuits' for boys. While teaching catechism and supplementing the inadequate lessons of Dijon's "dame schools," Anne gradually recognized clearly her vocation: to establish a religious community of women dedicated to the apostolate of education, "embracing rich and poor with the same love," consecrated by vows but not living in the cloister—a revolutionary ambition bitterly opposed by family, friends, and clergy. A decade of misunderstanding, persecution, and lonely struggle bore fruit on June 16, 1606, when with three companions she founded in Dôle the Society of St. Ursula, the first noncloistered teaching congregation. At her death there were six foundations in eastern France and Switzerland. In 1964 Anne de Xainctonge's daughters were continuing the formation of youth in Europe, Africa, and America, still inspired by the spirit of their foundress, who was declared venerable in 1900.

Bibliography: M. T. BRESLIN, *Anne de Xainctonge, Her Life and Spirituality* (Kingston, NY 1957). S. R. MARIE CELESTINE, *Review for Religious* 17 (1958) 201–210.

[M. T. BRESLIN]

XANTHOPULUS, NICEPHORUS CALLISTUS

Byzantine priest, ecclesiastical writer; b. Constantinople, shortly before 1260; d. Constantinople, *c.* 1335. Enrolled among the clergy of Santa Sophia as a child, he was later affiliated to the college of priests of this basilica and taught grammar and rhetoric, undoubtedly in the patriarchal school. His life thus combined the functions of active cleric and teacher. Despite some of the sources, it does not seem likely that he became a monk, although in his last hours he may have done so, taking the name of Nilus. Xanthopulus's many writings grew out of the practical demands of his ministry and his teaching. Hence, his works include a number of liturgical writings: SYNAXARIES for the chief feasts in the Triodion (i.e., the ten weeks before Easter) and for the feasts of the saints throughout the year; an explanation of the Mass of the Presanctified; a complete Office of Our Lady the Source of Life; commentaries on hymns; ten Marian poems; pious epigrams; and prose prayers. This group of works is of more than practical significance, for it outlines the writer's thinking on certain points of doctrine (Trinitarian theology, eschatology, Mariology) and delineates many liturgical practices current in his day. His works of exegesis, rhetoric, and history are the result of his career as a professor. The outstanding work in this group is his *Ecclesiastical History* in 18 books covering the beginnings of Christianity to the death of the Emperor Phocas (618). The summary announced five further books to cover the period through the reign of Leo VI (912). Krumbacher claims that this work was a simple plagiarism from another *History* written in the 9th century; but even in this case it is still useful as an account of the first centuries of Christianity, of the history of the Christological controversies, and of the development of the heresies, because it cites frequently and sometimes at length from annals since lost (e.g., that of THEODORE LECTOR, a 6th–century writer). Xanthopulus's thoroughness as a historian led him to compile—as part of his documentation—catalogues of the Fathers of the church, the emperors, patriarchs, melodists, and saints and synthesized explanations of events within specific periods. His secular writings were confined to some exercises in rhetoric and a eulogy on wine.

Bibliography: Sources. *Patrologia Graeca,* ed. J. P. MIGNE, 161 v. (Paris 1857–66) 145–147. For complete list of works including those not collected in *Patrologia Graeca, see* M. JUGIE, *Dictionnaire de théologie catholique,* ed. A. VACANT et al., 15 v. (Paris 1903–50; Tables générales 1951–) 11.1: 446–452, noting that the life of St. Andrew the Fool is not the work of Xanthopulus. Literature. N. GREGORAS, *Correspondance de Nicéphore Grégoras,* ed. and tr. R. GUILLAND (Paris 1927) 382–385. I. SYKOUTRIS, Περὶ τὸ σχίσμα τῶν Ἀρσενιατῶν 4 v. (Athens 1929–32) 3:29–33. V. LAURENT, *Lexikon für Theologie und Kirche,* ed. J. HOFER and K. RAHNER, 10 v. (2d, new ed. Freiburg 1957–65) 10:1007. H. G. BECK, *Kirche und theologische Literatur im byzantinischen Reich* (Munich 1959) 705–707. M. E. COLONNA, *Storici profani,* v.1 of *Gli storici bizantini dal sec. IV al sec. XV* (Naples 1956–) 137–138, for manuscripts of the *History.* G. MORAVCSIK, *Die byzantinischen Quellen der Geschichte der Türkvölker,* v.1 of *Byzantinoturcica,* 2 v. (2d ed. Berlin 1958) 459–60, for the *History.*

[V. LAURENT]

XAVERIAN BROTHERS

Brothers of St. Francis Xavier (CFX, Official Catholic Directory #1350), a congregation of lay religious founded by Theodore James RYKEN (BROTHER FRANCIS XAVIER) in Bruges, Belgium, 1839, for the education of youth, especially in America. Unable to carry out his plan to found a religious body in Holland for catechetical work, Ryken went to serve the American mission in 1831. Attracted to the Indian apostolate, he returned to Belgium to establish a religious community for that end. In 1837 he returned to the U.S. to seek the approbation of the American bishops for his plan but was persuaded by Bp. Joseph Rosati of St. Louis, Mo., to direct his enterprise toward the education of American children and to staff schools in his diocese. Returning to Belgium, Ryken began his foundation in June 1839 under Bp. Francis Boussen of Bruges.

Destitute and beset by many difficulties, the little community grew slowly. In 1843 an infant school was opened in Bruges, and Ryken with three others took the habit. In 1846 the 10 oldest pronounced vows. The first branch house was opened in Bury, Lancashire, England, in 1848 as a preparation for America. With the death of Rosati (1843) and the collapse of subsequent negotiations elsewhere, Ryken was forced to wait until 1854 to send his first colony to America. At the invitation of Bp. Martin John Spalding, six brothers arrived in Louisville, Ky, Aug. 11, 1854, and opened St. Patrick's school and a school at Immaculate Conception parish. For a time little progress was made in America, partly because of financial problems in Bruges. In 1860, at the request of the bishop of Bruges, Ryken resigned as superior general in favor of a younger man, Brother Vincent Terhoeven, who governed until 1895. Under his direction the congregation prospered, and in 1875 separate provinces were created in Belgium, England, and the U.S.

Schools in Belgium were few at first because of the foundations in England and America. St. Francis Xavier Institute, the central house at Bruges, evolved from a small school opened in 1844. In time primary and secondary schools were established throughout West Flanders. In England, where they were the first brotherhood from the continent, the Xaverian Brothers played an important role in the development of Catholic education, filling many parish schools in Lancashire and London and staffing for a time St. Mary's Training School, Hammersmith. Toward the end of the century they moved into secondary education, but the English province declined when elementary schools were abandoned.

In the U.S. the Xaverians staffed most of the parish schools of Louisville and opened St. Xavier's Institute (1864), their first secondary school in America. In 1866 they were invited by Spalding, now archbishop of Baltimore, Md., to open St. Mary's Industrial School, inaugurating a type of work for which the Xaverians in the U.S. were noted for many years. Under Brother Alexius, the first provincial (1875–1900), the brothers opened other schools in Baltimore, including Mt. St. Joseph's College, and expanded into Massachusetts and Virginia. During the provincialate of Brother Isidore Kuppel (1907–25) the brothers turned their attention to their own professional training and to secondary education. In 1920 the first of several schools was opened in New York. In 1927 the congregation received papal recognition, and in 1928 Brother Paul Scanlan, the American provincial, was elected superior general, the first American so honored in any religious institute of European origin.

The Belgian province was first to revive the missionary character of the congregation by sending a colony to the Belgian Congo in 1931. In 1949 the American Xaverians entered Uganda. Shortly after the division of the American province in 1960, the central province opened schools in Bolivia.

The Congregation underwent many changes in response to the developments stemming from the second Vatican Council. Membership decreased, but forms of ministerial activity and geographic dispersion increased greatly. In addition to education, the brothers undertook a variety of pastoral and social ministries, especially in poorer areas. Brothers from the US established new foundations in Haiti, Alaska, Kenya, Lithuania and Bolivia. The secondary schools in the United States were reorganized as "Xaverian Brothers Sponsored Schools," a network which now includes 12 schools in Massachusetts, Connecticut, New York, Maryland, Kentucky and Alabama. In 2001, the Brothers ministered in 11 different countries on five continents.

The structure of the Congregation was modified in 1995 with the dissolution of all provinces and the consolidation of the international membership under one general leadership group, with a Generalate in Baltimore, Maryland.

Bibliography: Brother JULIAN, *Men and Deeds* (New York 1930). J. J. DOWNEY (Brother Aubert), *March On! God Will Provide: The Life of Theodore James Ryken* (Boston 1961).

[D. SPALDING]

XAVERIAN MISSIONARY FATHERS

(SX, Official Catholic Directory #1360); officially known as the Saint Francis Xavier Foreign Mission Society; founded, 1898, at Parma, Italy; received papal approbation, first given in 1906, was made definite on Jan. 6, 1921. The founder, Guido Maria CONFORTI, became archbishop of Ravenna in 1902 and, later, bishop of Parma. The particular aim of the society is foreign mission work, to which the members bind themselves by a special vow. According to the desire of the founder, the characteristic spirit of the Xaverians should be a combination of faith, obedience, and brotherly love.

On May 13, 1906, the newly erected prefecture apostolic of Western Honan was entrusted to the Xaverians, who had been working in China since 1899. In 1948 they began work in Japan. Missions in Sierra Leone followed in 1950; Indonesia and Mexico, in 1951; Pakistan, in 1952; Brazil, in 1953; and the Congo, in 1958. In Italy the society is particularly active in promoting education and information about mission and evangelization through the mass media. Its publishing house is responsible for missionary magazines and reviews, and for several series of books. The Xaverian Missionary Sisters of Mary (Xaverian Sisters), founded at Parma in 1945, are the female branch of the society. The generalate is in Rome; the United States provincialate is in Wayne, New Jersey.

Bibliography: G. BONARDI, *Guido Maria Conforti* (Parma 1936). G. BARSOTTI, *Il servo di Dio Guido Maria Conforti* (Rome 1953).

[F. SOTTOCORNOLA/EDS.]

XAVIER, FRANCIS, ST.

Apostle of India and Japan (Spanish form, Francisco de Yasu y Javier); b. Castle of Xavier, near Sangüesa, Navarre, Spain, April 7, 1506; d. on the island of Sancian, near the coast of China, Dec. 3, 1552. After completing his preliminary studies in his own country, Francis Xavier went to Paris in 1525, where he entered the College of Sainte-Barbe. Here in 1526 he met the Savoyard, Pierre Favre, and a warm friendship sprang up between

St. Francis Xavier, painting by a Japanese Jesuit. (©The Granger Collection)

them. Ignatius Loyola, the future founder of the Society of Jesus, resided at this same college from September 1529 to March 1535. He won the confidence of the two young men. First Favre and later (1533) Xavier offered themselves as his companions and were the first to associate themselves with him in the formation of the society. Four others, Salmeron, Rodriguez, Laynez, and Bobadilla, having joined them, the seven made their well-known vow at Montmartre, Aug. 15, 1534, binding themselves to the service of God.

After completing his philosophical studies, Xavier received the degree of master of arts in March of 1530. He then filled the post of regent in the Beauvais College (1530–34), and afterward studied theology (1534–36). He left Paris with his companions Nov. 15, 1536, and made his way to Venice, where he expected to take ship for PALESTINE. On June 24, 1537, he received Holy Orders with Ignatius at Venice. Unable to proceed to Palestine, he spent the following autumn and winter in Bologna, and in April 1538 he went to Rome. From April to June 1539 he took part in the conferences Ignatius held with his companions to prepare the foundation of the Society of Jesus. The order received verbal approbation from Paul III, Sept. 3, 1539. Before written approval was secured, Xavier was appointed to substitute for the sick

Bobadilla, who, at the request of John III, King of Portugal, was to have gone to minister to the Christians of southeast India. Xavier left Rome, March 15, 1540, and reached Lisbon in June. There he remained nine months, occupying himself in giving catechetical instructions, hearing confessions, and tending to the prisoners of the Inquisition.

India and Malaya. On April 7, 1541, the king delivered to him a brief appointing him apostolic nuncio in the East, and he embarked for India. After a tedious and dangerous voyage, which was interrupted by winter spent in Mozambique, he landed at Goa 13 months after leaving Lisbon. He immediately busied himself learning the language, preaching and ministering to the sick, and composing a catechism.

In September he set out for the Pearl Fishery Coast, which extends from Cape Comorin to the isle of Mannar, opposite Ceylon. Christianity had been introduced into that area five to seven years earlier, but had almost disappeared owing to the lack of priests. Xavier devoted two years to the work of preaching to the Paravas, with notable success. Multitudes flocked to hear him, and at times he was so fatigued from administering the Sacrament of Baptism that he could scarcely move his arms, as he himself wrote in a letter dated Jan. 15, 1544. He had less success with the Brahmans than with the low-caste Paravas; only one Brahman convert rewarded a year's work.

Xavier had many trials and hardships to face. The Christians of Comorin and Tuticorin were attacked by Badagas from the north who robbed, butchered, and carried off captives into slavery. Six hundred Christians were slain by the ruler of Jaffna in northern Ceylon. Other trials stemmed from the avarice, debauchery, and cruelty of Portuguese merchants and officials.

Japan. At the end of August 1545, Xavier set off from Mylapore (Madras) for Malacca on the Malay Peninsula with the intention of going on to Macassar. He labored in Malacca for the last four months of the year. Hearing that there was another priest in Macassar, he left Malacca for Amboina and visited islands that he referred to as the Moluccas. In July 1547, he was back in Malacca, where he again spent four months, and where he met a Japanese called Anjiro. From him he gathered information about Japan. Xavier's zeal was at once aroused by the idea of introducing Christianity into Japan, but for the time being the work of the society required his presence at Goa, where he went, taking Anjiro with him. In the meantime other JESUIT missionaries sent from Europe by Ignatius and Simon Rodriguez had arrived at Goa in 1545 and 1546, and the little company there was augmented by a number of recruits who had entered the society in Goa. Thus, in 1548 and 1549 Xavier was able to send Jesuits to the principal centers of the Portuguese East, such as Ormuz, Bassein, Cochin, Quilon, and Malacca, to establish houses and colleges. Xavier received into the society a Spanish secular priest, Cosmas de Torres, whom he had met in the Moluccas. With him and Juan Fernandez of Cordova, a laybrother, Xavier set out on April 17, 1549, for Japan. They took with them the Japanese Anjiro, who had been baptized at Goa and had taken the name of Paul of Holy Faith.

They landed at Kagoshima in southern Japan, Aug. 15, 1549. The first year was devoted to learning the Japanese language and translating, with the help of Paul, a short catechism and explanation of the Creed that was to be used in preaching and catechizing. Xavier was welcomed by the daimyo (ruler), but after some time the bonzes (Buddhist monks and religious leaders) became troublesome. Leaving behind, under the care of Paul, a flock of about 100 converts, Xavier set out from Kagoshima at the end of August 1550 with the intention of penetrating to the center of Japan. He preached in Hirado and visited Hakata and Yamaguchi. Toward the end of the year he reached Sakai, and in January he was in Miyako (Kyoto), then the capital of the empire. Here he found it impossible to obtain audience with the mikado as he had hoped, and so much civil strife filled the capital city at that time that Xavier saw it would be fruitless to prolong his stay. Therefore, he returned to Yamaguchi. There he altered his methods somewhat. Apostolic poverty did not appear as attractive to the Japanese as it had to the low-caste Indians, so Xavier put on better clothing and disputed with the bonzes.

After an apostolate of about two years and three months in Japan the Christian community in that nation numbered some 2,000, and later increased rapidly. Leaving De Torres in charge of the mission, Xavier returned to Malacca, where, at the end of 1551, he was appointed provincial of the newly erected Province of India. He then continued his journey to Goa, where he arrived at the end of February 1552.

China. After settling certain domestic troubles at Goa and naming the Flemish Gaspar Berze vice provincial, Xavier turned his attention to China. He had heard much of that empire during his stay in Japan, and he knew what an important influence its conversion would have upon the Japanese. With the help of friends he arranged an embassy to the Chinese sovereign, and obtained from the Portuguese viceroy in India the appointment of Diogo Pereira as ambassador. Pereira awaited Xavier at Malacca, but the maritime authority there, because of a personal grudge, refused to permit Pereira to sail either as envoy or as a private trader. Xavier succeeded in persuading the authority to permit him to sail in Pereira's ship and to go on to China even though the embassy project had to be abandoned. In the last week of August 1552, the ship reached the desolate island of Sancian (Shang-chwan), near the Chinese coast and not far from Canton. There, while trying to arrange means of gaining entry into China, he was seized by a fever on November 21. He grew weaker, and at last, in the early morning of December 3 he died. He was buried the following day.

After more than two months the grave and coffin were opened, and his body was found to be incorrupt and fresh. It was taken first to Malacca and then to Goa, where it is still enshrined in the church of the Good Jesus. The Jesuit General Claudio ACQUAVIVA ordered the right arm to be severed at the elbow and brought to Rome, where an altar was erected to receive it in the church of the Gesù.

Xavier was beatified by Paul V, Oct. 21, 1619, and canonized by Gregory XV, March 12, 1622. In 1748 he was declared Patron of the Orient; in 1904, of the work of the Propagation of the Faith; in 1927, together with St. Thérèse de Lisieux, of all missions. He is honored also as patron of navigators.

Feast: Dec. 3.

Bibliography: *Epistolarum libri quatuor,* ed. Q. TORSELLINO (Antwerp 1657); *Epistolae S. Francisci Xaverii,* ed. G. SCHURHAMMER and J. WICKI, 2 v. (Monumenta Historica Societatis Jesu 67–68; Rome 1944–45); *The Letters and Instructions of Francis Xavier,* tr. M. J. COSTELLOE (St. Louis, Mo. 1992); *the Life and Letters of St. Francis Xavier,* tr. H. J. COLERIDGE (2d ed. New Delhi 1997). *Monumenta Xaveriana,* 2 v. (MonHistSJ; Madrid 1899–1914). J. WICKI, ed., *Documenta indica (Monumenta historica Societatis Jesu 70, 72, 74– ;* Rome 1948–). G. SCHURHAMMER, *Die zeitgenössischen Quellen zur Geschichte Portugiesisch Asiens . . . zur Zeit des Hl. Franz Xaver, 1538–1552* (Rome 1962). H. J. COLERIDGE, *Life and Letters of St. Francis Xavier,* 2 v. (new ed. London 1886). O. TORSELLINO, *De vita Francisci Xaverii* (Antwerp 1596); *The Admirable Life of S. Francis Xavier, 1632* (Ilkley, England 1976). D. BARTOLI, *Dell'historia della Compagnia di Giesú, l'Asia,* 3 v. (Rome 1653–63) 1.1–4. A. BROU, *Saint François Xavier, 1506–1548,* 2 v. (2d ed. Paris 1922). J. BRODRICK, *Saint Francis Xavier, 1506–1552* (New York 1952). G. SCHURHAMMER, *Franz Xaver* (Freiburg 1955–), exhaustive; *Xaveriana,* ed. L. SZILAS (Lisboa 1964); *Francis Xavier; His Life, His Times,* tr. M. J. COSTELLOE, 4 v. (Rome 1973–82). J. M. AZCONA, *Bibliografía de San Francisco de Javier* (Pamplona 1952). DON PETER, *Xavier as educator* (Delhi 1974); *Francis Xavier, teacher of nations : the educational aspects of the missionary career of St. Francis Xavier* (Colombo 1987). L. BOURDON, *La Compagnie de Jesus et le Japon* (Lisbon 1993) V. SERRÃO, *A lenda de São Francisco Xavier pelo pintor André Reinoso: estudo histórico, estético e iconológico de um ciclo barroco existente na Sacristía da Igreja de São Roque* (Lisbon 1993). I. P. NEWMAN FERNANDES, *St. Francis Xavier and Old Goa* (2d rev. ed. Avedem, Quepem, Goa 1994). J. F. BELLIDO, *Hasta los últimos confines* (Bilbao 1998). F. G. GUTIÉRREZ, *San Francisco Javier: en el arte de España y Japón* (Sevilla 1998). J. N. TYLENDA, *Jesuit Saints & Martyrs* (Chicago 1998), 421–26.

[J. WICKI]

XAVIER UNIVERSITY OF LOUISIANA

Founded in New Orleans by St. Katharine DREXEL and the Sisters of the Blessed Sacrament (S.B.S.), Xavier University of Louisiana is the first and only historically black and Roman Catholic school of higher learning in North America.

In 1915, at the request of local black Catholics and the Most Rev. James H. Blenk, Archbishop of New Orleans, Mother Katherine opened high school classes for black youth in the buildings of the old Southern University, a Louisiana state institution that had moved elsewhere. Under Catholic auspices, Xavier was open to students of all religious backgrounds. The school was given special permission by Catholic church officials to operate on a co-educational basis, making it among the earlier such Catholic institutions in the United States. In 1917, a teacher-training department was added and, in 1918, the school began awarding two-year postsecondary commercial, music, and industrial degrees.

In 1925, the full four-year undergraduate program was introduced, leading to the Bachelor of Arts, the Bachelor of Arts in Education, and the Bachelor of Science. There was also was a two-year Pre-Medical Course. With money from Mother Katharine's sister Louise Drexel Morrell, an annex was added. In 1927, a College of Pharmacy was opened. Mother Katharine and local African-American leaders founded a historical association to raise money to buy rare books and manuscripts about black history and culture for the university library. The first president of the college was the Reverend Edward J. Brunner, S.S.J., who in a consultative capacity, followed as President by Mother Agatha Ryan, a Sister of the Blessed Sacrament (S.B.S.).

In 1929, a program to enlarge the campus was implemented. The first buildings completed were a stadium (1930), the Administration Building (1932), a library (1937), and a gymnasium (1938). During the 1930s, a separate Negro History Department combined courses in history, literature, and social studies teaching methods, making it one of the first college-level programs in African-American Studies. At the same time, the Graduate School was inaugurated, conferring Master's degrees in education, science, history, English, and French.

In 1934, Xavier inaugurated a School of Social Service for training social workers and an opera program, which eventually produced singers who had major careers in Europe and America. The same year also witnessed Xavier's awarding of its first honorary degree, a Master of Arts, to the African-American sculptor Richmond Barthé. During the 1930s and 1940s, the College

Exterior of the auditorium of Xavier University of Louisiana.

ran an extension school for education majors in Lake Charles, Louisiana, that provided a large proportion of the teachers who staffed small black Catholic parochial schools in the Acadiana region of the state. Because of a shortage of priests and nuns, Xavier graduates ran the schools solely with lay people.

After World War II, the school constructed wood-frame men's and women's dorms and an Industrial Arts Education building. The number of Sisters of the Blessed Sacrament at Xavier reached their all-time high. Following the U.S. Supreme Court decision in *Brown v. Board Education* (1954), the school's charter was amended to permit non-black students. Previously, Xavier's affiliation with The Catholic University of America had enabled white nuns to attend afternoon classes at Xavier from the 1920s to 1956.

The death of Mother Katherine on March 3, 1955 marked a turning point in the university's history. The university could no longer draw upon Mother Katherine's inheritance from her father Francis Anthony Drexel. Under the terms of the bequest, the proceeds could be used only during her and her sisters' lifetimes.

The 1960s brought great change. Except for basketball and track and field, most of the intercollegiate athletic programs were ended in 1960 and the home economics and industrial arts programs in 1962. The Student Center (1962) and St. Joseph's Residence Hall for women (October 1965) were erected. During the high point of the modern Civil Rights Movement, when the Freedom Riders passed through New Orleans and had a hard time finding places to stay, Xavier University put them up. With the decline in enrollment of postwar veterans, the loss of Mother Katharine's income, the opening of two public colleges in New Orleans, and the recruitment of African Americans by formerly white-segregated colleges, only 775 students signed up for the 1963 to 1964 school year. The decision of Loyola University of New Orleans, a Jesuit institution, to close its pharmacy program in 1965 enhanced significantly Xavier's program and its non-black enrollment.

In 1965, Sr. Maris Stella Ross, S.B.S. became president. Sparked principally by the devastating impact of Hurricane Betsy in the same year, an expansion program was announced. In 1969, construction was completed on Katharine Drexel Residence Hall for women, the Blessed Sacrament House of Studies for women religious attending Xavier, the Central Plant, a new cafeteria wing for the Student Center, and the College of Pharmacy Building. Until 1966, Xavier had no separate existence apart from the S.B.S. Corporation of Louisiana. In 1966, the order reconstituted the University as a separate corporation and transferred all the real property to it. Norman C. Francis, a Xavier alumnus, became the first lay person and the first black person to be president of the university on June 26, 1968. He also became one of the earliest lay presidents of any Catholic college in America.

The 1970s and 1980s marked a comeback for the school. By the mid-1970s, the school was receiving major grants from federal agencies and private foundations. Enrollment was on the rise. The school developed further pre-medical and other science programs that brought new funds and better recruitment of students. By the mid-1980s, more than half of the enrollment of 2,000 consisted of science majors, a number of whom are preparing for medical school.

At the beginning of the 21st century, Xavier University offered 42 undergraduate major areas. The Institute for Black Catholic Studies, founded in 1980, grants the Master of Theology, and the College of Pharmacy grants a Doctor of Pharmacy degree. Of the total enrollment of 3,797 students, 72 percent were women. Black (non-Hispanic) students comprised nearly 89 percent, 5 percent white (non-Hispanic), and 6 percent Asian American and other. Asian Americans and Louisiana Creoles represented the only predominantly Roman Catholic part of the student body, with more than two-thirds of the other students being Protestant. About half of the students now come from outside Louisiana. Recipients of degrees have been largely teachers, medical doctors, and pharmacists, although Xavier's influence has been felt also in religious life, science, jurisprudence, social service, civil rights, and government. The full-time faculty number more than 200.

[L. SULLIVAN]

XIMÉNEZ DE CISNEROS, FRANCISCO

Franciscan archbishop of Toledo, cardinal, inquisitor general, and governor of Castile; b. Torrelaguna, New Castile, 1436; d. Roa, near Valladolid, Nov. 8, 1517. The name is also spelled Jiménez according to modern Spanish orthography. Little is known of his life before 1492. He studied at Alcalá and Salamanca, receiving a doctorate in both Canon and civil law, and also, for a while at Rome. Because of his claim to the archpriesthood of Uzeda, he was imprisoned by Archbishop Carillo of Toledo, who did not, however, succeed in getting him to resign this benefice. After being freed from prison, he exchanged the archpriesthood for the office of vicar general of Sigüenza. From a desire for greater solitude for prayer, he became an Observantine Franciscan in 1484, changing his first name from Gonzalo to Francisco.

The year 1492 marked a decisive change in this life. In that year, at the advice of Cardinal Pedro González de MENDOZA, who recognized Ximénez's outstanding ability, Queen ISABELLA I of Castile chose him as her confessor. In 1494 he was appointed vicar provincial of the Observantine Franciscans in Castile, and, after the death of Cardinal Mendoza in 1495, archbishop of Toledo. From then on, his activity, which constantly increased until his death, was amazing. Ferdinand and Isabella found in him a strong arm for the religious reformation of the religious orders, especially the Conventual Franciscans. In his archdiocese he renewed the ecclesiastical and Christian life, holding synods, rigorously administering the revenues, visiting the suffragan dioceses, and printing liturgical and devotional books. He endeavored unsuccessfully to have the cathedral chapter live a community life. By his efforts he saved the MOZARABIC RITE from extinction. In 1500 he had the Moors of Granada baptized, and gave orders to burn thousands of Qur'āns, but to save the Arabic books on medicine, philosophy, and history. His burning of the Qur'āns, which was approved by almost all his contemporaries, has been condemned by many modern critics who do not understand the circumstances of the time.

It was only after the death of Queen Isabella in 1504 that Ximénez took an active part in national and international politics. In that year he acted as mediator between Philip I the Handsome and Ferdinand the Catholic in their dispute over the succession to the throne of Castile. When Philip died in 1506, Ximénez was given charge of the government of Castile until Ferdinand returned from Naples in the following year, bringing back with him for Ximénez the cardinal's hat and the nomination to the office of inquisitor general. In 1509 Ximénez organized and directed the conquest of Oran in northwestern Algeria.

When Ferdinand died in January 1516, the government of Castile was again entrusted to Ximénez. By his splendid political activity he succeeded in saving the work of the "Catholic Kings," Ferdinand and Isabella. When he had Charles proclaimed king, he managed to prevent Spain from being badly governed from Flanders; he suppressed the haughty turbulence of certain nobles and the uprising in some cities that were opposed to the army that he established; he counteracted the intrigues of the clique of Prince Ferdinand; he lightened the people's tax load and improved their farmlands. For the Indies he drew up a plan of which the heart was the establishment of settlements for Christianizing and civilizing the native peoples, and although it failed, its norms served for the future. He was respectful, though forceful, in his relations with the Holy See. He defended Navarre from the attacks of the French; he continued, with varying success, the war in north Africa, and aided with his counsel the governor of Aragon, Archbishop Alfonso of Zaragoza. Yet his enemies induced the young king to send him a cold letter of dismissal, ungrateful despite its formal words of thanks. Some say that the cardinal died before the letter reached him.

With the income of his archbishopric, Ximénez supported innumerable good works. In the field of education he was the outstanding patron of the University of ALCALÁ de Henares, which he founded, and also the generous founder of the Major College of San Ildefonso with its cortege of minor colleges. He financed the printing of many religious books, notably the famous POLYGLOT BIBLE, known as the Complutensian (from *Complutum*, the Latin name of Alcalá), which contains the first printed edition of the Greek New Testament. In the field of religion and social works he endowed churches, monasteries, and convents; founded homes for the aged and for poor young women; and established public granaries, etc.

He left a reputation of sanctity. His austerity and love of poverty were proverbial. In his episcopal residence he lived as a Franciscan friar. His cause of beatification was introduced in 1626, but was suspended in 1746. Efforts are now being made to reintroduce it on the basis of ample documentary investigation. Although accused of excessive severity, he was one of Spain's great political geniuses, and in the field of religion he is rightly regarded as the reformer and renewer of the Spanish church before the Council of Trent.

Bibliography: A. GOMEZ DE CASTRO, *De rebus gestis a Francisco Ximenio Cisnerio* (Alcalá 1569), basic biography on which all later ones largely depend. P. DE QUINTANILLA Y MENDOZA, *Archetypo de virtudes* (Palermo 1653), important for use made of Alcalá archives. Letters. *Cartas del cardenal . . . Cisneros* (Madrid 1867). *Cartas de los secretarios del cardenal . . . Cisneros* (Madrid 1875). Other items. J. L. DE AYALA, *El cardenal Cisneros: Gobernador del reino*, 2 v. (Madrid 1921–28). L. FERNÁNDEZ DE RETANA, *Cisneros y su siglo*, 2 v. (Madrid 1929–30). J. MESEGUER FERNÁNDEZ, *Archivo Ibero-Americano* 2d época 13 (1953) 243–248, 353–357; 18 (1958) 257–286, 322–330. J. M. POU Y MARTÍ, "Proceso de beatificación del cardenal Cisneros," *ibid.* 17 (1922) 5–28. W. STARKIE, *Grand Inquisitor: Being an Account of Cardinal Ximénez de Cisneros and His Times* (London 1940), popular treatment.

[J. MESEGUER FERNÁNDEZ]

XIMÉNEZ DE RADA, RODRIGO

Reforming archbishop of Toledo, statesman, and historian; b. Navarre, before 1171; d. June 10, 1247. He was the son of a Navarrese noble and a graduate of Bologna and Paris; he became bishop elect of Osma and archbishop of Toledo in 1208. Rodrigo was chief adviser to FERDINAND III of Castile, participating in the victory over the Moors at Las Navas de Tolosa in 1212 and thereafter in the reconquest, repopulation, and ecclesiastical organization of Andalusia. He attended LATERAN COUNCIL IV in 1215 and introduced its reforms into Castile, preaching the crusade, holding synods, reforming the clergy, and sending missions to Morocco. He was a protector of the Jews, and a papal legate in Spain for ten years. For his see he secured the chancellorship of Castile (1230), the primacy of Spain (1239), and spiritual jurisdiction over La Mancha (1243). In 1227 he began to build the present cathedral and the archbishop's palace. He encouraged such scholars as Michael Scot, Diego García, and Mark of Toledo. His *Historia Gothica,* learned and nationalistic, based on Christian and Muslim documentary and epic sources, is a model for subsequent histories of Spain. Rodrigo wrote other histories, including the unpublished *Breviarium historiae catholicae.*

Bibliography: F. A. LORENZANA Y BUITRON, ed., *SS. PP. Toletanorum . . . opera,* 4 v. (Madrid–Rome 1782–97) v.3. E. DE AGUILERA Y GAMBOA, *El arzobispo D. Rodrigo Ximénez de Rada y el monasterio de Santa María de Huerta* (Madrid 1908). J. GOROSTERRATZU, *Don Rodrigo Jiménez de Rada* (Pamplona 1925). E. ESTELLA, *El fundador de la catedral de Toledo* (Toledo 1926). D. MANSILLA REOYO, *Iglesia castellano–leonesa y Curia romana en los tiempos del rey san Fernando* (Madrid 1945).

[D. W. LOMAX]

Y

YAHWEH

The full and proper name of the Lord of Israel, written with four consonants YHWH, known as the Tetragrammaton. Its form and meaning and the history of the sacred Tetragrammaton are considered in this article.

It appears only twice outside the Bible: in the 9th-century (B.C.) MESHA Inscription and in the 6th-century (B.C.) Lachis Letters (J. B. Pritchard, *Ancient Near Eastern Texts relating to the Old Testament* 320, 322). A shortened form *yhw* or *yāhû* appears at the end of names, e.g., Isaiah (*yeša'yāhû*), both in the Bible and in the 5th-century Elephantine Papyri. The form *yh* is used in names, e.g., *'ăbiyyâ*, and in poetical passages, or liturgical formulas, e.g., *halelûyāh* [Ps 103 (104).35]. The name occurs in other abbreviated forms (*yehô-, yô-, yē-*) in many compound proper names.

Judging from Greek transcriptions of the sacred name (ιαβε, ιαουαι), YHWH ought to be pronounced Yahweh. The pronunciation JEHOVAH was unknown in ancient Jewish circles, and is based upon a later misunderstanding of the scribal practice of using the vowels of the word Adonai with the consonants of YHWH.

Great diversity of opinion prevails as to the meaning of the word Yahweh. For some it is an acclamation (*Yah!*) meaning "It is he!" But this does scant justice to the revelatory character of the name. Others trace the word to *hyh* or *hwh*, the verb "to be." The Lord, speaking to Moses from the burning bush (Ex 3.14), revealed His name to Moses by saying "I am who am." In relaying this information to the people, Moses would have had to resort to the use of the third person singular form "He is who he is." Some scholars consider the Lord's reply a refusal to answer Moses' question (for an analogous reply in the negative, *see* Ex 33.19–23). This view however runs counter to Moses' subsequent behavior, for he proffers the divine name as justifying his mission; the name ought therefore to be considered a true reply, containing in it a revelation of the Lord's true nature (*see* GOD, NAME OF). Yahweh is not a blind force but a person. Because He is always what He is, He is perfectly reliable, unchanging. Always present, He manifests His saving interest in His people, and is ready to help them. The Egyptians and all other peoples shall know from His actions "that I am Yahweh" (*see* Ex 7.5 and *passim*).

Some translate the name by "I shall be what I was," which would bring out the Lord's eternity; but this view is not consistent with the context, or even a good translation, for as both verbs are in the imperfect, both should be rendered in the same way. Still others consider the divine answer to be a revelation of God's essential nature as an *Ens a se* in whom all being is to be found in all its fullness. This view, however, attributes to the Hebrews a philosophical awareness that they did not possess.

All these explanations, however, overlook the fact that in Ex 3.14 a merely folk etymology of the name, based on the *qal* form of the verb "to be," is given. Grammatically, because of its vocalization, *yahweh* can only be a *hi'phîl* or causative form of this verb, with the meaning "He causes to be, He brings into being." Probably, therefore, *yahweh* is an abbreviated form of the longer *yahweh 'ăšr yihweh,* "He brings into being whatever exists." The name, therefore, describes the God of Israel as the Creator of the universe.

According to many texts (Gn 4.26; 9.26; 12.8; 26.25, etc.) the name of Yahweh was known before the FLOOD and by the Patriarchs. These cases are scribal anticipations of the name revealed to Moses (*see* YAHWIST), and thus another way of affirming the identity of Yahweh with the God worshiped as El, or El-Shaddai, or Elohim. The name *yôkebed* in Moses' genealogy (Ex 6.20; Nm 26.59) is a Yahwistic theophoric name but *yō-* has probably been substituted for some other name of God by the PRIESTLY WRITERS. Hosea also suggests (12.9; 13.4) that God was known as Yahweh only from the time of the Exodus. A Madianite or Cinite origin of the name has not been proved.

Sometime after the end of the Exile, the name Yahweh began to be considered with special reverence, and the practice arose of substituting for it the word ADONAI or ELOHIM. Such reverence for the divine name may have been prompted by a religious scruple or by the fear that by being named, the Lord might seem to be put on a par with pagan deities, who also had personal names. In any case, the practice led in time to forgetfulness of the proper pronunciation of the name Yahweh. It is interesting to note that the name Yahweh does not appear in Ecclesiastes, is used in Daniel only in 9.1–20, and is often replaced by Elohim in Ps 41 (42)–82(83). In the Dead Sea Scrolls (1QS 6, 27 and 1QpHb) the name is written in archaic letters.

Bibliography: H. GROSS, *Lexikon für Theologie und Kirche,* ed. J. HOFER and K. RAHNER, 10 v. (2d, new ed. Freiburg 1957–65); suppl., *Das ZweiteVatikanische Konzil: Dokumente und kommentare,* ed. H. S. BRECHTER et al., pt. 1 (1966) 4:1127–29; 6:713. W. EICHRODT, *Theology of the Old Testament,* tr. J. A. BAKER (London 1961–). E. JACOB, *Theology of the Old Testament,* tr. A. W. HEATHCOTE and P. J. ALLCOCK (New York 1958). J. P. E. PEDERSEN, *Israel: Its Life and Culture,* 4 v. in 2 (New York 1926–40; reprint 1959). P. VAN IMSCHOOT, *Théologie de l'ancien Testament* (Tournai 1954–). T. VRIEZEN, *An Outline of Old Testament Theology,* tr. S. NEUIJEN (Newton Centre, MA 1958).

[R. T. A. MURPHY]

YAHWIST

Name (abbreviated ''J'' from its German form) given to what the literary critics consider the oldest of the Pentateuchal traditions. It received its definitive form(s) in the Southern Kingdom of Judah during the early period of the monarchy. After the destruction of the Northern Kingdom in 721 B.C., J was conflated with the ELOHIST (E) tradition to the benefit of the former. J is characterized by its anachronistic use of the name YAHWEH for God from the beginning of its history (whence its name). Its theological outlook, its style, and much of its vocabulary are all distinctive. Its history includes: the creation of man and woman, the Fall, the religious decline of mankind, the patriarchs and their descent into Egypt, the Exodus, and the wandering in the desert. J's history provides the basic narrative framework for the Pentateuch. Many critics think that the history continued with a description of the conquest and other events until the time of the monarchy, but there is no agreement concerning the precise identification of J in the later books. For more details and bibliography, *see* PENTATEUCH.

[E. H. MALY]

YAN GUODONG, JAMES, ST.

Servant, lay martyr, member of the Third Order of St. Francis; b. 1853, Jianhe, Yangqu Xian, Shanxi Prov-

ince, China; d. July 9, 1900, Taiyüan, Shanxi Province. James (Jacob) Yan Guodong (also spelled Yen Ku-tung or Ien-Ku-Tun) was the eldest child of the peasants Matthias Side and Maria Du. He cheerfully served the Franciscan community at Taiyüan as scullery servant. He was among the innumerable Christians martyred during the Boxer Rebellion and among the several dozen trapped inside the Taiyüan cathedral, arrested, and beheaded. James was beatified by Pope Pius XII (Nov. 24, 1946) and canonized (Oct. 1, 2000) by Pope John Paul II with Augustine Zhao Rong and companions.

Feast: July 4.

Bibliography: L. M. BALCONI, *Le Martiri di Taiyuen* (Milan 1945). *Acta Apostolicae Sedis* 47 (1955) 381–388; *Vita del b. A. Crescitelli* (Milan 1950). M. T. DE BLARER, *Les Bse Marie Hermine de Jésus et ses compagnes, franciscaines missionnaires de Marie, massacrées le 9 juillet 1900 à Tai-Yuan-Fou, Chine* (Paris 1947). *Les Vingt-neuf martyrs de Chine, massacrés en 1900, béatifiés par Sa Sainteté Pie XII, le 24 novembre, 1946* (Rome 1946). L. MINER, *China's Book of Martyrs: A Record of Heroic Martyrdoms and Marvelous Deliverances of Chinese Christians during the Summer of 1900* (Ann Arbor 1994). J. SIMON, *Sous le sabre des Boxers* (Lille 1955). C. TESTORE, *Sangue e palme sul fiume giallo. I beati martiri cinesi nella persecuzione della Boxe Celi Sud-Est, 1900* (Rome 1955). *L'Osservatore Romano,* Eng. Ed. 40 (2000): 1–2, 10.

[K. I. RABENSTEIN]

YAXLEY, RICHARD, BL.

Priest, martyr; b. ca. 1560 at Boston, Lincolnshire, England; hanged, drawn, and quartered July 5, 1589 at Oxford. Richard, the third son of William Yaxley and his wife Rose Langton, went to Rheims in 1582 to study for the priesthood. Ordained in 1585, he began his labors in and around Oxford in February 1586. He was arrested with Bl. George NICHOLS and two others. All were interrogated at Oxford. Sent to London for further questioning, they were imprisoned at Bridewell. Yaxley was sent to the Tower of London as a close prisoner on May 25, 1589, and appears to have been racked frequently until sent back to Oxford on June 30, to stand trial for treason. Following his execution, his head was placed on a pike at Oxford Castle and his other remains on the four gates of the city. He was beatified by Pope John Paul II on Nov. 22, 1987 with George Haydock and companions.

Feast of the English Martyrs: May 4 (England).

See Also: ENGLAND, SCOTLAND, AND WALES, MARTYRS OF.

Bibliography: R. CHALLONER, *Memoirs of Missionary Priests,* ed. J. H. POLLEN (rev. ed. London 1924). J. H. POLLEN, *Acts of English Martyrs* (London 1891).

[K. I. RABENSTEIN]

YBARRA DE VILLALONGA, RAFAELA, BL.

Widow, mother, and foundress of the Institute of Holy Guardian Angels; b. Bilbao, Spain, Jan. 16, 1843; d. Bilbao, Feb. 23, 1900. Born into a noble, pious family, Rafaela married while still young. With the approval of her husband, she pronounced vows of poverty, chastity, and obedience (1890). In order to assist abandoned girls, she founded the Holy Guardian Angels (Dec. 8, 1894) with three other women. Although her duties as the mother of seven children prevented her from living in community, Rafaela directed the formation of the first nuns, organized the community, built its first residential school in Bilbao at her own expense (1899), and wrote its first Rule. The institute provides moral and economic support for disadvantaged youth, especially young women, through schools and residences. Rafaela, known for her social conscience and activity, died at age fifty-seven following a serious illness. Pope John Paul II beatified her, Sept. 30, 1984.

Feast: March 8.

Bibliography: J. E. SCHENK, *Rafaela Ybarra* (Valencia, Spain 1984). *Acta Apostolicae Sedis* (1984): 1104. *L'Osservatore Romano,* English edition, no. 44 (1984): 6–7.

[K. I. RABENSTEIN]

William Butler Yeats. (©Bettmann/CORBIS)

YEATS, WILLIAM BUTLER

Irish poet and dramatist; b. Dublin, June 13, 1865; d. Cap Martin, France, Jan. 28, 1939. His father was the painter John Butler Yeats; his mother was Susan Pollexfen. Yeats attended art school but soon discovered that his true vocation was poetry. Yet, his narrative poem *The Wanderings of Oisin* (1889) is filled with painterly imagery, and his early lyric poetry is suffused with the sentiments of the Pre-Raphaelites. Their successors, the poets of the 1890s, were Yeats's associates and friends, but he was to grow beyond them into a new dimension.

Several influences served to exorcise *fin-de-siècle* languor from Yeats's poetry: his concern for Irish history and the life of the Irish peasantry; his friendship with Lady Isabella Augusta Gregory and through it an enhanced appreciation of the Anglo-Irish aristocracy; his experience with the Irish Literary Theatre, which he and Lady Gregory founded and the long course of his unrequited love for Maud Gonne (1865–1953). His failure in heroic love, "theatre business, management of men," and the attempt to relate the world of dream to harsh reality matured the poet and changed his style. He renounced the exotic colors that he claimed Shelley had brought out of Italy into English poetry and hoped instead that he might write poetry "as cold and passionate as the dawn."

Like others of his generation, Yeats was much concerned with the relation of art to religion, with the artist conceived as a priest of the imagination, and with the possibility that—now that science had made its shattering impact—poetry might have to substitute for religion. This lifelong concern arose early. As a youth he came to feel for science "a monkish hate," and, "deprived by Huxley and Tyndall . . . of the simple-minded religion" of his childhood, he was compelled, he tells us, to make up a "new religion" out of stories, personages, and emotions handed down by the poets and painters.

In 1917 Yeats married Georgie Hyde-Lees. His marriage brought to a head his new religion, for Mrs. Yeats was a medium, and through her automatic writing the "teaching spirits" gave him the material for a remarkable book, *A Vision* (1925). Yeats characterized the work as a "system of thought," but the spirits told Yeats that their purpose was to give him metaphors for his poetry, and Yeats told the reader that his own purpose was to "restore to the philosopher his mythology." Like BLAKE's prophetic books, *A Vision* is a personal mythology. Whether or not reading *A Vision* helps one to understand Yeats's poetry, writing the book was clearly helpful to Yeats: he told Lady Gregory that it enabled him to simplify his poetry.

In 1923 Yeats was awarded the Nobel prize, but it was not until the publication of *The Tower* (1928) that his greatness became generally recognized. His readers were driven to revalue the poems of earlier volumes, such as *The Wild Swans at Coole* (1917), and the plays, particularly those after 1917 modeled on the Japanese *nō* drama. At his death he was generally regarded as the greatest poet writing in English.

Yeats set his face against his age. Through a lifetime he warred against what he called "Whiggery"—a "levelling, rancorous, rational sort of mind / That never looked out of the eye of a saint / Or out of a drunkard's eye." The heroes of his poems are the aristocrat and the peasant, the artist and the saint; his great theme, the drama of the soul as it struggles with its own contrarieties to achieve its own truth. Christians, of course, cannot admit Yeats's claim that his refurbished religion is not anti-Christian but in fact includes Christianity; but Yeats's imagination was gripped by Christian symbols and his mind was constantly engaged with the historical and doctrinal problems of Christianity. He refuses to trivialize or simplify the human drama; he pushes aside timid Victorian pieties and Pre-Raphaelite softenings to invoke Christianity as the world-shaking force displayed in Byzantine art or in the intellectual history of the Western world. His poetry returns to Christianity the dimension of awe. But even when he sings the "Profane perfection of mankind," his poetry constantly asserts against the intellectual corruptions of our times the dignity and power of the human spirit.

Bibliography: *Autobiography* (New York 1953); *Collected Poems* (New York 1955); *Collected Plays* (New York 1953); *Letters*, ed. A. WADE (New York 1955); *A Vision* (New York 1956); *Essays and Introductions* (New York 1961); *Variorum Edition of the Poem*, ed. P. ALLT and R. K. ALSPACH (New York 1957). R. ELLMANN, *Yeats: The Man and the Masks* (New York 1948). A. N. JEFFARES, *W. B. Yeats: Man and Poet* (New Haven 1949).

[C. BROOKS]

YEMEN, THE CATHOLIC CHURCH IN

The Republic of Yemen is located in the southwest of the Arabian Peninsula. Its Arabic name is *al-Yaman,* "the righthand side," i.e., south of the Ka'aba in Mecca, since for Semites the south is at the right, the north at the left. It is bound by SAUDI ARABIA on the north, Oman on the northeast, the Gulf of Aden and the Arabian Sea on the south and southeast, and the Red Sea on the west. Primarily a desert region, the climate is hot and dry in the eastern desert, becoming humid near the southern coast. A narrow plain along the coast rises to flattened hills and

---

Capital: San'â.
Size: 74,000 sq. miles.
Population: 17,479,210 in 2000.
Languages: Arabic.
Religions: 3,000 Catholics (.02%), 17,472,210 Sunni and Shi'a Muslims (99.9%), 2,500 Protestants (.02%), 1,500 Hindus (.01%).
Apostolic vicariate: Arabia, with a seat in Abu Dhabi.

---

then to mountains, while the central region is a desert plain. Natural resources include petroleum, rock salt, marble and small quantities of coal, gold, nickel, copper and lead. The fertile interior highlands (7,000–9,000 ft. above sea level) are the seat of much of Yemen's agriculture and grazing, while the terraced mountain slopes in the west and the coastal plain of the Tihama also provide room for crops and livestock. Agricultural products include grains, fruit and vegetables, qat (a mild narcotic), coffee, cotton and dairy and livestock.

Northern Yemen broke free of the Ottoman Empire in November of 1918, and became North Yemen, while the southern region around the port of Aden, a strategic location as one of the world's most active shipping lanes, remained a protectorate of Great Britain until proclaiming independence on Nov. 30, 1967. North Yemen became the Yemen Arab Republic on Sept. 26, 1962; by 1970 the southern section had become the People's republic of Yemen, a Marxist state. During the 1970s and 1980s massive migrations of Yemeni from the south to the north occurred, increasing tensions between the two regions. In 1990 the two regions reunited as the Republic of Yemen, although secessionists began a short-lived agitation in 1994. One of the poorest nations in the Middle East, Yemen benefited from its oil reserves, but remained at the effect of oil prices. The government's efforts to modernize the economy and relieve its foreign debt were undercut by a high population growth and political instability. The population is overwhelmingly Muslim; most of the Jewish population was flown back to Israel after the founding of the State of Israel in 1948, leaving the 500 Jews remaining by 2000 scattered through several villages in the north.

Early History. In ancient times, the Sabaean kingdom with its capital Mârib, which is presently a small, almost deserted village on the eastern border of Yemen, flourished in the eastern center of Yemen, and the ruins of the ancient Minaean kingdom lie under a sandy mantel in the northeastern section of Yemen. The Old Testament depicts the Sabaeans both as wealthy traders of incense, perfumes, gold, etc., and as raiders [*see* SABA (SHEBA)]. In the course of history, the whole southwestern section of Arabia, described as *Arabia Felix* by ancient authors be-

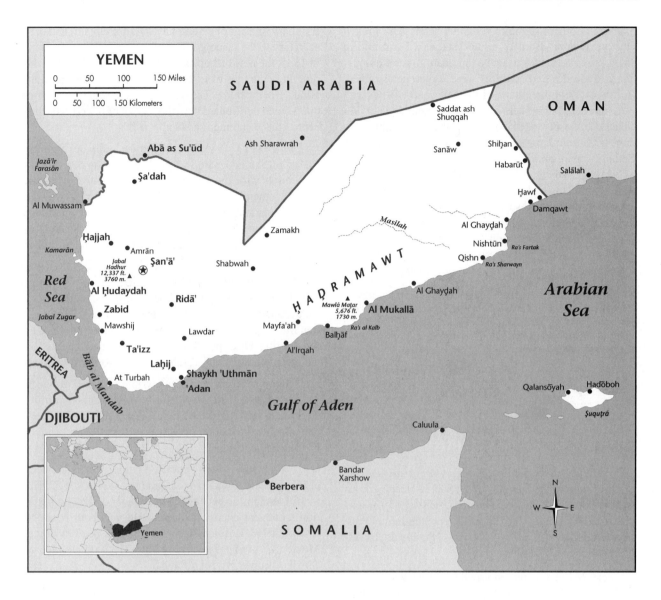

cause of its wealth, was under Sabaean rule. There were many Jewish communities in ancient Yemen and Christianity also gained followers, especially in Najrân (presently in southern Saudi Arabia). A persecution headed by a South Arabian provincial king who had embraced the Jewish faith, Masruk DhūNuwās, decimated the Christians in A.D. 523. The Sabaean power was, however, declining at an alarming rate, and Islam conquered the people in A.D. 628. From A.D. 893 until the revolution of 1962, Yemen was governed by IMAMS (Ar. 'imâm, exemplar) even during the Ottoman supremacy which lasted from the 16th century to the end of World War I.

Into the 21st Century. At the fall of the Soviet empire, the political friction between the communist government in the south and the non-communist north dissolved. On May 22, 1990 Yemen, divided since the 1960s, named Lt. Gen. Ali Abdallah Salih president of the new united republic. Under its new constitution, promulgated on May 16, 1991, Islam was the state religion, although people of other faiths were allowed to freely practice their religion. Shari'a, Islamic law, was the basis for much of the nation's civil law and all legislation; under the new system apostasy—conversion of a Muslim to another faith— was punishable by death, and the permission of the state was required before construction of any houses of worship.

By 2000 there were four parishes in Yemen, tended by four priests. Most Catholics were temporary foreign workers from Southeast Asia; most lived in the south and sent their children to small, private Catholic schools. The Missionaries of Charity—the order founded by Mother Teresa—were invited by the government to enter the country and operated homes for the poor and the handicapped in Sana'a and three other major cities, while the

Salesian Brothers attend to religious needs. The French Doctors without Borders group established a clinic in Aden. As a minority in an Islamic nation, relations between Catholics and Muslims were sometimes strained. In July of 1998 three nuns of the Missionary of Charity were murdered in western Yemen by a gunman later discovered to be deranged; the government took quick action in the murderer's capture and trial. Harassment of Catholics, particularly in the southern region, continued to occur sporadically through the 1990s due to a rise in Islamic fundamentalism, although the government remained quick to quell such acts. The Vatican established diplomatic relations with Yemen in October of 1998, and President Saleh visited with Pope John Paul II in April of 2000. An ecumenical Christian center was permitted to be constructed in Sana'a in the late 1990s.

Bibliography: L. FORRER, *Südarabien nach Al-Hamdānī's "Beschreibung der arabischen Halbinsel"* (Leipzig 1942). *Western Arabia and the Red Sea, Geographical Handbook* (London 1946). A. JAMME, *Research on Sabaean Rock Inscriptions from Southwestern Saudi Arabia* (Washington DC 1965).

[A. JAMME/EDS.]

YERMO Y PARRES, JOSÉ MARÍA DE, ST.

Founder of the Christian Mercy Program and the Congregation of the Servants of the Sacred Heart of Jesus and the Poor (*Congregación de las Servidoras del Sagrado Corazón*); b. Nov. 10, 1851, Hacienda de Jalmolonga, Malinalco, Mexico; d. Sept. 20, 1904, Puebla de los Angeles, Mexico.

José María was the only child of a lawyer, Manuel de Yermo y Soviñas, and his wife María Josefa Parres, who died 50 days after his birth. Under careful religious training by his father and his paternal aunt, José María soon discovered his vocation. He received his academic education from tutors, then by members of the Congregation of the Mission (VINCENTIANS) (1861–67). Emperor Maximilian gave him a medal for his academic excellence.

At age 16 he left home to join the Vincentians in Mexico City. In 1873, he founded a youth group called the "Angel of Purity." José María was sent to Paris for his theological studies. After his return to Mexico and a vocational crisis, he left the Vincentians to study in the diocesan seminary of León, Guerrero, and was ordained (Aug. 24, 1879).

Early in his career José María was known for his eloquence, promotion of catechesis for children, and care in fulfilling diocesan duties as secretary of the diocesan seminary, master of ceremonies, choir chaplain, and prosecretary to the bishop. When his health began to fail him in 1885, the new bishop assigned Father José María to the outlying churches of El Calvario (Calvary) and El Santo Niño (Holy Child). The young priest wanted to resign upon being confronted with the misery of poverty, but accepted his assignment as God's will.

On Dec. 13, 1885, he founded the Asilo del Sagrado Corazón (Sacred Heart Shelter) at the hilltop near Calvary Church with the help of four women and a doctor. These women became the nucleus of the Servants of the Sacred Heart of Jesus and the Poor as they began their novitiate (June 19, 1888). The following year the congregation was transferred to Puebla de los Angeles, where it grew rapidly and spread throughout Mexico.

Despite many tribulations during the rest of his short life, José María founded schools, hospitals, and homes for the elderly, orphans, and repentant women. His Christian Mercy program at Puebla freed women from lives of prostitution. On Sept. 20, 1904 he established the mission among the indigenous Tarahumaras of northern Mexico.

The saint left behind many writings, not all of which have been published, despite his having obtained printing equipment from Italy and France. He edited the first magazine for the formation of Mexican clergy (*El reproductor eleciástico*).

Father José María, known for his personal asceticism, obedience, and love of the poor, died at age 52. His mortal remains lie beneath the main altar of the congregation's convent chapel in Puebla. He was both beatified (May 6 1990, Basilica of Nuestra Señora de Guadalupe, Mexico City) and canonized (May 21, 2000, Jubilee of Mexico, Rome) by John Paul II.

[K. I. RABENSTEIN]

YEROVI, JOSÉ MARÍA

Franciscan bishop of Quito, noted for his sanctity; b. Quito, April 12, 1819; d. Quito, June 20, 1867. Yerovi received his intermediate education in the Colegio San Fernando, studied law in the University of St. Thomas, and received the title of attorney on Aug. 8, 1844. Shortly afterward, he sought admission to sacred orders and was ordained on May 31, 1845. After serving in two parishes, he was appointed chaplain of the monastery of Conceptas de Ibarra (February 1848). He remained there until 1852, with the exception of a brief term as deputy for Imbabura in the Constitutional Assembly in 1850. In December 1853, he was appointed vicar of Guayaquil, a post in which he showed extraordinary devotion. However, the regalistic regime put innumerable obstacles in the way of his pastoral work, and Yerovi was obliged to resign.

He fled to Pasto (1854), where he found refuge for his yearnings for penitence and piety in the Oratorio de San Felipe. He remained there until the political-religious storm provoked by General Mosquera broke out. He then entered the Franciscan Monastery of Cali (1862) and immediately began his novitiate, which was interrupted by the persecution. He was transferred to Lima, where he made his profession. The commisary, Friar Pedro Gual, took him as secretary on his visitation of the convents in Chile. When Yerovi returned to Lima to renew his life of mortification, he was appointed apostolic administrator of Ibarra. In this diocese, recently created by Pius IX at the request of President García Moreno, he increased his activity to care for the heavy work of organization, but very soon he was made coadjutor bishop of Quito, with the right of succession. On Aug. 5, 1866, he was consecrated.

Working zealously, he renewed the Eucharistic life in Quito, where it had been blighted by Jansenism, and spread the gospel as no other bishop had done. At his death he was widely mourned, for, as Juan Montalvo wrote, "such men as he come into the world only now and then." The case for his beatification was in progress in 1963.

Bibliography: J. TOBAR DONOSO, *Il Ilmo Padre Fray José María Yerovi, O.F.M., arzobispo de Quito* (Quito 1958). *Cartas Pastorales* (Publicadas por el Comité de Canonización; Quito 1954).

[J. TOBAR DONOSO]

YEṢIRAH, BOOK OF

The title of a work in Hebrew (*seper yᵉṣîrâ*, the Book of Creation), of disputed origin, constituting with the ZOHAR the pith of the medieval Jewish CABALA, thus giving a clue to Jewish GNOSTICISM. It occupies the center of cabalistic metaphysics, for it is through the instrumentality of this writing that the cabalistic movement studied the ancient doctrine of the genesis of the world through letters and numbers.

Origin. It was later than the Talmud, which was finished *c.* A.D. 500, and probably dates from the 7th century. SA'ADIA BEN JOSEPH, Judah BEN SAMUEL HA-LEVI, and Shabbataï Donnolo attributed the work to the Patriarch Abraham, who was thought to have been a learned astrologer. Others placed it in an Essenian milieu or ascribed it to Akiba. The work probably came from a Gnostic group in Palestine or Syria. It is couched in a style at once clear and mysterious. The greatest Jewish thinkers of the Middle Ages commented upon it: Ibn Gabirol (AVICEBRON), Moses NAHMANIDES, Abraham ben Meïr IBN EZRA, etc. Among contemporaries it has been examined from every possible point of view, and it has been translated and commented upon in almost all Occidental languages. Its success and influence are due to the importance of its doctrine as well as to the manner in which it is presented.

Doctrine. The author of the Yesirah asks the "how" of Creation. The origin of the creative act is for him God's free will. The first section delineates 32 ways by which the divine Will applied itself to the world's creation: the 22 letters of the sacred alphabet and the ten *sephiroth* (enumerations, entities designating divine attributes, and zones of their emanation). The beginning of the Yeṣirah reads, "According to 32 mysterious ways of wisdom, Yah, Lord of Hosts, the living God and King of the world, El Shaddaï, merciful and clement, superior and supreme (sacred is his Name!), has engraved and created His world through three *sepharim* . . . through *sephar* and through *sippur* and through *sepher*. 10 *sephiroth belima* and the 22 basic letters: 3 'mothers,' 7 'doubled,' and 12 'simple' ones."

The 10 *sephiroth* express the order in which beings are conceived: 1 is spirit or word of God; 2 is breath that comes from spirit; 3 is water that proceeds from breath or air; 4 is fire that comes from water; 5 is height; 6, depth; 7, East; 8, West; 9, South; 10, North.

The letters are divided in three classes: the 3 "mothers" (aleph, mem, shin), which represent air, fire, and water; the 7 "doubled ones," which represent antitheses such as good and evil, life and death, wisdom and folly, the two sexes. The 7 planets, the 7 days, the 7 heavens are the 7 letters b, g, d, k, p, t, r. The other letters represent the 12 frontiers of space, the 12 signs of the Zodiac, the 12 organs of the soul. The possible combinations of these letters are beyond the capacity of the imagination, but they are all absorbed in the One.

Thus the first 10 numbers and the letters (signs of thought) presided over the creation of the macrocosm (time and space) and the microcosm (man). "The union of language and philosophy constitute the system of the Sepher Yesirah, in which the study of articulated sounds forms the point of departure" (A. Epstein). This book, says Judah ha-Levi, "teaches us the existence of a single God by showing us unity and harmony amid variety and multiplicity, for such an accord could only come from a single Organizer" (*Kuzari* 4, 8, 25).

Relations between macrocosm and microcosm; between time, space, and man; speculations concerning letters—all these themes are echoes of late Hellenistic speculation. Attempts have been made to compare the Yeṣirah with the cosmogony of PROCLUS, but similarity with certain strains of Christian GNOSIS is much more evident, e.g., with the Clementine Homilies, whose redaction is placed in the Near East *c.* 350. In revealing new horizons to the mystical world this book exercised an enormous influence on Jewish thought.

See Also: NUMEROLOGY

Bibliography: K. SCHUBERT, *Lexikon für Theologie und Kirche,* ed. J. HOFER and K. RAHNER, 10 v. (2d, new ed. Freiburg 1957–65); suppl., *Das ZweiteVatikanische Konzil: Dokumente und kommentare,* ed. H. S. BRECHTER et al., pt. 1 (1966) 5:971. L. GINZBERG, *The Jewish Encyclopedia,* ed. J. SINGER 12:602–606. S. COHEN, *Universal Jewish Encyclopedia* (New York 1939–44) 10:596–597. A. EPSTEIN, ''Recherches sur le Sefer Yeçira,'' *Revue des études juives* 28–29 (Paris 1894).

[A. BRUNOT]

YEZIDI RELIGION

The Yezidis are an esoteric religious group inhabiting scattered villages in Iraq, Syria, Turkey, and southern Russia. Most are farmers and shepherds. Their faith prohibits unnecessary association with outsiders and their sacred books (*Resh* and *Jalwa*) are sealed to nonbelievers. They venerate the tomb of Shaikh Adi, son of Musafir, located in Lalish Valley in northern Iraq.

Yezidis recognize seven facets of God (Jesus, the sun, Adi, Yezid, Gabriel, etc.); each treated as a separate entity. One facet is Satan, hence they are called devil-worshippers. Each deity is represented by a copper standard (*Sanjaq*) to which they contribute financially.

Yezidis believe they are the sons of Shahid, who sprang from Adam's seed. Their society has sharply defined castes (princes, clergy, kochaks, faqirs, pirs, chanters, and commoners) between which marriage is prohibited. Every Yezidi must have a spiritual brother-sister from the clergy. They pray to the sun at dawn, observe three fasting days each year, make an annual pilgrimage to Adi's tomb, and have several feasts (Sari Sali, Qurban, Yezid, Ijwa, etc.). They practice baptism and circumcision and believe in the transmigration of souls. Their faith embodies countless dietary taboos (pork, fish, cabbage, cock and deer meat, lettuce), prohibits utterance of words containing ''sh'' and ''t'' sounds, and only family members of the clergy are permitted to acquire education.

Yezidism has borrowed heavily from other religions in the area (Babylonian, Mithraic, Zoroastrianism, Manichaean, Judaic, Christian, and Islamic), and thus embodies something of the entire religious experience of Western Asia.

Bibliography: S. S. AHMED, *The Yezidis, Their Life and Beliefs,* 2 v. (Baghdad 1971). I. CHOL, *The Yezidis Past and Present* (Beirut 1934). S. DAMLUJI, *The Yezidis* (Mosul 1949). E. S. DROWER, *Peacock Angel* (London 1941). R. H. W. EMPSEN, *The Cult of the Peacock Angel* (London 1928). H. FIELD and J. GLUBB, *The Yezidis, Sulubba and Other Tribes of Iraq and Adjacent Regions* (Manasha, Wis, 1943). J. ISYA, *Devil Worship, The Sacred Books of the Yezidis* (Boston 1919). M. J. MENANT, *Les Yezidis* (Paris 1892), T. MENZEL, ''Yezidi,'' *Encyclopedia of Islam* 4 (Leiden 1938).

[S. S. AHMED]

YOGA

Yoga is one of the most important and best known of the six *darshanas,* or schools of Hindu philosophy (*see* HINDUISM). The classical texts are the Yoga *Sutras.* These are attributed to Pātañjali, *c.* 200 B.C., although they probably date from A.D. 400 to 500.

Origins of Yoga. The doctrine and practice of yoga go back to a much earlier period than the texts, perhaps to the very beginning of Indian culture. A figure in the characteristic posture of a yogi was found among the excavations at Mohenjo-Daro, West Pakistan, where the remains date from the 2d millennium B.C. In any case, it is probable that yoga originated among the pre-Aryan peoples of India and has its roots in certain mystical and magical traditions of a very primitive character. The decisive development of yoga took place in about the 6th century B.C. when an ascetical movement arose, perhaps as a result of the doctrine of transmigration, which seems to have entered into Hindu tradition at this time. This ascetical movement was to have a permanent effect on Indian culture, for from it Buddhism and Jainism were born, and the doctrine of the Upanishads took shape under its influence.

The word used for asceticism in India is *tapas,* which meant literally ''heat.'' In the early stages of the development of Indian asceticism, effort was concentrated on acquiring ''interior heat'' by which, it was believed, magical powers could be obtained. Even in the early period of the Upanishads, yoga came to be regarded as a means of controlling the senses and the mind to attain a state of mystical union with the Divine Being and a liberation (*mokṣa*) from the wheel of life (*saṁsāra*). These two elements of magic and mysticism have always been closely interwoven in yoga, so that on the one hand it is regarded as a means of acquiring preternatural powers, and on the other, as a means of liberating the soul from the bondage of matter and restoring it to its original state as a pure spirit.

Classical Yoga. The yoga of Pātañjali, or classical yoga, is based on the doctrine of the Sānkhya school of philosophy, according to which the soul is by nature a pure spirit (*puruṣa*) that has become identified through ignorance (*avidyā*) with matter (*prakṛti*). The purpose of yoga is to set the soul free. Its method is a technique of control of body and mind, conscious and unconscious, until the mind (*chitta*) reaches the state of "concentration on a single point" (*ekāgrāta*) in which it is no longer subject to the influence of the body. There are eight states or "members" (*angas*) in this process, which together compose the system of classical yoga.

Counsels and Disciplines. The first two stages are of a moral nature, and may be compared with the precepts and counsels of Christian perfection. The precepts, literally "restraints" (*yama*), are not to kill (*ahiṁsā*), not to lie (*satya*), not to steal (*asteya*), not to be impure (*brahmacharya*), and not to be avaricious (*aparigraha*). The counsels, or disciplines (*niyama*), are cleanliness (*shauca*), serenity (*saṁtoṣa*), asceticism (*tapas*), the study of scriptures (*svādhyāya*), and devotion to God (*Īshvarapraṇidhāna*). The last two disciplines are of particular interest because, although they were of less importance in classical yoga, they provided the basis for the development of religious yoga (*bhakti yoga*) that took place in the Middle Ages.

Posture. The next two stages, posture (*āsana*) and control of breath (*prāṇāyāma*), were important in the development of Haṭha yoga. The position of the body is considered of cardinal significance in the control of the mind. The position, according to Pātañjali, should be both firm and pleasant (*sthirasukham*). The effort to attain the correct position may require considerable practice, but, once attained, it should become perfectly easy, so that the mind is in no way disturbed by the body. The ideal position is said to be *padmāsana,* the "lotus" pose in which the yogi is normally depicted; but any position is permitted in which body and mind can be calm and recollected.

Breath Control. The control of the breath (*prāṇāyāma*) is considered to be of even greater importance than the position of the body, since it is held to lead to control of consciousness. By control of the breath the yogi can not only gain control over the body, so as to be able even to suspend the breath altogether for a considerable time, but he can also penetrate into the deepest levels of the unconscious and control its effects. Even in the early stages it is said that *prāṇāyāma* brings about physical and psychological harmony.

Withdrawal of the Senses. This stage of yoga (*pratyāhāra*) consists of the detachment of the senses from their proper objects, so that the mind is no longer disturbed by any external object but remains recollected in itself. This leads to the three final stages of mental concentration by which the end of yoga is realized. The first of these is "concentration" (*dhāranā*), that is, fixing the attention on a single point, such as the tip of the nose, the sphere of the navel, or the "lotus of the heart." The lotus of the heart is not so much a physical point as a psychological "center," and the purpose of the exercise is to bring about a state of psychological unity. It is here that Pātañjali introduces the idea of God in yoga, by saying that the yogi may concentrate on the divine form or "Vishnu in the heart."

Meditation. The next stage is "meditation" (*dhyāna*), which is reached when concentration becomes continuous in a "unified current of thought." It should be observed that this is not meditation in the ordinary sense, but a concentration of the mind on an object of thought in such a way as to penetrate to its essence and to enter into the secrets of its nature. This leads to the final stage of "contemplation" (*samādhi*), which is a state of total absorption in the object of thought. In this state there is no longer any distinction between the object, the subject, and the act of thought. It is a knowledge by "identity," when the object reveals itself in its state of pure being. It must be observed that this is not a state of trance in the ordinary sense, in which the faculties are suspended, but a state of pure consciousness in which the mind, in perfect lucidity, retains control. Yet even this is not the ultimate state. As long as the mind remains in relation with any object, *samādhi* is said to be "with seed" (*bīja samādhi*); i.e., the seeds of differentiated thought (*saṁskāra*) still remain within the mind. It is only in the state of "seedless" *samādhi* (*nirbīja samādhi*), when the mind is withdrawn from all relation with any object and remains in a state of absolute isolation (*kaivalya*) reflecting the pure light of the Self (*puruṣa*), that the ultimate goal of yoga is attained and the yogi gains liberation (*mokṣa*). He is then what is called *jīvanmukta,* liberated while yet alive, having altogether transcended the condition of mortal life, and become identified with Being itself.

Though the ultimate purpose of yoga is to attain liberation in this way, yet in the course of yoga it is held that various supernatural, or more properly preternatural, powers (*siddhi*) are obtained. By penetrating into the different states of consciousness the yogi is said to be able to know his "former births" and to be able to read the thoughts of men. By penetrating to the essence of the object that he contemplates, and so into the secrets of nature, he is said to gain control over nature, and even to be able to control his body to such an extent that he can become invisible and "fly through the air." He also develops a whole organism of "subtle" senses, sight, hearing, smell, etc., so that he has powers of clairvoyance, clair-audition, etc., and of causing things to materialize. No doubt, there is much exaggeration in these claims, but it would seem that there is in this a systematic development of what has been called the *psi* faculty, through which very remarkable powers can be acquired. In later times great attention was paid to the development of these powers, and Pātañjali himself devotes a whole book to them. Yet he insists that these powers must be renounced by those who would attain to final liberation, as they are a form of bondage to the material world.

Such is the classical system of yoga, sometimes known as *Rāja yoga* (Royal yoga), which may be called the typical system of Indian yoga. But in addition to this, though largely based upon it, there are many other forms of yoga. Both Buddhism and Jainism developed their own systems of yoga, different not so much in method itself as in the doctrine underlying the method and the form of "realization" that was sought. For the Jain the purpose of yoga was the elimination of *karma,* that is, the effects on the soul of the actions of former lives, and its final purification. For the Buddhist it was the attainment of *nirvana,* the "blowing out" of life and the elimination of the self in the bliss of pure being.

Role of the *Bhagavad Gītā* in Yoga. One of the most important stages in the development of yoga is to be found in the *Bhagavad Gītā.* It is here that we can begin to discern the distinction between the three ways of yoga, *karma yoga, jñāna yoga,* and *bhakti yoga.* The yoga of Pātañjali is properly a form of jñāna yoga, a way of release by "knowledge." But such a way demanded a life of asceticism (*tapas*), which was not possible for the ordinary man. The *Bhagavad Gītā* declares that the way of release is open also to the ordinary householder by means of "action" (*karma*). If a man does the ordinary duties of his state of life in a spirit of detachment, without seeking the "fruits" of his action for himself, he can be saved no less than the ascetic. This is brought into relation with the new concept of *bhakti yoga,* the way of "devotion" to God, which is now declared to be the supreme way of obtaining liberation. If the ordinary actions of life are offered to God as a sacrifice they become a means of liberation, and it is devotion to God, that is to Krishna, the personal form of God, which is the essential means of liberation. Thus the devotion to God, which in the yoga of Pātañjali had played very little part, becomes the essential form of yoga, and liberation is conceived not as form of "isolation" achieved by the ascetic effort of the soul, but as a mystical union with a personal God achieved through his grace.

Haṭha Yoga. Opposite to this in every way is what is known as *Haṭha* yoga. This form of yoga relies entirely on physical exercises and aims primarily at bodily perfection. In modern times it is considered as a method of acquiring physical health and equilibrium, but in ancient times it was rather a method for acquiring preternatural powers. It belongs, in fact, to the school of tantric yoga, which developed in the Middle Ages (A.D. 500–1000).

Tantric Yoga. The aim of tantric yoga was to enable the body to attain to a supernatural condition; not to transcend the body, as in classical yoga, but to transform it. The purpose was to obtain a "diamond" body, that is a body free from all infirmities and virtually immortal. For this purpose the technique of *prāṇāyāma* was systematically developed, but various other techniques were added. There were methods of cleansing the body by swallowing a piece of cloth, which was left for some time in the stomach, and of drawing in and expelling water. But more important than this is what has been called a system of "mystical physiology." It was held that the body was made up of a multitude of veins or nerves (*nādīs*) and centers (*chakras*) in which its powers were concentrated. These are to be regarded not so much as physical but as psychological or "subtle" entities; the *chakras* are the various centers of psychic energy and the *nādīs* are the channels through which it is transmitted. It was held that the basic center is at the base of the spine, where the psychic energy is represented as being curled up like a serpent and known as *Kuṇḍalinī.* The purpose of *Kuṇḍalinī* yoga is to lead this energy through the different *chakras* from the base of the spine to the top of the head by a technique of breathing so that all the different regions of consciousness are awakened. When *Kuṇḍalinī,* the vital energy of *shakti,* reaches the ultimate center at the top of the head, it unites with Siva, the principle of pure spiritual consciousness, and the whole being is transformed. Whatever may be said of its physical basis, there can be no doubt that *Kuṇḍalinī* yoga is a profound method of psychological transformation, leading to that unification of being which is the ultimate goal of the practice of yoga.

Among the methods used in tantric yoga to reach the final state of equilibrium there are certain practices of a sexual nature. In some schools of tantric yoga a kind of "orgy" was practiced, in which all normal restraints were abandoned, but it is said that even this was often carried out only in a symbolic way. But the practice of intercourse (*maithuna*) between a yogi and a yogini was of a different nature. It was never an indulgence in passion, but, on the contrary, an attempt to control sex in such a way as to make it a means of spiritual liberation. The texts insist that in this practice the "semen must not be emitted." It was actually an attempt to control the flow of semen, so as to have complete mastery over the body. Thus by the control of the breath in *prāhāyāma,* the control of every movement of the mind, both conscious and unconscious, and finally by the control of the semen, the whole body was to be controlled and the whole nature transformed.

Purpose and Evaluation of Yoga. In all these forms of yoga, as Mircea Eliade has pointed out, there is a constant effort to return to the state of man before the Fall, to transcend the human state and become ''like God.'' In so far as it relies on human effort and a definite technique to attain this end, yoga may be regarded as a system of magic, and there can be no doubt that this element is often present. But, on the other hand, following the original impulse of the Indian mind in its search for God, there is also a definite desire to attain to spiritual freedom, to be freed from the effects of sin, and in certain schools, at least, to depend on the grace of God rather than on human effort. In this case the goal is not so much magical as mystical. The aim is to separate the soul from its subjection to the body and its passions, to free the mind from its subjection to the senses and the imagination, and to attain to a state of absolute freedom and spiritual consciousness. In this state, it is believed, man can be restored to his original state of unity, above the flux of time and change, free from bondage to the material world, and established in perfect freedom and immortality. It marks the deep aspiration of the Indian soul to return to God, to recover the lost state of Paradise; but, lacking the light of revelation, it is inevitably exposed to the dangers of illusion and of magic and superstition. Yet, on the whole, one must say that the desire to know God is the fundamental motive of yoga.

Bibliography: PĀTAÑJALI, *The Yoga-System of Pātañjali,* tr. J. H. WOODS (Harvard Oriental Series 17; Cambridge, Mass. 1914); *How to Know God: The Yoga Aphorisms,* tr. and ed. S. PRABHAVA-NANDA and C. ISHERWOOD (New York 1953). M. ELIADE, *Yoga: Immortality and Freedom,* tr. W. R. TRASK (New York 1958); *Die Religion in Geschichte und Gegenwart,* 7 v. (3d ed. Tübingen 1957–65) 6:1855–57. J. G. WOODROFEE, ed. and tr., *The Serpent Power* (Madras 1953).

[B. GRIFFITHS]

YORK, ANCIENT SEE OF

Metropolitan see located in northern England where it included all or part of the modern counties of Cumberland, Northumberland, Westmorland, Yorkshire, Lancashire, and Nottinghamshire within its shifting boundaries during the Anglo-Saxon and medieval periods.

Growth and Development. The Christian origins of the archdiocese are obscure, although York itself was an important center of Roman Britain, and it is known that a bishop of York attended the Council of Arles in 314. Christianity was presumably destroyed by the Anglo-Saxon invasions and was not restored until the 7th century following Augustine of Canterbury's mission to England, 597. Pope Gregory I the Great intended York to be a metropolitan see with 12 suffragans, a hope which,

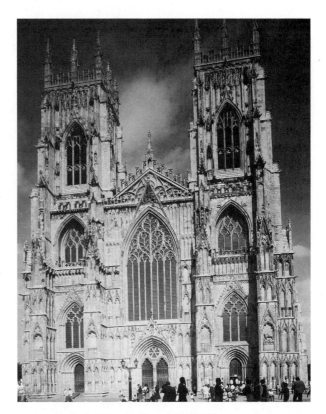

York Cathedral. (©Angelo Hornak/CORBIS)

although never realized, would seem to confirm York's importance earlier. Not until 625 was Augustine's disciple, PAULINUS OF YORK, consecrated bishop there, but his tenure proved short-lived. The Christian king of Northumbria, EDWIN, was killed in battle, 632, and Paulinus fled to Rochester, leaving York to the care of the Celtic bishop abbot of LINDISFARNE. The see was restored in 664, when the volatile Wilfrid was consecrated bishop and restored the church of York. With the accession of Egbert (Ecgbert) of York, brother of the Northumbrian king, the see was raised to metropolitan status; the PALLIUM arrived in 735. The 9th century brought the Scandinavian invasions and the destruction of the Northumbrian ecclesiastical organization. HEXHAM, Lindisfarne, and WHITHORN, all three suffragans of York, were ravaged, and the Scandinavians occupied York itself in 866, although it appears that Archbishop Wulfhere continued to reside in the city until his death in 900. The succession of archbishops was interrupted until Athelstan's liberation of the city in 927. Archbishop Wulfstan I (*c.* 931–956) began the awesome task of reestablishing Christianity in the north. The only 10th-century suffragan of York was Chester-le-Street, whose diocesan seat was removed permanently to DURHAM in 994. The poverty of the archdiocese was such, however, that York was frequently held in plurality with the bishopric of WORCES-

TER in the 10th and 11th centuries. Durham remained the only suffragan of York until well after the Norman Conquest of England, which brought, in its turn, terrible destruction to the north when King William the Conqueror exterminated the rebels of 1069 to 1070. In 1133, following the conquest of Cumberland by King William II Rufus (1087–1100), an additional suffragan was established at Carlisle. From that date no substantial changes occurred in the organization of the archdiocese until the reign of King HENRY VIII. York produced its share of outstanding personalities: the aforementioned Wilfrid (d. 709), that difficult but singularly vital figure in Northumbrian ecclesiastical history; JOHN OF BEVERLEY (d. 721), Bishop of York, canonized in the 11th century for his numerous miracles of healing; OSWALD OF YORK, the late 10th-century Bishop of Worcester and Archbishop of York, a significant contributor to the introduction of Cluniac monasticism in England; Wulfstan II, Archbishop of York, 1002 to 1023, one of the most notable homilists of his age; THOMAS OF BAYEUX (1070–1100), first Norman archbishop and builder of the great minster, which was pulled down in the 13th century to make way for the present one, begun 1227; JOHN LE ROMEYN (1286–96), largely responsible for the north transept and the tower; Thomas ARUNDEL (1388–96), opponent of Lollardy; Richard SCROPE (1398–1405); Cardinal Christopher BAINBRIDGE; and most famous (or infamous) of all, Cardinal Thomas WOLSEY (1514–30), the most powerful English ecclesiastic of the late Middle Ages, and the English Church's greatest single "abuse." Most of the archbishops were men of authority in both temporal and ecclesiastical affairs, and many were men of notable learning, but following the Norman Conquest, none were saints.

Culture. The most significant artistic monument of the archdiocese is certainly York Minster, dedicated to St. Peter. Its principal feature is its medieval stained glass, especially the collection of windows (c. 1260–65) in the north transept, the "Five Sisters window" of grisaille glass. Also noteworthy is the great east window of the 15th century, the work of a single craftsman. In fact, more than one-half of the extant medieval stained glass in England is in the churches of York. The cathedral's chapter house contains Saxon Gospels and a Saxon horn of Near Eastern provenance.

In education, York played its greatest role during the Anglo-Saxon period. Archbishop Egbert, who may have beenn Bede's pupil, founded school and library, both of which became famous in the 8th century and, through ALCUIN, greatly influenced intellectual life in Carolingian Europe. Despite invasions and internal struggles in Northumbria, the school, noted for its encyclopedism and systematization of knowledge rather than its intellectual creativity, maintained its essential continuity until the Norman Conquest; the library, greatest in western Europe during the 8th century, was burned in 1069. Neither school nor library was "replaced," and York was not an important intellectual center after 1066.

Monastic life in the archdiocese flourished during two widely separated periods: that of Northumbrian religious life in the 7th and 8th centuries, which produced CUTHBERT at Lindisfarne and BEDE at JARROW; and the period of the 12th-century revival that gave rise not only to great CISTERCIAN houses such as RIEVAULX, associated with Abbot AELRED, and FOUNTAINS, but also to foundations by other orders such as the large Benedictine house, St. Mary's Abbey, in York.

Jurisdiction. York's struggle with Canterbury over archiepiscopal primacy in England was, without doubt, York's single most important role on the broader stage of England's religious history. It began during the episcopate of Thomas of Bayeux (1070–1100). In 1071 with both archbishops, Thomas and LANFRANC, present, Pope ALEXANDER II decided for Canterbury over York, but in 1118 THURSTAN, Archbishop elect of York, refused to submit to Canterbury and appealed to Pope CALLISTUS II (1119–24), who consecrated him and released him and his successors from subordination to Canterbury. The struggle was renewed in the 14th century and was finally settled by Pope INNOCENT VI (1352–62), who decided that the archbishop of Canterbury was to have precedence and the title, "Primate of all England," while the archbishop of York was to be called "Primate of England." Both archbishops could carry their crosses in the other's province. This decision has ensured Canterbury's primacy ever since, both for the remainder of the Middle Ages and since the Henrician changes.

Bibliography: HUGH THE CHANTOR, *The History of the Church of York, 1066–1127,* tr. by C. JOHNSON (New York 1961). G. W. KITCHIN, ed., *The Records of the Northern Convocation* (Surtees Society Pub. 113; Durham 1907). J. RAINE, ed., *The Historians of the Church of York and Its Archbishops,* 3 v. (*Rerum Britannicarum medii aevi scriptores,* 71; London 1879-94). F. L. CROSS, *The Oxford Dictionary of the Christian Church* (London 1957) 1484–85. *The Victoria History of the County of Yorkshire,* ed. P. M. TILLOTT (London 1961). J. LENEVE, *Fasti Ecclesiae Anglicanae 1300–1541* (1716). Corrected and continued from 1215 by T. D. HARDY, 3 v. (Oxford 1854). New ed. by H. P. F. KING et al. (London 1962–): v.6, Northern Province (York, Carlisle and Durham) comp. B. JONES 6:vii–viii, 1–94.

[H. S. REINMUTH, JR./EDS.]

YORK USE

Christianity was established in York in the fourth century, but after the departure of the Romans the country relapsed into paganism. St. Paulinus (d.644), sent to England by Gregory the Great in 601, was bishop in 631 but fled from his see in the face of the new pagan invasion, and for a time the region was under the care of missionaries from Lindisfarne, sent by St. Aidan (d. 651). Traces of this Celtic interlude remained down to the time of the reorganization of the chapter by the Normans. Thus, up to that time the clergy of the cathedral at York was known as CULDEES or *Colidaei.*

The liturgy of York, like that of SARUM, was a Norman codification of existing practice with the addition of many Norman-French practices, particularly those of a ceremonial nature. For York, unlike Sarum, we know the precise source of many of these: it was the cathedral church of Rouen. In comparison with Sarum liturgical books, those of the York Use are comparatively rare, and there are only about a half dozen manuscript Missals in existence. The Missal was printed in 1509 at Rouen, and again in 1516, 1517, and 1530.

The general features of the Mass offered considerable similarities with those of Sarum Use. Thus the prayers at the foot of the altar were in the same short form, with Psalm 42 as part of the celebrant's private preparation on the way to the altar. There were some slight ritual differences between Sarum and York at such points as the Gospel and the Offertory. At York the celebrant was directed to wash his hands twice, once before touching the host and again after incensing the altar (on this occasion while saying the *Veni Creator*). The offerings of host and chalice were made simultaneously and the answer to the *Orate fratres et sorores,* to be made by the choir in a low voice, was the first three verses of Psalm 19. The Canon contained the mention of the king, as at Sarum, but was otherwise identical with the Roman form. At the kiss of peace the formula was not the usual *Pax tibi et ecclesiae* (Peace to you and the Church), but *Habete vinculum pacis et caritatis ut apti sitis sacrosanctis mysteriis Dei* (Keep the bond of peace and charity that you may be fit for the sacred mysteries of God). The Mass Propers included a large number of sequences (more than at Sarum), the majority of them of indifferent quality. The Breviary showed many variations, mostly of a slight character, from those of Rome and Sarum, but in its general features resembled that of Sarum.

The Manual, again while resembling the general pattern of the Sarum and other English Manuals, contained several small differences. For example, in the York marriage service, the troth plighting ran as follows: "Here I take thee, N., to my wedded wife, to have and to hold at bed and at board, for fairer for fouler, for better for worse, in sickness and in health, till death us do part and thereto I plight thee my troth" (the form omits "if holy Church

will it ordain" found commonly in England and elsewhere). The bridegroom, while placing the ring on his bride's finger, said: "With this ring I wed thee, and with this gold and silver I honour thee, and with this gift I dowe thee," omitting "with my body I thee worship" of the Sarum rite, words that have been retained in the marriage service of the English BOOK OF COMMON PRAYER. The color sequence resembled that of Sarum, but it is difficult to establish a really probable sequence from the scanty evidence.

Bibliography: W. MASKELL, *The Ancient Liturgy of the Church of England, According to the Uses of Sarum, Bangor, York and Herford, and the Modern Roman Liturgy* (3d ed. Oxford 1882). A. A. KING, *Liturgies of the Past* (Milwaukee 1959). W. H. ST. J. HOPE and E. G. ATCHLEY, *English Liturgical Colours* (London 1918). E. BISHOP, *Liturgica Historica,* ed. R. H. CONNOLLY and K. SISAM (Oxford 1918). S. W. LAWLEY, ed., *York Breviary* (Surtees Society 71; Newcastle, Eng. 1880). W. G. HENDERSON, ed., *York Manual and Processional* (Surtees Society 63; Newcastle, Eng. 1875). H. J. FEASEY, *Ancient English Holy Week Ceremonial* (London 1897).

[L. C. SHEPPARD/EDS.]

YORKE, PETER CHRISTOPHER

Priest, writer, social reformer; b. Galway, Ireland, Aug. 15, 1864; d. San Francisco, Calif., April 5, 1925. After study at St. Patrick's College, Maynooth, he was accepted for the Archdiocese of San Francisco, completed his training at St. Mary's Seminary, Baltimore, Md., and was ordained on Dec. 17, 1887. He attended the Catholic University of America, Washington, D.C. (1889–91), receiving an S.T.L. degree. The Holy See awarded him a doctorate in theology in 1906 in recognition of his publications.

In San Francisco, Yorke was soon involved in controversy. As editor (1894–99) of the *Monitor,* official newspaper of the archdiocese, he campaigned against the religious bigotry instigated by the AMERICAN PROTECTIVE ASSOCIATION (A.P.A.). To defend religious liberty against the A.P.A., he formed the American Women's Liberal League and the Catholic Truth Society of San Francisco. At the request of labor leaders in San Francisco, Yorke publicly defended the teamsters' strike of 1901. His emphasis upon the principles of the encyclical RERUM NOVARUM (1891), particularly on the right of collective bargaining, helped to turn public opinion in the workers' favor. When he denounced city officials for partiality toward the employers' association and prevailed upon the governor of California to withhold state intervention, the employers agreed to recognize union labor. In 1902 he founded the *Leader,* a weekly newspaper devoted to the cause of Irish nationalism and the rights of labor. Through this medium and by lectures he continued to defend the workers during the street railway strike of 1906–07, and during the prosecution for graft of municipal officials identified with the Union Labor Party. The right of churchmen to intervene in social matters was not generally conceded in his day, nor was *Rerum novarum* widely known or understood. Nevertheless, Yorke persisted in his efforts to persuade the government to assume its social responsibilities.

Yorke's activities were wide–ranging. He was a vice president of the Irish Sein Fein in the U.S.; the founder of Innesfael, a home for working girls; an advocate of temperance; the founder of the Catholic Truth Society of San Francisco; a regent of the University of California; and a vice president of the National Catholic Educational Association. The *Text Books of Religion,* which he published in 1901, became standard in the grade schools of many Western dioceses, and he was the author of such works as *Lectures on Ghosts* (1897), *Roman Liturgy* (1903), *Altar and Priest* (1913), and *The Mass* (1921). While contributing to the religious and social development of California, Yorke also served as chancellor of the Archdiocese of San Francisco (1894–99) and as pastor of St. Anthony's, Oakland (1903–13), and St. Peter's, San Francisco (1913–25), the largest parishes in their respective cities. Annually, on Palm Sunday, the anniversary of his death, a civic memorial service is held at his grave in San Francisco.

Bibliography: B.C. CRONIN, *Father Yorke and The Labor Movement in San Francisco, 1900–1910* (Washington, D.C. 1944).

[B. C. CRONIN]

YOUNG, BRIGHAM

Second president of the Mormon Church, colonizer of Utah; b. Whitingham, VT, June 1, 1801; d. Salt Lake City, UT, Aug. 29, 1877. His parents, John and Abigail (Howe) Young, were poor and could give him little formal education. After joining the Church of Jesus Christ of LATTER-DAY SAINTS (Mormons) in upstate New York in 1832, he rose steadily as a church official, doing missionary work in the East and in England, aiding the beleaguered Saints in Missouri, and organizing their exodus when they were driven from that state in 1838–39. When Joseph SMITH was murdered in 1844, Young became church leader and led the Mormon trek to the West. Arriving on July 24, 1847, in the Valley of the Great Salt Lake, he started a settlement based on agriculture and embodying Mormon economic and family ideals. Young brought some 70,000 emigrants from Europe, encouraged cooperative economic forms, and developed indigenous industry, with the exception of mining. He repressed internal dissent, advocated plural marriage, and resisted Federal opposition, building a cohesive Mormon community of 140,000 by the time of his death.

Bibliography: M. R. WERNER, *Brigham Young* (New York 1925). M. R. HUNTER, *Brigham Young the Colonizer* (Salt Lake City 1940). L. H. CREER, *Founding of an Empire* (Salt Lake City 1947). T. F. O'DEA *The Mormons* (Chicago 1957).

[T. F. O'DEA]

YOUVILLE, MARIE MARGUERITE D', ST.

Foundress; first native Canadian saint; b. Varennes, Canada, Oct. 15, 1701; d. Montreal, Canada, Dec. 23, 1771.

Marguerite was the eldest of six children born to Christophe Dufrost de Lajemmerais and Marie–Renée Gaultier. Her father died when she was seven years old, leaving this family of six in great poverty. Through the influence of her great grandfather, Pierre Boucher, she was enabled to study for two years at the URSULINES in Quebec. Upon her return home, she became an invaluable support to her mother and undertook the education of her brothers and sisters.

Marguerite married François d'Youville in 1722, and the young couple made their home with his mother, who made life miserable for her daughter–in–law. Marguerite soon came to realize that her husband had no interest in making a home life. His frequent absences and illegal trading with the natives caused her great suffering and brought him infamy. She was pregnant with their sixth child when François became seriously ill. She faithfully cared for him until his death in 1730.

By the age of 29, she had experienced desperate poverty and suffered the loss of her father and husband. Four of her six children had died in infancy. In all these sufferings, Marguerite grew in her belief of God's presence in her life and God's love for every human person. She, in turn, wanted to make known God's compassion to all, undertaking many charitable works with complete trust in God.

Marguerite provided for the education of her two sons, who later became priests. As a Lady of Charity in her parish, Madame d'Youville helped the sick, buried the bodies of hanged criminals, and welcomed a blind woman into her home. Marguerite was soon joined by three young women who shared her love and concern for the poor. On Dec. 31, 1737, they consecrated themselves to God and promised to serve God in the person of the poor. Marguerite, without realizing it, had founded a group that would become the Sisters of Charity of Montreal, "Grey Nuns."

D'Youville always fought for the rights of the poor and broke with the social conventions of her day, making her the object of ridicule and taunts by her own relatives. Her small society was publicly refused Holy Communion, stoned, and insulted. When fire destroyed their home, they pledged on Feb. 2, 1745 to put everything in common in order to help a greater number of persons in need.

In 1747, this "mother of the poor" as she was called, was asked to become director of the Charon Brothers Hospital in Montreal, which was falling into ruin. She and her sisters rebuilt the hospital and cared for those in most desperate human misery. With the help of lay collaborators, Marguerite laid the foundation for service to the poor of a thousand faces.

In 1765 a fire destroyed the hospital, but Marguerite's faith and courage remained firm. She asked her sisters and the poor who lived at the hospital to recognize the hand of God in the disaster and to offer praise. At the age of 64, she undertook the reconstruction of this shelter for those in need. Totally exhausted, she died six years later.

She was declared venerable in 1890, beatified on May 3, 1959 by Pope John XXIII, who called her "Mother of Universal Charity," and canonized by John Paul II on Dec. 9, 1990.

Feast Oct. 16 (Canada).

Bibliography: Archives, Grey Nuns of Montreal. A. FERLAND–ANGERS, *Mère d'Youville* (Montréal 1945), approved Fr. biog. for beatification. M. P. FITTS, *Hands to the Needy; Blessed Marguerite d'Youville, Apostle to the Poor* (Garden City, NY 1971), approved Eng. biog. for beatification. B. JETTÉ, *Vie de la vénérable mère d'Youville, fondatrice des Soeurs de la charité de Montréal, suivie d'un historique de son institut* (Montréal 1900). A. FAUTEUX, *Love Spans the Centuries*, 4 vols. (Montreal, 1987). E. MITCHELL, *Marguerite d'Youville, Foundress of the Grey Nuns,* tr. H. NANTAIS (Montreal 1965); *Le vrai visage de Marguerite d'Youville* (Montréal 1973); *The Spiritual Portrait of Saint Marguerite d'Youville* (Montreal 1993).

[S. FORGET]

Brigham Young.

YSAMBERT, NICOLAS

Theologian; b. Orléans, France, 1569; d. Paris, May 14, 1642. Ysambert studied at the Sorbonne, and upon the completion of his studies (1602) taught theology there (1603). A chair of theology for the study of questions disputed between Catholics and Protestants was established in 1616, and Ysambert was appointed to it by King Louis XIII. It was his custom to use the *Summa Theologiae* of St. Thomas Aquinas as the basis for his lectures. Publication of his voluminous *Commentarius in S. Thomae summam* was begun by him; it was completed posthumously (6 v. Paris 1639–48). He taught in particular on the doctrine of grace a distinct form of congruism. The exponent of a moderate form of ULTRAMONTANISM, Ysambert was a major opponent of E. Richer. He was also the instigator of the censure directed by the theological faculty against Marcantonio de DOMINIS, the apostate archbishop of Spalatro whose *De republica christiana* was subversive of ecclesiastical authority.

Bibliography: E. PUYOL, *Edmond Richer* (Paris 1876). U. HORST, *Papst Konzil Unfehlbarkeit* (Mainz 1978). L. W. BROCKLISS, *French Education in the Seventeenth and Eighteenth Centuries* (Oxford 1987). J. M. GRES-GAYER, *Le Jansénisme en Sorbonne* (Paris 1996). H. HURTER, *Nomenclator literarius theologiae catholicae* (Innsbruck 1926) 3:948–949. É. AMANN, *Dictionnaire de théologie catholique*, ed. A. VACANT et al., (Paris 1903–50) 15.2:3621.

[P. K. MEAGHER/J. M. GRES-GAYER]

YSARNUS, ST.

Benedictine monk, abbot of SAINT-VICTOR IN MARSEILLES; b. near Toulouse, France; d. Marseilles, Sept. 9, 1043. Attracted by its reputation, he became a monk at the Benedictine Abbey of Saint-Victor. He then became prior, and finally abbot (1021–43). His reputation for virtue, and particularly his charity and supernatural gifts, attracted many vocations. He reformed the abbey and carried this reformation to numerous monasteries in the center of France and in Catalonia. In spite of serious illness, he traveled to Spain in order to discuss with the Moslems the liberation of some monks imprisoned by them. He died at Saint-Victor; his tomb is located in the crypt of the abbatial church. His life, written soon after his death on the basis of accounts of credulous eyewitnesses, is not critical; his cult was approved by Pope Urban V.

Feast: Sept. 24.

Bibliography: J. MABILLION, *Acta sanctorum ordinis S. Benedict* (Venice 1733–40) 8:532–559. *Acta Sanctorum* (Paris 1863—) 6:728–749. G. DE REY, *Les Saints de Marseille* (Marseille 1885) 185–204. A. M. ZIMMERMANN, *Kalendarium Benedictinum: Die Heiligen und Seligen des Benediktinerorderns und seiner Zweige* (Metten 1933–38) 3:80–83. J. L. BAUDOT and L. CHAUSSIN, *Vies des saints et des bienheureux selon l'ordre du calendrier avec l'historique des fêtes*, ed. by the Benedictines of Paris (Paris 1935–56) 9:498–499.

[É. BROUETTE]

YVES DE PARIS

Capuchin theologian, humanist and spiritual writer; b. 1588 as Charles de la Rue; ordained to the priesthood 1630 or 1632; d. 1678. While there are few definite facts about his secular life, it is known that he was born into the lesser nobility (*petite noblesse de robe*) in Paris, he studied law at the University of Orléans and was admitted into the bar of the Parliament of Paris in 1608. While in Italy, he discovered the Neoplatonism of Marsilio FICINO (1433–1499), the chief scholar of the Platonic Academy founded by Cosimo de' Medici. In addition to Ficino, he appeared to have absorbed the writings of Ramón LULL (c.1232–1316), the Stoics, and the French Humanists.

After the collapse of his family's fortune and much soul searching, Charles de la Rue entered the Order of Friars Minor Capuchins in 1619 and took the name of Yves after St. Yves (1301–1347), a priest and lawyer. During the years of his formation for the priesthood (1620–1630), Yves studied scholastic theology according to the Capuchin synthesis of Aquinas and Bonaventure. He combined this scholastic training with the reading of Augustine and other spiritual authors, especially Francis de Sales (1567–1622).

The writings of Yves de Paris can be classified under four major headings: apologetical, philosophical-theological, spiritual, and moral. Among his apologetical works are *Les Heureux succèss de la piété* (1632)—a defense of religious priests as spiritual directors—and three anti–Jansenist writings: *Très humble remonstrance faite à la reyne* (1644), *Les misericordes de Dieu dans la conduite de l'homme* (1645), and *Le souverain pontife* (1645). In addition to these major headings, he co–authored two works on astrology under the pseudonym of François Allaeus, an Arab Christian. Of his philosophical-theological writings, two are noteworthy. The four volume *Digestum sapientiae* (1643–1674), written in Latin, attempts to unify all the sciences into one coherent system by making use of Platonic and scholastic categories. A more accessible text is Yves' four-volume *La théologie naturelle* (1633–1638), which seeks to answer the arguments of the radical fideists, skeptics, and learned freethinkers (*libertins érudits*) of his day. Yves' natural theology employs elements of reason and rhetorical persuasion in an effort to show the logical coherence of God, divine providence, and the truths of the Christian religion. His fundamental thesis is that human beings have a natural awareness of God (un sentiment naturel de Dieu). In this, he shows many affinities with the Augustinian tradition of divine illumination and the Neoplatonic theology of Ficino.

Two spiritual writings of Yves deserve mention: *Traité de l'indifference* (1638) and *Les Progrès de l'Amour divin* (4 vol., 1642 and re-edited in 1675). Yves' treatise on indifference points to total submission to the will of God as the key to human happiness. His integration of "indifference" with a complementary commitment to the moral life avoids the dangers of antinomianism that would later emerge in the Quietist controversy of the 1680's and 1690's. Yves' four-volume study of the progressions of divine love (beginning love, suffering love, active love and joyous love) combines elements of humanism, Stoicism, and Platonic illuminationism in an effort to counter the hyper-Augustinian pessimism of the Jansenists.

In his moral writings, Yves shows himself to be a Molinist in his emphasis on human freedom's cooperation with divine grace. His four-volume treatise, *Les morales chrétiene* (1638–1642) is later followed by a book on the cultivation of Christian virtues entitled *Le gentilhomme chrétien* (1666). His 1661 work on the "vain excuses of sinners" (*Les vaines excuses des pécheurs* [1661]) is more austere in tone.

Although Yves de Paris was a well-known apologist of the mid- to late-17th century, he fell into oblivion from the 18th century until the 20th century when Henri Bremond's *L'histoire littéraire du sentiment religieux en France* (1916–1933) assigned him a prominent place as one of the best representatives of "devout humanism." From 1936 to 1970, numerous articles and books on Yves de Paris were published by the Capuchin scholar, Julien-Eymard d'Angers.

Bibliography: YVES DE PARIS, *Les oeuvres françoises du P. Ives de Paris, capuchin,* 2 vols. (Paris 1675–1680); D'indifférence, édition critique, RENÉ BADY, ed. (Paris 1966). H. BREMOND, *L'histoire littériare du sentiment religieux en France, t. 1, l'Humanisme dévot* (Paris 1916), 421–512, Eng. tr. K. L. MONTGOMERY, *A Literary History of Religious Thought in France* (New York 1928), vol. 1, 331–396. B. CHÉDOZEAU, ''Yves de Paris'' in *Dictionnaire de Spiritualité,* vol. 16 (Paris 1994) 1566–1576. CHARLES CHESNEAU (Julien-Eymard d'Angers, O.F.M. Cap.), *Le Père Yves de Paris et son temps* (1590–1678), 2 vols. (Paris 1946). *L'apologétique en France de 1580 à 1670, Pascal et ses précurseurs* (Paris 1954). *Yves de Paris: introduction et choix de texts* (Paris 1965). *L'humanisme chrétien au XVIIe siècle: Saint Francois de Sales et Yves de Paris* (La Haye 1970). R. FASTIGGI, *The Natural Theology of Yves de Paris* (Atlanta 1991). I. GORBY, ed., *Mystiques franciscaines* (Paris 1959). C. VASOLI, ''Il digestum sapientiae di Yves di Parigi,'' *Rivista di filosofia Neo-Scholastica* (Gennaro-Giugno, 1978) 247–265.

[R. FASTIGGI]

Z

ZABARELLA, FRANCESCO

A distinguished canonist and ecclesiastical diplomat; b. Padua, Aug. 10, 1360; d. Constance, Sept. 26, 1417. He was trained in law at Bologna and taught Canon Law at Florence (1385–90) and at Padua (1390–1410). In 1398 he was made an archpriest of the cathedral of Padua. He carried out a number of diplomatic missions for that city and participated in the Council of Pisa as a councilor. The antipope John XXIII appointed him bishop of Florence, July 18, 1410, and the following year (June 6, 1411), cardinal deacon of SS. Cosmas and Damian at Rome. He never received major orders, but he was a man of upright character and an active promoter of ecclesiastical reform. He may be described as a moderate conciliarist. One of the staunchest supporters of the antipope JOHN XXIII, he acted as one of his legates to Emperor Sigismund and helped to bring about the opening of the Council of Constance, Nov. 1, 1414. In the interest of Church unity, he persuaded John XXIII to resign (April 1415), but opposed the Avignon antipope BENEDICT XIII. When John HUS, Jerome of Prague, and Jean Petit were cited before the Council, he urged Hus and Jerome to sign a milder form of retraction, but without success. His last days were spent in pressing the Council to elect a new pope as soon as possible. His chief works are: *De schismate sui temporis,* dealing with ways and means of ending the schism (written at intervals, 1403–08; printed at Strassburg 1545); *Lectura super Clementinis* (completed in 1402; printed at Rome 1477 and Venice 1481); *Commentaria in V libros Decretalium* (1396–1404; printed at Venice 1502); *Consilia* (printed at Pescia 1490 and Venice 1581).

Bibliography: J. BECKMANN, *Lexikon für Theologie und Kirche*[1] 10:1017. H. HURTER, *Nomenclator literarius theologiae catholicae* 2:766–769. C. J. VON HEFELE, *Histoire des conciles d'après les documents originaux* 7, *passim.* G. ZONTA, *Francesco Zabarella* (Padua 1915).

[M. R. P. MCGUIRE]

ZABARELLA, JACOPO

Renaissance philosopher; b. Padua, Sept. 7, 1533; d. there, Oct. 25, 1589. A count of the Holy Roman Empire and a citizen of the Venetian Republic, he was professor of logic and natural philosophy at Padua from 1564 until his death. His is the terminal and most lucid development of Renaissance ARISTOTELIANISM, especially in logic. Influenced in part by humanism and by the Latin AVERROISM stemming from JOHN OF JANDUN, Zabarella wrote rigorous commentaries on Aristotle's text and separate systematic treatises on his philosophy. His commentaries on the *Posterior Analytics, Physics,* and *De Anima* have been used by modern classicists, especially W. D. Ross, in editing and interpreting Aristotle. His collected logical treatises, the *Opera logica* (Venice 1578, 2d ed. 1586), contain, noteworthily, two books on the nature of logic and four on philosophic or scientific methodology, the *De methodis.* The latter criticizes the untidy neo–Galenian theory of methods, reducing them to two, the analytic, or resolutive, and the synthetic, or compositive. Also noteworthy is his treatise *De regressu,* a sort of theory of verification in physical science. His collected natural treatises, the *De rebus naturalibus* (Venice 1590), include the earlier *De naturalis scientiae constitutione* (1586) and, also of note, two books on primary matter; four on the discovery of the first mover; one on the agent sense (a problem bequeathed the Italians by John of Jandun); one each on the human mind, the intelligible species, and the agent mind; and one on methodology, the *De ordine intelligendi.* Zabarella's natural philosophy is of considerable historical interest, but his theories of logic and method are, in addition, of permanent systematic importance. Zabarella's transmontane impact was greater than his immediate influence upon his fellow Italians. GALILEO cites him only twice, once in general approval, once to oppose him on primary matter. Despite the Lyons edition of his logic in 1587, his influence in France seems negligible. But in Germany, thanks to the fourth edition of his logic (Basel 1594) and the fact that reforming theologians had been students of his at Padua, he was cited among the moderns as of at least equal authority with P. MELANCHTHON, and was rivaled only by the Portuguese Jesuit P. da FONSECA. He influenced J. Jungius (1587–1657), Leibniz's professor of logic, and was avidly studied by G. W. LEIBNIZ himself, A. G. Baumgarten (1714–62), and others.

See Also: RENAISSANCE PHILOSOPHY.

Bibliography: Works. *De natura logicae,* Eng. D. D. RUNES, ed., *Classics in Logic* (New York 1962). Literature. W. F. EDWARDS, *Enciclopedia filosofica,* 4 v. (Venice–Rome 1957) 4:1811–13; *The Logic of Iacopo Zabarella* (Doctoral Diss. Columbia U. 1961); "The Averroism of Iacopo Zabarella" *Atti del XII Congresso Internazionale de Filosofia* 9 (1960) 91–107. J. J. GLANVILLE, "Zabarella and Poinsot on the Object and Nature of Logic," in *Readings in Logic,* ed. R. HOUDE (Dubuque 1958). N. W. GILBERT, *Renaissance Concepts of Method* (New York 1960).

[J. J. GLANVILLE]

ZACCARIA, ANTHONY MARY, ST.

Physician and priest, founder of the BARNABITES and the Angelicals of St. Paul; b. Cremona, Italy, 1502; d. there, July 5, 1539. His mother, Antonietta Pescaroli, was 18 years old at the death of her husband, Lazzaro, and she subsequently gave her whole attention to the education of her infant son. After his first studies at Cremona and Pavia, Anthony obtained a doctorate in medicine at Padua in 1524. While exercising his profession among the poor of Cremona, he felt a growing attraction to a religious apostolate. Having already made a notarized renunciation of any future inheritance, he began teaching catechism in the church of S. Vitale, and in 1528 he became a priest. At his first Mass, celebrated contrary to custom without solemnity, angels appeared at the altar. After two years of ministry, he was transferred to Milan as chaplain to Countess Ludovica Torelli of Guastalla. There he joined the Confraternity of Eternal Wisdom together with Bartolomeo FERRARI and Giacomo Morigia. Under the inspiration of his confessor, Battista da Crema, OP, he and two friends laid the foundations of the Congregation of Clerks Regular of St. Paul, known generally as Barnabites and approved by Clement VII in 1533. With Countess Torelli he instituted the Angelicals of St. Paul for religious women. This too was approved, by Paul III in 1535. The ambition of these two religious families was to reform the decadent society of the 16th century, beginning with the clergy, and including a renewal of spiritual life in monasteries of men and women.

Inspired by St. Paul, for whom he had great devotion, Zaccaria preached in churches and in the streets; performed public penances, which impressed his audiences; and conducted missions throughout Lombardy and in

Venice. He did not fear to introduce innovations such as the collaboration of the laity in the apostolate; frequent, even daily Communion; the exposition of the Blessed Sacrament in the 40 Hours' Devotion; the ringing of bells at three o'clock each Friday afternoon: and so on. These new things stirred the people to much good, but they also provoked a reaction and persecution that resulted in the official ecclesiastical processes of 1534–35 and 1537. On both occasions the Barnabites were exonerated. In May 1539, Zaccaria, already ill, accepted the commission to restore peace to Guastalla, then under pontifical interdict. After two months of fatiguing labor Zaccaria, sensing that death was near, was brought to Cremona for a last visit with his mother; he died there, only 36 years of age.

The spirituality of Zaccaria, austere though open to human sentiment and characterized by ardent, apostolic activity, is well reflected in his writings (see *Bibliotheca sanctorum* 2:220). His popular cult was suspended by Urban VIII in 1634, but the process for his canonization was reintroduced in 1890. On May 27, 1897, he was canonized by Leo XIII. His body rests at Milan in the crypt of S. Barnaba. In his iconography he is represented either with his first two companions or with a lily or a symbol recalling his three devotions, the Eucharist, the Crucifixion, and St. Paul.

Feast: July 5.

Bibliography: A. M. TEPPA, *Vita del beato A. M. Zaccaria* (Milan 1897). F. T. MOLTEDO, *Vita di S. A. M. Zaccaria* (Florence 1897). G. CHASTEL, *Saint Antoine-Marie Zaccaria, Barnabite* (Paris 1930). E. CASPANI, *Dictionnaire de spiritualité ascétique et mystique. Doctrine et histoire,* ed. M. VILLER et al., (Paris 1932—) 1:720–723. G. BOFFITO, *Bibtioteca Barnabitica,* 4 v. (Florence 1933–37) 4:209–264, bibliog. and iconography. A. M. GENTILI, *Prontuario per lo spirito* (Milan 1994).

[U. M. FASOLA]

ZACCARIA, FRANCESCO ANTONIO

Jesuit theologian, historian, and prolific writer; b. Venice, March 27, 1714; d. Rome, Oct. 10, 1795. His father, Tancred, a noted jurist, and his mother, Teresa Ferretti, a distinguished and pious Venetian, gave him, their only son, a thorough Christian education under the tutelage of the Society of Jesus. He entered the Austrian province of that order on Oct. 18, 1731, and soon proved to be so accomplished in Latin and Greek that he was chosen to teach grammar, the humanities, and rhetoric in the College of Gorizia, where he remained until the end of 1738, when he was sent to Rome for his theological studies. He was ordained in Rome in 1740. In 1742 he began a correspondence with some of the leading literary figures of his time, even proposing to Cardinal Angelo

Maria Querini a critical evaluation of the latter's *Life of Pius II*. In 1742 he was appointed prefect of the library of the Roman College, much to the dismay of Querini, who thought him better suited for the pursuit of higher studies in history. In the same year he began to preach in the Diocese of Fermio, a work he continued for 30 years throughout northern and central Italy. His eloquence as a preacher and controversial lecturer gained him great renown.

In 1751 he was transferred from the Austrian to the Roman province of his order, where upon the recommendation of Querini he was appointed archivist and librarian for Francis III, Duke of Modena. He succeeded Muratori, who died in 1750. This appointment won the approval of many of the intellectuals of his day, both in Italy and elsewhere, with the exception, however, of the Febronians and Jansenists. The duke ignored their calumnies and retained him for several years. With his publication of *Antifebronio* in 1767, however, the powerful antipapists persuaded the duke to ask the superior general of the society, Lorenzo Ricci, to recall him to Rome under the pretext of entrusting to him the reorganization of the library of the Gesù in Rome and of continuing the work of the library of the writers of his own order. Clement XIII granted him a pension as a recompense for his work in defense of the papacy. After the suppression of the society in 1773, the pension was stopped and his manuscripts were confiscated. For a time he was imprisoned in Castel Sant' Angelo, where he endured considerable suffering. Pius VI, who had always held him in high esteem and often consulted him, restored his pension and appointed him professor of church history at the Sapienza and director of the Accademia de' Nobili Ecclesiastici.

Zaccaria was one of the most erudite and prolific writers of his time. Sommervogel enumerates 161 of his publications, not to mention the great number of his works that remained in manuscript form.

Bibliography: L. CUCCAGNI, *Elogio storico dell' abate Francescantonio Zaccaria* (Rome 1796). C. SOMMERVOGEL et al., *Bibliothèque de la Compagnie de Jésus,* 11 v. (Brussels–Paris 1890–1932; v. 12, suppl. 1960) 8:1381–1435. H. HURTER, *Nomenclator literarius theologiae catholicae,* 5 v. in 6 (3d ed. Innsbruck 1903–13); v. 1 (4th ed. 1926) 5.1:484–498. J. P. GRAUSEM, *Dictionnaire de théologie catholique,* ed. A. VACANT et al., 15 v. (Paris 1903–50; Tables générales 1951–) 15:3645–48.

[L. L. GOOLEY]

ZACHARIAE, JOHANN

Theologian, opponent of John Hus; b. Erfurt *c.* 1362; d. there, July 25, 1428. As an Augustinian he was sent to Oxford in 1384, where he was a lector (1384–91). Having obtained a doctorate of theology at Bologna, he was incorporated at the University of Erfurt by 1410. Johann's sermons (six are extant) at the Council of CONSTANCE, where he was the delegate of the University of Erfurt, were memorable. He is said to have convicted John HUS, whence his title "Hussomastix." Contrary to tradition, he did not receive the GOLDEN ROSE from MARTIN V, who brought it to the Augustinian house at Erfurt, March 6, 1418, for the Emperor SIGISMUND, who resided there.

Zachariae was provincial of the Saxon Province of Augustinians, 1419 to 1423 and 1425 to 1427. In 1419 he presided at the general chapter of Asti, which ended the division within the order caused by the WESTERN SCHISM; his vote decided in favor of Augustine Favaroni of Rome as general. Zachariae wrote an extensive commentary on the Apocalypse as well as *Notabilia* on Matthew, Mark, and Luke.

Bibliography: A. ZUMKELLER, "Manuskripte von Werken der Autoren des Augustiner–Eremitenordens in mitteleuropäischen Bibliotheken," *Augustiniana* 12 (1962) 335–340. T. KOLDE, *Die deutsche Augustiner–Congregation* (Gotha 1897). *Acta Concilii Constanciensis,* ed. H. FINKE, 4 v. (Münster 1896–1928) v.2. F. ROTH, "The Great Schism and the Augustinian Order," *Augustiniana* 8 (1958) 281–298. A. B. EMDEN, *A Biographical Register of the University of Oxford to A.D. 1500* 3:2142.

[F. ROTH]

ZACHARIAS, PATRIARCH OF JERUSALEM

B. probably Constantinople; d. Jerusalem, Feb. 21, 631. He was a priest and guardian of the sacred vessels in the HAGIA SOPHIA at Constantinople, who became patriarch of Jerusalem in 609 succeeding Isaac. During the Persian invasion of 614, after having attempted to prevent the seizure of Jerusalem and the massacre of its inhabitants, he was captured and sent in exile to Persia. He wrote an encyclical letter to the Church of Jerusalem exhorting its people to penance and patience. Liberated after the victory over the Persians by HERACLIUS in 628, he reentered Jerusalem with the relic of the true Cross. During his absence, with the aid of (St.) JOHN THE ALMSGIVER of Alexandria, a restoration of the sacred monuments had been started by the superior of the Monastery of St. Theodosius, the Abbot Modestus, who succeeded Zacharias as patriarch (631–634).

Bibliography: *Patrologia Graeca* 86.2:3227–34. *Acta Sanctorum* Feb. 3:250–251. O. BARDENHEWER, *Geschichte der altkirchlichen Literatur* 5:41. M. LE QUIEN, *Oriens Christianus* 3:249–258. H. G. BECK, *Kirche und theologische Literatur im byzantinischen Reich* 448, 450, 454.

[I. H. DALMAIS]

ZACHARY, POPE, ST.

Pontificate: Dec. 3, 741 to March 15, 752. Nothing is known of his early life except that he was the son of a Greek, Polychronius, of Calabria. His pontificate was marked by charity for the clergy and poor of Rome, but especially by vigorous diplomatic relations with the LOMBARDS, the Byzantine Empire, and the FRANKS. Under Zachary's predecessor, GREGORY III, the papacy had continually suffered the depredations of the Lombard King Liutprand. In line with his new political orientation, Zachary repudiated the alliance of the papacy with the duke of Spoleto against Liutprand and, instead, personally met with the king on two occasions, persuading him to return the four cities he had taken from the Duchy of Rome and to desist from attacking RAVENNA. Thus he achieved peace with the Lombards.

In accord with his desire to maintain friendly relations with Byzantium, Zachary immediately dispatched envoys to the church of CONSTANTINOPLE and to the iconoclastic Emperor CONSTANTINE V Copronymos to inform them of his election and to exhort the emperor to restore the use of sacred images. His envoys shrewdly withheld their letters from the usurper Artabasdus, who at that time had seized Constantine's throne while he campaigned against the Saracens. They finally presented their letters in November 743, after the rightful emperor had regained his throne; and he replied with a gift to Rome of two large estates in south Italy.

Zachary's close association with the Frankish church began immediately, as he received BONIFACE's renewed expressions of loyalty and submission to the Chair of Peter and confirmed for him the establishment of the bishoprics of Würzburg, Buraburg, and Erfurt. He also confirmed Boniface as a papal legate to a Frankish council in 742. Until his death Zachary corresponded with Boniface and the Frankish bishops and rulers, fostering ecclesiastical and moral discipline and extending papal jurisdiction among the Franks; e.g., in 743 a Roman synod confirmed the acts of the earlier Frankish council and dealt with a question of impediments to marriage referred by the Franks to his predecessor. Again in 745 Zachary held a council at Rome in which he confirmed the condemnation for heresy of ALDEBERT and Clement, previously condemned by a Frankish council under Boniface. Four years after CARLOMAN entered a monastery (747) and left his brother PEPIN III as sole ruler in France under a figurehead MEROVINGIAN, Childeric III, Pepin inaugurated a new era in church-state relations when he obtained the support of Zachary for the deposition of Childeric and for his own coronation (751). History has remembered Zachary for his part in creating the Carolingian-Papal alliance; in his own time he was noted for his

Greek translation of the *Dialogues* of Pope GREGORY I the Great.

Feast: March 5.

Bibliography: *Regesta pontificum romanorum ab condita ecclesia ad annum post Christum natum 1198*, ed. P. EWALD (Graz 1956) 1:262–270. *Monumenta Germaniae Historica: Epistolae* (Berlin 1826—) 3:479–487, two letters. *Liber pontificalis*, ed. L. DUCHESNE (Paris 1886–92) 1:426–439. H. K. MANN, *The Lives of the Popes in the Early Middle Ages from 590 to 1304* (London 1902–32) 1.2:225–288. E. CASPAR, *Geschichte de Papsttums von den Anfängen bis zur Höhe der Weltherrschaft* (Tübingen 1930–33) 2:710–740. É. AMANN, *Dictionnaire de thééologie catholique*, ed. A. VACANT et al. (Paris 1903–50) 15.2:3671–75. F. X. SEPPELT, *Geschichte der Päpste von den Anfängen bis zur Mitte des 20. Jh.* (Munich 1955) 2:108–119. A. FLICHE and V. MARTIN, *Histoire de L'église depuis les origines jusqu'à nos jours* (Paris 1935—) 5:418–423. A. ANGENENDT, *Lexikon für Theologie und Kirche* 2 (Freiburg 1994), s.v. "Concilium Germanicum (742/43)." A. BEAU, *Le culte et les reliques de Saint Benoît de de Sainte Scholastique* (Monserrat 1980). DE FRANCESCO, "Considerazioni storico-topografiche a proposito delle 'domuscultae' laziali," *Archivio della Società Romana di Storia Patria* 119 (Rome 1996) 5–47. I. HEIDRICH, "Synode und Hoftag in Düren im August 747," *Deutsches Archiv für Erforschung des Mittelalters* 50 (Köln-Wein 1994) 415–40. H. MORDEK-M. GLATTHAR, "Von Wahrsagerinnen und Zauberern. Ein Beitrag zur Religionspolitik Karls des Großen," *Archiv für Kulturgeschichte* 75 (Cologne-Vienna 1993) 33–64. B. SODARO, *Santi e beati di Calabria* (Rosarno 1996) 75–80. K. WOLF, "Mögliche Gründe für Karlmanns d. Ä Resignation 747. Ein kanonistischer Versuch," *Zeitschrift der Savigny-Stuftung für Rechtsgeschichte. Kanonistische Abteilung* 109 (Vienna 1992) 517–31. J. N. D. KELLY, *Oxford Dictionary of Popes* (New York 1986) 89–90.

[M. C. MCCARTHY]

ZACHARY THE RHETOR

Sixth-century metropolitan of Mytilene, Church historian; b. Maiuma, Palestine, *c.* 465; d. Constantinople, after 536. Educated in the famous school of Gaza, Zachary studied philosophy at Alexandria (485–487) and law at Beirut (487–491); he persuaded SEVERUS OF ANTIOCH to be baptized and to embrace a strictly ascetical life. In 492 Zachary migrated to Constantinople, practiced law, took part in the cultural life of the court, and was selected as metropolitan of Mytilene on the island of Lesbos. He participated in the Synod of Constantinople in 536 under MENNAS, which condemned the deposed patriarch ANTHIMUS, Severus of Antioch, PETER OF APAMEA, and the Monk Zoanas. Despite his original acceptance of the HENOTICON, Zachary followed the court theology and rallied to the Catholic position.

His *Ecclesiastical History,* written in Greek, was a memoir composed for an imperial administrator, Eupraxius; it contains accurate information on events in Egypt and Palestine from 450 to 491. Evagrius used it in books

2 and 3 of his history, and it was embodied in a 12–volume work in Syriac probably compiled by a monk of Amida in Armenia. Zachary's *Life of Severus of Antioch* is an apologetic biography covering his early friend's career to 512 and exonerating him of charges of paganism and idolatry. It is important for details of daily life, scholarship, and asceticism in sixth–century Alexandria and Beirut. This is true also of his *Life of the Monk Isaac,* a Palestinian ascetic (d. 488). Fragments of a *Life of Peter the Iberian* have been preserved in Syriac, but only the name of his *Life of Theodore, Bishop of Antinoë* is known. His *Disputatio de mundi officio* is a dialogue with the Alexandrian Sophist Ammonius defending the immortality of the soul and creation of the world in time. Fragments of a *Disputatio contra Manichaeos* are preserved.

Bibliography: ZACHARY THE RHETOR, *Vie de Séveère,* ed. and tr. M. A. KUGENER (*Patrologia orientalis* 2.1; 1907); *The Syriac Chronicle,* tr. F. J. HAMILTON and E. W. BROOKS (London 1899). G. BARDY, *Dictionnaire de théologie catholique,* ed. A. VACANT et al., 15 v. (Paris 1903–50; Tables générales 1951–) 15.2:3676–80. B. ALTANER, *Patrology,* tr. H. GRAEF from 5th Ger. ed. (New York 1950) 204. M. A. KUGENER, "Observations sur la vie de l'ascète Isaïe . . . par Zacharie le Scolastique," *Byzantinische Zeitschrift* 9 (1900) 464–470; "La Compilation de Pseudo–Zacharie le Rhéteur," *Revue d l'Orient chrétien* 5 (1900) 201–214, 461–480. E. W. BROOKS, ed. and tr., *Vitae virorum apud monophysitas celeberrimorum* (*Corpus scriptorum Christianorum orientalium* 3.25; 1907). SEVERUS OF ANTIOCH, *Les Homiliae cathedrales,* ed. and tr. M. BRIÈRE (*Patrologia orientalis,* 25.1; 1943). E. HONIGMANN, *Patristic Studies* (*Studi e Testi* 173; 1953) 194–204.

[F. X. MURPHY]

ZAGO, MARCELLO

Missionary to Laos and Cambodia, member and superior general of the Congregation of Missionary Oblates of Mary Immaculate (O.M.I.), and secretary of the Congregation for the EVANGELIZATION OF PEOPLES; b. Villorba in the northeastern Italian Province of Treviso, Aug. 9, 1932; d. Rome, March 1, 2001. Ordained in 1959, Zago was sent by the O.M.I. to Laos and Cambodia during a turbulent period in that region's history, i.e., at the height of the Vietnam War with its spillover effect on Laos and Cambodia. In Laos, he became deeply involved in Buddhist Christian dialogue and was highly knowledgeable in Buddhist thought and spirituality. Frequently invited by Buddhists to speak in their study centers, in 1971, at the request of the bishops of Laos, Zago established the Center for Study and Dialogue with Buddhists and in 1972 led a delegation of Laotian Buddhists to Assisi and Rome.

In 1974 Zago took part in the first plenary assembly of the Federation of Asian Bishops' Conferences in Taipei on "Evangelization in Modern-Day Asia." That same year he was elected to a six-year term as assistant superior general of the O.M.I. From 1983 to 1986 he served in the Vatican as secretary for what was then called the Secretariat for Relations with Non-Christians, the predecessor of the Pontifical Council for Interreligious Dialogue. In 1984, the Secretariat issued the statement "The Attitude of the Church Towards the Followers of Other Religions: Reflections and Orientations on Dialogue and Mission." This document bears the stamp of Zago's thinking in recognizing the evangelizing mission of the church as a "single but complex and articulated reality" that comprises: (1) presence and witness; (2) commitment to social development and human liberation; (3) liturgical life, prayer, and contemplation; (4) interreligious dialogue; and, finally, (5) proclamation and catechesis. Missiologists have acclaimed these five elements as the single most comprehensive statement of what Christian mission entails as a complex process directed toward the communication of salvific truth, while respecting the dignity of followers of other religious traditions. While at the Secretariat, Zago helped organize Pope John Paul II's meeting with leaders of many religious traditions at Assisi in October 1986, an event widely regarded as an ecumenical landmark.

Zago was elected superior general of the O.M.I. in 1986 and re-elected to that post in 1992, during which period the congregation began 13 new missions. As superior general, Zago was one of the key persons behind the writing of *REDEMPTORIS MISSIO,* an encyclical that refused to oversimplify mission's many dimensions or denigrate other religious traditions. On March 28, 1998 he was appointed secretary of the Congregation for the Evangelization of Peoples by Pope John Paul II and ordained bishop in St. Peter's Basilica by Cardinal Jozef Tomko, prefect of the Congregation for the Evangelization of Peoples on April 25, 1998. His appointment was the capstone of a career, but especially marked a period during which this humble but brilliant missionary helped the Congregation for the Evangelization of Peoples understand other religious traditions, evaluate them as worthy "others," and, at the same time, remain true to Christ's admonition to "teach all nations what I have commanded" (Matthew 28:18-2).

[W. R. BURROWS]

ZAHM, JOHN AUGUSTINE

Educator, apologist, and author of important studies on the relationship between science and religion, particularly the question of evolution; b. New Lexington, Ohio, June 14, 1851; d. Munich, Germany, Nov. 11, 1921. His father, Jacob M. Zahm, had immigrated to the U.S. from Oldsberg, Alsace; his Pennsylvania-born mother, Mary Ellen Zahm, was the grandniece of Maj. Gen. Edward Braddock. John's early education included formal schooling in a small Ohio log school and at SS. Peter and Paul School, Huntington, Ind. In 1867 he entered the University of Notre Dame, Ind., and received his A.B. (1871) and M.A. (1873) degrees. He joined the Congregation of Holy Cross and was ordained in 1875, along with Daniel Hudson, CSC, future editor of the *Ave Maria* magazine. From 1875 to 1892 Zahm served at Notre Dame as a professor of physics and held several administrative offices. His campus projects included the construction of a science building with the latest equipment for chemistry and physics. Through his efforts, Notre Dame became the first American college campus to be lighted by electricity and the first American Catholic college to abandon the dormitory system and inaugurate private residence halls. His first book, *Sound and Music* (1892), terminated his active interest in the physical sciences.

In 1892 he began writing on the relationship of Catholic dogma to modern science. Like St. George MIVART, he believed that theistic evolution, i.e., that God created the universe *in potentia* rather than *in actu,* was a distinct possibility. Zahm lectured on the theme of science and religion at the Catholic Summer School at Plattsburg, N.Y. (1893); the Brussels International Catholic Scientific Congress (1894); the Colombian Catholic Summer School at Madison, Wis. (1895); the Winter School at New Orleans, La. (1896); and at the Fribourg International Catholic Scientific Congress, Switzerland (1897). His essays in the religious and secular press and his books, notably, *Bible, Science and Faith* (1894) and *Evolution and Dogma* (1896), continued the theme that no conflict should exist between science and Catholicism. The latter book was prohibited by the Congregation of the Index in 1898 during the tense months of the AMERICANISM controversy.

As U.S. provincial of the Congregation of Holy Cross (1898–1906) and through his association with Abp. John IRELAND and Bps. John KEANE and Denis O'CONNELL, Zahm succeeded in preparing a community of scholarly priests and resources at the University of Notre Dame and at Holy Cross College, adjacent to the Catholic University of America, Washington, D.C. After 1906 he took two extended trips through the interior of South America, the second one with former President Theodore Roosevelt. Zahm's triology, *Following the Conquistadores* (1910, 1911, 1916), recounted his trips, South American history, and the Catholic contributions to its culture. Three additional books, *Woman in Science* (1913), *Great Inspirers* (1917), and *The Quest of El Dorado* (1917), were completed during these years. He died while completing the manuscript of his last book, *From Berlin to Bagdad and Babylon* (1922).

Bibliography: R. E. WEBER, *Notre Dame's John Zahm* (South Bend, Ind. 1961). T. T. MCAVOY, *The Great Crisis in American Catholic History, 1895–1900* (Chicago 1957). A. J. HOPE, *Notre Dame: One Hundred Years* (South Bend, Ind. 1943). J. A. O'BRIEN, *Evolution and Religion* (New York 1932). T. F. O'CONNOR, "John A. Zahm, C.S.C.: Scientist and Americanist," *Americas* 7 (1951) 435–462.

[R. E. WEBER]

ZAMBIA, THE CATHOLIC CHURCH IN

A landlocked country located in south central Africa, the Republic of Zambia is bordered on the north by the Democratic Republic of the Congo and Tanzania, on the east by Malawi and Mozambique, on the south by Zimbabwe and Namibia, and on the west by Angola. Zambia is the most urbanized country in Africa; over half its population live in cities and towns along the railroad line that links the copper belt in the north to the Victoria Falls in the south. The Zambezi and Kafue rivers provide hydroelectric power and are potential sources for agricultural irrigation. Most agricultural production, which includes corn, rice, peanuts, tobacco and cotton, is rain-fed, and intermittent but severe and prolonged droughts caused the country to rely occasionally on food aid from outside. The region's abundant natural resources include copper, cobalt, zinc, lead, coal, emeralds, gold, silver and uranium.

Known as Northern Rhodesia until 1964, Zambia was administered by the British South Africa Company from 1889 until 1924. From then until 1964 it was a British protectorate and, as such, was part of the Federation of Rhodesia and Nyasaland (1953–64). Independent since 1964, Zambia had one of the highest annual population growth rates in Africa, although its life expectancy was only 37 years in 2000. Over half the population was under the age of 15. The four largest linguistic groups were Bemba, Lozi, Nyanja and Tonga. Despite ethnic diversities, Zambia was notable for the climate of peace it maintained among all its population.

Early History. The region was originally the home of hunter-gatherer peoples, who were joined by more advanced migrating tribes *c.* 1000 BC. Bantu-speaking tribes entered the area from southern Zaire during the 15th century. Portuguese missionaries penetrated Zambia in the 16th and 17th centuries, but few traces of their work remained a century later. Europeans returned to the region in the mid-19th century, the most famous being British explorer David Livingstone who, in 1855, discovered the waterfalls of the Zambezi River. Livingstone named the falls after Queen Victoria; a town near the falls now bears his name.

Late in the 19th century Protestants, soon followed by Catholics, began organized mission activity. Jesuits came northward in the 1880s to southern Zambia, then part of the Zambezi mission established in 1879. In 1895 White Fathers under Joseph Dupont (1850–1930) established the first mission in the northern and eastern sections at Kayambi. The western region was first evangelized in 1931, when Italian Franciscans came to Ndola and Irish Capuchins opened missions at Livingstone and in the Barotseland protectorate. Growth was rapid, particularly in the two decades after World War II, when Catholic populations doubled. In 1959 the hierarchy was established, and Lusaka became an archdiocese and metropolitan see for the entire country.

In 1888 British entrepreneur Cecil Rhodes gained the right to mine in the region from local tribal leaders. Shortly thereafter Northern and Southern Rhodesia came into being under British governance. Southern Rhodesia (Zimbabwe) was annexed and gained autonomous status in 1923, while Northern Rhodesia (Zambia) became a protectorate a year later. In 1953 the Federation of Rhodesia and Nyasaland was formed by both regions and the area that is now Malawi. During the early 1960s demands for African nationalism conflicted with the British desire to retain power and preserve its economic interests in the area.

The Modern Era. In early 1963 Northern Rhodesia demanded complete autonomy and a new democratic constitution. On Dec. 31, 1963, the federation dissolved, and the Republic of Zambia came into being on Oct. 24, 1964. The nation's first president, Kenneth J. Kaunda, would govern for almost 30 years. A socialist, Kaunda established relationship with communist nations and developed a strong central government. Most of Zambia's industry, commerce and services were nationalized, and as the government became more authoritarian, the economy became more strained. Although the country possessed a wealth of natural resources, with the departure of the British, few Zambians were sufficiently trained or educated to run the country's industry or serve in its government.

Zambian support of independence movements in neighboring Southern Rhodesia, Angola and elsewhere led to economic problems by the 1980s. Under Kaunda's leadership, Zambia supported independence movements that led to the establishment of new governments in Zimbabwe (formerly Southern Rhodesia), Mozambique, Angola and Namibia, and hosted the offices of South Africa's exiled African National Congress. In addition to

Capital: Lusaka.
Size: 290,323 sq. miles.
Population: 9,582,415 in 2000.
Languages: English; over 70 African languages are spoken in various regions.
Religions: 2,683,075 Catholics (28%), 2,770 Hindus (.003%), 479,120 Muslims (5%), 3,449,670 Protestants (36%), 2,967,780 worship indigenous or other faiths.
Archdioceses: Kasama, with suffragans Mansa and Mpika; Lusaka, with suffragans Chipata, Livingston, Mongu, Monze, Ndola, and Solwezi.

military attacks from Rhodesia and South Africa, Kaunda's policy of support created economic problems due to export and import losses. Despite the economic strain it caused, Zambia welcomed thousands of refugees from the conflict areas of its neighbors. A drop in copper prices during the 1970s further undercut Zambian efforts to stabilize its slumping economy. The nation's economic woes resulted in it amassing over seven billion US dollars in debt by 1993. At US $800 for every man, woman and child in Zambia, this was one of the highest per-capita debts in the world.

The Church after Vatican II. Both during the colonial era and in the early years following independence, the Church was actively engaged mainly in education, health and development efforts. Responding to the call of the Second Vatican Council, in the late 1960s Church leaders began to promote an INCULTURATION or Africanization of the faith. Within the field of liturgy, the lectionary and prayer texts were translated into the main local languages. Liturgical music was composed using local melodies and traditional instruments such as drums, while traditional dances were incorporated into the liturgy, for example at the Gloria, the preparation of the gifts and the Eucharistic prayer. The Bible was translated into the local languages in a cooperative effort among the Catholic Church and several Protestant churches.

In the early 1970s Zambia's socialist government took over all mission schools and hospitals in the country, leaving only a few under Church management. This act expanded into a major conflict between the Church and the state by the late 1970s following a state effort to adopt "scientific socialism" as a governing ideology. School curricula were prepared with a strong Marxist interpretation of philosophy and history. Church leaders joined with Protestant and Evangelical leaders to protest against the imposition of this ideology in the form of joint pastoral letters, seminars and representations to the government. Their challenge was successful, as the curricula were never fully implemented.

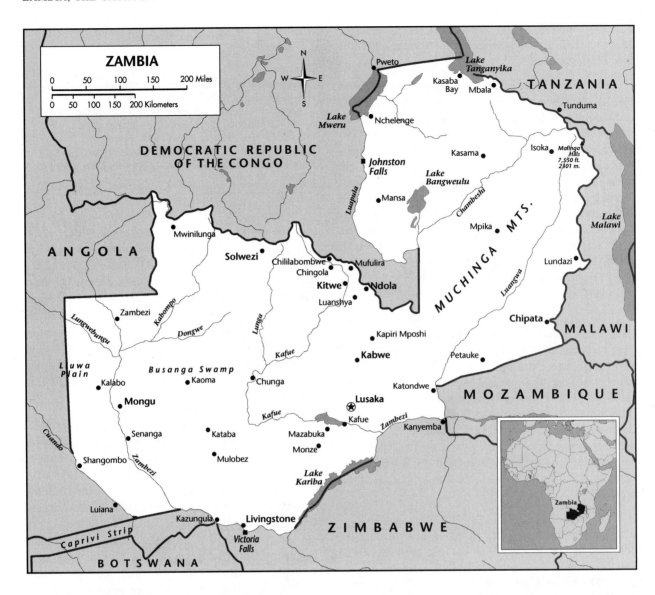

The role of the Church within Zambia remained politicized in the wake of continued government efforts to restrict social freedoms and negatively impact the welfare of Zambians. When Pope John Paul II visited Zambia in 1989, he praised the government's support of religious liberty, but he challenged the Church and society to address the increasingly severe problems of poverty more effectively. Following serious riots and an attempted coup in June of 1990 the bishops wrote a pastoral letter calling for greater accountability by the government and ruling party. This letter, *Economics, Politics, and Justice,* was seen by many as a catalyst in the struggle to end one-party rule and establish a multiparty democracy. The 1993 pastoral letter *Hear the Cry of the Poor* criticized the policy of the International Monetary Fund and the World Bank, and challenged the government to take stronger measures to protect Zambians who were experiencing economic hardships. Additional statements on economic justice were made by the bishops and by the National Catholic Commission for Justice and Peace.

Into the 21st Century. In 1991 the country ended one-party rule, although subsequent elections were fraught with accusations of fraud and harassment of opposition candidates. Concurrent with national elections, in 1996 the Zambian constitution was modified to proclaim the country a "Christian" nation while preserving religious freedom. The privatization of Zambian copper mining operations helped to shore up the unemployment and inflation rates.

By 2000 Zambia had 238 parishes tended by 217 diocesan and 376 religious priests, with approximately 160 brothers and 1,322 sisters at work throughout the country, both as teachers in the country's 22 primary schools and 37 secondary schools and as caregivers to the many thousands stricken with HIV/AIDS. Because of the scarcity of ordained priests, the active participation of the laity was strongly encouraged by the Church, and catechists played essential parts in the building of rural Christian communities. As part of Jubilee 2000, Great Britain canceled a portion of the debt service owed it by Zambia, and the European Union remained willing to aid the country's efforts toward economic recovery.

Bibliography: G. D. KITTLER, *The White Fathers* (New York 1957). B. P. CARMODY, *Conversion and Jesuit Schools in Zambia* (Leiden 1992). *Democracy in Zambia: Key Speeches of President Chiluba, 1991–92,* ed. D. CHANDA, (Lusaka 1992). *The Dynamics of the One-Party State in Zambia,* ed. C. GERTZEL (Manchester 1984). K. HANNECART, *''Intrepid Sowers'': From Nyasa to Fort Jameson: 1889–1946: Some Historical Notes* (Rome 1991). K. D. KAUNDA, *Humanism in Zambia and a Guide to Its Implementation* (Lusaka 1987). E. MILINGO, *The World in Between: Christian Healing and the Struggle for Spiritual Survival* (Maryknoll, NJ 1988). C. DILLON-MALONE, *Zambian Humanism, Religion and Social Morality* (Ndola 1989); *The October 1991 National Elections in Zambia* (Washington, DC 1992).

[J. F. O'DONOHUE/P. HENRIOT/EDS.]

ZAMOMETIČ, ANDREA

Croatian archbishop, imperial envoy, reform agitator; d. Basel, Nov. 13, 1484. Of Croatian origin, he took the Dominican habit in the friary of Udine, Italy. He became master of novices and taught at Padua, where he became a friend of Francesco della Rovere (later Pope SIXTUS IV). After becoming archbishop of Krajina in Albania (1476) the ambitious Andrea paid three visits to Rome in the year 1478 as the envoy of Emperor Frederick III to Sixtus IV. He went to Rome again in 1480, and this time openly attacked the abuses he saw there, e.g., the NEPOTISM of the Pope and the rapacity of the Rovere family. This led to his imprisonment in CASTEL SANT' ANGELO. Because of the Emperor and the intercession of the cardinal from Venice, the imprisonment was of short duration. Once released, Andrea allied himself with the Pope's enemies, such as Lorenzo de' MEDICI, King Louis XI of France, and Ferrante of Naples, and went to Basel, where he assumed the ironical title of Cardinal of Saint-Sixtus. On March 25, 1482, in the cathedral, this proud, rebellious churchman announced the convening of a Church council and demanded that the Pope cease all exercise of power until the council should have pronounced judgment on him. The bishops of Mainz and Constance seemed disposed to listen to Andrea; the bishop of Würzburg and the Franciscan Glazberger vigorously opposed him. Backed by the University of Basel, Andrea became more insulting and vituperative to the delight of the Pope's enemies, but Emperor Frederick had had enough and vainly ordered Andrea to return to the court. Basel, which had ignored a papal interdict, was influenced by

the Emperor's action and placed Andrea under arrest (December 1482). He hanged himself in his prison cell.

Bibliography: L. PASTOR, *The History of the Popes from the Close of the middle Ages* 4:358–363. R. COULON, *Dictionnaire d'histoire et de géographie ecclésiastiques* 2:1718–21. ''Zamometič, Andreas,'' *Lexikon für Theologie und Kirche*[2] v.10.

[T. C. CROWLEY]

ZAMORA, ALFONSO DE

Eminent Hebraist; b. Zamora, Spain, *c.* 1474; d. place unknown, *c.* 1531. Although born and reared a Jew and educated as a rabbi, he became a Catholic in 1506, taking in baptism the name Alfonso. He was the first professor of Hebrew at the University of Salamanca. While there he collaborated on the preparation of the Complutensian POLYGLOT BIBLE, editing the Hebrew text of the Old Testament and its Aramaic Targum. The Latin translation of the latter is from his pen, as is the sixth volume, containing a Hebrew-Aramaic-Latin dictionary. Among his writings, all in Latin, are the *Grammaticae hebraicae libri tres,* the *Catalogus iudicum, regum et sacerdotum atque prophetarum Veteris Legis,* and the *Epistula auctoris ad infideles Hebraeos urbis Romae,* which was written to prove that Jesus of Nazareth was the promised Messiah.

Bibliography: G. BARTOLOCCI, *Bibliotheca Magna Rabbinica,* 4 v. (Rome 1685–93) 2:31; 3:811. *Enciclopedia universal ilustrada Europeo–Americana,* 70 v. (Barcelona 1908–30; suppl. 1934) 4:614. H. HURTER, *Nomenclator literarius theologiae catholicae,* 5 v. in 6 (3d ed. Innsbruck 1903–13) 2:1134.

[S. M. POLAN]

ZAPATA DE CÁRDENAS, LUIS

Archbishop of Bogotá, Colombia, supporter of native vocations; b. Llerena, Spain, *c.* 1515; d. Bogotá, Jan. 24, 1590. Of a noble family, Luis Zapata fought in the Spanish infantry regiment. About 1542 he entered the Franciscan Order in Hornachos. He was commissary general in Peru in 1561 and provincial of San Miguel Province in 1566. Having been named bishop of Cartagena de Indias in 1569, he was designated archbishop of Bogotá on Nov. 8, 1570. He assumed that post on March 28, 1573, and then made the pastoral visit to the archdiocese.

In 1576 he made a new distribution of the native Columbian *doctrinas* and, to unify the missionary work, ordered Canon Miguel de Espejo to write a catechism, a practical pastoral manual containing detailed rules of unusual anthropological, social, and catechetical value with respect to the indigenous culture. He was noted for the establishment of the native clergy. He ordained more than 100 Creole and mestizo priests, in spite of attempts to prevent his doing so. In 1583 he founded the Colegio-Seminario de San Luis, the first seminary in Colombia, where he taught courses in the Muysca language, in compliance with the royal decree of Philip II of 1580, which forbade priests who did not know the language from being appointed to serve in native parishes. His substituting secular Creole clergy for religious from Spain in the native parishes caused disputes with Franciscans, Dominicans, and Augustinians, who were supported by the audiencia. In 1584 he convoked a provincial council, which he was not able to hold. During his episcopate the Poor Clares were established in Tunja and the Conceptionist Sisters in Bogotá. He approved the miraculous restoration of the painting of Our Lady of Chiquinquirá, patroness of Colombia. During the smallpox epidemic of 1587 his works of charity were distinguished.

Bibliography: J. RESTREPO POSADA, "Ilmo. Sr. Don Fray Luis Zapata de Cárdenas," *Revista javeriana* 46 (1956) 181–198. A. LEE LÓPEZ, "Clero indígena en el arzobispado de Santa Fé en el siglo XVI," *Boletín de historia y antigüedades* 50 (1963) 1–86.

[A. LEE LÓPEZ]

ZAPATA Y SANDOVAL, JUAN

Bishop of Guatemala and defender of the prerogatives of the creoles in the Spanish empire; b. Mexico City, date unknown; d. Guatemala City, Guatemala, Jan. 9, 1630. His surname, more properly written Sandoval y Zapata, has caused some difficulty in identification; he has been confused with his uncle Juan Zapata, OSA (d. 1606). His parents, both members of the aristocracy of New Spain (Mexico), were Manuel de Sandoval and María Alarcón. His maternal grandparents were Luis de Villanueva and Beatriz Zapata y Sandoval. Juan joined the Augustinians and made his religious profession in Mexico City on July 13, 1590. After his ordination he taught in the Colegio San Pablo, and later, having earned the degree of master of theology in the University of Mexico, he also taught in the university. In 1602 Juan went to Spain where for 11 years he taught theology and served as regent of studies and rector in the Colegio San Gabriel, Valladolid. On Sept. 1, 1613, he was nominated bishop of Chiapa, Mexico. Upon returning to New Spain the following year, he was consecrated bishop in Puebla de los Angeles. In 1621 Zapata y Sandoval was promoted to the See of Guatemala.

He is best remembered for his treatise *De justitia distributiva,* written while he was in Spain and published at Valladolid in 1609. In this work Zapata y Sandoval contended strongly that the civil and ecclesiastical offices of the overseas empire should be entrusted to native-born colonials, rather than to persons sent from Spain. He also maintained that the encomienda system should be made perpetual for the benefit of those who had built up the empire. Since he was a man of excellent education and wrote a polished Latin, he succeeded in gaining a hearing and helped to establish a good reputation for the colonials of New Spain. The subsequent appointment of the Creoles to civil and ecclesiastical positions in the Spanish empire is credited in large measure to his influence.

Bibliography: G. DE SANTIAGO VELA, *Ensayo de una biblioteca ibero-americana de la orden de San Agustín,* 7 v. in 8 (Madrid 1913–31) 7:287–292.

[A. J. ENNIS]

ZARLINO, GIOSEFFO

Leading Renaissance music theorist; b. Chioggia, Italy, March 22, 1517; d. Venice, Feb. 14, 1590. A promising Franciscan theologian at 24, he abandoned this calling in 1541 to study with the world-famous WILLAERT, *maestro di cappella* of St. Mark's in Venice. He succeeded Willaert in 1565 (three years after the latter's death) and remained in this post for the rest of his life. Although he composed occasional Masses and motets for affairs of state and church, and possibly other works now lost, his importance lies in three contributions to musical theory. The first, *Istituzioni harmoniche* (1558), contains the most comprehensive exposition of contrapuntal principles produced up to that time. His rules for the proper placement of text are still a model for editors of late 16th-century vocal music. The prominent place accorded the Ionian and Aeolian modes in book four of the *Istituzioni* anticipated their subsequent supremacy in the 18th century. While vigorously opposed by his own student Vincenzo Galilei, he favored the Ptolemaic rather than the older Pythagorean intonation. In his third treatise, *Sopplimenti musicali* (1588), written in part as a reply to Galilei's attacks, he proposed for the fretted lute a form of equal temperament commonly accepted only two centuries later.

Bibliography: G. ZARLINO, *Istituzioni armoniche: Books III and IV,* O. STRUNK, ed., *Source Readings in Music History* (New York 1950) 229–261. A. EINSTEIN, *The Italian Madrigal,* tr. A. H. KRAPPE et al., 3 v. (Princeton 1949). G. REESE, *Music in the Renaissance* (rev. ed. New York 1959). *Baker's Biographical Dictionary of Musicians,* ed. N. SLONIMSKY (5th, rev. ed. New York 1958) 1837–38. M. A. BURKHART, S.N.D., "Gioseffo Zarlino's Practice of Counterpoint: A Musical Supplement to Part III of *Le instituioni harmoniche, 1558*" (Ph.D. diss. Boston University, 1978). J. P. CLENDINNING, "Zarlino and the Helicon of Ptolemy: A Translation with Commentary of Book III, Chapter III of Gioseffo Zarlino's *Sopplimenti Musicalí,*" *Theoria: Historical Aspects of Music Theory* 2 (1987), 39–58. A. CŒURDEVEY, "Contrepoint et structure contrapuntique de Tinctoris à Zarlino,'' *Analyse Musicale* 31 (1993), 40–52. V. COHEN, ''Zarlino on Modes: An Annotated, Indexed Translation, with Introduction and Commentary, of Part IV of *Le istitutioni harmoniche*'' (Ph.D. diss. City University of New York, 1977). D. COLLINS, ''Zarlino and Berardi as Teachers of Canon,'' *Theoria: Historical Aspects of Music Theory* 7 (1993), 103–123. C. V. PALISCA, ''Gioseffo Zarlino'' in *The New Grove Dictionary of Music and Musicians*, vol. 20, ed. S. SADIE (New York 1980) 646–649. D. M. RANDEL, ed., *The Harvard Biographical Dictionary of Music* (Cambridge 1996) 1006. B. RIVERA, ''Zarlino's Approach to Counterpoint Modified and Transmitted by Seth Calvisius,'' *Theoria: Historical Aspects of Music Theory* 4 (1989), 1–9. N. SLONIMSKY, ed., *Baker's Biographical Dictionary of Musicians*, eighth edition (New York 1992) 2097.

[E. R. LERNER]

ZATVORNIK, THEOPHAN

Russian Orthodox bishop, spiritual writer; b. Černavsk, the Orel Region of Russia, Jan. 10, 1815; d. Pushkin, 1894. Theophan Zatvornik, born George Vasilievič Govorov, son of a priest, studied in the minor seminary of Livny and the major seminaries of Orel and Kiev. He was ordained in Kiev in 1841, and in the same year he became a monk, taking the name Theophan. He was superior of an ecclesiastical school at Kiev for a year and then prefect of discipline and professor of philosophy in the seminary of Novgorod. In 1844 he became professor of moral theology in the seminary of St. Petersburg. He left Russia in 1847 to found a Russian center in Palestine, where he remained seven years studying Greek and grounding himself in patristic traditions.

Back in Russia, in 1855 he became rector of the seminary of Olonets, and two years later rector of the seminary at St. Peterburg. In 1858 he was consecrated bishop of Tambov, whence he was translated to Vladimir in 1863. He obtained permission in 1866 to retire to the monastery of Vyšenskaja Pustyn, where he remained until his death, devoting his time to prayer and writing. In 1872 he became a complete recluse, shutting himself up in a small apartment in the monastery and refusing to see anyone, even members of his family. He lived thus for 22 years.

The works of Zatvornik include many books on the moral and ascetical life, several volumes of commentaries on the Epistles of St. Paul, and the five-volume *Dobrotoliubie* (a translation of the Greek *Philokalia*, with many of his own additions). He wrote also a monumental work on the monastic rules of Pachomius, Basil, Benedict, and Cassian. In addition, his letters of spiritual direction, published only in part, fill ten volumes.

His best moral work is *Natchertanie Khristianskavo nravooutchenia* (*An Outline of Christian Moral Teach-*

ing). As his sources he used the scriptures, the teachings of the Fathers, the examples of the saints, the moral teachings of the liturgical texts, rational speculation, and Christian psychology. A complementary work is his *Pout'k spasieniou* (*The Way to Salvation*).

In his works Zatvornik approached the Catholic doctrine on frequent Communion, which was contrary to the ordinary teaching of the Orthodox church during his lifetime. Except for a few doctrinal errors inherited from his Protestant–tinged professors, his general teaching is quite acceptable to Catholics. He did not copy from Catholic authors, but in his attempt to be faithful to patristic teachings he was close to Catholic doctrine drawn from the same sources, especially through the teachings of St. Thomas Aquinas. As to the dogmatic teachings of the church and his view of Rome in general, he repeated the prejudices of his environment. To him, the Catholic church was just another sect terrorized by the Inquisition and a despotic pope who attributed to himself divine qualities.

Zatvornik's works are thoroughly patristic in character. They contain the best traditional Orthodox teaching on the spiritual life and are, for the most part, also in harmony with the teachings of the Catholic church. He is an outstanding example of the best in Orthodox teaching in moral and ascetical theology, owing mainly to his dependence on the teachings of the Oriental Fathers.

Bibliography: T. F. BOSSUYT, *Théophane le reclus: Sa doctrine sur l'oraison* (Rome 1959), contains a complete bibliog. of his works. S. TYSZKIEWICZ, *Moralistes de Russie* (Rome 1951) 110–127; comp. and tr., *Écrits d'ascètes Russes* (Namur 1957). G. P. FEDOTOV, *A Treasury of Russian Spirituality* (New York 1948). E. KADLOUBOVSKY and G. E. H. PALMER, *Writings from the Philokalia on Prayer of the Heart* (New York 1952).

[G. A. MALONEY]

ZDISLAVA OF LEMBERK, ST.

Married member of the Dominican lay tertiary; b. Krizanov, Moravia (now Letomerice, Bohemia, Czech Republic), *c.* 1220; d. Jablonné v Podjestìdí, Bohemia, Jan. 1, 1252. Zdislava, daughter of Privislav, was born into the Czech aristocracy. Her mother Sibila was a lady-in-waiting to Queen Cunegunda of Hohenstaufen. About 1236, Zdislava married Count Havel of Lemberk (d. 1253), a soldier in command of the frontier fortress at Gabel (Jablonné v Podjestìdí), to whom she bore four children (Havel, Margarita, Jaroslav, and Zadislav).

Through the preaching of St. HYACINTH and Bl. CESLAUS OF SILESIA, Zdislava became the first Slavic Dominican tertiary. She encouraged her husband to build a hostel for homeless pilgrims, visited and interceded for prisoners, cared for the poor, taught the faith to her servants' children, and built a church and priories at Turnov and Jablonné.

Not content with merely funding charitable works, she personally bathed the sick and carried some of the materials for the church. During the Mongol invasions she eased the distress of the suffering who sought refuge with her.

According to her fourteenth-century chronicler Dalimil, Zdislava raised five dead men to life, healed many through her touch, and was gifted with visions and ecstasies. Her body is venerated in the church she had built, now called SS. Lawrence and Zdislava at Jablonné v Podjestìdí. Her cultus as a *beata* was confirmed in 1907. Zdislava was canonized by Pope John Paul II at Olomouc, Czech Republic, May 21, 1995, during his second pastoral visit. She is the patroness of the sick and poor of Bohemia, and of families in Bohemia and Moravia.

Feast: Jan. 4 (Dominicans); May 30 (Czech Republic).

Bibliography: M. J. DORCY, *Saint Dominic's Family* (Dubuque, Iowa 1964), 47–48. J. DURYCH, *Svetlo ve tmách: blahoslaven' Zdislava* (Rím, Czech Rep. 1988). T. EDEL, *Príbeh ztraceného klóstera blahoslavené Zdislavy* (Prague 1993). Z. KALISTA, *Blahoslavená Zdislava z Lemberka* (Rím 1969). J. SALLMANN, *Festschrift zum 200 jährigen Jubiläum der Dekanalkirche zum Hl. Laurentius in Deutsch Gabel* (Gabel 1929). *L'Osservatore Romano,* English edition, no. 21 (1995): 1–2, 12; no. 23 (1995): 9.

[K. I. RABENSTEIN]

ZEAL

From the Greek ζῆλος, which derives from a root meaning to be hot or to begin to boil, signifies a vehement intensity of emotion or of will with respect to a cause, coupled, as circumstances permit, with energetic activity in its service. In classical as well as Biblical usage the word was associated with the notions of emulation and JEALOUSY; the English word "jealousy" is in fact derived from "zeal." Zeal is a desirable or undesirable quality depending upon the merit of the cause toward which it is directed. The pejorative sense predominates in the derivative "zealot," which commonly designates a person with an excessive enthusiasm for a good cause or a fanatical dedication to an unworthy one. In Christian usage, however, zeal generally indicates an enthusiasm activated by a true good, and it is most commonly applied to a notable degree of fervor when this marks an individual's love of God and neighbor. A zealous person is not content to do the minimum to which he is strictly obliged, but strives rather to do the most that he can. It is a quality

manifested in many ways—in a strong desire to promote God's glory (1 Kgs 19.14), in the eagerness to do charitable service to others (2 Cor 9.2), in striving after better gifts (1 Cor 12.31), in the doing of good works (Ti 2.14). Above all, it is the love of Christ urging one on (2 Cor 5.14). As the fervor of charity, the excellence of zeal is that of CHARITY itself.

Bibliography: A. TANQUEREY, *The Spiritual Life,* tr. H. BRANDERIS (2d ed. Tournai 1930; repr. Westminster, MD 1945). X. LÉON-DUFOUR, ed., *Vocabulaire de théologie biblique* (Paris 1962) 1135–38.

[R. L. COLE]

ZEALOTS

A Jewish nationalist faction (ζηλωταί) of A.D. 6–73, founded "in the name of Yahweh" to enforce strict observance of the Law and, like the Maccabees (1 Mc 2.50), to labor and, if necessary, to die for independence from Roman domination. The zealots contended that Yahweh was the sole ruler in Israel, that the descendants of Abraham had never been slaves to any man (Jn 8.33) and ought never to be (Dt 17.15), and consequently, that rebellion was the Jew's religious duty. Realizing that open insurrection would fail (Acts 5.37), these extremists worked in secret to foster a spirit of bitterness against the Roman yoke. Rebellion became more and more the creed of the masses. Emboldened by success, they suppressed every moderating influence. By fanatical violence and rabid propaganda they caused the fatal insurrection against Rome and the catastrophe of 66 to 70. Soon after the destruction of the Holy City, the zealots disappeared from history. St. SIMON the Apostle had once, apparently, belonged to the group (Mt 10.4; Mk 3.18; Lk 6.15; Acts 1.13), although the designation may refer only to his religious zeal for the Law (cf. Acts 21.20; Gal 1.14).

Bibliography: W. R. FARMER, *Maccabees, Zealots and Josephus* (New York 1956); G. A. BUTTRICK, ed., *The Interpreters' Dictionary of the Bible* (Nashville 1962) 4:936–38. *Encyclopedic Dictionary of the Bible,* tr. and adap. by L. HARTMAN (New York 1963) 2627–28.

[J. M. DOUGHERTY]

ZECHARIAH, BOOK OF

Zechariah is the eleventh of the twelve minor Prophets. Zechariah's ministry extended at least from November 520 to November 518 B.C. and so partly coincided with that of Haggai [*see* HAGGAI, BOOK OF]. Both men campaigned after the return from the Exile for the reconstruction of the Temple. Zechariah's words, however, are confined to ch. 1–8 of the book bearing his name. The last six chapters were added later from various anonymous sources. This second section, in fact, may once have included the Book of MALACHI, because the original introduction to Malachi (Mal 1.1) seems to have been the same as in Zec 9.1 and 12.1, the simple phrase *maśśā'* (literally, burden, i.e., oracle). When the three chapters of Malachi were separated from Zechariah, possibly from a desire to divide the minor Prophets into the sacred number of 12, the name ''Malachi'' (Heb. *mal'ākî*, my messenger) was borrowed from a reference in Mal 3.1. The two major sections of Zechariah, ch. 1–8 and ch. 9–14, are here considered separately, both as to author and content, after a discussion of the Prophet himself.

The Prophet. Zechariah (Heb. *zᵉkaryâ,* Yahweh remembers) is called the ''son of Berechiah, son of Iddo'' (Zec 1.1). The phrase ''son of Berechiah'' is suspect, for it is missing in Ezr 5.1; 6.14; Neh 12.16; it probably slipped in here from Is 8.2, and the confusion continued in Mt 23.35. As a son of Iddo, Zechariah belonged to a priestly family (Neh 12.4, 6). This fact, coupled with the dominant influence of Ezekiel in postexilic Judaism, explains why priestly attitudes and interests deeply colored Zechariah's preaching. Zechariah's command of words, sweep of ideas, and sense of the practical reveal a gifted speaker. He was able to distract people's minds from ''the day of small beginnings'' all around them (Zec 4.10) by his effusive, apocalyptic writing, which included visions, mysterious knowledge of the future, angelic mediators, other ethereal beings, extensive symbolism, and expectation of the messianic breakthrough at any moment. Besides being an apocalyptist, Zechariah was also a reforming Prophet. Although primarily interested in the Temple and its liturgy, Zechariah defended the homeless, the orphan, and the widows (7.1–14). Moral integrity, he insisted, must accompany the worshiper at the sanctuary (ch. 3).

Zechariah preached from the 8th month of the 2nd year of Darius I (Oct. 27 to Nov. 25, 520 B.C.) to at least the 4th day of the 9th month of the 4th year of this king (Dec. 8, 518 B.C.; Zec 1.1; 7.1). DARIUS I, KING OF PERSIA (521–486 B.C.), governed a sprawling empire. The fact that he seized the throne amid palace intrigues and assassinations and that for two years he conducted vigorous military campaigns to suppress revolts may help to explain Zechariah's messianic concerns (*see* MESSIANISM), especially his hopes for Jewish independence and for the restoration of the Davidic monarchy under Zerubbabel (6.9–15).

In his preaching Zechariah gave first place to the reconstruction of the Temple and the worthy performance of its liturgy. [*See* TEMPLES (IN THE BIBLE).] The Temple is the place where God renews His great acts of salvation and where the messianic age will suddenly appear (1.16–17). It is not enough to observe ceremonial laws; moral wickedness must be atoned for and removed (3.1–10; 5.1–11). Zechariah witnesses to the postexilic devotion to angels (1.9, 12, 14; 2.7; 3.2); they are present not only to explain the strange, even weird, visions that fill his prophecy but also to impress upon the people the fatherly concern of Almighty God. In postexilic theology God is awesome and transcendent, but He sends His angels to protect and lead His people. Finally, a rather pronounced universalism extends the Prophet's thoughts to the salvation of all men (2.15; 8.21–22).

First Major Sections: Chapters 1–8. The anthology of Zechariah's preaching in ch. 1–8 begins with a description of the Prophet's vocation (1.1–6). There immediately follows an account of eight visions (1.7–6.8), told in highly apocalyptic language. This choice of style, in fact, makes us suspect that ''vision'' was more a literary medium than an actual fact. The first vision of the Four Horsemen (1.7–17) moves quickly from a report of tranquility and rest (perhaps that which settled upon the Persian Empire after Darius I crushed all resistance) to the sight of Israel's despondency over messianic frustrations and concludes with a glimpse of the new Jerusalem. The second vision of the four horns and the four blacksmiths [2.1–4; in the Septuagint (LXX) and Vulgate (Vulg) 1.18–21] remains extremely vague even for modern interpreters. The third vision of the new Jerusalem (2.5–17; in the LXX and Vulg 2.1–13) reviews the glorious prospects of Jerusalem, peaceful, prosperous, and reminiscent of the days of Moses, when God had led His people by columns of fiery clouds (Ex 13.21–22). The fourth vision (Zec 3.1–10; 4.4–10) presents no difficulty in its general sweep of thought: the high priest Joshua, son of Jehozadak, will be cleansed of moral guilt and ceremonial fault in order to represent the nation worthily before the throne of God. The Prophet thus recognizes the important messianic role of the priesthood. Either Zechariah or, what seems more probable, a later editor of this prophecy balances the priestly reference with a recognition of Zerubbabel and the messianic position of the Davidic family. The fifth vision, that of the lampstand and the two olive trees (4.1–3, 11–14), has various explanations: the lampstand can represent God, His providence, His universal power, the Jewish people as witnesses, or the Temple. The two olive trees probably symbolize the priestly and royal representatives, both of whom were consecrated with olive oil. While the sixth and seventh visions of the flying scroll and the flying bushel (ch. 5) announce the removal of sin from God's people, the eighth vision (6.1–8) seems to repeat the thought and imagery of the first vision.

It is difficult to decide whether the coronation of Zerubbabel (6.9–15) really took place or whether it is another symbolic vision. The Hebrew text, which seems to be garbled here, speaks of more than one crown and centers the action around the high priest Joshua. Because of surrounding phrases, however, most scholars feel that Zechariah was thinking exclusively of Zerubbabel. In the last two chapters of this section (ch. 7–8) is heard an echo of authentic prophetic preaching, in the insistence that faith, kindness, and compassion are far superior to fasting and liturgical ceremonies (7.1–14; 8.18–23). The ten separate, messianic oracles of ch. 8 also resound with familiar prophetic phrases, but the central position of the Temple and priesthood shows that the leadership in the prophetic movement had passed into priestly hands.

Second Major Section: Chapters 9–14. The second part of the book (ch. 9–14) reveals such differences of style and background that scholars are almost unanimous in attributing these chapters to one or more inspired authors other than Zechariah. Unlike ch. 1–8, these chapters do not provide any clear, historical allusion; precise dates and names are completely lacking. Nor are ch. 9–14 preoccupied with Temple reconstruction, the high priest Joshua, or the governor Zerubbabel. While ch. 1–8 are prosaic, redundant, and involved, ch. 9–14 are poetic, simple, and direct. The lack of specific historical references, however, often makes it impossible to identify the events alluded to, although these, no doubt, were evident to the original audience. What was of primary, messianic interest in the first part—Jerusalem and the revival of the Davidic dynasty—is reduced to a secondary position in the second part. The apocalyptic spirit of the first part, however, continues through these chapters and, in fact, reaches one of its most intense expressions in ch. 14.

The second part is often called "Deutero-Zechariah" (i.e., second Zechariah). It is best to explain Deutero-Zechariah as the end product of an inspired tradition, rather than as the work of a single author, for these chapters not only drew upon the texts and references of earlier Prophets but also developed and expanded through the years until they reached their present form. New sections were added and older ones were reworked and enlarged. For a while, as already mentioned, the three chapters of Malachi were probably included here.

The composition of this second part, therefore, extends through the entire 1st century of the Hellenistic Age (333–63 B.C.). The earliest references to foreigners seem friendly enough (9.7; 14.21); the Jews at first welcomed Alexander the Great as a divine instrument in delivering them from Persian oppression. Later additions, however, reflect hatred and hostility (9.13b; most of ch. 12–14). The historical details, here as always in postexilic Judaism, are very difficult to reconstruct. We sense a scourge of internal intrigue and external persecution that recall the teaching of the Songs of the SUFFERING SERVANT in Isaiah (*see* especially Is 52.13–53.12). Suffering, with its power to purify and strengthen (Zec 12.10–14), will issue in a perpetual messianic Feast of Tabernacles (14.8, 16), a constant thanksgiving for abundant joys.

Not only do ch. 9–14 weave in many quotations from, or allusions to, earlier prophetic writings (especially Isaiah, Deuteronomy, Jeremiah, Ezekiel, and Joel), but verses from the chapters of Zechariah are themselves frequently quoted in the New Testament: Zec 9.9a in Lk 1.28?; Zec 9.9b in Mt 21.5; Zec 11.12 in Mt 26.15; Zec 12.4 in Lk 20.17–18; Zec 12.10 in Jn 19.37 and Rev 1.7; Zec 13.7 in Mt 26.31; Zec 14.21b in Jn 2.16.

Bibliography: P. R. ACKROYD in *Peake's Commentary on the Bible,* ed. M. BLACK and H. H. ROWLEY (New York 1962) 646–655. S. BULLOUGH, *Catholic Commentary on Holy Scripture,* ed. B. ORCHARD et al. (London-New York 1957) 689–700. T. CHARY, *Les Prophètes et le culte à partir de l'exil* (Tournai 1955) 118–127. A. GELIN, *Aggée, Zacharie, Malachie* in *Bible de Jérusalem* (Paris 1957) 1960. R. T. SIEBENECK, ''The Messianism of Aggeus and Proto-Zacharias,'' *The Catholic Bible Quarterly* 19 (1957) 312–328. T. H. ROBINSON and F. HORST, *Die zwölf Kleinen Propheten* in *Handbuch zum Alten Testament,* ed. O. EISSFELDT (14; Tübingen 1954), with complete bibliog.

[C. STUHLMUELLER]

ZEGADA, ESCOLÁSTICO

Argentine priest and educator; b. Jujuy, Argentina, Feb. 10, 1813; d. there, 1871. Zegada was of noble birth, a nephew of GORRITI. He studied for the priesthood in Chuquisaca, Bolivia, was ordained in 1836, and was appointed almost immediately to Jujuy. Greatly concerned with the education of youth of both sexes, in 1858 he founded and supported the Colegio de Educandos, a boarding school for the training of teachers. He arranged for the Vincentian Sisters to come from France in 1864 to educate the girls and brought the Lazarist Fathers for the boys' school. At his own expense and with great sacrifice, he established the San Roque hospital in 1850. Zegada introduced the first printing press into Jujuy, rebuilt the ruined churches of San Francisco and La Merced, restored the original colonial church, and founded the *Recoba,* an organization for social and economic assistance. In 1849 he was appointed provincial governor of the state of Jujuy, served twice as representative, and was a member of the constituent parliament in 1855. His basic work on doctrine and social and moral ethics called *Instrucciones cristianas* was twice published by the national government and recommended as a school text. He later wrote his political and philosophical *Reflexiones.*

Bibliography: M. A. VERGARA, *Zegada: Sacerdote y patricio de Jujuy* (Jujuy, Argen. 1940).

[M. A. VERGARA]

ZEN

The Japanese translation of the Sanskrit word *dhyāna* (Chinese, *ch'an*), Zen designates the School of Meditation. It arose probably in the 6th century A.D. in China in Mahāyāna Buddhism, but with an influx of the native Taoism. In the 13th century it was transplanted to Japan; and down to the present in Japan, and recently also in America and Europe, it has exhibited a notable activity. Meditation is widespread among Buddhists, but the Zen School teaches a special and very effective manner of meditation, which is regarded by many (even by representatives of depth psychology) as the high point of Buddhist meditation.

Special Character of Zen Meditation. Zen is characterized by its radical orientation toward the experience of enlightenment (in Japanese, *satori*). Enlightenment is a super-clear experience of the reality or intuitive vision of the original unity of being. Experience is suddenly attained in the breakthrough of the stages of consciousness of the empirical "Ego." Basically, this inner realization can result spontaneously. However, the Zen School has developed a methodical way to enlightenment, a kind of psychic technique, which if practiced with intensity of purpose and perseverance, leads necessarily, according to most masters of Zen, to the experience intended.

Zen Technique: Zazen and Kōan. The most important elements in Zen technique are meditation in an upright sitting position with legs crossed (Japanese, *zazen*) and the practice of the *kōan*. The lotus sitting posture (*padmāsana*), which came from primitive Indian tradition and is employed in *zazen*, is regarded as superior to all other sitting positions taught in yoga. The many hours spent in continued meditation in this sitting position produces, in addition to physical and psychic relaxation, an emptying of the mind of all conscious content. It is combined frequently with the *kōan* practice. For *kōan* (assembled in *Kōan* collections), dialogues between master and disciple (called *mondō* in Japanese) are employed; paradoxical words and deeds, and all possible anecdotes from lives of the Zen masters of the ancient period are used also. These elements, one and all, contain the rationally insoluble factor of a logical contradiction. The disciple is requested to concentrate his mind completely on the *kōan* story in order that through the greatest possible application he may find the solution. However, all intellectual effort is in vain. The solution can be experienced only in the sudden flash of enlightenment.

Young monk of the Son (Zen) Buddhist order, To Son Sa temple, Seoul, Korea. (©G. John Renard)

History. The Indian monk Bodhidharma, who according to legend came from India to China in order to be the first to teach a new way of enlightenment, is regarded by the Zen School as its founder and the first Chinese Zen patriarch. Bodhidharma's biography is historically questionable in all details. Even the life story of the sixth Chinese Zen patriarch, Hui-neng (A.D. 638–713), is not fully certain historically; but the history proper of the Zen School in China begins with him. A large number of significant Zen masters marks the high point of Chinese Zen during the late T'ang Period (8th and 9th centuries). In the Sung Period that followed, five "houses" or schools assumed definite form in Chinese Zen. Of these, the Lin-chi (Japanese, *Rinzai*) and Ts'ao-tung (Japanese, *Sōtō*) schools were transplanted to Japan, where together with the Ōbaku School, which also was introduced at a later date from China (in the 17th century), they have continued to represent Japanese Zen Buddhism down to the present time.

One can hardly speak of doctrinal differences between the schools of Zen Buddhism, but Zen practice differs according to each school and monastery. The Sōtō School (founded in Japan by Dōgen, 1200–53) puts emphasis on meditation in the sitting position, the so-called *zazen*, which according to Dōgen's teaching on the unity of enlightenment and practice of Zen, demonstrates the original enlightenment of the Buddha nature. In the Japanese Rinzai School, Hakuin (1685–1768), the outstanding representative, is famous for his psychological insight and many ecstasies, and also for his educational influence on the people.

Effects in Art and Culture. Zen Buddhism, especially in Japan, has exercised a significant influence on culture. Of the arts or "ways" (Japanese, *dō*) inspired by the spirit of Zen, those of a warlike nature, as swordfighting, wrestling, and archery, and others of a domestic character, as flower arrangement, the tea ceremony, and gardening, and some also as arts in the Western sense, as poetic compositions, calligraphy, and painting, all have had the widest dissemination and often have reached high perfection. Even today the gardens near the Zen temples of the old capital Kyoto bear witness to the unique and strongly symbolic artistic sense of their creators. Zen art reached its zenith in painting, in which the ink drawings and watercolor pictures of Sesshū (1421–1506) are masterpieces of world art. The lyrical poetry of the greatest Japanese poet, Bashō (1644–94), whose immortal epigrams in 17 syllables (called *haiku* in Japanese) cannot be translated adequately, is deeply impressed with the spirit of Zen.

Zen and Christianity. A distinction must be made between the metaphysical background and the specific manner of meditation in Zen Buddhism. The Zen School possesses no special teaching, but since it arose in Mahāyāna Buddhism, it is impressed with the spirit of the Mahāyāna religion. The disciples of Zen, as believing Buddhists, are bound by Buddhist scripture and piety. The monastic discipline and cult of Buddhism play an important role in the Zen monasteries. All Zen Buddhists explain the enlightenment experience on the basis of the monistic or cosmotheistic metaphysics of Mahāyāna Buddhism, which is in manifest opposition to Christian theism.

On the other hand, the practice of specific Zen meditation (including the *satori* experience) could perhaps be compatible with Christian belief, but with a limitation as regards the *kōan* practice insofar as the *kōan* exercises, at least in the Zen understanding of them, express the monistic Mahāyāna *Weltanschauung*. Meditation in the required sitting position can produce entirely beneficial effects among Christians also. Enlightenment, as a natural experience of reality independent of all ideological interpretation, possesses a spiritual value. The endeavors to introduce Eastern forms of meditation into Christian spirituality, when proposed by experienced persons, deserve sympathetic attention and encouragement.

Bibliography: J. L. BROUGHTON, *The Bodhidharma Anthology: the Earliest Records of Zen* (Berkeley 1999). H. DUMOULIN, *Zen Buddhism: A History*, 2 vols. rev. ed. (New York 1988). H. DUMOULIN, *Zen Enlightenment: Origins and Meaning* (New York 1979). N. FOSTER and J. SHOEMAKER, *The Roaring Stream: A New Zen Reader* (Hopewell, N. J. 1996). P. KAPLEAU, *The Three Pillars of Zen*, rev. ed (New York 1980). K. KRAFT, ed. *Zen: Tradition and Transition* (New York 1988).

[H. DUMOULIN/EDS.]

ZENO, BYZANTINE EMPEROR

The Byzantine emperor Zeno (474–491) came from the village of Rusumblada in Isauria. Born *c.* 426/431, his original name was Tarasicodissa. During a military career, Zeno acquired papers in 466 showing the treachery of Aspar's son Ardabur. This brought him promotion to *comes domesticorum* and marriage to Leo's daughter Ariadne. He served as *magister militum per Thracias* (467–469) and *magister militum per Orientem* (469–471), before acting as *magister militum praesentalis* (?–474). He was also given the honors of the consulate (469) and *patricius*. Zeno's son Leo (born *c.* 467) was made Augustus with his grandfather in January 474. After Leo I's death, Jan. 18, 474, Zeno ruled as Augustus from February 9 with his young son. When Leo II died in November 474, Zeno ruled alone.

Revolts against him were launched by Basiliscus (475–476) Marcian (479), and Leontius (484–488). Basiliscus seized power in January 475, forcing Zeno to flee to Isauria. He returned to Constantinople in August 476, after Basiliscus lost the support of his conspirators Illus and Armatus. Marcian, his brother-in-law, was defeated by Illus in an attempt to storm the palace in 479. Lastly, Zeno's mother-in-law, Verina, revolted in 484 with the support of Illus. When Zeno sent Leontius against them in 484, Leontius deserted and was acclaimed emperor. The rebels were defeated near Antioch in 484, but it was not until 488 that they were finally suppressed in the Isaurian mountains. Beset by immediate problems, Zeno paid little attention to the west, though in 474 he declared Nepos emperor in Italy. He continued to recognize Nepos even after the latter had been forced into exile, but when Nepos died in 480, Zeno accepted Odoacer's authority in Italy. Until Theoderic Strabo's accidental death in 481, Zeno could set him against Theoderic the Amal, another Gothic leader in the Balkans. Then Theoderic the Amal became a grave threat, even attacking Constantinople in

487. In 488 Zeno sent him against Odoacer in Italy, thus removing most of the Goths from the Balkans.

In religious affairs, Zeno was faced with twin problems of western reluctance to accept a patriarchate at Constantinople and of Alexandrian rejection of Chalcedon. In 482 Zeno issued his Edict (subsequently known as the Henoticon) which was neutral on Chalcedon but supported the patriarch of Constantinople, Acacius. On both grounds this offended the pope, causing the Acacian Schism (484–519). Although extremists (Nestorians and Eutychians) rejected the Edict, it was accepted by most moderates. Zeno's subsequent actions tended towards anti-Chalcedonianism, appointing patriarchs like Peter the Fuller in Antioch who were sympathetic to monophysitism.

Zeno was unpopular, particularly in the capital. The frequent military crises placed great financial demands on the treasury, and Zeno raised money by selling offices. This, along with his patronage of Isaurians provoked widespread hostility. Despite the enormous challenges he faced, Zeno died in peace, Apr. 9, 491, leaving no heir.

Bibliography: E. W. BROOKS, "The Emperor Zenon and the Isaurians," *English Historical Review* 8 (1893) 209–238. A. CAMERON, et al., eds., *Cambridge Ancient History* vol. 14 (Cambridge 2000) 49–52. H. W. ELTON, "Illus and the Imperial Aristocracy under Zeno," *Byzantion* 70 (2000) 393–407.

[H. W. ELTON]

ZENO OF ELEA

Greek philosopher of the Parmenidean school; b. *c.* 489 B.C. While still quite young he wrote a series of 40 arguments designed to defend the Eleatic denial of motion and plurality. Only fragments of this book are extant. In about 450 B.C. he traveled to Athens and possibly taught there for some time. His political activities reputedly resulted in his being put to death by the tyrant Nearchus of Elea, although the date and details are not known. Aristotle called him the father of dialectics because of his ability to draw two contradictory conclusions from an opponent's assumptions.

Zeno's arguments against pluralism appear to be directed to the Pythagoreans who held that extended physical bodies are composed of nonextended mathematical points. Zeno argued that everything in the universe is both infinitely large and has no size at all, a blatant contradiction. The infinite divisibility of any physical body regardless of size means that it is composed of an infinite number of elements, and is thus infinitely large. On the other hand the body has no size at all because no number of nonextended units can produce an extended body. A parallel argument comes to the conclusion that any plurality is both finite and infinite.

Zeno's famous four paradoxes concerning motion, presented in Aristotle's *Physics* (239b 5–240a 18), are as follows: (1) It is impossible to traverse any finite distance because one must first reach the midpoint, then the next midpoint, then the next, etc., to infinity. (2) In the race between Achilles and the tortoise, who is given a head start, Achilles can never win because when he reaches the point from which the tortoise started, the tortoise has moved a short distance ahead, etc., to infinity. (3) A flying arrow is at rest, for at any moment it occupies some place, and when it is in a place it is at rest. (4) If two bodies, *A* and *B,* are traveling toward each other with equal velocity, then *A* passes *B* twice as fast as it passes another body *C* at rest. Therefore, a whole time is equal to half of itself.

The basic point behind Zeno's paradoxes is that the infinitely divisible becomes actually divided to infinity when traversed. His arguments emphasized the need for a more adequate theory of the continuum. Although his thought was more polemical than constructive, Zeno's intriguing paradoxes are a classic statement of the problems of the continuum and have won him a permanent place of importance in the history of philosophy and science.

See Also: CONTINUUM; MOTION.

Bibliography: Sources. H. DIELS, *Die Fragmente der Vorsokratiker: Griechisch und Deutsch,* ed. W. KRANZ, 3 v. (9th ed. Berlin 1956); v. 1 (10th ed. Berlin 1960–61). K. FREEMAN, tr., *Ancilla to the Pre–Socratic Philosophers* (Cambridge, Mass. 1957). Studies. H. D. R. LEE, *Zeno of Elea* (Cambridge, Eng. 1936). J. BURNET, *Early Greek Philosophy* (4th ed. London 1930; reprint New York 1957). F. C. COPLESTON, *History of Philosophy* (Westminster, Md. 1946–63) 1:54–59.

[R. J. BLACKWELL]

ZENO OF VERONA, ST.

Bishop of Verona; d. ca. 371. St. Ambrose (397) and his own anti-Arian writings indicate that Zeno flourished *c.* 362 to 371 or 372. His use of African authors, scriptural citations, and a sermon on St. Caesarius of Mauretania argue his African origin. Zeno is not mentioned in Jerome's *De viris illustribus,* and his vita, written four centuries later by Coronatus Notarius, is overburdened with legends. The sermons reveal a pastoral-minded bishop intent on instilling a liturgical and sacramental life in his flock. He insisted on liberality, hospitality, and care for the poor: "Your homes are open to all travelers. For a long time, here in Verona, no one alive or dead has gone naked. Our poor no longer know what it is to beg for food." Zeno's name is associated with the development of Western monasticism and with the founding of one of the first convents of nuns. Ninety-three of Zeno's ser-

St. Zeno of Verona, 13th-century polychrome statue in the Basilica of St. Zeno Major, Verona. (Alinari-Art Reference/Art Resource, NY)

mons (first printed in 1508) have been preserved: 63 deal primarily with Baptism and the Paschal mystery, and show a rich use of typology. His teaching on the Trinity and the Incarnation reveals the undeveloped status of theology in the West; but he insists on the complete virginity of Mary, before, in, and after giving birth. In art Zeno is represented with a fish on a string being drawn from the water; he is invoked as a patron against floods and drowning. The statue in the abbey church of St. Zeno Major in Verona marks him as "the saint who smiles."

Feast: April 12.

Bibliography: ZENO OF VERONA, *Tractatus, Patrologia Latina,* ed. J. P. MIGNE, 217 v. (Paris 1878–90) 11:253–528; *Sermones,* ed. J. B. C. GIULARI (Verona 1900); *The Day Has Come! : Easter and Baptism in Zeno of Verona,* ed. G. P. JEANES (Collegeville, Minn. 1995). *Studi zenoniani: in occasione del XVI centemario della morte di S. Zeno* (Verona 1974). D. G. MORIN, "Deux petits discours d'un évêque Petronius," *Revue Bénédictine* 14 (Maredsous 1897) 3–8. *Acta Sacntorum* (Paris 1863–) April 2:68–78. *Bibliotheca hagiographica latina antiquae et mediae aetatis,* 2 v. (Brussels 1898–1901; suppl. 1911) 9001–02. A. BIGELMAIR, *Zeno* (Münster 1904). G. BARDY, *Dictionnaire de théologie catholique,* ed. A. VACANT et al., (Paris 1903–50; Tables générales 1951–) 15.2:3685–90. M. F. STEPANICH, *The Christology of Zeno* (Washington 1948). L. PALANCA, *prose Artistry and Birth of Rhyme in St. Zeno of Verona* (2d ed. rev. New York 1972). G. P. MARCHI, *Il culto di San Zenonnel Veronese* (Verona 1972). B. LÖFSTEDT and D. W. PACKARD, *A Concordance to the Sermons of Bishop Zeno of Verona* (Urbana, Ill. 1975). F. SEGALA, *Il culto di san Zeno nella liturgia medioevale fino al secolo XII* (Verona 1982). C. TRUZZI, *Zeno, Gaudenzio e Cromazio: testi e contenuti della predicazione cristiana per le chiese di Verona, Brescia e Aquileia* (Brescia 1985). G. SGREVA, *La teologia di Zenone di Verona* (Vicenza 1989). W. MONTORSI, *Geminiano e Zenone: due santi per una leggenda* (Modena 1993). A. BUTLER, *The Lives of the Saints,* rev. ed. H. THURSTON and D. ATTWATER, 4 v. (New York 1956) 2:77–78.

[A. C. RUSH]

ZEPHANIAH, BOOK OF

This Old Testament book summarizes in its three chapters much of the prophetic teaching on the nature of true religion. Consideration of the contents and historical background of the book in this article will serve to highlight the Prophet's enduring message.

Contents. The uniquely Israelite concept of a God who involves Himself in human history is immediately evidenced in Zephaniah by its contents: prophetic woes, oracles against the nations, and predictions of hope. The punishments are to be accomplished by the power of Yahweh, but are provoked by the free choice of men. The rapidly approaching DAY OF THE LORD is the Prophet's major theme. Zephaniah's account of this day (1.2–2.16) inspired the *Dies Irae* (cf. 1.15–16) of the Requiem Mass. The day will bring universal devastation, especially for Juda and Jerusalem, whose condemnation is found in the book's first two oracles (1.2–2.3). Oracles against the nations (2.4–15) are followed by a third oracle against Jerusalem (3.1–8). Promises of restoration for the nations (3.9–10) and Jerusalem (3.11–20) end the book on a note of joy.

Interpretation. The inscription of the book (1.1) situates the prophecy in the reign of King Josiah (640–609 B.C.) and traces the Prophet's genealogy four generations to a certain Hezekiah, perhaps the same as King Hezekiah (both *ḥizqîyâ* in Hebrew). Some, rejecting this verse, have attempted to situate the prophecy in the reign of Joachim (609–598 B.C.), thus making the Chaldean destruction of 597–587 the fulfillment of the predictions of the Day of Yahweh; however, scholars, by general agreement, now place the prophecy in the early reign of Josiah before his Deuteronomic reform (*c.* 629 B.C.; cf. 2 Kgs ch. 22–23).

Assyria, which in the 8th century B.C. destroyed Samaria and laid waste much of Judah, maintained a world domination that reached the zenith of its power under King Assurbanipal (668–628 B.C.). Chaldea was building the kingdom that would eventually destroy Assyria (612

B.C.), but Judah lived under nearly complete subjection to Assyria through the 7th century to the years of Josiah's youth. This subjection led to religious syncretism, especially under Judah's "worst king," Manasseh, who introduced Assyrian rites into the Temple and revived Canaanite cults at the high places. The Prophet's attack on the worship of false gods (1.4–5) and condemnation of pro-Assyrian ministers at the court (1.8–9; 3.3) reflects this situation, which had continued into the early reign of Josiah.

Probably the general political complications rather than any one particular event, such as the Scythian invasion mentioned by Herodotus, led Zephaniah to recall the teaching of earlier Prophets on the Day of Yahweh and enabled him to see that the immorality, idolatry, and arrogant pride of Judah and the nations would make this a day of utter devastation. Yet mercy would be the final work of God. To a remnant of Israel composed of the "poor of the land," "a people humble and lowly" (3.12), the proclamation would resound: "Yahweh, your God, is in your midst, a mighty savior; he will rejoice over you with gladness, and renew you in his love, he will sing joyfully because of you as one sings at festivals" (3.17–18). Condemning the proud self-sufficiency of the rulers, Zephaniah directed his words of consolation to the poor who recognized their need of God and placed their entire hope in Yahweh alone. This message of humble trust and hope against hope the Prophet offers to any man who desires peace in the world. It is this message that Jesus Christ makes the basis of His own teaching and life: "Blessed are you poor, for yours is the kingdom of God" (Lk 6.20); "Learn from me, for I am meek and humble of heart" (Mt 11.29).

Bibliography: C. L. TAYLOR, JR., and H. THURMAN, G. A. BUTTRICK, ed., *The Interpreters' Dictionary of the Bible,* 4 v. (Nashville 1962) 6:1005–34. A. GEORGE, *Michée, Sophonie, Nahum* (*Bible de Jérusalem* 27; Paris 1952). G. GERLEMAN, *Zephanja* (Lund 1942). A. VAN HOONACKER, *Les Douze petits prophètes* (*Études bibliques,* Paris 1908). J. COPPENS, *Les Douze petits prophètes* (Bruges 1950). J. M. P. SMITH, et al., *A Critical and Exegetical Commentary on Micah, Zephaniah, Nahum, Habakkuk, Obadiah and Joel* (International Critical Commentary, New York 1911). J. P. HYATT, "The Date and Background of Zephaniah," *Journal of Near Eastern Studies* 7 (1948) 25–29. G. VON RAD, "The Origin of the concept of the Day of Yahweh," *Journal of Semitic Studies* 4 (1959) 97–108.

[D. J. MOELLER]

ZEPHYRINUS, POPE, ST.

Pontificate: 198 to 217. Eusebius records that Zephyrinus became pope *c.* 200 and reigned for 18 or 19 years. The *Annuario Pontificio* of 2000 begins his pontifi-

Illuminated initial "V" of the Book of Zephaniah in the "Great Bible of Demeter Neksei-Lipocz" (Pre. Acc. MS 1, v. 2, folio 192 v), executed in Hungary in an atelier headed by a Bolognese artist, c. 1350.

cate in 198. The *Liber pontificalis,* which gives several untrustworthy reports about him, states that he was a Roman, the son of Habundius, although his name is Greek. The persecution of the Christians under Septimius Severus during his pontificate was worse in the provinces than in Rome. He appointed CALLISTUS I curator of the cemetery in Rome. The learned and caustic HIPPOLYTUS, who became an antipope, depicts Zephyrinus as a dull, unlearned man, the puppet of his ambitious rival, Callistus. This is an overstatement, but Zephyrinus was a weak man who depended heavily upon Callistus. Zephyrinus would not condemn MONARCHIANISM and PATRIPASSIANISM as Hippolytus desired. According to HARNACK, the statements Hippolytus attributes to him form the oldest recorded, dogmatic definition of a Roman bishop.

During his pontificate, the adoptionist followers (*see* ADOPTIONISM) of Theodotus of Byzantium continued in Rome with a salaried bishop, Natalius, but they eventually returned to the Church. Tertullian accused Zephyrinus of having accepted Montanism initially, but then of having abandoned it. The learned Roman Gaius refuted the MONTANISM of Proclus, while the visit of the renowned ORIGEN, a correspondent of Hippolytus, "to see the most ancient church of Rome'' indicates the importance of the see at this time. The MARTYROLOGY OF ST. JEROME gives Zephyrinus's feast as December 20. His place of burial in the cemetery of Callistus is uncertain.

Feast: Aug. 26.

Bibliography: EUSEBIUS, *Historia Ecclesiastica* 2:25; 5:28; 6:14, 20. É. AMANN, *Dictionnaire de théologie catholique*, ed. A. VACANT et al., (Paris 1903–50) 15.2:3690–91. A. MERCATI and A. PELZER, *Dizionario ecclesiastico* (Turin 1954–58) 3:1400. E. FERGUSON, *Encyclopedia of Early Christianity* (New York 1997) 2.1187–88. J. N. D. KELLY, *Oxford Dictionary of Popes* (New York 1986) 12–13.

[E. G. WELTIN]

ZERVANISM

An Iranian religion that has *Zervan,* or ''Time,'' as its supreme god. It is not certain whether there is a reference to this god in the 12th-century B.C. text found in the Nuzi cuneiform tablets. He is not mentioned in Zoroaster's *Gāthās.* In the 4th century B.C. the Babylonian Berossus speaks of a ''mythical king Zerovanus,'' and Eudemus of Rhodes, a pupil of Aristotle, mentions a philosopher by that name. His account, preserved by the Neoplatonist Damascius, seems to be a reply to this question of a Greek impressed by Iranian dualism: ''What is the supreme and sole principle?'' The answer is ambiguous, for, besides Time, Space is also cited as a name of the ''infinite and intelligible all.''

The appearance of astral fatalism in Iran, some centuries after Zoroaster, was due apparently to Greco-Babylonian influence, which gave new vigor to the old faith in the Time-God. Zervanism had a great vogue under the Arsacids and Sassanids. Official Mazdaism had to sustain a long struggle against it in the Sassanid period, and Mazdaism's success varied. The supreme god of Manichaeism is Zervan, not Ormazd; the supremacy of Ormazd was more theoretical than real. Thus in the Acts of the Christian martyrs of Iran there is frequent mention of Zervan as the supreme god of the Persians.

Official doctrine, as reflected in the AVESTA, tries to place Time and Space under the supreme authority of Ahura Mazda. In the Vidēvdāt, ''Law against the Demons,'' one of the books of the Avesta, Zervan is more a principle than a god. He is described as imperishable and infinite. When he appears in more concrete form, it is as god of the three ages of man and as god of death. A distinction is made between Time ''without limit'' and Time ''long to rule.'' As a god of three ages of man he had a close parallel in the Hellenistic god Aion, whose birth was celebrated on January 6, the date later adopted for the Epiphany. This may account for the tradition representing the Magi of Bethlehem as a youth, an adult, and an old man.

Zervanism and Mazdaism could be combined in two ways: Zervan could be absorbed into official Mazdaism, or he could retain the highest position and assume certain Mazdean features. This is illustrated in the myth of Zervan giving birth to the twins Ormazd and Ahriman, as recorded by the Armenian Eznik (5th century A.D.). This myth however, was condemned as heretical by orthodox Mazdaism.

See Also: PERSIAN RELIGION, ANCIENT; ZOROASTER (ZARATHUSHTRA).

Bibliography: R. C. ZAEHNER, *Zurvan: A Zoroastrian Dilemma* (New York 1955). J. DUCHESNE-GUILLEMIN, *La Religion de l'Iran ancien* (Paris 1962). ''Die Weisen aus dem Morgenlande, in *Antaios* (1965).

[J. DUCHESNE-GUILLEMIN]

ZHANG BANNIU, PETER, ST.

Laborer, lay martyr, member of the Third Order of St. Francis; b. 1849, Tuling Village, Yangqu Xian, Shanxi Province, China; d. July 9, 1900, Taiyüan, Shanxi Province. Peter Zhang Banniu (also given as Chang Panniu or Tchang-Pan-Nieu) was born to the Catholic Zhang Yuke family in a Catholic village. During the last decade of his life, he moved from his farm to Taiyüan, where he did odd jobs for the Franciscan community. At the outbreak of persecution in June 1900, Peter refused to flee into hiding, because he desired martyrdom. He was captured in the Taiyüan cathedral (July 5, 1900) and beheaded with his bishop and the Franciscan Missionaries of Mary. A few days after his death, Peter appeared before his son who was praying in a chapel. He urged his son, who also became a martyr, to remain constant. Peter was beatified by Pope Pius XII (Nov. 24, 1946) and canonized (Oct. 1, 2000) by Pope John Paul II with Augustine Zhao Rong and companions.

Feast: July 4.

Bibliography: L. M. BALCONI, *Le Martiri di Taiyuen* (Milan 1945). *Acta Apostolicae Sedis* 47 (1955) 381–388; *Vita del b. A. Crescitelli* (Milan 1950). M. T. DE BLARER, *Les Bse Marie Hermine de Jésus et ses compagnes, franciscaines missionaires de Marie, massacrées le 9 juillet 1900 à Tai-Yuan-Fou, Chine* (Paris 1947). *Les Vingt-neuf martyrs de Chine, massacrés en 1900, béatifiés par Sa Sainteté Pie XII, le 24 novembre, 1946* (Rome 1946). L. MINER, *China's Book of Martyrs: A Record of Heroic Martyrdoms and Marvelous Deliverances of Chinese Christians during the Summer of 1900* (Ann Arbor 1994). J. SIMON, *Sous le sabre des Boxers* (Lille 1955). C. TESTORE, *Sangue e palme sul fiume giallo. I beati martiri cinesi nella persecuzione della Boxe Celi Sud-Est, 1900* (Rome 1955). *L'Osservatore Romano*, Eng. Ed. 40 (2000): 1–2, 10.

[K. I. RABENSTEIN]

ZHANG HE, THÉRÈSE, ST.

Lay martyr, also known as Thérèse Chang Ho-shih or Teresa Tchang-Hene-Cheu; b. 1864, Ningqin County, Hebei (Hopeh) Province, China; d. there, July 16, 1900. Thérèse, born into a Catholic family, had expressed a desire to die for the faith. When she came of age, she married into the local Zhang family. Thérèse was captured by the Boxers in the village kitchen garden. Together with her son and daughter she was taken to the local temple to apostatize. Upon her refusal, all three were stabbed to death. She was among the 2,072 killed between June and August 1900 whose causes were submitted to the Vatican of which 56 were beatified by Pope Pius XII (April 17, 1955) and canonized (Oct. 1, 2000) by Pope John Paul II with Augustine Zhao Rong and companions.

Feast: July 20.

Bibliography: L. MINER, *China's Book of Martyrs: A Record of Heroic Martyrdoms and Marvelous Deliverances of Chinese Christians during the Summer of 1900* (Ann Arbor 1994). J. SIMON, *Sous le sabre des Boxers* (Lille 1955). C. TESTORE, *Sangue e palme sul fiume giallo. I beati martiri cinesi nella persecuzione della Boxe Celi Sud-Est, 1900* (Rome 1955). *L'Osservatore Romano*, Eng. Ed. 40 (2000): 1–2, 10.

[K. I. RABENSTEIN]

ZHANG HUAILU, ST.

Martyred catechumen, also known as Chang Huai-lu or Tchang-Hoai-Lou; b. 1843, in the village of Zhukotian, Hengshui County, Hebei (Hopeh) Province, China; d. there, June 9, 1900. Zhang Huailu became a catechumen the same year that he shed his blood for the faith. Because he was born and lived in a village where there were only a few Christians, the 57-year-old suffered first as a confessor. Taking advantage of the animosity aroused against Christians by the Boxers, local criminals extorted 300 silver pieces from him to guarantee they would not denounce him as a Catholic. Forewarned, most Catholics escaped the village prior to the June 9 invasion of the Boxers. Zhang Huailu, however, was captured. Although the extortionists pleaded that he was not a Christian (he was not yet baptized), Zhang Huailu replied, "If I am not Catholic, why did you take money from me to ensure my freedom?" Thereafter he was beaten and beheaded. He was beatified by Pope Pius XII (Apr. 17, 1955) and canonized (Oct. 1, 2000) by Pope John Paul II with Augustine Zhao Rong and companions.

Feast: July 20.

Bibliography: L. MINER, *China's Book of Martyrs: A Record of Heroic Martyrdoms and Marvelous Deliverances of Chinese Christians during the Summer of 1900* (Ann Arbor 1994). J. SIMON,

Sous le sabre des Boxers (Lille 1955). C. TESTORE, *Sangue e palme sul fiume giallo. I beati martiri cinesi nella persecuzione della Boxe Celi Sud-Est, 1900* (Rome 1955). *L'Osservatore Romano*, Eng. Ed. 40 (2000): 1–2, 10.

[K. I. RABENSTEIN]

ZHANG HUAN, JOHN, ST.

Martyr, Franciscan seminarian; b. Aug. 18, 1882, Nanshe, Yangqu Xian, Shanxi Province; d. July 9, 1900, Taiyüan, Shanxi Province, China. John Zhang Huan (Chang or Tchang) was the son of the pious Catholics Simon Zhang Tianjun and Clare Wu. Even in childhood his life and play centered on the faith. He began his studies in the minor seminary of Ko-lao-kou in 1896 and four years later transferred to the seminary at Taiyüan, where he was guided by Fr. Elias Facchini. When he and his classmates were advised to flee into hiding at the beginning of the Boxer Rebellion, John returned home. Soon thereafter he decided he would rather die with his bishop, Francesco Fogolla than hide his faith. He was among those arrested in the Taiyüan cathedral and executed after a short imprisonment. John was beatified by Pope Pius XII (Nov. 24, 1946) and canonized (Oct. 1, 2000) by Pope John Paul II with Augustine Zhao Rong and companions.

Feast: July 4.

Bibliography: L. M. BALCONI, *Le Martiri di Taiyuen* (Milan 1945). *Acta Apostolicae Sedis* 47 (1955) 381–388; *Vita del b. A. Crescitelli* (Milan 1950). M. T. DE BLARER, *Les Bse Marie Hermine de Jésus et ses compagnes, franciscaines missionnaires de Marie, massacrées le 9 juillet 1900 à Tai-Yuan-Fou, Chine* (Paris 1947). *Les Vingt-neuf martyrs de Chine, massacrés en 1900, béatifiés par Sa Sainteté Pie XII, le 24 novembre, 1946* (Rome 1946). L. MINER, *China's Book of Martyrs: A Record of Heroic Martyrdoms and Marvelous Deliverances of Chinese Christians during the Summer of 1900* (Ann Arbor 1994). J. SIMON, *Sous le sabre des Boxers* (Lille 1955). C. TESTORE, *Sangue e palme sul fiume giallo. I beati martiri cinesi nella persecuzione della Boxe Celi Sud-Est, 1900* (Rome 1955). *L'Osservatore Romano*, Eng. Ed. 40 (2000): 1–2, 10.

[K. I. RABENSTEIN]

ZHANG JINGGUANG, ST.

Franciscan seminarian, martyr; b. 1878, Fujing Cun, Taigu Xian, Shanxi Province, China; d. July 9, 1900, Taiyüan, Shanxi Province. John Zhang Jinguang (also given as Chiang, Tchang, or Zhang Jingguang) was one of the five children of Maria Ren and Zhang Zhiqian, who died while his son was in the seminary at Dongergou. In 1893 John entered the major seminary at Taiyüan, where he was known for his piety, obedience to his superiors, and observance of the Rule. Bp. Francesco Fogolla installed him as acolyte in 1897. Thereafter he began his theological studies. Following the destruction of a Protestant church by the Boxers (June 17, 1900), most of the seminarians returned to their families. John remained with his bishop and was captured and martyred with him. He was beatified by Pope Pius XII (Nov. 24, 1946) and canonized (Oct. 1, 2000) by Pope John Paul II with Augustine Zhao Rong and companions.

Feast: July 4.

Bibliography: L. M. BALCONI, *Le Martiri di Taiyuen* (Milan 1945). *Acta Apostolicae Sedis* 47 (1955) 381–388; *Vita del b. A. Crescitelli* (Milan 1950). M. T. DE BLARER, *Les Bse Marie Hermine de Jésus et ses compagnes, franciscaines missionnaires de Marie, massacrées le 9 juillet 1900 à Tai-Yuan-Fou, Chine* (Paris 1947). *Les Vingt-neuf martyrs de Chine, massacrés en 1900, béatifiés par Sa Sainteté Pie XII, le 24 novembre, 1946* (Rome 1946). L. MINER, *China's Book of Martyrs: A Record of Heroic Martyrdoms and Marvelous Deliverances of Chinese Christians during the Summer of 1900* (Ann Arbor 1994). J. SIMON, *Sous le sabre des Boxers* (Lille 1955). C. TESTORE, *Sangue e palme sul fiume giallo. I beati martiri cinesi nella persecuzione della Boxe Celi Sud-Est, 1900* (Rome 1955). *L'Osservatore Romano*, Eng. Ed. 40 (2000): 1–2, 10.

[K. I. RABENSTEIN]

ZHANG RONG, FRANCIS, ST.

Farmer, lay martyr, member of the Third Order of St. Francis; b. 1838, Qizi Shawn, Yangqu Xian, Shanxi Province, China; d. July 9, 1900, Taiyüan, Shanxi Province. Francis Zhang Rong (also given as Tchang-Iun or Chang Yüan), born of Christian peasant stock, was a widowed farmer. For the last decade of his life, he served the Franciscan community at Taiyüan as doorkeeper and janitor. He was known for his frequent fasting and prayerful life. Although his son-in-law, Tian Wancheng, provided him the means to flee the persecution of the Boxers, he stayed with his Franciscan brethren, was captured with them in Taiyüan's cathedral (July 5, 1900), and beheaded four days later. Francis was beatified by Pope Pius XII (Nov. 24, 1946) and canonized (Oct. 1, 2000) by Pope John Paul II with Augustine Zhao Rong and companions.

Feast: July 4.

Bibliography: L. M. BALCONI, *Le Martiri di Taiyuen* (Milan 1945). *Acta Apostolicae Sedis* 47 (1955) 381–388; *Vita del b. A. Crescitelli* (Milan 1950). M. T. DE BLARER, *Les Bse Marie Hermine de Jésus et ses compagnes, franciscaines missionnaires de Marie, massacrées le 9 juillet 1900 à Tai-Yuan-Fou, Chine* (Paris 1947). *Les Vingt-neuf martyrs de Chine, massacrés en 1900, béatifiés par Sa Sainteté Pie XII, le 24 novembre, 1946* (Rome 1946). L. MINER, *China's Book of Martyrs: A Record of Heroic Martyrdoms and Marvelous Deliverances of Chinese Christians during the Summer of 1900* (Ann Arbor 1994). J. SIMON, *Sous le sabre des Boxers* (Lille 1955). C. TESTORE, *Sangue e palme sul fiume giallo. I beati martiri cinesi nella persecuzione della Boxe Celi Sud-Est, 1900* (Rome 1955). *L'Osservatore Romano*, Eng. Ed. 40 (2000): 1–2, 10.

[K. I. RABENSTEIN]

ZHANG ZHIHE, PHILIP, ST.

Franciscan seminarian, martyr; b. 1880, Shangqingyu, Lin Xian, Shanxi Province; d. July 9, 1900, Taiyüan, Shanxi Province, China. Both in the minor seminary at Dongergou and the major seminary at Taiyüan, Philip Zhang Zhihe (Chiang or Tchang) was regarded as a diligent, tenacious student. After the June 27 burning of the local Protestant church, the seminarians were advised to return home. Philip and four other seminarians stayed. He was corned in Taiyüan's cathedral with his bishop and several dozen other Christians, and martyred after a short imprisonment. He was beatified by Pope Pius XII (Nov. 24, 1946) and canonized (Oct. 1, 2000) by Pope John Paul II with Augustine Zhao Rong and companions.

Feast: July 4.

Bibliography: L. M. BALCONI, *Le Martiri di Taiyuen* (Milan 1945). *Acta Apostolicae Sedis* 47 (1955) 381–388; *Vita del b. A. Crescitelli* (Milan 1950). M. T. DE BLARER, *Les Bse Marie Hermine de Jésus et ses compagnes, franciscaines missionnaires de Marie, massacrées le 9 juillet 1900 à Tai-Yuan-Fou, Chine* (Paris 1947). *Les Vingt-neuf martyrs de Chine, massacrés en 1900, béatifiés par Sa Sainteté Pie XII, le 24 novembre, 1946* (Rome 1946). L. MINER, *China's Book of Martyrs: A Record of Heroic Martyrdoms and Marvelous Deliverances of Chinese Christians during the Summer of 1900* (Ann Arbor 1994). J. SIMON, *Sous le sabre des Boxers* (Lille 1955). C. TESTORE, *Sangue e palme sul fiume giallo. I beati martiri cinesi nella persecuzione della Boxe Celi Sud-Est, 1900* (Rome 1955). *L'Osservatore Romano*, Eng. Ed. 40 (2000): 1–2, 10.

[K. I. RABENSTEIN]

ZHAO, JOHN BAPTIST AND PETER, SS.

Lay martyrs, b. Beiwangtou, Shen County, Hebei (Hopeh) Province, China; d. there, July 3, 1900. Peter Zhao Mingzhen (Tchao-Ming, Chao Ming-hsi, Chao Mingxi, Zhao Mingxi, b. 1839) and his brother John Baptist (b. 1844) led a group of 18 family and friends in prayer in preparation for death following their capture by the Boxers. They intoned, ''God, please help us; give us constancy so that we may sincerely offer our humble lives on to you. Please open the gates of Heaven to us and receive our souls, so that we may enjoy eternal life with you.'' The brothers were among the 56 martyrs beatified by Pope Pius XII (April 17, 1955) and canonized (Oct. 1, 2000) by Pope John Paul II with Augustine Zhao Rong and companions.

Feast: July 20.

Bibliography: L. MINER, *China's Book of Martyrs: A Record of Heroic Martyrdoms and Marvelous Deliverances of Chinese Christians during the Summer of 1900* (Ann Arbor 1994). J. SIMON, *Sous le sabre des Boxers* (Lille 1955). C. TESTORE, *Sangue e palme* sul fiume giallo. I beati martiri cinesi nella persecuzione della Boxe Celi Sud-Est, 1900 (Rome 1955). *L'Osservatore Romano*, English Edition 40 (2000): 1–2, 10.

[K. I. RABENSTEIN]

ZHAO, MARY, MARY, AND ROSA, SS.

Lay martyrs, b. Zhaojiacun, Wuchiao County, Hebei (Hopeh) Province, China; d. there, July 28, 1900. Mary Zhao Guo (also given as Chao Kuo-shih, Zhao-Guo, or Tchao- Kouo-Cheu, b. 1840) and her virgin daughters Rose (catechist, b. 1878) and Mary (b. 1883) were unsuccessful in evading the pursuing Boxers by jumping into a well. Rose responded to their captors' demand for apostasy: ''We have already resolved that we would rather die than deny our faith,'' then led her family in prayer. At Rose's request, the three were decapitated in the Zhao family cemetery and their heads burned. They were among the 2,072 killed between June and August 1900 whose causes were submitted to the Vatican of which 56 were beatified by Pope Pius XII (April 17, 1955) and canonized (Oct. 1, 2000) by Pope John Paul II with Augustine Zhao Rong and companions.

Feast: July 20.

Bibliography: L. MINER, *China's Book of Martyrs: A Record of Heroic Martyrdoms and Marvelous Deliverances of Chinese Christians during the Summer of 1900* (Ann Arbor 1994). J. SIMON, *Sous le sabre des Boxers* (Lille 1955). C. TESTORE, *Sangue e palme sul fiume giallo. I beati martiri cinesi nella persecuzione della Boxe Celi Sud-Est, 1900* (Rome 1955). *L'Osservatore Romano*, English Edition 40 (2000): 1–2, 10.

[K. I. RABENSTEIN]

ZHAO QUANXIN, JAMES, ST.

Lay martyr; b. 1856, Luilinzhaung Cun, Taiyüan Xian, Shanxi Province, China; d. July 9, 1900, Taiyüan, Shanxi Province. James Zhao Quanxin (given also as Chao Ch'üan-hsin or James Tciao-Tciuen-Sin) was born into a Catholic family headed by Antonius Zhang Desheng and Martha Jia. After military service, James married. He moved with his mother, wife, and two sons to Taiyüan to work for the Franciscan community. Although he was not arrested on July 5, 1900 with Bps. Gregorio GRASSI and Francesco Fogolla, he visited them each day in prison and resolved that he would die with them. He was arrested. His former military colleagues pled on his behalf in court, but James continued to profess himself a Christian. He was beaten and slashed to death by the sword. James was beatified by Pope Pius XII (Nov. 24, 1946) and canonized (Oct. 1, 2000) by Pope John Paul II with Augustine Zhao Rong and companions.

Feast: July 4.

Bibliography: L. M. BALCONI, *Le Martiri di Taiyuen* (Milan 1945). *Acta Apostolicae Sedis* 47 (1955) 381–388; *Vita del b. A. Crescitelli* (Milan 1950). M. T. DE BLARER, *Les Bse Marie Hermine de Jésus et ses compagnes, franciscaines missionnaires de Marie, massacrées le 9 juillet 1900 à Tai-Yuan-Fou, Chine* (Paris 1947). *Les Vingt-neuf martyrs de Chine, massacrés en 1900, béatifiés par Sa Sainteté Pie XII, le 24 novembre, 1946* (Rome 1946). L. MINER, *China's Book of Martyrs: A Record of Heroic Martyrdoms and Marvelous Deliverances of Chinese Christians during the Summer of 1900* (Ann Arbor 1994). J. SIMON, *Sous le sabre des Boxers* (Lille 1955). C. TESTORE, *Sangue e palme sul fiume giallo. I beati martiri cinesi nella persecuzione della Boxe Celi Sud-Est, 1900* (Rome 1955). *L'Osservatore Romano*, Eng. Ed. 40 (2000): 1–2, 10.

[K. I. RABENSTEIN]

ZHU RIXIN, PETER, ST.

Lay martyr; b. 1881, East Zhujiahe, Qin County, Hebei (Hopeh) Province, China; d. there, July 18, 1900. Peter Zhu Rixin (also given as Chou Jih-hsin or Tchou-Jeu-Sinn), a promising 19-year-old student, was one of the martyrs killed with Mary Zhu Wu by the Boxers. The parishioners in the predominantly Catholic Village were gathered in the church, which was set aflame. Most who escaped the burning building were massacred outside. Fifty-one, including Peter, were bound, ordered to renounce the faith, and, upon refusal to comply, executed the following day. Peter was among the 2,072 killed between June and August 1900 whose causes were submitted to the Vatican, and among the 56 from this period who were beatified by Pope Pius XII (April 17, 1955) and canonized (Oct. 1, 2000) by Pope John Paul II with Augustine Zhao Rong and companions.

Feast: July 20.

Bibliography: L. MINER, *China's Book of Martyrs: A Record of Heroic Martyrdoms and Marvelous Deliverances of Chinese Christians during the Summer of 1900* (Ann Arbor 1994). J. SIMON, *Sous le sabre des Boxers* (Lille 1955). C. TESTORE, *Sangue e palme sul fiume giallo. I beati martiri cinesi nella persecuzione della Boxe Celi Sud-Est, 1900* (Rome 1955). *L'Osservatore Romano*, Eng. Ed. 40 (2000): 1–2, 10.

[K. I. RABENSTEIN]

ZHU WU, MARY, ST.

Lay martyr; b. *c.* 1850, Zhujiahe, Qin County, Hebei (Hopeh) Province, China; d. there, July 17, 1900. The exemplary Christian Mary Zhu Wu (also spelled Chu Wu-shih or Ts'I-U), wife of the village's Catholic leader Zhu Tianxuan, was shot to death by the Boxers in her besieged parish church. After the priest was killed, the church was set aflame with other Christians inside it.

Mary's faith was evident prior to her martyrdom: She was known for her charity and trust in God's providence. She was beatified by Pope Pius XII (April 17, 1955) and canonized (Oct. 1, 2000) by Pope John Paul II with Augustine Zhao Rong and companions.

Feast: July 20.

Bibliography: L. MINER, *China's Book of Martyrs: A Record of Heroic Martyrdoms and Marvelous Deliverances of Chinese Christians during the Summer of 1900* (Ann Arbor 1994). J. SIMON, *Sous le sabre des Boxers* (Lille 1955). C. TESTORE, *Sangue e palme sul fiume giallo. I beati martiri cinesi nella persecuzione della Boxe Celi Sud-Est, 1900* (Rome 1955). *L'Osservatore Romano,* Eng. Ed. 40 (2000): 1–2, 10.

[K. I. RABENSTEIN]

ZHU WURUI, JOHN BAPTIST, ST.

Lay martyr; b. 1883, Green Grass River Village, Qin County, Hebei (Hopeh) Province, China; d. there, Aug. 18, 1900. John Baptist Zhu Wurui (also given as Chu Wu-jui or Tchou-Ou-Joei) was born into a Catholic family. He was captured by the Boxers as he tried to escape his besieged village to warn Catholics in the vicinity. He remained steadfast in his faith under interrogation by the county prefect. After severing his head, the Boxers hung it on a tree as a warning to other Christians. John Baptist was among the 2,072 killed between June and August 1900 whose causes were submitted to the Vatican. Of these, 56, including John Baptist, were beatified by Pope Pius XII (April 17, 1955) and canonized (Oct. 1, 2000) by Pope John Paul II with Augustine Zhao Rong and companions.

Feast: July 20.

Bibliography: L. MINER, *China's Book of Martyrs: A Record of Heroic Martyrdoms and Marvelous Deliverances of Chinese Christians during the Summer of 1900* (Ann Arbor 1994). J. SIMON, *Sous le sabre des Boxers* (Lille 1955). C. TESTORE, *Sangue e palme sul fiume giallo. I beati martiri cinesi nella persecuzione della Boxe Celi Sud-Est, 1900* (Rome 1955). *L'Osservatore Romano,* Eng. Ed. 40 (2000): 1–2, 10.

[K. I. RABENSTEIN]

ZHUANGZI (CHUANG TZU)

Chinese philosopher, contemporary of MENGZI (Mencius); b. *c.* 370; d. *c.* 285 B.C. Unlike Mengzi, Zhuangzi did not travel far to preach his doctrine; yet his fame reached the Prince of Chu, who asked him to become his prime minister. Zhuangzi declined the invitation, preferring to live simply in a small village and discuss philosophy with his disciples and friends. The *Book of Zhuangzi,* written by his disciples, had 52 chapters, but only 33 are extant. His teachings on cosmology, ethics, and politics are similar to those of LAOZI (Lao Tzŭ). He taught that all values are relative and that all extremes will eventually meet because they are really different aspects of the same unique reality. He developed a technique of dialectics that he used effectively in discussions. After Laozi, Zhuangzi was considered the great master of Taoist philosophy.

Bibliography: B. WATSON, tr., *The Complete Works of Chuang Tzu* (New York 1968). A. C. GRAHAM, tr., *The Seven Inner Chapters and Other Writings from the Book of Chuang-Tzu* (London 1981); *Disputers of the Tao: Philosophical Argument in Ancient China* (La Salle, IL 1989). K. M. WU, *The Butterfly As Companion: Meditations of the First Three Chapters of the Chuang Tzu* (Albany 1990).

[A. A. TSEU]

ZIERIKZEE, CORNELIUS OF

Franciscan reformer in Scotland; b. Island of Schouwen, Zeeland, the Netherlands, 1405; d. Antwerp, Belgium, *c.* 1470. Since 1282 there had been at least one friary of FRANCISCANS on the Island of Schouwen, and whether Cornelius entered this house before he joined the Franciscan Observants is not known. King James I of Scotland (d. 1437) had asked the province of Cologne for learned and pious religious to reestablish Franciscan life in his country. Made aware of the King's wishes, the Vicar-General John of Maubert, at the close of the provincial congregation of Gouda (1447), sent James II a group of seven Franciscans under Cornelius's leadership. The choice was well-made, for the friars soon became popular, and Cornelius accepted into the order several young noblemen who had studied at the Universities of Paris and Cologne. At first he hesitated to accept the fine buildings in Edinburgh offered to him by the King, but in 1455 he consented when compelled to do so by PIUS II, who, at the request of the archbishop primate of SAINT ANDREWS, accepted the property for the Holy See. In 1458 a second friary was built at Saint Andrews by Robert Keith and a third at Perth in 1460 by Jerome Lindsay, and eventually Cornelius was put in charge of both of them. In 1462 he returned to the province of Cologne and subsequently died a saintly death in the monastery at Antwerp. His remains were burned by the Calvinists in 1566.

Bibliography: Sources. W. M. BRYCE, *The Scottish Grey Friars,* 2 v. (London 1909) v.2. *Collection d'etudes et de documents sur l'histoire religieuse et littéraire du moyen âge,* 7 v. (Paris 1898–1909) v.1. Literature. A. DU MONSTIER, *Martyrologium franciscanum* (2d ed. Paris 1753). S. SCHOUTENS, *Martyrologium minoritico-Belgicum* (Hoogstraten, Bel. 1902). P. SCHLAGER, *Beiträge zur Geschichte der kölnischen Franziskaner-Ordensprovinz im*

Mittelalter (Cologne 1904) 102–104. *Archivum Franciscanum historicum* 1 (1908) 309; 7 (1914) 572.

[J. CAMBELL]

ZIGABENUS, EUTHYMIUS

12th-century Byzantine theologian, exegete. Because of confusion with another monk, Zigabenus of Peribleptos, there is almost no biographical information preserved in regard to the author of the *Panoplia Dogmatike,* a work requested by the Emperor ALEXIUS COMNENUS as a refutation of all heresies. The *Panoplia* was highly praised by Anna Comnena, but modern research indicates that it was based upon patristic texts in florilegia rather than on firsthand knowledge. The first seven titles (chapters) are a positive exposition of theodicy and Christology; the following 21 titles combat heresies from those of the Jews to those of the author's contemporaries: Armenians, Paulicians, Messalians, Bogomils, and Musulmans. Zigabenus is a useful source for knowledge of the Bogomils and in the opinion of V. Grumel has probably excerpted a synodal document in their regard; but he presents a mere compilation of sources for the other heresies. His exegetical work is represented by commentaries On the Psalms, including the Canticle of Canticles; On the Gospels; and On the Pauline Epistles. He gives mainly a résumé of earlier exegetical opinion, particularly of St. John Chrysostom. Other dogmatic and rhetorical works and letters attributed to him are not authentic.

Bibliography: *Patrologia Graeca* v.128–131. N. KALOGERAS, ed., *Euthymii Zigabeni Commentarius in XIV epistolas Sancti Pauli,* 2 v. (Athens 1887). M. JUGIE, *Dictionnaire de théologie catholique* 5.2:1577–82. H. G. BECK, *Kirche und theologische Literatur im byzantinischen Reich* 614–616.

[P. CANART]

ZIGLIARA, TOMMASO

Dominican philosopher and theologian; b. Bonifacio, Corsica, Oct. 29, 1833; d. Rome, May 10, 1893. Having studied in Rome and Perugia, he taught at Viterbo (1861–70) and at the Collegium Divi Thomae in Rome (1870–79), where he became regent in 1873. In 1879 Leo XIII made him a cardinal, appointing him director of the critical edition of the works of St. Thomas Aquinas (Leonine ed.), president of the Roman Academy of St. Thomas Aquinas, and prefect of the Congregation of Studies. Highly esteemed by the pope, he was consulted on the question of ROSMINI-SERBATI and took part in the preparation of important documents, including *AETERNI PATRIS* and *RERUM NOVARUM.* Having a profound knowledge of the thought of St. Thomas, he was among the best qualified NEOTHOMISTS. His critique of current philosophical systems (traditionalism, ontologism, and positivism) was acute and forceful, yet free from the bitterness of polemics. Through his position in the Roman Curia and his widely used *Summa philosophica* (17 ed. in Latin) he effectively fostered the growth of Thomism. He also helped to establish modern fundamental theology. His major works include *Summa philosophica in usum scholarum* (3 v. Rome 1876), *De mente Concilii Viennensis* (Rome 1878), *Propaedeutica ad sacram theologiam* (Rome 1890), and notes in volume 1 of the Leonine edition.

Bibliography: A. FRÜHWIRTH, *Analecta Sacri Ordinis Praedicatorum* 1 (1893) 258–263. R. FEI, *Memorie Domenicane* 45 (1928) 265–275. O. F. TENCAJOLI, *ibid.* 52. (1935) 160–176. I. P. GROSSI, *ibid.* 78 (1961) 86–100.

[I. P. GROSSI]

ZIMARA, MARCO ANTONIO

Renaissance philosopher of the Paduan Averroist School; b. San Pietro di Galatina (Lecce) *c.* 1470; d. Padua, 1532. Of humble origin, he was sent by an uncle, a priest, to Padua, where he acquired a remarkable encyclopedic education and in 1501 received the doctorate in arts. He devoted his life to intensive publishing activity, compiling numerous treatises and editing the works of the most discussed philosophers of the time, including AVERROËS, St. ALBERT THE GREAT, HARVEY NEDELLEC, and JOHN OF JANDUN. In 1509, because of the war against Venice, he withdrew from Padua; in 1514 he was in his native town; in 1519 he taught at Salerno; in 1523 he was professor of metaphysics at the Conventual studium in Naples; in 1525 the Venetian Senate recalled him to Padua for three years; and from then on nothing is known of his activities. An expert on the entire *Corpus Aristotelicum* and the commentaries of Averroës, Zimara is of importance for his exposition and defense of ARISTOTELIANISM from the Averroistic point of view, against the errors of the Bolognese School, who espoused the cause of SIGER OF BRABANT, and later those of the so-called Simplicians, who followed the interpretation of the *De anima* by Simplicius. His most significant works are the *Solutiones contradictionum in dictis Averrois* (Venice 1508) and the *Tabula et dilucidationes in dicta Aristotelis et Averrois* (Venice 1537).

See Also: RENAISSANCE PHILOSOPHY.

Bibliography: G. SAITTA, *Il pensiero italiano nell'Umanesimo e nel Rinascimento,* 3 v. (Bologna 1949–51) v.2. B. NARDI, *Saggi sull'Aristotelismo Padovano dal secolo XIV al XVI* (Florence 1958) 321–363. F. CORVINO, "Le lezione di M. A. Zimara *In primum Posteriorum,*" *Atti del XII Congresso Internazionale di Filosofia* 9 (1960) 41–51.

[A. POPPI]

ZIMBABWE, THE CATHOLIC CHURCH IN

Formerly known as Southern Rhodesia, the Republic of Zimbabwe is an inland country in southern Africa, bordering Zambia on the northwest, Mozambique on the northeast and east, South Africa on the south and Botswana on the southwest and west. A plateau region possessing a tropical climate, Zimbabwe's high veld (plateau) rises in the center, while mountains stretch across to the east. The Victoria Falls are located at the country's northwest corner. Natural resources include coal, chromium, asbestos, gold, nickel, iron ore, copper, lithium and tin; agricultural products, grown in the veld region, consist of cotton, corn, tobacco, wheat, coffee, sugarcane, peanuts and livestock, although recurrent drought conditions make farming difficult.

Named after the British businessman Cecil Rhodes, the region formerly known as Rhodesia was explored by the British late in the 19th century, and it became a colony administered by Rhodes's British South Africa Company until 1923. The region was self-governing as part of the British Commonwealth, and from 1954 to 1963 it was part of the Federation of Rhodesia and Nyasaland. In 1965 the white government declared its independence from Great Britain and rejected political participation by blacks. In 1979, following U.N. sanctions and a militant uprising, the right wing government recognized the principle of black majority rule. In 1979 the government promulgated a new constitution and Robert Mugabe was elected prime minister of an independent Zimbabwe; the name was taken from that of an ancient city in the region. While tribal differences continued between Shona (Mugabe) and Ndebele (Joshua Nkomo), they were resolved by 1987 and the state of emergency was lifted in 1990. Mugabe retained control into 2000, as a severe drought and the AIDS epidemic continued to take its toll on the country. A land reform program instituted in 2001 further hurt the economy by forcing tenant farmers out of work when the government confiscated lands owned by whites.

History. The first attempt to evangelize the area was made in 1560 by the Portuguese missionary Gonçalo da Silveira, who followed the Zambezi River and established a mission in the region then known as Monomotapa. After baptizing a local chief and a few others, he was slain in 1561. Endeavors by later missionaries to reach this section were unsuccessful. In 1759 the mission was

---

Capital: Harare (formerly Salisbury).
Size: 150,333 sq. miles.
Population: 11,342,520 in 2000.
Languages: English, Shona, Sindebele; numerous tribal dialects are spoken in various regions.
Religions: 1,158,020 Catholics (10%), 145,500 Muslims (1%), 1,587,900 Protestants (14%), 5,671,260 syncretic (part Christian, part indigenous) (50%), 2,779,840 follow indigenous beliefs.
Archdioceses: Bulawago, with suffragans Gweru, Swange, and Masvingo; Harare, with suffragans Chinhoyi, Gokwe, and Mutare.

---

formally abandoned. Not until 1879 was a Zambezi mission successfully reopened; it encompassed all of Rhodesia, much of Zambia and part of Mozambique. The Jesuits, who had charge of the mission, were well received by the Matabele chief Lobengula, but they were unable to begin missionary activity before his death in 1893. Thereafter progress was steady and the hierarchy was established in 1955 with Salisbury (now Harare) as archdiocese and metropolitan see for the country.

Independence. In 1965 Prime Minister Ian Smith made a declaration of independence from Great Britain that was followed in 1969 by a new constitution designed to maintain the white governing elite. In a country where the racial imbalance was on the order of 20 blacks to one white, this was unjust, and was duly pronounced as such by Church leaders. Exacerbating the problem were several other factors. One was economic: land ownership was divided almost equally between blacks and whites, resulting in the fact that the black population, most of whom were landless, were relegated to the lower economic classes. The other factor stemmed from the fact that the country's borders—arbitrarily drawn—contained two broad ethnic/linguistic groups, the Ndebele and the Shona, as well as several minor tribal groups, which made political unity difficult. The conflict that was sparked by Smith's move was not simply black vs. white, but was complicated by tribal rivalries. By 1972 black nationalist leaders, Joshua Nkomo and Robert Mugabe, were leading guerrilla forces in what would become a seven-year civil war against the Smith regime.

During the civil war, the work of the Church was severely hampered and, in some areas, brought to a standstill. Missionaries in the villages remained supportive of guerilla forces, supplying them with food and medical supplies, with the consequence that some missions were the focus of government attack. Because of the increasing danger from both sides in the conflict, many missions were abandoned until peace was restored in 1979.

The concern of the Catholic Church for issues of social justice during the 1970s were expressed through the

ZIMBABWE

0 25 50 75 100 125 150 Miles

0 25 50 75 100 125 150 Kilometers

work of the Catholic Commission for Justice and Peace, an arm of the bishops' conference. The commission's episcopal chairman, Bishop Donal Lamont, was expelled from the country in 1977 after his Rhodesian citizenship was withdrawn because of his criticism of government policies. The commission accumulated evidence that government security forces used various propaganda tactics to repress its critics, even disguising government security personnel as guerillas. This tactic caused the guerillas to be blamed for inhumane treatment of villagers.

In 1979, after a civil war during which over 25,000 people lost their lives, a settlement was reached between Prime Minister Smith and three black leaders: Bishop Abel Muzorewa, the Reverend Ndabaningi Sithole and Chief Jeremiah Chirau. These four men constituted an executive office during a transition period, which ended when a new constitution was promulgated and general

elections were held. On April 18, 1980 the country proclaimed its independence as Zimbabwe, with former rebel leader Robert Mugabe, himself a practicing Roman Catholic, being elected as prime minister. Church schools, which were nationalized by the new government, were eventually returned to their founders due to inadequate resources. Although friction continued during the next seven years as Mugabe and rival rebel leader Joshua Nkomo battled over tribal differences, the two were reconciled when their political factions merged in 1987. That same year the country held its first free elections, in which Prime Minister Mugabe was also elected executive president. In 1997 a report was published by the country's bishops detailing human rights abuses perpetrated by the government from 1981 to 1987. Elections in 2000 were preceded by violence directed primarily against Mugabe's detractors during which 32 people were killed.

Into the 21st Century. By 2000 there were 142 parishes, tended by 148 diocesan and 270 religious priests. Other religious, which included approximately 100 brothers and 1,000 sisters, directed the country's hospitals, dispensaries and orphanages. In addition, religious served as teachers in Zimbabwe's 72 primary and 56 secondary schools, as well as at the Catholic University in Harare. Chief among the Church's concerns by 2000 was the spread of AIDS, which infected one out of every four citizens, reduced the life expectancy of the average Zimbabwean to 37 years of age, and had created orphans of almost a million infants and young children by 1999. The infection rate was the highest in the world, in part because the belief system of several indigenous faiths required healing by prayer rather than through modern medicine. Members of several Christian churches completed a long-running project, translating the Bible into the majority language Shona, in 2000.

Bibliography: S. C. RUPERT and R. K. RASMUSSEN *Historical Dictionary of Zimbabwe* (Metuchen, NJ 2001). P. MASON, *The Birth of a Dilemma: The Conquest and Settlement of Rhodesia* (New York 1982). C. F. HALLENCREUTZ, *Religion and Politics in Harare, 1890–1980* (New York 1982). N. BHEBE, *Christianity and Traditional Religion in Western Zimbabwe, 1859–1923* (Harare 1975). *Bilan du Monde*, 2:735–744. *Annuario Pontificio* has annual data on all dioceses.

[J. F. O'DONOHUE/EDS.]

ZIMMER, PATRICK

Anti-Kantian philosopher and theologian; b. Württemberg, Feb. 22, 1752; d. Landshut, Oct. 16, 1820. After his ordination (1775) he taught dogmatic theology at Dillingen (1783–95). There he was a colleague of the famous J. M. SAILER, with whom he also taught at Ingolstadt and Landshut, and who, upon Zimmer's death, wrote his biography and an appreciation of his work. Zimmer's pastorate at Steinheim was given as the reason for his removal from Dillingen, although the real reason seems to have been opposition to his philosophical ideas. He died as rector of the University of Landshut and a deputy to the Bavarian Parliament. His eloquence and enthusiastic teaching drew many students to his courses. Personally he was always sincerely orthodox in his belief and generous both to his doctrinal adversaries and to the poor. His writings are somewhat vitiated by excessive theoretical adherence to the pantheistic notions of F. SCHELLING. His chief works were: *Theologiae Christianae theoreticae systema* (Dillingen 1787), *Theologia Christiana dogmatica* (2 v. Vienna 1789–90), and *Theologia Christiana specialis* (4 v. Landshut 1802–06).

Bibliography: H. HURTER, *Nomenclator literarius theologiae catholicae* 5.1:647–649. J. MERCIER, *Dictionnaire de théologie catholique* 15.2:3694.

[A. ROCK]

ZINZENDORF, NIKOLAUS LUDWIG VON

German religious reformer; b. Dresden, May 26, 1700; d. Herrnhut, May 6, 1760. Zinzendorf was one of the most striking and influential leaders of the Protestant world in the 18th century. He was chiefly responsible for reviving the old Church of the Czech Brethren, later renamed the Moravian Church. Zinzendorf came from an old Austrian Lutheran noble family that had achieved landed wealth in Upper Lusatia. As a student he came under the influence of A. H. Francke and of the Halle school of Lutheran Pietism. Later, as a student at Utrecht, he made Calvinist contacts, and when visiting in Paris, he approached members of the French episcopate, among them Cardinal de Noailles, with whom he maintained a lengthy correspondence. In 1722 he received on his Lusatian estate of Herrnhut (The Lord's Protection) a number of refugees from Bohemia and Moravia who had maintained much of the teachings of the Czech Brethren. Their coming acquainted Zinzendorf with the history and theology of the Unitas Fratrum, though these had already had some influence upon earlier Pietism through the medium of the work of J. A. COMENIUS. It was Comenius's grandson Daniel Arnost Jablonsky (himself a bishop of the still surviving Polish Unitas) who in 1735 ordained the Moravian immigrant Nitzschmann and two years later Zinzendorf himself as bishops of the restored Church of the Brethren. As such, the Herrnhut group as well as a number of daughter communities in Prussia, the Netherlands, and England were recognized by the Prussian King Frederick William I as well as by Dr. Potter, Archbishop of Canterbury, as an ''ancient Protestant Episcopal Church.'' In England and especially in the regions of the Americas, under Zinzendorf's active direction and participation, the Moravians soon undertook a vigorous and widespread missionary activity. Zinzendorf visited the American colonies and founded Bethlehem, Pa., in 1741. His meeting with John Wesley (in 1738 and later) ended in disagreement, but Wesley was influenced by Zinzendorf's disciple Peter Böhler and Methodism soon reflected Moravian piety. Zinzendorf's pietistic theology with its often overemotional aspects, at times taking the character of a specific mystical veneration of Christ's wounds, differed considerably from the quieter, more ethically oriented teachings of the older Unitas Fratrum. Both emphasized strong and joyous Christocentrism; and the congregational character of the movement, with its

Exterior of stone building identified as site of the Last Supper, or Cenacle, Jerusalem. (©Richard T. Nowitz/CORBIS)

emphasis on communal cooperation, maintained much of the old heritage. Zinzendorf's ecumenical church policy failed to end sectarian disagreements. He could not even prevent an open break with the Lutheran church, within whose framework he had hoped to keep the Moravian church as a sort of daughter organization. Yet when he died in 1760, exhausted, partly at least, from years of overwork in the service of his church, the survival of the Moravian church as a small but spiritually and educationally strong and creative religious group was assured.

Bibliography: J. T. MÜLLER, *Zinzendorf als Erneuerer der alten Brüderkirche* (Leipzig 1900). O. STEINECKE, *Zinzendorf und der Katholicismus* (Halle 1902). O. PFISTER, *Die Frömmigkeit des Grafen Ludwig von Zinzendorf* (2d ed. Vienna 1925), a psychological study. J. R. WEINLICK, *Count Zinzendorf* (Nashville 1956). R. A. KNOX, *Enthusiasm* (New York 1961).

[F. G. HEYMANN]

ZION

Originally the name of the Jebusite fortress in Jerusalem, later applied to other sections of the city or to the whole city of JERUSALEM, and in the New Testament used of the heavenly Jerusalem.

Origin of the Term. The etymology of the word Zion (Heb. ṣîyôn) is uncertain. If it comes from a Semitic root, this may be the root ṣyw (to be dry), and ṣîyôn would then mean bleak hill; or the root may be ṣyn (to protect) and the name would then mean stronghold. It has also been suggested that the name is derived from the Hurrian word ṣeya, meaning running water and thus connected originally with the strong Spring of Gibon at the foot of Mt. Zion.

Location. Originally Zion referred to the Jebusite fortress at Jerusalem that David captured and renamed the City of David (2 Sm 5.7–9). It is archeologically certain that this was the section of the southeastern hill of the later enlarged Jerusalem, the region known also as Ophel (hillock, or citadel: Is 32.14; Mi 4.8), south of the Temple area (Josephus, *Bell. Jud.* 5.4.2). Later, Zion, or Mt. Zion, was often used as a poetic synonym for the whole city of Jerusalem, especially in the Prophets and Psalms, both names being frequently used in poetic parallelism (Is 2.3; 4.3; 30.19; 37.32; Jl 3.5; etc.). The poetic expression ''(virgin) daughter of Zion'' (Is 1.8; 10.32; 37.32; etc.) means simply ''(virgin) daughter Zion,'' i.e., Zion personified as a woman. Since Yahweh loved Mt. Zion [Ps 77(78).68] and chose it as His dwelling place

(Is 8.18; 18.7), Mt. Zion was used at times poetically for the Temple [Ps 19(20).3;133(134).2–3]. Hence, in Maccabean times Mt. Zion had become a topological term for the Temple area as distinct from the City of David (1 Mc 7.32–33) on which the Syrians had built their citadel (1 Mc 1.35). According to Josephus the latter was not on the southeastern but on the southwestern hill of Jerusalem (*Ant.* 7.3.1–2).

Early Christian tradition, however, located Mt. Zion on Jerusalem's southwestern hill, not only because of the wrong identification witnessed to by Josephus, but also because the CENACLE and the early events of the Church had made this hill especially sacred to Christians. Since the Church was regarded as the true Zion, its birthplace, the southwestern hill of Jerusalem, was known to the pilgrims of the 4th and later centuries as Christian Zion; and in the 4th century Bp. John of Jerusalem erected a basilica called *Sancta Sion* over the Cenacle. Consequently, Herod's palace on the northwest hill of Jerusalem (completely outside the preexilic city) became known as the Tower of David, and a spurious Tomb of David is still venerated near the Cenacle.

Figurative Usage. In the New Testament, Mt. Zion and Jerusalem are blended more and more into one concept dealing with the spiritual ideal and supernatural reality of New Testament times. Mt. Zion is represented as the place and Jerusalem as the capital city of the New Testament kingdom of God. In Gal 4.21–31 St. Paul makes reference to the Zion-Jerusalem concept. The contrast between the slavery of HAGAR and the freedom of Sarah illustrates the difference between the Old and New Covenants. The Old Covenant was established on Mt. Sinai, ''which corresponds to the present Jerusalem'' (Gal 4.25), the center of Judaism at Paul's time. But the New Covenant is not limited to the place of its birth, for it is ''that Jerusalem which is above'' that ''is free'' (Gal 4.26). It is the fulfillment of the ideal Jerusalem of which Isaiah spoke (Is 2.3) and which enjoys a God-given freedom and richness. It is a renewed Jerusalem enjoying the favor of God after its years of suffering affliction and a foreign yoke.

Zion is named in Heb 12.22 as the mount on which the Covenant of Mt. Sinai gave way to the Covenant based on Christ's sacrificial death: ''But you have come to Mount Zion and to the city of the living God, the heavenly Jerusalem.'' Here the heavenly mountain and the heavenly city are described as the haven of the company of many thousands of angels and the community of the firstborn who are enrolled in the heavens. Zion, the heavenly Jerusalem, is already present, for it is the community. The mountain is the firm foundation on which the new way of life rests. St. John closes his Revelation with a vision of the heavenly Jerusalem. In figurative language he describes how paradise returns to earth in the heavenly Jerusalem. He sees the fantastic city coming down from heaven to earth, and those marked with the sign of God and the Holy City enjoy the rights of citizenship in the new order. According to the eschatological hope of Judaism the Jerusalem of the final days would have a Temple of the Lord. But not so the Jerusalem that John sees in the Revelation. This new Jerusalem has no Temple, for the Lord God and the Lamb are its Temple.

Bibliography: D. CORREA, *De significatione montis Sion in Sacra Scriptura* (Rome 1954). *Encyclopedic Dictionary of the Bible,* translated and adapted by L. HARTMAN (New York 1963) 2241–46.

[S. MUSHOLT]

ZIRC, ABBEY OF

A Cistercian monastery in the Diocese of Veszprém, Hungary, founded by CLAIRVAUX ABBEY (1182) under King Béla III. In 1526 the Turks left Zirc in ruins for almost 200 years, destroying many of the records of its past. It became a commendatory abbey in 1609, was attached to the Cistercians of LILIENFELD in 1659, and in 1699 joined with those of Heinrichau (Silesia), who restored it. The new baroque church was consecrated in 1752. Zirc became independent in 1810 when Heinrichau was suppressed. In 1814 it incorporated Pilis (founded 1184) and Pásztó (founded 1190). With the addition of St. Gotthard (founded 1184) in 1878, Zirc became the most prosperous Cistercian congregation. In 1776 the abbey took over Jesuit *gymnasia,* and thereafter the monks devoted themselves to education, eventually caring for five schools, as well as 15 parishes. The abbey's great prosperity ended with World War II. The Communist regime confiscated the estates, secularized the schools (1948), and in 1950 suppressed Zirc and its affiliated institutions. Monks from Zirc in 1958 founded the Abbey of Our Lady of Dallas in Texas; it is affiliated with the University of Dallas.

Bibliography: U. CHEVALIER, *Répertoire des sources historiques du moyen-âge. Biobibliographie,* 2 v. (2d. ed. Paris 1905–07) 2:3380. L. H. COTTINEAU, *Répertoire topobibliographique des abbayes et prieurés,* 2 v. (Mâcon 1935–39) 2:3483. K. HORVÁTH, *Schematismus Congregationis de Zirc* (Budapest 1942); *Lexikon für Theologie und Kirche,* ed. M. BUCHBERGER, 10 v. (Freiburg 1930–38)[1] 10:1076–77.

[L. J. LEKAI]

ZITA, ST.

Virgin; b. Monsagrati, near Lucca, Italy, 1218; d. Lucca, April 27, 1278. At 12 Zita, reared religiously by poor, devout parents, entered the service of the Fatinelli family of Lucca, where she remained until her death. She performed her duties faithfully, and in addition rose at night for prayer, daily attended early Mass, fasted often, and distributed her portion of food to the poor. Although mistreated by her fellow servants, she at length overcame their envy by her humility and charity and became a friend and adviser of the whole family. She was buried in the church of San Frediano at Lucca. About May 1278 public veneration to Zita was authorized by the bishop of Lucca. Her coffin, opened in 1446, 1581, and 1652, revealed her body intact. Innocent XII confirmed her cult Sept. 5, 1696. She was declared patroness of domestic workers Sept. 26, 1953.

Feast: April 27.

Bibliography: *Acta Sanctorum* (Paris 1863—) 3:502–532. BENEDICT XIV, *De servorum Dei beatificatione et beatorum canonizatione,* v.1–7 of *Opera omnia,* 17 v. in 20 (Prato 1839–47) bk. 2, ch. 24, sec. 25. H. DELEHAYE et al., eds., *Propylaeum ad Acta Sanctorum Decembris* (Brussels 1940) 158–159. J. L. BAUDOT and L. CHAUSSIN, *Vies des saints et des bienheureux selon l'ordre du calendrier avec l'historique des fêtes,* ed. by the Benedictines of Paris, (Paris 1935–56) 4:675–679. A. BUTLER, *The Lives of the Saints,* rev. ed. H. THURSTON and D. ATTWATER (New York 1956) 2:173–174. E. REGGIO, *A Saint in the Kitchen; A Story of Saint Zita* (Notre Dame, Ind. 1955).

[M. G. MCNEIL]

ŽIŽKA, JOHN

Hussite leader; b. Trocnov *c.* 1358; d. Pribyslav (Czech.), Oct. 11, 1424. A member of the landed gentry, Žižka learned the art of war in the expedition of Emperor WENCESLAUS against the TEUTONIC KNIGHTS. As a royal courtier (1411–19) he became interested in the religious issues of the day. At the outbreak of the Hussite revolution under John Želivský (1419), he took charge of its military action. Seeing himself as *Zelator praecipuus* of the law of Christ, he considered his enemies "those who did not take the Body and Blood of Christ in both kinds," including the Emperor SIGISMUND, Germans, Catholics, compromising UTRAQUISTS, and extremists such as the PICARDS. In 1420 he assumed leadership of the radical HUSSITES, the TABORITES, transforming their theocratic community of Tabor into a military unit. Numerous victories brought him recognition (1422) as commander-in-chief of all Hussite forces. Although he represented a practical and political, rather than a moral, power he insisted on the *Four Articles of Prague* as a unifying factor for preserving the strength of the Hussites. When extremists became too influential at Tabor, he turned to the Orebites, transferring his army to Hradec Kralové (1423), known since as Lesser Tabor. From there he continued his militant defense of the "cause of the chalice." Recent research pictures him not as a radical adventurer, but as a leader conscious of the religious, national, and social issues at stake.

Bibliography: J. PEKAŘ, *Žižka a jeho doba,* 4 v. (Prague 1927–33). F. G. HEYMANN, *John Žižka and the Hussite Revolution* (Princeton 1955).

[L. NEMEC]

ZOBOR, ABBEY OF

Near Nitra, Slovakia. According to a tradition reported by Cosmas of Prague (d. 1125), it was founded *c.* 880 by Bp. Viching of Nitra, formerly a Benedictine, endowed by Prince Svatopluk, and settled by Benedictines as St. Hippolytus Abbey. The first historical notice dates from *c.* 1000. SS. ZOËRARDUS AND BENEDICT received monastic training here, and Benedict's martyrdom at Skalka in 1012 made Zobor a national shrine that flourished until 1468, when the bishop of Nitra dispersed the monks and occupied the abbey. In 1691 Bp. Jalkin of Nitra restored Zobor and gave it to Camaldolese monks, but Emperor JOSEPH II suppressed it in 1782. In 1936 Bp. K. Kmetko of Nitra rebuilt it as a novitiate for Divine Word missionaries, but in 1950 Communists suppressed it.

Bibliography: L. H. COTTINEAU, *Répertoire topobibliographique des abbayes et prieurés,* 2 v. (Mâcon 1935–39) 2:3483. B. HRIN, "Benedictine Monasteries in Slovakia," *Slovak Studies* 1 (1961) 51–60.

[L. NEMEC]

ZOËRARDUS AND BENEDICT, SS.

Hermits of Zobor, Hungary (the former known also as Svorad-Andrew or Andrej-Svorad), fl. *c.* 1000. Zoërardus came to Slovakia from Poland during the reign of King (St.) STEPHEN. He became a monk in ZOBOR, which until the 15th century was the center of Benedictine life in Slovakia. With his disciple, Benedict (Stojislav), he led a combined eremitico-cenobitical life in the cave of Skalka in the Diocese of Nitra. It is uncertain whether he was a Benedictine or Camaldolese monk. He excelled in mortification and penance; chains embedded in his flesh witnessed to his self-inflicted chastisement. His disciple was martyred three years after his master's death. He was strangled by robbers and thrown into the River Váh (Waag) in 1012. The relics of both holy hermits are preserved in the cathedral of Nitra, and both were proclaimed patrons of the diocese. St. Svorad-Andrew is patron of some well-known Slovak institutions, e.g.,

Svoradov in Bratislava and St. Andrew's Benedictine abbey in Cleveland, Ohio, spiritual center of the Slovaks in America. The cultus of Zoërardus and Benedict was approved in 1083.

Feast: July 17.

Bibliography: M. KAPISZEWSKI, ''Czerty źróda do źyvota Św. Świrada,'' *Nasza Przeszlosc* 19 (1964) 5–31, sketches of St. Svorad's Life. *Acta sanctorum* (Paris 1863—) 4:326–338. J. MELICH, *Collectanea Theologica* 15 (1934) 438–448. M. ŠPRINC, *Sv. Andrej-Svorad* (*St. Andrew-Svorad*) (Cleveland 1952). A. ZIMMERMANN, *Lexikon für Theologie und Kirche*, ed. M. BUCHBERGER (Freiburg 1930–38) 10:1086–87. A. M. ZIMMERMANN, *Kalendarium Benedictinum: Die Heiligen und Seligen des Benediktinerorderns und seiner Zweige* (Metten 1933–38) 2:445, 447–448. S. SÓLYMOS, *Szent Zoerard-András (Szórád) és Benedek remet ék élete és kultusza Magyarországon* (Budapest 1996).

[J. PAPIN]

ZOHAR

Principal literary production of the Jewish CABALA, mostly in the form of comments on parts of the Hebrew Bible. The term (Heb. *zōhar,* brightness) is taken from Ez 8.2: Dn 12.3.

Origin and Contents. The origin of the Zohar is shrouded in mystery. Toward the end of the 13th century a Spanish-Jewish mystic, Moses ben Shemtob de Leon (1250–1305), introduced the Zohar to the public, and at once there arose legends concerning its origin. Moses de Leon himself spoke of finding an ancient manuscript the authorship of which he attributed to Rabbi Simeon ben Yoḥai (or, bar Yochai), but his widow later denied the existence of such a manuscript and called her husband the real author of the Zohar. The controversy has continued ever since. Many great cabalists, among them contemporaries of the ''discoverer,'' subscribed to the authenticity of the Zohar, which they regarded as a deposit of mystical revelation at least equal to the written Law (the Bible) and the oral Law (the TALMUD). On the other hand, notable historians, particularly H. Graetz, have held the Zohar to be a forgery of Moses de Leon.

Viewed as a work of literature, the Zohar has no unity. The Zohar proper, the second part of the whole four-part work, is a midrash (*see* MIDRASHIC LITERATURE) on the Mosaic Law in the form of conversations between Simeon ben Yoḥai, a famous but mysterious Tanna (Mishnaic rabbi) of the 2d century, and his students on the mysteries of God and creation. The first part of the work is called *midrāš hanne'ēlām* (Interpretation of What Is Hidden); the third part, *rā'ayā meḥemenā'* (The Faithful Shepherd); the fourth part, *tiqqūnnê hazzōhor* (Emendations on the Zohar). The second (main) part con-

tains the *sipra' diṣenyūta'* (The Book of Mysteries) on the mysteries of creation in the form of *baraita,* the *idra' rabba'* (Large Assembly) and the *idra' zutā'* (Small Assembly), which contain dramatic accounts of mystic experiences, and other fragments, such as the *sitrê tôrâ* (Mysteries of the Law).

The language of the Zohar is Aramaic, with wide stylistic variations in the various parts of the work from the abbreviated, fragmented Talmudic style to a literary homiletic one. The vocabulary, in which neologisms are not wanting, is, however, rather poor compared to the Talmudic literature. The syntax and construction are strongly influenced by medieval rabbinical Hebrew.

Could the basis of the Zohar be (as in the case of ancient rabbinical literature) older documents that were gathered by one or more compilers and supplemented? This was long considered a very probable thesis. Professor G. Scholem of Jerusalem distinguishes in the composite work three redactional strata, of which at least two have the same author.

Leaving aside the question of authorship, in which regard Moses de Leon has recently again come into the foreground, it can be said that the Zohar, with all its lack of unity, is an elaborate synthesis of very old mystic-esoteric traditions in Judaism. The beginnings of such traditions can be found in the more recent Biblical literature, they become more common in the apocryphal and apocalyptical literature, and they have their undisputed place in the Mishnah and the Gemara. To this are to be added philosophical and mystical elements from the Hellenistic sphere and Gnostic speculation. After an initial appearance in Babylonia, cabalistic literature came into the open with the Book of Bahir (Splendor) and the Book of YEṢIRAH (creation), and then spread both to Germany, where a special school of mysticism arose, and to Spain. In the latter country mysticism came in contact with religious philosophy, and from Spain it finally passed to southern France, where, in the circle of Isaac the Blind (*c.* 1200), it developed into the cabalistic system, which has been employed as the basis of the Zohar.

Doctrine. Any attempt to present a consistent treatment of the doctrine of the Zohar and its supplementary tracts meets with difficulty because of the entirely unsystematic character of the work. Contrary to the traditional rabbinical notion, the Zohar assumes, in the realm of divine activity, variously graded powers, whose inner unity is established in an unreachably distant divine principle, the *'ên sôph* (the endless, infinite).

Since, in this perspective, creation cannot be considered the work of the divine prime principle, which, by definition, is static, the Zohar solves the difficulty by introducing a series of emanations through which, in the last instance, the passage from the prime principle to the created world is effected. The cosmic creation proceeds (analogously with Philo's LOGOS) from the first creature (*Adam qadmon,* First Man) and is effected in the four streams of creative power: *Aṣîlut* (emanation), *Ber'iah* (creating), *Yeṣîrah* (forming), and *'Aśiyah* (making). Before the present created world, in which man is the focal point, there existed other worlds, which have passed away and which, allegorically with haggadic reminiscences, are termed Kings of Edom.

The world of the *Aṣîlut* unfolds itself in the ten *Sephirot,* whose creative spiritual channels are concentrated in the 6th *Sephirah, Tiph'eret* (beauty), in order to arrive at visible creation in the 10th, *Malkut* (kingdom). Within the *Sephirot,* which all have various names, there are manifold structures and combinations, among which are a "most high trinity," which is often likened to the Plotinic trinity, and the constellation of the "three columns"—right, middle, and left column. The left column embodies the negative element, the *sitrā ăḥērā* (other side), the world of evil, while the right column embodies the positive element. The mutual relations between the positive and negative powers are often presented in the Zohar by the image of the relationship between the two sexes.

The center of all creation is man, who, as a microcosm in his structure, reflects the structure of the macrocosm. The souls of all mankind were contained in Adam's soul. Through the fall of man the human image was darkened; but through the divine plan for salvation, as expressed especially in the covenant of Sinai, man's reascent was initiated, and it will find its glorious completion in the Messiah. Since there is a mysterious relationship of exchange between the higher and lower worlds, man can exercise influence on the higher world by the purity of his intention (*kawwānah*).

Other peculiarities of the Zohar's teachings are transmigration of souls (*gilgul*), which is foreign to rabbinical literature, the large space that the Zohar gives to the world of the angels with its manifold gradations, and the significance that the Zohar gives to the letters of the Hebrew Bible as the direct results of the substantial sounds based on the "primeval sound." The mysticism of letters and numbers that follows from this idea is often used exegetically in the Zohar.

In the course of the centuries the Zohar became the true Bible of the cabalists, especially from the time of Isaac LURIA (1534–72) and the cabalistic circle founded by him at Safed. As early as 1557 it first appeared in print. From the time of Luria on, all Jewish life fell more and more under the influence of the cabala in the form pro-

posed by him. This was effective particularly in Jewish prayers, in which texts borrowed from the Zohar and its world of ideas gradually spread a luxuriant growth over the old trunk of the ancient prayers. Even in modern times, the traditional prayer book of the Synagogue has preserved many such elements.

After the study of the Zohar had fallen into discredit in rabbinical circles as a result of the spiritual confusion caused by the disturbances of SHABBATAIÏSM, it experienced a revival in the Hasidic movement (*see* HASIDISM) and it is still highly regarded in the eastern communities of the Jews.

The Zohar has always been of great interest to Christian authors also, chiefly because of the points of agreement that it contains (or is interpreted to contain) with Christian concepts, such as the Trinity and messianism. The Zohar has been repeatedly translated into other languages, though mostly in the form of excerpts.

Bibliography: G. G. SCHOLEM, *Major Trends in Jewish Mysticism* (3d ed. New York 1954; repr. pa. 1961) 156–243. H. SPERLING et al., trs., *The Zohar,* 5 v. (London 1931–34).

[K. HRUBY]

ZOÏLUS OF ALEXANDRIA

Chalcedonian patriarch, 540 to 551. He was a Palestinian monk, chosen patriarch of Alexandria by the Apocrisiarius Pelagius (later pope) after the deposition of Paul of Tabennisi at the Council of Gaza (540). He was a staunch Catholic, though not learned, and pursued the anti-Monophysite policies of his predecessor. Compelled to sign the Edict of JUSTINIAN I against the Three Chapters in 543 or 544, he sent two messengers to Pope VIGILIUS at Catania in Sicily early in 546 to protest that he had complied only under pressure and to excuse his weakness. He was forced to flee Alexandria during a local revolt and took refuge in Constantinople, where in July 551 Justinian had him deposed because of his refusal to condemn the THREE CHAPTERS.

Bibliography: J. MASPERO, *Histoire des patriarches d'Alexandrie* (Paris 1923) 150–156. E. STEIN, *Histoire du Bas-Empire,* tr. J. R. PALANQUE, 2 v. in 3 (Paris 1949–59), 2:391, 628, 637, 640, 647.

[V. RICCI]

ZOLA, GUISEPPE

Jansenist theologian; b. Concessio (near Brescia), 1739; d. same place, Nov. 5, 1806. He led a very agitated life and followed the politico-religious movements of the times. As a young man he was named professor of moral theology at the seminary of Brescia. He became a very close friend of Pietro Tamburini and with him championed the ideas of C. O. JANSEN and Richer in Northern Italy. Both Zola and Tamburini were relieved of their teaching duties in 1771 by the bishop of Brescia, because of their Jansenistic rigorism. Zola, called to Rome, was reinstated through the intervention of Cardinal Marefoschi. In 1774 he went to Pavia to teach Church history and to be director of the German College, which Joseph II had transferred there to serve as a general seminary. Upon the death of the emperor the Lombard bishops reestablished the episcopal seminaries in their dioceses and once again dismissed Zola and Tamburini. After the French invasion and the annexation of the Cisalpine Republic to France by Bonaparte (1796–99), Zola occupied the chair of diplomatic law at Pavia. He was interrupted by the brief return of the Austrians (1799–1800), but again reinstated after the victory of Marengo and the formation of the kingdom of Italy. His principal works were: *Theologicarum praelectionum specimen* (Brescia 1775), placed on the Index in 1797, and *De locis theologiae moralis* (Pavia 1785).

Bibliography: H. HURTER, *Nomenclator literarius theologiae catholicae* 5:710. A. MERCATI and A. PELZER, *Dizionario ecclesiastico* 3:1405.

[P. BROUTIN]

ZOLLI, EUGENIO

Semitic scholar, chief Rabbi of Rome, and convert to Catholicism; b. Brody, Austrian Galicia, Sept. 17, 1881; d. Rome, March 2, 1956. His original name was Israel Zoller. After graduating from the University of Florence and the Rabbinical College of that city, he became chief Rabbi of Trieste in 1914, where he changed his name to Zolli. From 1930 to 1938 he taught Hebrew at the University of Padua and in 1940 advanced to the post of chief Rabbi of Rome. When the German army occupied Rome in September 1943, Zolli in vain advised the Jewish community to disperse. Not sharing the optimism of other leaders and under pressure from friends, he himself went into hiding, where he remained effectively active, satisfying, with financial assistance from the Vatican, the ransom that the Germans demanded from the Roman Jews. On Feb. 13, 1945, after Italy had been liberated, Zolli entered the Catholic Church. His conversion attracted international interest, and some of his former coreligionists attributed it to base motives [see L. I. Newman, *A "Chief Rabbi" of Rome Becomes a Catholic: a Study in Fright and Spite* (New York 1945)]. Zolli's baptism, however, was clearly an ultimate result of his ardent interest, evident in his earlier writings, in Jesus Christ. The charity of Pope Pius XII, whose baptismal name he chose, contributed much to his conversion. From 1945 almost until his death he taught Semitics at the University of Rome and the Pontifical Biblical Institute. Best known among Zolli's numerous writings are *Il Nazareno* [(Udine 1938), in English translation, *The Nazarene*, tr. C. Vollert (St. Louis 1950)] and *Before the Dawn: Autobiographical Reflections* (New York 1954).

Bibliography: *Biblica* 37 (1956) 261–262. A. MERCATI and A. PELZER, *Dizionario ecclesiastico* 3:1405–06.

[G. WOOD]

ZONARAS, JOHN

Byzantine historian, canonist; b. toward the end of the 11th century; d. after 1160. After a career as a civil servant and court official under ALEXIUS I COMNENUS, he entered a monastery *c.* 1118 on Hagia Glykeria, in the Princes' Islands, where he wrote his history and other works. His Historical Epitome, recounting events from creation to 1118, stands upon a much higher level than the other Byzantine universal chronicles. Not only did he use sources no longer surviving, such as the complete text of Cassius Dio and several lost Byzantine historians, but he reproduced them in great length and detail, and treated them critically, up to a point. He is thus of value as a source for all periods from the early Roman Empire to his own day. The work was much read, excerpted, and translated—e.g., into Old Slavonic—in the later Middle Ages. His massive commentary on the canons of the Apostles (*see* APOSTOLIC CONSTITUTIONS), the councils and synods, and the Fathers is perhaps the greatest achievement of Byzantine Canon Law. It was closely followed by his 12th-century successors, Alexius Aristenos and Theodore Balsamon. His other works include discussions of particular points of Canon Law, homilies, lives of saints, commentaries on liturgical hymns, and a lexicon. Not all is yet published.

Bibliography: J. ZONARAS, *Epitomae historiarum libri*, ed. M. PINDER, 4 v. (Bonn 1841–97); *Lexicon*, ed. J. A. H. TITTMANN, 2 v. (Leipzig 1808); *Patrologia graeca*, ed. J. P. MIGNE (Paris 1857–66) 137–138, commentary on Canon Law. M. WEINGART, *Byzantské kroniky v literatuře církevněslovanské*, 2 v. (Bratislava 1923) 1:125–159. M. DIMAIO, "Zonaras Ecclesiasticus: Three Source Notes on the Epitome Historiarum," *Greek Orthodox Theological Review* 25 (1980) 77–82. I. GRIGORIADIS, *Linguistic and literary Studies in the Epitome Historion of John Zonaras*, (Thessalonike 1998)

[R. BROWNING/EDS.]

ZOROASTER (ZARATHUSHTRA)

The Greek form of the name of the prophet of ancient Iran. Like all great religious founders or reformers, he early became a legendary figure, endowed with all kinds of miraculous features. Only his hymns, the *GĀTHĀS*, furnish some evidence on him as a historical person, but they are allusive and obscure. According to the native tradition, and there is no sufficient reason to question it, he lived 258 years before Alexander conquered Iran in 331 B.C. No certain data are preserved regarding his birthplace, but the AVESTA seems to imply that his religion appeared first in northeastern Iran, that is, in what is now Afghanistan or perhaps farther north, and that it then spread southward and westward. The *Gāthās* make no allusions to the Babylonian, Greek, or Jewish cultures and completely ignore the Achaemenids. Prince Vishtaspa, whom Zoroaster won over to his new creed, has the same name as the father of Darius, but all attempts that have been made from antiquity to the present to identify the two have failed.

Scholars differ widely in the evaluation of his life, character, and doctrine. On the one hand, he is seen as a kind of primitive sorcerer or shaman, intoxicating himself with hemp fumes; on the other, he is represented as a lofty moralist and social reformer. His hymns receive some clarification from external sources, namely, from the later Zoroastrian tradition—which, however, may have modified his original teaching—or from comparison with the Vedic religion, a comparison that may well fail to do justice to his originality; or, finally, from comparison with the religions of other Indo–European peoples— an approach that is delicate but also rewarding.

The decisive event in the life of Zoroaster appears to have been his conversion of Vishtaspa, his first success after a difficult beginning. He then made converts in the royal court and also in his own family. The legend of his daughter's marriage with one of the great men of the realm may have a historical foundation. Sometimes— probably before he found these mighty protectors— Zoroaster had doubts on the success of his doctrine. On one occasion he ascribed the reason for his failure to the fact that he possessed few cattle and few men. He found consolation in AHURA MAZDA and his justice. He castigated the followers of false religion, the worshipers of the *daēvas*. He denounced in a stern and vivid manner a certain prince who had refused him hospitality and left him standing in the cold with his horses shivering. He preached a kind of holy war against such men.

His own ideas on true teaching and ritual seem to have come from visions in which the holiness and beneficence of Ahura Mazda, the Wise Lord, appeared to him. He is on rather familiar terms with Ahura Mazda, from whom he asks for the help that a friend would give to a friend. The chief tenets of his doctrine are the following. A choice must be made between good and evil, and there is a reward or punishment according to each one's choice and according to his thoughts, words, and actions. There will be a new world in which only the virtuous will have a place. Ahura Mazda, the Wise Lord, is alone worthy of worship, as the creator of light and darkness, heaven and earth, and the universe and its movements, and as the father of *Asha* (justice), *Vohu Manah* (good thought), and *Ārmati* (application). No cult should be given to the *daēvas* (evil spirits); the sacrifice of oxen is forbidden, and that of *haoma* is limited. The cult of fire is to be carried out because fire is an instrument of ordeal and, above all, a symbol of divine justice.

See Also: PERSIAN RELIGION, ANCIENT.

Bibliography: W. HENNING, *Zoroaster: Politician or Witch–Doctor?* (Oxford 195I). W. EILERS, *Die Religion in Geschichte und Gegenwart,* 7 v. (3d ed. Tübingen 1957–65) 6:1866–68, with bibliog. H. HUMBACH, *Die Gâthâs des Zarathustra* (Heidelberg 1960). M. MOLÉ, *Culte, mythe et cosmologie dans l'Iran ancien* (Paris 1963). J. DUCHESNE–GUILLEMIN, *La Religion de l'Iran ancien* (Paris 1962); *Symbols in Zoroastrianism* (New York 1966).

[J. DUCHESNE–GUILLEMIN]

ZOSIMUS, POPE, ST.

Pontificate: March 18, 417 to Dec. 26, 418. The short pontificate of Zosimus was stormy. The *Liber pontificalis* describes him as "of Greek origin, his father was Abram." The last name seems to indicate Jewish ancestry. He may have been recommended to the attention of INNOCENT I by St. JOHN CHRYSOSTOM; but his election seems to have affronted a part of the Roman clergy. The bishop of Arles, Patroclus, was in Rome at the time and seems to have had a hand in the election. In any case the first act of Zosimus was to reward him with a papal vicariate over Gaul on the grounds that St. Trophimus, a disciple of St. Peter, founded the See of Arles. No cleric was to present himself in Rome without a letter of communion from the metropolitan of Arles, who was authorized to consecrate all the bishops of the provinces of Vienne and the two Narbonnes and to decide all cases unless the matter had to be referred to Rome.

Such an arrangement was naturally resented in Gaul. Hilary of Narbonne was threatened by the Pope with excommunication for attempted resistance; Proculus of Marseilles and Simplicius of Vienne were both summoned to appear in Rome but refused to obey, whereupon Proculus was deposed; but Zosimus died before the sentence could be carried out. From a letter to Hesychius of Salona, the metropolitan of Dalmatia, it appears that the

Pope also contemplated erecting a vicariate for western Illyricum.

The Pope's handling of the Pelagian affair seriously if temporarily damaged Roman prestige. Augustine had no sooner uttered his famous words *Causa finita est* than the case of Pelagius was reopened in Rome. Pelagius sent a profession of faith to Innocent I that arrived after the latter's death, but Caelestius came in person to present his *libellus fidei*. Zosimus examined the *libellus* and its author at length in the church of St. Clement and finding no heresy in the statements of either Pelagius or Caelestius, he requested their accusers to appear before him and present their case within two months, although the matter had presumably been closed by Innocent I. The African bishops were naturally outraged and so informed the Pope (November 417).

Zosimus was compelled to reverse his stand, and in his reply, he informed the Africans that he had not yet made up his mind but that meanwhile the decision of his predecessor was to stand. He took the occasion, however, to read the Africans a lecture on the Roman primacy, stressing that "the tradition of the fathers has assigned such great authority to the Apostolic See that no one would dare to dispute its judgment" and asserting that "Peter is the head of such great authority and has confirmed the devotion of all the fathers who followed him, so that the Roman church is established by all laws and discipline, both human and divine. His place we rule. . . . And such being our authority, no one can revise our sentence."

It was a hollow gesture, intended to save face, but the African bishops would have none of it. They went above the pope's head to the Western Emperor Honorius, who issued a rescript condemning Pelagius, Caelestius, and their followers and banishing them as disturbers of the peace (April 30, 418). In a council at Carthage on May 1, 418, the African bishops drafted a letter to Zosimus informing him that they stood by the previous condemnation of Innocent I; and Zosimus then issued his *Epistola Tractoria* condemning PELAGIANISM (H. Denzinger, *Enchiridion symbolorum* 109a).

A new controversy threatened to disrupt relations between Rome and Africa when Zosimus entertained the appeal of an African priest Apiarius, who had been deprived by his bishop, Urbanus of Sicca Veneria. This contravened existing African Canon Law, which forbade such appeals by priests and deacons, though apparently not by bishops. The rule had been confirmed by a canon of the Council of Carthage (418) forbidding appeals to *transmarina iudicia*.

Instead of contenting himself with a letter, Zosimus sent three legates, including the tactless Bp. Faustinus of Potenza, to Africa with instructions demanding that the African bishops should not make such frequent appeals to the imperial court, that bishops were to be allowed to appeal to Rome, that priests and deacons could appeal to the bishops of neighboring sees, and that Urbanus was to be excommunicated unless he corrected the injustice he had caused to Apiarius. Zosimus based his contention regarding the appeals on the canons of the Council of Sardica, which he (and the Roman Church) mistakenly believed to belong to the Council of Nicaea. But since the African church knew these canons to be false, they did not honor the pope's reliance on them. Zosimus died before the Apiarius affair had been settled.

In Rome a section of the Roman clergy who resented the Pope's high-handed actions appealed to the court at Ravenna against him. Zosimus excommunicated his accusers and apparently would have taken sterner measures had he not died after a serious illness. He was buried in the basilica of St. Lawrence-outside-the-Walls; the exact location of his tomb is unknown. Presumably his remains are still there. The ninth-century Martyrology of Ado was the first to list him as a saint.

Feast: Dec. 26.

Bibliography: *Patrologia Latina,* ed. J. P. MIGNE (Paris 1878–90) 20:639–686; *Patrologiae cursus completus, series latina;* ed. A. HAMMAN 1:796–798. *Clavis Patrum latinorum,* ed. E. DEKKERS (2d. ed. Streenbrugge 1961) 1644–47. *Liber pontificalis,* ed. L. DUCHESNE, 1: 225–226 (Paris 1886–92). H. LECLERCQ, *Dictionnaire d'archéologie chrétienne et de liturgie,* ed. F. CHABROL, H. LECLERCQ, and H. I. MARROU, (Paris 1907–53) 13.1:1203. É. AMANN, *Dictionnaire de théologie catholique,* ed. A. VACANT et al., (Paris 1903–50; Tables générales 1951–) 15.2:3708–16. R. U. MONTINI, *Le tombe dei Papi* (Rome 1957) 97–98. J. P. BURNS, "Augustine's Role in the Imperial Action against Pelagius," *Journal of Theological Studies* 30: 67–83. A. DIBERARDINO, *Patrology* (Westminster, Md. 1986) 4:585–586. E. FERGUSON, ed., *Encyclopedia of Early Christianity* (New York 1997) 2:1189–1190. D. FRYE, "Bishops as Pawns in Early Fifth-Century Gaul" *Journal of Ecclesiastical History* 42: 349–361. H. JEDIN, *History of the Church* (New York 1980), 2:259–261. J. N. D. KELLY, *Oxford Dictionary of Popes* (New York 1986) 38–39. J. MERDINGER, *Rome and the African Church* (New Haven 1997) 111–153. C. OCKER, "Augustine, Imperial Interests, and the Papacy in Late Roman Africa," *Journal of Ecclesiastical History* 42: 179–201. C. PIETRI, *Rome Christiana* (Rome 1976) 1212–1258. O. WERMINGLER, *Rome und Pelagius* (Stuttgart 1975). M. E. KULIKOWSKI, "Two Councils of Turin," *The Journal of Theological Studies* 47: 159–68. B. SODARO, *Sant e beati di Calabria* (Rosarno 1996) 57–61.

[J. CHAPIN]

ZOUAVES, PAPAL

A corps of Catholic volunteer soldiers who served in the papal army under this name (1861–70). The army was formed at the beginning of 1860, when the very existence of the STATES OF THE CHURCH was menaced by the new Kingdom of Italy, determined to unify politically the entire peninsula. Pius IX chose one of his close friends, Monsignor de MÉRODE, a former Belgian army officer who had become priest, as minister of arms, with the task of reorganizing the papal army. De Mérode immediately placed in command of these forces Louis de LAMORICIÈRE, former general of the French army in Africa, war minister during the Second Republic, and an admitted political foe of Napoleon III. With an entourage of several legitimist French officers, such as the Marquis de Pimodan, De Charette, Chevigné, and Bourbon-Chalus, he organized in five regiments some 5,000 Austrian light-infantrymen, redistributed the 4,000 Swiss soldiers, formed St. Patrick's battalion of 3,000 Irish volunteers, and formed the French volunteers into a squadron of guides and a half-battalion of infantry. Belgian volunteers were incorporated into this last group. Under the leadership of Cathelineau, who was descended from a hero in the war of the Vendée, there arrived a little later a rather tumultuous French band wearing large crosses on their breasts and called "crusaders." Belgian "crusaders" accompanied them. They were incorporated into Franco-Belgian groups already constituted. This heterogeneous army received its baptism of fire at Castelfidardo (Sept. 18, 1860), where La Moricière maneuvered his troops very poorly and met defeat. His army was disbanded and the Marquis de Pimodan was killed.

The Franco-Belgian volunteers officially assumed the title of papal zouaves on Jan. 1, 1861, thanks to La Moricìre, who took the name from that of a light-infantry corps created for the Algerian wars. After Castelfidardo French Catholic opinion became more and more passionately eager to defend the Pope and his territories. The fallen at Castelfidardo were glorified as heroes and martyrs. Some overzealous bishops who blundered into making martyrs out of the living drew the mockery of the anti-Catholic press.

A lively recruiting program increased zouave members. Some came from as far away as Canada. After the capitulation of Ancona La Moricìre resigned and returned to France. Mérode fell into disgrace and quit his "ministry" in 1865. The papal army was then reorganized in 1865 by General Kanzler, a German. Zouaves were sufficiently numerous to form a regiment under Colonels Alhet and de Charette. Their mission was to prevent the outbreak of revolution in the States of the Church while they awaited the attacks of the Italian armies. This task they fulfilled. New recruits, notably Spanish Carlists, arrived between 1866 and 1870. After the surrender of Rome (Sept. 16, 1870) the papal zouaves were repatriated.

During the Franco-Prussian War (1870–71), De Charette came from Civitavecchia to Marseilles, offered to form a French corps in support of France, and succeeded in organizing the legion of volunteers from the west that fought courageously at Orléans, Patay, and Loigny. In western France the papal zouaves long retained the aureole of crusaders. Catholics had a custom of dressing children as zouaves for Catholic celebrations and processions.

Bibliography: L. A. DE BECDELIÈVRE, *Souvenirs de l'armée pontificate* (Paris 1867). O. DE POLI, *Les Soldats du pape* (4th ed. Paris 1868). F. RUSSELL-KILLOUGH, *Dix années au service pontifical* (Paris 1871). A. C. M. CHARETTE DE LA CONTRIE, *Souvenirs du régiment des zouaves pontificaux: Rome 1860–70, France 1870–71*, 2 v. (Paris 1877–78). R. BITTARD DES PORTES, *Histoire des zouaves pontificaux* (Paris 1894). *Matricule des zouaves pontificaux: Liste des zouaves*, 2 v. (Lille 1920). G. F. BERKELEY, *The Irish Battalion in the Papal Army of 1860* (Dublin 1929). H. DE MOREAU, *Le R. P. Hildebrand de Hemptinne* (Maredsous 1930). *Intermédiaire des chercheurs et curieux* 12 (1962) 440, 1072, 1178; 13 (1963) 54, 709; 14 (1964) 830, 1167, uniforms, families of the zouaves.

[E. JARRY]

ZUMÁRRAGA, JUAN DE

First bishop and archbishop of Mexico; b. Tavira de Durango, Vizcaya, Spain, c. 1468; d. Mexico City, June 3, 1548. Apparently while still young, he entered the Franciscan Order, taking the habit in the province of Concepción, of which he became provincial minister (1520–23). He was appointed first bishop of Mexico on Dec. 12, 1527.

By express order of Charles V, Zumárraga, as bishop elect but without episcopal consecration, embarked for Mexico, where he arrived Dec. 6, 1528. He immediately began to organize his newly established, extensive diocese, whose poorly defined limits extended from Michoacán and Jalisco on the northwest, up to and including Guatemala on the south. The Franciscan and Dominican missionaries who worked zealously on the conversion of the natives were of invaluable assistance in this difficult task of organization. The spiritual needs of the conquistadors and Spanish colonists were entrusted to the secular clergy whose lives, functions, and salaries were regulated by Zumárraga, though not without difficulty. Following the old authorized traditions, the bishop elect played an important role in the verification and approval of the appearances of Our Lady of Guadalupe in Tepeyac, in honor of which he erected the first hermitage (1531).

Protector of the Native Peoples. Zumárraga received the appointment and office of protector and defender of the native peoples. Unfortunately, the civil authorities not only failed to respect the wise provisions

937

made by Zumárraga in favor of the native peoples, but even impeded by force the exercise of his office of protector. Therefore Zumárraga excommunicated them and placed Mexico City under interdict. This severe measure brought the disapproval of the Spanish king, who instructed him to return to Spain to justify his actions. Zumárraga obeyed the royal order, returned to Spain in 1532, and succeeded in defending himself against his enemies' charges, many of them slanderous. The emperor, satisfied by this vindication, invited Zumárraga to receive the episcopal consecration; he was consecrated in Valladolid, Spain, on April 27, 1533.

Educational Work. The following year Zumárraga returned to Mexico and applied himself to the enormous task of strengthening ecclesiastical discipline, favoring the missionaries who were attempting to convert the natives, and dedicated himself effectively to the foundation of schools and colleges for native children of both sexes. He and Viceroy Antonio de Mendoza built the first seminary and high school in America, the Colegio de la Santa Cruz de Santiago Tlatelolco, in Mexico City (1536). Beginning in 1537, he also promoted the foundation of a university, which, though not completed during his lifetime, was opened in 1553.

First Press in America. Zumárraga played an important part in the introduction of the press into the New World. He worked toward its establishment from 1533 onward and succeeded in 1539, thanks again to the cooperation of Viceroy Mendoza. The activities of the bishop with respect to the publication and editing, at his own expense, of the first books of New Spain are outstanding: he published the first catechisms in the Castilian and Mexican languages, as well as ascetic and liturgical works for the benefit of his diocese. He himself wrote some of these works, e.g., *Doctrina breve muy provechosa . . .* Mexico City 1544) and *Regla christiana* (Mexico City 1544). These notable activities resulted from his literary and humanistic background. He was particularly influenced by the works of Erasmus of Rotterdam, some of whose orthodox Catholic ideas he adopted.

Diocesan Organization. Zumárraga placed great importance on the ecclesiastical organization of his diocese and of all New Spain. He promoted, together with the rulers of Mexico at that time, the establishment of the Dioceses of Chiapas, Oaxaca, Guatemala, and Michoacán and proposed as bishops such people as Bartolomé de LAS CASAS and Vasco de QUIROGA. Furthermore, in order to harmonize the missionary and ecclesiastical work of his and neighboring dioceses, he promoted important meetings of bishops in Mexico City, which, if they were not called provincial councils for lack of certain formalities, were nevertheless useful in the orderly

and peaceful development of the religious and social life in New Spain. Among these councils, that of 1536 deserves special mention. It was called to settle the controversies that had arisen among the clergy concerning the administration of the Sacraments of Baptism and Matrimony to newly converted natives. The decisions of this council were partially confirmed by the bull *O altitudo divini consilii* issued by Pope Paul III (1537).

Inquisitor. From 1535 to 1543 Zumárraga exercised the difficult office of inquisitor. In his great desire to protect the rudimentary faith of the new converts, he once carried his work to an extreme, condemning to death through the civil authorities the *cacique* Don Carlos de Tetzcoco (Nov. 30, 1534). His rigorous procedure was censured by the Spanish court, which, if it did not reprimand him formally, recognizing that Zumárraga had acted upon high motives of rigid ecclesiastical discipline, nevertheless relieved him of the office of inquisitor.

Historians recall with regret that Zumárraga permitted the destruction of many temples, idols, and writings of the ancient Mexicans. The motives that induced this action are to be found in that same zeal, at times too impetuous, of the vigorous prelate.

Personally, the first bishop of Mexico was a man of great moral rectitude and an excellent religious who made a constant effort to live in accordance with his Franciscan vocation and episcopal dignity. He was made first archbishop of Mexico in 1547, but he did not receive news of this until May of the following year. Because of his frequent and generous gifts and donations, he died poor and burdened with debts.

Zumárraga is the dominant figure of early church history of Mexico, as noted and demonstrated by the Jesuit historian Mariano Cuevas. At times he committed excesses of zeal in the execution of his delicate and arduous offices because of his energetic and vigorous character, but these defects must not outbalance his great merits as protector of the native peoples and promoter of the Christian and cultural life of Mexico.

Bibliography: J. GARCÍA ICAZBALCETA, *Don fray Juan de Zumárraga: Primer obispo y arzobispo de México*, 4 v. (Mexico City 1947). F. DE J. CHAUVET, *Fray Juan de Zumárraga* (Mexico City 1948). A. M. CARREÑO, *Don fray Juan de Zumárraga: Teólogo y editor, humanista e inquisidor* (Mexico City 1950). R. E. GREENLEAF, *Zumárraga and the Mexican Inquisition, 1536–1543* (Washington 1962).

[F. DE J. CHAUVET]

ZWETTL, ABBEY OF

Slavic for "clearing," *Claravallis,* Austrian Cistercian monastery in the Diocese of St. Pölten; founded from HEILIGENKREUZ (1138) by Hadmar I of Kuenring. It flourished until 1348 when decline set in. Hussites wreaked destruction in 1427, and the Reformation interrupted restoration with internal deterioration. Abbot Ulrich Hackl (1577–1607) revived the abbey, and under Melchior Zaunagg (1706–47) baroque construction was done on the church, the campanile, and the library. Earlier, the Romanesque church consecrated in 1159 had been redone (1343–83) in an early Gothic French modification (apse and 13 chapels). The Romanesque dormitory and the oldest Cistercian chapter house in existence were vaulted *c.* 1190. The cloister and well house (1128–1230) are late-Romanesque early-gothic transition with Burgundian influence. The late-gothic side altars have paintings by Jörg Breu the Elder (1500). Zwettl's scholarship can be noted in the chronicle originated by Abbot Ebro (d. 1305), in its 420 MSS, and in its library of 45,000 books. Abbot Bernhard Link (d. 1671) compiled the *Annales Austro Claravallenses* (Vienna 1723–25) and Leopold Janauschek published *Origines Cistercienses* (Vienna 1877). At its height in 1330, Zwettl had 110 monks.

Bibliography: J. LEUTGEB, *Lexikon für Theologie und Kirche,* ed. M. BUCHBERGER, 10 v. (Freiburg 1930–38) 10:1112–13. P. B. UBERL, *Die Kunstdenkmäler des Zisterzienser Klosters Zwettl* (Vienna 1940). H. HAHN, *Die frühe Kirchenbaukunts der Zisterzienser* (Berlin 1957).

[H. ÓZELT]

ZWIEFALTEN, ABBEY OF

The Abbey of Zwiefalten, or Zwiefaltach, former Benedictine monastery founded by Counts Cuno and Liutold of Achalm. The Benedictine rule was adopted on the advice of Bp. ADALBERO OF WÜRZBURG and Abbot WILLIAM OF HIRSAU; the document of foundation is dated Dec. 8, 1089, and Zwiefalten became an independent abbey two years later. The first prior, Wezilo, became the first abbot (1091) of SANKT PAUL in Carinthia. The first abbot of Zwiefalten was Nogger, a monk from Einsiedeln or Hirsau. The patrons of the monastery were SS. STEPHEN and AURELIUS, whose head was brought to Zwiefalten after the suppression of Hirsau. The reliquary of Stephen was especially famous. A monastery of women was associated with that for men until the 13th century. Many nobles entered Zwiefalten, and the monastery was characterized almost uninterruptedly by excellent discipline and admirable scholarly activity. It had a school of copyists and illuminators; two notable house chroniclers were Ortlieb and Reinhard. Renowned for their pastoral zeal, monks from Zwiefalten were postulated as abbots for ALPIRSBACH, Kladrau, Elchingen, SANKT GALLEN, NERESHEIM, St. Peter in the Black Forest, SCHEYERN and

WEINGARTEN. Monks were sent to reform Weingarten and REICHENAU in the 15th and 16th centuries. From the 16th to the 18th centuries the monks studied and were professors at the universities in TÜBINGEN, Dillingen, and Salzburg. The abbey church was originally Romanesque; the present edifice dates from 1738 and was consecrated in 1765. Plans drawn up by the Schneider brothers were probably based on preliminary sketches by Franz Beer; the construction was entrusted to Johann Michael Fischer (*see* CHURCH ARCHITECTURE, HISTORY OF, 7. BAROQUE) from 1741. There is a gigantic fresco by Franz Spiegler in the nave. Winged altars were executed by Italian and German artists. The great organ by Josef Martin of Hayingen is now in the Protestant cathedral of Stuttgart. The library, containing 466 manuscripts, some from the 9th century, and 762 incunabula, can be found today in the Württemberg Provincial Library, Stuttgart. The abbey was secularized in 1802; the cloister was remodeled in baroque style at the end of the 17th century by Thomaso Camaccio and Franz Beer; in 1812 it was converted into an insane asylum and the abbey church became the Catholic parish church.

Bibliography: P. LINDNER, *Professbuch der Benediktinerabtei Zwiefalten* (Kempten 1910). M. ERZBERGER, *Die Säkularisation in Württemberg von 1802–1810* (Stuttgart 1902). E. KÖNIG and K. O. MÜLLER, *Die Zwiefalter Chroniken Ortliebs und Bertholds* (Stuttgart 1941). J. N. VANOTTI, ''Beiträge zur Geschichte der Orden in der Diözese Rottenburg,'' *Freiburger Diözesan Archiv,* 19 (1887) 226–248. G. SPAHR, *Barock in Oberschwaben* (Weingarten 1963). J. N. HAUNTINGER, *Reise durch Schwaben und Bayern im Jahre 1784* (Weissenhorn 1964).

[G. SPAHR]

ZWINGLI, HULDRYCH

Swiss theologian, statesman, and reformer; b. Wildhaus in the Toggenburg Valley, Canton St. Gall, Switzerland, January 1, 1484; d. Kappel, October 11, 1531.

Early Career. At the age of ten Zwingli was entered in the Latin school of St. Theodor in Klein-Basel. He displayed such promise as a student that two years later (1496) he was sent to Bern, where he undertook more advanced studies under the direction of the celebrated humanist scholar Heinrich Wölflin. The Bern Dominicans urged Zwingli, who was exceptionally gifted as a musician and singer, to enter their monastery to further his study of music as well as to sing in the choir. He accepted the offer in 1497, but was withdrawn almost immediately by his family and sent to the university of Vienna, where he matriculated in 1498. For reasons as yet unknown, he was dismissed, but he was readmitted in 1500. After two years of a predominantly humanistic education, he returned to Switzerland and entered the university of Basel,

Huldrych Zwingli.

where he earned the degree of bachelor of arts in 1504 and master of arts in 1506. In that same year he was ordained at Constance and in December moved to Glarus, where he was pastor for the next decade. There he extended his studies, both classical and Christian; corresponded with a small circle of humanist friends; and taught himself Greek. He served also as chaplain to the Glarus mercenaries in the service of Julius II, and his personal experience of the catastrophic defeat of the Swiss at the battle of Marignano in September 1515 contributed greatly to the uncompromising opposition to the mercenary system that he thereafter maintained. His outspoken opposition to the mercenary trade was, in fact, so unpopular that he was forced to resign his pastorate. From Glarus he went as a preacher to the famous monastery of Einsiedeln in Canton Schwyz. Early in 1515 he had journeyed to Basel to meet ERASMUS, and henceforth, until late in 1522, the works of the great humanist were decisive in their influence on the intellectual and religious development of Zwingli as a reformer. While at Einsiedeln he steeped himself in the *Enchiridion* and the Greek New Testament, copying out and committing the Pauline corpus to memory; he read widely and deeply in the Fathers of the Church, Greek as well as Latin, especially Origen, Jerome, and Augustine, and eventually acquired a command of patristic literature greater than that of Luther or Calvin; and in his opposition to mercenary service he found welcome support in Erasmus's radical pacifism.

The Reformer. In 1518 his friend Oswald Myconius nominated him for the position of people's priest in the Great Minster at Zurich. His candidacy was opposed, primarily because Zwingli had broken his vow of celibacy two years earlier, a charge to which he candidly admitted. Myconius eventually overcame the opposition, however, and he was elected to the post on December 11, 1518. On January 1, 1519, he preached his first sermon in the city. The progress and success of the Reformation in Zurich was owing ultimately to the vigor and eloquence of Zwingli's preaching together with his willingness to cooperate with the conciliar government of the city. In 1522, two years after Zwingli had resigned his papal pension, the publisher Christopher Froschauer and some of his colleagues publicly ate meat during Lent, an action that Zwingli defended in a sermon, later enlarged and published, arguing that abstention from meat was not commanded by "the Law of Christ." The bishop of Constance intervened, and after some months of fruitless negotiations with the city, Zwingli issued his first major reformatory treatise, the *Archeteles,* indicting the whole ceremonial structure of the Church. This was followed (January 19, 1523) by the *Sixty-Seven Conclusions,* a full-scale program for reforming the Church, which was to be debated at a public disputation called by the Great Council of Zurich for January 29. There Zwingli won a conclusive victory against his opponent, the vicar-general of Constance: the sole authority of Scripture for the reform of the Church was upheld. The problem of interpreting Scripture soon arose, however, focusing itself primarily on the propriety of images and liturgical reform. Impelled by some iconoclastic demonstrations in September 1523, the Council called for a second disputation, held in October, as a result of which the decision was made to abolish both images and the Mass.

Accordingly, between June 20 and July 2, 1524, all images were removed from the city churches. The Mass was abolished on April 12, 1525, and in that same year a new baptismal formula was prepared. Zwingli, who had secretly married Anna Reinhard in 1522, openly announced the marriage in 1524. Significantly enough, therefore, was the establishment in May 1525 of a court for regulating marriages. The year 1525 marked also the beginning of ANABAPTIST opposition to Zwingli's reform and to the internal conflict with these dissidents within the city was added as well the extended and acrimonious controversy, primarily with Martin LUTHER, over the nature of the Real Presence in the Lord's Supper. The two theologians finally met in October 1529 at Marburg, but neither would yield his point of view on the question. Civil war between Zurich and Bern, won to the Reformation in 1528, and the five Forest Cantons that had remained staunchly Roman Catholic had barely been averted in 1529. The ill-concealed and rising tension between them broke in 1531, and on October 6 the armies of the Forest Cantons began their march on a Zurich unprepared for war. Five days later they met the Zurich army at Kappel, and in the ensuing battle Zwingli was slain.

Bibliography: O. FARNER, *Zwingli the Reformer,* tr. D. G. SEAR (New York 1952); *Huldrych Zwingli,* 4 v. (Zurich 1943–60). J. V. POLLET, *Huldrych Zwingli et la réforme en Suisse* (Paris 1963). W. KÖHLER, *Huldrych Zwingli* (Leipzig 1943). R. STAEHELIN, *Huldreich Zwingli,* 2 v. (Basel 1895–97). F. BLANKE and G. W. LOCHER, *Die Religion in Geschichte und Gegenwart,* 7 v. (3d ed. Tübingen 1957–65) 6:1952–69. L CHRISTIANI, *Dictionnaire de théologie catholique,* ed. A. VACANT, 15 v. (Paris 1903–50; Tables générales 1951–) 15.2:3716–44. H. JEDIN, *Lexikon für Theologie und Kirche,* ed. M. BUCHBERGER, 10 v. (Freiburg 1930–38) 10:1114–18. CHARLES GARSIDE, *Zwingli and the Arts* (New Haven 1966). G.R. POTTER, *Zwingli* (Cambridge 1976). W.P. STEPHENS, *Zwingli. An Introduction to His Thought* (Oxford 1992). W.P. STEPHENS *The Theology of Huldrych Zwingli* (Oxford 1986).

[C. GARSIDE, JR.]

ZWINGLIANISM

Although the reformed theology of Huldrych Zwingli shows the influence of scholasticism, it is primarily the product of the New Learning. In his early years Zwingli had a taste for the schoolmen, including Duns Scotus, but he departed from the *via antiqua* through the attraction of the humanism of the Parisian Jacques Lefèvre d'Étaples and the members of the Florentine Academy, particularly the Neoplatonist, Marsilio Ficino. Through association with Erasmus, he acquired a philological and exegetical interest in the Scriptures and the early witnesses of tradition, Origen, Jerome, Gregory of Nyssa, Gregory of Nazianzus, Cyril of Alexandria, and John Chrysostom; only later did he succumb to the spell of St. Augustine. As a result of this regard for the early centuries of the Church, Zwingli turned primitivist in his theological thought and was led to an iconoclastic rejection of statues, crucifixes, altars, organs, incense, and all the liturgical functions that arose during the Middle Ages. The pulpit replaced the altar, and a communion service performed on a bare wooden table with wooden vessels supplanted the Sacrifice of the Mass.

Bibliocentrism. In parallel development appeared his reliance upon the Scriptures as sole norm and authority in matters of faith; these were to be privately interpreted by all Christians, so that "the cottage of every peasant is a school where the Old and New Testament could be read; this is the supreme art (*der höchste Kunst*)." (*Corpus reformatorum* 3:463.3.) Distinguishing between the interior word (faith) and the exterior word (reading and preaching of the Gospel), Zwingli taught that faith is not directly illumined by the external word but by Christ Himself, already established in the human spirit through faith: *Sic verbum per nos praedicatum non facit credentes, sed Christus intus docens* (Schuler and Schulthess, 6:702). Thus he repudiated an objective magisterium, or any suprapersonal authority in scriptural interpretations, and in its place substituted the subjective factors of religious experience. In his own scriptural writings he adopted a metaphorical and rhetorical exegesis rather than one that was literal (as among the scholastics) or moral (as with Martin Luther).

Ecclesiology. In Zwinglian ecclesiology the Church has two aspects: it is invisible (ideal), embracing all the elect in God; and also visible or sensible (empirical), composed of those who profess their faith and are signed with Baptism in alliance with God. Impressed with the dynamism of the primitive Church, especially at Corinth, Zwingli discarded any hierarchical structure as a hindrance to the flow of grace throughout the Christian body. He admitted, however, the need of a pastor to teach and inspire. This pastor, like the Prophets of the Old Testament, would enjoy charism and become in effect a preacher-prophet (*Corpus reformatorum* 3:23.6; 3:25.16). A major characteristic of Zwinglianism was the congregational organization, with its close interrelation with the secular magistracy in ecclesiastical government. The Council of the Canton (province) was to carry out the policies of the pastor and the community, including decrees of excommunication for public sinners. At Zurich, which became the first of the state churches, this wedding of laic and ecclesiastical rights gave the pastor a wide influence in the political assemblies of the community and over the "godly magistrate."

Sacramental Theory. Of the seven Sacraments, Zwingli admits only Baptism and the Eucharist as instituted by Christ. These are not efficacious and instrumental causes of grace but mere symbols (*sacrae rei signa, nuda signa*) and commemorative ceremonies. Baptism is comparable to the rite of circumcision in the Old Law, and the Lord's Supper is a service like the Passover, which memorialized Israel's deliverance from the Egyptian pharao. His position on the symbolic presence of Christ in the elements of the Eucharist, *corpus et sanguinem nonnisi symbolicos accipi* (*Corpus reformatorum* 4:498.25), was a topic of lively debate among his contemporary reformers and led to several attempts to formulate a generally acceptable compromise statement. (*See* CONFESSIONS OF FAITH, PROTESTANT.) Marriage, though not considered a Sacrament, is placed in special honor because it is decreed by God as a sign of contract binding for life (*foedus vitae*). Confirmation, the confession of sins, and the anointing of the sick are simple acts of fraternity within the Christian community; the ceremony of orders does not constitute a permanent minister but indicates only a temporary assignment for prescribed functions (*Corpus reformatorum* 2:404.3: 2:124.3; 3:8:24.8). In general Zwingli's rejection of sacramental efficacy is founded upon his spiritualism, which could not admit the production of spiritual grace from a sensible, material thing; this to him was magic.

Providence and Predestination. Zwingli's interpretation of divine providence and predestination of man reveals a type of pantheism in which God is author of both good and evil and man is an emanation from God, foreordained to election or reprobation; his fate is fixed and his will powerless. Both elect and doomed glorify God, the one His goodness, the other His justice, according to the plan of providence. This view of God as a universal agent causing with infallible and inexorable finality both good and evil is expressed in both the *De vera et falsa religionis commentarius* (1525) and the *Sermo de providentia Dei* (1530). Emphasis, however, is placed upon God's goodness in rescuing man from original sin, which he calls a disease (*morbus, Präst*); thus the treatises take on a tone of optimism.

Although Zwingli's doctrine appears succinctly in the 67 articles drawn up on Jan. 19, 1523, and in the *Christianae fidei expositio* sent to Francis I, king of France, in 1531 and published posthumously by Heinrich BULLINGER in February 1536, it is in his tractates and pamphlets that appeared from 1523 that the subtleties and progression of his theology are discovered. These fall into three groups: the anti-Catholic polemics (1523–24) against monasticism, papal power, the invocation of the saints, purgatory, etc.; the diatribes against Lutherans and the charge that Zwinglianism was merely transplanted Lutheranism, and against the Anabaptists, with whom he quarreled particularly over the questions of Church and State (1525–27); and the didactic works and confessional statements of his last years (1528–31).

Bibliography: *Huldrich Zwinglis Werke,* ed. M. SCHULER and J. SCHULTHESS, 8 v. (Zurich 1828–42 with suppl. 1861). *Huldrich Zwingtis sämtliche Werke,* ed. E. EGLI et al. in *Corpus reformatorum* 88–97 (*Schriften* 1–6; *Briefe* 7–11). J. V. M. POLLET, *Dictionnaire de théologie catholique,* ed. A. VACANT, 15 v. (Paris 1903–50; Tables générales 1951–) 15.2:3745–3928, detailed study and bibliog. G. W. LOCHER, *Die Theologie Huldrych Zwinglis im Lichte seiner Christologie,* v. 1, *Die Gotteslehre* (Zurich 1952); "Die Prädestinationslehre Huldrych Zwinglis," *Theologische Zeitschrift* 12 (Basel 1956) 526–548. J. KREUTZER, *Zwinglis Lehre von der Obrigkeit* (Stuttgart 1909). W. KÖHLER, *Zwingli und Luther* (Leipzig 1924). P. WERNLE, *Der evangelische Glaube nach den Hauptschriften der Reformatoren,* 3 v. (Tübingen 1918–19) v.2. A. FARNER, *Die Lehre von Kirche und Staat bei Zwingli* (Tübingen 1930). O. FARNER, *Aus Zwinglis Predigten zu Jesaja und Jeremia, unbekannte Nachschriften* (Zurich 1957); *Aus Zwinglis Predigten zu Mattäus, Markus und Johannes* (Zurich 1957). A. RICH, *Die Anfänge der Theologie Huldrych Zwinglis* (Zurich 1949). H. WATT, J. HASTINGS, ed., *Encyclopedia of Religion & Ethics,* 13 v. (Edinburgh 1908–27) 12:873–876. J. ROGGE, *Zwingli und Erasmus* (Stuttgart 1962). H. SCHMID, *Zwinglis Lehre von der göttlichen und menschlichen Gerechtigkeit* (Zurich 1959). *Zwingliana. Beiträge zur Geschichte Zwinglis, der Reformation und des Protestantismus in der Schweiz* (Zurich 1897–), esp. the Jubilee years, 1919, 1931. H. A. E. VAN GELDER, *The Two Reformations in the 16th Century,* tr. J. F. FINLAY and A. HANHAM (The Hague 1961). G. W. BROMILEY, comp., *Zwingli und Bullinger* (Philadelphia 1953), trs. including *Exposition of the Faith.* G. W. LOCHER, "The Change in the Understanding of Zwingli in Recent Research," *Church History* 34 (Philadelphia 1965) 3–24.

[E. D. MCSHANE]

ISBN 0-7876-4018-2

90000